UNIVERSITY CASEBOOK SERIES®

FEDERAL COURTS AND THE LAW OF FEDERAL-STATE RELATIONS

NINTH EDITION

PETER W. LOW
Hardy Cross Dillard Professor of Law Emeritus
University of Virginia

JOHN C. JEFFRIES, JR.
David and Mary Harrison Distinguished Professor of Law
University of Virginia

CURTIS A. BRADLEY
William Van Alstyne Professor of Law
Duke University

FOUNDATION
PRESS

© 1987, 1989, 1994, 1998, 2004 FOUNDATION PRESS
© 2008, 2011 THOMSON REUTERS/FOUNDATION PRESS
© 2014 LEG, Inc. d/b/a West Academic
© 2018 LEG, Inc. d/b/a West Academic
    444 Cedar Street, Suite 700
    St. Paul, MN 55101
    1-877-888-1330

Printed in the United States of America

ISBN: 978-1-68328-006-4

PREFACE

There are differing conceptions of a course in Federal Courts. The subject began as Federal Jurisdiction, which typically focused on federal pleading and practice. That course served as a complement to Civil Procedure, which concentrated on pleading and practice in state courts. Today, that version of Federal Courts is largely obsolete. Increasingly, the Federal Rules of Civil Procedure provide the model for civil litigation in state as well as federal courts. In consequence, many aspects of federal pleading and practice, and even of federal subject matter jurisdiction, are now covered in Civil Procedure, and the modern Federal Courts course has a broader agenda.

Today, Federal Courts is closely allied to Constitutional Law. It includes not only the jurisdiction of the federal courts, but also their ability to resist congressional control, their participation in the creation of federal law, and their role in enforcing federal rights. Increasingly, as this book reflects, Federal Courts also includes intersections with international law.

The 9th edition is configured to facilitate teacher choice. In our opinion, the first six chapters of the book contain materials that almost everyone will wish to cover. There may be, however, differences about sequence. One co-author begins with *Erie* and choice of law in the federal system (Chapter I) and continues with the power of the federal courts to create federal law, either by common-law innovation or by inferring private rights of action from federal statutes or the Constitution (Chapter II). This teacher then addresses *Marbury v. Madison*, judicial review, and the various doctrines of justiciability (Chapter III) and proceeds to congressional control over the federal courts (Chapter IV).

Another co-author begins with *Marbury*, judicial review, and justiciability (Chapter III) and continues with congressional control of the federal courts (Chapter IV). At that point, this teacher's sequence goes back to Chapters I and II to pick up *Erie*, choice of law in the federal system, and the role of the federal courts in creating federal law.

Both approaches make sense intellectually, and both work equally well. The choice between them is essentially a matter of taste. We have therefore constructed the book to facilitate this choice by providing alternate beginnings (Chapter I or Chapter III), with materials flowing logically and naturally from that point.

Users of this book will note a bias toward recent decisions rather than old chestnuts, in situations where either would do. In continuation of that policy, we will publish annual Supplements, which provide generous treatment of post-publication developments. Indeed, we include in the Supplements many matters that may not warrant permanent inclusion in the casebook itself, because we believe that others may enjoy, as we do, teaching the most recent decisions.

PWL
JCJ JR.
CAB

January 2018

SUMMARY OF CONTENTS

TABLE OF CONTENTS

TABLE OF CASES

The principal cases are in bold type.

TABLE OF AUTHORITIES

UNIVERSITY CASEBOOK SERIES®

FEDERAL COURTS AND THE LAW OF FEDERAL-STATE RELATIONS

NINTH EDITION

CHAPTER I

CHOICE OF LAW IN THE FEDERAL SYSTEM

SECTION 1. STATE LAW IN FEDERAL COURT

Erie Railroad Company v. Tompkins

Supreme Court of the United States, 1938.
304 U.S. 64.

■ MR. JUSTICE BRANDEIS delivered the opinion of the Court.

The question for decision is whether the oft-challenged doctrine of Swift v. Tyson, 41 U.S. (16 Pet.) 1 (1842), shall now be disapproved.

Tompkins, a citizen of Pennsylvania, was injured on a dark night by a passing freight train of the Erie Railroad Company while walking along its right of way at Hughestown in that state. He claimed that the accident occurred through negligence in the operation, or maintenance, of the train; that he was rightfully on the premises as licensee because on a commonly used beaten footpath which ran for a short distance alongside the tracks; and that he was struck by something which looked like a door projecting from one of the moving cars. To enforce that claim he brought an action in the federal court for southern New York, which had jurisdiction because the company is a corporation of that state. It denied liability; and the case was tried by a jury.

The Erie insisted that its duty to Tompkins was no greater than that owed to a trespasser. It contended, among other things, that its duty to Tompkins, and hence its liability, should be determined in accordance with the Pennsylvania law; that under the law of Pennsylvania, as declared by its highest court, persons who use pathways along the railroad right of way—that is a longitudinal pathway as distinguished from a crossing—are to be deemed trespassers; and that the railroad is not liable for injuries to undiscovered trespassers resulting from its negligence, unless it be wanton or wilful. Tompkins denied that any such rule had been established by the decisions of the Pennsylvania courts; and contended that, since there was no statute of the state on the subject, the railroad's duty and liability is to be determined in federal courts as a matter of general law.

The trial judge refused to rule that the applicable law precluded recovery. The jury brought in a verdict of $30,000; and the judgment entered thereon was affirmed by the Circuit Court of Appeals, which held that it was unnecessary to consider whether the law of Pennsylvania was as contended, because the question was one not of local, but of general, law and that upon questions of general law the federal courts are free, in the absence of a local statute, to exercise their independent judgment as to what the law is; and it is well settled that the question of the responsibility of a railroad for injuries caused by its servants is one of general law. . . . Where the public has made open and notorious use of a railroad right of way for a long period of time and without objection, the company owes to persons on such permissive pathway a duty of care in the operation of its trains. . . . It is likewise generally recognized law that a jury may find that negligence exists toward a pedestrian using a permissive path on the railroad right of way if he is hit by some object projecting from the side of the train.

The Erie had contended that application of the Pennsylvania rule was required, among other things, by § 34 of the Federal Judiciary Act of September 24, 1789 [now 28 U.S.C. § 1652], which provides:

> The laws of the several states, except where the Constitution, treaties, or statutes of the United States otherwise require or provide, shall be regarded as rules of decision in trials at common law, in the courts of the United States, in cases where they apply.

Because of the importance of the question whether the federal court was free to disregard the alleged rule of the Pennsylvania common law, we granted certiorari.

First. *Swift v. Tyson* held that federal courts exercising jurisdiction on the ground of diversity of citizenship need not, in matters of general jurisprudence, apply the unwritten law of the state as declared by its highest court; that they are free to exercise an independent judgment as to what the common law of the state is—or should be; and that, as there stated by Mr. Justice Story:

> The true interpretation of the 34th section limited its application to state laws strictly local, that is to say, to the positive statutes of the state, and the construction thereof adopted by the local tribunals, and to rights and titles to things having a permanent locality, such as the rights and titles to real estate, and other matters immovable and intraterritorial in their nature and character. It never has been supposed by us, that the section did apply, or was intended to apply, to questions of a more general nature, not at all dependent upon local statutes or local usages of a fixed and permanent operation, as, for example, to the construction of ordinary contracts or other written instruments, and especially to questions of general commercial law, where the state tribunals are called upon to perform the like functions as ourselves, that is, to ascertain upon general reasoning and legal analogies, what is the true exposition of the contract or instrument, or what is the just rule furnished by the principles of commercial law to govern the case.

The Court in applying the rule of § 34 to equity cases, in Mason v. United States, 260 U.S. 545, 559 (1923), said: "The statute, however, is merely declarative of the rule which would exist in the absence of the statute." The federal courts assumed, in the broad field of "general law," the power to declare rules of decision which Congress was confessedly without power to enact as statutes. Doubt was repeatedly expressed as to the correctness of the construction given § 34, and as to the soundness of the rule which it introduced. But it was the more recent research of a competent scholar, who examined the original document, which established that the construction given to it by the Court was erroneous; and that the purpose of the section was merely to make certain that, in all matters except those in which some federal law is controlling, the federal courts exercising jurisdiction in diversity of citizenship cases would apply as their rules of decision the law of the state, unwritten as well as written.[5]

Criticism of the doctrine became widespread after the decision of Black & White Taxicab & Transfer Co. v. Brown & Yellow Taxicab & Transfer Co., 276 U.S. 518 (1928). There, Brown and Yellow, a Kentucky corporation owned by Kentuckians, and the Louisville and Nashville Railroad, also a Kentucky corporation, wished that the former should have the exclusive privilege of soliciting passenger and baggage transportation at the Bowling Green, Kentucky, railroad station; and that the Black and White, a competing Kentucky corporation, should be prevented from interfering with that privilege. Knowing that such a contract would be void under the common law of Kentucky, it was arranged that

---

[5] Charles Warren, New Light on the History of the Federal Judiciary Act of 1789, 37 Harv. L. Rev. 49, 51–52, 81–88, 108 (1923).

[Warren's principal evidence for this conclusion was a slip of paper he found in the Senate archives containing the original version of § 34, handwritten by Senator (later Chief Justice) Oliver Ellsworth:

> And be it further enacted, That the ~~statute law~~ [laws] of the several states ~~in force for the time being and their unwritten or common law now in use; whether by adoption from the common law of England, the ancient statutes of the same or otherwise~~, except where the Constitution, treaties or statutes of the United States shall otherwise require or provide, shall be regarded as rules of decision in the trials at common law in the courts of the United States in cases where they apply.

Before he submitted his proposal, Senator Ellsworth inserted the word "laws" where it appears in brackets above, and crossed out the words that are struck out above. Warren concluded:

> The meaning of this change was probably as follows: that the word[s] "laws of the several states" [were] intended to be a concise expression and a summary of the more detailed enumeration of the different forms of state law, set forth in the original draft. It seems clear that the word "laws" was not intended to be confined to "statute law," because Ellsworth expressly and evidently intentionally struck out the words "statute law" from his original draft, and broadened it by inserting the word "laws"; having so broadened it, he evidently concluded that the specific enumeration which followed in his original draft was unnecessary.

Warren further argued that unless the change from "statute law" to "laws" was meant to include both statutes and common law,

> then no meaning whatever can be given to the change. If Ellsworth had simply meant to strike out the provision that the state common law should be a rule of decision in federal courts and had intended to have only the state statute law apply, he would have left his original draft just as it stood, and would simply have struck out the clause following the words 'the several states,' in which case the section would have read precisely as Judge Story construed it. . . .]—[Addition to footnote by eds.]

the Brown and Yellow reincorporate under the law of Tennessee, and that the contract with the railroad should be executed there. The suit was then brought by the Tennessee corporation in the federal court for western Kentucky to enjoin competition by the Black and White; an injunction issued by the district court was sustained by the Court of Appeals; and this Court, citing many decisions in which the doctrine of *Swift v. Tyson* had been applied, affirmed the decree.

Second. Experience in applying the doctrine of *Swift v. Tyson* had revealed its defects, political and social; and the benefits expected to flow from the rule did not accrue. Persistence of state courts in their own opinions on questions of common law prevented uniformity; and the impossibility of discovering a satisfactory line of demarcation between the province of general law and that of local law developed a new well of uncertainties.[8]

On the other hand, the mischievous results of the doctrine had become apparent. Diversity of citizenship jurisdiction was conferred in order to prevent apprehended discrimination in state courts against those not citizens of the state. *Swift v. Tyson* introduced grave discrimination by non-citizens against citizens. It made rights enjoyed under the unwritten "general law" vary according to whether enforcement was sought in the state or in the federal court; and the privilege of selecting the court in which the right should be determined was conferred upon the non-citizen. Thus, the doctrine rendered impossible equal protection of the law. In attempting to promote uniformity of law throughout the United States, the doctrine had prevented uniformity in the administration of the law of the state.

The discrimination resulting became in practice far-reaching. This resulted in part from the broad province accorded to the so-called "general law" as to which federal courts exercised an independent judgment. In addition to questions of purely commercial law, "general law" was held to include the obligations under contracts entered into and to be performed within the state; the extent to which a carrier operating within a state may stipulate for exemption from liability for his own negligence or that of his employee; the liability for torts committed within the state upon persons resident or property located there, even where the question of liability depended upon the scope of a property right conferred by the state; and the right to exemplary or punitive damages. Furthermore, state decisions construing local deeds, mineral conveyances, and even devises of real estate were disregarded.

---

[8] Compare 2 Charles Warren, The Supreme Court in United States History 89 (rev. ed. 1935):

> Probably no decision of the Court has ever given rise to more uncertainty as to legal rights; and though doubtless intended to promote uniformity in the operation of business transactions, its chief effect has been to render it difficult for business men to know in advance to what particular topic the Court would apply the doctrine. . . .

The Federal Digest, through the 1937 volume, lists nearly 1000 decisions involving the distinction between questions of general and of local law.

In part the discrimination resulted from the wide range of persons held entitled to avail themselves of the federal rule by resort to the diversity of citizenship jurisdiction. Through this jurisdiction individual citizens willing to remove from their own state and become citizens of another might avail themselves of the federal rule. And, without even change of residence, a corporate citizen of the state could avail itself of the federal rule by re-incorporating under the laws of another state, as was done in the Taxicab Case.

The injustice and confusion incident to the doctrine of *Swift v. Tyson* have been repeatedly urged as reasons for abolishing or limiting diversity of citizenship jurisdiction. Other legislative relief has been proposed. If only a question of statutory construction were involved, we should not be prepared to abandon a doctrine so widely applied throughout nearly a century. But the unconstitutionality of the course pursued has now been made clear and compels us to do so.

Third. Except in matters governed by the federal Constitution or by acts of Congress, the law to be applied in any case is the law of the state. And whether the law of the state shall be declared by its legislature in a statute or by its highest court in a decision is not a matter of federal concern. There is no federal general common law. Congress has no power to declare substantive rules of common law applicable in a state whether they be local in their nature or "general," be they commercial law or a part of the law of torts. And no clause in the Constitution purports to confer such a power upon the federal courts. As stated by Mr. Justice Field when protesting in Baltimore & Ohio R. Co. v. Baugh, 149 U.S. 368, 401 (1893), against ignoring the Ohio common law of fellow servant liability:

> I am aware that what has been termed the general law of the country—which is often little less than what the judge advancing the doctrine thinks at the time should be the general law on a particular subject—has been often advanced in judicial opinions of this court to control a conflicting law of a state. I admit that learned judges have fallen into the habit of repeating this doctrine as a convenient mode of brushing aside the law of a state in conflict with their views. And I confess that, moved and governed by the authority of the great names of those judges, I have myself, in many instances, unhesitatingly and confidently, but I think now erroneously, repeated the same doctrine. But, notwithstanding the great names which may be cited in favor of the doctrine, and notwithstanding the frequency with which the doctrine has been reiterated, there stands, as a perpetual protest against its repetition, the Constitution of the United States, which recognizes and preserves the autonomy and independence of the states—independence in their legislative and independence in their judicial departments. Supervision over either the legislative or the judicial action of the states

is in no case permissible except as to matters by the Constitution specifically authorized or delegated to the United States. Any interference with either, except as thus permitted is an invasion of the authority of the state and, to that extent, a denial of its independence.

The fallacy underlying the rule declared in *Swift v. Tyson* is made clear by Mr. Justice Holmes.[15] The doctrine rests upon the assumption that there is "a transcendental body of law outside of any particular state but obligatory within it unless and until changed by statute," that federal courts have the power to use their judgment as to what the rules of common law are; and that in the federal courts "the parties are entitled to an independent judgment on matters of general law":

> But law in the sense in which courts speak of it today does not exist without some definite authority behind it. The common law so far as it is enforced in a state, whether called common law or not, is not the common law generally but the law of that state existing by the authority of that state without regard to what it may have been in England or anywhere else. . . .

> The authority and only authority is the state, and if that be so, the voice adopted by the state as its own [whether it be of its legislature or of its Supreme Court] should utter the last word.

Thus the doctrine of *Swift v. Tyson* is, as Mr. Justice Holmes said, "an unconstitutional assumption of powers by courts of the United States which no lapse of time or respectable array of opinion should make us hesitate to correct." In disapproving that doctrine we do not hold unconstitutional § 34 of the Federal Judiciary Act of 1789 or any other act of Congress. We merely declare that in applying the doctrine this Court and the lower courts have invaded rights which in our opinion are reserved by the Constitution to the several states.

Fourth. The defendant contended that by the common law of Pennsylvania as declared by its highest court, the only duty owed to the plaintiff was to refrain from wilful or wanton injury. The plaintiff denied that such is the Pennsylvania law. In support of their respective contentions the parties discussed and cited many decisions of the Supreme Court of the state. The Circuit Court of Appeals ruled that the question of liability is one of general law; and on that ground declined to decide the issue of state law. As we hold this was error, the judgment is reversed and the case remanded to it for further proceedings in conformity with our opinion.

Reversed.

■ MR. JUSTICE CARDOZO took no part in the consideration or decision of this case.

---

[15] Kuhn v. Fairmont Coal Co., 215 U.S. 349, 370–72 (1910); Black & White Taxicab Co. v. Brown & Yellow Taxicab Co., 276 U.S. 518, 532–36 (1929).

[Justice Butler, joined by Justice McReynolds, dissented from the Court's rationale but concurred in the result on the ground that the plaintiff was contributorily negligent as a matter of law. Justice Butler observed that "[n]o constitutional question was suggested or argued below or here" and that "[a]gainst the protest of those joining in this opinion, the Court declines to assign the case for reargument."]

■ MR. JUSTICE REED (concurring in part).

I concur in the conclusion reached in this case, in the disapproval of the doctrine of *Swift v. Tyson,* and in the reasoning of the majority opinion except in so far as it relies upon the unconstitutionality of the "course pursued" by the federal courts.

The "doctrine of *Swift v. Tyson,*" as I understand it, is that the words "the laws," as used in § 34 . . . do not include in their meaning "the decisions of the local tribunals." . . .

To decide the case now before us and to "disapprove" the doctrine of *Swift v. Tyson* requires only that we say that the words "the laws" include in their meaning the decisions of the local tribunals. As the majority opinion shows . . . that this Court is now of the view that "laws" includes "decisions," it is unnecessary to go further and declare that the "course pursued" was "unconstitutional," instead of merely erroneous.

The "unconstitutional" course referred to in the majority opinion is apparently the ruling in *Swift v. Tyson* that the supposed omission of Congress to legislate as to the effect of decisions leaves federal courts free to interpret general law for themselves. I am not at all sure whether, in the absence of federal statutory direction, federal courts would be compelled to follow state decisions. . . . Mr. Justice Holmes evidently saw nothing "unconstitutional" which required the overruling of *Swift v. Tyson,* for he said in the very opinion quoted by the majority, "I should leave *Swift v. Tyson* undisturbed, . . . but I would not allow it to spread the assumed dominion into new fields." If the opinion commits this Court to the position that the Congress is without power to declare what rules of substantive law shall govern the federal courts, that conclusion also seems questionable. The line between procedural and substantive law is hazy but no one doubts federal power over procedure. Wayman v. Southard, 23 U.S. (10 Wheat.) 1 (1825). The Judiciary Article and the "necessary and proper" clause may fully authorize legislation, such as this section of the Judiciary Act.

In this Court, stare decisis, in statutory construction, is a useful rule, not an inexorable command. It seems preferable to overturn an established construction of an act of Congress, rather than, in the circumstances of this case, to interpret the Constitution.

There is no occasion to discuss further the range or soundness of these few phrases of the opinion. It is sufficient now to call attention to them and express my own non-acquiescence.

NOTES ON STATE LAW IN FEDERAL COURTS

1. THE CASE OF SWIFT V. TYSON

Tyson purchased land from Nathaniel Norton (and one Jarius Keith) and paid by executing a negotiable instrument in favor of Norton, who endorsed it to Swift in payment of a prior obligation. When Swift sought to collect, Tyson refused to pay, claiming that Norton had defrauded him in the original transaction by purporting to convey land to which he did not have title. Swift sued Tyson in federal court, with jurisdiction based on diversity of citizenship. The issue was whether Tyson's defense against Norton was also good against Swift. The defense would fail if Swift could establish, among other things, that he was a purchaser for value. Whether Swift qualified as a purchaser for value turned on whether satisfaction of Norton's pre-existing debt to him constituted sufficient consideration.

In Swift v. Tyson, 41 U.S. (16 Pet.) 1 (1842), the Supreme Court held that this question should be decided by reference to "the general principles and doctrines of commercial jurisprudence." In reaching this conclusion, Justice Story had to consider whether the directive in § 34 of the Judiciary Act that federal courts should follow the "laws of the several states" included state decisional law. Story argued that "[i]n the ordinary use of language, it will hardly be contended that the decisions of courts constitute laws. They are, at most, only evidence of what the laws are, and are not, of themselves, laws." He therefore construed the word "laws" as limited to "state laws strictly local," which included statutes, court decisions governing titles to land, and the like. Under this reading, Section 34 did not apply to the issue in *Swift,* and Justice Story felt free to decide the case by independent inquiry into general commercial law.

Fifty years later, *Swift v. Tyson* was extended in Baltimore & Ohio RR. v. Baugh, 149 U.S. 368 (1893), which held that questions of tort liability were part of the "general" common law. Justice Field's extensive dissent was quoted by Justice Brandeis in *Erie. Swift* was expanded still further in Kuhn v. Fairmont Coal Co., 215 U.S. 349 (1910), which held that rights deriving from a deed to land were also within the "general" common law powers of the federal courts. Justice Holmes's dissent in *Kuhn* was also quoted in *Erie*, as was another forceful Holmes's dissent in Black & White Taxicab Co. v. Brown & Yellow Taxicab Co., 276 U.S. 518 (1928), which is fully described in *Erie.*

The *Taxicab* case became a lightning rod for criticism. In the decade following that decision, *Swift* seemed to be weakening. It had been extended far beyond the original domain of commercial law and the distinction between "local" and "general" law had become increasingly troublesome.

2. THE REGIME OF SWIFT V. TYSON

The regime of *Swift v. Tyson* is hard for modern students to understand. The task becomes easier if one remembers the paucity of published state decisions in the early days of the Republic, which would have made it very hard for federal courts to follow state decisions even if they had wanted to, and the prominence in the learning of that era of general principles (memorialized in influential treatises) rather than jurisdiction-specific precedents. These practicalities may help explain why the early federal courts found it natural to reach their own conclusions on matters of "general" law, whatever the conceptual underpinnings of that approach.

To one who seeks to understand the conceptual underpinnings of *Swift*, however, the regime seems strange. Indeed, the very concept of "general" law may be puzzling. Traditionally, *Swift v. Tyson* is described as "federal general common law." This label says a good deal. The rule of *Swift v. Tyson* was "federal" in the sense that it was created by, and applied in, the federal courts. It was "general" in the sense that it applied to generally applicable legal rules and not to jurisdiction-specific statutes or to peculiarly "local" issues, such as title to real estate. And it was "common law" because it was announced by judges. The difficulty lies in conceiving of substantive law that applies only in federal courts and is not binding on the states under the Supremacy Clause.

There is, however, another way to view pre-*Erie* law. "General" common law might be seen not as free-floating law of indeterminate origin but as *state* law. But if the "general" common law was recognized as state law existing by virtue of state sovereignty, why did the federal courts feel free to make their own assessments of its meaning? The answer, at least in the minds of some, is that state authority might have chosen to maintain the general rules and principles of the unwritten law rather than to displace that regime with a jurisdiction-specific rule or statute. In other words, a state might have chosen to maintain a general law that had not been made local. In that conception, a state court decision would be seen, under state law, as *evidence* of the unwritten law applicable in that state, not as a *binding declaration* of its meaning in that jurisdiction. Of course, lower state courts would have to respect the opinions of their highest state court on the meaning of the unwritten law, but courts outside that hierarchal relationship—including both federal courts and the courts of other states—would be free to reach their own interpretations. On this view, respect for state sovereignty did *not* require federal courts to defer to state court decisions on the meaning of general unwritten law, as *Swift v. Tyson* in fact held.

This way of looking at pre-*Erie* law is explicated in Caleb Nelson, A Critical Guide to *Erie Railroad Co. v. Tompkins*, 54 Wm. & Mary L. Rev. 921 (2013), which, in the course of a searching critique of *Erie*, attempts to rehabilitate the regime of *Swift*. See also Michael G. Collins, Justice Iredell, Choice of Law, and the Constitution—A Neglected Encounter, 23 Const. Comment. 163 (2006) (identifying sources that regarded the "general" common law as state law); Michael Steven Green, Law's Dark Matter, 54 Wm. & Mary L. Rev. 845 (2013) (arguing that *Swift*'s conception of general common law reflected the view that (as a matter of state law) state court decisions should not have "extrajurisdictional effect" in federal and other state courts). This way of thinking about pre-*Erie* general law may be unfamiliar to those educated in a post-*Erie* world, but it recognizes in the regime of *Swift v. Tyson* an intellectual coherence and integrity that are slighted in most modern accounts.

3. JUSTICE BRANDEIS'S HISTORY

Justice Brandeis's history, in particular his reliance on the research of Charles Warren (see footnote 5), has been attacked on several grounds. Most obvious is the question whether the single slip of paper found in Ellsworth's files was actually seen or relied on by the Senate. It may seem unlikely that a single handwritten copy was passed around from hand to hand, and there is no record that it was.

Also debatable is Warren's assumption that Oliver Ellsworth's rephrasing of what eventually became § 34 of the Judiciary Act was intended to condense and restate the original version, rather than to revise its meaning. Neither view is implausible. The lack of evidence on this point led one scholar to conclude that "there is no way to determine whether the change was . . . or was not intended to change the substantive meaning of the statute." Suzanna Sherry, Wrong, Out of Step, and Pernicious: *Erie* as the Worst Decision of All Time, 39 Pepp. L. Rev. 129 (2011).

Even if one assumes that Ellsworth's rephrasing was intended to preserve rather than alter the original meaning, that meaning is not as clear as Warren and Brandeis supposed. See, for example, the competing interpretation of § 34 in Wilfred J. Ritz, Wythe Holt, and L.H. LaRue, Rewriting the History of the Judiciary Act of 1789: Exposing Myths, Challenging Premises, and Using New Evidence (1990). The Ritz-Holt-LaRue thesis rests in part on the state of legal affairs in 1789. The hierarchal judicial system established in the First Judiciary Act was entirely new. In most states, an undifferentiated group of judges sometimes "rode circuit" to try cases at various places in the state and at other times gathered, usually in the capital, to try cases and hear "appeals." These appeals were really new trials, with a new jury. There were no separate trial and appellate courts, as are familiar today. The decisions of these state courts were not in print, and there was no easy way to obtain copies of state statutes, much less up-to-date collections of statutes organized in an orderly fashion. "No rational Congress," the authors conclude, "would have required federal courts to apply a nonexistent state common law, nor a virtually inaccessible state statute law."

This much may perhaps be conceded. But Ritz, Holt, and LaRue also analyze word usages of the day, and conclude that the phrase "laws of the several states" as used in § 34 probably referred to the laws of the American states *generally*, not to the laws of *specific* individual states. On this reading, the statute simply directed federal courts to use emerging American common law rather than British common law as the basis for their decisions. As the study explains:

> Section 34 is a direction to the national courts to apply American law, as distinguished from English law. American law is to be found in the "laws of the several states" viewed as a group of eleven states in 1789, and not viewed separately and individually. It is not a direction to apply the law of a particular state, for if it had been so intended, the section would have referred to the "laws of the respective states."

The authors argue that this difference between the words "several" (to refer to the aggregate) and "respective" (to refer to the particular) was fairly common in both the Constitution and other portions of the 1789 Judiciary Act.

While this distinction between "several" and "respective" has been influential,[a] it has also been contested. There are certainly examples of "several" used in precisely in the way Charles Warren supposed, including the constitutional command that the members of the House of Representatives be "chosen every second Year by the People of the several States." Art. I, § 2. Obviously, this must refer to the states individually rather than to some collective entity. Moreover, there is record of contemporary observers attributing that same meaning to the word "several" as used in § 34. A review of the available evidence led one scholar to conclude flatly that "Ritz was wrong about the original meaning of section 34." Caleb Nelson, A Critical Guide to *Erie Railroad Co. v. Tompkins*, 54 Wm. & Mary L. Rev. 921, 959 (2013).

Of course, the fact that Ritz may have been wrong does not make Brandeis right. On the contrary, there is reason to doubt Brandeis's (and Charles Warren's) history on grounds that have nothing to do with "several" versus "respective." Nelson, for example, accepts that § 34 is "naturally understood to refer to the laws of each state individually" and is even prepared to accept that "laws" may be read to include the unwritten law, but nevertheless contends that § 34 does not specify whether "federal courts must defer to each state's highest court about the content of the unwritten law in force within that state." That depends, to put the matter simply, on whether the decisions of a state supreme court *define* the unwritten law in that state, as we are inclined to think today, or are only one *interpretation* of the unwritten law, as lawyers at the Founding might have assumed. On that question, the history propounded by Warren and relied on by Brandeis has "no real bearing."

The disputes surrounding the historical basis for Brandeis's construction of § 34 are far more extended and elaborate than can be recounted here, but perhaps it suffices to say that history is no longer thought to provide a compelling justification for *Erie*'s outcome. If the decision is to rest on a secure foundation, one must look elsewhere.

4. THE CONSTITUTIONAL PREMISES OF *ERIE*

At the end of the second part of his *Erie* opinion, Brandeis observed:

> If only a question of statutory construction were involved, we should not be prepared to abandon a doctrine so widely applied throughout nearly a century. But the unconstitutionality of the course pursued has now been made clear and compels us to do so.

Although Brandeis plainly thought constitutional concerns important, he was famously opaque about their precise content. What exactly are the

---

[a]   See, e.g., Patrick J. Borchers, The Origins of Diversity Jurisdiction, The Rise of Legal Positivism and a Brave New World for *Erie* and *Klaxon*, 72 Tex. L. Rev. 79 (1993).

grounds for thinking that "the course pursued" under *Swift* was unconstitutional? The following notes explore this question.

(i) Equal Protection

Near the end of the paragraph beginning "On the other hand" in the "Second" part of his opinion, Brandeis said that the doctrine of *Swift* "rendered impossible equal protection of the law." Did the Court mean that the application of different legal rules in different forums would violate equal protection?

The answer is almost surely "no." A decade earlier, Justice Holmes had dismissed equal protection as "the usual last resort of constitutional arguments." Buck v. Bell, 274 U.S. 200 (1927). Although a few state laws had been invalidated on equal protection grounds before *Erie*,[b] the inequalities of *Swift* were not covered by those precedents—nor, indeed, by cases decided since that time. Another objection to an equal protection rationale for *Erie* is that the supposed culprits were federal courts—to which the Fourteenth Amendment does not in terms apply. Not until Bolling v. Sharpe, 347 U.S. 497 (1954) (forbidding school desegregation in the District of Columbia), were equal protection principles explicitly applied to the federal government through the Fifth Amendment Due Process Clause.

Moreover, there is a sense in which *Erie* merely substituted one kind of inequality for another. *Erie* restricted forum shopping between state and federal courts, but it did not prevent forum shopping between the courts of different states. Then, as now, a defendant frequently could be sued in more than one state. Often each state applied its own law. The resulting disparity among state courts was extended to federal courts in Klaxon Co. v. Stentor Electric Manufacturing Co., Inc., 313 U.S. 487 (1941), which directed federal courts to apply the conflict-of-laws principles of the state in which they sit. As applied in *Klaxon*, *Erie* eliminated forum-shopping between state and federal courts in the same state, but facilitated forum-shopping between federal courts in different states. (This point is explained more fully in the notes following *Klaxon*, which is the next main case.) The modern expansion of in personam jurisdiction has greatly exacerbated this kind of inequality, and constitutional arguments against it have been unavailing. For these reasons, it seems plain that the regime of *Swift v. Tyson* did not violate the equal protection rights of litigants and that *Erie* was not decided on that rationale.

(ii) Federalism

In the first paragraph of the "Third" part of his opinion, Justice Brandeis seemed to say that the Court was purporting to exercise power that Congress lacked:

> Congress has no power to declare substantive rules of common law applicable in a state whether they be local in their nature or "general," be they commercial law or a part of the law of torts. And

---

[b]   E.g., Strauder v. West Virginia, 100 U.S. 303 (10 Otto) (1879) (exclusion of African-Americans from juries); Yick Wo v. Hopkins, 118 U.S. 356 (1886) (purposeful discrimination against Chinese laundries).

no clause in the Constitution purports to confer such a power on the federal courts.

Today, of course, Congress has broad authority to pass laws governing commercial law, torts, and many other matters. Even in 1938, Congress would have had clear authority under the Commerce Clause to regulate the precise issue at stake in *Erie*, as the Court had long taken a generous view of Congress's power to regulate railroads. Nonetheless, *Swift* did authorize the federal courts to exercise powers that Congress lacked. At the time, Congress could not have regulated *all* activity that fell into the category of "general" common law. That is to say, Congress could not have regulated all activity that could be called commercial or tortious. Yet *Swift* had the effect of authorizing the federal courts to do just that. Though *Erie* itself was not an example, *Swift* led to cases where federal courts supplied rules of decision for matters arguably beyond federal legislative power. This was, the argument goes, the unconstitutional "course of conduct" authorized by *Swift*. When federal courts supplied "general" federal common law, they failed to ask whether the national government had the authority to regulate the activity in question. At the very least, *Erie* stands for the proposition that federal courts must respect constitutional limits on federal legislative power.[c]

Today, however, a rationale for *Erie* based strictly on principles of federalism would have little practical importance. Despite the rebirth of limits on federal legislative power in cases such as United States v. Lopez, 514 U.S. 549 (1995) (striking down the Gun-Free School Zones Act), Printz v. United States, 521 U.S. 898 (1997) (invalidating portions of the Brady Handgun Violence Prevention Act), and United States v. Morrison, 529 U.S. 598 (2000)

---

[c] See John Hart Ely, The Irrepressible Myth of *Erie*, 87 Harv. L. Rev. 693, 702–04 (1974); Henry J. Friendly, In Praise of *Erie*—And of the New Federal Common Law, 39 N.Y.U. L. Rev. 383, 394–95 (1964).

Compare the argument in Louise Weinberg, Back to the Future: The New General Common Law, 35 J. Mar. L. & Com. 523 (2004). The constitutional premise of *Erie*, she says, is the positivist view that law must find its source in the authority of a relevant sovereign. The law applied under *Swift* "was not state law, but it was not federal law, either. It was, you might say 'brooding omnipresence' law." She argues that application of a law that is not rooted in the authority, interests, and power of an identifiable sovereign should be regarded as a denial of due process.

Weinberg makes a comparison to the role of due process in horizontal, state-state choice-of-law situations. Alaska Packers Ass'n v. Indus. Accident Comm'n, 294 U.S. 532 (1935), permits a state court to apply its law only if the state has a "legitimate public interest" in the controversy. Consistent with that approach, Home Insurance Co. v. Dick, 281 U.S. 397 (1930), held that a state without an appropriate interest in the controversy cannot apply its own law. Weinberg argues that the same structure should apply to vertical, federal-state choice-of-law issues. Leaving aside international issues, federal and state courts have two choices when they decide whose law to apply: they may apply the law of a state that satisfies the *Alaska Packers* limitation; or they may apply federal law if the controversy lies within federal delegated powers. Weinberg concludes that the courts do not have a third option. They may not apply "brooding omnipresence" law, that is, they may not, as *Swift* did, apply abstract principles of law that are not rooted in the authority, interests, and power of an identified sovereign.

There is a wealth of other scholarship examining the jurisprudential premises and implications of *Erie*, including William Casto, The *Erie* Doctrine and the Structure of Constitutional Revolutions, 62 Tulane L. Rev. 907 (1988), and Jack Goldsmith and Steven Walt, *Erie* and the Irrelevance of Legal Positivism, 84 Va. L. Rev. 673 (1998) (arguing that the historical connection between *Erie* and legal positivism has not been shown and that "*Erie's* commitment to legal positivism is conceptually and normatively independent of its constitutional holding").

(striking down a section of the Violence Against Women Act), modern constitutional precedents give Congress very broad legislative authority over many subjects. If *Erie* meant only that federal courts could not supply federal rules of decision for matters beyond federal legislative control, it would have little practical bite.

(iii) Separation of Powers

In the first paragraph of the "Third" part of his opinion, Justice Brandeis observed that there "is no federal general common law" and that "no clause in the Constitution" confers power on the federal courts to "declare substantive rules of common law applicable in a state." This language suggests that *Erie* is based, at least in part, on separation of powers. In this view, the "course pursued" under *Swift v. Tyson* may have been unconstitutional because a federal court, rather than the federal legislature, was "making" law.

Although separation of powers as a rationale for *Erie* has undoubted force, it requires qualification. Historically, the federal legislature has enjoyed *primacy* but not *exclusivity* in making law. As illustrated in the next note, federal courts often make law. The notion that federal courts act unconstitutionally whenever they act as common-law courts is far more radical than anything said in *Erie* or supported by history and does not characterize contemporary practice.

Yet separation of powers remains an important strand in understanding *Erie*. In essence, separation of powers and federalism intersect to impose structural limits on the power of federal courts to override state law absent federal legislative authorization. As Henry Monaghan observed in a review of the Hart & Wechsler federal courts casebook, "*Erie* is, fundamentally, a limitation on the federal court's power to displace state law absent some relevant constitutional or statutory mandate which neither the general language of Article III nor the jurisdictional statute provides." 87 Harv. L. Rev. 889, 892 (1974).

A more elaborate articulation of this view appears in Paul Mishkin, Some Further Last Words on *Erie*: The Thread, 87 Harv. L. Rev. 1682, 1683–86 (1974). Mishkin argues that the "[p]rinciples related to the separation of powers impose [a] limit on the authority of federal courts to engage in lawmaking on their own (unauthorized by Congress)":

> The point may perhaps be made most easily by example. I take it there is little doubt that Congress could validly enact "no-fault" liability for all automobile accidents in the country—and no doubt at all about accidents on public thoroughfares carrying interstate traffic. At the same time I take it as equally clear that the federal courts would currently not seriously entertain the contention that they should adopt a federal "no-fault" liability rule even if the particular accident clearly involved interstate traffic. . . . I submit that this conclusion is of constitutional dimension, that any other course would be "unconstitutional" in the sense that term was used in the *Erie* opinion. . . . In my judgment, the clarity and strength with which the inappropriateness of federal judicial lawmaking on such

a base is perceived (even when congressional power is pellucid) is itself significant evidence of the constitutional nature of the limitation.

Consider Mishkin's argument carefully. It is based on both federalism and separation of powers. Specifically, it asserts that separation of powers places limits on the federal courts additional to, and distinct from, the limits that federalism imposes on the national government as a whole.[d]

5.   EXAMPLES OF FEDERAL COMMON LAW

Notwithstanding legislative primacy in law-making, there are occasions when federal courts make common law and when it is generally (though not unanimously) accepted that they should do so.[e] Consider the following examples.

---

[d]   Sustained and thoughtful defense of a constitutional basis for *Erie*, along lines broadly consistent with the excerpt from Mishkin, comes from the work of Bradford R. Clark. In Bradford R. Clark, *Erie's* Constitutional Source, 95 Calif. L. Rev. 1289 (2007), Clark concludes that "[t]he Supremacy Clause supplies specific textual, historical, and structural support for Mishkin's conclusions." One can infer from its structure that federal courts are precluded "from acting outside its terms to displace state law." For further development of these views, see Bradford R. Clark, Federal Law and the Role of Structure in Constitutional Interpretation, 96 Calif. L. Rev. 699 (2008), and Anthony J. Bellia Jr. and Bradford R. Clark, General Law in Federal Court, 54 Wm. & Mary L. Rev. 655 (2013). See also Ernest Young, Federalism as a Constitutional Principle, 83 U. Cin. L. Rev. 1057 (2015), and Ernest A. Young, A General Defense of *Erie Railroad Co. v. Tompkins*, 10 J. Law, Econ. & Policy 17 (2013). In the latter article, Young says in reinforcement of the Mishkin thesis that "the displacement of state law must be traceable to the valid exercise of federal lawmaking authority. Under the federal separation of powers, that authority generally belongs to Congress, which can legislate only by a difficult process in which the states are represented. . . . This interstitial view of federal law, with a broad national lawmaking jurisdiction circumscribed by political and procedural safeguards, remains the most promising model for maintaining our federal balance in the modem era."

Also important in this literature is the work of Craig Green. See Craig Green, Repressing *Erie's* Myth, 96 Calif. L. Rev. 595 (2008); Craig Green, *Erie* and Problems of Constitutional Structure, 96 Calif. L. Rev. 661 (2008); Craig Green, Can *Erie* Survive as Federal Common Law?, 54 Wm. & Mary L. Rev. 813 (2013).

Finally, see also Aaron Nielson, *Erie* as Nondelegation, 72 Ohio St. L.J. 239 (2011), which finds a constitutional foundation for *Erie* not on the grounds stated in the opinion but in the idea that Congress cannot delegate authority to the courts, over commercial law, for example, without providing meaningful standards for its exercise. It is argued in Doris DelTosto Brogan, Less Mischief, Not None: Respecting Federalism, Respecting States and Respecting Judges in Diversity Jurisdiction Cases, 51 Tulsa L. Rev. 39 (2015), that Nielson's argument is "persuasive and important but not sufficient." *Erie* "finds its constitutional anchor," she argues, "in 'the constitutional structure' ": "to quote Justice Kennedy in *Alden v. Maine* [527 U.S. 706, 729 (1999)], 'not by the text of [any article or amendment] alone but by fundamental postulates implicit in the constitutional design.' "

[e]   See generally Jay Tidmarsh and Brian J. Murray, A Theory of Federal Common Law, 100 Nw. U. L. Rev. 585 (2006); Anthony J. Bellia Jr., State Courts and the Making of Federal Common Law, 153 U. Pa. L. Rev. 825 (2005); Bradford R. Clark, Federal Common Law: A Structural Reinterpretation, 144 U. Pa. L. Rev. 1245 (1996); Martha A. Field, Sources of Law: The Scope of Federal Common Law, 99 Harv. L. Rev. 881 (1986); Paul Lund, The Decline of Federal Common Law, 76 B.U. L. Rev. 895 (1996); Thomas W. Merrill, The Common Law Powers of Federal Courts, 52 U. Chi. L. Rev. 1 (1985); Peter L. Strauss, 2001 Daniel J. Meador Lecture: Courts or Tribunals? Federal Courts and the Common Law, 53 Ala. L. Rev. 891 (2002); Louise Weinberg, Federal Common Law, 83 Nw. U. L. Rev. 805 (1989).

Caleb Nelson, The Persistence of General Law, 106 Colum. L. Rev. 503 (2006), argues that, even post-*Erie*, there is a substantial body of "general law" where a federal rule of decision will govern but it is not appropriate to incorporate the law of a particular state. In such situations, federal courts do much as the Court did in the *Swift* era and as is the goal of the ALI Restatements—they look to best practices or to consensus among the various states.

(i)   Lawsuits Between States

On the same day that the Court decided *Erie*, Justice Brandeis wrote a unanimous opinion holding that the apportionment of water rights in a stream controlled by an interstate compact presented "a question of 'federal common law' upon which neither the statutes nor the decisions of either state can be conclusive." Hinderlider v. La Plata River & Cherry Creek Ditch Co., 304 U.S. 92 (1938). *Hinderlider* is often cited in approval of federal judge-made law to resolve conflicts between states. The principle is involved where one state sues another over water rights or boundary disputes. Henry Monaghan has defended a federal common-law power to craft rules to resolve conflicts between states on practical grounds:

> The interstate dispute cases present a good example of author-
> ity to create federal common law gleaned by implication from the
> federal structure of the United States. Some tribunal must exist for
> settling interstate controversies; but it is a basic presumption of the
> Constitution that the state courts may be too parochial to adminis-
> ter fairly disputes in which important state interests are at
> issue. . . . An acceptable accommodation of interstate, to say noth-
> ing of national, interests in a given dispute dictates that the
> Supreme Court must possess power to fashion substantive law not
> tied to that of any particular state. [T]he authority to create federal
> common law springs of necessity from the structure of the Consti-
> tution. . . .[f]

For a modern application of this doctrine, see Virginia v. Maryland, 540 U.S. 5 (2003), where the Court said: "Federal common law governs interstate bodies of water, ensuring that the water is equitably apportioned between the States and that neither State harms the other's interest in the river." A similar argument can be made about admiralty law.[g]

---

[f]   Henry P. Monaghan, The Supreme Court, 1974 Term, Forward: Constitutional Common Law, 89 Harv. L. Rev. 1, 14 (1975).

[g]   For an example of the application of federal common law in an admiralty context, see Norfolk Southern Railway Co. v. Kirby, 543 U.S. 14 (2004). For academic commentary, compare David J. Bederman, Uniformity, Delegation and the Dormant Admiralty Clause, 28 J. Maritime Law & Commerce 1 (1997) (arguing that there are implied limits on state law in admiralty matters, even where Congress has been silent and indeed that there is a "non-delegable, consti-tutional core of admiralty law that not even Congress can make non-uniform."). See also Joel K. Goldstein, Federal Common Law in Admiralty: An Introduction to the Beginning of an Ex-change, 43 St. Louis U. L.J. 1337 (1999) (advocating "a fairly robust federal common law-making role for admiralty courts"); Ernest A. Young, The Last Brooding Omnipresence: *Erie Railroad Co. v. Tompkins* and the Unconstitutionality of Preemptive Federal Maritime Law, 43 St. Louis U. L.J. 1349 (1999) (arguing that the "broad role of maritime preemption is unconstitutional"); Robert Force, An Essay on Federal Common Law and Admiralty, 43 St. Louis U. L.J. 1367 (1999) (defending the "constitutional authority [of federal courts] to create substantive rules of maritime law"); Steven F. Friedell, The Diverse Nature of Admiralty Jurisdiction, 43 St. Louis U. L.J. 1389 (1999) (arguing that Congress has confirmed the law-making authority of the fed-eral admiralty courts on numerous occasions); Jonathan M. Gutoff, Federal Common Law and Congressional Delegation: A Reconceptualization of Admiralty, 61 U. Pitt. L. Rev. 367 (2000).

(ii) The Dormant Commerce Clause

In many cases, the Supreme Court has invalidated state legislation on the ground that it conflicts with unexercised federal power under the Commerce Clause. Most commonly, the Court strikes down state laws that discriminate against out-of-state interests, for example by limiting the opportunities of out-of-state firms or subjecting them to higher taxes. Such laws are said to violate the "dormant" or "negative" Commerce Clause. Of course, there is only one Commerce Clause; it appears in Art. I, Sec. 8 and authorizes federal regulation of interstate commerce. The limitations on state legislation based on the "dormant" or "negative" Commerce Clause are inferences drawn by courts from the existence of federal legislative power, even when it is unexercised.

The Supreme Court routinely describes these invalid state laws as "unconstitutional," but that term requires qualification since Congress (which is bound by the Constitution) could authorize the states to enact these laws. Consider the views of Henry Monaghan, who thought that "the most satisfactory explanation of the [dormant] Commerce Clause cases is that the Supreme Court is fashioning federal common law on the authority of the Commerce Clause. That clause embodies a national, free-trade philosophy which can be read as requiring the Court, in limited circumstances, to displace state-created trade barriers. . . ." Henry P. Monaghan, The Supreme Court, 1974 Term, Forward: Constitutional Common Law, 89 Harv. L. Rev. 1, 17 (1975).[h]

It is crucial to Monaghan's argument that the negative Commerce Clause cases are "wholly subject to congressional revision." This point is undisputed as a matter of precedent. Congress can authorize states to regulate interstate commerce in ways that would be struck down as "unconstitutional" absent federal legislation. See, e.g., Prudential Ins. Co. v. Benjamin, 328 U.S. 408 (1946) (approving discriminatory taxation of out-of-state insurers on the ground that Congress had authorized such taxation). The Court's willingness to strike down as "unconstitutional" what Congress can rehabilitate by legislation reveals the negative Commerce Clause decisions as something other than what is typically referred to as constitutional law. Congress cannot, for example, set aside restrictive Court rulings on free speech, due process, or equal protection. Treating the dormant Commerce Clause as another variant of federal common law (although derived from constitutionally based principles) may be the more accurate characterization.

---

[h] It is argued in Suzanna Sherry, Normalizing *Erie*, 69 Vand. L. Rev. 1161 (2016), that this view of the dormant Commerce Clause cases provides a model for all *Erie* questions. "The principal importance of the dormant commerce clause doctrine," she says, "is that it establishes as a first principle that courts have the authority to protect federal interests even when those interests are unprotected or unarticulated by Congress." She concludes that the *Erie* inquiry should be "normalized" by applying state law in all *Erie* situations unless it is "overcome by a sufficiently strong unarticulated federal interest."

For criticism of the Monaghan position, see Thomas S. Schrock and Robert C. Welsh, Reconsidering the Constitutional Common Law, 91 Harv. L. Rev. 1117, 1138–41 (1978). See also Patrick C. McGinley, Trashing the Constitution: Judicial Activism, the Dormant Commerce Clause, and the Federalism Mantra, 71 Ore. L. Rev. 409 (1992) (arguing that the dormant Commerce Clause decisions are inconsistent with the values underlying *Erie*).

(iii) Res Judicata Effect of Federal Court Decisions

What law controls the claim-preclusive effect of a federal-court judgment in a diversity case? State or federal? In Semtek International, Inc. v. Lockheed Martin Corp., 531 U.S. 497 (2001), a unanimous Supreme Court ruled that federal law controlled, even though no federal statute or rule of procedure spoke to the question. "In short," said Justice Scalia, "federal common law governs the claim-preclusive effect of a dismissal by a federal court sitting in diversity." In determining the federal rule on preclusion, however, the Supreme Court looked to the law of the state in which the federal court sat. State law thus applied indirectly, but the Supreme Court reserved "the last word on the claim-preclusive effect of *all* federal judgments." In other words, state law mattered only if, and to the extent that, federal law allowed.[i]

What is the source of res judicata rules if the first and successor cases are based on federal question jurisdiction? The Court held a restrictive Texas abortion law unconstitutional in Whole Woman's Health v. Hellerstedt, 579 U.S. ___, 136 S.Ct. 2292 (2016), but it first faced a res judicata problem. A prior federal decision upholding the law arguably precluded the attack that was before the Court. Over a dissent by Justice Alito joined by Chief Justice Roberts and Justice Thomas, the Court held that the case could be resolved on the merits. In the absence of an applicable federal statute, the Court relied for its conclusion on general principles derived from prior federal cases, ALI Restatements, treatises, and the like. The opinion did not mention the words "federal common law," nor did it refer to the laws of any state. The dissent came to a different res judicata conclusion in reliance on the same sources, also without reference to the concept of federal common law or the law of any state.

Is the *Whole Woman's Health* res judicata debate best regarded as a dispute over the proper outcome based on federal common law principles? Is there any reasonable alternative to federal common law in the *Whole Woman's Health* and *Semtek* situations? What else could the Supreme Court do?

(iv) Dice v. Akron, Canton & Youngstown Railroad

In Dice v. Akron, Canton & Youngstown Railroad Co., 342 U.S. 359 (1952), a railroad employee brought a Federal Employers Liability Act (FELA) action in state court against his employer.[j] The railroad's defense was that the employee had signed a release. The employee responded that

---

[i]   For an endorsement of the *Semtek* result, see Stephen B. Burbank, *Semtek*, Forum Shopping, and Federal Common Law, 77 Notre Dame L. Rev. 1027 (2002). See also Robert J. Pushaw, Jr., The Inherent Powers of Federal Courts and the Structural Constitution, 86 Iowa L. Rev. 735 (2001); John Harrison, The Power of Congress over the Rules of Precedent, 50 Duke L.J. 503 (2002). For consideration of the power of federal courts to make federal common law on "procedural" topics as a general matter, see Amy Coney Barrett, Procedural Common Law, 94 Va. L. Rev. 813 (2008).

[j]   The FELA authorizes negligence actions in federal court against railroads for injuries to its employees. It functions in lieu of relief under worker's compensation laws for this class of employees.

he had signed the release in reliance on the railroad's deliberately false statement that the document was merely a receipt for back wages.

On the question whether federal or state law controlled the validity of the purported release, the Supreme Court substituted the "correct federal rule" for the rule that had been applied in the state litigation. As to why it did so, the Court said:

> We . . . hold that validity of releases under the Federal Employers' Liability Act raises a federal question to be determined by federal rather than state law. Congress in § 1 of the act granted petitioner a right to recover against his employer for damages negligently inflicted. State laws are not controlling in determining what the incidents of this federal right shall be. Manifestly the federal rights affording relief to injured railroad employees under a federally declared standard could be defeated if states were permitted to have the final say as to what defenses could and could not be properly interposed to suits under the act. Moreover, only if federal law controls can the federal act be given that uniform application throughout the country essential to effectuate its purposes. Releases and other devices designed to liquidate or defeat injured employees' claims play an important part in the federal act's administration. Their validity is but one of the many interrelated questions that must constantly be determined in these cases according to a uniform federal law.

What the Court did in *Dice* has often been called "interstitial" lawmaking. The federal courts fill in the gaps of a comprehensive federal statutory scheme in a manner consistent with the policies Congress is seeking to promote.[k] Does *Dice* differ from the other examples of federal common law discussed above? Is it consistent with *Erie*?

6. CONCLUDING COMMENTS

The phenomenon of federal common law is front and center in Chapter II and just beneath the surface elsewhere in this book. The examples in the preceding note merely set the stage for asking whether the creation of federal common law in a particular setting can be reconciled with the understanding of *Erie* as a federalism/separation-of-powers limitation on the capacity of the federal courts to make law. Consider Judge Henry Friendly's famous comment:

> By focusing judicial attention on the nature of the right being enforced, *Erie* caused the principle of a specialized federal common law, binding in all courts because of its source, to develop within a quarter century into a powerful unifying force. Just as federal

---

[k] See Henry J. Friendly, In Praise of *Erie*—And of the New Federal Common Law, 39 N.Y.U. L. Rev. 383, 407 (1964) ("the normal filling of statutory interstices"). Another example of "interstitial" law-making is found in the federal criminal law. Generally applicable defenses, for example, such as entrapment and self-defense and at one point insanity, are derived from judge-made law that only in a highly attenuated sense could be described as "interpretations" of federal statutes. See, e.g., Dixon v. United States, 548 U.S. 1 (2006) (burden of proof on duress defense).

courts now conform to state decisions on issues properly for the states, state courts must conform to federal decisions in areas where Congress, acting within powers granted to it, has manifested, be it ever so lightly, an intention to that end. . . .

These complementary concepts—that federal courts must follow state decisions on matters of substantive law appropriately cognizable by the states and that state courts must follow federal decisions on subjects within national legislative power where Congress has so directed [or the basic scheme of the Constitution demands]—seem so beautifully simple, and so simply beautiful, that we must wonder why a century and a half were needed to discover them, and must wonder even more why anyone should want to shy away once the discovery was made. . . .[l]

Note that the *Erie* requirement that federal courts follow state law where applicable, as well as the requirement that they follow federal law when it should be applied, is not limited to diversity cases. One obvious example occurs when the Supreme Court reviews state court decisions. Long before *Erie*, the Court limited its review of state-court decisions to questions of federal law. See Murdock v. Memphis, 87 U.S. (20 Wall.) 590 (1875), a decision considered more fully later in this chapter. As *Murdock* makes plain, the relationship between state and federal law envisioned by *Erie* applies whether the case starts in federal or state court.

The same can be true when federal district courts hear cases under their federal question jurisdiction. In United Mine Workers of America v. Gibbs, 383 U.S. 715 (1966), the Supreme Court held that a federal court hearing a federal claim under federal question jurisdiction could also hear a related state claim arising out of the same facts by exercising what has come to be known as "supplemental" jurisdiction. Whenever such jurisdiction is exercised, *Erie* requires application of state law to the state claim, even though federal jurisdiction over the case is based on a federal question.[m]

In addition, even diversity cases can involve questions of federal law. The canonical examples are Francis v. Southern Pacific Co., 333 U.S. 445 (1948), and Sola Electric Co. v. Jefferson Electric Co., 317 U.S. 173 (1942). *Francis* was a diversity case based on common-law negligence. The plaintiff's decedent was a railroad employee killed while riding as a passenger on a free pass. The Court held that various federal decisions and statutes on the liability of railroads to their employees precluded recovery for ordinary negligence. *Sola* was a suit by a patentee under a licensing agreement. The agreement was governed by state law, and jurisdiction was based on diversity of citizenship. The defendant asserted that the patent covered by the

---

[l]   Henry J. Friendly, In Praise of *Erie*—And of the New Federal Common Law, 39 N.Y.U. L. Rev. 383, 405, 407, 422 (1964), also printed in Henry J. Friendly, Benchmarks (1967). The bracketed phrase in the last paragraph appears in the later book but not the essay as originally published in the N.Y.U. Law Review.—[Footnote by eds.]

[m]   A less obvious example of the relevance of *Erie* in non-diversity cases occurs in federal drug or firearm prosecutions where the crucial evidence is obtained by a state police officer following a motor vehicle stop. The validity of the stop will often be a matter of state law. For discussion of this problem, see Wayne A. Logan, *Erie* and Federal Criminal Courts, 63 Vand. L. Rev. 1243 (2010).

license was invalid and that the licensing agreement violated the Sherman Antitrust Act. Both defenses were controlled by federal law.

The result, as Judge Friendly said, is a system that is "beautifully simple, and . . . simply beautiful" in the sense that specific issues are governed by state law or federal law, as the case may be, no matter in what court the case is litigated and no matter the jurisdictional basis if it is brought in federal court. It is the *issue* that determines whether federal or state law will be applied, not the location of the court or the basis for its jurisdiction.[n]

Klaxon Co. v. Stentor Electric Manufacturing Co., Inc.

Supreme Court of the United States, 1941.
313 U.S. 487.

■ MR. JUSTICE REED delivered the opinion of the Court.

The principal question in this case is whether in diversity cases the federal courts must follow conflict of laws rules prevailing in the states in which they sit. . . .

In 1918 respondent, a New York corporation, transferred its entire business to petitioner, a Delaware corporation. Petitioner contracted to use its best efforts to further the manufacture and sale of certain patented devices covered by the agreement, and respondent was to have a share of petitioner's profits. The agreement was executed in New York, the assets were transferred there, and petitioner began performance there although later it moved its operations to other states. Respondent was voluntarily dissolved under New York law in 1919. Ten years later it instituted this action in the United States District Court for the District of Delaware, alleging that petitioner had failed to perform its agreement to use its best efforts. Jurisdiction rested on diversity of citizenship. In 1939 respondent recovered a jury verdict of $100,000, upon which judgment was entered. Respondent then moved to correct the judgment by adding interest at the rate of six per cent from June 1, 1929, the date the action had been brought. The basis of the motion was the provision in the New York Civil Practice Act directing that in contract actions interest be added to the principal sum "whether theretofore liquidated or unliquidated." The District Court granted the motion, taking the view that the rights of the parties were governed by New York law and that under New York law the addition of such interest was mandatory. The

---

[n] Friendly's *In Praise of Erie* article was the "lodestar, or at any rate an inspiration" for a Symposium on *Erie* published in the Journal of Law, Economics & Policy in 2013. See Michael S. Greve and Richard A. Epstein, Introduction: *Erie Railroad* at Seventy-Five, 10 J.L. Econ. & Pol'y 1 (2013); Ernest A. Young, A General Defense of *Erie Railroad Co. v. Tompkins*, 10 J. L., Econ. & Pol'y 17 (2013); Allan Erbsen, *Erie*'s Starting Points: The Potential Role of Default Rules in Structuring Choice of Law Analysis, 10 J.L. Econ. & Pol'y 125 (2013); Samuel Issacharoff, Federalized America: Reflections on *Erie v. Tompkins* and State-Based Regulation, 10 J.L. Econ. & Pol'y 199 (2013); Robert R. Gasaway and Ashley C. Parrish, In Praise of *Erie*—and its Eventual Demise, 10 J.L. Econ. & Pol'y 225 (2013). Other articles in the Symposium are cited where more directly relevant to the topic under discussion. See also Allan Erbsen, *Erie*'s Four Functions: Reframing Choice of Law in Federal Courts, 89 Notre Dame L. Rev. 579 (2013).

Circuit Court of Appeals affirmed and we granted certiorari, limited to the question whether the New York Civil Practice Act is applicable to an action in the federal court in Delaware.

The Circuit Court of Appeals was of the view that under New York law the right to interest before verdict went to the substance of the obligation, and that proper construction of the contract in suit fixed New York as the place of performance. It then concluded that [New York law] was applicable to the case because:

> it is clear by what we think is undoubtedly the better view of the law that the rules for ascertaining the measure of damages are not a matter of procedure at all, but are matters of substance which should be settled by reference to the law of the appropriate state according to the type of case being tried in the forum. The measure of damages for breach of a contract is determined by the law of the place of performance.

. . . Application of the New York statute apparently followed from the court's independent determination of the "better view" without regard to Delaware law, for no Delaware decision or statute was cited or discussed.

We are of opinion that the prohibition declared in Erie Railroad Co. v. Tompkins, 304 U.S. 64 (1938), against such independent determinations by the federal courts, extends to the field of conflict of laws. The conflict of laws rules to be applied by the federal court in Delaware must conform to those prevailing in Delaware's state courts. Otherwise the accident of diversity of citizenship would constantly disturb equal administration of justice in co-ordinate state and federal courts sitting side by side. Any other ruling would do violence to the principle of uniformity within a state, upon which the *Tompkins* decision is based. Whatever lack of uniformity this may produce between federal courts in different states is attributable to our federal system, which leaves to a state, within the limits permitted by the Constitution, the right to pursue local policies diverging from those of its neighbors. It is not for the federal courts to thwart such local policies by enforcing an independent "general law" of conflict of laws. Subject only to review by this Court on any federal question that may arise, Delaware is free to determine whether a given matter is to be governed by the law of the forum or some other law. This Court's views are not the decisive factor in determining the applicable conflicts rule. And the proper function of the Delaware federal court is to ascertain what the state law is, not what it ought to be. . . .

Accordingly, the judgment is reversed and the case remanded to the Circuit Court of Appeals for decision in conformity with the law of Delaware.

Reversed.

NOTES ON CHOICE OF STATE LAW BY FEDERAL COURTS

1. CONFLICT OF LAWS

Litigation often concerns events, transactions, or occurrences involving more than one state. This is not problematic if the law is the same in each of the involved states. But where there are significant differences, the law must develop rules to select which of the conflicting rules to apply. *Klaxon* has come to stand for the proposition that when federal courts are bound by *Erie* to use state law, they are also obligated to use the conflict-of-laws rules of the forum state. This is one of the most important applications of *Erie*.

Conflict of laws is a large and complicated subject that cannot be adequately summarized here. Perhaps it is sufficient to know two things. First, conflicts rules vary substantially from state to state. There is no unanimity among American jurisdictions in their approach to the rules governing choice of law. Second, in many if not most cases, conflicts rules are applied with a home-state bias. In a sense, this is predictable, as each judge has a natural inclination to follow the law with which he or she is familiar. Moreover, the primacy of the forum's law is reinforced by the rule that, even when another state's law would ordinarily apply, the forum need not enforce any rule against (its conception of) "public policy." The "public policy" limitation provides a doctrinal justification for preferring the law of the forum. It is not unusual for a plaintiff's choice of forum to turn on the expectation of gaining a favorable rule of law. The result is an opportunity for forum-shopping among state courts and, under *Klaxon*, among federal courts in different states.[a]

2. SUBSTANCE AND PROCEDURE IN CHOICE OF LAW

The law of conflicts embraces a substance/procedure distinction analogous to, but different from, the substance/procedure distinction in *Erie*. When federal courts apply state substantive law, they nevertheless follow federal procedures. See Hanna v. Plumer, 380 U.S. 460 (1965). Similarly, when state courts apply the substantive law of other states, they nevertheless follow forum state procedures. Thus, one of the most important questions in the law of conflicts is whether a particular rule is substantive (in which case the law of another state may apply) or procedural (in which case the forum state's law will prevail).

The interaction of these two substance/procedure distinctions can be surprising. Consider Sampson v. Channell, 110 F.2d 754 (1st Cir. 1940), a

---

[a] For criticism of this approach, see Patrick J. Borchers, The Origins of Diversity Jurisdiction, the Rise of Legal Positivism, and a Brave New World for *Erie* and *Klaxon*, 72 Texas L. Rev. 79 (1993) (arguing that *Erie* and *Klaxon* "should be replaced with an approach that calls on diversity courts to apply an independent choice-of-law approach" so that "diversity jurisdiction [can] fulfill its promise as an instrument of national harmony"). For a different version of this problem based on class action legislation enacted in 2005, see Patrick Woolley, *Erie* and Choice of Law after the Class Action Fairness Act, 80 Tul. L. Rev. 1723 (2006). For an argument that the *Klaxon* requirement that federal courts follow state choice of law rules should not necessarily apply to cases involving the decision whether to apply the laws of a foreign country, see Donald Earl Childress, III, When *Erie* Goes International, 105 Nw. U. L. Rev. 1531 (2011).

pre-*Klaxon* case which anticipated that decision. *Sampson* involved the burden of proof for contributory negligence. An automobile accident in Maine led to a federal diversity action in Massachusetts. Massachusetts required the defendant to prove contributory negligence, while Maine required the plaintiff to disprove it. Because the accident occurred in Maine, a Massachusetts court would have followed Maine law on all substantive issues. But Massachusetts regarded burden of proof as procedural. Hence, under the Massachusetts law of conflicts, a Massachusetts court would have followed its own rule and put the burden of proof on the defendant regardless of where the accident occurred. The question was what a federal court sitting in Massachusetts should do in this situation.

The First Circuit concluded that *Erie* required the federal courts to follow state law on questions of substantive law and that allocation of the burden of proof was substantive under *Erie*. The next question was which state's law should be used, Massachusetts or Maine? Anticipating the result in *Klaxon,* the First Circuit held that the federal court should apply the conflicts rules of the forum state. Since Massachusetts classified the burden of proof as procedural and therefore governed by the law of the forum, a federal court sitting in Massachusetts was required to reach the same result. The court admitted that it might seem a "surface incongruity" to apply Massachusetts law first because it was "substantive" and then because it was "procedural," but concluded that *Erie* commanded that result.

3.   *GRIFFIN V. MCCOACH*

It is possible under *Klaxon* that the laws of a forum state will be applied to suits that could not be litigated in that state's courts. The situation arose in Griffin v. McCoach, 313 U.S. 498 (1941), decided on the same day as *Klaxon*.

The personal representative of a deceased Texas citizen filed suit in a federal court in Texas to collect on an insurance policy issued by Prudential Life Insurance. Other claimants had acquired an interest in the policy in New York under contracts that were valid in that state. These claimants lacked an "insurable interest" in the decedent under Texas law. Prudential invoked the Federal Interpleader Act, joined all claimants to the policy, paid the money into court, and withdrew from the suit. The Supreme Court held that Texas choice of law rules should apply, and that "it is for Texas to say whether its public policy permits a beneficiary of an insurance policy on the life of a Texas citizen to recover where no insurable interest in the decedent exists in the beneficiary."

On the facts of *Griffin*, it appears that the Texas courts could not have exercised personal jurisdiction over the New York claimants. An ordinary in personam action to cut off their interests therefore could not have been brought in a Texas state court. Personal jurisdiction was available in federal court only because the Federal Interpleader Act authorizes nationwide service of process. This procedure brought the claimants into a federal court in Texas, where Texas law could be applied to foreclose their interests, even though Texas could not have reached them directly. The *Griffin* opinion made no mention of this anomaly.

Similar situations can arise when a federal statute authorizes nation-wide service of process and the federal court elects to hear a pendent state claim. Additionally, the problem can arise under the "bulge" provision of Federal Rule of Civil Procedure 4(k)(1)(B). That provision applies in Rule 14 impleader (where the defendant joins a third-party defendant who is or may be liable to the defendant if the plaintiff prevails) and Rule 19 joinder of necessary parties. In these situations, the third-party defendant or necessary party can be served anywhere within a 100-mile radius of the courthouse, even if that circle "bulges" into another state. Again, *Klaxon* might command that federal courts apply a state's law to litigants who could not be reached by that state's courts.

4. TRANSFER FOR CONVENIENCE: *VAN DUSEN V. BARRACK*

Section 1404(a) of title 28 provides that "[f]or the convenience of parties and witnesses, in the interest of justice, a district court may transfer any civil action to any other district or division where it might have been brought or to any district or division to which all parties have consented." Ordinarily, transfer is sought by defendants. Van Dusen v. Barrack, 376 U.S. 612 (1964), was such a case. It involved claims by the personal representatives of 40 Pennsylvania decedents killed in a plane crash in Boston. They filed an action in a federal District Court in Pennsylvania. More than 100 actions against the same defendants were pending in a District Court in Massachusetts. Massachusetts law limited recovery for wrongful death to $20,000. Pennsylvania had no such limitation. It was unclear whether the Pennsylvania state courts would apply their own law to the limitation question—as some other states had done—or whether they would apply the law of the place where the accident occurred (Massachusetts).

One of the questions before the Supreme Court was whether, if the case were transferred to Massachusetts, the federal court would apply the conflicts principles of the transferor forum (Pennsylvania) or the transferee forum (Massachusetts). The Court ruled that Pennsylvania conflicts rules should govern. Plaintiffs were entitled to retain whatever advantages they achieved in the forum they selected, and defendants should not be able to secure a change of law by changing venue.

The Court did not address the choice-of-law implications of a transfer under 28 U.S.C. § 1406(a), which provides for transfer "in the interest of justice" of a suit brought in a district without proper venue (unlike the forum non conveniens provision of § 1404(a), which requires proper venue in the transferor court). The *Van Dusen* Court also reserved decision on what would happen if the plaintiff requested transfer or if the transferor forum would have dismissed the action on grounds of forum non conveniens.[b]

---

[b]   For discussion of these issues, see Robert A. Ragazzo, Transfer and Choice of Federal Law: The Appellate Model, 93 Mich. L. Rev. 703 (1995); Louise Weinberg, Choosing Law: The Limitations Debates, 1991 U. Ill. L. Rev. 683; Joan Steinman, Law of the Case: A Judicial Puzzle in Consolidated and Transferred Cases and in Multidistrict Litigation, 135 Pa. L. Rev. 595 (1987).

5.   TRANSFER FOR CONVENIENCE BY PLAINTIFF: *FERENS V. JOHN DEERE CO.*

One of the questions left open in *Van Dusen*—whether the choice of law rules of the transferor forum would apply if the *plaintiff* moved for transfer under § 1404(a)—was answered in the affirmative in Ferens v. John Deere Co., 494 U.S. 516 (1990).

Ferens was injured in Pennsylvania by a John Deere product. He brought a diversity action in federal court in Pennsylvania. Since the suit was filed after expiration of Pennsylvania's two-year statute of limitations on torts, the plaintiff brought only contract and breach-of-warranty claims. Shortly thereafter, he filed a second diversity suit in a Mississippi federal court, where he raised his tort claims. The Mississippi statute of limitations, which would have applied in state court, was six years. As Justice Kennedy's opinion for the Court said, the issue before the Supreme Court "arose when the Ferenses took their forum shopping a step further: having chosen the federal court in Mississippi to take advantage of the state's limitations period, they next moved, under § 1404(a), to transfer the action to the federal court in Pennsylvania on the ground that Pennsylvania was a more convenient forum." The motion to transfer was granted, but the Pennsylvania District Court dismissed the action under the Pennsylvania statute of limitations. The Supreme Court reversed the dismissal, five to four.

(i)   The Majority Opinion

Speaking for the Court, Justice Kennedy derived three policies from *Van Dusen:*

> First, § 1404(a) should not deprive parties of state-law advantages that exist absent diversity jurisdiction. Second, § 1404(a) should not create or multiply opportunities for forum shopping. Third, the decision to transfer venue under § 1404(a) should turn on considerations of convenience and the interest of justice rather than on the possible prejudice resulting from a change of law.

The first policy supported using the law of the transferor forum to preserve the plaintiff's advantages in choosing the forum state, even when the plaintiff moved for transfer. Second, Justice Kennedy noted that application of the transferor law did not create or multiply the opportunities for forum-shopping. The plaintiff could not use transfer to obtain a law that could not have been obtained through selection of the initial forum. "If it does make selection of the most favorable law more convenient, it does no more than recognize a forum shopping choice that already exists." And the third policy also supported transferor law, as the administration of § 1404(a) would be much simpler if courts could focus solely on "convenience and the interest of justice" rather than difficult questions of choice of law. The Court concluded that "[f]oresight and judicial economy now seem to favor the simple rule that the law does not change following a transfer of venue under § 1404(a)," and added the following comments:

Some may object that a district court in Pennsylvania should not have to apply a Mississippi statute of limitations to a Pennsylvania cause of action. This point, although understandable, should have little to do with the outcome of this case. Congress gave the Ferenses the power to seek a transfer in § 1404(a) and our decision in *Van Dusen* already could require a district court in Pennsylvania to apply the Mississippi statute of limitations to Pennsylvania claims. Our rule may seem too generous because it allows the Ferenses to have both their choice of law and their choice of forum, or even to reward the Ferenses for conduct that seems manipulative. We nonetheless see no alternative rule that would produce a more acceptable result. Deciding that the transferee law should apply, in effect, would tell the Ferenses that they should have continued to litigate their warranty action in Pennsylvania and their tort action in Mississippi. Some might find this preferable, but we do not. We have made quite clear that "[t]o permit a situation in which two cases involving precisely the same issues are simultaneously pending in different district courts leads to the wastefulness of time, energy and money that § 1404(a) was designed to prevent." Continental Grain Co. v. Barge FBL-585, 364 U.S. 19, 26 (1960).

From a substantive standpoint, two further objections give us pause but do not persuade us to change our rule. First, one might ask why we require the Ferenses to file in the District Court in Mississippi at all. Efficiency might seem to dictate a rule allowing plaintiffs in the Ferenses' position not to file in an inconvenient forum and then to return to a convenient forum though a transfer of venue, but instead simply to file in the convenient forum and ask for the law of the inconvenient forum to apply. Although our rule may invoke certain formality, one must remember that § 1404(a) does not provide for an automatic transfer of venue. The section, instead, permits a transfer only when convenient and "in the interest of justice." Plaintiffs in the position of the Ferenses must go to the distant forum because they have no guarantee, until the court there examines the facts, that they may obtain a transfer. . . .

Second, one might contend that, because no per se rule requiring a court to apply either the transferor law or the transferee law will seem appropriate in all circumstances, we should develop more sophisticated federal choice of law rules for diversity actions involving transfers. To a large extent, however, state conflicts of law rules already ensure that appropriate laws will apply to diversity cases. Federal law, as a general matter, does not interfere with these rules. In addition, even if more elaborate federal choice of law rules would not run afoul of *Klaxon* and *Erie,* we believe that applying the law of the transferor forum effects the appropriate balance between fairness and simplicity. For the foregoing reasons, we conclude that Mississippi's statute of limitations should govern the Ferenses' action.

(ii) The Dissent

Justice Scalia, joined by Justices Brennan, Marshall, and Blackmun, dissented. The question, he said, was whether the normal result that would follow from *Erie* and *Klaxon* (here that a Pennsylvania District Court would apply Pennsylvania choice-of-law rules) should be displaced by § 1404(a). In *Van Dusen* such displacement was appropriate for two reasons:

> First, we thought it highly unlikely that Congress, in enacting § 1404(a), meant to provide defendants with a device by which to manipulate the substantive rules that would be applied. That conclusion rested upon the fact that the law grants the plaintiff the advantage of choosing the venue in which his action will be tried, with whatever state-law advantages accompany that choice. A defensive use of § 1404(a) in order to deprive the plaintiff of this "venue privilege" would allow the defendant to " 'get a change of law as a bonus for a change of venue' " and would permit the defendant to engage in forum shopping among states, a privilege that the *Klaxon* regime reserved for plaintiffs. Second, we concluded that the policies of *Erie* and *Klaxon* would be undermined by application of the transferee court's choice-of-law principles in the case of a defendant-initiated transfer because then "the 'accident' of federal diversity jurisdiction" would enable the defendant "to utilize a transfer to achieve a result in federal court which could not have been achieved in the courts of the state where the action was filed." The goal of *Erie* and *Klaxon,* we reasoned, was to prevent "forum shopping" as between state and federal systems; the plaintiff makes a choice of forum-law by filing the complaint, and that choice must be honored in federal court, just as it would have been honored in state court, where the defendant would not have been able to transfer the case to another state.

Scalia found these reasons inapplicable in *Ferens*:

> In my view, neither of [these] considerations is served—and indeed both are positively defeated—by a departure from *Klaxon* in [this] context. First, just as it is unlikely that Congress, in enacting § 1404(a), meant to provide the defendant with a vehicle by which to manipulate in his favor the substantive law to be applied in a diversity case, so too is it unlikely that Congress meant to provide the *plaintiff* with a vehicle by which to appropriate the law of a distant and inconvenient forum in which he does not intend to litigate, and to carry that prize back to the state in which he wishes to try the case. Second, application of the transferor court's law in this context would encourage forum-shopping between federal and state courts in the same jurisdiction on the basis of differential substantive law. It is true, of course, that the plaintiffs here did not select the *Mississippi* federal court in preference to the Mississippi state courts because of any differential substantive law; the former, like the latter, would have applied Mississippi choice-of-law rules, and thus the Mississippi statute of limitations. But one must be blind

to reality to say that it is the *Mississippi* federal court in which these plaintiffs have chosen to sue. That was merely a way station en route to suit in the *Pennsylvania* federal court. The plaintiffs were seeking to achieve exactly what *Klaxon* was designed to prevent: the use of a Pennsylvania federal court instead of a Pennsylvania state court in order to obtain application of a different substantive law. Our decision in *Van Dusen* compromised "the principle of uniformity within a state" [quoting *Klaxon*] only in the abstract, but today's decision compromises it precisely in the respect that matters—i.e., insofar as it bears upon the plaintiff's choice between a state and a federal forum. The significant federal judicial policy expressed in *Erie* and *Klaxon* is reduced to a laughing-stock if it can so readily be evaded through filing-and-transfer.[c]

6. TRANSFER FOR CONVENIENCE: CONTRACTUAL FORUM-SELECTION CLAUSE

The Court held in Atlantic Marine Construction Company, Inc. v. United States District Court for the Western District of Texas, 571 U.S. ___, 134 S.Ct. 568 (2013), that a forum-selection clause in a private contract can be enforced by a motion to transfer under 28 U.S.C. § 1404(a). Atlantic Marine, a Virginia corporation, contracted with the Army Corps of Engineers to build a child-development center in Texas. It then entered into a subcontract with a Texas corporation for a part of the project. One of the terms of the subcontract was that any dispute "shall be" litigated in a particular Virginia state or federal court. A payment dispute resulted in a diversity suit by the Texas corporation against Atlantic Marine in a federal court in Texas. Atlantic Marine moved to transfer the suit to Virginia under § 1404(a). The District Court denied the motion, and the Court of Appeals denied mandamus on the merits.

The Supreme Court unanimously reversed. It held that:

> When the parties have agreed to a valid forum-selection clause, a district court should ordinarily transfer the case to the forum specified in that clause. Only under extraordinary circumstances unrelated to the convenience of the parties should a § 1404(a) motion be denied.

It added that "the presence of a valid forum-selection clause requires district courts to adjust their usual § 1404(a) analysis in three ways." The first is that "the plaintiff's choice of forum merits no weight." The second is that arguments about the private interests of the parties should not be considered: "[A] district court should transfer [such a] case unless extraordinary circumstances unrelated to the convenience of the parties clearly disfavor a transfer." And third:

> [W]hen a party bound by a forum-selection clause flouts its contractual obligation and files suit in a different forum, a § 1404(a)

---

[c] For criticism of *Ferens* and the "double forum shopping" it allows, see Kimberly Jade Norwood, Double Forum Shopping and the Extension of *Ferens* to Federal Claims That Borrow State Limitations Periods, 44 Emory L.J. 501 (1995).—[Footnote by eds.]

transfer of venue will not carry with it the original venue's choice-of-law rules. . . .

The policies motivating our exception to the *Klaxon* rule for § 1404(a) transfers . . . do not support an extension to cases where a defendant's motion is premised on enforcement of a valid forum-selection clause. To the contrary, those considerations lead us to reject the rule that the law of the court in which the plaintiff inappropriately filed suit should follow the case to the forum contractually selected by the parties. In Van Dusen v. Barrack, 376 U.S. 612 (1964), we were concerned that, through a § 1404(a) transfer, a defendant could "defeat the state-law advantages that might accrue from the exercise of [the plaintiff's] venue privilege." But . . . a plaintiff who files suit in violation of a forum-selection clause enjoys no such "privilege" with respect to its choice of forum, and therefore it is entitled to no concomitant "state-law advantages." Not only would it be inequitable to allow the plaintiff to fasten its choice of substantive law to the venue transfer, but it would also encourage gamesmanship. Because "§ 1404(a) should not create or multiply opportunities for forum shopping," Ferens v. John Deere Co., 494 U.S. 516, 523 (1990), we will not apply the *Van Dusen* rule when a transfer stems from enforcement of a forum-selection clause: The court in the contractually selected venue should not apply the law of the transferor venue to which the parties waived their right.

When parties have contracted in advance to litigate disputes in a particular forum, courts should not unnecessarily disrupt the parties' settled expectations. A forum-selection clause, after all, may have figured centrally in the parties' negotiations and may have affected how they set monetary and other contractual terms; it may, in fact, have been a critical factor in their agreement to do business together in the first place. In all but the most unusual cases, therefore, "the interest of justice" is served by holding parties to their bargain.

7.   ASCERTAINING STATE LAW

Once it has been determined which state's law is to be applied, the analysis must turn to the content of that law. In the second sentence of the "Third" part of his *Erie* opinion, Justice Brandeis said that state law must be followed whether "declared by its legislature in a statute or by its highest court in a decision." What happens if the highest state court has not spoken? Do lower-court decisions control? In principle, the answer seems easy. A federal court should do its best to predict what the state's highest court would say if faced with the question (which, indeed, is exactly what a lower state court would do). Lower-court decisions should be followed if they are consistent with recent decisions by the highest court and appear to be accurate forecasts of what that court would say if presented with the issue.

The Supreme Court has not always followed this course. Its most radical departure was condemned by Henry J. Friendly, In Praise of *Erie*—And of the New Federal Common Law, 39 N.Y.U. L. Rev. 383, 400 (1964), as "the excesses of 311 U.S. as to the respect that federal judges must pay to decisions of lower state courts." Judge Friendly had in mind a series of cases decided by the Supreme Court in 1940. The "nadir," said Friendly, was Fidelity Union Trust Co. v. Field, 311 U.S. 169 (1940), where the Court required adherence to the decisions of two New Jersey trial judges with statewide jurisdiction, even though the decisions had no precedential effect on other judges of equal status and even though they appeared to be rather plainly wrong.

Recent decisions are more in line with Commissioner v. Estate of Bosch, 387 U.S. 456, 465 (1967), where the Court said:

> [T]he state's highest court is the best authority on its own law. If there be no decision by that court then federal authorities must apply what they find to be the state law after giving "proper regard" to relevant rulings of other courts of the state. In this respect, it may be said to be, in effect, sitting as a [lower] state court.[d]

This does not, of course, mean that determining the content of state law will be easy.

One possibility when determining the content of state law is especially difficult would be to refuse to adjudicate the case and remit the parties to a new lawsuit in state court. The Supreme Court, however, has categorically rejected this solution:

> Congress having adopted the policy of opening the federal courts to suitors in all diversity cases involving the jurisdictional amount, we can discern in its action no recognition of a policy which would exclude cases from the jurisdiction merely because they involve state law or because the law is uncertain or difficult to determine. . . .

---

[d]   For examinations of the meaning of *Bosch* and recommendations on its proper application, see Paul L. Caron, The Federal Courts of Appeals' Use of State Court Decisions in Tax Cases: "Proper Regard" Means "No Regard," 46 Okla. L. Rev. 443 (1993); Paul L. Caron, The Role of State Court Decisions in Federal Tax Litigation: *Bosch, Erie,* and Beyond, 71 Ore. L. Rev. 781 (1992). A related question is explored in Jonathan Remy Nash, Resuscitating Deference to Lower Federal Court Judges' Interpretations of State Law, 77 So. Calif. L. Rev. 975 (2004). For a different take on the role of federal courts in applying state law, see Robert A. Schapiro, Interjurisdictional Enforcement of Rights in a Post-*Erie* World, 46 Wm. & Mary L. Rev. 1399 (2005). For argument that the obligation to ascertain and follow state law includes a requirement that state statutory interpretation methodology be followed, see Abbe R. Gluck, Intersystemic Statutory Interpretation: Methodology as "Law" and the *Erie* Doctrine, 120 Yale L.J. 1898 (2011). For a response, see Michael Steven Green, *Erie*'s International Effect, 107 Nw. U. L. Rev. 165 (2013).

Suppose a state court follows a *Swift* approach and believes that courts of other jurisdictions are therefore as free as it was to determine the content of its law. Must a federal court in that state still follow state court precedent? For argument that the answer is "yes" and that *Erie* in effect stands for a nondiscrimination principle, see Michael Steven Green, *Erie*'s Suppressed Premise, 95 Minn. L. Rev. 1111 (2011): "A state supreme court may not free federal courts of the duty to follow its decisions concerning state law unless it is willing to free its own courts of the same duty." For a related argument that a state court interpreting the law of a sister state must decide the case as the sister state supreme court would, see Michael Steven Green, Horizontal *Erie* and the Presumption of Forum Law, 109 Mich. L. Rev. 1237 (2011).—[Footnote by eds.]

> *Erie* did not free the federal courts from the duty of deciding questions of state law in diversity cases. Instead it placed on them a greater responsibility for determining and applying state laws in all cases within their jurisdiction in which federal law does not govern.

Meredith v. Winter Haven, 320 U.S. 228, 236, 238 (1943). There is also an important practical reason supporting this result. Often one cannot determine until proceedings are well along whether a particular proposition of state law will be important. It can be difficult to make this prediction at the outset of litigation and inefficient to abort litigation in progress once an uncertain proposition of state law becomes determinative.

A second possibility would be to stay litigation in the federal court until a declaratory judgment proceeding or some other suitable state-court lawsuit could resolve any uncertain questions of state law. The inefficiencies of such abstention are apparent—two lawsuits going on at the same time to resolve one or more questions of state law. The Supreme Court has authorized this procedure in some specialized contexts, but the Court has never authorized abstention in routine diversity cases where the only concern is a lack of clarity in state law.

Finally there is the possibility of certification. Nearly all states plus the District of Columbia and Puerto Rico permit some form of certification of an uncertain question of local law by a federal court to a court empowered to make an authoritative decision. The Supreme Court has approved this procedure. See, e.g., Lehman Brothers v. Schein, 416 U.S. 386 (1974). *Lehman Brothers* was a shareholder's derivative suit filed in a New York federal court against a Florida corporation. Jurisdiction was based on diversity of citizenship. The District Court decided that Florida law would govern. Under Florida law, the question was whether the Florida courts would follow a New York precedent that supplied the theory of the plaintiff's cause of action, but this question was quite unclear. The Supreme Court vacated a guess by the lower federal courts and suggested that they consider certifying the question to the Florida Supreme Court:

> [*Meredith*] teaches that the mere difficulty in ascertaining local law is no excuse for remitting the parties to a state tribunal for the start of another lawsuit. We do not suggest that where there is doubt as to local law and where the certification procedure is available, resort to it is obligatory. It does, of course, in the long run save time, energy, and resources and helps build a cooperative judicial federalism. Its use in a given case rests in the sound discretion of the federal court.

> Here resort to it would seem particularly appropriate in view of the novelty of the question and the great unsettlement of Florida law, Florida being a distant state. When federal judges in New York attempt to predict uncertain Florida law, they act, as we have referred to ourselves on this Court in matters of state law, as "outsiders" lacking the common exposure to local law which comes from sitting in the jurisdiction.

Justice Rehnquist concurred, stating that "in a purely diversity case such as this one, the use of such a procedure is more a question of the considerable discretion of the federal court in going about the decision-making process than it is a question of a choice trenching upon the fundamentals of our federal-state jurisprudence." He also pointed out that the "other side of the certification coin is that it does in fact engender delay and create additional expense for litigants."[e]

SECTION 2. FEDERAL LAW IN STATE COURT

NOTES ON THE POWER OF STATE COURTS TO HEAR FEDERAL QUESTIONS

1. *GULF OFFSHORE CO.*

The power of state courts to hear federal questions was described in Gulf Offshore Co. v. Mobil Oil Corp., 453 U.S. 473 (1981):

> In considering the propriety of state-court jurisdiction over [a] federal claim, the Court begins with the presumption that state courts enjoy concurrent jurisdiction. Congress, however, may confine jurisdiction to the federal courts either explicitly or implicitly. Thus, the presumption of concurrent jurisdiction can be rebutted by an explicit statutory directive, by unmistakable implication from legislative history, or by a clear incompatibility between state-court jurisdiction and federal interests.

2. *TAFFLIN V. LEVITT*

Tafflin v. Levitt, 493 U.S. 455 (1990), concerned whether the state courts have concurrent jurisdiction to hear civil RICO[a] claims, a question on which the statute is completely silent. Speaking for a unanimous Court, Justice O'Connor framed the question as "whether state courts have been divested of jurisdiction to hear civil RICO claims 'by an explicit statutory directive, by unmistakable implication from legislative history, or by a clear incompatibility between state-court jurisdiction and federal interests'"

---

[e] For an example of unanimous use of the certification procedure by the Supreme Court seeking the answer to a question of state law that would shape the federal constitutional question presented by a petition for federal habeas corpus, see Fiore v. White, 528 U.S. 23 (1999). For academic commentary on this issue, see Gregory L. Acquaviva, The Certification of Unsettled Questions of State Law to State High Courts: The Third Circuit's Experience, 115 Penn St. L. Rev. 377 (2010); Bradford R. Clark, Ascertaining the Laws of the Several States: Positivism and Judicial Federalism after *Erie*, 145 U. Pa. L. Rev. 1459 (1997); Deborah J. Challener, Distinguishing Certification from Abstention in Diversity Cases: Postponement versus Abdication of the Duty to Exercise Jurisdiction, 38 Rutgers L.J. 847 (2007); Rebecca A. Cochran, Federal Court Certification of Questions of State Law to State Courts: A Theoretical and Empirical Study, 29 J. Legis. 157 (2003); Jonathan Remy Nash, Examining the Power of Federal Courts to Certify Questions of State Law, 88 Cornell L. Rev. 1672 (2003); Geri J. Yonover, A Kinder, Gentler *Erie*: Reigning in the Use of Certification, 47 Ark. L. Rev. 305 (1994); Benjamin C. Glassman, Making State Law in Federal Court, 41 Gonz. L. Rev. 237 (2005/06); Justin R. Long, Against Certification, 78 Geo. Wash. L. Rev. 114 (2009).

[a] "RICO" refers to the Racketeer Influenced and Corrupt Organizations Act, 18 U.S.C. §§ 1961–68. RICO is a criminal statute, but victims of RICO violations are permitted to sue the offenders for treble damages plus attorney's fees.

(quoting *Gulf Offshore*). Finding none of these factors, the Court concluded that state courts "retain their presumptive authority to adjudicate such claims." The Court also emphasized that its decision "creates no significant danger of inconsistent application of federal criminal law" because "federal courts . . . would not be bound by state court interpretations of the federal offenses constituting RICO's predicate acts" and "[s]tate courts adjudicating civil RICO claims will, in addition, be guided by federal court interpretations of the relevant federal criminal statutes, just as federal courts sitting in diversity are guided by state court interpretations of state law."

Justice Scalia, joined by Justice Kennedy, joined the Court's opinion but objected to the "dictum" in *Gulf Offshore*:

> State courts have jurisdiction over federal causes of action not because it is "conferred" upon them by the Congress; nor even because their inherent powers permit them to entertain transitory causes of action arising under the laws of foreign sovereigns; but because "[t]he laws of the United States are laws in the several states, and just as much binding on the citizens and courts thereof as the state laws are. . . . The two together form one system of jurisprudence, which constitutes the law of the land for the state; and the courts of the two jurisdictions are not foreign to each other." Claflin v. Houseman, 93 U.S. 130, 136–37 (1876).

> It therefore takes an affirmative act of power under the Supremacy Clause to oust the states of jurisdiction—an exercise of what one of our earliest cases referred to as "the power of Congress to *withdraw*" federal claims from state-court jurisdiction. Houston v. Moore, 18 U.S. (5 Wheat.) 1, 26 (1820) (emphasis added). . . .

> [I]n the standard fields of exclusive federal jurisdiction, the governing statutes specifically recite that suit may be brought "only" in federal court; that the jurisdiction of the federal courts shall be "exclusive"; or indeed even that the jurisdiction of the federal courts shall be "exclusive of the courts of the States."

> Assuming, however, that exclusion by implication is possible, surely what is required is implication in the text of the statute, and not merely, as the second part of the *Gulf Offshore* dictum would permit, through "unmistakable implication from legislative history." . . . [I]t is simply wrong in principle to assert that Congress can effect this affirmative legislative act by simply talking about it with unmistakable clarity. What is needed to oust the states of jurisdiction is congressional *action* (i.e., a provision of law), not merely congressional discussion.

> It is perhaps also true that implied preclusion can be established by the fact that a statute expressly mentions only federal courts, plus the fact that state-court jurisdiction would plainly disrupt the statutory scheme. That is conceivably what was meant by the third part of the *Gulf Offshore* dictum, "clear incompatibility between state-court jurisdiction and federal interests." If the phrase is interpreted more broadly than that, however—if it is

taken to assert some power on the part of this Court to exclude state-court jurisdiction when systemic federal interests make it undesirable—it has absolutely no foundation in our precedent. . . .

In sum: As the Court holds, the RICO cause of action meets none of the three tests for exclusion of state-court jurisdiction recited in *Gulf Offshore*. Since that is so, the proposition that meeting any one of the tests would have sufficed is dictum here, as it was there. In my view meeting the second test is assuredly not enough, and meeting the third may not be.[b]

INTRODUCTORY NOTES ON THE PROCEDURES TO BE FOLLOWED WHEN STATE COURTS HEAR FEDERAL CLAIMS

1. PRELIMINARY COMMENT

Plaintiffs who wish to assert a claim based on federal law will usually have the option of filing suit in state court. The state courts, naturally, will be inclined to follow their local procedures, a situation that can lead to potential clashes between those procedures and the obligation of the state courts to follow the substance of the federal law. This version of the familiar "substance-procedure" problem, as one would suspect, is not self-resolving.

2. *DICE V. AKRON, CANTON & YOUNGSTOWN RAILROAD CO.*

Most workers in this country are covered by worker's compensation statutes that exchange limited liability for certainty of recovery. Railroad workers must use the Federal Employers' Liability Act (FELA), under which they can obtain ordinary damages but only on proof of negligence. FELA cases can be litigated in state or federal court.

A well-known case in which the Supreme Court addressed the ensuing substance-procedure problem is Dice v. Akron, Canton & Youngstown Railroad Co., 342 U.S. 359 (1952). Dice involved a railroad fireman who was seriously injured when an engine jumped the track. He sued in state court under the FELA. The railroad defended on the ground that the plaintiff had signed a release, which the plaintiff said he had not read and which he claimed had been misrepresented as merely a receipt for back wages. The jury awarded the plaintiff $25,000, but the trial judge set aside the verdict, saying that the plaintiff had been "guilty of supine negligence" in failing to read the release and that the facts did not "sustain either in law or equity the allegations of fraud." The Ohio Supreme Court affirmed, ruling that Ohio, not federal, law governed on the validity of the release. The court also agreed that the relevant factual issues should have been, as they were, resolved by the judge and not the jury.

In an opinion by Justice Black, the Supreme Court reversed:

[Ohio] has provided jury trials for cases arising under the federal act but seeks to single out one phase of the question of fraudu-

---

b   For extensive consideration of the issues raised by *Tafflin* and *Gulf Offshore*, see Michael E. Solimine, Rethinking Exclusive Federal Jurisdiction, 52 U. Pitt. L. Rev. 383 (1991).

lent releases for determination by a judge rather than by a jury. . . . We have previously held that "[t]he right to trial by jury is 'a basic and fundamental feature of our system of federal jurisprudence'" and that it is "part and parcel of the remedy afforded railroad workers under the Employers' Liability Act." Bailey v. Central Vermont R. Inc., 319 U.S. 350, 354 (1943). We also recognized in that case that to deprive railroad workers of the benefit of a jury trial where there is evidence to support negligence "is to take away a goodly portion of the relief which Congress has afforded them." It follows that the right to trial by jury is too substantial a part of the rights accorded by the act to permit it to be classified as a mere "local rule of procedure" for denial in the manner that Ohio has here used.

Justice Frankfurter, joined by Justices Reed, Jackson, and Burton, dissented. Frankfurter agreed that federal law controlled the validity of the release, but disagreed that it governed allocation of that issue to judge or jury:

> Ohio, as do many other states, maintains the old division between law and equity as to the mode of trying issues, even though the same judge administers both. . . . To require Ohio to try a particular issue before a different fact-finder in negligence actions brought under the Employers' Liability Act from the fact-finder on the identical issue in every other negligence case disregards the settled distribution of judicial power between federal and state courts where Congress authorizes concurrent enforcement of federally-created rights. [A] state is under no duty to treat actions arising under that act differently from the way it adjudicates local actions for negligence, so far as the mechanics of litigation, the forms in which law is administered, are concerned. . . .

> Ohio and her sister states with a similar division of functions between law and equity are not trying to evade their duty under the Federal Employers' Liability Act; nor are they trying to make it more difficult for railroad workers to recover, than for those suing under local law. The states merely exercise a preference in adhering to historic ways of dealing with a claim of fraud. . . . The fact that Congress authorized actions under the Federal Employers' Liability Act to be brought in state as well as in federal courts seems a strange basis for the inference that Congress overrode state procedural arrangements controlling all other negligence suits in a state, by imposing upon state courts to which plaintiffs choose to go the rules prevailing in the federal courts regarding juries. Such an inference is admissible, so it seems to me, only on the theory that Congress included as part of the right created by the Employers' Liability Act an assumed likelihood that trying all issues to juries is more favorable to plaintiffs. . . .[c]

---

[c]   For interesting commentary on *Dice*, see Margaret G. Stewart, Federalism and Judicial Supremacy: Control of State Judicial Decision-Making, 68 Chi.-Kent L. Rev. 431 (1992).—[Footnote by eds.]

Justice Frankfurter had also dissented in a previous FELA case involving the strictness with which the plaintiff's complaint should be read. The Court held in Brown v. Western R. Co. of Ala., 338 U.S. 294 (1949), that the plaintiff had properly alleged negligence even though, under rules applied to all litigation by the Georgia courts, the complaint was deficient. Frankfurter's view, in dissent, was that "[i]f a litigant chooses to enforce a federal right in a state court, he cannot be heard to object if he is treated exactly as are plaintiffs who press like claims arising under state law with regard to the form in which the claim must be stated—the particularity, for instance, with which a cause of action must be described."

While an interesting illustration of the substance-procedure issue, FELA cases are arguably so idiosyncratic as to be of limited relevance to other contexts. In dissent in Bailey v. Central Vermont Ry., 319 U.S. 350 (1943), Justice Roberts explained what he thought the Court was up to in cases like *Dice* and *Brown*:

> I cannot concur in the intimation . . . that, as Congress has seen fit not to enact a workmen's compensation law, this Court will strain the law of negligence to accord compensation where the employer is without fault. I yield to none in my belief in the wisdom and equity of workmen's compensation laws, but I do not conceive it to be within our judicial function to write the policy which underlies compensation laws into acts of Congress when Congress has not chosen that policy but, instead, has adopted the common law doctrine of negligence.

If plaintiff-bias is indeed a part of the substantive federal policy, then it may not be appropriate to follow even "neutral" state procedures when they operate to benefit the defendant.

3. *FELDER V. CASEY*

In Felder v. Casey, 487 U.S. 131 (1988), the plaintiff filed a § 1983 action in state court alleging that nine months earlier he had been unlawfully beaten and arrested by Milwaukee police officers. In doing so, he failed to comply with a state notice-of-claim statute that required written notice of a claim against a governmental subdivision or its officers within 120 days of the incident giving rise to such claim. The highest state court dismissed the suit, but the Supreme Court reversed.

In an opinion by Justice Brennan, the Court held that "application of the notice requirement burdens the exercise of the federal right" in a manner "inconsistent in both design and effect with the compensatory aims of the federal civil rights laws." Among the arguments in support of enforcing the state requirement was the following:

> Respondents and their supporting amici urge that we approve the application of the notice-of-claim statute to § 1983 actions brought in state court as a matter of equitable federalism. They note that " '[t]he general rule, bottomed deeply in belief in the importance of state control of state judicial procedure, is that federal law takes the state courts as it finds them.' " Brief for Amici Curiae

8 (quoting Hart, The Relations Between State and Federal Law, 54 Colum. L. Rev. 489, 508 (1954)). Litigants who chose to bring their civil rights actions in state courts presumably do so in order to obtain the benefit of certain procedural advantages in those courts, or to draw their juries from urban populations. Having availed themselves of these benefits, civil rights litigants must comply as well with those state rules they find less to their liking.

The Court responded:

However equitable this bitter-with-the-sweet argument may appear in the abstract, it has no place under our Supremacy Clause analysis. Federal law takes state courts as it finds them only insofar as those courts employ rules that do not "impose unnecessary burdens upon rights of recovery authorized by federal laws." Brown v. Western Ry. of Alabama, 338 U.S. 294, 298–99 (1949). . . . [E]nforcement of the notice-of-claim statute in § 1983 actions brought in state court so interferes with and frustrates the substantive right Congress created that, under the Supremacy Clause, it must yield to the federal interest. . . .

Civil rights victims often do not appreciate the constitutional nature of their injuries and thus will fail to file a notice of injury or claim within the requisite time period, which in Wisconsin is a mere four months. Unless such claimants . . . file an itemized claim for damages, they must bring their § 1983 suits in federal court or not at all. Wisconsin, however, may not alter the outcome of federal claims it chooses to entertain in its courts by demanding compliance with outcome-determinative rules that are inapplicable when such claims are brought in federal court. . . . The state notice-of-claim statute is more than a mere rule of procedure: . . . the statute is a substantive condition on the right to sue governmental officials and entities, and the federal courts have therefore correctly recognized that the notice statute governs the adjudication of state-law claims in diversity actions. In Guaranty Trust Co. v. York, 326 U.S. 99 (1945), we held that, in order to give effect to a state's statute of limitations, a federal court could not hear a state-law action that a state court would deem time-barred. Conversely, a state court may not decline to hear an otherwise properly presented federal claim because that claim would be barred under a state law requiring timely filing of notice. State courts simply are not free to vindicate the substantive interests underlying a state rule of decision at the expense of the federal right.

Finally, in Wilson v. Garcia, 471 U.S. 261 (1985), we characterized § 1983 suits as claims for personal injuries because such an approach ensured that the same limitations period would govern all § 1983 actions brought in any given state, and thus comported with Congress's desire that the federal civil rights laws be given a uniform application within each state. A law that predictably alters the outcome of § 1983 claims depending solely on whether they are brought in state or federal court within the same state is obviously inconsistent with this federal interest in intra-state uniformity.

Justice White concurred on a different rationale, and Justice O'Connor, joined by Chief Justice Rehnquist, dissented.[d]

Johnson v. Fankell

Supreme Court of the United States, 1997.
520 U.S. 911.

■ JUSTICE STEVENS delivered the opinion of the Court.

The question presented is whether defendants in an action brought under 42 U.S.C. § 1983, in state court have a federal right to an interlocutory appeal from a denial of qualified immunity. We hold that they do not.

I

Petitioners are officials of the Idaho Liquor Dispensary. Respondent, a former liquor store clerk, brought this action for damages under § 1983 in the District Court for the County of Bonner, Idaho. She alleged that petitioners deprived her of property without due process of law in violation of the Fourteenth Amendment to the federal Constitution when they terminated her employment. Petitioners moved to dismiss the complaint on the ground that they were entitled to qualified immunity. They contended that, at the time of respondent's dismissal, they reasonably believed that she was a probationary employee who had no property interest in her job. Accordingly, petitioners argued, her termination did not violate clearly established law. The trial court denied the motion,[1] and petitioners filed a timely notice of appeal to the Supreme Court of the State of Idaho.

The state Supreme Court entered an order dismissing the appeal. The Court explained that an order denying a motion for summary judgment is not appealable under Idaho Appellate Rule 11(a)(1) "for the reason it is not from a final order or Judgment." It also rejected petitioners' arguments that the order was appealable under 42 U.S.C. § 1983. . . . We granted certiorari . . . and now affirm.

---

d   With *Felder v. Casey*, compare Engel v. Davenport, 271 U.S. 33 (1926). The case involved a seaman's claim against a shipowner under the Merchant Marine Act of 1920, a federal statute that incorporated by reference many provisions of the FELA, including its two-year statute of limitations for negligence actions. A California state court dismissed the claim as barred by the state's one-year statute of limitations for personal injury actions, but the Supreme Court reversed, holding that the two-year limitations period was part of the "substantive right, setting a limit to the existence of the obligation which the act creates." The shorter state statute therefore did not control. A similar result was reached on the authority of *Engel* in McAllister v. Magnolia Petroleum Co., 357 U.S. 221 (1958).

1   Because affidavits had been filed in support of the motion, the court treated it as a motion for summary judgment.

II

We have recognized a qualified immunity defense for both federal officials sued under the implied cause of action asserted in Bivens v. Six Unknown Fed. Narcotics Agents, 403 U.S. 388 (1971), and state officials sued under § 1983. In both situations, "officials performing discretionary functions, generally are shielded from liability for civil damages insofar as their conduct does not violate clearly established statutory or constitutional rights of which a reasonable person would have known." Harlow v. Fitzgerald, 457 U.S. 800, 818 (1982).

This "qualified immunity" defense is valuable to officials asserting it for two reasons. First, if it is found applicable at any stage of the proceedings, it determines the outcome of the litigation by shielding the official from damages liability. Second, when the complaint fails to allege a violation of clearly established law or when discovery fails to uncover evidence sufficient to create a genuine issue whether the defendant committed such a violation, it provides the defendant with an immunity from the burdens of trial as well as a defense to liability. Indeed, one reason for adopting the objective test announced in *Harlow* was to "permit the resolution of many insubstantial claims on summary judgment."

Consistent with that purpose, we held in Mitchell v. Forsyth, 472 U.S. 511, 524–30 (1985), that a federal district court order rejecting a qualified immunity defense on the ground that the defendant's actions— if proven—would have violated clearly established law may be appealed immediately as a "final decision" within the meaning of the general federal appellate jurisdiction statute, 28 U.S.C. § 1291.[3] If this action had been brought in a federal court, therefore, petitioners would have had a right to take an appeal from the trial court's order denying their motion for summary judgment.

Relying on the facts (a) that respondent has asserted a federal claim under a federal statute, and (b) that they are asserting a defense provided by federal law, petitioners submit that the Idaho courts must protect their right to avoid the burdens of trial by allowing the same interlocutory appeal that would be available in a federal court. They support this submission with two different arguments: First, that when the Idaho courts construe their own rules allowing appeals from final judgments, they must accept the federal definition of finality in cases brought under § 1983; and second, that if those rules do not authorize the appeal, they are preempted by federal law. We find neither argument persuasive.

III

We can easily dispense with petitioners' first contention that Idaho must follow the federal construction of a "final decision." Even if the Idaho and federal statutes contained identical language—and they do

---

[3] While Mitchell v. Forsyth, 472 U.S. 511 (1985), involved a *Bivens* action against a federal official, we have also construed § 1291 to authorize similar appeals in actions brought against state officials under § 1983. See, e.g., Johnson v. Jones, 515 U.S. 304 (1995).

not[4]—the interpretation of the Idaho statute by the Idaho Supreme Court would be binding on federal courts. Neither this Court nor any other federal tribunal has any authority to place a construction on a state statute different from the one rendered by the highest court of the state. This proposition, fundamental to our system of federalism, is applicable to procedural as well as substantive rules.

The definition of the term "final decision" that we adopted in *Mitchell* was an application of the "collateral order" doctrine first recognized in Cohen v. Beneficial Industrial Loan Corp., 337 U.S. 541 (1949). In that case, as in all of our cases following it, we were construing the federal statutory language of 28 U.S.C. § 1291. While some states have adopted a similar "collateral order" exception when construing their jurisdictional statutes, we have never suggested that federal law compelled them to do so. Indeed, a number of states employ collateral order doctrines that reject the limitations this Court has placed on § 1291. Idaho could, of course, place the same construction on its Appellate Rule 11(a)(1) as we have placed on § 1291. But that is clearly a choice for that court to make, not one that we have any authority to command.

IV

Petitioners also contend that, to the extent that Idaho Appellate Rule 11(a)(1) does not allow an interlocutory appeal, it is preempted by § 1983. Relying heavily on Felder v. Casey, 487 U.S. 131 (1988), petitioners first assert that pre-emption is necessary to avoid "different outcomes in § 1983 litigation based solely on whether the claim is asserted in state or federal court." Second, they argue that the state procedure "impermissibly burden[s]" the federal immunity from suit because it does not adequately protect their right to prevail on the immunity question in advance of trial.

For two reasons, petitioners have a heavy burden of persuasion in making this argument. First, our normal presumption against pre-emption is buttressed by the fact that the Idaho Supreme Court's dismissal of the appeal rested squarely on a neutral state rule regarding the administration of the state courts.[9] As we explained in Howlett v. Rose, 496 U.S. 356, 372 (1990):

> When a state court refuses jurisdiction because of a neutral
> state rule regarding the administration of the courts, we must

---

[4] "Final decision" is the operative term of § 1291, whereas "[j]udgments, orders and decrees which are final" is the language of Idaho Appellate Rule 11(a)(1).

[9] Unlike the notice-of-claim rule at issue in *Felder*, Idaho Appellate Rule 11(a)(1) does not target civil rights claims against the state. Instead, it generally permits appeals only of "[j]udgments, orders and decrees which are final," without regard to the identity of the party seeking the appeal or the subject matter of the suit. Petitioners claim that the rule is not neutral because it permits interlocutory appeals in certain limited circumstances but denies an appeal here. But we have never held that a rule must be monolithic to be neutral. Absent evidence that Appellate Rule 11(a)(1) discriminates against interlocutory appeals of § 1983 qualified immunity determinations by defendants—as compared with other types of appeals—we must deem the state procedure neutral.

act with utmost caution before deciding that it is obligated to entertain the claim. The requirement that a state court of competent jurisdiction treat federal law as the law of the land does not necessarily include within it a requirement that the state create a court competent to hear the case in which the federal claim is presented. The general rule, "bottomed deeply in belief in the importance of state control of state judicial procedure, is that federal law takes the state courts as it finds them." The states thus have great latitude to establish the structure and jurisdiction of their own courts.

A second barrier to petitioners' argument arises from the nature of the interest protected by the defense of qualified immunity. Petitioners' argument for pre-emption is bottomed on their claims that the Idaho rules are interfering with their federal rights. While it is true that the defense has its source in a federal statute (§ 1983), the ultimate purpose of qualified immunity is to protect the state and its officials from overenforcement of federal rights. The Idaho Supreme Court's application of the state's procedural rules in this context is thus less an interference with *federal* interests than a judgment about how best to balance the competing *state* interests of limiting interlocutory appeals and providing state officials with immediate review of the merits of their defense.[10]

Petitioner's arguments for pre-emption are not strong enough to overcome these considerable hurdles. Contrary to petitioners' assertions, Idaho's decision not to provide appellate review for the vast majority of interlocutory orders—including denials of qualified immunity in § 1983 cases—is not "outcome determinative" in the sense that we used that term when we held that Wisconsin's notice-of-claim statute could not be applied to defeat a federal civil rights action brought in state courts under § 1983. The failure to comply with the Wisconsin statute in *Felder* resulted in a judgment dismissing a complaint that would not have been dismissed—at least not without a judicial determination of the merits of the claim—if the case had been filed in a federal court. One of the primary grounds for our decision was that, because the notice-of-claim requirement would "frequently and predictably produce different outcomes" depending on whether § 1983 claims were brought in state or federal court, it was inconsistent with the federal interest in uniformity.

Petitioners' reliance on *Felder* is misplaced because "outcome," as we used the term there, referred to the ultimate disposition of the case. If

---

[10] It does warrant observation that Rule 12(a) of the Idaho Appellate Rules provides that the State Supreme Court may grant permission "to appeal from an interlocutory order or decree . . . which is not otherwise appealable under these rules, but which involves a controlling question of law as to which there is substantial grounds for difference of opinion and in which an immediate appeal . . . may materially advance the orderly resolution of the litigation." Presumably, petitioners could have sought review under this permissive provision, and the Idaho Supreme Court might have granted review if, in the view of that court, the officials' claim to immunity was so substantial that the suit should not proceed.

petitioners' claim to qualified immunity is meritorious, there is no suggestion that the application of the Idaho rules of procedure will produce a final result different from what a federal ruling would produce. Petitioners were able to argue their immunity from suit claim to the trial court, just as they would to a federal court. And the claim will be reviewable by the Idaho Supreme Court after the trial court enters a final judgment, thus providing the petitioners with a further chance to urge their immunity. Consequently, the postponement of the appeal until after final judgment will not affect the ultimate outcome of the case.

Petitioners' second argument for pre-emption of the state procedural rule is that the rule does not adequately protect their right to prevail in advance of trial. In evaluating this contention, it is important to focus on the precise source and scope of the federal right at issue. The right to have the trial court rule on the merits of the qualified immunity defense presumably has its source in § 1983, but the right to immediate appellate review of that ruling in a federal case has its source in § 1291. The former right is fully protected by Idaho. The latter right, however, is a federal procedural right that simply does not apply in a nonfederal forum.[11]

The locus of the right to interlocutory appeal in § 1291, rather than in § 1983 itself, is demonstrated by our holding in Johnson v. Jones, 515 U.S. 304 (1995). In that case, government officials asserting qualified immunity claimed entitlement to an interlocutory appeal of a District Court order denying their motion for summary judgment on the ground that the record showed a genuine issue of material fact whether the officials actually engaged in the conduct that constituted a clear violation of constitutional law. We concluded that this circumstance was different from that presented in *Mitchell*, in which the subject of the interlocutory appeal was whether a given set of facts showed a violation of clearly established law, and held that although § 1291 did allow an interlocutory appeal in the latter circumstance, such an appeal was not allowed in the former.

In so holding, we acknowledged that "whether a district court's denial of summary judgment amounts to (a) a determination about pre-existing 'clearly established' law, or (b) a determination about 'genuine' issues of fact for trial, it still forces public officials to trial." But we concluded that the strong "countervailing considerations" surrounding appropriate interpretation of § 1291 were of sufficient importance to outweigh the officials' interest in avoiding the burdens of litigation.

The "countervailing considerations" at issue here are even stronger than those presented in *Johnson*. When pre-emption of state law is at

---

[11] Petitioners' reliance on Dice v. Akron, C. & Y.R. Co., 342 U.S. 359 (1952), is therefore misplaced. In *Dice* we held that the Federal Employers' Liability Act (FELA) pre-empted a state rule denying a right to a jury trial. In that case, however, we made clear that Congress had provided in FELA that the jury trial procedure was to be part of claims brought under the act. In this case, by contrast, Congress has mentioned nothing about interlocutory appeals in § 1983; rather, the right to an immediate appeal in the federal court system is found in § 1291, which obviously has no application to state courts.

issue, we must respect the "principles [that] are fundamental to a system of federalism in which the state courts share responsibility for the application and enforcement of federal law." *Howlett*, 496 U.S. at 372–73. This respect is at its apex when we confront a claim that federal law requires a state to undertake something as fundamental as restructuring the operation of its courts. We therefore cannot agree with petitioners that § 1983's recognition of the defense of qualified immunity preempts a state's consistent application of its neutral procedural rules, even when those rules deny an interlocutory appeal in this context.

The judgment of the Supreme Court of the State of Idaho dismissing petitioners' appeal is therefore affirmed.

It is so ordered.

ADDITIONAL NOTES ON THE SUBSTANCE-PROCEDURE PROBLEM

1. QUESTIONS AND COMMENTS ON *JOHNSON V. FANKELL*

At an abstract level, the applicable rule seems straightforward. State courts are generally free to apply their own procedures to the litigation of federal claims, but they cannot undermine federal law by doing so. The reconciliation of these general principles, however, is sometimes difficult.[a]

In one view of *Fankell*, the defendants' federal right to avoid trial (assuming that summary judgment should have been granted) was undermined by denying interlocutory appeal. No judgment *after* trial could restore the right. In another view, there was no federal right to avoid trial but only a federal right to avoid liability in certain circumstances. The federal courts provided appropriate mechanisms for asserting the immunity defense; the state courts merely provided different, but also appropriate, mechanisms. So long as the issue is ultimately correctly resolved, the defendants have no complaint. Which is the better characterization of the rights at stake in *Fankell*?

2. FEDERAL CLAIMS RAISED BY DEFENDANTS

Fankell, *Felder*, and the FELA cases involved *plaintiffs* who asserted federal claims in a state court. Are the issues different when state *defendants* raise federal claims? Consider two illustrations.

(i) *Jackson v. Denno*

Jackson v. Denno, 378 U.S. 368 (1964), involved a New York procedure for adjudicating the voluntariness of a confession. New York allowed the trial

---

a   For general analysis of the topic, see Anthony J. Bellia Jr., Federal Regulation of State Court Procedures, 110 Yale L.J. 947 (2001), and Kevin M. Clermont, Reverse-*Erie*, 82 Notre Dame L. Rev. 1 (2006). For a comprehensive treatment of the litigation of § 1983 claims in a state court, see Steven Steinglass, The Emerging State Court § 1983 Action: A Procedural Review, 38 U. Miami L. Rev. 381 (1984). Finally, for a suggestion that state courts adjudicating federal claims should adhere to federal rather than state standards of justiciability, see Paul J. Katz, Standing in Good Stead: State Courts, Federal Standing Doctrine, and Reverse-*Erie* Analysis, 99 Nw. U. L. Rev. 1315 (2005).

judge to exclude a confession from evidence only if it was clearly involuntary. If the facts were disputed or the issue unclear, the question of voluntariness had to be submitted to the jury. The judge then instructed the jury to consider a confession found to be voluntary and to ignore a confession found to be involuntary. Exactly how the jurors dealt with that responsibility would often be unknown, as they returned only a general verdict of guilty or not guilty.

The Supreme Court held that a "defendant objecting to the admission of a confession is entitled to a fair hearing in which both the underlying factual issues and the voluntariness of his confession are actually and reliably determined." It found that the New York procedure failed this test and hence violated the Due Process Clause of the Fourteenth Amendment. Henceforth the judge was required to hold an independent hearing, resolve all factual disputes, and make an independent determination of voluntariness before a confession was submitted to the jury.

(ii) Chapman v. California

In Chapman v. California, 386 U.S. 18 (1967), the prosecutor commented on the defendants' failure to take the stand, and the jury was charged that it could take such comments into account. Subsequently the Supreme Court held such practices unconstitutional. The question before the Court in *Chapman* was whether California had properly applied its harmless error doctrine to uphold the convictions despite the error. Justice Black wrote for the Court:

> Before deciding the two questions here—whether there can ever be harmless constitutional error and whether the error here was harmless—we must first decide whether state or federal law governs. The application of a state harmless-error rule is, of course, a state question where it involves only errors of state procedure or state law. But the error from which these petitioners suffered was a denial of rights guaranteed against invasion by the Fifth and Fourteenth Amendments. . . . Whether a conviction for crime should stand when a state has failed to accord federal constitutionally guaranteed rights is every bit as much of a federal question as what particular federal constitutional provisions themselves mean, what they guarantee, and whether they have been denied. With faithfulness to the constitutional union of the states, we cannot leave to the states the formulation of the authoritative laws, rules, and remedies designed to protect people from infractions by the states of federally guaranteed rights. We have no hesitation in saying that the right of these [defendants] not to be punished for exercising their Fifth and Fourteenth Amendment right to be silent—expressly created by the federal Constitution itself—is a federal right which, in the absence of appropriate congressional action, it is our responsibility to protect by fashioning the necessary rule.

The Court went on to say that federal law required that federal constitutional errors required reversal unless "harmless beyond a reasonable doubt," and applying that standard, reversed the conviction.

Justice Harlan dissented. So long as the state's harmless-error rule was not itself unconstitutional, Harlan argued, the Supreme Court had no right to override it:

> I regard the Court's assumption of what amounts to a general supervisory power over the trial of federal constitutional issues in state courts as a startling constitutional development that is wholly out of keeping with our federal system and completely unsupported by the Fourteenth Amendment where the source of such a power must be found.

> [T]he Court has always been especially reluctant to interfere with state procedural practices. From the beginning of the federal union, state courts have had power to decide issues of federal law and to formulate "authoritative laws, rules, and remedies" for the trial of those issues. The primary responsibility for the trial of state criminal cases still rests upon the states, and the only constitutional limitation upon these trials is that the laws, rules, and remedies applied must meet constitutional requirements. If they do not, this Court may hold them invalid. The Court has no power, however, to declare which of many admittedly constitutional alternatives a state may choose. To impose uniform national requirements when alternatives are constitutionally permissible would destroy that opportunity for broad experimentation which is the genius of our federal system.

(iii) Questions and Comments on Claims Raised by Defendants

Are *Jackson* and *Chapman* analytically similar to *Fankell* and *Dice*? Arguably the answer is "yes," since all four cases involved state "procedures" that would have been perfectly valid had only state rights been at issue but that were seen in a different light because of their effect on federal rights. But a criminal defendant has no choice but to litigate federal claims in state court. Does this make it more justifiable for the Court to assess the impact of state procedures on federal substantive rights? Or is Justice Harlan right that the Court should not displace state procedures unless they are unconstitutional?

INTRODUCTORY NOTES ON THE DUTY OF STATE COURTS TO HEAR FEDERAL CLAIMS

1.   FROM POWER TO DUTY

Once a state court assumes jurisdiction over a federal claim, the Supremacy Clause requires it to resolve the claim consistently with federal law.[a] State courts cannot reject a required federal outcome on the ground

---

[a]   For discussion of how state courts should go about the business of interpreting federal statutes, see Anthony J. Bellia Jr., State Courts and the Interpretation of Federal Statutes, 59

that state policy calls for a different result. Nor can they follow state procedures that effectively undermine the controlling federal law. But it does not necessarily follow that state courts are *required* to hear federal claims in the first instance. The cases now to be considered ask whether state courts *must* hear federal claims when, for one reason or another, state law says they should not be heard.

2. *TESTA V. KATT*

The canonical citation on the duty of state courts to hear federal cases is Testa v. Katt, 330 U.S. 386 (1947). The plaintiff alleged that the defendant sold him a car for $1100, which was $210 above the ceiling price established under the World War II Emergency Price Control Act. That statute provided that suits for treble the overcharge, plus costs and a reasonable attorney's fee, could be brought "in any court of competent jurisdiction." It further specified that federal district courts had jurisdiction "concurrently with state and territorial courts." Plaintiff sued in state court, but the Rhode Island Supreme Court held that the treble-damages provision of the Price Control Act was "penal" in nature and that Rhode Island courts were not open to enforce the penal laws of a government that was foreign in the private international sense.

Justice Black wrote for a unanimous Court. He did not care whether the Emergency Price Control Act was penal in the "private international" or any other sense:

> [W]e cannot accept the basic premise on which the Rhode Island Supreme Court held that it has no more obligation to enforce a valid penal law of the United States than it has to enforce a penal law of another state or a foreign country. Such a broad assumption flies in the face of the fact that the states of the Union constitute a nation. It disregards the purpose and effect of [the Supremacy Clause]. . . .

> So here, the fact that Rhode Island has an established policy against enforcement by its courts of statutes of other states and the United States which it deems penal, cannot be accepted as a "valid excuse." Cf. Douglas v. New York, N.H. & H.R. Co., 279 U.S. 377, 388 (1929). For the policy of the federal act is the prevailing policy in every state. . . .

> It is conceded that this same type of claim arising under Rhode Island law would be enforced by that state's courts. . . . Thus the Rhode Island courts have jurisdiction adequate and appropriate under established local law to adjudicate this action. Under these circumstances the state courts are not free to refuse enforcement of petitioners' claim.[b]

Vand. L. Rev. 1501 (2006). For argument that state courts should be required to follow lower federal court precedent when resolving questions of federal law, see Amanda Frost, Inferiority Complex: Should State Courts Follow Lower Federal Court Precedent on the Meaning of Federal Law? 68 Vand. L. Rev. 53 (2015).

[b] Justice Black's opinion in *Testa* relied on Claflin v. Houseman, 93 U.S. (3 Otto) 130 (1876), even though the issue of a state-court *obligation* to hear federal claims was not there

3.   THE FELA CASES

Exploration of the concept of a "valid excuse" for not hearing federal claims came in a line of cases arising under the FELA. Three of them are summarized below. Several others are adequately described in the next main case.

(i)   Mondou

In Mondou v. New York, N.H. & H.R. Co., 223 U.S. 1 (1912), the Connecticut courts declined jurisdiction over an FELA action on the grounds that "the policy manifested by [the FELA] is not in accord with the policy of the state" and that "it would be inconvenient and confusing" for the state courts to apply federal standards in FELA cases and state standards in cases arising under state law. The question in the Supreme Court was whether the FELA could be "enforced, as of right, in the courts of the states when their jurisdiction, as fixed by local laws, is adequate to the occasion?" A unanimous Court answered "yes":

> [T]here is not here involved any attempt by Congress to enlarge or regulate the jurisdiction of state courts or to control or affect their modes of procedure, but only a question of the duty of such a court, when its ordinary jurisdiction as prescribed by local laws is appropriate to the occasion and is invoked in conformity with those laws, to take cognizance of an action to enforce a right of civil recovery arising under the act of Congress and susceptible of adjudication according to the prevailing rules of procedure.

At this point the Court said, in language later quoted in *Testa:*

> The suggestion that the act of Congress is not in harmony with the policy of the state and therefore that the courts of the state are free to decline jurisdiction, is quite inadmissible, because it presupposes what in legal contemplation does not exist. When Congress, in the exertion of the power confided to it by the Constitution, adopted that act, it spoke for all the people and all the states, and thereby established a policy for all. That policy is as much the policy of Connecticut as if the act had emanated from its own legislature, and should be respected accordingly in the courts of the state.

The Court concluded:

> We are not disposed to believe that the exercise of jurisdiction by the state courts will be attended by any appreciable inconvenience or confusion; but, be this as it may, it affords no reason for declining a jurisdiction conferred by law. The existence of the jurisdiction creates an implication of duty to exercise it, and that its exercise may be onerous does not militate against that implication. . . . We conclude that rights arising under the act in question

---

presented. The actual issue in *Claflin* was merely whether state courts were entitled to enforce federal rights. On that subject, *Claflin* provided an early statement of the principles of *Gulf Offshore* and was cited approvingly in that case. For discussion of *Claflin*, see Martin H. Redish and John E. Muench, Adjudication of Federal Causes of Action in State Court, 75 Mich. L. Rev. 311, 313–40 (1976).—[Footnote by eds.]

may be enforced, as of right, in the courts of the states when their jurisdiction, as prescribed by local laws, is adequate to the occasion.

(ii) Douglas

In Douglas v. New York, N.H. & H.R. Co., 279 U.S. 377 (1929), the New York courts refused to hear an FELA action brought by a Connecticut plaintiff against a Connecticut corporation for injuries that occurred in that state. The New York courts exercised a discretion available under local law to decline to hear nonresident suits against foreign corporations. In affirming that decision, the unanimous opinion by Justice Holmes treated the obligation of state courts to hear federal cases in a single paragraph:

> As to the grant of jurisdiction in the Employers' Liability Act, that statute does not purport to require state courts to entertain suits arising under it, but only to empower them to do so, so far as the authority of the United States is concerned. It may very well be that if the Supreme Court of New York were given no discretion, being otherwise competent, it would be subject to a duty. But there is nothing in the act of Congress that purports to force a duty upon such courts as against an otherwise valid excuse.

(iii) McKnett

McKnett v. St. Louis & S.F.R. Co., 292 U.S. 230 (1934), involved an FELA action brought in an Alabama court to recover for injuries incurred in Tennessee. The plaintiff resided in Tennessee and the defendant was a foreign corporation doing business in Alabama. The Alabama courts had consistently refused to take jurisdiction of a transitory cause of action arising in another state where the defendant was a foreign corporation. Under *Douglas*, such a refusal would have been permitted, but the Alabama legislature passed a law requiring its courts to accept jurisdiction over all such cases if the cause of action arose "by common law or the statutes of another state."

The Alabama courts read this statute to exclude causes of action arising in another state under *federal* law and accordingly dismissed the suit. The Supreme Court unanimously reversed. Speaking through Justice Brandeis, it said:

> The power of a state to determine the limits of the jurisdiction of its courts and the character of the controversies which shall be heard in them is, of course, subject to the restrictions imposed by the federal Constitution. . . . While Congress has not attempted to compel states to provide courts for the enforcement of the [FELA], the federal Constitution prohibits state courts of general jurisdiction from refusing to do so solely because the suit is brought under a federal law. The denial of jurisdiction by the Alabama court is based solely upon the source of law sought to be enforced. . . . A state may not discriminate against rights arising under federal laws.

4. *HOWLETT V. ROSE*

The plaintiff in Howlett v. Rose, 496 U.S. 356 (1990), was a former high school student who sued the school board (and three officials) under § 1983 for an allegedly illegal search of his car and a resulting suspension from school. School boards and other local governments are proper defendants under § 1983, Monell v. Department of Social Services, 436 U.S. 658 (1978), though states and state agencies are not. Will v. Michigan Dept. of State Police, 491 U.S. 58 (1989). Thus, so far as federal law was concerned, Howell was entitled to bring a § 1983 action (as well as related state-law claims) against the school board in either state or federal court. The Florida courts, however, concluded that Florida's statutory waiver of sovereign immunity applied only to state-law claims and thus barred suit against the school board in state court.

So phrased, the ruling of the Florida courts that the school board enjoyed an immunity not recognized by federal law seems a straightforward violation of the Supremacy Clause, and perhaps that is all that need have been said. The Supreme Court, however, wrote more elaborately to review the principles applicable in the area. The Court concluded: (1) that federal claims ordinarily are enforceable in state court; (2) that a "valid excuse" for declining to hear federal claims cannot violate or be inconsistent with federal law; but (3) that a state court ordinarily can refuse jurisdiction under "a neutral state rule regarding the administration of the courts." The attempt to characterize Florida's position as a neutral jurisdictional rule of this sort was unanimously rejected:

> The state of Florida has constituted the Circuit Court for Pinellas County as a court of general jurisdiction. It exercises jurisdiction over tort claims by private citizens against state entities (including school boards), of the size and type of petitioner's claim here, and it can enter judgment against them. That court also exercises jurisdiction over § 1983 actions against individual officers and is fully competent to provide the remedies the federal statute requires. Petitioner has complied with all the state law procedures for invoking the jurisdiction of that court.

The fact that the state called its immunity rule "jurisdictional" was of no consequence: "The force of the Supremacy Clause is not so weak that it can be evaded by mere mention of the word 'jurisdiction.' " The Court concluded that

> whether the question is framed in preemption terms, as petitioner would have it, or in the obligation to assume jurisdiction over a "federal" cause of action, as respondent would have it, the Florida court's refusal to entertain one discrete category of § 1983 claims, when the court entertains similar state law actions against state defendants, violates the Supremacy Clause.

Haywood v. Drown

Supreme Court of the United States, 2009.
556 U.S. 729.

■ JUSTICE STEVENS delivered the opinion of the Court.

. . . New York . . . prohibits the trial courts that generally exercise jurisdiction over § 1983 suits brought against other state officials from hearing virtually all such suits brought against state correction officers. The question presented is whether that exceptional treatment of a limited category of § 1983 claims is consistent with the Supremacy Clause of the United States Constitution.

I

Petitioner, an inmate in New York's Attica Correctional Facility, commenced two § 1983 actions against several correction employees alleging that they violated his civil rights in connection with three prisoner disciplinary proceedings and an altercation. Proceeding pro se, petitioner filed his claims in State Supreme Court and sought punitive damages and attorney's fees. The trial court dismissed the actions on the ground that, under N.Y. Correct. Law Ann. § 24 (West 1987) (hereinafter Correction Law § 24), it lacked jurisdiction to entertain any suit arising under state or federal law seeking money damages from correction officers for actions taken in the scope of their employment. The intermediate appellate court summarily affirmed the trial court. The New York Court of Appeals, by a 4-to-3 vote, also affirmed. . . . [W]e granted certiorari [and] now reverse.

II

Motivated by the belief that damages suits filed by prisoners against state correction officers were by and large frivolous and vexatious, New York passed Correction Law § 24. The statute employs a two-step process to strip its courts of jurisdiction over such damages claims and to replace those claims with the State's preferred alternative. The provision states in full:

> 1.   No civil action shall be brought in any court of the state, except by the attorney general on behalf of the state, against any officer or employee of the department, in his personal capacity, for damages arising out of any act done or the failure to perform any act within the scope of employment and in the discharge of the duties by such officer or employee.

> 2.   Any claim for damages arising out of any act done or the failure to perform any act within the scope of employment and in the discharge of the duties of any officer or employee of the department shall be brought and maintained in the court of claims as a claim against the state.

Thus, under this scheme, a prisoner seeking damages from a correction officer will have his claim dismissed for want of jurisdiction and will be left, instead, to pursue a claim for damages against an entirely different party (the State) in the Court of Claims—a court of limited jurisdiction.[4]

For prisoners seeking redress, pursuing the Court of Claims alternative comes with strict conditions. In addition to facing a different defendant, plaintiffs in that Court are not provided with the same relief, or the same procedural protections, made available in § 1983 actions brought in state courts of general jurisdiction. Specifically, under New York law, plaintiffs in the Court of Claims must comply with a 90-day notice requirement; are not entitled to a jury trial; have no right to attorney's fees; and may not seek punitive damages or injunctive relief.

We must decide whether Correction Law § 24, as applied to § 1983 claims, violates the Supremacy Clause.

III

This Court has long made clear that federal law is as much the law of the several States as are the laws passed by their legislatures. Federal and state law "together form one system of jurisprudence, which constitutes the law of the land for the State; and the courts of the two jurisdictions are not foreign to each other, nor to be treated by each other as such, but as courts of the same country, having jurisdiction partly different and partly concurrent." Claflin v. Houseman, 93 U.S. 130, 136–37 (1876). Although § 1983, a Reconstruction-era statute, was passed "to interpose the federal courts between the States and the people, as guardians of the people's federal rights," Mitchum v. Foster, 407 U.S. 225, 242 (1972), state courts as well as federal courts are entrusted with providing a forum for the vindication of federal rights violated by state or local officials acting under color of state law.

So strong is the presumption of concurrency that it is defeated only in two narrowly defined circumstances: first, when Congress expressly ousts state courts of jurisdiction; and second, "[w]hen a state court refuses jurisdiction because of a neutral state rule regarding the administration of the courts," Howlett v. Rose, 496 U.S. 356, 372 (1990). Focusing on the latter circumstance, we have emphasized that only a neutral jurisdictional rule will be deemed a "valid excuse" for departing from the default assumption that "state courts have inherent authority, and are thus presumptively competent, to adjudicate claims arising under the laws of the United States." Tafflin v. Levitt, 493 U.S. 455, 458 (1990).

In determining whether a state law qualifies as a neutral rule of judicial administration, our cases have established that a State cannot

---

4   Although the State has waived its sovereign immunity from liability by allowing itself to be sued in the Court of Claims, a plaintiff seeking damages against the State in that court cannot use § 1983 as a vehicle for redress because a State is not a "person" under § 1983. See Will v. Michigan Dept. of State Police, 491 U.S. 58, 66 (1989). [Thus, although state-law tort claims could be brought directly against the state, federal § 1983 damages actions (which include the availability of attorney's fees) could be brought only in federal court.—Addition to footnote by eds.]

employ a jurisdictional rule "to dissociate [itself] from federal law because of disagreement with its content or a refusal to recognize the superior authority of its source." *Howlett*, 496 U.S. at 371. In other words, although States retain substantial leeway to establish the contours of their judicial systems, they lack authority to nullify a federal right or cause of action they believe is inconsistent with their local policies. . . . "The suggestion that [an] act of Congress is not in harmony with the policy of the State, and therefore that the courts of the State are free to decline jurisdiction, is quite inadmissible, because it presupposes what in legal contemplation does not exist." Second Employers' Liability Cases, 223 U.S. 1, 57 (1912).

It is principally on this basis that Correction Law § 24 violates the Supremacy Clause. In passing Correction Law § 24, New York made the judgment that correction officers should not be burdened with suits for damages arising out of conduct performed in the scope of their employment. Because it regards these suits as too numerous or too frivolous (or both), the State's longstanding policy has been to shield this narrow class of defendants from liability when sued for damages.[5] The State's policy, whatever its merits, is contrary to Congress's judgment that *all* persons who violate federal rights while acting under color of state law shall be held liable for damages. . . . That New York strongly favors a rule shielding correction officers from personal damages liability and substituting the State as the party responsible for compensating individual victims is irrelevant. The State cannot condition its enforcement of federal law on the demand that those individuals whose conduct federal law seeks to regulate must nevertheless escape liability.

IV

While our cases have uniformly applied the principle that a State cannot simply refuse to entertain a federal claim based on a policy disagreement, we have yet to confront a statute like New York's that registers its dissent by divesting its courts of jurisdiction over a disfavored federal claim in addition to an identical state claim. The New York Court of Appeals' holding was based on the misunderstanding that this equal treatment of federal and state claims rendered Correction Law § 24 constitutional. To the extent our cases have created this misperception, we now make clear that equality of treatment does not ensure that a state law will be deemed a neutral rule of judicial administration and therefore a valid excuse for refusing to entertain a federal cause of action.

---

[5] In many respects, Correction Law § 24 operates more as an immunity-from-damages provision than as a jurisdictional rule. . . . In *Howlett*, we considered the question whether a Florida school board could assert a state-law immunity defense in a § 1983 action brought in state court when the defense would not have been available if the action had been brought in federal court. We unanimously held that the State's decision to extend immunity "over and above [that which is] already provided in § 1983 . . . directly violates federal law," and explained that the "elements of, and the defenses to, a federal cause of action are defined by federal law." Thus, if Correction Law § 24 were understood as offering an immunity defense, *Howlett* would compel the conclusion that it violates the Supremacy Clause.

Respondents correctly observe that, in the handful of cases in which this Court has found a valid excuse, the state rule at issue treated state and federal claims equally. In Douglas v. New York, N. H. & H. R. Co., 279 U.S. 377 (1929), we upheld a state law that granted state courts discretion to decline jurisdiction over state and federal claims alike when neither party was a resident of the State. Later, in Herb v. Pitcairn, 324 U.S. 117 (1945), a city court dismissed an action brought under the Federal Employers' Liability Act (FELA) for want of jurisdiction because the cause of action arose outside the court's territorial jurisdiction. We upheld the dismissal on the ground that the State's venue laws were not being applied in a way that discriminated against the federal claim. In a third case, Missouri ex rel. Southern R. Co. v. Mayfield, 340 U.S. 1 (1950), we held that a State's application of the forum non conveniens doctrine to bar adjudication of a FELA case brought by nonresidents was constitutionally sound as long as the policy was enforced impartially. And our most recent decision finding a valid excuse, Johnson v. Fankell, 520 U.S. 911 (1997), rested largely on the fact that Idaho's rule limiting interlocutory jurisdiction did not discriminate against § 1983 actions.

Although the absence of discrimination is necessary to our finding a state law neutral, it is not sufficient. A jurisdictional rule cannot be used as a device to undermine federal law, no matter how evenhanded it may appear. As we made clear in *Howlett*, "[t]he fact that a rule is denominated jurisdictional does not provide a court an excuse to avoid the obligation to enforce federal law if the rule does not reflect the concerns of power over the person and competence over the subject matter that jurisdictional rules are designed to protect." Ensuring equality of treatment is thus the beginning, not the end, of the Supremacy Clause analysis.

. . . Although Correction Law § 24 denies state courts authority to entertain damages actions against correction officers, this case does not require us to decide whether Congress may compel a State to offer a forum, otherwise unavailable under state law, to hear suits brought pursuant to § 1983. The State of New York has made this inquiry unnecessary by creating courts of general jurisdiction that routinely sit to hear analogous § 1983 actions. . . . For instance, if petitioner had attempted to sue a police officer for damages under § 1983, the suit would be properly adjudicated by a state supreme court. Similarly, if petitioner had sought declaratory or injunctive relief against a correction officer, that suit would be heard in a state supreme court. It is only a particular species of suits—those seeking damages relief against correction officers—that the State deems inappropriate for its trial courts.

We therefore hold that, having made the decision to create courts of general jurisdiction that regularly sit to entertain analogous suits, New York is not at liberty to shut the courthouse door to federal claims that it considers at odds with its local policy. A State's authority to organize its courts, while considerable, remains subject to the strictures of the Constitution. See, e.g., *McKnett v. St. Louis & San Francisco R. Co.*, 292 U.S. 230, 233 (1934). We have never treated a State's invocation of "jurisdiction" as a trump that ends the Supremacy Clause inquiry, and we decline to do so in this case. Because New York's supreme courts generally have personal jurisdiction over the parties in § 1983 suits brought by prisoners against correction officers and because they hear the lion's share of all other § 1983 actions, we find little concerning "power over the person and competence over the subject matter" in Correction Law § 24.[8]

Accordingly, the dissent's fear that "no state jurisdictional rule will be upheld as constitutional" is entirely unfounded. Our holding addresses only the unique scheme adopted by the State of New York—a law designed to shield a particular class of defendants (correction officers) from a particular type of liability (damages) brought by a particular class of plaintiffs (prisoners). Based on the belief that damages suits against correction officers are frivolous and vexatious, Correction Law § 24 is effectively an immunity statute cloaked in jurisdictional garb. Finding this scheme unconstitutional merely confirms that the Supremacy Clause cannot be evaded by formalism.

V

The judgment of the New York Court of Appeals is reversed, and the case is remanded to that court for further proceedings not inconsistent with this opinion. . . .

■ JUSTICE THOMAS, with whom THE CHIEF JUSTICE, JUSTICE SCALIA, and JUSTICE ALITO join as to Part III, dissenting.

. . . Because neither the Constitution nor our precedent requires New York to open its courts to § 1983 federal actions, I respectfully dissent.

I

Although the majority decides this case on the basis of the Supremacy Clause, the proper starting point is Article III of the Constitution. . . . The history of the drafting and ratification of this Article establishes that it leaves untouched the States' plenary authority to decide whether their local courts will have subject-matter jurisdiction over federal causes of action. . . .

---

[8] The dissent's proposed solution would create a blind spot in the Supremacy Clause. If New York had decided to employ a procedural rule to burden the enforcement of federal law, the dissent would find the scheme unconstitutional. Yet simply because New York has decided to impose an even greater burden on a federal cause of action by selectively withdrawing the jurisdiction of its courts, the dissent detects no constitutional violation. Thus, in the dissent's conception of the Supremacy Clause, a State could express its disagreement with (and even open hostility to) a federal cause of action, declare a desire to thwart its enforcement, and achieve that goal by removing the disfavored category of claims from its courts' jurisdiction. If this view were adopted, the lesson of our precedents would be that other States with unconstitutionally burdensome procedural rules did not go far enough "to avoid the obligation to enforce federal law." *Howlett*, 496 U.S. at 381.

There was sharp disagreement at the Philadelphia Convention . . . over the need for lower federal courts. . . . The so-called Madisonian Compromise . . . left to the wisdom of Congress the creation of lower federal courts. . . . The assumption that state courts would continue to exercise concurrent jurisdiction over federal claims was essential to this compromise. . . .

The Constitution's implicit preservation of state authority to entertain federal claims, however, did not impose a duty on state courts to do so. [T]here was at least one proposal to expressly require state courts to take original jurisdiction over federal claims . . . that was introduced in an attempt to forestall the creation of lower federal courts. But in light of the failure of this proposal—which was offered before the adoption of the Madisonian Compromise—the assertions by its supporters that state courts would ordinarily entertain federal causes of action cannot reasonably be viewed as an assurance that the States would never alter the subject-matter jurisdiction of their courts. . . . The Framers' decision to empower Congress to create federal courts that could either supplement or displace state-court review of federal claims, as well as the exclusion of any affirmative command requiring the States to consider federal claims in the text of Article III, confirm this understanding.[2]

The earliest decisions addressing this question, written by then-serving and future Supreme Court Justices, confirm that state courts remain "tribunals over which the government of the Union has no adequate control, and which may be closed to any claim asserted under a law of the United States." Osborn v. Bank of United States, 9 Wheat. 738, 821 (1824). . . .

Under our federal system, therefore, the States have unfettered authority to determine whether their local courts may entertain a federal cause of action. Once a State exercises its sovereign prerogative to deprive its courts of subject-matter jurisdiction over a federal cause of action, it is the end of the matter as far as the Constitution is concerned.

The present case can be resolved under this principle alone. New York Correction Law § 24 . . . erects a jurisdictional bar that prevents the state courts from entertaining petitioner's claim for damages under § 1983. Because New York's decision to withdraw jurisdiction over § 1983

---

[2]   See also Michael G. Collins, Article III Cases, State Court Duties, and the Madisonian Compromise, 1995 Wis. L. Rev. 39, 144 (1995) ("It is . . . extremely difficult to argue from the debatable assumption that state courts would be under an obligation to take all Article III judicial business in the first instance—as a quid pro quo for the Constitution's noninclusion of any reference to lower federal courts—to the conclusion that such a duty still existed when the second half of that bargain was decisively rejected (in the Madisonian Compromise, no less)"); James E. Pfander, Rethinking the Supreme Court's Original Jurisdiction in State-Party Cases, 82 Calif. L. Rev. 555, 596 (1994) ("The framers may well have assumed that the federal system would simply take the state courts as it found them; state courts could exercise a concurrent jurisdiction over any federal claims that fit comfortably within their pre-existing jurisdiction. . . . It seems unlikely, however, that the framers would have chosen to compel the state courts to entertain federal claims against their will and in violation of their own jurisdictional limits").

damages actions—or indeed, over any claims—does not offend the Constitution, the judgment below should be affirmed.

II

The Court has evaded Article III's limitations by finding that the Supremacy Clause constrains the States' authority to define the subject-matter jurisdiction of their own courts. In particular, the Court has held that "the Federal Constitution prohibits state courts of general jurisdiction from refusing" to entertain a federal claim "solely because the suit is brought under a federal law" as a "state may not discriminate against rights arising under federal laws." McKnett v. St. Louis & San Francisco R. Co., 292 U.S. 230, 233–34 (1934). There is no textual or historical support for the Court's incorporation of this antidiscrimination principle into the Supremacy Clause.

A

1

. . . As a textual matter . . . the Supremacy Clause does not address whether a state court must entertain a federal cause of action; it provides only a rule of decision that the state court must follow if it adjudicates the claim. . . .

The Supremacy Clause's path to adoption at the Convention confirms this focus. Its precursor was introduced as part of the New Jersey Plan. But, as explained above, the New Jersey Plan also included an entirely separate provision that [required state courts to hear federal claims. This provision and its Supremacy Clause counterpart] worked in tandem to require state courts to entertain federal claims and to decide the substantive dispute in favor of federal law if a conflict between the two arose.

After the adoption of the Madisonian Compromise and the defeat of the New Jersey Plan, the Framers returned to the question of federal supremacy. A proposal was introduced granting Congress the power to "'negative all laws passed by the several States (contravening in the opinion of [Congress] the articles of Union, or any treaties subsisting under the authority of [Congress]).'" James Madison believed the proposal "essential to the efficacy [and] security of the [federal] Gov[ernmen]t." But others at the Convention, including Roger Sherman, "thought it unnecessary . . . . In the end, Madison's proposal was defeated. But as a substitute for that rejected proposal, Luther Martin resurrected the Supremacy Clause provision from the New Jersey Plan and it was unanimously approved. This historical record makes clear that the Supremacy Clause's exclusive function is to disable state laws that are substantively inconsistent with federal law—not to require state courts to hear federal claims over which the courts lack jurisdiction. . . .

The Supremacy Clause's exclusive focus on substantive state law is also evident from the context in which it was [introduced]. . . .

[T]he timing of the Clause's adoption suggests that the Framers viewed it as achieving the same end as Madison's congressional "negative" proposal. Although Madison believed that Congress could most effectively countermand inconsistent state laws, the Framers decided that the Judiciary could adequately perform that function. There is no evidence that the Framers envisioned the Supremacy Clause as having a substantively broader sweep than the proposal it replaced. And, there can be no question that Madison's congressional "negative" proposal was entirely unconcerned with the dispute over whether state courts should be required to exercise jurisdiction over federal claims. Indeed, Madison's proposal did not require the States to become enmeshed in any federal business at all; it merely provided that state laws could be directly nullified if Congress found them to be inconsistent with the Constitution or laws of the United States. The role of the Supremacy Clause is no different. It does not require state courts to entertain federal causes of action. Rather, it only requires that in reaching the merits of such claims, state courts must decide the legal question in favor of the "law of the Land." . . .

The supremacy of federal law . . . therefore, is not impugned by a State's decision to strip its local courts of subject-matter jurisdiction to hear certain federal claims. Subject-matter jurisdiction determines only whether a court has the power to entertain a particular claim—a condition precedent to reaching the merits of a legal dispute. Although the line between subject-matter jurisdiction over a claim and the merits of that claim can at times prove difficult to draw, the distinction is crucial in the Supremacy Clause context. If the state court does not reach the merits of the dispute for lack of statutory or constitutional jurisdiction, the preeminence of federal law remains undiminished. . . .

2

The Court was originally faithful to this conception of federal supremacy. In Claflin v. Houseman, 93 U.S. 130 (1876), the Court concluded that because the federal statute under consideration did not deprive the state court of jurisdiction, the state court was competent to resolve the claim. . . . Then in Second Employers' Liability Cases, 223 U.S. 1 (1912), the Court applied the rule set forth in *Claflin* and correctly rejected a Connecticut court's refusal to enforce the 1908 Federal Employers' Liability Act (FELA). FELA neither provided for exclusive federal jurisdiction nor attempted to require state courts to entertain claims brought under it. Therefore, the statute was enforceable "as of right, in the courts of the States *when their jurisdiction, as prescribed by local laws, is adequate to the occasion.*" Id. at 55 (emphasis added). Connecticut had not deprived its courts of subject-matter jurisdiction over FELA claims; thus, the state court's refusal to hear the claim was "not because the ordinary jurisdiction of the Superior Courts, as defined by the constitution and laws of the State, was deemed inadequate or not adapted to the adjudication of such a case." Rather, the state court took the position that "it would be inconvenient and confusing for the same court, in dealing with cases of the same general class, to apply in some the standards of right established by the congressional act and in others the different standards recognized by the laws of the State."

The Court's reversal of such a decision is compatible with the original understanding of Article III and the Supremacy Clause. Because there was no question that the state court had subject-matter jurisdiction under state law to adjudicate the federal claim, the Court correctly observed that the state court's refusal to decide the case amounted to a policy dispute with federal law . . . . As the Court correctly noted, the existence of the jurisdiction creates an implication of duty to exercise it, and that its exercise may be onerous does not militate against that implication.

But nothing in *Second Employers'* suggested that the Supremacy Clause could pre-empt a state law that deprived the local court of subject-matter jurisdiction over the federal claim. Instead, the *Second Employers'* Court took exactly the opposite position on this question: "[W]e deem it well to observe that there is not here involved any attempt by Congress to enlarge or regulate the jurisdiction of state courts . . . but only a question of the duty of such a court, when its ordinary jurisdiction as prescribed by local laws is appropriate to the occasion."

The Court again confronted this issue in Douglas v. New York, N.H. & H.R. Co., 279 U.S. 377 (1929). There, the Court considered whether a New York court was required to hear a claim brought under FELA. Unlike the Connecticut court in *Second Employers'*, however, the New York court did not have jurisdiction under state law to entertain the federal cause of action. As a result, this Court upheld the state-court ruling that dismissed the claim. . . . [B]ecause the New York court lacked subject-matter jurisdiction under state law, it was not "otherwise competent" to adjudicate the federal claim.

In sum, *Claflin*, *Second Employers'*, and *Douglas* together establish that a state court's inability to entertain a federal claim because of a lack of state-law jurisdiction is an "otherwise valid excuse" that in no way denies the superiority of federal substantive law. It simply disables the state court from adjudicating a claim brought under that federal law.

3

It was not until five years after *Douglas* that the Court used the Supremacy Clause to strike down a state jurisdictional statute for its failure to permit state-court adjudication of federal claims. See McKnett v. St. Louis & San Francisco R. Co., 292 U.S. 230 (1934). The Court started by correctly noting that it "was settled" in *Second Employers'* "that a state court whose ordinary jurisdiction as prescribed by local laws is appropriate to the occasion, may not refuse to entertain suits under [FELA]." Yet, even though the Alabama court *lacked* such jurisdiction over the relevant federal claim pursuant to a state statute, the *McKnett* Court held that the state court had improperly dismissed the federal claim.

According to the Court, "[w]hile Congress has not attempted to compel states to provide courts for the enforcement of [FELA], the Federal Constitution prohibits state courts of general jurisdiction from refusing to do so solely because the suit is brought under a federal law. The denial of jurisdiction by the Alabama court is based solely upon the source of law sought to be enforced. The plaintiff is cast out because he is suing to enforce a federal act. A state may not discriminate against rights arising under federal laws."

For all the reasons identified above, *McKnett* cannot be reconciled with the decisions of this Court that preceded it. Unlike the Connecticut court in *Second Employers'*, the Alabama Supreme Court did not indulge its own bias against adjudication of federal claims in state court by refusing to hear a federal claim over which it had subject-matter jurisdiction. Rather, like the New York court decision affirmed in *Douglas*, the Alabama court's dismissal merely respected a jurisdictional barrier to adjudication of the federal claim imposed by state law. The fact that Alabama courts were competent to hear similar state-law claims should have been immaterial. Alabama had exercised its sovereign right to establish the subject-matter jurisdiction of its courts. Under *Claflin* and its progeny, that legislative judgment should have been upheld.

Despite *McKnett*'s infidelity to the Constitution and more than a century of Supreme Court jurisprudence, the Court's later decisions have repeated *McKnett*'s declaration that state jurisdictional statutes must be policed for antifederal discrimination. See, e.g., Testa v. Katt, 330 U.S. 386, 394 (1947) ("It is conceded that this same type of claim arising under Rhode Island law would be enforced by that State's courts. . . . Under these circumstances the State courts are not free to refuse enforcement of petitioners' claim"); Howlett v. Rose, 496 U.S. 356, 375 (1990) ("[W]hether the question is framed in pre-emption terms, as petitioner would have it, or in the obligation to assume jurisdiction over a 'federal' cause of action, . . . the Florida court's refusal to entertain one discrete category of § 1983 claims, when the court entertains similar state-law actions against state defendants, violates the Supremacy Clause"). The outcome in these cases, however, can be reconciled with first principles notwithstanding the Court's stated reliance on *McKnett*'s flawed interpretation of the Supremacy Clause.

In *Testa*, the Court struck down the Rhode Island Supreme Court's refusal to entertain a claim under the federal Emergency Price Control Act. There was no dispute that "the Rhode Island courts [had] jurisdiction adequate and appropriate under established local law to adjudicate this action." . . . Because the Rhode Island Supreme Court had invoked [a] common-law doctrine despite the existence of state-law statutory jurisdiction over the federal claims, this Court correctly ruled that the state court's "policy against enforcement . . . of statutes of other states and the United States which it deems penal, [could not] be accepted as a 'valid excuse.' "

Testa thus represents a routine application of the rule of law set forth in *Second Employers'*: As long as jurisdiction over a federal claim exists as a matter of state law, state-court judges cannot sua sponte refuse to enforce federal law because they disagree with Congress's decision to allow for adjudication of certain federal claims in state court.

In *Howlett*, the Court likewise correctly struck down a Florida Supreme Court decision affirming the dismissal of a § 1983 suit on state-law sovereign immunity grounds. The Florida court had interpreted the State's statutory "waiver of sovereign immunity" not to extend to federal claims brought in state court. According to the state court, absent a statutory waiver, Florida's pre-existing common-law sovereign immunity rule provided a "blanket immunity on [state] governmental entities from federal civil rights actions under § 1983" brought in Florida courts. Based on this rule, the Florida Supreme Court affirmed the dismissal with prejudice of the § 1983 suit against the state officials.

No antidiscrimination rule was required to strike down the Florida Supreme Court's decision. . . . First, because the Florida Supreme Court had dismissed the § 1983 lawsuit with prejudice, its decision was on the merits. Second, Florida's sovereign immunity rule violated the Supremacy Clause by operating as a state-law defense to a federal law. Resolving a federal claim with preclusive effect based on a state-law defense is far different from simply closing the door of the state courthouse to that federal claim. The first changes federal law by denying relief on the merits; the second merely dictates the forum in which the federal claim will be heard.

. . . [C]ontrary to *McKnett*, the Constitution does not require state courts to give equal billing to state and federal claims. To read the Supremacy Clause to include an anti-discrimination principle undermines the compromise that shaped Article III and contradicts the original understanding of Constitution. There is no justification for preserving such a principle. . . .

B

. . . [Section 1983] includes no substantive command requiring New York to provide a state judicial forum to a § 1983 plaintiff. . . . [Nor does] NYCLA § 24 . . . conflict with § 1983. . . . Congress did not grant § 1983 plaintiffs a "right" to bring their claims in state court or "guarantee" that the state forum would remain open to their suits. Moreover, Congress has created inferior federal courts that have the power to adjudicate all § 1983 actions. And this Court has expressly determined that § 1983 plaintiffs do not have to exhaust state-court remedies before proceeding in federal court. See Patsy v. Board of Regents of State of Fla., 457 U.S. 496, 516 (1982).

Therefore, even if every state court closed its doors to § 1983 plaintiffs, the plaintiffs could proceed with their claims in the federal forum. And because the dismissal of § 1983 claims from state court pursuant to

NYCLA § 24 is for lack of subject-matter jurisdiction, it has no preclusive effect on claims refiled in federal court . . . and thus does not alter the substance of the federal claim. Any contention that NYCLA § 24 conflicts with § 1983 therefore would be misplaced.

The Court nevertheless has relied on an expansive brand of "conflict" pre-emption to strike down state-court procedural rules that are perceived to "burde[n] the exercise of the federal right" in state court. Felder v. Casey, 487 U.S. 131, 141 (1988). In such cases, the Court has asked if the state-law rule, when applied "to § 1983 actions brought in state courts [is] consistent with the goals of the federal civil rights laws, or does the enforcement of such a requirement instead 'stand as an obstacle to the accomplishment and execution of the full purposes and objectives of Congress'?" See id. at 138 (quoting Hines v. Davidowitz, 312 U.S. 52, 67 (1941)). There has been no suggestion in this case, however, that NYCLA § 24 is a procedural rule that must be satisfied in order to bring the § 1983 action in state court. As explained above, petitioner's claim was not procedurally deficient; the state court simply lacked the power to adjudicate the claim. Thus, the *Felder* line of cases is inapplicable to this case.

But even if there were such a claim made in this case, the Supremacy Clause supplies this Court with no authority to pre-empt a state procedural law merely because it "burdens the exercise" of a federal right in state court. "Under the Supremacy Clause, state law is pre-empted only by federal law 'made in Pursuance' of the Constitution—not by extratextual considerations of the purposes underlying congressional inaction," such as a desire to ensure that federal law is not burdened by state-law procedural obligations. Wyeth v. Levine, 555 U.S. 555, 603 (2009) (Thomas, J., concurring in judgment). A sweeping approach to pre-emption based on perceived congressional purposes "leads to the illegitimate—and thus, unconstitutional—invalidation of state laws." Id. at 604. I cannot agree with the approach employed in *Felder* "that pre-empts state laws merely because they 'stand as an obstacle to the accomplishment and execution of the full purposes and objectives' of federal law . . . as perceived by this Court." Id.

III

Even accepting the entirety of the Court's precedent in this area of the law, however, I still could not join the majority's resolution of this case as it mischaracterizes and broadens this Court's decisions. . . .

A

. . . A jurisdictional statute simply deprives the relevant court of the power to decide the case altogether. Such a statute necessarily operates without prejudice to the adjudication of the matter in a competent forum. Jurisdictional statutes therefore by definition are incapable of undermining federal law. NYCLA § 24 no more undermines § 1983 than the amount-in-controversy requirement for federal diversity jurisdiction undermines state law. The relevant law (state or federal) remains fully operative in both circumstances. The sole consequence of the jurisdictional barrier is that the law cannot be enforced in one particular judicial forum.

As a result, the majority's focus on New York's reasons for enacting this jurisdictional statute is entirely misplaced. The States "remain independent and autonomous within their proper sphere of authority." *Printz v. United States*, 521 U.S. 898, 928 (1997). New York has the organic authority, therefore, to tailor the jurisdiction of state courts to meet its policy goals.

. . . Unlike the Florida immunity rule in *Howlett*, NYCLA § 24 is not a defense to a federal claim and the dismissal it authorizes is without prejudice. For this reason, NYCLA § 24 is not merely "denominated" as jurisdictional—it actually is jurisdictional. The New York courts, therefore, have not declared a "category" of § 1983 claims to be " 'frivolous' " or to have " 'no merit' " in order to " 'relieve congestion' " in the state-court system (quoting *Howlett*, 496 U.S. at 380). These courts have simply recognized that they lack the power to adjudicate this category of claims regardless of their merit.

The majority's failure to grapple with the clear differences between the immunity rule at issue in *Howlett* and NYCLA § 24 proves that its decision is untethered from precedent. And more broadly, the majority's failure to account for the important role of claim preclusion in evaluating whether a statute is jurisdictional undermines the important line drawn by this Court's decisions between subject-matter jurisdiction and the merits. . . .

The majority's principal response is that NYCLA § 24 "is effectively an immunity statute cloaked in jurisdictional garb." But this curious rejoinder resurrects an argument that the majority abandons earlier in its own opinion. The majority needs to choose. Either it should definitively commit to making the impossible case that a statute denying state courts the power to entertain a claim without prejudice to its reassertion in federal court is an immunity defense in disguise, or it should clearly explain why some other aspect of *Howlett* controls the outcome of this case. This Court has required Congress to speak clearly when it intends to "upset the usual constitutional balance of federal and state powers." *Gregory v. Ashcroft*, 501 U.S. 452, 460 (1991). It should require no less of itself. . . .[11]

---

[11] The majority also suggests that allowing jurisdictional neutrality to be the test "would create a blind spot in the Supremacy Clause" because a procedural rule that too heavily burdens a federal cause of action would be struck down as unconstitutional while "a State could express its disagreement with (and even open hostility to) a federal cause of action, declare a desire to thwart its enforcement, and achieve that goal by removing the disfavored category of claims from its courts' jurisdiction." . . . [T]he majority obscures important differences between procedural rules, like the notice-of-claim rule at issue in *Felder*, and neutral jurisdictional statutes like NYCLA § 24. Unlike a neutral jurisdictional statute, which merely prevents a state court from entertaining a federal claim, failure to comply with a state procedural rule will result in dismissal of a federal claim with prejudice. Contrary to the majority's assertion, therefore, it is

B

The majority also incorrectly concludes that NYCLA § 24 is not a neutral jurisdictional statute because it applies to a "narrow class of defendants" and because New York courts "hear the lion's share of all other § 1983 actions." A statute's jurisdictional status does not turn on its narrowness or on its breadth. Rather, as explained above, a statute's jurisdictional status turns on the grounds on which the state-law dismissal rests and the consequences that follow from such rulings. No matter how narrow the majority perceives NYCLA § 24 to be, it easily qualifies as jurisdictional under this established standard. Accordingly, it is immaterial that New York has chosen to allow its courts of general jurisdiction to entertain § 1983 actions against certain categories of defendants but not others (such as correction officers), or to entertain § 1983 actions against particular defendants for only certain types of relief.

Building on its assumption that a statute's jurisdictional status turns on its scope, the majority further holds that "having made the decision to create courts of general jurisdiction that regularly sit to entertain analogous suits, New York is not at liberty to shut the courthouse door to federal claims that it considers at odds with its local policy." But whether two claims are "analogous" is relevant only for purposes of determining whether a state jurisdictional statute discriminates against federal law. This inquiry necessarily requires an evaluation of the similarities between *federal* and *state* law claims to assess whether state-court jurisdiction is being denied to a federal claim simply because of its federal character.

In contrast, the majority limits its analysis to state-law claims, finding discrimination based solely on the fact that state law provides jurisdiction in state court for claims against state officials who serve in "analogous" roles to the correction officers. The majority's inquiry is not probative of antifederal discrimination, which is the concern that first led this Court in *McKnett* to find a Supremacy Clause limitation on state-court jurisdictional autonomy. Consequently, there is no support for the majority's assertion that New York's decision to treat police officers differently from correction officers for purposes of civil litigation somehow violates the Constitution.

Worse still, the majority concludes that § 1983 claims for damages against "other state officials" are "sufficiently analogous to petitioner's § 1983 claims" to trigger a Supremacy Clause violation. Under this reasoning, if a State grants its trial courts jurisdiction to hear § 1983 claims for damages against *any* state official, the State's decision to deny those

---

not that state courts with "unconstitutionally burdensome procedural rules did not go far enough"—it is instead that they went too far by placing an insurmountable procedural hurdle in the plaintiff's path that led to a judgment against him on the merits. As a result, the Court's assessment of whether a state procedural rule too heavily burdens a federal right does not have any bearing on the Court's continued adherence to the neutrality principle as the sole determinant in evaluating state-law jurisdictional statutes.

courts the power to entertain some narrower species of § 1983 claims—even on jurisdictionally neutral terms—a fortiori violates the Supremacy Clause. The majority's assurance that its holding is applicable only to New York's "unique scheme" thus rings hollow. The majority is forcing States into an all-or-nothing choice that neither the Constitution nor this Court's decisions require. . . .

ADDITIONAL NOTES ON THE DUTY OF STATE COURTS TO HEAR FEDERAL CLAIMS

1. QUESTIONS AND COMMENTS ON *HAYWOOD*

As the *Haywood* opinions reveal, the propositions for which these cases stand may be formulated in at least three ways. Most broadly, *Testa, Howlett*, and *Haywood* may be taken to stand for the proposition that state courts of general jurisdiction cannot decline to adjudicate federal claims for reasons reflecting disagreement with federal policy. Under this reading, *Haywood* was correctly decided, because New York's reasons for redirecting damages actions against corrections officers were contrary to the federal policy embodied in § 1983.

A second reading is slightly narrower. It would take the true principle to be only that state courts with jurisdiction to hear "analogous" state claims cannot discriminate against federal claims by excluding them from state-court jurisdiction. This formulation explains *Testa* and *Howlett* but arguably not *Haywood*. As Justice Thomas pointed out in Part III of his dissent (joined by Roberts, Scalia, and Alito), New York's law treated damage actions against corrections officers exactly the same, whether they were state or federal. Thus, if discrimination against federal claims were the only issue, *Haywood* arguably should have gone the other way.

The most narrow reading is apparently endorsed only by Justice Thomas. He argued in Parts I and II of his dissent that states should be free to discriminate against federal claims so long as the approach is genuinely jurisdictional. Put differently, Thomas believes that states should be free to exclude federal claims from state court so long as (1) Congress has not commanded otherwise (in a valid exercise of its constitutional authority) and (2) the resulting judgments are jurisdictional only, do not resolve the merits, and therefore do not preclude vindication of federal claims in federal court. Even this narrowest statement of the governing principles is sufficient to explain *Howlett*, which is perhaps why that decision was unanimous. It may also be sufficient to explain *Testa* if, like Justice Thomas, one takes the fact that there was no generally applicable, state legislative policy denying state-court jurisdiction as decisive. At the least, Thomas's dissent suggests that the broad proposition for which *Testa* is typically cited was not necessarily essential to its disposition.

2. QUESTIONS AND COMMENTS ON THE SOURCE OF THE DUTY

What is the source of the obligation of state courts to hear federal claims?[a] Justice Black in *Testa*, and Justice Stevens in both *Howlett* and *Haywood*, said that the requirement comes from the Supremacy Clause. Terrance Sandalow, *Henry v. Mississippi* and the Adequate State Ground: Proposals for a Revised Doctrine, 1965 Sup. Ct. Rev. 187, disagreed.

Sandalow noted that the federal courts were open to the plaintiffs in *Testa*, which meant that a refusal by the state courts to take the case would not have prevented enforcement of the underlying federal rights. He added that the federal substantive policy had to do with the adjustment of rights between the parties, not the uses to which state courts should be put. The burdens to be undertaken by the respective state and federal courts seem peculiarly a matter for the respective legislatures, he asserted, and allowing Congress to make the ultimately controlling judgment sufficiently protects any federal interests at stake. Sandalow concluded that "[i]n the absence of a declaration by Congress that state courts must enforce state rights that Congress has created, there appears to be no substantial reason why the Supreme Court should enforce such an obligation." Sandalow said that, in the end, the justification for *Testa* seems to come down to no more than that it is "unseemly" for state courts to refuse to hear federal claims where similar claims under state law would be heard. That justification, he argued, is insufficient.

Sandalow suggested that if the state courts are to have an obligation to hear federal claims, it should come from Congress not the Supreme Court. What should happen when Congress *permits* the states to exercise concurrent jurisdiction but does not *command* that they do so? At least three solutions seem possible. First, as Sandalow concluded, state courts could be required to hear a federal claim only when Congress explicitly says that they must. Second, the Supreme Court could require state courts to hear federal claims only when the purposes of the particular federal claim at issue would be undermined by a lack of state-court enforcement. Third, the Court could create a general obligation (with or without exceptions) that state courts hear all federal claims over which state jurisdiction is permitted. The Court seems to have chosen the third option. Is this the best choice?

3. *MONTGOMERY V. LOUISIANA*

In Montgomery v. Louisiana, 577 U.S. ___, 136 S.Ct. 718 (2016), the Court appeared to choose Sandalow's third option in the context of state post-conviction proceedings. The Court had held in Miller v. Alabama, 567 U.S. 460 (2012), that a juvenile convicted of homicide could not be subject to a mandatory sentence of life without parole. Consideration of a juvenile's diminished culpability and heightened capacity for reform was constitutionally required. Henry Montgomery was 69 when his claim that *Miller* should be applied retroactively came before the Supreme Court. He had been sentenced

---

[a]   Since questions of state sovereign immunity are often implicated, the issue of whether state courts are obligated to provide remedies for federal constitutional claims has been postponed to Chapter VIII.

to a mandatory term of life without parole for a murder committed in 1963 when he was 17.

Montgomery's retroactivity argument was based on Teague v. Lane, 489 U.S. 288 (1989). *Teague* held that new rules adopted after a state conviction had become final ordinarily should not be applied retroactively on federal habeas corpus. *Teague* then specified exceptions, described in *Montgomery* as follows:

> First, courts must give retroactive effect to new substantive rules of constitutional law. Substantive rules include "rules forbidding criminal punishment of certain primary conduct," as well as "rules prohibiting a certain category of punishment for a class of defendants because of their status or offense." Penry v. Lynaugh, 492 U.S. 302, 330 (1989). . . . Second, courts must give retroactive effect to new " 'watershed rules of criminal procedure' implicating the fundamental fairness and accuracy of the criminal proceeding." Schriro v. Summerlin, 542 U.S. 348, 352 (2004).

Before reaching the merits of Montgomery's retroactivity argument, the Court faced what it called a "jurisdictional" issue. *Teague* concerned the rules governing *federal* habeas corpus. Montgomery's case arose in a *state* collateral proceeding. The Louisiana courts had adopted the *Teague* analysis for application in state collateral proceedings, but had done so under what they regarded as a state-law choice, not a federal-law compulsion.[b] Presumably this would mean that they would be free to shape the *Teague* standards to their own purposes rather than having to follow what the federal courts would do. This possibility formed the crux of the argument that the Court lacked jurisdiction in *Montgomery*.[c] Specifically, the argument was

> that a State is under no obligation to give a new rule of constitutional law retroactive effect in its own collateral review proceedings. As those proceedings are created by state law and under the State's plenary control, . . . it is for state courts to define applicable principles of retroactivity. Under this view, the Louisiana Supreme Court's decision does not implicate a federal right; it only determines the scope of relief available in a particular type of state proceeding—a question of state law beyond this Court's power to review.

The Court was not persuaded:

> The Court now holds that when a new substantive rule of constitutional law controls the outcome of a case, the Constitution requires state collateral review courts to give retroactive effect to that rule. *Teague*'s conclusion establishing the retroactivity of new substantive rules is best understood as resting upon constitutional

---

[b] The Louisiana Supreme Court had adopted "the *Teague* standards for all cases on collateral review in our state courts," but said that "[i]n doing so, we recognize that we are not bound to adopt the *Teague* standards." Taylor v. Whitley, 606 So.2d 1292, 1296 (La. 1992)

[c] There is an argument that the Court could review the state court's application of the *Teague* standards even if the state courts had borrowed them for application as state law. This possibility is addressed in the Notes on Remote Federal Premise Cases following *Standard Oil Co. of California v. Johnson* in Section 3 below.

premises. That constitutional command is, like all federal law, binding on state courts. . . .

Substantive rules . . . set forth categorical constitutional guarantees that place certain criminal laws and punishments altogether beyond the State's power to impose. It follows that when a State enforces a proscription or penalty barred by the Constitution, the resulting conviction or sentence is, by definition, unlawful. . . . Where state collateral review proceedings permit prisoners to challenge the lawfulness of their confinement, States cannot refuse to give retroactive effect to a substantive constitutional right that determines the outcome of that challenge.

In adjudicating claims under its collateral review procedures a State may not deny a controlling right asserted under the Constitution, assuming the claim is properly presented in the case. Louisiana follows these basic Supremacy Clause principles in its post-conviction proceedings for challenging the legality of a sentence. The State's collateral review procedures are open to claims that a decision of this Court has rendered certain sentences illegal, as a substantive matter, under the Eighth Amendment. Montgomery alleges that *Miller* announced a substantive constitutional rule and that the Louisiana Supreme Court erred by failing to recognize its retroactive effect. This Court has jurisdiction to review that determination.

Having established its jurisdiction, the Court then held that *Miller* was "a substantive rule of constitutional law" that the Louisiana courts were bound to enforce.[d] Joined by Justices Thomas and Alito, Justice Scalia dissented on both the Court's jurisdictional holding and its conclusion that *Miller* announced a substantive rule requiring retroactive application. Justice Thomas dissented separately, arguing that the Court lacked jurisdiction because "nothing in the Constitution's text or in our constitutional tradition provides such a right to a remedy on collateral review."

The Court's decision in *Montgomery* might be taken to suggest that it is constitutionally mandatory for states to establish post-conviction review procedures that are at least as broad as federal habeas corpus. Or it could be taken for the narrower proposition that, once a state has adopted a process for collateral review, that review must extend to all valid federal constitutional claims. Both positions reject the idea that states are free to establish post-conviction relief in their own courts on their own terms. Why should this be so? If federal habeas is available as a backup, why should it matter if a state chooses to provide narrower collateral relief in its own courts? Are *Testa v. Katt* and *Haywood v. Drown* helpful in thinking about this question?

---

[d]   It mitigated the effect of its decision by adding that a "State may remedy a *Miller* violation by permitting juvenile homicide offenders to be considered for parole, rather than by resentencing them." It also added that its "holding is limited to *Teague*'s first exception for substantive rules; the constitutional status of *Teague*'s exception for watershed rules of procedure need not be addressed here."

The merits of the retroactivity issue in *Montgomery* are considered as part of the coverage of *Teague* in Chapter VII, Section 1, Subsection B.

The Court made no reference to this line of cases in *Montgomery*. Should it have? Is there an alternative explanation for the result?

The U.S. Solicitor General's amicus brief in *Montgomery* contained an appendix summarizing the various state court views on incorporating *Teague* into their regimes for state post-conviction review. It reported that 25 states—Louisiana among them—"use the framework in *Teague* to decide retroactivity on collateral review," 17 states and the District of Columbia "follow *Teague* in part to decide retroactivity on collateral review," five states use a different framework, and three states have not addressed the question. How might *Montgomery* apply in the 26 jurisdictions that do not fully incorporate *Teague* into their state processes for post-conviction review? Will those states be compelled to follow *Teague* at least for new rules that are "substantive"?

4.   QUESTIONS AND COMMENTS ON "VALID EXCUSE"

If state courts are required to hear federal claims, why should they be permitted to decline jurisdiction when they have a "valid excuse"? What exceptions to the obligation are appropriate?

Sandalow had a position on this question as well. If refusal to accept jurisdiction over a federal claim is somehow inconsistent with federal policy, why does it matter that the state courts would not have jurisdiction over a comparable state claim? The federal policy is undermined, Sandalow argued, no matter the rationale under state law for not hearing the claim. The Supremacy Clause, if that is the source of the obligation, seems equally offended by any reason for closing the state court doors. Is this position persuasive?[e]

5.   THE ANTI-COMMANDEERING PRINCIPLE

In Printz v. United States, 521 U.S. 898 (1997), the Supreme Court ruled that Congress could not constitutionally require local law enforcement to conduct background checks of firearms purchasers, as specified in the Brady Handgun Violence Prevention Act. The Court found the requirement violative of what has been called the anti-commandeering principle, namely, that "[t]he federal government may not compel the states to enact or administer a federal regulatory program." New York v. United States, 505 U.S. 144, 188 (1992).

Although the anti-commandeering principle in terms applies only to executive and legislative officers, there is some tension between that view of state sovereignty as a limit on federal legislative power and the requirement,

---

[e]   Compare Nicole A. Gordon and Douglas Gross, Justiciability of Federal Claims in State Court, 59 Notre Dame L. Rev. 1145 (1984) (arguing that "the supremacy clause . . . requires state courts to vindicate federal rights, even when similar rights under state law are held to be non-justiciable"). For a very different perspective on the jurisdictional autonomy of state courts, see Michael G. Collins, Article III Cases, State Court Duties, and the Madisonian Compromise, 1995 Wis. L. Rev. 39 (attacking the historical foundation of *Testa v. Katt* and calling for "curbs on Congress's ability further to conscript state courts in the administration of federal law"). See also Anthony J. Bellia Jr., Congressional Power and State Court Jurisdiction, 94 Geo. L.J. 949 (2006); Charlton C. Copeland, Federal Law in State Court: Judicial Federalism through a Relational Lens, 19 Wm. & Mary Bill of Rts J. 511 (2011); Samuel P. Jordan, Reverse Abstention, 92 B.U. L. Rev. 1771 (2012).

usually associated with *Testa v. Katt*, that state courts must hear federal claims. The *Printz* Court distinguished congressional "commandeering" of state judges on the ground that they are bound by the Supremacy Clause to enforce state law. This reasoning, though not the conclusion to which it leads, is questioned and its implications explored in Martin H. Redish and Steven G. Sklaver, Federal Power to Commandeer State Courts: Implications for the Theory of Judicial Federalism, 32 Ind. L. Rev. 71 (1998), and Vicki C. Jackson, The Infrastructure of Federal Supremacy, 32 Ind. L. Rev. 111 (1998). For an argument that Congress does not have the constitutional authority to vest state courts with jurisdiction and that, as a result, "if a state court lacks any courts of general jurisdiction, Congress would be helpless to mandate that the state courts hear a cause of action," see Josh Blackmun, State Judicial Sovereignty, 2016 U. Ill. L. Rev. 2033, 2128.

NOTES ON PRECLUDING STATE COURTS FROM HEARING FEDERAL QUESTIONS

1. BACKGROUND

State courts are precluded from hearing federal claims where Congress has provided that federal jurisdiction is exclusive. See, e.g., 28 U.S.C. § 1338 (patent cases).[a] In *Gulf Offshore* the Court said that state jurisdiction is also precluded if there is "a clear incompatibility between state-court jurisdiction and federal interests" The Court gave no examples of "clear incompatibility" but presumably had in mind situations where state court jurisdiction has been foreclosed without explicit statutory command. Examples of such situations are surveyed in the following notes.

2. *TARBLE'S CASE*

Tarble's Case, 80 U.S. (13 Wall.) 397 (1872), involved a habeas corpus petition filed before a state court commissioner in Dane County, Wisconsin. The defendant was a recruiting officer of the United States Army. The petition was filed by a father who alleged that his son, who was less than 18 years old, had enlisted under a false name without the father's consent and that the enlistment was therefore illegal. The commissioner issued the writ, and the Supreme Court of Wisconsin affirmed the order discharging the son from the custody of the Army.

The issue, according to the Supreme Court, was "[w]hether any judicial officer of a state has jurisdiction to issue a writ of habeas corpus, or to continue proceedings under the writ when issued, for the discharge of a person held under the authority, or under claim and color of the authority, of the United States, by an officer of that government." The response was categorical: "[N]o state can authorize one of its judges or courts to exercise judicial

---

[a]   See also 18 U.S.C. § 3231 (district court jurisdiction over federal crimes shall be "exclusive of the courts of the States"). There have been occasional proposals for the use of state courts to prosecute federal crimes. For examination of the constitutional and practical difficulties posed by such proposals and the conclusion that they should be rejected, see Michael G. Collins and Jonathan Remy Nash, Prosecuting Federal Crimes in State Courts, 97 Va. L. Rev. 243 (2011).

power, by habeas corpus or otherwise, within the jurisdiction of another and independent government." The Court explained:

> There are within the territorial limits of each state two governments, restricted in their spheres of action, but independent of each other, and supreme within their respective spheres. . . . Neither government can intrude within the jurisdiction . . . of the other. The two governments in each state stand in their respective spheres of action in the same independent relation to each other, except in one particular, that they would if their authority embraced distinct territories. That particular consists in the supremacy of the authority of the United States when any conflict arises between the two governments. . . . Whenever . . . any conflict arises . . . the national government must have supremacy until the validity of the different enactments and authorities can be finally determined by the tribunals of the United States. This temporary supremacy until judicial decision by the national tribunals, and the ultimate determination of the conflict by such decision, are essential to the preservation of order and peace, and the avoidance of forcible collision between the two governments.
>
> Such being the distinct and independent character of the two governments, . . . it follows that neither can intrude with its judicial process into the domain of the other, except so far as such intrusion may be necessary on the part of the national government to preserve its rightful supremacy in cases of conflict of authority.

The Court then shifted to more practical considerations:

> Now, among the powers assigned to the national government, is the power "to raise and support Armies" and the power "to [make Rules] for the Government and Regulation of the land and naval Forces." The execution of these powers falls within the line of its duties; and its control over the subject is plenary and exclusive. . . . No interference with the execution of this power of the national government in the formation, organization, and government of its armies by any state officials could be permitted without greatly impairing the efficiency, if it did not utterly destroy, this branch of the public service. Probably in every county and city in the several states there are one or more officers authorized by law to issue writs of habeas corpus on behalf of persons alleged to be illegally restrained of their liberty; and if soldiers could be taken from the army of the United States, and the validity of their enlistment inquired into by any one of these officers, such proceeding could be taken by all of them, and no movement could be made by the national troops without their commanders being subjected to constant annoyance and embarrassment from this source. The experience of the late rebellion has shown us that, in times of great popular excitement, there may be found in every state large numbers ready and anxious to embarrass the operations of the government, and easily persuaded to believe every step taken for the enforcement of its authority illegal and void. Power to issue writs of habeas corpus

for the discharge of soldiers in the military service, in the hands of parties thus disposed, might be used, and often would be used, to the great detriment of the public service. . . .

This limitation upon the power of state tribunals and state officers furnishes no just ground to apprehend that the liberty of the citizen will thereby be endangered. [The courts of the United States] are clothed with the power to issue the writ of habeas corpus in all cases, where a party is illegally restrained of his liberty by an officer of the United States. . . . And there is no just reason to believe that they will exhibit any hesitation to exert their power, when it is properly invoked. . . .

3. QUESTIONS AND COMMENTS ON *TARBLE'S CASE*

In a sense, *Tarble's Case* is the converse of *Haywood v. Drown*. Both cases concern whether the Supreme Court is justified, in the absence of Congressional command, in limiting state control over the cases to be heard in its own courts. In *Haywood* the question was whether a reluctant state court should be required to hear a federal claim; in *Tarble* the question was whether a willing state court should be foreclosed from hearing a federal claim.

What is the basis for the Court's conclusion in *Tarble*? Would the Court have reacted differently if habeas had not been available in the lower federal courts? Today, it is unlikely that *Tarble* would arise in precisely the same way, as the defendant-official could remove the case to a federal court. See 28 U.S.C. § 1442a, enacted in 1956.

4. *MCCLUNG V. SILLIMAN*

McClung claimed an interest in land owned by the federal government and sought to compel Silliman, the federal officer in charge of the land, to make a formal conveyance. Silliman refused, on the ground that the interest had already been conveyed to another. McClung first sought mandamus in the local federal court, which held that it did not have jurisdiction to award mandamus against a federal officer, and the Supreme Court affirmed. McIntire v. Wood, 11 U.S. (7 Cranch) 504 (1813). McClung then sought mandamus in state court, but the Supreme Court ruled that state courts lacked the authority to issue mandamus against a federal officer. McClung v. Silliman, 19 U.S. (6 Wheat.) 598 (1821). The Court reasoned:

It is not easy to conceive, on what legal ground, a state tribunal can, in any instance, exercise the power of issuing a mandamus to the register of a land-office. The United States have not thought proper to delegate that power to their own courts. But when, in the cases of Marbury v. Madison, 5 U.S. (1 Cranch) 137 (1803), and McIntire v. Wood, 11 U.S. (7 Cranch) 504 (1813), this Court decided against the exercise of that power, the idea never presented itself to any one, that it was not within the scope of the judicial powers of the United States, although not vested by law in the courts of the general government. And no one will seriously contend, it is presumed, that it is among the reserved powers of the states, because not communicated by law to the courts of the United States.

There is but one shadow of a ground on which such a power can be contended for, which is, the general rights of legislation which the states possess over the soil within their respective territories. It is not now necessary to consider that power, as to the soil reserved to the United States, in the states respectively. The question in this case is, as to the power of the state courts, over the officers of the general government, employed in disposing of that land, under the laws passed for that purpose. [The] conduct [of such an officer] can only be controlled by the power that created him; since, whatever doubts have from time to time been suggested, as to the supremacy of the United States in its legislative, judicial or executive powers, no one has ever contested its supreme right to dispose of its own property in its own way. And when we find it withholding from its own courts, the exercise of this controlling power over its ministerial officers, employed in the appropriation of its lands, the inference clearly is, that all violations of private right, resulting from the acts of such officers, should be the subject of actions for damages, or to recover the specific property (according to circumstances), in courts of competent jurisdiction. That is, that parties should be referred to the ordinary mode of obtaining justice, instead of resorting to the extraordinary and unprecedented mode of trying such questions on a motion for a mandamus.

Did the Court mean that it is inconsistent with the constitutional structure for a state court to issue a writ of mandamus against a federal officer? Or did the Court mean that Congress, by not conferring mandamus jurisdiction on federal courts, intended to deny the same power to state courts? Note that Congress did not expressly deny mandamus jurisdiction to the federal courts, but simply failed to make an affirmative grant of such jurisdiction. That defect was cured in 1962, when Congress authorized federal courts to issue mandamus against federal officers. See 28 U.S.C. § 1361. *McClung* is still taken to have established that state courts cannot do so.

5. OTHER SUITS AGAINST FEDERAL OFFICIALS IN STATE COURTS

Note the reference near the end of the *McClung* excerpt to the availability of more "ordinary" forms of relief against federal officers. Does this mean that state courts can award damages against a federal officer? Specific performance? An injunction? Or does the reasoning of *Tarble* and *McClung* extend to these forms of relief as well?

The law on this point was summarized in Richard S. Arnold, The Power of State Courts to Enjoin Federal Officers, 73 Yale L.J. 1385, 1397 (1964). Arnold found the cases clear on several points. State courts have jurisdiction to award damages and possession of specific property and to convict for crimes.[b] Habeas and mandamus are off limits. But the lower courts are divided on issuance of injunctions, though most deny state courts the authority to enjoin federal officers. The Supreme Court has not spoken to the issue.

Should state courts be permitted to enjoin federal officers? Contrary to the reasoning (though not necessarily the results) of *Tarble's Case* and *McClung,* Arnold argued that the state courts should have such jurisdiction. He started by observing that state courts frequently hear cases involving federal questions and, once they accept jurisdiction, are obligated by the Supremacy Clause to decide them consistently with federal law. In addition, state courts usually exercise jurisdiction concurrently with federal courts over any subject matter not reserved by statute to the federal courts. Congressional silence typically is taken to leave state court jurisdiction intact. He continued:

> Federal and state law are inseparable parts of one system of jurisprudence, binding alike on all persons within the boundaries of any given state. . . . For a state court, accordingly, to order a federal official to act according to federal law, or to obey valid state law that Congress has not displaced, is no usurpation, nor any assertion that state courts are superior to federal courts or federal officials. It is rather an assertion of the supremacy of law, and especially of federal law.

Are there practical reasons why state courts should not be allowed to interfere with federal officials by injunction? Are the state courts not to be trusted to follow federal law? Any fears in this respect, Arnold concluded, are adequately resolved by one of four responses: Supreme Court review; removal, which is now available to any federal officer sued in a state court "for any act under color of office or in the performance of his duties" (28 U.S.C. § 1442(a)(3)); federal habeas, which is available for persons in custody in violation of the federal Constitution or laws (28 U.S.C. § 2441(c)(3)); or specification by Congress that the jurisdiction of the federal courts is exclusive. Given these controls and the already extensive jurisdiction of state courts over federal officers in actions at law, he concluded, a prohibition of jurisdiction to issue an injunction (or for that matter mandamus or habeas corpus) cannot be defended.

6. *DONOVAN V. DALLAS*

The question presented in Donovan v. Dallas, 377 U.S. 408 (1964), was "whether a state court can validly enjoin a person from prosecuting an action

---

[b] The question whether federal officials can be prosecuted criminally in state courts is extensively discussed in Seth P. Waxman and Trevor W. Morrison, What Kind of Immunity? Federal Officers, State Criminal Law, and the Supremacy Clause, 112 Yale L.J. 2195 (2003). They take as their point of departure the prosecution of an FBI agent for involuntary manslaughter arising out of the Ruby Ridge incident. The case was removed to federal court under 28 U.S.C. § 1442(a)(1), and ultimately dismissed because the state dropped the charges. The authors conclude that "federal officers acting within the scope of their employment should be immune from state prosecution for taking any action they reasonably believe is necessary and proper to the performance of their federal functions. Properly applied, this standard is effectively coextensive with qualified immunity."

in personam in a district or appellate court of the United States which has jurisdiction both of the parties and of the subject matter."

The city of Dallas proposed to issue revenue bonds to finance an additional runway for its municipal airport. Forty-six Dallas citizens brought a class action in state court to prevent this initiative. Summary judgment was rendered for the city, the Texas appellate courts affirmed, and the United States Supreme Court denied certiorari. Knowing that the bonds could not be issued until all litigation involving their validity had concluded, 120 Dallas citizens, including 27 of the same people involved in the state suit, filed an action in federal court on the day bids for the sale of the bonds were to be opened. The city filed a motion to dismiss the federal suit on grounds of res judicata and applied to a Texas court for a writ of prohibition to bar the plaintiffs from further litigation. The Texas courts initially denied relief, but the Texas Supreme Court ordered that the writ be issued.

The plaintiffs not only opposed the city's motion to dismiss the federal suit but filed another federal action, this time against the city and all of the Texas judges who had been involved in issuing the writ, seeking an injunction against enforcement of the state court writ of prohibition. The federal District Court dismissed the first federal case and held the second one moot. When the federal plaintiffs appealed, the Texas courts promptly held them in contempt. Donovan served 20 days in jail, and the other plaintiffs were fined $200 each. The federal appeal was dismissed on a motion "made under duress." The Supreme Court then granted certiorari to review both the initial Texas Supreme Court decision ordering that the writ of prohibition be issued and the subsequent contempt citations.

Justice Black wrote for a six-three majority holding that the state courts had no authority to issue the writ of prohibition:

> Early in the history of our country a general rule was established that state and federal courts would not interfere with or try to restrain each other's proceedings. That rule has continued substantially unchanged to this time. An exception has been made in cases where a court has custody of property, that is, proceedings in rem or quasi in rem. In such cases this Court has said that the state or federal court having custody of such property has exclusive jurisdiction to proceed. . . . It may be that a full hearing in an appropriate court would justify a finding that the state-court judgment in favor of Dallas in the first suit barred the issues raised in the second suit, a question as to which we express no opinion. But plaintiffs in the second suit chose to file that case in the federal court. They had a right to do this, a right which is theirs by reason of congressional enactments passed pursuant to congressional policy. And whether or not a plea of res judicata in the second suit would be good is a question for the federal courts to decide. . . .

> Petitioners being properly in the federal court had a right granted by Congress to have the court decide the issues they presented, and to appeal to the Court of Appeals from the District

Court's dismissal. . . . The Texas courts were without power to take away this federal right by contempt proceedings or otherwise.

Justice Harlan, whose dissent was joined by Justices Clark and Stewart, stated the question quite differently: "May a state court enjoin resident state-court suitors from prosecuting in the federal courts vexatious, duplicative litigation which has the effect of thwarting a state court judgment already rendered against them?" He noted that the Texas Supreme Court made unchallenged findings amply supported by the record that the controversy had "reached the point of vexatious and harassing litigation." He then said:

> The power of a court in equity to enjoin persons subject to its jurisdiction from conducting vexatious and harassing litigation in another forum has not been doubted until now. . . . This Court, in 1941, expressly recognized the power of a state court to do precisely what the Texas court did here. In Baltimore & Ohio R. Co. v. Kepner, 314 U.S. 44, 51–52 (1941), the Court, although denying the state court's power to issue an injunction in that case, said:
>
>> The real contention of petitioner is that . . . respondent is acting in a vexatious and inequitable manner. . . . Under such circumstances, petitioner asserts power, abstractly speaking, in the Ohio court to prevent a resident under its jurisdiction from doing inequity. *Such power does exist.* [Emphasis supplied by Harlan.]

Harlan noted that none of the cases relied on by the majority involved vexatious litigation, and concluded:

> There can be no dispute, therefore, that all the weight of authority . . . is contrary to the position which the Court takes in this case. It is not necessary to comment on the Court's assertion that the petitioners "had a right granted by Congress" to maintain their suit in the federal court, for that is the very question at issue. In any event, the statutory boundaries of federal jurisdiction are hardly to be regarded as a license to conduct litigation in the federal courts for the purpose of harassment. The exception which the Court recognizes for in rem actions demonstrates that no such view of federal jurisdiction is tenable; for in those cases, too, the federal courts have statutory jurisdiction to proceed.

7.   QUESTIONS AND COMMENTS ON *DONOVAN*

In Richard Arnold, State Power to Enjoin Federal Court Proceedings, 51 Va. L. Rev. 59 (1965), the conclusion is that precedent supported Justice Black's position in *Donovan*. A number of cases in the mid-1800s squarely held the state courts without power to enjoin prosecution of a federal suit; the *Kepner* dicta in 1941 did not consider those decisions nor thoroughly canvass the issue; and such authority as there was after *Kepner* followed the old rule. On the question of what the result should be, Arnold thought that a state court injunction should be permitted only if adequate relief could not be obtained in a federal court. He defended this result as a proper "federal common law" solution to avoid unnecessary friction between the two court systems.

Is it relevant to the result in *Donovan* that Congress has forbidden the federal courts to enjoin state court suits in 28 U.S.C. § 2283? Note that § 2283 forbids injunctions only against *pending* litigation; it does not foreclose an injunction against the *institution* of litigation. Note also that § 2283 contains three exceptions, permitting a federal court to act "to protect or effectuate its judgments" and "where necessary in aid of its jurisdiction." These exceptions would have permitted a federal injunction against a pending state court suit if the facts in *Donovan* were reversed. Should that matter?[c]

SECTION 3. SUPREME COURT REVIEW OF STATE COURT DECISIONS

INTRODUCTORY NOTES ON THE POWER OF THE SUPREME COURT TO REVIEW STATE COURT DECISIONS

1. MARTIN V. HUNTER'S LESSEE

The Supreme Court's power to review state-court decisions was settled in Martin v. Hunter's Lessee, 14 U.S. (1 Wheat.) 304 (1816). The case involved when and whether an escheat of land to the state of Virginia had occurred. Hunter's lessee claimed the land under a grant from the state made in 1789. Martin claimed the land through the will of Lord Fairfax, a British subject who had previously owned the land. Two treaties, one in 1783 and one in 1794, prevented state governments from interfering with the normal rights of British subjects to land in the United States. If the land had escheated to Virginia before these treaties went into effect, the state's grant of the land was valid, and Hunter's lessee would prevail. If the land had not escheated until the treaties came into effect, then Virginia never acquired the land and the grant to Hunter was invalid.

The Virginia Court of Appeals (as the highest state court was then known) held in favor of Hunter's lessee, in part on the ground that the land had escheated to Virginia in 1782, before either of the treaties came into effect. The United States Supreme Court reversed, but the Virginia Court of Appeals declined to obey its mandate. The Virginia judges expressed their

---

[c]   Chief Justice Rehnquist thought it should. In dissent in General Atomic Co. v. Felter, 434 U.S. 12 (1977), he argued that *Donovan* should be re-examined and that a "general rule of parity" should be adopted under which "where a federal district court has power to enjoin the institution of proceedings in a state court, a state court must have a similar power to forbid the initiation of vexatious litigation in federal court." He inferred from § 2283 that Congress would not deny to state courts the authority it granted to federal courts. And "[n]either the Supremacy Clause . . . nor the congressional grants of jurisdiction to federal courts in any way militate against the conclusion that *both* state and federal courts possess the authority to protect jurisdiction which they have acquired from being undercut or nullified by suits later instituted in the courts of the other jurisdiction." But the Court held in a per curiam summary reversal that it was "clear from *Donovan* that the rights conferred by Congress to bring in personam actions in federal courts are not subject to abridgment by state-court injunctions, *regardless of whether the federal litigation is pending or prospective*." (Emphasis added.)

views individually, but joined in the unanimous conclusion "that the appellate power of the Supreme Court of the United States . . . does not extend to this court." The case then came back to the Supreme Court, which held that it had statutory authority to review state court decisions and that such authority was constitutional.

Justice Story wrote for the Court. He first addressed the question of constitutional power:

> The appellate power is not limited by the terms of the third article to any particular courts. The words are, "the judicial Power . . . shall extend *to all Cases*," . . . and "in all other Cases before mentioned the supreme Court shall have appellate Jurisdiction." It is the *case,* then, and not *the court,* that gives the jurisdiction. . . . If some of these cases might be entertained by state tribunals, and no appellate jurisdiction as to them should exist, then the appellate power would not extend to *all,* but to *some,* cases. . . .

> [I]t is plain that the framers of the Constitution did contemplate that cases within the judicial cognizance of the United States . . . would arise in the state courts [quoting the Supremacy Clause]. . . . It must, therefore, be conceded that the Constitution . . . meant to provide for cases within the scope of the judicial power of the United States, which might yet depend before state tribunals. It was foreseen that in the exercise of their ordinary jurisdiction, state courts would incidentally take cognizance of cases arising under the Constitution, the laws, and treaties of the United States. Yet to all these cases the judicial power, by the very terms of the Constitution, is to extend. It cannot extend by original jurisdiction if that was already rightfully and exclusively attached in the state courts . . . ; it must, therefore, extend by appellate jurisdiction. . . .

Story next turned to considerations of policy:

> It is further argued, that no great public mischief can result from a construction which shall limit the appellate power of the United States to cases in their own courts: first, because state judges are bound by an oath to support the Constitution of the United States, and must be presumed to be men of learning and integrity; and, secondly, because Congress must have an unquestionable right to remove all cases within the scope of the judicial power from the state courts to the courts of the United States, at any time before final judgment, though not after final judgment. As to the first reason—admitting that the judges of the state courts are, and always will be, of as much learning, integrity, and wisdom, as those of the courts of the United States, . . . it does not aid the argument. The Constitution has presumed . . . that state attachments, state prejudices, state jealousies, and state interests, might sometimes obstruct, or control, or be supposed to obstruct or control, the regular administration of justice. . . .

This is not all. A motive of another kind, perfectly compatible with the most sincere respect for state tribunals, might induce the grant of appellate power over their decisions. That motive is the importance, and even necessity of *uniformity* of decisions throughout the whole United States, upon all subjects within the purview of the Constitution. Judges of equal learning and integrity, in different states, might differently interpret a statute, or a treaty of the United States, or even the Constitution itself: If there were no revising authority to control these jarring and discordant judgments, and harmonize them into uniformity, the laws, the treaties, and the Constitution of the United States would be different in different states, and might, perhaps, never have precisely the same construction, obligation, or efficacy, in any two states. [T]he appellate jurisdiction must continue to be the only adequate remedy for such evils.

There is an additional consideration, which is entitled to great weight. The Constitution of the United States was designed for the common and equal benefit of all the people of the United States. The judicial power was granted for the same benign and salutary purposes. It was not to be exercised exclusively for the benefit of parties who might be plaintiffs, and would elect the national forum, but also for the protection of defendants who might be entitled to try their rights, or assert their privileges, before the same forum. Yet, if the construction contended for be correct, it will follow, that as the plaintiff may always elect the state court, the defendant may be deprived of all the security which the Constitution intended in aid of his rights. Such a state of things can, in no respect, be considered as giving equal rights. To obviate this difficulty, we are referred to the power which it is admitted Congress possess to remove suits from state courts to the national courts. . . .

The power of removal . . . presupposes an exercise of original jurisdiction to have attached elsewhere. . . . But [the power of removal] is always deemed . . . an exercise of appellate, and not of original jurisdiction. If, then, the right of removal be included in the appellate jurisdiction, it is only because it is one mode of exercising that power, and as Congress is not limited by the Constitution to any particular mode, . . . it may authorize a removal either before or after judgment. . . . A writ of error is, indeed, but a process which removes the record of one court to the possession of another court, and enables the other to inspect the proceedings, and give such judgment as its own opinion of the law and justice of the case may warrant. . . .

Finally, Story pointed to history:

Strong as this conclusion stands upon the general language of the Constitution, it may still derive support from other sources. It is an historical fact, that this exposition of the Constitution, extending its appellate power to state courts, was, previous to its adoption, uniformly and publicly avowed by its friends, and admitted by its enemies. . . . It is an historical fact, that at the time when the judiciary act was submitted to the deliberations of the first Congress, composed, as it was, not only of men who had acted a principal part in framing, supporting, or opposing that Constitution, the same exposition was explicitly declared and admitted by the friends and by the opponents of that system. It is an historical fact, that the Supreme Court of the United States have, from time to time, sustained this appellate jurisdiction in a great variety of cases, brought from the tribunals of many of the most important states in the union, and that no state tribunal has ever breathed a judicial doubt on the subject, or declined to obey the mandate of the Supreme Court, until the present occasion. This weight of contemporaneous exposition by all parties, this acquiescence of enlightened state courts, and these judicial decisions of the Supreme Court through so long a period, do, as we think, place the doctrine upon a foundation of authority which cannot be shaken. . . .

2.   *MURDOCK V. CITY OF MEMPHIS*

Murdock v. City of Memphis, 87 U.S. (20 Wall.) 590 (1875), is the *Erie* of appellate review. It held that only questions of federal law are open to Supreme Court review and that state court judgments are final on questions of state law. As in *Erie,* a number of subtleties are hidden in this simple statement. But unlike *Erie, Murdock* had no constitutional pretensions but was based solely on the relevant jurisdictional statute.

In July 1844, Murdock's ancestors conveyed land to the city of Memphis for a naval depot, providing specifically that the land would revert to the grantors or their heirs "in case the same shall not be appropriated by the United States for that purpose." In September 1844, the city conveyed the land unconditionally to the United States. The federal government took possession of the land for the purpose of establishing the naval depot, and made various improvements. Ten years later, it abandoned the project and, by act of Congress, conveyed the land back to the city "for the use and benefit of said city."

Murdock sued the city in state court, claiming that the abandonment of the naval depot triggered his reversionary interest in the land. The state court held that the deed of July 1844 gave Murdock a reversionary interest only if the land were never conveyed to the United States for establishment of the depot. The state court also held that the act of Congress reconveying the land back to the city was unconditional and that the city therefore held complete title to the land.

The case came to the Supreme Court by writ of error under a statute passed in 1867. The 1867 act amended the Judiciary Act of 1789, § 25 of which had established the appellate jurisdiction of the Supreme Court over state court decisions. Both statutes described certain categories of cases subject to Supreme Court review—e.g., cases where the state court held a federal statute unconstitutional, cases where the state court upheld the constitutionality of a state statute against a federal challenge, and cases where a federal right claimed under the Constitution or a statute was denied. The last sentence of the original § 25 provided:

> But no other error shall be assigned or regarded as a ground of reversal in any such case as aforesaid than such as appears on the face of the record and immediately respects the before-mentioned questions of validity or construction of the said Constitution, treaties, statutes, commissions, or authorities in dispute.

This language expressly limited review of state decisions to "questions, that for the sake of brevity, though not with strict verbal accuracy, we shall call federal questions, namely, those in regard to the validity or construction of the Constitution, treaties, statutes, commissions, or authority of the federal government."

The 1867 revision omitted the last sentence of § 25. The effect of this deletion, Murdock argued, was to open the entire case for review—including questions of state law. The Supreme Court disagreed:

> The 25th section of the act of 1789 has been the subject of innumerable decisions, some of which are to be found in almost every volume of the reports from that year down to the present. These form a system of appellate jurisprudence relating to the exercise of the appellate power of this Court over the courts of the states. That system has been based upon the fundamental principle that this jurisdiction was limited to the correction of errors relating solely to federal law. And though it may be argued with some plausibility that the reason of this is to be found in the restrictive clause of the act of 1789, which is omitted in the act of 1867, yet an examination of the cases will show that it rested quite as much on the conviction of this Court that without that clause and on general principles the jurisdiction extended no further. It requires a very bold reach of thought, and a readiness to impute to Congress a radical and hazardous change of a policy vital in its essential nature to the independence of the state courts, to believe that that body contemplated, or intended, what is claimed, by the mere omission of a clause in the substituted statute, which may well be held to have been superfluous, or nearly so, in the old one. . . .

> It is not difficult to discover what the purpose of Congress in the passage of this law was. In a vast number of cases the rights of the people of the Union, as they are administered in the courts of the states, must depend upon the construction which those courts gave to the Constitution, treaties, and laws of the United States. The highest courts of the states were sufficiently numerous, even in 1789, to cause it to be feared that, with the purest motives, this construction given in different courts would be various and conflicting. It was desirable, however, that whatever conflict of opinion might exist in those courts on other subjects, the rights which depended on the federal laws should be the same everywhere, and that their construction should be uniform. This could only be done by conferring upon the Supreme Court of the United States—the

appellate tribunal established by the Constitution—the right to decide these questions finally and in a manner which would be conclusive on all other courts, state or national. This was the first purpose of the statute, and it does not require that, in a case involving a variety of questions, any other should be decided than those described in the act.

[In addition, it] was no doubt the purpose of Congress to secure to every litigant whose rights depended on any question of federal law that that question should be decided for him by the highest federal tribunal if he desired it, when the decisions of the state courts were against him on that question. That rights of this character, guaranteed to him by the Constitution and laws of the Union, should not be left to the exclusive and final control of the state courts.

There may be some plausibility in the argument that these rights cannot be protected in all cases unless the Supreme Court has final control of the whole case. But the experience of 85 years of the administration of the law under the opposite theory would seem to be a satisfactory answer to the argument. It is not to be presumed that the state courts, where the rule is clearly laid down to them on the federal question, and its influence on the case fully seen, will disregard or overlook it, and this is all that the rights of the party claiming under it require. Besides, by the very terms of this statute, when the Supreme Court is of opinion that the question of federal law is of such relative importance to the whole case that it should control the final judgment, that court is authorized to render such judgment and enforce it by its own process. It cannot, therefore, be maintained that it is in any case necessary for the security of the rights claimed under the Constitution, laws, or treaties of the United States that the Supreme Court should examine and decide other questions not of a federal character.

On the merits, the Court held that the deed of conveyance from the United States to the city was unconditional and established no federal rights in Murdock. The question whether Murdock retained a reversionary interest based on the original conveyance to the city was held to be one of state law over which the Court had no jurisdiction.

3. COMMENTS

Murdock limited Supreme Court review of state court decisions to federal questions. The standard proposition is that the Court is not free to reexamine questions of state law decided by state courts.[a] Though this conclusion is well settled, complexities lurk within it. The next two main cases,

---

[a]   For an article that "challenges the longstanding notion that the Supreme Court should never reverse a state supreme court's judgment solely on state-law grounds" and "contends that there exists a narrow category of cases in which the justices can and should consider state-law reversals as an alternative to rulings that would otherwise rest on novel and contentious federal constitutional pronouncements," see Jonathan F. Mitchell, Reconsidering *Murdock*: State-Law Reversals as Constitutional Avoidance, 77 U. Chi. L. Rev. 1335 (2010).

Indiana ex rel. Anderson v. Brand, 303 U.S. 95 (1938), and Standard Oil Co. of California v. Johnson, 316 U.S. 481 (1942), involve instances where the Supreme Court did review issues of state law. The questions to be considered are whether and, if so, on what ground these decisions are consistent with *Murdock*.[b]

Indiana ex rel. Anderson v. Brand

Supreme Court of the United States, 1938.
303 U.S. 95.

■ MR. JUSTICE ROBERTS delivered the opinion of the Court.

[Dorothy Anderson filed an action in state court to compel her retention as a public school teacher. She had been teaching since 1924, and her contracts for the 1931–32 and 1932–33 school years contained a clause giving her tenure under the provisions of the 1927 Teacher Tenure Law. She was told in July 1933 that she was to be terminated for cause. This decision was confirmed after a hearing and an administrative appeal. She nonetheless was permitted to teach during the 1933–34 school year. This suit was filed because she was again threatened with termination when that school year was over.

[The defendant demurred on two grounds: first, that Anderson had already been terminated for cause; and second, that the application of the Teacher Tenure Act to teachers in township schools had been repealed. The demurrer was sustained. The state supreme court affirmed, but only on the second ground. The court did not reach the question of termination for cause, but held that Anderson had not been deprived of a vested property right and that repeal of the applicable portions of the Teacher Tenure Act was not an unconstitutional impairment of her contract with the school authorities. The Supreme Court granted certiorari.]

The court below holds . . . that in enacting laws for the government of public schools, the legislature exercises a function of sovereignty and the power to control public policy in respect of their management and operation cannot be contracted away by one legislature so as to create a permanent public policy unchangeable by succeeding legislatures. In the alternative the court declares that if the relationship be considered as controlled by the rules of private contract the provision for re-employment from year to year is unenforceable for want of mutuality.

As in most cases brought to this Court under the contract clause of the Constitution, the question is as to the existence and nature of the

---

[b]   *Murdock*'s place in the history of the times is comprehensively treated in Michael G. Collins, Reconstructing *Murdock v. Memphis*, 98 Va. L. Rev. 1439 (2012). Collins concludes that:

> *Murdock*'s . . . fundamental holding—to which the Court continues to adhere—that Congress did not give the Court a general ability to reconsider state law questions on direct review, is more than plausible. To the extent that Congress may have been concerned with state court decisions on questions of state law, it was likely concerned about such decisions only when they might thwart the Court's ability to exercise appellate review over state court denials of federal rights. And if so, *Murdock*'s . . . holding [in this respect] stands in need of no revision.

contract and not as to the construction of the law which is supposed to impair it. The principal function of a legislative body is not to make contracts but to make laws which declare the policy of the state and are subject to repeal when a subsequent legislature shall determine to alter that policy. Nevertheless, it is established that a legislative enactment may contain provisions which, when accepted as the basis of action by individuals, become contracts between them and the state or its subdivisions within the protection of article 1, § 10. If the people's representatives deem it in the public interest they may adopt a policy of contracting in respect of public business for a term longer than the life of the current session of the legislature. This the petitioner claims has been done with respect to permanent teachers. The Supreme Court has decided, however, that it is the state's policy not to bind school corporations by contract for more than one year.

On such a question, one primarily of state law, we accord respectful consideration and great weight to the views of the state's highest court but, in order that the constitutional mandate may not become a dead letter, we are bound to decide for ourselves whether a contract was made, what are its terms and conditions, and whether the state has, by later legislation, impaired its obligation. This involves an appraisal of the statutes of the state and the decisions of its courts.

The courts of Indiana have long recognized that the employment of school teachers was contractual and have afforded relief in actions upon teachers' contracts. An act adopted in 1899 required all contracts between teachers and school corporations to be in writing, signed by the parties to be charged, and to be made a matter of public record. A statute of 1921 enacted that every such contract should be in writing and should state the date of the beginning of the school term, the number of months therein, the amount of the salary for the term, and the number of payments to be made during the school year.

In 1927 the state adopted the Teachers' Tenure Act under which the present controversy arises. . . . By this act it was provided that a teacher who has served under contract for five or more successive years, and thereafter enters into a contract for further service with the school corporation, shall become a permanent teacher and the contract, upon the expiration of its stated term, shall be deemed to continue in effect for an indefinite period, shall be known as an indefinite contract, and shall remain in force unless succeeded by a new contract or canceled as provided in the act. The corporation may cancel the contract, after notice and hearing, for incompetency, insubordination, neglect of duty, immorality, justifiable decrease in the number of teaching positions, or other good or just cause, but not for political or personal reasons. The teacher may not cancel the contract during the school term nor for a period 30 days previous to the beginning of any term (unless by mutual agreement) and may cancel only upon five days' notice.

By an amendatory act of 1933 township school corporations were omitted from the provisions of the act of 1927. The court below construed this act as repealing the act of 1927 so far as township schools and teachers are concerned and as leaving the respondent free to terminate the petitioner's employment. But we are of opinion that the petitioner had a valid contract with the respondent, the obligation of which would be impaired by the termination of her employment.

Where the claim is that the state's policy embodied in a statute is to bind its instrumentalities by contract, the cardinal inquiry is as to the terms of the statute supposed to create such a contract. The state long prior to the adoption of the act of 1927 required the execution of written contracts between teachers and school corporations, specified certain subjects with which such contracts must deal, and required that they be made a matter of public record. These were annual contracts, covering a single school term. The act of 1927 announced a new policy that a teacher who had served for five years under successive contracts, upon the execution of another was to become a permanent teacher and the last contract was to be indefinite as to duration and terminable by either party only upon compliance with the conditions set out in the statute. The policy which induced the legislation evidently was that the teacher should have protection against the exercise of the right, which would otherwise inhere in the employer, of terminating the employment at the end of any school term without assigned reasons and solely at the employer's pleasure. The state courts in earlier cases so declared.

The title of the act is couched in terms of contract. It speaks of the making and cancelling of indefinite contracts. In the body the word "contract" appears 10 times in section 1, defining the relationship; 11 times in section 2, relating to the termination of the employment by the employer, and four times in section 4, stating the conditions of termination by the teacher.

The tenor of the act indicates that the word "contract" was not used inadvertently or in other than its usual legal meaning. By section 6 it is expressly provided that the act is a supplement to that of March 7, 1921, requiring teachers' employment contracts to be in writing. By section 1 it is provided that the written contract of a permanent teacher "shall be deemed to continue in effect for an indefinite period and shall be known as an indefinite contract." Such an indefinite contract is to remain in force unless succeeded by a new contract signed by both parties or canceled as provided in section 2. No more apt language could be employed to define a contractual relationship. By section 2 it is enacted that such indefinite contracts may be canceled by the school corporation only in the manner specified. The admissible grounds of cancellation, and the method by which the existence of such grounds shall be ascertained and made a matter of record, are carefully set out. Section 4 permits cancellation by the teacher only at certain times consistent with the convenient administration of the school system and imposes a sanction for violation of its requirements. Examination of the entire act convinces us that the teacher was by it assured of the possession of a binding and enforceable contract against school districts.

Until its decision in the present case the Supreme Court of the state had uniformly held that the teacher's right to continued employment by virtue of the indefinite contract created pursuant to the act was contractual. [For example, in] School City of Elwood v. State ex rel. Griffin, 203 Ind. 626, 634, 180 N.E. 471, 474 (1932), it was said:

> The position of a teacher in the public schools is not a public office, but an employment by contract between the teacher and the school corporation. The relation remains contractual after the teacher has, under the provisions of a Teachers' Tenure Law, become a permanent teacher—but the terms and conditions of the contract are thereafter governed primarily by the statute. . . .

We think the decision in this case runs counter to the policy evinced by the act of 1927, to its explicit mandate and to earlier decisions construing its provisions. . . .

The respondent urges that every contract is subject to the police power and that in repealing the Teachers' Tenure Act the legislature validly exercised that reserved power of the state. The sufficient answer is found in the statute. By section 2 of the act of 1927 power is given to the school corporation to cancel a teacher's indefinite contract for incompetency, insubordination (which is to be deemed to mean willful refusal to obey the school laws of the state or reasonable rules prescribed by the employer), neglect of duty, immorality, justifiable decrease in the number of teaching positions, or other good and just cause. The permissible reasons for cancellation cover every conceivable basis for such action growing out of a deficient performance of the obligations undertaken by the teacher, and diminution of the school requirements. Although the causes specified constitute in themselves just and reasonable grounds for the termination of any ordinary contract of employment, to preclude the assumption that any other valid ground was excluded by the enumeration, the legislature added that the relation might be terminated for any other good and just cause. Thus in the declaration of the state's policy, ample reservations in aid of the efficient administration of the school system were made. The express prohibitions are that the contract shall not be canceled for political or personal reasons. We do not think the asserted change of policy evidenced by the repeal of the statute is that school boards may be at liberty to cancel a teacher's contract for political or personal reasons. We do not understand the respondent so to contend. The most that can be said for his position is that, by the repeal, township school corporations were again put upon the basis of annual contracts, renewable at the pleasure of the board. It is significant that the act of 1933 left the system of permanent teachers and indefinite contracts untouched as respects school corporations in cities and towns of the state.

It is not contended, nor can it be thought, that the legislature of 1933 determined that it was against public policy for school districts in cities and towns to terminate the employment of teachers of five or more years' experience for political or personal reasons and to permit cancellation, for the same reasons, in townships.

Our decisions recognize that every contract is made subject to the implied condition that its fulfillment may be frustrated by a proper exercise of the police power but we have repeatedly said that, in order to have this effect, the exercise of the power must be for an end which is in fact public and the means adopted must be reasonably adapted to that end, and the Supreme Court of Indiana has taken the same view in respect of legislation impairing the obligation of the contract of a state instrumentality. The causes of cancellation provided in the act of 1927 and the retention of the system of indefinite contracts in all municipalities except townships by the act of 1933 are persuasive that the repeal of the earlier act by the later was not an exercise of the police power for the attainment of ends to which its exercise may properly be directed.

As the court below has not passed upon one of the grounds of demurrer which appears to involve no federal question, and may present a defense still open to the respondent, we reverse the judgment and remand the cause for further proceedings not inconsistent with this opinion.

So ordered.

■ MR. JUSTICE CARDOZO took no part in the consideration or decision of this case.

[Justice Black argued in dissent that the Court had misread the Indiana cases and that no "contract" under state law had ever been created.]

NOTES ON FEDERAL PROTECTION OF STATE-CREATED RIGHTS

1.   QUESTIONS AND COMMENTS ON BRAND

Application of the Art. I, § 10 provision that "no State shall . . . pass any . . . Law impairing the Obligation of Contracts" obviously presents a federal question. But state law governs whether there was a contract in the first place and, if so, what obligations it created. If there were no limits on the freedom of state courts to determine whether contractual obligations had been created, the federal limitation on impairment of those obligations might be easily evaded. On the other hand, if the Supreme Court were completely free to substitute its judgment for that of the state court on the state law questions involved, the result would be a federal common law of contracts and state law would no longer matter. Neither alternative seems tenable.

Does it help to ask what state law was at the time the parties were contracting? Is that different from determining the policies that should be followed in fixing the rights and obligations that flow from contracts? Is that what the Supreme Court was doing in *Brand*?

2. PROCEDURAL DUE PROCESS

Today, *Brand* likely would be litigated as a procedural due process case. Anderson's constitutional claim would be that the state deprived her of "liberty" or "property" without adequate procedural protections. Whose law creates the "liberty" or "property" protected by procedural due process?

Board of Regents of State Colleges v. Roth, 408 U.S. 564 (1972), said that federal law defines "liberty," but suggested that "property" is a creature of state law: "Property interests, of course, are not created by the Constitution. Rather they are created and their dimensions are defined by existing rules or understandings that stem from an independent source such as state law—rules or understandings that secure certain benefits and that support claims of entitlement to those benefits."

Suppose *Brand* came up today, Anderson claimed a right to a hearing before she was discharged, the school authorities answered that she had no right to a hearing because she had no "property" interest in her job, and the highest state court ruled that she was indeed terminable at will. Would the Supreme Court review that conclusion? By what standards?[a]

3. *BUSH V. GORE*

Bush v. Gore, 531 U.S. 98 (2000), at least in Chief Justice Rehnquist's view, involved an issue analogous to *Brand*. The case involved recount procedures in the close contest for Florida's electoral votes in the 2000 presidential election. A majority of the Supreme Court put an end to a messy recount process and therefore an end to the debate about the winner of the election. It did so in a per curiam opinion holding that vagaries in the recount process violated equal protection. Joined by Justices Scalia and Thomas, Chief Justice Rehnquist wrote separately to justify the outcome on a different rationale:

> In most cases, comity and respect for federalism compel us to defer to the decisions of state courts on issues of state law. That practice reflects our understanding that the decisions of state courts are definitive pronouncements of the will of the States as sovereigns. Cf. Erie R. Co. v. Tompkins, 304 U.S. 64 (1938). Of course, in ordinary cases, the distribution of powers among the branches of a State's government raises no questions of federal constitutional law . . . But there are a few exceptional cases in which the Constitution imposes a duty or confers a power on a particular branch of a State's government. This is one of them. Article II, § 1, cl. 2, provides that "each State shall appoint, in such Manner as the *Legislature*

---

[a] Two arguably analogous constitutional propositions are that "[f]ull Faith and Credit" must be given to the judgments of one state court by another and that state courts may not deny fair notice by the retroactive interpretation of criminal statutes. In both contexts, state law plays a part in the determination of the rights to which the federal constitutional protection attaches. See also Lucas v. South Carolina Coastal Council, 505 U.S. 1003 (1992) ("takings" issue controlled in part by the "bundle of rights" acquired under state law with title to property).

thereof may direct," electors for President and Vice President. (Emphasis added.) Thus, the text of the election law itself, and not just its interpretation by the courts of the States, takes on independent significance. . . . A significant departure from the legislative scheme for appointing Presidential electors presents a federal constitutional question.

Since the legislature was in charge of the electoral process by federal constitutional compulsion, interference by the state supreme court with the legislature's specifications presented a federal question. If the Florida Supreme Court interpreted and applied Florida law in a manner consistent with the legislative structure, there would be no problem. But if the Florida Court changed the rules and substituted its own views on what should happen, the *Brand* problem would be presented: A requirement of federal law would have been undermined by state court misapplication of state law. On this topic in general, Rehnquist had the following to say:

> In any election but a Presidential election, the Florida Supreme Court can give as little or as much deference to [the legislative structure] as it chooses, so far as Article II is concerned, and this Court will have no cause to question the court's actions. But, with respect to a Presidential election, the court must be both mindful of the legislature's role under Article II in choosing the manner of appointing electors and deferential to those bodies expressly empowered by the legislature to carry out its constitutional mandate.
>
> In order to determine whether a state court has infringed upon the legislature's authority, we necessarily must examine the law of the State as it existed prior to the action of the court. Though we generally defer to state courts on the interpretation of state law . . . , there are of course areas in which the Constitution requires this Court to undertake an independent, if still deferential, analysis of state law.
>
> For example, in NAACP v. Alabama ex rel. Patterson, 357 U.S. 449 (1958), it was argued that we were without jurisdiction because the petitioner had not pursued the correct appellate remedy in Alabama's state courts. Petitioners had sought a state-law writ of certiorari in the Alabama Supreme Court when a writ of mandamus, according to that court, was proper. We found this state-law ground inadequate to defeat our jurisdiction because we were "unable to reconcile the procedural holding of the Alabama Supreme Court" with prior Alabama precedent. The purported state-law ground was so novel, in our independent estimation, that "petitioner could not fairly be deemed to have been apprised of its existence."
>
> Six years later we decided Bouie v. City of Columbia, 378 U.S. 347 (1964), in which the state court had held, contrary to precedent, that the state trespass law applied to black sit-in demonstrators who had consent to enter private property but were then asked to leave. Relying upon *NAACP*, we concluded that the South Carolina

Supreme Court's interpretation of a state penal statute had impermissibly broadened the scope of that statute beyond what a fair
reading provided, in violation of due process. What we would do in
the present case is precisely parallel: Hold that the Florida Supreme Court's interpretation of the Florida election laws impermissibly distorted them beyond what a fair reading required, in violation of Article II.[1]

This inquiry does not imply a disrespect for state *courts* but
rather a respect for the constitutionally prescribed role of state *legislatures*. To attach definitive weight to the pronouncement of a
state court, when the very question at issue is whether the court
has actually departed from the statutory meaning, would be to ab-
dicate our responsibility to enforce the explicit requirements of
Article II.

The Chief Justice then proceeded to detail the ways in which the Florida
Supreme Court had departed from the legislative scheme for handling the
recount issue.

In three separate dissents, Justices Stevens, Souter, Ginsburg, and
Breyer disagreed with the Chief Justice's Article II position. Justice Ginsburg wrote in a part of her opinion joined by the other three dissenters:

No doubt there are cases in which the proper application of
federal law may hinge on interpretations of state law. Unavoidably,
this Court must sometimes examine state law in order to protect
federal rights. But we have dealt with such cases ever mindful of
the full measure of respect we owe to interpretations of state law
by a State's highest court. . . .

Rarely has this Court rejected outright an interpretation of
state law by a state high court. Fairfax's Devisee v. Hunter's Lessee, 11 U.S. (7 Cranch) 603 (1813), NAACP v. Alabama ex rel.
Patterson, 357 U.S. 449 (1958), and Bouie v. City of Columbia, 378
U.S. 347 (1964), cited by the Chief Justice are three such rare instances. But those cases are embedded in historical contexts hardly
comparable to the situation here. *Fairfax's Devisee*, which held that
the Virginia Court of Appeals had misconstrued its own forfeiture
laws to deprive a British subject of lands secured to him by federal
treaties, occurred amidst vociferous States' rights attacks on the
Marshall Court. The Virginia court refused to obey this Court's
Fairfax's Devisee mandate to enter judgment for the British subject's successor in interest. That refusal led to the Court's
pathmarking decision in Martin v. Hunter's Lessee, 14 U.S. (1
Wheat.) 304 (1816). *Patterson*, a case decided three months after

---

[1]　. . . In one of our oldest cases, we similarly made an independent evaluation of state law
in order to protect federal treaty guarantees. In Fairfax's Devisee v. Hunter's Lessee, 11 U.S. (7
Cranch) 603 (1813), we disagreed with the Supreme Court of Appeals of Virginia that a 1782
state law had extinguished the property interests of one Denny Fairfax, so that a 1789 ejectment
order against Fairfax supported by a 1785 state law did not constitute a future confiscation
under the 1783 peace treaty with Great Britain. See 11 U.S. at 623; Hunter v. Fairfax's Devisee,
15 Va. 218, 1 Munf. 218 (Va. 1809).

Cooper v. Aaron, 358 U.S. 1 (1958), in the face of Southern resistance to the civil rights movement, held that the Alabama Supreme Court had irregularly applied its own procedural rules to deny review of a contempt order against the NAACP arising from its refusal to disclose membership lists. We said that "our jurisdiction is not defeated if the nonfederal ground relied on by the state court is without any fair or substantial support' " *Bouie*, stemming from a lunch counter "sit-in" at the height of the civil rights movement, held that the South Carolina Supreme Court's construction of its trespass laws—criminalizing conduct not covered by the text of an otherwise clear statute—was "unforeseeable" and thus violated due process when applied retroactively to the petitioners.

The Chief Justice's casual citation of these cases might lead one to believe they are part of a larger collection of cases in which we said that the Constitution impelled us to train a skeptical eye on a state court's portrayal of state law. But one would be hard pressed, I think, to find additional cases that fit the mold. . . . [T]his case involves nothing close to the kind of recalcitrance by a state high court that warrants extraordinary action by this Court. The Florida Supreme Court concluded that counting every legal vote was the overriding concern of the Florida Legislature when it enacted the State's Election Code. The court surely should not be bracketed with state high courts of the Jim Crow South. . . .

4.   *BUSH V. GORE* AND SUPREME COURT REVIEW OF STATE LAW

In principle, it is hard to disagree with the proposition that manipulation of state law to defeat federal rights states a violation of federal law. Whether the Florida Supreme Court's recount decision could fairly be so characterized, however, was—and is—a matter of intense dispute. The weight of academic opinion seemed to lie with the dissenters,[b] though some commentators supported the Chief Justice's concurring opinion.[c]

---

[b]   See, e.g., Samuel Issacharoff, Political Judgments, 68 U. Chi. L. Rev. 637 (2001) (concluding that Rehnquist's argument "provides little basis for a robust approach to the problem of elections gone bad"); Frank I. Michelman, Suspicion, or the New Prince, 68 U. Chi. L. Rev. 679 (2001) (describing Rehnquist's argument in terms that may fairly be called dismissive); David A. Strauss, *Bush v. Gore*: What Were They Thinking?, 68 U. Chi. L. Rev. 737 (2001) (concluding that the Florida Supreme Court "was not acting in a fundamentally illegitimate way"); Harold J. Krent, Judging Judging: The Problem of Second-Guessing State Judges' Interpretation of State Law in *Bush v. Gore*, 29 Fla. State U. L. Rev. 493 (2001) (examining in detail the materials on which Rehnquist relied and concluding that the decision "flies in the face" of the Court's usual practice in deferring to state-court interpretations of state law); Robert A. Schapiro, Conceptions and Misconceptions of State Law Constitutional Law in *Bush v. Gore*, 29 Fla. State U. L. Rev. 661 (2001) (also providing detailed inquiry into the questions of Florida law); Erwin Chemerinsky, *Bush v. Gore* Was Not Justiciable, 76 Notre Dame L. Rev. 1094 (2001) (arguing, in addition to non-justiciability, that the Supreme Court "impermissibly usurped" the authority of the Florida courts to interpret state law).

[c]   See, e.g., Richard A. Posner, *Bush v. Gore*: Prolegomenon to an Assessment, 68 U. Chi. L. Rev. 718 (2001) (finding "rough justice" in the Supreme Court's decision, given the fact that the Florida Supreme Court "grievously erred" in interpreting state law); Richard A. Epstein, "In Such Manner as the Legislature Thereof May Direct": The Outcome of *Bush v. Gore* Defended, 68 U. Chi. L. Rev. 613 (2001) (concluding that the Florida Supreme Court's "peculiar determination to override . . . the decisions of Florida's canvassing boards, Secretary of State, and circuit

For present purposes, the most important articles are those that analyze *Bush v. Gore* in terms of the more general problem of Supreme Court review of state court interpretations of state law. One of the most interesting is Laura S. Fitzgerald, Suspecting the States: Supreme Court Review of State-Court State-Law Judgments, 101 Mich. L. Rev. 80 (2002). Fitzgerald defends a very narrow scope of Supreme Court review of state-court interpretations of state law, a review that she believes proper only when the Supreme Court "can identify and substantiate some concrete indication that the state court has deliberately manipulated state law to thwart federal law and then evade Supreme Court review." In her view, Supreme Court consideration of the merits of state law would require an articulation of distrust of the bona fides of the state court.

The opposing position is advanced in Henry Paul Monaghan, Supreme Court Review of State-Court Determinations of State Law in Constitutional Cases, 103 Colum. L. Rev. 1919 (2003). Monaghan argues that while deference to state-court interpretations of state-law generally makes sense, the authority of the Supreme Court should not be so limited. He argues that the Supreme Court has a kind of "ancillary jurisdiction" over state law "whenever the applicable federal constitutional provision directly constrains or incorporates state law. This jurisdiction most clearly exists when the federal petitioner asserts that the applicable constitutional provision imposes a duty of fidelity to state law at a given point in time in the past . . . and the petitioner claims that at some later point the time . . . that duty was materially and impermissibly breached." In these situations, Monaghan argues, the supremacy of federal law empowers the Supreme Court to make an "independent judgment" on the content of state law, whenever fidelity to state law is a matter of federal constitutional importance. In the context of *Bush v. Gore*, this approach would mean that it was clearly a federal question whether the Florida Supreme Court had impermissibly departed from state law, given the constraint on state law imposed (in Rehnquist's understanding) by Article II.[d]

Standard Oil Co. of California v. Johnson
Supreme Court of the United States, 1942.
316 U.S. 481.

■ MR. JUSTICE BLACK delivered the opinion of the Court.

The California Motor Vehicle Fuel License Tax Act imposes a license tax, measured by gallonage, on the privilege of distributing any motor

---

court judges crosses [the] line"); Michael W. McConnell, Two-and-a-Half Cheers for *Bush v. Gore*, 68 U. Chi. L. Rev. 657 (2001) (characterizing the Florida Supreme Court's rulings as "dubious at best and disingenuous at worst"); Michael Wells, Were There Adequate State Grounds in *Bush v. Gore*?, 18 Const. Commentary 403 (2001) (arguing that lack of Supreme Court deference to the Florida court's interpretation of state law was appropriate in light of Article II).

[d]   See also Michael E. Solimine, Supreme Court Monitoring of State Courts in the Twenty-First Century, 35 Ind. L. Rev. 335 (2002) (speculating that *Bush v. Gore*'s "aggressive review" of state law in *Bush v. Gore* might signal a new stance toward review of state-court cases), and Jeffrey A. Grove, Supreme Court Monitoring of State Courts in the Twenty-First Century: A Response to Professor Solimine, 35 Ind. L.J. 965 (2002) (commenting on the observations in the preceding article).

vehicle fuel. Section 10 states that the act is inapplicable "to any motor vehicle fuel sold to the government of the United States or any department thereof for official use of said government." The appellant, a "distributor" within the meaning of the act, sold gasoline to the United States Army Post Exchanges in California. The state levied a tax, and the appellant paid it under protest. The appellant then filed this suit in the Superior Court of Sacramento County seeking to recover the payment on two grounds: (1) that sales to the Exchanges were exempt from tax under § 10; (2) that if construed and applied to require payment of the tax on such sales the act would impose a burden upon instrumentalities or agencies of the United States contrary to the federal Constitution. Holding against the appellant on both grounds, the trial court rendered judgment for the state. The Supreme Court of California affirmed. Since validity of the state statute as construed was drawn in question on the ground of its being repugnant to the Constitution, we think the case is properly here on appeal. . . .

Since § 10 of the California act made the tax inapplicable "to any motor vehicle fuel sold to the government of the United States or any department thereof," it was necessary for the Supreme Court of California to determine whether the language of this exemption included sales to post exchanges. If the court's construction of § 10 of the act had been based purely on local law, this construction would have been conclusive, and we should have to determine whether the statute so construed and applied is repugnant to the federal Constitution. But in deciding that post exchanges were not "the government of the United States or any department thereof," the court did not rely upon the law of California. On the contrary, it relied upon its determination concerning the relationship between post exchanges and the government of the United States, a relationship which is controlled by federal law. For post exchanges operate under regulations of the Secretary of War pursuant to federal authority. These regulations and the practices under them establish the relationship between the post exchange and the United States government, and together with the relevant statutory and constitutional provisions from which they derive, afford the data upon which the legal status of the post exchange may be determined. It was upon a determination of a federal question, therefore, that the Supreme Court of California rested its conclusion that, by § 10, sales to a post exchange were not exempted from the tax. Since this determination of a federal question was by a state court, we are not bound by it. We proceed to consider whether it is correct.

On July 25, 1895, the Secretary of War, under authority of Congressional enactments promulgated regulations providing for the establishment of post exchanges. These regulations have since been amended from time to time and the exchange has become a regular feature of Army posts. That the establishment and control of post exchanges have been in accordance with regulations rather than specific statutory directions does not alter their status, for authorized War Department regulations have the force of law.

Congressional recognition that the activities of post exchanges are governmental has been frequent. Since 1903, Congress has repeatedly made substantial appropriations to be expended under the direction of the Secretary of War for construction, equipment, and maintenance of suitable buildings for post exchanges. In 1933 and 1934, Congress ordered certain moneys derived from disbanded exchanges to be handed over to the federal Treasury. And in 1936, Congress gave consent to state taxation of gasoline sold by or through post exchanges, when the gasoline was not for the exclusive use of the United States.

The commanding officer of an Army Post, subject to the regulations and the commands of his own superior officers, has complete authority to establish and maintain an exchange. He details a post exchange officer to manage its affairs. This officer and the commanding officers of the various company units make up a council which supervises exchange activities. None of these officers receives any compensation other than his regular salary. The object of the exchanges is to provide convenient and reliable sources where soldiers can obtain their ordinary needs at the lowest possible prices. Soldiers, their families, and civilians employed on military posts here and abroad can buy at exchanges. The government assumes none of the financial obligations of the exchange. But government officers, under government regulations, handle and are responsible for all funds of the exchange which are obtained from the companies or detachments composing its membership. Profits, if any, do not go to individuals. They are used to improve the soldiers' mess, to provide various types of recreation, and in general to add to the pleasure and comfort of the troops.

From all of this, we conclude that post exchanges as now operated are arms of the government deemed by it essential for the performance of governmental functions. They are integral parts of the War Department, share in fulfilling the duties entrusted to it, and partake of whatever immunities it may have under the Constitution and federal statutes. In concluding otherwise the Supreme Court of California was in error.

Whether the California Supreme Court would have construed the Motor Vehicle Fuel License Act as applicable to post exchanges if it had decided the issue of legal status of post exchanges in accordance with this opinion, we have no way of knowing. Hence, a determination here of the constitutionality of such an application of the act is not called for by the state of the record. Accordingly, we reverse the judgment and remand the cause to the court below for further proceedings not inconsistent with this opinion.

Reversed.

NOTES ON REMOTE FEDERAL PREMISE CASES

1. QUESTIONS AND COMMENTS ON *STANDARD OIL V. JOHNSON*

Standard Oil turned on the meaning of a state tax statute, surely a question of state law. Yet the Supreme Court felt free to examine a premise in the chain of reasoning that led the state court to its conclusion. Cases of this sort can be called "remote federal premise cases."

Suppose that on remand the California court thanked the Supreme Court for its opinion on the meaning of federal law, but reiterated its view that the post exchange was not exempt under the state tax statute. What options would the Supreme Court have then? Would it simply cite *Marbury v. Madison* and *Martin v. Hunter's Lessee* and reverse, accusing the California Supreme Court of ignoring the Supremacy Clause? Or, assuming that there was no federal-law reason for compelling a different answer, would it let the new California decision stand?

2. *CALIFORNIA V. BYERS*

In the words of Chief Justice Burger's plurality opinion, California v. Byers, 402 U.S. 424 (1971), presented "the narrow but important question whether the constitutional privilege against compulsory self-incrimination is infringed by California's so-called 'hit and run' statute which requires the driver of a motor vehicle involved in an accident to stop at the scene and give his name and address. Similar 'hit and run' statutes are in effect in all 50 states and the District of Columbia." The California Supreme Court held that compliance with the statute would have confronted Byers with "substantial hazards of self-incrimination" under federal constitutional decisions, but upheld the statute after interpreting it to impose a "use" restriction on the required disclosures. It then held that it would be "unfair" to punish Byers for failing to stop because he could not have reasonably anticipated judicial creation of the use restriction.

The Supreme Court granted certiorari, as the plurality put it, "to assess the validity of the California Supreme Court's premise that without a use restriction [the statute] would violate the privilege against compulsory self-incrimination." Writing for four Justices, Burger concluded that the privilege would not be violated by enforcement of the statute without the use restriction and that the decision below should be vacated and remanded for further proceedings "not inconsistent" with the Supreme Court's opinion. Justice Harlan concurred, agreeing that the privilege would not be violated by enforcing the statute without a use restriction but on a different analysis. During the course of his opinion, Justice Harlan observed that:

> Of course, after the federal law premise has been removed, the state is free to conclude as a matter of state constitutional or legislative policy that continued imposition of use restrictions with respect to this category of cases would still be appropriate in light of the state's own assessment of the relevant regulatory interests at stake and the personal values protected by the privilege against self-incrimination.

Justices Black, Douglas, Brennan, and Marshall dissented on the merits of the self-incrimination issue.

Byers and *Standard Oil* are analytically similar in that each concerned Supreme Court review of a federal "premise" underlying a state court's conclusion on a question of state law. Do the reasons the Supreme Court would want to exercise reviewing authority in these cases differ? Are they justifiable? On remand, could the California Supreme Court stick by its guns and impose a use restriction as a matter of state law?

3.   *MOORE V. CHESAPEAKE & OHIO RY. CO.*

Moore v. Chesapeake & Ohio Ry. Co., 291 U.S. 205 (1934), involved a railroad employee injured while working in *intra*state commerce. The cause of action came from a Kentucky statute, which precluded the defenses of contributory negligence and assumption of risk if the railroad had violated the Federal Safety Appliance Acts. Less clearly, it may also have said that violation of these federal laws constituted negligence per se.

The question before the Supreme Court was whether the case fell within the federal question jurisdiction of the district courts. The Court held that "the complaint set forth a cause of action under the Kentucky statute and, as to this cause of action, the suit is not to be regarded as one arising under the laws of the United States." In the course of its opinion, however, the Court said that "[q]uestions arising in actions in state courts to recover for injuries sustained by employees in intrastate commerce and relating to the scope of the Federal Safety Appliance Acts are, of course, federal questions which may appropriately be reviewed in this Court." Thus, the standards of the Federal Safety Appliance Act, as incorporated elements of state law, would not support original "arising under" jurisdiction of the federal district courts but would present a federal question subject to appellate review by the Supreme Court.

Note that federal law did not require Kentucky to use federal safety standards in state laws governing intrastate injuries. If the state voluntarily chooses to rely on federal standards, why does their meaning as applied by state law present a federal question? Assume that the Supreme Court reviewed a state case and construed the Safety Appliance Acts in a way that the Kentucky courts did not like. Would the Kentucky courts be free on remand to ignore the Supreme Court's decision and construe the state statute differently? Is the case for Supreme Court review in a *Moore* situation different from the case for review in *Standard Oil* or *Byers*? More or less justifiable?

Finally, does Supreme Court review in these cases result in the issuance of "advisory" opinions? See in this respect Justice Jackson's comments in Herb v. Pitcairn, 324 U.S. 117, 125–26 (1945):

> Our only power over state judgments is to correct them to the extent that they incorrectly adjudge federal rights. And our power is to correct wrong judgments, not to revise opinions. We are not permitted to render an advisory opinion, and if the same judgment would be rendered by the state court after we corrected its views of

federal laws, our review could amount to nothing more than an advisory opinion.

Does Jackson have a point? Is it applicable to *Standard Oil*? To *Byers*? To *Moore*?

4.   *MONTGOMERY V. LOUISIANA*

Darryl Tate pleaded guilty in a Louisiana state court to a murder committed when he was 17 years old. He was sentenced to a mandatory term of life without parole. The Supreme Court held in Miller v. Alabama, 567 U.S. 460 (2012), that a juvenile could not constitutionally be sentenced to life without parole for a homicide without consideration of the reduced culpability and enhanced capacity for reform of that particular offender. The question in State v. Tate, 130 So.3d 829 (La. 2013), was whether *Miller* applied retroactively to Tate's 1982 conviction.

The Supreme Court of Louisiana said that "the standards for determining retroactivity set forth in Teague v. Lane, 489 U.S. 288 (1989), apply to 'all cases on collateral review in our state courts.' Accordingly, our analysis is directed by the *Teague* inquiry." Relying almost exclusively on U.S. Supreme Court cases, the Louisiana court then applied the complicated *Teague* analysis,[a] concluding that it did not require that *Miller* be applied retroactively to a final judgment entered some 30 years earlier.

The Louisiana Supreme Court relied on *Tate* to support its conclusion in State v. Montgomery, 141 So.3d 264 (La. 2014) (Mem.), that *Miller* did not apply retroactively. Montgomery had been sentenced to a mandatory term of life without parole for a murder committed when he was 17. He was 69 when the retroactivity question came before the United States Supreme Court in Montgomery v. Louisiana, 577 U.S. ___, 136 S.Ct. 718 (2016).

The first issue addressed by Justice Kennedy's opinion for the Court was whether the case presented a federal question over which the Court had jurisdiction. The Court held that it did, reasoning that the applicable portion of *Teague* was a constitutionally mandated requirement of federal law that the Louisiana courts, which were otherwise open to hear federal constitutional claims on collateral attack, were bound by the Supremacy Clause to follow:

> If a state collateral proceeding is open to a claim controlled by federal law, the state court "has a duty to grant the relief that federal law requires." Yates v. Aiken, 484 U.S. 211, 218 (1988). Where state collateral review proceedings permit prisoners to challenge the lawfulness of their confinement, States cannot refuse to give retro-

---

[a]   *Teague* involved a federal collateral attack on a state court criminal conviction. *Teague* developed an elaborate analysis for determining when new rules must be applied retroactively to otherwise final state court judgments. The content of the *Teague* analysis is considered in detail in Chapter VII, Section 1, Subsection B, where the merits of the *Miller* retroactivity issue are also addressed.

active effect to a substantive constitutional right that determines the outcome of that challenge.[b]

Given this conclusion on the constitutional obligation to apply *Miller* retroactively, the Court's jurisdiction to review the Louisiana Supreme Court was clear.

In a dissent joined by Justices Thomas and Alito, Justice Scalia took a different view.[c] For him, the Louisiana Supreme Court "adopted *Teague*'s framework to govern the provision of post-conviction remedies available to *state* prisoners in its *state* courts as a matter of *state* law." As for the Louisiana court's obligation under the Supremacy Clause, he said:

> A state court need only apply the law as it existed at the time a defendant's conviction and sentence became final. And once final, "a new rule cannot reopen a door already closed." James B. Beam Distilling Co. v. Georgia, 501 U.S. 529, 541 (1991) (opinion of Souter, J.). Any relief a prisoner might receive in a state court after finality is a matter of grace, not constitutional prescription.

Justice Scalia's position that the state court adopted the *Teague* framework as a matter of state choice rather than federal compulsion followed the position of the Louisiana Supreme Court. It had said previously that it would "adopt the *Teague* standards for all cases on collateral review in our state courts," but that "[i]n doing so, we recognize that we are not bound to adopt the *Teague* standards." Taylor v. Whitley, 606 So.2d 1292, 1296 (La. 1992).

Does it follow from the dissent's view of the role of state law—as Scalia thought it did—that the United States Supreme Court had no jurisdiction to decide *Montgomery*? Could the Court have reviewed the analysis of the federal cases on which the Louisiana Supreme Court relied, reversed the state judgment on the ground that *Teague* was applied inaccurately, and remanded for further proceedings? Would this result have been supported by the jurisdictional rationale of *Standard Oil*, *Byers*, and *Moore*?

The U.S. Solicitor General argued for this result in an amicus brief that relied on *Standard Oil*. "[E]xercising jurisdiction based on the incorporated-federal-law principle permits the Court to avoid deciding the substantial constitutional question of whether the Constitution compels retroactivity in state collateral review when an exception to *Teague* applies."[d] And the state's

---

    [b]   This aspect of the Court's ruling is considered in the Additional Notes on the Duty of State Courts to Hear Federal Claims following *Haywood v. Drown* in Section 2 above.—[Footnote by eds.]

    [c]   Justice Thomas wrote a separate dissent on the jurisdictional issue. The Scalia dissent also disagreed with the majority on the merits of the retroactivity issue.

    [d]   The Solicitor General also argued that:

> [E]xercising jurisdiction based on the State's incorporation of federal law respects the role of the States in our federal system. This Court's review of the Louisiana Supreme Court's application of *Teague* would promote comity interests by avoiding intrusive federal habeas litigation. For prisoners in Louisiana, *Teague* principles will control the retroactivity of *Miller* on state collateral review and on federal habeas corpus review. If the Court finds jurisdiction and decides the merits in this case, it will provide a definitive interpretation that will apply in both forums. In the absence of a uniform rule, state prisoners will inevitably seek an intrusive round of federal habeas review in the hope that they will obtain *Miller* relief from federal courts after failing to obtain it in state court. But "it would be unseemly in our dual system of government

brief in *Montgomery* supported Supreme Court jurisdiction on the same ground, pointing out that the *Standard Oil* "principle applies here" because "[i]t is undisputed that the Louisiana Supreme Court relied exclusively on *Teague* and applied no independent state-law retroactivity standard."

This approach to the jurisdictional issue was not discussed in any of the Court's opinions in *Montgomery*. Should the Court have taken this route?

INTRODUCTORY NOTES ON THE ADEQUATE AND INDEPENDENT STATE GROUND DOCTRINE

1. THE DOCTRINE

The intersection of federal and state law in cases coming to the Supreme Court from state courts has led to emergence of the adequate and independent state ground doctrine. The doctrine is conceptually straightforward. It asks first whether the judgment of a state court rests on a proposition of state law that is "adequate" to support the decision below and second whether the state court's reasoning is "independent" of federal law. If the conclusion is that the state court decision rests on state law grounds that are adequate and independent, the Supreme Court will hold that it lacks jurisdiction to hear the case and will not examine any federal questions to see whether they were correctly decided.[a]

In practice, two sorts of questions arise. One is whether the state's rationale is "inadequate" in the sense that it is unconstitutional or that it unduly interferes with the enforcement of federal rights. The state law basis for the lower court decision, in other words, is not "adequate" if it conflicts with or undermines federal law. Mostly these issues occur when the state has relied on noncompliance with a state procedure to foreclose a federal claim. The question, then, is whether the state imposition of a procedural default is "adequate" to support the judgment denying the federal claim. Issues about the adequacy of state procedural grounds arise most frequently today in criminal cases where the defendant seeks to raise a federal constitutional defense. Not so long ago, contests over the adequacy of state procedural grounds were prominently featured in a number of civil rights cases coming to the Supreme Court from the South.

The second is whether the intertwining of federal and state law in the lower court's reasoning means that a purported state ground of decision is not really "independent" of influence from federal law. In the main these cases involve situations where the state court's decision is consistent with

---

for a federal district court to upset a state court conviction without an opportunity to the state courts to correct a constitutional violation." Coleman v. Thompson, 501 U.S. 722, 731 (1991). Correcting the state court's error affords the State the opportunity to provide a remedy for *Miller* violations in its own courts, thus avoiding the federalism costs of a second round of habeas litigation.

[a] See Michael G. Collins, Reconstructing *Murdock v. Memphis*, 98 Va. L. Rev. 1439 (2012), for an historical treatment of cases both before and immediately after *Murdock* on this issue. *Murdock* had endorsed a different order of decision under which the federal question was resolved first and the Court then examined the impact of state law on the judgment that should be rendered. Collins concludes that *Murdock* itself was a departure on the order-of-decision question that was "rather quickly abandoned."

recognition of a federal claim, but where the state court may or may not have rested exclusively on state law. It may be, for example, that—by analogy to the issues in *Standard Oil* and *Byers*—the state courts have resolved a question of state law based on a misimpression of a federal law premise. Or it may be that it is simply not clear whether the state court meant to rest its decision on state or federal law. The question in these cases, then, is whether the state decision rests on genuinely "independent" state grounds.

policy

The rationale for the adequate and independent state ground doctrine is at least prudential. In the ordinary case, it is not efficient for the Supreme Court to review state court decisions that are going to come out the same way no matter how a federal question in the case is resolved. Normally, at least, as Justice Jackson said (see the end of the preceding note), the Court sits to "correct wrong judgments, not to revise opinions." At least Justice Harlan, however, believed that the rule was constitutionally compelled. See Fay v. Noia, 372 U.S. 391, 464 (1963) (dissenting opinion) ("the rule is one of constitutional dimensions going to the heart of the division of judicial powers in a federal system").

Competing rationales for the doctrine are collected and criticized in Richard Matasar and Gregory Bruch, Procedural Common Law, Federal Jurisdictional Policy, and Abandonment of the Adequate and Independent State Grounds Doctrine, 86 Colum. L. Rev. 1291 (1986). They argue that the two principal reasons for the "case or controversy" and "advisory opinion" limitations—"ensuring an adversarial presentation of actual disputes" and "promoting finality of judicial action essential to the maintenance of separation of powers within the national government"—would not be undermined even if the adequate and independent state ground doctrine were not followed. They also argue that the doctrine is not mandated by the Constitution or by any federal statute but is a rule of federal "procedural common law" and as such "is a judicial creature, subject to judicial modification and experiment."[b]

2.   ADEQUATE STATE GROUNDS

As noted above, the "adequacy" question usually arises in the context of federal claims that have been rejected by a state court on the ground that the claimant has not followed the correct state procedure. Justice Frankfurter once described state prerogatives in this respect in terms that provide a good baseline for considering the "adequacy" issue:

> While the power to review the denial by a state court of a non-frivolous claim under the United States Constitution has been centered in this Court, carrying with it the responsibility to see that the opportunity to assert such a claim be not thwarted by any local procedural device, equally important is observance by this Court of the wide discretion in the States to formulate their own procedures

---

[b]   They also discuss other examples of federal "procedural common law," including the "well-pleaded complaint" rule, the abstention doctrines, and forum non conveniens. For an argument that "the Constitution dictates the boundaries" of the adequate and independent state ground doctrine, see Cynthia L. Fountaine, Article III and the Adequate and Independent State Grounds Doctrine, 48 Am. U. L. Rev. 1053 (1999).

for bringing issues appropriately to the attention of their local courts, either in shaping litigation or by appeal. Such methods and procedures may, when judged by the best standards of judicial administration, appear crude, awkward and even finicky or unnecessarily formal when judged in the light of modern emphasis on informality. But so long as the local procedure does not discriminate against the raising of federal claims and, in the particular case, has not been used to stifle a federal claim to prevent its eventual consideration here, this Court is powerless to deny to a State the right to have the kind of judicial system it chooses and to administer that system in its own way.

Staub v. City of Baxley, 355 U.S. 313, 329–30 (1958) (dissenting opinion).

The problem, of course, comes in the application. In *Staub* itself, the Court held that the state had applied its procedure by forcing "resort to an arid ritual of meaningless form."[c] Compare NAACP v. Alabama ex rel. Flowers, 377 U.S. 288 (1964), where the Court said that "it seems to us crystal clear that the rule invoked by [the Alabama Supreme Court] cannot reasonably be deemed applicable to this case" and that the "Alabama courts have not heretofore applied their rules respecting the preparation of briefs with the pointless severity noted here."[d]

The Court also said in *Staub* that it could review the federal question presented by the appellant because the state's procedure was "without any fair or substantial support." The Court may have meant "no support in prior state law," i.e., that the state procedural rule was invented for this case. But it may have meant to express a different idea, namely that in context a state procedural ground can be "adequate" to cut off review of a federal claim only if it serves legitimate state procedural purposes. This point has been stated explicitly in subsequent cases. In Henry v. Mississippi, 379 U.S. 443, 447–48 (1965), for example, the Court said that

> a litigant's procedural defaults in state proceedings do not prevent vindication of his federal rights unless the state's insistence on compliance with its procedural rule serves a legitimate state interest. In every case we must inquire whether the enforcement of a procedural forfeiture serves such a state interest. If it does not, the state procedural rule ought not be permitted to bar vindication of important federal rights.

rule)

---

c   *Staub* was a criminal case in which the defendant sought to challenge the constitutionality of a municipal ordinance that had nine sections. The state appellate court refused to consider the constitutional question because "[t]he attack should have been made against specific sections of the ordinance and not against the ordinance as a whole." The Supreme Court responded:

> The several sections of the ordinance are interdependent in their application to one in appellant's position and constitute but one complete act. . . . For that reason, no doubt, she challenged the constitutionality of the whole ordinance, and in her objections used language challenging the constitutional effect of all its sections. She did, thus, challenge all sections of the ordinance, though not by number. To require her, in these circumstances, to count off, one by one, the several sections of the ordinance would be to force resort to an arid ritual of meaningless form.

d   The state rule in this case had to do with the form of a brief: "where unrelated assignments of error are argued together and one is without merit, the others will not be considered."

See also James v. Kentucky, 466 U.S. 341, 349 (1984) (state ground inadequate that, among other things, "would further no perceivable state interest").

One might think this ground for setting aside a state ground of decision inconsistent with Frankfurter's dictum in *Staub* that it is acceptable for state procedures to "appear crude, awkward and even finicky or unnecessarily formal." The Supreme Court, it could be argued, should take state procedures as it finds them and should not second-guess the procedural policies that underlie them so long as they are announced in advance, consistently applied, and provide a fair opportunity to raise federal claims. Be that as it may, it is clear that state procedures that, as Frankfurter said, "stifle" federal claims or "thwart" or "discriminate against the raising of federal claims" will be held inadequate.

In NAACP v. Alabama ex rel. Patterson, 357 U.S. 449 (1957), for example, the merits of a federal claim were not resolved in a contentious civil rights case because review was sought in the state supreme court by certiorari rather than mandamus. The United States Supreme Court said that it was "unable to reconcile the procedural holding of the Alabama Supreme Court in the present case with its past unambiguous holdings" and that even though the rule that was applied "may now appear in retrospect to form part of a consistent pattern of procedures to obtain appellate review," it could not be applied to cut off review of the federal claim in this case because the NACCP

> could not fairly be deemed to have been apprised of its existence. Novelty in procedural requirements cannot be permitted to thwart review in this Court applied for by those who, in justified reliance upon prior decisions, seek vindication in state courts of their federal constitutional rights.

Similarly, the Court said in Hathorn v. Lovorn, 457 U.S. 255, 263 (1982), that "[s]tate courts may not avoid deciding federal issues by invoking procedures that they do not apply even-handedly to all similar claims." In Barr v. City of Columbia, 378 U.S. 146, 149 (1964), the Court said that "state procedural requirements which are not strictly or regularly followed cannot deprive us of the right to review." For yet another example of the same idea, see Wright v. Georgia, 373 U.S. 284, 291 (1963), where the Court found the state ground inadequate because, among other things, "no prior Georgia case which respondent has cited nor which we have found gives notice of the existence of any requirement" that the federal claimant follow the hypertechnical ground on which the state supreme court relied as the basis for refusing to consider the federal claim.[e]

needs to same apply state procedure to all cases

---

[e] The defendants in *Wright* argued that the statute under which they were convicted was unconstitutionally vague. The state supreme court refused to hear their claim because they did not explicitly relate their vagueness argument to the trial judge's failure to grant a motion for a new trial. The Supreme Court responded:

> In short the Georgia court would require the petitioners to say something like the following at the end of [their vagueness argument]: "A fortiori it was error for the trial court to overrule the motions for a new trial." As was said in a similar case coming to us from the Georgia courts, this "would be to force resort to an arid ritual of meaningless form."

The Court has applied in these cases what it has called "standards of state decisional consistency," Bouie v. City of Columbia, 378 U.S. 347, 354 (1964), that are similar to the questions it would ask in cases like *Indiana ex rel Anderson v. Brand*. In a *Brand* situation, the question is whether the state has manipulated prior state law in a manner that could undermine a federal claim. Or, to put the point another way, the question—not necessarily easy to determine—is whether the state law determination below was a reasonable application of previously established law or whether it was a retroactive creation of new law that changed the ground rules upon which the federal claim relies. The similar question here, in effect, is whether the state's application of its rules of procedural foreclosure is a consistent application of previously settled practice or a surprising entrapment.

An additional and obvious ground for holding a state procedure inadequate is that it is unconstitutional. In Saunders v. Shaw, 244 U.S. 317 (1917), and Brinkerhoff-Faris Trust & Savings Co. v. Hill, 281 U.S. 673 (1930), for example, the Court held that the state procedural rule violated due process by not providing a fair opportunity for a hearing on federal claims. And in Reece v. Georgia, 350 U.S. 85 (1955), the Court held it a violation of due process to allow an unrepresented and illiterate criminal defendant to challenge the racial composition of the grand jury only if the issue was raised prior to indictment.

3.   INDEPENDENT STATE GROUNDS

How the Supreme Court determines whether a state ground is "independent" is the subject of the next main case.

Michigan v. Long

Supreme Court of the United States, 1983.
463 U.S. 1032.

■ JUSTICE O'CONNOR delivered the opinion of the Court.

[In Terry v. Ohio, 392 U.S. 1 (1968), the Supreme Court held that a protective search of the person for weapons could be made in the absence of probable cause to arrest if a police officer had an "articulable suspicion" that an individual was armed and dangerous. *Michigan v. Long* involved whether such a protective search for weapons could extend beyond the person, specifically to the passenger compartment of a car the defendant was driving.

[The Michigan Supreme Court held the search invalid and reversed the resulting conviction for possession of marijuana. The United States Supreme Court granted certiorari. Part II of its opinion, excerpted below, addressed whether it had jurisdiction to reach the *Terry* question.]

Before reaching the merits, we must consider Long's argument that we are without jurisdiction to decide this case because the decision below rests on an adequate and independent state ground. The court below referred twice to the state constitution in its opinion, but otherwise relied exclusively on federal law. Long argues that the Michigan courts have provided greater protection from searches and seizures under the state constitution than is afforded under the Fourth Amendment, and the references to the state constitution therefore establish an adequate and independent ground for the decision below.

It is, of course, "incumbent upon this Court . . . to ascertain for itself . . . whether the asserted non-federal ground independently and adequately supports the judgment." Although we have announced a number of principles in order to help us determine whether various forms of references to state law constitute adequate and independent state grounds,[4] we openly admit that we have thus far not developed a satisfying and consistent approach for resolving this vexing issue. In some instances, we have taken the strict view that if the ground of decision was at all unclear, we would dismiss the case. In other instances, we have vacated or continued a case, in order to obtain clarification about the nature of a state court decision. In more recent cases, we have ourselves examined state law to determine whether state courts have used federal law to guide their application of state law or to provide the actual basis for the decision that was reached. In Oregon v. Kennedy, 456 U.S. 667, 670–71 (1982), we rejected an invitation to remand to the state court for clarification even when the decision rested in part on a case from the state court, because we determined that the state case itself rested upon federal grounds. We added that "[e]ven if the case admitted of more doubt as to whether federal and state grounds for decision were intermixed, the fact that the state court relied to the extent it did on federal grounds requires us to reach the merits."

This ad hoc method of dealing with cases that involve possible adequate and independent state grounds is antithetical to the doctrinal consistency that is required when sensitive issues of federal-state relations are involved. Moreover, none of the various methods of disposition that we have employed thus far recommends itself as the preferred method that we should apply to the exclusion of others, and we therefore determine that it is appropriate to reexamine our treatment of this jurisdictional issue in order to achieve the consistency that is necessary.

The process of examining state law is unsatisfactory because it requires us to interpret state laws with which we are generally unfamiliar,

---

[4]   For example, we have long recognized that "where the judgment of a state court rests upon two grounds, one of which is federal and the other nonfederal in character, our jurisdiction fails if the non-federal ground is independent of the federal ground and adequate to support the judgment." Fox Film Corp. v. Muller, 296 U.S. 207, 210 (1935). We may review a state case decided on a federal ground even if it is clear that there was an available state ground for decision on which the state court could properly have relied. Beecher v. Alabama, 389 U.S. 35, 37, n.3 (1967). Also, if, in our view, the state court " 'felt compelled by what it understood to be federal constitutional considerations to construe . . . its own law in the manner that it did,' " then we will not treat a normally adequate state ground as independent, and there will be no question about our jurisdiction. Delaware v. Prouse, 440 U.S. 648, 653 (1979). Finally, "where the non-federal ground is so interwoven with the [federal ground] as not to be an independent matter, or is not of sufficient breadth to sustain the judgment without any decision of the other, our jurisdiction is plain." Enterprise Irrigation District v. Farmers' Mutual Canal Company, 243 U.S. 157, 164 (1917).

and which often, as in this case, have not been discussed at length by the parties. Vacation and continuance for clarification have also been unsatisfactory both because of the delay and decrease in efficiency of judicial administration, see Dixon v. Duffy, 344 U.S. 143 (1952),[5] and, more important, because these methods of disposition place significant burdens on state courts to demonstrate the presence or absence of our jurisdiction. Finally, outright dismissal of cases is clearly not a panacea because it cannot be doubted that there is an important need for uniformity in federal law, and that this need goes unsatisfied when we fail to review an opinion that rests primarily upon federal grounds and where the *independence* of an alleged state ground is not apparent from the four corners of the opinion. We have long recognized that dismissal is inappropriate "where there is strong indication . . . that the federal Constitution as judicially construed controlled the decision below."

Respect for the independence of state courts, as well as avoidance of rendering advisory opinions, have been the cornerstones of this Court's refusal to decide cases where there is an adequate and independent state ground. It is precisely because of this respect for state courts, and this desire to avoid advisory opinions, that we do not wish to continue to decide issues of state law that go beyond the opinion that we review, or to require state courts to reconsider cases to clarify the grounds of their decisions. Accordingly, when, as in this case, a state court decision fairly appears to rest primarily on federal law, or to be interwoven with the federal law, and when the adequacy and independence of any possible state law ground is not clear from the face of the opinion, we will accept as the most reasonable explanation that the state court decided the case the way it did because it believed that federal law required it to do so. If a state court chooses merely to rely on federal precedents as it would on the precedents of all other jurisdictions, then it need only make clear by a plain statement in its judgment or opinion that the federal cases are being used only for the purpose of guidance, and do not themselves compel the result that the court has reached. In this way, both justice and judicial administration will be greatly improved. If the state court decision indicates clearly and expressly that it is alternatively based on bona fide separate, adequate, and independent grounds, we, of course, will not undertake to review the decision.

This approach obviates in most instances the need to examine state law in order to decide the nature of the state court decision, and will at the same time avoid the danger of our rendering advisory opinions.[6] It also avoids the unsatisfactory and intrusive practice of requiring state

---

[5]   Indeed, Dixon v. Duffy is also illustrative of another difficulty involved in our requiring state courts to reconsider their decisions for purposes of clarification. In *Dixon,* we continued the case on two occasions in order to obtain clarification, but none was forthcoming. "[T]he California court advised petitioner's counsel informally that it doubted its jurisdiction to render such a determination." We then vacated the judgment of the state court, and remanded.

[6]   There may be certain circumstances in which clarification is necessary or desirable, and we will not be foreclosed from taking the appropriate action.

courts to clarify their decisions to the satisfaction of this Court. We believe that such an approach will provide state judges with a clearer opportunity to develop state jurisprudence unimpeded by federal interference, and yet will preserve the integrity of federal law. "It is fundamental that state courts be left free and unfettered by us in interpreting their state constitutions. But it is equally important that ambiguous or obscure adjudications by state courts do not stand as barriers to a determination by this Court of the validity under the federal Constitution of state action." Minnesota v. National Tea Co., 309 U.S. 551, 557 (1940).

The principle that we will not review judgments of state courts that rest on adequate and independent state grounds is based, in part, on "the limitations of our own jurisdiction." Herb v. Pitcairn, 324 U.S. 117, 125 (1945).[7] The jurisdictional concern is that we not "render an advisory opinion, and if the same judgment would be rendered by the state court after we corrected its views of federal laws, our review could amount to nothing more than an advisory opinion." Our requirement of a "plain statement" that a decision rests upon adequate and independent state grounds does not in any way authorize the rendering of advisory opinions. Rather, in determining, as we must, whether we have jurisdiction to review a case that is alleged to rest on adequate and independent state grounds, we merely assume that there are no such grounds when it is not clear from the opinion itself that the state court relied upon an adequate and independent state ground and when it fairly appears that the state court rested its decision primarily on federal law.[8]

Our review of the decision below under this framework leaves us unconvinced that it rests upon an independent state ground. Apart from its

---

[7]　In Herb v. Pitcairn, 324 U.S. 117, 128 (1945), the Court also wrote that it was desirable that state courts "be asked rather than told what they have intended." It is clear that we have already departed from that view in those cases in which we have examined state law to determine whether a particular result was guided or compelled by federal law. Our decision today departs further from *Herb* insofar as we disfavor further requests to state courts for clarification, and we require a clear and express statement that a decision rests on adequate and independent state grounds. However, the "plain statement" rule protects the integrity of state courts for the reasons discussed above. The preference for clarification expressed in *Herb* has failed to be a completely satisfactory means of protecting the state and federal interests that are involved.

[8]　... In dissent, Justice Stevens proposes the novel view that this Court should never review a state court decision unless the Court wishes to vindicate a federal right that has been endangered. The rationale of the dissent is not restricted to cases where the decision is arguably supported by adequate and independent state grounds. Rather, Justice Stevens appears to believe that even if the decision below rests exclusively on federal grounds, this Court should not review the decision as long as there is no federal right that is endangered.

The state courts handle the vast bulk of all criminal litigation in this country. In 1982, more than 12 million criminal actions (excluding juvenile and traffic charges) were filed in the 50 state court systems and the District of Columbia. See 7 State Court Journal 18 (1983). By comparison, approximately 32,700 criminal suits were filed in federal courts during that same year. See Annual Report of the Director of the Administrative Office of the United States Courts 6 (1982). The state courts are required to apply federal constitutional standards, and they necessarily create a considerable body of "federal law" in the process. It is not surprising that this Court has become more interested in the application and development of federal law by state courts in the light of the recent significant expansion of federally created standards that we have imposed on the states.

two citations to the state constitution, the court below relied *exclusively* on its understanding of *Terry* and other federal cases. Not a single state case was cited to support the state court's holding that the search of the passenger compartment was unconstitutional. Indeed, the court declared that the search in this case was unconstitutional because "[t]he Court of Appeals erroneously applied the principles of *Terry v. Ohio* . . . to the search of the interior of the vehicle in this case." The references to the state constitution in no way indicate that the decision below rested on grounds in any way *independent* from the state court's interpretation of federal law. Even if we accept that the Michigan Constitution has been interpreted to provide independent protection for certain rights also secured under the Fourth Amendment, it fairly appears in this case that the Michigan Supreme Court rested its decision primarily on federal law.

Rather than dismissing the case, or requiring that the state court reconsider its decision on our behalf solely because of a mere possibility that an adequate and independent ground supports the judgment, we find that we have jurisdiction in the absence of a plain statement that the decision below rested on an adequate and independent state ground. It appears to us that the state court "felt compelled by what it understood to be federal constitutional considerations to construe . . . its own law in the manner it did."[10]

[The Court then held the search valid under federal standards. Accordingly, it reversed the state court decision and remanded "for further proceedings not inconsistent with this opinion."]

■ JUSTICE BLACKMUN, concurring in part and concurring in the judgment.

I join [all of the Court's opinion except the discussion reproduced above.] While I am satisfied that the Court has jurisdiction in this particular case, I do not join the Court . . . in fashioning a new presumption of jurisdiction over cases coming here from state courts. Although I agree with the Court that uniformity in federal law is desirable, I see little efficiency and an increased danger of advisory opinions in the Court's new approach.

---

[10] There is nothing unfair about requiring a plain statement of an independent state ground in this case. Even if we were to rest our decision on an evaluation of the state law relevant to Long's claim, as we have sometimes done in the past, our understanding of Michigan law would also result in our finding that we have jurisdiction to decide this case. Under state search and seizure law, a "higher standard" is imposed under Art. 1, § 11, of the 1963 Michigan Constitution. If, however, the item seized is, inter alia, a "narcotic drug . . . seized by a peace officer outside the curtilage of any dwelling house in this state," Art. 1, § 11 of the 1963 Michigan Constitution, then the seizure is governed by a standard identical to that imposed by the Fourth Amendment.

. . . At the time that the 1963 Michigan Constitution was enacted, it is clear that marijuana was considered a narcotic drug. We . . . conclude that the seizure of marijuana in Michigan is not subject to analysis under any "higher standard" than may be imposed on the seizure of other items. In the light of our holding in *Delaware v. Prouse* that an interpretation of state law in our view compelled by federal constitutional considerations is not an independent state ground, we would have jurisdiction to decide the case.

■ JUSTICE BRENNAN, with whom, JUSTICE MARSHALL joins, dissenting.

[Justice Brennan dissented on the merits of the *Terry* issue. As to the jurisdictional point, he said only: "I agree that the Court has jurisdiction to decide this case. See ante, at n.10."]

■ JUSTICE STEVENS, dissenting.

The jurisprudential questions presented in this case are far more important than the question whether the Michigan police officer's search of respondent's car violated the Fourth Amendment. The case raises profoundly significant questions concerning the relationship between two sovereigns—the state of Michigan and the United States of America.

The Supreme Court of the state of Michigan expressly held "that the deputies' search of the vehicle was proscribed by the Fourth Amendment of the United States Constitution and *Art. 1, § 11 of the Michigan Constitution.*" The state law ground is clearly adequate to support the judgment, but the question whether it is independent of the Michigan Supreme Court's understanding of federal law is more difficult. Four possible ways of resolving that question present themselves: (1) asking the Michigan Supreme Court directly, (2) attempting to infer from all possible sources of state law what the Michigan Supreme Court meant, (3) presuming that adequate state grounds are independent unless it clearly appears otherwise, or (4) presuming that adequate state grounds are *not* independent unless it clearly appears otherwise. This Court has, on different occasions, employed each of the first three approaches; never until today has it even hinted at the fourth. In order to "achieve the consistency that is necessary," the Court today undertakes a reexamination of all the possibilities. It rejects the first approach as inefficient and unduly burdensome for state courts, and rejects the second approach as an inappropriate expenditure of our resources. Although I find both of those decisions defensible in themselves, I cannot accept the Court's decision to choose the fourth approach over the third—to presume that adequate state grounds are intended to be dependent on federal law unless the record plainly shows otherwise. I must therefore dissent.

If we reject the intermediate approaches, we are left with a choice between two presumptions: one in favor of our taking jurisdiction, and one against it. Historically, the latter presumption has always prevailed. The rule, as succinctly stated in Lynch v. New York, 293 U.S. 52, 54–55 (1934), was as follows:

> Where the judgment of the state court rests on two grounds, one involving a federal question and the other not, or if it does not appear upon which of two grounds the judgment was based, and the ground independent of a federal question is sufficient in itself to sustain it, this Court will not take jurisdiction.

The Court today points out that in several cases we have weakened the traditional presumption by using the other two intermediate approaches identified above. Since those two approaches are now to be rejected, however, I would think that stare decisis would call for a return to historical principle. Instead, the Court seems to conclude that because some precedents are to be rejected, we must overrule them all.

Even if I agreed with the Court that we are free to consider as a fresh proposition whether we may take presumptive jurisdiction over the decisions of sovereign states, I could not agree that an expansive attitude makes good sense. It appears to be common ground that any rule we adopt should show "respect for state courts, and [a] desire to avoid advisory opinions." And I am confident that all members of this Court agree that there is a vital interest in the sound management of scarce federal judicial resources. All of those policies counsel against the exercise of federal jurisdiction. They are fortified by my belief that a policy of judicial restraint—one that allows other decisional bodies to have the last word in legal interpretation until it is truly necessary for this Court to intervene—enables this Court to make its most effective contribution to our federal system of government.

The nature of the case before us hardly compels a departure from tradition. These are not cases in which an American citizen has been deprived of a right secured by the United States Constitution or a federal statute. Rather, they are cases in which a state court has upheld a citizen's assertion of a right, finding the citizen to be protected under both federal and state law. The complaining party is an officer of the state itself, who asks us to rule that the state court interpreted federal rights too broadly and "overprotected" the citizen.

Such cases should not be of inherent concern to this Court. The reason may be illuminated by assuming that the events underlying this case had arisen in another country, perhaps the Republic of Finland. If the Finnish police had arrested a Finnish citizen for possession of marijuana, and the Finnish courts had turned him loose, no American would have standing to object. If instead they had arrested an American citizen and acquitted him, we might have been concerned about the arrest but we surely could not have complained about the acquittal, even if the Finnish Court had based its decision on its understanding of the United States Constitution. That would be true even if we had a treaty with Finland requiring it to respect the rights of American citizens under the United States Constitution. We would only be motivated to intervene if an American citizen were unfairly arrested, tried, and convicted by the foreign tribunal.

In this case the state of Michigan has arrested one of its citizens and the Michigan Supreme Court has decided to turn him loose. The respondent is a United States citizen as well as a Michigan citizen, but since there is no claim that he has been mistreated by the state of Michigan, the final outcome of the state processes offended no federal interest whatever. Michigan simply provided greater protection to one of its citizens than some other state might provide or, indeed, than this Court might require throughout the country.

I believe that in reviewing the decisions of state courts, the primary role of this Court is to make sure that persons who seek to *vindicate* federal rights have been fairly heard. That belief resonates with statements in many of our prior cases. In Abie State Bank v. Weaver, 282 U.S. 765 (1931), the Supreme Court of Nebraska had rejected a federal constitutional claim, relying in part on the state law doctrine of laches. Writing for the Court in response to the Nebraska governor's argument that the Court should not accept jurisdiction because laches provided an independent ground for decision, Chief Justice Hughes concluded that this Court must ascertain for itself whether the asserted nonfederal ground independently and adequately supported the judgment "in order that constitutional guarantees may appropriately be enforced." He relied on our earlier opinion in Union Pacific Railroad Co. v. Public Service Commission of Missouri, 248 U.S. 67 (1918), in which Justice Holmes had made it clear that the Court engaged in such an inquiry so that it would not "be possible for a state to impose an unconstitutional burden" on a private party. And both *Abie* and *Union Pacific* rely on Creswill v. Knights of Pythias, 225 U.S. 246, 261 (1912), in which the Court explained its duty to review the findings of fact of a state court "where a federal right has been denied."

Until recently we had virtually no interest in cases of this type. Thirty years ago, this Court reviewed only one. Nevada v. Stacher, 346 U.S. 906 (1953). Indeed, that appears to have been the only case during the entire 1952 term in which a state even sought review of a decision by its own judiciary. Fifteen years ago, we did not review any such cases, although the total number of requests had mounted to three. Some time during the past decade, perhaps about the time of the 5-to-4 decision in Zacchini v. Scripps-Howard Broadcasting Co., 433 U.S. 562 (1977), our priorities shifted. The result is a docket swollen with requests by states to reverse judgments that their courts have rendered in favor of their citizens.[3] I am confident that a future Court will recognize the error of this allocation of resources. When that day comes, I think it likely that the Court will also reconsider the propriety of today's expansion of our jurisdiction.

The Court offers only one reason for asserting authority over cases such as the one presented today: "an important need for uniformity in federal law [that] goes unsatisfied when we fail to review an opinion that rests primarily upon federal grounds and where the independence of an alleged state ground is not apparent from the four corners of the opinion." Of course, the supposed need to "review an opinion" clashes directly with

---

[3]   This year, we devoted argument time to [13 other cases, one of which was argued twice], as well as this case. And a cursory survey of the United States Law Week index reveals that so far this term at least 80 petitions for certiorari to state courts were filed by the states themselves.

our oft-repeated reminder that "our power is to correct wrong judgments, not to revise opinions." Herb v. Pitcairn, 324 U.S. 117, 126 (1945). The clash is not merely one of form: the "need for uniformity in federal law" is truly an ungovernable engine. That same need is no less present when it is perfectly clear that a state ground is both independent and adequate. In fact, it is equally present if a state prosecutor announces that he believes a certain policy of non-enforcement is commanded by federal law. Yet we have never claimed jurisdiction to correct such errors, no matter how egregious they may be, and no matter how much they may thwart the desires of the state electorate. We do not sit to expound our understanding of the Constitution to interested listeners in the legal community; we sit to resolve disputes. If it is not apparent that our views would affect the outcome of a particular case, we cannot presume to interfere.[4]

Finally, I am thoroughly baffled by the Court's suggestion that it must stretch its jurisdiction and reverse the judgment of the Michigan Supreme Court in order to show "[r]espect for the independence of state courts." Would we show respect for the Republic of Finland by convening a special sitting for the sole purpose of declaring that its decision to release an American citizen was based upon a misunderstanding of American law?

---

[4] In this regard, one of the cases overruled today deserves comment. In Minnesota v. National Tea Co., 309 U.S. 551 (1940), the Court considered a case much like this one—the Minnesota Supreme Court had concluded that both the Fourteenth Amendment to the United States Constitution and Art. 9, § 1, of the Minnesota Constitution prohibited a graduated income tax on chain store income. The state court stated that "the [ ] provisions of the federal and state Constitutions impose identical restrictions upon the legislative power of the state in respect to classification for purposes of taxation," and then adverted briefly to three of its former decisions which had interpreted the state provision. It then proceeded to conduct a careful analysis of the federal Constitution. It could justly be said that the decision rested primarily on federal law. The majority of the Court reasoned as follows:

> Enough has been said to demonstrate that there is considerable uncertainty as to the precise grounds for the decision. That is sufficient reason for us to decline at this time to review the federal question asserted to be present, consistently with the policy of not passing upon questions of a constitutional nature which are not clearly necessary to a decision of the case.

The Court therefore remanded to the state court for clarification.

Today's Court rejects that approach as intruding unduly on the state judicial process. One might therefore expect it to turn to Chief Justice Hughes's dissenting opinion in National Tea. In a careful statement of the applicable principles, he made an observation that I find unanswerable:

> The fact that provisions of the state and federal Constitutions may be similar or even identical does not justify us in disturbing a judgment of a state court which adequately rests upon its application of the provisions of its own constitution. That the state court may be influenced by the reasoning of our opinions makes no difference. The state court may be persuaded by majority opinions in this Court or it may prefer the reasoning of dissenting judges, but the judgment of the state court upon the application of its own constitution remains a judgment which we are without jurisdiction to review. Whether in this case we thought that the state tax was repugnant to the federal Constitution or consistent with it, the judgment of the state court that the tax violated the state constitution would still stand. It cannot be supposed that the Supreme Court of Minnesota is not fully conscious of its independent authority to construe the constitution of the state, whatever reasons it may adduce in so doing.

I respectfully dissent.

NOTE ON *MICHIGAN V. LONG*

Justice O'Connor stated in footnote 4 that "[w]e may review a state case decided on a federal ground even if it is clear that there was an available state ground for decision on which the state court could properly have relied." This is standard lore. The Court has traditionally based its jurisdiction to review state court judgments on the actual grounds of decision by the court below, not the potential grounds. See Caldwell v. Mississippi, 472 U.S. 320, 327 (1985); County Court of Ulster County, New York, et al. v. Allen, 442 U.S. 140, 152–54 (1979); Oregon v. Guzek, 546 U.S. 517 (2006).

Assume, for example, a criminal conviction in state court. Evidence is introduced that was arguably the product of an illegal search and seizure. Though the evidence may have been inadmissible under state law, the highest state court reverses the conviction on federal grounds without reaching the question of state law. The Supreme Court then grants certiorari and reverses, holding the evidence admissible under federal standards. Would the state court then be free on remand to hold that the conviction must nonetheless be set aside on grounds of state law? The settled answer is "yes."

If one concludes, as the Court has, that the practice of reviewing the actual grounds of decision below is desirable and permissible, how does *Michigan v. Long* differ? Does the presumption that a federal question was resolved by an ambiguous lower court opinion present different constitutional questions? Different policy questions? Does the possibility that the lower court may not have decided a federal question change the calculus?

Consider also the effect of the Supreme Court's decision in *Michigan v. Long* on the options open to the state courts on remand. In the search-and-seizure hypothetical above, the state court was free on remand to reinstate its judgment based on state law.[a] Is the autonomy of state courts over questions of state law different after *Michigan v. Long*? Does the decision intrude on the prerogatives of state courts? Does it violate the principles of *Erie* and *Murdock*?[b]

Justice Stevens said in his *Michigan v. Long* dissent that a case like this one "should not be of inherent concern to this Court." Are his arguments in favor of this position persuasive? Congress has provided since 1914 for Supreme Court review of state court decisions holding in favor of federal claims. Should this matter? And what does his reference to potential Finnish judicial

---

[a]   In fact, the Michigan Supreme Court's decision on remand in *Michigan v. Long* accepted the U.S. Supreme Court's conclusion that the search of the interior of the car was proper and did not try to stake out an independent state position on that question. But it proceeded to hold that the subsequent search of the trunk (where the police had found the marijuana) violated the federal Fourth Amendment, an issue that the U.S. Supreme Court had not addressed. See People v. Long, 419 Mich. 636, 359 N.W.2d 194 (1984). The case did not return to the U.S. Supreme Court, and the prosecutor later dropped all charges. See Edward A. Purcell, Jr., The Story of *Michigan v. Long*: Supreme Court Review and the Workings of American Federalism, in Federal Courts Stories 115, 136 (Vicki C. Jackson and Judith Resnik eds., 2010).

[b]   *Michigan v. Long* was subject to extensive academic commentary at the time of the decision. That work is referenced in Michael Esler, *Michigan v. Long*: A Twenty-Year Retrospective, 66 Alb. L. Rev. 835 (2003).

proceedings have to do with state court obligations under the Supremacy Clause to apply correct understandings of federal law?

CHAPTER II

THE POWER OF FEDERAL COURTS TO CREATE FEDERAL LAW

SECTION 1. FEDERAL COMMON LAW

United States v. Little Lake Misere Land Co., Inc.

Supreme Court of the United States, 1973.
412 U.S. 580.

■ MR. CHIEF JUSTICE BURGER delivered the opinion of the Court.

We granted the writ in this case to consider whether state law may retroactively abrogate the terms of written agreements made by the United States when it acquires land for public purposes explicitly authorized by Congress.

The United States initiated this litigation in 1969 in the United States District Court for the Western District of Louisiana, seeking to quiet title to two adjacent parcels of land in Cameron Parish, Louisiana, which the government had acquired pursuant to the Migratory Bird Conservation Act as part of the Lacassine Wildlife Refuge. Title to one parcel was acquired by the United States by purchase on July 23, 1937; to the other parcel by a judgment of condemnation entered August 30, 1939. Both the 1937 act of sale and the 1939 judgment of condemnation reserved to the respondent Little Lake Misere oil, gas, sulphur, and other minerals for a period of 10 years from the date of vesting of title in the United States. The reservation was to continue in effect "as long [after the initial 10-year period] as oil, gas, sulphur or other mineral is produced . . . or so long thereafter as [respondents] shall conduct drilling or reworking operations thereon with no cessation of more than 60 days consecutively until production results; and, if production results, so long as such mineral is produced." The deed and the judgment of condemnation further recited that at the end of 10 years or at the end of any period after 10 years during which the above conditions had not been met, "the right to mine, produce and market said oil, gas, sulphur or other mineral shall terminate . . . and the complete fee title to said lands shall thereby become vested in the United States."

The parties stipulated, and the District Court found, that as to both the parcels in issue here, no drilling, reworking, or other operations were conducted and no minerals were obtained for a period of more than 10 years following the act of sale and judgment of condemnation, respectively. Thus, under the terms of these instruments, fee title in the United

States ripened as of 1947 and 1949, respectively—10 years from the dates of creation. In 1955, the United States issued oil and gas leases applicable to the lands in question.

Respondents, however, continued to claim the mineral rights and accordingly entered various transactions purporting to dispose of those rights. Respondents relied upon Louisiana Act 315 of 1940, which provides:

> When land is acquired by conventional deed or contract, condemnation or expropriation proceedings by the United States of America, or any of its subdivisions or agencies from any person, firm or corporation, and by the act of acquisition, order or judgment, oil, gas or other minerals or royalties are reserved, or the land so acquired is by the act of acquisition conveyed subject to a prior sale or reservation of oil, gas or other minerals or royalties, still in force and effect, the rights so reserved or previously sold shall be imprescriptible.

Respondents contended that the 1940 enactment rendered inoperative the conditions set forth in 1937 and 1939 for the extinguishment of the reservations. . . .

I

[In this section of its opinion, the Court summarized more than 25 years of complex litigation dealing with federal land rights in Louisiana.]

II

The essential premise of the Court of Appeals' decision in [a related] case was that state law governs the interpretation of a federal land acquisition authorized by the Migratory Bird Conservation Act. The Court of Appeals did not set forth in detail the basis for this premise, but that court's opinion seems to say that state law governs this land acquisition because, at bottom, it is an "ordinary" "local" land transaction to which the United States happens to be a party. The suggestion is that this Court's decision in Erie R. Co. v. Tompkins, 304 U.S. 64 (1938), compels application of state law here because the Rules of Decisions Act requires application of state law in the absence of an explicit congressional command to the contrary. We disagree.

The federal jurisdictional grant over suits brought by the United States is not in itself a mandate for applying federal law in all circumstances. This principle follows from *Erie* itself, where, although the federal courts had jurisdiction over diversity cases, we held that the federal courts did not possess the power to develop a concomitant body of general federal law. It is true, too, that "[t]he great body of law in this country which controls acquisition, transmission, and transfer of property, and defines the rights of its owners in relation to the state or to private parties, is found in the statutes and decisions of the state." Even when federal general law was in its heyday, an exception was carved out for local laws of real property. Indeed, before *Erie*, this Court's opinions left open the possibility that even "the United States, while protected by the Constitution from discriminatory state action, and perhaps certain other special forms of state control, was nevertheless governed generally in its ordinary proprietary relations by state law." Henry M. Hart, The Relations between State and Federal Law, 54 Colum. L. Rev. 489, 533 (1954). See, e.g., Mason v. United States, 260 U.S. 545, 558 (1923).

Despite this arguable basis for its reasoning the Court of Appeals in the instant case seems not to have recognized that this land acquisition . . . is one arising from and bearing heavily upon a federal regulatory program. Here, the choice-of-law task is a federal task for federal courts, as defined by Clearfield Trust Co. v. United States, 318 U.S. 363 (1943). Since *Erie,* and as a corollary of that decision, we have consistently acted on the assumption that dealings which may be "ordinary" or "local" as between private citizens raise serious questions of national sovereignty when they arise in the context of a specific constitutional or statutory provision; particularly is this so when transactions undertaken by the federal government are involved, as in this case.[10] In such cases, the Constitution or acts of Congress "require" otherwise than that state law govern of its own force.

There will often be no specific federal legislation governing a particular transaction to which the United States is a party; here, for example, no provision of the Migratory Bird Conservation Act guides us to choose state or federal law in interpreting federal land acquisition agreements under the act. But silence on that score in federal legislation is no reason for limiting the reach of federal law. . . . To the contrary, the inevitable incompleteness presented by all legislation means that interstitial federal lawmaking is a basic responsibility of the federal courts. "At the very least, effective constitutionalism requires recognition of power in the federal courts to declare, as a matter of common law or 'judicial legislation,' rules which may be necessary to fill in interstitially or otherwise effectuate the statutory patterns enacted in the large by Congress. In other words, it must mean recognition of federal judicial competence to declare the governing law in an area comprising issues substantially related to an established program of government operation." Paul J. Mishkin, The Variousness of "Federal Law": Competence and Discretion in the Choice

---

[10] This is not a case where the United States seeks to oust state substantive law on the basis of "an amorphous doctrine of national sovereignty" divorced from any specific constitutional or statutory provision and premised solely on the argument "that every authorized activity of the United States represents an exercise of its governmental power," see United States v. Burnison, 339 U.S. 87, 91, 92 (1950); United States v. Fox, 94 U.S. 315 (1877). *Burnison* and *Fox* stand at the opposite end of the spectrum from cases where Congress explicitly displaces state law in the course of exercising clear constitutional regulatory power over a particular subject matter. See, e.g., Sunderland v. United States, 266 U.S. 226, 232–33 (1924) (United States may displace Oklahoma law by imposing restrictions on alienation of Indian property despite the "general rule . . . that the tenure, transfer, control and disposition of real property are matters which rest exclusively with the state where the property lies"). The present case falls between the poles of *Burnison* and *Sunderland.* Here we deal with an unquestionably appropriate and specific exercise of congressional regulatory power which fails to specify whether or to what extent it contemplates displacement of state law.

of National and State Rules for Decision, 105 U. Pa. L. Rev. 797, 800 (1957).

This, then, is what has aptly been described as the "first" of the two holdings of *Clearfield Trust*—that the right of the United States to seek legal redress for duly authorized proprietary transactions "is a federal right, so that the courts of the United States may formulate a rule of decision." Henry J. Friendly, In Praise of *Erie*—And of the New Federal Common Law, 39 N.Y.U. L. Rev. 383, 410 (1964). At least this first step of the *Clearfield* analysis is applicable here. We deal with the interpretation of a land acquisition agreement (a) explicitly authorized, though not precisely governed, by the Migratory Bird Conservation Act and (b) to which the United States itself is a party. Cf. Bank of America Nat. Trust & Savings Ass'n v. Parnell, 352 U.S. 29, 33 (1956). As in *Clearfield* and its progeny, "[t]he duties imposed upon the United States and the rights acquired by it . . . find their roots in the same federal sources. . . . In absence of an applicable act of Congress it is for the federal courts to fashion the governing rule of law according to their own standards."

III

The next step in our analysis is to determine whether the 1937 and 1939 land acquisition agreements in issue should be interpreted according to "borrowed" state law—Act 315 of 1940. The availability of this choice was explicitly recognized in *Clearfield Trust* itself and fully elaborated some years later in United States v. Standard Oil Co., 332 U.S. 301 (1947). There we acknowledged that "in many situations, and apart from any supposed influence of the *Erie* decision, rights, interests and legal relations of the United States are determined by application of state law, where Congress has not acted specifically." We went on to observe that whether state law is to be applied is a question "of federal policy, affecting not merely the federal judicial establishment and the groundings of its action, but also the government's legal interests and relations, a factor not controlling in the types of cases producing and governed by the *Erie* ruling. And the answer to be given necessarily is dependent upon a variety of considerations always relevant to the nature of the specific governmental interests and to the effects upon them of applying state law."

The government urges us to decide, virtually without qualification, that land acquisition agreements of the United States should be governed by federally created federal law. We find it unnecessary to resolve this case on such broad terms. For even if it be assumed that the established body of state property law should generally govern federal land acquisitions, we are persuaded that the particular rule of law before us today—Louisiana's Act 315 of 1940, as retroactively applied—may not. The "reasons which may make state law at times the appropriate federal rule are singularly inappropriate here."

The Court in the past has been careful to state that, even assuming in general terms the appropriateness of "borrowing" state law, specific aberrant or hostile state rules do not provide appropriate standards for federal law. In De Sylva v. Ballentine, 351 U.S. 570 (1956), we held that whether an illegitimate child was a "child" of the author entitled under the Copyright Act to renew the author's copyright was to be determined by whether, under state law, the child would be an heir of the author. But Mr. Justice Harlan's opinion for the Court took pains to caution that the Court's holding "does not mean that a state would be entitled to use the word 'children' in a way entirely strange to those familiar with its ordinary usage. . . ." In RFC v. Beaver County, 328 U.S. 204 (1946), the issue was whether the definition of "real property," owned by the RFC and authorized by Congress to be subject to state and local taxation, was to be derived from state law or to be fashioned as an independent body of federal law. The Court concluded that "the congressional purpose can best be accomplished by application of settled state rules as to what constitutes 'real property' "—but again the Court foresaw that its approach would be acceptable only "so long as it is plain, as it is here, that the state rules do not effect a discrimination against the government, or patently run counter to the terms of the act."

Under Louisiana's Act 315, land acquisitions of the United States, explicitly authorized by the Migratory Bird Conservation Act, are made subject to a rule of retroactive imprescriptibility, a rule that is plainly hostile to the interests of the United States. As applied to a consummated land transaction under a contract which specifically defined conditions for prolonging the vendor's mineral reservation, retroactive application of Act 315 to the United States deprives it of bargained-for contractual interests.

To permit state abrogation of the explicit terms of a federal land acquisition would deal a serious blow to the congressional scheme contemplated by the Migratory Bird Conservation Act and indeed all other federal land acquisition programs. These programs are national in scope. They anticipate acute and active bargaining by officials of the United States charged with making the best possible use of limited federal conservation appropriations. Certainty and finality are indispensable in any land transaction, but they are especially critical when, as here, the federal officials carrying out the mandate of Congress irrevocably commit scarce funds.

The legislative history of the Migratory Bird Conservation Act confirms the importance of contractual certainty to the federal land acquisition program it authorizes. As originally enacted in 1929, the act provided that land acquisitions might include reservations, easements, and rights of way but that these were to be subject to "such rules and regulations" as the Secretary of Agriculture might prescribe "from time to time." This sweeping statement of the Secretary's power to modify contract terms in favor of the government had an unsettling effect on potential vendors; in 1935, the act was amended to require the Secretary either to include his rules or regulations in the contract itself or to state in the contract that the reservation or easement would be subject to rules and regulations promulgated "from time to time." A Congress solicitous of the interests of private vendors in the certainty of contract would hardly condone state modification of the contractual terms specified by the United States itself as vendee, whether or not those terms may be characterized as "rules and regulations" within the meaning of the act.

Conceivably, our conclusion might be influenced if Louisiana's Act 315 of 1940, as applied retroactively, served legitimate and important state interests the fulfillment of which Congress might have contemplated through application of state law. But that is not the case. We do not deprecate Louisiana's concern with facilitating federal land acquisitions by removing uncertainty on the part of reluctant vendors over the duration of mineral reservations retained by them. From all appearances, this concern was a significant force behind the enactment of the 1940 legislation. But today we are not asked to consider Act 315 on its face, or as applied to transactions consummated after 1940; we are concerned with the application of Act 315 to a pair of acquisition agreements in 1937 and 1939. And however legitimate the state's interest in facilitating federal land acquisitions, that interest has no application to transactions already completed at the time of the enactment of Act 315: the legislature cannot "facilitate" transactions already consummated.

The Louisiana Supreme Court has candidly acknowledged two additional purposes which help to explain retroactive application of Act 315: to clarify the taxability by the state of mineral interests in the large federal land holdings in Louisiana, otherwise in doubt by virtue of the arcane and fluctuating doctrines of intergovernmental tax immunity; and to ensure that federal mineral interests could be subjected to state mineral conservation laws without federal pre-emption. We are not unsympathetic to Louisiana's concern for the consequences of a continuing substantial, even if contingent, federal interest in Louisiana minerals. Congress, however, could scarcely have viewed that concern as a proper justification for retroactive application of state legislation which effectively deprives the government of its bargained-for contractual interests. Our federal union is a complicated organism, but its legal processes cannot legitimately be simplified through the inviting expedient of special legislation which has the effect of confiscating interests of the United States. . . .

Were the terms of the mineral reservations at issue here less detailed and specific, it might be said that the government acknowledged and intended to be bound by unforeseeable changes in state law. But the mineral reservations before us are flatly inconsistent with the respondents' suggestion that the United States in fact expected that these reservations would be wholly subject to retroactive modification. Nor, given the absence of any reliable contemporaneous Louisiana signpost and the absence even today of any final resolution of the pertinent state law question, can we say that the United States ought to have anticipated that its deed contained an empty promise. . . . Years after the fact, state law may not redefine federal contract terminology "in a way entirely strange to those familiar with its ordinary usage. . . ."

IV

In speaking of the choice of law to be applied, the alternatives are plain although in this case identifying them in fixed categories is somewhat elusive. One "choice" would be to apply the law urged on us by respondents, i.e., Louisiana Act 315 of 1940. In some circumstances, . . . state law may be found an acceptable choice, possibly even when the United States itself is a contracting party. However, in a setting in which the rights of the United States are at issue in a contract to which it is a party and "the issue's outcome bears some relationship to a federal program, no rule may be applied which would not be wholly in accord with that program." Mishkin, 105 U. Pa. L. Rev. at 805–06.

Since Act 315 is plainly not in accord with the federal program implemented by the 1937 and 1939 land acquisitions, state law is not a permissible choice here. The choice of law merges with the constitutional demands of controlling federal legislation; we turn away from state law by default. Once it is clear that Act 315 has no application here, we need not choose between "borrowing" some residual state rule of interpretation or formulating an independent federal "common law" rule; neither rule is the law of Louisiana yet either rule resolves this dispute in the government's favor. The contract itself is unequivocal; the District Court concluded, and it is not disputed here, that by the clear and explicit terms of the contract reservations, "[respondents'] interests in the oil, gas, sulphur and other minerals terminated . . . no later than July 23, 1947, and August 30, 1949, unless Act 315 of 1940 has caused the reservations of the servitudes in favor of [respondents] to be imprescriptible."

We hold that, under settled principles governing the choice of law by federal courts, Louisiana's Act 315 of 1940 has no application to the mineral reservations agreed to by the United States and respondents in 1937 and 1939, and that, as a result, any contract interests of respondents expired on the dates identified by the District Court. Accordingly, we reverse the judgment of the Court of Appeals and remand the case for entry of an order consistent with this opinion.

Reversed and remanded.

■ MR. JUSTICE STEWART, concurring in the judgment.

I cannot agree with the Court that the mineral reservations agreed to by the United States and the respondents in 1937 and 1939 are governed by some brooding omnipresence labeled federal common law. It seems clear to me, as a matter of law, not a matter of "choice" or "borrowing," that when anyone, including the federal government, goes into a state and acquires real property, the nature and extent of the rights created are to be determined, in the absence of a specifically applicable federal statute, by the law of the state.

Since I think the government's property acquisitions here are controlled by state law, the decisive question for me is whether the retroactive application of Louisiana Act 315 of 1940 to those acquisitions is constitutional. The 1937 deed of purchase and the 1939 condemnation judgment were unequivocal: the mineral rights were reserved to the former owners of the land for a 10-year period, after which time—if certain conditions regarding exploration and production were not met—the reserved rights were to terminate, and complete fee title to the land, including the mineral rights, was to become vested in the United States. The federal government bargained for this contingent future interest in the minerals; it was clearly agreed to in the conveyances, and was thus reflected in the consideration paid by the government to the former owners.

Yet the Court of Appeals held that Louisiana Act 315, which was enacted subsequent to those conveyances, operated to abrogate the agreed-upon terms of the mineral reservations by eliminating the government's future interest. This retroactive application of Act 315, I believe, is a textbook example of a violation of art. I, § 10, cl. 1, of the Constitution, which provides that no state shall pass any law "impairing the Obligation of Contracts."[2]

Accordingly, I concur in the judgment of the Court.

■ MR. JUSTICE REHNQUIST, concurring in the judgment.

I agree with my Brother Stewart that the central question presented by this case is whether Louisiana has the constitutional power to make Act 315 applicable to this transaction, and not whether a judicially created rule of decision, labeled federal common law, should displace state law. The Migratory Bird Conservation Act does not establish a federal rule controlling the rights of the United States under the reservation. Whether Congress could enact such a provision is a question not now before us. In *Clearfield Trust,* this Court held that federal common law governed the rights and duties of the United States "on commercial paper which it issues. . . ." The interest in having those rights governed by a rule which is uniform across the nation was the basis of that decision. But the interest of the federal government in having real property acquisitions that it makes in the states pursuant to a particular federal program governed by a similarly uniform rule is too tenuous to invoke the *Clearfield* principle, especially in light of the consistent statements by this Court that state law governs real property transactions.

What for my Brother Stewart, however, is a "textbook example" of a violation of the obligation of contracts clause, is for me something more difficult. The scope of this clause has been restricted by past decisions of

---

2   This case is a far cry from Home Building & Loan Ass'n v. Blaisdell, 290 U.S. 398 (1934), which upheld, in the face of a challenge based on the contract clause, emergency state legislation enacted to cope with the extraordinary economic depression existing in 1934. The retroactive application of Louisiana Act 315 serves no such paramount state interest. Cf. City of El Paso v. Simmons, 379 U.S. 497 (1965).

the Court such as Home Building & Loan Ass'n v. Blaisdell, 290 U.S. 398 (1934), in which a Minnesota statute extending the period of time in which the mortgagor might redeem his equity following foreclosure was upheld in the face of vigorous arguments that the statute impaired a valid contract. Were there no simpler ground for disposing of the case, it would be necessary to resolve this very debatable question.

I believe that such another ground is present here, in view of the fact that Act 315 enacted by Louisiana by its terms applies only to transactions in which "the United States of America, or any of its subdivisions or agencies" is a party. While it is argued that Louisiana by other legislation made the same principle applicable to the state government, this proposition is . . . by no means demonstrated. And in any event the change in the period of prescriptibility was not made applicable to nongovernmental grantees.

Implicit in the holdings of a number of our cases dealing with state taxation and regulatory measures applied to the federal government is that such measures must be nondiscriminatory.

The doctrine of intergovernmental immunity enunciated in McCulloch v. Maryland, 17 U.S. (4 Wheat.) 316 (1819), however it may have evolved since that decision, requires at least that the United States be immune from discriminatory treatment by a state which in some manner interferes with the execution of federal laws. If the state of Pennsylvania could not impose a nondiscriminatory property tax on property owned by the United States, United States v. Allegheny County, 322 U.S. 174 (1944), a fortiori, the state of Louisiana may not enforce Act 315 against the property of the United States involved in this case. I therefore concur in the judgment of the Court.

NOTES ON THE LAW GOVERNING THE RIGHTS AND DUTIES OF THE UNITED STATES

1. BACKGROUND

Chief Justice Burger said that pre-*Erie* decisions "left open the possibility" that the proprietary activities of the United States were ordinarily governed by state law. That is a considerable understatement.

In Cotton v. United States, 52 U.S. (11 How.) 229 (1850), the United States brought a civil trespass action against Cotton for cutting timber from federal lands. Cotton claimed that federal law provided no civil remedy for damage to public lands, but the Supreme Court reasoned that it would be a "strange anomaly" if, "having the power to make contracts and hold property as other persons," the United States were not equally "entitled to the same remedies for their protection." Thus, whatever the constitutional limitations on the federal government as sovereign, the federal government as landowner was entitled to the protections of state law. "As an owner of property in almost every state of the Union, they have the same right to have it protected by the local laws that other persons have."

In Mason v. United States, 260 U.S. 545 (1923), the government sued for an accounting of oil and gas extracted by the defendants from public lands in Louisiana. One issue was whether federal law supplied the measure of damages for a suit in equity. The Supreme Court held that the "entire cause of action is . . . local, and the matter of damages within the controlling scope of state legislation."

The idea that state law governed the rights of the United States in the acquisition of property was confirmed by a pair of famous probate cases. The earlier decision was United States v. Fox, 94 U.S. (4 Otto) 315 (1877). Fox lived in New York City. He left all his real and personal property to the United States for the purpose of reducing the debt from the Civil War. His heirs challenged the devise, and the New York probate courts held under state law that the United States could not take property by will. The Supreme Court affirmed. The Court reasoned that the United States could acquire and hold real property as needed for the exercise of governmental powers and, where appropriate, could exercise a right of eminent domain. Otherwise, state law governed: "It is an established principle of law, everywhere recognized, arising from the necessity of the case, that the disposition of immovable property, whether by deed, descent, or any other mode, is exclusively subject to the government within whose jurisdiction the property is situated."

Fox was followed in United States v. Burnison, 339 U.S. 87 (1950). Two California decedents left property to the United States by will. The California Supreme Court voided both wills pursuant to a state statute prohibiting testamentary gifts to the United States, even though it did not prohibit such gifts to California or its subdivisions. The Supreme Court upheld the state law, saying that, "[w]ithin broad limits, the state has power to say what is devisable and to whom it may be given." The Court further found that it was not unconstitutional for California to discriminate against the United States in its regulation of testamentary dispositions. The decision to forbid inheritance by the United States but not by the state and its subdivisions was "justified by reason of the state's close relationship with its residents and their property. A state may by statute properly prefer itself in this way, just as states have always preferred themselves in escheat." The Court did not discuss the cases relied on by Justice Rehnquist in Lake Misere concerning intergovernmental immunity.

2.   CLEARFIELD TRUST CO. V. UNITED STATES

As the foregoing cases attest, the law used to be that the United States entered the marketplace as an ordinary citizen. Except where federal statutes explicitly displaced state law, the law governing the rights and duties of the United States in proprietary transactions was the same state law that would govern the rights and duties of a private party to the same transaction. Thus, if the Internal Revenue Service leased office space or if the United States bought or sold land or issued negotiable paper, state law governed the rights and obligations that flowed from the transaction. If anything, Erie might be thought to have reinforced that tradition.

The decisive break came in Clearfield Trust Co. v. United States, 318 U.S. 363 (1943). A check issued by the United States for Works Progress Administration (WPA) work was stolen and presented by an unknown person to a J.C. Penney's store. Penney's cashed the check and endorsed it to Clearfield Trust for payment. Clearfield in turn collected on the check through the Federal Reserve System. The original payee then informed the WPA that he had not been paid, and a second check was issued. The United States sued Clearfield Trust in a federal court, invoking jurisdiction under what is now 28 U.S.C. § 1345. The question before the Supreme Court concerned the effect of the government's delay in giving notice to Penney's and Clearfield Trust of the theft and forgery of the original payee's signature. Under Pennsylvania law, recovery was barred by an unreasonable delay in giving notice. The District Court therefore ruled in favor of Clearfield Trust, but the Circuit Court reversed. The Supreme Court affirmed. In an opinion by Justice Douglas, it said:

> We agree with the Circuit Court of Appeals that the rule of Erie Railroad Co. v. Tompkins, 304 U.S. 64 (1938), does not apply to this action. The rights and duties of the United States on commercial paper which it issues are governed by federal rather than local law. When the United States disburses its funds or pays its debts, it is exercising a constitutional function or power. This check was issued for services performed under the Federal Emergency Relief Act of 1935. The authority to issue the check had its origin in the Constitution and the statutes of the United States and was in no way dependent on the laws of Pennsylvania or of any other state. The duties imposed upon the United States and the rights acquired by it as a result of the issuance find their roots in the same federal sources.[2] In absence of an applicable act of Congress it is for the federal courts to fashion the governing rule of law according to their own standards. . . .

> In our choice of the applicable federal rule we have occasionally selected state law. But reasons which may make state law at times the appropriate federal rule are singularly inappropriate here. The issuance of commercial paper by the United States is on a vast scale and transactions in that paper from issuance to payment will commonly occur in several states. The application of state law, even without the conflict of laws rules of the forum, would subject the rights and duties of the United States to exceptional uncertainty. It would lead to great diversity in results by making identical transactions subject to the vagaries of the laws of the several states. The desirability of a uniform rule is plain. And while the federal law merchant, developed for about a century under the regime of *Swift v. Tyson,* represented general commercial law rather than a choice of a federal rule designed to protect a federal

---

[2] Various Treasury Regulations govern the payment and endorsement of government checks and warrants and the reimbursement of the Treasurer of the United States by Federal Reserve banks and member bank depositories on payment of checks or warrants bearing a forged endorsement. Forgery of the check was an offense against the United States.

right, it nevertheless stands as a convenient source of reference for fashioning federal rules applicable to these federal questions.

On examining the federal and state commercial law precedents, the Court held that the lack of prompt notice was a defense only if Clearfield and Penney's could show actual damages resulting from the lack of notification.

3.   FEDERAL OR STATE LAW

In part II of its opinion in *Lake Misere*, the Court concluded that the interpretation of the government's land acquisition agreements was governed by federal rather than state law. Resolution of this issue is often referred to as the "first" holding of *Clearfield Trust*, as noted by the Court in *Lake Misere* and described in the first paragraph of *Clearfield* quoted above in Note 2.

By contrast, the Court found that state law applied to various rights and obligations of the government in *Cotton, Mason, Fox,* and *Burnison*. Note that the answer to the question whether state or federal law applied did not depend on the court in which the case was heard. *Fox* and *Burnison* involved the rights of the United States in suits initiated in state courts, while *Cotton* and *Mason* arose in federal court. In none of these cases—nor in *Clearfield* or *Lake Misere*—did the Supreme Court make anything of the court in which the suit was filed.

The Court in *Lake Misere* explained that, since *Erie*, it has "consistently acted on the assumption that dealings which may be 'ordinary' or 'local' as between private citizens raise serious questions of national sovereignty when they arise in the context of a specific constitutional or statutory provision; particularly is this so when transactions undertaken by the federal government are involved, as in this case." Do *Clearfield Trust* and *Lake Misere* mean that henceforth federal law *always* governs the rights and obligations of the United States? The Court repeatedly emphasized in *Lake Misere* that the Migratory Bird Act "explicitly authorized" the transactions in question. Does this limit the reach of the decision?

4.   CONTENT OF FEDERAL COMMON LAW

Quoting from *Clearfield*, the Court concludes part II of *Lake Misere* by noting: " 'In absence of an applicable act of Congress it is for the federal courts to fashion the governing rule of law according to their own standards.' "[a] In fashioning such law, the Court may do one of two things.

First, it may develop a rule of federal common law applicable uniformly throughout the country. This is what happened in *Clearfield Trust*. In taking

---

[a]   This is the "second" holding of *Clearfield*, articulated in the second paragraph quoted in Note 2 above. Designation of the two paragraphs quoted in Note 2 as concerning the "first" and "second" holdings of *Clearfield Trust* originated in Henry J. Friendly, In Praise of *Erie*—And of the New Federal Common Law, 39 N.Y.U. L. Rev. 383 (1964), and has passed into the common vocabulary for discussing the case. For careful consideration of the implications of *Clearfield*, see Ernest A. Young, Preemption and Federal Common Law, 83 Notre Dame L. Rev. 1639 (2008).

this action, the Court may look to such Congressional policies as it can discern, to the common-law or statutory policies used by any state to solve related problems, or to any other source. The Court is acting in this instance as an ordinary common-law court. Its job is to formulate the best solution to the problem before it, consistent with any controlling legislative policy.[b]

Alternatively, the Court may incorporate or borrow state law as the federal rule of decision. This is the option referred to at the beginning of part III of the *Lake Misere* opinion. If state law is borrowed, federal law will differ depending on the state in which the controversy arises. The controlling federal policy, therefore, will be that it is better for federal law to mirror local law than for there to be a uniform federal rule.[c]

5. BORROWING STATE LAW: *DE SYLVA V. BALLENTINE*

The Federal Tort Claims Act provides that the United States can be sued, under certain conditions, for the negligent acts of its employees. Specifically, 28 U.S.C. § 1346(b) says that the United States can be sued in a federal district court for negligent or wrongful injury by an employee of the government, "under circumstances where the United States, if a private person, would be liable to the claimant in accordance with the law of the place where the act or omission occurred." This provision explicitly requires borrowing of state law.

More difficult questions arise when Congress is silent. This was the case in De Sylva v. Ballentine, 351 U.S. 570 (1956), which, although it does not involve the rights and obligations of the United States, was cited by the Chief Justice in *Lake Misere* because it is one of the best known instances of borrowing state law.

De Sylva involved the federal Copyright Act, which then provided that a copyright lasts for 28 years and can be renewed for an additional 28 years on application by "the author of such work, if still living, or the widow, widower, or children of the author, if he be dead. . . ." The author of the work in question had died, leaving a widow and an illegitimate child. The widow renewed the copyright, but proposed not to share the proceeds with the illegitimate child. Suit brought by the mother of the child against the widow raised two questions: whether the widow and children took as a class or in the order of enumeration in the statute; and, if they took as a class, whether the word "children" in the statute encompassed illegitimate children. The Court decided that both widows and children were entitled to share in the renewal term of the copyright, then addressed the meaning of the word "children":

> The scope of a federal right is, of course, a federal question, but that does not mean that its content is not to be determined by state, rather than federal law. This is especially true where a statute

b For a comprehensive analysis of the sources to which federal courts do and should look in determining the content of federal common law, see Caleb Nelson, The Persistence of General Law, 106 Colum. L. Rev. 503 (2006). See also Richard A. Epstein, Federal Preemption, and Federal Common Law, in Nuisance Cases, 102 Nw. U. L. Rev. 551 (2008).

c See Radha A. Pathak, Incorporated State Law, 61 Case W. Res. L. Rev. 823 (2011).

deals with a familial relationship; there is no federal law of domestic relations, which is primarily a matter of state concern.

If we look at the other persons who . . . are entitled to renew the copyright after the author's death, it is apparent that this is the general scheme of the statute. To decide who is the widow or widower of a deceased author, or who are his executors or next of kin, requires a reference to the law of the state which created those legal relationships. The word "children," although it to some extent describes a purely physical relationship, also describes a legal status not unlike the others. To determine whether a child has been legally adopted, for example, requires a reference to state law. We think it proper, therefore, to draw on the ready-made body of state law to define the word "children." . . . This does not mean that a state would be entitled to use the word "children" in a way entirely strange to those familiar with its ordinary usage, but at least to the extent that there are permissible variations in the ordinary concept of "children" we deem state law controlling.

. . . The evident purpose of [the copyright provisions] is to provide for the family of the author after his death. Since the author cannot assign his family's renewal rights, [the provision] takes the form of a compulsory bequest of the copyright to the designated persons. This is really a question of the descent of property, and we think the controlling question under state law should be whether the child would be an heir of the author. It is clear [under the applicable California law that] the child is . . . included within the term "children."[d]

Justice Douglas, joined by Justice Black, concurred in the judgment. He argued:

The meaning of the word "children" as used in . . . the Copyright Act is a federal question. Congress could of course give the word the meaning it has under the laws of the several states. But I would think the statutory policy of protecting dependents would be better served by uniformity, rather than by the diversity which

---

[d] See also *Astrue v. Capato*, 566 U.S. 541 (2012). As the Court said there, the federal Social Security Act "generally refers to state law to determine whether an applicant qualifies as a wife, widow, husband, widower, child or parent. . . ." *Capato* upheld the denial of survivors benefits to twins who, with the help of in vitro fertilization, were born 18 months after the death of the mother's husband. The case turned on whether the twins met the definition of "child" in the Social Security Act. After navigating through a maze of complex provisions in the federal law, the Court accepted the Social Security Administration's conclusion that the case turned on whether the twins would inherit under the applicable state intestacy law:

Reliance on state intestacy law to determine who is a "child" . . . serves the Act's driving objective [which is not to create a program generally benefitting needy persons but to provide dependent members of a wage earner's family with protection against hardship caused by loss of the insured's earnings]. True, the intestacy criterion yields benefits to some children outside the Act's central concern. Intestacy laws in a number of States . . . do provide for inheritance by posthumously conceived children. . . . It was nonetheless Congress's prerogative to legislate for the generality of cases. It did so here by employing eligibility to inherit under state intestacy law as a workable substitute for burdensome case-by-case determinations whether the child was, in fact, dependent on her father's earnings.—[Footnote by eds.]

would flow from incorporating into the act the laws of 48 states. I would . . . hold that illegitimate children were "children" within the meaning . . . of the Copyright Act, whether or not state law would allow them dependency benefits.

Should the Court have incorporated state law in *De Sylva*? What factors should control that decision? Are there valid generalizations about when state law ought to be borrowed, or is the question entirely contextual? Consider United States v. Kimbell Foods, 440 U.S. 715 (1979), where the Court said the following:

> Undoubtedly, federal programs that "by their nature are and must be uniform in character throughout the nation" necessitate formulation of controlling federal rules. Conversely, when there is little need for a nationally uniform body of law, state law may be incorporated as the federal rule of decision. Apart from considerations of uniformity, we must also determine whether application of state law would frustrate specific objectives of the federal programs. If so, we must fashion special rules solicitous of those federal interests. Finally, our choice-of-law inquiry must consider the extent to which application of a federal rule would disrupt commercial relationships predicated on state law.

Does this help?

Once the decision is made that state law should be borrowed, there is a second-order question: "Which state's law?" Suppose in a *De Sylva* situation, for example, the author lived in one state, the illegitimate child was born in another state, the mother and child lived in a third state, and the federal court that heard the case was sitting in yet a fourth state. Which state's law should be applied? Is this a matter to be determined by *Klaxon* (a main case in Chapter I, Section 1)? Or should the federal courts develop an independent body of federal common law to resolve questions of this sort? The Supreme Court noticed this question in *De Sylva*, but the issue was not contested there and has not been definitively resolved in subsequent cases. For an argument that an independent body of federal common law should be developed, see William Baude, Beyond DOMA: Choice of State Law in Federal Statutes, 64 Stan. L. Rev. 1371 (2012).

Finally, note that in both *De Sylva* and the Federal Tort Claims Act, there is no question of state law applying of its own force. The meaning of a federal statute is necessarily a matter of federal law. In *Lake Misere* and *Clearfield Trust*, by contrast, the Court had to decide initially that federal law applies. Would not the reasons for holding that federal law applies necessarily support a uniform federal rule of decision? To put the same question differently, does the borrowing of state law suggest that federal law should not have applied in the first place?

6. DOES THE THEORY MATTER?

Assume a case where everyone agrees that state law should apply to a particular issue involving the rights and obligations of the United States. The theories used by Justices Stewart and Rehnquist in *Lake Misere* would reach this result by holding that state law applies unless and until displaced by an applicable federal statute or by the Constitution. The theory used by Chief Justice Burger would reach the same result by holding that federal law applies but borrows state law as the rule of decision.

Does anything turn on the choice of reasoning? Is this theory run amok, or are there practical consequences that flow from whether state law applies of its own force or is borrowed by federal law? If state law applies of its own force, does this mean that federal courts will be obligated to apply, in the words of *De Sylva*, "entirely strange" state laws?

Now consider a situation, such as that in *Lake Misere*, where everyone agrees that state law should not apply. Is there any advantage in reaching this conclusion via the theoretical perspective of the Chief Justice rather than that of Justices Stewart or Rehnquist? Would it have been better simply to hold that this particular Louisiana law could not apply under the Supremacy Clause because it was inconsistent with the policies of the Migratory Bird Act?

7.   DEFERENCE TO CONGRESS: *UNITED STATES V. STANDARD OIL* AND *UNITED STATES V. GILMAN*

It does not necessarily follow that the federal government has access to remedies that may be available to private parties. Two older cases provide illustrations.

In United States v. Standard Oil Co. of California, 332 U.S. 301 (1947), a soldier was hit by a Standard Oil truck, hospitalized, and disabled for a short time. After the soldier settled his claim with Standard Oil, the United States sued the company to recover for the soldier's pay while incapacitated and for the cost of his stay in a military hospital. The Supreme Court's resolution of the case came in three steps.

It held first that federal and not state law applied:

> [A]s the federal government has the exclusive power to establish and define the relationship [between itself and its soldiers] by virtue of its military and other powers, equally clearly it has power in execution of the same functions to protect the relation once formed from harms inflicted by others. Since also the government's purse is affected, as well as its power to protect the relationship, its fiscal powers, to the extent that they are available to protect it against financial injury, add their weight to the military basis for excluding state intrusion. Indeed, in this aspect the case is not greatly different from the *Clearfield* case. . . .

The Court then held that state law should not be borrowed:

> [W]e know of no good reason why the government's right to be indemnified in these circumstances, or the lack of such a right, should vary in accordance with the different rulings of the several states, simply because the soldier marches or today perhaps as often flies across state lines. Furthermore, the liability sought is not essential or even relevant to protection of the state's citizens

against tortious harms, nor indeed for the soldier's personal indemnity or security . . . since his personal rights against the wrongdoer may be fully protected without reference to any indemnity for the government's loss. . . . The question, therefore, is chiefly one of federal fiscal policy, not of special or peculiar concern to the states or their citizens. And because those matters ordinarily are appropriate for uniform national treatment rather than diversified local disposition, . . . they are more fittingly determinable by independent federal judicial decision than by reference to varying state policies.

But in the end, the Court rejected common law tort analogies and deferred to Congress on the question of whether the federal government should be entitled to relief:

> [T]he issue comes down in final consequence to a question of federal fiscal policy. . . . The tort law analogy is brought forth . . . as the instrument for determining and establishing the federal fiscal and regulatory policies which the government's executive arm thinks should prevail. . . . [But whatever] the merits of the policy, its conversion into law is a proper subject for congressional action, not for any creative power of ours. Congress, not this Court . . . , is the custodian of the national purse. [I]t is the primary . . . arbiter of federal fiscal affairs. . . . Until it acts to establish the liability, this Court . . . should withhold creative touch.

Standard Oil was followed in United States v. Gilman, 347 U.S. 507 (1954). The question was whether the United States "may recover indemnity from one of its employees after it has been held liable under the Federal Tort Claims Act for the negligence of the employee." The statute made no express provision for such recovery. The Court refused to find a right of indemnification. The Court surveyed the "host of considerations" involved and concluded that the selection of the better rule was "more appropriately for those who write the laws, rather than for those who interpret them."

8.   CRIMINAL LAW

It has long been settled that federal courts may not rely on the common law as the basis for criminal prosecutions. See, e.g., United States v. Hudson & Goodwin, 11 U.S. (7 Cranch) 32 (1812). There are, in other words, no federal common law crimes. Federal courts have, however, allowed defendants to invoke common law *defenses* to federal crimes, such as the defenses of mistake, entrapment, duress, and necessity. This practice is based on the understanding that "Congress in enacting criminal statutes legislates against a background of Anglo-Saxon common law." United States v. Bailey, 444 U.S. 394, 415 n.11 (1980).

Some criminal statutes are also written in broad or vague terms and thus require substantial judicial interpretation. This interpretation can sometimes resemble the development of federal common law. Consider, for example, Skilling v. United States, 561 U.S. 358 (2010), where a criminal defendant challenged, as unconstitutionally vague, an amendment to the federal mail and wire fraud statutes that allowed for the prosecution of "a scheme or artifice to deprive another of the intangible right of honest services." This provision had been added in response to the Supreme Court's decision in McNally v. United States, 483 U.S. 350 (1987), which had construed the mail fraud statute as extending only to situations involving the deprivation of property rights. To avoid vagueness concerns associated with the honest services provision, the Court in *Skilling*, in an opinion by Justice Ginsburg, held that the provision could be used only to prosecute bribery and kickback schemes. The Court reasoned that Congress had intended to reinstate the pre-*McNally* lower court case law that had allowed for the prosecution of fraud involving the deprivation of honest services, and that this lower court case law had "consistently applied the fraud statute to bribery and kickback schemes," whereas "there was considerable disarray [in the courts] over the statute's application to conduct outside that core category." In a concurrence, Justice Scalia, joined by Justices Thomas and Kennedy, accused the majority of "replac[ing] a vague criminal standard that Congress adopted with a more narrow one (included within the vague one) that can pass constitutional muster," an action that he said involved "not interpretation but invention." In Justice Scalia's view, the Court should have simply held that the honest services provision was unconstitutionally vague.

At what point does statutory construction slide into the creation of federal common law? With statutory interpretation, the courts at least begin with a statutory text. Does that reduce the separation of powers and federalism issues otherwise implicated by the development of federal common law? For an argument that broadly worded criminal statutes should be viewed as implicitly delegating authority to the federal courts to develop federal common law, see Dan M. Kahan, Lenity and Federal Common Law Crimes, 1994 Sup. Ct. Rev. 345. Joined by Justice O'Connor, Justice Stevens had embraced this approach in his *McNally* dissent:

> Statutes like the Sherman Act, the civil rights legislation, and the mail fraud statute were written in broad general language on the understanding that the courts would have wide latitude in construing them to achieve the remedial purposes that Congress had identified. The wide open spaces in statutes such as these are most appropriately interpreted as implicit delegations of authority to the courts to fill in the gaps in the common-law tradition of case-by-case adjudication.

McNally, 483 U.S. at 372–73.

Boyle v. United Technologies Corp.

Supreme Court of the United States, 1988.
487 U.S. 500.

■ JUSTICE SCALIA delivered the opinion of the Court.

This case requires us to decide when a contractor providing military equipment to the federal government can be held liable under state tort law for injury caused by a design defect.

I

On April 27, 1983, David A. Boyle, a United States Marine helicopter pilot, was killed when the CH-53D helicopter in which he was flying crashed off the coast of Virginia Beach, Virginia, during a training exercise. Although Boyle survived the impact of the crash, he was unable to escape from the helicopter and drowned. Boyle's father, petitioner here, brought this diversity action in federal District Court against the Sikorsky Division of United Technologies Corporation (Sikorsky), which built the helicopter for the United States.

At trial, petitioner presented two theories of liability under Virginia tort law that were submitted to the jury. First, petitioner alleged that Sikorsky had defectively repaired a device called the servo in the helicopter's automatic flight control system, which allegedly malfunctioned and caused the crash. Second, petitioner alleged that Sikorsky had defectively designed the copilot's emergency escape system: the escape hatch opened out instead of in (and was therefore ineffective in a submerged craft because of water pressure), and access to the escape hatch handle was obstructed by other equipment. The jury returned a general verdict in favor of petitioner and awarded him $725,000. The District Court denied Sikorsky's motion for judgment notwithstanding the verdict.

Initial args.

The Court of Appeals reversed and remanded with directions that judgment be entered for Sikorsky. It found, as a matter of Virginia law, that Boyle had failed to meet his burden of demonstrating that the repair work performed by Sikorsky, as opposed to work that had been done by the Navy, was responsible for the alleged malfunction of the flight control system. It also found, as a matter of federal law, that Sikorsky could not be held liable for the allegedly defective design of the escape hatch because, on the evidence presented, it satisfied the requirements of the "military contractor defense," which the court had recognized the same day in Tozer v. LTV Corp., 792 F.2d 403 (4th Cir.1986).

Petitioner sought review here, challenging the Court of Appeals' decision on three levels: First, petitioner contends that there is no justification in federal law for shielding government contractors from liability for design defects in military equipment. Second, he argues in the alternative that even if such a defense should exist, the Court of Appeals' formulation of the conditions for its application is inappropriate. Finally, petitioner contends that the Court of Appeals erred in not remanding for a jury determination of whether the elements of the defense were met in this case. We granted certiorari.

Present args.

II

Petitioner's broadest contention is that [in the absence of legislation specifically immunizing government contractors from liability for design defects, there is no basis for judicial recognition of such a defense.] We disagree. In most fields of activity, to be sure, this Court has refused to find federal pre-emption of state law in the absence of either a clear statutory prescription or a direct conflict between federal and state law. But we have held that a few areas, involving "uniquely federal interests," Texas Industries, Inc. v. Radcliff Materials, Inc., 451 U.S. 630, 640 (1981), are so committed by the Constitution and laws of the United States to federal control that state law is pre-empted and replaced where necessary, by federal law of a content prescribed (absent explicit statutory directive) by the courts—so-called "federal common law." See, e.g., Howard v. Lyons, 360 U.S. 593, 597 (1959); Clearfield Trust Co. v. United States, 318 U.S. 363, 366–67 (1943).

The dispute in the present case borders upon two areas that we have found to involve such "uniquely federal interests." We have held that obligations to and rights of the United States under its contracts are governed exclusively by federal law. See, e.g., United States v. Little Lake Misere Land Co., 412 U.S. 580, 592–94 (1973); *Clearfield Trust.* The present case does not involve an obligation to the United States under its contract, but rather liability to third persons. That liability may be styled one in tort, but it arises out of performance of the contract—and traditionally has been regarded as sufficiently related to the contract that until 1962 Virginia would generally allow design defect suits only by the purchaser and those in privity with the seller.

Another area that we have found to be of peculiarly federal concern, warranting the displacement of state law, is the civil liability of federal officials for actions taken in the course of their duty. We have held in many contexts that the scope of that liability is controlled by federal law. See, e.g., Westfall v. Erwin, 484 U.S. 292, 295 (1988); *Howard*, 360 U.S. at 597; Barr v. Matteo, 360 U.S. 564 (1959). The present case involves an independent contractor performing its obligation under a procurement contract, rather than an official performing his duty as a federal employee, but there is obviously implicated the same interest in getting the government's work done.[2]

We think the reasons for considering these closely related areas to be of "uniquely federal" interest apply as well to the civil liabilities arising out of the performance of federal procurement contracts. [I]t is plain that the federal government's interest in the procurement of equipment is implicated by suits such as the present one—even though the dispute is one between private parties. It is true that where "litigation is purely between private parties and does not touch the rights and duties of the United States," Bank of America Nat. Trust & Savings Ass'n v. Parnell, 352 U.S. 29, 33 (1956), federal law does not govern. Thus, for example, in Miree v. DeKalb County, 433 U.S. 25, 30 (1977), which involved the question whether certain private parties could sue as third-party beneficiaries

---

[2] The dissent misreads our discussion here to "intimat[e] that the immunity [of federal officials] might extend . . . to nongovernment employees" such as a government contractor. But we do not address this issue, as it is not before us. We cite these cases merely to demonstrate that the liability of independent contractors performing work for the federal government, like the liability of federal officials, is an area of uniquely federal interest.

to an agreement between a municipality and the Federal Aviation Administration, we found that state law was not displaced because "the operations of the United States in connection with FAA grants such as these . . . would [not] be burdened" by allowing state law to determine whether third-party beneficiaries could sue, and because "any federal interest in the outcome of the [dispute] before us '[was] far too speculative, far too remote a possibility to justify the application of federal law to transactions essentially of local concern.'" [S]ee also Wallis v. Pan American Petroleum Corp., 384 U.S. 63, 69 (1966). But the same is not true here. The imposition of liability on government contractors will directly affect the terms of government contracts: either the contractor will decline to manufacture the design specified by the government, or it will raise its price. Either way the interests of the United States will be directly affected.

That the procurement of equipment by the United States is an area of uniquely federal interest does not, however, end the inquiry. That merely establishes a necessary, not a sufficient, condition for the displacement of state law.[4] Displacement will occur only where, as we have variously described, a "significant conflict" exists between an identifiable "federal policy or interest and the [operation] of state law," Wallis, 384 U.S. at 68, or the application of state law would "frustrate specific objectives" of federal legislation, Kimbell Foods, 440 U.S. at 728. The conflict with federal policy need not be as sharp as that which must exist for ordinary preemption when Congress legislates "in a field which the states have traditionally occupied." Rice v. Santa Fe Elevator Corp., 331 U.S. 218, 230 (1947). Or to put the point differently, the fact that the area in question is one of unique federal concern changes what would otherwise be a conflict that cannot produce pre-emption into one that can. But conflict there must be. In some cases, for example where the federal interest requires a uniform rule, the entire body of state law applicable to the area conflicts and is replaced by federal rules. See, e.g., Clearfield Trust, 318 U.S. at 366–67. . . . In others, the conflict is more narrow, and only particular elements of state law are superseded. See, e.g., Little Lake Misere, 412 U.S. at 595 . . . ; Howard, 360 U.S. at 597. . . .

In Miree, the suit was not seeking to impose upon the person contracting with the government a duty contrary to the duty imposed by the government contract. Rather, it was the contractual duty itself that the private plaintiff (as third party beneficiary) sought to enforce. Between

---

[4] We refer here to the displacement of state law, although it is possible to analyze it as the displacement of federal-law reference to state law for the rule of decision. Some of our cases appear to regard the area in which a uniquely federal interest exists as being entirely governed by federal law, with federal law deigning to "borro[w]," United States v. Little Lake Misere Land Co., 412 U.S. 580, 594 (1973), or "incorporat[e]" or "adopt," United States v. Kimbell Foods, Inc., 440 U.S. 715, 728, 729, 730 (1979), state law except where a significant conflict with federal policy exists. We see nothing to be gained by expanding the theoretical scope of the federal preemption beyond its practical effect, and so adopt the more modest terminology. If the distinction between displacement of state law and displacement of federal law's incorporation of state law ever makes a practical difference, it at least does not do so in the present case.

Miree and the present case, it is easy to conceive of an intermediate situation, in which the duty sought to be imposed on the contractor is not identical to one assumed under the contract, but is also not contrary to any assumed. If, for example, the United States contracts for the purchase and installation of an air conditioning unit, specifying the cooling capacity but not the precise manner of construction, a state law imposing upon the manufacturer of such units a duty of care to include a certain safety feature would not be a duty identical to anything promised the government, but neither would it be contrary. The contractor could comply with both its contractual obligations and the state-prescribed duty of care. No one suggests that state law would generally be pre-empted in this context.

Laws never directly contradictory

The present case, however, is at the opposite extreme from *Miree*. Here the state-imposed duty of care that is the asserted basis of the contractor's liability (specifically, the duty to equip helicopters with the sort of escape-hatch mechanism petitioner claims was necessary) is precisely contrary to the duty imposed by the government contract (the duty to manufacture and deliver helicopters with the sort of escape-hatch mechanism shown by the specifications). Even in this sort of situation, it would be unreasonable to say that there is always a "significant conflict" between the state law and a federal policy or interest. If, for example, a federal procurement officer orders, by model number, a quantity of stock helicopters that happen to be equipped with escape hatches opening outward, it is impossible to say that the government has a significant interest in that particular feature. That would be scarcely more reasonable than saying that a private individual who orders such a craft by model number cannot sue for the manufacturer's negligence because he got precisely what he ordered. . . .

There is . . . a statutory provision that demonstrates the potential for, and suggests the outlines of, "significant conflict" between federal interests and state law in the context of government procurement. In the Federal Tort Claims Act (FTCA), Congress authorized damages to be recovered against the United States for harm caused by the negligent or wrongful conduct of government employees, to the extent that a private person would be liable under the law of the place where the conduct occurred. 28 U.S.C. § 1346(b). It excepted from this consent to suit, however,

Federal tort claim exemption

> [a]ny claim . . . based upon the exercise or performance or the failure to exercise or perform a discretionary function or duty on the part of a federal agency or an employee of the Government, whether or not the discretion involved be abused.

28 U.S.C. § 2680(a).

We think that the selection of the appropriate design for military equipment to be used by our Armed Forces is assuredly a discretionary function within the meaning of this provision. It often involves not merely engineering analysis but judgment as to the balancing of many technical, military, and even social considerations, including specifically the trade-off between greater safety and greater combat effectiveness. And we are further of the view that permitting "second-guessing" of these judgments through state tort suits against contractors would produce the same effect sought to be avoided by the FTCA exemption. The financial burden of judgments against the contractors would ultimately be passed through, substantially if not totally, to the United States itself, since defense contractors will predictably raise their prices to cover, or to insure against, contingent liability for the government-ordered designs. To put the point differently: It makes little sense to insulate the government against financial liability for the judgment that a particular feature of military equipment is necessary when the government produces the equipment itself, but not when it contracts for the production. In sum, we are of the view that state law which holds government contractors liable for design defects in military equipment does in some circumstances present a "significant conflict" with federal policy and must be displaced.

We agree with the scope of displacement adopted by the Fourth Circuit here. . . . Liability for design defects in military equipment cannot be imposed, pursuant to state law, when (1) the United States approved reasonably precise specifications; (2) the equipment conformed to those specifications; and (3) the supplier warned the United States about the dangers in the use of the equipment that were known to the supplier but not to the United States. The first two of these conditions assure that the suit is within the area where the policy of the "discretionary function" would be frustrated—i.e., they assure that the design feature in question was considered by a government officer, and not merely by the contractor itself. The third condition is necessary because, in its absence, the displacement of state tort law would create some incentive for the manufacturer to withhold knowledge of risks, since conveying that knowledge might disrupt the contract but withholding it would produce no liability. We adopt this provision lest our effort to protect discretionary functions perversely impedes them by cutting off information highly relevant to the discretionary decision.

We have considered [an] alternative formulation of the government contractor defense, urged upon us by petitioner. . . . That would preclude suit only if (1) the contractor did not participate, or participated only minimally, in the design of the defective equipment; *or* (2) the contractor timely warned the government of the risks of the design and notified it of alternative designs reasonably known by it, *and* the government, although forewarned, clearly authorized the contractor to proceed with the dangerous design. While this formulation may represent a perfectly reasonable tort rule, it is not a rule designed to protect the federal interest embodied in the "discretionary function" exemption. The design ultimately selected may well reflect a significant policy judgment by government officials whether or not the contractor rather than those officials developed the design. In addition, it does not seem to us sound

[handwritten margin note: Important discussion on scope of displacement]

policy to penalize, and thus deter, active contractor participation in the design process, placing the contractor at risk unless it identifies all design defects.

III

[The case was remanded so that the Court of Appeals could determine whether the case should have gone to the jury or whether the evidence was such that no reasonable jury could find the government contractor defense inapplicable.]

So ordered.

■ JUSTICE BRENNAN, with whom JUSTICE MARSHALL and JUSTICE BLACKMUN join, dissenting.

Lieutenant David A. Boyle died when the CH-53D helicopter he was copiloting spun out of control and plunged into the ocean. We may assume, for purpose of this case, that Lt. Boyle was trapped under water and drowned because respondent United Technologies negligently designed the helicopter's escape hatch. We may further assume that any competent engineer would have discovered and cured the defects, but that they inexplicably escaped respondent's notice. Had respondent designed such a death trap for a commercial firm, Lt. Boyle's family could sue under Virginia tort law and be compensated for his tragic and unnecessary death. But respondent designed the helicopter for the federal government, and that, the Court tells us today, makes all the difference: Respondent is immune from liability so long as it obtained approval of "reasonably precise specifications"—perhaps no more than a rubberstamp from a federal procurement officer who might or might not have noticed or cared about the defects, or even had the expertise to discover them.

If respondent's immunity "bore the legitimacy of having been prescribed by the people's elected representatives," we would be duty bound to implement their will, whether or not we approved. Congress, however, has remained silent—and conspicuously so, having resisted a sustained campaign by government contractors to legislate for them some defense.[1] The Court—unelected and unaccountable to the people—has unabashedly stepped into the breach to legislate a rule denying Lt. Boyle's family the compensation that state law assures them. This time the injustice is of this Court's own making.

Worse yet, the injustice will extend far beyond the facts of this case, for the Court's newly discovered government contractor defense is breathtakingly sweeping. It applies not only to military equipment like the CH-53D helicopter, but (so far as I can tell) to any made-to-order gadget that the federal government might purchase after previewing plans—from NASA's Challenger space shuttle to the Postal Service's old mail cars. The contractor may invoke the defense in suits brought not

---

[1] [Justice Brennan cited six proposed bills that were not enacted.]

only by military personnel like Lt. Boyle, or government employees, but by anyone injured by a government contractor's negligent design, including, for example, the children who might have died had respondent's helicopter crashed on the beach. It applies even if the government has not intentionally sacrificed safety for other interests like speed or efficiency, and, indeed, even if the equipment is not of a type that is typically considered dangerous; thus, the contractor who designs a government building can invoke the defense when the elevator cable snaps or the walls collapse. And the defense is invocable regardless of how blatant or easily remedied the defect, so long as the contractor missed it and the specifications approved by the government, however unreasonably dangerous, were "reasonably precise."

In my view, this Court lacks both authority and expertise to fashion such a rule, whether to protect the Treasury of the United States or the coffers of industry. Because I would leave that exercise of legislative power to Congress, where our Constitution places it, I would reverse the Court of Appeals and reinstate petitioner's jury award. . . . [a]

II

Congress has not decided to supersede state law here (if anything, it has decided not to, see n.1, supra) and the Court does not pretend that its newly manufactured "government contractor defense" fits within any of the handful of "narrow areas," *Texas Industries*, 451 U.S. at 641, of "uniquely federal interests" in which we have heretofore done so. Rather, the Court creates a new category of "uniquely federal interests" out of a synthesis of two whose origins predate *Erie* itself: the interest in administering the "obligations to and rights of the United States under its contracts" and the interest in regulating the "civil liability of federal officials for actions taken in the course of their duty." This case is, however, simply a suit between two private parties. We have steadfastly declined to impose federal contract law on relationships that are collateral to a federal contract, or to extend the federal employee's immunity beyond federal employees. . . .

A

The proposition that federal common law continues to govern the "obligations to and rights of the United States under its contracts" is nearly as old as *Erie* itself. Federal law typically controls when the federal government is a party to a suit involving its rights or obligations under a contract, whether the contract entails procurement, see Priebe & Sons v. United States, 332 U.S. 407 (1947), a loan, see United States v. Kimbell Foods, Inc., 440 U.S. 715, 726 (1979), a conveyance of property, see *Little Lake Misere*, 412 U.S. at 591–94, or a commercial instrument issued by the government, see Clearfield Trust Co. v. United States, 318 U.S. 363, 366 (1943), or assigned to it, see D'Oench, Duhme & Co. v. FDIC, 315 U.S. 447, 457 (1942). But it is by now established that our

---

[a]   Part I of Justice Brennan's opinion has been omitted.—[Footnote by eds.]

power to create federal common law controlling the *federal government's* contractual rights and obligations does not translate into a power to prescribe rules that cover all transactions or contractual relationships collateral to government contracts.

In *Miree v. DeKalb County*, for example, the county was contractually obligated under a grant agreement with the Federal Aviation Administration (FAA) to " 'restrict the use of land adjacent to . . . the airport to activities and purposes compatible with normal airport operations including landing and takeoff of aircraft.' " At issue was whether the county breached its contractual obligation by operating a garbage dump adjacent to the airport, which allegedly attracted the swarm of birds that caused a plane crash. Federal common law would undoubtedly have controlled in any suit by the federal government to enforce the provision against the county or to collect damages for its violation. The diversity suit, however, was brought not by the government, but by assorted private parties injured in some way by the accident. We observed that "the operations of the United States in connection with FAA grants such as these are undoubtedly of considerable magnitude," and that "the United States has a substantial interest in regulating aircraft travel and promoting air travel safety." Nevertheless, we held that state law should govern the claim because "only the rights of private litigants are at issue here" and the claim against the county "will have *no direct effect upon the United States or its Treasury.*"

Miree relied heavily on Bank of America Nat. Trust & Savings Ass'n v. Parnell, 352 U.S. 29 (1956), and *Wallis*, the former involving commercial paper issued by the United States and the latter involving property rights in federal land. In the former case, Parnell cashed certain government bonds that had been stolen from their owner, a bank. It is beyond dispute that federal law would have governed the United States' duty to pay the value bonds upon presentation; we held as much in *Clearfield Trust*. But the central issue in *Parnell,* a diversity suit, was whether the victim of the theft could recover the money paid to Parnell. That issue, we held, was governed by state law, because the "litigation [was] purely between private parties and [did] *not touch the rights and duties of the United States.*" (Emphasis added.)

The same was true in *Wallis,* which also involved a government contract—a lease issued by the United States to a private party under the Mineral Leasing Act of 1920, 30 U.S.C. § 181 et seq.—governed entirely by federal law. Again, the relationship at issue in this diversity case was collateral to the government contract: it involved the validity of contractual arrangements between the lessee and other private parties, not between the lessee and the federal government. Even though a federal statute authorized certain assignments of lease rights and imposed certain conditions on their validity, we held that state law, not federal common law, governed their validity because application of state law would present "no significant threat to any identifiable federal policy or interest."

Here, as in *Miree, Parnell,* and *Wallis,* a government contract governed by federal common law looms in the background. But here, too, the United States is not a party to the suit and the suit neither "touch[es] the rights and duties of the United States," *Parnell,* 352 U.S. at 33, nor has a "direct effect upon the United States or its Treasury," *Miree,* 433 U.S. at 29. The relationship at issue is at best collateral to the government contract. We have no greater power to displace state law governing the collateral relationship in the government procurement realm than we had to dictate federal rules governing equally collateral relationships in the areas of aviation, government-issued commercial paper, or federal lands.

That the government might "have to pay higher prices for what it orders if delivery in accordance with the contract exposes the seller to potential liability" does not distinguish this case. Each of the cases just discussed declined to extend the reach of federal common law despite the assertion of comparable interests that would have affected the terms of the government contract—whether its price or its substance—just as "directly" (or indirectly). Third-party beneficiaries can sue under a county's contract with the FAA, for example, even though—as the Court's focus on the absence of "*direct* effect on the United States or its Treasury," *Miree,* 433 U.S. at 29 (emphasis added), suggests—counties will likely pass on the costs to the government in future contract negotiations. Similarly, we held that state law may govern the circumstances under which stolen federal bonds can be recovered, notwithstanding Parnell's argument that "the value of bonds to the first purchaser and hence their salability by the government would be materially affected." Brief for Respondent Parnell in Bank of America Nat. Trust & Savings Ass'n v. Parnell, O.T. 1956, No. 21, pp. 10–11. As in each of the cases declining to extend the traditional reach of federal law of contracts beyond the rights and duties of the *federal government,* "any federal interest in the outcome of the question before us 'is far too speculative, far too remote a possibility to justify the application of federal law to transactions essentially of local concern.' " *Miree,* 433 U.S. at 32–33, quoting *Parnell,* 352 U.S. at 33–34.

B

Our "uniquely federal interest" in the tort liability of affiliates of the federal government is equally narrow. The immunity we have recognized has extended no further than a subset of "officials of the federal government" and has covered only "discretionary" functions within the scope of their legal authority. See, e.g., Westfall v. Erwin, 484 U.S. 292 (1988); Howard v. Lyons, 360 U.S. 593 (1959); Barr v. Matteo, 360 U.S. 564, 571 (1959). Never before have we so much as intimated that the immunity (or the "uniquely federal interest" that justifies it) might extend beyond that narrow class to cover also nongovernment employees whose authority to act is independent of any source of federal law and that are as far removed from the "functioning of the federal government" as is a government contractor, *Howard*, 360 U.S. at 597.

The historical narrowness of the federal interest and the immunity is hardly accidental. A federal officer exercises statutory authority, which not only provides the necessary basis for the immunity in positive law, but also permits us confidently to presume that interference with the exercise of discretion undermines congressional will. In contrast, a government contractor acts independently of any congressional enactment. Thus, immunity for a contractor lacks both the positive law basis and the presumption that it furthers congressional will.

Moreover, even within the category of congressionally authorized tasks, we have deliberately restricted the scope of immunity to circumstances in which "the contributions of immunity to effective government in particular contexts outweigh the perhaps recurring harm to individual citizens," Doe v. McMillan, 412 U.S. 306, 320 (1973), because immunity "contravenes the basic tenet that individuals be held accountable for their wrongful conduct," *Westfall*, 484 U.S. at 295. . . . [A] grant of immunity to government contractors could not advance "the fearless, vigorous, and effective administration of policies of government" nearly as much as does the current immunity for government employees. Id. at 571. . . . [I]nhibition of the government official who actually sets government policy presents a greater threat to the "administration of policies of government," than does inhibition of a private contractor, whose role is devoted largely to assessing the technological feasibility and cost of satisfying the government's predetermined needs. Similarly, unlike tort suits against government officials, tort suits against government contractors would rarely "consume time and energies" that "would otherwise be devoted to governmental service." Id.

In short, because the essential justifications for official immunity do not support an extension to the government contractor, it is no surprise that we have never extended it that far. . . .

III

[T]he Court invokes the discretionary function exception of the Federal Tort Claims Act (FTCA), 28 U.S.C. § 2680(a). The Court does not suggest that the exception has any direct bearing here, for petitioner has sued a private manufacturer (not the federal government) under Virginia law (not the FTCA). [T]he Court [reasons] that federal common law must immunize government contractors from state tort law to prevent erosion of the discretionary function exception's *policy* of foreclosing judicial " 'second-guessing' " of discretionary governmental decisions. The erosion the Court fears apparently is rooted not in a concern that suits against government contractors will prevent them from designing, or the government from commissioning the design of, precisely the product the government wants, but in the concern that such suits might preclude the government from purchasing the desired product at the price it wants: "The financial burden of judgments against the contractors," the Court fears, "would ultimately be passed through, substantially if not totally, to the United States itself." . . .

IV

At bottom, the Court's analysis is premised on the proposition that any tort liability indirectly absorbed by the government so burdens governmental functions as to compel us to act when Congress has not. That proposition is by no means uncontroversial. The tort system is premised on the assumption that the imposition of liability encourages actors to prevent any injury whose expected cost exceeds the cost of prevention. If the system is working as it should, government contractors will design equipment to avoid certain injuries (like the deaths of soldiers or government employees), which would be certain to burden the government. The Court therefore has no basis for its assumption that tort liability will result in a net burden on the government (let alone a clearly excessive net burden) rather than a net gain.

Perhaps tort liability is an inefficient means of ensuring the quality of design efforts, but "[w]hatever the merits of the policy" the Court wishes to implement, "its conversion into law is a proper subject for congressional action, not for any creative power of ours." *Standard Oil*, 332 U.S. at 314–15. It is, after all, "Congress, not this Court or the other federal courts, [that] is the custodian of the national purse. By the same token [Congress] is the primary and most often the exclusive arbiter of federal fiscal affairs. And these comprehend, as we have said, securing the treasury or the government against financial losses *however inflicted.* . . ." Id. (emphasis added). If Congress shared the Court's assumptions and conclusion it could readily enact "A BILL to place limitations on the civil liability of government contractors to ensure that such liability does not impede the ability of the United States to procure necessary goods and services," H.R. 4765, 99th Cong., 2d Sess. (1986). It has not.

Were I a legislator, I would probably vote against any law absolving multibillion dollar private enterprises from answering for their tragic mistakes, at least if that law were justified by no more than the unsupported speculation that their liability might ultimately burden the United States Treasury. Some of my colleagues here would evidently vote otherwise (as they have here), but that should not matter here. We are judges not legislators, and the vote is not ours to cast.

I respectfully dissent.

■ JUSTICE STEVENS, dissenting.

When judges are asked to embark on a lawmaking venture, I believe they should carefully consider whether they, or a legislative body, are better equipped to perform the task at hand. There are instances of so-called interstitial lawmaking that inevitably become part of the judicial process. But when we are asked to create an entirely new doctrine—to answer "questions of policy on which Congress has not spoken," United

States v. Gilman, 347 U.S. 507, 511 (1954)—we have a special duty to identify the proper decisionmaker before trying to make the proper decision.

When the novel question of policy involves a balancing of the conflicting interests in the efficient operation of a massive governmental program and the protection of the rights of the individual—whether in the social welfare context, the civil service context, or the military procurement context—I feel very deeply that we should defer to the expertise of the Congress. . . . For in this case, as in *United States v. Gilman*, supra: "The selection of that policy which is most advantageous to the whole involves a host of considerations that must be weighed and appraised. That function is more appropriately for those who write the laws, rather than for those who interpret them."

I respectfully dissent.

NOTES ON THE LAW GOVERNING THE RIGHTS AND DUTIES OF PRIVATE PARTIES

1. BACKGROUND: SUITS BETWEEN PRIVATE PARTIES

Three major decisions provide background for *Boyle*.

(i) Bank of America v. Parnell

Bank of America Nat. Trust & Savings Ass'n v. Parnell, 352 U.S. 29 (1956), was the first major test of the implications of *Clearfield* for suits between private parties. The Bank of America brought a diversity case for the conversion of 73 government-issued bearer bonds held by four defendants, among them Parnell. The bonds had been stolen while Bank of America was preparing to present them for payment.

It was not alleged that Parnell and the other defendants stole the bonds. On the contrary, they apparently were acting for people who received the bonds for value. The question was whether they were "holders in due course" and as such were entitled to extinguish the rights of the original owner. The main issue at trial was whether the defendants took the bonds in good faith and without notice of the defect in their chain of title. The trial judge, following state law, charged that the defendants had the burden of persuasion on their good faith and lack of notice. The en banc Court of Appeals disagreed, holding that federal law applied under *Clearfield* and that federal law placed the burden of persuasion on the plaintiff to show notice and lack of good faith by the defendants. The Supreme Court reversed.

In an opinion by Justice Frankfurter, the Court said:

> Securities issued by the government generate immediate interests of the government. These were dealt with in *Clearfield Trust*. . . . But they also radiate interests in transactions between private parties. The present litigation is purely between private parties and does not touch the rights and duties of the United States. The only possible interest of the United States in a situation

like the one here, exclusively involving the transfer of government paper between private persons, is that the floating of securities of the United States might somehow or other be adversely affected by the local rule of a particular state regarding the liability of a converter. This is far too speculative, far too remote a possibility to justify the application of federal law to transactions essentially of local concern.

We do not mean to imply that litigation with respect to government paper necessarily precludes the presence of a federal interest, to be governed by federal law, in all situations merely because it is a suit between private parties, or that it is beyond the range of federal legislation to deal comprehensively with government paper. . . . Federal law of course governs the interpretation of the nature of the rights and obligations created by the government bonds themselves.[a] . . .

Justice Black, joined by Justice Douglas, dissented:

We believe that the "federal law merchant," which *Clearfield Trust* held applicable to transactions in the commercial paper of the United States, should be applicable to all transactions in that paper. . . . Not until today has a distinction been drawn between suits by the United States on that paper and suits by other parties to it. But the Court does not stop there. Because this is "essentially a private transaction," it is to be governed by local law. Yet the nature of the rights and obligations created by commercial paper of the United States government is said to be controlled by federal law. Thus, federal law is to govern some portion of a dispute between private parties, while that portion of the dispute which is "essentially of local concern" is to be governed by local law. The uncertainties which inhere in such a dichotomy are obvious.

The virtue of a uniform law governing bonds, notes, and other paper issued by the United States is that it provides a certain and definite guide to the rights of all parties rather than subjecting them to the vagaries of the laws of many states. The business of the United States will go on without that uniformity. But the policy surrounding our choice of law is concerned with the convenience, certainty, and definiteness in having one set of rules governing the rights of all parties to government paper, as contrasted to multiple rules. If the rule of the *Clearfield Trust* case is to be abandoned as to some parties, it should be abandoned as to all and we should start afresh on this problem.

(ii) *Wallis v. Pan American Petroleum Corp.*

Wallis v. Pan American Petroleum Corp., 384 U.S. 63 (1966), refused to apply federal law to dealings between private parties in an oil and gas lease

---

[a] For example, questions of when the bonds were due for payment or whether the government was obligated to pay, would be governed, under *Clearfield*, by federal law.—[Footnote by eds.]

issued under the Mineral Leasing Act of 1920. In the course of his opinion for the Court, Justice Harlan stated the criteria for applying federal law in suits between private parties:

In deciding whether rules of federal common law should be fashioned, normally the guiding principle is that a significant conflict between some federal policy or interest and the use of state law in the premises must first be specifically shown. It is by no means enough that, as we may assume, Congress could under the Constitution readily enact a complete code of law governing transactions in federal mineral leases among private parties. Whether latent federal power should be exercised to displace state law is primarily a decision for Congress. Even where there is related federal legislation in an area, as is true in this instance, it must be remembered that "Congress acts . . . against the background of the total corpus juris of the states. . . ." Henry Hart and Herbert Wechsler, The Federal Courts and the Federal System 435 (1953).[b] Because we find no significant threat to any identifiable federal policy or interest, we do not press on to consider other questions relevant to invoking federal common law, such as the strength of the state interest in having its own rules govern, cf. United States v. Yazell, 382 U.S. 341, 351–353 (1966),[c] the feasibility of creating a judicial substitute, cf. U.A.W. v. Hoosier Cardinal Corp., 383 U.S. 696, 701 (1966),[d] and other similar factors.

If there is a federal statute dealing with the general subject, it is a prime repository of federal policy and a starting point for federal common law. We find nothing in the Mineral Leasing Act of

---

[b]   The full passage from which this quotation is taken is well known:

Federal law is generally interstitial in nature. It rarely occupies a legal field completely, totally excluding all participation by the legal systems of the states. This was plainly true in the beginning when the federal legislative product (including the Constitution) was extremely small. It is significantly true today, despite the volume of Congressional enactments, and even within areas where Congress has been very active. Federal legislation, on the whole, has been conceived and drafted on an ad hoc basis to accomplish limited objectives. It builds upon legal relationships established by the states, altering or supplanting them only so far as necessary for the special purpose. Congress acts, in short, against the background of the total corpus juris of the states in much the same way that a state legislature acts against the background of the common law, assumed to govern unless changed by legislation.—[Footnote by eds.]

[c]   *Yazell* involved an effort by the Small Business Administration to foreclose on a disaster loan. The question was whether the Texas law of "coverture" prevented the government from seizing Mrs. Yazell's separate property. The Court held that the state law applied, which had the effect of insulating Mrs. Yazell's property even though she had signed the note when the money was borrowed. Among the factors emphasized by the Court were that these loans tend to be negotiated in light of local law and that the state had a strong interest in regulating property arrangements of this type. That *Yazell* may have been a "widows and orphans" case was suggested by the opening line to Justice Fortas's opinion: "[T]he question presented is whether the . . . federal government, in its zealous pursuit of the balance due on a disaster loan made by the Small Business Administration, may obtain judgment against Ethel Mae Yazell of Lampass, Texas."—[Footnote by eds.]

[d]   *Hoosier Cardinal* concerned the statute of limitations applicable to a suit brought under § 301 of the Taft-Hartley Act. Although the suit involved a federal cause of action, the Court looked to state law for the statute of limitations, in part because of the difficulty of determining a particular limitation period.—[Footnote by eds.]

1920 expressing policies inconsistent with state law in the area that concerns us here.

(iii) Miree v. DeKalb County

The facts of Miree v. DeKalb County, 433 U.S. 25 (1977), are described in Justice Brennan's dissent in *Boyle*. The survivors of deceased passengers and others sued under Georgia law as third-party beneficiaries to a federal contract between the Federal Aviation Administration (FAA) and a County airport. The county argued that federal law precluded third-party suits on FAA contracts. Justice Rehnquist spoke for the Court:

> [T]he resolution of petitioners' breach-of-contract claim against respondent will have no direct effect upon the United States or its Treasury. The Solicitor General [waived] his right to respond. . . .

> The operations of the United States in connection with FAA grants such as these are undoubtedly of considerable magnitude. However, we see no reason for concluding that these operations would be burdened or subjected to uncertainty by variant state-law interpretations regarding whether those with whom the United States contracts might be sued by third-party beneficiaries to the contracts. Since only the rights of private litigants are at issue here, we find the *Clearfield Trust* rationale inapplicable.

> . . . The parallel between *Parnell* and these cases is obvious. The question of whether petitioners may sue respondent does not require decision under federal common law since the litigation is among private parties and no substantial rights or duties of the United States hinge on its outcome. On the other hand, nothing we say here forecloses the applicability of federal common law in interpreting the rights and duties of the United States under federal contracts.

2. SUITS AGAINST FEDERAL OFFICERS

Another line of cases regarded as relevant in *Boyle* developed a federal defense to state-law tort suits against federal officials.

(i) Howard v. Lyons

In Howard v. Lyons, 360 U.S. 593 (1959), two civilian employees sued the Commander of the Boston Naval Shipyard for defamation. Justice Harlan's opinion for the Court asked "whether the extent of the privilege in respect of civil liability for statements allegedly defamatory under state law which may be claimed by officers of the federal government, acting in the course of their duties, is a question as to which the federal courts are bound to follow state law." His response was brief:

> We think that the very statement of the question dictates a negative answer. The authority of a federal officer to act derives from federal sources, and the rule which recognizes a privilege under appropriate circumstances as to statements made in the course of

duty is one designed to promote the effective functioning of the federal government. No subject could be one of more peculiarly federal concern, and it would deny the very considerations which give the rule of privilege its being to leave determination of its extent to the vagaries of the laws of the several states. Cf. Clearfield Trust Co. v. United States, 318 U.S. 363 (1943). We hold that the validity of petitioner's claim of absolute privilege must be judged by federal standards, to be formulated by the courts in the absence of legislative action by Congress.

The Court then held the Commander's statements absolutely privileged because made " 'in the discharge of [his] official duties and in relation to matters committed to him for determination.' "

(ii) Barr v. Matteo

Barr v. Matteo, 360 U.S. 564 (1959), was a companion case in which Justice Harlan's plurality opinion quoted Learned Hand on the reasons for recognizing a federal defense to state tort claims:

> It does indeed go without saying that an official, who is in fact guilty of using his powers to vent his spleen upon others, or for any other personal motive not connected with the public good, should not escape liability for the injuries he may cause; and, if it were possible in practice to confine such complaints to the guilty, it would be monstrous to deny recovery. The justification for doing so is that it is impossible to know whether the claim is well founded until the case has been tried, and that to submit all officials, the innocent as well as the guilty, to the burden of a trial and to the inevitable danger of its outcome, would dampen the ardor of all but the most resolute, or the most irresponsible, in the unflinching discharge of their duties. . . . In this instance it has been thought in the end better to leave unredressed the wrongs done by dishonest officers than to subject those who try to do their duty to the constant dread of retaliation. . . . Gregoire v. Biddle, 177 F.2d 579, 581 (2d Cir. 1949).

In *Barr*, the Court held that the privilege against liability for defamation should not be restricted to high-ranking officials, although the occasions for its invocation may increase with the broader discretion exercised by those in higher positions.[e]

(iii) Westfall v. Erwin

In Westfall v. Erwin, 484 U.S. 292 (1988), Erwin and his wife brought a state-law tort suit for injuries allegedly suffered through the negligence of federal officials. Erwin was a civilian warehouseman at an Army depot. The

---

[e]   Justice Harlan wrote for a plurality of four. Justice Black would have gone further: "So far as I am concerned, if federal employees are to be subjected to such suits in reporting their views about how to run the government better, the restraint will have to be imposed expressly by Congress and not by the general libel laws of the states. . . ." Chief Justice Warren and Justices Douglas, Brennan, and Stewart dissented.

defendants were supervisors at the depot. The question was the scope of absolute immunity enjoyed by these officials. Justice Marshall wrote for a unanimous Court that "absolute immunity does not shield official functions from state tort liability unless the challenged conduct is within the outer perimeter of an official's duties and is discretionary in nature":

> The purpose of such official immunity is not to protect an erring official, but to insulate the decisionmaking process from the harassment of prospective litigation. The provision of immunity rests on the view that the threat of liability will make federal officials unduly timid in carrying out their official duties, and that effective government will be promoted if officials are freed of the costs of vexatious and often frivolous damages suits. See Barr v. Matteo, 360 U.S. 564 (1959). This Court always has recognized, however, that official immunity comes at a great cost. An injured party with an otherwise meritorious tort claim is denied compensation simply because he had the misfortune to be injured by a federal official. Moreover, absolute immunity contravenes the basic tenet that individuals be held accountable for their wrongful conduct. We therefore have held that absolute immunity for federal officials is justified only when "the contributions of immunity to effective government in particular contexts outweigh the perhaps recurring harm to individual citizens." Doe v. McMillan, 412 U.S. 306, 320 (1973).[3] . . .

> The central purpose of official immunity, promoting effective government, would not be furthered by shielding an official from state-law tort liability without regard to whether the alleged tortious conduct is discretionary in nature. When an official's conduct is not the product of independent judgment, the threat of liability cannot detrimentally inhibit that conduct. It is only when officials exercise decisionmaking discretion that potential liability may shackle "the fearless, vigorous, and effective administration of policies of government." *Barr v. Matteo*, 360 U.S. at 571. Because it would not further effective governance, absolute immunity for nondiscretionary functions finds no support in the traditional justification for official immunity.

3. QUESTIONS AND COMMENTS

By the time of *Clearfield* and *Parnell*, every state had adopted the Uniform Negotiable Instruments Law, since superseded by Article 3 of the Uniform Commercial Code. Given the relative uniformity of state law, does the *Clearfield-Parnell* dichotomy make sense? Whatever the theory, would it be better simply to let state law apply to the rights and obligations of the federal government on its checks and bonds, as well as to the rights and obligations of private parties on the same instruments? Or would it have been

---

[3]   In determining the propriety of shielding an official from suit under the circumstances, this Court has long favored a "functional" inquiry—immunity attaches to particular official functions, not to particular offices. . . .

better, as Black and Douglas apparently preferred, for federal law to apply across the board?

From *Parnell, Wallis,* and *Miree,* one might conclude that federal law governs the rights and obligations of the federal government itself and that state law, except where displaced by Congress, governs the rights and obligations of private parties. The cases on the immunity of federal officials from state tort liability are exceptions to this generalization. *Boyle* further complicates the issue.[f] By what criteria does the Court determine when federal common law applies to disputes among private parties? Was the Court in *Boyle* in effect acting as a legislative body, as Justice Brennan charged?

In the end, should the question be whether the Constitution requires a uniform federal law (as in the case of admiralty, for example) or whether there are valid federal policies that require this result? If so, how is the Court to determine the relevant federal policies?

4. NARROWER CONCEPTION OF FEDERAL COMMON LAW: *O'MELVENY & MYERS V. FDIC*

Boyle represents a particularly expansive example of the Supreme Court's authority to develop federal common law. In some of its subsequent decisions, the Court has articulated a more restrained conception of when federal common law is appropriate. A good illustration is O'Melveny & Myers v. FDIC, 512 U.S. 79 (1994). In that case, the Federal Deposit Insurance Corporation (FDIC), acting as receiver for a federally insured bank in California, brought suit against a law firm that had represented the bank in real estate transactions. The FDIC alleged that the firm's failure to uncover fraudulent activities by the bank's officers constituted malpractice under California law. The firm responded that the FDIC was estopped from pursuing this claim because the knowledge of the bank's officers should be imputed to the corporation, and to the FDIC as receiver. The issue was whether the standard for imputation of knowledge should be determined by state law or federal common law. The Ninth Circuit held that federal common law governed the issue of imputation and that, as a matter of federal common law, the attributed knowledge of corporate officers acting against the corporation's interest could not be used as the basis for an estoppel defense against the FDIC as receiver.

The Supreme Court reversed. In an opinion by Justice Scalia, the Court began by sharply rejecting the proposition that federal common law should generally govern the imputation standard for federally insured banks. Quoting the statement in *Erie* that "[t]here is no federal general common law," and, citing *Parnell*, the Court noted that "the remote possibility that corporations may go into federal receivership is no conceivable basis for adopting a special federal common-law rule divesting States of authority over the entire law of imputation." As for the narrower argument that federal common law should apply in those situations in which the FDIC is acting as receiver,

---

f   For criticism of *Boyle*, see Michael D. Green and Richard A. Matasar, The Supreme Court and the Products Liability Crisis: Lessons from *Boyle*'s Government Contractor Defense, 63 So. Calif. L. Rev. 639 (1990).

the Court distinguished the *Clearfield* line of cases on the ground that, in bringing a suit as receiver, the FDIC steps into the shoes of the bank and thus is not asserting claims of the United States itself. Although a federal statute established some specialized rules for claims brought by the FDIC, it did not address the issue of imputation, and the Court concluded that adding federal common law rules would improperly alter the statutory scheme.

More generally, the Court emphasized that the instances in which federal common law is appropriate are "few and restricted" and that a prerequisite for the development of federal common law is a "significant conflict between some federal policy or interest and the use of state law." In this case, however, the Court saw no such conflict. As for "that most generic (and lightly invoked) of alleged federal interests, the interest in uniformity," the Court noted that, while "[u]niformity of law might facilitate the FDIC's nationwide litigation of these suits, eliminating state-by-state research and reducing uncertainty . . . if the avoidance of those ordinary consequences qualified as an identifiable federal interest, we would be awash in 'federal common-law' rules."

The Court further rejected the argument that federal common law was justified by the interest in not depleting the federal insurance fund. It said there "is no federal policy that the fund should always win," and, citing *Kimbell Foods* and other decisions, it observed that its prior decisions had "previously rejected 'more money' arguments remarkably similar to the one made here." Finally, the Court stated that a desire to insulate the federal program from particular state views about the scope of malpractice liability was "[e]ven less persuasive-indeed, positively probative of the dangers of respondent's facile approach to federal-common-law-making." "By presuming to judge what constitutes malpractice," observed the Court, "this argument demonstrates the runaway tendencies of 'federal common law' untethered to a genuinely identifiable (as opposed to judicially constructed) federal policy."

Justice Scalia was the author of the majority opinions in both *Boyle* and *O'Melveny*. Can the two decisions be reconciled? Were the requirements for federal common law articulated in *O'Melveny* met in *Boyle*?

5. *EMPIRE HEALTHCHOICE ASSURANCE, INC. V. MCVEIGH*

As authorized by a governing federal statute, health insurance for federal employees is provided pursuant to contract between the Office of Personnel Management (OPM) and private carriers. Payment of premiums is divided 75%–25% between the government and its employees. The premiums are paid into a special treasury account. The private carriers draw upon this fund to pay for covered benefits. They are paid a fee for administering the program and bear no risk of loss.

The contract provides for full subrogation rights in the name of the private carrier in the event that an employee recovers compensation for illness or injury for which benefits have been paid. Empire Healthchoice Assurance, Inc. v. McVeigh, 547 U.S. 677 (2006), involved such a suit by a private carrier against the estate of a covered employee to recover $157,309 in benefits paid for the decedent's medical care. The decedent was injured in an accident in

1997 and died in 2001. Tort litigation in state court led to a settlement in favor of the estate for $3,175,000. Any recovery in the subrogation suit would be deposited in the same treasury account that held the premiums.

Empire filed suit in federal court, alleging federal question jurisdiction based on § 1331. The District Court dismissed for want of subject matter jurisdiction, and the Circuit Court affirmed. Both lower courts concluded that the subrogation claim arose under state law and did not involve sufficient federal questions to warrant the exercise of federal court jurisdiction. The Supreme Court affirmed by a five to four vote. Since the majority opinion is largely a response to the dissent, the latter is covered first.

(i)   The Dissent

Joined by Justices Kennedy, Souter, and Alito, Justice Breyer wrote the dissent. "There is little about this case," he said, "that is not federal":

> [T]he statute [creating the program] is federal, the program it creates is federal, the program's beneficiaries are federal employees working throughout the country, the Federal Government pays all relevant costs, and the Federal Government receives all relevant payments. The private carrier's only role in this scheme is to administer the health benefits plan for the federal agency in exchange for a fixed service charge. . . .
>
> It seems clear to me that the petitioner's claim arises under federal common law. The dispute concerns the application of terms in a federal contract. This Court has consistently held that "obligations to and rights of the United States under its contracts are governed exclusively by federal law." Boyle v. United Technologies Corp., 487 U.S. 500, 504 (1988). This principle dates back at least as far as Clearfield Trust Co. v. United States, 318 U.S. 363, 366 (1943). . . .
>
> This Court has applied this principle, the principle embodied in *Clearfield Trust,* to Government contracts of all sorts. [Citations omitted.] In this case, the words that provide the right to recover are contained in the [explanatory] brochure [given to beneficiaries], which in turn explains the provisions of the contract between the Government and the carrier, provisions that were written by a federal agency acting pursuant to a federal statute that creates a federal benefit program for federal employees. At bottom, then, the petitioner's claim is based on the interpretation of a federal contract, and as such should be governed by federal common law. And because the petitioner's claim is based on federal common law, the federal courts have jurisdiction over it pursuant to § 1331.

Breyer added three reasons in support of this conclusion:

> First, although the nominal plaintiff in this case is the carrier, the real party in interest is the United States. Any funds that the petitioner recovers here it must pay directly to the United States, by depositing those funds in the [treasury] account managed by the federal agency. The carrier simply administers the reimbursement

proceeding for the United States, just as it administers the rest of the agency/carrier contract. Accordingly, this case, just like the *Clearfield Trust* cases, concerns the "rights of the United States under its contracts." *Boyle,* 487 U.S. at 504.

Second, the health insurance system FEHBA establishes is a federal program. The Federal Government pays for the benefits, receives the premiums, and resolves disputes over claims for medical services. Given this role, the Federal Government's need for uniform interpretation of the contract is great. Given the spread of Government employees throughout the Nation and the unfairness of treating similar employees differently, the employees' need for uniform interpretation is equally great. That interest in uniformity calls for application of federal common law to disputes about the meaning of the words in the agency/carrier contract and brochure. And that interest in uniformity also suggests that the doors of the federal courts should be open to decide such disputes.

uniformity argument

Third, as discussed above, the provisions at issue here are just a few scattered islands in a sea of federal contractual provisions, all of which federal courts will interpret and apply (when reviewing the federal agency's resolution of disputes regarding benefits). Given this context, why would Congress have wanted the courts to treat those islands any differently? I can find no convincing answer.

(ii) The Majority

The majority, in an opinion by Justice Ginsburg, disagreed:

[T]he dissent is mistaken in supposing that the *Clearfield* doctrine covers this case. *Clearfield* was a suit by the United States to recover from a bank the amount paid on a Government check on which the payee's name had been forged [and the] Court held that "[t]he rights and duties of the United States on commercial paper which it issues are governed by federal rather than [state] law." . . . Later, in *Boyle,* the Court telescoped the appropriate inquiry, focusing it on the straightforward question whether the relevant federal interest warrants displacement of state law. Referring simply to "the displacement of state law," the Court recognized that prior cases had treated discretely (1) the competence of federal courts to formulate a federal rule of decision, and (2) the appropriateness of declaring a federal rule rather than borrowing, incorporating, or adopting state law in point. The Court preferred "the more modest terminology," questioning whether "the distinction between displacement of state law and displacement of federal law's incorporation of state law ever makes a practical difference." *Boyle* made two further observations here significant. First, *Boyle* explained, the involvement of "an area of uniquely federal interest . . . establishes a necessary, not a sufficient, condition for the displacement of state law." Second, in some cases, an "entire body of state law" may conflict with the federal interest and therefore require replacement. But in others, the conflict is confined, and "only particular elements of state law are superseded."

The dissent describes this case as pervasively federal, and "the provisions . . . here [as] just a few scattered islands in a sea of federal contractual provisions." But there is nothing "scattered" about the provisions on reimbursement and subrogation in the . . . master contract. Those provisions are linked together and depend upon a recovery from a third party under terms and conditions ordinarily governed by state law.[4] The Court of Appeals, whose decision we review, trained on the matter of reimbursement, not, as the dissent does, on [the] authorized contracts at large. So focused, the appeals court determined that Empire has not demonstrated a "significant conflict . . . between an identifiable federal policy or interest and the operation of state law." Unless and until that showing is made, there is no cause to displace state law, much less to lodge this case in federal court.

This decision suggests that a majority of the Court is not particularly inclined to extend *Boyle*. The case also is a reminder that the determination of whether to apply federal common law can affect not only preemption of state law, but also federal court jurisdiction.

6. FEDERAL COMMON LAW AND FOREIGN AFFAIRS

In Banco Nacional de Cuba v. Sabbatino, 376 U.S. 398 (1964), the Cuban government sued in a federal court in New York to recover the proceeds from its sale of sugar from a factory in Cuba, which it had expropriated after Fidel Castro had come to power. The issue was whether the court could consider whether Cuba was the lawful owner of the sugar when it made the sale. In holding that the court was required to assume the validity of Cuba's title, the Supreme Court applied the "act of state doctrine," pursuant to which "the courts of one country will not sit in judgment on the acts of the government of another, done within its own territory." Underhill v. Hernandez, 168 U.S. 250, 252 (1897).

In an opinion by Justice Harlan, the Court in *Sabbatino* held that the act of state doctrine was a rule of post-*Erie* federal common law. The Court acknowledged that it "could, perhaps, in this diversity action, avoid the question of deciding whether federal or state law is applicable to this aspect of the litigation," since the New York state courts had embraced the act of state doctrine in terms similar to the relevant federal decisions. The Court nevertheless said that it was "constrained to make it clear that an issue concerned with a basic choice regarding the competence and function of the Judiciary and the National Executive in ordering our relationships with other members of the international community must be treated exclusively as an aspect of federal law." It is unclear what implications this decision has for other issues relating to foreign affairs. The potential relevance of the decision to

---

[4]   The dissent nowhere suggests that uniform, court-declared federal law would govern the carrier's subrogation claim against the tortfeasor. Nor does the dissent explain why the two linked provisions—reimbursement and subrogation—should be decoupled.

debates over the domestic status of "customary international law" (which arises out of certain practices of the international community) is considered below in Section 4.

7.   BIBLIOGRAPHY

For an early article praising the post-*Erie* development of federal common law, see Henry J. Friendly, In Praise of *Erie*—And of the New Federal Common Law, 39 N.Y.U. L. Rev. 383 (1964). Scholars in subsequent years have expressed a wide range of views about the proper scope of federal common law. See, for example, Thomas W. Merrill, The Common Law Powers of Federal Courts, 52 U. Chi. L. Rev. 1, 47 (1985) (courts should not develop federal common law rules of decision unless they are "necessary in order to preserve or effectuate some other federal policy that can be derived from the specific intentions of the draftsmen of an authoritative federal text"); Martha A. Field, Sources of Law: The Scope of Federal Common Law, 99 Harv. L. Rev. 881, 887 (1986) ("[T]he only limitation on courts' power to create federal common law is that the court must point to a federal enactment, constitutional or statutory, that it interprets as authorizing the federal common law rule."); Martin H. Redish, Federal Common Law, Political Legitimacy, and the Interpretive Process: An "Institutionalist" Perspective, 83 Nw. U. L. Rev. 761, 766 (1989) (contending that the Rules of Decision Act "limit[s] the situations in which federal substantive law displaces state law to those specific instances in which Congress-rather than the federal judiciary-chooses to do so"); Louise Weinberg, Federal Common Law, 83 Nw. U. L. Rev. 805, 813 (1989) ("[W]hat justifies an exercise of national lawmaking power is the existence of a legitimate national governmental interest. Courts must act, of course, within their constitutional and statutory jurisdiction. But no other 'authorization' is required."); Larry Kramer, The Lawmaking Power of the Federal Courts, 12 Pace L. Rev. 263, 288 (1992) ("[F]ederal judges must wait for Congress to take the first step. Once Congress has acted, however, federal courts can make any common law 'necessary and proper' to implement the statute."); Bradford R. Clark, Federal Common Law: A Structural Reinterpretation, 144 U. Pa. L. Rev. 1245, 1252 (1996) (defending some aspects of federal common law, especially in the area of foreign affairs, as "merely background rules that federal and state courts apply in order to avoid encroaching upon authority committed by the Constitution to Congress and the President"); and Jay Tidmarsh and Brian J. Murray, A Theory of Federal Common Law, 100 Nw. U. L. Rev. 585, 588 (2006) ("[P]otential bias in creating state law is a necessary condition for creating federal common law."). For a discussion of the role of *state* courts in making federal common law, and an argument that these courts should make federal common law "not on the basis of purely forward-looking policy considerations, but only as a consequence of their best efforts to enforce federal law as it existed at the time pertinent to the issue being resolved," see Anthony J. Bellia Jr., State Courts and the Making of Federal Common Law, 153 U. Pa. L. Rev. 825 (2005). A recent article by Caleb Nelson analyzes different types of federal common law and offers a strong defense of some of them. See Caleb Nelson, The Legitimacy of (Some) Federal Common Law, 101 Va. L. Rev. 1 (2015). Finally, Mark D. Rosen, Choice-of-Law as Non-Constitutional Federal Law, 99 Minn.

L. Rev. 1017 (2015), argues that choice of law, which after *Klaxon* generally is governed by state law even in federal court, should be reconceptualized as a species of federal common law applicable throughout the nation.

SECTION 2. IMPLIED RIGHTS OF ACTION TO ENFORCE FEDERAL STATUTES

Cort v. Ash

Supreme Court of the United States, 1975.
422 U.S. 66.

■ MR. JUSTICE BRENNAN delivered the opinion of the Court.

There are other questions, but the principal issue presented for decision is whether a private cause of action for damages against corporate directors is to be implied in favor of a corporate stockholder under 18 U.S.C. § 610, a criminal statute prohibiting corporations from making "a contribution or expenditure in connection with any election at which Presidential and Vice Presidential electors . . . are to be voted for."[1] We conclude that the implication of such a federal cause of action is not suggested by the legislative context of § 610 or required to accomplish Congress' purposes in enacting the statute. . . .

I

In August and September 1972, an advertisement with the caption "I say let's keep the campaign honest. Mobilize 'truth squads' " appeared in various national publications, including Time, Newsweek, and U.S. News and World Report, and in 19 local newspapers in communities where Bethlehem Steel Corp. (Bethlehem), a Delaware corporation, has plants. Reprints of the advertisement, which consisted mainly of quotations from a speech by petitioner Stewart S. Cort, chairman of the board of directors of Bethlehem, were included with the September 11, 1972, quarterly dividend checks mailed to the stockholders of the corporation.

---

[1]   Title 18 U.S.C. § 610 (1970 ed. and Supp. III) provided in part as follows when this suit was filed:

Contributions or expenditures by national banks, corporations, or labor organizations.

It is unlawful for any national bank, or any corporation organized by authority of any law of Congress, to make a contribution or expenditure in connection with any election to any political office, or in connection with any primary election or political convention or caucus held to select candidates for any political office, or for any corporation whatever, or any labor organization to make a contribution or expenditure in connection with any election at which Presidential and Vice Presidential electors or a Senator or Representative in, or a Delegate or Resident Commissioner to Congress are to be voted for, or . . .

Every corporation or labor organization which makes any contribution or expenditure in violation of this section shall be fined not more than $5,000; and every officer or director of any corporation, or officer of any labor organization, who consents to any contribution or expenditure by the corporation or labor organization, as the case may be, and any person who accepts or receives any contribution, in violation of this section, shall be fined not more than $1,000 or imprisoned not more than one year, or both; and if the violation was willful, shall be fined not more than $10,000 or imprisoned not more than two years, or both. . . .

The main text of the advertisement appealed to the electorate to "encourage responsible, honest, and truthful campaigning." It alleged that vigilance was needed because "careless rhetoric and accusations . . . are being thrown around these days—their main target being the business community." In italics, under a picture of Mr. Cort, the advertisement quoted "the following statement made by a political candidate: 'The time has come for a tax system that says to big business—you must pay your fair share.'" It then printed Mr. Cort's rejoinder to this in his speech, including his opinion that to say "large corporations [are] not carrying their fair share of the tax burden" is "baloney." The advertisement concluded with an offer to send, on request, copies of Mr. Cort's entire speech and a folder "telling how to go about activating *Truth Squads.*" These publications could be obtained free from the Public Affairs Department of Bethlehem. It is stipulated that the entire costs of the advertisements and various mailings were paid from Bethlehem's general corporate funds.

Respondent owns 50 shares of Bethlehem stock and was qualified to vote in the 1972 presidential election. He filed this suit in the United States District Court for the Eastern District of Pennsylvania on September 28, 1972, on behalf of himself and derivatively, on behalf of Bethlehem. The complaint . . . alleged jurisdiction under 28 U.S.C. § 1331, and sought to state a private claim for relief under 18 U.S.C. § 610, which, as mentioned, in terms provides only for a criminal penalty. . . . Immediate injunctive relief against further corporate expenditures in connection with the 1972 presidential election or any future campaign was sought, as well as compensatory and punitive damages in favor of the corporation.

The District Court . . . granted petitioner's motion for summary judgment without opinion. The Court of Appeals reversed. The Court of Appeals held that, since the [complaint] sought damages for the corporation for violation of § 610, the controversy was not moot, although the election which occasioned it was past. The Court of Appeals held further that "a private cause of action, whether brought by a citizen to secure injunctive relief or by a stockholder to secure injunctive or derivative damage relief [is] proper to remedy violation of § 610."

II

[In this part of its opinion, the Court determined that injunctive relief to enforce § 610 was in any event improper due to the subsequent enactment of the Federal Election Campaign Act of 1974, which established an administrative procedure for processing complaints of alleged violation of § 610 after January 1, 1975.]

III

[W]e turn next to the holding of the Court of Appeals that "a private cause of action . . . by a stockholder to secure . . . derivative damage relief

[is] proper to remedy violation of § 610." We hold that such relief is not available. . . .

In determining whether a private remedy is implicit in a statute not expressly provided one, several factors are relevant. First, is the plaintiff "one of the class for whose *especial* benefit the statute was enacted," Texas & Pacific R. Co. v. Rigsby, 241 U.S. 33 (1916) (emphasis supplied)—that is, does the statute create a federal right in favor of the plaintiff? Second, is there any indication of legislative intent, explicit or implicit, either to create such a remedy or to deny one? Third, is it consistent with the underlying purposes of the legislative scheme to imply such a remedy for the plaintiff? And finally, is the cause of action one traditionally relegated to state law, in an area basically the concern of the states, so that it would be inappropriate to infer a cause of action based solely on federal law?

The dissenting judge in the Court of Appeals and petitioners here suggest that where a statute provides a penal remedy alone, it cannot be regarded as creating a right in any particular class of people. . . .

Clearly, a provision of a criminal penalty does not necessarily *preclude* implication of a private cause of action for damages. [See] J.I. Case Co. v. Borak, 377 U.S. 426 (1964); *Texas & Pacific R. Co. v. Rigsby*. However in [*Borak* and *Rigsby*], there was at least a statutory basis for inferring that a civil cause of action of some sort lay in favor of someone.[11] Here, there was nothing more than a bare criminal statute, with absolutely no indication that civil enforcement of any kind was available to anyone.

We need not, however, go so far as to say that in this circumstance a bare criminal statute can *never* be deemed sufficiently protective of some special group so as to give rise to a private cause of action by a member of that group. For the intent to protect corporate shareholders particularly was at best a subsidiary purpose of § 610, and the other relevant factors all either are not helpful or militate against implying a private cause of action.

First, § 610 is derived from the Act of January 26, 1907, which "seems to have been motivated by two considerations. First, the necessity for destroying the influence over elections which corporations exercised through financial contribution. Second, the feeling that corporate officials had no moral right to use corporate funds for contribution to

---

[11] . . . In *Borak*, § 27 of the Securities Exchange Act of 1934 specifically granted jurisdiction to the district courts over civil actions to "enforce any liability or duty created by this title or the rules and regulations thereunder," and there seemed to be no dispute over the fact that at least a private suit for declaratory relief was authorized; the question was whether a derivative suit for recission and damages was also available. Further it was clear that the Securities and Exchange Commission could sue to enjoin violations of § 14(a) of the act, the section involved in *Borak*.

[I]n *Rigsby*, the Court noted that the statutes involved included language pertinent only to a private right of action for damages, although such a right of action was not expressly provided, thus rendering "[t]he inference of a private right of action . . . irresistible." 241 U.S. at 40.

political parties without the consent of stockholders." United States v. CIO, 335 U.S. 106, 113 (1948). Respondent bases his derivative action on the second purpose, claiming that the intent to protect stockholders from use of their invested funds for political purposes demonstrates that the statute set up a federal right in shareholders not to have corporate funds used for this purpose.

However, the legislative history of the 1907 act, recited at length in United States v. Auto Workers, 352 U.S. 567 (1957), demonstrates that the protection of ordinary stockholders was at best a secondary concern.[13] Rather, the primary purpose of the 1907 act . . . was to assure that federal elections are " 'free from the power of money,' " id. at 574, to eliminate " 'the apparent hold on political parties which business interests . . . seek and sometimes obtain by reason of liberal campaign contributions.' " Id. at 576. Thus, the legislation was primary concerned with corporations as a source of aggregated wealth and therefore of possible corrupting influence, and not directly with the internal relations between the corporations and their stockholders. . . .

Second, there is no indication whatever in the legislative history of § 610 which suggests a congressional intention to vest in corporate shareholders a federal right to damages for violation of § 610. True, in situations in which it is clear that federal law has granted a class of persons certain rights, it is not necessary to show an intention to *create* a private cause of action, although an explicit purpose to *deny* such cause of action would be controlling. But where, as here, it is at least dubious whether Congress intended to vest in the plaintiff class rights broader than those provided by state regulation of corporations, the fact that there is no suggestion at all that § 610 may give rise to a suit for damages reinforces the conclusion that the expectation, if any, was that the relationship between corporations and their stockholders would continue to be entrusted entirely to state law.

Third, while "it is the duty of the courts to be alert to provide such remedies as are necessary to make effective the congressional purpose," J.I. Case Co. v. Borak, 377 U.S. 426, 433 (1964), in this instance the remedy sought would not aid the primary congressional goal. Recovery of derivative damages by the corporation for violation of § 610 would not cure the influence which the use of corporate funds in the first instance may have had on a federal election. Rather, such a remedy would only permit directors in effect to "borrow" corporate funds for a time; the later compelled repayment might well not deter the initial violation and would certainly not decrease the impact of the use of such funds upon an election already past.

Fourth, and finally, for reasons already intimated, it is entirely appropriate in this instance to relegate respondent and others in his situation to whatever remedy is created by state law. . . . Corporations

---

[13]   Section 610 was later expanded to include labor unions within its prohibition. . . .

are creatures of state law, and investors commit their funds to corporate directors on the understanding that, except where federal law expressly requires certain responsibilities of directors with respect to stockholders, state law will govern the internal affairs of the corporation. If, for example, state law permits corporations to use corporate funds as contributions in state elections, shareholders are on notice that their funds may be so used and have no recourse under any federal statute. We are necessarily reluctant to imply a federal right to recover funds used in violation of a federal statute where the laws governing the corporation may put a shareholder on notice that there may be no such recovery. . . .

Because . . . implication of a federal right of damages on behalf of a corporation under § 610 would intrude into an area traditionally committed to state law without aiding the main purpose of § 610, we reverse.

It is so ordered.

NOTES ON IMPLIED RIGHTS OF ACTION TO ENFORCE FEDERAL STATUTES

1.   *J.I. CASE V. BORAK*

Although unanimously rejected by the Justices, the approach taken by the court of appeals in *Cort v. Ash* followed the Supreme Court's lead in J.I. Case Co. v. Borak, 377 U.S. 426 (1964). *J.I. Case* involved § 14 of the Securities and Exchange Act of 1934, which provided that it "shall be unlawful for any person . . . to solicit . . . any proxy . . . in contravention of such rules and regulations as the [Securities and Exchange] Commission may prescribe as necessary or appropriate in the public interest or for the protection of investors." Rule 14a–9 prohibited proxy solicitations containing any "false or misleading" statement. Additionally, § 27 of the act gave federal district courts "exclusive jurisdiction of violations of this title or the rules and regulations thereunder, and of all suits in equity and actions at law brought to enforce any liability or duty created by this title or the rules and regulations thereunder." Other sections of the act explicitly authorized private damages actions in other circumstances, but not for false or misleading proxy statements.

Borak owned stock in J.I. Case. He filed a stockholders' derivative action against the company to challenge the terms of a proposed merger. The question was "whether § 27 of the act authorizes a federal cause of action for recission or damages to a corporate stockholder with respect to a consummated merger which was authorized pursuant to the use of a proxy statement alleged to contain false and misleading statements violative of § 14(a) of the act." In a brief and unanimous opinion, the Court said yes. Justice Clark wrote:

> The purpose of § 14(a) is to prevent management or others from obtaining authorization for corporate action by means of deceptive or inadequate disclosure in proxy solicitation. . . . While [it]

makes no specific reference to a private right of action, among its chief purposes is "the protection of investors," which certainly implies the availability of judicial relief where necessary to achieve that result.

. . . Private enforcement of the proxy rules provides a necessary supplement to Commission action. As in antitrust treble damage litigation, the possibility of civil damages or injunctive relief serves as a most effective weapon in the enforcement of the proxy requirements. The Commission advises [in an amicus brief supporting the existence of a private cause of action] that it examines over 2,000 proxy statements annually and each of them must necessarily be expedited. Time does not permit an independent examination of the facts set out in the proxy material and this results in the Commission's acceptance of the representations contained therein at their face value, unless contrary to other material on file with it. Indeed, on the allegations of [Borak's] complaint, the proxy material failed to disclose alleged unlawful market manipulation of the stock [of the company with which J.I. Case merged], and this unlawful manipulation would not have been apparent to the Commission until after the merger.

We, therefore, believe that under the circumstances here it is the duty of the courts to be alert to provide such remedies as are necessary to make effective the congressional purpose. . . .

2.   *CANNON V. UNIVERSITY OF CHICAGO*

In both *J.I. Case* and *Cort v. Ash*, the Supreme Court assumed that it had the *power* to recognize private rights of action where appropriate. That assumption was challenged in Cannon v. University of Chicago, 441 U.S. 677 (1979).

In *Cannon*, the plaintiff alleged that she had been denied admission to medical school in violation of § 901 of Title IX of the Education Amendments of 1972. The statute provided that:

No person in the United States shall, on the basis of sex, be excluded from participation in, be denied the benefits of, or be subjected to discrimination under any education program or activity receiving federal financial assistance. . . .

The lower courts found no private right of action for injunctive relief, but a divided Supreme Court disagreed.

(i)   *The Majority*

In an opinion by Justice Stevens, the Court applied *Cort v. Ash*. The first factor was easily satisfied, as the statute clearly created a right not to be discriminated against on the basis of sex. Second, the Court thought Congress "rather plainly . . . intended to create" a private remedy. Title IX was patterned after Title VI of the Civil Rights Act of 1964, and the courts had already recognized a private remedy under Title VI when Title IX was enacted. "Moreover," Stevens continued, during the period between the enactment of Title VI in 1964 and the enactment of Title IX in 1972, this Court had consistently found implied remedies—often in cases much less clear than this. It was *after* 1972 that this Court decided *Cort v. Ash* [and other more restrictive cases]. We, of course, adhere to the strict approach followed in our recent cases, but our evaluation of congressional action in 1972 must take into account its contemporary legal context.

Third, the Court noted that Congress had two purposes in enacting Title IX: to prevent the use of federal funds to support discriminatory practices and to protect individual citizens against discrimination. The cut-off of funding would be so severe that it would not likely be invoked for an isolated violation. An injunction would be more effective, and there would be no inconsistency in permitting both remedies. The federal agency charged with enforcing the statute, moreover, had expressed its support of the private remedy as a supplementary means of enforcement.

Finally, the last *Cort* factor also supported recognition of a federal remedy. Ever since the Civil War, the Court said, the federal government has been the primary protector against discrimination. "In sum," the Court concluded, "there is no need in this case to weigh the four *Cort* factors, all of them support the same result."

Chief Justice Burger concurred in the judgment without opinion, while Justice Rehnquist, joined by Justice Stewart, wrote a separate concurrence. Rehnquist emphasized that the Court's approach was "quite different" from the analysis in *J.I. Case*. "The question of the existence of a private right of action is basically one of statutory construction." He concluded that while Congress may well have had reason in the past to believe that the courts would readily infer a private cause of action, the situation now was different. The lawmaking branch should be apprised "that the ball, so to speak, may well now be in its court. [T]his Court in the future should be extremely reluctant to imply a cause of action absent . . . specificity on the part of the legislative branch."

(ii) The Powell Dissent

In a dissent joined by Justice Blackmun, Justice White argued that Congress specifically intended that there *not* be a private cause of action in this case. In a separate dissent, Justice Powell agreed with that conclusion but launched a much broader attack, arguing that the "mode of analysis we have applied in the recent past cannot be squared with the doctrine of separation of powers":

> Under Article III, Congress alone has the responsibility for determining the jurisdiction of the lower federal courts. As the legislative branch, Congress also should determine when private parties are to be given causes of action under legislation it adopts. . . . When Congress chooses not to provide a private civil remedy, federal courts should not assume the legislative role of creating such a remedy and thereby enlarge their jurisdiction.

. . . The "four factor" analysis of *Cort* is an open invitation to federal courts to legislate causes of action not authorized by Congress. It is an analysis not faithful to constitutional principles and should be rejected. Absent the most compelling evidence of affirmative congressional intent, a federal court should not infer a private cause of action. . . .

Of the four factors mentioned in *Cort*, only one refers expressly to legislative intent. The other three invite independent judicial lawmaking. Asking whether a statute creates a right in favor of a private party, for example, begs the question at issue. What is involved is not the mere existence of a legal right, but a particular person's right to invoke the power of the courts to enforce that right. Determining whether a private action would be consistent with the "underlying purposes" of a legislative scheme permits a court to decide for itself what the goals of a scheme should be, and how those goals should be advanced. Finally, looking to state law for parallels to the federal right simply focuses inquiry on a particular policy consideration that Congress already may have weighed in deciding not to create a private action.

That the *Cort* analysis too readily permits courts to override the decision of Congress not to create a private action is demonstrated conclusively by the flood of lower-court decisions applying it. Although from the time *Cort* was decided until today this Court consistently has turned back attempts to create private actions, other federal courts have tended to proceed in exactly the opposite direction. In the four years since we decided *Cort*, no less than 20 decisions by the courts of appeals have implied private actions from federal statutes. It defies reason to believe that in each of these statutes Congress absentmindedly forgot to mention an intended private action. Indeed, the accelerating trend evidenced by these decisions attests to the need to re-examine the *Cort* analysis.

Powell then asserted that the approach of *Cort* was not only unwise but also unconstitutional. Echoing the famous passage in *Erie*, he said that "[i]f only a matter of statutory construction were involved," he might be inclined to refine *Cort* so as better to reflect congressional intent. " 'But the unconstitutionality of the course pursued has now been made clear' and compels us to abandon the implication doctrine of *Cort*":

Cort allows the judicial branch to assume a policymaking authority vested by the Constitution in the legislative branch. It also invites Congress to avoid resolution of the often controversial question whether a new regulatory statute should be enforced through private litigation. Rather than confronting the hard political choices involved, Congress is encouraged to shirk its constitutional obligation and leave the issue to the courts to decide. When this happens, the legislative process with its public scrutiny and participation has been bypassed, with attendant prejudice to everyone concerned. . . .

It is true that the federal judiciary necessarily exercises substantial powers to construe legislation, including, when appropriate, the power to prescribe substantive standards of conduct that supplement federal legislation. But this power normally is exercised with respect to disputes over which a court already has jurisdiction, and in which the existence of the asserted cause of action is established. Implication of a private cause of action, in contrast, involves a significant additional step. By creating a private action, a court of limited jurisdiction necessarily extends its authority to embrace a dispute Congress has not assigned it to resolve. This runs contrary to the established principle that "[t]he jurisdiction of the federal courts is carefully guarded against expansion by judicial interpretation . . . ," and conflicts with the authority of Congress under Article III to set the limits of federal jurisdiction.

The facts of this case illustrate how the implication of a right of action not authorized by Congress denigrates the democratic process. Title IX embodies a national commitment to the elimination of discrimination based on sex, a goal the importance of which has been recognized repeatedly by our decisions. But because Title IX applies to most of our nation's institutions of higher learning, it also trenches on the authority of the academic community to govern itself, an authority the free exercise of which is critical to the vitality of our society. Arming frustrated applicants with the power to challenge in court his or her rejection inevitably will have a constraining effect on admissions programs. The burden of expensive, vexatious litigation upon institutions whose resources often are severely limited may well compel an emphasis on objectively measured academic qualifications at the expense of more flexible admissions criteria that bring richness and diversity to academic life. If such a significant incursion into the arena of academic polity is to be made, it is the constitutional function of the legislative branch, subject as it is to the checks of the political process, to make this judgment.

. . . Henceforth, we should not condone the implication of any private action from a federal statute absent the most compelling evidence that Congress in fact intended such an action to exist. Where a statutory scheme expressly provides for an alternative mechanism for enforcing the rights and duties created, I would be especially reluctant ever to permit a federal court to volunteer its services for enforcement purposes.

Was Justice Powell right in suggesting that the approach of *Cort v. Ash* is unconstitutional? Are there good reasons to think that judicial creativity should be more limited here than with respect to other issues of federal common law? If courts have the power to create private remedies, how should that power be exercised?

In this connection, it may be useful to focus on the intersection between private rights of action and administrative law. The issue of judicial creation of private rights of action is largely a product of the administrative state. The problem usually arises when Congress authorizes administrative regulation of private activity without expressly authorizing private law suits. The question may then arise whether judicial recognition of a private right of action would aid or disrupt agency enforcement.

In some circumstances—*J.I. Case v. Borak* is an example—there is no real conflict. Given the numbers of proxy statements that the Securities and Exchange Commission must review and the limited opportunity the Commission has to know if those statements are false or misleading, a private right of action to enforce the proxy rules seemed a "necessary supplement" to agency action. No doubt that is why the Commission itself urged that result.

In other cases, a private right of action may disrupt agency action. This is especially likely where the underlying statute provides only vague and indefinite specification of substantive standards. In these circumstances, the effective role in defining substantive law, at least in the first instance, is left to the administrative agency. A private right of action by-passes the administrative structure in favor of direct resort to the courts. The two types of decisionmakers are importantly different. Agencies are typically expert and specialized; they usually follow a centralized enforcement agenda; and they are often designed to be politically accountable. In a private enforcement action, the courts have no specialized expertise; the enforcement agenda is decentralized among private plaintiffs; and the decisionmaking process is carefully insulated from political pressure. In some circumstances, therefore a legislature might sensibly prefer to rely solely on administrative enforcement.[a]

3.   POST-*CANNON* RESTRICTIONS

After *Cannon*, the Court became decidedly, but not consistently, more restrictive. A month after *Cannon*, the Court refused to infer a private remedy for damages in a complex securities case. Touche Ross & Co. v. Redington, 442 U.S. 560 (1979), all but rejected the four *Cort* factors, saying that "our task is limited solely to determining whether Congress intended to create the private right of action asserted. . . . The ultimate question is one of congressional intent, not one of whether this Court thinks it can improve upon the statutory scheme that Congress enacted into law."

Transamerica Mortgage Advisors, Inc. (TAMA) v. Lewis, 444 U.S. 11 (1979), continued that approach. The case involved the Investment Advisers Act of 1940. Section 206 of the act broadly proscribes fraudulent practices by investment advisers. Section 215 provides that contracts in violation of the act "shall be void . . . as regards the rights of" the violator and knowing successors in interest. The plaintiff was a shareholder of a company advised by TAMA. Alleging fraud and breach of fiduciary duty, the plaintiff sought damages and an injunction against further performance of the investment

---

[a]   For an extended analysis of these issues, see Richard Stewart and Cass Sunstein, Public Programs and Private Rights, 95 Harv. L. Rev. 1191 (1982). Stewart and Sunstein locate the controversy over implied rights of action in the larger context of judicial control of the administrative state and relate the private right of action to other potential remedies for administrative default.

adviser's contract. The Court, per Justice Stewart, began with the now customary remark that "[t]he question whether a statute creates a cause of
action, either expressly or by implication, is basically a matter of statutory
construction." With respect to § 215, however, the Court found that "the statutory language itself fairly implies a right to specific and limited relief in a
federal court":

> By declaring certain contracts void, § 215 by its terms necessarily
> contemplates that the issue of voidness under its criteria may be
> litigated somewhere. At the very least Congress must have as-
> sumed that § 215 could be raised defensively in private litigation to
> preclude the enforcement of an investment advisers contract. But
> the legal consequences of voidness are typically not so limited. A
> person with the power to void a contract ordinarily may resort to a
> court to have the contract rescinded and to obtain restitution of
> consideration paid. . . . For these reasons we conclude that when
> Congress declared in § 215 that certain contracts are void, it in-
> tended that the customary legal incidents of voidness would follow,
> including the availability of a suit for recission or for an injunction
> against continued operation of the contract, and for restitution.

The Court took a different view of plaintiff's claim for damages under
§ 206, which simply proscribed certain conduct without specifying any civil
liability. "If monetary liability to a private plaintiff is to be found, it must be
read into the act. Yet it is an elementary canon of statutory construction that
where a statute expressly provides a particular remedy or remedies [i.e., SEC
enforcement actions and criminal prosecutions], a court must be chary of
reading others into it. . . ."[b]

Texas Industries, Inc. v. Radcliff Materials, Inc., 451 U.S. 630 (1981), is
another post-*Cannon* decision taking a dim view of judicial creativity. The
question was whether a defendant held liable for an antitrust violation had
a right to contribution from other participants in the unlawful conspiracy.
The Supreme Court said no. Writing for a unanimous Court, Chief Justice
Burger found no indication that Congress had intended to create a right of
contribution. He recognized that the courts had played a large role in filling
in the meaning of the federal antitrust statutes but said the issues raised by
the suggested right of contribution were too far-reaching for judicial resolution.

Finally, Thompson v. Thompson, 484 U.S. 174 (1988), involved the Parental Kidnapping and Prevention Act of 1980 (PKPA), 28 U.S.C. § 1738A.
The statute requires states to enforce the child custody decrees of other
states if certain conditions are met in the rendering court. It focuses on enforcing custody decrees in *state* court and makes no explicit provision for
resort to federal court in the event that the courts of two states disagree.
That situation arose in *Thompson*, where California and Louisiana courts
entered conflicting custody decrees. The question was whether the California

---

[b]   Justice Powell concurred with the notation that he regarded the Court's opinion "as
compatible with my dissent in *Cannon*." Justice White, joined by Justices Brennan, Marshall,
and Stevens, dissented on the ground that the four *Cort* factors justified a damages remedy to
enforce § 206.

father could go to federal court to get an injunction against enforcement of the Louisiana decree. The Supreme Court agreed with the lower courts that the PKPA "does not create a private right of action in federal court to determine the validity of two conflicting custody decrees." Speaking for the Court, however, Justice Marshall did not reiterate the restrictive rhetoric of *Touche Ross* and *Transamerica Mortgage Advisors*, but instead spoke approvingly of *Cort v. Ash*, adding:

> Our focus on congressional intent does not mean that we require evidence that members of Congress, in enacting the statute, actually had in mind the creation of a private cause of action. The implied cause of action doctrine would be a virtual dead letter were it limited to correcting drafting errors when Congress simply forgot to codify its evident intention to provide a cause of action. Rather, as an *implied* cause of action doctrine suggests, "the legislative history of a statute that does not expressly create or deny a private remedy will typically be equally silent or ambiguous on the question" [quoting *Cannon*].

These words drew a riposte from Justice Scalia, joined in part by Justice O'Connor. Scalia pronounced himself "at a loss to imagine what congressional intent to create a private right of action might mean, if it does not mean that Congress had in mind the creation of a private right of action." He also objected to the emphasis on *Cort v. Ash*, for "[i]t could not be plainer that we effectively overruled the *Cort* analysis in *Touche Ross* and *Transamerica*, converting one of its four factors (congressional intent) into *the determinative factor*, with the other three merely indicative of its presence or absence." He added: "I have found the Court's dicta in the present case particularly provocative because it is my view that, if the current state of the law were to be changed, it should be moved in precisely the opposite direction—away from our current congressional intent test to the categorical position that federal private rights of action will not be implied."

4. LESS RESTRICTIVE DECISIONS

Despite the restrictive decisions noted above, the Court continued to recognize private rights of action in some contexts after *Cannon*. Most of them involved statutes passed at a time when private rights of action were routinely created or for which a private right of action had long been assumed.

A good example is Merrill Lynch, Pierce, Fenner & Smith v. Curran, 456 U.S. 353 (1982), which involved the Commodity Futures Trading Commission Act. The statute had been amended in 1974, and the Court focused on the prevailing judicial climate at that time. In 1974 the federal courts "routinely and consistently" recognized implied private rights of action without worrying much about actual legislative intent. Against this background of judicial creativity, the fact that Congress left intact statutory provisions that were thought to support a private right of action seemed to a majority of the Justices evidence of an affirmative intent to retain that remedy. Four Justices dissented.

The Court has also continued a tradition of judicial activism in cases under Rule 10b–5, the antifraud regulation promulgated under § 10(b) of the 1934 Securities Exchange Act. In Herman & MacLean v. Huddleston, 459 U.S. 375 (1983), a unanimous Court (Justice Powell not participating) approved a private damages action to enforce Rule 10b–5, despite the existence of an overlapping, though not completely congruent, civil remedy under § 11 of the 1933 Act. The Court noted that a private right of action to enforce Rule 10b–5 had been recognized in the lower courts for more than 35 years and concluded that "[t]he existence of this implied remedy is simply beyond peradventure."

In Musick, Peeler & Garrett v. Employers Insurance of Wausau, 508 U.S. 286 (1993), the Court followed this lead by creating a right of contribution from joint tortfeasors for 10b–5 liability. Speaking through Justice Kennedy, the Court distinguished *Texas Industries v. Radcliff Materials* (which had refused to create a right of contribution under the antitrust laws) on the ground that the cause of action involved in that case was statutory and that it was therefore up to Congress to provide (or withhold) a right of contribution. Rule 10b–5 was different: "Having implied the underlying liability in the first place, to now disavow any authority to allocate it on the theory that Congress has not addressed the issue would be most unfair to those against whom damages are assessed." Justice Thomas, joined by Justices Blackmun and O'Connor, dissented.

5.   CHOICE OF REMEDIES TO ENFORCE IMPLIED RIGHTS

In cases where the Supreme Court has found an implied cause of action, what are the available remedies? The Court held in *Cannon,* for example, that an implied cause of action for injunctive relief existed under Title IX of the Education Amendments of 1972, 20 U.S.C. §§ 1681–88. Does it follow that a Title IX plaintiff could also seek damages?

This issue arose in Franklin v. Gwinnett County Public Schools, 503 U.S. 60 (1992). Franklin alleged that a coach and teacher in the county school system sexually harassed her and that the school system responded inadequately to these events. Overruling the lower courts, the Supreme Court unanimously concluded that a private damages remedy was available under Title IX. Speaking through Justice White, the Court said:

> In *Cannon v. University of Chicago,* the Court held that Title IX is enforceable through an implied right of action. . . . [I]n this case we must decide what remedies are available in a suit brought pursuant to this implied right. As we have often stated, the question of what remedies are available under a statute that provides a private right of action is "analytically distinct" from the issue of whether such a right exists in the first place. Thus, although we examine the text and history of a statute to determine whether Congress intended to create a right of action, *Touche Ross & Co. v. Redington,* we presume the availability of all appropriate remedies unless Congress has expressly indicated otherwise.

Justice Scalia, joined by Chief Justice Rehnquist and by Justice Thomas, accepted the result because of subsequent legislation that assumed the availability of money damages for violation of Title IX, but disagreed with the general reasoning:

> In my view, when rights of action are judicially "implied," categorical limitations upon their remedial scope may be judicially implied as well. Although we have abandoned the expansive rights-creating approach exemplified by *Cannon*—and perhaps ought to abandon the notion of implied causes of action entirely—causes of action that came into existence under the ancien regime should be limited by the same logic that gave them birth. To require, with respect to a right that is not consciously and intentionally created, that any limitation of remedies must be express, is to provide, in effect, that the most questionable of private rights will also be the most expansively remediable. . . .

The issue of appropriate remedies surfaced again in Gebser v. Lago Vista Independent School District, 524 U.S. 274 (1998). *Gebser* involved a damages action against a school district for sexual harassment by a teacher. The teacher had sexual relations with an eighth-grade middle-school student, but neither the student nor anyone else reported the misconduct to the teacher's superiors. The matter came to light only when a policeman caught them in the act, after which the teacher was immediately fired. When the student and the student's parents subsequently sued the school district, the question was whether liability could rest on respondeat superior.

The dissenters in *Gebser* took the view that *Cannon* and *Franklin* had established a private right to enforce Title IX through actions for money damages and that no judicial restrictions were appropriate. Speaking for himself and for Justices Souter, Ginsburg, and Breyer, Justice Stevens referenced *Cannon*'s conclusion that Congress intended Title IX to be enforceable in the same way as Title VI of the 1964 Civil Rights Act, which had been judicially interpreted to authorize money damages. "As long as the intent of Congress is clear," said Stevens, "an implicit command has the same legal force as one that is explicit." He also noted the presumption asserted by Justice White, writing for the Court in *Franklin*, that "Congress intends to authorize 'all appropriate remedies' unless it expressly indicates otherwise":

> Because these constructions of the statute have been accepted by Congress and are unchallenged here, they have the same legal effect as if the private cause of action seeking damages had been explicitly, rather than implicitly, authorized by Congress. We should therefore seek guidance from the text of the statute and settled legal principles rather than from our views about sound policy.

The majority disagreed. Writing for the Court, Justice O'Connor said that, "[b]ecause the private right of action under Title IX is judicially implied, we have a measure of latitude to shape a sensible remedial scheme that best comports with the statute." Specifically, the Court concluded that it would be unwise to permit damages actions against a school district without actual notice of the misconduct:

> [I]n cases like this one that do not involve official policy of the recipient [of federal funds] entity, we hold that a damages remedy will not lie under Title IX unless an official who at a minimum has authority to address the alleged discrimination and to institute correction measures on the recipient's behalf has actual knowledge of the discrimination in the recipient's programs and fails adequately to respond.

As no responsible official had knowledge of the teacher's misconduct in *Gebser*, the school district was not liable.

In a sense, *Gebser* involves an unusual role reversal. Liberal Justices, who typically support judicial authority to recognize private rights of action, argued that the Court lacked authority to limit a right of action so recognized. Conservative Justices, who typically decry judicial creativity, argued that the fact that the damages action under Title IX was "implied" in the first place provided ample authority for limiting constructions to serve sound policy. Are both positions internally inconsistent? If not, who has the better side of the argument?

Alexander v. Sandoval

Supreme Court of the United States, 2001.
532 U.S. 275.

■ JUSTICE SCALIA delivered the opinion of the Court.

This case presents the question whether private individuals may sue to enforce disparate-impact regulations promulgated under Title VI of the Civil Rights Act of 1964.

I

The Alabama Department of Public Safety (Department), of which petitioner James Alexander is the Director, accepted grants of financial assistance from the United States Department of Justice (DOJ) and Department of Transportation (DOT) and so subjected itself to the restrictions of Title VI of the Civil Rights Act of 1964, as amended, 42 U.S.C. § 2000d et seq. Section 601 of that Title provides that no person shall, "on the ground of race, color, or national origin, be excluded from participation in, be denied the benefits of, or be subjected to discrimination under any program or activity" covered by Title VI. 42 U.S.C. § 2000d. Section 602 authorizes federal agencies "to effectuate the provisions of [§ 601] . . . by issuing rules, regulations, or orders of general applicability," 42 U.S.C. § 2000d–1, and the DOJ in an exercise of this authority promulgated a regulation forbidding funding recipients to "utilize criteria or methods of administration which have the effect of subjecting individuals to discrimination because of their race, color, or national origin . . . ." 28 CFR § 42.104(b)(2) (1999).

The State of Alabama amended its Constitution in 1990 to declare English "the official language of the state of Alabama." Pursuant to this provision and, petitioners have argued, to advance public safety, the Department decided to administer state driver's license examinations only in English. Respondent Sandoval, as representative of a class, brought suit in the United States District Court for the Middle District of Alabama to enjoin the English-only policy, arguing that it violated the DOJ regulation because it had the effect of subjecting non-English speakers to discrimination based on their national origin. The District Court agreed. It enjoined the policy and ordered the Department to accommodate non-English speakers. Petitioners appealed to the Court of Appeals for the Eleventh Circuit, which affirmed. Both courts rejected petitioners' argument that Title VI did not provide respondents a cause of action to enforce the regulation.

We do not inquire here whether the DOJ regulation was authorized by § 602, or whether the courts below were correct to hold that the English-only policy had the effect of discriminating on the basis of national origin. The petition for writ of certiorari raised, and we agreed to review, only the question posed in the first paragraph of this opinion: whether there is a private cause of action to enforce the regulation.

II

Although Title VI has often come to this Court, it is fair to say (indeed, perhaps an understatement) that our opinions have not eliminated all uncertainty regarding its commands. For purposes of the present case, however, it is clear from our decisions, from Congress's amendments of Title VI, and from the parties' concessions that three aspects of Title VI must be taken as given. First, private individuals may sue to enforce § 601 of Title VI and obtain both injunctive relief and damages. In Cannon v. University of Chicago, 441 U.S. 677 (1979), the Court held that a private right of action existed to enforce Title IX of the Education Amendments of 1972, as amended, 20 U.S.C. § 1681 et seq. The reasoning of that decision embraced the existence of a private right to enforce Title VI as well. . . . Congress has since ratified Cannon's holding. Section 1003 of the Rehabilitation Act Amendments of 1986, 42 U.S.C. § 2000d–7, expressly abrogated States' sovereign immunity against suits brought in federal court to enforce Title VI and provided that in a suit against a State "remedies (including remedies both at law and in equity) are available . . . to the same extent as such remedies are available . . . in the suit against any public or private entity other than a State," § 2000d–7(a)(2). We recognized in Franklin v. Gwinnett County Public Schools, 503 U.S. 60 (1992), that § 2000d–7 "cannot be read except as a validation of Cannon's holding." Id. at 72. It is thus beyond dispute that private individuals may sue to enforce § 601.

Second, it is similarly beyond dispute—and no party disagrees—that § 601 prohibits only intentional discrimination. . . .

Third, we . . . . assume for the purposes of deciding this case that the DOJ and DOT regulations proscribing activities that have a disparate impact on the basis of race are valid. . . .

We do not doubt that regulations applying § 601's ban on intentional discrimination are covered by the cause of action to enforce that section. Such regulations, if valid and reasonable, authoritatively construe the statute itself, and it is therefore meaningless to talk about a separate cause of action to enforce the regulations apart from the statute. A Congress that intends the statute to be enforced through a private cause of action intends the authoritative interpretation of the statute to be so enforced as well. The many cases that respondents say have "assumed" that a cause of action to enforce a statute includes one to enforce its regulations illustrate (to the extent that cases in which an issue was not presented can illustrate anything) only this point . . . .

It is clear now that the disparate-impact regulations do not simply apply § 601—since they indeed forbid conduct that § 601 permits—and therefore clear that the private right of action to enforce § 601 does not include a private right to enforce these regulations. That right must come, if at all, from the independent force of § 602. As stated earlier, we assume for purposes of this decision that § 602 confers the authority to promulgate disparate-impact regulations; the question remains whether it confers a private right of action to enforce them. If not, we must conclude that a failure to comply with regulations promulgated under § 602 that is not also a failure to comply with § 601 is not actionable.

Implicit in our discussion thus far has been a particular understanding of the genesis of private causes of action. Like substantive federal law itself, private rights of action to enforce federal law must be created by Congress. Touche Ross & Co. v. Redington, 442 U.S. 560, 578 (1979) (remedies available are those "that Congress enacted into law"). The judicial task is to interpret the statute Congress has passed to determine whether it displays an intent to create not just a private right but also a private remedy. Transamerica Mortgage Advisors, Inc. v. Lewis, 444 U.S. 11, 15 (1979). Statutory intent on this latter point is determinative. Without it, a cause of action does not exist and courts may not create one, no matter how desirable that might be as a policy matter, or how compatible with the statute. . . .

Respondents would have us revert in this case to the understanding of private causes of action that held sway 40 years ago when Title VI was enacted. That understanding is captured by the Court's statement in J.I. Case Co. v. Borak, 377 U.S. 426, 433 (1964), that "it is the duty of the courts to be alert to provide such remedies as are necessary to make effective the congressional purpose" expressed by a statute. We abandoned that understanding in Cort v. Ash, 422 U.S. 66, 78 (1975)—which itself interpreted a statute enacted under the *ancien regime*—and have not returned to it since. . . . Having sworn off the habit of venturing beyond

Congress's intent, we will not accept respondents' invitation to have one last drink.

Nor do we agree with the Government that our cases interpreting statutes enacted prior to *Cort* v. *Ash* have given "dispositive weight" to the "expectations" that the enacting Congress had formed "in light of the 'contemporary legal context.' " Only three of our legion implied-right-of-action cases have found this sort of "contemporary legal context" relevant, and two of those involved Congress's enactment (or reenactment) of the verbatim statutory text that courts had previously interpreted to create a private right of action. See Merrill Lynch, Pierce, Fenner & Smith, Inc. v. Curran, 456 U.S. 353, 378–79 (1982); *Cannon,* 441 U.S. at 698–99. In the third case, this sort of "contemporary legal context" simply buttressed a conclusion independently supported by the text of the statute. See Thompson v. Thompson, 484 U.S. 174 (1988). We have never accorded dispositive weight to context shorn of text. . . .

We therefore begin (and find that we can end) our search for Congress's intent with the text and structure of Title VI. Section 602 authorizes federal agencies "to effectuate the provisions of [§ 601] . . . by issuing rules, regulations, or orders of general applicability." 42 U.S.C. § 2000d–1. It is immediately clear that the "rights-creating" language so critical to the Court's analysis in *Cannon* of § 601, is completely absent from § 602. Whereas § 601 decrees that "no person . . . shall . . . be subjected to discrimination," 42 U.S.C. § 2000d, the text of § 602 provides that "each Federal department and agency . . . is authorized and directed to effectuate the provisions of [§ 601]," 42 U.S.C. § 2000d–1. Far from displaying congressional intent to create new rights, § 602 limits agencies to "effectuating" rights already created by § 601. And the focus of § 602 is twice removed from the individuals who will ultimately benefit from Title VI's protection. Statutes that focus on the person regulated rather than the individuals protected create "no implication of an intent to confer rights on a particular class of persons." California v. Sierra Club, 451 U.S. 287, 294 (1981). . . . When this is true, "there [is] far less reason to infer a private remedy in favor of individual persons," *Cannon, supra,* at 690–91. So far as we can tell, this authorizing portion of § 602 reveals no congressional intent to create a private right of action.

Nor do the methods that § 602 goes on to provide for enforcing its authorized regulations manifest an intent to create a private remedy; if anything, they suggest the opposite. Section 602 empowers agencies to enforce their regulations either by terminating funding to the "particular program, or part thereof," that has violated the regulation or "by any other means authorized by law," 42 U.S.C. § 2000d–1. No enforcement action may be taken, however, "until the department or agency concerned has advised the appropriate person or persons of the failure to comply with the requirement and has determined that compliance cannot be secured by voluntary means." Id. And every agency enforcement action is subject to judicial review. § 2000d–2. If an agency attempts to terminate program funding, still more restrictions apply. The agency head must "file with the committees of the House and Senate having legislative jurisdiction over the program or activity involved a full written report of the circumstances and the grounds for such action." § 2000d–1. And the termination of funding does not "become effective until thirty days have elapsed after the filing of such report." Id. Whatever these elaborate restrictions on agency enforcement may imply for the private enforcement of rights created *outside* of § 602, . . . they tend to contradict a congressional intent to create privately enforceable rights through § 602 itself. The express provision of one method of enforcing a substantive rule suggests that Congress intended to preclude others. . . . Sometimes the suggestion is so strong that it precludes a finding of congressional intent to create a private right of action, even though other aspects of the statute (such as language making the would-be plaintiff "a member of the class for whose benefit the statute was enacted") suggest the contrary. . . . In the present case, the claim of exclusivity for the express remedial scheme does not even have to overcome such obstacles. The question whether § 602's remedial scheme can overbear other evidence of congressional intent is simply not presented, since we have found no evidence anywhere in the text to suggest that Congress intended to create a private right to enforce regulations promulgated under § 602.

Both the Government and respondents argue that the *regulations* contain rights-creating language and so must be privately enforceable, but that argument skips an analytical step. Language in a regulation may invoke a private right of action that Congress through statutory text created, but it may not create a right that Congress has not. Thus, when a statute has provided a general authorization for private enforcement of regulations, it may perhaps be correct that the intent displayed in each regulation can determine whether or not it is privately enforceable. But it is most certainly incorrect to say that language in a regulation can conjure up a private cause of action that has not been authorized by Congress. Agencies may play the sorcerer's apprentice but not the sorcerer himself. . . .

Neither as originally enacted nor as later amended does Title VI display an intent to create a freestanding private right of action to enforce regulations promulgated under § 602. We therefore hold that no such right of action exists. . . .

The judgment of the Court of Appeals is reversed.

It is so ordered.

■ JUSTICE STEVENS, with whom JUSTICE SOUTER, JUSTICE GINSBURG, and JUSTICE BREYER join, dissenting. . . .

Today, in a decision unfounded in our precedent and hostile to decades of settled expectations, a majority of this Court carves out an important exception to the right of private action long recognized under Title VI. . . .

II

. . . The majority's statutory analysis does violence to both the text and the structure of Title VI. Section 601 does not stand in isolation, but rather as part of an integrated remedial scheme. Section 602 exists for the sole purpose of forwarding the antidiscrimination ideals laid out in § 601. The majority's persistent belief that the two sections somehow forward different agendas finds no support in the statute. Nor does Title VI anywhere suggest, let alone state, that for the purpose of determining their legal effect, the "rules, regulations, [and] orders of general applicability" adopted by the agencies are to be bifurcated by the judiciary into two categories based on how closely the courts believe the regulations track the text of § 601.

What makes the Court's analysis even more troubling is that our cases have already adopted a simpler and more sensible model for understanding the relationship between the two sections. For three decades, we have treated § 602 as granting the responsible agencies the power to issue broad prophylactic rules aimed at realizing the vision laid out in § 601, even if the conduct captured by these rules is at times broader than that which would otherwise be prohibited. . . .

This understanding is firmly rooted in the text of Title VI. As § 602 explicitly states, the agencies are authorized to adopt regulations to "effectuate" § 601's antidiscrimination mandate. 42 U.S.C. § 2000d–1. The plain meaning of the text reveals Congress' intent to provide the relevant agencies with sufficient authority to transform the statute's broad aspiration into social reality. So too does a lengthy, consistent, and impassioned legislative history.

This legislative design reflects a reasonable—indeed inspired—model for attacking the often-intractable problem of racial and ethnic discrimination. On its own terms, the statute supports an action challenging policies of federal grantees that explicitly or unambiguously violate antidiscrimination norms (such as policies that on their face limit benefits or services to certain races). With regard to more subtle forms of discrimination (such as schemes that limit benefits or services on ostensibly race-neutral grounds but have the predictable and perhaps intended consequence of materially benefiting some races at the expense of others), the statute does not establish a static approach but instead empowers the relevant agencies to evaluate social circumstances to determine whether there is a need for stronger measures. Such an approach builds into the law flexibility, an ability to make nuanced assessments of complex social realities, and an admirable willingness to credit the possibility of progress.

The "effects" regulations at issue in this case represent the considered judgment of the relevant agencies that discrimination on the basis of race, ethnicity, and national origin by federal contractees are significant social problems that might be remedied, or at least ameliorated, by

the application of a broad prophylactic rule. Given the judgment underlying them, the regulations are inspired by, at the service of, and
inseparably intertwined with § 601's antidiscrimination mandate. Contrary to the majority's suggestion, they "apply" § 601's prohibition on
discrimination just as surely as the intentional discrimination regulations the majority concedes are privately enforceable. . . .

III

The majority couples its flawed analysis of the structure of Title VI
with an uncharitable understanding of the substance of the divide between those on this Court who are reluctant to interpret statutes to allow
for private rights of action and those who are willing to do so if the claim
of right survives a rigorous application of the criteria set forth in Cort v.
Ash, 422 U.S. 66 (1975). As the majority narrates our implied right of
action jurisprudence, the Court's shift to a more skeptical approach represents the rejection of a common-law judicial activism in favor of a
principled recognition of the limited role of a contemporary "federal tribunal." According to its analysis, the recognition of an implied right of
action when the text and structure of the statute do not absolutely compel
such a conclusion is an act of judicial self-indulgence. As much as we
would like to help those disadvantaged by discrimination, we must resist
the temptation to pour ourselves "one last drink." To do otherwise would
be to "venture beyond Congress's intent."

Overwrought imagery aside, it is the majority's approach that blinds
itself to congressional intent. While it remains true that, if Congress intends a private right of action to support statutory rights, "the far better
course is for it to specify as much when it creates those rights," Cannon,
441 U.S. at 717, its failure to do so does not absolve us of the responsibility to endeavor to discern its intent. In a series of cases since Cort v. Ash,
we have laid out rules and developed strategies for this task.

The very existence of these rules and strategies assumes that we will
sometimes find manifestations of an implicit intent to create such a right.
Our decision in Cannon represents one such occasion. As the Cannon
opinion iterated and reiterated, the question whether the plaintiff had a
right of action that could be asserted in federal court was a "question of
statutory construction," 441 U.S. at 688, not a question of policy for the
Court to decide. Applying the Cort v. Ash factors, we examined the nature
of the rights at issue, the text and structure of the statute, and the relevant legislative history. Our conclusion was that Congress unmistakably
intended a private right of action to enforce both Title IX and Title VI.
Our reasoning—and, as I have demonstrated, our holding—was equally
applicable to intentional discrimination and disparate impact claims.

Underlying today's opinion is the conviction that Cannon must be
cabined because it exemplifies an "expansive rights-creating approach."
Franklin v. Gwinnett County Public Schools, 503 U.S. 60, 77 (1992)
(Scalia, J. concurring in judgment). But, as I have taken pains to explain,
it was Congress, not the Court, that created the cause of action, and it

was the Congress that later ratified the *Cannon* holding in 1986 and again in 1988.

In order to impose its own preferences as to the availability of judicial remedies, the Court today adopts a methodology that blinds itself to important evidence of congressional intent. It is one thing for the Court to ignore the import of our holding in *Cannon*, as the breadth of that precedent is a matter upon which reasonable jurists may differ. It is entirely another thing for the majority to ignore the reasoning of that opinion and the evidence contained therein, as those arguments and that evidence speak directly to the question at issue today. As I stated above, *Cannon* carefully explained that both Title VI and Title IX were intended to benefit a particular class of individuals, that the purposes of the statutes would be furthered rather than frustrated by the implication of a private right of action, and that the legislative histories of the statutes support the conclusion that Congress intended such a right. Those conclusions and the evidence supporting them continue to have force today.

Similarly, if the majority is genuinely committed to deciphering congressional intent, its unwillingness to even consider evidence as to the context in which Congress legislated is perplexing. Congress does not legislate in a vacuum. As the respondent and the Government suggest, and as we have held several times, the objective manifestations of congressional intent to create a private right of action must be measured in light of the enacting Congress' expectations as to how the judiciary might evaluate the question.

At the time Congress was considering Title VI, it was normal practice for the courts to infer that Congress intended a private right of action whenever it passed a statute designed to protect a particular class that did not contain enforcement mechanisms which would be thwarted by a private remedy. Indeed, the very year Congress adopted Title VI, this Court specifically stated that "it is the duty of the courts to be alert to provide such remedies as are necessary to make effective the congressional purpose." J.I. Case Co. v. Borak, 377 U.S. 426, 433 (1964). Assuming, as we must, that Congress was fully informed as to the state of the law, the contemporary context presents important evidence as to Congress' intent—evidence the majority declines to consider.

Ultimately, respect for Congress' prerogatives is measured in deeds, not words. Today, the Court coins a new rule, holding that a private cause of action to enforce a statute does not encompass a substantive regulation issued to effectuate that statute unless the regulation does nothing more than "authoritatively construe the statute itself." This rule might be proper if we were the kind of "common-law court" the majority decries, inventing private rights of action never intended by Congress. For if we are not construing a statute, we certainly may refuse to create a remedy for violations of federal regulations. But if we are faithful to the commitment to discerning congressional intent that all Members of this Court profess, the distinction is untenable. There is simply no reason to assume that Congress contemplated, desired, or adopted a distinction between regulations that merely parrot statutory text and broader regulations that are authorized by statutory text.

IV

Beyond its flawed structural analysis of Title VI and an evident antipathy toward implied rights of action, the majority offers little affirmative support for its conclusion that Congress did not intend to create a private remedy for violations of the Title VI regulations. The Court offers essentially two reasons for its position. First, it attaches significance to the fact that the "rights-creating" language in § 601 that defines the classes protected by the statute is not repeated in § 602. But, of course, there was no reason to put that language in § 602 because it is perfectly obvious that the regulations authorized by § 602 must be designed to protect precisely the same people protected by § 601. Moreover, it is self-evident that, linguistic niceties notwithstanding, any statutory provision whose stated purpose is to "effectuate" the eradication of racial and ethnic discrimination has as its "focus" those individuals who, absent such legislation, would be subject to discrimination.

Second, the Court repeats the argument advanced and rejected in *Cannon* that the express provision of a fund cut-off remedy "suggests that Congress intended to preclude others." In *Cannon*, we carefully explained why the presence of an explicit mechanism to achieve one of the statute's objectives (ensuring that federal funds are not used "to support discriminatory practices") does not preclude a conclusion that a private right of action was intended to achieve the statute's other principal objective ("to provide individual citizens effective protection against those practices"). In support of our analysis, we offered policy arguments, cited evidence from the legislative history, and noted the active support of the relevant agencies. In today's decision, the Court does not grapple with—indeed, barely acknowledges—our rejection of this argument in *Cannon*.

Like much else in its opinion, the present majority's unwillingness to explain its refusal to find the reasoning in *Cannon* persuasive suggests that today's decision is the unconscious product of the majority's profound distaste for implied causes of action rather than an attempt to discern the intent of the Congress that enacted Title VI of the Civil Rights Act of 1964. Its colorful disclaimer of any interest in "venturing beyond Congress's intent," has a hollow ring.

ADDITIONAL NOTES ON IMPLIED RIGHTS OF ACTION

1. QUESTIONS AND COMMENTS ON *ALEXANDER V. SANDOVAL*

According to the Court in *Sandoval*, what was it about § 602 of Title VI that suggested that, unlike § 601, it did not confer a private right of action? Why does the Court decline to take into account the fact that Congress enacted Title VI at a time when the Court was more permissive about recognizing private rights of action? What are the implications of the Court's statement that "[t]he express provision of one method of enforcing a substantive rule suggests that Congress intended to preclude others"?

Title 42 U.S.C. § 1983 authorizes a private right of action against anyone who violates a federal statute while acting "under color of" state law. The defendants in *Sandoval* were state officers and so could have been sued under § 1983 without resort to an "implied" cause of action directly under Title VI. It was this possibility that led Justice Stevens to remark, in dissent:

> [T]o the extent that the majority denies relief to the respondents merely because they neglected to mention 42 U.S.C. § 1983 in framing their Title VI claim, this case is something of a sport. Litigants who in the future wish to enforce the Title VI regulations against state actors in all likelihood must only reference § 1983 to obtain relief; indeed, the plaintiffs in this case (or other similarly situated individuals) presumably retain the option of re-challenging Alabama's English-only policy in a complaint that invokes § 1983 even after today's decision.

Is it conceivable that *Sandoval* actually involved only a pleading error in the plaintiffs' failure to invoke § 1983? Analytically, this position is tenable, as 42 U.S.C. § 1983 purports to provide a private right of action to enforce rights secured by the "Constitution *and laws*" of the United States (emphasis added). Under the broad reading of that language in Maine v. Thiboutot, 448 U.S. 1 (1980), § 1983 would provide an independent damages remedy any time that the person who violated a federal statute acted under color of state law. The Supreme Court, however, has been in retreat from this proposition almost since the day it was announced. In recent years, in particular, the Court has moved to align the use of § 1983 to enforce federal statutes with its more restrictive approach to inferring private rights of action directly from federal statutes. See generally Chapter IX, Section 4, which deals at length with the enforcement of non-constitutional rights under § 1983.

2. *STONERIDGE INVESTMENT PARTNERS, LLC V. SCIENTIFIC-ATLANTA, INC.*

The Court has long held that there is an implied right of action to sue for securities fraud under § 10(b) of the Securities Exchange Act of 1934. In Central Bank of Denver, N.A. v. First Interstate Bank of Denver, N.A., 511 U.S. 164 (1994), the Court held that this implied right of action does not extend to suits against mere aiders and abettors of securities fraud. In response to this decision, Congress provided for SEC enforcement against aiders and abettors but did not provide for a private right of action.

In Stoneridge Investment Partners, LLC v. Scientific-Atlanta, Inc., 532 U.S. 275 (2008), the issue was whether there was a private right of action under § 10(b) against aiders and abettors who also engage in deceptive actions that, although not directly relied upon by the plaintiffs, facilitate the securities fraud. In that case, it was alleged that a cable operator had fraudulently inflated its revenues and that this fraud was facilitated by sham financial arrangements with its suppliers. In an opinion by Justice Kennedy, the Court held that there was no implied right of action under § 10(b) against the suppliers.

The Court reasoned that allowing an implied right of action here would be inconsistent with Congress's decision to authorize only SEC enforcement against aiders and abettors. The Court also expressed federalism concerns about recognizing a federal cause of action under these circumstances. While securities regulation is predominantly federal, corporate law remains predominantly state. If § 10(b) liability were extended beyond the securities markets to "the realm of financing business," the Court explained, "there would be a risk that the federal power would be used to invite litigation beyond the immediate sphere of securities litigation and in areas already governed by functioning and effective state-law guarantees."

Finally, the Court expressed a more general reluctance to extend private rights of action: "Concerns with the judicial creation of a private cause of action caution against its expansion. The decision to extend the cause of action is for Congress, not for us. Though it remains the law, the § 10(b) private right should not be extended beyond its present boundaries."

Justice Stevens dissented and was joined by Justices Souter and Ginsburg. (Justice Breyer did not participate.) Stevens argued that *Central Bank* was distinguishable because in this case the defendants had themselves engaged in deceptive actions and thus were not merely aiders and abettors. He contended that Congress's decision "not to restore the aiding and abetting liability removed by *Central Bank* does not mean that Congress wanted to exempt from liability the broader range of conduct that today's opinion excludes." More generally, Stevens complained that the Court's modern reluctance to imply statutory rights of action was inconsistent with the approach followed by the Court throughout much of American history, whereby "[f]ashioning appropriate remedies for the violation of rules of law designed to protect a class of citizens was the routine business of judges."

Sandoval and *Stoneridge* demonstrate that the Court has come a long way from the days of *J.I. Case*, when private rights of action were more or less routinely created, especially in the area of securities law. While *J.I. Case* suggested that a private right of action would be recognized unless the defendant demonstrated a very good reason not to do so, a majority of the Court seems at least to have reversed the presumption. Today, the plaintiff who seeks to establish an "implied" right of action bears a heavy burden of grounding that argument in legislative design and intent.

Why do these decisions often seem to come down to a traditional conservative-versus-liberal divide among the Justices? Because conservative Justices are more wary about judicial creativity and liberal Justices are more comfortable with it? Because conservative Justices are more reluctant than liberal Justices to enable additional private litigation? Because conservative Justices are more attentive than liberal Justices to the potential federalism implications associated with finding federal statutory rights of action for conduct that might otherwise be regulated only by state law?

3. PRIVATE RIGHTS OF ACTION UNDER TREATIES

Litigants sometimes attempt to bring claims under treaties that have been ratified by the United States. To be judicially enforceable, a treaty provision must be "self-executing." A self-executing treaty, the Supreme Court has explained, "has automatic domestic effect as federal law upon ratification." Medellin v. Texas, 552 U.S. 491, 505 n.2 (2008). A non-self-executing treaty, by contrast, "does not by itself give rise to domestically enforceable federal law" but "depends upon implementing legislation passed by Congress" for domestic effect. Id. It is not entirely clear how courts are to distinguish between self-executing and non-self-executing treaties, but the Court has indicated that the text of the treaty should be consulted to discern whether the parties (or at least the United States) contemplated domestic judicial enforcement. Sometimes the Senate, when giving its advice and consent to a treaty, will issue a declaration stating whether the treaty is or is not self-executing, and to date courts have deferred to these declarations. Even if a treaty provision is self-executing and thus potentially subject to judicial application, it may not create a private right of action, such as the right to sue for damages. In fact, the Supreme Court, quoting from the Restatement (Third) of the Foreign Relations Law of the United States (1987), has stated that "the background presumption is that '[i]nternational agreements, even those directly benefitting private persons, generally do not create private rights or provide for a private cause of action in domestic courts.'" Id. at 506 n.3.

Should courts be more reluctant to infer private rights from treaties than from statutes? If so, why? Is it because, as the Court stated in Head Money Cases, 112 U.S. 580, 598 (1884), "[a] treaty is primarily a compact between independent nations" that "depends for the enforcement of its provisions on the interest and the honor of the governments which are parties to it"? See also Restatement (Fourth) of the Foreign Relations Law of the United States: Treaties, Tentative Draft No. 2, § 111(1) (Mar. 20, 2017) ("A treaty provision, even if it is self-executing, does not by virtue of that fact alone establish a private right of action or confer a right to seek particular remedies such as damages.").

4. BIBLIOGRAPHY

The subject of implied rights of action has generated an enormous literature. For articles generally supportive of a restrained approach, see George D. Brown, Of Activism and *Erie*—Implication Doctrine's Implications for the Nature and Role of the Federal Courts, 69 Iowa L. Rev. 617 (1984) (linking judicial to implied rights of action to a renewed emphasis on *Erie* as a limitation on the creativity of the federal courts); Richard W. Creswell, The Separation of Powers Implications of Implied Rights of Action, 34 Mercer L. Rev. 973 (1983) (linking the focus on congressional intent to separation-of-powers principles).

For articles supportive of judicial creativity, see H. Miles Foy III, Some Reflections on Legislation, Adjudication, and Implied Private Actions in the

State and Federal Courts, 71 Corn. L. Rev. 501 (1986) (arguing that recognizing private actions vindicates the "powerful and valuable political principle" of judicial availability to remedy all wrongs defined by law); Tamar Frankel, Implied Rights of Action, 67 Va. L. Rev. 553 (1981) (arguing that "no constitutional principle bars federal courts from recognizing by implication claims by private plaintiffs who are clearly members of the class the statute was designed to protect"); Susan J. Stabile, The Role of Congressional Intent in Determining the Existence of Implied Private Rights of Action, 71 Notre Dame L. Rev. 861 (1996) (arguing that congressional intent should be only "one of several factors" in determining whether to create a private right of action under a federal statute); Donald Zeigler, Rights Require Remedies: A New Approach to the Enforcement of Rights in the Federal Courts, 38 Hast. L.J. 665 (1987) (criticizing restrictive standards for recognition of private rights of action). For a consideration of the standards that should apply when a governmental entity, rather than a private party, sues under a statute or constitutional provision that does not specifically provide for a judicially-enforced remedy, see Seth Davis, Implied Public Rights of Action, 114 Colum. L. Rev. 1 (2014).

SECTION 3. RIGHTS OF ACTION TO ENFORCE CONSTITUTIONAL RIGHTS

Bivens v. Six Unknown Named Agents of Federal Bureau of Narcotics

Supreme Court of the United States, 1971.
403 U.S. 388.

■ MR. JUSTICE BRENNAN delivered the opinion of the Court. . . .

This case has its origin in an arrest and search carried out on the morning of November 26, 1965. Petitioner's complaint alleged that on that day respondents, agents of the Federal Bureau of Narcotics acting under claim of federal authority, entered his apartment and arrested him for alleged narcotics violations. The agents manacled petitioner in front of his wife and children, and threatened to arrest the entire family. They searched the apartment from stem to stern. Thereafter, petitioner was taken to the federal courthouse in Brooklyn, where he was interrogated, booked, and subjected to a visual strip search.

On July 7, 1967, petitioner brought suit in federal District Court. In addition to the allegations above, his complaint asserted that the arrest and search were effected without a warrant, and that unreasonable force was employed in making the arrest; fairly read, it alleges as well that the arrest was made without probable cause. Petitioner claimed to have suffered great humiliation, embarrassment, and mental suffering as a result of the agents' unlawful conduct, and sought $15,000 damages from each of them. The District Court, on respondents' motion, dismissed the complaint on the ground, inter alia, that it failed to state a cause of action.[2] The Court of Appeals . . . affirmed on that basis. We granted certiorari. We reverse.

I

Respondents do not argue that petitioner should be entirely without remedy for an unconstitutional invasion of his rights by federal agents. In respondents' view, however, the rights that petitioner asserts—primarily rights of privacy—are creations of state and not of federal law. Accordingly, they argue, petitioner may obtain money damages to redress invasion of these rights only by an action in tort, under state law, in the state courts. In this scheme the Fourth Amendment would serve merely to limit the extent to which the agents could defend the state law tort suit by asserting that their actions were a valid exercise of federal power: if the agents were shown to have violated the Fourth Amendment, such a defense would be lost to them and they would stand before the state law merely as private individuals. Candidly admitting that it is the policy of the Department of Justice to remove all such suits from the state to the federal courts for decision,[4] respondents nevertheless urge that we uphold dismissal of petitioner's complaint in federal court, and remit him to filing an action in the state courts in order that the case may properly be removed to the federal court for decision on the basis of state law.

We think that respondents' thesis rests upon an unduly restrictive view of the Fourth Amendment's protection against unreasonable searches and seizures by federal agents, a view that has consistently been rejected by this Court. Respondents seek to treat the relationship between a citizen and a federal agent unconstitutionally exercising his authority as no different from the relationship between two private citizens. In so doing, they ignore the fact that power, once granted, does not disappear like a magic gift when it is wrongfully used. An agent acting—albeit unconstitutionally—in the name of the United States possesses a far greater capacity for harm than an individual trespasser exercising no authority other than his own. Accordingly, as our cases make clear, the Fourth Amendment operates as a limitation upon the exercise of federal power regardless of whether the state in whose jurisdiction that power is

---

[2] The agents were not named in petitioner's complaint, and the District Court ordered that the complaint be served upon "those federal agents who it is indicated by the records of the United States Attorney participated in the November 25, 1965, arrest of the [petitioner]." Five agents were ultimately served.

[4] "[S]ince it is the present policy of the Department of Justice to remove to the federal courts all suits in state courts against federal officers for trespass or false imprisonment, a claim for relief, whether based on state common law or directly on the Fourth Amendment, will ultimately be heard in a federal court." Brief for Respondents 13. In light of this, it is difficult to understand our Brother Blackmun's complaint that our holding today "opens the door for another avalanche of new federal cases." In estimating the magnitude of any such "avalanche," it is worth noting that a survey [in 1968] of comparable actions against state officers under 42 U.S.C. § 1983 found only 53 reported cases in 17 years (1951–1967) that survived a motion to dismiss. Increasing this figure by 900% to allow for increases in rate and unreported cases, every federal district judge could expect to try one such case every 13 years.

exercised would prohibit or penalize the identical act if engaged in by a private citizen. It guarantees to citizens of the United States the absolute right to be free from unreasonable searches and seizures carried out by virtue of federal authority. And "where federally protected rights have been invaded, it has been the rule from the beginning that courts will be alert to adjust their remedies so as to grant the necessary relief."

First. Our cases have long since rejected the notion that the Fourth Amendment proscribes only such conduct as would, if engaged in by private persons, be condemned by state law. [R]espondents' argument that the Fourth Amendment serves only as a limitation on federal defenses to a state law claim, and not as an independent limitation upon the exercise of federal power, must [therefore] be rejected.

Second. The interests protected by state laws regulating trespass and the invasion of privacy, and those protected by the Fourth Amendment's guarantee against unreasonable searches and seizures, may be inconsistent or even hostile. Thus, we may bar the door against an unwelcome private intruder, or call the police if he persists in seeking entrance. The availability of such alternative means for the protection of privacy may lead the state to restrict imposition of liability for any consequent trespass. A private citizen, asserting no authority other than his own, will not normally be liable in trespass if he demands, and is granted, admission to another's house. But one who demands admission under a claim of federal authority stands in a far different position. The mere invocation of federal power by a federal law enforcement official will normally render futile any attempt to resist an unlawful entry or arrest by resort to the local police; and a claim of authority to enter is likely to unlock the door as well. "In such cases there is no safety for the citizen, except in the protection of the judicial tribunals, for rights which have been invaded by the officers of the government, professing to act in its name. There remains to him but the alternative of resistance, which may amount to crime." Nor is it adequate to answer that the state may take into account the different status of one clothed with the authority of the federal government. For just as state law may not authorize federal agents to violate the Fourth Amendment, neither may state law undertake to limit the extent to which federal authority can be exercised. The inevitable consequence of this dual limitation on state power is that the federal question becomes not merely a possible defense to the state law action, but an independent claim both necessary and sufficient to make out the plaintiff's cause of action.

Third. That damages may be obtained for injuries consequent upon a violation of the Fourth Amendment by federal officials should hardly seem a surprising proposition. Historically, damages have been regarded as the ordinary remedy for an invasion of personal interests in liberty. Of course, the Fourth Amendment does not in so many words provide for its enforcement by an award of money damages for the consequences of its violation. But "it is . . . well settled that where legal rights have been invaded, and a federal statute provides for a general right to sue for such invasion, federal courts may use any available remedy to make good the wrong done." Bell v. Hood, 327 U.S. 678, 684 (1946) (footnote omitted). The present case involves no special factors counseling hesitation in the absence of affirmative action by Congress. We are not dealing with a question of "federal fiscal policy," as in United States v. Standard Oil Co., 332 U.S. 301, 311 (1947). In that case we refused to infer from the government-soldier relationship that the United States could recover damages from one who negligently injured a soldier and thereby caused the government to pay his medical expenses and lose his services during the course of his hospitalization. Noting that Congress was normally quite solicitous where the federal purse was involved, we pointed out that "the United States [was] the party plaintiff to the suit. And the United States has power at any time to create the liability." Nor are we asked in this case to impose liability upon a congressional employee for actions contrary to no constitutional prohibition, but merely said to be in excess of the authority delegated to him by the Congress. Wheeldin v. Wheeler, 373 U.S. 647 (1963). Finally, we cannot accept respondents' formulation of the question as whether the availability of money damages is necessary to enforce the Fourth Amendment. For we have here no explicit congressional declaration that persons injured by a federal officer's violation of the Fourth Amendment may not recover money damages from the agents, but must instead be remitted to another remedy, equally effective in the view of Congress. The question is merely whether petitioner, if he can demonstrate an injury consequent upon the violation by federal agents of his Fourth Amendment rights, is entitled to redress his injury through a particular remedial mechanism normally available in the federal courts. Cf. J.I. Case Co. v. Borak, 377 U.S. 426, 433 (1964). "The very essence of civil liberty certainly consists in the right of every individual to claim the protection of the laws, whenever he receives an injury." Marbury v. Madison, 5 U.S. (1 Cranch) 137, 163 (1803). Having concluded that petitioner's complaint states a cause of action under the Fourth Amendment, we hold that petitioner is entitled to recover money damages for any injuries he has suffered as a result of the agents' violation of the amendment.

II

In addition to holding that petitioner's complaint had failed to state facts making out a cause of action, the District Court ruled that in any event respondents were immune from liability by virtue of their official position. This question was not passed upon by the Court of Appeals, and accordingly we do not consider it here. The judgment of the Court of Appeals is reversed and the case is remanded for further proceedings consistent with this opinion.

So ordered.

■ MR. JUSTICE HARLAN, concurring in the judgment. . . .

Chief Judge Lumbard's opinion [for the court below] reasoned, in essence, that: (1) the framers of the Fourth Amendment did not appear to contemplate a "wholly new federal cause of action founded directly on the Fourth Amendment," and (2) while the federal courts had power under a general grant of jurisdiction to imply a federal remedy for the enforcement of a constitutional right, they should do so only when the absence of alternative remedies renders the constitutional command a "mere 'form of words.'" The government takes essentially the same position here. And two members of the Court add the contention that we lack the constitutional power to accord Bivens a remedy for damages in the absence of congressional action creating "a federal cause of action for damages for an unreasonable search in violation of the Fourth Amendment."

For the reasons set forth below, I am of the opinion that federal courts do have the power to award damages for violation of "constitutionally protected interests" and I agree with the Court that a traditional judicial remedy such as damages is appropriate to the vindication of the personal interests protected by the Fourth Amendment.

I

I turn first to the contention that the constitutional power of federal courts to accord Bivens damages for his claim depends on the passage of a statute creating a "federal cause of action." Although the point is not entirely free of ambiguity, I do not understand either the government or my dissenting Brothers to maintain that Bivens's contention that he is entitled to be free from the type of official conduct prohibited by the Fourth Amendment depends on a decision by the state in which he resides to accord him a remedy. Such a position would be incompatible with the presumed availability of federal equitable relief, if a proper showing can be made in terms of the ordinary principles governing equitable remedies. However broad a federal court's discretion concerning equitable remedies, it is absolutely clear—at least after Erie R. Co. v. Tompkins, 304 U.S. 64 (1938)—that in a nondiversity suit a federal court's power to grant even equitable relief depends on the presence of a substantive right derived from federal law.

Thus the interest which Bivens claims—to be free from official conduct in contravention of the Fourth Amendment—is a federally protected interest. Therefore, the question of judicial *power* to grant Bivens damages is not a problem of the "source" of the "right"; instead, the question is whether the power to authorize damages as a judicial remedy for the vindication of a federal constitutional right is placed by the Constitution itself exclusively in Congress's hands.

II

The contention that the federal courts are powerless to accord a litigant damages for a claimed invasion of his federal constitutional rights until Congress explicitly authorizes the remedy cannot rest on the notion that the decision to grant compensatory relief involves a resolution of policy considerations not susceptible of judicial discernment. Thus, in suits for damages based on violations of federal statutes lacking any express authorization of a damage remedy, this Court has authorized such relief where, in its view, damages are necessary to effectuate the congressional policy underpinning the substantive provisions of the statute. J.I. Case Co. v. Borak, 377 U.S. 426 (1964).[4]

If it is not the nature of the remedy which is thought to render a judgment as to the appropriateness of damages inherently "legislative," then it must be the nature of the legal interest offered as an occasion for invoking otherwise appropriate judicial relief. But I do not think that the fact that the interest is protected by the Constitution rather than statute or common law justifies the assertion that federal courts are powerless to grant damages in the absence of explicit congressional action authorizing the remedy. Initially, I note that it would be at least anomalous to conclude that the federal judiciary—while competent to choose among the range of traditional judicial remedies to implement statutory and common law policies, and even to generate substantive rules governing primary behavior in furtherance of broadly formulated policies articulated by statute or Constitution, see Textile Workers v. Lincoln Mills, 353 U.S. 448 (1957); United States v. Standard Oil Co., 332 U.S. 301, 304–11 (1947); Clearfield Trust Co. v. United States, 318 U.S. 363 (1943)—is powerless to accord a damages remedy to vindicate social policies which, by virtue of their inclusion in the Constitution, are aimed predominantly at restraining the government as an instrument of the popular will.

More importantly, the presumed availability of federal equitable relief against threatened invasions of constitutional interests appears entirely to negate the contention that the status of an interest as constitutionally protected divests federal courts of the power to grant damages absent express congressional authorization. . . .

If explicit congressional authorization is an absolute prerequisite to the power of a federal court to accord compensatory relief regardless of the necessity or appropriateness of damages as a remedy simply because of the status of a legal interest as constitutionally protected, then it seems to me that explicit congressional authorization is similarly prerequisite to the exercise of equitable remedial discretion in favor of

---

[4]   The *Borak* case is an especially clear example of the exercise of federal judicial power to accord damages as an appropriate remedy in the absence of any express statutory authorization of a federal cause of action. There we "implied"—from what can only be characterized as an "exclusively procedural provision" affording access to a federal forum—a private cause of action for damages for violation of § 14(a) of the Securities Exchange Act of 1934. We did so in an area where federal regulation has been singularly comprehensive and elaborate administrative enforcement machinery had been provided. The exercise of judicial power involved in *Borak* simply cannot be justified in terms of statutory construction, see Alfred Hill, Constitutional Remedies, 69 Colum. L. Rev. 1109, 1120–21 (1969); nor did the *Borak* Court purport to do so. The notion of "implying" a remedy, therefore, as applied to cases like *Borak*, can only refer to a process whereby the federal judiciary exercises a choice among traditionally available judicial remedies according to reasons related to the substantive social policy embodied in an act of positive law.

constitutionally protected interests. Conversely, if a general grant of jurisdiction to the federal courts by Congress is thought adequate to empower a federal court to grant equitable relief for all areas of subject-matter jurisdiction enumerated therein, then it seems to me that the same statute is sufficient to empower a federal court to grant a traditional remedy at law.[6] Of course, the special historical traditions governing the federal equity system, might still bear on the comparative appropriateness of granting equitable relief as opposed to money damages. That possibility, however, relates, not to whether the federal courts have the power to afford one type of remedy as opposed to the other, but rather to the criteria which should govern the exercise of our power. To that question, I now pass.

III

The major thrust of the government's position is that, where Congress has not expressly authorized a particular remedy, a federal court should exercise its power to accord a traditional form of judicial relief at the behest of a litigant, who claims a constitutionally protected interest has been invaded, only where the remedy is "essential," or "indispensable for vindicating constitutional rights." While this "essentiality" test is most clearly articulated with respect to damages remedies, apparently the government believes the same test explains the exercise of equitable remedial powers. It is argued that historically the Court has rarely exercised the power to accord such relief in the absence of an express congressional authorization and that "[i]f Congress had thought that federal officers should be subject to a law different than state law, it would have had no difficulty in saying so, as it did with respect to state officers. . . ." See 42 U.S.C. § 1983. Although conceding that the standard of determining whether a damage remedy should be utilized to effectuate statutory policies is one of "necessity" or "appropriateness," see J.I. Case Co. v. Borak, 377 U.S. 426, 432 (1964), the government contends that questions concerning congressional discretion to modify judicial remedies relating to constitutionally protected interests warrant a more stringent constraint on the exercise of judicial power with respect to this class of legally protected interests.

---

[6]   Chief Judge Lumbard's opinion for the Court of Appeals in the instant case is, as I have noted, in accord with this conclusion:

> Thus even if the Constitution itself does not give rise to an inherent injunctive power to prevent its violation by governmental officials there are strong reasons for inferring the existence of this power under any general grant of jurisdiction to the federal courts by Congress.

The description of the remedy as "inferred" cannot, of course, be intended to assimilate the judicial decision to accord such a remedy to any process of statutory construction. Rather, as with the cases concerning remedies, implied from statutory schemes, see n.4, supra, the description of the remedy as "inferred" can only bear on the reasons offered to explain a judicial decision to accord or not to accord a particular remedy.

These arguments for a more stringent test to govern the grant of damages in constitutional cases[7] seem to be adequately answered by the point that the judiciary has a particular responsibility to assure the vindication of constitutional interests such as those embraced by the Fourth Amendment. To be sure, "it must be remembered that legislatures are ultimate guardians of the liberties and welfare of the people in quite as great a degree as the courts." But it must also be recognized that the Bill of Rights is particularly intended to vindicate the interests of the individual in the face of the popular will as expressed in legislative majorities; at the very least, it strikes me as no more appropriate to await express congressional authorization of traditional judicial relief with regard to these legal interests than with respect to interests protected by federal statutes.

The question then, is, as I see it, whether compensatory relief is "necessary" or "appropriate" to the vindication of the interest asserted. In resolving that question, it seems to me that the range of policy considerations we may take into account is at least as broad as the range of those a legislature would consider with respect to an express statutory authorization of a traditional remedy. In this regard I agree with the Court that the appropriateness of according Bivens compensatory relief does not turn simply on the deterrent effect liability will have on federal official conduct. Damages as a traditional form of compensation for invasion of a legally protected interest may be entirely appropriate even if no substantial deterrent effects on future official lawlessness might be thought to result. Bivens, after all, has invoked judicial processes claiming entitlement to compensation for injuries resulting from allegedly lawless official behavior, if those injuries are properly compensable in money damages. I do not think a court of law—vested with the power to accord a remedy— should deny him his relief simply because he cannot show that future lawless conduct will thereby be deterred.

And I think it is clear that Bivens advances a claim of the sort that, if proved, would be properly compensable in damages. The personal interests protected by the Fourth Amendment are those we attempt to capture by the notion of "privacy"; while the Court today properly points out that the type of harm which officials can inflict when they invade protected zones of an individual's life are different from the types of harm private citizens inflict on one another, the experience of judges in dealing with private trespass and false imprisonment claims supports the conclusion that courts of law are capable of making the types of judgment concerning causation and magnitude of injury necessary to accord meaningful compensation for invasion of Fourth Amendment rights.[9]

---

[7]   I express no view on the government's suggestion that congressional authority to simply discard the remedy the Court today authorizes might be in doubt; nor do I understand the Court's opinion today to express any view on that particular question.

[9]   The same, of course, may not be true with respect to other types of constitutionally protected interests, and therefore the appropriateness of money damages may well vary with the nature of the personal interest asserted.

On the other hand, the limitations on state remedies for violation of common-law rights by private citizens argue in favor of a federal damages remedy. The injuries inflicted by officials acting under color of law, while no less compensable in damages than those inflicted by private parties, are substantially different in kind, as the Court's opinion today discusses in detail. It seems to me entirely proper that these injuries be compensable according to uniform rules of federal law, especially in light of the very large element of federal law which must in any event control the scope of official defenses to liability. Certainly, there is very little to be gained from the standpoint of federalism by preserving different rules of liability for federal officers dependent on the state where the injury occurs.

Putting aside the desirability of leaving the problem of federal official liability to the vagaries of common-law actions, it is apparent that some form of damages is the only possible remedy for someone in Bivens's alleged position. It will be a rare case indeed in which an individual in Bivens's position will be able to obviate the harm by securing injunctive relief from any court. However desirable a direct remedy against the government might be as a substitute for individual official liability, the sovereign still remains immune to suit. Finally, assuming Bivens's innocence of the crime charged, the "exclusionary rule" is simply irrelevant. For people in Bivens's shoes, it is damages or nothing.

The only substantial policy consideration advanced against recognition of a federal cause of action for violation of Fourth Amendment rights by federal officials is the incremental expenditure of judicial resources that will be necessitated by this class of litigation. There is, however, something ultimately self-defeating about this argument. For if, as the government contends, damages will rarely be realized by plaintiffs in these cases because of jury hostility, the limited resources of the official concerned, etc., then I am not ready to assume that there will be a significant increase in the expenditure of judicial resources on these claims. Few responsible lawyers and plaintiffs are likely to choose the course of litigation if the statistical chances of success are truly de minimis. And I simply cannot agree with my Brother Black that the possibility of "frivolous" claims—if defined simply as claims with no legal merit—warrants closing the courthouse doors to people in Bivens's situation. There are other ways, short of that, of coping with frivolous lawsuits.

On the other hand, if—as I believe is the case with respect, at least, to the most flagrant abuses of official power—damages to some degree will be available when the option of litigation is chosen, then the question appears to be how Fourth Amendment interests rank on a scale of social values compared with, for example, the interests of stockholders defrauded by misleading proxies. See *J.I. Case Co. v. Borak*. Judicial resources, I am well aware, are increasingly scarce these days. Nonetheless, when we automatically close the courthouse door solely on this basis, we implicitly express a value judgment on the comparative importance of classes of legally protected interests. And current limitations upon the effective functioning of the courts arising from budgetary inadequacies should not be permitted to stand in the way of the recognition of otherwise sound constitutional principles.

Of course, for a variety of reasons, the remedy may not often be sought. And the countervailing interests in efficient law enforcement of course argue for a protective zone with respect to many types of Fourth Amendment violations. But, while I express no view on the immunity defense offered in the instant case, I deem it proper to venture the thought that at the very least such a remedy would be available for the most flagrant and patently unjustified sorts of police conduct. Although litigants may not often choose to seek relief, it is important, in a civilized society, that the judicial branch of the nation's government stand ready to afford a remedy in these circumstances. It goes without saying that I intimate no view on the merits of petitioner's underlying claim.

For these reasons, I concur in the judgment of the Court.

■ MR. JUSTICE BLACK, dissenting.

. . . There can be no doubt that Congress could create a federal cause of action for damages for an unreasonable search in violation of the Fourth Amendment. Although Congress [in 42 U.S.C. § 1983] has created such a federal cause of action against *state* officials acting under color of state law, it has never created such a cause of action against federal officials. If it wanted to do so, Congress could, of course, create a remedy against federal officials who violate the Fourth Amendment in the performance of their duties. But the point of this case and the fatal weakness in the Court's judgment is that neither Congress nor the State of New York has enacted legislation creating such a right of action. For us to do so is, in my judgment, an exercise of power that the Constitution does not give us.

Even if we had the legislative power to create a remedy, there are many reasons why we should decline to create a cause of action where none has existed since the formation of our Government. The courts of the United States as well as those of the States are choked with lawsuits. . . . We sit at the top of a judicial system accused by some of nearing the point of collapse. Many criminal defendants do not receive speedy trials and neither society nor the accused are assured of justice when inordinate delays occur. Citizens must wait years to litigate their private civil suits. Substantial changes in correctional and parole systems demand the attention of the lawmakers and the judiciary. If I were a legislator I might well find these and other needs so pressing as to make me believe that the resources of lawyers and judges should be devoted to them rather than to civil damage actions against officers who generally strive to perform within constitutional bounds. There is also a real danger that such suits might deter officials from the *proper* and honest performance of their duties.

[margin handwritten note: Argument that Congress has not created a cause of action against federal officials violating 4th]

[margin handwritten note: Qualified immunity arguments]

All of these considerations make imperative careful study and weighing of the arguments both for and against the creation of such a remedy under the Fourth Amendment. I would have great difficulty for myself in resolving the competing policies, goals, and priorities in the use of resources, if I thought it were my job to resolve those questions. But that is not my task. The task of evaluating the pros and cons of creating judicial remedies for particular wrongs is a matter for Congress and the legislatures of the States. Congress has not provided that any federal court can entertain a suit against a federal officer for violations of Fourth Amendment rights occurring in the performance of his duties. A strong inference can be drawn from creation of such actions against state officials that Congress does not desire to permit such suits against federal officials. Should the time come when Congress desires such lawsuits, it has before it a model of valid legislation, 42 U.S.C. § 1983, to create a damage remedy against federal officers. Cases could be cited to support the legal proposition which I assert, but it seems to me to be a matter of common understanding that the business of the judiciary is to interpret the laws and not to make them.

I dissent.

[Chief Justice Burger and Justice Blackmun filed separate dissents.]

NOTES ON PRIVATE RIGHTS OF ACTION AFTER BIVENS

1. INTRODUCTION

Prior to *Bivens*, 42 U.S.C. § 1983 provided a cause of action against *state* officials who violated federal rights. Additionally, a federal cause of action for injunctive relief could be asserted against a federal officer, notwithstanding the absence of express statutory authority. This cause of action stemmed from the decision in Ex parte Young, 209 U.S. 123 (1908), which is reproduced as a main case in Chapter VIII. The Court had also inferred a private cause of action for recission or damages from a federal statute that did not specifically authorize such relief. See J.I. Case Co. v. Borak, 377 U.S. 426 (1964), which is discussed elsewhere in this Chapter.[a] Moreover, in 1914 the Court decided that evidence obtained in violation of the Fourth Amendment must be excluded from federal criminal trials. See Weeks v. United States, 232 U.S. 383 (1914). It extended the Fourth Amendment exclusionary rule to state courts in 1961. See Mapp v. Ohio, 367 U.S. 643 (1961).

Does it follow from these decisions that the Court had the constitutional authority to do what it did in *Bivens*? *J.I. Case* was unanimous. What reason would Justice Black have for joining that decision, yet saying in *Bivens* that "[f]or us [to create the cause of action is] an exercise of power that the Constitution does not give us"? With respect to the Fourth Amendment, is the

---

[a] For elaboration of the appropriate role for a "cause of action" in federal law and for "an effort to bring some consistency to the understanding of the federal cause of action," see John F. Preis, How the Federal Cause of Action Relates to Rights, Remedies, and Jurisdiction, 67 Fla. L. Rev. 849 (2015).

exclusionary rule an adequate and sufficient remedy? It would not apply, of course, in cases where no evidence was obtained, where there was a guilty plea, or where criminal proceedings were not pursued. Without *Bivens*, how would Fourth Amendment violations be remedied in such cases?

Since *J.I. Case*, several Justices have taken the position that the Court should not—and perhaps constitutionally cannot—infer a cause of action from a federal statute in the absence of a clear indication of congressional intent. If this position is correct, does it follow that *Bivens* is wrong? Or is the Court more justified in supplying a remedy for a constitutional violation than for the violation of a federal statute? Or is it somehow more problematic, from the perspective of separation of powers, to create a private remedy for constitutional violations than for statutory violations?

Bivens left open whether, when *Bivens* remedies are proper, they are constitutionally required. If they are, then Congress cannot preclude them. If they are ordinary federal common law, however, then they can be overridden by Congress (leaving damage remedies to state law). Perhaps the answer is somewhere in between: Congress may have a lot of flexibility with respect to remedies, but not the ability completely to eliminate an adequate remedial option in suits against federal officials. If so, *Bivens* remedies would be a form of quasi-constitutional common law.

The subsequent history of *Bivens* is surprisingly complicated. The decision has never been reversed nor held inapplicable to the familiar and important situation of rights violated by federal law enforcement. The application of *Bivens* to other contexts, however, has been contested. While early decisions have extended *Bivens*, more recent ones have not. In some cases, the reluctance to extend *Bivens* stemmed from the adequacy of alternative remedies provided by Congress. In others, it reflected a special concern not to disrupt the military. More recently, the Court seems to evince a general disenchantment with *Bivens*, and perhaps doubt about whether it should ever be extended. This history is summarized in the notes below.

2.   *BIVENS* EXTENDED

Davis v. Passman, 442 U.S. 228 (1979), and Carlson v. Green, 446 U.S. 14 (1980), were early decisions that extended the *Bivens* remedy. *Davis v. Passman* involved Title VII of the 1964 Civil Rights Act, which prohibits gender discrimination in employment. Even though the statute specifically exempted discrimination against congressional employees, the Court found that the plaintiff—claiming that she had been discharged because she was a woman—could sue Congressman Otto Passman under *Bivens*. Four Justices dissented, chiefly on the ground that it was inappropriate for the Court to enforce a non-statutory damages remedy against a member of Congress when Congress had taken pains to exempt itself from the statutory remedy provided in Title VII.

Carlson v. Green involved a suit against the director of the Federal Bureau of Prisons for the death of an inmate owing to lack of medical care. Application of *Bivens* was complicated by the fact that the allegations would also have supported a suit directly against the United States under the Federal Tort Claims Act. Speaking through Justice Brennan, the Court repeated what it had said in *Passman*—that *Bivens* actions were precluded when "Congress has provided an alternative remedy which it explicitly declared to be a *substitute* for recovery directly under the Constitution and viewed it as equally effective." The Federal Tort Claims Act did not meet this test, as Congress had not explicitly indicated that it intended to displace *Bivens*. Moreover, the Court listed several advantages of *Bivens* actions, including the availability of punitive damages and jury trial, neither of which is available under the FTCA. The implication was that the requirement that an alternative remedy be "equally effective" would be taken very seriously.

Justices Powell and Stewart concurred in the judgment without endorsing the Court's reasoning. Chief Justice Burger dissented, saying that the FTCA provided an "adequate" remedy, and that "[f]or me, that is the end of the matter." Justice Rehnquist dissented on a broader ground that assumed increasing importance in later years. He argued, in line with Justice Black, that *Bivens* itself was an unconstitutional assumption of power by the Supreme Court. While federal courts historically had broad authority to fashion equitable remedies, Rehnquist thought damages required legislative authorization.

3.   *BIVENS* CURTAILED: ALTERNATIVE REMEDIES

Later decisions on the adequacy of alternative remedies proved less demanding. In Bush v. Lucas, 462 U.S. 367 (1983), the Court unanimously refused to allow a *Bivens* action by federal employee who claimed that his supervisor had discharged him for public criticism of the agency in which they worked. The Court said the employee had to be content with civil service remedies. While the civil service regime provided important advantages to the employee, it also precluded punitive damages, jury trial, and compensation for emotional and dignitary harms. The Court did not focus on these disadvantages. In an opinion by Justice Stevens, it said that the question was whether "an elaborate remedial system that has been constructed step by step, with careful attention to conflicting policy considerations, should be augmented by the creation of a new judicial remedy," and concluded that Congress was "in a far better position than a court" to make that decision.

Schweiker v. Chilicky, 487 U.S. 412 (1988), was decided on the same ground. The plaintiffs in *Schweiker* were individuals whose social security disability benefits had been terminated, allegedly in violation of due process. Eventually, the terminations were reversed and the benefits retroactively restored, but the plaintiffs claimed damages for the suffering they endured while their benefits were suspended. Congress subsequently enacted a variety of reforms, including a requirement that benefits be continued during the pendency of administrative appeals.

Speaking through Justice O'Connor, the Court declined to go farther than Congress: "When the design of a government program suggests that Congress has provided what it considers adequate remedial mechanisms for constitutional violations that may occur in the course of its administration, we have not created additional *Bivens* remedies. The court also said that the case "cannot reasonably be distinguished from *Bush v. Lucas*":

> Here, exactly as in *Bush*, Congress has failed to provide for "complete relief": respondents have not been given a remedy in damages for emotional distress or for other hardships suffered because of delays in their receipt of social security benefits. The creation of a *Bivens* remedy would obviously offer the prospect of relief for injuries that must now go unredressed. Congress, however, has not failed to provide meaningful safeguards or remedies for the rights of persons situation as respondents were. . . . The prospect of personal liability for official acts, moreover, would undoubtedly lead to new difficulties and expense in recruiting administrators for the programs Congress has established. Congressional competence at "balancing governmental efficiency and the rights of [individuals]" is no more questionable in the social welfare context than it is in the civil service context.

Joined by Justices Marshall and Blackmun, Justice Brennan dissented. He emphasized that the legislation governing *future* disability reviews in no way redressed the harms occasioned by *past* denials of benefits, nor did Congress suggest that it would. In his view, the "mere fact that Congress was aware of the prior injustices and failed to provide a form of redress for them, standing alone," did not counsel against a judicial remedy.

4.   *BIVENS* CURTAILED: SENSITIVE CONTEXTS

The Court said in *Bivens* that "[t]he present case involves no special factors counseling hesitation in the absence of affirmative action by Congress." This formula has assumed particular importance in subsequent cases. One of the "special factors counseling hesitation" is congressional provision of alternative remedies. Another is an especially sensitive context. In two cases, the Court has indicated that fear of judicial intrusion into the effective functioning of the military is a potent argument against *Bivens* remedies.

> The easier case was Chappell v. Wallace, 462 U.S. 296 (1983), where five enlisted men on a naval vessel tried to sue their officers for racial discrimination. The Supreme Court unanimously refused, saying that "the unique disciplinary structure of the Military Establishment and Congress's activity in the field constitute 'special factors' which dictate that it would be inappropriate to provide enlisted military personnel a *Bivens*-type remedy against their superior officers."

The more difficult case was United States v. Stanley, 483 U.S. 669 (1987). In 1958, Army Sgt. Stanley volunteered to participate in a program to test protective clothing. There he was secretly administered LSD, so that the Army could study the effects of the drug. Stanley alleged that he suffered severe adverse effects, leading to violent behavior toward his wife and children and a subsequent divorce. He learned about the LSD only in 1975, when the Army asked him to participate in a study of the long-term effects of LSD on the "volunteers" who had participated in the earlier tests.

Stanley's attempt to bring a *Bivens* action was rejected by the Supreme Court. This decision followed United States v. Johnson, 481 U.S. 681 (1987), which involved an FTCA suit by the widow of Coast Guard officer allegedly killed by the negligence of civilian officials. By a vote of five to four, the Court held that "the government is not liable under the Federal Tort Claims Act for injuries to servicemen where the injuries arise out of or are in the course of activity incident to service." This decision was not based on the language or legislative history of the FTCA, but on the appropriate relation of the judiciary to the military. In an opinion by Justice Scalia, the Court found that the same policies should control in *Stanley*. Accordingly, the Court held "that no *Bivens* remedy is available for injuries that 'arise out of or are in the course of activity incident to service.'" The presence or absence of an alternative remedy was irrelevant.

Justice Brennan, joined by Justice Marshall and in part by Justice Stevens, dissented. They thought the concern for the proper relationship of the courts to the military was outweighed on these facts by the need for a remedy for the intentional violation of constitutional rights in a context where the "special requirements of command that concerned us in *Chappell* are not implicated . . . ." Justice O'Connor dissented separately.

5.   APPLICATION TO DEFENDANTS OTHER THAN FEDERAL EMPLOYEES

Correctional Services Corp. v. Malesko, 534 U.S. 61 (2001), declined to extend *Bivens* to claims against a private corporation operating a halfway house under contract with the Federal Bureau of Prisons. An inmate with a heart condition was improperly denied the use of the elevator and had a heart attack after climbing stairs to the fifth floor. In a previous decision, FDIC v. Meyer, 510 U.S. 471 (1994), the Court had ruled that *Bivens* actions would not lie against federal agencies, as distinct from the individual officers employed by them. *Malesko* extended that reasoning to private corporations operating under federal contract. The Court noted that the plaintiff did not lack alternative remedies, as he could have sued the company for negligence under state law.

Joined by Justice Thomas, Justice Scalia concurred, condemning *Bivens* as "a relic of the heady days in which this Court assumed common-law powers to create causes of action—decreeing them to be 'implied' by the mere existence of a statutory or constitutional prohibition." Justices Stevens, Souter, Ginsburg, and Breyer dissented. Answering Scalia directly, Stevens said that "the driving force behind the Court's decision is a disagreement with the holding in *Bivens* itself" and called for respect for that precedent, whether or not the current Justices would have endorsed that rule when it was announced.

Malesko barred *Bivens* actions against private companies that ran federal prisons, but it left open the question whether the employees of those companies could be sued for inadequate medical care. Minneci v. Pollard, 565 U.S. 118 (2012), said "no." In a decision that was almost unanimous (only Justice Ginsburg dissented), the Court said the question was whether state-law remedies were generally comparable to *Bivens* actions—that is, whether they "provide roughly similar incentives for potential defendants to comply with the Eighth Amendment while also providing roughly similar compensation to victims of violations." The Court found that they did. The fact that the defendants were not federal employees was significant, as under the Westfall Act, prisoners "ordinarily *cannot* bring state-law tort actions against employees of the Federal Government," but ordinarily "*can* bring state law tort actions against employees of a private firm."

Wilkie v. Robbins

Supreme Court of the United States, 2007.
551 U.S. 537.

■ JUSTICE SOUTER delivered the opinion of the Court.

Officials of the Bureau of Land Management stand accused of harassment and intimidation aimed at extracting an easement across private property. The [question here is] whether the landowner has . . . a private action for damages of the sort recognized in Bivens v. Six Unknown Fed. Narcotics Agents, 403 U.S. 388 (1971) . . . . We hold that [he does not].

I

A

[Plaintiff] Frank Robbins owns and operates the High Island Ranch, a commercial guest resort in Hot Springs County, Wyoming, stretching across some 40 miles of territory. The ranch is a patchwork of mostly contiguous land parcels intermingled with tracts belonging to other private owners, the State of Wyoming, and the National Government. . . . In response to persistent requests by environmentalists and outdoor enthusiasts, the Bureau tried to induce the ranch's previous owner, George Nelson, to grant an easement for public use over South Fork Owl Creek Road . . . . [S]hortly after agreeing to sell the property to Robbins, in March 1994, Nelson signed a nonexclusive deed of easement giving the United States the right to use and maintain the road along a stretch of his property. In return, the Bureau agreed to rent Nelson a right-of-way to maintain a different section of the road as it runs across federal property and connects otherwise isolated parts of Robbins's holdings.

In May 1994, Nelson conveyed the ranch to Robbins, who continued to graze cattle and run guest cattle drives in reliance on grazing permits and a Special Recreation Use Permit (SRUP) issued by the Bureau. But Robbins knew nothing about Nelson's grant of the easement across South Fork Owl Creed Road, which the Bureau had failed to record, and upon recording his warranty deed in Hot Springs County, Robbins took title to the ranch free of the easement, by operation of Wyoming law.

When the Bureau's employee Joseph Vessels discovered, in June 1994, that the Bureau's inaction had cost it the easement, he telephoned Robbins and demanded an easement to replace Nelson's. Robbins refused but indicated that he would consider granting one in return for something. In a later meeting, Vessels allegedly told Robbins that "the Federal Government does not negotiate," and talks broke down. Robbins says that over the next several years the [defendants], who are current and former employees of the Bureau, carried on a campaign of harassment and intimidation aimed at forcing him to regrant the lost easement.

B

. . . The substance of Robbins's claim, and the degree to which existing remedies available to him were adequate, can be understood and assessed only by getting down to the details . . . .

In the summer of 1994, after the fruitless telephone conversation in June, Vessels wrote to Robbins for permission to survey his land in the area of the desired easement. Robbins said no, that it would be a waste of time for the Bureau to do a survey without first reaching agreement with him. Vessels went ahead with a survey anyway, trespassed on Robbins's land, and later boasted about it to Robbins. . . .

Vessels and his supervisor, defendant Charles Wilkie, continued to demand the easement, under threat to cancel the reciprocal maintenance right-of-way that Nelson had negotiated. When Robbins would not budge, the Bureau canceled the right-of-way, citing Robbins' refusal to grant the desired easement and failure even to pay the rental fee. Robbins did not appeal the cancellation to the Interior Board of Land Appeals (ILBA) or seek judicial review under the Administrative Procedure Act. . . .

In October 1995, the Bureau claimed various permit violations and changed the High Island Ranch's 5-year SRUP to a SRUP subject to annual renewal. According to Robbins, losing the 5-year SRUP disrupted his guest ranching business, owing to the resulting uncertainty about permission to conduct cattle drives. Robbins declined to seek administrative review, however, in part because Bureau officials told him that the process would be lengthy and that his permit would be suspended until the IBLA reached a decision.

Beginning in 1996, defendants brought administrative charges against Robbins for trespass and other land-use violations. Robbins claimed some of the charges were false, and others unfairly selective enforcement, and he took all of them to be an effort to retaliate for refusing the Bureau's continuing demands for the easement. He contested a number of these charges, but not all of them, administratively.

In the spring of 1997, the South Fork Owl Creed Road, the only way to reach [portions of the ranch], became impassable. When the Bureau refused to repair the section of the road across federal land, Robbins took matters into his own hands and fixed the public road himself, even though the Bureau had refused permission. The Bureau fined Robbins for trespass, but offered to settle the charge and entertain an application to renew the old maintenance right-of-way. Instead, Robbins appealed to the IBLA, which . . . upheld the fine and rejected Robbins's claim that the

Bureau was trying to "blackmail" him into providing the easement. It said that "[t]he record effectively shows . . . intransigence was the tactic of Robbins, not [the] BLM." Robbins did not seek judicial review of the IBLA's decision.

In July 1997, defendant Teryl Shryack and a colleague entered Robbins's property, claiming the terms of a fence easement as authority. Robbins accused Shryack of unlawful entry, tore up the written instrument, and ordered her off his property. Later that month . . . Michael Miller, a Bureau law enforcement officer questioned Robbins without advance notice and without counsel about the incident with Shryack. The upshot was a charge with two counts of knowingly and forcibly impeding and interfering with a federal employee, in violation of 18 U.S.C. § 111, a crime with a penalty of up to one year in prison. A jury acquitted Robbins in December, after deliberating less than 30 minutes. According to a news story, the jurors "were appalled at the actions of the government" and one said that "Robbins could not have been railroaded any worse . . . if he worked for the Union Pacific." . . .

In 1998, Robbins brought the lawsuit now before us, though there was further vexation to come. In June 1999, the Bureau denied Robbins's application to renew his annual SRUP, based on an accumulation of land-use penalties levied against him. Robbins appealed, the IBLA affirmed, and Robbins did not seek judicial review. Then, in August, the Bureau revoked the grazing permit for High Island Ranch, claiming that Robbins had violated its terms when he kept Bureau officials from passing over his property to reach public lands. Robbins appealed to the IBLA, which stayed the revocation pending resolution of the appeal.

The stay held for several years, despite periodic friction. Without a SRUP, Robbins was forced to redirect his guest cattle drives away from federal land and through a mountain pass with unmarked property boundaries. In August 2000, Vessels and defendants Darrell Barnes and Miller tried to catch Robbins trespassing in driving cattle over a corner of land administered by the Bureau. From a nearly hilltop, they videotaped ranch guests during the drive, even while the guests sought privacy to relieve themselves. That afternoon, Robbins alleges, Barnes and Miller broke into his guest lodge, left trash inside, and departed without closing the lodge gates.

The next summer, defendant David Wallace spoke with Preston Smith, an employee of the Bureau of Indian Affairs who manages land along the High Island Ranch's southern border, and pressured him to impound Robbins' cattle. Smith told Robbins, but did nothing more.

Finally, in January 2003, tension actually cooled to the point that Robbins and the Bureau entered into a settlement agreement that, among other things, established a procedure for informal resolution of future grazing disputes and stayed 16 pending administrative appeals with a view to their ultimate dismissal . . . . The settlement came apart,

however, in January 2004, when the Bureau began formal trespass proceedings against Robbins and unilaterally voided the settlement
agreement. Robbins tried to enforce the agreement in federal court, but
a district court denied relief in a decision affirmed by the Court of Appeals in February 2006.

C

In this lawsuit . . . , Robbins asks for compensatory and punitive
damages as well as declaratory and injunctive relief. . . . Defendants filed
a motion to dismiss on qualified immunity and failure to state a claim,
which the District Court granted, holding that . . . the APA and the Federal Tort Claims Act (FTCA) were effective alternative remedies that
precluded *Bivens* relief. The Court of Appeals for the Tenth Circuit reversed . . . , although it specified that *Bivens* relief was available only for
those "constitutional violations committed by individual federal employees unrelated to final agency action."

On remand, defendants again moved to dismiss . . . . [The District
Court dismissed some claims but] declined to dismiss the Fifth Amendment claim of retaliation for the exercise of Robbins's right to exclude the
Government from his property and to refuse any grant of a property interest without compensation. . . . [T]he Court of Appeals affirmed. . . . We
granted certiorari, and now reverse.

II

The . . . question is whether to devise a new *Bivens* damages action
for retaliating against the exercise of ownership rights, in addition to the
discrete administrative and judicial remedies available to a landowner
like Robbins in dealing with the Government's employees . . . .

Whatever the ultimate conclusion, . . . our consideration of a *Bivens*
request follows a familiar sequence, and on the assumption that a constitutionally recognized interest is adversely affected by the actions of
federal employees, the decision whether to recognize a *Bivens* remedy
may require two steps. In the first place, there is the question whether
any alternative, existing process for protecting the interest amounts to a
convincing reason for the Judicial Branch to refrain from providing and
new and freestanding remedy in damages. But even in the absence of an
alternative, a *Bivens* remedy is a subject of judgment: "the federal courts
must make the kind of remedial determination that is appropriate for a
common-law tribunal, paying particular heed, however, to any special
factors counselling hesitation before authorizing a new kind of federal
litigation." Bush v. Lucas, 462 U.S. 367, 378 (1983).

A

In this factually plentiful case, assessing the significance of any alternative remedies at step one has to begin by categorizing the difficulties
Robbins experienced in dealing with the Bureau. We think they can be
separated into four main groups: torts or tort-like injuries inflicted on

him, charges brought against him, unfavorable agency actions, and offensive behavior by Bureau employees falling outside these three categories. . . .

[The Court then examined the factual allegations in detail and concluded:] In sum, Robbins has an administrative, and ultimately a judicial, process for vindicating virtually all of his complaints. He suffered no charges of wrongdoing on his own part without an opportunity to defend himself . . . . And final agency action, as in canceling permits, for example, was open to administrative and judicial review . . . .

This state of the law gives Robbins no intuitively meritorious case for recognizing a new constitutional cause of action, but neither does it plainly answer no to the question whether he should have it. Like the combination of public and private land ownership around the ranch, the forums of defense and redress open to Robbins are a patchwork, an assemblage of state and federal, administrative and judicial benches applying regulations, statutes, and common law rules. It would be hard to infer that Congress expected the Judiciary to stay its *Bivens* hand, but equally hard to extract any clear lesson that *Bivens* ought to spawn a new claim.

B

This, then, is a case for *Bivens* step two, for weighing reasons for and against the creation of a new cause of action, the way common law judges have always done. Here, the competing arguments boil down to one on a side: from Robbins, the inadequacy of discrete, incident-by-incident remedies; and from the Government and its employees, the difficulty of defining limits to legitimate zeal on the public's behalf in situations where hard bargaining is to be expected in the back-and-forth between public and private interests that the Government's employees engage in every day.

1

As we have said, when the incidents are examined one by one, Robbins's situation does not call for creating a constitutional cause of action for want of other means of vindication . . . . But Robbins's argument for a remedy that looks at the course of dealing as a whole, not simply as so many individual incidents, has the force of the metaphor Robbins invokes, "death by a thousand cuts." It is one thing to be threatened with loss of grazing rights, or to be prosecuted, or to have one's lodge broken into, but something else to be subjected to this in combination over a period of six years, by a series of public officials bent on making life difficult. Agency appeals, lawsuits, and criminal defense take money, and endless battling depletes the spirit along with the purse. The whole where is greater than the sum of its parts.

2

On the other side of the ledger there is a difficulty in defining a workable cause of action. Robbins describes the wrong here as retaliation for standing on his right as a property owner to keep the Government out (by refusing a free replacement for the right-of-way it had lost), and the mention of retaliation brings with it a tailwind of support from our longstanding recognition that the Government may not retaliate for exercising First Amendment speech rights or others of constitutional rank.

But on closer look, the claim against the Bureau's employees fails to fit the prior retaliation cases. Those cases turn on an allegation of impermissible purpose and motivation; an employee who spoke out on matters of public concern and then was fired, for example, would need to "prove that the conduct at issue was constitutionally protected, and that it was a substantial or motivating factor in the termination." Board of Comm'rs v. Umbehr, 518 U.S. 668, 675 (1996). In its defense, the Government may respond that the firing had nothing to do with the protected speech, or that "it would have taken the same action even in the absence of the protected conduct." Ibid. In short, the outcome turns on "what for" questions: what was the Government's purpose in firing him and would he have been fired anyway? Questions like these have definite answers, and we have established methods for identifying the presence of an illicit reason (in competition with others), not only in retaliation cases but on claims of discrimination based on race or other characteristics.

But a *Bivens* case by Robbins could not be resolved merely by answering a "what for" question or two. All agree that the Bureau's employees intended to convince Robbins to grant an easement. But unlike punishing someone for speaking out against the Government, trying to induce someone to grant an easement for public use is a perfectly legitimate purpose: as a landowner the Government may have, and in this instance does have, a valid interest in getting access to neighboring lands. . . .

Robbins's challenge, therefore, is not to the object the Government seeks to achieve, and for the most part his argument is not that the means the Government used were necessarily illegitimate; rather, he says that defendants simply demanded too much and went too far. But as soon as Robbins's claim is framed this way, the line-drawing difficulties it creates are immediately apparent. A "too much" kind of liability standard (if standard at all) can never be as reliable a guide to conduct and to any subsequent liability as a "what for" standard, and that reason counts against recognizing freestanding liability in a case like this. . . .

The point here is not to deny that Government employees sometimes overreach, for of course they do, and they may have done so here if all the allegations are true. The point is the reasonable fear that a general *Bivens* cure would be worse than the disease.

C

. . . Robbins had ready at hand a wide variety of administrative and judicial remedies to redress his injuries. The proposal, nonetheless, to create a new *Bivens* remedy to redress such injuries collectively on a theory of retaliation for exercising his property right to exclude, or on a general theory of unjustifiably burdening his rights as a property owner, raises a serious difficulty of devising a workable cause of action. A judicial standard to identify illegitimate pressure going beyond legitimately hard bargaining would be endlessly knotty to work out, and a general provision for tortlike liability when Government employees are unduly zealous in pressing a government interest affecting property would invite an onslaught of *Bivens* actions.

We think accordingly that any damages remedy for actions by Government employees who push too hard for the Government's benefit may come better, if at all, through legislation. . . . The judgment . . . is reversed, and the case is remanded for further proceedings consistent with this opinion.

It is so ordered.

■ JUSTICE THOMAS, with whom JUSTICE SCALIA joins, concurring.

The Court correctly concludes that Bivens v. Six Unknown Fed. Narcotics Agents, 403 U.S. 388 (1971), does not supply a cause of action in this case. I therefore join its opinion. I write separately because I would not extend *Bivens* even if its reasoning logically applied to the case. "*Bivens* is a relic of the heady days in which this Court assumed common-law powers to create causes of action." Correctional Services Corp. v. Malesko, 534 U.S. 61, 75 (2001) (Scalia, J., joined by Thomas, J., concurring). Accordingly, in my view, *Bivens* and its progeny should be limited "to the precise circumstances that they involved." Ibid.

■ JUSTICE GINSBURG, with whom JUSTICE STEVENS, joins, . . . dissenting in [relevant] part.

Bureau of Land Management (BLM) officials in Wyoming made a careless error. They failed to record an easement obtained for the United States along a stretch of land on the privately owned High Island Ranch. [Plaintiff] Frank Robbins purchased the ranch knowing nothing about the easement granted by the prior owner. Under Wyoming law, Robbins took title to the land free of the easement. BLM officials, realizing their mistake, demanded from Robbins an easement—for which they did not propose to pay—to replace the one they carelessly lost. Their demand, one of them told Robbins, was nonnegotiable. Robbins was directed to provide the easement, or else. When he declined to follow that instruction, the BLM officials mounted a seven-year campaign of relentless harassment and intimidation to force Robbins to give in. They refused to maintain the road providing access to the ranch, trespassed on Robbins' property, brought unfounded criminal charges against him, canceled his special recreational use permit and grazing privileges, interfered with his business operations, and invaded the privacy of his ranch guests on cattle drives.

Robbins commenced this lawsuit to end the incessant harassment and intimidation he endured. He asserted that the Fifth Amendment's Takings Clause forbids government action calculated to acquire private property coercively and cost free. He further urged that federal officials dishonor their constitutional obligation when they act in retaliation for the property owner's resistance to an uncompensated taking. In support of his claim for relief, . . . The Court recognizes that the "remedy" to which the Government would confine Robbins—a discrete challenge to each offending action as it occurs—is inadequate. A remedy so limited would expose Robbins' business to "death by a thousand cuts." Nevertheless, the Court rejects his claim, for it fears the consequences. Allowing Robbins to pursue this suit, the Court maintains, would open the floodgates to a host of unworthy suits "in every sphere of legitimate governmental action affecting property interests."

But this is no ordinary case of "hard bargaining" or bureaucratic arrogance. Robbins charged "vindictive action" to extract property from him without paying a fair price. He complains of a course of conduct animated by an illegitimate desire to "get him." That factor is sufficient to minimize the Court's concern. Taking Robbins' allegations as true, as the Court must at this stage of the litigation, the case presents this question: Does the Fifth Amendment provide an effective check on federal officers who abuse their regulatory powers by harassing and punishing property owners who refuse to surrender their property to the United States without fair compensation? The answer should be a resounding "Yes."

I

The Court acknowledges that, at this stage of proceedings, the facts must be viewed in the light most favorable to Robbins. The full force of Robbins' complaint, however, is not quite captured in the Court's restrained account of his allegations. A more complete rendition of the saga that sparked this suit is in order. [Justice Ginsburg's "more complete" rendition of the facts included many details of overbearing and animosity by BLM employees.]

II

"The very essence of civil liberty certainly consists in the right of every individual to claim the protection of the laws, whenever he receives an injury." Marbury v. Madison, 5 U.S. (1 Cranch) 137, 163 (1803). In Bivens v. Six Unknown Fed. Narcotics Agents, 403 U.S. 388 (1971), the Court drew upon that venerable principle in holding that a victim of a Fourth Amendment violation by federal officers has a claim for relief in the form of money damages. "Historically," the Court observed, " damages have been regarded as the ordinary remedy for invasion of personal interests in liberty." 403 U.S. at 395.

The Court's decisions recognize that the reasoning underlying *Bivens* is not confined to Fourth Amendment claims [citing Davis v. Passman, 442 U.S. 228 (1979), and Carlson v. Green, 446 U.S. 14 (1980).] *Carlson* announced two exceptions to *Bivens'* rule: "The first [applies] when defendants demonstrate special factors counselling hesitation in the absence of affirmative action by Congress. The second [applies] when defendants show that Congress has provided an alternative remedy which it explicitly declared to be a *substitute* for recovery directly under the Constitution and viewed as equally effective." Prior decisions have invoked these exceptions to bar *Bivens* suits against federal officers in only three contexts. [Here Justice Ginsburg discussed Bush v. Lucas, 462 U.S. 367 (1983), Schweiker v. Chilicky, 487 U.S. 412 (1988), and the pair of cases dealing with the military, Chappell v. Wallace, 462 U.S. 296 (1983), and United States v. Stanley, 483 U.S. 669 (1987). Cases refusing to extend *Bivens* to actions against private prisons, Correctional Services Corp. v. Malesko, 534 U.S. 61 (2001), and against federal agencies, FDIC v. Meyer, 510 U.S. 471 (1994), were not to the contrary, she argued, as neither involved a suit against a federal officer.]

III

A

The Court does not hold that Robbins' *Bivens* suit is precluded by a carefully calibrated administrative regime like those at issue in *Bush*, *Chilicky*, *Chappell*, or *Stanley*, nor could it. As the Court recognizes, Robbins has no alternative remedy for the relentless torment he alleges. True, Robbins may have had discrete remedies for particular instances of harassment. But, in these circumstances, piecemeal litigation, the Court acknowledges, cannot forestall "death by a thousand cuts." For plaintiffs in Robbins' shoes, "it is damages or nothing." *Bivens*, 403 U.S. at 410 (Harlan, J., concurring in the judgment).

Despite the Court's awareness that Robbins lacks an effective alternative remedy, it nevertheless bars his suit. The Court finds, on the facts of this case, a special factor counseling hesitation quite unlike any we have recognized before. Allowing Robbins to seek damages for years of harassment, the Court says, "would invite an onslaught of *Bivens* actions" . . . .

The "floodgates" argument the Court today embraces has been rehearsed and rejected before. . . . The only serious policy argument against recognizing a right of action for Bivens, Justice Harlan observed, was the risk of inundating courts with Fourth Amendment claims. He found the argument unsatisfactory, 403 U.S. at 410–11:

> [T]he question appears to be how Fourth Amendment interests rank on a scale of social values compared with, for example, the interests of stockholders defrauded by misleading proxies. Judicial resources, I am well aware, are increasingly scarce these days. Nonetheless, when we automatically close the courthouse door solely on this basis, we implicitly express a value judgment on the comparative importance of classes of legally protected interests.

In attributing heavy weight to the floodgates concern pressed in this case, the Court today veers away from Justice Harlan's sound counsel.

B

In the Court's view Robbins' complaint poses an inordinate risk of imposing on vigilant federal officers, and inundating federal courts, for his pleading "fails to fit the [Court's] prior retaliation cases." "Those cases," the Court says, "turn[ed] on an allegation of [an] impermissible purpose and motivation." Robbins' suit, the Court maintains, raises a different sort of claim: that BLM employees went "too far" in their efforts to achieve an objective that "[a]ll agree" was "perfectly legitimate" . . . .

The Court's assertion that the BLM officials acted with a "perfectly legitimate" objective is a dubious characterization of the long campaign to "bury" Robbins. . . . Even if we allowed that the BLM employees had a permissible objective throughout their harassment of Robbins, and also that they pursued their goal through "legitimate tactics," it would not follow that Robbins failed to state a retaliation claim amenable to judicial resolution.

Impermissible retaliation may well involve lawful action in service of legitimate objectives. For example, in Board of Comm'rs v. Umbehr, 518 U.S. 668 (1996), this Court held that a county board of commissioners may cross into unconstitutional territory if it fires a contractors for speaking out against members of the Board on matters of public concern. The Court recognized that termination a contractor for public criticism of board practices might promote legitimate governmental objectives (e.g., maintaining relationships of trust with those from whom services are purchased). The Court, furthermore, instructed that even where the background law allows a government agency to terminate a contractor at will, the agency lacks carte blanche to do so in retaliation for constitutionally protected conduct. The same is true here: BLM officials may have had the authority to cancel Robbins' permits or penalize his trespasses, but they are not at liberty to do so selectively, in retaliation for his exercise of a constitutional right.

I therefore cannot join the Court in concluding that Robbins' allegations present questions more "knotty" than the mine-run of constitutional retaliation claims. Because "we have established methods for identifying the presence of an illicit reason . . . in retaliation cases," Robbins' suit can be resolved in familiar fashion. A court need only ask whether Robbins engaged in constitutionally protected conduct (resisting the surrender of his property sans compensation), and if so, whether that was the reason BLM agents harassed him.

C

The Court's opinion is driven by the "fear" that a "*Bivens* cure" for the retaliation Robbins experienced may be "worse than the disease." This concern seems to me exaggerated. Robbins' suit is predicated upon the agents' vindictive motive, and the presence of this element in his claim minimizes the risk of making everyday bureaucratic overreaching fare for constitutional litigation. . . .

Indeed, one could securely forecast that the flood the Court fears would not come to pass. . . . Because we have no reason to believe that state employees are any more or less respectful of Fifth Amendment rights than federal agents, 42 U.S.C. § 1983 provides a controlled experiment. If numerous *Bivens* claims would eventuate were courts to entertain claims like Robbins', then courts should already have encountered endeavors to mount Fifth Amendment Takings suits under § 1983. But the Court of Appeals, the Solicitor General, and Robbins all agree that there are no reported cases on charges of retaliation by state officials against the exercise of Takings Clause rights. Harassment of the sort Robbins alleges, it seems, is exceedingly rare. . . . Discrete episodes of hard bargaining that might be viewed as oppressive would not entitle a litigant to relief. But where a plaintiff could prove a pattern of severe and pervasive harassment in duration and degree well beyond the ordinary rough-and-tumble one expects in strenuous negotiations, a *Bivens* suit would provide a remedy. Robbins would have no trouble meeting that standard. . . .

* * *

Thirty-six years ago, the Court created the *Bivens* remedy. In doing so, it assured that federal officials would be subject to the same constraints as state officials in dealing with the fundamental rights of the people who dwell in this land. Today, the court decides that elaboration of *Bivens* to cover Robbins' case should be left to Congress. The *Bivens* analog to § 1983, however, is hardly an obscure part of the Court's jurisprudence. If Congress wishes to codify and further define the *Bivens* remedy, it may do so at any time. Unless and until Congress acts, however, the Court should not shy away from the effort to ensure that bedrock constitutional rights do not become "merely precatory."

ADDITIONAL NOTES ON PRIVATE RIGHTS OF ACTION AFTER BIVENS

1.   QUESTIONS AND COMMENTS ON *WILKIE V. ROBBINS*

The Supreme Court has not approved a new *Bivens* claim since 1980. Perhaps the most interesting thing about *Wilkie v. Robbins* is how far the Court has retreated in the intervening years from anything resembling a presumption in favor of damages for constitutional violations. Two Justices thought *Bivens* should be confined to its facts. Five others embrace an open-ended common-law approach, with no thumb on the scales one way or the other. The result is to transform "special factors counselling hesitation" from a limited list of exceptions to a general invitation to assess the context. In most new situations, one might infer, *Bivens* actions will not lie.

2. *ZIGLAR V. ABBASI*

The declining likelihood of *Bivens* being extended was reinforced in Ziglar v. Abbasi, 582 U.S. ___, 137 S.Ct. 615 (2017). The case involved complex litigation arising from the detention of deportable aliens, mostly Arab or Muslim, in the aftermath of September 11. The government adopted a "hold-until-cleared" policy that kept immigration detainees in custody until they were cleared of involvement in terrorist activities. The conditions of confinement were harsh and in many cases lasted a long time. Plaintiffs sued under *Bivens* to recover damages for unconstitutional conditions of confinement, including excessive force and racial and religious discrimination.

As the case came to the Supreme Court from the Second Circuit, *Bivens* claims had been upheld against a motion to dismiss for two categories of defendants. Attorney General John Ashcroft, FBI Director Robert Mueller, and Immigration and Naturalization Service Commissioner James Ziglar were the "executive officials." They were responsible for the general policy under which plaintiffs were detained. Other defendants, the "wardens," were responsible for the operation of the facility at which plaintiffs were held. By a vote of four to two,[a] the Supreme Court reversed with respect to the executive officials and remanded for reconsideration of the claims against the wardens.

Justice Kennedy's opinion for the Court (joined by Chief Justice Roberts and Justices Thomas and Alito) dwelt on the question, not previously prominent in *Bivens* cases, whether the claims arose in a "new context" not covered by prior Supreme Court decisions that allowed *Bivens* claims. This responded to the Second Circuit, which relied heavily on its finding that the case did *not* involve a "new context." That conclusion was unsurprising for the claims against the wardens, which were closely analogous to conditions-of-confinement claims by ordinary prisoners that were dealt with in Carlson v. Green, 446 U.S. 14 (1980). But it was more contentious for the claims against the executive officials. Ashcroft and Mueller were cabinet-level officers, sued for adopting an unconstitutional detention policy (as distinct from rogue officials accused of not following policy) in the immediate aftermath of a national emergency. The Second Circuit nevertheless concluded that the claims against the wardens did not arise in a "new context" and therefore did not trigger the traditional *Bivens* inquiry into "special factors counselling hesitation." Thus although the Second Circuit opinion was long and detailed, the result rested squarely on its conclusion that, because the claims presented no "new context," further analysis was not required.

The Supreme Court disagreed:

> The proper test for determining whether a case presents a new *Bivens* context is as follows. If the case is different in a meaningful way from previous *Bivens* cases decided by this Court, then the context is new. . . . In the present suit, [plaintiffs'] detention policy

---

[a] Justices Sotomayor, Kagan, and Gorsuch did not participate. Sotomayor was on the Second Circuit when the defendants unsuccessfully petitioned for en banc reconsideration of the panel decision, Kagan was involved in the case as Solicitor General, and Gorsuch joined the Court after the case was argued.

claims challenge the confinement conditions imposed on illegal aliens pursuant to a high-level executive policy created in the wake of a major terrorist attack on American soil. Those claims bear little resemblance to the . . . *Bivens* claims the Court has approved in the past. . . . The Court of Appeals therefore should have held that this was a new *Bivens* context. Had it done so, it would have recognized that a special factors analysis was required before allowing this damages suit to proceed.

The Court had no trouble finding special factors for the executive officials. A damages action against executive officers was thought not an appropriate vehicle for challenging general policy, especially in a sensitive national-security context. The Court also emphasized that Congress had remained silent about a damages remedy, despite public awareness of the "hold-until-cleared" policy and of complaints about its administration. Finally, the Court suggested that habeas corpus provided an alternative, and in these circumstances, superior remedy. The Court therefore reversed with respect to the executive officials and ordered the claims dismissed.

More surprisingly, the Court also found a "new context" for the claims against the wardens. Carlson v. Green, 446 U.S. 14 (1980), which had allowed a *Bivens* action for claims of prisoner mistreatment, was admittedly analogous:

> Yet even a modest extension is still an extension. And this case does seek to extend *Carlson* to a new context. . . . [A] case can present a new context for *Bivens* purposes if it implicates a different constitutional right; if judicial precedents provide a less meaningful guide for official misconduct; or if there are potential special factors that were not considered in prior *Bivens* cases.

Here the claims were made under the Due Process Clause of the Fifth Amendment rather than the Cruel and Unusual Punishment Clause of the Eighth Amendment (because the plaintiffs were detainees rather than convicted prisoners). Judicial guidance for wardens in such situations was "less developed." And the Prison Litigation Reform Act of 1995, passed after *Carlson* was decided, made changes in the litigation of prisoner abuse cases without explicitly authorizing a damages remedy.

The Court admitted that the "differences between this claim and the one in *Carlson* are perhaps small," but said they were nevertheless "meaningful": "Given this Court's expressed caution about extending the *Bivens* remedy . . . the new-context inquiry is easily satisfied." In the Court's view, alternative remedies and other factors counseling against judicial recognition of a damages remedy required consideration. The Court therefore vacated the judgment against the wardens and remanded for reconsideration.[b]

Instead of extending Bivens/Carlson the court said this was a "new-context"

Justice Breyer, joined by Justice Ginsburg, dissented. Again the "new context" question figured prominently:

---

[b]   Justice Thomas concurred in this judgment as to this disposition in order to allow a controlling decision, but his preferred approach would have been to reverse outright without remand.

The Court, in my view, is wrong to hold that permitting a constitutional tort action here would "extend" *Bivens*, applying it in a new context. To the contrary, I fear that the Court's holding would significantly shrink the existing *Bivens* contexts, diminishing the compensatory remedy constitutional tort law now offers to harmed individuals.

For the dissenters, the context was not "new," or "fundamentally different" from prior *Bivens* cases. The plaintiffs were civilians (albeit noncitizens), not members of the military. The defendants were government officers, not federal agencies or private employees. And the unconstitutional-conditions-of-confinement claims were familiar. The dissenters therefore agreed with the Second Circuit that no "new context" was presented.

Justice Breyer, however, did not rest there. He went on to address what he called "the Court's strongest argument," namely that "*Bivens* should not apply to policy-related actions taken in times of national-security need, for example, during war or national-security emergency." He admitted that prior decisions had not answered "the specific question the Court places at issue here: Should *Bivens* actions continue to exist in respect to policy-related actions taken in time of war or national emergency." His answer was that "they should":

> [T]here may well be a particular need for *Bivens* remedies when security-related Government actions are at issue. History tells us of far too many instances where the Executive or Legislative Branch took actions during time of war that, on later examination, turned out unnecessarily and unreasonably to have deprived American citizens of basic constitutional rights. We have read about the Alien and Sedition Acts, the thousands of civilians imprisoned during the Civil War, and the suppression of civil liberties during World War I. The pages of the U.S. Reports themselves recite this Court's refusal to set aside the Government's World War II action removing more than 70,000 American citizens of Japanese origin from their west coast homes and interning them in camps, see Korematsu v. United States, 323 U.S. 214 (1944)—an action that at least some officials knew at the time was unnecessary.

> Can we, in respect to actions taken during those periods, rely exclusively, at the Court seems to suggest, upon injunctive remedies or writs of habeas corpus, their retail equivalent? Complaints seeking that kind of relief typically come during the emergency itself, when emotions are strong, when courts may have too little or inaccurate information, and when courts may well prove particularly reluctant to interfere . . . .

> A damages action, however, is typically brought after the emergency is over, after emotions have cooled, and at a time when more factual information is available. In such circumstances, courts have more time to exercise such judicial virtues as clam reflection and dispassionate application of the law to the facts. We have applied the Constitution to actions taken during periods of

war and national-security emergency. See Boumediene v. Bush, 553 U.S. 723 (2008); Hamdi v. Rumsfeld, 542 U.S. 507 (2004). I should think that the wisdom of permitting courts to consider *Bivens* actions, later granting monetary compensation to those wrong at the time, would follow a fortiori.

Ziglar v. Abbasi is a divided decision rendered by a six-Justice Court in an unusual case with a long and difficult history. Its significance is not altogether clear. That said, two observations seem sound. First, the emphasis on "new context" introduces a new element into the traditional analysis of alternative remedies and special factors counseling hesitation. Those inquiries do not come into play unless a "new context" is found (which apparently will not be difficult). Second, once a "new context" is found, the chances of "extending" *Bivens* seem slim. The Court was explicit in rejecting *Bivens* actions for the claims against the executive officials, though its remand of the claims against the wardens raises at least the possibility that they could eventually be upheld.

3   PRE-*ZIGLAR* DECISIONS AND REACTIONS

Lower court decisions prior to *Ziglar* were unreceptive to *Bivens* actions relating to the "war on terror" or military actions in Iraq, generally on grounds of "special factors counselling hesitation." See, e.g., Vance v. Rumsfeld, 701 F.3d 193 (7th Cir. 2012) (en banc) (rejecting *Bivens* claim by U.S. citizens allegedly tortured in Iraq); Lebron v. Rumsfeld, 670 F.3d 540 (4th Cir. 2012) (rejecting *Bivens* claim by U.S. citizen for detention by the military); Arar v. Ashcroft, 585 F.3d 559 (2nd Cir. 2009) (en banc) (rejecting *Bivens* claim by noncitizens for alleged mistreatment in Syria); Rasul v. Myers, 563 F.3d 527 (D.C. Cir. 2009) (per curiam) (rejecting *Bivens* claim for detention at Guantanamo Bay).

Academic opinion prior to *Ziglar* was more supportive. See, e.g., Stephen I. Vladeck, National Security and *Bivens* After *Iqbal*, 14 Lewis & Clark L. Rev. 255 (2010); George D. Brown, "Counter-Counter-Terrorism via Lawsuit"—The *Bivens* Impasse, 82 S. Calif. L. Rev. 841 (2009); Peter Margulies, Judging Myopia in Hindsight: *Bivens* Actions, National Security Decisions and the Rule of Law, 96 Iowa L. Rev. 195 (2010).

4.   PREVALENCE OF *BIVENS* CLAIMS

Despite the Court's repeated unwillingness to recognize new *Bivens* claims, it has not shown any inclination to overturn its early decisions allowing such claims (including *Bivens* itself). As a result, *Bivens* claims are still very common, especially Fourth Amendments claims brought against federal law enforcement officials and Eighth Amendment claims brought against federal prison officials.

It is important to keep in mind, however, that plaintiffs asserting such claims face a variety of obstacles. For example, federal officials are typically entitled at least to qualified immunity, which means that they cannot be held liable for damages unless they violated clearly established law. (The scope of qualified immunity for state officials is explored in Section 2 of Chapter IX;

the qualified immunity of federal officials is essentially identical.) In addition, the plaintiff must still show that there has been a violation of the constitutional right and meet whatever test the Supreme Court has established for showing such violations, which may require proof of deliberate action or indifference rather than mere negligence. For these and other reasons, although many *Bivens* actions are filed, they are often dismissed.

A statistic that is often recited in the literature is that, between 1971 and 1985, approximately 12,000 *Bivens* actions had been filed, but only 30 of these cases had resulted in judgment for the plaintiff, and a number of those judgments were reversed on appeal. See, e.g., Perry M. Rosen, The *Bivens* Constitutional Tort, An Unfulfilled Promise, 67 N.C. L. Rev. 337, 343–44 (1989). What are the implications of that statistic? That the courts should be less worried about allowing *Bivens* actions? Or that it is not worth the trouble of allowing them in the first place? In any event, this statistic is too pessimistic. A recent empirical study of *Bivens* claims, based on "a detailed study of case dockets over three years in five district courts," finds that "*Bivens* cases are much more successful than has been assumed by the legal community." Alexander A. Reinert, Measuring the Success of *Bivens* Litigation and Its Consequences for the Individual Liability Model, 62 Stan. L. Rev. 809, 813 (2012).

5.   WESTFALL ACT

In 1988, Congress enacted the Federal Employees Liability Reform and Tort Compensation Act, also known as the "Westfall Act." See 28 U.S.C. § 2679. The Act was passed in response to the Supreme Court's decision in Westfall v. Erwin, 484 U.S. 292 (1988), which held that federal employees did not have absolute immunity from state tort claims for conduct within the scope of their employment. The Act provides that the Federal Tort Claims Act provides the exclusive remedy for injuries resulting from the "negligent or wrongful act or omission of any employee of the Government while acting within the scope of his office or employment," and it provides a mechanism for substituting the federal government as the defendant when such cases are brought against individual federal officials. There is an exception in the Act, however, for suits against federal officials "brought for a violation of the Constitution of the United States." In *Minneci*, the Supreme Court suggested that the Act generally precludes state tort actions against federal officials and that the exception for constitutional violations applies only to *Bivens* claims. See also Osborn v. Haley, 549 U.S. 225, 229 (2007) (noting that the Westfall Act "accords federal employees absolute immunity from common-law tort claims arising out of acts they undertake in the course of their official duties").

For consideration of the relationship between *Bivens* and the Westfall Act, see Carlos M. Vázquez and Stephen I. Vladeck, State Law, the Westfall Act, and the Nature of the *Bivens* Question, 161 U. Pa. L. Rev. 509 (2013). The authors argue that the *Bivens* line of cases was premised on the idea that, if a federal cause of action were not allowed for a federal official's violation of the Constitution, a state tort law remedy would still be available. They further contend that the Westfall Act should be understood, contrary to *Minneci*, as preserving state tort claims that seek to remedy a constitutional violation. If the Act is to be interpreted as preempting all state tort claims against federal officials, however, the authors argue that courts should be more receptive to *Bivens* claims than they currently are, given what the authors contend was Congress's intent in the Act to "(a) preserve the remedies available to victims of constitutional violations, (b) leave *Bivens* as it found it, and (c) avoid rather than provoke constitutional problems." For a response arguing that the Supreme Court has correctly construed the Westfall Act as preserving only *Bivens* claims, not state tort claims, see James E. Pfander and David P. Baltmanis, W(h)ither *Bivens?*, 161 U. Pa. L. Rev. PENNumbra 231 (2013). Despite this disagreement, Pfander and Baltmanis agree with Vázquez and Vladeck that courts should be more receptive to *Bivens* claims.

6.   BIBLIOGRAPHY

For a thoughtful argument in favor of the approach of *Bivens*, see Walter E. Dellinger, Of Rights and Remedies: The Constitution as Sword, 85 Harv. L. Rev. 1532 (1972). For the argument that Congress can limit *Bivens* actions, but only if it supplies constitutionally adequate alternative remedies, see Gene R. Nichol, Jr., *Bivens, Chilicky,* and Constitutional Damages Claims, 75 Va. L. Rev. 1117 (1989). Nichol criticizes the "special factors" exception to *Bivens* as inherently unmanageable and destructive of the judicial function and argues that it should be abandoned. For an examination of *Bivens* "in an aspirational sense"—that is, as standing for the principle that judicial enforcement of constitutional rights through money damages should not depend on action (or inaction) by the political branches—see Susan Bandes, Reinventing *Bivens*: The Self-Executing Constitution, 68 So. Calif. L. Rev. 289 (1995). For analysis of these cases and their role in a general conception of federal common law, see George D. Brown, Letting Statutory Tails Wag Constitutional Dogs—Have the *Bivens* Dissenters Prevailed?, 64 Ind. L.J. 263 (1989). For an article criticizing the case-by-case approach of current law and arguing for the presumptive availability of *Bivens* remedies, see James E. Pfander and David Baltmanis, Rethinking *Bivens*: Legitimacy and Constitutional Adjudication, 98 Geo. L.J. 117 (2009). Pfander and Baltmanis pay particular attention to post-*Bivens* legislation, which they interpret as reflecting Congress's desire to preserve and ratify the general availability of *Bivens* actions. Finally, for early commentary on *Minneci*, see Alexander A. Reinert and Lumen N. Mulligan, Asking the First Question: Reframing *Bivens* After *Minneci*, 90 Wash. U. L. Rev. 1473 (2013) (arguing, among other things, that the focus on the adequacy of state-law remedies destroys the long-established parallelism between *Bivens* remedies and § 1983).

SECTION 4. CUSTOMARY INTERNATIONAL LAW AND THE ALIEN TORT STATUTE

INTRODUCTORY NOTES ON CUSTOMARY INTERNATIONAL LAW AND THE ALIEN TORT STATUTE

1. WHAT IS "CUSTOMARY INTERNATIONAL LAW"?

There are two principal sources of international law—treaties and customary international law. Treaties are express agreements among nations. Customary international law, by contrast, is the law that "results from a general and consistent practice of states followed by them from a sense of legal obligation." Restatement (Third) of the Foreign Relations Law of the United States § 102(2) (1987). Historically, customary international law was referred to as part of the "law of nations."

In order for a nation to become bound by a treaty, it must expressly ratify the treaty. Under the U.S. Constitution, ratification of a treaty requires that the President obtain the advice and consent of two-thirds of the Senate. An act of ratification is not required, however, in order for customary international law to develop and become binding. Instead, it arises from a looser body of international practice and opinion, often informed by international agreements or declarations that may not have been adopted as binding by the United States.

Once a rule of customary international law develops, all nations are bound by it unless they persistently objected during the period of its formation. Although exactly what persistent objection entails is unclear, it must include active steps and (at least in the eyes of the international community) it is apparently rare. Increasingly, and importantly, customary international law is concerned not only with relations among states, but also with the relations between states and their own citizens. This new focus on human rights substantially increases the prospect of conflict between customary international law and domestic law.

The United States has resisted the direct incorporation of human rights *treaties* into its domestic law. For a long time, the United States declined to become a party to any of the major human rights treaties. When it eventually began ratifying some of these treaties starting in the late 1980s, it attached declarations stating that the treaty obligations are "non-self-executing," which courts have construed as precluding judicial application of the treaties in the absence of implementing legislation enacted by Congress.

2. "PART OF OUR LAW"

Article VI of the Constitution specifies that three types of law constitute the "the supreme law of the land": the Constitution itself, laws of the United States made in pursuance of the Constitution, and treaties. There is no specific mention of the law of nations in the Supremacy Clause. In fact, the only reference to the law of nations in the Constitution is a grant of power to Congress to "define and punish . . . Offences against the Law of Nations." U.S. Const. art. I, § 8, cl. 10.

In several pre-*Erie* decisions, however, the Supreme Court referred to the law of nations as "part of our law," or part of the "law of the land." The most famous such decision is The Paquete Habana, 175 U.S. 677 (1900). In that case, the U.S. Navy had seized two fishing vessels off the coast of Cuba during the Spanish-American War, and the owners of the vessels argued that the seizure violated the law of nations. The Supreme Court agreed and ordered that the owners be compensated for the seizure. The Court stated that "[i]nternational law is part of our law, and must be ascertained and administered by the courts of justice of appropriate jurisdiction, as often as questions of right depending upon it are duly presented for their determination." The Court also observed that, "where there is no treaty, and no controlling executive or legislative act or judicial decision, resort must be had to the customs and usages of civilized nations."

Most commentators agree that during this period U.S. courts were applying the law of nations as general common law. Indeed, the law merchant applied as general common law in *Swift v. Tyson* was considered in the 19th century to be part of the law of nations. Moreover, before *Erie*, the Supreme Court expressly referred to the law of nations as "general law" or "common law," and it declined in several cases to review state court determinations of the law of nations because the determinations did not raise a federal question. See, e.g., Oliver Am. Trading Co. v. Mexico, 264 U.S. 440, 442–43 (1924); New York Life Ins. Co. v. Hendren, 92 U.S. 286, 286–87 (1875). As general common law, customary international law would have been available to both federal and state courts as a potential rule of decision in cases in which the courts otherwise had jurisdiction and there was no controlling contrary authority. But federal court interpretations of this law would not bind state courts and cases arising under this law would not on that basis arise under federal law for purposes of federal court jurisdiction.

3. THE ALIEN TORT STATUTE

The Alien Tort Statute (ATS), also sometimes called the Alien Tort Claims Act, provides that: "The district courts shall have original jurisdiction of any civil action by an alien for a tort only, committed in violation of the law of nations or a treaty of the United States." 28 U.S.C. § 1350. First enacted as part of the Judiciary Act of 1789, the ATS successfully served as the basis for jurisdiction in only two reported cases before 1980—an admiralty case in the 1790s, and an international child custody case in the 1960s. There is almost no legislative history for the ATS, and its original purposes are uncertain. In 1975, Judge Henry Friendly, an expert on the jurisdiction of the federal courts, described the statute as "a kind of legal Lohengrin; although it has been with us since the first Judiciary Act . . . no one seems to know whence it came." IIT v. Vencap, Ltd., 519 F.2d 1001, 1015 (2d Cir. 1975).

A variety of theories have been proposed about why the First Congress enacted the ATS. One common theory is that the ATS was designed to ensure the availability of a federal forum in certain tort cases in which the United States would have had an obligation under international law to provide an adequate means of redress. Commentators cite to an incident in 1784 involving an assault on a French ambassador in Philadelphia, in which the Continental Congress was concerned that state authorities might not adequately prosecute the case.

For discussion of this and other theories about the original meaning of the ATS, see Anthony J. Bellia Jr. and Bradford R. Clark, The Alien Tort Statute and the Law of Nations, 78 U. Chi. L. Rev. 445 (2011); Curtis A. Bradley, The Alien Tort Statute and Article III, 42 Va. J. Int'l L. 587 (2002); Anne-Marie Burley (Slaughter), The Alien Tort Statute and the Judiciary Act of 1789: A Badge of Honor, 83 Am. J. Int'l L. 461 (1989); William R. Casto, The Federal Courts' Protective Jurisdiction Over Torts Committed in Violation of the Law of Nations, 18 Conn. L. Rev. 467 (1986); William S. Dodge, The Historical Origins of the Alien Tort Statute: A Response to the "Originalists," 19 Hastings Int'l & Comp. L. Rev. 221 (1996); Thomas H. Lee, The Safe Conduct Theory of the Alien Tort Statute, 106 Colum. L. Rev. 830 (2006); John M. Rogers, The Alien Tort Statute and How Individuals "Violate" International Law, 21 Vand. J. Transnat'l L. 47 (1988); Joseph Modeste Sweeney, A Tort Only in Violation of the Law of Nations, 18 Hastings Int'l & Comp. L. Rev. 445 (1995).

4.   *FILARTIGA V. PENA-IRALA*

In 1980, the U.S. Court of Appeals for the Second Circuit issued a seminal decision interpreting the ATS, Filartiga v. Pena-Irala, 630 F.2d 876 (2d Cir. 1980). In that case, two Paraguayan citizens sued a former Paraguayan police inspector under the ATS, alleging that he was responsible for the torture and murder of a family member. In allowing the action to proceed, the Second Circuit reasoned that the terms of the ATS were satisfied because the case was being brought by aliens, the plaintiffs were alleging a tort, and the tort of torture violated the modern law of nations. On the last point, the court explained:

> In light of the universal condemnation of torture in numerous international agreements, and the renunciation of torture as an instrument of official policy by virtually all of the nations of the world (in principle if not in practice), we find that an act of torture committed by a state official against one held in detention violates established norms of the international law of human rights, and hence the law of nations.

The Second Circuit also concluded that the exercise of federal court jurisdiction over this case was consistent with Article III of the Constitution. It has long been established that suits between aliens, even aliens from different countries, do not satisfy even the minimal diversity of citizenship required for purposes of Article III diversity jurisdiction. See Mossman v. Higginson, 4 U.S. (4 Dall.) 12, 14 (1800). In *Filartiga*, both the plaintiffs and the defendant were citizens of Paraguay, so Article III diversity jurisdiction was not available. The court in *Filartiga* concluded, however, that the case properly fell within Article III federal question jurisdiction because the law of nations had the status of federal common law.

For purposes of its decision, the Second Circuit assumed for the sake of argument that the ATS was merely jurisdictional and did not itself confer a private cause of action. It therefore left the source of the cause of action to be determined on remand. Some lower courts after *Filartiga*, however, construed the ATS as implicitly creating a cause of action for damages.

In 1992, Congress enacted the Torture Victim Protection Act (TVPA) and added it as a note to the ATS. The TVPA creates a cause of action for claims of torture and "extrajudicial killing" committed under color of foreign law, subject to certain limitations. In addition to providing a clear statutory basis for a cause of action for these two torts, the TVPA eliminates the Article III issue for cases that fall within its terms, because these cases arise under federal statutory law.

5.   CUSTOMARY INTERNATIONAL LAW AS FEDERAL COMMON LAW

The Restatement (Third) of the Foreign Relations Law of the United States (1987) declares, without qualification, that customary international law is federal common law, and that as such, "it supersedes inconsistent State law or policy whether adopted earlier or later." Numerous scholars similarly have taken the position that customary international law has the status of federal common law, and several lower courts, including the court in *Filartiga*, have endorsed this proposition for purposes of establishing federal court jurisdiction.

In addition to citing pre-*Erie* decisions such as *The Paquete Habana*, these scholars and courts often rely on Banco Nacional de Cuba v. Sabbatino, 376 U.S. 398 (1964). As noted above in Section 1 of this chapter, in *Sabbatino* the Cuban government was suing to recover the proceeds from the sale of a shipment of sugar made from a company that the Cuban government had expropriated in Cuba after Fidel Castro assumed power. The issue was whether Cuba should be barred from recovering the proceeds because of the illegality of its expropriation under customary international law. In an opinion by Justice Harlan, the Court held that Cuba's claim was not barred because, under the "act of state doctrine," U.S. courts are required to assume the validity of foreign government acts taken within their own territory. The Court explained that this doctrine is based on considerations of separation of powers relating to the Executive's role in conducting foreign affairs, and it made clear that the doctrine had the status of federal common law and thus was binding on state courts. The Court stated:

> [W]e are constrained to make it clear that an issue concerned with a basic choice regarding the competence and function of the Judiciary and the National Executive in ordering our relationships with other members of the international community must be treated exclusively as an aspect of federal law. It seems fair to assume that the Court did not have rules like the act of state doctrine in mind when it decided *Erie R. Co. v. Tompkins*. Soon thereafter, Professor Philip C. Jessup, now a judge of the International Court

of Justice, recognized the potential dangers were *Erie* extended to legal problems affecting international relations.[24] He cautioned that rules of international law should not be left to divergent and perhaps parochial state interpretations. His basic rationale is equally applicable to the act of state doctrine.

Justice White dissented. Quoting *The Paquete Habana*, he observed that customary international law is "part of our law," and he argued that the Court should have applied it to decide the merits of the case. He expressed "dismay[ ] that the Court has, with one broad stroke, declared the ascertainment and application of international law beyond the competence of the courts of the United States in a large and important category of cases."

Ironically, this decision, which declined to apply customary international law, is now cited for the proposition that customary international law is directly incorporated into the U.S. legal system as federal common law. How might it be used to support that claim? Proponents of this position emphasize, among other things, the Court's favorable citation to the essay by Philip Jessup. In that essay, Jessup had observed with concern that if *Erie* were "applied broadly, it would follow that hereafter a state court's determination of a rule of international law would be a finding regarding the law of the state and would not be reviewed by the Supreme Court of the United States." Jessup argued against this construction of *Erie*, reasoning that the Court in *Erie* was not thinking of international law and that it "would be as unsound as it would be unwise" to bind federal courts to state court interpretations of international law.

6.   BRADLEY AND GOLDSMITH: THE ATTACK ON CONVENTIONAL WISDOM

Today, the domestic status of customary international law is a subject of much academic dispute. The conventional wisdom about the domestic status of customary international law was challenged by Curtis A. Bradley and Jack L. Goldsmith, Customary International Law as Federal Common Law: A Critique of the Modern Position, 110 Harv. L. Rev. 815 (1997). Bradley and Goldsmith criticized *Filartiga*, the Restatement (Third), and the scholarly consensus in favor of the automatic domestic enforceability of customary international law, which they termed the "modern position." They explored at length the rapid expansion of customary international law (which they abbreviated as "CIL") into the area of human rights, where relations between states and their own citizens might be called into question. The foundation of their position, however, had less to do with the changing content of customary international law than with its uncertain relation to the powers of the federal courts:

> Courts and scholars generally agree that federal common law must be authorized in some fashion by the Constitution or by a federal statute. This principle flows from *Erie*'s requirement that all law applied by federal courts must derive from a domestic sovereign

---

[24]   The Doctrine of *Erie Railroad v. Tompkins* Applied to International Law, 33 Am. J. Int'l L. 740 (1939).

source. It is precisely the grounding of federal common lawmaking in a *federal* sovereign source that makes the new federal common law, unlike the pre-*Erie* general common law, binding on the states.

Is there domestic federal authorization for federal courts to interpret and apply CIL as federal law in the wholesale fashion contemplated by the modern position? Nothing on the face of the Constitution or any federal statute authorizes such a practice. Article III of the Constitution does not even list CIL as a basis for the exercise of federal judicial power, much less authorize federal courts to incorporate CIL wholesale into federal law. Nor does Article VI list CIL as a source of supreme federal law. Article I does authorize Congress to define and punish offenses against the law of nations, and Congress has exercised this and related powers to incorporate selected CIL principles into federal statutes. But Congress has never purported to incorporate all of CIL into federal law. . . .

Bradley and Goldsmith do not dispute that some doctrines of federal common law will justifiably be created by the federal courts to protect uniquely federal interests in foreign relations, but they object to the wholesale incorporation of *all* customary international law into federal law. Not only is wholesale incorporation inconsistent with the interstitial tradition of the common law, but also, and more fundamentally, it is at odds with the law-making powers of the federal courts. "If, according to the modern position, federal courts must apply whatever CIL requires," Bradley and Goldsmith reason, "then it is illogical also to assert that they exercise the political or legal authority that transforms CIL into federal law." In other words, federal courts cannot logically be bound by the entirety of customary international law if it becomes federal law only when specifically found to be necessary to protect federal interests.

Bradley and Goldsmith also attack the wholesale incorporation of customary international law into federal common law as "in tension with basic notions of American representative democracy. When a federal court applies customary international law as federal common law, it is not applying law generated by U.S. lawmaking processes. Rather, it is applying law derived from the views and practices of the international community." The tension is especially great when customary international law embraces a position that the United States government has expressly declined to ratify or adopt in its treaties.

Finally, Bradley and Goldsmith noted (with apparent reservation) the prominent role of academics in explaining and propounding customary international law. "Because of their relative unfamiliarity with international law and because of the special difficulties associated with determining international law rules, judges tend to be heavily influenced by academic sources in this context." Amicus curiae briefs and expert testimony become vehicles for academic participation in defining the legal obligations to be enforced in United States courts. In sum, Bradley and Goldsmith found "substantial reasons" to question the incorporation of customary international law into federal common law.

7.   THE KOH RESPONSE

The academic reaction to Bradley and Goldsmith was swift and hostile. Perhaps the most prominent response was Harold Hongju Koh, Is International Law Really State Law?, 111 Harv. L. Rev. 1824 (1998).[a] Koh was unpersuaded by the arguments against CIL's status as federal common law, and strongly defended *Filartiga*, which he had previously dubbed the "*Brown v. Board of Education*" of "transnational public law litiga[tion]." Harold Hongju Koh, Transnational Public Law Litigation, 100 Yale L.J. 2347, 2366 (1991).

In particular, Koh asked: If customary international law is not federal common law, what is it? One possibility was state law, but Koh could see no reason "why fifty state courts and legislatures should be free to reject, modify, reinterpret, incorporate or completely oust customary international law rules from domestic law." Koh emphasized the "distinct federal interest in foreign relations," and argued that reliance on *Erie* was misplaced. *Erie* required that "state law be the governing substantive law in diversity cases," because otherwise federal judge-made law might sweep beyond the authority of the federal legislature:

> But with respect to international and foreign affairs law, the Constitution envisions no similar role for state [law]. Federal judicial determination of most questions of customary international law transpires not in a zone of core state concerns, such as state tort law, but in a foreign affairs area in which the Tenth Amendment has reserved little or no power to the states.

111 Harv. L. Rev. at 1831.

Most alarming of all to Koh was the possibility that neither the federal nor state political branches would adopt customary international law. This prospect revealed the Bradley-Goldsmith position as "even more radical than it first appears. For if customary international law is neither federal nor state law (unless specifically incorporated by the state or federal political branches), then in most cases, customary international law is not United States law at all!" That customary international law might not, in itself, provide a rule of decision for U.S. courts seemed to Koh unthinkable.

8.   THE BRADLEY-GOLDSMITH REJOINDER

Nothing so clearly reveals the gap between these positions as the Bradley-Goldsmith rejoinder to Koh's last point. They cheerfully accepted the consequence that Koh found devastating:

> The title of Koh's article is somewhat misleading, for we have not in fact argued that CIL is state law. Rather . . . our view is that CIL should not be a source of law for courts in the United States unless the appropriate sovereign—the federal political branches or

---

[a]   See also Ryan Goodman and Derek P. Jinks, *Filartiga*'s Firm Footing: International Human Rights and Federal Common Law, 66 Fordham L. Rev. 463 (1997); Gerald L. Neuman, Sense and Nonsense about Customary International Law: A Response to Professors Bradley and Goldsmith, 66 Fordham L. Rev. 371 (1997); Beth Stephens, The Law of Our Land: Customary International Law as Federal Law after *Erie*, 66 Fordham L. Rev. 393 (1997).

the appropriate state entity—makes it so. If accepted, this argument would mean, as Koh states emphatically, that CIL in some instances "[would not be] United States law at all!"

Curtis A. Bradley and Jack L. Goldsmith, Federal Courts and the Incorporation of International Law, 111 Harv. L. Rev. 2260, 2260 (1998).

That Bradley and Goldsmith did not find this possibility bizarre or threatening reflects their nationalist (for want of a better term) approach to sovereignty. When the political branches of the national and state governments have not authorized the incorporation of customary international law—and especially when they have expressly precluded it—then it should not apply of its own force in the courts of the United States. Of course, federal courts would remain free to find that specific propositions approved by customary international law (having to do, for example, with amenability of heads of state to service of process) were part of the federal common law, and state courts would be free, according to the laws of the states, to incorporate customary international law in appropriate cases as state common law. But some action and decision by a sovereign source—a federal or state legislature or a federal or state court—would be required beyond simply a finding that a particular legal proposition was a part of customary international law.

9.   THE JUVENILE DEATH PENALTY

One illustration of the potential practical implications of the wholesale incorporation of customary international law into federal common law is the juvenile death penalty debate. Prior to 2005, more than 20 states in the United States permitted imposition of the death penalty on offenders who were under the age of 18 at the time of their offense. The United States came under increasing political and legal pressure from the international community to change this practice. International treaties, the International Covenant on Civil and Political Rights (ICCPR), Dec. 19, 1966, 999 U.N.T.S. 175, and the Convention on the Rights of the Child (CRC), Nov. 20, 1989, 28 I.L.M. 1448, specifically prohibited the juvenile death penalty. The United States ratified the ICCPR in 1992, but attached a reservation declining to accept the prohibition on the juvenile death penalty. The United States has not ratified the CRC, though almost every other nation has. Some scholars argued that these treaties conclusively demonstrated that the juvenile death penalty is a violation of customary international law.

As noted above, if customary international law is really federal common law, then it would be expected to preempt inconsistent state law. Under this view, if the juvenile death penalty is a violation of customary international law, then state statutes authorizing the death penalty for juveniles would be preempted. Critics challenged this conclusion on several grounds. One argument rejected the conclusion that the juvenile death penalty is a violation of customary international law. Another challenged CIL's status as federal common law.

In addition to the general arguments summarized above, the juvenile death penalty raised other specific concerns of separation of powers and federalism. First, the political branches, in their failure to ratify or sign international treaties prohibiting the juvenile death penalty, clearly indicated their stance on the issue. If the judicial branch were to apply an international norm as federal law in the face of contrary action by the political branches, it would raise separation-of-powers concerns. Second, criminal punishment traditionally has been regarded as belonging in a sphere of state authority that federal law is not readily interpreted to preempt. Even if Congress has the constitutional authority to preempt the states in this arena, judicial action having that effect—especially given the stance of the political branches on the question—would raise federalism as well as separation-of-powers concerns.

The issue is now moot. In Thompson v. Oklahoma, 487 U.S. 815 (1988), a plurality of four Justices held that offenders under the age of 16 at the time of the offense could not be executed. The next year, in Stanford v. Kentucky, 492 U.S. 361 (1989), the Court held five-to-four that the Eighth Amendment did not forbid the execution of juvenile offenders who were over 15 but under 18. The majority was clear in emphasizing that "it is *American* conceptions of decency that are dispositive" to the Eighth Amendment inquiry. The dissenters disagreed with the result, but like the majority did not address the argument that the juvenile death penalty was a violation of customary international law that preempted state law. Subsequent lower-court and state-court decisions addressed the customary international law argument, at least nominally,[b] but consistently rejected the argument, often relying heavily on *Stanford*. Scholars were particularly critical of this reliance. Not only did *Stanford* plainly not address the customary international law argument, but it was decided in 1989, before the international developments such as the ICCPR and CRC upon which human rights advocates relied.

The Supreme Court put the matter to rest in Roper v. Simmons, 543 U.S. 551 (2005). Justice Kennedy, a dissenter in *Stanford*, changed his mind and joined four other Justices to hold that "the death penalty is disproportionate punishment for offenders under 18" at the time of their offense.[c] Justice Kennedy discussed the international consensus at some length, saying that it was "instructive" but not controlling:

> Our determination that the death penalty is disproportionate punishment for offenders under 18 finds confirmation in the stark reality that the United States is the only country in the world that continues to give official sanction to the juvenile death penalty. This reality does not become controlling, for the task of interpreting the Eighth Amendment remains our responsibility. . . . [Yet it] is proper that we acknowledge the overwhelming weight of international opinion against the juvenile death penalty. . . .

---

[b]   The most notable case in this regard is Domingues v. Nevada, 114 Nev. 783 (1998). See also Ex parte Pressley, 770 So.2d 143 (Ala. 2000). But see Servin v. State, 117 Nev. 775 (2001) (citing the customary international law argument against the juvenile death penalty in dicta as an additional reason for vacating the defendant's death sentence).

[c]   Two new Justices had been appointed to the Court since *Stanford*, but they divided one-to-one on the issue as had their predecessors. Justice Thomas had replaced Justice Marshall and Justice Ginsburg had replaced Justice White.

Joined by Chief Justice Rehnquist and Justice Thomas, Justice Scalia's dissent objected strongly to the Court's reference to international opinion.[d]

10. CUSTOMARY INTERNATIONAL LAW AS POST-*ERIE* GENERAL COMMON LAW?

As mentioned in Note 2, most commentators now agree that, before *Erie*, customary international law was treated by the courts as part of the general common law. Some commentators have argued that, despite *Erie*'s announcement that "[t]here is no federal general common law," customary international law should continue to be treated by courts today as general common law. Ernest Young argues, for example, that customary international law "should be viewed as 'general' law, just as it was in the nineteenth century under *Swift v. Tyson*," and that federal courts should apply it like they apply foreign law, based on conflict of laws principles. See Ernest A. Young, Sorting Out the Debate over Customary International Law, 42 Va. J. Int'l L. 365, 467–68 (2002). Similarly, Alex Aleinikoff contends that customary international law should be considered "nonpreemptive, nonfederal law," such that "[a] federal court decision on [customary international law] would not bind states; it would simply announce the rule for the federal branches." T. Alexander Aleinikoff, International Law, Sovereignty, and American Constitutionalism: Reflections on the Customary International Law Debate, 98 Am. J. Int'l L. 91, 97 (2004). See also A. M. Weisburd, State Courts, Federal Courts, and International Cases, 20 Yale J. Int'l L. 1, 48–49 (1995). Compare Lea Brilmayer, Untethered Norms After *Erie Railroad Co. v. Tompkins*: Positivism, International Law, and the Return of the "Brooding Omnipresence," 54 Wm. & Mary L. Rev. 725 (2013) (suggesting that judicial application of customary international law may call into question *Erie*'s purported disallowance of general common law).

What would the implications be of adopting this conception of the domestic status of customary international law? Would the federal courts have the constitutional authority to exercise jurisdiction over a case like *Filartiga* involving a suit between foreign citizens for a violation of customary international law?

11. BIBLIOGRAPHY

Prior to the Bradley-Goldsmith and Koh debate, several scholars had written on the status of customary international law as federal law. A prominent early article is Louis Henkin, International Law as Law in the United States, 82 Mich. L. Rev. 1555 (1984), which argues that customary international law is "like" federal common law. According to Henkin, customary international law is different from other federal common law in that "federal courts find international law rather than make it . . . as is clearly not the case when federal judges make federal common law pursuant to constitutional or legislative delegation." For the view that customary international law has full preemptive effect on state law, see Lea Brilmayer, Federalism,

---

[d]   Justice O'Connor dissented separately.

State Authority, and the Preemptive Power of International Law, 1994 Sup. Ct. Rev. 295.

On the other side of the debate, see Philip R. Trimble, A Revisionist View of Customary International Law, 33 U.C.L.A. L. Rev. 665, 695 (1986), which argues that the courts have not applied and should not apply customary international law as a rule of decision in the United States absent "political branch intercession." For the view that customary international law should be treated as neither state nor federal law, but instead as a separate body of law analogous to the law of a foreign sovereign with application governed by conflict-of-laws principles, see A. M. Weisburd, State Courts, Federal Courts, and International Cases, 20 Yale J. Int'l L. 1 (1995).

For yet another perspective on the debate over the domestic status of customary international law, see Anthony J. Bellia Jr. and Bradford R. Clark, The Federal Common Law of Nations, 109 Colum. L. Rev. 1 (2009). Bellia and Clark posit an "allocation of powers approach" to the status of customary international law in the U.S. legal system. They explain that, throughout much of U.S. history, the Supreme Court enforced other nations' "perfect rights" under customary international law (and close analogues to those rights), covering topics related to territorial sovereignty, the conduct of diplomatic relations, treaty obligations, and freedom on the seas. They further explain that the breach of such rights was historically a just cause for war, and they argue that the Court enforced them in order to ensure that the decision to commit the United States to war would rest exclusively with the federal political branches, not the judiciary or the states. By their account, the Court applied customary international law not because it was viewed as inherently part of federal law, but rather because its application in these contexts was thought to be required by the Constitution's allocation of powers to Congress and the executive branch. When viewed in historical context, they contend, "the best reading of Supreme Court precedent . . . is that the law of nations does not apply as preemptive federal law by virtue of any general Article III power to fashion federal common law, but only when necessary to preserve and implement distinct Article I and Article II powers to recognize foreign nations, conduct foreign relations, and decide momentous questions of war and peace." For elaboration of their views, see Anthony J. Bellia Jr. and Bradford R. Clark, The Law of Nations and the United States Constitution (2017).

For a recent defense of a broad role for CIL as federal common law, see Carlos M. Vázquez, Customary International Law as U.S. Law: A Critique of the Revisionist and Intermediate Positions and a Defense of the Modern Position, 86 Notre Dame L. Rev. 1495 (2011). Vázquez contends that "[t]he basic case for the modern position relies on an inference from the constitutional structure very similar to the one advanced by Bellia and Clark: Violations of customary international law risk retaliation against the nation as a whole. Permitting States to violate it allows States to externalize the costs of such violations, thus likely producing excessive violations." For a more critical assessment contending that "the repudiation of general federal common law in *Erie* pushed courts (on the urging of prominent commentators) to see cases involving foreign states as governed by a special (and preemptive) federal common law of foreign affairs, which was then extended to cover international human rights claims," see Jeremy Rabkin, Off the Track or Just Down the Line? From *Erie Railroad* to Global Governance, 10 J.L. Econ. & Pol'y 251 (2013).

Sosa v. Alvarez-Machain

Supreme Court of the United States, 2004.
542 U.S. 692.

■ JUSTICE SOUTER delivered the opinion of the Court. . . .

I

We have considered the underlying facts before, United States v. Alvarez-Machain, 504 U.S. 655 (1992). In 1985, an agent of the Drug Enforcement Administration (DEA), Enrique Camarena-Salazar, was captured on assignment in Mexico and taken to a house in Guadalajara, where he was tortured over the course of a two-day interrogation, then murdered. Based in part on eyewitness testimony, DEA officials in the United States came to believe that respondent Humberto Alvarez-Machain (Alvarez), a Mexican physician, was present at the house and acted to prolong the agent's life in order to extend the interrogation and torture.

In 1990, a federal grand jury indicted Alvarez for the torture and murder of Camarena-Salazar, and the United States District Court for the Central District of California issued a warrant for his arrest. The DEA asked the Mexican Government for help in getting Alvarez into the United States, but when the requests and negotiations proved fruitless, the DEA approved a plan to hire Mexican nationals to seize Alvarez and bring him to the United States for trial. As so planned, a group of Mexicans, including petitioner Jose Francisco Sosa, abducted Alvarez from his house, held him overnight in a motel, and brought him by private plane to El Paso, Texas, where he was arrested by federal officers.

Once in American custody, Alvarez moved to dismiss the indictment on the ground that his seizure was "outrageous governmental conduct," *Alvarez-Machain,* 504 U.S. at 658, and violated the extradition treaty between the United States and Mexico. The District Court agreed, the Ninth Circuit affirmed, and we reversed, holding that the fact of Alvarez's forcible seizure did not affect the jurisdiction of a federal court. The case was tried in 1992, and ended at the close of the Government's case, when the District Court granted Alvarez's motion for a judgment of acquittal.

In 1993, after returning to Mexico, Alvarez began the civil action before us here. He sued Sosa, Mexican citizen and DEA operative Antonio Garate-Bustamante, five unnamed Mexican civilians, the United States, and four DEA agents. So far as it matters here, Alvarez sought damages from the United States under the [Federal Tort Claims Act (FTCA)], alleging false arrest, and from Sosa under the ATS, for a violation of the law of nations. The former statute authorizes suit "for . . . personal injury

. . . caused by the negligent or wrongful act or omission of any employee of the Government while acting within the scope of his office or employ-ment." 28 U.S.C. § 1346(b)(1). The latter provides in its entirety that "the district courts shall have original jurisdiction of any civil action by an alien for a tort only, committed in violation of the law of nations or a treaty of the United States." § 1350.

The District Court granted the Government's motion to dismiss the FTCA claim, but awarded summary judgment and $25,000 in damages to Alvarez on the ATS claim. A three-judge panel of the Ninth Circuit then affirmed the ATS judgment, but reversed the dismissal of the FTCA claim.

A divided en banc court came to the same conclusion. As for the ATS claim, the court called on its own precedent, "that [the ATS] not only pro-vides federal courts with subject matter jurisdiction, but also creates a cause of action for an alleged violation of the law of nations." The Circuit then relied upon what it called the "clear and universally recognized norm prohibiting arbitrary arrest and detention," to support the conclu-sion that Alvarez's arrest amounted to a tort in violation of international law. On the FTCA claim, the Ninth Circuit held that, because "the DEA had no authority to effect Alvarez's arrest and detention in Mexico," the United States was liable to him under California law for the tort of false arrest.

We granted certiorari . . . and . . . now reverse. . . .

II

[The Court reversed the judgment of liability under the FTCA on the ground that the statute excepts from its waiver of sovereign immunity claims "arising in a foreign country." 28 U.S.C. § 2680(k). The Court found that exception applicable to this case. Though the Justices were unanimous in this conclusion, Justice Ginsburg, joined by Justice Breyer, offered a somewhat different analysis in a concurrence in the result on the FTCA issue.]

III

Alvarez has also brought an action under the ATS against petitioner, Sosa, who argues (as does the United States supporting him) that there is no relief under the ATS because the statute does no more than vest federal courts with jurisdiction, neither creating nor authorizing the courts to recognize any particular right of action without further congres-sional action. Although we agree the statute is in terms only jurisdictional, we think that at the time of enactment the jurisdiction en-abled federal courts to hear claims in a very limited category defined by the law of nations and recognized at common law. We do not believe, however, that the limited, implicit sanction to entertain the handful of international law cum common law claims understood in 1789 should be taken as authority to recognize the right of action asserted by Alvarez here. . . .

The first Congress passed [the ATS] as part of the Judiciary Act of 1789, in providing that the new federal district courts "shall also have cognizance, concurrent with the courts of the several States, or the circuit courts, as the case may be, of all causes where an alien sues for a tort only in violation of the law of nations or a treaty of the United States."[6]

The parties and amici here advance radically different historical interpretations of this terse provision. Alvarez says that the ATS was intended not simply as a jurisdictional grant, but as authority for the creation of a new cause of action for torts in violation of international law. We think that reading is implausible. As enacted in 1789, the ATS gave the district courts "cognizance" of certain causes of action, and the term bespoke a grant of jurisdiction, not power to mold substantive law. The fact that the ATS was placed in § 9 of the Judiciary Act, a statute otherwise exclusively concerned with federal-court jurisdiction, is itself support for its strictly jurisdictional nature. . . . In sum, we think the statute was intended as jurisdictional in the sense of addressing the power of the courts to entertain cases concerned with a certain subject.

But holding the ATS jurisdictional raises a new question, this one about the interaction between the ATS at the time of its enactment and the ambient law of the era. Sosa would have it that the ATS was stillborn because there could be no claim for relief without a further statute expressly authorizing adoption of causes of action. Amici professors of federal jurisdiction and legal history take a different tack, that federal courts could entertain claims once the jurisdictional grant was on the books, because torts in violation of the law of nations would have been recognized within the common law of the time. Brief for Vikram Amar et al. as Amici Curiae. We think history and practice give the edge to this latter position.

"When the United States declared their independence, they were bound to receive the law of nations, in its modern state of purity and refinement." Ware v. Hylton, 3 U.S. (3 Dall.) 199, 281 (1796) (Wilson, J.). In the years of the early Republic, this law of nations comprised two principal elements, the first covering the general norms governing the behavior of national states with each other. . . . This aspect of the law of nations thus occupied the executive and legislative domains, not the judicial. See 4 W. Blackstone, Commentaries on the Laws of England 68 (1769) (hereinafter Commentaries) ("Offenses against" the law of nations are "principally incident to whole states or nations").

The law of nations included a second, more pedestrian element, however, that did fall within the judicial sphere, as a body of judge-made law regulating the conduct of individuals situated outside domestic boundaries and consequently carrying an international savor. To Blackstone, the

---

6   The statute has been slightly modified on a number of occasions since its original enactment. It now reads in its entirety: "The district courts shall have original jurisdiction of any civil action by an alien for a tort only, committed in violation of the law of nations or a treaty of the United States." 28 U.S.C. § 1350.

law of nations in this sense was implicated "in mercantile questions, such as bills of exchange and the like; in all marine causes, relating to freight, average, demurrage, insurances, bottomry . . . ; [and] in all disputes relating to prizes, to shipwrecks, to hostages, and ransom bills." Id. at 67. The law merchant [that] emerged from the customary practices of international traders and admiralty required its own transnational regulation. . . .

There was, finally, a sphere in which these rules binding individuals for the benefit of other individuals overlapped with the norms of state relationships. Blackstone referred to it when he mentioned three specific offenses against the law of nations addressed by the criminal law of England: violation of safe conducts, infringement of the rights of ambassadors, and piracy. 4 Commentaries 68. An assault against an ambassador, for example, impinged upon the sovereignty of the foreign nation and if not adequately redressed could rise to an issue of war. It was this narrow set of violations of the law of nations, admitting of a judicial remedy and at the same time threatening serious consequences in international affairs, that was probably on minds of the men who drafted the ATS with its reference to tort.

Before there was any ATS, a distinctly American preoccupation with these hybrid international norms had taken shape owing to the distribution of political power from independence through the period of confederation. The Continental Congress was hamstrung by its inability to "cause infractions of treaties, or of the law of nations to be punished," J. Madison, Journal of the Constitutional Convention 60 (E. Scott ed. 1893). . . . The Framers responded by vesting the Supreme Court with original jurisdiction over "all Cases affecting Ambassadors, other public ministers and Consuls," U.S. Const., Art. III, § 2, and the First Congress followed through. The Judiciary Act reinforced this Court's original jurisdiction over suits brought by diplomats, see § 13, created alienage jurisdiction, § 11 and, of course, included the ATS, § 9.

. . . There is no record of congressional discussion about private actions that might be subject to the jurisdictional provision, or about any need for further legislation to create private remedies; there is no record even of debate on the section. . . . [D]espite considerable scholarly attention, it is fair to say that a consensus understanding of what Congress intended has proven elusive.

Still, the history does tend to support two propositions. First, there is every reason to suppose that the First Congress did not pass the ATS as a jurisdictional convenience to be placed on the shelf for use by a future Congress or state legislature that might, some day, authorize the creation of causes of action or itself decide to make some element of the law of nations actionable for the benefit of foreigners. The anxieties of the preconstitutional period cannot be ignored easily enough to think that the statute was not meant to have a practical effect. . . .

2/2

The second inference to be drawn from the history is that Congress intended the ATS to furnish jurisdiction for a relatively modest set of actions alleging violations of the law of nations. Uppermost in the legislative mind appears to have been offenses against ambassadors, violations of safe conduct were probably understood to be actionable, and individual actions arising out of prize captures and piracy may well have also been contemplated. But the common law appears to have understood only those three of the hybrid variety as definite and actionable, or at any rate, to have assumed only a very limited set of claims. As Blackstone had put it, "offences against this law [of nations] are principally incident to whole states or nations," and not individuals seeking relief in court. 4 Commentaries 68. . . .

In sum, although the ATS is a jurisdictional statute creating no new causes of action, the reasonable inference from the historical materials is that the statute was intended to have practical effect the moment it became law. The jurisdictional grant is best read as having been enacted on the understanding that the common law would provide a cause of action for the modest number of international law violations with a potential for personal liability at the time.

What court thinks the ATS means

IV

We think it is correct, then, to assume that the First Congress understood that the district courts would recognize private causes of action for certain torts in violation of the law of nations, though we have found no basis to suspect Congress had any examples in mind beyond those torts corresponding to Blackstone's three primary offenses: violation of safe conducts, infringement of the rights of ambassadors, and piracy. We assume, too, that no development in the two centuries from the enactment of § 1350 to the birth of the modern line of cases beginning with Filartiga v. Pena-Irala, 630 F.2d 876 (2d Cir. 1980), has categorically precluded federal courts from recognizing a claim under the law of nations as an element of common law; Congress has not in any relevant way amended § 1350 or limited civil common law power by another statute. Still, there are good reasons for a restrained conception of the discretion a federal court should exercise in considering a new cause of action of this kind. Accordingly, we think courts should require any claim based on the present-day law of nations to rest on a norm of international character accepted by the civilized world and defined with a specificity comparable to the features of the 18th-century paradigms we have recognized. This requirement is fatal to Alvarez's claim.

Limited causes of action

A

A series of reasons argue for judicial caution when considering the kinds of individual claims that might implement the jurisdiction conferred by the early statute. First, the prevailing conception of the common law has changed since 1789 in a way that counsels restraint in judicially applying internationally generated norms. When § 1350 was enacted, the accepted conception was of the common law as "a transcendental

Why there needs to be caution when looking at individual claims

body of law outside of any particular State but obligatory within it unless and until changed by statute." Black and White Taxicab & Transfer Co. v. Brown and Yellow Taxicab & Transfer Co., 276 U.S. 518, 533 (1928) (Holmes, J., dissenting). Now, however, in most cases where a court is asked to state or formulate a common law principle in a new context, there is a general understanding that the law is not so much found or discovered as it is either made or created. . . . [A] judge deciding in reliance on an international norm will find a substantial element of discretionary judgment in the decision.

Second, along with, and in part driven by, that conceptual development in understanding common law has come an equally significant rethinking of the role of the federal courts in making it. Erie R. Co. v. Tompkins, 304 U.S. 64 (1938), was the watershed in which we denied the existence of any federal "general" common law, which largely withdrew to havens of specialty, some of them defined by express congressional authorization to devise a body of law directly. e.g., Textile Workers v. Lincoln Mills of Ala., 353 U.S. 448 (1957) (interpretation of collective-bargaining agreements). Elsewhere, this Court has thought it was in order to create federal common law rules in interstitial areas of particular federal interest. And although we have even assumed competence to make judicial rules of decision of particular importance to foreign relations, such as the act of state doctrine, see Banco Nacional de Cuba v. Sabbatino, 376 U.S. 398, 427 (1964), the general practice has been to look for legislative guidance before exercising innovative authority over substantive law. It would be remarkable to take a more aggressive role in exercising a jurisdiction that remained largely in shadow for much of the prior two centuries.

Third, this Court has recently and repeatedly said that a decision to create a private right of action is one better left to legislative judgment in the great majority of cases. Correctional Services Corp. v. Malesko, 534 U.S. 61, 68 (2001); Alexander v. Sandoval, 532 U.S. 275, 286–87 (2001). The creation of a private right of action raises issues beyond the mere consideration whether underlying primary conduct should be allowed or not, entailing, for example, a decision to permit enforcement without the check imposed by prosecutorial discretion. Accordingly, even when Congress has made it clear by statute that a rule applies to purely domestic conduct, we are reluctant to infer intent to provide a private cause of action where the statute does not supply one expressly. While the absence of congressional action addressing private rights of action under an international norm is more equivocal than its failure to provide such a right when it creates a statute, the possible collateral consequences of making international rules privately actionable argue for judicial caution.

Fourth, the subject of those collateral consequences is itself a reason for a high bar to new private causes of action for violating international law, for the potential implications for the foreign relations of the United

States of recognizing such causes should make courts particularly wary of impinging on the discretion of the Legislative and Executive Branches in managing foreign affairs. It is one thing for American courts to enforce constitutional limits on our own State and Federal Governments' power, but quite another to consider suits under rules that would go so far as to claim a limit on the power of foreign governments over their own citizens, and to hold that a foreign government or its agent has transgressed those limits. Yet modern international law is very much concerned with just such questions, and apt to stimulate calls for vindicating private interests in § 1350 cases. Since many attempts by federal courts to craft remedies for the violation of new norms of international law would raise risks of adverse foreign policy consequences, they should be undertaken, if at all, with great caution.

The fifth reason is particularly important in light of the first four. We have no congressional mandate to seek out and define new and debatable violations of the law of nations, and modern indications of congressional understanding of the judicial role in the field have not affirmatively encouraged greater judicial creativity. It is true that a clear mandate appears in the Torture Victim Protection Act of 1991, providing authority that "establishes an unambiguous and modern basis for" federal claims of torture and extrajudicial killing, H. R. Rep. No. 102–367, pt. 1, p. 3 (1991). But that affirmative authority is confined to specific subject matter, and although the legislative history includes the remark that § 1350 should "remain intact to permit suits based on other norms that already exist or may ripen in the future into rules of customary international law," Congress as a body has done nothing to promote such suits. Several times, indeed, the Senate has expressly declined to give the federal courts the task of interpreting and applying international human rights law, as when its ratification of the International Covenant on Civil and Political Rights declared that the substantive provisions of the document were not self-executing. 138 Cong. Rec. 8071 (1992).

B

These reasons argue for great caution in adapting the law of nations to private rights. Justice Scalia concludes that caution is too hospitable, and a word is in order to summarize where we have come so far and to focus our difference with him on whether some norms of today's law of nations may ever be recognized legitimately by federal courts in the absence of congressional action beyond § 1350. All Members of the Court agree that § 1350 is only jurisdictional. We also agree, or at least Justice Scalia does not dispute, that the jurisdiction was originally understood to be available to enforce a small number of international norms that a federal court could properly recognize as within the common law enforceable without further statutory authority. Justice Scalia concludes, however, that two subsequent developments should be understood to preclude federal courts from recognizing any further international norms as judicially enforceable today, absent further congressional action. As described before, we now tend to understand common law not as a discoverable reflection of universal reason but, in a positivistic way, as a product of human choice. And we now adhere to a conception of limited judicial power first expressed in reorienting federal diversity jurisdiction, see *Erie R. Co. v. Tompkins*, that federal courts have no authority to derive "general" common law.

Whereas Justice Scalia sees these developments as sufficient to close the door to further independent judicial recognition of actionable international norms, other considerations persuade us that the judicial power should be exercised on the understanding that the door is still ajar subject to vigilant doorkeeping, and thus open to a narrow class of international norms today. *Erie* did not in terms bar any judicial recognition of new substantive rules, no matter what the circumstances, and post-*Erie* understanding has identified limited enclaves in which federal courts may derive some substantive law in a common law way. For two centuries we have affirmed that the domestic law of the United States recognizes the law of nations. See, e.g., *Sabbatino*, 376 U.S. at 423 ("It is, of course, true that United States courts apply international law as a part of our own in appropriate circumstances"); The Paquete Habana, 175 U.S. 677, 700 (1900) ("International law is part of our law, and must be ascertained and administered by the courts of justice of appropriate jurisdiction, as often as questions of right depending upon it are duly presented for their determination"). It would take some explaining to say now that federal courts must avert their gaze entirely from any international norm intended to protect individuals.

We think an attempt to justify such a position would be particularly unconvincing in light of what we know about congressional understanding bearing on this issue lying at the intersection of the judicial and legislative powers. The First Congress, which reflected the understanding of the framing generation and included some of the Framers, assumed that federal courts could properly identify some international norms as enforceable in the exercise of § 1350 jurisdiction. We think it would be unreasonable to assume that the First Congress would have expected federal courts to lose all capacity to recognize enforceable international norms simply because the common law might lose some metaphysical cachet on the road to modern realism. Later Congresses seem to have shared our view. The position we take today has been assumed by some federal courts for 24 years, ever since the Second Circuit decided *Filartiga*. . . . Congress, however, has not only expressed no disagreement with our view of the proper exercise of the judicial power, but has responded to its most notable instance by enacting legislation supplementing the judicial determination in some detail [referring to the Torture Victim Protection Act].

While we agree with Justice Scalia to the point that we would welcome any congressional guidance in exercising jurisdiction with such

[handwritten margin note: Court believes door is not closed on judicial recognition of actionable norms]

obvious potential to affect foreign relations, nothing Congress has done is a reason for us to shut the door to the law of nations entirely. It is enough to say that Congress may do that at any time (explicitly, or implicitly by treaties or statutes that occupy the field) just as it may modify or cancel any judicial decision so far as it rests on recognizing an international norm as such.

C

We must still, however, derive a standard or set of standards for assessing the particular claim Alvarez raises, and for this case it suffices to look to the historical antecedents. Whatever the ultimate criteria for accepting a cause of action subject to jurisdiction under § 1350, we are persuaded that federal courts should not recognize private claims under federal common law for violations of any international law norm with less definite content and acceptance among civilized nations than the historical paradigms familiar when § 1350 was enacted. This limit upon judicial recognition is generally consistent with the reasoning of many of the courts and judges who faced the issue before it reached this Court. See *Filartiga,* 630 F.2d, at 890 ("For purposes of civil liability, the torturer has become—like the pirate and slave trader before him—hostis humani generis, an enemy of all mankind"). And the determination whether a norm is sufficiently definite to support a cause of action[20] should (and, indeed, inevitably must) involve an element of judgment about the practical consequences of making that cause available to litigants in the federal courts.[21]

Thus, Alvarez's detention claim must be gauged against the current state of international law, looking to those sources we have long, albeit cautiously, recognized.

> Where there is no treaty, and no controlling executive or legislative act or judicial decision, resort must be had to the customs and usages of civilized nations; and, as evidence of these, to the works of jurists and commentators, who by years of labor, research and experience, have made themselves peculiarly well acquainted with the subjects of which they treat. Such works are resorted to by judicial tribunals, not for the speculations of

---

[20] A related consideration is whether international law extends the scope of liability for a violation of a given norm to the perpetrator being sued, if the defendant is a private actor such as a corporation or individual. . . .

[21] This requirement of clear definition is not meant to be the only principle limiting the availability of relief in the federal courts for violations of customary international law, though it disposes of this case. For example, the European Commission argues as amicus curiae that basic principles of international law require that before asserting a claim in a foreign forum, the claimant must have exhausted any remedies available in the domestic legal system, and perhaps in other fora such as international claims tribunals. Cf. Torture Victim Protection Act of 1991, § 2(b) (exhaustion requirement). We would certainly consider this requirement in an appropriate case.

Another possible limitation that we need not apply here is a policy of case-specific deference to the political branches. . . .

their authors concerning what the law ought to be, but for trust-
worthy evidence of what the law really is.

The Paquete Habana, 175 U.S. at 700.

To begin with, Alvarez cites two well-known international agreements that, despite their moral authority, have little utility under the
standard set out in this opinion. He says that his abduction by Sosa was
an "arbitrary arrest" within the meaning of the Universal Declaration of
Human Rights (Declaration), G. A. Res. 217A (III), U. N. Doc. A/810
(1948). And he traces the rule against arbitrary arrest not only to the
Declaration, but also to article nine of the International Covenant on
Civil and Political Rights (Covenant), Dec. 19, 1996, 999 U.N.T.S. 171,[22]
to which the United States is a party, and to various other conventions
to which it is not. But the Declaration does not of its own force impose
obligations as a matter of international law. . . . And, although the Covenant does bind the United States as a matter of international law, the
United States ratified the Covenant on the express understanding that
it was not self-executing and so did not itself create obligations enforceable in the federal courts. Accordingly, Alvarez cannot say that the
Declaration and Covenant themselves establish the relevant and applicable rule of international law. He instead attempts to show that
prohibition of arbitrary arrest has attained the status of binding customary international law.

Here, it is useful to examine Alvarez's complaint in greater detail.
As he presently argues it, the claim does not rest on the cross-border feature of his abduction. Although the District Court granted relief in part
on finding a violation of international law in taking Alvarez across the
border from Mexico to the United States, the Court of Appeals rejected
that ground of liability for failure to identify a norm of requisite force
prohibiting a forcible abduction across a border. Instead, it relied on the
conclusion that the law of the United States did not authorize Alvarez's
arrest, because the DEA lacked extraterritorial authority under 21
U.S.C. § 878, and because Federal Rule of Criminal Procedure 4(d)(2)
limited the warrant for Alvarez's arrest to "the jurisdiction of the United
States."[25] It is this position that Alvarez takes now: that his arrest was
arbitrary and as such forbidden by international law not because it infringed the prerogatives of Mexico, but because no applicable law
authorized it.

Alvarez thus invokes a general prohibition of "arbitrary" detention
defined as officially sanctioned action exceeding positive authorization to

---

[22] Article nine provides that "no one shall be subjected to arbitrary arrest or detention,"
that "no one shall be deprived of his liberty except on such grounds and in accordance with such
procedure as are established by law," and that "anyone who has been the victim of unlawful
arrest or detention shall have an enforceable right to compensation." 999 U. N. T. S., at 175–76.

[25] The Rule has since been moved and amended and now provides that a warrant may also
be executed "anywhere else a federal statute authorizes an arrest." Fed. Rule Crim. Proc. 4(c)(2).

detain under the domestic law of some government, regardless of the circumstances. Whether or not this is an accurate reading of the Covenant, Alvarez cites little authority that a rule so broad has the status of a binding customary norm today. He certainly cites nothing to justify the federal courts in taking his broad rule as the predicate for a federal lawsuit, for its implications would be breathtaking. His rule would support a cause of action in federal court for any arrest, anywhere in the world, unauthorized by the law of the jurisdiction in which it took place, and would create a cause of action for any seizure of an alien in violation of the Fourth Amendment, supplanting the actions under 42 U.S.C. § 1983 and Bivens v. Six Unknown Fed. Narcotics Agents, 403 U.S. 388 (1971), that now provide damages remedies for such violations. It would create an action in federal court for arrests by state officers who simply exceed their authority; and for the violation of any limit that the law of any country might place on the authority of its own officers to arrest. And all of this assumes that Alvarez could establish that Sosa was acting on behalf of a government when he made the arrest, for otherwise he would need a rule broader still.

Alvarez's failure to marshal support for his proposed rule is underscored by the Restatement (Third) of Foreign Relations Law of the United States § 702 (1987), which says in its discussion of customary international human rights law that a "state violates international law if, as a matter of state policy, it practices, encourages, or condones . . . prolonged arbitrary detention." Although the Restatement does not explain its requirements of a "state policy" and of "prolonged" detention, the implication is clear. Any credible invocation of a principle against arbitrary detention that the civilized world accepts as binding customary international law requires a factual basis beyond relatively brief detention in excess of positive authority. . . .

Whatever may be said for the broad principle Alvarez advances, in the present, imperfect world, it expresses an aspiration that exceeds any binding customary rule having the specificity we require. Creating a private cause of action to further that aspiration would go beyond any residual common law discretion we think it appropriate to exercise. It is enough to hold that a single illegal detention of less than a day, followed by the transfer of custody to lawful authorities and a prompt arraignment, violates no norm of customary international law so well defined as to support the creation of a federal remedy.

The judgment of the Court of Appeals is reversed.

■ JUSTICE SCALIA, with whom THE CHIEF JUSTICE and JUSTICE THOMAS join, concurring in part and concurring in the judgment.

There is not much that I would add to the Court's detailed opinion, and only one thing that I would subtract: its reservation of a discretionary power in the Federal Judiciary to create causes of action for the enforcement of international-law-based norms. . . .

I

. . . At the time of its enactment, the ATS provided a federal forum in which aliens could bring suit to recover for torts committed in "violation of the law of nations." The law of nations that would have been applied in this federal forum was at the time part of the so-called general common law. See Ernest A. Young, Sorting out the Debate Over Customary International Law, 42 Va. J. Int'l L. 365, 374 (2002); Curtis A. Bradley and Jack L. Goldsmith, Customary International Law as Federal Common Law: A Critique of the Modern Position, 110 Harv. L. Rev. 815, 824 (1997).

General common law was not federal law under the Supremacy Clause, which gave that effect only to the Constitution, the laws of the United States, and treaties. Federal and state courts adjudicating questions of general common law were not adjudicating questions of federal or state law, respectively—the general common law was neither. . . .

This Court's decision in Erie R. Co. v. Tompkins, 304 U.S. 64 (1938), signaled the end of federal-court elaboration and application of the general common law. *Erie* repudiated the holding of Swift v. Tyson, 41 U.S. 1 (1842), that federal courts were free to "express our own opinion" upon "the principles established in the general commercial law." After canvassing the many problems resulting from "the broad province accorded to the so-called 'general law' as to which federal courts exercised an independent judgment," the *Erie* Court extirpated that law with its famous declaration that "there is no federal general common law." *Erie* affected the status of the law of nations in federal courts not merely by the implication of its holding but quite directly, since the question decided in *Swift* turned on the "law merchant," then a subset of the law of nations.

After the death of the old general common law in *Erie* came the birth of a new and different common law pronounced by federal courts. . . . Unlike the general common law that preceded it, however, federal common law was self-consciously "made" rather than "discovered," by judges. . . . Because post-*Erie* federal common law is made, not discovered, federal courts must possess some federal-common-law-making authority before undertaking to craft it. . . . The general rule as formulated in Texas Industries, Inc. v. Radcliff Materials, Inc., 451 U.S. 630, 640–41 (1981), is that "the vesting of jurisdiction in the federal courts does not in and of itself give rise to authority to formulate federal common law." This rule applies not only to applications of federal common law that would displace a state rule, but also to applications that simply create a private cause of action under a federal statute. Indeed, *Texas Industries* itself involved the petitioner's unsuccessful request for an application of the latter sort—creation of a right of contribution to damages assessed under the antitrust laws.

The rule against finding a delegation of substantive lawmaking power in a grant of jurisdiction is subject to exceptions, some better established than others. The most firmly entrenched is admiralty law, derived from the grant of admiralty jurisdiction in Article III, § 2, cl. 3, of the Constitution. . . . At the other extreme is Bivens v. Six Unknown Fed. Narcotics Agents, 403 U.S. 388 (1971), which created a private damages cause of action against federal officials for violation of the Fourth Amendment. We have said that the authority to create this cause of action was derived from "our general jurisdiction to decide all cases 'arising under the Constitution, laws, or treaties of the United States.' " Correctional Services Corp. v. Malesko, 534 U.S. 61, 66 (2001) (quoting 28 U.S.C. § 1331). While *Bivens* stands, the ground supporting it has eroded. For the past 25 years, "we have consistently refused to extend *Bivens* liability to any new context." *Correctional Services Corp.*, 534 U.S. at 68. *Bivens* is "a relic of the heady days in which this Court assumed common-law powers to create causes of action." Id. at 75 (Scalia, J., concurring).

II

With these general principles in mind, I turn to the question presented. The Court's detailed exegesis of the ATS conclusively establishes that it is "a jurisdictional statute creating no new causes of action." The Court provides a persuasive explanation of why respondent's contrary interpretation, that "the ATS was intended not simply as a jurisdictional grant, but as authority for the creation of a new cause of action for torts in violation of international law," is wrong. Indeed, the Court properly endorses the views of one scholar that this interpretation is " 'simply frivolous' " (quoting William Casto, The Federal Courts' Protective Jurisdiction Over Torts Committed in Violation of the Law of Nations, 18 Conn. L. Rev. 467, 479, 480 (1986)).

These conclusions are alone enough to dispose of the present case in favor of petitioner Sosa. None of the exceptions to the general rule against finding substantive lawmaking power in a jurisdictional grant apply. *Bivens* provides perhaps the closest analogy. That is shaky authority at best, but at least it can be said that *Bivens* sought to enforce a command of our *own* law—the *United States* Constitution. In modern international human rights litigation of the sort that has proliferated since Filartiga v. Pena-Irala, 630 F.2d 876 (2d Cir. 1980), a federal court must first *create* the underlying federal command. But "the fact that a rule has been recognized as [customary international law], by itself, is not an adequate basis for viewing that rule as part of federal common law." Daniel J. Meltzer, Customary International Law, Foreign Affairs, and Federal Common Law, 42 Va. J. Int'l L. 513, 519 (2002). In Benthamite terms, creating a federal command (federal common law) out of "international norms," and then constructing a cause of action to enforce that command through the purely jurisdictional grant of the ATS, is nonsense upon stilts.

III

The analysis in the Court's opinion departs from my own in this respect: After concluding in Part III that "the ATS is a jurisdictional statute creating no new causes of action," the Court addresses at length in Part

IV the "good reasons for a restrained conception of the *discretion* a federal court should exercise in considering a new cause of action" under the ATS (emphasis added). By framing the issue as one of "discretion," the Court skips over the antecedent question of authority. This neglects the "lesson of *Erie*," that "grants of jurisdiction alone" (which the Court has acknowledged the ATS to be) "are not themselves grants of law-making authority." Meltzer, at 541. On this point, the Court observes only that no development between the enactment of the ATS (in 1789) and the birth of modern international human rights litigation under that statute (in 1980) "has categorically *precluded* federal courts from recognizing a claim under the law of nations as an element of common law" (emphasis added). This turns our jurisprudence regarding federal common law on its head. The question is not what case or congressional action *prevents* federal courts from applying the law of nations as part of the general common law; it is what *authorizes* that peculiar exception from *Erie*'s fundamental holding that a general common law *does not exist*.

The Court would apparently find authorization in the understanding of the Congress that enacted the ATS, that "district courts would recognize private causes of action for certain torts in violation of the law of nations." But as discussed above, that understanding rested upon a notion of general common law that has been repudiated by *Erie*.

The Court recognizes that *Erie* was a "watershed" decision heralding an avulsive change, wrought by "conceptual development in understanding common law ... [and accompanied by an] equally significant rethinking of the role of the federal courts in making it." The Court's analysis, however, does not follow through on this insight, interchangeably using the unadorned phrase "common law" in Parts III and IV to refer to pre-*Erie* general common law and post-*Erie* federal common law. This lapse is crucial, because the creation of post-*Erie* federal common law is rooted in a positivist mindset utterly foreign to the American common-law tradition of the late 18th century. Post-*Erie* federal common lawmaking (all that is left to the federal courts) is so far removed from that general-common-law adjudication which applied the "law of nations" that it would be anachronistic to find authorization to do the former in a statutory grant of jurisdiction that was thought to enable the latter. Yet that is precisely what the discretion-only analysis in Part IV suggests.

Because today's federal common law is not our Framers' general common law, the question presented by the suggestion of discretionary authority to enforce the law of nations is not whether to extend old-school general-common-law adjudication. Rather, it is whether to create new federal common law. The Court masks the novelty of its approach when it suggests that the difference between us is that we would "close the door to further independent judicial recognition of actionable international norms," whereas the Court would permit the exercise of judicial power "on the understanding that the door is still ajar subject to vigilant door-keeping." The general common law was the old door. We do not close that door today, for the deed was done in *Erie*. Federal common law is a *new* door. The question is not whether that door will be left ajar, but whether this Court will open it.

Although I fundamentally disagree with the discretion-based framework employed by the Court, we seem to be in accord that creating a new federal common law of international human rights is a questionable enterprise. . . . [The considerations recited by the Court] are not, as the Court thinks them, reasons why courts must be circumspect in use of their extant general-common-law-making powers. They are reasons why courts cannot possibly be thought to have been given, and should not be thought to possess, federal-common-law-making powers with regard to the creation of private federal causes of action for violations of customary international law.

To be sure, today's opinion does not itself precipitate a direct confrontation with Congress by creating a cause of action that Congress has not. But it invites precisely that action by the lower courts. . . . In holding open the possibility that judges may create rights where Congress has not authorized them to do so, the Court countenances judicial occupation of a domain that belongs to the people's representatives. One does not need a crystal ball to predict that this occupation will not be long in coming, since the Court endorses the reasoning of "many of the courts and judges who faced the issue before it reached this Court," including the Second and Ninth Circuits.

The Ninth Circuit brought us the judgment that the Court reverses today. Perhaps its decision in this particular case, like the decisions of other lower federal courts that receive passing attention in the Court's opinion, "reflects a more assertive view of federal judicial discretion over claims based on customary international law than the position we take today." But the verbal formula it applied is the same verbal formula that the Court explicitly endorses. Endorsing the very formula that led the Ninth Circuit to its result in this case hardly seems to be a recipe for restraint in the future. . . .

Though it is not necessary to resolution of the present case, one further consideration deserves mention: Despite the avulsive change of *Erie*, the Framers who included reference to "the Law of Nations" in Article I, § 8, cl. 10, of the Constitution would be entirely content with the post-*Erie* system I have described, and quite terrified by the "discretion" endorsed by the Court. That portion of the general common law known as the law of nations was understood to refer to the accepted practices of nations in their dealings with one another (treatment of ambassadors, immunity of foreign sovereigns from suit, etc.) and with actors on the high seas hostile to all nations and beyond all their territorial jurisdictions (pirates). Those accepted practices have for the most part, if not in their entirety, been enacted into United States statutory law, so that insofar as they are concerned the demise of the general common law is inconsequential. The notion that a law of nations, redefined to mean the consensus of states on *any* subject, can be used by a private citizen to control a sovereign's treatment of *its own citizens* within *its own territory* is a 20th-century invention of internationalist law professors and human-rights advocates. See generally Bradley and Goldsmith, Critique of the Modern Position, 110 Harv. L. Rev., at 831–37. The Framers would, I am confident, be appalled by the proposition that, for example, the American peoples' democratic adoption of the death penalty, see, e.g., Tex. Penal Code Ann. § 12.31 (2003), could be judicially nullified because of the disapproving views of foreigners.

We Americans have a method for making the laws that are over us. We elect representatives to two Houses of Congress, each of which must enact the new law and present it for the approval of a President, whom we also elect. For over two decades now, unelected federal judges have been usurping this lawmaking power by converting what they regard as norms of international law into American law. Today's opinion approves that process in principle, though urging the lower courts to be more restrained.

This Court seems incapable of admitting that some matters—*any* matters—are none of its business. In today's latest victory for its Never Say Never Jurisprudence, the Court ignores its own conclusion that the ATS provides only jurisdiction, wags a finger at the lower courts for going too far, and then—repeating the same formula the ambitious lower courts *themselves* have used—invites them to try again.

It would be bad enough if there were some assurance that future conversions of perceived international norms into American law would be approved by this Court itself. (Though we know ourselves to be eminently reasonable, self-awareness of eminent reasonableness is not really a substitute for democratic election.) But in this illegitimate lawmaking endeavor, the lower federal courts will be the principal actors; we review but a tiny fraction of their decisions. And no one thinks that all of them are eminently reasonable.

American law—the law made by the people's democratically elected representatives—does not recognize a category of activity that is so universally disapproved by other nations that it is automatically unlawful here, and automatically gives rise to a private action for money damages in federal court. That simple principle is what today's decision should have announced.

[The separate opinions of Justice Ginsburg and Justice Breyer are omitted.]

NOTES ON SOSA V. ALVAREZ-MACHAIN

1.   QUESTIONS AND COMMENTS ON SOSA

All nine Justices in *Sosa* agreed that the Alien Tort Statute (ATS) is a "strictly jurisdictional" statute that does not by itself confer a cause of action.

On what basis, therefore, did the majority find that the ATS authorizes a cause of action for a "relatively modest set" of claims involving violations of the law of nations? The majority concluded that, when the ATS was first enacted in 1789, Congress would have assumed that some law of nations claims could have been brought without the need for a statutory cause of action. In applying the ATS today, should the Court be attempting to give effect to a congressional assumption about, in the Court's words, the "interaction between the ATS at the time of its enactment and the ambient law of the era"? Or do the arguments for judicial caution, also recited by the majority, suggest that Congress should be required to update the ATS before it is used as a vehicle for redressing modern violations of the law of nations? Does the fact that Congress had not acted to disapprove the *Filartiga* line of cases suggest that it had acquiesced in the modern uses of the ATS?

After *Sosa*, when should courts recognize a cause of action in an ATS case? The Court stated that a cause of action should not be recognized under the ATS "for violations of any international law norm with less definite content and acceptance among civilized nations than the historical paradigms familiar when [the ATS] was enacted." Does this test provide enough guidance to the lower courts? Will the test ensure, as the Court claims, that the use of the ATS will be limited to a "narrow class" of causes of action?

For an article contesting the Court's premise in *Sosa* that, when the ATS was enacted, Congress would have assumed that the common law would have supplied a cause of action for ATS cases, see Anthony J. Bellia Jr. and Bradford R. Clark, The Original Source of the Cause of Action in Federal Courts: The Example of the Alien Tort Statute, 101 Va. L. Rev. 609 (2015). The authors contend that, when the ATS was enacted, "there was no single body of 'common law' that applied throughout the United States" and that "Congress made no attempt to follow the states' lead by adopting its own version of the common law as a whole for the nation, in part because any such attempt would have exceeded enumerated federal powers as then understood." Instead, in the Process Acts of 1789 and 1792, Congress "directed federal courts to apply the same causes of action that local state courts applied in cases at law, and to apply traditional causes of action in equity and admiralty cases." It was therefore inappropriate, the authors maintain, for the Court in *Sosa* to rely on the "ambient law of the era" as support for allowing the development of modern federal common law causes of action in ATS cases.

2. IMPLICATIONS OF *SOSA* FOR THE DOMESTIC STATUS OF CUSTOMARY INTERNATIONAL LAW

What, if anything, does *Sosa* suggest about the domestic status of the law of nations, or customary international law, outside the context of ATS litigation? Some commentators have argued that *Sosa* provides support for the "modern position" that all of customary international law has the status of post-*Erie* federal common law. See, e.g., Ralph G. Steinhardt, Laying One Bankrupt Critique to Rest: *Sosa v. Alvarez-Machain* and the Future of International Human Rights Litigation in U.S. Courts, 57 Vand. L. Rev. 2241,

2255 (2004). Professors Bradley, Goldsmith, and Moore argue, to the contrary, that "the decision in *Sosa* cannot reasonably be read as embracing the modern position and, indeed, is best read as rejecting it." Curtis A. Bradley, Jack L. Goldsmith and David H. Moore, *Sosa, Customary International Law, and the Continuing Relevance of Erie*, 120 Harv. L. Rev. 869, 873 (2007). Among other things, these authors contend that "[c]ommentators who construe *Sosa* as embracing the modern position have confounded the automatic incorporation of [customary international law] as domestic federal law in the absence of congressional authorization (that is, the modern position) with the entirely different issue of whether and to what extent a particular statute, the Alien Tort Statute (ATS), authorizes courts to apply [customary international law] as domestic federal law." These authors make clear that they do not call for a rejection of all judicial incorporation of customary international law into federal common law, but they believe that "courts can domesticate [customary international law] only in accordance with the requirements and limitations of post-*Erie* federal common law," limitations that the authors maintain were reaffirmed by the Court in *Sosa*. For commentary on the Bradley-Goldsmith-Moore article, see William S. Dodge, *Customary International Law and the Question of Legitimacy*, 120 Harv. L. Rev. F. 19 (2007), and Ernest A. Young, *Sosa and the Retail Incorporation of International Law*, 120 Harv. L. Rev. F. 28 (2007). See also Carlos M. Vázquez, *Alien Tort Claims and the Status of Customary International Law*, 106 Am. J. Int'l L. 531 (2012) (discussing relevance of customary international law's status to ATS litigation).

3. SUITS AGAINST CORPORATIONS UNDER THE ATS

In recent years, a number of ATS suits have been brought against private corporations, on the theory that they either violated one of the few international human rights norms that apply to private actors (such as the prohibition on slavery) or that they "aided and abetted" violations of international human rights law committed by foreign governments. The allegations in these cases vary from case to case and range from merely doing business with an oppressive regime to knowingly participating in abuses. Should these corporate ATS cases be allowed under *Sosa*? Or should courts insist on more express authorization from Congress before allowing such suits?

In Kiobel v. Royal Dutch Petroleum Co., 621 F.3d 111 (2d Cir. 2010), the Second Circuit held that ATS suits could not be brought against private corporations. The court reasoned that, in order for a defendant's conduct to be actionable under the ATS, the conduct must violate international law, and the court concluded that international human rights law does not extend to conduct by corporations. This decision created a conflict in the circuits. The Supreme Court granted certiorari to resolve the conflict, but ultimately decided the case on other grounds. (Its decision in *Kiobel* is the next main case in this Section.) In the meantime, other circuit courts have disagreed with the Second Circuit. See Flomo v. Firestone Natural Rubber Co., 643 F.3d 1013 (7th Cir. 2011); Doe v. Exxon Mobil Corp., 654 F.3d 11 (D.C. Cir. 2011).

As noted earlier in this section, in 1992 Congress enacted the Torture Victim Protection Act (TVPA), which creates a cause of action for claims of torture and "extrajudicial killing" under color of foreign law. The TVPA, which is codified as a note to the ATS, refers to claims by an "individual" against another "individual." Because of this language, the Court held in Mohamad v. Palestinian Authority, 566 U.S. 449 (2012), that the TVPA authorizes suit only against natural persons. The Court observed that, because the ATS does not use the term "individual," it "offers no comparative value here regardless of whether corporate entities can be held liable in a federal common-law action brought under that statute."

For articles discussing the issue of corporate liability under the ATS, see Curtis A. Bradley, State Action and Corporate Human Rights Liability, 85 Notre Dame L. Rev. 1823 (2010); Doug Cassel, Corporate Aiding and Abetting of Human Rights Violations: Confusion in the Courts, 6 Nw. U.J. Int'l Hum. Rts. 304 (2008); Chimene Keitner, Conceptualizing Complicity in Alien Tort Cases, 60 Hastings L.J. 61 (2008); Julian G. Ku, The Curious Case of Corporate Liability under the Alien Tort Statute: A Flawed System of Judicial Lawmaking, 51 Va. J. Int'l L. 353 (2011); Michael D. Ramsey, International Law Limits on Investor Liability in Human Rights Litigation, 50 Harv. Int'l L.J. 271 (2009); Alan O. Sykes, Corporate Liability for Extraterritorial Torts under the Alien Tort Statute and Beyond: An Economic Analysis, 100 Geo. L.J. 2161 (2012).

4. FOREIGN OFFICIAL IMMUNITY

In most situations involving alleged human rights abuses committed by foreign governments, the governments will have immunity from suit in U.S. courts pursuant to the Foreign Sovereign Immunities Act (FSIA), which provides that, subject to certain specified exceptions, "a foreign state shall be immune from the jurisdiction of the courts of the United States." 28 U.S.C. § 1604. Although tort cases are excepted, the exception applies only if the damage or injury from the tort occurs in the United States. As a result, instead of suing foreign governments directly, plaintiffs in ATS cases often sue the individual foreign officials who were allegedly involved in or responsible for the abuses. This is what happened in the seminal *Filartiga* case, for example, in which the plaintiffs sued a former Paraguayan police inspector. Until recently, courts had not given much consideration to the possibility that suits against foreign officials might be barred by principles of immunity. In part this was due to the fact that the FSIA makes no specific mention of suits against individual officials, and, in defining "foreign state," merely states that this term "includes a political subdivision of a foreign state or an agency or instrumentality of a foreign state."

Despite the lack of clear support in the text of the FSIA, a number of circuit courts in non-ATS cases came to the conclusion that a suit against a foreign official for conduct that was carried out in his or her official capacity is a suit against an "agency or instrumentality" of a foreign state and thus is covered by the FSIA's immunity provisions. In Samantar v. Yousuf, 560 U.S. 305 (2010), however, the Supreme Court unanimously held that suits against individual foreign officials are not covered by the FSIA. In that case, a group of Somalis sued a former high-ranking Somali official under the ATS, alleging that during the 1980s the official exercised control over Somalia's military forces, and that these forces engaged in acts of torture, murder, and arbitrary detention. The defendant official argued that the suit was barred by the FSIA, either because the suit in effect was against the "foreign state" under the terms of the FSIA, or because the defendant qualified as an "agency or instrumentality" of the foreign state. In an opinion by Justice Stevens, the Court rejected these arguments. The Court found that there was insufficient evidence in the text of the FSIA to indicate that Congress intended to address suits against individual officials. While acknowledging that foreign officials had some immunity under the pre-FSIA common law, and that "in some circumstances the immunity of the foreign state extends to an individual for acts taken in his official capacity," the Court reasoned that "it does not follow from this premise that Congress intended to codify that immunity in the FSIA."

The Court described the pre-FSIA common law regime as involving a "two-step procedure":

> Under that procedure, the diplomatic representative of the sovereign could request a "suggestion of immunity" from the State Department. If the request was granted, the district court surrendered its jurisdiction. But "in the absence of recognition of the immunity by the Department of State," a district court "had authority to decide for itself whether all the requisites for such immunity existed." Ex parte Peru, 318 U.S. 578, 587 (1943).

The Court acknowledged that one of the purposes of the FSIA was "to transfer primary responsibility for deciding 'claims of foreign states to immunity' from the State Department to the courts," but it said that it had "been given no reason to believe that Congress saw as a problem, or wanted to eliminate, the State Department's role in determinations regarding individual official immunity."

The Court denied that its holding would allow plaintiffs to circumvent the FSIA through artful pleading:

> Even if a suit is not governed by the Act, it may still be barred by foreign sovereign immunity under the common law. And not every suit can successfully be pleaded against an individual official alone. Even when a plaintiff names only a foreign official, it may be the case that the foreign state itself, its political subdivision, or an agency or instrumentality is a required party, because that party has "an interest relating to the subject of the action" and "disposing of the action in the person's absence may . . . as a practical matter impair or impede the person's ability to protect the interest." Fed. Rule Civ. Proc. 19(a)(1)(B). If this is the case, and the entity is immune from suit under the FSIA, the district court may have to dismiss the suit, regardless of whether the official is immune or not under the common law. See Republic of Philippines v. Pimentel, 553 U.S. 851, 867 (2008) ("[W]here sovereign immunity is asserted, and the claims of the sovereign are not frivolous, dismissal of the

action must be ordered where there is a potential for injury to the interests of the absent sovereign"). Or it may be the case that some actions against an official in his official capacity should be treated as actions against the foreign state itself, as the state is the real party in interest. Cf. Kentucky v. Graham, 473 U.S. 159, 166 (1985) ("[A]n official-capacity suit is, in all respects other than name, to be treated as a suit against the entity. It is *not* a suit against the official personally, for the real party in interest is the entity.").

Emphasizing the "narrowness" of its ruling, the Court remanded the case to the district court so that it could consider "[w]hether [the defendant] may be entitled to immunity under the common law, and whether he may have other valid defenses to the grave charges against him."

This decision leaves open a number of questions that the lower courts will now need to address. In particular, they will need to determine the scope of the common law immunity that the Court says was not superseded by the FSIA. In making that determination, one issue will be the extent to which principles of customary international law should inform the common law of immunity. In *Samantar*, the Court said very little about international law, simply noting that "[b]ecause we are not deciding that the FSIA bars petitioner's immunity but rather that the Act does not address the question, we need not determine whether declining to afford immunity to petitioner would be consistent with international law."

Another issue will be how to distinguish between actions taken by foreign officials in their personal capacity from actions taken in their official capacity. On that issue, it may be relevant that the Court in *Samantar* cites as a "Cf." to Kentucky v. Graham, 473 U.S. 159 (1985). *Graham* was a domestic civil rights case in which the Court held that an attorney's fee award could not be imposed on a state based on the success of a suit brought against one of the state's officials in their personal capacity. The sentence from *Graham* that the Court quotes in *Samantar* came in the context of an effort to "unravel once again the distinctions between personal-and official-capacity suits," a distinction that the Court said "apparently continues to confuse lawyers and confound lower courts":

> Personal-capacity suits seek to impose personal liability upon a government official for actions he takes under color of state law. Official-capacity suits, in contrast, "generally represent only another way of pleading an action against an entity of which an officer is an agent." Monell v. New York City Dept. of Social Services, 436 U.S. 658, 690, n.55 (1978). As long as the government entity receives notice and an opportunity to respond, an official-capacity suit is, in all respects other than name, to be treated as a suit against the entity. It is *not* a suit against the official personally, for the real party in interest is the entity. Thus, while an award of damages against an official in his personal capacity can be executed only against the official's personal assets, a plaintiff seeking to recover on a damages judgment in an official-capacity suit must look to the government entity itself.

Does this discussion in *Graham* clarify the distinction between personal-capacity and official-capacity suits? In any event, is it relevant to suits against foreign officials?

As the citation to *Graham* indicates, and as discussed in Chapter VIII, potentially analogous issues of immunity arise in domestic civil rights litigation. State governments have broad immunity from private lawsuits under the Eleventh Amendment and related doctrines, but the Supreme Court has held that this immunity is not generally triggered by a lawsuit that is brought against a state official and seeks a damages award that will be enforceable only against the official's personal assets. This is true even if it is the state's policy to indemnify the official. If this jurisprudence were applied to suits against foreign officials, including international human rights suits brought under the ATS, it might suggest that there should be no immunity as long as the suit seeks only damages from the official. Domestic civil rights suits, however, do not present the same foreign relations and international law issues presented by suits against foreign officials. For consideration of these and other differences between domestic civil rights litigation and human rights litigation brought against foreign officials, see Curtis A. Bradley and Jack L. Goldsmith, Foreign Sovereign Immunity and Domestic Officer Suits, 13 Green Bag 2d 137 (2010).

In the wake of *Samantar*, the Executive Branch has claimed that courts should defer to its views about whether particular foreign officials should receive common law immunity. For a critique of that claim, see Ingrid Wuerth, Foreign Official Immunity Determinations in U.S. Courts: The Case against the State Department, 51 Va. J. Int'l L. 915 (2011). In a subsequent proceeding in *Samantar*, the Fourth Circuit held that absolute deference to the Executive Branch is appropriate only for the immunity of sitting heads of state, and that, for the immunity of other officials, the Executive Branch's view "carries substantial weight" but is not controlling. See Yousuf v. Samantar, 699 F.3d 763, 773 (4th Cir. 2012). The Fourth Circuit also held that former officials are entitled to immunity only for their official acts while in office and that this immunity does not extend to violations of "jus cogens" norms of international law, which consist of certain fundamental international limitations such as the prohibitions on war crimes, genocide, slavery, and torture. See id. at 777.

For additional discussion of the post-*Samantar* common law of foreign official immunity, see Curtis A. Bradley and Laurence R. Helfer, International Law and the U.S. Common Law of Foreign Official Immunity, 2010 Sup. Ct. Rev. 213; Chimene I. Keitner, Foreign Official Immunity after *Samantar*, 44 Vand. J. Transnat'l L. 837 (2011); Peter B. Rutledge, *Samantar*, Official Immunity and Federal Common Law, 15 Lewis & Clark L. Rev. 589 (2011); Beth Stephens, The Modern Common Law of Foreign Official Immunity, 79 Fordham L. Rev. 2669 (2011); and David P. Stewart, *Samantar* and the Future of Foreign Official Immunity, 15 Lewis & Clark L. Rev. 633 (2011). For discussion of the early history of foreign official immunity in the United States, see Chimene I. Keitner, The Forgotten History of Foreign Official Immunity, 87 N.Y.U. L. Rev. 704 (2012).

5. EXHAUSTION OF REMEDIES

Some defendants in ATS cases have argued that international law requires that a plaintiff exhaust local remedies before pursuing an action in a foreign court, and have sought to have U.S. courts apply this requirement. The Ninth Circuit considered this issue in Sarei v. Rio Tinto, PLC, 550 F.3d 822 (9th Cir. 2008) (en banc). In that case, former residents of Bougainville, Papua New Guinea, sued the Rio Tinto company under the ATS, alleging that, in connection with its mining operations in Bougainville, Rio Tinto was involved in or facilitated war crimes, crimes against humanity, racial discrimination, and environmental torts. In an en banc decision, the Ninth Circuit remanded the case to the District Court for consideration of whether to dismiss the claims as a result of a failure to exhaust local remedies. The lead plurality opinion found that "certain ATS claims are appropriately considered for exhaustion under both domestic prudential standards and core principles of international law," but it declined to impose an absolute requirement of exhaustion in ATS cases. Instead, it reasoned that an exhaustion requirement should be applied as a "prudential" matter in cases that have little connection to the United States, "particularly—but not exclusively—with respect to claims that do not involve matters of 'universal concern.' "

For additional discussion of the issue of exhaustion in ATS cases, see Note, The Alien Tort Statute, Forum Shopping, and the Exhaustion of Local Remedies Norm, 121 Harv. L. Rev. 2110 (2008). For an extension of the idea outside the ATS context to a case involving an alleged expropriation of property, see Cassirer v. Kingdom of Spain, 580 F.3d 1048 (9th Cir. 2009).

6. BIBLIOGRAPHY

For additional commentary on *Sosa* and its implications, see William R. Casto, The New Federal Common Law of Tort Remedies for Violations of International Law, 37 Rutgers L.J. 635 (2006); William S. Dodge, Bridging *Erie*: Customary International Law in the U.S. Legal System after *Sosa v. Alvarez-Machain*, 12 Tulsa J. Comp. & Int'l L. 87 (2004); William A. Fletcher, International Human Rights Law in American Courts, 93 Va. L. Rev. 653 (2007); Julian Ku and John Yoo, Beyond Formalism in Foreign Affairs: A Functional Approach to the Alien Tort Statute, 2004 Sup. Ct. Rev. 153; David H. Moore, An Emerging Uniformity for International Law, 75 Geo. Wash. L. Rev. 1 (2006); Pamela J. Stephens, Spinning *Sosa*: Federal Common Law, the Alien Tort Statute, and Judicial Restraint, 25 B.U. Int'l L.J. 1 (2007); G. Edward White, A Customary International Law of Torts, 41 Val. U. L. Rev. 755 (2006); Note, An Objection to *Sosa*—And to the New Federal Common Law, 119 Harv. L. Rev. 2077 (2006). For an argument that, in addressing the various issues that arise in ATS litigation after *Sosa*, courts should not understand themselves as presented with a binary choice between applying international law and applying federal common law, but should instead view the entire enterprise as governed by federal common law "with certain aspects of ATS litigation governed by federal common law that is tightly linked to international law, other aspects governed by federal common law that is not derived from international norms, and still others that fall somewhere in between," see Ingrid Wuerth, The Alien Tort Statute and Federal Common Law: A New Approach, 85 Notre Dame L. Rev. 1931 (2010). For consideration of how international human rights litigation might proceed if the courts restrict application of the ATS, see Donald Earl Childress III, The Alien Tort Statute, Federalism, and the Next Wave of Transnational Litigation, 100 Geo. L.J. 709 (2012). As the next main case illustrates, such a restriction has now occurred.

Kiobel v. Royal Dutch Petroleum Co.

Supreme Court of the United States, 2013.
569 U.S. 108.

■ CHIEF JUSTICE ROBERTS delivered the opinion of the Court.

Petitioners, a group of Nigerian nationals residing in the United States, filed suit in federal court against certain Dutch, British, and Nigerian corporations. Petitioners sued under the Alien Tort Statute, 28 U.S.C. § 1350, alleging that the corporations aided and abetted the Nigerian Government in committing violations of the law of nations in Nigeria. The question presented is whether and under what circumstances courts may recognize a cause of action under the Alien Tort Statute, for violations of the law of nations occurring within the territory of a sovereign other than the United States.

I

Petitioners were residents of Ogoniland, an area of 250 square miles located in the Niger delta area of Nigeria and populated by roughly half a million people. When the complaint was filed, respondents Royal Dutch Petroleum Company and Shell Transport and Trading Company, p.l.c., were holding companies incorporated in the Netherlands and England, respectively. Their joint subsidiary, respondent Shell Petroleum Development Company of Nigeria, Ltd. (SPDC), was incorporated in Nigeria, and engaged in oil exploration and production in Ogoniland. According to the complaint, after concerned residents of Ogoniland began protesting the environmental effects of SPDC's practices, respondents enlisted the Nigerian Government to violently suppress the burgeoning demonstrations. Throughout the early 1990s, the complaint alleges, Nigerian military and police forces attacked Ogoni villages, beating, raping, killing, and arresting residents and destroying or looting property. Petitioners further allege that respondents aided and abetted these atrocities by, among other things, providing the Nigerian forces with food, transportation, and compensation, as well as by allowing the Nigerian military to use respondents' property as a staging ground for attacks.

Following the alleged atrocities, petitioners moved to the United States where they have been granted political asylum and now reside as legal residents. They filed suit in the United States District Court for the Southern District of New York, alleging jurisdiction under the Alien Tort Statute and requesting relief under customary international law. The

ATS provides, in full, that "[t]he district courts shall have original jurisdiction of any civil action by an alien for a tort only, committed in violation of the law of nations or a treaty of the United States." 28 U.S.C. § 1350. According to petitioners, respondents violated the law of nations by aiding and abetting the Nigerian Government in committing (1) extrajudicial killings; (2) crimes against humanity; (3) torture and cruel treatment; (4) arbitrary arrest and detention; (5) violations of the rights to life, liberty, security, and association; (6) forced exile; and (7) property destruction. The District Court dismissed the first, fifth, sixth, and seventh claims, reasoning that the facts alleged to support those claims did not give rise to a violation of the law of nations. The court denied respondents' motion to dismiss with respect to the remaining claims, but certified its order for interlocutory appeal pursuant to § 1292(b).

The Second Circuit dismissed the entire complaint, reasoning that the law of nations does not recognize corporate liability. We granted certiorari to consider that question. After oral argument, we directed the parties to file supplemental briefs addressing an additional question: "Whether and under what circumstances the [ATS] allows courts to recognize a cause of action for violations of the law of nations occurring within the territory of a sovereign other than the United States." We heard oral argument again and now affirm the judgment below, based on our answer to the second question.

II

Passed as part of the Judiciary Act of 1789, the ATS was invoked twice in the late 18th century, but then only once more over the next 167 years. . . . The statute provides district courts with jurisdiction to hear certain claims, but does not expressly provide any causes of action. We held in Sosa v. Alvarez-Machain, 542 U.S. 692, 714 (2004), however, that the First Congress did not intend the provision to be "stillborn." The grant of jurisdiction is instead "best read as having been enacted on the understanding that the common law would provide a cause of action for [a] modest number of international law violations." We thus held that federal courts may "recognize private claims [for such violations] under federal common law." The Court in Sosa rejected the plaintiff's claim in that case for "arbitrary arrest and detention," on the ground that it failed to state a violation of the law of nations with the requisite "definite content and acceptance among civilized nations."

The question here is not whether petitioners have stated a proper claim under the ATS, but whether a claim may reach conduct occurring in the territory of a foreign sovereign. Respondents contend that claims under the ATS do not, relying primarily on a canon of statutory interpretation known as the presumption against extraterritorial application. That canon provides that "[w]hen a statute gives no clear indication of an extraterritorial application, it has none," Morrison v. National Australia Bank Ltd., 561 U.S. 247, 255 (2010), and reflects the "presumption that

United States law governs domestically but does not rule the world," Microsoft Corp. v. AT&T Corp., 550 U.S. 437, 454 (2007).

This presumption "serves to protect against unintended clashes between our laws and those of other nations which could result in international discord." EEOC v. Arabian American Oil Co., 499 U.S. 244, 248 (1991). . . .

We typically apply the presumption to discern whether an Act of Congress regulating conduct applies abroad. . . . The ATS, on the other hand, is "strictly jurisdictional." *Sosa*, 542 U.S. at 713. It does not directly regulate conduct or afford relief. It instead allows federal courts to recognize certain causes of action based on sufficiently definite norms of international law. But we think the principles underlying the canon of interpretation similarly constrain courts considering causes of action that may be brought under the ATS.

Indeed, the danger of unwarranted judicial interference in the conduct of foreign policy is magnified in the context of the ATS, because the question is not what Congress has done but instead what courts may do. This Court in *Sosa* repeatedly stressed the need for judicial caution in considering which claims could be brought under the ATS, in light of foreign policy concerns. . . . These concerns, which are implicated in any case arising under the ATS, are all the more pressing when the question is whether a cause of action under the ATS reaches conduct within the territory of another sovereign.

These concerns are not diminished by the fact that *Sosa* limited federal courts to recognizing causes of action only for alleged violations of international law norms that are "specific, universal, and obligatory." As demonstrated by Congress's enactment of the Torture Victim Protection Act of 1991, identifying such a norm is only the beginning of defining a cause of action. See id. § 3 (providing detailed definitions for extrajudicial killing and torture); id. § 2 (specifying who may be liable, creating a rule of exhaustion, and establishing a statute of limitations). Each of these decisions carries with it significant foreign policy implications.

The principles underlying the presumption against extraterritoriality thus constrain courts exercising their power under the ATS.

III

Petitioners contend that even if the presumption applies, the text, history, and purposes of the ATS rebut it for causes of action brought under that statute. It is true that Congress, even in a jurisdictional provision, can indicate that it intends federal law to apply to conduct occurring abroad. See, e.g., 18 U.S.C. § 1091(e) (providing jurisdiction over the offense of genocide "regardless of where the offense is committed" if the alleged offender is, among other things, "present in the United States"). But to rebut the presumption, the ATS would need to evince a "clear indication of extraterritoriality." *Morrison*, 561 U.S. at 265. It does not.

To begin, nothing in the text of the statute suggests that Congress intended causes of action recognized under it to have extraterritorial reach. The ATS covers actions by aliens for violations of the law of nations, but that does not imply extraterritorial reach—such violations affecting aliens can occur either within or outside the United States. Nor does the fact that the text reaches "*any* civil action" suggest application to torts committed abroad; it is well established that generic terms like "any" or "every" do not rebut the presumption against extraterritoriality. . . .

Petitioners make much of the fact that the ATS provides jurisdiction over civil actions for "torts" in violation of the law of nations. They claim that in using that word, the First Congress "necessarily meant to provide for jurisdiction over extraterritorial transitory torts that could arise on foreign soil." For support, they cite the common-law doctrine that allowed courts to assume jurisdiction over such "transitory torts," including actions for personal injury, arising abroad. . . .

Under the transitory torts doctrine, however, "the only justification for allowing a party to recover when the cause of action arose in another civilized jurisdiction is a well founded belief that it was a cause of action in that place." Cuba R. Co. v. Crosby, 222 U.S. 473, 479 (1912) (majority opinion of Holmes, J.). The question under *Sosa* is not whether a federal court has jurisdiction to entertain a cause of action provided by foreign or even international law. The question is instead whether the court has authority to recognize a cause of action under U.S. law to enforce a norm of international law. The reference to "tort" does not demonstrate that the First Congress "necessarily meant" for those causes of action to reach conduct in the territory of a foreign sovereign. In the end, nothing in the text of the ATS evinces the requisite clear indication of extraterritoriality.

Nor does the historical background against which the ATS was enacted overcome the presumption against application to conduct in the territory of another sovereign. We explained in *Sosa* that when Congress passed the ATS, "three principal offenses against the law of nations" had been identified by Blackstone: violation of safe conducts, infringement of the rights of ambassadors, and piracy. The first two offenses have no necessary extraterritorial application. . . .

Two notorious episodes involving violations of the law of nations occurred in the United States shortly before passage of the ATS. Each concerned the rights of ambassadors, and each involved conduct within the Union. In 1784, a French adventurer verbally and physically assaulted Francis Barbe Marbois—the Secretary of the French Legion—in Philadelphia. The assault led the French Minister Plenipotentiary to lodge a formal protest with the Continental Congress and threaten to leave the country unless an adequate remedy were provided. And in 1787, a New York constable entered the Dutch Ambassador's house and arrested one of his domestic servants. At the request of Secretary of Foreign Affairs John Jay, the Mayor of New York City arrested the constable in turn, but cautioned that because " 'neither Congress nor our [State] Legislature have yet passed any act respecting a breach of the privileges of Ambassadors,' " the extent of any available relief would depend on the common law. See Curtis A. Bradley, The Alien Tort Statute and Article III, 42 Va. J. Int'l L. 587, 641–642 (2002) (quoting 3 Dept. of State, The Diplomatic Correspondence of the United States of America 447 (1837)). The two cases in which the ATS was invoked shortly after its passage also concerned conduct within the territory of the United States. See Bolchos v. Darrell, 3 F. Cas. 810 (D.S.C. 1795) (No. 1607) (wrongful seizure of slaves from a vessel while in port in the United States); Moxon v. The Fanny, 17 F. Cas. 942 (D.C. Pa. 1793) (No. 9895) (wrongful seizure in United States territorial waters).

These prominent contemporary examples—immediately before and after passage of the ATS—provide no support for the proposition that Congress expected causes of action to be brought under the statute for violations of the law of nations occurring abroad.

The third example of a violation of the law of nations familiar to the Congress that enacted the ATS was piracy. Piracy typically occurs on the high seas, beyond the territorial jurisdiction of the United States or any other country. . . . This Court has generally treated the high seas the same as foreign soil for purposes of the presumption against extraterritorial application. . . . Petitioners contend that because Congress surely intended the ATS to provide jurisdiction for actions against pirates, it necessarily anticipated the statute would apply to conduct occurring abroad.

Applying U.S. law to pirates, however, does not typically impose the sovereign will of the United States onto conduct occurring within the territorial jurisdiction of another sovereign, and therefore carries less direct foreign policy consequences. Pirates were fair game wherever found, by any nation, because they generally did not operate within any jurisdiction. We do not think that the existence of a cause of action against them is a sufficient basis for concluding that other causes of action under the ATS reach conduct that does occur within the territory of another sovereign; pirates may well be a category unto themselves. . . .

Finally, there is no indication that the ATS was passed to make the United States a uniquely hospitable forum for the enforcement of international norms. As Justice Story put it, "No nation has ever yet pretended to be the custos morum of the whole world. . . ." United States v. The La Jeune Eugenie, 26 F. Cas. 832, 847 (No. 15,551) (CC Mass. 1822). It is implausible to suppose that the First Congress wanted their fledgling Republic—struggling to receive international recognition—to be the first. Indeed, the parties offer no evidence that any nation, meek or mighty, presumed to do such a thing.

The United States was, however, embarrassed by its potential inability to provide judicial relief to foreign officials injured in the United States. Bradley, 42 Va. J. Int'l L. at 641. Such offenses against ambassadors violated the law of nations, "and if not adequately redressed could rise to an issue of war." *Sosa*, 542 U.S. at 715. . . . The ATS ensured that the United States could provide a forum for adjudicating such incidents. Nothing about this historical context suggests that Congress also intended federal common law under the ATS to provide a cause of action for conduct occurring in the territory of another sovereign.

Indeed, far from avoiding diplomatic strife, providing such a cause of action could have generated it. Recent experience bears this out. See Doe v. Exxon Mobil Corp., 654 F.3d 11, 77–78 (D.C. Cir. 2011) (Kavanaugh, J., dissenting in part) (listing recent objections to extraterritorial applications of the ATS by Canada, Germany, Indonesia, Papua New Guinea, South Africa, Switzerland, and the United Kingdom). Moreover, accepting petitioners' view would imply that other nations, also applying the law of nations, could hale our citizens into their courts for alleged violations of the law of nations occurring in the United States, or anywhere else in the world. The presumption against extraterritoriality guards against our courts triggering such serious foreign policy consequences, and instead defers such decisions, quite appropriately, to the political branches.

We therefore conclude that the presumption against extraterritoriality applies to claims under the ATS, and that nothing in the statute rebuts that presumption. "[T]here is no clear indication of extraterritoriality here," *Morrison*, 561 U.S. at 265, and petitioners' case seeking relief for violations of the law of nations occurring outside the United States is barred.

IV

On these facts, all the relevant conduct took place outside the United States. And even where the claims touch and concern the territory of the United States, they must do so with sufficient force to displace the presumption against extraterritorial application. Corporations are often present in many countries, and it would reach too far to say that mere corporate presence suffices. If Congress were to determine otherwise, a statute more specific than the ATS would be required.

The judgment of the Court of Appeals is affirmed.

It is so ordered.

■ JUSTICE KENNEDY, concurring.

The opinion for the Court is careful to leave open a number of significant questions regarding the reach and interpretation of the Alien Tort Statute. In my view that is a proper disposition. Many serious concerns with respect to human rights abuses committed abroad have been addressed by Congress in statutes such as the Torture Victim Protection Act of 1991 (TVPA), 106 Stat. 73, note following 28 U.S.C. § 1350, and that class of cases will be determined in the future according to the detailed statutory scheme Congress has enacted. Other cases may arise with allegations of serious violations of international law principles protecting persons, cases covered neither by the TVPA nor by the reasoning and holding of today's case; and in those disputes the proper implementation of the presumption against extraterritorial application may require some further elaboration and explanation.

■ JUSTICE ALITO, with whom JUSTICE THOMAS joins, concurring.

I concur in the judgment and join the opinion of the Court as far as it goes. Specifically, I agree that when Alien Tort Statute (ATS) "claims touch and concern the territory of the United States, they must do so with sufficient force to displace the presumption against extraterritorial application." This formulation obviously leaves much unanswered, and perhaps there is wisdom in the Court's preference for this narrow approach. I write separately to set out the broader standard that leads me to the conclusion that this case falls within the scope of the presumption.

In Morrison v. National Australia Bank Ltd., 561 U.S. 247 (2010), we explained that "the presumption against extraterritorial application would be a craven watchdog indeed if it retreated to its kennel whenever *some* domestic activity is involved in the case." We also reiterated that a cause of action falls outside the scope of the presumption—and thus is not barred by the presumption—only if the event or relationship that was "the 'focus' of congressional concern" under the relevant statute takes place within the United States. . . .

The Court's decision in Sosa v. Alvarez-Machain, 542 U.S. 692 (2004), makes clear that when the ATS was enacted, "congressional concern" was " 'focus[ed],' " *Morrison*, 561 U.S. at 266, on the "three principal offenses against the law of nations" that had been identified by Blackstone: violation of safe conducts, infringement of the rights of ambassadors, and piracy. The Court therefore held that "federal courts should not recognize private claims under federal common law for violations of any international law norm with less definite content and acceptance among civilized nations than the historical paradigms familiar when [the ATS] was enacted." *Sosa*, 542 U.S. at 732. In other words, only conduct that satisfies *Sosa*'s requirements of definiteness and acceptance among civilized nations can be said to have been "the 'focus' of congressional concern," *Morrison*, 561 U.S. at 266, when Congress enacted the ATS. As a result, a putative ATS cause of action will fall within the scope of the presumption against extraterritoriality—and will therefore be barred—unless the domestic conduct is sufficient to violate an international law norm that satisfies *Sosa*'s requirements of definiteness and acceptance among civilized nations.

■ JUSTICE BREYER, with whom JUSTICE GINSBURG, JUSTICE SOTOMAYOR, and JUSTICE KAGAN join, concurring in the judgment.

I agree with the Court's conclusion but not with its reasoning. . . .

Unlike the Court, I would not invoke the presumption against extra-territoriality. Rather, guided in part by principles and practices of foreign relations law, I would find jurisdiction under this statute where (1) the alleged tort occurs on American soil, (2) the defendant is an American national, or (3) the defendant's conduct substantially and adversely affects an important American national interest, and that includes a distinct interest in preventing the United States from becoming a safe harbor (free of civil as well as criminal liability) for a torturer or other common enemy of mankind. . . . In this case, however, the parties and relevant conduct lack sufficient ties to the United States for the ATS to provide jurisdiction.

I

A

. . . Recognizing that Congress enacted the ATS to permit recovery of damages from pirates and others who violated basic international law norms as understood in 1789, *Sosa* essentially leads today's judges to ask: Who are today's pirates? We provided a framework for answering that question by setting down principles drawn from international norms and designed to limit ATS claims to those that are similar in character and specificity to piracy.

In this case we must decide the extent to which this jurisdictional statute opens a federal court's doors to those harmed by activities belonging to the limited class that *Sosa* set forth *when those activities take place abroad.* To help answer this question here, I would refer both to *Sosa* and, as in *Sosa,* to norms of international law.

B

In my view the majority's effort to answer the question by referring to the "presumption against extraterritoriality" does not work well. That presumption "rests on the perception that Congress ordinarily legislates with respect to domestic, not foreign matters." Morrison v. National Australia Bank Ltd., 561 U.S. 247, 255 (2010). The ATS, however, was enacted with "foreign matters" in mind. The statute's text refers explicitly to "alien[s]," "treat[ies]," and "the law of nations." The statute's purpose was to address "violations of the law of nations, admitting of a judicial remedy and at the same time threatening serious con-sequences in international affairs." *Sosa,* 542 U.S. at 715. And at least one of the three kinds of activities that we found to fall within the statute's scope, namely piracy, normally takes place abroad.

The majority cannot wish this piracy example away by emphasizing that piracy takes place on the high seas. That is because the robbery and murder that make up piracy do not normally take place in the water; they take place on a ship. And a ship is like land, in that it falls within the jurisdiction of the nation whose flag it flies. . . .

The majority nonetheless tries to find a distinction between piracy at sea and similar cases on land. It writes, "Applying U.S. law to pirates

. . . does not typically impose the sovereign will of the United States onto conduct occurring within the *territorial* jurisdiction of another sovereign and therefore carries less direct foreign policy consequences." But, as I have just pointed out, "[a]pplying U.S. law to pirates" *does* typically involve applying our law to acts taking place within the jurisdiction of another sovereign. Nor can the majority's words "territorial jurisdiction" sensibly distinguish land from sea for purposes of isolating adverse foreign policy risks, as the Barbary Pirates, the War of 1812, the sinking of the *Lusitania,* and the Lockerbie bombing make all too clear.

The majority also writes, "Pirates were fair game wherever found, by any nation, because they generally did not operate within any jurisdiction." I very much agree that pirates were fair game "wherever found." Indeed, that is the point. That is why we asked, in *Sosa,* who are today's pirates? Certainly today's pirates include torturers and perpetrators of genocide. And today, like the pirates of old, they are "fair game" where they are found. . . . And just as a nation that harbored pirates provoked the concern of other nations in past centuries, so harboring "common enemies of all mankind" provokes similar concerns today. . . .

II

In applying the ATS to acts "occurring within the territory of a[nother] sovereign," I would assume that Congress intended the statute's jurisdictional reach to match the statute's underlying substantive grasp. That grasp, defined by the statute's purposes set forth in *Sosa,* includes compensation for those injured by piracy and its modern-day equivalents, at least where allowing such compensation avoids "serious" negative international "consequences" for the United States. *Sosa,* 542 U.S. at 715. And just as we have looked to established international substantive norms to help determine the statute's substantive reach, so we should look to international jurisdictional norms to help determine the statute's jurisdictional scope.

The Restatement (Third) of Foreign Relations Law is helpful. Section 402 recognizes that, subject to § 403's "reasonableness" requirement, a nation may apply its law (for example, federal common law, not only (1) to "conduct" that "takes place [or to persons or things] within its territory" but also (2) to the "activities, interests, status, or relations of its nationals outside as well as within its territory," (3) to "conduct outside its territory that has or is intended to have substantial effect within its territory," and (4) to certain foreign "conduct outside its territory . . . that is directed against the security of the state or against a limited class of other state interests." In addition, § 404 of the Restatement explains that a "state has jurisdiction to define and prescribe punishment for certain offenses recognized by the community of nations as of universal concern, such as piracy, slave trade," and analogous behavior.

Considering these jurisdictional norms in light of both the ATS's basic purpose (to provide compensation for those injured by today's pirates) and *Sosa*'s basic caution (to avoid international friction), I believe that the statute provides jurisdiction where (1) the alleged tort occurs on American soil, (2) the defendant is an American national, or (3) the defendant's conduct substantially and adversely affects an important American national interest, and that includes a distinct interest in preventing the United States from becoming a safe harbor (free of civil as well as criminal liability) for a torturer or other common enemy of mankind.

I would interpret the statute as providing jurisdiction only where distinct American interests are at issue. Doing so reflects the fact that Congress adopted the present statute at a time when, as Justice Story put it, "No nation ha[d] ever yet pretended to be the custos morum of the whole world." United States v. La Jeune Eugenie, 26 F. Cas. 832, 847 (No. 15,551) (CC Mass. 1822). That restriction also should help to minimize international friction. Further limiting principles such as exhaustion, forum non conveniens, and comity would do the same. So would a practice of courts giving weight to the views of the Executive Branch. . . .

As I have indicated, we should treat this Nation's interest in not becoming a safe harbor for violators of the most fundamental international norms as an important jurisdiction-related interest justifying application of the ATS in light of the statute's basic purposes—in particular that of compensating those who have suffered harm at the hands of, e.g., torturers or other modern pirates. . . .

International norms have long included a duty not to permit a nation to become a safe harbor for pirates (or their equivalent). . . .

More recently two lower American courts have, in effect, rested jurisdiction primarily upon that kind of concern. In Filartiga v. Pena-Irala, 630 F.2d 876 (2d Cir. 1980), an alien plaintiff brought a lawsuit against an alien defendant for damages suffered through acts of torture that the defendant allegedly inflicted in a foreign nation, Paraguay. Neither plaintiff nor defendant was an American national and the actions underlying the lawsuit took place abroad. The defendant, however, "had . . . resided in the United States for more than ninth months" before being sued, having overstayed his visitor's visa. Id. at 878–79. Jurisdiction was deemed proper because the defendant's alleged conduct violated a well-established international law norm, and the suit vindicated our Nation's interest in not providing a safe harbor, free of damages claims, for those defendants who commit such conduct.

In *Marcos*, the plaintiffs were nationals of the Philippines, the defendant was a Philippine national, and the alleged wrongful act, death by torture, took place abroad. . . . A month before being sued, the defendant, "his family, . . . and others loyal to [him] fled to Hawaii," where the ATS case was heard. In re Estate of Marcos, Human Rights Litigation, 25 F.3d 1467, 1469 (9th Cir. 1994). As in *Filartiga*, the court found ATS jurisdiction.

And in *Sosa* we referred to both cases with approval, suggesting that the ATS allowed a claim for relief in such circumstances. . . . Not surprisingly, both before and after *Sosa*, courts have consistently rejected the notion that the ATS is categorically barred from extraterritorial application. . . .

Application of the statute in the way I have suggested is consistent with international law and foreign practice. Nations have long been obliged not to provide safe harbors for their own nationals who commit such serious crimes abroad. . . .

Many countries permit foreign plaintiffs to bring suits against their own nationals based on unlawful conduct that took place abroad. . . .

Other countries permit some form of lawsuit brought by a foreign national against a foreign national, based upon conduct taking place abroad and seeking damages. Certain countries, which find "universal" criminal "jurisdiction" to try perpetrators of particularly heinous crimes such as piracy and genocide, see Restatement § 404, also permit private persons injured by that conduct to pursue "actions civiles," seeking civil damages in the criminal proceeding. . . .

At the same time Congress has ratified treaties obliging the United States to find and punish foreign perpetrators of serious crimes committed against foreign persons abroad. . . .

And Congress has sometimes authorized civil damages in such cases. See generally note following 28 U.S.C. § 1350 (Torture Victim Protection Act of 1991 (TVPA) (private damages action for torture or extrajudicial killing committed under authority of a foreign nation)). . . .

Congress, while aware of the award of civil damages under the ATS—including cases such as *Filartiga* with foreign plaintiffs, defendants, and conduct—has not sought to limit the statute's jurisdictional or substantive reach. Rather, Congress has enacted other statutes, and not only criminal statutes, that allow the United States to prosecute (or allow victims to obtain damages from) foreign persons who injure foreign victims by committing abroad torture, genocide, and other heinous acts. See, e.g., 18 U.S.C. § 2340A(b)(2) (authorizing prosecution of torturers if "the alleged offender is present in the United States, irrespective of the nationality of the victim or alleged offender"); § 1091(e)(2)(D) (genocide prosecution authorized when, "regardless of where the offense is committed, the alleged offender is . . . present in the United States"); note following 28 U.S.C. § 1350, § 2(a) (private right of action on behalf of individuals harmed by an act of torture or extrajudicial killing committed "under actual or apparent authority, or color of law, of any foreign nation"). . . .

III

Applying these jurisdictional principles to this case, however, I agree with the Court that jurisdiction does not lie. The defendants are two foreign corporations. Their shares, like those of many foreign corporations, are traded on the New York Stock Exchange. Their only presence in the United States consists of an office in New York City (actually owned by a separate but affiliated company) that helps to explain their business to potential investors. The plaintiffs are not United States nationals but nationals of other nations. The conduct at issue took place abroad. And the plaintiffs allege, not that the defendants directly engaged in acts of torture, genocide, or the equivalent, but that they helped others (who are not American nationals) to do so.

Under these circumstances, even if the New York office were a sufficient basis for asserting general jurisdiction . . . it would be farfetched to believe, based solely upon the defendants' minimal and indirect American presence, that this legal action helps to vindicate a distinct American interest, such as in not providing a safe harbor for an "enemy of all mankind." Thus I agree with the Court that here it would "reach too far to say" that such "mere corporate presence suffices."

I consequently join the Court's judgment but not its opinion.

NOTES ON *KIOBEL V. ROYAL DUTCH PETROLEUM*

1. PRESUMPTION AGAINST EXTRATERRITORIALITY

The Supreme Court has held that federal statutes should be presumed not to apply to conduct occurring outside the United States. In EEOC v. Arabian American Oil Co., 499 U.S. 244 (1991), the Court applied this presumption in holding that Title VII did not apply to a U.S. corporation's alleged discriminatory treatment of a U.S. citizen in Saudi Arabia. In Morrison v. National Australia Bank Ltd., 561 U.S. 247 (2010), the Court applied the presumption in holding that Section 10(b) of the Securities Exchange Act did not apply to claims of alleged misconduct in connection with securities traded on foreign exchanges. The Court has explained that the presumption "rests on the perception that Congress ordinarily legislates with respect to domestic, not foreign matters," *Morrison*, 561 U.S. at 255, and that it also "serves to protect against unintended clashes between our laws and those of other nations which could result in international discord," *Arabian American Oil*, 499 U.S. at 248.

Despite the presumption against extraterritoriality, most lower courts had assumed before *Kiobel* that claims could be brought under the ATS for foreign conduct. One reason they may have made this assumption is that the ATS is limited to torts that violate international law. Since international law applies globally, it may not seem "extraterritorial" for a U.S. court to apply it to adjudicate a dispute concerning conduct abroad. In *Sosa*, however, the Supreme Court seemed to suggest that the cause of action in ATS cases was coming from federal common law that was authorized in some fashion by the ATS, a proposition confirmed by the Court in *Kiobel*. The issue in *Kiobel*, therefore, was whether the presumption against extraterritoriality applied to a claim under U.S. federal common law. The majority contends that, if anything, the justifications for the presumption apply with greater force in the context of a judicially developed rather than statutory cause of action.

2. QUESTIONS AND COMMENTS ON *KIOBEL*

After *Kiobel*, what is left of ATS litigation? It is clear that foreign corporations may not be sued under the ATS for torts they commit abroad. (Indeed, the Court was 9–0 on that point.) What about U.S. corporations? At the end of its opinion, the majority states that "where the claims touch and concern the territory of the United States, they must do so with sufficient force to displace the presumption against extraterritorial application," and that "mere corporate presence" in the United States is not enough. What, beyond mere corporate presence, might be enough? What answer was Justice Alito suggesting in his concurrence?

Recall the Second Circuit's decision in *Filartiga* (discussed in the introductory notes to this Section), which involved a suit against a former Paraguayan police inspector for acts committed in Paraguay. Does *Kiobel* suggest that *Filartiga* was wrongly decided? Importantly, the Torture Victim Protection Act (TVPA) now provides an alternative basis for a case, like *Filartiga*, that involves acts of torture or "extrajudicial killing." Justice Kennedy, who was part of the five-Justice majority, observed in his short concurrence that the decision left open "significant questions regarding the reach and interpretation of the Alien Tort Statute" and that "the presumption against extraterritorial application may require some further elaboration and explanation" in cases covered "neither by the TVPA nor by the reasoning and holding of today's case." What cases might he have had in mind?

In arguing that the presumption against extraterritoriality has been overcome in this case, Justice Breyer contends in his concurrence that the ATS was designed in part to allow suits against pirates, whose conduct would typically take place outside the United States. What is the majority's response to this argument? What evidence is there, if any, that the ATS was in fact designed for suits against pirates? Even if pirates could have historically been sued under the ATS, is Justice Breyer right in describing egregious human rights abuses as "modern-day equivalents" to piracy? In any event, isn't Justice Breyer correct that the United States has an interest in not being a safe haven for human rights abusers? Is it a sufficient answer to Breyer that Congress can provide for broader civil liability if it is dissatisfied with the decision in *Kiobel*?

In light of the Supreme Court's restriction of ATS litigation in *Kiobel*, plaintiffs may attempt to use state tort law as a vehicle for litigating claims that they might otherwise have attempted to litigate under the ATS. Cases based on state law typically cannot be brought in federal court unless there is diversity jurisdiction, which will not be available in cases between foreign parties. Whether brought in federal or state court, cases based on state tort law are likely to raise difficult choice-of-law questions. Also relevant to the choice-of-law question will be the fact that there are probably due process and other limitations on the extent to which states can apply their tort law to conduct in other countries. Plaintiffs may also face more significant forum non conveniens limitations if they lack a federal cause of action, especially where both the plaintiffs and the defendants are non-U.S. citizens.

3.   COMMENTARY ON *KIOBEL*

For an effort to situate ATS litigation "within the traditional federal-courts framework of implied rights of action and federal common law," see Ernest A. Young, Universal Jurisdiction, the Alien Tort Statute, and Transnational Public Law Litigation After *Kiobel*, 64 Duke L.J. 1023 (2015). Young contends that this framework supports the Supreme Court's disallowance in *Kiobel* of "universal jurisdiction" under the ATS. For additional discussion of the decision and its implications, see the Symposium articles in Volume 89, Issue 4 of the Notre Dame Law Review: Roger P. Alford, The Future of Human Rights Litigation After *Kiobel*, 89 Notre Dame L. Rev. 749 (2014); Anthony J. Bellia Jr. and Bradford R. Clark, Two Myths About the Alien Tort Statute, 89 Notre Dame L. Rev. 1609 (2014); William R. Casto, The ATS Cause of Action is *Sui Generis*, 89 Notre Dame L. Rev. 1545 (2014); Doug Cassel, Suing Americans for Human Rights Torts Overseas: The Supreme Court Leaves the Door Open, 89 Notre Dame L. Rev. 1773 (2014); William S. Dodge, Alien Tort Statute Litigation: The Road Not Taken, 89 Notre Dame L. Rev. 1577 (2014); Eugene Kontorovich, *Kiobel* Surprise: Unexpected by Scholars but Consistent with International Trends, 89 Notre Dame L. Rev. 1671 (2014); Thomas H. Lee, Three Lives of the Alien Tort Statute: The Evolving Role of the Judiciary in U.S. Foreign Relations, 89 Notre Dame L. Rev. 1645 (2014); Ralph G. Steinhardt, Determining Which Human Rights Claims "Touch and Concern" the United States: Justice Kennedy's *Filartiga*, 89 Notre Dame L. Rev. 1695 (2014); Beth Stephens, The Curious History of the Alien Tort Statute, 89 Notre Dame L. Rev. 1467 (2014); Carlos M. Vázquez, Things We Do with Presumptions: Reflections on *Kiobel v. Royal Dutch Petroleum*, 89 Notre Dame L. Rev. 1719 (2014). See also Roger P. Alford, Human Rights After *Kiobel*: Choice of Law and the Rise of Transnational Tort Litigation, 63 Emory L.J. 1089 (2014).

CHAPTER III

JUDICIAL REVIEW AND JUSTICIABILITY

The federal courts are courts of limited jurisdiction. Most fundamentally, this means that they are allowed to exercise their judicial power only in the cases and controversies specified in Article III of the Constitution. This proposition was confirmed by the Supreme Court in *Marbury v. Madison*. In addition, except for cases falling within the original jurisdiction of the Supreme Court, a federal court cannot hear a case unless Congress has authorized jurisdiction—that is, unless the court has statutory subject matter jurisdiction. The particular requirements for statutory subject matter jurisdiction, and the potential limitations on Congress's ability to restrict federal court jurisdiction, are explored in other chapters of the casebook. This chapter considers a different set of limitations on the ability of the federal courts to hear cases—limitations that come under the label "justiciability." Justiciability encompasses a variety of doctrines, many of which relate to the meaning of the terms "cases" and "controversies" in Article III, and others of which have been adopted by the Supreme Court as a matter of prudence. Section 1 deals with judicial review. The succeeding sections of this chapter cover the various doctrines of justiciability.

SECTION 1. JUDICIAL REVIEW

Marbury v. Madison
Supreme Court of the United States, 1803.
5 U.S. (1 Cranch) 137.

■ [T]he following opinion of the Court was delivered by THE CHIEF JUSTICE: . . .

At the last term on the affidavits then read and filed with the clerk, a rule was granted in this case, requiring the Secretary of State to show cause why a mandamus should not issue, directing him to deliver to William Marbury his commission as a justice of the peace for the county of Washington, in the District of Columbia.

No cause has been shown, and the present motion is for a mandamus. The peculiar delicacy of this case, the novelty of some of its circumstances, and the real difficulty attending the points which occur in it, require a complete exposition of the principles on which the opinion to be given by the Court, is founded.

These principles have been, on the side of the applicant, very ably argued at the bar. In rendering the opinion of the Court, there will be some departure in form, though not in substance, from the points stated in that argument.

In the order in which the Court has viewed this subject, the following questions have been considered and decided:

1st. Has the applicant a right to the commission he demands?

2dly. If he has a right, and that right has been violated, do the laws of this country afford him a remedy?

3dly. If they do afford him a remedy, is it a mandamus issuing from this Court?

The first object of inquiry is,

1st. Has the applicant a right to the commission he demands?

His right originates in an act of Congress passed in February 1801, concerning the District of Columbia. . . .

It appears, from the affidavits, that in compliance with this law, a commission for William Marbury as a justice of the peace for the county of Washington, was signed by John Adams, then President of the United States; after which the seal of the United States was affixed to it; but the commission has never reached the person for whom it was made out. . . .

It is . . . decidedly the opinion of the Court, that when a commission has been signed by the President, the appointment is made; and that the commission is complete, when the seal of the United States has been affixed to it by the Secretary of State. . . .

Mr. Marbury, then, since his commission was signed by the President, and sealed by the Secretary of State, was appointed; and as the law creating the office, gave the officer a right to hold for five years, independent of the executive, the appointment was not revocable; but vested in the officer legal rights, which are protected by the laws of his country.

To withhold his commission, therefore, is an act deemed by the Court not warranted by law, but violative of a vested legal right.

This brings us to the second inquiry; which is,

2dly. If he has a right, and that right has been violated, do the laws of his country afford him a remedy?

The very essence of civil liberty certainly consists in the right of every individual to claim the protection of the laws, whenever he receives an injury. One of the first duties of government is to afford that protection. . . .

The government of the United States has been emphatically termed a government of laws, and not of men. It will certainly cease to deserve this high appellation, if the laws furnish no remedy for the violation of a vested legal right.

If this obloquy is to be cast on the jurisprudence of our country, it must arise from the peculiar character of the case.

It behooves us then to enquire whether there be in its composition any ingredient which shall exempt it from legal investigation, or exclude the injured party from legal redress. . . .

Is it in the nature of the transaction? Is the act of delivering or withholding a commission to be considered as a mere political act, belonging to the executive department alone, for the performance of which entire confidence is placed by our Constitution in the supreme executive; and for any misconduct respecting which, the injured individual has no remedy.

That there may be such cases is not to be questioned; but that every act of duty, to be performed in any of the great departments of government, constitutes such a case, is not to be admitted. . . .

It follows, then, that the question, whether the legality of an act of the head of a department be examinable in a court of justice or not, must always depend on the nature of that act. . . .

By the Constitution of the United States, the President is invested with certain important political powers, in the exercise of which he is to use his own discretion, and is accountable only to his country in his political character, and to his own conscience. To aid him in the performance of these duties, he is authorized to appoint certain officers, who act by his authority and in conformity with his orders.

In such cases, their acts are his acts; and whatever opinion may be entertained of the manner in which executive discretion may be used, still there exists, and can exist, no power to control that discretion. The subjects are political. They respect the nation, not individual rights, and being entrusted to the executive, the decision of the executive is conclusive. . . .

But when the legislature proceeds to impose on that officer other duties; when he is directed peremptorily to perform certain acts; when the rights of individuals are dependent on the performance of those acts; he is so far the officer of the law; is amenable to the laws for his conduct; and cannot at his discretion sport away the vested rights of others.

The conclusion from this reasoning is, that where the heads of departments are the political or confidential agents of the executive, merely to execute the will of the President, or rather to act in cases in which the executive professes a constitutional or legal discretion, nothing can be more perfectly clear than that their acts are only politically examinable. But where a specific duty is assigned by law, and individual rights depend upon the performance of that duty, it seems equally clear that the individual who considers himself injured, has a right to resort to the laws of his country for a remedy. . . .

It is, then, the opinion of the Court [that Marbury has a] right to the commission; a refusal to deliver which, is a plain violation of that right, for which the laws of his country afford him a remedy.

It remains to be enquired whether,

3dly. He is entitled to the remedy for which he applies. This depends on,

1st. The nature of the writ applied for, and,

2dly. The power of this Court. . . .

[T]o render the mandamus a proper remedy, the officer to whom it is to be directed, must be one to whom, on legal principles, such writ may be directed; and the person applying for it must be without any other specific and legal remedy. . . .

With respect to the officer to whom it would be directed. The intimate political relation, subsisting between the President of the United States and the heads of departments, necessarily renders any legal investigation of the acts of one of those high officers peculiarly irksome, as well as delicate; and excites some hesitation with respect to the propriety of entering into such investigation. Impressions are often received without much reflection or examination, and it is not wonderful that in such a case as this, the assertion, by an individual, of his legal claims in a court of justice; to which claims it is the duty of that court to attend; should at first view be considered by some, as an attempt to intrude into the cabinet, and to intermeddle with the prerogatives of the executive.

It is scarcely necessary for the Court to disclaim all pretensions to such a jurisdiction. An extravagance, so absurd and excessive, could not have been entertained for a moment. The province of the Court is, solely, to decide on the rights of individuals, not to enquire how the executive, or executive officers, perform duties in which they have a discretion. Questions in their nature political, or which are, by the Constitution and laws, submitted to the executive, can never be made in this Court.

But if this be not such a question; . . . what is there in the exalted station of the officer, which shall bar a citizen from asserting, in a court of justice, his legal rights, or shall forbid a court to listen to the claim; or to issue a mandamus, directing the performance of a duty, not depending on executive discretion, but on particular acts of Congress and the general principles of law? . . .

It is not by the office of the person to whom the writ is directed, but the nature of the thing to be done that the propriety or impropriety of issuing a mandamus, is to be determined. Where the head of a department acts in a case, in which executive discretion is to be exercised; in which he is the mere organ of executive will; it is again repeated, that any application to a court to control, in any respect, his conduct, would be rejected without hesitation.

But where he is directed by law to do a certain act affecting the absolute rights of individuals, in the performance of which he is not placed under the particular direction of the President, and the performance of which, the President cannot lawfully forbid, and therefore is never presumed to have forbidden; as for example, to record a commission, or a patent for land, which has received all the legal solemnities; or to give a copy of such record; in such cases, it is not perceived on what ground the courts of the country are further excused from the duty of giving judgment, that right be done to an injured individual, than if the same services were to be performed by a person not the head of a department. . . .

This, then, is a plain case for a mandamus, either to deliver the commission, or a copy of it from the record; and it only remains to be enquired,

Whether it can issue from this Court.

The act to establish the judicial courts of the United States authorizes the Supreme Court "to issue writs of mandamus in cases warranted by the principles and usages of law, to any courts appointed, or persons holding office, under the authority of the United States."[a]

The Secretary of State, being a person holding an office under the authority of the United States, is precisely within the letter of the description; and if this Court is not authorized to issue a writ of mandamus to such an officer, it must be because the law is unconstitutional, and therefore absolutely incapable of conferring the authority, and assigning the duties which its words purport to confer and assign.

The Constitution vests the whole judicial power of the United States in one Supreme Court, and such inferior courts as Congress shall, from time to time, ordain and establish. This power is expressly extended to all cases arising under the laws of the United States; and, consequently, in some form, may be exercised over the present case; because the right claimed is given by a law of the United States.

In the distribution of this power it is declared that "the Supreme Court shall have original jurisdiction in all cases affecting ambassadors, other public ministers and consuls, and those in which a state shall be a

---

[a]   Section 13 of the Judiciary Act of 1789 provided:

And be it further enacted, That the Supreme Court shall have exclusive jurisdiction of all controversies of a civil nature, where a state is a party, except between a state and its citizens; and except also between a state and citizens of other states, or aliens, in which later case it shall have original but not exclusive jurisdiction. And shall have exclusively all such jurisdiction of suits or proceedings against ambassadors, or other public ministers, or their domestics, or domestic servants, as a court of law can have or exercise consistently with the law of nations; and original, but not exclusive jurisdiction of all suits brought by ambassadors, or other public ministers, or in which a consul, or vice consul, shall be a party. And the trial of issues of fact in the Supreme Court, in all actions at law against citizens of the United States, shall be by jury. The Supreme court shall also have appellate jurisdiction from the circuit courts and courts of the several states, in the cases hereinafter specially provided for; and shall have power to issue writs of prohibition to the district courts, when proceeding as courts of admiralty and maritime jurisdiction, and writs of mandamus, in cases warranted by the principles and usages of law, to any courts appointed, or persons holding office, under the authority of the United States.—[Footnote by eds.]

party. In all other cases, the Supreme Court shall have appellate jurisdiction."

It has been insisted, at the bar, that as the original grant of jurisdiction, to the supreme and inferior courts, is general, and the clause, assigning original jurisdiction to the Supreme Court, contains no negative or restrictive words; the power remains to the legislature, to assign original jurisdiction to that Court in other cases than those specified in the article which has been recited; provided those cases belong to the judicial power of the United States.

If it had been intended to leave it in the discretion of the legislature to apportion the judicial power between the supreme and inferior courts according to the will of that body, it would certainly have been useless to have proceeded further than to have defined the judicial power, and the tribunals in which it should be vested. The subsequent part of the section is mere surplusage, is entirely without meaning, if such is to be the construction. If Congress remains at liberty to give this Court appellate jurisdiction, where the Constitution has declared their jurisdiction shall be original; and original jurisdiction where the Constitution has declared it shall be appellate; the distribution of jurisdiction, made in the Constitution, is form without substance.

Affirmative words are often, in their operation, negative of other objects than those affirmed; and in this case, a negative or exclusive sense must be given to them or they have no operation at all.

It cannot be presumed that any clause in the Constitution is intended to be without effect; and, therefore, such a construction is inadmissible, unless the words require it.

If the solicitude of the convention, respecting our peace with foreign powers, induced a provision that the Supreme Court should take original jurisdiction in cases which might be supposed to affect them; yet the clause would have proceeded no further than to provide for such cases, if no further restriction on the powers of Congress had been intended. That they should have appellate jurisdiction in all other cases, with such exceptions as Congress might make, is no restriction; unless the words be deemed exclusive of original jurisdiction.

When an instrument organizing fundamentally a judicial system, divides into one supreme, and so many inferior courts as the legislature may ordain and establish; then enumerates its powers, and proceeds so far to distribute them, as to define the jurisdiction of the Supreme Court by declaring the cases in which it shall take original jurisdiction, and that in others it shall take appellate jurisdiction; the plain import of the words seems to be, that in one class of cases its jurisdiction is original, and not appellate; in the other it is appellate, and not original. If any other construction would render the clause inoperative, that is an additional reason for rejecting such other construction, and for adhering to their obvious meaning.

To enable this Court then to issue a mandamus, it must be shown to be an exercise of appellate jurisdiction, or to be necessary to enable them to exercise appellate jurisdiction.

It has been stated at the bar that the appellate jurisdiction may be exercised in a variety of forms, and that if it be the will of the legislature a mandamus should be used for that purpose, that will must be obeyed. This is true, yet the jurisdiction must be appellate, not original.

It is the essential criterion of appellate jurisdiction, that it revises and corrects the proceedings in a cause already instituted, and does not create that cause. Although, therefore, a mandamus may be directed to courts, yet to issue such a writ to an officer for the delivery of a paper, is in effect the same as to sustain an original action for that paper, and therefore seems not to belong to appellate, but to original jurisdiction. Neither is it necessary in such a case as this, to enable the Court to exercise its appellate jurisdiction.

The authority, therefore, given to the Supreme Court, by the act establishing the judicial courts of the United States, to issue writs of mandamus to public officers, appears not to be warranted by the Constitution; and it becomes necessary to enquire whether a jurisdiction, so conferred, can be exercised.

[handwritten margin note: issuing writs seems not warranted by the constitution]

The question, whether an act, repugnant to the Constitution, can become the law of the land, is a question deeply interesting to the United States; but, happily, not of an intricacy proportioned to its interest. It seems only necessary to recognize certain principles, supposed to have been long and well established, to decide it.

That the people have an original right to establish, for their future government, such principles as, in their opinion, shall most conduce to their own happiness, is the basis, on which the whole American fabric has been erected. The exercise of this original right is a very great exertion; nor can it, nor ought it to be frequently repeated. The principles, therefore, so established, are deemed fundamental. And as the authority, from which they proceed, is supreme, and can seldom act, they are designed to be permanent.

This original and supreme will organizes the government, and assigns to different departments their respective powers. It may either stop here; or establish certain limits not to be transcended by those departments.

The government of the United States is of the latter description. The powers of the legislature are defined, and limited; and that those limits may not be mistaken, or forgotten, the Constitution is written. To what purpose are powers limited, and to what purpose is that limitation committed to writing, if these limits may, at any time, be passed by those intended to be restrained? The distinction, between a government with limited and unlimited powers, is abolished, if those limits do not confine the persons on whom they are imposed, and if acts prohibited and acts

[handwritten margin note: slippery slope for gov't to have unlimited powers]

allowed, are of equal obligation. It is a proposition too plain to be contested, that the Constitution controls any legislative act repugnant to it; or, that the legislature may alter the Constitution by an ordinary act.

Between these alternatives there is no middle ground. The Constitution is either a superior, paramount law, unchangeable by ordinary means, or it is on a level with ordinary legislative acts, and like other acts, is alterable when the legislature shall please to alter it.

If the former part of the alternative be true, then a legislative act contrary to the Constitution is not law: if the latter part be true, then written constitutions are absurd attempts, on the part of the people, to limit a power in its own nature illimitable.

Certainly all those who have framed written constitutions contemplate them as forming the fundamental and paramount law of the nation, and consequently the theory of every such government must be, that an act of the legislature, repugnant to the Constitution, is void.

This theory is essentially attached to a written constitution, and is consequently to be considered, by this Court, as one of the fundamental principles of our society. It is not therefore to be lost sight of in the further consideration of this subject.

If an act of the legislature, repugnant to the Constitution, is void, does it, notwithstanding its invalidity, bind the courts, and oblige them to give it effect? Or, in other words, though it be not law, does it constitute a rule as operative as if it was a law? This would be to overthrow in fact what was established in theory; and would seem, at first view, an absurdity too gross to be insisted on. It shall, however, receive a more attentive consideration.

It is emphatically the province and duty of the judicial department to say what the law is. Those who apply the rule to particular cases, must of necessity expound and interpret that rule. If two laws conflict with each other, the courts must decide on the operation of each.

So if a law be in opposition to the Constitution; if both the law and the Constitution apply to a particular case, so that the court must either decide that case conformably to the law, disregarding the Constitution; or conformably to the Constitution, disregarding the law; the court must determine which of these conflicting rules governs the case. This is of the very essence of judicial duty.

If, then, the courts are to regard the Constitution; and the Constitution is superior to any ordinary act of the legislature; the Constitution, and not such ordinary act, must govern the case to which both apply.

Those then who controvert the principle that the Constitution is to be considered, in court, as a paramount law, are reduced to the necessity of maintaining that courts must close their eyes on the Constitution, and see only the law.

This doctrine would subvert the very foundation of all written constitutions. It would declare that an act, which, according to the principles and theory of our government, is entirely void; is yet, in practice, completely obligatory. It would declare, that if the legislature shall do what is expressly forbidden, such act, notwithstanding the express prohibition, is in reality effectual. It would be giving to the legislature a practical and real omnipotence, with the same breath which professes to restrict their powers within narrow limits. It is prescribing limits, and declaring that those limits may be passed at pleasure.

That it thus reduces to nothing what we have deemed the greatest improvement on political institutions—a written constitution—would of itself be sufficient, in America, where written constitutions have been viewed with so much reverence, for rejecting the construction. But the peculiar expressions of the Constitution of the United States furnish additional arguments in favour of its rejection.

The judicial power of the United States is extended to all cases arising under the Constitution.

Could it be the intention of those who gave this power, to say that, in using it the Constitution should not be looked into? That a case arising under the Constitution should be decided without examining the instrument under which it arises?

This is too extravagant to be maintained.

In some cases, then, the Constitution must be looked into by the judges. And if they can open it at all, what part of it are they forbidden to read, or to obey?

There are many other parts of the Constitution which serve to illustrate this subject.

It is declared that "no tax or duty shall be laid on articles exported from any state." Suppose a duty on the export of cotton, of tobacco, or of flour; and a suit instituted to recover it. Ought judgment to be rendered in such a case? Ought the judges to close their eyes on the Constitution and only see the law?

The Constitution declares that "no bill of attainder or ex post facto law shall be passed."

If, however, such a bill should be passed and a person should be prosecuted under it; must the court condemn to death those victims whom the Constitution endeavors to preserve?

"No person," says the Constitution, "shall be convicted of treason unless on the testimony of two witnesses to the same overt act, or on confession in open court."

Here the language of the Constitution is addressed especially to the courts. It prescribes, directly for them, a rule of evidence not to be departed from. If the legislature should change that rule, and declare *one* witness, or a confession *out* of court, sufficient for conviction, must the constitutional principle yield to the legislative act?

From these, and many other selections which might be made, it is apparent, that the framers of the Constitution contemplated that instrument, as a rule for the government of *courts*, as well as of the legislature.

Why otherwise does it direct the judges to take an oath to support it? This oath certainly applies, in an especial manner, to their conduct in their official character. How immoral to impose it on them, if they were to be used as the instruments, and the knowing instruments, for violating what they swear to support!

That oath of office, too, imposed by the legislature, is completely demonstrative of the legislative opinion on this subject. It is in these words, "I do solemnly swear that I will administer justice without respect to persons, and do equal right to the poor and to the rich; and that I will faithfully and impartially discharge all the duties incumbent on me as _____, according to the best of my abilities and understanding, agreeably to *the Constitution*, and laws of the United States."

Why does a judge swear to discharge his duties agreeably to the Constitution of the United States, if that Constitution forms no rule for his government? If it is closed upon him, and cannot be inspected by him?

If such be the real state of things, this is worse than solemn mockery. To prescribe, or to take this oath, becomes equally a crime.

It is also not entirely unworthy of observation, that in declaring what shall be the *supreme* law of the land, the *Constitution* itself is first mentioned; and not the laws of the United States generally, but those only which shall be made in *pursuance* of the Constitution, have that rank.

Thus, the particular phraseology of the Constitution of the United States confirms and strengthens the principle, supposed to be essential to all written constitutions, that a law repugnant to the Constitution is void; and that *courts*, as well as other departments, are bound by that instrument.

The rule must be discharged.

NOTES ON ARTICLE III, THE JUDICIARY ACT OF 1789, AND MARBURY V. MADISON

1.   THE MADISONIAN COMPROMISE

Between the time of Declaration of Independence in 1776 and the establishment of the Constitution in 1788–89, the United States operated without a national court system, other than a limited admiralty appellate tribunal. Instead, it relied on the judicial systems of the 13 states. This lack of a national court system was perceived by many as a defect that should be remedied by the establishment of a Constitution. In debates over the Constitution, however, there was controversy over whether to establish anything other than a national Supreme Court. The so-called Antifederalists were concerned that a system of national trial courts would displace too much state judicial authority. The solution—often called the Madisonian Compromise—was to establish a Supreme Court and to give Congress the authority to create lower federal courts.

2.   ARTICLE III

Read through Article III of the Constitution. Consistent with the Madisonian Compromise, Section 1 refers to a Supreme Court and "such inferior Courts as the Congress may from time to time ordain and establish." This section also says that federal judges are to "hold their Offices during good Behavior," which means life tenure as long as they do not do something impeachable. It also says that they shall not have their compensation diminished while in office. These provisions—lifetime tenure and salary protection—do not exist in many state court systems, the majority of which today have some sort of elections for judges. Why would the Framers have adopted them for the federal courts? Alexander Hamilton, in one of the Federalist Papers, explained that these protections would operate as a "barrier to the encroachments and oppressions of the representative body," i.e., Congress. Even with this protection, Hamilton contended that the judiciary would be the "least dangerous" branch of the government, since it would not have direct control over either the sword or the purse, i.e., over either the military or the revenue.

Section 2 of Article III lists nine categories of jurisdiction—three based on subject matter, referred to as "Cases," and six based on parties, referred to as "Controversies." At least today, the two most important categories are cases "arising under this Constitution, the Laws of the United States, and Treaties made, or which shall be made, under their Authority"—referred to as federal question jurisdiction—and controversies "between Citizens of different States"—referred to as diversity jurisdiction. Section 2 goes on to say that in certain types of cases the Supreme Court shall have original jurisdiction. For all other cases, the Court was to have appellate jurisdiction, either from the state courts or from lower federal courts to the extent that they were created. The Court's appellate jurisdiction, Section 2 further provides, is subject to "such Exceptions, and under such Regulations as the Congress shall make."

3.   THE JUDICIARY ACT OF 1789

Congress quickly decided to establish lower federal courts. In one of its earliest pieces of legislation—the Judiciary Act of 1789—Congress enacted extensive provisions concerning the structure and jurisdiction of both the lower federal courts and the Supreme Court. The federal court system that Congress established in 1789 differed in a number of respects from the one we have today. For example, the Judiciary Act set the number of Supreme Court Justices at six. It also directed that the circuit courts were to be composed of a mix of district court judges and Supreme Court justices who would "ride circuit." Moreover, the jurisdiction of the circuit courts was such that they would operate as trial courts for some matters and appellate courts for others. Perhaps surprisingly, the Judiciary Act did not contain any grant of general federal question jurisdiction. Such jurisdiction was not permanently enacted until 1875, and even then it had a jurisdictional amount requirement which was not eliminated until 1980. The Judiciary Act did provide for diversity jurisdiction, subject to a $500 amount in controversy requirement. It also provided for Supreme Court review of state court decisions, but only if the state court held against a federal claim.

4.   QUESTIONS AND COMMENTS ON *MARBURY V. MADISON*

Marbury argued, and the Court agreed, that Section 13 of the Judiciary Act (which is excerpted in a footnote added to *Marbury*) authorized mandamus actions to be brought directly in the Supreme Court. Is that the best reading of Section 13?[a] Should the Court have worked harder to construe Section 13 to avoid a constitutional problem? What, precisely, was the constitutional problem in *Marbury*? The Court concludes that Article III does not allow for a mandamus action to be brought directly in the Supreme Court—that is, in the Court's "original," as opposed to its "appellate," jurisdiction. Is Article III really clear on that point?[b] Note that, notwithstanding the categorical reasoning of *Marbury*, the Supreme Court in subsequent decisions has not interpreted Article III as disallowing the conferral of *appellate* jurisdiction on the Court with respect to cases that fall within its Article III original jurisdiction. The holding of *Marbury* that Congress cannot increase the Court's original jurisdiction, however, remains good law.

5.   CONSTITUTIONAL AVOIDANCE

Although not illustrated by *Marbury*, the federal courts often seek to avoid resolving constitutional questions when they can decide cases on other grounds. This idea was expressed most famously by Justice Brandeis in his concurrence in Ashwander v. Tennessee Valley Authority, 297 U.S. 288, 347 (1936), in which he outlined a variety of tools for constitutional avoidance, including the proposition that "[t]he Court will not pass upon a constitutional question, although properly presented by the record, if there is also present some other ground upon which the case may be disposed of."

---

[a]   For differing views, see William Van Alstyne, A Critical Guide to *Marbury v. Madison*, 1969 Duke L.J. 1, 15 ("No textual mangling is required to confine [the grant of mandamus authority to the Supreme Court in Section 13] to appellate jurisdiction."); Akhil Reed Amar, *Marbury*, Section 13, and the Original Jurisdiction of the Supreme Court, 56 U. Chi. L. Rev. 443, 456 (1989) ("[T]he mandamus clause is best read as simply giving the Court remedial authority—for both original and appellate jurisdiction cases—after jurisdiction (whether original or appellate) has been independently established."); and James E. Pfander, *Marbury*, Original Jurisdiction, and the Supreme Court's Supervisory Powers, 101 Colum. L. Rev. 1515, 1532 (2001) ("Carefully sifted, the evidence supports Marshall's conclusion that the drafters of section 13 gave the Court freestanding mandamus authority.").

[b]   Compare Van Alstyne, A Critical Guide, at 31 ("The clause readily supports a meaningful interpretation that the Court's original jurisdiction may not be *reduced* by Congress, but that it may be supplemented by adding to its original jurisdiction over some cases which would otherwise fall only within its appellate jurisdiction."), with Amar, *Marbury*, at 444 (arguing that "Article III delimits the maximum amount of original jurisdiction that the Supreme Court may exercise" because of concerns about the geographic inconvenience of forcing litigants to try cases before the Court).

The Supreme Court has invoked constitutional avoidance in its construction of federal statutes, in two ways. First, the Court has long stated that federal statutes should be construed, where possible, so that they do not violate the Constitution. See, e.g., Parsons v. Bedford, 28 U.S. (3 Pet.) 433, 448–449 (1830) ("No court ought, unless the terms of an act rendered it unavoidable, to give a construction to it which should involve a violation, however unintentional, of the constitution."). Part of the idea behind this canon of construction is that Congress presumably would rather have its enactments construed to avoid unconstitutionality rather than held invalid. See Richard A. Posner, Statutory Interpretation—In the Classroom and in the Courtroom, 50 U. Chi. L. Rev. 800, 814–15 (1983) ("This canon rests on the commonsense assumption that the legislators would rather not have the courts nullify their effort entirely unless the interpretation necessary to save it would pervert the goals of the legislature in enacting it.").

Second, the Court sometimes invokes a broader canon of construction to construe statutes, where possible, to avoid "serious constitutional questions" or "serious constitutional doubts." This canon, like the avoidance of unconstitutionality canon, reduces the instances in which the federal courts exercise their power of constitutional judicial review. But, unlike the unconstitutionality canon, it also allows the courts to avoid committing to a particular constitutional interpretation, since they need merely find serious doubt rather than actual unconstitutionality. Application of this canon has been criticized by some commentators, in part because it is likely to result in the under-enforcement of statutes even when such under-enforcement is not required by the Constitution. In any event, the Court has emphasized that "[s]tatutes should be interpreted to avoid *serious* constitutional doubts, . . . not to eliminate all possible contentions that the statute *might* be unconstitutional." Reno v. Flores, 507 U.S. 292, 314 n.9 (1993).

6.   MODERN FEDERAL-STATE COURT SYSTEM

There are currently 94 federal district courts. Each state has at least one district court, and many states have more than one, at different locations within the state. There are also district courts in Washington, D.C., Puerto Rico, and the U.S. territories of the Virgin Islands, Guam, and the Northern Mariana Islands. There are thirteen federal courts of appeal—11 regional circuit courts, a circuit court in Washington, D.C., and a Federal Circuit (also located in Washington, D.C.). The regional circuit courts hear appeals from district court decisions in their region. The D.C. Circuit hears appeals from the federal district court in Washington and also from various administrative agencies. The Federal Circuit hears appeals in certain specialized cases, such as those involving patent law and contract claims against the U.S. government. The number of judges on the circuit courts varies substantially, from a low of around six active judges on the First Circuit (which covers the Northeast) to almost thirty active judges on the Ninth Circuit (which includes California). The U.S. Supreme Court sits atop the federal court system. Although the size of the Court has varied throughout history, it has consisted of nine Justices since shortly after the Civil War. In addition to being able to hear certain cases directly (such as disputes between states), the Court can hear appeals from the various circuit courts. Today, its appellate jurisdiction is almost entirely discretionary, which means that it decides which cases it will hear. In recent years, the Court has received thousands of petitions for review each year but typically has granted review in only about 75–80 of these cases. Separate from the federal court system, each state (and Washington, D.C.) has its own court system, with trial and appellate courts. Unlike federal judges, many state judges are subject to some form of popular election. The state courts are courts of general jurisdiction, which means that they can hear essentially any type of case, including cases involving federal law (with some limited exceptions). The U.S. Supreme Court can hear appeals from the state courts, but only in cases that involve issues of federal law.

NOTE ON MARBURY V. MADISON AND JUDICIAL REVIEW

There is relatively little disagreement today with the general proposition, traceable to *Marbury*, that the federal courts properly exercise a power of judicial review.[a] The proper *scope* of that judicial review, however, has generated controversy. *Marbury* can be read in different ways. William Van Alstyne, author of A Critical Guide to *Marbury v. Madison*, 1969 Duke L.J. 1, identified three possible "specifications" of the holding of the case.

At its narrowest, *Marbury* could be limited to the kind of "defensive" use of judicial review actually presented by its facts:

> In litigation before the Supreme Court, the Court may refuse to give effect to an act of Congress where the act pertains to the judicial power itself. In deciding whether to give effect to such an act, the Court may determine its decision according to its own interpretation of constitutional provisions which describe the judicial power. (Italics omitted.)

So described, *Marbury* seeks only to "maintain the Court as a co-ordinate branch of government" and thus draws "considerable support from the concept of *separated* powers."

Perhaps *Marbury* could have stopped there, but in fact it said much more. Nothing in the text of Marshall's opinion appears to limit the assertion of the power of judicial review to the defensive context. Perhaps for this reason, a second and broader reading of *Marbury* has come to be generally accepted:

> In litigation before the Supreme Court, the Court may refuse to give effect to an act of Congress where, in the Court's own view, that act is repugnant to the Constitution.

In this view, *Marbury* stands for the proposition that it is the responsibility of the Supreme Court—and presumably all courts—to apply the Constitution

---

[a] For defenses of judicial review based on the constitutional text and Founding history, see John Harrison, The Constitutional Origins and Implications of Judicial Review, 84 Va. L. Rev. 333 (1998), and Saikrishna B. Prakash and John C. Yoo, The Origins of Judicial Review, 70 U. Chi. L. Rev. 887 (2003).

as the "supreme law of the land" to all cases properly presented for decision. Courts may not decide cases in contravention of the Constitution.

This view of *Marbury* stops considerably short of the most expansive reading of the opinion, which asserts judicial supremacy in interpreting the Constitution. Under this view, it is the responsibility of courts, and ultimately the Supreme Court, to provide authoritative interpretations of the Constitution and to ensure the enforcement of constitutional values. Van Alstyne notes that nothing in *Marbury* compels the view that "the only interpretation of the Constitution which all branches of the national government must employ is the interpretation which the Court may provide in the course of litigation." Yet this claim is often made, including by the Supreme Court itself. In Cooper v. Aaron, 358 U.S. 1, 18 (1958), for example, the Court reviewed *Marbury* and announced that:

> This decision declared the basic principle that the federal judiciary is supreme in the exposition of the law of the Constitution, and that principle has ever since been respected by this Court and the country as a permanent and indispensable feature of our constitutional system.

The same view was taken by Chief Justice Warren in Powell v. McCormack, 395 U.S. 486, 549 (1969), where, in writing for the Court, he cited *Marbury* in support of the proposition that "it is the responsibility of this Court to act as the ultimate interpreter of the Constitution." See also United States v. Morrison, 529 U.S. 598, 616 n.7 (2000) ("No doubt the political branches have a role in interpreting and applying the Constitution, but ever since *Marbury* this Court has remained the ultimate expositor of the constitutional text.").

This interpretation of *Marbury* is controversial. There is an ongoing debate in the academic literature between "departmentalists," who contend that each branch of government has the responsibility to interpret the Constitution independently, and "judicial supremacists," who argue that the Supreme Court's view is paramount. For a defense of departmentalism, see Michael Stokes Paulsen, The Most Dangerous Branch: Executive Power to Say What the Law Is, 83 Geo. L.J. 217 (1994). For a defense of the judicial supremacist view, see Larry Alexander & Frederick Schauer, On Extrajudicial Constitutional Interpretation, 110 Harv. L. Rev. 1359 (1997). For additional discussion of that debate, see Dawn E. Johnsen, Functional Departmentalism and Nonjudicial Interpretation: Who Determines Constitutional Meaning?, 67 Law & Contemp. Probs. 105 (2004), and Keith E. Whittington, Extrajudicial Constitutional Interpretation: Three Objections and Responses, 80 N.C. L. Rev. 773 (2002). For an "effort to sketch successive understandings of *Marbury* since its initial formulation, and to show how those understandings have been affected by changing views of the relationship of the courts to other actors in the American constitutional order," see G. Edward White, The Constitutional Journey of *Marbury v. Madison*, 89 Va. L. Rev. 1463, 1468 (2003).

SECTION 2. STANDING

INTRODUCTORY NOTE ON STANDING

Historically, standing required the plaintiff to show that his or her "legal interest" had been invaded by the defendant. Put this way, the issue of standing was embedded in the merits. Standing to sue was subsumed in the question whether the plaintiff had a cause of action for redress of injury to a legally protected interest.

The modern law of standing is far more elaborate and purports, at least, to be separate and apart from the merits. At bottom, this development was a response to changes in the objectives of litigation. No longer is litigation simply a method of resolving disputes between private parties. Today, it is often a vehicle for participating in the governance of the nation. This is especially true of suits challenging the constitutionality of government behavior. Although accomplished within the forms of ordinary litigation, such lawsuits are often importantly different in scope and content. The characteristics of this new kind of lawsuit and its departures from the classical model are summarized in Abram Chayes, Foreword: Public Law Litigation and the Burger Court, 96 Harv. L. Rev. 4, 4–5 (1982):

In the classical model, . . . [f]irst, litigation is bipolar; two parties are locked in a confrontational, winner-take-all controversy. Second, the process is retrospective, directed to determining the legal consequences of a closed set of past events. Third, right and remedy are linked in a close, mutually defining logical relationship. Fourth, the lawsuit is a self-contained entity. It is bounded in time: judicial involvement ends with the determination of the disputed issues. It is bounded in effect: the impact is limited to the (two) parties before the court. Finally, the whole process is party initiated and party controlled. The judge is passive, a neutral umpire. . . .

In the contemporary model, . . . [f]irst, the party structure and the matters in controversy are both amorphous, defined ad hoc as the proceedings unfold rather than exogenously determined by legal theories and concepts. Second, the temporal orientation of the lawsuit is prospective rather than historical. Third, because the relief sought looks to the future and is corrective rather than compensatory, it is not derived logically from the rights asserted. Instead, it is fashioned ad hoc, usually by a quasi-negotiating process. Fourth, prospective relief implies continuing judicial involvement. And because the relief is directed at government or corporate policies, it will have a direct impact that extends far beyond the immediate parties to the lawsuit.

Several factors have contributed to this development. First, there has been an explosion in the recognition of constitutional rights. The natural by-product has been proliferation of plausible legal theories that can be used to test the validity of government action. A second factor is the rise of the administrative state. Recognizing the need to supervise agency power, courts have allowed suit by persons adversely affected by agency action, even when there was no infringement of a traditional common-law interest. In particular, courts have allowed suit by the intended beneficiaries of government regulation, as well as by those whose conduct was directly constrained. Third, the protracted process of school desegregation introduced continuing judicial supervision of state and local governments. In many ways, school desegregation became the prototype for judicial supervision of government. And finally, the development of the class action facilitated large-scale litigation leading to system-wide relief.

By the 1960s a new style of lawsuit—often called "public law" or "structural reform"—had developed. Such lawsuits attempt to coerce reform or curtailment of government actions, and they create a potential nation of plaintiffs. Increasingly, it became important to decide who had the power to bring such actions. As Chayes pointed out, id. at 9–10:

> The ability to bring such lawsuits is ultimately the ability to elicit judicial pronouncements on the public policies and values implicated in the challenged official actions. Limitations on standing thus translate into limitations on the power of the courts, or at least on the occasions for its exercise.

In recent decades, therefore, the Supreme Court has become increasingly concerned with issues of standing. Eventually, the Court settled on the rather elaborate rendition of standing doctrine recounted in *Allen v. Wright,* the next main case. The law of standing is said to comprise both constitutional and prudential considerations. The most important prudential concern is the bar against litigating the rights of another, a topic considered in Section 3, Subsection A, of this Chapter.[a] The constitutional minimum derives from the Article III limitation of the judicial power to "cases" and "controversies" and has three requirements. First, the plaintiff must suffer an injury, either actual or threatened. Second, the injury must be fairly traceable to the defendant's conduct, a requirement of causation. Third is the closely related requirement of redressability; the injury must be likely to be redressed by a favorable judicial decision.[b]

---

[a] For a general treatment of the elusive subject of prudential standing, see S. Todd Brown, The Story of Prudential Standing, 42 Hastings Const. L. Q. 95 (2014). And for discussion of whether prudential standing requirements are "jurisdictional" or may be waived if a party fails to raise the issue, see Bradford C. Mank, Is Prudential Standing Jurisdictional?, 64 Case West. Res. L. Rev. 413 (2013).

[b] Almost all discussion of standing involves adversarial litigation, but there have long been instances in which federal law authorizes ex parte proceedings. Naturalization proceedings are one example. Another is the Foreign Intelligence Surveillance Act's requirement that the government obtain ex parte authorization from a court before conducting certain kinds of electronic surveillance. The basis for jurisdiction in such cases is explored at length in James E. Pfander and Daniel D. Birk, Article III Judicial Power, the Adverse-Party Requirement, and Non-Contentious Jurisdiction, 124 Yale L.J. 1346 (2015). They conclude that non-contentious jurisdiction is an inheritance from Roman law, picked up by admiralty and equity courts, and implicitly accepted in Article III. The historical basis of this claim is attacked in Ann Woolhandler, Adverse Interests and Article III, 111 Nw. U. L. Rev. 1025 (2017), which argues that most of the "non-contentious" proceedings involve adverse interests, even if not formally adverse parties. This criticism in turn prompted a rejoinder. James F. Pfander and Daniel Birk, Adverse Interests and Article III: A Reply, 111 Nw. U. L. Rev. 1067 (2017).

SUBSECTION A. CONSTITUTIONAL CORE

Allen v. Wright

Supreme Court of the United States, 1984.
468 U.S. 737.

■ JUSTICE O'CONNOR delivered the opinion of the Court.

Parents of black public school children allege in this nationwide class action that the Internal Revenue Service (IRS) has not adopted sufficient standards and procedures to fulfill its obligation to deny tax-exempt status to racially discriminatory private schools. They assert that the IRS thereby harms them directly and interferes with the ability of their children to receive an education in desegregated public schools. The issue before us is whether plaintiffs have standing to bring this suit. . . . We hold that they do not.

I

The Internal Revenue Service denies tax-exempt status under §§ 501(a) and (c)(3) of the Internal Revenue Code—and hence eligibility to receive charitable contributions deductible from income taxes under §§ 170(a)(1) and (c)(2) of the Code—to racially discriminatory private schools. Rev. Rul. 71–447, 1972–2 Cum. Bull. 230.[1] The IRS policy requires that a school applying for tax-exempt status show that it "admits the students of any race to all the rights, privileges, programs, and activities generally accorded or made available to students at that school and that the school does not discriminate on the basis of race in administration of its educational policies, admissions policies, scholarship and loan programs, and athletic and other school-administered programs." To carry out this policy, the IRS has established guidelines and procedures for determining whether a particular school is in fact racially nondiscriminatory. Failure to comply with the guidelines "will ordinarily result in the proposed revocation of" tax-exempt status.

The guidelines provide that "[a] school must show affirmatively both that it has adopted a racially nondiscriminatory policy as to students that is made known to the general public and that since the adoption of that policy it has operated in a bona fide manner in accordance therewith." The school must state its nondiscrimination policy in its organizational charter, and in all of its brochures, catalogues, and other advertisements to prospective students. The school must make its nondiscrimination policy known to the entire community served by the school and must publicly disavow any contrary representations made on its behalf once it

---

[1] As the Court explained last term in Bob Jones University v. United States, 461 U.S. 574, 577–79 (1983), the IRS announced this policy in 1970 and formally adopted it in 1971. This change in prior policy was prompted by litigation over tax exemptions for racially discriminatory private schools in the state of Mississippi, litigation that resulted in the entry of an injunction against the IRS largely if not entirely coextensive with the position the IRS had voluntarily adopted. Green v. Connally, 330 F. Supp. 1150 (D.D.C.), summarily aff'd sub nom. Coit v. Green, 404 U.S. 997 (1971) (entering permanent injunction).

becomes aware of them. The school must have nondiscriminatory policies concerning all programs and facilities, including scholarships and loans, and the school must annually certify, under penalty of perjury, compliance with these requirements.

The IRS rules require a school applying for tax-exempt status to give a breakdown along racial lines of its student body and its faculty and administrative staff, as well as of scholarships and loans awarded. They also require the applicant school to state the year of its organization, and to list "incorporators, founders, board members, and donors of land or buildings," and state whether any of the organizations among these have an objective of maintaining segregated public or private school education. The rules further provide that, once given an exemption, a school must keep specified records to document the extent of compliance with the IRS guidelines. Finally, the rules announce that any information concerning discrimination at a tax-exempt school is officially welcomed.

In 1976 respondents challenged these guidelines and procedures in a suit filed in federal District Court against the Secretary of the Treasury and the Commissioner of Internal Revenue. The plaintiffs named in the complaint are parents of black children who, at the time the complaint was filed, were attending public schools in seven states in school districts undergoing desegregation. They brought this nationwide class action "on behalf of themselves and their children, and . . . on behalf of all other parents of black children attending public school systems undergoing, or which may in the future undergo, desegregation pursuant to court order [or] HEW regulations and guidelines, under state law, or voluntarily." They estimated that the class they seek to represent includes several million persons.

Respondents allege in their complaint that many racially segregated private schools were created or expanded in their communities at the time the public schools were undergoing desegregation. According to the complaint, many such private schools, including 17 schools or school systems identified by name in the complaint (perhaps some 30 schools in all), receive tax exemptions either directly or through the tax-exempt status of "umbrella" organizations that operate or support the schools. Respondents allege that, despite the IRS policy of denying tax-exempt status to racially discriminatory private schools and despite the IRS guidelines and procedures for implementing that policy, some of the tax-exempt racially segregated private schools created or expanded in desegregating districts in fact have racially discriminatory policies. Respondents allege that the IRS grant of tax exemptions to such racially discriminatory schools is unlawful.

Respondents allege that the challenged government conduct harms them in two ways. The challenged conduct

   (a) constitutes tangible federal financial aid and other support for racially segregated educational institutions, and

(b) fosters and encourages the organization, operation and expansion of institutions providing racially segregated educational opportunities for white children avoiding attendance in desegregating public school districts and thereby interferes with the efforts of federal courts, HEW and local school authorities to desegregate public school districts which have been operating racially dual school systems.

Thus, respondents do not allege that their children have been the victims of discriminatory exclusion from the schools whose tax exemptions they challenge as unlawful. Indeed, they have not alleged at any stage of this litigation that their children have ever applied or would ever apply to any private school. Rather, respondents claim a direct injury from the mere fact of the challenged government conduct and, as indicated by the restriction of the plaintiff class to parents of children in desegregating school districts, injury to their children's opportunity to receive a desegregated education. The latter injury is traceable to the IRS grant of tax exemptions to racially discriminatory schools, respondents allege, chiefly because contributions to such schools are deductible from income taxes . . . and the "deductions facilitate the raising of funds to organize new schools and expand existing schools in order to accommodate white students avoiding attendance in desegregating public school districts."

Respondents request only prospective relief. They ask for a declaratory judgment that the challenged IRS tax-exemption practices are unlawful. They also ask for an injunction requiring the IRS to deny tax exemptions to a considerably broader class of private schools than the class of racially discriminatory private schools. Under the requested injunction, the IRS would have to deny tax-exempt status to all private schools

which have insubstantial or non-existent minority enrollments, which are located in or serve desegregating public school districts, and which either—

(1) were established or expanded at or about the time the public school district in which they are located or which they serve were desegregating;

(2) have been determined in adversary judicial or administrative proceedings to be racially segregated; or

(3) cannot demonstrate that they do not provide racially segregated educational opportunities for white children avoiding attendance in desegregating public school systems.

Finally, respondents ask for an order directing the IRS to replace its 1975 guidelines with standards consistent with the requested injunction.

In May 1977 the District Court permitted intervention as a defendant by petitioner Allen, the head of one of the private school systems identified in the complaint. Thereafter, progress in the lawsuit was stalled for several years. During this period, the Internal Revenue Service reviewed its challenged policies and proposed new Revenue Procedures to tighten requirements for eligibility for tax-exempt schools. In 1979, however, Congress blocked any strengthening of the IRS guidelines at least until October 1980.[16] The District Court thereupon considered and granted the defendants' motion to dismiss the complaint, concluding that respondents lack standing, that the judicial task proposed by respondents is inappropriately intrusive for a federal court, and that awarding the requested relief would be contrary to the will of Congress expressed in the 1979 ban on strengthening the IRS guidelines.

The United States Court of Appeals for the District of Columbia reversed, concluding that respondents have standing to maintain this lawsuit. . . . The Court of Appeals also held that the 1979 congressional actions were not intended to preclude judicial remedies and that the relief requested by respondents could be fashioned "without large scale judicial intervention in the administrative process." . . .

We granted certiorari and now reverse.

II

A

Article III of the Constitution confines the federal courts to adjudicating actual "cases" and "controversies." As the Court [has] explained . . . , the "case or controversy" requirement defines with respect to the judicial branch the idea of separation of powers on which the federal government is founded. The several doctrines that have grown up to elaborate that requirement are "founded in concern about the proper— and properly limited—role of the courts in a democratic society." Warth v. Seldin, 422 U.S. 490, 498 (1975). . . .

The Article III doctrine that requires a litigant to have "standing" to invoke the power of a federal court is perhaps the most important of these doctrines. . . . Standing doctrine embraces several judicially self-imposed limits on the exercise of federal jurisdiction, such as the general prohibition on a litigant's raising another person's legal rights, the rule barring adjudication of generalized grievances more appropriately addressed in the representative branches, and the requirement that a plaintiff's complaint fall within the zone of interests protected by the law invoked. The requirement of standing, however, has a core component derived directly

---

[16] Section 615 of the act, known as the Dornan Amendment, specifically forbade the use of funds to carry out the IRS's proposed Revenue Procedures. Section 103 of the act, known as the Ashbrook Amendment, more generally forbade the use of funds to make the requirements for tax-exempt status of private schools more stringent than those in effect prior to the IRS's proposal of its new Revenue Procedures.

These provisions expired on October 1, 1980, but [the] Dornan and Ashbrook Amendments were reinstated for the period December 16, 1980, through September 30, 1981. For fiscal year 1982, Congress specifically denied funding for carrying out not only administrative actions but also court orders entered after the date of the IRS's proposal of its first revised Revenue Procedure. No such spending restrictions are currently in force.

from the Constitution. A plaintiff must allege personal injury fairly traceable to the defendant's allegedly unlawful conduct and likely to be redressed by the requested relief. . . .

[T]he law of Article III standing is built on a single basic idea—the idea of separation of powers. It is this fact which makes possible the gradual clarification of the law through judicial application. . . .

Typically, . . . the standing inquiry requires careful judicial examination of a complaint's allegations to ascertain whether the particular plaintiff is entitled to an adjudication of the particular claims asserted. Is the injury too abstract, or otherwise not appropriate, to be considered judicially cognizable? Is the line of causation between the illegal conduct and injury too attenuated? Is the prospect of obtaining relief from the injury as a result of a favorable ruling too speculative? These questions and any others relevant to the standing inquiry must be answered by reference to the Article III notion that federal courts may exercise power only "in the last resort, and as a necessity," and only when adjudication is "consistent with a system of separated powers and [the dispute is one] traditionally thought to be capable of resolution through the judicial process." Flast v. Cohen, 392 U.S. 83, 97 (1968).

B

Respondents allege two injuries in their complaint to support their standing to bring this lawsuit. First, they say that they are harmed directly by the mere fact of government financial aid to discriminatory private schools. Second, they say that the federal tax exemptions to racially discriminatory private schools in their communities impair their ability to have their public schools desegregated. . . . We conclude that neither suffices to support respondents' standing. The first fails under clear precedents of this Court because it does not constitute judicially cognizable injury. The second fails because the alleged injury is not fairly traceable to the assertedly unlawful conduct of the IRS.

1

Respondents' first claim of injury can be interpreted in two ways. It might be a claim simply to have the government avoid the violation of law alleged in respondents' complaint. Alternatively, it might be a claim of stigmatic injury, or denigration, suffered by all members of a racial group when the government discriminates on the basis of race. Under neither interpretation is this claim of injury judicially cognizable.

This Court has repeatedly held that an asserted right to have the government act in accordance with law is not sufficient, standing alone, to confer jurisdiction on a federal court. In Schlesinger v. Reservists Committee to Stop the War, 418 U.S. 208 (1974), for example, the Court rejected a claim of citizen standing to challenge Armed Forces Reserve commissions held by members of Congress as violating the Incompatibility Clause of Art. I, § 6, cl. 2 of the Constitution. As citizens, the Court held, plaintiffs alleged nothing but "the abstract injury in nonobservance of the Constitution." . . . Respondents here have no standing to complain simply that their government is violating the law.

Neither do they have standing to litigate their claims based on the stigmatizing injury often caused by racial discrimination. There can be no doubt that this sort of noneconomic injury is one of the most serious consequences of discriminatory government action and is sufficient in some circumstances to support standing. Our cases make clear, however, that such injury accords a basis for standing only to "those persons who are personally denied equal treatment" by the challenged discriminatory conduct.

In Moose Lodge No. 107 v. Irvis, 407 U.S. 163 (1972), the Court held that the plaintiff had no standing to challenge a club's racially discriminatory membership policies because he had never applied for membership. In O'Shea v. Littleton, 414 U.S. 488 (1974), the Court held that the plaintiffs had no standing to challenge racial discrimination in the administration of their city's criminal justice system because they had not alleged that they had been or would likely be subject to the challenged practices. The Court denied standing on similar facts in Rizzo v. Goode, 423 U.S. 362 (1976). In each of those cases, the plaintiffs alleged official racial discrimination comparable to that alleged by respondents here. Yet standing was denied in each case because the plaintiffs were not personally subject to the challenged discrimination. Insofar as their first claim of injury is concerned, respondents are in exactly the same position. . . .

Personally subjected to challenged discrimination required

The consequences of recognizing respondents' standing on the basis of their first claim of injury illustrate why our cases plainly hold that such injury is not judicially cognizable. If the abstract stigmatic injury were cognizable, standing would extend nationwide to all members of the particular racial groups against which the government was alleged to be discriminating by its tax exemption to a racially discriminatory school, regardless of the location of that school. A black person in Hawaii could challenge the grant of a tax exemption to a racially discriminatory school in Maine. Recognition of standing in such circumstances would transform the federal courts into "no more than a vehicle for the vindication of the value interests of concerned bystanders." United States v. SCRAP, 412 U.S. 669, 687 (1973). Constitutional limits on the role of the federal courts preclude such a transformation.

2

It is in their complaint's second claim of injury that respondents allege harm to a concrete, personal interest that can support standing in some circumstances. The injury they identify—their children's diminished ability to receive an education in a racially integrated school—is, beyond any doubt, not only judicially cognizable but . . . one of the most serious injuries recognized in our legal system. Despite the constitutional importance of curing the injury alleged by respondents, however, the federal judiciary may not redress it unless standing requirements are met.

Court acknowledges injury, but needs standing

In this case, respondents' second claim of injury cannot support standing because the injury alleged is not fairly traceable to the government conduct respondents challenge as unlawful.

The illegal conduct challenged by respondents is the IRS's grant of tax exemptions to some racially discriminatory schools. The line of causation between that conduct and desegregation of respondents' schools is attenuated at best. From the perspective of the IRS, the injury to respondents is highly indirect and "results from the independent action of some third party not before the court." Simon v. Eastern Kentucky Welfare Rights Org., 426 U.S. 26, 42 (1976).

The diminished ability of respondents' children to receive a desegregated education would be fairly traceable to unlawful IRS grants of tax exemptions only if there were enough racially discriminatory private schools receiving tax exemptions in respondents' communities for withdrawal of those exemptions to make an appreciable difference in public-school integration. Respondents have made no such allegation. It is, first, uncertain how many racially discriminatory private schools are in fact receiving tax exemptions. Moreover, it is entirely speculative, as respondents themselves conceded in the Court of Appeals, whether withdrawal of a tax exemption from any particular school would lead the school to change its policies. It is just as speculative whether any given parent of a child attending such a private school would decide to transfer the child to public school as a result of any changes in educational or financial policy made by the private school once it was threatened with loss of tax-exempt status. It is also pure speculation whether, in a particular community, a large enough number of the numerous relevant school officials and parents would reach decisions that collectively would have a significant impact on the racial composition of the public schools. . . .

The idea of separation of powers that underlies standing doctrine explains why our cases preclude the conclusion that respondents' alleged injury "fairly can be traced to the challenged action" of the IRS. That conclusion would pave the way generally for suits challenging, not specifically identifiable government violations of law, but the particular programs agencies establish to carry out their legal obligations. . . .

> Carried to its logical end, [respondents'] approach would have the federal courts as virtually continuing monitors of the wisdom and soundness of executive action; such a role is appropriate for the Congress acting through its committees and the "power of the purse"; it is not the role of the judiciary, absent actual present or immediately threatened injury resulting from unlawful government action.

Laird v. Tatum, 408 U.S. 1, 15 (1972).

The same concern for the proper role of the federal courts is reflected in cases like *O'Shea v. Littleton, Rizzo v. Goode,* and City of Los Angeles v. Lyons, 461 U.S. 95 (1983). In all three cases plaintiffs sought injunctive relief directed at certain statewide law enforcement practices. The Court held in each case that, absent an allegation of a specific threat of being subject to the challenged practices, plaintiffs had no standing to ask for an injunction. Animating this Court's holdings was the principle that "[a] federal court . . . is not the proper forum to press" general complaints about the way in which government goes about its business. Id. at 111–12. . . . Most relevant to this case is the principle articulated in *Rizzo*, 423 U.S. at 378–79:

> When a plaintiff seeks to enjoin the activity of a government agency . . . his case must contend with "the well established rule that the government has traditionally been granted the widest latitude in the 'dispatch of its own internal affairs.' "

When transported into the Article III context, that principle, grounded as it is in the idea of separation of powers, counsels against recognizing standing in a case brought not to enforce specific legal obligations whose violation works a direct harm, but to seek a restructuring of the apparatus established by the executive branch to fulfill its legal duties. The Constitution, after all, assigns to the executive branch, and not to the judicial branch, the duty to "take Care that the Laws be faithfully executed." Art. II, § 3. We could not recognize respondents' standing in this case without running afoul of that structural principle.

C

The Court of Appeals relied for its contrary conclusion on Gilmore v. City of Montgomery, 417 U.S. 556 (1974), Norwood v. Harrison, 413 U.S. 455 (1973), and on Coit v. Green, 404 U.S. 997 (1971), summarily affirming Green v. Connally, 330 F. Supp. 1150 (D.D.C.). . . . None of these cases, however, requires that we find standing in this lawsuit.

In *Gilmore v. City of Montgomery*, the plaintiffs asserted a constitutional right, recognized in an outstanding injunction, to use the city's public parks on a nondiscriminatory basis. They alleged that the city was violating that equal protection right by permitting racially discriminatory private schools and other groups to use the public parks. The Court recognized plaintiffs' standing to challenge this city policy insofar as the policy permitted the exclusive use of the parks by racially discriminatory private schools: the plaintiffs had alleged direct cognizable injury to their right to nondiscriminatory access to the public parks. . . .

In *Norwood v. Harrison*, parents of public school children in Tunica County, Mississippi, filed a statewide class action challenging the state's provision of textbooks to students attending racially discriminatory private schools in the state. The Court held the state's practice unconstitutional because it breached "the state's acknowledged duty to establish a unitary school system." The Court did not expressly address the basis for the plaintiffs' standing.

Distinguishable situations

In *Gilmore,* however, the Court identified the basis for standing in *Norwood*: "The plaintiffs in *Norwood* were parties to a school desegregation order and the relief they sought was directly related to the concrete injury they suffered." Through the school-desegregation decree, the plaintiffs had acquired a right to have the state "steer clear" of any perpetuation of the racially dual school system that it had once sponsored. The interest acquired was judicially cognizable because it was a personal interest, created by law, in having the state refrain from taking specific actions. The plaintiffs' complaint alleged that the state directly injured that interest by aiding racially discriminatory private schools. Respondents in this lawsuit, of course, have no injunctive rights against the IRS that are allegedly being harmed by the challenged IRS action.

Unlike *Gilmore* and *Norwood, Coit v. Green,* cannot easily be seen to have based standing on an injury different in kind from any asserted by respondents here. The plaintiffs in *Coit,* parents of black school children in Mississippi, sued to enjoin the IRS grant of tax exemptions to racially discriminatory private schools in the state. Nevertheless, *Coit* in no way mandates the conclusion that respondents have standing.

First, the decision has little weight as a precedent on the law of standing. This Court's decision in *Coit* was merely a summary affirmance; for that reason alone it could hardly establish principles contrary to those set out in opinions issued after full briefing and argument. Moreover, when the case reached this Court, the plaintiffs and the IRS were no longer adverse parties; and the ruling that was summarily affirmed did not include a ruling on the issue of standing. . . .

Thus, we need not consider whether standing was properly found in *Coit*. Whatever the answer to that question, respondents' complaint . . . alleges no connection between the asserted desegregation injury and the challenged IRS conduct direct enough to overcome the substantial separation-of-powers barriers to a suit seeking an injunction to reform administrative procedures.

"The necessity that the plaintiff who seeks to invoke judicial power stand to profit in some personal interest remains an Article III requirement." *Simon,* 426 U.S. at 39. Respondents have not met this fundamental requirement. The judgment of the Court of Appeals is accordingly reversed, and the injunction issued by that court is vacated.

■ JUSTICE MARSHALL took no part in the decision of this case.

■ JUSTICE BRENNAN, dissenting. . . .

One could hardly dispute the proposition that Article III of the Constitution, by limiting the judicial power to "cases" or "controversies," embodies the notion that each branch of our national government must confine its actions to those that are consistent with our scheme of separated powers. But simply stating that unremarkable truism provides little, if any, illumination of the standing inquiry that must be undertaken by a federal court faced with a particular action filed by particular plaintiffs. . . .

The Court's attempt to obscure the standing question must be seen, therefore, as no more than a cover for its failure to recognize the nature of the specific claims raised by the respondents in these cases. By relying on generalities concerning our tripartite system of government, the Court is able to conclude that the respondents lack standing to maintain this action without acknowledging the precise nature of the injuries they have alleged. In so doing, the Court displays a startling insensitivity to the historical role played by the federal courts in eradicating race discrimination from our nation's schools. . . . Because I cannot join in such misguided decisionmaking, I dissent.

I

The respondents, suing individually and on behalf of their minor children, are parents of black children attending public schools in various school districts across the nation. Each of these school districts, the respondents allege, was once segregated and is now in the process of desegregating pursuant to court order, federal regulations or guidelines, state law, or voluntary agreement. Moreover, each contains one or more private schools that discriminate against black school children and that operate with the assistance of tax exemptions unlawfully granted to them by the Internal Revenue Service (IRS).

To eliminate this federal financial assistance for discriminating schools, the respondents seek a declaratory judgment that current IRS practices are inadequate both in identifying racially discriminatory schools and in denying requested tax exemptions or revoking existing exemptions for any schools so identified. In particular, they allege that existing IRS guidelines permit schools to receive tax exemptions simply by adopting and certifying—but not implementing—a policy of nondiscrimination. Pursuant to these ineffective guidelines, many private schools that discriminate on the basis of race continue to benefit illegally from their tax-exempt status and the resulting charitable deductions granted to taxpayers who contribute to such schools. The respondents therefore seek a permanent injunction requiring the IRS to deny tax exemptions [as described in the opinion of the Court]. The requested relief is substantially similar to the enforcement guidelines promulgated by the IRS itself in 1978 and 1979, before congressional action temporarily stayed, and the agency withdrew, the amended procedures.

II

Persons seeking judicial relief from an Article III court must have standing to maintain their cause of action. At a minimum, the standing requirement is not met unless the plaintiff has "such a personal stake in the outcome of the controversy as to assure that concrete adverseness which sharpens the presentation of issues upon which the court so largely depends. . . ." Baker v. Carr, 369 U.S. 186, 204 (1962). Under the Court's cases, this "personal stake" requirement is satisfied if the person seeking redress has suffered, or is threatened with, some "distinct and palpable injury," and if there is some causal connection between the asserted injury and the conduct being challenged.

A

In these cases, the respondents have alleged at least one type of injury that satisfies the constitutional requirement of "distinct and palpable injury."[3] In particular, they claim that the IRS' grant of tax-exempt status to racially discriminatory private schools directly injures their children's opportunity and ability to receive a desegregated education. . . . The Court acknowledges that this alleged injury is sufficient to satisfy constitutional standards. . . .

B

. . . Viewed in light of the injuries they claim, the respondents have alleged a direct causal relationship between the government action they challenge and the injury they suffer: their inability to receive an education in a racially integrated school is directly and adversely affected by the tax-exempt status granted by the IRS to racially discriminatory schools in their respective school districts. Common sense alone would recognize that the elimination of tax-exempt status for racially discriminatory private schools would serve to lessen the impact that those institutions have in defeating efforts to desegregate the public schools. . . .

Moreover, the Court has previously recognized the existence, and constitutional significance, of such direct relationships between unlawfully segregated school districts and government support for racially discriminatory private schools in those districts. In Norwood v. Harrison, 413 U.S. 455 (1973), for example, we considered a Mississippi program that provided textbooks to students attending both public and private schools, without regard to whether any participating school had racially discriminatory policies. In declaring that program constitutionally invalid, we noted that "a state may not induce, encourage or promote private persons to accomplish what it is constitutionally forbidden to accomplish." We then spoke directly to the financial aid provided by the state textbook program and the constitutional rights asserted by the students and their parents:

> The District Court laid great stress on the absence of a showing by appellants that "any child enrolled in private school, if deprived of free textbooks, would withdraw from private school and subsequently enroll in the public schools." . . . *We do not agree with the District Court in its analysis of the legal consequences of this uncertainty, for the Constitution does not*

---

[3] Because I conclude that the second injury alleged by the respondents is sufficient to satisfy constitutional requirements, I do not need to reach what the Court labels the "stigmatic injury." . . .

permit the state to aid discrimination even when there is no precise causal relationship between state financial aid to a private school and the continued well-being of that school. A state may not grant the type of tangible financial aid here involved if that aid has a significant tendency to facilitate, reinforce, and support private discrimination. (Emphasis added.)

Thus, *Norwood* explicitly stands for the proposition that government aid to racially discriminatory schools is a direct impediment to school desegregation.

The Court purports to distinguish *Norwood* from the present litigation because " '[t]he plaintiffs in *Norwood* were parties to a school desegregation order' " and therefore "had acquired a right to have the state 'steer clear' of any perpetuation of the racially dual school system that it had once sponsored," whereas the "[r]espondents in this lawsuit . . . have no injunctive rights against the IRS that are allegedly being harmed." . . . Given that many of the school districts identified in the respondents' complaint have also been the subject of court-ordered integration, the standing inquiry in these cases should not differ. And, although, the respondents do not specifically allege that they are named parties to any outstanding desegregation orders, that is undoubtedly due to the passage of time since the orders were issued, and not to any difference in the harm they suffer.

Even accepting the relevance of the Court's distinction, moreover, that distinction goes to the injury suffered by the respective plaintiffs and not to the causal connection between the harm alleged and the governmental action challenged. The causal relationship existing in *Norwood* between the alleged harm (i.e., interference with the plaintiffs' injunctive rights to a desegregated school system) and the challenged government action (i.e., free textbooks provided to racially discriminatory schools) is indistinguishable from the causal relationship existing in the present cases, unless the Court intends to distinguish the lending of textbooks from the granting of tax-exempt status. . . .

Similarly, although entitled to less weight than a decision after full briefing and oral argument on the merits, our summary affirmance in Coit v. Green, 404 U.S. 997 (1971), is directly relevant to the standing of the respondents in this litigation. . . .

Given these precedents, the Court is forced to place primary reliance on our decision in Simon v. Eastern Kentucky Welfare Rights Org., 426 U.S. 26 (1976). In that case, the Court denied standing to plaintiffs who challenged an IRS revenue ruling that granted charitable status to hospitals even though they failed to operate to the extent of their financial ability when refusing medical services for indigent patients. The Court found that the injury alleged was not one "that fairly can be traced to the challenged action of the defendant." In particular, it was "purely speculative" whether the denial of access to hospital services alleged by the plaintiffs fairly could be traced to the government's grant of tax-exempt status to the relevant hospitals, primarily because hospitals were likely making their service decisions without regard to the tax implications.

Even accepting the correctness of the causation analysis included in that decision, however, it is plainly distinguishable from the case at hand. The respondents in this case do not challenge the denial of any service by a tax-exempt institution; admittedly, they do not seek access to racially discriminatory private schools. Rather, the injury they allege, and the injury that clearly satisfies constitutional requirements, is the deprivation to their children's opportunity and ability to receive an education in a racially integrated school district. This injury, as the Court admits, and as we have previously held in *Norwood v. Harrison,* is of a kind that is directly traceable to the governmental action being challenged. . . .

III

More than one commentator has noted that the causation component of the Court's standing inquiry is no more than a poor disguise for the Court's view of the merits of the underlying claims. The Court today does nothing to avoid that criticism. What is most disturbing about today's decision, therefore, is not the standing analysis applied, but the indifference evidenced by the Court to the detrimental effects that racially segregated schools, supported by tax-exempt status from the federal government, have on the respondents' attempt to obtain an education in a racially integrated school system. I cannot join such indifference, and would give the respondents a chance to prove their case on the merits.

■ JUSTICE STEVENS, with whom JUSTICE BLACKMUN joins, dissenting.

Three propositions are clear to me: (1) respondents have adequately alleged "injury in fact"; (2) their injury is fairly traceable to the conduct that they claim to be unlawful; and (3) the "separation of powers" principle does not create a jurisdictional obstacle to the consideration of the merits of their claim.

I

Respondents, the parents of black school children, have alleged that their children are unable to attend fully desegregated schools because large numbers of white children in the areas in which respondents reside attend private schools which do not admit minority children. The Court, Justice Brennan, and I all agree that this is an adequate allegation of "injury in fact." . . .

II

In the final analysis, the wrong the respondents allege that the government has committed is to subsidize the exodus of white children from schools that would otherwise be racially integrated. The critical question in this case, therefore, is whether respondents have alleged that the government has created that kind of subsidy.

In answering that question, we must of course assume that respondents can prove what they have alleged. Furthermore, at this stage of the case we must put to one side all questions about the appropriateness of a nationwide class action. The controlling issue is whether the causal connection between the injury and the wrong has been adequately alleged.

... Only last term we explained the effect of ... preferential [tax] treatment:

> Both tax exemptions and tax deductibility are a form of subsidy that is administered through the tax system. A tax exemption has much the same effect as a cash grant to the organization of the amount of tax it would have to pay on its income. Deductible contributions are similar to cash grants of the amount of a portion of the individual's contributions.

Regan v. Taxation With Representation of Washington, Inc., 461 U.S. 540, 544 (1983). The purpose of this scheme, like the purpose of any subsidy, is to promote the activity subsidized. ... If the granting of preferential tax treatment would "encourage" private segregated schools to conduct their "charitable" activities, it must follow that the withdrawal of the treatment would "discourage" them, and hence promote the process of desegregation.

We have held that when a subsidy makes a given activity more or less expensive, injury can fairly be traced to the subsidy for purposes of standing analysis because of the resulting increase or decrease in the ability to engage in the activity. Indeed, we have employed exactly this causation analysis in the same context at issue here—subsidies given private schools that practice racial discrimination. Thus, in Gilmore v. City of Montgomery, 417 U.S. 556 (1974), we easily recognized the causal connection between official policies that enhanced the attractiveness of segregated schools and the failure to bring about or maintain a desegregated public school system. Similarly, in Norwood v. Harrison, 413 U.S. 455 (1973), we concluded that the provision of textbooks to discriminatory private schools "has a significant tendency to facilitate, reinforce, and support private discrimination." ...

This causation analysis is nothing more than a restatement of elementary economics: when something becomes more expensive, less of it will be purchased. ... If racially discriminatory private schools lose the "cash grants" that flow from the operation of the statutes, the education they provide will become more expensive and hence less of their services will be purchased. [T]he withdrawal of the subsidy for segregated schools means the incentive structure facing white parents who seek such schools for their children will be altered. Thus, the laws of economics, not to mention the laws of Congress embodied in §§ 170 and 501(c)(3), compel the conclusion that the injury respondents have alleged—the increased segregation of their children's schools because of the ready availability of private schools that admit whites only—will be redressed if these schools' operations are inhibited through the denial of preferential tax treatment.

III

Considerations of tax policy, economics, and pure logic all confirm the conclusion that respondents' injury in fact is fairly traceable to the government's allegedly wrongful conduct. The Court therefore is forced to introduce the concept of "separation of powers" into its analysis. The Court writes that the separation of powers "explains why our cases preclude the conclusion" that respondents' injury is fairly traceable to the conduct they challenge.

The Court could mean one of three things by its invocation of the separation of powers. First, it could simply be expressing the idea that if the plaintiff lacks Article III standing to bring a lawsuit, then there is no "case or controversy" within the meaning of Article III and hence the matter is not within the area of responsibility assigned to the judiciary by the Constitution. . . . While there can be no quarrel with this proposition, in itself it provides no guidance for determining if the injury respondents have alleged is fairly traceable to the conduct they have challenged.

Second, the Court could be saying that it will require a more direct causal connection when it is troubled by the separation of powers implications of the case before it. That approach confuses the standing doctrine with the justiciability of the issues that respondents seek to raise. The purpose of the standing inquiry is to measure the plaintiff's stake in the outcome, not whether a court has the authority to provide it with the outcome it seeks. . . .

Thus, the " 'fundamental aspect of standing' is that it focuses primarily on the *party* seeking to get his complaint before the federal court rather than 'on the issues he wishes to have adjudicated,' " United States v. Richardson, 418 U.S. 166, 174 (1974) (emphasis in original). The strength of the plaintiff's interest in the outcome has nothing to do with whether the relief it seeks would intrude upon the prerogatives of other branches of government; the possibility that the relief might be inappropriate does not lessen the plaintiff's stake in obtaining that relief. If a plaintiff presents a nonjusticiable issue, or seeks relief that a court may not award, then its complaint should be dismissed for those reasons, and not because the plaintiff lacks a stake in obtaining that relief and hence has no standing. Imposing an undefined but clearly more rigorous standard for redressability for reasons unrelated to the causal nexus between the injury and the challenged conduct can only encourage undisciplined, ad hoc litigation, a result that would be avoided if the Court straightforwardly considered the justiciability of the issues respondents seek to raise, rather than using those issues to obfuscate standing analysis.

Third, the Court could be saying that it will not treat as legally cognizable injuries that stem from an administration decision concerning how enforcement resources will be allocated. This surely is an important point. Respondents do seek to restructure the IRS' mechanisms for enforcing the legal requirement that discriminatory institutions not receive tax-exempt status. Such restructuring would dramatically affect the way in which the IRS exercises its prosecutorial discretion. The executive requires latitude to decide how best to enforce the law, and in general the Court may well be correct that the exercise of that discretion, especially in the tax context, is unchallengeable.

However, as the Court also recognizes, this principle does not apply when suit is brought "to enforce specific legal obligations whose violation works a direct harm." . . . Here, respondents contend that the IRS is violating a specific constitutional limitation on its enforcement discretion. There is a solid basis for that contention [quoting *Norwood* and *Gilmore*]. Respondents contend that these cases limit the enforcement discretion enjoyed by the IRS. They establish, respondents argue, that the IRS cannot provide "cash grants" to discriminatory schools through preferential tax treatment without running afoul of a constitutional duty to refrain from "giving significant aid" to these institutions. Similarly, respondents claim that the Internal Revenue Code itself, as construed in Bob Jones University v. United States, 461 U.S. 574 (1983), constrains enforcement discretion.[12] It has been clear since Marbury v. Madison, 5 U.S. (1 Cranch) 137 (1803), that "[i]t is emphatically the province and duty of the judicial department to say what the law is." Deciding whether the Treasury has violated a specific legal limitation on its enforcement discretion does not intrude upon the prerogative of the executive, for in so deciding we are merely saying "what the law is." Surely the question whether the Constitution or the Code limits enforcement discretion is one within the judiciary's competence, and I do not believe that the question whether the law, as enunciated in *Gilmore, Norwood,* and *Bob Jones,* imposes such an obligation upon the IRS is so insubstantial that respondents' attempt to raise it should be defeated for lack of subject-matter jurisdiction on the ground that it infringes the executive's prerogatives.

In short, I would deal with the question of the legal limitations on the IRS' enforcement discretion on the merits, rather than by making the untenable assumption that the granting of preferential tax treatment to segregated schools does not make those schools more attractive to white students and hence does not inhibit the process of desegregation. I respectfully dissent.

NOTES ON THE CONSTITUTIONAL REQUIREMENTS OF STANDING

1. THE REQUIREMENT OF INJURY: *SCHLESINGER V. RESERVISTS COMMITTEE TO STOP THE WAR*

Allen v. Wright states settled law in saying that mere objection to government conduct, however sincerely felt, does not constitute injury for pur-

---

[12] In *Bob Jones* we clearly indicated that the Internal Revenue Code not only permits but in fact requires the denial of tax-exempt status to racially discriminatory private schools. . . .

poses of standing. Obviously, individuals suffer injury when they are offended or distressed, but that does not count. There must be some more concrete interest that differentiates this plaintiff from those who merely dislike the government's action.

The rule against mere ideological objection also bars suits by those who have a completely undifferentiated interest in opposing government action, such as the mere fact of being a citizen. Often cited for this point is Schlesinger v. Reservists Committee to Stop the War, 418 U.S. 208 (1974). Art. I, § 6, cl. 2 says that "no Person holding any Office under the United States, shall be a Member of either House during his Continuance in Office." An anti-war group challenged the constitutionality of members of Congress holding reserve commissions in the armed forces. They alleged that reserve officers might be subject to undue influence by the executive branch. The District Court found that the plaintiffs had standing to sue as citizens of the United States. The court admitted that the injury alleged was "hypothetical," but thought it was precisely that potential injury, as distinct from any specific harm, that the constitutional provision was designed to prevent. The court also found that the parties were genuinely adverse and ably represented. Finally, the District Court noted that if these plaintiffs could not raise this issue, "then as a practical matter no one can."

The Court of Appeals affirmed, but the Supreme Court reversed. "[S]tanding to sue," said Chief Justice Burger in his opinion for the Court,

> may not be predicated upon an interest of the kind alleged here which is held in common by all members of the public, because of the necessarily abstract nature of the injury all citizens share. Concrete injury, whether actual or threatened, is that indispensable element of a dispute which serves in part to cast it in a form traditionally capable of judicial resolution. It adds the essential dimension of specificity to the dispute by requiring that the complaining party have suffered a particular injury caused by the action challenged as unlawful. . . .
>
> Moreover, when a court is asked to undertake constitutional adjudication, the most important and delicate of its responsibilities, the requirement of concrete injury further serves the function of insuring that such adjudication does not take place unnecessarily. . . . First, concrete injury removes from the realm of speculation whether there is a real need to exercise the power of judicial review in order to protect the interests of the complaining party. . . . Second, the discrete factual context within which the concrete injury occurred or is threatened insures the framing of relief no broader than required by the precise facts to which the court's ruling would be applied.

Most importantly, the Court rejected the idea that the lack of any other plaintiff justified relaxation of the requirements of standing: "The assumption that if respondents have no standing to sue, no one would have standing, is not a reason to find standing." Justices Douglas, Brennan, and Marshall dissented.

2. THE REQUIREMENTS OF CAUSATION AND REDRESSABILITY: *CLAPPER V. AMNESTY INTERNATIONAL*

If ideological objection counted as injury, there would no need to worry about causation. The plaintiff's statement would suffice. But since standing requires concrete injury, it becomes necessary to ensure that allegations of such injury are not fanciful or contrived. That is done chiefly by requiring that the alleged injury be "fairly traceable" to the defendant's conduct. Although this requirement of causation is settled doctrine, the kind of showing necessary is hotly contested. In many cases, as in *Allen v. Wright*, there is division over whether the plaintiffs' allegations of causation are sufficiently plausible to allow the case to proceed. Critics often suggest, as Justice Brennan argued in *Allen v. Wright*, that adjudications of causation are really merits rulings in disguise.

A recent example of a demanding approach to causation is Clapper v. Amnesty International, 568 U.S. 398 (2013). Plaintiffs objected to electronic eavesdropping by the National Security Agency, as authorized by the Foreign Intelligence Surveillance Act. As amended in 2008, that statute allows the "targeting of persons reasonably believed to be located outside the United States to acquire foreign intelligence information." 50 U.S.C. § 1881a. Specific targets and authorizations are not required. Rather, the Foreign Intelligence Surveillance Court can give blanket approval for interception of communications with targets located outside the United States, so long as certain statutory procedures are followed.

(i) The Majority

Speaking through Justice Alito, the Court described the respondents (plaintiffs in the action) and their interest as follows:

> Respondents are attorneys and human rights, labor, legal, and media organizations whose work allegedly requires them to engage in sensitive and sometimes privileged telephone and e-mail communications with colleagues, clients, sources, and other individuals located abroad. Respondents believe that some of the people with whom they exchange foreign intelligence information are likely targets of surveillance under § 1881a. Specifically, respondents claim that they communicate by telephone and e-mail with people the Government "believes or believed to be associated with terrorist organizations," "people located in geographic areas that are a special focus" of the Government's counterterrorism or diplomatic efforts, and activists who oppose governments that are supported by the United States Government.

> Respondents claim that § 1881a compromises their ability to locate witnesses, cultivate sources, obtain information, and communicate confidential information to their clients. Respondents also assert that they "have ceased engaging" in certain telephone and e-mail conversations. According to respondents, the threat of surveillance will compel them to travel abroad in order to have in-person conversations. In addition, respondents declare that they

have undertaken "costly and burdensome measures" to protect the confidentiality of sensitive communications.

The Second Circuit held that the plaintiffs had standing, both because of the "objectively reasonable likelihood" that their communications would be intercepted and because they were suffering "*present* injuries in fact— economic and professional harms—stemming from a reasonable fear of *future* harmful government conduct." The Supreme Court disagreed:

Respondents assert that they can establish injury in fact that is fairly traceable to § 1881a because there is an objectively reasonable likelihood that their communications with their foreign contacts will be intercepted under § 1881a at some point in the future. This argument fails. As an initial matter, the Second Circuit's "objectively reasonable likelihood" standard is inconsistent with our requirement that "threatened injury must be certainly impending to constitute injury in fact." Whitmore v. Arkansas, 495 U.S. 149, 158 (1990) (internal quotation marks omitted). Furthermore, respondents' argument rests on [a] highly speculative fear. . . .

First, it is speculative whether the Government will imminently target communications to which respondents are parties. Section 1881a expressly provides that respondents, who are U.S. persons, cannot be targeted for surveillance under § 1881a. . . . Accordingly, respondents' theory necessarily rests on their assertion that the Government will target *other individuals*—namely, their foreign contacts.

Yet respondents have no actual knowledge of the Government's § 1881a targeting practices. Instead, respondents merely speculate and make assumptions about whether their communications with their foreign contacts will be acquired under § 1881a. For example, journalist Christopher Hedges states: "I have no choice but to *assume* that any of my international communications *may* be subject to government surveillance, and I have to make decisions . . . in light of that *assumption*" (emphasis added and deleted). . . .

Second, even if respondents could demonstrate that the targeting of their foreign contacts is imminent, respondents can only speculate as to whether the Government will seek to use § 1881a-authorized surveillance (rather than other methods) to do so. The Government has numerous other methods of conducting surveillance, none of which is challenged here. . . .

Third, even if respondents could show that the Government will seek the Foreign Intelligence Surveillance Court's authorization to acquire the communications of respondents' foreign contacts under § 1881a, respondents can only speculate as to whether that court will authorize such surveillance. . . . We decline to abandon our usual reluctance to endorse standing theories that rest on speculation about the decisions of independent actors. Section 1881a mandates that the Government must obtain the Foreign Intelligence Surveillance Court's approval of targeting procedures, minimization procedures, and a governmental certification regarding proposed surveillance. . . . And, critically, the Court must also assess whether the Government's targeting and minimization procedures comport with the Fourth Amendment. § 1881a(i)(3)(A).

Fourth, even if the Government were to obtain the Foreign Intelligence Surveillance Court's approval to target respondents' foreign contacts under § 1881a, it is unclear whether the Government would succeed in acquiring the communications of respondents' foreign contacts. And fifth, even if the Government were to conduct surveillance of respondents' foreign contacts, respondents can only speculate as to whether *their own communications* with their foreign contacts would be incidentally acquired.

In sum, respondents' speculative chain of possibilities does not establish that injury based on potential future surveillance is certainly impending or is fairly traceable to § 1881a.[5]

Respondents' alternative argument—namely, that they can establish standing based on the measures that they have undertaken to avoid § 1881a-authorized surveillance—fares no better. Respondents assert that they are suffering ongoing injuries that are fairly traceable to § 1881a because the risk of surveillance under § 1881a requires them to take costly and burdensome measures to protect the confidentiality of their communications. Respondents claim, for instance, that the threat of surveillance sometimes compels them to avoid certain e-mail and phone conversations, to "tal[k] in generalities rather than specifics," or to travel so that they can have in-person conversations. The Second Circuit panel concluded that, because respondents are already suffering such ongoing injuries, the likelihood of interception under § 1881a is relevant only to the question whether respondents' ongoing injuries are "fairly traceable" to § 1881a. Analyzing the "fairly traceable" element of standing under a relaxed reasonableness standard, the Second Circuit then held that "plaintiffs have established that they suffered *present* injuries in fact—economic and professional harms—stemming from a reasonable fear of *future* harmful government conduct."

The Second Circuit's analysis improperly allowed respondents to establish standing by asserting that they suffer present costs and burdens that are based on a fear of surveillance, so long as that fear is not "fanciful, paranoid, or otherwise unreasonable." This improperly waters down the fundamental requirements of Article III.

---

[5] Our cases do not uniformly require plaintiffs to demonstrate that it is literally certain that the harms they identify will come about. In some instances, we have found standing based on a "substantial risk" that the harm will occur, which may prompt plaintiffs to reasonably incur costs to mitigate or avoid that harm. Monsanto Co. v. Geertson Seed Farms, 561 U.S. 139, 153–54 (2010). But to the extent that the "substantial risk" standard is relevant and is distinct from the "clearly impending" requirement, respondents fall short of even that standard, in light of the attenuated chain of inferences necessary to find harm here. In addition, plaintiffs bear the burden of pleading and proving concrete facts showing that the defendant's actual action has caused the substantial risk of harm. . . .

Respondents' contention that they have standing because they incurred certain costs as a reasonable reaction to a risk of harm is unavailing—because the harm respondents seek to avoid is not certainly impending. In other words, respondents cannot manufacture standing merely by inflicting harm on themselves based on their fears of hypothetical future harm that is not certainly impending. . . .

We hold that respondents lack Article III standing because they cannot demonstrate that the future injury they purportedly fear is certainly impending and because they cannot manufacture standing by incurring costs in anticipation of non-imminent harm.

(ii) The Dissent

Justice Breyer, joined by Justices Ginsburg, Sotomayor, and Kagan, disputed both the majority's standard and its application. Emphasis on the phrase "certainly impending" as used in *Whitmore v. Arkansas* was misplaced:

> [C]*ertainty* is not, and never has been the touchstone of standing. The future is inherently uncertain. Yet federal courts frequently entertain actions for injunctions and for declaratory relief aimed at preventing future activities that are reasonably likely or highly likely, but not absolutely certain, to take place. And that degree of certainty is all that is needed to support standing here.

Moreover, "the Court has often *found* standing where the occurrence of the relevant injury was far *less* certain than here." Among the cases adduced to support that proposition was Pennell v. San Jose, 485 U.S. 1 (1988):

> A city ordinance forbade landlords to raise the rent charged to a tenant by more than 8 percent where doing so would work an unreasonably severe hardship on that tenant. A group of landlords sought a judgment declaring the ordinance unconstitutional. The Court held that, to have standing, the landlords had to demonstrate a " *'realistic danger of sustaining a direct injury* as a result of the statute's operation.' " Id. at 8 (emphasis added). It found that the landlords had done so by showing a likelihood of enforcement and a "probability" that the ordinance would make the landlords charge lower rents—even though the landlords had not shown (1) that they intended to raise the relevant rents to the point of causing unreasonably severe hardship; (2) that the tenants would challenge those increases; or (3) that the city's hearing examiners and arbitrators would find against the landlords. Here, even more so than in *Pennell,* there is a *"realistic danger"* that the relevant harm will occur.

Precedents also supported finding *present* injury in the precautions taken to avoid reasonably probable *future* injury:

> Thus, in Monsanto Co. v. Geertson Seed Farms, 561 U.S. 139 (2010), plaintiffs, a group of conventional alfalfa growers, challenged an agency decision to deregulate genetically engineered alfalfa. They claimed that deregulation would harm them because

their neighbors would plant the genetically engineered seed, bees would obtain pollen from the neighbors' plants, and the bees would then (harmfully) contaminate their own conventional alfalfa with the genetically modified gene. The lower courts had found a "reasonable probability" that this injury would occur.

Without expressing views about that probability, we found standing because the plaintiffs would suffer present harm by trying to combat the threat. The plaintiffs, for example, "would have to conduct testing to find out whether and to what extent their crops have been contaminated." Id. at 154. And they would have to take "measures to minimize the likelihood of potential contamination and to ensure an adequate supply of non-genetically-engineered alfalfa." Id. We held that these "harms, which [the plaintiffs] will suffer even if their crops are not actually infected with" the genetically modified gene, "are sufficiently concrete to satisfy the injury-in-fact prong of the constitutional standing analysis." Id. at 155.

Virtually identical circumstances are present here. Plaintiff McKay [a lawyer representing clients accused of terrorism], for example, points out that, when he communicates abroad about, or in the interests of, a client (e.g., a client accused of terrorism), he must "make an assessment" whether his "client's interests would be compromised" should the Government "acquire the communications." If so, he must either forgo the communication or travel abroad.

Since travel is expensive, since forgoing communication can compromise the client's interests, since McKay's assessment itself takes time and effort, this case does not differ significantly from *Monsanto*. And that is so whether we consider the plaintiffs' present necessary expenditure of time and effort as a separate concrete, particularized, imminent harm, or consider it as additional evidence that the future harm (an interception) is likely to occur.

The dissenters had no trouble finding a "very high likelihood" that the NSA, acting under the authority of § 1881a, would intercept at least some of the plaintiffs' communications:

First, the plaintiffs have engaged, and continue to engage, in electronic communications of a kind that the 2008 amendment . . . authorizes the Government to intercept. These communications include discussions with family members of those detained at Guantanamo, friends and acquaintances of those persons, and investigators, experts and others with knowledge of circumstances related to terrorist activities. These persons are foreigners located outside the United States. . . .

Second, the plaintiffs have a strong *motive* to engage in, and the Government has a strong *motive* to listen to, conversations of the kind described. A lawyer representing a client normally seeks to learn the circumstances surrounding the crime (or the civil wrong) of which the client is accused. . . . Journalists and human rights workers have strong similar motives to conduct conversations of this kind.

At the same time, the Government has a strong motive to conduct surveillance of conversations that contain material of this kind. The Government, after all, seeks to learn as much as it can reasonably learn about suspected terrorists (such as those detained at Guantanamo), as well as about their contacts and activities, along with those of friends and family members. And the Government is motivated to do so, not simply by the desire to help convict those whom the Government believes guilty, but also by the critical, overriding need to protect America from terrorism.

Third, the Government's *past behavior* shows that it has sought, and hence will in all likelihood continue to seek, information about alleged terrorists and detainees through means that include surveillance of electronic communications. . . .

Fourth, the Government has the *capacity* to conduct electronic surveillance of the kind at issue. . . . Of course, to exercise this capacity the Government must have intelligence court authorization. But the Government rarely files requests that fail to meet the statutory criteria. As the intelligence court itself has stated, its review under § 1881a is "narrowly circumscribed." There is no reason to believe that the communications described would all fail to meet the conditions necessary for approval. . . .

The upshot is that (1) similarity of content, (2) strong motives, (3) prior behavior, and (4) capacity all point to a very strong likelihood that the Government will intercept at least some of the plaintiffs' communications. . . .

Consequently, we need only assume that the Government is doing its job (to find out about, and combat, terrorism) in order to conclude that there is a high probability that the Government will intercept at least some electronic communication to which at least some of the plaintiffs are parties. The majority is wrong when it describes the harm threatened plaintiffs as "speculative."

(iii) Questions and Comments

Clapper v. Amnesty International confirms the requirements of injury, causation, and redressability, as stated in *Allen v. Wright* and in many subsequent cases. Yet *Clapper* confirms that, just beneath the doctrinal surface, the law of standing remains deeply and durably controversial. Not only is the Court split five-to-four, but that split reflects a perfect "liberal"-"conservative" alignment.

Why should that be? Is there some reason why "conservatives" should be consistently more robust in construing the requirements of standing than their more "liberal" colleagues? If so, is the alignment consistent across cases? Or might, as is often alleged, the split over standing have something to do with the merits of the case? Are "conservatives" necessarily more sensitive to the potential national security costs of judicial review in *Clapper* and therefore more anxious to avoid a decision? Are "liberals" less concerned with national security or perhaps more concerned about invasions of privacy? Note how hard it is to make confident statements of this sort, given that neither opinion addresses the merits of the plaintiffs' claims.

Is it problematic for the government to argue both that (a) it will not disclose to the plaintiffs whether interception of their communications has occurred or is likely and that (b) the complaint should be dismissed because the plaintiffs cannot establish what the government will not disclose? Or is that oddity simply a natural consequence of the secrecy required for national security operations?

Finally, note that a plaintiff's injury must not only be "fairly traceable" to the defendant's conduct but also be "likely to be redressed by the requested relief." What does the last requirement add? On the evidence of the decided cases, the answer is "not much." There are very few cases that turn on redressability, probably because redressability does not support standing where causation is lacking.[a]

3. *DUKE POWER*

An extremely unusual standing decision that arguably involved redressability came in Duke Power Co. v. Carolina Environmental Study Group, Inc., 438 U.S. 59 (1978). The case concerned the constitutionality of the Price-Anderson Act, which limits the liability of utilities for nuclear accidents. Originally enacted in 1957, the statute was designed to encourage nuclear power by protecting the industry against the uninsurability of the risk of nuclear mishap.

Environmentalists sued Duke Power and the Nuclear Regulatory Commission to have the Price-Anderson Act declared unconstitutional. The District Court upheld plaintiffs' standing and struck down the statute on the ground that denial of compensation to the victims of a nuclear accident would violate due process and equal protection. On direct appeal, the Supreme Court affirmed as to standing and reversed on the merits.

Speaking through Chief Justice Burger, the Court found that plaintiffs had alleged specific injuries, including the adverse environmental and aesthetic effects of thermal pollution of the two lakes on which the plants were sited and the fear of damage resulting from low-level radiation. The Court then turned to "the more difficult step" of determining whether the injuries " 'fairly can be traced to the challenged action of the defendant,' or put otherwise, [whether] the exercise of the Court's remedial powers would redress the claimed injuries." The District Court had found that "there is a substantial likelihood that Duke would not be able to complete the construction and maintain the operation of the [plants] but for the protection of the Price-Anderson Act." The Court found this conclusion "not clearly erroneous."

Most interestingly, the Court rejected the contention that standing required a connection between the constitutional defect in the statute (which

---

[a]   For analysis and criticism of *Clapper*, see Vicki C. Jackson, Standing and the Role of Federal Courts: Triple Error Decisions in *Clapper v. Amnesty International USA* and *City of Los Angeles v. Lyons*, 23 Wm. & M. Bill of Rts J. 127 (2014).

concerned only potential accident victims) and the environmental and health injuries that allegedly affected the plaintiffs. The Court held that no "subject-matter nexus between the right asserted and the injury alleged" was necessary.

Justices Stevens and Stewart disputed the Court's handling of standing. Justice Stevens focused on causation:

> The string of contingencies that supposedly holds this litigation together is too delicate for me. We are told that but for the Price-Anderson Act there would be no financing of nuclear power plants, no development of those plants by private parties, and hence no present injury to persons such as [plaintiffs]; we are then asked to remedy an alleged due process violation that may possibly occur at some uncertain time in the future, and may possibly injure the appellees in a way that has no significant connection with any present injury. It is remarkable that such a series of speculations is considered sufficient . . . to establish appellees' standing. . . .

> The Court's opinion will serve the national interest in removing doubts concerning the constitutionality of the Price-Anderson Act. I cannot, therefore, criticize the statesmanship of the Court's decision to provide the country with an advisory opinion on an important subject. Nevertheless, my view of the proper function of this Court, or of any other federal court, in the structure of our government is more limited. We are not statesmen; we are judges. When it is necessary to resolve a constitutional issue in the adjudication of an actual case or controversy, it is our duty to do so. But whenever we are persuaded by reasons of expediency to engage in the business of giving legal advice, we chip away a part of the foundation of our independence and our strength.

Justice Stewart insisted that there should be some connection between the constitutional claim and the injury alleged for purposes of standing:

> [T]he Court relies on the "present" injuries of increased water temperatures and low-level radiation emissions [to establish standing]. Even assuming that but for the act the plant would not exist and therefore neither would its effects on the environment, I cannot believe that it follows that the [plaintiffs] have standing to attack the constitutionality of the act. Apart from the but-for connection in the loosest sense of that concept, there is no relationship at all between the injury alleged for standing purposes and the injury alleged [to support the claim on the merits].

> Surely a plaintiff does not have standing simply because his challenge, if successful, will remove the injury relied on for standing purposes *only* because it will put the defendant out of existence. Surely there must be *some* direct relationship between the plaintiff's federal claim and the injury relied on for standing. An interest in the local water temperature does not, in short, give these [plaintiffs] standing . . . to challenge the constitutionality of a law

limiting liability in an unrelated and as-yet-to-occur major nuclear accident.

Was *Duke Power* correctly decided? Is it consistent with *Allen*?

4. STANDING AND REMEDY

If a litigant who has standing to seek one kind of relief (say, damages) seeks another kind of relief (say, an injunction), one might conclude simply that the litigant is not entitled to the second relief sought. Or one might conclude that the litigant does not have *standing* to seek that relief. The latter formulation was invoked by the Court in City of Los Angeles v. Lyons, 461 U.S. 95 (1983). Lyons was injured when subjected to a chokehold by officers of the LAPD. His standing to seek damages was undoubted. But Lyons also sought a broad injunction against use of chokeholds in the future, and the Supreme Court said that the plaintiff had not shown any likelihood of future injury. The mere allegation that Los Angeles police used chokeholds unjustifiably "falls far short of the allegations that would be necessary to establish a case or controversy between these parties."

Lyons is sometimes thought of as a ripeness case and is discussed further in the materials on ripeness. But considered as a standing case, *Lyons* seems consistent with Town of Chester v. Laroe Estates, Inc., 581 U.S. ___, 137 S.Ct. 1645 (2017). *Laroe Estates* resolved a question that might have been thought obvious had not the Second Circuit ruled otherwise. An intervenor as of right, under Rule 24, who seeks exactly the same relief sought by the plaintiff, does not require Article III standing. In those circumstances, the intervenor functions more or less as an amicus curiae. But if the intervenor pursues relief different from or additional to that sought by the plaintiff, then the intervenor must have standing to seek that relief. Put simply, Rule 24 does not obviate the requirements of Article III.

5. BIBLIOGRAPHY

The modern law of standing has generated an enormous literature. Of particular interest is William A. Fletcher, The Structure of Standing, 98 Yale L.J. 221 (1988), which launches a broad conceptual attack on both the utility of, and necessity for, a law of standing:

policy

> I propose that we abandon the attempt to capture the question of who should be able to enforce legal rights in a single formula, abandon the idea that standing is a preliminary jurisdictional issue, and abandon the idea that Article III requires a showing of "injury in fact." Instead, standing should simply be a question on the merits of plaintiff's claim. If a duty is statutory, Congress should have essentially unlimited power to define the class of persons entitled to enforce that duty, for congressional power to create the duty should include the power to define those who have standing to enforce it. If a duty is constitutional, the constitutional clause should be seen not only as a source of the duty, but also as the primary description of those entitled to enforce it.

Thus, for Fletcher, the variation among constitutional standing cases is neither surprising nor, in itself, objectionable. In his view, the controlling question should not be any comprehensively stated requirement of standing, but rather the meaning and purpose of the underlying constitutional provision.[b]

Others attack standing law from different perspectives. Robert Pushaw argues that standing requirements are appropriate in bilateral disputes involving only the immediate parties, but should not be allowed to curtail exposition of the law in disputes of broader moment. See Robert J. Pushaw, Jr., Article III's Case/Controversy Distinction and the Dual Functions of the Federal Courts, 69 Notre Dame L. Rev. 447 (1994); and Robert J. Pushaw, Jr., Justiciability and Separation of Powers: A Neo-Federalist Approach, 81 Corn. L. Rev. 393 (1996). Edward Hartnett argues that federal criminal prosecutions demonstrate that "injury in fact," in the sense of "concrete and particularized" harm, need not exist for the United States as plaintiff and consequently that injury is not part of the "irreducible constitutional minimum" of Article III. See Edward A. Hartnett, The Standing of the United States: How Criminal Prosecutions Show That Standing Doctrine Is Looking for Answers in All the Wrong Places, 97 Mich. L. Rev. 2239 (1999). Finally, Richard Fallon links standing and other justiciability doctrines to questions of remedies, arguing that "concerns about remedies exert a nearly ubiquitous, often unrecognized, and little understood influence in the shaping and application of justiciability doctrines." See Richard H. Fallon, Jr., The Linkage between Justiciability and Remedies—And Their Connections to Substantive Rights, 92 Va. L. Rev. 633 (2006).

In an interesting argument that cuts across modern standing law, Richard Re concludes in Richard M. Re, Relative Standing, 102 Geo. L.J. 1191 (2014), that the Supreme Court should, and often does, focus on the "most interested plaintiff" as a gloss on existing doctrine. Under this "relative standing" approach, the courts should not be open to "inferior plaintiffs with relatively weak claims to standing," so long as "superior plaintiffs" with better claims are available. When that is not true, as in Federal Election Commission v. Akins, 524 U.S. 11 (1998), and Massachusetts v. Environmental Protection Agency, 549 U.S. 497 (2007) (both cases considered in the next subsection), the courts should loosen the traditional requirement of injury-in-fact in order to allow suit. "In practice," says Re, "each plaintiff's standing critically depends, not on a constant benchmark, but on how she compares with other would-be claimants."

---

[b] In 2013, Fletcher's article was the subject of a 25-year retrospective in a Symposium in the Alabama Law Review. The Symposium begins with Fletcher's restatement of his views in a student lecture, William A. Fletcher, Standing: Who Can Sue to Enforce a Legal Duty?, 65 Ala. L. Rev. 278 (2013). Articles exploring and supporting Fletcher's views include Jonathan R. Siegel, What If the Universal Injury-in-Fact Test Already is Normative?, 65 Ala. L. Rev. 403 (2013), and Ernest A. Young, In Praise of Judge Fletcher—And of General Standing Principles, 65 Ala. L. Rev. 473 (2013). More critical assessments include Robert J. Pushaw, Jr., Fortuity and the Article III "Case": A Critique of Fletcher's The Structure of Standing, 65 Ala. L. Rev. 289 (2013), and Maxwell L. Stearns, Grains of Sand or Butterfly Effect: Standing, the Legitimacy of Precedent, and Reflections on Hollingsworth and Windsor, 65 Ala. L. Rev. 349 (2013). Other contributions to the Symposium are noted where relevant elsewhere in these materials.

Among the valuable additional articles published since 2000 are Heather Elliott, Does the Supreme Court Ignore Standing Problems to Reach the Merits? Evidence (or Lack Thereof) from the Roberts Court, 23 Wm. & M. Bill of Rts J. 189 (2014); Heather Elliott, The Functions of Standing, 61 Stan. L. Rev. 459 (2008); Richard H. Fallon, Jr., The Fragmentation of Standing, 93 Tex. L. Rev. 1061 (2015); Tara Leigh Grove, Standing as an Article II Nondelegation Doctrine, 11 U. Pa. J. Const. L. 781 (2009); F. Andrew Hessick, The Separation-of-Powers Theory of Standing, 95 N.C. L. Rev. 673 (2017); F. Andrew Hessick, Standing, Injury in Fact, and Private Rights, 93 Corn. L. Rev. 275 (2008); Aziz Z. Huq, Standing for the Structural Constitution, 99 Va. L. Rev. 1325 (2013); Eugene Kontorovich, What Standing Is Good For, 93 Va. L. Rev. 1663 (2007); Bradford C. Mank, Prudential Standing and the Dormant Commerce Clause: Why the "Zone of Interests" Test Should Not Apply to Constitutional Cases, 48 Ariz. L. Rev. 23 (2006); Richard Murphy, Abandoning Standing: Trading a Rule of Access for a Rule of Deference, 60 Admin. L. Rev. 943 (2008); James E. Pfander, Standing to Sue: Lessons from Scotland's Actio Popularis, 66 Duke L.J. 1493 (2017); Jonathan R. Siegel, A Theory of Justiciability, 86 Tex. L. Rev. 73 (2007); Ann Woolhandler and Caleb Nelson, Does History Defeat Standing Doctrine?, 102 Mich. L. Rev. 689 (2004).

SUBSECTION B. STATUTORY STANDING

Lujan v. Defenders of Wildlife

Supreme Court of the United States, 1992.
504 U.S. 555.

■ JUSTICE SCALIA delivered the opinion of the Court with respect to parts I, II, III-A, and IV, and an opinion with respect to part III-B in which THE CHIEF JUSTICE, JUSTICE WHITE, and JUSTICE THOMAS join.

This case involves a challenge to a rule promulgated by the Secretary of the Interior interpreting § 7 of the Endangered Species Act of 1973 (ESA), 16 U.S.C. § 1536, in such fashion as to render it applicable only to actions within the United States or on the high seas. The preliminary issue, and the only one we reach, is whether the respondents here, plaintiffs below, have standing to seek judicial review of the rule.

I

The ESA seeks to protect species of animals against threats to their continued existence caused by man. The ESA instructs the Secretary of the Interior to promulgate by regulation a list of those species which are either endangered or threatened under enumerated criteria, and to define the critical habitat of these species. Section 7(a)(2) of the act then provides, in pertinent part:

> Each Federal agency shall, in consultation with and with the assistance of the Secretary [of the Interior], insure that any action authorized, funded, or carried out by such agency . . . is

not likely to jeopardize the continued existence of any endangered species or threatened species or result in the destruction or adverse modification of habitat of such species which is determined by the Secretary, after consultation as appropriate with affected States, to be critical.

16 U.S.C. § 1536(a)(2). In 1978, the Fish and Wildlife Service (FWS) and the National Marine Fisheries Service (NMFS), on behalf of the Secretary of the Interior and the Secretary of Commerce, respectively, promulgated a joint regulation stating that the obligations imposed by § 7(a)(2) extend to actions taken in foreign nations. The next year, however, the Interior Department began to reexamine its position. A revised joint regulation, reinterpreting § 7(a)(2) to require consultation only for actions taken in the United States or on the high seas, was promulgated in 1986.

Shortly thereafter, respondents, organizations dedicated to wildlife conservation and other environmental causes, filed this action against the Secretary of the Interior, seeking a declaratory judgment that the new regulation is in error as to the geographic scope of § 7(a)(2), and an injunction requiring the Secretary to promulgate a new regulation restoring the initial interpretation. The District Court ... ordered the Secretary to publish a revised regulation. The Eighth Circuit affirmed. We granted certiorari.

II

... Over the years, our cases have established that the irreducible constitutional minimum of standing contains three elements: First, the plaintiff must have suffered an "injury in fact"—an invasion of a legally-protected interest which is (a) concrete and particularized and (b) "actual or imminent, not 'conjectural' or 'hypothetical.'" Whitmore v. Arkansas, 495 U.S. 149, 155 (1990). Second, there must be a causal connection between the injury and the conduct complained of—the injury has to be "fairly trace[able] to the challenged action of the defendant, and not ... th[e] result [of] the independent action of some third party not before the court." Simon v. Eastern Kentucky Welfare Rights Org., 426 U.S. 26, 41–42 (1976). Third, it must be "likely," as opposed to merely "speculative," that the injury will be "redressed by a favorable decision." Id. at 38.

The party invoking federal jurisdiction bears the burden of establishing these elements. Since they are not mere pleading requirements but rather an indispensable part of the plaintiff's case, each element must be supported in the same way as any other matter on which the plaintiff bears the burden of proof, i.e., with the manner and degree of evidence required at successive stages of the litigation. At the pleading stage, general factual allegations of injury resulting from the defendant's conduct may suffice. ... In response to a summary judgment motion, however, the plaintiff can no longer rest on such "mere allegations," but must "set forth" by affidavit or other evidence "specific facts," Fed. Rule Civ. Proc. 56(e), which for purposes of the summary judgment motion will be taken to be true. And at the final stage, those facts (if controverted) must be "supported adequately by the evidence adduced at trial." Gladstone, Realtors v. Village of Bellwood, 441 U.S. 91, 115 n.31 (1979).

When the suit is one challenging the legality of government action or inaction, the nature and extent of facts that must be averred (at the summary judgment stage) or proved (at the trial stage) in order to establish standing depends considerably upon whether the plaintiff is himself an object of the action (or foregone action) at issue. If he is, there is ordinarily little question that the action or inaction has caused him injury, and that a judgment preventing or requiring the action will redress it. When, however, as in this case, a plaintiff's asserted injury arises from the government's allegedly unlawful regulation (or lack of regulation) of *someone else*, much more is needed. In that circumstance, causation and redressability ordinarily hinge on the response of the regulated (or regulable) third party to the government action or inaction—and perhaps on the response of others as well. The existence of one or more of the essential elements of standing "depends on the unfettered choices made by independent actors not before the courts and whose exercise of broad and legitimate discretion the courts cannot presume either to control or predict," ASARCO, Inc. v. Kadish, 490 U.S. 605, 615 (1989) (opinion of Kennedy, J.); and it becomes the burden of the plaintiff to adduce facts showing that these choices have been or will be made in such manner as to produce causation and permit redressability of injury. Thus, when the plaintiff is not himself the object of the government action or inaction he challenges, standing is not precluded, but it is ordinarily "substantially more difficult" to establish. Allen v. Wright, 468 U.S. 737, 758 (1984).

III

We think the Court of Appeals failed to apply the foregoing principles in denying the Secretary's motion for summary judgment. . . .

A

Respondents' claim to injury is that the lack of consultation with respect to certain funded activities abroad "increas[es] the rate of extinction of endangered and threatened species." Of course, the desire to use or observe an animal species, even for purely aesthetic purposes, is undeniably a cognizable interest for purpose of standing. See, e.g., Sierra Club v. Morton, 405 U.S. 727, 734 (1972). "But the 'injury in fact' test requires more than an injury to a cognizable interest. It requires that the party seeking review be himself among the injured." Id. at 734–35. To survive the Secretary's summary judgment motion, respondents had to submit affidavits or other evidence showing, through specific facts, not only that listed species were in fact being threatened by funded activities abroad, but also that one or more of respondents' members would thereby be "directly" affected apart from their " 'special interest' in th[e] subject." Id. at 735, 739.

With respect to this aspect of the case, the Court of Appeals focused on the affidavits of two Defenders' members—Joyce Kelly and Amy Skilbred. Ms. Kelly stated that she traveled to Egypt in 1986 and "observed the traditional habitat of the endangered Nile crocodile there and intend[s] to do so again, and hope[s] to observe the crocodile directly," and that she "will suffer harm in fact as a result of [the] American . . . role . . . in overseeing the rehabilitation of the Aswan High Dam on the Nile . . . and [in] develop[ing] . . . Egypt's . . . Master Water Plan." Ms. Skilbred averred that she traveled to Sri Lanka in 1981 and "observed th[e] habitat" of "endangered species such as the Asian elephant and the leopard" at what is now the site of the Mahaweli Project funded by the Agency for International Development (AID), although she "was unable to see any of the endangered species;" "this development project," she continued, "will seriously reduce endangered, threatened, and endemic species habitat including areas that I visited[, which] may severely shorten the future of these species;" that threat, she concluded, harmed her because she "intend[s] to return to Sri Lanka in the future and hope[s] to be more fortunate in spotting at least the endangered elephant and leopard." When Ms. Skilbred was asked at a subsequent deposition if and when she had any plans to return to Sri Lanka, she reiterated that "I intend to go back to Sri Lanka," but confessed that she had no current plans: "I don't know [when]. There is a civil war going on right now. I don't know. Not next year, I will say. In the future."

We shall assume for the sake of argument that these affidavits contain facts showing that certain agency-funded projects threaten listed species—though that is questionable. They plainly contain no facts, however, showing how damage to the species will produce "imminent" injury to Mss. Kelly and Skilbred. That the women "had visited" the areas of the projects before the projects commenced proves nothing. . . . And the affiants' profession of an "inten[t]" to return to the places they had visited before—where they will presumably, this time, be deprived of the opportunity to observe animals of the endangered species—is simply not enough. Such "some day" intentions—without any description of concrete plans, or indeed even any specification of when the some day will be—do not support a finding of the "actual or imminent" injury that our cases require.

Besides relying upon the Kelly and Skilbred affidavits, respondents propose a series of novel standing theories. The first, inelegantly styled "ecosystem nexus," proposes that any person who uses any part of a "contiguous ecosystem" adversely affected by a funded activity has standing even if the activity is located a great distance away. This approach, as the Court of Appeals correctly observed, is inconsistent with our opinion in Lujan v. National Wildlife Federation, 497 U.S. 871 (1990), which held that a plaintiff claiming injury from environmental damage must use the area affected by the challenged activity and not an area roughly "in the vicinity" of it. It makes no difference that the general-purpose section of the ESA states that the act was intended in part "to provide a means whereby the ecosystems upon which endangered species and threatened species depend may be conserved," 16 U.S.C. § 1531(b). To say that the act protects ecosystems is not to say that the act creates (if it were possible) rights of action in persons who have not been injured in fact, that is, persons who use portions of an ecosystem not perceptibly affected by the unlawful action in question.

Respondents' other theories are called, alas, the "animal nexus" approach, whereby anyone who has an interest in studying or seeing the endangered animals anywhere on the globe has standing; and the "vocational nexus" approach, under which anyone with a professional interest in such animals can sue. Under these theories, anyone who goes to see Asian elephants in the Bronx Zoo, and anyone who is a keeper of Asian elephants in the Bronx Zoo, has standing to sue because the Director of AID did not consult with the Secretary regarding the AID-funded project in Sri Lanka. This is beyond all reason. Standing is not "an ingenious academic exercise in the conceivable," United States v. Students Challenging Regulatory Agency Procedures (SCRAP), 412 U.S. 669, 688 (1973), but as we have said requires, at the summary judgment stage, a factual showing of perceptible harm. It is clear that the person who observes or works with a particular animal threatened by a federal decision is facing perceptible harm, since the very subject of his interest will no longer exist. It is even plausible—though it goes to the outermost limit of plausibility—to think that a person who observes or works with animals of a particular species in the very area of the world where that species is threatened by a federal decision is facing such harm, since some animals that might have been the subject of his interest will no longer exist, see Japan Whaling Assn. v. American Cetacean Society, 478 U.S. 221, 231 n.4 (1986). It goes beyond the limit, however, and into pure speculation and fantasy, to say that anyone who observes or works with an endangered species, anywhere in the world, is appreciably harmed by a single project affecting some portion of that species with which he has no more specific connection.

B

[Here Justice Scalia argued that the plaintiffs also failed the requirement of redressability, since the only remedy the Secretary of the Interior could give was consultation with other agencies. On this point, Scalia spoke only for a plurality of the Justices.]

IV

The Court of Appeals found that respondents had standing for an additional reason: because they had suffered a "procedural injury." The so-called "citizen-suit" provision of the ESA provides, in pertinent part, that "any person may commence a civil suit on his own behalf (A) to enjoin any person, including the United States and any other governmental instrumentality or agency . . . who is alleged to be in violation of any provision of this chapter." 16 U.S.C. § 1540(g). The court held that, because

§ 7(a)(2) requires interagency consultation, the citizen-suit provision creates a "procedural righ[t]" to consultation in all "persons"—so that anyone can file suit in federal court to challenge the Secretary's (or presumably any other official's) failure to follow the assertedly correct consultative procedure, notwithstanding their inability to allege any discrete injury flowing from that failure. To understand the remarkable nature of this holding one must be clear about what it does not rest upon: This is not a case where plaintiffs are seeking to enforce a procedural requirement the disregard of which could impair a separate concrete interest of theirs (e.g., the procedural requirement for a hearing prior to denial of their license application, or the procedural requirement for an environmental impact statement before a federal facility is constructed next door to them).[7] Nor is it simply a case where concrete injury has been suffered by many persons, as in mass fraud or mass tort situations. Nor, finally, is it the unusual case in which Congress has created a concrete private interest in the outcome of a suit against a private party for the government's benefit, by providing a cash bounty for the victorious plaintiff. Rather, the court held that the injury-in-fact requirement had been satisfied by congressional conferral upon all persons of an abstract, self-contained, noninstrumental "right" to have the executive observe the procedures required by law. We reject this view.

We have consistently held that a plaintiff raising only a generally available grievance about government—claiming only harm to his and every citizen's interest in proper application of the Constitution and laws, and seeking relief that no more directly and tangibly benefits him than it does the public at large—does not state an Article III case or controversy. . . .

[I]n Schlesinger v. Reservists Committee to Stop the War, 418 U.S. 208, 217 (1974), we dismissed . . . a citizen-taxpayer suit contending that it was a violation of the Incompatibility Clause, Art. I, § 6, cl. 2, for members of Congress to hold commissions in the military Reserves. We said that the challenged action, "standing alone, would adversely affect only the generalized interest of all citizens in constitutional governance. . . ." Since *Schlesinger* we have on two occasions held that an injury amounting only to the alleged violation of a right to have the government act in accordance with law was not judicially cognizable . . . . *Allen*, 468 U.S. at

---

[7]   There is this much truth to the assertion that "procedural rights" are special: The person who has been accorded a procedural right to protect his concrete interests can assert that right without meeting all the normal standards for redressability and immediacy. Thus, under our case-law, one living adjacent to the site for proposed construction of a federally licensed dam has standing to challenge the licensing agency's failure to prepare an environmental impact statement, even though he cannot establish with any certainty that the statement will cause the license to be withheld or altered, and even though the dam will not be completed for many years. (That is why we do not rely, in the present case, upon the government's argument that, even if the other agencies were obliged to consult with the Secretary, they might not have followed his advice.) What respondents' "procedural rights" argument seeks, however, is quite different from this: standing for persons who have no concrete interests affected—persons who live (and propose to live) at the other end of the country from the dam.

754; Valley Forge Christian College v. Americans United for Separation of Church and State, Inc., 454 U.S. 464, 483 (1982). . . .

To be sure, our generalized-grievance cases have typically involved government violation of procedures assertedly ordained by the Constitution rather than the Congress. But there is absolutely no basis for making the Article III inquiry turn on the source of the asserted right. Whether the courts were to act on their own, or at the invitation of Congress, in ignoring the concrete injury requirement described in our cases, they would be discarding a principle fundamental to the separate and distinct constitutional role of the third branch—one of the essential elements that identifies those "Cases" and "Controversies" that are the business of the courts rather than of the political branches. "The province of the court," as Chief Justice Marshall said in Marbury v. Madison, 5 U.S. (1 Cranch) 137, 170 (1803) "is, solely, to decide on the rights of individuals." Vindicating the *public* interest (including the public interest in government observance of the Constitution and laws) is the function of Congress and the chief executive. The question presented here is whether the public interest in proper administration of the laws (specifically, in agencies' observance of a particular, statutorily prescribed procedure) can be converted into an individual right by a statute that denominates it as such, and that permits all citizens (or, for that matter, a subclass of citizens who suffer no distinctive concrete harm) to sue. If the concrete injury requirement has the separation-of-powers significance we have always said, the answer must be obvious: To permit Congress to convert the undifferentiated public interest in executive officers' compliance with the law into an "individual right" vindicable in the courts is to permit Congress to transfer from the President to the courts the chief executive's most important constitutional duty, to "take Care that the Laws be faithfully executed," Art. II, § 3. It would enable the courts, with the permission of Congress, . . . to become " 'virtually continuing monitors of the wisdom and soundness of executive action.' " *Allen*, 468 U.S. at 760 (quoting Laird v. Tatum, 408 U.S. 1, 15 (1972)). We have always rejected that vision of our role. . . .

Nothing in this contradicts the principle that "[t]he . . . injury required by Article III may exist solely by virtue of 'statutes creating legal rights, the invasion of which creates standing.' " *Warth*, 422 U.S. at 500 (quoting Linda R. S. v. Richard D., 410 U.S. 614, 617, n.3 (1973)). Both of the cases used by *Linda R. S.* as an illustration of that principle involved Congress's elevating to the status of legally cognizable injuries concrete, de facto injuries that were previously inadequate in law (namely, injury to an individual's personal interest in living in a racially integrated community, see Trafficante v. Metropolitan Life Ins. Co., 409 U.S. 205, 208–12 (1972), and injury to a company's interest in marketing its product free from competition, see Hardin v. Kentucky Utilities Co., 390 U.S. 1, 6 (1968)). As we said in *Sierra Club*, "[Statutory] broadening [of] the categories of injury that may be alleged in support of standing is a different

matter from abandoning the requirement that the party seeking review must himself have suffered an injury." 405 U.S. at 738. . . .

* * *

We hold that respondents lack standing to bring this action and that the Court of Appeals erred in denying the summary judgment motion filed by the United States. The opinion of the Court of Appeals is hereby reversed, and the cause remanded for proceedings consistent with this opinion.

■ JUSTICE KENNEDY, with whom JUSTICE SOUTER joins, concurring in part and concurring in the judgment. . . .

I agree with the Court's conclusion in part III-A that, on the record before us, respondents have failed to demonstrate that they themselves are "among the injured." Sierra Club v. Morton, 405 U.S. 727, 735 (1972).

. . . In my view, Congress has the power to define injuries and articulate chains of causation that will give rise to a case or controversy where none existed before, and I do not read the Court's opinion to suggest a contrary view. In exercising this power, however, Congress must at the very least identify the injury it seeks to vindicate and relate the injury to the class of persons entitled to bring suit. The citizen-suit provision of the Endangered Species Act does not meet these minimal requirements, because while the statute purports to confer a right on "any person . . . to enjoin . . . the United States and any other governmental instrumentality or agency . . . who is alleged to be in violation of any provision of this chapter," it does not of its own force establish that there is an injury in "any person" by virtue of any "violation." 16 U.S.C. § 1540(g)(1)(A).

The Court's holding that there is an outer limit to the power of Congress to confer rights of action is a direct and necessary consequence of the case and controversy limitations found in Article III. I agree that it would exceed those limitations if, at the behest of Congress and in the absence of any showing of concrete injury, we were to entertain citizen-suits to vindicate the public's nonconcrete interest in the proper administration of the laws. . . .

■ JUSTICE STEVENS, concurring in the judgment.

Because I am not persuaded that Congress intended the consultation requirement in § 7(a)(2) of the Endangered Species Act (ESA) to apply to activities in foreign countries, I concur in the judgment of reversal. I do not, however, agree with the Court's conclusion that respondents lack standing . . . .

In my opinion a person who has visited the critical habitat of an endangered species, has a professional interest in preserving the species and its habitat, and intends to revisit them in the future has standing to challenge agency action that threatens their destruction. Congress has found that a wide variety of endangered species of fish, wildlife, and plants are of "aesthetic, ecological, educational, historical, recreational, and scientific value to the Nation and its people." 16 U.S.C. § 1531(a)(3). Given that finding, we have no license to demean the importance of the interest that particular individuals may have in observing any species or its habitat, whether those individuals are motivated by aesthetic enjoyment, an interest in professional research, or an economic interest in preservation of the species. . . .

If respondents are genuinely interested in the preservation of the endangered species and intend to study or observe these animals in the future, their injury will occur as soon as the animals are destroyed. Thus the only potential source of "speculation" in this case is whether respondents' intent to study or observe the animals is genuine. In my view, Joyce Kelly and Amy Skilbred have introduced sufficient evidence to negate petitioner's contention that their claims of injury are "speculative" or "conjectural." As Justice Blackmun explains, a reasonable finder of fact could conclude, from their past visits, their professional backgrounds, and their affidavits and deposition testimony, that Ms. Kelly and Ms. Skilbred will return to the project sites and, consequently, will be injured by the destruction of the endangered species and critical habitat. . . .

■ JUSTICE BLACKMUN, with whom JUSTICE O'CONNOR joins, dissenting.

I part company with the Court in this case in two respects. First, I believe that respondents have raised genuine issues of fact—sufficient to survive summary judgment—both as to injury and as to redressability. Second, I question the Court's breadth of language in rejecting standing for "procedural" injuries. I fear the Court seeks to impose fresh limitations on the constitutional authority of Congress to allow citizen-suits in the federal courts for injuries deemed "procedural" in nature. I dissent.

I

Article III of the Constitution confines the federal courts to adjudication of actual "cases" and "controversies." To ensure the presence of a "case" or "controversy," this Court has held that Article III requires, as an irreducible minimum, that a plaintiff allege (1) an injury that is (2) "fairly traceable to the defendant's allegedly unlawful conduct" and that is (3) "likely to be redressed by the requested relief." Allen v. Wright, 468 U.S. 737, 751 (1984).

A

To survive petitioner's motion for summary judgment on standing, respondents need not prove that they are actually or imminently harmed. They need show only a "genuine issue" of material fact as to standing. Fed. Rule Civ. Proc. 56(c). This is not a heavy burden. A "genuine issue" exists so long as "the evidence is such that a reasonable jury could return a verdict for the nonmoving party [respondents]." Anderson v. Liberty Lobby, Inc., 477 U.S. 242, 248 (1986). . . .

Were the Court to apply the proper standard for summary judgment, I believe it would conclude that the sworn affidavits and deposition testimony of Joyce Kelly and Amy Skilbred advance sufficient facts to create

a genuine issue for trial concerning whether one or both would be imminently harmed by the Aswan and Mahaweli projects. . . . A reasonable
finder of fact could conclude, based not only upon their statements of intent to return, but upon their past visits to the project sites, as well as
their professional backgrounds, that it was likely that Kelly and Skilbred
would make a return trip to the project areas. . . .

By requiring a "description of concrete plans" or "specification of
when the some day [for a return visit] will be," the Court, in my view,
demands what is likely an empty formality. No substantial barriers prevent Kelly or Skilbred from simply purchasing plane tickets to return to
the Aswan and Mahaweli projects. This case differs from other cases in
which the imminence of harm turned largely on the affirmative actions
of third parties beyond a plaintiff's control. See[, e.g.,] Los Angeles v. Lyons, 461 U.S. 95, 105 (1983) (harm dependent on police's arresting
plaintiff again and subjecting him to chokehold).

I fear the Court's demand for detailed descriptions of future conduct
will do little to weed out those who are genuinely harmed from those who
are not. . . .

B

[Here Justice Blackmun criticized the plurality's conclusion on redressability.]

II

The Court concludes that any "procedural injury" suffered by respondents is insufficient to confer standing. It rejects the view that the
"injury-in-fact requirement . . . [is] satisfied by congressional conferral
upon all person of an abstract, self-contained, noninstrumental 'right' to
have the executive observe the procedures required by law." Whatever
the Court might mean with that very broad language, it cannot be saying
that "procedural injuries" as a class are necessarily insufficient for purposes of Article III standing.

. . . The Court expresses concern that allowing judicial enforcement
of "agencies' observance of a particular, statutorily prescribed procedure"
would "transfer from the President to the courts the chief executive's
most important constitutional duty, to 'take Care that the Laws be faithfully executed,' Art. II, § 3." In fact, the principal effect of foreclosing
judicial enforcement of such procedures is to transfer power into the
hands of the executive at the expense—not of the courts—but of Congress, from which that power originates and emanates.

Under the Court's anachronistically formal view of the separation of
powers, Congress legislates pure, substantive mandates and has no business structuring the procedural manner in which the executive implements these mandates. To be sure, in the ordinary course, Congress
does legislate in black-and-white terms of affirmative commands or negative prohibitions on the conduct of officers of the executive branch. In
complex regulatory areas, however, Congress often legislates, as it were,

in procedural shades of gray. That is, it sets forth substantive policy goals and provides for their attainment by requiring executive branch officials to follow certain procedures, for example, in the form of reporting, consultation, and certification requirements. The Court recently has considered two such procedurally oriented statutes. In Japan Whaling Assn. v. American Cetacean Society, 478 U.S. 221 (1986), the Court examined a statute requiring the Secretary of Commerce to certify to the President that foreign nations were not conducting fishing operations or trading which "diminis[h] the effectiveness" of an international whaling convention. The Court expressly found standing to sue. In Robertson v. Methow Valley Citizens Council, 490 U.S. 332, 348 (1989), this Court considered injury from violation of the "action-forcing" procedures of the National Environmental Policy Act (NEPA), in particular the requirements for issuance of environmental impact statements.

The consultation requirement of § 7 of the Endangered Species Act is a similar, action-forcing statute. Consultation is designed as an integral check on federal agency action, ensuring that such action does not go forward without full consideration of its effects on listed species. Once consultation is initiated, the Secretary is under a duty to provide to the action agency "a written statement setting forth the Secretary's opinion, and a summary of the information on which the opinion is based, detailing how the agency action affects the species or its critical habitat." 16 U.S.C. § 1536(b)(3)(A). The Secretary is also obligated to suggest "reasonable and prudent alternatives" to prevent jeopardy to listed species. Id. . . . After the initiation of consultation, the action agency "shall not make any irreversible or irretrievable commitment of resources" which would foreclose the "formulation or implementation of any reasonable and prudent alternative measures" to avoid jeopardizing listed species. § 1536(d). These action-forcing procedures are "designed to protect some threatened concrete interest" of persons who observe and work with endangered or threatened species. That is why I am mystified by the Court's unsupported conclusion that "[t]his is not a case where plaintiffs are seeking to enforce a procedural requirement the disregard of which could impair a separate concrete interest of theirs."

Congress legislates in procedural shades of gray not to aggrandize its own power but to allow maximum executive discretion in the attainment of Congress's legislative goals. . . . Just as Congress does not violate separation of powers by structuring the procedural manner in which the executive shall carry out the laws, surely the federal courts do not violate separation of powers when, at the very instruction and command of Congress, they enforce these procedures.

To prevent Congress from conferring standing for "procedural injuries" is another way of saying that Congress may not delegate to the courts authority deemed "executive" in nature. Here Congress seeks not to delegate "executive" power but only to strengthen the procedures it has legislatively mandated. . . .

In short, determining "injury" for Article III standing purposes is a fact-specific inquiry. . . . There may be factual circumstances in which a congressionally imposed procedural requirement is so insubstantially connected to the prevention of a substantive harm that it cannot be said to work any conceivable injury to an individual litigant. But, as a general matter, the courts owe substantial deference to Congress's substantive purpose in imposing a certain procedural requirement. In all events, "[o]ur separation-of-powers analysis does not turn on the labeling of an activity as 'substantive' as opposed to 'procedural.'" Mistretta v. United States, 488 U.S. 361, 393 (1989). There is no room for a per se rule or presumption excluding injuries labeled "procedural" in nature.

III

In conclusion, I cannot join the Court on what amounts to a slash-and-burn expedition through the law of environmental standing. In my view, "[t]he very essence of civil liberty certainly consists in the right of every individual to claim the protection of the laws, whenever he receives an injury." Marbury v. Madison, 5 U.S. (1 Cranch) 137, 163 (1803).

I dissent.

NOTES ON STATUTORY STANDING

1. CITIZEN-SUIT PROVISIONS

The Endangered Species Act authorizes "any person [to] commence a civil suit . . . to enjoin any person, including the United States and any other governmental instrumentality or agency . . . who is alleged to be in violation of any provision of this chapter." 16 U.S.C. § 1536(g). Most federal environmental statutes (and many others) have such "citizen-suit" provisions. Their purpose is to augment agency enforcement of legal standards by permitting private suits. The most important aspect of *Lujan* was the Court's refusal to give effect to this provision.

In support of this holding, Justice Scalia relied on cases not involving a statutory grant of standing. He said it made no difference "[w]hether the courts were to act on their own, or at the invitation of Congress, in ignoring the concrete injury requirement. . . ." This accords with the Court's repeated statements that injury in fact, causation, and redressability are the "constitutional core" of standing, but before *Lujan* there were good reasons to think that Congress could relax or redefine these requirements. Historically, standing law focused not on injury in fact (an inquiry originally designed to broaden standing), but on the existence in the plaintiff of some "legal interest" invaded by the defendant's conduct. Under this older phrasing, it seemed obvious that Congress could create new "legal interests" and thus could expand the universe of potential plaintiffs. Some observers—including the

Congress—continued in this assumption after the emergence of injury, causation, and redressability as the doctrinal requirements of standing. And in fact there were modern cases supporting that view.[a]

2. QUESTIONS AND COMMENTS ON STATUTORY STANDING

In Standing to Sue: A Proposed Separation of Powers Analysis, 1984 Wis. L. Rev. 37, written before *Lujan*, David Logan found that plaintiffs claiming constitutional violations were more likely to be found to lack standing than plaintiffs asserting statutory claims. He suggested that the disparity made sense from a separation-of-powers perspective. The judicial reluctance to hear "generalized grievances" usually works to minimize friction with the elected branches. When Congress legislates a right to sue, however, separation-of-powers concerns cut the other way. Logan concluded that the courts should allow standing to anyone injured in a way contemplated by remedial legislation.

A more radical attack on statutory standing requirements appears in Cass R. Sunstein, What's Standing After *Lujan*? Of Citizen Suits, "Injuries," and Article III, 91 Mich. L. Rev. 163 (1992). Sunstein argues against requiring injury in fact. He notes that the existence of a judicially cognizable injury is not determined solely as a question of fact. Every person who brings a lawsuit believes that he or she has been injured. Some harms count as injury, and others are dismissed as purely ideological. Sunstein calls for the Court to "abandon the metaphysics of injury in fact [and] return to the question whether a cause of action has been conferred on the plaintiff." He added: "When Congress creates a cause of action enabling people to complain against racial discrimination, consumer fraud, or destruction of environmental assets, it is really giving people a kind of property right to a certain state of affairs. Invasion of that property right is the relevant injury."

Is Sunstein's analysis persuasive? Is it adequately answered in *Lujan*?

3. *FRIENDS OF THE EARTH V. LAIDLAW*

In several subsequent decisions involving citizen-suit provisions, the Supreme Court has been more receptive to standing than it was in *Lujan*. A notable example is Friends of the Earth, Inc. v. Laidlaw Environmental Services, Inc., 528 U.S. 167 (2000). Environmentalists sued Laidlaw under the citizen-suit provision of the Clean Water Act, 33 U.S.C. § 1251 et seq. They complained of mercury discharges into South Carolina's North Tyger River in amounts exceeding the stringent limitations imposed in a discharge permit held by the company. The District Court found that the discharge violations had caused "no demonstrated proof of harm to the environment." The court accordingly denied injunctive relief (noting that the company had been in substantial compliance for some time), but imposed a civil penalty of $405,800, payable to the United States Treasury, for the past violations. As

---

[a] See, e.g., Havens Realty Corp. v. Coleman, 455 U.S. 363 (1982) (finding standing under the Fair Housing Act of 1968 on the basis of a relaxed understanding of "injury in fact"); Gladstone Realtors v. Bellwood, 441 U.S. 91 (1979) (similar).

the case came to the Supreme Court, a key issue was whether the plaintiffs had standing to maintain a citizen-suit for this monetary remedy.

Under the Clean Water Act, a citizen suit is authorized by "a person or persons having an interest which is or may be adversely affected." 33 U.S.C. §§ 1365(a), (g). To establish "injury in fact," plaintiffs submitted affidavits recounting their environmental concerns:

> For example, . . . Kenneth Lee Curtis averred in an affidavit that he lived a half-mile from Laidlaw's facility; that he occasionally drove over the North Tyger River, and that it looked and smelled polluted; and that he would like to fish, camp, swim, and picnic in and near the river between three and 15 miles downstream from the facility, as he did when he was a teenager, but would not do so because he was concerned that the water was polluted by Laidlaw's discharges.

Speaking for the Court, Justice Ginsburg found such allegations sufficient under Article III: "We have held that environmental plaintiffs adequately allege injury in fact when they aver that they use the affected area and are persons 'for whom the aesthetic and recreational values of the area will be lessened' by the challenged activity" (quoting Sierra Club v. Morton, 405 U.S. 727, 735 (1972). *Lujan* was not to the contrary, because the allegations in that case were more "general" and "conclusory."

Justices Scalia and Thomas dissented. Justice Scalia emphasized the trial court's finding of no harm to the environment and argued that plaintiffs' "concerns" were not enough: "By accepting plaintiffs' vague, contradictory, and unsubstantiated allegations of 'concern' about the environment as adequate to prove injury in fact, and accepting them even in the face of a finding that the environment was not demonstrably harmed, the Court makes the injury-in-fact requirement a sham."

A related issue was redressability. The relief plaintiffs obtained was a civil penalty payable not to them, but to the United States. In Steel Co. v. Citizens for a Better Environment, 523 U.S. 83 (1998), the Court had said that civil penalties paid to the government do not redress environmental plaintiffs for their past injuries. *Steel Co.* was distinguished on the ground that the *Laidlaw* plaintiffs alleged continuing violations, which would be deterred by the monetary penalty:

> It can scarcely be doubted that, for a plaintiff who is injured or faces the threat of future injury due to illegal conduct ongoing at the time of suit, a sanction that effectively abates that conduct and prevents its recurrence provides a form of redress. Civil penalties can fit that description.

4. *FEDERAL ELECTION COMMISSION V. AKINS*

The Federal Election Campaign Act of 1971 imposed on "political committees," as therein defined, extensive record-keeping and disclosure obligations. The FEC read the statute not to apply to the American Israel Public Affairs Committee (AIPAC). Opponents of AIPAC, who sought disclosure of its donors and activities, sued the FEC when their complaint was dismissed.

The statute authorized "[a]ny person who believes a violation of this Act . . . has occurred" to file a complaint and "[a]ny party aggrieved by an order of the Commission dismissing a complaint filed by such party" to bring suit. 2 U.S.C. §§ 437g(a)(1) and 437g(8)(A).

In Federal Election Commission v. Akins, 524 U.S. 11 (1998), the Supreme Court, speaking through Justice Breyer, found these provisions sufficient to support standing. The "injury in fact" suffered by the plaintiffs was their "inability to obtain information-lists of AIPAC donors . . . and campaign-related contributions and expenditures." That this injury was shared by the public at large did not make it the kind of "generalized grievance" that rendered the dispute nonjusticiable. That language, said the Court, "invariably appears in cases where the harm at issue is not only widely shared, but is also of an abstract and indefinite nature." Here, the "informational injury" to the plaintiffs was "sufficiently concrete and specific such that the fact that it is widely shared does not deprive Congress of constitutional power to authorize its vindication in the federal courts."

Justice Scalia, joined by Justices O'Connor and Thomas, dissented. The dissenters focused on United States v. Richardson, 418 U.S. 166 (1974), where plaintiffs seeking disclosure of CIA expenditures were found to lack standing. Justice Scalia noted: "It was alleged in *Richardson* that the Government had denied a right conferred by the Constitution, whereas [plaintiffs] here assert a right conferred by a statute—but of course 'there is absolutely no basis for making the Article III inquiry turn on the source of the asserted right," quoting *Lujan*, 504 U.S. at 576. The dissenters then explained the broader issue they saw at stake:

> The Constitution's line of demarcation between the Executive power and the Judicial power presupposes a common understanding of the type of interest needed to sustain a "case or controversy" against the Executive in the courts. A system in which the citizenry at large could sue to compel Executive compliance with the law would be a system in which the courts, rather than the President, are given the primary responsibility to "take Care that the Laws be faithfully executed," Art. II, § 3. We do not have such a system because the common understanding of the interest necessary to sustain suit has included the requirement, affirmed in *Richardson*, that the complained-of injury be particularized and differentiated, rather than common to all the electorate. . . . "To permit Congress to convert the undifferentiated public interest in executive officers' compliance with the law into an 'individual right' vindicable in the courts is to permit Congress to transfer from the President to the courts the Chief Executive's most important constitutional duty."
> *Lujan*, 504 U.S. at 577.

5. *MASSACHUSETTS V. EPA*

Lujan was also disputed in Massachusetts v. Environmental Protection Agency, 549 U.S. 497 (2007), a suit brought by the Commonwealth of Massachusetts and others to force EPA to regulate the emission of carbon dioxide and other greenhouse gases that cause global warming. The agency had concluded that Congress had not empowered it to address global climate change and that even if it had such power, it would not act, given that the link between greenhouse gas emissions and global temperature "cannot be unequivocally established."

Standing to challenge that inaction was based on 42 U.S.C. § 7607(b)(1), which authorizes private suits to review agency decisions in the District of Columbia Circuit. Speaking for the Court, Justice Stevens found that authorization "of critical importance." He quoted Justice Kennedy's *Lujan* concurrence to the effect that "Congress has the power to define injuries and articulate chains of causation that will give rise to a case or controversy where none existed before." Massachusetts based its claim of injury in part on its ownership of coastal lands that might be submerged if water levels rose. Presumably, such potential injury would be shared by any coastal landowner, but the Court also emphasized that the Commonwealth's stake in protecting its "quasi-sovereign interests" entitled it to "special solicitude in our standing analysis." Thus, to some unspecified extent, the Court's conclusion may have rested on the fact that the plaintiff was a state. The fact that the risks of global climate change were "widely shared" did not vitiate Massachusetts's right to seek review. (On the merits, the majority concluded that the EPA's inaction was arbitrary and capricious and ordered further consideration.)

The Court's conclusion on standing was criticized in a lengthy dissent by Chief Justice Roberts, joined by Justices Scalia, Thomas, and Alito. They disputed whether Massachusetts's "quasi-sovereign interests" had anything to do with the requirements of Article III. The dissenters also claimed that the "very concept of global warming," which is "harmful to humanity at large," is inconsistent with the kind of particularized injury sufficient to support standing. As to the risk of inundation of state lands by rising sea levels, the Chief Justice dismissed the claim as "pure conjecture" supported by only a "single conclusory statement" in the plaintiffs' submissions.

The *Massachusetts* Court's reliance on some notion of "state standing" should not obscure the critical importance of Congressional authorization to the majority's reasoning. Of course, the same authorization was found unavailing in *Lujan*. *Massachusetts*, therefore, like *Laidlaw* and *Akins*, calls *Lujan* into question.[b]

6.   *SPOKEO, INC. V. ROBINS*

The Court said more about the relationship between statutory standing and the injury requirement in Spokeo, Inc. v. Robins, 587 U.S. ___, 136 S.Ct. 1540 (2016). That case involved a website, operated by Spokeo, Inc., that allows users to obtain information about a person after inputting the person's

---

[b]   For commentary on this decision, see Kimberly N. Brown, Justiciable Generalized Grievances, 68 Md. L. Rev. 221 (2008); Bradford Mank, Should States Have Greater Standing Rights Than Ordinary Citizens?: *Massachusetts v. EPA*'s New Standing Test for States, 49 Wm. & Mary L. Rev. 1701 (2008); Bradford Mank, Standing and Future Generations: Does *Massachusetts v. EPA* Open Standing for Generations to Come?, 34 Colum. J. Environ. L. 1 (2009); Calvin Massey, State Standing after *Massachusetts v. EPA*, 61 Fla. L. Rev. 249 (2009).

name, phone number, and e-mail address. A search for information about Robins generated incorrect information. In particular, the information incorrectly stated that he was in his 50s, was married, had a graduate degree, was employed in a professional or technical field, and was relatively affluent. Robins claimed that these errors harmed him in searching for employment by making him "appear overqualified for jobs he might have gained, expectant of a higher salary than employers would be willing to pay, and less mobile because of family responsibilities."

When Robins learned of the inaccuracies, he filed suit against Spokeo in a federal district court in California, on behalf of himself and others similarly situated. He sued under the Fair Credit Reporting Act of 1970 (FCRA), which imposes various procedural and other requirements on "consumer reporting agencies" and provides that "[a]ny person who willfully fails to comply with any requirement [of the Act] with respect to any [individual] is liable to that [individual]" for either actual or statutory damages, costs and attorney's fees, and potentially punitive damages. Robins claimed that Spokeo qualified as a consumer reporting agency and had failed to comply with requirements in the Act. The district court dismissed Robins' complaint for lack of standing, concluding that "Plaintiff has not suffered an injury in fact because Plaintiff has failed to allege that Defendant has caused him any actual or imminent harm." The Ninth Circuit reversed, reasoning that "[t]he violation of a statutory right is usually a sufficient injury in fact to confer standing"; that Robins "alleges that Spokeo violated his statutory rights, not just the statutory rights of other people"; and that "personal interests in the handling of the credit information are individualized rather than collective."

Concluding that the Ninth Circuit's analysis was "incomplete," the Supreme Court vacated and remanded for further proceedings. In an opinion by Justice Alito, the Court emphasized that "[p]articularization is necessary to establish an injury in fact, but it is not sufficient." The injury must also be "concrete," said the Court, which means that the injury "must be 'de facto': that is, it must actually exist." This does not mean, the Court explained, that the injury must be tangible: "Although tangible injuries are perhaps easier to recognize, we have confirmed in many of our previous cases that intangible injuries can nevertheless be concrete." The Court further observed that:

> In determining whether an intangible harm constitutes injury in fact, both history and the judgment of Congress play important roles. Because the doctrine of standing derives from the case-or-controversy requirement, and because that requirement in turn is grounded in historical practice, it is instructive to consider whether an alleged intangible harm has a close relationship to a harm that has traditionally been regarded as providing a basis for a lawsuit in English or American courts. . . . In addition, because Congress is well positioned to identify intangible harms that meet minimum Article III requirements, its judgment is also instructive and important.

Finally, the Court made clear that "Congress' role in identifying and elevating intangible harms does not mean that a plaintiff automatically satisfies the injury-in-fact requirement whenever a statute grants a person a statutory right and gives that person a right to sue. Article III standing requires a concrete injury even in the context of a statutory violation." As a result, said the Court, "Robins could not, for example, allege a bare procedural violation, divorced from any concrete harm, and satisfy the injury-in-fact requirement of Article III."

Applying these principles to the present case suggested "two things," said the Court:

> On the one hand, Congress plainly sought to curb the dissemination of false information by adopting procedures designed to decrease that risk. On the other hand, Robins cannot satisfy the demands of Article III by alleging a bare procedural violation. A violation of one of the FCRA's procedural requirements may result in no harm. For example, even if a consumer reporting agency fails to provide the required notice to a user of the agency's consumer information, that information regardless may be entirely accurate. In addition, not all inaccuracies cause harm or present any material risk of harm. An example that comes readily to mind is an incorrect zip code. It is difficult to imagine how the dissemination of an incorrect zip code, without more, could work any concrete harm.

Justice Thomas concurred, expressing the view that the standing analysis should depend on the nature of the right being asserted. Historically, he explained, common law courts required the allegation of actual injury only for violations of public rights (that is, "rights that involve duties owed 'to the whole community, considered as a community, in its social aggregate capacity'") not for private rights (that is, rights "belonging to individuals, considered as individuals"). Under that approach, said Thomas, "Robins has no standing to sue Spokeo, in his own name, for violations of the duties that Spokeo owes to the public collectively, absent some showing that he has suffered concrete and particular harm." But Thomas noted that one of the statutory provisions invoked by Robins requires that a consumer reporting agency "follow reasonable procedures to assure maximum possible accuracy of the information concerning the individual about whom the report relates." If this provision "created a private duty owed personally to Robins to protect his information, then the violation of the legal duty suffices for Article III injury in fact," said Thomas. On the other hand, if it "vests any and all consumers with the power to police the 'reasonable procedures' of Spokeo, without more, then Robins has no standing to sue for its violation absent an allegation that he has suffered individualized harm."

Joined by Justice Sotomayor, Justice Ginsburg dissented, arguing that Robins had sufficiently alleged a concrete injury. Ginsburg explained that Robins "seeks redress, not for harm to the citizenry, but for Spokeo's spread of misinformation specifically about him." "Far from an incorrect zip code," she noted, "Robins complains of misinformation about his education, family situation, and economic status, inaccurate representations that could affect his fortune in the job market." She therefore thought that there was "no utility" in returning the case to the Ninth Circuit.

What does this decision suggest about the extent to which Congress can confer standing on private parties to enforce statutory provisions? Under the majority's analysis, what must a plaintiff show beyond a "bare procedural violation"? How does the majority's approach compare with Justice Thomas's proposed approach?

7.   "PRUDENTIAL" LIMITATIONS ON STANDING

The Supreme Court has suggested at various times that, in addition to the requirements of Article III, there are also "prudential" limitations on standing. In Elk Grove Unified School Dist. v. Newdow, 542 U.S. 1, 12 (2004), the Court described these limitations:

> Although we have not exhaustively defined the prudential dimensions of the standing doctrine, we have explained that prudential standing encompasses "the general prohibition on a litigant's raising another person's legal rights, the rule barring adjudication of generalized grievances more appropriately addressed in the representative branches, and the requirement that a plaintiff's complaint fall within the zone of interests protected by the law invoked." Allen v. Wright, 468 U.S. 737, 751 (1984). . . . "Without such limitations—closely related to Art. III concerns but essentially matters of judicial self-governance—the courts would be called upon to decide abstract questions of wide public significance even though other governmental institutions may be more competent to address the questions and even though judicial intervention may be unnecessary to protect individual rights." Warth v. Seldin, 422 U.S. 490, 500 (1975).

In Lexmark Int'l, Inc. v. Static Control Components, Inc., 572 U.S. ___, 134 S.Ct. 1377 (2014), however, the Court held that the "zone of interests" limitation is not in fact a restriction on standing but is instead merely a matter of statutory interpretation. The issue there was whether Static Control—a company that refurbished and resold Lexmark printer cartridges—could sue Lexmark for false advertising under Section 43(a) of the Lanham Act. In a unanimous opinion by Justice Scalia, the Court began by noting that "Lexmark does not deny that Static Control's allegations of lost sales and damage to its business reputation give it standing under Article III to press its false advertising claim, and we are satisfied that they do." As for whether Static Control's claim nevertheless fell outside the "zone of interests" protected by Section 43(a), the Court explained that this was not a question of standing: "Whether a plaintiff comes within the 'zone of interests' is an issue that requires us to determine, using traditional tools of statutory interpretation, whether a legislatively conferred cause of action encompasses a particular plaintiff's claim." In a footnote, the Court seemed to call into question the remainder of the "prudential standing" concept, suggesting that the bar on bringing generalized grievances is in fact part of the limitations on Article III standing, and questioning whether the restriction on litigating the rights of third parties constitutes a limitation on standing as opposed to a question about whether the plaintiff has a cause of action. But the Court also observed that "[t]his case does not present any issue of third-party standing, and consideration of that doctrine's proper place in the standing firmament can await another day." (Issues of third-party standing are addressed below in Section 3A of this Chapter.) For a subsequent decision confirming that the "zone of interests" analysis is a matter of statutory interpretation, see Bank of America Corp. v. City of Miami, 581 U.S. ___, 137 S.Ct. 1296 (2017) (finding that the City of Miami was an "aggrieved person" authorized to sue under the Fair Housing Act).

8. BIBLIOGRAPHY

For extensive commentary on these decisions, see the Symposium on Citizen Suits and the Future of Standing in the 21st Century: From *Lujan* to *Laidlaw* and Beyond, published in a double-issue of the Duke Environmental Law & Policy Forum. Contributors included Gene R. Nichol, The Impossibility of *Lujan*'s Project, 11 Duke Env. L. & Pol. Forum 193 (2001); Richard J. Pierce, Jr., Issues Raised by *Friends of the Earth v. Laidlaw Environmental Services*: Access to the Court for Environmental Plaintiffs, id. at 207; William W. Buzbee, Standing and the Statutory Universe, id. at 247; John D. Echeverria, Critiquing *Laidlaw*: Congressional Power to Confer Standing and the Irrelevance of Mootness Doctrine to Civil Penalties, id. at 287; Maxwell L. Stearns, From *Lujan* to *Laidlaw*: A Preliminary Model of Environmental Standing, id. at 321; A. H. Barnett and Timothy D. Terrell, Economic Observations on Citizen-Suit Provisions of Environmental Legislation, 12 Duke Env. L. & Pol. Forum 1 (2001); Jonathan D. Adler, Stand or Deliver: Citizen Suits, Standing, and Environmental Protection, id at 39; Harold J. Krent, *Laidlaw*: Redressing the Law of Redressability, id. at 85; Robert V. Percival and Joanna B. Goger, Escaping the Common Law's Shadow: Standing in the Light of *Laidlaw*, id. at 119; Steven L. Winter, What If Justice Scalia Took History and the Rule of Law Seriously?, id. at 155; Michael S. Greve, *Friends of the Earth*, Foes of Federalism, id. at 167; Karl S. Coplan, Direct Environmental Standing for Chartered Conservation Corporations, id. at 183. See also Radha A. Pathak, Statutory Standing and the Tyranny of Labels, 62 Okla. L. Rev. 89 (2009); Evan Tsen Lee and Josephine Mason Ellis, The Standing Doctrine's Dirty Little Secret, 107 Nw. U. L. Rev. 169 (2012).

SUBSECTION C. TAXPAYER STANDING

INTRODUCTORY NOTE ON TAXPAYER STANDING

Recognition of ideological injury or "citizen standing" in cases such as *Allen v. Wright* would obviate the need for any more elaborate inquiry. As it is, the Court's refusal to allow litigation based on mere objection necessitates some more particularized allegation of injury by persons seeking to challenge government action. An inviting alternative is "taxpayer standing"—the assertion that a taxpayer is injured in the allocable share of tax revenues expended in illegal activity.

Functionally, citizen and taxpayer standing are similar. Under both theories, a vast number of persons would be empowered to contest government action on the basis of an injury shared generally and not otherwise relevant to any particular plaintiff. One might have thought, therefore, that taxpayer standing would be categorically disallowed on the same ground as citizen standing. Today that conclusion is very nearly true, but the doctrinal history is surprisingly complicated.

In Flast v. Cohen, 392 U.S. 83 (1968), the Supreme Court recognized an exception to the bar against taxpayer standing and allowed suit challenging the disbursement of federal funds to religious schools as a violation of the Establishment Clause. As a policy matter, *Flast* was supported by the fact that, absent some special rule, there might be no plaintiff with standing to challenge Establishment Clause violations, but the decision was not explained on that ground. Instead, the Court spoke of a confusing two-part test, the meaning of which is discussed below.

Later litigants have invoked *Flast* to support other claims of taxpayer standing. In most—but not all—cases, standing was denied. The twists and turns of taxpayer standing—and its continuing ability to divide the Court—are reflected in the next main case.

Hein v. Freedom From Religion Foundation, Inc.

Supreme Court of the United States, 2007.
551 U.S. 587.

■ JUSTICE ALITO announced the judgment of the Court and delivered an opinion in which THE CHIEF JUSTICE and JUSTICE KENNEDY joined.

This is a lawsuit in which it was claimed that conferences held as part of the President's Faith-Based and Community Initiatives program violated the Establishment Clause of the First Amendment because, among other things, President Bush and former Secretary of Education Paige gave speeches that used "religious imagery" and praised the efficacy of faith-based programs in delivering social services. The plaintiffs contend that they meet the standing requirements of Article III of the Constitution because they pay federal taxes.

It has long been established, however, that the payment of taxes is generally not enough to establish standing to challenge an action taken by the Federal Government. In light of the size of the federal budget, it is a complete fiction to argue that an unconstitutional federal expenditure causes an individual federal taxpayer any measurable economic harm. And if every federal taxpayer could sue to challenge any Government expenditure, the federal courts would cease to function as courts of law and would be cast in the role of general complaint bureaus.

In Flast v. Cohen, 392 U.S. 83 (1968), we recognized a narrow exception to the general rule against federal taxpayer standing. Under *Flast,* a plaintiff asserting an Establishment Clause claim has standing to challenge a law authorizing the use of federal funds in a way that allegedly violates the Establishment Clause. In the present case, Congress did not specifically authorize the use of federal funds to pay for the conferences or speeches that the plaintiffs challenged. Instead, the conferences and speeches were paid for out of general Executive Branch appropriations. The Court of Appeals, however, held that the plaintiffs have standing as taxpayers because the conferences were paid for with money appropriated by Congress.

The question that is presented here is whether this broad reading of *Flast* is correct. We hold that it is not. . . .

I

A

In 2001, the President issued an executive order creating the White House Office of Faith-Based and Community Initiatives within the Executive Office of the President. Exec. Order No. 13199, 3 CFR 752 (2001 Comp.). The purpose of this new office was to ensure that "private and charitable community groups, including religious ones . . . have the fullest opportunity permitted by law to compete on a level playing field, so long as they achieve valid public purposes" and adhere to "the bedrock principles of pluralism, nondiscrimination, evenhandedness, and neutrality." Id. The office was specifically charged with the task of eliminating unnecessary bureaucratic, legislative, and regulatory barriers that could impede such organizations' effectiveness and ability to compete equally for federal assistance.

By separate executive orders, the President also created Executive Department Centers for Faith-Based and Community Initiatives within several federal agencies and departments. These centers were given the job of ensuring that faith-based community groups would be eligible to compete for federal financial support without impairing their independence or autonomy, as long as they did "not use direct Federal financial assistance to support any inherently religious activities, such as worship, religious instruction, or proselytization." Exec. Order No. 13279, 3 CFR § 2(f), p. 260 (2002 Comp.). . . . Petitioners, who have been sued in their official capacities, are the directors of the White House Office and various Executive Department Centers.

No congressional legislation specifically authorized the creation of the White House Office or the Executive Department Centers. Rather, they were "created entirely within the executive branch . . . by Presidential executive order." Freedom From Religion Foundation, Inc. v. Chao, 433 F.3d 989, 997 (7th Cir. 2006). Nor has Congress enacted any law specifically appropriating money for these entities' activities. Instead, their activities are funded through general Executive Branch appropriations. For example, the Department of Education's Center is funded from money appropriated for the Office of the Secretary of Education, while the Department of Housing and Urban Development's Center is funded through that Department's salaries and expenses account.

B

The respondents are Freedom From Religion Foundation, Inc., a nonstock corporation "opposed to government endorsement of religion," and three of its members. Respondents brought suit in the United States District Court for the Western District of Wisconsin, alleging that petitioners violated the Establishment Clause by organizing conferences at which faith-based organizations allegedly "are singled out as being particularly worthy of federal funding . . . , and the belief in God is extolled as distinguishing the claimed effectiveness of faith-based social services." Respondents further alleged that the content of these conferences sent a message to religious believers "that they are insiders and favored members of the political community" and that the conferences sent the message to nonbelievers "that they are outsiders" and "not full members of the political community." In short, respondents alleged that the conferences were designed to promote, and had the effect of promoting, religious community groups over secular ones.

The only asserted basis for standing was that the individual respondents are federal taxpayers who are "opposed to the use of Congressional taxpayer appropriations to advance and promote religion." In their capacity as federal taxpayers, respondents sought to challenge Executive Branch expenditures for these conferences, which, they contended, violated the Establishment Clause. . . .

II

A

Article III of the Constitution limits the judicial power of the United States to the resolution of "Cases" and "Controversies" . . . "[O]ne of the controlling elements in the definition of a case or controversy under Article III" is standing. ASARCO Inc. v. Kadish, 490 U.S. 605, 613 (1989) (opinion of Kennedy, J.). The requisite elements of Article III standing are well established: "A plaintiff must allege personal injury fairly traceable to the defendant's allegedly unlawful conduct and likely to be redressed by the requested relief." Allen v. Wright, 468 U.S. 737, 751 (1984). . . .

B

As a general matter, the interest of a federal taxpayer in seeing that Treasury funds are spent in accordance with the Constitution does not give rise to the kind of redressable "personal injury" required for Article III standing. Of course, a taxpayer has standing to challenge the *collection* of a specific tax assessment as unconstitutional; being forced to pay such a tax causes a real and immediate economic injury to the individual taxpayer. But that is not the interest on which respondents assert standing here. Rather, their claim is that, having paid lawfully collected taxes into the Federal Treasury at some point, they have a continuing, legally cognizable interest in ensuring that those funds are not *used* by the Government in a way that violates the Constitution.

We have consistently held that this type of interest is too generalized and attenuated to support Article III standing. In Frothingham v. Mellon, 262 U.S. 447 (1923), a federal taxpayer sought to challenge federal appropriations for mothers' and children's health, arguing that federal involvement in this area intruded on the rights reserved to the States under the Tenth Amendment and would "increase the burden of future taxation and thereby take [the plaintiff's] property without due process of law." We concluded that the plaintiff lacked the kind of particularized injury required for Article III standing. . . .

In Doremus v. Board of Ed. of Hawthorne, 342 U.S. 429, 433 (1952), we reaffirmed this principle, explaining that "the interests of a taxpayer in the moneys of the federal treasury are too indeterminable, remote, uncertain and indirect to furnish a basis for an appeal to the preventive powers of the Court over their manner of expenditure." We therefore rejected a state taxpayer's claim of standing to challenge a state law authorizing public school teachers to read from the Bible because "the grievance which [the plaintiff] sought to litigate . . . is not a direct dollars-and-cents injury but is a religious difference." In so doing, we gave effect to the basic constitutional principle that "a plaintiff raising only a generally available grievance about government—claiming only harm to his and every citizen's interest in proper application of the Constitution and laws, and seeking relief that no more directly and tangibly benefits him than it does the public at large—does not state an Article III case or controversy." Lujan v. Defenders of Wildlife, 504 U.S. 555, 573–74 (1992).

C

In *Flast,* the Court carved out a narrow exception to the general constitutional prohibition against taxpayer standing. The taxpayer-plaintiff in that case challenged the distribution of federal funds to religious schools under the Elementary and Secondary Education Act of 1965, alleging that such aid violated the Establishment Clause. The Court set out a two-part test for determining whether a federal taxpayer has standing to challenge an allegedly unconstitutional expenditure:

> First, the taxpayer must establish a logical link between that status and the type of legislative enactment attacked. Thus, a taxpayer will be a proper party to allege the unconstitutionality only of exercises of congressional power under the taxing and spending clause of Art. I, § 8, of the Constitution. It will not be sufficient to allege an incidental expenditure of tax funds in the administration of an essentially regulatory statute. . . . Secondly, the taxpayer must establish a nexus between that status and the precise nature of the constitutional infringement alleged. Under this requirement, the taxpayer must show that the challenged enactment exceeds specific constitutional limitations imposed upon the exercise of the congressional taxing and spending power and not simply that the enactment is generally beyond the powers delegated to Congress by Art. I, § 8.

The Court held that the taxpayer-plaintiff in *Flast* had satisfied both prongs of this test: The plaintiff's "constitutional challenge [was] made to an exercise by Congress of its power under Art. I, § 8, to spend for the general welfare," and she alleged a violation of the Establishment Clause, which "operates as a specific constitutional limitation upon the exercise by Congress of the taxing and spending power conferred by Art. I, § 8."

III

A

Respondents argue that this case falls within the *Flast* exception, which they read to cover any "expenditure of government funds in violation of the Establishment Clause." But this broad reading fails to observe "the rigor with which the *Flast* exception to the *Frothingham* principle ought to be applied." Valley Forge Christian College v. Americans United for Separation of Church and State, 454 U.S. 464, 481 (1982). . . .

B

The link between congressional action and constitutional violation that supported taxpayer standing in *Flast* is missing here. Respondents do not challenge any specific congressional action or appropriation; nor do they ask the Court to invalidate any congressional enactment or legislatively created program as unconstitutional. That is because the expenditures at issue here were not made pursuant to any Act of Congress. Rather, Congress provided general appropriations to the Executive Branch to fund its day-to-day activities. These appropriations did not expressly authorize, direct, or even mention the expenditures of which respondents complain. Those expenditures resulted from executive discretion, not congressional action.

We have never found taxpayer standing under such circumstances. In *Valley Forge,* we held that a taxpayer lacked standing to challenge "a decision by [the federal Department of Health, Education and Welfare] to transfer a parcel of federal property" to a religious college because this transfer was "not a congressional action." . . . [W]e found that the plaintiffs lacked standing because *Flast* "limited taxpayer standing to challenges directed 'only [at] exercises of congressional power'" under the Taxing and Spending Clause. . . .

Bowen v. Kendrick, 487 U.S. 589 (1988), on which respondents rely heavily, is not to the contrary. In that case, we held that the taxpayer-plaintiffs had standing to mount an as-applied challenge to the Adolescent Family Life Act (AFLA), which authorized federal grants to private community service groups including religious organizations. The Court found "a sufficient nexus between the taxpayer's standing as a taxpayer and the congressional exercise of taxing and spending power," notwithstanding the fact that the "the funding authorized by Congress ha[d] flowed through and been administered" by an Executive Branch official.

But the key to that conclusion was the Court's recognition that AFLA was "at heart a program of disbursement of funds pursuant to Congress's taxing and spending powers," and that the plaintiffs' claims "call[ed] into question how the funds authorized by Congress [were] being disbursed *pursuant to the AFLA's statutory mandate*." (Emphasis added.) AFLA not only expressly authorized and appropriated specific funds for grant-making, it also expressly contemplated that some of those moneys might go to projects involving religious groups.[6] Unlike this case, *Kendrick* involved a "program of disbursement of funds pursuant to Congress's taxing and spending powers" that "Congress had created," "authorized," and "mandate[d]."

Respondents attempt to paint their lawsuit as a *Kendrick*-style as-applied challenge, but this effort is unavailing for the simple reason that they can cite no statute whose application they challenge. The best they can do is to point to unspecified, lump-sum "Congressional budget appropriations" for the general use of the Executive Branch. . . . It cannot be that every legal challenge to a discretionary Executive Branch action implicates the constitutionality of the underlying congressional appropriation. When a criminal defendant charges that a federal agent carried out an unreasonable search or seizure, we do not view that claim as an as-applied challenge to the constitutionality of the statute appropriating funds for the Federal Bureau of Investigation. Respondents have not established why the discretionary Executive Branch expenditures here, which are similarly funded by no-strings, lump-sum appropriations, should be viewed any differently.

In short, this case falls outside the "the narrow exception" that *Flast* "created to the general rule against taxpayer standing established in *Frothingham*." *Kendrick*, 487 U.S. at 618. Because the expenditures that respondents challenge were not expressly authorized or mandated by any specific congressional enactment, respondents' lawsuit is not directed at an exercise of congressional power, see *Valley Forge*, 454 U.S. at 479, and thus lacks the requisite "logical nexus" between taxpayer status "and the type of legislative enactment attacked." *Flast*, 392 U.S. at 102.

IV

A

1

Respondents argue that it is "arbitrary" to distinguish between money spent pursuant to congressional mandate and expenditures made in the course of executive discretion, because "the injury to taxpayers in

---

[6]   For example, the statute noted that the problems of adolescent premarital sex and pregnancy "are best approached through a variety of integrated and essential services provided to adolescents and their families" by "religious and charitable organizations," among other groups. 42 U.S.C. § 300z(a)(8)(B) (1982 ed.). . . . And it directed that demonstration projects funded by the government "shall . . . make use of support systems" such as religious organizations, § 300z–2(a), and required grant applicants to describe how they would "involve religious and charitable organizations" in their projects, § 300z–5(a)(21)(B).

both situations is the very injury targeted by the Establishment Clause and *Flast*—the expenditure for the support of religion of funds exacted from taxpayers."...

But *Flast* focused on congressional action, and we must decline this invitation to extend its holding to encompass discretionary Executive Branch expenditures. . . . It is significant that, in the four decades since its creation, the *Flast* exception has largely been confined to its facts. We have declined to lower the taxpayer standing bar in suits alleging violations of any constitutional provision apart from the Establishment Clause. See Tilton v. Richardson, 403 U.S. 672 (1971) (no taxpayer standing to sue under Free Exercise Clause of First Amendment); United States v. Richardson, 418 U.S. 166, 175 (1974) (no taxpayer standing to sue under Statement and Account Clause of Art. I); Schlesinger v. Reservists Comm. to Stop the War, 418 U.S. 208, 228 (1974) (no taxpayer standing to sue under Incompatibility Clause of Art. I); DaimlerChrysler Corp. v. Cuno, 547 U.S. 332, 349 (2006) (no taxpayer standing to sue under Commerce Clause). We have similarly refused to extend *Flast* to permit taxpayer standing for Establishment Clause challenges that do not implicate Congress's taxing and spending power. In effect, we have adopted the position set forth by Justice Powell in his concurrence in *United States v. Richardson* and have "limit[ed] the expansion of federal taxpayer and citizen standing in the absence of specific statutory authorization to an outer boundary drawn by the *results* in *Flast*. . . ." *Richardson*, 418 U.S. at 196.

2

. . . Because almost all Executive Branch activity is ultimately funded by some congressional appropriation, extending the *Flast* exception to purely executive expenditures would effectively subject every federal action—be it a conference, proclamation or speech—to Establishment Clause challenge by any taxpayer in federal court. . . . The rule respondents propose would enlist the federal courts to superintend, at the behest of any federal taxpayer, the speeches, statements, and myriad daily activities of the President, his staff, and other Executive Branch officials. . . .

B

Respondents set out a parade of horribles that they claim could occur if *Flast* is not extended to discretionary Executive Branch expenditures. For example, they say, a federal agency could use its discretionary funds to build a house of worship or to hire clergy of one denomination and send them out to spread their faith. Or an agency could use its funds to make bulk purchases of Stars of David, crucifixes, or depictions of the star and crescent for use in its offices or for distribution to the employees or the general public. Of course, none of these things has happened, even though *Flast* has not previously been expanded in the way that respondents urge. In the unlikely event that any of these executive actions did take place, Congress could quickly step in. And respondents make no effort to show that these improbable abuses could not be challenged in federal court by plaintiffs who would possess standing based on grounds other than taxpayer standing.

C

Over the years, *Flast* has been defended by some and criticized by others. But the present case does not require us to reconsider that precedent. The Court of Appeals did not apply *Flast;* it extended *Flast*. It is a necessary concomitant of the doctrine of stare decisis that a precedent is not always expanded to the limit of its logic. That was the approach that then-Justice Rehnquist took in his opinion for the Court in *Valley Forge,* and it is the approach we take here. We do not extend *Flast,* but we also do not overrule it. We leave *Flast* as we found it.

Justice Scalia says that we must either overrule *Flast* or extend it to the limits of its logic. His position is not "[in]sane," inconsistent with the "rule of law," or "utterly meaningless" [quoting Scalia's opinion]. But it is wrong. Justice Scalia does not seriously dispute either (1) that *Flast* itself spoke in terms of "legislative enactment[s]" and "exercises of congressional power," or (2) that in the four decades since *Flast* was decided, we have never extended its narrow exception to a purely discretionary Executive Branch expenditure. We need go no further to decide this case. Relying on the provision of the Constitution that limits our role to resolving the "Cases" and "Controversies" before us, we decide only the case at hand.

* * *

For these reasons, the judgment of the Court of Appeals for the Seventh Circuit is reversed.

■ JUSTICE KENNEDY, concurring. . . .

In my view the result reached in *Flast* is correct and should not be called into question. For the reasons set forth by Justice Alito, however, *Flast* should not be extended to permit taxpayer standing in the instant matter. . . .

Flast established a "narrow exception" to the rule against taxpayer standing. Bowen v. Kendrick, 487 U.S. 589, 618 (1988). To find standing in the circumstances of this case would make the narrow exception boundless. . . . The Court should not authorize the constant intrusion upon the executive realm that would result from granting taxpayer standing in the instant case. . . .

■ JUSTICE SCALIA, with whom JUSTICE THOMAS joins, concurring in the judgment.

Today's opinion is, in one significant respect, entirely consistent with our previous cases addressing taxpayer standing to raise Establishment Clause challenges to government expenditures. Unfortunately, the consistency lies in the creation of utterly meaningless distinctions which

separate the case at hand from the precedents that have come out differently, but which cannot possibly be (in any sane world) the reason it
comes out differently. If this Court is to decide cases by rule of law rather
than show of hands, we must surrender to logic and choose sides: Either
Flast v. Cohen, 392 U.S. 83 (1968), should be applied to (at a minimum)
all challenges to the governmental expenditure of general tax revenues
in a manner alleged to violate a constitutional provision specifically limiting the taxing and spending power, or *Flast* should be repudiated. For
me, the choice is easy. *Flast* is wholly irreconcilable with the Article III
restrictions on federal-court jurisdiction that this Court has repeatedly
confirmed are embodied in the doctrine of standing.

I

A

There is a simple reason why our taxpayer-standing cases involving
Establishment Clause challenges to government expenditures are notoriously inconsistent: We have inconsistently described the first element
of the "irreducible constitutional minimum of standing," which minimum
consists of (1) a "concrete and particularized" " 'injury in fact' " that is (2)
fairly traceable to the defendant's alleged unlawful conduct and (3) likely
to be redressed by a favorable decision. See Lujan v. Defenders of Wildlife, 504 U.S. 555, 560–61 (1992). We have alternately relied on two
entirely distinct conceptions of injury in fact, which for convenience I will
call "Wallet Injury" and "Psychic Injury."

Wallet Injury is the type of concrete and particularized injury one
would expect to be asserted in a *taxpayer* suit, namely, a claim that the
plaintiff's tax liability is higher than it would be, but for the allegedly
unlawful government action. The stumbling block for suits challenging
government expenditures based on this conventional type of injury is
quite predictable. The plaintiff cannot satisfy the traceability and redressability prongs of standing. It is uncertain what the plaintiff's tax
bill would have been had the allegedly forbidden expenditure not been
made, and it is even more speculative whether the government will, in
response to an adverse court decision, lower taxes rather than spend the
funds in some other manner.

Psychic Injury, on the other hand, has nothing to do with the plaintiff's tax liability. Instead, the injury consists of the taxpayer's *mental
displeasure* that money extracted from him is being spent in an unlawful
manner. This shift in focus eliminates traceability and redressability
problems. Psychic Injury is directly traceable to the improper *use* of taxpayer funds, and it is redressed when the improper use is enjoined,
regardless of whether that injunction affects the taxpayer's purse. *Flast*
and the cases following its teaching have invoked a peculiarly restricted
version of Psychic Injury, permitting taxpayer displeasure over unconstitutional spending to support standing *only if* the constitutional provision
allegedly violated is a specific limitation on the taxing and spending
power. Restricted or not, this conceptualizing of injury in fact in purely

mental terms conflicts squarely with the familiar proposition that a plaintiff lacks a concrete and particularized injury when his only complaint is the generalized grievance that the law is being violated. . . .

As the following review of our cases demonstrates, we initially denied taxpayer standing based on Wallet Injury, but then found standing in some later cases based on the limited version of Psychic Injury described above. The basic logical flaw in our cases is thus twofold: We have never explained why Psychic Injury was insufficient in the cases in which standing was denied, and we have never explained why Psychic Injury, however limited, is cognizable under Article III.

B

1

Two pre-*Flast* cases are of critical importance. In Frothingham v. Mellon, 262 U.S. 447 (1923), the taxpayer challenged the constitutionality of the Maternity Act of 1921, alleging in part that the federal funding provided by the Act was not authorized by any provision of the Constitution. The Court held that the taxpayer lacked standing. After emphasizing that "the effect upon future taxation . . . of any payment out of [Treasury] funds" was "remote, fluctuating and uncertain," the Court concluded that "[t]he party who invokes the power [of judicial review] must be able to show not only that the statute is invalid but that he has sustained or is immediately in danger of sustaining some direct injury as the result of its enforcement, and not merely that he suffers in some indefinite way in common with people generally." The Court was thus describing the traceability and redressability problems with Wallet Injury, and rejecting Psychic Injury as a generalized grievance rather than concrete and particularized harm.

The second significant pre-*Flast* case is Doremus v. Board of Ed. of Hawthorne, 342 U.S. 429 (1952). There the taxpayers challenged under the Establishment Clause a state law requiring public-school teachers to read the Bible at the beginning of each school day. Relying extensively on *Frothingham,* the Court denied standing. After first emphasizing that there was no allegation that the Bible reading increased the plaintiffs' taxes or the cost of running the schools, and then reaffirming that taxpayers must allege more than an indefinite injury suffered in common with people generally, the Court concluded that the "grievance which [the plaintiffs] sought to litigate here is not a direct dollars-and-cents injury but is a religious difference." . . . *Doremus* rejected Psychic Injury in unmistakable terms. The opinion's deprecation of a mere "religious difference," in contrast to a real "dollars-and-cents injury," can only be understood as a flat denial of standing supported only by taxpayer disapproval of the unconstitutional use of tax funds. If the Court had thought that Psychic Injury was a permissible basis for standing, it should have sufficed (as the dissenting Justices in *Doremus* suggested) that public employees were being paid in part to violate the Establishment Clause.

2

Sixteen years after *Doremus,* the Court took a pivotal turn. In *Flast v. Cohen*, taxpayers challenged the Elementary and Secondary Education Act of 1965, alleging that funds expended pursuant to the Act were being used to support parochial schools. They argued that either the Act itself proscribed such expenditures or that the Act violated the Establishment Clause. The Court held that the taxpayers had standing. Purportedly in order to determine whether taxpayers have the "personal stake and interest" necessary to satisfy Article III, a two-pronged nexus test was invented.

The first prong required the taxpayer to "establish a logical link between [taxpayer] status and the type of legislative enactment." The Court described what that meant as follows:

> [A] taxpayer will be a proper party to allege the unconstitutionality only of exercises of congressional power under the taxing and spending clause of Art. I, § 8, of the Constitution. It will not be sufficient to allege an incidental expenditure of tax funds in the administration of an essentially regulatory statute. This requirement is consistent with the limitation imposed upon state-taxpayer standing in federal courts in *Doremus*. . . .

The second prong required the taxpayer to "establish a nexus between [taxpayer] status and the precise nature of the constitutional infringement alleged." The Court elaborated that this required "the taxpayer [to] show that the challenged enactment exceeds specific constitutional limitations imposed upon the exercise of the congressional taxing and spending power and not simply that the enactment is generally beyond the powers delegated to Congress by Art. I, § 8." The Court held that the Establishment Clause was the type of specific limitation on the taxing and spending power that it had in mind because "one of the specific evils feared by" the Framers of that Clause was that the taxing and spending power would be used to favor one religion over another or to support religion generally.

Because both prongs of its newly minted two-part test were satisfied, *Flast* held that the taxpayers had standing. Wallet Injury could not possibly have been the basis for this conclusion, since the taxpayers in *Flast* were no more able to prove that success on the merits would reduce their tax burden than was the taxpayer in *Frothingham*. Thus, *Flast* relied on Psychic Injury to support standing, describing the "injury" as the taxpayer's allegation that "his tax money is being extracted and spent in violation of specific constitutional protections against such abuses of legislative power."

But that created a problem: If the taxpayers in *Flast* had standing based on Psychic Injury, and without regard to the effect of the litigation on their ultimate tax liability, why did not the taxpayers in *Doremus* and *Frothingham* have standing on a similar basis? Enter the magical two-pronged nexus test. It has often been pointed out, and never refuted, that the criteria in *Flast*'s two-part test are *entirely unrelated* to the purported goal of ensuring that the plaintiff has a sufficient "stake in the outcome of the controversy." See *Flast*, 392 U.S. at 121–24 (Harlan, J., dissenting); United States v. Richardson, 418 U.S. 166, 183 (1974) (Powell, J., concurring). In truth, the test was designed for a quite different goal. Each prong was meant to disqualify from standing one of the two prior cases that would otherwise contradict the holding of *Flast*. The first prong distinguished *Doremus* as involving a challenge to an "incidental expenditure of tax funds in the administration of an essentially regulatory statute," rather than a challenge to a taxing and spending statute. Did the Court proffer any reason why a taxpayer's Psychic Injury is less concrete and particularized, traceable, or redressable when the challenged expenditures are incidental to an essentially regulatory statute (whatever that means)? Not at all. *Doremus* had to be evaded, and so it was. In reality, of course, there is simply no material difference between *Flast* and *Doremus* as far as Psychic Injury is concerned: If taxpayers upset with the government's giving money to parochial schools had standing to sue, so should the taxpayers who disapproved of the government's paying public-school teachers to read the Bible.

Flast's dispatching of *Frothingham* via the second prong of the nexus test was only marginally less disingenuous. Not only does the relationship of the allegedly violated provision to the taxing and spending power have no bearing upon the concreteness or particularity of the Psychic Injury, but the existence of that relationship does not even genuinely distinguish *Flast* from *Frothingham*. It is impossible to maintain that the Establishment Clause is a more direct limitation on the taxing and spending power than the constitutional limitation invoked in *Frothingham, which is contained within the very provision creating the power to tax and spend.* Article I, § 8, cl. 1, provides: "The Congress shall have Power To lay and collect Taxes . . . , to pay the Debts and provide for the common Defence *and general Welfare* of the United States." (Emphasis added.) Though unmentioned in *Flast,* it was precisely this limitation upon the permissible purposes of taxing and spending upon which Mrs. Frothingham relied.

3

Coherence and candor have fared no better in our later taxpayer-standing cases. The three of them containing lengthy discussion of the Establishment Clause warrant analysis.

Flast was dismissively and unpersuasively distinguished just 13 years later in Valley Forge Christian College v. Americans United for Separation of Church and State, Inc., 454 U.S. 464 (1982). The taxpayers there challenged the decision of the Department of Health, Education, and Welfare to give a 77-acre tract of Government property, worth over half a million dollars, to a religious organization. The Court, adhering to the strict letter of *Flast*'s two-pronged nexus test, held that the taxpayers lacked standing. *Flast*'s first prong was not satisfied: Rather than challenging a congressional taxing and spending statute, the plaintiffs were attacking an agency decision to transfer federal property pursuant to Congress's power under the Property Clause, Art. IV, § 3, cl. 2.

In distinguishing between the Spending Clause and the Property Clause, *Valley Forge* achieved the seemingly impossible: It surpassed the high bar for irrationality set by *Flast*'s distinguishing of *Doremus* and *Frothingham.* Like the dissenters in *Valley Forge,* I cannot fathom why Article III standing should turn on whether the government enables a religious organization to obtain real estate by giving it a check drawn from general tax revenues or instead by buying the property itself and then transferring title. . . .

A mere six years later, *Flast* was resuscitated in Bowen v. Kendrick, 487 U.S. 589 (1988). The taxpayers there brought facial and as-applied Establishment Clause challenges to the Adolescent Family Life Act (AFLA), which was a congressional scheme that provided grants to public or nonprofit private organizations to combat premarital adolescent pregnancy and sex. The as-applied challenge focused on whether particular grantees selected by the Secretary of Health and Human Services were constitutionally permissible recipients. The Solicitor General argued that, under *Valley Forge*'s application of *Flast*'s first prong, the taxpayers lacked standing for their as-applied claim because that claim was really a challenge to executive decisionmaking, not to Congress's exercise of its taxing and spending power. The Court rejected this contention, holding that the taxpayers' as-applied claim was still a challenge to Congress's taxing and spending power even though disbursement of the funds authorized by Congress had been administered by the Secretary.

Kendrick, like *Flast* before it, was obviously based on Psychic Injury: The taxpayers could not possibly make, and did not attempt to make, the showing required for Wallet Injury. But by relying on Psychic Injury, *Kendrick* perfectly revealed the incompatibility of that concept with the outcome in *Doremus.* Just as *Kendrick* did not care whether the appropriated funds would have been spent anyway—given to a different, permissible recipient—so also *Doremus* should not have cared that the teachers would likely receive the same salary once their classroom activities were limited to secular conduct. *Flast* and *Kendrick*'s acceptance of Psychic Injury is fundamentally at odds with *Frothingham, Doremus,* and *Valley Forge.* . . .

[T]here are only two logical routes available to this Court. We must initially decide whether Psychic Injury is consistent with Article III. If it is, we should apply *Flast* to *all* challenges to government expenditures in violation of constitutional provisions that specifically limit the taxing and spending power; if it is not, we should overturn *Flast.*

II

A

The plurality today avails itself of neither principled option. Instead, . . . it limits *Flast* to challenges to expenditures that are "expressly authorized or mandated by . . . specific congressional enactment." It offers no intellectual justification for this limitation, except that "[i]t is a necessary concomitant of the doctrine of stare decisis that a precedent is not always expanded to the limit of its logic." That is true enough, but since courts purport to be engaged in *reasoned* decisionmaking, it is *only* true when (1) the precedent's logic is seen to require narrowing or readjustment in light of relevant distinctions that the new fact situation brings to the fore; or (2) its logic is fundamentally flawed, and so deserves to be limited to the facts that begot it. Today's plurality claims neither of these justifications. As to the first, the plurality offers no explanation of why the factual differences between this case and *Flast* are *material*. It virtually admits that express congressional allocation vel non has nothing to do with whether the plaintiffs have alleged an injury in fact that is fairly traceable and likely to be redressed. As the dissent correctly contends and I shall not belabor, *Flast* is *indistinguishable* from this case for purposes of Article III. Whether the challenged government expenditure is expressly allocated by a specific congressional enactment *has absolutely no relevance* to the Article III criteria of injury in fact, traceability, and redressability.

Yet the plurality is also unwilling to acknowledge that the logic of *Flast* (its Psychic Injury rationale) is simply wrong, and *for that reason* should not be extended to other cases. Despite the lack of acknowledgment, however, that is the only plausible explanation for the plurality's indifference to whether the "distinguishing" fact is legally material, and for its determination to limit *Flast* to its "*resul[t]*."[3] . . .

B

While I have been critical of the Members of the plurality, I by no means wish to give the impression that respondents' legal position is any more coherent. Respondents argue that *Flast* did not turn on whether Congress has expressly allocated the funds to the allegedly unconstitutional use, and their case plainly rests on Psychic Injury. They repeatedly emphasize that the injury in *Flast* was merely the governmental extraction and spending of tax money in aid of religion. Respondents refuse to admit that their argument logically implies, for the reasons already discussed, that *every* expenditure of tax revenues that is alleged to violate the Establishment Clause is subject to suit under *Flast*.

---

[3] This explanation does not suffice with regard to Justice Kennedy, who, unlike the other Members of the plurality, openly and avowedly contends both that *Flast* was correctly decided and that respondents should nevertheless lose this case. He thus has the distinction of being the only Justice who affirms both propositions. . . .

Of course, such a concession would run headlong into the denial of standing in *Doremus*. Respondents' only answer to *Doremus* is the cryptic assertion that the injury there was not fairly traceable to the unconstitutional conduct. This makes no sense. On *Flast*'s theory of Psychic Injury, the injury in *Doremus* was perfectly traceable and not in any way attenuated. It consisted of the psychic frustration that tax funds were being used in violation of the Establishment Clause, which was directly caused by the paying of teachers to read the Bible, and which would have been remedied by prohibition of that expenditure. . . .

The logical consequence of respondents' position finds no support in this Court's precedents or our Nation's history. Any taxpayer would be able to sue whenever tax funds were used in alleged violation of the Establishment Clause. So, for example, any taxpayer could challenge the fact that the Marshal of our Court is paid, in part, to call the courtroom to order by proclaiming "God Save the United States and this Honorable Court." As much as respondents wish to deny that this is what *Flast* logically entails, it blinks reality to conclude otherwise. If respondents are to prevail, they must endorse a future in which ideologically motivated taxpayers could "roam the country in search of governmental wrongdoing and . . . reveal their discoveries in federal court," transforming those courts into "ombudsmen of the general welfare" with respect to Establishment Clause issues. *Valley Forge,* 454 U.S. at 487.

C

Ultimately, the arguments by the parties in this case and the opinions of my colleagues serve only to confirm that *Flast*'s adoption of Psychic Injury has to be addressed head-on. Minimalism is an admirable judicial trait, but not when it comes at the cost of meaningless and disingenuous distinctions that hold the sure promise of engendering further meaningless and disingenuous distinctions in the future. The rule of law is ill served by forcing lawyers and judges to make arguments that deaden the soul of the law, which is logic and reason. Either *Flast* was correct, and must be accorded the wide application that it logically dictates, or it was not, and must be abandoned in its entirety. I turn, finally, to that question.

III

Is a taxpayer's purely psychological displeasure that his funds are being spent in an allegedly unlawful manner ever sufficiently concrete and particularized to support Article III standing? The answer is plainly no.

As I noted at the outset, *Lujan* explained that the "consisten[t]" view of this Court has been that "a plaintiff raising only a generally available grievance about government—claiming only harm to his and every citizen's interest in proper application of the Constitution and laws, and seeking relief that no more directly and tangibly benefits him than it does the public at large—does not state an Article III case or controversy." . . .

"To permit a complainant who has no concrete injury to require a court to rule on important constitutional issues in the abstract would create the potential for abuse of the judicial process, distort the role of the Judiciary in its relationship to the Executive and the Legislature and open the Judiciary to an arguable charge of providing 'government by injunction.'" Schlesinger v. Reservists Comm. to Stop the War, 418 U.S. 208, 222 (1974). . . . [O]nce a proper understanding of the relationship of standing to the separation of powers is brought to bear, Psychic Injury, even as limited in *Flast,* is revealed for what it is: a contradiction of the basic propositions that the function of the judicial power "is, solely, to decide on the rights of individuals," Marbury v. Madison, 5 U.S. (1 Cranch) 137, 170 (1803), and that generalized grievances affecting the public at large have their remedy in the political process.

Overruling prior precedents, even precedents as disreputable as *Flast,* is nevertheless a serious undertaking, and I understand the impulse to take a minimalist approach. But laying just claim to be honoring stare decisis requires more than beating *Flast* to a pulp and then sending it out to the lower courts weakened, denigrated, more incomprehensible than ever, and yet somehow technically alive. . . . We had an opportunity today to erase this blot on our jurisprudence, but instead have simply smudged it. . . . I can think of few cases less warranting of stare decisis respect. It is time—it is past time—to call an end. *Flast* should be overruled.

■ JUSTICE SOUTER, with whom JUSTICE STEVENS, JUSTICE GINSBURG, and JUSTICE BREYER join, dissenting.

Flast v. Cohen, 392 U.S. 83 (1968), held that plaintiffs with an Establishment Clause claim could "demonstrate the necessary stake as taxpayers in the outcome of the litigation to satisfy Article III requirements." Here, the controlling, plurality opinion declares that *Flast* does not apply, but a search of that opinion for a suggestion that these taxpayers have any less stake in the outcome than the taxpayers in *Flast* will come up empty: the plurality makes no such finding, nor could it. Instead, the controlling opinion closes the door on these taxpayers because the Executive Branch, and not the Legislative Branch, caused their injury. I see no basis for this distinction in either logic or precedent, and respectfully dissent.

I

We held in *Flast* . . . that the "'injury' alleged in Establishment Clause challenges to federal spending" is "the very 'extract[ion] and spen[ding]' of 'tax money' in aid of religion." DaimlerChrysler Corp. v. Cuno, 547 U.S. 332, 348 (2006) (quoting *Flast*). As the Court said in *Flast,* the importance of that type of injury has deep historical roots going back to the ideal of religious liberty in James Madison's Memorial and Remonstrance Against Religious Assessments, that the government in a free society may not "force a citizen to contribute three pence only of his property for the support of any one establishment" of religion. 2 Writings of

James Madison 183, 186 (G. Hunt ed.1901) (hereinafter Madison), quoted in *Flast*, 392 U.S. at 103. Madison thus translated into practical terms the right of conscience described when he wrote that "[t]he Religion . . . of every man must be left to the conviction and conscience of every man; and it is the right of every man to exercise it as these may dictate."

The right of conscience and the expenditure of an identifiable three pence raised by taxes for the support of a religious cause are therefore not to be split off from one another. The three pence implicates the conscience, and the injury from Government expenditures on religion is not accurately classified with the "Psychic Injury" that results whenever a congressional appropriation or executive expenditure raises hackles of disagreement with the policy supported. Justice Stewart recognized this in his concurring opinion in *Flast,* when he said that "every taxpayer can claim a personal constitutional right not to be taxed for the support of a religious institution," and thus distinguished the case from one in which a taxpayer sought only to air a generalized grievance in federal court.

Here, there is no dispute that taxpayer money in identifiable amounts is funding conferences, and these are alleged to have the purpose of promoting religion. The taxpayers therefore seek not to "extend" *Flast,* but merely to apply it. When executive agencies spend identifiable sums of tax money for religious purposes, no less than when Congress authorizes the same thing, taxpayers suffer injury. . . .

The plurality points to the separation of powers to explain its distinction between legislative and executive spending decisions, but there is no difference on that point of view between a Judicial Branch review of an executive decision and a judicial evaluation of a congressional one. We owe respect to each of the other branches, no more to the former than to the latter, and no one has suggested that the Establishment Clause lacks applicability to executive uses of money. It would surely violate the Establishment Clause for the Department of Health and Human Services to draw on a general appropriation to build a chapel for weekly church services (no less than if a statute required it), and for good reason: if the Executive could accomplish through the exercise of discretion exactly what Congress cannot do through legislation, Establishment Clause protection would melt away.

So in Bowen v. Kendrick, 487 U.S. 589 (1988), we recognized the equivalence between a challenge to a congressional spending bill and a claim that the Executive Branch was spending an appropriation, each in violation of the Establishment Clause. We held that the "claim that . . . funds [were] being used improperly by individual grantees [was no] less a challenge to congressional taxing and spending power simply because the funding authorized by Congress has flowed through and been administered by the Secretary," and we added that "we have not questioned the standing of taxpayer plaintiffs to raise Establishment Clause challenges, even when their claims raised questions about the administratively made grants."

The plurality points out that the statute in *Bowen* "expressly authorized and appropriated specific funds for grantmaking" and "expressly contemplated that some of those moneys might go to projects involving religious groups." That is all true, but there is no reason to think it should matter, and every indication in *Bowen* that it did not. In *Bowen* we already had found the statute valid on its face before we turned to the taxpayers' as-applied challenge, so the case cannot be read to hold that taxpayers have standing only to claim that congressional action, but not its implementation, violates the Establishment Clause. Thus, after *Bowen,* the plurality's distinction between a "congressional mandate" on the one hand and "executive discretion" on the other, is at once arbitrary and hard to manage: if the statute itself is constitutional, all complaints must be about the exercise of "executive discretion," so there is no line to be drawn between *Bowen* and the case before us today.

II

While *Flast* standing to assert the right of conscience is in a class by itself, it would be a mistake to think that case is unique in recognizing standing in a plaintiff without injury to flesh or purse. Cognizable harm takes account of the nature of the interest protected, which is the reason that "the constitutional component of standing doctrine incorporates concepts concededly not susceptible of precise definition," leaving it impossible "to make application of the constitutional standing requirement a mechanical exercise." Allen v. Wright, 468 U.S. 737, 751 (1984). The question, ultimately, has to be whether the injury alleged is "too abstract, or otherwise not appropriate, to be considered judicially cognizable." Id. at 752.

In the case of economic or physical harms, of course, the "injury in fact" question is straightforward. But once one strays from these obvious cases, the enquiry can turn subtle. Are esthetic harms sufficient for Article III standing? What about being forced to compete on an uneven playing field based on race (without showing that an economic loss resulted), or living in a racially gerrymandered electoral district? These injuries are no more concrete than seeing one's tax dollars spent on religion, but we have recognized each one as enough for standing. See Friends of Earth, Inc. v. Laidlaw Environmental Services (TOC), Inc., 528 U.S. 167, 183 (2000) (esthetic injury); United States v. Hays, 515 U.S. 737, 744–45 (1995) (living in a racially gerrymandered electoral district). This is not to say that any sort of alleged injury will satisfy Article III, but only that intangible harms must be evaluated case by case.[4]

Thus, *Flast* speaks for this Court's recognition (shared by a majority of the Court today) that when the Government spends money for religious purposes a taxpayer's injury is serious and concrete enough to be "judicially cognizable," *Allen,* 468 U.S. at 752. The judgment of sufficient

---

[4] Outside the Establishment Clause context, as the plurality points out, we have not found the injury to a taxpayer when funds are improperly expended to suffice for standing.

injury takes account of the Madisonian relationship of tax money and conscience, but it equally reflects the Founders' pragmatic "conviction that individual religious liberty could be achieved best under a government which was stripped of all power to tax, to support, or otherwise to assist any or all religions," Everson v. Board of Ed. of Ewing, 330 U.S. 1, 11 (1947), and the realization continuing to the modern day that favoritism for religion "sends the . . . message to . . . nonadherents that they are outsiders, not full members of the political community," McCreary County v. American Civil Liberties Union of Ky., 545 U.S. 844, 860 (2005).

Because the taxpayers in this case have alleged the type of injury this Court has seen as sufficient for standing, I would affirm.

NOTES ON TAXPAYER STANDING

1.   QUESTIONS AND COMMENTS ON TAXPAYER STANDING

Are citizen and taxpayer standing different? Should the answer depend on the dollar value of the taxpayer's share of the disputed expenditure, or on the nature of the taxpayer's objection to it?

If some instances of taxpayer standing are to be permitted, is there any way to distinguish the others? Several differentiations have been attempted, including the two-pronged nexus test of *Flast v. Cohen*, the interpretation of that approach in *Hein* and *Valley Forge*, and the claim that there should be a special rule for the Establishment Clause. Is any of these approaches persuasive? If, as Justice Scalia contends, the only sensible choice regarding taxpayer standing is all or nothing, which would be the better rule?[a]

2.   *ARIZONA CHRISTIAN SCHOOL TUITION ORG. V. WINN*

Taxpayer standing in Establishment Clause cases returned to the Supreme Court in Arizona Christian School Tuition Org. v. Winn, 563 U.S. 125 (2011), and produced yet another five-four split and yet another restrictive interpretation of *Flast v. Cohen*. The case involved an Arizona statute providing tax credits to taxpayers who contributed money to "school tuition organizations." The STOs used the contributions to fund scholarships for students attending private schools, many of which were religious. Arizona taxpayers challenged this tax credit as a violation of the Establishment Clause. Given the long history of decisions cabining *Flast* and given the Supreme Court's approval of tuition aid to parents who enroll their children in religious schools, see Zelman v. Simmons-Harris, 536 U.S. 639 (2002), it is not surprising that the taxpayers' challenge was rejected. It is, however, surprising that the Court did so on the ground that a tax credit, which enabled taxpayers to reduce their tax liability by the amount of their contributions, did not qualify as expenditure of government funds under *Flast*.

---

[a] For an amusing "dialogue" on *Hein* and taxpayer standing, see Eric J. Segall, The Taxing Law of Taxpayer Standing, 43 Tulsa L. Rev. 673 (2008), and for additional commentary on *Hein*, see Craig A. Stern, Another Sign from *Hein*: Does the Generalized Grievance Fail a Constitutional or a Prudential Test of Federal Standing to Sue?, 12 Lewis & Clark L. Rev. 1169 (2008).

Speaking for the Court, Justice Kennedy said that government appropriations and tax credits were not equivalent:

> When Arizona taxpayers choose to contribute to STOs, they spend their own money, not money the State has collected from respondents [plaintiffs below] or from other taxpayers. [The Arizona statute] does not extrac[t] and spen[d] a conscientious dissenter's funds in service of an establishment, [quoting *Flast v. Cohen*, 392 U.S. at 106], or force a citizen to contribute three pence only of his property to a sectarian organization, id. at 103 [quoting James Madison's Memorial and Remonstrance Against Religious Assessments]. On the contrary, respondents and other Arizona taxpayers remain free to pay their own tax bills, without contributing to an STO. Respondents are likewise able to contribute to an STO of their choice, either religious or secular. And respondents also have the option of contributing to other charitable organizations, in which case respondents may become eligible for a tax deduction or a different tax credit. The STO tax credit is not tantamount to a religious tax or to a tithe and does not visit the injury identified in *Flast*. It follows that respondents have neither alleged an injury for standing purposes under general rules nor met the *Flast* exception. Finding standing under these circumstances would be . . . a departure from *Flast*'s stated rationale.

The Court acknowledged that this conclusion differed from several cases reviewing Establishment Clause challenges to tax expenditures, but insisted that those cases had not directly confronted the question of standing.

Justice Scalia, joined by Justice Thomas, concurred. "Today's majority and dissent struggle with whether respondents' challenge to the Arizona tuition tax credit falls within [*Flast*'s] narrow exception [to the ban on taxpayer standing]. Under a principled reading of Article III, their struggles are unnecessary. *Flast* is an anomaly in our jurisprudence, irreconcilable with the Article III restrictions on federal judicial power that our opinions have established. I would repudiate that misguided decision and enforce the Constitution."

Justice Kagan, joined by Justices Ginsburg, Breyer, and Sotomayor, dissented. She attacked the "novel distinction in standing law between appropriations and tax expenditures." She cited prior cases treating tax credits as equivalent to direct appropriations, noting that "[u]ntil today, this Court has never so much as hinted that litigants in the same shoes as the plaintiffs lack standing under *Flast*." The reason, she said, was not merely precedent, but principle:

> Our taxpayer standing cases have declined to distinguish between appropriations and tax expenditures for a simple reason: Here, as in many contexts, the distinction is one in search of a difference. . . .
>
> For just this reason, government budgeting rules routinely insist on calculation of tax subsidies, in addition to appropriations. The President must provide information on the estimated cost of

tax expenditures in the budget he submits to Congress each year. Similarly, congressional budget committees must report to all Members on the level of tax expenditures in the federal budget. Many States—including Arizona—likewise compute the impact of targeted tax breaks on the public treasury, in recognition that these measures are just spending under a different name. . . .

And because these financing mechanisms result in the same bottom line, taxpayers challenging them can allege the same harm. . . . Whenever taxpayers have standing under *Flast* to challenge an appropriation, they should also have standing to contest a tax expenditure. Their access to the federal courts should not depend on which type of financial subsidy the State has offered.

She closed with an example:

Suppose a State desires to reward Jews—by, say, $500 per year—for their religious devotion. Should the nature of taxpayers' concern vary if the State allows Jews to claim the aid on their tax returns, in lieu of receiving an annual stipend? Or assume a State wishes to subsidize the ownership of crucifixes. It could purchase the religious symbols in bulk and distribute them to all takers. Or it could mail a reimbursement check to any individual who buys her own and submits a receipt for the purchase. Or it could authorize that person to claim a tax credit equal to the price she paid. Now, really—do taxpayers have less reason to complain if the State selects the last of these three options? The Court today says they do, but that is wrong. The effect of each form of subsidy is the same, on the public fisc and on those who contribute to it. Regardless of which mechanism the State uses, taxpayers have an identical stake in ensuring that the State's exercise of its taxing and spending power complies with the Constitution.

The example Justice Kagan gives of federal subsidies to specific religious beliefs is, on the merits, easily distinguishable from the Arizona tax credit for contributions to STOs. The latter is more nearly analogous to (though more generous than) the deductibility of contributions to churches and religious schools, as well as other charitable organizations. One may well think, therefore, that on the merits Justice Kagan's hypothetical would be unconstitutional and that the tax credits for contributions to STOs are not. But how is that relevant to the law of standing? If, as the majority insists, taxpayers lack standing to challenge tax expenditures on Establishment Clause grounds, then presumably the taxpayers would lack standing regardless of the constitutionality of the underlying program. Does that mean that the egregious example suggested by Justice Kagan would be insulated from review? Or does the Court's analysis of standing somehow reflect its view of the merits?[b]

---

[b]   For analysis and criticism of *Winn*, see William P. Marshall and Gene R. Nichol, Not a *Winn*-Win: Misconstruing Standing and the Establishment Clause, 2011 Sup. Ct. Rev. 215.

SUBSECTION D. LEGISLATIVE AND GOVERNMENTAL STANDING

INTRODUCTORY NOTES ON LEGISLATIVE AND STATE STANDING

1. INTRODUCTION

Law students are often surprised that disputes over the extent of federal legislative power vis-à-vis the states are typically litigated not in suits brought by the states themselves, but rather by private parties adversely affected by federal legislation. Sometimes, however, institutional actors—Congress, a state legislature, individual legislators, or a state government—attempt to have the courts assess the lawfulness of government action. Such attempts implicate justiciability concerns and are often unsuccessful, but the full history is more complex. Not only are there differences in the results of decided cases, but there is also uncertainty about exactly which justiciability doctrine is at stake. Most of the cases speak of standing, which generally concerns who is a proper plaintiff. But disputes between government institutions may also be thought to implicate the political question doctrine, which holds that certain kinds of disputes are inappropriate for judicial resolution and therefore non-justiciable even if the plaintiff has standing. The political question doctrine is covered at length in Section 4 of this Chapter.

2. *COLEMAN V. MILLER*

Coleman v. Miller, 307 U.S. 433 (1939), is usually considered in connection with the political-question doctrine, but it also involved a question of legislative standing. In 1925 the Kansas legislature voted not to ratify the proposed Child Labor Amendment to the United States Constitution. In 1937 a second effort resulted in a tie vote in the state senate. The lieutenant governor broke the tie and voted for ratification, as did the Kansas house. The losers in the state senate then sued, claiming that (1) the requirement in Article V of the Constitution that constitutional amendments be ratified by "the Legislatures of three fourths of the several States" did not allow action by the lieutenant governor, (2) the prior rejection of the amendment should preclude later ratification, and (3) in any event too much time had elapsed after proposal of the amendment for the ratification to be valid. In *Coleman*, the Supreme Court found these issues to be non-justiciable political questions, a result described more fully in Section 4.

Before addressing the political question doctrine, the Court concluded that the Kansas legislators had standing to sue. The holding on that subject was murky, partly because the Court rejected the case on political-question grounds and, as a result, whatever it said about standing arguably did not matter. The lead opinion for the Court, written by Chief Justice Hughes, reasoned that the complaining state senators had "a plain, direct and adequate interest in maintaining the effectiveness of their votes." But it is surprisingly hard to count the votes for this proposition. Justice Scalia gave it a try in his dissent in Arizona State Legislature v. Arizona Independent Redistricting

Commission, 576 U.S. ___, 135 S.Ct. 2652 (2015) (discussed in the notes after the next main case), and came up with the following:

The opinion discussing and finding standing, and going on to affirm the Kansas Supreme Court, was written by Chief Justice Hughes and announced by Justice Stone. Justice Frankfurter, joined by three other Justices, held there was no standing, and would have dismissed the petition (leaving the judgment of the Kansas Supreme Court in place). Justice Butler, joined by Justice McReynolds, dissented (neither joining Hughes's opinion nor separately discussing standing) and would have reversed the Kansas Supreme Court.

That adds up to two votes to affirm on the merits, two to reverse on the merits (without discussing standing) and four to dismiss for lack of standing. Justice Stanley Reed, who was on the Court and apparently participated in the case, is not mentioned in any of the opinions recorded in the United States Reports. So, in order to find *Coleman* a binding precedent on standing, rather than a four-to-four stand-off, one must assume that Justice Reed voted with Hughes. There is some reason to make that assumption: The four Justices rejecting standing went on to discuss the merits, because "the ruling of the Court just announced removes from the case the question of petitioners' standing to sue." 307 U.S. at 456 (Black, J., concurring). But then again, if nine Justices participated, how could it be that on one of the two issues in the case the Court was "equally divided and therefore . . . expresse[d] no opinion"?

Scalia concluded that *Coleman* was a "pretty shaky foundation" for concluding anything about the law of standing, but that it nevertheless stands as one of the few examples where legislators were allowed to sue. The meaning of *Coleman* was at issue in the following case.

Raines v. Byrd
Supreme Court of the United States, 1997.
521 U.S. 811.

■ CHIEF JUSTICE REHNQUIST delivered the opinion of the Court.*

The District Court for the District of Columbia declared the Line Item Veto Act unconstitutional. On this direct appeal, we hold that appellees lack standing to bring this suit, and therefore direct that the judgment of the district court be vacated and the complaint dismissed.

I

The appellees are six members of Congress, four of whom served as Senators and two of whom served as Congressmen in the 104th Congress (1995–1996). On March 27, 1996, the Senate passed a bill entitled the Line Item Veto Act by a vote of 69–31. All four appellee Senators voted

---

* Justice Ginsburg joins this opinion.

"nay." The next day, the House of Representatives passed the identical bill by a vote of 232–177. Both appellee Congressmen voted "nay." On April 4, 1996, the President signed the Line Item Veto Act into law. 2 U.S.C. §§ 691 et seq. (Supp. 1997). The act went into effect on January 1, 1997. The next day, appellees filed a complaint in the District Court for the District of Columbia against the two appellants, the Secretary of the Treasury and the Director of the Office of Management and Budget, alleging that the act was unconstitutional.

The provisions of the Line Item Veto Act do not use the term "veto." Instead, the President is given the authority to "cancel" certain spending and tax benefit measures after he has signed them into law. Specifically, [2 U.S.C. § 691(a)] provides:

> [T]he President may, with respect to any bill or joint resolution that has been signed into law pursuant to Article I, section 7, of the Constitution of the United States, cancel in whole—(1) any dollar amount of discretionary budget authority; (2) any item of new direct spending; or (3) any limited tax benefit; if the President—
>
>> (A) determines that such cancellation will—(i) reduce the Federal budget deficit; (ii) not impair any essential Governmental Functions; and (iii) not harm the national interest; and
>>
>> (B) notifies the Congress of such cancellation by transmitting a special message . . . within five calendar days (excluding Sundays) after the enactment of the law [to which the cancellation applies].

. . . With respect to dollar amounts of "discretionary budget authority," a cancellation means "to rescind." § 691e(4)(A). With respect to "new direct spending" items or "limited tax benefit[s]," a cancellation means that the relevant legal provision, legal obligation, or budget authority is "prevent[ed] from having legal force or effect." §§ 691e(4)(B), (C). . . .

The act provides that "[a]ny member of Congress or any individual adversely affected by [this act] may bring an action, in the United States District Court for the District of Columbia, for declaratory judgment and injunctive relief on the ground that any provision of this part violates the Constitution." § 692(a)(1). Appellees brought suit under this provision, claiming that . . . the act "unconstitutionally expands the President's power," and "violates the requirements of bicameral passage and presentment by granting to the President, acting alone, the authority to 'cancel' and thus repeal provisions of federal law." They alleged that the act injured them "directly and concretely . . . in their official capacities" in three ways:

> The act . . . (a) alter[s] the legal and practical effect of all votes they may cast on bills containing such separately vetoable items, (b) divest[s] the [appellees] of their constitutional role in

the repeal of legislation, and (c) alter[s] the constitutional balance of powers between the legislative and executive branches, both with respect to measures containing separately vetoable items and with respect to other matters coming before Congress.

. . . On April 10, 1997, the District Court (i) denied appellants' motion to dismiss, holding that appellees had standing to bring this suit and that their claim was ripe, and (ii) granted appellees' summary judgment motion, holding that the act is unconstitutional. . . .

The act provides for a direct, expedited appeal to this Court. . . . We established an expedited briefing schedule and heard oral argument on May 27. We now hold that appellees have no standing to bring this suit, and therefore direct that the judgment of the district court be vacated and the complaint dismissed.

II

[In part II, the Court reviewed and restated general standing principles, placing particular emphasis on Allen v. Wright, 468 U.S. 737 (1984), and Lujan v. Defenders of Wildlife, 504 U.S. 555 (1992).]

III

We have never had occasion to rule on the question of legislative standing presented here.[4] In Powell v. McCormack, 395 U.S. 486 (1969), we held that a member of Congress' constitutional challenge to his exclusion from the House of Representatives (and his consequent loss of salary) presented an Article III case or controversy. But *Powell* does not help appellees. First, appellees have not been singled out for specially unfavorable treatment as opposed to other members of their respective bodies. Their claim is that the act causes a type of institutional injury (the diminution of legislative power), which necessarily damages all members of Congress and both Houses of Congress equally. Second, appellees do not claim that they have been deprived of something to which they *personally* are entitled. . . . Rather, appellees' claim of standing is based on a loss of political power, not loss of any private right, which would make the injury more concrete. . . .

The one case in which we have upheld standing for legislators (albeit *state* legislators) claiming an institutional injury is Coleman v. Miller, 307 U.S. 433 (1939). . . . In *Coleman*, 20 of Kansas' 40 state senators voted not to ratify the proposed "Child Labor Amendment" to the federal Constitution. With the vote deadlocked 20–20, the Amendment ordinarily would not have been ratified. However, the state's lieutenant governor, the presiding officer of the state senate, cast a deciding vote in favor of the Amendment, and it was deemed ratified. . . . The 20 state senators who had voted against the Amendment, joined by a 21st state senator and three state house members, filed an action in the Kansas

---

[4] Over strong dissent, the Court of Appeals for the District of Columbia Circuit has held that members of Congress may have standing when (as here) they assert injury to their institutional power as legislators.

Supreme Court seeking a writ of mandamus that would compel the appropriate state officials to recognize that the legislature had not in fact ratified the Amendment. That court held that the members of the legislature had standing to bring their mandamus action, but ruled against them on the merits.

This Court affirmed. By a vote of five-four, we held that the members of the legislature had standing. In explaining our holding, we repeatedly emphasized that if these legislators (who were suing as a bloc) were correct on the merits, then their votes not to ratify the Amendment were deprived of all validity. . . . It is obvious, then, that our holding in *Coleman* stands (at most) for the proposition that legislators whose votes would have been sufficient to defeat (or enact) a specific legislative act have standing to sue if that legislative action goes into effect (or does not go into effect), on the ground that their votes have been completely nullified.

It should be equally obvious that appellees' claim does not fall within our holding in *Coleman*, as thus understood. They have not alleged that they voted for a specific bill, that there were sufficient votes to pass the bill, and that the bill was nonetheless deemed defeated. . . .

Nonetheless, appellees rely heavily on our statement in *Coleman* that the Kansas senators had "a plain, direct, and adequate interest in maintaining the effectiveness of their votes." Appellees claim that this statement applies to them because their votes on future appropriations bills . . . will be less "effective" than before, and that the "meaning" and "integrity" of their vote has changed. The argument goes as follows. Before the act, members of Congress could be sure than when they voted for, and Congress passed, an appropriations bill that included funds for project X, one of two things would happen: (i) the bill would become law and all of the projects listed in the bill would go into effect, or (ii) the bill would not become law and none of the projects listed in the bill would go into effect. . . . After the act, however, a vote for an appropriations bill that includes project X means something different. Now, in addition to the two possibilities listed above, there is a third option: the bill will become law and then the President will "cancel" project X.

[This] argument pulls *Coleman* too far from its moorings. Appellees' use of the word "effectiveness" to link their argument to *Coleman* stretches the word far beyond the sense in which the *Coleman* opinion used it. There is a vast difference between the level of vote nullification at issue in *Coleman* and the abstract dilution of institutional legislative power that is alleged here. To uphold standing here would require a drastic extension of *Coleman*. We are unwilling to take that step.

Not only do appellees lack support from precedent, but historical practice appears to cut against them as well. . . .

IV

In sum, appellees have alleged no injury to themselves as individuals (contra *Powell*), the institutional injury they allege is wholly abstract and widely dispersed (contra *Coleman*), and their attempt to litigate this dispute at this time and in this form is contrary to historical experience. We attach some importance to the fact that appellees have not been authorized to represent their respective houses of Congress in this action, and indeed both houses actively oppose this suit. We also note that our conclusion neither deprives members of Congress of an adequate remedy (since they may repeal the act or exempt appropriations bills from its reach), nor forecloses the act from constitutional challenge (by someone who suffers judicially cognizable injury as a result of the act). Whether the case would be different if any of these circumstances were different, we need not now decide. . . .

■ JUSTICE SOUTER, concurring in the judgment, with whom JUSTICE GINSBURG joins. . . .

As Justice Stevens points out, appellees essentially claim that, by granting the President power to repeal statutes, the act injures them by depriving them of their official role in voting on the provisions that become law. Under our precedents, it is fairly debatable whether this injury is sufficiently "personal" and "concrete" to satisfy the requirements of Article III. . . .

Because it is fairly debatable whether appellee's injury is sufficiently personal and concrete to give them standing, it behooves us to resolve the question under more general separation-of-powers principles underlying our standing requirements. [R]espect for the separation of powers requires the judicial branch to exercise restraint in deciding constitutional issues by resolving those implicating the powers of the three branches of government as a "last resort." . . .

While it is true that a suit challenging the constitutionality of this Act brought by a party from outside the Federal Government would also involve the Court in resolving the dispute over the allocation of power between the political branches, it would expose the Judicial Branch to a lesser risk. Deciding a suit to vindicate an interest outside the Government raises no specter of judicial readiness to enlist on one side of a political tug of war . . . .

The virtue of waiting for a private suit is only confirmed by the certainty that another suit can come to us. The parties agree, and I see no reason to question, that if the President "cancels" a conventional spending or tax provision pursuant to the act, the putative beneficiaries of that provision will likely suffer a cognizable injury and thereby have standing under Article III. . . .

■ JUSTICE STEVENS, dissenting.

The Line Item Veto Act purports to establish a procedure for the creation of laws that are truncated versions of bills that have been passed

by the Congress and presented to the President for signature. If the procedure were valid, it would deny every Senator and every Representative
any opportunity to vote for or against the truncated measure that survives the exercise of the President's cancellation authority. Because the
opportunity to cast such votes is a right guaranteed by the text of the
Constitution, I think it clear that the persons who are deprived of that
right by the act have standing to challenge its constitutionality. Moreover, because the impairment of that constitutional right has an immediate impact on their official powers, in my judgment they need not wait
until after the President has exercised his cancellation authority to bring
suit. . . .

In my judgment, the deprivation of [the right to vote on the precise
text that will ultimately become law] constitutes a sufficient injury to
provide every member of Congress with standing to challenge the constitutionality of the statute. If the dilution of an individual voter's power to
elect representatives provides that voter with standing—as surely it
does, see, e.g., Baker v. Carr, 369 U.S. 186, 204–08 (1962)—the deprivation of the right possessed by each Senator and Representative to vote
for or against the precise text of any bill before it becomes law must also
be a sufficient injury to create Article III standing for them. . . .

■ JUSTICE BREYER, dissenting. . . .

I concede that there would be no case or controversy here were the
dispute before us not truly adversary, or were it not concrete and focused.
But the interests that the parties assert are genuine and opposing, and
the parties are therefore truly adverse. . . .

Nonetheless, there remains a serious constitutional difficulty due to
the fact that this dispute about law-making procedures arises between
government officials and is brought by legislators. The critical question
is whether or not this dispute, for that reason, is so different in form from
those "matters that were the traditional concern of the courts at Westminster" that is falls outside the scope of Article III's judicial power.
Coleman v. Miller, 307 U.S. 433, 460 (1939) (Frankfurter, J., dissenting). . . . Justice Frankfurter dissented because, in his view, the "political" nature of the case, which involved legislators, placed the dispute outside the scope of Article III's "case" or "controversy" requirement. Nonetheless, the *Coleman* Court rejected his argument.

Although the majority today attempts to distinguish *Coleman*, I do
not believe that Justice Frankfurter's argument or variations on its
theme can carry the day here. First, . . . the jurisdictional statute before
us eliminates all but constitutional considerations. . . . Second, the Constitution does not draw an absolute line between disputes involving a
"personal" harm and those involving an "official" harm. . . . *Coleman* itself involved injuries in the plaintiff legislators' official capacity. . . .

Third, Justice Frankfurter's views were dissenting views, and the
dispute before us, when compared to *Coleman*, presents a much stronger

claim, not a weaker claim, for constitutional justiciability. The lawmakers in *Coleman* complained of a lawmaking procedure that, at worst, improperly counted Kansas as having ratified one proposed constitutional amendment, which had been ratified by only five other states, and rejected by 26, making it unlikely that it would ever become law. The lawmakers in this case complain of a lawmaking procedure that threatens the validity of many laws (for example, all appropriations laws) that Congress regularly and frequently enacts. . . .

The majority finds a difference in the fact that the validity of the legislators' votes was directly at issue in *Coleman*. . . . But since many of the present plaintiffs will likely vote in the majority for at least some appropriations bills that are then subject to presidential cancellation, I think that—on their view of the law—their votes are threatened with nullification too. . . .

In sum, I do not believe that the Court can find this case nonjusticiable without overruling *Coleman*. Since it does not do so, I need not decide whether the systematic nature, seriousness, and immediacy of the harm would make this dispute constitutionally justiciable even in *Coleman*'s absence. Rather, I can and would find this case justiciable on *Coleman*'s authority. I add that because the majority has decided that this dispute is not now justiciable and has expressed no view on the merits of the appeal, I shall not discuss the merits either, but reserve them for future argument

NOTES ON LEGISLATIVE AND GOVERNMENTAL STANDING

1.   QUESTIONS AND COMMENTS ON *RAINES*

The Court in *Raines* suggests that legislators might be able to sue for institutional injury in situations in which their votes have been "completely nullified." What would legislators need to show satisfy that standard? Why was the standard not met in *Raines*?

The effect of *Raines* is to sharply limit the circumstances under which individual members of Congress can raise judicial challenges to the validity of legislation or Executive Branch actions. Does this make sense from the perspective of separation of powers? Justice Souter's concurrence argues that it does. What is his concern?

Raines also illustrates the influence of broader justiciability concerns on questions of legislative standing. That the plaintiffs were actually injured may be thought fairly clear. What was not clear was that the courts should get involved in resolving disputes between the other branches unless absolutely necessary. That disinclination might be described as a restriction on standing, as it was in *Raines*, or it might be described as the related justiciability concern addressed by the political question doctrine, as it was in *Coleman*.

Standing was necessarily the preferred vocabulary in *Raines* in order to preserve the possibility that the same underlying issue could be raised by another plaintiff. That in fact happened in Clinton v. City of New York, 524 U.S. 417 (1998). Two months after *Raines*, President Clinton used the line-item veto to cancel provisions in two budgetary statutes. Various parties who were affected by those cancelations, including the City of New York, sued to have his actions reversed. The Court found that the plaintiffs had standing and concluded that the line-item veto authority was unconstitutional. Justices Scalia, O'Connor, and Breyer dissented.

2. INSTITUTIONAL AUTHORIZATION TO SUE

In *Raines*, the Court said that it "attach[ed] some importance to the fact that appellees have not been authorized to represent their respective houses of Congress in this action, and indeed both houses actively oppose this suit." To what extent does institutional authorization matter? The cases are unclear, although the Supreme Court has occasionally allowed houses of Congress to defend the constitutionality of legislation after the Executive Branch has declined to do so.

One such instance was INS v. Chadha, 462 U.S. 919 (1983). At issue was the constitutionality of a "legislative veto" provision that allowed a House of Congress to override an executive decision not to deport someone otherwise eligible for deportation. When someone facing deportation challenged the provision, the Executive Branch declined to defend its constitutionality, although it continued to act in accordance with the provision. The Supreme Court nevertheless concluded that there was a sufficient "case or controversy," noting that the House and Senate, which had been permitted to intervene in the Supreme Court proceedings, were defending the statute. The Court noted that it had "long held that Congress is the proper party to defend the validity of a statute when an agency of government, as a defendant charged with enforcing the statute, agrees with plaintiffs that the statute is inapplicable or unconstitutional."

This issue arose again in United States v. Windsor, 570 U.S. 744 (2013). *Windsor*, which is excerpted in the materials on standing to appeal in Subsection E, concerned the constitutionality of the Defense of Marriage Act (DOMA). DOMA, among other things disallowed federal marriage benefits for same sex married couples. The Supreme Court held that there was standing to appeal a decision invalidating DOMA, even though the Executive Branch had said that it agreed with that decision. The Court noted that the Executive was still enforcing DOMA and had formally filed the appeal. As for the concern that there would not be a truly adversarial presentation of arguments (since the government and the plaintiffs agreed on the merits), the Court reasoned that this was merely a prudential concern, and that it was sufficiently addressed by the fact that a group appointed by the House of Representatives (the Bipartisan Legal Advisory Group (BLAG), consisting of five members of the House leadership) had been permitted to intervene to argue in support of the Act. The Court said that it did not need to decide whether BLAG would have independent standing to appeal. The Court then proceeded to find that DOMA was unconstitutional.

In dissent, Justice Alito disagreed with the Court that the Executive Branch had standing in this situation, but he argued that BLAG did have standing, given that it was authorized to represent the House of Representatives, which he said was injured by having its law struck down. Alito relied heavily on *Chadha.* In a separate dissent, Justice Scalia criticized Alito, arguing that allowing suits by Congress to defend legislation would improperly pull the courts into political disputes between Congress and the Executive Branch and unduly interfere with the Executive Branch's constitutional obligation to take care that the laws are faithfully executed. Scalia distinguished *Chadha* as involving a situation in which "the House and Senate were threatened with destruction of what they claimed to be one of their institutional powers," whereas "[n]othing like that is present here."

An important lower court decision in this line is House of Representatives v. Burwell, 130 F. Supp. 3d 53 (D.D.C. 2015). In that case, the House of Representatives sued Executive Branch officials, arguing that they had acted unconstitutionally in spending unappropriated money from the Treasury to reimburse insurance companies under the Affordable Care Act and in delaying and narrowing the Act's employer mandate provisions through regulations. The suit was specifically authorized by a resolution passed by the House in 2014. The court concluded that the House had standing to challenge the allegedly unlawful use of funds, but not to challenge the regulations concerning the employer mandate. The court reasoned that the claim about spending was a constitutional claim: that the Executive Branch had violated the requirement in Article I, § 9, cl. 7, that "[n]o money shall be drawn from the Treasury, but in Consequence of Appropriations made by Law." If the Executive Branch usurps that authority, reasoned the court, it injures Congress. The court distinguished *Raines* as involving a suit only by individual members of Congress, whereas here the House was suing as an institution (cf. *Arizona State Legislature,* below). The court concluded, however, that the House did not have standing to pursue the claims relating to the employer mandate regulations because those claims were ultimately about statutory interpretation. Congress should not be allowed to challenge the Executive Branch's construction of statutes, reasoned the court, because that would improperly put the judiciary in the position of overseeing the Executive Branch's execution of the laws. The court subsequently held the Executive Branch's expenditures to be unconstitutional, but it stayed its decision pending appeal. During the pendency of the appeal, Donald Trump was elected President.

Even if Congress should not generally be able to sue the Executive Branch, should it be able to do so when it is attempting to enforce its institutional prerogatives, such as oversight? Consider Committee on the Judiciary v. Miers, 558 F. Supp. 2d 53 (D.D.C. 2008), where the court concluded that, notwithstanding *Raines,* a congressional committee could sue the Executive Branch to enforce a subpoena, which the Executive Branch had resisted on the ground of "executive privilege." The court reasoned: "A House committee has issued a subpoena to certain members of the executive branch who have refused to comply with it, and the House has authorized the Committee to proceed to court. The injury incurred by the Committee, for Article III purposes, is both the loss of information to which it is entitled and the institutional diminution of its subpoena power." For a similar conclusion, see Comm. on Oversight and Gov't Reform v. Holder, 979 F. Supp. 2d 1 (D.D.C. 2013).

3. *ARIZONA STATE LEGISLATURE V. ARIZONA IND. REDISTRICTING COMM'N*

Raines was distinguished in Arizona State Legislature v. Arizona Independent Redistricting Commission, 576 U.S. ___, 135 S.Ct. 2652 (2015). In an effort to stop gerrymandering, Arizona voters adopted an initiative depriving the state legislature of authority over redistricting and vesting that power in an independent redistricting commission. The initiative procedure was undoubtedly valid under state law. The legislature therefore accepted the result with respect to state legislative districts, but claimed that as applied to congressional districts, the independent commission violated federal law, specifically Art. I, § 4, cl. 1, the "Elections Clause," which provides that the "Times, Places and Manner of holding Elections for Senators and Representatives, shall be prescribed in each State by the Legislature thereof. . . ."

In an opinion by Justice Ginsburg, and over a powerful dissent by the Chief Justice, the majority found that the Elections Clause did not require action by the actual legislature but allowed redistricting by any entity in which the people had vested that power. To reach that conclusion, the Court necessarily found that the legislature had standing to raise the issue. The Court distinguished *Raines*:

> Raines v. Byrd, 521 U.S. 811 (1997), does not aid [the] argument that there is no standing here. In *Raines*, this Court held that six *individual Members* of Congress lacked standing to challenge the Line Item Veto Act. The Act, which gave the President authority to cancel certain spending and tax benefit measures after signing them into law, allegedly diluted the efficacy of the Congressmembers' votes. The "institutional injury" at issue, we reasoned, scarcely zeroed in on any individual Member. . . . None of the plaintiffs, therefore, could tenably claim a "personal stake" in the suit.

> In concluding that the individual Members lacked standing, the Court "attach[ed] some importance to the fact that [the *Raines* plaintiffs had] not been authorized to represent their respective Houses of Congress." "Indeed," the Court observed, "both houses actively oppose[d] their suit." Having failed to prevail in their own Houses, the suitors could not repair to the Judiciary to complain. The Arizona Legislature, in contrast, is an institutional plaintiff asserting an institutional injury, and it commenced this action after authorizing votes in both of its chambers. That "different circumstance[e]" was not sub judice in *Raines*.

Having distinguished *Raines*, the Court relied on Coleman v. Miller, 307 U.S. 433 (1939), and particularly on *Raines*'s description of *Coleman* as standing "for the proposition that legislatures whose votes would have been sufficient to defeat (or enact) a specific legislative Act have standing to sue if that legislative action goes into effect (or does not go into effect), on the ground that their votes have been completely nullified." That, said the Court, was precisely the effect of the amendment depriving the Arizona legislature of authority over congressional redistricting.[a]

Justices Scalia, Thomas, and Alito joined the Chief Justice's long dissent on the merits. "Nowhere," the Chief Justice said, "does the majority explain how a constitutional provision that vests redistricting authority in 'the Legislature' permits a State to wholly exclude 'the Legislature' from redistricting."

Additionally, Justice Scalia, joined by Justice Thomas, disputed justiciability:

> I do not believe that the question the Court answers is properly before us. Disputes between governmental branches or departments regarding the allocation of political power do not in my view constitute "cases" or "controversies" committed to our resolution by Art. III, § 2, of the Constitution. . . .
>
> We consult history and judicial tradition to determine whether [a dispute is justiciable]. What history and judicial tradition show is that courts do not resolve direct disputes between two political branches of the same government regarding their respective powers. Nearly every separation-of-powers case presents questions like the ones in this case. But we have *never* passed on a separation-of-powers question raised directly by a governmental subunit's complaint. We have *always* resolved those questions in the context of a private lawsuit in which the claim or defense depends on the constitutional validity of action by one of the governmental subunits that has caused a private party harm. . . .
>
> The sole precedent the Court relies upon is Coleman v. Miller, 307 U.S. 433 (1939). . . . But the reality is that the supposed holding of *Coleman* stands out like a sore thumb from the rest of our jurisprudence, which denies standing for intragovernmental disputes.[b]

Is the difference between *Raines* and *Arizona State Legislature* simply the fact of institutional authorization for the suit? Can the House of Representatives or the Senate become a plaintiff to challenge presidential action

---

[a]   In footnote 12 of its opinion, the Court noted:

The case before us does not touch or concern the question whether Congress has standing to bring a suit against the President. There is no federal analogue to Arizona's initiative power, and a suit between Congress and the President would raise separation-of-powers concerns absent here. The Court's standing analysis, we have noted, has been "especially rigorous when reaching the merits of the dispute would force [the Court] to decide whether an action taken by one of the other two branches of the Federal Government was unconstitutional." Raines v. Byrd, 521 U.S. 811, 819–20 (1997)

[b]   After reaching his conclusion on justiciability, Justice Scalia added:

Normally . . . I would express no opinion on the merits unless my vote was necessary to enable the Court to produce a judgment. In the present case, however, the majority's resolution of the merits question ("legislature" means "the people") is so outrageously wrong, so utterly devoid of textual or historic support, so flatly in contradiction of prior Supreme Court cases, so obviously the willful product of hostility to districting by state legislatures, that I cannot avoid adding my vote to the devastating dissent of the Chief Justice.—[Footnote by eds.]

whenever the body as a whole votes to do so? Or is "legislative standing" limited by the nature of the challenge that the legislature wishes to raise? Some light may be thrown on these questions by the standing-to-appeal cases in the next subsection.

Another potential distinction between *Raines* and *Arizona State Legislature* is that the former involved a dispute within the federal government, whereas the latter involved a dispute internal to a state. Perhaps the Supreme Court is more reluctant to address disputes involving other branches of the federal government than it is to address state disputes. Should it be?

Consider *Arizona State Legislature* from a different perspective. In an op-ed in the New York Times, Richard Pildes observed that establishing the Arizona Commission was based on "the need to take out of the hands of existing officeholders the power to control the rules under which they and their rivals compete for political power."[c] The pressure to redress this situation was similar, he said, to the pressure that led the Court to its famous "one person—one vote" ruling, namely to rectify "the self-interested temptations of power when legislators regulate the political process itself." The majority in *Arizona State Legislature* clearly was motivated by this policy in reaching its substantive conclusion. Is it likely that it also influenced the Court's holding on standing? Would there be other plaintiffs who could challenge the Arizona system if standing were denied to the Legislature? Should that matter?

4. STATE GOVERNMENT STANDING

There seems to be little question that states have standing to challenge federal actions that directly target states—for example, when the federal government imposes obligations on the states or cuts state funding. The Supreme Court has decided a number of important federalism cases in this posture. See, e.g., New York v. United States, 505 U.S. 144 (1992) (allowing the state of New York to challenge statutory provisions imposing obligations on states to dispose of radioactive waste). See generally Ann Woolhandler and Michael G. Collins, State Standing, 81 Va. L. Rev. 387 (1995); Stephen I. Vladeck, States' Rights and State Standing, 46 U. Rich. L. Rev. 845 (2012). The harder question is whether and to what extent states have standing to challenge federal government actions that merely *affect* them.

In Massachusetts v. EPA, 549 U.S. 497 (2007) (discussed in Subsection B), the Supreme Court (in a five-to-four decision) allowed the state of Massachusetts to challenge the EPA's decision that it did not have statutory authority to regulate greenhouse gas emissions. The Court found direct economic injury to Massachusetts as a coastal land owner, but the Court also said that Massachusetts had "quasi-sovereign interests" that it could seek to protect on behalf of its residents. The Court further observed that states are entitled to "special solicitude" in the standing analysis, although it did not spell out what that might mean. The degree to which states have standing where a similarly situated private party would not therefore remains murky.

---

c   Op-Ed, At the Supreme Court, A Win for Direct Democracy, N.Y. Times (June 29, 2015).

In an important lower court decision, Texas v. United States, 809 F.3d 134 (5th Cir. 2015), the U.S. Court of Appeals for the Fifth Circuit held that the state of Texas had standing to challenge the Obama Administration's Deferred Action for Parents of Americans and Lawful Permanent Residents (DAPA) program. Under DAPA, the Administration had extended lawful presence in the United States to approximately 4.3 million undocumented aliens and allowed them to seek federal work permits. Texas argued that DAPA violated federal statutory law and was inconsistent with the obligation of the Executive Branch to faithfully execute the law. In a two-to-one decision, the Fifth Circuit held that Texas had standing because Texas law allows anyone with federal work permits to seek a driver's license. Because Texas heavily subsidizes driver's licenses, DAPA would therefore have a meaningful financial impact on the state. The Fifth Circuit also relied heavily on *Massachusetts v. EPA* and its reference to the "special solicitude" owed to states in the standing analysis. Following the death of Justice Scalia in February 2016, the Supreme Court affirmed the Fifth Circuit by an equally divided vote, as usual without opinion. United States v. Texas, 579 U.S. ___, 136 S.Ct. 2271 (2016).

States have been allowed in some cases to sue the federal government or its officials to challenge federal preemption of state law when the preemption is alleged to invade certain "sovereign" prerogatives. See, e.g., Missouri v. Holland, 252 U.S. 416 (1920) (allowing a state to sue a federal game warden in an effort to enjoin enforcement of a federal migratory birds protection statute). See also Tara Leigh Grove, When Can a State Sue the United States?, 101 Cornell L. Rev. 851 (2016). The general ability of states to bring challenges to federal preemption, however, is unclear. States may of course defend state laws against federal preemption when the states are themselves sued, and they may appeal findings of federal preemption in such cases. But their standing to bring affirmative challenges against federal preemption of state law, absent direct economic injury or an interference with particular sovereign prerogatives, is unsettled.

Recently, one scholar called for expansion of state standing to circumstances where (i) the federal government has preempted state law and (ii) then failed to enforce adequately the preemptive legislation. See Jonathan R. Nash, Sovereign Preemption State Standing, 112 Nw. U. L. Rev. 201 (2017). What Nash calls "sovereign preemption state standing" is "neither purely economic nor purely sovereign; rather, it is a form of quasi-sovereign—or parens patriae—injury." Specifically, the state seeks to redress the injury to its citizens caused by federal preemption of state law without providing adequate enforcement of the federal alternative. Given the four-four split in *United States v. Texas*, acceptance of this kind of state standing remains very much in doubt.

5.   BIBLIOGRAPHY

For an argument that "Congress has the constitutional power to investigate the executive and judicially enforce subpoenas but that it cannot defend federal statutes in court," see Tara Leigh Grove and Neil Devins, Congress's (Limited) Power to Represent Itself in Court, 99 Cornell L. Rev. 571,

573 (2014). The authors contend that their conclusion is supported by historical practice:

> From 1789 until modern times, the House and the Senate asserted the power to conduct investigations and to litigate any disputes related to those investigations. By contrast, Congress historically delegated control over all other federal litigation to the executive. That was true even when the executive branch declined to defend a federal law. Although members of Congress occasionally participated as amici in such cases, neither Congress nor its components asserted the power to intervene on behalf of federal laws. This historical pattern remained unchanged until 1983, when the Supreme Court—with virtually no explanation—permitted intervention by the House and Senate counsel in *INS v. Chadha*.

Id. at 575. For a response to this article, see Jack Beermann, Congress's (Less) Limited Power to Represent Itself in Court: A Comment on Grove and Devins, 99 Cornell L. Rev. Online 166, 168 (2014) ("Contrary to Grove and Devins's view, there is no constitutional provision that can fairly be interpreted to prohibit Congress or one House of Congress from defending the constitutionality of a duly enacted federal statute."). For additional commentary on these issues, see Jonathan Remy Nash, A Functional Theory of Congressional Standing, 114 Mich. L. Rev. 339 (2015), which surveys past decisions and proposes a "functional" theory of congressional standing. Nash says that Congress should have standing in limited situations where litigation is needed to protect its primary functions of voting and information gathering. Allowing institutional standing in those cases, he argues, would broadly track the decided cases and bring a coherent theory to the field. For a broadly compatible approach, see Bradford C. Mank, Does a House of Congress Have Standing Over Appropriations?: The House of Representatives Challenges the Affordable Care Act, 19 J. of Const. L. 141 (2016), which argues that one House of Congress or a committee thereof should have standing to defend "core constitutional authority," such as the exclusivity of the appropriations process, but not merely to challenge implementation of federal statutes.

For another attempt to sort out this area, see Matthew I. Hall, Making Sense of Legislative Standing, 90 S. Calif. L. Rev. 1 (2016). Hall argues that legislators as individuals have standing when they can show individual injury and that legislatures as institutions have standing when they can show institutional injury. *Chadha* and *Arizona State Legislature* are examples. But legislatures do not have standing, Hall argues, to defend their "handiwork," enacted statutes, against constitutional attack.

For an argument that "States have broad standing to challenge federal statutes and regulations that preempt, or otherwise undermine the continued enforceability of, state law" but that they "do not have a special interest in the manner in which the federal executive enforces federal law," see Tara Leigh Grove, When Can a State Sue the United States?, 101 Cornell L. Rev. 851, 855 (2016). For more sympathetic consideration of a role for states in monitoring the Executive Branch, see Gillian E. Metzger, Federalism and Federal Agency Reform, 111 Colum. L. Rev. 1, 70–75 (2011).

SUBSECTION E. STANDING TO APPEAL

Before 2013, it is unlikely that any federal courts casebook would have included a section on "standing to appeal." The issue arises when the executive branch, which is charged with the duty of defending challenged statutes, acquiesces in a lower court's ruling that a statute is unconstitutional. In what circumstances and by whom could such a ruling be appealed to a higher court?

Variations on this question arose in the marriage-equality cases of 2013. The Supreme Court's answers were controversial and arguably inconsistent.

Hollingsworth v. Perry

Supreme Court of the United States, 2013.
570 U.S. 693.

■ CHIEF JUSTICE ROBERTS delivered the opinion of the Court.

The public is currently engaged in an active political debate over whether same-sex couples should be allowed to marry. That question has also given rise to litigation. In this case, petitioners, who oppose same-sex marriage, ask us to decide whether the Equal Protection Clause "prohibits the State of California from defining marriage as the union of a man and a woman." Respondents, same-sex couples who wish to marry, view the issue in somewhat different terms: For them, it is whether California—having previously recognized the right of same-sex couples to marry—may reverse that decision through a referendum.

Federal courts have authority under the Constitution to answer such questions only if necessary to do so in the course of deciding an actual "case" or "controversy." As used in the Constitution, those words do not include every sort of dispute, but only those "historically viewed as capable of resolution through the judicial process." Flast v. Cohen, 392 U.S. 83, 95 (1968). This is an essential limit on our power: It ensures that we act *as judges,* and do not engage in policymaking properly left to elected representatives.

For there to be such a case or controversy, it is not enough that the party invoking the power of the court have a keen interest in the issue. That party must also have "standing," which requires, among other things, that it have suffered a concrete and particularized injury. Because we find that petitioners do not have standing, we have no authority to decide this case on the merits, and neither did the Ninth Circuit.

I

In 2008, the California Supreme Court held that limiting the official designation of marriage to opposite-sex couples violated the equal protection clause of the California Constitution. In re Marriage Cases, 43 Calif. 4th 757 (2008). Later that year, California voters passed the ballot initiative at the center of this dispute, known as Proposition 8. That proposition amended the California Constitution to provide that "[o]nly marriage between a man and a woman is valid or recognized in California." Cal. Const., Art. I, § 7.5. Shortly thereafter, the California Supreme Court rejected a procedural challenge to the amendment, and held that the Proposition was properly enacted under California law. . . .

Respondents, two same-sex couples who wish to marry, filed suit in federal court, challenging Proposition 8 under the Due Process and Equal Protection Clauses of the Fourteenth Amendment to the Federal Constitution. The complaint named as defendants California's Governor, attorney general, and various other state and local officials responsible for enforcing California's marriage laws. Those officials refused to defend the law, although they have continued to enforce it throughout this litigation. The District Court allowed petitioners—the official proponents of the initiative—to intervene to defend it. After a 12-day bench trial, the District Court declared Proposition 8 unconstitutional, permanently enjoining the California officials named as defendants from enforcing the law, and "directing the official defendants that all persons under their control or supervision" shall not enforce it. Perry v. Schwarzenegger, 704 F. Supp. 2d 921, 1004 (N.D. Cal. 2010).

Those officials elected not to appeal the District Court order. When petitioners did, the Ninth Circuit asked them to address "why this appeal should not be dismissed for lack of Article III standing." After briefing and argument, the Ninth Circuit certified a question to the California Supreme Court:

> Whether under Article II, Section 8 of the California Constitution, or otherwise under California law, the official proponents of an initiative measure possess either a particularized interest in the initiative's validity or the authority to assert the State's interest in the initiative's validity, which would enable them to defend the constitutionality of the initiative upon its adoption or appeal a judgment invalidating the initiative, when the public officials charged with that duty refuse to do so.

The California Supreme Court agreed to decide the certified question, and answered in the affirmative. Without addressing whether the proponents have a particularized interest of their own in an initiative's validity, the court concluded that "[i]n a postelection challenge to a voter-approved initiative measure, the official proponents of the initiative are authorized under California law to appear and assert the state's interest in the initiative's validity and to appeal a judgment invalidating the measure when the public officials who ordinarily defend the measure or appeal such a judgment decline to do so." Perry v. Brown, 52 Cal. 4th 1116, 1127 (2011).

Relying on that answer, the Ninth Circuit concluded that petitioners had standing under federal law to defend the constitutionality of Proposition 8. California, it reasoned, " 'has standing to defend the constitutionality of its [laws],' " and States have the "prerogative, as independent sovereigns, to decide for themselves who may assert their interests." Perry v. Brown, 671 F.3d 1052, 1070, 1071 (9th Cir. 2012). "All a federal court need determine is that the state has suffered a harm sufficient to confer standing and that the party seeking to invoke the jurisdiction of the court is authorized by the state to represent its interest in remedying that harm." Id. at 1072.

On the merits, the Ninth Circuit affirmed the District Court. . . . We granted certiorari to review that determination, and directed that the parties also brief and argue "Whether petitioners have standing under Article III, § 2, of the Constitution in this case."

II

Article III of the Constitution confines the judicial power of federal courts to deciding actual "Cases" or "Controversies." One essential aspect of this requirement is that any person invoking the power of a federal court must demonstrate standing to do so. This requires the litigant to prove that he has suffered a concrete and particularized injury that is fairly traceable to the challenged conduct, and is likely to be redressed by a favorable judicial decision. Lujan v. Defenders of Wildlife, 504 U.S. 555, 560–61 (1992). . . .

Most standing cases consider whether a plaintiff has satisfied the requirement when filing suit, but Article III demands that an "actual controversy" persist throughout all stages of litigation. Already, LLC v. Nike, Inc., 568 U.S. 85, 90–91 (2013). That means that standing "must be met by persons seeking appellate review, just as it must be met by persons appearing in courts of first instance." Arizonans for Official English v. Arizona, 520 U.S. 43, 64 (1997). We therefore must decide whether petitioners had standing to appeal the District Court's order.

Respondents initiated this case in the District Court against the California officials responsible for enforcing Proposition 8. . . .

After the District Court declared Proposition 8 unconstitutional and enjoined the state officials named as defendants from enforcing it, however, the inquiry under Article III changed. Respondents no longer had any injury to redress—they had won—and the state officials chose not to appeal.

The only individuals who sought to appeal that order were petitioners, who had intervened in the District Court. But the District Court had not ordered them to do or refrain from doing anything. To have standing, a litigant must seek relief for an injury that affects him in a "personal and individual way." *Defenders of Wildlife*, 504 U.S. at 560 n.1. He must possess a "direct stake in the outcome" of the case. *Arizonans for Official English*, 530 U.S. at 64 (internal quotation marks omitted). Here, however, petitioners had no "direct stake" in the outcome of their appeal. Their only interest in having the District Court order reversed was to vindicate the constitutional validity of a generally applicable California law.

We have repeatedly held that such a "generalized grievance," no matter how sincere, is insufficient to confer standing. . . . Petitioners argue that the California Constitution and its election laws give them a " 'unique,' 'special,' and 'distinct' role in the initiative process—one 'involving both authority and responsibilities that differ from other supporters of the measure.' " True enough—but only when it comes to the process of enacting the law. Upon submitting the proposed initiative to the attorney general, petitioners became the official "proponents" of Proposition 8. Cal. Elec. Code Ann. § 342 (West 2003). As such, they were responsible for collecting the signatures required to qualify the measure for the ballot. After those signatures were collected, the proponents alone had the right to file the measure with election officials to put it on the ballot. Petitioners also possessed control over the arguments in favor of the initiative that would appear in California's ballot pamphlets.

But once Proposition 8 was approved by the voters, the measure became "a duly enacted constitutional amendment or statute." *Perry*, 52 Cal. 4th at 1147. Petitioners have no role—special or otherwise—in the enforcement of Proposition 8. They therefore have no "personal stake" in defending its enforcement that is distinguishable from the general interest of every citizen of California. . . .

III

A

Without a judicially cognizable interest of their own, petitioners attempt to invoke that of someone else. They assert that even if *they* have no cognizable interest in appealing the District Court's judgment, the State of California does, and they may assert that interest on the State's behalf. It is, however, a "fundamental restriction on our authority" that "[i]n the ordinary course, a litigant must assert his or her own legal rights and interests, and cannot rest a claim to relief on the legal rights or interests of third parties." Powers v. Ohio, 499 U.S. 400, 410 (1991). There are "certain, limited exceptions" to that rule.[a] But even when we have allowed litigants to assert the interests of others, the litigants themselves still "must have suffered an injury in fact, thus giving [them] a sufficiently concrete interest in the outcome of the issue in dispute." Id. at 411 (internal quotation marks omitted).

In *Diamond v. Charles,* for example, we refused to allow Diamond, a pediatrician engaged in private practice in Illinois, to defend the constitutionality of the State's abortion law. In that case, a group of physicians filed a constitutional challenge to the Illinois statute in federal court. The State initially defended the law, and Diamond, a professed "conscientious object[or] to abortions," intervened to defend it alongside the State.

After the Seventh Circuit affirmed a permanent injunction against enforcing several provisions of the law, the State chose not to pursue an

---

[a]   The general rule against raising someone else's rights is covered in the materials on third-party standing in Section 3, Subsection A of this Chapter.—[Footnote by eds.]

appeal to this Court. But when Diamond did, the state attorney general filed a " 'letter of interest,' " explaining that the State's interest in the proceeding was " 'essentially co-terminous with the position on the issues set forth by [Diamond].' " 476 U.S. at 61. That was not enough, we held, to allow the appeal to proceed. . . . As the Court explained, "[e]ven if there were circumstances in which a private party would have standing to defend the constitutionality of a challenged statute, this [was] not one of them," because Diamond was not able to assert an injury in fact of his own. Id. at 65 (footnote omitted). And without "any judicially cognizable interest," Diamond could not "maintain the litigation abandoned by the State." Id. at 71.

For the reasons we have explained, petitioners have likewise not suffered an injury in fact, and therefore would ordinarily have no standing to assert the State's interests.

B

Petitioners contend that this case is different, because the California Supreme Court has determined that they are "authorized under California law to appear and assert the state's interest" in the validity of Proposition 8. *Perry*, 52 Cal.4th at 1127. The court below agreed: "All a federal court need determine is that the state has suffered a harm sufficient to confer standing and that the party seeking to invoke the jurisdiction of the court is authorized by the state to represent its interest in remedying that harm." 671 F.3d at 1072. As petitioners put it, they "need no more show a personal injury, separate from the State's indisputable interest in the validity of its law, than would California's Attorney General or did the legislative leaders held to have standing in Karcher v. May, 484 U.S. 72 (1987)."

In *Karcher,* we held that two New Jersey state legislators—Speaker of the General Assembly Alan Karcher and President of the Senate Carmen Orechio—could intervene in a suit against the State to defend the constitutionality of a New Jersey law, after the New Jersey attorney general had declined to do so. "Since the New Jersey Legislature had authority under state law to represent the State's interests in both the District Court and the Court of Appeals," we held that the Speaker and the President, in their official capacities, could vindicate that interest in federal court on the legislature's behalf.

Far from supporting petitioners' standing, however, *Karcher* is compelling precedent against it. The legislators in that case intervened in their official capacities as Speaker and President of the legislature. No one doubts that a State has a cognizable interest "in the continued enforceability" of its laws that is harmed by a judicial decision declaring a state law unconstitutional. Maine v. Taylor, 477 U.S. 131, 137 (1986). To vindicate that interest or any other, a State must be able to designate agents to represent it in federal court. That agent is typically the State's attorney general. But state law may provide for other officials to speak for the State in federal court, as New Jersey law did for the State's presiding legislative officers in *Karcher*.

What is significant about *Karcher* is what happened after the Court of Appeals decision in that case. Karcher and Orechio lost their positions as Speaker and President, but nevertheless sought to appeal to this Court. We held that they could not do so. We explained that while they were able to participate in the lawsuit in their official capacities as presiding officers of the incumbent legislature, "since they no longer hold those offices, they lack authority to pursue this appeal." Id. at 81.

The point of *Karcher* is not that a State could authorize *private parties* to represent its interests; Karcher and Orechio were permitted to proceed only because they were state officers, acting in an official capacity. As soon as they lost that capacity, they lost standing. Petitioners here hold no office and have always participated in this litigation solely as private parties. . . .

C

Both petitioners and respondents seek support from dicta in Arizonans for Official English v. Arizona, 520 U.S. 43 (1997). The plaintiff in *Arizonans for Official English* filed a constitutional challenge to an Arizona ballot initiative declaring English " 'the official language of the State of Arizona.' " After the District Court declared the initiative unconstitutional, Arizona's Governor announced that she would not pursue an appeal. Instead, the principal sponsor of the ballot initiative—the Arizonans for Official English Committee—sought to defend the measure in the Ninth Circuit. Analogizing the sponsors to the Arizona Legislature, the Ninth Circuit held that the Committee was "qualified to defend [the initiative] on appeal," and affirmed the District Court. Id. at 58, 61.

Before finding the case mooted by other events, this Court expressed "grave doubts" about the Ninth Circuit's standing analysis. Id. at 66. We reiterated that "[s]tanding to defend on appeal in the place of an original defendant . . . demands that the litigant possess 'a direct stake in the outcome.' " Id. at 64 (quoting *Diamond,* 476 U.S. at 62). We recognized that a legislator authorized by state law to represent the State's interest may satisfy standing requirements, as in *Karcher,* but noted that the Arizona committee and its members were "not elected representatives, and we [we]re aware of no Arizona law appointing initiative sponsors as agents of the people of Arizona to defend, in lieu of public officials, the constitutionality of initiatives made law of the State." *Arizonans for Official English,* 520 U.S. at 65.

Petitioners argue that, by virtue of the California Supreme Court's decision, they *are* authorized to act " 'as agents of the people' of California." But that Court never described petitioners as "agents of the people," or of anyone else. Nor did the Ninth Circuit. The Ninth Circuit asked—and the California Supreme Court answered—only whether petitioners had "the authority to assert the State's interest in the initiative's valid-ity." 52 Cal. 4th at 1124. All that the California Supreme Court decision stands for is that, so far as California is concerned, petitioners may argue in defense of Proposition 8. This "does not mean that the proponents be-come de facto public officials"; the authority they enjoy is "simply the authority to participate as parties in a court action and to assert legal arguments in defense of the state's interest in the validity of the initiative measure." Id. at 1159. That interest is by definition a generalized one, and it is precisely because proponents assert such an interest that they lack standing under our precedents.

And petitioners are plainly not agents of the State—"formal" or oth-erwise. . . . [T]he most basic features of an agency relationship are missing here. Agency requires more than mere authorization to assert a particular interest. "An essential element of agency is the principal's right to control the agent's actions." 1 Restatement (Third) of Agency § 1.01, Comment f (2005) (hereinafter Restatement). Yet petitioners an-swer to no one; they decide for themselves, with no review, what arguments to make and how to make them. Unlike California's attorney general, they are not elected at regular intervals—or elected at all. No provision provides for their removal. . . . "If the relationship between two persons is one of agency . . . , the agent owes a fiduciary obligation to the principal." 1 Restatement § 1.01, Comment e. But petitioners owe noth-ing of the sort to the people of California. Unlike California's elected officials, they have taken no oath of office. . . . They are free to pursue a purely ideological commitment to the law's constitutionality without the need to take cognizance of resource constraints, changes in public opin-ion, or potential ramifications for other state priorities.

Finally, the California Supreme Court stated that "[t]he question of who should bear responsibility for any attorney fee award . . . is *entirely distinct* from the question" before it. 52 Cal. 4th at 1161 (emphasis added). But it is hornbook law that "a principal has a duty to indemnify the agent against expenses and other losses incurred by the agent in de-fending against actions brought by third parties if the agent acted with actual authority in taking the action challenged by the third party's suit." 2 Restatement § 8.14, Comment d. If the issue of fees is entirely distinct from the authority question, then authority cannot be based on agency.

Neither the California Supreme Court nor the Ninth Circuit ever de-scribed the proponents as agents of the State, and they plainly do not qualify as such.

IV

[We do not] question California's sovereign right to maintain an ini-tiative process, or the right of initiative proponents to defend their initiatives in California courts, where Article III does not apply. But as the dissent acknowledges, standing in federal court is a question of fed-eral law, not state law. And no matter its reasons, the fact that a State thinks a private party should have standing to seek relief for a generalized grievance cannot override our settled law to the contrary. . . .

We have never before upheld the standing of a private party to defend the constitutionality of a state statute when state officials have chosen not to. We decline to do so for the first time here. . . . The judgment of the Ninth Circuit is vacated, and the case is remanded with instructions to dismiss the appeal for lack of jurisdiction.

■ JUSTICE KENNEDY, with whom JUSTICE THOMAS, JUSTICE ALITO, and JUSTICE SOTOMAYOR join, dissenting.

The Court's opinion is correct to state, and the Supreme Court of California was careful to acknowledge, that a proponent's standing to defend an initiative in federal court is a question of federal law. Proper resolution of the justiciability question requires, in this case, a threshold determination of state law. The state-law question is how California defines and elaborates the status and authority of an initiative's proponents who seek to intervene in court to defend the initiative after its adoption by the electorate. Those state-law issues have been addressed in a meticulous and unanimous opinion by the Supreme Court of California.

Under California law, a proponent has the authority to appear in court and assert the State's interest in defending an enacted initiative when the public officials charged with that duty refuse to do so. The State deems such an appearance essential to the integrity of its initiative process. Yet the Court today concludes that this state-defined status and this state-conferred right fall short of meeting federal requirements because the proponents cannot point to a formal delegation of authority that tracks the requirements of the Restatement of Agency. But the State Supreme Court's definition of proponents' powers is binding on this Court. And that definition is fully sufficient to establish the standing and adversity that are requisites for justiciability under Article III of the United States Constitution. . . .

I

As the Court explains, the State of California sustained a concrete injury, sufficient to satisfy the requirements of Article III, when a United States District Court nullified a portion of its State Constitution. To determine whether justiciability continues in appellate proceedings after the State Executive acquiesced in the District Court's adverse judgment, it is necessary to ascertain what persons, if any, have "authority under state law to represent the State's interests" in federal court. Karcher v. May, 484 U.S. 72, 82 (1987).

As the Court notes, the California Elections Code does not on its face prescribe in express terms the duties or rights of proponents once the initiative becomes law. If that were the end of the matter, the Court's analysis would have somewhat more force. But it is not the end of the matter. It is for California, not this Court, to determine whether and to what extent the Elections Code provisions are instructive and relevant in determining the authority of proponents to assert the State's interest in postenactment judicial proceedings. And it is likewise not for this Court to say that a State must determine the substance and meaning of its laws by statute, or by judicial decision, or by a combination of the two. That, too, is for the State to decide.

This Court, in determining the substance of state law, is "bound by a state court's construction of a state statute." Wisconsin v. Mitchell, 508 U.S. 476, 483 (1993). And the Supreme Court of California, in response to the certified question submitted to it in this case, has determined that State Elections Code provisions directed to initiative proponents do inform and instruct state law respecting the rights and status of proponents in postelection judicial proceedings. Here, in reliance on these statutes and the California Constitution, the State Supreme Court has held that proponents do have authority "under California law to appear and assert the state's interest in the initiative's validity and appeal a judgment invalidating the measure when the public officials who ordinarily defend the measure or appeal such a judgment decline to do so." Perry v. Brown, 52 Cal. 4th 1116, 1127 (2011).

. . . [I]n California, proponents play a "unique role . . . in the initiative process." Id. at 1152. They "have a unique relationship to the voter-approved measure that makes them especially likely to be reliable and vigorous advocates for the measure and to be so viewed by those whose votes secured the initiative's enactment into law." Id. Proponents' authority under state law is not a contrivance. It is not a fictional construct. It is the product of the California Constitution and the California Elections Code. There is no basis for this Court to set aside the California Supreme Court's determination of state law. . . .

II

A

The Court concludes that proponents lack sufficient ties to the state government. It notes that they "are not elected," "answer to no one," and lack " 'a fiduciary obligation' " to the State. But what the Court deems deficiencies in the proponents' connection to the State government, the State Supreme Court saw as essential qualifications to defend the initiative system. The very object of the initiative system is to establish a lawmaking process that does not depend upon state officials. In California, the popular initiative is necessary to implement "the theory that all power of government ultimately resides in the people." Perry, 52 Cal. 4th at 1140 (internal quotation marks omitted). The right to adopt initiatives has been described by the California courts as "one of the most precious rights of [the State's] democratic process." Id. (internal quotation marks omitted). That historic role for the initiative system "grew out of dissatisfaction with the then governing public officials and a widespread belief that the people had lost control of the political process." Id. The initiative's "primary purpose," then, "was to afford the people the ability to propose and to adopt constitutional amendments or statutory provisions that their elected public officials had refused or declined to adopt." Id.

The California Supreme Court has determined that this purpose is undermined if the very officials the initiative process seeks to circumvent are the only parties who can defend an enacted initiative when it is challenged in a legal proceeding. Giving the Governor and attorney general this de facto veto will erode one of the cornerstones of the State's governmental structure. . . . As a consequence, California finds it necessary to vest the responsibility and right to defend a voter-approved initiative in the initiative's proponents when the State Executive declines to do so. . . .

B

Contrary to the Court's suggestion, this Court's precedents do not indicate that a formal agency relationship is necessary. In Karcher v. May, 484 U.S. 72 (1987), the Speaker of the New Jersey Assembly (Karcher) and President of the New Jersey Senate (Orechio) intervened in support of a school moment-of-silence law that the State's Governor and attorney general declined to defend in court. In considering the question of standing, the Court looked to New Jersey law to determine whether Karcher and Orechio "had authority under state law to represent the State's interest in both the District Court and Court of Appeals." Id. at 82. The Court concluded that they did. Because the "New Jersey Supreme Court ha[d] granted applications of the Speaker of the General Assembly and the President of the Senate to intervene as parties-respondent on behalf of the legislature in defense of a legislative enactment," the *Karcher* Court held that standing had been proper in the District Court and Court of Appeals. Id. By the time the case arrived in this Court, Karcher and Orechio had lost their presiding legislative offices, without which they lacked the authority to represent the State under New Jersey law. This, the Court held, deprived them of standing. Here, by contrast, proponents' authority under California law is not contingent on officeholder status, so their standing is unaffected by the fact that they "hold no office" in California's Government.

Arizonans for Official English v. Arizona, 520 U.S. 43 (1997), is consistent with the premises of this dissent, not with the rationale of the Court's opinion. There, the Court noted its serious doubts as to the aspiring defenders' standing because there was "no Arizona law appointing initiative sponsors as agents of the people of Arizona to defend, in lieu of public officials, the constitutionality of initiatives made law of the State." Id. at 65. The Court did use the word "agents"; but, read in context, it is evident that the Court's intention was not to demand a formal agency relationship in compliance with the Restatement. Rather, the Court used the term as shorthand for a party whom "state law authorizes" to "represent the State's interests" in court.

. . . Although [the Ninth Circuit] panel divided on the proper resolution of the merits of this case, it was unanimous in concluding that proponents satisfy the requirements of Article III. Its central premise, ignored by the Court today, was that the "State's highest court [had] held that California law provides precisely what the *Arizonans* Court found lacking in Arizona law: it confers on the official proponents of an initiative the authority to assert the State's interests in defending the constitutionality of that initiative, where state officials who would ordinarily assume that responsibility choose not to do so." 671 F.3d at 1072. The Court of Appeals and the State Supreme Court did not ignore *Arizonans for Official English*; they were faithful to it. . . .

III

There is much irony in the Court's approach to justiciability in this case. A prime purpose of justiciability is to ensure vigorous advocacy, yet the Court insists upon litigation conducted by state officials whose preference is to lose the case. The doctrine is meant to ensure that courts are responsible and constrained in their power, but the Court's opinion today means that a single district court can make a decision with far-reaching effects that cannot be reviewed. And rather than honor the principle that justiciability exists to allow disputes of public policy to be resolved by the political process rather than the courts, here the Court refuses to allow a State's authorized representatives to defend the outcome of a democratic election. . . .

In the end, what the Court fails to grasp or accept is the basic premise of the initiative process. And it is this. The essence of democracy is that the right to make law rests in the people and flows to the government, not the other way around. Freedom resides first in the people without need of a grant from government. The California initiative process embodies these principles and has done so for over a century. "Through the structure of its government, and the character of those who exercise government authority, a State defines itself as sovereign." *Gregory v. Ashcroft*, 501 U.S. 452, 460 (1991). In California and the 26 other States that permit initiatives and popular referendums, the people have exercised their own inherent sovereign right to govern themselves. The Court today frustrates that choice by nullifying, for failure to comply with the Restatement of Agency, a State Supreme Court decision holding that state law authorizes an enacted initiative's proponents to defend the law if and when the State's usual legal advocates decline to do so. The Court's opinion fails to abide by precedent and misapplies basic principles of justiciability. Those errors necessitate this respectful dissent.

United States v. Windsor

Supreme Court of the United States, 2013.
570 U.S. 744.

■ JUSTICE KENNEDY delivered the opinion of the Court.

Two women then resident in New York were married in a lawful ceremony in Ontario, Canada, in 2007. Edith Windsor and Thea Spyer returned to their home in New York City. When Spyer died in 2009, she left her entire estate to Windsor. Windsor sought to claim the estate tax exemption for surviving spouses. She was barred from doing so, however, by a federal law, the Defense of Marriage Act, which excludes a same-sex partner from the definition of "spouse" as that term is used in federal statutes. Windsor paid the taxes but filed suit to challenge the constitutionality of this provision. The United States District Court and the Court of Appeals ruled that this portion of the statute is unconstitutional and ordered the United States to pay Windsor a refund. This Court granted certiorari and now affirms the judgment in Windsor's favor.

I

In 1996, as some States were beginning to consider the concept of same-sex marriage, and before any State had acted to permit it, Congress enacted the Defense of Marriage Act (DOMA). DOMA contains two operative sections: Section 2, which has not been challenged here, allows States to refuse to recognize same-sex marriages performed under the laws of other States. See 28 U.S.C. § 1738C.

Section 3 is at issue here. It amends the Dictionary Act in Title 1, § 7, of the United States Code to provide a federal definition of "marriage" and "spouse." Section 3 of DOMA provides as follows:

> In determining the meaning of any Act of Congress, or of any ruling, regulation, or interpretation of the various administrative bureaus and agencies of the United States, the word "marriage" means only a legal union between one man and one woman as husband and wife, and the word "spouse" refers only to a person of the opposite sex who is a husband or a wife.

The definitional provision does not by its terms forbid States from enacting laws permitting same-sex marriages or civil unions or providing state benefits to residents in that status. The enactment's comprehensive definition of marriage for purposes of all federal statutes and other regulations or directives covered by its terms, however, does control over 1,000 federal laws in which marital or spousal status is addressed as a matter of federal law.

Edith Windsor and Thea Spyer met in New York City in 1963 and began a long-term relationship. Windsor and Spyer registered as domestic partners when New York City gave that right to same-sex couples in 1993. Concerned about Spyer's health, the couple made the 2007 trip to Canada for their marriage, but they continued to reside in New York City. The State of New York deems their Ontario marriage to be a valid one.

Spyer died in February 2009, and left her entire estate to Windsor. Because DOMA denies federal recognition to same-sex spouses, Windsor did not qualify for the marital exemption from the federal estate tax, which excludes from taxation "any interest in property which passes or has passed from the decedent to his surviving spouse." 26 U.S.C. § 2056(a). Windsor paid $363,053 in estate taxes and sought a refund.

The Internal Revenue Service denied the refund, concluding that, under DOMA, Windsor was not a "surviving spouse." Windsor commenced this refund suit in the United States District Court for the Southern District of New York. She contended that DOMA violates the guarantee of equal protection, as applied to the Federal Government through the Fifth Amendment.

While the tax refund suit was pending, the Attorney General of the United States notified the Speaker of the House of Representatives, pursuant to 28 U.S.C. § 530D, that the Department of Justice would no longer defend the constitutionality of DOMA's § 3. Noting that "the Department has previously defended DOMA against ... challenges involving legally married same-sex couples," the Attorney General informed Congress that "the President has concluded that given a number of factors, including a documented history of discrimination, classifications based on sexual orientation should be subject to a heightened standard of scrutiny." The Department of Justice has submitted many § 530D letters over the years refusing to defend laws it deems unconstitutional, when, for instance, a federal court has rejected the Government's defense of a statute and has issued a judgment against it. This case is unusual, however, because the § 530D letter was not preceded by an adverse judgment. The letter instead reflected the Executive's own conclusion, relying on a definition still being debated and considered in the courts, that heightened equal protection scrutiny should apply to laws that classify on the basis of sexual orientation.

Although "the President ... instructed the Department not to defend the statute in *Windsor*," he also decided "that Section 3 will continue to be enforced by the Executive Branch" and that the United States had an "interest in providing Congress a full and fair opportunity to participate in the litigation of those cases." The stated rationale for this dual-track procedure (determination of unconstitutionality coupled with ongoing enforcement) was to "recogniz[e] the judiciary as the final arbiter of the constitutional claims raised."

In response to the notice from the Attorney General, the Bipartisan Legal Advisory Group (BLAG) of the House of Representatives voted to intervene in the litigation to defend the constitutionality of § 3 of DOMA. . . .

On the merits of the tax refund suit, the District Court ruled against the United States. It held that § 3 of DOMA is unconstitutional and ordered the Treasury to refund the tax with interest. Both the Justice Department and BLAG filed notices of appeal, and the Solicitor General filed a petition for certiorari before judgment. Before this Court acted on the petition, the Court of Appeals for the Second Circuit affirmed the District Court's judgment. It applied heightened scrutiny to classifications based on sexual orientation, as both the Department and Windsor had urged. The United States has not complied with the judgment. Windsor has not received her refund, and the Executive Branch continues to enforce § 3 of DOMA.

In granting certiorari on the question of the constitutionality of § 3 of DOMA, the Court requested argument on two additional questions: whether the United States' agreement with Windsor's legal position precludes further review and whether BLAG has standing to appeal the case. All parties agree that the Court has jurisdiction to decide this case; and, with the case in that framework, the Court appointed Professor Vicki Jackson as amicus curiae to argue the position that the Court lacks jurisdiction to hear the dispute. She has ably discharged her duties. . . .

II

It is appropriate to begin by addressing whether either the Government or BLAG, or both of them, were entitled to appeal to the Court of Appeals and later to seek certiorari and appear as parties here.

There is no dispute that when this case was in the District Court it presented a concrete disagreement between opposing parties, a dispute suitable for judicial resolution. . . . Windsor suffered a redressable injury when she was required to pay estate taxes from which, in her view, she was exempt but for the alleged invalidity of § 3 of DOMA.

The decision of the Executive not to defend the constitutionality of § 3 in court while continuing to deny refunds and to assess deficiencies does introduce a complication. Even though the Executive's current position was announced before the District Court entered its judgment, the Government's agreement with Windsor's position would not have deprived the District Court of jurisdiction to entertain and resolve the refund suit; for her injury (failure to obtain a refund allegedly required by law) was concrete, persisting, and unredressed. The Government's position—agreeing with Windsor's legal contention but refusing to give it effect—meant that there was a justiciable controversy between the parties, despite what the claimant would find to be an inconsistency in that stance. Windsor, the Government, BLAG, and the amicus appear to agree upon that point. The disagreement is over the standing of the parties, or aspiring parties, to take an appeal in the Court of Appeals and to appear as parties in further proceedings in this Court.

The amicus's position is that, given the Government's concession that § 3 is unconstitutional, once the District Court ordered the refund the case should have ended; and the amicus argues the Court of Appeals should have dismissed the appeal. The amicus submits that once the President agreed with Windsor's legal position and the District Court issued its judgment, the parties were no longer adverse. From this standpoint the United States was a prevailing party below, just as Windsor was. Accordingly, the amicus reasons, it is inappropriate for this Court to grant certiorari and proceed to rule on the merits; for the United States seeks no redress from the judgment entered against it.

This position, however, elides the distinction between two principles: the jurisdictional requirements of Article III and the prudential limits on its exercise. See Warth v. Seldin, 422 U.S. 490, 498 (1975). The latter are "essentially matters of judicial self-governance." Id. at 500. . . . Rules of prudential standing [are] flexible "rule[s] . . . of federal appellate practice," Deposit Guaranty Nat. Bank v. Roper, 445 U.S. 326, 333 (1980), designed to protect the courts from "decid[ing] abstract questions of wide public significance even [when] other governmental institutions may be more competent to address the questions and even though judicial intervention may be unnecessary to protect individual rights." *Warth,* 422 U.S. at 500.

In this case the United States retains a stake sufficient to support Article III jurisdiction on appeal and in proceedings before this Court. The judgment in question orders the United States to pay Windsor the refund she seeks. An order directing the Treasury to pay money is "a real and immediate economic injury," Hein v. Freedom From Religion Foundation, Inc., 551 U.S. 587, 599 (2007), indeed as real and immediate as an order directing an individual to pay a tax. That the Executive may welcome this order to pay the refund if it is accompanied by the constitutional ruling it wants does not eliminate the injury to the national Treasury if payment is made, or to the taxpayer if it is not. The judgment orders the United States to pay money that it would not disburse but for the court's order. The Government of the United States has a valid legal argument that it is injured even if the Executive disagrees with § 3 of DOMA, which results in Windsor's liability for the tax. Windsor's ongoing claim for funds that the United States refuses to pay thus establishes a controversy sufficient for Article III jurisdiction. It would be a different case if the Executive had taken the further step of paying Windsor the refund to which she was entitled under the District Court's ruling.

This Court confronted a comparable case in INS v. Chadha, 462 U.S. 919 (1983). A statute by its terms allowed one House of Congress to order the Immigration and Naturalization Service (INS) to deport the respondent Chadha. There, as here, the Executive determined that the statute was unconstitutional, and "the INS presented the Executive's views on the constitutionality of the House action to the Court of Appeals." Id. at 930. The INS, however, continued to abide by the statute, and "the INS brief to the Court of Appeals did not alter the agency's decision to comply with the House action ordering deportation of Chadha." Id. This Court held "that the INS was sufficiently aggrieved by the Court of Appeals decision prohibiting it from taking action it would otherwise take," id. regardless of whether the agency welcomed the judgment. . . . In short, even where "the Government largely agree[s] with the opposing party on the merits of the controversy," there is sufficient adverseness and an "adequate basis for jurisdiction in the fact that the Government intended to enforce the challenged law against that party." Id. at 940 n.12.

It is true that "[a] party who receives all that he has sought generally is not aggrieved by the judgment affording the relief and cannot appeal from it." *Roper,* 445 U.S. at 333. But this rule "does not have its source in the jurisdictional limitations of Art. III. In an appropriate case, appeal may be permitted . . . at the behest of the party who has prevailed on the merits, so long as that party retains a stake in the appeal satisfying the requirements of Art. III." *Roper,* 445 U.S. at 333–34.

While these principles suffice to show that this case presents a justiciable controversy under Article III, the prudential problems inherent in the Executive's unusual position require some further discussion. The Executive's agreement with Windsor's legal argument raises the risk that instead of a " 'real, earnest and vital controversy,' " the Court faces a "friendly, non-adversary, proceeding . . . [in which] 'a party beaten in the legislature [seeks to] transfer to the courts an inquiry as to the constitutionality of the legislative act.' " Ashwander v. TVA, 297 U.S. 288, 346 (1936) (Brandeis, J., concurring) (quoting Chicago & Grand Trunk R. Co. v. Wellman, 143 U.S. 339, 345 (1892)). Even when Article III permits the exercise of federal jurisdiction, prudential considerations demand that the Court insist upon "that concrete adverseness which sharpens the presentation of issues upon which the court so largely depends for illumination of difficult constitutional questions." Baker v. Carr, 369 U.S. 186, 204 (1962).

There are, of course, reasons to hear a case and issue a ruling even when one party is reluctant to prevail in its position. Unlike Article III requirements—which must be satisfied by the parties before judicial consideration is appropriate—the relevant prudential factors that counsel against hearing this case are subject to "countervailing considerations [that] may outweigh the concerns underlying the usual reluctance to exert judicial power." *Warth,* 422 U.S. at 500–01. One consideration is the extent to which adversarial presentation of the issues is assured by the participation of amici curiae prepared to defend with vigor the constitutionality of the legislative act. With respect to this prudential aspect of standing as well, the *Chadha* Court encountered a similar situation. It noted that "there may be prudential, as opposed to Art. III, concerns about sanctioning the adjudication of [this case] in the absence of any participant supporting the validity of [the statute]. The Court of Appeals properly dispelled any such concerns by inviting and accepting briefs from both Houses of Congress." 462 U.S. at 940. *Chadha* was not an anomaly in this respect. The Court adopts the practice of entertaining arguments made by an amicus when the Solicitor General confesses error with respect to a judgment below, even if the confession is in effect an admission that an Act of Congress is unconstitutional. See, e.g., Dickerson v. United States, 530 U.S. 428 (2000).

In the case now before the Court the attorneys for BLAG present a substantial argument for the constitutionality of § 3 of DOMA. BLAG's sharp adversarial presentation of the issues satisfies the prudential concerns that otherwise might counsel against hearing an appeal from a decision with which the principal parties agree. Were this Court to hold that prudential rules require it to dismiss the case, and, in consequence, that the Court of Appeals erred in failing to dismiss it as well, extensive litigation would ensue. The district courts in 94 districts throughout the Nation would be without precedential guidance not only in tax refund suits but also in cases involving the whole of DOMA's sweep involving over 1,000 federal statutes and a myriad of federal regulations. . . . In these unusual and urgent circumstances, the very term "prudential" counsels that it is a proper exercise of the Court's responsibility to take jurisdiction. For these reasons, the prudential and Article III requirements are met here; and, as a consequence, the Court need not decide whether BLAG would have standing to challenge the District Court's ruling and its affirmance in the Court of Appeals on BLAG's own authority.

The Court's conclusion that this petition may be heard on the merits does not imply that no difficulties would ensue if this were a common practice in ordinary cases. The Executive's failure to defend the constitutionality of an Act of Congress based on a constitutional theory not yet established in judicial decisions has created a procedural dilemma. On the one hand, as noted, the Government's agreement with Windsor raises questions about the propriety of entertaining a suit in which it seeks affirmance of an order invalidating a federal law and ordering the United States to pay money. On the other hand, if the Executive's agreement with a plaintiff that a law is unconstitutional is enough to preclude judicial review, then the Supreme Court's primary role in determining the constitutionality of a law that has inflicted real injury on a plaintiff who has brought a justiciable legal claim would become only secondary to the President's. This would undermine the clear dictate of the separation-of-powers principle that "when an Act of Congress is alleged to conflict with the Constitution, '[i]t is emphatically the province and duty of the judicial department to say what the law is.' " Zivotofsky v. Clinton, 566 U.S. 189, 196 (2012) (quoting Marbury v. Madison, 5 U.S. (1 Cranch) 137, 177 (1803)). Similarly, with respect to the legislative power, when Congress has passed a statute and a President has signed it, it poses grave challenges to the separation of powers for the Executive at a particular moment to be able to nullify Congress's enactment solely on its own initiative and without any determination from the Court.

The Court's jurisdictional holding, it must be underscored, does not mean the arguments for dismissing this dispute on prudential grounds lack substance. Yet the difficulty the Executive faces should be acknowledged. When the Executive makes a principled determination that a statute is unconstitutional, it faces a difficult choice. Still, there is no suggestion here that it is appropriate for the Executive as a matter of course to challenge statutes in the judicial forum rather than making the case to Congress for their amendment or repeal. The integrity of the political process would be at risk if difficult constitutional issues were simply referred to the Court as a routine exercise. But this case is not routine. And the capable defense of the law by BLAG ensures that these prudential issues do not cloud the merits question, which is one of immediate importance to the Federal Government and to hundreds of thousands of persons. These circumstances support the Court's decision to proceed to the merits.

[In the remainder of its opinion, the Court examined DOMA and found that it lacked any legitimate purpose sufficient to outweigh "the purpose and effect to disparage and to injure those whom the State, by its marriage laws, sought to protect in personhood and dignity" and was therefore unconstitutional. The Court purported not to say whether a state statute similarly defining the institution of marriage would also be unconstitutional.]

The judgment of the Court of Appeals for the Second Circuit is affirmed.

■ JUSTICE SCALIA, with whom JUSTICE THOMAS joins, and with whom THE CHIEF JUSTICE joins as to Part I, dissenting.

This case is about power in several respects. It is about the power of our people to govern themselves, and the power of this Court to pronounce the law. Today's opinion aggrandizes the latter, with the predictable consequence of diminishing the former. We have no power to decide this case. And even if we did, we have no power under the Constitution to invalidate this democratically adopted legislation. The Court's errors on both points spring forth from the same diseased root: an exalted conception of the role of this institution in America.

I

A

The Court is eager—*hungry*—to tell everyone its view of the legal question at the heart of this case. Standing in the way is an obstacle, a technicality of little interest to anyone but the people of We the People, who created it as a barrier against judges' intrusion into their lives. They gave judges, in Article III, only the "judicial Power," a power to decide not abstract questions but real, concrete "Cases" and "Controversies." Yet the plaintiff and the Government agree entirely on what should happen in this lawsuit. They agree that the court below got it right; and they agreed in the court below that the court below that one got it right as well. What, then, are we *doing* here?

The answer lies at the heart of the jurisdictional portion of today's opinion, where a single sentence lays bare the majority's vision of our role. The Court says that we have the power to decide this case because if we did not, then our "primary role in determining the constitutionality of a law" (at least one that "has inflicted real injury on a plaintiff") would "become only secondary to the President's." But wait, the reader wonders—Windsor won below, and so *cured* her injury, and the President was glad to see it. True, says the majority, but judicial review must march on regardless, lest we "undermine the clear dictate of the separation-of-powers principle that when an Act of Congress is alleged to conflict with the Constitution, it is emphatically the province and duty of the judicial department to say what the law is." (Internal quotation marks and brackets omitted.)

That is jaw-dropping. It is an assertion of judicial supremacy over the people's Representatives in Congress and the Executive. It envisions a Supreme Court standing (or rather enthroned) at the apex of government, empowered to decide all constitutional questions, always and everywhere "primary" in its role.

This image of the Court would have been unrecognizable to those who wrote and ratified our national charter. . . . [W]e are quite forbidden to say what the law is whenever (as today's opinion asserts) " 'an Act of Congress is alleged to conflict with the Constitution.' " We can do so only when that allegation will determine the outcome of a lawsuit, and is contradicted by the other party. The "judicial Power" is not, as the majority believes, the power " 'to say what the law is,' " giving the Supreme Court the "primary role in determining the constitutionality of laws." . . . The judicial power as Americans have understood it (and their English ancestors before them) is the power to adjudicate, with conclusive effect, disputed government claims (civil or criminal) against private persons, and disputed claims by private persons against the government or other private persons. Sometimes (though not always) the parties before the court disagree not with regard to the facts of their case (or not *only* with regard to the facts) but with regard to the applicable law—in which event (and *only* in which event) it becomes the " 'province and duty of the judicial department to say what the law is.' "

In other words, declaring the compatibility of state or federal laws with the Constitution is not only not the "primary role" of this Court, it is not a separate, free-standing role *at all*. We perform that role incidentally—by accident, as it were—when that is necessary to resolve the dispute before us. Then, and only then, does it become " 'the province and duty of the judicial department to say what the law is.' " That is why, in 1793, we politely declined the Washington Administration's request to "say what the law is" on a particular treaty matter that was not the subject of a concrete legal controversy. 3 Correspondence and Public Papers of John Jay 486–489 (H. Johnston ed. 1893). And that is why, as our opinions have said, some questions of law will *never* be presented to this Court, because there will never be anyone with standing to bring a lawsuit. See Schlesinger v. Reservists Comm. to Stop the War, 418 U.S. 208, 227 (1974); United States v. Richardson, 418 U.S. 166, 179 (1974). . . . Our authority begins and ends with the need to adjudge the rights of an injured party who stands before us seeking redress. Lujan v. Defenders of Wildlife, 504 U.S. 555, 560 (1992).

That is completely absent here. Windsor's injury was cured by the judgment in her favor. And while, in ordinary circumstances, the United States is injured by a directive to pay a tax refund, this suit is far from ordinary. Whatever injury the United States has suffered will surely not be redressed by the action that it, as a litigant, asks us to take. The final sentence of the Solicitor General's brief on the merits reads: "For the foregoing reasons, the judgment of the court of appeals *should be affirmed*" (emphasis added). That will not cure the Government's injury, but carve it into stone. One could spend many fruitless afternoons ransacking our library for any other petitioner's brief seeking an affirmance of the judgment against it. What the petitioner United States asks us to do in the case before us is exactly what the respondent Windsor asks us to do: not to provide relief from the judgment below but to say that that judgment was correct. And the same was true in the Court of Appeals: Neither party sought to undo the judgment for Windsor, and so that court should have dismissed the appeal (just as we should dismiss) for lack of jurisdiction. Since both parties agreed with the judgment of the District Court for the Southern District of New York, the suit should have ended there. The further proceedings have been a contrivance, having no object in mind except to elevate a District Court judgment that has no precedential effect in other courts, to one that has precedential effect throughout the Second Circuit, and then (in this Court) precedential effect throughout the United States.

We have never before agreed to speak—to "say what the law is"—where there is no controversy before us. In the more than two centuries that this Court has existed as an institution, we have never suggested that we have the power to decide a question when every party agrees with both its nominal opponent *and the court below* on that question's answer. The United States reluctantly conceded that at oral argument.

The closest we have ever come to what the Court blesses today was our opinion in INS v. Chadha, 462 U.S. 919 (1983). But in that case, two parties to the litigation disagreed with the position of the United States and with the court below: the House and Senate, which had intervened in the case. Because *Chadha* concerned the validity of a mode of congressional action—the one-house legislative veto—the House and Senate were threatened with destruction of what they claimed to be one of their institutional powers. The Executive choosing not to defend that power,[2] we permitted the House and Senate to intervene. Nothing like that is present here.

---

[2]   There the Justice Department's refusal to defend the legislation was in accord with its longstanding (and entirely reasonable) practice of declining to defend legislation that in its view infringes upon Presidential powers. There is no justification for the Justice Department's abandoning the law in the present case. . . .

To be sure, the Court in *Chadha* said that statutory aggrieved-party status was "not altered by the fact that the Executive may agree with the holding that the statute in question is unconstitutional." Id. at 930–31. But in a footnote to that statement, the Court acknowledged Article III's separate requirement of a "justiciable case or controversy," and stated that *this* requirement was satisfied "because of the presence of the two Houses of Congress as adverse parties." Id. at 931 n.6. Later in its opinion, the *Chadha* Court remarked that the United States' announced intention to enforce the statute also sufficed to permit judicial review, even absent congressional participation. Id. at 939. That remark is true, as a description of the judicial review conducted in the Court of Appeals, where the Houses of Congress had not intervened. (The case originated in the Court of Appeals, since it sought review of agency action under 8 U.S.C. § 1105a(a) (1976 ed.).) There, absent a judgment setting aside the INS order, Chadha faced deportation. This passage of our opinion seems to be addressing that initial standing in the Court of Appeals, as indicated by its quotation from the lower court's opinion. But if it was addressing standing to pursue the appeal, the remark was both the purest dictum (as congressional intervention at that point made the required adverseness "beyond doubt," id. at 939), and quite incorrect. When a private party has a judicial decree safely in hand to prevent his injury, additional judicial action requires that a party injured by the decree *seek to undo it*. In *Chadha,* the intervening House and Senate fulfilled that requirement. Here no one does.

The majority's discussion of the requirements of Article III bears no resemblance to our jurisprudence. It accuses the amicus (appointed to argue against our jurisdiction) of "elid[ing] the distinction between . . . the jurisdictional requirements of Article III and the prudential limits on its exercise." It then proceeds to call the requirement of adverseness a "prudential" aspect of standing. *Of standing.* That is incomprehensible. A plaintiff (or appellant) can have all the standing in the world—satisfying all three standing requirements of *Lujan* that the majority so carefully quotes—and yet no Article III controversy may be before the court. Article III requires not just a plaintiff (or appellant) who has standing to complain but *an opposing party* who denies the validity of the complaint. It is not the amicus that has done the eliding of distinctions, but the majority, calling the quite separate Article III requirement of adverseness between the parties an element (which it then pronounces a "prudential" element) of standing. The question here is not whether, as the majority puts it, "the United States retains a stake sufficient to support Article III jurisdiction," the question is whether there is any controversy (which requires *contradiction*) between the United States and Ms. Windsor. There is not.

. . . The authorities the majority cites fall miles short of supporting the counterintuitive notion that an Article III "controversy" can exist without disagreement between the parties. In Deposit Guaranty Nat.

Bank v. Roper, 445 U.S. 326 (1980), the District Court had entered judgment in the individual plaintiff's favor based on the defendant bank's offer to pay the full amount claimed. The plaintiff, however, sought to appeal the District Court's denial of class certification under Federal Rule of Civil Procedure 23. There was a continuing dispute between the parties concerning the issue raised on appeal. . . . The majority can cite no case in which this Court entertained an appeal in which both parties urged us to affirm the judgment below. And that is because the existence of a controversy is not a "prudential" requirement that we have invented, but an essential element of an Article III case or controversy. The majority's notion that a case between friendly parties can be entertained so long as "adversarial presentation of the issues is assured by the participation of amici curiae prepared to defend with vigor" the other side of the issue, effects a breathtaking revolution in our Article III jurisprudence.

It may be argued that if what we say is true some Presidential determinations that statutes are unconstitutional will not be subject to our review. That is as it should be, when both the President and the plaintiff agree that the statute is unconstitutional. Where the Executive is enforcing an unconstitutional law, suit will of course lie; but if, in that suit, the Executive admits the unconstitutionality of the law, the litigation should end in an order or a consent decree enjoining enforcement. This suit saw the light of day only because the President enforced the Act (and thus gave Windsor standing to sue) even though he believed it unconstitutional. He could have equally chosen (more appropriately, some would say) neither to enforce nor to defend the statute he believed to be unconstitutional, see Presidential Authority to Decline to Execute Unconstitutional Statutes, 18 Op. Off. Legal Counsel 199 (Nov. 2, 1994)—in which event Windsor would not have been injured, the District Court could not have refereed this friendly scrimmage, and the Executive's determination of unconstitutionality would have escaped this Court's desire to blurt out its view of the law. The matter would have been left, as so many matters ought to be left, to a tug of war between the President and the Congress, which has innumerable means (up to and including impeachment) of compelling the President to enforce the laws it has written. Or the President could have evaded presentation of the constitutional issue to this Court simply by declining to appeal the District Court and Court of Appeals dispositions he agreed with. Be sure of this much: If a President wants to insulate his judgment of unconstitutionality from our review, he can. What the views urged in this dissent produce is not insulation from judicial review but insulation from Executive contrivance.

The majority brandishes the famous sentence from Marbury v. Madison, 5 U.S. (1 Cranch) 137, 177 (1803), that "[i]t is emphatically the province and duty of the judicial department to say what the law is." But that sentence neither says nor implies that it is always the province and duty of the Court to say what the law is—much less that its responsibility in that regard is a "primary" one. The very next sentence of Chief Justice

Marshall's opinion makes the crucial qualification that today's majority ignores: "*Those who apply the rule to particular cases*, must of necessity expound and interpret that rule." Id. at 177 (emphasis added). Only when a "particular case" is before us—that is, a controversy that it is our business to resolve under Article III—do we have the province and duty to pronounce the law. . . . There is, in the words of Marbury, no "necessity [to] expound and interpret" the law in this case; just a desire to place this Court at the center of the Nation's life.

B

A few words in response to the theory of jurisdiction set forth in Justice Alito's dissent: Though less far reaching in its consequences than the majority's conversion of constitutionally required adverseness into a discretionary element of standing, the theory of that dissent similarly elevates the Court to the "primary" determiner of constitutional questions involving the separation of powers, and, to boot, increases the power of the most dangerous branch: the "legislative department," which by its nature "draw[s] all power into its impetuous vortex." The Federalist, No. 48, at 309 (J. Madison). Heretofore in our national history, the President's failure to "take Care that the Laws be faithfully executed," U.S. Const., Art. II, § 3, could only be brought before a judicial tribunal by someone whose concrete interests were harmed by that alleged failure. Justice Alito would create a system in which Congress can hale the Executive before the courts not only to vindicate its own institutional powers to act, but to correct a perceived inadequacy in the execution of its laws.[3] . . . [This would create a] system in which Congress and the Executive can pop immediately into court, in their institutional capacity, whenever the President refuses to implement a statute he believes to be unconstitutional, and whenever he implements a law in a manner that is not to Congress's liking. . . .

To be sure, if Congress cannot invoke our authority in the way that Justice Alito proposes, then its only recourse is to confront the President directly. Unimaginable evil this is not. Our system is *designed* for confrontation. That is what "[a]mbition . . . counteract[ing] ambition," The Federalist, No. 51, at 322 (J. Madison), is all about. If majorities in both Houses of Congress care enough about the matter, they have available innumerable ways to compel executive action without a lawsuit—from refusing to confirm Presidential appointees to the elimination of funding.

---

[3] Justice Alito attempts to limit his argument by claiming that Congress is injured (and can therefore appeal) when its statute is held unconstitutional without Presidential defense, but is not injured when its statute is held unconstitutional despite Presidential defense. I do not understand that line. The injury to Congress is the same whether the President has defended the statute or not. And if the injury is threatened, why should Congress not be able to participate in the suit from the beginning, just as the President can? And if having a statute declared unconstitutional (and therefore inoperative) by a court is an injury, why is it not an injury when a statute is declared unconstitutional by the President and rendered inoperative by his consequent failure to enforce it? Or when the President simply declines to enforce it without opining on its constitutionality? If it is the inoperativeness that constitutes the injury—the "impairment of [the legislative] function," as Justice Alito puts it—it should make no difference which of the other two branches inflicts it, and whether the Constitution is the pretext. . . .

(Nothing says "enforce the Act" quite like ". . . or you will have money for little else.") But the condition is crucial; Congress must care enough to act against the President itself, not merely enough to instruct its lawyers to ask *us* to do so. Placing the Constitution's entirely anticipated political arm wrestling into permanent judicial receivership does not do the system a favor. And by the way, if the President loses the lawsuit but does not faithfully implement the Court's decree, just as he did not faithfully implement Congress's statute, what then? Only Congress can bring him to heel by . . . what do you think? Yes: a direct confrontation with the President.

For the reasons above, I think that this Court has, and the Court of Appeals had, no power to decide this suit. We should vacate the decision below and remand to the Court of Appeals for the Second Circuit, with instructions to dismiss the appeal. Given that the majority has volunteered its view of the merits, however, I proceed to discuss that as well.

[Justice Scalia's discussion of the merits, which Justice Thomas joined, is omitted.]

■ JUSTICE ALITO, dissenting.

Our Nation is engaged in a heated debate about same-sex marriage. That debate is, at bottom, about the nature of the institution of marriage. Respondent Edith Windsor, supported by the United States, asks this Court to intervene in that debate, and although she couches her argument in different terms, what she seeks is a holding that enshrines in the Constitution a particular understanding of marriage under which the sex of the partners makes no difference. The Constitution, however, does not dictate that choice. It leaves the choice to the people, acting through their elected representatives at both the federal and state levels. I would therefore hold that Congress did not violate Windsor's constitutional rights by enacting § 3 of the Defense of Marriage Act (DOMA), which defines the meaning of marriage under federal statutes that either confer upon married persons certain federal benefits or impose upon them certain federal obligations.

I

I turn first to the question of standing. In my view, the United States clearly is not a proper petitioner in this case. The United States does not ask us to overturn the judgment of the court below or to alter that judgment in any way. Quite to the contrary, the United States argues emphatically in favor of the correctness of that judgment. We have never before reviewed a decision at the sole behest of a party that took such a position, and to do so would be to render an advisory opinion, in violation of Article III's dictates. For the reasons given in Justice Scalia's dissent, I do not find the Court's arguments to the contrary to be persuasive.

Whether the Bipartisan Legal Advisory Group of the House of Representatives (BLAG) has standing to petition is a much more difficult question. It is also a significantly closer question than whether the intervenors in *Hollingsworth v. Perry,* which the Court also decides today—have standing to appeal. It is remarkable that the Court has simultaneously decided that the United States, which "receive[d] all that [it] ha[d] sought" below, Deposit Guaranty Nat. Bank v. Roper, 445 U.S. 326, 333 (1980), is a proper petitioner in this case but that the intervenors in *Hollingsworth,* who represent the party that lost in the lower court, are not. In my view, both the *Hollingsworth* intervenors and BLAG have standing.[1]

A party invoking the Court's authority has a sufficient stake to permit it to appeal when it has " 'suffered an injury in fact' that is caused by 'the conduct complained of' and that 'will be redressed by a favorable decision.' " Camreta v. Greene, 563 U.S. 692, 701 (2011) (quoting Lujan v. Defenders of Wildlife, 504 U.S. 555, 560–61 (1992)). In the present case, the House of Representatives, which has authorized BLAG to represent its interests in this matter, suffered just such an injury.

In INS v. Chadha, 462 U.S. 919 (1983), the Court held that the two Houses of Congress were "proper parties" to file a petition in defense of the constitutionality of the one-house veto statute, id. at 930 n.5 (internal quotation marks omitted). Accordingly, the Court granted and decided petitions by both the Senate and the House, in addition to the Executive's petition. That the two Houses had standing to petition is not surprising: The Court of Appeals' decision in *Chadha,* by holding the one-house veto to be unconstitutional, had limited Congress's power to legislate. In discussing Article III standing, the Court suggested that Congress suffered a similar injury whenever federal legislation it had passed was struck down, noting that it had "long held that Congress is the proper party to defend the validity of a statute when an agency of government, as a defendant charged with enforcing the statute, agrees with plaintiffs that the statute is inapplicable or unconstitutional." Id. at 940.

The United States attempts to distinguish *Chadha* on the ground that it "involved an unusual statute that vested the House and the Senate themselves each with special procedural rights—namely, the right effectively to veto Executive action." But that is a distinction without a difference: just as the Court of Appeals decision that the *Chadha* Court affirmed impaired Congress's power by striking down the one-house veto, so the Second Circuit's decision here impairs Congress's legislative power by striking down an Act of Congress. The United States has not explained why the fact that the impairment at issue in *Chadha* was "special" or "procedural" has any relevance to whether Congress suffered an injury.

---

[1] Our precedents make clear that, in order to support our jurisdiction, BLAG must demonstrate that it had Article III standing in its own right, quite apart from its status as an intervenor. See Arizonans for Official English v. Arizona, 520 U.S. 43, 64 (1997) ("Standing to defend on appeal in the place of an original defendant, no less than standing to sue, demands that the litigant possess a direct stake in the outcome" (internal quotation marks omitted)); id. at 65 ("An intervenor cannot step into the shoes of the original party unless the intervenor independently fulfills the requirements of Article III" (internal quotation marks omitted)).

Indeed, because legislating is Congress's central function, any impairment of that function is a more grievous injury than the impairment of a procedural add-on.

The Court's decision in Coleman v. Miller, 307 U.S. 433 (1939), bolsters this conclusion. In *Coleman,* we held that a group of state senators had standing to challenge a lower court decision approving the procedures used to ratify an amendment to the Federal Constitution. We reasoned that the senators' votes—which would otherwise have carried the day—were nullified by that action. See id. at 438 ("Here, the plaintiffs include twenty senators, whose votes against ratification have been overridden and virtually held for naught although if they are right in their contentions their votes would have been sufficient to defeat ratification. We think that these senators have a plain, direct and adequate interest in maintaining the effectiveness of their votes"). By striking down § 3 of DOMA as unconstitutional, the Second Circuit effectively "held for naught" an Act of Congress. Just as the state-senator-petitioners in *Coleman* were necessary parties to the amendment's ratification, the House of Representatives was a necessary party to DOMA's passage; indeed, the House's vote would have been sufficient to prevent DOMA's repeal if the Court had not chosen to execute that repeal judicially.

Both the United States and the Court-appointed amicus err in arguing that Raines v. Byrd, 521 U.S. 811 (1997), is to the contrary. In that case, the Court held that Members of Congress who had voted "nay" to the Line Item Veto Act did not have standing to challenge that statute in federal court. *Raines* is inapposite for two reasons. First, *Raines* dealt with individual Members of Congress and specifically pointed to the individual Members' lack of institutional endorsement as a sign of their standing problem: "We attach some importance to the fact that appellees have not been authorized to represent their respective Houses of Congress in this action, and indeed both Houses actively oppose their suit." Id. at 829; see also id. n.10 (citing cases to the effect that "members of collegial bodies do not have standing to perfect an appeal the body itself has declined to take" (internal quotation marks omitted)).

Second, the Members in *Raines*—unlike the state senators in *Coleman*—were not the pivotal figures whose votes would have caused the Act to fail absent some challenged action. Indeed, it is telling that *Raines* characterized *Coleman* as standing "for the proposition that legislators whose votes would have been sufficient to defeat (or enact) a specific legislative Act have standing to sue if that legislative action goes into effect (or does not go into effect), on the ground that their votes have been completely nullified." 521 U.S. at 823. Here, by contrast, passage by the House was needed for DOMA to become law.

I appreciate the argument that the Constitution confers on the President alone the authority to defend federal law in litigation, but in my view, as I have explained, that argument is contrary to the Court's holding in *Chadha,* and it is certainly contrary to the *Chadha* Court's endorsement of the principle that "Congress is the proper party to defend the validity of a statute" when the Executive refuses to do so on constitutional grounds. 462 U.S. at 940. Accordingly, in the narrow category of cases in which a court strikes down an Act of Congress and the Executive declines to defend the Act, Congress both has standing to defend the undefended statute and is a proper party to do so.

[Justice Alito's discussion of the merits, which Justice Thomas joined, is omitted.]

[The separate dissenting opinions of Chief Justice Roberts and Justice Thomas, which did not address justiciability, are omitted.]

NOTES ON STANDING TO APPEAL

1. *INS V. CHADHA*

Most of the precedents discussed in *Perry* and *Windsor* are adequately discussed in the opinions or elsewhere in these materials. INS v. Chadha, 462 U.S. 919 (1983), may be an exception. *Chadha* struck down the so-called legislative veto, a statutory mechanism that reserved to Congress (or to one house thereof) the power to overrule the executive's exercise of delegated power by passing a simple resolution. The Court found such schemes unconstitutional. Congressional power to override executive action by resolution, the Court held, undermined the President's constitutionally mandated opportunity to veto legislation with which the executive disagrees. If Congress wishes to overrule an executive action, the Court said, it must enact new law, which triggers the President's veto opportunity.

Of particular relevance here is an appellate standing issue. Chadha was a non-U.S. national who became eligible for deportation for overstaying his visa. Pursuant to authority granted by statute, the Immigration and Naturalization Service (INS) suspended Chadha's deportation (essentially for good behavior) and, as required, reported that action to Congress. The House of Representatives then exercised its power under the statute to overrule the INS decision. After agency adjudication, the INS ordered deportation. Chadha then petitioned the Ninth Circuit for review of the agency's order, claiming that the legislative veto provision under which the House had acted against him was unconstitutional. The INS agreed with that contention (in accord with long-standing Executive Branch hostility to the legislative veto) but announced that it would proceed with deportation unless ordered otherwise. When the Ninth Circuit agreed with the INS (and Chadha), struck down the legislative veto, and halted deportation, the INS appealed, presumably to obtain an authoritative Supreme Court ruling on the question.

Both the House and the Senate, which had been allowed to intervene before the Ninth Circuit and which thereby became parties to the litigation, objected that the INS could not seek appellate review of a decision granting the relief it had requested. Speaking through Chief Justice Burger, the Court responded as follows:

The INS was ordered by one House of Congress to deport Chadha. . . . [T]he INS brief to the Court of Appeals did not alter the agency's decision to comply with the House action ordering deportation of Chadha. . . . At least for purposes of deciding whether the INS is "any party" within the grant of appellate jurisdiction in [28 U.S.C.] § 1252, we hold that the INS was sufficiently aggrieved by the Court of Appeals decision prohibiting it from taking action it would otherwise take. . . . When an agency of the United States is a party to a case in which the Act of Congress it administers is held unconstitutional, it is an aggrieved party for purposes of taking an appeal under § 1252. The agency's status as an aggrieved party under § 1252 is not altered by the fact that the Executive may agree with the holding that the statute in question is unconstitutional.

At this point, the Court dropped a footnote, which contained its only discussion of justiciability as a question distinct from the statutory requirements for appeal by an agency:

In addition to meeting the statutory requisites of § 1252, of course, an appeal must present a justiciable case or controversy under Art. III. Such a controversy clearly exists [here], because of the presence of the two Houses of Congress as adverse parties.[a]

All of the opinions in *Windsor* discuss *Chadha*. The majority claims that *Chadha* supports the United States's standing to appeal a decision with which it entirely agreed. Justice Alito disagrees with respect to the United States ("the United States is clearly not a proper petitioner in this case") but says that *Chadha* supports BLAG's standing to appeal, an issue that the majority explicitly declined to address. Finally, Justice Scalia distinguished *Chadha* on the ground that the House and Senate were allowed to intervene because they "were threatened with destruction of what they claimed to be one of their institutional powers" and because "[n]othing like that is present here." Who has the better of this dispute?

2.   QUESTIONS AND COMMENTS

Why is the majority reluctant to embrace standing to appeal by BLAG? If BLAG's standing were accepted, would the consequences be as radical as Justice Scalia suggests, or is Justice Alito's attempt to limit the implications of his position persuasive? And if Congressional authorization to intervene (as existed for BLAG and in *Chadha*) suffices for justiciability, why did California's authorization of the proponents of Proposition 8 not also suffice? Are the cases distinguishable?

The Proposition 8 case (*Hollingsworth*) raises additional questions concerning the intersection of the federal law of standing with state law. The majority and dissent agree that the standing of the intervenors in that case is to be governed by federal law. They differ, however, over the extent to

---

[a]   There were dissenting opinions by Justices White and Rehnquist and a concurrence in the result by Justice Powell, but none of them disputed justiciability.—[Footnote by eds.]

which the application of federal law should be affected by the California Supreme Court's determination that the intervenors were authorized under state law to represent the state's interest in the validity of Proposition 8. Has the majority "set aside the California Supreme Court's determination of state law," as the dissent contends? Why must the intervenors have a formal agency relationship with the state in order to have standing to defend Proposition 8? Does it make sense to disallow appellate review of the invalidation of a public referendum when a state government, which did not even propose the referendum, declines to defend it on appeal? Note that, unlike many of the other decisions in this Section (including *Windsor*), *Hollingsworth* did not feature a clear liberal-conservative split. Why not? Why is this case a departure from the generally clear pattern of standing decisions?

Two years after its decision in *Hollingsworth*, the Court in another case held that the Constitution gives same-sex couples the right to marry. See Obergefell v. Hodges, 576 U.S. ___, 135 S.Ct. 2584 (2015).

3.   BIBLIOGRAPHY

For early commentary on *Perry* and *Windsor*, arguing that they "significantly reshaped the law of Article III standing to appeal," see Ryan W. Scott, Standing to Appeal and Executive Non-Defense of Federal Law after the Marriage Cases, 89 Ind. L.J. 67 (2014). See also Richard H. Fallon, Jr., How to Make Sense of Supreme Court Standing Cases—A Plea for the Right Kind of Realism, 23 Wm. & M. Bill of Rts J. 105 (2014) (seeking to identify "patterns" of decision that "offer relatively stable grounds for prediction" of future cases).

For discussion of the intersection of federal standing and state law in *Perry*, see Glenn S. Koppel, "Standing" in the Shadow of *Erie*: Federalism in the Balance in *Hollingsworth v. Perry*, 34 Pace L. Rev. 631 (2014), and Heather Elliott, Federalism Standing, 65 Ala. L. Rev. 435 (2013). On another aspect of federalism and standing, see F. Andrew Hessick, Standing in Diversity, 65 Ala. L. Rev. 417 (2013), which argues that state standing law should apply in federal courts hearing state causes of action.

For an interesting perspective on legislative standing, see Tara Leigh Grove, Standing Outside of Article III, 162 U. Pa. L. Rev. 1311 (2014). Grove argues that the standing of the executive and legislative branches cannot be determined solely by reference to Article III, but must be derived from the constitutional powers of those branches. In her view, the executive's power to "take Care that the Laws be faithfully executed" gives the executive standing when it asserts the government's interest in enforcing federal law, but not otherwise. When, as in *Windsor*, the government declines to defend federal law, she argues, it no longer has the right to invoke judicial review."

For another analysis that looks outside Article III, see Seth Davis, Standing Doctrine's State Action Problem, 91 Notre Dame L. Rev. 585 (2015). Davis criticizes the *Perry* Court's refusal to allow private parties to defend the constitutionality of California law. He argues that, "contra *Perry*, the Constitution does not require legislatures to limit the power of government standing to only traditional government employees and common law agents of the state." Instead, he says, the question should be one of the "constitutional accountability" of those who seek to stand for government. When mechanisms exist to assure that the private representation of government interests presents no potential for abuse, it should be allowed.

Finally, for historically grounded perspectives on governmental standing, see Ann Woolhandler & Michael G. Collins, State Standing, 81 Va. L. Rev. 387 (1995), and Ann Woolhandler, Governmental Sovereignty Actions, 23 Wm. & M. Bill of Rts J. 209 (2014).

SECTION 3. RELATED DOCTRINES

SUBSECTION A. THIRD-PARTY STANDING

Singleton v. Wulff
Supreme Court of the United States, 1976.
428 U.S. 106.

■ MR. JUSTICE BLACKMUN delivered the opinion of the Court (parts I [and] II-A . . .) together with an opinion (part II-B), in which MR. JUSTICE BRENNAN, MR. JUSTICE WHITE, and MR. JUSTICE MARSHALL joined.

[T]his case involves a claim of a state's unconstitutional interference with the decision to terminate pregnancy. The particular object of the challenge is a Missouri statute excluding abortions that are not "medically indicated" from the purposes for which Medicaid benefits are available to needy persons. In its present posture, [the issue] is whether the plaintiff-appellees, as physicians who perform nonmedically indicated abortions, have standing to maintain the suit, to which we answer that they do.

I

Missouri participates in the so-called Medicaid program, under which the federal government partially underwrites qualifying state plans for medical assistance to the needy. Missouri's plan . . . includes . . . a list of 12 categories of medical services that are eligible for Medicaid funding. The last is:

> (12) Family planning services as defined by federal rules and regulations; provided, however, that such family planning services shall not include abortions unless such abortions are medically indicated.

This provision is the subject of the litigation before us.

The suit was filed in the United States District Court for the Eastern District of Missouri by two Missouri-licensed physicians. Each plaintiff avers, in an affidavit filed in opposition to a motion to dismiss, that he "has provided, and anticipates providing abortions to welfare patients who are eligible for Medicaid payments." The plaintiffs further allege in their affidavits that all Medicaid applications filed in connection with abortions performed by them have been refused by the defendant, who is the responsible state official. . . . [E]ach plaintiff states that he antici- pates further refusals by the defendant to fund nonmedically indicated abortions. Each avers that such refusals "deter [him] from the practice of medicine in the manner he considers to be most expertise [sic] and bene- ficial for said patients . . . and chill and thwart the ordinary and custom- ary functioning of the doctor-patient relationship."

The complaint sought a declaration of the statute's invalidity and an injunction against its enforcement. . . . The defendant's sole pleading in District Court was a pre-answer motion to dismiss. [The District Court dismissed the case] "for lack of standing." The court saw no "logical nexus between the status asserted by the plaintiffs and the claim they seek to have adjudicated." The United States Court of Appeals for the Eighth Circuit reversed. . . . We granted certiorari. . . .

II

Although we are not certain that they have been clearly separated in the District Court's and Court of Appeals' opinions, two distinct stand- ing questions are presented. . . . First, whether the plaintiff-respondents allege "injury in fact," that is, a sufficiently concrete interest in the out- come of their suit to make it a case or controversy subject to a federal court's Article III jurisdiction, and, second, whether, as a prudential mat- ter, the plaintiff-respondents are proper proponents of the particular legal rights on which they base their suit.

A. The first of these questions needs little comment, for there is no doubt now that the respondent-physicians suffer concrete injury from the operation of the challenged statute. Their complaint and affidavits, de- scribed above, allege that they have performed and will continue to perform operations for which they would be reimbursed under the Medi- caid program, were it not for the limitation of reimbursable abortions to those that are "medically indicated." If the physicians prevail in their suit to remove this limitation, they will benefit, for they will then receive pay- ment for the abortions. The state (and federal government) will be out of pocket by the amount of the payments. The relationship between the par- ties is classically adverse, and there clearly exists between them a case or controversy in the constitutional sense.

B. The question of what rights the doctors may assert in seeking to resolve that controversy is more difficult. The Court of Appeals adverted to what it perceived to be the doctor's own "constitutional rights to prac- tice medicine." We have no occasion to decide whether such rights exist. Assuming that they do, the doctors, of course, can assert them. It ap- pears, however, that the Court of Appeals also accorded the doctors standing to assert . . . the rights of their patients. We must decide whether this assertion of jus tertii was a proper one.

Federal courts must hesitate before resolving a controversy, even one within their constitutional power to resolve, on the basis of the rights of third persons not parties to the litigation. The reasons are two. First, the courts should not adjudicate such rights unnecessarily, and it may be that in fact the holders of those rights either do not wish to assert them, or will be able to enjoy them regardless of whether the in-court litigant is successful or not. Second, third parties themselves usually will be the best proponents of their own rights. The courts depend on effective advocacy, and therefore should prefer to construe legal rights only when the most effective advocates of those rights are before them. The holders of the rights may have a like preference, to the extent they will be bound by the courts' decisions under the doctrine of stare decisis. These two considerations underlie the Court's general rule: "Ordinarily, one may not claim standing in this Court to vindicate the constitutional rights of some third party."

Like any general rule, however, this one should not be applied where its underlying justifications are absent. With this in mind, the Court has looked primarily to two factual elements to determine whether the rule should apply in a particular case. The first is the relationship of the litigant to the person whose right he seeks to assert. If the enjoyment of the right is inextricably bound up with the activity the litigant wishes to pursue, the court at least can be sure that its construction of the right is not unnecessary in the sense that the right's enjoyment will be unaffected by the outcome of the suit. Furthermore, the relationship between the litigant and the third party may be such that the former is fully, or very nearly, as effective a proponent of the right as the latter. Thus in Griswold v. Connecticut, 381 U.S. 479 (1965), where two persons had been convicted of giving advice on contraception, the Court permitted the defendants, one of whom was a licensed physician, to assert the privacy rights of the married persons whom they advised. The Court pointed to the "confidential" nature of the relationship between the defendants and the married persons, and reasoned that the rights of the latter were "likely to be diluted or adversely affected" if they could not be asserted in such a case. See also Eisenstadt v. Baird, 405 U.S. 438, 445–46 (1972); Barrows v. Jackson, 346 U.S. 249 (1953). . . .

The other factual element to which the Court has looked is the ability of the third party to assert his own right. Even where the relationship is close, the reasons for requiring persons to assert their own rights will generally still apply. If there is some genuine obstacle to such assertion, however, the third party's absence from court loses its tendency to suggest that his right is not truly at stake, or truly important to him, and the party who is in court becomes by default the right's best available proponent. Thus, in NAACP v. Alabama, 357 U.S. 449 (1958), the Court held that the National Association for the Advancement of Colored People, in resisting a court order that it divulge the names of its members, could assert the first and Fourteenth Amendment rights of those members to remain anonymous. The Court reasoned that "[t]o require that

[the right] be claimed by the members themselves would result in nullification of the right at the very moment of its assertion." See also
Eisenstadt, 405 U.S. at 446; *Barrows,* 346 U.S. at 259.[6]

Application of these principles to the present case quickly yields its
proper result. The closeness of the relationship is patent, as it was in
Griswold. . . . A woman cannot safely secure an abortion without the aid
of a physician, and an impecunious woman cannot easily secure an abortion without the physician's being paid by the state. The woman's
exercise of her right to an abortion, whatever its dimension, is therefore
necessarily at stake here. Moreover, the constitutionally protected abortion decision is one in which the physician is intimately involved.

As to the woman's assertion of her own rights, there are several obstacles. For one thing, she may be chilled from such assertion by a desire
to protect the very privacy of her decision from the publicity of a court
suit. A second obstacle is the imminent mootness, at least in the technical
sense, of any individual woman's claim. Only a few months, at the most,
after the maturing of the decision to undergo an abortion, her right
thereto will have been irrevocably lost, assuming, as it seems fair to assume, that unless the impecunious woman can establish Medicaid
eligibility she must forego abortion. It is true that these obstacles are not
insurmountable. Suit may be brought under a pseudonym, as so frequently has been done. A woman who is no longer pregnant may
nonetheless retain the right to litigate the point because it is " 'capable
of repetition yet evading review.' " Roe v. Wade, 410 U.S. 113, 124–25
(1973). And it may be that a class could be assembled, whose fluid membership always included some women with live claims. But if the
assertion of the right is to be "representative" to such an extent anyway,
there seems little loss in terms of effective advocacy from allowing its
assertion by a physician.

For these reasons, we conclude that it generally is appropriate to
allow a physician to assert the rights of women patients as against governmental interference with the abortion decision. [T]he judgment of the
Court of Appeals is affirmed . . . and the case is remanded with directions
that it be returned to the District Court so that petitioner may file an
answer to the complaint and the litigation proceed accordingly.

---

[6]   Mr. Justice Powell objects that such an obstacle is not enough, that our prior cases allow
assertion of third-party rights only when such assertion by the third parties themselves would
be "in all practicable terms impossible." Carefully analyzed, our cases do not go that far. The
Negro real-estate purchaser in *Barrows,* if he could prove that the racial covenant alone stood
in the way of his purchase (as presumably he could easily have done, given the amicable posture
of the seller in that case), could surely have sought a declaration of its invalidity or an injunction
against its enforcement. The Association members in *NAACP v. Alabama* could have obtained
a similar declaration or injunction, suing anonymously by the use of pseudonyms. The recipients
of contraceptives in *Eisenstadt* (or their counterparts in *Griswold* . . . , for that matter) could
have sought similar relief as necessary to the enjoyment of their constitutional rights. The point
is not that these were easy alternatives, but that they differed only in the degree of difficulty, if
they differed at all, from the alternative in this case of the women themselves seeking a declaration or injunction that would force the state to pay the doctors for their abortions.

It is so ordered.

■ MR. JUSTICE STEVENS, concurring in part.

In this case (1) the plaintiff-physicians have a financial stake in the outcome of the litigation, and (2) they claim that the statute impairs their own constitutional rights. They therefore clearly have standing to bring this action.

Because these two facts are present, I agree that the analysis in part II-B of Mr. Justice Blackmun's opinion provides an adequate basis for considering the arguments based on the effect of the statute on the constitutional rights of their patients. Because I am not sure whether the analysis in part II-B would, or should, sustain the doctor's standing, apart from those two facts, I join only parts I [and] II-A . . . of the Court's opinion.

■ MR. JUSTICE POWELL, with whom THE CHIEF JUSTICE, MR. JUSTICE STEWART, and MR. JUSTICE REHNQUIST join, concurring in part and dissenting in part.

The Court holds that the respondents have standing to bring this suit and to assert their own constitutional rights, if any, in an attack on [the Missouri statute]. I agree with [this holding] and therefore concur in parts I [and] II-A, . . . of Justice Blackmun's opinion, as well as in the first four sentences of part II-B.

The Court further holds that after remand to the District Court the respondents may assert, in addition to their own rights, the constitutional rights of their patients who would be eligible for Medicaid assistance in obtaining elective abortions but for the exclusion of such abortions in [the statute]. I dissent from this holding.

I

As the Court notes, respondents by complaint and affidavit established their Article III standing to invoke the judicial power of the District Court. They have performed abortions for which Missouri's Medicaid system would compensate them directly if the challenged statutory section did not preclude it. Respondents allege an intention to continue to perform such abortions, and that the statute deprives them of compensation. These arguments, if proved, would give respondents a personal stake in the controversy over the statute's constitutionality.

II

[T]he Article III standing inquiry often is only the first of two inquiries necessary to determine whether a federal court should entertain a claim at the instance of a particular party. The Article III question is one of power within our constitutional system, as courts may decide only actual cases and controversies between the parties who stand before the court. Beyond this question, however, lies the further and less easily defined inquiry of whether it is prudent to proceed to decision on particular issues even at the instance of a party whose Article III standing is clear.

This inquiry has taken various forms, including the one presented by this case: whether, in defending against or anticipatorily attacking state action, a party may argue that it contravenes someone else's constitutional rights.

This second inquiry is a matter of "judicial self-governance." The usual and wise stance of the federal courts when policing their own exercise of power in this manner is one of cautious reserve. This caution has given rise to the general rule that a party may not defend against or attack governmental action on the ground that it infringes the rights of some third party, and to the corollary that any exception must rest on specific factors outweighing the policies behind the rule itself.

The plurality acknowledges this general rule, but identifies "two factual elements"—thought to be derived from prior cases—that justify the adjudication of the asserted third-party rights: (i) obstacles to the assertion by the third party of her own rights, and (ii) the existence of some "relationship" such as the one between physician and patient. In my view these factors do not justify allowing these physicians to assert their patients' rights.

A

Our prior decisions are enlightening. In Barrows v. Jackson, 346 U.S. 249 (1953), a covenantor who breached a racially restrictive covenant by selling to Negroes was permitted to set up the buyers' rights to equal protection in defense against a damages action by the covenantees. See Shelley v. Kraemer, 334 U.S. 1 (1948). The Court considered the general rule outweighed by "the need to protect [these] fundamental rights" in a situation "in which it would be difficult if not impossible for the persons whose rights are asserted to present their grievance before any court." It would indeed have been difficult if not impossible for the rightholders to assert their own rights: the operation of the restrictive covenant and the threat of damages actions for its breach tended to insure they would not come into possession of the land, and there was at the time little chance of a successful suit based on a covenantor's failure to sell to them. In a second case, NAACP v. Alabama, 357 U.S. 449 (1958), an organization was allowed to resist an order to produce its membership list by asserting the associational rights of its members to anonymity because, as the plurality notes, the members themselves would have had to forgo the rights in order to assert them. And in Eisenstadt v. Baird, 405 U.S. 438 (1972), the Court considered it necessary to relax the rule and permit a distributor of contraceptives to assert the constitutional rights of the recipients because the statutory scheme operating to deny the contraceptives to the recipients appeared to offer them no means of challenge.

The plurality purports to derive from these cases the principle that a party may assert another's rights if there is "some genuine obstacle" to the third party's own litigation. But this understates the teaching of those cases: On their facts they indicate that such an assertion is proper,

not when there is merely some "obstacle" to the rightholder's own litigation, but when such litigation is in all practicable terms impossible. Thus,
in its framing of this principle, the plurality has gone far beyond our major precedents.

Moreover, on the plurality's own statement of this principle and on
its own discussion of the facts, the litigation of third-party rights cannot
be justified in this case. The plurality virtually concedes, as it must, that
the two alleged "obstacles" to the women's assertion of their rights are
chimerical. Our docket regularly contains cases in which women, using
pseudonyms, challenge statutes that allegedly infringe their right to exercise the abortion decision. Nor is there basis for the "obstacle" of incipi-
ent mootness when the plurality itself quotes from the portion of Roe v.
Wade, 410 U.S. 113, 124–25 (1973), that shows no such obstacle exists.
In short, in light of experience which we share regularly in reviewing
appeals and petitions for certiorari, the "obstacles" identified by the plurality as justifying departure from the general rule simply are not
significant. Rather than being a logical descendant of *Barrows, NAACP,*
and *Eisenstadt,* this case is much closer to Warth v. Seldin, 422 U.S. 490
(1975), in which taxpayers were refused leave to assert the constitutional
rights of low-income persons in part because there was no obstacle to
those low-income persons' asserting their own rights in a proper case.[4]

B

The plurality places primary reliance on a second element, the existence of a "confidential relationship" between the rightholder and the
party seeking to assert her rights.[5] Focusing on the professional [rela-
tionship] present in *Griswold,* the plurality suggests that allowing the
physicians in this case to assert their patients' rights flows naturally. . . .
Indeed, its conclusion is couched in terms of the general appropriateness

---

[4]   The plurality retrospectively analyzes the facts in *Barrows, NAACP,* and *Eisenstadt* in
an effort to show that litigation by the rightholders was possible in each case. [See] n.6. While
this technically may be true, it also is true that the Court in *Barrows* and *NAACP* expressly
emphasized the extreme difficulty of such litigation. Moreover, the plurality underestimates the
difficulty confronting a would-be Negro vendee in *Barrow's* who attempted to prove that race
alone blocked his deal with a covenantor. And the plurality denigrates the difficulty of the
NAACP members' assertion of their own right to anonymity when in the text on the same page
it quotes, approvingly, the very language in the *NAACP* case expressing the difficulty of such
litigation. As for *Eisenstadt,* allowing the assertion of third-party rights there was justified not
only because of the difficulty of rightholders' litigation, but also because the state directly interdicted a course of conduct that allegedly enjoyed constitutional protection. As explained infra,
part II–B, the Court rightly shows special solicitude in that situation.

In any event, as argued above in the text, my basic disagreement with the plurality rests
on the facts of *this case,* and the application of the plurality's *own* test—"some genuine obstacle"
to the rightholder's assertion of her own rights. There simply is *no* such obstacle here.

[5]   The plurality's primary emphasis upon this relationship is in marked contrast to the
Court's previous position that the relationship between litigant and rightholder was subordinate in importance to "the impact of the litigation on the third-party interests." Eisenstadt v.
Baird, 405 U.S. 438, 445 (1972). I suspect the plurality's inversion of the previous order results
from the weakness of the argument that this litigation is necessary to protect third-party interests. I would keep the emphasis where it has been before, and would consider the closeness of
any "relationship" only as a factor imparting confidence that third-party interests will be represented adequately in a case in which allowing their assertion is justified on other grounds.

of allowing physicians to assert the privacy interests of their patients in attacks on "governmental interference with the abortion decision."

With all respect, I do not read [*Griswold*] as merging the physician and his patient for constitutional purposes. The principle [it supports] turns not upon the confidential nature of a physician-patient relationship but upon the nature of the state's impact upon the relationship. [T]he state directly interdicted the normal functioning of the physician-patient relationship by criminalizing certain procedures. In the circumstances of direct interference, I agree that one party to the relationship should be permitted to assert the constitutional rights of the other, for a judicial rule of self-restraint should not preclude an attack on a state's proscription of constitutionally protected activity. But Missouri has not directly interfered with the abortion decision—neither the physicians nor their patients are forbidden to engage in the procedure. The only impact of [the statute] is that . . . it causes these doctors financial detriment. This affords them Article III standing because they aver injury in fact, but it does not justify abandonment of the salutary rule against assertion of third-party rights.

C

The physicians have offered no special reason for allowing them to assert their patients' rights in an attack on this welfare statute, and I can think of none. Moreover, there are persuasive reasons not to permit them to do so. It seems wholly inappropriate, as a matter of judicial self-governance, for a court to reach unnecessarily to decide a difficult constitutional issue in a case in which nothing more is at stake than remuneration for professional services. And second, this case may well set a precedent that will prove difficult to cabin. No reason immediately comes to mind, after today's holding, why any provider of services should be denied standing to assert his client's or customer's constitutional rights, if any, in an attack on a welfare statute that excludes from coverage his particular transaction.

Putting it differently, the Court's holding invites litigation by those who perhaps have the least legitimate ground for seeking to assert the rights of third parties. Before today I certainly would not have thought that an interest in being compensated for professional services, without more, would be deemed a sufficiently compelling reason to justify departing from a rule of restraint that well serves society and our judicial system. . . .

NOTES ON THIRD-PARTY STANDING

1. INTRODUCTION

The Supreme Court has often said that a litigant has standing to raise only his or her own rights. This rule is prudential only and has many exceptions. In those circumstances in which a litigant is allowed to raise another's rights, third-party standing or jus tertii is said to exist. The exceptions have been important in constitutional litigation. As the Court notes in *Singleton,* development of the right to marital privacy in *Griswold* arose under such an exception. Others are illustrated below.

The requirement of standing to sue and the rule against third-party standing are related but distinguishable. Both bar the litigation of hypotheticals. The requirement of standing to sue ensures that there be an actual case or controversy requiring judicial resolution. The rule against third-party standing ensures that the litigation be restricted to that case or controversy and does not become an excuse for adjudicating unrelated claims. Not surprisingly, refusal to allow third-party standing is most likely where the injury to third-party rights is imaginary or conjectural.

In other cases, however, the existence of actual injury to the rights of identifiable third parties can scarcely be doubted. In such circumstances, a litigant who has a concrete interest in the dispute and who will benefit from the vindication of third-party rights is sometimes allowed to raise those rights. Such a litigant may be a plaintiff or a defendant. In either case, the litigant typically seeks to avoid enforcement of a rule or statute on the ground that it violates another's rights.

Are the rationales articulated in *Singleton* for the general rule against third-party standing persuasive? What would be wrong with allowing third-party standing whenever the litigant before the court has a sufficiently concrete interest in the outcome of the suit to present a justiciable case or controversy? If the general rule is sound, is Justice Blackmun's rendition of the exceptions sound? Or is Justice Powell's more restrictive version to be preferred? Consider these questions in connection with the following cases.

2.   THE THIRD PARTY'S ABILITY TO RAISE HIS OR HER OWN RIGHTS

In *Singleton* both the plurality and the dissenters agreed that third-party standing might turn on the rightholder's ability to raise his or her own rights. This factor has figured largely in several cases.

(i)   *Barrows v. Jackson*

In the famous early case of Barrows v. Jackson, 346 U.S. 249 (1953), Los Angeles landowners had entered into a racially restrictive covenant on land in their neighborhood. Some of them brought an action at law for damages against a fellow landowner who had permitted occupancy of her property by non-Caucasians. The Supreme Court had held in Shelley v. Kraemer, 334 U.S. 1 (1948), that although racially restrictive covenants were not illegal per se, they could not be enforced in equity against black purchasers. The Court had reasoned that judicial enforcement of such an agreement constituted state action and converted private discrimination into a constitutional violation.

In *Barrows,* however, no one sought to enforce the covenant against blacks. Instead, the plaintiffs sued the white landowner for damages. The question thus arose whether the defendant landowner could raise the rights of her black purchasers to avoid her obligation under the covenant. The Court upheld third-party standing, describing the case as a "unique situation

... in which it would be difficult if not impossible for the persons whose rights are asserted to present their grievance before any court." Since the landowner was the only person in a position to resist this particular form of enforcement, the Court held that the "rule of practice" against litigating the rights of another would give way to "the need to protect the fundamental rights which would be denied by permitting the damages action to be maintained."

(ii) Eisenstadt v. Baird

A similar concern surfaced in Eisenstadt v. Baird, 405 U.S. 438 (1972). Baird gave a public lecture on contraception and afterwards distributed a contraceptive foam to unmarried persons in violation of a Massachusetts statute. *Griswold v. Connecticut* had struck down a ban against using contraceptives as an infringement of the right of "marital privacy," but had not decided whether single persons had similar rights. Baird was allowed to raise that issue in his own defense, largely because "unmarried persons denied access to contraceptives in Massachusetts . . . are not themselves subject to prosecution and, to that extent, are denied a forum in which to assert their own rights."

In *Schlesinger v. Reservists Committee to Stop the War* and *United States v. Richardson*, the absence of an alternative plaintiff was deemed irrelevant to the question of standing to sue. Can that conclusion be reconciled with *Barrows* and *Eisenstadt*?

3. RELATIONSHIP BETWEEN LITIGANT AND THIRD PARTY

Singleton v. Wulff also illustrates the significance of a pre-existing relationship between litigant and rightholder. The doctor-patient relationship involved in *Singleton* also figured in Doe v. Bolton, 410 U.S. 179 (1973), in which the Court allowed a physician to litigate the constitutionality of restrictions on abortion. In *Doe* the third-party standing issue was "of no great consequence," given that a woman who wanted an abortion was also a party to the suit. In Planned Parenthood v. Danforth, 428 U.S. 52 (1976), however, there was no such party, and the Supreme Court held, with virtually no discussion, that a physician could raise the abortion rights of women patients.

The standing of abortion providers to raise the rights of women who desire such services was also accepted, without discussion, by the Court in Whole Woman's Health v. Hellerstedt, 579 U.S. ___, 136 S.Ct. 2292 (2016), and by Justice Alito, author of the principal dissent. In a separate dissent, Justice Thomas explained at length his disagreement. Acknowledging that "third-party standing jurisprudence is no model of clarity," Thomas said that the Court had been "especially forgiving" in abortion cases: "Since *Singleton*, the Court has unquestioningly accepted doctors' and clinics' vicarious assertion of the constitutional rights of hypothetical patients, even as women seeking abortions have successfully and repeatedly asserted their own rights before this Court." Thomas found this especially troubling in light of the substantive standard of whether abortion laws "unduly burden" a woman's right to terminate her pregnancy:

There should be no surer sign that our jurisprudence has gone off the rails than this: After creating a constitutional right to abortion because it "involve[s] the most intimate and personal choices a person may make in a lifetime, choices central to personal dignity and autonomy," Planned Parenthood v. Casey, 505 U.S. 883, 851 (1992), the Court has created special rules that cede its enforcement to others.

The Court has also allowed schools to raise the constitutional rights of students and their parents. In Pierce v. Society of Sisters, 268 U.S. 510 (1925), private schools successfully challenged mandatory public school attendance as an unreasonable interference with "the liberty of parents and guardians to direct the upbringing and education of children under their control." In the same vein, Runyon v. McCrary, 427 U.S. 160 (1976), allowed a private school to claim, albeit unsuccessfully, that a law prohibiting racial discrimination in admissions violated the associational and privacy rights of students and their parents.

4. DILUTION OF THIRD-PARTY RIGHTS

In some cases the Court has suggested a much broader explanation for third-party standing—namely, that failure to vindicate the litigant's claim would "dilute" or "adversely affect" enjoyment of claimed rights by the third party. This rationale may obtain where there is no apparent obstacle to the rightholder's assertion of his or her own rights and where there is no pre-existing relationship between the litigant and the third party.

An example is Craig v. Boren, 429 U.S. 190 (1976), where a saloon-keeper was allowed to raise the equal protection rights of young men to buy beer at the same age as young women. The restriction on young men caused the saloon-keeper economic injury and therefore established standing to sue. Further, she was found "entitled to assert those concomitant rights of third parties that would be 'diluted or adversely affected' should her constitutional challenge fail and the statutes remain in force." Accordingly, the saloon-keeper came within the seemingly general rule that "vendors and those in like positions have been uniformly permitted to resist efforts at restricting their operations by acting as advocates for the rights of third parties who seek access to their market or function," citing *Eisenstadt v. Baird* and *Barrows v. Jackson*.

Craig v. Boren might be discounted on the ground that the litigation originally included an underage male (with respect to whom the case became moot when he reached the required age) and that the objection to the saloon-keeper's assertion of third-party rights was made for the first time in the Supreme Court. No such factors were present, however, in Carey v. Population Services International, 431 U.S. 678 (1977), which followed the same approach. In *Carey* a corporate seller of contraceptives challenged a New York statute that prohibited sale of contraceptives to persons under the age of 16. Speaking for a majority of seven, Justice Brennan declared that the corporation's standing to attack the statute, "not only in its own right but also on behalf of its potential customers, is settled by *Craig v. Boren.*"

Potentially, the rationale of *Craig* and *Carey* has a very broad reach. Indeed, would there be any case of actual injury to an identifiable third party in which the third-party's rights would not be "diluted or adversely affected" by failure to vindicate the litigant's claim? If not, the bar against third-party standing would be reduced to a prohibition against litigating purely hypothetical situations. Would that be sound? Would it be consistent with the Court's decisions on Article III standing to sue?

5.   *KOWALSKI V. TESMER*

Despite the tendency toward progressive liberalization of third-party standing, the Court pulled up short in Kowalski v. Tesmer, 543 U.S. 125 (2004). The case was triggered by a change in the Michigan constitution making appeal by an accused who had pleaded guilty available not as of right but only by leave of court. The legislature then eliminated (with some exceptions) appointed appellate counsel for indigents. Two lawyers filed suit in federal court to challenge the state law. Standing to sue was based on direct economic injury to the lawyers. The question was whether they could raise the rights of prospective indigent defendants to have appointed counsel on appeal.

In an opinion by Chief Justice Rehnquist, the Court said "no." For one thing, the lawyers were raising the rights of "hypothetical" clients and therefore did not have a "close relationship" with the third parties. Perhaps more important, the Court saw no particular obstacle to the indigents' advancing their own rights to appointed counsel on appeal. The fact that indigent defendants had done so in Michigan supported that supposition. Nevertheless, Justices Ginsburg, Stevens, and Souter dissented, principally on the ground that indigent defendants, "many of whom are likely to be unsophisticated and poorly educated," faced practical obstacles to raising complicated constitutional claims without a lawyer.

Is this decision consistent with *Singleton v. Wulff*? With *Craig v. Boren*? Note that in both *Craig* and *Carey v. Population Services International* the law directly regulated the plaintiffs' conduct (selling alcohol and contraceptives). By contrast, the law being challenged in *Kowalski* did not directly regulate the plaintiffs' conduct but only affected them economically. Does this help explain the Court's stricter approach to third-party standing?

Finally, note that *Kowalski* may have been influenced by Younger v. Harris, 401 U.S. 37 (1971) (considered at length in Chapter VI), which bars defendants in pending state criminal prosecutions from trying to raise their claims in federal court. *Younger* abstention was not in terms applicable to the lawyers in *Kowalski*, as no prosecutions were pending against them, but it had been applied to dismiss from the case three indigent defendants who had originally been co-plaintiffs. Nonetheless, the lawyers were plainly seeking a federal forum to attack pending (and non-pending) state prosecutions, and to that extent the policies of *Younger* might have been thought relevant. Whether the restrictive approach of *Kowalski* will extend outside that context remains to be seen.

6.   THE OVERBREADTH DOCTRINE

The instances of third-party standing discussed to this point have in common the allegation of concrete injury to the rights of identifiable third parties. None involves litigation of a purely hypothetical situation. In one context, however, the Supreme Court has endorsed the litigation of hypotheticals and has allowed a litigant to raise the rights of persons whose interest in the matter at hand is entirely conjectural. That context is the First Amendment overbreadth doctrine.

The word "overbreadth" refers to the substantive coverage of a statute that is challenged on First Amendment grounds. A law is said to be overbroad if its prohibition includes some protected speech. The heart of the overbreadth doctrine is the resulting posture of judicial review. The law may be challenged as unconstitutional "on its face." This means that a litigant whose conduct is covered by a statute but is not constitutionally protected may challenge the validity of the law as it might be applied to constitutionally protected conduct that falls within the statute.

Although overbreadth cases are not often cited as such, the overbreadth doctrine may be seen as a dramatic case of third-party standing. A litigant is allowed to attack the validity of a statute by raising someone else's rights. And unlike most instances of third-party standing, the overbreadth claimant is not required to show an obstacle to the third party's assertion of his or her own rights or a relationship between the litigant and the third party, or even to identify a third party whose rights would be infringed. In essence, the doctrine is the ultimate extension of a dilution-of-rights rationale. The mere existence of an overbroad law is assumed to "dilute or adversely affect" the First Amendment rights of those unidentified persons whose behavior may be "chilled" by the threat that the law will be enforced against them.

The Supreme Court has noted that overbreadth review is "strong medicine" and required that the excess coverage "not only be real, but substantial as well, judged in relation to the statute's plainly legitimate sweep." Broadrick v. Oklahoma, 413 U.S. 601, 613, 615 (1973). Even so constrained, however, the overbreadth doctrine is significantly more accommodating to the litigation of another's rights than most of the judicial pronouncements on third-party standing.

The usual explanation for this approach is the societal importance of the First Amendment. Does it suggest that other instances of third-party standing might also turn on the importance to society of the right being asserted? That a distinction might be made between rights that are significantly societal or "systemic" in their impact and those (perhaps the Fourth Amendment?) that are more "personal" in nature?[a]

---

[a]   For a revisionist analysis of third-party standing with particular attention to the overbreadth doctrine, see Brian Charles Lea, The Merits of Third-Party Standing, 24 Wm. & M. Bill of Rts J. 277 (2015). Lea argues that third-party standing should turn on whether the litigant has a right to the relief sought. On this view, Lea finds standing in overbreadth cases difficult to support.

7.   ASSIGNEE STANDING AND REDRESSABILITY

In the words of the Supreme Court, the question presented in Sprint Communications Co. v. APCC Services, Inc., 554 U.S. 269 (2008), was "whether an assignee of a legal claim for money owed has standing to pursue that claim in federal court, even when the assignee has promised to remit the proceeds of the litigation to the assignor." The assignors were payphone operators that were owed money for calls placed to toll-free numbers. The assignees were "aggregators," who aggregated such claims and sued to collect them from Sprint and other carriers that sponsored toll-free numbers. Recoveries were promised to the assignors, who then paid the aggregators a fee.

In an opinion by Justice Breyer, the Court found that the aggregators had standing. This conclusion rested squarely on history: "[H]istory and precedent are clear on the question before us: Assignees of a claim, including assignees for collection, have long been permitted to bring suit." Given the historical tradition of allowing suits by assignees, the Court looked for a "convincing reason" to do otherwise and, finding none, upheld standing. Controversy focused on the redressability requirement, for the aggregators were required to remit any recovery to the payphone operators. In the Court's view, however, redressability focused

> on whether the *injury* that a plaintiff alleges is likely to be redressed through the litigation—not on what the plaintiff ultimately intends to do with the money he recovers. Here, a legal victory would unquestionably redress the *injuries* for which the aggregators bring suit. . . . [I]f the aggregators prevail in this litigation, the long-distance carriers would write a check to the aggregators for the amount of . . . compensation owed. What does it matter what the aggregators do with the money afterward? The injuries would be redressed whether the agregators remit the litigation proceeds to the payphone operators, donate them to charity, or use them to build new corporate headquarters.

In dissent, Chief Justice Roberts, speaking for himself and for Justices Scalia, Thomas, and Alito, addressed redressasbility as follows:

> The Court goes awry when it asserts that the standing inquiry focuses on whether the *injury* is likely to be redressed, not whether the *complaining party's* injury is likely to be redressed. That could not be more wrong. We have never approved federal-court jurisdiction over a claim where the entire relief requested will run to a party not before the court. Never. . . .
>
> The majority finds that respondents have a sufficient stake in this litigation because the substantive recovery will initially go to them, and "[w]hat does it matter what the aggregators do with the money afterward?" The majority's assertion implies, incorrectly, that respondents have, or ever had, a choice of what to do with the recovery. It may be true that a plaintiff's *independent* decision to pledge his recovery to another . . . would not divest the plaintiff of Article III standing. But respondents never had the right to direct the disposition of the recovery; they have only the right to sue. The

hypothetical plaintiff who chooses to pledge her recovery to charity, by contrast, will secure a personal benefit from the recovery. . . . In that situation, the Article III requirement that a plaintiff demonstrate a personal stake in the outcome of the litigation is satisfied.

Who has the better of this exchange? More generally, what role should history play in such determinations? Should a long (though not uncomplicated) tradition of allowing suit by assignees suffice, or should historical practices be subjected to rigorous review under modern standing doctrine?

The majority also observed that, "as a practical matter, . . . it would be particularly unwise for us to abandon history and precedent in resolving the question before us" because a denial of standing "could easily be overcome." The majority noted, for example, that "the Agreement could be rewritten to give the aggregator a tiny portion of the assigned claim itself, perhaps only a dollar or two." The dissent responded that, while the majority might be right that there would be standing in that situation, "Article III is worth a dollar" and that, in any event, "the ease with which respondents can comply with the requirements of Article III is not a reason to abandon our precedents; it is a reason to adhere to them." Which view is more persuasive? Is there a value to insisting on standing requirements even if they can easily be bypassed, or does such insistence improperly elevate form over substance?

SUBSECTION B. RIPENESS

Poe v. Ullman

Supreme Court of the United States, 1961.
367 U.S. 497.

■ MR. JUSTICE FRANKFURTER announced the judgment of the Court in an opinion in which THE CHIEF JUSTICE, MR. JUSTICE CLARK and MR. JUSTICE WHITTAKER join.

These appeals challenge the constitutionality, under the Fourteenth Amendment, of Connecticut statutes which, as authoritatively construed by the Connecticut Supreme Court of Errors, prohibit the use of contraceptive devices and the giving of medical advice in the use of such devices. In proceedings seeking declarations of law, not on review of convictions for violation of the statutes, that court has ruled that these statutes would be applicable in the case of married couples and even under claim that conception would constitute a serious threat to the health or life of the female spouse.

[The appeals involved three separate actions for declaratory relief. The first, brought under the names of Paul and Pauline Poe, alleged that Mrs. Poe had given birth to three deformed children, each of whom died shortly thereafter; that the Poes' physician, Dr. Buxton, had determined "that the best and safest medical treatment which could be prescribed for their situation is advice in methods of preventing conception"; but that the Poes had been unable to obtain such information "for the sole reason that its delivery and use may or will be claimed by the defendant State's

Attorney (appellee in this Court) to constitute offenses against Connecticut law." The second suit was brought by a married woman who had endured an extremely difficult pregnancy and had been told by Dr. Buxton that she needed contraceptive advice. The third suit was brought by Dr. Buxton, who claimed that the statute interfered with his medical practice in a manner that violated due process.]

Appellants' complaints in these declaratory judgment proceedings do not clearly, and certainly do not in terms, allege that appellee Ullman threatens to prosecute them for use of, or for giving advice concerning, contraceptive devices. The allegations are merely that, in the course of his public duty, he intends to prosecute any offenses against Connecticut law, and that he claims that use of and advice concerning contraceptives would constitute offenses. The lack of immediacy of the threat described by these allegations might alone raise serious questions of nonjusticiability of appellants' claims. See United Public Workers v. Mitchell, 330 U.S. 75 (1947). But even were we to read the allegations to convey a clear threat of imminent prosecutions, we are not bound to accept as true all that is alleged on the face of the complaint and admitted, technically, by demurrer, any more than the Court is bound by stipulation of the parties. Formal agreement between parties that collide with plausibility is too fragile a foundation for indulging in constitutional adjudication.

The Connecticut law prohibiting the use of contraceptives has been on the state's books since 1879. During the more than three-quarters of a century since its enactment, a prosecution for its violation seems never to have been initiated, save in State v. Nelson, 126 Conn. 412, 11 A.2d 856 (1940). The circumstances of that case . . . only prove the abstract character of what is before us. There, a test case was brought to determine the constitutionality of the act as applied against two doctors and a nurse who had allegedly disseminated contraceptive information. After the Supreme Court of Errors sustained the legislation on appeal from a demurrer to the information, the state moved to dismiss the information. Neither counsel nor our own researches have discovered any other attempt to enforce the prohibition of distribution or use of contraceptive devices by criminal process. The unreality of these suits is illuminated by another circumstance. We were advised by counsel for appellants that contraceptives are commonly and notoriously sold in Connecticut drug stores. Yet no prosecutions are recorded; and certainly such ubiquitous, open, public sales would more quickly invite the attention of enforcement officials than the conduct in which the present appellants wish to engage—the giving of private medical advice by a doctor to his individual patients, and their private use of the devices prescribed. The undeviating policy of nullification by Connecticut of its anti-contraceptive laws throughout all the long years that they have been on the statute books bespeaks more than prosecutorial paralysis. What was said in another context is relevant here. "Deeply embedded traditional ways of carrying out state policy . . ."—or not carrying it out—"are often tougher and truer law than the dead words of the written text."

The restriction of our jurisdiction to cases and controversies within the meaning of Article III of the Constitution is not the sole limitation on the exercise of our appellate powers, especially in cases raising constitutional questions. The policy reflected in numerous cases and over a long period was thus summarized in the oft-quoted statement of Mr. Justice Brandeis: "The Court [has] developed, for its own governance in the cases confessedly within its jurisdiction, a series of rules under which it has avoided passing upon a large part of all the constitutional questions pressed upon it for decision." Ashwander v. Tennessee Valley Authority, 297 U.S. 288, 341 (1936) (concurring opinion). In part the rules summarized in the *Ashwander* opinion have derived from the historically defined, limited nature and function of courts and from the recognition that, within the framework of our adversary system, the adjudicatory process is most securely founded when it is exercised under the impact of a lively conflict between antagonistic demands, actively pressed, which make resolution of the controverted issue a practical necessity. In part they derive from the fundamental federal and tripartite character of our national government and from the role—restricted by its very responsibility—of the federal courts, and particularly this Court, within that structure.

These considerations press with special urgency in cases challenging legislative action or state judicial action as repugnant to the Constitution. "The best teaching of this Court's experience admonishes us not to entertain constitutional questions in advance of the strictest necessity." The various doctrines of "standing," "ripeness," and "mootness," which this Court has evolved with particular, though not exclusive, reference to such cases are but several manifestations—each having its own "varied application"—of the primary conception that federal judicial power is to be exercised to strike down legislation, whether state or federal, only at the instance of one who is himself immediately harmed, or immediately threatened with harm, by the challenged action. . . .

It is clear that the mere existence of a state penal statute would constitute insufficient grounds to support a federal court's adjudication of its constitutionality in proceedings brought against the state's prosecuting officials if real threat of enforcement is wanting. If the prosecutor expressly agrees not to prosecute, a suit against him for declaratory and injunctive relief is not such an adversary case as will be reviewed here. Eighty years of Connecticut history demonstrate a similar, albeit tacit agreement. The fact that Connecticut has not chosen to press the enforcement of this statute deprives these controversies of the immediacy which is an indispensable condition of constitutional adjudication. This Court cannot be umpire to debates concerning harmless, empty shadows. To find it necessary to pass on these statutes now, in order to protect appellants from the hazards of prosecution, would be to close our eyes to reality. . . .

Justiciability is of course not a legal concept with a fixed content or susceptible of scientific verification. Its utilization is the resultant of many subtle pressures, including the appropriateness of the issues for decision by this Court and the actual hardship to the litigants of denying them the relief sought. Both these factors justify withholding adjudication of the constitutional issue raised under the circumstances and in the manner in which they are now before the Court.

Dismissed.

■ MR. JUSTICE BLACK dissents because he believes that the constitutional questions should be reached and decided.

■ MR. JUSTICE BRENNAN, concurring in the judgment.

I agree that this appeal must be dismissed for failure to present a real and substantial controversy which unequivocally calls for adjudication of the rights claimed in advance of any attempt by the state to curtail them by criminal prosecution. I am not convinced, on this skimpy record, that these appellants are truly caught in an inescapable dilemma. The true controversy in this case is over the opening of birth-control clinics on a large scale; it is that which the state has prevented in the past, not the use of contraceptives by isolated and individual married couples. It will be time enough to decide the constitutional questions urged upon us when, if ever, that real controversy flares up again. Until it does, or until the state makes a definite and concrete threat to enforce these laws against individual married couples—a threat which it has never made in the past except under the provocation of litigation—this Court may not be compelled to exercise its most delicate power of constitutional adjudication.

■ MR. JUSTICE DOUGLAS, dissenting.

These cases are dismissed because a majority of the members of this Court conclude, for varying reasons, that this controversy does not present a justiciable question. That conclusion is too transparent to require an extended reply. The device of the declaratory judgment is an honored one. . . . If there is a case where the need for this remedy in the shadow of a criminal prosecution is shown, it is this one, as Mr. Justice Harlan demonstrates. . . .

What are these people—doctor and patients—to do? Flout the law and go to prison? Violate the law surreptitiously and hope they will not get caught? By today's decision we leave them no other alternatives. It is not the choice they need have under the regime of the declaratory judgment and our constitutional system. It is not the choice worthy of a civilized society. A sick wife, a concerned husband, a conscientious doctor seek a dignified, discrete [sic], orderly answer to the critical problem confronting them. We should not turn them away and make them flout the law and get arrested to have their constitutional rights determined. They are entitled to an answer to their predicament here and now. . . .

■ MR. JUSTICE HARLAN, dissenting. . . .

There can be no quarrel with the plurality opinion's statement that "Justiciability is of course not a legal concept with a fixed content or susceptible of scientific verification," but, with deference, the fact that justiciability is not precisely definable does not make it ineffable. . . .

[T]he Court, in the course of its decisions on matters of justiciability, has developed and given expression to a number of important limitations on the exercise of its jurisdiction, the presence or absence of which here should determine the justiciability of these appeals. Since all of them are referred to here in one way or another, it is well to proceed to a disclosure of those which are *not* involved in the present appeals, thereby focusing attention on the one factor on which reliance appears to be placed by both the plurality and concurring opinions in this instance.

First: It should by now be abundantly clear that the fact that only constitutional claims are presented in proceedings seeking *anticipatory* relief against state criminal statutes does not for that reason alone make the claims premature. . . .

Second: I do not think these appeals may be dismissed for want of "ripeness" as that concept has been understood in its "varied applications." There is no lack of "ripeness" in the sense that is exemplified by cases such as United Public Workers v. Mitchell, 330 U.S. 75 (1947); International Longshoremen's and Warehousemen's Union v. Boyd, 347 U.S. 222 (1954); [and others]. In all of these cases the lack of ripeness inhered in the fact that the need for some further procedure, some further contingency of application or interpretation, whether judicial administrative or executive, or some further clarification of the intentions of the claimant, served to make remote the issue which was sought to be presented to the Court. Certainly the appellants have stated in their pleadings fully and unequivocally what it is that they intend to do; no clarifying or resolving contingency stands in their way before they may embark on that conduct. Thus, there is no circumstance besides that of detection or prosecution to make remote the particular controversy. And it is clear beyond cavil that the mere fact that a controversy such as this is rendered still more unavoidable by an actual prosecution, is not *alone* sufficient to make the case too remote, not ideally enough "ripe" for adjudication, at the prior stage of anticipatory relief.

. . . I cannot see what further elaboration is required to enable us to decide the appellants' claims, and indeed neither the plurality opinion nor the concurring opinion—notwithstanding the latter's characterization of this record as "skimpy"—suggests what more grist is needed before the judicial mill could turn.

Third: This is not a feigned, hypothetical, friendly or colorable suit such as discloses "a want of a truly adversary contest." . . .

Fourth: The doctrine of the cases dealing with a litigant's lack of standing to raise a constitutional claim is said to justify the dismissal of these appeals. . . . There is no question but that appellants here are asserting rights which are peculiarly their own, and which, if they are to be raised at all, may be raised most appropriately by them. Nor do I understand the argument to be that this is the sort of claim which is too remote ever to be pressed by anyone, because no one is ever sufficiently involved. Thus, in truth, it is not the parties pressing this claim but the occasion chosen for pressing it which is objected to. But as has been shown the fact that it is anticipatory relief which is asked cannot of itself make the occasion objectionable.

We are brought, then, to the precise failing in these proceedings which is said to justify refusal to exercise our mandatory appellate jurisdiction: that there has been but one recorded Connecticut case dealing with a *prosecution* under the statute. The significance of this lack of recorded evidence of prosecutions is said to make the presentation of appellants' rights too remote, too contingent, too hypothetical for adjudication. . . .

As far as the record is concerned, I think it is pure conjecture, and indeed conjecture which to me seems contrary to realities, that an open violation of the statute by a doctor (or more obviously still by a birth-control clinic) would not result in a substantial threat of prosecution. Crucial to the opposite conclusion is the description of the 1940 prosecution instituted in *State v. Nelson* as a "test case" which, as it is viewed, scarcely even punctuates the uniform state practice of nonenforcement of this statute. I read the history of Connecticut enforcement in a very different light. The *Nelson* case, as appears from the state court's opinion, was a prosecution of two doctors and a nurse for aiding and abetting violations of this statute by married women in prescribing and advising the use of contraceptive materials by them. It is true that there is evidence of a customary unwillingness to enforce the statute prior to *Nelson*. . . . What must also be noted is that the prosecutor [in that case] stated that the purpose of the prosecution was:

> the establishment of the constitutional validity and efficacy of the statutes under which these accused are informed against. Henceforth any person, whether a physician or layman, who violates the provisions of these statutes, must expect to be prosecuted and punished in accordance with the literal provisions of the law. . . .

The plurality opinion now finds, and the concurring opinion must assume, that the only explanation of the absence of recorded prosecutions subsequent to the *Nelson* case is that Connecticut has renounced that intention to prosecute and punish "*any* person . . . in accordance with the literal provisions of the law" which it announced in *Nelson*. But if renunciation of the purposes of the *Nelson* prosecution is consistent with a lack of subsequent prosecutions, success of that purpose is no less consistent with that lack. . . . In short, I fear that the Court has indulged in a bit of sleight of hand to be rid of this case. It has treated the significance of the absence of prosecutions during the 20 years since *Nelson* as identical with that of the absence of prosecutions during the years before *Nelson*. It has ignored the fact that the very purpose of the *Nelson* prosecution was to change defiance into compliance. It has ignored the very possibility that this purpose may have been successful. The result is to postulate a security from prosecution for open defiance of the statute which I do not believe the record supports. . . .

The Court's disposition assumes that to decide the case now, in the absence of any consummated prosecutions, is unwise because it forces a difficult decision in advance of any exigent necessity therefor. Of course it is abundantly clear that this requisite necessity can exist prior to any actual prosecution, for that is the theory of anticipatory relief, and is by now familiar law. What must be relied on, therefore, is that the historical absence of prosecutions in some way leaves these appellants free to violate the statute without fear of prosecution, whether or not the law is constitutional, and thus absolves us from the duty of deciding if it is. Despite the suggestion of a "tougher and truer law" of immunity from criminal prosecution and despite speculation as to a "tacit agreement" that this law will not be enforced, there is, of course, no suggestion of an estoppel against the state if it should attempt to prosecute appellants. Neither the plurality nor the concurring opinion suggests that appellants have some legally cognizable right not to be prosecuted if the statute is constitutional. What is meant is simply that the appellants are more or less free to act without fear of prosecution because the prosecuting authorities of the state, in their discretion and at their whim, are, as a matter of prediction, unlikely to decide to prosecute.

Here is the core of my disagreement with the present disposition. [T]he most substantial claim which these married persons press is their right to enjoy the privacy of their marital relations free of the enquiry of the criminal law, whether it be in a prosecution of them or of a doctor whom they have consulted. And I cannot agree that their enjoyment of this privacy is not substantially impinged upon, when they are told that . . . the only thing which stands between them and being forced to render criminal account of their marital privacy is the whim of the prosecutor. . . .

I therefore think it is incumbent on us to consider the merits of appellants' constitutional claims. . . .

■ MR. JUSTICE STEWART, dissenting.

For the reasons so convincingly advanced by both Mr. Justice Douglas and Mr. Justice Harlan, I join them in dissenting from the dismissal of these appeals. . . . [a]

---

   [a]   In 1961, Dr. Buxton served as medical director of a birth-control clinic opened by the Planned Parenthood League in New Haven, Conn. His criminal prosecution and that of the

NOTES ON RIPENESS

1. RIPENESS IN CONTEXT

Since "ripeness" is the name given to prematurity in litigation, it usually arises in suits for anticipatory relief. Of course, anticipatory relief has long been available in the form of an injunction, but the equitable requirements of irreparable harm and no adequate remedy at law typically proved more restrictive than any Article III limitation on the exercise of judicial power. Nonetheless, one encounters "ripeness" in suits for injunctive relief, where it tends to merge with (or supersede) the traditional requirements of equity. This context is illustrated in Notes 4–7, below.

Additionally, "ripeness" arises in challenges to actions by administrative agencies. In these cases, the question is typically whether litigation should await some further agency action that may clarify or perhaps eliminate the dispute. In this application, ripeness is related to the doctrine of exhaustion of remedies. This context is discussed in Note 8, below.

As a problem distinct from the law of equity and from judicial review of administrative agencies, ripeness is chiefly a product of declaratory judgments. The Federal Declaratory Judgment Act, now codified in 28 U.S.C. §§ 2201–2202, was enacted in 1934.[a] Its purpose was to obviate the necessity "to violate or purport to violate a statute in order to obtain a judicial determination of its meaning or validity." S. Rep. No. 1005, 73rd Cong., 2d Sess., pp. 2–3. The statute authorized the courts of the United States "to declare rights and other legal relations" without regard to whether further relief was or could be asked for, but expressly limited this power to "cases of actual controversy." By providing a mechanism for anticipatory relief unburdened by the traditional requirements of equity, the Declaratory Judgment Act created a need for an independent doctrine of ripeness.

2. RIPENESS IN DECLARATORY JUDGMENTS: *AETNA LIFE INS. V. HAWORTH*

In Aetna Life Ins. Co. v. Haworth, 300 U.S. 227 (1937), the declaratory judgment procedure was challenged as inconsistent with Article III. The case involved a series of insurance policies providing benefits in the event of disability. The insured claimed such disability, but the company denied the claim and asserted that the policies had lapsed for non-payment of premiums. After some time, the company sued for a declaration of non-liability, contending that otherwise its ability to disprove the disability claim might be impaired by the disappearance, illness, or death of relevant witnesses. The trial court dismissed the complaint on the ground that it did not set forth

---

League's executive director led to the invalidation of the Connecticut statutes in Griswold v. Connecticut, 381 U.S. 479 (1965).—[Footnote by eds.]

[a] The current provision, 28 U.S.C. § 2201, reads as follows:

In a case of actual controversy within its jurisdiction, except with respect to federal taxes, any court of the United States, upon the filing of an appropriate pleading, may declare the rights and other legal relations of any interested party seeking such declaration, whether or not further relief is or could be sought. Any such declaration shall have the force and effect of a final judgment or decree and shall be reviewable as such.

a justiciable "controversy." That decision was affirmed by the Court of Appeals, but reversed by the Supreme Court. Speaking for a unanimous Court, Chief Justice Hughes said:

> The Constitution limits the exercise of the judicial power to "cases" and "controversies." . . . The Declaratory Judgment Act of 1934, in its limitation to "cases of actual controversy," manifestly has regard to the constitutional provision and is operative only in respect to controversies which are such in the constitutional sense. . . .

> A "controversy" in this sense must be one that is appropriate for judicial determination. A justiciable controversy is thus distinguished from a difference or dispute of a hypothetical or abstract character; from one that is academic or moot. The controversy must be definite and concrete, touching the legal relations of parties having adverse legal interests. It must be a real and substantial controversy admitting of specific relief through a decree of a conclusive character, as distinguished from an opinion advising what the law would be upon a hypothetical state of facts.

Applying these principles, the Court found that the insurer's suit was "manifestly susceptible of judicial determination." It called "not for an advisory opinion upon a hypothetical basis, but for an adjudication of present right upon established facts." If the insured had sued on the policies, the existence of a justiciable controversy would have been clear. That the company brought suit instead was of no consequence, for "[i]t is the nature of the controversy, not the method of its presentation or the particular party who presents it, that is determinative."

Note that the *Haworth* opinion did not use the word "ripeness." Yet today the considerations it requires would likely be known under that label.

3. QUESTIONS AND COMMENTS ON *POE*

Is *Poe* consistent with *Haworth*? Was the controversy in *Poe* more abstract, hypothetical, or academic than the controversy in *Haworth*? Or is the difference in result attributable to a difference in judicial attitude toward the claim being raised? Might the Court have been more chary to rule on the constitutionality of Connecticut's laws than to resolve the contractual rights of private parties? Is it proper for such considerations to figure in determinations of ripeness?

4. *UNITED PUBLIC WORKERS V. MITCHELL*

An early ripeness case, cited by both sides in *Poe*, is United Public Workers v. Mitchell, 330 U.S. 75 (1947). Federal workers sued to enjoin enforcement of a provision in the Hatch Act stating that "[n]o officer or employee in the executive branch of the federal government . . . shall take any active part in political management or in political campaigns." Only one of the plaintiffs had actually violated the Hatch Act. The rest alleged their desire to violate the rule against political activity and their conviction that the statute contravened their constitutional rights. The Supreme Court found their claims nonjusticiable. "We can only speculate," said Justice Reed, "as to the kinds of political activity the appellants desire to engage in or as to the contents of their proposed public statements or the circumstances of their publication." To this he added an influential statement of the case for judicial self-restraint:

> The Constitution allots the nation's judicial power to the federal courts. Unless these courts respect the limits of that unique authority, they intrude upon powers vested in the legislative or executive branches. Judicial adherence to the doctrine of the separation of powers preserves the courts for the decision of issues, between litigants, capable of effective determination. Judicial exposition upon political proposals is permissible only when necessary to decide definite issues between litigants. When the courts act continually within these constitutionally imposed boundaries of their power, their ability to perform their function as a balance for the people's protection against abuse of power by other branches of government remains unimpaired. Should the courts seek to expand their power so as to bring under their jurisdiction ill-defined controversies over constitutional issues, they would become the organ of political theories. Such abuse of judicial power would properly meet rebuke and restriction from other branches.

Do these remarks suggest a "prudential" component to ripeness, independent of the minimum requirements of Article III? Do they provide a rationale for the decision in *Poe*?

5. RIPENESS AND STANDING: *DUKE POWER*

In Duke Power Co. v. Carolina Environmental Study Group, Inc., 438 U.S. 59 (1978) (discussed in Section 1 of this chapter in the materials on standing), environmental activists sought to derail construction of nuclear power plants by attacking the constitutionality of the Price-Anderson Act, which limits total compensation to be paid by utility companies in the event of a major nuclear accident. Plaintiffs claimed that this limitation on compensation would violate their constitutional rights, but as no accident had yet occurred (or was likely to), plaintiffs could not show actual injury resulting from the limits on compensation in the event of an accident. Instead, plaintiffs established standing by pointing to injuries resulting from the ordinary operation of the plants, chiefly thermal and environmental pollution of lake waters used to cool the reactors. One of the objections to the case was the fact that the rights claimed to be violated were unrelated to the injuries that established standing, but the Supreme Court found that this presented no problem:

> To the extent that issues of ripeness involve, at least in part, the existence of a live "Case or Controversy," our conclusion that appellees will sustain immediate injury from the operation of the disputed power plants [thermal pollution] and that such injury would be redressed by the relief requested would appear to satisfy this requirement.

The prudential considerations embodied in the ripeness doctrine also argue strongly for a prompt resolution of the claims presented. Although it is true that no nuclear accident has yet occurred and that such an occurrence would eliminate much of the existing scientific uncertainty surrounding this subject, it would not, in our view, significantly advance our ability to deal with the legal issues presented nor aid us in their resolution. However, delayed resolution of these issues would foreclose any relief from the present injury suffered by appellees—relief that would be forthcoming if they were to prevail in their various challenges to the act. Similarly, delayed resolution would frustrate one of the key purposes of the Price-Anderson Act—the elimination of doubts concerning the scope of private liability in the event of major nuclear accident. In short, all parties would be adversely affected by a decision to defer definitive resolution of the constitutional validity vel non of the Price-Anderson Act. Since we are persuaded that "we will be in no better position later than we are now" to decide this question, we hold that it is presently ripe for adjudication.

Are these persuasive reasons for resolving the constitutionality of the statute? Did the decision on justiciability depend on an assessment of the merits? Should it have mattered that the alleged constitutional defect had no relation to plaintiffs' present injuries?

Consider the argument of Jonathan Varat, Variable Justiciability and the *Duke Power* Case, 58 Tex. L. Rev. 273 (1980). Varat asserts that the "unacknowledged result" of this decision is "to collapse the Article III ripeness inquiry into the Article III standing inquiry and to alter the primary policy of ripeness from a concern with the issues to a concern with the plaintiff's cognizable injury in fact":

> If ripeness, in the dimension of reasonable certainty of actual harm, is not to be a redundant inquiry into standing, the Court must focus on harm to the rights claimed to be unlawfully disregarded, not the concrete harm that gives the plaintiff a stake in the litigation. Ripeness is meaningful only if applied to the issue raised in the case. To be sure, relative certainty of harm to the plaintiff in most cases coincides with relative certainty of harm to the rights asserted in the suit. Most suits claim that present rights have been, or are being, unlawfully ignored. In the rare case like *Duke Power,* however, the inquiries are separate and should be treated as such. The Court's job is to protect rights that are threatened—not to redress any injury that incidentally might be redressed by adjudication of rights not in jeopardy and not legally related to that injury.

Does this criticism clarify an independent significance to questions of ripeness and standing? Is the focus here on ripeness, or on the adjudication of third-party rights? Or are they perhaps only two ways of looking at the same thing?

6. RIPENESS AND STANDING: *SUSAN B. ANTHONY LIST V. DRIEHAUS*

Ohio passed a statute making it illegal to publish or disseminate a false statement about a political candidate, with knowledge or reckless disregard of its falsity. Under the statute, a complaint filed with the Ohio Elections Commission triggered a hearing on falsity, which could result in mere reprimand or in misdemeanor prosecution.

The Susan B. Anthony List (SBA), a "pro-life advocacy organization," attacked then-Congressman Steve Driehaus for having supported the Affordable Care Act. Specifically, they alleged that in doing so "Driehaus voted FOR taxpayer-funded abortion." Driehaus filed a complaint with the Commission, a panel of which found probable cause that a violation had been committed. Before the full Commission could rule, SBA sued in federal court to declare the Ohio statute invalid under the First Amendment, but that suit was stayed under Younger v. Harris, 401 U.S. 37 (1971), pending completion of the state proceedings. The election intervened, Driehaus lost his seat, and he withdrew his complaint.

With the state proceeding resolved, SBA amended their complaint and renewed their federal action. The District Court dismissed the suit as non-justiciable, and the Sixth Circuit affirmed for lack of ripeness. That conclusion was based on analysis of "(1) the likelihood that the alleged harm would come to pass; (2) whether the factual record was sufficiently developed; and (3) the hardship to the parties if judicial relief were denied."

In Susan B. Anthony List v. Driehaus, 573 U.S. ___, 134 S.Ct. 2334 (2014), the Supreme Court unanimously reversed. Speaking through Justice Thomas, the Court paid almost no attention to ripeness as an independent doctrine. Instead, the Court analyzed the case as a problem of injury-in-fact under the law of standing. The Court had no trouble finding such injury, given that the plaintiff intended to engage in similar speech in the future, that the speech was proscribed by the Ohio law, and that there was a "credible threat of prosecution" by the Ohio Commission. See Babbitt v. Farm Workers, 442 U.S. 289, 298 (1979).

The existence of that credible threat of prosecution would seem to be the critical factor distinguishing this case from *Poe v. Ullman*, but the analysis rests on different doctrinal grounds. *Poe*, like the Sixth Circuit decision in *Susan B. Anthony List*, rested squarely on ripeness. The Supreme Court's opinion treated the same issue under the law of standing. Is there any real difference? Can every ripeness issue be recharacterized as a question of standing, or is this simply illustrative of a sub-set of cases in which the doctrines overlap?

7. RIPENESS IN STRUCTURAL REFORM LITIGATION: *O'SHEA V. LITTLETON*

O'Shea v. Littleton, 414 U.S. 488 (1974), involved a class action for injunctive relief against police, prosecutors, and judges in Cairo, Illinois. The plaintiffs alleged a continuing pattern of racial discrimination in law enforcement. Most of the complaint related to plaintiffs' effort to maintain an

economic boycott against certain white merchants and the defendants' allegedly unlawful interference with that effort. In the Supreme Court, attention
focused on a judge and a magistrate who were alleged, quite generally, to
engage in a continuing practice of illegal bond-setting and sentencing.
Speaking through Justice White, the Court rejected this suit:

> The complaint failed to satisfy the threshold requirement im-
> posed by Article III of the Constitution that those who seek to
> invoke the power of the federal courts must allege an actual case or
> controversy. . . . Neither the complaint nor [plaintiffs'] counsel sug-
> gested that any of the named plaintiffs at the time the complaint
> was filed were themselves serving an allegedly illegal sentence or
> were on trial or awaiting trial before [these defendants]. . . .

> Of course, past wrongs are evidence bearing on whether there
> is a real and immediate threat of repeated injury. But here the pro-
> spect of future injury rests on the likelihood that [plaintiffs] will
> again be arrested for and charged with violations of the criminal
> law and will again be subjected to bond proceedings, trial, or sen-
> tencing before [defendants]. . . . Apparently, the proposition is that
> *if* [plaintiffs] proceed to violate an unchallenged law and *if* they are
> charged, held to answer, and tried in any proceedings before [de-
> fendants], they will be subjected to the discriminatory practices
> that [defendants] are alleged to have followed. But it seems to us
> that attempting to anticipate whether and when these [plaintiffs]
> will be charged with crime and will be made to appear before either
> [defendant] takes us into the area of speculation and conjecture. . . .

> The foregoing considerations obviously shade into those deter-
> mining whether the complaint states a sound basis for equitable
> relief; and even if we were inclined to consider the complaint as
> presenting an existing case or controversy, we would firmly disa-
> gree . . . that an adequate basis for equitable relief against these
> [defendants] had been stated.

Justices Douglas, joined by Justices Brennan and Marshall, dissented.
He claimed that the allegations "of past and continuing wrongdoing clearly
state a case or controversy in the Article III sense" and argued that concerns
about the appropriateness of equitable relief should be delayed until trial.

As Justice White's comments suggest, if the doctrine of ripeness had
never been invented, essentially the same questions would have arisen under
the requirements of equity. In structural reform cases, ripeness blends Article III concerns with traditional equity concerns, and the whole is overlaid
by concerns about federalism.

8.   Ripeness in Structural Reform Litigation: *Los Angeles v.
     Lyons*

According to the findings of the District Court, Adolph Lyons was
stopped for a routine traffic offense and, without provocation or justification,
subjected to a department-authorized chokehold which left him unconscious,
spitting up blood, lying in his own urine. In City of Los Angeles v. Lyons, 461

U.S. 95 (1983), the Supreme Court held that, although Lyons was entitled to seek money damages for that event, he lacked standing to sue for injunctive relief against future use of such chokeholds. Speaking for the Court, Justice White said:

> Lyons's standing to seek the injunction requested depended on whether he was likely to suffer future injury from the use of the chokeholds by police officers. . . . That Lyons may have been illegally choked by the police on October 6, 1976, while presumably affording Lyons standing to claim damages . . . , does nothing to establish a real and immediate threat that he would again be stopped for a traffic violation, or for any other offense, by an officer or officers who would illegally choke him into unconsciousness without any provocation or resistance on his part. The additional allegation in the complaint that the police in Los Angeles routinely apply chokeholds in situations where they are not threatened by the use of deadly force falls far short of the allegations that would be necessary to establish a case or controversy between these parties.

As in *O'Shea*, Justice White also said that, even if Lyon's allegations were taken to establish an Article III case or controversy, they do not meet the equity requirement of irreparable injury.

Justice Marshall, joined by Justices Brennan, Blackmun, and Stevens, dissented. Marshall insisted that Lyons's injury gave him standing and that there was no authority for "fragmenting the standing inquiry and imposing a separate standing hurdle with respect to each form of relief sought." The propriety of an injunction, which Marshall thought justified, was in any event a remedial issue and should be resolved on that ground.

Lyons richly illustrates the plasticity and redundancy of the various categories of nonjusticiability. The Court conceived of the problem as standing: Lyons's past injury gave him standing to sue for damages but no standing to prevent future harms. If one conceives of standing as settled by the past injury, as Justice Marshall argued, the question might then be phrased in terms of ripeness: Was Lyons's attack against future chokeholds in unspecified circumstances ripe for adjudication? And, as usual, this question blends into the traditional equity requirement of irreparable injury. Finally, in *Lyons*, as in structural reform litigation generally, the various doctrinal categories are overlaid by the Supreme Court's concern not to allow judges to move too far or too fast in supplanting local authority.

9. RIPENESS IN THE ADMINISTRATIVE STATE: RELATED DOCTRINES

Ripeness is the main, but not the only, bar to premature litigation. Closely related are the requirements of finality and exhaustion of remedies, both of which operate to prevent premature judicial review of administrative decisions. As used in this context,[b] "finality" describes the usual statutory

---

[b] The word is also used to describe the limitation of appellate jurisdiction in 28 U.S.C. § 1291 to "final decisions" of the District Courts and the specification in 28 U.S.C. § 1257 that the Supreme Court has jurisdiction over "[f]inal judgments or decrees" of the highest state courts.

authorization of judicial review of final agency actions. See, e.g., 15 U.S.C. § 45(c) (authorizing judicial review of final "cease and desist" orders of the Federal Trade Commission). The generic provision is in the Administrative Procedure Act (APA), 5 U.S.C. § 704, which provides for judicial review of "final agency action for which there is no other adequate remedy in a court." Other agency action may be challenged if "made reviewable by statute." 5 U.S.C. § 701(a).

As the Supreme Court made clear in Abbott Laboratories v. Gardner, 387 U.S. 136 (1967), the APA does not bar pre-enforcement review by means of suits for declaratory or injunctive relief. That means that the doctrine of ripeness functions, in this context, "to prevent the courts, through avoidance of premature adjudication, from entangling themselves in abstract disagreements over administrative policies, and also to protect the agencies from judicial interference until an administrative decision has been formalized and its effects felt in a concrete way by the challenging parties." These goals could be served by a "pragmatic" administration of the statutory requirement. Specifically, said the Court, "finality" would depend on an evaluation of "the fitness of the issues for judicial decision" and "the hardship to the parties of withholding court consideration."

Of similar effect is the requirement of exhaustion of administrative remedies. See Myers v. Bethlehem Shipbuilding Corp., 303 U.S. 41 (1938). In that case the Court invoked the "long settled rule of judicial administration that no one is entitled to judicial relief for a supposed or threatened injury until the prescribed administrative remedy has been exhausted." The goal is to avoid disruption of agency action by premature judicial intervention.[c]

SUBSECTION C. MOOTNESS

INTRODUCTORY NOTES ON MOOTNESS

1. INTRODUCTION

As traditionally stated, mootness requires that a live controversy exist throughout the litigation. If a live controversy ceases to exist at trial, the case will be dismissed as moot. If the controversy disappears on appeal, the judgment below will be vacated and the case dismissed as moot. So stated, mootness sounds simple. In fact, the doctrine is complicated by a history of exceptions and uncertainty in its administration.

2. VOLUNTARY CESSATION OF ILLEGAL ACTIVITY

In United States v. W.T. Grant Co., 345 U.S. 629 (1953), the government brought an antitrust action to enjoin the use of interlocking directorates

---

[c] A variant of ripeness arises under the Takings Clause. Williamson County Regional Planning Commission v. Hamilton Bank of Johnson City, 473 U.S. 172 (1985), held that a federal plaintiff seeking to challenge a regulatory taking by a state or local authority must first seek compensation in state court. For discussion of the complexities of administering that requirement and a proposed "prudential" approach to the problem, see Katherine Mims Crocker, Justifying a Prudential Solution to the *Williamson County* Ripeness Puzzle, 49 Ga. L. Rev. 163 (2014).

among competing corporations. After the overlapping directors resigned, the defendants asked to have the suit dismissed as moot. The Supreme Court refused:

> Both sides agree to the abstract proposition that voluntary cessation of allegedly illegal conduct does not deprive the tribunal of power to hear and determine the case, i.e., does not make the case moot. A controversy may remain to be settled in such circumstances, e.g., a dispute over the legality of the challenged practices. The defendant is free to return to his old ways. This, together with a public interest in having the legality of the practices settled, militates against a mootness conclusion. For to say that the case has become moot means that the defendant is entitled to a dismissal as a matter of right. The courts have rightly refused to grant defendants such a powerful weapon against public law enforcement.

The Court went on to say that although a mere disclaimer of an intent to revive an illegal practice would not suffice, a case might become moot if the defendants could demonstrate that "there is no reasonable expectation that the wrong will be repeated."

For applications of this principle, see City of Mesquite v. Aladdin's Castle, Inc., 455 U.S. 283 (1982), and Northeastern Florida Chapter of Associated General Contractors v. City of Jacksonville, 508 U.S. 656 (1993). In *Aladdin's Castle*, a municipal ordinance was declared unconstitutionally vague after it had been repealed. The Supreme Court noted that if the decision below were vacated, the municipality would be free to reenact the same ordinance. Accordingly, the case was not moot.

In *Associated General Contractors*, the contractors challenged Jacksonville's minority set-aside program as unconstitutional. After the Supreme Court granted certiorari, the city repealed the set-aside ordinance and enacted a more carefully constructed replacement. Speaking through Justice Thomas, the Court said the case was not moot: "There is no mere risk that Jacksonville will repeat its allegedly wrongful conduct; it has already done so." That the new ordinance differed from the old one did not matter: "[I]f that were the rule, a defendant could moot a case by repealing the challenged statute and replacing it with one that differs only in some insignificant respect."

Justice O'Connor, joined by Justice Blackmun, dissented. She argued that *Aladdin's Castle* stated an exceptional rule for those rare cases "where circumstances demonstrate that the legislature will likely reinstate the old law." Other precedents established that, "where a challenged statute is replaced with more narrowly drawn legislation pending our review, and the plaintiff seeks only prospective relief, we generally should decline to decide the case. The controversy with respect to the old statute is moot, because a declaration of its invalidity or an injunction against the law's future enforcement would not benefit the plaintiff."

Who has the better of this argument? Should the courts assume that a repealed ordinance will be reenacted or that other allegedly illegal activity will be resumed? In making that assumption, are the courts reaching to adjudicate mere hypotheticals? Or is this stance necessary to prevent the kind of cat-and-mouse game described by Justice Thomas? Is it possible for a court to assess, on a case-by-case basis, the defendant's good faith?[a]

3. CONTROVERSIES "CAPABLE OF REPETITION, YET EVADING REVIEW"

Another exception to mootness is a question "capable of repetition, yet evading review." The phrase comes from Southern Pacific Terminal Co. v. Interstate Commerce Commission, 219 U.S. 498, 515 (1911), and is typically invoked where the specific dispute has been mooted by the passage of time but the same issue is likely to arise again between the same parties. There must be "a 'reasonable expectation' or a 'demonstrated probability' that the same controversy will recur." Murphy v. Hunt, 455 U.S. 478, 482 (1982) (per curiam). And traditionally, at least, it is not enough that the same *issue* will arise in the future; the controversy must be "capable of repetition, yet evading review" with respect to the same *claimant*.

This principle is illustrated by First National Bank of Boston v. Bellotti, 435 U.S. 765 (1978). In that case, Massachusetts corporations attacked a statute forbidding them from spending money to influence voter referenda on issues not materially affecting business interests. The statute specified that no issue concerning the taxation of individuals could be deemed materially affecting business interests. The corporations wanted to oppose a state constitutional amendment authorizing a graduated individual income tax. When informed that such expenditures would be illegal, the corporations challenged the statute as a violation of free speech. By the time the case reached the Supreme Court, the referendum had been held, and the proposed amendment defeated, but the Court nevertheless found a live controversy.

Similar amendments had been proposed by the legislature on four occasions. In each instance, the time between the legislative proposal and submission to the voters had been too short to allow complete judicial review of the restriction on corporate expenditure. There seemed little doubt that the proposal would be revived in the future and that the plaintiff corporations would again be subject to the statutory restriction. The case was therefore found to fall within that category of controversies "capable of repetition, yet evading review," and not moot.[b]

---

[a] For a recent application of this rule, see Already, LLC v. Nike, Inc., 568 U.S. 85 (2013). Nike sued Already for infringement of a trademark shoe design. Already counterclaimed for a declaration of trademark invalidity. After some preliminary proceedings, Nike apparently saw the handwriting on the wall, because it then moved to have its claims against Already dismissed with prejudice and eventually covenanted "unconditionally and irrevocably" to refrain from making any claims or demands of Already or its distributors for the allegedly infringing shoes or for "any colorable imitations thereof." Already nevertheless wanted to press its attack on Nike's trademark, but the Supreme Court found the case moot. The test was whether "the allegedly wrongful behavior [could] reasonably be expected to recur," and in light of the breadth and content of Nike's covenant, the answer was "no."

[b] See also Davis v. Federal Election Commission, 554 U.S. 724 (2008); Roe v. Wade, 410 U.S. 113 (1973); and Gerstein v. Pugh, 420 U.S. 103 (1975). In *Davis*, as in *Bellotti*, the dispute concerned campaign finance regulation that arguably became moot when the election occurred, but that would have recurred if, as seemed likely, the candidate ran again. In *Roe*, a pregnant

On what ground can this exception be justified? Can it be squared with the Court's statement, made in Schlesinger v. Reservists Committee to Stop the War, 418 U.S. 208 (1974), and repeated in other cases, that "[t]he assumption that if [plaintiffs] have no standing to sue, no one would have standing, is not a reason to find standing"?

4. *HONIG V. DOE*

The meaning and implications of "capable of repetition, yet evading review" were disputed in Honig v. Doe, 484 U.S. 305 (1988). The case involved the "stay-put" provision of the Education of the Handicapped Act. That provision directs that a disabled child "shall remain in [his or her] then current educational placement" pending administrative and judicial review of proposed changes. The question was whether emotionally disabled children in public school could be expelled for dangerous or disruptive conduct growing out of their disabilities.

The decision involved an application of the "stay-put" provision that seemed to have become moot. The majority, however, found the dispute "capable of repetition, yet evading review." Although the student had not returned to school, he still suffered from the emotional disability that led to his expulsion. The Court therefore found a "reasonable expectation" that the problem would recur and that any resulting claim would likely evade review.

This conclusion was disputed by Justice Scalia, with whom Justice O'Connor joined. There was no showing that the student would return to public school or that, if he did, he would be placed in an educational setting unable to accommodate his disruptive behavior. Therefore, Scalia argued, the traditional standard of "capable of repetition" had not been met.

Honig suggests—and it is not the only case to suggest—a certain laxity in the administration of "capable of repetition, yet evading review." In *Honig*, as in many other cases, an issue of limited duration was certain to recur, but not necessarily between the same parties. One way to look at *Honig* is as a dispute between those who would require a rigorous showing that *this plaintiff* will have the same claim again and those who would be satisfied with a showing that *this defendant* will face similar claims in the future.

An interesting concurrence was filed by Chief Justice Rehnquist. He called for reconsideration of mootness and its relation to Article III:

> If it were indeed Article III which—by reason of its requirement of a case or controversy for the exercise of federal judicial power—underlies the mootness doctrine, the "capable of repetition, yet evading" review exception relied upon by the Court in this case would be incomprehensible. Article III extends the judicial power of the United States only to cases and controversies; it does not except from this requirement other lawsuits which are "capable of repetition, yet evading review." If our mootness doctrine were

---

plaintiff was asserting a right to an abortion, but it took much longer than nine months for the case to get through the legal system to the Supreme Court. Similarly, in *Gerstein* criminal defendants were complaining about pre-trial detentions in cases that were long since over by the time the issue could be fully litigated.

forced upon us by the case or controversy requirement of Article III itself, we would have no more power to decide lawsuits which are "moot" but which also raise questions which are capable of repetition but evading review than we would to decide cases which are "moot" but raise no such questions. . . .

The logical conclusion to be drawn from [the precedents], and from the historical development of the principle of mootness, is that while an unwillingness to decide moot cases may be connected to the case or controversy requirement of Article III, it is an attenuated connection that may be overridden where there are strong reasons to override it. The "capable of repetition, yet evading review" exception is an example. So too is our refusal to dismiss as moot those cases in which the defendant voluntarily ceases, at some advanced stage of the appellate proceedings, whatever activity prompted the plaintiff to seek an injunction. I believe we should adopt an additional exception to our present mootness doctrine for those cases where the events which render the case moot have supervened since our grant of certiorari. . . . [Our] resources—the time spent preparing to decide the case by reading briefs, hearing oral arguments, and conferring—are squandered in every case in which it becomes apparent after the decisional process is underway that we may not reach the question presented. To me [that] is a sufficient reason either to abandon the doctrine of mootness altogether in cases which this Court has decided to review, or at least to relax the doctrine of mootness in such a manner as the dissent accuses the majority of doing here. I would leave the mootness doctrine as established by our cases in full force and effect when applied to the earlier stages of a lawsuit, but I believe that once this Court has undertaken a consideration of a case, an exception to that principle is just as much warranted as where a case is "capable of repetition, yet evading review."

Justice Scalia responded that he did not see how mootness, any more than standing, could be "merely prudential." "Both doctrines have equivalently deep roots in the common-law understanding, and hence the constitutional understanding, of what makes a matter appropriate for judicial disposition." As traditionally applied, "capable of repetition, yet evading review" was not to the contrary:

Where the conduct has ceased for the time being but there is a demonstrated probability that it *will* recur, a real-life controversy between parties with a personal stake in the outcome continues to exist, and Article III is no more violated than it is violated by entertaining a declaratory judgment action. But that is the limit of our power. I agree with the Chief Justice to this extent: the "yet evading review" portion of our "capable of repetition, yet evading review" test is prudential; whether or not that criterion is met, a justiciable controversy exists. But the probability of recurrence between the same parties is essential to our jurisdiction as a court, and it is that deficiency which the case before us presents.

Which understanding of the "capable of repetition, yet evading review" exception is more persuasive? Is it plausible to think of mootness as less closely related to constitutional requirements than other justiciability doctrines? If not, is there any way to avoid the waste of resources described by Rehnquist?

5. *DEFUNIS V. ODEGAARD*

A controversial application of mootness doctrine occurred in DeFunis v. Odegaard, 416 U.S. 312 (1974). Marco DeFunis was an unsuccessful white applicant for admission to the University of Washington Law School. He sued in state court, claiming that the school's minority admissions program violated equal protection. DeFunis won in the trial court and was admitted. That decision was overturned by the Washington Supreme Court, but the judgment was stayed pending final decision by the Supreme Court of the United States. By the time the case was argued, DeFunis was in his final term, and the law school had agreed that it would not seek to cancel registration for any term in which DeFunis was already enrolled. The Supreme Court therefore found the case moot. It explained:

> [A]ll parties agree that DeFunis is now entitled to complete his legal studies at the University of Washington and to receive his degree from that institution. A determination by this Court of the legal issues tendered by the parties is no longer necessary to compel that result, and could not serve to prevent it. DeFunis did not cast his suit as a class action, and the only remedy he requested was an injunction commanding his admission to the Law School.

Justice Brennan, joined by Justices Douglas, White, and Marshall, dissented:

> I can . . . find no justification for the Court's straining to rid itself of this dispute. . . . [T]here is no . . . want of an adversary contest in this case. Indeed, the Court concedes that, if petitioner has lost his stake in this controversy, he did so only when he registered for the spring term. But petitioner took that action only after the case had been fully litigated in the state courts, briefs had been filed in this Court, and oral argument had been heard. The case is thus ripe for decision on a fully developed factual record with sharply defined and fully canvassed legal issues.
>
> Moreover, in endeavoring to dispose of this case as moot, the Court clearly disserves the public interest. The constitutional issues which are avoided today concern vast numbers of people, organizations, and colleges and universities, as evidenced by the filing of 26 amicus curiae briefs. Few constitutional questions in recent history have stirred as much debate, and they will not disappear. . . .

The issues avoided in *DeFunis* returned to the Supreme Court in University of California Board of Regents v. Bakke, 438 U.S. 265 (1978). Does that suggest that Justice Brennan was right in disparaging the *DeFunis* dismissal? Or does it simply show that mootness is properly a doctrine concerned with particular cases, not the issues they raise? What weight, if any, should have been given to the fact that the mootness question arose late in the litigation, after the development of a record and after substantial investment of time by all concerned? Is the societal importance of the issues raised in *DeFunis* a relevant consideration? If so, does it argue for decision or delay?

Genesis Healthcare Corp. v. Symczyk

Supreme Court of the United States, 2013.
569 U.S. 66.

■ JUSTICE THOMAS delivered the opinion of the Court.

The Fair Labor Standards Act of 1938 (FLSA), 29 U.S.C. § 201 et seq., provides that an employee may bring an action to recover damages for specified violations of the Act on behalf of himself and other "similarly situated" employees. We granted certiorari to resolve whether such a case is justiciable when the lone plaintiff's individual claim becomes moot. We hold that it is not justiciable.

I

The FLSA establishes federal minimum-wage, maximum-hour, and overtime guarantees that cannot be modified by contract. Section 16(b) of the FLSA gives employees the right to bring a private cause of action on their own behalf and on behalf of "other employees similarly situated" for specified violations of the FLSA. A suit brought on behalf of other employees is known as a "collective action."

In 2009, respondent, who was formerly employed by petitioners as a registered nurse at Pennypack Center in Philadelphia, Pennsylvania, filed a complaint on behalf of herself and "all other persons similarly situated." Respondent alleged that petitioners violated the FLSA by automatically deducting 30 minutes of time worked per shift for meal breaks for certain employees, even when the employees performed compensable work during those breaks. Respondent, who remained the sole plaintiff throughout these proceedings, sought statutory damages for the alleged violations.

When petitioners answered the complaint, they simultaneously served upon respondent an offer of judgment under Federal Rule of Civil Procedure 68. The offer included $7,500 for alleged unpaid wages, in addition to "such reasonable attorneys' fees, costs, and expenses . . . as the Court may determine." Petitioners stipulated that if respondent did not accept the offer within 10 days after service, the offer would be deemed withdrawn.

After respondent failed to respond in the allotted time period, petitioners filed a motion to dismiss for lack of subject-matter jurisdiction. Petitioners argued that because they offered respondent complete relief on her individual damages claim, she no longer possessed a personal stake in the outcome of the suit, rendering the action moot. Respondent objected, arguing that petitioners were inappropriately attempting to "pick off" the named plaintiff before the collective-action process could unfold.

The District Court found that it was undisputed that no other individuals had joined respondent's suit and that the Rule 68 offer of judgment fully satisfied her individual claim. It concluded that petitioners' Rule 68 offer of judgment mooted respondent's suit, which it dismissed for lack of subject-matter jurisdiction.

The Court of Appeals reversed. The court agreed that no other potential plaintiff had opted into the suit, that petitioners' offer fully satisfied respondent's individual claim, and that, under its precedents, whether or not such an offer is accepted, it generally moots a plaintiff's claim. But the court nevertheless held that respondent's collective action was not moot. It explained that calculated attempts by some defendants to "pick off" named plaintiffs with strategic Rule 68 offers before certification could short circuit the process, and, thereby, frustrate the goals of collective actions. The court determined that the case must be remanded in order to allow respondent to seek "conditional certification"[1] in the District Court. If respondent were successful, the District Court was to relate the certification motion back to the date on which respondent filed her complaint.[2]

II

Article III, § 2, of the Constitution limits the jurisdiction of federal courts to "Cases" and "Controversies" . . . A corollary to this case-or-controversy requirement is that " 'an actual controversy must be extant at all stages of review, not merely at the time the complaint is filed.' " Arizonans for Official English v. Arizona, 520 U.S. 43, 67 (1997) (quoting Preiser v. Newkirk, 422 U.S. 395, 401 (1975)). If an intervening circumstance deprives the plaintiff of a "personal stake in the outcome of the lawsuit," at any point during litigation, the action can no longer proceed and must be dismissed as moot. Lewis v. Continental Bank Corp., 494 U.S. 472, 477–78 (1990) (internal quotation marks omitted).

In the proceedings below, both courts concluded that petitioners' Rule 68 offer afforded respondent complete relief on—and thus mooted—

---

[1] Lower courts have borrowed class-action terminology to describe the process of joining co-plaintiffs under 29 U.S.C. § 216(b). While we do not express an opinion on the propriety of this use of class-action nomenclature, we do note that there are significant differences between certification under Federal Rule of Civil Procedure 23 and the joinder process under § 216(b).

[2] The "relation back" doctrine was developed in the context of class actions under Rule 23 to address the circumstance in which a named plaintiff's claim becomes moot prior to certification of the class. This case raises two circumstances in which the Court has applied this doctrine. First, where a named plaintiff's claim is "inherently transitory," and becomes moot prior to certification, a motion for certification may "relate back" to the filing of the complaint. See, e.g., County of Riverside v. McLaughlin, 500 U.S. 44, 51–52 (1991). Second, we have held that where a certification motion is denied and a named plaintiff's claim subsequently becomes moot, an appellate reversal of the certification decision may relate back to the time of the denial. See United States Parole Comm'n v. Geraghty, 445 U.S. 388, 404 (1980).

her FLSA claim. Respondent now contends that these rulings were erroneous, because petitioners' Rule 68 offer lapsed without entry of judgment. . . .

While the Courts of Appeals disagree whether an unaccepted offer that fully satisfies a plaintiff's claim is sufficient to render the claim moot, we do not reach this question, or resolve the split, because the issue is not properly before us. The Third Circuit clearly held in this case that respondent's individual claim was moot. Acceptance of respondent's argument to the contrary now would alter the Court of Appeals' judgment, which is impermissible in the absence of a cross-petition from respondent. See Northwest Airlines, Inc. v. County of Kent, 510 U.S. 355, 364 (1994). Moreover, even if the cross-petition rule did not apply, respondent's waiver of the issue would still prevent us from reaching it. In the District Court, respondent conceded that "[a]n offer of complete relief will generally moot the [plaintiff's] claim, as at that point the plaintiff retains no personal interest in the outcome of the litigation." Respondent made a similar concession in her brief to the Court of Appeals, and failed to raise the argument in her brief in opposition to the petition for certiorari. We, therefore, assume, without deciding, that petitioners' Rule 68 offer mooted respondent's individual claim.

III

We turn, then, to the question whether respondent's action remained justiciable based on the collective-action allegations in her complaint. A straightforward application of well-settled mootness principles compels our answer. In the absence of any claimant's opting in, respondent's suit became moot when her individual claim became moot, because she lacked any personal interest in representing others in this action. While the FLSA authorizes an aggrieved employee to bring an action on behalf of himself and "other employees similarly situated," 29 U.S.C. § 216(b), the mere presence of collective-action allegations in the complaint cannot save the suit from mootness once the individual claim is satisfied.[4] In order to avoid this outcome, respondent relies almost entirely upon cases that arose in the context of Federal Rule of Civil Procedure 23 class actions, particularly United States Parole Comm'n v. Geraghty, 445 U.S. 388 (1980); Deposit Guaranty Nat. Bank v. Roper, 445 U.S. 326 (1980); and Sosna v. Iowa, 419 U.S. 393 (1975). But these cases are inapposite, both because Rule 23 actions are fundamentally different from collective

---

[4]   While we do not resolve the question whether a Rule 68 offer that fully satisfies the plaintiff's claims is sufficient by itself to moot the action, we note that Courts of Appeals on both sides of that issue have recognized that a plaintiff's claim may be satisfied even without the plaintiff's consent. Some courts maintain that an unaccepted offer of complete relief alone is sufficient to moot the individual's claim. E.g., Weiss v. Regal Collections, 385 F.3d 337, 340 (3d Cir. 2004); Greisz v. Household Bank (Ill.), N.A., 176 F.3d 1012, 1015 (7th Cir. 1999). Other courts have held that, in the face of an unaccepted offer of complete relief, district courts may "enter judgment in favor of the plaintiffs in accordance with the defendants' Rule 68 offer of judgment." O'Brien v. Ed Donnelly Enters., Inc., 575 F.3d 567, 575 (6th Cir. 2009); see also McCauley v. Trans Union, LLC, 402 F.3d 340, 342 (2d Cir. 2005). Contrary to the dissent's assertion, nothing in the nature of FLSA actions precludes satisfaction—and thus the mooting—of the individual's claim before the collective-action component of the suit has run its course.

actions under the FLSA, and because these cases are, by their own terms, inapplicable to these facts. It follows that this action was appropriately dismissed as moot.

A

Respondent contends that she has a sufficient personal stake in this case based on a statutorily created collective-action interest in representing other similarly situated employees under § 216(b). In support of her argument, respondent cites our decision in *Geraghty,* which in turn has its roots in *Sosna.* Neither case supports her position.

In *Sosna,* the Court held that a class action is not rendered moot when the named plaintiff's individual claim becomes moot *after* the class has been duly certified. The Court reasoned that when a district court certifies a class, "the class of unnamed persons described in the certification acquire[s] a legal status separate from the interest asserted by [the named plaintiff]," with the result that a live controversy may continue to exist, even after the claim of the named plaintiff becomes moot. 419 U.S. at 399–402. *Geraghty* narrowly extended this principle to *denials* of class certification motions. The Court held that where an action would have acquired the independent legal status described in *Sosna* but for the district court's erroneous denial of class certification, a corrected ruling on appeal "relates back" to the time of the erroneous denial of the certification motion.

Geraghty is inapposite, because the Court explicitly limited its holding to cases in which the named plaintiff's claim remains live at the time the district court denies class certification. Here, respondent had not yet moved for "conditional certification" when her claim became moot, nor had the District Court anticipatorily ruled on any such request. Her claim instead became moot prior to these events, foreclosing any recourse to *Geraghty.* There is simply no certification decision to which respondent's claim could have related back.

More fundamentally, essential to our decisions in *Sosna* and *Geraghty* was the fact that a putative class acquires an independent legal status once it is certified under Rule 23. Under the FLSA, by contrast, "conditional certification" does not produce a class with an independent legal status, or join additional parties to the action. The sole consequence of conditional certification is the sending of court-approved written notice to employees, who in turn become parties to a collective action only by filing written consent with the court, § 216(b). So even if respondent were to secure a conditional certification ruling on remand, nothing in that ruling would preserve her suit from mootness.

B

Respondent also advances an argument based on a separate, but related, line of cases in which the Court held that an "inherently transitory" class-action claim is not necessarily moot upon the termination of the named plaintiff's claim. Like our decision in *Geraghty,* this line of cases began with *Sosna* and is similarly inapplicable here.

After concluding that the expiration of a named plaintiff's claim following certification does not moot the class action, *Sosna* suggested that, where a named plaintiff's individual claim becomes moot before the district court has an opportunity to rule on the certification motion, and the issue would otherwise evade review, the certification might "relate back" to the filing of the complaint. 419 U.S. at 402, n.11. The Court has since held that the relation-back doctrine may apply in Rule 23 cases where it is "certain that other persons similarly situated" will continue to be subject to the challenged conduct and the claims raised are " 'so inherently transitory that the trial court will not have even enough time to rule on a motion for class certification before the proposed representative's individual interest expires.' " County of Riverside v. McLaughlin, 500 U.S. 44, 52 (1991) (quoting *Geraghty,* 445 U.S. at 399), in turn citing Gerstein v. Pugh, 420 U.S. 103, 110, n.11 (1975). Invoking this doctrine, respondent argues that defendants can strategically use Rule 68 offers to "pick off" named plaintiffs before the collective-action process is complete, rendering collective actions "inherently transitory" in effect.

Our cases invoking the "inherently transitory" relation-back rationale do not apply. The "inherently transitory" rationale was developed to address circumstances in which the challenged conduct was effectively unreviewable, because no plaintiff possessed a personal stake in the suit long enough for litigation to run its course. A plaintiff might seek, for instance, to bring a class action challenging the constitutionality of temporary pretrial detentions. In doing so, the named plaintiff would face the considerable challenge of preserving his individual claim from mootness, since pretrial custody likely would end prior to the resolution of his claim. See *Gerstein,* supra. To address this problem, the Court explained that in cases where the transitory nature of the conduct giving rise to the suit would effectively insulate defendants' conduct from review, certification could potentially "relate back" to the filing of the complaint. Id. at 110 n.11. But this doctrine has invariably focused on the fleeting nature of the challenged conduct giving rise to the claim, not on the defendant's litigation strategy.

In this case, respondent's complaint requested statutory damages. Unlike claims for injunctive relief challenging ongoing conduct, a claim for damages cannot evade review; it remains live until it is settled, judicially resolved, or barred by a statute of limitations. Nor can a defendant's attempt to obtain settlement insulate such a claim from review, for a full settlement offer addresses plaintiff's alleged harm by making the plaintiff whole. While settlement may have the collateral effect of foreclosing unjoined claimants from having their rights vindicated in *respondent's* suit, such putative plaintiffs remain free to vindicate their rights in their own suits. They are no less able to have their claims settled or adjudicated following respondent's suit than if her suit had never been filed at all.

C

Finally, respondent argues that the purposes served by the FLSA's collective-action provisions—for example, efficient resolution of common claims and lower individual costs associated with litigation—would be frustrated by defendants' use of Rule 68 to "pick off" named plaintiffs before the collective-action process has run its course. Both respondent and the Court of Appeals purported to find support for this position in our decision in *Roper*.

In *Roper,* the named plaintiffs' individual claims became moot after the District Court denied their motion for class certification under Rule 23 and subsequently entered judgment in their favor, based on the defendant bank's offer of judgment for the maximum recoverable amount of damages, in addition to interest and court costs. The Court held that even though the District Court had entered judgment in the named plaintiffs' favor, they could nevertheless appeal the denial of their motion to certify the class. The Court found that, under the particular circumstances of that case, the named plaintiffs possessed an ongoing, personal economic stake in the substantive controversy—namely, to shift a portion of attorney's fees and expenses to successful class litigants.[5] Only then, in dicta, did the Court underscore the importance of a district court's class certification decision and observe that allowing defendants to " 'pic[k] off' " party plaintiffs before an affirmative ruling was achieved "would frustrate the objectives of class actions." 445 U.S. at 339.

Roper's holding turned on a specific factual finding that the plaintiffs' possessed a continuing personal economic stake in the litigation, even after the defendants' offer of judgment. As already explained, here, respondent conceded that petitioners' offer "provided complete relief on her individual claims," and she failed to assert any continuing economic interest in shifting attorney's fees and costs to others. Moreover, *Roper*'s dictum was tethered to the unique significance of certification decisions in class-action proceedings. Whatever significance "conditional certification" may have in § 216(b) proceedings, it is not tantamount to class certification under Rule 23.

The Court of Appeals concluded that respondent's individual claim became moot following petitioners' Rule 68 offer of judgment. We have assumed, without deciding, that this is correct.

Reaching the question on which we granted certiorari, we conclude that respondent has no personal interest in representing putative, unnamed claimants, nor any other continuing interest that would preserve

---

[5] Because *Roper* is distinguishable on the facts, we need not consider its continuing validity in light of our subsequent decision in Lewis v. Continental Bank Corp., 494 U.S. 472 (1990). See id. at 480 ("[An] interest in attorney's fees is, of course, insufficient to create an Article III case or controversy where none exists on the merits of the underlying claim").

her suit from mootness. Respondent's suit was, therefore, appropriately dismissed for lack of subject-matter jurisdiction.

The judgment of the Court of Appeals for the Third Circuit is reversed.

■ JUSTICE KAGAN, with whom JUSTICE GINSBURG, JUSTICE BREYER, and JUSTICE SOTOMAYOR join, dissenting.

The Court today resolves an imaginary question, based on a mistake the courts below made about this case and others like it. The issue here, the majority tells us, is whether a " 'collective action' " brought under the Fair Labor Standards Act of 1938 (FLSA), 29 U.S.C. § 201 et seq., "is justiciable when the lone plaintiff's individual claim becomes moot." Embedded within that question is a crucial premise: that the individual claim *has* become moot, as the lower courts held and the majority assumes without deciding. But what if that premise is bogus? What if the plaintiff's individual claim here never became moot? And what if, in addition, no similar claim for damages will ever become moot? In that event, the majority's decision—founded as it is on an unfounded assumption—would have no real-world meaning or application. The decision would turn out to be the most one-off of one-offs, explaining only what (the majority thinks) should happen to a proposed collective FLSA action when something that in fact never happens to an individual FLSA claim is errantly thought to have done so. That is the case here, for reasons I'll describe. Feel free to relegate the majority's decision to the furthest reaches of your mind: The situation it addresses should never again arise.

Consider the facts of this case, keeping an eye out for anything that would render any part of it moot. Respondent Laura Symczyk brought suit under a provision of the FLSA, 29 U.S.C. § 216(b), "on behalf of herself and others similarly situated." Her complaint alleged that her former employer, petitioner Genesis Healthcare Corporation (Genesis), violated the FLSA by treating 30 minutes of every shift as an unpaid meal break, even when an employee worked during that time. Genesis answered the complaint and simultaneously made an offer of judgment under Federal Rule of Civil Procedure 68. That settlement proposal covered only Symczyk's individual claim, to the tune of $7,500 in lost wages. The offer, according to its terms, would "be deemed withdrawn" if Symczyk did not accept it within 10 days. That deadline came and went without any reply. The case then proceeded in the normal fashion, with the District Court setting a schedule for discovery. Pause here for a moment to ask whether you've seen anything yet that would moot Symczyk's individual claim. No? Neither have I.

Nevertheless, Genesis moved to dismiss Symczyk's suit on the ground that it was moot. The supposed logic went like this: We (i.e., Genesis) offered Symczyk complete relief on her individual damages claim; she "effectively reject[ed] the [o]ffer" by failing to respond; because she did so, she "no longer has a personal stake or legally cognizable interest in the outcome of this action"; accordingly, the court "should dismiss her claims." Relying on Circuit precedent, the District Court agreed; it dismissed the case for lack of jurisdiction—without awarding Symczyk any damages or other relief—based solely on the unaccepted offer Genesis had made. And finally, the Court of Appeals for the Third Circuit concurred that Genesis's offer mooted Symczyk's individual claim (though also holding that she could still proceed with a collective action).

That thrice-asserted view is wrong, wrong, and wrong again. We made clear earlier this Term that "[a]s long as the parties have a concrete interest, however small, in the outcome of the litigation, the case is not moot." Chafin v. Chafin, 568 U.S. 165, 172 (2012) (internal quotation marks omitted). "[A] case becomes moot only when it is impossible for a court to grant any effectual relief whatever to the prevailing party." Id. (internal quotation marks omitted). By those measures, an unaccepted offer of judgment cannot moot a case. When a plaintiff rejects such an offer—however good the terms—her interest in the lawsuit remains just what it was before. And so too does the court's ability to grant her relief. An unaccepted settlement offer—like any unaccepted contract offer—is a legal nullity, with no operative effect. As every first-year law student learns, the recipient's rejection of an offer "leaves the matter as if no offer had ever been made." Minneapolis & St. Louis R. Co. v. Columbus Rolling Mill, 119 U.S. 149, 151 (1886). Nothing in Rule 68 alters that basic principle; to the contrary, that rule specifies that "[a]n unaccepted offer is considered withdrawn." Fed. Rule Civ. Proc. 68(b). So assuming the case was live before—because the plaintiff had a stake and the court could grant relief—the litigation carries on, unmooted.

For this reason, Symczyk's individual claim was alive and well when the District Court dismissed her suit. Recall: Genesis made a settlement offer under Rule 68; Symczyk decided not to accept it; after 10 days, it expired and the suit went forward. Symczyk's individual stake in the lawsuit thus remained what it had always been, and ditto the court's capacity to grant her relief. After the offer lapsed, just as before, Symczyk possessed an unsatisfied claim, which the court could redress by awarding her damages. As long as that remained true, Symczyk's claim was not moot, and the District Court could not send her away empty-handed. So a friendly suggestion to the Third Circuit: Rethink your mootness-by-unaccepted-offer theory. And a note to all other courts of appeals: Don't try this at home.

To this point, what I have said conflicts with nothing in the Court's opinion. The majority does not attempt to argue, à la the Third Circuit, that the unaccepted settlement offer mooted Symczyk's individual damages claim. Instead, the majority hangs its hat on a finding of waiver. The majority notes—correctly—that Symczyk accepted the Third Circuit's rule in her briefs below, and also failed to challenge it in her brief in opposition to the petition for certiorari; she contested it first in her merits brief before this Court. That enables the majority to "assume, without deciding," the mootness of Symczyk's individual claim and reach the oh-so-much-more-interesting question relating to her proposed collective action.

But as this Court noted in a similar case, "assum[ing] what the facts will show to be ridiculous" about a predicate question—just because a party did not think to challenge settled Circuit precedent—runs "a risk that ought to be avoided." Lebron v. National Railroad Passenger Corporation, 513 U.S. 374, 382 (1995). The question Symczyk now raises ("Did an unaccepted settlement offer moot my individual FLSA claim?") is logically prior to—and thus inextricably intertwined with—the question the majority rushes to resolve ("If an unaccepted settlement offer mooted Symczyk's individual FLSA claim, could a court proceed to consider her proposed collective action?"). Indeed, the former is so much part and parcel of the latter that the question Genesis presented for our review—and on which we granted certiorari—actually looks more like Symczyk's than like the majority's. Genesis asked: "Whether a case becomes moot . . . when the lone plaintiff receives an offer from the defendants to satisfy all of the plaintiff's claims." Symczyk, of course, would respond "no," because merely receiving an offer does not moot any claim. The majority's refusal to consider that obviously correct answer impedes "intelligent resolution of the question presented." Ohio v. Robinette, 519 U.S. 33, 38 (1996) (internal quotation marks omitted). By taking a fallacy as its premise, the majority ensures it will reach the wrong decision.

Still, you might think, the majority's approach has at least this benefit: In a future FLSA case, when an individual claim for damages in fact becomes moot, a court will know what to do with the collective allegations. But no, even that much cannot be said for the majority's opinion. That is because the individual claims in such cases will *never* become moot, and a court will therefore never need to reach the issue the majority resolves. The majority's decision is fit for nothing: Aside from getting this case wrong, it serves only to address a make-believe problem.

To see why, consider how a collective FLSA action seeking damages unfolds. A plaintiff (just like Symczyk, but let us now call her Smith, to highlight her typicality) sues under § 216(b) on behalf of both herself and others. To determine whether Smith can serve as a representative party, the court considers whether the workplace policy her suit challenges has similarly affected other employees. If it has, the court supervises their discovery and notification, and then "oversee[s] the joinder" of any who want Smith to represent them. Hoffmann-La Roche Inc. v. Sperling, 493 U.S. 165, 171 (1989). During that period, as the majority observes, the class has no "independent legal status." At the same time, Smith's own claim is in perfect health. Because it is a damages claim for past conduct, the employer cannot extinguish it by adopting new employment practices. Indeed, the claim would survive even Smith's own demise, belonging then to her estate. Smith's individual claim, in short, is not going away on its own; it can easily wait out the time involved in assembling a collective action.

Now introduce a settlement offer into the picture: Assume that before the court finally decides whether to permit a collective action, the defendant proposes to pay Smith the value of her individual claim in exchange for her abandonment of the entire litigation. If Smith agrees, of course, all is over; like any plaintiff, she can assent to a settlement ending her suit. But assuming Smith does not agree, because she wishes to proceed on behalf of other employees, could the offer ever succeed in mooting her case? I have already shown that it cannot do so in the circumstances here, where the defendant makes an offer, the plaintiff declines it, and nothing else occurs: On those facts, Smith's claim is as it ever was, and the lawsuit continues onward. But suppose the defendant additionally requests that the court enter judgment in Smith's favor—though over her objection—for the amount offered to satisfy her individual claim. Could a court approve that motion and then declare the case over on the ground that Smith has no further stake in it? That course would be less preposterous than what the court did here; at least Smith, unlike Symczyk, would get some money. But it would be impermissible as well.

For starters, Rule 68 precludes a court from imposing judgment for a plaintiff like Smith based on an unaccepted settlement offer made pursuant to its terms. The text of the Rule contemplates that a court will enter judgment only when a plaintiff accepts an offer. See Rule 68(a) ("If . . . the [plaintiff] serves written notice accepting the offer, either party may then file the offer and notice of acceptance, plus proof of service. The clerk must then enter judgment"). And the Rule prohibits a court from considering an unaccepted offer for any purpose other than allocating litigation costs—including for the purpose of entering judgment for either party. See Rule 68(b) ("Evidence of an unaccepted offer is not admissible except in a proceeding to determine costs"). That injunction accords with Rule 68's exclusive purpose: to promote voluntary cessation of litigation by imposing costs on plaintiffs who spurn certain settlement offers. See Marek v. Chesny, 473 U.S. 1, 5 (1985). The Rule provides no appropriate mechanism for a court to terminate a lawsuit without the plaintiff's consent.

Nor does a court have inherent authority to enter an unwanted judgment for Smith on her individual claim, in service of wiping out her proposed collective action. To be sure, a court has discretion to halt a lawsuit by entering judgment for the plaintiff when the defendant unconditionally surrenders and only the plaintiff's obstinacy or madness prevents her from accepting total victory. But the court may not take that tack when the supposed capitulation in fact fails to give the plaintiff all the law authorizes and she has sought. And a judgment satisfying an individual claim does not give a plaintiff like Smith, exercising her right to sue on behalf of other employees, "all that [she] has . . . requested in the complaint (i.e., relief for the class)." Deposit Guaranty Nat. Bank v. Roper, 445 U.S. 326, 341 (1980) (Rehnquist, J., concurring). No more in a collective action brought under the FLSA than in any other class action may a court, prior to certification, eliminate the entire suit by acceding to a defendant's proposal to make only the named plaintiff whole. That course would short-circuit a collective action before it could begin, and thereby frustrate Congress's decision to give FLSA plaintiffs "the opportunity to proceed collectively." *Hoffmann-La Roche,* 493 U.S. at 170; see *Roper,* 445 U.S. at 339. It is our plaintiff Smith's choice, and not the defendant's or the court's, whether satisfaction of her individual claim, without redress of her viable classwide allegations, is sufficient to bring the lawsuit to an end.

And so, the question the majority answers should never arise— which means the analysis the majority propounds should never apply. The majority assumes that an individual claim has become moot, and then asks whether collective allegations can still proceed by virtue of the relation-back doctrine. But that doctrine comes into play only when a court confronts a jurisdictional gap—an individual claim becoming moot before the court can certify a representative action. And in an FLSA case for damages, that gap cannot occur (unless a court, as here, mistakenly creates it): As I have explained, the plaintiff's individual claim remains live all the way through the court's decision whether to join new plaintiffs to the litigation. Without any gap to span, the relation-back doctrine has no relevance. Neither, then, does the majority's decision.[3]

The Court could have resolved this case (along with a Circuit split) by correcting the Third Circuit's view that an unaccepted settlement offer mooted Symczyk's individual claim. Instead, the Court chose to address an issue predicated on that misconception, in a way that aids no one, now or ever. I respectfully dissent.

NOTES ON MOOTNESS IN CLASS ACTIONS

1. *GENESIS HEALTHCARE* AND OFFERS OF JUDGMENT

Justice Kagan's skepticism about the Third Circuit's rule that a mere offer of full satisfaction may render a case moot proved well founded. In

---

[3] And that is a good thing, because (just as a by-the-by) the majority's opinion also misconceives our decisions applying the relation-back doctrine. The majority painstakingly distinguishes those decisions on their individual facts, but misses their common take-away. In each, we confronted a situation where a would-be class representative's individual claim became moot before a court could make a final decision about the propriety of class litigation; and in each, we used relation-back principles to preserve the court's ability to adjudicate on the merits the classwide questions the representative raised. See, e.g., County of Riverside v. McLaughlin, 500 U.S. 44, 51–52 (1991); Swisher v. Brady, 438 U.S. 204, 213–14, n. 11 (1978); Gerstein v. Pugh, 420 U.S. 103, 110–11, n. 11 (1975); see also United States Parole Comm'n v. Geraghty, 445 U.S. 388, 399, 404, n.11 (1980); Sosna v. Iowa, 419 U.S. 393, 402, n.11 (1975). If, counterfactually, Symczyk's individual claim became moot when she failed to accept Genesis's offer of judgment, her case would fit comfortably alongside those precedents. Because the District Court would not then have had "enough time to rule on a motion" for certification under § 216(b), "the 'relation back' doctrine [would be] properly invoked to preserve the merits of the case for judicial resolution." *McLaughlin,* 500 U.S. at 52 (internal quotation marks omitted).

Campbell-Ewald Co. v. Gomez, 577 U.S. ___, 136 S.Ct. 663 (2016), the Supreme Court explicitly adopted Kagan's reasoning and held that "an unaccepted settlement offer has no force."

The question arose when Jose Gomez filed suit as the named plaintiff in a class action seeking statutory and treble damages for violation of the Telephone Consumer Protection Act, which prohibits automated telephone calls or text messages to cellular telephones without prior consent. Defendant Campbell-Ewald Co. allegedly sent an unconsented text message to Gomez as part of a marketing contract with the United States Navy. Prior to the deadline for filing a motion for class certification, Campbell-Ewald filed an offer of judgment, pursuant to Rule 68 of the Federal Rules of Civil Procedure, fully satisfying Gomez's individual claim. Gomez did not accept the offer, which lapsed after the 14 days specified in Rule 68. Campbell-Ewald then moved to dismiss the case, arguing that its offer mooted the individual claim and that, as Gomez had not yet moved for class certification, nothing else was before the court. Speaking through Justice Ginsburg, the Supreme Court rejected that argument, holding that "an unaccepted settlement offer or offer of judgment does not moot a plaintiff's case, so the District Court retained jurisdiction to adjudicate Gomez's complaint." Although Rule 68 provides that if a plaintiff ultimately obtains no more than a rejected settlement offer they must pay the other side's attorney's fees, the Court reasoned that this is a separate matter from mootness. Justice Thomas concurred in the judgment, and Chief Justice Roberts, joined by Justices Scalia and Alito, dissented.

What would have happened if the defendant in *Campbell-Ewald*, instead of merely offering full satisfaction, had asked for judgment to be entered against it?[a] The Supreme Court did not say:

> We need not, and do not, now decide whether the result would be different if a defendant deposits the full amount of the plaintiff's individual claim in an account payable to the plaintiff, and the court then enters judgment for the plaintiff in that amount. That question is appropriately reserved for a case in which it is not hypothetical.

This reservation led at least one of the dissenters (Justice Alito) to think that the Court's decision "does not prevent a defendant who actually pays complete relief—either directly to the plaintiff or to a trusted intermediary—from seeking dismissal on mootness grounds." Requiring an actual judgment in plaintiff's favor, as distinct from merely guaranteeing relief, Alito argued, would contradict Already, LLC v. Nike, Inc., 568 U.S. 85 (2013). In that case, Nike sued Already claiming a trademark violation in certain athletic shoes. Already counterclaimed that the trademark was invalid. Nike did not contest

---

[a]   It is interesting to speculate as to why that was not done. Perhaps the defendant feared that an actual judgment against it would have adverse precedential effect. Or perhaps the defendant doubted that the judge would enter judgment for plaintiff over plaintiff's objection, or at least that he would do so in advance of considering a motion for class certification. The authority of a court to enter judgment for plaintiff over plaintiff's objection, if the claim is fully satisfied, seems undoubted, but the question of timing would be a matter of discretion. If the court refused to enter judgment until after considering class certification, the defendant's purpose in offering individual relief would be defeated.

the counterclaim but instead issued a unilateral covenant not to sue Already, promising "unconditionally and irrevocably" not to make any trademark claims against Already based on current shoe designs. Nike then asked the court to dismiss the counterclaim as moot, which it did over Already's objection. The Supreme Court unanimously agreed that the counterclaim was moot, despite the absence of any judgment in the case, because Already had been given full relief. Given the unconditionality of Nike's covenant, the conduct to which Already objected was not likely to recur.

The Court in *Campbell-Ewald* distinguished *Already* in a footnote and never clearly said whether a judgment in plaintiff's favor would be necessary to render a case moot or, indeed, even whether it would be sufficient to do so. It may well be, therefore, that a plaintiff's individual claim becomes moot whenever the defendant actually *provides* rather than merely *offers* complete relief. On that interpretation, *Campbell-Ewald* is another narrow decision postponing the important question for another day.

2. *GENESIS HEALTHCARE* AND CLASS ACTIONS

The important question that *Genesis Healthcare* did not reach is whether the defendant in a putative class action can avoid that litigation by (one way or another) mooting the plaintiff's individual claim. Even the dissent concedes that a court has inherent authority to enter judgment over plaintiff's objection when the claim is completely satisfied and the plaintiff refuses to accept what the dissent calls "total victory." The fighting issue is whether satisfaction of the plaintiff's *individual* claim is in fact total victory, when the plaintiff seeks to bring a *collective* action. Put differently, the question is whether and when a plaintiff has a right to pursue a class action even though her individual interest has been mooted. The question of mootness in class actions has a long and interesting history.

3. *SOSNA V. IOWA* AND CERTIFIED CLASS ACTIONS

The easiest case is when the named plaintiff's claim becomes moot after the court has certified a class action. In that situation, the named plaintiff is not the only party before the court when his or her claim becomes moot. So long as the claims of other class members remain live, the class action is not moot.

This principle was settled in Sosna v. Iowa, 419 U.S. 393 (1975). *Sosna* involved a challenge to a one-year residency requirement for divorce. The plaintiff sought and obtained certification of her suit as a class action on behalf of all persons who had been residents of Iowa for less than one year and wanted to divorce. By the time the case reached the Supreme Court, the named plaintiff had not only satisfied the Iowa residency requirement but had obtained a divorce in another state. The case therefore had become moot with respect to the individual plaintiff but remained "very much alive" for the class she represented.[b]

---

[b]   Some language in *Sosna* suggested that the decision might be limited to class actions raising issues—such as durational residency requirements—that would not last long enough to

4. "INHERENTLY TRANSITORY" CLAIMS

Another relatively easy case is the class action raising "inherently transitory" clams. See County of Riverside v. McLaughlin, 500 U.S. 44 (1991). This is analogous to "capable of repetition, but evading review." "Inherently transitory" describes attempted class actions that raise claims of such limited duration that the named plaintiff's claim will predictably expire before a class action can be certified. Such issues might never be heard on the merits. The Court therefore adopted the rule that certification of the suit as a class action would "relate back" to the filing of the complaint, at which time the named plaintiff had a live interest. As of that time, therefore, the case would not be moot, and the class action (involving others with the same claim) could proceed.

5. *DEPOSIT GUARANTY NATIONAL BANK V. ROPER*

More difficult questions arise when the named plaintiff's claim is not "inherently transitory" but nonetheless becomes moot before certification of a class action. As the named plaintiff is the only party formally before the court when mootness arises, the whole case might be thought moot. The Supreme Court ruled otherwise in Deposit Guaranty National Bank v. Roper, 445 U.S. 326 (1980).

In *Roper,* two BankAmericard holders sued the issuing bank for charging usurious interest.[c] They sought to represent 90,000 cardholders, but the District Court refused to certify a class action. Instead, it entered judgment for the individual plaintiffs for $889.42 and $423.54, respectively, pursuant to a settlement offer made by the defendant. The question was whether the judgment for the plaintiffs for the entire amount to which they were individually entitled mooted the case, or whether the plaintiffs still retained a sufficient interest in representing the class to appeal the denial of class certification. The Supreme Court held that they did.

Chief Justice Burger's opinion for the Court noted that the general rule was that a "party who receives all that he has sought generally is not aggrieved by the judgment affording the relief and cannot appeal from it." But here, "the dismissal of the action over plaintiffs' objection [did not moot] the plaintiffs' claim on the merits so long as they retained an economic interest in class certification." Such an interest can be a sufficient "personal stake in the appeal," which was here satisfied because the plaintiffs claimed "a continuing interest in the resolution of the class certification question in their desire to shift part of the costs of litigation to those who will share in its benefits if the class is certified and ultimately prevails." A contrary ruling, the Chief Justice noted, would reduce the effectiveness of the class action as

---

allow complete judicial review. Any such limitation was discarded in Franks v. Bowman Transportation Co., 424 U.S. 747 (1976), which held that *Sosna* applied to class actions generally.

   c   The cause of action was based on the National Bank Act, which allows recovery of twice the interest paid in excess of that authorized by state law. The alleged violation of state law concerned the method by which monthly interest charges were assessed. The state law was changed to authorize the bank's practice after the suit was filed. Moreover, the statute of limitations for additional claims based on the alleged previous violations expired while the case was in litigation.

a device for obtaining relief for a multiplicity of small claims. Justices Rehnquist, Blackmun, and Stevens concurred separately.[d]

Justice Powell, joined by Justice Stewart, dissented. Justice Powell thought that the plaintiffs' " 'injury'—if any exists—is not one that 'fairly can be traced' " to the defendant. The plaintiffs had a 25 percent contingent fee arrangement with their attorneys, and "no one has explained how [their] obligation to pay 25 percent of their recovery to counsel could be reduced if a class is certified and its members became similarly obligated to pay 25 percent of their recovery":

> Apart from the persistence of the lawyers, this has been a noncase since the [defendant] tendered full satisfaction of the [plaintiffs'] individual claims. . . . I know of no decision by any court that holds that a lawyer's interest in a larger fee, to be paid by third persons not present in court, creates the personal stake in the outcome required by Article III.

6.   *UNITED STATES PAROLE COMMISSION V. GERAGHTY*

On the same day that it decided *Roper*, the Supreme Court reached a similar result in United States Parole Commission v. Geraghty, 445 U.S. 388 (1980). Geraghty was a federal prisoner who had twice been denied parole. He brought a class action to challenge the parole-release guidelines under which he had been unsuccessful. The trial court refused to certify a class action and rejected Geraghty's claim on the merits. Geraghty challenged both rulings on appeal but was released from custody while his appeal was pending. The question then became whether Geraghty could litigate class certification (and if a class was certified, the merits) even though he no longer had a direct stake in the issue. Speaking through Justice Blackmun, the Court said that he could still press his "procedural claim" that a class should have been certified, even though his substantive claim of injury from the challenged guidelines had lapsed:

> A plaintiff who brings a class action presents two separate issues for judicial resolution. One is the claim on the merits; the other is the claim that he is entitled to represent a class. "The denial of class certification stands as an adjudication of one of the issues litigated." We think that in determining whether the plaintiff may continue to press the class certification claim, after the claim on the merits "expires," we must look to the nature of the "personal stake" in the class certification claim. . . .
>
> Application of the personal-stake requirement to a procedural claim, such as the right to represent a class, is not automatic or readily resolved. . . . The justifications that led to the development of the class action include the protection of the defendant from inconsistent obligations, the protection of the interests of absentees,

---

[d]   Justice Stevens would have permitted the appeal on a different ground: "In my opinion, when a proper class action is filed, the absent members of the class should be considered parties to the case or controversy at least for the limited purpose of the court's Article III jurisdiction. If the district judge fails to certify the class, I believe they remain parties until a final determination has been made that the action may not be maintained as a class action."

the provision of a convenient and economical means for disposing of similar lawsuits, and the facilitation of the spreading of litigation costs among numerous litigants with similar claims. Although the named representative receives certain benefits from the class nature of the action, . . . these benefits generally are byproducts of the class-action device. In order to achieve the primary benefits of a class suit, the Federal Rules of Civil Procedure give the proposed class representative the right to have a class certified if the requirements of the rules are met. This "right" is more analogous to the private attorney general concept than to the type of interest traditionally thought to satisfy the "personal stake" requirement.

[T]he purpose of the "personal stake" requirement is to assure that the case is in a form capable of judicial resolution. The imperatives of a dispute capable of judicial resolution are sharply presented issues in a concrete factual setting and self-interested parties vigorously advocating opposing positions. We conclude that these elements can exist with respect to the class certification issue notwithstanding the fact that the named plaintiff's claim on the merits has expired. The question whether class certification is appropriate remains as a concrete, sharply presented issue. . . .

We therefore hold that an action brought on behalf of a class does not become moot upon expiration of the named plaintiff's substantive claim, even though class certification has been denied. The proposed representative retains a "personal stake" in obtaining class certification sufficient to assure that Article III values are not undermined. If the appeal results in reversal of the class certification denial, and a class subsequently is properly certified, the merits of the class claim then may be adjudicated pursuant to the holding in *Sosna*.

Justice Powell, joined by Chief Justice Burger and Justices Stewart and Rehnquist, dissented:

The Court makes no effort to identify any injury to respondent that may be redressed by, or any benefit to respondent that may accrue from, a favorable ruling on the certification question. Instead, respondent's "personal stake" is said to derive from two factors having nothing to do with concrete injury or stake in the outcome. First, the Court finds that the Federal Rules of Civil Procedure create a "right," "analogous to the private attorney general concept," to have a class certified. Second, the Court thinks that the case retains the "imperatives of a dispute capable of judicial resolution," which are identified as (i) a sharply presented issue, (ii) a concrete factual setting, and (iii) a self-interested party actually contesting the case.

The Court's reliance on some new "right" inherent in Rule 23 is misplaced. We have held that even Congress may not confer federal-court jurisdiction when Article III does not. Far less so may a rule of procedure which "shall not be construed to extend . . . the jurisdiction of the United States District Courts." Fed. Rule Civ. Proc. 82. Moreover, the "private attorney general concept" cannot supply the personal stake necessary to satisfy Article III. It serves only to permit litigation by a party who has a stake of his own [of claims that] otherwise might be barred by prudential standing rules.

In the dissenters' view, the fact that the issue was concretely presented and vigorously argued did not suffice for justiciability. There remained the requirement of a case or controversy:

> [T]his a case in which the putative class representative . . . no longer has the slightest interest in the injuries alleged in his complaint. . . . The case therefore lacks a plaintiff with the minimal personal stake that is a constitutional prerequisite to the jurisdiction of an Article III court.

7. QUESTIONS AND COMMENTS ON MOOTNESS IN CLASS ACTIONS

The progression from *Sosna* to *Roper* and *Geraghty* greatly increases the utility of the class action as a device for litigating claims that otherwise would be mooted by the expiration of the representative's individual claim. But have these cases abandoned—or redefined—the requirement of a "case or controversy"? How can they be reconciled with conventional mootness doctrine as it is applied outside class actions. In that context, a case becomes moot if the plaintiff's personal stake disappears, even though the issue is concretely presented and passionately argued and otherwise ready for judicial resolution. *DeFunis* is an illustration. Although the particular application of that rule in *DeFunis* was controversial, the rule that the plaintiff's interest must persist throughout the litigation is routinely applied and rarely contested in ordinary litigation. Why not also in class actions?

In this connection, consider the views expressed in Richard Greenstein, Bridging the Mootness Gap in Federal Court Class Actions, 35 Stan. L. Rev. 897 (1983). Greenstein argued that restrictions on the presentation of class claims by a representative party whose individual interest has become moot should be regarded as prudential only:

> In a class action suit, the function of the named plaintiff, with respect to the claims of the class, is to represent the interests of putative class members, not to supply the injury needed to satisfy the case-or-controversy requirement of Article III. This latter function is served by the class allegations themselves from the moment they are formally presented to the court in the pleadings. Because Article III concerns are met by the class claims, the question of the plaintiff's standing to litigate those claims has no constitutional significance. Nor does the mooting of the plaintiff's own claims. To be more precise, while the mooting of the plaintiff's claim does have constitutional consequences regarding the litigation of those specific claims, it has none regarding the litigation of the class claims.

Thus, the question of the plaintiff's standing to present the claims of the class—whether *his* claim is moot—raises purely prudential concerns. These concerns are addressed by the test for class representation set out in Federal Rule of Civil Procedure 23.

For the more radical argument that the class action attorney, not the class representative, should be regarded as the relevant focus for analyzing justiciability issues, see Sergio J. Campos, Class Actions and Justiciability, 66 Fla. L. Rev. 553 (2014).

Even more radical is the proposal that the entire mootness doctrine be "deconstitutionalized." Evan Tsen Lee, Reconstitutionalizing Justiciability: The Example of Mootness, 105 Harv. L. Rev. 605 (1992). "When confronted with a case that may be moot," Lee argues, "a federal court should ask whether the likely preclusive effect of a judgment or likely precedential effect of a decision on appeal justifies the expenditure of judicial resources necessary to adjudicate the merits." This question would turn chiefly on whether decision of the case "would give true and concrete meaning to constitutional or public values." If so, adjudication would be warranted, in Lee's view, despite apparent mootness.[e]

What light, if any, does *Genesis Healthcare* throw on these arguments? The fact that *Genesis Healthcare* involved a "collective action" under the Fair Labor Standards Act rather than a class action under Rule 23 allows the majority to keep the class action mootness precedents at arm's length. The Court emphasized the "particular circumstances" of *Roper* and declined to take a position on its "continuing validity." See footnote 5, supra. The Court did seem to accept the ruling in *Geraghty*, but with limitations. Specifically, the Court said that *Geraghty* is good only for Rule 23 class actions and only when the named plaintiff's claim remained live at the time when the case *should* have been certified. In that event, the eventual certification of the class action "relates back" to the date certification was improperly denied, at which time the named plaintiff had a personal interest, and the rule of *Sosna v. Iowa* applies.

These limitations distinguish *Geraghty* from *Genesis Healthcare*, but they do nothing to resolve the apparent conflict between *Geraghty* and mootness rules outside of class actions. Does *Genesis Healthcare*'s treatment of *Geraghty* suggest that mootness is in fact a sub-constitutional doctrine, as scholars and Rehnquist have argued? Or does *Genesis Healthcare* perhaps suggest that the class-action mootness doctrine is on thin ice? For the moment, the future is unclear, and the discrepancy between supposedly constitutional mootness requirements in and out of class actions continues.

---

[e] Cf. Matthew I. Hall, The Partially Prudential Doctrine of Mootness, 77 Geo. Wash. L. Rev. 562 (2009), which argues that mootness is properly considered prudential insofar as it concerns whether *this plaintiff* still has the necessary personal stake to raise a live issue, but is properly considered constitutional (and hence not subject to exceptions) when it concerns whether the *issue* itself remains live.

SUBSECTION D. APPEAL BY PREVAILING PARTIES

INTRODUCTORY NOTES ON APPEAL BY PREVAILING PARTIES

1. BACKGROUND

In Deposit Guaranty National Bank v. Roper, 445 U.S. 326 (1980), the Court held that class action plaintiffs whose individual claims had been fully satisfied could nevertheless appeal the denial of class certification. This decision followed its companion, United States Parole Commission v. Geraghty, 445 U.S. 388 (1980), which held that a representative plaintiff whose personal claim had become moot could nevertheless appeal denial of class certification. Speaking for the Court in *Geraghty*, Justice Blackmun explained that: "A plaintiff who brings a class action presents two separate issues for judicial resolution. One is the claim on the merits; the other is the claim that he is entitled to represent a class." The satisfaction of the plaintiff's claim on the merits did not bar him from continuing to litigate the issue of class certification, so long as there were "sharply presented issues in a concrete factual setting and self-interested parties vigorously advocating opposing positions."

2. APPEAL BY PREVAILING PARTIES IN CONSTITUTIONAL TORT CASES

The rule of *Geraghty* and *Roper* is controversial, but perhaps not of much practical importance. After all, the consequential player in a large consumer class action is not the representative plaintiff, but the class action attorney. If the lawyer selects more or better representative plaintiffs, the issue in *Roper* and *Geraghty* is unlikely to arise.

Something similar to the *Roper* issue, but arguably more important, occurs in constitutional tort actions against government officers. Although injunctive and declaratory relief are freely available, government officers are protected against the award of money damages by the doctrine of qualified immunity. Under that doctrine, they cannot be held liable in money damages unless they violated "clearly established" constitutional rights. Whether a right is "clearly established" is an inquiry conducted fairly close to the ground. In consequence, many rights that are clearly established in the abstract will not be found so in particular situations. The result is a shield against damages liability for reasonable mistake as to illegality.

Courts hearing constitutional tort cases are allowed (at one time were required) to rule on the merits of the plaintiff's claim before determining whether the defendant is protected by qualified immunity. See Pearson v. Callahan, 555 U.S. 223 (2009). Merits-first adjudication produces some decisions in which the defendant loses on the merits but nevertheless wins under qualified immunity. Sometimes, a defendant who prevails in that way may nevertheless want to challenge the ruling on the merits in order to avoid an adverse precedent condemning certain government conduct as unconstitutional. The question therefore arises whether a party who has prevailed in the lawsuit can nonetheless appeal. The next main case confronted that issue in the context of a petition for certiorari to the Supreme Court.

Camreta v. Greene

Supreme Court of the United States, 2011.
563 U.S. 692.

■ JUSTICE KAGAN delivered the opinion of the Court.

Almost a decade ago, a state child protective services worker and a county deputy sheriff interviewed a girl at her elementary school in Oregon about allegations that her father had sexually abused her. The girl's mother subsequently sued the government officials on the child's behalf for damages under 42 U.S.C. § 1983, claiming that the interview infringed the Fourth Amendment. The United States Court of Appeals for the Ninth Circuit agreed, ruling that the officials had violated the Constitution by failing to obtain a warrant to conduct the interview. But the Court of Appeals further held that qualified immunity shielded the officials from monetary liability because the constitutional right at issue was not clearly established under existing law.

The two officials sought this Court's review of the Ninth Circuit's ruling on the Fourth Amendment. We granted their petitions to examine two questions. First, may government officials who prevail on grounds of qualified immunity obtain our review of a court of appeals' decision that their conduct violated the Constitution? And second, if we may consider cases in this procedural posture, did the Ninth Circuit correctly determine that this interview breached the Fourth Amendment?

We conclude that this Court generally may review a lower court's constitutional ruling at the behest of a government official granted immunity. But we may not do so in this case for reasons peculiar to it. The case has become moot because the child has grown up and moved across the country, and so will never again be subject to the Oregon in-school interviewing practices whose constitutionality is at issue. We therefore do not reach the Fourth Amendment question in this case. In line with our normal practice when mootness frustrates a party's right to appeal, see United States v. Munsingwear, Inc., 340 U.S. 36, 39 (1950), we vacate the part of the Ninth Circuit's opinion that decided the Fourth Amendment issue.

I

In February 2003, police arrested Nimrod Greene for suspected sexual abuse of a young boy unrelated to him. During the investigation of that offense, the boy's parents told police that they suspected Greene of molesting his 9-year-old daughter S.G. The police reported this information to the Oregon Department of Human Services, which assigned petitioner Bob Camreta, a child protective services caseworker, to assess S.G.'s safety. Several days later, Camreta, accompanied by petitioner

James Alford, a Deschutes County deputy sheriff, went to S.G.'s elementary school and interviewed her about the allegations. Camreta and Alford did not have a warrant, nor had they obtained parental consent to conduct the interview. Although S.G. at first denied that her father had molested her, she eventually stated that she had been abused. Greene was indicted and stood trial for sexually abusing S.G., but the jury failed to reach a verdict and the charges were later dismissed.

Respondent Sarah Greene, S.G.'s mother, subsequently sued Camreta and Alford on S.G.'s behalf for damages under 42 U.S.C. § 1983, which authorizes suits against state officials for violations of constitutional rights. S.G. alleged that the officials' in-school interview had breached the Fourth Amendment's proscription on unreasonable seizures.

The District Court granted summary judgment to Camreta and Alford, and the Ninth Circuit affirmed. The Court of Appeals first ruled that the interview violated S.G.'s rights because Camreta and Alford had "seize[d] and interrogate[d] S.G. in the absence of a warrant, a court order, exigent circumstances, or parental consent." But the court further held that the officials were entitled to qualified immunity from damages liability because no clearly established law had warned them of the illegality of their conduct.

The Ninth Circuit explained why it had chosen to rule on the merits of the constitutional claim, rather than merely hold that the officials were immune from suit. By addressing the legality of the interview, the court said, it could "provide guidance to those charged with the difficult task of protecting child welfare within the confines of the Fourth Amendment." That guidance came in no uncertain terms: "[G]overnment officials investigating allegations of child abuse," the court warned, "should cease operating on the assumption that a 'special need' automatically justifies dispensing with traditional Fourth Amendment protections in this context."

Although the judgment entered was in their favor, Camreta and Alford petitioned this Court to review the Ninth Circuit's ruling that their conduct violated the Fourth Amendment. S.G. declined to cross-petition for review of the decision that the officials have immunity. We granted certiorari.

II

We first consider our ability to act on a petition brought by government officials who have won final judgment on grounds of qualified immunity, but who object to an appellate court's ruling that they violated the plaintiff's constitutional rights. Camreta and Alford are, without doubt, prevailing parties. The Ninth Circuit's decision shielded them from monetary liability, and S.G. chose not to contest that ruling. So whatever else follows, they will not have to pay S.G. the damages she sought. The question we confront is whether we may nonetheless review the Court of Appeals' holding that the officials violated the Constitution.

The statute governing this Court's jurisdiction authorizes us to adjudicate a case in this posture, and S.G. does not contend otherwise. The relevant provision confers unqualified power on this Court to grant certiorari "upon the petition of *any* party." 28 U.S.C. § 1254(1) (emphasis added). That language covers petitions brought by litigants who have prevailed, as well as those who have lost, in the court below.

S.G., however, alleges two impediments to our exercise of statutory authority here, one constitutional and the other prudential. First, she claims that Article III bars review because petitions submitted by immunized officials present no case or controversy. Second, she argues that our settled practice of declining to hear appeals by prevailing parties should apply with full force when officials have obtained immunity. We disagree on both counts.

A

Article III of the Constitution grants this Court authority to adjudicate legal disputes only in the context of "Cases" or "Controversies." To enforce this limitation, we demand that litigants demonstrate a "personal stake" in the suit. The party invoking the Court's authority has such a stake when three conditions are satisfied: The petitioner must show that he has "suffered an injury in fact" that is caused by "the conduct complained of" and that "will be redressed by a favorable decision." Lujan v. Defenders of Wildlife, 504 U.S. 555, 560–61 (1992) (internal quotation marks omitted). And the opposing party also must have an ongoing interest in the dispute, so that the case features "that concrete adverseness which sharpens the presentation of issues." Los Angeles v. Lyons, 461 U.S. 95, 101 (1983) (internal quotation marks omitted). To ensure a case remains "fit for federal-court adjudication," the parties must have the necessary stake not only at the outset of litigation, but throughout its course. Arizonans for Official English v. Arizona, 520 U.S. 43, 67 (1997).

We have previously recognized that an appeal brought by a prevailing party may satisfy Article III's case-or-controversy requirement. See Deposit Guaranty Nat. Bank v. Roper, 445 U.S. 326, 332–36 (1980). Indeed, we have twice before allowed a party for whom judgment was entered to challenge an unfavorable lower court ruling. See id.; Electrical Fittings Corp. v. Thomas & Betts Co., 307 U.S. 241 (1939).[3] In that context as in others, we stated, the critical question under Article III is whether the litigant retains the necessary personal stake in the appeal. *Deposit Guaranty*, 445 U.S. at 334. As we will explain, a court will usually

---

[3]   The dissent discusses *Deposit Guaranty* and *Electrical Fittings* at length in an effort to distinguish them from this suit. But we do not say those cases are foursquare with this one on their facts; we rely on them only for the proposition that this Court has previously identified no special Article III bar on review of appeals brought by parties who obtained a judgment in their favor below. The dissent does not, because it cannot, dispute that simple point.

invoke rules of "federal appellate practice" to decline review of a prevailing party's challenge even when he has the requisite stake. But in such a case, Article III is not what poses the bar; these rules of practice "d[o] not have [their] source in the jurisdictional limitations" of the Constitution. *Deposit Guaranty*, 445 U.S. at 333–34. So long as the litigants possess the personal stake discussed above, an appeal presents a case or controversy, no matter that the appealing party was the prevailing party below.

This Article III standard often will be met when immunized officials seek to challenge a ruling that their conduct violated the Constitution. That is not because a court has made a retrospective judgment about the lawfulness of the officials' behavior, for that judgment is unaccompanied by any personal liability. Rather, it is because the judgment may have prospective effect on the parties. The court in such a case says: "Although this official is immune from damages today, what he did violates the Constitution and he or anyone else who does that thing again will be personally liable." If the official regularly engages in that conduct as part of his job (as Camreta does), he suffers injury caused by the adverse constitutional ruling. So long as it continues in effect, he must either change the way he performs his duties or risk a meritorious damages action. Only by overturning the ruling on appeal can the official gain clearance to engage in the conduct in the future. He thus can demonstrate, as we demand, injury, causation, and redressability.[4] And conversely, if the person who initially brought the suit may again be subject to the challenged conduct, she has a stake in preserving the court's holding. See Erie v. Pap's A.M., 529 U.S. 277, 287–89 (2000); Honig v. Doe, 484 U.S. 305, 318–23 (1988). Only if the ruling remains good law will she have ongoing protection from the practice.

We therefore reject S.G.'s view that Article III bars us from adjudicating any and all challenges brought by government officials who have received immunity below. That the victor has filed the appeal does not deprive us of jurisdiction. The parties in such cases may yet have a sufficient "interest in the outcome of [a litigated] issue" to present a case or controversy. *Deposit Guaranty*, 445 U.S. at 336 n.7.

B

Article III aside, an important question of judicial policy remains. As a matter of practice and prudence, we have generally declined to consider cases at the request of a prevailing party, even when the Constitution allowed us to do so. Our resources are not well spent superintending each word a lower court utters en route to a final judgment in the petitioning party's favor. We therefore have adhered with some rigor to the principle that "[t]his Court reviews judgments, not statements in opinions." California v. Rooney, 483 U.S. 307, 311 (1987) (per curiam) (internal quota-

---

4   Contrary to the dissent's view, the injury to the official thus occurs independent of any future suit brought by a third party. Indeed, no such suit is likely to arise because the prospect of damages liability will force the official to change his conduct.

tion marks omitted). On the few occasions when we have departed from that principle, we have pointed to a "policy reaso[n] . . . of sufficient importance to allow an appeal" by the winner below. *Deposit Guaranty*, 445 U.S. at 336 n.7.

We think just such a reason places qualified immunity cases in a special category when it comes to this Court's review of appeals brought by winners. The constitutional determinations that prevailing parties ask us to consider in these cases are not mere dicta or "statements in opinions." *Rooney*, 483 U.S. at 311 (internal quotation marks omitted). They are rulings that have a significant future effect on the conduct of public officials—both the prevailing parties and their co-workers—and the policies of the government units to which they belong. And more: they are rulings self-consciously designed to produce this effect, by establishing controlling law and preventing invocations of immunity in later cases. And still more: they are rulings designed this way with this Court's permission, to promote clarity—and observance—of constitutional rules. We describe in more detail below these features of the qualified immunity world and why they came to be. We hold that taken together, they support bending our usual rule to permit consideration of immunized officials' petitions.

To begin, then, with the nature of these suits: Under § 1983 (invoked in this case) and Bivens v. Six Unknown Fed. Narcotics Agents, 403 U.S. 388 (1971), a plaintiff may seek money damages from government officials who have violated her constitutional or statutory rights. But to ensure that fear of liability will not "unduly inhibit officials in the discharge of their duties," Anderson v. Creighton, 483 U.S. 635, 638 (1987), the officials may claim qualified immunity; so long as they have not violated a "clearly established" right, they are shielded from personal liability, Harlow v. Fitzgerald, 457 U.S. 800, 818 (1982). That means a court can often avoid ruling on the plaintiff's claim that a particular right exists. If prior case law has not clearly settled the right, and so given officials fair notice of it, the court can simply dismiss the claim for money damages. The court need never decide whether the plaintiff's claim, even though novel or otherwise unsettled, in fact has merit.

And indeed, our usual adjudicatory rules suggest that a court *should* forbear resolving this issue. After all, a "longstanding principle of judicial restraint requires that courts avoid reaching constitutional questions in advance of the necessity of deciding them." Lyng v. Northwest Indian Cemetery Protective Assn., 485 U.S. 439, 445 (1988); see also Ashwander v. TVA, 297 U.S. 288, 346–47 (1936) (Brandeis, J., concurring). In this category of qualified immunity cases, a court can enter judgment without ever ruling on the (perhaps difficult) constitutional claim the plaintiff has raised. Small wonder, then, that a court might leave that issue for another day.

But we have long recognized that this day may never come—that our regular policy of avoidance sometimes does not fit the qualified immunity situation because it threatens to leave standards of official conduct permanently in limbo. Consider a plausible but unsettled constitutional claim asserted against a government official in a suit for money damages. The court does not resolve the claim because the official has immunity. He thus persists in the challenged practice; he knows that he can avoid liability in any future damages action, because the law has still not been clearly established. Another plaintiff brings suit, and another court both awards immunity and bypasses the claim. And again, and again, and again. So the moment of decision does not arrive.[5] Courts fail to clarify uncertain questions, fail to address novel claims, fail to give guidance to officials about how to comply with legal requirements. Qualified immunity thus may frustrate "the development of constitutional precedent" and the promotion of law-abiding behavior. Pearson v. Callahan, 555 U.S. 223, 237 (2009).

For this reason, we have permitted lower courts to avoid avoidance—that is, to determine whether a right exists before examining whether it was clearly established. Indeed, for some time we *required* courts considering qualified immunity claims to first address the constitutional question, so as to promote "the law's elaboration from case to case." Saucier v. Katz, 533 U.S. 194, 201 (2001). More recently, we have left this matter to the discretion of lower courts, and indeed detailed a range of circumstances in which courts should address only the immunity question. See Pearson v. Callahan, 555 U.S. 223, 236–42 (2009). In general, courts should think hard, and then think hard again, before turning small cases into large ones. But it remains true that following the two-step sequence—defining constitutional rights and only then conferring immunity—is sometimes beneficial to clarify the legal standards governing public officials.

Here, the Court of Appeals followed exactly this two-step process, for exactly the reasons we have said may in select circumstances make it "advantageous." Id. at 242. The court, as noted earlier, explained that it was "address[ing] both prongs of the qualified immunity inquiry . . . to provide guidance to those charged with the difficult task of protecting child welfare within the confines of the Fourth Amendment." To that end, the court adopted constitutional standards to govern all in-school interviews of suspected child abuse victims. And the court specifically instructed government officials to follow those standards going forward—to "cease operating on the assumption" that warrantless interviews are permitted. With the law thus clearly established, officials who conduct this kind of interview will not receive immunity in the Ninth Circuit. And

---

[5] The constitutional issue could arise in a case in which qualified immunity is unavailable—for example, "in a suit to enjoin future conduct, in an action against a municipality, or in litigating a suppression motion in a criminal proceeding." County of Sacramento v. Lewis, 523 U.S. 833, 841 n.5 (1998). A decision in such a case would break the repetitive cycle of qualified immunity defenses described above. But some kinds of constitutional questions do not often come up in these alternative settings. Id. (noting that "these avenues w[ill] not necessarily be open").

the State of Oregon has done just what we would expect in the wake of the court's decision: It has provided revised legal advice, consonant with the Ninth Circuit's ruling, to child protective services workers wishing to interview children in schools. The court thus accomplished what it set out to do: settle a question of constitutional law and thereby guide the conduct of officials.

Given its purpose and effect, such a decision is reviewable in this Court at the behest of an immunized official. No mere dictum, a constitutional ruling preparatory to a grant of immunity creates law that governs the official's behavior. If our usual rule pertaining to prevailing parties applied, the official would "fac[e] an unenviable choice": He must either acquiesce in a ruling he had no opportunity to contest in this Court, or "defy the views of the lower court, adhere to practices that have been declared illegal, and thus invite new suits and potential punitive damages." *Pearson*, 555 U.S. at 240–41 (internal quotation marks and brackets omitted). And if our usual bar on review applied, it would undermine the very purpose served by the two-step process, "which is to clarify constitutional rights without undue delay." Bunting v. Mellen, 541 U.S. 1019, 1024 (2004) (Scalia, J., dissenting from denial of certiorari). This Court, needless to say, also plays a role in clarifying rights. Just as that purpose may justify an appellate court in reaching beyond an immunity defense to decide a constitutional issue, so too that purpose may support this Court in reviewing the correctness of the lower court's decision.

We emphasize, however, two limits of today's holding. First, it addresses only our own authority to review cases in this procedural posture. The Ninth Circuit had no occasion to consider whether it could hear an appeal from an immunized official: In that court, after all, S.G. appealed the judgment in the officials' favor. We therefore need not and do not decide if an appellate court, too, can entertain an appeal from a party who has prevailed on immunity grounds.[7] Second, our holding concerns only what this Court *may* review; what we actually will choose to review is a different matter. That choice will be governed by the ordinary principles informing our decision whether to grant certiorari. . . . Our decision today does no more than exempt one special category of cases from our usual rule against considering prevailing parties' petitions. Going forward, we will consider these petitions one by one in accord with our usual standards.

---

[7] We note, however, that the considerations persuading us to permit review of petitions in this posture may not have the same force as applied to a district court decision. "A decision of a federal district court judge is not binding precedent in either a different judicial district, the same judicial district, or even upon the same judge in a different case." 18 J. Moore et al., Moore's Federal Practice § 134.02[1][d], p. 134–26 (3d ed. 2011). Many Courts of Appeals therefore decline to consider district court precedent when determining if constitutional rights are clearly established for purposes of qualified immunity. See, e.g., Kalka v. Hawk, 215 F.3d 90, 100 (D.C. Cir. 2000) (Tatel, J., concurring in part and concurring in judgment) (collecting cases). Otherwise said, district court decisions—unlike those from the courts of appeals—do not necessarily settle constitutional standards or prevent repeated claims of qualified immunity.

III

Although we reject S.G.'s arguments for dismissing this case at the threshold, we find that a separate jurisdictional problem requires that result: This case, we conclude, is moot.[8]

As we explained above, in a dispute of this kind, both the plaintiff and the defendant ordinarily retain a stake in the outcome. That is true of one defendant here: Camreta remains employed as a child protective services worker, so he has an interest in challenging the Ninth Circuit's ruling requiring him to obtain a warrant before conducting an in-school interview.[9] But S.G. can no longer claim the plaintiff's usual stake in preserving the court's holding because she is no longer in need of any protection from the challenged practice. After we granted certiorari, we discovered that S.G. has "moved to Florida, and ha[s] no intention of relocating back to Oregon." Brief for Respondent 13 n.13. What is more, S.G. is now only months away from her 18th birthday—and, presumably, from her high school graduation. S.G. therefore cannot be affected by the Court of Appeals' ruling; she faces not the slightest possibility of being seized in a school in the Ninth Circuit's jurisdiction as part of a child abuse investigation. When "subsequent events ma[ke] it absolutely clear that the allegedly wrongful behavior could not reasonably be expected to recur," we have no live controversy to review. United States v. Concentrated Phosphate Export Assn., Inc., 393 U.S. 199, 203 (1968); see, e.g., DeFunis v. Odegaard, 416 U.S. 312 (1974) (per curiam) (suit challenging law school admissions policy mooted when plaintiff neared graduation). Time and distance combined have stymied our ability to consider this petition. . . .

We thus must decide how to dispose of this case. When a civil suit becomes moot pending appeal, we have the authority to "direct the entry of such appropriate judgment, decree, or order, or require such further proceedings to be had as may be just under the circumstances." 28 U.S.C. § 2106. Our "established" (though not exceptionless) practice in this situation is to vacate the judgment below. "A party who seeks review of the merits of an adverse ruling, but is frustrated by the vagaries of circumstance," we have emphasized, "ought not in fairness be forced to acquiesce in" that ruling. U.S. Bancorp Mortgage Co. v. Bonner Mall Partnership, 513 U.S. 18, 25 (1994). The equitable remedy of vacatur ensures that "those who have been prevented from obtaining the review to

---

[8]   Justice Sotomayor maintains that, because this case is moot, "[t]here is no warrant for reaching th[e] question" whether immunized officials may obtain our consideration of an adverse constitutional ruling. But this Court has never held that it may consider only one threshold issue per case. And here, as we will explain, our discussion of reviewability is critical to our ultimate disposition of this suit. Moreover, that issue was fully litigated in this Court. We granted certiorari to consider whether "the Ninth Circuit's constitutional ruling [is] reviewable, notwithstanding that [the Court of Appeals] ruled in [the officials'] favor on qualified immunity grounds." And all the parties, as well as the United States as amicus curiae, addressed that question in their briefs and oral arguments.

[9]   The same cannot be said for Deputy Sheriff Alford. In their briefs, the parties informed us that Alford no longer works for Deschutes County or in law enforcement. . . .

which they are entitled [are] not . . . treated as if there had been a review." *Munsingwear*, 340 U.S. at 39.[10]

S.G. contends that vacatur is inappropriate in the qualified immunity context because that disposition would "undermine" the Court of Appeals' choice to "decide [a] constitutional questio[n]" to govern future cases. Far from counseling against vacatur, S.G.'s argument reveals the necessity of that procedural course. The point of vacatur is to prevent an unreviewable decision "from spawning any legal consequences," so that no party is harmed by what we have called a "preliminary" adjudication. *Munsingwear*, 340 U.S. at 40–41. As we have just explained, a constitutional ruling in a qualified immunity case is a legally consequential decision; that is the very reason we think it appropriate for review even at the behest of a prevailing party. When happenstance prevents that review from occurring, the normal rule should apply: Vacatur then rightly "strips the decision below of its binding effect," Deakins v. Monaghan, 484 U.S. 193, 200 (1988), and "clears the path for future relitigation," *Munsingwear*, 340 U.S. at 40.

In this case, the happenstance of S.G.'s moving across country and becoming an adult has deprived Camreta of his appeal rights. Mootness has frustrated his ability to challenge the Court of Appeals' ruling that he must obtain a warrant before interviewing a suspected child abuse victim at school. We therefore vacate the part of the Ninth Circuit's opinion that addressed that issue, and remand for further proceedings consistent with this opinion.[11]

It is so ordered.

---

[10] Our analysis of the proper disposition of this case follows from our conclusion that government officials who secure a favorable judgment on immunity grounds may obtain our review of an adverse constitutional holding. As just noted, *Munsingwear* justified vacatur to protect a litigant who had the right to appeal but lost that opportunity due to happenstance. We have therefore left lower court decisions intact when mootness did not deprive the appealing party of any review to which he was entitled. See, e.g., *U.S. Bancorp Mortgage Co.*, 513 U.S. at 25 (holding that the appealing party had "surrender[ed] his claim to the equitable remedy of vacatur" by settling the case and thus "voluntarily forfeit[ing] his legal remedy by the ordinary processes of appeal"); Karcher v. May, 484 U.S. 72, 83 (1987) (holding that vacatur in light of mootness was not warranted when the losing party declined to file an appeal). So if immunized officials could not challenge an appellate decision in this Court, we would choose not to exercise our equitable authority to vacate that decision, even if the case later became moot. But here, as we have just explained, the theory that underlies our prior cases applying *Munsingwear* is satisfied: Vacatur expunges an adverse decision that would be reviewable had this case not become moot.

[11] Our disposition of this case differs slightly from the normal *Munsingwear* order vacating the lower court's judgment and remanding the case with instructions to dismiss the relevant claim. We leave untouched the Court of Appeals' ruling on qualified immunity and its corresponding dismissal of S.G.'s claim because S.G. chose not to challenge that ruling. We vacate the Ninth Circuit's ruling addressing the merits of the Fourth Amendment issue because, as we have explained, that is the part of the decision that mootness prevents us from reviewing but that has prospective effects on Camreta. But we emphasize that this unique disposition follows from the unique posture of this case and signals no endorsement of deviations from the usual *Munsingwear* order in other situations.

■ JUSTICE SCALIA, concurring.

I join the Court's opinion, which reasonably applies our precedents, strange though they may be. The alternative solution, as Justice Kennedy suggests, is to end the extraordinary practice of ruling upon constitutional questions unnecessarily when the defendant possesses qualified immunity. The parties have not asked us to adopt that approach, but I would be willing to consider it in an appropriate case.

■ JUSTICE SOTOMAYOR, with whom JUSTICE BREYER joins, concurring in the judgment.

I agree with the Court's conclusion that this case is moot and that vacatur is the appropriate disposition; unlike the majority, however, I would go no further. As the exchange between the majority and Justice Kennedy demonstrates, the question whether Camreta, as a prevailing party, can obtain our review of the Ninth Circuit's constitutional ruling is a difficult one. There is no warrant for reaching this question when there is clearly no longer a genuine case or controversy between the parties before us. Indeed, it is improper for us to do so. Cf. U.S. Bancorp Mortgage Co. v. Bonner Mall Partnership, 513 U.S. 18, 21 (1994) ("[A] federal court [may not] decide the merits of a legal question not posed in an Article III case or controversy").

The majority suggests that we must decide whether Camreta has a "right to appeal" in order to vacate the judgment below under United States v. Munsingwear, Inc., 340 U.S. 36 (1950). But that view does not accord with our past practice. Nor is it consistent with the principles underlying our mootness jurisprudence. In accordance with our normal procedure for disposing of cases that have become moot through no fault of the party seeking review, we should simply vacate the portion of the Ninth Circuit's opinion Camreta sought to challenge and remand with instructions to dismiss.

■ JUSTICE KENNEDY, with whom JUSTICE THOMAS joins, dissenting.

Today's decision results from what is emerging as a rather troubling consequence from the reasoning of our recent qualified immunity cases. The Court is correct to note the problem presented when, on the one hand, its precedents permit or invite courts to rule on the merits of a constitutional claim even when qualified immunity disposes of the matter; and, on the other hand, jurisdictional principles prevent us from reviewing those invited rulings. It does seem that clarification is required. In my view, however, the correct solution is not to override jurisdictional rules that are basic to the functioning of the Court and to the necessity of avoiding advisory opinions. Dictum, though not precedent, may have its utility; but it ought not to be treated as a judgment standing on its own. So, while acknowledging the problem the Court confronts, my concern with the rule adopted for this case calls for this respectful dissent.

I

The Court acknowledges our "settled refusal to entertain an appeal," including a petition for certiorari, "by a party on an issue as to which he prevailed." At the outset, however, it is important to state this rule more fully to show its foundational character. A party that has already obtained the judgment it requested may not seek review to challenge the reasoning of a judicial decision. As we have said on many occasions, "This Court reviews judgments, not statements in opinions." California v. Rooney, 483 U.S. 307, 311 (1987) (per curiam) (internal quotation marks omitted). The rule has been noted and followed since the early years of this Court. "The question before an appellate Court is, was the *judgment* correct, not the *ground* on which the judgment professes to proceed." McClung v. Silliman, 19 U.S. (6 Wheat.) 598, 603 (1821).

The rule against hearing appeals or accepting petitions for certiorari by prevailing parties is related to the Article III prohibition against issuing advisory opinions. This principle underlies, for example, the settled rule against hearing cases involving a disputed judgment based on grounds of state law. As Justice Jackson explained for the Court: "[O]ur power is to correct wrong judgments, not to revise opinions. We are not permitted to render an advisory opinion, and if the same judgment would be rendered by the state court after we corrected its views of federal laws, our review could amount to nothing more than an advisory opinion." Herb v. Pitcairn, 324 U.S. 117, 125–26 (1945). . . .

The Court nonetheless holds that defendants who prevail in the Courts of Appeals based on qualified immunity may still obtain review in this Court. This point is put in perspective by the fact that the Court today, in an altogether unprecedented disposition, says that it vacates not a judgment but rather "part of the Ninth Circuit's opinion." The Court's conclusion is unsettling in its implications. Even on the Court's reading of our cases, the almost invariable rule is that prevailing parties are not permitted to obtain a writ of certiorari. Cf. Kalka v. Hawk, 215 F.3d 90, 96 n.9 (D.C. Cir. 2000) (concluding that the Supreme Court "has apparently never granted the certiorari petition of a party who prevailed in the appellate court"). After today, however, it will be common for prevailing parties to seek certiorari based on the Court's newfound exception. And that will be so even though the "admonition" against reviewing mere statements in opinions "has special force when the statements raise constitutional questions, for it is our settled practice to avoid the unnecessary decision of such issues." FCC v. Pacifica Foundation, 438 U.S. 726, 734 (1978).

The Court defends its holding with citations to just two of our cases. Neither provides support for the Court's result.

The first case is Electrical Fittings Corp. v. Thomas & Betts Co., 307 U.S. 241 (1939). There, a plaintiff alleged the infringement of two patent claims. The District Court found the plaintiff's first claim valid but not infringed and the second claim invalid. Rather than issuing a judgment "dismissing the bill without more," the District Court instead "entered a decree adjudging claim 1 valid" and "dismissing the bill for failure to prove infringement." The District Court thus issued a formal judgment regarding the validity of the first claim. The defendant appealed to dispute that claim's validity. This Court noted, without qualification, that a party "may not appeal from a judgment or decree in his favor, for the purpose of obtaining a review of findings he deems erroneous which are not necessary to support the decree." Id. at 242. "But," this Court went on to explain, "here the decree itself purports to adjudge the validity of claim 1, and though the adjudication was immaterial to the disposition of the cause, it stands as an adjudication of one of the issues litigated." In other words, the District Court had entered an unnecessary legal conclusion into the terms of the judgment itself, making it possible, for example, that the decree would have estoppel effect as to an issue whose resolution was unnecessary to the proper judgment of dismissal. *Electrical Fittings* therefore concluded that "the petitioners were entitled to have this portion of the decree eliminated." The sole relief provided was an order for the "reformation of the decree." That result accords with, indeed flows from, the settled rule that this Court reviews only judgments, not statements in opinions.

The second case is Deposit Guaranty Nat. Bank v. Roper, 445 U.S. 326 (1980). In that case plaintiffs attempted to bring a class action against a bank. After the District Court denied class certification, the defendant tendered to the plaintiffs the maximum value that they could recover as individuals. Of course, that offer did not amount to "all that ha[d] been requested in the complaint"—namely, "relief for the class." Id. at 341 (Rehnquist, J., concurring). It is therefore no surprise that the plaintiffs responded with "a counteroffer of judgment in which they attempted to reserve the right to appeal the adverse class certification ruling." Id. at 329 (opinion of the Court). But that proposal was denied. "Based on the bank's offer, the District Court entered judgment in respondents' favor, over their objection." Id. at 330. The District Court thus issued a judgment other than the one the plaintiffs had sought. The would-be class plaintiffs appealed, and this Court later granted certiorari. The Court held that appeal was not barred by the prevailing-party rule: "We view the denial of class certification as an example of a procedural ruling, collateral to the merits of a litigation, that is appealable after the entry of final judgment." As the Court explained, the plaintiffs had obtained only a judgment in their individual capacities. Yet the plaintiffs had "asserted as their personal stake in the appeal their desire to shift to successful class litigants a portion of those fees and expenses that have been incurred in this litigation." Because the purported prevailing parties were injured by their failure to obtain the class-based judgment they had sought, the Court held there was "jurisdiction to entertain the appeal only to review the asserted procedural error, not for the purpose of passing on the merits." The Court was clear that the District Court's denial of class certification had a direct effect on the judgment: "As in *Electrical Fittings*," the purported prevailing parties "were entitled to have [a] portion of the District Court's judgment reviewed."

Neither *Electrical Fittings* nor *Deposit Guaranty* provides support for the rule adopted today. Those decisions instead held that, in the unusual circumstances presented, particular parties who at first appeared to have prevailed below had in fact failed to obtain the judgments they had sought. This Court therefore had jurisdiction, including of course jurisdiction under Article III, to provide relief for the harm caused by the adverse judgments entered below. The parties seeking appeal in *Electrical Fittings* and *Deposit Guaranty* might be compared with plaintiffs who have requested $1,000 in relief but obtained only $500. Such parties have prevailed in part, but have not "receive[d] all that [they] ha[d] sought." *Deposit Guaranty*, 445 U.S. at 333. In contrast the Court appears to assume that the petitioners in the present case are true prevailing parties. They have obtained from the Court of Appeals the only formal judgment they requested: denial of respondent's claim for damages. . . .

The Court errs in reading *Electrical Fittings* and *Deposit Guaranty* to permit review and, indeed, the provision of relief disconnected from any judgment. The result is an erroneous and unbounded exception to an essential principle of judicial restraint. Parties who have obtained all requested relief may not seek review here.

II

As today's decision illustrates, our recent qualified immunity cases tend to produce decisions that are in tension with conventional principles of case-or-controversy adjudication. This Court has given the Courts of Appeals "permission" to find constitutional violations when ordering dismissal or summary judgment based on qualified immunity. See Pearson v. Callahan, 555 U.S. 223 (2009). This invitation, as the Court is correct to note, was intended to produce binding constitutional holdings on the merits. The goal was to make dictum precedent, in order to hasten the gradual process of constitutional interpretation and alter the behavior of government defendants. The present case brings the difficulties of that objective into perspective. In express reliance on the permission granted in *Pearson*, the Court of Appeals went out of its way to announce what may be an erroneous interpretation of the Constitution; and, under our case law, the Ninth Circuit must give that dictum legal effect as precedent in future cases.

In this way unnecessary merits decisions in qualified immunity cases could come to resemble declaratory judgments or injunctions. Indeed the United States as amicus curiae contends that the merits decision below "has an effect similar to an injunction or a declaratory judgment against the government as a whole." Today's opinion adopts that view, providing as relief the vacatur of "part of the Ninth Circuit's opinion"—namely, the part of the opinion that rules on the constitutional merits. For the first time, obiter dictum is treated not just as precedent for future cases but as a judgment in its own right.

The Court of Appeals in this case did not in fact issue a declaratory judgment or injunction embodying a determination on the merits, and it does not appear that a judgment of that kind could have issued. Plaintiffs must establish standing as to each form of relief they request, yet the plaintiff in this case had no separate interest in obtaining a declaratory judgment. See Los Angeles v. Lyons, 461 U.S. 95, 103–05 (1983). There was no likelihood that S.G., the plaintiff's daughter, would again be subjected to interrogation while at school, much less that she would be interrogated by petitioner-defendant Camreta, so S.G. would seem to have had no greater stake in obtaining a declaratory judgment than the plaintiff in *Lyons* had in obtaining an injunction. See 461 U.S. at 104 (noting the "actual controversy that must exist for a declaratory judgment to be entered"). Our qualified immunity cases should not permit plaintiffs in constitutional cases to make an end-run around established principles of justiciability. In treating dictum as though it were a declaratory judgment or an injunction, the Court appears to approve the issuance of such judgments outside the bounds of Article III jurisdiction.

The Court creates an exception to the prevailing party rule in order to solve the difficulties created by our qualified immunity jurisprudence, but the Court's solution creates new problems. Sometimes defendants in qualified immunity cases have no particular interest in disputing the constitutional merits. Acknowledging as much, the Court notes that petitioner Alford no longer works for the government and so "has lost his interest in the Fourth Amendment ruling." In concluding that Alford lacks Article III standing, the Court suggests that it would lack jurisdiction to review and perhaps even to vacate the merits decision of the Court of Appeals if respondent had sued only Alford. That suggestion is disconcerting. Under today's decision, it appears that the Court's ability to review merits determinations in qualified immunity cases is contingent on the defendant who has been sued. A defendant who has left the government's employ or otherwise lacks an interest in disputing the merits will be unable to obtain further review.

The Court today avoids this difficulty by concluding that petitioner Camreta has suffered an Article III injury. But the Court can reach that conclusion only because, "as part of his job," Camreta "regularly engages" in conduct made unlawful by the reasoning of the Court of Appeals. As discussed below, this conclusion is doubtful. In any event the Court's standing analysis will be inapplicable in most qualified immunity cases. When an officer is sued for taking an extraordinary action, such as using excessive force during a high-speed car chase, there is little possibility that a constitutional decision on the merits will again influence that officer's conduct. The officer, like petitioner Alford . . . , would have no interest in litigating the merits in the Court of Appeals and, under the Court's rule, would seem unable to obtain review of a merits ruling by petitioning for certiorari. This problem will arise with great frequency in qualified immunity cases. Once again, the decision today allows plaintiffs to obtain binding constitutional determinations on the merits that lie beyond this Court's jurisdiction to review. The Court thus fails to solve the problem it identifies.

III

It is most doubtful that Article III permits appeals by any officer to whom the reasoning of a judicial decision might be applied in a later suit. Yet that appears to be the implication of the Court's holding. The favorable judgment of the Court of Appeals did not in itself cause petitioner Camreta to suffer an Article III injury entitling him to appeal. On the contrary, Camreta has been injured by the decision below to no greater extent than have hundreds of other government officers who might argue that they too have been affected by the unnecessary statements made by the Court of Appeals. . . .

The Court's analysis appears to rest on the premise that the reasoning of the decision below in itself causes Camreta injury. Until today, however, precedential reasoning of general applicability divorced from a particular adverse judgment was not thought to yield "standing to appeal." Parr v. United States, 351 U.S. 513, 516, 517 (1956). That is why "[o]nly one injured by the judgment sought to be reviewed can appeal." Id. at 516. It is revealing that the Court creates an exception to the prevailing party rule while making clear that the Courts of Appeals are not to follow suit, in any context.

The conclusion that precedent of general applicability cannot in itself create standing to sue or appeal flows from basic principles. Camreta's asserted injury is caused not by the Court of Appeals or by respondent but rather by "the independent action of some third party not before the court"—that is, by the still-unidentified private plaintiffs whose lawsuits Camreta hopes to avoid. Lujan v. Defenders of Wildlife, 504 U.S. 555, 560–61 (1992) (internal quotation marks omitted). This circumstance distinguishes the present case from requests for declaratory or injunctive relief filed against officeholders who threaten legal enforcement. An inert rule of law does not cause particular, concrete injury; only the specific threat of its enforcement can do so. That is why the proper defendant in a suit for prospective relief is the party prepared to enforce the relevant legal rule against the plaintiff. Without an adverse judgment from which to appeal, Camreta has in effect filed a new declaratory judgment action in this Court against the Court of Appeals. This is no more consistent with Article III than filing a declaratory judgment action against this Court for its issuance of an adverse precedent or against Congress in response to its enactment of an unconstitutional law.

IV

If today's decision proves to be more than an isolated anomaly, the Court might find it necessary to reconsider its special permission that the Courts of Appeals may issue unnecessary merits determinations in qualified immunity cases with binding precedential effect.

Other dynamics permit the law of the Constitution to be elaborated within the conventional framework of a case or controversy. "[T]he development of constitutional law is by no means entirely dependent on cases in which the defendant may seek qualified immunity." *Pearson*, 555 U.S. at 242–43. For example, qualified immunity does not bar Fourth and Fifth Amendment suppression challenges. Nor does it prevent invocation of the Constitution as a defense against criminal prosecution, civil suit, or cruel and unusual punishment. Nor is qualified immunity available in constitutional suits against municipalities. . . .

The desire to resolve more constitutional questions ought not lead to altering our jurisdictional rules. That is the precise object that our legal tradition tells us we should resist. Haste to resolve constitutional issues has never been thought advisable. We instead have encouraged the Courts of Appeals to follow "that older, wiser judicial counsel not to pass on questions of constitutionality unless such adjudication is unavoidable." Scott v. Harris, 550 U.S. 372, 388 (2007) (Breyer, J., concurring) (internal quotation marks omitted); see generally Ashwander v. TVA, 297 U.S. 288, 347 (1936) (Brandeis, J., concurring). . . .

There will be instances where courts discuss the merits in qualified immunity cases. It is sometimes a better analytic approach and a preferred allocation of judicial time and resources to dismiss a claim on the merits rather than to dismiss based on qualified immunity. And "[i]t often may be difficult to decide whether a right is clearly established without deciding precisely what the existing constitutional right happens to be." *Pearson*, 555 U.S. at 236 (internal quotation marks omitted). This Court should not superintend the judicial decisionmaking process in qualified immunity cases under special rules, lest it make the judicial process more complex for civil rights suits than for other litigation. It follows, however, that the Court should provide no special permission to reach the merits. If qualified immunity cases were treated like other cases raising constitutional questions, settled principles of constitutional avoidance would apply. So would conventional rules regarding dictum and holding. Judicial observations made in the course of explaining a case might give important instruction and be relevant when assessing a later claim of qualified immunity. But as dicta those remarks would not establish law and would not qualify as binding precedent.

* * *

The distance our qualified immunity jurisprudence has taken us from foundational principles is made all the more apparent by today's decision. The Court must construe two of its precedents in so broad a manner that they are taken out of their proper and logical confines. To vacate the reasoning of the decision below, the Court accepts that obiter

dictum is not just binding precedent but a judgment susceptible to plenary review. I would dismiss this case and note that our jurisdictional
rule against hearing appeals by prevailing parties precludes petitioners'
attempt to obtain review of judicial reasoning disconnected from a judgment.

NOTE ON CAMRETA V. GREENE

Abstractly considered, *Deposit National Guaranty Bank v. Roper* and
Camreta v. Greene present similar problems. Both cases involve situations
in which the traditional model of litigation as dispute resolution between
named parties no longer fully accounts for modern practice. In consumer
class actions, the named or representative plaintiff is almost a secondary figure. The primary actor is the lawyer who seeks to certify a class and proceed
to settlement or litigation on that basis. One way to understand *Deposit
Guaranty* is that it protected the interest of the class action lawyer and the
other class members whom he or she might represent, even though the claim
of the named individual plaintiff had been fully satisfied.

In *Camreta v. Greene*, the Court confronted an analogous situation in
constitutional tort cases. Constitutional tort plaintiffs ordinarily must sue
government officers as individuals. Routinely, however, those officers are defended by the governments that employ them and any adverse judgments
are satisfied from public funds. See John C. Jeffries, Jr., In Praise of the
Eleventh Amendment and Section 1983, 84 Va. L. Rev. 47, 49–50 (1998)
("Very generally, a suit against a state officer is functionally a suit against
the state, for the state defends the action and pays any adverse judgment.").
Thus, the named defendant in a § 1983 case, such as Mr. Camreta, is not the
only party in interest. The government that employs that officer typically
has an interest not only in protecting its employee but also in defending government practices against constitutional attack and in challenging adverse
rulings against them. One way to understand *Camreta*, therefore, is that it
protected the interests of the state and local governments that stand behind
officer defendants. Whether these functional justifications can be squared
with the constraints of Article III and traditional understandings of the roles
of courts are questions that arise in both cases.

There are also more particular questions that arise within the four corners of *Camreta*. What is one to make of footnote 7, limiting the Court's
ruling to Supreme Court review? Are the policy considerations that support
appellate review of merits rulings in qualified immunity cases confined to
the Supreme Court? Justice Kennedy said that the Court had "create[d] an
exception to the prevailing party rule while making clear that the Courts of
Appeals are not to follow suit, in any context." Is that clear? Or has the question been left to another day?

Finally, *Camreta* is interesting as a mootness case as well. In a concurring opinion in Honig v. Doe, 484 U.S. 305, 327 (1988), Chief Justice
Rehnquist ventured the suggestion that mootness should be seen as having
only an "attenuated" connection to Article III. He viewed the doctrine as
largely prudential. Consistent with that view, he proposed an exception to

mootness for cases that became moot only after full consideration by the Supreme Court: "[Our] resources—the time spent preparing to decide the case by reading briefs, hearing oral arguments, and conferring—are squandered in every case in which it becomes apparent after the decisional process is underway that we may not reach the question presented." Rehnquist thought that a sufficient reason to abandon or reformulate mootness in the Supreme Court. Justice Scalia rebutted this suggestion, 484 U.S. at 332 (Scalia, J., dissenting), and it attracted no wider support. Does footnote 8 of the *Camreta* opinion belatedly adopt Rehnquist's view? Does it signal that mootness is now viewed as largely prudential?

SECTION 4. THE POLITICAL QUESTION

INTRODUCTORY NOTES ON THE HISTORY OF THE DOCTRINE

1. *MARBURY V. MADISON*

The political question doctrine asserts that some issues are appropriate for resolution only by the political branches of the government rather than the courts. Cases presenting such issues are said to be nonjusticiable. This idea has a long history. In Marbury v. Madison, 5 U.S. (1 Cranch) 137 (1803), the Supreme Court famously stated that it "is emphatically the province and duty of the Judicial Department to say what the law is." But the Court also observed that "[q]uestions, in their nature political or which are, by the Constitution and laws, submitted to the Executive, can never be made in this court." The Court further noted that "[t]he province of the Court is solely to decide on the rights of individuals, not to inquire how the Executive or Executive officers perform duties in which they have a discretion."

2. *LUTHER V. BORDEN*

The leading early case arose out of the Dorr Rebellion against the "charter" government of Rhode Island. After the United States separated from England, Rhode Island did not adopt a new constitution but instead continued the form of government established by a British charter. In 1842, Dorr was elected governor under a new state constitution, but the pre-existing charter government refused to admit the validity of these proceedings. Dorr tried to take power by force, but was repulsed. The charter government then called a constitutional convention, and a peaceful transition to the new government was made in 1843.

During the Rebellion, Borden and other charter officers, acting under the authority of martial law, broke into Luther's house. Luther sued for trespass, claiming that the charter government had been displaced and therefore could not authorize the defendants' acts. In this way, Luther sought to litigate the existence and authority of the charter government in the interval between the purported approval of a new constitution in 1842 and the actual transfer of authority to the new government in 1843. The lower court, however, declined to consider this issue and entered a verdict for defendants. In Luther v. Borden, 48 U.S. (7 How.) 1 (1849), the Supreme Court affirmed.

Speaking through Chief Justice Taney, the Court offered several reasons for refusing to inquire into the continued validity of the charter government. Grave practical difficulties would follow if all acts of the established government could be called into question. Moreover, the state courts had approved the charter government's authority during that period and accepted its acts as valid. Finally, as to Art. IV, § 4, which provides that the "United States shall guarantee to every State a Republican Form of Government," the Court held:

> Congress must necessarily decide what government is established in the state before it can determine whether it is republican or not. And when the senators and representatives of a state are admitted into the councils of the Union, the authority of the government under which they are appointed, as well as its republican character, is recognized by the proper constitutional authority. And its decision is binding on every other department of the government, and could not be questioned in a judicial tribunal.

Subsequent Supreme Court decisions confirmed that whether a state government constitutes a republican form of government for purposes of Art. IV, § 4 is to be determined exclusively by the political branches, not the courts. See, e.g., Ohio ex rel. Davis v. Hildebrant, 241 U.S. 565 (1916); Pacific States Telephone & Telegraph Co. v. Oregon, 223 U.S. 118 (1912).

3.   *COLEMAN V. MILLER*

In Coleman v. Miller, 307 U.S. 433 (1939), members of the Kansas state legislature brought an action to invalidate the state's ratification of a proposed Child Labor Amendment to the federal Constitution. The legislature had initially declined to ratify the amendment in 1925. In 1937, however, the state senate considered a new resolution to ratify the amendment and deadlocked on a vote of 20 to 20. Kansas' lieutenant governor then purported to cast a tie-breaking vote in favor of ratification. The state house of representatives subsequently approved the resolution.

Article V of the Constitution, which prescribes the process for amendment, refers to ratification by state "legislatures." The petitioners first argued that the lieutenant governor was not part of the state legislature and thus that his vote should not count. The Supreme Court divided four-four on whether this issue raised a political question and thus reached no conclusion on the merits.

The petitioners also argued that, since the state had already rejected the proposed amendment, it should not have been allowed to ratify the amendment at a later time. The Court concluded that "the question of the efficacy of ratifications by state legislatures, in the light of previous rejection or attempted withdrawal, should be regarded as a political question pertaining to the political departments, with the ultimate authority in the Congress in the exercise of its control over the promulgation of the adoption of the amendment."

Finally, the petitioners argued that too much time had elapsed between the proposal of the amendment and the state's ratification of it. The Court found that this issue, too, presented a political question. The determination of what constitutes a reasonable amount of time for ratification of a constitutional amendment "lies within the congressional province," said the Court. The Court expressed particular concern that there were no judicially manageable criteria for determining a reasonable time period:

> In determining whether a question falls within [the political question] category, the appropriateness under our system of government of attributing finality to the action of the political departments and also the lack of satisfactory criteria for a judicial determination are dominant considerations.

4.   *BAKER V. CARR*

After *Luther v. Borden,* Guarantee Clause questions were usually held nonjusticiable. This position eventually assumed great importance, for it blocked attempts to litigate the constitutionality of legislative malapportionment. In Colegrove v. Green, 328 U.S. 549 (1946), for example, the Court refused to reach the merits of a constitutional attack on Illinois's congressional districting. Speaking for a plurality, Justice Frankfurter described the issue as one "of a peculiarly political nature and therefore not meet for judicial determination." In subsequent cases, the Court followed *Colegrove* in turning aside constitutional attacks on legislative districting. See, e.g., South v. Peters, 339 U.S. 276 (1950).

All this was changed by Baker v. Carr, 369 U.S. 186 (1962). Plaintiffs claimed that the malapportionment of the Tennessee legislature denied equal protection to voters in the more populous districts. The trial court dismissed the suit on the authority of *Colegrove,* but the Supreme Court reversed. In an opinion by Justice Brennan, the Court said that "the mere fact that the suit seeks protection of a political right does not mean it presents a political question." The Court found the Guarantee Clause cases irrelevant. Their only significance was in holding that the particular constitutional provision there was "not a repository of judicially manageable standards." The Equal Protection Clause was different.

The Court reviewed "a number of political question cases, in order to expose the attributes of the doctrine—attributes which, in various settings, diverge, combine, appear, and disappear in seeming disorderliness." "That review reveals," the Court said, "that, in the Guaranty Clause cases and in the other 'political question' cases, it is the relationship between the judiciary and the coordinate branches of the Federal Government, and not the federal judiciary's relationship to the States, which gives rise to the 'political question.'"

Finally, in a famous passage the Court identified six ingredients of a "political question":

> Prominent on the surface of any case held to involve a political question is found a textually demonstrable constitutional commitment of the issue to a coordinate political department; or a lack of judicially discoverable and manageable standards for resolving it;

or the impossibility of deciding without an initial policy determination of a kind clearly for nonjudicial discretion; or the impossibility
of a court's undertaking independent resolution without expressing
lack of the respect due coordinate branches of government; or an
unusual need for unquestioning adherence to a political decision
already made; or the potentiality of embarrassment from multifarious pronouncements by various departments on one question.

Unless one of these factors is "inextricable from the case at bar," said the
Court, there should be no dismissal for nonjusticiability on the ground of a
political question. Accordingly, the case was remanded for trial on the merits.[a]

5. *POWELL V. MCCORMACK*

The question in Powell v. McCormack, 395 U.S. 486 (1969), was whether
the House of Representatives could refuse to seat Representative Adam
Clayton Powell, Jr., on the grounds that he had misused House funds. Powell
sued Speaker John W. McCormack and other officials, claiming that he could
not be excluded from the House for dishonesty but only for failure to meet
the three requirements of Art. I, § 2, cl. 2: "No Person shall be a Representative who shall not have attained to the Age of twenty five Years, and been
seven Years a Citizen of the United States, and who shall not, when elected,
be an Inhabitant of that State in which he shall be chosen." The defendants
claimed that the issue was a political question and therefore nonjusticiable.

In an opinion by Chief Justice Warren, the Supreme Court focused on
the first *Baker* factor—whether there was "a textually demonstrable constitutional commitment of the issue to a coordinate political department." The
defendants had a good candidate. Art. I, § 5, cl. 1 provides that "Each House
shall be the Judge of the Elections, Returns and Qualifications of its own
Members. . . ." The Chief Justice responded, however, that "[i]n order to determine the scope of any 'textual commitment' under Art. I, § 5, we necessarily must determine the meaning" of that provision. After examining the
history of the question, the Court concluded that "the Constitution leaves the
House without authority to *exclude* any person, duly elected by his constitu-
ents, who meets all the requirements for membership expressly prescribed
in the Constitution."[b]

Does the search for a textually demonstrable commitment turn on the
merits or on justiciability? In finding no such commitment in *Powell*, the
Court made a determination that the House lacked constitutional authority
to exclude Powell for dishonesty and thus that it had acted improperly. If the
Court had found that the House did have such authority, would it have gone
on to determine whether the House acted properly in this case? Or would it

---

[a] Two years later, in Reynolds v. Sims, 377 U.S. 533 (1964), the Court ruled that both
houses of a state legislature must be elected from districts "as nearly of equal population as is
practicable."

[b] A different question would have been presented had the House *expelled* Representative
Powell after he had been seated. Art. I, § 5, cl. 2 explicitly provides for the authority to expel a
Member but requires "the Concurrence of two thirds." Representative Powell was *excluded* on a
simple majority vote.

simply have decided that the propriety of the decision was not subject to judicial evaluation? Is there a difference?

6. *GILLIGAN V. MORGAN*

Gilligan v. Morgan, 413 U.S. 1 (1973), arose in the aftermath of the shootings by the Ohio National Guard at Kent State University in May 1970. Members of the student government sued to enjoin the governor from premature use of the National Guard and to enjoin the Guard from violating students' rights. Most aspects of the suit were dismissed, but the Court of Appeals ordered a trial on the claim that the training and leadership of the National Guard made the unnecessary use of deadly force "inevitable." In an opinion by Chief Justice Burger, the Supreme Court reversed. Finding a political question within the meaning of *Baker v. Carr*, the Court reasoned:

> It would be difficult to think of a clearer example of the type of governmental action that was intended by the Constitution to be left to the political branches directly responsible—as the Judicial Branch is not—to the electoral process. Moreover, it is difficult to conceive of an area of governmental activity in which the courts have less competence. The complex, subtle, and professional decisions as to the composition, training, equipping, and control of a military force are essentially professional military judgments, subject always to civilian control of the Legislative and Executive Branches. The ultimate responsibility for these decisions is appropriately vested in branches of the government which are periodically subject to electoral accountability.

The Court did not say specifically which *Baker* factors applied. What does the above passage suggest about that?

Nixon v. United States

Supreme Court of the United States, 1993.
506 U.S. 224.

■ CHIEF JUSTICE REHNQUIST delivered the opinion of the Court. . . .

Nixon, a former Chief Judge of the United States District Court for the Southern District of Mississippi, was convicted by a jury of two counts of making false statements before a federal grand jury and sentenced to prison. The grand jury investigation stemmed from reports that Nixon had accepted a gratuity from a Mississippi businessman in exchange for asking a local district attorney to halt the prosecution of the businessman's son. Because Nixon refused to resign from his office as a United States District Judge, he continued to collect his judicial salary while serving out his prison sentence.

On May 10, 1989, the House of Representatives adopted three articles of impeachment for high crimes and misdemeanors. The first two articles charged Nixon with giving false testimony before the grand jury and the third article charged him with bringing disrepute on the Federal Judiciary.

After the House presented the articles to the Senate, the Senate voted to invoke its own Impeachment Rule XI, under which the presiding officer appoints a committee of Senators to "receive evidence and take testimony." The Senate committee held four days of hearings, during which 10 witnesses, including Nixon, testified. Pursuant to Rule XI, the committee presented the full Senate with a complete transcript of the proceeding and a Report stating the uncontested facts and summarizing the evidence on the contested facts. Nixon and the House impeachment managers submitted extensive final briefs to the full Senate and delivered arguments from the Senate floor during the three hours set aside for oral argument in front of that body. Nixon himself gave a personal appeal, and several Senators posed questions directly to both parties. The Senate voted by more than the constitutionally required two-thirds majority to convict Nixon on the first two articles. The presiding officer then entered judgment removing Nixon from his office as United States District Judge.

Nixon thereafter commenced the present suit, arguing that Senate Rule XI violates the constitutional grant of authority to the Senate to "try" all impeachments because it prohibits the whole Senate from taking part in the evidentiary hearings. See Art. I, § 3, cl. 6. Nixon sought a declaratory judgment that his impeachment conviction was void and that his judicial salary and privileges should be reinstated. The District Court held that his claim was nonjusticiable, and the Court of Appeals for the District of Columbia Circuit agreed. We granted certiorari.

A controversy is nonjusticiable—i.e., involves a political question— where there is "a textually demonstrable constitutional commitment of the issue to a coordinate political department; or a lack of judicially discoverable and manageable standards for resolving it . . . ." Baker v. Carr, 369 U.S. 186 (1962). But the courts must, in the first instance, interpret the text in question and determine whether and to what extent the issue is textually committed. See id.; Powell v. McCormack, 395 U.S. 486, 519 (1969). As the discussion that follows makes clear, the concept of a textual commitment to a coordinate political department is not completely separate from the concept of a lack of judicially discoverable and manageable standards for resolving it; the lack of judicially manageable standards may strengthen the conclusion that there is a textually demonstrable commitment to a coordinate branch.

In this case, we must examine Art. I, § 3, cl. 6, to determine the scope of authority conferred upon the Senate by the Framers regarding impeachment. It provides:

The Senate shall have the sole Power to try all Impeachments. When sitting for that Purpose, they shall be on Oath or Affirmation. When the President of the United States is tried, the Chief Justice shall preside: And no Person shall be convicted without the Concurrence of two thirds of the Members present.

The language and structure of this Clause are revealing. The first sentence is a grant of authority to the Senate, and the word "sole" indicates that this authority is reposed in the Senate and nowhere else. The next two sentences specify requirements to which the Senate proceedings shall conform: The Senate shall be on oath or affirmation, a two-thirds vote is required to convict, and when the President is tried the Chief Justice shall preside.

Petitioner argues that the word "try" in the first sentence imposes by implication an additional requirement on the Senate in that the proceedings must be in the nature of a judicial trial. From there petitioner goes on to argue that this limitation precludes the Senate from delegating to a select committee the task of hearing the testimony of witnesses, as was done pursuant to Senate Rule XI. " 'Try' means more than simply 'vote on' or 'review' or 'judge.' In 1787 and today, trying a case means hearing the evidence, not scanning a cold record." Brief for Petitioner 25. Petitioner concludes from this that courts may review whether or not the Senate "tried" him before convicting him.

There are several difficulties with this position which lead us ultimately to reject it. The word "try," both in 1787 and later, has considerably broader meanings than those to which petitioner would limit it. Older dictionaries define try as "to examine" or "to examine as a judge." See 2 S. Johnson, A Dictionary of the English Language (1785). In more modern usage the term has various meanings. For example, try can mean "to examine or investigate judicially," "to conduct the trial of," or "to put to the test by experiment, investigation, or trial." Webster's Third New International Dictionary 2457 (1971). Petitioner submits that "try," as contained in T. Sheridan, Dictionary of the English Language (1796), means "to examine as a judge; to bring before a judicial tribunal." Based on the variety of definitions, however, we cannot say that the Framers used the word "try" as an implied limitation on the method by which the Senate might proceed in trying impeachments. . . .

The conclusion that the use of the word "try" in the first sentence of the Impeachment Trial Clause lacks sufficient precision to afford any judicially manageable standard of review of the Senate's actions is fortified by the existence of the three very specific requirements that the Constitution does impose on the Senate when trying impeachments: The Members must be under oath, a two-thirds vote is required to convict, and the Chief Justice presides when the President is tried. These limitations are quite precise, and their nature suggests that the Framers did not intend to impose additional limitations on the form of the Senate proceedings by the use of the word "try" in the first sentence. . . .

The history and contemporary understanding of the impeachment provisions support our reading of the constitutional language. The parties do not offer evidence of a single word in the history of the Constitutional Convention or in contemporary commentary that even alludes to the possibility of judicial review in the context of the impeachment powers. . . .

In addition to the textual commitment argument, we are persuaded that the lack of finality and the difficulty of fashioning relief counsel against justiciability. We agree with the Court of Appeals that opening the door of judicial review to the procedures used by the Senate in trying impeachments would "expose the political life of the country to months, or perhaps years, of chaos." This lack of finality would manifest itself most dramatically if the President were impeached. The legitimacy of any successor, and hence his effectiveness, would be impaired severely, not merely while the judicial process was running its course, but during any retrial that a differently constituted Senate might conduct if its first judgment of conviction were invalidated. Equally uncertain is the question of what relief a court may give other than simply setting aside the judgment of conviction. Could it order the reinstatement of a convicted federal judge, or order Congress to create an additional judgeship if the seat had been filled in the interim?

Petitioner finally contends that a holding of nonjusticiability cannot be reconciled with our opinion in Powell v. McCormack, 395 U.S. 486 (1969).

Our conclusion in *Powell* was based on the fixed meaning of "qualifications" set forth in Art. I, § 2. The claim by the House that its power to "be the Judge of the Elections, Returns and Qualifications of its own Members" was a textual commitment of unreviewable authority was defeated by the existence of this separate provision specifying the only qualifications which might be imposed for House membership. The decision as to whether a Member satisfied these qualifications *was* placed with the House, but the decision as to what these qualifications consisted of was not.

In the case before us, there is no separate provision of the Constitution that could be defeated by allowing the Senate final authority to determine the meaning of the word "try" in the Impeachment Trial Clause. . . .

For the foregoing reasons, the judgment of the Court of Appeals is affirmed.

[Justice Stevens concurred, observing that, for him, "the debate about the strength of the inferences to be drawn from the use of the words 'sole' and 'try' is far less significant than the central fact that the Framers decided to assign the impeachment power to the Legislative Branch."

[Joined by Justice Blackmun, Justice White concurred in the judgment. White disagreed with the majority that the case presented a political question, contending that judicial review should be available to "ensure that the Senate adhered to a minimal set of procedural standards in conducting impeachment trials." He voted to affirm the decision below, however, because he thought the Senate had met its constitutional obligation to "try" Nixon. He acknowledged that, "as a practical matter, it will likely make little difference whether the Court's or my view controls this case."

[Justice Souter also concurred in the judgment. Although he agreed with the majority that the case presented a political question, he thought it was possible to "envision different and unusual circumstances that might justify a more searching review of impeachment proceedings." In particular, he noted that "[i]f the Senate were to act in a manner seriously threatening the integrity of its results, convicting, say, upon a coin toss, or upon a summary determination that an officer of the United States was simply 'a bad guy,' judicial interference might well be appropriate."]

NOTES ON NIXON V. UNITED STATES

1.   QUESTIONS AND COMMENTS ON NIXON

What is the difference in *Nixon* between holding that the meaning of the word "try" is nonjusticiable and holding that the Senate has broad leeway under the Constitution in deciding how to conduct an impeachment trial? Both Justice White and Justice Souter wanted to leave open some possibility of judicial review in future cases. Is there an important difference between their positions?

When the first *Baker* factor applies to an issue, does it mean: (a) the Constitution gives a political actor complete discretion over the issue, so whatever action is taken concerning that issue is inherently constitutional; (b) the Constitution gives a political actor a range of discretion over the issue, so any action taken within that range is inherently constitutional; or (c) the action taken by the political actor concerning the issue may or may not be constitutional, but it is in any event not judicially reviewable? Both (a) and (b) would seem to be decisions on the merits rather than on justiciability. Is it clear which of these meanings the majority in *Nixon* had in mind?

2.   THE POLITICAL QUESTION DOCTRINE AND JUDICIAL REVIEW

There are fundamental questions concerning the relationship between the political question doctrine and the role of the courts in exercising judicial review. Is the doctrine a sensible way for the courts to manage their political capital and accord proper respect to the other branches of government, or is it an unprincipled evasion of judicial responsibility?

The significance of this question is almost invisible if one focuses on the Supreme Court, whose jurisdiction is in any event almost entirely discretionary. Considerations of timing, political context, and situational difficulty are everyday aspects of the decision to grant or deny certiorari. For the lower federal courts, however, a decision to decline jurisdiction must be explained. And difficult questions arise when "political" considerations preclude adjudication in *any* federal court of what might be a valid claim.

Concern on these points led Herbert Wechsler famously to advocate a narrow view of the doctrine of the political question:

> [A]ll the doctrine can defensibly imply is that the courts are called upon to judge whether the Constitution has committed to another agency of government the autonomous determination of the issue raised, a finding that itself requires interpretation. [T]he only proper judgment that may lead to an abstention from decision is that the Constitution has committed the determination of the issue to another agency of government than the courts. Difficult as it may be to make that judgment wisely, whatever factors may be rightly weighed in situations where the answer is not clear, what is involved is itself an act of constitutional interpretation, to be made and judged by standards that should govern the interpretive process generally. This, I submit, is toto caelo different from a broad discretion to abstain or intervene.

Herbert Wechsler, Toward Neutral Principles of Constitutional Law, 73 Harv. L. Rev. 1, 7–8 (1959). For Wechsler, this narrow approach followed from the fact that judicial review is "anchored in the Constitution" and therefore constitutes a "judicial obligation."

This argument produced a response from Alexander Bickel:

> [O]nly by means of a play on words can the broad discretion that the courts have in fact exercised be turned into an act of constitutional interpretation. The political-question doctrine simply resists being domesticated in this fashion. There is something different about it, in kind, not in degree, from the general "interpretive process"; something greatly more flexible, something of prudence, not construction and not principle. And it is something that cannot exist within the four corners of *Marbury v. Madison*.

Alexander Bickel, The Supreme Court, 1960 Term—Foreword: The Passive Virtues, 75 Harv. L. Rev. 40, 46 (1961).[a]

For Bickel, as for Wechsler, the scope of the political question doctrine was intimately related to the rationale for judicial review. For Bickel, however, judicial review was not so much a *duty* imposed by the Constitution on an obedient judiciary as a *power* to be used or withheld on the basis of discerning judgment. In Bickel's view, the task of the Court was to safeguard principle in a world of political expediency. "[T]he role of the Court and its raison d'etre are to evolve, to defend, and to protect principle." In some circumstances, it would be appropriate for the Court to attempt to coerce adherence to principle by the political branches. In others, "there ought to be discretion free of principled rules." After all, "no society, certainly not a large and heterogeneous one, can fail in time to explode if it is deprived of the arts of compromise, if it knows no way to muddle through." In such situations, the Court may have to tolerate unprincipled actions, but it should at least avoid "legitimating" them by pronouncements of constitutionality.

---

[a] Bickel later expanded these views in his book, The Least Dangerous Branch (1962).

It is in this frame of reference that Bickel placed his view of a political question:

> Such is the basis of the political question doctrine: the Court's sense of lack of capacity, compounded in unequal part of the strangeness of the issue and the suspicion that it will have to yield more often and more substantially to expediency than to principle; the sheer momentousness of it, which unbalances judgment and prevents one from subsuming the normal calculations of probabilities; the anxiety not so much that judicial judgment will be ignored, as that perhaps it should be, but won't; finally and in sum ("in a mature democracy"), the inner vulnerability of an institution which is electorally irresponsible and has no earth to draw strength from.

Which view is more persuasive? Are there important differences between when the political question doctrine would apply under these two positions? If, as Wechsler argued, the political question doctrine should not be applied for mere prudential reasons, would courts likely find other ways to limit their involvement in politically sensitive cases?

3. POLITICAL GERRYMANDERING

Despite being subject to a one-person, one-vote standard, there are various ways of drawing the lines of voting districts—for both state legislatures and for Congress—that can favor a particular political party. This sort of "political gerrymandering" (also known as "partisan gerrymandering") is widespread and consequential, and almost everyone agrees that unrestrained partisanship in drawing district lines is a bad thing. It is unclear, however, whether courts should get involved or on what basis.

(i) Davis v. Bandemer

In Davis v. Bandemer, 479 U.S. 109 (1986), which concerned a challenge to a Republican-led redistricting in Indiana, the Supreme Court held that challenges to political gerrymandering based on the Equal Protection Clause are justiciable. The Court reasoned:

> Disposition of this question does not involve us in a matter more properly decided by a coequal branch of our Government. There is no risk of foreign or domestic disturbance, and, in light of our cases since *Baker*, we are not persuaded that there are no judicially discernible and manageable standards by which political gerrymander cases are to be decided.

A majority of the Court also agreed that, to establish an equal protection violation, a claimant would have to prove "both intentional discrimination against an identifiable political group and an actual discriminatory effect on that group," meaning that exclusion of the disadvantaged party would persist over time. The six Justices who thought the case was justiciable, however, disagreed among themselves over how this demanding standard could be met.

Joined by Chief Justice Burger and Justice Rehnquist, Justice O'Connor concurred in the judgment, arguing that political gerrymandering claims brought by members of one of the two major political parties raise nonjusticiable political questions. O'Connor argued that "the legislative business of apportionment is fundamentally a political affair, and challenges to the manner in which an apportionment has been carried out—by the very parties that are responsible for this process—present a political question in the truest sense of the term."

(ii) Vieth v. Jubelirer

In Vieth v. Jubelirer, 541 U.S. 267 (2004), the Court considered an equal protection challenge to how the Republican-controlled Pennsylvania legislature had drawn the state's congressional districts. A plurality of the Court, through Justice Scalia, concluded that the case presented a political question because of the second *Baker* factor: a lack of judicially discoverable and manageable standards for resolving the issue. The plurality also emphasized that the Constitution provides a non-judicial remedy by giving Congress the power to make adjustments to the electoral districts drawn up by state legislatures.

The plurality further argued that it was time to overturn *Davis v. Bandemer* in light of the fact that "no judicially discernible and manageable standards for adjudicating political gerrymandering claims have emerged" since the decision. Justice Kennedy provided the controlling vote. He agreed that no workable standard had yet emerged for addressing political gerrymandering claims, but he declined to overturn *Davis*, reasoning that it might be appropriate for courts to intervene some day if they are ever able to develop workable standards: "If suitable standards with which to measure the burden a gerrymander imposes on representational rights did emerge, hindsight would show that the Court prematurely abandoned the field. That is a risk the Court should not take." The dissenting Justices (Stevens, Souter, Ginsburg, and Breyer) proposed various more-or-less complicated tests for evaluating equal protection challenges to political gerrymandering.

(iii) League of United Latin American Citizens v. Perry

The division of opinion in *Vieth* continued in League of United Latin American Citizens v. Perry, 548 U.S. 399 (2006). That case involved an appeal from a three-judge District Court involving an attack on a Republican-led redistricting in Texas in 2003. In a confusing array of opinions, the Court found one congressional district violative of § 2 of the Voting Rights Act but rejected a broader claim of statewide political gerrymandering.

Justice Kennedy, who waffled in *Vieth*, and the four dissenters from that decision agreed that the *League of United Latin American Citizens* claim was justiciable. Kennedy, however, concluded that the plaintiffs had not demonstrated a "reliable standard for identifying unconstitutional political gerrymanders." While this language may sound like nonjusticiability, it led Kennedy to conclude instead that "[plaintiffs] have established no legally impermissible use of political classifications. For this reason, they state no claim on which relief may be granted for their statewide challenge."

Joined by Justice Thomas, Justices Scalia adhered to his conclusion in *Vieth* that such a claim was non justiciable:

> Justice Kennedy's discussion of appellants' political-gerry-mandering claims ably demonstrates that, yet again, no party or judge has put forth a judicially discernible standard by which to evaluate them. Unfortunately, the opinion then concludes that the appellants have failed to state a claim as to political gerrymandering, without ever articulating what the elements of such a claim consist of. That is not an available disposition of this appeal. We must either conclude that the claim is nonjusticiable and dismiss it, or else set forth a standard and measure appellants' claim against it. Instead, we again dispose of this claim in a way that provides no guidance to lower-court judges and perpetuates a cause of action with no discernible content.

This left Chief Justice Roberts and Justice Alito, who were not on the Court when *Vieth* was decided. They joined Kennedy (and Scalia and Thomas) in rejecting the claim. They agreed with Justice Kennedy that no "reliable standard for identifying unconstitutional political gerrymanders" had been found, without joining his conclusion on justiciability. Writing for himself and Justice Alito, the Chief Justice declined to say whether the plaintiffs had failed to present a justiciable controversy or had merely failed to state a claim on which relief can be granted:

> I . . . take no position on that question which has divided the Court, and I join the Court's disposition . . . without specifying whether appellants have failed to state a claim on which relief can be granted, or have failed to present a justiciable controversy.

As if this were not complicated enough, the four dissenters in *Vieth* stuck to their position on justiciability but disagreed among themselves on the merits. Justice Stevens, joined by Justice Breyer, dissented, finding this a clear case of an unconstitutional political gerrymander. Justices Souter and Ginsburg joined Justice Kennedy in rejecting one line of attack but did not commit themselves on another. By way of explanation, Souter said, "I see nothing to be gained by working through these cases on the standard I would have applied in *Vieth*, because here as in *Vieth* we have no majority for any single criterion of permissible gerrymandering. . . ."

Thus, the lineup in *Vieth*, which might be described as four-one-four, degenerated in *League of United Latin American Citizens* to something approximating two-two-one-two-two.

Zivotofsky v. Clinton

Supreme Court of the United States, 2012.
566 U.S. 189.

■ CHIEF JUSTICE ROBERTS delivered the opinion of the Court. . . .

I

The State Department's Foreign Affairs Manual states that "[w]here the birthplace of the applicant is located in territory disputed by another country, the city or area of birth may be written in the passport." The manual specifically directs that passport officials should enter "JERU-SALEM" and should "not write Israel or Jordan" when recording the birthplace of a person born in Jerusalem on a passport.

Section 214(d) [of the Foreign Relations Authorization Act for Fiscal Year 2003] sought to override this instruction by allowing citizens born in Jerusalem to have "Israel" recorded on their passports if they wish. . . .

Petitioner Menachem Binyamin Zivotofsky was born in Jerusalem on October 17, 2002, shortly after § 214(d) was enacted. Zivotofsky's parents were American citizens and he accordingly was as well, by virtue of congressional enactment. Zivotofsky's mother filed an application for a consular report of birth abroad and a United States passport. She requested that his place of birth be listed as "Jerusalem, Israel" on both documents. U.S. officials informed Zivotofsky's mother that State Department policy prohibits recording "Israel" as Zivotofsky's place of birth. Pursuant to that policy, Zivotofsky was issued a passport and consular report of birth abroad listing only "Jerusalem."

Zivotofsky's parents filed a complaint on his behalf against the Secretary of State. Zivotofsky sought a declaratory judgment and a permanent injunction ordering the Secretary to identify his place of birth as "Jerusalem, Israel" in the official documents. . . .

II

The lower courts concluded that Zivotofsky's claim presents a political question and therefore cannot be adjudicated. We disagree.

In general, the Judiciary has a responsibility to decide cases properly before it, even those it "would gladly avoid." Cohens v. Virginia, 19 U.S. (6 Wheat) 264, 404 (1821). Our precedents have identified a narrow exception to that rule, known as the "political question" doctrine. We have explained that a controversy "involves a political question . . . where there is 'a textually demonstrable constitutional commitment of the issue to a coordinate political department; or a lack of judicially discoverable and manageable standards for resolving it.' " Nixon v. United States, 506 U.S. 224, 228 (1993) (quoting Baker v. Carr, 369 U.S. 186, 217 (1962)). In such a case, we have held that a court lacks the authority to decide the dispute before it. . . .

[The D.C. Circuit] concluded that "[o]nly the Executive—not Congress and not the courts—has the power to define U.S. policy regarding Israel's sovereignty over Jerusalem," and also to "decide how best to implement that policy." Because the Department's passport rule was adopted to implement the President's "exclusive and unreviewable constitutional power to keep the United States out of the debate over the status of Jerusalem," the validity of that rule was itself a "nonjusticiable political question" that "the Constitution leaves to the Executive alone." [T]he D.C. Circuit's opinion does not even mention § 214(d) until the fifth of its six paragraphs of analysis, and then only to dismiss it as irrelevant:

"That Congress took a position on the status of Jerusalem and gave Zivo-tofsky a statutory cause of action . . . is of no moment to whether the judiciary has [the] authority to resolve this dispute. . . ."

The existence of a statutory right, however, is certainly relevant to the Judiciary's power to decide Zivotofsky's claim. The federal courts are not being asked to supplant a foreign policy decision of the political branches with the courts' own unmoored determination of what United States policy toward Jerusalem should be. Instead, Zivotofsky requests that the courts enforce a specific statutory right. To resolve his claim, the Judiciary must decide if Zivotofsky's interpretation of the statute is cor-rect, and whether the statute is constitutional. This is a familiar judicial exercise.

Moreover, because the parties do not dispute the interpretation of § 214(d), the only real question for the courts is whether the statute is constitutional. At least since Marbury v. Madison, 5 U.S. (1 Cranch) 137 (1803), we have recognized that when an Act of Congress is alleged to conflict with the Constitution, "[i]t is emphatically the province and duty of the judicial department to say what the law is." That duty will some-times involve the "[r]esolution of litigation challenging the constitutional authority of one of the three branches," but courts cannot avoid their re-sponsibility merely "because the issues have political implications." INS v. Chadha, 462 U.S. 919, 943 (1983).

In this case, determining the constitutionality of § 214(d) involves deciding whether the statute impermissibly intrudes upon Presidential powers under the Constitution. If so, the law must be invalidated and Zivotofsky's case should be dismissed for failure to state a claim. If, on the other hand, the statute does not trench on the President's powers, then the Secretary must be ordered to issue Zivotofsky a passport that complies with § 214(d). Either way, the political question doctrine is not implicated. . . .

The Secretary contends that "there is 'a textually demonstrable con-stitutional commitment' " to the President of the sole power to recognize foreign sovereigns and, as a corollary, to determine whether an American born in Jerusalem may choose to have Israel listed as his place of birth on his passport. Perhaps. But there is, of course, no exclusive commit-ment to the Executive of the power to determine the constitutionality of a statute. The Judicial Branch appropriately exercises that authority, in-cluding in a case such as this, where the question is whether Congress or the Executive is "aggrandizing its power at the expense of another branch."

Our precedents have also found the political question doctrine impli-cated when there is " 'a lack of judicially discoverable and manageable standards for resolving' " the question before the court. Framing the is-sue as the lower courts did, in terms of whether the Judiciary may decide the political status of Jerusalem, certainly raises those concerns. They dissipate, however, when the issue is recognized to be the more focused one of the constitutionality of § 214(d). Indeed, both sides offer detailed legal arguments regarding whether § 214(d) is constitutional in light of powers committed to the Executive, and whether Congress's own powers with respect to passports must be weighed in analyzing this question. . . .

[The Court then reviewed the government's and the petitioner's arguments on the merits of the constitutionality of Section 214(d).]

Recitation of these arguments—which sound in familiar principles of constitutional interpretation—is enough to establish that this case does not "turn on standards that defy judicial application." Resolution of Zivotofksy's claim demands careful examination of the textual, structural, and historical evidence put forward by the parties regarding the nature of the statute and of the passport and recognition powers. This is what courts do. The political question doctrine poses no bar to judicial review of this case. . . .

Having determined that this case is justiciable, we leave it to the lower courts to consider the merits in the first instance.

The judgment of the Court of Appeals for the D.C. Circuit is vacated, and the case is remanded for further proceedings consistent with this opinion.

■ JUSTICE SOTOMAYOR, with whom JUSTICE BREYER joins as to Part I, concurring in part and concurring in the judgment. . . .

I

. . . In *Baker*, this Court identified six circumstances in which an issue might present a political question. . . . But *Baker* left unanswered when the presence of one or more factors warrants dismissal, as well as the interrelationship of the six factors and the relative importance of each in determining whether a case is suitable for adjudication.

In my view, the *Baker* factors reflect three distinct justifications for withholding judgment on the merits of a dispute. When a case would require a court to decide an issue whose resolution is textually committed to a coordinate political department, as envisioned by *Baker*'s first factor, abstention is warranted because the court lacks authority to resolve that issue. . . . In such cases, the Constitution itself requires that another branch resolve the question presented.

The second and third *Baker* factors reflect circumstances in which a dispute calls for decisionmaking beyond courts' competence. . . . When a court is given no standard by which to adjudicate a dispute, or cannot resolve a dispute in the absence of a yet-unmade policy determination charged to a political branch, resolution of the suit is beyond the judicial role envisioned by Article III. . . .

The final three *Baker* factors address circumstances in which prudence may counsel against a court's resolution of an issue presented. Courts should be particularly cautious before forgoing adjudication of a dispute on the basis that judicial intervention risks "embarrassment from multifarious pronouncements by various departments on one question," would express a "lack of the respect due coordinate branches of government," or because there exists an "unusual need for unquestioning adherence to a political decision already made." We have repeatedly rejected the view that these thresholds are met whenever a court is called upon to resolve the constitutionality or propriety of the act of another branch of Government. . . .

Rare occasions implicating *Baker*'s final factors, however, may present an " 'unusual case' " unfit for judicial disposition. *Baker*, 369 U.S. at 218 (quoting the argument of Daniel Webster in Luther v. Borden, 48 U.S. 1 (1849)). Because of the respect due to a coequal and independent department, for instance, courts properly resist calls to question the good faith with which another branch attests to the authenticity of its internal acts. . . . Likewise, we have long acknowledged that courts are particularly ill suited to intervening in exigent disputes necessitating unusual need for "attributing finality to the action of the political departments," Coleman v. Miller, 307 U.S. 433, 454 (1939), or creating acute "risk [of] embarrassment of our government abroad, or grave disturbance at home," *Baker*, 369 U.S. at 226. Finally, it may be appropriate for courts to stay their hand in cases implicating delicate questions concerning the distribution of political authority between coordinate branches until a dispute is ripe, intractable, and incapable of resolution by the political process. . . .

When such unusual cases arise, abstention accommodates considerations inherent in the separation of powers and the limitations envisioned by Article III, which conferred authority to federal courts against a common-law backdrop that recognized the propriety of abstention in exceptional cases. . . . The political questions envisioned by *Baker*'s final categories find common ground, therefore, with many longstanding doctrines under which considerations of justiciability or comity lead courts to abstain from deciding questions whose initial resolution is better suited to another time; or another forum. . . .

To be sure, it will be the rare case in which *Baker*'s final factors alone render a case nonjusticiable.[2] But our long historical tradition recognizes that such exceptional cases arise, and due regard for the separation of powers and the judicial role envisioned by Article III confirms that abstention may be an appropriate response.

II

The court below held that this case presented a political question because it thought petitioner's suit asked the court to decide an issue "textually committed" to a coordinate branch—namely, "to review a policy of the State Department implementing the President's decision" to keep the United States out of the debate over the status of Jerusalem.

---

[2]   Often when such factors are implicated in a case presenting a political question, other factors identified in *Baker* will likewise be apparent. . . .

Largely for the reasons set out by the Court, I agree that the Court of Appeals misapprehended the nature of its task. In two respects, however, my understanding of the political question doctrine might require a court to engage in further analysis beyond that relied upon by the Court.

First, the Court appropriately recognizes that petitioner's claim to a statutory right is "relevant" to the justiciability inquiry required in this case. In order to evaluate whether a case presents a political question, a court must first identify with precision the issue it is being asked to decide. Here, petitioner's suit claims that a federal statute provides him with a right to have "Israel" listed as his place of birth on his passport and other related documents. To decide that question, a court must determine whether the statute is constitutional, and therefore mandates the Secretary of State to issue petitioner's desired passport, or unconstitutional, in which case his suit is at an end. Resolution of that issue is not one "textually committed" to another branch; to the contrary, it is committed to this one. In no fashion does the question require a court to review the wisdom of the President's policy toward Jerusalem or any other decision committed to the discretion of a coordinate department. For that reason, I agree that the decision below should be reversed.

That is not to say, however, that no statute could give rise to a political question. It is not impossible to imagine a case involving the application or even the constitutionality of an enactment that would present a nonjusticiable issue. Indeed, this Court refused to determine whether an Ohio state constitutional provision offended the Republican Guarantee Clause, Art. IV, § 4, holding that "the question of whether that guarantee of the Constitution has been disregarded presents no justiciable controversy." Ohio ex rel. Davis v. Hildebrant, 241 U.S. 565, 569 (1916). A similar result would follow if Congress passed a statute, for instance, purporting to award financial relief to those improperly "tried" of impeachment offenses. To adjudicate claims under such a statute would require a court to resolve the very same issue we found nonjusticiable in *Nixon*. Such examples are atypical, but they suffice to show that the foreclosure altogether of political question analysis in statutory cases is unwarranted.

Second, the Court suggests that this case does not implicate the political question doctrine's concern with issues exhibiting "a lack of judicially discoverable and manageable standards," because the parties' arguments rely on textual, structural, and historical evidence of the kind that courts routinely consider. But that was equally true in *Nixon*. . . .

In my view, it is not whether the evidence upon which litigants rely is common to judicial consideration that determines whether a case lacks judicially discoverable and manageable standards. Rather, it is whether that evidence in fact provides a court a basis to adjudicate meaningfully the issue with which it is presented. The answer will almost always be yes, but if the parties' textual, structural, and historical evidence is inapposite or wholly unilluminating, rendering judicial decision no more than guesswork, a case relying on the ordinary kinds of arguments offered to courts might well still present justiciability concerns.

In this case, however, the Court of Appeals majority found a political question solely on the basis that this case required resolution of an issue "textually committed" to the Executive Branch. Because there was no such textual commitment, I respectfully concur in the Court's decision to reverse the Court of Appeals.

[Justice Alito concurred in the judgment. He reasoned: "Under our case law, determining the constitutionality of an Act of Congress may present a political question, but I do not think that the narrow question presented here falls within that category. Delineating the precise dividing line between the powers of Congress and the President with respect to the contents of a passport is not an easy matter, but I agree with the Court that it does not constitute a political question that the Judiciary is unable to decide."]

■ JUSTICE BREYER, dissenting. . . .

[As Justice Sotomayor notes,] the circumstances in which . . . prudential considerations lead the Court not to decide a case otherwise properly before it are rare. I agree. But in my view we nonetheless have before us such a case. Four sets of prudential considerations, *taken together*, lead me to that conclusion.

First, the issue before us arises in the field of foreign affairs. . . . The Constitution primarily delegates the foreign affairs powers "to the political departments of the government, Executive and Legislative," not to the Judiciary. Chicago & Southern Air Lines, Inc. v. Waterman S.S. Corp., 333 U.S. 103, 111 (1948). . . . And that fact is not surprising. Decisionmaking in this area typically is highly political. It is "delicate" and "complex." Id. It often rests upon information readily available to the Executive Branch and to the intelligence committees of Congress, but not readily available to the courts. It frequently is highly dependent upon what Justice Jackson called "prophecy." And the creation of wise foreign policy typically lies well beyond the experience or professional capacity of a judge. At the same time, where foreign affairs is at issue, the practical need for the United States to speak "with one voice and ac[t] as one," is particularly important. . . .

The result is a judicial hesitancy to make decisions that have significant foreign policy implications, as reflected in the fact that many of the cases in which the Court has invoked the political question doctrine have arisen in this area. . . .

Second, if the courts must answer the constitutional question before us, they may well have to evaluate the foreign policy implications of foreign policy decisions. The constitutional question focuses upon a statutory provision, § 214(d), that says: The Secretary of State, upon the request of a U.S. citizen born in Jerusalem (or upon the request of the citizen's legal guardian), shall "record" in the citizen's passport or consular birth report "the place of birth as Israel." And the question is whether this statute unconstitutionally seeks to limit the President's inherent constitutional authority to make certain kinds of foreign policy decisions. . . .

The Secretary of State argues that the President's constitutional authority to determine foreign policy includes the power to recognize foreign governments, that this Court has long recognized that the latter power belongs to the President exclusively, that the power includes the power to determine claims over disputed territory as well as the policy governing recognition decisions, and that the statute unconstitutionally limits the President's exclusive authority to exercise these powers. . . .

Zivotofsky, supported by several Members of Congress, points out that the Constitution also grants Congress powers related to foreign affairs, such as the powers to declare war, to regulate foreign commerce, and to regulate naturalization. They add that Congress may share some of the recognition power and its attendant power of determining claims over disputed territory. And they add that Congress may enact laws concerning travel into this country and concerning the citizenship of children born abroad to U.S. citizens. They argue that these powers include the power to specify the content of a passport (or consular birth report). And when such a specification takes the form of statutory law, they say, the Constitution requires the President (through the Secretary of State) to execute that statute.

Were the statutory provision undisputedly concerned only with purely administrative matters (or were its enforcement undisputedly to involve only major foreign policy matters), judicial efforts to answer the constitutional question might not involve judges in trying to answer questions of foreign policy. But in the Middle East, administrative matters can have implications that extend far beyond the purely administrative. Political reactions in that region can prove uncertain. And in that context it may well turn out that resolution of the constitutional argument will require a court to decide how far the statute, in practice, reaches beyond the purely administrative, determining not only whether but also the extent to which enforcement will interfere with the President's ability to make significant recognition-related foreign policy decisions.

Certainly the parties argue as if that were so. Zivotofsky, for example, argues that replacing "Jerusalem" on his passport with "Israel" will have no serious foreign policy significance. . . . Moreover, Zivotofsky says, it is unfair to allow the 100,000 or so Americans born in cities that the United States recognizes as under Israeli sovereignty, such as Tel Aviv or Haifa, the right to a record that mentions Israel, while denying that privilege to the 50,000 or so Americans born in Jerusalem.

At the same time, the Secretary argues that listing Israel on the passports (and consular birth reports) of Americans born in Jerusalem will have significantly adverse foreign policy effects. She says that doing so would represent "an official decision by the United States to begin to treat Jerusalem as a city located within Israel," that it "would be interpreted as an official act of recognizing Jerusalem as being under Israeli sovereignty," and that our "national security interests" consequently "would be significantly harmed." Such an action, she says, "would signal, symbolically or concretely, that" the United States "recognizes that Jerusalem is a city that is located within the sovereign territory of Israel," and doing so, "would critically compromise the ability of the United States to work with Israelis, Palestinians and others in the region to further the peace process." . . .

A judge's ability to evaluate opposing claims of this kind is minimal. At the same time, a judicial effort to do so risks inadvertently jeopardizing sound foreign policy decisionmaking by the other branches of Government. How, for example, is this Court to determine whether, or the extent to which, the continuation of the adjudication that it now orders will itself have a foreign policy effect?

Third, the countervailing interests in obtaining judicial resolution of the constitutional determination are not particularly strong ones. Zivotofsky does not assert the kind of interest, e.g., an interest in property or bodily integrity, which courts have traditionally sought to protect. Nor, importantly, does he assert an interest in vindicating a basic right of the kind that the Constitution grants to individuals and that courts traditionally have protected from invasion by the other branches of Government. . . .

The interest that Zivotofsky asserts, however, is akin to an ideological interest. . . . And insofar as an individual suffers an injury that is purely ideological, courts have often refused to consider the matter, leaving the injured party to look to the political branches for protection. . . .

Fourth, insofar as the controversy reflects different foreign policy views among the political branches of Government, those branches have nonjudicial methods of working out their differences. . . .

The upshot is that this case is unusual both in its minimal need for judicial intervention and in its more serious risk that intervention will bring about "embarrassment," show lack of "respect" for the other branches, and potentially disrupt sound foreign policy decisionmaking. For these prudential reasons, I would hold that the political question doctrine bars further judicial consideration of this case. And I would affirm the Court of Appeals' similar conclusion.

NOTES ON *ZIVOTOFSKY V. CLINTON*

1. THE POLITICAL QUESTION DOCTRINE IN FOREIGN AFFAIRS

In *Baker v. Carr*, the Court acknowledged that foreign affairs was an area where the political question doctrine might have particular salience.

The Court explained that, "[n]ot only does resolution of such issues frequently turn on standards that defy judicial application, or involve the exercise of a discretion demonstrably committed to the executive or legislature, but many such questions uniquely demand single-voiced statement of the Government's views." The Court also made clear, however, that "it is error to suppose that every case or controversy which touches foreign relations lies beyond judicial cognizance."

Although successful resort to the political question doctrine in purely domestic disputes is unusual, the lower federal courts often invoke the political question doctrine to defeat attempts to litigate the legality of U.S. foreign policy. See, e.g., Jaber v. United States, 861 F.3d 241 (D.C. Cir. 2017) (challenge to U.S. drone attack in Yemen held to be nonjusticiable); El-Shifa Pharmaceutical Industries Co. v. United States, 607 F.3d 836 (D.C. Cir. 2010) (en banc) (challenge to U.S. military action in Sudan that caused property damage held to be nonjusticiable); Corrie v. Caterpillar, 503 F.3d 974 (9th Cir. 2007) (claim against corporation for supplying bulldozers used by the Israeli army to demolish homes triggered political question doctrine because it implicated U.S. aid policy towards Israel); Gonzalez-Vera v. Kissinger, 449 F.3d 1260 (D.C. Cir. 2006) (claim against former Secretary of State and National Security Adviser for support of the Pinochet regime in Chile during the 1970s held to be nonjusticiable). During the Vietnam War, a number of lower courts invoked the political question doctrine in rejecting challenges to the legality of the war, and the Supreme Court denied certiorari. See, e.g., Atlee v. Richardson, 411 U.S. 911 (1973).

For criticism of the judicial affinity for the political question doctrine in foreign affairs, see Thomas M. Franck, Political Questions/Judicial Answers: Does the Rule of Law Apply to Foreign Affairs? (1992). For a defense, see Jide O. Nzelibe, The Uniqueness of Foreign Affairs, 89 Iowa L. Rev. 941 (2004).

2. *GOLDWATER V. CARTER*

A noteworthy invocation of the political question doctrine in the foreign affairs context occurred when members of Congress sued President Carter to challenge his authority to terminate a mutual defense treaty with Taiwan. The treaty included a right of termination but did not specify how that right could be exercised. The District Court held that the President could not act unilaterally. The Court of Appeals reversed. In Goldwater v. Carter, 444 U.S. 996 (1979), the Supreme Court ordered the complaint dismissed.

Speaking for himself and three others, Justice Rehnquist found a political question. Since the Constitution did not speak to the question of congressional participation in the termination of treaties, the issue should "be controlled by political standards." This was especially so because the question involved foreign relations, an area in which the courts have traditionally been reluctant to intervene. Rehnquist also observed that "[h]ere . . . we are asked to settle a dispute between coequal branches of our Government, each of which has resources available to protect and assert its interests, resources not available to private litigants outside the judicial forum."[a]

Justice Marshall concurred in the result without opinion. Justice Powell disagreed that the case presented a political question but nevertheless concluded that the dispute would not be ripe for adjudication "unless and until each branch has taken action asserting its constitutional authority" and the conflict has reached "constitutional impasse." Justices Blackmun and White voted to set the case for argument. Finally, Justice Brennan voted to affirm the judgment of the Court of Appeals on the ground that the President's action was supported by the established presidential authority to recognize foreign governments.

3. STATUTORY CHALLENGES TO EXECUTIVE BRANCH ACTION: *JAPAN WHALING*

Even in the context of foreign affairs, courts are less likely to apply the political question doctrine to cases that involve allegations that the Executive Branch has failed to comply with a federal statute. A good illustration is Japan Whaling Association v. American Cetacean Society, 478 U.S. 221 (1986). In that case, the Secretary of Commerce was alleged to have violated a federal statute in failing to certify that Japan was exceeding international whaling quotas, a finding that would have triggered mandatory sanctions. The Supreme Court held that no political question was implicated because the case presented only "a purely legal question of statutory interpretation." The Court explained that "under the Constitution, one of the Judiciary's characteristic roles is to interpret statutes, and we cannot shirk this responsibility merely because our decision may have significant political overtones." The Court then concluded that the statute had not been violated.

4. INDIVIDUAL RIGHTS CONTROVERSIES

The political question doctrine is also less likely to be applied to foreign affairs controversies that involve alleged infringements of individual rights. The Supreme Court did not apply the doctrine, for example, in the famous steel seizure case, Youngstown Sheet & Tube Co. v. Sawyer, 343 U.S. 579 (1952). There, the Court found that President Truman had acted unconstitutionally in seizing private steel mills in the United States, despite his claim that the seizure was needed in order to support the war effort in Korea. Similarly, the Supreme Court has decided a number of detention and military trial cases arising out of the post-September 11, 2001 "war on terror" without regard to the political question doctrine.[b]

---

[a]   In a footnote, Justice Rehnquist stated:

> This Court, of course, may not prohibit state courts from deciding political questions, any more than it may prohibit them from deciding questions that are moot . . . so long as they do not trench upon exclusively federal questions of foreign policy.

Is this right? If the political question doctrine stems only from Article III of the Constitution, then it would presumably apply only to the federal courts. But might the doctrine, at least in some cases, reflect other constitutional considerations?

[b]   See, e.g., Boumediene v. Bush, 553 U.S. 723 (2008); Hamdan v. Rumsfeld, 548 U.S. 557 (2006); Hamdi v. Rumsfeld, 542 U.S. 507 (2004).

5. QUESTIONS AND COMMENTS ON *ZIVOTOFSKY*

The majority in *Zivotofsky* refers only to the first two *Baker* factors. Is it suggesting that the other factors are irrelevant? Or that they are relevant only in cases in which one of the first two factors is arguably triggered? Justice Breyer contends in dissent that resolution of the issues will require the judiciary to engage in assessments of foreign policy for which it is ill equipped. Is he right? In deciding whether Congress can regulate the passport issue, the judiciary would not be deciding whether Congress's particular regulation here is good policy. On the other hand, in deciding whether Congress has intruded on an exclusive presidential power, a court is likely to take into account the potential foreign policy implications of the intrusion. Do considerations of this sort support non-justiciability?

Another prudential argument made by Justice Breyer is that there is no strong need for judicial review in this case because the political branches have their own tools for working it out. Is that persuasive?

The existence of a federal statutory right was a significant consideration in the majority's determination that there was no political question. Under the majority's analysis, could the constitutionality of a federal statute ever constitute a political question? What about the hypothetical situations posed by Justice Sotomayor? Cf. INS v. Chadha, 462 U.S. 919, 941–42 (1983) ("No policy underlying the political question doctrine suggests that Congress or the Executive, or both acting in concert and in compliance with Art. I, can decide the constitutionality of a statute; that is a decision for the courts.").

On remand, the court of appeals in *Zivotofsky* held that the passport statute was unconstitutional because it interfered with the exclusive power of the President. The Supreme Court affirmed in Zivotofsky v. Kerry, 576 U.S. ___, 135 S.Ct. 2076 (2015). In an opinion by Justice Kennedy, the Court inferred from the Constitution's text and structure that the President has the authority to determine whether the United States recognizes particular foreign nations or governments. The Court further concluded that this recognition power is exclusive to the President and cannot be exercised by Congress. The Court based this conclusion in part on what it referred to as "functional considerations," namely that "the Nation must have a single policy regarding which governments are legitimate in the eyes of the United States and which are not." It also invoked longstanding historical practice. While acknowledging that "history is not all on one side," the Court thought that "on balance it provides strong support for the conclusion that the recognition power is the President's alone." The passport statute conflicts with this exclusive presidential power, the Court further reasoned, because it requires the executive branch to contradict its policy of neutrality with respect to the status of Jerusalem. "If the power over recognition is to mean anything," said the Court, "it must mean that the President not only makes the initial, formal recognition determination but also that he may maintain that determination in his and his agent's statements."

Justice Breyer concurred, noting that he continued to think that the case presented a political question. Justice Thomas concurred in part. In a dissent joined by Justice Scalia, Chief Justice Roberts argued that the statute in question merely regulated identification of the passport holder and thus did not intrude on whatever recognition power the President may possess. In a separate dissent joined by the Chief Justice and Justice Alito, Justice Scalia argued that, although "the Constitution may well deny Congress power to recognize—the power to make an international commitment accepting a foreign entity as a state, a regime as its government, a place as part of its territory, and so on," the statute here "plainly does not make (or require the President to make) a commitment accepting Israel's sovereignty over Jerusalem."[c]

6.   ADDITIONAL BIBLIOGRAPHY

In addition to the articles cited above, recent articles focusing on the political question doctrine include Jesse Choper, The Political Question Doctrine: Suggested Criteria, 54 Duke L.J. 1457 (2005) (proposing criteria for invoking the political question doctrine and surveying their application to a variety of issues that might be thought nonjusticiable); Harlan Grant Cohen, A Politics-Reinforcing Political Question Doctrine, 49 Az. St. L.J. 1 (2017) (arguing for an approach to the political question doctrine that "counsels abstention or forbearance specifically when the President and Congress are in disagreement" and "eyes political settlement—speaking with one voice—more skeptically"); Tara Leigh Grove, The Lost History of the Political Question Doctrine, 90 N.Y.U. L. Rev. 1908 (2015) (arguing that the doctrine is of more recent vintage than is commonly supposed and that, as used today, it reinforces rather than undermines judicial supremacy); John Harrison, The Relation between Limitations on and Requirements of Article III Adjudication, 95 Calif. L. Rev. 1367 (2007) (attempting an integrated understanding of standing, the political question doctrine, procedural due process, and non-Article III courts); and Louis Michael Seidman, The Secret Life of the Political Question Doctrine, 37 John Marshall L. Rev. 441 (2004) (discussing when the political question doctrine matters and why).

---

[c]   In December 2017, President Donald Trump exercised the Executive's power of recognition and announced that the United States was formally recognizing Jerusalem as the capital of Israel.

CHAPTER IV

CONGRESSIONAL CONTROL OF THE FEDERAL COURTS

SECTION 1. POWER TO LIMIT FEDERAL COURT JURISDICTION

INTRODUCTORY NOTES ON CONGRESSIONAL POWER TO LIMIT FEDERAL COURT JURISDICTION

1. THE CONSTITUTIONAL TEXT

Article III provides in relevant part:

SECTION 1. The judicial Power of the United States, shall be vested in one supreme Court, and in such inferior Courts as the Congress may from time to time ordain and establish. The Judges, both of the supreme and inferior Courts, shall hold their Offices during good Behavior, and shall, at stated Times, receive for their Services, a Compensation, which shall not be diminished during their continuance in Office.

SECTION 2. The judicial Power shall extend to all Cases, in Law and Equity, arising under this Constitution, the Laws of the United States, and Treaties made, or which shall be made, under their Authority;—to all Cases affecting Ambassadors, other Public Ministers and Consuls;—to all cases of admiralty and maritime Jurisdiction;—to Controversies to which the United States shall be a Party;—to Controversies between two or more States;—between a State and Citizens of another State;—between Citizens of different States;—between Citizens of the same State claiming Lands under Grants of different States, and between a State, or the Citizens thereof, and foreign States, Citizens or Subjects.

In all Cases affecting Ambassadors, other public Ministers and Consuls, and those in which a State shall be a Party, the supreme Court shall have original Jurisdiction. In all the other Cases before mentioned, the supreme Court shall have appellate Jurisdiction, both as to Law and Fact, with such Exceptions, and under such Regulations as the Congress shall make.

Additionally, art. I, § 8, cl. 9 gives Congress the power "To constitute Tribunals inferior to the supreme Court."

2. QUESTIONS AND COMMENTS

The Constitution treats the Supreme Court and the lower federal courts differently.

487

(i) The Supreme Court

Section 1 of Article III vests the "judicial Power of the United States" in one Supreme Court. Section 2 seems to give the Supreme Court jurisdiction over all matters within the judicial power. It identifies the subjects to which the judicial power extends and then says that the Supreme Court "shall have original Jurisdiction" over certain cases and "shall have appellate Jurisdiction" over the rest.

The appellate jurisdiction, however, is conferred "with such Exceptions, and under such Regulations as the Congress shall make." The question raised by this language is whether the power to make exceptions is plenary or whether it is limited—by Article III itself, by other provisions of the Constitution, or by inferences drawn from the constitutional structure. This question is addressed below.

The Supreme Court has never had jurisdiction over the entire range of subjects to which the judicial power extends. The Court does not today review—and never has reviewed—diversity cases coming from state courts. Indeed, the First Judiciary Act limited Supreme Court review of state-court judgments to cases where a federal question was decided *against* the federal claimant. A state-court decision *in favor of* the federal claimant was not then eligible for Supreme Court review, though it is now.

(ii) The Lower Federal Courts

The power of Congress to create lower federal courts is stated in Article I, § 8, cl. 9 and in the first sentence of Article III, § 1. These provisions might be read to say that the Constitution vests the entire judicial power in whatever lower federal courts Congress chooses to create. The text provides that the power "shall be vested" in such lower courts as Congress may create. There is no explicit power to make exceptions.

But the Constitutional language has never been so read. Textually, one could say that Congress's power to decide whether to create lower federal courts implies a lesser power to confer on those courts less than full Article III jurisdiction. The fact is, in any event, that Congress has never given any lower federal court jurisdiction over the entire "judicial Power" and neither the Supreme Court nor the lower federal courts have viewed lower court jurisdiction as extending beyond that authorized by statute. The First Judiciary Act authorized diversity jurisdiction only for cases involving more than a specified amount. More importantly, the First Judiciary Act gave *no* federal trial court a general power to hear cases arising under federal law. The general federal question statute (28 U.S.C. § 1331) was first enacted in 1875.[a] Until 1980, it too contained a jurisdictional amount requirement, a limitation that continues to this day in the general diversity statute (28 U.S.C. § 1332).

If Congress need not confer the entire judicial power on every lower federal court nor distribute the entire judicial power among the lower federal

---

[a]   Congress had earlier provided for federal question jurisdiction in the Judiciary Act of 1801, but that grant of jurisdiction lasted only a year before being repealed.

courts as a group, does it follow that there are no limits on Congress's ability to contract the jurisdiction of the lower federal courts? This question is also addressed below.

3. *MARBURY V. MADISON*

Everyone agrees that the power to control jurisdiction does not include the power to dictate unconstitutional outcomes in decided cases. It is one thing for a court not to decide a case at all. It is quite another for the court to decide a case but be required to render a result inconsistent with the Constitution. For example, Congress might have the power to exclude all state criminal cases from Supreme Court review, but Congress would not have the power to withhold jurisdiction over all due process issues in state criminal cases that the Court hears on the merits.

This proposition follows from even the most limited view of *Marbury v. Madison*. At a minimum, that case supports the proposition that the courts cannot decide cases inconsistently with the Constitution. *Marbury* may or may not say anything about the kinds of cases courts should resolve, and it may or may not address their ultimate role in the constitutional plan. What it plainly does say is that courts are not free to ignore the Constitution in rendering decisions on the merits of cases that come before them. The principle underlying this reading of *Marbury* applies in state courts as well. The Supremacy Clause explicitly instructs them to decide cases in accordance with the federal Constitution.

A more difficult question would arise if Congress sought to limit only the judicial provision of remedies for constitutional violations. Consider, for example, a statute permitting federal courts to decide school desegregation cases but withholding authority to order busing as a remedy. Would such a statute be constitutional? Would it matter whether the statute was drafted as a rule of law governing remedies or as a limitation on jurisdiction? Suppose a statute provided for liquidated damages for unconstitutional searches and seizures by state officials and permitted Supreme Court review of state criminal cases, but denied authority to require the exclusion of evidence under *Mapp v. Ohio*? Would it matter whether the statute was drafted as a rule of law governing the admissibility of evidence or as a limitation on jurisdiction?

4. A TESTING HYPOTHETICAL: ABORTION

For the broader questions of congressional control of federal court jurisdiction, it is helpful to have a specific context in mind. Consider a woman who is early enough in pregnancy so that she has a clear constitutional right to an abortion under Roe v. Wade, 410 U.S. 113 (1973), and its progeny. Assume that she is confronted with a state criminal statute prohibiting all abortions. And assume further that Congress has passed a statute that denies jurisdiction to all courts—the Supreme Court, the lower federal courts, and the state courts—to hear any constitutional claim founded upon the right recognized in *Roe*. What can the courts do in the face of the federal statute? The materials in this section suggest a variety of possible answers to this question.

5. THE TRADITIONAL VIEW OF CONGRESSIONAL POWER TO LIMIT
    THE JURISDICTION OF THE FEDERAL AND STATE COURTS

Assume that the state courts have heard the abortion claim on the merits in one proceeding or another, but have decided the issue in direct contravention of *Roe v. Wade*. Could Congress foreclose Supreme Court review?

Many respected commentators—enough so that this can be called the traditional view—believe that Congress has the power to make exceptions to the jurisdiction of the Supreme Court over any category of cases, constitutional or otherwise. In this view, Congress has plenary power over the appellate jurisdiction of the Supreme Court (as well as the jurisdiction of the lower federal courts) as part of the checks and balances built into the constitutional framework. Traditionalists believe, however, that the Supremacy Clause forbids Congress from depriving the state courts of jurisdiction to decide constitutional questions that come before them in the ordinary course of litigation authorized by state law. Thus, in spite of the modern mindset that looks to federal courts as the primary source of federal constitutional decisions, under this view state courts could become the ultimate protectors of federal rights. In the abortion hypothetical discussed above, for example, Congress could not foreclose the state courts from exercising their jurisdiction consistently with the Constitution.

This position is defended in Herbert Wechsler, The Courts and the Constitution, 65 Colum. L. Rev. 1001 (1965). Wechsler recognized that some were of the view that "exceptions" should be narrowly defined to deny Congress the authority to exclude cases from federal courts that involve constitutional issues, and that some might cite the Supremacy Clause or the Fifth Amendment as a limit having the same effect. But he responded that these positions were "antithetical to the plan of the Constitution for the courts." The job of deciding how the federal judicial power should be exercised was given to Congress:

> Federal courts, including the Supreme Court, do not pass on constitutional questions because there is a special function vested in them to enforce the Constitution or police the other agencies of the government. They do so rather for the reason that they must decide a litigated issue that is otherwise within their jurisdiction and in doing so must give effect to the supreme law of the land. That is, at least, what *Marbury v. Madison* was all about.

A similar conclusion was stated in Henry Hart's famous dialogue, first published in Henry M. Hart, Jr., The Power of Congress to Limit the Jurisdiction of Federal Courts: An Exercise in Dialectic, 66 Harv. L. Rev. 1362 (1953). In response to the objection that Congress might leave constitutional rights without a remedy, the answer was that one could always fall back on the state courts. "[T]hey are the primary guarantors of constitutional rights." As to the argument that Congress could take jurisdiction away from the state courts, the answer was that the source of state court jurisdiction is the state legislature, not the Congress. Every state has courts of general jurisdiction, and the Supremacy Clause would require those courts to exercise that jurisdiction in conformity with the Constitution. Could the Supreme Court be ordered by Congress to reverse state-court decisions upholding a federal constitutional right? The answer was:

> Not lawfully, if the decisions were in accordance with the Constitution. Congress can't shut the Supreme Court off from the merits and give it jurisdiction simply to reverse. Not, anyway, if I'm right . . . that jurisdiction always is jurisdiction only to decide constitutionally.

Are these views persuasive? What consequences would they have for the meaning of modern constitutional rights? How, for example, could state courts be expected to react if the meaning of *Roe v. Wade* or some other controversial constitutional decision were left to them to resolve? One objection frequently made to the traditional view is that Congress would effectively have the power to amend the Constitution without following the prescribed procedures by permitting state and lower federal courts to deviate—perhaps inconsistently from court to court—from the Constitution as interpreted by the Supreme Court. Is this objection well taken?

One reason for not enacting jurisdiction-stripping legislation is practical. Congress needs the federal courts to carry out its programs. Consider, for example, the argument in Lawrence G. Sager, What Is a Nice Court Like You Doing in a Democracy Like This?, 36 Stan. L. Rev. 1087 (1984). Sager considered what would have happened if the New Deal Congress had deprived the federal courts of jurisdiction to resolve constitutional challenges to New Deal legislation. The result, he argued, would have been chaos. Some state courts would have been hostile, and any prospect of decisional uniformity would have been lost. "It is hard to imagine a more certain road to the collapse of the economic recovery program."

As apt as these comments might be for the New Deal context, would similar constraints operate in the context of abortion? Is there perhaps a greater need for constitutionally required federal-court supervision of the validity of state laws than for similar supervision of federal laws? Is the need for uniform answers to controversial constitutional questions only a practical constraint or does it rise to the level of a constitutional constraint?

6. CONGRESSIONAL POWER TO CURTAIL THE JURISDICTION OF STATE COURTS

All states have trial courts of general jurisdiction and at least one court with statewide jurisdiction to hear appeals. This jurisdiction is fixed by state law. Can Congress override these provisions? Can it make exceptions to the jurisdiction of the state courts?

The answer, generally, is yes. It is not uncommon for Congress to give the federal courts exclusive jurisdiction over certain cases involving federal law and thereby to preclude state court consideration of these cases. For example, 28 U.S.C. § 1338 provides that the jurisdiction of federal courts to hear patent and copyright cases "shall be exclusive of the courts of the states." Similarly, 28 U.S.C. § 1446(e) states that once a civil case has been removed from a state court to a federal district court "the State court shall proceed no further unless and until the case is remanded." Many other examples could be given, and their constitutionality is clear.

How far does this congressional power go? Suppose the woman in the problem posed above has an abortion and is charged with a crime. Could the state courts hear her *Roe* defense in the ensuing prosecution? Suppose it is possible under state law to get a declaratory judgment or an injunction against threatened criminal prosecution based on anticipated behavior that would be protected by the Constitution. Could the state courts issue the injunction?

7. CONCLUDING COMMENT

The traditional view is hotly disputed. It may be that the Constitution disallows Congress from singling out particular constitutional rights in its regulation of jurisdiction. The notes above are intended merely to introduce the problem, not to resolve it. The remaining materials in this section consider whether a contrary conclusion can or should be derived from cases decided by the Supreme Court or from different assumptions about the nature of our constitutional system.

Ex parte McCardle

United States Supreme Court, 1868.
74 U.S. (7 Wall.) 506.

[McCardle was editor of the Vicksburg Times. He was arrested by U.S. Army officials under the Military Reconstruction Act of 1867, which established military jurisdiction over much of the South following the Civil War. McCardle was charged with disturbing the peace, inciting to insurrection, libel, and impeding reconstruction for writing and publishing inflammatory editorials. He sought release by bringing an action for habeas corpus in the federal Circuit Court for the Southern District of Mississippi. The Circuit Court dismissed the writ and remanded McCardle to military custody. He was released on bail subject to the disposition of an appeal of that decision to the Supreme Court. His appeal raised a number of contentions, among them a frontal attack on the constitutionality of the Military Reconstruction Act itself.[a] The government moved to dismiss the appeal, but the Court upheld its jurisdiction. Ex parte McCardle, 73 U.S. (6 Wall.) 318 (1868). The case was then argued

---

[a] His major argument in this respect was that military court-martial of civilians was unconstitutional given the fact that the civil courts were then functioning. See William Van Alstyne, A Critical Guide to Ex parte McCardle, 15 Ariz. L. Rev. 229, 238 n.46 (1973), which quotes a letter written by Chief Justice Chase to the effect that "had the merits of the *McCardle* case been decided the Court would doubtless have held that this imprisonment for trial before a military commission was illegal." Van Alstyne's article reviews the historical context of *McCardle* and analyzes the Court's opinion. It is well worth reading. See also Daniel J. Meltzer, The Story of *Ex parte McCardle*: The Power of Congress to Limit the Supreme Court's Appellate Jurisdiction, *in* Federal Courts Stories (Vicki C. Jackson and Judith Resnik eds., 2010).

on the merits, after which the statute authorizing the appeal was repealed by Congress. The opinion reproduced below is the Court's reaction to the repealing statute.

[Understanding the Court's opinion requires more detailed explanation of the procedural background. The First Judiciary Act authorized federal trial courts to issue writs of habeas corpus, but only for persons in *federal* custody. There was no provision specifically authorizing appeals from lower federal courts in habeas actions, but appeals to the Supreme Court were generally available in civil cases (habeas corpus has always been regarded as a "civil" case) if a jurisdictional amount of $2000 was satisfied. Because the jurisdictional amount limitation appeared to be a bar to appellate review of habeas actions, the Court, which itself was authorized to issue writs of habeas corpus, developed the practice of issuing "original" writs of habeas corpus to review the habeas decisions of the lower federal courts. The practice was reconciled with the limitations of Article III by the rationalization that since the work of a lower court was being reviewed, the issuance of an "original" writ was nonetheless an exercise of "appellate" jurisdiction. The common-law writ of certiorari was often used in this procedure, and it too, being a writ used by appellate courts to call up the record from the court below, gave an "appellate" flavor to the proceedings.

[In February 1867, Congress expanded the writ of habeas corpus to encompass persons in the custody of *state* officials. It also specifically authorized appeals to the Supreme Court in habeas cases. The government's argument in the first *McCardle* decision was that McCardle's case was not appealable under this provision, in part because the new statute was limited by its context to appeals from decisions concerning detentions by *state* officials. The Court rejected the argument, holding that the 1867 statute authorizing appeals in habeas cases applied generally to any habeas decision by the lower courts. Thus, McCardle's case was properly before the Court on appeal.

[Three days after the case was argued on the merits, Congress repealed that part of the 1867 statute authorizing appeals in habeas cases. Two weeks later, President Johnson (who then was facing impeachment proceedings) vetoed the repealing statute, but the veto was overridden two days later (in March 1868). Argument on the effect of the repealing statute was postponed in the Supreme Court while Chief Justice Chase presided over the impeachment proceedings, but after further argument, the Court delivered the following opinion.]

■ THE CHIEF JUSTICE delivered the opinion of the Court.

The first question necessarily is that of jurisdiction; for, if the act of March, 1868, takes away the jurisdiction defined by the act of February, 1867, it is useless, if not improper, to enter into any discussion of other questions.

It is quite true, as was argued by the counsel for the petitioner, that the appellate jurisdiction of this Court is not derived from acts of Congress. It is, strictly speaking, conferred by the Constitution. But it is conferred "with such exceptions and under such regulations as Congress shall make."

It is unnecessary to consider whether, if Congress had made no exceptions and no regulations, this Court might not have exercised general appellate jurisdiction under rules prescribed by itself. For among the earliest acts of the first Congress, at its first session, was the act of September 24th, 1789, to establish the judicial courts of the United States. That act provided for the organization of this Court, and prescribed regulations for the exercise of its jurisdiction.

The source of that jurisdiction, and the limitations of it by the Constitution and by statute, have been on several occasions subjects of consideration here. In the case of Durousseau v. United States, 10 U.S. (6 Cranch) 307 (1810), particularly, the whole matter was carefully examined, and the Court held, that while "the appellate powers of this Court are not given by the judicial act, but are given by the Constitution," they are, nevertheless, "limited and regulated by that act, and by such other acts as have been passed on the subject." The court said, further, that the judicial act was an exercise of the power given by the Constitution to Congress "of making exceptions to the appellate jurisdiction of the Supreme Court." "They have described affirmatively," said the Court, "its jurisdiction, and this affirmative description has been understood to imply a negation of the exercise of such appellate power as is not comprehended within it."

The principle that the affirmation of appellate jurisdiction implies the negation of all such jurisdiction not affirmed having been thus established, it was an almost necessary consequence that acts of Congress, providing for the exercise of jurisdiction, should come to be spoken of as acts granting jurisdiction, and not as acts making exceptions to the constitutional grant of it.

The exception to appellate jurisdiction in the case before us, however, is not an inference from the affirmation of other appellate jurisdiction. It is made in terms. The provision of the act of 1867, affirming the appellate jurisdiction of this Court in cases of habeas corpus is expressly repealed. It is hardly possible to imagine a plainer instance of positive exception.

We are not at liberty to inquire into the motives of the legislature. We can only examine into its power under the Constitution; and the power to make exceptions to the appellate jurisdiction of this Court is given by express words.

What, then, is the effect of the repealing act upon the case before us? We cannot doubt as to this. Without jurisdiction the Court cannot proceed at all in any cause. Jurisdiction is power to declare the law, and when it ceases to exist, the only function remaining to the Court is that of announcing the fact and dismissing the cause. And this is not less clear upon authority than upon principle.

Several [state] cases were cited by the counsel for the petitioner in support of the position that jurisdiction of this case is not affected by the repealing act. But none of them, in our judgment, [affords] any support to it. They are all cases of the exercise of judicial power by the legislature, or of legislative interference with courts in the exercising of continuing jurisdiction.

On the other hand, the general rule, supported by the best elementary writers, is, that "when an act of the legislature is repealed, it must be considered, except as to transactions past and closed, as if it never existed." And the effect of repealing acts upon suits under acts repealed, has been determined by the adjudications of this Court. The subject was fully considered in [two decisions, both of which] held that no judgment could be rendered in a suit after the repeal of the act under which it was brought and prosecuted.

It is quite clear, therefore, that this Court cannot proceed to pronounce judgment in this case, for it has no longer jurisdiction of the appeal; and judicial duty is not less fitly performed by declining ungranted jurisdiction than in exercising firmly that which the Constitution and the laws confer.

Counsel seem to have supposed, if effect be given to the repealing act in question, that the whole appellate power of the Court, in cases of habeas corpus, is denied. But this is an error. The act of 1868 does not except from that jurisdiction any cases but appeals from Circuit Courts under the act of 1867. It does not affect the jurisdiction which was previously exercised.*

The appeal of the petitioner in this case must be dismissed for want of jurisdiction.

NOTES ON THE TRADITIONAL VIEW

1.   THE SOURCE OF THE SUPREME COURT'S APPELLATE JURISDICTION

It is generally accepted that Congress has "excepted" from the Supreme Court's appellate jurisdiction all cases that do not fall within an affirmative

---

*   Ex parte McCardle, 73 U.S. (6 Wall.) 318, 324 (1868). [The Court's reference is to that part of the first *McCardle* opinion discussing the former practice of reviewing lower federal court habeas decisions by issuing original writs of habeas corpus supplemented by common law writs of certiorari. Indeed, in Ex parte Yerger, 75 U.S. (8 Wall.) 85 (1869), decided after *McCardle,* the Court upheld its jurisdiction to review habeas corpus decisions by the lower federal courts, holding that the repealing statute had no effect on this alternative form of appellate review. *Yerger* was also a challenge to the Military Reconstruction Act by an arrested newspaper editor, but the merits were again left unresolved because the military released Yerger before the Court reached a decision.—Addition to footnote by eds.]

statutory grant of jurisdiction. Under this view, the Supreme Court's appellate jurisdiction must be specifically authorized. The constitutional text alone is not sufficient.

Why has the scope of the congressional power to make exceptions to the appellate jurisdiction of the Supreme Court not been more frequently litigated? Probably because the Court has felt little need to address the kinds of questions that have been excluded. For example, the Court has never had authority to review questions of state law decided by state supreme courts in cases where diversity of citizenship existed between the parties, but there is little reason why the Court would want to decide such questions. In cases where the Court has felt the need to act, it has found ways around statutory limitations. A good example, illustrated in the *McCardle* litigation, is the development of "original" habeas corpus as a mechanism for appellate review in early federal habeas corpus cases.

Today, any federal question litigated in the state courts can get to the Supreme Court by one means or another, as can any question litigated in a lower federal court. The scope of the exceptions clause would arise, therefore, only if Congress were to make a specific exclusion from the prevailing statutory pattern. On the few occasions when Congress has done so, the Court has construed the applicable statutes to permit constitutional claims to be heard.

2.   THE SIGNIFICANCE OF *MCCARDLE*

On its face, *McCardle* seems to affirm a broad power in the Congress to make exceptions to the appellate jurisdiction of the Supreme Court. Yet *McCardle* can also be read quite narrowly.

The Court was not anxious to hear the case. The Reconstruction legislation at stake had been passed over a presidential veto, and the President himself was facing impeachment. For the Court to have declared the legislation unconstitutional would have precipitated a confrontation with Congress at a time when the Court itself was under attack. Two years earlier, Congress had reduced the number of Justices from ten to seven (thereby depriving President Johnson of appointments) and the House had passed a bill requiring an extraordinary majority to invalidate an act of Congress. The Court had avoided decision on the constitutionality of Reconstruction legislation in two prior cases, Mississippi v. Johnson, 71 U.S. (4 Wall.) 475 (1866), and Georgia v. Stanton, 73 U.S. (6 Wall.) 50 (1867), and was to do so again in Ex parte Yerger, 75 U.S. (8 Wall.) 85 (1868). There thus may have been some attraction to the idea of not resolving the merits, so long as a ground for decision could be found that would do no institutional damage to the Court. As the Court was well aware,[a] no serious unfairness was being done to McCardle in the meantime. He was free on bail and had resumed his critical editorials.

These factors may help explain the last full paragraph of the Court's opinion. The act of 1868 cut off only one of two possible ways of getting a case such as McCardle's before the Supreme Court, leaving the other intact.

---

[a]   See William Van Alstyne, A Critical Guide to Ex Parte McCardle, 15 Ariz. L. Rev. 229, 248 (1973).

Given the last paragraph, the opinion can be read as approving the undoubted authority of Congress to foreclose only one of two avenues of review. On this reading, the Court ducked a sensitive constitutional problem, avoided a confrontation with Congress, and preserved its authority to adjudicate future cases.

On this view, *McCardle* neither supports nor refutes the traditional view of the congressional power to make exceptions to the jurisdiction of the Supreme Court.[b] But if the last paragraph of the opinion is not given special significance and the rest of *McCardle* is taken to mean what it says, the case would appear to provide direct Supreme Court support for the traditional view.

3. CONGRESSIONAL POWER OVER THE JURISDICTION OF THE LOWER FEDERAL COURTS: *SHELDON V. SILL*

Section 11 of the First Judiciary Act contained a so-called "assignee" clause.[c] Its purpose was to prevent parties from collusively creating federal diversity jurisdiction by selling or assigning claims to citizens of other states.

Sill was a citizen of New York. He brought a diversity action against Sheldon, a citizen of Michigan. Sheldon answered that the bond and mortgage that were the subject of the suit had been executed by him to a Michigan bank, which had assigned the claim to Sill for recovery. Sheldon therefore argued under § 11 that the federal court had no diversity jurisdiction. Sill responded:

> [T]he case before the Circuit Court was a controversy between citizens of different states, and to such a controversy the judicial power of the courts of the United States extends by the Constitution, and by the same Constitution that power is vested, except where the Supreme Court has original jurisdiction by the Constitution, in the inferior courts created by Congress. This judicial power, therefore, to take cognizance of this case, is, by the Constitution, vested in the Circuit Court, and the plaintiff claims the constitutional right to have his controversy with Mr. Sheldon . . . decided by that court. . . . Where does Congress get the power or authority to deprive the courts of the United States of the judicial power with which the Constitution has invested them? Congress may create the courts, but they are clothed with their powers by the Constitution. . . . Can it any more take away a constitutional power than it can confer an unconstitutional one? We submit that it cannot. [W]e respectfully submit, that it is of the utmost importance to citizens

---

[b] The only Supreme Court decision that arguably held unconstitutional an effort by Congress to make an "exception" to the Supreme Court's jurisdiction is United States v. Klein, 80 U.S. (13 Wall.) 128 (1871). *Klein* is considered in Section 2 of this Chapter.

[c] Section 11 precluded federal trial courts from taking "cognizance of any suit to recover the contents of any promissory note or other chose in action, in favor of an assignee, unless a suit might have been prosecuted in such court to recover the contents, if no assignment had been made, except in cases of foreign bills of exchange." A similar provision is found today, in considerably modified form, in 28 U.S.C. § 1359.

of the different states that the whole judicial power granted by the Constitution to the courts of the United States should be exercised.

The Supreme Court disagreed:

> It must be admitted, that if the Constitution had ordained and established the inferior courts, and distributed to them their respective powers, they could not be restricted or divested by Congress. But as it has made no such distribution, one of two consequences must result,—either that each inferior court created by Congress must exercise all the judicial powers not given to the Supreme Court, or that Congress, having the power to establish the courts, must define their respective jurisdictions. The first of these inferences has never been asserted, and could not be defended with any show of reason, and if not, the latter would seem to follow as a necessary consequence. And it would seem to follow, also, that, having a right to prescribe, Congress may withhold from any court of its creation jurisdiction of any of the enumerated controversies. Courts created by statute can have no jurisdiction but such as the statute confers. No one of them can assert a just claim to jurisdiction exclusively conferred on another, or withheld from all.

> The Constitution has defined the limits of the judicial power of the United States, but has not prescribed how much of it shall be exercised by the circuit court; consequently, the statute which does prescribe the limits of their jurisdiction, cannot be in conflict with the Constitution, unless it confers powers not enumerated therein.

Sheldon describes the power of Congress to control the jurisdiction of the lower federal courts in seemingly unlimited terms. It says that Congress "may withhold from any court of its creation jurisdiction of *any* of the enumerated controversies" (emphasis added), that no federal court can exercise jurisdiction "withheld from all" federal courts, and that a statute prescribing limits on lower federal court jurisdiction "cannot be in conflict with the Constitution, unless it confers powers not enumerated therein." Are there indeed no limits on the power of Congress to exclude controversies from litigation in the lower federal courts?

4. UNFAVORABLE CONGRESSIONAL REACTION TO SUPREME COURT DECISIONS

Politically unpopular Supreme Court decisions have often prompted proposals in Congress to curtail the jurisdiction of the federal courts. Such laws were first proposed in the 1820s in reaction to decisions by the Marshall Court. In the late 1950s, bills motivated by anti-communist sentiments were introduced to curb the Court's jurisdiction over contempt proceedings against congressional witnesses, dismissal of government employees for national security reasons, state subversive activities legislation, and state bar admission requirements. Decisions by the Warren Court in the areas of reapportionment, criminal procedure, and school desegregation prompted similar proposals. Decisions on school prayer, abortion, and school busing led to a series of new proposals in the early 1980s. More recent Congresses have been presented with similar bills. One example is proposed legislation to restrict jurisdiction over challenges to laws barring flag burning.

None of these proposed laws has been enacted, and there have therefore been no Supreme Court rulings on their constitutionality. On the rare occasions when jurisdiction stripping measures have been enacted, moreover, the Court's primary strategy has been to construe the jurisdictional limitation in a way that avoids the most difficult constitutional issues.[d] Illustrations of this approach are provided below.

There is, however, an enormous body of academic literature on the subject, literature described by one scholar as "choking on redundancy."[e] Given the lack of Supreme Court consideration and the voluminous academic literature, most discussions begin and end with arguments about the various theories advanced for limiting (or not limiting) congressional power.

5.　*WEBSTER V. DOE*

"Congress has to speak clearly for constitutional issues"

On its facts, *Sheldon* was an easy case. Surely Congress has the authority to protect the integrity of the diversity jurisdiction by preventing collusion. A more difficult question would arise if the lower federal courts were foreclosed from enforcing federal rights. The Supreme Court has not defined the authority of Congress in this respect. As noted above, its typical response when presented with apparently jurisdiction-stripping legislation has been to read the statute to permit the case to go forward. Webster v. Doe, 486 U.S. 592 (1988), is an important modern illustration.

John Doe was employed by the CIA as a covert electronics technician. He had consistently been rated excellent or outstanding until he voluntarily told a security officer that he was gay. He was promptly placed on administrative leave and was later fired because his "homosexuality presented a security threat." There was no evidence that his sexual orientation had compromised his job performance.

Doe sued the Director of Central Intelligence on a variety of statutory and constitutional claims. Debate centered on a provision in the National Security Act of 1947, 50 U.S.C. § 403(c), which states:

> [T]he Director of Central Intelligence may, in his discretion, terminate the employment of any officer or employee of the Agency whenever he shall deem such termination necessary or advisable in the interests of the United States. . . .

The question was whether the Director's discretion was reviewable in the federal courts.

---

[d]　An important exception is Boumediene v. Bush, 553 U.S. 723 (2008), discussed below, in which the Court held that Congress's effort to eliminate habeas corpus jurisdiction over alleged terrorists held by the U.S. military violated the Suspension Clause of the Constitution.

[e]　The comment was made by William Van Alstyne in a letter to Gerald Gunther. See Gerald Gunther, Congressional Power to Curtail Federal Court Jurisdiction: An Opinionated Guide to the Ongoing Debate, 36 Stan. L. Rev. 895, 897 n.9 (1984).

The Court was unanimous that the statute precluded judicial review of all statutory claims.[f] As to Doe's constitutional claims, the Court said:

> We do not think that § 403(c) can be read to exclude review of constitutional claims. We emphasized in Johnson v. Robison, 415 U.S. 361 (1974), that where Congress intends to preclude judicial review of constitutional claims its intent to do so must be clear. In Weinberger v. Salfi, 422 U.S. 749 (1975), we reaffirmed that view. We require this heightened showing in part to avoid the "serious constitutional question" that would arise if a federal statute were construed to deny any judicial forum for a colorable constitutional claim. See Bowen v. Michigan Academy of Family Physicians, 476 U.S. 667, 681 n.12 (1986). . . . On remand, the District Court should thus address respondent's constitutional claims and the propriety of the equitable remedies sought.

Justice O'Connor dissented from this part of the Court's holding:

> I disagree . . . with the Court's conclusion that a constitutional claim challenging the validity of an employment decision covered by § 403(c) may . . . be brought in a federal district court. Whatever may be the exact scope of Congress's power to close the lower federal courts to constitutional claims in other contexts, I have no doubt about its authority to do so here. The functions performed by the Central Intelligence Agency and the Director of Central Intelligence lie at the core of "the very delicate, plenary and exclusive power of the President as the sole organ of the federal government in the field of international relations." The authority of the Director of Central Intelligence to control access to sensitive national security information by discharging employees deemed to be untrustworthy flows primarily from this constitutional power of the President, and Congress may surely provide that the inferior federal courts are not used to infringe on the President's constitutional authority. Section 403(c) plainly indicates that Congress has done exactly that, and the Court points to nothing in the structure, purpose, or legislative history of the National Security Act that would suggest a different result. Accordingly, I respectfully dissent from the Court's decision to allow this lawsuit to go forward.

Justice Scalia's dissent was more elaborate:

> Before taking the reader through the terrain of the Court's holding that respondent may assert some constitutional claims in this suit, I would like to try to clear some of the underbrush, consisting primarily of the Court's ominous warning that "[a] 'serious constitutional question' . . . would arise if a federal statute were construed to deny any judicial forum for a colorable constitutional claim."
>
> The first response to the Court's grave doubt about the constitutionality of denying all judicial review to a "colorable consti-

---

[f]   Chief Justice Rehnquist wrote for the Court. Justice Scalia disagreed with the Court's rationale, but agreed with the result. Justice Kennedy did not participate.

tutional claim" is that the denial of all judicial review is not at issue here, but merely the denial of review in the United States district courts. As to that, the law is, and has long been, clear. . . . We long ago held that the power not to create any lower federal courts at all includes the power to invest them with less than all of the judicial power [citing *Sheldon v. Sill*]. Thus, if there is any truth to the proposition that judicial cognizance of constitutional claims cannot be eliminated, it is, at most, that they cannot be eliminated from state courts, and from this Court's appellate jurisdiction over cases from state courts (or cases from federal courts, should there be any) involving such claims. . . .

It can fairly be argued, however, that our interpretation of [the governing statute] indirectly implicates the constitutional question whether state courts can be deprived of jurisdiction, because if they cannot, then interpreting [the statute] to exclude relief here would impute to Congress the peculiar intent to let state courts review federal government action that it is unwilling to let federal district courts review—or, alternatively, the peculiar intent to let federal district courts review, upon removal from state courts pursuant to 28 U.S.C. § 1442(a)(1), claims that it is unwilling to let federal district courts review in original actions. I turn, then, to the substance of the Court's warning that judicial review of all "colorable constitutional claims" arising out of the respondent's dismissal may well be constitutionally required. What could possibly be the basis for this fear? Surely not some general principle that *all* constitutional violations must be remediable in the courts. The very text of the Constitution refutes that principle, since it provides that "[e]ach House shall be the Judge of the Elections, Returns and Qualifications of its own Members," art. I, § 5, and that "for any Speech or Debate in either House, [the Senators and Representatives] shall not be questioned in any other Place," art. I, § 6. Claims concerning constitutional violations committed in these contexts—for example, the rather grave constitutional claim that an election has been stolen—cannot be addressed to the courts. Even apart from the strict text of the Constitution, we have found some constitutional claims to be beyond judicial review because they involve "political questions." See, e.g., Coleman v. Miller, 307 U.S. 433, 446–53 (1939). The doctrine of sovereign immunity—not repealed by the Constitution, but to the contrary at least partly reaffirmed as to the states by the Eleventh Amendment—is a monument to the principle that some constitutional claims can go unheard. No one would suggest that, if Congress had not passed the Tucker Act, 28 U.S.C. § 1491(a)(1), the courts would be able to order disbursements from the treasury to pay for property taken under lawful authority (and subsequently destroyed) without just compensation. . . . In sum, it is simply untenable that there must be a judicial remedy for every constitutional violation. Members of Congress and the supervising officers of the executive branch take the same oath to uphold the

Constitution that we do, and sometimes they are left to perform that oath unreviewed, as we always are.

Perhaps, then, the Court means to appeal to a more limited principle, that although there may be areas where judicial review of a constitutional claim will be denied, the scope of those areas is fixed by the Constitution and judicial tradition, and cannot be affected by *Congress*, through the enactment of a statute such as § 403(c). That would be a rather counter-intuitive principle, especially since Congress has in reality been the principal determiner of the scope of review, for constitutional claims as well as all other claims, through its waiver of the pre-existing doctrine of sovereign immunity. On the merits of the point, however: It seems to me clear that courts would not entertain, for example, an action for backpay by a dismissed Secretary of State claiming that the reason he lost his government job was that the President did not like his religious views—surely a colorable violation of the First Amendment. I am confident we would hold that the President's choice of his Secretary of State is a "political question." But what about a similar suit by the Deputy Secretary of State? Or one of the Under Secretaries? Or an Assistant Secretary? Or the head of the European Desk? Is there really a constitutional line that falls at some immutable point between one and another of these offices at which the principle of unreviewability cuts in, and which cannot be altered by congressional prescription? I think not. I think Congress can prescribe, at least within broad limits, that for certain jobs the dismissal decision will be unreviewable. . . .

Once it is acknowledged, as I think it must be, (1) that not all constitutional claims require a judicial remedy, and (2) that the identification of those that do not can, even if only within narrow limits, be determined by Congress, then it is clear that the "serious constitutional question" feared by the Court is an illusion. . . . I think it entirely beyond doubt that if Congress intended . . . to exclude judicial review of the President's decision (through the Director of Central Intelligence) to dismiss an officer of the Central Intelligence Agency, that disposition would be constitutionally permissible.

Scalia then turned to the question whether the statute could be read to support a distinction between statutory and constitutional claims. He said that it could not, and concluded:

The harm done by today's decision is that, contrary to what Congress knows is preferable, it brings a significant decisionmaking process of our intelligence services into a forum where it does not belong. Neither the Constitution, nor our laws, nor common sense gives an individual a right to come into court to litigate the reasons for his dismissal as an intelligence agent. It is of course not just *valid* constitutional claims that today's decision makes the basis for judicial review of the Director's action, but all *colorable* constitutional claims, whether meritorious or not. And in determining whether what is colorable is in fact meritorious, a court will necessarily have to review the entire decision. If the Director denies, for example, respondent's contention in the present case that he was dismissed because he was a homosexual, how can a court possibly resolve the dispute without knowing what other good, intelligence-related reasons there might have been? I do not see how any "latitude to control the discovery process" could justify the refusal to permit such an inquiry, at least in camera.[g] Presumably, the court would be expected to evaluate whether the agent really did fail in this or that secret mission. The documents needed will make interesting reading for district judges (and perhaps others) throughout the country. Of course the Agency can seek to protect itself, ultimately, by an authorized assertion of executive privilege, United States v. Nixon, 418 U.S. 683 (1974), but that is a power to be invoked only in extremis, and any scheme of judicial review of which it is a central feature is extreme. I would, in any event, not like to be the agent who has to explain to the intelligence services of other nations, with which we sometimes cooperate, that they need have no worry that the secret information they give us will be subjected to the notoriously broad discovery powers of our courts, because, although we have to litigate the dismissal of our spies, we have available a protection of somewhat uncertain scope known as executive privilege, which the President can invoke if he is willing to take the political damage that it often entails.

Today's result, however, will have ramifications far beyond creation of the world's only secret intelligence agency that must litigate the dismissal of its agents. If constitutional claims can be raised in this highly sensitive context, it is hard to imagine where they cannot. The assumption that there are any executive decisions that cannot be hauled into the courts may no longer be valid. . . .

Given the sensitivity of the matters entrusted to the CIA, *Webster* might be seen as an unusually strong case for judicial deference to agency discretion. And as Scalia concluded, it is difficult to draw from the statutory text an exception for constitutional issues. Why, then, did denial of federal jurisdiction command only two votes? What was the "serious constitutional question" the majority avoided by its construction of the statute? Is it relevant to the abortion hypothetical raised above in the introductory notes to these materials?

---

[g] On this point, the Court had said:

Petitioner complains that judicial review even of constitutional claims will entail extensive "rummaging around" in the Agency's affairs to the detriment of national security. But petitioner acknowledges that title VII claims attacking the hiring and promotion policies of the Agency are routinely entertained in federal court, and the inquiry and discovery associated with those proceedings would seem to involve some of the same sort of rummaging. Furthermore, the District Court has the latitude to control any discovery process which may be instituted so as to balance respondent's need for access to proof which would support a colorable constitutional claim against the extraordinary needs of the CIA for confidentiality and the protection of its methods, sources, and mission.—[Footnote by eds.]

6.   *FELKER V. TURPIN*

The Court similarly avoided constitutional questions in Felker v. Turpin, 518 U.S. 651 (1996). That case concerned the Antiterrorism and Effective Death Penalty Act of 1996, in which Congress imposed a series of limitations on the availability of habeas corpus, one of which was that second or successive petitions must first be presented to the relevant Court of Appeals for a preliminary determination of whether the District Court could entertain the case. Congress further provided that "[t]he grant or denial of an authorization by a court of appeals to file a second or successive application shall not be appealable and shall not be the subject of a petition for rehearing or for a writ of certiorari." In rejecting the argument that this provision was an unconstitutional exception to the Supreme Court's jurisdiction, the Court relied on Ex parte Yerger, 75 U.S. (8 Wall.) 85 (1868), and stated: "The act does remove our authority to entertain an appeal or a petition for a writ of certiorari to review a decision of a court of appeals exercising its 'gatekeeping' function over a second petition. But since it does not repeal our authority to entertain [an original] petition for habeas corpus, there can be no plausible argument that the act has deprived this Court of appellate jurisdiction in violation of art. III, § 2."

7.   *IMMIGRATION AND NATURALIZATION SERVICE V. ST. CYR*

The Court once again engaged in constitutional avoidance in Immigration and Naturalization Service v. St. Cyr, 533 U.S. 289 (2001), and a companion case, Calcano-Martinez v. Immigration and Naturalization Service, 533 U.S. 348 (2003). These cases presented a potential conflict between a jurisdiction-stripping statute and the Suspension Clause in Article I, Section 9 of the Constitution. The Suspension Clause provides that "[t]he Privilege of the Writ of Habeas Corpus shall not be suspended, unless when in Cases of Rebellion or Invasion the public Safety may require it." Congress had enacted immigration reform legislation that seemed to withdraw from the Attorney General the authority, which that officer had previously possessed, to grant discretionary relief from deportation orders for aliens convicted of criminal offenses. The Attorney General therefore declined to consider requests for such relief.

In an effort to obtain judicial review of the Attorney General's authority to issue such relief, two deportable aliens filed petitions for habeas corpus. The Immigration and Naturalization Service argued that various statutory provisions precluded judicial review of the issue, including review in a habeas action. A five-four majority of the Supreme Court disagreed, noting that there was no "clear statement of congressional intent to repeal habeas jurisdiction" and that, in the absence of a such a clear statement, the Court should avoid the "substantial constitutional questions" that such jurisdiction-stripping would present. Justice Scalia dissented, joined by Chief Justice Rehnquist, Justice O'Connor, and Justice Thomas. Justice Scalia argued that the statutory provisions in question unambiguously precluded the exercise of habeas jurisdiction and that these provisions were constitutional.

8. *HAMDAN V. RUMSFELD*

Salim Ahmed Hamdan, a Yemeni national, was imprisoned at Guantanamo Bay after having been captured during hostilities in Afghanistan. He filed a petition for habeas corpus challenging the intention of the government to try him before a military tribunal. The District Court granted relief, but the Court of Appeals reversed. The Supreme Court granted certiorari on November 7, 2005. On December 30, 2005, Congress passed an amendment to 28 U.S.C. § 2241 that arguably stripped the Court of jurisdiction:

> (e)   Except as provided in section 1005 of the Detainee Treatment Act of 2005, no court, justice, or judge shall have jurisdiction to hear or consider—
>
>> (1)   an application for a writ of habeas corpus filed by or on behalf of an alien detained by the Department of Defense at Guantanamo Bay, Cuba. . . .

Section 1005 of the act conferred exclusive jurisdiction to review a "final decision" of a military commission in such cases on the District of Columbia Circuit Court, mentioning specifically constitutional issues that arise during the course of the proceeding. It also contained "effective date" language stating that the provisions of the act "shall take effect on the date of the enactment of this Act." A second subsection on "effective date" stated specifically that its provisions governing review in the District of Columbia Circuit Court "shall apply . . . to any claim . . . that is pending on or after the date of the enactment of this Act."

In Hamdan v. Rumsfeld, 548 U.S. 557 (2006), the Court upheld its jurisdiction to proceed by applying "[o]rdinary principles of statutory construction," including the negative inference that, since part of the statute was explicit about applying to pending cases, the rest—and in particular its jurisdiction-stripping feature—did not. It was therefore unnecessary to reach Hamdan's arguments that the amendment to § 2241 violated the Exceptions and/or the Suspension Clause. Justice Stevens wrote for a five-three majority.[h]

Speaking for himself and Justices Thomas and Alito, Justice Scalia dissented on the jurisdictional issue. Scalia thought the jurisdiction-stripping language "unambiguously" applicable, and the Court's contrary conclusion "patently erroneous." He concluded that "the Court has made a mess of this statute." Because he concluded that the Court lacked jurisdiction, he went on to confront the Exceptions and Suspension Clause arguments. There was no problem under either provision, he concluded, because Congress had provided an alternative remedy.[i] The statute "merely *defers* our jurisdiction" and "does not eliminate that jurisdiction." "The exclusive-review provisions provide a substitute for habeas review adequate to satisfy the Suspension

---

[h]   Chief Justice Roberts did not participate. Justice Kennedy wrote separately to disagree with a portion of the Court's rationale on the merits. Justices Thomas and Alito wrote separate dissenting opinions on the merits. Justices Scalia and Alito joined.

[i]   Justice Scalia pointed out that "the Government does not dispute that the [act] leaves unaffected our certiorari jurisdiction . . . to review the D.C. Circuit's decisions."

Clause" and "provide a substitute adequate to satisfy any implied substantive limitations, whether real or imaginary, upon the Exceptions Clause."

9. *BOUMEDIENE V. BUSH*

In response to *Hamdan*, Congress once again acted to preclude habeas jurisdiction over detainees in the "war on terror." In 2006, Congress enacted the Military Commissions Act, Section 7 of which amended the habeas statute to provide that "[n]o court, justice, or judge shall have jurisdiction to hear or consider an application for a writ of habeas corpus filed by or on behalf of an alien detained by the United States who has been determined by the United States to have been properly detained as an enemy combatant or is awaiting such determination." This time, Congress left no doubt that the habeas restriction was intended to apply to pending cases, stating that it "shall take effect on the date of the enactment of this Act, and shall apply to all cases, without exception, pending on or after the date of the enactment of this Act which relate to any aspect of the detention, transfer, treatment, trial, or conditions of detention of an alien detained by the United States since September 11, 2001." In place of habeas jurisdiction, Congress provided for limited review in the D.C. Circuit of the determination by military panels that the detainees qualified as enemy combatants.

In Boumediene v. Bush, 553 U.S. 723 (2008), the Supreme Court concluded, in a five-four decision, that this habeas restriction was unconstitutional as applied to the detainees at Guantanamo. In an opinion by Justice Kennedy, the Court noted that, although Guantanamo is not formally part of the United States, the United States exercises exclusive jurisdiction and control there. If the territorial reach of the Constitution was determined solely by formal sovereignty, the Court reasoned, the government could "govern without legal constraint" by "surrendering formal sovereignty over any unincorporated territory to a third party, while at the same time entering into a lease that grants total control over the territory back to the United States." "Our basic charter cannot be contracted away like this," said the Court. The Court thought this particularly true of the Suspension Clause: because "the writ of habeas corpus is itself an indispensable mechanism for monitoring the separation of powers . . . [t]he test for determining the scope of this provision must not be subject to manipulation by those whose power it is designed to restrain." The Court considered several factors that it said were relevant to the territorial reach of the Suspension Clause—"(1) the citizenship and status of the detainee and the adequacy of the process through which that status determination was made; (2) the nature of the sites where apprehension and then detention took place; and (3) the practical obstacles inherent in resolving the prisoner's entitlement to the writ"—and concluded that the Clause applied to Guantanamo. Finally, the Court found that the D.C. Circuit review provisions did not provide an adequate substitute for habeas review because of (among other things) limitations on the D.C. Circuit's ability to consider exculpatory evidence.

Chief Justice Roberts filed a dissent, which was joined by Justices Scalia, Thomas, and Alito, arguing that the D.C. Circuit review provisions provided an adequate substitute for habeas review. Justice Scalia filed a separate dissent, joined by Chief Justice Roberts and Justices Thomas and Alito, arguing that the Suspension Clause did not apply to Guantanamo.

Boumediene is a significant decision for a number of reasons, one of which is that it confirms that Congress does not have unlimited authority to control federal court jurisdiction. In considering the implications of the decision, it is important to keep in mind that the Court was addressing what was in effect a limitation on both federal and state court review, since it has long been settled that state courts are not allowed to grant habeas relief to federal prisoners.[j] It is also worth noting that the Court in *Boumediene* relied on a constitutional limitation that is external to Article III and therefore did not address potential limitations that may be internal to that provision.

NOTES ON COMPETING VIEWS OF CONGRESSIONAL POWER TO LIMIT THE JURISDICTION OF THE FEDERAL COURTS

1. INTRODUCTION

There are several major theories that advance limits on the congressional power to make exceptions to the jurisdiction of the Supreme Court and/or its power over the jurisdiction of the lower federal courts. The following is a brief summary of a voluminous literature.

2. JUSTICE STORY

Relying mainly on the text of Article III, Justice Story said in dicta in Martin v. Hunter's Lessee, 14 U.S. (1 Wheat.) 304 (1816), that Congress

> might establish one or more inferior courts; they might parcel out the jurisdiction among such courts from time to time, at their own pleasure. But the whole judicial power of the United States should be, at all times, vested, either in an original or an appellate form, in some courts created under its authority.

Story may have thought the obligation to which he referred was moral rather than legal—that is, something that Congress ought to do that was not legally enforceable. Whatever Story meant, cases such as *Sheldon v. Sill* and the fact that Congress has never conferred the entire judicial power on the federal courts belie Story's position. Indeed, some have concluded that Justice Story's view "no longer deserves to be taken seriously."[a]

Akhil Amar takes issue with this statement.[b] He argues that prior commentators have not sufficiently focused on the word "all" in Article III, § 2. He observes that Article III requires that "all" cases arising under federal law, "all" cases affecting ambassadors, and "all" cases of admiralty or maritime jurisdiction must be vested, either as an original or an appellate matter,

---

[j] This issue is addressed in the discussion of *Tarble's Case* in Chapter 1, Section 2.

[a] Paul Bator, Congressional Power over the Jurisdiction of the Federal Courts, 27 Vill. L. Rev. 1030, 1035 (1982).

[b] Akhil Amar, A Neo-Federalist View of Article III: Separating the Two Tiers of Federal Jurisdiction, 65 Boston U. L. Rev. 205 (1985).

in some federal court. The remaining controversies—since Article III does not say that they must "all" be vested in a federal court—may be excluded from the federal courts in Congress's discretion. Justice Story was thus partly right, Amar concludes, and his argument "deserves to be taken very seriously indeed."

3.   THE ESSENTIAL FUNCTIONS THESIS

Recall that Article III confers appellate jurisdiction on the Supreme Court "with such Exceptions, and under such Regulations as the Congress shall make." Henry Hart cryptically suggested at the beginning of his dialogue[c] that "exceptions" presuppose a rule and cannot be so broad as to engulf the rule itself: "[T]he exceptions must not be such as will destroy the essential role of the Supreme Court in the constitutional plan." He did not elaborate, but others have.

The best known proponent of the "essential functions thesis" is Leonard Ratner, who set forth his views in two major articles.[d] In the more recent, he defined the essential functions of the Supreme Court as:

> (i) ultimately to resolve inconsistent or conflicting interpretations of federal law, and particularly of the Constitution, by state and federal courts; (ii) to maintain the supremacy of federal law, and particularly the Constitution, when it conflicts with state law or is challenged by state authority. Interpreted in this context, the exceptions and regulations clause means, as Henry Hart first suggested: with such exceptions and under such regulations as Congress may make, not inconsistent with the essential functions of the Supreme Court under the Constitution.

Ratner conceded that this does not mean that a Supreme Court decision is needed in every case that presents a constitutional question. "But an avenue must remain open to permit ultimate resolution by the Supreme Court of persistent conflicts between the Constitution and state law or in the interpretation of federal law by lower courts."

In the earlier article, Ratner defended his thesis by relying on inferences from the constitutional debates and from early Supreme Court decisions. He also suggested that the term "exception" meant to the framers "that in a legal context an exception cannot destroy the essential characteristics of the subject to which it applies" and the term "regulation" meant that "authority to prescribe [regulations] does not ordinarily include the power to prohibit the entire sphere of activity that is subject to regulation." He also analyzed the early jurisdictional structure under which the Court operated and concluded that, "[d]espite some impediments in early statutes, the Supreme Court from its inception has performed the essential constitutional functions of maintaining the uniformity and supremacy of federal law."

---

c   See Henry M. Hart, Jr., The Power of Congress to Limit the Jurisdiction of Federal Courts: An Exercise in Dialectic, 66 Harv. L. Rev. 1362 (1953).

d   Leonard Ratner, Majoritarian Constraints on Judicial Review: Congressional Control of Supreme Court Jurisdiction, 27 Vill. L. Rev. 929 (1982); Leonard Ratner, Congressional Power over the Appellate Jurisdiction of the Supreme Court, 109 U. Pa. L. Rev. 157 (1960).

A version of this thesis appears in Lawrence Sager, Forward: Constitutional Limitations on Congress's Authority to Regulate the Jurisdiction of the Federal Courts, 95 Harv. L. Rev. 17 (1981). Sager relied on "the firm commitment to federal judicial supervision of the states reflected in the history and logic of the Constitution" to defend the "argument that supervision of state conduct to ensure general compliance with the Constitution is an essential function of the Supreme Court. . . ."[e] Sager argued that Congress does not have unlimited authority to allow cases within the federal judicial power to be decided by judges who do not have Article III protections. Since state judges are not so protected, Congress may not rely exclusively on state courts. This does not mean, he continued, that no Article III cases may be consigned to state courts. Diversity cases, for example, could surely be excluded from all federal courts. But "there must be limits," he concluded, and "those limits are surely crossed when Congress attempts to divest the Supreme Court, and all other federal courts, of jurisdiction at least to review state court decisions on constitutional challenges to governmental behavior."

The "essential functions" thesis was developed as a limit on congressional power to make "exceptions" to the jurisdiction of the Supreme Court. Versions of it have also been advanced to limit the power of Congress to control the jurisdiction of the lower federal courts.[f] The broadest statement of this position appears in Theodore Eisenberg, Congressional Authority to Restrict Lower Federal Court Jurisdiction, 83 Yale L.J. 498 (1974).

Eisenberg argues that the contemporary understanding by the framers was "that the federal courts, whatever their form, could be expected to hear any litigant whose case was within the federal constitutional jurisdiction, either at trial or on appeal." The framers assumed, he continued, that Supreme Court review could accomplish this objective. But with the increased caseloads of modern times, this assumption is no longer practical:

> It is thus no longer reasonable to assert that Congress may simply abolish the lower federal courts. When Supreme Court review of all cases within Article III jurisdiction was possible, lower federal courts were perhaps unnecessary. As federal caseloads grew, however, lower federal courts became necessary components of the national judiciary if the constitutional duty of case by case consideration of all federal cases was to be fulfilled. It can now be asserted that their existence in some form is constitutionally required.

Eisenberg does not argue that Congress must vest the entire Article III power in some federal court. He concedes that Congress may exclude cases

---

[e] Sager modified this statement somewhat in his subsequent discussion: "The Court must be available to superintend state compliance with federal law unless Congress provides effective review elsewhere within the federal judiciary."

[f] See, e.g., Lawrence Sager, Forward: Constitutional Limitations on Congress's Authority to Regulate the Jurisdiction of the Federal Courts, 95 Harv. L. Rev. 17 (1981). The "essential function" identified by Sager—"supervision of state conduct to ensure general compliance with the Constitution"—must be performed, he argues, by the federal judicial system as a whole. Congress may, therefore, withdraw Supreme Court jurisdiction over such an issue if it provides for jurisdiction in a lower federal court.

from federal jurisdiction for "neutral" policy reasons, such as to avoid case overloads or to promote the efficiency of federal justice. Thus, a jurisdictional amount limitation is defensible, as is the failure to provide for federal trial of state criminal cases in which federal issues might, but need not, arise.[g] He also concludes that Congress "has unfettered power to enact jurisdictional laws that accomplish what it could have accomplished by means of a substantive rule." This means, he asserts, that "it may enact any jurisdictional statute that does not prevent vindication of a constitutional right" but that it "cannot withdraw jurisdiction to issue any constitutionally required remedy."

Those who hold the traditional view have not been kind to the essential functions thesis. Martin Redish calls it "constitutional wishful thinking,"[h] and Gerald Gunther condemns it as "question-begging" reasoning that confuses the familiar with the necessary.[i] But is the essential functions thesis any more question-begging than the traditional view? How does one discover the premises from which to build an argument about the scope of the congressional power? Does argument about the meaning of *Marbury v. Madison* help? Does thinking about other potential legislative and executive controls on federal court outcomes?

If one views the essential functions theory favorably, how are the "essential functions" of the federal courts to be discovered? Do Ratner and Sager identify the right functions? Should they have included an obligation to act as a check on the majoritarian branches of government and thereby protect minority rights?

In the 1980s, the Justice Department endorsed the essential functions thesis as applied to the Supreme Court's appellate jurisdiction. In commenting on a proposal in Congress to restrict the Supreme Court's jurisdiction over cases involving voluntary prayer in public schools and public buildings, Attorney General William French Smith sent a letter to the Chairman of the Senate Judiciary Committee stating that Congress may not, "consistent with the Constitution, make 'exceptions' to Supreme Court jurisdiction which would intrude upon the core functions of the Supreme Court as an independent and equal branch in our system of separation of powers." This letter was deemed sufficiently important that it was made an official opinion of the Justice Department's Office of Legal Counsel.[j] Before Smith sent the letter, there was a robust debate within the Justice Department between the head of the Office of Legal Counsel (Ted Olson), who argued for the essential functions thesis, and a young John Roberts, who argued for the traditional view. See Curtis A. Bradley and Neil S. Siegel, Historical Gloss, Constitutional

---

[g] He is comforted in this latter conclusion by the availability of federal habeas corpus for the assertion of federal claims by those convicted of state crimes.

[h] Martin H. Redish, Congressional Power to Regulate Supreme Court Appellate Jurisdiction under the Exceptions Clause: An Internal and External Examination, 27 Vill. L. Rev. 900, 911 (1982).

[i] Gerald Gunther, Congressional Power to Curtail Federal Court Jurisdiction: An Opinionated Guide to the Ongoing Debate, 36 Stan. L. Rev. 895, 908 (1984).

[j] See Constitutionality of Legislation Withdrawing Supreme Court Jurisdiction to Consider Cases Relating to Voluntary Prayer, 6 Op. O.L.C. 13 (1982).

Conventions, and the Judicial Separation of Powers, 105 Geo. L.J. 255, 302–11 (2017).

4. INDEPENDENT UNCONSTITUTIONALITY

Most commentators accept the proposition that the congressional power to regulate the jurisdiction of the federal courts is, like all other congressional powers, subject to the specific limitations contained in other parts of the Constitution, for example, in the Suspension Clause and the Bill of Rights. Thus, it would be unconstitutional for Congress to exclude jurisdiction over a particular litigant by name, or to exclude all cases brought by members of a particular race. However, there is considerable dispute over how far this limitation extends. For example, suppose Congress excluded all members of a particular race from litigation in the Supreme Court *and* denied the Court jurisdiction to hear all cases alleging racial discrimination. Would these provisions be unconstitutional? What if the second part of the statute were enacted alone?[k]

5. DUE PROCESS: ACCESS TO COURTS

Many commentators recognize that due process sometimes requires judicial process. For example, they argue, it would violate due process—as well as other constitutional rights, such as the right to trial by jury—to convict someone of a crime without using a judicial process. Paul Bator—who adhered to the traditional view of Congress's power—accepted this proposition. But he argued that "the Constitution is indifferent to whether that access is to a federal or a state court."[l] Hence, Bator argued, where state courts remain available, Congress may freely foreclose access to lower federal courts.

Martin Redish and Curtis Woods disagree. They argue that "[t]here exists a due process right to an independent judicial determination of constitutional rights" and that state courts under some circumstances are *not* open to hear such claims. They conclude that due process requires access in such cases to a federal court.[m]

In a later article,[n] Redish advances a broader contention. He builds on Lawrence Sager's thesis that the Article III salary and tenure provisions require access to federal courts over cases involving challenges to the constitutionality of state official conduct. Redish suggests that the Due Process Clause could be construed—though it has not been—to preclude final adjudicatory authority by state judges over the constitutionality of actions by state government. The argument in support of this construction would be

---

    [k] This hypothetical was suggested by Kenneth R. Kay in a Symposium discussion reported in 27 Vill. L. Rev. 1042, 1044 (1982).

    [l] Bator, Congressional Power, at 1034. For further discussion of this issue, see Louise Weinberg, The Article III Box: The Power of "Congress" to Attack the "Jurisdiction" of "Federal Courts," 78 Tex. L. Rev. 1405 (2000).

    [m] Martin H. Redish and Curtis E. Woods, Congressional Power to Control the Jurisdiction of Lower Federal Courts: A Critical Review and a New Synthesis, 124 U. Pa. L. Rev. 45 (1975). Their authority for the proposition that state courts are sometimes closed to constitutional claims is Tarble's Case, 80 U.S. (13 Wall.) 397 (1872), and related holdings.

    [n] Martin H. Redish, Constitutional Limitations on Congressional Power to Control Federal Jurisdiction: A Reaction to Professor Sager, 77 Nw. U. L. Rev. 143 (1982).

that state judges are not sufficiently "independent" of the government they are expected to supervise. And since Supreme Court review is not routinely available, due process would require access to lower federal courts to hear these cases.

6.   DISCRIMINATION AGAINST CONSTITUTIONAL CLAIMS

Some commentators argue that jurisdiction-stripping legislation would almost always be unconstitutional if its object were to remove a particular class of constitutional litigants from the federal courts. Particular attention has been focused on equal protection principles, but the same argument could be made for rights derived from substantive due process. The claim is that congressional exclusion of particular classes of litigation from the Supreme Court's jurisdiction, identified by the nature of the constitutional claim (e.g., abortion), having an impact only on the class of litigants who would assert that right and motivated by congressional hostility to the underlying constitutional right involved should be subject to the same strict scrutiny as any other substantive regulation of that subject matter. Under this test, the Court should examine the rationale underlying the congressional exclusion and uphold the excision from jurisdiction only if it serves a compelling interest. It goes without saying that dissatisfaction with the constitutional right itself would not satisfy this standard.

The ultimate difficulty with this view, the critics respond, is that it assumes the point in issue.[o] Those who believe that congressional power is essentially plenary believe that dissatisfaction with Supreme Court decisions *is* a permissible basis for limiting jurisdiction. The constitutional plan left it to Congress to allocate judicial business among the state and federal courts; if Congress chooses to leave certain rights to state courts, that was a choice given to Congress to make.

It is argued by Lea Brilmayer and Stefan Underhill, Congressional Obligation to Provide a Forum for Constitutional Claims: Discriminatory Jurisdictional Rules and the Conflict of Laws, 69 Va. L. Rev. 819 (1983), that a series of conflict-of-laws cases stands for the proposition that Congress may not discriminate against constitutional claims when it enacts jurisdictional legislation.[p] They argue that "*in no other legal context* within our federal system has the power to establish and regulate courts carried with it the power to enact jurisdictional statutes that discriminate against claims arising from other sources of law within that system." They conclude that "door-closing rules that single out constitutional claims without valid reason are prohibited." Congressional hostility to a constitutional right, they argue, is not a "valid reason" to enact a jurisdiction-stripping statute. Nor can they think of a valid reason if a statute were facially to discriminate between some constitutional rights and others, or between constitutional rights and other federal

---

[o]   See, e.g., Gunther, Congressional Power, at 916–21.

[p]   They primarily rely on Hughes v. Fetter, 341 U.S. 609 (1951), Testa v. Katt, 330 U.S. 386 (1947), and a series of FELA cases. *Hughes* held that one state was obligated to hear a statutory claim asserted under the laws of another state. *Testa* and the FELA cases held that state courts were obligated to hear federal statutory claims.

rights. A somewhat similar argument is made by Laurence Tribe in Jurisdictional Gerrymandering: Zoning Disfavored Rights Out of the Federal Courts, 16 Harv. Civ. Rts.-Civ. Lib. L. Rev. 129 (1981).

7.   IMPLICATIONS OF *BOUMEDIENE*

Richard Fallon notes that, although the precise holding in *Boumediene* is narrow, the Court's "guarded recognition of the limitations of narrowly textual and rigidly originalist analysis . . . diverged notably from the originalist and textualist style of reasoning that has characterized nearly all leading academic writings on congressional control of jurisdiction." Richard H. Fallon, Jr., Jurisdiction-Stripping Reconsidered, 96 Va. L. Rev. 1043, 1047 (2010). In light of *Boumediene*, Fallon contends that "the time seems ripe for a general reconsideration of Congress's power to withdraw jurisdiction from the federal courts as a means of shielding questions about the legality of official conduct from judicial review." He proceeds to argue that:

> First, notwithstanding contrary language in the 1869 case of *Ex parte McCardle*, Congress's purpose or motive in enacting jurisdiction-stripping legislation may sometimes bear crucially on such legislation's constitutionality. . . .

> Second, Congress cannot use its power to control jurisdiction to preclude constitutionally necessary remedies for the violation of constitutional rights. . . .

> Third, as *Boumediene* teaches, issues involving congressional preclusion of judicial jurisdiction are often bound up with issues involving the permissible use of non-Article III federal tribunals such as legislative courts and administrative agencies [and] [e]ven when initial adjudication by a non-Article III tribunal is permissible, the Constitution may mandate the availability of either appellate review or some other mode of access to an Article III court.

More generally, Fallon contends that "it is impossible to think deeply about the preclusion of jurisdiction without thinking about constitutionally necessary remedies under modern constitutional doctrines, rooted in provisions of the Constitution other than Article III, that have sometimes diverged from original constitutional understandings."

Is Fallon reading too much into the *Boumediene* decision? To what extent are Fallon's arguments supported by other materials in this section? With respect to Fallon's first argument, how easy would it be for the Supreme Court to assess Congress's motives in enacting jurisdiction-stripping legislation, and, assuming it could do so, how would it know which motives were improper? Even in *Boumediene*, was it clear that the government had an improper purpose in housing the detainees at Guantanamo and limiting their access to federal court? As for Fallon's second argument, does it beg the questions of which remedies are constitutionally required and the extent to which state courts can adequately provide such remedies?

8. INSTITUTIONAL CHARACTERISTICS OF STATE AND FEDERAL COURTS

One question underlying the debate between the traditional view and the competing views is whether state court adjudication of federal rights is comparable to federal court adjudication of the same rights. This question is also relevant to a number of other topics in a Federal Courts course. It is important in thinking about it to consider what is meant by comparability and how one would identify the controlling characteristics.

Burt Neuborne, The Myth of Parity, 90 Harv. L. Rev. 1105 (1977), argues that state courts "are less likely [than federal courts] to be receptive to vigorous enforcement of federal constitutional doctrine" even though he disclaims "any intent to cast aspersions on the good faith of state judges." He says that the proper institutional comparison is between state and federal trial courts, both because of the importance of fact-finding in constitutional litigation and because the expense and delay of relying on appellate courts may deter prospective litigants from testing their claims.

Neuborne argues that federal trial judges tend to be more competent than their state counterparts, largely because of sheer numbers. There are about twice as many trial judges in California as there are in the entire federal system, and it is necessarily more difficult to maintain a high level of quality with so many positions. Moreover, he continues, federal judges are better paid and have more prestige. They also get better staff support, particularly in the number and quality of law clerks.

Neuborne also focuses on a series of psychological and attitudinal characteristics. He argues that federal judges seem to have a better sense of tradition and institutional mission and that they feel closer to, and more receptive to the concerns of, the Supreme Court. They are also less jaundiced by the fact patterns presented by the daily grist of their cases, and are chosen from a successful, homogeneous socioeconomic class that tends to be receptive to constitutional claims. Additionally, he notes that life tenure insulates federal judges from the majoritarian pressures to which elected state judges are subject.

Finally, Neuborne identifies three disadvantages of constitutional litigation in federal courts. First, federal judges may be "less sensitive to the social milieu" into which their decisions must fit. Second, federal courts are overburdened with litigation. And third, channeling important constitutional cases into the federal courts may perpetuate the "second-class status and performance" of the state trial courts.

Neuborne made these arguments in the context of explaining why civil liberties lawyers are likely to choose federal rather than state court. He did not address the extent to which his contentions might be relevant to questions of congressional power to limit the jurisdiction of the federal courts.

For an elaborate discussion of many of the issues raised by Neuborne, see Gil Seinfeld, The Federal Courts as a Franchise: Rethinking the Justifications for Federal Question Jurisdiction, 97 Calif. L. Rev. 95 (2009). Seinfeld critiques what he calls the traditional "bias-uniformity-expertise" mantra and offers a "Federal Franchise" model as an explanation for the uniqueness of federal courts. Federal courts are best seen as a "chain of dispute resolution forums with a set of basic characteristics held in common across branches, regardless of the location in which any particular branch sits." This way of looking at it, he says, "shifts attention away from what federal judges might do *to federal law*, and directs it, instead, to the experience of the lawyer and litigant *in federal court*. . . . It carries the promise . . . of inverting the dynamics of insider and outsider status that might otherwise be in play."

As explained in Brian T. Fitzpatrick, The Constitutionality of Federal Jurisdiction-Stripping Legislation and the History of State Judicial Selection and Tenure, 98 Va. L. Rev. 839 (2012), state judges at the time of the constitutional Founding were all appointed rather than elected, and they had life tenure. It was not until the mid-nineteenth century that states began moving towards elected judges and limited terms. "[T]he decline in the parity between state and federal judiciaries," the author suggests, "can persuade even those who give significant weight to original understanding to conclude that jurisdiction stripping is unconstitutional today even though it may not have been unconstitutional at the Founding."

9. BIBLIOGRAPHY

For additional commentary on Congress's authority to limit the jurisdiction of the federal courts, see Joseph Blocher, Amending the Exceptions Clause, 92 Minn. L. Rev. 971 (2008); Laurence Claus, The One Court That Congress Cannot Take Away: Singularity, Supremacy, and Article III, 96 Geo. L.J. 59 (2007); Tara Leigh Grove, The Article II Safeguards of Federal Jurisdiction, 112 Colum. L. Rev. 250 (2012); John Harrison, The Power of Congress to Limit the Jurisdiction of Federal Courts and the Text of Article III, 64 U. Chi. L. Rev. 203 (1997); James E. Pfander, Jurisdiction-Stripping and the Supreme Court's Power to Supervise Inferior Tribunals, 78 Tex. L. Rev. 1433 (2000); James E. Pfander, Federal Supremacy, State Court Inferiority, and the Constitutionality of Jurisdiction-Stripping Legislation, 101 Nw. U. L. Rev. 191 (2007); Mark Strasser, Taking Exception to Traditional Exceptions Clause Jurisprudence: On Congress's Power to Limit the Court's Jurisdiction, 2001 Utah L. Rev. 125; Gordon G. Young, A Critical Reassessment of the Case Law Bearing on Congress's Power to Restrict the Jurisdiction of the Lower Federal Courts, 54 Md. L. Rev. 132 (1995).

For commentary on Akhil Amar's theory of Article III (most of which has been critical), see, for example, William R. Casto, An Orthodox View of the Two-Tier Analysis of Congressional Control over Federal Jurisdiction, 7 Const. Commentary 89 (1990); William A. Fletcher, Congressional Power over the Jurisdiction of Federal Courts: The Meaning of the Word "All" in Article III, 59 Duke L.J. 929 (2010); Julian Velasco, Congressional Control Over Federal Court Jurisdiction: A Defense of the Traditional View, 46 Cath. U. L. Rev. 671 (1997); Ann Woolhandler, Power, Rights, and Section 25, 86 Notre Dame L. Rev. 1241 (2011). Amar's thesis is elaborated in Akhil Amar, The Two-Tiered Structure of the Judiciary Act of 1789, 138 U. Pa. L. Rev.

1499 (1990). Responses follow in the same issue of the University of Pennsylvania Law Review, as well as a rejoinder by Amar. See Daniel J. Meltzer, The History and Structure of Article III, 138 U. Pa. L. Rev. 1569 (1990); Martin H. Redish, Text, Structure, and Common Sense in the Interpretation of Article III, 138 U. Pa. L. Rev. 1633 (1990); Akhil Amar, Reports of My Death Are Greatly Exaggerated, 138 U. Pa. L. Rev. 1651 (1990). For a friendly elaboration of the Amar position, see Robert J. Pushaw, Jr., Congressional Power Over Federal Court Jurisdiction: A Defense of the Neo-Federalist Interpretation of Article III, 1997 B.Y.U. L. Rev. 847.

Additional debate was generated by Barry Friedman, A Different Dialogue: The Supreme Court, Congress, and Federal Jurisdiction, 85 Nw. U. L. Rev. 1 (1990). For responses to this article and Friedman's reply, see Akhil Amar, Taking Article III Seriously: A Reply to Professor Friedman, 85 Nw. U. L. Rev. 442 (1990); Mark Tushnet, The Law, Politics, and Theory of Federal Courts: A Comment, 85 Nw. U. L. Rev. 454 (1990); Michael Wells, Congress's Paramount Role in Setting the Scope of Federal Jurisdiction, 85 Nw. U. L. Rev. 465 (1990); Barry Friedman, Federal Jurisdiction and Legal Scholarship: A (Dialogic) Reply, 85 Nw. U. L. Rev. 478 (1990).

Also of interest in this debate is David E. Engdahl, Federal Question Jurisdiction under the 1789 Judiciary Act, 14 Okla. City Univ. L. Rev. 521 (1989), which disputes the traditional understanding that federal question jurisdiction was not fully conferred by the Judiciary Act of 1789. See also David E. Engdahl, Intrinsic Limits of Congress's Power Regarding the Judicial Branch, 1999 B.Y.U. L. Rev. 75. Engdahl criticizes Amar's analysis, suggests that one key to the scope of Congressional power over federal court jurisdiction lies in properly understanding the necessary and proper clause, and concludes that "[w]hile Congress may create or abolish inferior tribunals and may shuffle assignments among such federal courts as exist, no category of subject matter jurisdiction, once vested, may be divested from the judiciary as a whole, except by constitutional amendment."

For another defense of a view akin to Justice Story's, see Robert N. Clinton, A Mandatory View of Federal Court Jurisdiction: A Guided Quest for the Original Understanding of Article III, 132 U. Pa. L. Rev. 741 (1984). See also Robert N. Clinton, A Mandatory View of Federal Court Jurisdiction: Early Implementation of and Departures from the Constitutional Plan, 86 Colum. L. Rev. 1515 (1986).

Finally, for yet two more approaches to the jurisdiction-stripping issue, see Alex Glashausser, A Return to Form for the Exceptions Clause, 51 B.C. L. Rev. 1383 (2010), and Tara Leigh Grove, The Structural Safeguards of Federal Jurisdiction, 124 Harv. L. Rev. 869 (2011). Glashausser offers an unconventional interpretation of the Exceptions Clause. In his view, the word "exceptions" applies to "appellate," not "Jurisdiction." On this reading, the clause gives Congress only the power to shift cases falling within Article III from the Court's appellate to its original jurisdiction. Grove starts from a premise more in line with the traditional view of the Exceptions Clause. She attacks the proposition that effective limits on the ability of Congress to pass jurisdiction-stripping legislation must be judicially enforceable and asserts instead that the structural protections contained in Article I are sufficient to protect the Supreme Court's appellate role. In another article, Grove contends that "Congress has largely used its power over the Supreme Court's appellate jurisdiction to safeguard, not to undermine, the Court's constitutional role" (such as through an expansion of the Court's discretionary certiorari jurisdiction). See Tara Leigh Grove, The Exceptions Clause as a Structural Safeguard, 113 Colum. L. Rev. 929, 931 (2013). See also Tara Leigh Grove, Article III in the Political Branches, 90 Notre Dame L. Rev. 1835 (2015) (examining the relevance of the practices of the political branches in determining the scope of Article III).

SECTION 2. POWER TO REGULATE FEDERAL RULES OF DECISION AND JUDGMENTS

Plaut v. Spendthrift Farm, Inc.

Supreme Court of the United States, 1995.
514 U.S. 211.

■ JUSTICE SCALIA delivered the opinion of the Court.

The question presented in this case is whether § 27A(b) of the Securities Exchange Act of 1934, to the extent that it requires federal courts to reopen final judgments in private civil actions under § 10(b) of the Act, contravenes the Constitution's separation of powers or the Due Process Clause of the Fifth Amendment.

I

In 1987, petitioners brought a civil action against respondents in the United States District Court for the Eastern District of Kentucky. The complaint alleged that in 1983 and 1984 respondents had committed fraud and deceit in the sale of stock in violation of § 10(b) of the Securities Exchange Act of 1934 and Rule 10b–5 of the Securities and Exchange Commission. The case was mired in pretrial proceedings in the District Court until June 20, 1991, when we decided Lampf, Pleva, Lipkind, Prupis & Petigrow v. Gilbertson, 501 U.S. 350 (1991). *Lampf* held that "litigation instituted pursuant to § 10(b) and Rule 10b–5 . . . must be commenced within one year after the discovery of the facts constituting the violation and within three years after such violation." We applied that holding to the plaintiff-respondents in *Lampf* itself, found their suit untimely, and reinstated a summary judgment previously entered in favor of the defendant-petitioners. On the same day we decided James B. Beam Distilling Co. v. Georgia, 501 U.S. 529 (1991), in which a majority of the Court held, albeit in different opinions, that a new rule of federal law that is applied to the parties in the case announcing the rule must be applied as well to all cases pending on direct review. The joint effect of *Lampf* and *Beam* was to mandate application of the 1-year/3-year limitations period to petitioners' suit. The District Court, finding that petitioners' claims were untimely under the *Lampf* rule, dismissed their action with prejudice on August 13, 1991. Petitioners filed no appeal; the judgment accordingly became final 30 days later

On December 19, 1991, the President signed the Federal Deposit Insurance Corporation Improvement Act of 1991. Section 476 of the Act—a section that had nothing to do with FDIC improvements—became § 27A of the Securities Exchange Act of 1934. It provides:

(a)   Effect on pending causes of action

The limitation period for any private civil action implied under section 78j(b) of this title [§ 10(b) of the Securities Exchange Act of 1934] that was commenced on or before June 19, 1991, shall be the limitation period provided by the laws applicable in the jurisdiction, including principles of retroactivity, as such laws existed on June 19, 1991.

(b)   Effect on dismissed causes of action

Any private civil action implied under section 78j(b) of this title that was commenced on or before June 19, 1991—

(1)   which was dismissed as time barred subsequent to June 19, 1991, and

(2)   which would have been timely filed under the limitation period provided by the laws applicable in the jurisdiction, including principles of retroactivity, as such laws existed on June 19, 1991,

shall be reinstated on motion by the plaintiff not later than 60 days after December 19, 1991.

On February 11, 1992, petitioners returned to the District Court and filed a motion to reinstate the action previously dismissed with prejudice. The District Court found that the conditions set out in §§ 27A(b)(1) and (2) were met, so that petitioners' motion was required to be granted by the terms of the statute. It nonetheless denied the motion, agreeing with respondents that § 27A(b) is unconstitutional. The United States Court of Appeals for the Sixth Circuit affirmed. We granted certiorari.

II

[In this section of its opinion, the Court examined the statutory language and concluded that "there is no reasonable construction on which § 27A(b) does not require federal courts to reopen final judgments in suits dismissed with prejudice by virtue of *Lampf*."]

III

Respondents submit that § 27A(b) violates both the separation of powers and the Due Process Clause of the Fifth Amendment. Because the latter submission, if correct, might dictate a similar result in a challenge to state legislation under the Fourteenth Amendment, the former is the narrower ground for adjudication of the constitutional questions in the case, and we therefore consider it first. We conclude that in § 27A(b) Congress has exceeded its authority by requiring the federal courts to exercise "the judicial Power of the United States," U.S. Const., Art. III, § 1, in a manner repugnant to the text, structure, and traditions of Article III.

Our decisions to date have identified two types of legislation that require federal courts to exercise the judicial power in a manner that Article III forbids. The first appears in United States v. Klein, 80 U.S. (13 Wall.) 128 (1872), where we refused to give effect to a statute that was said "[to] prescribe rules of decision to the Judicial Department of the government in cases pending before it." Whatever the precise scope of *Klein*, however, later decisions have made clear that its prohibition does not take hold when Congress "amend[s] applicable law." Robertson v. Seattle Audubon Soc., 503 U.S. 429, 441 (1992). Section 27A(b) indisputably does set out substantive legal standards for the Judiciary to apply, and in that sense changes the law (even if solely retroactively). The second type of unconstitutional restriction upon the exercise of judicial power identified by past cases is exemplified by Hayburn's Case, 2 U.S. (2 Dall.) 409 (1792), which stands for the principle that Congress cannot vest review of the decisions of Article III courts in officials of the Executive Branch. Yet under any application of § 27A(b) only courts are involved; no officials of other departments sit in direct review of their decisions. Section 27A(b) therefore offends neither of these previously established prohibitions.

We think, however, that § 27A(b) offends a postulate of Article III just as deeply rooted in our law as those we have mentioned. Article III establishes a "judicial department" with the "province and duty . . . to say what the law is" in particular cases and controversies. Marbury v. Madison, 5 U.S. (1 Cranch) 137, 177 (1803). The record of history shows that the Framers crafted this charter of the judicial department with an expressed understanding that it gives the Federal Judiciary the power, not merely to rule on cases, but to *decide* them, subject to review only by superior courts in the Article III hierarchy—with an understanding, in short, that "a judgment conclusively resolves the case" because "a 'judicial Power' is one to render dispositive judgments." Frank Easterbrook, Presidential Review, 40 Case W. Res. L. Rev. 905, 926 (1990). By retroactively commanding the federal courts to reopen final judgments, Congress has violated this fundamental principle.

A

The Framers of our Constitution lived among the ruins of a system of intermingled legislative and judicial powers, which had been prevalent in the colonies long before the Revolution, and which after the Revolution had produced factional strife and partisan oppression. In the 17th and 18th centuries colonial assemblies and legislatures functioned as courts of equity of last resort, hearing original actions or providing appellate review of judicial judgments. Often, however, they chose to correct the judicial process through special bills or other enacted legislation. It was common for such legislation not to prescribe a resolution of the dispute, but rather simply to set aside the judgment and order a new trial or appeal. . . .

The vigorous, indeed often radical, populism of the revolutionary legislatures and assemblies increased the frequency of legislative correction of judgments. . . . Voices from many quarters, official as well as private, decried the increasing legislative interference with the private-law judgments of the courts. . . .

This sense of a sharp necessity to separate the legislative from the judicial power, prompted by the crescendo of legislative interference with private judgments of the courts, triumphed among the Framers of the new Federal Constitution. The Convention made the critical decision to establish a judicial department independent of the Legislative Branch by providing that "the judicial Power of the United States shall be vested in one supreme Court, and in such inferior Courts as the Congress may from time to time ordain and establish." . . .

B

Section 27A(b) effects a clear violation of the separation-of-powers principle we have just discussed. It is, of course, retroactive legislation, that is, legislation that prescribes what the law *was* at an earlier time, when the act whose effect is controlled by the legislation occurred—in this case, the filing of the initial Rule 10b–5 action in the District Court. When retroactive legislation requires its own application in a case already finally adjudicated, it does no more and no less than "reverse a determination once made, in a particular case." The Federalist No. 81, p. 545 (J. Cooke ed. 1961). Our decisions stemming from *Hayburn's Case*— although their precise holdings are not strictly applicable here—have uniformly provided fair warning that such an act exceeds the powers of Congress. [E.g.,] Pennsylvania v. Wheeling & Belmont Bridge Co., 59 U.S. (18 How.) 421, 431 (1856) ("It is urged, that the act of Congress cannot have the effect and operation to annul the judgment of the court already rendered, or the rights determined thereby. . . . This, as a general proposition, is certainly not to be denied, especially as it respects adjudication upon the private rights of parties. When they have passed into judgment the right becomes absolute, and it is the duty of the court to enforce it"). Today those clear statements must either be honored, or else proved false.

It is true, as petitioners contend, that Congress can always revise the judgments of Article III courts in one sense: When a new law makes clear that it is retroactive, an appellate court must apply that law in reviewing judgments still on appeal that were rendered before the law was enacted, and must alter the outcome accordingly. See United States v. Schooner Peggy, 5 U.S. (1 Cranch) 103 (1801); Landgraf v. USI Film Products, 511 U.S. 244 (1994). Since that is so, petitioners argue, federal courts must apply the "new" law created by § 27A(b) in finally adjudicated cases as well; for the line that separates lower court judgments that are pending on appeal (or may still be appealed), from lower court judgments that are final, is determined by statute, see, e.g., 28 U.S.C. § 2107(a) (30-day time limit for appeal to federal court of appeals), and so cannot possibly be a *constitutional* line. But a distinction between judgments from which all appeals have been forgone or completed, and judgments that remain on appeal (or subject to being appealed), is implicit in what Article III creates: not a batch of unconnected courts, but a judicial *department* composed of "inferior Courts" and "one supreme Court." Within that hierarchy, the decision of an inferior court is not (unless the time for appeal has expired) the final word of the department as a whole. It is the obligation of the last court in the hierarchy that rules on the case to give effect to Congress's latest enactment, even when that has the effect of overturning the judgment of an inferior court, since each court, at every level, must "decide according to existing laws." *Schooner Peggy*, 5 U.S. at 109. Having achieved finality, however, a judicial decision becomes the last word of the judicial department with regard to a particular case or controversy, and Congress may not declare by retroactive legislation that the law applicable *to that very case* was something other than what the courts said it was. Finality of a legal judgment is determined by statute, just as entitlement to a government benefit is a statutory creation; but that no more deprives the former of its constitutional significance for separation-of-powers analysis than it deprives the latter of its significance for due process purposes.

To be sure, § 27A(b) reopens (or directs the reopening of) final judgments in a whole class of cases rather than in a particular suit. We do not see how that makes any difference. The separation-of-powers violation here, if there is any, consists of depriving judicial judgments of the conclusive effect that they had when they were announced, not of acting in a manner—viz., with particular rather than general effect—that is unusual (though, we must note, not impossible) for a legislature. To be sure, a general statute such as this one may reduce the perception that legislative interference with judicial judgments was prompted by individual favoritism; but it is legislative interference with judicial judgments nonetheless. Not favoritism, nor even corruption, but *power* is the object of the separation-of-powers prohibition. The prohibition is violated when an individual final judgment is legislatively rescinded for even the *very best* of reasons, such as the legislature's genuine conviction (supported by all the law professors in the land) that the judgment was wrong; and it is violated 40 times over when 40 final judgments are legislatively dissolved.

It is irrelevant as well that the final judgments reopened by § 27A(b) rested on the bar of a statute of limitations. The rules of finality, both statutory and judge made, treat a dismissal on statute-of-limitations grounds the same way they treat a dismissal for failure to state a claim, for failure to prove substantive liability, or for failure to prosecute: as a judgment on the merits. Petitioners suggest, directly or by implication, two reasons why a merits judgment based on this particular ground may be uniquely subject to congressional nullification. First, there is the fact that the length and indeed even the very existence of a statute of limitations upon a federal cause of action is entirely subject to congressional control. But virtually *all* of the reasons why a final judgment on the merits is rendered on a federal claim are subject to congressional control. Congress can eliminate, for example, a particular element of a cause of action that plaintiffs have found it difficult to establish; or an evidentiary rule that has often excluded essential testimony; or a rule of offsetting wrong (such as contributory negligence) that has often prevented recovery. To distinguish statutes of limitations on the ground that they are mere creatures of Congress is to distinguish them not at all. The second supposedly distinguishing characteristic of a statute of limitations is that it can be extended, without violating the Due Process Clause, after the cause of the action arose and even after the statute itself has expired. But that also does not set statutes of limitations apart. To mention only one other broad category of judgment-producing legal rule: Rules of pleading and proof can similarly be altered after the cause of action arises, and even, if the statute clearly so requires, after they have been applied in a case but before final judgment has been entered. Petitioners' principle would therefore lead to the conclusion that final judgments rendered on the basis of a stringent (or, alternatively, liberal) rule of pleading or proof may be set aside for retrial under a new liberal (or, alternatively, stringent) rule of pleading or proof. This alone provides massive scope for undoing final judgments and would substantially subvert the doctrine of separation of powers. . . .

C

Apart from the statute we review today, we know of no instance in which Congress has attempted to set aside the final judgment of an Article III court by retroactive legislation. That prolonged reticence would be amazing if such interference were not understood to be constitutionally proscribed. The closest analogue that the Government has been able to put forward is the statute at issue in United States v. Sioux Nation, 448 U.S. 371 (1980). That law required the Court of Claims, " 'notwithstanding any other provision of law . . . [to] review on the merits, without regard to the defense of res judicata or collateral estoppel,' " a Sioux claim for just compensation from the United States—even though the Court of Claims had previously heard and rejected that very claim. We considered and rejected separation-of-powers objections to the statute based upon *Hayburn's Case* and *United States v. Klein*. The basis for our rejection was a line of precedent (starting with Cherokee Nation v. United States, 270 U.S. 476 (1926)) that stood, we said, for the proposition that "Congress has the power to waive the res judicata effect of a prior judgment entered in the Government's favor on a claim against the United States." . . .

The Solicitor General suggests that even if *Sioux Nation* is read in accord with its holding, it nonetheless establishes that Congress may require Article III courts to reopen their final judgments, since "if res judicata were compelled by Article III to safeguard the structural independence of the courts, the doctrine would not be subject to waiver by any party litigant." Brief for United States 27. But the proposition that legal defenses based upon doctrines central to the courts' structural independence can never be waived simply does not accord with our cases. Certainly one such doctrine consists of the "judicial Power" to disregard an unconstitutional statute, see *Marbury*, 5 U.S. at 177; yet none would suggest that a litigant may never waive the defense that a statute is unconstitutional. What may follow from our holding that the judicial power unalterably includes the power to render final judgments is not that waivers of res judicata are always impermissible, but rather that, as many federal Courts of Appeals have held, waivers of res judicata need not always be accepted—that trial courts may in appropriate cases raise the res judicata bar on their own motion. Waiver subject to the control of the courts themselves would obviously raise no issue of separation of powers, and would be precisely in accord with the language of the decision that the Solicitor General relies upon. . . .

Petitioners also rely on a miscellany of decisions upholding legislation that altered rights fixed by the final judgments of non-Article III courts, see, e.g., Sampeyreac v. United States, 32 U.S. (7 Pet.) 222, 238 (1833); Freeborn v. Smith, 69 U.S. (2 Wall.) 160 (1865), or administrative agencies, Paramino Lumber Co. v. Marshall, 309 U.S. 370 (1940), or that altered the prospective effect of injunctions entered by Article III courts, *Wheeling & Belmont Bridge Co.* These cases distinguish themselves; nothing in our holding today calls them into question. Petitioners rely on general statements from some of these cases that legislative annulment of final judgments is not an exercise of judicial power. But even if it were our practice to decide cases by weight of prior dicta, we would find the many dicta that reject congressional power to revise the judgments of Article III courts to be the more instructive authority.

Finally, petitioners liken § 27A(b) to Federal Rule of Civil Procedure 60(b), which authorizes courts to relieve parties from a final judgment for grounds such as excusable neglect, newly discovered evidence, fraud, or "any other reason justifying relief. . . ." We see little resemblance. Rule 60(b), which authorizes discretionary judicial revision of judgments in the listed situations and in other "extraordinary circumstances," does not impose any legislative mandate to reopen upon the courts, but merely reflects and confirms the courts' own inherent and discretionary power, "firmly established in English practice long before the foundation of our Republic," to set aside a judgment whose enforcement would work inequity. Hazel-Atlas Glass Co. v. Hartford-Empire Co., 322 U.S. 238, 244 (1944). Thus, Rule 60(b), and the tradition that it embodies, would be relevant refutation of a claim that reopening a final judgment is always a denial of property without due process; but they are irrelevant to the claim that legislative instruction to reopen impinges upon the independent constitutional authority of the courts.

The dissent promises to provide "[a] few contemporary examples" of statutes retroactively requiring final judgments to be reopened, "to demonstrate that [such statutes] are ordinary products of the exercise of legislative power." That promise is not kept. The relevant retroactivity, of course, consists not of the requirement that there be set aside a judgment that has been rendered *prior to its being setting aside*—for example, a statute passed today which says that all default judgments rendered in the future may be reopened within 90 days after their entry. In that sense, *all* requirements to reopen are "retroactive," and the designation is superfluous. Nothing we say today precludes a law such as that. The finality that a court can pronounce is no more than what the law in existence at the time of judgment will permit it to pronounce. If the law then applicable says that the judgment may be reopened for certain reasons, that limitation is built into the judgment itself, and its finality is so conditioned. The present case, however, involves a judgment that Congress subjected to a reopening requirement which did not exist when the judgment was pronounced. The dissent provides not a single clear prior instance of such congressional action. . . .

The dissent sets forth a number of hypothetical horribles flowing from our assertedly "rigid holding"—for example, the inability to set aside a civil judgment that has become final during a period when a natural disaster prevented the timely filing of a certiorari petition. That is horrible not because of our holding, but because the underlying statute *itself* enacts a "rigid" jurisdictional bar to entertaining untimely civil petitions. Congress could undoubtedly enact *prospective* legislation permitting, or indeed requiring, this Court to make equitable exceptions to an otherwise applicable rule of finality, just as district courts do pursuant to Rule 60(b). It is no indication whatever of the invalidity of the constitutional rule which we announce, that it produces unhappy consequences when a legislature lacks foresight, and acts belatedly to remedy a deficiency in the law. That is a routine result of constitutional rules. . . .

Finally, we may respond to the suggestion of the concurrence that this case should be decided more narrowly. . . . Ultimately, the concurrence agrees with our judgment only "because the law before us embodies risks of the very sort that our Constitution's 'separation of powers' prohibition seeks to avoid." But the doctrine of separation of powers is a *structural safeguard* rather than a remedy to be applied only when specific harm, or risk of specific harm, can be identified. In its major features (of which the conclusiveness of judicial judgments is assuredly one) it is a prophylactic device, establishing high walls and clear distinctions because low walls and vague distinctions will not be judicially defensible in the heat of interbranch conflict. . . . Separation of powers, a distinctively

American political doctrine, profits from the advice authored by a distinctively American poet: Good fences make good neighbors.

* * *

We know of no previous instance in which Congress has enacted retroactive legislation requiring an Article III court to set aside a final
judgment, and for good reason. The Constitution's separation of legislative and judicial powers denies it the authority to do so. Section 27A(b) is
unconstitutional to the extent that it requires federal courts to reopen
final judgments entered before its enactment. The judgment of the Court
of Appeals is affirmed.

It is so ordered.

[Justice Breyer concurred in the judgment, arguing that "the separation of powers inherent in our Constitution means that at least
sometimes Congress lacks the power under Article I to reopen an otherwise closed court judgment," and that "[t]hree features of [§ 27A(B)]—its
exclusively retroactive effect, its application to a limited number of individuals, and its reopening of closed judgments—taken together, show
that Congress here impermissibly tried to *apply*, as well as *make*, the
law." Justice Breyer noted, however, that "if Congress enacted legislation
that reopened an otherwise closed judgment but in a way that mitigated
some of the here relevant 'separation-of-powers' concerns, by also providing some of the assurances against 'singling out' that ordinary legislative
activity normally provides—say, prospectivity and general applicability—we might have a different case."]

■ JUSTICE STEVENS, with whom JUSTICE GINSBURG joins, dissenting. . . .

Section 27A is a statutory amendment to a rule of law announced by
this Court. The fact that the new rule announced in *Lampf* was a product
of judicial, rather than congressional, lawmaking should not affect the
separation-of-powers analysis. We would have the same issue to decide
had Congress enacted the *Lampf* rule but, as a result of inadvertence or
perhaps a scrivener's error, failed to exempt pending cases, as is customary when limitations periods are shortened. In my opinion, if Congress
had retroactively restored rights its own legislation had inadvertently or
unfairly impaired, the remedial amendment's failure to exclude dismissed cases from the benefited class would not make it invalid. The
Court today faces a materially identical situation and, in my view,
reaches the wrong result.

Throughout our history, Congress has passed laws that allow courts
to reopen final judgments. Such laws characteristically apply to judgments entered before as well as after their enactment. When they apply
retroactively, they may raise serious due process questions,[2] but the

---

[2]   Because the Court finds a separation-of-powers violation, it does not reach respondents'
alternative theory that § 27A(b) denied them due process under the Fifth Amendment. . . .
Given the existence of statutes and rules, such as Rule 60(b), that allow courts to reopen apparently "final" judgments in various circumstances, respondents cannot assert an inviolable

Court has never invalidated such a law on separation-of-powers grounds until today. . . .

The most familiar remedial measure that provides for reopening of final judgments is Rule 60(b) of the Federal Rules of Civil Procedure. That Rule both codified common-law grounds for relieving a party from a final judgment and added an encompassing reference to "any other reason justifying relief from the operation of the judgment." Not a single word in its text suggests that it does not apply to judgments entered prior to its effective date. On the contrary, the purpose of the Rule, its plain language, and the traditional construction of remedial measures all support construing it to apply to past as well as future judgments. Indeed, because the Rule explicitly abolished the common-law writs it replaced, an unintended gap in the law would have resulted if it did not apply retroactively.

Other examples of remedial statutes that resemble § 27A include the Soldiers' and Sailors' Civil Relief Act of 1940, which authorizes members of the Armed Forces to reopen judgments entered while they were on active duty; the Handicapped Children's Protection Act of 1986, which provided for recovery of attorney's fees under the Education for All Handicapped Children Act of 1975; and the federal habeas corpus statute, 28 U.S.C. § 2255, which authorizes federal courts to reopen judgments of conviction. The habeas statute, similarly to Rule 60(b), replaced a common-law writ, and thus necessarily applied retroactively. State statutes that authorize the reopening of various types of default judgments and judgments that became final before a party received notice of their entry, as well as provisions for motions to reopen based on newly discovered evidence, further demonstrate the widespread acceptance of remedial statutes that allow courts to set aside final judgments. As in the case of Rule 60(b), logic dictates that these statutes be construed to apply retroactively to judgments that were final at the time of their enactments. All of these remedial statutes announced generally applicable rules of law as well as establishing procedures for reopening final judgments.[5]

In contrast, in the examples of colonial legislatures' review of trial courts' judgments on which today's holding rests, the legislatures issued directives in individual cases without purporting either to set forth or to apply any legal standard. . . .

"vested right" in the District Court's post-*Lampf* dismissal of petitioners' claims. In addition, § 27A(b) did not upset any "settled expectations" of respondents. . . . Before 1991 no one could have relied either on the yet to be announced rule in *Lampf* or on the Court's unpredictable decision to apply that rule retroactively. All of the reliance interests that ordinarily support a presumption against retroactivity militate in favor of allowing retroactive application of § 27A.

[5]   The Court offers no explanation of why the Constitution should be construed to interpose an absolute bar against these statutes' retroactive application. Under the Court's reasoning, for example, an amendment that broadened the coverage of Rule 60(b) could not apply to any inequitable judgments entered prior to the amendment. The Court's rationale for this formalistic restriction remains elusive.

The Framers' disapproval of such a system of ad hoc legislative review of individual trial court judgments has no bearing on remedial measures such as Rule 60(b) or the 1991 amendment at issue today. The history on which the Court relies provides no support for its holding. . . .

Section 27A shares several important characteristics with the remedial statutes discussed above. It does not decide the merits of any issue in any litigation but merely removes an impediment to judicial decision on the merits. The impediment it removes would have produced inequity because the statute's beneficiaries did not cause the impediment. It requires a party invoking its benefits to file a motion within a specified time and to convince a court that the statute entitles the party to relief. Most important, § 27A(b) specifies both a substantive rule to govern the reopening of a class of judgments—the pre-*Lampf* limitations rule—and a procedure for the courts to apply in determining whether a particular motion to reopen should be granted. These characteristics are quintessentially legislative. They reflect Congress's fealty to the separation of powers and its intention to avoid the sort of ad hoc excesses the Court rightly criticizes in colonial legislative practice. In my judgment, all of these elements distinguish § 27A from "judicial" action and confirm its constitutionality. A sensible analysis would at least consider them in the balance.

Instead, the Court myopically disposes of § 27A(b) by holding that Congress has no power to "require an Article III court to set aside a final judgment." That holding must mean one of two things. It could mean that Congress may not impose a mandatory duty on a court to set aside a judgment even if the court makes a particular finding, such as a finding of fraud or mistake, that Congress has not made. Such a rule, however, could not be correct. Although Rule 60(b), for example, merely authorizes federal courts to set aside judgments after making appropriate findings, Acts of Congress characteristically set standards that judges are obligated to enforce. Accordingly, Congress surely could add to Rule 60(b) certain instances in which courts *must* grant relief from final judgments if they make particular findings—for example, a finding that a member of the jury accepted a bribe from the prevailing party. The Court, therefore, must mean to hold that Congress may not *unconditionally* require an Article III court to set aside a final judgment. That rule is both unwise and beside the point of this case. . . .

The majority's rigid holding unnecessarily hinders the Government from addressing difficult issues that inevitably arise in a complex society. This Court, for example, lacks power to enlarge the time for filing petitions for certiorari in a civil case after 90 days from the entry of final judgment, no matter how strong the equities. See 28 U.S.C. § 2101(c). If an Act of God, such as a flood or an earthquake, sufficiently disrupted communications in a particular area to preclude filing for several days, the majority's reasoning would appear to bar Congress from addressing the resulting inequity. If Congress passed remedial legislation that retroactively granted movants from the disaster area extra time to file petitions or motions for extensions of time to file, today's holding presumably would compel us to strike down the legislation as an attack on the finality of judgments. Such a ruling, like today's holding, would gravely undermine federal courts' traditional power "to set aside a judgment whose enforcement would work inequity." . . .

We have the authority to hold that Congress has usurped a judicial prerogative, but even if this case were doubtful I would heed Justice Iredell's admonition in Calder v. Bull, 3 U.S. (3 Dall.) 386, 399 (1798), that "the Court will never resort to that authority, but in a clear and urgent case." An appropriate regard for the interdependence of Congress and the judiciary amply supports the conclusion that § 27A(b) reflects constructive legislative cooperation rather than a usurpation of judicial prerogatives.

Accordingly, I respectfully dissent.

<h2 style="text-align:center">Miller v. French</h2>

Supreme Court of the United States, 2000.
530 U.S. 327.

■ JUSTICE O'CONNOR delivered the opinion of the Court.

The Prison Litigation Reform Act of 1995 (PLRA) establishes standards for the entry and termination of prospective relief in civil actions challenging prison conditions. If prospective relief under an existing injunction does not satisfy these standards, a defendant or intervenor is entitled to "immediate termination" of that relief. And under the PLRA's "automatic stay" provision, a motion to terminate prospective relief "shall operate as a stay" of that relief during the period beginning 30 days after the filing of the motion (extendable to up to 90 days for "good cause") and ending when the court rules on the motion. The superintendent of the Pendleton Correctional Facility, which is currently operating under an ongoing injunction to remedy violations of the Eighth Amendment regarding conditions of confinement, filed a motion to terminate prospective relief under the PLRA. Respondent prisoners moved to enjoin the operation of the automatic stay provision of § 3626(e)(2), arguing that it is unconstitutional. The District Court enjoined the stay, and the Court of Appeals for the Seventh Circuit affirmed. We must decide whether a district court may enjoin the operation of the PLRA's automatic stay provision and, if not, whether that provision violates separation of powers principles.

I

A

This litigation began in 1975, when four inmates at what is now the Pendleton Correctional Facility brought a class action under 42 U.S.C.

§ 1983, on behalf of all persons who were, or would be, confined at the facility against the predecessors in office of petitioners (hereinafter State). After a trial, the District Court found that living conditions at the prison violated both state and federal law, including the Eighth Amendment's prohibition against cruel and unusual punishment, and the court issued an injunction to correct those violations. While the State's appeal was pending, this Court decided Pennhurst State School and Hospital v. Halderman, 465 U.S. 89 (1984), which held that the Eleventh Amendment deprives federal courts of jurisdiction over claims for injunctive relief against state officials based on state law. Accordingly, the Court of Appeals for the Seventh Circuit remanded the action to the District Court for reconsideration. On remand, the District Court concluded that most of the state law violations also ran afoul of the Eighth Amendment, and it issued an amended remedial order to address those constitutional violations. The order also accounted for improvements in living conditions at the Pendleton facility that had occurred in the interim.

The Court of Appeals affirmed the amended remedial order as to those aspects governing overcrowding and double celling, the use of mechanical restraints, staffing, and the quality of food and medical services, but it vacated those portions pertaining to exercise and recreation, protective custody, and fire and occupational safety standards. This ongoing injunctive relief has remained in effect ever since, with the last modification occurring in October 1988, when the parties resolved by joint stipulation the remaining issues related to fire and occupational safety standards.

B

In 1996, Congress enacted the PLRA. As relevant here, the PLRA establishes standards for the entry and termination of prospective relief in civil actions challenging conditions at prison facilities. Specifically, a court "shall not grant or approve any prospective relief unless the court finds that such relief is narrowly drawn, extends no further than necessary to correct the violation of a Federal right, and is the least intrusive means necessary to correct the violation of the Federal right." 18 U.S.C. § 3626(a)(1)(A). The same criteria apply to existing injunctions, and a defendant or intervenor may move to terminate prospective relief that does not meet this standard. In particular, § 3626(b)(2) provides:

> In any civil action with respect to prison conditions, a defendant or intervener shall be entitled to the immediate termination of any prospective relief if the relief was approved or granted in the absence of a finding by the court that the relief is narrowly drawn, extends no further than necessary to correct the violation of the Federal right, and is the least intrusive means necessary to correct the violation of the Federal right.

A court may not terminate prospective relief, however, if it "makes written findings based on the record that prospective relief remains necessary to correct a current and ongoing violation of the Federal right, extends no further than necessary to correct the violation of the Federal right, and that the prospective relief is narrowly drawn and the least intrusive means necessary to correct the violation." § 3626(b)(3). The PLRA also requires courts to rule "promptly" on motions to terminate prospective relief, with mandamus available to remedy a court's failure to do so. § 3626(e)(1).

Finally, the provision at issue here, § 3626(e)(2), dictates that, in certain circumstances, prospective relief shall be stayed pending resolution of a motion to terminate. Specifically, subsection (e)(2), entitled "Automatic Stay," states:

> Any motion to modify or terminate prospective relief made under subsection (b) shall operate as a stay during the period—
>
> > (A)(i) beginning on the 30th day after such motion is filed, in the case of a motion made under paragraph (1) or (2) of subsection (b); . . . and
> >
> > (B) ending on the date the court enters a final order ruling on the motion.

As one of several 1997 amendments to the PLRA, Congress permitted courts to postpone the entry of the automatic stay for not more than 60 days for "good cause," which cannot include general congestion of the court's docket. 18 U.S.C. § 3626(e)(3).

C

On June 5, 1997, the State filed a motion under § 3626(b) to terminate the prospective relief governing the conditions of confinement at the Pendleton Correctional Facility. In response, the prisoner class moved for a temporary restraining order or preliminary injunction to enjoin the operation of the automatic stay, arguing that § 3626(e)(2) is unconstitutional as both a violation of the Due Process Clause of the Fifth Amendment and separation of powers principles. The District Court granted the prisoners' motion, enjoining the automatic stay. The State appealed, and the United States intervened pursuant to 28 U.S.C. § 2403(a) to defend the constitutionality of § 3626(e)(2).

The Court of Appeals for the Seventh Circuit affirmed the District Court's order, concluding that although § 3626(e)(2) precluded courts from exercising their equitable powers to enjoin operation of the automatic stay, the statute, so construed, was unconstitutional on separation of powers grounds. The court reasoned that Congress drafted § 3626(e)(2) in unequivocal terms, clearly providing that a motion to terminate under § 3626(b)(2) "*shall* operate" as a stay during a specified time period. While acknowledging that courts should not lightly assume that Congress meant to restrict the equitable powers of the federal courts, the Court of Appeals found "it impossible to read this language as doing anything less than that." Turning to the constitutional question, the court characterized § 3626(e)(2) as "a self-executing legislative determination that a specific decree of a federal court . . . must be set aside at least for a period of time." As such, it concluded that § 3626(e)(2) directly suspends a court order in violation of the separation of powers doctrine under *Plaut v. Spendthrift Farm, Inc.,* 514 U.S. 211 (1995), and mandates a particular rule of decision, at least during the pendency of the § 3626(b)(2) termination motion, contrary to *United States v. Klein,* 80 U.S. (13 Wall.) 128 (1872). Having concluded that § 3626(e)(2) is unconstitutional on separation of powers grounds, the Court of Appeals did not reach the prisoners' due process claims. Over the dissent of three judges, the court denied rehearing en banc.

We granted certiorari, to resolve a conflict among the Courts of Appeals as to whether § 3626(e)(2) permits federal courts, in the exercise of their traditional equitable authority, to enjoin operation of the PLRA's automatic stay provision and, if not, to review the Court of Appeals' judgment that § 3626(e)(2), so construed, is unconstitutional. . . .

II

We address the statutory question first. Both the State and the prisoner class agree, as did the majority and dissenting judges below, that § 3626(e)(2) precludes a district court from exercising its equitable powers to enjoin the automatic stay. The Government argues, however, that § 3626(e)(2) should be construed to leave intact the federal courts' traditional equitable discretion to "stay the stay," invoking two canons of statutory construction. First, the Government contends that we should not interpret a statute as displacing courts' traditional equitable authority to preserve the status quo pending resolution on the merits "absent the clearest command to the contrary." *Califano v. Yamasaki,* 442 U.S. 682, 705 (1979). Second, the Government asserts that reading § 3626(e)(2) to remove that equitable power would raise serious separation of powers questions, and therefore should be avoided under the canon of constitutional doubt. Like the Court of Appeals, we do not lightly assume that Congress meant to restrict the equitable powers of the federal courts, and we agree that constitutionally doubtful constructions should be avoided where "fairly possible." *Communications Workers v. Beck,* 487 U.S. 735, 762 (1988). But where Congress has made its intent clear, "we must give effect to that intent." *Sinclair Refining Co. v. Atkinson,* 370 U.S. 195, 215 (1962). . . .

[The Court concluded that § 3626(e)(2) could not reasonably be construed to permit federal courts, in the exercise of their traditional equitable authority, to enjoin operation of the PLRA's automatic stay provision.]

III

The Constitution enumerates and separates the powers of the three branches of Government in Articles I, II, and III, and it is this "very structure" of the Constitution that exemplifies the concept of separation of powers. *INS v. Chadha,* 462 U.S. 919, 946 (1983). While the boundaries between the three branches are not " 'hermetically' sealed," see id. at 951, the Constitution prohibits one branch from encroaching on the central prerogatives of another. . . . The powers of the Judicial Branch are set forth in Article III, § 1, which states that the "judicial Power of the United States shall be vested in one supreme Court and in such inferior Courts as Congress may from time to time ordain and establish," and provides that these federal courts shall be staffed by judges who hold office during good behavior, and whose compensation shall not be diminished during tenure in office. As we explained in *Plaut v. Spendthrift Farm, Inc.*, Article III "gives the Federal Judiciary the power, not merely to rule on cases, but to *decide* them, subject to review only by superior courts in the Article III hierarchy."

Respondent prisoners contend that § 3626(e)(2) encroaches on the central prerogatives of the Judiciary and thereby violates the separation of powers doctrine. It does this, the prisoners assert, by legislatively suspending a final judgment of an Article III court in violation of *Plaut* and Hayburn's Case, 2 U.S. (2 Dall.) 409 (1792). According to the prisoners, the remedial order governing living conditions at the Pendleton Correctional Facility is a final judgment of an Article III court, and § 3626(e)(2) constitutes an impermissible usurpation of judicial power because it commands the district court to suspend prospective relief under that order, albeit temporarily. An analysis of the principles underlying *Hayburn's Case* and *Plaut*, as well as an examination of § 3626(e)(2)'s interaction with the other provisions of § 3626, makes clear that § 3626(e)(2) does not offend these separation of powers principles. . . .

Unlike the situation in *Hayburn's Case*, § 3626(e)(2) does not involve the direct review of a judicial decision by officials of the Legislative or Executive Branches. Nonetheless, the prisoners suggest that § 3626(e)(2) falls within *Hayburn's* prohibition against an indirect legislative "suspension" or reopening of a final judgment, such as that addressed in *Plaut*. . . .

Plaut, however, was careful to distinguish the situation before the Court in that case—legislation that attempted to reopen the dismissal of a suit seeking money damages—from legislation that "altered the prospective effect of injunctions entered by Article III courts." We emphasized that "nothing in our holding today calls . . . into question" Congress's authority to alter the prospective effect of previously entered injunctions. Prospective relief under a continuing, executory decree remains subject to alteration due to changes in the underlying law. This conclusion follows from our decisions in Pennsylvania v. Wheeling & Belmont Bridge Co., 54 U.S. (13 How.) 518 (1852) (*Wheeling Bridge I*) and Pennsylvania v. Wheeling & Belmont Bridge Co., 59 U.S. (18 How.) 421 (1856) (*Wheeling Bridge II*). . . .

Applied here, the principles of *Wheeling Bridge II* demonstrate that the automatic stay of § 3626(e)(2) does not unconstitutionally "suspend" or reopen a judgment of an Article III court. Section § 3626(e)(2) does not by itself "tell judges when, how, or what to do." French v. Duckworth, 178

F.3d 437, 449 (7th Cir. 1999) (Easterbrook, J., dissenting from denial of rehearing en banc). Instead, § 3626(e)(2) merely reflects the change implemented by § 3626(b), which does the "heavy lifting" in the statutory scheme by establishing new standards for prospective relief. Section 3626 prohibits the continuation of prospective relief that was "approved or granted in the absence of a finding by the court that the relief is narrowly drawn, extends no further than necessary to correct the violation of the Federal right, and is the least intrusive means to correct the violation," § 3626(b)(2), or in the absence of "findings based on the record that prospective relief remains necessary to correct a current and ongoing violation of a Federal right, extends no further than necessary to correct the violation of the Federal right, and that the prospective relief is narrowly drawn and the least intrusive means necessary to correct the violation," § 3626(b)(3). Accordingly, if prospective relief under an existing decree had been granted or approved absent such findings, then that prospective relief must cease, see § 3626(b)(2), unless and until the court makes findings on the record that such relief remains necessary to correct an ongoing violation and is narrowly tailored, see § 3626(b)(3). The PLRA's automatic stay provision assists in the enforcement of §§ 3626(b)(2) and (3) by requiring the court to stay any prospective relief that, due to the change in the underlying standard, is no longer enforceable, i.e., prospective relief that is not supported by the findings specified in §§ 3626(b)(2) and (3).

By establishing new standards for the enforcement of prospective relief in § 3626(b), Congress has altered the relevant underlying law. The PLRA has restricted courts' authority to issue and enforce prospective relief concerning prison conditions, requiring that such relief be supported by findings and precisely tailored to what is needed to remedy the violation of a federal right. We note that the constitutionality of § 3626(b) is not challenged here; we assume, without deciding, that the new standards it pronounces are effective. As *Plaut* and *Wheeling Bridge II* instruct, when Congress changes the law underlying a judgment awarding prospective relief, that relief is no longer enforceable to the extent it is inconsistent with the new law. Although the remedial injunction here is a "final judgment" for purposes of appeal, it is not the "last word of the judicial department." *Plaut,* 514 U.S. at 227. The provision of prospective relief is subject to the continuing supervisory jurisdiction of the court, and therefore may be altered according to subsequent changes in the law. . . .

The entry of the automatic stay under § 3626(e)(2) helps to implement the change in the law caused by §§ 3626(b)(2) and (3). If the prospective relief under the existing decree is not supported by the findings required under § 3626(b)(2), and the court has not made the findings required by § 3626(b)(3), then prospective relief is no longer enforceable and must be stayed. The entry of the stay does not reopen or "suspend" the previous judgment, nor does it divest the court of authority to decide the merits of the termination motion. Rather, the stay merely reflects the changed legal circumstances—that prospective relief under the existing decree is no longer enforceable, and remains unenforceable unless and until the court makes the findings required by § 3626(b)(3).

For the same reasons, § 3626(e)(2) does not violate the separation of powers principle articulated in United States v. Klein, 80 U.S. (13 Wall.) 128 (1872). . . .

As we noted in *Plaut*, . . . "whatever the precise scope of *Klein*, . . . later decisions have made clear that its prohibition does not take hold when Congress 'amends applicable law.'" The prisoners concede this point but contend that, because § 3626(e)(2) does not itself amend the legal standard, *Klein* is still applicable. As we have explained, however, § 3626(e)(2) must be read not in isolation, but in the context of § 3626 as a whole. Section 3626(e)(2) operates in conjunction with the new standards for the continuation of prospective relief; if the new standards of § 3626(b)(2) are not met, then the stay "shall operate" unless and until the court makes the findings required by § 3626(b)(3). Rather than prescribing a rule of decision, § 3626(e)(2) simply imposes the consequences of the court's application of the new legal standard.

Finally, the prisoners assert that, even if § 3626(e)(2) does not fall within the recognized prohibitions of *Hayburn's Case*, *Plaut*, or *Klein*, it still offends the principles of separation of powers because it places a deadline on judicial decisionmaking, thereby interfering with core judicial functions. Congress's imposition of a time limit in § 3626(e)(2), however, does not in itself offend the structural concerns underlying the Constitution's separation of powers. For example, if the PLRA granted courts 10 years to determine whether they could make the required findings, then certainly the PLRA would raise no apprehensions that Congress had encroached on the core function of the Judiciary to decide "cases and controversies properly before them." United States v. Raines, 362 U.S. 17 (1960). Respondents' concern with the time limit, then, must be its relative brevity. But whether the time is so short that it deprives litigants of a meaningful opportunity to be heard is a due process question, an issue that is not before us. We leave open, therefore, the question whether this time limit, particularly in a complex case, may implicate due process concerns.

In contrast to due process, which principally serves to protect the personal rights of litigants to a full and fair hearing, separation of powers principles are primarily addressed to the structural concerns of protecting the role of the independent Judiciary within the constitutional design. In this action, we have no occasion to decide whether there could be a time constraint on judicial action that was so severe that it implicated these structural separation of powers concerns. The PLRA does not deprive courts of their adjudicatory role, but merely provides a new legal standard for relief and encourages courts to apply that standard promptly. . . .

Through the PLRA, Congress clearly intended to make operation of the automatic stay mandatory, precluding courts from exercising their equitable powers to enjoin the stay. And we conclude that this provision does not violate separation of powers principles. Accordingly, the judgment of the Court of Appeals for the Seventh Circuit is reversed, and the action is remanded for further proceedings consistent with this opinion.

It is so ordered.

[Justice Breyer dissented, joined by Justice Stevens. He argued for "a more flexible interpretation of the statute" whereby the federal courts would have the authority to suspend the automatic stay "when a party, in accordance with traditional equitable criteria, has demonstrated a need for such an exception."]

■ JUSTICE SOUTER, with whom JUSTICE GINSBURG joins, concurring in part and dissenting in part.

I agree that 18 U.S.C. § 3626(e)(2) is unambiguous and join Parts I and II of the majority opinion. I also agree that applying the automatic stay may raise the due process issue, of whether a plaintiff has a fair chance to preserve an existing judgment that was valid when entered. But I believe that applying the statute may also raise a serious separation-of-powers issue if the time it allows turns out to be inadequate for a court to determine whether the new prerequisite to relief is satisfied in a particular case. I thus do not join Part III of the Court's opinion and on remand would require proceedings consistent with this one. I respectfully dissent from the terms of the Court's disposition.

A prospective remedial order may rest on at least three different legal premises: the underlying right meant to be secured; the rules of procedure for obtaining relief, defining requisites of pleading, notice, and so on; and, in some cases, rules lying between the other two, such as those defining a required level of certainty before some remedy may be ordered, or the permissible scope of relief. At issue here are rules of the last variety.

Congress has the authority to change rules of this sort by imposing new conditions precedent for the continuing enforcement of existing, prospective remedial orders and requiring courts to apply the new rules to those orders. Cf. Plaut v. Spendthrift Farm, Inc., 514 U.S. 211, 232 (1995). If its legislation gives courts adequate time to determine the applicability of a new rule to an old order and to take the action necessary to apply it or to vacate the order, there seems little basis for claiming that Congress has crossed the constitutional line to interfere with the performance of any judicial function. But if determining whether a new rule applies requires time (say, for new factfinding) and if the statute provides insufficient time for a court to make that determination before the statute invalidates an extant remedial order, the application of the statute raises a serious question whether Congress has in practical terms assumed the judicial function. In such a case, the prospective order suddenly turns unenforceable not because a court has made a judgment to terminate it due to changed law or fact, but because no one can tell in the time allowed whether the new rule requires modification of the old order. One way to view this result is to see the Congress as mandating modification of an order that may turn out to be perfectly enforceable under the new rule, depending on judicial factfinding. If the facts are taken this way, the new statute might well be treated as usurping the judicial function of determining the applicability of a general rule in particular factual circumstances.[3] Cf. United States v. Klein, 80 U.S. (13 Wall.) 128 (1872).

Whether this constitutional issue arises on the facts of this action, however, is something we cannot yet tell, for the District Court did not address the sufficiency of the time provided by the statute to make the findings required by § 3626(b)(3) in this particular action. Absent that determination, I would not decide the separation-of-powers question, but simply remand for further proceedings. If the District Court determined both that it lacked adequate time to make the requisite findings in the period before the automatic stay would become effective, and that applying the stay would violate the separation of powers, the question would then be properly presented.

NOTES ON CONGRESSIONAL REGULATION OF FEDERAL RULES OF DECISION AND JUDGMENTS

1.   HAYBURN'S CASE

A 1792 statute authorized pensions for disabled veterans of the Revolutionary War. The statute provided that the federal circuit courts were to determine the appropriate disability payments, but that the Secretary of War had the discretion either to adopt or reject the courts' findings. The Supreme Court did not address the constitutionality of this arrangement, but the views of several circuit courts (reflecting the views of five Supreme Court Justices) were reported with the case, and these courts reasoned that the statute was unconstitutional because it asked the federal courts to do something that was not "judicial." See Hayburn's Case, 2 U.S. (2 Dall.) 409 (1792). In *Plaut v. Spendthrift Farm*, excerpted above, the Supreme Court said that *Hayburn's Case* "stands for the principle that Congress cannot vest review of

---

[3]   The constitutional question inherent in these possible circumstances does not seem to be squarely addressed by any of our cases. Congress did not engage in discretionary review of a particular judicial judgment, cf. Plaut v. Spendthrift Farm, Inc., 514 U.S. 211, 218, 226 (1995) (characterizing Hayburn's Case, 2 U.S. (2 Dall.) 409 (1792)), or try to modify a final, non-prospective judgment, cf. 514 U.S. at 218–19. Nor would a stay result from the judicial application of a change in the underlying law, cf. Pennsylvania v. Wheeling & Belmont Bridge Co., 59 U.S. (18 How.) 421 (1856); *Plaut*, 514 U.S. at 218 (characterizing United States v. Klein, 80 U.S. (13 Wall.) 128 (1872)). Instead, if the time is insufficient for a court to make a judicial determination about the applicability of the new rules, the stay would result from the inability of the Judicial Branch to exercise the judicial power of determining whether the new rules applied at all. Cf. Marbury v. Madison, 5 U.S. (1 Cranch) 137, 177 (1803) ("It is emphatically the province and duty of the judicial department to say what the law is").

the decisions of Article III courts in officials of the Executive Branch." *Hayburn's Case* is also often cited for the more general proposition that Article III courts may not issue advisory opinions.

2.   *PENNSYLVANIA V. WHEELING & BELMONT BRIDGE CO. II*

In the late 1840s, the state of Virginia (which at that time included what is now West Virginia) chartered a private company to build a bridge across the Ohio River. The state of Pennsylvania subsequently sued the company directly in the Supreme Court under the Court's original jurisdiction, arguing that the bridge would interfere with navigation on the river and seeking an injunction requiring that the bridge either be removed or elevated. The Court granted the requested injunction, concluding that the bridge was "an obstruction and nuisance." Pennsylvania v. Wheeling & Belmont Bridge Co., 54 U.S. 518, 626–27 (1852) (*Wheeling Bridge I*). Congress subsequently enacted a statute declaring the bridge to be a "lawful structure" and designating it as a "post road" for the passage of mail. Congress further stated that the bridge could be maintained at its present elevation "anything in the law or laws of the United States to the contrary notwithstanding." About two years later, the bridge was blown down in a storm, and the company began to rebuild it to its prior height. Pennsylvania returned to the Supreme Court, seeking to have the company held in contempt for violating the Court's injunction.

The Supreme Court denied the contempt motion and dissolved the injunction it had issued in *Wheeling Bridge I*. See Pennsylvania v. Wheeling & Belmont Bridge Co., 59 U.S. (18 How.) 421 (1856) (*Wheeling Bridge II*). The Court acknowledged that, "as a general proposition, [it] is certainly not to be denied" that an act of Congress "cannot have the effect and operation to annul the judgment of the court already rendered." Thus, the Court noted that, "if the remedy in this case had been an action at law, and a judgment rendered in favor of the plaintiff for damages, the right to these would have passed beyond the reach of the power of Congress." The Court explained, however, that the injunction at issue here was "executory, a continuing decree" that was based on the violation of a public right of free navigation, and that this public right was no longer being violated now that Congress had approved the bridge. In light of Congress's enactment, said the Court, "[t]here is no longer any interference with the enjoyment of the public right inconsistent with law."

Does this decision mean that Congress has unlimited authority to overturn injunctions issued by Article III courts? What if an injunction is based on the violation of a constitutional right? On the violation of a private property right?

3.   *UNITED STATES V. KLEIN*

During the Civil War, Congress authorized the Treasury Department to seize abandoned property in rebellious states. It also gave individuals the right to petition in the Court of Claims to recover the property or its proceeds if they could show that they had been loyal to the Union during the rebellion.

Union agents subsequently seized 600 bales of cotton belonging to Victor Wilson. Although there was evidence that Wilson had provided support to the Confederacy early in the War, he obtained a pardon pursuant to a proclamation issued by President Lincoln. Wilson died in 1865, and the administrator of his estate, John Klein, filed a petition in the Court of Claims seeking recovery of the proceeds from the Union's sale of the cotton.

In an unrelated but similar case, the Supreme Court held that a presidential pardon constituted sufficient evidence of loyalty during the rebellion, because a person covered by a pardon "is as innocent as if he had never committed the offence." United States v. Padelford, 76 U.S. 531, 542 (1870). Based on that precedent, the Court of Claims held in favor of Klein, awarding him $125,300. The government appealed the case to the Supreme Court. While the appeal was pending, Congress passed a statute that provided that in these property seizure cases a presidential pardon should not be treated as evidence of loyalty. The statute further provided that, when the pardon recited involvement in the rebellion or other acts of disloyalty, the pardon should be treated as "conclusive evidence that such person did take part in, and give aid and comfort to, the late rebellion." The statute also had two jurisdictional provisions. First, it provided that in cases in which a claimant had prevailed in the Court of Claims based on a presidential pardon, "the Supreme Court shall, on appeal, have no further jurisdiction of the cause, and shall dismiss the same for want of jurisdiction." Second, it provided that when proof of disloyalty was shown through the facts recited in a pardon, the jurisdiction of the Court of Claims over the case "shall cease, and the court shall forthwith dismiss the suit of such claimant." Based on this statute, the government sought to have the Supreme Court remand the case back to the Court of Claims with a mandate that the case be dismissed for lack of jurisdiction.

The Supreme Court concluded that the statute was unconstitutional, and it proceeded to affirm the Court of Claims' award in favor of Klein. See United States v. Klein, 80 U.S. (13 Wall.) 128 (1872). The Court first concluded that Klein still owned the property at the time of the pardon:

> We conclude . . . that the title to the proceeds of the property which came to the possession of the government by capture or abandonment . . . was in no case divested out of the original owner. It was for the government itself to determine whether these proceeds should be restored to the owner or not. The promise of restoration of all rights of property decides that question affirmatively as to all persons who availed themselves of the proffered pardon. It was competent for the President to annex to his offer of pardon any conditions or qualifications he should see fit; but after those conditions and qualifications had been satisfied, the pardon and its connected promises took full effect. The restoration of the proceeds became the absolute right of the persons pardoned, on application within two years from the close of the war.

It then considered whether the denial of jurisdiction in the Supreme Court should "be regarded as an exercise of the power of Congress to make 'such

exceptions from the appellate jurisdiction' as should seem to it expedient."
The Court responded:

> [T]he language of the [statute] shows plainly that it does not
> intend to withhold jurisdiction except as a means to an end. Its
> great and controlling purpose is to deny to pardons granted by the
> President the effect which this Court had adjudged them to have.
> [T]he denial of jurisdiction to this Court, as well as the Court of
> Claims, is founded solely on the application of a rule of decision, in
> cases pending, prescribed by Congress. The court has jurisdiction
> of the cause to a given point; but when it ascertains that a certain
> state of things exists, its jurisdiction is to cease and it is required
> to dismiss the cause for want of jurisdiction.

> It seems to us that this is not an exercise of the acknowledged
> power of Congress to make exceptions and prescribe regulations to
> the appellate power.

> The court is required to ascertain the existence of certain facts
> and thereupon to declare that its jurisdiction on appeal has ceased,
> by dismissing the bill. What is this but to prescribe a rule for the
> decision of a cause in a particular way? In the case before us, the
> Court of Claims has rendered judgment for the claimant and an
> appeal has been taken to this Court. We are directed to dismiss the
> appeal, if we find that the judgment must be affirmed, because of a
> pardon granted to the intestate of the claimants. Can we do so with-
> out allowing one party to the controversy to decide it in its own
> favor? Can we do so without allowing that the legislature may pre-
> scribe rules of decision to the judicial department of the govern-
> ment in cases pending before it? We think not. . . .

The Court distinguished *Wheeling Bridge II* on the ground that:

> No arbitrary rule of decision was prescribed in that case, but the
> Court was left to apply its ordinary rules to the new circumstances
> created by the act. In the case before us no new circumstances have
> been created by legislation. But the Court is forbidden to give the
> effect to evidence which, in its own judgment, such evidence should
> have, and is directed to give it an effect precisely contrary.

> We must think that Congress has inadvertently passed the
> limit which separates the legislative from the judicial power. . . .
> Congress has already provided that the Supreme Court shall have
> jurisdiction of the judgments of the Court of Claims on appeal. Can
> it prescribe a rule in conformity with which the Court must deny to
> itself the jurisdiction thus conferred, because and only because its
> decision, in accordance with settled law, must be adverse to the
> government and favorable to the suitor? This question seems to us
> to answer itself.

At this point, the Court shifted ground. It began by observing that "[t]he
rule prescribed is also liable to just exception as impairing the effect of a
pardon, and thus infringing the constitutional power of the executive." It
continued:

It is the intention of the Constitution that each of the great co-ordinate departments of the government—the legislative, the executive, and the judicial—shall be, in its sphere, independent of the others. To the executive alone is intrusted the power of pardon; and it is granted without limit. Pardon includes amnesty. It blots out the offence pardoned and removes all its penal consequences. It may be granted on conditions. In these particular pardons, that no doubt might exist as to their character, restoration of property was expressly pledged, and the pardon was granted on condition that the person who availed himself of it should take and keep a prescribed oath.

Now it is clear that the legislature cannot change the effect of such a pardon any more than the executive can change a law. Yet this is attempted by the provision under consideration. The court is required to receive special pardons as evidence of guilt and to treat them as null and void. It is required to disregard pardons granted by proclamation on condition, though the condition has been fulfilled, and to deny them their legal effect. This certainly impairs the executive authority and directs the court to be instrumental to that end.

Justice Miller, joined by Justice Bradley, dissented. He pointed out that the pardon in *Padelford* occurred *before* the property was seized by the government, whereas Klein's pardon came *after* the seizure. In his view, this made all the difference:

I have not been able to bring my mind to concur in the proposition that, under the act concerning captured and abandoned property, there remains in the former owner, who had given aid and comfort to the rebellion, any interest whatever in the property or its proceeds when it had been sold and paid into the treasury or had been converted to the use of the public under that act. . . . I hold now that as long as the possession or title of property remains in the party, the pardon or the amnesty remits all right in the government to forfeit or confiscate it. But where the property has already been seized and sold, and the proceeds paid into the treasury, and it is clear that the statute contemplates no further proceeding as necessary to divest the right of the former owner, the pardon does not and cannot restore that which has thus completely passed away.

4. QUESTIONS AND COMMENTS ON *KLEIN*

As many scholars have noted, it is difficult to parse the Court's reasoning in *Klein*. In fact, one scholar remarked that "*Klein* is sufficiently impenetrable that calling it opaque is a compliment." Barry Friedman, The History of the Countermajoritarian Difficulty, Part II: Reconstruction's Political Court, 91 Geo. L.J. 1, 34 (2002). Another scholar observed that the vague statements in *Klein* have allowed the decision "to be viewed as nearly all things to all men." Gordon G. Young, Congressional Regulation of Federal Courts' Jurisdiction and Processes: *United States v. Klein* Revisited, 1981

Wis. L. Rev. 1189, 1195. See also Gordon G. Young, *United States v. Klein,* Then and Now, 44 Loy. U. Chi. L.J. 265, 270–71 (2012).

Consider the following theories about the meaning of *Klein*:

"[I]f Congress directs an Article III court to decide a case . . . Article III [places] a limitation on the power of Congress to tell the court *how* to decide it." Henry M. Hart, Jr., The Power of Congress to Limit the Jurisdiction of Federal Courts: An Exercise in Dialectic, 66 Harv. L. Rev. 1362, 1373 (1953).

"The particular holding in *Klein* prohibits Congress from using its jurisdictional powers to manipulate federal courts so as to reach decisions which, if addressed in terms of substantive law, would be forbidden by the Constitution." Gordon G. Young, Congressional Regulation of Federal Courts' Jurisdiction and Processes: *United States v. Klein* Revisited, 1981 Wis. L. Rev. 1189, 1260.

"Congress may withhold jurisdiction. But it may not choose how much of the 'whole supreme law' an Article III court may apply to a case it has told the court to decide. Nor may it tell a court how to interpret that law. Nor, at the point when the court's constitutionally mandated choice of law and independent judgment are about to generate a decision and relief, may Congress pull the jurisdictional plug." James S. Liebman and William F. Ryan, "Some Effectual Power": The Quantity and Quality of Decisionmaking Required of Article III Courts, 98 Colum. L. Rev. 696, 822 (1998).

"The judiciary will not allow itself to be made to speak and act against its own best judgment on matters within its competence which have great consequence for our political community." Lawrence G. Sager, *Klein*'s First Principle: A Proposed Solution, 86 Geo. L.J. 2525, 2529 (1998).

"[W]hatever the breadth of Congress's power to regulate federal court jurisdiction, it may not exercise that power in a way that requires a federal court to act unconstitutionally." Daniel J. Meltzer, Congress, Courts, and Constitutional Remedies, 86 Geo. L.J. 2537, 2549 (1998).

"[T]he judiciary has the constitutional power and obligation to assure that Congress has not deceived the electorate as to the manner in which its legislation actually alters the preexisting legal, political, social, or economic topography." Martin H. Redish and Christopher R. Pudelski, Legislative Deception, Separation of Powers, and the Democratic Process: Harnessing the Political Theory of *United States v. Klein*, 100 Nw. U. L. Rev. 437, 438–39 (2006).

"[T]hree core principles emerge [from *Klein*]: (1) Congress cannot dictate to courts the outcome of particular litigation or command how courts should resolve particular legal and factual questions in a case; (2) Congress cannot compel courts to speak a 'constitutional untruth' by dictating how to understand and apply the Constitution where courts' independent judgment compels a different understanding or conclusion; and (3) Congress cannot enact legislation depriving individuals of their constitutional rights." Howard M. Wasserman, The Irrepressible Myth of *Klein*, 79 U. Cin. L. Rev. 53, 56 (2010).

Do these theories exhaust the possible meanings of *Klein*? Is *Klein*, in the end, nothing more or less than a reaffirmation of the unremarkable principle derived from *Marbury* that Congress may not regulate federal court jurisdiction in a way that causes a court to act unconstitutionally? Note that the government asked the Supreme Court to deny its own jurisdiction, but at the same time remand to the Court of Claims with a direction that it dismiss the case too. Could the Court have set aside the Court of Claims judgment without examining the merits and, in effect, resolving the case in an unconstitutional manner?

5.   *UNITED STATES V. SIOUX NATION*

In 1868, the United States entered into a treaty with the Sioux Nation tribes granting them territory in South Dakota as a reservation, including the Black Hills. In 1877, after gold was discovered in the Black Hills, Congress enacted a law removing the Black Hills from the territory of the reservation. In 1923, the Sioux Nation tribes petitioned the Court of Claims, arguing that the Black Hills had been taken from them without just compensation, in violation of the Fifth Amendment. The Court of Claims eventually dismissed this claim in 1942. Some years later, when the Sioux Nation tribes attempted to resubmit their takings claim, the Court of Claims held that it was barred by res judicata. In 1978, Congress directed the Court of Claims to consider the claim without regard to the defense of res judicata, and, acting pursuant to that statute, the Court of Claims held in favor of the tribes.

The Supreme Court affirmed, concluding that Congress's waiver of res judicata did not violate the doctrine of separation of powers. See United States v. Sioux Nation, 448 U.S. 371 (1980). The Court relied on a line of precedent, starting with Cherokee Nation v. United States, 270 U.S. 476 (1926), that stood for the proposition that "Congress has the power to waive the res judicata effect of a prior judgment entered in the Government's favor on a claim against the United States." The Court also distinguished *Klein* as follows:

> First, of obvious importance to the *Klein* holding was the fact that Congress was attempting to decide the controversy at issue in the Government's own favor. Thus, Congress's action could not be grounded upon its broad power to recognize and pay the Nation's debts. Second, and even more important, the proviso at issue in *Klein* had attempted "to prescribe a rule for the decision of a cause in a particular way." 80 U.S. at 146. The amendment at issue in the present case, however, like the Special Act at issue in *Cherokee Nation*, waived the defense of res judicata so that a legal claim could be resolved on the merits. Congress made no effort in either instance to control the Court of Claims' ultimate decision of that claim.

Consider these distinctions of *Klein* when reviewing the questions about *Plaut* in Note 7 below.

6.   *ROBERTSON V. SEATTLE AUDUBON SOCIETY*

Various groups brought lawsuits challenging the way in which the U.S. Forest Service was managing timber harvesting in the Pacific Northwest, with some groups (such as the Seattle Audubon Society) arguing that the Forest Service's approach provided too little protection to the spotted owl, and other groups (such as the Washington Contract Loggers Association) arguing that the approach provided too much protection. Seattle Audubon alleged violations of several federal statutes—the Migratory Bird Treaty Act, the National Environmental Policy Act, and the National Forest Management Act. In response to this litigation, Congress enacted the Northwest Timber Compromise, a statute that regulated timber harvesting in certain forests known to contain spotted owls. Subsection (b)(6)(A) of the Compromise provided that the regulations in the Compromise were "adequate consideration for the purpose of meeting the statutory requirements that are the basis for the consolidated cases captioned Seattle Audubon Society et al. v. F. Dale Robertson, Civil No. 89–160 and Washington Contract Loggers Assoc. et al. v. F. Dale Robertson, Civil No. 89–99 (order granting preliminary injunction) and the case Portland Audubon Society et al., v. Manuel Lujan, Jr., Civil No. 87–1160–FR."

The Seattle Audubon argued that subsection (b)(6)(A) violated *Klein* because it directed particular results in pending cases, and the U.S. Court of Appeals for the Ninth Circuit agreed. The Supreme Court reversed, reasoning that subsection (b)(6)(A) "compelled changes in law, not findings or results under old law." Robertson v. Seattle Audubon Society, 503 U.S. 429, 438 (1992). Although subsection (b)(6)(A) referred to specific cases, the Court concluded that these references were made in order to identify the statutory provisions being modified. As a result, explained the Court, "[t]o the extent that subsection (b)(6)(A) affected the adjudication of the cases, it did so by effectively modifying the provisions at issue in those cases." The Court concluded by stating:

> We have no occasion to address any broad question of Article III jurisprudence. The Court of Appeals held that subsection (b)(6)(A) was unconstitutional under *Klein* because it directed decisions in pending cases without amending any law. Because we conclude that subsection (b)(6)(A) *did* amend applicable law, we need not consider whether this reading of *Klein* is correct.

How is this case different from *Klein*? Why wasn't *Klein* also a case of amending applicable law? Is the only difference that in *Klein* Congress lacked the constitutional authority to make the amendment?

7.   QUESTIONS AND COMMENTS ON *PLAUT*

What was the specific constitutional problem in *Plaut*? To what extent were the decisions in *Hayburn's Case* and *Klein* relevant to the Court's analysis? How is *Plaut* distinguishable from *Wheeling Bridge II*? The Court in *Plaut* acknowledges that Congress has the authority to change the law that applies to a case while the case is pending, even while the case is pending on appeal after a judgment in the district court. Why is that sort of change allowed, but not the one in *Plaut*? Does the Court's holding deprive Congress of needed flexibility in remedying inequities, as argued by the dissent?

Consider Rule 60(b) of the Federal Rules of Civil Procedure, which provides:

> On motion and just terms, the court may relieve a party or its legal representative from a final judgment, order, or proceeding for the following reasons:
>
> > (1) mistake, inadvertence, surprise, or excusable neglect;
> >
> > (2) newly discovered evidence that, with reasonable diligence, could not have been discovered in time to move for a new trial under Rule 59(b);
> >
> > (3) fraud (whether previously called intrinsic or extrinsic), misrepresentation, or misconduct by an opposing party;
> >
> > (4) the judgment is void;
> >
> > (5) the judgment has been satisfied, released, or discharged; it is based on an earlier judgment that has been reversed or vacated; or applying it prospectively is no longer equitable; or
> >
> > (6) any other reason that justifies relief.

A motion under Rule 60(b) "must be made within a reasonable time—and for reasons (1), (2), and (3) no more than a year after the entry of the judgment or order or the date of the proceeding." Why doesn't this rule offend the principle of finality applied by the Court in *Plaut*? Because it is discretionary with the court? Is the dissent correct in arguing that "Congress surely could add to Rule 60(b) certain instances in which courts *must* grant relief from final judgments if they make particular findings—for example, a finding that a member of the jury accepted a bribe from the prevailing party"?

The majority in *Plaut* states that "the doctrine of separation of powers is a *structural safeguard* rather than a remedy to be applied only when specific harm, or risk of specific harm, can be identified." How does this conception of separation of powers differ from the one suggested by the concurrence and the dissent?

8.   STATUTORY RETROACTIVITY

At the backdrop of *Plaut* are more general issues concerning statutory retroactivity. As the Supreme Court has explained, a number of constitutional provisions limit statutory retroactivity:

> The Ex Post Facto Clause flatly prohibits retroactive application of penal legislation. Article I, § 10, cl. 1, prohibits States from passing another type of retroactive legislation, laws "impairing the Obligation of Contracts." The Fifth Amendment's Takings Clause prevents the Legislature (and other government actors) from depriving private persons of vested property rights except for a

"public use" and upon payment of "just compensation." The prohibitions on "Bills of Attainder" in Art. I, §§ 9–10, prohibit legislatures from singling out disfavored persons and meting out summary punishment for past conduct. The Due Process Clause also protects the interests in fair notice and repose that may be compromised by retroactive legislation. . . .

Landgraf v. USI Film Products, 511 U.S. 244, 266 (1994).

These constitutional limits are strongest with respect to criminal legislation. In the civil area, constitutional restrictions on retroactive legislation have been viewed as less robust, especially since the New Deal. In determining whether it is constitutional to apply a civil statute retroactively, courts will balance the public and private interests and will consider, among other things, whether retroactive application of the statute would interfere with settled expectations or reasonable reliance interests. Even when constitutional limits are not implicated, however, courts will presume that statutes do not operate retroactively, and thus will require that Congress "first make its intention clear" before a statute will be applied to conduct occurring prior to its enactment. *Landgraf*, 511 U.S. at 268. This presumption only applies, however, if the law "attaches new legal consequences to events completed before its enactment," id. at 269–70, and thus will not necessarily apply to jurisdictional and procedural changes.

Because the majority in *Plaut* found that the statute there violated the separation of powers, it did not address whether the statute was consistent with due process. Justice Stevens, in footnote 2 of his dissent, argued that the statute did not violate due process. Is his reasoning persuasive? Note that the majority in *Plaut* acknowledges that a statute of limitations "can be extended, without violating the Due Process Clause, after the cause of the action arose and even after the statute itself has expired." See also Chase Securities Corp. v. Donaldson, 325 U.S. 304, 316 (1945) ("[C]ertainly it cannot be said that lifting the bar of a statute of limitation so as to restore a remedy lost through mere lapse of time is per se an offense against the Fourteenth Amendment."). For additional discussion of statutory retroactivity, with an emphasis on the historic distinction between public and private rights, see Ann Woolhandler, Public Rights, Private Rights, and Statutory Retroactivity, 94 Geo. L.J. 1015 (2006).

9.   QUESTIONS AND COMMENTS ON *MILLER*

In what ways is *Miller* distinguishable from *Plaut*? The Court in *Miller* reasons that Congress in the Prison Litigation Reform Act (PLRA) was simply changing applicable law, similar to what Congress had done in *Robertson*. But wasn't the applicable law in *Miller* the Eighth Amendment prohibition against cruel and unusual punishments (as applied to the states through the Due Process Clause of the Fourteenth Amendment)? If so, was Congress in effect amending the Constitution? Under the PLRA, prospective relief may be continued if the court finds that the relief "remains necessary to correct a current and ongoing violation of the Federal right, extends no further than necessary to correct the violation of the Federal right, and that the prospective relief is narrowly drawn and the least intrusive means necessary to correct the violation." Does this allowance remove the concern about congressional amendment of the Constitution?

The Court in *Miller* leaves open the question whether the time limit on judicial decisionmaking associated with the automatic stay provision in the PLRA might violate due process under certain circumstances. Could such a time limit also raise separation of powers concerns, as argued by Justice Souter in his partial dissent? For a discussion of constitutional issues raised by time limits on judicial decisionmaking, see William F. Ryan, Rush to Judgment: A Constitutional Analysis of Time Limits on Judicial Decisions, 77 B.U. L. Rev. 761 (1997).

10. *BANK MARKAZI V. PETERSON*

The Foreign Sovereign Immunities Act, first enacted in 1976, regulates the immunity that foreign governments receive when sued in U.S. courts. Starting in 1996, Congress limited this immunity for certain suits brought against nations determined by the executive branch to be "state sponsors of terrorism." Relying on this exception to immunity, numerous plaintiffs obtained damage awards against Iran, which had been designated a state sponsor of terrorism. The plaintiffs subsequently sought to execute their judgments against Iranian state-owned property in the United States. In litigation over this issue involving Bank Markazi (the Central Bank of Iran), there was a dispute over the extent to which certain "blocked assets" of Iran (i.e., assets frozen by the executive branch) were subject to execution under federal law.

While the case was pending in a federal district court, Congress enacted 22 U.S.C. § 8772, providing that the assets at issue in that particular case, which the statute referred to by name, were subject to execution, as long as certain findings were made. The district court applied § 8772 and held that the assets should be turned over to the plaintiffs, and the court of appeals affirmed. Invoking *United States v. Klein*, Bank Markazi argued that § 8772 violated the separation of powers "by compelling the courts to reach a predetermined result in this case." In Bank Markazi v. Peterson, 578 U.S. ___, 136 S.Ct. 1310 (2016), the Supreme Court disagreed, with Justice Ginsburg writing for a six-to-two majority.

The Court construed § 8772 as having "changed the law by establishing new substantive standards, entrusting to the District Court application of those standards to the facts (contested or uncontested) found by the court." The Court explained that "Congress . . . may amend the law and make the change applicable to pending cases, even when the amendment is outcome determinative." "Any lingering doubts on that score," said the Court, "have been dispelled by *Robertson* and *Plaut*." Nor did it matter that Congress had referred to a pending case in the statute. Something similar had occurred in *Robertson*, the Court observed, and the Court also noted that it, and a number of lower courts, had "upheld as a valid exercise of Congress' legislative power diverse laws that governed one or a very small number of specific subjects." The Court denied that § 8772 was relevant to only one case, noting that "it covers a category of postjudgment execution claims filed by numerous plaintiffs." Finally, the Court emphasized the foreign affairs context of the case, "a realm that warrants respectful review by courts."

Chief Justice Roberts dissented and was joined by Justice Sotomayor. Roberts argued that in § 8772 Congress had changed the law simply to ensure that particular plaintiffs won a particular case, an action he contended improperly "assumes the role of the judge." He also argued that § 8772 was unprecedented: "Neither the majority nor respondents have identified another statute that changed the law for a pending case in an outcome-determinative way and explicitly limited its effect to particular judicial proceedings."

11. THE TERRI SCHIAVO CONTROVERSY

In 1990, Terri Schiavo, a Florida resident, suffered severe brain damage and was subsequently diagnosed as being in a persistent vegetative state. Her husband sought to have her disconnected from a life-sustaining feeding tube, but her parents opposed this action. Years of litigation ensued in the Florida state courts. In 2005, in response to a Florida court order to have the feeding tube removed, Congress enacted the "Act for the Relief of the Parents of Theresa Marie Schiavo," which purported to give a federal district court in Florida jurisdiction to hear "a suit or claim by or on behalf of Theresa Marie Schiavo for the alleged violation of any right of Theresa Marie Schiavo under the Constitution or laws of the United States relating to the withholding or withdrawal of food, fluids, or medical treatment necessary to sustain her life." The Act also purported to confer standing to Schiavo's parents, call for a de novo determination of the issues notwithstanding the state court proceedings, disallow judicial abstention, and remove any requirement the parents might have had to exhaust state remedies. Finally, the Act provided that "[n]othing in this Act shall be construed to create substantive rights not otherwise secured by the Constitution and laws of the United States or of the several States."

Notwithstanding the Act, the district court in Florida and the U.S. Court of Appeals for the Eleventh Circuit allowed the feeding tube to be removed, and Terri Schiavo died. The Eleventh Circuit also denied a motion for rehearing en banc. In concurring in the denial of rehearing, Judge Stanley Birch expressed the view that the Act was unconstitutional. Citing *Klein* and other cases, Judge Birch reasoned that, because the Act "constitute[s] legislative dictation of how a federal court should exercise its judicial functions (known as a 'rule of decision'), [it] invades the province of the judiciary and violates the separation of powers principle." Schiavo ex rel. Schindler v. Schiavo, 404 F.3d 1270, 1273–74 (11th Cir. 2005) (Birch, J., concurring).

Is it constitutionally problematic for Congress to override judicial doctrines such as issue preclusion, abstention, or exhaustion? Even if not normally problematic, does it become problematic if the override is directed at a single specified case? For discussion of these and other constitutional issues associated with the Schiavo controversy, see Michael P. Allen, Congress and Terri Schiavo: A Primer on the American Constitutional Order?, 108 W. Va. L. Rev. 309 (2005); Evan Caminker, *Schiavo* and *Klein*, 22 Const. Comm. 529 (2005); Edward A. Hartnett, Congress Clears Its Throat, 22 Const. Comm.

553 (2005); Steven G. Calabresi, The Terri Schiavo Case: In Defense of the Special Law Enacted by Congress and President Bush, 100 Nw. U. L. Rev. 151 (2006).

SECTION 3. POWER TO EXPAND FEDERAL JURISDICTION

INTRODUCTORY NOTES ON CONGRESSIONAL AUTHORITY TO CONFER FEDERAL QUESTION JURISDICTION ON THE DISTRICT COURTS

1.   ARTICLE III AS A CEILING: *TIDEWATER TRANSFER*

It is generally understood from *Marbury* and other decisions that Congress cannot give the federal courts more jurisdiction than is provided for in Article III. In other words, Article III acts as a ceiling on federal court jurisdiction. Several Supreme Court Justices challenged that proposition, however, in National Mutual Insurance Co. v. Tidewater Transfer Co., 337 U.S. 582 (1949).

Tidewater Transfer involved the constitutionality of the statutory provision (first enacted in 1940 and today codified in 28 U.S.C. § 1332(e)) that allows for diversity jurisdiction in suits between a citizen of a state and a citizen of the District of Columbia. Both the District Court and the Court of Appeals concluded that the statute was unconstitutional because the Article III diversity clause refers to suits "between citizens of different States," and they did not believe that the District of Columbia qualified as a "state" for purposes of this clause. The Supreme Court reversed, but the Justices were sharply divided on the rationale.

Justice Jackson, joined by Justices Black and Burton, agreed with the lower courts that the District of Columbia was not a state for purposes of Article III. In reaching this conclusion, Jackson relied heavily on an 1804 decision by the Court, which had concluded that a citizen of the District of Columbia was not a citizen of a state for purposes of the general diversity provision in the First Judiciary Act. See Hepburn & Dundas v. Ellzey, 6 U.S. (2 Cranch) 445 (1804). Jackson concluded, therefore, that "cases between citizens of the District and those of the states were not included in the catalogue of controversies over which the Congress could give jurisdiction to the federal courts by virtue of Art. III."

But that conclusion, said Jackson, "does not . . . determine that Congress lacks power under *other provisions* of the Constitution to enact this legislation." (Emphasis added.) Jackson noted that Congress has broad constitutional power under Article I of the Constitution to legislate for the District of Columbia and that it also has the power to enact laws that are necessary and proper to carry into execution this authority. While acknowledging that "there are limits to the nature of the duties which Congress may impose on the constitutional courts vested with the federal judicial power," he emphasized the limited nature of the diversity provision in question:

> It does not authorize or require either the district courts or this Court to participate in any legislative, administrative, political, or

other nonjudicial function or to render any advisory opinion. The jurisdiction conferred is limited to controversies of a justiciable nature, the sole feature distinguishing them from countless other controversies handled by the same courts being the fact that one party is a District citizen. Nor has the Congress, by this statute, attempted to usurp any judicial power. It has deliberately chosen the district courts as the appropriate instrumentality through which to exercise part of the judicial functions incidental to exertion of sovereignty over the District and its citizens.

Jackson concluded that "where Congress in the exercise of its powers under Article I finds it necessary to provide those on whom its power is exerted with access to some kind of court or tribunal for determination of controversies that are within the traditional concept of the justiciable, it may open the regular federal courts to them regardless of lack of diversity of citizenship."

In a concurrence, Justice Rutledge, joined by Justice Murphy, disagreed with Jackson that Congress had the authority to give federal courts jurisdiction not provided for in Article III. Among other things, Rutledge expressed the concern that, "[i]f Article III were no longer to serve as the criterion of district court jurisdiction, I should be at a loss to understand what tasks, within the constitutional competence of Congress, might not be assigned to district courts." Instead, Rutledge argued that, notwithstanding the *Hepburn* precedent, Congress could consider the District of Columbia a state for purposes of Article III. He reasoned that a construction of the Article III diversity clause as encompassing suits involving citizens of the District of Columbia is not foreclosed by either the text of the clause or its historical purposes, and is supported by pragmatic and equitable considerations.

There were two dissents, one by Chief Justice Vinson, joined by Justice Douglas, and the other by Justice Frankfurter, joined by Justice Reed. Both dissents argued that the District of Columbia is not a state for purposes of the Article III diversity clause and that Article III establishes the outer limits of permissible federal court jurisdiction.

Note the odd line-up in this decision. Seven Justices rejected the argument that the District of Columbia could be a "state" for purposes of Article III diversity jurisdiction. Six Justices rejected the alternate theory advanced by Justice Jackson, namely that Congress could assign to the federal courts suits involving citizens of the District of Columbia despite the absence of diversity. But the two Justices who lost on the first issue and the three Justices who lost on the second combined to make a five-Justice majority to uphold the constitutionality of diversity jurisdiction for District of Columbia citizens—even though decisive majorities had rejected both theories on which that result could be sustained. To this day, the fractured holding in *Tidewater Transfer* provides the basis on which citizens of the District of Columbia can be parties to diversity suits in federal courts.

Although the result survives, Justice Jackson's reasoning has been widely criticized. Most observers think it odd that cases not within any provision in Article III could be heard by the federal courts. The traditional view of the matter is that Article III, not Article I, provides the subject matter limitations on suits in a federal court. Moreover, it seems inconsistent to think, as Jackson did, that Article III limits federal courts to the decision of "cases or controversies" but that its subject matter limits can at least in some cases be exceeded.[a]

2. FEDERAL QUESTION JURISDICTION

Assuming that (*Tidewater* aside) Congress may not give the federal courts more jurisdiction than is provided for by Article III, the next question is how expansively the language of Article III can be read. The focus of the following materials is on the Article III "arising under" or "federal question" provision. This is the context in which the problem has most often arisen.

The "federal question" language of Article III[b] and the corresponding language in the general federal question statute[c] are nearly identical. It is settled, however, that the two provisions have different meanings. The constitutional language, augmented by the general powers of Congress and by the necessary and proper clause, confers a broad authority on the Congress to use the federal district courts to decide disputes involving federal policy. The statutory language has been construed far more narrowly. The meaning of the statute is postponed to Chapter V. The concern here is with congressional power and the outer limits of Article III.

3. *OSBORN V. BANK OF THE UNITED STATES*

The place to begin is Chief Justice Marshall's opinion in Osborn v. Bank of the United States, 22 U.S. (9 Wheat.) 738 (1824). Congress created the second Bank of the United States in 1816. In McCulloch v. Maryland, 17 U.S. (4 Wheat.) 316 (1819), the Supreme Court upheld the power of Congress to establish the bank and denied the power of the states to tax it. But Ohio did not give in easily. It assessed an annual tax of $50,000 on each office of the bank. After the federal Circuit Court enjoined collection of the tax, a state agent broke into the bank and took more than $120,000, most of which was given to the state treasurer. When the federal court ordered the money returned, the defendants appealed to the Supreme Court, claiming that the Circuit Court lacked jurisdiction.

At the time, there was no general federal question statute, and the parties lacked diversity of citizenship. The statute on which the bank relied for jurisdiction provided that the bank was "able and capable" to "sue and be sued, plead and be pleaded, answer and be answered, defend and be defended, in all state courts having competent jurisdiction, and in any circuit court of the United States." The defendants argued that this statute merely

---

[a] For a defense of Justice Jackson's position in *Tidewater*, and an argument that "the Supreme Court has shown no more enthusiasm for enforcing the enumeration of judicial powers in Article III, Section 2 than it has for policing the enumeration of legislative powers in Article I," see Gil Seinfeld, Article I, Article III, and the Limits of Enumeration, 108 Mich. L. Rev. 1389, 1391 (2010).

[b] "Cases, in Law and Equity, arising under this Constitution, the Laws of the United States, and Treaties made, or which shall be made, under their Authority."

[c] 28 U.S.C. § 1331: "The district courts shall have original jurisdiction of all civil actions arising under the Constitution, laws, or treaties of the United States."

conferred capacity to sue, but the Supreme Court ruled that it also established jurisdiction in the circuit courts over *any* suit involving the Bank of the United States.

Chief Justice Marshall began:

> In support of [jurisdiction], it is said, that the legislative, executive and judicial powers of every well-constructed government, are co-extensive with each other; that is, they are potentially co-extensive. The executive department may constitutionally execute every law which the legislature may constitutionally make, and the judicial department may receive from the legislature the power of construing every such law. All governments which are not extremely defective in their organization, must possess, within themselves, the means of expounding, as well as enforcing, their own laws. If we examine the Constitution of the United States, we find that its framers kept this great political principle in view. [Article III] enables the judicial department to receive jurisdiction to the full extent of the Constitution, laws, and treaties of the United States, when any question respecting them shall assume such a form that the judicial power is capable of acting on it. That power is capable of acting only when the subject is submitted to it by a party who asserts his rights in the form prescribed by law. It then becomes a case, and the Constitution declares, that the judicial power shall extend to all cases arising under the Constitution, laws and treaties of the United States.

Marshall rejected the argument that a case may not be heard in federal court if it presents questions "which depend upon the general principles of the law, not on any act of Congress":

> A cause may depend on several questions of fact and law. Some of these may depend on the construction of a law of the United States; others on principles unconnected with that law. If it be a sufficient foundation for jurisdiction, that the title or right set up by the party, may be defeated by one construction of the Constitution or law of the United States, and sustained by the opposite construction, provided the facts necessary to support the action be made out, then all the other questions must be decided as incidental to this, which gives that jurisdiction. . . . We think, then, that when a question to which the judicial power of the union is extended by the constitution, forms an ingredient of the original cause, it is in the power of Congress to give the circuit courts jurisdiction of that cause, although other questions of fact or of law may be involved in it.

Marshall concluded that in every case brought by the bank a series of federal questions necessarily would be involved—its capacity to sue as an entity, its capacity to engage in the behavior on which the suit is based, etc. These questions "exist in every possible case" brought by the bank. Even though the bank's capacity to sue was well settled and not disputed, it remained "an original ingredient in every cause." The right of the plaintiff to sue, he continued, "cannot depend on the defence which the defendant may choose to set up." The plaintiff's right to sue necessarily presented a federal question, whether or not the defendant chose to contest the issue.

Finally, Marshall answered the dissent's argument that the same reasoning could give every naturalized citizen the general right to sue in federal court, even though the suit involved state law only and even though diversity of citizenship was lacking:

> A naturalized citizen is, indeed, made a citizen under an act of Congress, but the act does not proceed to give, to regulate, or to prescribe his capacities. . . . The Constitution then takes him up, and, among other rights, extends to him the capacity of suing in the courts of the United States, precisely under the same circumstances under which a native might sue. . . . There is, then, no resemblance between the act incorporating the bank, and the general naturalization law.

Justice Johnson dissented. He argued that the federal courts should not assume jurisdiction "on a mere hypothesis" and claimed that cases do not arise under federal law until such a question "actually arise[s]." Johnson argued the case of the naturalized citizen. He was also troubled by another hypothetical. Suppose Congress passed a tax voiding all contracts not written upon stamped paper and giving federal courts jurisdiction over all contracts so written. Johnson thought that such a case could not be distinguished from the theory on which Marshall relied and that it would represent an unconstitutional effort to expand Article III jurisdiction.

4. THE CONCEPT OF PROTECTIVE JURISDICTION

Marshall's theory of decision in *Osborn* reached far beyond the circumstances of the case. On the facts of *Osborn,* Marshall could have said merely that Congress had the power to confer jurisdiction on the circuit courts to enforce the bank's federal right not to be taxed. But the theory Marshall actually used justified federal jurisdiction over *any* suit brought by the bank, including actions based entirely on state law. Indeed, in a companion case, Bank of United States v. Planters' Bank of Georgia, 22 U.S. (9 Wheat.) 904 (1824), the Court upheld a suit by the bank in federal court to collect on negotiable notes issued by a state bank.

The constitutional question raised by these cases is whether Congress can authorize "arising under" jurisdiction in the absence of a substantive federal claim. This is called "protective" jurisdiction: Congress gives federal courts jurisdiction over state-law claims asserted by non-diverse plaintiffs who need the "protection" of a federal forum. Such protection might be necessary if the neutrality of state courts is suspect, or because of procedural advantages in federal court, or for any other reason that Congress thinks good and sufficient. Of course, Congress can always confer federal-court jurisdiction where it has validly created a federal claim. The fighting issue is whether, where Congress has the power to create federal substantive rights but does not do so, it may exercise the (lesser?) power of permitting a state-law suit to be brought in federal court.

The argument against protective jurisdiction begins with the language of Article III, which specifies various forms of party-based jurisdiction. Diversity is an example. Arguably, the cases where Congress may use the federal courts to protect particular parties from the hazards or disadvantages of state courts are limited to those specified in Article III. Those who believe that protective jurisdiction is beyond the power of Congress believe that the diversity clauses and the other party-based provisions of Article III exhaust the capacity of Congress to provide for the protection of litigants who are not actually asserting federal rights.

In his *Osborn* dissent, Justice Johnson recognized the practicalities of the situation:

> I have very little doubt, that the public mind will be easily reconciled to the decision of the Court here rendered: for, whether necessary or unnecessary, originally, a state of things has grown up, in some of the states, which renders all the protection necessary, that the general government can give to this bank. The policy of the decision is obvious, that is, if the bank is to be sustained; and few will bestow upon its legal correctness, the reflection that it is necessary to test it by the Constitution and laws, under which it is rendered.

Did Marshall, as Johnson implied, sacrifice the Constitution on the altar of expediency? Or is congressional concern over the survival of the bank a constitutionally sufficient reason for providing federal jurisdiction over state-law claims? Could Congress have provided that federal law would govern all the bank's legal relations? If so, should Congress be required to take that step before it can permit suit in federal court? Which solution is the greater intrusion upon the states? The following case and its notes raise these questions in a more modern context.

Textile Workers Union v. Lincoln Mills

Supreme Court of the United States, 1957.
353 U.S. 448.

[Section 301 of the Labor Management Relations Act of 1947 provided:

(a) Suits for violation of contracts between an employer and a labor organization representing employees in an industry affecting commerce as defined in this chapter, or between any such labor organizations, may be brought in any district court of the United States having jurisdiction of the parties, without respect to the amount in controversy or without regard to the citizenship of the parties.

(b) Any labor organization which represents employees in an industry affecting commerce as defined in this chapter and any employer whose activities affect commerce as defined in this chapter shall be bound by the acts of its agents. Any such labor organization may sue or be sued as an entity and in behalf of the employees whom it represents in the courts of the United States. Any money judgment against a labor organization in a district court of the United States shall be enforceable only against the organization as an entity and its assets, and shall not be enforceable against any individual member or his assets.

[The Textile Workers Union entered into a collective bargaining agreement with Lincoln Mills. The agreement contained a no-strike clause and a grievance procedure ending in compulsory arbitration. The union filed several grievances, which were ultimately denied by the employer. When the employer refused to submit the grievances to arbitration, the union sued to compel arbitration. The District Court ordered the employer to comply with the contract, but the Court of Appeals reversed. It held that the District Court had no authority under either state or federal law to order such relief. The Supreme Court granted certiorari.

[In a majority opinion by Justice Douglas, the Court held that § 301(a) authorized the federal courts to develop a body of federal common law to enforce labor contracts.[a] The specific enforcement of arbitration agreements, moreover, was part of the federal common law that the courts were meant to enforce. The Court accordingly reversed the Court of Appeals' judgment.

[Justice Frankfurter dissented. He thought the statute should not be interpreted as directing the federal courts to fashion a body of federal common law out of whole cloth and suggested further that the courts might lack the power to do that, even if Congress so instructed. In his view, therefore, enforcement of the arbitration agreement depended on state law. Frankfurter then turned to the question whether Congress could confer jurisdiction on the federal district courts to hear non-diversity suits turning on questions of state law. The portion of his opinion addressing this issue is reproduced below.]

■ MR. JUSTICE FRANKFURTER, dissenting. . . .

Since I do not agree with the Court's conclusion that federal substantive law is to govern in actions under § 301, I am forced to consider . . . the constitutionality of a grant of jurisdiction to federal courts over contracts that came into being entirely by virtue of state substantive law, a jurisdiction not based on diversity of citizenship, yet one in which a federal court would, as in diversity cases, act in effect merely as another court of the state in which it sits. The scope of allowable federal judicial power that this grant must satisfy is constitutionally described as "Cases, in Law and Equity, arising under this Constitution, the Laws of the United States, and Treaties made, or which shall be made, under their Authority." Art. III, § 2. While interpretive decisions are legion under

---

[a]   One might think that giving courts such broad power would raise problems under the non-delegation doctrine, which generally requires legislative guidance as to the use of delegated powers by administrative agencies. For analysis of whether and how that doctrine should apply to courts, see Alexander Volokh, Judicial Non-Delegation, the Inherent-Powers Corollary, and Federal Common Law, 66 Emory L.J. 1391 (2017).

general statutory grants of jurisdiction strikingly similar to this constitutional wording, it is generally recognized that the full constitutional
power has not been exhausted by these statutes.

Almost without exception, decisions under the general statutory
grants have tested jurisdiction in terms of the presence, as an integral
part of plaintiff's cause of action, of an issue calling for interpretation or
application of federal law. E.g., Gully v. First National Bank, 299 U.S.
109 (1936). Although it has sometimes been suggested that the "cause of
action" must derive from federal law, see American Well Works Co. v.
Layne & Bowler Co., 241 U.S. 257, 260 (1916), it has been found sufficient
that some aspect of federal law is essential to plaintiff's success. Smith v.
Kansas City Title & Trust Co., 255 U.S. 180 (1921). The litigation-provoking problem has been the degree to which federal law must be in the
forefront of the case and not collateral, peripheral or remote.

In a few exceptional cases, arising under special jurisdictional
grants, the criteria by which the prominence of the federal question is
measured against constitutional requirements have been found satisfied
under circumstances suggesting a variant theory of the nature of these
requirements. The first, and the leading case in the field, is Osborn v.
Bank of the United States, 22 U.S. (9 Wheat.) 738 (1824). There, Chief
Justice Marshall sustained federal jurisdiction in a situation—hypothetical in the case before him but presented by the companion case of Bank
of the United States v. Planters' Bank, 22 U.S. (9 Wheat.) 904 (1824)—
involving suit by a federally incorporated bank upon a contract. Despite
the assumption that the cause of action and the interpretation of the contract would be governed by state law, the case was found to "arise under
the laws of the United States" because the propriety and scope of a federally granted authority to enter into contracts and to litigate might well
be challenged. This reasoning was subsequently applied to sustain jurisdiction in actions against federally chartered railroad corporations.
Pacific Railroad Removal Cases, 115 U.S. 1 (1885). The traditional interpretation of this series of cases is that federal jurisdiction under the
"arising" clause of the Constitution, though limited to cases involving potential federal questions, has such flexibility that Congress may confer it
whenever there exists in the background some federal proposition that
might be challenged, despite the remoteness of the likelihood of actual
presentation of such a federal question.[4]

The views expressed in *Osborn* and the *Pacific Railroad Removal
Cases* were severely restricted in constructing general grants of jurisdiction. But the Court later sustained this jurisdictional section of the
Bankruptcy Act of 1893 [§ 23]:

---

[4]   *Osborn* might possibly be limited on the ground that a federal instrumentality, the Bank
of the United States, was involved, see n.5, infra, but such an explanation could not suffice to
narrow the holding in the *Pacific Railroad Removal Cases*.

> The United States district courts shall have jurisdiction of all controversies at law and in equity, as distinguished from proceedings in bankruptcy, between trustees as such and adverse claimants concerning the property acquired or claimed by the trustees, in the same manner and to the same extent only as though bankruptcy proceedings had not been instituted and such controversies had been between the bankrupts and such adverse claimants.

Under this provision the trustee could pursue in a federal court a private cause of action arising under and wholly governed by state law. Schumacher v. Beeler, 293 U.S. 367 (1934); Williams v. Austrian, 331 U.S. 642 (1947). To be sure, the cases did not discuss the basis of jurisdiction. It has been suggested that they merely represent an extension of the approach of the *Osborn* case; the trustee's right to sue might be challenged on obviously federal grounds—absence of bankruptcy or irregularity of the trustee's appointment or of the bankruptcy proceedings. National Mutual Ins. Co. v. Tidewater Transfer Co., 337 U.S. 582, 611–13 (1949) (Rutledge, J., concurring). So viewed, this type of litigation implicates a potential federal question. . . .

With this background, many theories have been proposed to sustain the constitutional validity of § 301. In Textile Workers Union of America v. American Thread Co., 113 F. Supp. 137, 140 (1953), Judge Wyzanski suggested, among other possibilities, that § 301 might be read as containing a direction that controversies affecting interstate commerce should be governed by federal law incorporating state law by reference, and that such controversies would then arise under a valid federal law as required by Article III. Whatever may be said of the assumption regarding the validity of federal jurisdiction under an affirmative declaration by Congress that state law should be applied as federal law by federal courts to contract disputes affecting commerce, we cannot argumentatively legislate for Congress when Congress has failed to legislate. To do so disrespects legislative responsibility and disregards judicial limitations.

Another theory, relying on *Osborn* and the bankruptcy cases, has been proposed [in] Henry Hart and Herbert Wechsler, The Federal Courts and the Federal System 744–47 (1953) [and] Herbert Wechsler, Federal Jurisdiction and the Revision of the Judicial Code, 13 Law & Contemp. Prob. 216, 224–25 (1948). Called "protective jurisdiction," the suggestion is that in any case for which Congress has the constitutional power to prescribe federal rules of decision and thus confer "true" federal question jurisdiction, it may, without so doing, enact a jurisdictional statute, which will provide a federal forum for the application of state statute and decisional law. Analysis of the "protective jurisdiction" theory might also be attempted in terms of the language of Article III—construing "laws" to include jurisdictional statutes where Congress could have legislated substantively in a field. This is but another way of saying that because Congress could have legislated substantively and thereby could give rise to litigation under a statute of the United States, it can provide a federal forum for state-created rights although it chose not to adopt state law as federal law or to originate federal rights.

Surely the truly technical restrictions of Article III are not met or respected by a beguiling phrase that the greater power here must necessarily include the lesser. In the compromise of federal and state interests leading to distribution of jealously guarded judicial power in a federal system, it is obvious that very different considerations apply to cases involving questions of federal law and those turning solely on state law. It may be that the ambiguity of the phrase "arising under the laws of the United States" leaves room for more than traditional theory could accommodate. But, under the theory of "protective jurisdiction," the "arising under" jurisdiction of the federal courts would be vastly extended. For example, every contract or tort arising out of a contract affecting commerce might be a potential cause of action in the federal courts, even though only state law was involved in the decision of the case. At least in *Osborn* and the bankruptcy cases, a substantive federal law was present somewhere in the background. But this theory rests on the supposition that Congress could enact substantive federal law to govern the particular case. It was not held in those cases, nor is it clear, that federal law could be held to govern the transactions of all persons who subsequently become bankrupt, or of all suits of a bank of the United States.

"Protective jurisdiction," once the label is discarded, cannot be justified under any view of the allowable scope to be given to Article III. "Protective jurisdiction" is a misused label for the statute we are here considering. That rubric is properly descriptive of safeguarding some of the indisputable, staple business of the federal courts. It is a radiation of an existing jurisdiction. "Protective jurisdiction" cannot generate an independent source for adjudication outside of the Article III sanctions and what Congress has defined. The theory must have as its sole justification a belief in the inadequacy of state tribunals in determining state law. The Constitution reflects such a belief in the specific situation within which the diversity clause was confined. The intention to remedy such supposed defects was exhausted in this provision of Article III.[5] That this "protective" theory was not adopted by Chief Justice Marshall at a time when conditions might have presented more substantial justification strongly suggests its lack of constitutional merit. Moreover, Congress in its consideration of § 301 nowhere suggested dissatisfaction with the ability of

---

[5]   To be sure, the Court upheld the removal statute for suits or prosecutions commenced in a state court against federal revenue officers on account of any act committed under color of office. Tennessee v. Davis, 100 U.S. 257 (1879). The Court, however, construed the action of Congress in defining the powers of revenue agents as giving them a substantive defense against prosecution under state law for commission of acts "warranted by the federal authority they possess." That put federal law in the forefront as a defense. In any event, the fact that officers of the federal government were parties may be considered sufficient to afford access to the federal forum.

state courts to administer state law properly. Its concern was to provide access to the federal courts for easier enforcement of state-created rights.

Another theory also relies on *Osborn* and the bankruptcy cases as an implicit recognition of the propriety of the exercise of some sort of "protective jurisdiction" by the federal courts. Paul Mishkin, The Federal "Question" in the District Courts, 53 Colum. L. Rev. 157, 184 et seq. (1953). Professor Mishkin tends to view the assertion of such a jurisdiction, in the absence of any exercise of substantive powers, as irreconcilable with the "arising" clause since the case would then arise only under the jurisdictional statute itself, and he is reluctant to find a constitutional basis for the grant of power outside Article III. Professor Mishkin also notes that the only purpose of such a statute would be to insure impartiality to some litigant, an objection inconsistent with Article III's recognition of "protective jurisdiction" only in the specified situation of diverse citizenship. But where Congress has "an articulated and active federal policy regulating a field, the 'arising under' clause of Article III apparently permits the conferring of jurisdiction on the national courts of all cases in the area—including those substantively governed by state law." In such cases, the protection being offered is not to the suitor, as in diversity cases, but to the "congressional legislative program." Thus he supports § 301: "even though the rules governing collective bargaining agreements continue to be state-fashioned nonetheless the mode of their application and enforcement may play a very substantial part in the labor-management relations of interstate industry and commerce—an area in which the national government has labored long and hard."

Insofar as state law governs the case, Professor Mishkin's theory is quite similar to that advanced by Professors Hart and Wechsler and followed by the Court of Appeals for the First Circuit: The substantive power of Congress, although not exercised to govern the particular "case," gives "arising under" jurisdiction to the federal courts despite governing state law. The second "protective jurisdiction" theory has the dubious advantage of limiting incursions on state judicial power to situations in which the state's feelings may have been tempered by early substantive federal invasions.

Professor Mishkin's theory of "protective jurisdiction" may find more constitutional justification if there is not merely an "articulated and active" congressional policy regulating the labor field but also federal rights existing in the interstices of actions under § 301. Therefore, before resting on an interpretation of § 301 that would compel a declaration of unconstitutionality, we must . . . defer to the strong presumption—even as to such technical matters as federal jurisdiction—that Congress legislated in accordance with the Constitution. . . .

The contribution of federal law might consist in postulating the right of a union, despite its amorphous status as an unincorporated association, to enter into binding collective-bargaining contracts with an employer. The federal courts might also give sanction to this right by refusing to comply with any state law that does not admit that collective bargaining may result in an enforceable contract. It is hard to see what serious federal-state conflicts could arise under this view. . . .

Of course, the possibility of a state's law being counter to such a limited federal proposition is hypothetical, and to base an assertion of federal law on such a possibility, one never considered by Congress, is an artifice. And were a state ever to adopt a contrary attitude, its reasons for so doing might be such that Congress would not be willing to disregard them. But these difficulties are inherent in any attempt to expand § 301 substantively to meet constitutional requirements.

Even if this limited federal "right" were read into § 301, a serious constitutional question would still be present. It does elevate the situation to one closely analogous to that presented in *Osborn*.[6] Section 301 would, under this view, imply that a union is to be viewed as a juristic entity for purposes of acquiring contract rights under a collective-bargaining agreement, and that it has the right to enter into such a contract and to sue upon it. This was all that was immediately and expressly involved in the *Osborn* case, although the historical setting was vastly different, and the juristic entity in that case was completely the creature of federal law, one engaged in carrying out essential governmental functions. Most of these special considerations had disappeared, however, at the time and in the circumstances of the decision of the *Pacific Railroad Removal Cases*. There is force in the view that regards the latter as a "sport" and finds that the Court has so viewed it. See Mishkin, 53 Colum. L. Rev. at 160, n.24. The question is whether we should now so consider it and refuse to apply its holding to the present situation.

I believe that we should not extend the precedents of *Osborn* and the *Pacific Railroad Removal Cases* to this case, even though there be some elements of analytical similarity. *Osborn,* the foundation for the *Removal Cases,* appears to have been based on premises that today, viewed in the light of the jurisdictional philosophy of *Gully v. First National Bank* are subject to criticism. The basic premise was that every case in which a federal question might arise must be capable of being commenced in the federal courts, and when so commenced it might, because jurisdiction must be judged at the outset, be concluded there despite the fact that the federal question was never raised. Marshall's holding was undoubtedly influenced by his fear that the bank might suffer hostile treatment in the state courts that could not be remedied by an appeal on an isolated federal question. There is nothing in Article III that affirmatively supports the view that original jurisdiction over cases involving federal questions

---

6   Enunciation of such a requirement could in fact bring federal law somewhat further to the forefront than was true of *Osborn,* the *Pacific Railroad Removal Cases,* or the bankruptcy cases in the few cases where an assertion could be made that state law did not sufficiently recognize collective agreements as contracts. But there appears to be no state that today possesses such a rule. Most and probably all cases arising under § 301—certainly the present ones—would never present such a problem.

must extend to every case in which there is the potentiality of appellate jurisdiction. We also have become familiar with removal procedures that could be adapted to alleviate any remaining fears by providing for removal to a federal court whenever a federal question was raised. In view of these developments, we would not be justified in perpetuating a principle that permits assertion of original federal jurisdiction on the remote possibility of presentation of a federal question. Indeed, Congress, by largely withdrawing the jurisdiction that the *Pacific Railroad Removal Cases* recognized, and this Court, by refusing to perpetuate it under general grants of jurisdiction, see *Gully v. First National Bank,* have already done much to recognize the changed atmosphere.

Analysis of the bankruptcy power also reveals a superficial analogy to § 301. The trustee enforces a cause of action acquired under state law by the bankrupt. Federal law merely provides for the appointment of the trustee, vests the cause of action in him, and confers jurisdiction on the federal courts. Section 301 similarly takes the rights and liabilities which under state law are vested distributively in the individual members of a union and vests them in the union for purposes of actions in federal courts, wherein the unions are authorized to sue and be sued as an entity. While the authority of the trustee depends on the existence of a bankrupt and on the propriety of the proceedings leading to the trustee's appointment, both of which depend on federal law, there are similar federal propositions that may be essential to an action under § 301. Thus, the validity of the contract may in any case be challenged on the ground that the labor organization negotiating it was not the representative of the employees concerned, a question that has been held to be federal, or on the ground that subsequent change in the representative status of the union has affected the continued validity of the agreement. . . . Consequently, were the bankruptcy cases to be viewed as dependent solely on the background existence of federal questions, there would be little analytical basis for distinguishing actions under § 301. But the bankruptcy decisions may be justified by the scope of the bankruptcy power, which may be deemed to sweep within its scope interests analytically outside the "federal question" category, but sufficiently related to the main purpose of bankruptcy to call for comprehensive treatment. Also, although a particular suit may be brought by a trustee in a district other than the one in which the principal proceedings are pending, if all the suits by the trustee, even though in many federal courts, are regarded as one litigation for the collection and apportionment of the bankrupt's property, a particular suit by the trustee, under state law, to recover a specific piece of property might be analogized to the ancillary or pendent jurisdiction cases in which, in the disposition of a cause of action, federal courts may pass on state grounds for recovery that are joined to federal grounds.

If there is in the phrase "arising under the laws of the United States" leeway for expansion of our concepts of jurisdiction, the history of Article III suggests that the area is not great and that it will require the presence of some substantial federal interest, one of greater weight and dignity than questionable doubt concerning the effectiveness of state procedure. The bankruptcy cases might possibly be viewed as such an expansion. But even so, not merely convenient judicial administration but the whole purpose of the congressional legislative program—conservation and equitable distribution of the bankrupt's estate in carrying out the constitutional power over bankruptcy—required the availability of federal jurisdiction to avoid expense and delay. Nothing pertaining to § 301 suggests vesting the federal courts with sweeping power under the commerce clause comparable to that vested in the federal courts under the bankruptcy power.

In the wise distribution of governmental powers, this Court cannot do what a President sometimes does in returning a bill to Congress. We cannot return this provision to Congress and respectfully request that body to face the responsibility placed upon it by the Constitution to define the jurisdiction of the lower courts with some particularity and not to leave these courts at large. Confronted as I am, I regretfully have no choice. For all the reasons elaborated in this dissent, even reading into § 301 the limited federal rights consistent with the purposes of that section, I am impelled to the view that it is unconstitutional in cases such as the present ones where it provides the sole basis for exercise of jurisdiction by the federal courts.

NOTES ON THE CONSTITUTIONALITY OF PROTECTIVE JURISDICTION

1. *VERLINDEN B.V. V. CENTRAL BANK OF NIGERIA*

The Foreign Sovereign Immunities Act of 1976 included what is now 28 U.S.C. § 1330:

> (a) The district courts shall have original jurisdiction without regard to amount in controversy of any nonjury civil action against a foreign state as defined in section 1603(a) of this title as to any claim for relief in personam with respect to which the foreign state is not entitled to immunity either under sections 1605–1607 of this title or under any applicable international agreement.

In Verlinden B.V. v. Central Bank of Nigeria, 461 U.S. 480 (1983), the Court granted certiorari "to consider whether [this statute], by authorizing a foreign plaintiff to sue a foreign state in a United States district court on a non-federal cause of action, violates Article III of the Constitution."

Verlinden was a Dutch corporation which contracted with Nigeria for the delivery of cement. The contract specified that Dutch law would control its interpretation and that disputes would be resolved in a French forum. Verlinden filed suit in federal district court for anticipatory breach of the contract. The defendant was the Nigerian instrumentality responsible for the transaction. The District Court held that § 1330(a) authorized the suit, subject to whether the defendant was entitled to sovereign immunity under the terms of the statute. The court then upheld the defense of sovereign immunity and dismissed the case. The Court of Appeals affirmed on the entirely different ground that § 1330(a) was unconstitutional and that the trial court therefore lacked jurisdiction.

The Supreme Court upheld the statute. It first reviewed the history of the sovereign immunity granted to foreign governments under federal law. An early opinion by Chief Justice Marshall, Schooner Exchange v. McFaddon, 11 U.S. (7 Cranch) 116 (1812), established the basis for almost complete immunity for foreign sovereigns in U.S. courts. Starting in the late 1930s, the courts increasingly deferred to the views of the State Department about whether to grant immunity in particular cases. In 1952, the Department adopted the policy that foreign sovereigns should remain immune for their public acts but would no longer be immune for strictly commercial transactions, and the courts attempted to apply this distinction. At the same time, courts also continued to defer to the case-by-case views of the Department about whether to grant immunity, views that were inevitably influenced by political considerations. This led to inconsistent results and diplomatic pressure.

The Foreign Sovereign Immunities Act was passed to regularize the law in this area. It continued the immunity of foreign governments from suit in state or federal court, except in specified circumstances. Suits that satisfy one of the exceptions (including suits by foreign plaintiffs) can be brought either in state or federal court, but the defendant may remove any state-court action to federal court. The House Report stated that the removal authority was granted "in view of the political sensitivity of actions against foreign states and the importance of developing a uniform body of law in this area." This provision gave rise to the constitutional question, which a unanimous Court answered as follows:

> This Court's cases firmly establish that Congress may not expand the jurisdiction of the federal courts beyond the bounds established by the Constitution. Within Article III of the Constitution, we find two sources authorizing the grant of jurisdiction in the Foreign Sovereign Immunities Act: the diversity clause and the "arising under" clause.[17] The diversity clause, which provides that the judicial power extends to controversies between "a State, or the Citizens thereof, and foreign States," covers actions by citizens of states. Yet diversity jurisdiction is not sufficiently broad to support a grant of jurisdiction over actions by foreign plaintiffs. . . . We conclude, however, that the "arising under" clause of Article III provides an appropriate basis for the statutory grant of subject matter jurisdiction to actions by foreign plaintiffs under the act.

> The controlling decision on the scope of Article III "arising under" jurisdiction is Chief Justice Marshall's opinion for the Court in *Osborn v. Bank of the United States. In Osborn,* the Court upheld

---

[17] In view of our conclusion that proper actions by foreign plaintiffs under the Foreign Sovereign Immunities Act are within Article III "arising under" jurisdiction, we need not consider petitioner's alternative argument that the act is constitutional as an aspect of so-called "protective jurisdiction."

the constitutionality of a statute that granted the Bank of the United States the right to sue in federal court on causes of action based upon state law. . . . *Osborn* . . . reflects a broad conception of "arising under" jurisdiction, according to which Congress may confer on the federal courts jurisdiction over any case or controversy that might call for the application of federal law. The breadth of that conclusion has been questioned. It has been observed that, taken at its broadest, *Osborn* might be read as permitting "assertion of original federal jurisdiction on the remote possibility of presentation of a federal question," [citing Frankfurter's dissent in *Lincoln Mills*]. We need not now resolve that issue or decide the precise boundaries of Article III jurisdiction, however, since the present case does not involve a mere speculative possibility that a federal question may arise at some point in the proceeding. Rather, a suit against a foreign state under this act necessarily raises questions of substantive federal law at the very outset, and hence clearly "arises under" federal law, as that term is used in Article III.

By reason of its authority over foreign commerce and foreign relations, Congress has the undisputed power to decide, as a matter of federal law, whether and under what circumstances foreign nations should be amenable to suit in the United States. Actions against foreign sovereigns in our courts raise sensitive issues concerning the foreign relations of the United States, and the primacy of federal concerns is evident.

To promote these federal interests, Congress exercised its Article I powers by enacting a statute comprehensively regulating the amenability of foreign nations to suit in the United States. The statute must be applied by the district courts in every action against a foreign sovereign, since subject matter jurisdiction in any such action depends on the existence of one of the specified exceptions to foreign sovereign immunity. At the threshold of every action, therefore, the court must satisfy itself that one of the exceptions applies—and in doing so it must apply the detailed federal law standards set forth in the act. Accordingly, an action against a foreign sovereign arises under federal law, for purposes of Article III jurisdiction.

The Court responded to two arguments found persuasive by the Court of Appeals. The first was that decisions interpreting § 1331 required that the federal issue appear on the face of the plaintiff's well-pleaded complaint, whereas the issue of sovereign immunity would enter the case by way of defense. The Supreme Court responded that, "[a]lthough the language of § 1331 parallels that of the 'arising under' clause of Article III, this Court never has held that statutory 'arising under' jurisdiction is identical to Article III 'arising under' jurisdiction. Quite the contrary is true. . . . Article III 'arising under' jurisdiction is broader than federal question jurisdiction under § 1331. . . ."

The second argument accepted by the Court of Appeals was that a jurisdictional provision could not itself provide the basis for "arising under" jurisdiction—that this kind of bootstrapping should not be permitted. The Supreme Court rejected this argument on the ground that the Sovereign Immunities Act was more than a jurisdictional provision:

> The act . . . does not merely concern access to the federal courts. Rather, it governs the types of actions for which foreign sovereigns may be held liable in a court in the United States, federal or state. The act codifies the standards governing foreign sovereign immunity as an aspect of substantive federal law, and applying those standards will generally require interpretation of numerous points of federal law. . . . That the inquiry into foreign sovereign immunity is labeled under the act as a matter of jurisdiction does not affect the constitutionality of Congress's action in granting the federal courts jurisdiction over cases calling for application of this comprehensive regulatory statute.

> Congress, pursuant to its unquestioned Article I powers, has enacted a broad statutory framework governing assertions of foreign sovereign immunity. In so doing, Congress deliberately sought to channel cases against foreign sovereigns away from the state courts and into federal courts, thereby reducing the potential for a multiplicity of conflicting results among the courts of 50 states. The resulting jurisdictional grant is within the bounds of Article III, since every action against a foreign sovereign necessarily involves application of a body of substantive federal law, and accordingly "arises under" federal law, within the meaning of Article III.[a]

2.	QUESTIONS AND COMMENTS ON *LINCOLN MILLS* AND *VERLINDEN*

Did the *Verlinden* Court, despite the disclaimer in footnote 17, actually sustain protective jurisdiction? Suppose the foreign sovereign conceded that it was not entitled to immunity and the merits of the case involved no propositions of federal law. Would that matter? Since one cannot tell until the defendant has filed an answer whether sovereign immunity will be raised as a defense, is the Court upholding the Foreign Sovereign Immunities Act because of the *possibility* that federal questions will arise? Does it matter that the FSIA regulates even a waiver of immunity, and that courts have an obligation to ensure that there is an applicable exception to immunity (including potentially a waiver) in order to have subject matter jurisdiction under the FSIA? Are *Osborn, Lincoln Mills* (as Frankfurter saw the statute), and *Verlinden* based on the likelihood that federal questions actually will arise? Or is the critical question the nature of the interests involved, that is, whether the foreign relations issues in *Verlinden* and the survival of the bank in *Osborn* are more important than the policies involved in Frankfurter's version of *Lincoln Mills*?

---

[a]	In Argentine Republic v. Amerada Hess Shipping Corp., 488 U.S. 428 (1989), the Court held that § 1330 provides the exclusive basis for federal court jurisdiction over actions against a foreign state in spite of other possible bases on which such actions might be founded.—[Footnote by eds.]

3. MODERN VARIATIONS: CONSUMER PROTECTION, NUCLEAR POWER, AND THE RED CROSS

Consider a bill, introduced in 1969, to give the federal district courts jurisdiction, regardless of the amount in controversy and regardless of the citizenship of the parties, over civil class actions brought by consumers to redress "the violations of consumers' rights under State or Federal statutory or decisional law." Would such a statute be constitutional? A subsequent version of the bill responded to constitutional concerns by explicitly incorporating as federal law any state statutes or decisions relating to consumers' rights. Would that ploy help? In fact, neither version of the bill was enacted, so the courts never confronted the matter.

For an enacted statute raising similar problems, see 42 U.S.C. §§ 2210, 2014. Section 2210(2) provides:

> With respect to any public liability action arising out of or resulting from a nuclear incident, the United States district court in the district where the nuclear incident takes place, or in the case of a nuclear incident taking place outside the United States, the United States District Court for the District of Columbia, shall have original jurisdiction without regard to the citizenship of any party or the amount in controversy.

Section 2014(hh) adds:

> The term "public liability action," as used in section 2210 of this title, means any suit asserting public liability. A public liability action shall be deemed to be an action arising under section 2210 of this title, and the substantive rules for decision in such action shall be derived from the law of the State in which the nuclear incident involved occurs, unless such law is inconsistent with the provisions of such section.

Are these provisions constitutional?

Congress enacted the Air Transportation Safety and System Stabilization Act, Pub. Law No. 107–42, 115 Stat. 230, on September 22, 2001. Section 408(b) provides:

> (b) Federal Cause of Action.—
>
> (1) Availability of Action.—There shall exist a Federal cause of action for damages arising out of the hijacking and subsequent crashes of American Airlines flights 11 and 77, and United Airlines flights 93 and 175, on September 11, 2001. [T]his cause of action shall be the exclusive remedy for damages arising out of the hijacking and subsequent crashes of such flights.
>
> (2) Substantive Law.—The substantive law for decision in any such suit shall be derived from the law, including choice of law principles, of the State in which the crash occurred unless such law is inconsistent with or preempted by Federal law.

(3) Jurisdiction.—The United States District Court for the Southern District of New York shall have original and exclusive jurisdiction over all actions brought for any claim (including any claim for loss of property, personal injury, or death) resulting from or relating to the terrorist-related aircraft crashes of September 11, 2001.

Is this statute constitutional? It is argued in Eric J. Segall, Article III as a Grant of Power: Protective Jurisdiction, Federalism and the Federal Courts, 54 Fla. L. Rev. 361 (2002), that it is. Segall concludes that a "pure jurisdictional statute that furthers a legitimate Article I concern is properly a 'law' under which a claim may arise."

The statutory charter of the American National Red Cross permits it "to sue and be sued in courts of law and equity, State or Federal, within the jurisdiction of the United States." 36 U.S.C. § 2. In American National Red Cross v. S.G. & A.E., 505 U.S. 247 (1992), the Court held that this provision "confers original jurisdiction on federal courts over all cases to which the Red Cross is a party." Accordingly, the Red Cross was entitled to remove an action based on state law brought by persons who alleged that they had contracted AIDS from contaminated blood. The Court concluded that the grant of jurisdiction in question was "well within Article III's limits" in light of the Court's decision in *Osborn*, which was described as holding that Article III "arising under" jurisdiction "is broad enough to authorize Congress to confer federal-court jurisdiction over actions involving federally chartered corporations." Is the Red Cross case an example of protective jurisdiction? Cf. Anthony J. Bellia Jr., Article III and the Cause of Action, 89 Iowa L. Rev. 777, 814 (2004) ("If neither state nor federal law requires the Red Cross to prove its corporate existence and powers as part of a state-created cause of action that it brings, a federal question does not form an ingredient of the cause.").

The *Red Cross* decision adopted a rule that "a congressional charter's 'sue and be sued' provision may be read to confer federal court jurisdiction if, but only if, it specifically mentions the federal courts." Although that condition was satisfied in Lightfoot v. Cendant Mortgage Corp., 580 U.S. ___, 137 S.Ct. 553 (2017), the "sue and be sued" clause at issue there contained an additional component: "sue and . . . be sued . . . *in any court of competent jurisdiction*, State or Federal." (Emphasis added.) In a suit brought against it in state court based on state law, the Federal National Mortgage Association (Fannie Mae) sought removal to a federal court.[b] In a unanimous opinion by Justice Sotomayor, the Court held that, in light of the additional language in the "sue and be sued" clause, it should not be read as a grant of federal court jurisdiction, making removal improper. The Court explained that "a court of competent jurisdiction is a court with the power to adjudicate the case before it" and that the clause here merely "permits suit in any state or federal court *already endowed* with subject-matter jurisdiction over the suit."

---

[b] Fanny Mae was originally chartered as an entity wholly owned by the federal government. In a series of changes culminating in 1968, it became "a Government-sponsored private corporation." The "sue and be sued" language at issue in *Lightfoot* was adopted in a 1954 amendment. The original language had said simply that Fanny Mae could "sue and be sued . . . in any court of law or equity, State or Federal."

(Emphasis added.) The Court concluded: "The doors to federal court remain open to Fannie Mae through diversity and federal-question jurisdiction. . . . [T]he usual assumption is that state courts are up to the task of adjudicating their own laws."

4. *MESA V. CALIFORNIA*

In Mesa v. California, 489 U.S. 121 (1989), the state of California issued criminal complaints against two mail-truck drivers involved in serious accidents. Both defendants removed their cases to federal court under 28 U.S.C. § 1442(a)(1), which provides:

> A civil or criminal prosecution commenced in a State court against any of the following persons may be removed by them to the district court of the United States for the district and division embracing the place wherein it is pending:
>
> > (1) Any officer of the United States or any agency thereof, or person acting under him, for any act under color of such office. . . .

The District Court denied California's motions to remand, but the Ninth Circuit issued a writ of mandamus ordering remand of the cases to the California courts.

In the Supreme Court, the question was whether removal jurisdiction could be based on the mere fact that the defendants were federal officers or whether it was also required that they allege a federal defense. In an opinion by Justice O'Connor, the Court required a federal defense:

> The government's view, which would eliminate the federal defense requirement, raises serious doubt whether, in enacting § 1442(a), Congress would not have "expand[ed] the jurisdiction of the federal courts beyond the bounds established by the Constitution." Verlinden B.V. v. Central Bank of Nigeria, 461 U.S. 480, 491 (1983). In *Verlinden,* we discussed the distinction between "jurisdictional statutes" and "the federal law under which [an] action arises for Article III purposes," and recognized that pure jurisdictional statutes which seek "to do nothing more than grant jurisdiction over a particular class of cases" cannot support Article III "arising under" jurisdiction. . . .
>
> Section 1442(a), in our view, is a pure jurisdictional statute, seeking to do nothing more than grant district court jurisdiction over cases in which a federal officer is a defendant. Section 1442(a), therefore, cannot independently support Article III "arising under" jurisdiction. Rather, it is the raising of a federal question in the officer's removal petition that constitutes the federal law under which the action against the federal officer arises for Article III purposes. . . . Adopting the government's view would eliminate the substantive Article III foundation of § 1442(a)(1) and necessarily present grave constitutional problems. . . .

At oral argument the government urged upon us a theory of "protective jurisdiction" to avoid these Article III difficulties. . . . The government insists that the full protection of federal officers from interference by hostile state courts cannot be achieved if the averment of a federal defense must be a predicate to removal. More important, the government suggests that this generalized congressional interest in protecting federal officers from state court interference suffices to support Article III "arising under" jurisdiction.

We have, in the past, not found the need to adopt a theory of "protective jurisdiction" to support Article III "arising under" jurisdiction, and we do not see any need for doing so here because we do not recognize any federal interests that are not protected by limiting removal to situations in which a federal defense is alleged. In these prosecutions, no state court hostility or interference has even been alleged by petitioners and we can discern no federal interest in potentially forcing local district attorneys to choose between prosecuting traffic violations hundreds of miles from the municipality in which the violations occurred or abandoning those prosecutions.

. . . We are simply unwilling to credit the government's ominous intimations of hostile state prosecutors and collaborationist state courts interfering with federal officers by charging them with traffic violations and other crimes for which they would have no federal defense in immunity or otherwise. That is certainly not the case in the [present] prosecutions. . . .

Justice Brennan, joined by Justice Marshall, concurred. He wrote separately "to emphasize a point that might otherwise be overlooked":

In most traffic accident cases like those presented here, no significant federal interest is served by removal; it is, accordingly, difficult to believe that Congress would have intended the statute to reach so far. It is not at all inconceivable, however, that Congress's concern about local hostility to federal authority could come into play in some circumstances where the federal officer is unable to present any "federal defense." The days of widespread resistance by state and local government authorities to acts of Congress and to decisions of this Court in the areas of school desegregation and voting rights are not so distant that we should be oblivious to the possibility of harassment of federal agents by local law-enforcement authorities. Such harassment could well take the form of unjustified prosecution for traffic or other offenses, to which the federal officer would have no immunity or other federal defense. The removal statute, it would seem to me, might well have been intended to apply to such unfortunate and exceptional circumstances.

Brennan credited the Court with "leav[ing] open the possibility that where a federal officer is prosecuted because of local hostility to his function, 'careful pleading, demonstrating the close connection between the state prosecution and the federal officer's performance of his duty, might adequately replace the specific averment of a federal defense.'" Accordingly, he concurred in the Court's judgment and opinion "[w]ith the understanding that today's decision does not foreclose the possibility of removal in such circumstances even in the absence of a federal defense. . . ."

If the case that Brennan anticipated were to arise, on what theory could the Court uphold removal jurisdiction?

5. *GUTIERREZ DE MARTINEZ V. LAMAGNO*

The Federal Employees Liability Reform Act of 1988, commonly known as the Westfall Act, grants absolute immunity from common law tort claims to federal employees for acts undertaken in the course of their official duties. When an employee is sued for negligent conduct, the Attorney General is empowered to certify that the employee was acting within the scope of employment at the time of the incident on which the suit was based. 28 U.S.C. § 2679(d). Following certification, the individual defendant is dismissed from the case and cannot subsequently be sued based on the same transaction. The United States is then substituted as a defendant and the case is governed by the Federal Tort Claims Act. If the suit was filed in state court, certification is followed by removal of the case to federal court.

In Gutierrez de Martinez v. Lamagno, 515 U.S. 417 (1995), a car driven by Lamagno, a special agent of the Drug Enforcement Administration, had collided with another vehicle in Barranquilla, Colombia. The injured Colombians filed a diversity action against Lamagno in the federal district court of his residence in the belief that diplomatic immunity barred suit in Colombia. The local United States Attorney filed a Westfall Act certification. Normally a plaintiff might welcome the substitution of the deeper pocket of the United States, but the Federal Tort Claims Act exempts the United States from liability for "[a]ny claim arising in a foreign country." This provision appeared to leave the plaintiffs in this case without remedy. To counter this possibility, the plaintiffs argued that the certification was invalid because Lamagno was not acting within the scope of his employment at the time of the accident.

The Supreme Court granted certiorari to decide whether the factual basis of government certification under the Westfall Act was subject to judicial review. In a five-to-four decision written by Justice Ginsburg, the Court held the certification reviewable.[c] Of interest in the present context is the dissent's argument that the majority's decision might create a problem under Article III in removal cases. Joined by Chief Justice Rehnquist and Justices Scalia and Thomas, Justice Souter wrote:

> [A]n anomalous jurisdictional consequence of the Court's position should be enough to warn us away from treating the Attorney General's certification as reviewable. The Court recognizes that

---

[c] The Attorney General supported judicial review. The Court was influenced by the fact that the government had no incentive not to certify. The employee could challenge a failure to certify, and there would be little reason for a United States Attorney to litigate a "scope of employment" issue against a government employee where there was no prospect of United States liability.

there is nothing equivocal about the act's provision that once a state tort action has been removed to a federal court after a certification by the Attorney General, it may never be remanded to the state system: "certification of the Attorney General shall conclusively establish scope of office or employment for purposes of removal," 28 U.S.C. § 2679(d)(2). As the Court concedes, then, its reading supposes that Congress intended federal courts to retain jurisdiction over state-law tort claims between nondiverse parties even after determining that the Attorney General's certification (and thus the United States's presence as the defendant) was improper. But there is a serious problem, on the Court's reasoning, in requiring a federal district court, after rejecting the Attorney General's certification, to retain jurisdiction over a claim that does not implicate federal law in any way. Although we have declined recent invitations to define the outermost limit of federal court jurisdiction authorized by the "arising under" clause of Article III of the Constitution, see Mesa v. California, 489 U.S. 121, 136–37 (1989); Verlinden B.V. v. Central Bank of Nigeria, 461 U.S. 480 (1983), on the Court's reading this statute must at the very least approach the limit, if it does not cross the line. . . .

The Court . . . looks for jurisdictional solace in the theory that once the Attorney General has issued a scope-of-employment certification, the United States's (temporary) appearance as the sole defendant suffices forever to support jurisdiction in federal court, even if the district court later rejects the Attorney General's certification and resubstitutes as defendant the federal employee first sued in state court. Whether the employee was within the scope of his federal employment, the Court reasons, is itself a sufficient federal question to bring the case into federal court, and " 'considerations of judicial economy, convenience and fairness to litigate,' " are sufficient to keep it there even after a judicial determination that the United States is not the proper defendant.

But the fallacy of this conclusion appears as soon as one recalls the fact that substitution of the United States as defendant (which establishes federal-question jurisdiction) is exclusively dependant on the scope-of-employment certification. The challenge to the certification is thus the equivalent of a challenge to the essential jurisdictional fact that the United States is a party, and the federal court's jurisdiction to review scope of employment (on the Court's theory) is merely an example of any court's necessary authority to rule on a challenge to its own jurisdiction to try a particular action. To argue, as the Court does, that authority to determine scope of employment justifies retention of jurisdiction whenever evidence bearing on jurisdiction and liability overlaps, is therefore tantamount to saying the authority to determine whether a Court has jurisdiction over the cause of action supplies the very jurisdiction that is subject to challenge. . . .

It would never be sound to attribute such an aberrant concept of federal question jurisdiction to Congress; it is impossible to do so when we realize that Congress expressly provided that when a federal court considers a challenge to the Attorney General's refusal to certify (raised by an employee-defendant) and finds the act outside the scope of employment, a case that originated in a state court must be remanded back to the state court. See 28 U.S.C. § 2679(d)(3). In such a case, there will have been just as much overlap of jurisdictional evidence and liability evidence as there will be when the jurisdictional issue is litigated at the behest of a plaintiff (as here) who contests a scope-of-employment certification. If Congress thought the federal court should retain jurisdiction when it is revealed that none exists in this latter case, it should have thought so in the former. But it did not, and the reason it did not is obvious beyond any doubt. It assumed a federal court would never be in the position to retain jurisdiction over an action for which a tort plaintiff has shown there is no federal-question basis, and Congress was entitled to assume this, because it had provided that a certification was conclusive.

. . . The Court's . . . view implies a jurisdictional tenacity that Congress expressly declined to assert elsewhere in the act, and invites a difficult and wholly unnecessary constitutional adjudication about the limits of Article III jurisdiction. These are powerful reasons to recognize the unreviewability of certification, and the Court's contrary arguments fail to measure up to them.

Justice Ginsburg, writing at this point for herself and Justices Stevens, Kennedy, and Breyer, responded:[d]

[W]e do not think the Article III problem . . . is a grave one. There may no longer be a federal question once the federal employee is resubstituted as defendant, but [there would have been] a nonfrivolous federal question, certified by the local U.S. Attorney, when the case was removed to federal court. At that time, the United States was the defendant, and the action was thus under the FTCA. Whether the employee was acting within the scope of his federal employment is a significant federal question—and the Westfall Act was designed to assure that this question could be aired in a federal forum. Because a case under the Westfall Act thus "raises [a] questio[n] of substantive federal law at the very outset," it "clearly 'arises under' federal law, as that term is used in Article III." Verlinden B.V. v. Central Bank of Nigeria, 461 U.S. 480, 493 (1983).

In adjudicating the scope-of-federal-employment question "at the very outset," the court inevitably will confront facts relevant to the alleged misconduct, matters that bear on the state tort claims against the employee. Cf. Mine Workers v. Gibbs, 383 U.S. 715, 725 (1966) (approving exercise of pendent jurisdiction when federal and

---

d   Justice O'Connor did not join this part of the opinion.

state claims have "a common nucleus of operative fact" and would "ordinarily be expected to [be tried] all in one judicial proceeding"). "[C]onsiderations of judicial economy, convenience and fairness to litigants," id. at 726, make it reasonable and proper for the federal forum to proceed beyond the federal question to final judgment once it has invested time and resources on the initial scope-of-employment contest.

If, in preserving judicial review of scope-of-employment certifications, Congress "approach[ed] the limit" of federal court jurisdiction, [as the dissent argues]—and we do not believe it did—we find the exercise of federal court authority involved here less ominous than the consequences of declaring certifications of the kind at issue uncontestable: The local U.S. Attorney, whose conflict of interest is apparent, would be authorized to make final and binding decisions insulating both the United States and federal employees like Lamagno from liability while depriving plaintiffs of potentially meritorious tort claims. The Attorney General, having weighed the competing considerations, does not read the statute to confer on her such extraordinary authority. Nor should we assume that Congress meant federal courts to accept cases only to stamp them "Dismissed" on an interested executive official's unchallengeable representation. The statute is fairly construed to allow petitioners to present to the district court their objections to the Attorney General's scope-of-employment certification, and we hold that construction the more persuasive one.

6. BIBLIOGRAPHY

For historical examination of the original meaning of "arising under" jurisdiction, see Anthony J. Bellia Jr., The Origins of "Arising Under" Jurisdiction, 57 Duke L.J. 263 (2007). Bellia pays particular attention to *Osborn v. United States* and concludes, contrary to the modern understanding, that the Marshall Court's decisions do not support extending "arising under" jurisdiction beyond cases where "federal law would be determinative of the right or title asserted in the federal proceeding."

Discussion of protective jurisdiction can be found in George D. Brown, Beyond *Pennhurst*—Protective Jurisdiction, the Eleventh Amendment, and the Power of Congress to Enlarge Federal Jurisdiction in Response to the Burger Court, 71 Va. L. Rev. 343 (1985); Carole E. Goldberg-Ambrose, The Protective Jurisdiction of the Federal Courts, 30 U.C.L.A. L. Rev. 542 (1983); Linda Mullenix, Complex Litigation Reform and Article III Jurisdiction, 59 Fordham L. Rev. 169 (1990); James E. Pfander, Protective Jurisdiction, Aggregate Litigation, and the Limits of Article III, 95 Calif. L. Rev. 1423 (2007); Carlos M. Vázquez, The Federal "Claim" in the District Courts: *Osborn, Verlinden*, and Protective Jurisdiction, 95 Calif. L. Rev. 1731 (2007); Louise Weinberg, The Power of Congress over Courts in Nonfederal Cases, 1995 B.Y.U. L. Rev. 731; Ernest A. Young, Stalking the Yeti: Protective Jurisdiction, Foreign Affairs Removal, and Complete Preemption, 95 Calif. L. Rev.

1775 (2007); and Note, The Theory of Protective Jurisdiction, 57 N.Y.U. L. Rev. 933 (1982).

SECTION 4. POWER TO CREATE NON-ARTICLE III COURTS

INTRODUCTORY NOTES ON THE CREATION OF NON-ARTICLE III COURTS

1. ARTICLE III AND CONGRESSIONAL POWER

Article I of the Constitution expressly gives Congress the authority to establish the lower federal courts. Article II specifies the process for appointing judges to these courts: nomination by the President and approval by the Senate. Article III states that the judges are to hold their offices during good behavior (which has been interpreted to mean life tenure subject to impeachment) and shall not have their compensation diminished while in office. In the *Federalist Papers*, Alexander Hamilton explained that the federal courts needed these protections to ensure their independence. The judiciary was "beyond comparison the weakest of the three departments of power," said Hamilton, and therefore "all possible care is requisite to enable it to defend itself against" the other branches of government. Judges who have been appointed pursuant to the constitutional process and have the specified tenure and salary protections are referred to as "Article III judges." An obvious example of judges who are *not* Article III judges are the judges on the state courts, who are appointed through state court procedures (which in many states today involve elections) and typically have limited terms.

One might think from the constitutional provisions recited above that, when Congress establishes courts to hear the cases and controversies listed in Article III, it must staff them with Article III judges. As one prominent federal courts scholar explained: "The Constitution, in other words, seems to adopt a simple, majestic, and powerful model: Congress may leave the initial adjudication of some or all of article III's list of cases to the state courts, but if federal adjudication is felt to be needed, the requirements of article III automatically come into play and specify what sorts of courts Congress must employ for federal adjudication." Paul M. Bator, The Constitution as Architecture: Legislative and Administrative Courts Under Article III, 65 Ind. L.J. 233, 234 (1990).

There are at least three complications with this conclusion, however. First, it may not always be clear what constitutes a "court." For example, in applying the laws enacted by Congress, the Executive Branch (and its departments and agencies) may need to engage in fact-finding and legal interpretation, but this would not necessarily make it a court. Second, in addition to giving Congress the power to establish the federal courts, the Constitution gives Congress a variety of other powers, the exercise of which might entail the need to establish adjudicatory institutions. It is not self-apparent from the constitutional text that Article III must regulate those institutions. Third, and perhaps most importantly, Congress has long used non-Article III judges for adjudicating certain types of cases that otherwise would fall within the federal judicial power, and the Supreme Court has expressly approved some of these uses.

Despite these complications, there must be limitations on Congress's ability to staff adjudicatory institutions with non-Article III judges. Although fanciful, imagine if Congress, using its power to regulate interstate commerce, tried to establish the "shmederal courts" with all the jurisdiction of today's federal courts but staffed with judges who were subject to having their salaries reduced by Congress or being removed by the President at will. Even assuming such a scheme would otherwise fall within Congress's authority over commerce, it would clearly be unconstitutional because it would eviscerate the protections for federal judges specified in Article III. The difficult issue, of course, is figuring out how to draw the line between when Congress or the Executive Branch may use non-Article III judges and when they may not.

2. TERRITORIAL COURTS

The Supreme Court has long held that Congress has the authority to establish non-Article III courts in U.S. territorial possessions, pursuant to Congress's constitutional authority to "make all needful Rules and Regulations respecting the Territory or other Property belonging to the United States." U.S. Const. art. IV, § 3, cl. 2. In American Insurance Co. v. Canter, 26 U.S. (1 Pet.) 511 (1811), for example, a territorial court in Florida (before it became a state) had decided a maritime salvage case, something that otherwise would fall within the admiralty jurisdiction of the federal courts. Despite the fact that the Florida court was staffed by judges serving only four-year terms, the Court held that there was no violation of Article III. Speaking through Chief Justice Marshall, the Court explained:

> [The Florida courts] are legislative courts, created in virtue of the general right of sovereignty which exists in the government or in virtue of that clause which enables Congress to make all needful rules and regulations respecting the territory belonging to the United States. The jurisdiction with which they are invested is not a part of that judicial power which is defined in the 3d Article of the Constitution, but is conferred by Congress in the execution of those general powers which that body possesses over the territories of the United States. Although admiralty jurisdiction can be exercised in the states in those courts only which are established in pursuance of the 3d Article of the Constitution, the same limitation does not extend to the territories. In legislating for them, Congress exercises the combined powers of the general and of a state government.

The Supreme Court has similarly held that Congress has the authority to establish non-Article III courts in the District of Columbia. In Palmore v. United States, 411 U.S. 389 (1973), the Court explained that Congress's power to "exercise exclusive legislation in all cases ... over such District" (see U.S. Const. art I, § 8, cl. 17) is "plenary" and that it "permits [Congress] to legislate for the District in a manner with respect to subjects that would exceed its powers, or at least be very unusual, in the context of national legislation enacted under other powers delegated to it under Art. I, § 8." The Court also rejected the proposition "that an Art. III judge must preside over every proceeding in which a charge, claim, or defense is based on an Act of Congress or a law made under its authority." See also Kendall v. United States, 37 U.S. (12 Pet.) 524, 619 (1838) ("Congress has the entire control over the District for every purpose of government, and it is reasonable to suppose that, in organizing a judicial department here, all judicial power necessary for the purposes of government would be vested in the courts of justice.").

3. MILITARY COURTS-MARTIAL

The U.S. military has long used non-Article III courts to adjudicate criminal offenses committed by service personnel and others connected to the military. The jurisdiction and procedures of these "courts-martial" have historically been regulated by Congress, pursuant to its authority "to make Rules for the Government and Regulation of the land and naval Forces." U.S. Const., art. I, § 8, cl. 14. Since 1950, these regulations have been set forth in the Uniform Code of Military Justice, 10 U.S.C. § 801 et seq. Court-martial decisions are made by a panel of military officers. These decisions can be appealed first through the chain of command and then to the U.S. Court of Appeals for the Armed Forces, a non-Article III court composed of five civilian judges who serve fifteen-year terms. Decisions of that court can be reviewed by the Supreme Court on a petition for a writ of certiorari.

The Supreme Court has upheld the constitutionality of military courts-martial, reasoning that

> Congress has the power to provide for the trial and punishment of military and naval offences in the manner then and now practiced by civilized nations; and that the power to do so is given without any connection between it and the 3d article of the Constitution defining the judicial power of the United States; indeed, that the two powers are entirely independent of each other.

Dynes v. Hoover, 61 U.S. (20 How.) 65, 79 (1858). The Court has also held, however, that civilian U.S. citizens not employed by the military cannot be tried by courts-martial, even if they are dependents of a service member living with them on a military base abroad. See Reid v. Covert, 354 U.S. 1 (1957); Kinsella v. United States ex rel. Singleton, 361 U.S. 234 (1960). The Court has explained that "[t]he test for jurisdiction . . . is one of status, namely, whether the accused in the court-martial proceeding is a person who can be regarded as falling within the term 'land and naval Forces.'" *Kinsella*, 361 U.S. at 240–41. For analysis of the traditional exception to Article III for military courts in light of recent expansions in their jurisdiction, see Stephen I. Vladeck, Military Courts and Article III, 103 Geo. L.J. 933 (2015).

4. "PUBLIC RIGHTS" ADJUDICATION

The Supreme Court has suggested that Article III judges are not required for the adjudication of certain "public rights." The "public rights" doctrine can be traced to Murray's Lessee v. Hoboken Land & Improvement Co., 59 U.S. (18 How.) 272 (1856). In that case, the Solicitor of the Treasury, exercising authority granted by Congress, issued a warrant against property held by a federal customs collector, after an audit by the Treasury Department revealed substantial deficiencies in the collector's accounts. In response to the argument that the issuance of the warrant violated Article III, the Court acknowledged that, "if the auditing of this account, and the ascertainment of its balance, and the issuing of this process, was an exercise of the judicial power of the United States, the proceeding was void, for the officers who performed these acts could exercise no part of that judicial power." But the Court found no violation of Article III, explaining:

> [W]e do not consider Congress can either withdraw from judicial cognizance any matter which, from its nature, is the subject of a suit at the common law, or in equity, or admiralty, nor, on the other hand, can it bring under the judicial power a matter which, from its nature, is not a subject for judicial determination. At the same time, there are matters, involving public rights, which may be presented in such form that the judicial power is capable of acting on them, and which are susceptible of judicial determination, but which Congress may or may not bring within the cognizance of the courts of the United States, as it may deem proper.

Another decision emphasizing something like this distinction is Ex parte Bakelite Corp., 279 U.S. 438 (1929). In that case, the Court considered the constitutionality of the Court of Customs Appeals, a non-Article III court established by Congress to handle appeals from the Tariff Commission, which made recommendations to the President concerning potential sanctions against importers found to have engaged in unfair trading practices. The Court first concluded that, because the Court of Customs Appeals was a "legislative court," it could make determinations that might otherwise be considered improperly advisory if made by an Article III court. The Court next concluded that Congress had not violated Article III in creating the Court of Customs and Patent Appeals, explaining that the issues it addressed "include nothing which inherently or necessarily requires judicial determination, but only matters the determination of which may be, and, at times, has been, committed exclusively to executive officers." The Court also explained more generally why some disputes involving the government do not need to be assigned to Article III courts:

> Legislative courts also may be created as special tribunals to examine and determine various matters, arising between the government and others, which, from their nature, do not require judicial determination, and yet are susceptible of it. The mode of determining matters of this class is completely within congressional control. Congress may reserve to itself the power to decide, may

delegate that power to executive officers, or may commit it to judicial tribunals.

Conspicuous among such matters are claims against the United States. These may arise in many ways and may be for money, lands, or other things. They all admit of legislative or executive determination, and yet, from their nature, are susceptible of determination by courts; but no court can have cognizance of them except as Congress makes specific provision therefor. Nor do claimants have any right to sue on them unless Congress consents; and Congress may attach to its consent such conditions as it deems proper, even to requiring that the suits be brought in a legislative court specially created to consider them.

A similar decision is Williams v. United States, 289 U.S. 553, 58–81 (1933), which held that the Court of Claims, which heard monetary claims against the U.S. government, was properly constituted as a non-Article III court. The Court reasoned that, "since Congress, whenever it thinks proper, undoubtedly may, without infringing the Constitution, confer upon an executive officer or administrative board, or an existing or specially constituted court, or retain for itself, the power to hear and determine controversies respecting claims against the United States, it follows indubitably that such power, in whatever guise or by whatever agency exercised, is no part of the judicial power vested in the constitutional courts by the third article."[a]

5. *CROWELL V. BENSON* AND JURISDICTIONAL AND CONSTITUTIONAL FACTS

Crowell v. Benson, 285 U.S. 22 (1932), involved a compensation award made by a Deputy Commissioner of the U.S. Employees' Compensation Commission. The award was issued pursuant to a statute that authorized the Commission to determine the compensation that should be paid by employers when their employees suffered disability or death from an injury occurring on the navigable waters of the United States. Under the statutory scheme, these compensation awards could be set aside by federal district courts if found to be "not in accordance with law," but there was no provision in the statute for federal court review of the Commission's factual determinations. The lower courts nevertheless enjoined enforcement of the award on the ground that the Deputy Commissioner had erred in finding that there was an employment relationship at the time of the injury. In an opinion by Chief Justice Hughes, the Supreme Court affirmed.

The Court began by observing that, "[a]s to determinations of fact, the distinction is at once apparent between cases of private right and those which arise between the government and persons subject to its authority in

---

[a] Congress subsequently designated both the Court of Claims and the Court of Customs and Patent Appeals (the successor to the Court of Customs Appeals) as Article III courts, and the Supreme Court accepted that designation. See Glidden Co. v. Zdanok, 370 U.S. 530 (1962). In 1982, Congress merged the Court of Customs and Patent Appeals and the appellate division of the Court of Claims into a new U.S. Court of Appeals for the Federal Circuit, which was designated as an Article III court. The trial division of the Court of Claims, now called the Court of Federal Claims, was designated as a non-Article III court.

connection with the performance of the constitutional functions of the executive or legislative departments." The present case, the Court noted, involved private rights—"that is, of the liability of one individual to another under the law as defined." But the Court explained that, even in cases involving private rights, "there is no requirement that, in order to maintain the essential attributes of the judicial power, all determinations of fact in constitutional courts shall be made by judges." The Court further reasoned:

> In deciding whether the Congress, in enacting the statute under review, has exceeded the limits of its authority to prescribe procedure in cases of injury upon navigable waters, regard must be had, as in other cases where constitutional limits are invoked, not to mere matters of form, but to the substance of what is required.

> The statute has a limited application, being confined to the relation of master and servant, and the method of determining the questions of fact, which arise in the routine of making compensation awards to employees under the Act, is necessary to its effective enforcement. The Act itself, where it applies, establishes the measure of the employer's liability, thus leaving open for determination the questions of fact as to the circumstances, nature, extent, and consequences of the injuries sustained by the employee for which compensation is to be made in accordance with the prescribed standards. Findings of fact by the deputy commissioner upon such questions are closely analogous to the findings of the amount of damages that are made according to familiar practice by commissioners or assessors, and the reservation of full authority to the court to deal with matters of law provides for the appropriate exercise of the judicial function in this class of cases. For the purposes stated, we are unable to find any constitutional obstacle to the action of the Congress in availing itself of a method shown by experience to be essential in order to apply its standards to the thousands of cases involved, thus relieving the courts of a most serious burden while preserving their complete authority to insure the proper application of the law.

The Court explained, however, that different considerations apply to the determination of "jurisdictional facts," the existence of which are "a condition precedent to the operation of the statutory scheme." The Court elaborated:

> The recognition of the utility and convenience of administrative agencies for the investigation and finding of facts within their proper province, and the support of their authorized action, does not require the conclusion that there is no limitation of their use, and that the Congress could completely oust the courts of all determinations of fact by vesting the authority to make them with finality in its own instrumentalities or in the executive department. That would be to sap the judicial power as it exists under the federal Constitution, and to establish a government of a bureaucratic character alien to our system wherever fundamental rights depend, as not infrequently they do depend, upon the facts, and finality as to facts becomes in effect finality in law.

Some facts are not only jurisdictional, the Court explained, but their determination is also relevant to constitutional rights. Thus, in this case, "[i]f the person injured was not an employee of the person sought to be held, or if the injury did not occur upon the navigable waters of the United States, there is no ground for an assertion that the person against whom the proceeding was directed could constitutionally be subjected, in the absence of fault upon his part, to the liability which the statute creates."

To avoid constitutional doubts, the Court construed the statute as not giving the Commission exclusive authority to determine these jurisdictional and constitutional facts. As a result, the Court concluded that it was proper for the lower courts in this case to make their own determination of whether the claimant was employed by the defendant at the time of the injury.

Justice Brandeis dissented and was joined by Justices Stone and Roberts. Brandeis saw nothing in the statute supporting the Court's distinction between ordinary facts and jurisdictional facts. Nor did he think such a distinction was needed in order to avoid constitutional doubts:

> I see no basis for a contention that the denial of the right to a trial de novo upon the issue of employment is in any manner subversive of the independence of the federal judicial power. Nothing in the Constitution, or in any prior decision of this Court to which attention has been called, lends support to the doctrine that a judicial finding of any fact involved in any civil proceeding to enforce a pecuniary liability may not be made upon evidence introduced before a properly constituted administrative tribunal, or that a determination so made may not be deemed an independent judicial determination. Congress has repeatedly exercised authority to confer upon the tribunals which it creates, be they administrative bodies or courts of limited jurisdiction, the power to receive evidence concerning the facts upon which the exercise of federal power must be predicated, and to determine whether those facts exist. The power of Congress to provide by legislation for liability under certain circumstances subsumes the power to provide for the determination of the existence of those circumstances. It does not depend upon the absolute existence in reality of any fact.

Brandeis further argued that, to the extent that federal court review was required for certain issues, this would be because of the requirements of due process, not because of Article III:

> The "judicial power" of Article III of the Constitution is the power of the federal government, and not of any inferior tribunal. There is in that article nothing which requires any controversy to be determined as of first instance in the federal District Courts. The jurisdiction of those courts is subject to the control of Congress. Matters which may be placed within their jurisdiction may instead be committed to the state courts. If there be any controversy to which the judicial power extends that may not be subjected to the conclusive determination of administrative bodies or federal legislative courts, it is not because of any prohibition against the dimi-

nution of the jurisdiction of the federal District Courts as such, but because, under certain circumstances, the constitutional requirement of due process is a requirement of judicial process.

Note that, although not formally overruled, the distinction drawn in *Crowell* between ordinary facts and jurisdictional facts has not been consistently observed either in practice or in subsequent decisions. The special treatment of constitutional facts appears to have somewhat greater vitality, at least in cases involving issues of personal liberty. See, e.g., Frank R. Strong, The Persistent Doctrine of "Constitutional Fact," 46 N.C. L. Rev. 223 (1968).

6. *NORTHERN PIPELINE CONSTRUCTION CO. V. MARATHON PIPELINE CO.*

In 1978, after years of study, Congress substantially overhauled the federal bankruptcy system. Before this overhaul, federal district courts operated as bankruptcy courts with the assistance of non-Article III "referees." Claims involving the disposition to creditors of property in the possession of the court came within "summary" jurisdiction and were heard in the first instance by a bankruptcy referee. Other claims, including those for debts owed to the bankrupt by third parties, fell under "plenary" jurisdiction and could be heard by the referee only with the defendant's consent. Otherwise, such claims were tried separately in federal district court or in state court. This fragmentation of the proceedings resulted in costly and time-consuming jurisdictional disputes and in other inconveniences of administration. Additionally, because referees' recommendations had to be approved by a federal judge, bankruptcy proceedings were subject to long delays caused by crowded district court dockets.

The 1978 act responded to these problems by creating separate bankruptcy courts that were to serve as "adjuncts" to the district courts. The jurisdiction of the bankruptcy courts was much broader than under the referee system and extended to a wide variety of state and federal claims that might affect the property of the bankruptcy estate. These courts were also given the power to control their own dockets and to enter and enforce final judgments. Decisions of the bankruptcy courts could be appealed in various ways to the district courts or the courts of appeals. After long consideration, Congress decided not to give bankruptcy judges the protections of Article III. Prominent among the concerns that led to this result was the fear that staffing an independent court of equal rank would dilute the prestige and influence of district court judges. Instead, the judges on the bankruptcy courts were appointed for 14-year terms and were subject to removal by the judicial council of the circuit for "incompetency, misconduct, neglect of duty or physical or mental disability."

In Northern Pipeline Construction Co. v. Marathon Pipeline Co., 458 U.S. 50 (1982), the Supreme Court held that the new bankruptcy courts violated Article III. In that case, Northern Pipeline filed a petition for reorganization and then subsequently brought suit in the bankruptcy court against Marathon for alleged breaches of contract and warranty, as well as alleged misrepresentation, coercion, and duress. Marathon responded by arguing that the new bankruptcy court system was unconstitutional. The Supreme Court agreed. There was no majority opinion. Justice Brennan, writing for himself and Justices Marshall, Blackmun, and Stevens, authored the lead plurality opinion.

(i) Past Allowances of Non-Article III Courts

The plurality began by reviewing the past situations in which non-Article III courts had been allowed—namely, territorial courts, courts-martial, and public rights adjudication. The plurality explained that each of these past uses of non-Article III courts involved a "circumstance in which the grant of power to the Legislative and Executive Branches was historically and constitutionally so exceptional that the congressional assertion of a power to create legislative courts was consistent with, rather than threatening to, the constitutional mandate of separation of powers." For example, the allowance of non-Article III courts for U.S. territorial possessions "dates from the earliest days of the Republic, when it was perceived that the Framers intended that as to certain geographic areas, in which no State operated as sovereign, Congress was the exercise the general powers of government." Similarly, said the plurality, the use of non-Article III judges for courts-martial "involves a constitutional grant of power that has been historically understood as giving the political Branches of Government extraordinary control over the precise subject matter at issue."

(ii) Public Rights Doctrine

As for the "public rights" doctrine, the plurality had this to say:

> This doctrine may be explained in part by reference to the traditional principle of sovereign immunity, which recognizes that the Government may attach conditions to its consent to be sued. . . . But the public rights doctrine also draws upon the principle of separation of powers, and a historical understanding that certain prerogatives were reserved to the political Branches of Government. The doctrine extends only to matters arising "between the Government and persons subject to its authority in connection with the performance of the constitutional functions of the executive or legislative departments," Crowell v. Benson, 285 U.S. 22, 50 (1932), and only to matters that historically could have been determined exclusively by those departments, see Ex parte Bakelite Corp. The understanding of these cases is that the Framers expected that Congress would be free to commit such matters completely to nonjudicial executive determination, and that, as a result, there can be no constitutional objection to Congress's employing the less drastic expedient of committing their determination to a legislative court or an administrative agency.

The plurality acknowledged that "[t]he distinction between public rights and private rights has not been definitively explained in our precedents." But it argued that, at a minimum, matters of public rights arise between the government and others and do not extend to the liability of one individual to another. "Our precedents clearly establish," said the plurality, "that only controversies in the former category may be removed from Art. III courts and delegated to legislative courts or administrative agencies for their determination." By contrast, the plurality argued that "[p]rivate rights disputes . . . lie at the core of the historically recognized judicial power."

(iii) Inapplicability to Bankruptcy Courts

Ultimately, the plurality found that none of the historic uses of non-Article III courts provided support for the new bankruptcy courts:

> In each of these situations, the Court has recognized certain exceptional powers bestowed upon Congress by the Constitution or by historical consensus. Only in the face of such an exceptional grant of power has the Court declined to hold the authority of Congress subject to the general prescriptions of Art. III.

> We discern no such exceptional grant of power applicable in the cases before us. The courts created by the Bankruptcy Act of 1978 do not lie exclusively outside the States of the Federal Union, like those in the District of Columbia and the Territories. Nor do the bankruptcy courts bear any resemblance to courts-martial, which are founded upon the Constitution's grant of plenary authority over the Nation's military forces to the Legislative and Executive Branches. Finally, the substantive legal rights at issue in the present action cannot be deemed "public rights." Appellants argue that a discharge in bankruptcy is indeed a "public right," similar to such congressionally created benefits as "radio station licenses, pilot licenses, or certificates for common carriers" granted by administrative agencies. See Brief for United States 34. But the restructuring of debtor-creditor relations, which is at the core of the federal bankruptcy power, must be distinguished from the adjudication of state-created private rights, such as the right to recover contract damages that is at issue in this case. The former may well be a "public right," but the latter obviously is not. Appellant Northern's right to recover contract damages to augment its estate is "one of private right, that is, of the liability of one individual to another under the law as defined." *Crowell,* 285 U.S. at 51.

In response to the argument that Congress's power to "establish . . . uniform laws on the subject of bankruptcies throughout the United States" (U.S. Const. art. I, § 8, cl. 4) was sufficient authority to establish non-Article III courts, the plurality replied that this argument "provides no limiting principle" and thus "threatens to supplant completely our system of adjudication in independent Art. III tribunals and replace it with a system of 'specialized' legislative courts."

(iv) "Adjuncts"

The plurality also addressed the argument, based on *Crowell v. Benson* and *United States v. Raddatz* (a decision concerning magistrate judges that is discussed below in the Additional Notes on Non-Article III Adjudication), that the bankruptcy courts could be justified as "adjuncts" to Article III courts. The plurality acknowledged that "when Congress creates a substantive federal right, it possesses substantial discretion to prescribe the manner in which that right may be adjudicated—including the assignment to an adjunct of some functions historically performed by judges." Even then, said the plurality, "the functions of the adjunct must be limited in such a way that "the essential attributes" of judicial power are retained in the Art. III court." In any event, reasoned the plurality, this adjunct idea does not apply with much force to rights not created by Congress:

> . . . The constitutional system of checks and balances is designed to guard against "encroachment or aggrandizement" by Congress at the expense of the other branches of government. But when Congress creates a statutory right, it clearly has the discretion, in defining that right, to create presumptions, or assign burdens of proof, or prescribe remedies; it may also provide that persons seeking to vindicate that right must do so before particularized tribunals created to perform the specialized adjudicative tasks related to that right. Such provisions do, in a sense, affect the exercise of judicial power, but they are also incidental to Congress's power to define the right that it has created. No comparable justification exists, however, when the right being adjudicated is not of congressional creation. In such a situation, substantial inroads into functions that have traditionally been performed by the Judiciary cannot be characterized merely as incidental extensions of Congress's power to define rights that it has created. Rather, such inroads suggest unwarranted encroachments upon the judicial power of the United States, which our Constitution reserves for Art. III courts.

The plurality concluded that the Bankruptcy Act of 1978 "carries the possibility of such an unwarranted encroachment":

> Many of the rights subject to adjudication by the Act's bankruptcy courts . . . are not of Congress's creation. Indeed, the cases before us, which center upon appellant Northern's claim for damages for breach of contract and misrepresentation, involve a right created by state law, a right independent of and antecedent to the reorganization petition that conferred jurisdiction upon the Bankruptcy Court. Accordingly, Congress's authority to control the manner in which that right is adjudicated, through assignment of historically judicial functions to a non-Art. III "adjunct," plainly must be deemed at a minimum. Yet it is equally plain that Congress has vested the "adjunct" bankruptcy judges with powers over Northern's state-created right that far exceed the powers that it has vested in administrative agencies that adjudicate only rights of Congress's own creation.

(v)　Justice Rehnquist's Concurrence

Justice Rehnquist, joined by Justice O'Connor, concurred in the judgment. Rehnquist noted that "[t]he cases dealing with the authority of

Congress to create courts other than by use of its power under Art. III do not admit of easy synthesis." Whatever the boundaries of Congress's authority to establish non-Article III courts, he concluded that they were exceeded in this case, which he described as follows:

> From the record before us, the lawsuit in which Marathon was named defendant seeks damages for breach of contract, misrepresentation, and other counts which are the stuff of the traditional actions at common law tried by the courts at Westminster in 1789. There is apparently no federal rule of decision provided for any of the issues in the lawsuit; the claims of Northern arise entirely under state law. No method of adjudication is hinted, other than the traditional common law mode of judge and jury. The lawsuit is before the Bankruptcy Court only because the plaintiff has previously filed a petition for reorganization in that court.

(vi) Justice White's Dissent

Justice White dissented and was joined by Chief Justice Burger and Justice Powell. White argued that, "[i]n its attempt to pigeonhole [the Court's past] cases, the plurality does violence to their meaning and creates an artificial structure that itself lacks coherence." As for the plurality's suggestion that non-Article III adjudication is more problematic for claims under state law than under federal law, White thought that this approach "seems to turn the separation-of-powers doctrine, upon which the majority relies, on its head":

> Since state law claims would ordinarily not be heard by Art. III judges—i.e., they would be heard by state judges—one would think that there is little danger of a diminution of, or intrusion upon, the power of Art. III courts, when such claims are assigned to a non-Art. III court. The plurality misses this obvious point because it concentrates on explaining how it is that federally created rights can ever be adjudicated in Art. I courts—a far more difficult problem under the separation of powers doctrine. The plurality fumbles when it assumes that the rationale it develops to deal with the latter problem must also govern the former problem. In fact, the two are simply unrelated, and the majority never really explains the separation of powers problem that would be created by assigning state law questions to legislative courts or to adjuncts of Art. III courts.

Instead of the approach of the plurality, White proposed that Article III "should be read as expressing one value that must be balanced against competing constitutional values and legislative responsibilities." Under that approach, argued White, the bankruptcy courts are constitutional, for several reasons:

> First, ample provision is made for appellate review by Art. III courts. . . .

> Second, no one seriously argues that the Bankruptcy Act of 1978 represents an attempt by the political branches of government

to aggrandize themselves at the expense of the third branch or an attempt to undermine the authority of constitutional courts in general. . . .

Finally, I have no doubt that the ends that Congress sought to accomplish by creating a system of non-Art. III bankruptcy courts were at least as compelling as the ends found to be satisfactory in Palmore v. United States, 411 U.S. 389 (1973), or the ends that have traditionally justified the creation of legislative courts. . . .

(vii) Chief Justice Burger's Dissent

Chief Justice Burger dissented separately to argue that, when Brennan's plurality opinion was combined with Rehnquist's concurrence, the majority had decided only that "a 'traditional' state common-law action, not made subject to a federal rule of decision, and related only peripherally to an adjudication of bankruptcy under federal law, must, absent the consent of the litigants, be heard by an 'Art. III court' if it is to be heard by any court or agency of the United States."

(viii) Fallout from the Decision

The Supreme Court announced its decision in *Northern Pipeline* on June 28, 1982, but stayed its judgment until October 4 of that year. Arguing that Congress was unable to meet this deadline due to election-year pressures, the Solicitor General persuaded the Court to extend its stay until December 24, 1982. When it became clear that the second deadline would expire before Congressional action, the Solicitor General asked for another extension, but the Court refused. The Judicial Conference of the United States then attempted to restore order to the bankruptcy system by promulgating emergency rules. The interim rules were subsequently enacted by Congress, but not in exactly the form suggested by the Conference. Despite some resulting confusion, the emergency rules provided the operational basis for bankruptcy proceedings through 1984. Almost exactly two years after the Court announced its decision in *Northern Pipeline,* Congress passed the Bankruptcy Amendments and Federal Judgeship Act of 1984. The Act is described below in the excerpt of *Stern v. Marshall.*

7.   POSSIBLE RATIONALES FOR *NORTHERN PIPELINE*

The statute invalidated in *Northern Pipeline* was neither unimportant nor unconsidered. Instead, it was a recent act of Congress, passed after years of study and debate, and intended to accomplish major structural reform of the law of bankruptcy. For the Court to strike down such a statute was, by any reckoning, a notable exercise of judicial review. One might expect, therefore, that the fatal defect in the statutory scheme could be clearly stated. As is so often true in the arcane and confusing area of "non-Article III courts," however, the essential rationale of the decision is far from clear. At least four possible rationales have been suggested:

(i) Vindication of the Text

An obvious rationale for Northern Pipeline is vindication of the constitutional text. Article III is precise and apparently mandatory. Thus, it may be enough to say that the bankruptcy courts exercised the "judicial Power of the United States" without conforming to the requirements of Article III. The difficulty with this "Article III literalism" is not that it is in any demonstrable way wrong, but that its invocation is unaccountably selective. On its face, Article III admits of no exceptions. Nor is there textual basis for distinguishing among Congress's powers under Article I. Thus, if the constitutional text is sufficient to condemn non-Article III bankruptcy courts, it would seem equally conclusive with respect to territorial courts, District of Columbia local courts, courts-martial, and so forth. But if such exceptions are to be recognized, what reliance can fairly be placed on the language of Article III as a sufficient ground for invalidating the bankruptcy courts?

(ii) Separation of Powers

The plurality's concern with the "separation of powers" in *Northern Pipeline* was focused on the need for judicial independence. It described Article III as enunciating the "fundamental principle" that the judiciary must be independent, and it identified life tenure and guaranteed compensation as "institutional protections" designed to secure that independence. In this light, the problem with non-Article III courts is that they are not adequately shielded from legislative or executive interference. The ultimate evil to be avoided is tyrannous overreaching by the political branches.

Is this a persuasive rationale for *Northern Pipeline*? Is this a plausible context in which to raise the fear of outside meddling in judicial decision-making? In particular, is this fear more plausible here than in other contexts where non-Article III adjudication has been upheld?

Consider especially the military courts-martial. Military judges not only lack life tenure and guaranteed compensation; they are dependent for career advancement on the evaluation of their superiors and in some respects subject to direct command influence. See O'Callahan v. Parker, 395 U.S. 258, 264 (1969). Is it plausible to believe that a prophylaxis against governmental interference is more necessary in bankruptcy courts than in the administration of military justice?

Consider also the distinction between "public" and "private" rights. The plurality said that it was not permissible for a non-Article III court to settle a contract claim between private parties, in part because private-rights disputes "lie at the core of the historically recognized judicial power." In contrast, said the plurality, "when Congress creates a substantive federal right, it possesses substantial discretion to prescribe the manner in which that right may be adjudicated."

Can this distinction be reconciled with a concern for judicial independence? Consider the views of Maryellen Fullerton, who answered the *Northern Pipeline* plurality's notion of the "core" of Article III as follows:

[A] strong argument can be made that the core of judicial power includes public rights cases challenging the validity of legislative or executive actions. This broader description of the core of federal judicial power finds particular support in the checks and balances structure of the Constitution. A major role of the federal judiciary is to declare unlawful congressional or executive actions that exceed their powers under the Constitution. The Article III guarantees protect the judiciary in its exercise of the power to invalidate legislative or executive action. . . . Because the need to check unlawful acts by the executive or legislature is more likely to arise in suits challenging government actions rather than in litigation between private parties, allowing legislative courts to adjudicate public rights cases thwarts the policy of checks and balances.

Maryellen Fullerton, No Light at the End of the Pipeline: Confusion Surrounds Legislative Courts, 49 Brooklyn L. Rev. 207, 230–31 (1983). See also the more pointed comment by Martin Redish that if the dichotomy between public and private rights is to be used at all, "it would make considerably more sense to reverse it." Martin Redish, Legislative Courts, Administrative Agencies, and the *Northern Pipeline* Decision, 1983 Duke L.J. 197, 214.

(iii) Fairness to Litigants

A different rationale relates the requirements of Article III to an underlying concern for fairness to litigants. Judges who are inadequately shielded from political pressure may be less able to provide fair adjudication. In essence, this argument merges Article III and due process of law.

Does this rationale explain *Northern Pipeline*? Does the decision suggest that fundamental fairness requires judicial life tenure and guaranteed compensation? State judges typically lack these protections, and no one suggests that state court adjudication is unconstitutional. Congress could have left the resolution of "plenary" bankruptcy disputes to state courts, in which case they would have been resolved by judges who have no greater (and often much less) guarantee of judicial independence than do federal bankruptcy judges. Does that sufficiently answer the concern for fairness to litigants?

Is the following response by the plurality to a related point made by Justice White convincing?:

Justice White's dissent finds particular significance in the fact that Congress could have assigned all bankruptcy matters to the state courts. But, of course, virtually all matters that might be heard in Art. III courts could also be left by Congress to state courts. This fact is simply irrelevant to the question before us. Congress has no control over state court judges; accordingly the principle of separation of powers is not threatened by leaving the adjudication of federal disputes to such judges. . . . The Framers chose to leave to Congress the precise role to be played by the lower federal courts in the administration of justice. . . . But the Framers did not leave it to Congress to define the character of those courts—they were to be independent of the political branches and presided over by judges with guaranteed salary and life tenure.

(iv) Federalism

Lastly, there is some suggestion in the literature that the protections specified in Article III were designed not only to protect the federal judiciary against political interference but also to guard the states against encroachment by the national government. The idea seems to be that life tenure and guaranteed compensation for federal judges would assure an "impartial and independent forum" for adjudication of suits concerning the states and their laws and "ensure that any limitation of state prerogatives will occur by proper operation of law, rather than through legislative or executive coercion." Lucinda M. Finley, Note, Article III Limits on Article I Courts: The Constitutionality of the Bankruptcy Court and the 1979 Magistrate Act, 80 Colum. L. Rev. 560, 582–83 (1980).

Does federalism make sense as a rationale for Northern Pipeline? Perhaps some support for this view is implicit in the observation, made both by the plurality and the concurrence, that Congress did not create a federal rule of decision for Northern Pipeline's claim against Marathon, but merely authorized resolution of this state-law claim in a federal bankruptcy court. Yet everyone seems to agree that Congress could have authorized adjudication of this claim in a federal district court. Alternatively, Congress could have propounded a federal rule of decision governing this dispute, in which case, the plurality suggests, it could then have committed resolution of the dispute to a non-Article III tribunal. In light of these possibilities, what federalism interest can Northern Pipeline be said to vindicate?

As a way of further teasing out potential federalism concerns associated with non-Article III adjudication, consider this admittedly unlikely scenario: To relieve the federal courts of the burden of diversity jurisdiction, Congress establishes specialized "Diversity Courts" in each judicial district, staffed by non-Article III judges. Would such courts raise federalism concerns? If so, why?

8.   THOMAS V. UNION CARBIDE AGRICULTURAL PRODUCTS

One possible interpretation of *Northern Pipeline* was that the Court had decided to "go this far and no farther" in allowing non-Article III adjudication. Subsequent decisions proved that interpretation false.

Thomas v. Union Carbide Agricultural Products Co., 473 U.S. 568 (1985), involved a challenge to statutorily imposed binding arbitration. The Federal Insecticide, Fungicide, and Rodenticide Act established mandatory sharing of research data submitted to the Environmental Protection Agency to support new pesticide registration. The originator of a new pesticide was required, after a period of ten years, to allow competitors to use previously submitted research data for approval of their new products, but was entitled to compensation for the use of such data. Disputes about the appropriate amount of compensation proved extremely difficult for the EPA to handle, so in 1978 Congress amended the statute to require binding arbitration of compensation disputes, with judicial review only for "fraud, misrepresentation or other misconduct."

Following *Northern Pipeline,* several chemical companies charged that the mandatory arbitration procedure violated Article III. The Supreme Court disagreed. Speaking through Justice O'Connor, the Court explained that *Northern Pipeline* "establishes only that Congress may not vest in a non-Article III court the power to adjudicate, render final judgment, and issue binding orders in a traditional contract action arising under state law, without the consent of the litigants and subject only to ordinary appellate review." So construed, *Northern Pipeline* was distinguishable. Here the right to compensation did not arise under state law but was federally created. Moreover, although arguably a "private right" within the meaning of *Northern Pipeline,* it was enmeshed in a federal regulatory scheme and thus had "many characteristics of a 'public' right." Binding arbitration was therefore upheld. "To hold otherwise would be to erect a rigid and formalistic restraint on the ability of Congress to adopt innovative measures such as negotiation and arbitration with respect to rights created by a regulatory scheme." Justice Brennan, joined by Justices Marshall and Blackmun, and Justice Stevens, concurred in the judgment in separate opinions.

9. *COMMODITY FUTURES TRADING COMMISSION V. SCHOR*

A year later, the Supreme Court again considered the implications of *Northern Pipeline*, in Commodity Futures Trading Commission v. Schor, 478 U.S. 833 (1986). The issue in that case was the scope of the Commodity Future Trading Commission's jurisdiction in "reparation" proceedings brought under the Commodity Exchange Act. "Reparation" proceedings are brought by customers of professional commodity brokers for prohibited forms of fraudulent or manipulative conduct. The Commission, which is organized as an independent federal agency, is empowered to resolve such claims as an "inexpensive and expeditious" alternative to litigation. In 1976, the Commission by regulation authorized itself also to hear all counterclaims "aris[ing] out of the same transaction or occurrence" as the reparations claims. After *Northern Pipeline*, questions arose concerning the constitutionality of non-Article III adjudication of state-law counterclaims, but the Supreme Court approved the procedure.

Speaking through Justice O'Connor, the Court distinguished between the "personal" and "structural" interests protected by Article III. Any "personal" interest in securing Article III adjudication would be waived by the act of bringing a "reparation" proceeding rather than filing a lawsuit. A commodity customer who elected to forego litigation in favor of the quicker and less expensive administrative procedure "effectively agreed" to administrative adjudication of the entire controversy. To the extent, however, that Article III protects "structural" interests, the right to Article III adjudication could not be waived. Nevertheless, the Court saw no constitutional violation:

> The CFTC's adjudicatory powers depart from the traditional agency model in just one respect: the CFTC's jurisdiction over common law counterclaims. . . . The counterclaim asserted in this case

is a "private" right for which state law provides the rule of decision. It is therefore a claim of the kind assumed to be at the "core" of matters normally reserved to Article III courts. Yet this conclusion does not end our inquiry; just as this Court has rejected any attempt to make determinative for Article III purposes the distinction between public and private rights, *Thomas v. Union Carbide Agricultural Products*, there is no reason inherent in separation of powers principles to accord the state law character of a claim talismanic power in Article III inquiries. . . .

[W]here private, common law rights are at stake, our examination of the congressional attempt to control the manner in which those rights are adjudicated has been searching. See, e.g., *Northern Pipeline*. In this case, however, "[l]ooking beyond form to the substance of what" Congress has done, we are persuaded that the congressional authorization of limited CFTC jurisdiction over a narrow class of common law claims as an incident to the CFTC's primary, and unchallenged, adjudicative function does not create a substantial threat to the separation of powers.

It is clear that Congress has not attempted to "withdraw from judicial cognizance" the determination of [the counterclaim]. Congress gave the CFTC the authority to adjudicate such matters, but the decision to invoke this forum is left entirely to the parties and the power of the federal judiciary to take jurisdiction of these matters is unaffected. In such circumstances, separation of powers concerns are diminished, for it seems self-evident that just as Congress may encourage parties to settle a dispute out of court or resort to arbitration without impermissible incursions on the separation of powers, Congress may make available a quasi-judicial mechanism through which willing parties may, at their option, elect to resolve their differences. . . .

In such circumstances, the magnitude of any intrusion on the judicial branch can only be termed de minimis. Conversely, were we to hold that the legislative branch may not permit such limited cognizance of common law counterclaims at the election of the parties, it is clear that we would "defeat the obvious purpose of the legislation to furnish a prompt, continuous, expert and inexpensive method for dealing with a class of questions of fact which are peculiarly suited to examination and determination by an administrative agency specially assigned to that task." We do not think Article III compels this degree of prophylaxis.

Justice Brennan, with whom Justice Marshall joined, dissented. He urged that non-Article III adjudication be limited to the "few, well-established exceptions" detailed in his opinion in *Northern Pipeline* and charged that the majority had "far exceed[ed] the analytic framework of our precedents." In his view, the Court had improperly subordinated the command of Article III to the dictates of convenience.

Thomas and *Schor* seemed to suggest that the Court was pursuing a functional approach to the issue of non-Article III courts, similar to what Justice White had suggested in his dissent in *Northern Pipeline*. Instead of focusing on categorical distinctions, such as between public and private rights, the Court seemed to be assessing whether particular forms of non-Article III adjudication posed a threat to the separation of powers. The Court returned to a more formal approach, however, in *Stern v. Marshall*, which is excerpted below.

10. *GRANFINANCIERA, S.A. V. NORDBERG*

The Court elaborated on the distinction between public and private rights in Granfinanciera, S.A. v. Nordberg, 492 U.S. 33 (1989), in the context of determining whether someone who had not submitted a claim against a bankruptcy estate had a Seventh Amendment right to a jury trial when being sued by the bankruptcy trustee in a fraudulent conveyance action. In doing so, it signaled a possible shift back towards the formal, categorical approach to the constitutionality of non-Article III courts reflected in the plurality opinion in *Northern Pipeline*. The Court in *Granfinanciera*, in an opinion by Justice Brennan, explained that the Court's Seventh Amendment analysis overlapped with its jurisprudence on the use of non-Article III courts:

> [O]ur decisions point to the conclusion that, if a statutory cause of action is legal in nature, the question whether the Seventh Amendment permits Congress to assign its adjudication to a tribunal that does not employ juries as factfinders requires the same answer as the question whether Article III allows Congress to assign adjudication of that cause of action to a non-Article III tribunal: For if a statutory cause of action, such as respondent's right to recover a fraudulent conveyance . . . is not a "public right" for Article III purposes, then Congress may not assign its adjudication to a specialized non-Article III court lacking "the essential attributes of the judicial power." Crowell v. Benson, 285 U.S. 22, 51 (1932). And if the action must be tried under the auspices of an Article III court, then the Seventh Amendment affords the parties a right to a jury trial whenever the cause of action is legal in nature. Conversely, if Congress may assign the adjudication of a statutory cause of action to a non-Article III tribunal, then the Seventh Amendment poses no independent bar to the adjudication of that action by a nonjury factfinder.

While noting that "the issue admits of some debate," the Court concluded that a fraudulent conveyance action is "more accurately characterized as a private, rather than a public, right as we have used those terms in our Article III decisions." The Court explained that fraudulent conveyance actions "are quintessentially suits at common law that more nearly resemble state law contract claims brought by a bankrupt corporation to augment the bankruptcy estate than they do creditors' hierarchically ordered claims to a pro rata share of the bankruptcy res." Consequently, the Court concluded that the defendant in this case was entitled to a jury trial. Justice Scalia concurred, arguing that to qualify as a public rights case, the case must involve the government as a party. Scalia also critiqued the balancing approach to the non-Article III courts issue reflected in *Thomas* and *Schor*. Justice White dissented.[b]

Stern v. Marshall

Supreme Court of the United States, 2011.
564 U.S. 462.

■ CHIEF JUSTICE ROBERTS delivered the opinion of the Court.

. . . This is the second time we have had occasion to weigh in on this long-running dispute between Vickie Lynn Marshall and E. Pierce Marshall over the fortune of J. Howard Marshall II, a man believed to have been one of the richest people in Texas. The Marshalls' litigation has worked its way through state and federal courts in Louisiana, Texas, and California, and two of those courts—a Texas state probate court and the Bankruptcy Court for the Central District of California—have reached contrary decisions on its merits. The Court of Appeals below held that the Texas state decision controlled, after concluding that the Bankruptcy Court lacked the authority to enter final judgment on a counterclaim that Vickie brought against Pierce in her bankruptcy proceeding. To determine whether the Court of Appeals was correct in that regard, we must resolve two issues: (1) whether the Bankruptcy Court had the statutory authority under 28 U.S.C. § 157(b) to issue a final judgment on Vickie's counterclaim; and (2) if so, whether conferring that authority on the Bankruptcy Court is constitutional.

Although the history of this litigation is complicated, its resolution ultimately turns on very basic principles. Article III, § 1, of the Constitution commands that "[t]he judicial Power of the United States, shall be vested in one supreme Court, and in such inferior Courts as the Congress may from time to time ordain and establish." That Article further provides that the judges of those courts shall hold their offices during good behavior, without diminution of salary. Those requirements of Article III were not honored here. The Bankruptcy Court in this case exercised the judicial power of the United States by entering final judgment on a common law tort claim, even though the judges of such courts enjoy neither tenure during good behavior nor salary protection. We conclude that, although the Bankruptcy Court had the statutory authority to enter judgment on Vickie's counterclaim, it lacked the constitutional authority to do so.

I

Because we have already recounted the facts and procedural history of this case in detail [in our prior decision], we do not repeat them in full

---

[b]   For additional consideration of the relationship between the Seventh Amendment and the constitutionality of non-Article III courts, see Ellen E. Sward, Legislative Courts, Article III, and the Seventh Amendment, 77 N.C.L. Rev. 1037 (1999).

here. Of current relevance are two claims Vickie filed in an attempt to secure half of J. Howard's fortune. Known to the public as Anna Nicole Smith, Vickie was J. Howard's third wife and married him about a year before his death. Although J. Howard bestowed on Vickie many monetary and other gifts during their courtship and marriage, he did not include her in his will. Before J. Howard passed away, Vickie filed suit in Texas state probate court, asserting that Pierce—J. Howard's younger son—fraudulently induced J. Howard to sign a living trust that did not include her, even though J. Howard meant to give her half his property. Pierce denied any fraudulent activity and defended the validity of J. Howard's trust and, eventually, his will.

After J. Howard's death, Vickie filed a petition for bankruptcy in the Central District of California. Pierce filed a complaint in that bankruptcy proceeding, contending that Vickie had defamed him by inducing her lawyers to tell members of the press that he had engaged in fraud to gain control of his father's assets. The complaint sought a declaration that Pierce's defamation claim was not dischargeable in the bankruptcy proceedings. Pierce subsequently filed a proof of claim for the defamation action, meaning that he sought to recover damages for it from Vickie's bankruptcy estate. Vickie responded to Pierce's initial complaint by asserting truth as a defense to the alleged defamation and by filing a counterclaim for tortious interference with the gift she expected from J. Howard. As she had in state court, Vickie alleged that Pierce had wrongfully prevented J. Howard from taking the legal steps necessary to provide her with half his property.

On November 5, 1999, the Bankruptcy Court issued an order granting Vickie summary judgment on Pierce's claim for defamation. On September 27, 2000, after a bench trial, the Bankruptcy Court issued a judgment on Vickie's counterclaim in her favor. The court later awarded Vickie over $400 million in compensatory damages and $25 million in punitive damages.

In post-trial proceedings, Pierce argued that the Bankruptcy Court lacked jurisdiction over Vickie's counterclaim. In particular, Pierce renewed a claim he had made earlier in the litigation, asserting that the Bankruptcy Court's authority over the counterclaim was limited because Vickie's counterclaim was not a "core proceeding" under 28 U.S.C. § 157(b)(2)(C). As explained below, bankruptcy courts may hear and enter final judgments in "core proceedings" in a bankruptcy case. In non-core proceedings, the bankruptcy courts instead submit proposed findings of fact and conclusions of law to the district court, for that court's review and issuance of final judgment. The Bankruptcy Court in this case concluded that Vickie's counterclaim was "a core proceeding" under § 157(b)(2)(C), and the court therefore had the "power to enter judgment" on the counterclaim under § 157(b)(1).

The District Court disagreed. It recognized that "Vickie's counterclaim for tortious interference falls within the literal language" of the statute designating certain proceedings as "core," see § 157(b)(2)(C), but understood this Court's precedent to "suggest[ ] that it would be unconstitutional to hold that any and all counterclaims are core." The District Court accordingly concluded that a "counterclaim should not be characterized as core" when it "is only somewhat related to the claim against which it is asserted, and when the unique characteristics and context of the counterclaim place it outside of the normal type of set-off or other counterclaims that customarily arise."

Because the District Court concluded that Vickie's counterclaim was not core, the court determined that it was required to treat the Bankruptcy Court's judgment as "proposed[,] rather than final," and engage in an "independent review" of the record. Although the Texas state court had by that time conducted a jury trial on the merits of the parties' dispute and entered a judgment in Pierce's favor, the District Court declined to give that judgment preclusive effect and went on to decide the matter itself. Like the Bankruptcy Court, the District Court found that Pierce had tortiously interfered with Vickie's expectancy of a gift from J. Howard. The District Court awarded Vickie compensatory and punitive damages, each in the amount of $44,292,767.33.

The Court of Appeals reversed the District Court on a different ground, and we—in the first visit of the case to this Court—reversed the Court of Appeals on that issue. On remand from this Court, the Court of Appeals held that § 157 mandated "a two-step approach" under which a bankruptcy judge may issue a final judgment in a proceeding only if the matter both "meets Congress's definition of a core proceeding *and* arises under or arises in title 11," the Bankruptcy Code. The court also reasoned that allowing a bankruptcy judge to enter final judgments on all counterclaims raised in bankruptcy proceedings "would certainly run afoul" of this Court's decision in Northern Pipeline Construction Co. v. Marathon Pipe Line Co., 458 U.S. 50 (1982). With those concerns in mind, the court concluded that "a counterclaim under § 157(b)(2)(C) is properly a 'core' proceeding 'arising in a case under' the [Bankruptcy] Code only if the counterclaim is so closely related to [a creditor's] proof of claim that the resolution of the counterclaim is necessary to resolve the allowance or disallowance of the claim itself." The court ruled that Vickie's counterclaim did not meet that test. That holding made "the Texas probate court's judgment . . . the earliest final judgment entered on matters relevant to this proceeding," and therefore the Court of Appeals concluded that the District Court should have "afford[ed] preclusive effect" to the Texas "court's determination of relevant legal and factual issues."

We again granted certiorari.

II

A

With certain exceptions not relevant here, the district courts of the United States have "original and exclusive jurisdiction of all cases under title 11." 28 U.S.C. § 1334(a). Congress has divided bankruptcy proceedings into three categories: those that "aris[e] under title 11"; those that "aris[e] in" a Title 11 case; and those that are "related to a case under title 11." § 157(a). District courts may refer any or all such proceedings to the bankruptcy judges of their district, which is how the Bankruptcy Court in this case came to preside over Vickie's bankruptcy proceedings. District courts also may withdraw a case or proceeding referred to the bankruptcy court "for cause shown." § 157(d). Since Congress enacted the Bankruptcy Amendments and Federal Judgeship Act of 1984 (the 1984 Act), bankruptcy judges for each district have been appointed to 14-year terms by the courts of appeals for the circuits in which their district is located. § 152(a)(1).

The manner in which a bankruptcy judge may act on a referred matter depends on the type of proceeding involved. Bankruptcy judges may hear and enter final judgments in "all core proceedings arising under title 11, or arising in a case under title 11." § 157(b)(1). "Core proceedings include, but are not limited to" 16 different types of matters, including "counterclaims by [a debtor's] estate against persons filing claims against the estate." § 157(b)(2)(C).[3] Parties may appeal final judgments of a

---

3   In full, §§ 157(b)(1)–(2) provides:

    (1)   Bankruptcy judges may hear and determine all cases under title 11 and all core proceedings arising under title 11, or arising in a case under title 11, referred under subsection (a) of this section, and may enter appropriate orders and judgments, subject to review under section 158 of this title.

    (2)   Core proceedings include, but are not limited to—

        (A)   matters concerning the administration of the estate;

        (B)   allowance or disallowance of claims against the estate or exemptions from property of the estate, and estimation of claims or interests for the purposes of confirming a plan under chapter 11, 12, or 13 of title 11 but not the liquidation or estimation of contingent or unliquidated personal injury tort or wrongful death claims against the estate for purposes of distribution in a case under title 11;

        (C)   counterclaims by the estate against persons filing claims against the estate;

        (D)   orders in respect to obtaining credit;

        (E)   orders to turn over property of the estate;

        (F)   proceedings to determine, avoid, or recover preferences;

        (G)   motions to terminate, annul, or modify the automatic stay;

        (H)   proceedings to determine, avoid, or recover fraudulent conveyances;

        (I)   determinations as to the dischargeability of particular debts;

        (J)   objections to discharges;

        (K)   determinations of the validity, extent, or priority of liens;

        (L)   confirmations of plans;

        (M)   orders approving the use or lease of property, including the use of cash collateral;

        (N)   orders approving the sale of property other than property resulting from claims brought by the estate against persons who have not filed claims against the estate;

        (O)   other proceedings affecting the liquidation of the assets of the estate or the adjustment of the debtor-creditor or the equity security holder relationship, except personal injury tort or wrongful death claims; and

        (P)   recognition of foreign proceedings and other matters under chapter 15 of title 11.

bankruptcy court in core proceedings to the district court, which reviews them under traditional appellate standards. See § 158(a); Fed. Rule Bkrtcy. Proc. 8013.

When a bankruptcy judge determines that a referred "proceeding . . . is not a core proceeding but . . . is otherwise related to a case under title 11," the judge may only "submit proposed findings of fact and conclusions of law to the district court." § 157(c)(1). It is the district court that enters final judgment in such cases after reviewing de novo any matter to which a party objects.

B

[The Court concluded in this section that Vickie's counterclaim qualified as a "core proceeding" under § 157(b)(2)(C) and that the Bankruptcy Court therefore had statutory authority to enter a final judgment on the counterclaim.]

III

Although we conclude that § 157(b)(2)(C) permits the Bankruptcy Court to enter final judgment on Vickie's counterclaim, Article III of the Constitution does not.

A

. . . Article III could neither serve its purpose in the system of checks and balances nor preserve the integrity of judicial decisionmaking if the other branches of the Federal Government could confer the Government's "judicial Power" on entities outside Article III. That is why we have long recognized that, in general, Congress may not "withdraw from judicial cognizance any matter which, from its nature, is the subject of a suit at the common law, or in equity, or admiralty." Murray's Lessee v. Hoboken Land & Improvement Co., 59 U.S. (10 How.) 272, 284 (1856). When a suit is made of "the stuff of the traditional actions at common law tried by the courts at Westminster in 1789," Northern Pipeline, 458 U.S. at 90 (Rehnquist, J., concurring in judgment), and is brought within the bounds of federal jurisdiction, the responsibility for deciding that suit rests with Article III judges in Article III courts. The Constitution assigns that job—resolution of "the mundane as well as the glamorous, matters of common law and statute as well as constitutional law, issues of fact as well as issues of law"—to the Judiciary. Id. at 86–87 n.39 (plurality opinion).

B

. . . After our decision in Northern Pipeline, Congress revised the statutes governing bankruptcy jurisdiction and bankruptcy judges. In the 1984 Act, Congress provided that the judges of the new bankruptcy courts would be appointed by the courts of appeals for the circuits in which their districts are located. 28 U.S.C. § 152(a). And, as we have explained, Congress permitted the newly constituted bankruptcy courts to enter final judgments only in "core" proceedings.

With respect to such "core" matters, however, the bankruptcy courts under the 1984 Act exercise the same powers they wielded under the Bankruptcy Act of 1978. As in *Northern Pipeline,* for example, the newly constituted bankruptcy courts are charged under § 157(b)(2)(C) with resolving "[a]ll matters of fact and law in whatever domains of the law to which" a counterclaim may lead. As in *Northern Pipeline*, the new courts in core proceedings "issue final judgments, which are binding and enforceable even in the absence of an appeal." 458 U.S. at 85–86 (plurality opinion). And, as in *Northern Pipeline*, the district courts review the judgments of the bankruptcy courts in core proceedings only under the usual limited appellate standards. That requires marked deference to, among other things, the bankruptcy judges' findings of fact. See § 158(a); Fed. Rule Bkrtcy. Proc. 8013 (findings of fact "shall not be set aside unless clearly erroneous").

C

Vickie and the dissent argue that the Bankruptcy Court's entry of final judgment on her state common law counterclaim was constitutional, despite the similarities between the bankruptcy courts under the 1978 Act and those exercising core jurisdiction under the 1984 Act. We disagree. . . .

1

Vickie's counterclaim cannot be deemed a matter of "public right" that can be decided outside the Judicial Branch. [I]n *Northern Pipeline* we rejected the argument that the public rights doctrine permitted a bankruptcy court to adjudicate a state law suit brought by a debtor against a company that had not filed a claim against the estate. Although our discussion of the public rights exception since that time has not been entirely consistent, and the exception has been the subject of some debate, this case does not fall within any of the various formulations of the concept that appear in this Court's opinions. . . .

[At this point the Court summarized its prior decisions through *Thomas, Schor,* and *Granfinanciera.*]

Vickie's counterclaim—like the fraudulent conveyance claim at issue in *Granfinanciera*—does not fall within any of the varied formulations of the public rights exception in this Court's cases. It is not a matter that can be pursued only by grace of the other branches, as in *Murray's Lessee*, or one that "historically could have been determined exclusively by" those branches, *Northern Pipeline*, 458 U.S. at 68. The claim is instead one under state common law between two private parties. It does not "depend[ ] on the will of congress," *Murray's Lessee*, 59 U.S. at 284; Congress has nothing to do with it.

In addition, Vickie's claimed right to relief does not flow from a federal statutory scheme, as in *Thomas*. . . . It is not "completely dependent upon" adjudication of a claim created by federal law, as in *Schor*. And in contrast to the objecting party in *Schor*, Pierce did not truly consent to resolution of Vickie's claim in the bankruptcy court proceedings. He had nowhere else to go if he wished to recover from Vickie's estate. See *Granfinanciera*, 492 U.S. at 59 n.14 (noting that "[p]arallel reasoning [to *Schor*] is unavailable in the context of bankruptcy proceedings, because creditors lack an alternative forum to the bankruptcy court in which to pursue their claims").[8]

Furthermore, the asserted authority to decide Vickie's claim is not limited to a "particularized area of the law," as in *Thomas*, and *Schor*. We deal here not with an agency but with a court, with substantive jurisdiction reaching any area of the corpus juris. This is not a situation in which Congress devised an "expert and inexpensive method for dealing with a class of questions of fact which are particularly suited to examination and determination by an administrative agency specially assigned to that task." Crowell v. Benson, 285 U.S. 22, 46 (1932); see *Schor*, 478 U.S. at 855–56. The "experts" in the federal system at resolving common law counterclaims such as Vickie's are the Article III courts, and it is with those courts that her claim must stay.

The dissent reads our cases differently, and in particular contends that more recent cases view *Northern Pipeline* as " 'establish[ing] only that Congress may not vest in a non-Article III court the power to adjudicate, render final judgment, and issue binding orders in a traditional contract action arising under state law, without consent of the litigants, and subject only to ordinary appellate review.' " (quoting *Thomas*, 473 U.S. at 584). Just so: Substitute "tort" for "contract," and that statement directly covers this case.

We recognize that there may be instances in which the distinction between public and private rights—at least as framed by some of our recent cases—fails to provide concrete guidance as to whether, for example, a particular agency can adjudicate legal issues under a substantive regulatory scheme. Given the extent to which this case is so markedly distinct from the agency cases discussing the public rights exception in the context of such a regime, however, we do not in this opinion express any view on how the doctrine might apply in that different context.

What is plain here is that this case involves the most prototypical exercise of judicial power: the entry of a final, binding judgment *by a court* with broad substantive jurisdiction, on a common law cause of action, when the action neither derives from nor depends upon any agency regulatory regime. If such an exercise of judicial power may nonetheless be taken from the Article III Judiciary simply by deeming it part of some amorphous "public right," then Article III would be transformed from the

---

[8]   Contrary to the claims of the dissent, Pierce did not have another forum in which to pursue his claim to recover from Vickie's pre-bankruptcy assets, rather than take his chances with whatever funds might remain after the Title 11 proceedings. Creditors who possess claims that do not satisfy the requirements for nondischargeability under 11 U.S.C. § 523 have no choice but to file their claims in bankruptcy proceedings if they want to pursue the claims at all. That is why, as we recognized in *Granfinanciera*, the notion of "consent" does not apply in bankruptcy proceedings as it might in other contexts.

guardian of individual liberty and separation of powers we have long recognized into mere wishful thinking.

2

[In this section, the Court rejected the argument that Pierce's filing of a proof of claim in the bankruptcy proceedings distinguished the case from *Northern Pipeline* and *Granfinanciera,* noting, among other things, that "it is hard to see why Pierce's decision to file a claim should make any difference with respect to the characterization of Vickie's counterclaim."]

3

Vickie additionally argues that the Bankruptcy Court's final judgment was constitutional because bankruptcy courts under the 1984 Act are properly deemed "adjuncts" of the district courts. We rejected a similar argument in *Northern Pipeline*, see 458 U.S. at 84–86 (plurality opinion); id. at 91 (Rehnquist, J., concurring in judgment), and our reasoning there holds true today.

To begin, as explained above, it is still the bankruptcy court itself that exercises the essential attributes of judicial power over a matter such as Vickie's counterclaim. The new bankruptcy courts, like the old, do not "ma[k]e only specialized, narrowly confined factual determinations regarding a particularized area of law" or engage in "statutorily channeled factfinding functions." *Northern Pipeline*, 458 U.S. at 85 (plurality opinion). Instead, bankruptcy courts under the 1984 Act resolve "[a]ll matters of fact and law in whatever domains of the law to which" the parties' counterclaims might lead. Id. at 91 (Rehnquist, J., concurring in judgment).

In addition, whereas the adjunct agency in *Crowell v. Benson* "possessed only a limited power to issue compensation orders [that] could be enforced only by order of the district court," *Northern Pipeline*, 458 U.S. at 85, a bankruptcy court resolving a counterclaim under 28 U.S.C. § 157(b)(2)(C) has the power to enter "appropriate orders and judgments"—including final judgments—subject to review only if a party chooses to appeal, see §§ 157(b)(1), 158(a)–(b). It is thus no less the case here than it was in *Northern Pipeline* that "[t]he authority—and the responsibility—to make an informed, final determination ... remains with" the bankruptcy judge, not the district court. 458 U.S. at 81 (plurality opinion). Given that authority, a bankruptcy court can no more be deemed a mere "adjunct" of the district court than a district court can be deemed such an "adjunct" of the court of appeals. We certainly cannot accept the dissent's notion that judges who have the power to enter final, binding orders are the "functional[ ]" equivalent of "law clerks[ ] and the Judiciary's administrative officials." And even were we wrong in this regard, that would only confirm that such judges should not be in the business of entering final judgments in the first place.

It does not affect our analysis that, as Vickie notes, bankruptcy judges under the current Act are appointed by the Article III courts, rather than the President. If—as we have concluded—the bankruptcy court itself exercises "the essential attributes of judicial power [that] are reserved to Article III courts," *Schor*, 478 U.S. at 851, it does not matter who appointed the bankruptcy judge or authorized the judge to render final judgments in such proceedings. The constitutional bar remains. See The Federalist No. 78, at 471 ("Periodical appointments, however regulated, or by whomsoever made, would, in some way or other, be fatal to [a judge's] necessary independence").

D

Finally, Vickie and her amici predict as a practical matter that restrictions on a bankruptcy court's ability to hear and finally resolve compulsory counterclaims will create significant delays and impose additional costs on the bankruptcy process. It goes without saying that "the fact that a given law or procedure is efficient, convenient, and useful in facilitating functions of government, standing alone, will not save it if it is contrary to the Constitution." INS v. Chadha, 462 U.S. 919, 944 (1983).

In addition, we are not convinced that the practical consequences of such limitations on the authority of bankruptcy courts to enter final judgments are as significant as Vickie and the dissent suggest. The dissent asserts that it is important that counterclaims such as Vickie's be resolved "in a bankruptcy court," and that, "to be effective, a single tribunal must have broad authority to restructure [debtor-creditor] relations." But the framework Congress adopted in the 1984 Act already contemplates that certain state law matters in bankruptcy cases will be resolved by judges other than those of the bankruptcy courts. Section 1334(c)(2), for example, requires that bankruptcy courts abstain from hearing specified non-core, state law claims that "can be timely adjudicated[ ] in a State forum of appropriate jurisdiction." Section 1334(c)(1) similarly provides that bankruptcy courts may abstain from hearing any proceeding, including core matters, "in the interest of comity with State courts or respect for State law."

As described above, the current bankruptcy system also requires the district court to review de novo and enter final judgment on any matters that are "related to" the bankruptcy proceedings, § 157(c)(1), and permits the district court to withdraw from the bankruptcy court any referred case, proceeding, or part thereof, § 157(d). Pierce has not argued that the bankruptcy courts "are barred from 'hearing' all counterclaims" or proposing findings of fact and conclusions of law on those matters, but rather that it must be the district court that "finally decide[s]" them. We do not think the removal of counterclaims such as Vickie's from core bankruptcy jurisdiction meaningfully changes the division of labor in the current statute; we agree with the United States that the question presented here is a "narrow" one.

If our decision today does not change all that much, then why the fuss? Is there really a threat to the separation of powers where Congress has conferred the judicial power outside Article III only over certain counterclaims in bankruptcy? The short but emphatic answer is yes. A statute may no more lawfully chip away at the authority of the Judicial Branch than it may eliminate it entirely. "Slight encroachments create new boundaries from which legions of power can seek new territory to capture." Reid v. Covert, 354 U.S. 1, 39 (1957) (plurality opinion). Although "[i]t may be that it is the obnoxious thing in its mildest and least repulsive form," we cannot overlook the intrusion: "illegitimate and unconstitutional practices get their first footing in that way, namely, by silent approaches and slight deviations from legal modes of procedure." Boyd v. United States, 116 U.S. 616, 635 (1886). We cannot compromise the integrity of the system of separated powers and the role of the Judiciary in that system, even with respect to challenges that may seem innocuous at first blush.

* * *

Article III of the Constitution provides that the judicial power of the United States may be vested only in courts whose judges enjoy the protections set forth in that Article. We conclude today that Congress, in one isolated respect, exceeded that limitation in the Bankruptcy Act of 1984. The Bankruptcy Court below lacked the constitutional authority to enter a final judgment on a state law counterclaim that is not resolved in the process of ruling on a creditor's proof of claim. Accordingly, the judgment of the Court of Appeals is affirmed.

It is so ordered.

■ JUSTICE SCALIA, concurring.

I agree with the Court's interpretation of our Article III precedents, and I accordingly join its opinion. I adhere to my view, however, that—our contrary precedents notwithstanding—"a matter of public rights . . . must at a minimum arise between the government and others," Granfinanciera, S.A. v. Nordberg, 492 U.S. 33, 65 (1989) (Scalia, J., concurring in part and concurring in judgment).

The sheer surfeit of factors that the Court was required to consider in this case should arouse the suspicion that something is seriously amiss with our jurisprudence in this area. I count at least seven different reasons given in the Court's opinion for concluding that an Article III judge was required to adjudicate this lawsuit: that it was one "under state common law" which was "not a matter that can be pursued only by grace of the other branches"; that it was "not 'completely dependent upon' adjudication of a claim created by federal law"; that "Pierce did not truly consent to resolution of Vickie's claim in the bankruptcy court proceedings"; that "the asserted authority to decide Vickie's claim is not limited to a 'particularized area of the law' "; that "there was never any reason to believe that the process of adjudicating Pierce's proof of claim would necessarily resolve Vickie's counterclaim"; that the trustee was not "asserting a right of recovery created by federal bankruptcy law"; and that the Bankruptcy Judge "ha[d] the power to enter 'appropriate orders and judgments'—including final judgments—subject to review only if a party chooses to appeal."

Apart from their sheer numerosity, the more fundamental flaw in the many tests suggested by our jurisprudence is that they have nothing to do with the text or tradition of Article III. For example, Article III gives no indication that state-law claims have preferential entitlement to an Article III judge; nor does it make pertinent the extent to which the area of the law is "particularized." The multifactors relied upon today seem to have entered our jurisprudence almost randomly.

Leaving aside certain adjudications by federal administrative agencies, which are governed (for better or worse) by our landmark decision in Crowell v. Benson, 285 U.S. 22 (1932), in my view an Article III judge is required in *all* federal adjudications, unless there is a firmly established historical practice to the contrary. For that reason—and not because of some intuitive balancing of benefits and harms—I agree that Article III judges are not required in the context of territorial courts, courts-martial, or true "public rights" cases. See Northern Pipeline Constr. Co. v. Marathon Pipe Line Co., 458 U.S. 50, 71 (1982) (plurality opinion). Perhaps historical practice permits non-Article III judges to process claims against the bankruptcy estate, see, e.g., Thomas E. Plank, Why Bankruptcy Judges Need Not and Should Not Be Article III Judges, 72 Am. Bankr. L.J. 567, 607–09 (1998); the subject has not been briefed, and so I state no position on the matter. But Vickie points to no historical practice that authorizes a non-Article III judge to adjudicate a counterclaim of the sort at issue here.

■ JUSTICE BREYER, with whom JUSTICE GINSBURG, JUSTICE SOTOMAYOR, and JUSTICE KAGAN join, dissenting. . . .

I

[Part I of the dissent summarized the Court's prior decisions concerning non-Article III courts, and stated:]

. . . The majority, in my view, overemphasizes the precedential effect of the plurality opinion in Northern Pipeline Construction Co. v. Marathon Pipe Line Co., 458 U.S. 50 (1982). . . .

Rather than leaning so heavily on the approach taken by the plurality in *Northern Pipeline*, I would look to this Court's more recent Article III cases *Thomas* and *Schor*—cases that commanded a clear majority. In both cases the Court took a more pragmatic approach to the constitutional question. It sought to determine whether, in the particular instance, the challenged delegation of adjudicatory authority posed a genuine and serious threat that one branch of Government sought to aggrandize its own constitutionally delegated authority by encroaching upon a field of authority that the Constitution assigns exclusively to another branch. . . .

II

A

This case law, as applied in *Thomas* and *Schor*, requires us to determine pragmatically whether a congressional delegation of adjudicatory authority to a non-Article III judge violates the separation-of-powers principles inherent in Article III. That is to say, we must determine through an examination of certain relevant factors whether that delegation constitutes a significant encroachment by the Legislative or Executive Branches of Government upon the realm of authority that Article III reserves for exercise by the Judicial Branch of Government. Those factors include (1) the nature of the claim to be adjudicated; (2) the nature of the non-Article III tribunal; (3) the extent to which Article III courts exercise control over the proceeding; (4) the presence or absence of the parties' consent; and (5) the nature and importance of the legislative purpose served by the grant of adjudicatory authority to a tribunal with judges who lack Article III's tenure and compensation protections. The presence of "private rights" does not automatically determine the outcome of the question but requires a more "searching" examination of the relevant factors. *Schor*, 478 U.S. at 854.

Insofar as the majority would apply more formal standards, it simply disregards recent, controlling precedent. *Thomas*, 473 U.S. at 587 ("[P]ractical attention to substance rather than doctrinaire reliance on formal categories should inform application of Article III"); *Schor*, 478 U.S. at 851 ("[T]he Court has declined to adopt formalistic and unbending rules" for deciding Article III cases).

B

Applying *Schor*'s approach here, I conclude that the delegation of adjudicatory authority before us is constitutional. A grant of authority to a bankruptcy court to adjudicate compulsory counterclaims does not violate any constitutional separation-of-powers principle related to Article III.

First, I concede that *the nature of the claim to be adjudicated* argues against my conclusion. Vickie Marshall's counterclaim—a kind of tort suit—resembles "a suit at the common law." Murray's Lessee v. Hoboken Land & Improvement Co., 59 U.S. (10 How.) 272, 284 (1856). Although not determinative of the question, see *Schor*, 478 U.S. at 853, a delegation of authority to a non-Article III judge to adjudicate a claim of that kind poses a heightened risk of encroachment on the Federal Judiciary, id. at 854.

At the same time the significance of this factor is mitigated here by the fact that bankruptcy courts often decide claims that similarly resemble various common-law actions. Suppose, for example, that ownership of 40 acres of land in the bankruptcy debtor's possession is disputed by a creditor. If that creditor brings a claim in the bankruptcy court, resolution of that dispute requires the bankruptcy court to apply the same state property law that would govern in a state court proceeding. This kind of dispute arises with regularity in bankruptcy proceedings.

Of course, in this instance the state-law question is embedded in a debtor's counterclaim, not a creditor's claim. But the counterclaim is "compulsory." It "arises out of the transaction or occurrence that is the subject matter of the opposing party's claim." Fed. Rule Civ. Proc. 13(a); Fed. Rule Bkrtcy. Proc. 7013. Thus, resolution of the counterclaim will often turn on facts identical to, or at least related to, those at issue in a creditor's claim that is undisputedly proper for the bankruptcy court to decide.

Second, *the nature of the non-Article III tribunal* argues in favor of constitutionality. That is because the tribunal is made up of judges who enjoy considerable protection from improper political influence. Unlike the 1978 Act which provided for the appointment of bankruptcy judges by the President with the advice and consent of the Senate, current law provides that the federal courts of appeals appoint federal bankruptcy judges, § 152(a)(1). Bankruptcy judges are removable by the circuit judicial counsel (made up of federal court of appeals and district court judges) and only for cause. § 152(e). Their salaries are pegged to those of federal district court judges, § 153(a), and the cost of their courthouses and other work-related expenses are paid by the Judiciary, § 156. Thus, although Congress technically exercised its Article I power when it created bankruptcy courts, functionally, bankruptcy judges can be compared to magistrate judges, law clerks, and the Judiciary's administrative officials, whose lack of Article III tenure and compensation protections do not endanger the independence of the Judicial Branch.

Third, *the control exercised by Article III judges over bankruptcy proceedings* argues in favor of constitutionality. Article III judges control and supervise the bankruptcy court's determinations—at least to the same degree that Article III judges supervised the agency's determinations in *Crowell*, if not more so. Any party may appeal those determinations to the federal district court, where the federal judge will review all determinations of fact for clear error and will review all determinations of law *de novo*. . . . And, as *Crowell* noted, "there is no requirement that, in order to maintain the essential attributes of the judicial power, all determinations of fact in constitutional courts shall be made by judges." 285 U.S. at 51.

Moreover, in one important respect Article III judges maintain greater control over the bankruptcy court proceedings at issue here than they did over the relevant proceedings in any of the previous cases in which this Court has upheld a delegation of adjudicatory power. The District Court here may "withdraw, in whole or in part, any case or proceeding referred [to the Bankruptcy Court] . . . on its own motion or on timely motion of any party, for cause shown." 28 U.S.C. § 157(d); cf.

Northern Pipeline, 458 U.S. at 80 n.31 (plurality opinion) (contrasting pre-1978 law where "power to withdraw the case from the [bankruptcy] referee" gave district courts "control" over case with the unconstitutional 1978 statute, which provided no such district court authority).

Fourth, the fact that *the parties have consented* to Bankruptcy Court jurisdiction argues in favor of constitutionality, and strongly so. Pierce Marshall, the counterclaim defendant, is not a stranger to the litigation, forced to appear in Bankruptcy Court against his will. Cf. id. at 91 (Rehnquist, J., concurring in judgment) (suit was litigated in Bankruptcy Court "over [the defendant's] objection"). Rather, he appeared voluntarily in Bankruptcy Court as one of Vickie Marshall's creditors, seeking a favorable resolution of his claim against Vickie Marshall to the detriment of her other creditors. He need not have filed a claim, perhaps not even at the cost of bringing it in the future, for he says his claim is "nondischargeable," in which case he could have litigated it in a state or federal court after distribution. See 11 U.S.C. § 523(a)(6). Thus, Pierce Marshall likely had "an alternative forum to the bankruptcy court in which to pursue [his] clai[m]." *Granfinanciera, S.A. v. Nordberg*, 492 U.S. 33, 59 n.14 (1989). . . .

Fifth, *the nature and importance of the legislative purpose served* by the grant of adjudicatory authority to bankruptcy tribunals argues strongly in favor of constitutionality. Congress's delegation of adjudicatory powers over counterclaims asserted against bankruptcy claimants constitutes an important means of securing a constitutionally authorized end. Article I, § 8, of the Constitution explicitly grants Congress the "Power To . . . establish . . . uniform Laws on the subject of Bankruptcies throughout the United States." James Madison wrote in the Federalist Papers that the

> power of establishing uniform laws of bankruptcy is so intimately connected with the regulation of commerce, and will prevent so many frauds where the parties or their property may lie or be removed into different States, that the expediency of it seems not likely to be drawn into question. The Federalist No. 42, p. 271 (C. Rossiter ed. 1961).

Congress established the first Bankruptcy Act in 1800. From the beginning, the "core" of federal bankruptcy proceedings has been "the restructuring of debtor-creditor relations." *Northern Pipeline*, 458 U.S. at 71 (plurality opinion). And, to be effective, a single tribunal must have broad authority to restructure those relations, "having jurisdiction of the parties to controversies brought before them," "decid[ing] all matters in dispute," and "decree[ing] complete relief." *Katchen v. Landy*, 382 U.S. 323, 335 (1966).

The restructuring process requires a creditor to file a proof of claim in the bankruptcy court. In doing so, the creditor "triggers the process of 'allowance and disallowance of claims,' thereby subjecting himself to the bankruptcy court's equitable power." *Langenkamp v. Culp*, 498 U.S. 42,

44 (1990) (quoting *Granfinanciera*, 492 U.S. at 58). By filing a proof of claim, the creditor agrees to the bankruptcy court's resolution of that claim, and if the creditor wins, the creditor will receive a share of the distribution of the bankruptcy estate. When the bankruptcy estate has a related claim against that creditor, that counterclaim may offset the creditor's claim, or even yield additional damages that augment the estate and may be distributed to the other creditors.

The consequent importance to the total bankruptcy scheme of permitting the trustee in bankruptcy to assert counterclaims against claimants, *and resolving those counterclaims in a bankruptcy court*, is reflected in the fact that Congress included "counterclaims by the estate against persons filing claims against the estate" on its list of "[c]ore proceedings." 28 U.S.C. § 157(b)(2)(C). . . .

Consequently a bankruptcy court's determination of such matters has more than [what the majority describes as] "some bearing on a bankruptcy case." It plays a critical role in Congress's constitutionally based effort to create an efficient, effective federal bankruptcy system. At the least, that is what Congress concluded. We owe deference to that determination, which shows the absence of any legislative or executive motive, intent, purpose, or desire to encroach upon areas that Article III reserves to judges to whom it grants tenure and compensation protections.

Considering these factors together, I conclude that, as in *Schor*, "the magnitude of any intrusion on the Judicial Branch can only be termed *de minimis*." 478 U.S. at 856. I would similarly find the statute before us constitutional.

NOTES ON STERN V. MARSHALL

1. QUESTIONS AND COMMENTS

Stern is a significant decision in that it represents an endorsement by a majority of the Court of the approach followed by a plurality in *Northern Pipeline*. The dissent in *Stern* accuses the majority of deviating from the pragmatic approach to non-Article III courts issues followed in the subsequent *Thomas* and *Schor* decisions. Is this a fair criticism? In any event, can the result in *Stern* be supported by even a narrow reading of the holding in *Northern Pipeline*, as the majority contends?

What reasons does the Court give in *Stern* for finding Congress's allowance of bankruptcy court adjudication of the counterclaim to be unconstitutional? How do those reasons differ from the factors invoked by the dissent? The majority and dissent both seem to accept that a litigant's consent is relevant when considering whether a non-Article III adjudication is constitutional, but they disagree about the extent to which there was relevant consent in this case. Which opinion is more persuasive on this point? The dissent further emphasizes the control that Article III judges were given over the bankruptcy courts in the 1984 Bankruptcy Act and contends that, in light of these controls, "functionally, bankruptcy judges can be compared to magistrate judges, law clerks, and the Judiciary's administrative officials." Why does the majority reject this analogy? If the district courts exercised more searching review of the bankruptcy courts' factual findings in cases such as this one, would that resolve the constitutional problem?

Although he joins the majority opinion, Justice Scalia expresses frustration with the multiple factors invoked by the majority. He proposes that, except for adjudications by federal administrative agencies, an Article III judge should be required "in *all* federal adjudications, unless there is a firmly established historical practice to the contrary." Is this approach workable? Desirable? Why would Justice Scalia allow an exception for "firmly established historical practice"? Consider this appraisal made by an observer some years ago:

> There is a sense in which the strongest argument for the validity of legislative and administrative courts is history. For two hundred years our legislature has acted on the assumption that it has power to create these institutions. For two hundred years, it has been sustained in this by the very courts whose independence and integrity is supposedly subverted by its actions. . . . Virtually all of the great figures of the American judicial pantheon—Marshall and Hughes, Brandeis and Holmes, Frankfurter and Jackson—have participated in this process of validation. A large number of eminently useful and successful institutions have been created by virtue of this; and these are now deeply imbedded in the texture of our political and economic life. In a word, a huge body of precedent and experience validates our legislative and administrative tribunals.

Paul M. Bator, The Constitution as Architecture: Legislative and Administrative Courts Under Article III, 65 Ind. L.J. 233, 260 (1990).

In enacting the statutory provision at issue in *Stern*, was Congress attempting to diminish the authority or independence of the federal judiciary? Should Congress's motive matter in evaluating whether an assignment of authority to a non-Article III tribunal is constitutional? Similarly, to what extent, if at all, should Congress's interest in establishing an effective and efficient bankruptcy system be relevant to the constitutional analysis? The majority seems to acknowledge that the statutory provision at issue in this case does not by itself pose a significant threat to the authority or independence of the federal courts, but it contends that unless the judiciary polices even relatively innocuous delegations of authority to non-Article III courts, Congress might incrementally erode the separation of powers. Is this is legitimate concern? Cf. Daniel J. Meltzer, Legislative Courts, Legislative Power, and the Constitution, 65 Ind. L.J. 291, 292 (1990) ("I suspect that judicial independence is less likely to be subverted by 'wholesale transfers of jurisdiction' or by a Congress with destructive intent than by the accretion of measures, each of which creates a significant jurisdiction in a non-Article III tribunal.").

The dissent in *Stern* argued for a consideration of various factors when assessing the constitutionality of a non-Article III court. Assuming this approach were followed, did the dissent identify all the relevant factors? If the relevant factors do not all point in one direction, how should they be weighted? Would a multi-factored approach make the law in this area too uncertain and unpredictable? On the other hand, how certain and predictable is it now?

For commentary on *Stern*, see, for example, Susan Block-Lieb, What Congress Had to Say: Legislative History as a Rehearsal of Congressional Response to *Stern v. Marshall*, 86 Am. Bankr. L.J. 55 (2012); Ralph Brubaker, A "Summary" Statutory and Constitutional Theory of Bankruptcy Judges' Core Jurisdiction after *Stern v. Marshall*, 86 Am. Bankr. L.J. 121 (2012); Erwin Chemerinsky, Formalism without a Foundation: *Stern v. Marshall*, 2011 Sup. Ct. Rev. 183; and Troy A. McKenzie, Getting to the Core of *Stern v. Marshall*: History, Expertise, and the Separation of Powers, 86 Am. Bankr. L.J. 23 (2012).

2.   THE EFFECT OF PARTY CONSENT

In Executive Benefits Insurance Agency v. Arkinson, 573 U.S. ___, 134 S.Ct. 2165 (2014), the Supreme Court unanimously held that a bankruptcy court has the statutory authority to treat claims covered by *Stern* as "non-core" proceedings and to enter proposed findings of fact and conclusions of law on these claims, which can then be reviewed de novo by a federal district court. While the bankruptcy court had not expressly followed that route in this case, the federal district court had nevertheless reviewed the petitioner's fraudulent conveyance claim de novo. As a result, the Court concluded that, even assuming that a fraudulent conveyance claim is covered by *Stern*, "the District Court's de novo review and entry of its own valid final judgment cured any error." Because of this conclusion, the Court declined to consider whether the petitioner had consented to the bankruptcy court's adjudication, and, if so, whether party consent renders constitutional a bankruptcy court's resolution of a claim covered by *Stern*.

The Supreme Court subsequently addressed the effect of party consent in Wellness Int'l Network, Ltd. v. Sharif, 575 U.S. ___, 135 S.Ct. 1932 (2015). *Sharif* concerned a default judgment entered by a bankruptcy judge. The judge accepted a creditor's claim that a trust administered by the bankruptcy petitioner was the petitioner's alter ego, such that the trust's assets should be considered part of the bankruptcy estate. Prior to the entry of the judgment, the petitioner seemed to accept the authority of the bankruptcy judge to resolve the matter. An appeals court nevertheless held that the bankruptcy judge lacked constitutional authority under *Stern* to enter the judgment.

The Supreme Court reversed and remanded, holding that, even if bankruptcy judges normally would be barred under *Stern* from adjudicating the type of claim at issue here, they may do so when they have the parties' consent. In an opinion by Justice Sotomayor, the Court noted that it had treated consent as a significant factor in non-Article III adjudication outside the bankruptcy context, including in Commodity Futures Trading Comm'n v.

Schor, 478 U.S. 833 (1986), described as "[t]he foundational case in the modern era." The Court explained that "[t]he lesson of [these decisions] and the history that preceded them is plain: The entitlement to an Article III adjudicator is 'a personal right' and thus ordinarily 'subject to waiver.'" (quoting *Schor*, 478 U.S. at 848). While acknowledging that Article III also serves structural purposes, the Court observed that "allowing Article I adjudicators to decide claims submitted to them by consent does not offend the separation of powers so long as Article III courts retain supervisory authority over the process."

Ultimately, reasoned the Court, the question was "whether allowing bankruptcy courts to decide *Stern* claims by consent would 'impermissibly threate[n] the institutional integrity of the Judicial Branch.'" (quoting *Schor*, 478 U.S. at 851). To decide this question, the Court considered the following factors outlined in *Schor*:

> the extent to which the essential attributes of judicial power are reserved to Article III courts, and, conversely, the extent to which the non-Article III forum exercises the range of jurisdiction and powers normally vested only in Article III courts, the origins and importance of the right to be adjudicated, and the concerns that drove Congress to depart from the requirements of Article III.

Applying those factors, the Court concluded that "allowing bankruptcy litigants to waive the right to Article III adjudication of *Stern* claims does not usurp the constitutional prerogatives of Article III courts." Among other things, the Court noted that bankruptcy judges are subject to appointment and removal by Article III judges; that they hear matters only upon reference by a federal district court; that their ability to hear claims traditionally heard by Article III courts is limited to a narrow class of claims relating to bankruptcy proceedings; and that there is no indication that Congress gave them jurisdiction in an effort to aggrandize congressional authority or undermine the federal judiciary. The Court therefore determined that, "[s]o long as those judges are subject to control by the Article III courts, their work poses no threat to the separation of powers."

The Court further concluded that, although consent for these purposes must be "knowing and voluntary," it need not be express. Noting that a prior decision had accepted the possibility of implied consent for adjudication of civil matters by magistrate judges, the Court observed that "[a]pplied in the bankruptcy context, that standard possesses the same pragmatic virtues— increasing judicial efficiency and checking gamesmanship—that motivated our adoption of it for consent-based adjudications by magistrate judges." The Court remanded the case to the court of appeals to determine whether the bankruptcy petitioner in this case had "evinced the requisite knowing and voluntary consent."

Justice Alito concurred in part and concurred in the judgment, agreeing with the Court that *Schor* supports allowing *Stern* claims to be heard by bankruptcy judges with the parties' consent. Alito did not think it appropriate to decide, however, whether consent could be implied, because in his view the petitioner in this case had forfeited any *Stern* argument by failing to present it properly in the lower courts.

Chief Justice Roberts dissented and was joined by Justice Scalia and also, in the first part of the dissent, by Justice Thomas. Roberts began by arguing that the claim at issue in this case was not in fact a "*Stern* claim" requiring final adjudication by an Article III judge, and that the claim therefore could properly be resolved by a bankruptcy judge regardless of the parties' consent. Roberts noted, among other things, that "[i]dentifying property that constitutes the estate has long been a central feature of bankruptcy adjudication."

Roberts then proceeded to argue, at this point joined only by Justice Scalia, that bankruptcy judges should not be allowed to adjudicate claims covered by *Stern*. Noting that the Constitution's separation-of-powers structure is designed to protect individual liberty and promote governmental accountability, Roberts pointed out that the Court does not allow separation-of-powers constraints to be bypassed merely by the consent of the affected branch of government. "If a branch of the Federal Government may not consent to a violation of the separation of powers," he reasoned, "surely a private litigant may not do so." Even if one accepts that a litigant can consent to a deviation from Article III that affects only a "personal right," Roberts contended, the prohibition in *Stern* is structural because it helps protect the institutional integrity of the federal judiciary. Roberts further argued that the parties' consent cannot be relied upon to serve this role, because "such parties are unlikely to weigh the long-term structural independence of the Article III judiciary against their own short-term priorities." Finally, Roberts noted that even if the particular encroachment on Article III authority in this case might seem harmless by itself, "the fact remains that Congress controls the salary and tenure of bankruptcy judges, and the Legislature's present solicitude provides no guarantee of its future restraint."

Justice Thomas dissented separately to explain why the issue of "[w]hether parties may consent to bankruptcy court adjudication of *Stern* claims is a difficult constitutional question," and one that "turns on issues that are not adequately considered by the Court or briefed by the parties." Thomas concluded that this question "cannot—and should not—be resolved through a cursory reading of *Schor*, which itself is hardly a model of careful constitutional interpretation."

ADDITIONAL NOTES ON NON-ARTICLE III ADJUDICATION

1.   ADMINISTRATIVE AGENCIES: THE EXAMPLE OF THE NLRB

Lurking behind the debate over Article I courts is the problem of administrative agencies. Many federal agencies exercise rule-making or licensing authority not directly comparable to judicial decision-making. Others, however, make case-by-case determinations of the rights and liabilities of private parties. Such agencies would seem to be exercising the "judicial Power of the United States" within the meaning of Article III, that is, they are deciding "cases" arising under federal law. Plausibly, they should be subject to the constraints imposed on Article III courts. In fact, however, administrative agencies operate very differently from Article III courts and yet are widely accepted as constitutionally valid mechanisms of dispute resolution. Why? What is it about agency adjudication that makes Article III inapplicable?

Consider, for example, the National Labor Relations Board. The Board administers and interprets the unfair labor practice and representation provisions of the National Labor Relations Act. As provided in 29 U.S.C. § 153, the Board consists of five members appointed by the president for staggered, five-year terms. The Board itself sits as an appellate body, ordinarily in panels of three. Trial is had before an administrative law judge, who issues a recommended decision and order, which is automatically issued as a Board order if no one objects. If objection is raised, the case is transferred to the Board for final decision. Although charges of unfair labor practices are made by private parties, no case is brought to the Board unless a "complaint" is filed. This prosecutorial function is fulfilled by a General Counsel appointed by the president and by regional directors appointed by, and responsible to, the General Counsel.

The Board itself has no coercive power. Instead, Board orders are enforced in the United States Courts of Appeals on petition by the Board or reviewed by any person aggrieved by a final Board order. Under the statute, a Board finding of fact is conclusive "if supported by substantial evidence." 29 U.S.C. § 160(e) and (f). As elaborated in Universal Camera Corp. v. NLRB, 340 U.S. 474 (1951), this means that courts must give special deference to findings within the Board's area of expertise. Even outside that area, a court is not free to "displace the Board's choice between fairly conflicting views, even though the court would justifiably have made a different choice had the matter been before it de novo." Id. at 488. The standard of review for application of law to fact and for unmixed questions of law is not specified in the statute, and the approach of reviewing courts varies with context. As one authority put it, "[a]ll that can be said with confidence is that courts tend to believe that their own competence matches that of the Board, and finally surpasses it, as the finding moves from 'pure' fact, to mixed questions to issues of 'pure' statutory construction and then finally to issues of constitutional dimension." Robert A. Gorman, Basic Text on Labor Law 13 (1976).

Interestingly, although the NLRB also has rule-making authority, it is notoriously reluctant to use it. Despite repeated pleas from judges, practitioners, and academics, the Board consistently eschews formal rule-making in favor of case-by-case adjudication. The reasons for this practice may be many, but one factor repeatedly cited by experts is the agency's desire to insulate itself from effective judicial review by submerging its judgments in the facts of particular cases. Perhaps not entirely unrelated is the widespread perception that NLRB adjudication is ideological and politicized, characterized by sharp swings in enforcement perspective as annual presidential appointments remake the Board's composition.

Obviously, the NLRB falls very far short of the model of judicial independence established by Article III. Indeed, the Board's structure suggests, and the history of the National Labor Relations Act confirms, that the Board was not intended to provide impartial, apolitical adjudication of labor disputes. Instead, it was created to enforce certain policy objectives and constituted so that the President, acting with the advice and consent of the Senate, can assert relatively short-term political control over Board membership.

2. QUESTIONS AND COMMENTS ON AGENCY ADJUDICATION AND ARTICLE III

Given the incentive and opportunity for political interference, why is the Supreme Court so tolerant of NLRB adjudication? Or, to put the same question another way, if the Court is prepared to countenance adjudication by the NLRB and other administrative agencies, why is it so concerned with the structure of the bankruptcy courts?

One answer is that Article III pertains to courts and the NLRB is not a court. This kind of simplistic nominalism is not often stated, but some such notion seems implicit in any argument against the constitutionality of an "Article I court" that does not take account of administrative agencies. Is there any reason to suppose that Article III should limit only institutions called "courts"?

A different argument identifies functional differences between courts and agencies, chiefly that administrative agencies typically lack enforcement authority. Most agencies, like the compensation commission in *Crowell v. Benson* and like the NLRB, must go to court to have their orders enforced. The argument is developed most fully in Thomas G. Krattenmaker, Article III and Judicial Independence: Why the New Bankruptcy Courts Are Unconstitutional, 70 Geo. L.J. 297, 308–09 (1981). In commenting on *Northern Pipeline*, Krattenmaker notes that before enactment of the Bankruptcy Reform Act, bankruptcy judges had only limited of powers and operated under the supervision of United States District Courts. The new bankruptcy judges, in contrast, operated independently with the power to "conduct jury trials, to punish certain contempts of court, and to enter final judgments and issue writs of execution." According to Krattenmaker, these increased powers explain "why the new bankruptcy courts are not analogous to the federal administrative agencies":

> Proponents of the Bankruptcy Reform Act would be correct to argue that no neat, bright-line distinction exists—or could be tolerated in the modern bureaucratic state—between executive and judicial power. Many officials must be charged with interpreting congressional statutes and determining violations of them. . . . Not all people exercising such authority need be tenured or protected from salary cuts.

> But Article III, § 1 speaks only of "Courts" exercising "judicial Power." Looking to the purposes the framers had in mind in crafting that section, only a virtually willful inattention to detail could cause one to miss the difference between officers who are and officers who are not empowered to issue final judgments, to enforce

their own monetary awards, to conduct all manner of civil proceedings that federal district courts may conduct, including jury trials, and to exercise all these powers in disputes over liabilities between private citizens.

Is this persuasive? Consider the rebuttal in Martin H. Redish, Legislative Courts, Administrative Agencies, and the *Northern Pipeline* Decision, 1983 Duke L.J. 197, 217–18. Redish acknowledges that the chief difference between administrative agencies and legislative courts is that agencies "generally cannot issue automatically enforceable orders," but argues that "elevating this distinction to a status of constitutional significance places form over substance":

> When an agency seeks enforcement of an order in federal court, the court is required by both statute and precedent to defer to the findings and conclusions of the agency. . . . [O]ne may question whether there is any difference, in terms of satisfying the Article III provisions, between the requirement that the non-Article III agency seek enforcement in an Article III court where that agency's findings are subject to a minimal level of review, and the roughly comparable appellate review of the automatically enforceable orders of a bankruptcy or other legislative court. . . . In both situations, the non-Article III body conducts the primary adjudication, makes the basic legal and factual findings, and is subject to some level of review in an Article III court.

Finally, consider whether the constitutional tolerance of administrative adjudication might be justified on other grounds. Would NLRB cases, for example, fall within the "public rights" doctrine? Charges of unfair labor practices arise "between the government and others" in the sense that the regional director must decide to prosecute a complaint. Additionally, the agency is a party to judicial enforcement proceedings. On the other hand, NLRB cases do not involve claims against the government. On the contrary, the underlying dispute is between private parties, and Board adjudication determines their rights and liabilities "under the law as defined." Even if unfair labor practice cases do not involve "public rights," they do arise under federal law. Does that explain why agency adjudication is constitutional? If so, what is left of Article III? Does Article III matter only when a federal agency or court adjudicates cases arising under state law? Does that make sense?

3. ARTICLE III REVIEW OF NON-ARTICLE III DECISIONS

A number of commentators have suggested that review by the Article III judiciary can go a long way towards addressing any constitutional concerns associated with non-Article III adjudication. Perhaps most notably, Richard Fallon has argued that "adequately searching appellate review of the judgments of legislative courts and administrative agencies is both necessary and sufficient to satisfy the requirements of article III." Richard H. Fallon, Jr. , Of Legislative Courts, Administrative Agencies, and Article III, 101 Harv. L.

Rev. 915, 918 (1988). In terms of judicial precedent, Fallon relies in particular on *Crowell v. Benson* (discussed above in the *Introductory Notes on the Creation of Non-Article III Courts*). Fallon explains that

> As the *Crowell* tradition implicitly recognizes, to accept that article III courts need not adjudicate in the first instance is not to despair of the capacity of article III courts to protect and promote article III values. Appellate review can provide an effective check against politically influenced adjudication, arbitrary and self-interested decisionmaking, and other evils that the separation of powers was designed to prevent.

Id. at 947.

Is it true that Article III review is always necessary? What about in the public rights area? In any event, to provide an effective protection of judicial independence, how robust must the Article III review be? Federal courts often give deference to factual determinations made by non-Article III courts and administrative agencies. Sometimes they even give deference to legal determinations, most notably under the *Chevron* doctrine in administrative law (which under certain circumstances requires judicial acceptance of reasonable interpretations of ambiguous statutes adopted by the agencies that administer them). Can the relevant Article III values be protected in light of such deference? Even without deference, is it true that all the Article III values are protected by review? Consider this contention by the plurality in *Northern Pipeline*: "Our precedents make it clear that the constitutional requirements for the exercise of the judicial power must be met at all stages of adjudication, and not only on appeal, where the court is restricted to considerations of law, as well as the nature of the case as it has been shaped at the trial level." (Emphasis added.)

For a theory that is somewhat complementary to Fallon's, see James E. Pfander, Article I Tribunals, Article III Courts, and the Judicial Power of the United States, 118 Harv. L. Rev. 643, 650 (2004) (arguing that "all tribunals that Congress constitutes, including both Article III courts and Article I tribunals, must remain inferior to the Supreme Court").

4. MAGISTRATE JUDGES

The Federal Magistrates Act of 1968, codified at 28 U.S.C. § 631 et seq., created the office of magistrate with the power of appointment in the district court. The specification of a magistrate's duties was intentionally open-ended. Magistrates were authorized to serve as special masters under Federal Rule of Civil Procedure 53, to assist district judges in pretrial or discovery proceedings, to review prisoner applications for post-conviction relief, and to perform "such additional duties as are not inconsistent with the Constitution and laws of the United States." The usual mode of operation was a judicial reference to the magistrate who, after holding the necessary hearings or inquiries, reported back a recommended disposition.

The use of this procedure in habeas cases was temporarily curtailed in Wingo v. Wedding, 418 U.S. 461 (1974), which held that habeas corpus evidentiary hearings had to be conducted by federal judges personally. The

Court based this conclusion on the terms of the habeas statute, which the more recently enacted Magistrates Act had not purported to change.

Congress evidently disagreed, for it promptly amended the Magistrates Act to overrule *Wingo*. In addition to specifying that magistrates could hold evidentiary hearings on habeas corpus applications, the 1976 amendments also clarified magistrates' powers with respect to pretrial and other matters. Magistrates were allowed to "hear and determine" non-dispositive pretrial motions, subject only to overruling where the magistrate's order was "clearly erroneous or contrary to law." So-called "dispositive" motions, however, could be referred to magistrates only for proposed findings of fact and recommended disposition, and the presiding judge was required to make a "de novo determination" of any matter to which objection was made. Thus, the 1976 amendments sanctioned a recommended disposition procedure, but with an important limitation in certain cases.

The constitutionality of the recommended disposition procedure was contested in United States v. Raddatz, 447 U.S. 667 (1980). *Raddatz* involved a criminal prosecution that hinged on the admissibility of a confession. The defendant moved to suppress on the ground that the confession was involuntary. This motion was referred to a magistrate, who found that the statements had been made knowingly and voluntarily and recommended that the suppression motion be denied. The District Court accepted this recommendation after reviewing the transcript and receiving arguments of counsel, but without hearing live testimony. The Court of Appeals found this procedure authorized by statute and consistent with Article III, but violative of due process. The Supreme Court reversed.

Speaking for the Court, Chief Justice Burger found first that the statute required only a de novo determination of the suppression motion, not a de novo hearing. This requirement was satisfied if the "ultimate adjudicatory determination" was reserved to the judge, who was entitled to give the magistrate's proposed findings and recommendation as much weight as "sound judicial discretion" might indicate. The Court also found no violation of due process. The Court drew attention to the common administrative practice, as in the NLRB, of agency findings of fact based on evidence presented to a hearing officer. The Court concluded that an analogous procedure was acceptable for a suppression motion. The Court noted that the district judge retained broad discretion to hear live witnesses and to accept, reject, or modify proposed findings. Finally, the Court found no violation of Article III. Congress had not attempted to vest final disposition of a suppression motion in a non-Article III officer. On the contrary, the district court had "plenary discretion" to decide to use a magistrate and to review a magistrate's recommendation. "Therefore, the entire process takes place under the district court's total control and jurisdiction."

The year before *Raddatz* was announced, Congress again expanded the duties of magistrates. The Magistrates Act of 1979 authorizes civil trial by magistrate upon consent of the parties. See 28 U.S.C. § 636(c). The district court selects those cases appropriate for trial by magistrate, and the parties are notified of their opportunity to consent. Procedures are required to protect the voluntariness of the parties' choice. The district court can later revoke the reference for "good cause," but otherwise will not supervise the proceeding. The magistrate's determination leads automatically to entry of judgment. Appeal may be had as of right to the court of appeals or, if all parties have previously agreed thereto, an expedited appeal is available in the district court.

The nonconsensual use of magistrates was limited in Gomez v. United States, 490 U.S. 858 (1989). A district judge assigned a magistrate to conduct voir dire examination and jury selection for a felony prosecution and agreed to review any disputes de novo. The defendants objected, although without alleging any specific prejudice. The Second Circuit found the assignment within the statutory authorization of "such additional duties as are not inconsistent with the Constitution and the laws of the United States," 28 U.S.C. § 636(b)(3), but the Supreme Court reversed.

Speaking for a unanimous Court, Justice Stevens admitted that the statute literally allowed assignment of any duty not explicitly prohibited by statute or the Constitution, but invoked "our settled policy . . . to avoid an interpretation of a federal statute that engenders constitutional issues." Thus motivated, the Court found that the "carefully defined grant of authority to conduct trials of civil matters and minor criminal cases shall be construed as an implicit withholding of the authority to preside at a felony trial." Voir dire and jury selection were too important to the felony prosecution to allow nonconsensual reference to a magistrate.

In Peretz v. United States, 501 U.S. 923 (1991), the Court, in a 5–4 decision, held that the Federal Magistrates Act permits magistrate judges to preside over jury selection in felony criminal trials if the parties consent. The Court reasoned that, to the extent defendants have a constitutional right to have an Article III judge preside over jury selection, they can waive that right, just as they can waive many other constitutional rights. Even if a litigant may not waive the structural protections provided by Article III, the Court was "convinced that no such structural protections are implicated by the procedure followed in this case." Noting that magistrates are appointed and subject to removal by Article III judges, and that the district court decides whether to invoke the magistrate's assistance and whether to empanel the jury selected by the magistrate, the Court concluded that "there is no danger that the use of the magistrate involves a 'congressional attempt "to transfer jurisdiction [to non-Article III tribunals] for the purpose of emasculating" constitutional courts. . . .' "

In Roell v. Withrow, 538 U.S. 580 (2003), defendants in a § 1983 action were told of their option to have the case tried before a District Judge but instead proceeded to trial and jury verdict before a magistrate. Only when they lost did they point out (on appeal) that they had never expressly consented to the designation of a magistrate judge, as is required by 28 U.S.C. § 636(c)(1). In an opinion written by Justice Souter, the Supreme Court held that consent could be inferred from a party's conduct in the litigation. Decisive for the majority was the "risk of gamesmanship" if the parties could wait for the outcome before denying the magistrate judge's authority. Justice Thomas dissented in an opinion joined by Justices Stevens, Scalia, and Kennedy. They treated the lack of express consent as a jurisdictional defect that could not be waived by the conduct of the parties in proceeding with the litigation and emphasized the "strong policy" that waiver of the right to Article III adjudication be knowing and voluntary.

In Gonzalez v. United States, 553 U.S. 242 (2008), the Court held that the requisite consent of the criminal defendant for this use of magistrates may be provided by the defendant's counsel, without any express consent by the defendant personally. The Court reasoned that "acceptance of a magistrate judge at the jury selection phase is a tactical decision that is well suited for the attorney's own decision. . . . Requiring the defendant to consent to a magistrate judge only by way of an on-the-record personal statement . . . would burden the trial process, with little added protection for the defendant." The only dissent came from Justice Thomas, who argued that *Peretz* should be overruled.

For commentary on the Article III implications of the use of magistrate judges, see Lucinda M. Finley, Article III Limits on Article I Courts: The Constitutionality of the Bankruptcy Court and the 1979 Magistrate Act, 80 Colum. L. Rev. 560 (1980); Mark S. Kende, The Constitutionality of New Contempt Powers for Federal Magistrate-Judges, 53 Hastings L.J. 567 (2002); Reinier H. Kraakman, Article III Constraints and the Expanding Civil Jurisdiction of Federal Magistrates: A Dissenting View, 88 Yale L.J. 1023 (1979); and Linda J. Silberman, Masters and Magistrates, Part II: The American Analogue, 50 N.Y.U. L. Rev. 1297 (1975). For investigation and defense of the constitutionality of allowing magistrate judges to adjudicate petty offenses (maximum sentence of six months) without consent, see Stephen I. Vladeck, Petty Offenses and Article III, 19 Green Bag 2d 67 (2015).

5. MILITARY COMMISSIONS

Unlike courts-martial, military commissions have not traditionally been regulated by Congress but rather have been established pursuant to the President's commander-in-chief authority. That is, they have been "Article II courts" rather than "Article I courts." "Throughout U.S. history, military commissions have been used for three basic purposes: to administer justice in territories occupied by the United States; to replace civilian courts in parts of the United States where martial law has been declared; and to try enemy belligerents for violations of the laws of war." Curtis A. Bradley, The Story of Ex parte Milligan: Military Trials, Enemy Combatants, and Congressional Authorization, in Presidential Power Stories 95–96 (Christopher H. Schroeder and Curtis A. Bradley eds., 2009). These commissions were used extensively by the Union military during the Civil War and also in the occupied South during the Reconstruction period following the War. The Supreme Court held in 1866, however, that a civilian who is not connected to the military cannot be tried by a military commission in the absence of a valid declaration of martial law, reasoning that such a trial would violate both Article III and the jury trial rights of the accused. See Ex parte Milligan, 71 U.S. 2 (1866). During World War II, the Court upheld President Roosevelt's use of a military commission to try eight Nazi agents (including at least one U.S. citizen) for violations of the laws of war, after they had surreptitiously entered the United States with plans to commit sabotage. See Ex parte Quirin, 317 U.S. 1 (1942).

After the September 11, 2001 terrorist attacks in the United States, President George W. Bush authorized the use of military commissions to try certain non-U.S. citizens connected with terrorism. In 2006, however, the Supreme Court held that the military commission system that the Bush administration had established violated requirements that Congress had imposed on the use of military commissions—in particular, a requirement that "the rules applied to military commissions must be the same as those applied to courts-martial unless such uniformity proves impracticable." Hamdan v. Rumsfeld, 548 U.S. 557, 619 (2006). Congress responded to this decision by enacting the Military Commissions Act of 2006, which authorized the use of military commissions for certain terrorist detainees, detailed the procedures for these commissions, and defined the crimes that could be prosecuted before them. In 2009, after President Obama had taken office, Congress enacted a revised Military Commissions Act, which, among other things, increased the procedural protections for defendants. The judgments of the military commissions are subject to review within the military system and are also reviewable by the U.S. Court of Appeals for the D.C. Circuit with respect to "matters of law, including the sufficiency of the evidence to support the verdict."

For discussion of the history of the use of military commissions, see David J. Bederman, Article II Courts, 44 Mercer L. Rev. 825 (1993); David W. Glazier, Note, Kangaroo Court or Competent Tribunal?: Judging the 21st-Century Military Commission, 89 Va. L. Rev. 2005 (2003); Detlev F. Vagts, Military Commissions: The Forgotten Reconstruction Chapter, 23 Am. U. Int'l L. Rev. 231 (2008). For discussion of the use of military commissions in the war on terror, see Curtis A. Bradley and Jack L. Goldsmith, The Constitutional Validity of Military Commissions, 5 Green Bag 2d 249 (2002); Neal K. Katyal and Laurence H. Tribe, Waging War, Deciding Guilt: Trying the Military Tribunals, 111 Yale L.J. 1259 (2002); Detlev F. Vagts, Military Commissions: Constitutional Limits on Their Role in the War on Terror, 102 Am. J. Int'l L. 573 (2008).

6.   ADDITIONAL BIBLIOGRAPHY

For additional commentary on non-Article III courts, see George D. Brown, Article III as a Fundamental Value—The Demise of *Northern Pipeline* and Its Implications for Congressional Power, 49 Ohio St. L.J. 55 (1988); John T. Cross, Congressional Power to Extend Federal Jurisdiction to Disputes outside Article III: A Critical Analysis from the Perspective of Bankruptcy, 87 Nw. U. L. Rev. 1188 (1983); Richard B. Saphire and Michael E. Solimine, Shoring Up Article III: Legislative Court Doctrine in the Post *CFTC v. Schor* Era, 68 B.U. L. Rev. 85 (1988); Ralph U. Whitten, Consent, Caseload, and Other Justifications for Non-Article-III Courts and Judges: A Comment on *Commodities Futures Trading Commission v. Schor*, 20 Creighton L. Rev. 11 (1986); and Gordon G. Young, Public Rights and the Federal Judicial Power: From *Murray's Lessee* to *Crowell* to *Schor*, 35 Buff.

L. Rev. 765 (1986). For an ambitious discussion relating Article I courts to other constitutional issues, including standing, the doctrine of the political question, and the requirements of procedural due process, see John Harrison, The Relation between Limitations on and Requirements of Article III Adjudication, 95 Calif. L. Rev. 1367 (2007). For an interesting account of the historical origins of the appellate review model of the relationship between the Article III judiciary and administrative agencies, see Thomas W. Merrill, Article III, Agency Adjudication, and the Origins of the Appellate Review Model of Administrative Law, 111 Colum. L. Rev. 939 (2011). For a challenge to the assumption that using non-Article III tribunals allows for more customized dispute resolution processes, as well as a critical assessment of the role of consent in legitimizing the use of such tribunals, see Jaime Dodge, Reconceptualizing Non-Article III Tribunals, 99 Minn. L. Rev. 905 (2015).

SECTION 5. INTERNATIONAL TRIBUNALS

Medellin v. Texas

Supreme Court of the United States, 2008.
552 U.S. 491.

■ CHIEF JUSTICE ROBERTS delivered the opinion of the Court.

The International Court of Justice (ICJ), located in the Hague, is a tribunal established pursuant to the United Nations Charter to adjudicate disputes between member states. In the Case Concerning Avena and Other Mexican Nationals (Mex. v. U.S.), 2004 I.C.J. 12 (Judgment of Mar. 31) (*Avena*), that tribunal considered a claim brought by Mexico against the United States. The ICJ held that, based on violations of the Vienna Convention [on Consular Relations], 51 named Mexican nationals were entitled to review and reconsideration of their state-court convictions and sentences in the United States. This was so regardless of any forfeiture of the right to raise Vienna Convention claims because of a failure to comply with generally applicable state rules governing challenges to criminal convictions.

In *Sanchez-Llamas* v. *Oregon*, 548 U.S. 331 (2006)—issued after *Avena* but involving individuals who were not named in the *Avena* judgment—we held that, contrary to the ICJ's determination, the Vienna Convention did not preclude the application of state default rules. After the *Avena* decision, President George W. Bush determined, through a Memorandum to the Attorney General (Feb. 28, 2005), that the United States would "discharge its international obligations" under *Avena* "by having State courts give effect to the decision."

Petitioner José Ernesto Medellin, who had been convicted and sentenced in Texas state court for murder, is one of the 51 Mexican nationals named in the *Avena* decision. Relying on the ICJ's decision and the President's Memorandum, Medellin filed an application for a writ of habeas corpus in state court. The Texas Court of Criminal Appeals dismissed

Medellin's application as an abuse of the writ under state law, given Medellin's failure to raise his Vienna Convention claim in a timely manner under state law. We granted certiorari to decide two questions. First, is the ICJ's judgment in *Avena* directly enforceable as domestic law in a state court in the United States? Second, does the President's Memorandum independently require the States to provide review and reconsideration of the claims of the 51 Mexican nationals named in *Avena* without regard to state procedural default rules? We conclude that neither *Avena* nor the President's Memorandum constitutes directly enforceable federal law that pre-empts state limitations on the filing of successive habeas petitions. We therefore affirm the decision below.

I

A

In 1969, the United States, upon the advice and consent of the Senate, ratified the Vienna Convention, and the Optional Protocol Concerning the Compulsory Settlement of Disputes to the Vienna Convention (Optional Protocol or Protocol). Article 36 of the Convention . . . provides that if a person detained by a foreign country "so requests, the competent authorities of the receiving State shall, without delay, inform the consular post of the sending State" of such detention, and "inform the [detainee] of his righ[t]" to request assistance from the consul of his own state.

The Optional Protocol provides a venue for the resolution of disputes arising out of the interpretation or application of the Vienna Convention. Under the Protocol, such disputes "shall lie within the compulsory jurisdiction of the International Court of Justice" and "may accordingly be brought before the [ICJ] . . . by any party to the dispute being a Party to the present Protocol."

The ICJ is "the principal judicial organ of the United Nations." United Nations Charter, Art. 92. It was established in 1945 pursuant to the United Nations Charter. The ICJ Statute—annexed to the U.N. Charter—provides the organizational framework and governing procedures for cases brought before the ICJ.

Under Article 94(1) of the U.N. Charter, "[e]ach Member of the United Nations undertakes to comply with the decision of the [ICJ] in any case to which it is a party." The ICJ's jurisdiction in any particular case, however, is dependent upon the consent of the parties. The ICJ Statute delineates two ways in which a nation may consent to ICJ jurisdiction: It may consent generally to jurisdiction on any question arising under a treaty or general international law, or it may consent specifically to jurisdiction over a particular category of cases or disputes pursuant to a separate treaty. The United States originally consented to the general jurisdiction of the ICJ . . . in 1946. The United States withdrew from general ICJ jurisdiction in 1985. By ratifying the Optional Protocol to the

Vienna Convention, the United States consented to the specific jurisdiction of the ICJ with respect to claims arising out of the Vienna Convention. On March 7, 2005, subsequent to the ICJ's judgment in *Avena*, the United States gave notice of withdrawal from the Optional Protocol to the Vienna Convention. . . .

II

Medellin first contends that the ICJ's judgment in *Avena* constitutes a "binding" obligation on the state and federal courts of the United States. He argues that "by virtue of the Supremacy Clause, the treaties requiring compliance with the *Avena* judgment are *already* the 'Law of the Land' by which all state and federal courts in this country are 'bound.' " Accordingly, Medellin argues, *Avena* is a binding federal rule of decision that pre-empts contrary state limitations on successive habeas petitions.

No one disputes that the *Avena* decision—a decision that flows from the treaties through which the United States submitted to ICJ jurisdiction with respect to Vienna Convention disputes—constitutes an *international* law obligation on the part of the United States. But not all international law obligations automatically constitute binding federal law enforceable in United States courts. The question we confront here is whether the *Avena* judgment has automatic *domestic* legal effect such that the judgment of its own force applies in state and federal courts.

This Court has long recognized the distinction between treaties that automatically have effect as domestic law, and those that—while they constitute international law commitments—do not by themselves function as binding federal law. The distinction was well explained by Chief Justice Marshall's opinion in Foster v. Neilson, 27 U.S. 253 (1829), overruled on other grounds, United States v. Percheman, 32 U.S. 51 (1833), which held that a treaty is "equivalent to an act of the legislature," and hence self-executing, when it "operates of itself without the aid of any legislative provision." When, in contrast, "[treaty] stipulations are not self-executing they can only be enforced pursuant to legislation to carry them into effect." Whitney v. Robertson, 124 U.S. 190, 194 (1888). In sum, while treaties "may comprise international commitments . . . they are not domestic law unless Congress has either enacted implementing statutes or the treaty itself conveys an intention that it be 'self-executing' and is ratified on these terms." Igartua-De La Rosa v. United States, 417 F.3d 145, 150 (CA1 2005) (en banc) (Boudin, C. J.).[2]

A treaty is, of course, "primarily a compact between independent nations." Head Money Cases, 112 U.S. 580, 598 (1884). It ordinarily "depends for the enforcement of its provisions on the interest and the

---

[2]   The label "self-executing" has on occasion been used to convey different meanings. What we mean by "self-executing" is that the treaty has automatic domestic effect as federal law upon ratification. Conversely, a "non-self-executing" treaty does not by itself give rise to domestically enforceable federal law. Whether such a treaty has domestic effect depends upon implementing legislation passed by Congress.

honor of the governments which are parties to it." . . . Only "[i]f the treaty contains stipulations which are self-executing, that is, require no legislation to make them operative, [will] they have the force and effect of a legislative enactment." Whitney v. Robertson, 124 U.S. 190, 194 (1888).

Medellin and his amici nonetheless contend that the Optional Protocol, United Nations Charter, and ICJ Statute supply the "relevant obligation" to give the *Avena* judgment binding effect in the domestic courts of the United States. Because none of these treaty sources creates binding federal law in the absence of implementing legislation, and because it is uncontested that no such legislation exists, we conclude that the *Avena* judgment is not automatically binding domestic law.

A

The interpretation of a treaty, like the interpretation of a statute, begins with its text. Air France v. Saks, 470 U.S. 392, 396–97 (1985). Because a treaty ratified by the United States is "an agreement among sovereign powers," we have also considered as "aids to its interpretation" the negotiation and drafting history of the treaty as well as "the postratification understanding" of signatory nations. Zicherman v. Korean Air Lines Co., 516 U.S. 217, 226 (1996).

As a signatory to the Optional Protocol, the United States agreed to submit disputes arising out of the Vienna Convention to the ICJ. The Protocol provides: "Disputes arising out of the interpretation or application of the [Vienna] Convention shall lie within the compulsory jurisdiction of the International Court of Justice." Of course, submitting to jurisdiction and agreeing to be bound are two different things. A party could, for example, agree to compulsory nonbinding arbitration. Such an agreement would require the party to appear before the arbitral tribunal without obligating the party to treat the tribunal's decision as binding.

The most natural reading of the Optional Protocol is as a bare grant of jurisdiction. It provides only that "[d]isputes arising out of the interpretation or application of the [Vienna] Convention shall lie within the compulsory jurisdiction of the International Court of Justice" and "may accordingly be brought before the [ICJ] . . . by any party to the dispute being a Party to the present Protocol." The Protocol says nothing about the effect of an ICJ decision and does not itself commit signatories to comply with an ICJ judgment. The Protocol is similarly silent as to any enforcement mechanism.

The obligation on the part of signatory nations to comply with ICJ judgments derives not from the Optional Protocol, but rather from Article 94 of the United Nations Charter—the provision that specifically addresses the effect of ICJ decisions. Article 94(1) provides that "[e]ach Member of the United Nations *undertakes to comply* with the decision of the [ICJ] in any case to which it is a party." (Emphasis added.) The Executive Branch contends that the phrase "undertakes to comply" is not "an acknowledgement that an ICJ decision will have immediate legal effect in the courts of U.N. members," but rather "a *commitment* on the part of U.N. Members to take *future* action through their political branches to comply with an ICJ decision."

We agree with this construction of Article 94. The Article is not a directive to domestic courts. It does not provide that the United States "shall" or "must" comply with an ICJ decision, nor indicate that the Senate that ratified the U.N. Charter intended to vest ICJ decisions with immediate legal effect in domestic courts. Instead, "[t]he words of Article 94 . . . call upon governments to take certain action." Committee of United States Citizens Living in Nicaragua v. Reagan, 859 F.2d 929, 938 (CADC 1988). In other words, the U.N. Charter reads like "a compact between independent nations" that "depends for the enforcement of its provisions on the interest and the honor of the governments which are parties to it." *Head Money Cases*, 112 U.S. at 598.

The remainder of Article 94 confirms that the U.N. Charter does not contemplate the automatic enforceability of ICJ decisions in domestic courts. Article 94(2)—the enforcement provision—provides the sole remedy for noncompliance: referral to the United Nations Security Council by an aggrieved state.

The U.N. Charter's provision of an express diplomatic—that is, non-judicial—remedy is itself evidence that ICJ judgments were not meant to be enforceable in domestic courts. See *Sanchez-Llamas*, 548 U.S. at 347. And even this "quintessentially *international* remed[y]," id. at 355, is not absolute. First, the Security Council must "dee[m] necessary" the issuance of a recommendation or measure to effectuate the judgment. Second, as the President and Senate were undoubtedly aware in subscribing to the U.N. Charter and Optional Protocol, the United States retained the unqualified right to exercise its veto of any Security Council resolution. . . .

If ICJ judgments were instead regarded as automatically enforceable domestic law, they would be immediately and directly binding on state and federal courts pursuant to the Supremacy Clause. Mexico or the ICJ would have no need to proceed to the Security Council to enforce the judgment in this case. Noncompliance with an ICJ judgment through exercise of the Security Council veto—always regarded as an option by the Executive and ratifying Senate during and after consideration of the U.N. Charter, Optional Protocol, and ICJ Statute—would no longer be a viable alternative. There would be nothing to veto. In light of the U.N. Charter's remedial scheme, there is no reason to believe that the President and Senate signed up for such a result.

In sum, Medellin's view that ICJ decisions are automatically enforceable as domestic law is fatally undermined by the enforcement structure established by Article 94. His construction would eliminate the option of noncompliance contemplated by Article 94(2), undermining the ability of the political branches to determine whether and how to comply with an ICJ judgment. Those sensitive foreign policy decisions would instead be transferred to state and federal courts charged with applying an ICJ judgment directly as domestic law. And those courts would not be empowered to decide whether to comply with the judgment—again, always regarded as an option by the political branches—any more than courts may consider whether to comply with any other species of domestic law. This result would be particularly anomalous in light of the principle that "[t]he conduct of the foreign relations of our Government is committed by the Constitution to the Executive and Legislative—'the political'—Departments." Oetjen v. Central Leather Co., 246 U.S. 297, 302 (1918).

The ICJ Statute, incorporated into the U.N. Charter, provides further evidence that the ICJ's judgment in *Avena* does not automatically constitute federal law judicially enforceable in United States courts. To begin with, the ICJ's "principal purpose" is said to be to "arbitrate particular disputes between national governments." *Sanchez-Llamas*, 548 U.S. at 355. Accordingly, the ICJ can hear disputes only between nations, not individuals. More important, Article 59 of the statute provides that "[t]he decision of the [ICJ] has *no binding force* except between the parties and in respect of that particular case." (Emphasis added.) The dissent does not explain how Medellin, an individual, can be a party to the ICJ proceeding.

Medellin argues that because the *Avena* case involves him, it is clear that he—and the 50 other Mexican nationals named in the *Avena* decision—should be regarded as parties to the *Avena* judgment. But cases before the ICJ are often precipitated by disputes involving particular persons or entities, disputes that a nation elects to take up as its own. That has never been understood to alter the express and established rules that only nation-states may be parties before the ICJ, and—contrary to the position of the dissent—that ICJ judgments are binding only between those parties. . . .

It is, moreover, well settled that the United States' interpretation of a treaty "is entitled to great weight." Sumitomo Shoji America, Inc. v. Avagliano, 457 U.S. 176, 184–85 (1982); see also El Al Israel Airlines, Ltd. v. Tsui Yuan Tseng, 525 U.S. 155, 168 (1999). The Executive Branch has unfailingly adhered to its view that the relevant treaties do not create domestically enforceable federal law. . . .

C

Our conclusion that *Avena* does not by itself constitute binding federal law is confirmed by the "postratification understanding" of signatory nations. There are currently 47 nations that are parties to the Optional Protocol and 171 nations that are parties to the Vienna Convention. Yet neither Medellin nor his amici have identified a single nation that treats ICJ judgments as binding in domestic courts. In determining that the Vienna Convention did not require certain relief in United States courts in *Sanchez-Llamas*, we found it pertinent that the requested relief would not be available under the treaty in any other signatory country. So too here the lack of any basis for supposing that any other country would treat ICJ judgments as directly enforceable as a matter of their domestic law strongly suggests that the treaty should not be so viewed in our courts.

Moreover, the consequences of Medellin's argument give pause. An ICJ judgment, the argument goes, is not only binding domestic law but is also unassailable. As a result, neither Texas nor this Court may look behind a judgment and quarrel with its reasoning or result. (We already know, from *Sanchez-Llamas*, that this Court disagrees with both the reasoning and result in *Avena*.) Medellin's interpretation would allow ICJ judgments to override otherwise binding state law; there is nothing in his logic that would exempt contrary federal law from the same fate. And there is nothing to prevent the ICJ from ordering state courts to annul criminal convictions and sentences, for any reason deemed sufficient by the ICJ. Indeed, that is precisely the relief Mexico requested. . . .

Medellin and the dissent cite Comegys v. Vasse, 26 U.S. 193 (1828), for the proposition that the judgments of international tribunals are automatically binding on domestic courts. That case, of course, involved a different treaty than the ones at issue here; it stands only for the modest principle that the terms of a treaty control the outcome of a case. We do not suggest that treaties can never afford binding domestic effect to international tribunal judgments—only that the U.N. Charter, the Optional Protocol, and the ICJ Statute do not do so. And whether the treaties underlying a judgment are self-executing so that the judgment is directly enforceable as domestic law in our courts is, of course, a matter for this Court to decide.

D

Our holding does not call into question the ordinary enforcement of foreign judgments or international arbitral agreements. Indeed, we agree with Medellin that, as a general matter, "an agreement to abide by the result" of an international adjudication—or what he really means, an agreement to give the result of such adjudication domestic legal effect— can be a treaty obligation like any other, so long as the agreement is consistent with the Constitution. The point is that the particular treaty obligations on which Medellin relies do not of their own force create domestic law.

The dissent worries that our decision casts doubt on some 70-odd treaties under which the United States has agreed to submit disputes to the ICJ according to "roughly similar" provisions. Again, under our established precedent, some treaties are self-executing and some are not, depending on the treaty. That the judgment of an international tribunal might not automatically become domestic law hardly means the underlying treaty is "useless." Such judgments would still constitute international obligations, the proper subject of political and diplomatic negotiations. And Congress could elect to give them wholesale effect (rather than the judgment-by-judgment approach hypothesized by the dissent) through implementing legislation, as it regularly has.

Further, that an ICJ judgment may not be automatically enforceable in domestic courts does not mean the particular underlying treaty is not. Indeed, we have held that a number of the "Friendship, Commerce, and Navigation" Treaties cited by the dissent are self-executing—based on "the language of the[se] Treat[ies]." See *Sumitomo Shoji America, Inc.*, 457 U.S. at 180, 189–90. . . . Contrary to the dissent's suggestion, neither our approach nor our cases require that a treaty provide for self-execution in so many talismanic words; that is a caricature of the Court's opinion. Our cases simply require courts to decide whether a treaty's terms reflect a determination by the President who negotiated it and the Senate that confirmed it that the treaty has domestic effect.

In addition, Congress is up to the task of implementing non-self-executing treaties, even those involving complex commercial disputes. The judgments of a number of international tribunals enjoy a different status because of implementing legislation enacted by Congress. . . . Such language [in the relevant statutes] demonstrates that Congress knows how to accord domestic effect to international obligations when it desires such a result.

Further, Medellin frames his argument as though giving the *Avena* judgment binding effect in domestic courts simply conforms to the proposition that domestic courts generally give effect to foreign judgments. But Medellin does not ask us to enforce a foreign-court judgment settling a typical commercial or property dispute. Rather, Medellin argues that the *Avena* judgment has the effect of enjoining the operation of state law. . . .

For the reasons we have stated, the *Avena* judgment is not domestic law. . . . The judgment of the Texas Court of Criminal Appeals is affirmed.

It is so ordered

■ JUSTICE BREYER, with whom JUSTICE SOUTER and JUSTICE GINSBURG join, dissenting. . . .

[T]his Court has frequently held or assumed that particular treaty provisions are self-executing, automatically binding the States without more. . . .

Of particular relevance to the present case, the Court has held that the United States may be obligated by treaty to comply with the judgment of an international tribunal interpreting that treaty, despite the absence of any congressional enactment specifically requiring such compliance. See Comegys v. Vasse, 26 U.S. 193, 211–12 (1828) (holding that decision of tribunal rendered pursuant to a United States-Spain treaty, which obliged the parties to "undertake to make satisfaction" of treaty-based rights, was "conclusive and final" and "not re-examinable" in

American courts); see also Meade v. United States, 76 U.S. 691 725 (1870) (holding that decision of tribunal adjudicating claims arising under United States-Spain treaty "was final and conclusive, and bar[red] a recovery upon the merits" in American court). . . .

I would find the relevant treaty provisions self-executing as applied to the ICJ judgment before us (giving that judgment domestic legal effect) for the following reasons, taken together.

First, the language of the relevant treaties strongly supports direct judicial enforceability, at least of judgments of the kind at issue here. The Optional Protocol bears the title "Compulsory Settlement of Disputes," thereby emphasizing the mandatory and binding nature of the procedures it sets forth. The body of the Protocol says specifically that "any party" that has consented to the ICJ's "compulsory jurisdiction" may bring a "dispute" before the court against any other such party. And the Protocol contrasts proceedings of the compulsory kind with an alternative "conciliation procedure," the recommendations of which a party may decide "not" to "accep[t]." Thus, the Optional Protocol's basic objective is not just to provide a forum for *settlement* but to provide a forum for *compulsory* settlement.

Moreover, in accepting Article 94(1) of the Charter, "[e]ach Member . . . undertakes to comply with the decision" of the ICJ "in any case to which it is a party." And the ICJ Statute (part of the U.N. Charter) makes clear that, a decision of the ICJ between parties that have consented to the ICJ's compulsory jurisdiction has "*binding force* . . . between the parties and in respect of that particular case." Enforcement of a court's judgment that has "binding force" involves quintessential judicial activity. . . .

I . . . recognize, as the majority emphasizes, that the U.N. Charter says that "[i]f any party to a case fails to perform the obligations incumbent upon it under a judgment rendered by the [ICJ], the other party may have recourse to the Security Council." And when the Senate ratified the charter, it took comfort in the fact that the United States has a veto in the Security Council.

But what has that to do with the matter? To begin with, the Senate would have been contemplating politically significant ICJ decisions, not, e.g., the bread-and-butter commercial and other matters that are the typical subjects of self-executing treaty provisions. And in any event, both the Senate debate and U.N. Charter provision discuss and describe what happens (or does not happen) when a nation decides *not* to carry out an ICJ decision. The debates refer to remedies for a breach of our promise to carry out an ICJ decision. The Senate understood, for example, that Congress (unlike legislatures in other nations that do not permit domestic legislation to trump treaty obligations) can block through legislation self-executing, as well as non-self-executing determinations. The debates nowhere refer to the method we use for affirmatively carrying out an ICJ obligation that no political branch has decided to dishonor, still less to a decision that the President (without congressional dissent) seeks to enforce. . . .

The upshot is that treaty language says that an ICJ decision is legally binding, but it leaves the implementation of that binding legal obligation to the domestic law of each signatory nation. In this Nation, the Supremacy Clause, as long and consistently interpreted, indicates that ICJ decisions rendered pursuant to provisions for binding adjudication must be domestically legally binding and enforceable in domestic courts *at least sometimes.* And for purposes of this argument, that conclusion is all that I need. The remainder of the discussion will explain why, if ICJ judgments *sometimes* bind domestic courts, then they have that effect here.

Second, the Optional Protocol here applies to a dispute about the meaning of a Vienna Convention provision that is itself self-executing and judicially enforceable. The Convention provision is about an individual's "rights," namely, his right upon being arrested to be informed of his separate right to contact his nation's consul. The provision language is precise. The dispute arises at the intersection of an individual right with ordinary rules of criminal procedure; it consequently concerns the kind of matter with which judges are familiar. The provisions contain judicially enforceable standards. And the judgment itself requires a further hearing of a sort that is typically judicial. . . .

Third, logic suggests that a treaty provision providing for "final" and "binding" judgments that "settl[e]" treaty-based disputes is self-executing insofar as the judgment in question concerns the meaning of an underlying treaty provision that is itself self-executing. Imagine that two parties to a contract agree to binding arbitration about whether a contract provision's word "grain" includes rye. They would expect that, if the arbitrator decides that the word "grain" does include rye, the arbitrator will then simply read the relevant provision as if it said "grain including rye." They would also expect the arbitrator to issue a binding award that embodies whatever relief would be appropriate under that circumstance.

Why treat differently the parties' agreement to binding ICJ determination about, e.g., the proper interpretation of the Vienna Convention clauses containing the rights here at issue? Why not simply read the relevant Vienna Convention provisions as if (between the parties and in respect to the 51 individuals at issue) they contain words that encapsulate the ICJ's decision? Why would the ICJ judgment not bind in precisely the same way those words would bind if they appeared in the relevant Vienna Convention provisions—just as the ICJ says, for purposes of this case, that they do?. . . .

I am not aware of any satisfactory answer to these questions. It is no answer to point to the fact that in Sanchez-Llamas v. *Oregon,* 548 U.S. 331 (2006), this Court interpreted the relevant Convention provisions differently from the ICJ in *Avena.* This Court's *Sanchez-Llamas* interpretation binds our courts with respect to individuals whose rights were not espoused by a state party in *Avena*. Moreover, as the Court itself recognizes, and as the President recognizes, see President's Memorandum, the question here is the very different question of applying the ICJ's *Avena* judgment to the very parties whose interests Mexico and the United States espoused in the ICJ *Avena* proceeding. It is in respect to these individuals that the United States has promised the ICJ decision will have binding force. . . .

Nor does recognition of the ICJ judgment as binding with respect to the individuals whose claims were espoused by Mexico in any way derogate from the Court's holding in *Sanchez-Llamas*. This case does not implicate the general interpretive question answered in *Sanchez-Llamas*: whether the Vienna Convention displaces state procedural rules. We are instead confronted with the discrete question of Texas's obligation to comply with a binding judgment issued by a tribunal with undisputed jurisdiction to adjudicate the rights of the individuals named therein. . . .

Fourth, the majority's very different approach has seriously negative practical implications. The United States has entered into at least 70 treaties that contain provisions for ICJ dispute settlement similar to the Protocol before us. Many of these treaties contain provisions similar to those this Court has previously found self-executing—provisions that involve, for example, property rights, contract and commercial rights, trademarks, civil liability for personal injury, rights of foreign diplomats, taxation, domestic-court jurisdiction, and so forth. If the Optional Protocol here, taken together with the U.N. Charter and its annexed ICJ Statute, is insufficient to warrant enforcement of the ICJ judgment before us, it is difficult to see how one could reach a different conclusion in any of these other instances. And the consequence is to undermine longstanding efforts in those treaties to create an effective international system for interpreting and applying many, often commercial, self-executing treaty provisions. . . .

Nor can the majority look to congressional legislation for a quick fix. Congress is unlikely to authorize automatic judicial enforceability of *all* ICJ judgments, for that could include some politically sensitive judgments and others better suited for enforcement by other branches: for example, those touching upon military hostilities, naval activity, handling of nuclear material, and so forth. Nor is Congress likely to have the time available, let alone the will, to legislate judgment-by-judgment enforcement of, say, the ICJ's (or other international tribunals') resolution of non-politically-sensitive commercial disputes. And as this Court's prior case law has avoided laying down bright-line rules but instead has adopted a more complex approach, it seems unlikely that Congress will find it easy to develop legislative bright lines that pick out those provisions (addressed to the Judicial Branch) where self-execution seems warranted. But, of course, it is not necessary for Congress to do so—at least not if one believes that this Court's Supremacy Clause cases *already* embody criteria likely to work reasonably well. It is those criteria that I would apply here.

Fifth, other factors, related to the particular judgment here at issue, make that judgment well suited to direct judicial enforcement. The specific issue before the ICJ concerned " 'review and reconsideration' " of the "possible prejudice" caused in each of the 51 affected cases by an arresting State's failure to provide the defendant with rights guaranteed by the Vienna Convention. This review will call for an understanding of how criminal procedure works, including whether, and how, a notification failure may work prejudice. As the ICJ itself recognized, "it is the judicial process that is suited to this task." Courts frequently work with criminal procedure and related prejudice. Legislatures do not. Judicial standards are readily available for working in this technical area. Legislative standards are not readily available. Judges typically determine such matters, deciding, for example, whether further hearings are necessary, after reviewing a record in an individual case. Congress does not normally legislate in respect to individual cases. Indeed, to repeat what I said above, what kind of special legislation does the majority believe Congress ought to consider?

Sixth, to find the United States' treaty obligations self-executing as applied to the ICJ judgment (and consequently to find that judgment enforceable) does not threaten constitutional conflict with other branches; it does not require us to engage in nonjudicial activity; and it does not require us to create a new cause of action. The only question before us concerns the application of the ICJ judgment as binding law applicable to the parties in a particular criminal proceeding that Texas law creates independently of the treaty. . . .

Seventh, neither the President nor Congress has expressed concern about direct judicial enforcement of the ICJ decision. To the contrary, the President favors enforcement of this judgment. Thus, insofar as foreign policy impact, the interrelation of treaty provisions, or any other matter within the President's special treaty, military, and foreign affairs responsibilities might prove relevant, such factors *favor*, rather than militate against, enforcement of the judgment before us. . . .

In sum, a strong line of precedent . . . indicates that the treaty provisions before us and the judgment of the International Court of Justice address themselves to the Judicial Branch and consequently are self-executing. In reaching a contrary conclusion, the Court has failed to take proper account of that precedent and, as a result, the Nation may well break its word even though the President seeks to live up to that word and Congress has done nothing to suggest the contrary.

For the reasons set forth, I respectfully dissent.

NOTES ON INTERNATIONAL TRIBUNALS

1. JUDICIAL ENFORCEMENT OF TREATIES

Article II of the Constitution provides that the President has the authority to make treaties "by and with the Advice and Consent of the Senate . . . provided two thirds of the Senators present concur." The Supremacy Clause of the Constitution provides that such treaties (along with the Constitution itself and "Laws of the United States") "shall be the supreme Law of the Land; and the Judges in every State shall be bound thereby, any Thing in the Constitution or Laws of any State to the Contrary notwithstanding." And Article III of the Constitution provides that the judicial power shall extend to all cases arising under treaties.

Despite these constitutional provisions, it has long been settled that U.S. courts will enforce a treaty only if it is "self-executing." The doctrine of treaty self-execution is usually traced to Foster v. Neilson, 27 U.S. (2 Pet.) 253 (1829). That case involved an 1819 treaty between the United States and Spain that ceded certain disputed territory east of the Mississippi River to the United States. The petitioners claimed title to a tract of land within the territory based on an 1804 grant from Spain, and on that basis sought to eject the respondent from the tract. The treaty provided in relevant part that all grants of land made by Spain in the ceded territory prior to the treaty "shall be ratified and confirmed to the persons in possession of the lands to the same extent that the same grants would be valid if the territories had remained under the dominion" of Spain. In concluding that U.S. courts should not give effect to the land grants protected by the treaty, the Court, in an opinion by Chief Justice Marshall, reasoned as follows:

> A treaty is in its nature a contract between two nations, not a legislative act. It does not generally effect, of itself, the object to be accomplished, especially so far as its operation is infra-territorial; but is carried into execution by the sovereign power of the respective parties to the instrument.

> In the United States a different principle is established. Our constitution declares a treaty to be the law of the land. It is, consequently, to be regarded in courts of justice as equivalent to an act of the legislature, whenever it operates of itself without the aid of any legislative provision. But when the terms of the stipulation import a contract, when either of the parties engages to perform a particular act, the treaty addresses itself to the political, not the judicial department; and the legislature must execute the contract before it can become a rule for the Court.

> The article [of the treaty] under consideration does not declare that all the grants made by [Spain] before the [treaty] shall be valid to the same extent as if the ceded territories had remained under [its] dominion. It does not say that those grants are hereby confirmed. Had such been its language, it would have acted directly on the subject, and would have repealed those acts of Congress which were repugnant to it; but its language is that those grants shall be

ratified and confirmed to the persons in possession, & c. By whom shall they be ratified and confirmed? This seems to be the language of contract; and if it is, the ratification and confirmation which are promised must be the act of the Legislature. Until such act shall be passed, the Court is not at liberty to disregard the existing laws on the subject.

Several years after *Foster*, the Supreme Court changed its mind about the effect of the treaty provision at issue there. After examining the Spanish version of the provision, the English translation of which provided that the grants of land "shall remain ratified and confirmed," the Court concluded that the provision was in fact self-executing. See United States v. Percheman, 32 U.S. (7 Pet.) 51, 88–89 (1833).

For additional discussion of the doctrine of treaty self-execution, see Curtis A. Bradley, Self-Execution and Treaty Duality, 2008 Sup. Ct. Rev. 131; Carlos Manuel Vázquez, Treaties as Law of the Land: The Supremacy Clause and the Judicial Enforcement of Treaties, 122 Harv. L. Rev. 599 (2008); Tim Wu, Treaties' Domains, 93 Va. L. Rev. 571 (2007).

2.   International Court of Justice

The International Court of Justice (ICJ) is a fifteen-judge court that sits in The Hague, in the Netherlands. The ICJ was established by a treaty, the United Nations Charter, and is declared by the Charter to be the "principal judicial organ of the United Nations." Under Article 94(1) of the UN Charter, "[e]ach Member of the United Nations undertakes to comply with the decision of the International Court of Justice in any case to which it is a party." Under Article 94(2) of the Charter, if a party fails to perform the obligations imposed by an ICJ judgment, "the other party may have recourse to the [UN] Security Council, which may, if it deems necessary, make recommendations or decide upon measures to be taken to give effect to the judgment." The jurisdiction of the ICJ is regulated by another, related treaty—the Statute of the International Court of Justice. The United States became a party to both the Charter and the Statute in 1945.

The ICJ hears only disputes between nation-states, and only if the parties to the dispute have consented to the ICJ's jurisdiction. Nations can consent to the ICJ's jurisdiction in any one of three ways: by filing a declaration with the United Nations agreeing to be generally subject to the ICJ's jurisdiction "in relation to any other state accepting the same obligation"; by agreeing in a treaty to have disputes under the treaty resolved by the ICJ; or by agreeing at the time of a dispute to refer the dispute to the ICJ for resolution. For many years, the United States consented generally to the ICJ's jurisdiction, subject to certain limitations. The United States withdrew this general consent in 1985, however, after the ICJ exercised jurisdiction over a controversial case involving U.S. covert activities in Nicaragua.[a] Nevertheless, the United States is still a party to approximately 70 treaties that

---

[a]   The ICJ proceeded to rule against the United States on the merits in the Nicaragua case. The D.C. Circuit subsequently held that the obligation under Article 94 of the UN Charter to comply with the ICJ's judgment in that case was not self-executing. See Committee of United States Citizens Living in Nicaragua v. Reagan, 859 F.2d 929, 937–38 (D.C. Cir. 1988).

have clauses providing for ICJ jurisdiction over disputes arising under the treaties.

3. VIENNA CONVENTION LITIGATION

The Vienna Convention on Consular Relations is a treaty that regulates the establishment and functions of consulates and the immunity of consular officials.[b] Article 36 of the Convention provides that, when one party country arrests someone from another party country, the arrested individual shall have the right to have their consulate notified of their arrest and to communicate with their consulate. It further provides that the arresting authorities "shall inform the person concerned without delay" of these rights. Finally, it provides that these rights "shall be exercised in conformity with the laws and regulations of the receiving State, subject to the proviso, however, that the said laws and regulations must enable full effect to be given to the purposes for which the[se] rights . . . are intended." The United States became a party to the Vienna Convention in 1969. At the same time, the United States also became a party to an Optional Protocol to the Convention that gives the ICJ jurisdiction to hear disputes arising under the Convention. Today, approximately 171 nations are parties to the Vienna Convention, and approximately 47 are parties to the Optional Protocol.

State and local law enforcement personnel in the United States have often failed to provide arrested foreign nationals with the notice required by Article 36 of the Vienna Convention. Starting in the late 1990s, a series of cases were brought against the United States in the ICJ seeking relief for these treaty violations. The first case was brought by Paraguay on behalf of Angel Breard, a Paraguayan national on death row in Virginia. Although the ICJ issued a preliminary order in that case requesting that the United States "take all measures at its disposal" to stay the execution while the ICJ adjudicated the dispute, Breard was executed on schedule, and Paraguay subsequently abandoned its suit. In declining to stay Breard's execution, the U.S. Supreme Court found that Breard had procedurally defaulted his Vienna Convention claim by failing to raise it in state courts. In Breard v. Greene, 523 U.S. 371, 375 (1998), the Court explained:

> [W]hile we should give respectful consideration to the interpretation of an international treaty rendered by an international court with jurisdiction to interpret such, it has been recognized in international law that, absent a clear and express statement to the contrary, the procedural rules of the forum State govern the implementation of the treaty in that State. This proposition is embodied in the Vienna Convention itself, which provides that the rights expressed in the Convention "shall be exercised in conformity with the laws and regulations of the receiving State," provided that "said

---

[b] Like embassies, consulates are official outposts of a nation (the "sending state") located in the territory of another nation (the "receiving state"). Whereas embassies handle political relations and are typically located in the receiving state's capital, consulates typically handle economic and trade issues, and also provide certain assistance to the sending state's nationals, and they often have locations outside the capital.

laws and regulations must enable full effect to be given to the purposes for which the rights accorded under this Article are intended." It is the rule in this country that assertions of error in criminal proceedings must first be raised in state court in order to form the basis for relief in habeas. Claims not so raised are considered defaulted. By not asserting his Vienna Convention claim in state court, Breard failed to exercise his rights under the Vienna Convention in conformity with the laws of the United States and the Commonwealth of Virginia. Having failed to do so, he cannot raise a claim of violation of those rights now on federal habeas review.

The second case was brought by Germany on behalf of two German brothers on death row in Arizona, Walter and Karl LaGrand. Once again, the executions were carried out before the ICJ had resolved the dispute. Germany nevertheless persisted in its suit, and the ICJ eventually issued a final decision. In its decision, the ICJ held that the United States had violated the Vienna Convention and that in future situations in which German nationals "have been subjected to prolonged detention or convicted and sentenced to severe penalties," the United States would be required "to allow the review and reconsideration of the conviction and sentence by taking account of the violation of the rights set forth in the Convention." The ICJ also suggested that state authorities were responsible for any procedural default of the Vienna Convention claims, since they had failed to provide the requisite notice under Article 36. See LaGrand Case (Germany v. U.S.), ICJ, No. 104 (June 27, 2001), 40 I.L.M. 1069.

The third case, *Avena*, was brought by Mexico on behalf of 54 Mexican nationals on death row in a number of U.S. states. This time none of the individuals in question was executed during the pendency of the case. The ICJ ultimately concluded that the United States had violated the Vienna Convention with respect to 51 of the Mexican nationals. As in *LaGrand*, the ICJ held that, when there has been a violation of the Convention and severe penalties have been imposed, the United States is obligated to provide "review and reconsideration" of the defendant's conviction and sentence. The ICJ further explained that such review and reconsideration should "guarantee that the violation and the possible prejudice caused by that violation will be fully examined and taken into account in the review and reconsideration process." The ICJ also said that this review and reconsideration "should occur within the overall judicial proceedings relating to the individual defendant concerned." Finally, the ICJ suggested that U.S. procedural default rules should not be applied to bar review and reconsideration, at least in certain circumstances, because the application of such rules would deprive the rights in Article 36 from being given "full effect." See Case Concerning Avena and Other Mexican Nationals (Mexico v. U.S.), ICJ, No. 128 (Mar. 31, 2004), 43 I.L.M. 581.

Some months after the *Avena* decision, in February 2005, President Bush wrote a memorandum to the Attorney General stating that:

> I have determined, pursuant to the authority vested in me as President by the Constitution and the laws of the United States of

America, that the United States will discharge its international obligations under the decision of the International Court of Justice in [*Avena*], by having State courts give effect to the decision in accordance with general principles of comity in cases filed by the 51 Mexican nationals addressed in that decision.

Shortly thereafter, the United States announced that it was withdrawing from the Optional Protocol that had given the ICJ jurisdiction to hear the Vienna Convention cases.

4. *SANCHEZ-LLAMAS V. OREGON*

In Sanchez-Llamas v. Oregon, 548 U.S. 331 (2006), the Court considered two consolidated cases involving foreign nationals who had not been advised of their rights under Article 36 of the Vienna Convention. In one of the cases, a Mexican national, Moises Sanchez-Llamas, was seeking to have incriminating evidence suppressed as a result of the treaty violation. In the other case, a Honduran national, Mario Bustillo, was seeking to obtain review and reconsideration of his conviction and sentence, despite state procedural default rules that would normally have barred the claim because it was not raised either at trial or on direct appeal. Neither Sanchez-Llamas nor Bustillo was among the 51 individuals directly covered by the *Avena* judgment.

In an opinion by Chief Justice Roberts, the Court held that, even assuming that Article 36 of the Vienna Convention is self-executing and confers judicially enforceable rights, suppression of evidence is not an appropriate remedy for violation of the Convention, and a state may apply its regular procedural default rules to a claim brought under the Convention. With respect to the suppression issue, the Court reasoned that "it would be startling if the Convention were read to require suppression," given that the exclusionary rule as applied in the United States "is an entirely American legal creation." The Court also reasoned that the reasons for the exclusionary rule are not substantially implicated in the consular notice context, since a violation of the treaty is unlikely to produce unreliable confessions, and the police will not be tempted to violate the treaty in order to obtain practical advantages. The Court also made clear that the creation of a suppression remedy in this context did not fall within the Court's supervisory powers, since the Court does not have supervisory power over the state courts. As a result, said the Court, "our authority to create a judicial remedy applicable in state court must lie, if anywhere, in the treaty itself."

With respect to the procedural default issue, the Court relied on its decision in *Breard* for the proposition that procedural default rules are not inconsistent with the Vienna Convention. The Court also rejected the argument that it was bound by the ICJ's conclusion in *LaGrand* and *Avena* that Article 36 of the Vienna Convention overrides procedural default rules. The Court explained:

> Under our Constitution, "[t]he judicial Power of the United States" is "vested in one supreme Court, and in such inferior Courts as the Congress may from time to time ordain and establish."

Art. III, § 1. That "judicial Power . . . extend[s] to . . . Treaties." Id., § 2. And, as Chief Justice Marshall famously explained, that judicial power includes the duty "to say what the law is." Marbury v. Madison, 5 U.S. 137, 160 (1803). If treaties are to be given effect as federal law under our legal system, determining their meaning as a matter of federal law "is emphatically the province and duty of the judicial department," headed by the "one supreme Court" established by the Constitution. Id. . . . . It is against this background that the United States ratified, and the Senate gave its advice and consent to, the various agreements that govern referral of Vienna Convention disputes to the ICJ.

Nothing in the structure or purpose of the ICJ suggests that its interpretations were intended to be conclusive on our courts. The ICJ's decisions have "*no binding force* except between the parties and in respect of that particular case," Statute of the International Court of Justice, Art. 59 (1945) (emphasis added). Any interpretation of law the ICJ renders in the course of resolving particular disputes is thus not binding precedent *even as to the ICJ itself;* there is accordingly little reason to think that such interpretations were intended to be controlling on our courts. The ICJ's principal purpose is to arbitrate particular disputes between national governments. . . . While each member of the United Nations has agreed to comply with decisions of the ICJ "in any case to which it is a party," United Nations Charter, Art. 94(1) (1945), the Charter's procedure for noncompliance—referral to the Security Council by the aggrieved state—contemplates quintessentially *international* remedies, Art. 94(2).

In addition, "[w]hile courts interpret treaties for themselves, the meaning given them by the departments of government particularly charged with their negotiation and enforcement is given great weight." Kolovrat v. Oregon, 366 U.S. 187, 194 (1961). Although the United States has agreed to "discharge its international obligations" in having state courts give effect to the decision in *Avena*, it has not taken the view that the ICJ's interpretation of Article 36 is binding on our courts. Moreover, shortly after *Avena*, the United States withdrew from the Optional Protocol concerning Vienna Convention disputes. Whatever the effect of *Avena* and *LaGrand* before this withdrawal, it is doubtful that our courts should give decisive weight to the interpretation of a tribunal whose jurisdiction in this area is no longer recognized by the United States.

The reasoning in *LaGrand* and *Avena* therefore were entitled only to "respectful consideration," said the Court. Even with that consideration, the Court concluded that the best interpretation of Article 36 was one that allowed for the application of procedural default rules.

Justice Breyer dissented, joined by Joined by Justices Stevens and Souter, and joined in part by Justice Ginsburg. Justice Breyer argued that suppression of evidence should not be ruled out as a remedy for a violation of Article 36 because it may sometimes be the only effective remedy, and Article 36 requires effective remedies. He further argued, based on the text and drafting history of Article 36 and the ICJ's decisions in *LaGrand* and *Avena*, that Article 36 should be interpreted as sometimes displacing state procedural default rules. *Breard* was not dispositive, he contended, because it concerned a federal rather than state procedural default rule, it predated *LaGrand* and *Avena*, and it was a per curiam decision issued under a compressed time schedule. While Justice Breyer accepted the "respectful consideration" standard applied by the majority, he suggested that the majority had failed to take sufficient account of the ICJ's expertise in matters of treaty interpretation and the desirability of having a uniform treaty interpretation.

5. QUESTIONS AND COMMENTS ON *MEDELLIN V. TEXAS*

Unlike *Sanchez-Llamas*, the *Medellin* case concerned an individual who was specifically covered by the ICJ's judgment in *Avena*. Should that difference have led to a different outcome? Note that, whereas the United States was not under a treaty obligation to accept the ICJ's *reasoning* in *Avena*, it was undisputed that it was under a treaty obligation to comply with the ICJ's *judgment*, which required that review and reconsideration be provided in the 51 cases covered by the judgment.

The majority in *Medellin* acknowledges that the ICJ's judgment in *Avena* is binding on the United States internationally, but it concludes that the judgment does not have domestic legal force because the treaty provisions requiring the United States to comply with the judgment are non-self-executing. On what basis does the Court find a lack of self-execution? Does the phrase "undertakes to comply" in Article 94(1) of the UN Charter suggest that the issue of compliance was to be determined by the political branches rather than the courts? Does the provision in Article 94(2) for enforcement of ICJ decisions by the Security Council suggest this?

In addition to finding textual and other evidence of non-self-execution, the majority in *Medellin* expresses concern about the policy implications of allowing ICJ judgments to have direct effect in U.S. courts. The Court notes that "Medellin's interpretation would allow ICJ judgments to override otherwise binding state law" and that "there is nothing in his logic that would exempt contrary federal law from the same fate." The Court further observes that "there is nothing to prevent the ICJ from ordering state courts to annul criminal convictions and sentences, for any reason deemed sufficient by the ICJ." If Article 94(1) of the UN Charter were construed to be self-executing, would these implications necessarily follow? Even if they would, did the United States in effect agree to give the ICJ this authority when the United States consented to allow the ICJ to resolve disputes arising under the Vienna Convention, which is a treaty and thus part of the supreme law of the land?

As discussed in Section 4 of this chapter, in a series of domestic cases the Supreme Court has staked out rather uncertain boundaries on the proper use of non-Article III tribunals. International courts like the ICJ are non-

Article III tribunals in the sense that their judges are not appointed pursuant to the senatorial consent process in the Constitution and do not have the tenure and salary protections of federal judges. Moreover, as *Sanchez-Llamas* and *Medellin* illustrate, the jurisdictional authority of these tribunals sometimes overlaps with the jurisdictional authority of the federal courts. What implications, if any, do the domestic non-Article III tribunal decisions have for the constitutionality of delegations of adjudicative authority to international tribunals like the ICJ? More generally, does the growth of international tribunals present a threat to the power and independence of the federal judiciary?

Medellin was executed by the State of Texas in August 2008, after the Supreme Court denied him a stay of execution. In denying the stay, the Court observed in a per curiam opinion that "[i]t is up to Congress whether to implement obligations undertaken under a treaty which (like this one) does not itself have the force and effect of domestic law sufficient to set aside the judgment or the ensuing sentence, and Congress has not progressed beyond the bare introduction of a bill in the four years since the ICJ ruling and the four months since our ruling. . . ." The Court also noted: "The Department of Justice of the United States is well aware of these proceedings and has not chosen to seek our intervention. Its silence is no surprise: The United States has not wavered in its position that petitioner was not prejudiced by his lack of consular access." See Medellin v. Texas, 554 U.S. 759 (2008).

For additional discussion of *Medellin* and its implications, see Curtis A. Bradley, Intent, Presumptions, and Non-Self-Executing Treaties, 102 Am. J. Int'l L. 540 (2008); Julian G. Ku, *Medellin*'s Clear Statement Rule: A Solution for International Delegations, 77 Fordham L. Rev. 609 (2008); Janet Koven Levit, Does *Medellin* Matter?, 77 Fordham L. Rev. 617 (2008); John T. Parry, A Primer on Treaties and § 1983 after *Medellin v. Texas*, 13 Lewis & Clark L. Rev. 35 (2009); Jordan J. Paust, *Medellin*, *Avena*, the Supremacy of Treaties, and Relevant Executive Authority, 31 Suffolk Transnat'l L. Rev. 301 (2008); John Quigley, President Bush's Directive to Foreigners under Arrest: A Critique of *Medellin v. Texas*, 22 Emory Int'l L. Rev. 423 (2008); Paul B. Stephan, Open Doors, 13 Lewis & Clark L. Rev. 11 (2009); D.A. Jeremy Telman, *Medellin* and Originalism, 68 Md. L. Rev. 377 (2009); Carlos Manuel Vázquez, Less Than Zero?, 102 Am. J. Int'l L. 563 (2008).

6.   WORLD TRADE ORGANIZATION

Another important international tribunal is the Dispute Settlement Body (DSB) of the World Trade Organization (WTO), which adjudicates trade disputes between the member countries using appointed panels and a standing Appellate Body. The DSB's decisions are binding, and, if the losing party does not comply with a decision, the DSB may authorize the prevailing party to impose trade sanctions on the losing party. The United States is a party to the relevant WTO treaties, and it regularly participates in cases before the DSB, both as a plaintiff and as a defendant. As defendant, the United States has lost a number of significant cases, including a case challenging clean air regulations issued by the Environmental Protection Agency, a case challenging U.S. limits on shrimp imports designed to protect sea turtles, and a case challenging U.S. tax treatment of foreign sales corporations. In 1994, while the United States was considering the WTO treaties, Congress approved a "Statement of Administrative Action," which provides that WTO decisions "have no binding effect under the law of the United States and do not represent an expression of U.S. foreign or trade policy." In subsequent legislation implementing the WTO treaties, Congress deemed this Statement "an authoritative expression by the United States concerning the interpretation and application of the [WTO] Agreements and this Act in any judicial proceeding in which a question arises concerning such interpretation or application." As a result, WTO decisions are regarded as non-self-executing in the U.S. legal system.[c]

In the absence of such legislative guidance, should courts (a) presume that international decisions are self-executing, (b) presume that such decisions are not self-executing, or (c) apply no presumption one way or the other? What, if anything, does *Medellin* suggest about this question?

7. NAFTA ARBITRATION

In 1993, the United States became a party, along with Canada and Mexico, to the North American Free Trade Agreement (NAFTA). NAFTA provides for two types of arbitration that may raise constitutional issues. First, Chapter 19 of NAFTA allows certain import decisions of member countries (relating to the application of "antidumping laws" and the imposition of "countervailing duties") to be reviewed by binational arbitral panels. These panels apply the standard of review and substantive law of the importing country, and their decisions are binding and final. Thus, in the case of the United States, the panels can exercise final review over the application of U.S. trade law by the International Trade Commission (a federal administrative agency), whose decisions would otherwise be subject to review by the Court of International Trade, an Article III court. In situations in which a matter is referred by a panel back to the International Trade Commission, the Commission is bound by federal statute to "take action not inconsistent with the decision" of the panel. The panel members, however, need not be Article III judges, and their selection is not subject to the appointments process for such judges.

Does this scheme violate constitutional limitations on the use of non-Article III courts? Does it fall within the "public rights" category discussed in *Northern Pipeline*? Does the narrow and specialized nature of its jurisdiction help avoid constitutional concerns? The Chapter 19 arrangement has been challenged in U.S. courts on Article III and other constitutional grounds, but the challenges have to date been dismissed for lack of standing, see American Coalition for Competitive Trade v. Clinton, 128 F.3d 761 (D.C.

---

[c] An additional complication with the WTO treaties is that, like the NAFTA treaty discussed in Note 7, they were concluded as "congressional-executive agreements"—that is, they were concluded for the United States by the President and a majority of Congress, not the President and two-thirds of the Senate as specified in Article II of the Constitution. While there has been some academic debate over the legitimacy of the congressional-executive agreement process, this process has been used for the vast majority of international agreements concluded by the United States since the late 1930s.

Cir. 1997), and for lack of jurisdiction, see Coalition for Fair Lumber Imports v. United States, 471 F.3d 1329 (D.C. Cir. 2006).

Second, Chapter 11 of NAFTA requires each country to accord investors of the other two countries certain minimum standards of treatment, including protection against uncompensated expropriation. Investors who allege a violation of Chapter 11 may submit claims to a panel of three private arbitrators who can award monetary damages but not injunctive relief. A particularly interesting Chapter 11 case, brought in the late 1990s and resolved in 2003, concerned the treatment that a Canadian company, The Loewen Group, had received from Mississippi state courts. In that case, the owner of a funeral home in Mississippi had sued Loewen in a Mississippi trial court for unfair and deceptive trading practices and breach of contract. The plaintiff sought approximately $26 million in damages, but the jury awarded a total of $500 million, which included $400 million in punitive damages. Under Mississippi state law, Loewen was required to post a bond in the amount of 125% of the judgment (i.e., $625 million) in order to appeal, and the Mississippi Supreme Court refused to waive that requirement. Loewen settled the case for $175 million.

In its Chapter 11 proceeding, Loewen alleged that the plaintiffs' attorneys in the Mississippi case had been allowed to appeal to anti-Canadian, racial, and class biases, and that these biases had affected the verdict. Loewen argued that the unfairness of the Mississippi proceedings and the bond requirement violated Chapter 11 because they constituted an expropriation of property, unequal treatment of a foreign company, and a denial of justice. Loewen sought damages in the amount of $725 million, which included not only what it paid out in the settlement but also compensation for business losses allegedly sustained as a result of the verdict. It sought these damages directly from the U.S. government rather than from Mississippi, since it is the United States as a whole, not Mississippi, that is a party to NAFTA, and nations are generally responsible under international law for the actions of their constituent states.

In a preliminary ruling on jurisdiction, the arbitration panel held that a nation's judicial proceedings may be challenged under Chapter 11. The panel noted that Chapter 11 applies to "measures adopted or maintained by a party," and that "measure" is defined by NAFTA as "any law, regulation, procedure, requirement or practice." The panel reasoned that these terms could reasonably be read as encompassing judicial decisions:

> "Law" comprehends judge-made as well as statute-based rules. "Procedure" is apt to include judicial as well as legislative procedure. "Requirement" is capable of covering a court order which requires a party to do an act or to pay a sum of money, while "practice" is capable of denoting the practice of courts as well as the practice of other bodies.

The panel further reasoned that allowing for challenges to judicial decisions would be consistent with the purposes of NAFTA, since judicial decisions, like other governmental acts, have the potential to undermine free trade and investment. Finally, the panel noted that construing Chapter 11 in this way would be consistent with international law principles, which generally hold nations responsible for the actions of their judicial organs. See Decision on Hearing of Respondent's Objection to Competence and Jurisdiction, The Loewen Group, Inc. and United States of America, Case No. ARB(AF)/98/3 (Jan. 5, 2001), at http://www.state.gov/documents/organization/3921.pdf.

The arbitration panel ultimately ruled in favor of the United States, however, because it concluded that Loewen's assignment of its NAFTA claims to a Canadian corporation owned and controlled by a United States corporation had destroyed the diversity of nationality required for NAFTA arbitration. The panel also concluded that the claims should be dismissed on the merits because the claimants had failed to show that they had no reasonably available and adequate remedy under United States law. While concluding that the trial and verdict in the Mississippi case "were clearly improper and discreditable and cannot be squared with minimum standards of international law and fair and equitable treatment," the panel noted that Loewen had failed to appeal the Mississippi trial court's decision either to the Mississippi Supreme Court or the U.S. Supreme Court, and it reasoned that "a court decision which can be challenged through the judicial process does not amount to a denial of justice at the international level." See Award, The Loewen Group, Inc. and United States of America, Case No. ARB(AF)/98/3 (June 26, 2003), at http://www.state.gov/documents/organization/22094.pdf.

When applied to review the fairness of U.S. judicial proceedings, does Chapter 11 constitute a delegation of Article III judicial power to an international body? Does it constitute a displacement of the Supreme Court's role in the U.S. judicial system? Does it improperly undermine state judicial authority?

8. OTHER INTERNATIONAL ARBITRATION

In a number of instances throughout history, the United States has participated in international arbitration to resolve disputes with other countries. These disputes have sometimes concerned claims by the nations themselves and at other times have concerned claims by citizens of the respective nations. An early example of the use of such arbitration occurred in connection with the Jay Treaty of 1794, which established several arbitral tribunals to resolve claims between the United States and Great Britain, including claims by British creditors. Another prominent example was the Alabama Claims Arbitration after the Civil War, in which the United States sought damages against Great Britain for allowing British ports to be used during the War for the construction of Confederate ships. A more recent example was the establishment in 1981 of the Iran-United States Claims Tribunal, which, as part of the resolution of the Iranian hostage crisis, was charged with resolving various claims by U.S. citizens and companies against Iran as well as certain claims by Iran against the United States. In Dames & Moore v. Regan, 453 U.S. 654 (1981), the Supreme Court upheld presidential authority to suspend claims pending in U.S. courts and require that the claims be presented to this claims tribunal.

The dissent in *Medellin* refers to Comegys v. Vasse, 26 U.S. 193 (1828). In that case, Spain had agreed by treaty (in a different provision of the same treaty at issue in *Foster v. Neilson*, discussed above in Note 1) to pay up to a total of $5 million to resolve various damage claims by U.S. citizens. The treaty provided that the allocation of damage awards would be made by an arbitral commission consisting of three U.S. citizens, appointed by the President with the advice and consent of the Senate, that would sit in Washington, D.C. In *Comegys*, the Court observed, in an opinion by Justice Story, that:

> The object of the treaty was to invest the commissioners with full power and authority to receive, examine, and decide upon the amount and validity of the asserted claims upon Spain, for damages and injuries. Their decision, within the scope of this authority, is conclusive and final. If they pronounce the claim valid or invalid, if they ascertain the amount, their award in the premises is not re-examinable. The parties must abide by it, as the decree of a competent tribunal of exclusive jurisdiction. A rejected claim cannot be brought again under review, in any judicial tribunal; an amount once fixed, is a final ascertainment of the damages or injury.

Are the circumstances of that case distinguishable from those of *Medellin*?

Private parties also frequently agree to resolve their disputes through arbitration. The Federal Arbitration Act, 9 U.S.C. § 1 et seq., states that arbitration agreements are to be enforced like other contracts and provides for expedited judicial review to enforce arbitration awards. The Supreme Court has described this Act as "establish[ing] a national policy favoring arbitration when the parties contract for that mode of dispute resolution." Preston v. Ferrer, 552 U.S. 346 (2008). The United States is also a party to the New York Convention on the Recognition and Enforcement of Foreign Arbitral Awards, pursuant to which it is obligated to enforce arbitration judgments issued in the territory of other party nations, subject to narrow exceptions. Is dispute resolution by the ICJ analogous to such private-party arbitration, as suggested by the dissent in *Medellin*? For discussion of this issue, see Mark L. Movsesian, Commercial Arbitration and International Courts, 18 Duke J. Comp. & Int'l L. 423 (2008), and Ernest A. Young, Supranational Rulings as Judgments and Precedents, 18 Duke J. Comp. & Int'l L. 477 (2008).

9. ENFORCEMENT OF FOREIGN JUDGMENTS

Federal and state courts in the United States often enforce the civil judgments of other countries as a matter of comity. Before *Erie,* the standards for enforcing foreign civil judgments were regarded as part of the "general common law" that could be applied differently by federal and state courts. Today, the standards are generally regarded as matters of state law, which means that, pursuant to *Erie*, federal district courts asked to enforce foreign civil judgments look to the law of the state in which they sit. More than half the states have adopted the Uniform Foreign Money Judgments Recognition Act, which broadly allows for the enforcement of foreign civil judgments, subject to modest procedural and jurisdictional requirements.

Other states enforce foreign civil judgments as a matter of state common law. Both in the Act and as a matter of common law, states may decline to enforce a foreign civil judgment if it violates some fundamental public policy of the state. For example, courts have declined to enforce libel awards from Great Britain because British libel law accords less protection to free speech than does the First Amendment (as it has been construed by the Supreme Court). See, e.g., Matusevitch v. Telnikoff, 877 F.Supp. 1 (D.D.C. 1995); Bachchan v. India Abroad Publications, Inc., 585 N.Y.S.2d 661 (N.Y. Sup. Ct. 1992).

Are foreign civil judgments distinguishable from the judgments of international tribunals? If so, how? What does the majority say about this in *Medellin*? Should there be a public policy limitation on the enforcement of the judgments of international tribunals? Would such a limitation have addressed some of the concerns of the majority in *Medellin*?

Unlike foreign civil judgments, U.S. courts do not enforce foreign penal or revenue judgments. Judge Learned Hand explained the basis for this limitation:

> Even in the case of ordinary municipal liabilities, a court will not recognize those arising in a foreign state, if they run counter to the "settled public policy" of its own. Thus a scrutiny of the liability is necessarily always in reserve, and the possibility that it will be found not to accord with the policy of the domestic state. This is not a troublesome or delicate inquiry when the question arises between private persons, but it takes on quite another face when it concerns the relations between the foreign state and its own citizens or even those who may be temporarily within its borders. To pass upon the provisions for the public order of another state is, or at any rate should be, beyond the powers of a court; it involves the relations between the states themselves, with which courts are incompetent to deal, and which are intrusted to other authorities. It may commit the domestic state to a position which would seriously embarrass its neighbor. Revenue laws fall within the same reasoning; they affect a state in matters as vital to its existence as its criminal laws. No court ought to undertake an inquiry which it cannot prosecute without determining whether those laws are consonant with its own notions of what is proper.

Moore v. Mitchell, 30 F.2d 600, 604 (2d Cir. 1929) (Hand, J., concurring), aff'd on other grounds, 281 U.S. 18 (1930). Is this explanation persuasive? For a critique of this limitation on the enforcement of foreign judgments, see William S. Dodge, Breaking the Public Law Taboo, 43 Harv. Int'l L.J. 161 (2002).

10. BIBLIOGRAPHY

Ernest Young contends that insights about the proper relationship between domestic and international courts can and should be gleaned from the principles governing Federal Courts law, which have been developed to regulate the somewhat analogous relationship between federal and state courts. As he explains, in the federal-state system, "[b]oth constitutional values of federalism and the practical realities of the system—in particular, the inability of the federal courts to handle even all cases raising questions of federal law—mandate an emphasis on preserving both sets of courts as viable and respected institutions." Ernest A. Young, Institutional Settlement in a Globalizing Judicial System, 54 Duke L.J. 1143 (2005). Young suggests that "[i]f we are now to graft another layer of courts onto this system—the ICJ, NAFTA and WTO panels, perhaps an International Criminal Court (ICC)— then we will need to develop a comparable set of tools to mediate the new set of conflicts that will surely arise." Young argues in particular that, in thinking about the relationship between international and domestic courts, more attention should be paid to the principle of "institutional settlement"—that is, the principle that "law should allocate decisionmaking to the institutions best suited to decide particular questions, and that the decisions arrived at by those institutions must then be respected by other actors in the system, even if those actors would have reached a different conclusion."

Curtis Bradley suggests that delegations of adjudicative authority to international institutions are more likely to raise constitutional issues than delegations of legislative or regulatory authority. Among other things, he notes that "whereas delegations of legislative or regulatory authority involve voluntary transfers of authority from the branches of government that would normally exercise that authority, with adjudicative delegations the political branches are delegating another branch's (i.e., the judiciary's) authority" and therefore "[a]rguments about institutional consent and accountability for the initial delegation are . . . less applicable here." Curtis A. Bradley, The Federal Judicial Power and the International Legal Order, 2006 Sup. Ct. Rev. 59, 88. Bradley also contends that, "as a predictive matter, one can expect that the federal courts will be more solicitous in preventing the loss of their own authority than that of the other branches. In other modern contexts, the Supreme Court has resisted what it has perceived as political branch challenges to its judicial authority."

Henry Monaghan argues, by contrast, that arbitral tribunals, such as the panels used under NAFTA "raise no serious problems under Article III and are sanctioned by an ancient lineage," and that the Supreme Court is unlikely more generally to find that the Constitution places significant limits on international judicial review. Henry Paul Monaghan, Article III and Supranational Judicial Review, 107 Colum. L. Rev. 833, 842 (2007). Among other things, Monaghan contends:

> While in the beginning of our constitutional history it was quite possible to claim that Our Federalism invested our national government with less legal authority in the international sphere than that possessed by other nation-states, any such conception has no purchase now. Indeed, the Court insists that the national government possesses an apparently freestanding "foreign affairs" power. That being the case, *and assuming here the general validity of supranational lawmaking*, it seems unlikely that the Court will understand the Constitution to seriously impede the manner by which supranational disputes are resolved.

Monaghan also observes that "the history of our jurisprudence governing the rise of the modern administrative state demonstrates that the factfinding and law-application functions of the district courts (except in criminal and common law trials) can be curtailed." While he notes that "one important systemic role for the Article III courts remains: the power to confine other organs of government within the bounds of their authority," he argues that "[i]f NAFTA-like arbitration processes compromise that function, they do so only at the margin."

For additional discussion of the issues raised by delegations of adjudicative authority to international tribunals, see Curtis A. Bradley, International Delegations, the Structural Constitution, and Non-Self-Execution, 55 Stan. L. Rev. 1557 (2003); Jim C. Chen, Appointments with Disaster: The Unconstitutionality of Binational Arbitral Review under the United States-Canada Free Trade Agreement, 49 Wash. & Lee L. Rev. 1455 (1992); David M. Golove, The New Confederalism: Treaty Delegations of Legislative, Executive, and Judicial Authority, 55 Stan. L. Rev. 1697 (2003); Brian F. Havel, The Constitution in an Era of Supranational Adjudication, 78 N.C.L. Rev. 257 (2000); Eugene Kontorovich, The Constitutionality of International Courts: The Forgotten Precedent of Slave-Trade Tribunals, 158 U. Pa. L. Rev. 39 (2009); Julian G. Ku, The Delegation of Federal Power to International Organizations: New Problems with Old Solutions, 85 Minn. L. Rev. 71 (2000); Jenny S. Martinez, Towards an International Judicial System, 56 Stan. L. Rev. 429 (2003); Jenny S. Martinez, International Courts and the U.S. Constitution: Reexamining the History, 159 U. Pa. L. Rev. 1069 (2011); Mark L. Movsesian, Judging International Judgments, 48 Va. J. Int'l L. 65 (2007); A. Mark Weisburd, International Courts and American Courts, 21 Mich. J. Int'l L. 877 (2000).

CHAPTER V

SUBJECT MATTER JURISDICTION

SECTION 1. FEDERAL QUESTION JURISDICTION

INTRODUCTORY NOTES ON FEDERAL QUESTION JURISDICTION

1. FEDERAL QUESTION STATUTES

The general federal question statute, 28 U.S.C. § 1331, provides that "[t]he district courts shall have original jurisdiction of all civil actions arising under the Constitution, laws, or treaties of the United States." Section 1331 is a catch-all provision. It covers all claims based on federal statutes as well as those founded on federal common law.[a]

Other jurisdictional provisions deal with specific kinds of federal claims. For example, suits "arising under any act of Congress regulating commerce" may be brought under 28 U.S.C. § 1337, and suits "arising under any act of Congress relating to patents, plant variety protection, copyrights, and trademarks" may be brought under 28 U.S.C. § 1338. Additionally, statutes creating substantive rights often have their own jurisdictional provisions.

The materials in this Section focus on § 1331. For the most part, the principles and limitations developed for § 1331 also apply to the more specific federal question statutes. For all of these provisions, it is standard lore that the statutory meaning of when a case "arises" under federal law is more narrowly circumscribed than is the same concept in the Constitution.

2. THE FACE-OF-THE-COMPLAINT RULE

Jurisdiction under § 1331 requires that the plaintiff's claim be based on federal law. Federal defenses do not count. Therefore, the first step in determining § 1331 jurisdiction is to ascertain those matters that the plaintiff must plead to state a claim.

A famous application of this rule came in Louisville & Nashville Railroad Co. v. Mottley, 211 U.S. 149 (1908). Mr. and Mrs. Mottley received lifetime passes on the L&N Railroad in settlement of a personal injury claim. Thereafter Congress outlawed free passes. When the railroad refused to honor the settlement contract, the Mottleys sued in federal court for specific performance. Their arguments were, first, that the statute did not affect their preexisting contract of settlement and, second, if it did, the statute was to that extent unconstitutional. They grounded jurisdiction on these federal questions and won at trial.

---

[a] See Illinois v. Milwaukee, 406 U.S. 91 (1972).

On its own motion, the Supreme Court raised the question of jurisdiction:

> There was no diversity of citizenship and it is not and cannot be suggested that there was any ground of jurisdiction, except that the case was a "suit . . . arising under the Constitution and laws of the United States." It is the settled interpretation of these words, as used in this statute, conferring jurisdiction, that a suit arises under the Constitution and laws of the United States only when the plaintiff's statement of his own cause of action shows that it is based upon those laws or that Constitution. It is not enough that the plaintiff alleges some anticipated defense to his cause of action and asserts that the defense is invalidated by some provision of the Constitution of the United States. Although such allegations show that very likely, in the course of the litigation, a question under the Constitution would arise, they do not show that the suit, that is, the plaintiff's original cause of action, arises under the Constitution.

Note that what the complaint actually said was not determinative. What a properly pleaded complaint would have said controlled. A court is thus required to reformulate the complaint by identifying the elements of the plaintiff's "cause of action"—that is, the minimum allegations that would justify a judgment in favor of the plaintiff if the defendant did not contest the case. In *Mottley*, the well-pleaded complaint would have said that the parties had a valid contract, which the defendant refused to honor. Whether the defendant had a justification for refusing to honor the contract was not part of a properly pleaded complaint, but would enter the case only by way of defense. And whether the defendant's justification was based on an unconstitutional statute would enter the case only in the third round of proper pleading.

As the Court pointed out in Franchise Tax Board of California v. Construction Laborers Vacation Trust for Southern California, 463 U.S. 1, 10–11 n.9 (1983):

> The well-pleaded complaint rule applies to the original jurisdiction of the district courts as well as to their removal jurisdiction.[b]
>
> It is possible to conceive of a rational jurisdictional system in which the answer as well as the complaint would be consulted before a determination was made whether the case "arose under" federal law, or in which original and removal jurisdiction were not co-extensive. Indeed, until the 1887 amendments to the 1875 Act, the well-pleaded complaint rule was not applied in full force to cases removed from state court; the defendant's petition for removal could furnish the necessary guarantee that the case necessarily presented a substantial question of federal law. See Railroad

---

[b]   Section 1441(a) of Title 28 provides that a suit may be removed from a state trial court to the federal district court sitting in the same location if the district court would have had "original jurisdiction" over the case had it been brought there as an initial matter.—[Footnote by eds.]

Co. v. Mississippi, 102 U.S. 135, 140 (1880); Gold-Washing & Water Co. v. Keyes, 96 U.S. 199, 203–204 (1877). Commentators have repeatedly proposed that some mechanism be established to permit removal of cases in which a federal defense may be dispositive. See, e.g., American Law Institute, Study of the Division of Jurisdiction Between State and Federal Courts § 1312, at 188–94 (1969) (ALI Study); Herbert Wechsler, Federal Jurisdiction and the Revision of the Judicial Code, 13 Law & Contemp. Prob. 216, 233–34 (1948). But those proposals have not been adopted.

What is the rationale for the rule of the well-pleaded complaint? In Osborn v. Bank of the United States, 22 U.S. (9 Wheat.) 738 (1824), Chief Justice Marshall said: "The right of the plaintiff to sue cannot depend on the defence which the defendant may choose to set up. His right to sue is anterior to that defence, and must depend on the state of things when the action is brought." Does that adequately explain the rule?

3. *MIMS V. ARROW FINANCIAL SERVICES, LLC*

Mims v. Arrow Financial Services, LLC, 565 U.S. 368 (2012), involved a provision of the Telephone Consumer Protection Act (TCPA) that authorized private actions for damages in state courts to enforce the federal rights created by the Act. The question was whether this meant that state courts were the exclusive arbiters of such actions or whether a private plaintiff could also seek damages in a federal court under the general federal question statute. Justice Ginsburg wrote the opinion for a unanimous Court:

> Arrow agrees that this action arises under federal law, but urges that Congress vested exclusive adjudicatory authority over private TCPA actions in state courts. In cases "arising under" federal law, we note, there is a "deeply rooted presumption in favor of concurrent state court jurisdiction," rebuttable if "Congress affirmatively ousts the state courts of jurisdiction over a particular federal claim." Tafflin v. Levitt, 493 U.S. 455, 458–59 (1990). . . . The presumption of concurrent state-court jurisdiction, we have recognized, can be overcome "by an explicit statutory directive, by unmistakable implication from legislative history, or by a clear incompatibility between state-court jurisdiction and federal interests." Gulf Offshore Co. v. Mobil Oil Corp., 453 U.S. 473, 478 (1981).

> Arrow readily acknowledges the presumption of concurrent state-court jurisdiction, but maintains that 28 U.S.C. § 1331 creates no converse presumption in favor of federal-court jurisdiction. Instead, Arrow urges, the TCPA, a later, more specific statute, displaces § 1331, an earlier, more general prescription.

> Section 1331, our decisions indicate, is not swept away so easily. . . . [W]hen federal law creates a private right of action and furnishes the substantive rules of decision, the claim arises under federal law, and district courts possess federal-question jurisdiction under § 1331. That principle endures unless Congress divests federal courts of their § 1331 adjudicatory authority.

"[D]ivestment of district court jurisdiction" should be found no more readily than "divestmen[t] of state court jurisdiction," given "the longstanding and explicit grant of federal question jurisdiction in 28 U.S.C. § 1331." ErieNet, Inc. v. Velocity Net, Inc., 156 F.3d 513, 523 (3d Cir. 1998) (Alito, J., dissenting). Accordingly, the District Court retains § 1331 jurisdiction over Mims's complaint unless the TCPA, expressly or by fair implication, excludes federal-court adjudication.

After extensive examination of the interstices of the TCPA, the Court concluded:

Nothing in the text, structure, purpose, or legislative history of the TCPA calls for displacement of the federal-question jurisdiction U.S. district courts ordinarily have under 28 U.S.C. § 1331. In the absence of direction from Congress stronger than any Arrow has advanced, we apply the familiar default rule: Federal courts have § 1331 jurisdiction over claims that arise under federal law. Because federal law gives rise to the claim for relief Mims has stated and specifies the substantive rules of decision, [it was error to dismiss] Mims's case for lack of subject-matter jurisdiction.

4.   PENDENT JURISDICTION: *UNITED MINE WORKERS V. GIBBS*

Once "arising under" jurisdiction has been established, the plaintiff may assert additional state claims under pendent (or supplemental) jurisdiction. The leading case is United Mine Workers of America v. Gibbs, 383 U.S. 715 (1966), where the Court said that:

Pendent jurisdiction, in the sense of judicial *power,* exists whenever there is a claim "arising under [federal law]," and the relationship between that claim and the state claim permits the conclusion that the entire action before the court comprises but one constitutional "case." The federal claim must have substance sufficient to confer subject matter jurisdiction on the court.[c] The state and federal claims must derive from a common nucleus of operative fact. But if, considered without regard to their federal or state character, a plaintiff's claims are such that he would ordinarily be expected to try them all in one judicial proceeding, then, assuming substantiality of the federal issues, there is *power* in federal courts to hear the whole.

However, the Court added:

That power need not be exercised in every case in which it is found to exist. It has consistently been recognized that pendent jurisdiction is a doctrine of discretion, not of plaintiff's right. Its justification lies in considerations of judicial economy, convenience

---

[c]   The reference here is to the requirement that any federal question be "substantial," that is, non-frivolous, in order to confer jurisdiction on a federal court. The traditional citation for this proposition is Bell v. Hood, 327 U.S. 678 (1946). For an attack on the *Bell* principle, see Howard M. Wasserman, Jurisdiction, Merits, and Substantiality, 42 Tulsa L. Rev. 579 (2007).— [Footnote by eds.]

and fairness to litigants; if these are not present a federal court should hesitate to exercise jurisdiction over state claims, even though bound to apply state law to them. Needless decisions of state law should be avoided both as a matter of comity and to promote justice between the parties, by procuring for them a surer-footed reading of applicable law. Certainly, if the federal claims are dismissed before trial, even though not insubstantial in a jurisdictional sense, the state claims should be dismissed as well. Similarly, if it appears that the state issues substantially predominate, whether in terms of proof, of the scope of the issues raised, or of the comprehensiveness of the remedy sought, the state claims may be dismissed without prejudice and left for resolution to state tribunals. . . . Finally, there may be reasons independent of jurisdictional considerations, such as the likelihood of jury confusion in treating divergent legal theories of relief, that would justify separating state and federal claims for trial. If so, jurisdiction should ordinarily be refused.

The question of power will ordinarily be resolved on the pleadings. But the issue whether pendent jurisdiction has been properly assumed is one which remains open throughout the litigation. . . .[d]

5. PENDENT PARTY JURISDICTION: 28 U.S.C. § 1367

In Finley v. United States, 490 U.S. 545 (1989), the plaintiff sued the United States under the Federal Tort Claims Act, which provides for exclusive federal jurisdiction. The plaintiff later sought to add two pendent state-law claims involving additional defendants. All claims arose out of the death of plaintiff's husband and two children in an airplane crash, but the Supreme Court held, five-to-four, that pendent jurisdiction did not extend to additional parties.

Overruling *Finley* was the major purpose of 28 U.S.C. § 1367, enacted in 1990. That statute uses the generic term "supplemental" jurisdiction to refer to what lawyers previously had called "pendent" and "ancillary" jurisdiction. Subsection (a) provides that district courts shall have supplemental jurisdiction over all claims so related to claims within their original jurisdiction "that they form part of the same case or controversy" under Article III. This formula approximates the *Gibbs* test of "common nucleus of operative fact." The statute then adds: "Such supplemental jurisdiction shall include claims that involve the joinder or intervention of additional parties." Limitations are imposed on supplemental jurisdiction in diversity cases, and the court's option to decline to exercise supplemental jurisdiction in appropriate circumstances is preserved in Subsection (c).

---

[d] The authority of the district courts to refuse to hear pendent state claims when the federal claim has been disposed of early in the litigation was reaffirmed in Carnegie-Mellon University v. Cohill, 484 U.S. 343 (1988). After the defendant removed plaintiff's state-court action to federal court, the plaintiff amended the complaint to delete the federal claim that provided the basis for federal jurisdiction. In spite of language in Thermtron Products, Inc. v. Hermansdorfer, 423 U.S. 336 (1976), to the effect that remand was only permissible in situations specifically authorized by the removal statute, the Court voted five to three to permit the remand back to state court.—[Footnote by eds.]

There are many other situations when federal courts, having assumed proper jurisdiction over one claim, are entitled to hear related claims. Perhaps the most familiar example is the compulsory counterclaim, which need not independently meet the requirements of federal jurisdiction. Thus, if the plaintiff's claim arises under federal law, a state claim over which there is no other available basis of jurisdiction can be heard in federal court if it is raised by the plaintiff and it meets the *Gibbs* test or if it is raised by the defendant and it meets the test for a compulsory counterclaim established by the Federal Rules of Civil Procedure.[e] (Before § 1367, the former would have been called "pendent jurisdiction" and the latter "ancillary jurisdiction"; today both are called "supplemental jurisdiction.") Note that the test for when a counterclaim is compulsory under Rule 13(a) of the Federal Rules of Civil Procedure—a claim that "arises out of the transaction or occurrence that is the subject matter of the opposing party's claim"—is closely related to, if not the same as, the test for when the federal courts have power to hear supplemental claims asserted by a plaintiff.

SUBSECTION A. "ARISING UNDER" JURISDICTION

INTRODUCTORY NOTES ON WHEN A CASE "ARISES UNDER" FEDERAL LAW

1.   EARLY DECISIONS

The plaintiff's claim in most cases will rest entirely on state or federal law and there will no possibility of confusion. Sometimes, however, the law is mixed. A federal cause of action may incorporate elements of state law or a state cause of action may incorporate elements of federal law. Justice Brennan had such a case in mind in Franchise Tax Board of California v. Construction Laborers Vacation Trust for Southern California, 463 U.S. 1, 8 (1983), when he wrote for a unanimous Court:

> Since the first version of § 1331 was enacted [in 1875], the statutory phrase "arising under the Constitution, laws, or treaties of the United States" has resisted all attempts to frame a single, precise definition for determining which cases fall within, and which cases fall outside, the original jurisdiction of the district courts. [T]he phrase "arising under" masks a welter of issues regarding the interrelation of federal and state authority and the proper management of the federal judicial system.

Four well-known early cases illustrate what can happen when federal law and state law are mixed.

(i)   American Well Works

Analysis of "arising under" jurisdiction can usefully start with the opinion by Justice Holmes in American Well Works Co. v. Layne & Bowler Co.,

---

[e]   With exceptions not here relevant, the test is that the counterclaim "arises out of the transaction or occurrence that is the subject matter of the opposing party's claim." Fed. R. Civ. Proc. 13(1)(1)(A).

241 U.S. 257 (1916). The plaintiff manufactured and sold pumps on which it held, or had applied for, patents. The defendant claimed that the plaintiff's pump infringed defendant's patent and filed lawsuits against (or threatened to sue) several users of the plaintiff's pump. In the present action, the plaintiff sued for libel and slander to the title to its pump. The question was whether this business libel case arose under the predecessor to 28 U.S.C. § 1338, which provides for exclusive jurisdiction in federal district courts over "any civil action arising under any Act of Congress relating to patents."

The Court said no. Justice Holmes reasoned that "[a] suit arises under the law that creates the cause of action." Whether business libel by the defendant was actionable was entirely up to state law. Nothing in the federal patent laws imposed liability for such conduct. Hence the case did not "arise under" federal law, even though resolution of the plaintiff's claim would ultimately turn on a federal issue.[a]

(ii) Shoshone Mining Co. v. Rutter

While *American Well Works* states a reliable rule of thumb, it does not follow that *every* cause of action created by federal law presents a case arising under federal law. A well-known exception is Shoshone Mining Co. v. Rutter, 177 U.S. 505 (1900).

Congress created a system for issuing mining patents on federal lands. The statute provided that an "adverse suit" could be filed "in a court of competent jurisdiction" by a person who claimed a right of possession to a mine also claimed by another person. Such disputes were to be resolved by "local customs or rules of miners in the several mining districts, so far as the same are applicable and not inconsistent with the laws of the United States" and "by the statute of limitations for mining claims of the State or Territory where the same may be situated." The question was whether a suit under these provisions could be brought in federal court under the general federal question statute. The Court said it could not:

> [T]he "adverse suit" to determine the right of possession may not involve any question as to the construction or effect of the Constitution or laws of the United States, but may present simply a question of fact as to the time of the discovery of mineral, the location of the claim on the ground, or a determination of the meaning and effect of certain local rules and customs prescribed by the miners of the district, or the effect of state statutes. . . .

---

[a]   For elaboration of the appropriate role for a "cause of action" in federal law and for "an effort to bring some consistency to the understanding of the federal cause of action," see John F. Preis, How the Federal Cause of Action Relates to Rights, Remedies, and Jurisdiction, 67 Fla. L. Rev. 849 (2015).

See also Lumen N. Mulligan, You Can't Go Holmes Again, 107 Nw. U. L. Rev. 237 (2012), which argues that a better description of the results reached under current law as well as a better test for determining when a case arises under federal law is provided by Mims v. Arrow Financial Services, LLC, 565 U.S. 368, 378 (2012) ("when federal law creates a private right of action and furnishes the substantive rules of decision, the claim arises under federal law").

(iii) Smith v. Kansas City Title & Trust Co.

As *Shoshone Mining* illustrates, *American Well Works* sometimes (though rarely) fails as a test of inclusion. That it also sometimes fails as a test of exclusion is illustrated by Smith v. Kansas City Title & Trust Co., 255 U.S. 180 (1921). A stockholder in a corporation created by state law sued to enjoin the corporation from investing in certain federally authorized bonds. The federal statute provided that the bonds were lawful investments for corporations, and state law authorized the corporation to invest in all lawfully issued government bonds. The plaintiff's position was that the federal statute authorizing the sale of the bonds was unconstitutional.

Predictably, Justice Holmes argued that the case did not arise under federal law. The right of the stockholder to sue the corporate defendant, he reasoned, derived solely from state law:

> It is evident that the cause of action arises not under any law of the United States but wholly under Missouri law. The defendant is a Missouri corporation and the right claimed is that of a stockholder to prevent the directors from doing an act, that is, making an investment, alleged to be contrary to their duty. But the scope of their duty depends upon the charter of their corporation and other laws of Missouri. . . . If the Missouri law authorizes or forbids the investment according to the determination of this Court upon a point under the Constitution or acts of Congress, still that point is material only because the Missouri law saw fit to make it so. The whole foundation of the duty is Missouri law, which at its sole will incorporated the other law as it might incorporate a document. . . .

> But it seems to me that a suit cannot be said to arise under any other law than that which creates the cause of action. It may be enough that the law relied upon creates a part of the cause of action although not the whole, as held in *Osborn v. Bank of United States.* . . . I am content to assume this to be so, although the *Osborn* case has been criticized and regretted. But the law must create at least a part of the cause of action by its own force, for it is the suit, not a question in the suit, that must arise under the law of the United States. The mere adoption by a state law of a United States law as a criterion or test, when the law of the United States has no force ex proprio vigore, does not cause a case under the state law to be also a case under the law of the United States. . . .

Justice Holmes, however, was in dissent. The majority held that the case arose under federal law:

> The general rule is that, where it appears from the bill or statement of the plaintiff that the right to relief depends upon the construction or application of the Constitution or laws of the United States, and that such federal claim is not merely colorable, and rests upon a reasonable foundation, the district court has jurisdiction. . . .

> In the instant case the averments of the bill show that the directors were proceeding to make the investments in view of the act

authorizing the bonds about to be purchased, maintaining that the act authorizing them was constitutional and the bonds valid and desirable investments. The objecting shareholder avers in the bill that the securities were issued under an unconstitutional law, and hence of no validity. It is therefore apparent that the controversy concerns the constitutional validity of an act of Congress which is directly drawn in question. The decision depends upon the determination of this issue.

(iv) Moore v. Chesapeake & Ohio Ry.

One might infer from *Smith* that federal question jurisdiction can be founded on a state cause of action that incorporates a question of federal law. In Moore v. Chesapeake & Ohio Ry. Co., 291 U.S. 205 (1934), however, the Court reached the opposite conclusion.

Moore was a railroad worker. He sued the railroad in federal court under a Kentucky statute covering injuries in *intra*state commerce. That statute incorporated portions of the Federal Safety Appliance Acts, which covered railroad injuries in *inter*state commerce. Under the Kentucky statute, violation of the federal acts would constitute negligence per se and bar the railroad from relying on contributory negligence or assumption of risk. The Court nevertheless held that Moore's claim did not arise under federal law. The Court noted, however, that questions concerning the meaning of the Federal Safety Appliance Act arising in such state court litigation would be reviewable on appeal in the Supreme Court. But the case did not arise under federal law for purposes of trial court jurisdiction.

2. QUESTIONS AND COMMENTS ON THE EARLY DECISIONS

Can these results be reconciled? Consider William Cohen, The Broken Compass: The Requirement That a Case Arise "Directly" Under Federal Law, 115 U. Pa. L. Rev. 890 (1967). Cohen argues that the search for analytical or verbal formulas to determine when a case arises under federal law is misguided. In his view, the courts have established "pragmatic standards for a pragmatic problem." He invites contrast of the issues in *Smith v. Kansas City Title & Trust Co.* and *Shoshone Mining Co. v. Rutter*. In *Smith*, federal constitutional issues were central to the case, and there was little fear that considering such cases would have significant workload implications. By contrast, the practical considerations at stake in cases like *Shoshone* were "overwhelming." Almost all such cases would involve complicated factual questions intertwined with local customs and rules. No federal interests were likely to come up, the volume of such litigation would be burdensome, and the location of witnesses, the land, and the litigants would in many cases be a burdensome distance from the federal court that would hear the case. Cohen concluded:

> It is not startling that these practical considerations precipitated the results in *Smith* and *Shoshone*. Nor is it unusual that the Court in the two cases applied contradictory analytical formulas to explain the results, rather than resting squarely on those factors which, no doubt, influenced the actual decisions. What is surprising

is the continuing belief that there is, or should be, a single, all-purpose, neutral analytical concept which marks out federal question jurisdiction. A frank recognition of the pragmatic nature of the decision-making process would help throw light on the factors which actually induce decision. It would, moreover, reduce the danger that a judge would be beguiled by one of the numerous analytical tests into reaching an indefensible result.

Is Cohen right? Could it be argued to the contrary that an easy-to-apply verbal formula is precisely what is needed in determining questions of subject matter jurisdiction?[b] Consider the well-known passage from Justice Cardozo's opinion in Gully v. First National Bank in Meridian, 299 U.S. 109 (1936):

> How and when a case arises "under the Constitution or laws of the United States" has been much considered in the books. Some tests are well established. To bring a case within the statute, a right or immunity created by the Constitution or laws of the United States must be an element, and an essential one, of the plaintiff's cause of action. . . . The right or immunity must be such that it will be supported if the Constitution or laws of the United States are given one construction or effect, and defeated if they receive another. . . . A genuine and present controversy, not merely a possible or conjectural one, must exist with reference thereto . . . and the controversy must be disclosed upon the face of the complaint. . . .

Does this help?

3. *MERRELL DOW PHARMACEUTICALS, INC. V. THOMPSON*

The Court cast doubt on the continued vitality of *Smith* in Merrell Dow Pharmaceuticals, Inc. v. Thompson, 478 U.S. 804 (1986). The plaintiffs sued in state court for birth defects caused by a woman's use of defendant's drug during pregnancy. One theory of relief was common law negligence, based in part on the allegation that the drug did not contain adequate label warnings and was therefore "misbranded" in violation of the Federal Food, Drug, and Cosmetic Act (FDCA). The defendant removed the case to federal court, which was proper only if plaintiff's claim could have been brought originally in federal court. Relying on *Smith*, the defendant claimed that plaintiff would have had jurisdiction under § 1331.

The Supreme Court found no jurisdiction. The FDCA provided no federal cause of action, and all Justices agreed that this was not a situation where the federal courts would create an "implied" private right of action

---

[b]   Linda Hirshman, Whose Law Is It Anyway? A Reconsideration of Federal Question Jurisdiction over Cases of Mixed State and Federal Law, 60 Ind. L.J. 17 (1984), supports a return to the Holmes test. For an historical analysis concluding that the Holmes view in *Smith v. Kansas City Title & Trust Co.* was the anomaly, not the position of the majority, see Ann Woolhandler and Michael G. Collins, Federal Question Jurisdiction and Justice Holmes, 84 Notre Dame L. Rev. 2151 (2009). Indeed, they say, that "cases along the model of *Smith* were, historically, quite familiar to the federal courts and may even have been a primary focus of the 1875 federal question statute." For an article that "probes the anatomy and context" of *Smith v. Kansas City Title & Trust Co.*, see Larry Yackle, Federal Banks and Federal Jurisdiction in the Progressive Era: A Case Study of *Smith v. K.C. Title & Trust Co.*, 62 U. Kan. L. Rev. 255 (2013).

under federal law. Speaking for the Court, Justice Stevens emphasized that fact:

> The significance of the . . . assumption that there is no federal private cause of action . . . cannot be overstated. For the ultimate import of such a conclusion . . . is that it would flout congressional intent to provide a private remedy for the violation of the federal statute. We think it would similarly flout, or at least undermine, congressional intent to conclude that the federal courts might nevertheless exercise federal-question jurisdiction and provide remedies for violation of that federal statute solely because the violation of the federal statute is said to be [an element of a state cause of action], rather than a federal action under federal law.
>
> . . . Given the significance of the assumed congressional determination to preclude federal private remedies, the presence of the federal issue as an element of the state tort is not the kind of adjudication for which jurisdiction would serve congressional purposes and the federal system. We simply conclude that the congressional determination that there should be no federal remedy for the violation of this federal statute is tantamount to a congressional conclusion that the presence of a claimed violation of this statute as an element of a state cause of action is insufficiently "substantial" to confer federal question jurisdiction.

The Court then said in an important footnote (footnote 12):

> Several commentators have suggested that our § 1331 decisions can best be understood as an evaluation of the nature of the federal interest at stake. See, e.g., David L. Shapiro, Jurisdiction and Discretion, 60 N.Y.U. L. Rev. 543, 668 (1985); Charles Alan Wright, Federal Courts 96 (4th ed. 1983); William Cohen, The Broken Compass: The Requirement That a Case Arise "Directly" Under Federal Law, 115 U. Pa. L. Rev. 890, 916 (1967).[c] . . .
>
> Focusing on the nature of the federal interest, moreover, suggests that the widely perceived "irreconcilable" conflict between the finding of federal jurisdiction in Smith v. Kansas City Title & Trust Co., 255 U.S. 180 (1921), and the finding of no jurisdiction in Moore v. Chesapeake & Ohio R. Co., 291 U.S. 205 (1934), see, e.g., Martin H. Redish, Federal Jurisdiction: Tensions in the Allocation of Judicial Power 67 (1980), is far from clear. For the difference in results can be seen as manifestations of the differences in the nature of the federal issues at stake. In *Smith*, as the Court emphasized, the issue was the constitutionality of an important federal statute. . . . In *Moore*, in contrast, the Court emphasized that the violation of the federal standard as an element of state tort recovery did not fundamentally change the state tort nature of the action.
>
> The importance of the nature of the federal issue in federal-question jurisdiction is highlighted by the fact that, despite the

---

c   See also Daniel J. Meltzer, Jurisdiction and Discretion Revisited, 79 Notre Dame L. Rev. 1891, 1911–15 (2004).—[Footnote by eds.]

usual reliability of the Holmes test as an inclusionary principle, this Court has sometimes found that formally federal causes of action were not properly brought under federal-question jurisdiction because of the overwhelming predominance of state-law issues. See . . . Shoshone Mining Co. v. Rutter, 177 U.S. 505, 507 (1900). . . .

Justice Brennan, joined by Justices White, Marshall, and Blackmun, dissented. He thought the case appropriately in federal court under *Smith*. He pronounced *Smith* and *Moore* "irreconcilable" and described the latter decision as a "sport" that had "long been in a state of innocuous desuetude" and "ought to be overruled."

As to the relevance of the lack of a private right of action, Brennan noted that the FDA was given no independent enforcement authority, but was required to ask the Justice Department to enforce the statute in federal court by seeking an injunction, bringing a criminal prosecution, or other means. He reasoned:

> It may be that a decision by Congress not to create a private remedy is intended to preclude all private enforcement. If that is so, then a state cause of action that makes relief available to private individuals for violations of the FDCA is preempted. But if Congress's decision not to provide a private federal remedy does *not* preempt such a state remedy, then, in light of the FDCA's clear policy of relying on the federal courts for enforcement, it also should not foreclose federal jurisdiction over that state remedy. Both § 1331 and the enforcement provisions of the FDCA reflect Congress's strong desire to utilize the federal courts to interpret and enforce the FDCA, and it is therefore at odds with both these statutes to recognize a private state law remedy for violating the FDCA but to hold that this remedy cannot be adjudicated in the federal courts.

> The Court's contrary conclusion requires inferring from Congress's decision not to create a private federal remedy that, while some private enforcement is permissible in state courts, it is "bad" if that enforcement comes from the *federal* courts. But that is simply illogical. Congress's decision to withhold a private right of action and to rely instead on public enforcement reflects congressional concern with obtaining more accurate implementation and more coordinated enforcement of a regulatory scheme. These reasons are closely related to the Congress's reasons for giving federal courts original federal question jurisdiction. Thus, if anything, Congress's decision not to create a private remedy *strengthens* the argument in favor of finding federal jurisdiction over a state remedy that is not preempted.[d]

---

[d]   For criticism of this decision, see Patti Alleva, Prerogative Lost: The Trouble with Statutory Federal Question Doctrine after *Merrell Dow*, 52 Ohio St. L.J. 1477 (1991).—[Footnote by eds.]

4. CONCLUDING COMMENT

The continued viability of *Smith* and the implications of *Merrell Dow* were revisited in the next main case.

Grable & Sons Metal Products, Inc. v. Darue Engineering & Manufacturing

Supreme Court of the United States, 2005.
545 U.S. 308.

■ JUSTICE SOUTER delivered the opinion of the Court.

The question is whether want of a federal cause of action to try claims of title to land obtained at a federal tax sale precludes removal to federal court of a state action with non-diverse parties raising a disputed issue of federal title law. We answer no, and hold that the national interest in providing a federal forum for federal tax litigation is sufficiently substantial to support the exercise of federal question jurisdiction over the disputed issue on removal, which would not distort any division of labor between the state and federal courts, provided or assumed by Congress.

I

In 1994, the Internal Revenue Service seized Michigan real property belonging to petitioner Grable & Sons Metal Products, Inc., to satisfy Grable's federal tax delinquency. Title 26 U.S.C. § 6335 required the IRS to give notice of the seizure, and there is no dispute that Grable received actual notice by certified mail before the IRS sold the property to respondent Darue Engineering & Manufacturing. Although Grable also received notice of the sale itself, it did not exercise its statutory right to redeem the property within 180 days of the sale, § 6337(b)(1), and after that period had passed, the Government gave Darue a quitclaim deed. § 6339.

Five years later, Grable brought a quiet title action in state court, claiming that Darue's record title was invalid because the IRS had failed to notify Grable of its seizure of the property in the exact manner required by § 6335(a), which provides that written notice must be "given by the Secretary to the owner of the property [or] left at his usual place of abode or business." Grable said that the statute required personal service, not service by certified mail.

Darue removed the case to Federal District Court as presenting a federal question, because the claim of title depended on the interpretation of the notice statute in the federal tax law. The District Court declined to remand the case at Grable's behest after finding that the "claim does pose a significant question of federal law," and ruling that Grable's lack of a federal right of action to enforce its claim against Darue did not bar the exercise of federal jurisdiction. On the merits, the court granted summary judgment to Darue, holding that although § 6335 by its terms required personal service, substantial compliance with the statute was enough.

The Court of Appeals for the Sixth Circuit affirmed. On the jurisdictional question, the panel thought it sufficed that the title claim raised an issue of federal law that had to be resolved, and implicated a substantial federal interest (in construing federal tax law). The court went on to affirm the District Court's judgment on the merits. We granted certiorari on the jurisdictional question alone, to resolve a split within the Courts of Appeals on whether Merrell Dow Pharmaceuticals Inc. v. Thompson, 478 U.S. 804 (1986), always requires a federal cause of action as a condition for exercising federal-question jurisdiction. We now affirm.

II

Darue was entitled to remove the quiet title action if Grable could have brought it in federal district court originally, 28 U.S.C. § 1441(a), as a civil action "arising under the Constitution, laws, or treaties of the United States," § 1331. This provision for federal-question jurisdiction is invoked by and large by plaintiffs pleading a cause of action created by federal law (e.g., claims under 42 U.S.C. § 1983). There is, however, another longstanding, if less frequently encountered, variety of federal "arising under" jurisdiction, this Court having recognized for nearly 100 years that in certain cases federal question jurisdiction will lie over state-law claims that implicate significant federal issues. E.g., Hopkins v. Walker, 244 U.S. 486, 490–91 (1917). The doctrine captures the commonsense notion that a federal court ought to be able to hear claims recognized under state law that nonetheless turn on substantial questions of federal law, and thus justify resort to the experience, solicitude, and hope of uniformity that a federal forum offers on federal issues, see ALI, Study of the Division of Jurisdiction Between State and Federal Courts 164–66 (1968).

The classic example is Smith v. Kansas City Title & Trust Co., 255 U.S. 180 (1921), a suit by a shareholder claiming that the defendant corporation could not lawfully buy certain bonds of the National Government because their issuance was unconstitutional. Although Missouri law provided the cause of action, the Court recognized federal-question jurisdiction because the principal issue in the case was the federal constitutionality of the bond issue. *Smith* thus held, in a somewhat generous statement of the scope of the doctrine, that a state-law claim could give rise to federal-question jurisdiction so long as it "appears from the [complaint] that the right to relief depends upon the construction or application of [federal law]."

The *Smith* statement has been subject to some trimming to fit earlier and later cases recognizing the vitality of the basic doctrine, but shying away from the expansive view that mere need to apply federal law in a state-law claim will suffice to open the "arising under" door. As early as 1912, this Court had confined federal-question jurisdiction over state-law claims to those that "really and substantially involv[e] a dispute or controversy respecting the validity, construction or effect of [federal] law." Shulthis v. McDougal, 225 U.S. 561, 569 (1912). This limitation was the ancestor of Justice Cardozo's later explanation that a request to exercise federal-question jurisdiction over a state action calls for a "common-sense accommodation of judgment to [the] kaleidoscopic situations" that present a federal issue, in "a selective process which picks the substantial causes out of the web and lays the other ones aside." Gully v. First Nat. Bank in Meridian, 299 U.S. 109, 117–18 (1936). It has in fact become a constant refrain in such cases that federal jurisdiction demands not only a contested federal issue, but a substantial one, indicating a serious federal interest in claiming the advantages thought to be inherent in a federal forum.

But even when the state action discloses a contested and substantial federal question, the exercise of federal jurisdiction is subject to a possible veto. For the federal issue will ultimately qualify for a federal forum only if federal jurisdiction is consistent with congressional judgment about the sound division of labor between state and federal courts governing the application of § 1331. Thus, Franchise Tax Bd. of Cal. v. Construction Laborers Vacation Trust for Southern Cal., 463 U.S. 1, 28 (1983), explained that the appropriateness of a federal forum to hear an embedded issue could be evaluated only after considering the "welter of issues regarding the interrelation of federal and state authority and the proper management of the federal judicial system." Because arising-under jurisdiction to hear a state-law claim always raises the possibility of upsetting the state-federal line drawn (or at least assumed) by Congress, the presence of a disputed federal issue and the ostensible importance of a federal forum are never necessarily dispositive; there must always be an assessment of any disruptive portent in exercising federal jurisdiction.

These considerations have kept us from stating a "single, precise, all-embracing" test for jurisdiction over federal issues embedded in state-law claims between nondiverse parties. Christianson v. Colt Industries Operating Corp., 486 U.S. 800, 821 (1988) (Stevens, J., concurring). We have not kept them out simply because they appeared in state raiment, as Justice Holmes would have done, see *Smith*, 255 U.S. at 214 (dissenting opinion), but neither have we treated "federal issue" as a password opening federal courts to any state action embracing a point of federal law. Instead, the question is, does a state-law claim necessarily raise a stated federal issue, actually disputed and substantial, which a federal forum may entertain without disturbing any congressionally approved balance of federal and state judicial responsibilities.

III

A

This case warrants federal jurisdiction. Grable's state complaint must specify "the facts establishing the superiority of [its] claim," Mich. Ct. Rule 3.411(B)(2)(c) (West 2005), and Grable has premised its superior title claim on a failure by the IRS to give it adequate notice, as defined by federal law. Whether Grable was given notice within the meaning of the federal statute is thus an essential element of its quiet title claim, and the meaning of the federal statute is actually in dispute; it appears to be the only legal or factual issue contested in the case. The meaning of the federal tax provision is an important issue of federal law that sensibly belongs in a federal court. The Government has a strong interest in the "prompt and certain collection of delinquent taxes," United States v. Rodgers, 461 U.S. 677, 709 (1983), and the ability of the IRS to satisfy its claims from the property of delinquents requires clear terms of notice to allow buyers like Darue to satisfy themselves that the Service has touched the bases necessary for good title. The Government thus has a direct interest in the availability of a federal forum to vindicate its own administrative action, and buyers (as well as tax delinquents) may find it valuable to come before judges used to federal tax matters. Finally, because it will be the rare state title case that raises a contested matter of federal law, federal jurisdiction to resolve genuine disagreement over federal tax title provisions will portend only a microscopic effect on the federal-state division of labor.

This conclusion puts us in venerable company, quiet title actions having been the subject of some of the earliest exercises of federal-question jurisdiction over state-law claims. In *Hopkins*, 244 U.S. at 490–91, the question was federal jurisdiction over a quiet title action based on the plaintiffs' allegation that federal mining law gave them the superior claim. Just as in this case, "the facts showing the plaintiffs' title and the existence and invalidity of the instrument or record sought to be eliminated as a cloud upon the title are essential parts of the plaintiffs' cause of action."[3] As in this case again, "it is plain that a controversy respecting the construction and effect of the [federal] laws is involved and is sufficiently real and substantial." This Court therefore upheld federal jurisdiction in *Hopkins*, as well as in the similar quiet title matters of Northern Pacific R. Co. v. Soderberg, 188 U.S. 526, 528 (1903), and Wilson Cypress Co. v. Del Pozo Y Marcos, 236 U.S. 635, 643–44 (1915). Consistent with those cases, the recognition of federal jurisdiction is in order here.

B

Merrell Dow Pharmaceuticals Inc. v. Thompson, 478 U.S. 804 (1986), on which Grable rests its position, is not to the contrary. *Merrell Dow* considered a state tort claim resting in part on the allegation that the

---

[3] The quiet title cases also show the limiting effect of the requirement that the federal issue in a state-law claim must actually be in dispute to justify federal-question jurisdiction. In Shulthis v. McDougal, 225 U.S. 561 (1912), this Court found that there was no federal question jurisdiction to hear a plaintiff's quiet title claim in part because the federal statutes on which title depended were not subject to "any controversy respecting their validity, construction, or effect." As the Court put it, the requirement of an actual dispute about federal law was "especially" important in "suit[s] involving rights to land acquired under a law of the United States," because otherwise "every suit to establish title to land in the central and western states would so arise [under federal law], as all titles in those States are traceable back to those laws."

defendant drug company had violated a federal misbranding prohibition, and was thus presumptively negligent under Ohio law. The Court assumed that federal law would have to be applied to resolve the claim, but after closely examining the strength of the federal interest at stake and the implications of opening the federal forum, held federal jurisdiction unavailable. Congress had not provided a private federal cause of action for violation of the federal branding requirement, and the Court found "it would . . . flout, or at least undermine, congressional intent to conclude that federal courts might nevertheless exercise federal-question jurisdiction and provide remedies for violations of that federal statute solely because the violation . . . is said to be a . . . 'proximate cause' under state law."

Because federal law provides for no quiet title action that could be brought against Darue, Grable argues that there can be no federal jurisdiction here, stressing some broad language in *Merrell Dow* (including the passage just quoted) that on its face supports Grable's position, see Note, Mr. Smith Goes to Federal Court: Federal Question Jurisdiction over State Law Claims Post-*Merrell Dow,* 115 Harv. L. Rev. 2272, 2280–82 (2002) (discussing split in Circuit Courts over private right of action requirement after *Merrell Dow*). But an opinion is to be read as a whole, and *Merrell Dow* cannot be read whole as overturning decades of precedent, as it would have done by effectively adopting the Holmes dissent in *Smith,* and converting a federal cause of action from a sufficient condition for federal-question jurisdiction[5] into a necessary one.

In the first place, *Merrell Dow* disclaimed the adoption of any bright-line rule, as when the Court reiterated that "in exploring the outer reaches of § 1331, determinations about federal jurisdiction require sensitive judgments about congressional intent, judicial power, and the federal system." The opinion included a lengthy footnote explaining that questions of jurisdiction over state-law claims require "careful judgments," about the "nature of the federal interest at stake." And as a final indication that it did not mean to make a federal right of action mandatory, it expressly approved the exercise of jurisdiction sustained in *Smith,* despite the want of any federal cause of action available to *Smith's* shareholder plaintiff. *Merrell Dow* then, did not toss out, but specifically retained the contextual enquiry that had been *Smith's* hallmark for over 60 years. At the end of *Merrell Dow,* Justice Holmes was still dissenting.

Accordingly, *Merrell Dow* should be read in its entirety as treating the absence of a federal private right of action as evidence relevant to, but not dispositive of, the "sensitive judgments about congressional intent" that § 1331 requires. The absence of any federal cause of action affected *Merrell Dow's* result two ways. The Court saw the fact as worth some consideration in the assessment of substantiality. But its primary

---

[5]   For an extremely rare exception to the sufficiency of a federal right of action, see Shoshone Mining Co. v. Rutter, 177 U.S. 505, 507 (1900).

importance emerged when the Court treated the combination of no federal cause of action and no preemption of state remedies for misbranding as an important clue to Congress's conception of the scope of jurisdiction to be exercised under § 1331. The Court saw the missing cause of action not as a missing federal door key, always required, but as a missing welcome mat, required in the circumstances, when exercising federal jurisdiction over a state misbranding action would have attracted a horde of original filings and removal cases raising other state claims with embedded federal issues. For if the federal labeling standard without a federal cause of action could get a state claim into federal court, so could any other federal standard without a federal cause of action. And that would have meant a tremendous number of cases.

One only needed to consider the treatment of federal violations generally in garden variety state tort law. "The violation of federal statutes and regulations is commonly given negligence per se effect in state tort proceedings."[6] Restatement (Third) of Torts (proposed final draft) § 14, Comment a. . . . A general rule of exercising federal jurisdiction over state claims resting on federal mislabeling and other statutory violations would thus have heralded a potentially enormous shift of traditionally state cases into federal courts. Expressing concern over the "increased volume of federal litigation," and noting the importance of adhering to "legislative intent," *Merrell Dow* thought it improbable that the Congress, having made no provision for a federal cause of action, would have meant to welcome any state-law tort case implicating federal law "solely because the violation of the federal statute is said to [create] a rebuttable presumption [of negligence] . . . under state law." In this situation, no welcome mat meant keep out. *Merrell Dow's* analysis thus fits within the framework of examining the importance of having a federal forum for the issue, and the consistency of such a forum with Congress's intended division of labor between state and federal courts.

As already indicated, however, a comparable analysis yields a different jurisdictional conclusion in this case. Although Congress also indicated ambivalence in this case by providing no private right of action to Grable, it is the rare state quiet title action that involves contested issues of federal law, see n.3, supra. Consequently, jurisdiction over actions like Grable's would not materially affect, or threaten to affect, the normal currents of litigation. Given the absence of threatening structural consequences and the clear interest the Government, its buyers, and its delinquents have in the availability of a federal forum, there is no good reason to shirk from federal jurisdiction over the dispositive and contested federal issue at the heart of the state-law title claim.[7]

---

[6]   Other jurisdictions treat a violation of a federal statute as evidence of negligence or, like Ohio itself in Merrell Dow Pharmaceuticals Inc. v. Thompson, 478 U.S. 804 (1986), as creating a rebuttable presumption of negligence. Restatement (Third) of Torts (proposed final draft) § 14, Comment c. Either approach could still implicate issues of federal law.

[7]   At oral argument Grable's counsel espoused the position that after *Merrell Dow*, federal-question jurisdiction over state-law claims absent a federal right of action, could be recognized

IV

The judgment of the Court of Appeals, upholding federal jurisdiction over Grable's quiet title action, is affirmed.

It is so ordered.

■ JUSTICE THOMAS, concurring.

The Court faithfully applies our precedents interpreting 28 U.S.C. § 1331 to authorize federal-court jurisdiction over some cases in which state law creates the cause of action but requires determination of an issue of federal law, e.g., Smith v. Kansas City Title & Trust Co., 255 U.S. 180 (1921); Merrell Dow Pharmaceuticals Inc. v. Thompson, 478 U.S. 804 (1986). In this case, no one has asked us to overrule those precedents and adopt the rule Justice Holmes set forth in American Well Works Co. v. Layne & Bowler Co., 241 U.S. 257 (1916), limiting § 1331 jurisdiction to cases in which federal law creates the cause of action pleaded on the face of the plaintiff's complaint. In an appropriate case, and perhaps with the benefit of better evidence as to the original meaning of § 1331's text, I would be willing to consider that course.*

Jurisdictional rules should be clear. Whatever the virtues of the *Smith* standard, it is anything but clear. [As the Court states at various points of its opinion,] the standard "calls for a 'common-sense accommodation of judgment to [the] kaleidoscopic situations' that present a federal issue, in 'a selective process which picks the substantial causes out of the web and lays the other ones aside' " (quoting Gully v. First Nat. Bank in Meridian, 299 U.S. 109, 117–18 (1936)); "[T]he question is, does a state-law claim necessarily raise a stated federal issue, actually disputed and substantial, which a federal forum may entertain without disturbing any congressionally approved balance of federal and state judicial responsibilities"; " '[D]eterminations about federal jurisdiction require sensitive judgments about congressional intent, judicial power, and the federal system' "; "the absence of a federal private right of action [is] evidence relevant to, but not dispositive of, the 'sensitive judgments about congressional intent' that § 1331 requires" (quoting *Merrell Dow*, 478 U.S. at 810).

---

only where a constitutional issue was at stake. There is, however, no reason in text or otherwise to draw such a rough line. As *Merrell Dow* itself suggested, constitutional questions may be the more likely ones to reach the level of substantiality that can justify federal jurisdiction. But a flat ban on statutory questions would mechanically exclude significant questions of federal law like the one this case presents.

    *   This Court has long construed the scope of the statutory grant of federal-question jurisdiction more narrowly than the scope of the constitutional grant of such jurisdiction. See Merrell Dow Pharmaceuticals Inc. v. Thompson, 478 U.S. 804, 807–08 (1986). I assume for present purposes that this distinction is proper—that is, that the language of 28 U.S.C. § 1331, "[t]he district courts shall have original jurisdiction of all *civil actions arising under* the Constitution, laws, or treaties of the United States" (emphasis added), is narrower than the language of Art. III, § 2, cl. 1, of the Constitution, "[t]he judicial Power shall extend to all *Cases,* in Law and Equity, *arising under* this Constitution, the Laws of the United States, and Treaties made, or which shall be made, under their Authority . . ." (emphases added).

Whatever the vices of the *American Well Works* rule, it is clear. Moreover, it accounts for the " 'vast majority' " of cases that come within § 1331 under our current case law, *Merrell Dow*, 478 U.S. at 808—further indication that trying to sort out which cases fall within the smaller *Smith* category may not be worth the effort it entails. Accordingly, I would be willing in appropriate circumstances to reconsider our interpretation of § 1331.

FURTHER NOTES ON WHEN A CASE "ARISES UNDER" FEDERAL LAW

1.   *EMPIRE HEALTHCHOICE ASSURANCE, INC. V. MCVEIGH*

The issue in Empire Healthchoice Assurance, Inc. v. McVeigh, 547 U.S. 677 (2006), is described in Note 2 of the Notes on the Law Governing the Rights and Duties of Private Parties in Chapter II. For the reasons there set forth, the Court concluded by a five-to-four margin that federal law did not create the claim on which the subrogation suit at issue was based. It followed that there was no federal question jurisdiction under § 1331.

Empire made an additional argument for federal jurisdiction based on *Grable & Sons v. Darue*. The majority disagreed:[a]

> This case is poles apart from *Grable*. The dispute there centered on the action of a federal agency (IRS) and its compatibility with a federal statute, the question qualified as "substantial," and its resolution was both dispositive of the case and would be controlling in numerous other cases. Here, the reimbursement claim was triggered, not by the action of any federal department, agency, or service, but by the settlement of a personal-injury action launched in state court, and the bottom-line practical issue is the share of that settlement properly payable to Empire.

> *Grable* presented a nearly "pure issue of law," one "that could be settled once and for all and thereafter would govern numerous tax sale cases." In contrast, Empire's reimbursement claim, McVeigh's counsel represented without contradiction, is fact-bound and situation-specific. . . . The state court in which the personal-injury suit was lodged is competent to apply federal law, to the extent it is relevant. . . .

> The United States no doubt "has an overwhelming interest in attracting able workers to the federal workforce," and "in the health and welfare of the federal workers upon whom it relies to carry out its functions." But those interests, we are persuaded, do not warrant turning into a discrete and costly "federal case" an insurer's contract-derived claim to be reimbursed from the proceeds of a federal worker's state-court-initiated tort litigation.

---

[a]   The dissenters did not address this question.

In sum, *Grable* emphasized that it takes more than a federal element "to open the 'arising under' door." This case cannot be squeezed into the slim category *Grable* exemplifies.

2.   *GUNN V. MINTON*

Minton lost a patent infringement case in federal court when his patent was declared invalid. He then filed a malpractice action against his lawyers in state court, arguing that his patent would have been upheld had they not been dilatory in arguing for an exception to the rule that led to the invalidation. The state trial court granted summary judgment against him on the ground that the lawyers had acted properly because the exception did not apply to his patent. Minton appealed on the ground that the state courts lacked jurisdiction over his malpractice suit because it fell within the exclusive federal jurisdiction over claims "arising under" federal patent law created by 28 U.S.C. § 1338(a). His argument was that his case "arose under" federal law because it turned on a question of federal law—whether his patent fit an exception to the normal federal rule. The state supreme court agreed with Minton that his case fell within the exclusive jurisdiction of the federal district courts.

The Supreme Court reversed in a unanimous opinion by Chief Justice Roberts. Gunn v. Minton, 568 U.S. 251 (2013). The Court set the table in the now-traditional manner:

> For statutory purposes, a case can "aris[e] under" federal law in two ways. Most directly, a case arises under federal law when federal law creates the cause of action asserted. . . . As a rule of inclusion, this "creation" test admits of only extremely rare exceptions, and accounts for the vast bulk of suits that arise under federal law. Minton's original patent infringement suit . . . , for example, arose under federal law in this manner.

> But even where a claim finds its origins in state rather than federal law—as Minton's legal malpractice claim indisputably does—we have identified a "special and small category" of cases in which arising under jurisdiction still lies. In outlining the contours of this slim category, we do not paint on a blank canvas. Unfortunately, the canvas looks like one that Jackson Pollock got to first.

The Court characterized *Grable* as "an effort to bring some order to this unruly doctrine," and described its test as involving four questions: "federal jurisdiction over a state law claim will lie if a federal issue is: (1) necessarily raised, (2) actually disputed, (3) substantial, and (4) capable of resolution in federal court without disrupting the federal-state balance approved by Congress."

The first two questions were satisfied: the case necessarily raised a federal question and it was actually disputed. But "Minton's argument founders on *Grable*'s next requirement, . . . for the federal issue in this case is not substantial in the relevant sense":

> [I]t is not enough that the federal issue be significant to the particular parties in the immediate suit; that will *always* be true

when the state claim "necessarily raise[s]" a disputed federal issue, as *Grable* separately requires. The substantiality inquiry under *Grable* looks instead to the importance of the issue to the federal system as a whole.

Here, the Court said, that importance was lacking. No matter how the federal question was decided in the malpractice action, Minton's patent would remain invalid. That question was settled in the prior federal litigation. Nor will the adjudication of such an issue in a state court malpractice action have any effect on the development of a uniform body of federal patent law. It will not establish binding precedent that will control future federal court decisions, nor (under current Patent Office rules) will state court decisions in such lawsuits have any preclusive effect on future patent decisions. "But even assuming that a state court's . . . adjudication [in a case like this] may be preclusive under some circumstances," the Court continued, "the result would be limited to the parties and patents that had been before the state court. Such 'fact-bound and situation-specific' effects are not sufficient to establish federal arising under jurisdiction."

It followed from this reasoning that the fourth *Grable* factor was also not met:

> That requirement is concerned with the appropriate "balance of federal and state judicial responsibilities." We have already explained the absence of a substantial federal issue within the meaning of *Grable*. The States, on the other hand, have "a special responsibility for maintaining standards among members of the licensed professions." . . . We have no reason to suppose that Congress—in establishing exclusive federal jurisdiction over patent cases—meant to bar from state courts state legal malpractice claims simply because they require resolution of a hypothetical patent issue.

> . . . In this case, although the state courts must answer a question of patent law to resolve Minton's legal malpractice claim, their answer will have no broader effects. It will not stand as binding precedent for any future patent claim; it will not even affect the validity of Minton's patent. Accordingly, there is no "serious federal interest in claiming the advantages thought to be inherent in a federal forum," [quoting *Grable*].

3.   BIBLIOGRAPHY

For a general essay on uncertainty and complexity in many aspects of federal jurisdiction, including federal question cases, see Martha Field, The Uncertain Nature of Federal Jurisdiction, 22 Wm. & M. L. Rev. 683 (1981). For an equally wide-ranging Symposium on the relevance of separation of powers concerns to the scope of federal-question jurisdiction, abstention, and other issues concerning the failure of federal courts to exercise the full range of their authorized jurisdiction, see Donald L. Doernberg, "You Can Lead a Horse to Water . . .": The Supreme Court's Refusal to Allow the Exercise of Original Jurisdiction Conferred by Congress, 40 Case Western Res. L. Rev.

999 (1989–90); Martin H. Redish, Judge-Made Abstention and the Fashionable Art of "Democracy Bashing", 40 Case Western Res. L. Rev. 1023 (1989–90); Ann Althouse, The Humble and the Treasonous: Judge-Made Jurisdiction Law, 40 Case Western Res. L. Rev. 1035 (1989–90); Jack M. Beermann, "Bad" Judicial Activism and Liberal Federal-Courts Doctrine: A Comment on Professor Doernberg and Professor Redish, 40 Case Western Res. L. Rev. 1053 (1989–90). For historically grounded analysis of the concept of "cause of action," with particular attention to "arising under" jurisdiction, standing, and implied rights of action, see Anthony J. Bellia Jr., Article III and the Cause of Action, 89 Iowa L. Rev. 777 (2004).

For a detailed historical comparison of "arising under" jurisdiction in civil cases and in criminal prosecutions, see Donald H. Zeigler, Twins Separated at Birth: A Comparative History of the Civil and Criminal Arising Under Jurisdiction of the Federal Courts and Some Proposals for Change, 19 Vermont L. Rev. 673 (1995). Zeigler suggests that criminal "arising under" jurisdiction be made more like its civil counterpart by allowing state courts to try some federal criminal prosecutions and by allowing federal courts to exercise supplemental jurisdiction over related state crimes.

For a general discussion of how to determine the existence of federal question jurisdiction using as the point of departure *Merrell Dow*, *Franchise Tax Board*, and the less well known cases of City of Chicago v. International College of Surgeons, 522 U.S. 156 (1997), and Christianson v. Colt Industries Operating Corp., 486 U.S. 800 (1988), see John B. Oakley, Federal Jurisdiction and the Problem of the Litigative Unit: When Does What "Arise Under" Federal Law, 76 Texas L. Rev. 1829 (1998).

For post-*Grable* discussions of the reach of federal question jurisdiction in situations where a state claim has a federal ingredient, see Richard D. Freer, Of Rules and Standards: Reconciling Statutory Limitations on "Arising Under" Jurisdiction, 82 Ind. L.J. 309 (2007); Rachel M. Janutis, The Road Forward from *Grable*: Separation of Powers and the Limits of "Arising Under" Jurisdiction, 69 La. L. Rev. 99 (2008); Douglas D. McFarland, The True Compass: No Federal Question in a State Law Claim, 55 U. Kan. L. Rev. 1 (2006); Rory Ryan, No Welcome Mat, No Problem? Federal-Question Jurisdiction after *Grable*, 80 St. John's L. Rev. 621 (2006). See also John F. Preis, Reassessing the Purposes of Federal Question Jurisdiction, 42 Wake Forest L. Rev. 247 (2007), which discusses the objectives of federal question jurisdiction in light of a survey of state-court disposition of federal issues. And see Robert J. Pushaw, Jr., A Neo-Federalist Analysis of Federal Question Jurisdiction, 95 Calif. L. Rev. 1515 (2007), which argues for an expansive interpretation of federal question jurisdiction to encompass all cases "that will likely depend on the resolution of a genuine dispute over the interpretation, application, or enforcement of federal law" and a contraction of jurisdiction over cases that are likely only to involve state law. For an interesting discussion of principles that control the jurisdiction of federal district courts, including speculative application of the federal ingredient theory, see Howard M. Wesserman, A Jurisdictional Perspective on *New York Times v. Sullivan*, 107 Nw. U. L. Rev. 901 (2013). For criticism of the "mechanical,

test-driven approach to doctrine" represented by *Gunn v. Minton* and its fail-
ure to "redirect the jurisdictional analysis back to the fundamental principles
that once animated the Court's arising-under jurisprudence," see Simona
Grossi, A Modified Theory of the Law of Federal Courts: The Case of Arising-
Under Jurisdiction, 88 Wash. L. Rev. 961 (2013). For a response, see Lumen
N. Mulligan, *Gully* and the Failure to Stake a 28 U.S.C. Section 1331
"Claim," 89 Wash. L. Rev. 441 (2014). See also Amelia Smith Rinehart, The
Federal Question in Patent-License Cases, 90 Ind. L.J. 659 (2015), for exten-
sive discussion of *Gunn* and a proposal for increasing the scope of federal
question jurisdiction in patent cases.

Finally, for a fresh attempt to bring order to the Supreme Court's decisions on the scope of § 1331 jurisdiction, see Lumen N. Mulligan, A Unified
Theory of U.S.C. Section 1331 Jurisdiction, 61 Vand. L. Rev. 1667 (2008).
Mulligan argues that "§ 1331 jurisdiction is best understood as a function of
the viability of the federal right a plaintiff asserts in relation to other indicia
of congressional permission to bring such a claim in federal court, which is
often expressed by the creation of causes of action." This offers, he asserts,
an appropriate focus on congressional intent, a means of reconciling existing
precedent, and "greater clarity for adjudicating tough cases."

NOTES ON FEDERAL QUESTION JURISDICTION AND DECLARATORY JUDGMENTS

1. SKELLY OIL CO. V. PHILLIPS PETROLEUM CO.

The federal declaratory judgment statute, now codified in 28 U.S.C.
§§ 2201, 2202, permits a federal court to issue a declaratory judgment "[i]n a
case of actual controversy within its jurisdiction." The interaction between
this statute and § 1331 is complex. As interpreted in Skelly Oil Co. v. Phillips
Petroleum Co., 339 U.S. 667 (1950), the declaratory judgment statute provides a federal cause of action, but does not expand federal subject matter
jurisdiction. Jurisdiction in declaratory judgment cases is therefore not
judged by the normal rule of the well-pleaded (declaratory judgment) complaint. Instead, one must ask whether some other suit—an ordinary coercive
action on the same facts—would come within the ordinary federal question
jurisdiction of a district court. If so, then either party may seek declaratory
relief. If not, then neither party may do so.

To see how this works, recall the face-of-the-compaint ruling in Louisville & Nashville Railroad Co. v. Mottley, 211 U.S. 149 (1908). The railroad
had canceled lifetime free passes awarded to the Mottleys in settlement of a
personal injury claim. It did so after Congress passed legislation outlawing
free passes, legislation which the Mottleys claimed did not affect preexisting
contracts and was unconstitutional if it did. The Mottleys' breach of contract
claim was held to contain no federal ingredient and therefore not to fall
within the federal question jurisdiction of the district courts.

Had declaratory judgments been available in 1908, could the Mottleys
or the railroad have sought a declaratory judgment in federal court on the

applicability and validity of the act of Congress? It seems clear that the statute is literally satisfied. There surely was "a case of actual controversy" between the Mottleys and the railroad that involved several important federal questions. But *Skelly Oil* says that neither the Mottleys nor the railroad could seek such relief because neither of them could have filed a suit seeking traditional coercive relief in federal court. Instead, the only coercive action that could have been filed between the parties was the one the Mottleys actually filed, an action that did not satisfy the well-pleaded complaint requirement.

Contrast the situation in Shaw v. Delta Airlines, Inc., 463 U.S. 85 (1983). Although federal defenses are not sufficient to satisfy the well-pleaded complaint rule, a potential defendant may be able to go to federal court to enjoin a state law or regulation on federal grounds. As the Court unanimously said in *Shaw*:

> It is beyond dispute that federal courts have jurisdiction over suits to enjoin state officials from interfering with federal rights. See Ex parte Young, 209 U.S. 123, 160–62 (1908). A plaintiff who seeks injunctive relief from state regulation, on the ground that such regulation is pre-empted by a federal statute which, by virtue of the Supremacy Clause of the Constitution, must prevail, thus presents a federal question which the federal courts have jurisdiction under 28 U.S.C. § 1331 to resolve. See Smith v. Kansas City Title & Trust Co., 255 U.S. 180, 199–200 (1921); Louisville & Nashville R. Co. v. Mottley, 211 U.S. 149, 152 (1908). . . .

This proposition would permit declaratory judgment actions in situations where injunctive relief would be available in federal court. Indeed, this was the case in *Shaw*. The plaintiffs there—various airlines and other companies—had filed declaratory judgment actions alleging that provisions in New York's Human Rights Law and Disability Benefits Law were preempted by the federal Employee Retirement Income Security Act.[a]

2. QUESTIONS AND COMMENTS ON *SKELLY OIL*

Does the *Skelly Oil* approach make sense? Could it be argued that a controversy such as existed between the Mottleys and the railroad is exactly the kind of suit for which declaratory relief ought to be available in federal court? Consider William Cohen's argument that it is wrongheaded to seek "a

---

[a] For a more recent application of the *Skelly* principle, see Medtronic, Inc. v. Mikrowski Family Ventures, LLC., 571 U.S. ___, 134 S.Ct. 843 (2014). Mikrowski owned patents that it licensed to Medtronic. Medtronic brought a declaratory judgment action seeking a ruling that it was not infringing the patents. The Court looked to the form of coercive relief that the declaratory judgment defendant could have asserted. If Medtronic stopped paying royalties, Mikrowski could bring an ordinary patent infringement action. "Such an action," the Court said, "would arise under federal patent law because 'federal patent law creates the cause of action.' " "Consequently," it continued, "this declaratory judgment action, which avoids that threatened action, also 'arises under' federal patent law."

The Court also held that since the burden of proving infringement would fall on Mikrowski were it to bring an infringement action, it also fell on Mikrowski to prove infringement in the declaratory judgment action—even though it was the defendant in that suit. The decision on both issues was unanimous.

single, all-purpose, neutral analytical concept which marks out federal question jurisdiction." Rather, a "frank recognition of the pragmatic nature of the decision-making process would help throw light on the factors which actually induce decision."[b] Should either the Mottleys or the railroad be able to seek a declaratory judgment in federal court under this conception of "arising under" jurisdiction?

Application of the Cohen approach to *Skelly Oil* itself may lead to the Court's result in that case by a different route. *Skelly Oil* involved a private contract that allowed termination if an event controlled by federal law did not occur on or before a certain date. Resolution of the questions of federal law that determined whether the event had occurred was unavailable in a federal declaratory judgment action, the Court held, because the federal question could enter the case in a coercive suit only by way of defense to an action for breach of contract. Would this federal question have warranted the exercise of federal district court jurisdiction even without any special rules for declaratory judgments?

Cohen himself said "no." The presence of an issue involving federal law, he admitted, provides some support for federal question jurisdiction. But there are countervailing considerations. It is not entirely clear in *Skelly*, for example, that the contract used the federal trigger—issuance of a "certificate of public convenience and necessity"—in exactly the same sense that the relevant federal law (contained in the Natural Gas Act) used it. Construction of the contract under applicable principles of state law may make the federal issue go away. In addition, there is little federal interest in adjudicating the private contract rights at stake in a case like *Skelly*, even if a federal question must be resolved. Consider finally, he suggested, the incentives to private parties that are provided if incorporating a proposition of federal law in a private contract authorized federal court jurisdiction. There is no reason in federal policy that the opportunity to manufacture federal jurisdiction should be delegated to private parties in this manner. Perhaps there will be some cases, Cohen concluded, where it is important for federal courts to decide issues of this type, but they will be rare and a general rule forbidding district court jurisdiction will work well most of the time. And besides, certiorari from the state courts to the Supreme Court is available to correct an aberrational interpretation of an important question of federal law.[c]

3. *FRANCHISE TAX BOARD*

The Construction Laborers Vacation Trust for Southern California (CLVT) was a trust established for the purpose of collecting funds from employers to provide vacation benefits for construction workers. A prescribed amount per hour worked was placed into an account in each worker's name, and then paid to the worker once a year as a vacation benefit. The Franchise

---

[b] William Cohen, The Broken Compass: The Requirement That a Case Arise "Directly" Under Federal Law, 115 U. Pa. L. Rev. 890, 907 (1967). Cohen's argument is set forth more fully above in Note 2 of the Introductory Notes on When a Case "Arises Under" Federal Law.

[c] For analysis of the legislative history of the Declaratory Judgment Act and criticism of the Court's interpretation, see Donald Doernberg and Michael Mushlin, The Trojan Horse: How the Declaratory Judgment Act Created a Cause of Action and Expanded Federal Jurisdiction While the Supreme Court Wasn't Looking, 36 U.C.L.A. L. Rev. 529 (1989).

Tax Board was the state agency charged with collecting the state's personal income tax. California law authorized the Tax Board to pursue any "credits or other personal property belonging to a taxpayer" that were held by a third party and permitted a suit for damages against any third party that refused to pay a proper claim for such property over to the Tax Board. The Tax Board filed a suit in state court against CLVT under this provision based on unpaid taxes due from three individuals for whom the trust was holding vacation benefits. CLVT's defense was grounded on an opinion letter from the Department of Labor which concluded that the state law under which the Franchise Tax Board sought to proceed was preempted by § 514 of the Employment Retirement Income Security Act of 1974 (ERISA), 29 U.S.C. § 1000 et seq. The Tax Board sought damages under California law for the failure to make payments from the trust accounts and also invoked state declaratory judgment law seeking a declaration that CLVT was obligated to make the payments.

CLVT removed the case to federal court. The issue before the Supreme Court in Franchise Tax Board of California v. Construction Laborers Vacation Trust for Southern California, 463 U.S. 1 (1983), was whether the suit fit within the District Court's original jurisdiction and was therefore subject to removal. Justice Brennan's unanimous opinion for the Court had the following to say on the declaratory judgment aspect of the suit:

> Even though state law creates appellant's causes of action, its case might still "arise under" the laws of the United States if a well-pleaded complaint established that its right to relief under state law requires resolution of a substantial question of federal law in dispute between the parties. For appellant's first cause of action— to enforce its levy . . .—a straightforward application of the well-pleaded complaint rule precludes original federal court jurisdiction. California law establishes a set of conditions, without reference to federal law, under which a tax levy may be enforced; federal law becomes relevant only by way of a defense to an obligation created entirely by state law, and then only if appellant has made out a valid claim for relief under state law. The well-pleaded complaint rule was framed to deal with precisely such a situation. [S]ince 1887 it has been settled law that a case may not be removed to federal court on the basis of a federal defense, including the defense of preemption, even if the defense is anticipated in the plaintiff's complaint, and even if both parties admit that the defense is the only question truly at issue in the case.

> Appellant's declaratory judgment action poses a more difficult problem. Whereas the question of federal preemption is relevant to appellant's first cause of action only as a potential defense, it is a necessary element of the declaratory judgment claim. Under Cal. Proc. Code § 1060, a party with an interest in property may bring an action for a declaration of another party's legal rights and duties with respect to that property upon showing that there is an "actual controversy relating to the respective rights and duties" of the parties. The only questions in dispute between the parties in this case

concern the rights and duties of CLVT and its trustees under ERISA. Not only does appellant's request for a declaratory judgment under California law clearly encompass questions governed by ERISA, but appellant's complaint identifies no other questions as a subject of controversy between the parties. Such questions must be raised in a well-pleaded complaint for a declaratory judgment. Therefore, it is clear on the face of its well-pleaded complaint that appellant may not obtain the relief it seeks in its second cause of action ("[t]hat the court declare defendants legally obligated to honor all future levies by the board upon [CLVT]") without a construction of ERISA and/or an adjudication of its preemptive effect and constitutionality—all questions of federal law.

Appellant argues that original federal court jurisdiction over such a complaint is foreclosed by our decision in Skelly Oil Co. v. Phillips Petroleum Co., 339 U.S. 667 (1950). As we shall see, however, *Skelly Oil* is not directly controlling.

In *Skelly Oil,* Skelly Oil and Phillips had a contract, for the sale of natural gas, that entitled the seller—Skelly Oil—to terminate the contract at any time after December 1, 1946, if the Federal Power Commission had not yet issued a certificate of convenience and necessity to a third party, a pipeline company to whom Phillips intended to resell the gas purchased from Skelly Oil. Their dispute began when the Federal Power Commission informed the pipeline company on November 30 that it would issue a conditional certificate, but did not make its order public until December 2. By this time Skelly Oil had notified Phillips of its decision to terminate their contract. Phillips brought an action in United States District Court under the federal Declaratory Judgment Act, 28 U.S.C. § 2201, seeking a declaration that the contract was still in effect.

There was no diversity between the parties, and we held that Phillips's claim was not within the federal question jurisdiction conferred by § 1331. We reasoned:

> "[T]he operation of the Declaratory Judgment Act is procedural only." Congress enlarged the range of remedies available in the federal courts but did not extend their jurisdiction. When concerned as we are with the power of the inferior federal courts to entertain litigation within the restricted area to which the Constitution and acts of Congress confine them, "jurisdiction" means the kinds of issues which give right of entrance to federal courts. Jurisdiction in this sense was not altered by the Declaratory Judgment Act. Prior to that act, a federal court would entertain a suit on a contract only if the plaintiff asked for an immediate enforceable remedy like money damages or an injunction, but such relief could only be given if the requisites of jurisdiction, in the sense of a federal right or diversity, provided foundation for the resort to the federal courts. The Declaratory Judgment Act allowed relief to be given by way of recognizing the plaintiff's right even though

no immediate enforcement of it was asked. But the requirements of jurisdiction—the limited subject matters which alone
Congress had authorized the district courts to adjudicate—
were not impliedly repealed or modified.

We then observed that, under the well-pleaded complaint rule, an
action by Phillips to enforce its contract would not present a federal
question. *Skelly Oil* has come to stand for the proposition that "if,
but for the availability of the declaratory judgment procedure, the
federal claim would arise only as a defense to a state created action
jurisdiction is lacking." 10A Charles Alan Wright, Arthur R. Miller
and Mary Kay Kane, Federal Practice and Procedure § 2767, at
744–45 (2d ed. 1983). Cf. Public Service Comm'n v. Wycoff Co., 344
U.S. 237, 248 (1952) (dictum).[14]

The Court then broke its analysis into two parts. The first had to do with
whether *Skelly Oil* applied to a declaratory judgment action brought under
a *state* declaratory judgment statute:

> . . . As an initial matter, we must decide whether the doctrine
> of *Skelly Oil* limits original federal court jurisdiction under
> § 1331—and by extension removal jurisdiction under § 1441—
> when a question of federal law appears on the face of a well-pleaded
> complaint for a state law declaratory judgment. Apparently, it is a
> question of first impression. As the passage quoted above makes
> clear, *Skelly Oil* relied significantly on the precise contours of the
> federal Declaratory Judgment Act as well as of § 1331. . . . The
> Court's emphasis that the Declaratory Judgment Act was intended
> to affect only the remedies available in a federal district court, not
> the court's jurisdiction, was critical to the Court's reasoning. Our
> interpretation of the federal Declaratory Judgment Act in *Skelly
> Oil* does not apply of its own force to *state* declaratory judgment
> statutes, many of which antedate the federal statute.
>
> Yet while *Skelly Oil* itself is limited to the federal Declaratory
> Judgment Act, fidelity to its spirit leads us to extend it to state de-
> claratory judgment actions as well. If federal district courts could
> take jurisdiction, either originally or by removal, of state declara-
> tory judgment claims raising questions of federal laws, without
> regard to the doctrine of *Skelly Oil,* the federal Declaratory Judg-
> ment Act—with the limitations *Skelly Oil* read into it—would
> become a dead letter. For any case in which a state declaratory
> judgment action was available, litigants could get into federal court
> for a declaratory judgment despite our interpretation of § 2201,

---

[14] In *Wycoff,* [we said]:

Where the complaint in an action for declaratory judgment seeks in essence to
assert a defense to an impending or threatened state court action, it is the character of
the threatened action, and not of the defense, which will determine whether there is
federal-question jurisdiction in the district court. . . . Federal courts will not seize liti-
gations from state courts merely because one, normally a defendant, goes to federal
court to begin his federal-law defense before the state court begins the case under state
law.

simply by pleading an adequate state claim for a declaration of federal law. Having interpreted the Declaratory Judgment Act of 1934 to include certain limitations on the jurisdiction of federal district courts to entertain declaratory judgment suits, we should be extremely hesitant to interpret the Judiciary Act of 1875 and its 1887 amendments in a way that renders the limitations in the later statute nugatory. Therefore, we hold that under the jurisdictional statutes as they now stand[17] federal courts do not have original jurisdiction, nor do they acquire jurisdiction on removal, when a federal question is presented by a complaint for a state declaratory judgment, but *Skelly Oil* would bar jurisdiction if the plaintiff had sought a federal declaratory judgment.

The Court then turned to application of the *Skelly Oil* rule to the *Franchise Tax Board* facts. On this point it reasoned:

> . . . The question, then, is whether a federal district court could take jurisdiction of appellant's declaratory judgment claim had it been brought under 28 U.S.C. § 2201.[18] The application of *Skelly Oil* to such a suit is somewhat unclear. Federal courts have regularly taken original jurisdiction over declaratory judgment suits in which, if the declaratory judgment *defendant* brought a coercive action to enforce its rights, that suit would necessarily present a federal question.[19] Section 502(a)(3) of ERISA specifically grants trustees of ERISA-covered plans like CLVT a cause of action for injunctive relief when their rights and duties under ERISA are at issue, and that action is exclusively governed by federal law.[20] If CLVT could have sought an injunction under ERISA against application to it of state regulations that require acts inconsistent with

---

[17] It is not beyond the power of Congress to confer a right to a declaratory judgment in a case or controversy arising under federal law—within the meaning of the Constitution or of § 1331—without regard to *Skelly Oil*'s particular application of the well-pleaded complaint rule. The 1969 ALI report strongly criticized the *Skelly Oil* doctrine: "If no other changes were to be made in federal question jurisdiction, it is arguable that such language, and the historical test it seems to embody, should be repudiated." ALI Study § 1311, at 170–71. Nevertheless, Congress has declined to make such a change. At this point, any adjustment in the system that has evolved under the *Skelly Oil* rule must come from Congress.

[18] It may seem odd that, for purposes of determining whether removal was proper, we analyze a claim brought under state law, in state court, by a party who has continuously objected to district court jurisdiction over its case, as if that party had been trying to get original federal court jurisdiction all along. That irony, however, is a more-or-less constant feature of the removal statute, under which a case is removable if a federal district court could have taken jurisdiction had the same complaint been filed. See Herbert Wechsler, Federal Jurisdiction and the Revision of the Judicial Code, 13 Law & Contemp. Prob. 216, 234 (1948).

[19] For instance, federal courts have consistently adjudicated suits by alleged patent infringers to declare a patent invalid, on the theory that an infringement suit by the declaratory judgment defendant would raise a federal question over which the federal courts have exclusive jurisdiction. . . .

[20] . . . Even if ERISA did not expressly provide jurisdiction, CLVT might have been able to obtain federal jurisdiction under the doctrine applied in some cases that a person subject to a scheme of federal regulation may sue in federal court to enjoin application to him of conflicting state regulations, and a declaratory judgment action by the same person does not necessarily run afoul of the *Skelly Oil* doctrine. See, e.g., Lake Carriers' Assn. v. MacMullan, 406 U.S. 498, 506–08 (1972).

ERISA,[21] does a declaratory judgment suit by the state "arise under" federal law?

Given the analysis thus far, the answer to the Court's question, it would appear, is "yes." Since a coercive action could be brought in federal court by one of the parties, either may seek a declaratory judgment in federal court. And since the case could have been brought as a declaratory judgment in federal court, it is removable.

But not so fast. The Court answered its question in the next paragraph of its opinion:

> We think not. . . . There are good reasons why the federal courts should not entertain suits by the states to declare the validity of their regulations despite possibly conflicting federal law. States are not significantly prejudiced by an inability to come to federal court for a declaratory judgment in advance of a possible injunctive suit by a person subject to federal regulation. They have a variety of means by which they can enforce their own laws in their own courts, and they do not suffer if the preemption questions such enforcement may raise are tested there.[22] The express grant of federal jurisdiction in ERISA is limited to suits brought by certain parties, as to whom Congress presumably determined that a right to enter federal court was necessary to further the statute's purposes.[23] It did not go so far as to provide that any suit *against* such parties must also be brought in federal court when they themselves did not choose to sue. The situation presented by a state's suit for a declaration of the validity of state law is sufficiently removed from the spirit of necessity and careful limitation of district court jurisdiction that informed our statutory interpretation in *Skelly Oil* to convince us that, until Congress informs us otherwise, such a suit is not within the original jurisdiction of the United States district courts. Accordingly, the same suit brought originally in state court is not removable either.

---

[21] We express no opinion, however, whether a party in CLVT's position could sue under ERISA to enjoin or to declare invalid a state tax levy, despite the Tax Injunction Act, 28 U.S.C. § 1341. See California v. Grace Brethren Church, 457 U.S. 393 (1982). To do so, it would have to show either that state law provided no "speedy and efficient remedy" or that Congress intended § 502 of ERISA to be an exception to the Tax Injunction Act.

[22] Indeed, as appellant's strategy in this case shows, they may often be willing to go to great lengths to avoid federal-court resolution of a preemption question. Realistically, there is little prospect that states will flood the federal courts with declaratory judgment actions; most questions will arise, as in this case, because a state has sought a declaration in state court and the defendant has removed the case to federal court. Accordingly, it is perhaps appropriate to note that considerations of comity make us reluctant to snatch cases which a state has brought from the courts of that state, unless some clear rule demands it.

[23] Alleged patent infringers, for example, have a clear interest in swift resolution of the federal issue of patent validity—they are liable for damages if it turns out they are infringing a patent, and they frequently have a delicate network of contractual arrangements with third parties that is dependent on their right to sell or license a product. Parties subject to conflicting state and federal regulatory schemes also have a clear interest in sorting out the scope of each government's authority, especially where they face a threat of liability if the application of federal law is not quickly made clear.

Say again? Assume that *Skelly Oil* is right, or at least that it should be followed until Congress says otherwise. As the Court recognizes, a plaintiff should be able to seek a declaratory judgment in federal court in situations where either the plaintiff or the defendant could have brought a coercive action under federal law. Since the trust fund could have filed an action under ERISA for an injunction to prevent the tax assessments, either the trust or the taxing authority should have been able to seek declaratory relief in federal court. It should not matter, moreover, whether the federal declaratory judgment statute or the state declaratory judgment statute was used. In both situations, it seems clear that the case would "arise under" federal law under the applicable tests. And since the case could have been filed in federal court, it was removable when filed in state court.

This result seems supported, not undermined, by the fact that Congress has provided a cause of action to covered trust funds. Such actions are governed by federal common law and are to be heard exclusively in federal courts. Presumably this means that Congress believes it important that the *questions* involved in such lawsuits be heard in federal courts. And presumably this also means that Congress would not look favorably on the use of state courts to litigate such questions simply because a party challenging an ERISA entity won a race to the state courthouse. That, presumably, is what the removal statute is designed to prevent.

Why was this argument rejected? What does the last paragraph of the Court's opinion have to do with the rest of its opinion? But consider a different perspective. Does *Franchise Tax Board* confirm that what is going on here is a case-by-case balance of policies and not an analytical test? If so, does the Court get the policies right?[d]

4.   ARBITRATION ANALOGY?: *VADEN V. DISCOVER BANK*

Discover Bank filed an action in state court against Vaden, seeking to recover past due charges on a credit card. The action arose entirely under state law. Vaden counterclaimed, asserting that Discover's finance charges, late fees, and interest violated state law. Vaden's counterclaim was styled as a class action. Discover then filed a petition in federal court seeking an order under a clause in the credit card agreement to compel arbitration of the issues raised in the counterclaim.[e]

Section 4 of the Federal Arbitration Act, 9 U.S.C. § 4, provides:

> A party aggrieved by the alleged failure, neglect, or refusal of another to arbitrate under a written agreement for arbitration may petition any United States district court which, save for such agreement, would have jurisdiction under title 28, in a civil action or in

---

[d]   For an effort to reconcile *Skelly Oil* and *Franchise Tax Board*, see Paul E. Salamanca, Another Look at *Skelly Oil* and *Franchise Tax Board*, 80 Alb. L. Rev. 53 (2016/2017).

[e]   One reason Discover wanted arbitration is that the arbitration clause in the credit card agreement contained a provision precluding presentation of "any claims as a representative or member of a class."

admiralty of the subject matter of a suit arising out of the controversy between the parties, for an order directing that such
arbitration proceed in the manner provided for in such agreement.

To supply the federal question to demonstrate that a federal court "would
have jurisdiction" over the controversy, Discover argued that the issues
raised in Vaden's counterclaim were preempted by provisions of the Federal
Deposit Insurance Act (FDIA). To be successful, therefore, Discover argued—
and Vaden ultimately agreed—that Vaden's counterclaims would have to
rely on federal law.

The District Court accepted jurisdiction and ordered arbitration. The
Circuit Court affirmed. In Vaden v. Discover Bank, 556 U.S. 49 (2009), the
Supreme Court reversed. Even if it was appropriate to recharacterize Vaden's counterclaims as arising under federal law, Justice Ginsburg said for
the Court, the case seemed to present a classic "face of the complaint" issue:

> A *complaint* purporting to rest on state law, we have recog-
> nized, can be recharacterized as one "arising under" federal law if
> the law governing the complaint is exclusively federal. See Benefi-
> cial Nat. Bank v. Anderson, 539 U.S. 1, 8 (2003). Under this so-
> called "complete preemption doctrine," a plaintiff's "state cause of
> action [may be recast] as a federal claim for relief, making [its] re-
> moval [by the defendant] proper on the basis of federal question
> jurisdiction." 14B Wright and Miller § 3722.1, p. 511. A state-law-
> based *counterclaim*, however, even if similarly susceptible to re-
> characterization, would remain nonremovable. Under our prece-
> dent construing § 1331 . . . counterclaims, even if they rely exclu-
> sively on federal substantive law, do not qualify a case for federal-
> court cognizance.[f]

In dissent, joined by Justices Stevens, Breyer, and Alito, Chief Justice
Roberts argued in favor of district court jurisdiction based on the language
of § 4:

> The statute provides a clear and sensible answer: The court may
> consider the § 4 petition if the court "would have" jurisdiction over
> "the subject matter of a suit arising out of the controversy between
> the parties."
>
> The § 4 petition in this case explains that the controversy Dis-
> cover seeks to arbitrate is whether "Discover Bank charged illegal
> finance charges, interest and late fees." Discover contends in its pe-
> tition that the resolution of this dispute is controlled by federal
> law. . . . Vaden agrees that the legality of Discover's charges and
> fees is governed by the FDIA.[*] A federal court therefore "would

---

[f] *Beneficial National Bank* is the next main case, following which the implications of the
"complete preemption" doctrine are explored. At the end of the day, the Court found it unnecessary to determine whether the "complete preemption" doctrine applied in this setting.—
[Footnote by eds.]

[*] Vaden has conceded that the FDIA completely pre-empts her state-law counterclaims.
What is significant about that concession is not Vaden's agreement on the jurisdictional question of complete pre-emption (which we need not and do not address), but rather her agreement
that federal law—the FDIA—governs her allegation that Discover's charges and fees are illegal.

have jurisdiction . . . of the subject matter of a suit arising out of the controversy" Discover seeks to arbitrate. That suit could be an action by Vaden asserting that the charges violate the FDIA, or one by Discover seeking a declaratory judgment that they do not. . . . [This result] is closely analogous to the jurisdictional analysis in a typical declaratory judgment action. See Franchise Tax Bd. of Cal. v. Construction Laborers Vacation Trust for Southern Cal., 463 U.S. 1, 19 (1983) (jurisdiction over a declaratory judgment action exists when, "*if* the declaratory judgment defendant brought a coercive action to enforce its rights, that suit would necessarily present a federal question" (emphasis added)).

But the majority disagreed:

> [W]e read § 4 to convey that a party seeking to compel arbitration may gain a federal court's assistance only if, "save for" the agreement, the entire, actual "controversy between the parties," as they have framed it, could be litigated in federal court. We conclude that the parties' actual controversy, here precipitated by Discover's state-court suit for the balance due on Vaden's account, is not amenable to federal-court adjudication. Consequently, the § 4 petition Discover filed in the United States District Court . . . must be dismissed.

The Court explained:

> Under the well-pleaded complaint rule, a completely preempted counterclaim remains a counterclaim and thus does not provide a key capable of opening a federal court's door. . . .

> There is a fundamental flaw in the dissent's analysis: In lieu of focusing on the whole controversy as framed by the parties, the dissent hypothesizes discrete controversies of its own design. As the parties' state-court filings reflect, the originating controversy here concerns Vaden's alleged debt to Discover. Vaden's responsive counterclaims challenging the legality of Discover's charges are a discrete aspect of the whole controversy Discover and Vaden brought to state court. Whether one might imagine a federal-question suit involving the parties' disagreement over Discover's charges is beside the point. The relevant question is whether the whole controversy between the parties—not just a piece broken off from that controversy—is one over which the federal courts would have jurisdiction.

> The dissent would have us treat a § 4 petitioner's statement of the issues to be arbitrated as the relevant controversy even when that statement does not convey the full flavor of the parties' entire dispute. Artful dodges by a § 4 petitioner should not divert us from recognizing the actual dimensions of that controversy. The text of § 4 instructs federal courts to determine whether they would have jurisdiction over "a suit arising out of *the* controversy between the parties"; it does not give § 4 petitioners license to recharacterize an

existing controversy, or manufacture a new controversy, in an effort to obtain a federal court's aid in compelling arbitration. . . .

In sum, § 4 . . . instructs district courts asked to compel arbitration to inquire whether the court would have jurisdiction, "save for [the arbitration] agreement," over "a suit arising out of the controversy between the parties." We read that prescription in light of the well-pleaded complaint rule and the corollary rule that federal jurisdiction cannot be invoked on the basis of a defense or counterclaim. Parties may not circumvent those rules by asking a federal court to order arbitration of the portion of a controversy that implicates federal law when the court would not have federal-question jurisdiction over the controversy as a whole. It does not suffice to show that a federal question lurks somewhere inside the parties' controversy, or that a defense or counterclaim would arise under federal law. Because the controversy between Discover and Vaden, properly perceived, is not one qualifying for federal-court adjudication, § 4 . . . does not empower a federal court to order arbitration of that controversy, in whole or in part.[19]

Discover, we note, is not left without recourse. Under the Federal Arbitration Act, state courts as well as federal courts are obliged to honor and enforce agreements to arbitrate. Discover may therefore petition a Maryland court for aid in enforcing the arbitration clause of its contracts with Maryland cardholders.[g]

5. FOOTNOTE ON *AMERICAN WELL WORKS*

In footnote 19 of its opinion in *Franchise Tax Board*, the Court approves a line of lower-court patent cases that would allow the *American Well Works*

---

[19] This Court's declaratory judgment jurisprudence in no way undercuts our analysis. Discover, the dissent implies, could have brought suit in federal court seeking a declaration that its charges conform to federal law. Again, the dissent's position rests on its misconception of "the controversy between the parties." Like § 4 itself, the Declaratory Judgment Act does not enlarge the jurisdiction of the federal courts; it is "procedural only." Aetna Life Ins. Co. v. Haworth, 300 U.S. 227, 240 (1937). Thus, even in a declaratory judgment action, a federal court could not entertain Discover's state-law debt-collection claim. Cf. 10B Wright and Miller § 2758, pp. 519–521 ("The Declaratory Judgment Act was not intended to enable a party to obtain a change of tribunal from a state to federal court, and it is not the function of the federal declaratory action merely to anticipate a defense that otherwise could be presented in a state action.").

[g] *Vaden* resolved a Circuit split. A majority of the Circuits had held that a § 4 petition only raised questions about the validity and scope of the agreement to arbitrate. In *Vaden*, that approach would have involved only questions of state law—whether the agreement to arbitrate was a valid contract, to what issues it extended, whether the agreement had been breached, and the like. The minority position was that it was appropriate, in Justice Ginsburg's words, to " 'look through' the petition and grant the requested relief if the court would have federal-question jurisdiction over the underlying controversy." The entire Court concluded that it was appropriate to "look through" the petition. It split over where to look.

Another question lurking in the background in *Vaden*, again to use Justice Ginsburg's language, was the " 'antiquated and arcane' ouster notion. . . . [C]ourts traditionally viewed arbitration clauses as unworthy attempts to 'oust' them of jurisdiction; accordingly, to guard against encroachment on their domain, they refused to order specific enforcement of agreements to arbitrate." This doctrine was put to rest, the Court concluded, by enactment of the Federal Arbitration Act in 1925. For discussion of an issue not addressed specifically in *Vaden*, namely how arbitration can be regarded as consistent with Article III, see Peter B. Rutledge, Arbitration and Article III, 61 Vand. L. Rev. 1189 (2008)—[Footnote by eds.]

complaint to be heard in federal court if it were filed as a declaratory judgment seeking a determination of the validity of the defendant's patent. Is this consistent with *Skelly Oil*? Could a plaintiff in the *American Well Works* situation now seek such declaratory relief and then justify district court jurisdiction over its slander of title claim on a theory of pendent jurisdiction?

SUBSECTION B. PREEMPTION AS A BASIS FOR FEDERAL QUESTION JURISDICTION

Beneficial National Bank v. Anderson

Supreme Court of the United States, 2003.
539 U.S. 1.

■ JUSTICE STEVENS delivered the opinion of the Court.

The question in this case is whether an action filed in a state court to recover damages from a national bank for allegedly charging excessive interest in violation of both "the common law usury doctrine" and an Alabama usury statute may be removed to a federal court because it actually arises under federal law. We hold that it may.

I

Respondents are 26 individual taxpayers who made pledges of their anticipated tax refunds to secure short-term loans obtained from petitioner Beneficial National Bank, a national bank chartered under the National Bank Act. Respondents brought suit in an Alabama court against the bank and the two other petitioners that arranged the loans, seeking compensatory and punitive damages on the theory, among others, that the bank's interest rates were usurious. Their complaint did not refer to any federal law.

Petitioners removed the case to the United States District Court for the Middle District of Alabama. In their notice of removal they asserted that the National Bank Act, 12 U.S.C. § 85, is the exclusive provision governing the rate of interest that a national bank may lawfully charge, that the rates charged to respondents complied with that provision, that § 86 provides the exclusive remedies available against a national bank charging excessive interest,[2] and that the removal statute, 28 U.S.C. § 1441, therefore applied. The District Court denied respondents' motion to remand the case to state court but certified the question whether it

---

[2]   Section 86 provides:

     Usurious interest; penalty for taking; limitations

     The taking, receiving, reserving, or charging a rate of interest greater than is allowed by section 85 of this title, when knowingly done, shall be deemed a forfeiture of the entire interest which the note, bill, or other evidence of debt carries with it, or which has been agreed to be paid thereon. In case the greater rate of interest has been paid, the person by whom it has been paid, or his legal representatives, may recover back, in an action in the nature of an action of debt, twice the amount of the interest thus paid from the association taking or receiving the same: *Provided,* That such action is commenced within two years from the time the usurious transaction occurred.

had jurisdiction to proceed with the case to the Court of Appeals pursuant to 28 U.S.C. § 1292(b).

A divided panel of the Eleventh Circuit reversed. The majority held that under our "well-pleaded complaint" rule, removal is generally not permitted unless the complaint expressly alleges a federal claim and that the narrow exception from that rule known as the "complete preemption doctrine" did not apply because it could "find no clear congressional intent to permit removal under §§ 85 and 86." Because this holding conflicted with an Eighth Circuit decision, we granted certiorari.

II

A civil action filed in a state court may be removed to federal court if the claim is one "arising under" federal law. § 1441(b). To determine whether the claim arises under federal law, we examine the "well pleaded" allegations of the complaint and ignore potential defenses. . . . Thus, a defense that relies on the preclusive effect of a prior federal judgment, Rivet v. Regions Bank of La., 522 U.S. 470 (1998), or the preemptive effect of a federal statute, Franchise Tax Bd. of Cal. v. Construction Laborers Vacation Trust for Southern Cal., 463 U.S. 1 (1983), will not provide a basis for removal. As a general rule, absent diversity jurisdiction, a case will not be removable if the complaint does not affirmatively allege a federal claim.

Congress has, however, created certain exceptions to that rule. For example, the Price-Anderson Act contains an unusual preemption provision, 42 U.S.C. § 2014(hh), that not only gives federal courts jurisdiction over tort actions arising out of nuclear accidents but also expressly provides for removal of such actions brought in state court even when they assert only state-law claims. See El Paso Natural Gas Co. v. Neztsosie, 526 U.S. 473, 484–85 (1999).

We have also construed § 301 of the Labor Management Relations Act, 1947 (LMRA), 29 U.S.C. § 185, as not only preempting state law but also authorizing removal of actions that sought relief only under state law. Avco Corp. v. Machinists, 390 U.S. 557 (1968). We later explained that holding as resting on the unusually "powerful" preemptive force of § 301:

> The . . . petitioner's action "arose under" § 301, and thus could be removed to federal court, although the petitioner had undoubtedly pleaded an adequate claim for relief under the state law of contracts and had sought a remedy available *only* under state law. The necessary ground of decision was that the preemptive force of § 301 is so powerful as to displace entirely any state cause of action "for violation of contracts between an employer and a labor organization." Any such suit is purely a creature of federal law, notwithstanding the fact that state law would provide a cause of action in the absence of § 301. *Avco*

stands for the proposition that if a federal cause of action completely preempts a state cause of action any complaint that comes within the scope of the federal cause of action necessarily "arises under" federal law.

Franchise Tax Bd., 463 U.S. at 23–24.

Similarly, in Metropolitan Life Ins. Co. v. Taylor, 481 U.S. 58 (1987), we considered whether the "complete preemption" approach adopted in *Avco* also supported the removal of state common-law causes of action asserting improper processing of benefit claims under a plan regulated by the Employee Retirement Income Security Act of 1974 (ERISA), 29 U.S.C. § 1001 et seq. For two reasons, we held that removal was proper even though the complaint purported to raise only state-law claims. First, the statutory text in § 502(a), 29 U.S.C. § 1132, not only provided an express federal remedy for the plaintiffs' claims, but also in its jurisdiction subsection, § 502(f), used language similar to the statutory language construed in *Avco,* thereby indicating that the two statutes should be construed in the same way. Second, the legislative history of ERISA unambiguously described an intent to treat such actions "as arising under the laws of the United States in similar fashion to those brought under section 301 of the Labor-Management Relations Act of 1947."

Thus, a state claim may be removed to federal court in only two circumstances—when Congress expressly so provides, such as in the Price-Anderson Act, or when a federal statute wholly displaces the state-law cause of action through complete preemption.[3] When the federal statute completely preempts the state-law cause of action, a claim which comes within the scope of that cause of action, even if pleaded in terms of state law, is in reality based on federal law. This claim is then removable under 28 U.S.C. § 1441(b), which authorizes any claim that "arises under" federal law to be removed to federal court. In the two categories of cases where this Court has found complete preemption—certain causes of action under the LMRA and ERISA—the federal statutes at issue provided the exclusive cause of action for the claim asserted and also set forth procedures and remedies governing that cause of action. . . .

III

Count IV of respondents' complaint sought relief for "usury violations" and claimed that petitioners "charged . . . excessive interest in violation of the common law usury doctrine" and violated "Alabama Code. § 8–8–1, et seq. by charging excessive interest." Respondents' complaint thus expressly charged petitioners with usury. *Metropolitan Life, Avco,* and *Franchise Tax Board* provide the framework for answering the dispositive question in this case: Does the National Bank Act provide the exclusive cause of action for usury claims against national banks? If so,

---

[3]   Of course, a state claim can also be removed through the use of the supplemental jurisdiction statute, 28 U.S.C. § 1367(a), provided that another claim in the complaint is removable.

then the cause of action necessarily arises under federal law and the case is removable. If not, then the complaint does not arise under federal law and is not removable.

Sections 85 and 86 serve distinct purposes. The former sets forth the substantive limits on the rates of interest that national banks may charge. The latter sets forth the elements of a usury claim against a national bank, provides for a 2-year statute of limitations for such a claim, and prescribes the remedies available to borrowers who are charged higher rates and the procedures governing such a claim. If, as petitioners asserted in their notice of removal, the interest that the bank charged to respondents did not violate § 85 limits, the statute unquestionably preempts any common-law or Alabama statutory rule that would treat those rates as usurious. The section would therefore provide the petitioners with a complete federal defense. Such a federal defense, however, would not justify removal. Caterpillar Inc. v. Williams, 482 U.S. 386, 393 (1987). Only if Congress intended § 86 to provide the exclusive cause of action for usury claims against national banks would the statute be comparable to the provisions that we construed in the *Avco* and *Metropolitan Life* cases.[5]

In a series of cases decided shortly after the Act was passed, we endorsed that approach. [Citations omitted.]

In addition to this Court's longstanding and consistent construction of the National Bank Act as providing an exclusive federal cause of action for usury against national banks, this Court has also recognized the special nature of federally chartered banks. Uniform rules limiting the liability of national banks and prescribing exclusive remedies for their overcharges are an integral part of a banking system that needed protection from "possible unfriendly State legislation." Tiffany v. National Bank of Mo., 85 U.S. (18 Wall.) 409, 412 (1874). The same federal interest that protected national banks from the state taxation that Chief Justice Marshall characterized as the "power to destroy," McCulloch v. Maryland, 17 U.S. (4 Wheat.) 316, 431 (1819), supports the established interpretation of §§ 85 and 86 that gives those provisions the requisite preemptive force to provide removal jurisdiction. In actions against national banks for usury, these provisions supersede both the substantive and the remedial provisions of state usury laws and create a federal remedy for overcharges that is exclusive, even when a state complainant, as here, relies entirely on state law. Because §§ 85 and 86 provide the exclusive cause of action for such claims, there is, in short, no such thing as a state-law claim of usury against a national bank. Even though the complaint makes no mention of federal law, it unquestionably and unambiguously claims that petitioners violated usury laws. This cause of action

---

[5] Because the proper inquiry focuses on whether Congress intended the federal cause of action to be exclusive rather than on whether Congress intended that the cause of action be removable, the fact that these sections of the National Bank Act were passed in 1864, 11 years prior to the passage of the statute authorizing removal, is irrelevant, contrary to respondents' assertions.

against national banks only arises under federal law and could, therefore, be removed under § 1441.

The judgment of the Court of Appeals is reversed.

It is so ordered.

■ JUSTICE SCALIA, with whom JUSTICE THOMAS joins, dissenting.

. . . "[F]ederal question" jurisdiction has long been governed by the well-pleaded-complaint rule, which provides that "federal jurisdiction exists only when a federal question is presented on the face of the plaintiff's properly pleaded complaint." Caterpillar Inc. v. Williams, 482 U.S. 386, 392 (1987). A federal question "is presented" when the complaint invokes federal law as the basis for relief. It does not suffice that the facts alleged in support of an asserted state-law claim would *also* support a federal claim. "The [well-pleaded-complaint] rule makes the plaintiff the master of the claim; he or she may avoid federal jurisdiction by exclusive reliance on state law." Id. Nor does it even suffice that the facts alleged in support of an asserted state-law claim *do not support* a state-law claim and would *only* support a federal claim. "Jurisdiction may not be sustained on a theory that the plaintiff has not advanced." Merrell Dow Pharmaceuticals Inc. v. Thompson, 478 U.S. 804, 809 n.6 (1986).

Under the well-pleaded-complaint rule, "a federal court does not have original jurisdiction over a case in which the complaint presents a state-law cause of action, but also asserts that federal law deprives the defendant of a defense he may raise, . . . or that a federal defense the defendant may raise is not sufficient to defeat the claim." Franchise Tax Bd. of Cal. v. Construction Laborers Vacation Trust for Southern Cal., 463 U.S. 1, 10 (1983). Of critical importance here, the rejection of a federal defense as the basis for original federal-question jurisdiction applies with equal force when the defense is one of federal preemption. "By unimpeachable authority, a suit brought upon a state statute does not arise under an act of Congress or the Constitution of the United States because prohibited thereby." Gully v. First Nat. Bank in Meridian, 299 U.S. 109, 116 (1936). "[A] case may *not* be removed to federal court on the basis of . . . the defense of preemption. . . ." *Caterpillar*, 482 U.S. at 393. To be sure, preemption requires a state court to *dismiss* a particular claim that is filed under state law, but it does not, as a general matter, provide grounds for *removal*.

This Court has twice recognized exceptions to the well-pleaded-complaint rule, upholding removal jurisdiction notwithstanding the absence of a federal question on the face of the plaintiff's complaint. First, in Avco Corp. v. Machinists, 390 U.S. 557 (1968), we allowed removal of a state-court action to enforce a no-strike clause in a collective-bargaining agreement. The complaint concededly did not advance a federal claim, but was subject to a defense of preemption under § 301 of the Labor Management Relations Act. The well-pleaded-complaint rule notwithstanding, we treated the plaintiff's state-law contract claim as one arising under § 301, and held that the case could be removed to federal court.

The only support mustered by the *Avco* Court for its conclusion was a statement wrenched out of context from our decision in Textile Workers v. Lincoln Mills, 353 U.S. 448, 457 (1957), that "[a]ny state law applied [in a § 301 case] will be absorbed as federal law and will not be an independent source of private rights." To begin with, this statement is entirely unnecessary to the landmark holding in *Lincoln Mills*—that § 301 not only gives federal courts jurisdiction to decide labor relations cases but also supplies them with authority to create the governing substantive law. More importantly, understood in the context of that holding, the quoted passage in no way supports the proposition for which it is relied upon in *Avco*—that state-law claims relating to labor relations necessarily *arise under* § 301. If one reads *Lincoln Mills* with any care, it is clear beyond doubt that the relevant passage merely confirms that when, in deciding cases arising under § 301, courts employ legal rules that overlap with, or are even explicitly borrowed from, state law, such rules are nevertheless rules of federal law. It is in this sense that "[a]ny state law applied [in a § 301 case] will be absorbed as federal law"—in the sense that federally adopted state rules become federal rules, not in the sense that a state-law claim becomes a federal claim.

Other than its entirely misguided reliance on *Lincoln Mills,* the opinion in *Avco* failed to clarify the analytic basis for its unprecedented act of jurisdictional alchemy. The Court neglected to explain *why* state-law claims that are preempted by § 301 of the LMRA are exempt from the strictures of the well-pleaded-complaint rule, nor did it explain *how* such a state-law claim can plausibly be said to "arise under" federal law. Our subsequent opinion in *Franchise Tax Board,* struggled to prop up *Avco's* puzzling holding:

> The necessary ground of decision [in *Avco*] was that the preemptive force of § 301 is so powerful as to displace entirely any state cause of action "for violation of contracts between an employer and a labor organization." Any such suit is purely a creature of federal law, notwithstanding the fact that state law would provide a cause of action in the absence of § 301. *Avco* stands for the proposition that if a federal cause of action completely preempts a state cause of action any complaint that comes within the scope of the federal cause of action necessarily "arises under" federal law.

This passage has repeatedly been relied upon by the Court as an explanation for its decision in *Avco*. See, e.g., Metropolitan Life Ins. Co. v. Taylor, 481 U.S. 58, 64 (1987). Of course it is not an explanation at all. It provides nothing more than an account of what *Avco* accomplishes, rather than a justification (unless ipse dixit is to count as justification) for the radical departure from the well-pleaded-complaint rule, which demands rejection of the defense of federal preemption as a basis for federal jurisdiction. Neither the excerpt quoted above, nor any other fragment of the decision in *Franchise Tax,* explains how or why the nonviability (due to preemption) of the state-law contract claim in *Avco* magically transformed that claim into one "arising under" federal law.

Metropolitan Life Ins. Co. v. Taylor was our second departure from the prohibition against resting federal "arising under" jurisdiction upon the existence of a federal defense. . . . [T]he *Taylor* Court broke no new analytic ground; its opinion follows the exception established in *Avco* and described in *Franchise Tax Board,* but says nothing to commend that exception to logic or reason. . . .[1]

It is noteworthy that the straightforward (though similarly unsupported) rule announced in today's opinion—under which (1) removal is permitted "[w]hen [a] federal statute completely preempts a state-law cause of action," and (2) a federal statute is completely preemptive when it "provide[s] the exclusive cause of action for the claim asserted"—is nowhere to be found in either *Avco* or *Taylor.* To the contrary, the analysis in today's opinion implicitly contradicts (by rendering inexplicable) *Taylor*'s discussion of preemption and removal. (*Avco,* as I observed earlier, has no discussion to be contradicted.) Had it thought that today's decision was the law, the *Taylor* Court need not have taken pains to emphasize the "clos[e] parallels" between § 502(a)(1)(B) of ERISA and § 301 of the LMRA and need not have pored over the legislative history of § 502(a) to show that Congress expected ERISA to be treated like the LMRA. Instead, it could have rested after noting the "unique preemptive force of ERISA." Indeed, it could even have spared itself the trouble of adding the adjective "unique." While there is something unique about statutes whose preemptive force is closely patterned after that of the LMRA (which we had held to support removal), there is nothing whatever unique about a federal cause of action that displaces state causes of action. Displacement alone, if today's opinion is to be believed, would have sufficed to establish the existence of removal jurisdiction. . . .

[T]oday's holding also represents a sharp break from our long tradition of respect for the autonomy and authority of state courts. . . .[2] and effectuates a significant shift in decisional authority from state to federal courts.

---

[1]   This is not to say that *Taylor* was wrongly decided. Having been informed through the *Avco Corp. v. Machinists,* 390 U.S. 557 (1968), decision that the language of § 301 triggered "arising under" jurisdiction even with respect to certain state-law claims, Congress's subsequent decision to insert language into ERISA that "closely parallels" the text of § 301 can be viewed to be, as we said, a "specific reference to the *Avco* rule." *Taylor,* in other words, rests upon a sort of statutory incorporation of *Avco. Avco* itself, on the other hand, continues to rest upon nothing.

[2]   Our traditional regard for the role played by state courts in interpreting and enforcing federal law has other doctrinal manifestations. We indulge, for example, a "presumption of concurrent [state and federal] jurisdiction," which can be rebutted only "by an explicit statutory directive, by unmistakable implication from legislative history, or by a clear incompatibility between state-court jurisdiction and federal interests." Gulf Offshore Co. v. Mobil Oil Corp., 453 U.S. 473, 478 (1981).

In an effort to justify this shift, the Court explains that "[b]ecause §§ 85 and 86 [of the National Bank Act] provide the exclusive cause of action for such claims, there is . . . no such thing as a state-law claim of usury against a national bank." . . . The proper response to the presentation of a nonexistent claim to a state court is *dismissal,* not the "federalize-and-remove" dance authorized by today's opinion. For even if the Court is correct that the National Bank Act obliterates entirely any state-created right to relief for usury against a national bank, that does not explain how or why the claim of such a right is transmogrified into the claim of a federal right. Congress's mere act of creating a federal right and eliminating all state-created rights *in no way* suggests an expansion of federal jurisdiction so as to wrest from state courts the authority to decide questions of preemption under the National Bank Act. . . .

[T]here is no more reason to fear state-court error with respect to federal preemption accompanied by creation of a federal cause of action than there is with respect to federal preemption unaccompanied by creation of a federal cause of action—or, for that matter, than there is with respect to *any* federal defense to a state-law claim. The rational response to the . . . concern [that state courts will make errors of federal law] is to eliminate the well-pleaded-complaint rule entirely. . . . [I]t is up to Congress, not the federal courts, to decide when the risk of state-court error with respect to a matter of federal law becomes so unbearable as to justify divesting the state courts of authority to decide the federal matter. Unless and until we receive instruction from Congress that claims preempted under the National Bank Act—in contrast to almost all other claims that are subject to federal preemption—"arise under" federal law, we simply lack authority to "avoi[d] . . . potential errors" by permitting removal.

* * *

Today's opinion has succeeded in giving to our *Avco* decision a theoretical foundation that neither *Avco* itself nor *Taylor* provided. Regrettably, that theoretical foundation is itself without theoretical foundation. That is to say, the more general proposition that (1) the existence of a preemptive federal cause of action causes the invalid assertion of a state cause of action to raise a federal question, has no more logic or precedent to support it than the very narrow proposition that (2) the LMRA *(Avco)* and statutes modeled after the LMRA *(Taylor)* cause invalid assertions of state causes of action preempted by those particular statutes to raise federal questions. Since I believe that, as between an inexplicable narrow holding and an inexplicable broad one, the former is the lesser evil, I would adhere to the approach taken by *Taylor* and on the basis of stare decisis simply affirm, without any real explanation, that the LMRA and statutes modeled after it have a "unique preemptive force" that (quite illogically) suspends the normal rules of removal jurisdiction. Since no one asserts that the National Bank Act is modeled after the LMRA, the state-law claim pleaded here cannot be removed, and it is left to the state

courts to dismiss it. From the Court's judgment to the contrary, I respectfully dissent.

NOTES ON PREEMPTION AS A BASIS FOR FEDERAL QUESTION JURISDICTION

1. AVCO CORP. V. MACHINISTS

Avco Corp. v. Machinists, 390 U.S. 557 (1968), is the origin of the
preemption rule the Court applies in *Beneficial National Bank*. An employer
filed suit in state court seeking an injunction to enforce a "no-strike" clause
in a collective bargaining agreement. The agreement provided that the dispute over which the union had called the strike was subject to binding
arbitration. Under the collective bargaining culture of the day, the union's
agreement not to strike over a dispute was the typical quid pro quo for the
employer's agreement to subject the dispute to binding arbitration.

It had been established in Textile Workers Union v. Lincoln Mills, 353
U.S. 448 (1957), that § 301 of the Labor Management Relations Act of 1947
required that federal common law govern the interpretation of labor contracts. *Lincoln Mills* also held that an employer's agreement to submit a
dispute to binding arbitration was specifically enforceable in a suit brought
by a union in federal court.

The rub came in the decision in Sinclair Refining Co. v. Atkinson, 370
U.S. 195 (1962). *Sinclair* was an action in federal court brought by an employer to enforce the "no-strike" side of such a collective bargaining agreement. If we can be compelled to arbitrate, the company reasoned, we ought
to be able to compel the union not to strike. Not so, the Court held in *Sinclair*.
Congress had enacted the Norris-LaGuardia Act in 1932, one provision of
which stated that "[n]o court of the United States shall have jurisdiction to
issue any restraining order or temporary or permanent injunction in any
case involving or growing out of any labor dispute to prohibit any person"
from engaging in a peaceful strike. 29 U.S.C. § 104. The *Sinclair* Court said
that it is not for courts to rewrite policy in the face of such a clear statutory
mandate. Section 301 did not repeal the Norris-LaGuardia Act, expressly or
by implication. Norris-LaGuardia therefore required that the employer's
complaint be dismissed "for lack of jurisdiction."

This was the state of the law when *Avco* was litigated. It explains why
the employer wanted to be in state court. And it explains why the union
wanted to be in federal court. Unusually, the choice of forum dictated the
result. Justice Douglas, who was in dissent in *Sinclair*, wrote the unanimous
opinion in *Avco*.[a] His rationale was cryptic:

> An action arising under § 301 is controlled by federal substan-
> tive law even though it is brought in a state court. . . . It is thus
> clear that the claim under this collective bargaining agreement is

---

[a] Justice Stewart, joined by Justices Harlan and Brennan, wrote a short concurrence noting that "[t]he Court will, no doubt, have an opportunity to consider the scope and continuing
validity of *Sinclair* upon an appropriate future occasion." The dissenters in *Sinclair* were Brennan, Douglas, and Harlan. Justice Stewart was in the majority.

one arising under the "laws of the United States" within the meaning of the removal statute. It likewise seems clear that this suit is within the "original jurisdiction" of the District Court. . . . It is true that the Court . . . in Sinclair Refining Co. v. Atkinson, 370 U.S. 195 (1962), held that although a case was properly in the federal district court by reason of § 301, the Norris-LaGuardia Act bars that court from issuing an injunction in the labor dispute. The nature of the relief available after jurisdiction attaches is, of course, different from the question whether there is jurisdiction to adjudicate the controversy. . . . But the breadth or narrowness of the relief which may be granted under federal law in § 301 cases is a distinct question from whether the court has jurisdiction over the parties and the subject matter. Any error in granting or designing relief "does not go to the jurisdiction of the court." Swift & Co. v. United States, 276 U.S. 311, 331 (1928). When the Court in *Sinclair* said that dismissal of a count in the complaint asking for an injunction was correct "for lack of jurisdiction under the Norris-LaGuardia Act," it meant only that the Federal District Court lacked the general equity power to grant the particular relief.

The Court thus achieved uniformity of outcome by denying effect to the employer's choice of forum.

2. POST-*AVCO* DEVELOPMENTS

Sinclair was overruled in Boys Markets, Inc. v. Retail Clerks Union, Local 770, 398 U.S. 235 (1970).[b] The Court said that federal labor law should be uniform across the country. And it should not matter whether suit is filed in state or federal court. Accordingly, either the *Sinclair* limitation on injunctions should be extended to state courts or the holding in *Sinclair* should be modified. The outcome was described in Chicago District Council of Carpenters Pension Fund v. K&I Construction, Inc., 270 F.3d 1060 (7th Cir. 2001):[c]

> Two statutes influence the availability of the kind of injunction K&I wants: the Norris-LaGuardia Act (NLA), which imposes strict limits on the ability of courts to enjoin labor disputes; and the Labor Management Relations Act (LMRA), which establishes a strong policy in favor of arbitrating labor-management disputes. In *Boys Markets*, the Supreme Court addressed the tension that can arise between these two enactments. The Court recognized that one of the most important benefits employers gain when they agree to mandatory arbitration is the avoidance of strikes and other disruptive labor actions. In order to ensure that employers have an

---

     b   Justice Brennan, who wrote the *Sinclair* dissent, also wrote the overruling opinion. Justice Black, who wrote the majority opinion in *Sinclair*, dissented in *Boys Markets*. Justice White also dissented, and Justice Stewart wrote to say that he had changed his mind in the interim.

     c   See also the summary of the law and a proposed reform in Michael A. Berenson, Labor Injunctions Pending Arbitration: A Proposal to Amend Norris-LaGuardia, 63 Tul. L. Rev. 1681 (1989).

incentive to agree to arbitration (which, to the extent it occurs, fosters the social interest in industrial peace . . .), the Court determined that it was necessary to recognize a narrow exception to the NLA's anti-injunction provisions. If the employer has contractually obligated itself to arbitrate a given dispute, by the same token that employer must be able to enjoin the union from striking over that dispute. *Boys Markets* accordingly held that a court may "issue [an] injunctive order [if] it first holds that the contract *does* have [the] effect" of binding both parties to arbitrate the dispute at issue and that "an injunction would be warranted under ordinary principles of equity." It is in that sense that an employer seeking to enjoin a labor action is subject to an extra burden: it must both satisfy the normal requirements for an injunction and also demonstrate that the contract language binds the union to arbitrate the dispute that precipitated the strike.

After *Boys Markets*, the Court underscored that the relevant issue is not simply whether the labor action violates the collective bargaining agreement, but more specifically whether the dispute that gave rise to the labor action was also one that the parties specifically agreed would be the subject of mandatory arbitration. As the Court said in Jacksonville Bulk Terminals, Inc. v. International Longshoremen's Ass'n, 457 U.S. 702, 723 (1982), "in agreeing to broad arbitration and no-strike clauses, the parties do not bargain for injunctive relief to restore the status quo pending an arbitrator's decision on the legality of the strike under the collective bargaining agreement, without regard to what triggered the strike. Instead, they bargain only for specific enforcement of the union's promise to arbitrate the underlying grievance before resorting to a strike." A sympathy strike, for example, may be a violation of the collective bargaining agreement's no-strike clause, but it may not be enjoined pending arbitration of the propriety of the strike unless the union specifically obligated itself to arbitrate the issue that caused the walkout. See Buffalo Forge Co. v. United Steelworkers, 428 U.S. 397 (1976).

Had the law been in this posture when *Avco* was decided, is it likely that removal would have been permitted? Is the peculiar history of *Avco* sufficient reason to limit it to the labor context?

Note that a federal court cannot issue an injunction on the *Buffalo Forge* facts. That is, although the run-of-the-mill labor dispute will be handled by *Boys Markets*, that case does not extend to the unusual situation where a strike does not involve an issue subject to binding arbitration but nonetheless may be in violation of a no-strike clause. Sympathy strikes (*Buffalo Forge*) and political strikes (*Jacksonville Bulk Terminals*) may be examples. Is the potential of different outcomes in state and federal court more tolerable in those situations than it was in *Boys Markets*? Is *Avco* still the right outcome for them?

3. *FRANCHISE TAX BOARD*

Franchise Tax Board of California v. Construction Laborers Vacation Trust for Southern California, 463 U.S. 1 (1983), is discussed in detail in Note 3 of "Notes on Federal Question Jurisdiction and Declaratory Judgments" in Subsection A of this Section. It involved—among other issues—an application of *Avco*. There were two causes of action, both based on state law and filed in state court: one was a claim for damages; the second for a declaratory judgment that the defendants were legally obligated to pay trust funds to a state tax collection agency that were held by the trust on behalf of delinquent taxpayers. The question was whether one or both of these claims was removable, which in turn depended on whether they stated a claim that could originally have been brought in federal court. One of the removal theories was that original district court jurisdiction was justified under *Avco*. The District Court ruled that ERISA did not preempt the state's authority to obtain delinquent taxes from the trust fund, but the Court of Appeals reversed. The Supreme Court held the case not removable, and remanded for its return to state court without resolution of the preemption question.[d] In an opinion by Justice Brennan, a unanimous Court responded to the *Avco* argument:

> [ERISA] neither creates nor expressly denies any cause of action in favor of state governments, to enforce tax levies or for any other purpose. It . . . makes clear that Congress did not intend to preempt entirely every state cause of action relating to such plans. . . . [It is therefore] clear that a suit by state tax authorities [in a suit like this one] does not "arise under" ERISA. Unlike the contract rights at issue in *Avco,* the state's right to enforce its tax levies is not of central concern to the federal statute. For that reason . . . on the face of a well-pleaded complaint there are many reasons completely unrelated to the provisions and purposes of ERISA why the state may or may not be entitled to the relief it seeks.[29] Furthermore, ERISA does not provide an alternative cause of action in favor of the state to enforce its rights, while § 301 expressly supplied the plaintiff in *Avco* with a federal cause of action to replace its preempted state contract claim. Therefore, even though the Court of Appeals may well be correct that ERISA precludes enforcement of the state's levy in the circumstances of this case, an action to enforce the levy is not itself preempted by ERISA.

4. *METROPOLITAN LIFE INS. CO. V. TAYLOR*

Taylor was an employee of General Motors, which had established a disability plan insured by Metropolitan. A dispute arose about whether Taylor was disabled from working. General Motors took the position that Taylor was

---

[d] The Court subsequently held in Mackey v. Lanier Collection Agency & Service, Inc., 486 U.S. 825 (1988), that Georgia garnishment procedures could be used by a collection agency to reach employee welfare benefits covered by ERISA.

[29] In theory (looking only at the complaint), it may turn out that the levy was improper under state law, or that in fact the defendant had complied with the levy. Furthermore, a levy on CLVT might be for something like property taxes on real estate it owned. CLVT's trust agreement authorizes its trustees to pay such taxes.

malingering and fired him. Taylor responded by filing suit in state court against both General Motors and Metropolitan for breach of his employment contract, for wrongful termination, for the insurance benefits to which he believed himself entitled, and for other grievances. General Motors and Metropolitan removed the case to federal court, alleging that the claim for disability benefits presented a federal claim by virtue of ERISA and asserting pendent jurisdiction over the other claims. The District Court found the case removable and granted summary judgment for the defendants. The Court of Appeals reversed on the ground that "Taylor's complaint stated only state law causes of action subject to the federal defense of ERISA preemption, and that the 'well-pleaded complaint' rule of *Mottley* precluded removal on the basis of a federal defense." In Metropolitan Life Insurance Co. v. Taylor, 481 U.S. 58 (1987), the Supreme Court granted certiorari and, in an opinion by Justice O'Connor, reversed.

In a companion case, Pilot Life Ins. Co. v. Dedeaux, 481 U.S. 41 (1987), the Court had held that state common-law causes of action claiming benefits under plans regulated by ERISA were preempted. It followed in *Taylor* that his claim for disability benefits, "as a suit by a beneficiary to recover benefits from a covered plan . . . falls directly under § 502(a)(1)(B) of ERISA, which provides an exclusive federal cause of action for resolution of such disputes." The Court continued:

> Federal preemption is ordinarily a federal defense to the plaintiff's suit. As a defense, it does not appear on the face of a well-pleaded complaint, and, therefore, does not authorize removal to a federal court. One corollary of the well-pleaded complaint rule developed in the case law, however, is that Congress may so completely preempt a particular area, that any civil complaint raising this select group of claims is necessarily federal in character. . . .

> There is no dispute in this case that Taylor's complaint, although preempted by ERISA, purported to raise only state law causes of action. The question, therefore, resolves itself into whether or not the *Avco* principle can be extended to statutes other than the [Labor Management Relations Act] in order to recharacterize a state law complaint displaced by § 502(a)(1)(B) as an action arising under federal law. In Franchise Tax Bd. of Cal. v. Construction Laborers Vacation Trust for Southern Cal., 463 U.S. 1 (1983), the Court held that ERISA preemption, without more, does not convert a claim into an action arising under federal law. The Court suggested, however, that a state action that was not only preempted by ERISA, but also came "within the scope of § 502 of ERISA" might fall within the *Avco* rule. The claim in this case, unlike the state tax collection suit in *Franchise Tax Board,* is within the scope of § 502(a) and we therefore must face the question specifically reserved by *Franchise Tax Board.*

The Court observed that "[i]n the absence of explicit direction from Congress, this question would be a close one." But it found in the legislative history of ERISA express references to the Labor Management Relations Act and inferred from this that Congress wanted the two statutes to be interpreted similarly.[e]

Justice Brennan, joined by Justice Marshall, concurred. He said:

> While I join the Court's opinion, I note that our decision should not be interpreted as adopting a broad rule that *any* defense premised on congressional intent to preempt state law is sufficient to establish removal jurisdiction. The Court holds only that removal jurisdiction exists when, as here, "Congress has *clearly* manifested an intent to make causes of action . . . *removable to federal court.*" In future cases involving other statutes, the prudent course for a federal court that does not find a *clear* congressional intent to create removal jurisdiction will be to remand the case to state court.

5. *CATERPILLAR, INC. V. WILLIAMS*

Justice Brennan subsequently wrote the Court's unanimous opinion in Caterpillar, Inc. v. Williams, 482 U.S. 386 (1987), where the Court held the *Avco* rule applicable to claims founded on collective bargaining agreements, but not to claims founded on individual employment contracts. The employer had other preemption arguments, namely that the individual contracts were preempted by the principle of exclusive union representation protected by federal law, that enforcement of the individual contracts were preempted as an unfair labor practice, and that state law claims were preempted by federal defenses requiring interpretation of a collective bargaining agreement. The Court responded:

> It is true that when a defense to a state claim is based on the terms of a collective-bargaining agreement, the state court will have to interpret that agreement to decide whether the state claim survives. But the presence of a federal question, even a § 301 question, in a defensive argument does not overcome the paramount policies embodied in the well-pleaded complaint rule—that the plaintiff is the master of the complaint, that a federal question must appear on the face of the complaint, and that the plaintiff may, by eschewing claims based on federal law, choose to have the cause heard in state court. When a plaintiff invokes a right created by a collective-bargaining agreement, the plaintiff has *chosen* to plead what we have held must be regarded as a federal claim, and removal is at the defendant's option. But a *defendant* cannot, merely by injecting a federal question into an action that asserts what is plainly a state-law claim, transform the action into one arising under federal law, thereby selecting the forum in which the claim shall be litigated. If a defendant could do so, the plaintiff would be master of nothing. Congress has long since decided that federal defenses do not provide a basis for removal.

---

[e]   The Court followed *Metropolitan Life Ins. v. Taylor* in Aetna Health Inc. v. Davila, 542 U.S. 200 (2004). *Aetna Health Inc.* also involved ERISA claims.

6.   QUESTIONS AND COMMENTS

The Court said in *Franchise Tax Board*, that although normally " 'the party who brings the suit is master to decide what law he will rely upon,' it is an independent corollary of the well-pleaded complaint rule that a plaintiff may not defeat removal by omitting to plead necessary federal questions in a complaint." Does the Court in *Beneficial National Bank* correctly resolve the tension between these two statements? Or does Justice Scalia have the better of it?

The assertion of a federal preemption defense to a state law claim filed in state court is likely to occur with some frequency. After these cases, how are the lower courts to determine whether such a claim is removable? Must they decide the merits of the preemption claim before they can determine whether they have jurisdiction? Although the Court was unanimous in *Pilot Life* that ERISA preempted claims of the sort raised in *Taylor,* the answer to that question, as Justice Brennan also said in his *Taylor* concurrence, "was not obvious."[f] How would the Supreme Court have decided *Taylor* had it not decided *Pilot Life* on the same day?

Consider the debate initiated by Gil Seinfeld, The Puzzle of Complete Preemption, 155 U. Pa. L. Rev. 537 (2007), responded to in Trevor W. Morrison, Complete Preemption and the Separation of Powers, 155 U. Pa. L. Rev. Pennumbra 186 (2007), http://www.pennlawreview.com/responses/index.php?id=13, and in Paul E. McGreal, In Defense of Complete Preemption, 155 U. Pa. L. Rev. Pennumbra 147 (2007), http://www.pennlaw review.com/responses/index.php?id=24.

Seinfeld argues that, out of respect for the core values underlying federal question jurisdiction, "the jurisprudence of complete preemption might stand on firmer ground if the availability of federal defense removal turned on the breadth of the preemptive statute relied upon by the defendant." This requires, in his view, a case-by-case determination that "distinguishes those federal statutes that are so robustly preemptive as to merit special jurisdictional treatment from those that are not." Morrison's response is that this is all well and good, but "[c]ourts are ill-suited to perform this sort of policy-based balancing. Congress, in contrast, is well suited to the task." McGreal argues that they are both wrong. They conceive the doctrine as an exception to the well-pleaded complaint rule that requires special justification. He believes it is a corollary to that rule, a doctrine that "recharacterizes preempted state law claims according to their true federal nature." He concludes that the complete preemption doctrine "eliminates [a plaintiff's] perverse incentive" and therefore "ought to be retained."

See also Ernest A. Young, Stalking the Yeti: Protective Jurisdiction, Foreign Affairs Removal, and Complete Preemption, 95 Calif. L. Rev. 1775

---

[f]   Justice O'Connor responded on this point: "[T]he touchstone of the federal district court's removal jurisdiction is not the 'obviousness' of the preemption defense but the intent of Congress. Indeed, . . . even an 'obvious' preemption defense does not, in most cases, create removal jurisdiction. In this case, however, Congress has clearly manifested an intent to make causes of action within the scope of the civil enforcement provisions of § 502(a) removable to a federal court. . . . Accordingly, this suit, though it purports to raise only state law claims, is necessarily federal in character by virtue of the clearly manifested intent of Congress."

(2007), and Margaret Tarkington, Rejecting the Touchstone: Complete Preemption and Congressional Intent after *Beneficial National Bank v. Anderson*, 59 S.C. L. Rev. 225 (2008). Young analogizes complete preemption to protective jurisdiction: "Like protective jurisdiction, complete preemption ultimately rests on the notion that 'arising under' federal law should be interpreted expansively to cover not only cases in which federal law provides the rule of decision but also cases in which a federal forum for *state* claims is deemed necessary to protect federal interests stemming from a federal regulatory scheme." Tarkington rejects the Seinfeld position, and aligns herself more closely with Morrison. She argues that *Beneficial National Bank* "creates a policy-bankrupt allocation of state and federal jurisdiction" and that the proper "test for complete preemption [should be] based on congressional intent of removability."[g]

CONCLUDING NOTES ON THE PRIMACY OF SUBJECT MATTER JURISDICTION

1. INTRODUCTION

Rule 12(h)(3) of the Federal Rules of Civil Procedure provides that "[w]henever it appears by suggestion of the parties or otherwise that the court lacks jurisdiction of the subject matter, the court shall dismiss the action." This requirement operates at all levels of adjudication. If an appellate court notices at any stage of the proceedings that the district court lacked subject matter jurisdiction, it is obliged to order dismissal of the case for lack of jurisdiction and is foreclosed from reaching the merits of the case.

2. HYPOTHETICAL JURISDICTION: *STEEL CO. V. CITIZENS FOR A BETTER ENVIRONMENT*

In Steel Co. v. Citizens for a Better Environment, 523 U.S. 83 (1998), six Justices concluded that the plaintiff lacked Article III standing to bring suit under a federal statute. In the course of its opinion on the standing question, the Court, in an opinion by Justice Scalia, described a jurisdictional practice that had grown up in the Courts of Appeals:

---

[g] For an analysis of how the issue had been approached prior to *Taylor,* see Mary Twitchell, Characterizing Federal Claims: Preemption, Removal, and the Arising-Under Jurisdiction of the Federal Courts, 54 Geo. Wash. L. Rev. 812 (1986). Twitchell proposes a three-part test: "whether Congress has given plaintiff an express cause of action" for some of the relief sought in state court; if so, "whether defendant could reasonably argue that Congress intended that the regulatory scheme preempt plaintiff's asserted state law claim"; and if so, whether in fact the state claim is preempted. Applying her approach, she correctly predicted the result in *Taylor.*

See also Michael G. Collins, The Unhappy History of Federal Question Removal, 71 Iowa L. Rev. 717 (1986), which argues that the Court's federal defense removal cases incorrectly interpret the congressional intent; Garrick B. Pursley, Rationalizing Complete Preemption after *Beneficial National Bank v. Anderson*: A New Rule, a New Justification, 54 Drake L. Rev. 371 (2006), which applauds the decision as a "useful revision" of this area of the law; Robert A. Ragazzo, Reconsidering the Artful Pleading Doctrine, 44 Hastings L.J. 273 (1993), which argues that the Court "should reconsider its ill-advised departure from the traditional jurisdictional principles in *Avco*"; A. Mark Segreti, The Federal Preemption Question—A Federal Question? An Analysis of Federal Jurisdiction over Supremacy Clause Issues, 33 Cleve. St. L. Rev. 653 (1984–85), concluding that "[i]f federal law has preemptive force, the dispute 'arises under' federal law."

> [S]everal Courts of Appeals . . . find it proper to proceed imme-
> diately to the merits . . . despite jurisdictional objections, at least
> where (1) the merits question is more readily resolved, and (2) the
> prevailing party on the merits would be the same as the prevailing
> party were jurisdiction denied. The Ninth Circuit has denominated
> this practice—which it characterizes as "assuming" jurisdiction for
> the purpose of deciding the merits—the "doctrine of hypothetical
> jurisdiction."

The Court made it clear that such a doctrine was unacceptable:[a]

> We decline to endorse such an approach because it carries the
> courts beyond the bounds of authorized judicial action and thus of-
> fends fundamental principles of separation of powers. . . . This
> Court's insistence that proper jurisdiction appear begins at least as
> early as 1804, when we set aside a judgment for the defendant at
> the instance of the losing plaintiff *who had himself* failed to allege
> the basis for federal jurisdiction. Capron v. Van Noorden, 6 U.S. (2
> Cranch) 126 (1804). . . . Hypothetical jurisdiction produces nothing
> more than a hypothetical judgment—which comes to the same
> thing as an advisory opinion, disapproved by this Court from the
> beginning. Much more than legal niceties are at stake here. The
> statutory and (especially) constitutional elements of jurisdiction
> are an essential ingredient of separation and equilibration of pow-
> ers, restraining the courts from acting at certain times, and even
> restraining them from acting permanently regarding certain sub-
> jects. For a court to pronounce upon the meaning or the constitu-
> tionality of a state or federal law when it has no jurisdiction to do
> so is, by very definition, for a court to act ultra vires.

> Justice Breyer disagreed: "The Constitution does not impose a rigid ju-
> dicial 'order of operations,' when doing so would cause serious practical
> problems. . . . I would not make the ordinary sequence an absolute require-
> ment."

3.   IN PERSONAM VS. SUBJECT MATTER JURISDICTION: *RUHRGAS AG
     V. MARATHON OIL CO.*

In Ruhrgas AG v. Marathon Oil Co., 526 U.S. 574 (1999), Justice Ginsburg wrote for a unanimous Court:

> If as Steel Co. v. Citizens for a Better Environment, 523 U.S. 83
> (1998), held, jurisdiction generally must precede merits in disposi-
> tional order, must subject-matter jurisdiction precede personal
> jurisdiction on the decisional line? . . .

> We hold that . . . there is no unyielding jurisdictional hierar-
> chy. Customarily, a federal court first resolves doubts about its
> jurisdiction over the subject matter, but there are circumstances in

---

   [a]   For extensive consideration of *Steel*, see Scott C. Idelman, The Demise of Hypothetical
Jurisdiction in the Federal Courts, 52 Vand. L. Rev. 235 (1999); Joan Steinman, After *Steel Co.*:
"Hypothetical Jurisdiction" in the Federal Appellate Courts, 58 Wash. & Lee L. Rev. 855 (2001).

which a district court appropriately accords priority to a personal jurisdiction inquiry. The proceeding before us is such a case. . . .

The Court of Appeals accorded priority to the requirement of subject-matter jurisdiction because it is nonwaivable and delimits federal-court power, while restrictions on a court's jurisdiction over the person are waivable and protect individual rights. The character of the two jurisdictional bedrocks unquestionably differs. Subject-matter limitations on federal jurisdiction serve institutional interests. They keep the federal courts within the bounds the Constitution and Congress have prescribed. Accordingly, subject-matter delineations must be policed by the courts on their own initiative even at the highest level. . . .

These distinctions do not mean that subject-matter jurisdiction is ever and always the more "fundamental." . . . While *Steel Co.* reasoned that subject-matter jurisdiction necessarily precedes a ruling on the merits, the same principle does not dictate a sequencing of jurisdictional issues. . . . It is hardly novel for a federal court to choose among threshold grounds for denying audience to a case on the merits. [D]istrict courts do not overstep Article III limits when they decline jurisdiction of state-law claims on discretionary grounds without determining whether those claims fall within their pendent jurisdiction, see Moor v. County of Alameda, 411 U.S. 693, 715–16 (1973), or abstain under Younger v. Harris, 401 U.S. 37 (1971), without deciding whether the parties present a case or controversy, see Ellis v. Dyson, 421 U.S. 426, 433–34 (1975). . . .

Where, as here, . . . a district court has before it a straightforward personal jurisdiction issue presenting no complex question of state law, and the alleged defect in subject-matter jurisdiction raises a difficult and novel question, the court does not abuse its discretion by turning directly to personal jurisdiction.

4. FORUM NON CONVENIENS AND SUBJECT MATTER JURISDICTION: *SINOCHEM INTERNATIONAL V. MALAYSIA INT'L SHIPPING*

The *Ruhrgas* result was affirmed in another context in Sinochem International v. Malaysia International Shipping, 549 U.S. 422 (2007). The case involved a Malaysian corporation that sued a Chinese corporation in a U.S. federal court over a controversy that was then in litigation in a Chinese court. In an opinion by Justice Ginsburg, the Court unanimously concluded:

This is a textbook case for immediate forum non conveniens dismissal. The District Court's subject-matter jurisdiction presented an issue of first impression in the Third Circuit, and was considered at some length by the courts below. Discovery concerning personal jurisdiction would have burdened Sinochem with expense and delay. And all to scant purpose: The District Court inevitably would dismiss the case without reaching the merits, given its well-considered forum non conveniens appraisal. Judicial economy is disserved by continuing litigation in the Eastern District of

Pennsylvania given the proceedings long launched in China. And the gravamen of Malaysia International's complaint . . . is an issue best left for determination by the Chinese courts.

If, however, a court can readily determine that it lacks jurisdiction over the cause or the defendant, the proper course would be to dismiss on that ground. In the mine run of cases, jurisdiction "will involve no arduous inquiry" and both judicial economy and the consideration ordinarily accorded the plaintiff's choice of forum "should impel the federal court to dispose of [those] issue[s] first." *Ruhrgas*, 526 U.S. at 587–88. But where subject-matter or personal jurisdiction is difficult to determine, and forum non conveniens considerations weigh heavily in favor of dismissal, the court properly takes the less burdensome course.

SECTION 2. DIVERSITY JURISDICTION

INTRODUCTORY NOTES ON DIVERSITY JURISDICTION

1.   THE DEBATE

Congress conferred diversity jurisdiction on the federal courts in the Judiciary Act of 1789. Despite frequent calls for its abolition, diversity jurisdiction has been a feature of the federal court system since then. But surprisingly, there is no consensus on why the authorizing clause was included in Article III, why the first Congress included diversity cases in the Judiciary Act of 1789, or whether the diversity jurisdiction should be retained.

The generally accepted rationale for diversity jurisdiction is protection of the nonresident litigant from local prejudice. Yet Henry J. Friendly, The Historic Basis of Diversity Jurisdiction, 41 Harv. L. Rev. 483 (1928), reported that the diversity clause "was not a product of difficulties that had been acutely felt under the Confederation" and that "such information as we are able to gather . . . entirely fails to show the existence of prejudice on the part of the state judges."[a] Friendly did find two concerns.

First, said Friendly, "a careful reading of the arguments of the time will show that the real fear was not of state courts so much as of state legislatures." A particular concern was that local legislation would favor resident debtors: "the desire to protect creditors against legislation favorable to debtors was a principal reason for the grant of diversity jurisdiction, and that . . . reason . . . was by no means without validity."

---

[a]   John P. Frank, The Case for Diversity Jurisdiction, 16 Harv. J. Legis. 403, 406 (1979), argued in response that fear of local prejudice "was largely a gloomy anticipation of things to come rather than an experienced evil. . . ." See also James William Moore and Donald T. Weckstein, Diversity Jurisdiction: Past, Present, and Future, 43 Tex. L. Rev. 1, 15 (1964); E. Farish Percy, Making a Federal Case of It: Removing Civil Cases to Federal Court Based on Fraudulent Joinder, 91 Iowa L. Rev. 189 (2005). Deirdre Mask and Paul MacMahon, The Revolutionary War Prize Cases and the Origins of Diversity Jurisdiction, 63 Buff. L. Rev. 477 (2015), conclude that "the Prize Case experience rehabilitates the view that geographic bias was a driving force behind the grant of diversity jurisdiction to the federal courts."

Second, although hostility to out-of-state litigants was not apparent, "there were other grounds for distrust of the local courts. The method of appointment and the tenure of the judges were not of the sort to invite confidence." In all but two states, judges were selected by the legislatures, and in many the legislatures could also remove them. The "practical workings of the system" also were suspect. In Connecticut, for example, all judges were appointed by members of the Council, who then felt free to appear as advocates before the courts. In addition, the Council acted as the Supreme Court, thus reviewing cases which some of its members had tried. To make matters worse, Council members would occasionally argue their cases before the Council itself, and on some occasions Council members were appointed judges of lower courts and later permitted to sit in review of their own decisions. Friendly concluded:

> Not unnaturally the commercial interests of the country were reluctant to expose themselves to the hazards of litigation before such courts as these. They might be good enough for the inhabitants of their respective states, but merchants from abroad felt themselves entitled to something better. There was a vague feeling that the new courts would be strong courts, creditors' courts, business men's courts.[b]

Today, of course, local law cannot be avoided by resort to federal courts. Erie R. Co. v. Tompkins, 304 U.S. 64 (1938). Some have argued, however, that cases should be channeled to federal courts because they are better than state courts and that since out-of-state litigants have no opportunity to participate in reforms of local courts, they should not be required to appear before them.[c] It has also been argued that "diversity jurisdiction is an indispensable condition to the free flow of capital from one part of the nation to another."[d]

---

[b]   Robert L. Jones, Finishing a Friendly Argument: The Jury and the Historical Origins of Diversity Jurisdiction, 82 N.Y.U. L. Rev. 997 (2007), examines the historical sources at length and concludes that it was the prospect of controlling the composition of federal juries that was the primary motivation for establishing the diversity jurisdiction.—[Footnote by eds.]

[c]   See, e.g., David L. Shapiro, Federal Diversity Jurisdiction: A Survey and A Proposal, 91 Harv. L. Rev. 317, 329 (1977). Shapiro adds that there "may also be warrant for affording an out-of-state lawyer a procedure with which he is likely to be familiar because it is in force in the federal court in his own state."

[d]   Chief Justice Taft argued before the American Bar Association in 1922 that "no single element in our governmental system has done so much to secure capital for the legitimate development of enterprise, throughout the West and South." 47 Reports of the American Bar Association 250, 259 (1922). Compare the comments in Adrienne Marsh, Diversity Jurisdiction: Scapegoat of Overcrowded Federal Courts, 48 Brooklyn L. Rev. 197, 208–09 (1982) (which contains extensive citations to the relevant literature):

> In the 1980s, the corporate entity is a major force in interstate investments and development. Large corporations have come to rely on the unified system of federal jurisprudence. They customarily retain major law firms, who, from time-to-time, are called upon to represent their corporate clients in federal courts throughout the country. If national corporations were compelled to litigate in state courts, it would become necessary for them to retain numerous local attorneys. The inconvenience and increased costs of litigation caused by the use of correspondent attorneys would be compounded by trials held in county courthouses, which are often remote from air terminals.

2.   THE TRADITIONAL CASE FOR RETENTION

John P. Frank, an influential attorney from Arizona, has been a prominent spokesman for the retention of diversity jurisdiction. See John P. Frank, The Case for Diversity Jurisdiction, 16 Harv. J. Legis. 403 (1979), which suggests that there "is no reason to suppose that any appreciable group of private practitioners in the United States" supports abolition; the "position of the private practitioners is solid regardless of the interests they represent."[e] He elaborates:

> There is no substantial reason that is or can be advanced for [abolition of diversity jurisdiction] except the commendable desire to lighten the load on the federal courts. The difficulty with lightening that load is that necessarily the load must be increased on the state courts. Yet there is no profit in transferring cases from one logjam to another. Diversity jurisdiction must be seen for what it is, a social service of the federal government provided for the people of the United States. A primary function of the legal profession is to settle disputes. The diversity jurisdiction provides an opportunity for settling those disputes. In one sense, it can be compared to the school lunch program or the federal highway program or any other program by which the federal government serves the general public. . . . It is the oldest single federal social service. It comes to us quite literally from the hands of George Washington, James Madison, and Oliver Ellsworth.

Frank added two points. First, there is the number of cases disposed of, on the order of 30,000 when Frank wrote in 1979, and many more today. The general manner in which these cases have been tried and settled has led to the "general feeling that justice in federal courts is being well administered. There is no widespread, obvious abuse to be corrected." Second, there is "the educational value of having two systems in interaction." The development of the Federal Rules of Civil Procedure has had a positive impact on state procedures and, he continues, the fact that federal courts must constantly look to state law has led to positive changes in federal procedures. Moreover, the diversity jurisdiction "puts the whole litigation bar" into federal courts, rather than limiting dual exposure to those specialists who tend to litigate federal question cases. This in turn, he concludes, has an educational effect on the bar, which feeds law reform in both systems.

---

[e]   Charles Allen Wright has characterized the bar's strong support of diversity as follows:

I believe the basis for their position is not that they love the state courts less but that they love a choice of forum more. Of course it is tactically advantageous to be able to choose, and to pick for each case the system of courts in which a favorable result seems more likely. But surely our dual court structure was created to serve some loftier purpose than tactical maneuvering. It is dismaying to see respected bar groups asserting a vested interest in preserving jurisdictional statutes that have developed quite fortuitously and that are demonstrably irrational, unclear, inefficient, and productive of unnecessary friction.

Charles Alan Wright, Restructuring Federal Jurisdiction: The American Law Institute Proposals, 26 Wash. & Lee L. Rev. 185, 207 (1969).

3. The Traditional Case for Abolition

Charles Allen Wright stated the case against diversity jurisdiction in testimony before the Senate in 1978.[f] He made three major points. The first was the burden that diversity cases place on federal courts. A time study in 1969–70, he pointed out, showed that while diversity cases constituted 26.2 per cent of the civil docket of the district courts, 37.9 per cent of the time district judges spent on civil cases was devoted to diversity litigation. Given the other demands on the federal courts, he concluded, "diversity cases are a luxury we can no longer afford." Second, he argued that prejudice against out-of-state litigants is no longer a significant factor in the administration of justice in state court systems, even though there may be anecdotal evidence of an occasional abuse. Finally, he argued that the complexity of diversity cases is largely a function of their litigation in federal courts; many such cases could be much more straightforwardly resolved in state court:

> It was Mr. Frank himself . . . who made the penetrating insight that a case is a series of decision points, and that the goal of law reform must be to reduce the number and complexity of these decision points.
>
> Whether a case is properly within the diversity jurisdiction of the federal courts is a wholly useless decision point that vanishes if the case is brought in state court. This is a decision point of great complexity, because the rules of federal jurisdiction are far from being bright lines. Lawyers can easily be mistaken about those rules, and judges frequently must spend much time deciding and writing lengthy opinions about whether jurisdiction exists. In my multi-volume treatise, my collaborators and I devote 414 pages to the rules on diversity jurisdiction. . . . Amount in controversy has always been almost entirely a problem in diversity litigation. . . . [These rules] detain us for another 156 pages. We have a 32-page section on removal in diversity cases, and much of the rest of the 257-page chapter on removal deals with problems that are peculiar to diversity cases. . . .

Wright also noted that most of the 199 pages in his treatise devoted to venue concerned diversity problems, and that the task of ascertaining local law under *Erie* presents perhaps the most imposing difficulty. He concluded that abolition of diversity jurisdiction would mean "that litigants and judges no longer need be concerned about these problems and can go immediately to the merits of the case, rather than wasting time on unnecessary preliminary issues of this kind."[g]

---

[f] Hearings before the Subcommittee on Improvements in Judicial Machinery of the Committee on the Judiciary, United States Senate, 95th Cong., 2d Sess. 45–48 (1978).

[g] For an important addition to the abolition side of the debate, see Thomas Rowe, Abolish Diversity Jurisdiction: Positive Side Effects and Potential for Further Reforms, 92 Harv. L. Rev. 963 (1979). Rowe argued that "the considerable simplification in federal practice resulting from abolition would be an important benefit," as would "decisional developments and statutory and rule reforms that are now difficult or impossible because of problems that flow from diversity jurisdiction." See also David Crump, The Case for Restricting Diversity Jurisdiction: The Undeveloped Arguments, From the Race to the Bottom to the Substitution Effect, 62 Me. L. Rev. 1

Finally, note the concluding observations, which could as well have been written yesterday, made by Henry Friendly in his 1928 article quoted above:

> The steady expansion of the jurisdiction of the federal courts, especially since Reconstruction days, has been but a reflex of the general growth of federal political power. That growth will not abate, since it is responsive to deep social and economic causes. Only one aspect of the work of the federal courts is out of the current of these nationalizing forces—the jurisdiction based on diversity of citizenship. . . . The unifying tendencies of America here make for a recession of jurisdiction to the states, rather than an extension of federal authority. The pressure of distinctly federal litigation may call for relief of business that intrinsically belongs to the state courts. How far, if at all, the United States courts should be left with jurisdiction merely because the parties are citizens of different states is a question which calls for critical re-examination of the practical bases of diversity jurisdiction.

4.   STRAWBRIDGE V. CURTISS

Strawbridge v. Curtiss, 7 U.S. (3 Cranch) 267 (1806), established an important modern premise of diversity jurisdiction. Citizens of Massachusetts sued a citizen of Vermont and other citizens of Massachusetts. The question was whether "complete" diversity was required, that is, whether the presence of Massachusetts citizens on both sides of the case was fatal to the jurisdiction. In a brief and cryptic opinion, the Court held that complete diversity was required. This holding survives as an interpretation of the general diversity statute, though it is well settled that complete diversity is not constitutionally required. See State Farm Fire & Cas. Co. v. Tashire, 386

(2010); Robert J. Sheran and Barbara Isaacman, State Cases Belong in State Courts, 12 Creighton L. Rev. 1 (1978).

Larry Kramer, Diversity Jurisdiction, 1990 B.Y.U. L. Rev. 97, concluded that with three exceptions (aliens, interpleader, complex multistate litigation), diversity should be abolished. As a fall-back position, he suggested limitations. These included limiting the types of damages that count in satisfying the jurisdictional amount (e.g., eliminating punitive damages, attorney fees, and pain and suffering), barring plaintiffs from invoking diversity in their own states, and expanding corporate citizenship so as to limit the range of cases in which complete diversity can be shown.

It is concluded in Debra Lyn Bassett, The Hidden Bias in Diversity Jurisdiction, 81 Wash. U. L.Q. 119 (2003), that "[w]hat has been missed in [the diversity] debate is that, far from being an antidote to local bias, diversity jurisdiction today embodies, and indeed promotes, a form of bias by its very existence—a bias against rural areas so pervasive as to require the abolition of diversity jurisdiction."

U.S. 523 (1967).[h] And the fetish for "complete diversity" does not always prevail.[i]

5.   INTERPRETATION OF THE DIVERSITY STATUTE

As Charles Alan Wright said in his Senate testimony, the details of litigation concerning when diversity jurisdiction exists involve complex and often arcane issues that would require many pages to unfold, too many to justify complete treatment here. There may be value, however, in a brief overview of general principles.

Aliens aside, a person must be a "citizen of a state" in order to invoke diversity jurisdiction. Citizenship for this purpose has two prerequisites: one must be a citizen of the United States, and must be domiciled in a particular state. A person can have only one domicile at a time.[j] Diversity is determined

---

[h]   Indeed, the one context in which everyone agrees that diversity jurisdiction should be retained requires only "minimal" diversity. Interpleader suits typically involve an effort to resolve multiple claims to a single fund in one lawsuit. Since the multiple claimants may be from different states and may not all be subject to service of process in any single state, sometimes no state court can adjudicate such a suit. The Federal Interpleader Act provides for nationwide service of process and for federal subject matter jurisdiction where any two claimants are diverse. See 28 U.S.C. §§ 1335, 2361. For discussion of the theory and mechanics of interpleader, see Geoffrey C. Hazard, Jr. and Myron Moscovitz, An Historical and Critical Analysis of Interpleader, 52 Calif. L. Rev. 706 (1964); Werner Ilsen and William Sardell, Interpleader in the Federal Courts, 35 St. John's L. Rev. 1 (1960). For the proposal of an analogous new type of diversity jurisdiction for complex multi-state tort and products liability claims, see Thomas D. Rowe, Jr. and Kenneth D. Sibley, Beyond Diversity: Federal Multiparty, Multiform Jurisdiction, 135 U. Pa. L. Rev. 7 (1986). For a response to Rowe and Sibley and criticism of an ALI proposal based on their work, see C. Douglas Floyd, The Limits of Minimal Diversity, 55 Hastings L.J. 613 (2004).

In the Class Action Fairness Act of 2005, PL 109–2, 119 Stat. 4, Congress provided for diversity jurisdiction in certain kinds of cases based on incomplete diversity. It included amendments to 28 U.S.C. § 1332 and 28 U.S.C. § 1335, and added 28 U.S.C. § 1453.

[i]   In Caterpillar Inc. v. Lewis, 519 U.S. 61 (1996), complete diversity did not exist at the time of removal. But it did at the time of trial, and the Court held unanimously that a jury verdict should not be set aside. "[C]onsiderations of finality, efficiency, and economy . . . overwhelm[ed]" the technical arguments for dismissal.

The *Caterpillar* rationale did not prevail, however, in Grupo Dataflux v. Atlas Global Group, L.P., 541 U.S. 567 (2004). In that case the Court held, by a five-to-four vote, that a post-filing change in citizenship that cured a defect in diversity jurisdiction did not save the verdict. At the time of filing, Atlas was a partnership with members in Mexico, Texas, and Delaware. It sued Grupo, a citizen of Mexico. Three years later, a six-day trial resulted in a verdict for Atlas. Because partnerships are citizens of each place in which any of its partners is a citizen, diversity was lacking when the suit was filed. In a transaction unrelated to the suit, the Mexican partners left the partnership a month before the trial. The jurisdictional issue was not identified until after the verdict. Justice Scalia for the majority held that there should be no exception on these facts to the rule that "jurisdiction . . . depends on the state of things at the time of the action brought." For herself and the other dissenters (Stevens, Souter, and Breyer), Justice Ginsburg said that "salvage operations are ordinarily preferable to the wrecking ball."

[j]   Determination of domicile is often difficult. Its formal definition is "that place where he has his true, fixed, and permanent home and principal establishment, and to which he has the intention of returning whenever he is absent therefrom." Charles Alan Wright, The Law of Federal Courts 146 (4th ed. 1983). A citizen of the United States who is domiciled abroad cannot be a "citizen of a state" for purposes of diversity. A citizen of the United States who has two homes and who divides his or her time equally between them must nonetheless be found to be "domiciled" in one of them. For discussion of some of the difficulties of the concept, see Donald T. Weckstein, Citizenship for Purposes of Diversity Jurisdiction, 26 Sw. L.J. 360 (1972); David P. Currie, The Federal Courts and the American Law Institute, 36 U. Chi. L. Rev. 1, 8–12 (1968). By what standard of proof are contested facts determined on issues related to subject matter jurisdiction? See Kevin M. Clermont, Jurisdictional Fact, 91 Cornell L. Rev. 973 (2006).

as of the time the suit is filed and must be alleged in the pleadings and proved if challenged. A later change of domicile will not affect the court's jurisdiction. As with any question of subject matter jurisdiction, a failure of diversity can be noticed at any point in the litigation—even on appeal—and requires dismissal of the case. With three exceptions—in rem actions involving property already in the custody of a state court, domestic relations cases, and probate cases[k]—a diversity action can involve any kind of dispute. It is the status of the parties rather than the subject matter of the lawsuit that determines jurisdiction.[l]

Among the many potentially complicated details of diversity jurisdiction is determining the citizenship of a corporation. Section 1332(c) provides that "a corporation shall be deemed to be a citizen of any State by which it has been incorporated and of the State where it has its principal place of business." The circuits diverged in their treatment of the principal place of business, some focusing on the volume of business activity in a state and others looking to the location of the corporate headquarters or "nerve center." In Hertz Corp. v. Friend, 559 U.S. 77 (2010), two California citizens sued Hertz, a Delaware corporation with its headquarters in New Jersey, for violations of California law. Hertz tried to remove the case to federal court, but the court found that, because Hertz did more business in California than in any other single state, California was its principal place of business. The Supreme Court unanimously disagreed. Speaking through Justice Breyer, the Court reasoned that the nerve center approach was consistent with the statutory language referencing a particular place within a state. The business activities test, in contrast, led some courts "to look, not at a particular place within a State, but incorrectly at the State itself, measuring the total amount

---

[k] In Marshall v. Marshall, 547 U.S. 293 (2006), Justice Stevens wrote "separately to explain why I do not believe there is any 'probate exception' that ousts a federal court of jurisdiction it otherwise possesses." The Court held in *Marshall* that Texas could not oust the jurisdiction of a federal bankruptcy court by conferring exclusive jurisdiction on its probate courts to hear related claims of tortious interference. It also said that "the probate exception reserves to the state probate courts the probate or annulment of a will and the administration of a decedent's estate; it also precludes federal courts from endeavoring to dispose of property that is in the custody of a probate court. But it does not bar federal courts from adjudicating matters outside those confines and otherwise within federal jurisdiction."

In Ankenbrandt v. Richards, 504 U.S. 689 (1992), the Court reaffirmed the exception to diversity jurisdiction in cases of "divorce, alimony, and child custody decrees." The exception was held inapplicable to a tort action seeking damages for physical and sexual abuse of two children. In an opinion by Justice White, the Court rested the exception "on Congress's apparent acceptance of this construction of the diversity jurisdiction" as it reenacted the statute over the years. Justice Blackmun thought the older cases "precedent at most for continued discretionary abstention rather than mandatory limits on federal jurisdiction." Justice Stevens, joined by Justice Thomas, concurred in the judgment on the ground that the Court should not have speculated about the continued vitality of an exception that everyone agreed would not apply.

James E. Pfander and Emily K. Damrau, A Non-Contentious Account of Article III's Domestic Relations Exception, 92 Notre Dame L. Rev. 117 (2016), considers *Ankenbrandt* in the broader context of offering "a novel non-contentious view of the domestic relations exception."

[l] Many have argued against allowing a local plaintiff to file a diversity action in federal court against an out-of-state defendant. Perhaps as much as 50 percent of diversity litigation would be eliminated if this rule were changed. See Adrienne Marsh, Diversity Jurisdiction: Scapegoat of Overcrowded Federal Courts, 48 Brooklyn L. Rev. 197, 222 (1982). The statute permits in-state plaintiffs to file diversity suits in federal court, even though it does not permit in-state defendants who are sued to state court by out-of-state plaintiffs to remove such actions to federal court.

of business activities that the corporation conducts there and determining whether they are 'significantly larger' than in the next-ranking State." On that analysis, every national retailer would be deemed a citizen of California.

The Court also cited ease of administration. While a corporation's business activities might be scattered across the entire country, focusing on the corporate nerve center suggests a single location. Administrative simplicity was thought particularly important for a jurisdictional statute:

> Complex jurisdictional tests complicate a case, eating up time and money as the parties litigate, not the merits of their claims, but which court is the right court to decide those claims. Complex tests produce appeals and reversals, encourage gamesmanship, and, again, diminish the likelihood that results and settlements will reflect a claim's legal and factual merits. Judicial resources too are at stake. Courts have an independent obligation to determine whether subject-matter jurisdiction exists, even when no party challenges it. So courts benefit from straightforward rules under which they can readily assure themselves of their power to hear a case.

The Court acknowledged that there might be hard cases, but thought that the nerve center approach "nonetheless points courts in a single direction, towards the center of overall direction, control, and coordination."

There are many rules about whose citizenship counts. For example, in Navarro Savings Association v. Lee, 446 U.S. 458 (1980), the Supreme Court faced the question "whether the trustees of a business trust may invoke the diversity jurisdiction of the federal courts on the basis of their own citizenship, rather than that of the trust's beneficial shareholders." The Court held that the trustees could sue because they were the real parties in interest. They held legal title to the trust assets, managed the assets, and had legal power to control the litigation.[m] Similar problems arose in the context of estate administration, until that question was specifically resolved in 1988 by a statutory amendment stating that the legal representative of a decedent's estate "shall be deemed to be a citizen only of the same State as the decedent." See 28 U.S.C. § 1332(c)(2). The same is true of the representative of an infant or an incompetent. Unincorporated associations are citizens of each state of which any member is a citizen.[n]

Note that the alignment of the parties in the pleadings is not conclusive. The court is obligated to examine the "real interests" of the parties, place them on one side or another of the dispute, and determine the existence of

---

[m] In Carden v. Arkoma Associates, 494 U.S. 185 (1990), a divided Court, rejecting an analogy to *Navarro*, held that the citizenship of limited as well as general partners counts in determining the existence of complete diversity. In Americold Realty Trust v. Conagra Foods, Inc., 577 U.S. ___, 136 S.Ct. 1012 (2016), the Court also rejected an analogy to *Navarro*, holding unanimously that the citizenship of a real estate investment trust was measured by the citizenship of its shareholders. A similar problem arises in the interpretation of § 1332(a)(2), which establishes federal court jurisdiction for suits between "citizens of a State and citizens or subjects of a foreign state." In JPMorgan Chase Bank v. Traffic Stream (BVI) Infrastructure Ltd., 536 U.S. 88 (2002), the court held unanimously that a corporation organized under the laws of the British Virgin Islands was a "citizen . . . of a foreign state" even though the British Virgin Islands is a British Overseas Territory rather than a separately recognized sovereign state.

[n] United Steelworkers of America AFL-CIO v. R.H. Bouligny, Inc., 382 U.S. 145 (1965).

complete diversity based on the proper alignment. The leading case is City of Indianapolis v. Chase National Bank, 314 U.S. 63 (1941). A gas company had issued bonds, which were secured by a mortgage on which the bank was trustee. The bank, a citizen of New York, sued the gas company, a citizen of Indiana, and the city of Indianapolis, also a citizen of Indiana. The issue was whether the city had become a party to a lease from the gas company that made it, the city, liable for interest on the bonds. The Court held that the "primary" issue was whether the city was bound by the lease, and that on this issue the bank and the gas company were on the same side. Hence it realigned the parties and held that diversity jurisdiction did not exist.[o]

Finally, there is the required jurisdictional amount. The original diversity statute in 1789 fixed a jurisdictional amount of $500, which was raised over the years to the current figure of $75,000. It is not required that the plaintiff actually recover that amount—such a requirement would make the initial jurisdiction of the court turn on the ultimate resolution of the merits of the controversy. What is required is that the plaintiff make a good faith claim for a sum in excess of $75,000.

6. SUPPLEMENTAL JURISDICTION

In the traditional terminology, "pendent" jurisdiction referred to the ability of the plaintiff to attach a claim over which the court would not have independent subject matter jurisdiction to a claim over which the court did have jurisdiction. "Ancillary" jurisdiction referred to the ability of the defendant to assert claims that would not themselves satisfy the court's subject matter jurisdiction to a plaintiff's claims that did. In 1990 Congress codified both pendent and ancillary jurisdiction under the new label of "supplemental" jurisdiction. See 28 U.S.C. § 1367. The statute's primary purpose was to overrule Finley v. United States, 490 U.S. 545 (1989), which refused to allow pendent party jurisdiction in federal question cases.

The statutory scheme is to grant supplemental jurisdiction in subsection (a) over "all other claims that are so related to claims in the action within [the district court's] original jurisdiction that they form part of the same case or controversy under Article III." Subsection (b) then withdraws supplemental jurisdiction in some diversity cases. The next main case concerns the meaning and scope of the 1990 statute.

---

[o]   Realignment difficulties occur in shareholder's derivative suits, particularly on the question of whether a corporation named as a defendant should be realigned as a plaintiff. See Smith v. Sperling, 354 U.S. 91 (1957); Comment, Director's Failure to Bring Suit, Demand, and the Business Judgment Rule, 3 J. Corp. L. 208 (1977).

Exxon Mobil Corporation v.
Allapattah Services, Inc.

Supreme Court of the United States, 2005.
545 U.S. 546.

■ JUSTICE KENNEDY delivered the opinion of the Court.

These consolidated cases present the question whether a federal court in a diversity action may exercise supplemental jurisdiction over additional plaintiffs whose claims do not satisfy the minimum amount-in-controversy requirement, provided the claims are part of the same case or controversy as the claims of plaintiffs who do allege a sufficient amount in controversy. Our decision turns on the correct interpretation of 28 U.S.C. § 1367. . . .

We hold that, where the other elements of jurisdiction are present and at least one named plaintiff in the action satisfies the amount-in-controversy requirement, § 1367 does authorize supplemental jurisdiction over the claims of other plaintiffs in the same Article III case or controversy, even if those claims are for less than the jurisdictional amount specified in the statute setting forth the requirements for diversity jurisdiction. . . .

I

In 1991, about 10,000 Exxon dealers filed a class-action suit against the Exxon Corporation in the United States District Court for the Northern District of Florida. The dealers alleged an intentional and systematic scheme by Exxon under which they were overcharged for fuel purchased from Exxon. The plaintiffs invoked the District Court's § 1332(a) diversity jurisdiction. After a unanimous jury verdict in favor of the plaintiffs, the District Court certified the case for interlocutory review, asking whether it had properly exercised § 1367 supplemental jurisdiction over the claims of class members who did not meet the jurisdictional minimum amount in controversy. The Court of Appeals for the Eleventh Circuit upheld the District Court's extension of supplemental jurisdiction to these class members. . . .

In the other case now before us the Court of Appeals for the First Circuit took a different position on the meaning of § 1367(a). In that case, a 9-year-old girl sued Star-Kist in a diversity action in the United States District Court for the District of Puerto Rico, seeking damages for unusually severe injuries she received when she sliced her finger on a tuna can. Her family joined in the suit, seeking damages for emotional distress and certain medical expenses. The District Court granted summary judgment to Star-Kist, finding that none of the plaintiffs met the minimum amount-in-controversy requirement. The Court of Appeals for the First Circuit, however, ruled that the injured girl, but not her family members, had made allegations of damages in the requisite amount. . . . The court held that § 1367 authorizes supplemental jurisdiction only when the district court has original jurisdiction over the action, and that in a diversity case original jurisdiction is lacking if one plaintiff fails to satisfy the amount-in-controversy requirement. . . .

II

A

. . . In order to provide a neutral forum for what have come to be known as diversity cases, Congress . . . has granted district courts original jurisdiction in civil actions between citizens of different States, between U.S. citizens and foreign citizens, or by foreign states against U.S. citizens. To ensure that diversity jurisdiction does not flood the federal courts with minor disputes, § 1332(a) requires that the matter in controversy in a diversity case exceed a specified amount, currently $75,000.

Although the district courts may not exercise jurisdiction absent a statutory basis, it is well established—in certain classes of cases—that, once a court has original jurisdiction over some claims in the action, it may exercise supplemental jurisdiction over additional claims that are part of the same case or controversy. The leading modern case for this principle is Mine Workers v. Gibbs, 383 U.S. 715 (1966). In *Gibbs*, the plaintiff alleged the defendant's conduct violated both federal and state law. The District Court, *Gibbs* held, had original jurisdiction over the action based on the federal claims. *Gibbs* confirmed that the District Court had the additional power (though not the obligation) to exercise supplemental jurisdiction over related state claims that arose from the same Article III case or controversy.

As we later noted, the decision allowing jurisdiction over pendent state claims in *Gibbs* did not mention, let alone come to grips with, the text of the jurisdictional statutes and the bedrock principle that federal courts have no jurisdiction without statutory authorization. Finley v. United States, 490 U.S. 545, 548 (1989). In *Finley,* we nonetheless reaffirmed and rationalized *Gibbs* and its progeny by inferring from it the interpretive principle that, in cases involving supplemental jurisdiction over additional claims between parties properly in federal court, the jurisdictional statutes should be read broadly, on the assumption that in this context Congress intended to authorize courts to exercise their full Article III power to dispose of an "entire action before the court [which] comprises but one constitutional 'case.' "

We have not, however, applied *Gibbs's* expansive interpretive approach to other aspects of the jurisdictional statutes. For instance, we have consistently interpreted § 1332 as requiring complete diversity: In a case with multiple plaintiffs and multiple defendants, the presence in the action of a single plaintiff from the same State as a single defendant deprives the district court of original diversity jurisdiction over the entire action. Strawbridge v. Curtiss, 7 U.S. (3 Cranch) 267 (1806); Owen Equipment & Erection Co. v. Kroger, 437 U.S. 365, 375 (1978). The complete diversity requirement is not mandated by the Constitution, State Farm

Fire & Casualty Co. v. Tashire, 386 U.S. 523, 530–31 (1967), or by the plain text of § 1332(a). The Court, nonetheless, has adhered to the complete diversity rule in light of the purpose of the diversity requirement, which is to provide a federal forum for important disputes where state courts might favor, or be perceived as favoring, home-state litigants. The presence of parties from the same State on both sides of a case dispels this concern, eliminating a principal reason for conferring § 1332 jurisdiction over any of the claims in the action. The specific purpose of the complete diversity rule explains both why we have not adopted *Gibbs's* expansive interpretive approach to this aspect of the jurisdictional statute and why *Gibbs* does not undermine the complete diversity rule. In order for a federal court to invoke supplemental jurisdiction under *Gibbs,* it must first have original jurisdiction over at least one claim in the action. Incomplete diversity destroys original jurisdiction with respect to all claims, so there is nothing to which supplemental jurisdiction can adhere.

In contrast to the diversity requirement, most of the other statutory prerequisites for federal jurisdiction, including the federal-question and amount-in-controversy requirements, can be analyzed claim by claim. True, it does not follow by necessity from this that a district court has authority to exercise supplemental jurisdiction over all claims provided there is original jurisdiction over just one. Before the enactment of § 1367, the Court declined in contexts other than the pendent-claim instance to follow *Gibbs's* expansive approach to interpretation of the jurisdictional statutes. The Court took a more restrictive view of the proper interpretation of these statutes in so-called pendent-party cases involving supplemental jurisdiction over claims involving additional parties—plaintiffs or defendants—where the district courts would lack original jurisdiction over claims by each of the parties standing alone.

Thus, with respect to plaintiff-specific jurisdictional requirements, the Court held in Clark v. Paul Gray, Inc., 306 U.S. 583 (1939), that every plaintiff must separately satisfy the amount-in-controversy requirement. Though *Clark* was a federal-question case, at that time federal-question jurisdiction had an amount-in-controversy requirement analogous to the amount-in-controversy requirement for diversity cases. "Proper practice," *Clark* held, "requires that where each of several plaintiffs is bound to establish the jurisdictional amount with respect to his own claim, the suit should be dismissed as to those who fail to show that the requisite amount is involved." The Court reaffirmed this rule, in the context of a class action brought invoking § 1332(a) diversity jurisdiction, in Zahn v. International Paper Co., 414 U.S. 291 (1973). It follows "inescapably" from *Clark,* the Court held in *Zahn,* that "any plaintiff without the jurisdictional amount must be dismissed from the case, even though others allege jurisdictionally sufficient claims."

The Court took a similar approach with respect to supplemental jurisdiction over claims against additional defendants that fall outside the district courts' original jurisdiction. In Aldinger v. Howard, 427 U.S. 1 (1976), the plaintiff brought a 42 U.S.C. § 1983 action against county officials in district court pursuant to the statutory grant of jurisdiction in 28 U.S.C. § 1343(3). The plaintiff further alleged the court had supplemental jurisdiction over her related state-law claims against the county, even though the county was not suable under § 1983 and so was not subject to § 1343(3)'s original jurisdiction. The Court held that supplemental jurisdiction could not be exercised because Congress, in enacting § 1343(3), had declined (albeit implicitly) to extend federal jurisdiction over any party who could not be sued under the federal civil rights statutes. "Before it can be concluded that [supplemental] jurisdiction [over additional parties] exists," *Aldinger* held, "a federal court must satisfy itself not only that Art[icle] III permits it, but that Congress in the statutes conferring jurisdiction has not expressly or by implication negated its existence."

In Finley v. United States, 490 U.S. 545 (1989), we confronted a similar issue in a different statutory context. The plaintiff in *Finley* brought a Federal Tort Claims Act negligence suit against the Federal Aviation Administration in District Court, which had original jurisdiction under § 1346(b). The plaintiff tried to add related claims against other defendants, invoking the District Court's supplemental jurisdiction over so-called pendent parties. We held that the District Court lacked a sufficient statutory basis for exercising supplemental jurisdiction over these claims. Relying primarily on *Zahn, Aldinger,* and *Kroger,* we held in *Finley* that "a grant of jurisdiction over claims involving particular parties does not itself confer jurisdiction over additional claims by or against different parties." While *Finley* did not "limit or impair" *Gibbs's* liberal approach to interpreting the jurisdictional statutes in the context of supplemental jurisdiction over additional claims involving the same parties, *Finley* nevertheless declined to extend that interpretive assumption to claims involving additional parties. *Finley* held that in the context of parties, in contrast to claims, "we will not assume that the full constitutional power has been congressionally authorized, and will not read jurisdictional statutes broadly."

As the jurisdictional statutes existed in 1989, then, here is how matters stood: First, the diversity requirement in § 1332(a) required complete diversity; absent complete diversity, the district court lacked original jurisdiction over all of the claims in the action. Second, if the district court had original jurisdiction over at least one claim, the jurisdictional statutes implicitly authorized supplemental jurisdiction over all other claims between the same parties arising out of the same Article III case or controversy. Third, even when the district court had original jurisdiction over one or more claims between particular parties, the jurisdictional statutes did not authorize supplemental jurisdiction over additional claims involving other parties.

B

In *Finley* we emphasized that "[w]hatever we say regarding the scope of jurisdiction conferred by a particular statute can of course be changed by Congress." In 1990, Congress accepted the invitation. It passed the Judicial Improvements Act, 104 Stat. 5089, which enacted § 1367, the provision which controls these cases.

Section 1367 provides, in relevant part:

> (a) Except as provided in subsections (b) and (c) or as expressly provided otherwise by Federal statute, in any civil action of which the district courts have original jurisdiction, the district courts shall have supplemental jurisdiction over all other claims that are so related to claims in the action within such original jurisdiction that they form part of the same case or controversy under Article III of the United States Constitution. Such supplemental jurisdiction shall include claims that involve the joinder or intervention of additional parties.

> (b) In any civil action of which the district courts have original jurisdiction founded solely on section 1332 of this title, the district courts shall not have supplemental jurisdiction under subsection (a) over claims by plaintiffs against persons made parties under Rule 14, 19, 20, or 24 of the Federal Rules of Civil Procedure, or over claims by persons proposed to be joined as plaintiffs under Rule 19 of such rules, or seeking to intervene as plaintiffs under Rule 24 of such rules, when exercising supplemental jurisdiction over such claims would be inconsistent with the jurisdictional requirements of section 1332.

All parties to this litigation and all courts to consider the question agree that § 1367 overturned the result in *Finley*. There is no warrant, however, for assuming that § 1367 did no more than to overrule *Finley* and otherwise to codify the existing state of the law of supplemental jurisdiction. We must not give jurisdictional statutes a more expansive interpretation than their text warrants; but it is just as important not to adopt an artificial construction that is narrower than what the text provides. No sound canon of interpretation requires Congress to speak with extraordinary clarity in order to modify the rules of federal jurisdiction within appropriate constitutional bounds. Ordinary principles of statutory construction apply.[a] In order to determine the scope of supplemental jurisdiction authorized by § 1367, then, we must examine the statute's text in light of context, structure, and related statutory provisions.

Section 1367(a) is a broad grant of supplemental jurisdiction over other claims within the same case or controversy, as long as the action is one in which the district courts would have original jurisdiction. The last

---

[a] For an article challenging this statement, see Debra Lyn Bassett, Statutory Interpretation in the Context of Federal Jurisdiction, 76 Geo. Wash. L. Rev. 52 (2007).—[Footnote by eds.]

sentence of § 1367(a) makes it clear that the grant of supplemental jurisdiction extends to claims involving joinder or intervention of additional
parties. The single question before us, therefore, is whether a diversity
case in which the claims of some plaintiffs satisfy the amount-in-controversy requirement, but the claims of others plaintiffs do not, presents a
"civil action of which the district courts have original jurisdiction." If the
answer is yes, § 1367(a) confers supplemental jurisdiction over all claims,
including those that do not independently satisfy the amount-in-controversy requirement, if the claims are part of the same Article III case or
controversy. If the answer is no, § 1367(a) is inapplicable and, in light of
our holdings in *Clark* and *Zahn,* the district court has no statutory basis
for exercising supplemental jurisdiction over the additional claims.

We now conclude the answer must be yes. When the well-pleaded
complaint contains at least one claim that satisfies the amount-in-controversy requirement, and there are no other relevant jurisdictional
defects, the district court, beyond all question, has original jurisdiction
over that claim. The presence of other claims in the complaint, over which
the district court may lack original jurisdiction, is of no moment. If the
court has original jurisdiction over a single claim in the complaint, it has
original jurisdiction over a "civil action" within the meaning of § 1367(a),
even if the civil action over which it has jurisdiction comprises fewer
claims than were included in the complaint. Once the court determines
it has original jurisdiction over the civil action, it can turn to the question
whether it has a constitutional and statutory basis for exercising supplemental jurisdiction over the other claims in the action.

Section 1367(a) commences with the direction that §§ 1367(b) and
(c), or other relevant statutes, may provide specific exceptions, but otherwise § 1367(a) is a broad jurisdictional grant, with no distinction drawn
between pendent-claim and pendent-party cases. In fact, the last sentence of § 1367(a) makes clear that the provision grants supplemental
jurisdiction over claims involving joinder or intervention of additional
parties. The terms of § 1367 do not acknowledge any distinction between
pendent jurisdiction and the doctrine of so-called ancillary jurisdiction.
Though the doctrines of pendent and ancillary jurisdiction developed separately as a historical matter, the Court has recognized that the doctrines
are "two species of the same generic problem," *Kroger,* 437 U.S. at 370.
Nothing in § 1367 indicates a Congressional intent to recognize, preserve,
or create some meaningful, substantive distinction between the jurisdictional categories we have historically labeled pendent and ancillary.

If § 1367(a) were the sum total of the relevant statutory language,
our holding would rest on that language alone. The statute, of course,
instructs us to examine § 1367(b) to determine if any of its exceptions
apply, so we proceed to that section. While § 1367(b) qualifies the broad
rule of § 1367(a), it does not withdraw supplemental jurisdiction over the
claims of the additional parties at issue here. The specific exceptions to
§ 1367(a) contained in § 1367(b), moreover, provide additional support for

our conclusion that § 1367(a) confers supplemental jurisdiction over these claims. Section 1367(b), which applies only to diversity cases, withholds supplemental jurisdiction over the claims of plaintiffs proposed to be joined as indispensable parties under Federal Rule of Civil Procedure 19, or who seek to intervene pursuant to Rule 24. Nothing in the text of § 1367(b), however, withholds supplemental jurisdiction over the claims of plaintiffs permissively joined under Rule 20 (like the additional plaintiffs in [one of the cases before us]) or certified as class-action members pursuant to Rule 23 (like the [others]). The natural, indeed the necessary, inference is that § 1367 confers supplemental jurisdiction over claims by Rule 20 and Rule 23 plaintiffs. This inference, at least with respect to Rule 20 plaintiffs, is strengthened by the fact that § 1367(b) explicitly excludes supplemental jurisdiction over claims against defendants joined under Rule 20.

We cannot accept the view, urged by some of the parties, commentators, and Courts of Appeals, that a district court lacks original jurisdiction over a civil action unless the court has original jurisdiction over every claim in the complaint. As we understand this position, it requires assuming either that all claims in the complaint must stand or fall as a single, indivisible "civil action" as a matter of definitional necessity—what we will refer to as the "indivisibility theory"—or else that the inclusion of a claim or party falling outside the district court's original jurisdiction somehow contaminates every other claim in the complaint, depriving the court of original jurisdiction over any of these claims—what we will refer to as the "contamination theory."

The indivisibility theory is easily dismissed, as it is inconsistent with the whole notion of supplemental jurisdiction. If a district court must have original jurisdiction over every claim in the complaint in order to have "original jurisdiction" over a "civil action," then in *Gibbs* there was no civil action of which the district court could assume original jurisdiction under § 1331, and so no basis for exercising supplemental jurisdiction over any of the claims. The indivisibility theory is further belied by our practice—in both federal-question and diversity cases—of allowing federal courts to cure jurisdictional defects by dismissing the offending parties rather than dismissing the entire action. . . . If the presence of jurisdictionally problematic claims in the complaint meant the district court was without original jurisdiction over the single, indivisible civil action before it, then the district court would have to dismiss the whole action rather than particular parties.

We also find it unconvincing to say that the definitional indivisibility theory applies in the context of diversity cases but not in the context of federal-question cases. The broad and general language of the statute does not permit this result. The contention is premised on the notion that the phrase "original jurisdiction of all civil actions" means different things in § 1331 and § 1332. It is implausible, however, to say that the identical phrase means one thing (original jurisdiction in all actions where at least one claim in the complaint meets the following requirements) in § 1331 and something else (original jurisdiction in all actions where every claim in the complaint meets the following requirements) in § 1332.

The contamination theory, as we have noted, can make some sense in the special context of the complete diversity requirement because the presence of nondiverse parties on both sides of a lawsuit eliminates the justification for providing a federal forum. The theory, however, makes little sense with respect to the amount-in-controversy requirement, which is meant to ensure that a dispute is sufficiently important to warrant federal-court attention. The presence of a single nondiverse party may eliminate the fear of bias with respect to all claims, but the presence of a claim that falls short of the minimum amount in controversy does nothing to reduce the importance of the claims that do meet this requirement.

It is fallacious to suppose, simply from the proposition that § 1332 imposes both the diversity requirement and the amount-in-controversy requirement, that the contamination theory germane to the former is also relevant to the latter. There is no inherent logical connection between the amount-in-controversy requirement and § 1332 diversity jurisdiction. After all, federal-question jurisdiction once had an amount-in-controversy requirement as well. If such a requirement were revived under § 1331, it is clear beyond peradventure that § 1367(a) provides supplemental jurisdiction over federal-question cases where some, but not all, of the federal-law claims involve a sufficient amount in controversy. In other words, § 1367(a) unambiguously overrules the holding and the result in *Clark.* If that is so, however, it would be quite extraordinary to say that § 1367 did not also overrule *Zahn,* a case that was premised in substantial part on the holding in *Clark.* . . .

We also reject the argument . . . that while the presence of additional claims over which the district court lacks jurisdiction does not mean the civil action is outside the purview of § 1367(a), the presence of additional parties does. The basis for this distinction is not altogether clear, and it is in considerable tension with statutory text. Section 1367(a) applies by its terms to any civil action of which the district courts have original jurisdiction, and the last sentence of § 1367(a) expressly contemplates that the court may have supplemental jurisdiction over additional parties. So it cannot be the case that the presence of those parties destroys the court's original jurisdiction, within the meaning of § 1367(a), over a civil action otherwise properly before it. Also, § 1367(b) expressly withholds supplemental jurisdiction in diversity cases over claims by plaintiffs joined as indispensable parties under Rule 19. If joinder of such parties were sufficient to deprive the district court of original jurisdiction over the civil action within the meaning of § 1367(a), this specific limitation on supplemental jurisdiction in § 1367(b) would be superfluous. The argument that the presence of additional parties removes the civil action from the scope of § 1367(a) also would mean that § 1367 left the *Finley* result undisturbed. *Finley,* after all, involved a Federal Tort Claims Act suit against a federal defendant and state-law claims against additional defendants not otherwise subject to federal jurisdiction. Yet all concede that one purpose of § 1367 was to change the result reached in *Finley.*

Finally, it is suggested that our interpretation of § 1367(a) creates an anomaly regarding the exceptions listed in § 1367(b): It is not immediately obvious why Congress would withhold supplemental jurisdiction over plaintiffs joined as parties "needed for just adjudication" under Rule 19 but would allow supplemental jurisdiction over plaintiffs permissively joined under Rule 20. The omission of Rule 20 plaintiffs from the list of exceptions in § 1367(b) may have been an "unintentional drafting gap." If that is the case, it is up to Congress rather than the courts to fix it. The omission may seem odd, but it is not absurd. An alternative explanation for the different treatment of Rule 19 and Rule 20 is that Congress was concerned that extending supplemental jurisdiction to Rule 19 plaintiffs would allow circumvention of the complete diversity rule: A nondiverse plaintiff might be omitted intentionally from the original action, but joined later under Rule 19 as a necessary party. The contamination theory described above, if applicable, means this ruse would fail, but Congress may have wanted to make assurance double sure. More generally, Congress may have concluded that federal jurisdiction is only appropriate if the district court would have original jurisdiction over the claims of all those plaintiffs who are so essential to the action that they could be joined under Rule 19.

To the extent that the omission of Rule 20 plaintiffs from the list of § 1367(b) exceptions is anomalous, moreover, it is no more anomalous than the inclusion of Rule 19 plaintiffs in that list would be if the alternative view of § 1367(a) were to prevail. If the district court lacks original jurisdiction over a civil diversity action where any plaintiff's claims fail to comply with all the requirements of § 1332, there is no need for a special § 1367(b) exception for Rule 19 plaintiffs who do not meet these requirements. Though the omission of Rule 20 plaintiffs from § 1367(b) presents something of a puzzle on our view of the statute, the inclusion of Rule 19 plaintiffs in this section is at least as difficult to explain under the alternative view.

And so we circle back to the original question. When the well-pleaded complaint in district court includes multiple claims, all part of the same case or controversy, and some, but not all, of the claims are within the court's original jurisdiction, does the court have before it "any civil action of which the district courts have original jurisdiction"? It does. Under § 1367, the court has original jurisdiction over the civil action comprising the claims for which there is no jurisdictional defect. No other reading of § 1367 is plausible in light of the text and structure of the jurisdictional statute. Though the special nature and purpose of the diversity requirement mean that a single nondiverse party can contaminate every other claim in the lawsuit, the contamination does not occur with respect to jurisdictional defects that go only to the substantive importance of individual claims.

It follows from this conclusion that the threshold requirement of § 1367(a) is satisfied in cases, like those now before us, where some, but not all, of the plaintiffs in a diversity action allege a sufficient amount in controversy. We hold that § 1367 by its plain text overruled *Clark* and *Zahn* and authorized supplemental jurisdiction over all claims by diverse parties arising out of the same Article III case or controversy, subject only to enumerated exceptions not applicable in the cases now before us.

C

The proponents of the alternative view of § 1367 insist that the statute is at least ambiguous and that we should look to other interpretive tools, including the legislative history of § 1367, which supposedly demonstrate Congress did not intend § 1367 to overrule *Zahn*. We can reject this argument at the very outset simply because § 1367 is not ambiguous. For the reasons elaborated above, interpreting § 1367 to foreclose supplemental jurisdiction over plaintiffs in diversity cases who do not meet the minimum amount in controversy is inconsistent with the text, read in light of other statutory provisions and our established jurisprudence. Even if we were to stipulate, however, that the reading these proponents urge upon us is textually plausible, the legislative history cited to support it would not alter our view as to the best interpretation of § 1367.

Those who urge that the legislative history refutes our interpretation rely primarily on the House Judiciary Committee Report on the Judicial Improvements Act. H. R. Rep. No. 101–734 (1990) (House Report or Report). This Report explained that § 1367 would "authorize jurisdiction in a case like *Finley*, as well as essentially restore the pre-*Finley* understandings of the authorization for and limits on other forms of supplemental jurisdiction." . . . The Report then remarked that § 1367(b) "is not intended to affect the jurisdictional requirements of [§ 1332] in diversity-only class actions, as those requirements were interpreted prior to Finley," citing, without further elaboration, *Zahn* and Supreme Tribe of Ben-Hur v. Cauble, 255 U. S. 356 (1921). . . .

As we have repeatedly held, the authoritative statement is the statutory text, not the legislative history or any other extrinsic material. Extrinsic materials have a role in statutory interpretation only to the extent they shed a reliable light on the enacting Legislature's understanding of otherwise ambiguous terms. Not all extrinsic materials are reliable sources of insight into legislative understandings, however, and legislative history in particular is vulnerable to two serious criticisms. First, legislative history is itself often murky, ambiguous, and contradictory. Judicial investigation of legislative history has a tendency to become, to borrow Judge Leventhal's memorable phrase, an exercise in " 'looking over a crowd and picking out your friends.' " See Wald, Some Observations on the Use of Legislative History in the 1981 Supreme

Court Term, 68 Iowa L. Rev. 195, 214 (1983). Second, judicial reliance on legislative materials like committee reports, which are not themselves subject to the requirements of Article I, may give unrepresentative committee members—or, worse yet, unelected staffers and lobbyists—both the power and the incentive to attempt strategic manipulations of legislative history to secure results they were unable to achieve through the statutory text. We need not comment here on whether these problems are sufficiently prevalent to render legislative history inherently unreliable in all circumstances, a point on which Members of this Court have disagreed. It is clear, however, that in this instance both criticisms are right on the mark. . . .

[T]he worst fears of critics who argue legislative history will be used to circumvent the Article I process were realized in this case. The telltale evidence is the statement, by three law professors who participated in drafting § 1367 that § 1367 "on its face" permits "supplemental jurisdiction over claims of class members that do not satisfy section 1332's jurisdictional amount requirement, which would overrule [*Zahn*]. [There is] a disclaimer of intent to accomplish this result in the legislative history. . . . It would have been better had the statute dealt explicitly with this problem, and the legislative history was an attempt to correct the oversight." Rowe, Burbank, & Mengler, Compounding or Creating Confusion About Supplemental Jurisdiction? A Reply to Professor Freer, 40 Emory L.J. 943, 960, n. 90 (1991). The professors were frank to concede that if one refuses to consider the legislative history, one has no choice but to "conclude that section 1367 has wiped *Zahn* off the books." So there exists an acknowledgment, by parties who have detailed, specific knowledge of the statute and the drafting process, both that the plain text of § 1367 overruled *Zahn* and that language to the contrary in the House Report was a post hoc attempt to alter that result. One need not subscribe to the wholesale condemnation of legislative history to refuse to give any effect to such a deliberate effort to amend a statute through a committee report. . . .

D

Finally, we note that the Class Action Fairness Act (CAFA), Pub.L. 109–2, 119 Stat. 4, enacted this year, has no bearing on our analysis of these cases. Subject to certain limitations, the CAFA confers federal diversity jurisdiction over class actions where the aggregate amount in controversy exceeds $5 million. It abrogates the rule against aggregating claims, a rule this Court recognized in *Ben-Hur* and reaffirmed in *Zahn*. The CAFA, however, is not retroactive, and the views of the 2005 Congress are not relevant to our interpretation of a text enacted by Congress in 1990. The CAFA, moreover, does not moot the significance of our interpretation of § 1367, as many proposed exercises of supplemental jurisdiction, even in the class-action context, might not fall within the CAFA's ambit. The CAFA, then, has no impact, one way or the other, on our interpretation of § 1367.

* * *

The judgment of the Court of Appeals for the Eleventh Circuit is affirmed. The judgment of the Court of Appeals for the First Circuit is reversed, and the case is remanded for proceedings consistent with this opinion.

It is so ordered.

■ JUSTICE STEVENS, with whom JUSTICE BREYER joins, dissenting.

[Justice Stevens quoted extensively from the House Judiciary Committee Report and emphasized its disclaimer of an intent to overturn *Zahn* and its description of the purpose of § 1367 as simply to overturn *Finley*. That some people involved in the drafting process thought that the natural reading of the text was to overturn *Zahn* "only highlights the fact that the statute is ambiguous," said Stevens, and "[w]hat is determinative is that the House Report explicitly rejected that broad reading of the statutory text." As for the article by the three law professors that was discussed by the Court, Stevens described it as "merely saying that the text of the statute was susceptible to an overly broad (and simplistic) reading, and that clarification in the House Report was therefore appropriate."]

■ JUSTICE GINSBURG, with whom JUSTICE STEVENS, JUSTICE O'CONNOR, and JUSTICE BREYER join, dissenting.

. . . The Court reads § 1367 to overrule Clark v. Paul Gray, Inc., 306 U.S. 583, 589 (1939), and Zahn v. International Paper Co., 414 U.S. 291 (1973), thereby allowing access to federal court by co-plaintiffs or class members who do not meet the now in excess of $75,000 amount-in-controversy requirement, so long as at least one co-plaintiff, or the named class representative, has a jurisdictionally sufficient claim.

The Court adopts a plausibly broad reading of § 1367, a measure that is hardly a model of the careful drafter's art. There is another plausible reading, however, one less disruptive of our jurisprudence regarding supplemental jurisdiction. If one reads § 1367(a) to instruct, as the statute's text suggests, that the district court must first have "original jurisdiction" over a "civil action" before supplemental jurisdiction can attach, then *Clark* and *Zahn* are preserved, and supplemental jurisdiction does not open the way for joinder of plaintiffs, or inclusion of class members, who do not independently meet the amount-in-controversy requirement. For the reasons that follow, I conclude that this narrower construction is the better reading of § 1367.

I

. . . Shortly before the Court decided Finley v. United States, 490 U.S. 545, 548 (1989), Congress had established the Federal Courts Study Committee to take up issues relating to "the federal courts' congestion, delay, expense, and expansion." Judicial Conference of the United States,

Report of the Federal Courts Study Committee 3 (Apr. 2, 1990). The Committee's charge was to conduct a study addressing the "crisis" in federal courts caused by the "rapidly growing" caseload.

Among recommendations, the Committee urged Congress to "authorize federal courts to assert pendent jurisdiction over parties without an independent federal jurisdictional base." If adopted, this recommendation would overrule *Finley*. Earlier, a subcommittee had recommended that Congress overrule both *Finley* and *Zahn*. Report of the Subcommittee on the Role of the Federal Courts and Their Relationship to the States 547, 561 n.33 (Mar. 12, 1990), reprinted in 1 Judicial Conference of the United States, Federal Courts Study Committee, Working Papers and Subcommittee Reports (July 1, 1990). In the subcommittee's view, "[f]rom a policy standpoint," *Zahn* "ma[de] little sense."[3] The full Committee, however, urged only the overruling of *Finley* and did not adopt the recommendation to overrule *Zahn*.

As a separate matter, a substantial majority of the Committee "strongly recommend[ed]" the elimination of diversity jurisdiction, save for "complex multi-state litigation, interpleader, and suits involving aliens." "[N]o other step," the Committee's Report maintained, "will do anywhere nearly as much to reduce federal caseload pressures and contain the growth of the federal judiciary."

Congress responded by adopting, as part of the Judicial Improvements Act of 1990, 104 Stat. 5089, recommendations of the Federal Courts Study Committee ranked by the House Committee on the Judiciary as "modest" and "noncontroversial." H.R. Rep. No. 101–734, pp. 15–16 (1990). Congress did not take up the Study Committee's immodest proposal to curtail diversity jurisdiction. It did, however, enact a supplemental jurisdiction statute, codified as 28 U.S.C. § 1367.

II

A

Section 1367, by its terms, operates only in civil actions "of which the district courts have original jurisdiction." The "original jurisdiction" relevant here is diversity-of-citizenship jurisdiction, conferred by § 1332. The character of that jurisdiction is the essential backdrop for comprehension of § 1367.

The Constitution broadly provides for federal-court jurisdiction in controversies "between Citizens of different States." Art. III, § 2, cl. 1. This Court has read that provision to demand no more than "minimal diversity," i.e., so long as one party on the plaintiffs' side and one party

---

[3] Anomalously, in holding that each class member "must satisfy the jurisdictional amount," Zahn v. International Paper Co., 414 U.S. 291, 301 (1973), the *Zahn* Court did not refer to Supreme Tribe of Ben-Hur v. Cauble, 255 U.S. 356, 366 (1921), which established that in a class action, the citizenship of the named plaintiff is controlling. But see *Zahn*, 414 U.S. at 309–10 (Brennan, J., dissenting) (urging *Zahn*'s inconsistency with *Ben-Hur*).

on the defendants' side are of diverse citizenship, Congress may authorize federal courts to exercise diversity jurisdiction. Further, the Constitution includes no amount-in-controversy limitation on the exercise of federal jurisdiction. But from the start, Congress, as its measures have been construed by this Court, has limited federal court exercise of diversity jurisdiction in two principal ways. First, unless Congress specifies otherwise, diversity must be "complete," i.e., all parties on plaintiffs' side must be diverse from all parties on defendants' side. Second, each plaintiff's stake must independently meet the amount-in-controversy specification: "When two or more plaintiffs, having separate and distinct demands, unite for convenience and economy in a single suit, it is essential that the demand of each be of the requisite jurisdictional amount." Troy Bank v. G.A. Whitehead & Co., 222 U.S. 39, 40 (1911).

The statute today governing federal court exercise of diversity jurisdiction in the generality of cases, § 1332, like all its predecessors, incorporates both a diverse-citizenship requirement and an amount-in-controversy specification.[5] . . . This Court has long held that, in determining whether the amount-in-controversy requirement has been satisfied, a single plaintiff may aggregate two or more claims against a single defendant, even if the claims are unrelated. See, e.g., Edwards v. Bates County, 163 U.S. 269, 273 (1896). But in multiparty cases, including class actions, we have unyieldingly adhered to the nonaggregation rule stated in *Troy Bank.*

This Court most recently addressed "[t]he meaning of [§ 1332's] 'matter in controversy' language" in *Zahn. Zahn,* like Snyder v. Harris, 394 U.S. 332 (1969) decided four years earlier, was a class action. In *Snyder,* no class member had a claim large enough to satisfy the jurisdictional amount. But in *Zahn,* the named plaintiffs had such claims. Nevertheless, the Court declined to depart from its "longstanding construction of the 'matter in controversy' requirement of § 1332." The *Zahn* Court stated:

> *Snyder* invoked the well-established rule that each of several plaintiffs asserting separate and distinct claims must satisfy the jurisdictional-amount requirement if his claim is to survive a motion to dismiss. This rule plainly mandates not only that there may be no aggregation and that the entire case must be dismissed where none of the plaintiffs claims [meets the amount-in-controversy requirement] but also requires that any

---

[5]   Endeavoring to preserve the "complete diversity" rule . . ., the Court's opinion drives a wedge between the two components of 28 U.S.C. § 1332, treating the diversity-of-citizenship requirement as essential, the amount-in-controversy requirement as more readily disposable. Section 1332 itself, however, does not rank order the two requirements. What "[o]rdinary princip[e] of statutory construction" or "sound canon of interpretation" allows the Court to slice up § 1332 this way? In partial explanation, the Court asserts that amount in controversy can be analyzed claim-by-claim, but the diversity requirement cannot. It is not altogether clear why that should be so. The cure for improper joinder of a nondiverse party is the same as the cure for improper joinder of a plaintiff who does not satisfy the jurisdictional amount. In both cases, original jurisdiction can be preserved by dismissing the nonqualifying party.

plaintiff without the jurisdictional amount must be dismissed from the case, even though others allege jurisdictionally sufficient claims.

The rule that each plaintiff must independently satisfy the amount-in-controversy requirement, unless Congress expressly orders otherwise, was thus the solidly established reading of § 1332 when Congress enacted the Judicial Improvements Act of 1990, which added § 1367 to Title 28.

B

The Court divides . . . on the impact of § 1367(a) on diversity cases controlled by § 1332. Under the majority's reading, § 1367(a) permits the joinder of related claims cut loose from the nonaggregation rule that has long attended actions under § 1332. Only the claims specified in § 1367(b) would be excluded from § 1367(a)'s expansion of § 1332's grant of diversity jurisdiction. And because § 1367(b) contains no exception for joinder of plaintiffs under Rule 20 or class actions under Rule 23, the Court concludes, *Clark* and *Zahn* have been overruled.[8]

The Court's reading is surely plausible, especially if one detaches § 1367(a) from its context and attempts no reconciliation with prior interpretations of § 1332's amount-in-controversy requirement. But § 1367(a)'s text, as the First Circuit held, can be read another way, one that would involve no rejection of *Clark* and *Zahn*.

As explained by the First Circuit . . . , § 1367(a) addresses "civil action[s] of which the district courts have original jurisdiction," a formulation that, in diversity cases, is sensibly read to incorporate the rules on joinder and aggregation tightly tied to § 1332 at the time of § 1367's enactment. On this reading, a complaint must first meet that "original jurisdiction" measurement. If it does not, no supplemental jurisdiction is authorized. If it does, § 1367(a) authorizes "supplemental jurisdiction" over related claims. In other words, § 1367(a) would preserve undiminished, as part and parcel of § 1332 "original jurisdiction" determinations, both the "complete diversity" rule and the decisions restricting aggregation to arrive at the amount in controversy.[9] Section 1367(b)'s office, then, would be "to prevent the erosion of the complete diversity [and amount-in-controversy] requirement[s] that might otherwise result from an expansive application of what was once termed the doctrine of ancillary jurisdiction." See James E. Pfander, Supplemental Jurisdiction and Section 1367: The Case for a Sympathetic

---

[8] Under the Court's construction of § 1367, Beatriz Ortega's family members can remain in the action because their joinder is merely permissive, see Fed. Rule Civ. Proc. 20. If, however, their presence was "needed for just adjudication," Rule 19, their dismissal would be required. The inclusion of those who may join, and exclusion of those who should or must join, defies rational explanation. . . .

[9] On this reading of § 1367(a), it is immaterial that § 1367(b) "does not withdraw supplemental jurisdiction over the claims of the additional parties at issue here." Because those claims would not come within § 1367(a) in the first place, Congress would have had no reason to list them in § 1367(b).

Textualism, 148 U. Pa. L. Rev. 109, 114 (1999). In contrast to the Court's construction of § 1367, which draws a sharp line between the diversity and amount-in-controversy components of § 1332, the interpretation presented here does not sever the two jurisdictional requirements.

The more restrained reading of § 1367 just outlined would yield affirmance of the First Circuit's judgment . . . and reversal of the Eleventh Circuit's judgment. . . . It would not discard entirely, as the Court does, the judicially developed doctrines of pendent and ancillary jurisdiction as they existed when *Finley* was decided. Instead, it would recognize § 1367 essentially as a codification of those doctrines, placing them under a single heading, but largely retaining their substance, with overriding *Finley* the only basic change: Supplemental jurisdiction, once the district court has original jurisdiction, would now include "claims that involve the joinder or intervention of additional parties." § 1367(a).

Pendent jurisdiction . . . applied only in federal-question cases and allowed plaintiffs to attach nonfederal claims to their jurisdiction-qualifying claims. Ancillary jurisdiction applied primarily, although not exclusively, in diversity cases and "typically involve[d] claims *by a defending party* haled into court against his will." *Kroger*, 437 U.S. at 376 (emphasis added). As the First Circuit observed, neither doctrine permitted a plaintiff to circumvent the dual requirements of § 1332 (diversity of citizenship and amount in controversy) "simply by joining her [jurisdictionally inadequate] claim in an action brought by [a] jurisdictionally competent diversity plaintiff."

Not only would the reading I find persuasive "alig[n] statutory supplemental jurisdiction with the judicially developed doctrines of pendent and ancillary jurisdiction," it would also synchronize § 1367 with the removal statute, 28 U.S.C. § 1441. As the First Circuit carefully explained:

> Section 1441, like § 1367, applies only if the "civil action" in question is one "of which the district courts . . . have original jurisdiction." § 1441(a). Relying on that language, the Supreme Court has interpreted § 1441 to prohibit removal unless the entire action, as it stands at the time of removal, could have been filed in federal court in the first instance. See, e.g., Syngenta Crop Protection, Inc. v. Henson, 537 U.S. 28, 33 (2002). Section 1441 has thus been held to incorporate the well-pleaded complaint rule;[11] the complete diversity rule; and rules for calculating the amount in controversy.

The less disruptive view I take of § 1367 also accounts for the omission of Rule 20 plaintiffs and Rule 23 class actions in § 1367(b)'s text. If

---

[11] The point of the Court's extended discussion of City of Chicago v. International College of Surgeons, 522 U.S. 156, 163 (1997), in the instant cases slips from my grasp. There was no disagreement in that case, and there is none now, that 28 U.S.C. § 1367(a) is properly read to authorize the exercise of supplemental jurisdiction in removed cases. *International College of Surgeons* was unusual in that the federal court there was asked to review a decision of a local administrative agency. Such review, it was unsuccessfully argued, was "appellate" in character, and therefore outside the ken of a court empowered to exercise "original" jurisdiction.

one reads § 1367(a) as a plenary grant of supplemental jurisdiction to federal courts sitting in diversity, one would indeed look for exceptions in § 1367(b). Finding none for permissive joinder of parties or class actions, one would conclude that Congress effectively, even if unintentionally, overruled *Clark* and *Zahn*. But if one recognizes that the nonaggregation rule delineated in *Clark* and *Zahn* forms part of the determination whether "original jurisdiction" exists in a diversity case, then plaintiffs who do not meet the amount-in-controversy requirement would fail at the § 1367(a) threshold. Congress would have no reason to resort to a § 1367(b) exception to turn such plaintiffs away from federal court, given that their claims, from the start, would fall outside the court's § 1332 jurisdiction. See Pfander, 148 U. Pa. L. Rev. at 148.

Nor does the more moderate reading assign different meanings to "original jurisdiction" in diversity and federal-question cases. As the First Circuit stated:

> "[O]riginal jurisdiction" in § 1367(a) has the same meaning in every case: [An] underlying statutory grant of original jurisdiction must be satisfied. What differs between federal question and diversity cases is not the meaning of "original jurisdiction" but rather the [discrete] requirements of sections 1331 and 1332. Under § 1331, the sole issue is whether a federal question appears on the face of the plaintiff's well-pleaded complaint; the [citizenship] of the parties and the amounts they stand to recover [do not bear on that determination]. Section 1332, by contrast, predicates original jurisdiction on the identity of the parties (i.e., [their] complete diversity) and their [satisfaction of the amount-in-controversy specification]. [In short,] the 'original jurisdiction' language in § 1367 operates differently in federal-question and diversity cases not because the meaning of that term varies, but because the [jurisdiction-granting] statutes are different.

What is the utility of § 1367(b) under my reading of § 1367(a)? Section 1367(a) allows parties other than the plaintiff to assert *reactive* claims once entertained under the heading ancillary jurisdiction. ([E.g.,] compulsory counterclaims and impleader claims, over which federal courts routinely exercised ancillary jurisdiction). As earlier observed, § 1367(b) stops plaintiffs from circumventing § 1332's jurisdictional requirements by using another's claim as a hook to add a claim that the plaintiff could not have brought in the first instance. *Kroger* is the paradigm case. There, the Court held that ancillary jurisdiction did not extend to a plaintiff's claim against a nondiverse party who had been impleaded by the defendant under Rule 14. Section 1367(b), then, is corroborative of § 1367(a)'s coverage of claims formerly called ancillary, but provides exceptions to assure that accommodation of added claims would not fundamentally alter "the jurisdictional requirements of section 1332." See Pfander, 148 U. Pa. L. Rev. at 135–37.

While § 1367's enigmatic text[12] defies flawless interpretation,[13] the precedent-preservative reading, I am persuaded, better accords with the historical and legal context of Congress's enactment of the supplemental jurisdiction statute and the established limits on pendent and ancillary jurisdiction. It does not attribute to Congress a jurisdictional enlargement broader than the one to which the legislators adverted, and it follows the sound counsel that "close questions of [statutory] construction should be resolved in favor of continuity and against change." David L. Shapiro, Continuity and Change in Statutory Interpretation, 67 N.Y.U. L. Rev. 921, 925 (1992).[14]

* * *

For the reasons stated, I would hold that § 1367 does not overrule *Clark* and *Zahn*. I would therefore affirm the judgment of the Court of Appeals for the First Circuit and reverse the judgment of the Court of Appeals for the Eleventh Circuit.[b]

NOTES ON SUPPLEMENTAL JURISDICTION

1. *OWEN EQUIPMENT & ERECTION CO. V. KROGER*

Owen Equipment & Erection Co. v. Kroger, 437 U.S. 365 (1978), was decided before the enactment of the supplemental jurisdiction statute. James Kroger was killed when he was walking next to a steel crane that came too close to an electric power line. His widow filed a wrongful death action against the Omaha Public Power District (OPPD). OPPD in turn filed a third-party complaint under Rule 14(a) against the owner of the crane, the

---

[12] The Court notes the passage this year of the Class Action Fairness Act (CAFA), only to dismiss that legislation as irrelevant. Subject to several exceptions and qualifications, CAFA provides for federal-court adjudication of state-law-based class actions in which diversity is "minimal" (one plaintiff's diversity from one defendant suffices), and the "matter in controversy" is an aggregate amount in excess of $5,000,000. Significant here, CAFA's enlargement of federal-court diversity jurisdiction was accomplished, "clearly and conspicuously," by amending § 1332.

[13] If § 1367(a) itself renders unnecessary the listing of Rule 20 plaintiffs and Rule 23 class actions in § 1367(b), then it is similarly unnecessary to refer, as § 1367(b) does, to "persons proposed to be joined as plaintiffs under Rule 19." On one account, Congress bracketed such persons with persons "seeking to intervene as plaintiffs under Rule 24" to modify pre-§ 1367 practice. Before enactment of § 1367, courts entertained, under the heading ancillary jurisdiction, claims of Rule 24(a) intervenors "of right," but denied ancillary jurisdiction over claims of "necessary" Rule 19 plaintiffs. Congress may have sought simply to underscore that those seeking to join as plaintiffs, whether under Rule 19 or Rule 24, should be treated alike, i.e., denied joinder when "inconsistent with the jurisdictional requirements of section 1332." See H.R. Rep., at 29 ("Subsection (b) makes one small change in pre-*Finley* practice," i.e., it eliminates the Rule 19/Rule 24 anomaly.).

[14] While the interpretation of § 1367 described in this opinion does not rely on the measure's legislative history, that history, as Justice Stevens has shown, is corroborative of the statutory reading set out above.

[b] For a comprehensive treatment of the line of Supreme Court cases through *Exxon Mobil* and *Empire Healthchoice*, see Richard D. Freer, Of Rules and Standards: Reconciling Statutory Limitations on "Arising Under" Jurisdiction, 82 Ind. L.J. 309 (2007). See also Adam N. Steinman, Sausage-Making, Pigs' Ears, and Congressional Expansions of Federal Jurisdiction: *Exxon Mobil v. Allapattah* and Its Lessons for the Class Action Fairness Act, 81 Wash. L. Rev. 279 (2006).—[Footnote by eds.]

Owen Equipment & Erection Co., alleging that it was their negligence in operating the crane that caused Kroger's death. While OPPD's motion for summary judgment was pending, Kroger amended her complaint to add Owen as a defendant. Summary judgment was granted in favor of OPPD, leaving the complaint by Kroger against Owen to be litigated at trial.

Kroger was a citizen of Iowa and OPPD was a citizen of Nebraska. Kroger's amended complaint against Owen alleged that Owen was a Nebraska corporation with its principal place of business in Nebraska. Owen answered, admitting that it was "a corporation organized and existing under the laws of the state of Nebraska" and denying everything else. On the third day of the trial it was learned that Owen's principal place of business was in Iowa,[a] which meant that both the plaintiff and the defendant were from the same state. Owen moved to dismiss. The District Court reserved judgment, and later denied the motion after the jury returned a verdict for Kroger. The Court of Appeals affirmed on the authority of United Mine Workers v. Gibbs, 383 U.S. 715 (1966). The Supreme Court granted certiorari and reversed.

For the Court,[b] Justice Stewart observed first that, although the Federal Rules of Civil Procedure authorized the rounds of pleadings involved in the case, "it is axiomatic that the Federal Rules of Civil Procedure do not create or withdraw federal jurisdiction." The issue, therefore, turned on the meaning of the diversity statute. As to that, he wrote:

> . . . Over the years Congress has repeatedly re-enacted or amended the statute conferring diversity jurisdiction, leaving intact [the] rule of complete diversity. Whatever may have been the original purposes of diversity-of-citizenship jurisdiction, this subsequent history clearly demonstrates a congressional mandate that diversity jurisdiction is not to be available when any plaintiff is a citizen of the same state as any defendant.
>
> Thus it is clear that the respondent could not originally have brought suit in federal court naming Owen and OPPD as codefendants, since citizens of Iowa would have been on both sides of the litigation. Yet the identical lawsuit resulted when she amended her complaint. Complete diversity was destroyed just as surely as if she had sued Owen initially. . . .
>
> It is a fundamental precept that federal courts are courts of limited jurisdiction. The limits upon federal jurisdiction, whether imposed by the Constitution or by Congress, must be neither disregarded nor evaded. Yet under the reasoning of the Court of Appeals in this case, a plaintiff could defeat the statutory requirement of complete diversity by the simple expedient of suing only those defendants who were of diverse citizenship and waiting for them to

---

[a] How could this happen so late? Justice Stewart's opinion for the Court offered this explanation: "The problem apparently was one of geography. Although the Missouri River generally marks the boundary between Iowa and Nebraska, Carter Lake, Iowa, where the accident occurred and where Owen had its main office, lies west of the river, adjacent to Omaha, Neb. Apparently the river once avulsed at one of its bends, cutting Carter Lake off from the rest of Iowa."

[b] Joined by Justice Brennan, Justice White dissented.

implead nondiverse defendants.[17] If, as the Court of Appeals thought, a "common nucleus of operative fact" were the only requirement for ancillary jurisdiction in a diversity case, there would be no principled reason why the respondent in this case could not have joined her cause of action against Owen in her original complaint as ancillary to her claim against OPPD. Congress's requirement of complete diversity would thus have been evaded completely.

It is true, as the Court of Appeals noted, that the exercise of ancillary jurisdiction over nonfederal claims has often been upheld in situations involving impleader, cross-claims or counterclaims. But in determining whether jurisdiction over a nonfederal claim exists, the context in which the nonfederal claim is asserted is crucial. And the claim here arises in a setting quite different from the kinds of nonfederal claims that have been viewed in other cases as falling within the ancillary jurisdiction of the federal courts.

First, the nonfederal claim in this case was simply not ancillary to the federal one in the same sense that, for example, the impleader by a defendant of a third-party defendant always is. A third-party complaint depends at least in part upon the resolution of the primary lawsuit. Its relation to the original complaint is thus not mere factual similarity but logical dependence. The respondent's claim against the petitioner, however, was entirely separate from her original claim against OPPD, since the petitioner's liability to her depended not at all upon whether or not OPPD was also liable. Far from being an ancillary and dependent claim, it was a new and independent one.

Second, the nonfederal claim here was asserted by the plaintiff, who voluntarily chose to bring suit upon a state-law claim in a federal court. By contrast, ancillary jurisdiction typically involves claims by a defending party haled into court against his will, or by another person whose rights might be irretrievably lost unless he could assert them in an ongoing action in a federal court. A plaintiff cannot complain if ancillary jurisdiction does not encompass all of his possible claims in a case such as this one, since it is he who has chosen the federal rather than the state forum and must thus accept its limitations. "[T]he efficiency plaintiff seeks so avidly is

---

[17] This is not an unlikely hypothesis, since a defendant in a tort suit such as this one would surely try to limit his liability by impleading any joint tortfeasors for indemnity or contribution. Some commentators have suggested that the possible abuse of third-party practice could be dealt with under 28 U.S.C. § 1359, which forbids collusive attempts to create federal jurisdiction. Note, Rule 14 Claims and Ancillary Jurisdiction, 57 Va. L. Rev. 265, 274–75 (1971). The dissenting opinion today also expresses this view. But there is nothing necessarily collusive about a plaintiff's selectively suing only those tortfeasors of diverse citizenship, or about the named defendants' desire to implead joint tortfeasors. Nonetheless, the requirement of complete diversity would be eviscerated by such a course of events.

available without question in the state courts." Kenrose Mfg. Co. v. Fred Whitaker Co., 512 F.2d 890, 894 (4th Cir. 1972).[20]

It is not unreasonable to assume that, in generally requiring complete diversity, Congress did not intend to confine the jurisdiction of federal courts so inflexibly that they are unable to protect legal rights or effectively to resolve an entire, logically entwined lawsuit. Those practical needs are the basis of the doctrine of ancillary jurisdiction. But neither the convenience of litigants nor considerations of judicial economy can suffice to justify extension of the doctrine of ancillary jurisdiction to a plaintiff's cause of action against a citizen of the same state in a diversity case. Congress has established the basic rule that diversity jurisdiction exists under 28 U.S.C. § 1332 only when there is complete diversity of citizenship. "The policy of the statute calls for its strict construction." Snyder v. Harris, 394 U.S. 332, 340 (1969). To allow the requirement of complete diversity to be circumvented as it was in this case would simply flout the congressional command.[21]

2.   COLLUSION: *KRAMER V. CARIBBEAN MILLS*

The dissenters in *Kroger* suggested that 28 U.S.C. § 1359 could be invoked to prevent collusion between the plaintiff and the defendant to manufacture jurisdiction on facts such as those presented by the *Kroger* case. The majority, as it states in footnote 17, thought § 1359 an insufficient protection.

Kramer v. Caribbean Mills, Inc., 394 U.S. 823 (1969), illustrates the classic situation to which § 1359 applies. In *Kramer* a Haitian corporation agreed to purchase stock in a Panamanian corporation for $85,000 in cash and $165,000 in 12 annual installments. The installments were not paid. The Panamanian corporation assigned its entire interest in the installment payments to a Texas attorney for $1. On the same day, the Texas attorney agreed to pay 95 percent of any net recovery to the Panamanian corporation "solely as a bonus." A diversity suit was then filed by the Texas attorney in a Texas federal district court.

The Supreme Court had little difficulty in finding that the assignment fell "within [the] very core" of § 1359:

> If federal jurisdiction could be created by assignments of this kind, which are easy to arrange and involve few disadvantages for the assignor, then a vast quantity of ordinary contract and tort litigation could be channeled into the federal courts at the will of one of the parties. Such "manufacture of federal jurisdiction" was the very

---

[20]   Whether Iowa's statute of limitations would now bar an action by the respondent in an Iowa court is, of course, entirely a matter of state law.

[21]   Our holding is that the District Court lacked power to entertain the respondent's lawsuit against the petitioner. Thus, the asserted inequity in the respondent's alleged concealment of its citizenship is irrelevant. Federal judicial power does not depend upon "prior action or consent of the parties." American Fire & Cas. Co. v. Finn, 341 U.S. 6, 17–18 (1951).

thing which Congress intended to prevent when it enacted § 1359 and its predecessors.[c]

3.   SANDBAGGING

In *Kroger* the plaintiff did not learn until the trial was well underway that its defendant was a citizen of the same state. Should Owen then have been permitted to make a motion to dismiss? Could Owen have been sandbagging? The majority of the Supreme Court seemed unconcerned. In footnote 21, it said that "the asserted inequity in the respondent's alleged concealment of its citizenship is irrelevant." In footnote 20, it said that whether the plaintiff's suit was now barred by the state statute of limitations "is, of course, entirely a matter of state law."

Compare American Fire & Casualty Co. v. Finn, 341 U.S. 6 (1951). Finn filed suit for a fire loss against his insurance company in a Texas state court. The insurance company removed the case to federal court over Finn's objection. The case went to trial, and Finn won. The *insurance company* then appealed on the ground that the removal was improper. The Supreme Court agreed, vacated the judgment, and ordered that, if the jurisdictional error were not cured,[d] the case be remanded to the state courts. Three Justices dissented on the ground that the insurance company "having asked for and obtained the removal of the case to the federal District Court, and having lost its case in that court, is now estopped from having it remanded to the state court."

The standard doctrine, as *Finn* illustrates and *Kroger* also says, is that the parties cannot confer subject matter jurisdiction on the federal courts:

> The jurisdiction of the federal courts is carefully guarded against expansion by judicial interpretation or by prior action or consent of the parties. To permit a federal trial court to enter a judgment . . . where the federal court could not have original jurisdiction . . . would by the act of the parties work a wrongful extension of federal jurisdiction and give district courts power the Congress has denied them.

The American Law Institute disagrees. See ALI, Study of the Division of Jurisdiction Between State and Federal Courts § 1386 (Official Draft, 1969). With certain exceptions in cases of collusion or where the facts were unavailable before trial, it proposed that neither the parties nor the courts be able to raise objections going to subject matter jurisdiction after the beginning of the trial on the merits. It also proposed that state statutes of limitation be tolled for claims asserted in a federal suit while the suit was pending and for a prescribed period after a jurisdictional dismissal.[e]

---

[c]   See generally, William L. Daniels, Judicial Control of Manufactured Diversity Pursuant to § 1359, 9 Rutgers-Camden L.J. 1 (1977).—[Footnote by eds.]

[d]   As it happened, the jurisdictional error was easily cured by dismissing an additional party who had destroyed complete diversity.

[e]   After observing that "a wily defendant may conceal a known jurisdictional defect until the period of the statute of limitations has run, then obtain dismissal, and achieve total immunity from suit" and that "[s]ome decisions indicate that he may even do this by controverting jurisdictional facts previously alleged or admitted," the ALI commentary concludes that "this

Would the American Law Institute proposal be constitutional if adopted by Congress and applied to a case such as *Kroger*? Should the Supreme Court adopt the ALI view even if Congress does not?

4. THE SCOPE OF TRADITIONAL ANCILLARY JURISDICTION

Freeman v. Howe, 65 U.S. (24 How.) 450 (1860), was an important early recognition of the concept of ancillary jurisdiction. *Freeman* held that a state court could not entertain an action brought by claimants to property if the property had previously been attached in a federal diversity action. The state-court plaintiffs had objected to this result by arguing that it would leave them without a remedy, since their joinder in the federal suit would destroy complete diversity. The Court responded that the non-diverse state-court plaintiffs could nonetheless join the federal litigation since their claim was "ancillary and dependent, supplementary entirely to the original suit."

The *Freeman* Court faced a dilemma. In order to afford the state-court plaintiffs any opportunity to assert their claims, the Court either had to permit the state court to interfere with property already before a federal court or it had to allow the state-court plaintiffs to participate in the federal suit notwithstanding their impact on diversity. The doctrine of *Freeman* was therefore born of necessity. It has since become a doctrine of convenience and efficiency. It is now standard lore that a defendant who asserts a compulsory counterclaim in a diversity action may do so even though the jurisdictional amount is not satisfied.[f] And under Rule 14, a defendant may implead a third party even though the defendant and the third party are citizens of the same state. The rationale for these exceptions to the normal requirements of diversity jurisdiction obviously goes beyond *Freeman,* but there are good reasons for extending jurisdiction to these situations. Both examples involve litigation of closely related issues that will arise in a subsequent lawsuit if not the present one. The time of courts, parties, and witnesses, and the other expenses of litigation, support some mechanism for disposing of the matter

---

fetish of federal jurisdiction is wholly inconsistent with sound judicial administration and can only serve to diminish respect for a system that tolerates it." ALI, Study of the Division of Jurisdiction between State and Federal Courts § 1386, p. 366 (Official Draft, 1969). The commentary cites Page v. Wright, 116 F.2d 449 (7th Cir.1940), and Ramsey v. Mellon Nat'l Bank & Trust Co., 350 F.2d 874 (3d Cir.1965), as enforcing the "fetish," and DiFrischia v. New York Cent. R.R. Co., 279 F.2d 141 (3d Cir.1960), as running counter to the trend. For additional commentary, see Dan A. Dobbs, Beyond Bootstrap: Foreclosing the Issue of Subject-Matter Jurisdiction before Final Judgment, 51 Minn. L. Rev. 491 (1967); H.A. Stephens, Jr., Estoppel to Deny Jurisdiction—*Klee* and *DiFrischia* Break Ground, 68 Dick. L. Rev. 39 (1963).

     [f]   Under pre-§ 1367 law, *permissive* counterclaims did not fall within the ancillary jurisdiction of the federal courts. But since § 1337 establishes as a test for supplemental jurisdiction that a claim is "so related" as to fall within "the same case or controversy under Article III," it is arguable that at least some permissive counterclaims have a sufficient relationship to the plaintiff's claim that they should now be regarded as falling within federal court jurisdiction even though jurisdictional limitations are not independently satisfied. Some lower courts have so concluded, but the Supreme Court has not yet spoken. For an argument that § 1367 should not be regarded as changing the traditional answer to this question, see Douglas D. McFarland, Supplemental Jurisdiction over Permissive Counterclaims and Set Offs: A Misconception, 64 Mercer L. Rev. 437 (2013).

in one suit. In the case of impleader, moreover, there is a possibility of inconsistent results that cannot be dealt with by the traditional doctrines of res judicata or collateral estoppel.[g]

Although the *Kroger* result is preserved by subsection (b) of the supplemental jurisdiction statute, *Exxon Mobil*, as it explains, changes the landscape significantly in other respects. Who has the better of it, the majority or the dissent?

5.   CLASS ACTION FAIRNESS ACT

In 2005, in response to concerns about abuses of the class action device and the perception that, as a result of limitations on diversity jurisdiction, class actions of nationwide significance were improperly being kept out of the federal courts, Congress enacted the Class Action Fairness Act (CAFA). Subject to certain limitations, the CAFA authorizes federal courts to exercise jurisdiction over class actions based on state law as long as any member of the class has diverse citizenship from any defendant, there are at least 100 class members, and there is at least $5,000,000 in controversy. See 28 U.S.C. § 1332(d). It also allows the claims of the class members to be aggregated in order to satisfy the amount in controversy requirement. In addition, it facilitates removal of these class actions from state to federal court—by, for example, allowing removal even if one or more of the defendants is a citizen of the state in which the suit is brought. See 28 U.S.C. § 1453.

The scholarship on the CAFA includes a valuable set of Symposium articles published in the Pennsylvania Law Review. These articles include Stephen B. Burbank, The Class Action Fairness Act of 2005 in Historical Context: A Preliminary View, 156 U. Pa. L. Rev. 1439 (2008); Kevin M. Clermont and Theodore Eisenberg, CAFA Judicata: A Tale of Waste and Politics, 156 U. Pa. L. Rev. 1553 (2008); Geoffrey C. Hazard, Jr., Has the *Erie* Doctrine Been Repealed by Congress?, 156 U. Pa. L. Rev. 1629 (2008); Emery G. Lee III and Thomas E. Willging, The Impact of the Class Action Fairness Act on the Federal Courts: An Empirical Analysis of Filings and Removals, 156 U. Pa. L. Rev. 1723 (2008); Richard L. Marcus, Assessing CAFA's Stated Jurisdictional Policy, 156 U. Pa. L. Rev. 1765 (2008); and Edward A. Purcell, Jr., The Class Action Fairness Act in Perspective: The Old and the New in Federal Jurisdictional Reform, 156 U. Pa. L. Rev. 1823 (2008). For additional articles on the CAFA, see, for example, Nan S. Ellis, The Class Action Fairness Act of 2005: The Story behind the Statute, 35 J. Legis. 76 (2009), David Marcus, *Erie*, the Class Action Fairness Act, and Some Federalism Implications of Diversity Jurisdiction, 48 Wm. & Mary L. Rev. 1247 (2007), and Mark Moller, A New Look at the Original Meaning of the Diversity Clause, 51 Wm. & Mary L. Rev. 1113 (2009).

---

[g]   Assume, for example, that *A* sues *B,* and *B* claims that *C* is responsible to *B* for any liability to *A*. Judgment for *A* would bind *B,* but *B* would not be able to use that judgment against *C* in a subsequent suit. In litigation between *B* and *C,* the same issue might be resolved differently, resulting in inconsistent verdicts.

6. BIBLIOGRAPHY

There is an extensive literature on § 1367, including commentary from those who participated in its drafting. See Thomas M. Mengler, Stephen B. Burbank and Thomas D. Rowe, Jr., Congress Accepts Supreme Court's Invitation to Codify Supplemental Jurisdiction, 74 Judicature 213 (1991); Thomas M. Mengler, Stephen B. Burbank and Thomas D. Rowe, Jr., A Coda on Supplemental Jurisdiction, 40 Emory L.J. 993 (1991). There has also been criticism. See Richard D. Freer, Compounding Confusion and Hampering Diversity: Life after *Finley* and the Supplemental Jurisdiction Statute, 40 Emory L.J. 445 (1991); Thomas C. Arthur and Richard D. Freer, Grasping at Burnt Straws: The Disaster of the Supplemental Jurisdiction Statute, 40 Emory L.J. 963 (1991); Thomas C. Arthur and Richard D. Freer, Close Enough for Government Work: What Happens When Congress Doesn't Do Its Job, 40 Emory L.J. 1007 (1991). Rebuttal appears in Thomas D. Rowe, Jr., Stephen B. Burbank and Thomas M. Mengler, Compounding or Creating Confusion about Supplemental Jurisdiction? A Reply to Professor Freer, 40 Emory L.J. 943 (1991).

There is an extensive pre-*Exxon Mobil* literature on ancillary jurisdiction. See Michael A. Berch, The Erection of a Barrier against Assertion of Ancillary Claims: An Examination of *Owen Equipment and Erection Company v. Kroger,* 1979 Ariz. St. L.J. 253; Howard W. Brill, Federal Rule of Civil Procedure 14 and Ancillary Jurisdiction, 59 Neb. L. Rev. 631 (1980); Richard D. Freer, A Principled Statutory Approach to Supplemental Jurisdiction, 1987 Duke L.J. 34; John Garvey, The Limits of Ancillary Jurisdiction, 57 Texas L. Rev. 697 (1979); Rex E. Lee and Richard G. Wilkins, An Analysis of Supplemental Jurisdiction and Abstention with Recommendations for Legislative Action, 1990 B.Y.U. L. Rev. 321; Richard A. Matasar, A Pendent and Ancillary Jurisdiction Primer: The Scope and Limits of Supplemental Jurisdiction, 17 U.C. Davis L. Rev. 103 (1983); Mary Brigid McManamon, Dispelling the Myths of Pendent and Ancillary Jurisdiction: The Ramifications of a Revised History, 46 Wash. & Lee L. Rev. 863 (1989); Thomas M. Mengler, The Demise of Pendent and Ancillary Jurisdiction, 1990 B.Y.U. L. Rev. 247; Arthur R. Miller, Ancillary and Pendent Jurisdiction, 26 S. Tex. L.J. 1 (1985); Pamela J. Stephens, Ancillary Jurisdiction: Plaintiffs' Claims against Nondiverse Third-Party Defendants, 14 Loy. U. Chi. L.J. 419 (1983).

For discussion of the law prior to *Exxon Mobil* on the issue of aggregating the jurisdictional amount by combining the claims of multiple plaintiffs, see Mildred B. Bell, Jurisdictional Requirements in Suits for which Class Action Status is Sought Under Rule 23(b)(3), 8 Valparaiso L. Rev. 237 (1974); Mayo L. Coiner, Class Actions: Aggregation of Claims for Federal Jurisdiction, 4 Memphis St. L. Rev. 427 (1974); Brian Mattis and James S. Mitchell, The Trouble With *Zahn*: Progeny of *Snyder v. Harris* Further Cripples Class Actions, 53 Neb. L. Rev. 137 (1974); William H. Theis, *Zahn v. International Paper Co.*: The Non-Aggregation Rule in Jurisdictional Amount Cases, 35 La. L. Rev. (1974); Note, Ancillary Jurisdiction and the Jurisdictional Amount Requirement, 50 Notre Dame L. Rev. 346 (1974); Note, The Federal Jurisdictional Amount and Rule 20 Joinder of Parties: Aggregation of Claims, 53 Minn. L. Rev. 94 (1968).

SECTION 3. THE SUBSTANCE/PROCEDURE PROBLEM

INTRODUCTORY NOTES ON THE SUBSTANCE/PROCEDURE PROBLEM

1.   BACKGROUND

Two important events occurred in 1938. The Supreme Court held in *Erie* that federal courts were required to apply state substantive law in large categories of cases where federal courts had previously supplied the rules of decision as a matter of general common law. The same year saw the adoption of the Federal Rules of Civil Procedure, which for the first time provided uniform rules of procedure for the federal district courts. Before *Erie*, federal courts had been free under *Swift v. Tyson* to develop independent substantive rules of decision in many cases that would have been controlled by state law if litigated in a state court. As to procedure, the Conformity Act of 1872 had provided that procedure in federal district court, other than in equity and admiralty cases, should "conform, as near as may be" to the procedures of the state in which the court sat. The combined effect of *Erie* and the Federal Rules was, therefore, to reverse former practice with respect to both substance and procedure.

The Federal Rules were adopted pursuant to the 1934 Rules Enabling Act, now found in 28 U.S.C. § 2072, which gave the Supreme Court power to "prescribe general rules of practice and procedure" for the federal courts. It also specified that, "[s]uch rules shall not abridge, enlarge or modify any substantive right. . . ." Proposed drafts of the Rules were prepared by an Advisory Committee composed of law professors and practicing lawyers. After making some revisions to these proposals, the Supreme Court sent them to Congress. Under the terms of the Enabling Act, the Rules automatically took effect after Congress failed to disapprove them.

These two events created questions about how federal courts should handle issues that were arguably procedural in cases governed by state substantive law. As an initial matter, there is sometimes a fine line between substance and procedure. Even rules that are commonly understood as procedural can affect the outcome of a case. Consequently, if procedural rules vary depending on whether a case is heard in state or federal court, *Erie*'s concerns about forum shopping and inequitable administration of the laws might be implicated. Nonetheless, it is clear that the Federal Rules of Civil Procedure, which were promulgated with authorization from Congress, were designed to create a uniform system of procedure for the federal courts.

In deciding what law to apply to an arguably procedural issue in a case otherwise governed by state substantive law, there are at least three questions that a federal court might face. First, does a Federal Rule of Civil Procedure govern the issue? Second, if so, is the Rule valid under the Rules Enabling Act? Third, if the issue is not governed by a Federal Rule, is a federal court required under *Erie* to apply state law?

2. *SIBBACH V. WILSON*

Relying on diversity jurisdiction, Sibbach filed a tort action against Wilson & Company in a federal court in Illinois for injuries allegedly sustained in an automobile accident in Indiana. At Wilson's request, and consistent with Rule 35 of the Federal Rules of Civil Procedure, the court ordered the plaintiff to submit to a physical examination by a court-appointed physician, even though an Illinois state court would not have issued such an order. Sibbach sought review in the Supreme Court, arguing that Rule 35 was inconsistent with the Rules Enabling Act because it modified a substantive right.

In Sibbach v. Wilson, 312 U.S. 1 (1941), the Supreme Court upheld the validity of Rule 35. The Court noted that "Congress has undoubted power to regulate the practice and procedure of federal courts, and may exercise that power by delegating to this or other federal courts authority to make rules not inconsistent with the statutes or Constitution of the United States." It concluded that the issue of court-ordered physical examinations was procedural and that, in regulating that issue, Rule 35 did not modify substantive rights in violation of the Rules Enabling Act. The Court said that the right not to undergo a physical examination "is no more important than many others enjoyed by litigants in District Courts sitting in the several states, before the Federal Rules of Civil Procedure altered and abolished old rights or privileges and created new ones in connection with the conduct of litigation." More to the point, the Court rejected the idea that the test for determining whether a right was substantive should turn on whether the right is "important," noting that such an approach would "invite endless litigation and confusion worse confounded." Instead, said the Court, "[t]he test must be whether a rule really regulates procedure—the judicial process for enforcing rights and duties recognized by substantive law, and for justly administering remedy and redress for disregard or infraction of them."

3. *GUARANTY TRUST CO. V. YORK*

Although *Sibbach* settled the general validity of the Federal Rules, those rules do not cover all matters that could be termed procedural. Does *Erie* require the federal courts to follow state law on procedural matters not governed by the Federal Rules? In Cities Service Oil Co. v. Dunlap, 308 U.S. 208 (1939), the Court held that a Texas rule on burden of proof (a matter not covered by the Federal Rules) must be followed because it "relate[d] to a substantial right" and was not merely "one of practice." In Palmer v. Hoffman, 318 U.S. 109 (1943), the Court considered whether Rule 8(c), which provides that contributory negligence must be pleaded as an affirmative defense, also meant that the defendant had the burden of proof on that issue. The Court held that "Rule 8(c) covers only the matter of pleading. The question of the burden of establishing contributory negligence is a question of local law which federal courts in diversity of citizenship cases must apply."

These early decisions did not make an effort to develop general guidelines for interpreting the Federal Rules or for administering the line between substance and procedure. The first major decision to do so was Guaranty

Trust Co. v. York, 326 U.S. 99 (1945), which involved a class action filed in federal court based on diversity jurisdiction. The suit was brought in equity to recover for an alleged breach of trust in violation of state law. The question was whether the federal court was free, in a suit seeking equitable relief, to ignore the statute of limitations of the state whose substantive law controlled the controversy. *Guaranty Trust* is important for two reasons. First, the Court made it clear that the policy of *Erie* applied to suits in equity as well as law.[a] Second, Justice Frankfurter's opinion for the Court advanced a general test for determining when *Erie* required resort to state law:

> Here we are dealing with a right to recover derived not from the United States but from one of the states. When, because the plaintiff happens to be a non-resident, such a right is enforceable in a federal as well as in a state court, the forms and mode of enforcing the right may at times, naturally enough, vary because the two judicial systems are not identic. But since a federal court adjudicating a state-created right solely because of the diversity of citizenship of the parties is for that purpose, in effect, only another court of the state, it cannot afford recovery if the right to recover is made unavailable by the state nor can it substantially affect the enforcement of the right as given by the state.

> And so the question is not whether a statute of limitations is deemed a matter of "procedure" in some sense. The question is whether such a statute concerns merely the manner and the means by which a right to recover, as recognized by the state, is enforced, or whether such statutory limitation is a matter of substance in the aspect that alone is relevant to our problem, namely, does it significantly affect the result of a litigation for a federal court to disregard a law of a state that would be controlling in an action upon the same claim by the same parties in a state court?

> It is therefore immaterial whether statutes of limitation are characterized either as "substantive" or "procedural" in state court opinions in any use of those terms unrelated to the specific issue before us. *Erie R. Co. v. Tompkins* was not an endeavor to formulate scientific legal terminology. It expressed a policy that touches vitally the proper distribution of judicial power between state and federal courts. In essence, the intent of that decision was to insure that, in all cases where a federal court is exercising jurisdiction solely because of the diversity of citizenship of the parties, the outcome of the litigation in the federal court should be substantially the same, so far as legal rules determine the outcome of a litigation, as it would be if tried in a state court. The nub of the policy that underlies *Erie R. Co. v. Tompkins* is that for the same transaction the accident of a suit by a non-resident litigant in a federal court

---

[a]   For an interesting treatment of pre-*Erie* equity practice in the federal courts, see Kristin A. Collins, "A Considerable Surgical Operation": Article III, Equity, and Judge-Made Law in the Federal Courts, 60 Duke L.J. 249 (2010).

instead of in a state court a block away should not lead to a substantially different result.

The Court concluded that state law should be applied to determine the statute of limitations in a case otherwise governed by state law: "Plainly enough, a statute that would completely bar recovery in a suit if brought in a State court bears on a State-created right vitally, and not merely formally or negligibly. As to consequences that so intimately affect recovery or nonrecovery, a federal court in a diversity case should follow State law."

In attempting to distinguish between substance and procedure, is it useful to focus on whether the rule in question is likely to affect the outcome of the litigation? Could not any rule affect the outcome, if a party failed to comply with it?

4. *RAGAN V. MERCHANTS TRANSFER*

Four years after *Guaranty Trust*, the Court decided a trio of cases that were particularly deferential to state law. Ragan v. Merchants Transfer & Warehouse Co., 337 U.S. 530 (1949); Woods v. Interstate Realty Co., 337 U.S. 535 (1949); Cohen v. Beneficial Industrial Loan Corporation, 337 U.S. 541 (1949). *Ragan* illustrates the Court's approach.

It involved a suit brought in federal court in Kansas concerning an automobile accident that had occurred on October 1, 1943. Federal Rule of Civil Procedure 3 provides that "a civil action is commenced by filing a complaint with the court." This was done on September 4, 1945, well within the two-year statute of limitations established by Kansas law. A summons was issued on September 7 and duly served, but it was later quashed, presumably because of some irregularity. A valid summons was finally served on December 28, after the statute of limitations had run.

Under Kansas law, the statute of limitations is not tolled until the summons is served. The plaintiff claimed that "the Federal Rules of Civil Procedure determine when an action is commenced in the federal courts—a matter of procedure which the principle of *Erie* does not control." Accordingly, the plaintiff argued, the suit should have been allowed to continue since it was properly filed in federal court within the applicable statute of limitations.

The Supreme Court disagreed. It held that the "theory of *Guaranty Trust*" required the federal court to follow the Kansas rule:

> [T]here can be no doubt that the suit was properly commenced in the federal court. But in the present case we look to local law to find the cause of action on which the suit is brought. Since that cause of action is created by local law, the measure of it is to be found only in local law. It carries the same burden and is subject to the same defenses in federal court as in the state court. It accrues and comes to an end when local law so declares. Where local law qualifies or abridges it, the federal court must follow suit. . . . We cannot give it longer life in the federal court than it would have had in the state court without adding something to the cause of action. We may not do that consistently with *Erie*.

5.   *BYRD V. BLUE RIDGE*

In part because of considerations relating to the role of the jury in the federal courts, the Court was less deferential to state law in Byrd v. Blue Ridge Rural Elec. Cooperative, Inc., 356 U.S. 525 (1958). On the merits, the question was whether the plaintiff was a "statutory employee" of the defendant under South Carolina law. If so, he could recover only workmen's compensation. If not, he was permitted to sue for negligence. The *Erie* issue was whether the "statutory employee" question should be tried to a jury or, as required by South Carolina law, to the judge. In an opinion by Justice Brennan, the Court began by describing the state rule as "merely a form and mode of enforcing the immunity, and not a rule intended to be bound up with the definition of the rights and obligations of the parties." The Court then turned to the legacy of *Guaranty Trust*:

> But cases following *Erie* have evinced a broader policy to the effect that the federal courts should conform as near as may be—in the absence of other considerations—to state rules even of form and mode where the state rules may bear substantially on the question whether the litigation would come out one way in the federal court and another way in the state court if the federal court failed to apply a particular local rule. Concededly the nature of the tribunal which tries issues may be important in the enforcement of the parcel of rights making up a cause of action or defense, and bear significantly upon achievement of uniform enforcement of the right. It may well be that in the instant personal-injury case the outcome would be substantially affected by whether the issue . . . is decided by a judge or a jury. Therefore, were "outcome" the only consideration, a strong case might appear for saying that the federal court should follow the state practice.

> But there are affirmative countervailing considerations at work here. The federal system is an independent system for administering justice to litigants who properly invoke its jurisdiction. An essential characteristic of that system is the manner in which, in civil common-law actions, it distributed trial functions between judge and jury and, under the influence—if not the command[10]—of the Seventh Amendment, assigns the decisions of disputed questions of fact to the jury. The policy of uniform enforcement of state-created rights and obligations, see, e.g., *Guaranty Trust v. York*, cannot in every case exact compliance with a state rule—not bound up with rights and obligations—which disrupts the federal system of allocating functions between judge and jury.

The Court concluded that the federal court should not follow the state rule in this case, in light of the "strong federal policy against allowing state rules to disrupt the judge-jury relationship in the federal courts" and the fact that

---

[10]   Our conclusion makes unnecessary the consideration of—and we intimate no view upon—the constitutional question whether the right of jury trial protected in the federal courts by the Seventh Amendment embraces the factual issue of statutory immunity when asserted, as here, as an affirmative defense in a common-law negligence action.

it was far from clear that following the federal jury practice would change the outcome.

6.   CONCLUDING COMMENT

To this point, the Court's "substance-procedure" jurisprudence had not clearly distinguished between situations in which the Federal Rules purported to govern an issue and situations in which they did not. In *Hanna v. Plumer*, the Court drew a sharp distinction between these two situations and modified the outcome-determinative test of *Guaranty Trust*.

Hanna v. Plumer

Supreme Court of the United States, 1965.
380 U.S. 460.

■ MR. CHIEF JUSTICE WARREN delivered the opinion of the Court.

The question to be decided is whether, in a civil action where the jurisdiction of the United States district court is based upon diversity of citizenship between the parties, service of process shall be made in the manner prescribed by state law or that set forth in Rule 4(d)(1) of the Federal Rules of Civil Procedure.

On February 6, 1963, petitioner, a citizen of Ohio, filed her complaint in the District Court for the District of Massachusetts, claiming damages in excess of $10,000 for personal injuries resulting from an automobile accident in South Carolina, allegedly caused by the negligence of one Louise Plumer Osgood, a Massachusetts citizen deceased at the time of the filing of the complaint. Respondent, Mrs. Osgood's executor and also a Massachusetts citizen, was named as defendant. On February 8, service was made by leaving copies of the summons and the complaint with respondent's wife at his residence, concededly in compliance with Rule 4(d)(1), which provides:

> The summons and complaint shall be served together. The plaintiff shall furnish the person making service with such copies as are necessary. Service shall be made as follows:
>
> > (1)   Upon an individual other than an infant or an incompetent person, by delivering a copy of the summons and of the complaint to him personally or by leaving copies thereof at his dwelling house or usual place of abode with some person of suitable age and discretion then residing therein. . . .

Respondent filed his answer on February 26, alleging, inter alia, that the action could not be maintained because it had been brought "contrary to and in violation of the provisions of Massachusetts General Laws (Ter. Ed.) Chapter 197, Section 9." That section provides:

> Except as provided in this chapter, an executor or administrator shall not be held to answer to an action by a creditor of

the deceased which is not commenced within one year from the time of his giving bond for the performance of his trust, or to such an action which is commenced within said year unless before the expiration thereof the writ in such action has been served by delivery in hand upon such executor or administrator or service thereof accepted by him or a notice stating the name of the estate, the name and address of the creditor, the amount of the claim and the court in which the action has been brought has been filed in the proper registry of probate. . . .

On October 17, 1963, the District Court granted respondent's motion for summary judgment, citing Ragan v. Merchants Transfer & Warehouse Co., 337 U.S. 530 (1949), and Guaranty Trust Co. v. York, 326 U.S. 99 (1945), in support of its conclusion that the adequacy of the service was to be measured by § 9, with which, the court held, petitioner had not complied. On appeal, petitioner admitted noncompliance with § 9, but argued that Rule 4(d)(1) defines the method by which service of process is to be effected in diversity actions. The Court of Appeals for the First Circuit, finding that "relatively recent amendments [to § 9] evince a clear legislative purpose to require personal notification within the year," concluded that the conflict of state and federal rules was over "a substantive rather than a procedural matter," and unanimously affirmed. Because of the threat to the goal of uniformity of federal procedure posed by the decision below, we granted certiorari.

We conclude that the adoption of Rule 4(d)(1), designed to control service of process in diversity actions, neither exceeded the congressional mandate embodied in the Rules Enabling Act nor transgressed constitutional bounds, and that the Rule is therefore the standard against which the District Court should have measured the adequacy of the service. Accordingly, we reverse the decision of the Court of Appeals.

The Rules Enabling Act, 28 U.S.C. § 2702, provides, in pertinent part:

> The Supreme Court shall have the power to prescribe, by general rules, the forms of process, writs, pleadings, and motions, and the practice and procedure of the district courts of the United States in civil actions.

> Such rules shall not abridge, enlarge or modify any substantive right and shall preserve the right of trial by jury. . . .

Under the cases construing the scope of the Enabling Act, Rule 4(d)(1) clearly passes muster. Prescribing the manner in which a defendant is to be notified that a suit has been instituted against him, it relates to the "practice and procedure of the district courts."

> The test must be whether a rule really regulates procedure,— the judicial process for enforcing rights and duties recognized by substantive law and for justly administering remedy and redress for disregard or infraction of them.

Sibbach v. Wilson & Co., 312 U.S. 1, 14 (1941). . . .

[W]ere there no conflicting state procedure, Rule 4(d)(1) would clearly control. However, respondent, focusing on the contrary Massachusetts rule, calls to the Court's attention another line of cases, a line which—like the Federal Rules—had its birth in 1938. Erie R. Co. v. Tompkins, 304 U.S. 64 (1938), overruling Swift v. Tyson, 41 U.S. (16 Pet.) 1 (1842), held that federal courts sitting in diversity cases, when deciding questions of "substantive" law, are bound by state court decisions as well as state statutes. The broad command of *Erie* was therefore identical to that of the Enabling Act: federal courts are to apply state substantive law and federal procedural law. However, as subsequent cases sharpened the distinction between substance and procedure, the line of cases following *Erie* diverged markedly from the line construing the Enabling Act. *Guaranty Trust Co. v. York* made it clear that *Erie*-type problems were not to be solved by reference to any traditional or common-sense substance-procedure distinction:

> And so the question is not whether a statute of limitations is deemed a matter of "procedure" in some sense. The question is . . . does it significantly affect the result of a litigation for a federal court to disregard a law of a state that would be controlling in an action upon the same claim by the same parties in a state court?

Respondent, by placing primary reliance on *York* and *Ragan*, suggests that the *Erie* doctrine acts as a check on the Federal Rules of Civil Procedure, that despite the clear command of Rule 4(d)(1), *Erie* and its progeny demand the application of the Massachusetts rule. Reduced to essentials, the argument is: (1) *Erie*, as refined in *York*, demands that federal courts apply state law whenever application of federal law in its stead will alter the outcome of the case. (2) In this case, a determination that the Massachusetts service requirements obtain will result in immediate victory for respondent. If, on the other hand, it should be held that Rule 4(d)(1) is applicable, the litigation will continue, with possible victory for petitioner. (3) Therefore, *Erie* demands application of the Massachusetts rule. The syllogism possesses an appealing simplicity, but is for several reasons invalid.

In the first place, it is doubtful that, even if there were no Federal Rule making it clear that in-hand service is not required in diversity actions, the *Erie* rule would have obligated the District Court to follow the Massachusetts procedure. "Outcome-determination" analysis was never intended to serve as a talisman. Byrd v. Blue Ridge Rural Elec. Cooperative, 356 U.S. 525, 537 (1958). Indeed, the message of *York* itself is that choices between state and federal law are to be made not by application of any automatic, "litmus paper" criterion, but rather by reference to the policies underlying the *Erie* rule.

The *Erie* rule is rooted in part in a realization that it would be unfair for the character or result of a litigation materially to differ because the suit had been brought in a federal court. . . . The decision was also in part a reaction to the practice of "forum-shopping" which had grown up in response to the rule of *Swift v. Tyson*. That the *York* test was an attempt to effectuate these policies is demonstrated by the fact that the opinion framed the inquiry in terms of "substantial" variations between state and federal litigation. Not only are nonsubstantial, or trivial, variations not likely to raise the sort of equal protection problems which troubled the Court in *Erie*; they are also unlikely to influence the choice of a forum. The "outcome-determination" test therefore cannot be read without reference to the twin aims of the *Erie* rule: discouragement of forum-shopping and avoidance of inequitable administration of the laws.[9]

The difference between the conclusion that the Massachusetts rule is applicable, and the conclusion that it is not, is of course at this point "outcome-determinative" in the sense that if we hold the state rule to apply, respondent prevails, whereas if we hold that Rule 4(d)(1) governs, the litigation will continue. But in this sense *every* procedural variation is "outcome-determinative." For example, having brought suit in a federal court, a plaintiff cannot then insist on the right to file subsequent pleadings in accord with the time limits applicable in the state courts, even though enforcement of the federal timetable will, if he continues to insist that he must meet only the state time limit, result in determination of the controversy against him. So it is here. Though choice of the federal or state rule will at this point have a marked effect upon the outcome of the litigation, the difference between the two rules would be of scant, if any, relevance to the choice of a forum. Petitioner, in choosing her forum, was not presented with a situation where application of the state rule would wholly bar recovery;[10] rather, adherence to the state rule would have resulted only in altering the way in which process was served.[11] Moreover, it is difficult to argue that permitting service of defendant's

---

[9]   The Court of Appeals seemed to frame the inquiry in terms of how "important" § 9 is to the State. In support of its suggestion that § 9 serves some interest the State regards as vital to its citizens, the court noted that something like § 9 has been on the books in Massachusetts a long time, that § 9 has been amended a number of times, and that § 9 is designed to make sure that executors receive actual notice. The apparent lack of relation among these three observations is not surprising, because it is not clear to what sort of question the Court of Appeals was addressing itself. One cannot meaningfully ask how important something is without first asking "important for what purpose?" *Erie* and its progeny make clear that when a federal court sitting in a diversity case is faced with a question of whether or not to apply state law, the importance of a state rule is indeed relevant, but only in the context of asking whether application of the rule would make so important a difference to the character or result of the litigation that failure to enforce it would unfairly discriminate against citizens of the forum State, or whether application of the rule would have so important an effect upon the fortunes of one or both of the litigants that failure to enforce it would be likely to cause a plaintiff to choose the federal court.

[10]   See *Guaranty Trust Co. v. York*; *Ragan v. Merchants Transfer Co.;* Woods v. Interstate Realty Co., 337 U.S. 535 (1949). Similarly, a federal court's refusal to enforce the New Jersey rule involved in Cohen v. Beneficial Loan Corp., 337 U.S. 541 (1949), requiring the posting of security by plaintiffs in stockholders' derivative actions, might well impel a stockholder to choose to bring suit in the federal, rather than the state, court.

[11]   We cannot seriously entertain the thought that one suing an estate would be led to choose the federal court because of a belief that adherence to Rule 4(d)(1) is less likely to give the executor actual notice than § 9, and therefore more likely to produce a default judgment. Rule 4(d)(1) is well designed to give actual notice, as it did in this case.

wife to take the place of in-hand service of defendant himself alters the mode of enforcement of state-created rights in a fashion sufficiently "substantial" to raise the sort of equal protection problems to which the *Erie* opinion alluded.

There is, however, a more fundamental flaw in respondent's syllogism: the incorrect assumption that the rule of *Erie R. Co. v. Tompkins* constitutes the appropriate test of the validity and therefore the applicability of a Federal Rule of Civil Procedure. The *Erie* rule has never been invoked to void a Federal Rule. It is true that there have been cases where this Court has held applicable a state rule in the face of an argument that the situation was governed by one of the Federal Rules. But the holding of each such case was not that *Erie* commanded displacement of a Federal Rule by an inconsistent state rule, but rather that the scope of the Federal Rule was not as broad as the losing party urged, and therefore, there being no Federal Rule which covered the point in dispute, *Erie* commanded the enforcement of state law. . . . (Here, of course, the clash is unavoidable; Rule 4(d)(1) says—implicitly, but with unmistakable clarity—that in-hand service is not required in federal courts.) At the same time, in cases adjudicating the validity of Federal Rules, we have not applied the *York* rule or other refinements of *Erie*, but have to this day continued to decide questions concerning the scope of the Enabling Act and the constitutionality of specific Federal Rules in light of the distinction set forth in *Sibbach*.

Nor has the development of two separate lines of cases been inadvertent. The line between "substance" and "procedure" shifts as the legal context change. . . . It is true that both the Enabling Act and the *Erie* rule say, roughly, that federal courts are to apply state "substantive" law and federal "procedural" law, but from that it need not follow that the tests are identical. For they were designed to control very different sorts of decisions. When a situation is covered by one of the Federal Rules, the question facing the court is a far cry from the typical, relatively unguided *Erie* choice: the court has been instructed to apply the Federal Rule, and can refuse to do so only if the Advisory Committee, this Court, and Congress erred in their prima facie judgment that the Rule in question transgresses neither the terms of the Enabling Act nor constitutional restrictions.

We are reminded by the *Erie* opinion that neither Congress nor the federal courts can, under the guise of formulating rules of decision for federal courts, fashion rules which are not supported by a grant of federal authority contained in Article I or some other section of the Constitution; in such areas state law must govern because there can be no other law. But the opinion in *Erie*, which involved no Federal Rule and dealt with a question which was "substantive" in every traditional sense (whether the railroad owed a duty of care to Tompkins as a trespasser or a licensee), surely neither said nor implied that measures like Rule 4(d)(1) are unconstitutional. For the constitutional provision for a federal court system (augmented by the Necessary and Proper Clause) carries with it congressional power to make rules governing the practice and pleading in those courts, which in turn includes a power to regulate matters which, though falling within the uncertain area between substance and procedure, are rationally capable of classification as either. Cf. M'Culloch v. Maryland, 17 U.S. (4 Wheat.) 316, 421 (1819). Neither *York* nor the cases following it ever suggested that the rule there laid down for coping with situations where no Federal Rule applies is coextensive with the limitation on Congress to which *Erie* had adverted. . . .

Erie and its offspring cast no doubt on the long-recognized power of Congress to prescribe housekeeping rules for federal courts even though some of those rules will inevitably differ from comparable state rules. . . . Thus, though a court, in measuring a Federal Rule against the standards contained in the Enabling Act and the Constitution, need not wholly blind itself to the degree to which the Rule makes the character and result of the federal litigation stray from the course it would follow in state courts, it cannot be forgotten that the *Erie* rule, and the guidelines suggested in *York*, were created to serve another purpose altogether. To hold that a Federal Rule of Civil Procedure must cease to function whenever it alters the mode of enforcing state-created rights would be to disembowel either the Constitution's grant of power over federal procedure or Congress's attempt to exercise that power in the Enabling Act. Rule 4(d)(1) is valid and controls the instant case.

Reversed.

■ MR. JUSTICE BLACK concurs in the result.

■ MR. JUSTICE HARLAN, concurring.

It is unquestionably true that up to now *Erie* and the cases following it have not succeeded in articulating a workable doctrine governing choice of law in diversity actions. I respect the Court's effort to clarify the situation in today's opinion. However, in doing so I think it has misconceived the constitutional premises of *Erie* and has failed to deal adequately with those past decisions upon which the courts below relied.

Erie was something more than an opinion which worried about "forum-shopping and avoidance of inequitable administration of the laws," although to be sure these were important elements of the decision. I have always regarded that decision as one of the modern cornerstones of our federalism, expressing policies that profoundly touch the allocation of judicial power between the state and federal systems. *Erie* recognized that there should not be two conflicting systems of law controlling the primary activity of citizens, for such alternative governing authority must necessarily give rise to a debilitating uncertainty in the planning of everyday affairs.[1] And it recognized that the scheme of our Constitution envisions

---

[1]   Since the rules involved in the present case are parallel, rather than conflicting, this first rationale does not come into play here.

an allocation of law-making functions between state and federal legislative processes which is undercut if the federal judiciary can make substantive law affecting state affairs beyond the bounds of congressional legislative powers in this regard. Thus, in diversity cases *Erie* commands that it be the state law governing primary private activity which prevails.

The shorthand formulations which have appeared in some past decisions are prone to carry untoward results that frequently arise from oversimplification. The Court is quite right in stating that the "outcome-determinative" test of *Guaranty Trust Co. v. York*, if taken literally, proves too much, for any rule, no matter how clearly "procedural," can affect the outcome of litigation if it is not obeyed. In turning from the "outcome" test of *York* back to the unadorned forum-shopping rationale of *Erie*, however, the Court falls prey to like oversimplification, for a simple forum-shopping rule also proves too much; litigants often choose a federal forum merely to obtain what they consider the advantages of the Federal Rules of Civil Procedure or to try their cases before a supposedly more favorable judge. To my mind the proper line of approach in determining whether to apply a state or a federal rule, whether "substantive" or "procedural," is to stay close to basic principles by inquiring if the choice of rule would substantially affect those primary decisions respecting human conduct which our constitutional system leaves to state regulation.[2] If so, *Erie* and the Constitution require that the state rule prevail, even in the face of a conflicting federal rule.

The Court weakens, if indeed it does not submerge, this basic principle by finding, in effect, a grant of substantive legislative power in the constitutional provision for a federal court system (compare *Swift v. Tyson*), and through it, setting up the Federal Rules as a body of law inviolate. . . . So long as a reasonable man could characterize any duly adopted federal rule as "procedural," the Court, unless I misapprehend what is said, would have it apply no matter how seriously it frustrated a State's substantive regulation of the primary conduct and affairs of its citizens. Since the members of the Advisory Committee, the Judicial Conference, and this Court who formulated the Federal Rules are presumably reasonable men, it follows that the integrity of the Federal Rules is absolute. Whereas the unadulterated outcome and forum-shopping tests may err too far toward honoring state rules, I submit that the Court's "arguably procedural, ergo constitutional" test moves too fast and far in the other direction. . . .

It remains to apply what has been said to the present case. The Massachusetts rule provides that an executor need not answer suits unless in-hand service was made upon him or notice of the action was filed in the proper registry of probate within one year of his giving bond. The

---

[2] Byrd v. Blue Ridge Rural Elec. Cooperative, Inc., 356 U.S. 525, 536–40 (1958), indicated that state procedures would apply if the State had manifested a particularly strong interest in their employment. However, this approach may not be of constitutional proportions.

evident intent of this statute is to permit an executor to distribute the estate which he is administering without fear that further liabilities may be outstanding for which he could be held personally liable. If the Federal District Court in Massachusetts applies Rule 4(d)(1) of the Federal Rules of Civil Procedure instead of the Massachusetts service rule, what effect would that have on the speed and assurance with which estates are distributed? As I see it, the effect would not be substantial. It would mean simply that an executor would have to check at his own house or the federal courthouse as well as the registry of probate before he could distribute the estate with impunity. As this does not seem enough to give rise to any real impingement on the vitality of the state policy which the Massachusetts rule is intended to serve, I concur in the judgment of the Court.

NOTES ON SUBSTANCE AND PROCEDURE AFTER HANNA

1.   QUESTIONS AND COMMENTS ON HANNA

The Court's opinion in *Hanna* addresses two situations. The first is when a Federal Rule of Civil Procedure conflicts with state law. The question then, the Court says, is whether the federal rule is "rationally capable of classification" as procedure. If so, the Federal Rule is valid and must be applied. Is this approach consistent with the Rules Enabling Act? With more general considerations of federalism?

The second situation to which *Hanna* speaks is when there is no Federal Rule of Civil Procedure on point. The Court's discussion of the "twin aims of *Erie*" in footnote 9 and its accompanying text[a] suggests that the test for determining whether to follow state law in such a situation is twofold. State law is to be followed if

> the rule would make so important a difference to the character or result of the litigation that failure to enforce it would unfairly discriminate against citizens of the forum State, or . . . application of the rule would have so important an effect upon the fortunes of one or both of the litigants that failure to enforce it would be likely to cause a plaintiff to choose the federal court.

Is this a meaningful inquiry? Is Justice Harlan correct that this inquiry, like the "outcome" test, "proves too much"? As a thought experiment, consider the following approach:

---

[a]   For the argument that the "twin aims" are "unrelated to the concerns about federalism and state interests that motivated *Erie*" but "are instead justified by the federal interests standing behind the statute giving the federal court jurisdiction," see Michael Steven Green, The Twin Aims of *Erie*, 88 Notre Dame L. Rev. 1865 (2013). Green argues that this view of the "twin aims" has consequences in numerous contexts. For one example, the question in *York* "was not the applicability of state law, but whether the forum state's rule should be incorporated into federal common law to serve the federal purposes standing behind the diversity statute." It is argued in Jeffrey L. Rensberger, *Erie* and Preemption: Killing One Bird with Two Stones, 90 Ind. L.J. 1591 (2015), that the division of the substance-procedure problem into two categories turning on whether a federal rule is involved is wrong. In both cases, the author contends, the issues should be examined through the lens of preemption doctrine: "*Erie* and preemption are the same problem, albeit in somewhat different contexts."

(i)   If there is an applicable Federal Rule of Civil Procedure, follow it.

(ii)   If not, but there is a discernible federal policy, follow it.

(iii) If there is no applicable federal rule or policy, follow state law.

Would step (i) be consistent with the Rules Enabling Act? Does step (ii) give enough weight to the concerns articulated by the Court in *Erie*?

In the substance-procedure cases that have been decided by the Supreme Court since *Hanna*, there is frequently a dispute over whether a Federal Rule applies. In making this determination, what attitude should the federal courts bring to their interpretation of the Federal Rules? Should the Federal Rules be narrowly construed to avoid conflicts with state law? Or is the desirability of a uniform system of federal procedure—applicable to diversity and federal question cases alike—so strong that the possibility of conflict with state law should be ignored?

2. *WALKER V. ARMCO STEEL CORP.*

As illustrated by Walker v. Armco Steel Corp., 446 U.S. 740 (1980), considerations of substance vs. procedure can affect the determination of whether a Federal Rule applies to a particular issue. Walker, a carpenter, injured his eye when a nail he was hammering shattered. He filed a federal diversity suit against the manufacturer of the nail. The injury occurred on August 22, 1975. The complaint was filed on August 19, 1977. The record is ambiguous as to whether the summons was issued on August 19 or August 20, but in any event it was not delivered to the marshal for service until December 1, 1977, when it was served on the defendant.

The Oklahoma statute of limitations was two years. Oklahoma law provided that an action was "commenced" for purposes of tolling the statute of limitations by service of the summons, or in the alternative by filing the complaint if the summons was served within 60 days. Rule 3 of the Federal Rules, however, provides that, "A civil action is commenced by filing a complaint with the court." The plaintiff conceded that the Oklahoma law was not followed, but argued that Rule 3 should govern in federal court. The District Court dismissed the complaint, citing *Ragan,* and the Supreme Court agreed in a unanimous opinion by Justice Marshall.

After reviewing *Erie, Guaranty Trust, Ragan,* and *Hanna,* the Court noted that "the instant action is barred by the statute of limitations unless *Ragan* is no longer good law." The Court continued:

> This Court in *Hanna* distinguished *Ragan* rather than overruled it, and for good reason. Application of the *Hanna* analysis is premised on a "direct collision" between the federal rule and the state law. In *Hanna* itself the "clash" between Rule 4(d)(1) and the state in-hand service requirement was "unavoidable." The first question must therefore be whether the scope of the federal rule in fact is sufficiently broad to control the issue before the Court. It is

only if that question is answered affirmatively that the *Hanna* analysis applies.[9]

. . . There is no indication that [Rule 3] was intended to toll a state statute of limitations, much less that it purported to displace state tolling rules for purposes of state statutes of limitations. In our view, in diversity actions Rule 3 governs the date from which various timing requirements of the federal rules begin to run, but does not affect state statutes of limitations.

In contrast to Rule 3, the Oklahoma statute is a statement of a substantive decision by that state that actual service on, and accordingly actual notice by, the defendant is an integral part of the several policies served by the statute of limitations. The statute of limitations establishes a deadline after which the defendant may legitimately have peace of mind; it also recognizes that after a certain period of time it is unfair to require the defendant to attempt to piece together his defense to an old claim. A requirement of actual service promotes both of those functions of the statute. It is these policy aspects which make the service requirement an "integral" part of the statute of limitations both in this case and in *Ragan*. As such, the service rule must be considered part and parcel of the statute of limitations. Rule 3 does not replace such policy determinations found in state law. Rule 3 and [the Oklahoma law] can exist side-by-side, therefore, each controlling its own intended sphere of coverage without conflict.

Since there is no direct conflict between the federal rule and the state law, the *Hanna* analysis does not apply.[14] Instead, the policies behind *Erie* and *Ragan* control the issue whether, in the absence of a federal rule directly on point, state service requirements which are an integral part of the state statute of limitations should control in an action based on state law which is filed in federal court under diversity jurisdiction. The reasons for the application of such a state service requirement in a diversity action in the absence of a conflicting federal rule are well explained in *Erie* and *Ragan,* and need not be repeated here. It is sufficient to note that although in this case failure to apply the state service law might not create any problem of forum shopping,[15] the result would be an "inequitable administration" of the law. *Hanna*, 380 U.S. at 468. There is simply no reason why, in the absence of a controlling federal rule, an action based on state law which concededly would

---

[9]   This is not to suggest that the Federal Rules of Civil Procedure are to be narrowly construed in order to avoid a "direct collision" with state law. The Federal Rules should be given their plain meaning. If a direct collision with state law arises from that plain meaning, then the analysis developed in *Hanna v. Plumer* applies.

[14]   Since we hold that Rule 3 does not apply, it is unnecessary for us to address the second question posed by the *Hanna* analysis: whether Rule 3, if applied, would be outside the scope of the Rules Enabling Act or beyond the power of Congress under the Constitution.

[15]   There is no indication that when petitioner filed his suit in federal court he had any reason to believe that he would be unable to comply with the service requirements of Oklahoma law or that he chose to sue in federal court in an attempt to avoid those service requirements.

be barred in the state courts by the statute of limitations should proceed through litigation to judgment in federal court solely because of the fortuity that there is diversity of citizenship between the litigants. The policies underlying diversity jurisdiction do not support such a distinction between state and federal plaintiffs, and *Erie* and its progeny do not permit it.

Is *Walker* consistent with *Hanna*? What is the Court assuming when interpreting Rule 3? Does *Walker* imply, contrary to the Court's assertion, that the Federal Rules should be narrowly construed to avoid a "direct collision" with state law?

3. *GASPERINI V. CENTER FOR HUMANITIES*

In Gasperini v. Center for Humanities, 518 U.S. 415 (1996), the Court addressed a situation in which, at least in the view of the majority, no Federal Rule was potentially applicable. As a result, the Court was operating under the "twin aims of *Erie*" analysis articulated in *Hanna*.

Gasperini, a journalist, brought a diversity action against the Center for Humanities in a federal district court in New York, alleging that the Center had lost a set of 300 photographic slides that it had borrowed from him. The Center conceded liability, and the issue of damages was tried before a jury. After hearing expert testimony, the jury awarded Gasperini $1500 for each lost slide, for a total of $450,000. The Circuit Court reversed, concluding that the award was excessive. The court reached this conclusion after applying a New York statute that directs New York appellate courts to review the size of jury verdicts and order new trials when the jury's award "deviates materially from what would be reasonable compensation." This standard is more intrusive than the common law standard traditionally applied by the federal courts in reviewing jury awards, under which the award would not be disturbed unless so exorbitant that it "shocked the conscience of the court."

The Supreme Court vacated the decision below and remanded for further proceedings. In an opinion by Justice Ginsburg, the Court began by observing that "[c]lassification of a law as 'substantive' or 'procedural' for *Erie* purposes is sometimes a challenging endeavor." After reviewing the relevant decisions, it said that "we address the question whether New York's 'deviates materially' standard . . . is outcome affective in this sense: Would 'application of the [standard] . . . have so important an effect upon the fortunes of one or both of the litigants that failure to [apply] it would [unfairly discriminate against citizens of the forum State, or] be likely to cause a plaintiff to choose the federal court"?

The Court noted that even the plaintiff acknowledged that if New York had enacted a statutory cap on damages, this would be "substantive" for purposes of the *Erie* doctrine, and added that the New York law in question "was designed to provide an analogous control." The Court further observed that although New York law "contains a procedural instruction, . . . the State's objective is manifestly substantive." Finally, the Court said that if federal courts ignored the state law standard, there would likely be substantial variations between state and federal monetary judgments. The conclusion, therefore, was that the New York law implicated the twin aims of *Erie* articulated in *Hanna*.

The Court went on to explain, however, that there was a countervailing interest here that stemmed from the Seventh Amendment. This Amendment "bears not only on the allocation of trial functions between judge and jury, the issue in *Byrd*; it also controls the allocation of authority to review verdicts, the issue of concern here." Application of the New York standard by a federal appeals court, it was reasoned, "would be out of sync with the federal system's division of trial and appellate court functions, an allocation weighted by the Seventh Amendment." This concern led to the conclusion that federal district courts, rather than the federal circuit court should apply New York's "deviates materially" standard, subject to review by the circuit court for abuse of discretion.

Justice Scalia dissented, joined by Chief Justice Rehnquist and Justice Thomas. He argued that "changing the standard by which trial judges review jury verdicts . . . disrupt[s] the federal system, and is plainly inconsistent with the 'strong federal policy against allowing state rules to disrupt the judge-jury relationship in the federal court.' Byrd v. Blue Ridge Rural Elec. Cooperative, Inc., 356 U.S. 525, 538 (1958)." He rejected the majority's analogy to a statutory cap on damages, arguing that "[t]here is an absolutely fundamental distinction between a *rule of law* such as that, which would ordinarily be imposed upon the jury in the trial court's instructions, and a *rule of review*, which simply determines how closely the jury verdict will be scrutinized for compliance with the instructions." He also accused the majority of "commit[ting] the classic *Erie* mistake of regarding whatever changes the outcome as substantive." Finally, he argued that the Court should not even have reached the *Erie* question because Rule 59 of the Federal Rules of Civil Procedure provides that "[a] new trial may be granted . . . for any of the reasons for which new trials have heretofore been granted in actions at law in the courts of the United States." Because "[i]t is simply not possible to give controlling effect both to the federal standard and the state standard in reviewing the jury's award, . . . the court has no choice but to apply the Federal Rule."

4.   *SEMTEK INTERNATIONAL INC. V. LOCKHEED MARTIN CORP.*

As in *Gasperini*, the Court in Semtek International Inc. v. Lockheed Martin Corp., 531 U.S. 497 (2001), found that no Federal Rule applied to the issue before it. In that case, Semtek's suit against Lockheed, based on diversity jurisdiction, had been dismissed by a California federal district court as barred by the California two-year statute of limitations. A suit alleging the same claims was then filed in a Maryland state court, based on the Maryland three-year limitations period. The Maryland courts held that the preclusive effect of the California federal court judgment was to be determined by federal law and that, under the applicable federal law, the suit was barred.

The Supreme Court unanimously reversed. In an opinion by Justice Scalia, the Court found no answer in the Federal Rules of Civil Procedure. Although Rule 41(b) deems dismissals such as this one to be a judgment "on the merits," the Court concluded that it does not address the res judicata effect of such judgments. Among other things, the reasoning was that construing Rule 41(a) to give more res judicata effect to dismissals of state law claims than is provided for under the state law in which the federal court sits would arguably violate the Rules Enabling Act by affecting substantive rights, and would run afoul of the twin aims of *Erie* (by creating a claim preclusive judgment in cases removed to federal court but not cases litigated in state court). So instead Rule 41(b) was interpreted as simply barring the return of the losing party *to the same court.*

There was one prior Supreme Court case on point, Dupasseur v. Rochereau, 88 U.S. (21 Wall.) 130 (1875), which held that state law controlled the res judicata effect of a federal trial court exercising diversity jurisdiction. But *Dupasseur* was "not dispositive because it was decided under the Conformity Act of 1872, which required federal courts to apply the procedural law of the forum State in nonequity cases." What, then, to do? The Court's answer was that "federal common law governs the claim-preclusive effect of a dismissal by a federal court sitting in diversity. . . . It is left to us, then, to determine the appropriate federal rule."

And what should "the appropriate federal rule" be? The answer was:

> [D]espite the sea change that has occurred in the background law since *Dupasseur* was decided—not only repeal of the Conformity Act but also the watershed decision of this Court in *Erie*—we think the result decreed by *Dupasseur* continues to be correct for diversity cases. Since state, rather than federal, substantive law is at issue there is no need for a uniform federal rule. And indeed, nationwide uniformity in the substance of the matter is better served by having the same claim-preclusive rule (the state rule) apply whether the dismissal has been ordered by a state or a federal court. This is, it seems to us, a classic case for adopting, as the federally prescribed rule of decision, the law that would be applied by state courts in the State in which the federal diversity court sits. [A]ny other rule would produce the sort of "forum-shopping . . . and . . . inequitable administration of the laws" that *Erie* seeks to avoid, Hanna v. Plumer, 380 U.S. 460, 468 (1965), since filing in, or removing to, federal court would be encouraged by the divergent effects that the litigants would anticipate from likely grounds of dismissal.

> This federal reference to state law will not obtain, of course, in situations in which the state law is incompatible with federal interests. If, for example, state law did not accord claim-preclusive effect to dismissals for willful violation of discovery orders, federal courts' interest in the integrity of their own processes might justify a contrary federal rule. No such conflict with potential federal interests exists in the present case. Dismissal of this state cause of action was decreed by the California federal court only because the California statute of limitations so required; and there is no conceivable federal interest in giving that time bar more effect in other courts than the California courts themselves would impose.

The case was accordingly remanded so that the Maryland courts could determine the applicable California preclusion rules.[b]

5.   *SHADY GROVE ORTHOPEDIC ASSOCIATES V. ALLSTATE INSURANCE CO.*

The Court returned to the first part of the *Hanna* analysis, which governs what to do when a Federal Rule is potentially applicable, in Shady Grove Orthopedic Associates v. Allstate Insurance Co., 559 U.S. 393 (2010). After Shady Grove provided medical care to Sonia Galvez, it was assigned her rights to insurance benefits under a policy issued in New York by Allstate Insurance Co. Shady Grove tendered its claim to Allstate, which under New York law had 30 days in which to pay it. Allstate eventually paid, but not on time, and it refused to pay the statutory interest mandated by New York law. Shady Grove then filed a diversity class action in federal court in New York, alleging that Allstate routinely refused to pay interest on overdue benefits. After concluding that statutory interest constituted a "penalty," the District Court dismissed the suit on the basis of a New York law providing that "[u]nless a statute creating or imposing a penalty . . . specifically authorizes the recovery thereof in a class action, an action to recover a penalty . . . created or imposed by statute may not be maintained as a class action." The court reached this conclusion notwithstanding Rule 23 of the Federal Rules of Civil Procedure, which provides that "[a] class action may be maintained" if certain conditions, all of which were satisfied, are met.

(i)   *Interpretive Principles*

In an opinion by Justice Scalia, a five-to-four majority described the starting point of its analysis:

> We must first determine whether Rule 23 answers the question in dispute. If it does, it governs—New York's law notwithstanding— unless it exceeds statutory authorization or Congress's rulemaking power. We do not wade into *Erie*'s murky waters unless the federal rule is inapplicable or invalid.

The Court began its discussion of this issue as follows:

> The question in dispute is whether Shady Grove's suit may proceed as a class action. Rule 23 provides an answer. . . . By its terms [it] creates a categorical rule entitling a plaintiff whose suit meets the specified criteria to pursue his claim as a class action. [It] provides a one-size-fits-all formula for deciding the class-action question. Because [New York law] attempts to answer the same question—i.e., it states that Shady Grove's suit "may *not* be maintained as a class action" (emphasis added) because of the relief it seeks—it cannot apply in diversity suits unless Rule 23 is ultra vires.

Joined by Justices Kennedy, Breyer, and Alito, Justice Ginsburg argued in dissent that there was no conflict between Rule 23 and the New York law.

---

[b]   In Taylor v. Sturgell, 553 U.S. 880 (2008), the Court observed that "[f]or judgments in federal-question cases . . . federal courts participate in developing 'uniform federal rule[s]' of res judicata, which this Court has ultimate authority to determine and declare."

Her characterization of the situation was that the New York law effectively provided a cap on damages:

> Sensibly read, Rule 23 governs procedural aspects of class litigation, but allows state law to control the size of a monetary award a class plaintiff may pursue. . . . Rule 23 describes a method of enforcing a claim for relief, while [New York law] defines the dimensions of the claim itself.

She also argued that the Court should "interpret Federal Rules with awareness of, and sensitivity to, important state regulatory policies." It should avoid "immoderate interpretations of the Federal Rules that would trench on state prerogatives without serving any countervailing federal interest." She accused the majority of "veer[ing] away from that approach . . . in favor of a mechanical reading of Federal Rules, insensitive to state interests and productive of discord." She read New York law as designed to "prevent the exorbitant inflation of penalties," and disagreed with the majority that Rule 23 should be construed to conflict with that effort. "Sensibly read," she concluded, "Rule 23 governs procedural aspects of class litigation, but allows state law to control the size of a monetary award a class plaintiff may pursue."

The Court responded at length. The purpose of the New York law, it said, "cannot override the statute's clear text." Even if this was the aim of the New York law, it "achieves that end by limiting a plaintiff's power to maintain a class action," and "[w]e cannot rewrite that to reflect our perception of legislative purpose." The Court also rejected consideration of the "subjective intentions of the state legislature" in determining whether there was a conflict between a state law and a Federal Rule:

> It would mean, to begin with, that one State's statute could survive preemption (and accordingly affect the procedures in federal court) while another State's identical law would not, merely because its authors had different aspirations. It would also mean that district courts would have to discern, in every diversity case, the purpose behind any putatively preempted state procedural rule, even if its text squarely conflicts with federal law. That task will often prove arduous. Many laws further more than one aim, and the aim of others may be impossible to discern. Moreover, to the extent the dissent's purpose-driven approach depends on its characterization of [the New York law] as substantive, it would apply to many state rules ostensibly addressed to procedure. Pleading standards, for example, often embody policy preferences about the types of claims that should succeed—as do rules governing summary judgment, pretrial discovery, and the admissibility of certain evidence. Hard cases will abound. It is not even clear that a state supreme court's pronouncement of the law's purpose would settle the issue, since existence of the factual predicate for avoiding federal pre-emption is ultimately a federal question. Predictably, federal judges would be condemned to poring through state legislative history—which may be less easily obtained, less thorough, and less familiar than its federal counterpart.

The "central difficulty" of the dissent's focus on legislative intent, the Court continued, is that by their terms Rule 23 and New York law are in conflict:

> *Whatever* the policies they pursue, they flatly contradict each other. [It is argued that] we can (and must) interpret Rule 23 in a manner that avoids overstepping its authorizing statute. If the Rule were susceptible of two meanings—one that would violate [the Rules Enabling Act] and another that would not—we would agree. But it is not. Rule 23 unambiguously authorizes any plaintiff, in any federal civil proceeding, to maintain a class action if the Rule's prerequisites are met. We cannot contort its text, even to avert a collision with state law that might render it invalid.

A footnote to this passage added:

> If all the dissent means is that we should read an ambiguous Federal Rule to avoid "substantial variations [in outcomes] between state and federal litigation," Semtek Int'l Inc. v. Lockheed Martin Corp., 531 U.S. 497, 504 (2001), we entirely agree. We should do so not to avoid doubt as to the Rule's validity—since a Federal Rule that fails *Erie*'s forum-shopping test is not ipso facto invalid, see Hanna v. Plumer, 380 U.S. 460, 469–72 (1965)—but because it is reasonable to assume that "Congress is just as concerned as we have been to avoid significant differences between state and federal courts in adjudicating claims," Stewart Organization, Inc. v. Ricoh Corp., 487 U.S. 22, 37–38 (1988) (Scalia, J., dissenting). The assumption is irrelevant here, however, because there is only one reasonable reading of Rule 23.

(ii) Validity Under Rules Enabling Act

Justice Scalia concluded his opinion for the Court with the observation that "[w]e must therefore confront head-on whether Rule 23 falls within the statutory authorization." His affirmative answer to this question was provided in an opinion joined only by Chief Justice Roberts and Justices Thomas and Sotomayor. He began with these observations:

> *Erie* involved the constitutional power of federal courts to supplant state law with judge-made rules. In that context, it made no difference whether the rule was technically one of substance or procedure; the touchstone was whether it "significantly affect[s] the result of a litigation." Guaranty Trust Co. v. York, 326 U.S. 99, 109 (1945). That is not the test for either the constitutionality or the statutory validity of a Federal Rule of Procedure. Congress has undoubted power to supplant state law, and undoubted power to prescribe rules for the courts it has created, so long as those rules regulate matters "rationally capable of classification" as procedure. Hanna v. Plumer, 380 U.S. 460, 472 (1965). In the Rules Enabling Act, Congress authorized this Court to promulgate rules of procedure subject to its review, but with the limitation that those rules "shall not abridge, enlarge or modify any substantive right."

We have long held that this limitation means that the Rule must "really regulat[e] procedure,—the judicial process for enforcing rights and duties recognized by substantive law and for justly administering remedy and redress for disregard or infraction of them," Sibbach v. Wilson & Co., 312 U.S. 1, 14 (1941). The test is not whether the rule affects a litigant's substantive rights; most procedural rules do. What matters is what the rule itself regulates: If it governs only "the manner and the means" by which the litigants' rights are "enforced," it is valid; if it alters "the rules of decision by which [the] court will adjudicate [those] rights," it is not. Mississippi Publishing Corp. v. Murphree, 326 U.S. 438, 446 (1946). . . .

Applying that criterion, we think it obvious that rules allowing multiple claims (and claims by or against multiple parties) to be litigated together are also valid. Such rules neither change plaintiffs' separate entitlements to relief nor abridge defendants' rights; they alter only how the claims are processed. For the same reason, Rule 23—at least insofar as it allows willing plaintiffs to join their separate claims against the same defendants in a class action— falls within [the Rules Enabling Act's] authorization. A class action, no less than traditional joinder (of which it is a species), merely enables a federal court to adjudicate claims of multiple parties at once, instead of in separate suits. And like traditional joinder, it leaves the parties' legal rights and duties intact and the rules of decision unchanged.

It did not matter, Scalia continued, that the New York law may have had a substantive purpose:

The . . . substantive nature of New York's law, or its substantive purpose, *makes no difference*. A Federal Rule of Procedure is not valid in some jurisdictions and invalid in others—or valid in some cases and invalid in others—depending upon whether its effect is to frustrate a state substantive law (or a state procedural law enacted for substantive purposes). [I]t is not the substantive or procedural nature or purpose of the affected state law that matters, but the substantive or procedural nature of the Federal Rule. We have held since *Sibbach*, and reaffirmed repeatedly, that the validity of a Federal Rule depends entirely upon whether it regulates procedure. If it does, it is authorized by [the Rules Enabling Act] and is valid in all jurisdictions, with respect to all claims, regardless of its incidental effect upon state-created rights.

Scalia acknowledged that "keeping the federal-court door open to class actions that cannot proceed in state court will produce forum shopping." But, while such forum shopping "is unacceptable when it comes as the consequence of judge-made rules created to fill supposed 'gaps' in positive federal law," he concluded that "divergence from state law, with the attendant consequence of forum shopping, is the inevitable (indeed, one might say the intended) result of a uniform system of federal procedure."

Justice Stevens concurred in the result reached by Justice Scalia and his three colleagues. But he approached the case differently. He described his disagreement in the following terms:

> The New York law at issue is a procedural rule that is not part of New York's substantive law. Accordingly, I agree with Justice Scalia that Federal Rule of Civil Procedure 23 must apply in this case. . . . But I also agree with Justice Ginsburg that there are some state procedural rules that federal courts must apply in diversity cases because they function as a part of the State's definition of substantive rights and remedies. . . . Unlike Justice Scalia, I believe that an application of a federal rule that effectively abridges, enlarges, or modifies a state-created right or remedy violates [the command of the Rules Enabling Act]. Congress may have the constitutional power "to supplant state law" with rules that are "rationally capable of classification as procedure," but we should generally presume that it has not done so. Indeed, the mandate that federal rules "shall not abridge, enlarge or modify any substantive right" evinces the opposite intent, as does Congress's decision to delegate the creation of rules to this Court rather than to a political branch.

In response, Justice Scalia—on this point joined only by Chief Justice Roberts and Justice Thomas—argued that the approach that Justice Stevens was suggesting was ruled out by *Sibbach*. Scalia acknowledged that there is tension between *Sibbach* and the text of the Rules Enabling Act:

> In reality, the concurrence seeks not to apply *Sibbach*, but to overrule it (or, what is the same, to rewrite it). Its approach, the concurrence insists, gives short shrift to the statutory text forbidding the Federal Rules from "abridg[ing], enlarg[ing], or modify[ing] any substantive right." There is something to that. It is possible to understand how it can be determined whether a Federal Rule "enlarges" substantive rights without consulting State law: If the Rule creates a substantive right, even one that duplicates some state-created rights, it establishes a new *federal* right. But it is hard to understand how it can be determined whether a Federal Rule "abridges" or "modifies" substantive rights without knowing what state-created rights would obtain if the Federal Rule did not exist. *Sibbach*'s exclusive focus on the challenged Federal Rule— driven by the very real concern that Federal Rules which vary from State to State would be chaos—is hard to square with [the Rules Enabling Act's] terms.

But he noted that "*Sibbach* has been settled law . . . for nearly seven decades."

6.   QUESTIONS AND COMMENTS ON *SHADY GROVE*

The specific holding in *Shady Grove* may be relatively inconsequential, in that the majority does not dispute that the outcome might have been different if the New York law had simply been framed as a limitation on remedies rather than as a limitation on the use of class actions. The opinions in the case nevertheless reveal fundamental disagreements over how to interpret the Federal Rules in the face of a potential conflict with state law and over how to assess their validity under the Rules Enabling Act. Does the majority opinion evidence a retreat by the Court from construing the Federal Rules with sensitivity to state interests? Was the majority correct in concluding that "there is only one reasonable reading of Rule 23"? In evaluating the validity of a Federal Rule under the Enabling Act, to what extent, if at all, should a court take account of either the nature of the state law that is being displaced by the Federal Rule, or the danger that application of the Federal Rule will promote forum shopping?

For an article that "seeks to redeem the missed opportunities of *Shady Grove* and provide the clarifying accounts of the Enabling Act and Rule 23 that the opinions fail to offer," see Stephen B. Burbank and Tobias Barrington Wolff, Redeeming the Missed Opportunities of *Shady Grove,* 159 U. Pa. L. Rev. 17 (2010). Building on prior work, the authors "identify the need for a more dynamic approach to the text of Federal Rules than the Court has exhibited—one that recognizes the indeterminacy inherent in prospective rulemaking, the role of federal common law in the interpretation of the Rules, and the role of the Rules in federal common law—and the need to revisit the line between 'procedure' and 'substance' in light of practical experience and evolving legal norms." Among other things, the authors contend that the Court has erred over the years in grounding its understanding of the Rules Enabling Act in considerations of federalism rather than separation of powers. With respect to *Shady Grove,* the authors argue that the Court got the outcome wrong because "Rule 23 does not set policy on the propriety of aggregate remedies as a means of accomplishing regulatory goals—and it could not possibly do so." Rather, New York law set the policy and "[t]he Court did violence to the Enabling Act when it concluded that Rule 23 could supersede that policy."

For a collection of articles in the Creighton Law Review, in which the contributors were asked to write their own proposed opinions in *Shady Grove,* see Debra Lyn Bassett, Enabling the Federal Rules, 44 Creighton L. Rev. 7 (2010); Patrick J. Borchers, The Real Risk of Forum Shopping: A Dissent from *Shady Grove,* 44 Creighton L. Rev. 29 (2010); Stan Cox, Putting *Hanna* to Rest in *Shady Grove,* 44 Creighton L. Rev. 43 (2010); Richard D. Freer and Thomas C. Arthur, The Irrepressible Influence of *Byrd,* 44 Creighton L. Rev. 61 (2010); John B. Oakley, Illuminating *Shady Grove*: A General Approach to Resolving *Erie* Problems, 44 Creighton L. Rev. 79 (2010); Jeffrey L. Rensberger, *Hanna*'s Unruly Family: An Opinion for *Shady Grove Orthopedic Associates v. Allstate Insurance,* 44 Creighton L. Rev. 89 (2010); Thomas D. Rowe, Jr., Sonia, What's a Nice Person Like You Doing in Company Like That?, 44 Creighton L. Rev. 107 (2010); and Ralph U. Whitten, Justice Whitten, Nagging in Part and Declaring a Pox on All Houses, 44 Creighton L. Rev. 115 (2010).

Not surprisingly, *Shady Grove* continues to receive extensive treatment in the law reviews. See, e.g., Joseph P. Bauer, Shedding Light on *Shady Grove*: Further Reflections on the *Erie* Doctrine from a Conflicts Perspective,

86 Notre Dame L. Rev. 939 (2011); Stephen R. Brown, For Lack of a Better Rule: Using the Concept of Transsubstantivity to Solve the *Erie* Problem in *Shady Grove*, 80 U. Cin. L. Rev. 1 (2011); Sergio J. Campos, *Erie* as a Choice of Enforcement Defaults, 64 Fla. L. Rev. 1573 (2012); Kevin M. Clermont, The Repressible Myth of *Shady Grove*, 86 Notre Dame L. Rev. 987 (2011); Donald L. Doernberg, "The Tempest": *Shady Grove Orthopedic Associates, P.A. v. Allstate Insurance Co.*: The Rules Enabling Act Decision That Added to the Confusion—But Should Not Have, 44 Akron L. Rev. 1147 (2011); Jack Friedenthal, Defining the Word "Maintain"; Context Counts, 44 Akron L. Rev. 1139 (2011); Mark P. Gaber, Maintaining Uniform Federal Rules: Why the *Shady Grove* Plurality Was Right, 44 Akron L. Rev. 979 (2011); Bernadette Bollas Genetin, Reassessing the Avoidance Canon in *Erie* Cases, 44 Akron L. Rev. 1067 (2011); Jennifer S. Hendricks, In Defense of the Substance-Procedure Dichotomy, 89 Wash. U. L. Rev. 103 (2011); Helen Hershkoff, *Shady Grove*: Duck-Rabbits, Clear Statements, and Federalism, 74 Alb. L. Rev. 1703 (2010/2011); Allan Ides, The Standard for Measuring the Validity of a Federal Rule of Civil Procedure: The *Shady Grove* Debate between Justices Scalia and Stevens, 86 Notre Dame L. Rev. 1041 (2011); Glenn S. Koppel, The Fruits of *Shady Grove*: Seeing the Forest for the Trees, 44 Akron L. Rev. 999 (2011); Matthew R. Lyon, *Shady Grove*, the Rules Enabling Act, and the Application of State Summary Judgment Standards in Federal Diversity Cases, 85 St. John's L. Rev. 1011 (2011); Richard A. Nagareda, The Litigation-Arbitration Dichotomy Meets the Class Action, 86 Notre Dame L. Rev. 1069 (2011); Kermit Roosevelt, III, Choice of Law in Federal Courts: From *Erie* and *Klaxon* to CAFA and *Shady Grove*, 106 Nw. U. L. Rev. 1 (2012); Adam N. Steinman, Our Class Action Federalism: *Erie* and the Rules Enabling Act after *Shady Grove*, 86 Notre Dame L. Rev. 1131 (2011); Jeffrey W. Stempel, *Shady Grove* and the Potential Democracy-Enhancing Benefits of *Erie* Formalism, 44 Akron L. Rev. 907 (2011); Catherine T. Struve, Institutional Practice, Procedural Uniformity, and As-Applied Challenges under the Rules Enabling Act, 86 Notre Dame L. Rev. 1181 (2011); Jay Tidmarsh, Foreword: *Erie*'s Gift, 44 Akron L. Rev. 897 (2011); Jay Tidmarsh, Procedure, Substance, and *Erie*, 64 Vand. L. Rev. 877 (2011).

The Rules Enabling Act was limited to "civil actions" until it was amended to its present form in 1988 and made applicable to all cases in the lower federal courts. The Supreme Court has not addressed the extent to which the injunction in § 2072(b) against abridging, enlarging, or modifying "any substantive right" applies to the Federal Rules of *Criminal* Procedure. For a study of this question including the relevance of *Shady Grove* to its answer, see Max Minzner, The Criminal Rules Enabling Act, 46 U. Rich. L. Rev. 1047 (2012).

7.   BIBLIOGRAPHY

There is an extensive literature on the substance/procedure issues presented by both *Erie* and the Federal Rules. The most famous article is John Hart Ely, The Irrepressible Myth of *Erie*, 87 Harv. L. Rev. 693 (1974). In that article, Ely argued, consistent with the Court's decision in *Hanna*, that the validity of the Federal Rules should be evaluated solely under the Rules Enabling Act, not under the *Erie* jurisprudence. He also argued, however, that, contrary to the Court's suggestion in *Sibbach*, a Federal Rule should not be considered valid under the Enabling Act merely because it is procedural. The Rules Enabling Act makes clear, he contended, that the Rule must also not abridge or modify a substantive right. He proposed the following approach to the substance/procedure issue:

> When there is no Federal Rule, and as a result the Rules of Decision Act constitutes the controlling text, the court need ordinarily not concern itself with whether the federal rule urged by one party, or the state rule urged by the other, is most fairly designated substantive or procedural. The test is whether the choice between the two is material in the sense *Hanna* indicated, and that is not a function of the goals the rulemakers on either side were pursuing. . . . Where there is [a Federal] Rule, however, the designation substantive and procedural become important, for the Enabling Act has made them so. Its first sentence, tracking the constitutional requirement, demands that the Federal Rule be procedural. Its second sentence (the one the Court and the commentators have ignored) add to this checklist restriction the further, and considerably more significant, enclave-type proviso that the Rule not abridge, enlarge or modify any substantive right.

Ely's article provoked two responses in the Harvard Law Review. See Abram Chayes, Some Further Last Words on *Erie*: The Bead Game, 87 Harv. L. Rev. 741 (1974); Paul J. Mishkin, Some Further Last Words on *Erie*: The Thread, 87 Harv. L. Rev. 1682 (1974). Ely responded to Chayes in The Necklace, 87 Harv. L. Rev. 753 (1974).

For additional scholarship on this topic, see Amy Coney Barrett, Procedural Common Law, 94 Va. L. Rev. 813 (2008); Joseph P. Bauer, The *Erie* Doctrine Revisited: How a Conflicts Perspective Can Aid the Analysis, 74 Notre Dame L. Rev. 1235 (1999); Paul D. Carrington, "Substance" and "Procedure" in the Rules Enabling Act, 1989 Duke L.J. 281; Donald L. Doernberg, The Unseen Track of *Erie Railroad*: Why History and Jurisprudence Suggest a More Straightforward Form of *Erie* Analysis, 109 W. Va. L. Rev. 611 (2007); Earl C. Dudley, Jr. and George Rutherglen, Deforming the Federal Rules: An Essay on What's Wrong with the Recent *Erie* Decisions, 92 Va. L. Rev. 707 (2006); Richard D. Freer, Some Thoughts on the State of *Erie* after *Gasperini*, 76 Tex. L. Rev. 1637 (1998); Leslie M. Kelleher, Taking "Substantive Rights" (in the Rules Enabling Act) More Seriously, 74 Notre Dame L. Rev. 47 (1998); John C. McCoid, II, *Hanna v. Plumer*: The *Erie* Doctrine Changes Shape, 51 Va. L. Rev. 884 (1965); Martin H. Redish and Carter G. Phillips, *Erie* and the Rules of Decision Act: In Search of the Appropriate Dilemma, 91 Harv. L. Rev. 356 (1977); Thomas D. Rowe, Jr., Not Bad for Government Work: Does Anyone Else Think the Supreme Court Is Doing a Halfway Decent Job in Its *Erie-Hanna* Jurisprudence?, 73 Notre Dame L. Rev. 963 (1998); Ralph Whitten, *Erie* and the Federal Rules: A Review and Reappraisal after *Burlington Northern Railroad Co. v. Woods*, 21 Creighton L. Rev. 1 (1987); Richard C. Worf, Jr., The Effect of State Law on the Judge-

Jury Relationship in Federal Court, 30 N. Ill. U. L. Rev. 109 (2009). For more recent scholarship on the substance/procedure problem, see Robert J. Condlin, Is the Supreme Court Disabling the Enabling Act, or is *Shady Grove* Just Another Bad Opera, 47 Seton Hall L. Rev. 1 (2016); William H.J. Hubbard, An Empirical Study of the Effect of *Shady Grove v. Allstate* on Forum Shopping in the New York Courts, 10 J.L. Econ. & Pol'y 151 (2013); Suzanna Sherry, A Pox on Both Your Houses: Why the Court Can't Fix the *Erie* Doctrine, 10 J.L. Econ. & Pol'y 173 (2013); David E. Shipley, The Preliminary Injunction Standard in Diversity: A Typical Unguided *Erie* Choice, 50 Ga. L. Rev. 1169 (2016); Alan M. Trammell, Toil and Trouble: How the *Erie* Doctrine Became Structurally Incoherent (And How Congress Can Fix It), 82 Fordham L. Rev. 3249 (2014); Diane P. Wood, Back to the Basics of *Erie*, 18 Lewis & Clark L. Rev. 673 (2014); Patrick Woolley, The Role of State Law in Determining the Construction and Validity of Federal Rules of Civil Procedure, 35 Rev. Litig. 207 (2016).

Finally, see Alexander A. Reinert, *Erie* Step Zero, 85 Fordham L. Rev. 2341 (2017). Reinert argues that the *Erie* substance-procedure analysis should be subtly different depending on the basis for federal court jurisdiction. He considers two situations where state-law questions can arise in a federal question case: supplemental state claims based on a common core of facts; and cases where state and federal law are intertwined. These situations involve different considerations, he concludes, than those that would govern a diversity case the substance of which involves only questions of state law.

SECTION 4. FINALITY AND APPELLATE REVIEW

SUBSECTION A. SUPREME COURT REVIEW OF STATE COURT DECISIONS

INTRODUCTORY NOTES ON SUPREME COURT REVIEW OF STATE COURT DECISIONS

1. INITIATING REVIEW

The first Congress enacted the Judiciary Act of 1789, which established the federal court system and conferred jurisdiction on the Supreme Court to review state court decisions. That statute gave the Supreme Court jurisdiction over federal questions decided by the highest court of a state against a person claiming a federal right.[a] One of the concerns raised in Murdock v.

---

[a] It was not until 1914 that the successor statute was modified to extend the Court's jurisdiction to state-court decisions in favor of federal claimants. It is generally understood that the appellate jurisdiction established by the Judiciary Act of 1789 extended to both civil and criminal cases. The exercise of such jurisdiction in a criminal case is often said to have begun with Cohens v. Virginia, 19 U.S. (6 Wheat.) 264 (1821). But it is argued in Kevin C. Walsh, In the Beginning There Was None: Supreme Court Review of State Criminal Prosecutions, 90 Notre Dame L. Rev. 1867 (2015), that this is quite wrong. *Cohens*, Walsh argues, held only that Article III *permitted* direct review of state criminal convictions, not that the 1789 Judiciary Act *authorized* or *required* such review. He defends the conclusion that "the best interpretation of

City of Memphis, 87 U.S. (20 Wall.) 590 (1875), was how the Court should deal with frivolous federal issues raised in this context. *Murdock* came to the Court on a writ of error, a procedure under which the Court was required to review federal questions properly before it. As the Court noted, cases involving frivolous federal questions had become "such a burden and abuse that we either refuse to hear, or hear only one side of many such, and stop the argument, and have been compelled to adopt a rule that when a motion is made to dismiss it shall only be heard on printed argument." More formal procedures to deal with this problem have since been developed.[b]

The institution of review by writ of certiorari was an early answer. Under Supreme Court Rule 17, "review on writ of certiorari is not a matter of right, but of judicial discretion, and will be granted only when there are special and important reasons therefor." That discretion is exercised after the petitioner has filed a formal "petition for a writ of certiorari" and the respondent has had an opportunity to file a response. The Court then acts on the petition.[c] If the petition is granted, full briefs and oral argument usually follow.

Until 1988, appeals remained available as of right, at least as a formal matter, in two classes of cases coming from the state courts.[d] Under Supreme Court Rule 12(3), the formal requirements for docketing an appeal included the filing of a "jurisdictional statement" by the appellant. Rule 15 required that this document contain a "statement of the reasons why the questions presented are so substantial as to require plenary consideration, with briefs on the merits and oral argument, for their resolution." The opposing party was then given an opportunity to file a motion to dismiss or affirm, after which the Court in most cases would either "note probable jurisdiction" (indicating that it would hear the case on the merits) or "dismiss for want of a substantial federal question."[e] The latter disposition was an indication that the standard of Rule 15 had not been met.[f]

---

section 25 [of the 1789 Judiciary Act] is that it did not encompass Supreme Court appellate review of state criminal convictions."

    [b]   For a thoughtful treatment of many of the issues discussed below, see Herbert Wechsler, The Appellate Jurisdiction of the Supreme Court: Reflections on the Law and Logistics of Direct Review, 34 Wash. & Lee L. Rev. 1043 (1977).

    [c]   By tradition, four votes are sufficient to grant certiorari. The Court may limit the grant to only some of the issues presented in the petition. See Scott Bice, The Limited Grant of Certiorari and the Justification of Judicial Review, 1975 Wis. L. Rev. 343.

    [d]   Specifically, appeals were permitted if "the validity of a treaty or statute of the United States" was drawn in question "and the decision [was] against its validity" and if "the validity of a statute of any state" was drawn in question "on the ground of its being repugnant to the Constitution, treaties or laws of the United States, and the decision [was] in favor of its validity."

    [e]   Occasionally, the Court would summarily reverse at this stage, a disposition for which it has been criticized. See Henry M. Hart, Jr., Foreword: The Time Chart of the Justices, 73 Harv. L. Rev. 84, 89 & n.13 (1959); cf. Ernest J. Brown, Foreword: Process of Law, 72 Harv. L. Rev. 77 (1958).

    [f]   For an extensive analysis of the Court's management of its docket, see Arthur Hellman, The Supreme Court, the National Law, and the Selection of Cases for the Plenary Docket, 44 U. Pitt. L. Rev. 521 (1983), and Arthur Hellman, Error Correction, Lawmaking, and the Supreme Court's Exercise of Discretionary Review, 44 U. Pitt. L. Rev. 795 (1983). See also Samuel Estreicher and John Sexton, A Managerial Theory of the Supreme Court's Responsibilities, 59 N.Y.U. L. Rev. 681 (1984), which addresses the criteria the Court should use in selecting cases for review.

Congress amended 28 U.S.C. § 1257 in 1988 to make certiorari the exclusive method of reviewing state court decisions.[g] Thus the Court no longer is compelled by the language of § 1257 to hear any case that comes from a state court.

2.   THE MEANING OF SUMMARY DISPOSITION OF APPEALS

Denial of a petition for certiorari is not a decision on the merits and accordingly has no precedential value.[h] A more difficult question was posed by the pre-1988 provision of appeal for some state court cases (as well as some cases coming from federal courts). Many of these cases were disposed of summarily, without full briefing and oral argument, either by summary affirmance or reversal or (more commonly) by dismissal of the appeal for want of a substantial federal question. What is the precedential value of such dispositions? Must the Supreme Court and the lower state and federal courts treat these decisions as resolving the merits of the issues presented?

Since both petitions for certiorari and pre-1988 appeals required the filing of a preliminary document on the basis of which the Court decided whether to hear the case, one could have taken the position that the refusal to hear an appeal should be treated the same as the refusal to hear a case on a writ of certiorari. Indeed, for a substantial period of time, many courts and a substantial segment of the bar probably so regarded the summary disposition of an appeal.[i]

That situation was clarified, however, in Hicks v. Miranda, 422 U.S. 332 (1975). A three-judge District Court held that it was not bound by a prior Supreme Court dismissal of an appeal. The Court responded:

> [T]he District Court was in error in holding that it could disregard the decision [dismissing the prior case for want of a substantial federal question]. That case was an appeal from a decision by a state court upholding a state statute against federal constitutional attack. A federal constitutional issue was properly presented, it was within our appellate jurisdiction under § 1257(2),

---

[g]   There were also cases coming from the federal Circuit Courts that 28 U.S.C. § 1254 required to be heard by appeal before the 1988 amendment, specifically where a state statute had been held "invalid as repugnant to the Constitution, treaties or laws of the United States." The 1988 amendment also removed the Court's obligatory jurisdiction over these cases. For discussion of the history of the Supreme Court's mandatory jurisdiction and a description of the 1988 changes, see Bennett Boskey and Eugene Gressman, The Supreme Court Bids Farewell to Mandatory Appeals, 109 S.Ct. lxxxi (1988).

[h]   On this view, no inferences can be drawn from denials of certiorari. For an extensive analysis of this proposition, see Peter Linzer, The Meaning of Certiorari Denials, 79 Colum. L. Rev. 1227 (1979). Linzer concluded that "the orthodox view is oversimplified, and in some cases, false" and that "[u]nderstanding how to use denials of certiorari can be of great use to writers, practitioners, and judges."

[i]   In 1954, Chief Justice Warren told the American Law Institute that it was "only accurate to a degree to say that our jurisdiction in cases on appeal is obligatory as distinguished from discretionary on certiorari." Frederick Bernays Wiener, The Supreme Court's New Rules, 68 Harv. L. Rev. 20, 51 (1954). And Justice Clark said in a concurring opinion in a case on which he was sitting by designation after he retired from the Court that throughout his tenure on the Court, appeals from state courts "received treatment similar to that accorded petitions for certiorari and were given about the same precedential weight." Hogge v. Johnson, 526 F.2d 833, 836 (4th Cir.1975).

and we had no discretion to refuse adjudication of the case on its merits as would have been true had the case been brought here under our certiorari jurisdiction. We were not obligated to grant the case plenary consideration, and we did not; but we were required to deal with its merits. We did so by concluding that the appeal should be dismissed because the constitutional challenge was not a substantial one. The three-judge court was not free to disregard this pronouncement. . . .

The Supreme Court has been clear that *it* may reconsider prior summary decisions in the light of subsequent plenary presentation of the issues presented. But there has been no departure from the message of *Hicks* that lower state and federal courts are not free to disregard summary decisions by the Supreme Court.

3. DECISION BY THE "HIGHEST STATE COURT"

The requirement in § 1257 that any decision to be reviewed must have been "rendered by the highest court of a State in which a decision could be had" in effect enacts an obligation that the parties exhaust all available direct review remedies in the state courts before going to the Supreme Court.[j] Supreme Court review of a state trial court decision is thus permissible if no further (obligatory or discretionary) review is available within the state court system, as happened in the famous "no evidence" case, Thompson v. City of Louisville, 362 U.S. 199 (1960) (police court conviction for minor offense set aside as violation of due process on the ground that there was "no evidence" in the record to support the conviction).

4. FEDERAL QUESTION RAISED PROPERLY, PRESERVED, AND DECIDED

No federal question is open to review unless it has been raised properly, preserved, and decided under the procedures used by the courts from which the case has come. Thus, a question litigated at the trial level may not be open to Supreme Court review if no appeal is sought within the state court system on that question, even though the case is otherwise considered by the state supreme court. Similarly, if the question is not raised at all at trial or is raised too late or is raised for the first time on appeal or in a petition for rehearing, Supreme Court review also may be unavailable.

The word "may" in the preceding sentences has been used advisedly. There are two circumstances where the Court may regard it appropriate to consider an issue even though these rules have not been followed. First, if the state courts overlook procedural defaults and decide the issue on the merits, the Supreme Court will not refuse to consider the question on the ground that local procedures have not been followed. Review is unavailable only in those cases where the state courts rely on a "procedural foreclosure," that is, where they foreclose review of the merits of a question because it has

---

[j] It is not required, however, that a discretionary rehearing be sought in a state supreme court after that court has disposed of the case on the merits. See Local 174, Teamsters Union v. Lucas Flour Co., 369 U.S. 95 (1962).

not been properly raised and preserved, or where the issue was not raised at all in the "highest" state court.

The second exception is based on the fairness of the opportunity which the local procedural rules give for raising the question. If a question is raised at the first realistically available opportunity, if no fair chance is given to the parties to raise the issue, or if it appears that local rules have been applied in a manner that suggests evasion of the federal question, the Supreme Court may overlook the failure and regard the issue as appropriate for review. These conclusions are reached through application of the adequate and independent state ground doctrine.

5. THE RELEVANCE OF FEDERAL RULES OF STANDING: *ASARCO, INC. V. KADISH*

State courts are not bound by federal rules of standing. They are free to decide cases in situations where the limitations of Article III would preclude a federal court from hearing the case. What happens if a state court hears such a case and review is sought in the Supreme Court? Can the Supreme Court exercise its appellate jurisdiction?

This situation arose in ASARCO, Inc. v. Kadish, 490 U.S. 605 (1989). The plaintiffs were Arizona taxpayers and the Arizona Education Association, a group representing some 20,000 Arizona public school teachers. They sought a declaration that a state statute governing mineral leases on state lands was invalid because it did not comply with the methods Congress required the state to follow when it granted the land to the state in 1910. The defendants, among others, were a class of all present and future mineral lessees. The plaintiffs alleged that the invalid leasing practices deprived school trust funds of millions of dollars and unnecessarily increased taxes. The trial court upheld the Arizona leasing practices, but the state Supreme Court reversed and remanded with directions to enter a declaratory judgment invalidating the leasing system. Certiorari was granted at the instance of various members of the defendant class of mineral lessees.

A plurality held that neither group of plaintiffs had standing under Article III and that the case could not have been heard if filed originally in federal court.[k] But a majority (excepting only Rehnquist and Scalia) held that review in the Supreme Court was nevertheless appropriate:

> [T]he state judiciary . . . , as was their right, . . . took no account of federal standing rules in letting the case go to final judgment in the Arizona courts. That result properly follows from the allocation of authority in the federal system. We have recognized often that the constraints of Article III do not apply to state courts, and accordingly the state courts are not bound by the limitations of a case or controversy or other federal rules of justiciability even when they address issues of federal law. . . .

---

[k] The opinion was written by Justice Kennedy. Justice Brennan, joined by Justices White, Marshall, and Blackmun, dissented from this part of the opinion on the grounds that resolution of the standing question was unnecessary to the decision and that, particularly as to the teachers group, it was wrong anyway. Justice O'Connor did not participate in the decision.

Although the state courts are not bound to adhere to federal standing requirements, they possess the authority, absent a provision for exclusive federal jurisdiction, to render binding judicial decisions that rest on their own interpretations of federal law. . . .

The question now arises whether a judgment rendered by the state courts in these circumstances can support jurisdiction in this Court to review the case. At this juncture, petitioners allege a specific injury stemming from the state court decree, a decree which rests on principles of federal law. . . .

Although respondents would not have standing to commence suit in federal court based on the allegations in the complaint, they are not the party attempting to invoke the federal judicial power. Instead, it is petitioners, the defendants in the case and the losing parties below, who bring the case here and thus seek entry to the federal courts for the first time in the lawsuit. We determine that petitioners have standing to invoke the authority of a federal court and that this dispute now presents a justiciable case or controversy for resolution here.

Petitioners hold mineral leases that were granted under the state law the Arizona Supreme Court invalidated. [I]t is undisputed that the decision to be reviewed poses a serious threat to the continuing validity of those leases by virtue of its holding that they were granted under improper procedures and an invalid law. The state proceedings ended in a declaratory judgment adverse to petitioners, an adjudication of legal rights which constitutes the kind of injury cognizable in this Court on review from the state courts. . . .

If we were to vacate the judgment below on the ground that respondents lacked federal standing when they brought suit initially, that disposition would render nugatory the entire proceedings in the state court. The clear effect would be to impose federal standing requirements on the state courts whenever they adjudicate issues of federal law, if those judgments are to be conclusive on the parties. That result, however, would be contrary to established traditions and to our prior decisions recognizing that the state courts are not bound by Article III and yet have it within both their power and their proper role to render binding judgments on issues of federal law, subject only to review by this Court. . . .

If we were merely to dismiss this case and leave the judgment below undisturbed, a different set of problems would ensue. Although the judgment of a state court on issues of federal law normally binds the parties in any future suit even if that suit is brought separately in federal court, we have occasionally cautioned that such a judgment may well *not* bind the parties if the state court's conclusions about federal law were not subject to any federal review. . . . The predominant interest promoted by this apparent exception to normal preclusion doctrines is to assure that the binding application of federal law is uniform and subject to control by this Court. . . .

Given the likelihood that dismissal in this case would defeat the normal preclusive effects of the state court's judgment, however, the effect again would be to impose federal standing requirements on a state court that sought to render a binding decision on issues of federal law. It also would denigrate the authority of the state courts by creating a peculiar anomaly in the normal channels of appellate review. [Ordinarily,] direct review in the lower federal courts of a decision reached by the highest state court [is barred], for such authority is vested solely in this Court. . . .

[W]e adopt the following rationale for our decision on this jurisdictional point: When a state court has issued a judgment in a case where plaintiffs in the original action had no standing to sue under the principles governing the federal courts, we may exercise our jurisdiction on certiorari if the judgment of the state court causes direct, specific, and concrete injury to the parties who petition for our review, where the requisites of a case or controversy are met.

We are not unmindful of the paradox that would result if respondents (plaintiffs below) prevail on the merits, for then they will have succeeded in obtaining a federal determination here that was unavailable if the action had been filed initially in federal court. Nonetheless, [t]he rule we adopt is necessary in deference to the states and in response to the petitioning parties who seek this forum to redress a real and current injury stemming from the application of federal law. . . .

The Court then addressed the merits, held that the court below was correct in its conclusions about the applicable federal requirements, and affirmed the judgment. The respondents (plaintiffs below) thus did indeed prevail on the merits.[1]

---

[1]   Chief Justice Rehnquist, joined by Justice Scalia, dissented on the reviewability issue. The Court also held the judgment below "final" within two of the exceptions in Cox Broadcasting Corp. v. Cohn, 420 U.S. 469 (1975), namely that the federal issue was conclusively determined and the outcome of any further proceedings preordained. *Cox* is considered in the next set of Notes. For further debate among the Justices on the meaning of ASARCO, see United States Department of Labor v. Triplett, 494 U.S. 715 (1990), and Nike, Inc. v. Karsky, 539 U.S. 654 (2003). *Nike* also involved a *Cox* issue.

For consideration of *ASARCO* in connection with an argument that state courts hearing federal questions should be required to adhere to the federal requirement of a "case or controversy," see William A. Fletcher, The "Case or Controversy" Requirement in State Court Adjudication of Federal Questions, 78 Calif. L. Rev. 263 (1990).

NOTES ON SUPREME COURT REVIEW OF FINAL DECISIONS BY STATE COURTS

1. *COX BROADCASTING CORP. V. COHN:* THE MAJORITY

The current statute authorizing the Supreme Court to review state court decisions is 28 U.S.C. § 1257, which provides for review by certiorari of all "[f]inal judgments or decrees rendered by the highest court of a State in which a decision could be had. . . ." Cox Broadcasting Corp. v. Cohn, 420 U.S. 469 (1975), attempted to rationalize the law on when a state court decision is "final" for purposes of Supreme Court review.

The issue in *Cox* was whether the First Amendment allowed Georgia to award money damages for publication of the name of a deceased rape victim. A Georgia trial court recognized such a cause of action and entered summary judgment against a TV newsman, his station, and its corporate owner. The newsman had learned the identity of the rape victim from indictments in a pending prosecution. These indictments were available for public inspection as part of the court records in the criminal case. The state supreme court agreed that a cause of action for publication of the victim's name could be asserted, but reversed the summary judgment and remanded the case for trial on various factual issues. The Supreme Court reversed on the merits, holding that the First and Fourteenth Amendments precluded the state from recognizing a cause of action under these circumstances. En route to that result, the Supreme Court held that the judgment of the Georgia Supreme Court was "final" and therefore reviewable at this stage of the proceedings. It began by summarizing prior decisions on finality:

> Since 1789, Congress has granted this Court appellate jurisdiction with respect to state litigation only after the highest state court in which judgment could be had has rendered a "[f]inal judgment or decree." . . . The Court has noted that "[c]onsiderations of English usage as well as those of judicial policy" would justify an interpretation of the final-judgment rule to preclude review "where anything further remains to be determined by a state court. . . ." Radio Station WOW, Inc. v. Johnson, 326 U.S. 120, 124 (1945). But the Court there observed that the rule had not been administered in such a mechanical fashion and that there were circumstances in which there has been "a departure from this requirement of finality for federal appellate jurisdiction."

> These circumstances were said to be "very few"; but as the cases have unfolded, the Court has recurringly encountered situations in which the highest court of a state has finally determined the federal issue present in a particular case, but in which there are further proceedings in the lower state courts to come. There are now at least four categories of such cases in which the Court has treated the decision on the federal issue as a final judgment for the purposes of 28 U.S.C. § 1257. . . . In most, if not all, of the cases in these categories, these additional proceedings would not require

the decision of other federal questions that might also require review by the Court at a later date, and immediate rather than delayed review would be the best way to avoid "the mischief of economic waste and of delayed justice," as well as precipitate interference with state litigation. In the cases in the first two categories considered below, the federal issue would not be mooted or otherwise affected by the proceedings yet to be had because those proceedings have little substance, their outcome is certain, or they are wholly unrelated to the federal question. In the other two categories, however, the federal issue would be mooted if the petitioner or appellant seeking to bring the action here prevailed on the merits in the later state-court proceedings, but there is nevertheless sufficient justification for immediate review of the federal question finally determined in the state courts.

The Court then described the four categories of cases.

(i) Federal Issue Conclusive or Outcome Preordained

The first consisted of "those cases in which there are further proceedings—even entire trials—yet to occur in the state courts but where for one reason or another the federal issue is conclusive or the outcome of further proceedings preordained. In these circumstances, because the case is for all practical purposes concluded, the judgment of the state court on the federal issue is deemed final."

Mills v. Alabama, 384 U.S. 214 (1966), was cited as illustrative:

> [A] demurrer to a criminal complaint was sustained on federal constitutional grounds by a state trial court. The state Supreme Court reversed, remanding for jury trial. This Court took jurisdiction on the reasoning that the appellant had no defense other than his federal claim and could not prevail at trial on the facts or any nonfederal ground. To dismiss the appeal "would not only be an inexcusable delay of the benefits Congress intended to grant by providing for appeal to this Court, but it would also result in a completely unnecessary waste of time and energy in judicial systems already troubled by delays due to congested dockets."

(ii) Federal Issue Will Survive Anyway

The second category included cases "in which the federal issue, finally decided by the highest court in the state, will survive and require decision regardless of the outcome of future state-court proceedings." Among the Court's illustrations of this category was Brady v. Maryland, 373 U.S. 83 (1963), where

> the Maryland courts had ordered a new trial in a criminal case but on punishment only, and the petitioner asserted here that he was entitled to a new trial on guilt as well. We entertained the case, saying that the federal issue was separable and would not be mooted by the new trial on punishment ordered in the state courts.

(iii) Federal Issue Cannot Be Reviewed Later

The third category consisted of

> those situations where the federal claim has been finally decided, with further proceedings on the merits in the state courts to come, but in which later review of the federal issue cannot be had, whatever the ultimate outcome of the case. Thus, in these cases, if the party seeking interim review ultimately prevails on the merits, the federal issue will be mooted; if he were to lose on the merits, however, the governing state law would not permit him again to present his federal claims for review.

This category was illustrated by North Dakota State Board of Pharmacy v. Snyder's Drug Stores, Inc., 414 U.S. 156 (1973). There,

> the pharmacy board rejected an application for a pharmacy operating permit relying on a state statute specifying ownership requirements which the applicant did not meet. The state supreme court held the statute unconstitutional and remanded the matter to the board for further consideration of the application, freed from the constraints of the ownership statute. The board brought the case here, claiming that the statute was constitutionally acceptable under modern cases. After reviewing the various circumstances under which the finality requirement has been deemed satisfied despite the fact that litigation had not terminated in the state courts, we entertained the case over claims that we had no jurisdiction. The federal issue would not survive the remand, whatever the result of the state administrative proceedings. The board might deny the license on state-law grounds, thus foreclosing the federal issue, and the Court also ascertained that under state law the board could not bring the federal issue here in the event the applicant satisfied the requirements of state law except for the invalidated ownership statute. Under these circumstances, the issue was ripe for review.[a]

---

[a] For a more recent application of this exception, see Kansas v. Marsh, 548 U.S. 163 (2006). Marsh was convicted of murder and sentenced to death. The Kansas Supreme Court held a portion of the statute authorizing the death penalty unconstitutional and remanded for a new trial. The Supreme Court held the statute constitutional by a five-to-four vote. As to its jurisdiction to do so, the majority said:

> Here, although Marsh will be retried on the capital murder and aggravated arson charges, the Kansas Supreme Court's determination that Kansas's death penalty statute is facially unconstitutional is final and binding on the lower state courts. Thus, the State will be unable to obtain further review of its death penalty law later in this case. If Marsh is acquitted of capital murder, double jeopardy and state law will preclude the State from appealing. If he is reconvicted, the State will be prohibited under the Kansas Supreme Court's decision from seeking the death penalty, and there would be no opportunity for the State to seek further review of that prohibition.

The four dissenters did not object to the exercise of jurisdiction, although Justices Scalia and Stevens engaged in an interesting debate about whether certiorari should have been granted. Stevens's position was:

> [T]he State of Kansas petitioned us to review a ruling of its own Supreme Court on the grounds that the Kansas court had granted more protection to a Kansas litigant than the Federal Constitution required. A policy of judicial restraint would allow the highest court of the State to be the final decisionmaker in a case of this kind.

(iv) Later Review Would Seriously Erode Federal Policy

The final category was the one in which *Cox* itself was thought to fit. It was described as

> those situations where the federal issue has been finally decided in the state courts with further proceedings pending in which the party seeking review here might prevail on the merits on nonfederal grounds, thus rendering unnecessary review of the federal issue by this Court, and where reversal of the state court on the federal issue would be preclusive of any further litigation on the relevant cause of action rather than merely controlling the nature and character of, or determining the admissibility of evidence in, the state proceedings still to come. In these circumstances, if a refusal immediately to review the state-court decision might seriously erode federal policy, the Court has entertained and decided the federal issue, which itself has been finally determined by the state courts for purposes of the state litigation.

The Court illustrated this fourth category by reference to Mercantile National Bank at Dallas v. Langdeau, 371 U.S. 555 (1963), where

> two national banks were sued, along with others, in the courts of Travis County, Tex. The claim asserted was conspiracy to defraud an insurance company. The banks as a preliminary matter asserted that a special federal venue statute immunized them from suit in Travis County and that they could properly be sued only in another county. Although trial was still to be had and the banks might well prevail on the merits, the Court, relying on *Curry,* entertained the issue as a "separate and independent matter, anterior to the merits and not enmeshed in the factual and legal issues comprising the plaintiff's cause of action." Moreover, it would serve the policy of the federal statute "to determine now in which state court appellants may be tried rather than to subject them . . . to long and complex litigation which may all be for naught if consideration of the preliminary question of venue is postponed until the conclusion of the proceedings."

The Court also referred to Miami Herald Publishing Co. v. Tornillo, 418 U.S. 241 (1974), as "the latest case in this category":

> There a candidate for public office sued a newspaper for refusing, allegedly contrary to a state statute, to carry his reply to the paper's editorial critical of his qualifications. The trial court held the act unconstitutional, denying both injunctive relief and damages. The state supreme court reversed, sustaining the statute against the challenge based upon the First and Fourteenth Amendments and remanding the case for a trial and appropriate relief, including damages. The newspaper brought the case here. We sustained our

---

Scalia responded at length. Two of his points were: "Our principal responsibility . . . and a primary basis for the Constitution's allowing us to be accorded jurisdiction to review state-court decisions . . . is to ensure the integrity and uniformity of federal law." And: "When we correct a state court's federal errors, *we return power to the State, and to its people.*"

jurisdiction, relying on the principles elaborated in the *North Dakota* case and observing:

> Whichever way we were to decide on the merits, it would be intolerable to leave unanswered, under these circumstances, an important question of freedom of the press under the First Amendment; an uneasy and unsettled constitutional posture of [the state statute] could only further harm the operation of a free press.

Against this background, the Court concluded that the judgment in *Cox* was final:

> The Georgia Supreme Court's judgment is plainly final on the federal issue and is not subject to further review in the state courts. Appellants will be liable for damages if the elements of the state cause of action are proved. They may prevail at trial on nonfederal grounds, it is true, but if the Georgia court erroneously upheld the statute, there should be no trial at all. Moreover, even if appellants prevailed at trial and made unnecessary further consideration of the constitutional question, there would remain in effect the unreviewed decision of the state supreme court that a civil action for publishing the name of a rape victim disclosed in a public judicial proceeding may go forward despite the First and Fourteenth Amendments. Delaying final decision of the First Amendment claim until after trial will "leave unanswered . . . an important question of freedom of the press under the First Amendment," "an uneasy and unsettled constitutional posture [that] could only further harm the operation of a free press." *Tornillo*. On the other hand, if we now hold that the First and Fourteenth Amendments bar civil liability for broadcasting the victim's name, this litigation ends. Given these factors—that the litigation could be terminated by our decision on the merits and that a failure to decide the question now will leave the press in Georgia operating in the shadow of the civil and criminal sanctions of a rule of law and a statute the constitutionality of which is in serious doubt—we find that reaching the merits is consistent with the pragmatic approach that we have followed in the past in determining finality.

Chief Justice Burger concurred without opinion, and Justices Powell and Douglas wrote separately on the First Amendment question.

2. *COX BROADCASTING CORP. V. COHN:* THE DISSENT

Justice Rehnquist dissented on the finality issue. He regretted the gradual erosion of the finality requirement, saying that he would take a narrower approach to finality in Supreme Court review of state court judgments than he would on finality within the federal system:

> Were judicial efficiency the only interest at stake there would be less inclination to challenge the Court's resolution in this case, although, as discussed below, I have serious reservations that the standards the Court has formulated are effective for achieving even this single goal. The case before us, however, is an appeal from a

state court, and this fact introduces additional interests which must be accommodated in fashioning any exception to the literal application of the finality requirement. I consider § 1257 finality to be one of a number of congressional provisions reflecting concern that uncontrolled federal judicial interference with state administrative and judicial functions would have untoward consequences for our federal system.[4]

That comity and federalism are significant elements of § 1257 finality has been recognized by other members of the Court as well, perhaps most notably by Justice Harlan. In [his dissent in *Langdeau*], he argued that one basis of the finality rule was that it foreclosed "this Court from passing on constitutional issues that may be dissipated by the final outcome of a case, thus helping to keep to a minimum undesirable federal-state conflicts." [W]e have in recent years emphasized and re-emphasized the importance of comity and federalism in dealing with a related problem, that of district court interference with ongoing state judicial proceedings. See Younger v. Harris, 401 U.S. 37 (1971). Because these concerns are important, and because they provide "added force" to § 1257's finality requirement, I believe that the Court has erred by [limiting its] concern [to] efficient judicial administration.

Justice Rehnquist charged the Court with adopting in its fourth category "a virtually formless exception to the finality requirement, one which differs in kind from those previously carved out." He found five problems with the Court's test. First, it required a preliminary judgment on the merits as part of the finality inquiry. Second, he could not distinguish this case from any other in which a state court had rejected a federal claim at an intermediate stage of the proceedings. Third, he thought the right at stake not important enough to justify a departure from normal procedures. Fourth, he thought the Court had abandoned the salutary "principle that constitutional issues are too important to be decided save when absolutely necessary, and are to be avoided if there are grounds for decision of lesser dimension":

> In this case there has yet to be an adjudication of liability against appellants, and . . . they do not concede that they have no non-federal defenses. Nonetheless, the Court rules on their constitutional defense. Far from eschewing a constitutional holding in advance of the necessity for one, the Court construes § 1257 so that it may virtually rush out and meet the prospective constitutional litigant as he approaches our doors.

Finally, he speculated

> that after the Court has studied briefs and heard oral argument, it has an understandable tendency to proceed to a decision on the merits in preference to dismissing for want of jurisdiction. It is thus

---

[4]   See, e.g., 28 U.S.C. § 1341 (limitation on power of district courts to enjoin state taxing systems); 28 U.S.C. § 1739 (requiring that state judicial proceedings be accorded full faith and credit in federal courts); 28 U.S.C. §§ 2253–54 (prescribing various restrictions on federal habeas corpus for state prisoners); 28 U.S.C. § 2281 (three judge court requirement); 28 U.S.C. § 2283 (restricting power of federal courts to enjoin state-court proceedings).

especially disturbing that the rule of this case, unlike the more workable and straightforward exceptions which the Court has previously formulated, will seriously compound the already difficult task of accurately determining, at a preliminary stage, whether an appeal from a state-court judgment is a "final judgment or decree."

Rehnquist elaborated this point by examining the awkward position in which the Court's rule placed the practicing attorney and the potential impact of the decision on the Court's docket. Faced with an uncertain rule, attorneys could be expected to seek interlocutory review in order to assure that an issue would not be lost for lack of timely filing. "The inevitable result will be totally unnecessary additions to our docket and serious interruptions and delays of the state adjudicatory process."

3. *HATHORN V. LOVORN*

Hathorn v. Lovorn, 457 U.S. 255 (1982), involved the requirement in the Voting Rights Act of 1965 that states seek preclearance from the federal government for changes in electoral procedures. The Mississippi Supreme Court reversed a trial court decision invalidating a new election procedure and remanded for further proceedings. Compliance with the federal preclearance requirement was raised for the first time in a petition for rehearing. The court denied the petition without comment, and the United States Supreme Court denied certiorari. The state trial court then ordered an election under the new procedure, subject to approval by the United States Attorney General. The Attorney General declined to approve the new procedure, and after some complicated maneuvering the case was again appealed to the Mississippi Supreme Court. That court held that its prior decision constituted "the law of the case" upholding the procedure and not conditioning its use on prior approval by federal authorities. It accordingly ordered an election under the new procedure.

The Supreme Court reversed. Before reaching the merits, it considered the argument that the lower court's reliance on the "law of the case" doctrine barred review at this stage of the proceedings:

It has long been established . . . that "[w]e have jurisdiction to consider all of the substantial federal questions determined in the earlier stages of [state proceedings] and our right to re-examine such questions is not affected by a ruling that the first decision of the state court became the law of the case. . . ." Reece v. Georgia, 350 U.S. 85 (1955). Because we cannot review a state court judgment until it is final, a contrary rule would insulate interlocutory state court rulings on important federal questions from our consideration.

In this case the Mississippi Supreme Court's first decision plainly did not appear final at the time it was rendered. The court's remand . . . together with its failure to address expressly the Voting Rights Act issue, suggested that the [trial court] could still consider the federal issue on remand. . . . Under these circumstances, the Mississippi Supreme Court's subsequent reliance on the law of the case cannot prevent us from reviewing federal questions determined in the first appeal.

4.   QUESTIONS AND COMMENTS

Does the Court in *Cox* develop a coherent picture of what constitutes a "final" judgment? In particular, is its fourth category—the one involved in *Cox* itself—sufficiently well-defined to be meaningful? See Note, The Finality Rule for Supreme Court Review of State Court Orders, 91 Harv. L. Rev. 1004, 1025 (1978) (suggesting that the fourth *Cox* category is "virtually limitless" because it turns on ad hoc assessment of the importance of rights).

Consider also the resolution in *Hathorn*. Is it clear that the first decision by the Mississippi Supreme Court would not be reviewable under the Court's third category? If it would be, does that undermine the Court's reasoning? Or is this a situation in which the state court judgment became "final" at two different stages and could have been reviewed by the Supreme Court at either?[b] But if it was "final" the first time, why is it reviewable the second?

Also, consider whether *Cox* is consistent with the rationale underlying the adequate and independent state ground rule. It is argued in Richard A. Matasar and Gregory S. Bruch, Procedural Common Law, Federal Jurisdictional Policy, and Abandonment of the Adequate and Independent State Grounds Doctrine, 86 Colum. L. Rev. 1291, 1355 (1986), that: "[T]he finality exceptions . . . *are* inconsistent with the adequacy doctrine, but justifiably so, because they further the primary mission Congress contemplated for the Court as a vigilant guardian of federal supremacy and uniformity. It is not the finality exceptions, but the adequate and independent state grounds doctrine that flies in the face of federal jurisdictional policy." Are they right? Should the Court be free to decide federal questions that may not control the outcome of further proceedings to be conducted in the state courts?

NOTES ON THE SUPREME COURT'S GVR PRACTICE

1.   INTRODUCTION

For many years the Supreme Court has engaged in the practice of granting certiorari, vacating the judgment before it, and remanding for further action by the court below. The practice is common enough to have its own acronym—GVR—and, as illustrated below, for the acronym to have become a verb.

Perhaps the most common example is the Court's practice of holding cases presenting the same issue as a pending case and remanding the held

---

[b]   The policies underlying the final judgment requirement are explored in Timothy Dyk, Supreme Court Review of Interlocutory State-Court Decisions: "The Twilight Zone of Finality," 19 Stan. L. Rev. 907 (1967), which was written before *Cox* but which considers many of the cases on which it relies. For subsequent caselaw on the debate over the breadth of the *Cox* exceptions, see Pennsylvania v. Ritchie, 480 U.S. 39 (1987) (5–4 decision on finality issue); Goodyear Atomic Corp. v. Miller, 486 U.S. 174 (1988) (accepting review under fourth category); Fort Wayne Books v. Indiana, 489 U.S. 46 (1989) (accepting review under the fourth category); Jefferson v. City of Tarrant, 522 U.S. 75 (1997) (confining *Ritchie* to its precise circumstances). See also Southland Corp. v. Keating, 465 U.S. 1 (1984) (review under fourth category accepted without debate).

cases for reconsideration once the Court has decided the issue. One practical reason for this approach—a reason that could be regarded by the lower courts as an opportunity or an imposition—is that it gets the Supreme Court out of the messy and time-consuming task of applying its new decision case-by-case. It is not a significant extension of this practice to apply the GVR technique to other situations where an event of potential significance to the proper outcome intervenes between a decision below and Supreme Court review. For example, the Supreme Court might well make a GVR disposition if a Circuit Court makes a decision involving a question of state law and the state Supreme Court decides the question differently while a certiorari petition is pending, or if a potentially controlling act of Congress intervenes between the decision below and the disposition of a pending petition for certiorari. "Intervening event" remands are, in the main, well accepted, not controversial, and not particularly interesting. They are employed in cases coming to the Supreme Court from both state and federal courts.

But to say that GVR practice is sometimes justified is not to say that it always is.

2. *LAWRENCE V. CHATER*

Lawrence v. Chater, 516 U.S. 163 (1996), involved a claim to Social Security benefits. Lawrence alleged that she was the unmarried minor "child" of a deceased beneficiary. Under the applicable federal statute, the determination of whether one is a "child" for this purpose involves an application of "such law as would be applied in determining the devolution of intestate personal property by the courts of the State in which [the] insured individual . . . was domiciled at the time of his death." North Carolina supplied the relevant law in this case, and Lawrence admitted that she could not meet its procedural requirements on proof of paternity. She argued, however, that the North Carolina law was unconstitutional. The Circuit Court held, as the government had argued, "that the constitutionality of a state paternity law need not be considered before applying it to determine entitlement to benefits under the federal statutory scheme." The Supreme Court's per curiam opinion explained what happened next:

> In his response [to the petition for certiorari], the Solicitor General advises us that the "Social Security Administration has re-examined" the role of state paternity and intestacy laws in the federal benefits scheme, and now interprets the Social Security Act as "requir[ing] a determination, at least in some circumstances, of whether the state intestacy statute is constitutional." He also correctly notes that the Act directs the Commissioner of Social Security—not, in the first instance, the courts—to "apply such law as would be applied . . . by the courts of the State" concerned. Without conceding Lawrence's ultimate entitlement to benefits, he invites us to grant certiorari, vacate the judgment below, and remand the case (GVR) so that the Court of Appeals may either decide it in light of the Commissioner's new statutory interpretation or remand the case to the Commissioner for reconsideration in light of that interpretation. We conclude both that we have the power to

issue a GVR order, and that such an order is an appropriate exercise of our discretionary certiorari jurisdiction.

. . . Although . . . the *exercise* of our GVR power was, until recent times, rare, its infrequent early use may be explained in large part by the smaller size of our certiorari docket in earlier times. Regardless of its earlier history, however, the GVR order has, over the past 50 years, become an integral part of this Court's practice, accepted and employed by all sitting and recent Justices. . . .

The feature of this case that, in our view, makes a GVR order appropriate is the new interpretation of the Social Security Act that the Solicitor General informs us that the Social Security Administration, the agency charged with implementing that Act, has adopted. As Justice Scalia's dissent notes, we have not settled whether and to what extent deference is due to an administrative interpretation—its "lega[l] cognizab[ility]"—in a case that has already reached the appeal or certiorari stage when that interpretation is adopted. But in our view, such uncertainty does not preclude a GVR. Indeed, it is precisely because we are uncertain, without undertaking plenary analysis, of the legal impact of a new development, especially one, such as the present, which the lower court has had no opportunity to consider, that we GVR. [T]he Solicitor General has recommended judicial reconsideration of the merits, while not conceding the petitioner's ultimate entitlement to statutory benefits, based on a new statutory interpretation that will apparently be applied, and will probably be entitled to deference, in future cases nationwide. [O]ur summary review leads us to the conclusion that there is a reasonable probability that the Court of Appeals would conclude that the timing of the agency's interpretation does not preclude the deference that it would otherwise receive, and that it may be outcome determinative in this case. A GVR order is, therefore, appropriate, subject to the equities.

As to the equities, it seems clear that they favor a GVR order here. That disposition has the Government's express support, notwithstanding that its purpose is to give the Court of Appeals the opportunity to consider an administrative interpretation that appears contrary to the Government's narrow self-interest. And the Government has informed us that it intends to apply that interpretation to future cases nationwide. Giving Lawrence a chance to benefit from it furthers fairness by treating Lawrence like other future benefits applicants. We acknowledge the dissent's concern that postlitigation interpretations may be the product of unfair or manipulative Government litigating strategies, and we therefore view late changes of position by the Government with some skepticism. That *general* concern does not, however, appear to us to require that we deprive Lawrence of the benefit of a favorable administrative reinterpretation in these *particular* circumstances. We believe, therefore, that the equities and legal uncertainties of this case together merit a GVR order.

All Justices agreed that 28 U.S.C. § 2106 appears on its face to authorize a broad GVR power.[a] But the Court's disposition prompted a dissent by Justice Scalia.[b] He recognized three categories of GVR dispositions with which he was willing to concur: "(1) where an intervening factor has arisen that has a legal bearing upon the decision, (2) where, in a context not governed by *Michigan v. Long* clarification of the opinion below is needed to assure our jurisdiction, and (3) (in acknowledgment of established practice, though not necessarily in agreement with its validity) where the respondent or appellee confesses error in the judgment below." But he was not willing to adopt a more open-ended view:

> What is at issue here . . . is a . . . creature . . . which might be called "no-fault V&R": vacation of a judgment and remand *without* any determination of error in the judgment below. . . . The question presented . . . is whether there is any limitation (other than the mandate "do what is fair") upon this practice. The Court's per curiam opinions[c] answer "no"; I disagree.
>
> [The] facially unlimited statutory text [of § 2106] is subject to the implicit limitations imposed by traditional practice and by the nature of the appellate system created by the Constitution and laws of the United States. [The Court] acknowledges . . . no constitutional limitation on our power to vacate lower court orders properly brought before us. This presumably means that the constitutional grant of "appellate Jurisdiction" over "Cases . . . arising under [the] Constitution [and] Laws of the United States," Art. III, § 2, empowers the Court to vacate a state supreme court judgment, and remand the case, because it finds the opinion, though arguably correct, incomplete and unworkmanlike; or because it observes that there has been a postjudgment change in the personnel of the state supreme court, and wishes to give the new state justices a shot at the case. I think that is not so. When the Constitution divides our jurisdiction into "original Jurisdiction" and "appellate Jurisdiction," I think it conveys, with respect to the latter, the traditional accoutrements of appellate power. There doubtless is room for some innovation, particularly such as may be necessary to adapt to a

---

[a]   "The Supreme Court or any other court of appellate jurisdiction may . . . vacate . . . any judgment, decree, or order of a court lawfully brought before it for review, and may remand the cause and . . . require such further proceedings to be had as may be just under the circumstances."

[b]   He was joined by Justice Thomas. Chief Justice Rehnquist concurred in the judgment in a separate opinion. Justice Stevens also wrote a separate concurrence:

> The Court persuasively explains why we have "the power to remand to a lower federal court any case raising a federal issue that is properly before us in our appellate capacity." That conclusion comports with a primary characteristic—and, I believe, virtue—of our discretionary authority to manage our certiorari docket: our ability to apply the "totality-of-the-circumstances" approach that Justice Scalia finds objectionable. The Court's wise disposition of these petitions falls squarely within the best traditions of its administration of that docket. I therefore join the Court's opinions.

[c]   Scalia was dissenting from both *Lawrence* and another GVR disposition in *Stutson v. United States*, which is considered in the next Note.—[Footnote by eds.]

novel system of federalism; but the innovation cannot be limitless without altering the nature of the power conferred.

Not only does the Court reject any constitutional limitation upon its power to vacate; it is unwilling to submit to any prudential constraint as well. Even while acknowledging the potential for "unfair[ness] or manipulat[ion]" and professing to agree that "our GVR power should be exercised sparingly," the Court commits to no standard that will control that power, other than that cloak for all excesses, "the equities." We may, as the Court now pronounces, set aside valid judgments not merely when they are wrong, not merely when intervening events require that someone (either the lower court or we) reconsider them on new facts or under new legal criteria, not merely when it is ambiguous whether we have power to review them, not merely when the United States concedes that the judgment below (or one of the points of law relied upon below, or even one of the points of law *possibly* relied upon below) is wrong; but whenever there is "a reasonable probability that the decision below rests upon a premise that the lower court would reject if given the opportunity for further consideration." The power to "revis[e] and correc[t]" for error, Marbury v. Madison, 5 U.S. (1 Cranch) 137 (1803), has become a power to void for suspicion. Comparing the modest origins of the Court's "no-fault V & R" policy with today's expansive dénouement should make even the most Pollyannish reformer believe in camel's noses, wedges, and slippery slopes.

The Court justifies its approach on the ground that it "alleviates the potential for unequal treatment that is inherent in our inability to grant plenary review of all pending cases raising similar issues." I do not see how it can promote equal treatment to announce a practice that we cannot possibly pursue in every case. If we were to plumb the "equities" and ponder the "errors" for all the petitions that come before us . . . we would have no time left for the cases we grant to consider on the merits. Of course we do not *purport* to conduct such inquiries, not even the basic one of whether the decision below is probably in "error"—which is why we insist that our denial of certiorari does not suggest a view on the merits. Moreover, even if we tried applying the Court's "totality-of-the-circumstances" evaluation to all the petitions coming before us, we would be unlikely to achieve equal treatment. Such a plastic criterion is liable to produce inconsistent results in any series of decisions; it is virtually *guaranteed* to do so in a series of decisions made without benefit of adversary presentation (whether we should GVR is rarely briefed, much less argued—as it has not been here) and announced without accompaniment of a judicial opinion (we almost never give reasons as the Court has done today). The need to afford equal treatment argues precisely *against* the "totality-of-the-circumstances" approach embraced by the Court, and in favor of a more modest but standardized GVR practice.

This case, he concluded, did not fit any of the three categories he was prepared to recognize:

> The Court's failure to comprehend why it should make any difference that the Government's changed litigating position may not be entitled to deference displays a lamentable lack of appreciation of the concept of adding insult to injury. It is disrespectful enough of a lower court to set its considered judgment aside because the Government has altered the playing field on appeal; it is downright insulting to do so when the Government's bait-and-switch performance *has not for a certainty altered any factor relevant to the decision.* In that situation, at least, we should let the Government live with the consequences of its fickleness or inattention.

3. *STUTSON V. UNITED STATES*

Stutson v. United States, 516 U.S. 193 (1996), was decided by GVR on the same day as *Lawrence*, again in a per curiam opinion. The situation was this:

> Stutson, the petitioner in this case, is currently serving a federal prison sentence of 292 months for cocaine possession. He has had no appellate review of his legal arguments against conviction and sentence. The District Court held that his appeal was untimely and that the untimeliness was not the result of "excusable neglect" within the meaning of Rule 4(b) of the Federal Rules of Appellate Procedure, because his lawyer's office mailed his notice of appeal so that it arrived one working day late for the 10-day deadline, and at the Court of Appeals, when it should have been sent to the District Court. The District Court's opinion did not advert to our decision in Pioneer Investment Services Co. v. Brunswick Associates Ltd. Partnership, 507 U.S. 380 (1993), rendered one day before Stutson's brief was due in the District Court and not cited in the briefs before that court. In *Pioneer,* we held that a party could in some circumstances rely on his attorney's inadvertent failure to file a proof of claim in a timely manner in bankruptcy proceedings as "excusable neglect" under the bankruptcy rules.
>
> . . . In their briefs to the Court of Appeals for the Eleventh Circuit, the parties disputed the applicability of *Pioneer*'s liberal understanding of "excusable neglect" to the Rule 4(b) criminal appeal context, the Government contending that it applied only in bankruptcy cases. The Court of Appeals . . . dismissed Stutson's appeal without hearing oral argument or writing an opinion. Now, in his response to Stutson's petition for certiorari, the Solicitor General has reversed the Government's position. This change of position follows the unanimous view of the six Courts of Appeals

that, unlike the Eleventh Circuit in this case, have expressly addressed this new and important issue, and have held that the *Pioneer* standard applies in Rule 4 cases.[d]

The Court held that the GVR disposition was justified by an "exceptional combination of circumstances" and that there was "at least a reasonable probability" that the Circuit Court would reach a different conclusion on remand. The "equities clearly favor a GVR order" because:

> [T]his is a case where (1) the prevailing party below, the Government, has now repudiated the legal position that it advanced below; (2) the only opinion below did not consider the import of a recent Supreme Court precedent that both parties now agree applies; (3) the Court of Appeals summarily affirmed that decision; (4) all six Courts of Appeals that have addressed the applicability of the Supreme Court decision that the District Court did not apply in this case have concluded that it applies to Rule 4 cases; and (5) the petitioner is in jail having, through no fault of his own, had no plenary consideration of his appeal. [I]t is not insignificant that this is a criminal case. When a litigant is subject to the continuing coercive power of the Government in the form of imprisonment, our legal traditions reflect a certain solicitude for his rights, to which the important public interests in judicial efficiency and finality must occasionally be accommodated. . . . "[D]ry formalism should not sterilize procedural resources which Congress has made available to the federal courts." In this case, as in *Lawrence v. Chater,* a GVR order guarantees to the petitioner full and fair consideration of his rights in light of all pertinent considerations, and is also satisfactory to the Government. In this case, as in *Lawrence,* a GVR order both promotes fairness and respects the dignity of the Court of Appeals by enabling it to consider potentially relevant decisions and arguments that were not previously before it.

Justice Scalia's *Lawrence* dissent applied also to *Stutson*.[e] As to the Court's disposition in *Stutson*, he said:

> [T]he [*Pioneer*] decision "in light of" which [the Court vacates and remands] had been on the books for well more than a year before the Eleventh Circuit announced the judgment under review, and for almost two years before that court denied rehearing. Moreover, the parties *specifically argued* to the Court of Appeals the question whether *Pioneer* established the standard applicable to petitioner's claim of "excusable neglect" under Federal Rule of Appellate Procedure 4(b), with the United States disagreeing with petitioner and taking the position that *Pioneer* was *not* controlling. The Eleventh Circuit ruled against petitioner on the merits of his

---

[d] Four of the decisions in the other Circuits came after the Eleventh Circuit denied a petition for rehearing in this case. The other two were decided after the District Court decision in this case but before the decision by the Court of Appeals.—[Footnote by eds.]

[e] Justice Thomas joined the Scalia dissent in both cases. Chief Justice Rehnquist wrote a separate opinion in which he concurred in *Lawrence* but dissented in *Stutson*.

claim; its one-sentence order contained neither a reference to *Pioneer* nor any suggestion that the court viewed the case as turning on which party's proffered standard was applied.

The United States has now revised its legal position and—though it makes no suggestion that the Court of Appeals' judgment was incorrect—is of the view that *Pioneer does* establish the standard governing petitioner's claim. But the fact that the party who won below repudiates on certiorari its position on a particular point of law does not give rise to any "intervening," postjudgment factor that must be considered. The law is the law, whatever the parties, including the United States, may have argued. . . . We do not know in this case whether the Eleventh Circuit even *agreed* with the Government's position that has now been repudiated; for all we know, the court *applied Pioneer* and found against petitioner under that standard. The judgment is declared invalid because the Eleventh Circuit *might* (or might not) have relied on a standard (non-*Pioneer*) that might (or might not) be wrong, that *might* (or might not) have affected the outcome, and that the Eleventh Circuit *might* (or might not) abandon (whether or not it is wrong) because the Government has now abandoned it. This seems to me beyond all reason. . . . In my view we have no power to make such a tutelary remand, as to a schoolboy made to do his homework again.

4.　*YOUNGBLOOD V. WEST VIRGINIA*

The Court also granted, vacated, and remanded in a per curiam opinion in Youngblood v. West Virginia, 547 U.S. 867 (2006). Youngblood had been sentenced to 26 to 60 years' imprisonment following his conviction for abducting three young women and sexually assaulting one of them. Several months after his conviction, he filed a motion to set aside the verdict in the state court where he had been convicted. His claim was that he had uncovered exculpatory evidence which, though known to the state before his trial, had not been disclosed to him. The evidence was a note, written by two of the abducted women (but not the victim of the sexual assault), that taunted Youngblood for having been played for a fool, acknowledged that they had vandalized the house to which Youngblood took them, and thanked him for performing a sexual act with the third woman. Youngblood claimed that the note was shown to a state trooper who was investigating the sexual assault allegations. The trooper was said to have read the note but declined to take possession of it. Allegedly, he told the person who produced it to destroy it.

The defendant based his claim of entitlement to the evidence on Brady v. Maryland, 373 U.S. 83 (1963). The trial court denied the motion for new trial, responding that the note provided only impeachment and not exculpatory evidence. *Brady* was not specifically discussed, but the court said that the investigating officer attached no importance to the note and that, because he did not give it to the prosecutor, the state could not be faulted for failing to share it with Youngblood's attorney. A bare majority of the state Supreme Court of Appeals affirmed. The majority found no abuse of discretion, and did not specifically discuss any constitutional claims associated with non-disclosed evidence. The dissenters relied on *Brady* and viewed the note in context as supporting Youngblood's trial defense that the alleged sexual assault had been consensual. It was, they concluded, significantly at odds with the testimony of the three women at Youngblood's trial.

The U.S. Supreme Court began its analysis with a brief review of *Brady* doctrine, pointing out that it applies to impeachment as well as exculpatory evidence and to evidence known to investigators but not to the prosecutor. It then justified its disposition in the following paragraph, without further elaboration:

> Youngblood clearly presented a federal constitutional *Brady* claim to the State Supreme Court, as he had to the trial court. And, as noted, the dissenting justices discerned the significance of the issue raised. If this Court is to reach the merits of this case, it would be better to have the benefit of the views of the full Supreme Court of Appeals of West Virginia on the *Brady* issue. We, therefore, grant the petition for certiorari, vacate the judgment of the State Supreme Court, and remand the case for further proceedings not inconsistent with this opinion.

Joined by Justice Thomas, Justice Scalia dissented.[f] He had predicted in *Lawrence*, he said, that "GVR'd for clarification of _____" would "become a common form of order, drastically altering the role of this Court." "Today," he continued, "by vacating the judgment of a state court simply because '[i]f this Court is to reach the merits of this case, it would be better to have the benefit of the views of the full Supreme Court of Appeals of West Virginia on the *Brady* issue,' the Court brings this prediction to fulfillment." He then repeated the three categories of cases he accepted in *Lawrence* as suitable bases for a GVR disposition, noted that "today's novel GVR order falls into none of these categories," and continued:

> . . . Here, the Court vacates and remands *in light of nothing.* [T]he Court remarks tersely that it would be "better" to have "the benefit" of the West Virginia court's views on petitioner's *Brady* claim, should we eventually decide to take the case. The Court thus purports to conscript the judges of the Supreme Court of Appeals of West Virginia to write what is essentially an amicus brief on the merits of an issue they have already decided, in order to facilitate our *possible* review of the merits at some later time. It is not at all clear why it would be so much "better" to have the full court below address the *Brady* claim. True, we often prefer to review reasoned opinions that facilitate our consideration—though we *may* review even a summary disposition. But the dissenting judges in the case below discussed petitioner's *Brady* claim at some length (indeed, at

---

[f]   Justice Kennedy also wrote a brief dissent:

The Court's order to grant, vacate, and remand (GVR) in Lawrence v. Chater, 516 U.S. 163 (1996) (per curiam), had my assent. In that case there was a new administrative interpretation that the Court of Appeals did not have an opportunity to consider. The Court today extends the GVR procedure well beyond *Lawrence* and the traditional practice of issuing a GVR order in light of some new development. Since the issuance of a GVR order simply for further explanation is, as Justice Scalia explains, both improper and contrary to our precedents, I respectfully dissent.

greater length than appears in many of the decisions we agree to review), and argued that it was meritorious. Since we sometimes review judgments with no opinion, and often review judgments with opinion only on one side of the issue, it is not clear why we need opinions on *both* sides here.

To tell the truth, there is only one obvious sense in which it might be "better" to have the West Virginia court revisit the *Brady* issue: If the majority suspects that the court below erred, there is a chance that the GVR-in-light-of-nothing will induce it to change its mind on remand, sparing us the trouble of correcting the suspected error. [T]he Court does not invoke even the flabby standard adopted in *Lawrence,* namely whether there is "a reasonable probability that the decision below rests upon a premise that the lower court would reject if given the opportunity for further consideration." That is because (there being no relevant intervening event to create such a probability) the only *possibility* that the West Virginia court will alter its considered judgment *is created by this Court's GVR order itself.* . . . Those whose judgments we review have sometimes viewed even our legitimate, intervening-event GVR orders as polite directives that they reverse themselves. See, e.g., Sharpe v. United States, 712 F.2d 65, 67 (4th Cir. 1983) (Russell, J., dissenting) ("Once again, I think the majority has mistaken gentleness in instruction for indefiniteness in command. The Supreme Court was seeking to be gentle with us but there is, I submit, no mistaking what they expected us to do"). How much more is that suspicion justified when the GVR order rests on nothing more than our statement that it would be "better" for the lower court to reconsider its decision (much as a mob enforcer might suggest that it would be "better" to make protection payments).

Even when we suspect error, we may have many reasons not to grant certiorari outright in a case such as this—an overcrowded docket, a reluctance to correct "the misapplication of a properly stated rule of law," this Court's Rule 10, or (in this particular case) even a neo-Victorian desire to keep the lurid phrases of the "graphically explicit note" out of the U.S. Reports. But none of these reasons justifies "a tutelary remand, as to a schoolboy made to do his homework again." In "the nature of the appellate system created by the Constitution and laws of the United States," state courts and lower federal courts are constitutionally distinct tribunals, independently authorized to decide issues of federal law. They are not, as we treat them today, "the creatures and agents of this body." If we suspect that a lower court has erred and wish to correct its error, we should grant certiorari and decide the issue ourselves in accordance with the traditional exercise of our appellate jurisdiction.

It is particularly ironic that the Court inaugurates its "GVR-in-light-of-nothing" practice by vacating the judgment of a *state* court. Our no-fault GVR practice had its origins "in situations calling forth the special deference owed to state law and state courts in our system of federalism." . . . In vacating the judgment of a state court for no better reason than our own convenience, we not only fail to observe, but positively flout the "special deference owed to . . . state courts." Like the Ouroboros swallowing its tail, our GVR practice has ingested its own original justification. . . . At best, today's unprecedented decision rests on a finding that the state court's "opinion, though arguably correct, [is] incomplete and unworkmanlike,"—which all Members of the Court in *Lawrence* agreed was an illegitimate basis for a GVR. At worst, it is an implied threat to the lower court, not backed by a judgment of our own, that it had "better" reconsider its holding.

I suppose it would be available to the West Virginia Supreme Court of Appeals, on remand, simply to reaffirm its judgment without further elaboration. Or it could instead enter into a full discussion of the *Brady* issue, producing either a reaffirmance or a revision of its judgment. The latter course will of course encourage and stimulate our new "GVR-in-light-of-nothing" jurisprudence. Verb. sap.[g]

5. QUESTIONS AND COMMENTS

What are the appropriate limits to the Court's GVR practice? Justice Scalia at least hints, if not argues, that there are constitutional problems with the Court's use of this technique in its most extreme, and to him unacceptable, forms. The "facially unlimited statutory text" in § 2106, he says, "is subject to the implicit limitations imposed by traditional practice and by the nature of the appellate system created by the Constitution and laws of the United States." What are those limits? For a textualist, where do they come from? Scalia is clear enough about his conclusions. Is it easy to spell out the details of the argument that gets him there?

Aside from potential constitutional issues, how should the prudential issues be resolved? Does it matter that *Youngblood*, like *Stutson*, was a criminal case involving a substantial prison sentence? Scalia comments in *Lawrence* that mere "equities" are a "cloak for all excesses." Is this a situation where clearer rules are required? Or ought it to be sufficient for the Court to invoke the practice whenever five or six justices (recall that four can grant certiorari) think it will promote justice to do so?

However one responds to these issues and whatever one thinks of the results in *Lawrence* and *Stutson*, it is hard not to be astonished by the disposition in *Youngblood*. Is Scalia right that the Court is issuing a none-too-subtle hint that the West Virginia Supreme Court of Appeals ought to find a *Brady* violation and get on with it? Is there any other convincing rationale for the Court's GVR disposition? In Williams v. Georgia, 349 U.S. 375 (1955), the Georgia courts had invoked a procedural foreclosure in a death case to

---

[g]   From the Latin "verbum sapienti sat est" ("a word to the wise is sufficient").—[Footnote by eds.]

cut off a jury discrimination claim that was clearly valid. The Supreme Court found an intervening event to justify a remand:

> [T]here is an important factor which has intervened since the affirmance by the Georgia Supreme Court which impels us to remand for that court's further consideration. This is the acknowledgment by the state before this Court that, as a matter of substantive law, Williams has been deprived of his constitutional rights. The Solicitor General of Fulton County . . . had urged before the Georgia Supreme Court that no denial of equal protection was involved, and that court may well have been influenced by the contention. Moreover, if there is another remedy open to Williams, as the Attorney General of the state intimated in his brief to the Georgia Supreme Court, that court should have an opportunity to designate the appropriate remedy.

The Georgia Supreme Court would have none of this. On remand, it quoted the Tenth Amendment and said:

> Even though executives and legislators, not being constitutional lawyers, might often overstep the foregoing unambiguous constitutional prohibition of federal invasion of state jurisdiction, there can never be an acceptable excuse for judicial failure to strictly observe it. This court bows to the Supreme Court on all federal questions of law but we will not supinely surrender sovereign powers of this state.

The Georgia court concluded that it would re-enter its prior judgment "[n]ot in recognition of any jurisdiction of the Supreme Court to influence or in any manner to interfere with the functioning of this court on strictly state questions, but solely for the purpose of completing the record." The Supreme Court then called it a day. See Williams v. State, 211 Ga. 763, 88 S.E.2d 376 (1954), cert. denied, 350 U.S. 950 (1956).

To quote Justice Scalia, might the West Virginia Supreme Court of Appeals be tempted to respond in similar fashion to the United States Supreme Court's "tutelary remand" in *Youngblood*, "as to a schoolboy made to do his homework again"?[h]

---

[h] Joined by Justice Thomas, Justice Scalia returned to his "schoolboy" analogy in his dissent from a per curiam GVR in Wellons v. Hall, 558 U.S. 220 (2010): "Today the Court adds another beast to our growing menagerie: the SRIE, Summary Remand for Inconsequential Error—or, as the Court would have it, the SRTAEH, Summary Remand to Think About an Evidentiary Hearing. It disrespects the judges of the Courts of Appeals, who are appointed and confirmed as we are, to vacate and send back their authorized judgments for inconsequential imperfection of opinion—as though we were schoolmasters grading their homework." Justice Alito, joined by Chief Justice Roberts, also objected to the Court's disposition. As he read the decision below, the Circuit Court decision rested on two independent grounds: a procedural foreclosure and a merits decision that assumed the claim was not procedurally foreclosed. An intervening decision made clear that the procedural foreclosure dimension of the Circuit Court's opinion was wrong. Alito concluded: "What the Court has done—using a GVR as a vehicle for urging the Court of Appeals to reconsider its holding on a question that is entirely independent of the ground for the GVR—is extraordinary and, in my view, improper."

SUBSECTION B. CIRCUIT COURT REVIEW OF DISTRICT COURT DECISIONS

INTRODUCTORY NOTE ON CIRCUIT COURT REVIEW OF DISTRICT COURT DECISIONS

The statute authorizing appeals from federal district courts to federal circuit courts, 28 U.S.C. § 1291, also limits review to "final decisions."[a] The Supreme Court has given the § 1291 language a more rigid construction than its counterpart in § 1257 (Supreme Court review of decisions by the highest state court). Recall that Justice Rehnquist argued for the opposite result in *Cox*.

One difference between the two review structures is the availability of alternative avenues of review in the federal system. Whether this difference sufficiently explains the Court's construction of § 1291—as well as whether Rehnquist was right or wrong—should be considered in connection with the materials in this Subsection.

Coopers & Lybrand v. Livesay

Supreme Court of the United States, 1978.
437 U.S. 463.

■ MR. JUSTICE STEVENS delivered the opinion of the Court.

The question in this case is whether a District Court's determination that an action may not be maintained as a class action pursuant to Fed. Rule Civ. Proc. 23 is a "final decision" within the meaning of 28 U.S.C. § 1291[2] and therefore appealable as a matter of right. [W]e granted certiorari and now hold that such an order is not appealable under § 1291.

Petitioner, Coopers & Lybrand, is an accounting firm that certified the financial statements in a prospectus issued in connection with a 1972 public offering of securities in Punta Gorda Isles for an aggregate price of over $18 million. Respondents purchased securities in reliance on that prospectus. In its next annual report to shareholders, Punta Gorda restated the earnings that had been reported in the prospectus for 1970 and 1971 by writing down its net income for each year by over $1 million. Thereafter, respondents sold their Punta Gorda securities and sustained a loss of $2,650 on their investment.

---

[a]   Litigants have 30 days from the entry of judgment within which to initiate an appeal, 28 U.S.C. § 2107(a), a time that can be extended for up to 14 days on certain conditions under § 2107(c) and Rule 4 of the Federal Rules of Appellate Procedure. In Bowles v. Russell, 551 U.S. 205 (2007), the District Court extended the period but mistakenly gave the appellant 17 days within which to file the appeal. The appellant filed within the 17 days, but after 14 days had passed. The Court said by a five-to-four vote that "the timely filing of a notice of appeal in a civil case is a jurisdictional requirement" and, overruling a 1962 decision, "this Court has no authority to create equitable exceptions to jurisdictional requirements."

[2]   "The courts of appeals shall have jurisdiction of appeals from all final decisions of the district courts of the United States . . . except where a direct review may be had in the Supreme Court."

Respondents filed this action on behalf of themselves and a class of similarly situated purchasers. They alleged that petitioner and other defendants had violated various sections of the Securities Act of 1933 and the Securities Exchange Act of 1934. The District Court first certified, and then, after further proceedings, decertified the class.

Respondents did not request the District Court to certify its order for interlocutory review under 28 U.S.C. § 1292(b).[5] Rather, they filed a notice of appeal pursuant to § 1291.[6] The Court of Appeals regarded its appellate jurisdiction as depending on whether the decertification order had sounded the "death knell" of the action. After examining the amount of respondents' claims in relation to their financial resources and the probable cost of the litigation, the court concluded that they would not pursue their claims individually.[a] The Court of Appeals therefore held that it had jurisdiction to hear the appeal and, on the merits, reversed the order decertifying the class.

Federal appellate jurisdiction generally depends on the existence of a decision by the District Court that "ends the litigation on the merits and leaves nothing for the court to do but execute the judgment." Catlin v. United States, 324 U.S. 229, 233 (1945).[8] An order refusing to certify, or decertifying, a class does not of its own force terminate the entire litigation because the plaintiff is free to proceed on his individual claim. Such an order is appealable, therefore, only if it comes within an appropriate exception to the final-judgment rule. In this case respondents rely on the "collateral order" exception articulated by this Court in Cohen v.

---

[5]   Section 1292(b) provides:

When a district judge, in making in a civil action an order not otherwise appealable under this section, shall be of the opinion that such order involves a controlling question of law as to which there is substantial ground for difference of opinion and that an immediate appeal from the order may materially advance the ultimate termination of the litigation, he shall so state in writing in such order. The Court of Appeals may thereupon, in its discretion, permit an appeal to be taken from such order, if application is made to it within ten days after the entry of the order: *Provided, however,* That application for an appeal hereunder shall not stay proceedings in the district court unless the district judge or the Court of Appeals or a judge thereof shall so order.

[6]   Respondents also petitioned for a writ of mandamus directing the District Court to recertify the class. Since the Court of Appeals accepted appellate jurisdiction, it dismissed the petition for a writ of mandamus.

[a]   The plaintiffs had an aggregate annual income of $26,000 and a net worth of $75,000 and had already paid $1,200 of some $15,000 in accumulated legal expenses. If tried, the case, which was filed in of Missouri, would require extensive discovery in Florida and the retention of expert witnesses.—[Footnote by eds.]

[8]   For a unanimous Court in Cobbledick v. United States, 309 U.S. 323, 325 (1940), Mr. Justice Frankfurter wrote:

Since the right to a judgment from more than one court is a matter of grace and not a necessary ingredient of justice, Congress from the very beginning has, by forbidding piecemeal disposition on appeal of what for practical purposes is a single controversy, set itself against enfeebling judicial administration. Thereby is avoided the obstruction to just claims that would come from permitting the harassment and cost of a succession of separate appeals from the various rulings to which a litigation may give rise, from its initiation to entry of judgment. To be effective, judicial administration must not be leaden-footed. Its momentum would be arrested by permitting separate reviews of the component elements in a unified cause.

Beneficial Industrial Loan Corp., 337 U.S. 541 (1949), and on the "death knell" doctrine adopted by several circuits to determine the appealability of orders denying class certification.

I

In *Cohen,* the District Court refused to order the plaintiff in a stockholder's derivative action to post the security for costs required by a New Jersey statute. The defendant sought immediate review of the question whether the state statute applied to derivative suits in federal court. This Court noted that the purpose of the finality requirement "is to combine in one review all stages of the proceeding that effectively may be reviewed and corrected if and when final judgment results." Because immediate review of the District Court's order was consistent with this purpose, the Court held it appealable as a "final decision" under § 1291. The ruling had "settled conclusively the corporation's claim that it was entitled by state law to require the shareholder to post security for costs [and] concerned a collateral matter that could not be reviewed effectively on appeal from the final judgment."

To come within the "small class" of decisions excepted from the final-judgment rule by *Cohen,* the order must conclusively determine the disputed question, resolve an important issue completely separate from the merits of the action, and be effectively unreviewable on appeal from a final judgment. An order passing on a request for class certification does not fall in that category. First, such an order is subject to revision in the District Court. Fed. Rule Civ. Proc. 23(c)(1).[11] Second, the class determination generally involves considerations that are "enmeshed in the factual and legal issues comprising the plaintiff's cause of action." Mercantile Nat. Bank v. Langdeau, 371 U.S. 555, 558 (1963). Finally, an order denying class certification is subject to effective review after final judgment at the behest of the named plaintiff or intervening class members. For these reasons, . . . the collateral-order doctrine is not applicable to the kind of order involved in this case.

II

Several circuits, including the Court of Appeals in this case, have held that an order denying class certification is appealable if it is likely to sound the "death knell" of the litigation. The "death knell" doctrine assumes that without the incentive of a possible group recovery the individual plaintiff may find it economically imprudent to pursue his lawsuit to a final judgment and then seek appellate review of an adverse class determination. Without questioning this assumption, we hold that orders relating to class certification are not independently appealable under § 1291 prior to judgment.

---

[11] The rule provides that an order involving class status may be "altered or amended before the decision on the merits." Thus, a district court's order denying or granting class status is inherently tentative.

In addressing the question whether the "death knell" doctrine supports mandatory appellate jurisdiction of orders refusing to certify class actions, the parties have devoted a portion of their argument to the desirability of the small-claim class action. Petitioner's opposition to the doctrine is based in part on criticism of the class action as a vexatious kind of litigation. Respondents, on the other hand, argue that the class action serves a vital public interest and, therefore, special rules of appellate review are necessary to ensure that district judges are subject to adequate supervision and control. Such policy arguments, though proper for legislative consideration, are irrelevant to the issue we must decide.

There are special rules relating to class actions and, to that extent, they are a special kind of litigation. Those rules do not, however, contain any unique provisions governing appeals. The appealability of any order entered in a class action is determined by the same standards that govern appealability in other types of litigation. Thus, if the "death knell" doctrine has merit, it would apply equally to the many interlocutory orders in ordinary litigation—rulings on discovery, on venue, on summary judgment—that may have such tactical economic significance that a defeat is tantamount to a "death knell" for the entire case.

Though a refusal to certify a class is inherently interlocutory, it may induce a plaintiff to abandon his individual claim. On the other hand, the litigation will often survive an adverse class determination. What effect the economic disincentives created by an interlocutory order may have on the fate of any litigation will depend on a variety of factors.[15] Under the "death knell" doctrine, appealability turns on the court's perception of that impact in the individual case. Thus, if the court believes that the plaintiff has adequate incentive to continue, the order is considered interlocutory; but if the court concludes that the ruling, as a practical matter, makes further litigation improbable, it is considered an appealable final decision.

The finality requirement in § 1291 evinces a legislative judgment that "[r]estricting appellate review to 'final decisions' prevents the debilitating effect on judicial administration caused by piecemeal appeal disposition of what is, in practical consequence, but a single controversy." Eisen v. Carlisle & Jacquelin, 417 U.S. 156, 170 (1978). Although a rigid insistence on technical finality would sometimes conflict with the purposes of the statute, *Cohen v. Beneficial Industrial Loan Corp.*, even adherents of the "death knell" doctrine acknowledge that a refusal to certify a class does not fall in that limited category of orders which, though nonfinal, may be appealed without undermining the policies served by the general rule. It is undisputed that allowing an appeal from such an order in the ordinary case would run "directly contrary to the policy of

---

[15] E.g., the plaintiff's resources; the size of his claim and his subjective willingness to finance prosecution of the claim; the probable cost of the litigation and the possibility of joining others who will share that cost; and the prospect of prevailing on the merits and reversing an order denying class certification.

the final judgment rule embodied in 28 U.S.C. § 1291 and the sound reasons for it. . . ."[16] Yet several Courts of Appeals have sought to identify on a case-by-case basis those few interlocutory orders which, when viewed from the standpoint of economic prudence, may induce a plaintiff to abandon the litigation. These orders, then, become appealable as a matter of right.

In administering the "death knell" rule, the courts have used two quite different methods of identifying an appealable class ruling. Some courts have determined their jurisdiction by simply comparing the claims of the named plaintiffs with an arbitrarily selected jurisdictional amount;[17] others have undertaken a thorough study of the possible impact of the class order on the fate of the litigation before determining their jurisdiction. Especially when consideration is given to the consequences of applying these tests to pretrial orders entered in non-class-action litigation, it becomes apparent that neither provides an acceptable basis for the exercise of appellate jurisdiction.

The formulation of an appealability rule that turns on the amount of the plaintiff's claim is plainly a legislative, not a judicial, function. While Congress could grant an appeal of right to those whose claims fall below a specific amount in controversy, it has not done so. Rather, it has made "finality" the test of appealability. Without a legislative prescription, an amount-in-controversy rule is necessarily an arbitrary measure of finality because it ignores the variables that inform a litigant's decision to proceed, or not to proceed, in the face of an adverse class ruling.[18] Moreover, if the jurisdictional amount is to be measured by the aggregated claims of the named plaintiffs, appellate jurisdiction may turn on the joinder decisions of counsel rather than the finality of the order.

While slightly less arbitrary, the alternative approach to the "death knell" rule would have a serious debilitating effect on the administration of justice. It requires class-action plaintiffs to build a record in the trial court that contains evidence of those factors deemed relevant to the "death knell" issue and district judges to make appropriate findings. And one Court of Appeals has even required that the factual inquiry be extended to all members of the class because the policy against interlocutory appeals can be easily circumvented by joining "only those whose individual claims would not warrant the cost of separate litigation"; to avoid this possibility, the named plaintiff is required to prove that no member of the purported class has a claim that warrants individual litigation.

---

[16] Korn v. Franchard Corp., 443 F.2d 1301, 1305 (2d Cir.1971).

[17] Thus, orders denying class certification have been held nonappealable because the plaintiffs alleged damages in the $3,000–$8,000 range. Smaller claims, however, have been held sufficient to support appellate jurisdiction in other cases.

[18] . . . The arbitrariness of this approach is exacerbated by the fact that the Courts of Appeals have not settled on a specific jurisdictional amount; rather, they have simply determined on an ad hoc basis whether the plaintiff's claim is too small to warrant individual prosecution.

A threshold inquiry of this kind may, it is true, identify some orders that would truly end the litigation prior to final judgment; allowing an immediate appeal from those orders may enhance the quality of justice afforded a few litigants. But this incremental benefit is outweighed by the impact of such an individualized jurisdictional inquiry on the judicial system's overall capacity to administer justice.

The potential waste of judicial resources is plain. The district court must take evidence, entertain argument, and make findings; and the court of appeals must review that record and those findings simply to determine whether a discretionary class determination is subject to appellate review. And if the record provides an inadequate basis for this determination, a remand for further factual development may be required. Moreover, even if the court makes a "death knell" finding and reviews the class-designation order on the merits, there is no assurance that the trial process will not again be disrupted by interlocutory review. For even if a ruling that the plaintiff does not adequately represent the class is reversed on appeal, the district court may still refuse to certify the class on the ground that, for example, common questions of law or fact do not predominate. Under the "death knell" theory, plaintiff would again be entitled to an appeal as a matter of right pursuant to § 1291. And since other kinds of interlocutory orders may also create the risk of a premature demise, the potential for multiple appeals in every complex case is apparent and serious.

Perhaps the principal vice of the "death knell" doctrine is that it authorizes indiscriminate interlocutory review of decisions made by the trial judge. The Interlocutory Appeals Act of 1958, 28 U.S.C. § 1292(b), was enacted to meet the recognized need for prompt review of certain nonfinal orders. However, Congress carefully confined the availability of such review. Nonfinal orders could never be appealed as a matter of right. Moreover, the discretionary power to permit an interlocutory appeal is not, in the first instance, vested in the courts of appeals.[24] A party seeking review of a nonfinal order must first obtain the consent of the trial judge. This screening procedure serves the dual purpose of ensuring that such review will be confined to appropriate cases and avoiding time-consuming jurisdictional determinations in the court of appeals.[25] Finally,

---

[24] Thus, Congress rejected the notion that the courts of appeals should be free to entertain interlocutory appeals whenever, in their discretion, it appeared necessary to avoid unfairness in the particular case. H.R. Rep. No. 1667, 85th Cong., 2d Sess., 4–6 (1958); Note, Interlocutory Appeals in the Federal Courts under 28 U.S.C. § 1292(b), 88 Harv. L. Rev. 607, 610 (1975).

[25] Rep. No. 1667, at 5–6:

    ... The problem ... is to provide a procedural screen through which only the desired cases may pass, and to avoid the wastage of a multitude of fruitless applications to invoke the amendment contrary to its purpose.

    ... Requirement that the trial court certify the case as appropriate for appeal serves the double purpose of providing the appellate court with the best informed opinion that immediate review is of value, and at once protects appellate dockets against a flood of petitions in inappropriate cases. [A]voidance of ill-founded applications in the courts of appeals for piecemeal review is of particular concern. If the consequence of

even if the district judge certifies the order under § 1292(b), the appellant still "has the burden of persuading the court of appeals that exceptional circumstances justify a departure from the basic policy of postponing appellate review until after the entry of a final judgment." Fisons, Ltd. v. United States, 458 F.2d 1241, 1248 (7th Cir.1972). The appellate court may deny the appeal for any reason, including docket congestion. By permitting appeals of right from class-designation orders after jurisdictional determinations that turn on questions of fact, the "death knell" doctrine circumvents these restrictions.[27]

Additional considerations reinforce our conclusion that the "death knell" doctrine does not support appellate jurisdiction of prejudgment orders denying class certification. First, the doctrine operates only in favor of plaintiffs even though the class issue—whether to certify, and if so, how large the class should be—will often be of critical importance to defendants as well. Certification of a large class may so increase the defendant's potential damages liability and litigation costs that he may find it economically prudent to settle and to abandon a meritorious defense. Yet the courts of appeals have correctly concluded that orders granting class certification are interlocutory. Whatever similarities or differences there are between plaintiffs and defendants in this context involve questions of policy for Congress. Moreover, allowing appeals of right from nonfinal orders that turn on the facts of a particular case thrusts appellate courts indiscriminately into the trial process and thus defeats one vital purpose of the final-judgment rule—"that of maintaining the appropriate relationship between the respective courts. . . . This goal, in the absence of most compelling reasons to the contrary, is very much worth preserving."[29]

Accordingly, we hold that the fact that an interlocutory order may induce a party to abandon his claim before final judgment is not a sufficient reason for considering it a "final decision" within the meaning of § 1291.[30] The judgment of the Court of Appeals is reversed with directions to dismiss the appeal.

---

change is to be crowded appellate dockets as well as any substantial number of unjustified delays in the trial court, the benefits to be expected from the amendment may well be outweighed by the lost motion of preparation, consideration, and rejection of unwarranted applications for its benefits.

[27] Several courts of appeals have heard appeals from discretionary class determinations pursuant to § 1292(b). As Judge Friendly has noted: "[T]he best solution is to hold that appeals from the grant or denial of class action designation can be taken only under the procedure for interlocutory appeals provided by 28 U.S.C. § 1292(b). . . . Since the need for review of class action orders turns on the facts of the particular case, this procedure is preferable to attempts to formulate standards which are necessarily so vague as to give rise to undesirable jurisdictional litigation with concomitant expense and delay." Parkinson v. April Industries, Inc., 520 F.2d 650, 660 (2d Cir.1975) (concurring opinion).

[29] Parkinson, 529 F.2d at 654.

[30] Respondents also suggest that the Court's decision in Gillespie v. United States Steel Corp., 379 U.S. 148 (1964), supports appealability of a class-designation order as a matter of right. We disagree. In Gillespie, the Court upheld an exercise of appellate jurisdiction of what it considered a marginally final order that disposed of an unsettled issue of national significance because review of that issue unquestionably "implemented the same policy Congress sought to

It is so ordered.

NOTES ON WHEN DISTRICT COURT DECISIONS ARE "FINAL"

1. THE "COLLATERAL ORDER" DOCTRINE: *COHEN V. BENEFICIAL INDUSTRIAL LOAN CORP.*

The only clearly recognized exception to the finality requirement of § 1291 was created in Cohen v. Beneficial Industrial Loan Corp., 337 U.S. 541 (1949). *Cohen* was a stockholder's derivative action based on diversity jurisdiction. The applicable state law required the plaintiff shareholders to post security for costs in order to discourage harassment by strike suits. As the Federal Rules of Civil Procedure did not speak to the issue, the issue was whether, in a diversity action otherwise governed by state law, the state se-curity-for-costs provision should be applied.

The District Court refused to require security, and the Supreme court held that this action was a "final" judgment and therefore immediate appeal-able under § 1291:

> The effect of the statute is to disallow appeal from any decision which is tentative, informal or incomplete. Appeal gives the upper court a power of review, not one of intervention. So long as the matter remains open, unfinished or inconclusive, there may be no intrusion by appeal. But the District Court's action upon this appli-cation was concluded and closed and its decision final in that sense before the appeal was taken.

> Nor does the statute permit appeals, even from fully consum-mated decisions, where they are but steps towards final judgment in which they will merge. The purpose is to combine in one review all stages of the proceeding that effectively may be reviewed and corrected if and when final judgment results. But this order of the District Court did not make any step toward final disposition of the merits of the case and will not be merged in final judgment. When that time comes, it will be too late effectively to review the present order and the rights conferred by the statute, if it is applicable, will have been lost, probably irreparably. We conclude that the matters embraced in the decision appealed from are not of such an interloc-utory nature as to affect, or to be affected by, decision of the merits of this case.

> This decision appears to fall in that small class which finally determine claims of right separate from, and collateral to, rights asserted in the action, too important to be denied review and too

---

promote in § 1292(b)" and the arguable finality issue had not been presented to this Court until argument on the merits, thereby ensuring that none of the policies of judicial economy served by the finality requirement would be achieved were the case sent back with the important issue undecided. In this case, in contrast, respondents sought review of an inherently nonfinal order that tentatively resolved a question that turns on the facts of the individual case; and, as noted above, the indiscriminate allowance of appeals from such discretionary orders is plainly incon-sistent with the policies promoted by § 1292(b). If *Gillespie* were extended beyond the unique facts of that case § 1291 would be stripped of all significance.

independent of the cause itself to require that appellate consideration be deferred until the whole case is adjudicated. The Court has
long given this provision of the statute this practical rather than a
technical construction.

We hold this order appealable because it is a final disposition
of a claimed right which is not an ingredient of the cause of action
and does not require consideration with it. But we do not mean that
every order fixing security is subject to appeal. Here it is the right
to security that presents a serious and unsettled question. If the
right were admitted or clear and the order involved only an exercise
of discretion as to the amount of security, a matter the statute
makes subject to reconsideration from time to time, appealability
would present a different question.

As *Coopers & Lybrand* illustrates, with the possible exception of the *Gillespie* case cited in footnote 30 of Justice Stevens's opinion in *Coopers &
Lybrand*, the Court has refused to broaden the *Cohen* exception to the final
decision requirement. For examples in the context of disqualification of counsel, see Firestone Tire & Rubber Co. v. Risjord, 449 U.S. 368 (1981),
Flanagan v. United States, 465 U.S. 259 (1984), and Richardson-Merrell, Inc.
v. Koller, 472 U.S. 424 (1985). For examples of cases held to meet the *Cohen*
standard, see Moses H. Cone Memorial Hospital v. Mercury Constr. Corp.,
460 U.S. 1 (1983) (involving a stay of federal proceedings in favor of on-going
litigation in state court), and Quackenbush v. Allstate Insurance Company,
517 U.S. 706 (1996) (application of *Moses H. Cone* to justify immediate appealability of remand based on *Burford* abstention of a case removed from
state court).

The *Cohen* exception also applies in criminal cases, although "with the
utmost strictness." Flanagan v. United States, 465 U.S. 259, 265 (1984). In
Midland Asphalt Corp. v. United States, 489 U.S. 794 (1989), a unanimous
Court noted:

Although we have had numerous opportunities in the 40 years
since *Cohen* to consider the appealability of prejudgment orders in
criminal cases, we have found denials of only three types of motions
to be immediately appealable: motions to reduce bail, motions to
dismiss on double jeopardy grounds, and motions to dismiss under
the speech or debate clause. These decisions, along with the far
more numerous ones in which we have refused to permit interlocutory appeals, manifest the general rule that the third prong of the
Coopers & Lybrand test is satisfied only where the order at issue
involves "an asserted right the legal and practical value of which
would be destroyed if it were not vindicated before trial."

The reference to the "third prong" of the *Coopers & Lybrand* test is to the
requirement that the order "be effectively unreviewable on appeal from a
final judgment."

2. *Will v. Hallock*

Will v. Hallock, 546 U.S. 345 (2006), involved further refinement of the *Cohen* standard. Susan Hallock owned a computer software business that she and her husband operated from home. They were victims of identity theft, which resulted in her husband's credit card being used to purchase child pornography from a web site. U.S. Customs Service investigators traced the purchase through the web site and obtained a search warrant for the Hallock residence. They seized the Hallocks' computer equipment, software, and disk drives. No criminal charges were filed against the Hallocks. But when the computer equipment was returned, several disk drives were damaged, all stored data was lost (including account files and trade secrets), and the Hallocks were forced to shut down their business. Two suits resulted.

In the first, Susan and her company sued the United States under the Federal Tort Claims Act. This case was terminated when the District Court granted the government's motion to dismiss on the ground that the case fell within an exception to the Act's waiver of sovereign immunity. The second suit was filed while the first was pending. It was a *Bivens* action against the individual agents. The Federal Tort Claims Act contains a judgment bar stating that a judgment under the section of the act under which the first suit was brought "shall constitute a complete bar to any action by the claimant, by reason of the same subject matter, against the employee of the government whose act or omission gave rise to the claim." 28 U.S.C. § 2676. After the first suit was dismissed, the defendants in the *Bivens* action moved for dismissal in the second suit under this provision. The District Court denied the motion on the ground that the first-suit dismissal was on a procedural ground and was not a resolution of the merits of the controversy. The question was whether the District Court's decision was immediately appealable under the collateral-order doctrine.

In an opinion by Justice Souter, the Court held unanimously that it was not. Souter started with the three familiar conditions for invoking the doctrine: that the order "[1] conclusively determine the disputed question, [2] resolve an important issue completely separate from the merits of the action, and [3] be effectively unreviewable on appeal from a final judgment." These conditions, he said, are "stringent" and "unless they are kept so, the underlying doctrine will overpower the substantial . . . interests § 1291 is meant to further. . . ." The Court's reasoning and holding follow:

> Prior cases mark the line between rulings within the class and those outside. On the immediately appealable side are orders rejecting absolute immunity, Nixon v. Fitzgerald, 457 U.S. 731 (1982), and qualified immunity, Mitchell v. Forsyth, 472 U.S. 511, 530 (1985).[a] A State has the benefit of the doctrine to appeal a decision denying its claim to Eleventh Amendment immunity, Puerto

---

[a]   *Mitchell* is considered in context in the Notes on Immunity From the Award of Damages in Chapter 9, Section 2.—[Footnote by eds.]

Rico Aqueduct, 506 U.S. 139, 144–45 (1993),[b] and a criminal defendant may collaterally appeal an adverse ruling on a defense of double jeopardy, Abney v. United States, 431 U.S. 651, 660 (1977).

[These] examples admittedly raise the lawyer's temptation to generalize. In each case, the collaterally appealing party was vindicating or claiming a right to avoid trial, in satisfaction of the third condition: unless the order to stand trial was immediately appealable, the right would be effectively lost. Those seeking immediate appeal therefore naturally argue that any order denying a claim of right to prevail without trial satisfies the third condition. But this generalization is too easy to be sound and, if accepted, would leave the final order requirement of § 1291 in tatters. . . .

"Allowing immediate appeals to vindicate every such right would move § 1291 aside for claims that the district court lacks personal jurisdiction, that the statute of limitations has run, that the movant has been denied his Sixth Amendment right to a speedy trial, that an action is barred on claim preclusion principles, that no material fact is in dispute and the moving party is entitled to judgment as a matter of law, or merely that the complaint fails to state a claim. Such motions can be made in virtually every case." Digital Equipment Corp. v. Desktop Direct, Inc., 511 U.S. 863, 873 (1994). . . .

Since only some orders denying an asserted right to avoid the burdens of trial qualify, . . . the cases have to be combed for some further characteristic that merits appealability under Cohen; . . . that something . . . boils down to "a judgment about the value of the interests that would be lost through rigorous application of a final judgment requirement." Digital Equipment, 511 U.S. at 878–79.

Thus, in Nixon we stressed the "compelling public ends . . . rooted in . . . the separation of powers" that would be compromised by failing to allow immediate appeal of a denial of absolute Presidential immunity. In explaining collateral order treatment when a qualified immunity claim was at issue in Mitchell, we spoke of the threatened disruption of governmental functions, and fear of inhibiting able people from exercising discretion in public service if a full trial were threatened whenever they acted reasonably in the face of law that is not "clearly established." Puerto Rico Aqueduct explained the immediate appealability of an order denying a claim of Eleventh Amendment immunity by adverting not only to the burdens of litigation but to the need to ensure vindication of a State's dignitary interests. And although the double jeopardy claim given Cohen treatment in Abney did not implicate a right to be free of all proceedings whatsoever (since prior jeopardy is essential to the defense), we described the enormous prosecutorial power of the Government to subject an individual "to embarrassment, expense

---

[b]   Puerto Rico Aqueduct is considered in context in the Notes on State Immunity Against Award of Damages in Chapter 7, Section 1.—[Footnote by eds.]

and ordeal . . . compelling him to live in a continuing state of anxiety"; the only way to alleviate these consequences of the Government's superior position was by collateral order appeal.

In each case, some particular value of a high order was marshaled in support of the interest in avoiding trial. . . . That is, it is not mere avoidance of a trial, but avoidance of a trial that would imperil a substantial public interest, that counts when asking whether an order is "effectively" unreviewable if review is to be left until later. . . .

Does the claim of the customs agents in this case serve such a weighty public objective that the judgment bar should be treated as an immunity demanding the protection of a collateral order appeal? One can argue, of course, that if the *Bivens* action goes to trial the efficiency of Government will be compromised and the officials burdened and distracted, as in the qualified immunity case: if qualified immunity gets *Cohen* treatment, so should the judgment bar to further litigation in the aftermath of the Government's success under the Tort Claims Act. But the cases are different. Qualified immunity is not the law simply to save trouble for the Government and its employees; it is recognized because the burden of trial is unjustified in the face of a colorable claim that the law on point was not clear when the official took action, and the action was reasonable in light of the law as it was. The nub of qualified immunity is the need to induce officials to show reasonable initiative when the relevant law is not "clearly established"; a quick resolution of a qualified immunity claim is essential.

There is, however, no such public interest at stake simply because the judgment bar is said to be applicable. It is not the preservation of initiative but the avoidance of litigation for its own sake that supports the judgment bar, and if simply abbreviating litigation troublesome to Government employees were important enough for *Cohen* treatment, collateral order appeal would be a matter of right whenever the government lost a motion to dismiss under the Tort Claims Act, or a federal officer lost one on a *Bivens* action, or a state official was in that position in a case under 42 U.S.C. § 1983, or Ex parte Young, 209 U.S. 123 (1908). In effect, 28 U.S.C. § 1291 would fade out whenever the government or an official lost an early round that could have stopped the fight.

Another difference between qualified immunity and the judgment bar lies in the bar's essential procedural element. While a qualified immunity claim is timely from the moment an official is served with a complaint, the judgment bar can be raised only after a case under the Tort Claims Act has been resolved in the Government's favor. If a *Bivens* action alone is brought, there will be no possibility of a judgment bar, nor will there be so long as a *Bivens* action against officials and a Tort Claims Act against the Government are pending simultaneously (as they were for a time here). In the present case, if Susan Hallock had brought her *Bivens* action and no other, the agents could not possibly have invoked the judgment bar in claiming a right to be free of trial. The closer analogy to the judgment bar, then, is not immunity but the defense of claim preclusion, or res judicata.

Although the statutory judgment bar is arguably broader than traditional res judicata, it functions in much the same way, with both rules depending on a prior judgment as a condition precedent[*] and neither reflecting a policy that a defendant should be scot free of any liability. The concern behind both rules is a different one, of avoiding duplicative litigation. . . . But this rule of respecting a prior judgment by giving a defense against relitigation has not been thought to protect values so great that only immediate appeal can effectively vindicate them. [I]n the usual case, absent particular reasons for discretionary appeal by leave of the trial court, a defense of claim preclusion is fairly subordinated to the general policy of deferring appellate review to the moment of final judgment.

3. *RAY HALUCH GRAVEL CO. V. CENTRAL PENSION FUND*

The *Cohen* problem occurs when a party seeks an appeal on one or more issues when other issues remain unresolved. A contrasting problem occurred in Ray Haluch Gravel Co. v. Central Pension Fund, 571 U.S. ___, 134 S.Ct. 773 (2014).

Under a collective bargaining agreement, Haluch was obligated to contribute to various union-affiliated benefit funds. The funds sued Haluch in federal district court for failure to make required contributions. The funds also sought attorney's fees under the terms of the collective bargaining agreement. The trial judge entered judgment against Haluch on the contribution issues on June 17, 2011. It deferred the ruling on attorney's fees until June 25, when the plaintiffs' motion for such fees and costs was granted in a prescribed amount.

The timely filing of a notice of appeal is jurisdictional. See Bowles v. Russell, 551 U.S. 205, 214 (2007). Under Rule 4 of the Federal Rules of Appellate Procedure, parties have 30 days in which to file a notice of appeal. As the Court observed:

> The parties in this case agree that notice of appeal was not given within 30 days of the June 17 decision but that it was given within 30 days of the July 25 decision. The question is whether the June 17 order was a final decision for purposes of § 1291.

In an opinion by Justice Kennedy, the Court held unanimously that the June 17 order was a final decision on the merits and that the appeal on the contribution issues was therefore not timely.

---

[*] The right to be free of double jeopardy is subject to an analogous condition, that jeopardy have attached in a prior proceeding, a characteristic that distinguishes the Fifth Amendment right from other immunities mentioned above. But . . . double jeopardy deserves immunity treatment under § 1291 owing to the enormous advantage of a government prosecutor who chooses to go repeatedly against an individual.

The Court had held in a prior case, Budinich v. Becton Dickinson & Co., 486 U.S. 196 (1988), that a decision on the merits was "final" even though attorney's fees remained to be resolved. In *Haluch*, the Court said of *Budinich*:

> The Court noted that awards of attorney's fees do not remedy the injury giving rise to the action, are often available to the party defending the action, and were regarded at common law as an element of "costs" awarded to a prevailing party, which are generally not treated as part of the merits judgment. Though the Court acknowledged that the statutory or decisional law authorizing the fees might sometimes treat the fees as part of the merits, it held that considerations of "operational consistency and predictability in the overall application of § 1291" favored a "uniform rule that an unresolved issue of attorney's fees for the litigation in question does not prevent judgment on the merits from being final."

Budinich involved attorney's fees available under a Colorado statute. The question in *Haluch* was whether the answer should be different if the fees were sought under the provisions of a contract. The Court of Appeals had held that it did matter and that the June 17 decision was not a final appealable order. The Supreme Court applied the rationale of *Budinich* and disagreed.

4. INTERLOCUTORY REVIEW

Interlocutory review is permitted as of right by 28 U.S.C. § 1292(a) for orders "granting, continuing, modifying, refusing or dissolving injunctions, or refusing to dissolve or modify injunctions," for certain orders concerning receiverships, and for certain orders in admiralty cases. Section 1292(b), the purpose of which is discussed in *Coopers & Lybrand,* permits interlocutory appeal if the district judge certifies a "controlling question of law" under criteria stated in the statute.

The Supreme Court's approach to finality under § 1291 is undoubtedly influenced by the availability of discretionary interlocutory review under § 1292(b). In Van Cauwenberghe v. Biard, 486 U.S. 517 (1988), for example, the Court held that the *Cohen* collateral order doctrine did not permit immediate appeal from denial of a motion to dismiss for forum non conveniens. It added:

> Our conclusion . . . is fortified by the availability of interlocutory review pursuant to 28 U.S.C. § 1292(b). Under § 1292(b), a district court may certify a nonfinal order for interlocutory review when the order "involves a controlling question of law as to which there is substantial ground for difference of opinion and . . . an immediate appeal from the order may materially advance the ultimate termination of the litigation." A court of appeals may then, in its discretion, determine whether the order warrants prompt review. Section 1292(b) therefore provides an avenue for review of forum non conveniens determinations in appropriate cases.

5.   RULE 23(f)

An amendment to the Rules Enabling Act, enacted in 1990, authorized the Supreme Court to develop rules for defining when a district court's judgment is final for purposes of 28 U.S.C. § 1291. See 28 U.S.C. § 2072(c). A subsequent amendment to 28 U.S.C. § 1292 authorized the Supreme Court to use this rulemaking authority to allow for interlocutory appeals in situations not otherwise provided for in § 1292. See 28 U.S.C. § 1292(e). In 1998, the Court relied on this rulemaking authority to amend Rule 23 of the Federal Rules of Civil Procedure to give the courts of appeals discretion to hear appeals from grants or denials of class certification orders. See Rule 23(f). This Rule largely overrules the effect of *Coopers & Lybrand* as to class actions.

6.   RULE 54(b)

Rule 54(b) of the Federal Rules of Civil Procedure provides:

> When more than one claim for relief is presented in an action, whether as a claim, counterclaim, cross-claim, or third-party claim, or when multiple parties are involved, the court may direct the entry of a final judgment as to one or more but fewer than all the claims or parties only upon an express determination that there is no just reason for delay and upon an express direction for the entry of judgment. In the absence of such determination and direction, any order or other form of decision, however designated, which adjudicates fewer than all the claims or the rights and liabilities of fewer than all the parties shall not terminate the action as to any of the claims or parties, and the order or other form of decision is subject to revision at any time before the entry of judgment adjudicating all the claims and the rights and liabilities of all the parties.

The requirement of an "express determination" by the district judge that the matter is severable and appropriate for appeal brings clarity to the situations governed by this provision. The validity of Rule 54(b) was confirmed in Sears, Roebuck & Co. v. Mackey, 351 U.S. 427 (1956).[c]

The Court held in Curtiss-Wright Corp. v. General Electric Co., 446 U.S. 1 (1980), that a determination that Rule 54(b) should be invoked to permit an immediate appeal could be overturned by a court of appeals "only if it can say that the judge's conclusion was clearly unreasonable." By the very terms of § 1292(b), of course, the interlocutory appeal must be acceptable to both

---

[c]   A variation on the Rule 54(b) problem occurred in Gelboim v. Bank of America Corp., 574 U.S. ___, 135 S.Ct. 897 (2015). The petitioners filed a federal class action complaint raising a single claim against the Bank of America. The suit was consolidated with 60 other cases that had been commenced in different districts under 28 U.S.C. § 1407(a). The District Court then dismissed the claim without leave to amend. The question was whether this action was "final" and could be appealed even though discrete claims remained in the other cases with which it had been consolidated. The Supreme Court held unanimously that the order dismissing the complaint "had the hallmarks of a final decision" and was immediately appealable. The "§ 1407 consolidation offered convenience for the parties and promoted efficient judicial administration, but did not meld [this] action and [the] others . . . into a single unit." Rule 54(b) was irrelevant because it "is designed to permit acceleration of appeals in multiple-claim cases, not to retard appeals in single-claim cases."

the district court and the court of appeals before it can go forward. A district judge who refuses to invoke either procedure can be corrected only by extraordinary writ unless the court of appeals is prepared to hold that a "final" decision has been made.

7. MANDAMUS

Mandamus, which the courts of appeal are authorized to grant by 28 U.S.C. § 1651(a), is another mechanism for interlocutory appeal. Obviously, if mandamus were routinely available, the "final judgment" requirement of § 1291 would be undermined, and there would be no point to Rule 54(b) or § 1292(b). It is not surprising, therefore, that mandamus is regarded as an extraordinary writ designed only for extraordinary situations.

The cases defy convenient categorization, although there are pockets of the law where mandamus has been used with some frequency.[d] There is a sense in which the writ functions like the grant or denial of certiorari in the Supreme Court. A litigant who seeks mandamus bears the burden of showing that there are important reasons for *immediate* appellate intervention. It also functions like certiorari in the sense that intervention may be justified in order to correct errors on questions of significance beyond the immediate case.

Will v. United States, 389 U.S. 90 (1967), illustrates the kinds of arguments that might be persuasive. The District Court had ordered the government to give the defendant certain documents in a criminal trial. The government refused. The court then indicated that it would dismiss the indictment, but the government was able to get a writ of mandamus in the Court of Appeals to forestall that action. On certiorari the Supreme Court recited traditional platitudes about the scope of the writ: "it is clear that only exceptional circumstances amounting to a judicial 'usurpation of power' will justify the invocation of this extraordinary remedy"; mandamus is appropriate only "to confine an inferior court to a lawful exercise of its prescribed jurisdiction or to compel it to exercise its authority when it is its duty to do so."

More importantly, the *Will* Court seemed to accept the premise of the government's argument, though it held it inapplicable to the facts presented. The government argued that the district judge had displayed a "pattern of manifest noncompliance with the rules governing federal criminal trials"— in effect that he had committed the same error in many cases and that it would be expensive and inefficient to correct them one by one. The Court conceded that the writ serves "a vital corrective and didactic function" and could be used for "expository and supervisory" purposes.

8. *GULFSTREAM AEROSPACE CORP. V. MAYACAMAS CORP.*

Gulfstream sued Mayacamas in state court for breach of contract. Mayacamas answered and counterclaimed, declining to remove the case

---

d   For example, the improper denial of a jury trial is usually correctable by application for a writ of mandamus in the court of appeals. See Charles Alan Wright, The Law of Federal Courts 712 (4th ed. 1983).

although it could have done so on diversity grounds. One month later Mayacamas filed a diversity action in federal court against Gulfstream alleging breach of the same contract. Gulfstream moved for a stay or dismissal of the federal court action based on Colorado River Water Conservation District v. United States, 424 U.S. 800 (1976).[e] The District Court denied the motion. The Court of Appeals held that decision unreviewable on appeal and refused to issue a writ of mandamus. In Gulfstream Aerospace Corp. v. Mayacamas Corp., 485 U.S. 271 (1988), the Supreme Court unanimously affirmed. Three grounds were advanced for review of the District Court decision.

(i) Appeal Under § 1291

Gulfstream argued that the order was appealable under the *Cohen* collateral order doctrine, but the Court disagreed:

> In denying [a motion to dismiss or stay under *Colorado River*], the district court may well have determined only that it should await further developments before concluding that the balance of factors to be considered under *Colorado River* warrants a dismissal or stay. . . . Thus, whereas the granting of a *Colorado River* motion necessarily implies an expectation that the state court will resolve the dispute, the denial of such a motion may indicate nothing more than that the district court is not completely confident of the propriety of a stay or dismissal at that time. . . . Because an order denying a *Colorado River* motion is "inherently tentative" in this critical sense—because it is not "made with the expectation that it will be the final word on the subject addressed"—the order is not a conclusive determination within the meaning of the collateral-order doctrine and therefore is not appealable under § 1291.

Justice Scalia thought this analysis incomplete. He said it "oversimplifies somewhat to assign as the reason merely that the order is 'inherently tentative.'" *Cohen* was inapplicable, in his view, not only because the motion was likely to be renewed and reconsidered, but also because "the relief will be just as effective, or nearly as effective, if accorded at a later date—that is, the harm caused during the interval between initial denial and reconsideration will not be severe. Moreover, since these two conditions will almost always be met when the asserted basis for an initial stay motion is the pendency of state proceedings, the more general conclusion that initial orders denying *Colorado River* motions are never immediately appealable is justified." He also added the following observations:

> I note that today's result could also be reached by application of the rule adopted in the First Circuit, that to come within the *Cohen* exception the issue on appeal must involve "an important and unsettled question of controlling law," not merely a question of the proper exercise of the trial court's discretion. This approach has some support in our opinions [citing *Cohen* and *Coopers &*

---

[e] *Colorado River*, which is a main case in Chapter 6, states the general principles governing concurrent litigation in state and federal court. Generally, the fact that a proceeding is pending in state court is no bar to contemporaneous federal adjudication, but exceptional circumstances do exist that justify dismissal or stay of the federal suit.

Lybrand], as well as in policy. This rationale has not been argued here, and we should not embrace it without full adversarial exploration of its consequences. I do think, however, that our finality jurisprudence is sorely in need of further limiting principles, so that *Cohen* appeals will be, as we originally announced they would be, a "small class [of decisions] too important to be denied review."

(ii) Appeal Under § 1292(a)(1)

Section 1292(a)(1) of title 28 authorizes appeals from interlocutory orders granting or denying injunctions. Ordinarily, the Court said, "[a]n order by a federal court that relates only to the conduct or progress of litigation before that court . . . is not considered an injunction and therefore is not appealable under § 1292(a)(1)." But the *Enelow-Ettelson* doctrine,[f] it was argued, created an exception to this principle and allowed an appeal in this instance.

The *Enelow-Ettelson* doctrine derived from the separation of law and equity. If a plaintiff filed an action at law and the defendant sought to stay the proceedings in order to resolve an equitable defense, the "Court likened the stay to an injunction issued by an equity court to restrain an action at law." On that reasoning, an appeal from the denial of such a stay was allowed under § 1291(a)(1), even after the merger of law and equity.

The Court held in *Gulfstream Aerospace* that the *Enelow-Ettelson* doctrine was a "total fiction" that was "divorced from any rational or coherent appeals policy." It accordingly overruled the cases that gave rise to the doctrine and refused to permit the appeal on this ground.

(iii) Mandamus

Gulfstream also argued that the Court of Appeals should have reviewed the District Court decision by issuing a writ of mandamus. The Court made short work of this contention. It reiterated the standard doctrine that "mandamus is an extraordinary remedy, to be reserved for extraordinary situations" and held:

> Petitioner has failed to satisfy this stringent standard. This Court held in *Colorado River* that a federal court should stay or dismiss an action because of the pendency of a concurrent state-court proceeding only in "exceptional" circumstances and with "the clearest of justifications." Petitioner has failed to show that the District Court clearly overstepped its authority in holding that the circumstances of this case were not so exceptional as to warrant a stay or dismissal under *Colorado River*. This Court never has intimated acceptance of petitioner's view that the decision of a party to spurn removal and bring a separate suit in federal court invariably warrants the stay or dismissal of the suit under the *Colorado River* doctrine. . . . Petitioner . . . has failed to show that the District

---

[f]   See Enelow v. New York Life Ins. Co., 293 U.S. 379 (1935); Ettelson v. Metropolitan Life Ins. Co., 317 U.S. 188 (1942).

Court's order denying a stay or dismissal of the federal-court suit warranted the issuance of a writ of mandamus.

9. *MOHAWK INDUSTRIES, INC. V. CARPENTER*

A former employee of Mohawk Industries sued the company, alleging that his employment had been unlawfully terminated. During discovery, the district judge ordered Mohawk to turn over materials that were subject to the attorney-client privilege on the ground that Mohawk had implicitly waived the privilege. Mohawk sought immediate review under the collateral order doctrine, but the Court of Appeals held that doctrine inapplicable and the Supreme Court affirmed. Mohawk Industries, Inc. v. Carpenter, 558 U.S. 100 (2009).

In an opinion by Justice Sotomayor, the Court concluded that Mohawk had not satisfied the third requirement of the collateral order doctrine—that the interlocutory decision be "effectively unreviewable on appeal from the final judgment." In response to Mohawk's argument that discovery rulings implicating the attorney-client privilege "differ in kind from run-of-the-mill discovery orders because of the important institutional interests at stake," the Court "readily acknowledged the importance of the attorney-client privilege." The Court explained, however, that "[t]he crucial question . . . is not whether an interest is important in the abstract; it is whether deferring review until final judgment so imperils the interest as to justify the cost of allowing immediate appeal of the entire class of relevant orders." The Court found that this test was not met, because "[a]ppellate courts can remedy the improper disclosure of privileged material in the same way they remedy a host of other erroneous evidentiary rulings: by vacating an adverse judgment and remanding for a new trial in which the protected material and its fruits are excluded from evidence."

The Court also was unpersuaded by Mohawk's argument that forcing litigants to wait until final judgment to appeal discovery orders like this one would unduly chill attorney-client communications. The Court reasoned that, "in deciding how freely to speak, clients and counsel are unlikely to focus on the remote prospect of an erroneous disclosure order, let alone on the timing of a possible appeal." Moreover, the Court said that it is already the case that "clients and counsel must account for the possibility that they will later be required by law to disclose their communications for a variety of reasons—for example, because they misjudged the scope of the privilege, because they waived the privilege, or because their communications fell within the privilege's crime-fraud exception." The Court further noted that litigants confronted with a potentially injurious discovery order have other options for attempting to seek immediate review, either by asking the district court to certify, and the court of appeals to accept, an interlocutory appeal under 28 U.S.C. § 1292(b), or (in extraordinary situations) through seeking a writ of mandamus.

Finally, the Court emphasized that "the class of collaterally appealable orders must remain 'narrow and selective in its membership'" (quoting Will v. Hallock, 546 U.S. 345, 350 (2006)). The Court said that this was particularly true in light of legislation enacted in 1990 and 1992 that authorizes the

Court to promulgate rules that clarify which orders are final for purposes of § 1291 and that provide for interlocutory appeals not otherwise provided for by § 1292. The Court described this legislatively-authorized rulemaking process "as the preferred means for determining whether and when prejudgment orders should be immediately appealable."

Justice Thomas concurred in part and concurred in the judgment, arguing that the Court should not extend the collateral order doctrine any further and should instead rely solely on the rulemaking process specified by Congress. Further application of the collateral order doctrine, he argued, "needlessly perpetuates a judicial policy that we for many years have criticized and struggled to limit."

10. FOOTNOTE ON SUPREME COURT REVIEW OF CASES IN THE COURTS OF APPEALS

As Justice Harlan pointed out in *Gillespie*, review by the Supreme Court of a court of appeals decision is not constrained by a finality requirement. Section 1254 of title 28 provides that cases "in" the courts of appeals may be reviewed by the Supreme Court. Thus, if a court of appeals remands for further proceedings in the district court, review in the Supreme Court is available even though the court of appeals' order is not a "final" disposition of the case. Moreover, once a case has been docketed in a court of appeals, § 1254 provides that certiorari may be granted by the Supreme Court "before or after rendition of judgment or decree." Certiorari before judgment is rarely granted.[g]

11. BIBLIOGRAPHY

For general treatment of the various methods by which district court judgments can be reviewed, see Martin H. Redish, The Pragmatic Approach to Appealability in the Federal Courts, 75 Colum. L. Rev. 89 (1975), and Note, Appealability in the Federal Courts, 75 Harv. L. Rev. 351 (1961). See also Theodore Frank, Requiem for the Final Judgment Rule, 45 Tex. L. Rev. 292 (1966). For a comprehensive effort to restate the law on 28 U.S.C. §§ 1291, 1292, and 1651 with accompanying commentary, see Civil Appellate Jurisdiction, Parts I and II, in the Spring and Summer editions of 47 Law & Contemp. Probs. (1984). Discussion of finality in specific contexts can be found in Note, Interlocutory Appeal of Orders Granting or Denying Stays of Arbitration, 80 Mich. L. Rev. 153 (1981); Note, A Test for Appealability: The Final Judgment Rule and Closure Orders, 65 Minn. L. Rev. 1110 (1981); Note, Interlocutory Appeals in the Federal Courts under 28 U.S.C. § 1292(b), 88 Harv. L. Rev. 607 (1975).

For treatments of the availability of mandamus as a form of interlocutory review, see Griffin Bell, The Federal Appellate Courts and the All Writs

---

[g] For a study of pre-judgment certiorari, see James Lindgren and William P. Marshall, The Supreme Court's Extraordinary Power to Grant Certiorari before a Judgment of the Court of Appeals, 1986 Sup. Ct. Rev. 259. For an empirical study of the Supreme Court's certiorari policy, including analysis of various factors associated with the decision to review, see Kevin H. Smith, Certiorari and the Supreme Court Agenda: An Empirical Analysis, 54 Okla. L. Rev. 727 (2001).

Act, 23 Sw. L.J. 858 (1969); Edmund Kitch, Section 1404(a) of the Judicial Code: In the Interest of Justice or Injustice, 40 Ind. L.J. 99, 110–31 (1965); Note, The Use of Extraordinary Writs for Interlocutory Appeals, 44 Tenn. L. Rev. 137 (1976); Note, Supervisory and Advisory Mandamus under the All Writs Act, 86 Harv. L. Rev. 595 (1973); Note, Mandamus Proceedings in the Federal Courts of Appeals: A Compromise with Finality, 52 Calif. L. Rev. 1036 (1964); Note, The Effect of Mandamus on the Final Decision Rule, 57 Nw. L. Rev. 709 (1963).

For an exhaustive consideration of the "final judgment" rule past and present, see Robert J. Martineau, Defining Finality and Appealability by Court Rule: Right Problem, Wrong Solution, 54 U. Pitt. L. Rev. 717 (1993).[h] See also Thomas D. Rowe, Jr., Defining Finality and Appealability by Court Rule: A Comment on Martineau's "Right Problem, Wrong Solution," 54 U. Pitt. L. Rev. 795 (1993). Martineau endorses an approach to finality based on a Wisconsin statute that permits non-final decisions to be appealed upon leave granted by the appellate court if an appeal will "[m]aterially advance the termination of the litigation or clarify further proceedings in the litigation," "[p]rotect the petitioner from substantial or irreparable injury," or "[c]larify an issue of general importance in the administration of justice." Rowe endorses this approach, and recommends that it be adopted by court rule under the authority granted in the 1990 amendment to the Rules Enabling Act, 28 U.S.C. § 2072(c) ("Such rules may define when a ruling of a district court is final for the purposes of appeal under section 1291 of this title."), and the 1992 amendment to the interlocutory appeals statute, 28 U.S.C. § 1292(e) ("The Supreme Court may prescribe rules, in accordance with section 2072 of this title, to provide for an appeal of an interlocutory decision to the courts of appeals that is not otherwise provided for under subsection (a), (b), (c), or (d).").

---

[h] For discussion of pendent appellate jurisdiction in appeals permitted by *Cohen*, see Note, The Proper Scope of Pendent Appellate Jurisdiction in the Collateral Order Context, 100 Yale L.J. 511 (1990). For a rejection of a pendent appeal in the context of municipal liability under § 1983, see Swint v. Chambers County Commission, 514 U.S. 35 (1995). For an elaborate criticism of *Swint* and an argument in favor of a properly circumscribed doctrine of pendent appellate jurisdiction applicable to all categories of interlocutory review, see Joan Steinman, The Scope of Appellate Jurisdiction: Pendent Appellate Jurisdiction before and after *Swint*, 49 Hastings L.J. 1337 (1998).

CHAPTER VI

ABSTENTION

SECTION 1. INTRODUCTION

INTRODUCTORY NOTES ON FEDERAL COURT ABSTENTION

1. THE BASELINE OBLIGATION

In Cohens v. Virginia, 19 U.S. (6 Wheat.) 264, 404 (1821), Chief Justice Marshall said that the federal judiciary has "no more right to decline the exercise of jurisdiction which is given, than to usurp that which is not given. The one or the other would be treason to the Constitution." The classic illustration of the obligation of the federal courts to exercise the jurisdiction granted by Congress is Meredith v. City of Winter Haven, 320 U.S. 228 (1943). *Meredith* stands for the proposition that even in diversity cases, where the federal interest in exercising jurisdiction is very slight, a federal court may not decline to hear the case "merely because the state law is uncertain or difficult to determine."

2. ABSTENTION

Notwithstanding this baseline obligation, there are exceptional situations where jurisdiction is declined in favor of pending or prospective litigation elsewhere. The cases considered in this chapter concern these exceptional situations—usually lumped under the label of "abstention." In Colorado River Water Conservation District v. United States, 424 U.S. 800, 813 (1976), the Court structured the issue as follows:

> Abstention from the exercise of federal jurisdiction is the exception, not the rule. "The doctrine of abstention, under which a district court may decline to exercise or postpone the exercise of its jurisdiction, is an extraordinary and narrow exception to the duty of a district court to adjudicate a controversy properly before it. Abdication of the obligation to decide cases can be justified under this doctrine only in the exceptional circumstances where the order to the parties to repair to [another] court would clearly serve an important countervailing interest." County of Allegheny v. Frank Mashuda Co., 360 U.S. 185, 188–89 (1959).

Abstention is not a unitary concept. Instead, discrete abstention doctrines have evolved to deal with the various circumstances thought to justify the abdication or postponement of the exercise of federal court jurisdiction. They fall into two general categories.

(i) Statute-Based Abstention

Congress by statute has required the federal courts to abstain in certain classes of cases that otherwise would fall within a generally worded grant of jurisdiction. The question in these situations is simple enough in principle, though sometimes difficult to apply in practice. Most statute-based abstention doctrines are narrow and context-specific.[a] They defy generalization, and are of little interest beyond the specific categories of cases to which they apply. For this reason, they do not receive extensive treatment in these materials.

There is, however, one abstention statute of more general interest. Section § 2283 of Title 28, sometimes referred to as the "Anti-Injunction Act," provides:

> A court of the United States may not grant an injunction to stay proceedings in a State court except as expressly authorized by Act of Congress, or where necessary in aid of its jurisdiction, or to protect or effectuate its judgments.

The most litigated issues under § 2283 have to do with the scope of the statutory exceptions. One important exception is covered in Section 1 of this chapter. A number of others are considered in Section 5.

(ii)   Judge-Based Abstention

The Supreme Court has also identified exceptional circumstances that justify exceptions to generally worded jurisdictional statutes. Here the Supreme Court is the policymaker. Whether based on implied legislative intent, constitutional considerations, or general good sense about the administration of the federal courts, these decisions carve out additional exceptions to "the duty of a district court to adjudicate a controversy properly before it."

At the outset, two types of cases should be noted—those involving domestic relations and probate—where by tradition federal courts decline to exercise diversity jurisdiction based on the subject matter of the lawsuit.[b] In addition, there are two situations where concurrent litigation involving the same parties and the same issues usually requires deference to another court. The first is when a suit would interfere with the control of property already in formal custody of another court. In such a case, the normal rule is that the second court must defer to the court already in "possession" of the property. This is the traditional basis for in rem jurisdiction. The second situation is peculiar to the relationship among federal courts. It has long been the rule that the lower federal courts have discretion to defer to pending *federal* litigation involving the same parties and issues. See, e.g., Kerotest Manufacturing Co. v. C-O-Two Fire Equipment Co., 342 U.S. 180 (1952).[c] But the rule is different when contemporaneous in personam litigation is being pursued in a *state* court. The usual federal rule is that the federal court

---

[a]   E.g., the Tax Injunction Act, 28 U.S.C. § 1341, which provides that "[t]he district courts shall not enjoin, suspend or restrain the assessment, levy or collection of any tax under State law where a plain, speedy and efficient remedy may be had in the courts of such State." See also 28 U.S.C. §§ 1334 (involving bankruptcy cases), 1342 (involving state rate-making agencies).

[b]   See the brief discussion of these exceptions to diversity jurisdiction in the Note on Interpretation of the Diversity Statute in Section 2 of Chapter V.

[c]   A federal district court has the option in such a situation of transferring the case to the other federal district court "[f]or the convenience of parties and witnesses, in the interest of justice." 28 U.S.C. § 1404(a).

will proceed to judgment, despite the pendency of the same claim in state court, subject to the application of appropriate res judicata principles if the state proceeding becomes final before the federal suit is concluded. See, e.g., Kline v. Burke Constr. Co., 260 U.S. 226 (1922).

The next four sections of this chapter deal with judicially adopted abstention doctrines. They are treated prior to statute-based abstention because they are more frequently in play and because they cut across a much broader array of situations than do § 2283 and its statutory brethren.[d]

3. CONNECTION TO EQUITY PRINCIPLES

In explaining the propriety of abstention, the Court has noted that, in conferring jurisdiction on the federal courts, Congress has acted against the backdrop of a common-law tradition in which the courts had discretion over the exercise of jurisdiction when sitting in equity. In Quackenbush v. Allstate Insurance Co., 517 U.S. 706, 717 (1996), the Court said that "[t]his tradition informs our understanding of the jurisdiction Congress has conferred upon the federal courts and explains the development of our abstention doctrines." Based on this rationale, the Court added that it is generally not appropriate for the federal courts to dismiss (as opposed to stay) damages actions pursuant to judicially-developed abstention doctrines:

> We have thus held in cases where the relief being sought is equitable in nature or otherwise discretionary, federal courts not only have the power to stay the action based on abstention principles, but can also, in otherwise appropriate circumstances, decline to exercise jurisdiction altogether by either dismissing the suit or remanding it to state court. By contrast, while we have held that federal courts may stay actions for damages based on abstention principles, we have not held that those principles support the outright dismissal or remand of damages actions.

SECTION 2. *YOUNGER* ABSTENTION

INTRODUCTORY NOTES ON FEDERAL INJUNCTIONS AGAINST STATE CRIMINAL PROCEEDINGS

1. INTRODUCTION

Current law on federal injunctions against state criminal prosecutions begins with *Younger v. Harris,* the next main case. *Younger* held that, absent prosecutorial bad faith or harassment, a federal court normally cannot enjoin a pending state criminal prosecution. Prior developments provide necessary context for the Court's decision.

---

[d] It can be argued that judicially developed abstention doctrines violate the fundamental *Cohens* dictum that jurisdiction once given cannot be declined. For consideration—and rejection—of this claim, see Richard H. Fallon, Jr., Why Abstention Is Not Illegitimate: An Essay on the Distinction between "Legitimate" and "Illegitimate" Statutory Interpretation and Judicial Lawmaking, 107 Nw. U. L. Rev. 847 (2013), and William P. Marshall, Abstention, Separation of Powers, and Recasting the Meaning of Judicial Restraint, 107 Nw. U. L. Rev. 881 (2013).

(i) Douglas v. City of Jeannette

A group of Jehovah's Witnesses distributed religious literature without a permit in violation of a criminal ordinance in Jeannette, Pennsylvania. They filed a class action in federal District Court seeking an injunction against threatened prosecution under the ordinance. In Douglas v. City of Jeannette, 319 U.S. 157 (1943), the Court held the injunction unavailable:

> It is a familiar rule that courts of equity do not ordinarily restrain criminal prosecutions. No person is immune from prosecution in good faith for his alleged criminal acts. Its imminence, even though alleged to be in violation of constitutional guarantees, is not a ground for equity relief since the lawfulness or constitutionality of the statute or ordinance may be determined as readily in the criminal case as in a suit for an injunction. Where the threatened prosecution is by state officers for alleged violations of a state law, the state courts are the final arbiters of its meaning and application, subject only to review by this Court on federal grounds appropriately asserted. Hence the arrest by the federal courts of the processes of the criminal law within the states, and the determination of questions of criminal liability under state law by a federal court of equity, are to be supported only on a showing of danger of irreparable injury "both great and immediate." . . . It does not appear from the record that petitioners have been threatened with any injury other than that incidental to every criminal proceeding brought lawfully and in good faith, or that a federal court of equity by withdrawing the determination of guilt from the state courts could rightly afford the petitioners any protection which they could not secure by prompt trial and appeal pursued to this Court. . . .

(ii) The Habeas Exhaustion Requirement

Federal habeas corpus is a post-conviction remedy sometimes available to state prisoners who can establish federal constitutional defects in their state court prosecutions. Federal habeas is unavailable if state court remedies have not been exhausted. The exhaustion requirement dates from Ex parte Royall, 117 U.S. 241 (1886).

Royall was in jail awaiting trial on state criminal charges. He sought federal habeas on the ground that the statutes under which he was being prosecuted violated the Contract Clause of the federal Constitution. The Supreme Court held that, absent special circumstances, the federal courts should not intervene until both the state trial and appellate courts had an opportunity to rule on the federal claim. The federal habeas court "was not at liberty . . . to presume that the decision of the state court[s] would be otherwise than is required by the fundamental law of the land, or that it would disregard the settled principles of constitutional law announced by this Court."

The requirement that state prisoners exhaust available state remedies prior to seeking federal habeas corpus was codified in 1948, see 28 U.S.C. § 2254(b), and remains an essential feature of federal habeas jurisprudence.

2. *DOMBROWSKI V. PFISTER*

Taken together, *Douglas* and the habeas exhaustion requirement seemed to leave little room for federal court intervention in state criminal proceedings prior to their final disposition in the state courts. The functional justification for this rule was to avoid piecemeal review and the inevitable disruption of on-going state proceedings. This situation was arguably changed in Dombrowski v. Pfister, 380 U.S. 479 (1965).

A civil rights organization, the Southern Conference Educational Fund (SCEF), and several of its officers sought a federal court injunction against the enforcement of two Louisiana statutes, the Subversive Activities and Communist Control Law and the Communist Propaganda Control Law. The complaint alleged that state authorities were threatening prosecution of the plaintiffs under these laws, not with any expectation of securing valid convictions, but in order to harass the SCEF and to dissuade its members from civil rights activities. To the extent that the complaint was based on bad-faith harassment, it stated a basis for federal court relief that could well have been justified under the Court's reasoning in *Douglas*. But Justice Brennan's opinion for the Court offered a much broader basis for federal court intervention:

> [T]he Court has recognized that federal interference with a state's good faith administration of its criminal laws is peculiarly inconsistent with our federal framework. It is generally to be assumed that state courts and prosecutors will observe constitutional limitations as expounded by this Court, and that the mere possibility of erroneous initial application of constitutional standards will usually not amount to the irreparable injury necessary to justify a disruption of orderly state proceedings. [But] the allegations of this complaint depict a situation in which defense of the state's criminal prosecution will not assure adequate vindication of constitutional rights. They suggest that a substantial loss or impairment of freedoms of expression will occur if appellants must await the state court's disposition and ultimate review in this Court of any adverse determination. These allegations, if true, clearly show irreparable injury.

The Court said that "[t]he assumption that defense of a criminal prosecution will generally assure ample vindication of constitutional rights is unfounded" where a statute is challenged on First Amendment overbreadth grounds. "The chilling effect upon the exercise of First Amendment rights may derive from the fact of the prosecution, unaffected by the prospects of its success or failure." The Court then held certain portions of the Louisiana statutes unconstitutionally overbroad on their face, and ordered the lower court to enter an injunction against enforcement of those provisions. The plaintiffs' allegations of bad faith were left to later resolution following a hearing on the merits of the claim in the lower court.

A subsidiary aspect of *Dombrowski* was relied on in *Younger*. The question was whether a statute held unconstitutionally overbroad could ever be used as the basis for a subsequent prosecution. The Court said:

> The state must, if it is to invoke the statute after injunctive relief has been sought, assume the burden of obtaining a permissible narrow construction in a noncriminal proceeding before it may seek modification of the injunction to permit future prosecutions.[7] [T]he settled rule of our cases is that district courts retain power to modify injunctions in light of changed circumstances. Our view of the proper operation of the vagueness doctrine does not preclude district courts from modifying injunctions to permit prosecutions in light of subsequent state court interpretation clarifying the application of the statute to particular conduct.

3.   THE EFFECT OF *DOMBROWSKI*

Joined by Justice Clark, Justice Harlan dissented in *Dombrowski*. "In practical effect," he said, "the Court's decision means that a state may no longer carry on prosecutions under statutes challengeable for vagueness on 'First Amendment' grounds without the prior approval of the federal courts." Harlan found such supervision unwarranted:

> Underlying the Court's major premise that criminal enforcement of an overly broad statute affecting rights of speech and association is in itself a deterrent to the free exercise thereof seems to be the unarticulated assumption that state courts will not be as prone as federal courts to vindicate constitutional rights promptly and effectively. Such an assumption should not be indulged in the absence of a showing that such is apt to be so in a given case.

Civil rights plaintiffs and their attorneys shared Harlan's view of the implications of the decision. *Dombrowski* was regarded as signaling a new receptivity by federal courts to suits seeking injunctions against criminal proceedings based on overbroad state statutes. Many suits—literally hundreds, though few were successful—were brought to exploit this new opportunity. One such suit was *Younger v. Harris*.

Younger v. Harris
Supreme Court of the United States, 1971.
401 U.S. 37.

■ MR. JUSTICE BLACK delivered the opinion of the Court.

Appellee, John Harris, Jr., was indicted in a California state court, charged with violation of the California Penal Code §§ 11400 and 11401, known as the California Criminal Syndicalism Act.[a] . . . He then filed a

---

[7]   Our cases indicate that once an acceptable limiting construction is obtained, it may be applied to conduct occurring prior to the construction, provided such application affords fair warning to the defendants.

[a]   Harris had been distributing leaflets in response to the shooting by a white police officer of an African-American resident of Los Angeles. The leaflets referred to the shooting as a "murder," described south Los Angeles as a "concentration camp," and stated that the members of

complaint in the federal District Court, asking that court to enjoin the appellant, Younger, the District Attorney of Los Angeles County, from prosecuting him, and alleging that the prosecution and even the presence of the act inhibited him in the exercise of his rights of free speech and press, rights guaranteed him by the First and Fourteenth Amendments. Appellees Jim Dan and Diane Hirsch intervened as plaintiffs in the suit, claiming that the prosecution of Harris would inhibit them as members of the Progressive Labor Party from peacefully advocating the program of their party, which was to replace capitalism with socialism and to abolish the profit system of production in this country. Appellee Farrell Broslawsky, an instructor in history at Los Angeles Valley College, also intervened claiming that the prosecution of Harris made him uncertain as to whether he could teach about the doctrines of Karl Marx or read from the Communist Manifesto as part of his classwork. All claimed that unless the United States court restrained the state prosecution of Harris each would suffer immediate and irreparable injury. A three-judge federal District Court[b] . . . held that it had jurisdiction and power to restrain the District Attorney from prosecuting, held that the state's Criminal Syndicalism Act was void for vagueness and overbreadth in violation of the First and Fourteenth Amendments, and accordingly restrained the District Attorney from "further prosecution of the currently pending action against plaintiff Harris for alleged violation of the act."

The case is before us on appeal by the state's District Attorney Younger. . . . In his notice of appeal and his jurisdictional statement appellant presented two questions: (1) whether the decision of this Court in Whitney v. California, 274 U.S. 357 (1927), holding California's law constitutional in 1927 was binding on the District Court and (2) whether the state's law is constitutional on its face. In this Court the brief for the state of California, filed at our request, also argues that only Harris, who was indicted, has standing to challenge the state's law, and that issuance of the injunction was a violation of a longstanding judicial policy and of 28 U.S.C. § 2283, which provides:

> A court of the United States may not grant an injunction to stay proceedings in a State court except as expressly authorized

---

the police department "must all be wiped out before there is complete freedom." California Penal Code § 11400 defined "criminal syndicalism" to include "any doctrine or precept advocating, teaching or aiding and abetting the commission of crime, sabotage . . ., or unlawful acts of force and violence . . . as a means of accomplishing a change in industrial organization or control, or effecting any political change." Section 11401 punished, inter alia, one who "[b]y spoken or written words or personal conduct advocates, teaches or aids and abets criminal syndicalism . . .," or who "[p]rints, publishes, edits, issues or circulates or publicly displays any book, paper, pamphlet, document, poster or written or printed matter in any other form" advocating or advising criminal syndicalism.—[Footnote by eds.]

    b   Congress passed the Three-Judge Court Act in 1910 in response to the decision in Ex parte Young, 209 U.S. 123 (1908). The statute required three federal judges—usually two district judges and a circuit judge—to act as the trial court in cases brought to seek an injunction against a statute of statewide applicability. Appeal in such cases was available directly to the Supreme Court. These provisions were repealed in 1976.—[Footnote by eds.]

by Act of Congress, or where necessary in aid of its jurisdiction, or to protect or effectuate its judgments.

Without regard to the questions raised about *Whitney v. California*, since overruled by Brandenburg v. Ohio, 395 U.S. 444 (1969), or the constitutionality of the state law, we have concluded that the judgment of the District Court, enjoining appellant Younger from prosecuting under these California statutes, must be reversed as a violation of the national policy forbidding federal courts to stay or enjoin pending state court proceedings except under special circumstances. We express no view about the circumstances under which federal courts may act when there is no prosecution pending in state courts at the time the federal proceeding is begun.

I

Appellee Harris has been indicted, and was actually being prosecuted by California for a violation of its Criminal Syndicalism Act at the time this suit was filed. He thus has an acute, live controversy with the state and its prosecutor. But none of the other parties plaintiff in the District Court, Dan, Hirsch, or Broslawsky, has such a controversy. None has been indicted, arrested, or even threatened by the prosecutor. . . . Whatever right Harris, who is being prosecuted under the state syndicalism law may have, Dan, Hirsch, and Broslawsky cannot share it with him. If these three had alleged that they would be prosecuted for the conduct they planned to engage in, and if the District Court had found this allegation to be true—either on the admission of the state's District Attorney or on any other evidence—then a genuine controversy might be said to exist. But here appellees Dan, Hirsch, and Broslawsky do not claim that they have ever been threatened with prosecution, that a prosecution is likely, or even that a prosecution is remotely possible. They claim the right to bring this suit solely because, in the language of their complaint, they "feel inhibited." We do not think this allegation, even if true, is sufficient to bring the equitable jurisdiction of the federal courts into play to enjoin a pending state prosecution. A federal lawsuit to stop a prosecution in a state court is a serious matter. And persons having no fears of state prosecution except those that are imaginary or speculative, are not to be accepted as appropriate plaintiffs in such cases. Since Harris is actually being prosecuted under the challenged laws, however, we proceed with him as a proper party.

II

Since the beginning of this country's history Congress has, subject to few exceptions, manifested a desire to permit state courts to try state cases free from interference by federal courts. In 1793 an act unconditionally provided: "[N]or shall a writ of injunction be granted to stay proceedings in any court of a state. . . ." A comparison of the 1793 act with 28 U.S.C. § 2283, its present-day successor, graphically illustrates how few and minor have been the exceptions granted from the flat, prohibitory language of the old act. During all this lapse of years from 1793 to

1970 the statutory exceptions to the 1793 congressional enactment have been only three: (1) "except as expressly authorized by Act of Congress"; (2) "where necessary in aid of its jurisdiction"; and (3) "to protect or effectuate its judgments." . . .

The precise reasons for this longstanding public policy against federal court interference with state court proceedings have never been specifically identified but the primary sources of the policy are plain. One is the basic doctrine of equity jurisprudence that courts of equity should not act, and particularly should not act to restrain a criminal prosecution, when the moving party has an adequate remedy at law and will not suffer irreparable injury if denied equitable relief. The doctrine may originally have grown out of circumstances peculiar to the English judicial system and not applicable in this country, but its fundamental purpose of restraining equity jurisdiction within narrow limits is equally important under our Constitution, in order to prevent erosion of the role of the jury and avoid a duplication of legal proceedings and legal sanctions where a single suit would be adequate to protect the rights asserted. This underlying reason for restraining courts of equity from interfering with criminal prosecutions is reinforced by an even more vital consideration, the notion of "comity," that is, a proper respect for state functions, a recognition of the fact that the entire country is made up of a Union of separate state governments, and a continuance of the belief that the national government will fare best if the states and their institutions are left free to perform their separate functions in their separate ways. This, perhaps for lack of a better and clearer way to describe it, is referred to by many as "Our Federalism," and one familiar with the profound debates that ushered our federal Constitution into existence is bound to respect those who remain loyal to the ideals and dreams of "Our Federalism." The concept does not mean blind deference to "states' rights" any more than it means centralization of control over every important issue in our national government and its courts. The framers rejected both these courses. What the concept does represent is a system in which there is sensitivity to the legitimate interests of both state and national governments, and in which the national government, anxious though it may be to vindicate and protect federal rights and federal interests, always endeavors to do so in ways that will not unduly interfere with the legitimate activities of the state. It should never be forgotten that this slogan, "Our Federalism," born in the early struggling days of our union of states, occupies a highly important place in our nation's history and its future.

This brief discussion should be enough to suggest some of the reasons why it has been perfectly natural for our cases to repeat time and time again that the normal thing to do when federal courts are asked to enjoin pending proceedings in state courts is not to issue such injunctions. In Fenner v. Boykin, 271 U.S. 240 (1926), suit had been brought in the federal District Court seeking to enjoin state prosecutions under a recently enacted state law that allegedly interfered with the free flow of interstate commerce. The Court, in a unanimous opinion made clear that such a suit, even with respect to state criminal proceedings not yet formally instituted, could be proper only under very special circumstances:

> Ex parte Young, 209 U.S. 123 (1908), and following cases have established the doctrine that when absolutely necessary for protection of constitutional rights courts of the United States have power to enjoin state officers from instituting criminal actions. But this may not be done except under extraordinary circumstances where the danger of irreparable loss is both great and immediate. Ordinarily, there should be no interference with such officers; primarily, they are charged with the duty of prosecuting offenders against the laws of the state and must decide when and how this is to be done. The accused should first set up and rely upon his defense in the state courts, even though this involves a challenge of the validity of some statute, unless it plainly appears that this course would not afford adequate protection.

These principles, made clear in the *Fenner* case, have been repeatedly followed and reaffirmed in other cases involving threatened prosecutions. See, e.g., Watson v. Buck, 313 U.S. 387 (1941); Douglas v. City of Jeannette, 319 U.S. 157 (1943).

In all of these cases the Court stressed the importance of showing irreparable injury, the traditional prerequisite to obtaining an injunction. In addition, however, the Court also made clear that in view of the fundamental policy against federal interference with state criminal prosecutions, even irreparable injury is insufficient unless it is "both great and immediate." Certain types of injury, in particular, the cost, anxiety, and inconvenience of having to defend against a single criminal prosecution, could not by themselves be considered "irreparable" in the special legal sense of that term. Instead, the threat to the plaintiff's federally protected rights must be one that cannot be eliminated by his defense against a single criminal prosecution. Thus, in the *Buck* case we stressed:

> Federal injunctions against state criminal statutes, either in their entirety or with respect to their separate and distinct prohibitions, are not to be granted as a matter of course, even if such statutes are unconstitutional. "No citizen or member of the community is immune from prosecution, in good faith, for his alleged criminal acts. The imminence of such a prosecution even though alleged to be unauthorized and hence unlawful is not alone ground for relief in equity which exerts its extraordinary powers only to prevent irreparable injury to the plaintiff who seeks its aid."

And similarly, in *Douglas*, we made clear, after reaffirming this rule, that:

> It does not appear from the record that petitioners have been threatened with any injury other than that incidental to every criminal proceeding brought lawfully and in good faith. . . .

This is where the law stood when the Court decided Dombrowski v. Pfister, 380 U.S. 479 (1965), and held that an injunction against the enforcement of certain state criminal statutes could properly issue under the circumstances presented in that case. In *Dombrowski,* unlike many of the earlier cases denying injunctions, the complaint made substantial allegations that:

> the threats to enforce the statutes against appellants are not made with any expectation of securing valid convictions, but rather are part of a plan to employ arrests, seizures, and threats of prosecution under color of the statutes to harass appellants and discourage them and their supporters from asserting and attempting to vindicate the constitutional rights of Negro citizens of Louisiana.

The appellants in *Dombrowski* had offered to prove that their offices had been raided and all their files and records seized pursuant to search and arrest warrants that were later summarily vacated by a state judge for lack of probable cause. They also offered to prove that despite the state court order quashing the warrants and suppressing the evidence seized, the prosecutor was continuing to threaten to initiate new prosecutions of appellants under the same statutes, was holding public hearings at which photostatic copies of the illegally seized documents were being used, and was threatening to use other copies of the illegally seized documents to obtain grand jury indictments against the appellants on charges of violating the same statutes. These circumstances, as viewed by the Court, sufficiently establish the kind of irreparable injury, above and beyond that associated with the defense of a single prosecution brought in good faith, that had always been considered sufficient to justify federal intervention. Indeed, after quoting the Court's statement in *Douglas* concerning the very restricted circumstances under which an injunction could be justified, the Court in *Dombrowski* went on to say:

> But the allegations in this complaint depict a situation in which defense of the state's criminal prosecution will not assure adequate vindication of constitutional rights. They suggest that a substantial loss of or impairment of freedoms of expression will occur if appellants must await the state court's disposition and ultimate review in this Court of any adverse determination. These allegations, if true, clearly show irreparable injury.

. . . It is against the background of these principles that we must judge the propriety of an injunction under the circumstances of the present case. Here a proceeding was already pending in the state court, affording Harris an opportunity to raise his constitutional claims. There is no suggestion that this single prosecution against Harris is brought in bad faith or is only one of a series of repeated prosecutions to which he

will be subjected. In other words, the injury that Harris faces is solely
"that incidental to every criminal proceeding brought lawfully and in
good faith," *Douglas*, supra, and therefore under the settled doctrine we
have already described he is not entitled to equitable relief "even if such
statutes are unconstitutional," *Buck*, supra.

The District Court, however, thought that the *Dombrowski* decision
substantially broadened the availability of injunctions against state
criminal prosecutions and that under that decision the federal courts
may give equitable relief, without regard to any showing of bad faith or
harassment, whenever a state statute is found "on its face" to be vague
or overly broad, in violation of the First Amendment. We recognize that
there are some statements in the *Dombrowski* opinion that would seem
to support this argument. But, as we have already seen, such statements
were unnecessary to the decision of that case, because the Court found
that the plaintiffs had alleged a basis for equitable relief under the long-
established standards. In addition, we do not regard the reasons adduced
to support this position as sufficient to justify such a substantial departure from the established doctrines regarding the availability of
injunctive relief. It is undoubtedly true, as the Court stated in *Dombrowski* that "[a] criminal prosecution under a statute regulating expression usually involves imponderables and contingencies that themselves
may inhibit the full exercise of First Amendment freedoms." But this sort
of "chilling effect," as the Court called it, should not by itself justify federal intervention. In the first place, the chilling effect cannot be
satisfactorily eliminated by federal injunctive relief. In *Dombrowski* itself
the Court stated that the injunction to be issued there could be lifted if
the state obtained an "acceptable limiting construction" from the state
courts. The Court then made clear that once this was done, prosecutions
could then be brought for conduct occurring before the narrowing construction was made, and proper convictions could stand so long as the
defendants were not deprived of fair warning. The kind of relief granted
in *Dombrowski* thus does not effectively eliminate uncertainty as to the
coverage of the state statute and leaves most citizens with virtually the
same doubts as before regarding the danger that their conduct might
eventually be subjected to criminal sanctions. The chilling effect can, of
course, be eliminated by an injunction that would prohibit any prosecution whatever for conduct occurring prior to a satisfactory rewriting of
the statute. But the states would then be stripped of all power to prosecute even the socially dangerous and constitutionally unprotected
conduct that had been covered by the statute, until a new statute could
be passed by the state legislature and approved by the federal courts in
potentially lengthy trial and appellate proceedings. Thus, in *Dombrowski*
itself the Court carefully reaffirmed the principle that even in the direct
prosecution in the state's own courts, a valid narrowing construction can
be applied to conduct occurring prior to the date when the narrowing construction was made, in the absence of fair warning problems.

Moreover, the existence of a "chilling effect," even in the area of First Amendment rights, has never been considered a sufficient basis, in and of itself, for prohibiting state action. Where a statute does not directly abridge free speech, but—while regulating a subject within the state's power—tends to have the incidental effect of inhibiting First Amendment rights, it is well settled that the statute can be upheld if the effect on speech is minor in relation to the need for control of the conduct and the lack of alternative means for doing so. Just as the incidental "chilling effect" of such statutes does not automatically render them unconstitutional, so the chilling effect that admittedly can result from the very existence of certain laws on the statute books does not in itself justify prohibiting the state from carrying out the important and necessary task of enforcing these laws against socially harmful conduct that the state believes in good faith to be punishable under its laws and the Constitution.

Beyond all this is another, more basic consideration. Procedures for testing the constitutionality of a statute "on its face" in the manner apparently contemplated by *Dombrowski,* and for then enjoining all action to enforce the statute until the state can obtain court approval for a modified version, are fundamentally at odds with the function of the federal courts in our constitutional plan. The power and duty of the judiciary to declare laws unconstitutional is in the final analysis derived from its responsibility for resolving concrete disputes brought before the courts for decision; a statute apparently governing a dispute cannot be applied by judges, consistently with their obligations under the Supremacy Clause, when such an application of the statute would conflict with the Constitution. But this vital responsibility, broad as it is, does not amount to an unlimited power to survey the statute books and pass judgment on laws before the courts are called upon to enforce them. Ever since the constitutional convention rejected a proposal for having members of the Supreme Court render advice concerning pending legislation it has been clear that, even when suits of this kind involve a "case or controversy" sufficient to satisfy the requirements of Article III of the Constitution, the task of analyzing a proposed statute, pinpointing its deficiencies, and requiring correction of these deficiencies before the statute is put into effect, is rarely if ever an appropriate task for the judiciary. The combination of the relative remoteness of the controversy, the impact on the legislative process of the relief sought, and above all the speculative and amorphous nature of the required line-by-line analysis of detailed statutes, ordinarily results in a kind of case that is wholly unsatisfactory for deciding constitutional questions, whichever way they might be decided. In light of this fundamental conception of the framers as to the proper place of the federal courts in the governmental processes of passing and enforcing laws, it can seldom be appropriate for these courts to exercise any such power of prior approval or veto over the legislative process.

For these reasons, fundamental not only to our federal system but also to the basic functions of the judicial branch of the national government under our Constitution, we hold that the *Dombrowski* decision should not be regarded as having upset the settled doctrines that have always confined very narrowly the availability of injunctive relief against state criminal prosecutions. We do not think that opinion stands for the proposition that a federal court can properly enjoin enforcement of a statute solely on the basis of a showing that the statute "on its face" abridges First Amendment rights. There may, of course, be extraordinary circumstances in which the necessary irreparable injury can be shown even in the absence of the usual prerequisites of bad faith and harassment. For example, as long ago as the *Buck* case, we indicated:

> It is of course conceivable that a statute might be flagrantly and patently violative of express constitutional prohibitions in every clause, sentence and paragraph, and in whatever manner and against whomever an effort might be made to apply it.

Other unusual situations calling for federal intervention might also arise, but there is no point in our attempting now to specify what they might be. It is sufficient for purposes of the present case to hold, as we do, that the possible unconstitutionality of a statute "on its face" does not in itself justify an injunction against good-faith attempts to enforce it, and that appellee Harris has failed to make any showing of bad faith, harassment, or any other unusual circumstance that would call for equitable relief. Because our holding rests on the absence of the factors necessary under equitable principles to justify federal intervention, we have no occasion to consider whether 28 U.S.C. § 2283, which prohibits an injunction against state court proceedings "except as expressly authorized by Act of Congress" would in and of itself be controlling under the circumstances of this case.

The judgment of the District Court is reversed, and the case is remanded for further proceedings not inconsistent with this opinion.

Reversed.

■ MR. JUSTICE STEWART, with whom MR. JUSTICE HARLAN joins, concurring.

The questions the Court decides today are important ones. Perhaps as important, however, is a recognition of the areas into which today's holdings do not necessarily extend. [T]he Court deals only with the proper policy to be followed by a federal court when asked to intervene by injunction or declaratory judgment[c] in a criminal prosecution which is contemporaneously pending in a state court.

---

c   The declaratory judgment reference has to do with the Court's holding in a companion case, *Samuels v. Mackell*, discussed in the Notes following *Younger*.—[Footnote by eds.]

In basing its decisions on policy grounds, the Court does not reach any questions concerning the independent force of the federal anti-injunction statute, 28 U.S.C. § 2283. Thus we do not decide whether the word "injunction" in § 2283 should be interpreted to include a declaratory judgment, or whether an injunction to stay proceedings in a state court is "expressly authorized" by § 1 of the Civil Rights Act of 1871, now 42 U.S.C. § 1983. And since all of these cases involve state criminal prosecutions, we do not deal with the considerations that should govern a federal court when it is asked to intervene in state civil proceedings, where, for various reasons, the balance might be struck differently.[2] Finally, the Court today does not resolve the problems involved when a federal court is asked to give injunctive or declaratory relief from *future* state criminal prosecutions.

The Court confines itself to deciding the policy considerations that in our federal system must prevail when federal courts are asked to interfere with pending state prosecutions. Within this area, we hold that a federal court must not, save in exceptional and extremely limited circumstances, intervene by way of either injunction or declaration in an existing state criminal prosecution. . . .

■ MR. JUSTICE BRENNAN, with whom MR. JUSTICE WHITE and MR. JUSTICE MARSHALL join, concurring in the result.

I agree that the judgment of the District Court should be reversed. Appellee Harris had been indicted for violations of the California Criminal Syndicalism Act before he sued in federal court. He has not alleged that the prosecution was brought in bad faith to harass him. His constitutional contentions may be adequately adjudicated in the state criminal proceeding, and federal intervention at his instance was therefore improper.

Appellees Hirsch and Dan have alleged that they "feel inhibited" by the statute and the prosecution of Harris from advocating the program of the Progressive Labor Party. Appellee Broslawsky has alleged that he "is uncertain" whether as an instructor in college history he can under the statute give instruction relating to the Communist Manifesto and similar revolutionary works. None of these appellees has stated any ground for a reasonable expectation that he will actually be prosecuted under the statute for taking the actions contemplated. . . . In short, there is no reason to think that California has any ripe controversy with them.

■ MR. JUSTICE DOUGLAS, dissenting.

The fact that we are in a period of history when enormous extrajudicial sanctions are imposed on those who assert their First Amendment rights in unpopular causes emphasizes the wisdom of Dombrowski v.

---

[2] Courts of equity have traditionally shown greater reluctance to intervene in criminal prosecutions than in civil cases. The offense to state interests is likely to be less in a civil proceeding. A state's decision to classify conduct as criminal provides some indication of the importance it has ascribed to prompt and unencumbered enforcement of its law. By contrast, the state might not even be a party in a proceeding under a civil statute. . . .

Pfister, 380 U.S. 479 (1965). There we recognized that in times of repression, when interests with powerful spokesmen generate symbolic pogroms against nonconformists, the federal judiciary, charged by Congress with special vigilance for protection of civil rights, has special responsibilities to prevent an erosion of the individual's constitutional rights.

Dombrowski represents an exception to the general rule that federal courts should not interfere with state criminal prosecutions. The exception does not arise merely because prosecutions are threatened to which the First Amendment will be the proffered defense. *Dombrowski* governs statutes which are a blunderbuss by themselves or when used en masse—those that have an "overbroad" sweep. "If the rule were otherwise, the contours of regulation would have to be hammered out case by case—and tested only by those hardy enough to risk criminal prosecution to determine the proper scope of regulation." Id. at 487. It was in the context of overbroad state statutes that we spoke of the "chilling effect upon the exercise of First Amendment rights" caused by state prosecutions. . . .

The special circumstances when federal intervention in a state criminal proceeding is permissible are not restricted to bad faith on the part of state officials or the threat of multiple prosecutions. They also exist where for any reason the state statute being enforced is unconstitutional on its face. . . .

If the "advocacy" which Harris used was an attempt at persuasion through the use of bullets, bombs, and arson, we would have a different case. But Harris is charged only with distributing leaflets advocating political action toward his objective. He tried unsuccessfully to have the state court dismiss the indictment on constitutional grounds. He resorted to the state appellate court for writs of prohibition to prevent the trial, but to no avail. He went to the federal court as a matter of last resort in an effort to keep this unconstitutional trial from being saddled on him. . . .

NOTES ON *YOUNGER V. HARRIS*

1. *SAMUELS V. MACKELL*

Samuels v. Mackell, 401 U.S. 66 (1971), was a companion case decided on the same day as *Younger*. The issue was whether the policies of *Younger* also foreclosed federal *declaratory* relief against pending state prosecutions. Again Justice Black spoke for the Court:

> [O]rdinarily a declaratory judgment will result in precisely the same interference with and disruption of state proceedings that the longstanding policy limiting injunctions was designed to avoid. This is true for at least two reasons. In the first place the Declaratory Judgment Act provides that after a declaratory judgment is

issued the district court may enforce it by granting "further necessary or proper relief," and therefore a declaratory judgment issued while state proceedings are pending might serve as the basis for a subsequent injunction against those proceedings to "protect or effectuate" the declaratory judgment, 28 U.S.C. § 2283, and thus result in a clearly improper interference with the state proceedings. Secondly, even if the declaratory judgment is not used as a basis for actually issuing an injunction, the declaratory relief alone has virtually the same practical impact as a formal injunction would. As we said in Public Service Comm'n of Utah v. Wycoff Co., 344 U.S. 237, 247 (1952):

> Is the declaration contemplated here to be res judicata, so that the [state court] cannot hear evidence and decide any matter for itself? If so, the federal court has virtually lifted the case out of the state [court] before it could be heard. If not, the federal judgment serves no useful purpose as a final determination of rights.

We therefore hold that, in cases where the state criminal prosecution was begun prior to the federal suit, the same equitable principles relevant to the propriety of an injunction must be taken into consideration by federal district courts in determining whether to issue a declaratory judgment, and that where an injunction would be impermissible under these principles, declaratory relief should ordinarily be denied as well. . . . We, of course, express no views on the propriety of declaratory relief when no state proceeding is pending at the time the federal suit is begun.

2.   THE POLICIES OF *YOUNGER*

What policies support the result in *Younger*? Consider a simple case. Assume a pending *federal* criminal prosecution under an arguably overbroad statute for conduct the defendant has committed once and does not propose to engage in again. The defendant seeks an injunction against the prosecution from a different federal district judge sitting in the same district. Should the injunction be issued if the second judge thinks the statute unconstitutional? If not, should it matter if the criminal case is pending in a different federal district? In a state court?

Another way to look at *Younger* is that it is a necessary corollary of the exhaustion requirement for federal habeas corpus. Could a contrary result in *Younger* be reconciled with the habeas exhaustion requirement?

3.   THE *YOUNGER* EXCEPTIONS

Owen Fiss concluded six years after *Younger* that "the universe of bad-faith harassment claims that can be established is virtually empty." Owen M. Fiss, *Dombrowski*, 86 Yale L.J. 1103 (1977). Why might this still be so?

Younger also recognized an exception for a law "flagrantly and patently violative of express constitutional prohibitions in every clause, sentence and paragraph, in whatever manner and against whomever an effort might be

made to apply it." Reported instances of the successful assertion of this
ground were also rare, see Aviam Soifer and H.C. Macgill, The *Younger* Doctrine: Reconstructing Reconstruction, 55 Texas L. Rev. 1141, 1204–06 n.259
(1977), and still are. Why, in any event, should patent unconstitutionality be
a ground for immediate federal intervention? Is it unlikely that a state court
will afford prompt and adequate relief in such a case? If such an exception is
to exist, should the statute at issue in *Younger* have come within it?

4.   *MITCHUM V. FOSTER*

The *Younger* Court quoted the Anti-Injunction Act but did not rest on
that ground:

> Because our holding rests on the absence of the factors neces-
> sary under equitable principles to justify federal intervention, we
> have no occasion to consider whether 28 U.S.C. § 2283, which pro-
> hibits an injunction against state court proceedings "except as
> expressly authorized by Act of Congress" would in and of itself be
> controlling under the circumstances of this case.

In Mitchum v. Foster, 407 U.S. 225 (1972), a Florida prosecutor brought
a "public nuisance" proceeding to close down a bookstore. After a preliminary
order against continued operation of the bookstore but while the state trial
court proceedings were still pending, the owner of the bookstore asked a federal court to enjoin the state proceedings on the ground that they violated
the First and Fourteenth Amendments. A federal three-judge court concluded that § 2283 prohibited such an injunction, but the Supreme Court
reversed. In an opinion by Justice Stewart, a unanimous Court (with Justices
Powell and Rehnquist not participating) stated the issue as follows:

> An act of Congress, 42 U.S.C. § 1983, expressly authorizes a
> "suit in equity" to redress "the deprivation," under color of state
> law, "of any rights, privileges, or immunities secured by the Con-
> stitution. . . ."[a] The question before us is whether this "Act of
> Congress" comes within the "expressly authorized" exception of the
> anti-injunction statute so as to permit a federal court in a § 1983
> suit to grant an injunction to stay a proceeding pending in a state
> court.

The Court began by remarking on the implications of *Younger*:

> While the Court in *Younger* and its companion cases expressly
> disavowed deciding the question now before us—whether § 1983

---

[a]   Section 1983 provides in full:

> Every person who, under color of any statute, ordinance, regulation, custom, or
> usage, of any State or Territory or the District of Columbia, subjects, or causes to be
> subjected, any citizen of the United States or other person within the jurisdiction
> thereof to the deprivation of any rights, privileges, or immunities secured by the Con-
> stitution and laws, shall be liable to the party injured in an action at law, suit in equity,
> or other proper proceeding for redress, except that in any action brought against a
> judicial officer for an act or omission taken in such officer's judicial capacity, injunctive
> relief shall not be granted unless a declaratory decree was violated or declaratory relief
> was unavailable. For the purposes of this section, any Act of Congress applicable ex-
> clusively to the District of Columbia shall be considered to be a statute of the District
> of Columbia.—[Footnote by eds.]

comes within the "expressly authorized" exception of the anti-injunction statute—it is evident that our decisions in those cases cannot be disregarded in deciding this question. In the first place, if § 1983 is not within the statutory exception, then the anti-injunction statute would have absolutely barred the injunction issued in *Younger* . . . , and there would have been no occasion whatever for the Court to decide that case upon the "policy" ground of "Our Federalism." Secondly, if § 1983 is not within the "expressly authorized" exception of the anti-injunction statute, then we must overrule *Younger* and its companion cases insofar as they recognized the permissibility of injunctive relief against pending criminal prosecutions in certain limited and exceptional circumstances.

The Court reviewed the legislative history of § 2283 and § 1983. As to § 1983, it said:

This legislative history makes evident that Congress clearly conceived that it was altering the relationship between the states and the nation with respect to the protection of federally created rights; it was concerned that state instrumentalities could not protect those rights; it realized that state officers might, in fact, be antipathetic to the vindication of those rights; and it believed that these failings extended to the state courts.

The Court continued:

Section 1983 was thus a product of a vast transformation from the concepts of federalism that had prevailed in the late 18th century when the anti-injunction statute was enacted. The very purpose of § 1983 was to interpose the federal courts between the states and the people, as guardians of the people's federal rights—to protect the people from unconstitutional action under color of state law, "whether that action be executive, legislative, or judicial." Ex parte Virginia, 100 U.S. 339, 346 (1879). In carrying out that purpose, Congress plainly authorized the federal courts to issue injunctions in § 1983 actions, by expressly authorizing a "suit in equity" as one of the means of redress. And this Court long ago recognized that federal injunctive relief against a state court proceeding can in some circumstances be essential to prevent great, immediate, and irreparable loss of a person's constitutional rights. Ex parte Young, 209 U.S. 123 (1908). For these reasons we conclude that . . . § 1983 is an act of Congress that falls within the "expressly authorized" exception of that law.

In so concluding, we do not question or qualify in any way the principles of equity, comity, and federalism that must restrain a federal court when asked to enjoin a state court proceeding. These principles, in the context of state criminal prosecutions, were canvassed at length last term in Younger v. Harris, 401 U.S. 37 (1971), and its companion cases. They are principles that have been emphasized by this Court many times in the past. Today we decide only that the District Court in this case was in error in holding that, because of the anti-injunction statute, it was absolutely without power in this § 1983 action to enjoin a proceeding pending in a state court under any circumstances whatsoever.[b]

5. QUESTIONS AND COMMENTS ON *MITCHUM*

The Court's opinion in *Mitchum* emphasizes the extent to which § 1983 was intended to change the relationship between federal and state courts. Does this view of § 1983, which was the basis for the plaintiff's cause of action in *Younger*, cast doubt on the correctness of *Younger*? What is the Court's authority, given the conclusion in *Mitchum*, for limiting the occasions for federal intervention in state criminal proceedings to the "exceptions" recognized in *Younger* and its companion cases? To ask the same question from the other direction, could it be argued on the basis of *Younger* that *Mitchum* was wrongly decided?

Of what relevance is the pendency of state proceedings to these questions? Note that § 2283 has been interpreted not to preclude federal court interference with the *institution* of litigation in the state courts. It only prohibits interference with state proceedings that are pending or that have been concluded when the federal suit is filed. If this reading of § 2283 is correct, does the fact that § 1983 is an "express exception" to § 2283 mean that it is precisely in pending or concluded state proceedings that federal injunctive relief *ought* to be available? In other words, could one reasonably conclude that injunctive relief ought to be available under § 1983 both against the institution of state court proceedings (because § 2283 is not applicable) and against the continuation of pending state proceedings or the implementation of concluded state proceedings (because § 1983 is an "express exception" to § 2283)?

6. BIBLIOGRAPHY

Younger is the subject of a large body of mostly contemporaneous comment. For a sample, see Douglas Laycock, Federal Interference with State Prosecutions: The Need for Prospective Relief, 1977 Sup. Ct. Rev. 193; Gene R. Nichol, Jr., Federalism, State Courts and Section 1983, 73 Va. L. Rev. 959 (1987); Martin H. Redish, The Doctrine of *Younger v. Harris*: Deference in Search of a Rationale, 63 Corn. L. Rev. 463 (1977); Louise Weinberg, The New Judicial Federalism, 29 Stan. L. Rev. 1191 (1977); Ralph Whitten, Federal Declaratory and Injunctive Interference with State Court Proceedings: The Supreme Court and the Limits of Judicial Discretion, 53 N.C.L. Rev. 591 (1975); Donald H. Zeigler, Rights Require Remedies: A New Approach to the

---

[b]   Chief Justice Burger's concurrence emphasized that the Court was not foreclosing the possibility that *Younger* could still prevent an injunction against the state proceedings:

> We have not yet reached or decided exactly how great a restraint is imposed by [*Younger*] principles on a federal court asked to enjoin state *civil* proceedings. Therefore, on remand in this case, it seems to me the District Court, before reaching a decision on the merits of appellant's claim, should properly consider whether general notions of equity or principles of federalism, similar to those invoked in *Younger*, prevent the issuance of an injunction against the state 'nuisance abatement' proceedings in the circumstances of this case.

The relevance of *Younger* to civil proceedings is considered below.—[Footnote by eds.]

Enforcement of Rights in the Federal Courts, 38 Hast. L.J. 665, 682–708 (1987); and Donald H. Zeigler, An Accommodation of the *Younger* Doctrine and the Duty of the Federal Court to Enforce Constitutional Safeguards in the State Criminal Process, 125 U. Pa. L. Rev. 266 (1976). For a more recent analysis of *Younger* and its progeny, see James E. Pfander and Nassim Nazemi, The Anti-Injunction Act and the Problem of Federal-State Jurisdictional Overlap, 92 Tex. L. Rev. 1, 59–67 (2013).

Steffel v. Thompson

Supreme Court of the United States, 1974.
415 U.S. 452.

■ MR. JUSTICE BRENNAN delivered the opinion of the Court.

. . . This case presents the important question reserved in Samuels v. Mackell, 401 U.S. 66 (1971), whether declaratory relief is precluded when a state prosecution has been threatened, but is not pending, and a showing of bad-faith enforcement or other special circumstances has not been made.

Petitioner . . . filed a complaint in the District Court for the Northern District of Georgia [seeking] a declaratory judgment . . . that [the Georgia criminal trespass statute] was being applied in violation of petitioner's First and Fourteenth Amendment rights, and an injunction restraining respondents—the solicitor of the Civil and Criminal Court of DeKalb County, the chief of the DeKalb County Police, the owner of the North DeKalb Shopping Center, and the manager of that shopping center—from enforcing the statute so as to interfere with petitioner's constitutionally protected activities.

The parties stipulated to the relevant facts: On October 8, 1970, while petitioner and other individuals were distributing handbills protesting American involvement in Vietnam on an exterior sidewalk of the North DeKalb Shopping Center, shopping center employees asked them to stop handbilling and leave. They declined to do so, and police officers were summoned. The officers told them that they would be arrested if they did not stop handbilling. The group then left to avoid arrest. Two days later petitioner and a companion returned to the shopping center and again began handbilling. The manager of the center called the police, and petitioner and his companion were once again told that failure to stop their handbilling would result in their arrests. Petitioner left to avoid arrest. His companion stayed, however, continued handbilling, and was arrested and subsequently arraigned on a charge of criminal trespass. . . . [3] Petitioner alleged in his complaint that, although he desired to return to the shopping center to distribute handbills, he had not done so because of his concern that he, too, would be arrested. . . .

---

[3]   We were advised at oral argument that the trial of petitioner's companion, Sandra Lee Becker, has been stayed pending decision of this case.

After hearing, the District Court denied all relief and dismissed the action. . . . The Court of Appeals . . . affirmed. . . . We granted certiorari and now reverse.

I

At the threshold we must consider whether petitioner presents an "actual controversy," a requirement imposed by Article III of the Constitution and the express terms of the Federal Declaratory Judgment Act, 28 U.S.C. § 2201.[9]

Unlike three of the appellees in *Younger v. Harris*, 401 U.S. 37 (1971), petitioner has alleged threats of prosecution that cannot be characterized as "imaginary or speculative." He has been twice warned to stop handbilling that he claims is constitutionally protected and has been told by the police that if he again handbills at the shopping center and disobeys a warning to stop he will likely be prosecuted. The prosecution of petitioner's handbilling companion is ample demonstration that petitioner's concern with arrest has not been "chimerical." In these circumstances, it is not necessary that petitioner first expose himself to actual arrest or prosecution to be entitled to challenge a statute that he claims deters the exercise of his constitutional rights. Moreover, petitioner's challenge is to those specific provisions of state law which have provided the basis for threats of criminal prosecution against him. . . .

II

We now turn to the question of whether the District Court and the Court of Appeals correctly found petitioner's request for declaratory relief inappropriate.

Sensitive to principles of equity, comity, and federalism, we recognized in *Younger v. Harris* that federal courts should ordinarily refrain from enjoining ongoing state criminal prosecutions. We were cognizant that a pending state proceeding, in all but unusual cases, would provide the federal plaintiff with the necessary vehicle for vindicating his constitutional rights, and, in that circumstance, the restraining of an ongoing prosecution would entail an unseemly failure to give effect to the principle that state courts have the solemn responsibility, equally with the federal courts "to guard, enforce, and protect every right granted or secured by the Constitution of the United States. . . ." Robb v. Connolly, 111 U.S. 624 (1884). In *Samuels v. Mackell*, the Court also found that the

---

[9]   Section 2201 provides:

In a case of actual controversy within its jurisdiction, except with respect to Federal taxes, any court of the United States, upon the filing of an appropriate pleading, may declare the rights and other legal relations of any interested party seeking such declaration, whether or not further relief is or could be sought. Any such declaration shall have the force and effect of a final judgment or decree and shall be reviewable as such.

Section 2202 further provides:

Further necessary or proper relief based on a declaratory judgment or decree may be granted, after reasonable notice and hearing, against any adverse party whose rights have been determined by such judgment.

same principles ordinarily would be flouted by issuance of a federal declaratory judgment when a state proceeding was pending, since the intrusive effect of declaratory relief "will result in precisely the same interference with and disruption of state proceedings that the long-standing policy limiting injunctions was designed to avoid."[11] We therefore held in *Samuels* that, "in cases where the state criminal prosecution was begun prior to the federal suit, the same equitable principles relevant to the propriety of an injunction must be taken into consideration by federal district courts in determining whether to issue a declaratory judgment. . . ."

Neither *Younger* nor *Samuels,* however, decided the question whether federal intervention might be permissible in the absence of a pending state prosecution. . . . When no state criminal proceeding is pending at the time the federal complaint is filed, federal intervention does not result in duplicative legal proceedings or disruption of the state criminal justice system; nor can federal intervention, in that circumstance, be interpreted as reflecting negatively upon the state court's ability to enforce constitutional principles. In addition, while a pending state prosecution provides the federal plaintiff with a concrete opportunity to vindicate his constitutional rights, a refusal on the part of the federal courts to intervene when no state proceeding is pending may place the hapless plaintiff between the Scylla of intentionally flouting state law and the Charybdis of forgoing what he believes to be constitutionally protected activity in order to avoid becoming enmeshed in a criminal proceeding.

When no state proceeding is pending and thus considerations of equity, comity, and federalism have little vitality, the propriety of granting federal declaratory relief may properly be considered independently of a request for injunctive relief. Here, the Court of Appeals held that, because injunctive relief would not be appropriate since petitioner failed to demonstrate irreparable injury—a traditional prerequisite to injunctive relief—it followed that declaratory relief was also inappropriate. Even if the Court of Appeals correctly viewed injunctive relief as inappropriate—a question we need not reach today since petitioner has abandoned his request for that remedy—the court erred in treating the requests for injunctive and declaratory relief as a single issue. "[W]hen no state prosecution is pending and the only question is whether declaratory relief is appropriate, . . . the congressional scheme that makes the federal courts the primary guardians of constitutional rights, and the express congressional authorization of declaratory relief, afforded because it is a less harsh and abrasive remedy than the injunction, become the factors of primary significance." Perez v. Ledesma, 401 U.S. 82, 104 (1971) (separate opinion of Brennan, J.).

---

[11] The Court noted that under 28 U.S.C. § 2202 a declaratory judgment might serve as the basis for issuance of a later injunction to give effect to the declaratory judgment, see n.9, supra, and that a declaratory judgment might have a res judicata effect on the pending state proceeding. 401 U.S. at 72.

. . . That Congress plainly intended declaratory relief to act as an alternative to the strong medicine of the injunction and to be utilized to test the constitutionality of state criminal statutes in cases where injunctive relief would be unavailable is amply evidenced by the legislative history of the act. . . .[18] It was this history that formed the backdrop to our decision in Zwickler v. Koota, 389 U.S. 241 (1967), where a state criminal statute was attacked on grounds of unconstitutional overbreadth and no state prosecution was pending against the federal plaintiff. There, we found error in a three-judge district court's considering, as a single question, the propriety of granting injunctive and declaratory relief. Although we noted that injunctive relief might well be unavailable under principles of equity jurisprudence canvassed in Douglas v. City of Jeannette, 319 U.S. 157 (1943), we held that "a federal district court has the duty to decide the appropriateness and the merits of the declaratory request irrespective of its conclusion as to the propriety of the issuance of the injunction." Only one year ago, we reaffirmed the *Zwickler v. Koota* holding in Roe v. Wade, 410 U.S. 113 (1973), and Doe v. Bolton, 410 U.S. 179 (1973). In those two cases, we declined to decide whether the district courts had properly denied to the federal plaintiffs, against whom no prosecutions were pending, injunctive relief restraining enforcement of the Texas and Georgia criminal abortion statutes; instead, we affirmed the issuance of declaratory judgments of unconstitutionality, anticipating that these would be given effect by state authorities. We said:

> The Court has recognized that *different considerations* enter into a federal court's decision as to declaratory relief, on the one hand, and injunctive relief, on the other. Zwickler v. Koota, 389 U.S. 241, 252–255 (1967); Dombrowski v. Pfister, 380 U.S. 479 (1965).

Roe, 410 U.S. at 166 (emphasis added).

The "different considerations" entering into a decision whether to grant declaratory relief have their origins in the preceding historical summary. First, as Congress recognized in 1934, a declaratory judgment will have a less intrusive effect on the administration of state criminal law. As we observed in *Perez*, 401 U.S. at 124–26 (separate opinion of Brennan, J.):

---

[18] As Professor Borchard, a principal proponent and author of the Federal Declaratory Judgment Act, said in a written statement introduced at the hearings on the act:

> It often happens that courts are unwilling to grant injunctions to restrain the enforcement of penal statutes or ordinances, and relegate the plaintiff to his option, either to violate the statute and take his chances in testing constitutionality on a criminal prosecution, or else to forgo, in the fear of prosecution, the exercise of his claimed rights. Into this dilemma no civilized legal system operating under a constitution should force any person. The court, in effect, by refusing an injunction informs the prospective victim that the only way to determine whether the suspect is a mushroom or a toadstool, is to eat it. Assuming that the plaintiff has a vital interest in the enforcement of the challenged statute or ordinance, there is no reason why a declaratory judgment should not be issued, instead of compelling a violation of the statute as a condition precedent to challenging its constitutionality.

Of course, a favorable declaratory judgment may nevertheless be valuable to the plaintiff though it cannot make even an unconstitutional statute disappear. [T]he declaration does not necessarily bar prosecutions under the statute, as a broad injunction would. Thus, where . . . a federal court declares the statute unconstitutionally vague or overbroad, it may well be open to a state prosecutor, after the federal court decision, to bring a prosecution under the statute if he reasonably believes that the defendant's conduct is not constitutionally protected and that the state courts may give the statute a construction so as to yield a constitutionally valid conviction. . . . The persuasive force of the court's opinion and judgment may lead state prosecutors, courts, and legislators to reconsider their respective responsibilities toward the statute. Enforcement policies or judicial construction may be changed, or the legislature may repeal the statute and start anew. Finally, the federal court judgment may have some res judicata effect, though this point is not free from difficulty and the governing rules remain to be developed with a view to the proper workings of a federal system. What is clear, however, is that even though a declaratory judgment has "the force and effect of a final judgment" it is a much milder form of relief than an injunction. Though it may be persuasive, it is not ultimately coercive; noncompliance with it may be inappropriate, but is not contempt.[19]

Second, engrafting upon the Declaratory Judgment Act a requirement that all of the traditional equitable prerequisites to the issuance of an injunction be satisfied before the issuance of a declaratory judgment is considered would defy Congress's intent to make declaratory relief available in cases where an injunction would be inappropriate. . . . Thus, the Court of Appeals was in error when it ruled that a failure to demonstrate irreparable injury—a traditional prerequisite to injunctive relief, having no equivalent in the law of declaratory judgments—precluded the granting of declaratory relief.

. . . In the instant case, principles of federalism not only do not preclude federal intervention, they compel it. Requiring the federal courts totally to step aside when no state criminal prosecution is pending against the federal plaintiff would turn federalism on its head. When federal claims are premised on 42 U.S.C. § 1983 and 28 U.S.C. § 1343(3)—as they are here—we have not required exhaustion of state judicial or administrative remedies, recognizing the paramount role Congress has assigned to the federal courts to protect constitutional rights. See, e.g.,

---

[19] The pending prosecution of petitioner's handbilling companion does not affect petitioner's action for declaratory relief. In Roe v. Wade, 410 U.S. 113 (1973), while the pending prosecution of Dr. Hallford under the Texas abortion law was found to render his action for declaratory and injunctive relief impermissible, this did not prevent our granting plaintiff Roe, against whom no action was pending, a declaratory judgment that the statute was unconstitutional.

McNeese v. Board of Education, 373 U.S. 668 (1963); Monroe v. Pape, 365 U.S. 167 (1961). But exhaustion of state remedies is precisely what would be required if both federal injunctive and declaratory relief were unavailable in a case where no state prosecution had been commenced.

III

. . . We therefore hold that, regardless of whether injunctive relief may be appropriate, federal declaratory relief is not precluded when no state prosecution is pending and a federal plaintiff demonstrates a genuine threat of enforcement of a disputed state criminal statute. . . . The judgment of the Court of Appeals is reversed, and the case is remanded for further proceedings consistent with this opinion.

It is so ordered.[a]

■ MR. JUSTICE WHITE, concurring.

. . . I would anticipate that a final declaratory judgment entered by a federal court holding particular conduct of the federal plaintiff to be immune on federal constitutional grounds from prosecution under state law should be accorded res judicata effect in any later prosecution of that very conduct. . . .

Neither can I at this stage agree that the federal court, having rendered a declaratory judgment in favor of the plaintiff, could not enjoin a later state prosecution for conduct that the federal court has declared immune. The Declaratory Judgment Act itself provides that a "declaration shall have the force and effect of a final judgment or decree," 28 U.S.C. § 2201; eminent authority anticipated that declaratory judgments would be res judicata, E. Borchard, Declaratory Judgments 10–11 (2d ed. 1941); and there is every reason for not reducing declaratory judgments to mere advisory opinions. . . . The statute provides for "[f]urther necessary or proper relief . . . against any adverse party whose rights have been determined by such judgment," 28 U.S.C. § 2202, and it would not seem improper to enjoin local prosecutors who refuse to observe adverse federal judgments. . . .

■ MR. JUSTICE REHNQUIST, with whom CHIEF JUSTICE BURGER joins, concurring.

. . . The Court quite properly leaves for another day whether the granting of a declaratory judgment by a federal court will have any subsequent res judicata effect or will perhaps support the issuance of a later federal injunction. But since possible resolutions of those issues would substantially undercut the principles of federalism reaffirmed in Younger v. Harris, 401 U.S. 37 (1971), and preserved by the decision today, I feel it appropriate to add a few remarks.

---

[a]   The separate concurring opinion by Justice Stewart, joined by Chief Justice Burger, is omitted.—[Footnote by eds.]

First, the legislative history of the Declaratory Judgment Act and the Court's opinion in this case both recognize that the declaratory judgment procedure is an alternative to pursuit of the arguably illegal activity. There is nothing in the act's history to suggest that Congress intended to provide persons wishing to violate state laws with a federal shield behind which they could carry on their contemplated conduct. . . .

Second, I do not believe that today's decision can properly be raised to support the issuance of a federal injunction based upon a favorable declaratory judgment. The Court's description of declaratory relief as . . . having a "less intrusive effect on the administration of state criminal laws" than an injunction indicates to me critical distinctions which make declaratory relief appropriate where injunctive relief would not be. . . .

A declaratory judgment is simply a statement of rights, not a binding order supplemented by continuing sanctions. State authorities may choose to be guided by the judgment of a lower federal court, but they are not compelled to follow the decision by threat of contempt or other penalties. If the federal plaintiff pursues the conduct for which he was previously threatened with arrest and is in fact arrested, he may not return the controversy to federal court, although he may, of course, raise the federal declaratory judgment in the state court for whatever value it may prove to have.[3] In any event, the defendant at that point is able to present his case for full consideration by a state court charged, as are the federal courts, to preserve the defendant's constitutional rights. Federal interference with this process would involve precisely the same concerns discussed in *Younger* and recited in the Court's opinion in this case.

Third, attempts to circumvent *Younger* by claiming that enforcement of a statute declared unconstitutional by a federal court is per se evidence of bad faith should not find support in the Court's decision in this case. . . .

If the declaratory judgment remains, as I think the Declaratory Judgment Act intended, a simple declaration of rights without more, it will not be used merely as a dramatic tactical maneuver on the part of any state defendant seeking extended delays. Nor will it force state officials to try cases time after time, first in the federal courts and then in the state courts. I do not believe Congress desired such unnecessary results, and I do not think that today's decision should be read to sanction them. Rather the act, and the decision, stand for the sensible proposition that both a potential state defendant, threatened with prosecution but not charged, and the state itself, confronted by a possible violation of its criminal laws, may benefit from a procedure which provides for a declaration of rights without activation of the criminal process. If the federal

---

[3]   The Court's opinion notes that the possible res judicata effect of a federal declaratory judgment in a subsequent state court prosecution is a question " 'not free from difficulty.' " I express no opinion on that issue here. However, I do note that the federal decision would not be accorded the stare decisis effect in state court that it would have in a subsequent proceeding within the same federal jurisdiction. Although the state court would not be compelled to follow the federal holding, the opinion might, of course, be viewed as highly persuasive.

court finds that the threatened prosecution would depend upon a statute it judges unconstitutional, the state may decide to forgo prosecution of similar conduct in the future, believing the judgment persuasive. Should the state prosecutors not find the decision persuasive enough to justify forbearance, the successful federal plaintiff will at least be able to bolster his allegations of unconstitutionality in the state trial with a decision of the federal district court in the immediate locality. The state courts may find the reasoning convincing even though the prosecutors did not. Finally, of course, the state legislature may decide, on the basis of the federal decision, that the statute would be better amended or repealed. All these possible avenues of relief would be reached voluntarily by the states and would be completely consistent with . . . concepts of federalism. . . . Other more intrusive forms of relief should not be routinely available.

These considerations should prove highly significant in reaching future decisions based upon the decision rendered today. For the present it is enough to say, as the Court does, that petitioner . . . may maintain an action for a declaratory judgment in the District Court.

NOTES ON THE APPLICATION OF YOUNGER TO CRIMINAL CASES

1. EXHAUSTION OF STATE REMEDIES IN § 1983 SUITS

Monroe v. Pape, 365 U.S. 167 (1961), the case most responsible for modern § 1983 litigation, established that state judicial remedies need not be exhausted prior to filing a federal § 1983 suit: "The federal remedy is supplementary to the state remedy, and the latter need not be first sought and refused before the federal one is invoked."[a] As the Court said in *Samuels*, requiring *Younger* abstention in the *Samuels* situation would be inconsistent with *Monroe*: "exhaustion of state remedies is precisely what would be required if both federal injunctive and declaratory relief were unavailable in a case where no state prosecution had been commenced."

The *Younger* doctrine therefore aligns abstention law with the Court's exhaustion precedents. If no state criminal proceeding is pending, exhaustion of state remedies is not required and *Younger* does not require abstention in favor of potential state remedies in a federal § 1983 suit. Habeas corpus at this point in time, however, is precluded by the habeas exhaustion doctrine. If a state criminal proceeding *is* pending, the habeas corpus exhaustion requirement precludes federal habeas relief prior to the

---

[a]   The same principle has been applied to the exhaustion of state *administrative* remedies, notwithstanding the well-recognized rule that administrative remedies normally must be pursued before going to court. In a long series of cases beginning with McNeese v. Board of Education, 373 U.S. 668 (1963), the Court declined to require dismissal of § 1983 suits for failure to exhaust state administrative remedies. It addressed the issue fully in Patsy v. Board of Regents, 457 U.S. 496 (1982), holding that "exhaustion of state administrative remedies should not be required as a prerequisite to bringing an action pursuant to § 1983." As to whether *Younger* might require federal court deference to state administrative proceedings, see Hawaii Housing Authority v. Midkiff, 467 U.S. 229 (1984): "Since *Younger* is not a bar to federal action when state judicial proceedings have not themselves commenced, abstention [in favor of] administrative proceedings was not required."

conclusion of the state proceedings, and the *Younger* doctrine limits the ability of the federal courts to disrupt the state proceedings by declaratory judgment or injunction. In addition, for reasons discussed in Section 5, Subsection B, of Chapter VII, suits under § 1983 are not available to provide relief from state court convictions *after* the state criminal process has concluded. Federal habeas provides the exclusive avenue of federal relief at that point.

2. *HICKS V. MIRANDA*

Hicks v. Miranda, 422 U.S. 332 (1975), blurred the pending/nonpending line established by *Younger* and *Steffel*. The dispute began when the police, acting pursuant to warrants, seized four copies of the film "Deep Throat" from an adult theater. Criminal charges were brought against two employees of the cinema. Separate judicial proceedings were begun to have the film declared legally obscene. And, after a hearing, the court determined that the film was obscene and ordered all copies found at the theater to be seized. The theater owners did not appeal this judgment but went straight to federal court for a declaration of the obscenity statute's unconstitutionality, an injunction against its continued enforcement, and an order requiring return of the films. A three-judge court convened to consider the constitutionality of the statute, at which point the state court criminal complaint was amended to name the theater owners as additional defendants in the criminal charges. The federal court nevertheless proceeded to judgment and granted the relief sought. On appeal, the Supreme Court reversed in an opinion by Justice White:

> [O]n the day following the completion of service of the complaint, [the owners] were charged along with their employees in Municipal Court. Neither *Steffel v. Thompson* nor any other case in this Court has held that for *Younger v. Harris* to apply, the state criminal proceedings must be pending on the day the federal case is filed. Indeed, the issue has been left open; and we now hold that where state criminal proceedings are begun against the federal plaintiffs after the federal complaint is filed but before any proceedings of substance on the merits have taken place in the federal court, the principles of *Younger v. Harris* should apply in full force. . . .

This holding provoked a dissent from Justice Stewart, joined by Justices Douglas, Brennan, and Marshall:

> There is, to be sure, something unseemly about having the applicability of the *Younger* doctrine turn solely on the outcome of a race to the courthouse. The rule the Court adopts today, however, does not eliminate that race; it merely permits the state to leave the mark later, run a shorter course, and arrive first at the finish line. This rule seems to me to result from a failure to evaluate the state and federal interests as of the time the state prosecution was commenced.

As of the time when its jurisdiction is invoked in a *Steffel* situation, a federal court is called upon to vindicate federal constitutional rights when no other remedy is available to the federal plaintiff. The Court has recognized that at this point in the proceedings no substantial state interests counsel the federal court to stay its hand. . . . But there is nothing in our decision in *Steffel* that requires a state to stay its hand during the pendency of the federal litigation. If, in the interest of efficiency, the state wishes to refrain from actively prosecuting the criminal charge pending the outcome of the federal declaratory judgment suit, it may, of course, do so. But no decision of this Court requires it to make the choice.

The Court today, however, goes much further than simply recognizing the right of the state to proceed with the orderly administration of its criminal law; it ousts the federal courts from their historic role as the "primary reliances" for vindicating constitutional freedoms. This is no less offensive to "Our Federalism" than the federal injunction restraining pending state criminal proceedings condemned in *Younger v. Harris*.

The Court's new rule creates a reality which few state prosecutors can be expected to ignore. It is an open invitation to state officials to institute state proceedings in order to defeat federal jurisdiction. One need not impugn the motives of state officials to suppose that they would rather prosecute a criminal suit in state court than defend a civil case in a federal forum. . . .

The doctrine of *Younger v. Harris* reflects an accommodation of competing interests. The rule announced today distorts that balance beyond recognition.

3.   *DORAN V. SALEM INN*

Doran v. Salem Inn, Inc., 422 U.S. 922 (1975), was decided six days after *Hicks v. Miranda*. It involved three corporations operating topless bars in North Hempstead, Long Island. The town passed an ordinance against topless dancing, after which the corporations clad their dancers in bikini tops and brought a federal suit under § 1983 to declare the ordinance invalid and to enjoin its enforcement. The day after the complaint was filed, one of the bars resumed topless entertainment and was prosecuted under the ordinance. The District Court thereafter ruled the ordinance unconstitutional on its face under the First Amendment and issued a preliminary injunction restraining its enforcement against all three corporations. The Court of Appeals affirmed, and the Supreme Court granted certiorari.

Justice Rehnquist wrote for the Court. With respect to the corporation that had been prosecuted, the Court held that *Younger* and *Hicks* barred both injunctive and declaratory relief. That the federal action was actually begun first did not matter, for it was still "in an embryonic stage and no contested matter had been decided." Only Justice Douglas dissented from this portion of the opinion.

With respect to the other two corporations, the Court unanimously held that they were entitled to relief:

> Under *Steffel* they . . . could at least have obtained a declaratory judgment upon an ordinary showing of entitlement to that relief. The District Court, however, did not grant declaratory relief . . . , but instead granted them preliminary injunctive relief. . . . We now hold that on the facts of this case the issuance of a preliminary injunction is not subject to the restrictions of *Younger*. [P]rior to final judgment there is no established declaratory remedy comparable to a preliminary injunction; unless preliminary relief is available upon a proper showing, plaintiffs in some situations may suffer unnecessary and substantial irreparable harm. Moreover, neither declaratory nor injunctive relief can directly interfere with enforcement of contested statutes or ordinances except with respect to the particular federal plaintiffs, and the state is free to prosecute others who may violate the statute.
>
> The traditional standard for granting a preliminary injunction requires the plaintiff to show that in the absence of its issuance he will suffer irreparable injury and also that he is likely to prevail on the merits. . . . Although only temporary, the injunction does prohibit state and local enforcement activities against the federal plaintiff pending final resolution of his case in the federal court. [W]hile the standard to be applied by the District Court in deciding whether a plaintiff is entitled to a preliminary injunction is stringent, the standard of appellate review is simply whether the issuance of the injunction . . . constituted an abuse of discretion. . . .

The Court then held that, while the question was "a close one," the District Court did not abuse its discretion as to either of the two elements that justified relief. The two corporations had sufficiently shown that they would suffer a substantial loss of business—"and perhaps even bankruptcy"—if they were not able to resume topless entertainment. And the ordinance was sufficiently broad so as to make out a "sufficient showing of the likelihood of ultimate success on the merits."

4.   QUESTIONS AND COMMENTS

The Court was nearly unanimous on the results in both *Younger* and *Steffel*. *Hicks* produced the first close split. How should that case have been resolved? Does it create improper incentives for state prosecutors? Does it undermine the authority of the federal courts?

Given *Hicks,* the unanimity of the Court in *Doran* is surprising. It would appear that—if irreparable harm and the likelihood of success on the merits can be shown—a person who has not yet violated a criminal statute may obtain a preliminary injunction and then engage in the conduct under the protection of the injunction until the federal case is resolved on the merits. Of course, the plaintiff risks prosecution if the federal case is lost. But if declaratory relief is ultimately obtained, the plaintiff has successfully avoided state court resolution of the controversy and at the same time enjoyed the benefits of engaging in the conduct prohibited by the state statute. Is this consistent with *Hicks*? Would the same strategy be permitted by one who has violated the statute but seeks to repeat his or her conduct? The next Note deals with this situation.

5.   *WOOLEY V. MAYNARD*

In Huffman v. Pursue, Ltd., 420 U.S. 592 (1975), the Court concluded that there was a pending state proceeding, even though final judgment had been entered in the trial court. In an opinion by Justice Rehnquist, the Court explained:

> Virtually all of the evils at which *Younger* is directed would inhere in federal intervention prior to completion of state appellate proceedings, just as surely as they would if such intervention occurred at or before trial. Intervention at the later stage is if anything more highly duplicative, since an entire trial has already taken place, and it is also a direct aspersion on the capabilities and good faith of state appellate courts. . . .

Huffman was distinguished in Wooley v. Maynard, 430 U.S. 705 (1977). George and Maxine Maynard had religious objections to the "Live Free or Die" motto displayed on state license plates. George put tape over those words and was three times convicted of obscuring a license. None of these convictions was appealed. The Maynards then successfully sued in federal court under § 1983 to enjoin future enforcement of the statute.

In the Supreme Court, the state argued that *Huffman* required abstention until the defendant exhausted state appellate remedies, but the Court disagreed. Speaking for the Court, Chief Justice Burger noted that in *Huffman*, the plaintiff had sought to prevent enforcement of a state court judgment declaring a theater a public nuisance. In *Wooley,* by contrast, plaintiffs sought only prospective relief. Mr. Maynard's sentences had been served, and he sought no revision of his record or other retrospective relief. Since the Maynards sought "only to be free from prosecutions for future violations," the fact that he had been prosecuted in the past did not bar federal relief.[b]

6.   MILITARY DETOUR: *HAMDAN V. RUMSFELD*

Salim Ahmed Hamdan, a Yemeni national, was imprisoned at Guantanamo Bay after having been captured during hostilities in Afghanistan. He filed a petition for habeas corpus challenging the intention of the government to try him before a military tribunal. The District Court granted relief, but the Court of Appeals reversed. In Hamdan v. Rumsfeld, 548 U.S. 557 (2006), the Supreme Court concluded that the military commission lacked power to proceed. Justice Stevens wrote for a five-three majority.

Hamdan invited a direct analogy to *Ex Parte Royall* and *Younger v. Harris*. Hamdan sought federal habeas corpus to stop a criminal proceeding against him before the charges had been litigated in the trial tribunal. The

---

[b]   Justice White, joined by Justices Rehnquist and Blackmun, dissented.

Court divided by the same five-to-three vote on whether he should have been permitted to do so.[c]

For the majority, Justice Stevens identified two considerations "that together favor abstention pending completion of ongoing court-martial proceedings against service personnel." The first related to military discipline and efficient operation of the armed forces. The second concerned respect for the military court system:

> Just as abstention in the face of ongoing state criminal proceedings is justified by our expectation that state courts will enforce federal rights, so abstention in the face of ongoing court-martial proceedings is justified by our expectation that the military court system established by Congress—with its substantial procedural protections and provision for appellate review by independent civilian judges—"will vindicate servicemen's constitutional rights."

But neither of these factors was applicable here:

> First, Hamdan is not a member of our Nation's Armed Forces, so concerns about military discipline do not apply. Second, the tribunal convened to try Hamdan is not part of the integrated system of military courts, complete with independent review panels, that Congress has established. . . . [T]he Government has identified no other "important countervailing interest" that would permit federal courts to depart from their general "duty to exercise the jurisdiction that is conferred upon them by Congress." To the contrary, Hamdan and the Government both have a compelling interest in knowing in advance whether Hamdan may be tried by a military commission that arguably is without any basis in law and operates free from many of the procedural rules prescribed by Congress for courts-martial—rules intended to safeguard the accused and ensure the reliability of any conviction. While we certainly do not foreclose the possibility that abstention may be appropriate in some cases seeking review of ongoing military commission proceedings (such as military commissions convened on the battlefield), the foregoing discussion makes clear that . . . abstention is not justified here.

Joined by Justices Thomas and Alito, Justice Scalia dissented on this issue. Congress had provided for post-conviction review in the District of Columbia Circuit Court, with certiorari apparently available to the Supreme Court. "In light of Congress's provision of an alternate avenue for petitioner's claims . . . [,] equitable principles counsel that we abstain from exercising jurisdiction in this case." He disagreed with the Court on the application of both of the principles it identified. There were serious issues of military effectiveness here, and Congress had established a process that included ultimate access to Article III courts. There was also a third important factor:

> [C]onsiderations of *interbranch* comity at the federal level weigh heavily against our exercise of equity jurisdiction in this case. Here, apparently for the first time in history, a District Court

---

c   The case also involved a jurisdiction-stripping issue that is considered in the Notes on the Traditional View in Chapter IV, Section 1.

enjoined ongoing military commission proceedings, which had been deemed "necessary" by the President "[t]o protect the United States and its citizens, and for the effective conduct of military operations and prevention of terrorist attacks." Such an order brings the Judicial Branch into direct conflict with the Executive in an area where the Executive's competence is maximal and ours is virtually nonexistent. We should exercise our equitable discretion to *avoid* such conflict. Instead, the Court rushes headlong to meet it. Elsewhere, we have deferred exercising habeas jurisdiction until state courts have "the first opportunity to review" a petitioner's claim, merely to "reduc[e] friction between the state and federal court systems." The "friction" created today between this Court and the Executive Branch is many times more serious.

NOTES ON *YOUNGER* ABSTENTION IN CIVIL PROCEEDINGS

1. APPLICATION TO CIVIL ENFORCEMENT PROCEEDINGS

Does *Younger* abstention apply to pending civil proceedings to which the state is a party? The answer is at least partially "yes." In a series of early cases, the Supreme Court applied *Younger* to a variety of civil proceedings closely allied to enforcement of the criminal law.

The first example was Huffman v. Pursue, Ltd., 420 U.S. 592 (1975), in which local officials brought a civil action to close an adult theater as a public nuisance. The theater lost in the state court but did not appeal. Instead, it filed a § 1983 action in federal court to enjoin enforcement of the nuisance statute. Speaking for himself and five others, Justice Rehnquist found *Younger* applicable: "[W]e deal here with a state proceeding which in important respects is more akin to a criminal prosecution than are most civil cases." The state was a party, and the public nuisance action was "both in aid of and closely related to" criminal obscenity statutes. The fact that the theater, if condemned, would have no subsequent access to the federal courts through federal habeas corpus was thought immaterial.

Judice v. Vail, 430 U.S. 327 (1977), applied *Huffman* to civil contempt proceedings. The federal plaintiff was a state judgment debtor. He had been held in contempt for failing to honor a subpoena to uncover his assets. When he did not pay the fine, the judge issued an ex parte commitment order. The debtor then challenged this procedure by bringing a class action in federal court. Speaking again for himself and five others, Justice Rehnquist said that "[w]hether disobedience of a court-sanctioned subpoena, and the resulting process leading to a finding of contempt, is labeled civil, quasi-criminal, or criminal in nature," the state's interest was of "sufficiently great import" to require *Younger* abstention.

Trainor v. Hernandez, 431 U.S. 434 (1977), involved a civil proceeding slightly more distant from the criminal law. The Illinois Department of Public Aid (IDPA) sued Juan and Maria Hernandez for return of public assistance money they had wrongfully received by concealing their assets. An attachment proceeding brought concurrently with the civil suit froze money in their credit union account pending resolution of the underlying dispute. The couple did not respond to the attachment or seek a hearing in state court. Instead, they filed a § 1983 action in federal court, claiming that the attachment statute and its procedures violated procedural due process. In an opinion by Justice White, a closely divided Court held that *Younger* abstention was required:

> The District Court thought that *Younger* policies were irrelevant because suits to recovery money and writs of attachment were available to private parties as well as the state; it was only because of the coincidence that the state was a party that the suit was "arguably" in aid of the criminal law. But the fact remains that the state was a party to the suit in its role of administering its public assistance programs. . . .
>
> For a federal court to proceed with its case rather than to remit appellees to their remedies in a pending state enforcement suit would confront the state with a choice of engaging in duplicative litigation, thereby risking a temporary federal injunction, or of interrupting its enforcement proceedings pending decision of the federal court at some unknown time in the future. It would also foreclose the opportunity of the state court to construe the challenged statute in the face of the actual federal constitutional challenges that would also be pending for decision before it, a privilege not wholly shared by the federal courts. . . . This disruption of suits by the state in its sovereign capacity, when combined with the negative reflection on the state's ability to adjudicate federal claims that occurs whenever a federal court enjoins a pending state proceeding, leads us to the conclusion that the interests of comity and federalism on which *Younger* and *Samuels v. Mackell* primarily rest apply in full force here.

Finally, *Younger* was applied to state bar disciplinary proceedings in Middlesex County Ethics Committee v. Garden State Bar Association, 457 U.S. 423 (1982). New Jersey had an elaborate administrative system for reviewing charges of attorney misconduct. Ultimate authority rested with the New Jersey Supreme Court, which issued rules governing the administrative procedure and which reviewed all serious sanctions. Rather than contest charges in the state system, an attorney and certain bar organizations sued in federal court to have the disciplinary rules declared invalid. The Supreme Court, however, held that the policies underlying *Younger* were "fully applicable" to state bar disciplinary proceedings. Those proceedings were essentially "judicial" in nature and afforded ample opportunity for federal constitutional objections to be raised and heard. Abstention was therefore required. There was no dissent.

2.   LIMITING *YOUNGER* TO "JUDICIAL" PROCEEDINGS

The uniformity of result in these early cases might have led one to conclude that *Younger* would apply to *any* pending civil proceeding to which the state was a party. New Orleans Public Service, Inc. v. Council of the City of New Orleans, 491 U.S. 350 (1989), showed that not to be true.

The case involved a utility's petition to the New Orleans City Council for a rate increase. The increase was to cover costs imposed on the utility by the Federal Energy Regulatory Commission (FERC). After protracted proceedings, the council found some of the costs unjustified and refused to allow the utility to pass them along to its consumers. The utility then sued in federal court, claiming that the FERC determination preempted the council's decision that the costs were unjustified and effectively required the council to allow the utility to recoup its costs. At the same time, the utility petitioned to review the council's order in the appropriate state court. The district court invoked *Younger* abstention and refused to address the merits of the federal suit, a position supported by the New Orleans City Council.

Although fractured as to reasoning, the Justices were unanimous in concluding that abstention was not required. Justice Scalia spoke for the Court:

> [The utility's] challenge must stand or fall upon the answer to the question whether the Louisiana court action is the type of proceeding entitled to *Younger* abstention. Viewed in isolation, it plainly is not. Although our concern for comity and federalism has led us to expand the protection of *Younger* beyond state criminal prosecutions . . . , it has never been suggested that *Younger* requires abstention in deference to a state judicial proceeding reviewing legislative or executive action.

The council argued that the state judicial proceedings should be viewed as a mere extension of the council action, and that *Younger* should therefore apply to the state proceedings viewed as a whole. The Court responded:

> Respondents' case for abstention still requires, however, that the *Council proceeding* be the sort of proceeding entitled to *Younger* treatment. We think it is not. While we have expanding *Younger* beyond criminal proceedings, and even beyond proceedings in courts, we have never extended it to proceedings that are not "judicial in nature."

The council's rate-making proceedings were not "judicial in nature." They were rate-making proceedings, which had long been understood as "legislative" in nature. It was true, said the Court, that Prentis v. Atlantic Coat Line Co., 211 U.S. 210 (1908), required that federal review of ratemaking must await the conclusion of that process, but here the "legislative" process was completed. All that remained was judicial review of the result.

> As a challenge to completed legislative action, [the utility's] suit represents neither the interference with ongoing judicial proceedings against which *Younger* was directed, nor interference with an ongoing legislative process against which our ripeness holding in *Prentis* was directed. It is, insofar as our policies of federal comity are concerned, no different in substance from a facial challenge to an allegedly unconstitutional statute or zoning ordinance— which we would assuredly not require to be brought in state courts.

3. *SPRINT COMMUNICATIONS V. JACOBS*

The Court's most ambitious attempt to delineate the boundary of *Younger* abstention came in Sprint Communications v. Jacobs, 571 U.S. ___, 134 S.Ct. 584 (2013). The case involved a complicated dispute between Sprint and Windstream, an Iowa communications company, over fees owned by Sprint for long distance Voice Over Internet Protocol (VoIP) calls made to Windstream's Iowa customers. Sprint argued that federal law preempted state regulation of VoIP traffic. Windstream, and ultimately the Iowa Utilities Boad (IUB), disagreed. Sprint filed two suits, one in federal court to declare that federal law controlled, and one in state court to challenge the Utilities Board's decision. The lower federal courts abstained under *Younger*, but the Supreme Court disagreed.

Speaking for a unanimous Court, Justice Ginsburg said that the federal-court suit against the Utility Board (actually against the individual members thereof in their official capacity) was not the type of civil proceeding to which *Younger* applied. She identified three circumstances appropriate for *Younger* abstention. The first precluded federal intrusion into ongoing state criminal prosecutions. The third prohibited disruption of "civil proceedings involving certain orders . . . uniquely in furtherance of the state courts' ability to perform their judicial functions," such as the contempt proceedings in *Juidice v. Vail*. The second circumstance, and the one claimed here, involved application of *Younger* to pending "civil enforcement proceedings." The Court found this case outside that category:

> Our decisions applying *Younger* to instances of civil enforcement have generally concerned state proceedings "akin to a criminal prosecution" in "important respects." Huffman v. Pursue, Ltd., 420 U.S. 592, 604 (1975). Such enforcement actions are characteristically initiated to sanction the federal plaintiff, i.e., the party challenging the state action for some wrong act. In cases of this genre, a state actor is routinely a party to the state proceeding and often initiates the action. Investigations are commonly involved, often culminating in the filing of a formal complaint or charges.

> The IUB proceeding does not resemble the state enforcement actions this Court has found appropriate for *Younger* abstention. It is not "akin to a criminal prosecution." Ibid. Nor was it initiated by "the State in its sovereign capacity." Trainor v. Hernandez, 431 U.S. 434, 444 (1977). A private corporation, Sprint, initiated the action. No state authority conducted an investigation into Sprint's activities, and no state actor lodged a formal complaint against Sprint. . . .

> In holding that abstention was the proper course, the Eighth Circuit relied heavily on this Court's decision in Middlesex County Ethics committee v. Garden State Bar Ass'n, 457 U.S. 423 (1982). *Younger* abstention was warranted, the Court of Appeals read *Middlesex* to say, whenever three conditions are met: There is (1) "an ongoing state judicial proceeding, which (2) implicates important

state interests, and (3) . . . provide[s] an adequate opportunity to raise [federal] challenges. Before this Court, the IUB has endorsed the Eighth Circuit's approach.

The Court of Appeals and the IUB attribute to this Court's decision in *Middlesex* extraordinary breadth. We invoked *Younger* in *Middlesex* to bar a federal court from entertaining a lawyer's challenge to a New Jersey state ethics committee's pending investigation of the lawyer. Unlike the IUB proceeding here, the state ethics committee's hearing in *Middlesex* was indeed "akin to a criminal proceeding." As we noted, an investigation and formal complaint preceded the hearing, and the purpose of the hearing was to determine whether the lawyer should be disciplined for his failure to meet the State's standards of professional conduct. . . . The three *Middlesex* conditions recited above were not dispositive; they were, instead, *additional* factors appropriately considered by the federal court before invoking *Younger*.

Divorced from their quasi-criminal context, the three *Middlesex* conditions would extend *Younger* to virtually all parallel state and federal proceedings, at least where a party could identify a plausibly important state interest. That result is irreconcilable with our dominant instruction that, even in the presence of parallel state proceedings, abstention from the exercise of federal jurisdiction is the "exception, not the rule." In short, to guide other federal courts, we today clarify and affirm that *Younger* extends to the three "exceptional circumstances" identified [above], but no further.

Has the Court in *Sprint Communications* drawn an identifiable line between the civil proceedings to which *Younger* applies and those to which it does not? If so, is it sensible?

SECTION 3. THE COMITY DOCTRINE

Levin v. Commerce Energy, Inc.

Supreme Court of the United States, 2010.
560 U.S. 413.

■ JUSTICE GINSBURG delivered the opinion of the Court.

This case presents the question whether a federal district court may entertain a complaint of allegedly discriminatory state taxation, framed as a request to increase a commercial competitor's tax burden. Relevant to our inquiry is the Tax Injunction Act (TIA or Act), 28 U.S.C. § 1341, which prohibits lower federal courts from restraining "the assessment, levy or collection of any tax under State law where a plain, speedy and efficient remedy may be had in the courts of such State." More embracive than the TIA, the comity doctrine applicable in state taxation cases restrains federal courts from entertaining claims for relief that risk disrupting state tax administration. See Fair Assessment in Real Estate

Assn., Inc. v. McNary, 454 U.S. 100 (1981). The comity doctrine, we hold, requires that a claim of the kind here presented proceed originally in state court. In so ruling, we distinguish Hibbs v. Winn, 542 U.S. 88 (2004), in which the Court held that neither the TIA nor the comity doctrine barred a federal district court from adjudicating an Establishment Clause challenge to a state tax credit that allegedly funneled public funds to parochial schools.

I

A

Historically, all natural gas consumers in Ohio purchased gas from the public utility, known as a local distribution company (LDC), serving their geographic area. In addition to selling gas as a commodity, LDCs own and operate networks of distribution pipelines to transport and deliver gas to consumers. LDCs offer customers a single, bundled product comprising both gas and delivery.

Today, consumers in Ohio's major metropolitan areas can alternatively contract with an independent marketer (IM) that competes with LDCs for retail sales of natural gas. IMs do not own or operate distribution pipelines; they use LDCs' pipelines. When a customer goes with an IM, therefore, she purchases two "unbundled" products: gas (from the IM) and delivery (from the LDC).

Ohio treats LDCs and IMs differently for tax purposes. Relevant here, Ohio affords LDCs three tax exemptions that IMs do not receive. First, LDCs' natural gas sales are exempt from sales and use taxes. LDCs owe instead a gross receipts excise tax, which is lower than the sales and use taxes IMs must collect. Second, LDCs are not subject to the commercial activities tax imposed on IMs' taxable gross receipts. Ohio law excludes inter-LDC natural gas sales from the gross receipts tax, which IMs must pay when they purchase gas from LDCs.

B

Plaintiffs-respondents Commerce Energy, Inc., a California corporation, and Interstate Gas Supply, Inc., an Ohio company, are IMs that market and sell natural gas to Ohio consumers. Plaintiff-respondent Gregory Slone is an Ohio citizen who has purchased natural gas from Interstate Gas Supply since 1999. Alleging discriminatory taxation of IMs and their patrons in violation of the Commerce and Equal Protection Clauses, respondents sued Richard A. Levin, Tax Commissioner of Ohio (Commissioner), in the U.S. District Court for the Southern District of Ohio. Invoking that court's federal-question jurisdiction under 28 U.S.C. § 1331, respondents sought declaratory and injunctive relief invalidating the three tax exemptions LDCs enjoy and ordering the Commissioner to stop "recognizing and/or enforcing" the exemptions. Respondents named the Commissioner as sole defendant; they did not extend the litigation to include the LDCs whose tax burden their suit aimed to increase.

The District Court granted the Commissioner's motion to dismiss the complaint. The TIA did not block the suit, the District Court initially held, because respondents, like the plaintiffs in *Hibbs,* were "third-parties challenging the constitutionality of [another's] tax benefit," and their requested relief "would not disrupt the flow of tax revenue" to the State.

Nevertheless, the District Court "decline[d] to exercise jurisdiction" as a matter of comity. Ohio's Legislature, the District Court observed, chose to provide the challenged tax exemptions to LDCs. Respondents requested relief that would "requir[e] Ohio to collect taxes which its legislature has not seen fit to impose." Such relief, the court said, would draw federal judges into "a particularly inappropriate involvement in a state's management of its fiscal operations." A state court, the District Court recognized, could extend the exemptions to IMs, but the TIA proscribed this revenue-reducing relief in federal court. "Where there would be two possible remedies," the Court concluded, a federal court should not "impose its own judgment on the state legislature mandating which remedy is appropriate."

The U.S. Court of Appeals for the Sixth Circuit reversed. . . . We granted the Commissioner's petition for certiorari. . . .

II

A

Comity considerations, the Commissioner dominantly urges, preclude the exercise of lower federal-court adjudicatory authority over this controversy, given that an adequate state-court forum is available to hear and decide respondents' constitutional claims. We agree.

The comity doctrine counsels lower federal courts to resist engagement in certain cases falling within their jurisdiction. The doctrine reflects

> a proper respect for state functions, a recognition of the fact that the entire country is made up of a Union of separate state governments, and a continuance of the belief that the National Government will fare best if the States and their institutions are left free to perform their separate functions in separate ways.

Fair Assessment, 454 U.S. at 112 (quoting Younger v. Harris, 401 U.S. 37, 44 (1971)).

Comity's constraint has particular force when lower federal courts are asked to pass on the constitutionality of state taxation of commercial activity. For "[i]t is upon taxation that the several States chiefly rely to obtain the means to carry on their respective governments, and it is of the utmost importance to all of them that the modes adopted to enforce the taxes levied should be interfered with as little as possible." Dows v. Chicago, 78 U.S. (11 Wall.) 108 (1871).

"An examination of [our] decisions," this Court wrote more than a century ago, "shows that a proper reluctance to interfere by prevention with the fiscal operations of the state governments has caused [us] to refrain from so doing in all cases where the Federal rights of the persons could otherwise be preserved unimpaired." Boise Artesian Hot & Cold Water Co. v. Boise City, 213 U.S. 276, 282 (1909). Accord Matthews v. Rodgers, 284 U.S. 521, 525–26 (1932) (So long as the state remedy was "plain, adequate, and complete," the "scrupulous regard for the rightful independence of state governments which should at all times actuate the federal courts, and a proper reluctance to interfere by injunction with their fiscal operations, require that such relief should be denied in every case where the asserted federal right may be preserved without it.").[2]

Statutes conferring federal jurisdiction, we have repeatedly cautioned, should be read with sensitivity to "federal-state relations" and "wise judicial administration." Quackenbush v. Allstate Ins. Co., 517 U.S. 706, 716 (1996). But by 1937, in state tax cases, the federal courts had moved in a different direction: they "had become free and easy with injunctions." Fair Assessment, 454 U.S. at 129 (Brennan, J., concurring in judgment).[3] Congress passed the TIA to reverse this trend.

Our post-Act decisions, however, confirm the continuing sway of comity considerations, independent of the Act. Plaintiffs in Great Lakes Dredge & Dock Co. v. Huffman, 319 U.S. 293 (1943), for example, sought a federal judgment declaring Louisiana's unemployment compensation tax unconstitutional. Writing six years after the TIA's passage, we emphasized the Act's animating concerns: A "federal court of equity," we reminded, "may in an appropriate case refuse to give its special protection to private rights when the exercise of its jurisdiction would be prejudicial to the public interest, [and] should stay its hand in the public

---

[2] Justice Brennan cogently explained, in practical terms, "the special reasons justifying the policy of federal noninterference with state tax collection":

> The procedures for mass assessment and collection of state taxes and for administration and adjudication of taxpayers' disputes with tax officials are generally complex and necessarily designed to operate according to established rules. State tax agencies are organized to discharge their responsibilities in accordance with the state procedures. If federal declaratory relief were available to test state tax assessments, state tax administration might be thrown into disarray, and taxpayers might escape the ordinary procedural requirements imposed by state law. During the pendency of the federal suit the collection of revenue under the challenged law might be obstructed, with consequent damage to the State's budget, and perhaps a shift to the State of the risk of taxpayer insolvency. Moreover, federal constitutional issues are likely to turn on questions of state tax law, which, like issues of state regulatory law, are more properly heard in the state courts.

Perez v. Ledesma, 401 U.S. 82, 128 n.17 (1971) (opinion concurring in part and dissenting in part).

[3] Two features of federal equity practice accounted for the courts' willingness to grant injunctive relief. First, the Court had held that, although "equity jurisdiction does not lie where there exists an adequate legal remedy[,] . . . the 'adequate legal remedy' must be one cognizable in federal court." Fair Assessment, 454 U.S. at 129 n.15 (Brennan, J., concurring in judgment). Second, federal courts, "construing strictly the requirement that the remedy available at law be 'plain, adequate and complete,' had frequently concluded that the procedures provided by the State were not adequate." Id.

interest when it reasonably appears that private interests will not suffer." In enacting the TIA, we noted, "Congress recognized and gave sanction to this practice." We could not have thought Congress intended to cabin the comity doctrine, for we went on to instruct dismissal in *Great Lakes* on comity grounds without deciding whether the Act reached declaratory judgment actions.[4]

Decades later, in *Fair Assessment,* we ruled, based on comity concerns, that 42 U.S.C. § 1983 does not permit federal courts to award damages in state taxation cases when state law provides an adequate remedy. We clarified in *Fair Assessment* that "the principle of comity which predated the Act was not restricted by its passage." And in National Private Truck Council, Inc. v. Oklahoma Tax Comm'n, 515 U.S. 582, 590 (1995), we said, explicitly, that "the [TIA] may be best understood as but a partial codification of the federal reluctance to interfere with state taxation."

B

Although our precedents affirm that the comity doctrine is more embracive than the TIA, several Courts of Appeals, including the Sixth Circuit in the instant case, have comprehended *Hibbs* to restrict comity's compass. *Hibbs,* however, has a more modest reach.

Plaintiffs in *Hibbs* were Arizona taxpayers who challenged a state law authorizing tax credits for payments to organizations that disbursed scholarship grants to children attending private schools. These organizations could fund attendance at institutions that provided religious instruction or gave admissions preference on the basis of religious affiliation. Ranking the credit program as state subsidization of religion, incompatible with the Establishment Clause, plaintiffs sought declaratory and injunctive relief and an order requiring the organizations to pay sums still in their possession into the State's general fund.

The Director of Arizona's Department of Revenue sought to escape suit in federal court by invoking the TIA. We held that the litigation fell outside the TIA's governance. Our prior decisions holding suits blocked by the TIA, we noted, were tied to the Act's "state-revenue-protective moorings." The Act, we explained, "restrain[ed] state taxpayers from instituting federal actions to contest their [own] liability for state taxes," suits that, if successful, would deplete state coffers. But "third parties" like the *Hibbs* plaintiffs, we concluded, were not impeded by the TIA "from pursuing constitutional challenges to tax benefits in a federal forum." The case, we stressed, was "not rationally distinguishable" from a procession of pathmarking civil-rights controversies in which federal courts had entertained challenges to state tax credits without conceiving of the TIA as a jurisdictional barrier. See, e.g., Griffin v. School Bd. of

---

[4]   We later held that the Act indeed does proscribe suits for declaratory relief that would thwart state tax collection. California v. Grace Brethren Church, 457 U.S. 393, 411 (1982).

Prince Edward Cty., 377 U.S. 218 (1964) (involving, inter alia, tax credits for contributions to private segregated schools).

Arizona's Revenue Director also invoked comity as cause for dismissing the action. We dispatched the Director's comity argument in a spare footnote that moved the Sixth Circuit here to reverse the District Court's comity-based dismissal. [T]he footnote stated: "[T]his Court has relied upon 'principles of comity' to preclude original federal-court jurisdiction only when plaintiffs have sought district-court aid in order to arrest or countermand state tax collection."

Relying heavily on our footnote in *Hibbs*, respondents urge that "comity should no more bar this action than it did the action in *Hibbs*." As we explain below, however, the two cases differ markedly in ways bearing on the comity calculus. We have had no prior occasion to consider, under the comity doctrine, a taxpayer's complaint about allegedly discriminatory state taxation framed as a request to increase a competitor's tax burden. Now squarely presented with the question, we hold that comity precludes the exercise of original federal-court jurisdiction in cases of the kind presented here.

III

A

Respondents complain that they are taxed unevenly in comparison to LDCs and their customers. Under either an equal protection or dormant Commerce Clause theory, respondents' root objection is the same: State action, respondents contend, "selects [them] out for discriminatory treatment by subjecting [them] to taxes not imposed on others of the same class." Hillsborough v. Cromwell, 326 U.S. 620, 623 (1946) (equal protection); see Dennis v. Higgins, 498 U.S. 439, 447–48 (1991) (dormant Commerce Clause).

When economic legislation does not employ classifications subject to heightened scrutiny or impinge on fundamental rights, courts generally view constitutional challenges with the skepticism due respect for legislative choices demands. And "in taxation, even more than in other fields, legislatures possess the greatest freedom in classification."

Of key importance, when unlawful discrimination infects tax classifications or other legislative prescriptions, the Constitution simply calls for *equal treatment*. How equality is accomplished—by extension or invalidation of the unequally distributed benefit or burden, or some other measure—is a matter on which the Constitution is silent.

On finding unlawful discrimination, we have affirmed, courts may attempt, within the bounds of their institutional competence, to implement what the legislature would have willed had it been apprised of the constitutional infirmity. The relief the complaining party requests does not circumscribe this inquiry. With the State's legislative prerogative firmly in mind, this Court, upon finding impermissible discrimination in a State's allocation of benefits or burdens, generally remands the case, leaving the remedial choice in the hands of state authorities. . . . Our remand leaves the interim solution in state-court hands, subject to subsequent definitive disposition by the State's legislature.

If lower federal courts were to give audience to the merits of suits alleging uneven state tax burdens, however, recourse to state court for the interim remedial determination would be unavailable. That is so because federal tribunals lack authority to remand to the state court system an action initiated in federal court. Federal judges, moreover, are bound by the TIA; absent certain exceptions, the Act precludes relief that would diminish state revenues, even if such relief is the remedy least disruptive of the state legislature's design.[7] These limitations on the remedial competence of lower federal courts counsel that they refrain from taking up cases of this genre, so long as state courts are equipped fairly to adjudicate them.[8]

B

Comity considerations, as the District Court determined, warrant dismissal of respondents' suit. Assuming, arguendo, that respondents could prevail on the merits of the suit, the most obvious way to achieve parity would be to reduce respondents' tax liability. Respondents did not seek such relief, for the TIA stands in the way of any decree that would "enjoin . . . collection of [a] tax under State law." 28 U.S.C. § 1341. A more ambitious solution would reshape the relevant provisions of Ohio's tax code. Were a federal court to essay such relief, however, the court would engage in the very interference in state taxation the comity doctrine aims to avoid. Respondents' requested remedy, an order invalidating the exemptions enjoyed by LDCs, may be far from what the Ohio Legislature would have willed. In short, if the Ohio scheme is indeed unconstitutional, surely the Ohio courts are better positioned to determine—unless and until the Ohio Legislature weighs in—how to comply with the mandate of equal treatment.

As earlier noted, our unelaborated footnote on comity in *Hibbs* led the Sixth Circuit to conclude that we had diminished the force of that doctrine and made it inapplicable here. We intended no such consequential ruling. *Hibbs* was hardly a run-of-the-mine tax case. It was essentially an attack on the allocation of state resources for allegedly unconstitutional purposes. In *Hibbs,* the charge was state aid in alleged violation of the Establishment Clause; in other cases of the same genre, the attack was on state allocations to maintain racially segregated schools. The plaintiffs in *Hibbs* were outsiders to the tax expenditure, "third parties" whose own tax liability was not a relevant factor. In this

---

[7]   State courts also have greater leeway to avoid constitutional holdings by adopting "narrowing constructions that might obviate the constitutional problem and intelligently mediate federal constitutional concerns and state interests." Moore v. Sims, 442 U.S. 415, 429–30 (1979).

[8]   Any substantial federal question, of course, "could be reviewed when the case [comes to this Court] through the hierarchy of state courts." McNeese v. Board of Ed. for Community Unit School Dist. 187, 373 U.S. 668, 673 (1963).

case, by contrast, the very premise of respondents' suit is that they are taxed differently from LDCs. Unlike the *Hibbs* plaintiffs, respondents do object to their own tax situation, measured by the allegedly more favorable treatment accorded LDCs.

Hibbs held that the TIA did not preclude a federal challenge by a third party who objected to a tax credit received by others, but in no way objected to her own liability under any revenue-raising tax provision. In context, we clarify, the *Hibbs* footnote comment on comity is most sensibly read to affirm that, just as the case was a poor fit under the TIA, so it was a poor fit for comity. The Court, in other words, did not deploy the footnote to recast the comity doctrine; it intended the note to convey only that the Establishment Clause-grounded case cleared both the TIA and comity hurdles.

Respondents steadfastly maintain that this case is fit for federal-court adjudication because of the simplicity of the relief they seek, i.e., invalidation of exemptions accorded the LDCs. But as we just explained, even if respondents' Commerce Clause and equal protection claims had merit, respondents would have no entitlement to their preferred remedy. In *Hibbs,* however, if the District Court found the Arizona tax credit impermissible under the Establishment Clause, only one remedy would redress the plaintiffs' grievance: invalidation of the credit, which inevitably would increase the State's tax receipts. Notably, redress in state court similarly would be limited to an order ending the allegedly impermissible state support for parochial schools.[12] Because state courts would have no greater leeway than federal courts to cure the alleged violation, nothing would be lost in the currency of comity or state autonomy by permitting the *Hibbs* suit to proceed in a federal forum.

Comity, in sum, serves to ensure that "the National Government, anxious though it may be to vindicate and protect federal rights and federal interests, always endeavors to do so in ways that will not unduly interfere with the legitimate activities of the States." *Younger,* 401 U.S. at 44. A confluence of factors in this case, absent in *Hibbs,* leads us to conclude that the comity doctrine controls here. First, respondents seek federal-court review of commercial matters over which Ohio enjoys wide regulatory latitude; their suit does not involve any fundamental right or classification that attracts heightened judicial scrutiny. Second, while respondents portray themselves as third-party challengers to an allegedly unconstitutional tax scheme, they are in fact seeking federal-court aid in an endeavor to improve their competitive position. Third, the Ohio courts are better positioned than their federal counterparts to correct any violation because they are more familiar with state legislative preferences and because the TIA does not constrain their remedial options. Individually,

---

[12] No refund suit (or other taxpayer mechanism) was open to the plaintiffs in *Hibbs,* who were financially disinterested "third parties"; they did not, therefore, improperly bypass any state procedure. Respondents here, however, could have asserted their federal rights by seeking a reduction in their tax bill in an Ohio refund suit.

these considerations may not compel forbearance on the part of federal district courts; in combination, however, they demand deference to the state adjudicative process.

C

The Sixth Circuit expressed concern that application of the comity doctrine here would render the TIA "effectively superfluous." This concern overlooks Congress' point in enacting the TIA. The Act was passed to plug two large loopholes courts had opened in applying the comity doctrine. See supra note 3. By closing these loopholes, Congress secured the doctrine against diminishment. Comity, we further note, is a prudential doctrine. "If the State voluntarily chooses to submit to a federal forum, principles of comity do not demand that the federal court force the case back into the State's own system." Ohio Bureau of Employment Servs. v. Hodory, 431 U.S. 471 (1977).

IV

Because we conclude that the comity doctrine justifies dismissal of respondents' federal-court action, we need not decide whether the TIA would itself block the suit. . . .

For the reasons stated, the Sixth Circuit's judgment is reversed, and the case is remanded for further proceedings consistent with this opinion.

It is so ordered.

■ JUSTICE KENNEDY, concurring.

The Court's rationale in *Hibbs v. Winn*, 542 U.S. 88 (2004), seems to me still doubtful. Nothing in the Court's opinion today expands *Hibbs'* holding further, however, and on that understanding I join the opinion of the Court.

■ JUSTICE THOMAS, with whom JUSTICE SCALIA joins, concurring in the judgment.

Although I, too, remain skeptical of the Court's decision in Hibbs v. Winn, 542 U.S. 88 (2004), I agree that it is not necessary for us to revisit that decision to hold that this case belongs in state court. As the Court rightly concludes, *Hibbs* permits not just the application of comity principles to the litigation here, but also application of the Tax Injunction Act (TIA or Act), 28 U.S.C. § 1341. I concur only in the judgment because where, as here, the same analysis supports both jurisdictional and non-jurisdictional grounds for dismissal (the TIA imposes a jurisdictional bar), the "proper course" under our precedents is to dismiss for lack of jurisdiction.

Congress enacted the TIA's prohibition on federal jurisdiction over certain cases involving state tax issues because federal courts had proved unable to exercise jurisdiction over such cases in the restrained manner that comity requires. As the Court explains, Congress' decision to prohibit federal jurisdiction over cases within the Act's scope did not disturb that jurisdiction, or the comity principles that guide its exercise, in cases outside the Act's purview. I therefore agree with the Court that nothing in the Act or in *Hibbs* affects the application of comity principles to cases not covered by the Act. I disagree that this conclusion moots the need for us to decide "whether the TIA would itself block th[is] suit."

The Court posits that because comity is available as a ground for dismissal even where the Act is not, the Act's application to this case is irrelevant if comity would also support sending the case to state court. . . . I see only one explanation for the Court's decision to dismiss on a "prudential" ground (comity), rather than a mandatory one (jurisdiction): The Court wishes to leave the door open to doing in future cases what it did in *Hibbs,* namely, retain federal jurisdiction over constitutional claims that the Court simply does not believe Congress should have entrusted to state judges under the Act.

That is not a legitimate approach to this important area of the law, and the Court's assertion that our civil rights precedents require it does not withstand scrutiny. If it is indeed true (which it may have been in the civil rights cases) that federal jurisdiction is necessary to ensure a fair forum in which to litigate an allegedly unconstitutional state tax scheme, the Act itself permits federal courts to retain jurisdiction on the ground that "a plain, speedy and efficient remedy" cannot be had in state court. But where, as here and in *Hibbs,* such a remedy can be had in state court, the Court should apply the Act as written.

Because I believe the Act forbids the approach to federal jurisdiction over state tax issues that the Court adopted in *Hibbs,* I would not decide this case in a way that leaves the door open to it even if the Court could find a doorstop that accords with, rather than upends, the settled principle that judges presented with multiple nonmerits grounds for dismissal should dismiss on jurisdictional grounds first. But the tension the Court's decision creates with this settled principle should be enough to convince even those who do not share my view of the TIA that the proper course here is to dismiss this case for lack of jurisdiction because *Hibbs'* construction of the Act applies at most to the type of true third-party suit that *Hibbs* describes, and thus does not save this case from the statute's jurisdictional bar.

■ JUSTICE ALITO, concurring in the judgment.

I agree with the Court that principles of comity bar the present action. I am doubtful about the Court's efforts to distinguish Hibbs v. Winn, 542 U.S. 88 (2004), but whether today's holding undermines *Hibbs'* foundations is a question that can be left for another day.

NOTES ON THE TAX INJUNCTION ACT AND THE COMITY DOCTRINE

1. INTRODUCTION

The Tax Injunction Act, codified in 28 U.S.C. § 1341, provides that "[t]he district courts shall not enjoin, suspend or restrain the assessment, levy or collection of any tax under State law where a plain, speedy and efficient remedy may be had in the courts of such State." This statute was enacted in 1937 for the reasons stated in *Levin*. Its legislative history is extensively discussed in Rosewell v. LaSalle National Bank, 450 U.S. 503 (1981).

As *Levin* indicates, the Supreme Court has adopted a broader comity principle resulting in deference to state courts not required by the text of the Tax Injunction Act. In Great Lakes Dredge & Dock Co. v. Huffman, 319 U.S. 293 (1943), for example, the Court applied the comity principle to prohibit declaratory judgments in situations where the Act forbade an injunction:

> [W]e find it unnecessary to inquire whether the words of the statute may be so construed as to prohibit a declaration by federal courts concerning the invalidity of a state tax. For we are of the opinion that those considerations which have led federal courts of equity to refuse to enjoin the collection of state taxes, save in exceptional cases, require a like restraint in the use of the declaratory judgment procedure.[a]

In Fair Assessment in Real Estate Assn., Inc. v. McNary, 454 U.S. 100 (1981), the Court applied the same comity bar to § 1983 damages actions that would interfere with the collection of state taxes:

> [D]espite the ready access to federal courts provided by Monroe v. Pape, 365 U.S. 167 (1961), and its progeny, we hold that taxpayers are barred by the principle of comity from asserting § 1983 actions against the validity of state tax systems in federal courts. Such taxpayers must seek protection of their federal rights by state remedies, provided of course that those remedies are plain, adequate, and complete, and may ultimately seek review of the state decisions in this Court.

And in National Private Truck Council, Inc. v. Oklahoma Tax Commission, 515 U.S. 582 (1995), the Court held that *state* courts could not enjoin the enforcement of a state tax or declare its invalidity in a proceeding filed under § 1983, so long as an adequate refund remedy was available under state law.

There is a judicially crafted exception to the Tax Injunction Act for cases where the United States sues to protect itself or one of its instrumentalities from state taxation. See Arkansas v. Farm Credit Services of Central Arkansas, 520 U.S. 821 (1997) (exception does not apply to a federally chartered Production Credit Association).

Given that the Tax Injunction Act expressly addressed the issue of federal court interference with state taxation, is it appropriate for the federal courts to develop an additional comity restriction not found in the statute? Even though application of that restriction will result in the dismissal of some cases falling within the courts' statutorily-conferred jurisdiction?

---

[a]   As the Court noted in *Levin*, it held later that this result was compelled by the text of the Tax Injunction Act. See California v. Grace Brethren Church, 457 U.S. 393 (1982).—[Footnote by eds.]

2. *HIBBS V. WINN*

The Court took great pains in *Levin* to distinguish Hibbs v. Winn, 542 U.S. 88 (2004), and four Justices made clear their discomfort with that decision. *Hibbs* involved a federal suit by Arizona taxpayers attacking a tax credit system that permitted a prescribed amount of state taxes to be paid instead to a "school tuition organization" (STO), which then could use them for scholarship grants to religious schools.[b] They sought three forms of relief: an injunction disallowing the tax credit; a declaration that the scheme violated the Establishment Clause on its face and as applied; and an order requiring that all funds in the hands of STOs be paid into the State general fund. The District Court dismissed the suit on the ground that it would restrain the "assessment" of state taxes in violation of the Tax Injunction Act (TIA). The Circuit Court reversed, and the Supreme Court granted certiorari and affirmed.

(i) *The Majority*

Justice Ginsburg wrote for the Court:

Plaintiffs-respondents do not contest their own tax liability. Nor do they seek to impede Arizona's receipt of tax revenues. Their suit, we hold, is not the kind § 1341 proscribes.

In decisions spanning a near half century, courts in the federal system, including this Court, have entertained challenges to tax credits authorized by state law, without conceiving of § 1341 as a jurisdictional barrier. On this first occasion squarely to confront the issue, we confirm the authority federal courts exercised in those cases.

It is hardly ancient history that States, once bent on maintaining racial segregation in public schools, and allocating resources disproportionately to benefit white students to the detriment of black students, fastened on tuition grants and tax credits as a promising means to circumvent Brown v. Board of Education, 347 U.S. 483 (1954). The federal courts, this Court among them, adjudicated the ensuing challenges, instituted under 42 U.S.C. § 1983, and upheld the Constitution's equal protection requirement. See, e.g., Griffin v. School Bd. of Prince Edward Cty., 377 U.S. 218, 233 (1964) (faced with unconstitutional closure of county public schools and tuition grants and tax credits for contributions to private segregated schools, District Court could require county to levy taxes to fund nondiscriminatory public schools). . . .

In the instant case, petitioner Hibbs, Director of Arizona's Department of Revenue, argues, in effect, that we and other federal courts were wrong in those civil-rights cases. The TIA, petitioner maintains, trumps § 1983; the Act, according to petitioner, bars all

---

b   "In effect," the Court said, the law "gives Arizona taxpayers an election. They may direct $500 (or, for joint-return filers, $625) to an STO, or to the Arizona Department of Revenue. As long as donors do not give STOs more than their total tax liability, their $500 or $625 contributions are costless."

lower federal-court interference with state tax systems, even when the challengers are not endeavoring to avoid a tax imposed on them, and no matter whether the State's revenues would be raised or lowered should the plaintiffs prevail. The alleged jurisdictional bar, which petitioner asserts has existed since the TIA's enactment in 1937, was not even imagined by the jurists in the pathmarking civil-rights cases just cited, or by the defendants in those cases, litigants with every interest in defeating federal-court adjudicatory authority. Our prior decisions command no respect, petitioner urges, because they constitute mere "sub silentio holdings." We reject that assessment.

All of the Justices agreed that the case turned on the meaning of the word "assessment" in the TIA. For the majority, "[i]n § 1341 and tax law generally, an assessment is closely tied to the collection of a tax, i.e., the assessment is the official recording of liability that triggers levy and collection efforts." If "assessment" was meant to refer to the entire tax collection scheme, "the TIA would not need the words 'levy' or 'collection'; the term 'assessment,' alone, would do all the necessary work." Accordingly, the majority read the TIA as "direct[ing] taxpayers to pursue refund suits instead of attempting to restrain collections." The legislative history established

> that the Act had two closely related, state-revenue-protective objectives: (1) to eliminate disparities between taxpayers who could seek injunctive relief in federal court—usually out-of-state corporations asserting diversity jurisdiction—and taxpayers with recourse only to state courts, which generally required taxpayers to pay first and litigate later; and (2) to stop taxpayers, with the aid of a federal injunction, from withholding large sums, thereby disrupting state government finances. In short, in enacting the TIA, Congress trained its attention on taxpayers who sought to avoid paying their tax bill by pursuing a challenge route other than the one specified by the taxing authority. . . .

> In sum, this Court has interpreted and applied the TIA only in cases Congress wrote the Act to address, i.e., cases in which state taxpayers seek federal-court orders enabling them to avoid paying state taxes. We have read harmoniously the § 1341 instruction conditioning the jurisdictional bar on the availability of "a plain, speedy and efficient remedy" in state court. The remedy inspected in our decisions was not one designed for the universe of plaintiffs who sue the State. Rather, it was a remedy tailormade for taxpayers.

(ii) The Dissent

Joined by Chief Justice Rehnquist and Justices Scalia and Thomas, Justice Kennedy dissented. For him, the purpose of the TIA was not (quoting from dicta in a prior case) just "to bar suits that might interrupt the process of collecting taxes," but "to prohibit courts from restraining any aspect of the tax laws' administration." The word "assessment" accordingly referred to "the recording of a taxpayer's ultimate tax liability." The TIA's purpose, the dissent continued, "is not only to protect the fisc but also to protect the State's tax system administration and tax policy implementation. . . . [The TIA is meant to protect] the operation of the whole tax collection system and the implementation of entire tax policy, not just a part of it." The dissent relied on numerous statements in prior cases that supported these conclusions. The majority responded that all of the cases "involved plaintiffs who mounted federal litigation to avoid paying state taxes (or to gain a refund of such taxes)."

The dissent also argued that:

> The Act is designed to respect not only the administration of state tax systems but also state-court authority to say what state law means. "[F]ederal constitutional issues are likely to turn on questions of state tax law, which, like issues of state regulatory law, are more properly heard in the state courts." California v. Grace Brethren Church, 457 U.S. 393, 410 (1982). This too establishes that the TIA's purpose is not solely to ensure that the State's fisc is not decreased. . . . The TIA protects the responsibility of the States and their courts to administer their own tax systems and to be accountable to the citizens of the State for their policies and decisions. The majority objects that "there is no disagreement as to the meaning of" state law in this case. . . . [But] the majority's ruling has implications far beyond this case and will most certainly result in federal courts in other States and in other cases being required to interpret state tax law in order to complete their review of challenges to state tax statutes.

> Our heretofore consistent interpretation of the Act's legislative history to prohibit interference with state tax systems and their administration accords with the direct, broad, and unqualified language of the statute. The Act bars all orders that enjoin, suspend, or restrain the assessment of any tax under state law. In effecting congressional intent we should give full force to simple and broad proscriptions in the statutory language.

> . . . Congress has said district courts are barred from disrupting the State's tax operations. It is immaterial whether the State's collection is raised or lowered. A court order will thwart and replace the State's chosen tax policy if it causes either result. No authority supports the proposition that a State lacks an interest in reducing its citizens' tax burden. It is a troubling proposition for this Court to proceed on the assumption that the State's interest in limiting the tax burden on its citizens to that for which its law provides is a secondary policy, deserving of little respect from us.

At bottom the majority and the dissent clashed on a more fundamental question about the role of the federal courts. The dissent began with the following observations:

> In this case, the Court shows great skepticism for the state courts' ability to vindicate constitutional wrongs. . . . [T]oday's

holding should probably be attributed to the concern the Court candidly shows animates it. See [the discussion quoted above] (noting it was the federal courts that "upheld the Constitution's equal protection requirement" when States circumvented Brown v. Board of Education, 347 U.S. 483 (1954), by manipulating their tax laws). The concern, it seems, is that state courts are second rate constitutional arbiters, unequal to their federal counterparts. State courts are due more respect than this. Dismissive treatment of state courts is particularly unjustified since the TIA, by express terms, provides a federal safeguard: The Act lifts its bar on federal-court intervention when state courts fail to provide "a plain, speedy, and efficient remedy." § 1341.

In view of the TIA's text, the congressional judgment that state courts are qualified constitutional arbiters, and the respect state courts deserve, I disagree with the majority's superseding the balance the Act strikes between federal- and state-court adjudication.

(iii) Questions and Comments on Hibbs

The *Hibbs* result aligns with numerous decisions upholding the primacy of federal courts in protecting federal constitutional rights. Do the observations written or joined by Justices Kennedy, Scalia, Thomas, and Alito in *Levin* suggest that *Hibbs* is in trouble? Do related developments on topics studied in other portions of this course reinforce that conjecture? Or are there peculiarities in this context that confine the *Hibbs* debate to disputes involving the implementation of state taxes?

3.   DIRECT MARKETING ASSOCIATION V. BROHL

As *Levin* illustrates, the Supreme Court has endorsed a non-statutory comity doctrine applicable to litigation that may interfere with state taxation and perhaps other policies integral to state government. Direct Marketing Association v. Brohl, 575 U.S. ___, 135 S.Ct. 1124 (2015), is another potential example.

The Court set the table in *Direct Marketing* as follows:

> [U]nder our negative Commerce Clause precedents, Colorado may not require retailers who lack a physical presence in the State to collect [sales or use] taxes. . . . See Quill Corp. v. North Dakota, 504 U.S. 298, 315–18 (1992).[c] Thus, Colorado requires its consumers who purchase tangible personal property from a retailer that does not collect these taxes (a "noncollecting retailer") to fill out a return and remit the taxes . . . directly.

---

[c]   The holding in *Quill* was based on a 1967 decision. Justice Kennedy wrote a separate concurring opinion in which he invited reconsideration of *Quill* and the prior case on the ground that the internet has been a game-changer and has made substantial inroads on the ability of states to collect taxes on goods purchased by their citizens from out-of-state sources.—[Footnote by eds.]

Voluntary compliance with the latter requirement is relatively low, leading to a significant loss of tax revenue, especially as Internet retailers have increasingly displaced their brick-and-mortar kin. . . . In hopes of stopping this trend, Colorado enacted legislation in 2010 imposing notice and reporting obligations on noncollecting retailers whose gross sales in Colorado exceed $100,000.

Specifically, the legislation required noncollecting retailers to notify Colorado purchasers that sales or use taxes were due on certain purchases and that the purchaser was required to file a sales or use tax return; to send a detailed report to all Colorado purchasers who bought more than $500 in taxable goods listing the purchases and informing the purchasers that a tax return must be filed; and to send an annual report to the Colorado taxing agency listing the names of all Colorado customers and the amounts they purchased.

The Direct Marketing Association, a trade association representing affected sellers, filed suit in federal court to enjoin enforcement of the notice and reporting obligations. The District Court entered the injunction, but the Court of Appeals reversed on the ground that it was forbidden by the Tax Injunction Act.

The Supreme Court was unanimous[d] in finding the Tax Injunction Act inapplicable:

Because an injunction is clearly a form of equitable relief barred by the TIA, the question becomes whether the enforcement of the notice and reporting requirements is an act of "assessment, levy or collection." We need not comprehensively define these terms to conclude that they do not encompass enforcement of the notice and reporting requirements at issue. . . . [T]hese three terms refer to discrete phases of the taxation process that do not include informational notices or private reports of information relevant to tax liability. . . .

Enforcement of the notice and reporting requirements may improve Colorado's ability to assess and ultimately collect its sales and use taxes from consumers, but the TIA is not keyed to all activities that may improve a State's ability to assess and collect taxes. Such a rule would be inconsistent not only with the text of the statute, but also with our rule favoring clear boundaries in the interpretation of jurisdictional statutes. See Hertz Corp. v. Friend, 559 U.S. 77, 94 (2010). The TIA is keyed to the acts of assessment, levy, and collection themselves, and enforcement of the notice and reporting requirements is none of these.

---

[d]   Justice Thomas wrote the opinion. Justice Ginsburg concurred separately to make two observations. The first one, in which she was joined by Justices Breyer and Sotomayor, was that her conclusion might be different if the relief sought by the plaintiff could be obtained in a suit in state court for a refund. The second, in which she was joined only by Justice Breyer, was that the Court's "decision in this case . . . is entirely consistent with our decision in *Hibbs*."

But it left the door open for application of the comity doctrine:

> We take no position on whether a suit such as this one might nevertheless be barred under the "comity doctrine," which "counsels lower federal courts to resist engagement in certain cases falling within their jurisdiction." Levin v. Commerce Energy, Inc., 560 U.S. 413, 421 (2010). Under this doctrine, federal courts refrain from "interfer[ing] . . . with the fiscal operations of the state governments . . . in all cases where the Federal rights of the persons could otherwise be preserved unimpaired." Id. at 422.

> Unlike the TIA, the comity doctrine is nonjurisdictional. [Although] Colorado did not seek comity from either of the courts below . . . we leave it to the Tenth Circuit to decide on remand whether the comity argument remains available. . . .

What is the scope of the Court's comity doctrine? Is *Direct Marketing* a candidate for its application? Notice the technical and textual orientation of *Direct Marketing*'s application of the Tax Injunction Act. In contrast, the comity doctrine—a prudential rather than a jurisdictional[e] limitation—is confined by policy not text. Are the policies clear? Is the Court correct to confine the statute narrowly to its text but more broadly to implement a policy of abstention? Does doing so suggest a route for changing the result in *Hibbs*?

4.   THE JOHNSON ACT

A second specialized abstention statute worthy of note is the Johnson Act, now codified at 28 U.S.C. § 1342:

> The district courts shall not enjoin, suspend or restrain the operation of, or compliance with any order affecting rates chargeable by a public utility and made by a State administrative agency or a rate-making body of a State political subdivision, where:

> > (1)   Jurisdiction is based solely on diversity of citizenship or repugnance of the order to the Federal Constitution; and,

> > (2)   The order does not interfere with interstate commerce; and

> > (3)   The order has been made after reasonable notice and hearing; and,

> > (4)   A plain, speedy and efficient remedy may be had in the courts of such State.

This statute derives from the Johnson Act of 1934. Contemporaneous comments on the statute can be found in Note, The Johnson Act: Defining a

---

[e]   The conventional wisdom is that the Tax Injunction Act is jurisdictional, as Justice Thomas says in *Direct Marketing*. For an interesting challenge to this view, see Erin Morrow Hawley, The Equitable Anti-Injunction Act, 90 Notre Dame L. Rev. 81 (2014). The focus of discussion is 26 U.S.C. § 7421(a), which provides with certain exceptions that "no suit for the purpose of restraining the assessment or collection of any [federal] tax shall be maintained in any court by any person, whether or not such person is the person against whom such tax was assessed." The argument is that principles of equity jurisdiction should govern the application of this statute—as well as, perhaps, the series of other anti-injunction acts that Congress has enacted in other contexts.

"Plain, Speedy, and Efficient" Remedy in the State Courts, 50 Harv. L. Rev. 813 (1937); and Comment, Limitation of Lower Federal Court Jurisdiction Over Public Utility Rate Cases, 44 Yale L.J. 119 (1934). Note the common threads running between the Tax Injunction Act, the Johnson Act, and the Court-developed comity doctrine.

In *Hibbs*, the Court distinguished the reach of the Johnson Act from the TIA in a footnote:

> The language of the TIA differs significantly from that of the Johnson Act, which provides in part: "The district courts shall not enjoin, suspend or restrain *the operation of, or compliance with,*" public-utility rate orders made by state regulatory bodies. 28 U.S.C. § 1342 (emphasis added). The TIA does not prohibit interference with "the operation of, or compliance with," state tax laws; rather, § 1341 proscribes interference only with those aspects of state tax regimes that are needed to produce revenue—*i.e.,* assessment, levy, and collection.

Does this linguistic difference suggest that the result in *Hibbs* was right? Does it suggest that greater deference to state court litigation is appropriate under the Johnson Act than under the Tax Injunction Act?

SECTION 4. *PULLMAN* ABSTENTION

Railroad Commission of Texas v. Pullman Co.

Supreme Court of the United States, 1941.
312 U.S. 496.

■ MR. JUSTICE FRANKFURTER delivered the opinion of the Court.

In those sections of Texas where the local passenger traffic is slight, trains carry but one sleeping car. These trains, unlike trains having two or more sleepers, are without a Pullman conductor; the sleeper is in charge of a porter who is subject to the train conductor's control. As is well known, porters on Pullmans are colored and conductors are white. Addressing itself to this situation, the Texas Railroad Commission after due hearing ordered that "no sleeping car shall be operated on any line of railroad in the state of Texas . . . unless such cars are continuously in the charge of an employee . . . having the rank and position of Pullman conductor." Thereupon, the Pullman Company and the railroads affected brought this action in a federal district court to enjoin the commission's order. Pullman porters were permitted to intervene as complainants, and Pullman conductors entered the litigation in support of the order. Three judges having been convened, the court enjoined enforcement of the order. From this decree, the case came here directly.[a]

The Pullman Company and the railroads assailed the order as unauthorized by Texas law as well as violative of the Equal Protection, the

---

[a]   At the time, a statute (since repealed) required that the case be decided by a three-judge district court, followed by direct appeal as of right to the Supreme Court.—[Footnote by eds.]

Due Process and the Commerce Clauses of the Constitution. The intervening porters adopted these objections but mainly objected to the order as a discrimination against Negroes in violation of the Fourteenth Amendment.

The complaint of the Pullman porters undoubtedly tendered a substantial constitutional issue. It is more than substantial. It touches a sensitive area of social policy upon which the federal courts ought not to enter unless no alternative to its adjudication is open. Such constitutional adjudication plainly can be avoided if a definitive ruling on the state issue would terminate the controversy. It is therefore our duty to turn to a consideration of questions under Texas law.

The commission found justification for its order in a Texas statute which we quote in the margin.[1] It is common ground that if the order is within the commission's authority its subject matter must be included in the commission's power to prevent "unjust discrimination . . . and to prevent any and all other abuses" in the conduct of railroads. Whether arrangements pertaining to the staffs of Pullman cars are covered by the Texas concept of "discrimination" is far from clear. What practices of the railroads may be deemed to be "abuses" subject to the commission's correction is equally doubtful. Reading the Texas statutes and the Texas decisions as outsiders without special competence in Texas law, we would have little confidence in our independent judgment regarding the application of that law to the present situation. The lower court did deny that the Texas statutes sustained the commission's assertion of power. And this represents the view of an able and experienced circuit judge of the circuit which includes Texas and of two capable district judges trained in Texas law. Had we or they no choice in the matter but to decide what is the law of the state, we should hesitate long before rejecting their forecast of Texas law. But no matter how seasoned the judgment of the District Court may be, it cannot escape being a forecast rather than a determination. The last word on the meaning of article 6445 of the Texas Civil Statutes, and therefore the last word on the statutory authority of the Railroad Commission in this case, belongs neither to us nor to the District Court but to the Supreme Court of Texas. In this situation a federal court of equity is asked to decide an issue by making a tentative answer which may be displaced tomorrow by a state adjudication. The reign of law is hardly promoted if an unnecessary ruling of a federal court is thus supplanted by a controlling decision of a state court. The resources of

---

[1]   Vernon's Anno. Texas Civil Statutes, Article 6445: "Power and authority are hereby conferred upon the Railroad Commission of Texas over all railroads . . . and it is hereby made the duty of the said Commission to adopt all necessary rates, charges and regulations, to govern and regulate such railroads . . . and to correct abuses and prevent unjust discrimination in the rates, charges and tolls of such railroads . . . and to fix division of rates, charges and regulations between railroads and other utilities and common carriers where a division is proper and correct, and to prevent any and all other abuses in the conduct of their business and to do and perform such other duties and details in connection therewith as may be provided by law."

equity are equal to an adjustment that will avoid the waste of a tentative decision as well as the friction of a premature constitutional adjudication.

An appeal to the chancellor . . . is an appeal to the "exercise of the sound discretion, which guides the determination of courts of equity." The history of equity jurisdiction is the history of regard for public consequences in employing the extraordinary remedy of the injunction. There have been as many and as variegated applications of this supple principle as the situations that have brought it into play. . . . Few public interests have a higher claim upon the discretion of a federal chancellor than the avoidance of needless friction with state policies, whether the policy relates to the enforcement of the criminal law, Fenner v. Boykin, 271 U.S. 240 (1926); Spielman Motor Sales Co. v. Dodge, 295 U.S. 89 (1935); or the administration of a specialized scheme for liquidating embarrassed business enterprises, Pennsylvania v. Williams, 294 U.S. 176 (1935); or the final authority of a state court to interpret doubtful regulatory laws of the state, Gilchrist v. Interborough Rapid Transit Co., 279 U.S. 159 (1929); cf. Hawks v. Hamill, 288 U.S. 52, 61 (1933). These cases reflect a doctrine of abstention appropriate to our federal system whereby the federal courts, "exercising a wise discretion," restrain their authority because of "scrupulous regard for the rightful independence of the state governments" and for the smooth working of the federal judiciary. This use of equitable powers is a contribution of the courts in furthering the harmonious relation between state and federal authority without the need of rigorous congressional restriction of those powers. Compare [the Three-Judge Court Act, the Tax-Injunction Act, the Johnson Act, and the Norris-LaGuardia Act.]

Regard for these important considerations of policy in the administration of federal equity jurisdiction is decisive here. If there was no warrant in state law for the commission's assumption of authority there is an end of the litigation; the constitutional issue does not arise. The law of Texas appears to furnish easy and ample means for determining the commission's authority. Article 6453 of the Texas Civil Statutes gives a review of such an order in the state courts. Or, if there are difficulties in the way of this procedure of which we have not been apprised, the issue of state law may be settled by appropriate action on the part of the state to enforce obedience to the order. In the absence of any showing that these obvious methods for securing a definitive ruling in the state courts cannot be pursued with full protection of the constitutional claim, the District Court should exercise its wise discretion by staying its hands.

We therefore remand the cause to the District Court, with directions to retain the bill pending a determination of proceedings, to be brought with reasonable promptness, in the state court in conformity with this opinion.

Reversed.

■ MR. JUSTICE ROBERTS took no part in the consideration or decision of this case.

NOTES ON PULLMAN ABSTENTION

1. SILER V. LOUISVILLE & NASHVILLE R. CO.

In Siler v. Louisville & Nashville R. Co., 213 U.S. 175 (1909), a railroad sued to enjoin enforcement of an order of the Kentucky railroad commission fixing maximum rates on commodities transported to and from points within the state. The railroad argued that the rates violated the federal Constitution and also that they were unauthorized by state law. The federal court enjoined enforcement of the rates on the federal ground.

The Supreme Court first held that the lower court had jurisdiction:

> The federal questions . . . gave the Circuit Court jurisdiction, and, having properly obtained it, that court had the right to decide all the questions in the case, even though it decided the federal questions adversely to the party raising them, or even if it omitted to decide them at all, but decided the case on local or state questions only.

It next addressed the order in which the questions in the case should be decided:

> Where a case in this Court can be decided without reference to questions arising under the federal Constitution, that course is usually pursued and is not departed from without important reasons. In this case we think it much better to decide it with regard to the question of a local nature, involving the construction of the state statute and the authority therein given to the commission to make the order in question, rather than to unnecessarily decide the various constitutional questions appearing in the record. . . .

> In this case we are without the benefit of a construction of the statute by the highest state court of Kentucky, and we must proceed in the absence of state adjudication upon the subject. Nevertheless, we are compelled to the belief that the statute does not grant to the commission any such great and extensive power as it has assumed to exercise in making the order in question. . . .

The Court then explained why it thought the state statute did not authorize the rate-making at issue and upheld the injunction.[a]

2. QUESTIONS AND COMMENTS ON PULLMAN

Why did the *Pullman* Court not follow *Siler*? Note that the decree in *Siler* could have been modified by the trial court if, in light of subsequent

---

[a]   *Siler* was distinguished and limited in Pennhurst State School and Hospital v. Halderman, 465 U.S. 89 (1984). *Pennhurst* held that the Eleventh Amendment precluded a federal court injunction against a state official for violation of state law. *Siler* was cited as contrary authority, but the Court said that *Siler* assumed the Eleventh Amendment away without discussion and that it was "contrary to the principles established in our Eleventh Amendment decisions" to assume that the Eleventh Amendment did not apply to pendent state claims. In a dissent joined by Justices Brennan, Marshall, and Blackmun, dissented, Justice Stevens found the Eleventh Amendment inapplicable and said that the *Siler* approach was "strongly supported by the interest in avoiding duplicative litigation and the unnecessary decision of federal constitutional questions."

state court decisions, the "forecast" of state law turned out to be wrong.[b] At that point, of course, the federal constitutional issue would have to be resolved and the injunction reissued if the state practice were found unconstitutional.

What should be done in these situations? Would it be better to assume that state law authorizes the challenged practice and proceed at once to decide the federal constitutional issue? Should the plaintiff be entitled to interim relief if abstention is ordered? Are there other options?[c]

3. VIOLATION OF STATE CONSTITUTION

Pullman abstention will not be granted if the state law in question is clear. In Wisconsin v. Constantineau, 400 U.S. 433 (1971), for example, the Supreme Court held that abstention was not proper in a case challenging, under the Due Process Clause, a Wisconsin statute that allowed for public posting of the identity of individuals deemed ineligible to purchase alcohol as a result of excessive drinking. The Court explained:

> In the present case, the Wisconsin Act does not contain any provision whatsoever for notice and hearing. There is no ambiguity in the state statute. There are no provisions which could fairly be taken to mean that notice and hearing might be given under some circumstances or under some construction, but not under others. . . . Where there is no ambiguity in the state statute, the federal court should not abstain, but should proceed to decide the federal constitutional claim.

This proposition generally holds true even if the state law might violate the state's own constitution. Otherwise, abstention might be triggered by most federal constitutional challenges to state laws, since many state constitutions have provisions similar to the federal ones. In Examining Board of Engineers v. Otero, 426 U.S. 572 (1976), for example, the Court held that abstention was not proper in a case challenging a Puerto Rican statute that allowed only U.S. citizens to become civil engineers, even though the statute might have violated equal protection provisions in the Puerto Rican constitution. The Court explained that, "to hold that abstention is required because [the statute] might conflict with the cited broad and sweeping constitutional provisions would convert abstention from an exception into a general rule."

---

     [b]   See, e.g., Martha A. Field, Abstention in Constitutional Cases: The Scope of the *Pullman* Abstention Doctrine, 122 U. Pa. L. Rev. 1071, 1094 n.90 (1974): "When a federal court rests its decision on a state question and thereby avoids a federal constitutional question, the decree will often include a provision expressly authorizing reopening in the event that the question of state law is subsequently decided differently in the state court. Even if the federal judge neglects to insert such a provision, the decree can be modified when the state court has authoritatively spoken. It is this possibility of modification that led Justice Frankfurter to fear in *Pullman* that a federal ruling on the state issue would be 'tentative.' "

     [c]   Martha A. Field, The Abstention Doctrine Today, 125 U. Pa. L. Rev. 590, 605–06 & n. 56 (1977), suggests that certification of unclear questions of state law to the state supreme courts may be the answer. For states without a certification procedure, "Congress could dispense with the need for state authorization and require states to entertain certified questions. . . . Congressional power would stem from Article III in conjunction with the necessary and proper clause. It may also be that Article III gives the federal courts power, without any congressional authorization, to compel certification."

In some cases, however, the state constitutional provisions will be sufficiently unique, or sufficiently intertwined with the challenged state law, that abstention will be warranted. In Reetz v. Bozanich, 397 U.S. 82 (1970), for example, the Court held that abstention was proper in a case involving a challenge, brought under the Equal Protection Clause and the Alaska constitution, to a set of laws and regulations in that state limiting licenses for commercial salmon fishing. The Court noted that "the provisions of the Alaska constitution at issue have never been interpreted by an Alaska court" and that these provisions "relate to fish resources, an asset unique in its abundance in Alaska." See also Harris County Commissioners Court v. Moore, 420 U.S. 77 (1975) (holding that abstention was proper in a case where "the uncertain status of local law stems from the unsettled relationship between the state constitution and a statute").

NOTES ON ADMINISTRATION OF PULLMAN ABSTENTION

1. INTRODUCTION

In most *Pullman* cases, the debate is whether state law is sufficiently "unclear" to justify abstention. Other considerations are whether an adequate state remedy is available to the federal plaintiff, whether a single state proceeding is likely to clear up the difficulty,[a] and whether there are special reasons for prompt federal intervention.[b] *Pullman* abstention is usually thought to be an offspring of equity and is usually limited to suits for injunctive relief.

Beyond these generalizations, the cases do not fit any consistent pattern. The propriety of abstention in any given situation is therefore likely to be unclear. This, in fact, is one of the major difficulties in the administration of the doctrine. On appeal, moreover, the *Pullman* question is reviewed de novo and can even be raised sua sponte. Abstention may thus be ordered even though time and money have already been expended in litigating the merits in lower federal courts.

One of the consequences of *Pullman* abstention is substantial delay in the adjudication of federal claims. Indeed, Martha Field has suggested that:

A survey of abstention decisions . . . raises the question whether delay is not sometimes the *aim* of the abstention procedure, and the desirability of obtaining a clarifying state decision simply the *excuse* for the delay. When, for example, a lawsuit presents a federal constitutional attack on a state program that does not seem politic at the moment to resolve, abstention may appear a convenient device for removing the parties from federal court, for the time being

---

[a] See, e.g., Dombrowski v. Pfister, 380 U.S. 479 (1965) (First Amendment vagueness and overbreadth challenge), and Baggett v. Bullitt, 377 U.S. 360 (1964) (vagueness challenge to loyalty oath). The Court held abstention inappropriate in both cases because the state statutes could only have been clarified in a series of lawsuits.

[b] See, e.g., Pike v. Bruce Church, Inc., 397 U.S. 137, 140 n. 3 (1970): "In view of the emergency situation presented, and the fact that only a narrow and specific application of the act was challenged as unconstitutional, the court was fully justified in not abstaining. . . ." The suit concerned the validity of packing regulations for the shipping of cantaloupes. The emergency was that if the regulations were enforced, a $700,000 crop would be lost.

at least. Even if they persist in demanding a federal forum to resolve their federal claims, abstention will put them off for a number of years.[c]

For these reasons, as well as the problems developed in connection with the remainder of these notes, most commentators oppose *Pullman* abstention. Over the years, the doctrine has ebbed and flowed, perhaps partly in response to the Court's view of the importance of the constitutional values at stake.

2. *GOVERNMENT EMPLOYEES V. WINDSOR*

Government and Civic Employees Organizing Committee v. Windsor, 353 U.S. 364 (1957), caused considerable confusion over how state law questions should be submitted to the state courts after a *Pullman* abstention. The suit in *Windsor* was filed in 1953, and a three-judge court abstained. That decision was affirmed by the Supreme Court, after which proceedings were begun in the state courts. The state trial court held the challenged statute applicable to the plaintiffs' activity, and the state Supreme Court affirmed. The plaintiffs then returned to the three-judge federal court. That court held the statute constitutional as applied, and dismissed the case. The case then came back to the Supreme Court, which in a unanimous per curiam opinion (Justice Black not participating) said:

> We do not reach the constitutional issues. . . . The bare adjudication by the Alabama Supreme Court . . . does not suffice, since that court was not asked to interpret the statute in light of the constitutional objections presented to the District Court. If appellants' [constitutional] arguments had been presented to the state court, it might have construed the statute in a different manner. Accordingly, the judgment of the District Court is vacated, and this cause is remanded to it with directions to retain jurisdiction until efforts to obtain an appropriate adjudication in the state courts have been exhausted.

Apparently the plaintiffs were themselves exhausted by the Supreme Court's disposition. See Martha A. Field, Abstention in Constitutional Cases: The Scope of the *Pullman* Abstention Doctrine, 122 U. Pa. L. Rev. 1071, 1086 n.65 (1974), which reports that the District Court remanded the "case to state court a second time, after which the plaintiff abandoned suit, having failed to obtain a decision on the merits after four years of litigation, including one trip to the Alabama Supreme Court and two to the United States Supreme Court."

3. *ENGLAND V. LOUISIANA STATE BOARD OF MEDICAL EXAMINERS*

The Court addressed the implications of *Windsor* in England v. Louisiana State Board of Medical Examiners, 375 U.S. 411 (1964). The Board of Medical Examiners insisted that chiropractors adhere to prescribed educational requirements. A group of chiropractors sought a federal injunction on

---

[c]   Martha A. Field, The Abstention Doctrine Today, 125 U. Pa. L. Rev. 590, 602 (1977).

the ground that the requirements violated the Fourteenth Amendment. A
federal judge dismissed the complaint for failure to state a substantial federal question, but the circuit court reversed. A three-judge federal court was
then convened to hear the claim. When that court abstained under *Pullman*,
an action was brought in the state courts, which ruled for the Board of Medical Examiners after the chiropractors "unreservedly submitted for decision"
both their federal and their state claims. The chiropractors did not appeal
this adverse state court ruling to the Supreme Court, but instead returned
to the federal three-judge court. That court then dismissed the claim on the
ground that all issues had been resolved in the state-court litigation.

The Supreme Court reversed and remanded for a resolution of the merits of the plaintiffs' Fourteenth Amendment claims. In an opinion by Justice
Brennan, the Court began with a statement of the governing principles:

> There are fundamental objections to any conclusion that a lit-
> igant who has properly invoked the jurisdiction of a federal district
> court to consider federal constitutional claims can be compelled,
> without his consent and through no fault of his own, to accept in-
> stead a state court's determination of those claims. . . . Abstention
> is a judge-fashioned vehicle for according appropriate deference to
> the "respective competence of the state and federal court systems."
> Louisiana P. & L. Co. v. City of Thibodaux, 360 U.S. 25, 29 (1959).
> Its recognition of the role of state courts as the final expositors of
> state law implies no disregard for the primacy of the federal judici-
> ary in deciding questions of federal law. Accordingly, we have on
> several occasions explicitly recognized that abstention "does not, of
> course, involve the abdication of federal jurisdiction, but only the
> postponement of its exercise." Harrison v. NAACP, 360 U.S. 167,
> 177 (1959).

> It is true that, after a post-abstention determination and re-
> jection of his federal claims by the state courts, a litigant could seek
> direct review in this Court. But such review, even when available
> by appeal rather than only by discretionary writ of certiorari, is an
> inadequate substitute for the initial district court determination—
> often by three judges—to which the litigant is entitled in the fed-
> eral courts. This is true as to issues of law; it is especially true as
> to issues of fact. Limiting the litigant to review here would deny
> him the benefit of a federal trial court's role in constructing a record
> and making fact findings. How the facts are found will often dictate
> the decision of federal claims. . . . Thus in cases where, but for the
> application of the abstention doctrine, the primary fact determina-
> tion would have been by the district court, a litigant may not be
> unwillingly deprived of that determination. The possibility of ap-
> pellate review by this Court of a state court determination may not
> be substituted, against a party's wishes, for his right to litigate his
> federal claims fully in the federal courts. . . .

This did not mean, however, that litigants could not elect to forego federal-court resolution of their claims by choosing to have them resolved in
state court. In such cases, the "line drawn should be bright and clear, so that

litigants shunted from federal to state courts by application of the abstention doctrine will not be exposed, not only to unusual expense and delay, but also to procedural traps operating to deprive them of their right to a district court determination of their federal claims." Accordingly:

> We now explicitly hold that if a party freely and without reservation submits his federal claims for decision by the state courts, litigates them there, and has them decided there, then—whether or not he seeks direct review of the state decision in this Court—he has elected to forgo his right to return to the district court.

As to the continuing effect of *Windsor*:

> The case does not mean that a party must litigate his federal claims in the state courts, but only that he must inform those courts what his federal claims are, so that the state statute may be construed "in light of" those claims. Thus mere compliance with *Windsor* will not support a conclusion, much less create a presumption, that a litigant has freely and without reservation litigated his federal claims in the state courts and so elected not to return to the district court.
>
> We recognize that in the heat of litigation a party may find it difficult to avoid doing more than is required by *Windsor*. This would be particularly true in the typical case, such as the instant one, where the state courts are asked to construe a state statute against the backdrop of a federal constitutional challenge. The litigant denying the statute's applicability may be led not merely to state his federal constitutional claim but to argue it, for if he can persuade the state court that application of the statute to him would offend the federal Constitution, he will ordinarily have persuaded it that the statute should not be construed as applicable to him. In addition, the parties cannot prevent the state court from rendering a decision on the federal question if it chooses to do so; and even if such a decision is not explicit, a holding that the statute is applicable may arguably imply, in view of the constitutional objections to such a construction, that the court considers the constitutional challenge to be without merit.
>
> Despite these uncertainties arising from application of *Windsor*—which decision, we repeat, does not require that federal claims be actually litigated in the state courts—a party may readily forestall any conclusion that he has elected not to return to the district court. He may accomplish this by making on the state record [a] reservation to the disposition of the entire case by the state courts. . . . That is, he may inform the state courts that he is exposing his federal claims there only for the purpose of complying with *Windsor*, and that he intends, should the state courts hold against him on the question of state law, to return to the district court for disposition of his federal contentions. Such an explicit reservation is not indispensable; the litigant is in no event to be denied his right

to return to the district court unless it clearly appears that he voluntarily did more than *Windsor* required and fully litigated his federal claims in the state courts.[12] When the reservation has been made, however, his right to return will in all events be preserved.[13]

The Court ultimately concluded, however, that it would be inappropriate to apply the Court's holding to these plaintiffs because they might reasonably have been misled by *Windsor*. The case was therefore remanded to the lower federal court for decision on the merits of the federal claim.

Justice Douglas concurred. He thought the majority decision created "something of a Frankenstein" and called for reappraisal of *Pullman*. Justice Black concurred in part and dissented in part. He thought "that the dismissal should be affirmed on the grounds relied upon by Judge J. Skelly Wright sitting alone in the District Court when the action first was brought: that the complaint failed to state a substantial federal question warranting exercise of jurisdiction." And dismissal, indeed, was the ultimate disposition. The suit was originally filed in 1957. In 1965, it was dismissed on remand by the three-judge federal court. The opinion was again written by Judge Wright, who again concluded that the constitutional claims lacked merit.

4.   *HARRIS COUNTY COMMISSIONERS V. MOORE*

Harris County Commissioners Court v. Moore, 420 U.S. 77 (1975), involved a suit by three justices of the peace and two constables who lost their jobs before the end of their terms because of the midterm adoption of a redistricting plan. They alleged that the redistricting plan violated equal protection and also that it violated their state constitutional right to complete an elected term unless removed for cause. Two local voters also joined as plaintiffs. A three-judge court granted relief, but the Supreme Court held that the lower court should have abstained. The Court's opinion concluded:

---

[12] It has been suggested that state courts may "take no more pleasure than do federal courts in deciding cases piecemeal . . ." and "probably prefer to determine their questions of law with complete records of cases in which they can enter final judgments before them." Clay v. Sun Ins. Office, 363 U.S. 207, 227 (1960) (dissenting opinion). We are confident that state courts, sharing the abstention doctrine's purpose of "[f]urthering the harmonious relation between state and federal authority," Railroad Comm'n v. Pullman Co., 312 U.S. 496, 501 (1941), will respect a litigant's reservation of his federal claims for decision by the federal courts. However, evidence that a party has been compelled by the state courts to litigate his federal claims there will of course preclude a finding that he has voluntarily done so. And if the state court has declined to decide the state question because of the litigant's refusal to submit without reservation the federal question as well, the district court will have no alternative but to vacate its order of abstention.

[13] The reservation may be made by any party to the litigation. Usually the plaintiff will have made the original choice to litigate in the federal court, but the defendant also, by virtue of the removal jurisdiction, 28 U.S.C. § 1441(b), has a right to litigate the federal question there. Once issue has been joined in the federal court, no party is entitled to insist, over another's objection, upon a binding state court determination of the federal question.

[For an example of a situation where a return to federal court was not permitted because petitioners had "phrased their state claims in language that sounded in the rules and standards established and refined by this Court's takings jurisprudence" and had thereby "effectively asked the state court to resolve the same federal issues they asked it to reserve," see San Remo Hotel, L.P. v. City and County of San Francisco, 545 U.S. 323, 331, 341 (2005).—Addition to Footnote by eds.]

In order to remove any possible obstacles to state court jurisdiction, we direct the District Court to dismiss the complaint. The
dismissal should be without prejudice so that any remaining federal claim may be raised in a federal forum after the Texas courts
have been given the opportunity to address the state law questions
in the case. England v. Louisiana State Board of Medical Examiners, 375 U.S. 411 (1964).

The Court then added in a footnote:

Ordinarily the proper course in ordering *"Pullman* abstention"
is to remand with instructions to retain jurisdiction but to stay the
federal suit pending determination of the state law questions in
state court. The Texas Supreme Court has ruled, however, that it
cannot grant declaratory relief under state law if a federal court
retains jurisdiction over the federal claim. United Services Life Ins.
Co. v. Delaney, 396 S.W.2d 855 (Tex. 1965).[d]

We have adopted the unusual course of dismissing in this case
solely in order to avoid the possibility that some state law remedies
might otherwise be foreclosed to appellees on their return to state
court. Obviously, the dismissal must not be used as a means to defeat the appellees' federal claims if and when they return to federal
court.[e]

5.   QUESTIONS AND COMMENTS ON THE PROCEDURAL
     CONSEQUENCES OF ABSTENTION

England requires a procedure that substantially increases the delay,
complexity, and expense of litigation. Is the problem worth such an elaborate
solution? If not, what should be done?

The Court said in *England* that "[l]imiting the litigant to review here
would deny him the benefit of a federal trial court's role in constructing a
record and making fact findings." Suppose the state court must resolve factual disputes before it can determine the state-law issue. Is the plaintiff
entitled to a retrial of the facts on return to federal court? If so, what is to be
done if the issues of state law might have been resolved differently in light
of the facts as found in federal court? Or should the state-court findings of
fact be given preclusive effect in the subsequent federal-court proceedings?

Another aspect of the problem is how the state courts are likely to react
to litigants who make the kind of explicit reservation contemplated by *England*. Is the reaction of the Texas court in *Delaney* surprising? Does *England*
promote or undermine harmonious federal-state relations? The Texas Constitution was amended in 1985 to give the Texas Supreme Court and Court
of Criminal Appeals "jurisdiction to answer questions of state law certified

---

[d]   *Delaney* held that declaratory relief could not be obtained because it would require an
advisory opinion.—[Footnote by eds.]

[e]   Justice Douglas was the lone dissenter. He pointed out that the suit had already been
in litigation for two years, that the term of office of the three justices of the peace had expired
before the lower court rendered its judgment, and that the term of the two constables would
expire ten months after the Supreme Court's remand. He argued that they had suffered enough
delay.—[Footnote by eds.]

from a federal *appellate* court." Tex. Const., art. 5, § 3–c (emphasis added). Did this change how a federal *district* court should have reacted to an abstention situation in Texas?

6.   BIBLIOGRAPHY

For a sample of the voluminous literature on *Pullman* abstention, see Randall P. Bezanson, Abstention: The Supreme Court and Allocation of Judicial Power, 27 Vand. L. Rev. 1107 (1974); Julie Davies, *Pullman* and *Burford* Abstention: Clarifying the Roles of State and Federal Courts in Constitutional Cases, 20 U.C. Davis L. Rev. 1 (1986); Martha A. Field, Abstention in Constitutional Cases: The Scope of the *Pullman* Abstention Doctrine, 122 U. Pa. L. Rev. 1071 (1974); Lisa A. Kloppenberg, Measured Constitutional Steps, 71 Ind. L.J. 297 (1996); Lisa A. Kloppenberg, Avoiding Constitutional Questions, 35 B.C. L. Rev. 1003 (1994); and Sidney Shapiro, Abstention and Primary Jurisdiction: Two Chips off the Same Block?—A Comparative Analysis, 60 Corn. L. Rev. 75, 83–91 (1974). See also Ann Woolhandler, Between the Acts: Federal Court Abstention in the 1940s and '50s, 59 N.Y.L.S.L. Rev. 211 (2014–15) ("showing ways in which the reasoning supporting abstention corresponded to the Court's reasoning in substantive decisions as to the validity of statutes" and "traces the decline of the doctrine, in part spurred by civil rights cases").

NOTES ON *BURFORD* AND OTHER FORMS OF ABSTENTION

1.   *BURFORD* ABSTENTION

In Burford v. Sun Oil Co., 319 U.S. 315 (1943), Sun Oil filed an action in federal court to enjoin the Texas Railroad Commission from granting Burford a permit to drill four oil wells. Jurisdiction was based on diversity and the alleged unconstitutionality of the Railroad Commission's order. Over a vigorous dissent by Justice Frankfurter, the Court, in an opinion by Justice Black, decided that the federal suit should have been dismissed. Since "the important constitutional issues have . . . been fairly well settled from the beginning," the Court treated the case as presenting the question whether federal district courts sitting in diversity should be permitted to intervene by injunction in the Texas regulatory scheme.

The case involved the East Texas oil field, an area approximately 40 miles long and five to nine miles wide, split into many small tracts and containing more than 26,000 wells. "Since the oil moves through the entire field," the Court explained, "one operator can not only draw the oil from under his own surface area, but can also, if he is advantageously located, drain oil from the most distant parts of the reservoir." It was important, therefore, for the oil field to be regulated as a unit and for a single regulatory agency to handle the complex problems of apportionment. That task had been assigned to the Texas Railroad Commission. The Court examined the state interests in efficient regulation and concluded:

> To prevent the confusion of multiple review of the same general issues, the legislature provided for concentration of all direct

review of the commission's orders in the state district courts of Travis County. [Yet the] very "confusion" which the Texas legislature . . . feared might result from review by many state courts of the Railroad Commission's orders has resulted from the exercise of federal equity jurisdiction. As a practical matter, the federal courts can make small contribution to the well organized system of regulation and review which the Texas statutes provide. Texas courts can give fully as great relief . . . as the federal courts. Delay, misunderstanding of local law, and needless federal conflict with the state policy, are the most inevitable product of this double system of review. [F]ederal court decisions on state law have created a constant task for the Texas Governor, the Texas legislature, and the Railroad Commission. . . . Special sessions of the legislature have been occupied with consideration of federal court decisions. . . . The instant case [raises] a number of problems of no general significance on which a federal court can only try to ascertain state law. . . . These questions of regulation of the industry by the state administrative agency . . . so clearly [involve] basic problems of Texas policy that equitable discretion should be exercised to give the Texas courts the first opportunity to consider them. . . .

The state provides a unified method for the formation of policy and determination of cases by the commission and by the state courts. The judicial review of the commission's decisions in the state courts is expeditious and adequate. Conflicts in the interpretation of state law, dangerous to the success of state policies, are almost certain to result from the intervention of lower federal courts. On the other hand, if the state procedure is followed from the commission to the state supreme court, ultimate review of the federal questions is [fully preserved here.] Under such circumstances, a sound respect for the independence of state action requires the federal equity court to stay its hand.

Abstention under *Burford* has not been widely invoked, and there has been little Supreme Court discussion of its meaning.[a] Another case frequently associated with *Burford* abstention is Alabama Public Service Comm'n v. Southern Ry. Co., 341 U.S. 341 (1951). In that case, also based on diversity jurisdiction and a federal constitutional claim, the federal court was asked to enjoin the Commission's refusal to permit discontinuance of two local trains. The Court, again over a vigorous dissent by Justice Frankfurter, held that the suit should have been dismissed. The regulation of local train service, Chief Justice Vinson said, is "primarily the concern of the state." As in *Burford,* review of commission decisions was concentrated in a single state entity. The Chief Justice characterized the case as involving an

---

    [a] For a rare exception, see New Orleans Public Service, Inc. v. Council of City of New Orleans, 491 U.S. 350 (1989), considered in the Notes on the Application of *Younger* to Civil Proceedings in Section 2 of this Chapter. The Court held that *Burford* abstention was not appropriate primarily because the federal court's preemption inquiry "would not unduly intrude into the processes of state government or undermine the state's ability to maintain desired uniformity" in a rate-making context.

"essentially local problem" and concluded that "[a]s adequate state court review of an administrative order based upon predominantly local factors is available . . . , intervention of a federal court is not necessary for the protection of federal rights."[b]

2.   A CONFUSING INTERLUDE

Two decisions rendered on the same day led to considerable confusion about the obligation of federal courts to hear diversity cases. Seven Justices thought the cases indistinguishable, though they disagreed on whether abstention was appropriate. Two justices thought abstention warranted in one case but not the other.

(i)   *Mashuda*

In Allegheny County v. Frank Mashuda Co., 360 U.S. 185 (1959), Mashuda's land had been taken by the county for the purpose of improving and enlarging the Pittsburgh airport. Mashuda was awarded compensation under the applicable state procedure, and both parties appealed the award to the appropriate state court. Mashuda then learned that the land had been leased to a corporation, allegedly for its private business use. Under state law, private property could not be taken for private use under eminent domain. While the appeal in the condemnation proceeding was still pending, Mashuda filed a diversity action in federal court against the county and the corporation, seeking damages and their ouster from the land. The District Court dismissed the suit on the ground that it should not interfere with the ongoing condemnation proceedings. The Court of Appeals reversed, noting that the validity of the taking could not be challenged in the compensation proceeding and that, since an independent suit was required in any event, the federal diversity action should proceed. The Supreme Court granted certiorari and affirmed.

Speaking for the Court, Justice Brennan said that abstention was "an extraordinary and narrow exception to the duty of a district court to adjudicate a controversy properly before it," justified "only in the exceptional circumstances where the order to the parties to repair to the state court would clearly serve an important countervailing interest." There was no such interest here. The case involved the resolution of a question of fact under settled state law and could not have been brought as part of the original condemnation proceedings. Moreover, federal courts routinely hear eminent

---

[b]   See also Prentis v. Atlantic Coast Line Co., 211 U.S. 210 (1908), where the Supreme Court held that a federal court should have refused to review a rate order of the Virginia State Corporation Commission because that body was acting in a legislative capacity and review by the Virginia Supreme Court of Appeals should have been sought first. Review in the Virginia court, which was available as of right, was regarded as a continuation of the legislative process because of the powers of revision which that court had been given. The Court explicitly said that—since the Virginia court would act in a legislative capacity—no res judicata effect should be given to its decision in the event of a subsequent federal suit.

The *Prentis* doctrine is analogous to exhaustion of administrative remedies. In effect, because of its power to revise the agency order, the Virginia court was a part of the state's administrative process.

domain proceedings under the diversity jurisdiction. *Burford* was not applicable, and there was no unusual likelihood of federal-state friction that would follow from district court resolution of the case.

(ii) *Thibodaux*

Though *Mashuda* seemed fairly straightforward, four Justices dissented. These four joined with two members of the *Mashuda* majority to approve abstention in Louisiana Power & Light Co. v. City of Thibodaux, 360 U.S. 25 (1959).[c]

The city filed a condemnation proceeding in a state court. The power company removed the case to federal court, invoking diversity jurisdiction. After a pre-trial conference, the District Court, on its own motion, stayed the case pending institution of a declaratory judgment proceeding in state court to determine whether the city had the power to make the kind of expropriation involved. If the state courts upheld the action, the case would return to federal court for assessment of the compensation.

The city then appealed the District Court's decision. The corporation—the party that had removed the case to federal court in the first place—supported the District Court's decision to defer to additional state proceedings. The Court of Appeals reversed, holding the stay inappropriate. The corporation then successfully obtained certiorari in the Supreme Court, arguing that the stay order was proper. A majority of the Court agreed, and the case was remanded to await the outcome of a state suit.

In an opinion by Justice Frankfurter, the Court argued that the differences between eminent domain proceedings and ordinary diversity litigation were "relevant and important." Eminent domain cases are of a "special and peculiar nature" that are "intimately involved with sovereign prerogative." This was especially true in this case, where the city's power to condemn was challenged. At stake was "the apportionment of governmental powers between city and state." Avoiding "the hazards of serious disruption by federal courts of state government" and "needless friction between state and federal authorities" justified deference to the state courts, particularly since the issues of state law were unclear. The district judge was "[c]aught between the language of an old but uninterpreted statute [that appeared to authorize the taking] and the pronouncement of the attorney general [which in an analogous case ruled that the city did not have the claimed power]." The judge "was thus exercising a fair and well-considered judicial discretion" in staying the proceedings pending resolution of the question by the state supreme court.

The Court did not mention *Mashuda*. Among those who voted for abstention, only Justice Stewart spoke to the difference between the two cases. He said:

---

[c] Specifically, the *Mashuda* majority was composed of Chief Justice Warren and Justices Brennan, Douglas, Stewart, and Whittaker. The dissenters in *Mashuda* were Justices Clark, Frankfurter, Black, and Harlan. Stewart and Whittaker joined the *Mashuda* dissenters in voting for abstention in *Thibodaux*.

In a conscientious effort to do justice the District Court deferred immediate adjudication of this controversy pending authoritative clarification of a controlling state statute of highly doubtful meaning. Under the circumstances presented, I think the course pursued was clearly within the District Court's allowable discretion. For that reason I concur in the judgment.

This case is totally unlike *Mashuda* . . . except for the coincidence that both cases involve eminent domain proceedings. In *Mashuda* the Court holds that it was error for the District Court to dismiss the complaint. The Court further holds in that case that, since the controlling state law is clear and only factual issues need be resolved, there is no occasion in the interest of justice to refrain from prompt adjudication.

Justice Brennan dissented at length. He focused in part on the alignment of the parties:

[T]he state of Louisiana, represented by its constituent organ the city of Thibodaux, urges the District Court to adjudicate the state law issue. How, conceivably, can the Court justify the abdication of responsibility to exercise jurisdiction on the ground of avoiding interference and conflict with the state when the state itself desires the federal court's adjudication? It is obvious that the abstention in this case was for the convenience of the District Court, not for the state. . . . The Power and Light Company, which escaped a state court decision by removing the city's action to the District Court, is now wholly content with the sua sponte action of the District Court. This is understandable since the longer decision is put off . . . the longer the Power and Light Company will enjoy the possession of [its property]. Resolution of the legal question of the city's authority, already delayed over two years due to no fault of the city, will be delayed . . . a minimum of two additional years before a decision may be obtained from the state supreme court in the declaratory judgment action. [A]t best the District Court will finally dispose of this case only after prolonged delay and considerable additional expense for the parties. . . . I think it is more than coincidence that both in this case and in *Mashuda* the party supporting abstention is the one presently in possession of the property in question. I cannot escape the conclusion in these cases that delay in the reaching of a decision is more important to those parties than the tribunal which ultimately renders the decision. [T]he Power and Light Company's strategy of delay . . . has succeeded, I dare say, past the fondest expectation of counsel who conceived it.

Can these cases be reconciled? If not, which one is right?

3.   *KAISER STEEL CORP. V. W.S. RANCH CO.*

Kaiser Steel Corp. v. W.S. Ranch Co., 391 U.S. 593 (1968) (per curiam), was a diversity action seeking damages and an injunction for trespass. Kaiser had entered the plaintiff's land to use water under the authority of a New

Mexico statute. The plaintiff claimed that the statute, if construed to permit Kaiser's action, would violate the New Mexico Constitution, which permitted the taking of private property only for a public use. The District Court and the Court of Appeals disagreed on the merits, but both courts agreed that the action should not be stayed pending resolution of the state constitutional issue by the state courts. The Supreme Court summarily reversed, explaining its rationale in a single paragraph:

> The Court of Appeals erred in refusing to stay its hand. The state law issue which is crucial in this case is one of vital concern to the arid state of New Mexico, where water is one of the most valuable natural resources. The issue, moreover, is a truly novel one. The question will eventually have to be resolved by the New Mexico courts, and since a declaratory judgment action is actually pending there, in all likelihood that resolution will be forthcoming soon. Sound judicial administration requires that the parties in this case be given the benefit of the same rule of law which will apply to all other businesses and landowners concerned with the use of this vital state resource.

No cases were cited. The Court remanded "with directions that the action be stayed. . . . Federal jurisdiction will be retained in the District Court in order to insure a just disposition of this litigation should anything prevent a prompt state court determination."

What is the rationale for the result in *Kaiser*? Does it follow from *Burford*? From *Mashuda* and *Thibodaux*?

4. *QUACKENBUSH V. ALLSTATE INS. CO.*

Quackenbush was the insurance commissioner of California and was appointed trustee to gather the assets of an insolvent company. In Quackenbush v. Allstate Insurance Company, 517 U.S. 706 (1996), he sued Allstate in state court seeking contract and tort damages for breach of various reinsurance agreements and a declaratory judgment of Allstate's obligations under those agreements. Allstate removed to federal court on grounds of diversity and moved to compel arbitration. Quackenbush sought a remand to state court based on *Burford*, arguing that federal court resolution of the case would interfere with California's regulation of the insolvency at issue. In particular, he argued that Allstate would seek to set off its own contract claims against the insolvent company and that its right to do so involved a disputed question of state law that should be resolved by state courts. In fact, this question was pending in state court in another case arising out of the same insolvency.

The District Court remanded the case to state court, but the Circuit Court vacated the remand and ordered arbitration. The Supreme Court unanimously affirmed. The Court, in an opinion by Justice O'Connor, summarized the cases discussed in the preceding notes as follows:

> We have . . . held that in cases where the relief being sought is equitable in nature or otherwise discretionary, federal courts not only have the power to stay the action based on abstention principles,

but can also, in otherwise appropriate circumstances, decline to exercise jurisdiction altogether by either dismissing the suit or remanding it to state court. By contrast, while we have held that federal courts may stay actions for damages based on abstention principles, we have not held that those principles support the outright dismissal or remand of damages actions.

As to this case, the Court concluded:

> *Burford* might support a federal court's decision to postpone adjudication of a damages action pending the resolution by the state courts of a disputed question of state law. For example, given the situation the District Court faced in this case, a stay order might have been appropriate: The setoff issue was being decided by the state courts at the time the District Court ruled, and in the interest of avoiding inconsistent adjudications on that point, the District Court might have been justified in entering a stay to await the outcome of the state court litigation.

> . . . Under our precedents, federal courts have the power to dismiss or remand cases based on abstention principles only where the relief being sought is equitable or otherwise discretionary. Because this was a damages action, we conclude that the District Court's remand order was an unwarranted application of the *Burford* doctrine.[d]

Justice Kennedy concurred, observing that "[w]e ought not rule out, though, the possibility that a federal court might dismiss a suit for damages in a case where a serious affront to the interests of federalism could be averted in no other way. We need not reach that question here." Justice Scalia answered that he "would not have joined today's opinion if [he] believed it left such discretionary dismissal available."

5.　BIBLIOGRAPHY

For a sample of the literature related to the topics considered above, see Randall P. Bezanson, Abstention: The Supreme Court and Allocation of Judicial Power, 27 Vand. L. Rev. 1107 (1974); Julie Davies, *Pullman* and *Burford* Abstention: Clarifying the Roles of State and Federal Courts in Constitutional Cases, 20 U.C. Davis L. Rev. 1 (1986); Michael Wells, The Role of Comity in the Law of Federal Courts, 60 N.C. L. Rev. 59 (1981); Ann Woolhandler and Michael G. Collins, Judicial Federalism and the Administrative

---

[d]　The Court added that it had "recognized that federal courts have discretion to dismiss damages actions, in certain narrow circumstances, under the common law doctrine of forum non conveniens." It explained:

> But our abstention doctrine is of a distinct historical pedigree, and the traditional considerations behind dismissal for forum non conveniens differ markedly from those informing the decision to abstain. Federal courts abstain out of deference to the paramount interests of another sovereign, and the concern is with principles of comity and federalism. Dismissal for forum non conveniens, by contrast, has historically reflected a far broader range of considerations, most notably the convenience to the parties and the practical difficulties that can attend the adjudication of a dispute in a certain locality.—[Footnote by eds.]

States, 87 Calif. L. Rev. 613 (1999); Gordon G. Young, Federal Court Abstention and State Administrative Law from *Burford* to *Ankenbrandt*: Fifty Years of Judicial Federalism under *Burford v. Sun Oil Co.* and Kindred Doctrines, 42 Depaul L. Rev. 859 (1993); and Donald Zeigler, Rights Require Remedies: A New Approach to the Enforcement of Rights in the Federal Courts, 38 Hastings L.J. 665 (1987).

SECTION 5. CONCURRENT LITIGATION

Colorado River Water Conservation District v. United States

Supreme Court of the United States, 1976.
424 U.S. 800.

■ MR. JUSTICE BRENNAN delivered the opinion of the Court.

The McCarran Amendment, 43 U.S.C. § 666, provides that consent is hereby given to join the United States as a defendant in any suit

(1) for the adjudication of rights to the use of water of a river system or other source, or

(2) for the administration of such rights, where it appears that the United States is the owner of or is in the process of acquiring water rights by appropriation under State law, by purchase, by exchange, or otherwise, and the United States is a necessary party to such suit.

The questions presented by this case concern the effect of the McCarran Amendment upon the jurisdiction of the federal district courts under 28 U.S.C. § 1345 over suits for determination of water rights brought by the United States as trustee for certain Indian tribes and as owner of various non-Indian government claims.[1]

I

It is probable that no problem of the southwest section of the nation is more critical than that of scarcity of water. As southwestern populations have grown, conflicting claims to this scarce resource have increased. To meet these claims, several southwestern states have established elaborate procedures for allocation of water and adjudication of conflicting claims to that resource. In 1969, Colorado enacted its Water Rights Determination and Administration Act in an effort to revamp its legal procedures for determining claims to water within the state.

Under the Colorado act, the state is divided into seven water divisions, each division encompassing one or more entire drainage basins for

---

[1] ... Title 28 U.S.C. § 1345 provides: "Except as otherwise provided by Act of Congress, the district courts shall have original jurisdiction of all civil actions, suits or proceedings commenced by the United States, or by any agency or officer thereof expressly authorized to sue by Act of Congress."

the larger rivers in Colorado. Adjudication of water claims within each division occurs on a continuous basis. Each month, water referees in each division rule on applications for water rights filed within the preceding five months or refer those applications to the water judge of their division. Every six months, the water judge passes on referred applications and contested decisions by referees. A state engineer and engineers for each division are responsible for the administration and distribution of the waters of the state according to the determinations in each division.

Colorado applies the doctrine of prior appropriation in establishing rights to the use of water. Under that doctrine, one acquires a right to water by diverting it from its natural source and applying it to some beneficial use. Continued beneficial use of the water is required in order to maintain the right. In periods of shortage, priority among confirmed rights is determined according to the date of initial diversion.

The reserved rights of the United States extend to Indian reservations, and other federal lands, such as national parks and forests. The reserved rights claimed by the United States in this case affect waters within Colorado Water Division No. 7. On November 14, 1972, the government instituted this suit in the United States District Court for the District of Colorado, invoking the court's jurisdiction under 28 U.S.C. § 1345. The District Court is located in Denver, some 300 miles from Division 7. The suit, against some 1,000 water users, sought declaration of the government's rights to waters in certain rivers and their tributaries located in Division 7. In the suit, the government asserted reserved rights on its own behalf and on behalf of certain Indian tribes, as well as rights based on state law. It sought appointment of a water master to administer any waters decreed to the United States. Prior to institution of this suit, the government had pursued adjudication of non-Indian reserved rights and other water claims based on state law in Water Divisions 4, 5, and 6, and the government continues to participate fully in those divisions.

Shortly after the federal suit was commenced, one of the defendants in that suit filed an application in the state court for Division 7, seeking an order directing service of process on the United States in order to make it a party to proceedings in Division 7 for the purpose of adjudicating all of the government's claims, both state and federal. On January 3, 1973, the United States was served pursuant to authority of the McCarran Amendment. Several defendants and intervenors in the federal proceeding then filed a motion in the District Court to dismiss on the ground that under the amendment, the court was without jurisdiction to determine federal water rights. Without deciding the jurisdictional question, the District Court, on June 21, 1973, granted the motion in an unreported oral opinion stating that the doctrine of abstention required deference to the proceedings in Division 7. On appeal, the Court of Appeals for the Tenth Circuit reversed, holding that the suit of the United States was within district court jurisdiction under 28 U.S.C. § 1345, and that abstention was inappropriate. We granted certiorari to consider the important questions of whether the McCarran Amendment terminated jurisdiction of federal courts to adjudicate federal water rights and whether, if that jurisdiction was not terminated, the District Court's dismissal in this case was nevertheless appropriate. We reverse.

II

We first consider the question of district court jurisdiction under 28 U.S.C. § 1345. That section provides that the district courts shall have original jurisdiction over all civil actions brought by the federal government "[e]xcept as otherwise provided by Act of Congress." It is thus necessary to examine whether the McCarran Amendment is such an act of Congress excepting jurisdiction under § 1345. . . .

In view of the McCarran Amendment's language and legislative history, controlling principles of statutory construction require the conclusion that the amendment did not constitute an exception "provided by Act of Congress" that repealed the jurisdiction of district courts under § 1345 to entertain federal water suits. . . . Not only do the terms and legislative history of the McCarran Amendment not indicate an intent to repeal § 1345, but also there is no irreconcilability in the operation of both statutes. The immediate effect of the amendment is to give consent to jurisdiction in the state courts concurrent with jurisdiction in the federal courts over controversies involving federal rights to the use of water. There is no irreconcilability in the existence of concurrent state and federal jurisdiction. Such concurrency has, for example, long existed under federal diversity jurisdiction. Accordingly, we hold that the McCarran Amendment in no way diminished federal district court jurisdiction under § 1345 and that the District Court had jurisdiction to hear this case.[15]

III

We turn next to the question whether this suit nevertheless was properly dismissed in view of the concurrent state proceedings in Division 7.

A

First, we consider whether the McCarran Amendment provided consent to determine federal reserved rights held on behalf of Indians in state court. [G]iven the claims for Indian water rights in this case, dismissal clearly would have been inappropriate if the state court had no jurisdiction to decide those claims. We conclude that the state court had jurisdiction over Indian water rights under the amendment. . . .

---

[15] The District Court also would have had jurisdiction of this suit under the general federal question jurisdiction of 28 U.S.C. § 1331. For the same reasons, the McCarran Amendment did not affect jurisdiction under § 1331 either.

B

Next, we consider whether the District Court's dismissal was appropriate under the doctrine of abstention. We hold that the dismissal cannot be supported under that doctrine in any of its forms.

[Abstention from the exercise of federal jurisdiction is the exception, not the rule.] "The doctrine of abstention, under which a district court may decline to exercise or postpone the exercise of its jurisdiction, is an extraordinary and narrow exception to the duty of a district court to adjudicate a controversy properly before it. Abdication of the obligation to decide cases can be justified under this doctrine only in the exceptional circumstances where the order to the parties to repair to the state court would clearly serve an important countervailing interest." County of Allegheny v. Frank Mashuda Co., 360 U.S. 185, 188–89 (1959). "[I]t was never a doctrine of equity that a federal court should exercise its judicial discretion to dismiss a suit merely because a state court could entertain it." Alabama Pub. Serv. Comm'n v. Southern R. Co., 341 U.S. 341, 361 (1951) (Frankfurter, J., concurring in result). Our decisions have confined the circumstances appropriate for abstention to three general categories.

(a) Abstention is appropriate "in cases presenting a federal constitutional issue which might be mooted or presented in a different posture by a state court determination of pertinent state law." County of Allegheny v. Frank Mashuda Co., 360 U.S. at 189. See, e.g., Railroad Comm'n of Texas v. Pullman Co., 312 U.S. 496 (1941). This case, however, presents no federal constitutional issue for decision.

(b) Abstention is also appropriate where there have been presented difficult questions of state law bearing on policy problems of substantial public import whose importance transcends the result in the case then at bar. Louisiana Power & Light Co. v. City of Thibodaux, 360 U.S. 25 (1959), for example, involved such a question. In particular, the concern there was with the scope of the eminent domain power of municipalities under state law. See also Kaiser Steel Corp. v. W.S. Ranch Co., 391 U.S. 593 (1968). In some cases, however, the state question itself need not be determinative of state policy. It is enough that exercise of federal review of the question in a case and in similar cases would be disruptive of state efforts to establish a coherent policy with respect to a matter of substantial public concern. In Burford v. Sun Oil Co., 319 U.S. 315 (1943), for example, the Court held that a suit seeking review of the reasonableness under Texas state law of a state commission's permit to drill oil wells should have been dismissed by the District Court. The reasonableness of the permit in that case was not of transcendent importance, but review of reasonableness by the federal courts in that and future cases, where the state had established its own elaborate review system for dealing with the geological complexities of oil and gas fields, would have had an impermissibly disruptive effect on state policy for the management of those fields. See also *Alabama Pub. Serv. Comm'n v. Southern R. Co.*[21]

The present case clearly does not fall within this second category of abstention. While state claims are involved in the case, the state law to be applied appears to be settled. No questions bearing on state policy are presented for decision. Nor will decision of the state claims impair efforts to implement state policy as in *Burford*. To be sure, the federal claims that are involved in the case go to the establishment of water rights which may conflict with similar rights based on state law. But the mere potential for conflict in the results of adjudications, does not, without more, warrant staying exercise of federal jurisdiction. See Meredith v. Winter Haven, 320 U.S. 228 (1943); Kline v. Burke Constr. Co., 260 U.S. 226 (1922); McClellan v. Carland, 217 U.S. 268 (1910). The potential conflict here, involving state claims and federal claims, would not be such as to impair impermissibly the state's effort to effect its policy respecting the allocation of state waters. . . .

(c)   Finally, abstention is appropriate where, absent bad faith, harassment, or a patently invalid state statute, federal jurisdiction has been invoked for the purpose of restraining state criminal proceedings, *Younger v. Harris*, 401 U.S. 37 (1971); Douglas v. City of Jeannette, 319 U.S. 157 (1943); state nuisance proceedings antecedent to a criminal prosecution, which are directed at obtaining the closure of places exhibiting obscene films, Huffman v. Pursue, Ltd., 420 U.S. 592 (1975); or collections of state taxes, Great Lakes Dredge & Dock Co. v. Huffman, 319 U.S. 293 (1943). Like the previous two categories, this category also does not include this case. We deal here neither with a criminal proceeding, nor such a nuisance proceeding, nor a tax collection. We also do not deal with an attempt to restrain such actions or to seek a declaratory judgment as to the validity of a state criminal law under which criminal proceedings are pending in a state court.

C

Although this case falls within none of the abstention categories, there are principles unrelated to considerations of proper constitutional adjudication and regard for federal-state relations which govern in situations involving the contemporaneous exercise of concurrent jurisdictions, either by federal courts or by state and federal courts. These principles rest on considerations of "[w]ise judicial administration, giving

---

[21] We note that *Burford v. Sun Oil Co.* and *Alabama Pub. Serv. Comm'n v. Southern R. Co.* differ from *Louisiana Power & Light Co. v. City of Thibodaux* and *County of Allegheny v. Frank Mashuda Co.* in that the former two cases, unlike the latter two, raised colorable constitutional claims and were therefore brought under federal question, as well as diversity, jurisdiction. While abstention in *Burford* and *Alabama Pub. Serv.* had the effect of avoiding a federal constitutional issue, the opinions indicate that this was not an additional ground for abstention in those cases. We have held, of course, that the opportunity to avoid decision of a constitutional question does not alone justify abstention by a federal court. . . . Indeed, the presence of a federal basis for jurisdiction may raise the level of justification needed for abstention.

regard to conservation of judicial resources and comprehensive disposition of litigation." Kerotest Mfg. Co. v. C-O-Two Fire Equipment Co., 342 U.S. 180, 183 (1952). Generally, as between state and federal courts, the rule is that "the pendency of an action in the state court is no bar to proceedings concerning the same matter in the federal court having jurisdiction. . . ." *McClellan*, 217 U.S. at 282. As between federal district courts, however, though no precise rule has evolved, the general principle is to avoid duplicative litigation. See *Kerotest Mfg. Co. v. C-O-Two Fire Equipment Co.* This difference in general approach between state-federal concurrent jurisdiction and wholly federal concurrent jurisdiction stems from the virtually unflagging obligation of the federal courts to exercise the jurisdiction given them. Given this obligation, and the absence of weightier considerations of constitutional adjudication and state-federal relations, the circumstances permitting the dismissal of a federal suit due to the presence of a concurrent state proceeding for reasons of wise judicial administration are considerably more limited than the circumstances appropriate for abstention. The former circumstances, though exceptional, do nevertheless exist.

It has been held, for example, that the court first assuming jurisdiction over property may exercise that jurisdiction to the exclusion of other courts. This has been true even where the government was a claimant in existing state proceedings and then sought to invoke district court jurisdiction under the jurisdictional provision antecedent to 28 U.S.C. § 1345. In assessing the appropriateness of dismissal in the event of an exercise of concurrent jurisdiction, a federal court may also consider such factors as the inconvenience of the federal forum; the desirability of avoiding piecemeal litigation; and the order in which jurisdiction was obtained by the concurrent forums. No one factor is necessarily determinative; a carefully considered judgment taking into account both the obligation to exercise jurisdiction and the combination of factors counseling against that exercise is required. Only the clearest of justifications will warrant dismissal.

Turning to the present case, a number of factors clearly counsel against concurrent federal proceedings. The most important of these is the McCarran Amendment itself. The clear federal policy evinced by that legislation is the avoidance of piecemeal adjudication of water rights in a river system. This policy is akin to that underlying the rule requiring that jurisdiction be yielded to the court first acquiring control of property, for the concern in such instances is with avoiding the generation of additional litigation through permitting inconsistent dispositions of property. This concern is heightened with respect to water rights, the relationships among which are highly interdependent. Indeed, we have recognized that actions seeking the allocation of water essentially involve the disposition of property and are best conducted in unified proceedings. The consent to jurisdiction given by the McCarran Amendment bespeaks a policy that recognizes the availability of comprehensive state systems for adjudication of water rights as the means for achieving these goals.

As has already been observed, the Colorado Water Rights Determination and Administration Act established such a system for the adjudication and management of rights to the use of the state's waters. As the government concedes . . . , the act established a single continuous proceeding for water rights adjudication which antedated the suit in District Court. . . . Additionally, the responsibility of managing the state's waters, to the end that they be allocated in accordance with adjudicated water rights, is given to the state engineer.

Beyond the congressional policy expressed by the McCarran Amendment and consistent with furtherance of that policy, we also find significant (a) the apparent absence of any proceedings in the District Court, other than the filing of the complaint, prior to the motion to dismiss, (b) the extensive involvement of state water rights occasioned by this suit naming 1,000 defendants, (c) the 300-mile distance between the District Court in Denver and the court in Division 7, and (d) the existing participation by the government in Divisions 4, 5, and 6 proceedings. We emphasize, however, that we do not overlook the heavy obligation to exercise jurisdiction. We need not decide, for example, whether, despite the McCarran Amendment, dismissal would be warranted if more extensive proceedings had occurred in the District Court prior to dismissal, if the involvement of state water rights were less extensive than it is here, or if the state proceeding were in some respect inadequate to resolve the federal claims. But the opposing factors here, particularly the policy underlying the McCarran Amendment, justify the District Court's dismissal in this particular case.[26]

The judgment of the Court of Appeals is reversed and the judgment of the District Court dismissing the complaint is affirmed for the reasons here stated.

It is so ordered.

■ MR. JUSTICE STEWART, with whom Mr. Justice Blackmun and MR. JUSTICE STEVENS concur, dissenting.

The Court says that the United States District Court for the District of Colorado clearly had jurisdiction over this lawsuit. I agree. The Court further says that the McCarran Amendment "in no way diminished" the District Court's jurisdiction. I agree. The Court also says that federal courts have a "virtually unflagging obligation . . . to exercise the jurisdiction given them." I agree. And finally, the Court says that nothing in the abstention doctrine "in any of its forms" justified the District Court's dismissal of the Government's complaint. I agree. These views would seem to lead ineluctably to the conclusion that the District Court was wrong in

---

[26] Whether similar considerations would permit dismissal of a water suit brought by a private party in federal district court is a question we need not now decide.

dismissing the complaint. Yet the Court holds that the order of dismissal was "appropriate." With that conclusion I must respectfully disagree.

In holding that the United States shall not be allowed to proceed with its lawsuit, the Court relies principally on cases reflecting the rule that where "control of the property which is the subject of the suit [is necessary] in order to proceed with the cause and to grant the relief sought, the jurisdiction of one court must of necessity yield to that of the other." Penn General Casualty Co. v. Pennsylvania ex rel. Schnader, 294 U.S. 189, 195 (1935). But, as [*Penn General* and similar cases] make clear, this rule applies only when exclusive control over the subject matter is necessary to effectuate a court's judgment. Here the federal court did not need to obtain in rem or quasi in rem jurisdiction in order to decide the issues before it. The court was asked simply to determine as a matter of federal law whether federal reservations of water rights had occurred, and, if so, the date and scope of the reservations. The District Court could make such a determination without having control of the river. . . .

The Court's principal reason for deciding to close the doors of the federal courthouse to the United States in this case seems to stem from the view that its decision will avoid piecemeal adjudication of water rights.[6] To the extent that this view is based on the special considerations governing in rem proceedings, it is without precedential basis. . . . To the extent that the Court's view is based on the realistic practicalities of this case, it is simply wrong, because the relegation of the government to the state courts will not avoid piecemeal litigation.

The Colorado courts are currently engaged in two types of proceedings under the state's water-rights law. First, they are processing new claims to water based on recent appropriations. Second, they are integrating these new awards of water rights with all past decisions awarding such rights into one all-inclusive tabulation for each water source. The claims of the United States that are involved in this case have not been adjudicated in the past. Yet they do not involve recent appropriations of water. In fact, these claims are wholly dissimilar to

---

[6]   The Court lists four other policy reasons for the "appropriateness" of the District Court's dismissal of this lawsuit. All of those reasons are insubstantial. First, the fact that no significant proceedings had yet taken place in the federal court at the time of the dismissal means no more than that the federal court was prompt in granting the defendants' motion to dismiss. At that time, of course, no proceedings involving the government's claims had taken place in the state court either. Second, the geographic distance of the federal court from the rivers in question is hardly a significant factor in this age of rapid and easy transportation. Since the basic issues here involve the determination of the amount of water the government intended to reserve rather than the amount it actually appropriated on a given date, there is little likelihood that live testimony by water district residents would be necessary. In any event, the federal District Court in Colorado is authorized to sit at Durango, the headquarters of Water Division 7. Third, the government's willingness to participate in some of the state proceedings certainly does not mean that it had no right to bring this action, unless the Court has today unearthed a new kind of waiver. Finally, the fact that there were many defendants in the federal suit is hardly relevant. It only indicates that the federal court had all the necessary parties before it in order to issue a decree finally settling the government's claims. . . .

normal state water claims, because they are not based on actual beneficial use of water but rather on an intention formed at the time the federal land use was established to reserve a certain amount of water to support the federal reservations. The state court will, therefore, have to conduct separate proceedings to determine these claims. And only after the state court adjudicates the claims will they be incorporated into the water source tabulations. If this suit were allowed to proceed in federal court the same procedures would be followed, and the federal court decree would be incorporated into the state tabulation, as other federal court decrees have been incorporated in the past. Thus, the same process will occur regardless of which forum considers these claims. Whether the virtually identical separate proceedings take place in a federal court or a state court, the adjudication of the claims will be neither more nor less "piecemeal." Essentially the same process will be followed in each instance.

Same process will be followed!

As the Court says, it is the virtual "unflagging obligation" of a federal court to exercise the jurisdiction that has been conferred upon it. Obedience to that obligation is particularly "appropriate" in this case, for at least two reasons.

First, the issues involved are issues of federal law. A federal court is more likely than a state court to be familiar with federal water law and to have had experience in interpreting the relevant federal statutes, regulations, and Indian treaties. Moreover, if tried in a federal court, these issues of federal law will be reviewable in a federal appellate court, whereas federal judicial review of the state courts' resolution of issues of federal law will be possible only on review by this Court in the exercise of its certiorari jurisdiction.

Second, some of the federal claims in this lawsuit relate to water reserved for Indian reservations. It is not necessary to determine that there is no state court jurisdiction of these claims to support the proposition that a federal court is a more appropriate forum than a state court for determination of questions of life-and-death importance to Indians. This Court has long recognized that " '[t]he policy of leaving Indians free from state jurisdiction and control is deeply rooted in the Nation's history.' " McClanahan v. Arizona State Tax Comm'n, 411 U.S. 164, 168 (1973), quoting Rice v. Olson, 324 U.S. 786, 789 (1945).

The Court says that "[o]nly the clearest of justifications will warrant dismissal" of a lawsuit within the jurisdiction of a federal court. In my opinion there was no justification at all for the District Court's order of dismissal in this case.

I would affirm the judgment of the Court of Appeals.

■ MR. JUSTICE STEVENS, dissenting.

While I join Mr. Justice Stewart's dissenting opinion, I add three brief comments:

First, I find the holding that the United States may not litigate a federal claim in a federal court having jurisdiction thereof particularly anomalous. I could not join such a disposition unless commanded to do so by an unambiguous statutory mandate or by some other clearly identifiable and applicable rule of law. The McCarran Amendment . . . announces no such rule.

Second, the federal government surely has no lesser right of access to the federal forum than does a private litigant, such as an Indian asserting his own claim. If this be so, today's holding will necessarily restrict the access to federal court of private plaintiffs asserting water rights claims in Colorado. This is a rather surprising byproduct of the McCarran Amendment; for there is no basis for concluding that Congress intended that amendment to impair the private citizen's right to assert a federal claim in a federal court.

Third, even on the Court's assumption that this case should be decided by balancing the factors weighing for and against the exercise of federal jurisdiction, I believe we should defer to the judgment of the Court of Appeals rather than evaluate those factors in the first instance ourselves. In this case the District Court erroneously dismissed the complaint on abstention grounds and the Court of Appeals found no reason why the litigation should not go forward in a federal court. Facts such as the number of parties, the distance between the courthouse and the water in dispute, and the character of the Colorado proceedings are matters which the Court of Appeals sitting in Denver is just as able to evaluate as are we. . . .

NOTES ON CONCURRENT LITIGATION IN STATE AND FEDERAL COURTS

1.   QUESTIONS AND COMMENTS ON *COLORADO RIVER*

Recall the observation in Note 2(ii) of the Introductory Notes to this chapter that "[t]he usual federal rule is that the federal court will proceed to judgment, despite the pendency of the same claim in state court, subject to the application of appropriate res judicata principles if the state proceeding becomes final before the federal suit is concluded." Three clusters of questions about this rule are spawned by *Colorado River*:

First, is it generally correct to require federal courts to continue in personam litigation when the same parties are already litigating the same issues in state court? Would it not be more efficient if the federal judge had discretion to defer to the state proceeding? Indeed, should the rule be that the federal judge is *required* to defer to a pending state proceeding unless there are good reasons not to?

Second, if there is a general obligation to hear the case in spite of the pending state proceeding, when is it appropriate to make an exception to that rule? Should the discretion be limited by the factors recited in *Colorado*

River? Or should district judges have a broader discretion to defer to a pending state proceeding?

Third, if there are to be exceptions, which court should control their administration? Should appellate courts be free to weigh the relevant criteria themselves? Or should "abuse of discretion" be the standard of review?

2. DECLARATORY JUDGMENTS

Federal courts are authorized by 28 U.S.C. §§ 2201 and 2202 to grant declaratory relief in cases of "actual controversy" otherwise within the scope of a jurisdictional statute. These statutes were passed in 1934. Shortly thereafter, the Court made it clear that declaratory relief was discretionary and that one reason for withholding such relief might be that the same issues were already pending in another court. See Brillhart v. Excess Ins. Co. of America, 316 U.S. 491 (1942).

Withhold disc to pending case

The breadth of Justice Frankfurter's opinion in *Brillhart* led to uncertainty about its applicability outside the declaratory judgment context. Speaking for himself and for Justices Stewart, White, and Stevens, Justice Rehnquist expressed the view in Will v. Calvert Fire Ins. Co., 437 U.S. 655 (1978), that federal district courts had much broader discretion to abstain in favor of pending state-court litigation than was recognized in *Colorado River*:

Discretion to abstain much broader that whet we saw in Colorado

> It is well established that "the pendency of an action in the state court is no bar to proceedings concerning the same matter in the federal court having jurisdiction." McClellan v. Carland, 217 U.S. 268, 282 (1910). It is equally well settled that a district court is "under no compulsion to exercise that jurisdiction," Brillhart v. Excess Ins. Co., 316 U.S. 491, 494 (1942), where the controversy may be settled more expeditiously in the state court. Although most of our decisions discussing the propriety of stays or dismissals of duplicative actions have concerned conflicts of jurisdiction between two federal district courts, we have recognized the relevance of these cases [where state and federal courts are involved.] See Colorado River Water Conservation District et al. v. United States, 424 U.S. 800, 817–19 (1976). In both situations, the decision is largely committed to the "carefully considered judgment" of the district court. . . .

> It is true that *Colorado River* emphasized "the virtually unflagging obligation of the federal courts to exercise the jurisdiction given them." That language underscores our conviction that a district court should exercise its discretion with this factor in mind, but it in no way undermines the conclusion of *Brillhart* that the decision whether to defer to the concurrent jurisdiction of a state court is, in the last analysis, a matter committed to the district court's discretion. . . . There are sound reasons for . . . the rule that a district court's decision to defer proceedings because of concurrent state litigation is generally committed to the discretion of that court. No one can seriously contend that a busy federal trial judge confronted both with competing demands on his time for matters

properly within his jurisdiction and with inevitable scheduling difficulties because of the unavailability of lawyers, parties, and witnesses, is not entrusted with a wide latitude in setting his own calendar.

Five Justices disagreed with this position, and in Moses H. Cone Memorial Hospital v. Mercury Constr. Corp., 460 U.S. 1 (1983), the Court confirmed that *Colorado River* stated a narrow exception to the normal obligation of federal district courts to decide cases properly before them. Indeed, the strength of the Court's reaffirmation that *Colorado River* was an exceptional situation led to speculation that even discretion to deny declaratory relief in favor of concurrent state court litigation had been narrowed. This speculation was put to rest in Wilton v. Seven Falls Co., 515 U.S. 277 (1995). In an opinion by Justice O'Connor, a unanimous Court[a] said:

> Relying on these post-*Brillhart* developments, [it is contended] that the *Brillhart* regime, under which district courts have substantial latitude in deciding whether to stay or to dismiss a declaratory judgment suit in light of pending state proceedings (and need not point to "exceptional circumstances" to justify their actions), is an outmoded relic of another era. We disagree. Neither *Colorado River*, which upheld the dismissal of federal proceedings, nor *Moses H. Cone*, which did not, dealt with actions brought under the declaratory judgment act. Distinct features of the declaratory judgment act, we believe, justify a standard vesting district courts with greater discretion in declaratory judgment actions than that permitted under the "exceptional circumstances" test of *Colorado River* and *Moses H. Cone*. . . .

> On its face, the statute provides that a court "*may* declare the rights and other legal relations of any interested party seeking such declaration," 28 U.S.C. § 2201(a). The statute's textual commitment to discretion, and the breadth of leeway we have always understood it to suggest, distinguish the declaratory judgment context from other areas of the law in which concepts of discretion surface. . . . By the declaratory judgment act, Congress . . . created an opportunity, rather than a duty, to grant a new form of relief to qualifying litigants.[2] . . . In the declaratory judgment context, the normal principle that federal courts should adjudicate claims within their jurisdiction yields to considerations of practicality and wise judicial administration. [P]roper application of the abuse of discretion standard on appellate review can, we think, provide appropriate guidance to district courts.

---

[a]   Justice Breyer did not participate.

[2]   We note that where the basis for declining to proceed is the pendency of a state proceeding, a stay will often be the preferable course, insofar as it assures that the federal action can proceed without risk of a time bar if the state case, for any reason, fails to resolve the matter in controversy.

3. BIBLIOGRAPHY

For a considerations of the *Colorado River* issue, see Barry Friedman, A Revisionist Theory of Abstention, 88 Mich. L. Rev. 530 (1989); Michael Gibson, Private Concurrent Litigation in Light of *Younger, Pennzoil,* and *Colorado River*, 14 Okla. City L. Rev. 185 (1989); Linda Mullenix, A Branch Too Far: Pruning the Abstention Doctrine, 75 Geo. L.J. 99 (1986); David Shapiro, Jurisdiction and Discretion, 60 N.Y.U. L. Rev. 543 (1985); and David A. Sonenshein, Abstention: The Crooked Course of *Colorado River,* 59 Tulane L. Rev. 651 (1985).

NOTES ON THE *ROOKER-FELDMAN* DOCTRINE

1. THE *ROOKER-FELDMAN* DOCTRINE

A different dimension of the problem of multiple litigation in state and federal courts was dealt with in a pair of cases decided 60 years apart. In Rooker v. Fidelity Trust Co., 263 U.S. 413 (1923), and District of Columbia Court of Appeals v. Feldman, 460 U.S. 462 (1983), the Court gave birth to a doctrine that it confined to a narrow role in Exxon Mobil Corporation v. Saudi Basic Industries Corporation, 544 U.S. 280 (2005), and Lance v. Dennis, 546 U.S. 459 (2006). In *Lance*, the Court described *Rooker* and *Feldman* as follows:

> In *Rooker,* a party who had lost in the Indiana Supreme Court, and failed to obtain review in this Court, filed an action in federal district court challenging the constitutionality of the state-court judgment. We viewed the action as tantamount to an appeal of the Indiana Supreme Court decision, over which only this Court had jurisdiction, and said that the "aggrieved litigant cannot be permitted to do indirectly what he no longer can do directly." *Feldman,* decided 60 years later, concerned slightly different circumstances, with similar results. The plaintiffs there had been refused admission to the District of Columbia bar by the District of Columbia Court of Appeals, and sought review of these decisions in federal district court. Our decision held that to the extent plaintiffs challenged the Court of Appeals decisions themselves—as opposed to the bar admission rules promulgated nonjudicially by the Court of Appeals—their sole avenue of review was with this Court.[a]

---

[a] The doctrine derived from these cases was the subject of a Symposium in the Notre Dame Law Review. See Thomas D. Rowe, Jr., *Rooker-Feldman*: Worth Only the Powder to Blow It Up?, 74 Notre Dame L. Rev. 1081 (1999); Suzanna Sherry, Judicial Federalism in the Trenches: The *Rooker-Feldman* Doctrine in Action, 74 Notre Dame L. Rev. 1085 (1999); Barry Friedman and James E. Gaylord, *Rooker-Feldman*, From the Ground Up, 74 Notre Dame L. Rev. 1129 (1999); Susan Bandes, The *Rooker-Feldman* Doctrine: Evaluating Its Jurisdictional Status, 74 Notre Dame L. Rev. 1175 (1999); Jack M. Beermann, Comments on *Rooker-Feldman* or Let State Law Be Our Guide, 74 Notre Dame L. Rev. 1209 (1999). The doctrine was revisited after *Exxon Mobil* and *Lance* in Dustin E. Buehler, Revisiting *Rooker-Feldman*: Extending the Doctrine to State Court Interlocutory Orders, 36 Fla. St. U. L. Rev. 373–414 (2009) and Dustin E. Buehler, Jurisdiction, Abstention, and Finality: Articulating a Unique Role for the *Rooker-Feldman* Doctrine, 42 Seton Hall L. Rev. 553 (2012). See also Steven N. Baker, The Fraud Exception to the *Rooker-Feldman* Doctrine: How It Almost Wasn't (and Probably Shouldn't Be), 5 Fed. Cts. L. Rev. 139 (2011).—[Footnote by eds.]

2. *EXXON MOBIL V. SABIC*

Saudi Basic Industries Corporation (SABIC) sued Exxon Mobil in state court seeking a declaratory judgment that certain royalty charges were proper under a joint venture agreement. Two weeks later, Exxon Mobil sued SABIC in federal court alleging that it had been overcharged. In due course, it answered the state court complaint and filed counterclaims in state court asserting the same claims on which it had sued in federal court. The state court proceedings went to judgment first, resulting in a verdict of over $400 million in favor of Exxon Mobil. SABIC appealed to the state Supreme Court. A panel of that court affirmed the state court judgment, and rehearing en banc was denied. The federal action reached the Supreme Court in Exxon Mobil Corp. v. Saudi Basic Industries Corp. 544 U.S. 280 (2005).

Jurisdiction in the concurrent federal court proceedings was based on 28 U.S.C. § 1330, which authorizes federal courts to hear actions against foreign states. Prior to the state court trial, SABIC claimed sovereign immunity and moved to dismiss the federal action. The District Court denied the motion, and SABIC filed an interlocutory appeal.

By the time the Circuit Court heard the appeal, the state court jury had returned its verdict. As described by the Supreme Court, the Circuit Court on its own motion "raised the question whether 'subject matter jurisdiction over this case fails under the *Rooker-Feldman* doctrine because Exxon Mobil's claims have already been litigated in state court.' The court did not question the District Court's possession of subject matter jurisdiction at the outset of the suit, but held that federal jurisdiction terminated when the Delaware Superior Court entered judgment on the jury verdict." The Supreme Court granted certiorari.[b]

Speaking for a unanimous Court, Justice Ginsburg pointed out that "[s]ince *Feldman*, this Court has never applied *Rooker-Feldman* to dismiss an action for want of jurisdiction. The few decisions that have mentioned *Rooker* and *Feldman* have done so only in passing or to explain why those cases did not dictate dismissal." She then discussed the rationale for the doctrine and why it did not apply in this case:

> The *Rooker-Feldman* doctrine, we hold today, is confined to cases of the kind from which the doctrine acquired its name: cases brought by state-court losers complaining of injuries caused by state-court judgments rendered before the district court proceedings commenced and inviting district court review and rejection of those judgments. *Rooker-Feldman* does not otherwise override or supplant preclusion doctrine or augment the circumscribed doctrines that allow federal courts to stay or dismiss proceedings in deference to state-court actions. . . .
>
> *Rooker* and *Feldman* exhibit the limited circumstances in which this Court's appellate jurisdiction over state-court judgments, 28 U.S.C. § 1257, precludes a United States district court

---

[b] At oral argument, SABIC declared its intention to seek certiorari from the Delaware Supreme Court decision upholding the jury verdict, but had not yet done so. The controversy was therefore not moot.

from exercising subject-matter jurisdiction in an action it would otherwise be empowered to adjudicate under a congressional grant of authority. In both cases, the losing party in state court filed suit in federal court after the state proceedings ended, complaining of an injury caused by the state-court judgment and seeking review and rejection of that judgment. Plaintiffs in both cases, alleging federal-question jurisdiction, called upon the District Court to overturn an injurious state-court judgment. Because § 1257, as long interpreted, vests authority to review a state court's judgment solely in this Court, the District Courts in *Rooker* and *Feldman* lacked subject-matter jurisdiction. . . .

When there is parallel state and federal litigation, *Rooker-Feldman* is not triggered simply by the entry of judgment in state court. This Court has repeatedly held that "the pendency of an action in the state court is no bar to proceedings concerning the same matter in the Federal court having jurisdiction." McClellan v. Carland, 217 U.S. 268, 282 (1910). Comity or abstention doctrines may, in various circumstances, permit or require the federal court to stay or dismiss the federal action in favor of the state-court litigation. See, e.g., Colorado River Water Conservation Dist. v. United States, 424 U.S. 800 (1976); Younger v. Harris, 401 U.S. 37 (1971); Burford v. Sun Oil Co., 319 U.S. 315 (1943); Railroad Comm'n of Tex. v. Pullman Co., 312 U.S. 496 (1941). But neither *Rooker* nor *Feldman* supports the notion that properly invoked concurrent jurisdiction vanishes if a state court reaches judgment on the same or related question while the case remains sub judice in a federal court.

Disposition of the federal action, once the state-court adjudication is complete, would be governed by preclusion law. The Full Faith and Credit Act, 28 U.S.C. § 1738, requires the federal court to "give the same preclusive effect to a state-court judgment as another court of that State would give." Parsons Steel, Inc. v. First Alabama Bank, 474 U.S. 518, 523 (1986). Preclusion, of course, is not a jurisdictional matter. In parallel litigation, a federal court may be bound to recognize the claim- and issue-preclusive effects of a state-court judgment, but federal jurisdiction over an action does not terminate automatically on the entry of judgment in the state court.

Nor does § 1257 stop a district court from exercising subject-matter jurisdiction simply because a party attempts to litigate in federal court a matter previously litigated in state court. If a federal plaintiff "present[s] some independent claim, albeit one that denies a legal conclusion that a state court has reached in a case to which he was a party . . . , then there is jurisdiction and state law determines whether the defendant prevails under principles of preclusion." GASH Assocs. v. Village of Rosemont, 995 F.2d 726, 728 (7th Cir. 1993).

. . . Exxon Mobil plainly has not repaired to federal court to undo the Delaware judgment in its favor. Rather, it appears Exxon Mobil filed suit in Federal District Court (only two weeks after SABIC filed in Delaware and well before any judgment in state court) to protect itself in the event it lost in state court on grounds (such as the state statute of limitations) that might not preclude relief in the federal venue.[9] *Rooker-Feldman* did not prevent the District Court from exercising jurisdiction when Exxon Mobil filed the federal action, and it did not emerge to vanquish jurisdiction after Exxon Mobil prevailed in the Delaware courts.

3.   *LANCE V. DENNIS*

Lance concerned redistricting in Colorado after the state gained a seat in the House of Representatives following the 2000 census. The legislature failed to enact a redistricting plan to govern the 2002 elections. The elections were eventually held under a court-ordered plan that resulted from state-court litigation. Subsequently, the legislature passed a plan in the spring of 2003 to govern future elections. This led to an original action in the Colorado Supreme Court filed by the state Attorney General against the Secretary of State seeking a decree that the court-ordered plan nonetheless must be followed. The legislature intervened as a defendant. The Colorado Supreme Court read the state constitution to require use of the court-ordered plan and ordered the Secretary of State to comply. People ex rel. Salazar v. Davidson, 79 P.3d 1221 (2003).[c]

The litigation at issue in *Lance* was filed in federal court by four Colorado citizens who were unhappy with the result in *Salazar*. They sought use of the legislature's plan on the argument that the provision of the Colorado constitution on which *Salazar* was based violated two clauses of the federal Constitution. The defendant—the Colorado Secretary of State—argued that *Rooker-Feldman* required dismissal, and a three-judge federal District Court agreed. While the plaintiffs in this action were not parties to the prior state court litigation, the District Court held it was enough that they were in privity with parties to that suit.

The plaintiffs appealed to the Supreme Court. In Lance v. Dennis, 546 U.S. 459 (2006) (per curiam), the Court held *Rooker-Feldman* inapplicable:

This Court is vested, under 28 U.S.C. § 1257, with jurisdiction over appeals from final state-court judgments. We have held that this grant of jurisdiction is exclusive: "Review of such judgments may be had *only* in this Court." Accordingly, under what has come to be known as the *Rooker-Feldman* doctrine, lower federal courts are precluded from exercising appellate jurisdiction over final state-court judgments. . . .

---

[9]   The Court of Appeals criticized Exxon Mobil for pursuing its federal suit as an "insurance policy" against an adverse result in state court. There is nothing necessarily inappropriate, however, about filing a protective action.

[c]   Additional litigation seeking a judgment that the court-ordered plan must be used was filed concurrently with the *Salazar* in state court by several proponents of the plan. This suit was removed to federal court and ultimately dismissed based on the resolution in *Salazar*.

In the case before us, plaintiffs were plainly not parties to the underlying state-court proceeding in *Salazar*. *Salazar* was an action brought by the state Attorney General against the Secretary of State, in which the Colorado General Assembly intervened. The four citizen-plaintiffs here did not participate in *Salazar*, and were not in a "position to ask this Court to review the state court's judgment." . . .

Although the District Court recognized the "general rule" that "*Rooker-Feldman* may not be invoked against a federal-court plaintiff who was not actually a party to the prior state-court judgment," it nevertheless followed Tenth Circuit precedent in allowing application of *Rooker-Feldman* against parties who were in privity with a party to the earlier state-court action. In determining whether privity existed, the court looked to cases concerning the preclusive effect that state courts are required to give federal-court judgments. It concluded that—for *Rooker-Feldman* as well as preclusion purposes—"the outcome of the government's litigation over a matter of public concern binds its citizens."

The District Court erroneously conflated preclusion law with *Rooker-Feldman*. Whatever the impact of privity principles on preclusion rules, *Rooker-Feldman* is not simply preclusion by another name. The doctrine applies only in "limited circumstances," *Exxon Mobil*, 544 U.S. at 291, where a party in effect seeks to take an appeal of an unfavorable state-court decision to a lower federal court. The *Rooker-Feldman* doctrine does not bar actions by nonparties to the earlier state-court judgment simply because, for purposes of preclusion law, they could be considered in privity with a party to the judgment.[2]

A more expansive *Rooker-Feldman* rule would tend to supplant Congress's mandate, under the Full Faith and Credit Act, 28 U.S.C. § 1738, that federal courts " 'give the same preclusive effect to state court judgments that those judgments would be given in the courts of the State from which the judgments emerged.' " Baker v. General Motors Corp., 522 U.S. 222, 246. Congress has directed federal courts to look principally to state law in deciding what effect to give state-court judgments. Incorporation of preclusion principles into *Rooker-Feldman* risks turning that limited doctrine into a uniform federal rule governing the preclusive effect of state-court judgments, contrary to the Full Faith and Credit Act.

Justice Stevens dissented. He concluded that the suit should have been dismissed, but not because of *Rooker-Feldman*. One of the federal constitutional claims on which the suit was based was identical to the claim rejected in *Salazar*. As to that issue, "all of the requirements under Colorado law for issue preclusion have been met" because the plaintiffs here were in privity

---

[2] In holding that *Rooker-Feldman* does not bar plaintiffs here from proceeding, we need not address whether there are any circumstances, however limited, in which *Rooker-Feldman* may be applied against a party not named in an earlier state proceeding—e.g., where an estate takes a de facto appeal in a district court of an earlier state decision involving the decedent.

with both the state attorney general and the state legislature. The other federal constitutional claim, Stevens thought, was frivolous and therefore correctly dismissed "because it fails to state a claim on which relief may be granted." As to *Rooker-Feldman*, Stevens pulled no punches:

> *Rooker* and *Feldman* are strange bedfellows. *Rooker,* a unanimous, three-page opinion written by Justice Van Devanter in 1923, correctly applied the simple legal proposition that only this Court may exercise appellate jurisdiction over state-court judgments. *Feldman,* a nonunanimous, 25-page opinion written by Justice Brennan in 1983, was incorrectly decided and generated a plethora of confusion and debate among scholars and judges.[d] Last Term, in Justice Ginsburg's lucid opinion in *Exxon Mobil Corp.*, the Court finally interred the so-called "*Rooker-Feldman* doctrine." And today, the Court quite properly disapproves of the District Court's resuscitation of a doctrine that has produced nothing but mischief for 23 years.[e]

Joined by Justice Souter, Justice Ginsburg concurred. She agreed "in full" with the Court's disposition of the *Rooker-Feldman* issue. She noted the persuasiveness of Justice Stevens's issue preclusion argument, but thought that question best resolved by the District Court on remand.

SECTION 6. INTERNATIONAL COMITY ABSTENTION

Royal and Sun Alliance Ins. Co. of Canada v. Century International Arms, Inc.

U.S. Court of Appeals for the Second Circuit, 2006.
466 F.3d 88.

■ Before MCLAUGHLIN and CALABRESI, CIRCUIT JUDGES, and LYNCH, DISTRICT JUDGE [sitting by designation].

■ GERALD E. LYNCH, DISTRICT JUDGE. . . .

Century America is in the business of manufacturing and distributing firearms and munitions. In connection with that business, Century America and its affiliate Century Canada obtained liability insurance policies from Royal and Sun Alliance Insurance Company of Canada ("RSA") for the time period between June 12, 1991, and March 25, 1994. During the policy period, Century America was sued by a number of individuals who alleged that they had suffered injuries caused by defects in Century America's products. RSA defended these lawsuits pursuant to

---

d   Stevens dissented in *Feldman.*—[Footnote by eds.]

e   In another case decided the same Term, Justice Stevens wrote separately to "explain why I do not believe there is any 'probate exception' that ousts a federal court of jurisdiction it otherwise possesses." He concluded by saying: "Rather than preserving whatever vitality that the 'exception' has retained . . ., I would provide the creature with a decent burial in a grave adjacent to the resting place of the *Rooker-Feldman* doctrine." Marshall v. Marshall, 547 U.S. 293 (2006).—[Footnote by eds.]

the terms of the insurance policies, and eventually negotiated settlements with the various plaintiffs and paid the settlement amounts on behalf of Century America. At the conclusion of the actions, RSA requested reimbursement for defense expenses and deductibles it claimed to be owed under the policies. No payment was received.

RSA and Century Canada are both Canadian corporations, and under the insurance policies Century Canada is named as the first insured party while Century America is listed as an additional insured. Accordingly, when RSA did not receive the money it believed it was owed under the policies, RSA filed an action in Superior Court, Province of Quebec, District of Montreal, Canada, against Century Canada, seeking payment for its expenses and deductibles. In its response to the Canadian action, Century Canada asserted that the expenses and deductibles for which RSA sought reimbursement "relate[d] to events which occurred in the United States and claims asserted against name[d] insureds other than . . . [Century Canada]," and that under the terms of the policies, the rights and obligations of RSA, Century Canada, and Century America apply "[s]eparately to each insured against whom claim is made or 'action' is brought."

Given Century Canada's averment that RSA had, in effect, sued the wrong insured party in the Canadian action, RSA filed the present complaint in the Southern District of New York against Century America. Soon after the case was filed, Century America moved to dismiss the complaint in favor of RSA's pending action against Century Canada. The District Court granted Century America's motion to dismiss, stating that it had "the inherent power to stay or dismiss an action based on the pendency of a related proceeding in a foreign jurisdiction," but recognizing that its discretion was "limited by its obligation to exercise jurisdiction." In exercising its discretion, the District Court concluded that the existence of a parallel proceeding in Canada involving Century America's affiliate, coupled with Century America's consent to jurisdiction in Canada, militated in favor of dismissal. This appeal followed. . . .

Century America argues that the District Court's decision was supported by the doctrine of international comity abstention. International comity is "the recognition which one nation allows within its territory to the legislative, executive or judicial acts of another nation, having due regard both to international duty and convenience." Hilton v. Guyot, 159 U.S. 113, 163–64 (1895). While the doctrine can be stated clearly in the abstract, in practice we have described its boundaries as "amorphous" and "fuzzy." JP Morgan Chase Bank v. Altos Hornos de Mexico, 412 F.3d 418, 423 (2d Cir. 2005), quoting Harold G. Maier, Extraterritorial Jurisdiction at a Crossroads: An Intersection Between Public and Private International Law, 76 Am. J. Int'l L. 280, 281 (1982). In addition to its imprecise application, even where the doctrine clearly applies it "is not an imperative obligation of courts but rather is a discretionary rule of 'practice, convenience, and expediency.'" Id., quoting Pravin Banker Associates., Ltd. v. Banco Popular Del Peru, 109 F.3d 850, 854 (2d Cir. 1997). . . .

Generally, concurrent jurisdiction in United States courts and the courts of a foreign sovereign does not result in conflict. China Trade & Dev. Corp. v. M.V. Choong Yong, 837 F.2d 33, 36 (2d Cir. 1987). Rather, "'[p]arallel proceedings in the same in personam claim should ordinarily be allowed to proceed simultaneously, at least until a judgment is reached in one which can be pled as res judicata in the other.'" Id., quoting Laker Airways, Ltd. v. Sabena Belgian World Airlines, 731 F.2d 909, 926–27 (D.C. Cir. 1984), citing Colorado River Water Conservation Dist. v. United States, 424 U.S. 800, 817 (1976). The mere existence of parallel foreign proceedings does not negate the district courts' "virtually unflagging obligation . . . to exercise the jurisdiction given them." *Colorado River*, 424 U.S. at 817.

We have recognized one discrete category of foreign litigation that generally requires the dismissal of parallel district court actions—foreign bankruptcy proceedings. A foreign nation's interest in the "equitable and orderly distribution of a debtor's property" is an interest deserving of particular respect and deference, and accordingly we have followed the general practice of American courts and regularly deferred to such actions. Outside the bankruptcy context, we have yet to articulate a list of factors a district court should consider when exercising its discretion to abstain in deference to pending litigation in a foreign court. However, whatever factors weigh in favor of abstention, "[o]nly the clearest of justifications will warrant dismissal." *Colorado River*, 424 U.S. at 819. The task of a district court evaluating a request for dismissal based on a parallel foreign proceeding is not to articulate a justification *for* the exercise of jurisdiction, but rather to determine whether exceptional circumstances exist that justify the surrender of that jurisdiction. Moses H. Cone Mem'l Hosp. v. Mercury Constr. Corp., 460 U.S. 1, 25–26 (1983). The exceptional circumstances that would support such a surrender must, of course, raise considerations which are not generally present as a result of parallel litigation, otherwise the routine would be considered exceptional, and a district court's unflagging obligation to exercise its jurisdiction would become merely a polite request.

Appellees contend that the above standards, articulated by the Supreme Court in *Colorado River* and *Moses H. Cone*, do not apply to the present matter because those cases involved abstention in favor of parallel state proceedings while the parallel action here at issue is pending in a foreign jurisdiction. Appellees' effort to distinguish these precedents is accurate, as far as it goes, but it does not go far. The factors a court must weigh in exercising its discretion to abstain in deference to parallel proceedings will indeed differ depending on the nature of the proceedings. For example, if the parallel proceeding is in a foreign jurisdiction, the district court need not consider the balance between state and federal power dictated by our Constitution. Conversely, if the parallel proceeding is in a state court, the district court need not concern itself with issues of international relations. However, while the relevant factors to be considered differ depending on the posture of the case, the starting point for the inquiry remains unchanged: a district court's "virtually unflagging obligation" to exercise its jurisdiction. In weighing the considerations for and against abstention, a court's "heavy obligation to exercise jurisdiction" exists regardless of what factors are present on the other side of the balance.

Obligation to exercise unchged

The Supreme Court has recognized that a decision to abstain from exercising jurisdiction based on the existence of parallel litigation "does not rest on a mechanical checklist, but on a careful balancing of the important factors . . . as they apply in a given case, with the balance heavily weighted in favor of the exercise of jurisdiction." *Moses H. Cone*, 460 U.S. at 16. "No one factor is necessarily determinative; a carefully considered judgment taking into account both the obligation to exercise jurisdiction and the combination of factors counselling against that exercise is required." *Colorado River*, 424 U.S. at 818–19.

★ Rule

In the context of parallel proceedings in a foreign court, a district court should be guided by the principles upon which international comity is based: the proper respect for litigation in and the courts of a sovereign nation, fairness to litigants, and judicial efficiency. Proper consideration of these principles will no doubt require an evaluation of various factors, such as the similarity of the parties, the similarity of the issues, the order in which the actions were filed, the adequacy of the alternate forum, the potential prejudice to either party, the convenience of the parties, the connection between the litigation and the United States, and the connection between the litigation and the foreign jurisdiction. This list is not exhaustive, and a district court should examine the "totality of the circumstances," Finova Capital Corp. v. Ryan Helicopters U.S.A., Inc. 180 F.3d 896, 900 (7th Cir. 1999), to determine whether the specific facts before it are sufficiently exceptional to justify abstention.

factors

totality of circumstances

In the present case, the District Court did not identify any exceptional circumstances that would support abstention, and therefore the dismissal of the action was an abuse of discretion. The District Court's decision to dismiss the action was based on four factors: the existence of the Canadian action against Century Canada, Century America's consent to jurisdiction in Canada, the affiliation between Century America and Century Canada, and the adequacy of Canadian judicial procedures. These factors led the District Court to conclude that the action in Canada was a parallel action that provided an adequate forum for RSA's claims, and that therefore a dismissal of the case was warranted. . . .

The existence of a parallel action in an adequate foreign jurisdiction must be the beginning, not the end, of a district court's determination of whether abstention is appropriate. As we explained above, circumstances that routinely exist in connection with parallel litigation cannot reasonably be considered exceptional circumstances, and therefore the mere existence of an adequate parallel action, by itself, does not justify the dismissal of a case on grounds of international comity abstention. Rather, additional circumstances must be present—such as a foreign nation's interest in uniform bankruptcy proceedings—that outweigh the district court's general obligation to exercise its jurisdiction. The District Court did not identify any such special circumstances.

Finally, both parties address the question of whether, as an alternative to dismissing the action, the District Court should have considered staying proceedings in deference to the Canadian litigation. Because the propriety of a temporary stay was not raised in the District Court, we do not decide whether the entry of such a stay would have been appropriate. However, on remand the District Court may consider the propriety of a stay based on the pending Canadian action.

In the context of abstention in deference to parallel state-court litigation, the Supreme Court has cautioned that "a stay is as much a refusal to exercise federal jurisdiction as a dismissal," because the decision to grant a stay "necessarily contemplates that the federal court will have nothing further to do in resolving any substantive part of the case." *Moses H. Cone*, 460 U.S. at 28. However, a measured temporary stay need not result in a complete forfeiture of jurisdiction. As a lesser intrusion on the principle of obligatory jurisdiction, which might permit the district court a window to determine whether the foreign action will in fact offer an efficient vehicle for fairly resolving all the rights of the parties, such a stay is an alternative that normally should be considered before a comity-based dismissal is entertained. . . .

Accordingly, on remand the District Court may consider whether its obligation to exercise jurisdiction over this action could be satisfied despite the entry of a brief stay to allow the Canadian court to determine if, for example, Century Canada is liable for the money RSA claims to be owed under the policies. We do not now decide that such a stay would necessarily be appropriate, or that other bases for a temporary stay would not be proper. Those questions are left to the District Court in the first instance. . . .

The judgment of the District Court is vacated and remanded for further proceedings.

NOTES ON INTERNATIONAL COMITY ABSTENTION

1. INTERNATIONAL COMITY

At its most general level, "international comity" refers to the respect that U.S. courts give to the laws, acts, and decisions of foreign countries. This respect is not mandated by international law, but it can help promote reciprocity and reduce friction in foreign relations. As the Supreme Court

famously explained in a case involving an attempt to enforce a foreign judgment in a U.S. court:

> "Comity," in the legal sense, is neither a matter of absolute
> obligation, on the one hand, nor of mere courtesy and good will,
> upon the other. But it is the recognition which one nation allows
> within its territory to the legislative, executive, or judicial acts of
> another nation, having due regard both to international duty and
> convenience, and to the rights of its own citizens or of other persons
> who are under the protection of its laws.

*Comity
def.*

Hilton v. Guyot, 159 U.S. 113, 163–64 (1895). The recognition and enforcement of foreign judgments by U.S. courts is discussed elsewhere, specifically
in Note 9 of the Notes on International Tribunals following *Medellin v. Texas*
in Section 5 of Chapter IV.

2. DISMISSAL OR STAY OF U.S. LITIGATION

In some situations, U.S. courts will stay or dismiss litigation in the
United States when similar or related litigation is pending in a foreign country. Courts disagree about the precise standards for this "international
comity abstention," with some courts holding that it is appropriate only in
exceptional circumstances and other courts holding that there is broad discretion to avoid duplicative litigation. See Turner Entertainment Co. v.
Degeto Film GmbH, 25 F.3d 1512, 1518 (11th Cir. 1994) (describing the differing approaches). In the *Royal and Sun Alliance* decision excerpted above,
the court applies the exceptional circumstances approach. In doing so, it relies heavily on *Colorado River* and related cases, which concern situations in
which there are pending state court proceedings.

*Courts disagree
on standard*

To what extent do the abstention considerations differ when the proceedings are pending instead in a foreign court? On the one hand, the
federalism considerations applicable in the *Colorado River* situation, which
might support federal court abstention, are absent in the international context. On the other hand, many of the international cases involve the application of state law or foreign law rather than federal law and thus there might
be less of an interest in exercising federal jurisdiction. In *Royal and Sun
Alliance*, for example, the relevant law was either state contract law or Canadian law. In addition, the international cases present foreign relations
considerations that might also support abstention. In light of these differences, should the court in *Royal and Sun Alliance* have been more receptive
to abstention? Cf. Posner v. Essex Ins. Co., 178 F.3d 1209, 1223 (11th Cir.
1999) ("[T]he Supreme Court's admonition that courts generally must exercise their non-discretionary authority in cases over which Congress has
granted them jurisdiction can apply only to those abstention doctrines addressing the unique concerns of federalism. . . . The relationship between the
federal courts and the states (grounded in federalism and the Constitution)
is different from the relationship between federal courts and foreign nations
(grounded in the historical notion of comity).").

Courts consider a variety of factors in deciding whether to apply international comity abstention. In *Royal and Sun Alliance*, the court refers to

Factors used in Royal Sun

"the similarity of the parties, the similarity of the issues, the order in which the actions were filed, the adequacy of the alternate forum, the potential prejudice to either party, the convenience of the parties, the connection between the litigation and the United States, and the connection between the litigation and the foreign jurisdiction." Other circuits apply similar lists of factors. See, e.g., Finova Capital Corp. v. Ryan Helicopters U.S.A., Inc., 180 F.3d 896, 898–99 (7th Cir. 1999). Cf. Mujica v. AirScan Inc., 771 F.3d 580, 603 (9th Cir. 2014) (noting that "courts have struggled to apply a consistent set of factors in their comity analyses"). What weight should courts give to these various factors? Are some more important than others? The court in *Royal and Sun Alliance* notes that international comity abstention is particularly appropriate when the parallel foreign proceedings involve bankruptcy. Why should this be so?

more discretion for stay discussed

The court in *Royal and Sun Alliance* also suggests that district courts should have more discretion to issue a temporary stay rather than outright dismissal in the face of parallel foreign proceedings. The court agreed in Ingersoll Milling Machine Co. v. Granger, 833 F.2d 680, 686 (7th Cir. 1987):

> Moreover, it is not insignificant—indeed, it is very significant—that the District Court's action in this case was a decidedly measured one. The court did not dismiss the action; it simply stayed further proceedings until the Belgian appeals were concluded. This approach protects the substantial rights of the parties while permitting the District Court to manage its time effectively.

Under the *Colorado River* line of cases, by contrast, the Supreme Court has indicated that "a stay is as much a refusal to exercise federal jurisdiction as a dismissal" because "the decision to invoke *Colorado River* necessarily contemplates that the federal court will have nothing further to do in resolving any substantive part of the case, whether it stays or dismisses." Moses H. Cone Mem'l Hosp. v. Mercury Constr. Corp., 460 U.S. 1, 28 (1983). A stay of litigation is more common, however, under the *Pullman* abstention doctrine (see Section 3 of this chapter). If an international case involves the application of foreign law or implicates important policy interests of a foreign nation, might a stay be warranted based on considerations analogous to those underlying *Pullman*? Or does the lack of an underlying constitutional question in the international cases serve to distinguish *Pullman*? Is *Burford* abstention (see the Notes on *Burford* in Section 3 of this chapter) a better analogy in this situation? Note that the Supreme Court has held that a dismissal under *Burford* is warranted only if the relief being sought is equitable or otherwise discretionary in nature, and is not appropriate when the claim is for damages. See Quackenbush v. Allstate Ins. Co., 517 U.S. 706, 731 (1996). The Court has also noted, however, that "*Burford* might support a federal court's decision to postpone adjudication of a damages action pending the resolution by the state courts of a disputed question of state law." Id. at 730–31.

3. ANTI-SUIT INJUNCTIONS

Occasionally, U.S. courts will issue a so-called "anti-suit" injunction to prevent persons or entities subject to their personal jurisdiction from pursuing litigation in a foreign country. See, e.g., Laker Airways, Ltd. v. Sabena, Belgian World Airlines, 731 F.2d 909, 927–31 (D.C. Cir. 1984). In this context, international comity considerations provide a reason for caution before entering the injunction. As with international comity abstention, courts disagree about the precise standards for issuing anti-suit injunctions. Some courts hold that they are appropriate whenever there is a duplication of parties and issues and the prosecution of simultaneous proceedings would frustrate the speedy and efficient determination of the case. Others focus more narrowly on whether the foreign action imperils the jurisdiction of the forum court or threatens some strong national policy. See Quaak v. Klynveld Peat Marwick Goerdeler Bedrijfsrevisoren, 361 F.3d 11, 17–19 (1st Cir. 2004) (describing differing approaches). To what extent might the considerations underlying *Younger* abstention, which limits the issuance of injunctive relief directed at state court proceedings (see Section 2 of this chapter), apply to injunctions directed at foreign court proceedings?

[handwritten margin note: differing standards]

4. RESPECT FOR FOREIGN LAWS

International comity abstention can involve respect not only for foreign judicial proceedings, but also for foreign laws. Consider, for example, Bi v. Union Carbide Chemical and Plastics Co., 984 F.2d 582 (2d Cir. 1993). In 1984, deadly gas escaped from a pesticide plant in Bhopal, India, killing thousands of people. The plant was operated by an Indian subsidiary of a U.S. company. India subsequently enacted a statute giving the Indian government exclusive standing to represent the victims of the disaster in India. Pursuant to this statute, the Indian government brought suit in Indian courts against the U.S. company and its subsidiary, and entered into a comprehensive settlement that was approved by the Indian Supreme Court. The suit in *Bi* was an attempt by plaintiffs who were unhappy with the Indian settlement to litigate their claims in the United States. In affirming a dismissal of the suit, the Court of Appeals described the case as raising "an issue of comity among nations." The court reasoned that "were we to pass on the validity of India's response to a disaster that occurred within its borders, it would disrupt our relations with the country and frustrate the efforts of the international community to develop methods to deal with problems of this magnitude in the future." As a result, the court concluded that "when a recognized democracy determines that the interests of the victims of a mass tort that occurred within its borders will be best served if the foreign government exclusively represents the victims in courts around the world, we will not pass judgment on that determination." Why should an Indian statute rather than U.S. law determine the exercise of jurisdiction by a U.S. federal court in a case involving the actions of a U.S. corporation and its subsidiary? Should it matter that India is a democracy?

5.   RESPECT FOR ALTERNATIVE DISPUTE RESOLUTION EFFORT

Considerations of comity can also arise when courts are asked to abstain not in the face of a foreign judicial proceeding or law, but rather in the face of some alternate foreign or international effort to resolve issues related to the litigation. For example, in Pravin Banker Assocs. v. Banco Popular Del Peru, 109 F.3d 850 (2d Cir. 1997), a Peruvian bank that had defaulted on loans from U.S. financial institutions sought to stay enforcement proceedings in U.S. courts while it attempted to restructure its commercial debt under a plan worked out by U.S. Treasury Secretary Nicholas Brady. In affirming the denial of a stay, the court noted that there were two competing U.S. government policy interests in the case: foreign debt resolution under the Brady plan and ensuring the enforceability of valid debts. The District Court had previously granted a six-month stay, thus serving to some degree the first interest. The Court of Appeals concluded that a further stay would unduly prejudice the second interest, reasoning that "courts will not extend comity to foreign proceedings when doing so would be contrary to the policies or prejudicial to the interests of the United States."

For a decision that was more receptive to granting international comity abstention based on the existence of an alternative dispute resolution effort, see Ungaro-Benages v. Dresdner Bank AG, 379 F.3d 1227 (11th Cir. 2004). In that case, the plaintiff sued two German banks, alleging that, during the 1930s and 1940s, they had stolen her family's interest in a company, pursuant to the Nazi program of "Aryanization" of Jewish assets. In upholding a dismissal of the suit, the court explained that international comity abstention can operate either retrospectively or prospectively:

> When applied retrospectively, domestic courts consider whether to respect the judgment of a foreign tribunal or to defer to parallel foreign proceedings. . . .

> When applied prospectively, domestic courts consider whether to dismiss or stay a domestic action based on the interests of our government, the foreign government and the international community in resolving the dispute in a foreign forum.

In concluding that abstention was proper in this case, the court noted that the United States and Germany had concluded an agreement in 2000 that established a private foundation to hear claims brought by victims of the Nazi regime. The court found that both the U.S. government and the German government had a strong interest in having the foundation operate as the exclusive basis for recovery, and that the foundation offered an adequate forum for resolving the claims. The court reached this conclusion even though nothing in the foundation agreement expressly precluded litigation in U.S. courts. But cf. Gross v. German Foundation Industrial Initiative, 456 F.3d 363, 394 (3d Cir. 2006) ("We remain skeptical of this broad application of the international comity doctrine [in *Ungaro-Benages*], noting our 'virtually unflagging obligation' to exercise the jurisdiction granted to us, Colorado River v. United States, 424 U.S. 800, 817 (1976), which is not diminished simply because foreign relations might be involved. . . .").

6. COMPARISON WITH FORUM NON CONVENIENS

International comity abstention is similar in some ways to forum non conveniens. Under that doctrine, federal district courts have discretion to dismiss a case if they determine that various private and public interest factors weigh in favor of adjudicating the case in an alternate forum and that the forum is adequate. See Piper Aircraft Co. v. Reyno, 454 U.S. 235 (1981). The private interest factors to be considered include "the 'relative ease of access to sources of proof; availability of compulsory process for attendance of unwilling, and the cost of obtaining attendance of willing, witnesses; possibility of view of premises, if view would be appropriate to the action; and all other practical problems that make trial of a case easy, expeditious and inexpensive.'" Id. at 241 n.6 (quoting Gulf Oil Corp. v. Gilbert, 330 U.S. 501, 508 (1947)). The public interest factors include "the administrative difficulties flowing from court congestion; the 'local interest in having localized controversies decided at home'; the interest in having the trial of a diversity case in a forum that is at home with the law that must govern the action; the avoidance of unnecessary problems in conflict of laws, or in the application of foreign law; and the unfairness of burdening citizens in an unrelated forum with jury duty." Id. (quoting *Gilbert*, 330 U.S. at 508, 509). In considering these factors, courts apply a presumption in favor of the plaintiff's choice of forum, although less of a presumption is given when the plaintiff is a foreign citizen. In determining whether an alternate forum is "adequate," courts look primarily at whether the forum would have jurisdiction to hear the dispute and the ability to provide a remedy. Ordinarily, an alternate forum will not be considered inadequate merely because its laws or procedures are less favorable to the plaintiff than those of the United States.

[handwritten: Presumption in favor of P choice]

Because of statutory provisions allowing for transfer of venue between federal district courts, the forum non conveniens doctrine is applied by federal courts today only in international cases. How does international comity abstention differ from applying forum non conveniens? Is there a need to have both doctrines? Consider this observation by the Supreme Court about the differences between domestic abstention and forum non conveniens:

> [T]he abstention doctrines and the doctrine of forum non conveniens proceed from a similar premise: In rare circumstances, federal courts can relinquish their jurisdiction in favor of another forum. But our abstention doctrine is of a distinct historical pedigree, and the traditional considerations behind dismissal for forum non conveniens differ markedly from those informing the decision to abstain. . . . Federal courts abstain out of deference to the paramount interests of another sovereign, and the concern is with principles of comity and federalism. Dismissal for forum non conveniens, by contrast, has historically reflected a far broader range of considerations. . . .

[handwritten: Abstension more narrow, different considerations]

Quackenbush v. Allstate Ins. Co., 517 U.S. 706, 723 (1996).

7. INTERNATIONAL COMITY AND PERSONAL JURISDICTION

The Supreme Court invoked considerations of international comity in limiting personal jurisdiction over foreign corporations in Daimler AG v. Bauman, 571 U.S. ___, 134 S.Ct. 746 (2014). In that case, residents of Argentina brought suit against a German corporation, Daimler AG, in a federal district court in California. The suit alleged that Daimler's Argentinian subsidiary had collaborated with state security forces in the 1970s and 1980s in carrying out human rights violations against the plaintiffs or their relatives. Personal jurisdiction was premised on the California contacts of Daimler's U.S. subsidiary, which was incorporated in Delaware and had its principal place of business in New Jersey. In an opinion by Justice Ginsburg, the Court held that the Due Process Clause precluded the district court from exercising personal jurisdiction over the defendant in this case. The Court noted that the case involved the exercise of "general" rather than "specific" jurisdiction, since the defendant's allegedly wrongful activities were not connected to California. Quoting Goodyear Dunlop Tires Operations v. Brown, 564 U.S. 915 (2011), the Court reasoned that " '[a] court may assert general jurisdiction over foreign (sister-state or foreign-country) corporations to hear any and all claims against them when their affiliations with the State are so 'continuous and systematic' as to render them essentially at home in the forum State.' " The Court concluded that this test was not met under the facts of this case, "for Daimler's slim contacts with the State hardly render it at home there." In its analysis, the Court noted that the "transnational context" of the dispute "bears attention." "Considerations of international rapport," the Court observed, "reinforce our determination that subjecting Daimler to the general jurisdiction of courts in California would not accord with the 'fair play and substantial justice' due process demands." Justice Sotomayor concurred in the judgment.

8. BIBLIOGRAPHY

For general discussions of international comity, see Harold G. Maier, Extraterritorial Jurisdiction at a Crossroads: An Intersection Between Public and Private International Law, 76 Am. J. Int'l L. 280 (1982); Joel R. Paul, Comity in International Law, 32 Harv. Int'l L.J. 1 (1991); and Michael D. Ramsey, Escaping "International Comity," 83 Iowa L. Rev. 893 (1998). For specific discussions of international comity abstention and antisuit injunctions, see George A. Bermann, The Use of Anti-Suit Injunctions in International Litigation, 28 Colum. J. Transnat'l L. 589 (1990); N. Jansen Calamita, Rethinking Comity: Towards a Coherent Treatment of International Parallel Proceedings, 27 U. Pa. J. Int'l Econ. L. 601 (2006); Austen L. Parrish, Duplicative Foreign Litigation, 78 Geo. Wash. L. Rev. 237 (2010); William L. Reynolds, The Proper Forum for a Suit: Transnational Forum Non Conveniens and Counter-Suit Injunctions in the Federal Courts, 70 Tex. L. Rev. 1663 (1992); and Steven R. Swanson, The Vexatiousness of a Vexation Rule: International Comity and Antisuit Injunctions, 30 Gw. J. Int'l & Econ. 1 (1996). For a more recent and comprehensive account of how U.S. courts apply the concept of international comity, see William S. Dodge, International Comity in American Law, 115 Colum. L. Rev. 2071 (2015).

SECTION 7. STATUTE-BASED ABSTENTION

Atlantic Coast Line Railroad Co. v. Brotherhood of Locomotive Engineers

Supreme Court of the United States, 1970.
398 U.S. 281.

■ MR. JUSTICE BLACK delivered the opinion of the Court.

Congress in 1793, shortly after the American colonies became one united nation, provided that in federal courts "a writ of injunction [shall not] be granted to stay proceedings in any court of a state." Act of March 2, 1793, § 5. Although certain exceptions to this general prohibition have been added, that statute, directing that state courts shall remain free from interference by federal courts, has remained in effect until this time. Today that amended statute provides:

> A court of the United States may not grant an injunction to stay proceedings in a State court except as expressly authorized by Act of Congress, or where necessary in aid of its jurisdiction, or to protect or effectuate its judgments.

28 U.S.C. § 2283. Despite the existence of this longstanding prohibition, in this case a federal court did enjoin the petitioner, Atlantic Coast Line Railroad Co. (ACL), from invoking an injunction issued by a Florida state court which prohibited certain picketing by respondent Brotherhood of Locomotive Engineers (BLE). The case arose in the following way.

In 1967 BLE began picketing the Moncrief yard, a switching yard located near Jacksonville, Florida, and wholly owned and operated by ACL.[2] As soon as this picketing began ACL went into federal court seeking an injunction. When the federal judge denied the request, ACL immediately went into state court and there succeeded in obtaining an injunction. No further legal action was taken in this dispute until two years later in 1969, after this Court's decision in Brotherhood of Railroad Trainmen v. Jacksonville Terminal Co., 394 U.S. 369 (1969). In that case the Court considered the validity of a state injunction against picketing by the BLE and other unions at the Jacksonville Terminal, located immediately next to Moncrief Yard. The Court reviewed the factual situation surrounding the Jacksonville Terminal picketing and concluded that the unions had a federally protected right to picket under the Railway Labor Act, 45 U.S.C. § 151 et seq., and that that right could not be interfered with by state court injunctions. Immediately after a petition for rehearing was denied in that case, the respondent BLE filed a motion in state court to dissolve the Moncrief yard injunction, arguing that under

---

[2] There is no present labor dispute between the ACL and the BLE or any other ACL employees. ACL became involved in this case as a result of a labor dispute between the Florida East Coast Railway Co. (FEC) and its employees. FEC cars are hauled into and out of Moncrief Yard and switched around to make up trains in that yard. The BLE picketed the yard, encouraging ACL employees not to handle any FEC car.

the *Jacksonville Terminal* decision the injunction was improper. The state judge refused to dissolve the injunction, holding that this Court's *Jacksonville Terminal* decision was not controlling. The union did not elect to appeal that decision directly, but instead went back into the federal court and requested an injunction against the enforcement of the state court injunction. The district judge granted the injunction and upon application a stay of that injunction, pending the filing and disposition of a petition for certiorari, was granted. The Court of Appeals summarily affirmed on the parties' stipulation, and we granted a petition for certiorari to consider the validity of the federal court's injunction against the state court.

In this Court the union contends that the federal injunction was proper either "to protect or effectuate" the District Court's denial of an injunction in 1967, or as "necessary in aid of" the District Court's jurisdiction. Although the questions are by no means simple and clear, and the decision is difficult, we conclude that the injunction against the state court was not justified under either of these two exceptions to the anti-injunction statute. We therefore hold that the federal injunction in this case was improper.

I

Before analyzing the specific legal arguments advanced in this case, we think it would be helpful to discuss the background and policy that led Congress to pass the anti-injunction statute in 1793. While all the reasons that led Congress to adopt this restriction on federal courts are not wholly clear, it is certainly likely that one reason stemmed from the essentially federal nature of our national government. When this nation was established by the Constitution, each state surrendered only a part of its sovereign power to the national government. But those powers that were not surrendered were retained by the states and unless a state was restrained by "the supreme Law of the Land" as expressed in the Constitution, laws, or treaties of the United States, it was free to exercise those retained powers as it saw fit. One of the reserved powers was the maintenance of state judicial systems for the decision of legal controversies. Many of the framers of the Constitution felt that separate federal courts were unnecessary and that the state courts could be entrusted to protect both state and federal rights. Others felt that a complete system of federal courts to take care of federal legal problems should be provided for in the Constitution itself. This dispute resulted in compromise. One "supreme Court" was created by the Constitution, and Congress was given the power to create other federal courts. In the first Congress this power was exercised and a system of federal trial and appellate courts with limited jurisdiction was created by the Judiciary Act of 1789.

While the lower federal courts were given certain powers in the 1789 act, they were not given any power to review directly cases from state courts, and they have not been given such powers since that time. Only the Supreme Court was authorized to review on direct appeal the decisions of state courts. Thus from the beginning we have had in this country two essentially separate legal systems. Each system proceeds independently of the other with ultimate review in this Court of the federal questions raised in either system. Understandably this dual court system was bound to lead to conflicts and frictions. Litigants who foresaw the possibility of more favorable treatment in one or the other system would predictably hasten to invoke the powers of whichever court it was believed would present the best chance of success. Obviously this dual system could not function if state and federal courts were free to fight each other for control of a particular case. Thus, in order to make the dual system work and "to prevent needless friction between state and federal court," it was necessary to work out lines of demarcation between the two systems. Some of these limits were spelled out in the 1789 act. Others have been added by later statutes as well as judicial decisions. The 1793 anti-injunction act was at least in part a response to these pressures.

On its face the present act is an absolute prohibition against enjoining state court proceedings, unless the injunction falls within one of three specifically defined exceptions. The respondents here have intimated that the act only establishes a "principle of comity," not a binding rule on the power of the federal courts. The argument implies that in certain circumstances a federal court may enjoin state court proceedings even if that action cannot be justified by any of the three exceptions. We cannot accept any such contention. In 1955 when this Court interpreted this statute, it stated: "This is not a statute conveying a broad general policy for appropriate ad hoc application. Legislative policy is here expressed in a clear-cut prohibition qualified only by specifically defined exceptions." Amalgamated Clothing Workers v. Richman Bros., 348 U.S. 511, 515–16 (1955). Since that time Congress has not seen fit to amend the statute and we therefore adhere to that position and hold that any injunction against state court proceedings otherwise proper under general equitable principles must be based on one of the specific statutory exceptions to § 2283 if it is to be upheld. Moreover since the statutory prohibition against such injunctions in part rests on the fundamental constitutional independence of the states and their courts, the exceptions should not be enlarged by loose statutory construction. Proceedings in state courts should normally be allowed to continue unimpaired by intervention of the lower federal courts, with relief from error, if any, through the state appellate courts and ultimately this Court.

II

In this case the Florida Circuit Court enjoined the union's intended picketing, and the United States District Court enjoined the railroad "from giving effect to or availing [itself] of the benefits of" that state court order. Both sides agree that although this federal injunction is in terms directed only at the railroad it is an injunction "to stay proceedings in a State court." It is settled that the prohibition of § 2283 cannot be evaded by addressing the order to the parties or prohibiting utilization of the results of a completed state proceeding. Oklahoma Packing Co. v. Gas & Electric Co., 309 U.S. 4, 9 (1940); Hill v. Martin, 296 U.S. 393, 403 (1935). Thus if the injunction against the Florida court proceedings is to be upheld, it must be "expressly authorized by Act of Congress," "necessary in aid of [the District Court's] jurisdiction," or "to protect or effectuate [that court's] judgments."

Neither party argues that there is any express congressional authorization for injunctions in this situation and we agree with that conclusion. The respondent does contend that the injunction was proper either as a means to protect or effectuate the District Court's 1967 order, or in aid of that court's jurisdiction. We do not think that either alleged basis can be supported.

A

[The federal District Court declined to enjoin the picketing in 1967 in part on the ground that under federal law the union was "free to engage in self-help." The union asserted in the Supreme Court that the] determination that it was "free to engage in self-help" was a determination that it had a federally protected right to picket and that state law could not be invoked to negate that right. The railroad, on the other hand, argues that the order merely determined that the *federal* court could not enjoin the picketing, in large part because of the general prohibition in the Norris-LaGuardia Act, 29 U.S.C. § 101 et seq., against issuance by federal courts of injunctions in labor disputes. Based solely on the state of the record when the order was entered, we are inclined to believe that the District Court did not determine whether federal law precluded an injunction based on state law. Not only was that point never argued to the court, but there is no language in the order that necessarily implies any decision on that question. In short we feel that the District Court in 1967 determined that federal law could not be invoked to enjoin the picketing at Moncrief Yard, and that the union did have a right "to engage in self-help" as far as the federal courts were concerned. But that decision is entirely different from a decision that the Railway Labor Act precludes state regulation of the picketing as well, and this latter decision is an essential prerequisite for upholding the 1969 injunction as necessary "to protect or effectuate" the 1967 order. [W]e think it highly unlikely that the brief statements in the order conceal a determination of a disputed legal point that later was to divide this Court in a four to three vote in *Jacksonville Terminal* in opinions totaling 29 pages. . . .

This record, we think, conclusively shows that neither the parties themselves nor the District Court construed the 1967 order as the union now contends it should be construed. Rather we are convinced that the union in effect tried to get the federal District Court to decide that the state court judge was wrong in distinguishing the *Jacksonville Terminal* decision.[a] Such an attempt to seek appellate review of a state decision in the federal District Court cannot be justified as necessary "to protect or effectuate" the 1967 order. The record simply will not support the union's contention on this point.

B

This brings us to the second prong of the union's argument in which it is suggested that even if the 1967 order did not determine the union's right to picket free from state interference, once the decision in *Jacksonville Terminal* was announced, the District Court was then free to enjoin the state court on the theory that such action was "necessary in aid of [the District Court's] jurisdiction." [T]he argument is somewhat unclear, but it appears to go in this way: The District Court had acquired jurisdiction over the labor controversy in 1967 when the railroad filed its complaint, and it determined at that time that it did have jurisdiction. The dispute involved the legality of picketing by the union and the *Jacksonville Terminal* decision clearly indicated that such activity was not only legal, but was protected from state court interference. The state court had interfered with that right, and thus a federal injunction was "necessary in aid of [the District Court's] jurisdiction." For several reasons we cannot accept the contention.

First, a federal court does not have inherent power to ignore the limitations of § 2283 and to enjoin state court proceedings merely because those proceedings interfere with a protected federal right or invade an area pre-empted by federal law, even when the interference is unmistakably clear. This rule applies regardless of whether the federal court itself has jurisdiction over the controversy, or whether it is ousted from jurisdiction for the same reason that the state court is. This conclusion is required because Congress itself set forth the only exceptions to the statute, and those exceptions do not include this situation. Second, if the District Court does have jurisdiction, it is not enough that the requested injunction is related to that jurisdiction, but it must be "*necessary in aid of*" that jurisdiction. While this language is admittedly broad, we conclude that it implies something similar to the concept of injunctions to "protect or effectuate" judgments. Both exceptions to the general prohibition of § 2283 imply that some federal injunctive relief may be necessary to prevent a state court from so interfering with a federal court's consideration or disposition of a case as to seriously impair the federal court's flexibility and authority to decide that case. Third, no such situation is presented here. Although the federal court did have jurisdiction of the railroad's complaint based on federal law, the state court also had jurisdiction over the complaint based on state law and the union's asserted federal defense as well. While the railroad could probably have based its federal case on the pendent state law claims as well, United

---

[a] In an omitted footnote, the Court said that it was prepared to "assume, without deciding, that the Florida Circuit Court's decision was wrong in light of our decision in *Jacksonville Terminal*."—[Footnote by eds.]

Mine Workers v. Gibbs, 383 U.S. 715 (1966), it was free to refrain from doing so and leave the state law questions and the related issue concerning preclusion of state remedies by federal law to the state courts. Conversely, although it could have tendered its federal claims to the state court, it was also free to restrict the state complaint to state grounds alone. In short, the state and federal courts had concurrent jurisdiction in this case, and neither court was free to prevent either party from simultaneously pursuing claims in both courts. Kline v. Burke Constr. Co., 260 U.S. 226 (1922); cf. Donovan v. Dallas, 377 U.S. 408 (1964). Therefore the state court's assumption of jurisdiction over the state law claims and the federal preclusion issue did not hinder the federal court's jurisdiction so as to make an injunction *necessary* to aid that jurisdiction. Nor was an injunction necessary because the state court may have taken action which the federal court was certain was improper under the *Jacksonville Terminal* decision. Again, lower federal courts possess no power whatever to sit in direct review of state court decisions. If the union was adversely affected by the state court's decision, it was free to seek vindication of its federal right in the Florida appellate courts and ultimately, if necessary, in this Court. Similarly if, because of the Florida Circuit Court's action, the union faced the threat of immediate irreparable injury sufficient to justify an injunction under usual equitable principles, it was undoubtedly free to seek such relief from the Florida appellate courts, and might possibly in certain emergency circumstances seek such relief from this Court as well. Unlike the federal District Court, this Court does have potential appellate jurisdiction over federal questions raised in state court proceedings, and that broader jurisdiction allows this Court correspondingly broader authority to issue injunctions "necessary in aid of its jurisdiction."

III

This case is by no means an easy one. The arguments in support of the union's contentions are not insubstantial. But whatever doubts we may have are strongly affected by the general prohibition of § 2283. Any doubts as to the propriety of a federal injunction against state court proceedings should be resolved in favor of permitting the state courts to proceed in an orderly fashion to finally determine the controversy. The explicit wording of § 2283 itself implies as much, and the fundamental principle of a dual system of courts leads inevitably to that conclusion.

The injunction issued by the District Court must be vacated. Since that court has not yet proceeded to a final judgment in the case, the cause is remanded to it for further proceedings in conformity with this opinion.

It is so ordered.

■ MR. JUSTICE MARSHALL took no part in the consideration or decision of this case.

■ MR. JUSTICE HARLAN, concurring.

I join the Court's opinion on the understanding that its holding implies no retreat from Brotherhood of Railroad Trainmen v. Jacksonville Terminal Co., 394 U.S. 369 (1969). Whether or not that case controls the underlying controversy here is a question that will arise only on review of any final judgment entered in the state court proceedings respecting that controversy.

■ MR. JUSTICE BRENNAN, with whom MR. JUSTICE WHITE joins, dissenting.

My disagreement with the Court in this case is a relatively narrow one. I do not disagree with much that is said concerning the history and policies underlying 28 U.S.C. § 2283. Nor do I dispute the Court's holding on the basis of Amalgamated Clothing Workers v. Richman Bros., 348 U.S. 511 (1955), that federal court courts do not have authority to enjoin state proceedings merely because it is asserted that the state court is improperly asserting jurisdiction in an area pre-empted by federal law or federal procedures. Nevertheless, in my view the District Court had discretion to enjoin the state proceedings in the present case because it acted pursuant to an explicit exception to the prohibition of § 2283, that is, "to protect or effectuate [the District Court's] judgments." . . .

In my view, what the District Court decided in 1967 was that BLE had a federally protected right to picket at the Moncrief Yard and, by necessary implication, that this right could not be subverted by resort to state proceedings. I find it difficult indeed to ascribe to the district judge the views that the Court now says he held, namely, that ACL, merely by marching across the street to the state court, could render wholly nugatory the district judge's declaration that BLE had a federally protected right to strike at the Moncrief Yard.

Moreover, it is readily apparent from the District Court's 1969 order enjoining the state proceedings that the district judge viewed his 1967 order as delineating the rights of the respective parties, and more particularly, as establishing BLE's right to conduct the picketing in question under paramount federal law. This interpretation should be accepted as controlling, for certainly the district judge is in the best position to render an authoritative interpretation of his own order. . . .

In justifying its niggardly construction of the District Court's orders, the Court takes the position that any doubts concerning the propriety of an injunction against state proceedings should be resolved against the granting of injunctive relief. Unquestionably § 2283 manifests a general design on the part of Congress that federal courts not precipitately interfere with the orderly determination of controversies in state proceedings. However, this policy of nonintervention is by no means absolute, as the explicit exceptions in § 2283 make entirely clear. Thus, § 2283 itself evinces a congressional intent that resort to state proceedings not be permitted to undermine a prior judgment of a federal court. But that is exactly what has occurred in the present case. Indeed, the federal determination that BLE may picket at the Moncrief Yard has been rendered wholly ineffective by the state injunction. The crippling restrictions that the Court today places upon the power of the District Court to effectuate and protect its orders are totally inconsistent with both the plain language of § 2283 and the policies underlying that statutory provision.

Accordingly, I would affirm the judgment of the Court of Appeals sustaining the District Court's grant of injunctive relief against petitioner's giving effect to, or availing itself of, the benefit of the state court injunction.[b]

NOTES ON THE ANTI-INJUNCTION ACT

1.   TOUCEY V. NEW YORK LIFE INS. CO.

As Justice Black observed in *Atlantic Coast Line,* the Anti-Injunction Act stems from a 1793 statute that flatly prohibited federal courts from issuing an injunction to stay proceedings in a state court. The statute was enacted in its present form in 1948.[a] Prior to that date, the Supreme Court had permitted the issuance of injunctions in many situations that were literally barred by the statute. A sharp break with this practice occurred in Toucey v. New York Life Ins. Co., 314 U.S. 118 (1941).[b]

Toucey sued the New York Life Insurance Company in state court for monthly disability benefits. Based on diversity of citizenship, the insurance company removed to a federal district court, which resolved the case in its favor. Toucey then assigned his claim to Shay, who filed a second action on

---

[b] For a comment on *Atlantic Coast Line* shortly after it was decided, see John Daniel Reaves and David S. Golden, The Federal Anti-Injunction Statute in the Aftermath of *Atlantic Coast Line Railroad,* 5 Ga. L. Rev. 294 (1971).—[Footnote by eds.]

[a] There is no helpful legislative history of the original statute, and little in its subsequent re-enactments that explains the intended scope of the statutory exceptions. Various limiting constructions have been suggested in the literature. For example, William T. Mayton, Ersatz Federalism under the Anti-Injunction Statute, 78 Colum. L. Rev. 330 (1978), argues that the statute was intended only as a limitation on the powers of an individual Supreme Court justice to grant injunctions. But the accepted view is that stated in *Atlantic Coast Line.* For evaluation of the current statute and a proposed revision, see Diane P. Wood, Fine-Tuning Judicial Federalism: A Proposal for Reform of the Anti-Injunction Act, 1990 B.Y.U. L. Rev. 289. See also James E. Pfander and Nassim Nazemi, The Anti-Injunction Act and the Problem of Federal-State Jurisdictional Overlap, 92 Tex. L. Rev. 1 (2013). Pfander and Nazemi argue "for a thorough reassessment of the law of federal-state concurrency" based on their examination of the legal backdrop against which the anti-injunction act was enacted. They find a

> fairly straightforward rule of priority: when the state proceeding began first and the parties went to federal court for a stay on equitable grounds, the federal action was barred. But when the parties first brought suit in federal court and that court obtained jurisdiction, the federal court could stay subsequently filed state proceedings where necessary as a matter of judicial self-defense.

A more detailed historical account of the origins of their theory is presented in James E. Pfander and Nassim Nazemi, *Morris v. Allen* and the Lost History of the Anti-Injunction Act of 1793, 108 Nw. U. L. Rev. 187 (2013).

[b] At the time of *Toucey,* the statute read: "The writ of injunction shall not be granted by any court of the United States to stay proceedings in any court of a State, except in cases where such injunction may be authorized by any law relating to proceedings in bankruptcy." The bankruptcy exception had been added in 1875.

the policy in state court. As diversity was now lacking, the insurance company could not remove the second suit. Instead, it asked the federal court to enjoin Shay and Toucey from proceeding further in state court. The injunction was issued, and the Court of Appeals affirmed.

The Supreme Court granted certiorari to decide whether "a federal court ha[s] power to stay a proceeding in a state court simply because the claim in controversy has previously been adjudicated in the federal court?" The Court answered "no," in language signaling a much stricter construction of the statute. "We must be scrupulous," Justice Frankfurter said for the Court, "in our regard for the limits within which Congress has confined the authority of the courts of its own creation."

In reaction to *Toucey*, Congress enacted the three exceptions to the Anti-Injunction Act. The authorization of a federal court to issue an injunction "to protect or effectuate its judgments" was specifically designed to overrule *Toucey*. What remained unclear was whether the 1948 revision was meant to preclude the recognition of exceptions not specifically covered by the statutory language.

2.   EARLY LITIGATION UNDER THE 1948 REVISION

Three cases provide the background for *Atlantic Coast Line:*

(i)   *Capital Service*

In Capital Service, Inc. v. NLRB, 347 U.S. 501 (1954), an employer obtained a state-court injunction against picketing by a union. The employer then filed an unfair labor practice charge against the union with the National Labor Relations Board and the Board issued a formal complaint. The Board went to federal court to enjoin the union from picketing until the complaint was adjudicated on the merits and, additionally, to restrain the employer from taking any further steps to enforce its state court injunction. The District Court awarded the requested relief, and both the Court of Appeals and the Supreme Court affirmed. The Supreme Court held that the injunction against enforcement of the state court order was "necessary in aid of" the District Court's jurisdiction, since the District Court was required to enforce valid orders by the NLRB and needed to be free of any restraints set by the state court injunction.

(ii) *Amalgamated Clothing Workers*

Amalgamated Clothing Workers v. Richman Bros., 348 U.S. 511 (1955), also involved a labor dispute. The employer obtained a state court injunction against union picketing. The union sued in federal court to block enforcement of the state court order, arguing that the subject matter of the dispute was exclusively within the control of the NLRB and that state court adjudication was pre-empted by the federal labor laws.[c] The federal injunction was denied

---

c   The Supreme Court assumed, as seemed clear, that the state-court proceeding was pre-empted under Garner v. Teamsters, Chauffeurs and Helpers Local Union No. 776, 346 U.S. 485 (1953).

by the lower courts, and the Supreme Court affirmed in an opinion by Justice Frankfurter:

> In the face of this carefully considered enactment [the 1948 revision of the Anti-Injunction Act], we cannot accept the argument of petitioner and the Board, as amicus curiae, that § 2283 does not apply whenever the moving party in the district court alleged that the state court is "wholly without jurisdiction over the subject matter, having invaded a field pre-empted by Congress." No such exception had been established by judicial decision under [the former statute]. In any event, Congress has left no justification for its recognition now. This is not a statute conveying a broad general policy for appropriate ad hoc application. Legislative policy is here expressed in a clear-cut prohibition qualified only by specifically defined exceptions.

The Court then considered the exceptions. It found no "express" exception, and there was no former federal court judgment to be protected. As to the "necessary in aid of jurisdiction" exception, it said:

> In no lawyer-like sense can the present proceeding be thought to be in aid of the District Court's jurisdiction. Under no circumstances has the District Court jurisdiction to enforce rights and duties which call for recognition by the Board. Such non-existent jurisdiction therefore cannot be aided.
>
> Insofar as protection is needed for the Board's exercise of its jurisdiction, Congress has . . . specifically provided for resort, but only by the Board, to the District Court's equity powers. [A]ny aid that is needed to protect jurisdiction is the aid which the Board may need for the safeguarding of its authority. Such aid only the Board could seek, and only if, in a case pending before it, it has satisfied itself as to the adequacy of the complaint.[d]

Chief Justice Warren and Justices Black and Douglas dissented. Justice Douglas said:

> The Court has been ready to imply other exceptions to § 2283, where the common sense of the situation required it. Thus, if the federal court first takes possession of a res, it may protect its control over it, even to the extent of enjoining a state court from interfering with the property. That result flies in the face of the literal words of § 2283. Yet the injunction is allowed to issue as the

---

[d]   The employer had filed no unfair labor practice charge against the union with the NLRB, and there was no such charge available to the union unless the employer had committed an unfair labor practice by the act of filing the state-court suit. At the time that was unclear. Hence there may have been no way the union could get the dispute before the Labor Board, and no basis for the Board itself to seek an injunction against the state court proceedings. For later developments on this issue, see Bill Johnson's Restaurants, Inc. v. NLRB, 461 U.S. 731 (1983) (The Board may regard it as an unfair labor practice if a state suit is filed in retaliation for the exercise of federally protected rights *and* if the suit "lacks a reasonable basis in fact or law.")— [Footnote by eds.]

preferable way of avoiding unseemly clashes between state and federal authorities.[e] . . .

A like exception is needed here, if the state suit is not to dislocate severely the federal regulatory scheme. Under the present decision, an employer can move in the state courts for an injunction against the strike. The injunction, if granted, may for all practical purposes settle the matter. There is no way for the union to transfer the dispute to the federal Board, for it seems to be assumed by both parties that the employer has committed no unfair labor practice. By today's decision the federal court is powerless to enjoin the state action. The case lingers in the state court. There can be no appeal to this Court from the temporary injunction. It may take substantial time in the trial court to prepare a record to support a permanent injunction. Once one is granted, the long, drawn-out appeal through the state hierarchy and on to this Court commences. Yet by the time this Court decides that from the very beginning the state court had no jurisdiction, . . . a year or more has passed; and time alone has probably defeated the claim.

(iii) Leiter Minerals

Amalgamated Clothing Workers seemed to put an end to the argument that there were exceptions to § 2283 beyond those specifically stated in the statute. The Court found an additional exception, however, in Leiter Minerals, Inc. v. United States, 352 U.S. 220 (1957). The United States had leased mineral rights in federally owned land to certain private parties. Leiter claimed that it owned the mineral rights and sued the federal lessees in state court. The United States then filed an action against Leiter in federal court to quiet title to the mineral rights, and also sought to enjoin continuation of the state proceedings. The Supreme Court, in another opinion by Justice Frankfurter, held that the injunction could issue even though it did not fit within any of the statutory exceptions to § 2283:

> The frustration of superior federal interests that would ensue from precluding the federal government from obtaining a stay of state court proceedings except under the severe restrictions of § 2283 would be so great that we cannot reasonably impute such a purpose to Congress from the general language of § 2283 alone. It is always difficult to feel confident about construing an ambiguous statute

---

[e]   Contrary to Justice Douglas's comments, the "in rem" exception is normally regarded as comfortably within the "in aid of its jurisdiction" language of § 2283. It is clear, however—as Justice Black said in *Atlantic Coast Line*—that this statutory exception does not permit a federal court to enjoin state court proceedings merely because concurrent in personam actions are underway in both court systems. See Vendo Co. v. Lektro-Vend Corp., 433 U.S. 623, 641–43 (1977) (plurality opinion); Kline v. Burke Constr. Co., 260 U.S. 226 (1922); Charles Alan Wright, The Law of Federal Courts 283–84 (4th ed. 1983). The situation may be different if a state in personam action is pending on a matter within the exclusive jurisdiction of the federal courts. See David R. Kochery, Conflict of Jurisdiction: 28 U.S.C.A. § 2283 and Exclusive Federal Jurisdiction, 4 Buff. L. Rev. 269 (1955); Comment, Power of a Federal Court to Enjoin State Court Action in Aid of Its Exclusive Jurisdiction, 48 Nw. L. Rev. 383 (1953).—[Footnote by eds.]

... but the interpretation excluding the United States from the coverage of the statute seems to us preferable in the context of healthy federal-state relations.

3.   *NLRB V. NASH-FINCH CO.*

Some of the language in *Atlantic Coast Line* may have been intended to restrict the implication of *Leiter Minerals* that further exceptions to § 2283 might be recognized. Yet the rationale of *Leiter Minerals* was extended in NLRB v. Nash-Finch Co., 404 U.S. 138 (1971). In that case an employer again had obtained an injunction restraining picketing by a union. The NLRB then sued in federal court to restrain enforcement of the state court injunction. Its rationale for doing so is contained in the following excerpt from Justice Douglas's opinion for the Court:

> The action in the instant case does not seek an injunction to restrain specific activities upon which the Board has issued a complaint but is based upon the general doctrine of pre-emption. We therefore do not believe this case falls within the narrow exception contained in § 2283 for matter "necessary in aid of its jurisdiction." There is in the act no express authority for the Board to seek injunctive relief against pre-empted state action. The question remains whether there is implied authority to do so.

> It has long been held that the Board, though not granted express statutory remedies, may obtain appropriate and traditional ones to prevent frustration of the purposes of the act. . . . We conclude that there is . . . an implied authority of the Board, in spite of the command of § 2283, to enjoin state action where its federal power pre-empts the field. . . . The purpose of § 2283 was to avoid unseemly conflict between the state and the federal courts where the litigants were private persons, not to hamstring the federal government and its agencies in the use of federal courts to protect federal rights. We can no more conclude here than in *Leiter* that a general statute, limiting the power of federal courts to issue injunctions, had as its purpose the frustration of federal systems of regulation. . . .

Justices White and Brennan dissented.

4.   THE STATUTORY EXCEPTIONS

The exceptions in § 2283 have been construed in several important cases.[f]

---

[f]   The Supreme Court has held that § 2283 does not foreclose injunctions against the institution of litigation in a state court. See Dombrowski v. Pfister, 380 U.S. 479, 484 n.2 (1965). It only prohibits interference with state proceedings that are pending or that have been concluded when the federal suit is filed. For criticism of the Court's treatment of the statutory exceptions, see Martin H. Redish, The Anti-Injunction Statute Reconsidered, 44 U. Chi. L. Rev. 717 (1977). Problems posed by § 2283 in the class action context are discussed in Steven Larimore, Exploring the Interface between Rule 23 Class Actions and the Anti-Injunction Act, 18 Ga. L. Rev. 259 (1984). The exception to "protect or effectuate its judgments" is considered in

(i)   Mitchum v. Foster

One might think that the "expressly authorized by Act of Congress" exception would be fairly straightforward. Mitchum v. Foster, 407 U.S. 225 (1972), demonstrates otherwise. The question in *Mitchum* was whether 42 U.S.C. § 1983 provided "express" authority to enjoin state court proceedings in the face of § 2283. Section 1983 provides:

> Every person who, under color of any statute, ordinance, regulation, custom, or usage, of any state or territory, subjects, or causes to be subjected, any citizen of the United States or other person within the jurisdiction thereof to the deprivation of any rights, privileges, or immunities secured by the Constitution and laws, shall be liable to the party injured in an action at law, suit in equity, or other proper proceeding for redress.

On its face, § 1983 seems to do no more than supply, inter alia, a federal equitable cause of action in general terms. But the Court found that it was an "express" exception to § 2283.

First the Court observed that, "in order to qualify under the 'expressly authorized' exception of the anti-injunction statute, a federal law need not contain an express reference to that statute. . . . Indeed, none of the previously recognized statutory exceptions contains any such reference." The Court also said that "a federal law need not expressly authorize an injunction of a state court proceeding in order to qualify as an exception." The relevant inquiry was:

> [I]n order to qualify as an "expressly authorized" exception to the anti-injunction statute, an act of Congress must have created a specific and uniquely federal right or remedy, enforceable in a federal court of equity, which could be frustrated if the federal court were not empowered to enjoin a state court proceeding. This is not to say that in order to come within the exception an act of Congress must, on its face and in every one of its provisions, be totally incompatible with the prohibition of the anti-injunction statute. The test, rather, is whether an act of Congress, clearly creating a federal right or remedy enforceable in a federal court of equity, could be given its intended scope only by the stay of a state court proceeding.

Under this test, the Court concluded that § 1983 was indeed an "express" exception.[g] Justices Powell and Rehnquist did not participate in the decision. There was no dissent.

(ii)   Vendo Co. v. Lektro-Vend Corp.

The implication of *Mitchum* for other acts of Congress authorizing equitable relief was raised in Vendo Co. v. Lektro-Vend Corp., 433 U.S. 623 (1977). The case involved an agreement not to compete entered into by

---

George A. Martinez, The Anti-Injunction Act: Fending Off the New Attack on the Relitigation Exception, 72 Neb. L. Rev. 643 (1993).

[g]   The determination that § 2283 does not bar § 1983 injunctions against state proceedings does not mean that injunctions routinely issue in such cases. *Younger v. Harris* and its progeny impose limitations quite apart from the Anti-Injunction Act.

Stoner when he sold his vending machine company to Vendo. Vendo filed a state court suit against Stoner and Lektro-Vend Corp., a competing vending machine company that had entered into a business relationship with Stoner. After nine years of litigation, Vendo won a judgment in excess of $7 million. Shortly after the state suit was filed, Stoner and Lektro-Vend filed an action in federal court against Vendo alleging that the agreement not to compete violated the federal antitrust laws and that the state court suit was filed to harass the plaintiffs and to eliminate their competition with Vendo. This suit lay dormant throughout the state court litigation, but after the state judgment became final, Stoner and Lektro-Vend persuaded the federal judge to enjoin its enforcement. The Court of Appeals affirmed, and the Supreme Court granted certiorari.

The issue was whether § 16 of the Clayton Act was an "express" exception to § 2283. That statute provides:

> Any person . . . shall be entitled to sue for and have injunctive relief, in any court of the United States having jurisdiction over the parties, against threatened loss or damage by violation of the antitrust laws . . . when and under the same conditions and principles as injunctive relief against threatened conduct that will cause loss or damage is granted by courts of equity, under the rules governing such proceedings . . .

The fractured vote of the Court can best be understood by focusing first on the dissent by Justice Stevens, joined by Justices Brennan, White, and Marshall. In Stevens's view, "litigation in state courts may constitute an antitrust violation," and that was exactly what the federal District Court found to have happened in this case. Since this was so, "[t]he language in § 16 of the Clayton Act which expressly authorizes injunctions against violations of the antitrust laws" constitutes an express exception to § 2283 and authorized the federal injunction.

Justice Blackmun, joined by Chief Justice Burger, agreed that § 16 was an express exception to § 2283, but only "under narrowly limited circumstances" that were not satisfied in the present case:

> [N]o injunction may issue against currently pending state court proceedings unless those proceedings are themselves part of a "pattern of baseless, repetitive claims" that are being used as an anti-competitive device, all the traditional prerequisites for equitable relief are satisfied, and the only way to give the antitrust laws their intended scope is by staying the state proceedings.

Here there was only one state court lawsuit, not a "pattern of baseless, repetitive claims," and hence "§ 16 itself did not authorize the injunction below."

Justice Rehnquist, writing for himself and Justices Stewart and Powell, said that § 2283 "is an absolute prohibition against any injunction of any state court proceedings, unless the injunction falls within one of the three specifically defined exceptions in the act." Section 16 was not an "express" exception for three reasons. First, the last clause in the statute (beginning "under the same conditions and principles") means that § 16, unlike § 1983, "may fairly be read as virtually incorporating the prohibitions of the Anti-Injunction Act. . . ." Second, unlike in *Mitchum,* the legislative history of the Clayton Act could not cure the omission of express reference in the statute to the possibility of enjoining state court proceedings. Third, reading § 16 as an "express" exception would mean that "§ 2283 would be completely eviscerated since the ultimate logic of this position can mean no less than that virtually *all* federal authorizing injunctive relief statutes are exceptions to § 2283."

At this point Rehnquist cited 26 federal statutes that authorized equitable relief in general terms. Justice Stevens responded:

> I am not now persuaded that the concept of federalism is necessarily inconsistent with the view that the 1793 act should be considered wholly inapplicable to later enacted federal statutes that are enforceable exclusively in federal litigation. If a fair reading of the jurisdictional grant in any such statute does authorize an injunction against state court litigation frustrating the federal policy, nothing in our prior cases would foreclose the conclusion that it is within the "expressly authorized" exception to § 2283.

He also noted that these other statutes were relatively obscure, and "it is extremely doubtful that they would generate as much, or as significant, litigation as either the Civil Rights Act or the antitrust laws."

(iii) Parsons Steel, Inc. v. First Alabama Bank

Parsons Steel, Inc. v. First Alabama Bank, 474 U.S. 518 (1986), involved the intersection between § 2283 and 28 U.S.C. § 1738 (requiring that federal courts give full faith and credit to state court judgments). Simultaneous suits on related subjects were pending in both state and federal courts. Parsons was the plaintiff and the bank was the defendant in both actions. The federal suit was concluded first, in favor of the bank. The bank then pleaded res judicata as a defense to the state court action, but the state court held that the federal judgment did not preclude continuation of the state suit. Judgment for some $4 million was then awarded against the bank, after which the bank sought an injunction from the federal court to preclude enforcement of the state court judgment. The injunction was entered and the Court of Appeals affirmed.

The Supreme Court unanimously reversed. It agreed that *Toucey* had been overruled by the 1948 amendment to § 2283, but held that the "relitigation exception" to § 2283 is limited "to those situations in which the state court has not yet ruled on the merits of the res judicata issue." The bank may have been entitled to an injunction while the state court proceeding was pending, but once the res judicata issue was raised in state court and decided against the bank, it could "not return to federal court for another try."[h]

---

[h] Can a defendant in state court remove to federal court on the ground that the plaintiff's claim is precluded by a prior federal court judgment? The Court said "no" in Rivet v. Regions Bank of Louisiana, 522 U.S. 470 (1998): "Under the well-pleaded complaint rule, [claim] preclusion [is] a defensive plea involving no recasting of the plaintiff's complaint, and is therefore not a proper basis for removal."

NOTE ON THE AFFORDABLE CARE ACT

The "individual mandate" of the Patient Protection and Affordable Care Act of 2010, 26 U.S.C. § 5000A, imposed a financial sanction on certain individuals who decline to purchase health insurance. The constitutionality of this provision was upheld five-to-four in National Federation of Independent Business v. Sebelius, 567 U.S. 519 (2012). Since the mandate was not to go into effect until 2014, a provision of the Internal Revenue Code, 26 U.S.C. § 7421(a) (the Anti-Injunction Act), provided a potential obstacle to litigation of its constitutionality before then: "no suit for the purpose of restraining the assessment or collection of any tax shall be maintained in any court by any person, whether or not such person is the person against whom such tax was assessed."[a] Chief Justice Roberts wrote for the Court on this question:

> Before turning to the merits, we need to be sure we have the authority to do so. The Anti-Injunction Act . . . protects the Government's ability to collect a consistent stream of revenue, by barring litigation to enjoin or otherwise obstruct the collection of taxes. Because of the Anti-Injunction Act, taxes can ordinarily be challenged only after they are paid, by suing for a refund. . . .

> The text of the pertinent statutes suggests [that the suit can go forward.] Congress . . . chose to describe the "[s]hared responsibility payment" imposed on those who forgo health insurance not as a "tax," but as a "penalty." There is no immediate reason to think that a statute applying to "any tax" would apply to a "penalty." . . .

> [It is argued] that even though Congress did not label the shared responsibility payment a tax, we should treat it as such under the Anti-Injunction Act because it functions like a tax. It is true that Congress cannot change whether an exaction is a tax or a penalty for constitutional purposes simply by describing it as one or the other. . . . The Anti-Injunction Act and the Affordable Care Act, however, are creatures of Congress's own creation. How they relate to each other is up to Congress, and the best evidence of Congress's intent is the statutory text. . . .

> The Affordable Care Act does not require that the penalty for failing to comply with the individual mandate be treated as a tax for purposes of the Anti-Injunction Act. The Anti-Injunction Act therefore does not apply to this suit, and we may proceed to the merits.

On the merits, the Government had argued that the statute was constitutional because within Congress's authority under the Commerce Clause or, alternatively, under the power to "lay and collect Taxes." The Court's response was fractured. In an unusual joint dissent, Justices Scalia, Kennedy, Thomas, and Alito rejected both arguments and concluded that the Act was unconstitutional. Chief Justice Roberts agreed with them that the statute

---

[a]   For extensive consideration of Section 7421(a) and an argument that the statute should not be seen as a jurisdictional limitation but should be governed by equitable principles, see Erin Morrow Hawley, The Equitable Anti-Injunction Act, 90 Notre Dame L. Rev. 81 (2014).

did not fall within the powers of Congress under the Commerce Clause.[b] But, joined by Justices Breyer, Ginsburg, Sotomayor, and Kagan, he said for the Court that the individual mandate fell within Congress's taxing power and that it was therefore constitutional. On the apparent inconsistency between treating the levy as a tax for purposes of Congress's power under Article I but not for purposes of the Anti-Injunction Act, he said for the Court:

> It is of course true that the Act describes the payment as a "penalty," not a "tax." But while that label is fatal to the application of the Anti-Injunction Act, it does not determine whether the payment may be viewed as an exercise of Congress's taxing power. It is up to Congress whether to apply the Anti-Injunction Act to any particular statute, so it makes sense to be guided by Congress's choice of label on that question. That choice does not, however, control whether an exaction is within Congress's constitutional power to tax.

This reasoning brought a stinging rebuke from the joint dissent:

> What the Government would have us believe in these cases is that the very same textual indications that show this is not a tax under the Anti-Injunction Act show that it is a tax under the Constitution. That carries verbal wizardry too far, deep into the forbidden land of the sophists.

---

[b]   Joined by Justices Breyer, Sotomayor, and Kagan, Justice Ginsburg wrote separately in support of the authority of Congress to adopt the individual mandate under the Commerce Clause.

CHAPTER VII

HABEAS CORPUS

SECTION 1. REVIEW OF STATE COURT DECISIONS ON THE MERITS: JUDICIAL LIMITATIONS

INTRODUCTORY NOTES ON THE HISTORY OF HABEAS CORPUS

1. HABEAS CORPUS FOR STATE PRISONERS: BASIC PRINCIPLES

The "Suspension Clause" of the Constitution, in Article I, Section 9, provides that "[t]he privilege of the Writ of Habeas Corpus shall not be suspended, unless when in Cases of Rebellion or Invasion the public Safety may require it." The ancient writ of habeas corpus—the form of the writ the Framers had in mind when they wrote the Suspension Clause—provided for judicial review of the legality of executive detention. Today, the most litigated form of habeas corpus concerns post-conviction review—that is, federal determination of the legality of confinement *after* judicial prosecution and conviction. The issues raised by this form of habeas are quite different from those involved when the executive acts without judicial oversight.[a]

Post-conviction habeas is in form a new lawsuit, separate from the underlying criminal prosecution, in which a person in custody challenges the custodian to defend the legality of the detention. The prisoner is the plaintiff, the warden or other custodian the defendant. The requested relief is release from custody (although the successful habeas petitioner may be subject to a retrial or a new sentencing proceeding). Because it is a separate lawsuit, habeas corpus is often called a "collateral attack," resulting in "collateral review" of the underlying conviction. Appeal following a criminal conviction provides "direct" review.

It is settled that the normal rules of res judicata and collateral estoppel do not apply to convictions attacked in federal habeas corpus proceedings. Issues decided on the merits in the direct proceedings may be subject to relitigation on habeas corpus. As subsequent materials demonstrate, however, there are many limitations on the availability of federal collateral relief, limitations found in an evolving, distinctive, and often arcane body of habeas corpus doctrine.

Most habeas petitioners are convicted criminals who allege a federal constitutional defect in the proceedings that led to their conviction or their sentence. Federal habeas cannot be sought until the trial and all appeals

---

[a] For discussions of the history of habeas corpus, including its operation in pre-revolutionary England and in the United States during the 19th and 20th centuries, see William F. Duker, A Constitutional History of Habeas Corpus (1980); Eric M. Freedman, Habeas Corpus: Rethinking the Great Writ of Liberty (2001); Paul D. Halliday, Habeas Corpus: From England to Empire (2010); and Amanda L. Tyler, Habeas Corpus in Wartime: From the Tower of London to Guantanamo Bay (2017).

within the chain of direct review have been exhausted.[b] If the claim was not resolved in those proceedings, a person convicted in a state court who wishes to pursue the claim in a federal habeas court must first exhaust in the state courts any opportunity that remains available for its litigation on the merits. All states have a post-conviction process, not always called habeas corpus, through which—under procedures and limitations unique to each state—federal constitutional claims that were not resolved at trial and the direct review process can be raised. Only after the state courts have been given an opportunity to pass on the merits of the claim may the petitioner turn to the federal courts on habeas.

The cases that arrive in a federal habeas court tend to fall into two patterns: Either the state courts decided a federal constitutional claim that the petitioner now wishes to relitigate in federal court; or the state courts refused to hear on the merits in direct or collateral proceedings (usually because of a failure to follow state procedures) a claim that the petitioner now wishes to litigate for the first time in federal court. Complex rules have been developed for each of these categories, frequently overlaid in both by a third issue: How should newly developed constitutional principles be applied to old convictions if the defendant is still in prison? Although normal principles of res judicata are not invoked to foreclose challenges to current custody based on new rules, there are, again, independent doctrines that apply in such situations to limit the availability of federal habeas relief.

2.   GOVERNING STATUTES

Statutory authority to grant habeas corpus was conferred on the federal courts by the Judiciary Act of 1789—but only for federal prisoners. Not until 1867 was federal habeas corpus made available to state prisoners. As currently codified, 28 U.S.C. § 2254(a) extends the writ to any prisoner who is "in custody in violation of the Constitution or laws or treaties of the United States."[c]

The precise conditions under which federal habeas is available were determined chiefly by judicial decision until the enactment of the Antiterrorism and Effective Death Penalty Act of 1996 (AEDPA). Today, that statute has a lot to say about the availability of habeas corpus. According to AEDPA's legislative history, the new provisions aimed "to curb the abuse of the statutory

---

[b]   The first case to state this requirement was Ex parte Royall, 117 U.S. 241 (1886), in which habeas was sought in a federal court to stop a state trial that had not begun. The Court held that the federal courts should not intervene until the state trial and appellate courts had an opportunity to rule on the constitutional claim.

Notice the relationship of this conclusion to the holding in Younger v. Harris, 401 U.S. 37 (1971), that federal courts in general may not enjoin pending state criminal proceedings. *Younger* is considered in Chapter VI, Section 2.

The exhaustion requirement begun in *Ex parte Royall* was later codified in what is now 28 U.S.C. § 2254(b)(1). Its modern substance is considered further in Section 3 of this Chapter.

[c]   The limitation of federal habeas to a person in "custody" once meant that habeas was open only to one then imprisoned. Beginning with Jones v. Cunningham, 371 U.S. 236 (1963), this requirement has been relaxed so that any "significant restraints on . . . liberty" now suffice. Thus, a person on probation or one whose sentence has been suspended on condition of good behavior is in "custody" and may challenge the underlying conviction in a habeas corpus proceeding.

writ of habeas corpus, and to address the acute problems of unnecessary delay and abuse in capital cases." H.R. Report 104–518, 104th Cong., 2d Sess., p. 111. The provisions designed to achieve these goals are complex and poorly drafted, and their relationship to prior Supreme Court decisions in the area is often unclear. Nonetheless, the overall purpose is plain. Congress wanted to curtail access to federal habeas corpus, especially in capital cases. To that end, the new legislation codified many restrictive doctrines developed by the Supreme Court and added new limitations unknown to prior law.

3. COLLATERAL RELIEF FOR FEDERAL PRISONERS

Section 2255 of Title 28 was enacted in 1948 as an alternative to habeas corpus for *federal* prisoners. Essentially, it is a venue provision. The proper venue in a habeas proceeding is the place where the prisoner is in custody. Before the enactment of § 2255, the burdens of habeas corpus for federal prisoners fell unevenly on federal judges. Those who sat in districts where federal prisons were located heard all habeas applications from federal prisoners incarcerated in their districts, whereas those who sat in districts without federal prisons heard none. Moreover, witnesses needed for habeas hearings typically lived near the place of the original trial, which was often far from the place of detention. Section 2255 addresses these problems by requiring that a federal prisoner seek collateral relief from the sentencing court.

As a formal matter, habeas corpus remains available to a federal prisoner, but the remedy provided by § 2255 must be sought first. Since the relief afforded by § 2255 is the same as that available in habeas, the need for a federal prisoner to resort to habeas corpus is unlikely to arise. In practice, therefore, a state prisoner will seek habeas corpus under § 2254, whereas a federal prisoner will file an analogous action under § 2255. For most purposes, the proceedings can be regarded as fungible, with the precedents for one fully applicable to the other. The phrase "2255 proceeding" has entered the vocabulary of defense attorneys and federal prisoners as the functional equivalent of habeas corpus. Importantly, AEDPA contains restrictions on § 2255 proceedings for federal prisoners analogous to those enacted for their state counterparts.

4. FEDERAL HABEAS REVIEW OF STATE COURT DECISIONS ON THE MERITS

Federal habeas corpus for persons in custody following conviction of a crime initially was limited to situations where the convicting court lacked "jurisdiction." This limit was applied until the middle of the 20th century to both federal and state prisoners.

Over time, the concept of "jurisdiction" was expanded to include a few situations where the court had jurisdiction in a technical sense but where fundamental rights were denied. The extreme to which this was taken is illustrated by Johnson v. Zerbst, 304 U.S. 458, 467–68 (1938), where the Court held with respect to a prior federal criminal conviction:

Since the Sixth Amendment constitutionally entitles one charged with crime to the assistance of counsel, compliance with this constitutional mandate is an essential jurisdictional prerequisite to a federal court's authority to deprive an accused of his life or liberty. . . . If the accused . . . is not represented by counsel and has not competently and intelligently waived his constitutional right, the Sixth Amendment stands as a jurisdictional bar to a valid conviction and sentence . . . . If this requirement of the Sixth Amendment is not complied with, the court no longer has jurisdiction to proceed. The judgment of conviction pronounced by a court without jurisdiction is void, and one imprisoned thereunder may obtain release by habeas corpus.

With respect to state prisoners, two major departures from the requirement that federal habeas corpus be limited to "jurisdictional" errors should be noted. The first occurred before *Johnson v. Zerbst*. The claim in Frank v. Magnum, 237 U.S. 309 (1915), was that Frank was denied Due Process because his trial was mob dominated. The Court accepted the validity of the claim in principle:

We, of course, agree that if a trial is in fact dominated by a mob, so that the jury is intimidated and the trial judge yields, and so that there is an actual interference with the course of justice, there is, in that court, a departure from due process of law in the proper sense of that term. And if the state, *supplying no corrective process*, carries into execution a judgment of death or imprisonment based upon a verdict thus produced by mob domination, the state deprives the accused of his life or liberty without due process of law. (Emphasis added.)

But it denied relief because the state courts had provided a process for hearing Frank's claim and had found "his allegations of fact . . . to be unfounded." Had the state courts not supplied a "corrective process" capable of addressing the claim, Frank would have been entitled to such a process in a federal habeas court.

The second major change came in Brown v. Allen, 344 U.S. 443 (1953), where the Court went much further. It held that the Habeas Corpus Act of 1867 authorized federal courts to *reconsider de novo* the merits of federal constitutional claims already heard and decided in state court. Principles of finality that ordinarily precluded relitigation of claims already heard and decided did not apply. The federal courts were authorized to decide federal constitutional claims anew.

Note the breadth of the *Brown v. Allen* holding. In effect, it turned the federal district courts into an avenue of appellate review of decisions by the state supreme courts. Federal district courts at trial and circuit courts on appeal were to decide de novo whether state courts had correctly resolved federal constitutional claims that arose in state criminal convictions and that had been decided by the state courts on the merits.[d] Judicial narrowing of *Brown*'s reach began in the Supreme Court 23 years later with the next main case.

SUBSECTION A. SEARCH AND SEIZURE CLAIMS

Stone v. Powell
Supreme Court of the United States, 1976.
428 U.S. 465.

■ MR. JUSTICE POWELL delivered the opinion of the Court.

Respondents in these cases were convicted of criminal offenses in state courts, and their convictions were affirmed on appeal. The prosecution in each case relied upon evidence obtained by searches and seizures alleged by respondents to have been unlawful. Each respondent subsequently sought relief in a federal district court by filing a petition for a writ of federal habeas corpus under 28 U.S.C. § 2254. The question presented is whether a federal court should consider, in ruling on a petition for habeas corpus relief filed by a state prisoner, a claim that evidence obtained by an unconstitutional search or seizure was introduced at his trial, when he has previously been afforded an opportunity for full and fair litigation of his claim in the state courts. . . .

[In Part I of his opinion, Justice Powell recited the facts of two cases that had been consolidated for review. In both, the state courts rejected search and seizure claims on the merits at trial and on direct appeal. The defendants in both cases obtained habeas relief from the lower federal courts, and the Supreme Court granted certiorari.

[Justice Powell rehearsed the history of federal habeas in Part II. He noted that initially the Court "defined the scope of the writ in accordance with the common law and limited it to an inquiry as to the jurisdiction of the sentencing tribunal." After the writ was extended to state prisoners in 1867, "the limitation of federal habeas corpus . . . to consideration of the jurisdiction of the sentencing court persisted." He noted that *Frank v. Mangum* and *Brown v. Allen* extended the writ beyond this narrow

---

d   See Carlos M. Vázquez, Habeas as Forum Allocation: A New Synthesis, 71 U. Miami L. Rev. 645 (2017):

> [T]he [pre-*Brown v. Allen*] debate was not about whether state prisoners' constitutional claims should be relegated to state court; it was instead about whether federal review should be undertaken in the Supreme Court or the lower federal courts. The Court eventually concluded that it could not hope to monitor state court compliance with the constitutional rights of state court criminal defendants and accordingly expanded the lower federal courts' power to do so via habeas.

The effect of AEDPA, he concludes, is to "shift[ ] back to the Supreme Court the responsibility for monitoring state court decisions and granting relief for wrong but reasonable state court convictions." But, he suggests, "allocating such a role to the Supreme Court would be even more dysfunctional today" than it was in the pre-*Brown v. Allen* era.

focus, the latter encompassing full reconsideration of constitutional claims decided by state courts on the merits.[a]]

III

The Fourth Amendment assures the "right of the people to be secure in their persons, houses, papers, and effects, against unreasonable searches and seizures." The amendment was primarily a reaction to the evils associated with the use of the general warrant in England and the writs of assistance in the Colonies, and was intended to protect the "sanctity of a man's home and the privacies of life" from searches under unchecked general authority.

The exclusionary rule was a judicially created means of effectuating the rights secured by the Fourth Amendment. Prior to the Court's decisions in Weeks v. United States, 232 U.S. 383 (1914), and Gouled v. United States, 255 U.S. 298 (1921), there existed no barrier to the introduction in criminal trials of evidence obtained in violation of the amendment. In *Weeks* the Court held that the defendant could petition before trial for the return of property secured through an illegal search or seizure conducted by federal authorities. In *Gouled* the Court held broadly that such evidence could not be introduced in a federal prosecution. Thirty-five years after *Weeks* the Court held in Wolf v. Colorado, 338 U.S. 25 (1949), that the right to be free from arbitrary intrusion by the police that is protected by the Fourth Amendment is "implicit in 'the concept of ordered liberty' and as such enforceable against the states through the [Fourteenth Amendment] Due Process Clause." The Court concluded, however, that the *Weeks* exclusionary rule would not be imposed upon the states as "an essential ingredient of [that] right." The full force of *Wolf* was eroded in subsequent decisions, and a little more than a decade later the exclusionary rule was held applicable to the states in Mapp v. Ohio, 367 U.S. 643 (1961).

Decisions prior to *Mapp* advanced two principal reasons for application of the rule in federal trials. The Court in Elkins v. United States, 364 U.S. 206 (1960), for example, in the context of its special supervisory role over the lower federal courts, referred to the "imperative of judicial integrity," suggesting that exclusion of illegally seized evidence prevents contamination of the judicial process. But even in that context a more pragmatic ground was emphasized:

> The rule is calculated to prevent, not to repair. Its purpose is to deter—to compel respect for the constitutional guaranty in the only effectively available way—by removing the incentive to disregard it.

---

[a]   The Court added this footnote: "Despite the expansion of the scope of the writ, there has been no change in the established rule with respect to nonconstitutional claims. The writ of habeas corpus and its federal counterpart, 28 U.S.C. § 2255, 'will not be allowed to do service for an appeal.' Sunal v. Large, 332 U.S. 174, 178 (1947). For this reason, nonconstitutional claims that could have been raised on appeal, but were not, may not be asserted in collateral proceedings. . . ."—[Footnote by eds.]

The *Mapp* majority justified the application of the rule to the states on several grounds, but relied principally upon the belief that exclusion would deter future unlawful police conduct.

Although our decisions often have alluded to the "imperative of judicial integrity," they demonstrate the limited role of this justification in the determination whether to apply the rule in a particular context. Logically extended this justification would require that courts exclude unconstitutionally seized evidence despite lack of objection by the defendant, or even over his assent. It also would require abandonment of the standing limitations on who may object to the introduction of unconstitutionally seized evidence, Alderman v. United States, 394 U.S. 165 (1969), and retreat from the proposition that judicial proceedings need not abate when the defendant's person is unconstitutionally seized, Gerstein v. Pugh, 420 U.S. 103, 119 (1975). Similarly, the interest in promoting judicial integrity does not prevent the use of illegally seized evidence in grand jury proceedings. United States v. Calandra, 414 U.S. 338 (1974). Nor does it require that the trial court exclude such evidence from use for impeachment of a defendant, even though its introduction is certain to result in conviction in some cases. Walder v. United States, 347 U.S. 62 (1954). The teaching of these cases is clear. While courts, of course, must ever be concerned with preserving the integrity of the judicial process, this concern has limited force as a justification for the exclusion of highly probative evidence. The force of this justification becomes minimal where federal habeas corpus relief is sought by a prisoner who previously has been afforded the opportunity for full and fair consideration of his search-and-seizure claim at trial and on direct review.

The primary justification for the exclusionary rule then is the deterrence of police conduct that violates Fourth Amendment rights. Post-*Mapp* decisions have established that the rule is not a personal constitutional right. It is not calculated to redress the injury to the privacy of the victim of the search or seizure, for any "[r]eparation comes too late." Linkletter v. Walker, 381 U.S. 618, 637 (1965). Instead, "the rule is a judicially created remedy designed to safeguard Fourth Amendment rights generally through its deterrent effect. . . ." *Calandra*, 414 U.S. at 348.

Mapp involved the enforcement of the exclusionary rule at state trials and on direct review. . . . But despite the broad deterrent purpose of the exclusionary rule, it has never been interpreted to proscribe the introduction of illegally seized evidence in all proceedings or against all persons. As in the case of any remedial device, "the application of the rule has been restricted to those areas where its remedial objectives are thought most efficaciously served." Id. Thus, our refusal to extend the exclusionary rule to grand jury proceedings was based on a balancing of the potential injury to the historic role and function of the grand jury by such extension against the potential contribution to the effectuation of the Fourth Amendment through deterrence of police misconduct:

> Any incremental deterrent effect which might be achieved by extending the rule to grand jury proceedings is uncertain at best. Whatever deterrence of police misconduct may result from the exclusion of illegally seized evidence from criminal trials, it is unrealistic to assume that application of the rule to grand jury proceedings would significantly further that goal. Such an extension would deter only police investigation consciously directed toward the discovery of evidence solely for use in a grand jury investigation. . . . We therefore decline to embrace a view that would achieve a speculative and undoubtedly minimal advance in the deterrence of police misconduct at the expense of substantially impeding the role of the grand jury.

Id. at 351.

The same pragmatic analysis of the exclusionary rule's usefulness in a particular context was evident earlier in *Walder v. United States*, where the Court permitted the government to use unlawfully seized evidence to impeach the credibility of a defendant who had testified broadly in his own defense. The Court held, in effect, that the interests safeguarded by the exclusionary rule in that context were outweighed by the need to prevent perjury and to assure the integrity of the trial process. The judgment in *Walder* revealed most clearly that the policies behind the exclusionary rule are not absolute. Rather, they must be evaluated in light of competing policies. In that case, the public interest in determination of truth at trial was deemed to outweigh the incremental contribution that might have been made to the protection of Fourth Amendment values by application of the rule.

The balancing process at work in these cases also finds expression in the standing requirement. Standing to invoke the exclusionary rule has been found to exist only when the government attempts to use illegally obtained evidence to incriminate the victim of the illegal search. Brown v. United States, 411 U.S. 223 (1973); Alderman v. United States, 394 U.S. 165 (1969). The standing requirement is premised on the view that the "additional benefits of extending the . . . rule" to defendants other than the victim of the search or seizure are outweighed by the "further encroachment upon the public interest in prosecuting those accused of crime and having them acquitted or convicted on the basis of all the evidence which exposes the truth." *Alderman*, 394 U.S. at 174–75.[26]

IV

We turn now to the specific question presented by these cases. Respondents allege violations of Fourth Amendment rights guaranteed

---

[26] Cases addressing the question whether search-and-seizure holdings should be applied retroactively also have focused on the deterrent purpose served by the exclusionary rule, consistently with the balancing analysis applied generally in the exclusionary rule context. See Desist v. United States, 394 U.S. 244, 249–51, 253–54 and n.21 (1969); Linkletter v. Walker, 381 U.S. 618, 636–37 (1965). The "attenuation-of-the-taint" doctrine also is consistent with the balancing approach. See Brown v. Illinois, 422 U.S. 590 (1975); Wong Sun v. United States, 371 U.S. 471, 491–92 (1963).

them through the Fourteenth Amendment. The question is whether state prisoners—who have been afforded the opportunity for full and fair consideration of their reliance upon the exclusionary rule with respect to seized evidence by the state courts at trial and on direct review—may invoke their claim again on federal habeas corpus review. The answer is to be found by weighing the utility of the exclusionary rule against the costs of extending it to collateral review of Fourth Amendment claims.

The costs of applying the exclusionary rule even at trial and on direct review are well known: the focus of the trial, and the attention of the participants therein, are diverted from the ultimate question of guilt or innocence that should be the central concern in a criminal proceeding. Moreover, the physical evidence sought to be excluded is typically reliable and often the most probative information bearing on the guilt or innocence of the defendant. As Justice Black emphasized in his dissent in *Kaufman*:

> A claim of illegal search and seizure under the Fourth Amendment is crucially different from many other constitutional rights; ordinarily the evidence seized can in no way have been rendered untrustworthy by the means of its seizure and indeed often this evidence alone establishes beyond virtually any shadow of a doubt that the defendant is guilty.

Application of the rule thus deflects the truthfinding process and often frees the guilty. The disparity in particular cases between the error committed by the police officer and the windfall afforded a guilty defendant by application of the rule is contrary to the idea of proportionality that is essential to the concept of justice. Thus, although the rule is thought to deter unlawful police activity in part through the nurturing of respect for Fourth Amendment values, if applied indiscriminately it may well have the opposite effect of generating disrespect for the law and administration of justice. These long-recognized costs of the rule persist when a criminal conviction is sought to be overturned on collateral review on the ground that a search-and-seizure claim was erroneously rejected by two or more tiers of state courts.[31]

Evidence obtained by police officers in violation of the Fourth Amendment is excluded at trial in the hope that the frequency of future violations will decrease. Despite the absence of supportive empirical evidence, we have assumed that the immediate effect of exclusion will be to

---

[31] Resort to habeas corpus, especially for purposes other than to assure that no innocent person suffers an unconstitutional loss of liberty, results in serious intrusions on values important to our system of government. They include "(i) the most effective utilization of limited judicial resources, (ii) the necessity of finality in criminal trials, (iii) the minimization of friction between our federal and state systems of justice, and (iv) the maintenance of the constitutional balance upon which the doctrine of federalism is founded." Schneckloth v. Bustamonte, 412 U.S. 218, 250, 259 (1973) (Powell, J., concurring). We nevertheless afford broad habeas corpus relief, recognizing the need in a free society for an additional safeguard against compelling an innocent man to suffer an unconstitutional loss of liberty. . . .

discourage law enforcement officials from violating the Fourth Amendment by removing the incentive to disregard it. More importantly, over the long term, this demonstration that our society attaches serious consequences to violation of constitutional rights is thought to encourage those who formulate law enforcement policies, and the officers who implement them, to incorporate Fourth Amendment ideals into their value system.

We adhere to the view that these considerations support the implementation of the exclusionary rule at trial and its enforcement on direct appeal of state-court convictions. But the additional contribution, if any, of the consideration of search-and-seizure claims of state prisoners on collateral review is small in relation to the costs. To be sure, each case in which such claim is considered may add marginally to an awareness of the values protected by the Fourth Amendment. There is no reason to believe, however, that the overall educative effect of the exclusionary rule would be appreciably diminished if search-and-seizure claims could not be raised in federal habeas corpus review of state convictions. Nor is there reason to assume that any specific disincentive already created by the risk of exclusion of evidence at trial or the reversal of convictions on direct review would be enhanced if there were the further risk that a conviction obtained in state court and affirmed on direct review might be overturned in collateral proceedings often occurring years after the incarceration of the defendant. The view that the deterrence of Fourth Amendment violations would be furthered rests on the dubious assumption that law enforcement authorities would fear that federal habeas review might reveal flaws in a search or seizure that went undetected at trial and on appeal.[35] Even if one rationally could assume that some additional incremental deterrent effect would be present in isolated cases, the resulting advance of the legitimate goal of furthering Fourth Amendment rights would be outweighed by the acknowledged costs to other values vital to a rational system of criminal justice.

In sum, we conclude that where the state has provided an opportunity for full and fair litigation of a Fourth Amendment claim, a state prisoner may not be granted federal habeas corpus relief on the ground

---

[35] The policy arguments that respondents marshal in support of the view that federal habeas corpus review is necessary to effectuate the Fourth Amendment stem from a basic mistrust of the state courts as fair and competent forums for the adjudication of federal constitutional rights. The argument is that state courts cannot be trusted to effectuate Fourth Amendment values through fair application of the rule, and the oversight jurisdiction of this Court on certiorari is an inadequate safeguard. The principal rationale for this view emphasizes the broad differences in the respective institutional settings within which federal judges and state judges operate. Despite differences in institutional environment and the unsympathetic attitude to federal constitutional claims of some state judges in years past, we are unwilling to assume that there now exists a general lack of appropriate sensitivity to constitutional rights in the trial and appellate courts of the several states. State courts, like federal courts, have a constitutional obligation to safeguard personal liberties and to uphold federal law. Moreover, the argument that federal judges are more expert in applying federal constitutional law is especially unpersuasive in the context of search-and-seizure claims, since they are dealt with on a daily basis by trial level judges in both systems. . . .

that evidence obtained in an unconstitutional search or seizure was introduced at his trial.[37] In this context the contribution of the exclusionary rule, if any, to the effectuation of the Fourth Amendment is minimal and the substantial societal costs of application of the rule persist with special force.

Accordingly, the judgments of the Courts of Appeals are

Reversed.

■ MR. JUSTICE BRENNAN, with whom MR. JUSTICE MARSHALL concurs, dissenting. . . .

Under *Mapp,* as a matter of federal constitutional law, a state court *must* exclude evidence from the trial of an individual whose fourth and Fourteenth Amendment rights were violated by a search or seizure that directly or indirectly resulted in the acquisition of that evidence. . . . When a state court admits such evidence, it has committed a *constitutional* error, and unless that error is harmless under federal standards, it follows ineluctably that the defendant has been placed "in custody in violation of the Constitution" within the comprehension of 28 U.S.C. § 2254. [I]t escapes me as to what logic can support the assertion that the defendant's unconstitutional confinement obtains during the process of direct review, no matter how long that process takes, but that the unconstitutionality then suddenly dissipates at the moment the claim is asserted in a collateral attack on the conviction.

The only conceivable rationale upon which the Court's "constitutional" thesis might rest is the statement that "the [exclusionary] rule is not a personal constitutional right. . . . Instead, 'the rule is a judicially created remedy designed to safeguard Fourth Amendment rights generally through its deterrent effect.' " . . . However the Court reinterprets *Mapp,* and whatever the rationale now attributed to *Mapp*'s holding or the purpose ascribed to the exclusionary rule, the prevailing constitutional *rule* is that unconstitutionally seized evidence *cannot be admitted* in the criminal trial of a person whose federal constitutional rights were violated by the search or seizure. The erroneous admission of such evidence is a violation of the federal Constitution—*Mapp* inexorably means at least this much, or there would be no basis for applying the exclusionary rule in state criminal proceedings—and an accused against whom such evidence is admitted has been convicted in derogation of rights mandated by, and is "in custody in violation of," the Constitution of the United States. Indeed, since state courts violate the strictures of the federal Constitution by admitting such evidence, then even if federal habeas review did not directly effectuate Fourth Amendment values, a proposition I

---

[37] [W]e hold only that a federal court need not apply the exclusionary rule on habeas review of a Fourth Amendment claim absent a showing that the state prisoner was denied an opportunity for a full and fair litigation of that claim at trial and on direct review. Our decision does not mean that the federal court lacks jurisdiction over such a claim, but only that the application of the rule is limited to cases in which there has been both such a showing and a Fourth Amendment violation.

deny, that review would nevertheless serve to effectuate what is concededly a constitutional principle concerning admissibility of evidence at trial.

The Court, assuming without deciding that respondents were convicted on the basis of unconstitutionally obtained evidence erroneously admitted against them by the state trial courts, acknowledges that respondents had the right to obtain a reversal of their convictions on appeal in the state courts or on certiorari to this Court. [T]he basis for reversing those convictions would of course have to be that the states, in rejecting respondents' Fourth Amendment claims, had deprived them of a right in derogation of the federal Constitution. It is simply inconceivable that that constitutional deprivation suddenly vanishes after the appellate process has been exhausted. And as between this Court on certiorari, and federal district courts on habeas, it is for *Congress* to decide what the most efficacious method is for enforcing *federal* constitutional rights and asserting the primacy of federal law. The Court, however, simply ignores the settled principle that for purposes of adjudicating constitutional claims Congress, which has the power to do so under Art. III of the Constitution, has effectively cast the district courts sitting in habeas in the role of surrogate Supreme Courts.[10]

. . . This Court's precedents have been "premised in large part on a recognition that the availability of collateral remedies is necessary to insure the integrity of proceedings at and before trial where constitutional rights are at stake. Our decisions leave no doubt that the federal habeas remedy extends to state prisoners alleging that unconstitutionally obtained evidence was admitted against them at trial." Kaufman v. United States, 394 U.S. 217, 225 (1969). Some of those decisions explicitly considered and rejected the "policies" referred to by the Court. There were no "assumptions" with respect to the construction of the habeas statutes,

---

[10] The failure to confront this fact forthrightly is obviously a core defect in the Court's analysis. For to the extent Congress has accorded the federal district courts a role in our constitutional scheme functionally equivalent to that of the Supreme Court with respect to review of state court resolutions of federal constitutional claims, it is evident that the Court's direct/collateral review distinction for constitutional purposes simply collapses. Indeed, logically extended, the Court's analysis, which basically turns on the fact that law enforcement officials cannot anticipate a second court's finding constitutional errors after one court has fully and fairly adjudicated the claim and found it to be meritless, would preclude any Supreme Court review on direct appeal or even state appellate review if the trial court fairly addressed the Fourth Amendment claim on the merits. . . .

The Court's arguments respecting the cost/benefit analysis of applying the exclusionary rule on collateral attack also have no merit. For all of the "costs" of applying the exclusionary rule on habeas *should already have been incurred* at the trial or on direct review if the state court had not misapplied federal constitutional principles. As such, these "costs" were evaluated and deemed to be outweighed when the exclusionary rule was fashioned. The only proper question on habeas is whether federal courts, acting under congressional directive to have the last say as to enforcement of federal constitutional principles, are to permit the states free enjoyment of the fruits of a conviction which by definition were only obtained through violations of the Constitution as interpreted in *Mapp*. And as to the question whether any "educative" function is served by such habeas review, today's decision will certainly provide a lesson that, tragically for an individual's constitutional rights, will not be lost on state courts. . . .

but reasoned decisions that those policies were an insufficient justification for shutting the federal habeas door to litigants with federal constitutional claims in light of such countervailing considerations as "the necessity that federal courts have the 'last say' with respect to questions of federal law, the inadequacy of state procedures to raise and preserve federal claims, the concern that state judges may be unsympathetic to federally created rights, [and] the institutional constraints on the exercise of this Court's certiorari jurisdiction to review state convictions," as well as the fundamental belief "that adequate protection of constitutional rights relating to the criminal trial process requires the continuing availability of a mechanism for relief." Id. at 225, 226. As Justice Harlan, who had dissented from many of the cases initially construing the habeas statutes, readily recognized, habeas jurisdiction as heretofore accepted by this Court was "not only concerned with those rules which substantially affect the fact-finding apparatus of the original trial. Under the prevailing notions, *the threat of habeas serves as a necessary additional incentive for trial and appellate courts throughout the land to conduct their proceedings in a manner consistent with established constitutional standards*." Desist v. United States, 394 U.S. 244, 262–63 (1969) (dissenting) (emphasis supplied). The availability of collateral review assures "that the lower federal and state courts toe the constitutional line." Id. at 264. . . . In effect, habeas jurisdiction is a deterrent to unconstitutional actions by trial and appellate judges, and a safeguard to ensure that rights secured under the Constitution and federal laws are not merely honored in the breach. . . .

At least since *Brown v. Allen,* detention emanating from judicial proceedings in which constitutional rights were denied has been deemed "contrary to fundamental law," and all constitutional claims have thus been cognizable on federal habeas corpus. . . . I can find no adequate justification elucidated by the Court for concluding that habeas relief for all federal constitutional claims is no longer compelled. . . .

I would address the Court's concerns for effective utilization of scarce judicial resources, finality principles, federal-state friction, and notions of "federalism" only long enough to note that such concerns carry no more force with respect to non-"guilt-related" constitutional claims than they do with respect to claims that affect the accuracy of the factfinding process. . . .

The Court . . . argues that habeas relief for non-"guilt-related" constitutional claims is not mandated because such claims do not affect the "basic justice" of a defendant's detention; this is presumably because the "ultimate goal" of the criminal justice system is "truth and justice." This denigration of constitutional guarantees and *constitutionally mandated procedures,* relegated by the Court to the status of mere utilitarian tools, must appall citizens taught to expect judicial respect and support for their constitutional rights. Even if punishment of the "guilty" were society's highest value—and procedural safeguards denigrated to this end—

in a constitution that a majority of the members of this Court would prefer, that is not the ordering of priorities under the Constitution forged by the framers, and this Court's sworn duty is to uphold that Constitution and not to frame its own. The procedural safeguards mandated in the framers' Constitution are not admonitions to be tolerated only to the extent they serve functional purposes that ensure that the "guilty" are punished and the "innocent" freed; rather, every guarantee enshrined in the Constitution, our basic charter and the guarantor of our most precious liberties, is by it endowed with an independent vitality and value, and this Court is not free to curtail those constitutional guarantees even to punish the most obviously guilty. Particular constitutional rights that do not affect the fairness of factfinding procedures cannot for that reason be denied at the trial itself. What possible justification then can there be for denying vindication of such rights on federal habeas when state courts do deny those rights at trial? To sanction disrespect and disregard for the Constitution in the name of protecting society from lawbreakers is to make the government itself lawless and to subvert those values upon which our ultimate freedom and liberty depend. . . . Enforcement of *federal* constitutional rights that redress constitutional violations directed against the "guilty" is a particular function of *federal* habeas review, lest judges trying the "morally unworthy" be tempted not to execute the supreme law of the land. State judges popularly elected may have difficulty resisting popular pressures not experienced by federal judges given lifetime tenure designed to immunize them from such influences, and the federal habeas statutes reflect the congressional judgment that such detached federal review is a salutary safeguard against *any* detention of an individual "in violation of the Constitution or laws . . . of the United States."

Federal courts have the duty to carry out the congressionally assigned responsibility to shoulder the ultimate burden of adjudging whether detentions violate federal law, and today's decision substantially abnegates that duty. The Court does not, because it cannot, dispute that institutional constraints totally preclude any possibility that this Court can adequately oversee whether state courts have properly applied federal law, and does not controvert the fact that federal habeas jurisdiction is partially designed to ameliorate that inadequacy. Thus, although I fully agree that state courts "have a constitutional obligation to safeguard personal liberties and to uphold federal law," and that there is no "general lack of appropriate sensitivity to constitutional rights in the trial and appellate courts of the several states," I cannot agree that it follows that, as the Court today holds, federal court determination of almost all Fourth Amendment claims of state prisoners should be barred and that state court resolution of those issues should be insulated from the federal review Congress intended. . . .

In any event, respondents' contention that Fourth Amendment claims, like all other constitutional claims, must be cognizable on habeas, does not rest on the ground attributed to them by the Court—that the state courts are rife with animosity to the constitutional mandates of this Court. It is one thing to assert that state courts, as a general matter, accurately decide federal constitutional claims; it is quite another to generalize from that limited proposition to the conclusion that, despite congressional intent that federal courts sitting in habeas must stand ready to rectify any constitutional errors that are nevertheless committed, federal courts are to be judicially precluded from ever considering the merits of whole categories of rights that are to be accorded less procedural protection merely because the Court proclaims that they do not affect the accuracy or fairness of the factfinding process. . . . To the extent state trial and appellate judges faithfully, accurately, and assiduously apply federal law and the constitutional principles enunciated by the federal courts, such determinations will be vindicated on the merits when collaterally attacked. But to the extent federal law is erroneously applied by the state courts, there is no authority in this Court to deny defendants the right to have those errors rectified by way of federal habeas; indeed, the Court's reluctance to accept Congress's desires along these lines can only be a manifestation of this Court's mistrust for *federal* judges. Furthermore, some might be expected to dispute the academic's dictum seemingly accepted by the Court that a federal judge is not necessarily more skilled than a state judge in applying federal law. For the Supremacy Clause of the Constitution proceeds on a different premise, and Congress, as it was constitutionally empowered to do, made federal judges (and initially federal district court judges) "the *primary* and powerful reliances for vindicating every right given by the Constitution, the laws, and treaties of the United States." Zwickler v. Koota, 389 U.S. 241, 247 (1967). . . .

I would affirm the judgments of the Courts of Appeals.

■ MR. JUSTICE WHITE, dissenting.

For many of the reasons stated by Mr. Justice Brennan, I cannot agree that the writ of habeas corpus should be any less available to those convicted of state crimes where they allege Fourth Amendment violations than where other constitutional issues are presented to the federal court. . . . I cannot distinguish between Fourth Amendment and other constitutional issues.

Suppose, for example, that two confederates in crime, Smith and Jones, are tried separately for a state crime and convicted on the very same evidence, including evidence seized incident to their arrest allegedly made without probable cause. Their constitutional claims are fully aired, rejected, and preserved on appeal. Their convictions are affirmed by the state's highest court. Smith, the first to be tried, does not petition for certiorari, or does so but his petition is denied. Jones, whose conviction was considerably later, is more successful. His petition for certiorari is granted and his conviction reversed because this Court, without making any new rule of law, simply concludes that on the undisputed facts the arrests were made without probable cause and the challenged evidence was therefore seized in violation of the Fourth Amendment. The state must either retry Jones or release him, necessarily because he is deemed in custody in violation of the Constitution. It turns out that without the evidence illegally seized, the state has no case; and Jones goes free. Smith then files his petition for habeas corpus. He makes no claim that he did not have a full and fair hearing in the state courts, but asserts that his Fourth Amendment claim had been erroneously decided and that he is being held in violation of the federal Constitution. He cites this Court's decision in Jones's case to satisfy any burden placed on him by § 2254 to demonstrate that the state court was in error. Unless the Court's reservation, in its present opinion, of those situations where the defendant has not had a full and fair hearing in the state courts is intended to encompass all those circumstances under which a state criminal judgment may be re-examined under § 2254—in which event the opinion is essentially meaningless and the judgment erroneous—Smith's petition would be dismissed, and he would spend his life in prison while his colleague is a free man. I cannot believe that Congress intended this result. . . .

I feel constrained to say, however, that I would join four or more other Justices in substantially limiting the reach of the exclusionary rule as presently administered under the Fourth Amendment in federal and state criminal trials. . . . I am of the view that the rule should be substantially modified so as to prevent its application in those many circumstances where the evidence at issue was seized by an officer acting in the good-faith belief that his conduct comported with existing law and having reasonable grounds for this belief.[b]

INTRODUCTORY NOTES ON THE SCOPE OF HABEAS CORPUS REVIEW AFTER STONE V. POWELL

1.   QUESTIONS AND COMMENTS ON STONE V. POWELL

The decision in *Stone* implicates two distinct lines of argument about the proper scope of federal habeas. The first concerns the value of finality in the criminal law: whether federal habeas corpus should be available to relitigate questions already heard and decided in the original trial and affirmed on appeal. Can relitigation be justified as a device for correcting error? Does the argument presuppose that the second (i.e., federal) court necessarily will produce more reliable results than its state counterparts?

Second, if relitigation is to be available in at least some cases, for what particular constitutional violations is it an appropriate remedy? In his famous article, Is Innocence Irrelevant? Collateral Attack on Criminal Judgments, 38 U. Chi. L. Rev. 142 (1970), Henry Friendly suggested that the

---

[b]   Chief Justice Burger wrote a separate concurrence in which he noted that he would also substantially limit the reach of the exclusionary rule at trial and on direct appeal.—[Footnote by eds.]

availability of federal habeas relief should depend on the petitioner's ability to make a "colorable showing of innocence." That requirement would distinguish the Fourth Amendment from many other constitutional rights. Is such a differentiation sound?

The same two lines of argument can be approached from another direction. Few would dispute the correctness of the proposition for which *Frank* is usually cited: federal habeas corpus should be available where the state has not provided an adequate procedural opportunity to raise a federal constitutional claim. *Brown v. Allen* goes much farther: all federal constitutional challenges litigated in state court can be relitigated on federal habeas corpus regardless of the adequacy of the state proceeding. There is lively debate on whether *Frank* states the norm that should be followed, whether *Brown* does, or whether the best position is somewhere in between.

2. EXTENSION OF *STONE V. POWELL* TO OTHER CONSTITUTIONAL CLAIMS

In omitted portions of his *Stone v. Powell* dissent, Justice Brennan expressed the fear that the case was the first step in a broad dismantling of federal habeas review of state criminal convictions. An early indication to the contrary came in Rose v. Mitchell, 443 U.S. 545 (1979). There the Court held that racial discrimination in the selection of a grand jury was not harmless error even though a properly constituted petit jury had found the defendant guilty. *Stone v. Powell* did not foreclose habeas review of such a claim. Writing for the Court, Justice Blackmun said that federal habeas review was "necessary to ensure that constitutional defects in the state judiciary's grand jury selection procedure are not overlooked by the very state judges who operate that system." The concern for "judicial integrity," deprecated in *Stone,* was more important where the integrity of the judicial system itself was called into question. Moreover, quashing an indictment did not preclude retrial and therefore was less costly to the administration of justice than is suppression of evidence. Finally, a claim of racial discrimination in grand jury selection raised interests "substantially more compelling than those at issue in *Stone.*" In dissent, Justices Powell and Rehnquist argued that *Stone* should have foreclosed habeas review.

It was 17 years before the Court ruled on the applicability of *Stone* to *Miranda.* In Withrow v. Williams, 507 U.S. 680 (1993), the Court held *Miranda* claims open to relitigation on habeas. *Miranda* was different from *Stone,* Justice Souter said for the Court, because *Miranda* involved a "trial right" that was not "necessarily divorced from the correct ascertainment of guilt":

> [A] system of criminal law enforcement which comes to depend on the "confession" will, in the long run, be less reliable and more subject to abuses than a system relying on independent investigation." Michigan v. Tucker, 417 U.S. 433, 448 n.23 (1974). By bracing against "the possibility of unreliable statements in every instance of in-custody interrogation," *Miranda* serves to guard against "the use of unreliable statements at trial." Johnson v. New Jersey, 384 U.S. 719, 730 (1966). . . .

Finally, and most importantly, eliminating review of *Miranda* claims would not significantly benefit the federal courts in their exercise of habeas jurisdiction, or advance the cause of federalism in any substantial way. As [the United States] concedes, eliminating habeas review of *Miranda* issues would not prevent a state prisoner from simply converting his barred *Miranda* claim into a due process claim that his conviction rested on an involuntary confession. Indeed, although counsel could provide us with no empirical basis for projecting the consequence of adopting petitioner's position, it seems reasonable to suppose that virtually all *Miranda* claims would simply be recast in this way.

If that is so, the federal courts would certainly not have heard the last of *Miranda* on collateral review. Under the due process approach, as we have already seen, courts look to the totality of circumstances to determine whether a confession was voluntary. Those potential circumstances include not only the crucial element of police coercion; the length of the interrogation; its location; its continuity; the defendant's maturity; education; physical condition; and mental health. They also include the failure of police to advise the defendant of his rights to remain silent and to have counsel present during custodial interrogation. We could lock the front door against *Miranda*, but not the back.

We thus fail to see how abdicating *Miranda*'s bright-line (or, at least, brighter-line) rules in favor of an exhaustive totality-of-circumstances approach on habeas would do much of anything to lighten the burdens placed on busy federal courts. . . . We likewise fail to see how purporting to eliminate *Miranda* issues from federal habeas would go very far to relieve such tensions as *Miranda* may now raise between the two judicial systems. Relegation of habeas petitioners to straight involuntariness claims would not likely reduce the amount of litigation . . . .

Chief Justice Rehnquist and Justices O'Connor, Scalia, and Thomas dissented.[a]

3.   NON-CONSTITUTIONAL CLAIMS: *REED V. FARLEY*

Note that § 2254(a) authorizes habeas corpus for persons in custody under the judgment of a state court "on the ground that he is in custody in violation of the Constitution *or laws* or treaties of the United States" (emphasis added). But as Justice Powell said in a footnote in Part II of his opinion in *Stone*, non-constitutional claims usually cannot be raised on habeas corpus.

In Hill v. United States, 368 U.S. 424, 428 (1962), the Court had recognized a small window of opportunity for errors amounting to "a fundamental

---

[a]   For an argument that the principles of *Stone* should govern *Miranda* and "prophylactic" rights generally, see William A. Schroeder, Federal Habeas Review of State Prisoner Claims Based on Alleged Violations of Prophylactic Rules of Constitutional Criminal Procedure: Reviving and Extending Stone v. Powell, 60 U. Kan. L. Rev. 231 (2011).

defect which inherently results in a complete miscarriage of justice, [or] an omission inconsistent with the rudimentary demands of fair procedure." *Hill* involved a *federal* prisoner seeking relief under § 2255.

Reed v. Farley, 512 U.S. 339 (1994), raised the question whether the *Hill* standard should be applied to *state* prisoners seeking federal habeas relief based on violation of the terms of an interstate compact.[b] In two opinions, a majority of five held that it did, but that the petitioner had failed to meet that standard. The four dissenters argued that the § 2255 standard should not be applied in state cases:

> . . . In a federal trial and appeal, virtually any procedural error, however minor, will violate a "law" of the United States. In this context, it is both impracticable and unnecessary to allow collateral review of all claims of error, particularly since the defendant has had the opportunity both to raise them in and to appeal them to a federal forum. It is hardly surprising, therefore, that the *Hill* . . . screening device, which sorts the substantial errors from the mere technical violations, was developed in § 2255. A state trial, by contrast, implicates few federal laws outside the Constitution. On the extraordinary occasions when Congress does consider a federal law to be so important as to warrant its application in state proceedings, this alone counsels an approach other than *Hill* . . . to determine whether a violation of that law warrants federal court review and enforcement.
>
> [A]t least until today, this Court never had held that a properly preserved claim of a violation of a federal statute should be treated differently in a § 2254 proceeding from a claim of a violation of the Constitution. Nor is there any reason to do so. Congress's decision to apply a federal statute to state criminal proceedings, which ordinarily are the exclusive province of state legislatures, generally should be read to reflect the congressional determination that important national interests are at stake. Where Congress has made this determination, the federal courts should be open to ensure the uniform enforcement and interpretation of these interests. It should be clear, then, that [there should be no distinction in this context] between constitutional and statutory violations.[c]

4. BIBLIOGRAPHY

Stone v. Powell has been widely discussed. For a representative sample of the literature, see Robert Cover and T. Alexander Aleinikoff, Dialectical Federalism: Habeas Corpus and the Court, 86 Yale L.J. 1035 (1977); J. Patrick Green, *Stone v. Powell*: The Hermeneutics of the Burger Court, 10 Creighton L. Rev. 655 (1977); Philip Halpern in Federal Habeas Corpus and the *Mapp* Exclusionary Rule after *Stone v. Powell,* 82 Colum. L. Rev. 1

---

[b] Prior decisions had established that a congressionally sanctioned interstate compact is a "law of the United States."

[c] For an argument that the distinction between constitutional and non-constitutional claims should not necessarily govern the availability of various forms of judicial relief, see Michael Coenen, Constitutional Privileging, 99 Va. L. Rev. 683 (2013).—[Footnote by eds.]

(1982); Ira Robbins and James Sanders, Judicial Integrity, the Appearance of Justice, and the Great Writ of Habeas Corpus: How to Kill Two Thirds (or More) with One Stone, 15 Am. Crim. L. Rev. 63 (1977); Louis Michael Seidman, Factual Guilt and the Burger Court: An Examination of Continuity and Change in Criminal Procedure, 80 Colum. L. Rev. 436 (1980); Mark Tushnet, Constitutional and Statutory Analyses in the Law of Federal Jurisdiction, 25 U.C.L.A. L. Rev. 1301 (1978).

SUBSECTION B. RETROACTIVE APPLICATION OF NEW CONSTITUTIONAL RIGHTS

INTRODUCTORY NOTE ON RETROACTIVE APPLICATION OF NEW CONSTITUTIONAL RIGHTS

The background assumption of our legal system, adapted from the common law and accepted by the Supreme Court today, is that constitutional rights, once declared, apply to all pending and future litigation. Thus, for example, the right-to-counsel holding of Gideon v. Wainwright, 372 U.S. 335 (1963), applied not only to future trials, but also to trials then in progress and to convictions then on appeal. If that required starting over, then new trial or release was the only option.

The expansion of habeas corpus in *Brown v. Allen* raised the possibility of retroactive application of newly discovered constitutional rights to the much larger category of persons whose convictions had become final but who remained in custody. *Brown* was not limited on its face to the protection of newly developed rights as fundamental as the right to counsel. Potentially, *all* newly recognized procedural rights based on the federal Constitution could be invoked by anyone whose case was open to relitigation on habeas corpus—that is, anyone still in custody.

The potential for habeas relief in such cases prompted the Supreme Court to develop a doctrine of non-retroactivity. The initial step came in Linkletter v. Walker, 381 U.S. 618 (1965). *Linkletter* held that the rule requiring the exclusion of evidence obtained from an unconstitutional search and seizure developed in *Mapp v. Ohio* would not apply to convictions that became final before *Mapp* was decided.[a] *Linkletter* led to a complex series of decisions announcing that some newly declared constitutional rights could not be invoked retroactively. Others, such as the holding in *Gideon*, could be.

As these cases evolved, Justice Harlan came to the view that ultimately informed the Court's position. He thought it correct that new rules of constitutional law should continue to apply in all cases still open on direct review. But, he thought, it is "sounder, in adjudicating habeas petitions, generally to apply the law prevailing at the time a conviction became final than it is to seek to dispose of [habeas] cases on the basis of intervening changes in constitutional interpretation." Mackey v. United States, 401 U.S. 667, 689 (1971) (opinion of Harlan, J.). Thus, for Harlan, retroactive application of

---

[a]   "Final" was defined as after direct review had concluded.

constitutional criminal procedure rights did not depend on the right asserted but on the remedy sought.

With this as the starting point, Harlan proposed two exceptions. First, rules that placed "certain kinds of primary, private individual conduct beyond the power of the criminal law-making authority to proscribe" should be applied retroactively. Second, "those procedures that . . . are 'implicit in the concept of ordered liberty,' " should also be applied retroactively. *Gideon*, for example, established such a rule. *Mapp v. Ohio* did not.

Teague v. Lane, 489 U.S. 288 (1989), is the groundbreaking decision that governs current law on this subject. *Teague* was written by Justice O'Connor, who was joined in the relevant part of her opinion only by Chief Justice Rehnquist and Justices Scalia and Kennedy. The *Teague* plurality on retroactivity became a majority when Justice White added his vote to O'Connor's approach later that term in Penry v. Lynaugh, 492 U.S. 302 (1989). The cases since then have embedded *Teague* as a central tenet of federal habeas corpus. The next main case describes *Teague* and illustrates its approach.

Welch v. United States

Supreme Court of the United States, 2016.
578 U.S. ___, 136 S.Ct. 1257.

■ JUSTICE KENNEDY delivered the opinion of the Court.

Last Term, this Court decided Johnson v. United States, 576 U.S. ___, 135 S.Ct. 2551 (2015). *Johnson* considered the residual clause of the Armed Career Criminal Act of 1984, 18 U.S.C. § 924(e)(2)(B)(ii). The Court held that provision void for vagueness. The present case asks whether *Johnson* is a substantive decision that is retroactive in cases on collateral review.

I

Federal law prohibits any felon—meaning a person who has been convicted of a crime punishable by more than a year in prison—from possessing a firearm. 18 U.S.C. § 922(g). A person who violates that restriction can be sentenced to prison for up to 10 years. § 924(a)(2). For some felons, however, the Armed Career Criminal Act imposes a much more severe penalty. Under the Act, a person who possesses a firearm after three or more convictions for a "serious drug offense" or a "violent felony" is subject to a minimum sentence of 15 years and a maximum sentence of life in prison. § 924(e)(1). Because the ordinary maximum sentence for a felon in possession of a firearm is 10 years, while the minimum sentence under the Armed Career Criminal Act is 15 years, a person sentenced under the Act will receive a prison term at least five years longer than the law otherwise would allow.

The Act defines "violent felony" as

any crime punishable by imprisonment for a term exceeding one year . . . that—

(i) has as an element the use, attempted use, or threatened use of physical force against the person of another; or

(ii) is burglary, arson, or extortion, involves use of explosives, or otherwise involves conduct that presents a serious potential risk of physical injury to another. § 924(e)(2)(B).

Subsection (i) of this definition is known as the elements clause. The end of subsection (ii)—"or otherwise involves conduct that presents a serious potential risk of physical injury to another"—is known as the residual clause. It is the residual clause that *Johnson* held to be vague and invalid. . . .

II

Petitioner Gregory Welch is one of the many offenders sentenced under the Armed Career Criminal Act before *Johnson* was decided. Welch pleaded guilty in 2010 to one count of being a felon in possession of a firearm. The Probation Office prepared a presentence report finding that Welch had three prior violent felony convictions, including a Florida conviction for a February 1996 "strong-arm robbery." The relevant Florida statute prohibits taking property from the person or custody of another with "the use of force, violence, assault, or putting in fear." Fla. Stat. § 812.13(1) (1994). . . . The District Court . . . concluded that the Florida offense of strong-arm robbery qualified as a violent felony both under the elements clause and the residual clause. The District Court proceeded to sentence Welch to the Act's mandatory minimum sentence of 15 years in prison.

The Court of Appeals for the Eleventh Circuit affirmed. That court did not decide whether the conviction at issue could qualify as a violent felony under the elements clause. Instead, it held only that the conviction qualified under the residual clause. This Court denied certiorari, and Welch's conviction became final.

In December 2013, Welch appeared pro se before the District Court and filed a collateral challenge to his conviction and sentence through a motion under 28 U.S.C. § 2255. . . . The District Court denied the motion and denied a certificate of appealability. [The Circuit Court also denied a certificate of appealability, even though *Johnson* was pending at the time. It also denied a motion for reconsideration after *Johnson* was decided.] Welch then filed a pro se petition for certiorari. . . . This Court granted the petition. Because the United States, as respondent, agrees with Welch that *Johnson* is retroactive, the Court appointed Helgi C. Walker as amicus curiae in support of the judgment of the Court of Appeals. She has ably discharged her responsibilities.

III

A

[The Court decided in this part of its opinion that the retroactivity of *Johnson* should be resolved.]

B

The normal framework for determining whether a new rule applies to cases on collateral review stems from the plurality opinion in Teague v. Lane, 489 U.S. 288 (1989). That opinion in turn drew on the approach outlined by the second Justice Harlan in his separate opinions in Mackey v. United States, 401 U.S. 667 (1971), and Desist v. United States, 394 U.S. 244 (1969). The parties here assume that the *Teague* framework applies in a federal collateral challenge to a federal conviction as it does in a federal collateral challenge to a state conviction, and we proceed on that assumption. . . . Under *Teague*, as a general matter, "new constitutional rules of criminal procedure will not be applicable to those cases which have become final before the new rules are announced." *Teague* and its progeny recognize two categories of decisions that fall outside this general bar on retroactivity for procedural rules. First, "[n]ew *substantive* rules generally apply retroactively." Schriro v. Summerlin, 542 U.S. 348, 351 (2004). Second, new "watershed rules of criminal procedure," which are procedural rules "implicating the fundamental fairness and accuracy of the criminal proceeding," will also have retroactive effect. Saffle v. Parks, 494 U.S. 484, 495 (1990).

It is undisputed that *Johnson* announced a new rule. See *Teague*, 489 U.S. at 301 ("[A] case announces a new rule if the result was not *dictated* by precedent existing at the time the defendant's conviction became final"). The question here is whether that new rule falls within one of the two categories that have retroactive effect under *Teague*. The parties agree that *Johnson* does not fall into the limited second category for watershed procedural rules. Welch and the United States contend instead that *Johnson* falls into the first category because it announced a substantive rule.

"A rule is substantive rather than procedural if it alters the range of conduct or the class of persons that the law punishes." *Schriro*, 542 U.S. at 353. "This includes decisions that narrow the scope of a criminal statute by interpreting its terms, as well as constitutional determinations that place particular conduct or persons covered by the statute beyond the State's power to punish." Id. at 351–52. Procedural rules, by contrast, "regulate only the *manner of determining* the defendant's culpability." *Schriro*, 542 U.S. at 353. Such rules alter "the range of permissible methods for determining whether a defendant's conduct is punishable." Id. "They do not produce a class of persons convicted of conduct the law does not make criminal, but merely raise the possibility that someone convicted with use of the invalidated procedure might have been acquitted otherwise." Id. at 352.

Under this framework, the rule announced in *Johnson* is substantive. By striking down the residual clause as void for vagueness, *Johnson* changed the substantive reach of the Armed Career Criminal Act, altering "the range of conduct or the class of persons that the [Act] punishes." Id. at 353. Before *Johnson,* the Act applied to any person who possessed a firearm after three violent felony convictions, even if one or more of those convictions fell under only the residual clause. An offender in that situation faced 15 years to life in prison. After *Johnson,* the same person engaging in the same conduct is no longer subject to the Act and faces at most 10 years in prison. The residual clause is invalid under *Johnson,* so it can no longer mandate or authorize any sentence. *Johnson* establishes, in other words, that "even the use of impeccable factfinding procedures could not legitimate" a sentence based on that clause. United States v. United States Coin & Currency, 401 U.S. 715, 724 (1971). It follows that *Johnson* is a substantive decision.

By the same logic, *Johnson* is not a procedural decision. *Johnson* had nothing to do with the range of permissible methods a court might use to determine whether a defendant should be sentenced under the Armed Career Criminal Act. It did not, for example, "allocate decision-making authority" between judge and jury, *Schriro*, 542 U.S. at 353, or regulate the evidence that the court could consider in making its decision, see Whorton v. Bockting, 549 U.S. 406, 413–14, 417 (2007). Unlike those cases, *Johnson* affected the reach of the underlying statute rather than the judicial procedures by which the statute is applied. *Johnson* is thus a substantive decision and so has retroactive effect under *Teague* in cases on collateral review.

C

Amicus urges the Court to adopt a different understanding of the *Teague* framework. She contends courts should apply that framework by asking whether the constitutional right underlying the new rule is substantive or procedural. Under that approach, amicus concludes that *Johnson* is a procedural decision because the void-for-vagueness doctrine that *Johnson* applied is based, she asserts, on procedural due process.

Neither *Teague* nor its progeny support that approach. As described above, this Court has determined whether a new rule is substantive or procedural by considering the function of the rule, not its underlying constitutional source. That is for good reason. The *Teague* framework creates a balance between, first, the need for finality in criminal cases, and second, the countervailing imperative to ensure that criminal punishment is imposed only when authorized by law. That balance turns on the function of the rule at issue, not the constitutional guarantee from which the rule derives. If a new rule regulates only the procedures for determining culpability, the *Teague* balance generally tips in favor of finality. The chance of a more accurate outcome under the new procedure normally does not justify the cost of vacating a conviction whose only flaw is that its procedures "conformed to then-existing constitutional standards."

Teague, 489 U.S. at 310. On the other hand, if a new rule changes the scope of the underlying criminal proscription, the balance is different. A change of that character will "necessarily carry a significant risk that a defendant stands convicted of 'an act that the law does not make criminal.' " Bousley v. United States, 523 U.S. 614, 620 (1998). By extension, where the conviction or sentence in fact is not authorized by substantive law, then finality interests are at their weakest. As Justice Harlan wrote, "[t]here is little societal interest in permitting the criminal process to rest at a point where it ought properly never to repose." *Mackey,* 401 U.S. at 693 (opinion of Harlan, J.).

The *Teague* balance thus does not depend on whether the underlying constitutional guarantee is characterized as procedural or substantive. It depends instead on whether the new rule itself has a procedural function or a substantive function—that is, whether it alters only the procedures used to obtain the conviction, or alters instead the range of conduct or class of persons that the law punishes. The emphasis by amicus on the constitutional guarantee behind the new rule, then, would untether the *Teague* framework from its basic purpose. . . .

Amicus next relies on language from this Court's cases describing substantive decisions as those that "place particular conduct or persons . . . beyond the State's power to punish," *Schriro,* 542 U.S. at 352, or that "prohibi[t] a certain category of punishment for a class of defendants because of their status or offense," *Saffle,* 494 U.S. at 494. Cases such as these, in which the Constitution deprives the Government of the power to impose the challenged punishment, "represen[t] the clearest instance" of substantive rules for which retroactive application is appropriate. *Mackey*, 401 U.S. at 693 (opinion of Harlan, J.). Drawing on those decisions, amicus argues that *Johnson* is not substantive because it does not limit Congress' power: Congress is free to enact a new version of the residual clause that imposes the same punishment on the same persons for the same conduct, provided the new statute is precise enough to satisfy due process.

Although this Court has put great emphasis on substantive decisions that place certain conduct, classes of persons, or punishments beyond the legislative power of Congress, the Court has also recognized that some substantive decisions do not impose such restrictions. The clearest example comes from *Bousley,* supra. In *Bousley,* the Court was asked to determine what retroactive effect should be given to its decision in Bailey v. United States, 516 U.S. 137 (1995). *Bailey* considered the "use" prong of 18 U.S.C. § 924(c)(1), which imposes increased penalties on the use of a firearm in relation to certain crimes. The Court held as a matter of statutory interpretation that the "use" prong punishes only "active employment of the firearm" and not mere possession. The Court in *Bousley* had no difficulty concluding that *Bailey* was substantive, as it was a decision "holding that a substantive federal criminal statute does not reach certain conduct." *Bousley*, 523 U.S. at 620; see *Schriro*, supra, at 354 ("A decision that modifies the elements of an offense is normally substantive rather than procedural"). The Court reached that conclusion even though Congress could (and later did) reverse Bailey by amending the statute to cover possession as well as use. See United States v. O'Brien, 560 U.S. 218, 232–33 (2010) (discussing statutory amendment known as the "*Bailey* fix"). *Bousley* thus contradicts the contention that the *Teague* inquiry turns only on whether the decision at issue holds that Congress lacks some substantive power. . . .

* * *

It may well be that the Court of Appeals on remand will determine on other grounds that the District Court was correct to deny Welch's motion to amend his sentence. For instance, the parties continue to dispute whether Welch's strong-arm robbery conviction qualifies as a violent felony under the elements clause of the Act, which would make Welch eligible for a 15-year sentence regardless of *Johnson*. On the present record, however, and in light of today's holding that *Johnson* is retroactive in cases on collateral review, reasonable jurists at least could debate whether Welch is entitled to relief. For these reasons, the judgment of the Court of Appeals is vacated, and the case is remanded for further proceedings consistent with this opinion.

It is so ordered.

■ JUSTICE THOMAS, dissenting.

. . . The majority . . . misconstrues the retroactivity framework developed in Teague v. Lane, 489 U.S. 288 (1989), and its progeny, thereby undermining any principled limitation on the finality of federal convictions. I respectfully dissent.

I

[Justice Thomas addressed a procedural issue in Part I of his dissent.]

II

. . . The retroactivity rules the Court adopted in Teague v. Lane, 489 U.S. 288 (1989), generally foreclose prisoners from collaterally challenging their convictions based on new decisions that postdate their convictions and sentences. The only exceptions to that bar are for decisions that announce a new substantive rule or a new "watershed" procedural rule. All agree that *Johnson* announced a new rule and that it is not a "watershed" procedural rule. But the rule in *Johnson* also does not satisfy our criteria for substantive rules. The majority concludes otherwise, but its approach fails under *Teague*'s own terms and erodes any meaningful limits on what a "substantive" rule is.

A

The Court has identified two types of substantive rules, and *Johnson*'s rule of decision fits neither description. It is not a new substantive

constitutional rule, nor does it narrow the scope of a criminal statute
through statutory construction.

1

Time and again, the Court has articulated the test for defining a
substantive constitutional rule as follows: The rule must "place particular conduct or persons covered by the statute beyond the State's power to
punish." Schriro v. Summerlin, 542 U.S. 348, 352 (2004); see also Beard
v. Banks, 542 U.S. 406, 416 (2004) (similar); Penry v. Lynaugh, 492 U.S.
302, 330 (1989) (rule is substantive if "the Constitution itself deprives the
State of the power to impose a certain penalty"). This is also the test the
Court has purported to apply in case after case. See, e.g., Sawyer v.
Smith, 497 U.S. 227, 233, 241 (1990) (prohibiting prosecutors from misleading the jury to believe that it was not responsible for a death sentence
was a nonsubstantive rule that did not "place an entire category of primary conduct beyond the reach of the criminal law" or "prohibit imposition of a certain type of punishment for a class of defendants because of
their status or offense"). Our precedents thus make clear the distinction
between substantive and nonsubstantive constitutional rules. A rule that
"*because* [a State] has made a certain fact essential to the death penalty,
that fact must be found by a jury," is not substantive; it had no effect on
the "range of conduct a State may criminalize." *Schriro*, 542 U.S. at 353–
54. But a rule in which this Court "ma[de] a certain fact essential to the
death penalty . . . would be substantive"; it would change the range of
conduct warranting a death sentence. Id. at 354.

Under these principles, *Johnson* announced a new constitutional
rule, but it is not substantive. . . . It does not preclude the Government
from prohibiting particular conduct or deem any conduct constitutionally
protected. The Government remains as free to enhance sentences for federal crimes based on the commission of previous violent felonies after
Johnson as it was before. Nor does *Johnson*'s vagueness rule place any
class of persons or punishment off limits. There is no category of offender
that Congress cannot subject to an enhanced sentence after *Johnson*. The
only constraint *Johnson* imposes is on the *manner* in which the Government can punish offenders. To avoid "fail[ing] to give ordinary people fair
notice" or "invit[ing] arbitrary enforcement," 576 U.S. at ___, 135 S.Ct. at
2556, Congress must be clearer in describing what conduct "otherwise
. . . presents a serious potential risk of physical injury to another." 18
U.S.C. § 924(e)(2)(B)(ii).

2

Johnson also does not fit within the second type of substantive rule
this Court has recognized, which consists of "decisions that narrow the
scope of a criminal statute by interpreting its terms." *Schriro*, 542 U.S.
at 351.

The Court has invoked this subset of new rules just once, in Bousley
v. United States, 523 U.S. 614 (1998). *Bousley* held that Bailey v. United

States, 516 U.S. 137 (1995), which interpreted a federal firearms sentencing enhancement to require proof of "active employment of the firearm" as an element, applied retroactively. The Court explained that *Teague*'s bar on retroactively applying "procedural rules" is "inapplicable to the situation in which this Court decides the meaning of a criminal statute enacted by Congress." Moreover, the Court reasoned, "decisions of this Court holding that a substantive federal criminal statute does not reach certain conduct" share a key commonality with "decisions placing conduct beyond the power of the criminal law-making authority to proscribe": both "necessarily carry a significant risk that a defendant stands convicted of an act that the law does not make criminal." The Court thus classified decisions "holding that a substantive federal criminal statute does not reach certain conduct" as substantive.

I would not so readily assume that *Bousley* applies here. Until today, *Bousley* applied only to new rules reinterpreting the text of federal criminal statutes in a way that narrows their reach. *Johnson* announced no such rule. It announced only that there is no way in which to narrow the reach of the residual clause without running afoul of the Due Process Clause. . . .

III

Today's opinion underscores a larger problem with our retroactivity doctrine: The Court's retroactivity rules have become unmoored from the limiting principles that the Court invoked to justify the doctrine's existence. Under *Teague* itself, the question whether *Johnson* applies retroactively would be a straightforward "No." If this question is close now, that is only because the Court keeps moving the goalposts.

As the majority observes, the foundations of our approach to retroactivity in collateral review come from Justice Harlan's separate opinions in Desist v. United States, 394 U.S. 244 (1969), and Mackey v. United States, 401 U.S. 667 (1971). There, Justice Harlan confronted a now-familiar problem: how to address the consequences of an ever-evolving Constitution. He responded with an approach to retroactivity that placed at the forefront the need for finality in the criminal process. In his view, very few rules that emerged after a prisoner's conviction—including constitutional rules—warranted disturbing that conviction. Justice Harlan saw only "two exceptions": "bedrock procedural" rules and "[n]ew 'substantive due process' rules" removing "certain kinds of primary, private individual conduct beyond the power of the criminal law-making authority to proscribe." As examples of the latter category, he cited such rules as that the First Amendment forbids criminalizing flag burning, that the right to privacy precludes the Government from prosecuting distributors of contraception, and that the "freedom to marry" and equal protection principles immunize couples from being punished for entering into interracial marriages. These " 'substantive due process' rules," Justice Harlan explained, were "on a different footing" because "the writ has historically been available for attacking convictions on such grounds." Moreover, society has an "obvious interest in freeing individuals for punishment for conduct that is constitutionally protected." And granting relief for such claims would not require retrials.

When *Teague* adopted Justice Harlan's approach, it agreed that to preserve "the principle of finality which is essential to the operation of our criminal justice system," "new rules generally should not be applied retroactively to cases on collateral review." *Teague* thus adopted Justice Harlan's two exceptions for "watershed rules of criminal procedure" and rules that "accord constitutional protection to . . . primary activity."

The Court then swiftly discarded the limitations that *Teague* adopted. *Penry* proclaimed the retroactivity of rules barring certain *punishments,* even though the Court's constant revision of the Eighth Amendment produces an "ever-moving target of impermissible punishments." Montgomery v. Louisiana, 577 U.S. ___, ___, 136 S.Ct. 718, 742 (2016) (Scalia, J., dissenting). *Bousley* extended retroactive relief for federal prisoners raising statutory claims, not just constitutional ones. *Montgomery* extended *Teague* to state post-conviction proceedings, enshrined *Teague* as a constitutional command, and redefined substantive rules to include rules that require sentencers to follow certain procedures in punishing juveniles. Now the majority collapses *Teague*'s substantive-procedural distinction further, allowing any rule that has the incidental effect of invalidating substantive provisions of a criminal statute to become a substantive rule.

Today's decision, like those that preceded it, professes to venerate Justice Harlan's theory of retroactivity. This rings hollow; these decisions spell its ruin. The Court adopted Justice Harlan's approach to retroactivity because it shared his conviction that "there [must] be a visible end to the litigable aspect of the criminal process." *Mackey*, 401 U.S. at 690. With the Court's unprincipled expansion of *Teague,* every end is instead a new beginning.

* * *

For these reasons, I respectfully dissent.

NOTES ON RETROACTIVE APPLICATION OF "NEW" RULES OF CONSTITUTIONAL LAW

1. *TEAGUE V. LANE*

The Court held in Taylor v. Louisiana, 419 U.S. 522 (1975), that the Sixth Amendment required that the jury venire be drawn from a fair cross section of the community. The question in Teague v. Lane, 489 U.S. 288 (1989), was whether this requirement should be extended to the petit jury. The case came to the Supreme Court after lower federal courts had denied habeas corpus relief following the affirmance of Taylor's state court convictions for six serious felonies.

Writing for four Justices,[a] Justice O'Connor began by noting that the Court had in the past adopted new constitutional rules of criminal procedure in habeas cases. Although the new rule was always applied in the case before the Court, it was sometimes held non-retroactive and therefore unavailable to later habeas petitioners. These "non-retroactivity" pronouncements were usually left to later cases, but occasionally the Court addressed retroactivity when announcing the new rule. Hereafter, O'Connor said, the approach should be different:

> Retroactivity is properly treated as a threshold question, for, once a new rule is applied to the defendant in the case announcing the rule, evenhanded justice requires that it be applied retroactively to all who are similarly situated. Thus, before deciding whether the fair cross section requirement should be extended to the petit jury, we should ask whether such a rule would be applied retroactively to the case at issue.

O'Connor then applied the analysis outlined in *Welch*, holding that the petitioner's claim sought a "new" rule that should not be applied retroactively. The lower court denial of relief, she concluded, was therefore correct regardless of the merits of the underlying Sixth Amendment question.

Administration of the *Teague* doctrine involves two distinct inquiries. The first is whether the rule on which the habeas applicant relies is "new." If it is not, then *Teague* does not foreclose federal habeas (though there may be other limitations on relief). If the rule is "new," then it will not be retroactively applied to the habeas petitioner unless it fits one of the two *Teague* exceptions. The following Notes address the meaning of "new" and application of the two *Teague* exceptions.

2. "NEW" RULES OF CONSTITUTIONAL LAW: *CHAIDEZ V. UNITED STATES*

When, under *Teague*, is a rule "new"? Justice O'Connor said in *Teague* that "[i]n general . . . a case announces a new rule when it breaks new ground or imposes a new obligation on the States or the Federal Government. . . . To put it differently, a case announces a new rule if the result was not dictated by precedent existing at the time the defendant's conviction became final."

The Court elaborated in Lambrix v. Singletary, 520 U.S. 518 (1997). Justices Stevens, Ginsburg, and Breyer had argued that the rule sought to be applied by the habeas applicant was "nothing more than an application of well-settled principles." Speaking for a majority of five (Justice O'Connor dissented on other grounds), Justice Scalia responded:

> Most of [the] dissent is devoted to making a forceful case that [the decision on which the habeas applicant relied] was a reasonable interpretation of prior law—perhaps even the most reasonable one. But the *Teague* inquiry—which is applied to Supreme Court

---

[a]   She was joined by Chief Justice Rehnquist and Justices Scalia and Kennedy. The O'Connor approach became the Court's view when Justice White added his support in Penry v. Lynaugh, 492 U.S. 302 (1989).

decisions that are, one must hope, usually the most reasonable interpretation of prior law—requires more than that. It asks whether [the decision] was *dictated* by precedent—i.e., whether *no other* interpretation was reasonable.

The Court affirmed this approach in Chaidez v. United States, 568 U.S. 342 (2013). Padilla v. Kentucky, 559 U.S. 356 (2010), held that the Sixth Amendment right to effective assistance of counsel requires that a defendant's attorney provide advice about the risk of deportation arising from a guilty plea. The issue in *Chaidez* was whether *Padilla* applied retroactively to cases that had already become final.

In an opinion by Justice Kagan, the Court said "no." The majority began by noting that the mere application of a settled principle to a new set of facts does not produce a new rule. That was not, however, the situation here. *Padilla* did not involve merely an application of the standard set forth in the Court's canonical ineffectiveness assistance of counsel decision, Strickland v. Washington, 466 U.S. 668 (1984). Before addressing whether an attorney's failure to provide advice about deportation "fell below an objective standard of reasonableness" under *Strickland*, the majority explained, *Padilla* decided a "threshold question" of whether advice about deportation even falls within the Sixth Amendment right to effective assistance of counsel. Prior to *Padilla*, courts had held that the right to effective assistance of counsel did not apply to advice about "collateral" consequences of a conviction, including deportation, and the Court itself had left that question open. "[W]hen we decided *Padilla*," the majority observed, "we answered a question about the Sixth Amendment's reach that we had left open, in a way that altered the law of most jurisdictions."

3. NEW "WATERSHED" PROCEDURES

The *Teague* plurality premised the second exception to its non-retroactivity rule on Justice Harlan's view that it should be "reserved for watershed rules of criminal procedure":

> [W]e believe that . . . the scope of the second exception [should be limited] to those new procedures without which the likelihood of an accurate conviction is seriously diminished. Because we operate from the premise that such procedures would be so central to an accurate determination of innocence or guilt, we believe it unlikely that many such components of basic due process have yet to emerge.

Subsequent cases confirm that this exception to the general non-retroactivity of new constitutional rules is extremely rare. In Whorton v. Bockting, 549 U.S. 406 (2007), a unanimous Court observed that "in the years since *Teague*, we have rejected every claim that a new rule satisfied the requirements for watershed status," and then derived a two-part test from prior decisions: "the rule must be necessary to prevent 'an impermissibly large risk' of an inaccurate conviction" and it "must 'alter our understanding of the bedrock procedural elements essential to the fairness of a proceeding.'"

Schriro v. Summerlin, 542 U.S. 348 (2004), provides another example. At issue was whether the rule of Ring v. Arizona, 536 U.S. 584 (2002), applied retroactively. *Ring* extended Apprendi v. New Jersey, 530 U.S. 466 (2000), to sentencing criteria applicable in capital cases. *Apprendi* had held that "[o]ther than the fact of a prior conviction, any fact that increases the penalty for a crime beyond the prescribed statutory maximum must be submitted to a jury, and proved beyond a reasonable doubt." Arizona law authorized the death penalty only where there was an aggravating factor. *Ring* held that the *Apprendi* jury-trial and beyond-a-reasonable-doubt requirements applied to such aggravating factors.

One question in *Schriro* was whether *Ring* should be retroactively applied as a new "watershed" rule of criminal procedure. In an opinion by Justice Scalia, the Court introduced the topic by saying:

> New rules of procedure . . . generally do not apply retroactively. They do not produce a class of persons convicted of conduct the law does not make criminal, but merely raise the possibility that someone convicted with use of the invalidated procedure might have been acquitted otherwise. Because of this more speculative connection to innocence, we give retroactive effect to only a small set of " 'watershed rules of criminal procedure' implicating the fundamental fairness and accuracy of the criminal proceeding." That a new procedural rule is "fundamental" in some abstract sense is not enough; the rule must be one "without which the likelihood of an accurate conviction is *seriously* diminished." This class of rules is extremely narrow, and "it is unlikely that any 'ha[s] yet to emerge.' "

The Court then declined to give *Ring* retroactive effect:

> The question here is not . . . whether the Framers believed that juries are more accurate factfinders than judges (perhaps so—they certainly thought juries were more independent). Nor is the question whether juries actually *are* more accurate factfinders than judges (again, perhaps so). Rather, the question is whether judicial factfinding so "*seriously* diminishe[s]" accuracy that there is an "impermissibly large risk" of punishing conduct the law does not reach. Teague v. Lane, 489 U.S. 288, 312–13 (1989). The evidence is simply too equivocal to support that conclusion.

> First, for every argument why juries are more accurate factfinders, there is another why they are less accurate. The [lower court] dissent noted several, including juries' tendency to become confused over legal standards and to be influenced by emotion or philosophical predisposition. . . . Members of this Court have opined that judicial sentencing may yield more consistent results because of judges' greater experience. Finally, the mixed reception that the right to jury trial has been given in other countries, though irrelevant to the meaning and continued existence of that right under our Constitution, surely makes it implausible that judicial factfinding so "*seriously* diminishe[s]" accuracy as to produce an

"impermissibly large risk" of injustice. When so many presumably reasonable minds continue to disagree over whether juries are better factfinders *at all,* we cannot confidently say that judicial factfinding *seriously* diminishes accuracy.[b]

4. NEW "SUBSTANTIVE" RULES

While the procedural "watershed" exception to *Teague* is reasonably settled, the scope of the "substantive" exception has been actively disputed. In describing the new "substantive" rule exception to its limitation on retroactivity, the *Teague* plurality said that "a new rule should be applied retroactively if it places 'certain kinds of primary, private individual conduct beyond the power of the criminal law-making authority to proscribe.'" The Court added in Penry v. Lynaugh, 492 U.S. 302, 330 (1989), that:

> the first exception set forth in *Teague* should be understood to cover not only rules forbidding criminal punishment of certain primary conduct but also rules prohibiting a certain category of punishment for a class of defendants because of their status or offense. Thus, if we held, as a substantive matter, that the Eighth Amendment prohibits the execution of mentally retarded persons . . . regardless of the procedures followed, such a rule would fall under the first exception to the general rule of non-retroactivity and would be applicable to defendants on collateral review.

(i) Schriro v. Summerlin

Schriro v. Summerlin, 542 U.S. 348 (2004), discussed in Note 3 above, also raised the issue whether the rule of Ring v. Arizona, 536 U.S. 584 (2002), fell within the new "substantive" rule exception to *Teague* non-retroactivity. The Court said:

> When a decision of this Court results in a "new rule," that rule applies to all criminal cases still pending on direct review. Griffith v. Kentucky, 479 U.S. 314, 328 (1987). As to convictions that are already final, however, the rule applies only in limited circumstances. New *substantive* rules generally apply retroactively. This includes decisions that narrow the scope of a criminal statute by interpreting its terms, see Bousley v. United States, 523 U.S. 614, 620–621 (1998), as well as constitutional determinations that place particular conduct or persons covered by the statute beyond the State's power to punish. Such rules apply retroactively because they "necessarily carry a significant risk that a defendant stands convicted of 'an act that the law does not make criminal'" or faces a punishment that the law cannot impose upon him.

---

[b] The Court was also influenced by DeStefano v. Woods, 392 U.S. 631 (1968) (per curiam). Duncan v. Louisiana, 391 U.S. 145 (1968), held that the Sixth Amendment jury-trial guarantee applied to the states. Applying the pre-*Teague* retroactivity analysis, *DeStefano* held that *Duncan* was not retroactive.

Joined by Justices Stevens, Souter, and Ginsburg, Justice Breyer dissented. He concluded that *Ring* was a " 'watershed' procedural ruling" for reasons closely associated with the fact that the death penalty was at stake.—[Footnote by eds.]

The *Ring* rule might well have been considered "substantive." The effect of *Apprendi*, one could argue, was to transform the sentencing factors to which it applied into "elements" of the offense, thus changing the substantive definition of the crime for which the defendant was convicted. Indeed, the Court in *Ring* had said that "[b]ecause Arizona's enumerated aggravating factors operate as 'the functional equivalent of an element of a greater offense,' the Sixth Amendment requires that they be found by a jury."

In an opinion by Justice Scalia, the Court disagreed:

> A decision that modifies the elements of an offense is normally substantive rather than procedural. New elements alter the range of conduct the statute punishes, rendering some formerly unlawful conduct lawful or vice versa. But that is not what *Ring* did; the range of conduct punished by death in Arizona was the same before *Ring* as after. *Ring* held that, *because* Arizona's statutory aggravators restricted (as a matter of state law) the class of death-eligible defendants, those aggravators *effectively were* elements for federal constitutional purposes, and so were subject to the procedural requirements the Constitution attaches to trial of elements. This Court's holding that, *because Arizona* has made a certain fact essential to the death penalty, that fact must be found by a jury, is not the same as *this Court's* making a certain fact essential to the death penalty. The former was a procedural holding; the latter would be substantive.

(ii) Bousley v. United States

Bousley v. United States, 523 U.S. 614 (1998), was cited in *Schriro* and again in *Welch* as an illustration of the substantive-new-rule exception to the *Teague* limitation on retroactivity. An enhanced penalty is provided in 18 U.S.C. § 924(c)(1)(A) for "any person who, during and in relation to any crime of violence or drug trafficking crime . . . for which the person may be prosecuted in a court of the Unites States, uses . . . a firearm. . . ." The Supreme Court held in Bailey v. United States, 516 U.S. 137 (1995), that the phrase "uses . . . a firearm" means "active employment of the firearm," not bare possession. One question in *Bousley* was whether *Bailey* should be applied retroactively to a conviction that occurred five years before *Bailey* was decided. The weapons involved were in close proximity to the site of the drug trafficking, but were not in active use.

The case came to the Supreme Court in review of Bousley's application for post-conviction relief under 28 U.S.C. § 2255. The Court held that "petitioner's claim is not *Teague*-barred":

> [P]etitioner contends that the record reveals that neither he, nor his counsel, nor the court correctly understood the essential elements of the crime with which he was charged. Were this contention proved, petitioner's plea would be . . . constitutionally invalid. . . .
>
> Amicus urges us to apply the rule of *Teague v. Lane* to petitioner's claim that his plea was not knowing and intelligent. In

Teague, we held that "new constitutional rules of criminal procedure will not be applicable to those cases which have become final before the new rules are announced," unless the new rule "places 'certain kinds of primary, private individual conduct beyond the power of the criminal law-making authority to proscribe,' " or could be considered a "watershed rul[e] of criminal procedure." But we do not believe that *Teague* governs this case. The only constitutional claim made here is that petitioner's guilty plea was not knowing and intelligent. There is surely nothing new about this principle . . . . And because *Teague* by its terms applies only to procedural rules, we think it is inapplicable to the situation in which this Court decides the meaning of a criminal statute enacted by Congress.

This distinction between substance and procedure is an important one in the habeas context. The *Teague* doctrine is founded on the notion that one of the "principal functions of habeas corpus [is] 'to assure that no man has been incarcerated under a procedure which creates an impermissibly large risk that the innocent will be convicted.' Teague v. Lane, 489 U.S. 288, 312 (1989). Consequently, unless a new rule of criminal procedure is of such a nature that "without [it] the likelihood of an accurate conviction is seriously diminished," id. at 313, there is no reason to apply the rule retroactively on habeas review. By contrast, decisions of this Court holding that a substantive federal criminal statute does not reach certain conduct, like decisions placing conduct " 'beyond the power of the criminal law-making authority to proscribe,' " id. at 311, necessarily carry a significant risk that a defendant stands convicted of "an act that the law does not make criminal." Davis v. United States, 417 U.S. 333, 346 (1974). For under our federal system it is only Congress, and not the courts, which can make conduct criminal. Accordingly, it would be inconsistent with the doctrinal underpinnings of habeas review to preclude petitioner from relying on our decision in *Bailey* in support of his claim that his guilty plea was constitutionally invalid.

(iii) Montgomery v. Louisiana

Henry Montgomery was convicted in 1963 of a murder committed when he was 17. He was sentenced to a mandatory term of life without parole. Many years later, the Court held in Miller v. Alabama, 567 U.S. 460 (2012), that life without parole could not be imposed on a juvenile for a homicide offense without consideration of the particular circumstances of each juvenile offender. The question in Montgomery v. Louisiana, 577 U.S. ___, 136 S.Ct. 718 (2016), was whether *Miller* fit *Teague's* substantive-new-rule exception to non-retroactivity. Speaking through Justice Kennedy, the Court held that it did:

Miller requires that before sentencing a juvenile to life without parole, the sentencing judge take into account "how children are different, and how those differences counsel against irrevocably sentencing them to a lifetime in prison." The Court recognized that a sentencer might encounter the rare juvenile offender who exhibits such irretrievable depravity that rehabilitation is impossible and life without parole is justified. But in light of "children's diminished culpability and heightened capacity for change," *Miller* made clear that "appropriate occasions for sentencing juveniles to this harshest possible penalty will be uncommon."

Miller, then, did more than require a sentencer to consider a juvenile offender's youth before imposing life without parole . . . . Because *Miller* determined that sentencing a child to life without parole is excessive for all but " 'the rare juvenile offender whose crime reflects irreparable corruption,' " it rendered life without parole an unconstitutional penalty for "a class of defendants because of their status"—that is, juvenile offenders whose crimes reflect the transient immaturity of youth. As a result, *Miller* announced a substantive rule of constitutional law. Like other substantive rules, *Miller* is retroactive because it " 'necessarily carr[ies] a significant risk that a defendant' "—here, the vast majority of juvenile offenders—" 'faces a punishment that the law cannot impose upon him.' " Schriro v. Summerlin, 542 U.S. 348, 352 (2004) (quoting Bousley v. United States, 523 U.S. 614, 620 (1998)).[c]

5. QUESTIONS AND COMMENTS ON *TEAGUE* AND *WELCH*

The first *Teague* exception was based on Justice Harlan's notion that new rules should be retroactive if they placed "certain kinds of primary, private individual conduct beyond the power of the criminal law-making authority to proscribe." Mackey v. United States, 401 U.S. 667, 692 (1971) (opinion of Harlan, J.). It is hard to fit *Johnson*'s holding that the residual clause of the Armed Career Criminal Act was unconstitutionally vague into this language. The statement in Schriro v. Summerlin, 542 U.S. 348 (2004), that the substantive exception applies to "constitutional determinations that place particular conduct or persons covered by the statute beyond the State's power to punish" also does not appear to embrace the *Johnson* holding. The majority in *Welch*, however, concluded that *Johnson* fell within the first *Teague* exception because *Johnson* "affected the reach of the underlying statute rather than the judicial procedures by which the statute is applied." Accordingly, it was "a substantive decision and so has retroactive effect under *Teague* in cases on collateral review." Which side has the better of the debate between the Court and Justice Thomas in *Welch*? Should *Johnson* have been given retroactive effect?

---

[c]   The Court also spoke to the appropriate remedy:

> A State may remedy a *Miller* violation by permitting juvenile homicide offenders to be considered for parole, rather than by resentencing them. Allowing those offenders to be considered for parole ensures that juveniles whose crimes reflected only transient immaturity—and who have since matured—will not be forced to serve a disproportionate sentence in violation of the Eighth Amendment.

Joined by Justices Thomas and Alito, Justice Scalia dissented. Justice Thomas also wrote a separate dissent on another issue.

Consider also the holding in *Montgomery* that *Miller* announced a new "substantive" rule. It is argued in Dov Fox and Alex Stein, Constitutional Retroactivity in Criminal Procedure, 91 Wash. L. Rev. 463, 468 (2016), that:

> The *Montgomery* majority reached a just result for the wrong reason. Justice required that the constitutional rule announced in *Miller* apply retroactively to prisoners who did not get the benefit of that rule by the time that their sentences were finalized. But the reason underlying this intuition is not that a right to individualized sentencing places particular conduct or persons beyond the power to punish. Rather, it is that *Miller* afforded juvenile defendants a fundamentally important due process protection. . . . The Court's "rewriting" of the *Miller* rule from procedural to substantive made that constitutional holding retroactive through the back door that its *Teague* jurisprudence left open.

Is their point well taken?[d]

Finally, how does *Bousley* fit the Court's approach to post-conviction relief? Is it an application of the "substantive" exception to *Teague* (as *Schriro* and *Welch* seem to assume) or is it better explained as resting on a different rationale? Is the content of the substantive exception clear? Evolving? More broadly, is the *Teague* regime the right approach to the availability in habeas proceedings of constitutional decisions that go beyond previously established law? A related question is the appropriate impact of *Teague* in *state* post-conviction proceedings. That topic is postponed for now but addressed in Subsection A of Section 5 of this Chapter.

6. BIBLIOGRAPHY

Teague prompted extensive commentary, including: Marc M. Arkin, The Prisoner's Dilemma: Life in the Lower Federal Courts after *Teague v. Lane,* 69 N.C. L. Rev. 371 (1991); Susan Bandes, Taking Justice to its Logical Extreme: A Comment on *Teague v. Lane,* 66 So. Calif. L. Rev. 2453 (1993); Vivian Berger, Justice Delayed or Justice Denied?—A Comment on Recent Proposals to Reform Death Penalty Habeas Corpus, 90 Colum. L. Rev. 1665 (1990); David R. Dow, *Teague* and Death: The Impact of Current Retroactivity Doctrine on Capital Defendants, 19 Hastings Const. L.Q. 23 (1991); Markus Dirk Dubber, Prudence and Substance: How the Supreme Court's New Habeas Retroactivity Doctrine Mirrors and Affects Substantive Constitutional Law, 30 Am. Crim. L. Rev. 1 (1992); Lyn S. Entzeroth, Reflections on Fifteen Years of the *Teague v. Lane* Retroactivity Paradigm: A Study of the Persistence, the Pervasiveness, and the Perversity of the Court's Doctrine, 35 N.M. L. Rev. 161 (2005); Stephen M. Feldman, Diagnosing Power: Postmodernism in Legal Scholarship and Judicial Practice (With an Emphasis on the *Teague* Rule Against New Rules in Habeas Corpus Cases), 88 Nw.

---

[d] After noting that new "watershed" procedural rulings by the Supreme Court have been an empty set, Fox and Stein also argue "that the universally-perceived irrelevance of the watershed doctrine misses its fundamental role in constitutional criminal procedure." They use "the dynamic concentration model of game theory to show how this doctrine quietly encourages courts to align their state's criminal procedures, beyond existing protections, with projections about the more generous vision of trial fairness that those protections represent."

U. L. Rev. 1046 (1994); Barry Friedman, Failed Enterprise: The Supreme Court's Habeas Reform, 83 Calif. L. Rev. 485 (1995); Barry Friedman, Pas de Deux: The Supreme Court and the Habeas Courts, 66 So. Calif. L. Rev. 2467 (1993); Barry Friedman, Habeas and Hubris, 45 Vanderbilt L. Rev. 797 (1992); Marshall J. Hartman, To Be or Not to Be a "New Rule:" The Non-Retroactivity of Newly Recognized Constitutional Rights after Conviction, 29 Cal. W. L. Rev. 53 (1992); Paul J. Heald, Retroactivity, Capital Sentencing, and the Jurisdictional Contours of Habeas Corpus, 42 Ala. L. Rev. 1273 (1991); Patrick E. Higgenbotham, Notes on *Teague*, 66 So. Calif. L. Rev. 2433 (1993); Joseph L. Hoffmann, The Supreme Court's New Vision of Federal Habeas Corpus for State Prisoners, 1989 Sup. Ct. Rev. 165; Joseph L. Hoffmann, Retroactivity and the Great Writ: How Congress Should Respond to *Teague v. Lane,* 1990 Brigham Young U. L. Rev. 183; Joseph L. Hoffmann, Is Innocence Sufficient? An Essay on the U.S. Supreme Court's Continuing Problems with Federal Habeas Corpus and the Death Penalty, 68 Ind. L.J. 817 (1993); Mary C. Hutton, Retroactivity in the States: The Impact of *Teague v. Lane* on State Post-conviction Remedies, 44 Ala. L. Rev. 421 (1993); Andrew Chongseh Kim, Beyond Finality: How Making Criminal Judgments Less Final Can Further the "Interests of Finality," 2013 Utah L. Rev. 561; Daniel J. Meltzer, Habeas Corpus Jurisdiction: The Limits of Models, 66 So. Calif. L. Rev. 2507 (1993); Linda Meyer, "Nothing We Say Matters": *Teague* and New Rules, 61 U. Chi. L. Rev. 423 (1994); Kermit Roosevelt, III, A Retroactivity Retrospective, with Thoughts for the Future: What the Supreme Court Learned from Paul Mishkin, and What It Might, 95 Calif. L. Rev. 1677 (2007); Larry W. Yackle, The Habeas Hagioscope, 66 So. Calif. L. Rev. 2331 (1993); Jason M. Zarrow and William H. Milliken, The Retroactivity of Substantive Rules to Cases on Collateral Review and the AEDPA, with a Special Focus on *Miller v. Alabama*, 48 Ind. L. Rev. 931 (2015).

Two articles relate the question of "new" law in denial of habeas corpus to legal uncertainty as a defense to constitutional tort liability. Richard Fallon and Daniel Meltzer, New Law, Non-Retroactivity, and Constitutional Remedies, 104 Harv. L. Rev. 1731 (1991); Kit Kinports, Habeas Corpus, Qualified Immunity, and Crystal Balls: Predicting the Course of Constitutional Law, 33 Ariz. L. Rev. 115 (1991). For a broader perspective on the role of "context" in lawmaking and on the Court's rhetorical stance in these cases, see Ann Althouse, Saying What Rights Are—In and Out of Context, 1991 Wis. L. Rev. 929. For an argument that the *Teague* retroactivity bar is inconsistent with the historical roots of habeas corpus in principles of equity, and that the Supreme Court should adopt equitable exceptions to the bar, see Erica Hashimoto, Reclaiming the Equitable Heritage of Habeas, 108 Nw. U. L. Rev. 139 (2013).

SECTION 2. REVIEW OF STATE COURT DECISIONS ON THE MERITS: AEDPA

INTRODUCTORY NOTES ON THE STANDARD OF REVIEW UNDER AEDPA FOR STATE-COURT MERITS DECISIONS

1. THE STATUTE

Under *Brown v. Allen*, federal judges were required to review de novo a state court's adjudication of a federal habeas petitioner's constitutional claims. This requirement extended both to pure questions of law and issues involving the application of law to facts (so-called "mixed" questions of law and fact). Functionally, as Justice Brennan pointed out in *Stone v. Powell*, this transformed the lower federal courts into appellate overseers of state supreme court rulings on federal constitutional claims. Federal district courts were broadly authorized to retry issues of fact, moreover, adding further assurance that state criminal convictions were obtained in compliance with federal constitutional limitations.

The Supreme Court substantially modified this structure in *Stone v. Powell*. So long as the states provided a fair opportunity for the litigation of Fourth Amendment claims, state court decisions on such claims were excluded from the *Brown* de novo review requirement. They were exempt from federal habeas review. Because certiorari review in the Supreme Court is so rare, state courts therefore became the effective final arbiters of the meaning of the Fourth Amendment in state criminal proceedings.

Teague v. Lane introduced another important limitation on the scope of federal review of state court merits decisions. *Teague* said that state courts were required only to conduct criminal proceedings in compliance with constitutional limitations that were "dictated" by precedent prior to completion of direct review of a conviction. With limited exceptions, new developments were not to be given retroactive effect in federal habeas proceedings. *Stone* excluded from federal habeas review decisions by state courts on search and seizure claims. Absent an exception, *Teague* excluded from federal habeas review state court decisions on *all* constitutional claims that were based on legal developments that emerged after the state criminal process had concluded.

The Antiterrorism and Effective Death Penalty Act of 1996 (AEDPA) added further limitations on the availability of federal habeas corpus. With respect to federal review of state court decisions on the merits of federal constitutional questions, § 2254(d)(1) provides:

> (d) An application for a writ of habeas corpus on behalf of a person in custody pursuant to the judgment of a State court shall not be granted with respect to any claim that was adjudicated on the merits in State court proceedings unless the adjudication of the claim—
>
> > (1) resulted in a decision that was contrary to, or involved an unreasonable application of, clearly established

Federal law, as determined by the Supreme Court of the United States. . . .

Subsequent materials elaborate on the meaning of this provision. It is useful first, however, to consider its relationship to *Stone v. Powell* and *Teague v. Lane.*

2.   IMPACT OF AEDPA ON SEARCH AND SEIZURE CLAIMS

The Supreme Court has yet to address the intersection of AEDPA with *Stone v. Powell.* How it interacts with the case is likely to turn on the meaning of "an opportunity for full and fair litigation of a Fourth Amendment claim."

(i) *Narrow Reading of "Opportunity for a Full and Fair Hearing"*

Stone v. Powell excluded Fourth Amendment claims from consideration on federal habeas corpus so long as the federal petitioner was given an "opportunity for full and fair litigation" of the claim. "Full and fair litigation" could mean only a fair opportunity to raise the claim so it could be considered by the state court on the merits. It could mean only that the state *procedures* were open and fair.[a]

If this is what "opportunity for a full and fair hearing" means, then search and seizure claims cannot be raised on federal habeas under *Stone v. Powell* if the defendant was given a procedural opportunity to assert the

---

[a] See, e.g., Capellan v. Riley, 975 F.2d 67, 70 (2d Cir. 1992):

> In the wake of *Powell,* this Circuit has developed a litmus test to discern when a state prisoner has been denied an opportunity for full and fair litigation of his fourth amendment claims. [We noted in a prior case] that "all that the [Supreme] Court required was that the state [ ] provide[ ] the *opportunity* to the state prisoner for a full and fair litigation of the Fourth Amendment claim. . . ." We concluded that review of fourth amendment claims in habeas petitions would be undertaken in only one of two instances: (a) if the state has provided no corrective procedures at all to redress the alleged fourth amendment violations; or (b) if the state has provided a corrective mechanism, but the defendant was precluded from using that mechanism because of an unconscionable breakdown in the underlying process.

See also Hampton v. Wyant, 296 F.3d 560, 563–64 (7th Cir. 2002):

> [Our test for] full and fair opportunity to litigate [is]:
>
> (1) he has clearly informed the state court of the factual basis for that claim and has argued that those facts constitute a violation of his fourth amendment rights and (2) the state court has carefully and thoroughly analyzed the facts and (3) applied the proper constitutional case law to the facts.
>
> [The state] wonders how the third of these considerations can be appropriate, given the way *Stone* itself handled a claim of error. The state's concern supposes, however, that [the requirement is that the state] decide the issue *correctly.* But this is not what we meant. What a state has to do is look to the appropriate body of decisional law. . . . It is impossible to see how the problem could be identified without paying *some* attention to how the state court dealt with the merits. But this must not be confused with a search for error. It takes an "egregious error" to imply that the state judges have closed their ears and minds to argument—and it is the latter circumstance, not the error itself, that would justify relief under *Stone.* Even an "egregious error" thus is not enough to support a writ of habeas corpus (that's what it means to say that the exclusionary rule does not apply on collateral attack); a blunder, no matter how obvious, matters only in conjunction with other circumstances that imply refusal by the state judiciary to take seriously its obligation to adjudicate claims under the fourth amendment.

claim in state court and if the state court stood ready to resolve the claim on the merits. It would not matter, on this view, how wrong the state court might have been in its merits decision. Search and seizure claims are left to the state courts for resolution, subject only to the possibility of direct review by certiorari in the Supreme Court.

Does AEPDA change this result? Suppose a state court fails to exclude evidence in clear contravention of applicable Supreme Court Fourth Amendment precedent. Literally, § 2254(d)(1) would seem to require a federal habeas court to set aside a resulting conviction because the state court decision was "contrary to . . . clearly established Federal law, as determined by the Supreme Court of the United States." On this reading, the language of AEDPA could be taken to have opened the door to federal habeas review of Fourth Amendment claims that *Stone v. Powell* closed. A statute plainly intended to curtail habeas relief would be read to permit an important new category of claims to be litigated on federal habeas.

The Supreme Court has yet to address this possibility, but the circuit courts have not been receptive. Consider, for example, Hampton v. Wyant, 296 F.3d 560, 562–63 (7th Cir. 2002):

> It is . . . not possible to move from a conclusion that seizure of evidence violated the Fourth Amendment to a holding that a writ of habeas corpus must issue. The exclusionary rule is not enforced on collateral attack. Put otherwise, a person imprisoned following a trial that relies, in part, on unlawfully seized evidence is not "in custody in violation of the Constitution or laws or treaties of the United States." 28 U.S.C. § 2254(a). The *seizure* may have violated the Constitution, but the *custody* does not, because the exclusionary rule is a social device for deterring official wrongdoing, not a personal right of defendants. This also means, by the way, that the Antiterrorism and Effective Death Penalty Act does not affect *Stone*. The AEDPA's changes to § 2254(d) apply only to cases within the scope of § 2254(a), which was not amended in 1996, and *Stone* is based on an interpretation of § 2254(a) that treats inaccurate administration of the exclusionary rule as outside the scope of that statute.

(ii) Broad Reading of "Opportunity for a Full and Fair Hearing"

The *Stone v. Powell* opportunity-for-a-hearing requirement could mean more than merely a fair procedural chance to raise a Fourth Amendment claim. It could require an "opportunity for full and fair litigation" in the sense that the merits were resolved by the state courts in fair compliance with the substantive meaning of the Fourth Amendment. It could be read to require reasonable and fair application of the governing Fourth Amendment law.[b]

---

[b]   See Gamble v. State of Oklahoma, 583 F.2d 1161, 1165 (10th Cir. 1978):

> "Opportunity for full and fair consideration" includes, but is not limited to, the procedural opportunity to raise or otherwise present a Fourth Amendment claim. . . . Furthermore, it contemplates recognition and at least colorable application of the correct Fourth Amendment constitutional standards. Thus, a federal court is not precluded from considering Fourth Amendment claims in habeas corpus proceedings

If this is what *Stone v. Powell* means, then search and seizure claims on federal habeas are reviewable if the state courts did not "fairly" resolve them on the merits. This reading is close to if not convergent with the standard stated in § 2254(d)(1): Did the state court resolution result "in a decision that . . . involved an unreasonable application of, clearly established Federal law, as determined by the Supreme Court of the United States"? If this is what *Stone v. Powell* means, then AEDPA may have introduced a subtle but not fundamental change in the meaning of *Stone v. Powell*. It would have come closer to codifying *Stone* than dramatically changing its meaning.[c]

3.   DOES *TEAGUE* SURVIVE AEDPA?

It would have been possible—and perhaps desirable—for the Court to conclude that the habeas regime established by AEDPA displaced *Teague*. But such was not to be the case. In Horn v. Banks, 536 U.S. 266 (2002), and the successor decision in the same case, Beard v. Banks, 542 U.S. 406 (2004), the Court held that federal habeas courts are required to apply *Teague* even though a state post-conviction court addressed the criminal defendant's claims on the merits and even though the state court decision may have made an "unreasonable" mistake in its application of federal law that would allow review under AEDPA. In *Horn*, the Court said in a unanimous per curiam opinion:

> While it is of course a necessary prerequisite to federal habeas relief that a prisoner satisfy the AEDPA standard of review set forth in 28 U.S.C. § 2254(d) . . ., none of our post-AEDPA cases have suggested that a writ of habeas corpus should automatically issue if a prisoner satisfies the AEDPA standard, or that AEDPA relieves courts from the responsibility of addressing properly raised *Teague* arguments. To the contrary, if our post-AEDPA cases suggest anything about AEDPA's relationship to *Teague,* it is that the AEDPA and *Teague* inquiries are distinct. . . . Thus, in addition to performing any analysis required by AEDPA, a federal court considering a habeas petition must conduct a threshold *Teague* analysis when the issue is properly raised by the state.

On remand, the Circuit Court held that the habeas petitioner's claim did not rely on a "new" rule and that the state Supreme Court had unreasonably applied the state of the law existing at the time of conviction. The Supreme Court reversed again. In a five-to-four decision, the majority concluded that the petitioner's claim was indeed based on a "new" rule and that neither *Teague* exception applied. Habeas was therefore foreclosed under *Teague* without regard to whether AEDPA would have allowed review.

---

where the state court wilfully refuses to apply the correct and controlling constitutional standards. Deference to state court consideration of Fourth Amendment claims does not require federal blindness to a state court's wilful refusal to apply the appropriate constitutional standard.

c   See, e.g., the Tenth Circuit's post-AEDPA holding in Harding v. McCollum, 565 Fed. Appx. 764 (10th Cir. 2014) (state court's Fourth Amendment holding not open on federal habeas because it "displayed 'recognition and at least colorable application of the correct Fourth Amendment constitutional standard' ").

4. *WILLIAMS V. TAYLOR*

Williams v. Taylor, 529 U.S. 362 (2000), was the Supreme Court's first attempt to explain the meaning of the AEDPA standard of review. In an opinion by Justice O'Connor, it concluded:

> In sum, § 2254(d)(1) places a new constraint on the power of a federal habeas court to grant a state prisoner's application for a writ of habeas corpus with respect to claims adjudicated on the merits in state court. Under § 2254(d)(1), the writ may issue only if one of the following two conditions is satisfied—the state-court adjudication resulted in a decision that (1) "was contrary to . . . clearly established Federal law, as determined by the Supreme Court of the United States," or (2) "involved an unreasonable application of . . . clearly established Federal law, as determined by the Supreme Court of the United States." Under the "contrary to" clause, a federal habeas court may grant the writ if the state court arrives at a conclusion opposite to that reached by this Court on a question of law or if the state court decides a case differently than this Court has on a set of materially indistinguishable facts. Under the "unreasonable application" clause, a federal habeas court may grant the writ if the state court identifies the correct governing legal principle from this Court's decisions but unreasonably applies that principle to the facts of the prisoner's case.

The words "clearly established Federal law, as determined by the Supreme Court of the United States," the Court added, refer "to the holdings, as opposed to the dicta, of this Court's decisions as of the time of the relevant state-court decision." The "contrary to" clause is violated when the state court decision is "substantially different from the relevant precedent of this Court" or if the state court "applies a rule that contradicts the governing law set forth in our cases." The statute requires more than a conclusion that the state court decision was "incorrect." For "[i]f a federal habeas court can, under the 'contrary to' clause, issue the writ whenever it concludes that the state court's application of clearly established federal law was incorrect, the 'unreasonable application' clause becomes a nullity":

> [T]he most important point is that an unreasonable application of federal law is different from an incorrect application of federal law. . . . Congress specifically used the word "unreasonable," and not a term like "erroneous" or "incorrect." Under § 2254(d)(1)'s "unreasonable application" clause, then, a federal habeas court may not issue the writ simply because that court concludes in its independent judgment that the relevant state-court decision applied clearly established federal law erroneously or incorrectly. Rather, that application must also be unreasonable.

One of the issues explicitly left unresolved in *Williams v. Taylor* was whether § 2254(d)(1) permits federal habeas relief when a state court "unreasonably" failed to extend Supreme Court precedents to a logical conclusion that technically went beyond their narrow holdings. The next main case resolves that issue and also illustrates the governing standard of federal review under AEDPA.

White v. Woodall

Supreme Court of the United States, 2014.
572 U.S. ___, 134 S.Ct. 1697.

■ JUSTICE SCALIA delivered the opinion of the Court.

Respondent brutally raped, slashed with a box cutter, and drowned a 16-year-old high-school student. After pleading guilty to murder, rape, and kidnaping, he was sentenced to death. The Kentucky Supreme Court affirmed the sentence, and we denied certiorari. Ten years later, the Court of Appeals for the Sixth Circuit granted respondent's petition for a writ of habeas corpus on his Fifth Amendment claim. In so doing, it disregarded the limitations of 28 U.S.C. § 2254(d)—a provision of law that some federal judges find too confining, but that all federal judges must obey. We reverse.

I

On the evening of January 25, 1997, Sarah Hansen drove to a convenience store to rent a movie. When she failed to return home several hours later, her family called the police. Officers eventually found the vehicle Hansen had been driving a short distance from the convenience store. They followed a 400 to 500 foot trail of blood from the van to a nearby lake, where Hansen's unclothed, dead body was found floating in the water. Hansen's "throat had been slashed twice with each cut approximately 3.5 to 4 inches long," and "[h]er windpipe was totally severed."

Authorities questioned respondent when they learned that he had been in the convenience store on the night of the murder. Respondent gave conflicting statements regarding his whereabouts that evening. Further investigation revealed that respondent's "fingerprints were on the van the victim was driving," "[b]lood was found on [respondent's] front door," "[b]lood on his clothing and sweatshirt was consistent with the blood of the victim," and "DNA on . . . vaginal swabs" taken from the victim "was consistent with" respondent's.

Faced with overwhelming evidence of his guilt, respondent pleaded guilty to capital murder. He also pleaded guilty to capital kidnaping and first-degree rape, the statutory aggravating circumstance for the murder. At the ensuing penalty-phase trial, respondent called character witnesses but declined to testify himself. Defense counsel asked the trial judge to instruct the jury that "[a] defendant is not compelled to testify and the fact that the defendant did not testify should not prejudice him in any way." The trial judge denied the request, and the Kentucky Supreme Court affirmed that denial. While recognizing that the Fifth Amendment requires a no-adverse-inference instruction to protect a nontestifying defendant at the guilt phase, see Carter v. Kentucky, 450 U.S. 288 (1981), the court held that Carter and our subsequent cases did not require such an instruction here. We denied respondent's petition for a writ of certiorari from that direct appeal.

In 2006, respondent filed this petition for habeas corpus in Federal District Court. The District Court granted relief, holding, as relevant here, that the trial court's refusal to issue a no-adverse-inference instruction at the penalty phase violated respondent's Fifth Amendment privilege against self-incrimination. The Court of Appeals affirmed and ordered Kentucky to either resentence respondent within 180 days or release him. . . . We granted certiorari.

II

A

Section 2254(d) of Title 28 provides that "[a]n application for a writ of habeas corpus on behalf of a person in custody pursuant to the judgment of a State court shall not be granted with respect to any claim that was adjudicated on the merits in State court proceedings unless the adjudication of the claim . . . resulted in a decision that was contrary to, or involved an unreasonable application of, clearly established Federal law, as determined by the Supreme Court of the United States." "This standard," we recently reminded the Sixth Circuit, "is 'difficult to meet.'" Metrish v. Lancaster, 569 U.S. 351, 357–58 (2013). "'[C]learly established Federal law'" for purposes of § 2254(d)(1) includes only "'the holdings, as opposed to the dicta, of this Court's decisions.'" Howes v. Fields, 565 U.S. 499, 505 (2012) (quoting Williams v. Taylor, 529 U.S. 362, 412 (2000)). And an "unreasonable application of" those holdings must be "'objectively unreasonable,'" not merely wrong; even "clear error" will not suffice. Lockyer v. Andrade, 538 U.S. 63, 75–76 (2003). Rather, "[a]s a condition for obtaining habeas corpus from a federal court, a state prisoner must show that the state court's ruling on the claim being presented in federal court was so lacking in justification that there was an error well understood and comprehended in existing law beyond any possibility for fairminded disagreement." Harrington v. Richter, 562 U.S. 86, 103 (2011).

Both the Kentucky Supreme Court and the Court of Appeals identified as the relevant precedents in this area our decisions in *Carter,* Estelle v. Smith, 451 U.S. 454 (1981), and Mitchell v. United States, 526 U.S. 314 (1999). *Carter* held that a no-adverse-inference instruction is required at the *guilt* phase. *Estelle* concerned the introduction at the penalty phase of the results of an involuntary, un-*Mirandized* pretrial psychiatric examination. And *Mitchell* disapproved a trial judge's drawing of an adverse inference from the defendant's silence at sentencing "with regard to factual determinations respecting the circumstances and details of the crime."

It is clear that the Kentucky Supreme Court's conclusion is not "contrary to" the actual holding of any of these cases. The Court of Appeals

held, however, that the "Kentucky Supreme Court's denial of this constitutional claim was an unreasonable application of" those cases. In its
view, "reading *Carter, Estelle,* and *Mitchell* together, the only reasonable
conclusion is that" a no-adverse-inference instruction was required at the
penalty phase.[2]

We need not decide here, and express no view on, whether the conclusion that a no-adverse-inference instruction was required would be
correct in a case not reviewed through the lens of § 2254(d)(1). For we are
satisfied that the issue was, at a minimum, not "beyond any possibility
for fairminded disagreement." *Harrington,* 562 U.S. at 103.

We have, it is true, held that the privilege against self-incrimination
applies to the penalty phase. But it is not uncommon for a constitutional
rule to apply somewhat differently at the penalty phase than it does at
the guilt phase. . . .

Indeed, *Mitchell* itself leaves open the possibility that some inferences might permissibly be drawn from a defendant's penalty-phase
silence. In that case, the District Judge had actually *drawn* from the defendant's silence an adverse inference about the drug quantity attributable to the defendant. We held that this ran afoul of the defendant's
"right to remain silent at sentencing." But we framed our holding narrowly, in terms implying that it was limited to inferences pertaining to
the facts of the crime: "We decline to adopt an exception for the sentencing phase of a criminal case *with regard to factual determinations
respecting the circumstances and details of the crime.*" *Mitchell,* 526 U.S.
at 328 (emphasis added). "The Government retains," we said, "*the burden
of proving facts relevant to the crime* . . . and cannot enlist the defendant
in this process at the expense of the self-incrimination privilege." Id. at
330 (emphasis added). And *Mitchell* included an express reservation of
direct relevance here: "Whether silence bears upon the determination of
a lack of remorse, or upon acceptance of responsibility for purposes of the
downward adjustment provided in § 3E1.1 of the United States Sentencing Guidelines (1998), is a separate question. It is not before us, and we
express no view on it." Id.[3]

Mitchell's reservation is relevant here for two reasons. First, if
Mitchell suggests that *some* actual inferences might be permissible at the

---

[2]   The Court of Appeals also based its conclusion that respondent "was entitled to receive
a no adverse inference instruction" on one of its own cases. That was improper. As we cautioned
the Sixth Circuit two Terms ago, a lower court may not "consul[t] its own precedents, rather
than those of this Court, in assessing" a habeas claim governed by § 2254. Parker v. Matthews,
567 U.S. 37, 48 (2012) (per curiam).

[3]   The Courts of Appeals have recognized that *Mitchell* left this unresolved; their diverging
approaches to the question illustrate the possibility of fairminded disagreement. . . .

Indeed, the Sixth Circuit itself has previously recognized that *Mitchell* "explicitly limited
its holding regarding inferences drawn from a defendant's silence to facts about the substantive
offense and did not address other inferences that may be drawn from a defendant's silence."
United States v. Kennedy, 499 F.3d 547, 552 (6th Cir. 2007). *Kennedy* upheld under *Mitchell* a
sentencing judge's consideration of the defendant's refusal to complete a court-ordered psycho-
sexual examination.

penalty phase, it certainly cannot be read to require a *blanket* no-adverse-inference instruction at every penalty-phase trial. And it was a blanket instruction that was requested and denied in this case; respondent's requested instruction would have informed the jury that "[a] defendant is not compelled to testify and the fact that the defendant did not testify should not prejudice him *in any way*." Counsel for respondent conceded at oral argument that remorse was at issue during the penalty-phase trial, yet the proposed instruction would have precluded the jury from considering respondent's silence as indicative of his lack of remorse. Indeed, the trial judge declined to give the no-adverse-inference instruction precisely because he was "aware of no case law that precludes the jury from considering the defendant's lack of expression of remorse . . . in sentencing." This alone suffices to establish that the Kentucky Supreme Court's conclusion was not "objectively unreasonable."

Second, regardless of the scope of respondent's proposed instruction, any inferences that could have been drawn from respondent's silence would arguably fall within the class of inferences as to which *Mitchell* leaves the door open. Respondent pleaded guilty to all of the charges he faced, including the applicable aggravating circumstances. Thus, Kentucky could not have shifted to respondent its "burden of proving facts relevant to the crime," *Mitchell*, 526 U.S. at 330: Respondent's own admissions had already established every relevant fact on which Kentucky bore the burden of proof. There are reasonable arguments that the logic of *Mitchell* does not apply to such cases. See, e.g., United States v. Ronquillo, 508 F.3d 744, 749 (5th Cir. 2007) ("*Mitchell* is inapplicable to the sentencing decision in this case because 'the facts of the offense' were based entirely on Ronquillo's admissions, not on any adverse inference. . . . Ronquillo, unlike the defendant in *Mitchell,* admitted all the predicate facts of his offenses").

The dissent insists that *Mitchell* is irrelevant because it merely declined to create an exception to the "normal rule," supposedly established by *Estelle,* "that a defendant is entitled to a requested no-adverse-inference instruction" at sentencing. That argument disregards perfectly reasonable interpretations of *Estelle* and *Mitchell* and hence contravenes § 2254(d)'s deferential standard of review. *Estelle* did not involve an adverse inference based on the defendant's silence or a corresponding jury instruction. Thus, whatever *Estelle* said about the Fifth Amendment, its holding[4]—the only aspect of the decision relevant here—does not "requir[e]" the categorical rule the dissent ascribes to it. Likewise,

---

    [4] The dissent says *Estelle* "held that 'so far as the protection of the Fifth Amendment is concerned,' it could 'discern no basis to distinguish between the guilt and penalty phases of a defendant's 'capital murder trial.' " Of course, it did not "hold" that. Rather, it held that the defendant's Fifth Amendment "rights were abridged by the State's introduction of" a pretrial psychiatric evaluation that was administered without the preliminary warning required by Miranda v. Arizona, 384 U.S. 436 (1966). In any event, even *Estelle*'s dictum did not assume an entitlement to a blanket no-adverse-inference instruction. The quoted language is reasonably read as referring to the availability of the Fifth Amendment privilege at sentencing rather than the precise scope of that privilege when applied in the sentencing context. Indeed, it appears in

fairminded jurists could conclude that *Mitchell*'s reservation regarding remorse and acceptance of responsibility would have served no meaningful purpose if *Estelle* had created an across-the-board rule against adverse inferences; we are, after all, hardly in the habit of reserving "separate question[s]," *Mitchell*, 526 U.S. at 330, that have already been definitively answered. In these circumstances, where the " 'precise contours' " of the right remain " 'unclear,' " state courts enjoy "broad discretion" in their adjudication of a prisoner's claims. *Lockyer*, 538 U.S. at 76.

B

In arguing for a contrary result, respondent leans heavily on the notion that a state-court " 'determination may be set aside . . . if, under clearly established federal law, the state court was unreasonable in refusing to extend the governing legal principle to a context in which the principle should have controlled.' " Brief for Respondent 21 (quoting Ramdass v. Angelone, 530 U.S. 156, 166 (2000) (plurality opinion)). The Court of Appeals and District Court relied on the same proposition in sustaining respondent's Fifth Amendment claim. . . . [T]his Court has never adopted the unreasonable-refusal-to-extend rule on which respondent relies. It has not been so much as endorsed in a majority opinion, let alone relied on as a basis for granting habeas relief. [W]e [now] reject it. Section 2254(d)(1) provides a remedy for instances in which a state court unreasonably *applies* this Court's precedent; it does not require state courts to *extend* that precedent or license federal courts to treat the failure to do so as error. Thus, "if a habeas court must extend a rationale before it can apply to the facts at hand," then by definition the rationale was not "clearly established at the time of the state-court decision." *Yarborough*, 541 U.S. at 666. AEDPA's carefully constructed framework "would be undermined if habeas courts introduced rules not clearly established under the guise of extensions to existing law." Ibid.

This is not to say that § 2254(d)(1) requires an " 'identical factual pattern before a legal rule must be applied.' " Panetti v. Quarterman, 551 U.S. 930, 953 (2007). To the contrary, state courts must reasonably apply the rules "squarely established" by this Court's holdings to the facts of each case. Knowles v. Mirzayance, 556 U.S. 111, 122 (2009). "[T]he difference between applying a rule and extending it is not always clear," but "[c]ertain principles are fundamental enough that when new factual permutations arise, the necessity to apply the earlier rule will be beyond doubt." *Yarborough*, 541 U.S. at 666. The critical point is that relief is available under § 2254(d)(1)'s unreasonable-application clause if, and only if, it is so obvious that a clearly established rule applies to a given set of facts that there could be no "fairminded disagreement" on the question, *Harrington*, 562 U.S. at 103.

---

a passage responding to the State's argument that the defendant "was not entitled to the protection of the Fifth Amendment" in the first place.

Perhaps the logical next step from *Carter, Estelle,* and *Mitchell* would be to hold that the Fifth Amendment requires a penalty-phase no-adverse-inference instruction in a case like this one; perhaps not. Either way, we have not yet taken that step, and there are reasonable arguments on both sides—which is all Kentucky needs to prevail in this AEDPA case. The appropriate time to consider the question as a matter of first impression would be on direct review, not in a habeas case governed by § 2254(d)(1).

* * *

Because the Kentucky Supreme Court's rejection of respondent's Fifth Amendment claim was not objectively unreasonable, the Sixth Circuit erred in granting the writ. . . . The judgment of the Court of Appeals is reversed, and the case is remanded for further proceedings consistent with this opinion.

It is so ordered.

■ JUSTICE BREYER, with whom JUSTICE GINSBURG and JUSTICE SOTOMAYOR join, dissenting.

During the penalty phase of his capital murder trial, respondent Robert Woodall asked the court to instruct the jury not to draw any adverse inferences from his failure to testify. The court refused, and the Kentucky Supreme Court agreed that no instruction was warranted. The question before us is whether the Kentucky courts unreasonably applied clearly established Supreme Court law in concluding that the Fifth Amendment did not entitle Woodall to a no-adverse-inference instruction. In my view, the answer is yes.

I

This Court's decisions in Carter v. Kentucky, 450 U.S. 288 (1981), and Estelle v. Smith, 451 U.S. 454 (1981), clearly establish that a criminal defendant is entitled to a requested no-adverse-inference instruction in the penalty phase of a capital trial. First consider *Carter.* The Court held that a trial judge "has the constitutional obligation, upon proper request," to give a requested no-adverse-inference instruction in order "to minimize the danger that the jury will give evidentiary weight to a defendant's failure to testify." This is because when "the jury is left to roam at large with only its untutored instincts to guide it," it may "draw from the defendant's silence broad inferences of guilt." A trial court's refusal to give a requested no-adverse-inference instruction thus "exacts an impermissible toll on the full and free exercise of the [Fifth Amendment] privilege."

Now consider *Estelle.* The Court held that "so far as the protection of the Fifth Amendment privilege is concerned," it could "discern no basis to distinguish between the guilt and penalty phases" of a defendant's "capital murder trial." The State had introduced at the penalty phase the defendant's compelled statements to a psychiatrist, in order to show the defendant's future dangerousness. Defending the admission of those statements, the State argued that the defendant "was not entitled to the protection of the Fifth Amendment because [his statements were] used only to determine punishment after conviction, not to establish guilt." This Court rejected the State's argument on the ground that the Fifth Amendment applies equally to the penalty phase and the guilt phase of a capital trial.

What is unclear about the resulting law? If the Court holds in Case A that the First Amendment prohibits Congress from discriminating based on viewpoint, and then holds in Case B that the Fourteenth Amendment incorporates the First Amendment as to the States, then it is clear that the First Amendment prohibits the States from discriminating based on viewpoint. By the same logic, because the Court held in *Carter* that the Fifth Amendment requires a trial judge to give a requested no-adverse-inference instruction during the guilt phase of a trial, and held in *Estelle* that there is no basis for distinguishing between the guilt and punishment phases of a capital trial for purposes of the Fifth Amendment, it is clear that the Fifth Amendment requires a judge to provide a requested no-adverse-inference instruction during the penalty phase of a capital trial.

II

[In Part II of his dissent, Justice Breyer argued that the Court read *Estelle* and *Mitchell* too narrowly. As to *Estelle*, he said:

> The reason that *Estelle* concluded that the Fifth Amendment applies to the penalty phase of a capital trial is that the Court saw "no basis to distinguish between the guilt and penalty phases of [a defendant's] capital murder trial so far as the protection of the Fifth Amendment privilege is concerned." And as there is no basis to distinguish between the two contexts for Fifth Amendment purposes, there is no basis for varying either the application or the content of the Fifth Amendment privilege in the two contexts.

Mitchell, he said, "held, simply and only, that the normal rule of *Estelle* applied in the circumstances of the particular case before the Court. That holding does not destabilize settled law beyond its reach."]

III

In holding that the Kentucky courts did not unreasonably apply clearly established law, the majority declares that if a court must "extend" the rationale of a case in order to apply it, the rationale is not clearly established. I read this to mean simply that if there may be "fair-minded disagreement" about whether a rationale applies to a certain set of facts, a state court will not unreasonably apply the law by failing to apply that rationale, and I agree. I do not understand the majority to suggest that reading two legal principles together would necessarily "extend" the law, which would be a proposition entirely inconsistent with our case law. As long as fairminded jurists would conclude that two (or more) legal rules considered together would dictate a particular outcome, a state court unreasonably applies the law when it holds otherwise.

That is the error the Kentucky Supreme Court committed here. Failing to consider together the legal principles established by *Carter* and *Estelle,* the state court confined those cases to their facts. It held that *Carter* did not apply because Woodall had already pleaded guilty—that is, because Woodall requested a no-adverse-inference instruction at the penalty phase rather than the guilt phase of his trial. And it concluded that *Estelle* did not apply because *Estelle* was not a "jury instruction case." The Kentucky Supreme Court unreasonably failed to recognize that together *Carter* and *Estelle* compel a requested no-adverse-inference instruction at the penalty phase of a capital trial. And reading *Mitchell* to rein in the law in contemplation of never-before-recognized exceptions to this normal rule would be an unreasonable *retraction* of clearly established law, not a proper failure to "extend" it. Because the Sixth Circuit correctly applied clearly established law in granting Woodall's habeas petition, I would affirm.

With respect I dissent from the Court's contrary conclusion.

NOTES ON RELITIGATION UNDER AEDPA

1. FEDERAL RULES THAT CONFER DISCRETION

The AEDPA standard of review is deferential to reasonable state court decisions. It is doubly deferential in situations where the federal rule itself confers discretion on a decisionmaker.

One example is state-court applications of Strickland v. Washington, 466 U.S. 668 (1984), the case that sets the standard for ineffective assistance of counsel. The Court said in Burt v. Titlow, 571 U.S. ___, ___, 134 S.Ct. 10, 16 (2013), that when "a state prisoner asks a federal court to set aside a sentence due to ineffective assistance of counsel . . . , our cases require that the federal court use a 'doubly deferential' standard of review that gives both the state court and the defense attorney the benefit of the doubt." In Cullen v. Pinholster, 563 U.S. 170, 189 (2011), it had said similarly that the standard required "a 'highly deferential' look at counsel's performance . . . through the 'deferential lens of § 2254(d).' " The Court had previously elaborated:

> In *Strickland* we said that "[j]udicial scrutiny of a counsel's performance must be highly deferential" and that "every effort [must] be made to eliminate the distorting effects of hindsight, to reconstruct the circumstances of counsel's challenged conduct, and to evaluate the conduct from counsel's perspective at the time." Thus, even when a court is presented with an ineffective-assistance claim not subject to § 2254(d)(1) deference, a defendant must overcome the "presumption that, under the circumstances, the challenged action 'might be considered sound trial strategy.' "

> For respondent to succeed [on habeas], however, he must do more than show that he would have satisfied *Strickland*'s test if his claim were being analyzed in the first instance, because under § 2254(d)(1), it is not enough to convince a federal habeas court that, in its independent judgment, the state-court decision applied *Strickland* incorrectly. Rather, he must show that the [state court] applied *Strickland* to the facts of his case in an objectively unreasonable manner.

Bell v. Cone, 535 U.S. 685, 698–99 (2002). The result is that it is particularly difficult to obtain federal habeas relief based on a claim of ineffective assistance of counsel.

Renico v. Lett, 559 U.S. 766 (2010), provides another example of deference to discretion. Lett's first trial for murder resulted in a deadlocked jury and a mistrial. After conviction in a second trial, Lett sought review in the Michigan courts on the ground that the mistrial had been declared without a "manifest necessity" for doing so and that his second trial therefore violated the Double Jeopardy Clause. The intermediate Michigan appeals court agreed with Lett and reversed his conviction. The Michigan Supreme Court reinstated the conviction, holding that the trial judge had not abused her discretion in granting the mistrial and that federal double jeopardy limitations did not preclude the second trial. A District Court set aside the conviction on federal habeas, and the Circuit Court affirmed. In an opinion by Chief Justice Roberts, the Supreme Court reversed. The Court's analysis began:

> It is important at the outset to define the question before us. That question is not whether the trial judge should have declared a mistrial. It is not even whether it was an abuse of discretion for her to have done so—the applicable standard on direct review. The question under AEDPA is instead whether the determination of the Michigan Supreme Court that there was no abuse of discretion was "an unreasonable application of . . . clearly established Federal law." [Section 2254(d)(1)] creates "a substantially higher threshold" for obtaining relief than de novo review. Schriro v. Landrigan, 550 U.S. 465, 473 (2007). AEDPA thus imposes a "highly deferential standard for evaluating state-court rulings," Lindh v. Murphy, 521 U.S. 320, 333 n.7 (1997), and "demands that state-court decisions be given the benefit of the doubt," Woodford v. Visciotti, 537 U.S. 19, 24 (2002).

The Court then noted that the clearly established federal law in this area reserved to the trial judge a "broad discretion" and was entitled to "great deference" on review:

> The legal standard applied by the Michigan Supreme Court in this case was whether there was an abuse of the "broad discretion" reserved to the trial judge. This type of general standard triggers another consideration under AEDPA. When assessing whether a state court's application of federal law is unreasonable, "the range

of reasonable judgment can depend in part on the nature of the relevant rule" that the state court must apply. Yarborough v. Alvarado, 541 U.S. 652, 664 (2004). Because AEDPA authorizes federal courts to grant relief only when state courts act unreasonably, it follows that "[t]he more general the rule" at issue—and thus the greater the potential for reasoned disagreement among fair-minded judges—"the more leeway [state] courts have in reaching outcomes in case-by-case determinations." Id.

Under this standard, the Court concluded, the Michigan Supreme Court decision was not an unreasonable application of federal law.

Joined by Justices Breyer and Sotomayor, Justice Stevens dissented. Stevens analyzed the record, and concluded that the Court "denies Lett relief by applying a level of deference to the state court's ruling that effectively effaces the role of the federal courts." In a part of his opinion joined only by Justice Sotomayor, he added that the ruling by the Michigan Supreme Court "was not only incorrect but also unreasonable by any fair measure." Moreover, "[a]ny attempt to prevent federal courts from exercising independent review of habeas applications would have been a radical reform of dubious constitutionality. . . ." He continued:

> So on two levels, it is absolutely "necessary for us to decide whether the Michigan Supreme Court's decision . . . was right or wrong." If a federal judge were firmly convinced that such a decision were wrong, then in my view not only would he have no statutory duty to uphold it, but he might also have a constitutional obligation to reverse it. And regardless of how one conceptualizes the distinction between an incorrect and an "unreasonable" state-court ruling under § 2254(d)(1), one must always determine whether the ruling was wrong to be able to test the magnitude of any error. Substantive and methodological considerations compel federal courts to give habeas claims a full, independent review—and then to decide for themselves. Even under AEDPA, there is no escaping the burden of judgment.

2. RELEVANCE OF CIRCUIT COURT DECISIONS

Recall footnote 2 in *White v. Woodall*, where the Court quoted a prior case to the effect that "a lower court may not 'consul[t] its own precedents, rather than those of this Court . . . .' " A subsidiary debate in *Renico v. Lett* raised the same issue, and the majority repeated the standard mantra:

> The Court of Appeals . . . relied upon its own [precedent] to buttress its conclusion that the Michigan Supreme Court erred in concluding that the trial judge had exercised sound discretion. [A Circuit Court decision], however, does not constitute "clearly established Federal law, as determined by the Supreme Court," § 2254(d)(1), so any failure to apply that decision cannot independently authorize habeas relief under AEDPA.

In *Marshall v. Rodgers*, 569 U.S. 58, 64 (2013), the Court elaborated:

> Although an appellate panel may, in accordance with its usual law-of-the-circuit procedures, look to circuit precedent to ascertain whether it has already held that the particular point in issue is clearly established by Supreme Court precedent, it may not canvass circuit decisions to determine whether a particular rule of law is so widely accepted among the Federal Circuits that it would, if presented to this Court, be accepted as correct.

The dissent in *Renico v. Lett* disagreed:

> . . . I do not agree that the . . . Court of Appeals "erred" by "rel[ying] upon its own decision." . . . The Sixth Circuit . . . panel examined its own precedents not as the relevant "clearly established Federal law" under AEDPA, but as a tool for illuminating the precise contours of that law. Lower courts routinely look to circuit cases to "provide evidence that Supreme Court precedents ha[ve] clearly established a rule as of a particular time or [to] shed light on the 'reasonableness' of the state courts' application of existing Supreme Court precedents." This is a healthy practice—indeed, a vital practice, considering how few cases this Court decides—and we have never disapproved it.

3. QUESTIONS AND COMMENTS

Does the language of AEDPA require the extreme deference to state court judgments endorsed by the Supreme Court? Speaking for himself and Justices Souter, Ginsburg, and Breyer, Justice Stevens argued in *Williams v. Taylor* that:

> The inquiry mandated by [AEDPA] relates to the way in which a federal habeas court exercises its duty to decide constitutional questions; the [statute] does not alter the underlying grant of jurisdiction in § 2254(a). When federal judges exercise their federal-question jurisdiction under the "judicial Power" of Article III of the Constitution, it is "emphatically the province and duty" of those judges to "say what the law is." Marbury v. Madison, 5 U.S. (1 Cranch) 137, 177 (1803). At the core of this power is the federal courts' independent responsibility—independent from its coequal branches in the Federal Government, and independent from the separate authority of the several States—to interpret federal law. A construction of AEDPA that would require the federal courts to cede this authority to the courts of the States would be inconsistent with the practice that federal judges have traditionally followed in discharging their duties under Article III of the Constitution. If Congress had intended to require such an important change in the exercise of our jurisdiction, we believe it would have spoken with much greater clarity than is found in the text of AEDPA.

He read the non-retroactivity rule recognized in Teague v. Lane, 489 U.S. 288 (1989), as the functional equivalent of the "clearly established" component of the AEDPA standard:

Because there is no reason to believe that Congress intended to require federal courts to ask both whether a rule sought on habeas is "new" under *Teague*—which remains the law—and also whether it is "clearly established" under AEDPA, it seems safe to assume that Congress had congruent concepts in mind. It is perfectly clear that AEDPA codifies *Teague* to the extent that *Teague* requires federal habeas courts to deny relief that is contingent upon a rule of law not clearly established at the time the state conviction became final. . . . *Teague* established . . . guidance for making this determination, explaining that a federal habeas court operates within the bounds of comity and finality if it applies a rule "dictated by precedent existing at the time the defendant's conviction became final." A rule that "breaks new ground or imposes a new obligation on the States or the Federal Government," falls outside this universe of federal law.

For Stevens and his colleagues in dissent, AEDPA established "a 'mood' that the federal judiciary must respect." Congress expected federal judges "to attend with the utmost care to state-court decisions, including all of the reasons supporting their decisions, before concluding that those proceedings were infected by constitutional error sufficiently serious to warrant the issuance of the writ." Stevens concluded that the words "contrary to" are

surely capacious enough to include a finding that the state-court "decision" is simply "erroneous" or wrong. . . . And there is nothing in the phrase "contrary to" . . . that implies anything less than independent review by the federal courts. . . . We all agree that state-court judgments must be upheld unless, after the closest examination of the state-court judgment, a federal court is firmly convinced that a federal constitutional right has been violated. Our difference is as to the cases in which, at first-blush, a state-court judgment seems entirely reasonable, but thorough analysis by a federal court produces a firm conviction that that judgment is infected by constitutional error. In our view, such an erroneous judgment is "unreasonable" within the meaning of the act even though that conclusion was not immediately apparent.

In sum, the statute directs federal courts to attend to every state-court judgment with utmost care, but it does not require them to defer to the opinion of every reasonable state-court judge on the content of federal law. If, after carefully weighing all the reasons for accepting a state court's judgment, a federal court is convinced that a prisoner's custody—or, as in this case, his sentence of death—violates the Constitution, that independent judgment should prevail. Otherwise the federal "law as determined by the Supreme Court of the United States" might be applied by the federal courts one way in Virginia and another way in California. In light of the well-recognized interest in ensuring that federal courts interpret federal law in a uniform way, we are convinced that Congress did not intend the statute to produce such a result.

Is this a better reading of the statute? What accounts for the different approaches to AEDPA?

4. BIBLIOGRAPHY

A Symposium in the Georgetown Law Journal entitled Congress and the Courts: Jurisdiction and Remedies contains six articles provoked in part by AEDPA: Vicki C. Jackson, Introduction: Congressional Control of Jurisdiction and the Future of the Federal Courts—Opposition, Agreement, and Hierarchy, 86 Geo. L.J. 2445 (1998); David Cole, Jurisdiction and Liberty: Habeas Corpus and Due Process as Limits on Congress's Control of Federal Jurisdiction, 86 Geo. L.J. 2481 (1998); John Harrison, Jurisdiction, Congressional Power, and Constitutional Remedies, 86 Geo. L.J. 2513 (1998); Lawrence G. Sager, *Klein*'s First Principle: A Proposed Solution, 86 Geo. L.J. 2525 (1998); Daniel J. Meltzer, Congress, Courts, and Constitutional Remedies, 86 Geo. L.J. 2537 (1998); Judith Resnick, The Federal Courts and Congress: Additional Sources, Alternative Texts, and Altered Aspirations, 86 Geo. L.J. 2589 (1998). For other literature on the statute, see Melissa M. Berry, Seeking Clarity in the Federal Habeas Fog: Determining What Constitutes "Clearly Established" Law under the Antiterrorism and Effective Death Penalty Act, 54 Cath. U. L. Rev. 747 (2005); Lyn Entzeroth, Federal Habeas Review of Death Sentences, Where Are We Now?: A Review of *Wiggins v. Smith* and *Miller-El v. Cockrell*, 39 Tulsa L. Rev. 49 (2003); Aziz Z. Huq, Habeas and the Roberts Court, 81 U. Chi. L. Rev. 519 (2014); Allan Ides, Habeas Standards of Review under 28 U.S.C. § 2254(d)(1): A Commentary on Statutory Text and Supreme Court Precedent, 60 Wash. & Lee L. Rev. 677 (2003); Lee Kovarsky, AEDPA's Wrecks: Comity, Finality, and Federalism, 82 Tul. L. Rev. 443 (2007); Evan Tsen Lee, Section 2254(d) of the New Habeas Statute: An (Opinionated) User's Manual, 51 Vand. L. Rev. 103 (1998); James S. Liebman and William F. Ryan, "Some Effectual Power": The Quantity and Quality of Decisionmaking Required of Article III Courts, 98 Colum. L. Rev. 696 (1998); Justin F. Marceau, Deference and Doubt: The Interaction of AEDPA Section 2254(d)(2) and (e)(1), 82 Tul. L. Rev. 385 (2007); Kent S. Scheidegger, Habeas Corpus, Relitigation, and the Legislative Power, 98 Colum. L. Rev. 888 (1998) (response to Liebman and Ryan); Kimberly A. Thomas, Substantive Habeas, 63 Am. U. L. Rev. 1749 (2014); Mark Tushnet and Larry Yackle, Symbolic Statutes and Real Laws: The Pathologies of the Antiterrorism and Effective Death Penalty Act and the Prison Litigation Reform Act, 47 Duke L.J. 1 (1997); Larry W. Yackle, State Convicts and Federal Courts: Reopening the Habeas Corpus Debate, 91 Cornell L. Rev. 541 (2006); Larry Yackle, A Primer on the New Habeas Corpus Statute, 44 Buffalo L. Rev. 381 (1996). Finally, for extensive consideration of *Bell v. Cone*, see William B. Rubenstein, Finality in Class Action Litigation: Lessons from Habeas, 82 N.Y.U. L. Rev. 790 (2007).

A number of commentators have expressed the view that the current federal habeas corpus system, which is both extremely complicated and highly unlikely to grant relief in any particular case, needs substantial reform. See, for example, Larry W. Yackle, State Convicts and Federal Courts: Reopening the Habeas Corpus Debate, 91 Cornell L. Rev. 541, 553 (2006)

("[W]e need to take a deep breath, recognize the mess we have made of things, and start over."); Joseph L. Hoffmann and Nancy J. King, Rethinking the Federal Role in State Criminal Justice, 84 N.Y.U. L. Rev. 791, 793 (2009) ("In 99.99% of all state felony cases—excluding those cases in which the defendant is sentenced to death—the time, money, and energy spent on federal habeas litigation is wasted, generating virtually no benefit for anyone."); Lynn Adelman, Federal Habeas Review of State Court Convictions: Incoherent Law but an Essential Right, 64 Me. L. Rev. 379 (2012) (reaction of a sitting federal judge to the Hoffmann-King article); John H. Blume, Sheri Lynn Johnson and Keir M. Weyble, In Defense of Noncapital Habeas: A Response to Hoffmann and King, 96 Cornell L. Rev. 435 (2011) (rebutting the argument of Hoffmann and King and calling for "more habeas, not less"); Justin F. Marceau, Challenging the Habeas Process Rather Than the Result, 69 Wash. & Lee L. Rev. 85 (2012) ("Because federal oversight of the merits of state review is substantially diminished, it is increasingly important that there be some minimal federal review of state procedures."); Eve Brensike Primus, A Structural Vision of Habeas Corpus, 98 Calif. L. Rev. 1, 3 (2010) ("Reconfiguring federal habeas to focus on systemic state violations—those that recur in a pattern across multiple cases—could reduce waste and better protect defendants' rights while showing greater respect for autonomous state decision-making."); Samuel R. Wiseman, What is Federal Habeas Worth?, 67 Fla. L. Rev. 1157 (2015) (calculating the cost of federal habeas at roughly $327 million per year, "a tiny fraction of criminal justice spending and barely a blip in state and federal budgets" that "places recent reform proposals in a new light" and suggests "more modest measures to make the current system more functional.").[a]

NOTES ON ADDITIONAL AEDPA ISSUES

1.   INTRODUCTION

AEDPA addresses a number of additional issues, complete coverage of which would unduly lengthen these materials. The following notes contain a menu of some of the Supreme Court decisions in this area. They begin with the important topic of harmless error.

2.   HARMLESS ERROR

(i)   Pre-AEDPA Law

The Court summarized the pre-AEDPA harmless error rules in Davis v. Ayala, 576 U.S. ___, 135 S.Ct. 2187 (2015):

> The test for whether a federal constitutional error was harmless depends on the procedural posture of the case. On direct appeal, the harmlessness standard is the one prescribed in Chapman v. California, 386 U.S. 18, 24 (1967): "[B]efore a federal con-

---

[a]   Today, Supreme Court consideration of habeas almost invariably involves appellate review of a habeas decision by a lower federal court. Technically, the Supreme Court also retains the authority to issue *original* writs of habeas corpus. For analysis of how that power has been and could be used, see Lee Kovarsky, Original Habeas Redux, 97 Va. L. Rev. 61 (2011).

stitutional error can be held harmless, the court must be able to declare a belief that it was harmless beyond a reasonable doubt." In a collateral proceeding, the test is different. For reasons of finality, comity, and federalism, habeas petitioners "are not entitled to habeas relief based on trial error unless they can establish that it resulted in 'actual prejudice.'" Brecht v. Abrahamson, 507 U.S. 619, 637 (1993).

In an opinion by Chief Justice Rehnquist, the *Brecht* Court noted that some constitutional errors involve

> "structural defects in the constitution of the trial mechanism, which defy analysis by 'harmless-error' standards." The existence of such defects—deprivation of the right to counsel, for example—requires automatic reversal of the conviction because they infect the entire trial process.

But "trial error," by contrast:

> occur[s] during the presentation of the case to the jury, and is amenable to harmless-error analysis because it "may . . . be quantitatively assessed in the context of other evidence presented in order to determine [the effect it had on the trial]."

These kinds of mistakes require reversal only if the

> error "had substantial and injurious effect or influence in determining the jury's verdict." Kotteakos v. United States, 328 U.S. 750, 776 (1946). The *Kotteakos* harmless-error standard is better tailored to the nature and purpose of collateral review than the *Chapman* standard, and application of a less onerous harmless-error standard on habeas promotes the considerations underlying our habeas jurisprudence. . . .[9]

(ii) Ineffective Assistance of Counsel

Strickland v. Washington, 466 U.S. 668, 687 (1984), established the criteria for reversal of a conviction based on ineffectiveness of counsel:

> A convicted defendant's claim that counsel's assistance was so defective as to require reversal . . . has two components. First, the defendant must show that counsel's performance was deficient. This requires showing that counsel made errors so serious that counsel was not functioning as the "counsel" guaranteed the defendant by the Sixth Amendment. Second, the defendant must show that the deficient performance prejudiced the defense. This requires showing that counsel's errors were so serious as to deprive the defendant of a fair trial, a trial whose result is reliable. Unless

---

[9]   Our holding does not foreclose the possibility that in an unusual case, a deliberate and especially egregious error of the trial type, or one that is combined with a pattern of prosecutorial misconduct, might so infect the integrity of the proceeding as to warrant the grant of habeas relief, even if it did not substantially influence the jury's verdict. Cf. Greer v. Miller, 483 U.S. 756, 769 (1987) (Stevens, J., concurring in judgment). We, of course, are not presented with such a situation here.

> a defendant makes both showings, it cannot be said that the con-
> viction . . . resulted from a breakdown in the adversary process that
> renders the result unreliable.

The first part of the *Strickland* inquiry establishes the basis for determining
when attorney behavior is constitutionally deficient. Functionally, the second part establishes a harmless error standard. The defendant is not entitled
to relief unless the attorney error so affected the result as to call into question its reliability.

Recall Chief Justice Rehnquist's dicta in *Brecht*, quoted in Note 2(i)
above, that "structural" errors require automatic reversal without reference
to a harmless error standard. In a separate opinion concurring in the judgment in Weaver v. Massachusetts, 582 U.S. ___, 137 S.Ct. 1899 (2017),
Justice Alito described the category of cases in which prejudice need not be
shown as falling into

> a very narrow set of cases in which the accused has effectively been
> denied counsel altogether: These include the actual or constructive
> denial of counsel, state interference with counsel's assistance, or
> counsel that labors under actual conflicts of interest.

In Sullivan v. Louisiana, 508 U.S. 275 (1993), the Court, in a unanimous
opinion by Justice Scalia, added a constitutionally deficient beyond-a-reasonable-doubt instruction to the list of "structural" errors, and referred to
other cases holding that trial by a biased judge and denial of the right to self-
representation also qualified. Chief Justice Rehnquist's opinion for the Court
in Arizona v. Fulminante, 499 U.S. 311 (1991), cited cases holding that unlawful exclusion of members of the defendant's race from a grand jury and
denial of the right to public trial should also lead to automatic reversal.

Weaver v. Massachusetts involved the latter type of error. The courtroom
was closed to the public for two days during jury selection for Kentel
Weaver's trial on state criminal charges. "In the direct review context," the
Court said, courtroom closure "has been treated by this Court as a structural
error, i.e., an error entitling the defendant to automatic reversal without any
inquiry into prejudice." The question in *Weaver* was whether a showing of
prejudice was required when the public closure issue was raised five years
after the conviction. Weaver claimed, and the Court assumed he was right,
that his lawyer's failure to object to the courtroom closure constituted ineffective assistance of counsel. In an opinion by Justice Kennedy, the Court
held:

> [W]hen a defendant raises a public-trial violation via an inef-
> fective-assistance-of-counsel claim, *Strickland* prejudice is not
> shown automatically. Instead, the burden is on the defendant to
> show either a reasonable probability of a different outcome in his
> or her case or . . . to show that the particular public-trial violation
> was so serious as to render his or her trial fundamentally unfair.[a]

---

[a]   Justice Kennedy assumed without deciding that the second inquiry focusing on funda-
mental fairness should be a part of the *Strickland* standard. Joined by Justice Gorsuch, Justice
Thomas objected to the addition of the "fundamental fairness" inquiry. He said he agreed with
Justice Alito's separate analysis of the case, which was also joined by Justice Gorsuch, that

Weaver was unable to make either showing.

(iii) Harmless Error After AEDPA

The question in Fry v. Pliler, 551 U.S. 112 (2007), was whether the *Brecht v. Abrahamson* "substantial-and-injurious-effect" standard for harmless error on habeas survived the enactment of AEDPA. The Court had two choices. First, the text of § 2254(d)(1) suggests that the federal habeas court should examine whether the state courts "unreasonably" applied *Chapman*, the standard required on direct review. Alternatively, *Brecht* could survive AEDPA, in which case *Brecht* rather than AEDPA would state the applicable test for federal habeas review.

The Court chose the latter in *Fry*. John Fry argued that the exclusion of proffered testimony at his trial deprived him of a fair opportunity to defend himself in violation of Chambers v. Mississippi, 410 U.S. 284 (1973). The claim was rejected on direct appeal on the grounds that the trial court had not abused its discretion in excluding the evidence and "no possible prejudice" could have resulted since the testimony would have been "merely cumulative." The state appellate court did not specify the nature of the harmless error standard that it was applying, and made no reference to *Chapman*. Fry later sought federal habeas, which was denied by the lower federal courts based on *Brecht*. The Supreme Court granted certiorari and affirmed.

Fry argued that the state court's failure to apply the *Chapman* standard on direct review "resulted in a decision that was contrary to, or involved an unreasonable application of, clearly established Federal law, as determined by the Supreme Court of the United States" in violation of the explicit standards of § 2254(d)(1) of AEDPA. In a unanimous opinion by Justice Scalia, the Court said this result was not

> suggested by the text of AEDPA, which sets forth a precondition to the grant of habeas relief ("a writ of habeas corpus . . . shall not be granted" unless the conditions of § 2254(d) are met), not an entitlement to it. Given our frequent recognition that AEDPA limited rather than expanded the availability of habeas relief, it is implausible that, without saying so, AEDPA replaced the *Brecht* standard of "actual prejudice," with the more liberal AEDPA/*Chapman* standard which requires only that the state court's harmless-beyond-a-reasonable-doubt determination be unreasonable. That said, it certainly makes no sense to require formal application of *both* tests (AEDPA/*Chapman* and *Brecht*) when the latter obviously subsumes the former. Accordingly, the [lower federal courts were] correct to apply the *Brecht* standard of review in assessing the prejudicial impact of federal constitutional error in a state-court criminal trial.

---

applied only the "reasonable-probability-of-a-different-outcome" standard to determine that Weaver was not entitled to relief.

Joined by Justice Kagan, Justice Breyer dissented: "A showing that an attorney's constitutionally deficient performance produced a structural error should . . . be enough to entitle a defendant to relief."—[Footnote by eds.]

Does this mean that AEDPA has no effect in harmless error cases? The Court addressed that issue in Davis v. Ayala, 576 U.S. ___, 135 S.Ct. 2187 (2015). Ayala's death sentence was upheld on direct appeal by the California Supreme Court. He had claimed that the procedure used by the trial judge to rule on some of the prosecutor's peremptory challenges to prospective jurors violated Batson v. Kentucky, 476 U.S. 79 (1986). The California court applied *Chapman*, holding that even if his claims stated a constitutional violation, the error was harmless beyond a reasonable doubt. In subsequent federal habeas proceedings, the Ninth Circuit held that the error was not harmless.

In an opinion by Justice Alito, over a dissent by Justice Sotomayor (joined by Justices Ginsburg, Breyer, and Kagan), the Supreme Court reversed. It held that "[a]ssuming without deciding that a federal constitutional error occurred, the error was harmless under Brecht v. Abrahamson, 507 U.S. 619 (1993), *and* the Antiterrorism and Effective Death Penalty Act of 1996 (AEDPA), 28 U.S.C. § 2254(d)." (Emphasis added.) The Court elaborated:

> Because Ayala seeks federal habeas corpus relief, he must meet the *Brecht* standard, but that does not mean, as the Ninth Circuit thought, that a state court's harmlessness determination has no significance under *Brecht*. In *Fry* v. *Pliler*, we held that the *Brecht* standard "subsumes" the requirements that § 2254(d) imposes when a federal habeas petitioner contests a state court's determination that a constitutional error was harmless under *Chapman*. The *Fry* Court did not hold—and would have had no possible basis for holding—that *Brecht* somehow abrogates the limitation on federal habeas relief that § 2254(d) plainly sets out. While a federal habeas court need not "formal[ly]" apply both *Brecht* and "AEDPA/*Chapman,*" AEDPA nevertheless "sets forth a precondition to the grant of habeas relief." *Fry*, 551 U.S. at 119–20. . . .

> Section 2254(d) thus demands an inquiry into whether a prisoner's "claim" has been "adjudicated on the merits" in state court; if it has, AEDPA's highly deferential standards kick in.

> . . . There is no dispute that the California Supreme Court held that any federal error was harmless beyond a reasonable doubt under *Chapman*, and this decision undoubtedly constitutes an adjudication of Ayala's constitutional claim "on the merits." Accordingly, a federal habeas court cannot grant Ayala relief unless the state court's rejection of his claim (1) was contrary to or involved an unreasonable application of clearly established federal law, or (2) was based on an unreasonable determination of the facts. Because the highly deferential AEDPA standard applies, we may not overturn the California Supreme Court's decision unless that court applied *Chapman* "in an 'objectively unreasonable' manner." Mitchell v. Esparza, 540 U.S. 12, 18 (2003) (per curiam). When a *Chapman* decision is reviewed under AEDPA, "a federal court may not

award habeas relief under § 2254 unless *the harmlessness determination itself* was unreasonable." *Fry*, 551 U.S. at 119 (emphasis in original). And a state-court decision is not unreasonable if " 'fair-minded jurists could disagree' on [its] correctness." Harrington v. Richter, 562 U.S. 86, 101 (2011). Ayala therefore must show that the state court's decision to reject his claim "was so lacking in justification that there was an error well understood and comprehended in existing law beyond any possibility for fair-minded disagreement." Ibid.

In sum, a prisoner who seeks federal habeas corpus relief must satisfy *Brecht*, and if the state court adjudicated his claim on the merits, the *Brecht* test subsumes the limitations imposed by AEDPA.

The Court then analyzed the record and concluded that "[t]here is no basis for finding that Ayala suffered actual prejudice, and the decision of the California Supreme Court represented an entirely reasonable application of controlling precedent."

Fry appeared to hold that, since the *Brecht* test required a more persuasive showing of prejudicial error than *Chapman*, it should be applied after AEDPA *instead of* asking whether a state court's decision was "contrary to" or "an unreasonable application of" the requirements of *Chapman*. *Ayala* appears to say that *both Brecht* and AEDPA must be satisfied.

Is *Ayala* consistent with *Fry*? Does it make sense even to think about AEDPA or *Chapman* if the ultimate test for harmless error is stated by *Brecht*?[b]

3. WHAT COUNTS AS A STATE-COURT ADJUDICATION ON THE MERITS

Section 2254(d) applies to any claim that "was adjudicated on the merits in State court proceedings." The Supreme Court has been required on several occasions to determine what "adjudicated on the merits" means.

(i) *Harrington v. Richter*

The question in Harrington v. Richter, 562 U.S. 86 (2011), was "whether § 2254(d) applies when a state court's order is unaccompanied by an opinion explaining the reasons relief has been denied." The Court held that it did:

By its terms § 2254(d) bars relitigation of any claim "adjudicated on the merits" in state court, subject only to the exceptions in §§ 2254(d)(1) and (2). There is no text in the statute requiring a statement of reasons. The statute refers only to a "decision," which

---

[b]   The Court's approach to harmless error is described in John M. Greabe, The Riddle of Harmless Error Revisited, 54 Houston L. Rev. 59 (2016), as a "quagmire." Greabe adds that "the tests for determining whether an error should be excused as harmless on habeas are extraordinarily difficult to understand and administer." He examines the history of harmless error doctrine and its relation to 28 U.S.C. § 2111 and other potential legal origins, and proposes that the Court initiate reform by adopting a "unitary harmless error test" and "simplifying and clarifying its approach to harmless-error review on collateral review."

resulted from an "adjudication." As every Court of Appeals to consider the issue has recognized, determining whether a state court's decision resulted from an unreasonable legal or factual conclusion does not require that there be an opinion from the state court explaining the state court's reasoning. . . . Where a state court's decision is unaccompanied by an explanation, the habeas petitioner's burden still must be met by showing there was no reasonable basis for the state court to deny relief. . . .

[R]equiring a statement of reasons could undercut state practices designed to preserve the integrity of the case-law tradition. The issuance of summary dispositions in many collateral attack cases can enable a state judiciary to concentrate its resources on the cases where opinions are most needed.

There is no merit . . . in Richter's argument that § 2254(d) is inapplicable because the California Supreme Court did not say it was adjudicating his claim "on the merits." The state court did not say it was denying the claim for any other reason. When a federal claim has been presented to a state court and the state court has denied relief, it may be presumed that the state court adjudicated the claim on the merits in the absence of any indication or state-law procedural principles to the contrary. . . .

(ii) *Johnson v. Williams*

A related issue arose in Johnson v. Williams, 568 U.S. 289 (2013):

[T]his case requires us to ascertain the meaning of the adjudication-on-the merits requirement. This issue arises when a defendant convicted in state court attempts to raise a federal claim, either on direct appeal or in a collateral state proceeding, and a state court rules against the defendant and issues an opinion that addresses some issues but does not expressly address the federal claim in question. If this defendant then raises the same claim in a federal habeas proceeding, should the federal court regard the claim as having been adjudicated on the merits by the state court and apply deference under § 2254(d)? . . .

We believe that the answer to this question follows logically from our decision in *Harrington v. Richter*. In that case, we held that, when a state court issues an order that summarily rejects without discussion *all* the claims raised by a defendant, including a federal claim that the defendant subsequently presses in a federal habeas proceeding, the federal habeas court must presume (subject to rebuttal) that the federal claim was adjudicated on the merits. We see no reason why this same rule should not apply when the state court addresses some of the claims raised by a defendant but not a claim that is later raised in a federal habeas proceeding.

(iii) Greene v. Fisher

In Greene v. Fisher, 565 U.S. 34 (2011), an intermediate state appellate court had adjudicated a federal claim on the merits and the state Supreme Court had dismissed an appeal from that ruling without reaching the merits. A new Supreme Court decision changing the law on which the intermediate court had relied intervened between these two state court decisions. The question was which state court disposition counted as the "adjudication" against which AEDPA standards should be applied.

The details were these. The Supreme Court held in Bruton v. United States, 391 U.S. 123 (1968), that the Confrontation Clause is violated when a codefendant's confession is introduced in evidence against the defendant and the codefendant does not testify. Greene was convicted of second degree murder, robbery, and conspiracy in a joint trial with four other defendants. Two of them confessed. Their confessions referred to Greene, but his name was redacted when they were admitted at the trial. The confessing defendants did not testify.

Greene appealed his conviction to the Pennsylvania Superior Court. His *Bruton* claim was rejected on the ground that the redaction cured the problem. He then sought discretionary review in the Pennsylvania Supreme Court. While his petition was pending, Gray v. Maryland, 523 U.S. 185 (1998), held that redaction did not cure a *Bruton* error. The Pennsylvania Supreme Court then granted Greene's petition for appeal, limiting argument to the *Bruton-Gray* issue. But after briefs were filed by both parties, the court without reaching the merits—dismissed the appeal as improvidently granted. Greene then raised the *Bruton-Gray* issue on federal habeas corpus.

The Court upheld the denial of relief in a unanimous opinion by Justice Scalia. The issue was whether any of the state court decisions was "contrary to, or . . . an unreasonable application of, clearly established" law. The Court concluded that none was:

> Greene [appeals] to our decision in Teague v. Lane, 489 U.S. 288 (1989). *Teague* held that, with two exceptions not pertinent here, a prisoner seeking federal habeas relief may rely on new constitutional rules of criminal procedure announced before the prisoner's conviction became final. Finality occurs when direct state appeals have been exhausted and a petition for writ of certiorari from this Court has become time barred or has been disposed of. Greene contends that, because finality marks the temporal cutoff for *Teague* purposes, it must mark the temporal cutoff for "clearly established Federal law" under AEDPA.
>
> . . . The retroactivity rules that govern federal habeas review on the merits—which include *Teague*—are quite separate from the relitigation bar imposed by AEDPA; neither abrogates or qualifies the other. . . . [W]e see no reason why *Teague* should alter AEDPA's plain meaning.* Greene . . . contends that the relevant "decision" to

---

* Whether § 2254(d)(1) would bar a federal habeas petitioner from relying on a decision that came after the last state-court adjudication on the merits, but fell within one of the exceptions recognized in Teague is a question we need not address to resolve this case.

which the "clearly established Federal law" criterion must be applied is the decision of the state supreme court that disposes of a direct appeal from a defendant's conviction or sentence, even when (as here) that decision does not adjudicate the relevant claim on the merits. This is an implausible reading of § 2254(d)(1). [A] decision by the state supreme court not to hear the appeal—that is, not to decide at all [is not an adjudication "on the merits"].

The Third Circuit held . . . that the last state-court adjudication on the merits of Greene's Confrontation Clause claim occurred on direct appeal to the Pennsylvania Superior Court. The Pennsylvania Superior Court's decision predated our decision in *Gray* by nearly three months. The Third Circuit thus correctly held that *Gray* was not "clearly established Federal law" against which it could measure the Pennsylvania Superior Court's decision. . . .

We must observe that Greene's predicament is an unusual one of his own creation. Before applying for federal habeas, he missed two opportunities to obtain relief under *Gray*: After the Pennsylvania Supreme Court dismissed his appeal, he did not file a petition for writ of certiorari from this Court, which would almost certainly have produced a remand in light of the intervening *Gray* decision. . . . Nor did Greene assert his *Gray* claim in a petition for state postconviction relief. Having forgone two obvious means of asserting his claim, Greene asks us to provide him relief by interpreting AEDPA in a manner contrary to both its text and our precedents. We decline to do so. . . .

4.   FACTUAL RECORD FOR § 2254(d)(1) REVIEW

Scott Pinholster had been convicted in a California state court on two counts of first-degree murder and was sentenced to death. He subsequently sought habeas relief in the California Supreme Court, alleging that his counsel had been ineffective in failing to investigate and present certain mitigating evidence during the penalty phase of his trial. After the California court twice denied his habeas petitions, a federal District Court held an evidentiary hearing and granted relief. The Ninth Circuit Court of Appeals affirmed en banc, concluding that, in light of the evidence adduced in the District Court, the California Supreme Court's denial of relief "was contrary to, or involved an unreasonable application of, clearly established Federal law."

In Cullen v. Pinholster, 563 U.S. 170 (2011), the Supreme Court reversed. Justice Thomas wrote for the Court:

We now hold that review under § 2254(d)(1) is limited to the record that was before the state court that adjudicated the claim on the merits. Section 2254(d)(1) refers, in the past tense, to a state-court adjudication that "resulted in" a decision that was contrary to, or "involved" an unreasonable application of, established law. This backward-looking language requires an examination of the state-court decision at the time it was made. It follows that the rec-ord under review is limited to the record in existence at that same time, i.e., the record before the state court.

. . . Our cases emphasize that review under § 2254(d)(1) fo-cuses on what a state court knew and did. State-court decisions are measured against this Court's precedents as of "the time the state court renders its decision." Lockyer v. Andrade, 538 U.S. 63, 71–72 (2003). To determine whether a particular decision is "contrary to" then-established law, a federal court must consider whether the de-cision "applies a rule that contradicts [such] law" and how the decision "confronts [the] set of facts" that were before the state court. Williams v. Taylor, 529 U.S. 362, 405, 406 (2000). If the state-court decision "identifies the correct governing legal principle" in existence at the time, a federal court must assess whether the de-cision "unreasonably applies that principle to the facts of the pris-oner's case." Id. at 413. It would be strange to ask federal courts to analyze whether a state court's adjudication resulted in a decision that unreasonably applied federal law to facts not before the state court.

5.   PERMISSION FROM THE CIRCUIT COURT TO APPEAL

AEDPA also contains special limitations on appeals from district to cir-cuit courts in habeas and § 2255 cases. Section 2253(b) provides that there "shall be no right of appeal" in such cases, and § 2253(c)(1) adds that appeals can be taken from final district court orders only if a "circuit justice or circuit judge"c issues a "certificate of appealability" (COA). Section 2253(c)(2) elab-orates that a COA "may issue . . . only if the applicant has made a substantial showing of the denial of a constitutional right" and § 2253(c)(3) requires that the applicant "indicate which specific issue or issues satisfy the showing."

In finding that a circuit court should have issued a COA on a denied *Batson* claim, the Supreme Court described the nature of the inquiry in Mil-ler-El v. Cockrell, 537 U.S. 322 (2003):

The COA determination under § 2253(c) requires an overview of the claims in the habeas petition and a general assessment of their merits. We look to the District Court's application of AEDPA

---

c   This is the language of the statute. But Rule 22(b) of the Federal Rules of Appellate Procedure, modified by Congress at the same time, says that "[i]f an applicant files a notice of appeal, the district judge who rendered the judgment must either issue a certificate of appeala-bility or state why a certificate should not issue. . . . If the district judge has denied the certificate, the applicant may request a circuit judge to issue the certificate." The Rule also as-sumes that the COA application can be submitted to the circuit court itself, and referred by the court to a panel or single judge. Although the statute applies in terms to either party, Rule 22(b)(3) says that "[a] certificate of appealability is not required when a state or its representa-tive or the United States or its representative appeals." For consideration of the tension between Rule 22 and the COA process, see Christopher Q. Cutler, Friendly Habeas Reform—Reconsid-ering a District Court's Threshold Role in the Appellate Habeas Process, 43 Willamette L. Rev. 281 (2007).

to petitioner's constitutional claims and ask whether that resolution was debatable amongst jurists of reason.[d] This threshold inquiry does not require full consideration of the factual or legal bases adduced in support of the claims. In fact, the statute forbids it. When a court of appeals side steps this process by first deciding the merits of an appeal, and then justifying its denial of a COA based on its adjudication of the actual merits, it is in essence deciding an appeal without jurisdiction.

To that end, our opinion in Slack v. McDaniel, 529 U.S. 473 (2000), held that a COA does not require a showing that the appeal will succeed. Accordingly, a court of appeals should not decline the application for a COA merely because it believes the applicant will not demonstrate an entitlement to relief. . . . It is consistent with § 2253 that a COA will issue in some instances where there is no certainty of ultimate relief. . . .

Our holding should not be misconstrued as directing that a COA always must issue. Statutes such as AEDPA have placed more, rather than fewer, restrictions on the power of federal courts to grant writs of habeas corpus to state prisoners. . . . By enacting AEDPA, . . . Congress confirmed the necessity and the requirement of differential treatment for those appeals deserving of attention from those that plainly do not. It follows that issuance of a COA must not be pro forma or a matter of course.

A prisoner seeking a COA must prove " 'something more than the absence of frivolity' " or the existence of mere "good faith" on his or her part. Barefoot v. Estelle, 463 U.S. 880, 893 (1983). We do not require petitioner to prove, before the issuance of a COA, that some jurists would grant the petition for habeas corpus. Indeed, a claim can be debatable even though every jurist of reason might agree, after the COA has been granted and the case has received full consideration, that petitioner will not prevail. As we stated in *Slack*, "[w]here a district court has rejected the constitutional claims on the merits, the showing required to satisfy § 2253(c) is straightforward: The petitioner must demonstrate that reasonable jurists would find the district court's assessment of the constitutional claims debatable or wrong."[e]

A related problem arose in Gonzalez v. Thaler, 565 U.S. 134 (2012):

In this case, the Court of Appeals judge granted a COA that identified a debatable procedural ruling, but did not "indicate" the issue on which Gonzalez had made a substantial showing of the

---

[d] Justice Scalia had a nit to pick with this sentence. He noted that the statute referred only to a "substantial showing of the denial of a constitutional right," whereas the Court referred to whether application of the AEDPA was debatable. Scalia accepted this formulation, however, because he regarded the statutory language as a necessary but not sufficient condition. It says that the COA "may be" issued "only if" there is a substantial showing of the denial of a constitutional right. Making such a showing in itself, he concluded, "*does not entitle* an applicant to a COA." The Court is free to impose additional requirements.—[Footnote by eds.]

[e] For a sequel decision applying the standard announced in *Slack* and *Miller-El*, see Tennard v. Dretke, 542 U.S. 274 (2004).—[Footnote by eds.]

denial of a constitutional right, as required by § 2253(c)(3). The question before us is whether that defect deprived the Court of Appeals of the power to adjudicate Gonzalez's appeal. We hold that it did not. . . . [T]he failure to obtain a COA is jurisdictional, while a COA's failure to indicate an issue is not. A defective COA is not equivalent to the lack of any COA.[f]

SECTION 3. PROCEDURAL LIMITATIONS

INTRODUCTORY NOTE

In addition to limitations on the substantive claims that can be heard and the standard of review governing those claims, federal habeas law contains a variety of procedural requirements and limitations. The most important, dealt with in Subsection A below, concerns claims that were not raised in state court under the procedures required by state law and that may therefore be barred from federal review. This is called a "procedural default" or a "procedural foreclosure." The effect of state procedural default on federal habeas relief has a long and controversial history, as recounted in detail below.

Other significant procedural requirements are dealt with more summarily in Subsection B. The requirement of "exhaustion" is considered first. This requirement means that, if an opportunity is available and the merits have not previously been addressed by the state courts, federal constitutional claims must be raised in the appropriate state courts before they can be considered on federal habeas corpus. Additionally, Subsection B deals with a body of law on "successive petitions," which places sharp limits on the claims that can be raised in a second or successive federal habeas petition. Finally, Subsection B addresses the federal statutory limitations period for bringing a habeas petition. These requirements are important in themselves and interact in subtle and complex ways.

SUBSECTION A. PROCEDURAL FORECLOSURE

INTRODUCTORY NOTE ON THE HISTORY OF PROCEDURAL FORECLOSURE

Recall that Brown v. Allen, 344 U.S. 443 (1953), held that federal habeas courts were required to consider de novo federal constitutional claims that were decided on the merits by the state courts. In effect, federal district courts exercised appellate review over state-court adjudication of federal rights.

On the same day and in the same set of opinions, the Court also decided the companion case of *Daniels v. Allen*. Brown and Daniels raised similar claims of coerced confession and racial discrimination in jury selection. While

---

[f]   Justice Scalia was the lone dissenter. In Erin Morrow Hawley, The Supreme Court's Quiet Revolution: Redefining the Meaning of Jurisdiction, 56 Wm. & Mary L. Rev. 2027 (2015), the author uses *Thaler* to illustrate a modern shift in the Court's use of the concept of "jurisdiction."—[Footnote by eds.]

Brown's claims had been heard and rejected on the merits in state court, Daniels' claims had been rejected without consideration of the merits because his lawyer failed to perfect a timely appeal as required by state law. On direct review, the failure to comply with valid state appeal procedures would have provided an adequate and independent state ground that would bar Supreme Court consideration of the merits. Although the opinion did not rely directly on this rationale, in effect *Daniels* held that the same rule should apply on collateral review.

There is a certain logic to saying that a federal district court hearing a habeas petition should have no broader authority than the Supreme Court of the United States would have on direct review of the state court decision. But, as noted by Justice Black in dissent, many found it "difficult to agree with the soundness of a philosophy which prompts this Court to grant a second review where the state has granted one but to deny any review at all where the state has granted none."

Dissatisfaction with *Daniels*, fueled by concern over the rate and effect of state-court procedural foreclosures, led to its overruling in Fay v. Noia, 372 U.S. 391 (1963). *Fay* held, over an anguished dissent by Justice Harlan, that the adequate-and-independent-state-ground doctrine had no application on collateral review. Hence habeas consideration of defaulted claims was not categorically barred. Instead, *Fay* held, habeas review was foreclosed only if the defendant had waived his constitutional claim, and waiver— which was to be measured under the standard of Johnson v. Zerbst, 304 U.S. 458 (1938)—required the intentional relinquishment of a known right. Applying this standard, the Court said that federal habeas courts could refuse to hear claims that had been procedurally defaulted in state court only if the defendant had "deliberately bypassed state procedures."

While *Daniels* foreclosed federal habeas review of most claims defaulted under state law (assuming that the state procedures were valid and not discriminatorily applied), *Fay* flipped the scales by allowing habeas review of most defaulted claims. Defaults are generally due to error, usually attorney error, not strategic choice. "Deliberate bypass" of a procedure for raising a federal constitutional claim that is known and readily available is unlikely and district courts rarely found that it had occurred. Default under valid state procedures therefore usually did not constrain federal habeas review.

The same pressures that led to the narrowing of the substantive reach of federal habeas led to dissatisfaction with *Fay*. As *Brown* was narrowed, so was *Fay*, its procedural counterpart. The most important result was Wainwright v. Sykes, 433 U.S. 72 (1977), which is the next main case. *Wainwright* laid the foundation for the modern law of procedural foreclosure. Unlike many other areas of habeas law, the judicial decisions on procedural foreclosure have not been touched by statute. AEDPA does not speak to the subject.

Wainwright v. Sykes

Supreme Court of the United States, 1977.

433 U.S. 72.

■ MR. JUSTICE REHNQUIST delivered the opinion of the Court.

We granted certiorari to consider the availability of federal habeas corpus to review a state convict's claim that testimony was admitted at his trial in violation of his rights under Miranda v. Arizona, 384 U.S. 436 (1966), a claim which the Florida courts have previously refused to consider on the merits because of noncompliance with a state contemporaneous-objection rule. Petitioner Wainwright, on behalf of the State of Florida, here challenges a decision of the Court of Appeals for the Fifth Circuit ordering a hearing in state court on the merits of respondent's contention.

Respondent Sykes was convicted of third-degree murder after a jury trial in the Circuit Court of DeSoto County. He testified at trial that on the evening of January 8, 1972, he told his wife to summon the police because he had just shot Willie Gilbert. Other evidence indicated that when the police arrived at respondent's trailer home, they found Gilbert dead of a shotgun wound, lying a few feet from the front porch. Shortly after their arrival, respondent came from across the road and volunteered that he had shot Gilbert, and a few minutes later respondent's wife approached the police and told them the same thing. Sykes was immediately arrested and taken to the police station.

Once there, it is conceded that he was read his *Miranda* rights, and that he declined to seek the aid of counsel and indicated a desire to talk. He then made a statement, which was admitted into evidence at trial through the testimony of the two officers who heard it, to the effect that he had shot Gilbert from the front porch of his trailer home. There were several references during the trial to respondent's consumption of alcohol during the preceding day and to his apparent state of intoxication, facts which were acknowledged by the officers who arrived at the scene. At no time during the trial, however, was the admissibility of any of respondent's statements challenged by his counsel on the ground that respondent had not understood the *Miranda* warnings. Nor did the trial judge question their admissibility on his own motion or hold a factfinding hearing bearing on that issue.

Respondent appealed his conviction, but apparently did not challenge the admissibility of the inculpatory statements. He later filed in the trial court a motion to vacate the conviction and, in the State District Court of Appeals and Supreme Court, petitions for habeas corpus. These filings, apparently for the first time, challenged the statements made to police on grounds of involuntariness. In all of these efforts respondent was unsuccessful.

Having failed in the Florida courts, respondent initiated the present action under 28 U.S.C. § 2254, asserting the inadmissibility of his statements by reason of his lack of understanding of the *Miranda* warnings. The United States District Court for the Middle District of Florida ruled that Jackson v. Denno, 378 U.S. 368 (1964), requires a hearing in a state criminal trial prior to the admission of an inculpatory out-of-court statement by the defendant. It held further that respondent had not lost his right to assert such a claim by failing to object at trial or on direct appeal, since only "exceptional circumstances" of "strategic decisions at trial" can create such a bar to raising federal constitutional claims in a federal habeas action. The court stayed issuance of the writ to allow the state court to hold a hearing on the "voluntariness" of the statements.

Petitioner warden appealed this decision to the United States Court of Appeals for the Fifth Circuit. That court first considered the nature of the right to exclusion of statements made without a knowing waiver of the right to counsel and the right not to incriminate oneself. It noted that *Jackson v. Denno*, guarantees a right to a hearing on whether a defendant has knowingly waived his rights as described to him in the *Miranda* warnings, and stated that under Florida law "[t]he burden is on the State to secure [a] prima facie determination of voluntariness, not upon the defendant to demand it."

The court then directed its attention to the effect on respondent's right of Florida Rule Crim. Proc. 3.190(i),[5] which it described as "a contemporaneous objection rule" applying to motions to suppress a defendant's inculpatory statements. It focused on this Court's decisions in Henry v. Mississippi, 379 U.S. 443 (1965); Davis v. United States, 411 U.S. 233 (1973); and Fay v. Noia, 372 U.S. 391 (1963), and concluded that the failure to comply with the rule requiring objection at the trial would only bar review of the suppression claim where the right to object was deliberately bypassed for reasons relating to trial tactics. . . . Concluding that "[t]he failure to object in this case cannot be dismissed as a trial tactic, and thus a deliberate by-pass," the court affirmed the District Court order that the State hold a hearing on whether respondent knowingly waived his *Miranda* rights at the time he made the statements.

[At this point, the Court discussed its prior habeas jurisprudence, noting its "historic willingness to overturn or modify its earlier views of

---

[5] Rule 3.190(i):

Motion to Suppress a Confession or Admissions Illegally Obtained.

(1)*Grounds.* Upon motion of the defendant or upon its own motion, the court shall suppress any confession or admission obtained illegally from the defendant.

(2)*Time for Filing.* The motion to suppress shall be made prior to trial unless opportunity therefor did not exist or the defendant was not aware of the grounds for the motion, but the court in its discretion may entertain the motion or an appropriate objection at the trial.

(3)*Hearing.* The court shall receive evidence on any issue of fact necessary to be decided in order to rule on the motion.

the scope of the writ, even where the statutory language authorizing judicial action has remained unchanged." It added that the "area of controversy which has developed" over the adequate-and-independent-state-ground doctrine "has concerned the reviewability of federal claims which the state court has declined to pass on because not presented in the manner prescribed by its procedural rules." It then reviewed *Daniels v. Allen* and *Fay v. Noia* and continued:]

A decade [after *Fay v. Noia*] we decided Davis v. United States, 411 U.S. 233 (1973), in which a federal prisoner's application under 28 U.S.C. § 2255 sought for the first time to challenge the makeup of the grand jury which indicted him. The government contended that he was barred by the requirement of Fed. Rule Crim. Proc. 12(b)(2) providing that such challenges must be raised "by motion before trial." The rule further provides that failure to so object constitutes a waiver of the objection, but that "the court for cause shown may grant relief from the waiver." We noted that the rule "promulgated by this Court and, pursuant to 18 U.S.C. § 3771, 'adopted' by Congress, governs by its terms the manner in which the claims of defects in the institution of criminal proceedings may be waived," and held that this standard contained in the rule, rather than the *Fay v. Noia* concept of waiver, should pertain in federal habeas as on direct review. Referring to previous constructions of Rule 12(b)(2), we concluded that review of the claim should be barred on habeas, as on direct appeal, absent a showing of cause for the noncompliance and some showing of actual prejudice resulting from the alleged constitutional violation.

Last term, in Francis v. Henderson, 425 U.S. 536 (1976), the rule of *Davis* was applied to the parallel case of a state procedural requirement that challenges to grand jury composition be raised before trial. The Court noted that there was power in the federal courts to entertain an application in such a case, but rested its holding on "considerations of comity and concerns for the orderly administration of criminal justice. . . ." While there was no counterpart provision of the state rule which allowed an exception upon some showing of cause, the Court concluded that the standard derived from the federal rule should nonetheless be applied in that context since " '[t]here is no reason to . . . give greater preclusive effect to procedural defaults by federal defendants than to similar defaults by state defendants.' " As applied to the federal petitions of state convicts, the *Davis* cause-and-prejudice standard was thus incorporated directly into the body of law governing the availability of federal habeas corpus review.

To the extent that the dicta of *Fay v. Noia* may be thought to have laid down an all-inclusive rule rendering state contemporaneous objection rules ineffective to bar review of underlying federal claims in federal habeas proceedings—absent a "knowing waiver" or a "deliberate bypass" of the right to so object—its effect was limited by *Francis,* which applied a different rule and barred a habeas challenge to the makeup of a grand jury. Petitioner Wainwright in this case urges that we further confine its effect by applying the principle enunciated in *Francis* to a claimed error in the admission of a defendant's confession. . . .

We . . . come to the crux of this case. Shall the rule of *Francis v. Henderson* barring federal habeas review absent a showing of "cause" and "prejudice" attendant to a state procedural waiver, be applied to a waived objection to the admission of a confession at trial? We answer that question in the affirmative.

. . . [S]ince Brown v. Allen, 344 U.S. 443 (1953), it has been the rule that the federal habeas petitioner who claims he is detained pursuant to a final judgment of a state court in violation of the United States Constitution is entitled to have the federal habeas court make its own independent determination of his federal claim, without being bound by the determination on the merits of that claim reached in the state proceedings. This rule of *Brown v. Allen* is in no way changed by our holding today. Rather, we deal only with contentions of federal law which were *not* resolved on the merits in the state proceeding due to respondent's failure to raise them there as required by state procedure. We leave open for resolution in future decisions the precise definition of the "cause"-and "prejudice" standard, and note here only that it is narrower than the standard set forth in dicta in Fay v. Noia, 372 U.S. 391 (1963), which would make federal habeas review generally available to state convicts absent a knowing and deliberate waiver of the federal constitutional contention. It is the sweeping language of *Fay v. Noia,* going far beyond the facts of the case eliciting it, which we today reject.

The reasons for our rejection of it are several. The contemporaneous-objection rule itself is by no means peculiar to Florida, and deserves greater respect than *Fay* gives it, both for the fact that it is employed by a coordinate jurisdiction within the federal system and for the many interests which it serves in its own right. A contemporaneous objection enables the record to be made with respect to the constitutional claim when the recollections of witnesses are freshest, not years later in a federal habeas proceeding. It enables the judge who observed the demeanor of those witnesses to make the factual determinations necessary for properly deciding the federal constitutional question. . . .

A contemporaneous-objection rule may lead to the exclusion of the evidence objected to, thereby making a major contribution to finality in criminal litigation. Without the evidence claimed to be vulnerable on federal constitutional grounds, the jury may acquit the defendant, and that will be the end of the case; or it may nonetheless convict the defendant, and he will have one less federal constitutional claim to assert in his federal habeas petition. . . . An objection on the spot may force the prosecution to take a hard look at its hole card, and even if the prosecutor thinks that the state trial judge will admit the evidence he must contemplate the possibility of reversal by the state appellate courts or the ultimate issuance of a federal writ of habeas corpus based on the impropriety of the state courts rejection of the federal constitutional claim.

We think that the rule of *Fay v. Noia,* broadly stated, may encourage "sandbagging" on the part of defense lawyers, who may take their chances on a verdict of not guilty in a state trial court with the intent to raise their constitutional claims in a federal habeas court if their initial gamble does not pay off. The refusal of federal habeas courts to honor contemporaneous-objection rules may also make state courts themselves less stringent in their enforcement. Under the rule of *Fay v. Noia,* state appellate courts know that a federal constitutional issue raised for the first time in the proceeding before them may well be decided in any event by a federal habeas tribunal. Thus, their choice is between addressing the issue notwithstanding the petitioner's failure to timely object, or else face the prospect that the federal habeas court will decide the question without the benefit of their views.

The failure of the federal habeas courts generally to require compliance with a contemporaneous-objection rule tends to detract from the perception of the trial of a criminal case in state court as a decisive and portentous event. A defendant has been accused of a serious crime, and this is the time and place set for him to be tried by a jury of his peers and found either guilty or not guilty by that jury. To the greatest extent possible all issues which bear on this charge should be determined in this proceeding: the accused is in the courtroom, the jury is in the box, the judge is on the bench, and the witnesses, having been subpoenaed and duly sworn, await their turn to testify. Society's resources have been concentrated at that time and place in order to decide, within the limits of human fallibility, the question of guilt or innocence of one of its citizens. Any procedural rule which encourages the result that those proceedings be as free of error as possible is thoroughly desirable, and the contemporaneous-objection rule surely falls within this classification.

We believe the adoption of the *Francis* rule in this situation will have the salutary effect of making the state trial on the merits the "main event," so to speak, rather than a "tryout on the road" for what will later be the determinative federal habeas hearing. There is nothing in the Constitution or in the language of § 2254 which requires that the state trial on the issue of guilt or innocence be devoted largely to the testimony of fact witnesses directed to the elements of the state crime, while only later will there occur in a federal habeas hearing a full airing of the federal constitutional claims which were not raised in the state proceedings. If a criminal defendant thinks that an action of the state trial court is about to deprive him of a federal constitutional right there is every reason for his following state procedure in making known his objection.

The "cause"-and-"prejudice" exception of the *Francis* rule will afford an adequate guarantee, we think, that the rule will not prevent a federal habeas court from adjudicating for the first time the federal constitutional claim of a defendant who in the absence of such an adjudication will be the victim of a miscarriage of justice. Whatever precise content may be given those terms by later cases, we feel confident in holding without further elaboration that they do not exist here. Respondent has advanced no explanation whatever for his failure to object at trial, and, as the proceeding unfolded, the trial judge is certainly not to be faulted for failing to question the admission of the confession himself. The other evidence of guilt presented at trial, moreover, was substantial to a degree that would negate any possibility of actual prejudice resulting to the respondent from the admission of his inculpatory statement.

We accordingly conclude that the judgment of the Court of Appeals for the Fifth Circuit must be reversed, and the cause remanded to the United States District Court for the Middle District of Florida with instructions to dismiss respondent's petition for a writ of habeas corpus.[a]

■ MR. JUSTICE BRENNAN, with whom MR. JUSTICE MARSHALL joins, dissenting. . . .

I begin with the threshold question: What is the meaning and import of a procedural default? If it could be assumed that a procedural default more often than not is the product of a defendant's conscious refusal to abide by the duly constituted, legitimate processes of the state courts, then I might agree that a regime of collateral review weighted in favor of a State's procedural rules would be warranted. *Fay,* however, recognized that such rarely is the case; and therein lies *Fay*'s basic unwillingness to embrace a view of habeas jurisdiction that results in "an airtight system of [procedural] forfeitures."

This, of course, is not to deny that there are times when the failure to heed a state procedural requirement stems from an intentional decision to avoid the presentation of constitutional claims to the state forum. *Fay* was not insensitive to this possibility. Indeed, the very purpose of its bypass test is to detect and enforce such intentional procedural forfeitures of outstanding constitutionally based claims. *Fay* does so through application of the longstanding rule used to test whether action or inaction on the part of a criminal defendant should be construed as a decision to surrender the assertion of rights secured by the Constitution: To be an effective waiver, there must be "an intentional relinquishment or abandonment of a known right or privilege." Johnson v. Zerbst, 304 U.S. 458, 464 (1938). Incorporating this standard, *Fay* recognized that if one "understandingly and knowingly forewent the privilege of seeking to vindicate his federal claims in the state courts, whether for strategic, tactical or any other reasons that can fairly be described as the deliberate bypassing of state procedures, then it is open to the federal court on habeas

---

[a] Chief Justice Burger and Justice Stevens each wrote a separate concurrence. Justice White concurred in the judgment. Although he agreed with the result reached by the majority, he did not see the need for a change in vocabulary: "In terms of the necessity for Sykes to show prejudice, it seems to me that the harmless error rule provides ample protection to the state's interest. . . . With respect to the necessity to show cause for noncompliance with the state rule, I think the deliberate bypass rule of Fay v. Noia affords adequate protection to the state's interest in insisting that defendants not flout the rules of evidence."—[Footnote by eds.]

to deny him all relief. . . ." For this reason, the Court's assertion that it "think[s]" that the *Fay* rule encourages intentional "sandbagging" on the part of the defense lawyers is without basis; certainly the Court points to no cases or commentary arising during the past 15 years of actual use of the *Fay* test to support this criticism. Rather, a consistent reading of case law demonstrates that the bypass formula has provided a workable vehicle for protecting the integrity of state rules in those instances when such protection would be both meaningful and just.

But having created the bypass exception to the availability of collateral review, *Fay* recognized that intentional, tactical forfeitures are not the norm upon which to build a rational system of federal habeas jurisdiction. In the ordinary case, litigants simply have no incentive to slight the state tribunal, since constitutional adjudication on the state and federal levels are not mutually exclusive. Under the regime of collateral review recognized since the days of *Brown v. Allen,* and enforced by the *Fay* bypass test, no rational lawyer would risk the "sandbagging" feared by the Court. If a constitutional challenge is not properly raised on the state level, the explanation generally will be found elsewhere than in an intentional tactical decision.

In brief then, any realistic system of federal habeas corpus jurisdiction must be premised on the reality that the ordinary procedural default is born of the inadvertence, negligence, inexperience, or incompetence of trial counsel. See, e.g., Alfred Hill, The Inadequate State Ground, 65 Colum. L. Rev. 943, 997 (1965). The case under consideration today is typical. The Court makes no effort to identify a tactical motive for the failure of Sykes's attorney to challenge the admissibility or reliability of a highly inculpatory statement. . . .

Fay's answer thus is plain: the bypass test simply refuses to credit what is essentially a lawyer's mistake as a forfeiture of constitutional rights. I persist in the belief that the interests of Sykes and the State of Florida are best rationalized by adherence to this test, and by declining to react to inadvertent defaults through the creation of an "airtight system of forfeitures."

What are the interests that Sykes can assert in preserving the availability of federal collateral relief in the face of his inadvertent state procedural default? Two are paramount.

As is true with any federal habeas applicant, Sykes seeks access to the federal court for the determination of the validity of his federal constitutional claim. Since at least *Brown v. Allen,* it has been recognized that the "fair effect [of] the habeas corpus jurisdiction as enacted by Congress" entitles a state prisoner to such federal review. *Brown,* 344 U.S. at 500 (opinion of Frankfurter, J.). While some of my Brethren may feel uncomfortable with this congressional choice of policy, see, e.g., Stone v. Powell, 428 U.S. 465 (1976), the Legislative Branch nonetheless remains entirely free to determine that the constitutional rights of an individual subject to state custody, like those of the civil rights plaintiff suing under

42 U.S.C. § 1983, are best preserved by "interpos[ing] the federal courts between the States and the people, as guardians of the peoples federal rights. . . ." Mitchum v. Foster, 407 U.S. 225, 242 (1972).

With respect to federal habeas corpus jurisdiction, Congress explicitly chose to effectuate the federal courts' primary responsibility for preserving federal rights and privileges by authorizing the litigation of constitutional claims and defenses in a district court after the State vindicates its own interest through trial of the substantive criminal offense in the state courts. . . .

Certainly, we can all agree that once a state court has assumed jurisdiction of a criminal case, the integrity of its own process is a matter of legitimate concern. The *Fay* bypass test, by seeking to discover intentional abuses of the rules of the state forum, is, I believe, compatible with this state institutional interest. But whether *Fay* was correct in penalizing a litigant solely for his intentional forfeitures properly must be read in light of Congress's desired norm of widened post-trial access to the federal courts. If the standard adopted today is later construed to require that the simple mistakes of attorneys are to be treated as binding forfeitures, it would serve to subordinate the fundamental rights contained in our constitutional charter to inadvertent defaults of rules promulgated by state agencies, and would essentially leave it to the States, through the enactment of procedure and the certification of the competence of local attorneys, to determine whether a habeas applicant will be permitted the access to the federal forum that is guaranteed him by Congress.

Thus, I remain concerned that undue deference to local procedure can only serve to undermine the ready access to a federal court to which a state defendant otherwise is entitled. But federal review is not the full measure of Sykes's interest, for there is another of even greater immediacy: assuring that his constitutional claims can be addressed to *some* court. For the obvious consequence of barring Sykes from the federal courthouse is to insulate Florida's alleged constitutional violation from any and all judicial review because of a lawyer's mistake. From the standpoint of the habeas petitioner, it is a harsh rule indeed that denies him "any review at all where the state has granted none," *Brown*, 344 U.S. at 552 (Black, J., dissenting)—particularly when he would have enjoyed both state and federal consideration had his attorney not erred. . . .

A regime of federal habeas corpus jurisdiction that permits the reopening of state procedural defaults does not invalidate any state procedural rule as such; Florida's courts remain entirely free to enforce their own rules as they choose, and to deny any and all state rights and remedies to a defendant who fails to comply with applicable state procedure. The relevant inquiry is whether more is required—specifically, whether the fulfillment of important interests of the State necessitates that federal courts be called upon to impose additional sanctions for inadvertent noncompliance with state procedural requirements such as the contemporaneous-objection rule involved here. . . .

Punishing a lawyer's unintentional errors by closing the federal courthouse door to his client is both a senseless and misdirected method of deterring the slighting of state rules. It is senseless because unplanned and unintentional action of any kind generally is not subject to deterrence; and, to the extent that it is hoped that a threatened sanction addressed to the defense will induce greater care and caution on the part of trial lawyers, thereby forestalling negligent conduct or error, the potential loss of all valuable state remedies would be sufficient to this end. And it is a misdirected sanction because even if the penalization of incompetence or carelessness will encourage more thorough legal training and trial preparation, the habeas applicant, as opposed to his lawyer, hardly is the proper recipient of such a penalty. Especially with fundamental constitutional rights at stake, no fictional relationship of principal-agent or the like can justify holding the criminal defendant accountable for the naked errors of his attorney. This is especially true when so many indigent defendants are without any realistic choice in selecting who ultimately represents them at trial. Indeed, if responsibility for error must be apportioned between the parties, it is the State, through its attorneys' admissions and certification policies, that is more fairly held to blame for the fact that practicing lawyers too often are ill-prepared or ill-equipped to act carefully and knowledgeably when faced with decisions governed by state procedural requirements.

NOTES ON PROCEDURAL FORECLOSURE AND INEFFECTIVE ASSISTANCE OF COUNSEL

1.   QUESTIONS AND COMMENTS ON *WAINWRIGHT V. SYKES*

One way of understanding Fay v. Noia, 372 U.S. 391 (1963), is that it made federal habeas review an alternative to claims of ineffective assistance of counsel. If every attorney omission and oversight could be corrected on habeas, then resort to the independent constitutional claim of ineffective assistance of counsel became less important.

In overruling *Fay*,[a] *Wainwright v. Sykes* returned ineffective assistance claims to the spotlight. Ineffective assistance claims derive from the Sixth Amendment right to counsel. Under Strickland v. Washington, 466 U.S. 668

---

[a]   Technically *Wainwright* did not result in a complete overruling of the deliberate bypass standard of *Fay*. In a portion of the opinion not reproduced above, it left open the possibility that *Fay* could still be applied in a factually identical case. But the Court completed the overruling process in Coleman v. Thompson, 501 U.S. 722, 750 (1991):

> We now make it explicit: In all cases in which a state prisoner has defaulted his federal claims in state court pursuant to an independent and adequate state procedural rule, federal habeas review of the claims is barred unless the prisoner can demonstrate cause for the default and actual prejudice as a result of the alleged violation of federal law, or demonstrate that failure to consider the claims will result in a fundamental miscarriage of justice.

The latter demonstration—"that failure to consider the claims will result in a fundamental miscarriage of justice"—was added to the *Wainwright* formula by *Murray v. Carrier*, which is covered in the next Note.

(1984), a claimant must make two showings: first, that the lawyer's performance fell below an objective standard of reasonableness—a judgment not made with 20–20 hindsight but in recognition of the lawyer's "wide latitude" in making tactical choices; and second, that there was a "reasonable probability" that, but for the lawyer's errors, the result would have been different.

The definition of ineffective assistance of counsel is unaffected by the law of habeas corpus, but the role of ineffective assistance claims assuredly is. A key perspective to keep in mind in evaluating *Wainwright* and its progeny is the degree to which they protect against miscarriages of justice caused by lawyer error. Which is the better approach—to hear procedurally foreclosed claims on the merits in a federal habeas court or to rely on the quality of counsel to get it right in state court?

2. THE MEANING OF "CAUSE": *MURRAY V. CARRIER*

The Court defined "cause" in Murray v. Carrier, 477 U.S. 478 (1986). Carrier had been convicted of rape and abduction. His court-appointed counsel moved twice for discovery of the victim's statements to the police, but the trial judge denied the motions. The notice of appeal filed by his lawyer in the state Supreme Court listed denial of these motions as a ground for appeal, but this ground was omitted in the subsequently filed petition for appeal. The state Supreme Court therefore refused to hear the appeal, and the United States Supreme Court denied certiorari. Carrier argued on state habeas that withholding the victim's statements denied him due process, but that claim was foreclosed by the procedural default on direct appeal. His federal habeas petition raised the same claim.

The Supreme Court held that ordinary attorney oversight or inadvertence did not constitute "cause" and that the claim was therefore procedurally foreclosed:

> [T]he mere fact that counsel failed to recognize the factual or legal basis for a claim, or failed to raise the claim despite recognizing it, does not constitute cause for a procedural default. . . . So long as a defendant is represented by counsel whose performance is not constitutionally ineffective under the standard established in Strickland v. Washington, 466 U.S. 668 (1984), we discern no inequity in requiring him to bear the risk of attorney error that results in a procedural default. Instead, we think that the existence of cause for a procedural default must ordinarily turn on whether the prisoner can show that some objective factor external to the defense impeded counsel's efforts to comply with the state's procedural rule. Without attempting an exhaustive catalog of such objective impediments to compliance with a procedural rule, we note that a showing that the factual or legal basis for a claim was not reasonably available to counsel, see Reed v. Ross, 468 U.S. 1, 16 (1984), or that "some interference by officials," Brown v. Allen, 344 U.S. 443, 486 (1953), made compliance impracticable, would constitute cause under this standard.

> [Attorney error rising to the level of ineffective assistance of counsel] is cause for a procedural default. However, we think that the exhaustion doctrine . . . generally requires that a claim of ineffective assistance be presented to the state courts as an independent claim before it may be used to establish cause for a procedural default.

The Court did, however, recognize an escape valve:

> "[I]n appropriate cases" the principles of comity and finality that inform the concepts of cause and prejudice "must yield to the imperative of correcting a fundamentally unjust incarceration." We remain confident that, for the most part, "victims of a fundamental miscarriage of justice will meet the cause-and-prejudice standard." But we do not pretend that this will always be true. Accordingly, we think that in an extraordinary case, where a constitutional violation has probably resulted in the conviction of one who is actually innocent, a federal habeas court may grant the writ even in the absence of a showing of cause for the procedural default.

3. INEFFECTIVE ASSISTANCE OF COUNSEL AND PROCEDURAL DEFAULT

Suppose an ineffective assistance of counsel claim could have been presented to the state court but was not. Exhaustion requires that habeas relief not be granted on a claim that has not been presented to state court, if there is still an opportunity to do so. Does the failure to exhaust an ineffective-assistance claim mean that it cannot be asserted as cause for the procedural default of another claim? In Edwards v. Carpenter, 529 U.S. 446 (2000), the Court said "yes." A habeas petitioner must exhaust an ineffective-assistance claim in order to raise ineffective assistance as an independent constitutional violation or as "cause" for defaulting other claims in state court.

(i) Ineffective Assistance in Federal Courts: Massaro v. United States

Massaro v. United States, 538 U.S. 500 (2003), held, in the context of a § 2255 proceeding by a federal prisoner, that ineffective-assistance-of-counsel claims are not procedurally foreclosed by failure to raise them on direct appeal, even if the claims were based on record evidence available to the appellate court. Speaking through Justice Kennedy, a unanimous Court said:

> The background for our discussion is the general rule that claims not raised on direct appeal may not be raised on collateral review unless the petitioner shows cause and prejudice. The procedural default rule is neither a statutory nor a constitutional requirement, but it is a doctrine adhered to by the courts to conserve judicial resources and to respect the law's important interest in the finality of judgments. We conclude that requiring a criminal defendant to bring ineffective-assistance-of-counsel claims on direct appeal does not promote these objectives.

As Judge Easterbrook has noted, "[r]ules of procedure should be designed to induce litigants to present their contentions to the right tribunal at the right time." Guinan v. United States, 6 F.3d 468, 474 (7th Cir. 1993) (concurring opinion). Applying the usual procedural-default rule to ineffective-assistance claims would have the opposite effect, creating the risk that defendants would feel compelled to raise the issue before there has been an opportunity fully to develop the factual predicate for the claim. Furthermore, the issue would be raised for the first time in a forum not best suited to assess those facts. This is so even if the record contains some indication of deficiencies in counsel's performance. The better-reasoned approach is to permit ineffective-assistance claims to be brought in the first instance in a timely motion in the district court under § 2255. We hold that an ineffective-assistance-of-counsel claim may be brought in a collateral proceeding under § 2255, whether or not the petitioner could have raised the claim on direct appeal.

. . . When an ineffective-assistance claim is brought on direct appeal, appellate counsel and the court must proceed on a trial record not developed precisely for the object of litigating or preserving the claim and thus often incomplete or inadequate for this purpose. Under Strickland v. Washington, 466 U.S. 668 (1984), a defendant claiming ineffective counsel must show that counsel's actions were not supported by a reasonable strategy and that the error was prejudicial. The evidence introduced at trial, however, will be devoted to issues of guilt or innocence, and the resulting record in many cases will not disclose the facts necessary to decide either prong of the *Strickland* analysis. If the alleged error is one of commission, the record may reflect the action taken by counsel but not the reasons for it. The appellate court may have no way of knowing whether a seemingly unusual or misguided action by counsel had a sound strategic motive or was taken because the counsel's alternatives were even worse. . . . The trial record may contain no evidence of alleged errors of omission, much less the reasons underlying them. And evidence of alleged conflicts of interest might be found only in attorney-client correspondence or other documents that, in the typical criminal trial, are not introduced. Without additional factual development, moreover, an appellate court may not be able to ascertain whether the alleged error was prejudicial.

Under the rule we adopt today, ineffective-assistance claims ordinarily will be litigated in the first instance in the district court, the forum best suited to developing the facts necessary to determining the adequacy of representation during an entire trial. The court may take testimony from witnesses for the defendant and the prosecution and from the counsel alleged to have rendered the deficient performance. In addition, the § 2255 motion often will be ruled upon by the same district judge who presided at trial. The judge, having observed the earlier trial, should have an advantageous perspective for determining the effectiveness of counsel's conduct and whether any deficiencies were prejudicial.

Kennedy noted complexities that may be encountered in the future:

> We do not hold that ineffective-assistance claims must be reserved for collateral review. There may be cases in which trial counsel's ineffectiveness is so apparent from the record that appellate counsel will consider it advisable to raise the issue on direct appeal. There may be instances, too, when obvious deficiencies in representation will be addressed by an appellate court sua sponte. In those cases, certain questions may arise in subsequent proceedings under § 2255 concerning the conclusiveness of determinations made on the ineffective-assistance claims raised on direct appeal; but these matters of implementation are not before us. We do hold that failure to raise an ineffective-assistance-of-counsel claim on direct appeal does not bar the claim from being brought in a later, appropriate proceeding under § 2255.

(ii) Ineffective Assistance in State Courts

The Court held in Coleman v. Thompson, 501 U.S. 722 (1991), that, subject to the "cause and prejudice" rule, procedural defaults in state post-conviction proceedings bar federal habeas relief. There is, however, an important difference in what constitutes "cause" for procedural default at trial or on appeal and what constitutes "cause" on collateral review. Since there is no constitutional right to an attorney in state post-conviction proceedings, ineffective assistance of counsel in such a proceeding cannot constitute "cause" for procedural default. AEDPA codified part of the *Coleman* holding by providing in § 2254(i) that: "The ineffectiveness or incompetence of counsel during Federal or State collateral post-conviction proceedings shall not be a ground for relief in a proceeding arising under section 2254."

In Martinez v. Ryan, 566 U.S. 1 (2012), the Court recognized a "narrow exception" to *Coleman. Martinez* involved an Arizona rule that permitted challenges to the effectiveness of trial counsel only in a collateral proceeding that was filed after the direct review process had concluded. Ineffective assistance of counsel at "initial-review" collateral proceedings, the Court said, may constitute "cause" for default of a claim of ineffective assistance at trial. By "initial-review" the Court meant situations where a collateral proceeding was the prisoner's first opportunity to raise a claim. Joined by Justice Thomas, Justice Scalia dissented.

A variation on *Martinez* arose in Trevino v. Thaler, 569 U.S. 413 (2013). The Texas law at issue there did not "on its face *require* a defendant initially to raise an ineffective-assistance-of-trial-counsel claim in a state collateral review proceeding," but was structured to make it "virtually impossible" for an ineffective assistance claim to be presented on direct review. The Court concluded that "where, as here, state procedural framework, by reason of its design and operation, makes it highly unlikely in a typical case that a defendant will have a meaningful opportunity to raise a claim of ineffective assistance of trial counsel on direct appeal, our holding in *Martinez* applies." Chief Justice Roberts (joined by Justice Alito) and Justice Scalia (joined by Justice Thomas) dissented.

Yet another variation on this problem was presented in Davila v. Davis, 582 U.S. ___, 137 S.Ct. 2058 (2017). Both *Martinez* and *Trevino* involved defaulted claims of ineffective assistance of counsel at trial. *Davila* involved a defaulted claim of ineffective assistance on appeal. Davila's lawyer objected to a jury instruction at trial but did not challenge the instruction on appeal. His lawyer in a state habeas proceeding raised neither the challenged jury instruction nor the ineffective assistance said to arise from its omission from the direct appeal. Davila then filed a federal habeas petition. Speaking through Justice Thomas, the Court said that the claim of ineffective assistance on appeal was procedurally defaulted when not raised in the state post-conviction proceeding. And ineffective assistance in the state post-conviction proceeding did not establish "cause" to excuse that default. *Martinez* was described as a "narrow exception" to *Coleman*, dependent on "the unique importance of protecting a defendant's trial rights, particularly the right to effective assistance of trial counsel." The Court accordingly "declin[ed] to expand the *Martinez* exception to the distinct context of ineffective assistance of appellate counsel." The equitable considerations that supported ineffective assistance as "cause" for trial defaults did not weigh as heavily when the ineffective assistance occurred on direct review, where the underlying question (here the challenged instruction) had at least been reviewed on the merits by the trial court. Justice Breyer, joined by Justices Ginsburg, Sotomayor, and Kagan, dissented.

Finally, still a different twist on the *Coleman* issue arose in Maples v. Thomas, 565 U.S. 266 (2012). Maples failed to file a timely appeal of the denial of state post-conviction relief because, unknown to him, the denial occurred and the time to appeal ran out after his two pro bono attorneys abandoned his case. His subsequent federal habeas petition was denied at the district and circuit levels because of the resulting procedural default. By a 7–2 vote, Justice Ginsburg writing for the Court and Justices Scalia and Thomas dissenting, the Supreme Court held that Maples had established "cause" for the default: "We agree that, under agency principles, a client cannot be charged with the acts or omissions of an attorney who has abandoned him. Nor can a client be faulted for failing to act on his own behalf when he lacks reason to believe his attorneys of record, in fact, are not representing him." As *Davila* makes clear, the result in *Maples* would have been different if, instead of abandoning him, his counsel had acted negligently in failing to file the appeal. This is a very fine line. Is it a sensible one?

ADDITIONAL NOTES ON PROCEDURAL FORECLOSURE

1. CONTINUING ROLE OF THE ADEQUATE-AND-INDEPENDENT-STATE-GROUND DOCTRINE AFTER *WAINWRIGHT V. SYKES*

The Supreme Court does not have jurisdiction to review the merits of a federal claim that is denied by a state court for procedural reasons that constitute an adequate and independent state ground. Fay v. Noia, 372 U.S. 391

(1963), held that an adequate and independent state ground did not deprive a federal court of the power to review procedurally defaulted claims on federal habeas corpus. Instead, the "deliberate bypass" formula provided the only basis on which federal courts could enforce a state procedural foreclosure. The adequate-and-independent-state-ground-doctrine was no longer applicable on federal habeas corpus.

As was made clear in Coleman v. Thompson, 501 U.S. 722 (1991), *Wainwright* reinstated a role for the adequate and independent state ground in federal habeas cases. "The independent and adequate state ground doctrine," the Court said, "ensures that the States' interest in correcting their own mistakes is respected in all federal habeas cases." A procedural foreclosure in state court based on an adequate and independent state ground would now have an effect in a federal habeas proceeding.

But the effect would be different. On direct review by the Supreme Court of a state court decision, a procedural foreclosure based on an adequate and independent state ground would continue to preclude the Court's jurisdiction. On federal habeas, however, a district court would have jurisdiction to apply the "cause and prejudice" and "miscarriage of justice" formulas of *Wainwright v. Sykes* and *Murray v. Carrier* as a basis for *not* enforcing a procedural default that otherwise would be required by the adequate-and-independent-state-ground-doctrine. If the habeas petitioner could demonstrate cause and prejudice or a miscarriage of justice, a federal habeas court could hear a claim on the merits in spite of the adequacy and independence of the procedural ground on which the state courts denied relief.[a]

A logical corollary of this way of thinking about the matter is that a state ground that was *in*adequate would also not stand in the way of federal habeas review. There would be no need for a finding of cause and prejudice or a miscarriage of justice, in other words, if the procedural ground on which a state court relied was inadequate to support a federal court's refusal to examine the merits of the petitioner's constitutional claim.

This post-*Wainwright* approach to an inadequate state ground was confirmed in Lee v. Kemna, 534 U.S. 362 (2002). Lee was tried in a Missouri court for first-degree murder. His sole defense was that he was in California at the time. When his counsel sought to present the supporting testimony of three members of Lee's family, they were not in the courthouse. His counsel moved for a continuance so that he could find the missing witnesses. The trial judge denied the motion, and Lee was found guilty. On appeal, the Missouri Court of Appeals held that the denial of the motion was proper because Lee's counsel had failed to comply with two Missouri Supreme Court Rules—Rule 24.09, which requires that applications for a continuance be in written

---

[a] Speaking for the Court, Justice Thomas began his opinion in Davila v. Davis, 582 U.S. ___, 137 S.Ct. 2058 (2017):

Federal habeas courts reviewing convictions from state courts will not consider claims that a state court refused to hear based on an adequate and independent state procedural ground. A state prisoner may be able to overcome this bar, however, if he can establish "cause" to excuse the procedural default and demonstrate that he suffered actual prejudice from the alleged error.

form and accompanied by an affidavit, and Rule 24.10, which lists the showings required in a continuance request that is based on the absence of witnesses. The trial court had not invoked either of these rules.

In an opinion by Justice Ginsburg, the Supreme Court held that the Missouri Rules did not constitute a state ground that was adequate to bar federal habeas review. After a detailed examination of the proceedings below, the Court concluded that Lee "substantially complied" with Rule 24.09 and that the "essential requirements" of Rule 24.10 "were substantially met":

> To summarize, there was in this case no reference whatever in the trial court to Rules 24.09 and 24.10, the purported procedural impediments the Missouri Court of Appeals later pressed. Nor is there any indication that formally perfect compliance with the Rules would have changed the trial court's decision. Furthermore, no published Missouri decision demands unmodified application of the Rules in the urgent situation Lee's case presented. Finally, the purpose of the Rules was served by Lee's submissions both immediately before and at the short trial. Under the special circumstances so combined, we conclude that no adequate state-law ground hinders consideration of Lee's federal claim.[b]

Justice Kennedy, joined by Justices Scalia and Thomas, dissented. He had this to say about the Court's finding of "substantial compliance" with Rule 24.10:

> The Court acknowledges, as it must, that Rule 24.10 does not discriminate against federal law or deny defendants a reasonable opportunity to assert their rights. . . . Nor is there any doubt Lee did not comply with the Rule . . . . The Court's acceptance of these two premises should lead it to conclude that Lee's violation of the Rule was an adequate state ground for the Missouri court's decision. . . .
>
> [T]he Court deems Lee's default inadequate because, it says, to the extent feasible under the circumstances, he substantially complied with the Rule's essential requirements. These precise terms have not been used in the Court's adequacy jurisprudence before, and it is necessary to explore their implications. The argument is not that Missouri has no interest in enforcing compliance with the Rule in general, but rather that it had no interest in enforcing full compliance in this particular case. . . .
>
> [This use of a] case-by-case approach is contrary to the principles of federalism underlying our habeas corpus jurisprudence. Procedural rules, like the substantive laws they implement, are the products of sovereignty and democratic processes. The States have weighty interests in enforcing rules that protect the integrity and uniformity of trials, even when "the reason for the rule does not

---

[b] A much more difficult problem would be raised if a state procedural foreclosure was challenged as not independent. The problem is discussed following the Note on Foster v. Chatman, 578 U.S. ___, 136 S.Ct. 1737 (2016), in Subsection A of Section 5 of this Chapter.— [Footnote by eds.]

clearly apply." Staub v. City of Baxley, 355 U.S. 313, 333 (1958) (Frankfurter, J., dissenting). Regardless of the particular facts in extraordinary cases, then, Missouri has a freestanding interest in Rule 24.10 as a rule.

By ignoring that interest, the majority's approach invites much mischief at criminal trials, and the burden imposed upon States and their courts will be heavy. . . . [T]he State's sound judgment on these matters can now be overridden by a federal court, which may determine for itself, given its own understanding of the rule's purposes, whether a requirement was essential or compliance was substantial in the unique circumstances of any given case. Henceforth, each time a litigant does not comply with an established state procedure, the judge must inquire, even "in the midst of trial, . . . whether noncompliance should be excused because some alternative procedure might be deemed adequate in the particular situation." The trial courts, then the state appellate courts, and, in the end, the federal habeas courts in numerous instances must comb through the full transcript and trial record, searching for ways in which the defendant might have substantially complied with the essential requirements of an otherwise broken rule. . . .

A federal court could consider the merits of Lee's defaulted federal claim if he had shown cause for the default and prejudice therefrom, see Wainwright v. Sykes, 433 U.S. 72, 90–91 (1977), or made out a compelling case of actual innocence, see Schlup v. Delo, 513 U.S. 298, 314–15 (1995). He has done neither. . . .c

2.   THE "ACTUAL INNOCENCE" EXCEPTION TO *WAINWRIGHT V. SYKES*: *HOUSE V. BELL*

As discussed below in Section 4, a claim of "actual innocence" may not, by itself, entitle a habeas petitioner to relief. Such a claim can, however, help a petitioner overcome certain procedural obstacles that would otherwise bar review of other claims. Recall in particular that *Murray v. Carrier* established an "actual innocence" exception to procedural foreclosure under *Wainwright v. Sykes*: "[W]e think that in an extraordinary case, where a constitutional violation has probably resulted in the conviction of one who is actually innocent, a federal habeas court may grant the writ even in the absence of a showing of cause for the procedural default."

---

c   In Beard v. Kindler, 558 U.S. 53 (2009), a unanimous Court answered "no" to the following question: "Is a state procedural rule automatically 'inadequate' under the adequate-state-grounds doctrine—and therefore unenforceable on federal habeas review—because the state rule is discretionary rather than mandatory?"

California does not have a fixed statutory deadline for habeas petitions, but requires that known claims be filed "as promptly as the circumstances allow." The California courts also have discretion to deny untimely petitions on the merits or as untimely. The California Supreme Court summarily dismissed Charles Martin's habeas petition as untimely. The Ninth Circuit "held that California's standard lacked the clarity and certainty necessary to constitute an adequate state bar." In Walker v. Martin, 562 U.S. 307 (2011), a unanimous Court—"[g]uided by" *Beard v. Kindler*—reversed, holding that federal habeas should have been denied because the California decision was based on an *adequate* and independent state ground.—[Footnote by eds.]

In House v. Bell, 547 U.S. 518 (2006), a majority of five Justices found, over three dissenting votes, that the habeas petitioner had made a sufficient showing of actual innocence to justify setting aside a state procedural default and hearing his federal claim on the merits. House had been sentenced to death for the murder of a neighbor. After two tries at state habeas, in the second of which his claim of ineffective assistance of counsel was procedurally defaulted, he sought habeas in federal court. After an extensive evidentiary hearing, the District Court found that a sufficient showing of actual innocence had not been made. The Circuit Court affirmed en banc, but the Supreme Court reversed.

In an opinion by Justice Kennedy, the Court first addressed the standard of review:

> In Schlup v. Delo, 513 U.S. 298, 319–22 (1995), the Court ... held that prisoners asserting innocence as a gateway to defaulted claims must establish that, in light of new evidence, "it is more likely than not that no reasonable juror would have found petitioner guilty beyond a reasonable doubt." ... Our review in this case [is] based on a fully developed record, and with respect to that inquiry *Schlup* makes plain that the habeas court must consider "all the evidence," old and new, incriminating and exculpatory, without regard to whether it would necessarily be admitted under "rules of admissibility that would govern at trial." Based on this total record, the court must make "a probabilistic determination about what reasonable, properly instructed jurors would do." ...
>
> [T]he state argues that [AEDPA] has replaced the *Schlup* standard with a stricter test based on Sawyer v. Whitley, 505 U.S. 333, 336 (1992), which permits consideration of successive, abusive, or defaulted sentencing-related claims only if the petitioner "show[s] by clear and convincing evidence that, but for a constitutional error, no reasonable juror would have found the petitioner eligible for the death penalty under the applicable state law." One AEDPA provision establishes a similar standard for second or successive petitions involving no retroactively applicable new law, 28 U.S.C. § 2244(b)(2)(B)(ii); another sets it as a threshold for obtaining an evidentiary hearing on claims the petitioner failed to develop in state court, § 2254(e)(2). Neither provision addresses the type of petition at issue here—a first federal habeas petition seeking consideration of defaulted claims based on a showing of actual innocence. Thus, the standard of review in these provisions is inapplicable.

Against these general comments, Kennedy examined the new evidence offered by House and concluded: "[A]lthough the issue is close, we conclude that this is the rare case where—had the jury heard all the conflicting testimony—it is more likely than not that no reasonable juror viewing the record as a whole would lack reasonable doubt. . . . House has satisfied the gateway standard set forth in *Schlup* and may proceed on remand with procedurally defaulted constitutional claims."

Joined by Justices Scalia and Thomas, Chief Justice Roberts dissented. He pointed out that the question is "not whether House was prejudiced at his trial because the jurors were not aware of the new evidence, but whether all the evidence, considered together, proves that House was actually innocent, so that no reasonable juror would vote to convict him." For the dissenters, that standard had not been met.[d]

3. HEARING ON THE FACTS OF PROCEDURALLY FORECLOSED CLAIMS: *MICHAEL WAYNE WILLIAMS V. TAYLOR*

Townsend v. Sain, 372 U.S. 293 (1963), decided on the same day as Fay v. Noia, 372 U.S. 391 (1963), held that federal habeas courts had considerable discretion to hold a new hearing and to redetermine the facts underlying a federal constitutional claim. The Court listed six situations in which an evidentiary hearing was mandatory,[e] adding that: "In all other cases where the material facts are in dispute, the holding of such a hearing is in the discretion of the district judge."[f]

In situations where the state courts held a hearing and resolved the federal constitutional claim on the merits, AEDPA replaces *Townsend* by restricting the ability of federal courts to hold a new hearing. A state court's determination of a factual issue is "presumed to be correct," and the habeas petitioner has the "burden of rebutting the presumption of correctness by clear and convincing evidence." 28 U.S.C. § 2254(e)(1). The precise impact of AEDPA in this respect remains very much dependent on case-by-case assessments by federal district judges. But AEDPA has plainly shifted evidentiary hearings from presumptively mandatory under *Townsend* to unavailable without an affirmative showing of necessity by the habeas petitioner.

Under the regime of *Fay v. Noia* and *Townsend v. Sain*, federal habeas courts also had generous discretion to hold hearings on the facts underlying

---

d   In McQuiggin v. Perkins, 569 U.S. 383 (2013), the petitioner filed a habeas petition 11 years after his conviction became final. Over four dissents, the Court held that "actual innocence, if proved, serves as a gateway through which a petitioner may pass whether the impediment is a procedural bar, as it was in *Schlup* and *House*, or, as in this case, expiration of the statute of limitations." In assessing whether no reasonable juror would have found guilt beyond a reasonable doubt, the Court added, the timing of the habeas petition was a factor in assessing the evidence: "A federal habeas court, faced with an actual-innocence gateway claim, should count unjustifiable delay on a habeas petitioner's part, not as an absolute barrier to relief, but as a factor in determining whether actual innocence has been reliably shown."

e   "We hold that a federal court must grant an evidentiary hearing to a habeas applicant under the following circumstances: if (1) the merits of the factual dispute were not resolved in the state hearing; (2) the state factual determination is not fairly supported by the record as a whole; (3) the factfinding procedure employed by the state was not adequate to afford a full and fair hearing; (4) there is a substantial allegation of newly discovered evidence; (5) the material facts were not adequately developed at the state court hearing; or (6) for any reason, it appears that the trier of fact did not afford the habeas applicant a full and fair fact hearing."

f   When combined with *Brown v. Allen* and *Fay v. Noia*, *Townsend* completed a powerful trifecta. If the state courts resolved the constitutional claim on the merits after a fact-finding hearing, the federal courts could retry the facts under *Townsend* and review the merits of the claim de novo under *Brown*. Claims that were procedurally defaulted in state court were open to fact-finding and merits resolution in federal court under *Townsend* and *Fay*.

These three cases created the most expansive regime for federal habeas review of state criminal convictions in the nation's history. It survived for a generation, but has been dismantled as recounted in these pages by the combination of restrictive Supreme Court decisions and AEDPA.

procedurally defaulted claims. In cases where the state courts do not hold a hearing because of a procedural foreclosure, AEDPA again adopts a much more restrictive standard that replaces the open-ended authority granted by *Townsend*. Section 2254(e)(2) provides:

> If the applicant has failed to develop the factual basis of a claim in State court proceedings, the court shall not hold an evidentiary hearing on the claim unless the applicant shows that—
>
> (A) the claim relies on—
>
> (i) a new rule of constitutional law, made retroactive to cases on collateral review by the Supreme Court, that was previously unavailable; or
>
> (ii) a factual predicate that could not have been previously discovered through the exercise of due diligence; and
>
> (B) the facts underlying the claim would be sufficient to establish by clear and convincing evidence that but for constitutional error, no reasonable factfinder would have found the applicant guilty of the underlying offense.

Should Lee have been required to satisfy the terms of this statute in order for his federal claims to be heard? Why was House entitled to a hearing on his procedurally defaulted claims?

The answer is found in Justice Kennedy's opinion for a unanimous Court in Michael Wayne Williams v. Taylor, 529 U.S. 420 (2000). Williams was sentenced to death following his conviction for multiple murders. His federal habeas petition made three claims: a *Brady* violation for failure by the prosecutor to disclose potentially favorable evidence; a claim that a juror was biased; and a claim of prosecutorial misconduct for failure to disclose prior knowledge of the potential juror bias.

The Court began by focusing on the word "failed" in the introductory clause of § 2254(e)(2):

> Section 2254(e)(2) begins with a conditional clause, "[i]f the applicant has failed to develop the factual basis of a claim in State court proceedings," which directs attention to the prisoner's efforts in state court. We ask first whether the factual basis was indeed developed in state court, a question susceptible, in the normal course, of a simple yes or no answer. Here the answer is no.
>
> The Commonwealth would have the analysis begin and end there. Under its no-fault reading of the statute, if there is no factual development in the state court, the federal habeas court may not inquire into the reasons for the default when determining whether the opening clause of § 2254(e)(2) applies. We do not agree with the Commonwealth's interpretation of the word "failed."

The word "failed," the Court held, implies fault:

> To say a person has failed in a duty implies he did not take the necessary steps to fulfill it. He is, as a consequence, at fault and

bears responsibility for the failure. In this sense, a person is not at fault when his diligent efforts to perform an act are thwarted, for example, by the conduct of another or by happenstance. Fault lies, in those circumstances, either with the person who interfered with the accomplishment of the act or with no one at all. We conclude Congress used the word "failed" in the sense just described. Had Congress intended a no-fault standard, it would have had no difficulty in making its intent plain. It would have had to do no more than use, in lieu of the phrase "has failed to," the phrase "did not."

Under the opening clause of § 2254(e)(2), a failure to develop the factual basis of a claim is not established unless there is lack of diligence, or some greater fault, attributable to the prisoner or the prisoner's counsel.

The Court then addressed the relation between this standard and the "cause and prejudice" inquiry found in its prior decisions. Keeney v. Tamayo-Reyes, 504 U.S. 1 (1992), a case decided four years before AEDPA's enactment, concerned a "state prisoner's failure to develop material facts in state court." To address this issue, *Keeney* borrowed the "cause and prejudice" standard from *Wainwright v. Sykes*, reasoning that there was no reason "to distinguish between failing to properly assert a federal claim in state court and failing in state court to properly develop such a claim."

As to the impact of AEDPA, the Court said:

To be sure, in requiring that prisoners who have not been diligent satisfy § 2254(e)(2)'s provisions rather than show cause and prejudice, and in eliminating a freestanding "miscarriage of justice" exception, Congress raised the bar *Keeney* imposed on prisoners who were not diligent in state-court proceedings. Contrary to the Commonwealth's position, however, there is no basis in the text of § 2254(e)(2) to believe Congress used "fail" in a different sense than the Court did in *Keeney* or otherwise intended the statute's further, more stringent requirements to control the availability of an evidentiary hearing in a broader class of cases than were covered by *Keeney*'s cause and prejudice standard.

Section 2254(e)(2)(A)(ii) itself contains a due diligence standard. Is that inconsistent with the Court's interpretation of the introductory clause? The Court said "no":

The Commonwealth argues a reading of "failed to develop" premised on fault empties § 2254(e)(2)(A)(ii) of its meaning. To treat the prisoner's lack of diligence in state court as a prerequisite for application of § 2254(e)(2), the Commonwealth contends, renders a nullity of the statute's own diligence provision requiring the prisoner to show "a factual predicate [of his claim] could not have been previously discovered through the exercise of due diligence." § 2254(e)(2)(A)(ii). We disagree.

The Commonwealth misconceives the inquiry mandated by the opening clause of § 2254(e)(2). The question is not whether the facts could have been discovered but instead whether the prisoner was diligent in his efforts. The purpose of the fault component of "failed" is to ensure the prisoner undertakes his own diligent search for evidence. Diligence for purposes of the opening clause depends upon whether the prisoner made a reasonable attempt, in light of the information available at the time, to investigate and pursue claims in state court; it does not depend, as the Commonwealth would have it, upon whether those efforts could have been successful. Though lack of diligence will not bar an evidentiary hearing if efforts to discover the facts would have been in vain, see § 2254(e)(2)(A)(ii), and there is a convincing claim of innocence, see § 2254(e)(2)(B), only a prisoner who has neglected his rights in state court need satisfy these conditions. The statute's later reference to diligence pertains to cases in which the facts could not have been discovered, whether there was diligence or not. In this important respect § 2254(e)(2)(A)(ii) bears a close resemblance to (e)(2)(A)(i), which applies to a new rule that was not available at the time of the earlier proceedings. . . . In these two parallel provisions Congress has given prisoners who fall within § 2254(e)(2)'s opening clause an opportunity to obtain an evidentiary hearing where the legal or factual basis of the claims did not exist at the time of state-court proceedings.

And finally, the Court said, its interpretation of the statute was consistent with principles of comity, finality, and federalism:

It is consistent with these principles to give effect to Congress's intent to avoid unneeded evidentiary hearings in federal habeas corpus, while recognizing the statute does not equate prisoners who exercise diligence in pursuing their claims with those who do not. Principles of exhaustion are premised upon recognition by Congress and the Court that state judiciaries have the duty and competence to vindicate rights secured by the Constitution in state criminal proceedings. Diligence will require in the usual case that the prisoner, at a minimum, seek an evidentiary hearing in state court in the manner prescribed by state law. . . . For state courts to have their rightful opportunity to adjudicate federal rights, the prisoner must be diligent in developing the record and presenting, if possible, all claims of constitutional error. If the prisoner fails to do so, himself or herself contributing to the absence of a full and fair adjudication in state court, § 2254(e)(2) prohibits an evidentiary hearing to develop the relevant claims in federal court, unless the statute's other stringent requirements are met. Federal courts sitting in habeas are not an alternative forum for trying facts and issues which a prisoner made insufficient effort to pursue in state proceedings. Yet comity is not served by saying a prisoner "has failed to develop the factual basis of a claim" where he was unable to develop his claim in state court despite diligent effort. In that circumstance, an evidentiary hearing is not barred by § 2254(e)(2).

The Court then applied these conclusions to the claims raised by Williams. The *Brady* claim was foreclosed because, with ordinary diligence, the defense lawyers could have discovered the situation in time to present it to the state courts. Since defense counsel "failed" to present the claim in state courts, and since the defendant admitted before the Supreme Court that he could not satisfy the provisions of § 2254(e)(2)(B), the 1996 legislation precluded federal habeas consideration of that claim.

The juror bias and prosecutor misconduct claims, however, were another matter. One of the jurors had been married for 17 years (with four children) to the prosecution's lead witness. They had been divorced for 15 years at the time of trial. One of the prosecutors, moreover, had represented the juror in the uncontested divorce. None of these facts came to light in the judge's questioning of the juror prior to the trial, during the trial, or in subsequent state post-conviction proceedings. They were discovered by happenstance when the defendant's federal habeas counsel interviewed two other jurors who referred to the juror in question by the same last name as the lead prosecution witness. The Court found that there had been no failure of diligence on the part of the prisoner or his counsel and that Section 2254(e)(2) therefore did not apply to those claims.

4.   BIBLIOGRAPHY

A predictive discussion of the issues in *Wainwright v. Sykes,* focusing in particular on the implications of a system of forfeiture of constitutional claims based on attorney error, may be found in Robert Cover and T. Alexander Aleinikoff, Dialectical Federalism: Habeas Corpus and the Court, 86 Yale L.J. 1035, 1069–86 (1977). An early explication of the possible meanings of "cause" and "prejudice" appears in Alfred Hill's article, The Forfeiture of Constitutional Rights in Criminal Cases, 78 Colum. L. Rev. 1050 (1978). For a preliminary survey of the reactions of lower courts, see Saul B. Goodman and Jonathan B. Sallett, *Wainwright v. Sykes*: The Lower Federal Courts Respond, 30 Hastings L.J. 1683 (1979). The effect of state waiver rules is explored by Lea Brilmayer in State Forfeiture Rules and Federal Review of State Criminal Convictions, 49 U. Chi. L. Rev. 741 (1982). The right-to-counsel dimension of the controversy is explored in Peter W. Tague, Federal Habeas Corpus and Ineffective Representation of Counsel: The Supreme Court Has Work to Do, 31 Stan. L. Rev. 1 (1978). For an empirical study examining, inter alia, the exhaustion doctrine, procedural default rules, and successive habeas petitions, see Richard Faust, Tina J. Rubenstein, and Larry Yackle, The Great Writ in Action: Empirical Light on the Federal Habeas Corpus Debate, 18 N.Y.U. Review of Law & Social Change 637 (1990–91). For an attempt to integrate procedural foreclosure and the right to counsel in an analysis grounded in *Stone*'s concern for protecting the arguably innocent, see John C. Jeffries, Jr. and William J. Stuntz, Ineffective Assistance and Procedural Default in Federal Habeas Corpus, 57 U. Chi. L. Rev. 679 (1990). For focus on "the Court's growing preoccupation with procedural fairness—that is, a requirement of a meaningful, or full and fair, opportunity to challenge one's conviction," see Justin F. Marceau, Is Guilt Dispositive? Federal Habeas After *Martinez*, 55 Wm. & Mary L. Rev. 2071 (2014).

For highly critical assessments of *Wainwright v. Sykes*, see Yale Rosenberg, Jettisoning *Fay v. Noia*: Procedural Defaults by Reasonably Incompetent Counsel, 62 Minn. L. Rev. 341 (1978), and Yale Rosenberg, Constricting Federal Habeas Corpus: From Great Writ to Exceptional Remedy, 12 Hastings L.J. 597 (1985). Special mention should be made of Maria Marcus, Federal Habeas Corpus After State Court Default: A Definition of Cause and Prejudice, 53 Fordham L. Rev. 663 (1985), which explores the values and choices at stake in defining "cause" and "prejudice" and proposes carefully crafted definitions of the terms.

SUBSECTION B. EXHAUSTION OF STATE REMEDIES AND TIMELINESS OF PETITIONS

NOTES ON EXHAUSTION AND SUCCESSIVE PETITIONS

1. HISTORY OF THE EXHAUSTION REQUIREMENT

Shortly after Congress extended federal habeas corpus to state prisoners, the Supreme Court ruled that federal relief should be withheld until available state remedies had been exhausted. Ex parte Royall, 117 U.S. 241 (1886). Royall was in jail awaiting trial on state criminal charges when he sought federal relief. The Supreme Court held that, absent special circumstances, a federal habeas court should not intervene until the state trial and appellate courts had an opportunity to rule on the petitioner's claims:

> The [habeas statute's authorization] to hear the case . . . does not deprive the court of discretion as to the time and mode in which it will exert the powers conferred upon it. That discretion should be exercised in light of the relations existing, under our system of government, between the judicial tribunals of the union and of the states, and in recognition of the fact that the public good requires that those relations not be disturbed by unnecessary conflict between courts equally bound to guard and protect rights secured by the Constitution.

The exhaustion requirement thus began as a judicially crafted limitation on federal habeas, designed to avoid disruption of state judicial proceedings by premature federal intervention. Exhaustion remained a purely judicial doctrine until it was codified in 1948.

Royall itself prohibited habeas intervention before trial,[a] but the limitation was soon extended to cover the entire process of state trial and appeal. Subsequent cases made plain that the exhaustion requirement also requires resort to state post-conviction procedures for claims that had not previously been considered by the state courts. Exhaustion requires that each claim raised in federal habeas must have been presented *once* to the state courts. Claims presented once need not be presented again. And the petitioner need not go through the motions if it is completely clear that state law provides no remedy. Finally, exhaustion is required only if an opportunity to present the claim to the state courts is currently available. That there was such an

---

[a] Notice the functional similarity to the abstention doctrine of Younger v. Harris, 401 U.S. 37 (1971), which generally prohibits federal courts from enjoining pending state criminal proceedings. *Younger* is covered in Chapter VI.

opportunity in the past does not mean that the claim is barred for failure to exhaust. This holding by Fay v. Noia, 372 U.S. 391 (1963), remains intact.

Claims that are decided on the merits by the state courts as a result of the exhaustion process are subject to the judicial and AEDPA limitations on merits review covered in Section 1 of this Chapter. A claim not raised in timely fashion and therefore defaulted under state law presents a question of procedural foreclosure to be analyzed under the adequate-and-independent-state-ground doctrine and the "cause and prejudice" and miscarriage of justice standards of Wainwright v. Sykes, 433 U.S. 72 (1977), and Murray v. Carrier, 477 U.S. 478, 496 (1986), as discussed at length in the preceding subsection of these materials. As held in Coleman v. Thompson, 501 U.S. 722 (1991), the *Wainwright* approach applies to claims that are defaulted at trial, on direct review, or during a state post-conviction process.

2.   EXHAUSTION CODIFIED

The exhaustion requirement is currently codified in 28 U.S.C. § 2254, which provides:

> (b) (1) An application for a writ of habeas corpus on behalf of a person in custody pursuant to the judgment of a State court shall not be granted unless it appears that—
>
> > (A) the applicant has exhausted the remedies available in the courts of the State; or
> >
> > (B) (i)   there is an absence of available State corrective process; or
> >
> > > (ii) circumstances exist that render such process ineffective to protect the rights of the applicant.
>
> (2) An application for a writ of habeas corpus may be denied on the merits, notwithstanding the failure of the applicant to exhaust the remedies available in the courts of the State.
>
> (3) A State shall not be deemed to have waived the exhaustion requirement or be estopped from reliance upon the requirement unless the State, through counsel, expressly waives the requirement.
>
> (c) An applicant shall not be deemed to have exhausted the remedies available in the courts of the State, within the meaning of this section, if he has the right under the law of the State to raise, by any available procedure, the question presented.

3.   *ROSE V. LUNDY* AND THE PROBLEM OF MIXED PETITIONS

Perhaps the most difficult problem in the law of exhaustion is what to do with a "mixed petition." The phrase refers to a habeas petition that contains both exhausted and unexhausted claims. This is extremely common. If exhaustion is to mean anything, a federal court obviously cannot consider unexhausted claims simply because they are presented together with claims that have been exhausted. But what should the court do with the exhausted claims that are ripe for review when other claims in the petition are not?

In Rose v. Lundy, 455 U.S. 509 (1982), a divided Supreme Court embraced a rule of total exhaustion. Speaking through Justice O'Connor, the Court held that a federal habeas court must dismiss mixed petitions, "leaving the prisoner with the choice of returning to state court to exhaust his claims or of amending or resubmitting the habeas petition to present only exhausted claims to the district court." The result was what the Court described as "a simple and clear instruction to potential litigants: before you bring any claims to federal court, be sure that you first have taken each one to state court." Three justices (White, Blackmun, and Stevens) would have preferred a rule that allowed the district court to hear the exhausted claims, even though accompanied by claims not yet ripe for federal review.

4. SUCCESSIVE PETITIONS: 28 U.S.C. § 2244(b)(2)

The significance of *Rose v. Lundy* depends on the rules for successive petitions. If a prisoner can cure a mixed petition simply by deleting the unexhausted claims and bringing them later in a second petition, the rule of total exhaustion is a little more than a formality of timing. Underlying the division of opinion in *Rose v. Lundy* was a dispute over whether the petitioner who deleted unexhausted claims should face obstacles to bringing them later.[b] At the time, this issue was governed by the doctrine of "abuse of the writ." Basically, that doctrine adapted the "cause and prejudice" standard to require justification for omitting claims from the first habeas petition.[c]

AEDPA clarified and tightened the rules for successive petitions. As summarized by the Court in Tyler v. Clain, 533 U.S. 656 (2001), the rules now are:

> If the prisoner asserts a claim that he has already presented in a previous federal habeas petition, the claim must be dismissed in all cases. And if the prisoner asserts a claim that was *not* presented in a previous petition, the claim must be dismissed unless it falls within two narrow exceptions. One of these exceptions is for claims predicated on newly discovered facts that call into question the accuracy of a guilty verdict. The other is for certain claims relying on new rules of constitutional law.

The exceptional circumstances described by the Court are spelled out in § 2244(b)(2):

---

[b] This division surfaced in a confusing array of separate opinions: Justice Blackmun concurring in the judgment but disagreeing about successive petitions; Justices Brennan (joined by Marshall) and White, concurring and dissenting; and Justice Stevens dissenting. These justices divided on the rule of total exhaustion but seemed to agree on a relaxed approach to successive petitions.

[c] See, e.g., McCleskey v. Zant, 499 U.S. 467 (1991), where the Court held, six-to-three, that "abuse of the writ" was not confined to instances of intentional abandonment but applied as well where the omission of an unexhausted claim from the first habeas petition was not excused by a showing of "cause and prejudice."

(2)   A claim presented in a second or successive habeas corpus application under section 2254 that was not presented in a prior application shall be dismissed unless—

(A)   the applicant shows that the claim relies on a new rule of constitutional law, made retroactive to cases on collateral review by the Supreme Court, that was previously unavailable; or

(B)   (i)   the factual predicate for the claim could not have been discovered previously through the exercise of due diligence; and

(ii)   the facts underlying the claim, if proven and viewed in light of the evidence as a whole, would be sufficient to establish by clear and convincing evidence that, but for constitutional error, no reasonable factfinder would have found the applicant guilty of the underlying offense.

Under these rules, the effect of *Rose v. Lundy* is greatly increased. Now a petitioner who deletes unexhausted claims in order to avoid a mixed petition very likely loses those claims forever. Absent one of the exceptional circumstances stated above, claims omitted from a prior petition are barred. It may be likely that the potentially meritorious claims are identified early and exhausted, in which case the additional unexhausted claims may be just a collection of long-shots. But whatever their merits, omitted claims are ordinarily barred from a second petition. That means that a prisoner who files a mixed petition must either dismiss the whole (in which case no claims are barred so long as the second petition is timely filed[d]) or proceed with the exhausted claims in the knowledge that the others are likely foreclosed.

5.   CERTIFICATION REQUIRED: 28 U.S.C. § 2244(b)(3)

In addition to these substantive restrictions, AEDPA also created an elaborate procedure for successive petitions. The requirements are stated in § 2244(b)(3):

(3)   (A)   Before a second or successive application permitted by this section is filed in the district court, the applicant shall move in the appropriate court of appeals for an order authorizing the district court to consider the application.

(B)   A motion in the court of appeals for an order authorizing the district court to consider a second or successive application shall be determined by a three-judge panel of the court of appeals.

(C)   The court of appeals may authorize the filing of a second or successive application only if it determines that the

---

d   See Slack v. McDaniel, 529 U.S. 473 (2000): "a habeas petition which is filed after an initial petition was dismissed without adjudication on the merits for failure to exhaust state remedies is not a 'second or successive' petition as that term is understood in the habeas corpus context."

application makes a prima facie showing that the application satisfies the requirements of this subsection.

(D) The court of appeals shall grant or deny the authorization to file a second or successive application not later than 30 days after the filing of the motion.

(E) The grant or denial of an authorization by a court of appeals to file a second or successive application shall not be appealable and shall not be the subject of a petition for rehearing or for a writ of certiorari.

(4) A district court shall dismiss any claim presented in a second or successive application that the court of appeals has authorized to be filed unless the applicant shows that the claim satisfies the requirements of this section.

Thus both substantively (§ 2244(b)(2)) and procedurally (§ 2244(b)(3)), successive petitions are strongly disfavored.

6. NEW RULES OF CONSTITUTIONAL LAW: *TYLER V. CAIN*

As noted, § 2254(b)(2)(A) provides an exception to foreclosure of a successive petition for claims that rely on a "new rule of constitutional law made retroactive to cases on collateral review by the Supreme Court, that was previously unavailable." Does that apply to a "new rule" that, under Supreme Court precedents, is likely to be found retroactive to cases on collateral review, or is it limited to a "new rule" that the Supreme Court has actually held to apply retroactively on collateral review? In Tyler v. Cain, 533 U.S. 656 (2001), the Supreme Court opted for the stricter interpretation.

Louisiana prosecuted and convicted Melvin Tyler for killing his infant daughter. The jury instruction on proof-beyond-a-reasonable-doubt said, among other things, that a reasonable doubt is "one that is founded upon a real tangible substantial basis and not upon mere caprice and conjecture. It must be such doubt as would give rise to a grave uncertainty, raised in your mind by reasons of the unsatisfactory character of the evidence or lack thereof." Some years later, Cage v. Louisiana, 498 U.S. 39 (1990), held this instruction unconstitutional. Tyler then filed petitions, first in state court and then in federal court, claiming that *Cage* gave him a right to a new trial. The question was whether the "new rule" of *Cage v. Louisiana* came within § 2254(b)(2)(A)'s requirement that it be "made retroactive to cases on collateral review by the Supreme Court."

Tyler's argument was aided by Sullivan v. Louisiana, 508 U.S. 275 (1993). After *Cage*, several lower courts held that the reasonable-doubt instruction disapproved in *Cage* could, on appropriate facts, be harmless error. In *Sullivan*, the Supreme Court disagreed, saying that misdescription of the reasonable-doubt standard deprived the defendant of a basic structural protection and could never be harmless error. The Court's analysis in *Sullivan* tracked the "watershed" exception in Teague v. Lane, 489 U.S. 288 (1989), for new procedures "without which the likelihood of an accurate conviction is seriously diminished." The effect of finding *Cage* within the "watershed" exception in *Teague* would be to render *Cage* retroactively applicable on collateral review. Tyler argued, therefore, that the Supreme Court's analysis in *Sullivan* made it quite clear that *Cage* should apply retroactively and therefore that a claim based on *Cage* was not barred as a successive petition.

Four Justices agreed, but five did not. Speaking through Justice Thomas, the Court held that the "plain meaning" of § 2244(b)(2)(A) commanded a different result. The only way the Supreme Court can "make" a new rule retroactive on collateral review, said the Court, is "through a holding":

> The Supreme Court does not "ma[k]e a rule retroactive when it merely establishes principles of retroactivity and leaves the application of those principles to the lower courts. . . . We thus conclude that a new rule is not "made retroactive to cases on collateral review" unless the Supreme Court holds it to be retroactive.

The Court also declined the invitation to hold *Cage* retroactive in this very case. Because Tyler had filed a successive petition, the district court was required to dismiss it unless *Cage* had *already* been made retroactive. Finding *Cage* retroactive now would not affect that outcome of this case and would therefore be mere dictum. Justice Breyer's dissent was joined by Justices Stevens, Souter, and Ginsburg.

7.　QUESTIONS AND COMMENTS

That the rule requiring total exhaustion of mixed petitions and the AEDPA provisions limiting successive petitions interact to form a highly restrictive regime cannot be denied. It is also very complicated. How well is this system likely to operate in the frequently pro-se world of habeas petitioners?

NOTES ON THE AEDPA STATUTE OF LIMITATIONS

1.　28 U.S.C. § 2244(d)

Until AEDPA, habeas corpus had no statute of limitations. Petitions could be filed as long as the petitioner remained in custody. AEDPA enacted § 2244(d) (and an analogous provision for federal prisoners in § 2255) imposing a limitations period of one year. Subsection (d)(1) provides:

> . . . The limitation period shall run from the latest of—
>
> (A)　the date on which the judgment became final by the conclusion of direct review or the expiration of the time for seeking such review;
>
> (B)　the date on which the impediment to filing an application created by State action in violation of the Constitution or laws of the United States is removed, if the applicant was prevented from filing by such State action;
>
> (C)　the date on which the constitutional right asserted was initially recognized by the Supreme Court, if the right has

been newly recognized by the Supreme Court and made retroactively applicable to cases on collateral review; or

(D) the date on which the factual predicate of the claim
or claims presented could have been discovered through the
exercise of due diligence.

2. WHEN THE STATUTE RUNS

In the ordinary case, the limitations period begins to run on "the date
on which the judgment became final by the conclusion of direct review or the
expiration of the time for seeking such review." § 2244(d)(1)(A). Does this
include a petition for certiorari to the Supreme Court? The answer is: "it depends."

In Lawrence v. Florida, 549 U.S. 327 (2007), the Supreme Court interpreted "the expiration of the time for seeking such review" to include a
petition for certiorari from direct review by the state courts. Thus for a claim
that is exhausted on direct review, the habeas petitioner has one year, measured from the date of the final decision by the state's highest court *or* from
the date of the denial of certiorari by the United States Supreme Court if
such relief is requested.

Of course, prisoners may also seek certiorari review of state post-conviction proceedings, but these petitions do *not* affect the habeas statute of
limitations. Section 2244(d)(2) says that the one-year limit will be tolled during the time that "a properly filed application for State post-conviction or
other collateral review ... is pending." But in contrast to the situation on
direct review, a petition for certiorari from the denial of state post-conviction
relief does not extend the limitation period. Thus, the limitations period for
federal habeas begins to run when direct review (including a petition for certiorari) is final; is suspended for so long as a state petition for collateral
review is pending; but resumes running as soon as the highest state court
rules on collateral review, regardless of any subsequent petition for certiorari.

As mentioned, § 2244(d)(2) provides that time does not run during the
pendency of any properly filed application for state post-conviction review.
What about a federal habeas petition? Does that suspend the one-year limitations period so that subsequent habeas petitions remain timely? In the
statutory language, the question is whether a federal habeas petition is a
"properly filed application for State post-conviction or *other collateral review*"
within the meaning of § 2244(d)(2) (emphasis added). In Duncan v. Walker,
533 U.S. 167 (2001), the Court said "no." The Court held that "other collateral
review" referred only to other *state* collateral review. Under this interpretation, a *federal* petition, although valid if timely filed, did not suspend
operation of the statute of limitations while it was pending.

The significance of this ruling comes into focus in the case of a mixed
petition. If the exhausted claims in the mixed petition are timely filed, consideration of them can proceed once the others are dismissed. But the
limitations period on those other claims continues to run while the habeas
proceeding is pending. Does the timely misfiling of unexhausted claims in

the original petition have no effect on the statute of limitations? That was the question presented in the case below.

3.   "STAY AND ABEYANCE": *RHINES V. WEBER*

Russell Rhines was convicted of murder and sentenced to death. The Supreme Court denied certiorari. Within three days of that denial, Rhines sought state habeas relief. Less than a month after the state petition was denied, he filed a federal habeas petition asserting 35 constitutional claims. At this point, he was well within (indeed barely into) the one-year limitation period imposed by AEDPA.

Eighteen months later, the federal habeas court determined that eight of the 35 claims had not been exhausted. Since under *Duncan* the AEDPA statute of limitations was not tolled during the pendency of the federal habeas petition, Rhines faced a problem. If the court dismissed the unexhausted claims, as required by *Rose v. Lundy*, they would be time barred by the AEDPA statute of limitations.[a] Thus, he could proceed in federal court with the 27 exhausted claims only at the cost of foregoing federal review of the eight unexhausted claims.

To avoid this result, Rhines asked the district court to hold his pending mixed petition "in abeyance" while he exhausted his state remedies on the eight claims, and then to let him return to federal court, if necessary, to litigate all 35 claims. The District Court granted his motion, provided that he moved promptly. The Court of Appeals held this procedure impermissible, and remanded for a determination of whether Rhines could proceed on his exhausted claims only. In Rhines v. Weber, 544 U.S. 269 (2005), the Supreme Court adopted a middle ground.

In an opinion by Justice O'Connor, the Court first addressed the question of a district court's power:

> District courts do ordinarily have authority to issue stays, where such a stay would be a proper exercise of discretion. AEDPA does not deprive district courts of that authority, but it does circumscribe their discretion. Any solution to this problem must therefore be compatible with AEDPA's purposes.

The Court then identified two relevant purposes: to reduce delays in achieving finality for state court judgments; and to encourage litigation in state courts first. It continued:

> Stay and abeyance, if employed too frequently, has the potential to undermine these twin purposes. Staying a federal habeas petition frustrates AEDPA's objective of encouraging finality by allowing a petitioner to delay the resolution of the federal proceedings. It also undermines AEDPA's goal of streamlining federal habeas proceedings by decreasing a petitioner's incentive to exhaust all his claims in state court prior to filing his federal petition.

---

[a]   If the court dismissed the entire petition, the situation would be even worse. Then all 35 claims would be barred.

For these reasons, stay and abeyance should be available only in limited circumstances. Because granting a stay effectively excuses a petitioner's failure to present his claims first to the state courts, stay and abeyance is only appropriate when the district court determines there was good cause for the petitioner's failure to exhaust his claims first in state court. Moreover, even if a petitioner had good cause for that failure, the district court would abuse its discretion if it were to grant him a stay when his unexhausted claims are plainly meritless. Cf. 28 U.S.C. § 2254(b)(2) ("An application for a writ of habeas corpus may be denied on the merits, notwithstanding the failure of the applicant to exhaust the remedies available in the courts of the State").

Even where stay and abeyance is appropriate, the district court's discretion in structuring the stay is limited by the timeliness concerns reflected in AEDPA. . . . Thus, district courts should place reasonable time limits on a petitioner's trip to state court and back. See, e.g., Zarvela v. Artuz, 254 F.3d 374, 381 (2d Cir. 2001) ("[District courts] should explicitly condition the stay on the prisoner's pursuing state court remedies within a brief interval, normally 30 days, after the stay is entered and returning to federal court within a similarly brief interval, normally 30 days after state court exhaustion is completed"). And if a petitioner engages in abusive litigation tactics or intentional delay, the district court should not grant him a stay at all.

On the other hand, it likely would be an abuse of discretion for a district court to deny a stay and to dismiss a mixed petition if the petitioner had good cause for his failure to exhaust, his unexhausted claims are potentially meritorious, and there is no indication that the petitioner engaged in intentionally dilatory litigation tactics. In such circumstances, the district court should stay, rather than dismiss, the mixed petition.

Justice Souter, joined by Justices Ginsburg and Breyer, concurred in part and concurred in the judgment. He had "one reservation":

[N]ot doctrinal but practical. Instead of conditioning stay-and-abeyance on "good cause" for delay, I would simply hold the order unavailable on a demonstration of "intentionally dilatory litigation tactics." The trickiness of some exhaustion determinations promises to infect issues of good cause when a court finds a failure to exhaust; pro se petitioners (as most habeas petitioners are) do not come well trained to address such matters. I fear that threshold enquiries into good cause will give the district courts too much trouble to be worth the time; far better to wait for the alarm to sound when there is some indication that a petitioner is gaming the system.

4. EQUITABLE TOLLING

Some have argued that the concept of "equitable tolling" could suspend operation of the AEDPA statute of limitations in certain circumstances. In Pace v. DiGuglielmo, 544 U.S. 408 (2005), the Court defined "equitable tolling" generally as requiring a litigant to establish "two elements: (1) that he has been pursuing his rights diligently, and (2) that some extraordinary circumstance stood in his way." In Holland v. Florida, 560 U.S. 631 (2010), the Court held that equitable tolling, so defined, was available under AEDPA. Justice Breyer's opinion for the Court reiterated that the circumstances must be "extraordinary," as *Pace* had said, and that the risk of attorney error ordinarily remains on the client where, as in post-conviction proceedings, there is no constitutional right to counsel. But equitable tolling would be allowed in "extraordinary circumstances" of "egregious" attorney misconduct. The Court did not spell out what those circumstances might be, remanding the case for initial consideration by the lower courts. A separate opinion by Justice Alito indicated that, at least in his view, extraordinary circumstances would be made out where the state attempted to hold a prisoner responsible for the actions of an attorney who had abandoned the representation. Justices Scalia and Thomas dissented.

5. CLAIMS OF INNOCENCE

In McQuiggin v. Perkins, 569 U.S. 383 (2013), the Court granted certiorari to determine "whether AEDPA's statute of limitations can be overcome by a showing of actual innocence." Perkins's conviction of murder became final in May of 1997. He filed for habeas relief more than 11 years later, claiming ineffective assistance by his trial attorney. To overcome the AEDPA one-year statute of limitations, he made a claim of actual innocence based on three affidavits that pointed to another person as the killer.

In an opinion by Justice Ginsburg, the Court said:

> In Holland v. Florida, 560 U.S. 631 (2010), this Court addressed the circumstances in which a federal habeas petitioner could invoke the doctrine of "equitable tolling." *Holland* held that "a [habeas] petitioner is entitled to equitable tolling only if he shows (1) that he has been pursuing his rights diligently, and (2) that some extraordinary circumstance stood in his way and prevented timely filing." As the courts below comprehended, Perkins does not qualify for equitable tolling. In possession of all three affidavits by July 2002, he waited nearly six years to seek federal post-conviction relief. [As the District Court held,] "[s]uch a delay falls far short of demonstrating the . . . diligence" required to entitle a petitioner to equitable tolling.

> Perkins, however, does not assert an excuse for filing after the statute of limitations has run. Instead, he maintains that a plea of actual innocence can overcome AEDPA's one-year statute of limitations. He thus seeks an equitable *exception* to § 2244(d)(1), not an extension of the time statutorily prescribed.

Decisions of this Court support Perkins's view of the significance of a convincing actual-innocence claim. We have not resolved whether a prisoner may be entitled to habeas relief based on a freestanding claim of actual innocence. Herrera v. Collins, 506 U.S. 390, 404–05 (1993). We have recognized, however, that a prisoner "otherwise subject to defenses of abusive or successive use of the writ [of habeas corpus] may have his federal constitutional claim considered on the merits if he makes a proper showing of actual innocence." Id. at 404. In other words, a credible showing of actual innocence may allow a prisoner to pursue his constitutional claims (here, ineffective assistance of counsel) on the merits notwithstanding the existence of a procedural bar to relief. "This rule, or fundamental miscarriage of justice exception, is grounded in the 'equitable discretion' of habeas courts to see that federal constitutional errors do not result in the incarceration of innocent persons." Id.

The state objected that it would be disadvantaged by delays in the presentation of new evidence. The Court responded:

Unexplained delay in presenting new evidence bears on the determination whether the petitioner has made the requisite showing. . . . Considering a petitioner's diligence, not discretely, but as part of the assessment whether actual innocence has been convincingly shown, attends to the State's concern that it will be prejudiced by a prisoner's untoward delay in proffering new evidence. . . . The timing of such a petition . . . should seriously undermine the credibility of the actual-innocence claim. . . . Focusing on the merits of a petitioner's actual-innocence claim and taking account of delay in that context, rather than treating timeliness as a threshold inquiry, is tuned to the rationale underlying the miscarriage of justice exception—i.e., ensuring "that federal constitutional errors do not result in the incarceration of innocent persons." Id.

Joined by Chief Justice Roberts and Justices Thomas and Alito, Justice Scalia dissented. Characteristically, he began with the statute's text:

The gaping hole in today's opinion for the Court is its failure to answer the crucial question upon which all else depends: What is the source of the Court's power to fashion what it concedes is an "exception" to this clear statutory command?

That question is unanswered because there is no answer. This Court has no such power, and not one of the cases cited by the opinion says otherwise. The Constitution vests legislative power only in Congress, which never enacted the exception the Court creates today. That inconvenient truth resolves this case.

He thought *Holland* different:

Equitable tolling—extending the deadline for a filing because of an event or circumstance that deprives the filer, through no fault of his own, of the full period accorded by the statute—seeks to vindicate what might be considered the genuine intent of the statute.

By contrast, suspending the statute because of a separate policy that the court believes should trump it ("actual innocence") is a blatant overruling. . . .

American courts' . . . adoption of the English equitable tolling practice need not be regarded as a violation of the separation of powers, but can be seen as a reasonable assumption of genuine legislative intent. . . . "It is hornbook law that limitations periods are customarily subject to equitable tolling, unless tolling would be inconsistent with the text of the relevant statute. Congress must be presumed to draft limitations periods in light of this background principle." Young v. United States, 535 U.S. 43, 49–50 (2002). Congress, being well aware of the longstanding background presumption of equitable tolling, "may provide otherwise if it wishes to do so." Irwin v. Department of Veterans Affairs, 498 U.S. 89, 96 (1990). The majority and dissenting opinions in *Holland* disputed whether that presumption had been overcome, but all agreed that the presumption existed and was a legitimate tool for construing statutes of limitations.

Here, by contrast, the Court has ambushed Congress with an utterly unprecedented (and thus unforeseeable) maneuver. Congressional silence, "while permitting an inference that Congress intended to apply ordinary background" principles, "cannot show that it intended to apply an unusual modification of those rules." Meyer v. Holley, 537 U.S. 280, 286 (2003). Because there is no plausible basis for inferring that Congress intended or could have anticipated this exception, its adoption here amounts to a pure judicial override of the statute Congress enacted.

Is Justice Scalia's distinction of *Holland* persuasive? Whether it is or is not, what is the answer to his question about the Court's authority to recognize an actual innocence exception in *Perkins*? Could it be argued that such an exception is warranted because it avoids a serious constitutional concern and that Congress would presumably prefer to have its statute limited rather than invalidated?

6.   RETROACTIVE NEW RULES AND THE STATUTE OF LIMITATIONS: *DODD V. UNITED STATES*

AEDPA establishes a one-year statute of limitations for § 2255 applications that usually begins to run upon completion of the direct review process after conviction. An alternative provision (analogous to § 2244(d)(1)(C)) starts the clock from "the date on which the right asserted was initially recognized by the Supreme Court, if that right has been newly recognized by the Supreme Court and made retroactively applicable to cases on collateral review." 28 U.S.C. § 2255, ¶ 6(3). Is the trigger for that provision the date on which a new right was recognized or the date on which it was made retroactively applicable on collateral review? The issue was considered in Dodd v. United States, 545 U.S. 353 (2005).

The "new rule" at issue in *Dodd* was established in Richardson v. United States, 526 U.S. 813 (1999), which held that a jury must agree unanimously on each of the predicate crimes that satisfy the multiple-crime requirement for conviction of engaging in a continuing criminal enterprise in violation of 21 U.S.C. § 848. As is its usual practice, the Court did not announce in *Richardson* whether this was a new rule to be applied retroactively on collateral review. *Richardson* was decided on June 1, 1999. The Eleventh Circuit held it retroactive on April 19, 2002.[b]

Dodd's conviction became final on August 6, 1997. He raised a *Richardson* claim in a § 2255 petition filed on April 4, 2001. If the statute of limitations exception was triggered by the date of the Circuit Court retroactivity holding, his petition was timely. If it was triggered by the date of the *Richardson* decision, it was not.

Justice O'Connor's opinion for the Court chose the date *Richardson* was decided:

> We believe that the text of ¶ 6(3) settles this dispute. It unequivocally identifies one, and only one, date from which the 1-year limitation period is measured: "the date on which the right asserted was initially recognized by the Supreme Court." . . . [I]f this Court decides a case recognizing a new right, a federal prisoner seeking to assert that right will have one year from this Court's decision within which to file his § 2255 motion. He may take advantage of the date in the first clause of ¶ 6(3) only if the conditions in the second clause are met.

Joined by Justices Souter, Ginsburg, and Breyer, Justice Stevens dissented. He thought the Court's interpretation "anomalous":

> Because a significant amount of time may elapse during the interval between the triggering event and the point at which a petitioner may actually be able to file an action seeking relief under the statute, there is a real risk that the 1-year limitation period will expire before the cause of action accrues. In my judgment, the probable explanation for statutory text that creates this risk is Congress's apparent assumption that our recognition of the new right and our decision to apply it retroactively would be made at the same time. Otherwise it seems nonsensical to assume that Congress deliberately enacted a statute that recognizes a cause of action, but wrote the limitation period in a way that precludes an individual from ever taking advantage of the cause of action. . . .
>
> Under the majority's interpretation, the statute of limitations . . . expired on June 1, 2000, one year after we recognized the new

---

[b] An issue that lay in the background in *Dodd* was whether retroactivity decisions must be made by the Supreme Court to satisfy the provisions of ¶ 6(3) or whether circuit court retroactivity decisions counted. Justice Stevens was the only one to give an answer. The case was decided on the assumption, without resolving the question, that a circuit court decision was sufficient. Justice Stevens said that "[w]hile I recognize that every Circuit to have addressed the issue has made the same assumption, I am satisfied that . . . the requirement that 'the right has been newly recognized by the Supreme Court and made retroactively applicable to cases on collateral review' is met only if the *Supreme Court* has made the right retroactive."

rule. The Eleventh Circuit, however, did not decide whether *Richardson* was retroactive until April 19, 2002. Thus, Dodd would not, under the majority's interpretation, have been able to raise his claim at all, since the statute of limitations expired before he could have taken advantage of ¶ 6(3)'s 1-year grace period. . . .

To avoid this result, I would interpret ¶ 6(3) to begin to run only when the Supreme Court has initially recognized the new right *and* when that right has been held to be retroactive. Under this interpretation, the statute of limitation would not begin to run until the prisoner was actually able to file a petition under ¶ 6(3), which is the only interpretation Congress could have intended. Although in enacting AEDPA Congress was clearly concerned with finality, ¶ 6(3) is an explicit exception to that general preference. Congress surely intended to allow habeas petitioners to take advantage of the new rights that this Court deems retroactive. Otherwise, there would have been no reason to include that section in the statute.

SECTION 4. CLAIMS OF INNOCENCE

Herrera v. Collins
Supreme Court of the United States, 1993.
506 U.S. 390.

■ CHIEF JUSTICE REHNQUIST delivered the opinion of the Court.

Petitioner Leonel Torres Herrera was convicted of capital murder and sentenced to death in January 1982. He unsuccessfully challenged the conviction on direct appeal and state collateral proceedings in the Texas state courts, and in a federal habeas petition. In February 1992— 10 years after his conviction—he urged in a second federal habeas petition that he was "actually innocent" of the murder for which he was sentenced to death, and that the Eighth Amendment's prohibition against cruel and unusual punishment and the Fourteenth Amendment's guarantee of due process of law therefore forbid his execution. He supported this claim with affidavits tending to show that his now-dead brother, rather than he, had been the perpetrator of the crime. Petitioner urges us to hold that this showing of innocence entitles him to relief in this federal habeas proceeding. We hold that it does not.

Shortly before 11 p.m. on an evening in late September 1981, the body of Texas Department of Public Safety Officer David Rucker was found by a passerby on a stretch of highway about six miles east of Los Fresnos, Texas, a few miles north of Brownsville in the Rio Grande Valley. Rucker's body was lying beside his patrol car. He had been shot in the head.

At about the same time, Los Fresnos Police Officer Enrique Carrisalez observed a speeding vehicle traveling west towards Los Fresnos, away from the place where Rucker's body had been found, along the same road. Carrisalez, who was accompanied in his patrol car by Enrique Hernandez, turned on his flashing red lights and pursued the speeding vehicle. After the car had stopped briefly at a red light, it signaled that it would pull over and did so. The patrol car pulled up behind it. Carrisalez took a flashlight and walked toward the car of the speeder. The driver opened his door and exchanged a few words with Carrisalez before firing at least one shot at Carrisalez' chest. The officer died nine days later.

Petitioner Herrera was arrested a few days after the shootings and charged with the capital murder of both Carrisalez and Rucker. He was tried and found guilty of the capital murder of Carrisalez in January 1982, and sentenced to death. In July 1982, petitioner pleaded guilty to the murder of Rucker.

At petitioner's trial for the murder of Carrisalez, Hernandez, who had witnessed Carrisalez' slaying from the officer's patrol car, identified petitioner as the person who had wielded the gun. A declaration by Officer Carrisalez to the same effect, made while he was in the hospital, was also admitted. Through a license plate check, it was shown that the speeding car involved in Carrisalez' murder was registered to petitioner's "live-in" girlfriend. Petitioner was known to drive this car, and he had a set of keys to the car in his pants pocket when he was arrested. Hernandez identified the car as the vehicle from which the murderer had emerged to fire the fatal shot. He also testified that there had been only one person in the car that night.

The evidence showed that Herrera's Social Security card had been found alongside Rucker's patrol car on the night he was killed. Splatters of blood on the car identified as the vehicle involved in the shootings, and on petitioner's blue jeans and wallet were identified as type A blood—the same type which Rucker had. (Herrera has type O blood.) Similar evidence with respect to strands of hair found in the car indicated that the hair was Rucker's and not Herrera's. A handwritten letter was also found on the person of petitioner when he was arrested, which strongly implied that he had killed Rucker.[1]

---

[1]   The letter read:

   To whom it may concern: I am terribly sorry for those I have brought grief to their lives. Who knows why? We cannot change the future's problems with problems from the past. What I did was for a cause and purpose. One law runs others, and in the world we live in, that's the way it is.

   I'm not a tormented person. . . . I believe in the law. What would it be without this [sic] men that risk their lives for others, and that's what they should be doing—protecting life, property, and the pursuit of happiness. Sometimes, the law gets too involved with other things that profit them. The most laws that they make for people to break them, in other words, to encourage crime.

   What happened to Rucker was for a certain reason. I knew him as Mike Tatum. He was in my business, and he violated some of its laws and suffered the penalty, like the one you have for me when the time comes.

   My personal life, which has been a conspiracy since my high school days, has nothing to do with what has happened. The other officer that became part of our lives, me and Rucker's (Tatum), that night had not to do in this [sic]. He was out to do what he

Petitioner appealed his conviction and sentence, arguing, among other things, that Hernandez' and Carrisalez' identifications were unreliable and improperly admitted. The Texas Court of Criminal Appeals affirmed, and we denied certiorari. Petitioner's application for state habeas relief was denied. Petitioner then filed a federal habeas petition, again challenging the identifications offered against him at trial. This petition was denied, and we again denied certiorari.

Petitioner next returned to state court and filed a second habeas petition, raising, among other things, a claim of "actual innocence" based on newly discovered evidence. In support of this claim petitioner presented the affidavits of Hector Villarreal, an attorney who had represented petitioner's brother, Raul Herrera, Sr., and of Juan Franco Palacious, one of Raul Sr.'s former cellmates. Both individuals claimed that Raul Sr., who died in 1984, had told them that he—and not petitioner—had killed Officers Rucker and Carrisalez.[2] The state District Court denied this application, finding that "no evidence at trial remotely suggest[ed] that anyone other than [petitioner] committed the offense." The Texas Court of Criminal Appeals affirmed, and we denied certiorari.

In February 1992, petitioner lodged the instant habeas petition—his second—in federal court, alleging, among other things, that he is innocent of the murders of Rucker and Carrisalez, and that his execution would thus violate the Eighth and Fourteenth Amendments. In addition to proffering the above affidavits, petitioner presented the affidavits of Raul Herrera, Jr., Raul Sr.'s son, and Jose Ybarra, Jr., a schoolmate of the Herrera brothers. Raul Jr. averred that he had witnessed his father shoot Officers Rucker and Carrisalez and petitioner was not present. Raul Jr. was nine years old at the time of the killings. Ybarra alleged that Raul Sr. told him one summer night in 1983 that he had shot the

---

had to do, protect, but that's life. There's a lot of us that wear different faces in lives every day, and that is what causes problems for all. [Unintelligible word].

You have wrote all you want of my life, but think about yours, also. [Signed Leonel Herrera].

I have tapes and pictures to prove what I have said. I will prove my side if you accept to listen. You [unintelligible word] freedom of speech, even a criminal has that right. I will present myself if this is read word for word over the media, I will turn myself in; if not, don't have millions of men out there working just on me while others— robbers, rapists, or burglars—are taking advantage of the law's time. Excuse my spelling and writing. It's hard at times like this.

[2]   Villarreal's affidavit is dated December 11, 1990. He attested that while he was representing Raul Sr. on a charge of attempted murder in 1984, Raul Sr. had told him that he, petitioner, their father, Officer Rucker, and the Hidalgo County Sheriff were involved in a drug-trafficking scheme; that he was the one who had shot Officers Rucker and Carrisalez; that he didn't tell anyone about this because he thought petitioner would be acquitted; and that after petitioner was convicted and sentenced to death, he began blackmailing the Hidalgo County Sheriff. According to Villarreal, Raul Sr. was killed by Jose Lopez, who worked with the sheriff on drug-trafficking matters and was present when Raul Sr. murdered Rucker and Carrisalez, to silence him.

Palacious's affidavit is dated December 10, 1990. He attested that while he and Raul Sr. shared a cell together in the Hidalgo County jail in 1984, Raul Sr. told him that he had shot Rucker and Carrisalez.

two police officers.[3] Petitioner alleged that law enforcement officials were aware of this evidence, and had withheld it in violation of Brady v. Maryland, 373 U.S. 83 (1963).

The District Court dismissed most of petitioner's claims as an abuse of the writ. However, "in order to ensure that petitioner can assert his constitutional claims and out of a sense of fairness and due process," the District Court granted petitioner's request for a stay of execution so that he could present his claim of actual innocence, along with the Raul Jr. and Ybarra affidavits, in state court. Although it initially dismissed petitioner's *Brady* claim on the ground that petitioner had failed to present "any evidence of withholding exculpatory material by the prosecution," the District Court also granted an evidentiary hearing on this claim after reconsideration.

The Court of Appeals vacated the stay of execution. It agreed with the District Court's initial conclusion that there was no evidentiary basis for petitioner's *Brady* claim, and found disingenuous petitioner's attempt to couch his claim of actual innocence in *Brady* terms. Absent an accompanying constitutional violation, the Court of Appeals held that petitioner's claim of actual innocence was not cognizable because, under Townsend v. Sain, 372 U.S. 293, 317 (1963), "the existence merely of newly discovered evidence relevant to the guilt of a state prisoner is not a ground for relief on federal habeas corpus."[4] We granted certiorari, and the Texas Court of Criminal Appeals stayed petitioner's execution. We now affirm.

Petitioner asserts that the Eighth and Fourteenth Amendments to the United States Constitution prohibit the execution of a person who is innocent of the crime for which he was convicted. This proposition has an elemental appeal, as would the similar proposition that the Constitution prohibits the imprisonment of one who is innocent of the crime for which he was convicted. After all, the central purpose of any system of criminal justice is to convict the guilty and free the innocent. But the evidence upon which petitioner's claim of innocence rests was not produced at his trial, but rather eight years later. In any system of criminal justice, "innocence" or "guilt" must be determined in some sort of a judicial proceeding. Petitioner's showing of innocence, and indeed his constitutional claim for relief based upon that showing, must be evaluated in the light of the previous proceedings in this case, which have stretched over a span of 10 years.

---

[3] Raul Jr.'s affidavit is dated January 29, 1992. Ybarra's affidavit is dated January 9, 1991. It was initially submitted with Petitioner's Reply to State's Brief in Response to Petitioner's Petition for Writ of Habeas Corpus filed January 18, 1991, in the Texas Court of Criminal Appeals.

[4] After the Court of Appeals vacated the stay of execution, petitioner attached a new affidavit by Raul Jr. to his Petition for Rehearing, which was denied. The affidavit alleges that during petitioner's trial, various law enforcement officials and the Hidalgo County Sheriff told Raul Jr. not to say what happened on the night of the shootings and threatened his family.

A person when first charged with a crime is entitled to a presumption of innocence, and may insist that his guilt be established beyond a reasonable doubt. [But] once a defendant has been afforded a fair trial and convicted of the offense for which he was charged, the presumption of innocence disappears. . . . Here, it is not disputed that the state met its burden of proving at trial that petitioner was guilty of the capital murder of Officer Carrisalez beyond a reasonable doubt. Thus, in the eyes of the law, petitioner does not come before the Court as one who is "innocent," but on the contrary as one who has been convicted by due process of law of two brutal murders.

Based on affidavits here filed, petitioner claims that evidence never presented to the trial court proves him innocent notwithstanding the verdict reached at his trial. Such a claim is not cognizable in the state courts of Texas. For to obtain a new trial based on newly discovered evidence, a defendant must file a motion within 30 days after imposition or suspension of sentence. The Texas courts have construed this 30-day time limit as jurisdictional.

Claims of actual innocence based on newly discovered evidence have never been held to state a ground for federal habeas relief absent an independent constitutional violation occurring in the underlying state criminal proceeding. Chief Justice Warren made this clear in *Townsend*, 372 U.S. at 317 (emphasis added):

> Where newly discovered evidence is alleged in a habeas application, evidence which could not reasonably have been presented to the state trier of facts, the federal court must grant an evidentiary hearing. Of course, such evidence must bear upon the constitutionality of the applicant's detention; *the existence merely of newly discovered evidence relevant to the guilt of a state prisoner is not a ground for relief on federal habeas corpus.*

This rule is grounded in the principle that federal habeas courts sit to ensure that individuals are not imprisoned in violation of the Constitution—not to correct errors of fact. . . Few rulings would be more disruptive of our federal system than to provide for federal habeas review of free-standing claims of actual innocence.

Our decision in Jackson v. Virginia, 443 U.S. 307 (1979), comes as close to authorizing evidentiary review of a state court conviction on federal habeas as any of our cases. There, we held that a federal habeas court may review a claim that the evidence adduced at a state trial was not sufficient to convict a criminal defendant beyond a reasonable doubt. But in so holding, we emphasized:

> [T]his inquiry does not require a court to "ask itself whether *it* believes that the evidence at the trial established guilt beyond a reasonable doubt." Instead, the relevant question is whether, after viewing the evidence in the light most favorable to the

prosecution, *any* rational trier of fact could have found the essential elements of the crime beyond a reasonable doubt. This familiar standard gives full play to the responsibility of the trier of fact fairly to resolve conflicts in the testimony, to weigh the evidence, and to draw reasonable inferences from basic facts to ultimate facts.

We specifically noted that "the standard announced . . . does not permit a court to make its own subjective determination of guilt or innocence."

The type of federal habeas review sought by petitioner here is different in critical respects than that authorized by *Jackson*. First, the *Jackson* inquiry is aimed at determining whether there has been an independent constitutional violation—i.e., a conviction based on evidence that fails to meet the . . . standard [of proof required by In re Winship, 397 U.S. 358 (1970)]. Thus, federal habeas courts act in their historic capacity—to assure that the habeas petitioner is not being held in violation of his or her federal constitutional rights. Second, the sufficiency of the evidence review authorized by *Jackson* is limited to "record evidence." *Jackson* does not extend to nonrecord evidence, including newly discovered evidence. Finally, the *Jackson* inquiry does not focus on whether the trier of fact made the correct guilt or innocence determination, but rather whether it made a rational decision to convict or acquit.

Petitioner is understandably imprecise in describing the sort of federal relief to which a suitable showing of actual innocence would entitle him. In his brief he states that the federal habeas court should have "an important initial opportunity to hear the evidence and resolve the merits of petitioner's claim." Acceptance of this view would presumably require the habeas court to hear testimony from the witnesses who testified at trial as well as those who made the statements in the affidavits which petitioner has presented, and to determine anew whether or not petitioner is guilty of the murder of Officer Carrisalez. Indeed, the dissent's approach differs little from that hypothesized here.

The dissent would place the burden on petitioner to show that he is "probably" innocent. Although petitioner would not be entitled to discovery "as a matter of right," the district court would retain its "discretion to order discovery . . . when it would help the court make a reliable determination with respect to the prisoner's claim." And although the district court would not be required to hear testimony from the witnesses who testified at trial or the affiants upon whom petitioner relies, it would allow the district court to do so "if the petition warrants a hearing." At the end of the day, the dissent would have the district court "make a case-by-case determination about the reliability of newly discovered evidence under the circumstances," and then "weigh the evidence in favor of the prisoner against the evidence of his guilt."

The dissent fails to articulate the relief that would be available if petitioner were to meets [sic] its "probable innocence" standard. Would it

be commutation of petitioner's death sentence, new trial, or unconditional release from imprisonment? The typical relief granted in federal
habeas corpus is a conditional order of release unless the state elects to
retry the successful habeas petitioner, or in a capital case a similar conditional order vacating the death sentence. Were petitioner to satisfy the
dissent's "probable innocence" standard, therefore, the district court
would presumably be required to grant a conditional order of relief, which
would in effect require the state to retry petitioner 10 years after his first
trial, not because of any constitutional violation which had occurred at
the first trial, but simply because of a belief that in light of petitioner's
new found evidence a jury might find him not guilty at a second trial.

Yet there is no guarantee that the guilt or innocence determination
would be any more exact. To the contrary, the passage of time only diminishes the reliability of criminal adjudications. Under the dissent's
approach, the district court would be placed in the even more difficult
position of having to weigh the probative value of "hot" and "cold" evidence on petitioner's guilt or innocence.

This is not to say that our habeas jurisprudence casts a blind eye
towards innocence. In a series of cases culminating with Sawyer v. Whitley, 505 U.S. 333 (1992), decided last term, we have held that a petitioner
otherwise subject to defenses of abusive or successive use of the writ may
have his federal constitutional claim considered on the merits if he makes
a proper showing of actual innocence. This rule, or fundamental miscarriage of justice exception, is grounded in the "equitable discretion" of
habeas courts to see that federal constitutional errors do not result in the
incarceration of innocent persons. But this body of our habeas jurisprudence makes clear that a claim of "actual innocence" is not itself a
constitutional claim, but instead a gateway through which a habeas petitioner must pass to have his otherwise barred constitutional claim
considered on the merits.

Petitioner in this case is simply not entitled to habeas relief based
on the reasoning of this line of cases. For he does not seek excusal of a
procedural error so that he may bring an independent constitutional
claim challenging his conviction or sentence, but rather argues that he is
entitled to habeas relief because newly discovered evidence shows that
his conviction is factually incorrect. The fundamental miscarriage of justice exception is available "only where the prisoner *supplements* his
constitutional claim with a colorable showing of factual innocence."
Kuhlmann v. Wilson, 477 U.S. 436, 454 (1986) (emphasis added). We
have never held that it extends to free-standing claims of actual innocence. Therefore, the exception is inapplicable here.

Petitioner asserts that this case is different because he has been sentenced to death. But we have "refused to hold that the fact that a death
sentence has been imposed requires a different standard of review on
federal habeas corpus." Murray v. Giarratano, 492 U.S. 1, 9 (1989) (plurality opinion). We have, of course, held that the Eighth Amendment

requires increased reliability of the process by which capital punishment may be imposed. But petitioner's claim does not fit well into the doctrine of these cases, since, as we have pointed out, it is far from clear that a second trial 10 years after the first trial would produce a more reliable result.

Perhaps mindful of this, petitioner urges not that he necessarily receive a new trial, but that his death sentence simply be vacated if a federal habeas court deems that a satisfactory showing of "actual innocence" has been made. But such a result is scarcely logical; petitioner's claim is not that some error was made in imposing a capital sentence upon him, but that a fundamental error was made in finding him guilty of the underlying murder in the first place. It would be a rather strange jurisprudence, in these circumstances, which held that under our Constitution he could not be executed, but that he could spend the rest of his life in prison. . . .

This is not to say, however, that petitioner is left without a forum to raise his actual innocence claim. For under Texas law, petitioner may file a request for executive clemency. Clemency is deeply rooted in our Anglo-American tradition of law, and is the historic remedy for preventing miscarriages of justice where judicial process has been exhausted. . . . Today, all 36 States that authorize capital punishment have constitutional or statutory provisions for clemency. . . .

As the foregoing discussion illustrates, in state criminal proceedings the trial is the paramount event for determining the guilt or innocence of the defendant. Federal habeas review of state convictions has traditionally been limited to claims of constitutional violations occurring in the course of the underlying state criminal proceedings. Our federal habeas cases have treated claims of "actual innocence," not as an independent constitutional claim, but as a basis upon which a habeas petitioner may have an independent constitutional claim considered on the merits, even though his habeas petition would otherwise be regarded as successive or abusive. History shows that the traditional remedy for claims of innocence based on new evidence, discovered too late in the day to file a new trial motion, has been executive clemency.

We may assume, for the sake of argument in deciding this case, that in a capital case a truly persuasive demonstration of "actual innocence" made after trial would render the execution of a defendant unconstitutional, and warrant federal habeas relief if there were no state avenue open to process such a claim. But because of the very disruptive effect that entertaining claims of actual innocence would have on the need for finality in capital cases, and the enormous burden that having to retry cases based on often stale evidence would place on the states, the threshold showing for such an assumed right would necessarily be extraordinarily high. The showing made by petitioner in this case falls far short of any such threshold.

Petitioner's newly discovered evidence consists of affidavits. In the new trial context, motions based solely upon affidavits are disfavored because the affiants' statements are obtained without the benefit of cross-examination and an opportunity to make credibility determinations. Petitioner's affidavits are particularly suspect in this regard because, with the exception of Raul Herrera, Jr.'s, affidavit, they consist of hearsay. Likewise, in reviewing petitioner's new evidence, we are mindful that defendants often abuse new trial motions "as a method of delaying enforcement of just sentences." United States v. Johnson, 327 U.S. 106, 112 (1946). Although we are not presented with a new trial motion per se, we believe the likelihood of abuse is as great—or greater—here.

The affidavits filed in this habeas proceeding were given over eight years after petitioner's trial. No satisfactory explanation has been given as to why the affiants waited until the 11th hour—and, indeed, until after the alleged perpetrator of the murders himself was dead—to make their statements. Equally troubling, no explanation has been offered as to why petitioner, by hypothesis an innocent man, pleaded guilty to the murder of Rucker.

Moreover, the affidavits themselves contain inconsistencies, and therefore fail to provide a convincing account of what took place on the night Officers Rucker and Carrisalez were killed. For instance, the affidavit of Raul Jr., who was nine years old at the time, indicates that there were three people in the speeding car from which the murderer emerged, whereas Hector Villarreal attested that Raul Sr. told him that there were two people in the car that night. Of course, Hernandez testified at petitioner's trial that the murderer was the only occupant of the car. The affidavits also conflict as to the direction in which the vehicle was heading when the murders took place, and petitioner's whereabouts on the night of the killings.

Finally, the affidavits must be considered in light of the proof of petitioner's guilt at trial—proof which included two eyewitness identifications, numerous pieces of circumstantial evidence, and a handwritten letter in which petitioner apologized for killing the officers and offered to turn himself in under certain conditions. That proof, even when considered alongside petitioner's belated affidavits, points strongly to petitioner's guilt.

This is not to say that petitioner's affidavits are without probative value. Had this sort of testimony been offered at trial, it could have been weighed by the jury, along with the evidence offered by the state and petitioner, in deliberating upon its verdict. Since the statements in the affidavits contradict the evidence received at trial, the jury would have had to decide important issues of credibility. But coming 10 years after petitioner's trial, this showing of innocence falls far short of that which would have to be made in order to trigger the sort of constitutional claim which we have assumed, arguendo, to exist.

The judgment of the Court of Appeals is affirmed.

■ JUSTICE O'CONNOR, with whom JUSTICE KENNEDY joins, concurring.

I cannot disagree with the fundamental legal principle that executing the innocent is inconsistent with the Constitution. Regardless of the verbal formula employed—"contrary to contemporary standards of decency," "shocking to the conscience," or offensive to a "principle of justice so rooted in the traditions and conscience of our people as to be ranked as fundamental,"—the execution of a legally and factually innocent person would be a constitutionally intolerable event. Dispositive to this case, however, is an equally fundamental fact: Petitioner is not innocent, in any sense of the word.

As the Court explains, petitioner is not innocent in the eyes of the law because, in our system of justice, "the trial is the paramount event for determining the guilt or innocence of the defendant." In petitioner's case, that paramount event occurred 10 years ago. He was tried before a jury of his peers, with the full panoply of protections that our Constitution affords criminal defendants. At the conclusion of that trial, the jury found petitioner guilty beyond a reasonable doubt. Petitioner therefore does not appear before us as an innocent man on the verge of execution. He is instead a legally guilty one who, refusing to accept the jury's verdict, demands a hearing in which to have his culpability determined once again.

Consequently, the issue before us is not whether a state can execute the innocent. It is, as the Court notes, whether a fairly convicted and therefore legally guilty person is constitutionally entitled to yet another judicial proceeding in which to adjudicate his guilt anew, 10 years after conviction, notwithstanding his failure to demonstrate that constitutional error infected his trial. In most circumstances, that question would answer itself in the negative. Our society has a high degree of confidence in its criminal trials, in no small part because the Constitution offers unparalleled protections against convicting the innocent. The question similarly would be answered in the negative today, except for the disturbing nature of the claim before us. Petitioner contends not only that the Constitution's protections "sometimes fail," but that their failure in his case will result in his execution—even though he is factually innocent and has evidence to prove it.

Exercising restraint, the Court and Justice White assume for the sake of argument that, if a prisoner were to make an exceptionally strong showing of actual innocence, the execution could not go forward. Justice Blackmun, in contrast, would expressly so hold; he would also announce the precise burden of proof. . . Resolving the issue is neither necessary nor advisable in this case. The question is a sensitive and, to say the least, troubling one. It implicates not just the life of a single individual, but also the state's powerful and legitimate interest in punishing the guilty, and the nature of state-federal relations. Indeed, as the Court persuasively demonstrates, throughout our history the federal courts have assumed that they should not and could not intervene to prevent an execution so long as the prisoner had been convicted after a constitutionally adequate trial. The prisoner's sole remedy was a pardon or clemency.

Nonetheless, the proper disposition of this case is neither difficult nor troubling. No matter what the Court might say about claims of actual innocence today, petitioner could not obtain relief. The record overwhelmingly demonstrates that petitioner deliberately shot and killed Officers Rucker and Carrisalez the night of September 29, 1981; petitioner's new evidence is bereft of credibility. Indeed, despite its stinging criticism of the Court's decision, not even the dissent expresses a belief that petitioner might possibly be actually innocent. Nor could it: The record makes it abundantly clear that petitioner is . . . the established perpetrator of two brutal and tragic [murders]. . . .

* * *

Ultimately, two things about this case are clear. First is what the Court does not hold. Nowhere does the Court state that the Constitution permits the execution of an actually innocent person. Instead, the Court assumes for the sake of argument that a truly persuasive demonstration of actual innocence would render any such execution unconstitutional and that federal habeas relief would be warranted if no state avenue were open to process the claim. Second is what petitioner has not demonstrated. Petitioner has failed to make a persuasive showing of actual innocence. Not one judge—no state court judge, not the District Court Judge, none of the three Judges of the Court of Appeals, and none of the Justices of this Court—has expressed doubt about petitioner's guilt. Accordingly, the Court has no reason to pass on, and appropriately reserves, the question whether federal courts may entertain convincing claims of actual innocence. That difficult question remains open. If the Constitution's guarantees of fair procedure and the safeguards of clemency and pardon fulfill their historical mission, it may never require resolution at all.

■ JUSTICE SCALIA, with whom JUSTICE THOMAS joins, concurring.

We granted certiorari on the question whether it violates due process or constitutes cruel and unusual punishment for a state to execute a person who, having been convicted of murder after a full and fair trial, later alleges that newly discovered evidence shows him to be "actually innocent." I would have preferred to decide that question, particularly since, as the Court's discussion shows, it is perfectly clear what the answer is: There is no basis in text, tradition, or even in contemporary practice (if that were enough), for finding in the Constitution a right to demand judicial consideration of newly discovered evidence of innocence brought forward after conviction. In saying that such a right exists, the dissenters apply nothing but their personal opinions to invalidate the rules of more than two thirds of the states, and a Federal Rule of Criminal Procedure for which this Court itself is responsible. If the system that has been in place for 200 years (and remains widely approved) "shocks" the dissenters' consciences, perhaps they should doubt the calibration of their consciences, or, better still, the usefulness of "conscience-shocking" as a legal test.

I nonetheless join the entirety of the Court's opinion, including the final portion—because there is no legal error in deciding a case by assuming arguendo that an asserted constitutional right exists, and because I can understand, or at least am accustomed to, the reluctance of the present Court to admit publicly that Our Perfect Constitution* lets stand any injustice, much less the execution of an innocent man who has received, though to no avail, all the process that our society has traditionally deemed adequate. With any luck, we shall avoid ever having to face this embarrassing question again, since it is improbable that evidence of innocence as convincing as today's opinion requires would fail to produce an executive pardon.

My concern is that in making life easier for ourselves we not appear to make it harder for the lower federal courts, imposing upon them the burden of regularly analyzing newly-discovered-evidence-of-innocence claims in capital cases (in which event such federal claims, it can confidently be predicted, will become routine and even repetitive). A number of Courts of Appeals have hitherto held, largely in reliance on our unelaborated statement in Townsend v. Sain, 372 U.S. 293, 317 (1963), that newly discovered evidence relevant only to a state prisoner's guilt or innocence is not a basis for federal habeas corpus relief. I do not understand it to be the import of today's decision that those holdings are to be replaced with a strange regime that assumes permanently, though only "arguendo," that a constitutional right exists, and expends substantial judicial resources on that assumption. The Court's extensive and scholarly discussion of the question presented in the present case does nothing but support our statement in *Townsend*, and strengthen the validity of the holdings based upon it.

■ JUSTICE WHITE, concurring in the judgment.

In voting to affirm, I assume that a persuasive showing of "actual innocence" made after trial, even though made after the expiration of the time provided by law for the presentation of newly discovered evidence, would render unconstitutional the execution of petitioner in this case. To be entitled to relief, however, petitioner would at the very least be required to show that based on proffered newly discovered evidence and the entire record before the jury that convicted him, "no rational trier of fact could [find] proof of guilt beyond a reasonable doubt." Jackson v. Virginia, 443 U.S. 307, 324 (1979). For the reasons stated in the Court's opinion,

---

* My reference is to an article by Professor Monaghan, which discusses the unhappy truth that not every problem was meant to be solved by the United States Constitution, nor can be. See Henry P. Monaghan, Our Perfect Constitution, 56 N.Y.U. L. Rev. 353 (1981).

petitioner's showing falls far short of satisfying even that standard, and I therefore concur in the judgment.

■ JUSTICE BLACKMUN, with whom JUSTICE STEVENS and JUSTICE SOUTER join with respect to Parts I–IV, dissenting.

Nothing could be more contrary to contemporary standards of decency or more shocking to the conscience than to execute a person who is actually innocent.

I therefore must disagree with the long and general discussion that precedes the Court's disposition of this case. That discussion, of course, is dictum because the Court assumes, "for the sake of argument in deciding this case, that in a capital case a truly persuasive demonstration of 'actual innocence' made after trial would render the execution of a defendant unconstitutional." Without articulating the standard it is applying, however, the Court then decides that this petitioner has not made a sufficiently persuasive case. Because I believe that in the first instance the District Court should decide whether petitioner is entitled to a hearing and whether he is entitled to relief on the merits of his claim, I would reverse the order of the Court of Appeals and remand this case for further proceedings in the District Court.

I

. . . We . . . are being asked to decide whether the Constitution forbids the execution of a person who has been validly convicted and sentenced but who, nonetheless, can prove his innocence with newly discovered evidence. Despite the state of Texas's astonishing protestation to the contrary, I do not see how the answer can be anything but "yes."

A

The Eighth Amendment prohibits "cruel and unusual punishments." This proscription is not static but rather reflects evolving standards of decency. I think it is crystal clear that the execution of an innocent person is "at odds with contemporary standards of fairness and decency." Spaziano v. Florida, 468 U.S. 447, 465 (1984). Indeed, it is at odds with any standard of decency that I can imagine.

This Court has . . . held that death is an excessive punishment for rape, Coker v. Georgia, 433 U.S. 584 (1977), and for mere participation in a robbery during which a killing takes place. Enmund v. Florida, 458 U.S. 782 (1982). If it is violative of the Eighth Amendment to execute someone who is guilty of those crimes, then it plainly is violative of the Eighth Amendment to execute a person who is actually innocent. . . .

The Court . . . suggests that allowing petitioner to raise his claim of innocence would not serve society's interest in the reliable imposition of the death penalty because it might require a new trial that would be less accurate than the first. This suggestion misses the point entirely. The question is not whether a second trial would be more reliable than the first but whether, in light of new evidence, the result of the first trial is sufficiently reliable for the state to carry out a death sentence. Furthermore, it is far from clear that a state will seek to retry the rare prisoner who prevails on a claim of actual innocence. As explained in part III, infra, I believe a prisoner must show not just that there was probably a reasonable doubt about his guilt but that he is probably actually innocent. I find it difficult to believe that any state would chose to retry a person who meets this standard. [I believe] that petitioner may raise an Eighth Amendment challenge to his punishment on the ground that he is actually innocent. . . .

II

The majority's discussion of petitioner's constitutional claims is even more perverse when viewed in the light of this Court's recent habeas jurisprudence. Beginning with a trio of decisions in 1986, this Court shifted the focus of federal habeas review of successive, abusive, or defaulted claims away from the preservation of constitutional rights to a fact-based inquiry into the habeas petitioner's guilt or innocence. The Court sought to strike a balance between the state's interest in the finality of its criminal judgments and the prisoner's interest in access to a forum to test the basic justice of his sentence. In striking this balance, the Court adopted the view of Judge Friendly that there should be an exception to the concept of finality when a prisoner can make a colorable claim of actual innocence. Henry J. Friendly, Is Innocence Irrelevant? Collateral Attack on Criminal Judgments, 38 U. Chi. L. Rev. 142, 160 (1970). . . .

Having adopted an "actual innocence" requirement for review of abusive, successive, or defaulted claims, however, the majority would now take the position that "the claim of 'actual innocence' is not itself a constitutional claim, but instead a gateway through which a habeas petitioner must pass to have his otherwise barred constitutional claim considered on the merits." In other words, having held that a prisoner who is incarcerated in violation of the Constitution must show he is actually innocent to obtain relief, the majority would now hold that a prisoner who is actually innocent must show a constitutional violation to obtain relief. The only principle that would appear to reconcile these two positions is the principle that habeas relief should be denied whenever possible.

III

The Eighth and Fourteenth Amendments, of course, are binding on the states, and one would normally expect the states to adopt procedures to consider claims of actual innocence based on newly discovered evidence. The majority's disposition of this case, however, leaves the states uncertain of their constitutional obligations.

A

Whatever procedures a state might adopt to hear actual innocence claims, one thing is certain: The possibility of executive clemency is not sufficient to satisfy the requirements of the Eighth and Fourteenth

Amendments. . . . The vindication of rights guaranteed by the Constitution has never been made to turn on the unreviewable discretion of an executive official or administrative tribunal. . . .

B

Like other constitutional claims, Eighth and Fourteenth Amendment claims of actual innocence advanced on behalf of a state prisoner can and should be heard in state court. If a state provides a judicial procedure for raising such claims, the prisoner may be required to exhaust that procedure before taking his claim of actual innocence to federal court. Furthermore, state-court determinations of factual issues relating to the claim would be entitled to a presumption of correctness in any subsequent federal habeas proceeding.

Texas provides no judicial procedure for hearing petitioner's claim of actual innocence and his habeas petition was [therefore] properly filed in district court. . . . If, as is the case here, the petition raises factual questions and the state has failed to provide a full and fair hearing, the district court is required to hold an evidentiary hearing.

Because the present federal petition is petitioner's second, he must either show cause for and prejudice from failing to raise the claim in his first petition or show that he falls within the "actual-innocence" exception to the cause and prejudice requirement. McCleskey v. Zant, 499 U.S. 467, 494–95 (1991). If petitioner can show that he is entitled to relief on the merits of his actual-innocence claim, however, he certainly can show that he falls within the "actual-innocence" exception to the cause and prejudice requirement and *McCleskey* would not bar relief.

C

The question that remains is what showing should be required to obtain relief on the merits of an Eighth or Fourteenth Amendment claim of actual innocence. I agree with the majority that "in state criminal proceedings the trial is the paramount event for determining the guilt or innocence of the defendant." I also think that "a truly persuasive demonstration of 'actual innocence' made after trial would render the execution of a defendant unconstitutional." The question is what "a truly persuasive demonstration" entails, a question the majority's disposition of this case leaves open.

In articulating the "actual-innocence" exception in our habeas jurisprudence, this Court has adopted a standard requiring the petitioner to show a " 'fair probability that, in light of all the evidence . . . , the trier of facts would have entertained a reasonable doubt of his guilt.' " Kuhlmann v. Wilson, 477 U.S. 436, 455 n.17 (1986). In other words, the habeas petitioner must show that there probably would be a reasonable doubt. See also Murray v. Carrier, 477 U.S. 478, 496 (1986) (exception applies when a constitutional violation has "probably resulted" in a mistaken conviction); *McCleskey*, 499 U.S. at 494 (exception applies when a constitutional violation "probably has caused" a mistaken conviction).

I think the standard for relief on the merits of an actual-innocence claim must be higher than the threshold standard for merely reaching that claim or any other claim that has been procedurally defaulted or is successive or abusive. I would hold that, to obtain relief on a claim of actual innocence, the petitioner must show that he probably is innocent. This standard is supported by several considerations. First, new evidence of innocence may be discovered long after the defendant's conviction. Given the passage of time, it may be difficult for the state to retry a defendant who obtains relief from his conviction or sentence on an actual-innocence claim. The actual-innocence proceeding thus may constitute the final word on whether the defendant may be punished. In light of this fact, an otherwise constitutionally valid conviction or sentence should not be set aside lightly. Second, conviction after a constitutionally adequate trial strips the defendant of the presumption of innocence. The government bears the burden of proving the defendant's guilt beyond a reasonable doubt, but once the government has done so, the burden of proving innocence must shift to the convicted defendant. The actual-innocence inquiry is therefore distinguishable from review for sufficiency of the evidence, where the question is not whether the defendant is innocent but whether the government has met its constitutional burden of proving the defendant's guilt beyond a reasonable doubt. When a defendant seeks to challenge the determination of guilt after he has been validly convicted and sentenced, it is fair to place on him the burden of proving his innocence, not just raising doubt about his guilt.

In considering whether a prisoner is entitled to relief on an actual-innocence claim, a court should take all the evidence into account, giving due regard to its reliability. Because placing the burden on the prisoner to prove innocence creates a presumption that the conviction is valid, it is not necessary or appropriate to make further presumptions about the reliability of newly discovered evidence generally. Rather, the court charged with deciding such a claim should make a case-by-case determination about the reliability of the newly discovered evidence under the circumstances. The court then should weigh the evidence in favor of the prisoner against the evidence of his guilt. Obviously, the stronger the evidence of the prisoner's guilt, the more persuasive the newly discovered evidence of innocence must be. A prisoner raising an actual-innocence claim in a federal habeas petition is not entitled to discovery as a matter of right. The district court retains discretion to order discovery, however, when it would help the court make a reliable determination with respect to the prisoner's claim.

It should be clear that the standard I would adopt would not convert the federal courts into " 'forums in which to relitigate state trials.' " It would not "require the habeas court to hear testimony from the witnesses who testified at the trial," though, if the petition warrants a hearing, it may require the habeas court to hear the testimony of "those who made the statements in the affidavits which petitioner has presented." I believe that if a prisoner can show that he is probably actually innocent, in light of all the evidence, then he has made "a truly persuasive demonstration," and his execution would violate the Constitution. I would so hold.

IV

In this case, the District Court determined that petitioner's newly discovered evidence warranted further consideration. Because the District Court doubted its own authority to consider the new evidence, it thought that petitioner's claim of actual innocence should be brought in state court, but it clearly did not think that petitioner's evidence was so insubstantial that it could be dismissed without any hearing at all. I would reverse the order of the Court of Appeals and remand the case to the District Court to consider whether petitioner has shown, in light of all the evidence, that he is probably actually innocent. . . .

V

I have voiced disappointment over this Court's obvious eagerness to do away with any restriction on the states' power to execute whomever and however they please. I have also expressed doubts about whether, in the absence of such restrictions, capital punishment remains constitutional at all. Of one thing, however, I am certain. Just as an execution without adequate safeguards is unacceptable, so too is an execution when the condemned prisoner can prove that he is innocent. The execution of a person who can show that he is innocent comes perilously close to simple murder.

NOTES ON HERRERA V. COLLINS AND ACTUAL INNOCENCE

1. HOUSE V. BELL

One aspect of House v. Bell, 547 U.S. 518 (2006), is considered in Section 3 above. The issue considered there concerned application of the "actual innocence" justification for ignoring a procedural default under *Wainwright v. Sykes*. A majority of five Justices found that the habeas petitioner had made a sufficient showing of actual innocence to justify setting aside a state procedural default. But the Court unanimously rejected a free-standing actual innocence claim. Justice Kennedy said in this respect for the majority:

> In addition to his gateway claim under *Schlup,* House argues that he has shown freestanding innocence and that as a result his imprisonment and planned execution are unconstitutional. In *Herrera* . . . the Court assumed without deciding that "in a capital case a truly persuasive demonstration of 'actual innocence' made after trial would render the execution of a defendant unconstitutional, and warrant federal habeas relief if there were no state avenue open to process such a claim." "[T]he threshold showing for such an assumed right would necessarily be extraordinarily high," the Court explained. . . . House urges the Court to answer the question left open in *Herrera* and hold not only that freestanding innocence claims are possible but also that he has established one.

We decline to resolve this issue. We conclude here, much as in *Herrera,* that whatever burden a hypothetical freestanding innocence claim would require, this petitioner has not satisfied it. To be sure, House has cast considerable doubt on his guilt—doubt sufficient to satisfy *Schlup*'s gateway standard for obtaining federal review despite a state procedural default. [Taken together, however, *Herrera* and *Schlup* imply] that *Herrera* requires more convincing proof of innocence than *Schlup*. It follows, given the closeness of the *Schlup* question here, that House's showing falls short of the threshold implied in *Herrera*.

2. *BOUSLEY V. UNITED STATES*

Bousley was charged with two federal offenses—possession of methamphetamine with intent to distribute and "knowingly and intentionally [using] . . . firearms during and in relation to a drug trafficking crime" in violation of 18 U.S.C. § 924(c)(1). After pleading guilty to both charges, he was sentenced to over six years in prison. He appealed the sentence but did not challenge the validity of the plea. He later filed a habeas petition in federal court, which was treated as a motion under 28 U.S.C. § 2255. The court denied relief. While his appeal from this denial was pending, the Supreme Court held in Bailey v. United States, 516 U.S. 137 (1995), that a conviction for use of a firearm under § 924(c)(1) requires the government to show "active employment of the firearm" rather than mere possession. Bousley argued that his guilty plea was involuntary because he had been misinformed about the required elements for a violation of § 924(c)(1). The Court of Appeals nonetheless affirmed the dismissal of his § 2255 motion.

In Bousley v. United States, 523 U.S. 614 (1998), the Supreme Court reversed and remanded. In an opinion by Chief Justice Rehnquist, the Court first concluded that the case was not governed by the limitation on applying "new rules" in habeas proceedings set forth in *Teague v. Lane*. The Court explained that Bousley's constitutional claim was that his guilty plea was not knowing and intelligent, which the Court said did not involve a new rule. Moreover, the Court observed that *Teague* "by its terms applies only to procedural rules [and thus] is inapplicable to the situation in which this Court decides the meaning of a criminal statute enacted by Congress."

The Court held, however, that Bousley was required to meet the cause and prejudice standard for overcoming a procedural default, and it found that he had not met the cause requirement. The Court noted that, "at the time of petitioner's plea, the Federal Reporters were replete with cases involving challenges to the notion that 'use' is synonymous with mere 'possession.'" Nor was it an excuse that the courts in his case would have rejected the claim, because "futility cannot constitute cause if it means simply that a claim was 'unacceptable to that particular court at that particular time.'" Engle v. Isaac, 456 U.S. 107, 130 (1982).

Nevertheless, the Court remanded to allow Bousley an opportunity to meet the actual innocence exception, and the Court elaborated on what would be required:

It is important to note in this regard that "actual innocence" means factual innocence, not mere legal insufficiency. See Sawyer v. Whitley, 505 U.S. 333, 339 (1992). In other words, the government is not limited to the existing record to rebut any showing that petitioner might make. Rather, on remand, the government should be permitted to present any admissible evidence of petitioner's guilt even if that evidence was not presented during petitioner's plea colloquy and would not normally have been offered before our decision in *Bailey*. In cases where the government has forgone more serious charges in the course of plea bargaining, petitioner's showing of actual innocence must also extend to those charges.

In this case, the government maintains that petitioner must demonstrate that he is actually innocent of both "using" and "carrying" a firearm in violation of § 924(c)(1). But petitioner's indictment charged him only with "using" firearms in violation of § 924(c)(1). And there is no record evidence that the government elected not to charge petitioner with "carrying" a firearm in exchange for his plea of guilty. Accordingly, petitioner need demonstrate no more than that he did not "use" a firearm as that term is defined in *Bailey*.

If, on remand, petitioner can make that showing, he will then be entitled to have his defaulted claim of an unintelligent plea considered on its merits. The judgment of the Court of Appeals is therefore reversed, and the case is remanded for further proceedings consistent with this opinion.[a]

3.   *DRETKE V. HALEY*

Haley was arrested in Texas after stealing a calculator from a Wal-Mart and attempting to exchange it for other merchandise. Because he already had two prior theft convictions, this offense was classified as a "state jail felony" punishable by up to two years in prison. Haley was also charged as an habitual felony offender on the ground that he had two prior felony convictions, one for delivery of drugs and the other for robbery. The habitual offender law allowed for punishment by up to 20 years in prison. Haley was convicted of both the theft offense and as an habitual offender and was sentenced to over 16 years in prison.

Texas's habitual offender statute applies when a defendant is convicted of a felony and has "previously been finally convicted of two felonies, *and* the second previous felony conviction is for an offense that occurred subsequent to the first previous conviction having become final" (emphasis added). Neither the prosecution nor the defense noticed that the records of Haley's prior two felony convictions showed that he had committed the second felony three days *before* his first felony conviction had become final, which meant that he should not have been subject to the habitual offender statute. Haley raised

---

    a   Justice Stevens concurred in part, arguing that "the burden is on the Government to prove his unlawful use of a firearm" because, since his guilty plea "was constitutionally invalid" Bousley "remains presumptively innocent of [the] offense." Joined by Justice Thomas, Justice Scalia dissented.—[Footnote by eds.]

this issue for the first time in a state post-conviction proceeding, and the state courts held that it was procedurally defaulted because Haley had not raised it at trial or on direct appeal. A federal district court subsequently granted habeas relief based on the "actual innocence" exception to the "cause and prejudice" standard, and the court of appeals affirmed.

In Dretke v. Haley, 541 U.S. 386 (2004), the Supreme Court granted certiorari to decide whether the actual innocence exception extends to non-capital sentencing error. In an opinion by Justice O'Connor, the Court decided not to answer that question, holding instead that "a federal court faced with allegations of actual innocence, whether of the sentence or of the crime charged, must first address all nondefaulted claims for comparable relief and other grounds for cause to excuse the procedural default." Here, the Court reasoned, Haley had a viable ineffective assistance of counsel claim and "[s]uccess on the merits would give respondent all of the relief that he seeks—i.e., resentencing . . . [and] would also provide cause to excuse the procedural default of his sufficiency of the evidence claim."

In a dissent joined by Justices Kennedy and Souter, Justice Stevens argued that "[b]ecause, as all parties agree, there is no factual basis for respondent's conviction as an habitual offender, it follows inexorably that respondent has been denied due process of law." Furthermore, they contended, "because that constitutional error clearly and concededly resulted in the imposition of an unauthorized sentence, it also follows that respondent is a 'victim of a miscarriage of justice,' Wainwright v. Sykes, 433 U.S. 72, 91 (1977), entitled to immediate and unconditional release." "If there were some uncertainty about the merits of respondent's claim that he has been incarcerated unjustly," they conceded, "it might make sense to require him to pursue other avenues for comparable relief before deciding the claim." "But in this case," they argued, "it is universally acknowledged that respondent's incarceration is unauthorized. The miscarriage of justice is manifest."

4. BIBLIOGRAPHY

Herrera has provoked widespread treatment in the literature. For a representative sample, see Arleen Anderson, Responding to the Challenge of Actual Innocence Claims after *Herrera v. Collins*, 71 Temple L. Rev. 489 (1998) (proposing that it is "in the states' best interests to provide their own post-conviction procedures for reviewing claims of actual innocence"); Vivian Berger, *Herrera v. Collins*: The Gateway of Innocence for Death-Sentenced Prisoners Leads Nowhere, 35 William & Mary L. Rev. 943 (1994) (pointing out that Herrera was executed on May 12, 1993; the Court's decision was rendered on January 25); Roger Berkowitz, Error-Centricity, Habeas Corpus, and the Rule of Law as the Law of Rulings, 64 La. L. Rev. 477 (2004) ("this paper shows how the great writ of habeas corpus is in danger of losing its once mythical connection to justice"); David Dow, Jared Tyler, Frances Bourliot and Jennifer Jeans, Is It Constitutional to Execute Someone Who Is Innocent (And If It Isn't, How Can It Be Stopped Following *House v. Bell*)?, 42 Tulsa L. Rev. 277 (2006) (identifying questions that remain open after *House* and containing detailed appendices covering state habeas and clemency procedures); Barry Friedman, Failed Enterprise: The Supreme Court's

Habeas Reform, 83 Calif. L. Rev. 485 (1995) (*Herrera* "may epitomize all that has gone wrong with the Supreme Court's 'reform' efforts"); Lisa Griffin, The Correction of Wrongful Convictions: A Comparative Perspective, 16 Am. U. Int'l L. Rev. 1241 (2001) (comparing the English and American approaches to the resolution of post-conviction claims of innocence); Joseph L. Hoffmann and William J. Stuntz, Habeas after the Revolution, 1993 Sup. Ct. Rev. 65 (proposing a two-track system of habeas focusing on innocence and deterrence); Paige Kaneb, Innocence Presumed: A New Analysis of Innocence as a Constitutional Claim, 50 Cal. W. L. Rev. 171 (2014) ("Modern consensus and widely shared practice now demonstrate that innocence claims are entitled to the constitutional protections of the Eighth and the Fourteenth Amendments."); Charles I. Lugosi, Executing the Factually Innocent: The U.S. Constitution, Habeas Corpus, and the Death Penalty: Facing the Embarrassing Question at Last, 1 Stan. J. C.R. & C.L. 473 (2005); Emanuel Margolis, Habeas Corpus: The No-Longer Great Writ, 98 Dickinson L. Rev. 557 (1994); Todd E. Pettys, Killing Roger Coleman: Habeas, Finality, and the Innocence Gap, 48 Wm. & Mary L. Rev. 2313 (2007); Robert J. Smith, Recalibrating Constitutional Innocence Protection, 87 Wash. L. Rev. 139 (2012) (proposing different standards of proof for freestanding innocence claims, vacating a death sentence, and relief from procedural default); Jordan Steiker, Innocence and Federal Habeas, 41 U.C.L.A. L. Rev. 303 (1993) ("the Court should permit habeas petitioners to litigate bare-innocence claims when the state courts have not afforded such claims full and fair review," "whether or not they are of constitutional dimension."); J. Thomas Sullivan, "Reforming" Federal Habeas Corpus: The Cost to Federalism; The Burden for Defense Counsel; And the Loss of Innocence, 61 U.M.K.C. L. Rev. 291 (1992).

For different takes on the factual innocence question, see Brandon L. Garrett, Innocence, Harmless Error, and Federal Wrongful Conviction Law, 2005 Wis. L. Rev. 35 (exploring wrongful conviction suits under § 1983); D. Michael Risinger, Unsafe Verdicts: The Need for Reformed Standards for the Trial and Review of Factual Innocence Claims, 41 Hous. L. Rev. 1281 (2004) (proposing reforms in the trial and direct review process); Laura Denvir Stith, A Contrast of State and Federal Court Authority to Grant Habeas Relief, 38 Val. U. L. Rev. 421 (2004) (Missouri Supreme Court Judge exploring one state's decision to inquire more broadly into actual innocence claims in state habeas proceedings than federal habeas law would allow). For an analysis of avenues of state-court relief for post-conviction claims of innocence, see Daniel S. Medwed, Up the River without a Procedure: Innocent Prisoners and Newly Discovered Non-DNA Evidence in State Courts, 47 Ariz. L. Rev. 655 (2005). For discussion of a non-judicial approach to the assessment of post-conviction claims of innocence, see David Wolitz, Innocence Commissions and the Future of Post-Conviction Review, 52 Ariz. L. Rev. 1027 (2010).

SECTION 5. INTERSECTING ISSUES

SUBSECTION A. APPLICABILITY OF *TEAGUE* IN STATE COURTS

NOTES ON TEAGUE IN STATE COURTS

1. INTRODUCTION

Recall, as developed previously in this Chapter, that Teague v. Lane, 489 U.S. 288 (1989), held that "new" rules of constitutional law adopted (discovered?) by the Supreme Court should not be applied retroactively in federal post-conviction proceedings if the conviction had become final before the decision announcing the new rule. The default is non-retroactivity. There are two exceptions: for new "substantive" rules; and for new "watershed" rules of criminal procedure that affect the fundamental fairness and accuracy of the underlying conviction. Litigation over application of the first exception is active and controversial. New "substantive" rules continue to be announced. Litigation over application of the second exception is pretty much settled. There have been no new "watershed" rules of criminal procedure for some time.

Teague was developed in the context of federal habeas corpus for state prisoners. It also applies in § 2255 proceedings for federal prisoners. The first two cases discussed below involve the relevance of *Teague* to *state* post-conviction proceedings. Must the state courts follow *Teague*? Or are the states free to chart their own course? Subsection A concludes by considering application of the independence prong of the adequate-and-independent-state-ground doctrine in both state and federal post-conviction proceedings.

2. *DANFORTH V. MINNESOTA*

Obviously, a state court may *deny* state post-conviction relief where *Teague* requires that federal habeas relief be denied. The question whether a state may *grant* relief where *Teague* forecloses it arose in Danforth v. Minnesota, 552 U.S. 264 (2008).

Danforth had been convicted of first-degree sexual assault of a minor based in part on videotaped testimony from the victim. After his conviction became final, the Supreme Court decided in Crawford v. Washington, 541 U.S. 36 (2004), that the Confrontation Clause was violated by such a procedure. Danforth then sought post-conviction relief in the state courts, arguing both that *Crawford* was retroactive under *Teague* and that, even if it was not, the state courts should apply a broader retroactivity standard than that required by *Teague*. The state supreme court held, correctly as a later U.S. Supreme Court decision confirmed, that *Crawford* was not retroactive under *Teague* because it did not establish a "watershed" rule of criminal procedure. With respect to Danforth's second claim, the state court held that it was not "free to give a Supreme Court decision of federal constitutional criminal procedure broader retroactive application than that given by the Supreme

Court" and that it "cannot apply state retroactivity principles when determining the retroactivity of a new rule of federal constitutional criminal procedure if the Supreme Court has already provided relevant federal principles."

(i)   The Majority

In an opinion by Justice Stevens, the Supreme Court disagreed. *Teague*, it said, was about remedies, not rights:

> "Retroactivity" suggests that when we declare that a new constitutional rule of criminal procedure is "nonretroactive," we are implying that the right at issue was not in existence prior to the date the "new rule" was announced. But this is incorrect. . . . [T]he source of a "new rule" is the Constitution itself, not any judicial power to create new rules of law. Accordingly, the underlying right necessarily pre-exists our articulation of the new rule.[a] What we are actually determining when we assess the "retroactivity" of a new rule is . . . whether a violation of the right that occurred prior to the announcement of the new rule will entitle a criminal defendant to the relief sought. . . .

> [O]ur jurisprudence concerning the "retroactivity" of "new rules" of constitutional law is primarily concerned, not with the question whether a constitutional violation occurred, but with the availability or nonavailability of remedies. A decision by this Court that a new rule does not apply retroactively under *Teague* does not imply that there was no right and thus no violation of that right at the time of trial—only that no remedy will be provided in federal habeas courts. . . .

> States that give broader retroactive effect to this Court's new rules of criminal procedure do not do so by misconstruing the federal *Teague* standard. Rather, they have developed *state* law to govern retroactivity in state post-conviction proceedings. The issue in this case is whether there is a federal rule, either implicitly announced in *Teague*, or in some other source of federal law, that prohibits them from doing so.

---

[a]   At a later point in its opinion, the Court quoted Justice Scalia's support for this position in American Trucking Assns., Inc. v. Smith, 496 U.S. 167, 201 (1990) (Scalia, J., concurring in the judgment):

> [P]rospective decisionmaking is incompatible with the judicial role, which is to say what the law is, not to prescribe what [the law] shall be. The very framing of the issue . . .—whether [a decision] shall "apply" retroactively—presupposes a view of our decisions as *creating* the law, as opposed to *declaring* what the law already is. . . . To hold a governmental Act to be unconstitutional is not to announce that *we* forbid it, but that the *Constitution* forbids it; and when, as in this case, the constitutionality of a state statute is placed in issue, the question is not whether some decision of ours "applies" in the way that a law applies; the question is whether the Constitution, as interpreted in that decision, invalidates the statute. Since the Constitution does not change from year to year; since it does not conform to our decisions, but our decisions are supposed to conform to it; the notion that our interpretation of the Constitution in a particular decision could take prospective form does not make sense.—[Footnote by eds.]

The Court's answer was that no such federal rule exists. It accordingly remanded the case for further proceedings consistent with this conclusion.[b]

(ii) The Dissent

Joined by Justice Kennedy, Chief Justice Roberts dissented. "The majority's decision," the Chief Justice said, "is grounded on the erroneous view that retroactivity is a remedial question." Instead, he argued, the retroactivity decision under *Teague* defines the nature of the federal right itself. When the Court adopts a "new" rule of law in *Teague* terms, it replaces an old federal law with a new one.[c] From this perspective, once the Supreme Court holds that a new federal rule is not retroactive, final state court convictions should be judged against the old law that was in effect when the conviction occurred. The new decision establishes no federal right for the state (or federal) courts to enforce against previously final convictions because it applies only prospectively. This leaves the state courts in the following position:

> Our precedents made clear that States could give greater substantive protection under their own laws than was available under federal law, and could give whatever retroactive effect to *those* laws they wished. . . . States [can] apply their own retroactivity rules only to new substantive rights "under their own law," not to new federal rules announced by this Court. . . . A State alone may "evaluate, and weigh the importance of" finality interests when it decides which substantive rules of criminal procedure *state law* affords; it is quite a leap to hold, as the Court does, that they . . . can do so in the name of the Federal Constitution.

> . . . The relevant inquiry is not about remedy; it is about choice of law—new or old. There is no reason to believe, either legally or intuitively, that States should have any authority over this question when it comes to which *federal* constitutional rules of criminal procedure to apply. Indeed, when the question is what federal rule of decision from this Court should apply to a particular case, no Court but this one should have final say over the answer. . . . Retroactivity is a question of federal law, and our final authority to construe it cannot, at this point in the Nation's history, be reasonably doubted. . . .

---

[b] On remand, the Minnesota Supreme Court noted that it was free to adopt a more generous standard under state law, but concluded that "[w]e elect to retain *Teague*." Danforth v. State, 761 N.W.2d 493, 498 (Minn. 2009). Two Justices dissented, arguing in favor of an approach based on *Teague* but applied more generously, as had been adopted by the Nevada Supreme Court in Colwell v. State, 118 Nev. 807, 59 P.3d 463 (2002).

[c] As the Chief Justice put it:

> Suppose . . . that a defendant, whose conviction became final before we announced our decision in *Crawford* argues (correctly) on collateral review that he was convicted in violation of both *Crawford* and . . . the case that *Crawford* overruled. . . . [T]he "new" rule announced in *Crawford* would not apply retroactively to the defendant. But I take it to be uncontroversial that the defendant would nevertheless get the benefit of the "old" rule . . . even under the view that the rule not only is but always has been an incorrect reading of the Constitution. Thus, the question whether a particular federal rule will apply retroactively is, in a very real way, a choice between new and old law.

Lurking behind today's decision is of course the question of just how free state courts are to define the retroactivity of our decisions interpreting the Federal Constitution. I do not see any basis in the majority's logic for concluding that States are free to hold our decisions retroactive when we have held they are not, but not free to hold that they are not when we have held they are. Under the majority's reasoning, in either case the availability of relief in state court is a question for those courts to evaluate independently. The majority carefully reserves that question, confirming that the majority regards it as open.[d]

(iii) Questions and Comments

The disagreement between the majority and the dissent in *Danforth* is narrow, if not esoteric. Both the majority and the dissent would permit state courts to provide relief based on a federal decision establishing a new rule that is not retroactive under *Teague*, albeit under different theories. From the majority perspective, states may establish state *remedies* for non-retroactive federal rights. Under the dissent, states may not do this, but they may, using the merits of the new non-retroactive federal decision as a model if they wish, provide relief by establishing both the *right* and the *remedy* under state law. Is there a practical difference between these two positions? In either case, the state may deny relief if it wants to. And in either case it may grant relief by following or establishing the state law needed to do so. Should it matter which they do?[e]

Consider *Danforth* from another perspective. The Chief Justice speculates in the last paragraph quoted above that states may be free under the majority's reasoning to deny relief in situations where the Supreme Court has held that a new federal rule should be applied retroactively. Is he right? *Danforth* established that state courts are free to *grant* relief where *Teague* denies it. Should state courts be free to *deny* relief where *Teague* allows it? This was the issue in *Montgomery v. Louisiana*.

3.   *MONTGOMERY V. LOUISIANA*

The issue in *Montgomery* was whether Miller v. Alabama, 567 U.S. 460 (2012), should have been applied retroactively in a state post-conviction proceeding. The state court had declined to do so.

Miller barred a sentence of mandatory life without parole for juvenile offenders who had been convicted of a homicide offense. As a matter of federal law, deciding whether *Miller* applied retroactively required consideration of whether it was a "new" rule that fell within one of the *Teague* exceptions to non-retroactivity. That is one of the issues debated and decided in the opinion below. That aspect of the decision is discussed above in the Notes

---

[d]   The reservation referred to by the Chief Justice was contained in a footnote to the majority opinion reading: "We note at the outset that this case does not present the question[ ] whether States are required to apply 'watershed' rules in state post-conviction proceedings . . . . Accordingly, we express no opinion on [this issue]."—[Footnote by eds.]

[e]   For analysis of the effects of *Danforth* on decisions by state courts, see Jason Mazzone, Rights and Remedies in State Habeas Proceedings, 74 Alb. L. Rev. 1749 (2010–11).

following *Welch v. United States* in Subsection B of Section 3 of this Chapter. The Court held that *Miller* fit the "substantive" *Teague* exception and therefore was applicable retroactively.

A separate question was whether a state court is permitted to deny collateral relief in a case where a *Teague* exception to non-retroactivity applies. Must the state court grant relief if a federal habeas court would be required to do so under a proper application of *Teague*? This issue was resolved by the opinion reproduced below, but with a confusing lack of attention to prominent precedents.

The first question addressed by the Supreme Court in *Montgomery* was whether it had jurisdiction to review the state court decision. Conventional analysis would suggest that the answer to this question would depend on whether the state court denial of relief was based on the decision of a federal question, and if not whether the state court decision rested on an adequate and independent state ground. As addressed in Section 3 of Chapter I, the Supreme Court is said to lack jurisdiction to review a state court judgment if the decision below was based on a state-law ground that was adequate to support the judgment and independent of federal law. But, surprisingly, while the Court did identify a federal question that was erroneously resolved by the decision below, it did not address the very real possibility that the state court decision rested on an adequate and independent state ground.

There are two lines of established precedent that could have been cited in favor of Supreme Court jurisdiction in *Montgomery*, both of which were ignored. The first is based on Testa v. Katt, 330 U.S. 386 (1947). *Testa* held that a state court open to hearing analogous state-law claims cannot decline to hear a federal claim because of disagreement with federal policy. The Court had not previously applied *Testa* to state post-conviction remedies, and it did not explicitly do so in *Montgomery*. Yet it held that the state courts violated federal law when they refused to apply *Miller* retroactively. If *Testa*'s reasoning underlies the jurisdictional conclusion in *Montgomery*, the state's refusal to grant collateral relief would not rest on an "adequate" state ground because it violated federal law. This approach to the question of jurisdiction in *Montgomery* is discussed in the Notes following *Haywood v. Drown* in Section 2 of Chapter I.

A second line of analysis would look to Standard Oil of California v. Johnson, 316 U.S. 481 (1942), for guidance and hold that the state-law ground for decision was not "independent" because federal and state law were intertwined. The Louisiana state courts thought they were deciding *Montgomery* on state-law grounds, but advertently borrowed federal law in doing so. *Johnson* held that when state courts choose to incorporate federal law into state law, the Supreme Court may review the state court's application of federal precedent. This potential approach to the *Montgomery* jurisdictional issue is discussed in the Notes following *Standard Oil v. Johnson* in Section 3 of Chapter I. See also *Foster v. Chatman* which is excerpted in the Notes below following *Montgomery*.

Johnson might well have supported Supreme Court *jurisdiction* over the Louisiana Supreme Court decision, but it would not have supported the

Court's result. Under *Johnson*, when the Supreme Court reviews a federal issue incorporated into state law and finds that the state court misunderstood the federal issue, it clarifies the question of federal law and then remands to the state court for further proceedings. The Supreme Court's interpretation of federal law is given as guidance to a state court, which may or may not choose to accept it. As shown below, the *Montgomery* Court was far more coercive.

In the end, therefore, the Court's jurisdiction could have been supported on a *Testa* rationale or a *Johnson* rationale. The decision to address the merits could have been explained as a holding that the state court relied on a ground of decision that was not "adequate" because it violated federal law or that was not "independent" because it relied on an erroneous understanding of federal law.

But neither the Court nor the dissenters speak in these terms. This leaves two questions: What did the Justices think they were doing? What did they actually do?

Montgomery v. Louisiana
Supreme Court of the United States, 2016.
577 U.S. ___, 136 S.Ct. 718.

■ JUSTICE KENNEDY delivered the opinion of the Court.

This is another case in a series of decisions involving the sentencing of offenders who were juveniles when their crimes were committed. In Miller v. Alabama, 567 U.S. 460 (2012), the Court held that a juvenile convicted of a homicide offense could not be sentenced to life in prison without parole absent consideration of the juvenile's special circumstances in light of the principles and purposes of juvenile sentencing. In the wake of *Miller*, the question has arisen whether its holding is retroactive to juvenile offenders whose convictions and sentences were final when *Miller* was decided. Courts have reached different conclusions on this point. Certiorari was granted in this case to resolve the question.

I

Petitioner is Henry Montgomery. In 1963, Montgomery killed Charles Hurt, a deputy sheriff in East Baton Rouge, Louisiana. Montgomery was 17 years old at the time of the crime. He was convicted of murder and sentenced to death, but the Louisiana Supreme Court reversed his conviction after finding that public prejudice had prevented a fair trial.

Montgomery was retried. The jury returned a verdict of "guilty without capital punishment." Under Louisiana law, this verdict required the trial court to impose a sentence of life without parole. The sentence was automatic upon the jury's verdict, so Montgomery had no opportunity to present mitigation evidence to justify a less severe sentence. That evidence might have included Montgomery's young age at the time of the crime; expert testimony regarding his limited capacity for foresight, self-discipline, and judgment; and his potential for rehabilitation. Montgomery, now 69 years old, has spent almost his entire life in prison.

Almost 50 years after Montgomery was first taken into custody, this Court decided *Miller v. Alabama. Miller* held that mandatory life without parole for juvenile homicide offenders violates the Eighth Amendment's prohibition on "cruel and unusual punishments." . . . *Miller* required that sentencing courts consider a child's "diminished culpability and heightened capacity for change" before condemning him or her to die in prison. Although *Miller* did not foreclose a sentencer's ability to impose life without parole on a juvenile, the Court explained that a lifetime in prison is a disproportionate sentence for all but the rarest of children, those whose crimes reflect "irreparable corruption."

After this Court issued its decision in *Miller*, Montgomery sought collateral review of his mandatory life-without-parole sentence. . . . [Louisiana law] allows a prisoner to bring a collateral attack on his or her sentence by filing a motion to correct an illegal sentence. . . . In the ordinary course Louisiana courts will not consider a challenge to a disproportionate sentence on collateral review; rather, as a general matter, it appears that prisoners must raise Eighth Amendment sentencing challenges on direct review.

Louisiana's collateral review courts will, however, consider a motion to correct an illegal sentence based on a decision of this Court holding that the Eighth Amendment to the Federal Constitution prohibits a punishment for a type of crime or a class of offenders. When, for example, this Court held in Graham v. Florida, 560 U.S. 48 (2010), that the Eighth Amendment bars life-without-parole sentences for juvenile nonhomicide offenders, Louisiana courts heard *Graham* claims brought by prisoners whose sentences had long been final. Montgomery's motion argued that *Miller* rendered his mandatory life-without-parole sentence illegal.

The trial court denied Montgomery's motion on the ground that *Miller* is not retroactive on collateral review. Montgomery then filed an application for a supervisory writ. The Louisiana Supreme Court denied the application. The court relied on its earlier decision in State v. Tate, 130 So.3d 829 (2013), which held that *Miller* does not have retroactive effect in cases on state collateral review. . . .

This Court granted Montgomery's petition for certiorari. The petition presented the question "whether *Miller* adopts a new substantive rule that applies retroactively on collateral review to people condemned as juveniles to die in prison." In addition, the Court directed the parties to address the following question: "Do we have jurisdiction to decide whether the Supreme Court of Louisiana correctly refused to give retroactive effect in this case to our decision in *Miller*?"

II

The parties agree that the Court has jurisdiction to decide this case. To ensure this conclusion is correct, the Court appointed Richard D.

Bernstein as amicus curiae to brief and argue the position that the Court lacks jurisdiction. He has ably discharged his assigned responsibilities.

Amicus argues that a State is under no obligation to give a new rule of constitutional law retroactive effect in its own collateral review proceedings. As those proceedings are created by state law and under the State's plenary control, amicus contends, it is for state courts to define applicable principles of retroactivity. Under this view, the Louisiana Supreme Court's decision does not implicate a federal right; it only determines the scope of relief available in a particular type of state proceeding—a question of state law beyond this Court's power to review.

If, however, the Constitution establishes a rule and requires that the rule have retroactive application, then a state court's refusal to give the rule retroactive effect is reviewable by this Court. States may not disregard a controlling, constitutional command in their own courts. See Martin v. Hunter's Lessee, 14 U.S. (1 Wheat.) 304, 340–41, 344 (1816); see also Yates v. Aiken, 484 U.S. 211, 218 (1988) (when a State has not "placed any limit on the issues that it will entertain in collateral proceedings . . . it has a duty to grant the relief that federal law requires"). Amicus' argument therefore hinges on the premise that this Court's retroactivity precedents are not a constitutional mandate.

Justice O'Connor's plurality opinion in Teague v. Lane, 489 U.S. 288 (1989), set forth a framework for retroactivity in cases on federal collateral review. Under *Teague,* a new constitutional rule of criminal procedure does not apply, as a general matter, to convictions that were final when the new rule was announced. *Teague* recognized, however, two categories of rules that are not subject to its general retroactivity bar. First, courts must give retroactive effect to new substantive rules of constitutional law. Substantive rules include "rules forbidding criminal punishment of certain primary conduct," as well as "rules prohibiting a certain category of punishment for a class of defendants because of their status or offense." Penry v. Lynaugh, 492 U.S. 302, 330 (1989). . . . Second, courts must give retroactive effect to new " ' "watershed rules of criminal procedure" implicating the fundamental fairness and accuracy of the criminal proceeding.' " Id. at 352.

It is undisputed, then, that *Teague* requires the retroactive application of new substantive and watershed procedural rules in federal habeas proceedings. Amicus, however, contends that *Teague* was an interpretation of the federal habeas statute, not a constitutional command; and so, the argument proceeds, *Teague*'s retroactivity holding simply has no application in a State's own collateral review proceedings.

To support this claim, amicus points to language in *Teague* that characterized the Court's task as " 'defin[ing] the scope of the writ.' " 489 U.S. at 308 (quoting Kuhlmann v. Wilson, 477 U.S. 436, 447 (1986) (plurality opinion)). . . . In addition, amicus directs us to Danforth v. Minnesota, 552 U.S. 264 (2008), in which a majority of the Court held that *Teague* does not preclude state courts from giving retroactive effect to a broader set of new constitutional rules than *Teague* itself required. The *Danforth* majority concluded that *Teague*'s general rule of nonretroactivity for new constitutional rules of criminal procedure "was an exercise of this Court's power to interpret the federal habeas statute." 552 U.S. at 278. Since *Teague*'s retroactivity bar "limit[s] only the scope of *federal* habeas relief," the *Danforth* majority reasoned, States are free to make new procedural rules retroactive on state collateral review.

Amicus, however, reads too much into these statements. Neither *Teague* nor *Danforth* had reason to address whether States are required as a constitutional matter to give retroactive effect to new substantive or watershed procedural rules. *Teague* originated in a federal, not state, habeas proceeding; so it had no particular reason to discuss whether any part of its holding was required by the Constitution in addition to the federal habeas statute. And *Danforth* held only that *Teague*'s general rule of nonretroactivity was an interpretation of the federal habeas statute and does not prevent States from providing greater relief in their own collateral review courts. The *Danforth* majority limited its analysis to *Teague*'s general retroactivity bar, leaving open the question whether *Teague*'s two exceptions are binding on the States as a matter of constitutional law.

In this case, the Court must address part of the question left open in *Danforth*. The Court now holds that when a new substantive rule of constitutional law controls the outcome of a case, the Constitution requires state collateral review courts to give retroactive effect to that rule. *Teague*'s conclusion establishing the retroactivity of new substantive rules is best understood as resting upon constitutional premises. That constitutional command is, like all federal law, binding on state courts. This holding is limited to *Teague*'s first exception for substantive rules; the constitutional status of *Teague*'s exception for watershed rules of procedure need not be addressed here. . . .

Substantive rules . . . set forth categorical constitutional guarantees that place certain criminal laws and punishments altogether beyond the State's power to impose. It follows that when a State enforces a proscription or penalty barred by the Constitution, the resulting conviction or sentence is, by definition, unlawful. . . . [It would] have the automatic consequence of invalidating a defendant's conviction or sentence. . . . A conviction or sentence imposed in violation of a substantive rule is not just erroneous but contrary to law and, as a result, void. It follows, as a general principle, that a court has no authority to leave in place a conviction or sentence that violates a substantive rule, regardless of whether the conviction or sentence became final before the rule was announced.

[Our prior cases] do not directly control the question the Court now answers for the first time. These precedents did not involve a state court's post-conviction review of a conviction or sentence and so did not address whether the Constitution requires new substantive rules to have retroactive effect in cases on state collateral review. These decisions, however, have important bearing on the analysis necessary in this case.

In support of its holding that a conviction obtained under an unconstitutional law warrants habeas relief, the [Court in Ex parte Siebold, 100 U.S. 371, 376 (1880)] explained that "[a]n unconstitutional law is void, and is as no law." A penalty imposed pursuant to an unconstitutional law is no less void because the prisoner's sentence became final before the law was held unconstitutional. There is no grandfather clause that permits States to enforce punishments the Constitution forbids. To conclude otherwise would undercut the Constitution's substantive guarantees. . . .

If a State may not constitutionally insist that a prisoner remain in jail on federal habeas review, it may not constitutionally insist on the same result in its own post-conviction proceedings. Under the Supremacy Clause of the Constitution, state collateral review courts have no greater power than federal habeas courts to mandate that a prisoner continue to suffer punishment barred by the Constitution. If a state collateral proceeding is open to a claim controlled by federal law, the state court "has a duty to grant the relief that federal law requires." Yates v. Aiken, 484 U.S. 211, 218 (1988). Where state collateral review proceedings permit prisoners to challenge the lawfulness of their confinement, States cannot refuse to give retroactive effect to a substantive constitutional right that determines the outcome of that challenge. . . .

In adjudicating claims under its collateral review procedures a State may not deny a controlling right asserted under the Constitution, assuming the claim is properly presented in the case. Louisiana follows these basic Supremacy Clause principles in its post-conviction proceedings for challenging the legality of a sentence. The State's collateral review procedures are open to claims that a decision of this Court has rendered certain sentences illegal, as a substantive matter, under the Eighth Amendment. Montgomery alleges that *Miller* announced a substantive constitutional rule and that the Louisiana Supreme Court erred by failing to recognize its retroactive effect. This Court has jurisdiction to review that determination.

III

This leads to the question whether *Miller*'s prohibition on mandatory life without parole for juvenile offenders indeed did announce a new substantive rule that, under the Constitution, must be retroactive. . . . [This aspect of the Court's holding in *Montgomery* is considered in the Notes following *Welch v. United States* in Subsection B of Section 2 of this Chapter. The Court concluded:]

The Court now holds that *Miller* announced a substantive rule of constitutional law. . . . Giving *Miller* retroactive effect, moreover, does not require States to relitigate sentences, let alone convictions, in every case where a juvenile offender received mandatory life without parole. A State may remedy a *Miller* violation by permitting juvenile homicide offenders to be considered for parole, rather than by resentencing them. Allowing those offenders to be considered for parole ensures that juveniles whose crimes reflected only transient immaturity—and who have since matured—will not be forced to serve a disproportionate sentence in violation of the Eighth Amendment. . . .

* * *

Henry Montgomery has spent each day of the past 46 years knowing he was condemned to die in prison. Perhaps it can be established that, due to exceptional circumstances, this fate was a just and proportionate punishment for the crime he committed as a 17-year-old boy. In light of what this Court has said in *Roper, Graham,* and *Miller* about how children are constitutionally different from adults in their level of culpability, however, prisoners like Montgomery must be given the opportunity to show their crime did not reflect irreparable corruption; and, if it did not, their hope for some years of life outside prison walls must be restored.

The judgment of the Supreme Court of Louisiana is reversed, and the case is remanded for further proceedings not inconsistent with this opinion.

It is so ordered.

■ JUSTICE SCALIA, with whom JUSTICE THOMAS and JUSTICE ALITO join, dissenting.

The Court has no jurisdiction to decide this case, and the decision it arrives at is wrong. I respectfully dissent.

I.   Jurisdiction

Louisiana post-conviction courts willingly entertain Eighth Amendment claims but, with limited exceptions, apply the law as it existed when the state prisoner was convicted and sentenced. Shortly after this Court announced Teague v. Lane, 489 U.S. 288 (1989), the Louisiana Supreme Court adopted *Teague*'s framework to govern the provision of post-conviction remedies available to *state* prisoners in its *state* courts as a matter of *state* law. Taylor v. Whitley, 606 So.2d 1292 (La.1992). In doing so, the court stated that it was "not bound" to adopt that federal framework. One would think, then, that it is none of our business that a 69-year-old Louisiana prisoner's state-law motion to be resentenced according to Miller v. Alabama, 567 U.S. 460 (2012), a case announced almost half a century after his sentence was final, was met with a firm rejection on state-law grounds by the Louisiana Supreme Court. But a majority of this Court, eager to reach the merits of this case, resolves the question of our jurisdiction by deciding that the Constitution *requires* state post-conviction courts to adopt *Teague*'s exception for so-called "substantive" new rules and to provide state-law remedies for the violations of those rules to prisoners whose sentences long ago became final. This conscription into federal service of state post-conviction courts is nothing short of astonishing.

A

Teague announced that federal courts could not grant habeas corpus to overturn state convictions on the basis of a "new rule" of constitutional law—meaning one announced after the convictions became final—*unless* that new rule was a "substantive rule" or a "watershed rul[e] of criminal procedure." 489 U.S. at 311. The *Teague* prescription followed from Justice Harlan's view of the "retroactivity problem". . . .

The Court in the mid-20th century . . . vacated and remanded many cases in the wake of Gideon v. Wainwright, 372 U.S. 335 (1963). Justice Harlan called upon the Court to engage in "informed and deliberate consideration" of "whether the States are constitutionally required to apply [*Gideon's*] new rule retrospectively, which may well require the reopening of cases long since finally adjudicated in accordance with then applicable decisions of this Court." Pickelsimer v. Wainwright, 375 U.S. 2, 3 (1963) (Harlan, J., dissenting). The Court answered that call in Linkletter v. Walker, 381 U.S. 618 (1965). *Linkletter* began with the premise "that we are neither required to apply, nor prohibited from applying, a decision retrospectively" and went on to adopt an equitable rule-by-rule approach to retroactivity, considering "the prior history of the rule in question, its purpose and effect, and whether retrospective operation will further or retard its operation."

The *Linkletter* framework proved unworkable when the Court began applying the rule-by-rule approach not only to cases on collateral review but also to cases on direct review, rejecting any distinction "between convictions now final" and "convictions at various stages of trial and direct review." Stovall v. Denno, 388 U.S. 293, 300 (1967). It was this rejection that drew Justice Harlan's reproach in Desist v. United States, 394 U.S. 244, 256 (1969) (dissenting opinion), and later in Mackey v. United States, 401 U.S. 667, 675 (1971) (opinion dissenting in part). He urged that "all 'new' rules of constitutional law must, at a minimum, be applied to all those cases which are still subject to direct review by this Court at the time the 'new' decision is handed down." *Desist,* 394 U.S. at 258. "Simply fishing one case from the stream of appellate review, using it as a vehicle for pronouncing new constitutional standards, and then permitting a stream of similar cases subsequently to flow by unaffected by that new rule constitute an indefensible departure from th[e] model of judicial review." *Mackey,* 401 U.S. at 679.

The decision in Griffith v. Kentucky, 479 U.S. 314 (1987), heeded this constitutional concern. The Court jettisoned the *Linkletter* test for cases pending on direct review and adopted for them Justice Harlan's rule of redressability: "[F]ailure to apply a newly declared constitutional rule to criminal cases pending on direct review violates basic norms of *constitutional* adjudication." Id. at 322 (emphasis added). . . .

When *Teague* followed on *Griffith*'s heels two years later, the opinion contained no discussion of "basic norms of constitutional adjudication," nor any discussion of the obligations of state courts. Doing away with *Linkletter* for good, the Court adopted Justice Harlan's solution to "the retroactivity problem" for cases pending on collateral review—which he described not as a constitutional problem but as "a problem as to the *scope of the habeas writ*." *Mackey*, 401 U.S. at 684 (emphasis added). *Teague* held that federal habeas courts could no longer upset state-court convictions for violations of so-called "new rules," not yet announced when the conviction became final. But it allowed for the previously mentioned exceptions to this rule of nonredressability: substantive rules placing "certain kinds of primary, private individual conduct beyond the power of the criminal law-making authority to proscribe" and "watershed rules of criminal procedure." Then in Penry v. Lynaugh, 492 U.S. 302 (1989), the Court expanded this first exception for substantive rules to embrace new rules "prohibiting a certain category of punishment for a class of defendants because of their status or offense."

Neither *Teague* nor its exceptions are constitutionally compelled. Unlike today's majority, the *Teague*-era Court understood that cases on collateral review are fundamentally different from those pending on direct review because of "considerations of finality in the judicial process." Shea v. Louisiana, 470 U.S. 51, 59–60 (1985). That line of finality demarcating the constitutionally required rule in *Griffith* from the habeas rule in *Teague* supplies the answer to the not-so-difficult question whether a state post-conviction court must remedy the violation of a new substantive rule: No. A state court need only apply the law as it existed at the time a defendant's conviction and sentence became final. . . . Any relief a prisoner might receive in a state court after finality is a matter of grace, not constitutional prescription.

B

The majority can marshal no case support for its contrary position. It creates a constitutional rule where none had been before: "*Teague*'s conclusion establishing the retroactivity of new substantive rules is best understood as resting upon constitutional premises" binding in both federal and state courts. "Best understood." Because of what? Surely not because of its history and derivation.

Because of the Supremacy Clause, says the majority. But the Supremacy Clause cannot possibly answer the question before us here. It only elicits another question: What federal law is supreme? Old or new? . . . [W]e have clarified time and again—recently in Greene v. Fisher, 565 U.S. 34, 36–39 (2011)—that *federal* habeas courts are to review state-court decisions against the law and factual record that existed at the time the decisions were made. "Section 2254(d)(1) [of the federal habeas statute] refers, in the past tense, to a state-court adjudication that 'resulted in' a decision that was contrary to, or 'involved' an unreasonable application of, established law. This backward-looking language requires an examination of the state-court decision at the time it was made." *Cullen v. Pinholster,* 563 U.S. 170 (2011). How can it possibly be, then, that the Constitution requires a *state* court's review of its own convictions to be governed by "new rules" rather than (what suffices when federal courts review state courts) "old rules"? . . .

The majority's sorry acknowledgment that [the Court's prior cases] ". . . do not directly control the question the Court now answers for the first time," is not nearly enough of a disclaimer. It is not just that they "do not directly control," but that the dicta cherry picked from those cases are irrelevant; they addressed circumstances fundamentally different from those to which the majority now applies them. . . .

The majority's maxim that "state collateral review courts have no greater power than federal habeas courts to mandate that a prisoner continue to suffer punishment barred by the Constitution," begs the question rather than contributes to its solution. Until today, no federal court was *constitutionally obliged* to grant relief for the past violation of a newly announced substantive rule. Until today, it was Congress's prerogative to do away with *Teague*'s exceptions altogether. Indeed, we had left unresolved the question whether Congress had already done that when it amended a section of the habeas corpus statute to add backward-looking language governing the review of state-court decisions. See Antiterrorism and Effective Death Penalty Act of 1996, § 104, codified at 28 U.S.C. § 2254(d)(1); *Greene,* 565 U.S. at 39, n. A maxim shown to be more relevant to this case, by the analysis that the majority omitted, is this: The Supremacy Clause does not impose upon state courts a constitutional obligation it fails to impose upon federal courts.

C

All that remains to support the majority's conclusion is that all-purpose Latin canon: ipse dixit. The majority opines that because a substantive rule eliminates a State's power to proscribe certain conduct or impose a certain punishment, it has "the automatic consequence of invalidating a defendant's conviction or sentence." What provision of the Constitution could conceivably produce such a result? The Due Process Clause? It surely cannot be a denial of due process for a court to pronounce a final judgment which, though fully in accord with federal constitutional law at the time, fails to anticipate a change to be made by this Court half a century into the future. The Equal Protection Clause? Both statutory and (increasingly) constitutional laws change. If it were a denial of equal protection to hold an earlier defendant to a law more stringent than what exists today, it would also be a denial of equal protection to hold a later defendant to a law more stringent than what existed 50 years ago. No principle of equal protection requires the criminal law of all ages to be the same.

The majority grandly asserts that "[t]here is no grandfather clause that permits States to *enforce punishments the Constitution forbids*" (emphasis added). Of course the italicized phrase begs the question. There most certainly is a grandfather clause—one we have called *finality*—which says that the Constitution does not require States to revise punishments that were lawful when they were imposed. Once a conviction has become final, whether new rules or old ones will be applied to revisit the conviction is a matter entirely within the State's control; the Constitution has nothing to say about that choice. . . .

The majority's imposition of *Teague*'s first exception upon the States is all the worse because it does not adhere to that exception as initially conceived by Justice Harlan—an exception for rules that "place, as a matter of constitutional interpretation, certain kinds of primary, private individual *conduct* beyond the power of the criminal lawmaking authority to proscribe." *Mackey,* 401 U.S. at 692 (emphasis added). Rather, it endorses the exception as expanded by *Penry,* to include "rules prohibiting a certain category of punishment for a class of defendants because of their status or offense." 492 U.S. at 330. That expansion empowered and obligated federal (and after today state) habeas courts to invoke this Court's Eighth Amendment "evolving standards of decency" jurisprudence to upset punishments that were constitutional when imposed but are "cruel and unusual" in our newly enlightened society. The "evolving standards" test concedes that in 1969 the State had the power to punish Henry Montgomery as it did. Indeed, Montgomery could at that time have been sentenced to death by our yet unevolved society. Even 20 years later, this Court reaffirmed that the Constitution posed no bar to death sentences for juveniles. Stanford v. Kentucky, 492 U.S. 361 (1989). Not until our People's "standards of decency" evolved a mere 10 years ago—nearly 40 years after Montgomery's sentence was imposed—did this Court declare the death penalty unconstitutional for juveniles. Roper v. Simmons, 543 U.S. 551 (2005). Even then, the Court reassured States that "the punishment of life imprisonment without the possibility of parole is itself a severe sanction," implicitly still available for juveniles. And again five years ago this Court left in place this severe sanction for juvenile homicide offenders. Graham v. Florida, 560 U.S. 48, 69 (2010). So for the five decades Montgomery has spent in prison, not one of this Court's precedents called into question the legality of his sentence—until the People's "standards of decency," as perceived by five Justices, "evolved" yet again in *Miller*.

Teague's central purpose was to do away with the old regime's tendency to "*continually* force the States to marshal resources in order to keep in prison defendants whose trials and appeals conformed to then-existing constitutional standards." 489 U.S. at 310. Today's holding thwarts that purpose with a vengeance. . . .

II.   The Retroactivity of *Miller*

Having created jurisdiction by ripping *Teague*'s first exception from its moorings, converting an equitable rule governing federal habeas relief to a constitutional command governing state courts as well, the majority proceeds to the merits. And here it confronts a second obstacle to its de-sired outcome. *Miller*, the opinion it wishes to impose upon state post-conviction courts, simply does not decree what the first part of the ma-jority's opinion says *Teague*'s first exception requires to be given retroactive effect: a rule "set[ting] forth *categorical* constitutional guar-antees that place certain criminal laws and punishments *altogether* beyond the State's power to impose" (emphasis added). No problem. Hav-ing distorted *Teague,* the majority simply proceeds to rewrite *Miller.* . . .

On the issue of whether *Miller* rendered life-without-parole penal-ties unconstitutional, it is impossible to get past *Miller*'s unambiguous statement that "[o]ur decision does not categorically bar a penalty for a class of offenders" and "mandates only that a sentencer follow a certain process . . . before imposing a particular penalty." It is plain as day that the majority is not applying *Miller*, but rewriting it.

And the rewriting has consequences beyond merely making *Miller*'s procedural guarantee retroactive. If, indeed, a State is categorically pro-hibited from imposing life without parole on juvenile offenders whose crimes do not "reflect permanent incorrigibility," then even when the pro-cedures that *Miller* demands are provided the constitutional requirement is not necessarily satisfied. It remains available for the defendant sen-tenced to life without parole to argue that his crimes did not in fact "reflect permanent incorrigibility." . . .

How wonderful. Federal and (like it or not) state judges are hence-forth to resolve the knotty "legal" question: whether a 17-year-old who murdered an innocent sheriff's deputy half a century ago was at the time of his trial "incorrigible." Under *Miller*, bear in mind, the inquiry is whether the inmate was seen to be incorrigible when he was sentenced—not whether he has proven corrigible and so can safely be paroled today. What silliness. (And how impossible in practice.). . . .

But have no fear. The majority does not seriously expect state and federal collateral-review tribunals to engage in this silliness, probing the evidence of "incorrigibility" that existed decades ago when defendants were sentenced. What the majority expects (and intends) to happen is set forth in the following not-so-subtle invitation: "A State may remedy a *Miller* violation by permitting juvenile homicide offenders to be consid-ered for parole, rather than by resentencing them." Of course. This whole exercise, this whole distortion of *Miller*, is just a devious way of eliminat-ing life without parole for juvenile offenders. The Court might have done that expressly (as we know, the Court can decree *anything*), but that would have been something of an embarrassment. After all, one of the justifications the Court gave for decreeing an end to the death penalty for murders (no matter how many) committed by a juvenile was that life without parole was a severe enough punishment. See *Roper,* 543 U.S. at 572. How could the majority—in an opinion written by the very author of *Roper*—now say *that* punishment is *also* unconstitutional? The Court ex-pressly refused to say so in *Miller*. So the Court refuses again today, but merely makes imposition of that severe sanction a practical impossibility. And then, in Godfather fashion, the majority makes state legislatures an offer they can't refuse: Avoid all the utterly impossible nonsense we have prescribed by simply "permitting juvenile homicide offenders to be considered for parole." Mission accomplished.

■ JUSTICE THOMAS, dissenting. . . .

[T]he issue in this case is not whether prisoners who received mandatory life-without-parole sentences for crimes they committed decades ago as juveniles had an Eighth Amendment right not to receive such a sentence. Rather, the question is how, when, and in what forum that newfound right can be enforced.

The Court . . . says that state post-conviction and federal habeas courts are constitutionally required to supply a remedy because a sentence or conviction predicated upon an unconstitutional law is a legal nullity. But nothing in the Constitution's text or in our constitutional tradition provides such a right to a remedy on collateral review. . . .

No provision of the Constitution supports the Court's holding. The Court invokes only the Supremacy Clause, asserting that the Clause deprives state and federal post-conviction courts alike of power to leave an unconstitutional sentence in place. But that leaves the question of what provision of the Constitution supplies that underlying prohibition.

The Supremacy Clause does not do so. That Clause merely supplies a rule of decision: *If* a federal constitutional right exists, that right supersedes any contrary provisions of state law. . . . [T]he Supremacy Clause is no independent font of substantive rights.

Nor am I aware of any other provision in the Constitution that would support the Court's new constitutional right to retroactivity. Of the natural places to look—Article III, the Due Process Clauses of the Fifth and Fourteenth Amendments, and the Equal Protection Clause of the Fourteenth Amendment—none establishes a right to void an unconstitutional sentence that has long been final.

To begin, Article III does not contain the requirement that the Court announces today. . . . Article III . . . defines the scope of *federal* judicial power. It cannot compel *state* post-conviction courts to apply new substantive rules retroactively. . . .

The Court's holding also cannot be grounded in the Due Process Clause's prohibition on "depriv[ations] . . . of life, liberty, or property, without due process of law." . . . We have never understood due process to require further proceedings once a trial ends. The Clause "does not establish any right to an appeal . . . and certainly does not establish any right to collaterally attack a final judgment of conviction." United States v. MacCollom, 426 U.S. 317, 323 (1976) (plurality opinion); Pennsylvania v. Finley, 481 U.S. 551, 557 (1987) ("States have no obligation to provide [post-conviction] relief"). Because the Constitution does not require post-conviction remedies, it certainly does not require post-conviction courts to revisit every potential type of error

Nor can the Equal Protection Clause justify requiring courts on collateral review to apply new substantive rules retroactively. . . . The disparity the Court eliminates today—between prisoners whose cases were on direct review when this Court announced a new substantive constitutional rule, and those whose convictions had already become final—is one we have long considered rational. "[T]he notion that different standards should apply on direct and collateral review runs throughout our recent habeas jurisprudence." Wright v. West, 505 U.S. 277, 292 (1992). . . .

Today's decision repudiates established principles of finality. It finds no support in the Constitution's text, and cannot be reconciled with our Nation's tradition of considering the availability of post-conviction remedies a matter about which the Constitution has nothing to say. I respectfully dissent.

NOTES ON MONTGOMERY V. LOUISIANA

1. QUESTIONS AND COMMENTS ON MONTGOMERY

No one would disagree that state courts are bound by *Miller* in all prosecutions conducted after that decision. By compulsion of the Supremacy Clause, state courts are indisputably bound by the federal Constitution in applying their criminal laws. Whether state courts should be obligated to apply *Miller* retroactively in post-conviction proceedings, as *Montgomery* holds, presents a more difficult question.

The conventional wisdom is that states are not constitutionally required to provide any post-conviction review.[a] If that is true, the state's greater power to have no post-conviction process seemingly would entail the lesser power to have limited post-conviction review.[b] Does *Montgomery* reject the premise of this argument? Carlos M. Vázquez and Stephen I. Vladeck, The Constitutional Right to Collateral Post-Conviction Review, 103 Va. L. Rev.

---

[a] At least the Supreme Court has not previously recognized such an obligation. The issue arose in Case v. Nebraska, 381 U.S. 336 (1965), in the context of a federal constitutional challenge that could not have been raised at trial. After certiorari was granted and briefs on the merits were submitted, Nebraska enacted a post-conviction procedure and the Court remanded the case for consideration under the new procedure. It has had no occasion since then to address the issue because all states now have some form of post-conviction process.

Justice Alito reiterated the conventional wisdom in his separate opinion in Foster v. Chatman, 578 U.S. ___, ___,136 S.Ct. 1737, 1759 (2016), quoted in Note 2 below. See also Pennsylvania v. Finley, 481 U.S. 551, 557 (1987), where, speaking of post-conviction relief in a case involving the right to counsel, Chief Justice Rehnquist said in an opinion for the Court: "States have no obligation to provide this avenue of relief." For additional consideration of the issue, see Chapter VIII, Section 3, and in particular the note on *Jackson v. Denno*.

[b] "[I]n the post-conviction context, the greater power—to abolish the process—should include the lesser power to limit and restrict the grounds on which relief may be sought." Stephen R. McAllister, Federalism and Retroactivity in State Post-conviction Proceedings, 18 Green Bag 271, 278 (2015) (consideration of *Montgomery* issues while the case was pending).

905 (2017), argues exactly that. The authors read *Montgomery* as "recognizing, for the first time in the Court's history, that there are circumstances in which [post-conviction] review is constitutionally *required*." Specifically, they say that *Montgomery* inferred from *Teague v. Lane* a "mandatory *constitutional* obligation on state courts to give retroactive effect in collateral post-conviction proceedings to new substantive rules of constitutional law," a proposition they describe as "both novel and momentous."

What about the federal courts? According to Vázquez and Vladeck, they have a similar obligation for federal prisoners, who are ordinarily not subject to state habeas corpus.[c] And what about the various restrictions on federal habeas imposed by AEDPA, such as the one-year statute of limitations for habeas petitions and the strict restrictions on second or successive petitions? If, as *Montgomery* seems to say, there is a constitutional right to have new substantive rules of constitutional law applied in cases that become final, then restrictions in the federal statutes that undermine this obligation presumably must give way.

Is it plausible to think that the Court in *Montgomery* meant all this? If not, is there some other way to read the decision? One possibility is that the Court means to present states with an all-or-nothing choice. They are free not to permit post-conviction review. But if they do (and all states have some form of post-conviction review), they may not discriminate among federal claims. They may not pick and choose among the federal claims they elect to enforce.

The majority in *Montgomery* appears to embrace this conclusion:

> . . . [W]hen a new substantive rule of constitutional law controls the outcome of a case, the Constitution requires state collateral review courts to give retroactive effect to that rule.

> . . . If a state collateral proceeding is open to a claim controlled by federal law, the state court "has a duty to grant the relief that federal law requires." . . . Where state collateral review proceedings permit prisoners to challenge the lawfulness of their confinement, States cannot refuse to give retroactive effect to a substantive constitutional right that determines the outcome of that challenge. . . .

> In adjudicating claims under its collateral review procedures a State may not deny a controlling right asserted under the Constitution, assuming the claim is properly presented in the case.

This reasoning might be based on the *Testa v. Katt* line of decisions, which as noted was not mentioned in *Montgomery*. But it is not obvious how *Testa* should apply to post-conviction review. If a state generally allows post-conviction review of some but not all federal constitutional claims, is it improperly discriminating against the excluded claims? Would an anti-discrimination rationale for *Montgomery* apply to all claims that might warrant relief in a federal habeas proceeding or only those that involve a retroactively applicable "substantive constitutional right"?

---

c   See Tarble's Case, 80 U.S. (13 Wall.) 397 (1872).

At the end of the day, what is the majority's underlying rationale? Is it begging the question, as Justice Scalia contends? Of what relevance is the fact that federal habeas is available for valid claims not enforced on collateral review by the state courts?[d]

2.   INDEPENDENCE OF PROCEDURAL GROUND: *FOSTER V. CHATMAN*

The Supreme Court does not have jurisdiction to review a state court decision if the disposition below rested on a state-law ground that was adequate (i.e., did not violate federal law) and independent (i.e., was not intertwined with federal law). The "independence" prong of this doctrine can present issues analogous to those involved in *Montgomery*. Foster v. Chatman, 578 U.S. ___, 136 S.Ct. 1737 (2016), provides an example.

Foster was convicted of capital murder and sentenced to death. His pretrial claim that the state's peremptory challenges were racially motivated in violation of Batson v. Kentucky, 476 U.S. 79 (1986), was rejected by the trial court and, on direct appeal, by the Georgia Supreme Court. He renewed his *Batson* claim in a state habeas corpus proceeding. While the habeas proceeding was pending, he gained access to the state's trial file. Its content, he claimed, constituted newly discovered evidence that confirmed the presence of racial bias. The state habeas court considered the new evidence, but denied relief. The Georgia Supreme Court summarily affirmed, and the U.S. Supreme Court granted certiorari.

The Court began by addressing its jurisdiction. The state habeas court denied the *Batson* claim based on Georgia res judicata principles because it had been resolved against Foster at trial and on direct review. But it nonetheless examined the claim to see whether it triggered an exception. This examination led the Supreme Court to conclude that it had jurisdiction:

> To determine whether Foster had alleged a sufficient "change in the facts," the habeas court engaged in four pages of what it termed a "*Batson* . . . analysis," in which it evaluated the original trial record and habeas record, including the newly uncovered prosecution file. Ultimately, that court concluded that Foster's "renewed *Batson* claim is *without merit.*"

> In light of the foregoing, it is apparent that the state habeas court's application of res judicata to Foster's *Batson* claim was not independent of the merits of his federal constitutional challenge. That court's invocation of res judicata therefore poses no impediment to our review of Foster's *Batson* claim.

The Court then upheld the claim on the merits, and made its traditional disposition: "The order of the Georgia Supreme Court is reversed, and the case is remanded for further proceedings not inconsistent with this opinion."

---

[d]   On remand, the Supreme Court of Louisiana sent the case back to the trial court for resentencing. State v. Montgomery, 194 So.3d 606 (2016). The trial court was directed to "determine whether relator was 'the rare juvenile offender whose crime reflects irreparable corruption' " as required by *Miller* or whether "he will be eligible for parole under the conditions established" by Louisiana law.

Chief Justice Roberts wrote the Court's opinion over a sole dissent by Justice Thomas.[e] Justice Alito concurred in the judgment, writing separately "to explain my understanding of the role of state law in the proceedings that must be held on remand." He elaborated:

> States are under no obligation to permit collateral attacks on convictions that have become final, and if they allow such attacks, they are free to limit the circumstances in which claims may be relitigated.
>
> To the extent that the decision of the Georgia Supreme Court was based on a state rule restricting the relitigation of previously rejected claims, the decision has a state-law component, and we have no jurisdiction to review a state court's decision on a question of state law. . . . [But] I agree that we cannot conclude from the brief order issued by the Supreme Court of Georgia that its decision was based wholly on state law. It is entirely possible that the State Supreme Court reached a conclusion about the effect of the state res judicata bar based in part on an assessment of the strength of Foster's *Batson* claim or the extent to which the new evidence bolstered that claim. And if that is what the State Supreme Court held, the rule that the court applied was an amalgam of state and federal law. . . .
>
> Our cases chart the path that we must follow in a situation like the one present here. When "a state court's interpretation of state law has been influenced by an accompanying interpretation of federal law," the proper course is for this Court to "revie[w] the federal question on which the state-law determination appears to have been premised. If the state court has proceeded on an incorrect perception of federal law, it has been this Court's practice to vacate the judgment of the state court and remand the case so that the court may reconsider the state-law question free of misapprehensions about the scope of federal law." Three Affiliated Tribes of Fort Berthold Reservation v. Wold Engineering, P.C., 467 U.S. 138, 152 (1984). In a situation like the one presented here, the correct approach is for us to decide the question of federal law and then to remand the case to the state court so that it can reassess its decision on the state-law question in light of our decision on the underlying federal issue.

Alito added in a footnote that the Court's opinion "does not preclude consideration of state law issues on remand." Is this what the Court should have done in *Montgomery*?

---

[e] Justice Thomas disagreed on the merits of the *Batson* claim. As to jurisdiction, he argued that this was a situation where the Court should have followed the option permitted by Michigan v. Long, 463 U.S. 1032 (1983), of vacating the Georgia Supreme Court's ruling and seeking clarification of its rationale. That court had affirmed the trial court's habeas decision in a one-line order without explanation.

3.   PROCEDURAL FORECLOSURE HYPOTHETICAL

A more difficult problem—perhaps a sinkhole—is posed by a variation of the *Foster v. Chatman* situation. Suppose the Supreme Court denied certiorari and Foster then filed a federal habeas petition raising his *Batson* issue. How should the lack of independence of the state ground be handled?

One response might be to accept that the state disposition was based on a procedural foreclosure and apply the *Wainwright v. Sykes* inquiries. Relief on the *Batson* claim could then be granted if the habeas petitioner could show cause and prejudice or a miscarriage of justice.

But the habeas petitioner could respond that the *Wainwright v. Sykes* hurdles are only applicable if there was a state-law based procedural foreclosure to begin with. Here there was no legitimate procedural foreclosure because the state decision was not based on an adequate and *independent* state ground. The habeas court would have jurisdiction to hear the *Batson* claim, the argument would conclude, for the same reason the Supreme Court did in the actual case. The lack of independence of the state ground would deprive the procedural foreclosure of its preclusive force on habeas just as it did in the actual case on direct review.

If this analysis is right, to what disposition would it lead? Would it be proper for the habeas court to ignore *Wainwright v. Sykes*, resolve the *Batson* claim on the merits, and, if the claim was valid, order the petitioner released or retried?

Perhaps not. In *Foster* itself the Court remanded to allow the state court to adjust its state law, if it chose to do so, in light of the Court's correction of its mistake as to the applicable federal law. Could a federal habeas court shape an analogous remedy? Should it? Must it?

One possibility is that the federal court could hold the case in abeyance while the petitioner returned to state court. This would give the state courts the opportunity to reassess their state-law res judicata holding in light of the federal district court's *Batson* analysis.

If this route were to be followed, by what standard should the federal habeas court measure the asserted *Batson* error? The state courts relied on their view of the *Batson* case law in reaching their decision. Must the federal habeas court review this decision by applying the "contrary to, or involved an unreasonable application of, clearly established Federal law, as determined by the Supreme Court of the United States" language of AEDPA § 2254(d)(1)? Or would it be free to resolve the *Batson* issues de novo and provide the state courts with its best judgment as to the applicable federal law that the state courts could then use in determining the meaning of state res judicata law?

If the state courts stuck to their guns and again enforced a procedural foreclosure based on state law, the foreclosure would at this point be supported by an independent state ground and the federal habeas court could move to the *Wainwright v. Sykes* inquiries and provide or deny relief accordingly.

But wait a minute. Since the *Batson* claim was based in part on after-discovered evidence, a state holding that denied any effect to such evidence could be interpreted as failing to provide a corrective process for a constitutional error. That in turn might make the state ground *inadequate*. If a habeas petitioner has no state forum in which to present a federal claim, a federal habeas court—going all the way back to Frank v. Magnum, 237 U.S. 309 (1915)—may then be obligated to provide a forum for its determination. Or, perhaps, the failure of the state to provide a corrective process should be assessed against the "cause" prong of the *Wainwright* inquiry.

And those who wish to seek post-conviction relief must figure all this stuff out without a right to counsel.

SUBSECTION B. RELATION OF § 1983 TO HABEAS CORPUS

INTRODUCTORY NOTE ON THE RELATION OF § 1983 TO HABEAS CORPUS

The Civil Rights Act of 1871 provides, in its current form, that:

> Every person who, under color of any statute, ordinance, regulation, custom, or usage, of any State or Territory or the District of Columbia, subjects, or causes to be subjected, any citizen of the United States or other person within the jurisdiction thereof to the deprivation of any rights, privileges, or immunities secured by the Constitution and laws, shall be liable to the party injured in an action at law, suit in equity, or other proper proceeding for redress
> . . . .

42 U.S.C. § 1983. There is, as the following case illustrates, a tension between the literal text of this statute and the restrictions applicable to federal habeas corpus for state prisoners.

Preiser v. Rodriguez
Supreme Court of the United States, 1973.
411 U.S. 475.

■ MR. JUSTICE STEWART delivered the opinion of the Court.

The respondents in this case were state prisoners who were deprived of good-conduct-time credits by the New York State Department of Correctional Services as a result of disciplinary proceedings. They then brought actions in a federal district court, pursuant to the Civil Rights Act of 1871, 42 U.S.C. § 1983. Alleging that the department had acted unconstitutionally in depriving them of the credits, they sought injunctive relief to compel restoration of the credits, which in each case would result in their immediate release from confinement in prison. [The District Court granted the requested relief, the Court of Appeals affirmed, and the Supreme Court granted certiorari.] The question before us is whether state prisoners seeking such redress may obtain equitable relief under the Civil Rights Act, even though the federal habeas corpus statute, 28 U.S.C. § 2254, clearly provides a specific federal remedy.

The question is of considerable practical importance. For if a remedy under the Civil Rights Act is available, a plaintiff need not first seek redress in a state forum. If, on the other hand, habeas corpus is the exclusive federal remedy in these circumstances, then a plaintiff cannot seek the intervention of a federal court until he has first sought and been denied relief in the state courts, if a state remedy is available and adequate. . . .

It is clear . . . that the essence of habeas corpus is an attack by a person in custody upon the legality of that custody, and that the traditional function of the writ is to secure release from illegal custody. . . . In the case before us, the respondents' suits in the District Court fell squarely within this traditional scope of habeas corpus. They alleged that the deprivation of their good-conduct-time credits was causing or would cause them to be in illegal physical confinement, i.e., that once their conditional-release date had passed, any further detention of them in prison was unlawful; and they sought restoration of those good-time credits, which, by the time the District Court ruled on their petitions, meant their immediate release from physical custody.

Even if the restoration of the respondents' credits would not have resulted in their immediate release, but only in shortening in length of their actual confinement in prison, habeas corpus would have been their appropriate remedy. For recent cases have established that habeas corpus relief is not limited to immediate release from illegal custody, but that the writ is available as well to attack future confinement and obtain future releases. . . . So, even if restoration of respondents' good-time credits had merely shortened the length of their confinement, rather than required immediate discharge from that confinement, their suits would still have been within the core of habeas corpus in attacking the very duration of their physical confinement itself. It is beyond doubt, then, that the respondents could have sought and obtained fully effective relief through federal habeas corpus proceedings.

Although conceding that they could have proceeded by way of habeas corpus, the respondents argue that the Court of Appeals was correct in holding that they were nonetheless entitled to bring their suits under § 1983 so as to avoid the necessity of first seeking relief in a state forum. Pointing to the broad language of § 1983, they argue that since their complaints plainly came within the literal terms of that statute, there is no justifiable reason to exclude them from the broad remedial protection provided by that law. According to the respondents, state prisoners seeking relief under the Civil Rights Act should be treated no differently from any other civil rights plaintiffs, when the language of the act clearly covers their causes of action.

The broad language of § 1983, however, is not conclusive of the issue before us. The statute is a general one, and, despite the literal applicability of its terms, the question remains whether the specific federal habeas corpus statute, explicitly and historically designed to provide the means for a state prisoner to attack the validity of his confinement, must be understood to be the exclusive remedy available in a situation like this where it so clearly applies. The respondents' counsel acknowledged at oral argument that a state prisoner challenging his underlying conviction and sentence on federal constitutional grounds in a federal court is limited to habeas corpus. It was conceded that he cannot bring a § 1983 action, even though the literal terms of § 1983 might seem to cover such a challenge, because Congress has passed a more specific act to cover that situation, and, in doing so, has provided that a state prisoner challenging his conviction must first seek relief in a state forum, if a state remedy is available. It is clear to us that the result must be the same in the case of a state prisoner's challenge to the fact or duration of his confinement, based, as here, upon the alleged unconstitutionality of state administrative action. Such a challenge is just as close to the core of habeas corpus as an attack on the prisoner's conviction, for it goes directly to the constitutionality of his physical confinement itself and seeks either immediate release from that confinement or the shortening of its duration.

In amending the habeas corpus laws in 1948, Congress clearly required exhaustion of adequate state remedies as a condition precedent to the invocation of federal judicial relief under those laws. It would wholly frustrate explicit congressional intent to hold that the respondents in the present case could evade this requirement by the simple expedient of putting a different label on their pleadings. In short, Congress has determined that habeas corpus is the appropriate remedy for state prisoners attacking the validity of the fact or length of their confinement, and that specific determination must override the general terms of § 1983.

The policy reasons underlying the habeas corpus statute support this conclusion. The respondents concede that the reason why only habeas corpus can be used to challenge a state prisoner's underlying conviction is the strong policy requiring exhaustion of state remedies in that situation—to avoid the unnecessary friction between the federal and state court systems that would result if a lower federal court upset a state court conviction without first giving the state court system an opportunity to correct its own constitutional errors. But they argue that this concern applies only to federal interference with state court convictions . . . .

In the respondents' view, the whole purpose of the exhaustion requirement, now codified in § 2254(b), is to give state *courts* the first chance at remedying *their own* mistakes, and thereby to avoid "the unseemly spectacle of federal district courts trying the regularity of proceedings had in *courts* of coordinate jurisdiction." This policy, the respondents contend, does not apply when the challenge is not to the action of a state court, but, as here, to the action of a state administrative body.

In that situation, they say, the concern with avoiding unnecessary interference by one court with the courts of another sovereignty with concurrent powers, and the importance of giving state courts the first opportunity to correct constitutional errors made by them, do not apply; and hence the purpose of the exhaustion requirement of the habeas corpus statute is inapplicable.

We cannot agree. The respondents, we think, view the reasons for the exhaustion requirement of § 2254(b) far too narrowly. The rule of exhaustion in federal habeas corpus actions is rooted in considerations of federal-state comity. That principle was defined in Younger v. Harris, 401 U.S. 37, 44 (1971), as "a proper respect for state functions," and it has as much relevance in areas of particular state administrative concern as it does where state judicial action is being attacked. . . .

It is difficult to imagine an activity in which a state has a stronger interest, or one that is more intricately bound up with state laws, regulations, and procedures, than the administration of its prisoners. The relationship of state prisoners and the state officers who supervise their confinement is far more intimate than that of a state and a private citizen. For state prisoners, eating, sleeping, dressing, washing, working, and playing are all done under the watchful eye of the state, and so the possibilities for litigation under the Fourteenth amendment are boundless. What for a private citizen would be a dispute with his landlord, with his employer, with his tailor, with his neighbor, or with his banker becomes, for the prisoner, a dispute with the state. Since these internal problems of state prisons involve issues so peculiarly within state authority and expertise, the states have an important interest in not being bypassed in the correction of these problems. Moreover, because most potential litigation involving state prisoners arises on a day-to-day basis, it is most efficiently and properly handled by the state administrative bodies and state courts, which are, for the most part, familiar with the grievances of state prisoners and in a better physical and practical position to deal with those grievances. In New York, for example, state judges sit on a regular basis at all but one of the state's correctional facilities, and thus inmates may present their grievances to a court at the place of their confinement, where the relevant records are available and where potential witnesses are located. The strong considerations of comity that require giving a state court system that has convicted a defendant the first opportunity to correct its own errors thus also require giving the states the first opportunity to correct the errors made in the internal administration of their prisons.[10]

---

[10] The dissent argues that the respondents' attacks on the actions of the prison administration here are no different, in terms of the potential for exacerbating federal-state relations, from the attacks made by the petitioners in McNeese v. Board of Education, 373 U.S. 668 (1963), Damico v. California, 389 U.S. 416 (1967), and Monroe v. Pape, 365 U.S. 167 (1961), on the various state administrative actions there. Thus, it is said, since exhaustion of state remedies was not required in those cases, it is anomalous to require it here. The answer, of course, is that in those cases, brought pursuant to § 1983, no other, more specific federal statute was involved that might have reflected a different congressional intent. In the present case, however, the

[T]he respondents contend that confining state prisoners to federal habeas corpus, after first exhausting state remedies, could deprive those prisoners of any damages remedy to which they might be entitled for their mistreatment, since damages are not available in federal habeas corpus proceedings, and New York provides no damages remedy at all for state prisoners. In the respondents' view, if habeas corpus is the exclusive federal remedy for a state prisoner attacking his confinement, damages might never be obtained, at least where the state makes no provision for them. They argue that even if such a prisoner were to bring a subsequent federal civil rights action for damages, that action could be barred by principles of res judicata where the state courts had previously made an adverse determination of his underlying claim, even though a federal habeas court had later granted him relief on habeas corpus.

The answer to this contention is that the respondents here sought no damages, but only equitable relief—restoration of their good-time credits—and our holding today is limited to that situation. If a state prisoner is seeking damages, he is attacking something other than the fact or length of his confinement, and he is seeking something other than immediate or more speedy release—the traditional purpose of habeas corpus. In the case of a damages claim, habeas corpus is *not* an appropriate or available federal remedy. Accordingly, as petitioners themselves concede, a damages action by a state prisoner could be brought under the Civil Rights Act in federal court without any requirement of prior exhaustion of state remedies. . . .

Principles of res judicata are, of course, not wholly applicable to habeas corpus proceedings. Hence, a state prisoner in the respondents' situation who has been denied relief in the state courts is not precluded from seeking habeas relief on the same claims in federal court. On the other hand, res judicata has been held to be fully applicable to a civil rights action brought under § 1983. Accordingly, there would be an inevitable incentive for a state prisoner to proceed at once in federal court by way of a civil rights action, lest he lose his right to do so. This would have the unfortunate dual effect of denying the state prison administration and the state courts the opportunity to correct the errors committed in the state's own prisons, and of isolating those bodies from an understanding of and hospitality to the federal claims of state prisoners in situations such as those before us. Federal habeas corpus, on the other hand, serves the important function of allowing the state to deal with these peculiarly local problems on its own, while preserving for the state prisoner an expeditious federal forum for the vindication of his federally protected rights, if the state has denied redress.

The respondents place a great deal of reliance on our recent decisions upholding the right of state prisoners to bring federal civil rights actions

---

respondents' actions fell squarely within the traditional purpose of federal habeas corpus, and Congress has made the specific determination in § 2254(b) that requiring the exhaustion of adequate state remedies in such cases will best serve the policies of federalism.

to challenge the conditions of their confinement. Cooper v. Pate, 378 U.S. 546 (1964); Houghton v. Shafer, 392 U.S. 639 (1968); Wilwording v. Swenson, 404 U.S. 249 (1971); Haines v. Kerner, 404 U.S. 519 (1972). But none of the state prisoners in those cases was challenging the fact or duration of his physical confinement itself, and none was seeking immediate release or a speedier release from that confinement—the heart of habeas corpus. In *Cooper,* the prisoner alleged that, solely because of his religious beliefs, he had been denied permission to purchase certain religious publications and had been denied other privileges enjoyed by his fellow prisoners. In *Houghton,* the prisoner's contention was that prison authorities had violated the Constitution by confiscating legal materials which he had acquired for pursuing his appeal, but which, in violation of prison rules, had been found in the possession of another prisoner. In *Wilwording,* the prisoners' complaints related solely to their living conditions and disciplinary measures while confined in maximum security. And in *Haines,* the prisoner claimed that prison officials had acted unconstitutionally by placing him in solitary confinement as a disciplinary measure, and he sought damages for claimed physical injuries sustained while so segregated. It is clear then, that in all those cases, the prisoners' claims related solely to the states' alleged unconstitutional treatment of them while in confinement. None sought, as did the respondents here, to challenge the very fact or duration of the confinement itself. Those cases, therefore, merely establish that a § 1983 action is a proper remedy for a state prisoner who is making a constitutional challenge to the conditions of his prison life, but not to the fact or length of his custody. Upon that understanding, we reaffirm those holdings.[14]

This is not to say that habeas corpus may not also be available to challenge such prison conditions. See Johnson v. Avery, 393 U.S. 483 (1969); *Wilwording v. Swenson.* When a prisoner is put under additional and unconstitutional restraints during his lawful custody, it is arguable that habeas corpus will lie to remove the restraints making the custody illegal.

But we need not in this case explore the appropriate limits of habeas corpus as an alternative remedy to a proper action under § 1983. That question is not before us. What is involved here is the extent to which § 1983 is a permissible alternative to the traditional remedy of habeas corpus. Upon that question, we hold today that when a state prisoner is challenging the very fact or duration of his physical imprisonment, and the relief he seeks is a determination that he is entitled to immediate release or a speedier release from that imprisonment, his sole federal remedy is a writ of habeas corpus. Accordingly, we reverse the judgment before us.

---

[14] If a prisoner seeks to attack both the conditions of his confinement and the fact or length of that confinement, his latter claim, under our decision today, is cognizable only in federal habeas corpus, with its attendant requirement of exhaustion of state remedies. But, consistent with our prior decisions, that holding in no way precludes him from simultaneously litigating in federal court, under § 1983, his claim relating to the conditions of his confinement.

It is so ordered.

■ MR. JUSTICE BRENNAN with whom MR. JUSTICE DOUGLAS and MR. JUS-
TICE MARSHALL join, dissenting. . . .

[T]he Court's holding today rests on an understandable apprehension that the no-exhaustion rule of § 1983 might, in the absence of some
limitation, devour the exhaustion rule of the habeas corpus statute. The
problem arises because the two statutes necessarily overlap. Indeed,
every application by the state prisoner for federal habeas corpus relief
against his jailers could, as a matter of logic and semantics, be viewed as
an action under [§ 1983] to obtain injunctive relief against "the deprivation," by one acting under color of state law, "of any rights, privileges, or
immunities secured by the Constitution and laws" of the United States.
To prevent state prisoners from nullifying the habeas corpus exhaustion
requirement by invariably styling their petitions as pleas for relief under
§ 1983, the Court today devises an ungainly and irrational scheme that
permits some prisoners to sue under § 1983, while others may proceed
only by way of petition for habeas corpus. And the entire scheme operates
in defiance of the purposes underlying both the exhaustion requirement
of habeas corpus and the absence of a comparable requirement under
§ 1983.

I

[In part I, Justice Brennan noted that the majority left Wilwording
v. Swenson, 404 U.S. 249 (1971), "unimpaired" where the challenge is
solely to conditions of confinement.]

II

Putting momentarily to one side the grave analytic shortcomings of
the Court's approach, it seems clear that the scheme's unmanageability
is sufficient reason to condemn it. For the unfortunate but inevitable legacy of today's opinion is a perplexing set of uncertainties and anomalies.
And the nub of the problem is the definition of the Court's new-found and
essentially ethereal concept, the "core of habeas corpus." . . .

Between a suit for damages and an attack on the conviction itself or
on the deprivation of good-time credits are cases where habeas corpus is
an appropriate and available remedy, but where the action falls outside
the "core of habeas corpus" because the attack is directed at the conditions of confinement, not at its fact or duration. Notwithstanding today's
decision, a prisoner may challenge, by suit under § 1983, prison living
conditions and disciplinary measures, or confiscation of legal materials,
or impairment of the right to free exercise of religion, even though federal
habeas corpus is available as an alternative remedy. It should be plain
enough that serious difficulties will arise whenever a prisoner seeks to
attack in a single proceeding both the conditions of his confinement and
the deprivation of good-time credits. And the addition of a plea for monetary damages exacerbates the problem.

If a prisoner's sole claim is that he was placed in solitary confinement pursuant to an unconstitutional disciplinary procedure, he can obtain federal injunctive relief and monetary damages in an action under § 1983. The unanswered question is whether he loses the right to proceed under § 1983 if, as punishment for his alleged misconduct, his jailers have not only subjected him to unlawful segregation and thereby inflicted an injury that is compensable in damages, but have compounded the wrong by improperly depriving him of good-time credits. Three different approaches are possible.

First, we might conclude that jurisdiction under § 1983 is lost whenever good-time credits are involved, even where the action is based primarily on the need for monetary relief or an injunction against continued segregation. If that is the logic of the Court's opinion, then the scheme creates an undeniable, and in all likelihood irresistible, incentive for state prison officials to defeat the jurisdiction of the federal courts by adding the deprivation of good-time credits to whatever other punishment is imposed. And if all of the federal claims must be held in abeyance pending exhaustion of state remedies, a prisoner's subsequent effort to assert a damages claim under § 1983 might arguably be barred by principles of res judicata. To avoid the loss of his damages claim, a prisoner might conclude that he should make no mention of the good-time issue and instead seek only damages in a § 1983 action. That approach (assuming it would not be disallowed as a subterfuge to circumvent the exhaustion requirement) creates its own distressing possibilities. For, having obtained decision in federal court on the issue of damages, the prisoner would presumably be required to repair to state court in search of his lost good-time credits, returning once again to federal court if his state court efforts should prove unavailing.

Moreover, a determination that no federal claim can be raised where good-time credits are at stake would give rise to a further anomaly. If the prisoner is confined in an institution that does not offer good-time credits, and therefore cannot withdraw them, his prison-conditions claims could always be raised in a suit under § 1983. On the other hand, an inmate in an institution that uses good-time credits as reward and punishment, who seeks a federal hearing on the identical legal and factual claims, would normally be required to exhaust state remedies and then proceed by way of federal habeas corpus. The rationality of that difference in treatment is certainly obscure. Yet that is the price of permitting the availability of a federal forum to be controlled by the happenstance (or stratagem) that good-time credits are at stake.

As an alternative, we might reject outright the premises of the first approach and conclude that a plea for money damages or for an injunction against continued segregation is sufficient to bring all related claims, including the question of good-time credits, under the umbrella of § 1983. That approach would, of course, simplify matters considerably. And it would make unnecessary the fractionation of the prisoner's claims into a number of different issues to be resolved in duplicative proceedings in state and federal courts. Nevertheless, the approach would seem to afford a convenient means of sidestepping the basic thrust of the Court's opinion, and we could surely expect state prisoners routinely to add to their other claims a plea for monetary relief. So long as the prisoner could formulate at least a colorable damages claim, he would be entitled to litigate all issues in federal court without first exhausting state remedies.

In any event, the Court today rejects, perhaps for the reasons suggested above, both of the foregoing positions. Instead, it holds that insofar as a prisoner's claim relates to good-time credits, he is required to exhaust state remedies; but he is not precluded from simultaneously litigating in federal court, under § 1983, his claim for monetary damages or an injunction against continued segregation. Under that approach, state correctional authorities have no added incentive to withdraw good-time credits, since that action cannot, standing alone, keep the prisoner out of federal court. And, at the same time, it does not encourage a prisoner to assert an unnecessary claim for damages or injunctive relief as a means of bringing his good-time claim under the purview of § 1983. Nevertheless, this approach entails substantial difficulties—perhaps the greatest difficulties of the three. In the first place, its extreme inefficiency is readily apparent. For in many instances a prisoner's claims will be under simultaneous consideration in two distinct forums, even though the identical legal and factual questions are involved in both proceedings. Thus, if a prisoner's punishment for some alleged misconduct is both a term in solitary and the deprivation of good-time credits, and if he believes that the punishment was imposed pursuant to unconstitutional disciplinary procedures, he can now litigate the legality of those procedures simultaneously in state court (where he seeks restoration of good-time credits) and in federal court (where he seeks damages or an injunction against continued segregation). Moreover, if the federal court is the first to reach decision, and if that court concludes that the procedures are, in fact, unlawful, then the entire state proceeding must be immediately aborted, even though the state court may have devoted substantial time and effort to its consideration of the case. By the same token, if traditional principles of res judicata are applicable to suits under § 1983, the prior conclusion of the state court suit would effectively set at naught the entire federal court proceeding. This is plainly a curious prescription for improving relations between state and federal courts.

Since some of the ramifications of this new approach are still unclear, the unfortunate outcome of today's decision—an outcome that might not be immediately surmised from the seeming simplicity of the basic concept, the "core of habeas corpus"—is almost certain to be the further complication of prison-conditions litigation. In itself that is disquieting enough. But it is especially distressing that the remaining questions will have to be resolved on the basis of pleadings, whether in habeas corpus or suit under § 1983, submitted by state prisoners, who will often have to cope with these questions without even minimal assistance of counsel.

III

. . . The concern that § 1983 not be used to nullify the habeas corpus exhaustion doctrine is, of course, legitimate. But our effort to preserve the integrity of the doctrine must rest on an understanding of the purposes that underlie it. In my view, the Court misapprehends these fundamental purposes and compounds the problem by paying insufficient attention to the reasons why exhaustion of state remedies is not required in suits under § 1983. As a result, the Court mistakenly concludes that allowing suit under § 1983 would jeopardize the purposes of the exhaustion rule.

By enactment of [§ 1983] in 1871, and again by the grant in 1875 of original federal-question jurisdiction to the federal courts, Congress recognized important interests in permitting a plaintiff to choose a federal forum in cases arising under federal law. . . .

This grant of jurisdiction was designed to preserve and enhance the expertise of federal courts in applying federal law; to achieve greater uniformity of results; and, since federal courts are "more likely to apply federal law sympathetically and understandingly than are state courts," to minimize misapplications of federal law.

In the service of the same interests, we have taken care to emphasize that there are

> fundamental objections to any conclusion that a litigant who has properly invoked the jurisdiction of a federal district court to consider federal constitutional claims can be compelled, without his consent and through no fault of his own, to accept instead a state court's determination of those claims. Such a result would be at war with the unqualified terms in which Congress, pursuant to constitutional authorization, has conferred specific categories of jurisdiction upon the federal courts, and with the principle that "When a federal court is properly appealed to in a case over which it has by law jurisdiction, it is its duty to take such jurisdiction. . . . The right of a party plaintiff to choose a federal court where there is a choice cannot be properly denied."

England v. Louisiana State Board of Medical Examiners, 375 U.S. 411, 415 (1964). We have also recognized that review by this Court of state decisions, "even when available by appeal rather than only by discretionary writ of certiorari, is an inadequate substitute for the initial district court determination . . . to which the litigant is entitled in the federal courts." The federal courts are, in short, the "primary and powerful reliances for vindicating every right given by the Constitution, the laws, and treaties of the United States." F. Frankfurter and J. Landis, The Business of the Supreme Court: A Study in the Federal Judicial System 65 (1928).

These considerations, applicable generally in cases arising under federal law, have special force in the context of [§ 1983]. In a suit to enforce fundamental constitutional rights, the plaintiff's choice of a federal forum has singular urgency. The statutory predecessor to § 1983 was, after all, designed "to afford a federal right in federal courts because, by reason of prejudice, passion, neglect, intolerance or otherwise, state laws might not be enforced and the claims of citizens to the rights, privileges, and immunities guaranteed by the Fourteenth Amendment might be denied by the state agencies." Monroe v. Pape, 365 U.S. 167, 180 (1961). And the statute's legislative history

> makes evident that Congress clearly conceived that it was altering the relationship between the states and the nation with respect to the protection of federally created rights; it was concerned that state instrumentalities could not protect those rights; it realized that state officers might, in fact, be antipathetic to the vindication of those rights; and it believed that these failings extended to the state courts. . . . The very purpose of § 1983 was to interpose the federal courts between the states and the people, as guardians of the people's federal rights—to protect the people from unconstitutional action under color of state law, "whether that action be executive, legislative or judicial."

Mitchum v. Foster, 407 U.S. 225, 242 (1972).

It is against this background that we have refused to require exhaustion of state remedies by civil rights plaintiffs. . . .

Our determination that principles of federalism do not require the exhaustion of state remedies in cases brought under [§ 1983] holds true even where the state agency or process under constitutional attack is intimately tied to the state judicial machinery. Indeed, only last term we held in *Mitchum v. Foster* that § 1983 operates as an exception to the federal anti-injunction statute, 28 U.S.C. § 2283, which prohibits federal court injunctions against ongoing state judicial proceedings and which is designed to prevent "needless friction between state and federal courts." Although the anti-injunction statute rests in part on considerations as fundamental as the "constitutional independence of the states and their courts," and although exceptions will "not be enlarged by loose statutory construction," we nevertheless unanimously concluded that § 1983 is excepted from the statute's prohibition—that the anti-injunction statute does not, in other words, displace federal jurisdiction under [§ 1983].

In sum, the absence of an exhaustion requirement in § 1983 is not an accident of history or the result of careless oversight by Congress or this Court. On the contrary, the no-exhaustion rule is an integral feature of the statutory scheme. Exhaustion of state remedies is not required precisely because such a requirement would jeopardize the purposes of the act. For that reason, the imposition of such a requirement, even if done indirectly by means of a determination that jurisdiction under § 1983 is displaced by an alternative remedial device, must be justified by a clear statement of congressional intent, or, at the very least, by the presence of the most persuasive considerations of policy. In my view, no such justification can be found.

Crucial to the Court's analysis of the case before us is its understanding of the purposes that underlie the habeas corpus exhaustion requirement. But just as the Court pays too little attention to the reasons for a no-exhaustion rule in actions under § 1983, it also misconceives the purposes of the exhaustion requirement in habeas corpus. As a result, the Court reaches what seems to me the erroneous conclusion that the purposes of the exhaustion requirement are fully implicated in respondents' actions, even though respondents sought to bring these actions under § 1983.

"The rule of exhaustion in federal habeas corpus actions is," according to today's opinion, "rooted in considerations of federal-state comity. That principle was defined in Younger v. Harris, 401 U.S. 37, 44 (1971), as 'a proper respect for state functions,' and it has as much relevance in areas of particular state administrative concern as it does where state judicial action is being attacked." Moreover, the Court reasons that since the relationship between state prisoners and state officers is especially intimate, and since prison issues are peculiarly within state authority and expertise, "the states have an important interest in not being bypassed in the correction of those problems." With all respect, I cannot accept either the premises or the reasoning that lead to the Court's conclusion.

Although codified in the habeas corpus statute in 1948, the exhaustion requirement is a "judicially crafted instrument which reflects a careful balance between important interests of federalism and the need to preserve the writ of habeas corpus as a 'swift and imperative remedy in all cases of illegal restraint or confinement.' " Braden v. 30th Judicial Circuit, 410 U.S. 484, 490 (1973). The indisputable concern of all our decisions concerning the doctrine has been the relationship "between the *judicial tribunals* of the union and of the states. [T]he public good requires that those relations be not disturbed by unnecessary conflict between *courts* equally bound to guard and protect rights secured by the Constitution." *Ex parte Royall*, 117 U.S. at 251 (emphasis added). . . .

That is not to say, however, that the purposes of the doctrine are implicated only where an attack is directed at a state court *conviction* or *sentence*. *Ex parte Royall* itself did not involve a challenge to a state conviction, but rather an effort to secure a prisoner's release on habeas corpus "in advance of his trial in the [state] court in which he [was] indicted." But there, too, the focus was on relations between the state and federal *judiciaries*. It is a fundamental purpose of the exhaustion doctrine to preserve the "orderly administration of state judicial business, preventing the interruption of state adjudication by federal habeas proceedings. It is important that petitioners reach state appellate courts, which can develop and correct errors of state and federal law and most effectively supervise and impose uniformity on trial courts." . . .

With these considerations in mind, it becomes clear that the Court's decision does not serve the fundamental purposes behind the exhaustion doctrine. For although respondents were confined pursuant to the judgment of a state judicial tribunal, their claims do not relate to their convictions or sentences, but only to the administrative action of prison officials who subjected them to allegedly unconstitutional treatment, including the deprivation of good-time credits. This is not a case, in other words, where federal intervention would interrupt a state proceeding or jeopardize the orderly administration of state judicial business. Nor is it a case where an action in federal court might imperil the relationship between state and federal courts. The "regularity of proceedings had in courts of coordinate jurisdiction" is not in any sense at issue.

To be sure, respondents do call into question the constitutional validity of action by state officials, and friction between those officials and the federal court is by no means an inconceivable result. But standing alone, that possibility is simply not enough to warrant application of an exhaustion requirement. First, while we spoke in Younger v. Harris, 401 U.S. 37, 44 (1971), of the need for federal courts to maintain a "proper respect for state functions," neither that statement nor our holding there supports the instant application of the exhaustion doctrine. Our concern in *Younger* was the "longstanding public policy against federal court interference with *state court proceedings*" by means of a federal injunction against the continuation of those proceedings. *Younger* is thus an instructive illustration of the very proposition that the Court regrettably misconstrues. It does not in any sense demand, or even counsel, today's decision.

Second, the situation that exists in the case before us—an attack on state administrative rather than judicial action—is the stereotypical situation in which relief under § 1983 is authorized. See, e.g., McNeese v. Board of Education, 373 U.S. 668 (1963) (attack on school districting scheme); Damico v. California, 389 U.S. 416 (1967) (attack on welfare requirements); *Monroe*, 365 U.S. at 183 (attack on police conduct). In each of these cases the exercise of federal jurisdiction was potentially offensive to the state and its officials. In each of these cases the attack was directed at an important state function in an area in which the state has wide powers of regulation. Yet in each of these cases we explicitly held that exhaustion of state remedies was not required. And in comparable cases we have taken pains to insure that the abstention doctrine is not used to defeat the plaintiff's initial choice of a federal forum, even though the plaintiff could reserve the right to litigate the federal claim in federal court at the conclusion of the state proceeding. England v. Louisiana State Board of Medical Examiners, 375 U.S. 411 (1964). Like Judge Kaufman, who concurred in the affirmance of the cases now before us, "I cannot believe that federal jurisdiction in cases involving prisoner rights is any more offensive to the state than federal jurisdiction in the areas" where the exhaustion requirement has been explicitly ruled inapplicable.

Third, if the Court is correct in assuming that the exhaustion requirement must be applied whenever federal jurisdiction might be a source of substantial friction with the state, then I simply do not understand why the Court stops where it does in rolling back the district courts' jurisdiction under § 1983. Application of the exhaustion doctrine now turns on whether or not the action is directed at the fact or duration of the prisoner's confinement. It seems highly doubtful to me that a constitutional attack on prison conditions is any less disruptive of federal-state relations than an attack on prison conditions joined with a plea for restoration of good-time credits. . . . Yet the Court holds today that exhaustion is required where a prisoner attacks the deprivation of good-time credits, but not where he challenges only the conditions of his confinement. It seems obvious to me that both of those propositions cannot be correct.

Finally, the Court's decision may have the ironic effect of turning a situation where state and federal courts are not initially in conflict into a situation where precisely such conflict does result. Since respondents' actions would neither interrupt a state judicial proceeding nor, even if successful, require the invalidation of a state judicial decision, "[t]he question is simply whether one court or another is going to decide the case." Note, Exhaustion of State Remedies under the Civil Rights Act, 68 Colum. L. Rev. 1201, 1205–06 (1968). If we had held, consistently with our prior cases, that the plaintiff has the right to choose a federal forum, the exercise of that right would not offend or embarrass a state court with concurrent jurisdiction. Now, however, a prisoner who seeks restoration of good-time credits must proceed first in state court, although he has the option of petitioning the federal court for relief if his state suit is unsuccessful. . . . [I]t seems a good deal premature to proclaim today's decision a major victory in our continuing effort to achieve a harmonious and healthy federal-state system.

IV

In short, I see no basis for concluding that jurisdiction under § 1983 is, in this instance, pre-empted by the habeas corpus remedy. Respondents' effort to bring these suits under the provisions of [§ 1983] should not be viewed as an attempted circumvention of the exhaustion requirement of the habeas corpus statute, for the effort does not in any sense conflict with the policies underlying that requirement. By means of these suits, they demand an immediate end to action under color of state law that has the alleged effect of violating fundamental rights guaranteed by the federal Constitution. [Section 1983] was designed to afford an expeditious federal hearing for the resolution of precisely such claims as these. Since I share the Court's view that exhaustion of state judicial remedies is not required in any suit properly brought in federal court under § 1983 and since I am convinced that respondents have properly invoked the jurisdictional grant of § 1983, I would affirm the judgment of the Court of Appeals.

NOTES ON THE RELATION OF § 1983 TO HABEAS CORPUS

1. QUESTIONS AND COMMENTS ON *PREISER*

Federal habeas corpus requires that available state judicial remedies be exhausted before resort to federal court. One consequence of this requirement is that federal habeas is generally unavailable until state criminal proceedings have been concluded. Younger v. Harris, 401 U.S. 37 (1971), establishes a similar limitation on § 1983 suits. It too forecloses federal judicial relief that would pretermit or undermine pending state criminal proceedings.

Once a state conviction is final, however, habeas and § 1983 diverge. Habeas continues to require exhaustion of claims not heard in state court. But § 1983 does not require further exhaustion of state remedies, nor is it constrained by the many limitations on the availability of federal habeas corpus surveyed in this Chapter. Some line must be drawn between the two remedies if both are to retain independent functions and if § 1983 is not to displace habeas. Does *Preiser* draw the right line?[a]

2. RELATION OF *PREISER* TO § 1983 ACTIONS FOR DAMAGES: *HECK V. HUMPHREY*

The disposition of § 1983 suits for damages involving issues relevant to pending or completed state criminal proceedings was addressed in Heck v. Humphrey, 512 U.S. 477 (1994). Heck was convicted in an Indiana court of voluntary manslaughter. While the appeal from his conviction was pending, he filed suit in federal district court under § 1983 against the prosecutors and a police investigator, alleging that they had engaged in an "unlawful, unreasonable, and arbitrary investigation" leading to his arrest, "knowingly destroyed" evidence "which was exculpatory in nature and could have proved [his] innocence," and caused "an illegal and unlawful voice identification procedure" to be used at his trial. The complaint sought, among other things, compensatory and punitive damages.

In an opinion by Justice Scalia, the Court held that the § 1983 suit could not be maintained.[b] "The issue with respect to monetary damages challenging conviction is not, it seems to us, exhaustion; but rather, the same as the issue was with respect to injunctive relief challenging conviction in *Preiser*: whether the claim is cognizable under § 1983 at all." To answer this question,

---

[a] For extensive analysis of a considerable body of decisional law and some proposed solutions, see Martin Schwartz, The *Preiser* Puzzle: Continued Frustrating Conflict between the Civil Rights and Habeas Corpus Remedies for State Prisoners, 37 DePaul L. Rev. 85 (1988). The administration of the *Preiser* holding after the Antiterrorism and Effective Death Penalty Act (AEDPA) is explored and proposed reforms suggested in Nancy J. King and Suzanna Sherry, Habeas Corpus and State Sentencing Reform: A Story of Unintended Consequences, 58 Duke L.J. 1 (2008).

[b] Justice Souter concurred in the judgment, joined by Justices Blackmun, Stevens and O'Connor.

the Court turned to the common law of torts, concluding that the law of malicious prosecution provided the best analogy: "One element that must be alleged and proved in a malicious prosecution action is termination of the prior criminal proceeding in favor of the accused."

Several rationales supported this requirement. It "avoids parallel litigation over the issues of probable cause and guilt . . . and it precludes the possibility of the claimant . . . succeeding in the tort action after having been convicted in the underlying criminal prosecution, in contravention of a strong judicial policy against the creation of two conflicting resolutions arising out of the same or identical transaction." And "to permit a convicted criminal defendant to proceed with a malicious prosecution claim would permit a collateral attack on the conviction through the vehicle of a civil suit." The Court concluded:

> We hold that, in order to recover damages for allegedly unconstitutional conviction or imprisonment, or for other harm caused by actions whose unlawfulness would render a conviction or sentence invalid, a § 1983 plaintiff must prove that the conviction or sentence has been reversed on direct appeal, expunged by executive order, declared invalid by a state tribunal authorized to make such determination, or called into question by a federal court's issuance of a writ of habeas corpus. A claim for damages bearing that relationship to a conviction or sentence that has not been so invalidated is not cognizable under § 1983. Thus, when a state prisoner seeks damages in a § 1983 suit, the district court must consider whether a judgment in favor of the plaintiff would necessarily imply the invalidity of his conviction or sentence; if it would, the complaint must be dismissed unless the plaintiff can demonstrate that the conviction or sentence has already been invalidated. But if the district court determines that the plaintiff's action, even if successful, will not demonstrate the invalidity of any outstanding criminal judgment against the plaintiff, the action should be allowed to proceed,[7] in the absence of some other bar to the suit.[8]

---

[7] For example, a suit for damages attributable to an allegedly unreasonable search may lie even if the challenged search produced evidence that was introduced in a state criminal trial resulting in the § 1983 plaintiff's still-outstanding conviction. Because of doctrines like independent source and inevitable discovery, and especially harmless error, such a § 1983 action, even if successful, would not necessarily imply that the plaintiff's conviction was unlawful. In order to recover compensatory damages, however, the § 1983 plaintiff must prove not only that the search was unlawful, but that it caused him actual, compensable injury, see Memphis Community School Dist. v. Stachura, 477 U.S. 299, 308 (1986), which, we hold today, does not encompass the "injury" of being convicted and imprisoned (until his conviction has been overturned).

[8] For example, if a state criminal defendant brings a federal civil-rights lawsuit during the pendency of his criminal trial, appeal, or state habeas action, abstention may be an appropriate response to the parallel state-court proceedings. See Colorado River Water Conservation Dist. v. United States, 424 U.S. 800 (1976). Moreover, we do not decide whether abstention might be appropriate in cases where a state prisoner brings a § 1983 damages suit raising an issue that also could be grounds for relief in a state-court challenge to his conviction or sentence.

3.   QUESTIONS AND COMMENTS ON *HECK V. HUMPHREY*

Joseph L. Hoffmann and Lauren K. Robel, Federal Court Supervision of State Criminal Justice Administration, 543 Annals Am. Acad. Pol. & Soc. 154 (1996), concludes that the "apparent breadth" of the holding in *Heck v. Humphrey* is "misleading" and that *Heck* actually "does very little to restrict § 1983 actions that might interfere with the policies of habeas law." As is suggested by the examples in Justice Scalia's footnote 7 and by his repeated use of the word "necessarily" as a descriptor of the potential undermining effect of the § 1983 judgment on the criminal conviction, there will be many situations in which § 1983 damages litigation can proceed (or at least where the plaintiff can argue that it should proceed) even though it involves an issue that is in some sense part of a state criminal prosecution or conviction. Simultaneous litigation will still be possible "so long as the plaintiff seeks to recover not for imprisonment, but instead only for those damages resulting directly from the unconstitutional conduct." As Justice Scalia implies in footnote 7, it may be difficult for the plaintiff to show an "actual, compensable injury" in some such cases, but there will be situations where physical injuries are alleged and there is always the possibility of punitive damages against individual defendants.

Are these big holes? Should the Court have gone further? Hoffmann and Robel say "yes." They argue that the issue should be whether the criminal defendant had a meaningful opportunity to get a merits resolution of the federal claim in a habeas proceeding. If so (and even if the opportunity was not pursued), they think a § 1983 action should be barred.

4.   *EDWARDS V. BALISOK*

The Supreme Court reaffirmed and perhaps extended *Heck* in Edwards v. Balisok, 520 U.S. 641 (1997). Balisok, a state prisoner, sought damages under § 1983 for the allegedly unconstitutional procedures used to take away his good-time credits. He did not seek damages for that result. The Ninth Circuit ruled *Heck* inapplicable on the ground that a claim challenging only the procedures used in a disciplinary hearing can always be brought under § 1983, but the Supreme Court unanimously reversed. In an opinion by Justice Scalia, the Court said that the Ninth Circuit's reasoning "disregards the possibility, clearly envisioned by *Heck*, that the nature of the challenge to the procedures could be such as necessarily to imply the invalidity of the judgment." Here, Balisok had alleged deceit and bias by the prison hearing officer, allegations that, if proved, would imply the invalidity of the disciplinary action taken against him. *Heck* therefore controlled.

5.   *WILKINSON V. DOTSON*

William Dotson and Rogerico Johnson were serving lengthy prison sentences in Ohio state prisons. Dotson was sentenced to life in 1981. He sought parole in 2000. The parole board denied relief and postponed further consideration for five years. Johnson began a 10–30 year term in 1992. He was considered and rejected for parole in 1999.

In both cases the parole board applied standards that were adopted in 1998, well after the two prisoners were convicted and sentenced. Both sought an injunction under § 1983 on the ground that retroactive application of the 1998 guidelines denied them due process and violated the Ex Post Facto clause. The District Court held the case cognizable only on habeas. In an opinion by Justice Breyer, the Supreme Court disagreed. Wilkinson v. Dotson, 544 U.S. 74 (2005).

In the course of holding that the suit could proceed under § 1983, Breyer summarized the prior cases and applied their principles:

> Throughout the legal journey from *Preiser* to *Balisok*, the Court has focused on the need to ensure that state prisoners use only habeas corpus (or similar state) remedies when they seek to invalidate the duration of their confinement—either directly through an injunction compelling speedier release or indirectly through a judicial determination that necessarily implies the unlawfulness of the State's custody. . . . [The cases], taken together, indicate that a state prisoner's § 1983 action is barred (absent prior invalidation)—no matter the relief sought (damages or equitable relief), no matter the target of the prisoner's suit (state conduct leading to conviction or internal prison proceedings)—if success in that action would necessarily demonstrate the invalidity of confinement or its duration.

> Applying these principles to the present case, we conclude that respondents' claims are cognizable under § 1983, i.e., they do not fall within the implicit habeas exception. Dotson and Johnson seek relief that will render invalid the state procedures used to deny parole eligibility (Dotson) and parole suitability (Johnson). Neither respondent seeks an injunction ordering his immediate or speedier release into the community. And . . . a favorable judgment will not "necessarily imply the invalidity of [their] conviction[s] or sentence[s]." Heck v. Humphrey, 512 U.S. 477, 487 (1994). Success for Dotson does not mean immediate release from confinement or a shorter stay in prison; it means at most new eligibility review, which at most will speed consideration of a new parole application. Success for Johnson means at most a new parole hearing at which Ohio parole authorities may, in their discretion, decline to shorten his prison term. Because neither prisoner's claim would necessarily spell speedier release, neither lies at "the core of habeas corpus." Preiser v. Rodriguez, 411 U.S. 475, 489 (1973). Finally, the prisoners' claims for future relief (which, if successful, will not necessarily imply the invalidity of confinement or shorten its duration) are yet more distant from that core.

Joined by Justice Thomas, Justice Scalia joined the Court's opinion but wrote separately to state his conclusion that habeas should not be available for these claims. "[A] contrary holding would require us to broaden the scope of habeas relief beyond recognition." Only Justice Kennedy dissented.

6.   ACCESS TO DNA EVIDENCE

In District Attorney's Office v. Osborne, 557 U.S. 52 (2009), the Court deferred decision on whether § 1983 or habeas was the correct route for asserting a constitutional right of post-conviction access to DNA testing. It could do so, the Court held, because the plaintiff's due process claim lacked merit in any event. Joined by Justice Kennedy, Justice Alito wrote a separate concurrence in which he concluded that the § 1983 remedy could not be used for this purpose:

> It is no answer to say, as respondent does, that he simply wants to use § 1983 as a discovery tool to lay the foundation for a future state post-conviction application, a state clemency petition, or a request for relief by means of "prosecutorial consent." Such tactics implicate precisely the same federalism and comity concerns that motivated our decisions (and Congress') to impose exhaustion requirements and discovery limits in federal habeas proceedings. If a petitioner can evade the habeas statute's exhaustion requirements in this way, I see no reason why a state prisoner asserting an ordinary *Brady* claim—i.e., a state prisoner who claims that the prosecution failed to turn over exculpatory evidence prior to trial— could not follow the same course.

> What respondent seeks was accurately described in his complaint—the discovery of evidence that has a material bearing on his conviction. Such a claim falls within "the core" of habeas. Preiser v. Rodriguez, 411 U.S. 475, 489 (1973). Recognition of a constitutional right to post-conviction scientific testing of evidence in the possession of the prosecution would represent an expansion of *Brady* and a broadening of the discovery rights now available to habeas petitioners. We have never previously held that a state prisoner may seek discovery by means of a § 1983 action, and we should not take that step here. I would hold that respondent's claim (like all other *Brady* claims) should be brought in habeas.[c]

The issue returned in Skinner v. Switzer, 562 U.S. 521 (2011). Skinner was sentenced to death in 1995 for murdering his live-in girlfriend and her two sons. A significant amount of biological evidence was collected and preserved by the police, but was untested at the time of trial.[d] The state enacted a statute in 2001 allowing post-conviction testing on application by prisoners in limited circumstances. Skinner moved for testing under these procedures in 2001 and again in 2007, but both motions were denied. He then filed a § 1983 suit for injunctive relief against the local prosecutor who had custody of the biological evidence. His claim was that the state statute denied him

---

[c]   In a prior footnote, Alito said: "This case is quite different from *Dotson*. In that case, two state prisoners filed § 1983 actions challenging the constitutionality of Ohio's parole procedures and seeking 'a new parole hearing that may or may not result in release, prescription of the composition of the hearing panel, and specification of the procedures to be followed.' Regardless of whether such remedies fall outside the authority of federal habeas judges, there is no question that the relief respondent seeks in this case—'exculpatory' evidence that tends to prove his innocence—lies 'within the core of habeas corpus.' "—[Footnote by eds.]

[d]   His lawyer testified during state post-conviction proceedings that he had not asked for testing prior to trial because he was afraid the results would implicate Skinner.

procedural due process because it completely foreclosed post-conviction DNA testing in cases where the prisoner could have sought testing prior to trial but did not.

In an opinion by Justice Ginsburg, the Court declined to address the merits of Skinner's due process claim, but did hold that it was cognizable under § 1983. After summarizing *Heck* and *Dotson*, the Court continued:

> Measured against our prior holdings, Skinner has properly invoked § 1983. Success in his suit for DNA testing would not "necessarily imply" the invalidity of his conviction. While test results might prove exculpatory, that outcome is hardly inevitable; . . . results might prove inconclusive or they might further incriminate Skinner. . . . Although Skinner's *immediate* plea is simply for an order requiring DNA testing, his ultimate aim, Switzer urges, is to use the test results as a platform for attacking his conviction. It suffices to point out that Switzer has found no case, nor has the dissent, in which the Court has recognized habeas as the sole remedy, or even an available one, where the relief sought would "neither terminat[e] custody, accelerat[e] the future date of release from custody, nor reduc[e] the level of custody." Wilkinson v. Dotson, 544 U.S. 74, 86 (Scalia, J., concurring).

Switzer argued that allowing § 1983 suits in this context would lead to a "vast expansion" of federal jurisdiction seeking discovery and other relief associated with prior convictions. The Court responded that there was no evidence in Circuits that allowed § 1983 DNA suits "of any litigation flood or even rainfall." Two reasons for this were the rejection in *Osborne* of substantive due process as the basis for DNA testing claims and significant limitations on prisoner litigation contained in the Prison Litigation Reform Act of 1995. Finally, the Court responded to the argument that its holding would open the doors to § 1983 suits for *Brady* claims:

> Unlike DNA testing, which may yield exculpatory, incriminating, or inconclusive results, a *Brady* claim, when successful post-conviction, necessarily yields evidence undermining a conviction: *Brady* evidence is, by definition, always favorable to the defendant and material to his guilt or punishment. And parties asserting *Brady* violations post-conviction generally do seek a judgment qualifying them for "immediate or speedier release" from imprisonment. Accordingly, *Brady* claims have ranked within the traditional core of habeas corpus and outside the province of § 1983.

Joined by Justices Kennedy and Alito, Justice Thomas dissented. He did not attempt to bring the situation into precise analytic alignment with *Preiser v. Rodriguez*'s focus on the fact or duration of custody. Rather, he described the case as a due process challenge to state collateral review procedures (under which DNA testing had been denied), and concluded that post-conviction challenges to such procedures should proceed under habeas corpus: "Challenges to all state procedures for reviewing the validity of a conviction should be treated the same as challenges to state trial procedures, which we have already recognized may not be brought under § 1983. . . . For purposes of deciding which claims fall within the bounds of § 1983, I think it makes sense to treat similarly all constitutional challenges to procedures concerning the validity of a conviction." *Wilkinson v. Dotson* was distinguished on the ground that the due process attack on state parole procedures involved in that case did not impeach the validity of the underlying criminal conviction or sentence. Justice Thomas added:

> In truth, the majority provides a roadmap for any unsuccessful state habeas petitioner to relitigate his claim under § 1983: After state habeas is denied, file a § 1983 suit challenging the state habeas process rather than the result.[3] . . .

> This Court has struggled to limit § 1983 and prevent it from intruding into the boundaries of habeas corpus. In crafting these limits, we have recognized that suits seeking "immediate or speedier release" from confinement fall outside its scope. *Dotson*, 544 U.S. at 82. We found another limit when faced with a civil action in which "a judgment in favor of the plaintiff would necessarily imply the invalidity of his conviction or sentence." *Heck*, 512 U.S. at 487. This case calls for yet another: due process challenges to state procedures used to review the validity of a conviction or sentence. Under that rule, Skinner's claim is not cognizable under § 1983. . . .

Who has the better of this argument?

---

[3]   Nor is there any reason to believe that the Court's holding will be cabined to collateral review procedures. . . . Just as any unsuccessful state habeas petitioner will now resort to § 1983 and challenge state collateral review procedures, so, too, will unsuccessful appellants turn to § 1983 to challenge the state appellate procedures.

CHAPTER VIII

STATE SOVEREIGN IMMUNITY AND THE ELEVENTH AMENDMENT

SECTION 1. NATURE OF THE LIMITATION

INTRODUCTORY NOTES ON THE ELEVENTH AMENDMENT

1. *CHISHOLM V. GEORGIA*

Shortly after ratification of the Constitution, the executor of a South Carolina merchant sued to recover for supplies furnished under a contract with the state of Georgia. Original jurisdiction in the Supreme Court was based on the Article III specification of federal judicial power over "Controversies . . . between a State and Citizens of another State" and on its implementation in § 13 of the Judiciary Act of 1789.[a] In Chisholm v. Georgia, 2 U.S. (2 Dall.) 419 (1793), the Court held that Georgia could be sued despite its claim of sovereign immunity.

In the manner of the time, each Justice wrote separately. Justices Blair and Cushing thought the suit authorized by the language of Article III. Justice Wilson added that in any event state sovereign immunity would be incompatible with the ultimate sovereignty of the people. By creating the national government and vesting in its courts the power to hear controversies involving states, he said, the people bound the states to answer legal claims against them. Wilson made particular reference to Art. I, § 10, prohibiting laws impairing the obligation of contracts: "What good purpose could this constitutional provision secure, if a state might pass a law impairing the obligation of its own contracts; and be amenable, for such a violation of right, to no controlling judiciary power?" Chief Justice Jay agreed.

Justice Iredell dissented. He argued that Congress must pass an authorizing statute before any federal court can exercise jurisdiction,[b] and he found no federal statute authorizing a compulsory action for the recovery of money from a state. He interpreted § 13 of the Judiciary Act to confer jurisdiction only over such "controversies of a civil nature" as were recognized by the principles and usages of the common law. As there was no precedent for an

---

[a] "[T]he supreme court shall have exclusive jurisdiction of all controversies of a civil nature, where a state is a party, except between a state and its citizens; and except also, between a state and citizens of other states, or aliens, in which latter case it shall have original, but not exclusive jurisdiction."

[b] Today, it is widely accepted that the Article III provisions on the original jurisdiction of the Supreme Court are self-executing.

action of assumpsit against a state, Iredell concluded that the Court lacked jurisdiction.c

2.   REACTION TO *CHISHOLM*

The reaction to *Chisholm* was swift and hostile. The concern, according to Charles Warren, was not merely the affront to state sovereignty but a practical fear of exhausting state treasuries: "In the crucial condition of the finances of most of the states at that time, only disaster was to be expected if suits could be successfully maintained by holders of state issues of paper and other credits, or by Loyalist refugees to recover property confiscated or sequestered by the states; and that this was no theoretical danger was shown by the immediate institution of such suits against the states in South Carolina, Georgia, Virginia and Massachusetts." 1 Charles Warren, The Supreme Court in United States History 99 (1922).d The state of Massachusetts adopted a resolution calling for the overturn of *Chisholm*, and the Georgia House of Representatives passed a bill to the effect that any persons attempting to execute process in the *Chisholm* case "are hereby declared to be guilty of felony, and shall suffer death, without the benefit of clergy, by being hanged." Id. at 100–01.

Constitutional amendments were proposed in the House of Representatives immediately after *Chisholm* was announced. One became the basis for the resolution adopted by Congress in the next session and ultimately ratified as the Eleventh Amendment to the Constitution:

> The Judicial power of the United States shall not be construed to extend to any suit in law or equity, commenced or prosecuted against one of the United States by Citizens of another State, or by Citizens or Subjects of any Foreign State.

3.   THE NEXT HUNDRED YEARS

For three-quarters of a century, the Eleventh Amendment was of little consequence. In Osborn v. Bank of the United States, 22 U.S. (9 Wheat.) 738 (1824), Chief Justice Marshall said that the amendment applied only when a state was "party of record." Thus, the effect of the amendment could be avoided simply by suing an appropriate state officer rather than the state itself.

This convenient evasion survived until the end of Reconstruction. The Civil War left the southern states economically destitute, yet saddled with debt. As the northern armies withdrew, one of the first goals of the restored local leadership was to repudiate at least part of their public bonds. The bondholders sought to hold the states to their obligations by resort to the federal courts. Given the similar history of *Chisholm,* the Eleventh Amendment was an obvious problem, and the bondholders tried a variety of ways

---

c   For an analysis of Iredell's opinion, see John V. Orth, The Truth about Justice Iredell's Dissent in *Chisholm v. Georgia* (1793), 73 N.C. L. Rev. 255 (1994); William R. Casto, James Iredell and the American Origins of Judicial Review, 27 Conn. L. Rev. 329 (1995).

d   The significance of this factor is disputed in Clyde Edward Jacobs, The Eleventh Amendment and Sovereign Immunity 67–74 (1972).

to avoid it. These included mandamus actions against state officials, Louisiana ex rel. Elliott v. Jumel, 107 U.S. 711 (1883); suits by other states, State of New Hampshire v. State of Louisiana, 108 U.S. 76 (1883); attachment of state property, Christian v. Atlantic & North Carolina R., 133 U.S. 233 (1890); and suit against a state by one of its own citizens, Hans v. Louisiana, 134 U.S. 1 (1890). None of these strategies worked. With some significant (and difficult to explain) exceptions, the Supreme Court refurbished and extended the Eleventh Amendment to defeat recovery.

John V. Orth, The Interpretation of the Eleventh Amendment, 1798–1908: A Case Study of Judicial Power, 1983 U. Ill. L. Rev. 423, argues that the post-Reconstruction cases can most plausibly be explained as reactions to the limited enforceability of judicial decisions once the northern armies withdrew: "A ruling in favor of the creditors of [southern states] would have required the collection of taxes and the disbursal of funds. The subjects of the orders would have been officers elected to prevent the payment of those very debts. Only overwhelming force could have availed, and the national will to coerce the South was lacking."

4. *HANS V. LOUISIANA*

The most famous case of this period remains a cornerstone of Eleventh Amendment law. In Hans v. Louisiana, 134 U.S. 1 (1890), a citizen of Louisiana sued to recover unpaid interest on bonds issued by the state. Louisiana had issued the bonds in 1874, but subsequently amended its Constitution to disclaim the obligation to pay the interest due in 1880. Hans claimed that the state constitutional amendment was a "Law impairing the Obligation of Contracts" in violation of Art. I, § 10, of the federal Constitution.

In an opinion by Justice Bradley, the Court stated the question as "whether a state can be sued in a Circuit Court of the United States by one of its own citizens upon a suggestion that the case is one that arises under the Constitution or laws of the United States." Hans had argued that the statute authorizing the federal courts to hear cases "arising under" the Constitution or laws of the United States made "no exception" based on "the character of the parties, and, therefore, that a state can claim no exemption from suit, if the case is really one arising under the Constitution, laws or treaties of the United States." The Court responded:

> That a state cannot be sued by a citizen of another state, or of a foreign state, on the mere ground that the case is one arising under the Constitution or laws of the United States, is clearly established by the decisions of this Court in several recent cases. . . . This Court held that the suits were virtually against the states themselves and were consequently violative of the Eleventh Amendment of the Constitution, and could not be maintained. It was not denied that they presented cases arising under the Constitution; but, notwithstanding that, they were held to be prohibited by the amendment referred to.

> In the present case [Hans] contends that he, being a citizen of Louisiana, is not embarrassed by the obstacle of the Eleventh

Amendment, inasmuch as that amendment only prohibits suits against a state which are brought by the citizens of another state, or by citizens or subjects of a foreign state. It is true, the amendment does so read: and if there were no other reason or ground for abating his suit, it might be maintainable; and then we should have this anomalous result, that in cases arising under the Constitution or laws of the United States, a state may be sued in the federal courts by its own citizens, though it cannot be sued for a like cause of action by the citizens of other states, or of a foreign state; and may be thus sued in the federal courts, although not allowing itself to be sued in its own courts. If this is the necessary consequence of the language of the Constitution and the law, the result is no less startling and unexpected than was the original decision of this Court [in] Chisholm v. Georgia, 2 U.S. (2 Dall.) 419 (1793), [which] created such a shock of surprise throughout the country that, at the first meeting of Congress thereafter, the Eleventh Amendment was proposed, and was in due course adopted by the legislatures of the states. This amendment . . . did not in terms prohibit suits by individuals against the states, but declared that the Constitution should not be construed to import any power to authorize the bringing of such suits. The language of the amendment is that "the Judicial power of the United States shall *not be construed to extend* to any suit in law or equity, commenced or prosecuted against one of the United States by Citizens of another State, or by Citizens or Subjects of any Foreign State." The Supreme Court had construed the judicial power as extending to such a suit, and its decision was thus overruled.

The Court embraced Justice Iredell's dissenting view in *Chisholm* "that it was not the intention [in the original Constitution] to create new and unheard of remedies, by subjecting sovereign states to actions at the suit of individuals, (which [Justice Iredell] conclusively showed was never done before), but only, by proper legislation, to invest the federal courts with jurisdiction to hear and determine controversies and cases . . . that were properly susceptible of litigation in courts." Justice Bradley quoted Hamilton, Madison, and Marshall to the effect that it is "inherent in the nature of sovereignty" that the state cannot be sued without its consent:

It seems to us that these views of those great advocates and defenders of the Constitution were most sensible and just. [The argument by Hans] is an attempt to strain the Constitution and the law to a construction never imagined or dreamed of. Can we suppose that, when the Eleventh Amendment was adopted, it was understood to be left open for citizens of a state to sue their own state in the federal courts, whilst the idea of suits by citizens of other states, or of foreign states, was indignantly repelled? Suppose that Congress, when proposing the Eleventh Amendment, had appended to it a proviso that nothing therein contained should prevent a state from being sued by its own citizens in cases arising under the Constitution or laws of the United States: can we imagine that it would have been adopted by the states? The supposition that it would is almost an absurdity on its face.

The truth is, that the cognizance of suits and actions unknown to the law, and forbidden by the law, was not contemplated by the Constitution when establishing the judicial power of the United States. . . .

To avoid misapprehension it may be proper to add that, although the obligations of a state rest for their performance upon its honor and good faith, and cannot be made the subjects of judicial cognizance unless the state consents to be sued, or comes itself into court; yet where property or rights are enjoyed under a grant or contract made by a state, they cannot wantonly be invaded. Whilst the state cannot be compelled by suit to perform its contracts, any attempt on its part to violate property or rights acquired under its contracts, may be judicially resisted; and any law impairing the obligation of contracts under which such property or rights are held is void and powerless to affect their enjoyment. . . . [e]

5. THE IMMUNITY INTERPRETATION

Hans is usually read to adopt the immunity interpretation of the Eleventh Amendment. This interpretation treats the Eleventh Amendment as reestablishing the state sovereign immunity implicitly recognized by Article III and erroneously abrogated by *Chisholm*. On this theory, the Eleventh Amendment constitutionalized state sovereign immunity.

There is, of course, a textual difficulty. The Eleventh Amendment applies in terms only to suits by citizens of other states or of foreign countries; it does not mention a state's own citizens. The *Hans* Court surmounted this difficulty by saying that the idea that the Eleventh Amendment left the federal courts open to suit against a state by its own citizens was "almost an absurdity on its face." Despite the limitations of its text, the *Hans* Court read the amendment as evidencing a comprehensive policy of state sovereign immunity in the federal courts.[f]

Although the *Hans* Court cited Hamilton, Madison, and Marshall as saying that state sovereign immunity was implicit in the original structure of Article III, they were not the only framers who spoke to the issue. Others

---

[e] For a critical reexamination of *Hans* in its historical context, see Edward A. Purcell, Jr., The Particularly Dubious Case of *Hans v. Louisiana*: An Essay on Law, Race, History, and "Federal Courts," 81 N.C. L. Rev. 1927 (2003). For analysis of state consent to suit and the (arguably distinct) doctrine of state waiver of sovereign immunity, see Jonathan R. Siegel, Waivers of State Sovereign Immunity and the Ideology of the Eleventh Amendment, 52 Duke L.J. 1167 (2003).—[Footnote by eds.]

[f] Later decisions have applied this policy in other contexts not covered by the language of the amendment. See, e.g., Ex parte New York, 256 U.S. 490 (1921) (state immunity may be invoked in admiralty actions, notwithstanding that the amendment applies in terms only to suits "in law or equity"); Monaco v. Mississippi, 292 U.S. 313 (1934) (immunity applies in action by foreign country). But see Rhode Island v. Massachusetts, 37 U.S. (12 Pet.) 657 (1838) (Eleventh Amendment does not bar suit by another state); United States v. Texas, 143 U.S. 621, 645 (1892) (Eleventh Amendment does not bar suit by the United States).

reached exactly the opposite conclusion. Patrick Henry and George Mason saw in Article III an abrogation of state sovereign immunity and opposed the Constitution partly on that ground. James (later Justice) Wilson agreed that the Constitution made states amenable to suits by individuals and regarded that as a virtue supporting ratification. Edmund Randolph, who while serving as Attorney General of the United States, argued the case for Chisholm, also read Article III as abrogating state sovereign immunity and also approved that result.[g]

6.   CONCLUDING COMMENTS

The stakes involved in interpreting the Eleventh Amendment are potentially very high. If broadly applied, the immunity theory could prohibit any suit against a state in federal court. Since a state can only act through its officers, the immunity approach could logically be extended to prohibit suits against any state official. And it could easily be extended further to suits against cities, counties, and other components of state government, as well as to suits against local officials. If all this were true, virtually the entire class of modern civil rights litigation would be excluded from the federal courts. There would be no *Brown v. Board of Education* (school desegregation) and no *Reynolds v. Sims* (reapportionment). There could be no damages against state officials for violation of the Constitution, and no injunctions to secure future compliance with constitutional limitations. The Constitution could be used as a defensive shield against state enforcement proceedings, but not as a sword to force state compliance with the Constitution.

Obviously, this extreme reading of the Eleventh Amendment has not been adopted. One way of stating the challenge facing the modern Supreme Court has been to accommodate the immunity interpretation suggested by *Hans* with the need for some means of enforcing civil rights against states.

Ex parte Young

Supreme Court of the United States, 1908.
209 U.S. 123.

[When Minnesota enacted legislation fixing railroad rates, shareholders of a railroad company brought a derivative suit in federal Circuit Court to challenge the rates as confiscatory under the Fourteenth Amendment. The federal court issued a preliminary injunction prohibiting the railroad from putting the new rates into effect and restraining Edward T. Young, Attorney General of the state of Minnesota, from taking any action to enforce the state law. Young nevertheless commenced a mandamus action in state court to compel compliance with the new rates

---

[g]   These and other statements of the framers are discussed by Martha Field in The Eleventh Amendment and Other Sovereign Immunity Doctrines: Part One, 126 U. Pa. L. Rev. 515, 527–36 (1978) (concluding that *Chisholm*'s construction of Article III "was not therefore the clear contravention of a general understanding that it has long been said to be"). For an argument that *Hans* should not be read to bar federal claims against states because the case involved only a common-law contract claim held to be barred by common-law sovereign immunity, see William Burnham, Taming the Eleventh Amendment Without Overruling *Hans v. Louisiana*, 40 Case Western Res. L. Rev. 931 (1989–90).

and was promptly adjudged in contempt of the federal court. The dispute came to the Supreme Court on Young's original application for writs of habeas corpus and certiorari.]

■ MR. JUSTICE PECKHAM . . . delivered the opinion of the Court. . . .

For disobedience to the freight act the officers, directors, agents and employees of the company are made guilty of a misdemeanor, and upon conviction each may be punished by imprisonment in the county jail for a period not exceeding 90 days. Each violation would be a separate offense, and therefore, might result in imprisonment of the various agents of the company who would dare disobey for a term of 90 days for each offense. Disobedience to the passenger rate act renders the party guilty of a felony and subject to a fine not exceeding $5,000 or imprisonment in the state prison for a period not exceeding five years, or both fine and imprisonment. The sale of each ticket above the price permitted by the act would be a violation thereof. It would be difficult, if not impossible, for the company to obtain officers, agents or employees willing to carry on its affairs except in obedience to the act and orders in question. . . . The company, in order to test the validity of the acts, must find some agent or employee to disobey them at the risk stated. The necessary effect and result of such legislation must be to preclude a resort to the courts (either state or federal) for the purpose of testing its validity. The officers and employees could not be expected to disobey any of the provisions of the acts or orders at the risk of such fines and penalties being imposed upon them, in case the court should decide that the law was valid. The result would be a denial of any hearing to the company. . . .

We hold, therefore, that the provisions of the acts relating to the enforcement of the rates, either for freight or passengers, by imposing such enormous fines and possible imprisonment as a result of an unsuccessful effort to test the validity of the laws themselves, are unconstitutional on their face, without regard to the question of the insufficiency of the rates. . . .

We have, therefore, upon this record the case of an unconstitutional act of the state legislature and an intention by the Attorney General of the state to endeavor to enforce its provisions. . . . The question that arises is whether there is a remedy that the parties interested may resort to, by going into a federal court of equity, in a case involving a violation of the federal Constitution, and obtaining a judicial investigation of the problem, and pending its solution obtain freedom from suits, civil or criminal, by a temporary injunction, and if the question be finally decided favorably to the contention of the company, a permanent injunction restraining all such actions or proceedings.

This inquiry necessitates an examination of the most material and important objection made to the jurisdiction of the Circuit Court, the objection being that the suit is, in effect, one against the state of Minnesota. . . . This objection is to be considered with reference to the Eleventh [Amendment] to the federal Constitution. The Eleventh

Amendment prohibits the commencement or prosecution of any suit against one of the United States by citizens of another state or citizens or subjects of any foreign state. . . .

[W]e naturally must give to the Eleventh Amendment all the effect it naturally would have, without cutting it down or rendering its meaning any more narrow than the language, fairly interpreted, would warrant. [We have] ample justification for the assertion that individuals, who, as officers of the state, are clothed with some duty in regard to the enforcement of the laws of the state, and who threaten and are about to commence proceedings, either of a civil or criminal nature, to enforce against parties affected an unconstitutional act, violating the federal Constitution, may be enjoined by a federal court of equity from such action. . . .

It is contended that the complainants do not complain and they care nothing about any action which Mr. Young might take or bring as an ordinary individual, but that he was complained of as an officer, to whose discretion is confided the use of the name of the state of Minnesota so far as litigation is concerned, and that when or how he shall use it is a matter resting in his discretion and cannot be controlled by any court.

The answer to all this is the same as made in every case where an official claims to be acting under the authority of the state. The act to be enforced is alleged to be unconstitutional, and if it be so, the use of the name of the state to enforce an unconstitutional act to the injury of complainants is a proceeding without the authority of and one which does not affect the state in its sovereign or governmental capacity. It is simply an illegal act upon the part of a state official in attempting by the use of the name of the state to enforce a legislative enactment which is void because unconstitutional. If the act which the state Attorney General seeks to enforce be a violation of the federal Constitution, the officer in proceeding under such enactment comes into conflict with the superior authority of the Constitution, and he is in that case stripped of his official or representative character and is subjected in his person to the consequences of his individual conduct. The state has no power to impart to him any immunity from responsibility to the supreme authority of the United States. . . .

It is further objected (and the objection really forms part of the contention that the state cannot be sued) that a court of equity has no jurisdiction to enjoin criminal proceedings, by indictment or otherwise, under the state law. This, as a general rule, is true. But there are exceptions. When such indictment or proceeding is brought to enforce an alleged unconstitutional statute, which is the subject matter of inquiry in a suit already pending in a federal court, the latter court having first obtained jurisdiction over the subject matter, has the right, in both civil and criminal cases, to hold and maintain such jurisdiction, to the exclusion of all other courts, until its duty is fully performed. But the federal court cannot, of course, interfere in a case where the proceedings were already pending in a state court. . . .

It is further objected that there is a plain and adequate remedy at law open to the complainants and that a court of equity, therefore, has no jurisdiction in such case. It has been suggested that the proper way to test the constitutionality of the act is to disobey it, at least once, after which the company might obey the act pending subsequent proceedings to test its validity. But in the event of a single violation the prosecutor might not avail himself of the opportunity to make the test, as obedience to the law was thereafter continued, and he might think it unnecessary to start an inquiry. If, however, he should do so while the company was thereafter obeying the law, several years might elapse before there was a final determination of the question, and if it should be determined that the law was invalid the property of the company would have been taken during that time without due process of law, and there would be no possibility of its recovery.

Another obstacle to making the test on the part of the company might be to find an agent or employee who would disobey the law, with a possible fine and imprisonment staring him in the face if the act should be held valid. . . . To await proceedings against the company in a state court grounded upon a disobedience of the act, and then, if necessary, obtain a review in this Court by writ of error to the highest state court, would place the company in peril of large loss and its agents in great risk of fines and imprisonment if it should be finally determined that the act was valid. This risk the company ought not to be required to take. . . .

[The supreme authority of the United States], which arises from the specific provisions of the Constitution itself, is nowhere more fully illustrated than in the series of decisions under the federal habeas corpus statute, in some of which cases persons in the custody of state officers for alleged crimes against the state have been taken from that custody and discharged by a federal court or judge, because the imprisonment was adjudged to be in violation of the federal Constitution. The right to so discharge has not been doubted by this Court, and it has never been supposed there was any suit against the state by reason of serving the writ upon one of the officers of the state in whose custody the person was found. In some of the cases the writ has been refused as a matter of discretion, but in others it has been granted, while the power has been fully recognized in all.

It is somewhat difficult to appreciate the distinction which, while admitting that the taking of such a person from the custody of the state by virtue of service of the writ on the state officer in whose custody he is found, is not a suit against the state, and yet service of a writ on the Attorney General to prevent his enforcing an unconstitutional enactment of a state legislature is a suit against the state. . . .

The rule to show cause is discharged and the petition for writs of habeas corpus and certiorari is dismissed.

■ MR. JUSTICE HARLAN, dissenting. . . .

Let it be observed that the suit instituted . . . in the Circuit Court of the United States was, as to the defendant Young, one against him *as, and only because he was,* Attorney General of Minnesota. No relief was sought against him individually but only in his capacity as Attorney General. And the manifest, indeed the avowed and admitted, object of seeking such relief was *to tie the hands* of the *state* so that it could not in any manner or by any mode of proceeding, *in its own courts,* test the validity of the statutes and orders in question. It would therefore seem clear that within the true meaning of the Eleventh Amendment the suit brought in the federal court was one, in legal effect, against the state—as much so as if the state had been formally named on the record as a party—and therefore it was a suit to which, under the [Eleventh] Amendment, so far as the state or its Attorney General was concerned, the judicial power of the United States did not and could not extend. . . .

[T]he intangible thing, called a state, however extensive its powers, can never appear or be represented or known in any court in a litigated case, except by and through its officers. When, therefore, the federal court forbade the defendant Young, as Attorney General of Minnesota, from taking any action, suit, step or proceeding whatever looking to the enforcement of the statutes in question, it said in effect to the state of Minnesota: "It is true that the powers not delegated to the United States by the Constitution, nor prohibited by it to the states, are reserved to the states respectively or to its people, and it is true that under the Constitution the judicial power of the United States does not extend to any suit brought against a state by a citizen of another state or by a citizen or subject of a foreign state, yet the federal court adjudges that you, the state, although a sovereign for many important governmental purposes, shall not appear in your own courts, by your law officer, with the view of enforcing, or even for determining the validity of the state enactments which the federal court has, upon a preliminary hearing, declared to be in violation of the Constitution of the United States."

This principle, if firmly established, would work a radical change in our governmental system. It would inaugurate a new era in the American judicial system and in the relations of the national and state governments. It would enable the subordinate federal courts to supervise and control the official action of the states as if they were "dependencies" or provinces. It would place the states of the Union in a condition of inferiority never dreamed of when the Constitution was adopted or when the Eleventh Amendment was made a part of the supreme law of the land. . . . Too little consequence has been attached to the fact that the courts of the states are under an obligation equally strong with that resting upon the courts of the Union to respect and enforce the provisions of the federal Constitution as the supreme law of the land, and to guard rights secured or guaranteed by that instrument. We must assume—a decent respect for the states requires us to assume—that the state courts will enforce every right secured by the Constitution. If they fail to do so, the party complaining has a clear remedy for the protection of his rights; for, he can come by writ of error, in an orderly, judicial way, from the highest court of the state to this tribunal for redress in respect of every right granted or secured by that instrument and denied by the state court. . . .

I dissent from the opinion and judgment.[a]

NOTES ON ALTERNATIVE INTERPRETATIONS OF THE ELEVENTH AMENDMENT

1. INJUNCTIVE RELIEF AGAINST STATE OFFICERS

Ex parte Young creates a substantial, if circumlocutory, exception to state sovereign immunity. For most purposes, the exception can be summarized by saying that a state can be sued in federal court for prospective relief by the simple expedient of naming the appropriate state officer as the defendant.[a] The official is "stripped" of any "official or representative character" if the enforcement of state law violates the federal Constitution, even though the official's conduct is still regarded as "state action" under the Fourteenth Amendment.[b] If it were not, there would be no unconstitutionality of which to complain.

Is it possible to reconcile *Young* with the theory of the Eleventh Amendment adopted in *Hans*? If not, should *Hans* itself be modified? Consider the following notes in connection with these questions.[c]

---

[a] A Symposium on *Ex parte Young* in the Toledo Law Review included the following articles: Rochelle Bobroff, *Ex parte Young* as a Tool to Enforce Safety-Net and Civil-Rights Statutes, 40 U. Tol. L. Rev. 819 (2009); Charlton C. Copeland, *Ex parte Young*: Sovereignty, Immunity, and the Constitutional Structure of American Federalism, 40 U. Tol. L. Rev. 843 (2009); James Leonard, *Ex parte Young* and Hard Times, 40 U. Tol. L. Rev. 889 (2009); Marcia L. McCormick, Solving the Mystery of How *Ex parte Young* Escaped the Federalism Revolution, 40 U. Tol. L. Rev. 909 (2009); Edward A. Purcell, Jr., *Ex parte Young* and the Transformation of the Federal Courts, 1890–1917, 40 U. Tol. L. Rev. 931 (2009); Michael E. Solimine, *Ex parte Young*: An Interbranch Perspective, 40 U. Tol. L. Rev. 999 (2009).—[Footnote by eds.]

[a] *Ex parte Young* was a watershed case in the sense that it clearly established for the first time a general basis for prospective relief against state officials. Older cases permitted some forms of such relief but not others. For example, before *Young* a citizen could sue to recover specific property wrongfully seized by state officials, see e.g., Osborn v. Bank of the United States, 22 U.S. (9 Wheat.) 738 (1824) (ordering the return of money seized from the bank and kept separately in a trunk), but not to enjoin the attorney general from instituting proceedings that allegedly would have violated the Contracts Clause. In re Ayers, 123 U.S. 443 (1887).

[b] See, e.g., Home Telephone & Telegraph Co. v. City of Los Angeles, 227 U.S. 278 (1913).

[c] The questions raised in the text reflect the widely accepted account of *Ex parte Young* as an exception to sovereign immunity. This understanding is challenged in John Harrison, *Ex parte Young*, 60 Stan. L. Rev. 989 (2008). Harrison's claims are summarized in the editorial introduction to the article as follows: "*Ex parte Young* does not represent an exception to ordinary principles of sovereign immunity, it does not employ a legal fiction, it does not imply a novel cause of action under the Constitution or other federal law, and it does not create a paradox by treating officers as state actors for one purpose and private persons for another." Instead, Harrison sees *Ex parte Young* as a traditional use of equity power to restrain proceedings at law and argues that a proper understanding curtails many of the modern inferences drawn from that decision. Accord Ann Woolhandler, The Common Law Origins of Constitutionally Compelled Remedies, 107 Yale L.J. 77 (1997) (concluding, after a comprehensive examination of

2. The Diversity Interpretation

One response to the difficulty of reconciling *Hans* with modern civil rights litigation is the "diversity" interpretation of the Eleventh Amendment. This approach reads the amendment as a restriction on the federal courts only when jurisdiction is based on diversity of citizenship. Under this interpretation, the Eleventh Amendment does not enshrine sovereign immunity as a constitutional concept. It only prohibits diversity suits *against* states, thus restricting the state-citizen diversity jurisdiction to suits *by* states. It does not affect suits arising under federal law. Under this view, the function of the Eleventh Amendment—and the reason it addresses only suits by out-of-state citizens—was merely to repeal a segment of the diversity jurisdiction originally authorized by Article III.

This interpretation assumes that Article III was intended to be neutral with respect to sovereign immunity—that is, neither to adopt state sovereign immunity as a limitation on federal power nor to abrogate state sovereign immunity simply because a case might be brought in federal court. The error of *Chisholm* was its treatment of the mere fact of diversity jurisdiction as an abrogation of state sovereign immunity *for a claim based on state law*. In this view, the Eleventh Amendment was designed not to constitutionalize state sovereign immunity, but merely to repudiate the idea that state sovereign immunity had been abrogated by diversity of citizenship. On this reading, the failure of the amendment to prohibit suits by a state's own citizens is perfectly understandable, as such suits would not in any event have come within the state-citizen diversity provision of Article III.

Note, however, that the text of the amendment is not limited to diversity cases. Taken literally, it would preclude *all* suits against a state by a citizen of another state, including those based on federal law. The usual response to this observation is that the failure to distinguish federal question cases is not surprising, given that there was at the time no statute generally authorizing the federal courts to hear cases arising under federal law and no disposition by the national legislature to impose federal liability upon the states. The question whether a suit based on federal law should be prohibited by the Eleventh Amendment, in other words, was simply not in view.

In summary, the diversity interpretation sees the Eleventh Amendment as simply rejecting the erroneous idea that diversity jurisdiction abrogated the common-law immunity of states. State sovereign immunity survived as

---

history, that *Ex parte Young* "did not fundamentally alter the role of the federal courts" in enforcing constitutional rights). For wide-ranging discussion of these and other views of *Young*, see David L. Shapiro, *Ex Parte Young* and the Uses of History, 67 N.Y.U. Ann. Surv. Am. L. 69 (2011).

Harrison's position is criticized in Larry Yackle, *Young* Again, 35 U. Haw. L. Rev. 51 (2013). Yackle's position is that "[t]he right of action in *Young* was an aspect of federal equity jurisprudence and general law applied in the federal courts at the time, which permitted shareholders to sue their own companies as well as parties with whom their companies had dealings, seeking injunctive relief protecting the shareholders' interests." It "must be understood," he says, "within a tradition in which corporations systematically employed shareholder suits to press constitutional claims. It is a familiar irony that in our time *Young* is revered as an essential ingredient of arrangements by which personal civil rights and civil liberties may be vindicated, but that, in its own day, *Young* was an instrument used by industry to forestall regulation that threatened corporate profits."

a non-constitutional doctrine, which can be asserted against state causes of action under state law. It can also be asserted against federal causes of action to the extent permitted by federal law as fashioned by Congress or the courts. Under this view, *Ex parte Young* was easy. Since the plaintiff's case was based on federal law, the Eleventh Amendment did not apply.

No Justice of the Supreme Court wholly accepted the diversity interpretation until Justice Brennan's dissent, joined by Justices Marshall, Blackmun, and Stevens, in Atascadero State Hospital v. Scanlon, 473 U.S. 234, 289–90 (1985). In Brennan's view:

> The language of the Eleventh Amendment, its legislative history, and the attendant historical circumstances all strongly suggest that the amendment was intended to remedy an interpretation of the Constitution that would have had the state-citizen and state-alien diversity clauses of Article III abrogating the state law of sovereign immunity on state-law causes of action brought in federal courts. . . .

> The *Chisholm* Court had interpreted the state-citizen clause of Article III to work a major change in state law, or at least in those cases arising under state law that found their way to federal court. The Eleventh Amendment corrected that error, and henceforth required that the party-based heads of jurisdiction in Article III be construed not to work this kind of drastic modification of state law. . . .

> Article III grants a federal question jurisdiction to the federal courts that is as broad as is the lawmaking authority of Congress. If Congress acting within its Article I or other powers creates a legal right and remedy, and if neither the right nor the remedy violates any provision of the Constitution outside Article III, then Congress may entrust adjudication of claims based on the newly created right to the federal courts—even if the defendant is a state. Neither Article III nor the Eleventh Amendment impose an independent limit on the lawmaking authority of Congress.

Practically speaking, the diversity interpretation reads the Eleventh Amendment to mean almost nothing. The only cases it would cover would be suits brought by out-of-state plaintiffs to enforce state-law obligations. No suits brought under federal law would be affected.

Academics have divided on the diversity interpretation of the Eleventh Amendment. An early explication of this view is Martha Field, The Eleventh Amendment and Other Sovereign Immunity Doctrines: Part One, 126 U. Pa. L. Rev. 515 (1978) . The most extensive historical investigation of the basis of the diversity interpretation appears in William A. Fletcher, A Historical Interpretation of the Eleventh Amendment: A Narrow Construction of an Affirmative Grant of Jurisdiction Rather than a Prohibition Against Jurisdiction, 35 Stan. L. Rev. 1033 (1983), and Akhil Reed Amar, Of Sovereignty and Federalism, 96 Yale L.J. 1425, 1466–92 (1987). For articles criticizing the diversity interpretation, see William Marshall, The Diversity Theory of the Eleventh Amendment: A Critical Evaluation, 102 Harv. L. Rev. 1372

(1989), and Calvin Massey, State Sovereignty and the Tenth and Eleventh Amendments, 56 U. Chi. L. Rev. 61 (1989). For a reply, see William Fletcher, The Diversity Explanation of the Eleventh Amendment: A Reply to Critics, 56 U. Chi. L. Rev. 1261 (1989).

A different rationale for a similarly constrained interpretation of the Eleventh Amendment appears in Thomas H. Lee, Making Sense of the Eleventh Amendment: International Law and State Sovereignty, 96 Nw. U. L. Rev. 1027 (2002). Lee extensively examines the history and concludes that the purpose of the Eleventh Amendment was to embrace "the classical international law rule that only states have rights against other states." It follows that "a foreign citizen may not sue a sovereign state." In Lee's view, "because the Amendment was intended, like the international law rule, to govern only interstate or international disputes between private parties and States, it logically makes no statement about the rights of citizens to sue their own States in federal court."

3. THE SEPARATION-OF-POWERS INTERPRETATION

Another view of the Eleventh Amendment reads the provision as stating a limitation on the federal courts derived from principles of federalism and separation of powers. The error of *Chisholm,* according to this theory, lay in its judicial creativity. That creativity can be explained in either of two ways. One is that in enforcing a state-created cause of action, the Court set aside the accompanying state law of sovereign immunity. The other is that in effect the Court created a new federal cause of action to enforce the constitutional obligation of the states not to impair their contracts. The purpose of the Eleventh Amendment, according to this view, was to curb the capacity of the federal courts to impose legal liabilities on the states in either manner.

This view holds that the Eleventh Amendment was not designed to speak to the powers of Congress. The balance of power between the state and federal legislatures was struck in the Constitution by the relationship between Article I and the Tenth Amendment. Article III, moreover—and particularly that part authorizing jurisdiction over cases arising under federal law—was designed to permit the Congress to use the federal courts for any purpose legitimately within its Article I powers.[d] The controversy surrounding *Chisholm* was not concerned with federal legislation, and the

---

[d] Compare Chief Justice Marshall in Osborn v. Bank of the United States, 22 U.S. (9 Wheat.) 738 (1824):

> [I]t is said, that the legislative, executive and judicial powers of every well-constructed government, are co-extensive with each other; that is, they are potentially co-extensive. The executive department may constitutionally execute every law which the legislature may constitutionally make, and the judicial department may receive from the legislature the power of construing every such law. All governments which are not extremely defective in their organization, must possess . . . the means of expounding, as well as enforcing, their own laws. If we examine the Constitution of the United States, we find that its framers kept this great political principle in view. [Article III] enables the judicial department to receive jurisdiction to the full extent of the Constitution, laws, and treaties of the United States, when any question respecting them shall assume such a form that the judicial power is capable of acting on it. That power is capable of acting only when the subject is submitted to it by a party who asserts his

debates leading to the Eleventh Amendment show no attention to whether the powers of Congress should be curtailed. The Eleventh Amendment should therefore be interpreted as a limitation on the law-making capacity of the federal courts in cases where the state or a state official is the defendant. It should not be interpreted as a restriction of Congress's powers under the Constitution.

Aspects of this argument appear in John Nowak, The Scope of Congressional Power to Create Causes of Action against State Governments and the History of the Eleventh and Fourteenth Amendments, 75 Colum. L. Rev. 1413 (1975), and Laurence Tribe, Intergovernmental Immunities in Litigation, Taxation, and Regulation: Separation of Powers Issues in Controversies about Federalism, 89 Harv. L. Rev. 682 (1976). Both rely on the policy perception, as Nowak phrased it, "that the pragmatic problems of federalism posed by the Eleventh Amendment should be resolved by Congress, not by the judiciary." Thus, both build on the premise that since the states as such are represented in the federal legislature, the courts should be reluctant to limit congressional power in the name of federalism. Martha Field has criticized this position on the ground "that it derives from nothing peculiar to the Eleventh Amendment," but rests instead on a *"general* limitation upon judicial power in relation to legislative power, at least in areas involving federal-state relations." Field, The Eleventh Amendment and Other Sovereign Immunity Doctrines: Congressional Imposition of Suit upon the States, 126 U. Pa. L. Rev. 1203, 1258–61 (1978).

4. CONCLUDING COMMENTS

The Supreme Court has not adopted, in its pure form, the immunity interpretation of the Eleventh Amendment, the diversity interpretation, or the separation-of-powers interpretation. In an important sense, the debate between the immunity and the diversity approaches to the Eleventh Amendment puts an all-or-nothing choice. One response might be to adopt the separation-of-powers interpretation. Yet it too has a central difficulty. Taken to its extreme, it would limit the capacity of the federal courts to engage in creative law-making in order to enforce constitutional limitations on state government. A separation-of-powers approach may explain *Hans,* but it is difficult to reconcile with *Ex parte Young.* More broadly speaking, the lines of cases based on *Mapp v. Ohio* (exclusionary rule), *Brown v. Board of Education* (school desegregation), and *Reynolds v. Sims* (reapportionment) involved the judicial development of remedies against state government, remedies the creation of which, if one adhered to a strict separation-of-powers limitation on judicial lawmaking, should have been left to Congress. Yet the necessities that led the Court to these actions were in large part the result of legislative default.

The Court's response to this situation, as *Ex parte Young* and subsequent materials illustrate, has been to adopt an amalgam of fictions and theories that have turned the Eleventh Amendment into "an arcane specialty

---

rights in the form prescribed by law. It then becomes a case, and the Constitution declares, that the judicial power shall extend to all cases arising under the Constitution, laws and treaties of the United States.

of lawyers and federal judges," "replete with historical anomalies, internal inconsistencies, and senseless distinctions."[e]

5.   ADDITIONAL BIBLIOGRAPHY

The literature on the Eleventh Amendment is too voluminous to survey here. Among articles published since 2000, reference is made to Bradford R. Clark, The Eleventh Amendment and the Nature of the Union, 123 Harv. L. Rev. 1817 (2010) (arguing that the oddity of barring suits by citizens of other states but not by citizens of the defendant state made sense in historical context, because the Framers did not expect that suits against states would arise under the laws of the United States); Erwin Chemerinsky, Against Sovereign Immunity, 53 Stan. L. Rev. 1201 (2001) (criticizing expansions of state sovereign immunity); Alfred Hill, In Defense of Our Law of Sovereign Immunity, 42 B.C. L. Rev. 485 (2001) (rebutting academic criticism of the constitutionalization of sovereign immunity); Mark Strasser, *Hans*, *Ayers*, and Eleventh Amendment Jurisprudence: On Justification, Rationalization, and Sovereign Immunity, 10 Geo. Mason L. Rev. 251 (2001) (concluding that *Hans* made sense at the time but that it does not justify modern Eleventh Amendment jurisprudence); John F. Manning, The Eleventh Amendment and the Reading of Precise Constitutional Texts, 113 Yale L.J. 1663 (2004) (criticizing the Court's willingness to read the Eleventh Amendment to mean much more than it says); Kurt T. Lash, Leaving the *Chisholm* Trail: The Eleventh Amendment and the Background Principle of Strict Construction, 50 Wm. & Mary L. Rev. 1577 (2009) (arguing that *Chisholm* was in fact only one of a number of suits dramatizing the "*concept* of an individual compelling a state to answer in federal court" and that hostility to this concept drove the Eleventh Amendment); Caleb Nelson, Sovereign Immunity as a Doctrine of Personal Jurisdiction, 115 Harv. L. Rev. 1561 (2002) (arguing that historically the concept of sovereign immunity traveled in the orbit of *personal* jurisdiction rather than *subject matter* jurisdiction and that unconsenting states should continue to enjoy some exemptions from compulsory process).

Finally, for articles that examine the Eleventh Amendment in the context of alternative means of enforcing federal rights, see John C. Jeffries, Jr., In Praise of the Eleventh Amendment and Section 1983, 84 Va. L. Rev. 47 (1998) (focusing on enforcement of federal rights through damages actions against state officers); Jesse H. Choper and John C. Yoo, Who's Afraid of the Eleventh Amendment? The Limited Impact of the Court's Sovereign Immunity Rulings, 106 Colum. L. Rev. 213 (2006) (concluding that "[p]reventing private plaintiffs from suing states for retrospective money damages poses, at most, a minor barrier" to the enforcement of federal law); Jesse H. Choper and John C. Yoo, Effective Alternatives to Causes of Action Barred by the Eleventh Amendment, 50 N.Y. L. Rev. 715 (2005–06); Michael E. Solimine, The Fall and Rise of Specialized Federal Constitutional Courts, 17 J. Const. L. 115 (2014) (analyzing three-judge courts as "specialized" constitutional courts and recommending against their use).

---

[e]   John Orth, The Judicial Power of the United States 11 (1987).

ADDITIONAL NOTES ON EX PARTE YOUNG

1.   SUBSEQUENT LEGISLATIVE LIMITATIONS ON *EX PARTE YOUNG*

Political reaction to *Ex parte Young* was not favorable. Particular objection was made to the power of a single federal judge to enjoin the enforcement of state law. Congress responded to this concern in 1910 by limiting the availability of temporary restraining orders and by requiring that applications for certain kinds of preliminary injunctive relief against state officials be heard by special three-judge district courts, with direct review by appeal to the United States Supreme Court.

The three-judge court requirement was extended in 1925 to the issuance of final injunctions against enforcement of unconstitutional state laws, and in 1937 an analogous provision required three-judge courts for suits attacking the constitutionality of federal legislation. These provisions spawned an exceedingly vexed and complicated body of law concerning such questions as the precise circumstances requiring the convening of a three-judge court, the powers of the single district judge before whom the case was initially filed, the kinds of additional claims that could be heard by the three-judge court once convened, the court to which issues that could have been resolved by a single judge should be appealed, etc.

Most of these questions have been mooted by the 1976 repeal of the general three-judge court provisions (formerly 28 U.S.C. §§ 2281 and 2282), a reform brought about in large part because of the burdens on lower court judges, the disproportionate share of the Supreme Court's docket consumed by direct appeals from three-judge courts, and by the perception that such courts were no longer necessary. Today, outside of certain highly specific statutory cases, three-judge courts are required only "when an action is filed challenging the constitutionality of the apportionment of congressional districts or the apportionment of any statewide legislative body." 28 U.S.C. § 2284. See generally Michael E. Solimine, Congress, *Ex parte Young*, and the Fate of the Three-Judge District Court, 70 U. Pitt. L. Rev. 101 (2008).

2.   FOOTNOTE ON THE CAUSE OF ACTION

The complainants in *Ex parte Young* sought affirmative relief to prevent violation of rights guaranteed by the Fourteenth Amendment to the federal Constitution. No statute was advanced to support such a suit. Where did the plaintiff's cause of action come from?

Though the answer to this question is not entirely clear, *Ex parte Young* has come to be cited for the proposition that such cause of action to require compliance with the Constitution exists independent of explicit congressional authorization. Two subsequent developments should be noted. First, Monroe v. Pape, 365 U.S. 167 (1961), rediscovered 42 U.S.C. § 1983 as creating a cause of action to enforce the Constitution, whether by equitable relief or actions for damages, against officials acting under color of *state* law. Second, Bivens v. Six Unknown Named Agents of Federal Bureau of Narcotics, 403 U.S. 388 (1971), authorized damages actions against *federal* officers for violation of the Fourth Amendment. A cause of action for equitable relief against both state and federal officers had previously been thought to exist under the authority of *Ex parte Young.*

Edelman v. Jordan

Supreme Court of the United States, 1974.
415 U.S. 651.

[Respondent Jordan brought a class action to challenge the practices of certain Illinois officials in administering federal-state programs under the Aid to the Aged, Blind, or Disabled Act (AABD). The District Court found that the defendant officials had failed to process AABD applications within applicable time limits and had failed to make the benefits retroactive to the date of initial eligibility, as required by federal regulations issued by the Department of Health, Education and Welfare under the Social Security Act. The court enjoined any future violations and ordered the state officials to refund all wrongfully withheld past benefits. The Seventh Circuit affirmed over the defendants' objection that the Eleventh Amendment barred the award of retroactive benefits. The Supreme Court granted certiorari.]

■ MR. JUSTICE REHNQUIST delivered the opinion of the Court. . . .

While the [Eleventh] Amendment by its terms does not bar suits against a state by its own citizens, this Court has consistently held that an unconsenting state is immune from suits brought in federal courts by her own citizens as well as by citizens of another state. Hans v. Louisiana, 134 U.S. 1 (1890); Parden v. Terminal Ry. Co., 377 U.S. 184 (1964); Employees v. Department of Public Health and Welfare, 411 U.S. 279 (1973). It is also well established that even though a state is not named a party to the action, the suit may nonetheless be barred by the Eleventh Amendment. In Ford Motor Co. v. Department of the Treasury, 323 U.S. 459, 464 (1945), the Court said:

> [W]hen the action is in essence one for the recovery of money from the state, the state is the real, substantial party in interest and is entitled to invoke its sovereign immunity from suit even though individual officials are nominal defendants.

Thus the rule has evolved that a suit by private parties seeking to impose a liability which must be paid from public funds in the state treasury is barred by the Eleventh Amendment.

The Court of Appeals in this case, while recognizing that the *Hans* line of cases permitted the state to raise the Eleventh Amendment as a defense to suit by its own citizens, nevertheless concluded that the amendment did not bar the award of retroactive payments of the statutory benefits found to have been wrongfully withheld. The Court of Appeals held that the above-cited cases, when read in light of this Court's landmark decision in Ex parte Young, 209 U.S. 123 (1908), do not preclude the grant of such a monetary award in the nature of equitable restitution.

Petitioner [the present Director of the Illinois Department of Public Aid] concedes that *Ex parte Young* is no bar to that part of the District Court's judgment that prospectively enjoined petitioner's predecessors for failing to process applications within the time limits established by the federal regulations. Petitioner argues, however, that *Ex parte Young* does not extend so far as to permit a suit which seeks the award of an accrued monetary liability which must be met from the general revenues of a state, absent consent or waiver by the state of its Eleventh Amendment immunity, and that therefore the award of retroactive benefits by the District Court was improper.

Ex parte Young was a watershed case in which this Court held that the Eleventh Amendment did not bar an action in the federal courts seeking to enjoin the Attorney General of Minnesota from enforcing a statute claimed to violate the Fourteenth Amendment of the United States Constitution. This holding has permitted the Civil War amendments to the Constitution to serve as a sword, rather than merely as a shield, for those whom they were designed to protect. But the relief awarded in *Ex parte Young* was prospective only; the Attorney General of Minnesota was enjoined to conform his future conduct of that office to the requirement of the Fourteenth Amendment. Such relief is analogous to that awarded by the District Court in the prospective portion of its order under review in this case.

But the retroactive portion of the District Court's order here, which requires the payment of a very substantial amount of money which that court held should have been paid, but was not, stands on quite a different footing. These funds will obviously not be paid out of the pocket of petitioner Edelman. Addressing himself to a similar situation in Rothstein v. Wyman, 467 F.2d 226 (2d Cir.1972), Judge McGowan observed for the court:

> It is not pretended that these payments are to come from the personal resources of these appellants. Appellees expressly contemplate that they will, rather, involve substantial expenditures from the public funds of the state. . . .

> It is one thing to tell the Commissioner of Social Services that he must comply with the federal standards for the future if the state is to have the benefit of federal funds in the programs he administers. It is quite another thing to order the Commissioner to use state funds to make reparation for the past. The latter would appear to us to fall afoul of the Eleventh Amendment if that basic constitutional provision is to be conceived of has having any present force.

We agree with Judge McGowan's observations. The funds to satisfy the award in this case must inevitably come from the general revenues of the state of Illinois, and thus the award resembles far more closely the monetary award against the state itself, *Ford Motor Co. v. Department of*

Treasury than it does the prospective injunctive relief awarded in *Ex parte Young. . . .*[11]

As in most areas of the law, the difference between the type of relief barred by the Eleventh Amendment and that permitted under *Ex parte Young* will not in many instances be that between day and night. The injunction issued in *Ex parte Young* was not totally without effect on the state's revenues, since the state law which the Attorney General was enjoined from enforcing provided substantial monetary penalties against railroads which did not conform to its provisions. Later cases from this Court have authorized equitable relief which has probably had greater impact on state treasuries than did that awarded in *Ex parte Young*. In Graham v. Richardson, 403 U.S. 365 (1971), Arizona and Pennsylvania welfare officials were prohibited from denying welfare benefits to otherwise qualified recipients who were aliens. In Goldberg v. Kelly, 397 U.S. 254 (1970), New York City welfare officials were enjoined from following New York state procedures which authorized the termination of benefits paid to welfare recipients without prior hearing. But the fiscal consequences to state treasuries in these cases were the necessary result of compliance with decrees which by their terms were prospective in nature. Such officials, in order to shape their official conduct to the mandate of the Court's decrees, would more likely have to spend money from the state treasury than if they had been left free to pursue their previous course of conduct. Such an ancillary effect on the state treasury is a permissible and often an inevitable consequence of the principle announced in *Ex parte Young*.

But that portion of the District Court's decree which petitioner challenges on Eleventh Amendment grounds goes much further than any of the cases cited. It requires payment of state funds, not as a necessary consequence of compliance in the future with a substantive federal-question determination, but as a form of compensation to those whose applications were processed on the slower time schedule at a time when petitioner was under no court-imposed obligation to conform to a different standard. While the Court of Appeals described this retroactive award of monetary relief as a form of "equitable restitution," it is in practical effect indistinguishable in many aspects from an award of damages against the state. It will to a virtual certainty be paid from state funds, and not from the pockets of the individual state officials who were the

---

[11] It may be true, as stated by our Brother Douglas in dissent, that "[m]ost welfare decisions by federal courts have a financial impact on the states." But we cannot agree that such a financial impact is the same where a federal court applies *Ex parte Young* to grant prospective declaratory and injunctive relief, as opposed to an order of retroactive payments as was made in the instant case. It is not necessarily true that "[w]hether the decree is prospective only or requires payments for the weeks or months wrongfully skipped over by the state officials, the nature of the impact on the state treasury is precisely the same." This argument neglects the fact that where the state has a definable allocation to be used in the payment of public aid benefits, and pursues a certain course of action such as the processing of applications within certain time periods as did Illinois here, the subsequent ordering by a federal court of retroactive payments to correct delays in such processing will invariably mean there is less money available for payments for the continuing obligations of the public aid system. . . .

defendants in the action. It is measured in terms of a monetary loss resulting from a past breach of a legal duty on the part of the defendant state officials.

Were we to uphold this portion of the District Court's decree, we would be obligated to overrule the Court's holding in *Ford Motor Co. v. Department of Treasury*. There a taxpayer, who had, under protest, paid taxes to the state of Indiana, sought a refund of those taxes from the Indiana state officials who were charged with their collection. The taxpayer claimed that the tax had been imposed in violation of the United States Constitution. The term "equitable restitution" would seem even more applicable to the relief sought in that case, since the taxpayer had at one time had the money, and paid it over to the state pursuant to an allegedly unconstitutional tax exaction. Yet this Court had no hesitation in holding that the taxpayer's action was a suit against the state, and barred by the Eleventh Amendment. We reach a similar conclusion with respect to the retroactive portion of the relief awarded by the District Court in this case. . . .

Three fairly recent District Court judgments requiring state directors of public aid to make the type of retroactive payments involved here have been summarily affirmed by this Court notwithstanding Eleventh Amendment contentions made by state officers who were appealing from the District Court judgments. Shapiro v. Thompson, 394 U.S. 618 (1969), is the only instance in which the Eleventh Amendment objection to such retroactive relief was actually presented to this Court in a case which was orally argued. The three-judge District Court in that case had ordered the retroactive payment of welfare benefits found by that court to have been unlawfully withheld because of residence requirements held violative of equal protection. This Court, while affirming the judgment, did not in its opinion refer to or substantively treat the Eleventh Amendment argument. Nor, of course, did the summary dispositions of the three District Court cases contain any substantive discussion of this or any other issues raised by the parties.

This case, therefore, is the first opportunity the Court has taken to fully explore and treat the Eleventh Amendment aspects of such relief in a written opinion. *Shapiro v. Thompson* and these three summary affirmances obviously are of precedential value in support of the contention that the Eleventh Amendment does not bar the relief awarded by the District Court in this case. Equally obviously, they are not of the same precedential value as would be an opinion of this Court treating the question on the merits. Since we deal with a constitutional question, we are less constrained by the principle of stare decisis than we are in other areas of the law. Having now had an opportunity to more fully consider the Eleventh Amendment issue after briefing and argument, we disapprove the Eleventh Amendment holdings of those cases to the extent that they are inconsistent with our holding today.

The Court of Appeals held in the alternative that even if the Eleventh Amendment be deemed a bar to the retroactive relief awarded respondent in this case, the state of Illinois had waived its Eleventh Amendment immunity and consented to the bringing of such a suit by participating in the federal AABD program. The Court of Appeals relied upon our holdings in Parden v. Terminal Ry. Co., 377 U.S. 184 (1964), and Petty v. Tennessee-Missouri Bridge Comm'n, 359 U.S. 275 (1959), and on the dissenting opinion of Judge Bright in Employees v. Department of Public Health and Welfare, 452 F.2d 820, 827 (8th Cir. 1971). While the holding in the latter case was ultimately affirmed by this Court in 411 U.S. 279 (1973), we do not think that the answer to the waiver question turns on the distinction between *Parden* and *Employees*. Both *Parden* and *Employees* involved a congressional enactment which by its terms authorized suit by designated plaintiffs against a general class of defendants which literally included states or state instrumentalities. Similarly, *Petty v. Tennessee-Missouri Bridge Comm'n* involved congressional approval, pursuant to the Compact Clause, of a compact between Tennessee and Missouri, which provided that each compacting state would have the power "to contract, to sue, and be sued in its own name." The question of waiver or consent under the Eleventh Amendment was found in those cases to turn on whether Congress had intended to abrogate the immunity in question, and whether the state by its participation in the program authorized by Congress had in effect consented to the abrogation of that immunity.

But in this case the threshold fact of congressional authorization to sue a class of defendants which literally includes states is wholly absent. Thus respondent is not only precluded from relying on this Court's holding in *Employees,* but on this Court's holdings in *Parden* and *Petty* as well.

The Court of Appeals held that as a matter of federal law Illinois had "constructively consented" to this suit by participating in the federal AABD program and agreeing to administer federal and state funds in compliance with federal law. Constructive consent is not a doctrine commonly associated with the surrender of constitutional rights, and we see no place for it here. In deciding whether a state has waived its constitutional protection under the Eleventh Amendment, we will find waiver only where stated "by the most express language or by such overwhelming implications from the text as [will] leave no room for any other reasonable construction." Murray v. Wilson Distilling Co., 213 U.S. 151, 171 (1909). We see no reason to retreat from the Court's statement in Great Northern Life Ins. Co. v. Read, 322 U.S. 47, 54 (1944):

> [W]hen we are dealing with the sovereign exemption from judicial interference in the vital field of financial administration a clear declaration of the state's intention to submit its fiscal problems to other courts than those of its own creation must be found.

The mere fact that a state participates in a program through which the federal government provides assistance for the operation by the state of a system of public aid is not sufficient to establish consent on the part of the state to be sued in the federal courts. And while this Court has, in cases such as J.I. Case Co. v. Borak, 377 U.S. 426 (1964), authorized suits by one private party against another in order to effectuate a statutory purpose, it has never done so in the context of the Eleventh Amendment and a state defendant. Since *Employees* where Congress had expressly authorized suits against a general class of defendants and the only thing left to implication was whether the described class of defendants included states, was decided adversely to the putative plaintiffs on the waiver question, surely this respondent must also fail on that issue. The only language in the Social Security Act which purported to provide a federal sanction against a state which did not comply with federal requirements for the distribution of federal monies was found in former 42 U.S.C. § 1384 (now replaced by substantially similar provisions in 42 U.S.C. § 804), which provided for termination of future allocations of federal funds when a participating state failed to conform with federal law. This provision by its terms did not authorize suit against anyone, and standing alone, fell far short of a waiver by a participating state of its Eleventh Amendment immunity.

Our Brother Marshall argues in dissent, and the Court of Appeals held, that although the Social Security Act itself does not create a private cause of action, the cause of action created by 42 U.S.C. § 1983, coupled with the enactment of the AABD program, and the issuance by HEW of regulations which require the states to make corrective payments after successful "fair hearings" and provide for federal matching funds to satisfy federal court orders of retroactive payments, indicate that Congress intended a cause of action for public aid recipients such as respondent. It is, of course, true that Rosado v. Wyman, 397 U.S. 397 (1970), held that suits in federal court under § 1983 are proper to secure compliance with the provisions of the Social Security Act on the part of participating states. But it has not heretofore been suggested that § 1983 was intended to create a waiver of a state's Eleventh Amendment immunity merely because an action could be brought under that section against state officers, rather than against the state itself. Though a § 1983 action may be instituted by public aid recipients such as respondent, a federal court's remedial power, consistent with the Eleventh Amendment, is necessarily limited to prospective injunctive relief, *Ex parte Young* and may not include a retroactive award which requires the payment of funds from the state treasury, *Ford Motor Co. v. Department of Treasury.*

Respondent urges that since the various Illinois officials sued in the District Court failed to raise the Eleventh Amendment as a defense to the relief sought by respondent, petitioner is therefore barred from raising the Eleventh Amendment defense in the Court of Appeals or in this

Court. The Court of Appeals apparently felt that the defense was proper-ly presented, and dealt with it on the merits. We approve of this resolution, since it has been well settled since the decision in *Ford Motor Co. v. Department of Treasury* that the Eleventh Amendment defense sufficiently partakes of the nature of a jurisdictional bar so that it need not be raised in the trial court:

> [The Attorney General of Indiana] appeared in the federal District Court and the Circuit Court of Appeals and defended the suit on the merits. The objection to petitioner's suit as a vi-olation of the Eleventh Amendment was first made and argued by Indiana in this Court. This was in time, however. The Elev-enth Amendment declares a policy and sets forth an explicit limitation on federal judicial power of such compelling force that this Court will consider the issue arising under this amendment in this case even though urged for the first time in this Court.

For the foregoing reasons we decide that the Court of Appeals was wrong in holding that the Eleventh Amendment did not constitute a bar to that portion of the District Court decree which ordered retroactive pay-ment of benefits found to have been wrongfully withheld. The judgment of the Court of Appeals is therefore reversed and the cause remanded for further proceedings consistent with this opinion.

So ordered.

■ MR. JUSTICE DOUGLAS, dissenting.

Congress provided in 42 U.S.C. § 1983 that:

> Every person who, under color of any statute, ordinance, regulation, custom, or usage, of any state or territory, subjects, or causes to be subjected, any citizen of the United States or other person within the jurisdiction thereof to the deprivation of any rights, privileges, or immunities secured by the Constitu-tion and laws, shall be liable to the party injured in an action at law, suit in equity, or other proper proceeding for redress.

In this class action respondent sought to enforce against state aid officials of Illinois provisions of the Social Security Act, 42 U.S.C. §§ 1381–1385, known as the Aid to the Aged, Blind, or Disabled (AABD) program. The complaint alleges violations of the Equal Protection Clause of the Fourteenth Amendment and also violations of the Social Security Act. Hence § 1983 is satisfied in haec verba, for a deprivation of "rights" which are "secured by the Constitution and laws" is alleged. The Court of Appeals, though ruling that the alleged constitutional violations had not occurred, sustained federal jurisdiction because federal "rights" were violated. The main issue tendered us is whether that ruling of the Court of Appeals is consistent with the Eleventh Amendment. . . .

As the complaint in the instant case alleges violations by officials of Illinois of the Equal Protection Clause of the Fourteenth Amendment, it seems that the case is governed by *Ex parte Young* so far as injunctive relief is concerned. The main thrust of the argument is that the instant case asks for relief which if granted would affect the treasury of the state.

Most welfare decisions by federal courts have a financial impact on the states. Under the existing federal state cooperative system, a state desiring to participate, submits a "state plan" to HEW for approval; once HEW approves the plan the state is locked into the cooperative scheme until it withdraws, all as described in King v. Smith, 392 U.S. 309, 316 (1968). The welfare cases coming here have involved ultimately the financial responsibility of the state to beneficiaries claiming they were deprived of federal rights. *King v. Smith* required payment to children even though their mother was cohabiting with a man who could not pass muster as a "parent." Rosado v. Wyman, 397 U.S. 397 (1970), held that under this state-federal cooperative program a state could not reduce its standard of need in conflict with the federal standard. It is true that *Rosado* did not involve retroactive payments as are involved here. But the distinction is not relevant or material because the result in every welfare case coming here is to increase or reduce the financial responsibility of the participating state. In no case when the responsibility of the state is increased to meet the lawful demand of the beneficiary, is there any levy on state funds. Whether the decree is prospective only or requires payments for the weeks or months wrongfully skipped over by the state officials, the nature of the impact on the state treasury is precisely the same.

We have granted relief in other welfare cases which included retroactive assistance benefits or payments. [Here Justice Douglas discussed *Shapiro v. Thompson* and the three summary affirmances mentioned in the majority opinion.]

It is said however, that the Eleventh Amendment is concerned, not with immunity of states from suit, but with the jurisdiction of the federal courts to entertain the suit. The Eleventh Amendment does not speak of "jurisdiction"; it withholds the "judicial power" of federal courts "to any suit in law or equity . . . against one of the United States. . . ." If that "judicial power," or "jurisdiction" if one prefers that concept, may not be exercised even in "any suit in . . . equity" then *Ex parte Young* should be overruled. But there is none eager to take the step. Where a state has consented to join a federal-state cooperative project, it is realistic to conclude that the state has agreed to assume its obligations under that legislation. There is nothing in the Eleventh Amendment to suggest a difference between suits at law and suits in equity, for it treats the two without distinction. If common sense has any role to play in constitutional adjudication, once there is a waiver of immunity it must be true that it is complete so far as effective operation of the state-federal joint welfare program is concerned. . . .

We have not always been unanimous in concluding when a state has waived its immunity. In Parden v. Terminal Ry. Co., 377 U.S. 184 (1964), where Alabama was sued by some of its citizens for injuries suffered in

1120 STATE SOVEREIGN IMMUNITY AND THE ELEVENTH AMENDMENT CHAPTER VIII

the interstate operation of an Alabama railroad, the state defended on the grounds of the Eleventh Amendment. The Court held that Alabama was liable as a carrier under the Federal Employers' Liability Act, saying:

> Our conclusion is simply that Alabama, when it began operation of an interstate railroad approximately 20 years after enactment of the FELA, necessarily consented to such suit as was authorized by that act.

The Court added:

> Our conclusion that this suit may be maintained is in accord with the common sense of this nation's federalism. A state's immunity from suit by an individual without its consent has been fully recognized by the Eleventh Amendment and by subsequent decisions of this Court. But when a state leaves the sphere that is exclusively its own and enters into activities subject to congressional regulation, it subjects itself to that regulation as fully as if it were a private person or corporation.

As the Court of Appeals in the instant case concluded, Illinois by entering into the joint federal-state welfare plan just as surely "[left] the sphere that is exclusively its own."

It is argued that participation in the program of federal financial assistance is not sufficient to establish consent on the part of the state to be sued in federal courts. But it is not merely participation which supports a finding of Eleventh Amendment waiver, but participation in light of the existing state of the law as exhibited in such decisions as Shapiro v. Thompson, 394 U.S. 618 (1969), which affirmed judgments ordering retroactive payment of benefits. Today's holding that the Eleventh Amendment forbids court-ordered retroactive payments, as the Court recognizes, necessitates an express overruling of several of our recent decisions. But it was against the background of those decisions that Illinois continued its participation in the federal program, and it can hardly be claimed that such participation was in ignorance of the possibility of court-ordered retroactive payments. The decision to participate against the background of precedent can only be viewed as a waiver of immunity from such judgments.

I would affirm the judgment of the Court of Appeals.

■ MR. JUSTICE BRENNAN, dissenting.

This suit is brought by Illinois citizens against Illinois officials. In that circumstance, Illinois may not invoke the Eleventh Amendment, since that amendment bars only federal court suits against states by citizens of other states. Rather, the question is whether Illinois may avail itself of the nonconstitutional but ancient doctrine of sovereign immunity as a bar to respondent's claim for retroactive AABD payments. In my view Illinois may not assert sovereign immunity for the reason I expressed in dissent in Employees v. Department of Public Health and

Welfare, 411 U.S. 279, 298 (1973): the states surrendered that immunity in Hamilton's words, "in the plan of the Convention," that formed the Union, at least insofar as the states granted Congress specifically enumerated powers. Congressional authority to enact the Social Security Act, of which AABD is a part, is to be found in Art. I, § 8, cl. 1, one of the enumerated powers granted Congress by the states in the Constitution. I remain of the opinion that "because of its surrender, no immunity exists that can be the subject of a congressional declaration or a voluntary waiver," and thus have no occasion to inquire whether or not Congress authorized an action for AABD retroactive benefits, or whether or not Illinois voluntarily waived the immunity by its continued participation in the program against the background of precedents which sustained judgments ordering retroactive payments.

I would affirm the judgment of the Court of Appeals.

■ MR. JUSTICE MARSHALL, with whom MR. JUSTICE BLACKMUN joins, dissenting.

The Social Security Act's categorical assistance programs, including the Aid to the Aged, Blind, or Disabled (AABD) program involved here, are fundamentally different from most federal legislation. Unlike the Fair Labor Standards Act involved in last term's decision in Employees v. Department of Public Health and Welfare, 411 U.S. 279 (1973), or the Federal Employers' Liability Act at issue in Parden v. Terminal Ry. Co., 377 U.S. 184 (1964), the Social Security Act does not impose federal standards and liability upon all who engage in certain regulated activities, including often unwilling state agencies. Instead, the act seeks to induce state participation in the federal welfare programs by offering federal matching funds in exchange for the state's voluntary assumption of the act's requirements. I find this basic distinction crucial: it leads me to conclude that by participation in the programs, the states waive whatever immunity they might otherwise have from federal court orders requiring retroactive payment of welfare benefits.[1]

In agreeing to comply with the requirements of the Social Security Act and HEW regulations, I believe that Illinois has also agreed to subject itself to suit in the federal courts to enforce these obligations. I recognize, of course, that the Social Security Act does not itself provide for a cause of action to enforce its obligations. As the Court points out, the only sanction expressly provided in the act for a participating state's failure to comply with federal requirements is the cutoff of federal funding by the Secretary of HEW.

But a cause of action is clearly provided by 42 U.S.C. § 1983, which in terms authorizes suits to redress deprivations of rights secured by the "laws" of the United States. And we have already rejected the argument

---

[1]   In view of my conclusion on this issue, I find it unnecessary to consider whether the Court correctly treats this suit as one against the state rather than as a suit against a state officer permissible under the rationale of Ex parte Young, 209 U.S. 123 (1908).

that Congress intended the funding cutoff to be the sole remedy for non-compliance with federal requirements. In Rosado v. Wyman, 397 U.S. 397, 420–23 (1970), we held that suits in federal court were proper to enforce the provisions of the Social Security Act against participating states. . . .

I believe that Congress also intended the full panoply of traditional judicial remedies to be available to the federal courts in these § 1983 suits. There is surely no indication of any congressional intent to restrict the courts' equitable jurisdiction. . . . In particular I am firmly convinced that Congress intended the restitution of wrongfully withheld assistance payments to be a remedy available to the federal courts in these suits. Benefits under the categorical assistance programs "are a matter of statutory entitlement for persons qualified to receive them." Goldberg v. Kelly, 397 U.S. 254, 262 (1970). Retroactive payment of benefits secures for recipients this entitlement which was withheld in violation of federal law. Equally important, the courts' power to order retroactive payments is an essential remedy to insure future state compliance with federal requirements. No other remedy can effectively deter states from the strong temptation to cut welfare budgets by circumventing the stringent requirements of federal law. The funding cutoff is a drastic sanction, one which HEW has proved unwilling or unable to employ to compel strict compliance with the act and regulations. Moreover, the cutoff operates only prospectively; it in no way deters the states from even a flagrant violation of the act's requirements for as long as HEW does not discover the violation and threaten to take such action. . . .

Illinois chose to participate in the AABD program with its eyes wide open. Drawn by the lure of federal funds, it voluntarily obligated itself to comply with the Social Security Act and HEW regulations, with full knowledge that Congress had authorized assistance recipients to go into federal court to enforce these obligations and to recover benefits wrongfully denied. Any doubts on this score must surely have been removed by our decisions in *Rosado v. Wyman* and Shapiro v. Thompson, 394 U.S. 618 (1969), where we affirmed a district court retroactive payment order. I cannot avoid the conclusion that, by virtue of its knowing and voluntary decision to nevertheless participate in the program, the state necessarily consented to subject itself to these suits. I have no quarrel with the Court's view that the waiver of constitutional rights should not lightly be inferred. But I simply cannot believe that the state could have entered into this essentially contractual agreement with the federal government without recognizing that it was subjecting itself to the full scope of the § 1983 remedy provided by Congress to enforce the terms of the agreement.

Of course, § 1983 suits are nominally brought against state officers, rather than the state itself, and do not ordinarily raise Eleventh Amendment problems in view of this Court's decision in Ex parte Young, 209 U.S. 123 (1908). But to the extent that the relief authorized by Congress in an action under § 1983 may be open to Eleventh Amendment objections, these objections are waived when the state agrees to comply with federal requirements enforceable in such an action. I do not find persuasive the Court's reliance in this case on the fact that "congressional authorization to sue a class of defendants which literally includes states" is absent. While true, this fact is irrelevant here, for this is simply not a case "literally" against the state. While the Court successfully knocks down the strawman it has thus set up, it never comes to grips with the undeniable fact that Congress has "literally" authorized this suit within the terms of § 1983. Since there is every reason to believe that Congress intended the full panoply of judicial remedies to be available in § 1983 equitable actions to enforce the Social Security Act, I think the conclusion is inescapable that Congress authorized and the state consented to § 1983 actions in which the relief might otherwise be questioned on Eleventh Amendment grounds. . . .

Congress undoubtedly has the power to insist upon a waiver of sovereign immunity as a condition of [the state's] consent to such a federal-state agreement. Since I am satisfied that Congress has in fact done so here, at least to the extent that the federal courts may do "complete rather than truncated justice," in § 1983 actions authorized by Congress against state welfare authorities, I respectfully dissent.

NOTES ON STATE IMMUNITY AGAINST AWARD OF DAMAGES

1. *FORD MOTOR CO. V. DEPARTMENT OF THE TREASURY*

The suit in *Edelman v. Jordan* was brought not against the state itself but against state officials charged with administration of the welfare laws. Should it therefore have been permissible as a suit against wrongdoing individuals and not against the state?

The Court's answer was based on Ford Motor Co. v. Department of Treasury of Indiana, 323 U.S. 459 (1945). In that case, Ford claimed that income taxes had been collected in violation of the Commerce Clause and the Fourteenth Amendment. Indiana law provided that refund suits could be filed in state court under certain conditions, all of which had been satisfied. Ford, however, filed its suit in federal court. The defendants were the state's department of the treasury and its governor, treasurer, and auditor, who collectively constituted the board of the department. Justice Reed framed the issue for a unanimous Court (Murphy not participating) by observing that where "relief is sought under general law from wrongful acts of state officials, the sovereign's immunity under the Eleventh Amendment does not extend to wrongful individual action, and the citizen is allowed a remedy against the wrongdoer personally. Where, however, an action is authorized by statute against a state officer in his official capacity and constituting an action against the state, the Eleventh Amendment operates to bar suit except in so far as the statute waives state immunity from suit." Accordingly, Ford's right to bring the suit "depends first, upon whether the action is against the state of Indiana or against an individual. Secondly, if the action is against the state, whether the state has consented to be sued in the federal courts."

On the first question, the Court said:

> We are of the opinion that petitioner's suit in the instant case against the department and the individuals as the board constitutes an action against the state of Indiana. A state statute prescribed the procedure for obtaining refund of taxes illegally exacted, providing that a taxpayer first file a timely application for a refund with the state department of treasury. Upon denial of such claim, the taxpayer is authorized to recover the illegal exaction in an action against the "department." Judgment obtained in such action is to be satisfied by payment "out of any funds in the state treasury." This section clearly provides for an action against the state, as opposed to one against the collecting official individually. . . .

> We have previously held that the nature of a suit as one against the state is to be determined by the essential nature and effect of the proceeding. And when the action is in essence one for the recovery of money from the state, the state is the real, substantial party in interest and is entitled to invoke its sovereign immunity from suit even though individual officials are nominal defendants. We are of the opinion, therefore, that the present proceedings was brought in reliance on [the state statute] and is a suit against the state.

Turning to the question of consent, the Court said that the fact that the state had consented to refund suits in its own courts was not determinative. The state had not thereby waived its Eleventh Amendment immunity in federal court. Accordingly, Ford was remitted to the state courts for assertion of its refund claim, with the possibility of review by the Supreme Court of any federal questions that might arise.

2.   *MILLIKEN V. BRADLEY (II)*

Justice Douglas argued in his *Edelman* dissent that the financial impact of an *Ex parte Young* injunction was in principle indistinguishable from an award of monetary relief. Even the *Edelman* majority admitted that "the difference between the type of relief barred by the Eleventh Amendment and that permitted under *Ex parte Young* will not in many instances be that between day and night." But in the end, the Court felt constrained by principle and precedent to draw a line between *Ford*-type relief and *Ex parte Young*-type relief.

Just how shadowy that line can become is suggested in Milliken v. Bradley (II), 433 U.S. 267 (1977), where the Court upheld a school desegregation order requiring the expenditure of state (as well as local) funds for educational components of the desegregation decree, including remedial reading programs. The Court disposed of the state's Eleventh Amendment objection as follows:

The decree to share the future costs of educational components in this case fits squarely within the prospective-compliance exception reaffirmed by *Edelman*. That exception, which had its genesis in *Ex parte Young,* permits federal courts to enjoin state officials to conform their conduct to requirements of federal law, notwithstanding a direct and substantial impact on the state treasury. The order challenged here does no more than that. The decree requires state officials, held responsible for unconstitutional conduct, in findings which are not challenged, to eliminate a de jure segregated school system. . . . The educational components, which the District Court ordered into effect *prospectively,* are plainly designed to wipe out continuing conditions of inequality produced by the inherently unequal dual school system long maintained by Detroit. . . . That the programs are also "compensatory" in nature does not change the fact that they are part of a plan that operates *prospectively* to bring about the delayed benefits of a unitary school system. We therefore hold that such prospective relief is not barred by the Eleventh Amendment.

Could the award of past payments at issue in *Edelman* be fairly described as "part of a plan that operates *prospectively* to bring about the delayed benefits of" the federally required payment schedule? Is there a meaningful distinction between the two cases?[a]

3.   *ROSADO V. WYMAN*

The plaintiff's cause of action in *Ford* was based on the Indiana refund statute. The underlying constitutional right was federal, but the cause of action was based on state law.[b] Does this fact distinguish *Ford* from *Edelman*? What was the source of the plaintiffs' cause of action in *Edelman*?

The answer appears to be 42 U.S.C. § 1983. Recall that the Court admitted that it "is, of course, true that Rosado v. Wyman, 397 U.S. 397 (1970), held that suits in federal court under § 1983 are proper to secure compliance with the provisions of the Social Security Act on the part of participating states." But it went on to say that § 1983 did not displace the state's Eleventh Amendment immunity. Thus, although § 1983 in terms authorizes both legal and equitable relief, it must in this context be limited to equitable relief.[c]

---

[a]   For other cases in which the line between prospective and retrospective relief proved troublesome, see Cory v. White, 457 U.S. 85 (1982); Papasan v. Allain, 478 U.S. 265 (1986); Green v. Mansour, 474 U.S. 64 (1985); Quern v. Jordan, 440 U.S. 332 (1979).

[b]   Recall that the plaintiff chooses the legal theory on which to base requested relief. The cause of action in *Ford* was based on state law not because it necessarily had to be, but because the plaintiff so pleaded it.

[c]   *Rosado* itself is obscure on this point. *Rosado* did approve an injunction by a federal court prohibiting enforcement of a New York welfare statute deemed inconsistent with the Social Security Act, but § 1983 was not mentioned in that opinion nor in a number of other welfare cases in which equitable relief against state officials was approved by the Supreme Court. Indeed, as Justice Rehnquist recognized, in Shapiro v. Thompson, 394 U.S. 618 (1969), and in three other summary actions, the Court affirmed an order awarding retroactive monetary relief to welfare claimants. In none of these cases was § 1983 explicitly relied on. Prior to *Edelman,* therefore, it was clear that welfare claimants could sue state officials to enforce federal law, but it was not clear whether their right to sue found its source in the Social Security Act itself, in

4. *WILL V. MICHIGAN DEPARTMENT OF STATE POLICE*

The Eleventh Amendment does not apply in state courts. If § 1983 supplies a cause of action for a welfare claimant in the *Edelman* situation in all instances except those foreclosed by the Eleventh Amendment, could the *Edelman* plaintiffs have avoided defeat by filing their case in state court?

This question was resolved in Will v. Michigan Department of State Police, 491 U.S. 58 (1989), where the Supreme Court held that "neither a state or its officials acting in their official capacities are 'persons' under § 1983." In an opinion by Justice White, the Court argued that the intent to make states directly liable had not been shown with the clarity required to support the conclusion that Congress meant to alter the "usual constitutional balance" between the states and the national government. It found nothing in the text, history, or purpose of § 1983 clearly evidencing such intent. As to state officials, it said:

> Obviously, state officials literally are persons. But a suit against a state official in his or her official capacity is not a suit against the official but rather is a suit against the official's office. As such, it is no different from a suit against the state itself. We see no reason to adopt a different rule in the present context, particularly when such a rule would allow petitioner to circumvent congressional intent by a mere pleading device.

This holding created an obvious tension with *Ex parte Young*. The Court addressed that tension in a footnote:

> Of course a state official in his or her official capacity, when sued for injunctive relief, would be a person under § 1983 because "official-capacity actions for prospective relief are not treated as actions against the state." Kentucky v. Graham, 473 U.S. 159, 167 n.14 (1985); Ex parte Young, 209 U.S. 123 (1908). This distinction is "commonplace in sovereign immunity doctrine," L. Tribe, American Constitutional Law § 3–27, p. 190 n.3 (2d ed. 1988), and would not have been foreign to the 19th-century Congress that enacted § 1983. . . .

Does that clarify the matter?

Justice Brennan dissented in an opinion joined by Justices Marshall, Blackmun, and Stevens. Brennan saw the Court's decision as improperly relying on the Eleventh Amendment, which, although admittedly inapplicable, nevertheless "lurks everywhere in today's decision and, in truth, determines its outcome." In a separate dissent, Justice Stevens emphasized the inconsistency of recognizing a § 1983 cause of action against states and state officials for prospective relief but not for compensatory damages.

---

§ 1983, or in some other source. *Edelman* confirmed that § 1983 can be used to enforce this corner of federal law, albeit not for relief barred by the Eleventh Amendment. *Edelman*'s recognition of this role for § 1983 was acknowledged in Maine v. Thiboutot, 448 U.S. 1 (1980), where the Court held that § 1983 supplied a cause of action to enforce federal statutes against state officials.

5.　*HAFER V. MELO*

James Melo brought a § 1983 damages action against Barbara Hafer, the Auditor General of Pennsylvania, for terminating his employment. Hafer argued that, because she had authority to fire Melo only because of her office, his suit complained of actions taken in her "official capacity" and was therefore not against a "person" who could be sued under § 1983. In an opinion by Justice O'Connor in Hafer v. Melo, 502 U.S. 21 (1991), the Court replied that the distinction between official capacity and personal capacity does not turn on the capacity in which the defendant *acted* when injuring the plaintiff, but rather on the capacity in which the defendant had been *sued*. Suits seeking to recover damages from a government officer personally are therefore suits against that officer in his or her personal capacity and may be brought under § 1983. Plaintiffs therefore have substantial ability to avoid state sovereign immunity by suing state officers rather than the state itself. Nominally, such suits can recover only from the officer's personal assets, but state indemnification against adverse judgments is routine. More importantly, officer defendants can usually assert a defense of qualified immunity, which precludes liability for actions not forbidden by clearly established law.

6.　APPEALABILITY OF IMMUNITY DENIALS: *PUERTO RICO AQUEDUCT AND SEWER AUTHORITY V. METCALF & EDDY, INC.*

Generally speaking, only "final decisions" of district courts are appealable under 28 U.S.C. § 1291. In Cohen v. Beneficial Industrial Loan Corp., 337 U.S. 541 (1949), however, the Supreme Court held that certain "collateral orders" are immediately appealable. Famously, *Cohen* held that a decision is "final" for purposes of appeal if it falls within "that small class which finally determine claims of right separable from, and collateral to, rights asserted in the action, too important to be denied review and too independent of the cause itself to require that appellate consideration be deferred until the whole case is adjudicated." Does this apply to a denial of Eleventh Amendment immunity?

In Puerto Rico Aqueduct and Sewer Authority v. Metcalf & Eddy, Inc., 506 U.S. 139 (1993), the Court said "yes." The Puerto Rico Aqueduct and Sewer Authority (PRASA) was sued for damages for breach of contract and damage to business reputation by an engineering firm hired to assist in upgrading its wastewater treatment plants. PRASA moved to dismiss on Eleventh Amendment grounds.[d] The District Court denied the motion because it thought state funds not implicated by the lawsuit. PRASA immediately appealed. The First Circuit held that it lacked jurisdiction over the appeal because no final decision had been rendered by the District Court. The Supreme Court reversed in an opinion by Justice White:

> Once it is established that a state and its "arms" are, in effect, immune from suit in federal court, it follows that the elements of

---

[d]　PRASA alleged that it was an "arm of the state" for Eleventh Amendment purposes. The case was tried under a First Circuit ruling that Puerto Rico is to be treated as a state for purposes of Eleventh Amendment immunity. The correctness of this ruling was not before the Supreme Court.

the *Cohen* collateral order doctrine are satisfied. "To come within the 'small class' of . . . *Cohen*, the order must [1] conclusively determine the disputed question, [2] resolve an important issue completely separate from the merits of the action, and [3] be effectively unreviewable on appeal from a final judgment." Coopers & Lybrand v. Livesay, 437 U.S. 463, 468 (1978). Denials of states' and state entities' claims to Eleventh Amendment immunity purport to be conclusive determinations that they have no right not to be sued in federal court. Moreover, a motion by a state or its agents to dismiss on Eleventh Amendment grounds involves a claim to a fundamental constitutional protection, whose resolution generally will have no bearing on the merits of the underlying action. Finally, the value to the states of their Eleventh Amendment immunity, like the benefit conferred by qualified immunity to individual officials, is for the most part lost as litigation proceeds past motion practice.

This decision brought immediate appealability as a "collateral order" of denials of state sovereign immunity into line with the immediate appealability of denials of qualified immunity for officers sued under § 1983. See Mitchell v. Forsyth, 472 U.S. 511 (1985). The collateral order doctrine is considered further in Section 4 of Chapter V.

7. ELEVENTH AMENDMENT IMMUNITY FOR LOCAL GOVERNMENTS

On the same day it decided *Hans v. Louisiana,* the Supreme Court held in Lincoln County v. Luning, 133 U.S. 529 (1890), that the Eleventh Amendment does not protect counties from suit in federal court. Subsequent cases have extended this holding to other units of local government. See, e.g., Workman v. New York, 179 U.S. 552 (1900) (cities); Mount Healthy City School District v. Doyle, 429 U.S. 274 (1977) (school boards); Northern Ins. Co. v. Chatham County, 547 U.S. 189 (2006) (reaffirming lack of immunity for counties).

Today, the different treatment of states and their political subdivisions seems anomalous, but it appears to have a foundation in history. At the time the Eleventh Amendment was adopted, municipal corporations were analogized to private corporations and were deemed to lack the attributes of sovereignty possessed by states. By the time that the municipal corporation came to be seen as a distinct governmental unit exercising powers delegated by the state, the amenability of local governments to suit in federal court had long been established.

For many years, the distinction between states and their political subdivisions was inconsequential. Prospective relief could be had against either under *Ex parte Young.* Damage awards against states were barred by the Eleventh Amendment, and in most instances, damages awards against localities were barred by the assumed unavailability of a cause of action authorizing such relief. All this changed in 1978, when the Supreme Court held, contrary to its earlier view, that a municipal corporation was a "person" who could be sued under § 1983. Monell v. Department of Social Services, 436 U.S. 658 (1978). Today, therefore, the distinction matters a great deal. States and state agencies are protected against damage actions in federal court under *Edelman v. Jordan* and in state court under *Will v. Michigan Department of State Police*. Local governments, by contrast, have no immunity and may be held liable in damages under § 1983 in either state or federal court for violations of federal law.

Although this line is clear in principle, its application to particular situations is sometimes not obvious. A unit of local government, although not in itself entitled to claim immunity, may be shielded by state sovereign immunity if an award of damages against it would operate directly against the state treasury. In *Edelman v. Jordan,* for example, the action was brought against both state and local welfare officials. Because the locality was merely disbursing state funds according to state policy, both levels of government were deemed to be protected. In contrast, *Milliken v. Bradley (II)* also involved both state and local defendants. In that case, however, the locality was guilty of an independent constitutional violation, and no immunity could be claimed.

NOTES ON THE INTERSECTION OF THE ELEVENTH AMENDMENT AND STATE LAW

1. SUITS AGAINST ONE STATE IN THE COURTS OF ANOTHER: *NEVADA V. HALL*

California residents were injured when their car was struck by a vehicle being driven on official business by an employee of the state of Nevada. The accident occurred in California. The plaintiffs sued in a California state court, naming as defendants the Nevada employee's estate (he was killed in the accident) and the state. Personal jurisdiction was acquired over the state under a California statute authorizing service of process on nonresident motorists. The California courts upheld a jury verdict against Nevada for more than $1 million, notwithstanding a Nevada statute limiting recoveries against the state to $25,000. In Nevada v. Hall, 440 U.S. 410 (1979), the Supreme Court affirmed.

Speaking for the Court, Justice Stevens denied that California was bound by federal law to respect Nevada's sovereign immunity. The Eleventh Amendment applied only in federal court, and neither the Full Faith and Credit Clause nor the overall scheme of the Constitution prohibited California from following its own law.

Justice Blackmun, joined by Chief Justice Burger and by Justice Rehnquist, dissented, saying that he would find "a constitutional doctrine of interstate sovereign immunity" implied as an essential component of the federal system. Justice Rehnquist, joined by the Chief Justice wrote separately, adding that the result reached by the majority "destroys the framers' careful allocation of responsibility among the state and federal judiciaries, and makes nonsense of the effort embodied in the Eleventh Amendment to preserve the doctrine of sovereign immunity."

Is *Nevada v. Hall* consistent with the Eleventh Amendment? The result is that a (constitutionally based?) principle of sovereign immunity prohibits (certain kinds of) suits against states to enforce federal rights in a federal court. Yet there is no such principle that prohibits suits against state *A* to enforce the laws of state *B* in state *B*'s own courts. Does this make sense? As a matter of policy, might the Court have it backwards?[a]

2. SUITS AGAINST ONE STATE IN THE COURTS OF ANOTHER: *FRANCHISE TAX BOARD V. HYATT*

Nevada v. Hall was upheld but limited in Franchise Tax Board of California v. Hyatt, 578 U.S. ___, 136 S.Ct. 1277 (2016). Gilbert Hyatt moved from California (with a high state income tax) to Nevada (with no state income tax) in 1991. The Franchise Tax Board claimed that he had not effected that move until 1992 and assessed $10 million in taxes, penalties, and interest. Hyatt filed suit in Nevada against the aggressive enforcement and investigative tactics of the California tax authorities and won a jury award for $388 million. The Nevada Supreme Court rejected most of that award (including all punitive damages) but upheld a $1 million judgment against the Franchise Tax Board for fraud and emotional distress.

In the Supreme Court of the United States, California argued that the sovereign immunity of the Franchise Tax Board under California law precluded an award of damages by Nevada. Justice Scalia passed away after the oral argument but before the decision was announced. The then eight-member Court was "equally divided" over whether to overturn *Nevada v. Hall* and thus left it in place.

California also argued that its liability in Nevada courts was in any event limited by a $50,000 cap that Nevada imposed on similar suits against its own agencies. The Supreme Court accepted this claim, by a vote of six to two, implicitly limiting *Nevada v. Hall*. Writing for the Court, Justice Breyer relied on language from Carroll v. Lanza, 349 U.S. 408 (1955). In *Carroll* the Court upheld, as consistent with the Full Faith and Credit Clause, a state's refusal to apply "the statute of another State reflecting a conflicting and opposed policy" but noted that the state had not adopted a "policy of hostility" to the public acts of a sister state. Here, the Court found such hostility:

> Nevada has not applied the principles of Nevada law ordinarily applicable to suits against Nevada's own agencies. Rather, it has applied a special rule of law applicable only in lawsuits against its sister States, such as California. . . . The Nevada Supreme Court explained [its position] by describing California's system of controlling its own agencies as failing to provide "adequate" recourse to Nevada's citizens. It expressed concerns about the fact that California's agencies " 'operat[e] outside' " the systems of " 'legislative control, administrative oversight, and public accountability' " that Nevada applies to its own agencies. Such an explanation, which amounts to little more than a conclusory statement disparaging California's own legislative, judicial, and administrative controls,

---
a   For criticism of *Nevada v. Hall*, see Ann Woolhandler, Interstate Sovereign Immunity, 2006 Sup. Ct. Rev. 249. For a defense of *Hall*, see William Baude, Sovereign Immunity and the Constitutional Text, 103 Va. L. Rev. 1 (2017). For discussion of the case in the broader context of choice of law generally, see Patrick J. Borchers, Is the Supreme Court Really Going to Regulate Choice of Law Involving States?, 50 Creighton L. Rev. 7 (2016).

cannot justify the application of a special and discriminatory rule. Rather, viewed through a full faith and credit lens, a State that disregards its own ordinary legal principles on this ground *is* hostile to another State.

Although the Court did not say so, its reasoning seems analogous to the established rule of federal common law that states cannot discriminate against federal interests. See, e.g., United States v. Little Lake Misere Land Co., Inc., 412 U.S. 580, 606 (1973) (Rehnquist, J., concurring in the judgment) (excerpted in Section 1 of Chapter II). *Hyatt* might be read as applying the same rule to state choice of law when the case involves another state.

In dissent, Chief Justice Roberts, joined by Justice Thomas, disputed the majority's position on choice of law. *Carroll's* reference to a "policy of hostility," Roberts argued, meant only that a "State may not refuse to apply another State's law where there are '*no* sufficient policy considerations to warrant such refusal,'" (quoting *Carroll*, 349 U.S. at 413). Applying that standard Roberts found that Nevada had a "sufficient" policy interest in protecting Nevada residents from injury and that the majority was not entitled to disregard the state court's reasons: "Nevada is not . . . required to treat its sister State as equally committed to the protection of Nevada citizens." Roberts also disputed the Court's remedy:

> The majority concludes that in the sovereign immunity context, the Full Faith and Credit Clause is not a choice of law provision, but a create-your-own-law provision: The Court does not require the Nevada Supreme court to apply either Nevada law (no immunity for the Board) or California law (complete immunity for the Board), but instead requires a hybrid rule, under which the Board enjoys partial immunity.

> The majority's approach is nowhere to be found in the Full Faith and Credit Clause. Where the Clause applies, it expressly requires a State to give *full* faith and credit to another State's laws. If the majority is correct that Nevada has no sufficient policy justification for applying Nevada immunity law, then California law applies. And under California law, the Board is entitled to *full* immunity. Or, if Nevada has a sufficient policy reason to apply its own law, then Nevada law applies, and the Board is subject to *full* liability.

On the public record, there is no way of knowing whether the dissenters voted to uphold or overturn *Nevada v. Hall*. Can an answer be discerned from the Roberts' dissent?

3.   FEDERAL INJUNCTIONS TO ENFORCE STATE LAW: *PENNHURST STATE SCHOOL AND HOSPITAL V. HALDERMAN*

The Pennhurst State School and Hospital was a Pennsylvania institution for the care of the mentally retarded. A class action was brought in federal court on behalf of residents of Pennhurst against the Hospital, some of its officials, the state Department of Public Welfare, and a number of other defendants to enforce rights alleged to arise from the federal Constitution, from federal legislation, and from state legislation. After long and complex litigation, the Circuit Court approved an injunction requiring comprehensive changes in living conditions at the Hospital on the basis of rights found to have been created by the *state* legislation.

In Pennhurst State School and Hospital v. Halderman, 465 U.S. 89 (1984), the Supreme Court held the injunction forbidden by the Eleventh Amendment:

> We first address the contention that respondents' state law claim is not barred by the Eleventh Amendment because it seeks only prospective relief as defined in *Edelman v. Jordan*. The Court of Appeals held that if the judgment below rested on federal law, it could be entered against petitioner state officials under the doctrine established in *Edelman* and *Ex parte Young* even though the prospective financial burden was substantial and on-going. The court assumed, and respondents assert, that this reasoning applies as well when the official acts in violation of state law. This argument misconstrues the basis of the doctrine established in *Young* and *Edelman*.

> [T]he injunction in *Ex parte Young* was justified, notwithstanding the obvious impact on the state itself, on the view that sovereign immunity does not apply because an official who acts unconstitutionally is "stripped of his official or representative character." . . . Our decisions repeatedly have emphasized that the *Young* doctrine rests on the need to promote the vindication of federal rights.

> The Court also has recognized, however, that the need to promote the supremacy of federal law must be accommodated to the constitutional immunity of the states. This is the significance of *Edelman v. Jordan*. We recognized that the prospective relief authorized by *Young* "has permitted the Civil War amendments to the Constitution to serve as a sword, rather than merely a shield, for those whom they were designed to protect." But we declined to extend the fiction of *Young* to encompass retroactive relief, for to do so would effectively eliminate the constitutional immunity of the states. . . . In sum *Edelman*'s distinction between prospective and retroactive relief fulfills the underlying purpose of *Ex parte Young* while at the same time preserving to an important degree the constitutional immunity of the states.

> The need to reconcile competing interests is wholly absent, however, when a plaintiff alleges that a state official has violated *state* law. In such a case the entire basis for the doctrine of *Young* and *Edelman* disappears. A federal court's grant of relief against state officials on the basis of state law, whether prospective or retroactive, does not vindicate the supreme authority of federal law. On the contrary, it is difficult to think of a greater intrusion on state sovereignty than when a federal court instructs state officials on how to conform their conduct to state law. Such a result conflicts

directly with the principles of federalism that underlie the Eleventh Amendment. We conclude that *Young* and *Edelman* are inapplicable in a suit against state officials on the basis of state law.

Justice Stevens, joined by Justices Brennan, Marshall, and Blackmun, dissented.

A footnote in Justice Powell's *Pennhurst* opinion states that "[a]t the time the suit was filed, suits against Pennsylvania were permitted only where expressly authorized by the legislature," and further that Pennsylvania later enacted a statute on sovereign immunity, "including an express preservation of its immunity from suit in federal court." The dissent made no mention of this point, but as David Shapiro points out in Comment, Wrong Turns: The Eleventh Amendment and the *Pennhurst* Case, 98 Harv. L. Rev. 61, 76–78 (1984), the story is more complicated than at first appears.

The *Pennhurst* litigation began in 1974. At that time, Pennsylvania's sovereign immunity was apparently intact. In 1978, however, the state Supreme Court abrogated the doctrine retroactively. The legislature overturned that decision, but the Pennsylvania Supreme Court held that the statute could not bar litigation of a cause of action that had already accrued at the time of its passage. Thus, it is at least arguable that, under the decisions of the Pennsylvania Supreme Court (and contrary to the wishes of the legislature), there was no state doctrine of sovereign immunity applicable to the *Pennhurst* litigation.

Should state law have mattered? *Erie* would seem to require that federal courts use state law to decide questions of state sovereign immunity from state law claims. Martha Field takes exactly that position. See Field, The Eleventh Amendment and Other Sovereign Immunity Doctrines: Congressional Imposition of Suit upon the States, 126 U. Pa. L. Rev. 1203, 1254 n.240 (1978). Does it follow that if state law permits an action against the state, the federal courts should be free to entertain it? In Atascadero State Hospital v. Scanlon, 473 U.S. 234, 241 (1985), the Court said:

> The test for determining whether a state has waived its immunity from federal-court jurisdiction is a stringent one. Although a state's general waiver of sovereign immunity may subject it to suit in state court, it is not enough to waive the immunity guaranteed by the Eleventh Amendment. As we explained just last term, "a state's constitutional interest in immunity encompasses not merely *whether* it may be sued, but *where* it may be sued." Pennhurst State School and Hospital v. Halderman, 465 U.S. 89, 99 (1984). Thus, in order for a state statute or constitutional provision to constitute a waiver of Eleventh Amendment immunity, it must specify the state's intention to subject itself to suit in *federal court*.

Does it follow from *Atascadero* that *Pennhurst* was right?

NOTES ON FEDERAL SOVEREIGN IMMUNITY

1.   INTRODUCTION

State sovereign immunity is broadly analogous to the immunity of the federal government. Although Article III extends the judicial power "to Controversies which the United States shall be a Party," the first Judiciary Act implemented that provision only where the United States was the plaintiff. This limitation reflects what Chief Justice Marshall described as the "universally received opinion" that "no suit be commenced or prosecuted against the United States" without its consent. Cohens v. Virginia 19 U.S. (6 Wheat.) 264, 411–12 (1821).

There are obvious tensions between the tradition of sovereign immunity inherited from British law and the ideal of popular sovereignty embedded in the Constitution. Sovereign immunity has therefore long been controversial. As with state immunity, one way around federal sovereign immunity has been to allow officer suits. Ex parte Young, 209 U.S. 123 (1908), created an effective if circumlocutory way of enforcing the Constitution prospectively by enjoining violations by state officers. The same remedy is available against federal officers, although with the usual limitations on obtaining equitable relief.

Suits seeking money from the United States are much more difficult. The direct application of sovereign immunity prohibits such actions against the government itself absent consent. Actions seeking money from the federal treasury are therefore barred, much as Edelman v. Jordan, 415 U.S. 651 (1974), barred retrospective relief against states. This is true even if the suit is nominally brought against government officials. Claimants in contractual disputes with the federal government historically had no remedy other than applying to Congress for a so-called "private bill" granting relief. Obviously, the willingness of Congress to grant such relief, even for meritorious claims, was neither reliable nor immediate. Eventually, as discussed below, Congress waived the government's immunity on contract claims, subject to various limitations.

Damages actions for tortious misconduct stand on a somewhat different footing. Damages actions against state and local officers for violations of the Constitution were authorized by the Civil Rights Act of 1871, now 42 U.S.C. § 1983. An analogous remedy against federal officers was recognized, in the context of Fourth Amendment violations, by Bivens v. Six Unknown Named Agents of the Federal Bureau of Narcotics, 403 U.S. 388 (1971). In *Bivens* actions, as under § 1983, judgments run against the officers personally, though the government employers generally foot the bills through indemnification policies. *Bivens* and its progeny are examined in detail in Chapter II. As those materials confirm, *Bivens* has not been extended to all constitutional violations. Tort suits brought against the federal government itself, as opposed to its officers, are barred by sovereign immunity absent waiver. Today, waiver of sovereign immunity is chiefly governed by the Federal Tort Claims Act, discussed below.

2. *UNITED STATES V. LEE*

In at least one respect, the Constitution itself seems to imply an exception to the federal government's immunity. The Fifth Amendment ends with the words, "nor shall private property be taken for public use, without just compensation." If that provision is to be legally enforceable, it implies that courts must be able to order the United States either to pay compensation when property is taken or to return the property if compensation is not paid. Some such understanding probably underlies the famously difficult old case of United States v. Lee, 106 U.S. 196 (1882).

Early in the Civil War, Union troops occupied the Arlington, Virginia, estate of Robert E. Lee. In 1864, the government purchased the property at a tax sale, after non-payment of taxes. In fact, Lee's wife tried to have an agent pay the taxes, but the government refused, saying that only the owner in person could do so. After the war, the Lees' son sued the government officials in charge of the property, seeking to have them ejected and to have himself declared rightful owner. By a vote of five to four, the Supreme Court agreed. The Court noted that a jury had found that private property had been taken "without any process of law and without any compensation," and concluded that "those provisions of the Constitution are of that character which it is intended the courts shall enforce. . . ." More generally, the majority dismissed the defense of sovereign immunity as "opposed to all the principles upon which the rights of the citizen, when brought in collision with the acts of the government, must be determined."

This did not persuade four dissenters. They argued that the "sovereign is not liable to be sued in any judicial tribunal without its consent." Since the "sovereign cannot hold property except by agents," allowing "an action for the recovery of possession of property held by the sovereign through its agents . . . is to invade the possession of the sovereign and to disregard the fundamental maxim that the sovereign cannot be sued." As this view did not prevail, the government had to pay a substantial sum for the Lees' old home, which became the Arlington National Cemetery.

The meaning of *United States v. Lee* was disputed at length in Larson v. Domestic & Foreign Commerce Corp., 337 U.S. 682 (1949), where a divided Court rejected the authority of *Lee* and refused to allow an officer suit to recover from the federal government property claimed by the plaintiff. *Larson*, like *Lee*, is a difficult case. One possible resolution is that by the time of *Larson*, the Tucker Act (see Note 5, below) had provided a statutory avenue for compensation in the Court of Claims, thus rendering the government's taking of property not "without just compensation." In any event, *Lee* and *Larson* are useful reminders of the possibility of officer suits as a means of avoiding sovereign immunity and of the absence (illustrated as well by *Edelman v. Jordan*) of any analytically exact formulation of when they will be available. As Justice Frankfurter said in his *Larson* dissent, the "unexpressed feeling" that sovereign immunity "runs counter to prevailing notions of reason and justice" surfaces "[i]n varying degrees, at different times" in decisions allowing officer suits. Saying anything more precise is a challenge.[a]

3. STATUTORY WAIVERS

One reason the theoretical boundaries of sovereign immunity have been allowed to remain unclear is that the government has waived so much of its protection. The Administrative Procedure Act, the Tucker Act, the Federal Tort Claims Act, and the statutes authorizing federal habeas corpus have gone a long way toward allowing litigation that might be barred by sovereign immunity. In consequence, old disputes about the scope of sovereign immunity and the alternative of officer suits have largely been displaced by disputes about the meaning of the statutory waivers. The underlying issues remain important and controversial, but they surface today as questions of statutory interpretation. Although the details of these statutes are beyond the scope of this book, introductory summaries are provided below.[b]

4. ADMINISTRATIVE PROCEDURE ACT

For federal officers, the Ex parte Young, 209 U.S. 123 (1908) line of cases, which allow officer suits seeking prospective relief, has largely been superseded by the Administrative Procedure Act, 5 U.S.C. §§ 701–706. That statute allows suits against an agency or officer of the United States for "relief other than money damages." § 702. More generally, the Act authorizes judicial review of various agency actions, including the promulgation of regulations and the adjudication of claims. § 705.

These provisions allow injunctive or declaratory relief but not "money damages." What about suits for specific equitable relief involving money? In Bowen v. Massachusetts, 487 U.S. 879 (1988), the Court allowed a state to obtain reimbursement for expenditures made under the federal Medicaid program, saying:

> Our cases have long recognized the distinction between an action at law for damages—which are intended to provide a victim with monetary compensation for an injury to his person, property, or reputation—and an equitable action for specific relief—which may include an order providing for the reinstatement of an employee with backpay, or for "the recovery of specific property *or monies*, ejectment from land, or injunction either direction or restraining the defendant officer's actions." Larson v. Domestic & Foreign Commerce Corp., 337 U.S. 682, 688 (1949) (emphasis added). The fact

---

[a]   Though not, perhaps, impossible. Frankfurter's *Larson* dissent offers a comprehensive survey of the law at that time. The Supreme Court returned to the task in Malone v. Bowdoin, 369 U.S. 643 (1962), which followed *Larson* and rejected *Lee.* Today, both *Larson* and *Malone* would be decided under the Administrative Procedure Act. See Note 4, infra. Academic summary of these cases appears in Gregory C. Sisk, Litigation With the Federal Government § 2.3, pp. 73–84 (2016).

[b]   For detail, the reader is again referred to Gregory C. Sisk, Litigation with the Federal Government (2016), which provides comprehensive analysis of all the statutes waiving federal sovereign immunity.

that a judicial remedy may require one party to pay money to another is not a sufficient reason to characterize the relief as "money damages."

As so construed, the APA provides a broad waiver of sovereign immunity that renders obsolete many of the older decisions regarding the availability of officer suits.

5.   COURT OF CLAIMS AND THE TUCKER ACT

In 1855 Congress created the Court of Claims to hear contractual claims against the federal government. At first, the Court of Claims only had the power to make recommendations to Congress, but in 1863 it was authorized to issue final judgments. In 1887, Congress enacted the Tucker Act, which broadly waived federal sovereign immunity for claims "not sounding in tort." The current version of that statute appears in 28 U.S.C. § 1991, which authorizes the U.S. Court of Federal Claims (successor to the original Court of Claims) to "render judgment upon any claim against the United States," whether based on the Constitution, statute, or administrative regulation, so long as the claim sounds in contract rather than tort. This provision applies only to actions for money judgments and not to suits for equitable relief, which are covered by the Administrative Procedure Act.[c]

6.   FEDERAL TORT CLAIMS ACT

Historically, a person injured by the negligence of a federal employee could only sue the employee personally. Often, individual employees lacked the resources to provide compensation, and in any event the government might be thought ultimately responsible. To address these problems, Congress sometimes enacted "private bills" to compensate victims and indemnify employees, but that remedy was difficult to obtain and not consistently available. In 1946 Congress addressed the problem in the Federal Tort Claims Act. The statute waives sovereign immunity for tort claims generally and allows recovery from the government "in the same manner and to the same extent as a private individual under like circumstances." 28 U.S.C. § 2674. This imposes respondeat superior liability on the government for acts for which a private party would be liable under the laws of the state where the tort occurred.

The FTCA's waiver of sovereign immunity is by no means complete. For one thing, intentional torts (assault, battery, false imprisonment, libel, slander, etc.) are generally excluded, although a 1974 amendment allowed suits for such acts when committed by law enforcement personnel. 28 U.S.C. § 2680(h). Other exceptions include claims arising in foreign countries, § 2680(k), and claims arising from a variety of specific activities, such as the fiscal operations of the Treasury or the activities of the Tennessee Valley Authority. § 2680(i) and (l).

---

[c]   The United States Court of Federal Claims, like the original Court of Claims, is a non-Article III institution. Today, however, its decisions can be reviewed on appeal by the United States Court of Appeals for the Federal Circuit, which is an Article III court.

Most important is the "discretionary function" exception, § 2680(a), which excludes from the FTCA any claim "based upon the exercise or performance or the failure to exercise or perform a discretionary function or duty on the part of a federal agency or an employee of the Government, whether or not the discretion involved be abused." The idea behind this provision is to prevent judicial second-guessing of government policy, United States v. Varig Airlines, 467 U.S. 797, 814 (1984), but its implementation is difficult. As almost any act could be said to involve discretion, the exception threatens to swallow the rule. The Supreme Court has therefore construed the discretionary function exception to have two requirements. First, the act must involve discretion. That is, it must not be subject to a mandatory statute or regulation (usually using the verb "shall") that imposes a strict duty. Second, the discretion must require judgment based on considerations of public policy. Not all discretionary acts meet this test. Thus, while driving a motor vehicle involves discretionary decisions, they do not turn on considerations of public policy and so are not excluded from governmental liability under the FTCA. Berkovitz v. United States, 486 U.S. 531 (1988). The Court has made clear, however, that the discretionary function exception "is not confined to the policy or planning level," but also extends to questions of implementation, if they depend on considerations of public policy. United States v. Gaubert, 499 U.S. 315, 322 (1991). Broadly speaking, the general effect of the discretionary function exception is to shift lawsuits attacking government policy away from the damages remedy of the FTCA and toward the injunctive and declaratory relief allowed by the Administrative Procedure Act and *Ex parte Young*.

Finally, in addition to the long list of statutory exceptions to the FTCA, there is an important judicial exception for suits by members of the armed forces. Torts that "arise out of or are in the course of activity incident to service" are not actionable. Feres v. United States, 340 U.S. 135, 146 (1950). The fear is that allowing torts actions by service personnel would undermine military discipline. Consequently, the Court has interpreted the FTCA not to encompass suits by or on behalf of service members for "service-related injuries." United States v. Johnson, 481 U.S. 681, 691 (1987). This rule, called the "*Feres* doctrine," has been criticized by scholars, but has been left unchanged by Congress.[d]

7.   WESTFALL ACT

In Westfall v. Erwin, 484 U.S. 292 (1988), a civilian employee at a federal Army Depot was injured after coming into contact with toxic materials stored there. He brought a state tort action against his supervisors, who removed to federal court, as is routine in such cases,[e] and claimed official

---

[d]   The *Feres* doctrine is of a piece with decisions precluding *Bivens* actions for service-related injuries, see Chappell v. Wallace, 462 U.S. 296 (1983), and United States v. Stanley, 483 U.S. 669 (1987), and with the creation of a military contractor defense as a matter of federal common law. Boyle v. United Technologies Corp., 487 U.S. 500 (1988). These decisions are discussed in Chapter II.

[e]   In Mesa v. California, 489 U.S. 121 (1989) (discussed in Chapter IV), the Court held that 28 U.S.C. § 1442(a)(1), which authorizes removal by federal officers, requires something more

immunity. The Supreme Court rejected that claim, holding that federal officials had tort immunity only if it was shown that they were acting within the scope of their official duties *and* that the conduct at issue was discretionary in nature: "It is only when officials exercise decisionmaking discretion that potential liability may shackle 'the fearless, vigorous, and effective administration of policies of government. Barr v. Matteo, 360 U.S. 564, 571 (1969)."

Congress disagreed. The Federal Employees Liability Reform and Tort Compensation Act, 28 U.S.C. § 2679, also known as the Westfall Act, expanded the applicability of the FTCA to state tort actions against federal employees. When a tort action is brought against a federal employee and the Attorney General certifies that he or she was acting within the scope of employment at the time of the incident in question, "any civil action or proceeding commenced upon such claim in a United States District Court shall be deemed an action against the United States . . . and the United States shall be substituted as the party defendant." If the Attorney General declines to make that certification, the employee may petition the court to do so. By this means, the FTCA is made the exclusive remedy for state tort claims relating to official employee conduct. Importantly, the Westfall Act does not apply to constitutional claims, leaving *Bivens* and its progeny unaffected.[f]

8. HABEAS CORPUS

Finally, federal sovereign immunity has never been thought to bar habeas corpus actions by those in federal custody. As discussed in Chapter VII, habeas corpus is a civil action that requires a custodian to show that detention is lawful. The Judiciary Act of 1789 authorized the federal courts to issue writs of habeas corpus, a power continued in 28 U.S.C. § 2441 et seq. The availability of federal habeas corpus to test the legality of federal executive detention—as distinct from its more common use as a collateral attack on judicial convictions—is probably constitutionally compelled, see Boumediene v. Bush, 553 U.S. 723 (2008), and to that extent, the traditional understanding that habeas actions against federal custodians do not implicate sovereign immunity continues to matter.

---

than the mere fact of being a federal officer. But that something is easily satisfied by the claim of a federal defense, even if the defense is ultimately unavailing.

    [f]   In Gutierrez de Martinez v. Lamagno, 515 U.S. 417 (1995), the Court held that the Attorney General's certifications under the Westfall Act are subject to judicial review. The Court subsequently held that a district court retains jurisdiction over a case removed to federal court under the Westfall Act, even if the scope-of-employment certification is denied and further that denial of such certification is immediately appealable under the collateral order doctrine. See Osborn v. Haley, 549 U.S. 225 (2007).

SECTION 2. CONSENT AND CONGRESSIONAL ABROGATION

INTRODUCTORY NOTES ON STATE CONSENT TO SUIT AND CONGRESSIONAL ABROGATION OF STATE SOVEREIGN IMMUNITY

1.   STATE CONSENT

Recall that in *Edelman*, the Eleventh Amendment issue was raised for the first time on appeal. The Court of Appeals nevertheless considered the issue, and the Supreme Court approved on the ground that "the Eleventh Amendment defense sufficiently partakes of the nature of a jurisdictional bar so that it need not be raised in the trial court." This view is based on an analogy to subject matter jurisdiction, which can be raised by any party or by the court at any time. It is also well settled, however, that a state can waive its Eleventh Amendment immunity and consent to suit in federal court.[a] Consent (although apparently revocable during the course of the litigation)[b] may be given by the state's legal representative or by statute. Such statutes, however, will be narrowly construed, and the state is free to consent to suit only in its own courts.[c] Obviously, this rule departs from the model of subject matter jurisdiction, which consenting parties are powerless to confer, but is consistent with the tradition of sovereign immunity, which the sovereign may choose to waive.

2.   CONGRESSIONAL ABROGATION: *PARDEN V. TERMINAL RY.*

Parden v. Terminal Ry., 377 U.S. 184 (1964), involved an FELA action against a state-owned railway, which was treated as an arm of the state. The Supreme Court nevertheless permitted the action. In an opinion by Justice Brennan, the Court advanced two seemingly independent rationales for that result.

First, the Court said that the states had "surrendered a portion of their sovereignty when they granted Congress the power to regulate commerce":

> By empowering Congress to regulate commerce, . . . the states necessarily surrendered any portion of their sovereignty that would stand in the way of such regulation. Since imposition of the FELA

---

[a]   See Hans v. Louisiana, 134 U.S. 1, 17 (1890) ("Undoubtedly a state may be sued by its own consent"). See also Lauren K. Robel, Sovereignty and Democracy: The States' Obligations to Their Citizens under Federal Statutory Law, 78 Ind. L.J. 543 (2003) (exploring "how states should make . . . waiver decisions, and what constraints—both political and legal—states face in doing so").

[b]   For criticism of this rule, see Gil Seinfeld, Waiver-in-Litigation: Eleventh Amendment Immunity and the Voluntariness Question, 63 Ohio St. L.J. 871 (2002).

[c]   Port Authority Trans-Hudson Corp. v. Feeney, 495 U.S. 299 (1990); Atascadero State Hospital v. Scanlon, 473 U.S. 234, 241 (1985). A state that has consented to suit in its own courts and removes such a suit to federal court has thereby waived its Eleventh Amendment immunity. Lapides v. Board of Regents of the University System of Georgia, 535 U.S. 613 (2002). *Lapides* left unresolved whether a state that would be immune in state court waives that immunity by removing the case to federal court. See Jessica Wagner, Waiver by Removal? An Analysis of State Sovereign Immunity, 102 Va. L. Rev. 549 (2016), for an examination of the issue and a proposed solution.

right of action upon interstate railroads is within the congressional regulatory power, it must follow that application of the act to such a railroad cannot be precluded by sovereign immunity.

Second, the Court noted that Alabama had begun operation of the railroad some 20 years after enactment of the FELA and concluded that the state had thereby consented to suit:

> Congress conditioned the right to operate a railroad in interstate commerce upon amenability to suit in federal court as provided by the act; by thereafter operating a railroad in interstate commerce, Alabama must be taken to have accepted that condition and thus to have consented to suit.

Justices White, Douglas, Harlan, and Stewart dissented. They argued that although it was within Congress's power to require a waiver of state sovereign immunity in order to engage in the interstate transportation business, such a design must be more clearly stated than was true in the FELA.

3. CONGRESSIONAL ABROGATION: *FITZPATRICK V. BITZER*

The idea that Congress could override Eleventh Amendment immunity was unequivocally embraced in Fitzpatrick v. Bitzer, 427 U.S. 445 (1976), insofar as Congress was acting to enforce Fourteenth Amendment rights. *Fitzpatrick* involved a 1972 amendment to title VII of the Civil Rights Act of 1964. The amendment explicitly authorized federal courts to award money damages against a state found to have engaged in employment discrimination by reason of "race, color, religion, sex, or national origin." Plaintiffs sued to recover retroactive retirement benefits of the sort precluded in *Edelman v. Jordan*, but the Court nevertheless ruled in their favor.

In an opinion by Justice Rehnquist, the Court stated the issue as "whether, as against the shield of sovereign immunity afforded the state by the Eleventh Amendment, Congress has the power to authorize federal courts to enter such an award against the state as a means of enforcing the substantive guarantees of the Fourteenth Amendment." The Court's answer was yes:

> [W]e think that the Eleventh Amendment, and the principle of state sovereignty which it embodies, are necessarily limited by the enforcement provisions of § 5 of the Fourteenth Amendment. In that section Congress is expressly granted authority to enforce "by appropriate legislation" the substantive provisions of the Fourteenth Amendment, which themselves embody significant limitations on state authority. When Congress acts pursuant to § 5, not only is it exercising legislative authority that is plenary within the terms of the constitutional grant, it is exercising that authority under one section of a constitutional amendment whose other sections by their own terms embody limitations on state authority. We think that Congress may, in determining what is "appropriate legislation" for the purpose of enforcing the provisions of the Fourteenth Amendment, provide for private suits against states or state officials which are constitutionally impermissible in other contexts.

Justices Brennan and Stevens wrote separately to concur in the judgment.[d]

4. STATE LIABILITY UNDER § 1983: *QUERN V. JORDAN* AND *WILL V. MICHIGAN DEPARTMENT OF STATE POLICE*

On remand from *Edelman v. Jordan,* the court ordered state officials to notify aid applicants of a state administrative procedure to apply for past benefits. In Quern v. Jordan, 440 U.S. 332 (1979), the Court unanimously rejected the contention that this required notice violated the Eleventh Amendment. Additionally, the Court (over two dissents) reaffirmed *Edelman's* conclusion that 42 U.S.C. § 1983 did not abrogate Eleventh Amendment immunity:

> [Section] 1983 does not explicitly and by clear language indicate on its face an intent to sweep away the immunity of the states; nor does it have a history which focuses directly on the question of state liability and which shows that Congress considered and firmly decided to abrogate the Eleventh Amendment immunity of the states.

A decade later, the Court faced the question of the amenability of states to § 1983 actions in *state* court, where the Eleventh Amendment in terms does not apply. Section 1983 imposes liability upon a "person" who denies rights under color of state law. In Will v. Michigan Department of State Police, 491 U.S. 58 (1989), the Court held that the word "person" in § 1983 does not include states or state agencies. The Court thus reaffirmed the *Quern* result for § 1983 suits in state courts, but by a different route.

5. ATTORNEY'S FEES: *HUTTO V. FINNEY*

Also permissible are attorney's fees awarded against a state under the Civil Rights Attorney's Fees Awards Act of 1976, 42 U.S.C. § 1988. Hutto v. Finney, 437 U.S. 678 (1978). The statute provides for attorney's fees in successful actions under various civil rights statutes, including 42 U.S.C. § 1983. Although states are not explicitly mentioned in the obligation to pay fees, the act is in terms unqualified, and the legislative history indicated that fees may be assessed, in an appropriate case, against states and state officials. Citing *Fitzpatrick,* the Court rejected an Eleventh Amendment challenge to fee awards on the grounds that congressional intent was plain and that attorney's fees were imposed "as part of the costs" and thus were distinguishable from retroactive liability for prelitigation conduct. No express statutory abrogation of state immunity was required.

---

[d] Perhaps because *Fitzpatrick* was unanimously decided, its correctness has been widely assumed. This assumption is questioned in John Harrison, State Sovereign Immunity and Congress's Enforcement Powers, 2006 Sup. Ct. Rev. 353. Harrison argues from history that the people who framed and ratified the Fourteenth and Fifteenth Amendments "probably did not believe that the amendments gave Congress power to create private causes of action against states." He also examines the question from the perspective of modern decisions and concludes that, if the doctrine of *Seminole Tribe* (excerpted as the next main case) is correct, *Fitzpatrick* is not.

Justice Powell, joined by Chief Justice Burger and Justices White and Rehnquist, dissented on the Eleventh Amendment holding. Powell returned to the language of *Edelman* emphasizing that "the threshold fact of congressional authorization to sue a class of defendants which literally includes states is wholly absent" and insisted that congressional override of state immunity be clearly stated.

6. THE REQUIREMENT OF CLEAR STATEMENT: *ATASCADERO STATE HOSPITAL V. SCANLON*

The Court's elevated its "clear statement" requirement to new heights in Atascadero State Hospital v. Scanlon, 473 U.S. 234 (1985). Scanlon claimed that he had been denied employment as a recreational therapist at a California state hospital because he was diabetic and blind in one eye. He brought suit under § 504 of the Rehabilitation Act of 1973. That statute prohibits employment discrimination against "otherwise qualified" handicapped persons by "any recipient of federal assistance." It was undisputed that California was a recipient of federal assistance. Additionally, the legislative history seemed to indicate that Congress intended, or at least assumed, that the remedies authorized by the act would be available against states. Nonetheless, the Court found the action barred:

> We . . . affirm that Congress may abrogate the states' constitutionally secured immunity from suit in federal court only by making its intention unmistakably clear in the language of the statute. . . . A general authorization for suit in federal court is not the kind of unequivocal statutory language sufficient to abrogate the Eleventh Amendment. When Congress chooses to subject the states to federal jurisdiction, it must do so specifically.

Justices Brennan, Marshall, Blackmun, and Stevens dissented.

There is an obvious tension between the clear statement required by *Atascadero* and *Parden v. Terminal Ry.*, which allowed something less. This tension was resolved in Welch v. Texas Department of Highways and Public Transportation, 483 U.S. 468 (1987), which involved state liability for injuries to seamen covered by the Jones Act, 46 U.S.C. § 688(a). The Court ruled, as in *Atascadero*, that Congress had not made states liable in "unmistakable statutory language" and that insofar as *Parden* promised a more lenient approach, it was expressly overruled.[e]

7. *PENNSYLVANIA V. UNION GAS CO.*

Fitzpatrick v. Bitzer settled that Congress could override Eleventh Amendment immunity to enforce Fourteenth Amendment rights, but the

---

[e] *Parden* was nonetheless followed, on very similar facts, in Hilton v. South Carolina Public Railways Commission, 502 U.S. 197 (1991). Hilton filed a state-court FELA action against the Commission, which was a state agency operating a railroad in interstate commerce. The South Carolina courts invoked the clear statement rule to bar Hilton's action, but the Supreme Court disagreed. Decisive for the majority was the longevity of *Parden* and the reliance on it by FELA plaintiffs and the states. The precise result in *Parden* was therefore reaffirmed, even though the majority doubted its correctness and plainly indicated its intention to require a clear statement in all future circumstances. Justices O'Connor and Scalia dissented.

question remained whether Congress had similar power under the Commerce Clause. *Welch* specifically reserved judgment on that question. The Court finally reached the issue in Pennsylvania v. Union Gas Company, 491 U.S. 1 (1989).

The case involved the Comprehensive Environmental Response, Compensation, and Liability Act of 1980 (CERCLA), 42 U.S.C. § 9601 et seq., as amended by the Superfund Amendments and Reauthorization Act of 1986 (SARA). A fractured Court found that this statute permitted damages actions against states in federal court and that Congress had the power to authorize such relief when legislating under the Commerce Clause. Speaking for himself and three others, Justice Brennan followed *Fitzpatrick* in concluding that Congress could override state sovereign immunity. Justice White concurred with the cryptic comment that "I agree with the conclusion reached by Justice Brennan . . . , although I do not agree with much of his reasoning." Four Justices dissented.

As the next case makes clear, the split decision in *Union Gas* was not to be the last word on Congress's power to abrogate Eleventh Amendment immunity.

Seminole Tribe of Florida v. Florida
Supreme Court of the United States, 1996.
517 U.S. 44.

■ CHIEF JUSTICE REHNQUIST delivered the opinion of the Court.

The Indian Gaming Regulatory Act provides that an Indian tribe may conduct certain gaming activities only in conformance with a valid compact between the tribe and the state in which the gaming activities are located. 25 U.S.C. § 2710(d)(1)(C). The act, passed by Congress under the Indian Commerce Clause, Art. I, § 10, cl. 3, imposes upon the states a duty to negotiate in good faith with an Indian tribe toward the formation of a compact, § 2710(d)(3)(A), and authorizes a tribe to bring suit in federal court against a state in order to compel performance of that duty, § 2710(d)(7). We hold that notwithstanding Congress's clear intent to abrogate the states' sovereign immunity, the Indian Commerce Clause does not grant Congress that power, and therefore § 2710(d)(7) cannot grant jurisdiction over a state that does not consent to be sued. We further hold that the doctrine of Ex parte Young, 209 U.S. 123 (1908), may not be used to enforce § 2710(d)(3) against a state official.

I

Congress passed the Indian Gaming Regulatory Act in 1988 in order to provide a statutory basis for the operation and regulation of gaming by Indian tribes. The act divides gaming on Indian lands into three classes—I, II, and III—and provides a different regulatory scheme for each class. Class III gaming—the type with which we are here concerned—. . . includes such things as slot machines, casino games, banking card games, dog racing, and lotteries. It is the most heavily regulated of the three classes. The act provides that class III gaming is lawful only where it is: (1) authorized by an ordinance or resolution that (a) is adopted by the governing body of the Indian tribe, (b) satisfies certain statutorily prescribed requirements, and (c) is approved by the National Indian Gaming Commission; (2) located in a state that permits such gaming for any purpose by any person, organization, or entity; and (3) "conducted in conformance with a Tribal-State compact entered into by the Indian tribe and the state under paragraph (3) that is in effect." § 2710(d)(1).

The "paragraph (3)" to which the last prerequisite of § 2710(d)(1) refers is § 2710(d)(3), which . . . describes the process by which a state and an Indian tribe begin negotiations toward a tribal-state compact [and provides that] "the State shall negotiate with the Indian tribe in good faith to enter into such a compact."

The state's obligation to "negotiate with the Indian tribe in good faith," is made judicially enforceable by § 2710(d)(7)(A)(i). . . :

> (A) The United States district courts shall have jurisdiction over—(i) any cause of action initiated by an Indian tribe arising from the failure of a State to enter into negotiations with the Indian tribe for the purpose of entering into a Tribal-State compact under paragraph (3) or to conduct such negotiations in good faith. . . .

Sections 2710(d)(7)(B)(ii)–(vii) describe an elaborate remedial scheme designed to ensure the formation of a tribal-state compact. [This scheme progressed to court-ordered negotiation, which, if unsuccessful, was followed by each side's submission of its "last best offer" to a mediator. The mediator recommended one of the two proposals. If the state still refused to agree, the mediator notified the Secretary of the Interior, who was then empowered to "prescribe . . . procedures . . . under which class III gaming may be conducted on the Indian lands over which the Indian tribe has jurisdiction."]

In September 1991, the Seminole Tribe of Indians, petitioner, sued the state of Florida and its governor, Lawton Chiles, respondents. Invoking jurisdiction under 25 U.S.C. § 2710(d)(7)(A), as well as 28 U.S.C. §§ 1331 and 1362, petitioner alleged that respondents had "refused to enter into any negotiation for inclusion of [certain gaming activities] in a tribal-state compact," thereby violating the "requirement of good faith negotiation" contained in § 2710(d)(3). Respondents moved to dismiss the complaint, arguing that the suit violated the state's sovereign immunity from suit in federal court. The District Court denied respondents' motion, and the respondents took an interlocutory appeal of that decision. See Puerto Rico Aqueduct and Sewer Authority v. Metcalf & Eddy, Inc., 506 U.S. 139 (1993) (collateral order doctrine allows immediate appellate review of order denying claim of Eleventh Amendment immunity).

The Court of Appeals for the Eleventh Circuit reversed the decision of the District Court, holding that the Eleventh Amendment barred petitioner's suit against respondents. . . . We . . . affirm the Eleventh Circuit's dismissal of petitioner's suit. . . .

Although the text of the amendment would appear to restrict only the Article III diversity jurisdiction of the federal courts, "we have understood the Eleventh Amendment to stand not so much for what it says, but for the presupposition . . . which it confirms." Blatchford v. Native Village of Noatak, 501 U.S. 775 (1991). That presupposition, first observed over a century ago in Hans v. Louisiana, 134 U.S. 1 (1890), has two parts: first, that each state is a sovereign entity in our federal system; and second, that " 'it is inherent in the nature of sovereignty not to be amenable to the suit of an individual without its consent.' " Id. at 13. For over a century we have reaffirmed that federal jurisdiction over suits against unconsenting states "was not contemplated by the Constitution when establishing the judicial power of the United States." Id. at 15 n.7 [and other cases].

Here, petitioner has sued the state of Florida and it is undisputed that Florida has not consented to the suit. Petitioner nevertheless contends that its suit is not barred by state sovereign immunity. First, it argues that Congress through the act abrogated the states' sovereign immunity. Alternatively, petitioner maintains that its suit against the governor may go forward under *Ex parte Young*. We consider each of those arguments in turn.

II

Petitioner argues that Congress through the act abrogated the states' immunity from suit. In order to determine whether Congress has abrogated the states' sovereign immunity, we ask two questions: first, whether Congress has "unequivocally expressed its intent to abrogate the immunity," Green v. Mansour, 474 U.S. 64, 68 (1985); and second, whether Congress has acted "pursuant to a valid exercise of power." Id.

A

[In this part of its opinion, the Court found "that Congress has in § 2710(d)(7) provided an 'unmistakably clear' statement of its intent to abrogate" state sovereign immunity.]

B

[W]e turn now to consider whether the act was passed "pursuant to a valid exercise of power." Id. Before we address that question here, however, we think it necessary first to define the scope of our inquiry.

Petitioner suggests that one consideration weighing in favor of finding the power to abrogate here is that the act authorizes only prospective injunctive relief rather than retroactive monetary relief. But we have often made it clear that the relief sought by a plaintiff suing a state is irrelevant to the question whether the suit is barred by the Eleventh

Amendment. . . . The Eleventh Amendment does not exist solely in order to "prevent federal court judgments that must be paid out of a state's treasury," Hess v. Port Authority Trans-Hudson Corporation, 513 U.S. 30 (1994); it also serves to avoid "the indignity of subjecting a state to the coercive process of judicial tribunals at the instance of private parties," Id. at 146 (internal quotation marks omitted).

Similarly, petitioner argues that the abrogation power is validly exercised here because the act grants the states a power that they would not otherwise have, viz., some measure of authority over gaming on Indian lands. It is true enough that the act extends to the states a power withheld from them by the Constitution. See California v. Cabazon Band of Mission Indians, 480 U.S. 202 (1987). Nevertheless, we do not see how that consideration is relevant to the question whether Congress may abrogate state sovereign immunity. The Eleventh Amendment immunity may not be lifted by Congress unilaterally deciding that it will be replaced by grant of some other authority.

Thus our inquiry into whether Congress has the power to abrogate unilaterally the states' immunity from suit is narrowly focused on one question: Was the act in question passed pursuant to a constitutional provision granting Congress the power to abrogate? Previously, in conducting that inquiry, we have found authority to abrogate under only two provisions of the Constitution. In Fitzpatrick v. Bitzer, 427 U.S. 445 (1976), we recognized that the Fourteenth Amendment, by expanding federal power at the expense of state autonomy, had fundamentally altered the balance of state and federal power struck by the Constitution. We noted that § 1 of the Fourteenth Amendment contained prohibitions expressly directed at the states and that § 5 of the amendment expressly provided that "The Congress shall have the power to enforce, by appropriate legislation, the provisions of this article." We held that through the Fourteenth Amendment, federal power extended to intrude upon the province of the Eleventh Amendment and therefore that § 5 of the Fourteenth Amendment allowed Congress to abrogate the immunity from suit guaranteed by that amendment.

In only one other case has congressional abrogation of the states' Eleventh Amendment immunity been upheld. In Pennsylvania v. Union Gas Co., 491 U.S. 1 (1989), a plurality of the Court found that the interstate Commerce Clause, Art. I, § 8, cl. 3, granted Congress the power to abrogate state sovereign immunity, stating that the power to regulate interstate commerce would be "incomplete without the authority to render states liable in damages." Justice White added the fifth vote necessary to the result in that case, but wrote separately in order to express that he "[did] not agree with much of [the plurality's] reasoning." . . .

The Court in *Union Gas* reached a result without an expressed rationale agreed upon by a majority of the Court. . . . The plurality's rationale . . . deviated sharply from our established federalism jurisprudence and essentially eviscerated our decision in *Hans*. It was well established in 1989 when *Union Gas* was decided that the Eleventh Amendment stood for the constitutional principle that state sovereign immunity limited the federal courts' jurisdiction under Article III. . . .

Never before the decision in *Union Gas* had we suggested that the bounds of Article III could be expanded by Congress operating pursuant to any constitutional provision other than the Fourteenth Amendment. Indeed, it had seemed fundamental that Congress could not expand the jurisdiction of the federal courts beyond the bounds of Article III. Marbury v. Madison, 5 U.S. (1 Cranch) 137 (1803). . . .

The [*Union Gas*] plurality's extended reliance upon our decision in *Fitzpatrick v. Bitzer* that Congress could under the Fourteenth Amendment abrogate the states' sovereign immunity was also, we believe, misplaced. *Fitzpatrick* was based upon a rationale wholly inapplicable to the interstate Commerce Clause, viz., that the Fourteenth Amendment, adopted well after the adoption of the Eleventh Amendment and the ratification of the Constitution, operated to alter the pre-existing balance between state and federal power achieved by Article III and the Eleventh Amendment. As the dissent in *Union Gas* made clear, *Fitzpatrick* cannot be read to justify "limitation of the principle embodied in the Eleventh Amendment through appeal to antecedent provisions of the Constitution."

. . . Reconsidering the decision in *Union Gas*, we conclude that none of the policies underlying stare decisis [requires] our continuing adherence to its holding. The decision has, since its issuance, been of questionable precedential value, largely because a majority of the Court expressly disagreed with the rationale of the plurality. The case involved the interpretation of the Constitution and therefore may be altered only by constitutional amendment or revision by this Court. Finally, both the result in *Union Gas* and the plurality's rationale depart from our established understanding of the Eleventh Amendment and undermine the accepted function of Article III. We feel bound to conclude that *Union Gas* was wrongly decided and that it should be, and now is, overruled.

The dissent makes no effort to defend the decision in *Union Gas*, but nonetheless would find congressional power to abrogate in this case.[11] Contending that our decision is a novel extension of the Eleventh Amendment, the dissent chides us for "attending" to dicta. We adhere in this case, however, not to mere obiter dicta, but rather to the well-established rationale upon which the Court based the results of its earlier decisions. . . . For over a century, we have grounded our decisions in the oft-repeated understanding of state sovereign immunity as an essential part of the Eleventh Amendment. In Principality of Monaco v. Mississippi, 292 U.S. 313 (1934), the Court held that the Eleventh Amendment barred

---

[11] Unless otherwise indicated, all references to the dissent are to the dissenting opinion authored by Justice Souter.

a suit brought against a state by a foreign state. Chief Justice Hughes wrote for a unanimous Court:

> [A]lthough a case may arise under the Constitution and laws of the United States, the judicial power does not extend to it if the suit is sought to be prosecuted against a state, without her consent, by one of her own citizens. . . .

Manifestly, we cannot rest with a mere literal application of the words of § 2 of Article III, or assume that the letter of the Eleventh Amendment exhausts the restrictions upon suits against non-consenting states. Behind the words of the constitutional provisions are postulates which limit and control. There is the essential postulate that the controversies, as contemplated, shall be found to be of a justiciable character. There is also the postulate that states of the Union, still possessing attributes of sovereignty, shall be immune from suits, without their consent, save where there has been a "surrender of this immunity in the plan of the convention."

It is true that we have not had occasion previously to apply established Eleventh Amendment principles to the question whether Congress has the power to abrogate state sovereign immunity (save in *Union Gas*). But consideration of that question must proceed with fidelity to this century-old doctrine.

The dissent, to the contrary, disregards our case law in favor of a theory cobbled together from law review articles and its own version of historical events. The dissent cites not a single decision since *Hans* (other than *Union Gas*) that supports its view of state sovereign immunity, instead relying upon the now-discredited decision in Chisholm v. Georgia, 2 U.S. (2 Dall.) 419 (1793). Its undocumented and highly speculative extralegal explanation of the decision in *Hans* is a disservice to the Court's traditional method of adjudication. . . .

Hans—with a much closer vantage point than the dissent—recognized that the decision in *Chisholm* was contrary to the well-understood meaning of the Constitution. . . . The dissent's lengthy analysis of the text of the Eleventh Amendment is directed at a straw man—we long have recognized that blind reliance upon the text of the Eleventh Amendment is " 'to strain the Constitution and the law to a construction never imagined or dreamed of.' " *Monaco*, 292 U.S. at 326, quoting *Hans*. The text dealt in terms only with the problem presented by the decision in *Chisholm*; in light of the fact that the federal courts did not have federal question jurisdiction at the time the amendment was passed (and would not have it until 1875), it seems unlikely that much thought was given to the prospect of federal question jurisdiction over the states. . . . [T]he lack of any statute vesting general federal question jurisdiction in the federal courts until much later makes the dissent's demand for greater specificity about a then-dormant jurisdiction overly exacting.[13]

In putting forward a new theory of state sovereign immunity, the dissent develops its own vision of the political system created by the framers, concluding with the statement that "the framers' principal objectives in rejecting English theories of unitary sovereignty . . . would have been impeded if a new concept of sovereign immunity had taken its place in federal question cases, and would have been substantially thwarted if that new immunity had been held untouchable by any congressional effort to abrogate it." This sweeping statement ignores the fact that the nation survived for nearly two centuries without the question of the existence of such power ever being presented to this Court. And Congress itself waited nearly a century before even conferring federal question jurisdiction on the lower federal courts.

In overruling *Union Gas* today, we reconfirm that the background principle of state sovereign immunity embodied in the Eleventh Amendment is not so ephemeral as to dissipate when the subject of the suit is an area, like the regulation of Indian commerce, that is under the exclusive control of the federal government. Even when the Constitution vests in Congress complete law-making authority over a particular area, the Eleventh Amendment prevents congressional authorization of suits by private parties against unconsenting states. The Eleventh Amendment restricts the judicial power under Article III, and Article I cannot be used to circumvent the constitutional limitations placed upon federal jurisdiction. Petitioner's suit against the state of Florida must be dismissed for a lack of jurisdiction.

III

Petitioner argues that we may exercise jurisdiction over its suit to enforce § 2710(d)(3) against the governor notwithstanding the jurisdictional bar of the Eleventh Amendment. Petitioner notes that since our decision in Ex parte Young, 209 U.S. 123 (1908), we often have found federal jurisdiction over a suit against a state official when that suit seeks only prospective injunctive relief in order to "end a continuing violation of federal law." *Green*, 474 U.S. at 68. The situation presented here, however, is sufficiently different from that giving rise to the traditional *Ex parte Young* action so as to preclude the availability of that doctrine.

Here, the "continuing violation of federal law" alleged by petitioner is the governor's failure to bring the state into compliance with § 2710(d)(3). But the duty to negotiate imposed upon the state by that statutory provision does not stand alone. Rather, as we have seen, Congress passed § 2710(d)(3) in conjunction with the carefully crafted and intricate remedial scheme set forth in § 2710(d)(7).

---

[13] Although the absence of any discussion dealing with federal question jurisdiction is therefore unremarkable, what is notably lacking in the framers' statements is any mention of Congress's power to abrogate the states' immunity. . . .

Where Congress has created a remedial scheme for the enforcement of a particular federal right, we have, in suits against federal officers, refused to supplement that scheme with one created by the judiciary. Schweiker v. Chilicky, 487 U.S. 412, 423 (1988) ("When the design of a government program suggests that Congress has provided what it considers adequate remedial mechanisms for constitutional violations that may occur in the course of its administration, we have not created additional . . . remedies"). Here, of course, the question is not whether a remedy should be created, but instead is whether the Eleventh Amendment bar should be lifted, as it was in *Ex parte Young*, in order to allow a suit against a state officer. Nevertheless, we think that the same general principle applies: therefore, where Congress has prescribed a detailed remedial scheme for the enforcement against a state of a statutorily created right, a court should hesitate before casting aside those limitations and permitting an action against a state officer based upon *Ex parte Young*.

Here, Congress intended § 2710(d)(3) to be enforced against the state in an action brought under § 2710(d)(7); the intricate procedures set forth in that provision show that Congress intended therein not only to define, but also significantly to limit, the duty imposed by § 2710(d)(3). [Even after court-ordered negotiation and submission of competing proposals to a mediator, the only sanction for the state's failure to accept the mediator's recommendation] is that the mediator shall notify the Secretary of the Interior who then must prescribe regulations governing Class III gaming on the tribal lands at issue. By contrast with this quite modest set of sanctions, an action brought against a state official under *Ex parte Young* would expose that official to the full remedial powers of a federal court, including, presumably, contempt sanctions. If § 2710(d)(3) could be enforced in a suit under *Ex parte Young*, § 2710(d)(7) would have been superfluous; it is difficult to see why an Indian tribe would suffer through the intricate scheme of § 2710(d)(7) when more complete and more immediate relief would be available under *Ex parte Young*.[17]

Here, of course, we have found that Congress does not have authority under the Constitution to make the state suable in federal court under § 2710(d)(7). Nevertheless, the fact that Congress chose to impose upon the state a liability which is significantly more limited than would be the liability imposed upon the state officer under *Ex parte Young* strongly indicates that Congress had no wish to create the latter under § 2710(d)(3). Nor are we free to rewrite the statutory scheme in order to approximate what we think Congress might have wanted had it known that § 2710(d)(7) was beyond its authority. If that effort is to be made, it should be made by Congress, and not by the federal courts. We hold that *Ex parte Young* is inapplicable to petitioner's suit against the governor of

---

[17] Contrary to the claims of the dissent, we do not hold that Congress cannot authorize federal jurisdiction under *Ex parte Young* over a cause of action with a limited remedial scheme. We find only that Congress did not intend that result in the Indian Gaming Regulatory Act. . . .

Florida, and therefore that suit is barred by the Eleventh Amendment and must be dismissed for a lack of jurisdiction. . . .

It is so ordered.

[The dissenting opinion of Justice Stevens has been omitted.]

■ JUSTICE SOUTER, with whom JUSTICE GINSBURG and JUSTICE BREYER join, dissenting.

In holding the state of Florida immune to suit under the Indian Gaming Regulatory Act, the Court today holds for the first time since the founding of the republic that Congress has no authority to subject a state to the jurisdiction of a federal court at the behest of an individual asserting a federal right. . . . I am convinced that its decision is fundamentally mistaken, and for that reason I respectfully dissent.

I

. . . There are two plausible readings of [the text of the Eleventh Amendment.] Under the first, it simply repeals the citizen-state diversity clauses of Article III for all cases in which the state appears as a defendant. Under the second, it strips the federal courts of jurisdiction in any case in which a state defendant is sued by a citizen not its own, even if jurisdiction might otherwise rest on the existence of a federal question in the suit. Neither reading of the amendment, of course, furnishes authority for the Court's view in today's case, but we need to choose between the competing readings for the light that will be shed on the *Hans* doctrine and the legitimacy of inflating that doctrine to the point of constitutional immutability as the Court has chosen to do.

The history and structure of the Eleventh Amendment convincingly show that it reaches only to suits subject to federal jurisdiction exclusively under the citizen-state diversity clauses.[8] In precisely tracking the language in Article III providing for citizen-state diversity jurisdiction, the text of the amendment does, after all, suggest to common sense that only the diversity clauses are being addressed. . . .

---

[8]   The great weight of scholarly commentary agrees. See, e.g., Vicki C. Jackson, The Supreme Court, the Eleventh Amendment, and State Sovereign Immunity, 98 Yale L.J. 1 (1988); Akhil Amar, Of Sovereignty and Federalism, 96 Yale L.J. 1425 (1987); William A. Fletcher, A Historical Interpretation of the Eleventh Amendment: A Narrow Construction of an Affirmative Grant of Jurisdiction Rather than a Prohibition Against Jurisdiction, 35 Stan. L. Rev. 1033 (1983); John J. Gibbons, The Eleventh Amendment and State Sovereign Immunity: A Reinterpretation, 83 Colum. L. Rev. 1889 (1983); Martha A. Field, The Eleventh Amendment and Other Sovereign Immunity Doctrines: Congressional Imposition of Suit upon the States, 126 U. Pa. L. Rev. 1203 (1978). While a minority has adopted the second view set out above, see, e.g., Lawrence C. Marshall, Fighting the Words of the Eleventh Amendment, 102 Harv. L. Rev. 1342 (1989); Calvin R. Massey, State Sovereignty and the Tenth and Eleventh Amendments, 56 U. Chi. L. Rev. 61 (1989), and others have criticized the diversity theory, see, e.g., William P. Marshall, The Diversity Theory of the Eleventh Amendment: A Critical Evaluation, 102 Harv. L. Rev. 1372 (1989), I have discovered no commentator affirmatively advocating the position taken by the Court today. As one scholar has observed, the literature is "remarkably consistent in its evaluation of the historical evidence and text of the amendment as not supporting a broad rule of constitutional immunity for states." Jackson, at 44 n.179.

It should accordingly come as no surprise that the weightiest commentary following the amendment's adoption described it simply as constricting the scope of the citizen-state diversity clauses. In Cohens v. Virginia, 19 U.S. (6 Wheat.) 264, 383 (1821), . . . Chief Justice Marshall, writing for the Court, emphasized that the amendment had no effect on federal courts' jurisdiction grounded on the "arising under" provision of Article III and concluded that "a case arising under the constitution or laws of the United States, is cognizable in the Courts of the Union, whoever may be the parties to that case." The point of the Eleventh Amendment, according to *Cohens*, was to bar jurisdiction in suits at common law by Revolutionary War debt creditors, not "to strip the government of the means of protecting, by the instrumentality of its courts, the constitution and laws from active violation." . . .

In sum, reading the Eleventh Amendment solely as a limit on citizen-state diversity jurisdiction has the virtue of coherence with this Court's practice, with the views of John Marshall, with the history of the amendment's drafting, and with its allusive language. Today's majority does not appear to disagree, at least insofar as the constitutional text is concerned; the Court concedes, after all, that "the text of the amendment would appear to restrict only the Article III diversity jurisdiction of the federal courts."

Thus, regardless of which of the two plausible readings one adopts, the further point to note here is that there is no possible argument that the Eleventh Amendment, by its terms, deprives federal courts of jurisdiction over all citizen lawsuits against the states. Not even the Court advances that proposition, and there would be no textual basis for doing so. Because the plaintiffs in today's case are citizens of the state that they are suing, the Eleventh Amendment simply does not apply to them. We must therefore look elsewhere for the source of that immunity by which the Court says their suit is barred from a federal court.[13]

II

The obvious place to look elsewhere, of course, is Hans v. Louisiana, 134 U.S. 1 (1890), and *Hans* was indeed a leap in the direction of today's holding, even though it does not take the Court all the way. The parties in *Hans* raised, and the Court in that case answered, only . . . the . . . question . . . whether the Constitution, without more, permits a state to plead sovereign immunity to bar the exercise of federal question jurisdiction. Although the Court invoked a principle of sovereign immunity to cure what it took to be the Eleventh Amendment's anomaly of barring only those state suits brought by noncitizen plaintiffs, the *Hans* Court

---

[13] The majority chides me that the "lengthy analysis of the text of the Eleventh Amendment is directed at a straw man." But plain text is the Man of Steel in a confrontation with "background principles" and " 'postulates which limit and control.' " . . . That the Court thinks otherwise is an indication of just how far it has strayed beyond the boundaries of traditional constitutional analysis.

had no occasion to consider whether Congress could abrogate that background immunity by statute. Indeed (except in the special circumstance of Congress's power to enforce the Civil War amendments), this question never came before our Court until Pennsylvania v. Union Gas Co., 491 U.S. 1 (1989), and any intimations of an answer in prior cases were mere dicta. In *Union Gas* the Court held that the immunity recognized in *Hans* had no constitutional status and was subject to congressional abrogation. Today the Court overrules *Union Gas* and holds just the opposite. In deciding how to choose between these two positions, the place to begin is with *Hans*'s holding that a principle of sovereign immunity derived from the common law insulates a state from federal question jurisdiction at the suit of its own citizen. A critical examination of that case will show that it was wrongly decided, as virtually every recent commentator has concluded. It follows that the Court's further step today of constitutionalizing *Hans*'s rule against abrogation by Congress compounds and immensely magnifies the century-old mistake of *Hans* itself and takes its place with other historic examples of textually untethered elevations of judicially derived rules to the status of inviolable constitutional law.

A

... *Hans* ... addressed the issue implicated (though not directly raised) in the preratification debate about the citizen-state diversity clauses and implicitly settled by Chisholm v. Georgia, 2 U.S. (2 Dall.) 419 (1793): whether state sovereign immunity was cognizable by federal courts on the exercise of federal question jurisdiction. According to *Hans*, and contrary to *Chisholm*, it was. But that is all that *Hans* held. Because no federal legislation purporting to pierce state immunity was at issue, it cannot fairly be said that *Hans* held state sovereign immunity to have attained some constitutional status immunizing it from abrogation.

Taking *Hans* only as far as its holding, its vulnerability is apparent. The Court rested its opinion on avoiding the supposed anomaly of recognizing jurisdiction to entertain a citizen's federal question suit, but not one brought by a noncitizen. There was, however, no such anomaly at all. As already explained, federal question cases are not touched by the Eleventh Amendment, which leaves a state open to federal question suits by citizens and noncitizens alike. . . .

Although there was thus no anomaly to be cured by *Hans*, the case certainly created its own anomaly in leaving federal courts entirely without jurisdiction to enforce paramount federal law at the behest of a citizen against a state that broke it. It destroyed the congruence of the judicial power under Article III with the substantive guarantees of the Constitution, and with the provisions of statutes passed by Congress in the exercise of its power under Article I: when a state injured an individual in violation of federal law no federal forum could provide direct relief. . . .

How such a result could have been threatened on the basis of a principle not so much as mentioned in the Constitution is difficult to understand. But history provides the explanation. [Justice Souter then explained *Hans* as the Supreme Court's extra-legal reaction to its perceived inability to enforce judgments against southern states after the end of Reconstruction.]

B

The majority does not dispute the point that *Hans* had no occasion to decide whether Congress could abrogate a state's immunity from federal question suits. The Court insists, however, that the negative answer to that question that it finds in *Hans* and subsequent opinions is not "mere obiter dicta, but rather . . . the well-established rationale upon which the Court based the results of its earlier decisions." The exact rationale to which the majority refers, unfortunately, is not easy to discern. The Court's opinion says, immediately after its discussion of stare decisis, that "for over a century, we have grounded our decisions in the oft-repeated understanding of state sovereign immunity as an essential part of the Eleventh Amendment." This cannot be the "rationale," though, because this Court has repeatedly acknowledged that the Eleventh Amendment standing alone cannot bar a federal question suit against a state brought by a state citizen. See, e.g., Edelman v. Jordan, 415 U.S. 651, 662 (1974) (acknowledging that "the amendment by its terms does not bar suits against a state by its own citizens"). . . .

The "rationale" which the majority seeks to invoke is, I think, more nearly stated in its quotation from Principality of Monaco v. Mississippi, 292 U.S. 313, 321–23 (1934). There, the Court said that "we cannot rest with a mere literal application of the words of § 2 of Article III, or assume that the letter of the Eleventh Amendment exhausts the restrictions upon suits against non-consenting states." This statement certainly is true to *Hans*, which clearly recognized a pre-existing principle of sovereign immunity, broader than the Eleventh Amendment itself, that will ordinarily bar federal question suits against a nonconsenting state. That was the "rationale" which was sufficient to decide *Hans* and all of its progeny prior to *Union Gas*. But leaving aside the indefensibility of that rationale . . . , that was as far as it went.

The majority, however, would read the "rationale" of *Hans* and its line of subsequent cases as answering the further question whether the "postulate" of sovereign immunity that "limits and controls" the exercise of Article III jurisdiction is constitutional in stature and therefore unalterable by Congress. It is true that there are statements in the cases that point toward just this conclusion. See, e.g., Pennhurst State School and Hospital v. Halderman, 465 U.S. 89, 98 (1984) ("In short, the principle of sovereign immunity is a constitutional limitation on the federal judicial power established in Article III"). . . . These statements, however, are dicta in the classic sense, that is, sheer speculation about what would happen in cases not before the court. . . . More generally, the proponents of the Court's theory have repeatedly referred to state sovereign immunity as a "background principle," "postulate," *Hall*, 440 U.S. at 437 (Rehnquist, J., dissenting), or "implicit limitation," Welch v. Texas Dept. of Highways and Public Transp., 483 U.S. 468, 496 (1987) (Scalia, J., concurring in part and concurring in judgment). . . .

The most damning evidence for the Court's theory that *Hans* rests on a broad rationale of immunity unalterable by Congress, however, is the Court's proven tendency to disregard the post-*Hans* dicta in cases where that dicta would have mattered. If it is indeed true that "private suits against states [are] not permitted under Article III (by virtue of the understanding represented by the Eleventh Amendment)," *Union Gas*, 491 U.S. at 40 (Scalia, J., concurring in part and dissenting in part), then it is hard to see how a state's sovereign immunity may be waived any more than it may be abrogated by Congress. See, e.g., Atascadero State Hospital v. Scanlon, 473 U.S. 234, 238 (1985) (recognizing that immunity may be waived). After all, consent of a party is in all other instances wholly insufficient to create subject-matter jurisdiction where it would not otherwise exist. Likewise, the Court's broad theory of immunity runs doubly afoul of the appellate jurisdiction problem. . . . If "the whole sum of the judicial power granted by the Constitution to the United States does not embrace the authority to entertain a suit brought by a citizen against his own state without its consent," Duhne v. New Jersey, 251 U.S. 311, 313 (1920), and if consent to suit in state court is not sufficient to show consent in federal court, see *Atascadero*, 473 U.S. at 241, then Article III would hardly permit this Court to exercise appellate jurisdiction over issues of federal law arising in lawsuits brought against the states in their own courts. We have, however, quite rightly ignored any post-*Hans* dicta in that sort of case and exercised the jurisdiction that the plain text of Article III provides. . . .

III

Three critical errors in *Hans* weigh against constitutionalizing its holding as the majority does today. The first we have already seen: the *Hans* Court misread the Eleventh Amendment. It also misunderstood the conditions under which common-law doctrines were received or rejected at the time of the founding, and it fundamentally mistook the very nature of sovereignty in the young republic that was supposed to entail a state's immunity to federal question jurisdiction in a federal court. While I would not, as a matter of stare decisis, overrule *Hans* today, an understanding of its failings on these points will show how the Court today simply compounds already serious error in taking *Hans* the further step of investing its rule with constitutional inviolability against the considered judgment of Congress to abrogate it.

A

There is and could be no dispute that the doctrine of sovereign immunity that *Hans* purported to apply had its origins in the "familiar doctrine of the common law," The Siren, 74 U.S. 152, 153 (1869), "derived from the laws and practices of our English ancestors," United States v.

Lee, 106 U.S. 196, 205 (1882). Although statutes came to affect its importance in the succeeding centuries, the doctrine was never reduced to codification, and Americans took their understanding of immunity doctrine from Blackstone, see 3 W. Blackstone, Commentaries on the Laws of England ch. 17 (1768). Here, as in the mother country, it remained a common-law rule.

This fact of the doctrine's common-law status in the period covering the founding and the later adoption of the Eleventh Amendment should have raised a warning flag to the *Hans* Court and it should do the same for the Court today. For although the Court has persistently assumed that the common law's presence in the minds of the early framers must have functioned as a limitation on their understanding of the new nation's constitutional powers, this turns out not to be so at all. One of the characteristics of the founding generation, on the contrary, was its joinder of an appreciation of its immediate and powerful common-law heritage with caution in settling that inheritance on the political systems of the new republic. . . .

While the states had limited their reception of English common law to principles appropriate to American conditions, the 1787 draft Constitution contained no provision for adopting the common law at all. This omission stood in sharp contrast to the state constitutions then extant, virtually all of which contained explicit provisions dealing with common-law reception. Since the experience in the states set the stage for thinking at the national level, this failure to address the notion of common-law reception could not have been inadvertent. Instead, the framers chose to recognize only particular common-law concepts, such as the writ of habeas corpus, Art. I, § 9, cl. 2, and the distinction between law and equity, Amendment VII, by specific reference in the constitutional text. This approach reflected widespread agreement that ratification would not itself entail a general reception of the common law of England. . . .

B

Given the refusal to entertain any wholesale reception of common law [and] given the failure of the new Constitution to make any provision for adoption of common law as such . . . , the *Hans* Court and the Court today cannot reasonably argue that something like the old immunity doctrine somehow slipped in as a tacit but enforceable background principle. The evidence is even more specific, however, that there was no pervasive understanding that sovereign immunity had limited federal question jurisdiction. . . .

[T]he framers and their contemporaries did not agree about the place of common-law state sovereign immunity even as to federal jurisdiction resting on the citizen-state diversity clauses. Edmund Randolph argued in favor of ratification on the ground that the immunity would not be recognized, leaving the states subject to jurisdiction. Patrick Henry opposed ratification on the basis of exactly the same reading. On the other hand, James Madison, John Marshall, and Alexander Hamilton all appear to have believed that the common-law immunity from suit would survive the ratification of Article III, so as to be at a state's disposal when jurisdiction would depend on diversity. This would have left the states free to enjoy a traditional immunity as defendants without barring the exercise of judicial power over them if they chose to enter the federal courts as diversity plaintiffs or to waive their immunity as diversity defendants. As Hamilton stated in Federalist 81,

> It is inherent in the nature of sovereignty, not to be amenable to the suit of an individual without its consent. This is the general sense and the general practice of mankind; and the exemption, as one of the attributes of sovereignty, is now enjoyed by the government of every state in the Union. Unless therefore, there is a surrender of this immunity in the plan of the convention, it will remain with the states, and the danger intimated must be merely ideal.

The Federalist No. 81, pp. 548–49 (J. Cooke ed. 1961). The majority sees in these statements, and chiefly in Hamilton's discussion of sovereign immunity in Federalist No. 81, an unequivocal mandate "which would preclude all federal jurisdiction over an unconsenting state." But there is no such mandate to be found. [T]he immediate context of Hamilton's discussion in Federalist No. 81 has nothing to do with federal question cases. It addresses a suggestion "that an assignment of the public securities of one state to the citizens of another, would enable them to prosecute that state in the federal courts for the amount of those securities." Federalist No. 81, at 548. Hamilton is plainly talking about a suit subject to a federal court's jurisdiction under the citizen-state diversity clauses of Article III. . . .

Thus, the Court's attempt to convert isolated statements by the framers into answers to questions not before them is fundamentally misguided. The Court's difficulty is far more fundamental however, than inconsistency with a particular quotation, for the Court's position runs afoul of the general theory of sovereignty that gave shape to the framers' enterprise. An enquiry into the development of that concept demonstrates that American political thought had so revolutionized the concept of sovereignty itself that calling for the immunity of a state as against the jurisdiction of the national courts would have been sheer illogic.

. . . [T]he adoption of the Constitution made [the states] members of a novel federal system that sought to balance [their] exercise of some sovereign prerogatives delegated from their own people with the principle of a limited but centralizing federal supremacy.

As a matter of political theory, this federal arrangement of dual delegated sovereign powers truly was a more revolutionary turn than the late war had been. Before the new federal scheme appeared, 18th-century political theorists had assumed that "there must reside somewhere in every political unit a single, undivided, final power, higher in legal authority than any other power, subject to no law, a law unto itself." B. Bailyn, The Ideological Origins of the American Revolution 198 (1967). The American development of divided sovereign powers, which "shattered ... the categories of government that had dominated Western thinking for centuries," id. at 385, was made possible only by a recognition that the ultimate sovereignty rests in the people themselves. The people possessing this plenary bundle of specific powers were free to parcel them out to different governments and different branches of the same government as they saw fit. . . .

Given this metamorphosis of the idea of sovereignty in the years leading up to 1789, the question whether the old immunity doctrine might have been received as something suitable for the new world of federal question jurisdiction is a crucial one. The answer is that sovereign immunity as it would have been known to the framers before ratification thereafter became inapplicable as a matter of logic in a federal suit raising a federal question. The old doctrine, after all, barred the involuntary subjection of a sovereign to the system of justice and law of which it was itself the font, since to do otherwise would have struck the common-law mind from the Middle Ages onward as both impractical and absurd. But the ratification demonstrated that state governments were subject to a superior regime of law in a judicial system established, not by the state, but by the people through a specific delegation of their sovereign power to a national government that was paramount within its delegated sphere. When individuals sued states to enforce federal rights, the government that corresponded to the "sovereign" in the traditional common-law sense was not the state but the national government, and any state immunity from the jurisdiction of the nation's courts would have required a grant from the true sovereign, the people, in their Constitution, or from the Congress that the Constitution had empowered. . . .

State immunity to federal question jurisdiction would, moreover, have run up against the common understanding of the practical necessity for the new federal relationship. According to Madison, the "multiplicity," "mutability," and "injustice" of then-extant state laws were prime factors requiring the formation of a new government. . . .

Given the framers' general concern with curbing abuses by state governments, it would be amazing if the scheme of delegated powers embodied in the Constitution had left the national government powerless to render the states judicially accountable for violations of federal rights. . . .

This sketch of the logic and objectives of the new federal order is confirmed by what we have previously seen of the preratification debate on state sovereign immunity, which in turn becomes entirely intelligible both in what it addressed and what it ignored. It is understandable that reasonable minds differed on the applicability of the immunity doctrine in suits that made it to federal court only under the original diversity clauses, for their features were not wholly novel. While they were, of course, in the courts of the new and, for some purposes, paramount national government, the law that they implicated was largely the old common law (and in any case was not federal law). It was not foolish, therefore, to ask whether the old law brought the old defenses with it. But it is equally understandable that questions seem not to have been raised about state sovereign immunity in federal question cases. The very idea of a federal question depended on the rejection of the simple concept of sovereignty from which the immunity doctrine had developed; under the English common law, the question of immunity in a system of layered sovereignty simply could not have arisen. The framers' principal objectives in rejecting English theories of unitary sovereignty, moreover, would have been impeded if a new concept of sovereign immunity had taken its place in federal question cases, and would have been substantially thwarted if that new immunity had been held to be untouchable by any congressional effort to abrogate it.

Today's majority discounts this concern. Without citing a single source to the contrary, the Court dismisses the historical evidence regarding the framers' vision of the relationship between national and state sovereignty, and reassures us that "the nation survived for nearly two centuries without the question of the existence of [the abrogation] power ever being presented to this Court." But we are concerned here not with the survival of the nation but the opportunity of its citizens to enforce federal rights in a way that Congress provides. . . .

C

. . . Although for reasons of stare decisis I would not today disturb the century-old [*Hans*] precedent, I surely would not extend its error by placing the common-law immunity it mistakenly recognized beyond the power of Congress to abrogate. . . . [It is] remarkable that as we near the end of this century the Court should choose to open a new constitutional chapter in confining legislative judgments on these matters by resort to textually unwarranted common-law rules, for it was just this practice in the century's early decades that brought this Court to the nadir of competence that we identify with Lochner v. New York, 198 U.S. 45 (1905).

It was the defining characteristic of the *Lochner* era, and its characteristic vice, that the Court treated the common-law background (in those days, common-law property rights and contractual autonomy) as paramount, while regarding congressional legislation to abrogate the common law on these economic matters as constitutionally suspect. And yet the superseding lesson that seemed clear after West Coast Hotel Co. v. Parrish, 300 U.S. 379 (1937), that action within the legislative power is not subject to greater scrutiny merely because it trenches upon the case law's ordering of economic and social relationships, seems to have been lost on the Court. . . .

IV

The Court's holding that the states' *Hans* immunity may not be abrogated by Congress leads to the final question in this case, whether federal question jurisdiction exists to order prospective relief enforcing IGRA against a state officer, respondent Chiles, who is said to be authorized to take the action required by the federal law. . . . The answer to this question is an easy yes, the officer is subject to suit under the rule in Ex parte Young, 209 U.S. 123 (1908), and the case could, and should, readily be decided on this point alone. . . .

It should be no cause for surprise that *Young* itself appeared when it did in the national law. It followed as a matter of course after the *Hans* Court's broad recognition of immunity in federal question cases. . . . *Young* provided, as it does today, a sensible way to reconcile the Court's expansive view of immunity expressed in *Hans* with the principles embodied in the Supremacy Clause and Article III. . . .

No clear statement of intent to displace the doctrine of *Ex parte Young* occurs in IGRA, and the Court is instead constrained to rest its effort to skirt *Young* on a series of suggestions thought to be apparent in Congress's provision of "intricate procedures" for enforcing a state's obligation under the act. The procedures are said to implicate a rule against judicial creativity in devising supplementary procedures; it is said that applying *Young* would nullify the statutory procedures; and finally the statutory provisions are said simply to reveal a congressional intent to preclude the application of *Young*.

The Court cites Schweiker v. Chilicky, 487 U.S. 412, 423 (1988), in support of refraining from what it seems to think would be judicial creativity in recognizing the applicability of *Young*. The Court quotes from *Chilicky* for the general proposition that when Congress has provided what it considers adequate remedial mechanisms for violations of federal law, this Court should not "create" additional remedies. The Court reasons that Congress's provision in IGRA of "intricate procedures" shows that it considers its remedial provisions to be adequate, with the implication that courts as a matter of prudence should provide no "additional" remedy under *Ex parte Young*.

Chilicky's remoteness from the point of this case is, however, apparent from its facts. In *Chilicky*, Congress had addressed the problem of erroneous denials of certain government benefits by creating a scheme of appeals and awards that would make a successful claimant whole for all benefits wrongly denied. The question was whether this Court should create a further remedy on the model of Bivens v. Six Unknown Fed. Narcotics Agents, 403 U.S. 388 (1971), for such harms as emotional distress, when the erroneous denial of benefits had involved a violation of procedural due process. . . .

The *Bivens* issue in *Chilicky* . . . is different from the *Young* issue here in every significant respect. *Young* is not an example of a novel rule that a proponent has a burden to justify affirmatively on policy grounds in every context in which it might arguably be recognized; it is a general principle of federal equity jurisdiction that has been recognized throughout our history and for centuries before our own history began. *Young* does not provide retrospective monetary relief but allows prospective enforcement of federal law that is entitled to prevail under the Supremacy Clause. It requires, not money payments from a government employee's personal pocket, but lawful conduct by a public employee acting in his official capacity. *Young* would not function here to provide a merely supplementary regime of compensation to deter illegal action, but the sole jurisdictional basis for an Article III court's enforcement of a clear federal statutory obligation, without which a congressional act would be rendered a nullity in a federal court. One cannot intelligibly generalize from *Chilicky*'s standards for imposing the burden to justify a supplementary scheme of tort law, to the displacement of *Young*'s traditional and indispensable jurisdictional basis for ensuring official compliance with federal law when a state itself is immune from suit. . . .

Next, the Court suggests that it may be justified in displacing *Young* because *Young* would allow litigants to ignore the "intricate procedures" of IGRA in favor of a menu of streamlined equity rules from which any litigant could order as he saw fit. But there is no basis in law for this suggestion, and the strongest authority to reject it. *Young* did not establish a new cause of action and it does not impose any particular procedural regime in the suits it permits. It stands, instead, for a jurisdictional rule by which paramount federal law may be enforced in a federal court by substituting a non-immune party (the state officer) for an immune one (the state itself). *Young* does no more and furnishes no authority for the Court's assumption that it somehow pre-empts procedural rules devised by Congress for particular kinds of cases that may depend on *Young* for federal jurisdiction. . . .

The Court's third strand of reasoning for displacing *Ex parte Young* is a supposed inference that Congress so intended. Since the Court rests this inference in large part on its erroneous assumption that the statute's procedural limitations would not be applied in a suit against an officer for which *Young* provided the jurisdictional basis, the error of that assumption is enough to show the unsoundness of any inference that Congress meant to exclude *Young*'s application. . . .

Finally, one must judge the Court's purported inference by stepping back to ask why Congress could possibly have intended to jeopardize the enforcement of the statute by excluding application of *Young*'s traditional jurisdictional rule, when that rule would make the difference between success or failure in the federal court if state sovereign immunity was recognized. Why would Congress have wanted to go for broke on the issue of state immunity in the event the state pleaded immunity as a jurisdictional bar? Why would Congress not have wanted IGRA to be enforced by means of a traditional doctrine giving federal courts jurisdiction over state officers, in an effort to harmonize state sovereign immunity with federal law that is paramount under the Supremacy Clause? There are no plausible answers to these questions. . . .

V

. . . I should add a word about my reasons for continuing to accept *Hans*'s holding as a matter of stare decisis.

The *Hans* doctrine was erroneous, but it has not previously proven to be unworkable or to conflict with later doctrine or to suffer from the effects of facts developed since its decision (apart from those indicating its original errors). I would therefore treat *Hans* as it has always been treated in fact until today, as a doctrine of federal common law. For, as so understood, it has formed one of the strands of the federal relationship for over a century now, and the stability of that relationship is itself a value that stare decisis aims to respect.

In being ready to hold that the relationship may still be altered, not by the Court but by Congress, I would tread the course laid out elsewhere in our cases. The Court has repeatedly stated its assumption that insofar as the relative positions of states and nation may be affected consistently with the Tenth Amendment, they would not be modified without deliberately expressed intent. The plain statement rule . . . is particularly appropriate in light of our primary reliance on "the effectiveness of the federal political process in preserving the states' interests." Garcia v. San Antonio Metropolitan Transit Authority, 469 U.S. 528, 552 (1985). Hence, we have required such a plain statement when Congress preempts the historic powers of the states, Rice v. Santa Fe Elevator Corp., 331 U.S. 218, 230 (1947), imposes a condition on the grant of federal moneys, South Dakota v. Dole, 483 U.S. 203, 207 (1987), or seeks to regulate a state's ability to determine the qualifications of its own officials. Gregory v. Ashcroft, 501 U.S. 452, 464 (1991).

When judging legislation passed under unmistakable Article I powers, no further restriction could be required. Nor does the Court explain why more could be demanded. In the past, we have assumed that a plain statement requirement is sufficient to protect the states from undue federal encroachments upon their traditional immunity from suit. It is hard to contend that this rule has set the bar too low, for (except in *Union Gas*) we have never found the requirement to be met outside the context of laws passed under § 5 of the Fourteenth Amendment. The exception I would recognize today proves the rule, moreover, because the federal abrogation of state immunity comes as part of a regulatory scheme which is itself designed to invest the states with regulatory powers that Congress need not extend to them. This fact suggests to me that the political safeguards of federalism are working, that a plain statement rule is an adequate check on congressional overreaching, and that today's abandonment of that approach is wholly unwarranted. . . . Because neither text, precedent, nor history supports the majority's abdication of our responsibility to exercise the jurisdiction entrusted to us in Article III, I would reverse the judgment of the Court of Appeals.

NOTES ON SUBSEQUENT DECISIONS

1.   FOOTNOTE ON *EX PARTE YOUNG*

Of all the oddities in Eleventh Amendment jurisprudence, none is stranger than *Seminole Tribe*'s treatment of *Ex parte Young*. For nearly a century, *Ex parte Young* has allowed prospective relief against states by resort to the fiction of suing a state officer. The *Seminole Tribe* Court purported not to question *Ex parte Young* but only to hold that Congress intended to preclude that option in the Indian Gaming Regulatory Act. Since prospective enforcement against state officers, as *Young* allows, would have implemented precisely the intention manifest in the statute, the Court's insistence that Congress actually intended to forbid this solution struck academic observers as "singularly unpersuasive," Daniel J. Meltzer, The *Seminole* Decision and State Sovereign Immunity, 1996 Sup. Ct. Rev. 1, 43, and "wilfully perverse." John C. Jeffries, Jr., In Praise of the Eleventh Amendment and Section 1983, 84 Va. L. Rev. 47, 52 n.19 (1998).

From all that appears, Congress could overrule *Seminole Tribe* simply by clarifying its intention to allow—or more accurately not to disallow—officer suits. The Supreme Court seems to have confirmed that understanding by declaring that, "[i]n determining whether the doctrine of *Ex parte Young* avoids an Eleventh Amendment bar to suit, a court need only conduct a 'straightforward inquiry into whether [the] complaint alleges an ongoing violation of federal law and seeks relief properly characterized as prospective.'" Verizon Maryland, Inc. v. Public Service Commission, 535 U.S. 635, 644 (2002) (quoting and citing various opinions collecting the views of seven Justices in Idaho v. Coeur d'Alene Tribe, 521 U.S. 261 (1997)). Accord: Frew v. Hawkins, 540 U.S. 431 (2004). So long as *Ex parte Young* remains intact, the practical significance of *Seminole Tribe* for questions of injunctive relief will be limited. As subsequent cases reveal, however, *Seminole Tribe* may be very consequential indeed in prohibiting damage awards against states and state agencies.

2.   *ALDEN V. MAINE*

What happens after *Seminole Tribe* if Congress expressly abolishes sovereign immunity in *state* courts over a cause of action to enforce federal law?

The answer came in Alden v. Maine, 527 U.S. 706 (1999). A group of Maine probation officers filed an action for compensation and liquidated damages in federal court under the Fair Labor Standards Act of 1938 (FLSA). They claimed that the State had violated FLSA overtime provisions. *Seminole Tribe* was decided while the suit was pending, and the District Court dismissed on the authority of that decision. After the Court of Appeals affirmed, the plaintiffs re-filed their action in state court. The state trial court dismissed on grounds of sovereign immunity, and the Maine Supreme Court affirmed. The United States Supreme Court affirmed five to four.

(i) The Majority Opinion

In an opinion by Justice Kennedy, the Court stated its conclusion up front:

> We hold that the powers delegated to Congress under Article I of the United States Constitution do not include the power to subject nonconsenting states to private suits for damages in state courts.

In support of this proposition, the Court began by reaffirming the broad principle underlying *Seminole Tribe*:

> The Eleventh Amendment confirmed rather than established sovereign immunity as a constitutional principle; it follows that the scope of the states' immunity from suit is demarcated not by the text of the amendment alone but by fundamental postulates implicit in the constitutional design. . . .
>
> The Constitution, by delegating to Congress the power to establish the supreme law of the land when acting within its enumerated powers, does not foreclose a state from asserting immunity to claims arising under federal law merely because that law derives not from the state itself but from the national power. . . . Nor can we conclude that the specific Article I powers delegated to Congress necessarily include, by virtue of the Necessary and Proper Clause or otherwise, the incidental authority to subject the states to private suits as a means of achieving objectives otherwise within the scope of the enumerated powers. Although some of our decisions had endorsed this contention, they have since been overruled [citing *Seminole Tribe* and the demise of Parden v. Terminal R. Co., 377 U.S. 184 (1964)]. . . . The logic of [these] decisions . . . does not turn on the forum in which the suits were prosecuted but extends to state-court suits as well.

The Court then dealt with "isolated statements in some of our cases suggesting that the Eleventh Amendment is inapplicable in state courts." Particularly troubling was Hilton v. South Carolina Public Railways Comm'n, 502 U.S. 197 (1991), which, in reliance on *Parden*, held "that an injured employee of a state-owned railroad could sue his employer (an arm of the state) in state court under the Federal Employers' Liability Act (FELA)":

> Our decision was "controlled and informed" by stare decisis. A generation earlier we had held that because the FELA made clear that all who operated railroads would be subject to suit by injured workers, states that chose to enter the railroad business after the statute's enactment impliedly waived their sovereign immunity from such suits. See Parden v. Terminal R. Co., 377 U.S. 184 (1964). Some states had excluded railroad workers from the coverage of their workers' compensation statutes on the assumption that FELA

provided adequate protection for those workers. Closing the courts to FELA suits against state employers would have dislodged settled expectations and required an extensive legislative response.

. . . The respondent in *Hilton*, the South Carolina Public Railways Commission, neither contested Congress's constitutional authority to subject it to suits for money damages nor raised sovereign immunity as an affirmative defense. Nor was the state's litigation strategy surprising. *Hilton* was litigated and decided in the wake of Pennsylvania v. Union Gas, 491 U.S. 1 (1989), and before this Court's decision[ ] in . . . *Seminole Tribe*. At that time it may have appeared to the state that Congress's power to abrogate its immunity from suit in any court was not limited by the Constitution at all, so long as Congress made its intent sufficiently clear.

Furthermore, our decision in *Parden* was based on concepts of waiver and consent. Although later decisions have undermined the basis of *Parden*'s reasoning, . . . we have not questioned the general proposition that a state may waive its sovereign immunity and consent to suit.

Hilton, then, must be read in light of the doctrinal basis of *Parden*, the issues presented and argued by the parties, and the substantial reliance interests drawn into question by the litigation. When so read, we believe the decision is best understood not as recognizing a congressional power to subject nonconsenting states to private suits in their own courts, nor even as endorsing the constructive waiver theory of *Parden*, but as simply adhering, as a matter of stare decisis and presumed historical fact, to the narrow proposition that certain states had consented to be sued by injured workers covered by the FELA, at least in their own courts.

This led to the conclusion that "[w]hether Congress has authority under Article I to abrogate a state's immunity from suit in its own courts is, then, a question of first impression." To answer that question, the Court turned to "history, practice, precedent, and the structure of the Constitution":

We look first to evidence of the original understanding of the Constitution. Petitioners contend that because the ratification debates and the events surrounding the adoption of the Eleventh Amendment focused on the states' immunity from suit in federal courts, the historical record gives no instruction as to the founding generation's intent to preserve the states' immunity from suit in their own courts.

We believe, however, that the founders' silence is best explained by the simple fact that no one, not even the Constitution's most ardent opponents, suggested the document might strip the states of the immunity. . . . In light of the historical record it is difficult to conceive that the Constitution would have been adopted if it had been understood to strip the states of immunity from suit in their own courts and cede to the federal government a power to subject nonconsenting states to private suits in these fora.

The Court also found support in *Ex parte Young*:

> [T]he exception to our sovereign immunity doctrine recognized in Ex parte Young, 209 U.S. 123 (1908), is based in part on the premise that sovereign immunity bars relief against states and their officers in both state and federal courts, and that certain suits for declaratory or injunctive relief against state officers must therefore be permitted if the Constitution is to remain the supreme law of the land. . . . Had we not understood the states to retain a constitutional immunity from suit in their own courts, the need for the *Ex parte Young* rule would have been less pressing, and the rule would not have formed so essential a part of our sovereign immunity doctrine.

The Court's "final consideration" was the "structure of the Constitution":

> Although the Constitution grants broad powers to Congress, our federalism requires that Congress treat the states in a manner consistent with their status as residuary sovereigns and joint participants in the governance of the nation. . . . In some ways, of course, a congressional power to authorize private suits against nonconsenting states in their own courts would be even more offensive to state sovereignty than a power to authorize the suits in a federal forum. Although the immunity of one sovereign in the courts of another has often depended in part on comity or agreement, the immunity of a sovereign in its own courts has always been understood to be within the sole control of the sovereign itself. . . .

> Underlying constitutional form are considerations of great substance. Private suits against nonconsenting states—especially suits for money damages—may threaten the financial integrity of the states. It is indisputable that, at the time of the founding, many of the states could have been forced into insolvency but for their immunity from private suits for money damages. Even today, an unlimited congressional power to authorize suits in state court to levy upon the treasuries of the states for compensatory damages, attorney's fees, and even punitive damages could create staggering burdens, giving Congress a power and a leverage over the states that is not contemplated by our constitutional design. . . .

> A general federal power to authorize private suits for money damages would place unwarranted strain on the states' ability to govern in accordance with the will of their citizens. Today, as at the time of the founding, the allocation of scarce resources among competing needs and interests lies at the heart of the political process. While the judgment creditor of the state may have a legitimate claim for compensation, other important needs and worthwhile ends compete for access to the public fisc. Since all cannot be satisfied in full, it is inevitable that difficult decisions involving the most sensitive and political of judgments must be made. If the principle of representative government is to be preserved to the states, the

> balance between competing interests must be reached after delib-
> eration by the political process established by the citizens of the
> state, not by judicial decree mandated by the federal government
> and invoked by the private citizen. . . .

> Congress cannot abrogate the states' sovereign immunity in
> federal court; were the rule to be different here, the national gov-
> ernment would wield greater power in the state courts than in its
> own judicial instrumentalities.

> The resulting anomaly cannot be explained by reference to the
> special role of the state courts in the constitutional design. Alt-
> hough Congress may not require the legislative or executive
> branches of the states to enact or administer federal regulatory pro-
> grams, see Printz v. United States, 521 U.S. 898, 935 (1997), it may
> require state courts of "adequate and appropriate" jurisdiction,
> Testa v. Katt, 330 U.S. 386, 394 (1947), "to enforce federal prescrip-
> tions, insofar as those prescriptions relate to matters appropriate
> for the judicial power," Printz, 521 U.S. at 907. It would be an un-
> precedented step, however, to infer from the fact that Congress may
> declare federal law binding and enforceable in state courts the fur-
> ther principle that Congress's authority to pursue federal objectives
> through the state judiciaries exceeds not only its power to press
> other branches of the state into its service but even its control over
> the federal courts themselves. . . .

The Court added, however, that:

> The constitutional privilege of a state to assert its sovereign
> immunity in its own courts does not confer upon the state a con-
> comitant right to disregard the Constitution or valid federal law.
> The states and their officers are bound by obligations imposed by
> the Constitution and by federal statutes that comport with the con-
> stitutional design. We are unwilling to assume the states will
> refuse to honor the Constitution or obey the binding laws of the
> United States. The good faith of the states thus provides an im-
> portant assurance that "this Constitution, and the Laws of the
> United States which shall be made in Pursuance thereof . . . shall
> be the supreme Law of the Land." U.S. Const., Art. VI.

Moreover, sovereign immunity "does not bar all judicial review of state compliance with the Constitution and valid federal law." Alternative remedies
included suits against states by consent, suits brought by other states and
by the federal government, suits to enforce the Fourteenth Amendment,
suits against municipalities and other units of local government, suits based
on Ex parte Young, and § 1983 damages actions against state officers.

(ii) The Dissent

Joined by Justices Stevens, Ginsburg, and Breyer, Justice Souter dissented. The dissenters disagreed with the majority on the history and
contemporaneous understandings, as well as on structure and policy:

[T]he general scheme of delegated sovereignty as between the two component governments of the federal system was clear, and was succinctly stated by Chief Justice Marshall: "In America, the powers of sovereignty are divided between the government of the union, and those of the states. They are each sovereign, with respect to the objects committed to it, and neither sovereign with respect to the objects committed to the other." McCulloch v. Maryland, 17 U.S. (4 Wheat.) 316, 410 (1819).

Hence the flaw in the Court's appeal to federalism. The state of Maine is not sovereign with respect to the national objective of the FLSA.[33] It is not the authority that promulgated the FLSA, on which the right of action in this case depends. That authority is the United States acting through the Congress, whose legislative power under Article I of the Constitution to extend FLSA coverage to state employees has already been decided and is not contested here.

Nor can it be argued that because the state of Maine creates its own court system, it has authority to decide what sorts of claims may be entertained there, and thus in effect to control the right of action in this case. Maine has created state courts of general jurisdiction; once it has done so, the Supremacy Clause of the Constitution, which requires state courts to enforce federal law and state-court judges to be bound by it, requires the Maine courts to entertain this federal cause of action. Maine has advanced no " 'valid excuse,' " Howlett v. Rose, 496 U.S. 356, 369 (1990), for its courts' refusal to hear federal-law claims in which Maine is a defendant, and sovereign immunity cannot be that excuse, simply because the state is not sovereign with respect to the subject of the claim against it. The Court's insistence that the federal structure bars Congress from making states susceptible to suit in their own courts is, then, plain mistake. . . .

It is equally puzzling to hear the Court say that "federal power to authorize private suits for money damages would place unwarranted strain on the states' ability to govern in accordance with the will of their citizens." So long as the citizens' will, expressed through state legislation, does not violate valid federal law, the strain will not be felt; and to the extent that state action does violate federal law, the will of the citizens of the United States already trumps that of the citizens of the state: the strain then is not only expected, but necessarily intended.

---

[33] It is therefore sheer circularity for the Court to talk of the "anomaly" that would arise if a state could be sued on federal law in its own courts, when it may not be sued under federal law in federal court. The short and sufficient answer is that the anomaly is the Court's own creation: the Eleventh Amendment was never intended to bar federal-question suits against the states in federal court. The anomaly is that *Seminole Tribe*, an opinion purportedly grounded in the Eleventh Amendment, should now be used as a lever to argue for state sovereign immunity in state courts, to which the Eleventh Amendment by its terms does not apply.

Least of all does the Court persuade by observing that "other important needs" than that of the "judgment creditor" compete for public money. The "judgment creditor" in question is not a dunning bill-collector, but a citizen whose federal rights have been violated, and a constitutional structure that stints on enforcing federal rights out of an abundance of delicacy toward the states has substituted politesse in place of respect for the rule of law. . . .

The Court apparently believes that because state courts have not historically entertained Commerce Clause-based federal-law claims against the states, such an innovation carries a presumption of unconstitutionality. At the outset, it has to be noted that this approach assumes a more cohesive record than history affords. In Hilton v. South Carolina Public Railways Comm'n, 502 U.S. 197, 205 (1991) (Kennedy, J.), a case the Court labors mightily to distinguish, we held that a state-owned railroad could be sued in state court under the Federal Employers' Liability Act notwithstanding the lack of an express congressional statement, because " 'the Eleventh Amendment does not apply in state courts.' " . . . But even if the record were less unkempt, the problem with arguing from historical practice in this case is that past practice, even if unbroken, provides no basis for demanding preservation when the conditions on which the practice depended have changed in a constitutionally relevant way. . . .

Least of all is it to the point for the Court to suggest that because the framers would be surprised to find states subjected to a federal-law suit in their own courts under the commerce power, the suit must be prohibited by the Constitution. . . . If the framers would be surprised to see states subjected to suit in their own courts under the commerce power, they would be astonished by the reach of Congress under the Commerce Clause generally. The proliferation of government, state and federal, would amaze the framers, and the administrative state with its reams of regulations would leave them rubbing their eyes. But the framers' surprise at, say, the FLSA, or the Federal Communications Commission, or the Federal Reserve Board is no threat to the constitutionality of any one of them, for a very fundamental reason:

> When we are dealing with words that also are a constituent act, like the Constitution of the United States, we must realize that they have called into life a being the development of which could not have been foreseen completely by the most gifted of its begetters. It was enough for them to realize or to hope that they had created an organism; it has taken a century and has cost their successors much sweat and blood to prove that they created a nation. The case before us must be considered in the light of our whole experience and not merely in that of what was said a hundred years ago.

Missouri v. Holland, 252 U.S. 416, 433 (1920) (Holmes, J.). . . .

[T]here is much irony in the Court's profession that it grounds its opinion on a deeply rooted historical tradition of sovereign immunity, when the Court abandons a principle nearly as inveterate, and much closer to the hearts of the framers: that where there is a right, there must be a remedy. . . .

[T]oday the Court has no qualms about saying frankly that the federal right to damages afforded by Congress under the FLSA cannot create a concomitant private remedy. . . . It will not do for the Court to respond that a remedy was never available where the right in question was against the sovereign. A state is not the sovereign when a federal claim is pressed against it, and even the English sovereign opened itself to recovery and, unlike Maine, provided the remedy to complement the right. . . . Far from defaulting on debt to eyes-open creditors, Maine is simply withholding damages from private citizens to whom they appear to be due. . . .

[I]f the present majority had a defensible position one could at least accept its decision with an expectation of stability ahead. As it is, any such expectation would be naive. The resemblance of today's state sovereign immunity to the *Lochner* era's industrial due process is striking. The Court began this century by imputing immutable constitutional status to a conception of economic self-reliance that was never true to industrial life and grew insistently fictional with the years, and the Court has chosen to close the century by conferring like status on a conception of state sovereign immunity that is true neither to history nor to the structure of the Constitution. I expect the Court's late essay into immunity doctrine will prove the equal of its earlier experiment in laissez-faire, the one being as unrealistic as the other, as indefensible, and probably as fleeting.

3. *COLLEGE SAVINGS BANK V. FLORIDA PREPAID POSTSECONDARY EDUCATION EXPENSE BOARD*

After *Seminole Tribe* and *Alden v. Maine*, it became important to distinguish between Congress's exercise of Article I powers, which cannot override state sovereign immunity against private claims, and Congress's exercise of Fourteenth Amendment powers, which can. One of the earliest cases to present that distinction was College Savings Bank v. Florida Prepaid Postsecondary Education Expense Board, 527 U.S. 666 (1999). The Fourteenth Amendment issue is considered after the next main case. Of interest here is the analysis under Article I.

The College Savings Bank, chartered in New Jersey, marketed and sold CollegeSure certificates of deposit designed to finance college education costs. It sued Florida Prepaid, an agency of the State of Florida, under the Trademark Remedy Clarification Act (TRCA). The TRCA expressly abolished Eleventh Amendment immunities for remedies available under the Lanham Act for false and misleading advertising and extended such remedies to state agencies "to the same extent" as available against private entities. The case was filed in federal court, and its dismissal by the District

Court was affirmed by the Court of Appeals. In College Savings Bank v. Florida Prepaid Postsecondary Education Expense Board, 527 U.S. 666 (1999), the Supreme Court affirmed.

(i)   The Majority Opinion

Plaintiff based its case on a reformulated version of Parden v. Terminal R. Co. of Ala. Docks Dept., 377 U.S. 184 (1964), an argument summarized by the Court as follows:

> First, Congress must provide unambiguously that the state will be subject to suit if it engages in certain specified conduct governed by federal regulation. Second, the state must voluntarily elect to engage in the federally regulated conduct that subjects it to suit. In this latter regard, their argument goes, a state is never deemed to have constructively waived its sovereign immunity by engaging in activities that it cannot realistically choose to abandon, such as the operation of a police force; but constructive waiver is appropriate where a state runs an enterprise for profit, operates in a field traditionally occupied by private persons or corporations, engages in activities sufficiently removed from "core [state] functions" or otherwise acts as a "market participant" in interstate commerce. On this theory, Florida Prepaid constructively waived its immunity from suit by engaging in the voluntary and nonessential activity of selling and advertising a for-profit educational investment vehicle in interstate commerce after being put on notice by the clear language of the TRCA that it would be subject to Lanham Act liability for doing so.

In an opinion by Justice Scalia, the Court rejected any reliance on *Parden*, including in the commercial context:

> We think that the constructive-waiver experiment of *Parden* was ill conceived, and see no merit in attempting to salvage any remnant of it. . . . Whatever may remain of our decision in *Parden* is expressly overruled.

> Nor do we think that the constitutionally grounded principle of state sovereign immunity is any less robust where, as here, the asserted basis for constructive waiver is conduct that the state realistically could choose to abandon, that is undertaken for profit, that is traditionally performed by private citizens and corporations, and that otherwise resembles the behavior of "market participants." . . . Since sovereign immunity itself was not traditionally limited by these factors, and since they have no bearing upon the voluntariness of the waiver, there is no principled reason why they should enter into our waiver analysis. . . .

(ii)   The Dissent

Writing for himself and Justices Stevens, Souter, and Ginsburg, Justice Breyer thought the commercial context important:

Far from being anomalous, *Parden*'s holding finds support in reason and precedent. When a state engages in ordinary commercial ventures, it acts like a private person, outside the area of its "core" responsibilities, and in a way unlikely to prove essential to the fulfillment of a basic governmental obligation. A Congress that decides to regulate those state commercial activities rather than to exempt the state likely believes that an exemption, by treating the state differently from identically situated private persons, would threaten the objectives of a federal regulatory program aimed primarily at private conduct. And a Congress that includes the state not only within its substantive regulatory rules but also (expressly) within a related system of private remedies likely believes that a remedial exemption would similarly threaten that program. It thereby avoids an enforcement gap which, when allied with the pressures of a competitive marketplace, could place the state's regulated private competitors at a significant disadvantage.

These considerations make Congress's need to possess the power to condition entry into the market upon a waiver of sovereign immunity (as "necessary and proper" to the exercise of its commerce power) unusually strong, for to deny Congress that power would deny Congress the power effectively to regulate *private* conduct. At the same time they make a state's need to exercise sovereign immunity unusually weak, for the state is unlikely to *have to* supply what private firms already supply, nor may it fairly demand special treatment, even to protect the public purse, when it does so. Neither can one easily imagine what the Constitution's founders would have thought about the assertion of sovereign immunity in this special context. These considerations, differing in kind or degree from those that would support a general congressional "abrogation" power, indicate that *Parden*'s holding is sound, irrespective of this Court's decisions in Seminole Tribe of Fla. v. Florida, 517 U.S. 44 (1996), and Alden v. Maine, 527 U.S. 706 (1999).

4. *FEDERAL MARITIME COMMISSION V. SOUTH CAROLINA STATE PORTS AUTHORITY*

Federal Maritime Commission v. South Carolina State Ports Authority, 535 U.S. 743 (2002), extended Eleventh Amendment protection to federal agency adjudication. The Federal Maritime Commission protects maritime terminal users against discrimination by maritime terminal operators. The Commission hears complaints through an adjudicative process that begins with an administrative law judge. If the complainant prevails, the Commission can issue an order to the terminal operator to "cease and desist" discrimination and to pay "reparations" for past acts. Commission orders, however, can be enforced only through judicial enforcement actions brought by the federal government.

In this case, the South Carolina State Ports Authority repeatedly refused to allow Charleston port facilities to be used by a cruise ship operator that offered gambling in international waters. When the operator filed a complaint with the Federal Maritime Commission, the state invoked Eleventh Amendment immunity against agency adjudication, even though that provision does not bar federal enforcement actions directly against states. The Fourth Circuit agreed with the state, and the Supreme Court affirmed. In an opinion by Justice Thomas, the Court said that the fact that the Commission's orders were not self-executing did not convert agency adjudication into direct enforcement against a state by the federal government: "The Attorney General's decision to bring an enforcement action against a State after the conclusion of the Commission's proceedings . . . does not retroactively convert [agency] adjudication initiated and pursued by a private party into one initiated and pursued by the Federal Government." Agency adjudication was therefore barred.

Justice Breyer, joined by Justices Stevens, Souter, and Ginsburg, dissented. Breyer argued that even if the Court's prior Eleventh Amendment decisions were correct, which he did not concede, they should not be extended to agency adjudication: "The Commission, but not a private party, may assess a penalty against the State for noncompliance [with the federal statute], and only a court acting at the Commission's request can compel compliance with a penalty order. In sum, no one can legally compel the State's obedience to [the statute] without a court order, and in no case would a court issue such an order . . . absent the request of a federal agency or other federal instrumentality." Breyer therefore saw agency adjudication as analogous to direct enforcement actions by the federal government, to which state sovereign immunity is no bar.

5.   THE BANKRUPTCY POWER: *CENTRAL VIRGINIA COMMUNITY COLLEGE V. KATZ*

Statements in *Seminole Tribe* reflected an assumption that the decision applied to the Bankruptcy Clause. In Central Virginia Community College v. Katz, 546 U.S. 356 (2006), the Supreme Court held otherwise. The Court ruled, five-four, that states could not assert sovereign immunity against actions by trustees in bankruptcy.

Central Virginia Community College involved educational institutions regarded as arms of the state. When a private bookseller went bankrupt, the trustee appointed to liquidate the company tried to recover "preferential transfers" made to state schools while the debtor was insolvent.[a] The schools invoked *Seminole Tribe* and claimed sovereign immunity. The Court found, however, that the Bankruptcy Clause gave Congress the power to override state sovereign immunity, because the states had "agreed in the plan of the Convention not to assert that immunity" in bankruptcy proceedings.

As the dissent noted, this conclusion sharply departed from—if it did not directly contradict—the reasoning of *Seminole Tribe*. In an opinion by

---

[a]   See 11 U.S.C. § 547(b). Generally speaking, preferential transfers are payments made to a creditor when the debtor was insolvent and within 90 days of the filing of the bankruptcy petition. They can be recovered by the debtor's estate and put into the pool of assets used to satisfy (to the extent possible) the claims of all creditors.

Justice Stevens, the Court grounded its decision in the origins of the Bankruptcy Clause. At the time of the Framing, bankruptcy was subject to a "patchwork" of state laws on insolvency and bankruptcy. These laws affected not only whether debts would be forgiven but also, in some jurisdictions, whether debtors would be imprisoned. Thus one jurisdiction's discharge in bankruptcy did not necessarily protect the debtor in another. The Bankruptcy Clause was a response to that problem.

As to the interaction of the Bankruptcy Clause and state sovereign immunity, the Court said:

> Bankruptcy jurisdiction, as understood today and at the time of the framing, is principally in rem jurisdiction. See Tennessee Student Assistance Corp. v. Hood, 541 U.S. 440, 447 (2004). In bankruptcy, "the court's jurisdiction is premised on the debtor and his estate, and not on the creditors." Id. As such, its exercise does not, in the usual case, interfere with state sovereignty even when States' interests are affected.

> The text of Article I, § 8, cl. 4, of the Constitution, however, provides that Congress shall have the power to establish "uniform Laws on the subject of Bankruptcies throughout the United States." Although the interest in avoiding unjust imprisonment for debt and making federal discharges in bankruptcy enforceable in every State was a primary motivation for the adoption of that provision, its coverage encompasses the entire "subject of Bankruptcies." The power granted to Congress by that Clause is a unitary concept rather than an amalgam of discrete segments.

> The Framers would have understood that laws "on the subject of Bankruptcies" included laws providing, in certain limited respects, for more than simple adjudication of rights in the res. [I]t is not necessary to decide whether actions to recover preferential transfers . . . are themselves properly characterized as in rem. Whatever the appropriate appellation, those who crafted the Bankruptcy Clause would have understood it to give Congress the power to authorize courts to avoid preferential transfers and to recover the transferred property. [Such] authority has been a core aspect of the administration of bankrupt estates since at least the eighteenth century. . . .

> Insofar as orders ancillary to the bankruptcy courts' in rem jurisdiction, like orders directing turnovers of preferential transfers, implicate States' sovereign immunity from suit, the States agreed in the plan of the Convention not to assert that immunity. So much is evidenced not only by the history of the Bankruptcy Clause, which shows that the Framers' primary goal was to prevent competing sovereigns' interference with the debtor's discharge, but also by legislation considered and enacted in the immediate wake of the Constitution's ratification. [The first Bankruptcy Act was passed in 1800, not long after the ratification of the Eleventh Amendment,] yet there appears to be no record of any objection to

the bankruptcy legislation . . . based on an infringement of sovereign immunity. . . .

[T]he Framers, in adopting the Bankruptcy Clause, plainly intended to give Congress the power to redress the rampant injustice resulting from States' refusal to respect one another's discharge orders. As demonstrated by [the nearly contemporaneous] enactment of a provision granting federal courts the authority to release debtors from state prisons, the power to enact bankruptcy legislation was understood to carry with it the power to subordinate state sovereignty, albeit within a limited sphere. The ineluctable conclusion, then, is that States agreed in the plan of the Convention not to assert any sovereign immunity defense they might have had in proceedings brought pursuant to "Laws on the subject of Bankruptcies."

None of this was persuasive to the dissent. Justice Thomas, joined by Chief Justice Roberts and Justices Scalia and Kennedy, insisted that the Bankruptcy Clause was no different from any other Article I power:

It is difficult to discern an intention to abrogate state sovereign immunity through the Bankruptcy Clause when no such intention has been found in any of the other clauses in Article I. . . .

The majority supports its break from precedent by relying on historical evidence that purportedly reveals the Framers' intent to eliminate state sovereign immunity in bankruptcy proceedings. The Framers undoubtedly wanted to give Congress the power to enact a national law of bankruptcy, as the text of the Bankruptcy Clause confirms. But the majority goes further, contending that the Framers . . . must have intended to waive the States' sovereign immunity against suit.

In contending that the States waived their immunity from suit by adopting the Bankruptcy Clause, the majority conflates two distinct attributes of sovereignty: the authority of a sovereign to enact legislation regulating its own citizens, and sovereign immunity against suit by private citizens. Nothing in the history of the Bankruptcy Clause suggests that, by including that clause in Article I, the founding generation intended to waive the latter aspect of sovereignty. These two attributes of sovereignty often do not run together—and for purposes of enacting a uniform law of bankruptcy, they need not run together.

Justice Thomas pointed out that Congress's powers to regulate interstate commerce and to protect copyrights and patents were also motivated by a desire for "nationally uniform legislation," yet the enforcement of those powers had been limited by state sovereign immunity. Abrogation of such immunity, he continued, is not necessary "to the enactment of nationally uniform bankruptcy laws. The sovereign immunity of the States against suit does not undermine the objective of a uniform national law of bankruptcy, any more than does any differential treatment between different categories of creditors."

The dissent concluded by emphasizing the inconsistency between *Central Virginia Community College* and *Seminole Tribe* and its progeny:

> It would be one thing if the majority simply wanted to overrule *Seminole Tribe* altogether. That would be wrong, but at least the terms of our disagreement would be transparent. The majority's action today, by contrast, is difficult to comprehend. Nothing in the text, structure, or history of the Constitution indicates that the Bankruptcy Clause, in contrast to all of the other provisions of Article I, manifests the States's consent to be sued by private citizens.

It remains to be seen whether this interpretation of the Bankruptcy Clause will be durable. For now, at least, the decision adds to the long list of vagaries and contradictions in the jurisprudence on state sovereign immunity.[b]

6. *SOSSAMON V. TEXAS*

After the Supreme Court struck down the Religious Freedom Restoration Act (see *City of Boerne v. Flores*, summarized in a Note following the next main case), Congress passed the Religious Land Use and Institutionalized Persons Act of 2000. Enacted under the spending power, RLUIPA prohibits a substantial burden on the religious exercise of an institutionalized person, absent a compelling state interest, if "the substantial burden is imposed in a program or activity that receives Federal financial assistance." 42 U.S.C. § 2000cc–1. The statute also provides an express private cause of action for "appropriate relief against a government," if such rights are violated. 42 U.S.C. § 2000cc–2(a). Under this provision, a Texas prisoner brought a damages action against the state, claiming that various prison policies violated RLUIPA. The question before the Supreme Court was whether the phrase "appropriate relief against a government" was sufficiently unambiguous to require a state waiver of sovereign immunity.

Speaking for the Court in Sossamon v. Texas, 563 U.S. 277 (2011), Justice Thomas said that it was not:

> "Appropriate relief" is open-ended and ambiguous about what types of relief it includes, as many lower courts have recognized. Far from clearly identifying money damages, the word "appropriate" is inherently context-dependent. The context here—where the defendant is a sovereign—suggests, if anything that monetary damages are not "suitable" or "proper."

---

b   For extensive commentary on *Katz* from a variety of perspectives, see Richard Lieb, Federal Supremacy and State Sovereignty: The Supreme Court's Early Jurisprudence, 15 Am. Bankruptcy Inst. L. Rev. 3 (2007); Martin H. Redish and Daniel M. Greenfield, Bankruptcy, Sovereign Immunity and the Dilemma of Principled Decision Making: The Curious Case of *Central Virginia Community College v. Katz*, 15 Am. Bankruptcy Inst. L. Rev. 13 (2007); Thomas E. Plank, State Sovereignty in Bankruptcy After *Katz*, 15 Am. Bankruptcy Inst. L. Rev. 59 (2007); Ralph Brubaker, Explaining *Katz*'s New Bankruptcy Exception to State Sovereign Immunity: The Bankruptcy Power as a Federal Forum Power, 15 Am. Bankruptcy Inst. L. Rev. 95 (2007); Randolph J. Haines, Federalism Principles in Bankruptcy After *Katz*, 15 Am. Bankruptcy Inst. L. Rev. 135 (2007); Susan M. Freeman and Marvin C. Ruth, The Scope of Bankruptcy Ancillary Jurisdiction After *Katz* as Informed by Pre-*Katz* Ancillary Jurisdiction Cases, 15 Am. Bankruptcy Inst. L. Rev. 155 (2007).

Because RLUIPA did not "expressly and unequivocally" so provide, the statute did not subject states to actions for money damages.

Justice Sotomayor, joined by Justice Breyer, dissented:

No one disputes that, in accepting federal funds, the States consent to suit for violations of RLUIPA's substantive provisions; the only question is what relief is available to plaintiffs asserting injury from such violations. That monetary damages are "appropriate relief" is, in my view, self-evident. Under general remedies principles, the usual remedy for a violation of a legal right is damages.

The Court's refusal to allow damages actions, Sotomayor argued, was not only wrong as a matter of general remedial principles, but also undermined Congress's aim to provide broad protection for religious exercise.[c]

Armstrong v. Exceptional Child Center

Supreme Court of the United States, 2015.
575 U.S. ___, 135 S.Ct. 1378.

■ JUSTICE SCALIA delivered the opinion of the Court, except as to Part IV.

We consider whether Medicaid providers can sue to enforce § (30)(A) of the Medicaid Act (codified as amended at 42 U.S.C. § 1396a(30)(A)).

I

Medicaid is a federal program that subsidizes the States' provision of medical services to "families with dependent children and of aged, blind, or disabled individuals, whose income and resources are insufficient to meet the costs of necessary medical services." § 1396–1. Like other Spending Clause legislation, Medicaid offers the States a bargain: Congress provides federal funds in exchange for the States' agreement to spend them in accordance with congressionally imposed conditions.

In order to qualify for Medicaid funding, the State of Idaho adopted, and the Federal Government approved, a Medicaid "plan," § 1396a(a), which Idaho administers through its Department of Health and Welfare. Idaho's plan includes "habilitation services"—in-home care for individuals who, "but for the provision of such services . . . would require the level of care provided in a hospital or a nursing facility or intermediate care facility for the mentally retarded the cost of which could be reimbursed under the State plan," § 1396n(c) and (c)(1). Providers of these services are reimbursed by the Department of Health and Welfare.

Section 30(A) of the Medicaid Act requires Idaho's plan to:

provide such methods and procedures relating to the utilization of, and the payment for, care and services available under the plan . . . as may be necessary to safeguard against unnecessary

---

[c]   For analysis of *Sossamon* before the case was decided, see Stephen I. Vladeck, State Sovereign Immunity and the Roberts Court, 5 Charleston L. Rev. 99 (2010).

utilization of such care and services and to assure that payments are consistent with efficiency, economy, and quality of
care and are sufficient to enlist enough providers so that care
and services are available under the plan at least to the extent
that such care and services are available to the general population in the geographic area. . . .

Respondents are providers of habilitation services to persons covered by
Idaho's Medicaid plan. They sued petitioners—two officials in Idaho's Department of Health and Welfare—in the United States District Court for
the District of Idaho, claiming that Idaho violates § 30(A) by reimbursing
providers of habilitation services at rates lower than § 30(A) permits.
They asked the court to enjoin petitioners to increase these rates.

The District Court entered summary judgment for the providers,
holding that Idaho had not set rates in a manner consistent with § 30(A).
The Ninth Circuit affirmed. It said that the providers had "an implied
right of action under the Supremacy Clause to seek injunctive relief
against the enforcement or implementation of state legislation." We
granted certiorari.

II

The Supremacy Clause, Art. VI, cl. 2, reads:

This Constitution, and the Laws of the United States which
shall be made in Pursuance thereof; and all Treaties made, or
which shall be made, under the Authority of the United States,
shall be the supreme Law of the Land; and the Judges in every
State shall be bound thereby, any Thing in the Constitution or
Laws of any State to the Contrary notwithstanding.

It is apparent that this Clause creates a rule of decision: Courts "shall"
regard the "Constitution," and all laws "made in Pursuance thereof," as
"the supreme Law of the Land." They must not give effect to state laws
that conflict with federal laws. It is equally apparent that the Supremacy
Clause is not the " 'source of any federal rights,' " Golden State Transit
Corp. v. Los Angeles, 493 U.S. 103, 107 (1989) (quoting Chapman v. Houston Welfare Rights Organization, 441 U.S. 600, 613 (1979)), and certainly does not create a cause of action. It instructs courts what to do when
state and federal law clash, but is silent regarding who may enforce federal laws in court, and in what circumstances they may do so. . . .

[I]t is important to read the Supremacy Clause in the context of the
Constitution as a whole. Article I vests Congress with broad discretion
over the manner of implementing its enumerated powers, giving it authority to "make all Laws which shall be necessary and proper for
carrying [them] into Execution." Art. I, § 8. We have said that this confers
upon the Legislature "that discretion, with respect to the means by which
the powers [the Constitution] confers are to be carried into execution,
which will enable that body to perform the high duties assigned to it,"

McCulloch v. Maryland, 17 U.S. 316 (1819). It is unlikely that the Constitution gave Congress such broad discretion with regard to the enactment of laws, while simultaneously limiting Congress's power over the manner of their implementation, making it impossible to leave the enforcement of federal law to federal actors. If the Supremacy Clause includes a private right of action, then the Constitution *requires* Congress to permit the enforcement of its laws by private actors, significantly curtailing its ability to guide the implementation of federal law. It would be strange indeed to give a clause that makes federal law supreme a reading that *limits* Congress's power to enforce that law, by imposing mandatory private enforcement—a limitation unheard-of with regard to state legislatures.

To say that the Supremacy Clause does not confer a right of action is not to diminish the significant role that courts play in assuring the supremacy of federal law. For once a case or controversy properly comes before a court, judges are bound by federal law. Thus, a court may not convict a criminal defendant of violating a state law that federal law prohibits. Similarly, a court may not hold a civil defendant liable under state law for conduct federal law requires. And, as we have long recognized, if an individual claims federal law immunizes him from state regulation, the court may issue an injunction upon finding the state regulatory actions preempted. Ex parte Young, 209 U.S. 123, 155–56 (1908).

Respondents contend that our preemption jurisprudence—specifically, the fact that we have regularly considered whether to enjoin the enforcement of state laws that are alleged to violate federal law—demonstrates that the Supremacy Clause creates a cause of action for its violation. They are incorrect. It is true enough that we have long held that federal courts may in some circumstances grant injunctive relief against state officers who are violating, or planning to violate, federal law. See, e.g., Osborn v. Bank of United States, 22 U.S. 738 (1824); *Ex parte Young*, 209 U.S. at 150–51. But that has been true not only with respect to violations of federal law by state officials, but also with respect to violations of federal law by federal officials. Thus, the Supremacy Clause need not be (and in light of our textual analysis above, cannot be) the explanation. What our cases demonstrate is that, "in a proper case, relief may be given in a court of equity . . . to prevent an injurious act by a public officer." Carroll v. Safford, 44 U.S. 441, 463 (1845).

The ability to sue to enjoin unconstitutional actions by state and federal officers is the creation of courts of equity, and reflects a long history of judicial review of illegal executive action, tracing back to England. It is a judge-made remedy, and we have never held or even suggested that, in its application to state officers, it rests upon an implied right of action contained in the Supremacy Clause. That is because, as even the dissent implicitly acknowledges, it does not. The Ninth Circuit erred in holding otherwise.

III

A

We turn next to respondents' contention that, quite apart from any cause of action conferred by the Supremacy Clause, this suit can proceed against Idaho in equity.

The power of federal courts of equity to enjoin unlawful executive action is subject to express and implied statutory limitations. See, e.g., Seminole Tribe of Fla. v. Florida, 517 U.S. 44, 74 (1996). . . . In our view the Medicaid Act implicitly precludes private enforcement of § 30(A), and respondents cannot, by invoking our equitable powers, circumvent Congress's exclusion of private enforcement.

Two aspects of § 30(A) establish Congress's "intent to foreclose" equitable relief. Verizon Md. Inc. v. Public Serv. Comm'n of Md., 535 U.S. 635, 647 (2002). First, the sole remedy Congress provided for a State's failure to comply with Medicaid's requirements—for the State's "breach" of the Spending Clause contract—is the withholding of Medicaid funds by the Secretary of Health and Human Services. 42 U.S.C. § 1396c. As we have elsewhere explained, the "express provision of one method of enforcing a substantive rule suggests that Congress intended to preclude others." Alexander v. Sandoval, 532 U.S. 275, 290 (2001).

The provision for the Secretary's enforcement by withholding funds might not, *by itself*, preclude the availability of equitable relief. But it does so when combined with the judicially unadministrable nature of § 30(A)'s text. It is difficult to imagine a requirement broader and less specific than § 30(A)'s mandate that state plans provide for payments that are "consistent with efficiency, economy, and quality of care," all the while "safeguard[ing] against unnecessary utilization of . . . care and services." Explicitly conferring enforcement of this judgment-laden standard upon the Secretary alone establishes, we think, that Congress "wanted to make the agency remedy that it provided exclusive," thereby achieving "the expertise, uniformity, widespread consultation, and resulting administrative guidance that can accompany agency decisionmaking," and avoiding "the comparative risk of inconsistent interpretations and misincentives that can arise out of an occasional inappropriate application of the statute in a private action." Gonzaga Univ. v. Doe, 536 U.S. 273, 292 (2002) (Breyer, J., concurring in judgment). The sheer complexity associated with enforcing § 30(A), coupled with the express provision of an administrative remedy, § 1396c, shows that the Medicaid Act precludes private enforcement of § 30(A) in the courts.

B

The dissent agrees with us that the Supremacy Clause does not provide an implied right of action, and that Congress may displace the equitable relief that is traditionally available to enforce federal law. It disagrees only with our conclusion that such displacement has occurred here.

The dissent insists that, "because Congress is undoubtedly aware of the federal courts' long-established practice of enjoining preempted state action, it should generally be presumed to contemplate such enforcement unless it *affirmatively* manifests a contrary intent." But a "long-established practice" does not justify a rule that denies statutory text its fairest reading. Section 30(A), fairly read in the context of the Medicaid Act, "display[s] a[n] intent to foreclose" the availability of equitable relief. *Verizon*, 535 U.S. at 647. We have no warrant to revise Congress's scheme simply because it did not "affirmatively" preclude the availability of a judge-made action at equity. See *Seminole Tribe*, 517 U.S. at 75 (inferring, in the absence of an "affirmative" statement by Congress, that equitable relief was unavailable). . . .

Finally, the dissent speaks as though we leave these plaintiffs with no resort. That is not the case. Their relief must be sought initially through the Secretary rather than through the courts. The dissent's complaint that the sanction available to the Secretary (the cut-off of funding) is too massive to be a realistic source of relief seems to us mistaken. We doubt that the Secretary's notice to a State that its compensation scheme is inadequate will be ignored.

IV

The last possible source of a cause of action for respondents is the Medicaid Act itself. They do not claim that, and rightly so. Section 30(A) lacks the sort of rights-creating language needed to imply a private right of action. *Sandoval*, 532 U.S. at 286–87. It is phrased as a directive to the federal agency charged with approving state Medicaid plans, not as a conferral of the right to sue upon the beneficiaries of the State's decision to participate in Medicaid. . . .

Our precedents establish that a private right of action under federal law is not created by mere implication, but must be "unambiguously conferred," *Gonzaga*, 536 U.S. at 283. Nothing in the Medicaid Act suggests that Congress meant to change that for the commitments made under § 30(A).

* * *

The judgment of the Ninth Circuit Court of Appeals is reversed.

It is so ordered.

■ JUSTICE BREYER, concurring in part and concurring in the judgment.

I join Parts I, II, and III of the Court's opinion. . . .

I believe that several characteristics of the federal statute before us, when taken together, make clear that Congress intended to foreclose respondents from bringing this particular action for injunctive relief.

For one thing, as the majority points out, § 30(A) of the Medicaid Act, sets forth a federal mandate that is broad and nonspecific. But, more than that, § 30(A) applies its broad standards to the setting of rates. The history of ratemaking demonstrates that administrative agencies are far better suited to this task than judges. More than a century ago, Congress created the Interstate Commerce Commission, the first great federal regulatory rate-setting agency, and endowed it with authority to set "reasonable" railroad rates. It did so in part because judicial efforts to maintain reasonable rate levels had proved inadequate.

Reading § 30(A) underscores the complexity and nonjudicial nature of the rate-setting task. That provision requires State Medicaid plans to "assure that payments are consistent with efficiency, economy, and quality of care and are sufficient to enlist enough providers" to assure "care and services" equivalent to that "available to the general population in the geographic area." § 1396a(a)(30)(A). The methods that a state agency, such as Idaho's Department of Health and Welfare, uses to make this kind of determination may involve subsidiary determinations of, for example, the actual cost of providing quality services, including personnel and total operating expenses; changes in public expectations with respect to delivery of services; inflation; a comparison of rates paid in neighboring States for comparable services; and a comparison of any rates paid for comparable services in other public or private capacities.

At the same time, § 30(A) applies broadly, covering reimbursements provided to approximately 1.36 million doctors, serving over 69 million patients across the Nation. And States engage in time-consuming efforts to obtain public input on proposed plan amendments.

I recognize that federal courts have long become accustomed to reviewing for reasonableness or constitutionality the rate-setting determinations made by agencies. But this is not such an action. Instead, the lower courts here . . . required the State to set rates that "approximate the cost of quality care provided efficiently and economically." To find in the law a basis for courts to engage in such direct rate-setting could set a precedent for allowing other similar actions, potentially resulting in rates set by federal judges (of whom there are several hundred) outside the ordinary channel of federal judicial review of agency decision-making. The consequence, I fear, would be increased litigation, inconsistent results, and disorderly administration of highly complex federal programs that demand public consultation, administrative guidance and coherence for their success. I do not believe Congress intended to allow a statute-based injunctive action that poses such risks (and that has the other features I mention).

I recognize that courts might in particular instances be able to resolve rate-related requests for injunctive relief quite easily. But I see no easy way to separate in advance the potentially simple sheep from the more harmful rate-making goats. In any event, this case, I fear, belongs in the latter category. . . .

For another thing, like the majority, I would ask why, in the complex rate-setting area, other forms of relief are inadequate. If the Secretary of Health and Human Services concludes that a State is failing to follow legally required federal rules, the Secretary can withhold federal funds.

If withholding funds does not work, the federal agency may be able to sue a State to compel compliance with federal rules.

Moreover, why could respondents not ask the federal agency to interpret its rules to respondents' satisfaction, to modify those rules, to promulgate new rules or to enforce old ones? Normally, when such requests are denied, an injured party can seek judicial review of the agency's refusal on the grounds that it is "arbitrary, capricious, an abuse of discretion, or otherwise not in accordance with law." 5 U.S.C. §§ 702, 706(2)(A). And an injured party can ask the court to "compel agency action unlawfully withheld or unreasonably delayed." §§ 702, 706(1).

I recognize that the law may give the federal agency broad discretionary authority to decide when and how to exercise or to enforce statutes and rules. As a result, it may be difficult for respondents to prevail on an APA claim unless it stems from an agency's particularly egregious failure to act. But, if that is so, it is because Congress decided to vest broad discretion in the agency to interpret and to enforce § 30(A). I see no reason for this Court to circumvent that congressional determination by allowing this action to proceed.

■ JUSTICE SOTOMAYOR, with whom JUSTICE KENNEDY, JUSTICE GINSBURG, and JUSTICE KAGAN join, dissenting.

Suits in federal court to restrain state officials from executing laws that assertedly conflict with the Constitution or with a federal statue are not novel. To the contrary, this Court has adjudicated such requests for equitable relief since the early days of the Republic. Nevertheless, today the Court holds that Congress has foreclosed private parties from invoking the equitable powers of the federal courts to require States to comply with § 30(A) of the Medicaid Act. It does so without pointing to the sort of detailed remedial scheme we have previously deemed necessary to establish congressional intent to preclude resort to equity. Instead, the Court relies on Congress' provision for agency enforcement of § 30(A)— an enforcement mechanism of the sort we have already definitively determined *not* to foreclose private actions—and on the mere fact that § 30(A) contains relatively broad language. As I cannot agree that these statutory provisions demonstrate the requisite congressional intent to restrict the equitable authority of the federal courts, I respectfully dissent.

I

A

That parties may call upon the federal courts to enjoin unconstitutional government action is not subject to serious dispute. Perhaps the most famous exposition of this principle is our decision in Ex parte Young, 209 U.S. 123 (1908), from which the doctrine derives its usual name. . . .

A suit, like this one, that seeks relief against state officials acting pursuant to a state law allegedly preempted by a federal statute falls comfortably within this doctrine. A claim that a state law contravenes a federal statute is "basically constitutional in nature, deriving its force from the operation of the Supremacy Clause," Douglas v. Seacoast Products, Inc., 431 U.S. 265, 271–72 (1977), and the application of preempted state law is therefore "unconstitutional," Crosby v. National Foreign Trade Council, 530 U.S. 363, 388 (2000); accord, e.g., McCulloch v. Maryland, 17 U.S. 316, 436 (1819) (that States have "no power" to enact laws interfering with "the operations of the constitutional laws enacted by Congress" is the "unavoidable consequence of that supremacy which the constitution has declared"; such a state law "is unconstitutional and void"). We have thus long entertained suits in which a party seeks prospective equitable protection from an injurious and preempted state law without regard to whether the federal statute at issue itself provided a right to bring an action. . . . Indeed, for this reason, we have characterized "the availability of prospective relief of the sort awarded in *Ex parte Young*" as giving "life to the Supremacy Clause." Green v. Mansour, 474 U.S. 64, 68 (1985).

Thus, even though the Court is correct that it is somewhat misleading to speak of "an implied right of action contained in the Supremacy Clause," that does not mean that parties may not enforce the Supremacy Clause by bringing suit to enjoin preempted state action. As the Court also recognizes, we "have long held that federal courts may in some circumstances grant injunctive relief against state officers who are violating, or planning to violate, federal law."

B

Most important for purposes of this case is not the mere existence of this equitable authority, but the fact that it is exceedingly well established—supported, as the Court puts it, by a "long history." Congress may, if it so chooses, either expressly or implicitly preclude *Ex parte Young* enforcement actions with respect to a particular statute or category of lawsuit. See, e.g., 28 U.S.C. § 1341 (prohibiting federal judicial restraints on the collection of state taxes); Seminole Tribe of Fla. v. Florida, 517 U.S. 44, 75–76 (1996) (comprehensive alternative remedial scheme can establish Congress' intent to foreclose *Ex parte Young* actions). But because Congress is undoubtedly aware of the federal courts' long-established practice of enjoining preempted state action, it should generally be presumed to contemplate such enforcement unless it affirmatively manifests a contrary intent. . . .

In this respect, equitable preemption actions differ from suits brought by plaintiffs invoking 42 U.S.C. § 1983 or an implied right of action to enforce a federal statute. Suits for "redress designed to halt or prevent the constitutional violation rather than the award of money damages" seek "traditional forms of relief." United States v. Stanley, 483 U.S. 669, 683 (1987). By contrast, a plaintiff invoking § 1983 or an implied statutory cause of action may seek a variety of remedies—including damages—from a potentially broad range of parties. Rather than simply pointing to background equitable principles authorizing the action that

Congress presumably has not overridden, such a plaintiff must demonstrate specific congressional intent to *create* a statutory right to these remedies. . . . For these reasons, the principles that we have developed to determine whether a statute creates an implied right of action, or is enforceable through § 1983, are not transferable to the *Ex parte Young* context.

II

In concluding that Congress has "implicitly preclude[d] private enforcement of § 30(A)," the Court ignores this critical distinction and threatens the vitality of our *Ex parte Young* jurisprudence. The Court identifies only a single prior decision—*Seminole Tribe*—in which we have ever discerned such congressional intent to foreclose equitable enforcement of a statutory mandate. Even the most cursory review of that decision reveals how far afield it is from this case.

In *Seminole Tribe*, the plaintiff Indian Tribe had invoked *Ex parte Young* in seeking to compel the State of Florida to "negotiate in good faith with [the] tribe toward the formation of a compact" governing certain gaming activities, as required by a provision of the Indian Gaming Regulatory Act. We rejected this effort, observing that "Congress passed [the provision] in conjunction with the carefully crafted and intricate remedial scheme set forth in [another part of the statute]." That latter provision allowed a tribe to sue for violations of the duty to negotiate 180 days after requesting such negotiations, but specifically limited the remedy that a court could grant to "an order directing the State and the Indian tribe to conclude a compact within 60 days," and provided that the only sanction for the violation of such an order would be to require the parties to "submit a proposed compact to a mediator." The statute further directed "that if the State should fail to abide by the mediator's selected compact, the sole remedy would be for the Secretary of the Interior, in consultation with the tribe, to prescribe regulations governing gaming." We concluded that Congress must have intended this procedural route to be the exclusive means of enforcing [the statutory duty to negotiate]. As we explained: . . . [It] is difficult to see why an Indian tribe would suffer through the intricate scheme of § 2710(d)(7) when more complete and more immediate relief would be available under *Ex parte Young.*" *Seminole Tribe*, 517 U.S. at 75.

What is the equivalent "carefully crafted and intricate remedial scheme" for enforcement of § 30(A)? The Court relies on two aspects of the Medicaid Act, but, whether considered separately or in combination, neither suffices.

First, the Court cites 42 U.S.C. § 1396c, which authorizes the Secretary of Health and Human Services (HHS) to withhold federal Medicaid payments to a State in whole or in part if the Secretary determines that the State has failed to comply with the obligations set out in § 1396a, including § 30(A). But in striking contrast to the remedial provision set out in the Indian Gaming Regulatory Act, § 1396c provides no specific procedure that parties actually affected by a State's violation of its statutory obligations may invoke in lieu of *Ex parte Young*—leaving them without any other avenue for seeking relief from the State. Nor will § 1396c always provide a particularly effective means for redressing a State's violations: If the State has violated § 30(A) by refusing to reimburse medical providers at a level "sufficient to enlist enough providers so that care and services are available" to Medicaid beneficiaries to the same extent as they are available to "the general population," agency action resulting in a reduced flow of federal funds to that State will often be self-defeating. § 1396a(30)(A). Far from rendering § 1396c "superfluous," then, *Ex parte Young* actions would seem to be an anticipated and possibly necessary supplement to this limited agency-enforcement mechanism. . . .

Second, perhaps attempting to reconcile its treatment of § 1396c with this longstanding precedent, the Court focuses on the particular language of § 30(A), contending that this provision, at least, is so "judicially unadministrable" that Congress must have intended to preclude its enforcement in private suits. Admittedly, the standard set out in § 30(A) is fairly broad. . . . But mere breadth of statutory language does not require the Court to give up all hope of judicial enforcement—or, more important, to infer that Congress must have done so. . . .

Of course, the broad scope of § 30(A)'s language is not irrelevant. But rather than compelling the conclusion that the provision is wholly unenforceable by private parties, its breadth counsels in favor of interpreting § 30(A) to provide substantial leeway to States, so that only in rare and extreme circumstances could a State actually be held to violate its mandate. The provision's scope may also often require a court to rely on HHS, which is "comparatively expert in the statute's subject matter." Douglas v. Independent Living Center of Southern Cal., Inc., 565 U.S. 606, 614 (2012). When the agency has made a determination with respect to what legal standard should apply, or the validity of a State's procedures for implementing its Medicaid plan, that determination should be accorded the appropriate deference. And if faced with a question that presents a special demand for agency expertise, a court might call for the views of the agency, or refer the question to the agency under the doctrine of primary jurisdiction. Finally, because the authority invoked for enforcing § 30(A) is equitable in nature, a plaintiff is not entitled to relief as of right, but only in the sound discretion of the court. Given the courts' ability to both respect States' legitimate choices and defer to the federal agency when necessary, I see no basis for presuming that Congress believed the Judiciary to be completely incapable of enforcing § 30(A).

* * *

In sum, far from identifying a "carefully crafted . . . remedial scheme" demonstrating that Congress intended to foreclose *Ex parte Young* enforcement of § 30(A), *Seminole Tribe,* 517 U.S. at 73–74, the

Court points only to two provisions. The first is § 1396c, an agency-enforcement provision that, given our precedent, cannot preclude private actions. The second is § 30(A) itself, which, while perhaps broad, cannot be understood to manifest congressional intent to preclude judicial involvement.

The Court's error today has very real consequences. Previously, a State that set reimbursement rates so low that providers were unwilling to furnish a covered service for those who need it could be compelled by those affected to respect the obligation imposed by § 30(A). Now, it must suffice that a federal agency, with many programs to oversee, has authority to address such violations through the drastic and often counterproductive measure of withholding the funds that pay for such services. Because a faithful application of our precedents would have led to a contrary result, I respectfully dissent.

NOTES ON ARMSTRONG V. EXCEPTIONAL CHILD CENTER

1.   COMMENTS AND QUESTIONS ON ARMSTRONG

All of the Justices in *Armstrong* agree that there is no implied right of action under the Supremacy Clause and that the authority of federal courts to enjoin the enforcement of state law on the basis of preemption stems from the courts' historic powers of equity. So, what are the majority and the dissent disagreeing about? The dissent contends that, "because Congress is undoubtedly aware of the federal courts' long-established practice of enjoining preempted state action, it should generally be presumed to contemplate such enforcement unless it affirmatively manifests a contrary intent." What is the majority's response? Why might Congress *not* want federal courts to enjoin the enforcement of state law or executive action when it conflicts with federal law? According to the majority, what in Section 30(A) of the Medicaid Act showed Congress's intent to preclude a private injunctive remedy? What does Justice Breyer's concurrence add to that analysis? Would the result in *Armstrong* have been different if the requirements in Section 30(A) for state Medicaid plans had been more specific?

The dissent contends that the majority's approach "threatens the vitality of our *Ex parte Young* jurisprudence." In assessing this charge, it is important to keep in mind that the majority acknowledges that the Supremacy Clause provides a "rule of decision" for cases in which there is a conflict between federal and state law. The majority thus accepts that there are situations in which private parties may argue that a federal statute preempts state law or executive action, regardless of whether the statute confers a cause of action. One of these situations, the majority notes, was presented by *Ex parte Young*: a private party subject to a state regulatory requirement argued that the requirement was preempted by federal law and sought to enjoin enforcement of the requirement on that basis. In light of these concessions, the majority's analysis appears to be limited to situations, like the one in *Armstrong*, where the state law or executive action that is said to be preempted does not impose obligations on the plaintiff. Is the dissent never-theless correct in arguing that the majority's approach to injunctive relief is more restrictive than the approach in *Seminole Tribe*?

Whatever its implications in the statutory area, *Armstrong* appears to leave untouched the general ability of plaintiffs to sue to enjoin state actors (and federal actors) from violating the Constitution. Why is the Court more willing to imply injunctive relief for violations of the Constitution than for federal statutes?

2.   RELATION TO JURISDICTION AND IMPLIED RIGHTS OF ACTION

As discussed in Chapter V, there is statutory federal question jurisdic-tion under 28 U.S.C. § 1331 where, as in *Armstrong*, the plaintiff contends that a state law or executive action is preempted by federal law. See Shaw v. Delta Airlines, Inc., 463 U.S. 85, 96 n.14 (1983). Jurisdiction, however, con-cerns only the power of a federal court to hear a case, not its power to issue a remedy in favor of the plaintiff. To obtain a remedy, a plaintiff must state a cause of action that justifies the remedy sought. Some federal statutes ex-pressly give private parties a cause of action—for example, a cause of action for damages. But many statutes do not expressly provide for private party enforcement, and as discussed in Chapter II, in recent years the Supreme Court has been reluctant to imply statutory causes of action in favor of pri-vate parties. The majority in *Armstrong* seems to acknowledge that a statutory cause of action is not required in order for a court to enjoin the violation of a federal statute, but it notes that a statute can *preclude* such equitable relief, and it concludes that Section 30(A) of the Medicaid Act has that effect. Presumably, it is easier to find that a federal statute lacks an implied right of action than it is to find that the statute precludes a court from granting equitable relief. But how, precisely, does the analysis differ as between those two issues? What does *Armstrong* suggest? (Note that the statutory cause of action issue is addressed separately in Part IV of the opin-ion, which is not joined by Justice Breyer.)

INTRODUCTORY NOTES ON ABROGATION OF STATE SOVEREIGN IMMUNITY UNDER SECTION 5 OF THE FOURTEENTH AMENDMENT

1.   *CITY OF BOERNE V. FLORES*

The decisions discussed above did not disturb the holding in Fitzpatrick v. Bitzer, 427 U.S. 445 (1976), that Congress can abrogate state sovereign immunity by exercise of its authority under Section 5 of the Fourteenth Amendment "to enforce, by appropriate legislation" the provisions of the Amendment. Numerous cases after *Seminole Tribe* have tested the scope of this authority.

Each of these cases took an approach first developed in a case that did not involve the Eleventh Amendment. City of Boerne v. Flores, 521 U.S. 507 (1997), was a challenge to the constitutionality of the Religious Freedom Res-toration Act (RFRA). The RFRA prohibited federal, state, and local governments from substantially burdening the exercise of religion, absent a compelling government interest, even through application of laws of general applicability. In the usual course of zoning decisions, the city of Boerne, Texas, denied a permit to enlarge a church. The church challenged that decision under RFRA. In an opinion by Justice Kennedy, the Court held that, insofar as it sought to control state and local governments, RFRA exceeded Congress's powers under Section 5 of the Fourteenth Amendment.

The Court first considered the nature of the Congressional power. Section 5 does not, the Court said, confer upon Congress the power to define or enlarge constitutional rights. Rather, Congressional power is limited to the provision of remedies for the rights that the Constitution itself (as construed by the courts) protects:

> Congress's power under § 5 . . . extends only to "enforc[ing]" the provisions of the Fourteenth Amendment. The Court has described this power as "remedial". . . . The design of the Amendment and the text of § 5 are inconsistent with the suggestion that Congress has the power to decree the substance of the Fourteenth Amendment's restrictions on the States. Legislation which alters the meaning of the Free Exercise Clause cannot be said to be enforcing the Clause. Congress does not enforce a constitutional right by changing what the right is. It has been given the power "to enforce," not the power to determine what constitutes a constitutional violation.

The Court then addressed whether RFRA could be justified as enforcement legislation. While Congress cannot redefine the rights protected by the Fourteenth Amendment, it can legislate to prevent or redress violations of established rights. On this subject the Court said:

> While preventive rules are sometimes appropriate remedial measures, there must be a congruence between the means used and the ends to be achieved. The appropriateness of remedial measures must be considered in light of the evil presented. Strong measures appropriate to address one harm may be an unwarranted response to another, lesser one.

This reasoning and the test that it spawned have been captured in the words *congruence* and *proportionality*. These words describe a requirement of means-end fit between a judicially recognized constitutional violation and remedial legislation adopted by Congress under the authority of Section 5. The required fit is much more demanding than mere "rationality." Rather, there must be "congruence and proportionality between the injury to be prevented or remedied and the means adopted to that end."

The *Boerne* Court's application of this standard to RFRA demonstrated that the requirement of congruence and proportionality has real teeth:

> . . . RFRA cannot be considered remedial, preventive legislation, if those terms are to have any meaning. RFRA is so out of proportion to a supposed remedial or preventive object that it cannot be understood as responsive to, or designed to prevent, unconstitutional behavior. It appears, instead, to attempt a substantive

change in constitutional protections. Preventive measures prohibiting certain types of laws may be appropriate when there is reason to believe that many of the laws affected by the congressional enactment have a significant likelihood of being unconstitutional. [But] RFRA is not so confined. Sweeping coverage ensures its intrusion at every level of government, displacing laws and prohibiting official actions of almost every description and regardless of subject matter. . . . RFRA applies to all federal and state law, statutory or otherwise, whether adopted before or after its enactment. . . . Any law is subject to challenge at any time by any individual who alleges a substantial burden on his or her free exercise of religion. . . . Simply put, RFRA is not designed to identify and counteract state laws likely to be unconstitutional because of their treatment of religion. In most cases, the state laws to which RFRA applies are not ones which will have been motivated by religious bigotry. . . . When the exercise of religion has been burdened in an incidental way by a law of general application, it does not follow that the persons affected have been burdened any more than other citizens, let alone burdened because of their religious beliefs.

City of Boerne did not implicate state sovereign immunity, since (among other things) it involved a suit against a city. But it did define the outer limits of legislative authority under Section 5 of the Fourteenth Amendment. Accordingly, it states the test that Congress must meet when using its Section 5 authority to abrogate state immunity for conduct that does not itself violate the Constitution but that Congress wishes to prohibit for preventative or remedial reasons. The test is not relevant when Congress sanctions actual constitutional violations. It clearly has the authority to do that. But when Congress seeks to authorize damage actions against states for prophylactic reasons, the congruence-and-proportionality test of *City of Boerne* must be met. As the Court said in Nevada Department of Human Resources v. Hibbs, 538 U.S. 721, 728 (2003):

> *City of Boerne* . . . confirmed . . . that it falls to this Court, not Congress, to define the substance of constitutional guarantees. "The ultimate interpretation and determination of the Fourteenth Amendment's substantive meaning remains the province of the Judicial Branch." Kimel v. Florida Bd. of Regents, 528 U.S. 62, 81 (2000). Section 5 legislation reaching beyond the scope of § 1's actual guarantees must be an appropriate remedy for identified constitutional violations, not "an attempt to substantively redefine the States' legal obligations." Id. at 88. We distinguish appropriate prophylactic legislation from "substantive redefinition of the Fourteenth Amendment right at issue," id. at 81, by applying the test set forth in *City of Boerne*: Valid § 5 legislation must exhibit "congruence and proportionality between the injury to be prevented or remedied and the means adopted to that end."

2.   IDENTIFYING THE CONSTITUTIONAL RIGHT

Three cases applying *City of Boerne* to attempts by Congress to abrogate state sovereign immunity illustrate the centrality to that approach of focusing on the nature of the constitutional right at stake.

(i)   *Florida Prepaid Postsecondary Education Expense Board v. College Savings Bank*

One of the earliest decisions to trace the limits of Congressional power to override state sovereign immunity was Florida Prepaid Postsecondary Education Expense Board v. College Savings Bank, 527 U.S. 627 (1999). The College Savings Bank, organized in New Jersey, sold savings instruments designed to finance the costs of college education. It claimed patent infringement by the Florida Prepaid Postsecondary Education Expense Board, a state agency. By a vote of five to four, the Supreme Court upheld state sovereign immunity.

Writing for the Court, Chief Justice Rehnquist agreed that Congress had expressly abrogated sovereign immunity in the Patent Remedy Act, but found it had no power to do so:

> Congress justified the Patent Remedy Act under three sources of constitutional authority: the Patent Clause, Art. I, § 8, cl. 8; the Interstate Commerce Clause, Art. I, § 8, cl. 3; and § 5 of the Fourteenth Amendment. . . . *Seminole Tribe* makes clear that Congress may not abrogate state sovereign immunity pursuant to its Article I powers; hence the Patent Remedy Act cannot be sustained under either the Commerce Clause or the Patent Clause. . . .
>
> Can the Patent Remedy Act be viewed as remedial or preventive legislation aimed at securing the protections of the Fourteenth Amendment for patent owners? . . . The underlying conduct at issue here is state infringement of patents and the use of sovereign immunity to deny patent owners compensation for the invasion of their patent rights. It is this conduct then—unremedied patent infringement by the states—that must give rise to the Fourteenth Amendment violation that Congress sought to redress in the Patent Remedy Act.
>
> In enacting the Patent Remedy Act, however, Congress identified no pattern of patent infringement by the states, let alone a pattern of constitutional violations. . . . Though patents may be considered "property" for purposes of our analysis, the legislative record still provides little support for the proposition that Congress sought to remedy a Fourteenth Amendment violation in enacting the Patent Remedy Act. This Court has . . . held that "in procedural due process claims, the deprivation by state action of a constitutionally protected interest . . . is not in itself unconstitutional; what is unconstitutional is the deprivation of such an interest without due process of law." Zinermon v. Burch, 494 U.S. 113, 125 (1990).

Thus, under the plain terms of the clause and the clear import of our precedent, a state's infringement of a patent, though interfering with a patent owner's right to exclude others, does not by itself violate the Constitution. Instead, only where the state provides no remedy, or only inadequate remedies, to injured patent owners for its infringement of their patent could a deprivation of property without due process result. See Parratt v. Taylor, 451 U.S. 527, 539–31 (1981).

Congress, however, barely considered the availability of state remedies for patent infringement and hence whether the states' conduct might have amounted to a constitutional violation under the Fourteenth Amendment. . . . The primary point made by [its] witnesses . . . was not that state remedies were constitutionally inadequate, but rather that they were less convenient than federal remedies, and might undermine the uniformity of patent law. . . .

The historical record and the scope of coverage therefore make it clear that the Patent Remedy Act cannot be sustained under § 5 of the Fourteenth Amendment. The examples of states avoiding liability for patent infringement by pleading sovereign immunity in a federal-court patent action are scarce enough, but any plausible argument that such action on the part of the state deprived patentees of property and left them without a remedy under state law is scarcer still. The statute's apparent and more basic aims were to provide a uniform remedy for patent infringement and to place states on the same footing as private parties under that regime. These are proper Article I concerns, but that article does not give Congress the power to enact such legislation after *Seminole Tribe.*

Justice Stevens dissented, joined by Justices Souter, Ginsburg, and Breyer.[a]

(ii) *Kimel v. Florida Board of Regents*

The *College Savings Bank* case was followed by Kimel v. Florida Board of Regents, 528 U.S. 62 (2000), which held that Congress could not constitutionally authorize damage actions against states for violation of the Age Discrimination in Employment Act (ADEA). As originally passed in 1967, that statute covered only private employers. A 1974 amendment extended the statute to public agencies, including states. In an opinion by Justice O'Connor, the Court held that the ADEA, although undoubtedly within Congress's Article I power, was not "appropriate legislation" under § 5 of the Fourteenth Amendment. The Court reasoned that since age discrimination generally does not violate equal protection (unless irrational), legislation to prohibit age discrimination in employment could not be justified as "responsive to, or designed to prevent, unconstitutional behavior." While the Court

---

a   In a companion case with a similar name, College Savings Bank v. Florida Prepaid Postsecondary Education Expense Board, 527 U.S. 666 (1999), the Court, by the same five-four majority, reached the same conclusion regarding Congress's attempt in the Trademark Remedy Clarification Act to make states liable in money damages for violations of trademark. This case is discussed at length in the notes following *Seminole Tribe.*

acknowledged that in some instances Section 5 can authorize remedial legislation that goes beyond the prohibition of conduct that is itself a violation of the Fourteenth Amendment, it concluded from its examination of the legislative record that "Congress's 1974 extension of the Act to the States was an unwarranted response to a perhaps inconsequential problem." The fact that Congress found discrimination in the private sector was "beside the point," said the Court, since "Congress made no such findings with respect to the States." Justices Stevens, Souter, Ginsburg, and Breyer dissented.

(iii) Board of Trustees of the University of Alabama v. Garrett

Board of Trustees of the University of Alabama v. Garrett, 531 U.S. 356 (2001), raised the question whether employees of the State of Alabama could recover money damages for the state's failure to abide by the Americans With Disabilities Act (ADA). The Court held the suit barred by state sovereign immunity.

"The first step" in the analysis, wrote Chief Justice Rehnquist for a five-to-four majority, "is to identify with some precision the scope of the constitutional right at issue." Prior decisions had established that a disability issue "incurs only the minimum 'rational-basis' review applicable to general social and economic legislation." "Thus," he concluded, "States are not required by the Fourteenth Amendment to make special accommodations for the disabled, so long as their actions towards such individuals are rational. They could quite hardheadedly—and perhaps hardheartedly—hold to job-qualification requirements which do not make allowance for the disabled. If special accommodations for the disabled are to be required, they have to come from positive law and not through the Equal Protection Clause." The question, then, was whether "Congress identified a history and pattern of unconstitutional employment discrimination by the States against the disabled." The conclusion, not surprisingly, was that "[t]he legislative record of the ADA . . . simply fails to show that Congress did in fact identify a pattern of irrational state discrimination in employment against the disabled." Justice Kennedy wrote a separate concurrence, joined by Justice O'Connor. Justice Breyer, joined by Justices Stevens, Souter, and Ginsburg, dissented.

Coleman v. Court of Appeals of Maryland
Supreme Court of the United States, 2012.
566 U.S. 30.

■ JUSTICE KENNEDY announced the judgment of the Court and delivered an opinion, in which THE CHIEF JUSTICE, JUSTICE THOMAS, and JUSTICE ALITO joined.

The question in this case is whether a state employee is allowed to recover damages from the state entity that employs him by invoking one of the provisions of a federal statute that, in express terms, seeks to abrogate the States' immunity from suits for damages. The statute in question is the Family and Medical Leave Act of 1993, 29 U.S.C. § 2601 et seq. The provision at issue requires employers, including state employers, to grant unpaid leave for self care for a serious medical condition, provided other statutory requisites are met, particularly requirements that the total amount of annual leave taken under all the Act's provisions does not exceed a stated maximum. In agreement with every Court of Appeals to have addressed this question, this Court now holds that suits against States under this provision are barred by the States' immunity as sovereigns in our federal system. . . .

I

A

The Family and Medical Leave Act of 1993 (FMLA or Act) entitles eligible employees to take up to 12 work weeks of unpaid leave per year. An employee may take leave under the FMLA for: (A) "the birth of a son or daughter . . . in order to care for such son or daughter," (B) the adoption or fostercare placement of a child with the employee, (C) the care of a "spouse . . . son, daughter, or parent" with "a serious health condition," and (D) the employee's own serious health condition when the condition interferes with the employee's ability to perform at work. 29 U.S.C. § 2612(a)(1). The Act creates a private right of action to seek both equitable relief and money damages "against any employer (including a public agency) in any Federal or State court of competent jurisdiction." As noted, subparagraph (D) is at issue here.

This Court considered subparagraph (C) in Nev. Dep't of Human Res. v. Hibbs, 538 U.S. 721 (2003). Subparagraph (C), like (A) and (B), grants leave for reasons related to family care, and those three provisions are referred to here as the family-care provisions. *Hibbs* held that Congress could subject the States to suit for violations of subparagraph (C). That holding rested on evidence that States had family-leave policies that differentiated on the basis of sex and that States administered even neutral family-leave policies in ways that discriminated on the basis of sex. Subparagraph (D), the self-care provision, was not at issue in *Hibbs*.

B

Petitioner Daniel Coleman was employed by the Court of Appeals of the State of Maryland. When Coleman requested sick leave, he was informed he would be terminated if he did not resign. Coleman then sued the state court in the United States District Court for the District of Maryland, alleging, inter alia, that his employer violated the FMLA by failing to provide him with self-care leave.

The District Court dismissed the suit on the basis that the Maryland Court of Appeals, as an entity of a sovereign State, was immune from the suit for damages. The parties do not dispute the District Court's ruling that the Maryland Court of Appeals is an entity or instrumentality of the State for purposes of sovereign immunity. The District Court concluded the FMLA's self-care provision did not validly abrogate the State's immunity from suit. The Court of Appeals for the Fourth Circuit affirmed, reasoning that, unlike the family-care provision at issue in *Hibbs*, the self-care provision was not directed at an identified pattern of gender-based discrimination and was not congruent and proportional to any pattern of sex-based discrimination on the part of States.

II

A

A foundational premise of the federal system is that States, as sovereigns, are immune from suits for damages, save as they elect to waive that defense. See Kimel v. Florida Bd. of Regents, 528 U.S. 62, 72–73 (2000); Alden v. Maine, 527 U.S. 706 (1999). As an exception to this principle, Congress may abrogate the States' immunity from suit pursuant to its powers under § 5 of the Fourteenth Amendment. See, e.g., Fitzpatrick v. Bitzer, 427 U.S. 445 (1976).

Congress must "mak[e] its intention to abrogate unmistakably clear in the language of the statute." *Hibbs*, 538 U.S. at 726. On this point the Act does express the clear purpose to abrogate the States' immunity. . . .

The question then becomes whether the self-care provision and its attempt to abrogate the States' immunity are a valid exercise of congressional power under § 5 of the Fourteenth Amendment. Section 5 grants Congress the power "to enforce" the substantive guarantees of § 1 of the Amendment by "appropriate legislation." The power to enforce " 'includes the authority both to remedy and to deter violation[s] of rights guaranteed' " by § 1. See Board of Trustees of Univ. of Ala. v. Garrett, 531 U.S. 356, 365 (2001) (quoting *Kimel*, 528 U.S. at 81). To ensure Congress's enforcement powers under § 5 remain enforcement powers, as envisioned by the ratifiers of the Amendment, rather than powers to redefine the substantive scope of § 1, Congress "must tailor" legislation enacted under § 5 " 'to remedy or prevent' " "conduct transgressing the Fourteenth Amendment's substantive provisions." Florida Prepaid Postsecondary Ed. Expense Bd. v. College Savings Bank, 527 U.S. 627, 639 (1999).

Whether a congressional Act passed under § 5 can impose monetary liability upon States requires an assessment of both the " 'evil' or 'wrong' that Congress intended to remedy," id., and the means Congress adopted to address that evil, see City of Boerne v. Flores, 521 U.S. 507, 520 (1997). Legislation enacted under § 5 must be targeted at "conduct transgressing the Fourteenth Amendment's substantive provisions." *Florida Prepaid*, 527 U.S. at 639; see *Kimel*, 528 U.S. at 88; *City of Boerne*, 521 U.S. at 525. And "[t]here must be a congruence and proportionality between the injury to be prevented or remedied and the means adopted to that end." Id. at 520.

Under this analysis *Hibbs* permitted employees to recover damages from States for violations of subparagraph (C). In enacting the FMLA, Congress relied upon evidence of a well-documented pattern of sex-based discrimination in family-leave policies. States had facially discriminatory leave policies that granted longer periods of leave to women than to men.

applying (or seeming to apply) the test, we must scour the legislative record in search of evidence that supports the congressional action. This grading of Congress's homework is a task we are ill suited to perform and ill advised to undertake.

I adhere to my view that we should instead adopt an approach that is properly tied to the text of § 5, which grants Congress the power "to *enforce*, by appropriate legislation," the other provisions of the Fourteenth Amendment. (Emphasis added.) As I have explained in greater detail elsewhere, see *Lane*, 541 U.S. at 558–60, outside of the context of racial discrimination (which is different for stare decisis reasons), I would limit Congress's § 5 power to the regulation of conduct that *itself* violates the Fourteenth Amendment. Failing to grant state employees leave for the purpose of self-care-or any other purpose, for that matter-does not come close.

Accordingly, I would affirm the judgment of the Court of Appeals.

■ JUSTICE GINSBURG, with whom JUSTICE BREYER joins, and with whom JUSTICE SOTOMAYOR and JUSTICE KAGAN join as to all but footnote 1, dissenting. . . .

Even accepting this Court's view of the scope of Congress's power under § 5 of the Fourteenth Amendment, I would hold that the self-care provision, validly enforces the right to be free from gender discrimination in the workplace.[1]

I

. . . The first step of the now-familiar *Boerne* inquiry calls for identification of the constitutional right Congress sought to enforce. The FMLA's self-care provision, Maryland asserts, trains not on the right to be free from gender discrimination, but on an "equal protection right to be free from irrational state employment discrimination based on a medical condition." Brief for Respondents 14. The plurality agrees, concluding that the self-care provision reveals "a concern for discrimination on the basis of illness, not sex." In so declaring, the plurality undervalues the language, purpose, and history of the FMLA, and the self-care provision's important role in the statutory scheme. As well, the plurality underplays the main theme of our decision in Nevada Dep't of Human Res. v. Hibbs, 538 U.S. 721 (2003): "The FMLA aims to protect the right to be free from genderbased discrimination in the workplace." Id. at 728.

I begin with the text of the statute, which repeatedly emphasizes gender discrimination. One of the FMLA's stated purposes is to "entitle employees to take reasonable leave," "in a manner that, consistent with

---

[1] I remain of the view that Congress can abrogate state sovereign immunity pursuant to its Article I Commerce Clause power. See Seminole Tribe of Fla. v. Florida, 517 U.S. 44, 100 (1996) (Souter, J., dissenting). Beyond debate, [the self-care provision] is valid Commerce Clause legislation. I also share the view that Congress can abrogate state immunity pursuant to § 5 of the Fourteenth Amendment where Congress could reasonably conclude that legislation "constitutes an appropriate way to enforce [a] basic equal protection requirement." Board of Trustees of Univ. of Ala. v. Garrett, 531 U.S. 356, 377 (2001) (Breyer, J., dissenting).

the Equal Protection Clause of the Fourteenth Amendment, minimizes the potential for employment discrimination on the basis of sex by ensuring generally that leave is available for eligible medical reasons (including maternity-related disability) and for compelling family reasons, on a gender-neutral basis." Another identified aim is "to promote the goal of equal employment opportunity for women and men, pursuant to [the Equal Protection Clause]." "[E]mployment standards that apply to one gender only," Congress expressly found, "have serious potential for encouraging employers to discriminate against employees and applicants for employment who are of that gender."

The FMLA's purpose and legislative history reinforce the conclusion that the FMLA, in its entirety, is directed at sex discrimination. Indeed, the FMLA was originally envisioned as a way to guarantee—without singling out women or pregnancy—that pregnant women would not lose their jobs when they gave birth. The self-care provision achieves that aim.

[Justice Ginsburg then reviewed the history surrounding the enactment of the FMLA, focusing in particular on the legislation as a response to demands by "equal-treatment feminists" for gender-neutral leave requirements that would not single out pregnancy or childbirth. From this history, she found, contrary to the plurality, that "it is impossible to conclude that 'nothing in particular about self-care leave . . . connects it to gender discrimination.' "]

II

A

Boerne next asks "whether Congress had evidence of a pattern of constitutional violations on the part of the States." *Hibbs*, 538 U.S. at 729. See also *Boerne*, 521 U.S. at 530–32. Beyond question, Congress had evidence of a well documented pattern of workplace discrimination against pregnant women. Section 2612(a)(1)(D) [the self-care provision] can therefore "be understood as responsive to, or designed to prevent, unconstitutional behavior." Id. at 532.

Although the [Pregnancy Discrimination Act of 1978] proscribed blatant discrimination on the basis of pregnancy, the Act is fairly described as a necessary, but not a sufficient measure. FMLA hearings conducted between 1986 and 1993 included illustrative testimony from women fired after becoming pregnant or giving birth. . . .

These women's experiences, Congress learned, were hardly isolated incidents. . . .

"Many pregnant women have been fired when their employer refused to provide an adequate leave of absence," Congress had ample cause to conclude. See H.R. Rep. No. 99–699, pt. 2, p. 22 (1986). Pregnancy, Congress also found, has a marked impact on women's earnings. One year after childbirth, mothers' earnings fell to $1.40 per hour less than those of women who had not given birth. See 1991 Senate Report 28.

Congress heard evidence tying this pattern of discrimination to the States. A 50-state survey by the Yale Bush Center Infant Care Leave Project concluded that "[t]he proportion and construction of leave policies available to public sector employees differs little from those offered private sector employees." *Hibbs*, 538 U.S. at 730 n.3 (quoting 1986 House Hearing 33 (statement of Meryl Frank)). Roughly 28% of women employed in the public sector did not receive eight weeks of job-protected medical leave to recover from childbirth. See 1987 Senate Hearings, pt. 1, pp. 31, 39 (statement of James T. Bond, National Counsel of Jewish Women). A South Carolina state legislator testified: "[I]n South Carolina, as well as in other states . . . no unemployment compensation is paid to a woman who is necessarily absent from her place of employment because of pregnancy or maternity." See id., pt. 2, p. 361 (statement of Rep. Irene Rudnick). According to an employee of the State of Georgia, if state employees took leave, it was held against them when they were considered for promotions: "It is common practice for my Department to compare the balance sheets of workers who have and have not used [leave] benefits in determining who should and should not be promoted." Hearing on H.R. 2 before the Subcommittee on Labor-Management Relations of the House Committee on Education and Labor, 102d Cong., 1st Sess., 36 (1991) (statement of Robert E. Dawkins). In short, Congress had every reason to believe that a pattern of workplace discrimination against pregnant women existed in public-sector employment, just as it did in the private sector. . . .

B

"[A] state's refusal to provide pregnancy leave to its employees," Maryland responds, is "not unconstitutional." Brief for Respondents 23 (citing Geduldig v. Aiello, 417 U.S. 484, 495 (1974)). *Aiello*'s footnote 20 proclaimed that discrimination on the basis of pregnancy is not discrimination on the basis of sex. In my view, this case is a fit occasion to revisit that conclusion. . . .

[C]hildbearing is not only a biological function unique to women. It is also inextricably intertwined with employers' "stereotypical views about women's commitment to work and their value as employees." *Hibbs*, 538 U.S. at 736. Because pregnancy discrimination is inevitably sex discrimination, and because discrimination against women is tightly interwoven with society's beliefs about pregnancy and motherhood, I would hold that *Aiello* was egregiously wrong to declare that discrimination on the basis of pregnancy is not discrimination on the basis of sex.

C

Boerne's third step requires " 'a congruence and proportionality between the injury to be prevented or remedied and the means adopted to that end.' " Section 2612(a)(1)(D), I would conclude, is an appropriate response to pervasive discriminatory treatment of pregnant women. In separating self-care leave for the physical disability following childbirth,

§ 2612(a)(1)(D), which affects only women, from family-care leave for par-enting a newborn baby, § 2612(a)(1)(A), for which men and women are equally suited, Congress could attack gender discrimination and chal-lenge stereo-types of women as lone childrearers. Cf. *Hibbs*, 538 U.S. at 731 (States' extended "maternity" leaves, far exceeding a woman's phys-ical disability following childbirth, were attributable "to the pervasive sex-role stereotype that caring for family members is women's work.").

It would make scant sense to provide job-protected leave for a woman to care for a newborn, but not for her recovery from delivery, a miscar-riage, or the birth of a stillborn baby. And allowing States to provide no pregnancy-disability leave at all, given that only women can become pregnant, would obviously "exclude far more women than men from the workplace." Id. at 738.

The plurality's statement that Congress lacked "wide-spread evi-dence of sex discrimination . . . in the administration of sick leave," misses the point. So too does the plurality's observation that state em-ployees likely "could take leave for pregnancy-related illnesses"—pre-sumably severe morning sickness, toxemia, etc. under paid sick-leave plans. Congress heard evidence that existing sick-leave plans were inad-equate to ensure that women were not fired when they needed to take time out to recover their strength and stamina after childbirth. The self-care provision responds to that evidence by requiring employers to allow leave for "ongoing pregnancy, miscarriages, . . . the need for prenatal care, childbirth, and recovery from childbirth." S. Rep. No. 103–3, p. 29 (1993).

That § 2612(a)(1)(D) entitles all employees to up to 12 weeks of un-paid, job-protected leave for a serious health condition, rather than singling out pregnancy or child-birth, does not mean that the provision lacks the requisite congruence and proportionality to the identified con-stitutional violations. As earlier noted, Congress made plain its rationale for the prescription's broader compass: Congress sought to ward off the unconstitutional discrimination it believed would attend a pregnancy-only leave requirement. . . .

Finally, as in *Hibbs*, it is important to note the moderate cast of the FMLA, in particular, the considerable limitations Congress placed on §§ 2612(a)(1)(A)–(D)'s leave requirement. FMLA leave is unpaid. It is limited to employees who have worked at least one year for the employer and at least 1,250 hours during the past year. High-ranking employees, including state elected officials and their staffs, are not within the Act's compass. Employees must provide advance notice of foreseeable leaves. Employers may require a doctor's certification of a serious health condi-tion. And, if an employer violates the FMLA, the employees' recoverable damages are "strictly defined and measured by actual monetary losses." *Hibbs*, 538 U.S. at 740. The self-care provision, I would therefore hold, is congruent and proportional to the injury to be prevented.

III

But even if *Aiello* senselessly holds sway, and impedes the conclusion that § 2612(a)(1)(D) is an appropriate response to the States' unconstitutional discrimination against pregnant women, I would nevertheless conclude that the FMLA is valid § 5 legislation. For it is a meet response to "the States' record of unconstitutional participation in, and fostering of, gender-based discrimination in the administration of [parental and family-care] leave benefits." *Hibbs*, 538 U.S. at 735.

Requiring States to provide gender-neutral parental and family-care leave alone, Congress was warned, would promote precisely the type of workplace discrimination Congress sought to reduce. The "pervasive sex-role stereo-type that caring for family members is women's work," id. at 731, Congress heard, led employers to regard required parental and family-care leave as a woman's benefit. . . .

Congress therefore had good reason to conclude that the self-care provision—which men no doubt would use—would counter employers' impressions that the FMLA would otherwise install female leave. Providing for self-care would thus reduce employers' corresponding incentive to discriminate against women in hiring and promotion. . . .

The plurality therefore gets it wrong in concluding that "[o]nly supposition and conjecture support the contention that the self-care provision is necessary to make the family-care provisions effective." Self-care leave, I would hold, is a key part of Congress's endeavor to make it feasible for women to work and have families. By reducing an employer's perceived incentive to avoid hiring women, § 2612(a)(1)(D) lessens the risk that the FMLA as a whole would give rise to the very sex discrimination it was enacted to thwart. The plurality offers no legitimate ground to dilute the force of the Act. . . .

NOTES ON ABROGATION OF STATE SOVEREIGN IMMUNITY UNDER SECTION 5 OF THE FOURTEENTH AMENDMENT

1. NEVADA DEPARTMENT OF HUMAN RESOURCES V. HIBBS

At the center of the dispute in *Coleman* was the Court's prior decision in Nevada Department of Human Resources v. Hibbs, 538 U.S. 721 (2003). There a state employee sought damages for violation of the family medical leave provision of the Family and Medical Leave Act, which entitles eligible employees to take up to 12 weeks of unpaid leave a year "[i]n order to care for the spouse, or a son, daughter, or parent, of the employee, if such spouse, son, daughter, or parent has a serious health condition." Hibbs was discharged after taking extensive leave from state employment to care for his wife while she recovered from a car accident and consequent neck surgery. The District Court granted summary judgment against him on grounds of state sovereign immunity, but the Supreme Court upheld the statute.

(i)   The Majority

Writing for a six-to-three majority, Chief Justice Rehnquist explained that "Congress may enact so-called prophylactic legislation that proscribes facially constitutional conduct, in order to prevent and deter unconstitutional conduct," but that such legislation "must exhibit 'congruence and proportionality between the injury to be prevented or remedied and the means adopted to that end' ":

> The FMLA aims to protect the right to be free from gender-based discrimination in the workplace. We have held that statutory classifications that distinguish between males and females are subject to heightened scrutiny. See, e.g., Craig v. Boren, 429 U.S. 190, 197–99 (1976). For a gender-based classification to withstand such scrutiny, it must "serv[e] important governmental objectives," and "the discriminatory means employed [must be] substantially related to the achievement of those objectives." United States v. Virginia, 518 U.S. 515, 533 (1996). The State's justification for such a classification "must not rely on overbroad generalizations about the different talents, capacities, or preferences of males and females." Id. We now inquire whether Congress had evidence of a pattern of constitutional violations on the part of the States in this area.
>
> The history of the many state laws limiting women's employment opportunities is chronicled in—and, until relatively recently, was sanctioned by—this Court's own opinions. For example, in Bradwell v. State, 83 U.S. (16 Wall.) 130 (1873) (Illinois), and Goesaert v. Cleary, 335 U.S. 464, 466 (1948) (Michigan), the Court upheld state laws prohibiting women from practicing law and tending bar, respectively. State laws frequently subjected women to distinctive restrictions, terms, conditions, and benefits for those jobs they could take. . . .
>
> Congress responded to this history of discrimination by abrogating States' sovereign immunity in Title VII of the Civil Rights Act of 1964, and we sustained this abrogation in Fitzpatrick v. Bitzer, 427 U.S. 445 (1976). But state gender discrimination did not cease. . . . According to evidence that was before Congress when it enacted the FMLA, States continue to rely on invalid gender stereotypes in the employment context, specifically in the administration of leave benefits. Reliance on such stereotypes cannot justify the States' gender discrimination in this area. The long and extensive history of sex discrimination prompted us to hold that measures that differentiate on the basis of gender warrant heightened scrutiny; here, as in *Fitzpatrick*, the persistence of such unconstitutional discrimination by the States justifies Congress's passage of prophylactic § 5 legislation.

The Court cited three types of evidence before the Congress. The first concerned "stereotype-based beliefs about the allocation of family duties" that lead to "widespread" differences between maternity and paternity leave policies. The second involved "differential leave policies" that "were not attributable to any differential physical needs of men and women, but rather to the pervasive sex-role stereotype that caring for family members is women's work." The third was "evidence that, even where state laws and policies were not facially discriminatory, they were applied in discriminatory ways." The Court concluded that "[i]n sum, the States' record of unconstitutional participation in, and fostering of, gender-based discrimination in the administration of leave benefits is weighty enough to justify the enactment of prophylactic § 5 legislation":

> We believe that Congress's chosen remedy, the family-care leave provision of the FMLA, is "congruent and proportional to the targeted violation." . . . By creating an across-the-board, routine employment benefit for all eligible employees, Congress sought to ensure that family-care leave would no longer be stigmatized as an inordinate drain on the workplace caused by female employees, and that employers could not evade leave obligations simply by hiring men. By setting a minimum standard of family leave for *all* eligible employees, irrespective of gender, the FMLA attacks the formerly state-sanctioned stereotype that only women are responsible for family caregiving, thereby reducing employers' incentives to engage in discrimination by basing hiring and promotion decisions on stereotypes.

Importantly, the Court added:

> We reached the opposite conclusion in Board of Trustees of the University of Alabama v. Garrett, 531 U.S. 356 (2001), and Kimel v. Florida Board of Regents, 528 U.S. 62 (2000). In those cases, the § 5 legislation under review responded to a purported tendency of state officials to make age-or disability-based distinctions. Under our equal protection case law, discrimination on the basis of such characteristics is not judged under a heightened review standard, and passes muster if there is "a rational basis for doing so at a class-based level, even if it 'is probably not true' that those reasons are valid in the majority of cases." *Kimel,* 528 U.S. at 86. Thus, in order to impugn the constitutionality of state discrimination against the disabled or the elderly, Congress must identify, not just the existence of age-or disability-based state decisions, but a "widespread pattern" of irrational reliance on such criteria. We found no such showing with respect to the ADEA and Title I of the Americans with Disabilities Act of 1990 (ADA).

> Here, however, Congress directed its attention to state gender discrimination, which triggers a heightened level of scrutiny. Because the standard for demonstrating the constitutionality of a gender-based classification is more difficult to meet than our rational-basis test—it must "serv[e] important governmental objectives" and be "substantially related to the achievement of those objectives," United States v. Virginia, 518 U.S. 515, 533 (1996)—it was easier for Congress to show a pattern of state constitutional violations.

(ii) The Dissent

In a dissent joined by Justices Scalia and Thomas, Justice Kennedy offered a point-by-point refutation of the arguments made by the majority and an exhaustive analysis of the evidence on which the majority relied. He claimed that FMLA's findings of purpose "are devoid of any discussion of the relevant evidence." In the main, "the evidence considered by Congress concerned discriminatory practices of the private sector, not those of state employers." The majority's "reliance on evidence suggesting States provided men and women with the parenting leave of different length . . . is too attenuated to justify the family leave provision [and] sets the contours of the inquiry at too high a level of abstraction." Kennedy concluded that "[c]onsidered in its entirety, the evidence fails to document a pattern of unconstitutional conduct sufficient to justify the abrogation of States' sovereign immunity" and continued:

> The paucity of evidence to support the case the Court tries to make demonstrates that Congress was not responding with a congruent and proportional remedy to a perceived course of unconstitutional conduct. Instead, it enacted a substantive entitlement program of its own. If Congress had been concerned about different treatment of men and women with respect to family leave, a congruent remedy would have sought to ensure the benefits of any leave program enacted by a State are available to men and women on an equal basis. Instead, the Act imposes, across the board, a requirement that States grant a minimum of 12 weeks of leave per year. This requirement may represent Congress's considered judgment as to the optimal balance between the family obligations of workers and the interests of employers, and the States may decide to follow these guidelines in designing their own family leave benefits. It does not follow, however, that if the States choose to enact a different benefit scheme, they should be deemed to engage in unconstitutional conduct and forced to open their treasuries to private suits for damages.

Kennedy added that Nevada had established a family leave policy well before the federal statute was enacted, but that it "did not track that devised by the [FMLA] in all respects." But even if it was deficient when measured against the standards of the federal statute, a

> congruent remedy to any discriminatory exercise of discretion . . . is the requirement that the grant of leave be administered on a gender-equal basis, not the displacement of the State's scheme by a federal one. . . .

> [T]he abrogation of state sovereign immunity pursuant to Title VII was a legitimate congressional response to a pattern of gender-based discrimination in employment. Fitzpatrick v. Bitzer, 427 U.S. 445 (1976). The family leave benefit conferred by the Act is, by contrast, a substantive benefit Congress chose to confer upon state employees. . . .

(iii) Justice Scalia

Justice Scalia joined the Kennedy dissent, but wrote separately to make "one further observation":

> The constitutional violation that is a prerequisite to "prophylactic" congressional action to "enforce" the Fourteenth Amendment is a violation *by the State against which the enforcement action is taken.* There is no guilt by association, enabling the sovereignty of one State to be abridged under § 5 of the Fourteenth Amendment because of violations by another State, or by most other States, or even by 49 other States. Congress has sometimes displayed awareness of this self-evident limitation. That is presumably why the most sweeping provisions of the Voting Rights Act of 1965 . . . were restricted to States "with a demonstrable history of intentional racial discrimination in voting," City of Rome v. United States, 446 U.S. 156, 177 (1980).

> Today's opinion for the Court does not even attempt to demonstrate that each one of the 50 States covered by [the FMLA] was in violation of the Fourteenth Amendment. It treats "the States" as some sort of collective entity which is guilty or innocent as a body. "[T]he States' record of unconstitutional participation in, and fostering of, gender-based discrimination," it concludes, "is weighty enough to justify the enactment of prophylactic § 5 legislation." This will not do. Prophylaxis in the sense of extending the remedy beyond the violation is one thing; prophylaxis in the sense of extending the remedy beyond the violator is something else. . . .

> When a litigant claims that legislation has denied him individual rights secured by the Constitution, the court ordinarily asks first whether the legislation is constitutional *as applied to him.* When, on the other hand, a federal statute is challenged as going beyond Congress's enumerated powers, under our precedents the court first asks whether the statute is unconstitutional *on its face.* If the statute survives this challenge, however, it stands to reason that the court may, if asked, proceed to analyze whether the statute (constitutional on its face) can be validly applied to the litigant. In the context of § 5 prophylactic legislation applied against a State, this would entail examining whether the State has itself engaged in discrimination sufficient to support the exercise of Congress's prophylactic power.

> It seems, therefore, that for purposes of defeating petitioner's challenge, it would have been enough for respondents to demonstrate that [the challenged section of the FMLA] was *facially* valid—i.e., that it could constitutionally be applied to *some* jurisdictions. (Even that demonstration, for the reasons set forth by Justice Kennedy, has not been made.) But when it comes to an as-applied challenge, I think Nevada will be entitled to assert that the mere facts that (1) it is a State, and (2) some States are bad actors,

is not enough; it can demand that *it* be shown to have been acting in violation of the Fourteenth Amendment.

2.   IS THE COURT TAKING THE RIGHT APPROACH?

In addition to the argument by Justice Scalia in his separate opinion in *Hibbs*, there have been two other challenges to the "congruence and proportionality" approach consistently taken by the Court's majority in this line of cases.

(i)   The Breyer Dissent in Garrett

The Court's holding in Board of Trustees of the University of Alabama v. Garrett, 531 U.S. 356 (2001), is summarized in the notes preceding *Coleman*. In dissent, Justice Breyer, joined by Justices Stevens, Souter, and Ginsburg, criticized the Court's approach:

> As the Court recognizes, state discrimination in employment against persons with disabilities might "run afoul of the Equal Protection Clause" where there is no "rational relationship between the disparity of treatment and some legitimate governmental purpose." In my view, Congress reasonably could have concluded that the remedy before us constitutes an "appropriate" way to enforce this basic equal protection requirement. And that is all the Constitution requires.
>
> . . . Congress expressly found substantial unjustified discrimination against persons with disabilities. . . . Moreover, it found that such discrimination typically reflects "stereotypic assumptions" or "purposeful unequal treatment." . . . The evidence in the legislative record bears out Congress's finding that the adverse treatment of persons with disabilities was often arbitrary or invidious . . . and thus unjustified. . . .
>
> The problem with the Court's approach is that [a] rule of restraint applicable to judges [should not apply] to Congress when it exercises its § 5 power. . . .
>
> There is simply no reason to require Congress, seeking to determine facts relevant to the exercise of its § 5 authority, to adopt rules or presumptions that reflect a court's institutional limitations. Unlike courts, Congress can readily gather facts from across the Nation, assess the magnitude of a problem, and more easily find an appropriate remedy. Unlike courts, Congress directly reflects public attitudes and beliefs, enabling Congress better to understand where, and to what extent, refusals to accommodate a disability amount to behavior that is callous or unreasonable to the point of lacking constitutional justification. . . . To apply a rule designed to restrict courts as if it restricted Congress's legislative power is to stand the underlying principle—a principle of judicial restraint—on its head. But without the use of this burden of proof rule or some other unusually stringent standard of review, it is difficult to see how the Court can find the legislative record here

inadequate. Read with a reasonably favorable eye, the record indicates that state governments subjected those with disabilities to seriously adverse, disparate treatment. . . .

The Court's harsh review of Congress's use of its § 5 power is reminiscent of the similar (now-discredited) limitation that it once imposed upon Congress's Commerce Clause power. Compare Carter v. Carter Coal Co., 298 U.S. 238 (1936), with United States v. Darby, 312 U.S. 100 (1941) (rejecting *Carter Coal*'s rationale). I could understand the legal basis for such review were we judging a statute that discriminated against those of a particular race or gender . . . or a statute that threatened a basic constitutionally protected liberty such as free speech. The legislation before us, however, does not discriminate against anyone, nor does it pose any threat to basic liberty. And it is difficult to understand why the Court, which applies "minimum 'rational-basis' review" to statutes that burden persons with disabilities subjects to far stricter scrutiny a statute that seeks to help those same individuals.

I recognize nonetheless that this statute imposes a burden upon States in that it removes their Eleventh Amendment protection from suit, thereby subjecting them to potential monetary liability. Rules for interpreting § 5 that would provide States with special protection, however, run counter to the very object of the Fourteenth Amendment. By its terms, that Amendment prohibits States from denying their citizens equal protection of the laws. Hence "principles of federalism that might otherwise be an obstacle to congressional authority are necessarily overridden by the power to enforce the Civil War Amendments 'by appropriate legislation.' Those Amendments were specifically designed as an expansion of federal power and an intrusion on state sovereignty." City of Rome v. United States, 446 U.S. 156, 179 (1980). And, ironically, the greater the obstacle the Eleventh Amendment poses to the creation by Congress of the kind of remedy at issue here—the decentralized remedy of private damages actions—the more Congress, seeking to cure important national problems, such as the problem of disability discrimination before us, will have to rely on more uniform remedies, such as federal standards and court injunctions, which are sometimes draconian and typically more intrusive. . . . I doubt that today's decision serves any constitutionally based federalism interest.

The Court, through its evidentiary demands, its non-deferential review, and its failure to distinguish between judicial and legislative constitutional competencies, improperly invades a power that the Constitution assigns to Congress. Its decision saps § 5 of independent force, effectively "confin[ing] the legislative power . . . to the insignificant role of abrogating only those state laws that the judicial branch [is] prepared to adjudge unconstitutional." Katzenbach v. Morgan, 384 U.S. 641, 648–49 (1966). Whether the Commerce Clause does or does not enable Congress to enact this provision, in my view, § 5 gives Congress the necessary authority.

(ii) The Scalia Dissent in Lane

The Court's holding in Tennessee v. Lane, 541 U.S. 509 (2004), a five-to-four disagreement about application of the *City of Boerne* test to a Congressional abrogation of state sovereign immunity under a different provision of the ADA, is summarized in the next Note. For present purposes, consider the separate dissent by Justice Scalia:

> I joined the Court's opinion in *Boerne* with some misgiving. I have generally rejected tests based on such malleable standards as "proportionality," because they have a way of turning into vehicles for the implementation of individual judges' policy preferences. . . . The "congruence and proportionality" standard, like all such flabby tests, is a standing invitation to judicial arbitrariness and policy-driven decisionmaking. Worse still, it casts the Court in the role of Congress's taskmaster. Under it, the courts (and ultimately this Court) must regularly check Congress's homework to make sure that it has identified sufficient constitutional violations to make its remedy congruent and proportional. As a general matter, we are ill advised to adopt or adhere to constitutional rules that bring us into constant conflict with a coequal branch of Government. When conflict is unavoidable, we should not come to do battle with the United States Congress armed only with a test ("congruence and proportionality") that has no demonstrable basis in the text of the Constitution and cannot objectively be shown to have been met or failed. . . .
>
> I would replace "congruence and proportionality" with another test—one that provides a clear, enforceable limitation supported by the text of § 5. Section 5 grants Congress the power "to *enforce*, by appropriate legislation," the other provisions of the Fourteenth Amendment (emphasis added). . . . [O]ne does not, within any normal meaning of the term, "enforce" a prohibition by issuing a still broader prohibition directed to the same end. One does not, for example, "enforce" a 55-mile-per-hour speed limit by imposing a 45-mile-per-hour speed limit—even though that is indeed directed to the same end of automotive safety and will undoubtedly result in many fewer violations of the 55-mile-per-hour limit. . . . That is simply not what the power to enforce means—or ever meant. . . .

In short, Scalia concluded, "[n]othing in § 5 allows Congress to go *beyond* the provisions of the Fourteenth Amendment to proscribe, prevent, or 'remedy' conduct that does not *itself* violate any provision of the Fourteenth Amendment. So-called 'prophylactic legislation' is reinforcement rather than enforcement."

Finally, Scalia attempted to reconcile his approach with the precedents, or rather most of them, by excepting racial discrimination:

[A]ll of our later cases except *Hibbs* that give an expansive meaning to "enforce" in § 5 of the Fourteenth Amendment, and all of our earlier cases that even suggest such an expansive meaning in dicta, involved congressional measures that were directed exclusively against, or were used in the particular case to remedy, *racial discrimination. . . .* Giving § 5 more expansive scope with regard to measures directed against racial discrimination by the States accords to practices that are distinctively violative of the principal purpose of the Fourteenth Amendment a priority of attention that this Court envisioned from the beginning, and that has repeatedly been reflected in our opinions. . . .

Thus, principally for reasons of stare decisis, I shall henceforth apply the permissive *McCulloch* standard to congressional measures designed to remedy racial discrimination by the States. . . . I shall leave it to Congress, under constraints no tighter than those of the Necessary and Proper Clause, to decide what measures are appropriate under § 5 to prevent or remedy racial discrimination by the States. . . . I shall also not subject to "congruence and proportionality" analysis congressional action under § 5 that is not directed to racial discrimination. Rather, I shall give full effect to that action when it consists of "enforcement" of the provisions of the Fourteenth Amendment, within the broad but not unlimited meaning of that term I have described above. When it goes beyond enforcement to prophylaxis, however, I shall consider it ultra vires.

3. *TENNESSEE V. LANE*

In Tennessee v. Lane, 541 U.S. 509 (2004), the Court applied the *City of Boerne* approach to uphold Congressional abrogation legislation—in this instance with respect to Title II of the ADA, which concerns public services and programs.[a] Plaintiffs were paraplegics who complained of state courthouses without elevator facilities. One of them crawled up two flights of stairs to answer criminal charges. When he returned to the courthouse for a hearing, he refused to repeat that effort or to be carried by officers to the courtroom. In consequence, he was arrested and jailed for failing to appear.

In an opinion by Justice Stevens, the Court distinguished *Garrett* on two grounds. First, *Garrett* involved the equal protection right to like treatment for persons similarly situated, a right triggering "mere rationality" review. *Lane*, in contrast, implicated the due process right of access to the courts and the Sixth Amendment's Confrontation Clause. These claims, said the Court, were "subject to a more searching standard of judicial review" than mere rationality. Consequently, remedial legislation seeking to prevent these harms would be more closely related to an underlying constitutional violation. Of

---

[a] Specifically, the statute provides that "no qualified individual with a disability shall, by reason of such disability, be excluded from participation in or be denied the benefits of the services, programs or activities of a public entity. . . ." 42 U.S.C. § 12131.

course, many claims arising under Title II of the ADA would not involve access to the courts, but the Court thought that irrelevant to the resolution of this case.

Second, the Court found a difference in evidentiary support for Congress's action. According to the majority, most of the evidence concerning disability discrimination by governments concerned public services and public accommodations, which are governed by Title II, rather than employment, which is the subject of Title I. Congress made an explicit finding that "discrimination against individuals with disabilities persists in such critical areas as . . . access to public services." 42 U.S.C. § 12101(a)(3). The "extensive record" that underlay this finding made it "clear beyond peradventure that inadequate provision of public services and access to public facilities was an appropriate subject for prophylactic legislation" under Section 5.

Neither of these grounds persuaded the four dissenters. Justice Scalia dissented for reasons noted in the preceding Note. Speaking for himself and for Justices Kennedy and Thomas, the Chief Justice reprised the "congruence and proportionality" analysis of *City of Boerne* and found Title II wanting. In particular, Rehnquist objected to the Court's reliance on wide-ranging evidence of societal discrimination against the disabled. He thought the proper inquiry whether Congress had identified a "history and pattern" of discrimination regarding access to the courts. Besides, he argued, the mere fact of an architecturally inaccessible courthouse, at least for older buildings, did not make out a constitutional violation. As he put it, "the fact that the State may need to assist an individual to attend a hearing has no bearing on whether the individual successfully exercises his due process right to be present at the proceeding." Viewed in this way, the congressional record behind Title II revealed a "near-total lack of actual constitutional violations." Consequently, Rehnquist found that Title II could not be justified as remedial legislation but amounted to an attempt by Congress to enact substantive legislation imposing new liability on the states.

4.   QUESTIONS AND COMMENTS

Is the *City of Boerne* standard a cohesive and understandable basis for deciding these cases? Who has the best of the debate between the plurality and the dissent in *Coleman*? Does the plurality persuasively distinguish *Hibbs*?

More broadly, is the *City of Boerne* formula the right approach? Is there a separation-of-powers issue when courts examine the sufficiency of the legislative record in such detail? If so, is the answer to disallow prophylactic legislation, as Justice Scalia suggests, or to relax the Section 5 standard and defer to the judgment of Congress as Justice Breyer would have it?

5.   BIBLIOGRAPHY

The post-*Seminole Tribe* decisions have produced an enormous scholarly reaction, including an entire issue of the Notre Dame Law Review on *Alden*. See James E. Pfander, Once More Unto the Breach: Eleventh Amendment Scholarship and the Court, 75 Notre Dame L. Rev. 817 (2000) (exploring the implications of *Alden* for Eleventh Amendment scholarship); Carlos Manuel Vázquez, Eleventh Amendment Schizophrenia, 75 Notre Dame L. Rev. 859 (2000) (exploring the "schizophrenia" of forbidding private damages actions against states, yet allowing private suits against state officers); Ann Woolhandler, Old Property, New Property, and Sovereign Immunity, 75 Notre Dame L. Rev. 919 (2000) (arguing that due process requires damages remedies against states or state officers for deprivations of traditional property interests but not for "statutorily created expectations of compliance with federal law"); Vicki C. Jackson, Principle and Compromise in Constitutional Adjudication: The Eleventh Amendment and State Sovereign Immunity, 75 Notre Dame L. Rev. 953 (2000) (criticizing Woolhandler's view); Daniel J. Meltzer, State Sovereign Immunity: Five Authors in Search of a Theory, 75 Notre Dame L. Rev. 1011 (2000) (criticizing the Court's efforts to promote federalism by limiting the enforcement of valid federal laws); John Nowak, The Gang of Five & the Second Coming of an Anti-Reconstruction Supreme Court, 75 Notre Dame L. Rev. 1091 (2000) (comparing modern decisions to those that dismantled Reconstruction-era legislation); Suzanna Sherry, States Are People Too, 75 Notre Dame L. Rev. 1121 (2000) (criticizing analogies between state sovereign immunity and individuals rights); Daniel A. Farber, Pledging a New Allegiance: An Essay on Sovereignty and the New Federalism, 75 Notre Dame L. Rev. 1133 (2000) (examining *Alden* as reflecting a "new federalism" credo of state sovereignty); John V. Orth, History and the Eleventh Amendment, 75 Notre Dame L. Rev. 1147 (2000) (examining the use of history to justify various positions on state sovereign immunity); Jay Tidmarsh, A Dialogic Defense of *Alden*, 75 Notre Dame L. Rev. 1161 (2000) (defending the result in *Alden* as "within the range of permissible constitutional choice").

Other reactions to these decisions include Pamela S. Karlan, The Irony of Immunity: The Eleventh Amendment, Irreparable Injury, and Section 1983, 53 Stan. L. Rev. 1311 (2001) (pointing out that precluding money damages for violations of federal statutes creates "irreparable injury" justifying injunctive relief); Carlos Manuel Vázquez, Sovereign Immunity, Due Process, and the *Alden* Trilogy, 109 Yale L.J. 1927 (2000) (suggesting that *Florida Prepaid v. College Savings Bank* may have undermined *Alden* by interpreting due process to require remedies for intentional deprivations of (at least some forms of) liberty or property in violation of federal law); Jonathan R. Siegel, Congress's Power to Authorize Suits against States, 68 Geo. Wash. L. Rev. 44 (1999) (arguing that Congress could avoid these problems by authorizing the federal government to espouse claims by private parties in suits against states); Ann Althouse, Vanguard States, Laggard States: Federalism and Constitutional Rights, 152 U. Pa. L. Rev. 1745 (2004) (analyzing recent decisions in terms of a concern for the behavior of "laggard states" and the impact of such perceptions on judicial views of federalism); Steven G. Gey, The Myth of State Sovereignty, 63 Ohio St. L.J. 1601 (2002) (asking "whether concepts of state sovereignty used to deny the federal government access to some enforcement mechanisms against lawbreaking states make sense in a context in which the Court itself repeatedly stresses that 'sovereign' states are not allowed to disobey federal law."); Michael T.

Gibson, Congressional Authority to Induce Waivers of State Sovereign Immunity: The Conditional Spending Power (And Beyond), 29 Hastings Const. L.Q. 439 (2002) (arguing that Congress has ample means to coerce state waiver of Eleventh Amendment immunity); Marcia L. McCormick, Federalism Re-Constructed: The Eleventh Amendment's Illogical Impact on Congress's Power, 37 Ind. L. Rev. 345 (2004) (arguing that the Court's decisions impose dangerous and unwarranted limitations on Congress's power to remedy civil rights violations by the states); Rebecca E. Zietlow, Federalism's Paradox: The Spending Power and Waiver of Sovereign Immunity, 37 Wake Forest L. Rev. 141 (2002) (examining the Spending Power as a means of Congressional inducement of sovereign immunity waiver).

These decisions continue to generate commentary. For critical reactions, see Erwin Chemerinsky, The Hypocrisy of *Alden v. Maine*: Judicial Review, Sovereign Immunity, and the Rehnquist Court, 33 Loy. L. Rev. 1283 (2000) (condemning the Court's preference for state power over individual rights); Michael Wells, Available State Remedies and the Fourteenth Amendment: Comments on *Florida Prepaid v. College Savings Bank*, 33 Loy. L. Rev. 1665 (2000) (asking how one determines whether state remedies for violations of federal rights are "available and adequate"); Daniel J. Meltzer, Overcoming Immunity: The Case of Federal Regulation of Intellectual Property, 53 Stan. L. Rev. 1331 (2001) (outlining strategies for enforcement of federal intellectual property statutes in light of Eleventh Amendment decisions); Vicki C. Jackson, Holistic Interpretation: *Fitzpatrick v. Bitzer* and Our Bifurcated Constitution, 53 Stan. L. Rev. 1259 (2001) (suggesting that the Fourteenth Amendment should be construed to have broadened the original grants of federal legislative power under Article I, with consequent expansion of Congress's ability to override state sovereign immunity); Michael E. Solimine, Formalism, Pragmatism, and the Conservative Critique of the Eleventh Amendment, 101 Mich. L. Rev. 1463 (2003) (wide-ranging review essay); Louise Weinberg, Of Sovereignty and Union: The Legends of *Alden*, 76 Notre Dame L. Rev. 1113 (2001) (criticizing *Alden* and related decisions as intellectually unsupportable and misguided).

For rare expressions of qualified support for the Court's decisions, see Ernest A. Young, State Sovereign Immunity and the Future of Federalism, 1999 Sup. Ct. Rev. 1 (offering "a critique of the Court's state sovereign immunity decisions from a perspective that is highly sympathetic to states' rights and interests"); Roderick M. Hills, Jr., The Eleventh Amendment as Curb on Bureaucratic Power, 53 Stan. L. Rev. 1225 (2001) (suggesting that a ban on damages liability and a consequent reliance on injunctions might have the salutary effect of allowing state legislatures to exert better control over state agencies).

Finally, for an imaginative attempt to find a middle ground on these questions, see James E. Pfander and Jessica Dwinell, A Declaratory Theory of State Accountability, 102 Va. L. Rev. 153 (2016). They accept (not endorse) restrictive decisions, but propose that the federal courts should remain open for declaratory relief against state officials. Relief beyond a declaration of rights would depend on current law, which would generally allow injunctive relief but might preclude access to the state's treasury.

SECTION 3. CONSTITUTIONALLY REQUIRED REMEDIES IN STATE COURT

McKesson Corp. v. Division of Alcoholic Beverages and Tobacco

Supreme Court of the United States, 1990.
496 U.S. 18.

■ JUSTICE BRENNAN delivered the opinion of the Court.

Petitioner McKesson Corporation brought this action in Florida state court, alleging that Florida's liquor excise tax violated the Commerce Clause of the United States Constitution. The Florida Supreme Court agreed with petitioner that the tax scheme unconstitutionally discriminated against interstate commerce because it provided preferences for distributors of certain local products. Although the court enjoined the state from giving effect to those preferences in the future, the court also refused to provide petitioner a refund or any other form of relief for taxes it had already paid.

Our precedents establish that if a state penalizes taxpayers for failure to remit their taxes in timely fashion, thus requiring them to pay first and obtain review of the tax's validity later in a refund action, the Due Process Clause requires the state to afford taxpayers a meaningful opportunity to secure postpayment relief for taxes already paid pursuant to a tax scheme ultimately found unconstitutional. We therefore agree with petitioner that the state court's decision denying such relief must be reversed.

I

For several decades until 1985, Florida's liquor excise tax scheme, which imposes taxes on manufacturers, distributors, and in some cases vendors of alcoholic beverages, provided for preferential treatment of beverages that were manufactured from certain "Florida-grown" citrus and other agricultural crops and then bottled in-state. After this Court held in Bacchus Imports, Ltd. v. Dias, 468 U.S. 263 (1984), that a similar preference scheme employed by the state of Hawaii violated the Commerce Clause (because it had both the purpose and effect of discriminating in favor of local products), the Florida Legislature revised its excise tax scheme and enacted the statutory provisions at issue in this litigation. See Fla.Stat. §§ 564.06, 565.12 (1985) (hereafter Liquor Tax). The legislature deleted the previous express preferences for "Florida-grown" products and replaced them with special rate reductions for certain specified citrus, grape, and sugarcane products, all of which are commonly grown in Florida and used in alcoholic beverages produced there.

Petitioner McKesson Corporation is a licensed wholesale distributor of alcoholic beverages whose products did not qualify for the rate reductions. Petitioner paid the applicable taxes every month as required after the revised Liquor Tax went into effect, but in June 1986, petitioner filed an application with the Florida Office of the Comptroller seeking a refund on the ground that the tax scheme was unlawful. In September, after the Comptroller denied its application, petitioner (along with other distributors not present here) brought suit in Florida state court against respondents Division of Alcoholic Beverages and Tobacco, Department of Business Regulation, and Officer of the Comptroller. Petitioner challenged the constitutionality of the tax under the Commerce Clause as well as under various other provisions of the United States and Florida Constitutions, and petitioner sought both declaratory and injunctive relief against the continued enforcement of the discriminatory tax scheme. Pursuant to Florida's "Repayment of Funds" statute, which provides for a refund of "[a]n overpayment of any tax, license or account due" and "[a]ny payment made into the state Treasury in error" and in apparent compliance with the statutory requisites for preserving a claim thereunder, petitioner also sought a refund in the amount of the excess taxes it had paid as a result of its disfavored treatment.

On petitioner's motion for partial summary judgment, the Florida trial court invalidated the discriminatory tax scheme on Commerce Clause grounds because the revised "legislation failed to surmount the constitutional violations addressed in *Bacchus*." The trial court enjoined future enforcement of the preferential rate reductions, leaving all distributors subject to the Liquor Tax's nonpreferred rates. The court, however, declined to order a refund or any other form of relief for the taxes previously paid and timely challenged under the discriminatory scheme. The court's order of prospective relief was stayed pending respondents' appeal of the Commerce Clause ruling to the Florida Supreme Court.

Petitioner McKesson cross-appealed the trial court's ruling, arguing that as a matter of both federal and state law it was entitled at least to "a refund of the difference between the disfavored product's tax rate and the favored product's tax rate." The state Supreme Court affirmed the trial court's ruling that the Liquor Tax unconstitutionally discriminated against interstate commerce and upheld the trial court's order that the preferential rate reductions be given no future operative effect. The Supreme Court also affirmed the trial court's refusal to order a tax refund, declaring that "the prospective nature of the rulings below was proper in light of the equitable considerations present in this case." The court noted that the Division of Alcoholic Beverages and Tobacco had collected the liquor tax in "good faith reliance on a presumptively valid statute." Moreover, the court suggested that, "if given a refund, [petitioner] would in all probability receive a windfall, since the cost of the tax has likely been passed on to [its] customers."

After petitioner's request for rehearing was denied, petitioner filed a petition for writ of certiorari in this Court, presenting the question whether federal law entitles it to a partial tax refund. We granted the petition. . . .

II

Respondents first ask us to hold that, though the Florida courts accepted jurisdiction over this suit which sought monetary relief from various state entities, the Eleventh Amendment nevertheless precludes our exercise of appellate jurisdiction in this case. We reject respondents' suggestion. Almost 170 years ago, Chief Justice Marshall, writing for the Court, rejected a state's Eleventh Amendment challenge to this Court's power on writ of error to review the judgment of a state court involving an issue of federal law. See Cohens v. Virginia, 19 U.S. (6 Wheat.) 264, 412 (1821). Although *Cohens* involved a proceeding commenced in the first instance by the state itself against a citizen, such that the Court's holding might be read as limited to that circumstance, the decision has long been understood as supporting a broader proposition: "[I]t was long ago settled that a writ of error to review the final judgment of a state court, even when a state is a formal party [defendant] and is successful in the inferior court, is not a suit within the meaning of the amendment." General Oil Co. v. Crain, 209 U.S. 211, 233 (1908) (Harlan, J., concurring). Our consistent practice since *Cohens* confirms this broader understanding. . . . We recognize what has long been implicit in our consistent practice and uniformly endorsed in our cases: the Eleventh Amendment does not constrain the appellate jurisdiction of the Supreme Court over cases arising from state courts. Accordingly, we turn to the merits of petitioner's claim.

III

It is undisputed that the Florida Supreme Court, after holding that the Liquor Tax unconstitutionally discriminated against interstate commerce because of its preferences for liquor made from "crops which Florida is adapted to growing" acted correctly in awarding petitioner declaratory and injunctive relief against continued enforcement of the discriminatory provisions. The question before us is whether prospective relief, by itself, exhausts the requirements of federal law. The answer is no: if a state places a taxpayer under duress promptly to pay a tax when due and relegates him to a postpayment refund action in which he can challenge the tax's legality, the Due Process Clause of the Fourteenth Amendment obligates the state to provide meaningful backward-looking relief to rectify any unconstitutional deprivation.

A

We have not had occasion in recent years to explain the scope of a state's obligation to provide retrospective relief as part of its postdeprivation procedure in cases such as this.[16] Our approach today, however, is rooted firmly in precedent dating back to at least early this century. [Justice Brennan's description of the precedents is omitted.]

B

These cases demonstrate the traditional legal analysis appropriate for determining Florida's constitutional duty to provide relief to petitioner McKesson for its payment of an unlawful tax. Because exaction of a tax constitutes a deprivation of property, the state must provide procedural safeguards against unlawful exactions in order to satisfy the commands of the Due Process Clause. The state may choose to provide a form of "predeprivation process," for example, by authorizing taxpayers to bring suit to enjoin imposition of a tax prior to its payment, or by allowing taxpayers to withhold payment and then interpose their objections as defenses in a tax enforcement proceeding initiated by the state. However, whereas "[w]e have described 'the root requirement' of the Due Process Clause as being 'that an individual be given an opportunity for a hearing before he is deprived of any significant property interest,' " Cleveland Board of Education v. Loudermill, 470 U.S. 532, 542 (1985), it is well established that a state need not provide predeprivation process for the exaction of taxes. Allowing taxpayers to litigate their tax liabilities prior to payment might threaten a government's financial security, both by creating unpredictable interim revenue shortfalls against which the state cannot easily prepare, and by making the ultimate collection of validly imposed taxes more difficult. To protect government's exceedingly strong interest in financial stability in this context, we have long held that a state may employ various financial sanctions and summary remedies such as distress sales in order to encourage taxpayers to make timely payments prior to resolution of any dispute over the validity of the tax assessment.

Florida has availed itself of this approach, establishing various sanctions and summary remedies designed so that liquor distributors tender tax payments before their objections are entertained and resolved. As a result, Florida does not purport to provide taxpayers like petitioner with a meaningful opportunity to withhold payment and to obtain a predeprivation determination of the tax assessment's validity;[21] rather, Florida

---

[16] In the recent past, after invalidating a state tax scheme on Commerce Clause grounds, we have left state courts with the initial duty upon remand of crafting appropriate relief in accord with both federal and state law.

[21] We have long held that, when a tax is paid in order to avoid financial sanctions or a seizure of real or personal property, the tax is paid under "duress" in the sense that the state has not provided a fair and meaningful predeprivation procedure. . . . In contrast, if a state chooses not to secure payments under duress and instead offers a meaningful opportunity for taxpayers to withhold contested tax assessments and to challenge their validity in a predeprivation hearing, payments tendered may be deemed "voluntary." The availability of a predepriva-

requires taxpayers to raise their objections to the tax in a postdeprivation refund action. To satisfy the requirements of the Due Process Clause, therefore, in this refund action the state must provide taxpayers with, not only a fair opportunity to challenge the accuracy and legal validity of their tax obligation, but also a "clear and certain remedy" for any erroneous or unlawful tax collection to ensure that the opportunity to contest the tax is a meaningful one.

Had the Florida courts declared the Liquor Tax invalid either because (other than its discriminatory nature) it was beyond the state's power to impose . . . or because the taxpayers were absolutely immune from the tax . . . , no corrective action by the state could cure the invalidity of the tax during the contested tax period. The state would have had no choice but to "undo" the unlawful deprivation by refunding the tax previously paid under duress, because allowing the state to "collect these unlawful taxes by coercive means and not incur any obligation to pay them back . . . would be in contravention of the Fourteenth Amendment." Ward v. Board of County Commissioners of Love County, Oklahoma, 253 U.S. 17, 24 (1920).

Here, however, the Florida courts did not invalidate the Liquor Tax in its entirety; rather, they declared the tax scheme unconstitutional only insofar as it operated in a manner that discriminated against interstate commerce. The state may, of course, choose to erase the property deprivation itself by providing petitioner with a full refund of its tax payments. But . . . a state found to have imposed an impermissibly discriminatory tax retains flexibility in responding to this determination. Florida may reformulate and enforce the Liquor Tax during the contested tax period in any way that treats petitioner and its competitors in a manner consistent with the dictates of the Commerce Clause. Having done so, the state may retain the tax appropriately levied upon petitioner pursuant to this reformulated scheme because this retention would deprive petitioner of its property pursuant to a tax scheme that is valid under the Commerce Clause. In the end, the state's postdeprivation procedure would provide petitioner with all of the process it is due: an opportunity to contest the validity of the tax and a "clear and certain remedy" designed to render the opportunity meaningful by preventing any permanent unlawful deprivation of property.

More specifically, the state may cure the invalidity of the Liquor Tax by refunding to petitioner the difference between the tax it paid and the tax it would have been assessed were it extended the same rate reductions that its competitors actually received. . . . Alternatively, to the extent consistent with other constitutional restrictions, the state may assess and collect back taxes from petitioner's competitors who benefitted from the rate reductions during the contested tax period, calibrating the

---

tion hearing constitutes a procedural safeguard against unlawful deprivations sufficient by itself to satisfy the Due Process Clause, and taxpayers cannot complain if they fail to avail themselves of this procedure.

retroactive assessment to create in hindsight a nondiscriminatory scheme. . . .[23] Finally, a combination of a partial refund to petitioner and a partial retroactive assessment of tax increases on favored competitors, so long as the resultant tax actually assessed during the contested tax period reflects a scheme that does not discriminate against interstate commerce, would render petitioner's resultant deprivation lawful and therefore satisfy the Due Process Clause's requirement of a fully adequate postdeprivation procedure. . . .

C

The Florida Supreme Court cites two "equitable considerations" as grounds for providing petitioner only prospective relief, but neither is sufficient to override the constitutional requirement that Florida provide retrospective relief as part of its postdeprivation procedure. The Florida court first mentions that "the tax preference scheme [was] implemented by the [Division of Alcoholic Beverages and Tobacco] in good faith reliance on a presumptively valid statute." This observation bespeaks a concern that a state's obligation to provide refunds for what later turns out to be an unconstitutional tax would undermine the state's ability to engage in sound fiscal planning. However, leaving aside the fact that the state might avoid any such disruption by choosing (consistent with constitutional limitations) to collect back taxes from favored distributors rather than to offer refunds, we do not find this concern weighty in these circumstances. A state's freedom to impose various procedural requirements on actions for postdeprivation relief sufficiently meets this concern with respect to future cases. The state might, for example, provide by statute that refunds will be available only to those taxpayers paying under protest or providing some other timely notice of complaint; execute any refunds on a reasonable installment basis; enforce relatively short statutes of limitation applicable to such actions; refrain from collecting taxes pursuant to a scheme that has been declared invalid by a court or other competent tribunal pending further review of such declaration on appeal; and/or place challenged tax payments into an escrow account or employ other accounting devices such that the state can predict with greater accuracy the availability of undisputed treasury funds. The state's ability in the future to invoke such procedural protections suffices

---

[23] We previously have held that the retroactive assessment of a tax increase does not necessarily deny due process to those whose taxes are increased, though beyond some temporal point the retroactive imposition of a significant tax burden may be "so harsh and oppressive as to transgress the constitutional limitation," depending on "the nature of the tax and the circumstances in which it is laid." Welch v. Henry, 305 U.S. 134, 147 (1938). . . .

Because we do not know whether the state will choose in this case to assess and collect back taxes from previously favored distributors, we need not decide whether this choice would violate due process by unduly interfering with settled expectations.

Should the state choose this remedial alternative, the state's effort to collect back taxes from previously favored distributors may not be perfectly successful. Some of these distributors, for example, may no longer be in business. But a good-faith effort to administer and enforce such a retroactive assessment likely would constitute adequate relief, to the same extent that a tax scheme would not violate the Commerce Clause merely because tax collectors inadvertently missed a few in-state taxpayers.

to secure the state's interest in stable fiscal planning when weighed against its constitutional obligation to provide relief for an unlawful tax.

And in the present case, Florida's failure to avail itself of certain of these methods of self-protection weakens any "equitable" justification for avoiding its constitutional obligation to provide relief. Moreover, even were we to assume that the state's reliance on a "presumptively valid statute" was a relevant consideration to Florida's obligation to provide relief for its unconstitutional deprivation of property, we would disagree with the Florida court's characterization of the Liquor Tax as such a statute. The Liquor Tax reflected only cosmetic changes from the prior version of the tax scheme that itself was virtually identical to the Hawaii scheme invalidated in Bacchus Imports, Ltd. v. Dias, 468 U.S. 263 (1984). The state can hardly claim surprise at the Florida courts' invalidation of the scheme.

The Florida Supreme Court also speculated that "if given a refund, [petitioner] would in all probability receive a windfall, since the cost of the tax has likely been passed on to [its] customers." The court's premise seems to be that the state, faced with an obligation to cure its discrimination during the contested tax period and choosing to meet that obligation through a refund, could legitimately choose to avoid generating a "windfall" for petitioner by refunding only that portion of the tax payment not "passed on" to customers (or even suppliers). Even were we to accept this premise, the state could not refuse to provide a refund based on sheer speculation that a "pass-on" occurred. . . . In any event, however, we reject respondents' premise that "equitable considerations" justify a state's attempt to avoid bestowing this so-called "windfall" when redressing a tax that is unconstitutional because discriminatory. [P]etitioner does not challenge here a tax assessment that merely exceeded the amount authorized by statute; petitioner's complaint was that the Florida tax scheme unconstitutionally discriminated against interstate commerce. The tax injured petitioner not only because it left petitioner poorer in an absolute sense than before (a problem that might be rectified to the extent petitioner passed on the economic incidence of the tax to others), but also because it placed petitioner at a relative disadvantage in the marketplace vis-a-vis competitors distributing preferred local products. To whatever extent petitioner succeeded in passing on the economic incidence of the tax through higher prices to its customers, it most likely lost sales to the favored distributors or else incurred other costs (e.g., for advertising) in an effort to maintain its market share. The state cannot persuasively claim that "equity" entitles it to retain tax moneys taken unlawfully from petitioner due to its pass-on of the tax where the pass-on itself furthers the very competitive disadvantage constituting the Commerce Clause violation that rendered the deprivation unlawful in the first place. We thus reject respondents' reliance on a pass-on defense in this context.[34]

D

Respondents assert that requiring the state to rectify its unconstitutional discrimination during the contested tax period "would plainly cause serious economic and administrative dislocation for the state." We agree that, within our due process jurisprudence, state interests traditionally have and may play some role in shaping the contours of the relief that the state must provide to illegally or erroneously deprived taxpayers, just as such interests play a role in shaping the procedural safeguards that the state must provide in order to ensure the accuracy of the initial determination of illegality or error. See generally Mathews v. Eldridge, 424 U.S. 319, 347–48 (1976). We have already noted that states have a legitimate interest in sound fiscal planning and that this interest is sufficiently weighty to allow states to withhold predeprivation relief for allegedly unlawful tax assessments, providing postdeprivation relief only. But even if a state chooses to provide partial refunds as a means of curing the unlawful discrimination (as opposed to increasing the tax assessment of those previously favored), the state's interest in financial stability does not justify a refusal to provide relief. As noted earlier, the state here does not and cannot claim that the Florida courts' invalidation of the Liquor Tax was a surprise, and even after the trial court found a Commerce Clause violation the state failed to take reasonable precautions to reduce its ultimate exposure for the unconstitutional tax. And in the future, states may avail themselves of a variety of procedural protections against any disruptive effects of a tax scheme's invalidation, such as providing by statute that refunds will be available to only those taxpayers paying under protest, or enforcing relatively short statutes of limitation applicable to refund actions. Such procedural measures would sufficiently protect states' fiscal security when weighed against their obligation to provide meaningful relief for their unconstitutional taxation.

Respondents also observe that the state's choice of relief may entail various administrative costs (apart from the "cost" of any refund itself[35]). Cf. Mathews, 424 U.S. at 348 ("[T]he government's interest . . . in conserving scarce fiscal and administrative resources is a factor that must be weighed" when determining precise contours of process due). The state

---

[34] Respondents suggest that a pass-on defense may nevertheless be invoked as a matter of state law. While they concede that the state waived any sovereign immunity from suit through [its] authorization of a state-court refund action, they contend that this waiver extends only to refunds sought where the taxpayer has borne the actual economic burden of the tax. We need not consider the import of this contention, however, because respondents misdescribe state law. In this case, the Florida Supreme Court characterized its concern about petitioner receiving a "windfall" due to the alleged pass-on of its tax burden as only an "equitable consideration," not a state-law prohibition on relief. . . .

[35] We reject respondents' intimation that the cost of any refund considered by the state might justify a decision to withhold it. Just as a state may not object to an otherwise available remedy providing for the return of real property unlawfully taken or criminal fines unlawfully imposed simply because it finds the property or moneys useful, so also Florida cannot object to a refund here just because it has other ideas about how to spend the funds.

may, of course, consider such costs when choosing between the various avenues of relief open to it. Because the Florida Supreme Court did not recognize in its refund proceeding the state's obligation under the Due Process Clause to rectify the invalidity of its deprivation of petitioner's property, the court did not consider how any administrative costs might influence the selection and fine-tuning of the relief afforded petitioner. We leave this to the state court on remand.

IV

When a state penalizes taxpayers for failure to remit their taxes in timely fashion, thus requiring them to pay first before obtaining review of the tax's validity, federal due process principles long recognized by our cases require the state's postdeprivation procedure to provide a "clear and certain remedy" for the deprivation of tax moneys in an unconstitutional manner. In this case, Florida may satisfy this obligation through any form of relief, ranging from a refund of the excess taxes paid by petitioner to an offsetting charge to previously favored distributors, that will cure any unconstitutional discrimination against interstate commerce during the contested tax period. The state is free to choose which form of relief it will provide, so long as that relief satisfies the minimum federal requirements we have outlined. The judgment of the Florida Supreme Court is reversed, and the case is remanded for further proceedings not inconsistent with this opinion.

It is so ordered.

NOTES ON THE DUTY OF STATE COURTS TO REMEDY CONSTITUTIONAL VIOLATIONS

1. GENERAL OIL V. CRAIN

General Oil v. Crain, 209 U.S. 211 (1908), is a well-known early case on the obligation of state courts to remedy constitutional violations. Crain was an oil inspector employed by the state of Tennessee. His job was to inspect stored oil and to collect a fee of 25 cents per barrel. General Oil objected to paying the fee on oil that was temporarily stored in Tennessee en route to other states for sale, taking the position that taxation of goods in transit would violate the Commerce Clause. General Oil sued in state court to enjoin collection of the fees. The Tennessee trial court entered an injunction covering part of the oil in controversy, but on appeal the Tennessee Supreme Court held that the trial court did not have jurisdiction because of a state statute barring injunctions against state officials in such circumstances.

Crain was decided on the same day as *Ex parte Young*. In *Crain,* the Court seemed to say that the equitable cause of action available in federal court under *Ex parte Young* could also be asserted in state court—irrespective, it appeared, of jurisdictional limitations imposed by the state on its own courts. Justice Harlan disagreed:

The oil company seeks a reversal of the decree of the state court, contending that it was denied a right arising under the Commerce Clause of the Constitution. But back of any question of that kind was the question before the Supreme Court of Tennessee whether the inferior state court, under the law of its organization, that is, under the law of Tennessee, could entertain jurisdiction of the suit. The question, we have seen, was determined adversely to jurisdiction. That certainly is a state, not a federal question. Surely, Tennessee has the right to say of what class of suits its own courts may take cognizance, and it was peculiarly the function of the Supreme Court of Tennessee to determine such a question. . . . It seems to me that this Court, accepting the decision of the highest court of Tennessee, as to the meaning of the Tennessee statute in question, as I think it must, has no alternative but to affirm the judgment, on the ground simply that the ground upon which it is placed is broad enough to support the judgment without any reference to any question raised or discussed [concerning the Commerce Clause].

By contrast, the opinion of the Court said:

Necessarily to give adequate protection to constitutional rights a distinction must be made between valid and invalid state laws, as determining the character of the suit against state officers. And the suit at bar illustrates the necessity. If a suit against state officers is precluded in the national courts by the Eleventh Amendment to the Constitution, and may be forbidden by a state to its courts, as it is contended in the case at bar that it may be, without power of review by this Court, it must be evident that an easy way is open to prevent the enforcement of many provisions of the Constitution, and the Fourteenth Amendment, which is directed at state action, could be nullified as to much of its operation. And it will not do to say that the argument is drawn from extremes. Constitutional provisions are based on the possibility of extremes. There need not, however, be imagination of extremes, if by extremes be meant a deliberate purpose to prevent the assertion of constitutional rights. . . .

It being then the right of a party to be protected against a law which violates a constitutional right, whether by its terms or the manner of its enforcement, it is manifest that a decision which denies such protection gives effect to the law, and the decision is reviewable by this court.

On the merits, the Court held that the Tennessee inspection law did not violate the Commerce Clause. Accordingly, the judgment of the Tennessee Supreme Court was affirmed.

2.   WARD V. LOVE COUNTY

One of the tax cases discussed by Justice Brennan in the omitted portions of the *McKesson* opinion was Ward v. Board of County Commissioners of Love County, Oklahoma, 253 U.S. 17 (1920). Members of the Choctaw Indian Tribe held lands in Oklahoma allotted to them by act of Congress. The statute provided that the lands were exempt from local taxation, but Congress later repealed the exemption. Love County then taxed the lands. A number of suits were filed to enjoin collection of the taxes, resulting in a decision by the Supreme Court that the original statutory exemption was a vested property right protected against legislative repeal by the Fifth Amendment.

In the meantime, Love County collected taxes in the amount of $7,823.35 from Ward and 66 other Indians by threatening to impose a penalty of 18 per cent and to sell their land unless the taxes were paid. After the Supreme Court decision upholding their right not to be taxed, Ward and the others filed suit in state court to get their money back. Relief was ultimately denied by the Oklahoma Supreme Court on two grounds:

> [That court] held, first, that the taxes were not collected by coercive means, but were paid voluntarily, and could not be recovered back as there was no statutory authority therefor; and, secondly, that there was no statute making the county liable for taxes collected and then paid over to the state and municipal bodies other than the county—which it was assumed was true of a portion of these taxes—and that the petition did not show how much of the taxes was retained by the county, or how much paid over to the state and other municipal bodies, and therefore it could not be the basis of any judgment against the county.

The Supreme Court unanimously reversed:

> We accept so much of the [Oklahoma] Supreme Court's decision as held that, if the payment was voluntary, the moneys could not be recovered back in the absence of a permissive statute, and that there was no such statute. But we are unable to accept its decision in other respects.
>
> The right to the exemption was a federal right, and was specially set up and claimed as such in the petition. Whether the right was denied, or not given due recognition, by the [Oklahoma] Supreme Court is a question as to which the claimants were entitled to invoke our judgment, and this they have done in the appropriate way. It therefore is within our province to inquire not only whether the right was denied in express terms, but also whether it was denied in substance and effect, as by putting forward nonfederal grounds of decision that were without any fair or substantial support. Of course, if nonfederal grounds, plainly untenable, may be thus put forward successfully, our power to review easily may be avoided. With this qualification, it is true that a judgment of a state court, which is put on independent nonfederal grounds broad enough to sustain it, cannot be reviewed by us. But the qualification is a material one and cannot be disregarded without neglecting

or renouncing a jurisdiction conferred by law and designed to protect and maintain the supremacy of the Constitution and the laws made in pursuance thereof.

The facts set forth in the petition, all of which were admitted by the demurrer whereon the county elected to stand, make it plain, as we think, that the finding or decision that the taxes were paid voluntarily was without any fair or substantial support. The claimants were Indians just emerging from a state of dependency and wardship. Through the pending suits and otherwise they were objecting and protesting that the taxation of their lands was forbidden by a law of Congress. But, notwithstanding this, the county demanded that the taxes be paid, and by threatening to sell the lands of these claimants and actually selling other lands similarly situated made it appear to the claimants that they must choose between paying the taxes and losing their lands. To prevent a sale and to avoid the imposition of a penalty of 18 per cent they yielded to the county's demand and paid the taxes, protesting and objecting at the time that the same were illegal. The moneys thus collected were obtained by coercive means—by compulsion. The county and its officers reasonably could not have regarded it otherwise; much less the Indian claimants.

It followed that the Indians were entitled to a refund:

As the payment was not voluntary, but made under compulsion, no statutory authority was essential to enable or require the county to refund the money. It is a well-settled rule that "money got through imposition" may be recovered back; and, as this court has said on several occasions, "the obligation to do justice rests upon all persons, natural and artificial, and if a county obtains the money or property of others without authority, the law, independent of any statute, will compel restitution or compensation." Marsh v. Fulton County, 77 U.S. (10 Wall.) 676, 684 (1870). To say that the county could collect these unlawful taxes by coercive means and not incur any obligation to pay them back is nothing short of saying that it could take or appropriate the property of these Indian allottees arbitrarily and without due process of law. Of course this would be in contravention of the Fourteenth Amendment, which binds the county as an agency of the state.

If it be true, as the [state] Supreme Court assumed, that a portion of the taxes was paid over, after collection, to the state and other municipal bodies, we regard it as certain that this did not alter the county's liability to the claimants. The county had no right to collect the money, and it took the same with notice that the rights of all who were to share in the taxes were disputed by these claimants and were being contested in the pending suits. In these circumstances it could not lessen its liability by paying over a portion of the money to others whose rights it knew were disputed and were no better than its own. In legal contemplation it received the money for the use and benefit of the claimants and should respond to them accordingly.

3. *REICH V. COLLINS*

Reich v. Collins, 513 U.S. 106 (1994), is a sequel to *McKesson*. Reich, a federal retiree, filed for a refund of taxes invalidated by Davis v. Michigan Dept. of Treasury, 489 U.S. 803 (1989). The basis for his suit was a Georgia statute that provided: "A taxpayer shall be refunded any and all taxes or fees which are determined to have been erroneously or illegally assessed and collected from him under the laws of this state, whether paid voluntarily or involuntarily." Ga. Code Ann. § 48–2–35(a) (Supp. 1994). The Georgia Supreme Court denied relief under this statute because it found that Reich had "ample" predeprivation remedies that he did not pursue. Certiorari was granted "to consider whether it was proper for the Georgia Supreme Court to deny Reich relief on the basis of Georgia's predeprivation remedies."

In an unanimous opinion by Justice O'Connor, the Court said:

> In a long line of cases, this Court has established that due process requires a "clear and certain" remedy for taxes collected in violation of federal law. A state has the flexibility to provide that remedy before the disputed taxes are paid (predeprivation), after they are paid (postdeprivation), or both. But what it may not do, and what Georgia did here, is hold out what plainly appears to be a "clear and certain" postdeprivation remedy and then declare, only after the disputed taxes have been paid, that no such remedy exists.

The Court observed that prior cases established that " 'a denial by a state court of a recovery of taxes exacted in violation of the laws or Constitution of the United States by compulsion is itself in contravention of the Fourteenth Amendment,' the sovereign immunity states traditionally enjoy in their own courts notwithstanding." As an aside, it added that "[w]e should note that the sovereign immunity states enjoy in federal court, under the Eleventh Amendment, does generally bar tax refund claims from being brought in that forum. See Ford Motor Co. v. Department of Treasury of Ind., 323 U.S. 459 (1945)." The Court then analyzed the Georgia situation:

> The Georgia Supreme Court is no doubt right that, under *McKesson*, Georgia has the flexibility to maintain an exclusively predeprivation remedial scheme, so long as that scheme is "clear and certain." Due process, we should add, also allows the state to maintain an exclusively postdeprivation regime, see, e.g., Bob Jones Univ. v. Simon, 416 U.S. 725, 746–48 (1974), or a hybrid regime. A state is free as well to reconfigure its remedial scheme over time, to fit its changing needs. Such choices are generally a matter only of state law.

> But what a state may *not* do, and what Georgia did here, is to reconfigure its scheme, unfairly, in *mid-course*—to "bait and switch," as some have described it. Specifically, in the mid-1980s, Georgia held out what plainly appeared to be a "clear and certain" postdeprivation remedy, in the form of its tax refund statute, and

then declared, only after Reich and others had paid the disputed taxes, that no such remedy exists. In this regard, the Georgia Supreme Court's reliance on Georgia's predeprivation procedures was entirely beside the point (and thus error), because even assuming the constitutional adequacy of these procedures—an issue on which we express no view—no reasonable taxpayer would have thought that they represented, in light of the apparent applicability of the refund statute, the exclusive remedy for unlawful taxes.

Nor can there be any question that . . . Georgia did appear to hold out a "clear and certain" postdeprivation remedy. To recall, the Georgia refund statute says that the State "*shall*" refund "*any and all* taxes or fees which are determined to have been erroneously or *illegally assessed* and collected from [a taxpayer] under the laws of this state, whether paid voluntarily or involuntarily." In our view, the average taxpayer reading this language would think it obvious that state taxes assessed in violation of federal law are "illegally assessed" taxes. . . . Respondents, moreover, do not point to any Georgia Supreme Court cases . . . that put any limiting construction on the statute's sweeping language; indeed, the cases we have found are all entirely consistent with that language's apparent breadth. [Citations omitted.] Even apart from the statute and the cases, we find it significant that, for obvious reasons, states ordinarily prefer that taxpayers pursue only postdeprivation remedies, i.e., that taxpayers "pay first, litigate later." This preference is significant in that it would seem especially unfair to penalize taxpayers who may have ignored the possibility of pursuing predeprivation remedies out of respect for that preference.

The Court with an analogy to NAACP v. Alabama ex rel. Patterson, 357 U.S. 449 (1958), where the Court ignored an Alabama procedural rule advanced as an "adequate and independent state ground" to bar review of a federal constitutional claim. In effect, the Court held in *Patterson*, Alabama had changed its procedures in mid-stream in order to preclude review of the federal claim: "Novelty in procedural requirements," the Court said, "cannot be permitted to thwart review in this Court applied for by those who, in justified reliance upon prior decisions, seek vindication in state courts of their federal constitutional rights."

4. QUESTIONS AND COMMENTS ON THE DUTY OF STATE COURTS TO REMEDY CONSTITUTIONAL VIOLATIONS

The Supreme Court has been notably imprecise about the source of the plaintiff's claim in cases such as *McKesson, Crain,* and *Ward.* In *Ward,* for example, the Court said that the county had to provide a refund because "the law" required restitution or compensation. What law? Since *Ward* was decided before *Erie,* the Court may not have focused on this question. Today, however, it would be necessary to ask whether the plaintiffs' cause of action in *Ward* found its source in state or federal law. If the answer was federal law, one would ask further whether it came from the Constitution, from an act of Congress, or from a common-law obligation implied by the Supreme

Court. If the cause of action did not stem directly from federal law, the question then would be whether it had previously existed in voluntarily adopted state law or whether the state in effect was required by the Supreme Court to create a state-law remedy where none existed before. Is there a difference between creating a federal cause of action and requiring the state to create one? If so, why might the Court do one or the other? Which was done in *Ward*?

McKesson contains the same ambiguity. Parts of the Court's opinion seem based on the premise that Florida chose to provide a refund mechanism and to waive sovereign immunity in refund suits. See especially footnote 34 of the Court's opinion. Contrast Justice O'Connor's comments for the plurality in American Trucking Associations, Inc. v. Smith, 496 U.S. 167 (1990). She said that "[o]ur decision in *McKesson* indicates that federal law sets certain minimum requirements that states must meet but may exceed in providing appropriate relief" and that *McKesson* held "that a ruling that a tax is unconstitutionally discriminatory under the Commerce Clause places substantial obligations on the states to provide relief." What would the Court do if the state courts held that there was no available remedy under state law?

Is the potential availability of suit in federal court relevant to the *McKesson-Crain-Ward* problem? It seems clear that *McKesson*-type suits would be barred by the Eleventh Amendment if brought in federal court.[a] But the Eleventh Amendment would not bar federal court actions analogous to *Crain* (recall *Ex parte Young*) or *Ward* (remember that the Eleventh Amendment does not protect local governments). Which way do these observations point? Does the Eleventh Amendment make it *more* imperative that there be a mandatory avenue of relief in state court in a *McKesson* situation, or does it make it *less* likely that the Supreme Court would initiate such an imposition on the state treasury?[b] How important is it that state courts be

---

[a]   Indeed, Ford Motor Co. v. Department of Treasury of Indiana, 323 U.S. 459 (1945)—discussed at length by the Court in *Edelman*—was just such a suit. In *Ford*, a taxpayer sued in *federal* court for a refund of state taxes on the ground that they violated the Commerce Clause. The suit was filed under an Indiana statutory refund procedure that authorized suit against the department of taxation "in any court of competent jurisdiction." The Supreme Court nonetheless held the suit barred by the Eleventh Amendment. It was a suit for monetary relief against the state. And the consent to suit in the statutory refund procedure did "not contain any clear indication that the state intended to consent to suit in federal courts" and hence was not a waiver of the state's Eleventh Amendment immunity.

[b]   Notice also the parallel with actions brought under 42 U.S.C. § 1983. As decided in *Edelman* and *Quern*, § 1983 is not a congressional abrogation of a state's Eleventh Amendment immunity. Moreover, under *Will v. Michigan Department of State Police*, a state is not a "person" which can be sued under that statute. Thus, § 1983 suits against a state are barred by the Eleventh Amendment in federal court and are not permitted by the language of the statute in state court.

By contrast, a local government is not protected by the Eleventh Amendment and, unlike a state, is a "person" within the meaning of § 1983. Monell v. Department of Social Services, 436 U.S. 658 (1978). And suits seeking equitable relief against state officials are permitted under § 1983 because of *Ex parte Young*.

The net result, therefore, is that a *McKesson*-type suit seeking monetary relief against a state could go forward in *neither* federal nor state court under § 1983. But actions analogous to *Ward* or *Crain* could be filed against a state official or a unit of local government in *either* state or federal court under § 1983.

open to hear cases where the Due Process Clause requires some avenue for affirmative relief?

Finally, consider the relevance of 28 U.S.C. § 1341 to these issues. Section 1341 provides:

> The district courts shall not enjoin, suspend or restrain the assessment, levy or collection of any tax under State law where a plain, speedy and efficient remedy may be had in the courts of such State.

Which way does this cut?

5. *JACKSON V. DENNO*

McKesson, *Crain*, and *Ward* involve situations where a *plaintiff* sought to assert federal rights in a state court. Is the situation different when a remedy is sought by a state court *defendant?*

Jackson v. Denno, 378 U.S. 368 (1964), involved New York procedures for contesting the voluntariness of a confession. New York allowed the jury to determine the voluntariness of a confession at the same time that it resolved the question of guilt. *Jackson* is interesting in the present context for two points. First, the Court held that New York was required to hold an independent hearing, out of the presence of the trial jury, at which the voluntariness of a confession would be determined. It thus imposed upon the state the obligation to provide a remedy in all future cases to test the violation of federal rights before admitting a confession into evidence in a criminal case. Is this holding problematical?

The second point concerns the remedy ordered in *Jackson.* Jackson had been tried under the invalid procedure. His conviction had been affirmed in appeals through the New York courts. The case came to the Supreme Court following a habeas corpus petition filed in a federal district court. Relief had been denied by the lower federal courts. After holding the New York confession procedures unconstitutional, the Court then faced what should be done. Jackson's allegations required a factual hearing in order to determine what happened at the time of the confession. As to where this hearing should be held, the Court said:

> [W]e think that the further proceedings to which Jackson is entitled should occur initially in the state courts rather than in the federal habeas corpus court. Jackson's trial did not comport with constitutional standards and he is entitled to a determination of the voluntariness of his confession in the state courts in accordance with valid state procedures; the state is also entitled to make this determination before this Court considers a case on direct review or a petition for habeas corpus is filed in a federal district court. . . .
>
> It is New York, therefore, not the federal habeas corpus court, which should first provide Jackson with that which he has not yet had and to which he is constitutionally entitled—an adequate evidentiary hearing productive of reliable results concerning the voluntariness of his confession.

The Court then said that the state should have the option of retrying Jackson or holding a hearing on the voluntariness of the confession. If the confession were found involuntary, a new trial would be required. But if the confession were found voluntary, the fact that the voluntariness determination was made by the jury at Jackson's trial could be regarded as harmless error. The Supreme Court concluded:

> Accordingly, the judgment denying [Jackson's] writ of habeas corpus is reversed and the case is remanded to the District Court to allow the state a reasonable time to afford Jackson a hearing or a new trial, failing which Jackson is entitled to his release.

Why was Jackson entitled to release if the state refused to hold a new hearing? Should it not first be determined whether his confession was actually involuntary?

Suppose a defendant convicted in state court claimed that appointed counsel was drunk during the entire trial and otherwise engaged in incompetent representation. Such a claim, if true, would entitle the defendant to a new trial, but a hearing must be held in order to determine whether it is true. If the state affords no procedure by which such a hearing can be held, does it follow from *Jackson* (or from *McKesson*, *Crain*, or *Ward*) that the defendant is automatically entitled to release or a new trial? Even if the claim is in fact not true? Is a failure by the state to provide an adequate corrective process—a failure to provide an adequate remedy for an asserted violation of federal law—itself a sufficient basis for Supreme Court reversal of a state criminal conviction?[c] Of what relevance is the fact that a federal court could hold a hearing on habeas corpus to determine the truth of the allegations?

---

[c] This question—whether the state must provide a post-conviction procedure for the consideration of federal constitutional challenges that could not have been raised at trial—was presented to the Court in Case v. Nebraska, 381 U.S. 336 (1965). After the Court granted certiorari and briefs on the merits were submitted, Nebraska enacted a post-conviction procedure. The Court remanded the case for a hearing under the new procedure without deciding what would have happened had the new statute not been enacted.

CHAPTER IX

42 U.S.C. § 1983

Section 1. "Under Color of" Law

Monroe v. Pape

Supreme Court of the United States, 1961.
365 U.S. 167.

■ Mr. Justice Douglas delivered the opinion of the Court.

This case presents important questions concerning the construction of R.S. § 1979, 42 U.S.C. § 1983,[a] which reads as follows:

> Every person who, under color of any statute, ordinance, regulation, custom, or usage, of any State or Territory, subjects, or causes to be subjected, any citizen of the United States or other person within the jurisdiction thereof to the deprivation of any rights, privileges, or immunities secured by the Constitution and laws, shall be liable to the party injured in an action at law, suit in equity, or other proper proceeding for redress.

The complaint alleges that 13 Chicago police officers broke into petitioners' home in the early morning, routed them from bed, made them stand naked in the living room, and ransacked every room, emptying drawers and ripping mattress covers. It further alleges that Mr. Monroe was then taken to the police station and detained on "open" charges for 10 hours, while he was interrogated about a two-day-old murder, that he was not taken before a magistrate, though one was accessible, that he was not permitted to call his family or attorney, that he was subsequently released without criminal charges being preferred against him. It is alleged that the officers had no search warrant and no arrest warrant and that they acted "under color of the statutes, ordinances, regulations, customs and usages" of Illinois and of the city of Chicago. Federal jurisdiction was asserted under 42 U.S.C. § 1983, which we have set out above, and 28 U.S.C. § 1343[20] and 28 U.S.C. § 1331.

---

[a] Subsequent citations in the Court's opinion to § 1979 of the Revised Statutes have been replaced with the now more conventional reference to title 42 of the United States Code, § 1983.—[Footnote by eds.]

[20] This section provides in material part:

The district courts shall have original jurisdiction of any civil action authorized by law to be commenced by any person . . .

(3) To redress the deprivation, under color of any state law, statute, ordinance, regulation, custom or usage, of any right, privilege or immunity secured by the Constitution of the United States or by any act of Congress providing for equal rights of citizens or of all persons within the jurisdiction of the United States.

[D]efendants moved to dismiss, alleging that the complaint alleged no cause of action under those acts or the federal Constitution. The District Court dismissed the complaint. The Court of Appeals affirmed. . . .

I

Petitioners claim that the invasion of their home and the subsequent search without a warrant and the arrest and detention of Mr. Monroe without a warrant and without arraignment constituted a deprivation of their "rights, privileges, or immunities secured by the Constitution" within the meaning of § 1983. . . .

Section 1983 came onto the books as § 1 of the Ku Klux Act of April 20, 1871. . . . Its purpose is plain from the title of the legislation, "An Act to enforce the Provisions of the Fourteenth Amendment to the Constitution of the United States, and for other Purposes." Allegation of facts constituting a deprivation under color of state authority of a right guaranteed by the Fourteenth Amendment satisfies to that extent the requirement of § 1983. See Douglas v. City of Jeannette, 319 U.S. 157 (1943). So far petitioners are on solid ground. For the guarantee against unreasonable searches and seizures contained in the fourth amendment has been made applicable to the states by reason of the Due Process Clause of the Fourteenth Amendment. Wolf v. Colorado, 338 U.S. 25 (1949).

II

There can be no doubt at least since Ex parte Virginia, 100 U.S. 339 (1879), that Congress has the power to enforce provisions of the Fourteenth Amendment against those who carry a badge of authority of a state and represent it in some capacity, whether they act in accordance with their authority or misuse it. See Home Tel. & Tel. Co. v. Los Angeles, 227 U.S. 278, 287–96 (1913). The question with which we now deal is the narrower one of whether Congress, in enacting § 1983, meant to give a remedy to parties deprived of constitutional rights, privileges and immunities by an official's abuse of his position. We conclude that it did so intend.

It is argued that "under color of" enumerated state authority excludes acts of an official or policeman who can show no authority under state law, state custom, or state usage to do what he did. In this case it is said that these policemen, in breaking into petitioners' apartment, violated the Constitution and laws of Illinois. It is pointed out that under Illinois law a simple remedy is offered for that violation and that, so far as it appears, the courts of Illinois are available to give petitioners that full redress which the common law affords for violence done to a person; and it is earnestly argued that no "statute, ordinance, regulation, custom or usage" of Illinois bars that redress. . . .

The legislation—in particular the section with which we are now concerned—had several purposes. There are threads of many thoughts running through the debates. One who reads them in their entirety sees that the present section had three main aims.

First, it might, of course, override certain kinds of state laws. Mr. Sloss of Alabama, in opposition, spoke of that object and emphasized that it was irrelevant because there were no such laws:

> The first section of this bill prohibits any invidious legislation by states against the rights or privileges of citizens of the United States. The object of this section is not very clear, as it is not pretended by its advocates on this floor that any state has passed any laws endangering the rights or privileges of colored people.

Second, it provided a remedy where state law was inadequate. That aspect of the legislation was summed up by Senator Sherman of Ohio:

> [I]t is said the reason is that any offense may be committed upon a negro by a white man, and a negro cannot testify in any case against a white man, so that the only way by which any conviction can be had in Kentucky in those cases is in the United States courts, because the United States courts enforce the United States laws by which negroes may testify.

But the purposes were much broader. The third aim was to provide a federal remedy where the state remedy, though adequate in theory, was not available in practice. . . .

This Act of April 20, 1871, sometimes called "the third 'force bill,' " was passed by a Congress that had the Klan "particularly in mind." The debates are replete with references to the lawless conditions existing in the South in 1871. There was available to the Congress during these debates a report, nearly 600 pages in length, dealing with the activities of the Klan and the inability of the state governments to cope with it. This report was drawn on by many of the speakers. It was not the unavailability of state remedies but the failure of certain states to enforce the laws with an equal hand that furnished the powerful momentum behind this "force bill." Mr. Lowe of Kansas said:

> While murder is stalking abroad in disguise, while whippings and lynchings and banishment have been visited upon unoffending American citizens, the local administrations have been found inadequate or unwilling to apply the proper corrective. Combinations, darker than the night that hides them, conspiracies, wicked as the worst of felons could devise, have gone unwhipped of justice. Immunity is given to crime, and the records of the public tribunals are searched in vain for any evidence of effective redress. . . .

While one main scourge of the evil—perhaps the leading one—was the Ku Klux Klan, the remedy created was not a remedy against it or its members but against those who representing a state in some capacity were *unable* or *unwilling* to enforce a state law. . . . There was, it was said, no quarrel with the state laws on the books. It was their lack of enforcement that was the nub of the difficulty. . . .

Senator Pratt of Indiana spoke of the discrimination against Union sympathizers and Negroes in the actual enforcement of the laws:

Plausibly and sophistically it is said [that] the laws of North Carolina do not discriminate against them; that the provisions in favor of rights and liberties are general; that the courts are open to all; that juries, grand and petit, are commanded to hear and redress without distinction as to color, race, or political sentiment.

But it is a fact, asserted in the report, that of the hundreds of outrages committed upon loyal people through the agency of this Ku Klux organization not one has been punished. This defect in the administration of the laws does not extend to other cases. Vigorously enough are the laws enforced against Union people. They only fail in efficiency when a man of known Union sentiments, white or black, invokes their aid. Then Justice closes the door of her temple.

It was precisely that breadth of the remedy which the opposition emphasized. . . . Senator Thurman of Ohio [said] about the section we are now considering:

It authorizes any person who is deprived of any right, privilege, or immunity secured to him by the Constitution of the United States, to bring an action against the wrongdoer in the federal courts, and that without any limit whatsoever as to the amount in controversy. The deprivation may be of the slightest conceivable character, the damages in the estimation of any sensible man may not be five dollars or even five cents; they may be what lawyers call merely nominal damages; and yet by this section jurisdiction of that civil action is given to the federal courts instead of its being prosecuted as now in the courts of the states.

The debates were long and extensive. It is abundantly clear that one reason the legislation was passed was to afford a federal right in federal courts because, by reason of prejudice, passion, neglect, intolerance or otherwise, state laws might not be enforced and the claims of citizens to the enjoyment of rights, privileges, and immunities guaranteed by the Fourteenth Amendment might be denied by the state agencies. . . .

Although the legislation was enacted because of the conditions that existed in the South at that time, it is cast in general language and is as applicable to Illinois as it is to the states whose names were mentioned over and again in the debates. It is no answer that the state has a law which if enforced would give relief. The federal remedy is supplementary to the state remedy, and the latter need not be first sought and refused before the federal one is invoked. Hence the fact that Illinois by its Constitution and laws outlaws unreasonable searches and seizures is no barrier to the present suit in the federal court.

We had before us in United States v. Classic, 313 U.S. 299 (1941), 18 U.S.C. § 242, which provides a criminal punishment for anyone who "under color of any law, statute, ordinance, regulation, or custom" subjects any inhabitant of a state to the deprivation of "any rights, privileges, or immunities secured by the Constitution or laws of the United States." Section 242 first came into the law as § 2 of the Civil Rights Act, Act of April 9, 1866. After passage of the Fourteenth Amendment, this provision was re-enacted and amended by §§ 17, 18, Act of May 31, 1870. The right involved in the *Classic* case was the right of voters in a primary to have their votes counted. The laws of Louisiana required the defendants "to count the ballots, to record the result of the count, and to certify the result of the election." But according to the indictment they did not perform their duty. In an opinion written by Mr. Justice (later Chief Justice) Stone, in which Mr. Justice Roberts, Mr. Justice Reed, and Mr. Justice Frankfurter joined, the Court ruled, "Misuse of power, possessed by virtue of state law and made possible only because the wrongdoer is clothed with the authority of state law, is action taken 'under color of' state law." There was a dissenting opinion; but the ruling as to the meaning of "under color of" state law was not questioned.

That view of the meaning of the words "under color of" state law, 18 U.S.C. § 242, was reaffirmed in Screws v. United States, 325 U.S. 91 (1945).[b] . . .

We conclude that the meaning given "under color of" law in the *Classic* case and in the *Screws* . . . was the correct one; and we adhere to it.

In the *Screws* case we dealt with a statute that imposed criminal penalties for acts "wilfully" done. We construed that word in its setting to mean the doing of an act with "a specific intent to deprive a person of a federal right." We do not think that gloss should be placed on § 1983 which we have here. The word "wilfully" does not appear in § 1983. Moreover, § 1983 provides a civil remedy while in the *Screws* case we dealt with a criminal law challenged on the ground of vagueness. Section 1983 should be read against the background of tort liability that makes a man responsible for the natural consequences of his actions.

---

[b] Screws was a Georgia sheriff who, with two other law enforcement officers, brutally beat an African-American man in the course of an apparently bogus arrest, then threw him in jail without medical care. The man died within the hour. When prosecuted under 18 U.S.C. § 242, the defendants claimed that their actions were not "under color of" law because they had not been commanded or authorized by state law. The Supreme Court rejected that argument in favor of the construction of § 242 adopted in *Classic*.—[Footnote by eds.]

So far, then, the complaint states a cause of action. . . . [S]ince the complaint should not have been dismissed against the officials[c] the judgment must be and is

Reversed.

■ MR. JUSTICE HARLAN, whom MR. JUSTICE STEWART joins, concurring.

Were this case here as one of first impression, I would find the "under color of any statute" issue very close indeed. However, in *Classic* and *Screws* this Court considered a substantially identical statutory phrase to have a meaning which, unless we now retreat from it, requires that issue to go for the petitioners here. . . .

Those aspects of Congress's purpose which are quite clear in the earlier congressional debates, as quoted by my Brothers Douglas and Frankfurter in turn, seem to me to be inherently ambiguous when applied to the case of an isolated abuse of state authority by an official. One can agree with the Court's opinion that

> [i]t is abundantly clear that one reason the legislation was passed was to afford a federal right in federal courts because, by reason of prejudice, passion, neglect, intolerance or otherwise, state laws might not be enforced and the claims of citizens to the enjoyment of rights, privileges, and immunities guaranteed by the Fourteenth Amendment might be denied by the state agencies

without being certain that Congress meant to deal with anything other than abuses so recurrent as to amount to "custom, or usage." One can agree with my Brother Frankfurter in dissent, that Congress had no intention of taking over the whole field of ordinary state torts and crimes, without being certain that the enacting Congress would not have regarded actions by an official, made possible by his position, as far more serious than an ordinary state tort, and therefore as a matter for federal concern. If attention is directed at the rare specific references to isolated abuses of state authority, one finds them neither so clear nor so disproportionately divided between favoring the positions of the majority or the dissent as to make either position seem plainly correct. . . .

The dissent considers that the "under color of" provision of § 1983 distinguishes between unconstitutional actions taken without state authority, which only the state should remedy, and unconstitutional actions authorized by the state, which the federal act was to reach. If so, then the controlling difference for the enacting legislature must have been either that the state remedy was more adequate for unauthorized actions than for authorized ones or that there was, in some sense, greater harm from unconstitutional actions authorized by the full panoply of state power and approval than from unconstitutional actions not so authorized

---

c   The Court's treatment of the plaintiff's claim against the City of Chicago, as distinct from his claims against its officers, is postponed until Section 3 of this Chapter, where the issue of municipal liability under § 1983 is considered in detail.—[Footnote by eds.]

or acquiesced in by the state. I find less than compelling the evidence that either distinction was important to that Congress.

I

If the state remedy was considered adequate when the official's unconstitutional act was unauthorized, why should it not be thought equally adequate when the unconstitutional act was authorized? . . .

Since the suggested narrow construction of § 1983 presupposes that state measures were adequate to remedy unauthorized deprivations of constitutional rights and since the identical state relief could be obtained for state-authorized acts with the aid of Supreme Court review, this narrow construction would reduce the statute to having merely a jurisdictional function, shifting the load of federal supervision from the Supreme Court to the lower courts and providing a federal tribunal for fact findings in cases involving authorized action. Such a function could be justified on various grounds. It could, for example, be argued that the state courts would be less willing to find a constitutional violation in cases involving "authorized action" and that therefore the victim of such action would bear a greater burden in that he would more likely have to carry his case to this Court, and once here, might be bound by unfavorable state court findings. But the legislative debates do not disclose congressional concern about the burdens of litigation placed upon the victims of "authorized" constitutional violations contrasted to the victims of unauthorized violations. Neither did Congress indicate an interest in relieving the burden placed on this Court in reviewing such cases.

The statute becomes more than a jurisdictional provision only if one attributes to the enacting legislature the view that a deprivation of a constitutional right is significantly different from and more serious than a violation of a state right and therefore deserves a different remedy even though the same act may constitute both a state tort and the deprivation of a constitutional right. This view, by no means unrealistic as a commonsense matter,[5] is, I believe, more consistent with the flavor of the legislative history than is a view that the primary purpose of the state was to grant a lower court forum for fact findings. . . .

II

I think this limited interpretation of § 1983 fares no better when viewed from the other possible premise for it, namely that state-approved

---

[5]   There will be many cases in which the relief provided by the state to the victim of a use of state power which the state either did not or could not constitutionally authorize will be far less than what Congress may have thought would be a fair reimbursement for deprivation of a constitutional right. I will venture only a few examples. There may be no damage remedy for the loss of voting rights or for the harm from psychological coercion leading to a confession. And what is the dollar value of the right to go to unsegregated schools? Even the remedy for such an unauthorized search and seizure as Monroe was allegedly subjected to may be only the nominal amount of damages to physical property allowable in an action for trespass to land. It would indeed be the purest coincidence if the state remedies for violation of common-law rights by private citizens were fully appropriate to redress those injuries which only a state official can cause and against which the Constitution provides protection.

constitutional deprivations were considered more offensive than those not so approved. For one thing, the enacting Congress was not unaware of the fact that there was a substantial overlap between the protections granted by state constitutional provisions and those granted by the Fourteenth Amendment. Indeed one opponent of the bill, Senator Trumbull, went so far as to state in a debate with Senators Carpenter and Edmunds that his research indicated a complete overlap in every state, at least as to the protections of the due process clause. Thus, in one very significant sense, there was no ultimate state approval of a large portion of otherwise authorized actions depriving a person of due-process rights. . . .

These difficulties in explaining the basis of a distinction between authorized and unauthorized deprivations of constitutional rights fortify my view that the legislative history does not bear the burden which stare decisis casts upon it. For this reason and for those stated in the opinion of the Court, I agree that we should not now depart from the holdings of the *Classic* and *Screws* cases.

■ MR. JUSTICE FRANKFURTER, dissenting. . . .

This case squarely presents the question whether the intrusion of a city policeman for which that policeman can show no such authority at state law as could be successfully interposed in defense to a state-law action against him, is nonetheless to be regarded as "under color" of state authority within the meaning of § 1983. Respondents, in breaking into the Monroe apartment, violated the laws of the state of Illinois. Illinois law appears to offer a civil remedy for unlawful searches; petitioners do not claim that none is available. Rather they assert that they have been deprived of due process of law and of equal protection of the laws under color of state law, although from all that appears the courts of Illinois are available to give them the fullest redress which the common law affords for the violence done them, nor does any "statute, ordinance, regulation, custom, or usage" of the state of Illinois bar that redress. Did the enactment by Congress of § 1 of the Ku Klux Act of 1871 encompass such a situation?

That section, it has been noted, was patterned on the similar criminal provision of § 2, Act of April 9, 1866 [now 18 U.S.C. § 242]. The earlier act had as its primary object the effective nullification of the Black Codes, those statutes of the Southern legislatures which had so burdened and disqualified the Negro as to make his emancipation appear illusory. The act had been vetoed by President Johnson, whose veto message describes contemporary understanding of its second section; the section, he wrote

> seems to be designed to apply to some existing or future law of a state or territory which may conflict with the provisions of the bill. . . . It provides for counteracting such forbidden legislation by imposing fine and imprisonment upon the legislators who may pass such conflicting laws, or upon the officers or agents who shall put, or attempt to put, them into execution. It means an official offense, not a common crime committed against law

upon the persons or property of the black race. Such an act may deprive the black man of his property, but not of the right to hold property. It means a deprivation of the right itself, either by the state judiciary or the state legislature.

And Senator Trumbull, then Chairman of the Senate Judiciary Committee, in his remarks urging its passage over the veto, expressed the intendment of the second section as those who voted for it read it:

> If an offense is committed against a colored person simply because he is colored, in a state where the law affords him the same protection as if he were white, this act neither has nor was intended to have anything to do with his case, because he has adequate remedies in the state courts; but if he is discriminated against under color of state laws because he is colored, then it becomes necessary to interfere for his protection. . . .

The original text of the present § 1983 contained words, left out in the Revised Statutes, which clarified the objective to which the provision was addressed:

> That any person who, under color of any law, statute, ordinance, regulation, custom, or usage of any state, shall subject or cause to be subjected, any person within the jurisdiction of the United States to the deprivation of any rights, privileges, or immunities secured by the Constitution of the United States, shall, *any such law, statute, ordinance, regulation, custom, or usage of the state to the contrary notwithstanding*, be liable to the party injured. . . .

The Court now says, however, that "It was not the unavailability of state remedies but the failure of certain states to enforce the laws with an equal hand that furnished the powerful momentum behind this 'force bill.'" Of course, if the notion of "unavailability" of remedy is limited to mean an absence of statutory, paper right, this is in large part true. Insofar as the Court undertakes to demonstrate—as the bulk of its opinion seems to do—that § 1983 was meant to reach some instances of action not specifically authorized by the avowed, apparent, written law inscribed in the statute books of the states, the argument knocks at an open door. No one would or could deny this, for by its express terms the statute comprehends deprivations of federal rights under color of any "statute, ordinance, regulation, *custom, or usage*" of a state. (Emphasis added.) The question is, *what* class of cases other than those involving state statute law were meant to be reached. And, with respect to this question, the Court's conclusion is undermined by the very portions of the legislative debates which it cites. For surely the misconduct of individual municipal police officers, subject to the effective oversight of appropriate state administrative and judicial authorities, presents a situation which differs toto coelo from one in which "Immunity is given to crime, and the records of the public tribunals are searched in vain for any evidence of effective redress," or in which murder rages while a state makes "no successful

effort to bring the guilty to punishment or afford protection or redress.". . . These statements indicate that Congress—made keenly aware
by the post-bellum conditions in the South that states through their authorities could sanction offenses against the individual by settled practice
which established state law as truly as written codes—designed § 1983
to reach, as well, official conduct which, because engaged in "permanently and as a rule," or "systematically," came through acceptance by
law-administering officers to constitute "custom, or usage" having the
cast of law. They do not indicate an attempt to reach, nor does the statute
by its terms include, instances of acts in defiance of state law and which
no settled state practice, no systematic pattern of official action or inaction, no "custom, or usage, of any state," insulates from effective and
adequate reparation by the state authorities.

Rather, all the evidence converges to the conclusion that Congress
by § 1983 created a civil liability enforceable in the federal courts only in
instances of injury for which redress was barred in the state courts because some "statute, ordinance, regulation, custom, or usage" sanctioned
the grievance complained of. . . .

The present case comes here from a judgment sustaining a motion
to dismiss petitioners' complaint. That complaint, insofar as it describes
the police intrusion, makes no allegation that that intrusion was authorized by state law other than the conclusory and unspecific claim that
"[d]uring all times herein mentioned the individual defendants and each
of them were acting under color of the statutes, ordinances, regulations,
customs, and usages of the state of Illinois, of the county of Cook and of
the defendant city of Chicago." In the face of Illinois decisions holding
such intrusions unlawful and in the absence of more precise factual averments to support its conclusion, such a complaint fails to state a claim
under § 1983.

However, the complaint does allege, as to the 10-hour detention of
Mr. Monroe, that "it was, and it is now, the custom or usage of the Police
Department of the city of Chicago to arrest and confine individuals in the
police stations and jail cells of the said department for long periods of
time on 'open' charges." . . . Such averments do present facts which, admitted as true for purposes of a motion to dismiss, seem to sustain
petitioners' claim that Mr. Monroe's detention—as contrasted with the
night-time intrusion into the Monroe apartment—was "under color" of
state authority. . . .[d]

---

[d]   In a portion of his opinion omitted here, Justice Frankfurter said that he thought *Classic*
and *Screws* had been wrongly decided and that stare decisis did not require that he perpetuate
the error.—[Footnote by eds.]

NOTES ON 42 U.S.C. § 1983

1. BACKGROUND

Before *Monroe v. Pape*, § 1983 was remarkable for its insignificance. Indeed, one commentator found only 21 suits brought under this provision in the years between 1871 and 1920.[a] During the 1920s and 30s, the statute was invoked in a handful of cases involving racial discrimination and the franchise.[b] The prospect of broader application was signaled in Hague v. Committee for Industrial Organization, 307 U.S. 496 (1939), where the Court affirmed an injunction against a local ordinance used to harass labor organizers. In all of these cases, however, the acts complained of were affirmatively authorized by statute or local ordinance and thus fit even the narrowest reading of "under color of" law. None raised the issue of unauthorized misconduct by state officials. *Monroe v. Pape* was the first Supreme Court vindication of the use of § 1983 as an independent federal remedy against acts that violated both state law and the federal Constitution.

(i) Civil Rights Cases

Monroe did not overrule precedent, but it did overturn a long-standing assumption that § 1983 reached only misconduct either officially authorized or so widely tolerated as to amount to "custom or usage." The origins of this assumption apparently lay in restrictive constitutional interpretations of the 19th century. In a number of cases, the Supreme Court insisted that federal legislative power to enforce the guarantees of the Fourteenth Amendment could be exercised only against "state action" and held unconstitutional Reconstruction-era efforts to reach private misconduct.[c] In the famous Civil Rights Cases, 109 U.S. 3 (1883), the Court struck down the attempt in the Civil Rights Act of 1875 to prohibit racial discrimination by private parties in the provision of public accommodations:

> [U]ntil some state law has been passed or some state action through its officers and agents has been taken, adverse to the rights of citizens sought to be protected by the Fourteenth Amendment, no legislation of the United States under said amendment, nor any proceeding under such legislation, can be called into activity; for the prohibitions of the amendment are against state laws and acts done under state authority. . . . In this connection it is proper to state that civil rights, such as are guaranteed by the Constitution against state aggression, cannot be impaired by the wrongful acts

---

[a] Comment, The Civil Rights Act: Emergence of an Adequate Federal Civil Remedy?, 26 Ind. L.J. 361, 363 (1951).

[b] See, e.g., Nixon v. Herndon, 273 U.S. 536 (1927) (awarding damages against Texas officials for enforcing a statute barring African-Americans from the Democratic primary); Lane v. Wilson, 307 U.S. 268 (1939) (vindicating rights of African-Americans against enforcement of racially discriminatory laws governing the franchise).

[c] This was the fate of that part of § 2 of the Act of 1871 (of which § 1983 was originally § 1) that imposed criminal penalties for private conspiracy to deprive any person of "the equal protection of the laws, or of equal privileges or immunities under the law." United States v. Harris, 106 U.S. 629 (1882).

of individuals, unsupported by state authority in the shape of laws, customs or judicial or executive proceedings.

Nowhere did the Court explicitly say that the acts of a state officer in violation of state law could not constitute the required state action, but this decision, and others, seemed to imply as much.[d] In fact, several lower courts explicitly so concluded.[e] In light of this background, a nineteenth-century observer might reasonably have thought that § 1983 would be unconstitutional unless it were limited to acts explicitly or impliedly authorized by state law.[f]

(ii) Home Telephone & Telegraph

By 1961 the notion of a *constitutional* incapacity to reach unauthorized misconduct of state officials had long since died. The demise of this idea dates from Home Telephone & Telegraph Co. v. Los Angeles, 227 U.S. 278 (1913) (cited in *Monroe*). In that case, the telephone company went to federal court to enjoin enforcement of a city ordinance setting telephone rates. The company charged that the rates were so unreasonably low as to be confiscatory and hence violative of the Fourteenth Amendment guarantee of due process of law. The city answered that, if that were true, the rates would also violate a parallel provision of the state constitution. In that event, said the city, the rates would be forbidden by state law and therefore their adoption would not constitute "state action." Since the Fourteenth Amendment guarantees due process only against state action, the city argued, the federal court would have no power to consider the matter "until, by final action of an appropriate state court, it was decided that such acts were authorized by the state. . . ." The Supreme Court rejected this view and embraced a much broader conception of "state action."

"To speak broadly," said the Court, "the difference between the proposition insisted upon and the true meaning of the amendment is this, that the one assumes that the amendment virtually contemplates alone wrongs authorized by a state, and gives only power accordingly, while in truth the amendment contemplates the possibility of state officers abusing the powers lawfully conferred upon them by doing wrongs prohibited by the amendment." The Court therefore concluded that the Fourteenth Amendment reached not only unconstitutional acts authorized by state law but also those committed when "state powers [were] abused by those who possessed them."

---

[d] Cf. Virginia v. Rives, 100 U.S. 313 (1879), in which the Supreme Court considered a provision of the Civil Rights Act of 1866 authorizing removal to federal court of a state criminal prosecution "[a]gainst any person who is denied or cannot enforce in the courts of such state a right under any law providing for the equal civil rights of citizens of the United States, or of all persons within the jurisdiction thereof." The Court held that the right to removal applied only where the denial of equal rights was accomplished by legislation rather than by the unauthorized acts of a state official. See also Barney v. New York, 193 U.S. 430 (1904).

[e] See the cases cited in Developments in the Law—Section 1983 and Federalism, 90 Harv. L. Rev. 1133, 1160–61 n.138 (1977), which summarizes the grounds for thinking that acts violative of state law could not be state action.

[f] For other factors that contributed to the pre-*Monroe* insignificance of § 1983, see Michael G. Collins, "Economic Rights," Implied Constitutional Actions, and the Scope of Section 1983, 77 Geo. L.J. 1493, 1499–1506 (1989); Louise Weinberg, The *Monroe* Mystery Solved: Beyond the "Unhappy History" Theory of Civil Rights Litigation, 1991 B.Y.U. L. Rev. 737.

Home Telephone & Telegraph established that conduct violative of state law could constitute state action within the meaning of the Fourteenth Amendment. This decision undermined the notion of a constitutional bar to a broad reading of § 1983, but it gave no indication whether the statute should in fact be so read. That possibility was first raised in *United States v. Classic* and *United States v. Screws*, both of which broadly interpreted the parallel "under color of" law language in 18 U.S.C. § 242 (quoted in *Monroe*). As the *Monroe* opinion recounts, 18 U.S.C. § 242 is a criminal provision, originally enacted as § 2 of the Civil Rights Act of 1866. The statute that ultimately became § 1983 was modeled on this earlier law, and provided civil remedies for conduct that had been prohibited by the penal statute. Given the close historical and textual association of the two provisions, it is not surprising that the interpretation placed on one would also be applied to the other.

The upshot of all this is that the degree of innovation involved in the *Monroe* decision is hard to pin down. The majority's reading of the statute may well have been consistent with the intent of its drafters, though that issue is certainly debatable.[g] The decision was foreshadowed by *Classic* and *Screws* and should therefore have been predictable. On the other hand, during much of the life of the statute, the interpretation placed on it in *Monroe v. Pape* would have been thought at least surprising and probably unconstitutional. And it seems plain that the bar generally was not aware of the potentialities of § 1983 until *Monroe* pointed the way. Thus, in an important sense, and regardless of whether it restored or perverted the original intention, *Monroe v. Pape* began a new chapter in federal court supervision of state officials.

2. QUESTIONS AND COMMENTS ON *MONROE V. PAPE*

Justice Douglas identified three main aims for § 1983: (1) to "override certain kinds of state laws," (2) to provide "a remedy where state law was inadequate," and (3) most importantly, "to provide a federal remedy where the state remedy, though adequate in theory, was not available in practice." Which of these purposes applies to the facts of *Monroe*? More generally, why did the Court declare that "the federal remedy is supplementary to the state remedy, and the latter need not be first sought and refused before the federal one is invoked?" What is the rationale for a "supplementary" federal remedy that does not depend on the inadequacy of state law? Does the *Monroe* opinion provide an answer? Under Justice Frankfurter's view, the federal courts would have to distinguish between an isolated abuse of authority by a state official and an abuse so widely practiced or tolerated as to amount to "custom

---

[g] For conflicting interpretations of that history, see Eric H. Zagrans, "Under Color of" *What* Law: A Reconstructed Model of § 1983 Liability, 71 Va. L. Rev. 499 (1985) (concluding that, "[a]s a matter of statutory construction, *Monroe* is flatly wrong"); Steven L. Winter, The Meaning of "Under Color of" Law, 91 Mich. L. Rev. 323 (1992) (concluding that the "Frankfurter-Zagrans misinterpretation of section 1983 is not only wrong, but wildly ahistorical"); David Achtenberg, A "Milder Measure of Villainy": The Unknown History of 42 U.S.C. § 1983 and the Meaning of "Under Color of" Law, 1999 Utah L. Rev. 1 (concluding that history "should dispel the remarkably persistent myth that the Forty-Second Congress never intended the provision to cover constitutional wrongs unless those wrongs were actually authorized by state law").

or usage." Do the difficulties in making this inquiry justify across-the-board federal relief?

A different rationale for an independent federal remedy was suggested by Justice Harlan. He "attribute[d] to the enacting legislature the view that a deprivation of a constitutional right is significantly different from and more serious than a violation of a state right and therefore deserves a different remedy even though the same act may constitute both a state tort and the deprivation of a constitutional right." Is this persuasive? Is deprivation of a constitutional right always more serious than the kinds of injuries against which state law protects? And why is a separate remedy needed when the same act accomplishes both wrongs?

3.   JURISDICTION OVER CIVIL RIGHTS ACTIONS

The jurisdictional counterpart of § 1983 is 28 U.S.C. § 1343(3), which was also derived from Section 1 of the 1871 Civil Rights Act and which is quoted in footnote 1 of the *Monroe* opinion. A related provision is 28 U.S.C. § 1343(4), which provides jurisdiction over suits brought under "any act of Congress providing for the protection of civil rights." Of course, these cases are also covered by the general "federal question" statute, 28 U.S.C. § 1331, but until 1980 that provision required a minimum amount in controversy. The elimination of the amount-in-controversy requirement of § 1331 has made the special jurisdictional provisions for civil rights actions redundant and unnecessary.

Under whatever statute, the plaintiff's option to sue in federal court is significant. Comparison between state and federal judiciaries is inevitably subjective, but differences can arise. Federal judges may be more qualified, more expert in the adjudication of federal claims, more independent of popular sentiment, more sympathetic to federal rights, and less reluctant to award damages against state officials. Or they may be none of these things. It seems clear, however, that for whatever reason civil rights plaintiffs typically prefer federal court and that at certain times and in certain places the advantage of federal court may be real and substantial. See Burt Neuborne, The Myth of Parity, 90 Harv. L. Rev. 1105 (1977). Whether there is "parity" between state and federal judges with respect to the adjudication of federal claims is explored further in Section 1 of Chapter IV.

Whatever the perceived advantages of the choice to litigate in federal court, § 1983 actions may also be brought in state court.[h] Indeed, in recent years, resort to state court has become increasingly common.[i]

4. IMPACT OF *MONROE V. PAPE*

Some crude measure of the impact of *Monroe v. Pape* can be derived from the annual statistics on the business of the federal courts. In the year of the *Monroe* decision, fewer than 300 suits were brought in federal court under all the civil rights acts. Ten years later, that figure had risen to 8,267, including 3,129 civil rights actions filed by prisoners. In the year ending on September 30, 2016, approximately 38,000 suits were brought under civil rights acts (chiefly § 1983, but also under statutes like the Americans with Disabilities Act). In addition, prisoners filed more than 28,000 civil rights cases (including conditions of confinement claims).[j]

Qualitatively, the assessment is more difficult. Since Ex parte Young, 209 U.S. 123 (1908), injunctive relief against unconstitutional state action had been available simply by the expedient of naming the appropriate state officer as defendant. With respect to prospective relief, therefore, *Monroe* recharacterized rather than created the opportunity for federal litigation. What was really new was the prospect of damage actions against government officials. Of course, § 1983 applies only to persons acting under color of statute, etc., "of any state or territory or the District of Columbia."[k] It creates no right of action against federal officers, unless they act in concert with state officials and under the authority of state law. See Dombrowski v. Eastland, 387 U.S. 82 (1967).[l] Moreover, the states as such are immune from damages

---

[h] Absent congressional direction to the contrary, state courts are *permitted* to hear federal claims. Accordingly, the Supreme Court has recognized the authority of state courts to hear § 1983 cases. A different question is whether state courts are *required* to hear § 1983 claims even when they would prefer not to do so. This question was resolved in Howlett v. Rose, 496 U.S. 356 (1990), where the Court held that state courts *must* hear § 1983 claims brought in a court otherwise competent to hear that type of claim. The state courts may refuse to hear a § 1983 case only if, under local law, they have a "valid excuse." A "valid excuse" must be a neutral procedural policy (the standard example is forum non conveniens) applicable to all cases (not just federal ones) heard in the court in question and not otherwise inconsistent with any governing federal policy. See Chapter II, Section 1.

[i] For analysis of possible tactical advantages in the choice of a state court and specific issues that may arise there, see Steven H. Steinglass, Section 1983 Litigation in State Courts (1989), and Susan Herman, Beyond Parity: Section 1983 and the State Courts, 54 Brooklyn L. Rev. 1057 (1989).

[j] These figures are extrapolated from the Annual Reports on the Judicial Business of the United States Courts published each year by the Administrative Office of the U.S. Courts. For one of the few empirical studies of § 1983 litigation, see Theodore Eisenberg and Stewart Schwab, The Reality of Constitutional Tort Litigation, 72 Cornell L. Rev. 641 (1987).

[k] In 1979, the statute was amended to treat the District of Columbia as a state for suit under § 1983. The amendment also declares that "any act of Congress applicable exclusively to the District of Columbia shall be considered to be a statute of the District of Columbia" for this purpose. Before that, the District of Columbia was outside the scope of § 1983, see District of Columbia v. Carter, 409 U.S. 418 (1973), even though the statute had been interpreted to cover acts under the laws of Puerto Rico. See Marin v. University of Puerto Rico, 377 F. Supp. 613 (D.P.R. 1973).

[l] Parallel damages actions against federal officers are known as "*Bivens* actions," a label derived from the Supreme Court's decision in Bivens v. Six Unknown Named Agents, 403 U.S. 388 (1971). The availability of *Bivens* actions against federal officers is extensively considered in Section 3 of Chapter II.

under the Eleventh Amendment. See Edelman v. Jordan, 415 U.S. 651 (1974). And state officials enjoy various kinds of (usually qualified) immunity, as is detailed in the next section. Thus, although the damage remedy is importantly qualified, the availability of money damages for the unconstitutional acts of government officials is the heart of § 1983.

Finally, mention should be made that § 1983 is not limited to constitutional violations. It applies in terms to deprivation of rights, privileges, or immunities "secured by the Constitution *and laws*" of the United States. Thus, it seems to create a private right of action for every violation of federal statute or regulation by a person acting under color of state authority. The extent to which this is true is a complicated question, examined at length in *Maine v. Thiboutot* and the notes following, in Section 4 of this chapter.

NOTES ON ATTORNEY'S FEES

1. LEGAL REPRESENTATION IN CIVIL RIGHTS CASES

The cost of litigating a constitutional claim can be substantial. When the plaintiff cannot afford a lawyer, there are several ways in which such litigation might be financed.

First, the government might provide lawyers for indigent civil rights claimants the same way that it does for indigent criminal defendants. The Supreme Court has held, however, that the Constitution does not require appointed counsel in civil cases. Lassiter v. Department of Social Services, 452 U.S. 18 (1981). While the government does fund legal services programs that provide aid to indigent individuals, these programs do not begin to meet the need for private counsel in civil rights cases.[a]

Second, one might rely on private attorneys, either recruited voluntarily or appointed as a condition of admission to the bar, to provide services free of charge or at reduced rates. In Mallard v. United States District Court, 490 U.S. 296 (1989), a federal district court directed Mallard, a recently admitted attorney, to represent indigent inmates in a § 1983 lawsuit against prison officials. Mallard objected, and the Supreme Court held that 28 U.S.C. § 1915(d) (now codified as § 1915(e)(1)), does not authorize the court to require an unwilling attorney to represent an indigent in a civil case. While many states follow the American Bar Association's recommendation that attorneys provide some number of hours of pro bono service, see ABA Model Rules of Professional Conduct Rule 6.1 (2004) (suggesting fifty hours of service per year), this recommendation is not an enforceable obligation. Whatever the actual amount of pro bono representation, unmet needs remain.

---

[a] Indeed, there may be statutory restrictions on the kinds of cases that government-funded legal aid services can take. See, e.g., 42 U.S.C. § 2996f(b)(9) (forbidding legal services organizations from using federal legal services funds to litigate any case involving school desegregation). Of course, specific limitations on what legal aid attorneys can do, as distinct from general underfunding, may raise constitutional concerns. See, e.g., Legal Services Corp. v. Velasquez, 531 U.S. 533 (2001) (holding that a federal funding restriction that prevented attorneys representing clients in welfare-related proceedings from challenging the constitutionality of state or federal law violates the First Amendment).

Third, civil rights plaintiffs might enter into contingent fee agreements, under which the attorney agrees to represent the plaintiff in return for receiving a portion of any recovery. This is the usual arrangement for ordinary tort litigation and would likely work for many constitutional torts as well. Other civil rights cases, however, will be seeking only prospective relief or will yield monetary recoveries too small to attract competent counsel for a contingent fee.

Fourth, one might adopt a fee-shifting regime in which the litigation expenses of the winning party (whether plaintiff or defendant) are assessed against the loser. This is the so-called "English Rule." While the English Rule would make clearly meritorious civil rights claims more attractive, it would also increase the cost of any losing effort. Whether such off-setting incentives would secure wider representation to civil rights plaintiffs generally is unclear.

In contrast to the English Rule, the "American Rule" requires each party to pay its own attorney, win or lose. Although this is norm for American law, courts in the past made many exceptions, especially where the plaintiffs can be seen as rendering a public service by enforcing their individual rights. On that rationale, many modern civil rights statutes explicitly authorize attorneys' fees, and courts sometimes invoked their inherent equitable powers to award fees even without express statutory authorization. In Alyeska Pipeline Service Co. v. Wilderness Society, 421 U.S. 240 (1975), the Supreme Court put a stop to this practice, stating that, in light of the traditional reliance on the American Rule, "it would be inappropriate for the judiciary, without legislative guidance, to reallocate the burdens of litigation."

2. THE CIVIL RIGHTS ATTORNEY'S FEE AWARD ACT

The chief consequence of *Alyeska Pipeline* was to preclude award of attorney's fees under § 1983 and other Reconstruction-Era civil rights statutes. Since attorney's fees were authorized by statute under modern civil rights laws, the disparity seemed anomalous. Congress responded by enacting the Civil Rights Attorneys' Fees Awards Act of 1976, now codified in 42 U.S.C. § 1988(b):

> In any action or proceeding to enforce a provision of §§ 1981, 1982, 1983, 1985, and 1986 of this Title, Title IX of Public Law 92–318 [the Education Amendments of 1972, 20 U.S.C. § 1681 et seq.], or Title VI of the Civil Rights Act of 1964 [42 U.S.C. § 2000d et seq.], the court, in its discretion, may allow the prevailing party, other than the United States, a reasonable attorney's fee as part of the costs.

Congress based this statute on analogous provisions in Titles II and VII of the 1964 Civil Rights Act. The legislative history indicates that Congress intended that the standard for awarding fees under these provisions "be generally the same." S. Rep. No. 1011, 94th Cong., 2d Sess., at 3 (1976). This history accounts for two important glosses on the text of the statute.

(i) "In Its Discretion"

The text of § 1988(b) seems to make fee awards discretionary with the court. In fact, award of fees to the successful civil rights plaintiff is required, absent a very narrow set of "special circumstances [that] would render such an award unjust." This interpretation comes from Newman v. Piggie Park Enterprises, Inc., 390 U.S. 400 (1968), which found in the 1964 Civil Rights Act a legislative intention routinely to award attorney's fees to prevailing plaintiffs in order to encourage and reward private enforcement of civil rights. *Piggie Park* was specially cited in the legislative history of § 1988(b), and its limitation of judicial discretion is taken to control the application of § 1988(b).

Under the cases, there seem to be only two circumstances where fees can be denied to a prevailing plaintiff. First, a pro se litigant is not entitled to fees, even if the litigant happens to be a lawyer. See Kay v. Ehrler, 499 U.S. 432 (1991). Second, there are cases in which, even though the plaintiff formally prevails, the judgment is so trivial relative to the relief originally sought that a court may deny the plaintiff fees. See Farrar v. Hobby, 506 U.S. 103 (1992). Otherwise, prevailing plaintiffs recover fees.

(ii) "Prevailing Party"

Section 1988(b) seems to say that plaintiffs and defendants would be equally entitled to recover fees as a "prevailing party." Such balanced incentives, however, presumably would do little to encourage private enforcement of the civil rights acts. The increased return on winning might be offset by the penalty for losing. The words of the statute have therefore been rejected in favor of a sharp differentiation between plaintiffs and defendants. A prevailing plaintiff almost always recovers fees. A prevailing defendant may recover fees only if the suit is unreasonable, frivolous, meritless, or vexatious. The term "meritless" has been construed to mean "groundless or without foundation, rather than [that] the plaintiff has ultimately lost his case." Christiansburg Garment Co. v. Equal Employment Opportunity Commission, 434 U.S. 412, 421 (1974) (involving an analogous issue under the 1964 Civil Rights Act).[b] In essence, "meritless" has been construed to echo rather to expand the meaning of "frivolous."

3. DETERMINING FEE AWARDS: THE LODESTAR

Hensley v. Eckerhart, 461 U.S. 424 (1983), set the standard for determining fee awards, It said that "[t]he most useful starting for determining the amount of a reasonable fee is the number of hours reasonably expended on the litigation multiplied by a reasonable hourly rate." Id. at 433. This figure is known as the "lodestar." It has become more than a "useful starting

---

[b]   In Fox v. Vice, 563 U.S. 826 (2011), the Court held that in cases involving both frivolous and non-frivolous claims, § 1988 "allows a defendant to recover reasonable attorney's fees incurred because of, but *only because of*, a frivolous claim." (Emphasis added.) Expenses that the defendant would have incurred anyway in defending against non-frivolous claims cannot be shifted to the plaintiff.

point" for calculating attorney's fees. In most cases, the lodestar *is* the fee award.

The calculation begins by determining the number of hours reasonably expended on the claims on which the plaintiff prevailed. The plaintiff does not have to win on all or the most important claim in order to recover fees. So long as the plaintiff succeeds on "any significant issue" and achieves "some of the benefit" sought in the suit, plaintiff is entitled to fees. Texas State Teachers Ass'n v. Garland Ind. School District, 489 U.S. 782 (1989). But the hours spent on unsuccessful claims are not compensated. Where a successful claim and an unsuccessful claim are unrelated, the court simply discards the hours spent on the unsuccessful claim. But where successful and unsuccessful claims overlap, allocation of effort is required. Generalizations are treacherous, but courts often seem to count for purposes of fee awards all hours relevant to *both* winning and losing claims and to exclude only those hours solely related to the unsuccessful claims.

For those hours attributable to prevailing claims, plaintiffs are required to exercise "billing judgment." That means they must subtract from the total number of hours expended those which are duplicative, unproductive, excessive, or otherwise unnecessary. *Hensley*, 461 U.S. at 434 ("Hours that are not properly billed to one's client are not properly billed to one's adversary. . . ."). As will be seen, however, that does not mean that lawyers must limit their efforts by the dollar value of the controversy, as would be true in billing a private client.

Obviously, there are judgments to be made about reasonable hourly rates as well as about the number of hours reasonably expended. A reasonable hourly rate depends on the experience and qualifications of the lawyer and on the particular market in which the lawyer is employed and perhaps on a particular professional specialty within that market. Courts cannot rely on published hourly rates as necessarily reasonable. The nominal rate may be discounted by not counting all the hours worked or by agreeing up front to a lump-sum compensation for a particular legal task.

In any event, unless the parties agree on a fee award, the district judge (or more likely the magistrate judge) has the responsibility for determining the lodestar. Although a trial court generally has no discretion not to award fees to a prevailing plaintiff, the calculation of hours reasonably spent and the reasonable hourly rate at which they should be compensated are necessarily evaluative and judgmental. And while fee awards can be appealed, the standard of review for the determination of a reasonable fee is abuse of discretion.

4.   LIMITING THE LODESTAR?: PROPORTIONALITY

Although there are many complexities in the administration of attorney's fees, two large questions stand out. One is whether, in an action for money damages, the lodestar should be limited by a requirement of proportionality to the damages won. The other, covered in the next note, is whether the lodestar should be enhanced or "multiplied" to offset the risk of non-payment if the plaintiff loses.

Should a civil rights attorney, litigating for money damages, be compensated for all of the time that the issues require, even if that sum greatly exceeds the value of the recovery? Put differently, is it reasonable to demand compensation for $100,000 of attorney time on a claim worth only $10,000? In City of Riverside v. Rivera, 477 U.S. 561 (1986), the Supreme Court said "yes." The case arose when police officers broke up a loud party and arrested four of its participants. Plaintiffs claimed violations of the First, Fourth, and Fourteenth Amendment rights and ultimately recovered $13,000 on their federal claims (approximately $29,000 in 2017 dollars) and an additional $20,050 on state-law claims (for which attorney's fees are not available). The fee award approved by the District Court and ultimately upheld by the Supreme Court was $245,456.25 (or approximately $550,000 in 2017 dollars). Speaking through Justice Brennan, the Court "rejected the notion that a civil rights action for damages constitutes nothing more than a private tort suit benefitting only the individual plaintiffs whose rights were violated." On the contrary, "a successful civil rights plaintiff often secures important social benefits that are not reflected in nominal or relatively small damage awards." The Court found that Congress's purpose in recruiting lawyers for civil rights claimants would be undermined by limiting the fee award. Instead, "Congress determined that it would be necessary to compensate lawyers for all time reasonably expended on a case." Chief Justice Burger and Justices White, Rehnquist, and O'Connor dissented.

Under the rule of City of Riverside, the potential liability for attorney's fees often dwarfs the potential liability for the underlying constitutional violation. Obviously, the availability of fees unconstrained by the concept of proportionality encourages litigation of otherwise non-economic civil rights claims. Whether trial courts deciding such claims will always be as generous as the award in City of Riverside may be doubted, but there can be no doubt that the availability of attorney's fees makes constitutional tort actions vastly more attractive than they would otherwise be.

5.   INCREASING THE LODESTAR?: FEE ENHANCEMENT

Defendants pay fees only to *prevailing* plaintiffs under the Civil Rights Attorney's Fees Award Act (and other fee-shifting statutes). The plaintiff's lawyer gets nothing if the plaintiff loses. This disparity led some lower courts to adopt "multipliers"—calculations that enhanced the lodestar to compensate the plaintiff's attorney for having run the risk of recovering no fee award in the event of an adverse judgment.

In City of Burlington v. Dague, 505 U.S. 557 (1992), this practice was disapproved. Speaking through Justice Scalia, the Court said:

> [A]n enhancement for contingency would likely duplicate in substantial part factors already subsumed in the lodestar. The risk of loss in a particular case (and therefore, the attorney's contingent risk) is the product of two factors: (1) the legal and factual merits of the claim, and (2) the difficulty of establishing these merits. The second factor, however, is ordinarily reflected in the lodestar—either in the higher number of hours expended to overcome the difficulty, or in the higher hourly rate of the attorney skilled and

experienced enough to do so. Taking account of it again in through lodestar enhancement amounts to double-counting.

The first factor (relative merits of the claim) is not reflected in the lodestar, but there are good reasons why it should pay no part in the calculation of the award. . . . [T]he consequence of awarding contingency enhancement to take account of this "merits" factor would be to provide attorneys with the same incentive to bring relatively meritless claims as relatively meritorious ones. Assume, for example, two claims, one with underlying merit of 20 percent, the other of 80 percent. Absent any contingency arrangement, a contingent-fee attorney would prefer to take the latter, since he is four times more likely to be paid. But with a contingency enhancement, this preference will disappear: the enhancement for the 20 percent claim would be a multiplier of 5 (100/20), which is quadruple the 1.25 multiplier (100/80) that would attach to the 80 percent claim. Thus, enhancement for the contingency risk posed by each case would encourage meritorious claims to be brought, but only at the social cost of indiscriminately encouraging nonmeritorious claims to be brought as well. We think that an unlikely objective of the "reasonable fees" provisions. "These statutes were not designed as a form of economic relief to improve the financial lot of lawyers." Pennsylvania v. Delaware Valley Citizens Council for Clean Air, 478 U.S. 546, 656 (1986).

The Court also rejected the suggestion that fees should be enhanced, not based on an individualized assessment of potential merit, but on the "difference in market treatment for contingent fee cases as a class." The Court doubted whether any coherent assessment of market treatment could be made for a class of litigation that would not occur in the private market.

The practical effect of denying fee enhancement—like the effect of rejecting any requirement of proportionality—depends heavily on how the lodestar is administered. Julie Davies, Federal Civil Rights Practice in the 1900s: The Dichotomy Between Reality and Practice, 48 Hastings L.J. 197 (1997), reports, perhaps surprisingly, that many civil rights practitioners regarded the loss of multipliers as relatively insignificant. According to Davies, the loss of multipliers does lessen the leverage of plaintiffs' lawyers in settlement negotiations, but several "stated that under the lodestar formulation, they are paid at a high hourly rate, and that courts have adjusted for the lack of a multiplier by awarding them a greater percentage of the hours billed." This empirical conclusion may not stand for all cases, but it draws attention once again to the importance of the trial court in administering the lodestar.

6.   CIVIL RIGHTS ACTIONS AGAINST FEDERAL DEFENDANTS

Section 1988(b) applies to suits under certain specified statutes. None of them covers suits against the United States or federal officers. Attorney's fees in such actions may be available under the Equal Access to Justice Act (EAJA), 28 U.S.C. § 2412(d)(1)(A), which authorizes attorney's fees to prevailing parties "other than the United States" in "any civil action (other than cases sounding in tort) . . . brought by or against the United States in any court having jurisdiction of that action. . . ." That provision, however, precludes a fee award when "the court finds that the position of the United States was substantially justified or that special circumstances make an award unjust."

The United States has waived its sovereign immunity with respect to claims "seeking relief other than money damages," 5 U.S.C. § 702, and permits actions for declaratory or injunctive relief to be brought either against the United States or against federal officers in their official capacity. Thus, in a lawsuit seeking declaratory or injunctive relief against federal officials, prevailing plaintiffs may be able to obtain fees. But federal courts of appeals have refused to award fees under the EAJA to prevailing plaintiffs in *Bivens* actions—the analogous common-law damages actions against individuals acting under color of federal law. Because *Bivens* actions are brought against federal officers in their personal or individual capacities, they are not considered civil actions against the United States.

SECTION 2. OFFICIAL IMMUNITIES

Scheuer v. Rhodes

Supreme Court of the United States, 1974.
416 U.S. 232.

■ MR. CHIEF JUSTICE BURGER delivered the opinion of the Court.

We granted certiorari in these cases to resolve whether the District Court correctly dismissed civil damage actions, brought under 42 U.S.C. § 1983, on the ground that these actions were, as a matter of law, against the state of Ohio, and hence barred by the Eleventh Amendment to the Constitution and, alternatively, that the actions were against state officials who were immune from liability for the acts alleged in the complaints. These cases arise out of the . . . period of alleged civil disorder on the campus of Kent State University in Ohio during May 1970. . . .

In these cases the personal representatives of the estates of three students who died in that episode seek damages against the governor, the adjutant general, and his assistant, various named and unnamed officers and enlisted members of the Ohio National Guard, and the president of Kent State University. The complaints in both cases allege a cause of action under the Civil Rights Act of 1871, 42 U.S.C. § 1983. . . .

The District Court dismissed the complaints for lack of jurisdiction over the subject matter on the theory that these actions, [although in form against the named individuals, were, in substance and effect, against the state of Ohio and thus barred by the Eleventh Amendment.] The Court of Appeals affirmed the action of the District Court, agreeing that the suit was in legal effect one against the state of Ohio and, alternatively, that the common-law doctrine of executive immunity barred action against the state officials who are respondents here. We are confronted with the narrow threshold question whether the District Court properly dismissed the complaints. We hold that dismissal was inappropriate at this stage of the litigation and accordingly reverse the judgments and remand for further proceedings. We intimate no view on the merits of the allegations since there is no evidence before us at this stage.

No view on the merits

I

The complaints in these cases are not identical but their thrust is essentially the same. In essence, the defendants are alleged to have "intentionally, recklessly, wilfully and wantonly" caused an unnecessary deployment of the Ohio National Guard on the Kent State campus and, in the same manner, ordered the Guard members to perform allegedly illegal actions which resulted in the death of plaintiffs' decedents. Both complaints allege that the action was taken "under color of state law" and that it deprived the decedents of their lives and rights without due process of law. Fairly read, the complaints allege that each of the named defendants, in undertaking such actions, acted either outside the scope of his respective office, or, if within the scope, acted in an arbitrary manner, grossly abusing the lawful powers of office. . . .

II

The Eleventh Amendment to the Constitution of the United States provides: "The Judicial power of the United States shall not be construed to extend to any suit in law or equity, commenced or prosecuted against one of the United States by Citizens of another State. . . ." It is well established that the amendment bars suits not only against the state when it is the named party but also when it is the party in fact. . . .

However, since Ex parte Young, 209 U.S. 123 (1908), it has been settled that the Eleventh Amendment provides no shield for a state official confronted by a claim that he had deprived another of a federal right under the color of state law. . . .

Ex Parte Young
↓
Dealt w/ injunctive relief not damages

Ex parte Young involved a question of the federal courts' injunctive power, not, as here, a claim for monetary damages. While it is clear that the doctrine of *Ex parte Young* is of no aid to a plaintiff seeking damages from the public treasury, Edelman v. Jordan, 415 U.S. 651 (1974), damages against individual defendants are a permissible remedy in some circumstances notwithstanding the fact that they hold public office. In some situations a damage remedy can be as effective a redress for the infringement of a constitutional right as injunctive relief might be in another.

Analyzing the complaints in light of these precedents, we see that petitioners allege facts that demonstrate they are seeking to impose individual and personal liability on the *named defendants* for what they claim—but have not yet established by proof—was a deprivation of federal rights by these defendants under color of state law. Whatever the plaintiffs may or may not be able to establish as to the merits of their allegations, their claims, as stated in the complaints, given the favorable reading required by the Federal Rules of Civil Procedure, are not barred by the Eleventh Amendment. . . .

III

The Court of Appeals relied upon the existence of an absolute "executive immunity" as an alternative ground for sustaining the dismissal of the complaints by the District Court. If the immunity of a member of the executive branch is absolute and comprehensive as to all acts allegedly performed within the scope of official duty, the Court of Appeals was correct; if, on the other hand, the immunity is not absolute but rather one that is qualified or limited, an executive officer may or may not be subject to liability depending on all the circumstances that may be revealed by the evidence. The concept of the immunity of government officers from personal liability springs from the same root considerations that generated the doctrine of sovereign immunity. While the latter doctrine—that the "king can do no wrong"—did not protect all government officers from personal liability, the common law soon recognized the necessity of permitting officials to perform their official functions free from the threat of suits for personal liability. This official immunity apparently rested, in its genesis, on two mutually dependent rationales: (1) the injustice, particularly in the absence of bad faith, of subjecting to liability an officer who is required, by the legal obligations of his position, to exercise discretion; (2) the danger that the threat of such liability would deter his willingness to execute his office with the decisiveness and the judgment required by the public good. . . .

Although the development of the general concept of immunity, and the mutations which the underlying rationale has undergone in its application to various positions are not matters of immediate concern here, it is important to note, even at the outset, that one policy consideration seems to pervade the analysis: the public interest requires decisions and action to enforce laws for the protection of the public. Mr. Justice Jackson expressed this general proposition succinctly, stating "it is not a tort for government to govern." Public officials, whether governors, mayors or police, legislators or judges, who fail to make decisions when they are needed or who do not act to implement decisions when they are made do not fully and faithfully perform the duties of their offices. Implicit in the idea that officials have some immunity—absolute or qualified—for their acts, is a recognition that they may err. The concept of immunity assumes this and goes on to assume that it is better to risk some error and possible injury from such error than not to decide or act at all. In Barr v. Matteo, 360 U.S. 564, 572–73 (1959), the Court observed, in the somewhat parallel context of the privilege of public officers from defamation actions, "The privilege is not a badge or emolument of exalted office, but an expression of a policy designed to aid in the effective functioning of government."

For present purposes we need determine only whether there is an absolute immunity, as the Court of Appeals determined, governing the specific allegations of the complaint against the chief executive officer of a state, the senior and subordinate officers and enlisted personnel of that state's National Guard, and the president of a state-controlled university. If the immunity is qualified, not absolute, the scope of that immunity will necessarily be related to facts as yet not established either by affidavits, admissions or a trial record. Final resolution of this question must take into account the functions and responsibilities of these particular defendants in their capacities as officers of the state government, as well as the purposes of 42 U.S.C. § 1983. . . .

Soon after *Monroe v. Pape*, Mr. Chief Justice Warren noted in Pierson v. Ray, 386 U.S. 547 (1967), that the "legislative record [of § 1983] gives no clear indication that Congress meant to abolish wholesale all common-law immunities." The Court had previously recognized that the Civil Rights Act of 1871 does not create civil liability for legislative acts by legislators "in a field where legislators traditionally have power to act." Tenney v. Brandhove, 341 U.S. 367 (1951). . . .

In similar fashion, *Pierson v. Ray* examined the scope of judicial immunity under this statute. Noting that the record contained no "proof or specific allegation" that the trial judge had "played any role in these arrests and convictions other than to adjudge petitioners guilty when their cases came before his court," the Court concluded that, had the Congress intended to abolish the common-law "immunity of judges for acts within the judicial role," it would have done so specifically. . . .

The *Pierson* Court was also confronted with whether immunity was available to that segment of the executive branch of a state government that is most frequently and intimately involved in day-to-day contacts with the citizenry and, hence, most frequently exposed to situations which can give rise to claims under § 1983—the local police officer. . . . The Court noted that the "common law has never granted police officers an absolute and unqualified immunity," but that "the prevailing view in this country [is that] a peace officer who arrests someone with probable cause is not liable for false arrest simply because the innocence of the suspect is later proved"; the Court went on to observe that a "policeman's lot is not so unhappy that he must choose between being charged with dereliction of duty if he does not arrest when he has probable cause, and being mulcted in damages if he does." The Court then held:

> that the defense of good faith and probable cause, which the Court of Appeals found available to the officers in the common-law action for false arrest and imprisonment, is also available to them in the action under 1983.

When a court evaluates police conduct relating to an arrest its guideline is "good faith and probable cause." In the case of higher officers of the executive branch, however, the inquiry is far more complex since the range of decisions and choices—whether the formulation of policy, of legislation, of budgets, or of day-to-day decisions—is virtually infinite. In common with police officers, however, officials with a broad range of duties and authority must often act swiftly and firmly at the risk that action

Police officer reasoning

deferred will be futile or constitute virtual abdication of office. Like legislators and judges, these officers are entitled to rely on traditional sources for the factual information on which they decide and act. When a condition of civil disorder in fact exists, there is obvious need for prompt action, and decisions must be made in reliance on factual information supplied by others. While both federal and state laws plainly contemplate the use of force when the necessity arises, the decision to invoke military power has traditionally been viewed with suspicion and skepticism since it often involves the temporary suspension of some of our most cherished rights—government by elected civilian leaders, freedom of expression, of assembly, and of association. Decisions in such situations are more likely than not to arise in an atmosphere of confusion, ambiguity, and swiftly moving events and when, by the very existence of some degree of civil disorder, there is often no consensus as to the appropriate remedy. In short, since the options which a chief executive and his principal subordinates must consider are far broader and far more subtle than those made by officials with less responsibility, the range of discretion must be comparably broad. . . .

These considerations suggest that, in varying scope, a qualified immunity is available to officers of the executive branch of government, the variation being dependent upon the scope of discretion and responsibilities of the office and all the circumstances as they reasonably appeared at the time of the action on which liability is sought to be based. It is the existence of reasonable grounds for the belief formed at the time and in light of all the circumstances, coupled with good-faith belief, that affords a basis for qualified immunity of executive officers for acts performed in the course of official conduct. . . .

Where immunity comes from

IV

These cases, in their present posture, present no occasion for a definitive exploration of the scope of immunity available to state executive officials nor, because of the absence of a factual record, do they permit a determination as to the applicability of the foregoing principles to the respondents here. The District Court acted before answers were filed and without any evidence other than the copies of the proclamations issued by respondent [Governor] Rhodes and brief affidavits of the adjutant general and his assistant. In dismissing the complaints, the District Court and the Court of Appeals erroneously accepted as a fact the good faith of the governor, and took judicial notice that "mob rule existed at Kent State University." There was no opportunity afforded petitioners to contest the facts assumed in that conclusion. There was no evidence before the courts from which such a finding of good faith could be properly made and, in the circumstances of these cases, such a dispositive conclusion could not be judicially noticed. We can readily grant that a declaration of emergency by the chief executive of a state is entitled to great weight but it is not conclusive.

Dismissed too soon

The documents properly before the District Court at this early pleading stage specifically placed in issue whether the governor and his subordinate officers were acting within the scope of their duties under the Constitution and laws of Ohio; whether they acted within the range of discretion permitted the holders of such office under Ohio law and whether they acted in good faith both in proclaiming an emergency and as to the actions taken to cope with the emergency so declared. Similarly, the complaints place directly in issue whether the lesser officers and enlisted personnel of the Guard acted in good-faith obedience to the orders of their superiors. Further proceedings, either by way of summary judgment or by trial on the merits, are required. . . .

The judgments of the Court of Appeals are reversed and the cases are remanded for further proceedings consistent with this opinion.

■ MR. JUSTICE DOUGLAS took no part in the decision of these cases.[a]

NOTES ON IMMUNITY FROM AWARD OF DAMAGES

1. BACKGROUND

Scheuer discusses two important early cases. Tenney v. Brandhove, 341 U.S. 367 (1951), held that persons engaged in legitimate legislative activity are absolutely immune from civil liability under § 1983. The Court reasoned that legislative immunity was so well established at common law that Congress would have explicitly said so if it had meant to abolish such immunity under § 1983. Pierson v. Ray, 386 U.S. 547 (1967), extended this reasoning to judges, but held that police officers sued for unconstitutional arrest of civil rights demonstrators were entitled only to a "qualified" defense of "good faith and probable cause."

Thus, by the time of *Scheuer v. Rhodes*, it was established, despite the complete absence of statutory language to this effect, that liability for damages under § 1983 is limited by official immunity and that the immunity may be either absolute or qualified. Persons performing legislative or judicial functions are absolutely immune, and, as the Court subsequently decided, certain core prosecutorial functions also trigger absolute immunity. Imbler v. Pachtman, 424 U.S. 409 (1976). Law enforcement personnel, however, are entitled only to a qualified defense.

Scheuer v. Rhodes was perhaps the first decision in which the Court devoted more attention to the merits of the immunity issue than to its common-law antecedents. Is the opinion persuasive? Does it explain why damages liability under § 1983 should be limited by official immunity? If so, does it

---

a   Following the Supreme Court's remand in *Scheuer,* the cases were tried on the merits. After a trial lasting nearly four months, the jury returned a verdict in favor of all defendants. This verdict was set aside on appeal because of threats made against a juror by some unknown person. Krause v. Rhodes, 570 F.2d 563 (6th Cir. 1977). The cases were then remanded for a second trial, but were eventually settled out of court. See Krause v. Rhodes, 535 F.Supp. 338 (N.D. Ohio 1979).—[Footnote by eds.]

demonstrate that the appropriate level of immunity for high executive officers is qualified rather than absolute? Why is absolute immunity less appropriate for a governor than for a judge or legislator?

2.   THE MEANING OF ABSOLUTE IMMUNITY

"Absolute" immunity refers to the level of immunity, not to its scope. For one thing, immunity from award of damages may not extend to declaratory or injunctive relief. Even with respect to damages, absolute immunity may not be completely comprehensive. There is always the requirement that the act complained of be within the sphere of activity for which the immunity has been recognized.

Generally speaking, the determinative factor is the function performed, not the office held. Individual city council members, although absolutely immune for legislative acts, were amenable to an award of damages when they urged discharge of the town's police chief. Miller v. City of Mission, 705 F.2d 368 (10th Cir. 1983). Similarly, a judge acting as such is absolutely immune from award of damages, but a judge acting in an administrative capacity (for example, in firing a court employee) enjoys only qualified immunity. Forrester v. White, 484 U.S. 219 (1988). And a judge who ordered a sandwich vendor to be handcuffed and brought before him for selling "putrid" coffee was held liable for compensatory and punitive damages on the sensible ground that monitoring matters of taste is no part of the business of judging. Zarcone v. Perry, 572 F.2d 52 (2d Cir. 1978). Most importantly, prosecutors are absolutely immune from the award of damages for acts "intimately associated with the judicial phase of the criminal process," but have only qualified immunity for investigative or administrative activities. Imbler v. Pachtman, 424 U.S. 409 (1976).

It is sometimes necessary to make close calls concerning the particular function performed. In Cleavinger v. Saxner, 474 U.S. 193 (1985), the Supreme Court considered the status of corrections officers who sat as members of a disciplinary committee to hear charges that inmates had violated prison rules. The Court found that the officers were not fulfilling a "classic" adjudicatory function. They were not independent adjudicators but only prison employees "temporarily diverted from their usual duties." As such, they were "under obvious pressure to resolve a disciplinary dispute in favor of the institution and their fellow employee." The officers were therefore entitled only to a qualified immunity from civil liability. Three Justices dissented.

Decisions on prosecutorial immunity also require line-drawing. In Burns v. Reed, 500 U.S. 478 (1991), Cathy Burns was charged with shooting her two sons while under the influence of a multiple personality, but the charges were dropped after the trial court suppressed incriminating statements obtained under hypnosis. She then sued the prosecutor, claiming two constitutional violations. First, the prosecutor had approved a police request to use hypnosis. Second, in a probable cause hearing to obtain a search warrant, he had elicited testimony of Burn's confession without mentioning the hypnosis. The Supreme Court held that absolute immunity extended only to the second claim, which was "intimately associated with the judicial phase of the criminal process" under *Imbler v. Pachtman*. For the first claim, involving faulty legal advice to the police, the prosecutor enjoyed only qualified immunity.

In Van de Kamp v. Goldstein, 555 U.S. 335 (2009), the Supreme Court ruled that some prosecutorial administrative responsibilities trigger absolute immunity. After securing his release from prison under federal habeas corpus, Goldstein sued the former Los Angeles County District Attorney and his chief deputy, asserting that they were liable for failure to train and supervise subordinates, who had failed to disclose impeachment material to the accused, as required by Giglio v. United States, 405 U.S. 150 (1972). The trial court ruled that the defendants were not entitled to absolute immunity, as their alleged failings were "administrative," not "prosecutorial," in nature. The Ninth Circuit affirmed. Although the Supreme Court agreed that the wrongs complained of involved administrative procedures, the Court unanimously upheld absolute immunity. In an opinion by Justice Breyer, the Court said:

> [W]e conclude that prosecutors involved in such supervision or training or information-system management enjoy absolute immunity from the kind of legal claims at issue here. Those claims focus upon a certain kind of administrative obligation—a kind that itself is directly connected with the conduct of a trial. Here, unlike with other claims related to administrative decisions, an individual prosecutor's error in the plaintiff's specific criminal trial constitutes an essential element of the plaintiff's claim. The administrative obligations at issue here are thus unlike administrative duties concerning, for example, workplace hiring, payroll administration, the maintenance of physical facilities, and the like. Moreover, the types of activities on which Goldstein's claims focus necessarily require legal knowledge and the exercise of related discretion, e.g., in determining what information should be included in the training or the supervision or the information-system management. And in that sense also Goldstein's claims are unlike claims of, say, unlawful discrimination in hiring employees. [We therefore] believe absolute immunity must follow.

Under *Van de Kamp*, even within the broad category of "administrative" responsibilities, some prosecutorial failings will be subject to absolute immunity. In every circumstance, one must ask how closely associated was the alleged misconduct with the "judicial phase" of criminal prosecution.

Where applicable, absolute immunity protects against damage actions, no matter how wrongful the act or malicious the motivation. The results can be extreme. Thus, for example, a justice of the peace was held immune from damages, even though he had convicted the defendant of a non-existent crime. Turner v. Raynes, 611 F.2d 92 (5th Cir. 1980). And in Stump v. Sparkman, 435 U.S. 349 (1978), a divided Supreme Court upheld the immunity of a state judge who ordered a tubal ligation on a 15-year-old girl who was told she was having an appendectomy. Obviously, the effect of absolute immunity is to vindicate fully the public's interest in unintimidated decisionmaking by

its officials, but only at a correspondingly complete sacrifice of the interests
of those who may be disadvantaged by abuse.

3. THE MEANING OF QUALIFIED IMMUNITY: *WOOD V. STRICKLAND*

The meaning of qualified immunity is more problematic. Not only is
there the same limitation as to scope of activity, but the level of protection is
itself qualified.

In *Pierson v. Ray,* the Court held that police sued for making unconstitutional arrests were entitled to a defense of "good faith and probable cause."
Obviously, this formulation of qualified immunity has particular relevance
to a charge of false arrest. In *Scheuer* the Court noted that "the inquiry is far
more complex" for higher level executive officials, but the Court followed
Pierson in making a two-pronged inquiry with both objective and subjective
components. Specifically, the Court asked whether an executive official had
"reasonable grounds for the belief formed at the time and in light of all the
circumstances, coupled with good-faith belief."

The Court returned to the issue of qualified immunity in Wood v. Strickland, 420 U.S. 308 (1975). Two teenage girls sued school board members who
expelled them for "spiking" the punch served at a high school event. Under
pressure from a teacher, the girls confessed to the principal, who suspended
them from school for two weeks, subject to review by the school board. That
night the school board met with neither the girls nor their parents present.
The board members heard recommendations of leniency and were preparing
to act when they received a phone call stating that a third participant in the
spiking incident had been involved in a fight at a basketball game. The board
then voted to expel all the girls for the rest of the semester, a period of about
three months. Two weeks later, the board held another meeting with the
girls, their parents, and counsel present, and affirmed its earlier decision.

The District Court instructed the jury that the school board members
could be held liable only if they acted with "malice," defined to mean "ill will
against a person—a wrongful act done intentionally without just cause or
excuse." The jury were unable to agree, and the court entered judgment for
defendants on the ground that there was no evidence of "malice." The Court
of Appeals reversed. It ruled that intent to harm was not required and that
the defendants' liability should be determined by an "objective," rather than
"subjective," test of good faith. The Supreme Court, in an opinion by Justice
White, said the following:

> The disagreement between the Court of Appeals and the Dis-
> trict Court over the immunity standard in his case has been put in
> terms of an "objective" versus a "subjective" test of good faith. As
> we see it, the appropriate standard necessarily contains elements
> of both. The official himself must be acting sincerely and with a
> belief that he is doing right, but an act violating a student's consti-
> tutional rights can be no more justified by ignorance or disregard
> of settled, indisputable law on the part of one entrusted with super-
> vision of students' daily lives than by the presence of actual malice.
> To be entitled to a special exemption from the categorical remedial

language of § 1983 in a case in which his action violated a student's constitutional rights, a school board member, who has voluntarily undertaken the task of supervising the operation of the school and the activities of the students, must be held to a standard of conduct based not only on permissible intentions, but also on knowledge of the basic, unquestioned constitutional rights of his charges. . . . Therefore, in the specific context of school discipline, we hold that a school board member is not immune from liability for damages under § 1983 if he knew or reasonably should have known that the action he took within his sphere of official responsibility would violate the constitutional rights of the student affected, or if he took the action with the malicious intention to cause a deprivation of constitutional rights or other injury to the students.

These remarks prompted a dissent by Justice Powell, in which the Chief Justice and Justices Blackmun and Rehnquist joined. The dissenters objected particularly to the majority's insistence that liability could be based on a school official's lack of knowledge of constitutional rights, as distinct from subjective bad faith:

This harsh standard, requiring knowledge of what is characterized as "settled, indisputable law," leaves little substance to the doctrine of qualified immunity. The Court's decision appears to rest on an unwarranted assumption as to what lay school officials know or can know about the law and constitutional rights. These officials will now act at the peril of some judge or jury subsequently finding that a good-faith belief as to the applicable law was mistaken and hence actionable.

The Court states the standard of required knowledge in two cryptic phrases: "settled, indisputable law" and "unquestioned constitutional rights." Presumably these are intended to mean the same thing, although the meaning of neither phrase is likely to be self-evident to constitutional law scholars—much less the average school board member. . . .

One problem with this standard concerns the knowledge of the law that a lay official should be expected to have. Obviously, it is not realistic to expect lay officials to have a lawyer's skills, but it is reasonable to demand that a lay official exercising government power know more about the limitations on the use of that power than would an ordinary citizen. Where is the line to be drawn? Is ignorance unreasonable if one fails to consult a lawyer? Should it depend on whether the official has ready access to legal advice? Is acting on a lawyer's advice automatically reasonable?

4.   *HARLOW V. FITZGERALD*

Though the *Wood v. Strickland* dissenters anticipated difficulty with the objective branch of qualified immunity, the subjective inquiry proved more troublesome. Problems arose with the substantial pre-trial proceedings sometimes required to determine whether an allegation of subjective bad faith had adequate foundation to proceed to trial. The Court addressed this problem in Harlow v. Fitzgerald, 457 U.S. 800 (1982).

Fitzgerald was a notorious "whistle-blower" in the Department of Defense. Following the elimination of his job in an Air Force reorganization, Fitzgerald brought a damage action[a] against a number of people, including Harlow, a presidential aide primarily responsible for congressional relations. Fitzgerald claimed that Harlow and others conspired to discharge Fitzgerald in retaliation for testifying to Congress concerning cost overruns in the Air Force. The alleged conspiracy took place in the years preceding Fitzgerald's dismissal in 1970. Fitzgerald filed suit in 1973, and Harlow was added as a defendant in an amended complaint in 1978. Harlow denied any involvement in the decision to fire Fitzgerald, and at the conclusion of extensive discovery, the evidence of Harlow's involvement "remained inferential." The trial court denied a motion for summary judgment, and a "collateral order" appeal was taken before trial to resolve the disputed issue of Harlow's immunity. The Supreme Court discussed that issue as follows:

> The resolution of immunity questions inherently requires a balance between the evils inevitable in any available alternative. In situations of abuse of office, an action for damages may offer the only realistic avenue for vindication of constitutional guarantees. It is this recognition that has required the denial of absolute immunity to most public officers. At the same time, however, it cannot be disputed seriously that claims frequently run against the innocent as well as the guilty—at a cost not only to the defendant officials, but to society as a whole. . . .

> In identifying qualified immunity as the best attainable accommodation of competing values, in Butz v. Economou, 438 U.S. 478 (1978) [holding federal executive officials entitled to qualified immunity in Bivens actions], and Scheuer v. Rhodes we relied on the assumption that this standard would permit "[i]nsubstantial lawsuits [to] be quickly terminated." Yet petitioners advance persuasive arguments that the dismissal of insubstantial lawsuits without trial—a factor presupposed in the balance of competing interests struck by our prior cases—requires an adjustment of the "good faith" standard established by our decisions.

> Qualified or "good faith" immunity is an affirmative defense that must be pleaded by a defendant official. Decisions of this Court have established that the "good faith" defense has both an "objective" and a "subjective" aspect. The objective element involves a presumptive knowledge of and respect for "basic, unquestioned constitutional rights." Wood v. Strickland, 420 U.S. 308, 322 (1975). The subjective component refers to "permissible intentions." Id. Characteristically, the Court has defined these elements by identifying the circumstances in which qualified immunity would *not* be

---

[a]   Since § 1983 applies in terms only to persons acting under color of *state* law, this action was a *Bivens*-type action brought directly under the Constitution. For present purposes, the distinction is immaterial, since the same concept of qualified immunity applies in both contexts.

available. Referring both to the objective and subjective elements, we have held that qualified immunity would be defeated if an official *"knew or reasonably should have known* that the action he took within his sphere of official responsibility would violate the constitutional rights of the [plaintiff], or if he took the action *with the malicious intention* to cause a deprivation of constitutional rights or other injury. . . ." Id. (emphasis added).

The subjective element of the good-faith defense frequently has proved incompatible with our admonition in *Butz* that insubstantial claims should not proceed to trial. Rule 56 of the Federal Rules of Civil Procedure provides that disputed questions of fact ordinarily may not be decided on motions for summary judgment. And an official's subjective good faith has been considered to be a question of fact that some courts have regarded as inherently requiring resolution by a jury.

In the context of *Butz*'s attempted balancing of competing values, it now is clear that substantial costs attend the litigation of the subjective good faith of government officials. Not only are there the general costs of subjecting officials to the risks of trial—distraction of officials from their governmental duties, inhibition of discretionary action, and deterrence of able people from public service. There are special costs to "subjective" inquiries of this kind. Immunity generally is available only to officials performing discretionary functions. In contrast with the thought processes accompanying "ministerial" tasks, the judgments surrounding discretionary action almost inevitably are influenced by the decisionmaker's experiences, values, and emotions. These variables explain in part why questions of subjective intent so rarely can be decided by summary judgment. Yet they also frame a background in which there often is no clear end to the relevant evidence. Judicial inquiry into subjective motivation therefore may entail broad-ranging discovery and the deposing of numerous persons, including an official's professional colleagues. Inquiries of this kind can be peculiarly disruptive of effective government.

Consistently with the balance at which we aimed in *Butz*, we conclude today that bare allegations of malice should not suffice to subject government officials either to the costs of trial or to the burdens of broad-reaching discovery. We therefore hold that government officials performing discretionary functions generally are shielded from liability for civil damages insofar as their conduct does not violate clearly established statutory or constitutional rights of which a reasonable person would have known.

Reliance on the objective reasonableness of an official's conduct, as measured by reference to clearly established law, should avoid excessive disruption of government and permit the resolution of many insubstantial claims on summary judgment. On summary judgment, the judge appropriately may determine, not only the currently applicable law, but whether that law was clearly established at the time an action occurred. If the law at that time was not clearly established, an official could not reasonably be expected to anticipate subsequent legal developments, nor could he fairly be said to "know" that the law forbade conduct not previously identified as unlawful. Until this threshold immunity question is resolved, discovery should not be allowed.

5. ANDERSON V. CREIGHTON

Harlow was revisited in Anderson v. Creighton, 483 U.S. 635 (1987). Anderson was an FBI agent who, when sued for making an unlawful search, filed a pre-trial motion for summary judgment. Ultimately, the Supreme Court ruled that he was entitled to summary judgment if, in light of the clearly established principles, a reasonable officer in Anderson's situation could have believed that the search was lawful.

In an opinion by Justice Scalia, the Court acknowledged the "driving force behind *Harlow*'s substantial reformulation of qualified-immunity principles—that 'insubstantial claims' against government officials be resolved prior to discovery and on summary judgment if possible." *Harlow* required an inquiry into the "objective legal reasonableness" of the action taken, judged in light of "clearly established" legal rules. In this case, the relevant issue was "the objective (albeit fact-specific) question whether a reasonable officer could have believed Anderson's warrantless search to be lawful, in light of clearly established law and the information the searching officers possessed." The Court explicitly stated that "Anderson's subjective beliefs about the search are irrelevant." In a concluding footnote, the Court added:

> Thus, on remand, it should first be determined whether the actions the Creightons allege Anderson to have taken are actions that a reasonable officer could have believed lawful. If they are, then Anderson is entitled to dismissal prior to discovery. If they are not, and if the actions Anderson claims he took are different from those the Creightons allege (and are actions that a reasonable officer could have believed lawful), then discovery may be necessary before Anderson's motion for summary judgment on qualified immunity grounds can be resolved. Of course, any such discovery should be tailored specifically to the question of Anderson's qualified immunity.

Justice Stevens, joined by Justices Brennan and Marshall, dissented at length. First, Stevens disputed the applicability of *Harlow*. Here there was no uncertainty in the legal standards, but only in their application to particular facts. Stevens therefore thought pre-trial summary judgment inappropriate:

> In this Court, Anderson has not argued that any relevant rule of law—whether the probable-cause requirement or the exigent-circumstances exception to the warrant requirement—was not "clearly established" in November 1983. Rather, he argues that a competent officer might have concluded that the particular set of

facts he faced did constitute "probable cause" and "exigent circumstances," and that his own reasonable belief that the conduct engaged in was within the law suffices to establish immunity. But the factual predicate for Anderson's argument is not found in the [plaintiffs'] complaint, but rather in the affidavits that he has filed in support of his motion for summary judgment. Obviously, the [plaintiffs] must be given an opportunity to have discovery to test the accuracy and completeness of the factual basis for the immunity claim.

Stevens emphasized that denial of *Harlow* immunity would not necessarily mean that the defendant would be liable. It would merely require that the case go to trial. The defendant official would still have a chance at trial to raise a reasonable good-faith defense, if adequately supported by the evidence.

Finally, Stevens argued with specific reference to the Fourth Amendment that qualified immunity should not be available to officers accused of conducting unlawful searches. In his view, tolerance for reasonable police error was already built into the constitutional standard: "[T]he probable cause standard itself recognizes the fair leeway that law enforcement officers must have in carrying out their dangerous work. The concept of probable cause leaves room for mistakes, provided always that they are mistakes that could have been made by a reasonable officer." Immunity for reasonable mistakes about whether probable cause existed struck Stevens as unwise:

> The argument that police officers need special immunity to encourage them to take vigorous enforcement action when they are uncertain about their right to make a forcible entry into a private home has already been accepted in our jurisprudence. We have held that the police act reasonably in entering a house when they have probable cause to believe a fugitive is in the house and exigent circumstances make it impracticable to obtain a warrant. This interpretation of the Fourth Amendment allows room for police intrusion, without a warrant, on the privacy of even innocent citizens. . . .

> Thus, until now the Court has not found intolerable the use of a probable-cause standard to protect the police officer from exposure to liability simply because his reasonable conduct is subsequently shown to have been mistaken. Today, however, the Court counts the law enforcement interest twice and the individual's privacy interest only once.

> The Court's double-counting approach reflects understandable sympathy for the plight of the officer and an overriding interest in unfettered law enforcement. It ascribes a far lesser importance to the privacy interest of innocent citizens than did the framers of the Fourth Amendment. The importance of that interest and the possible magnitude of its invasion are both illustrated by the facts of this case. The home of an innocent family was invaded by several officers without a warrant, without the owner's consent, with a substan-

tial show of force, and with blunt expressions of disrespect for the law and for the rights of the family members. As the case comes to us, we must assume that the intrusion violated the Fourth Amendment. Proceeding on that assumption, I see no reason why the family's interest in the security of its own home should be accorded a lesser weight than the government's interest in carrying out an invasion that was unlawful. . . .

6.   *CRAWFORD-EL V. BRITTON*

The question in Crawford-El v. Britton, 523 U.S. 574 (1998), was whether *Harlow*-inspired protections against discovery and trial should be deployed when improper motivation is required, not to disprove qualified immunity, but to establish the underlying constitutional violation. Examples are racial discrimination, which requires proof of discriminatory animus, and First Amendment retaliation, which requires proof of a retaliatory motive. In such cases, subjective motivation is relevant, not to qualified immunity but to the existence of a constitutional violation.

The *Crawford-El* Court made clear, if there had been any doubt, that the subjective branch of qualified immunity was completely eliminated. Under *Harlow*, said the Court, "a defense of qualified immunity may not be rebutted by evidence that the defendant's conduct was malicious or otherwise improperly motivated. Evidence concerning the defendant's subjective intent is simply irrelevant to that defense."

The Court, however, refused to make any analogous change in the proof of improper motivation where required by the underlying constitutional claim. The specific question at issue was the D.C. Circuit's ruling that a plaintiff alleging a constitutional violation requiring proof of improper motive had to prove that motive by clear and convincing evidence. By a vote of five to four, the Supreme Court disapproved that requirement. The Court did say, however, that trial judges could order a reply or more definite statement from the plaintiff and could "insist that the plaintiff 'put forward specific, nonconclusory factual allegations' that establish improper motive causing cognizable injury in order to survive a prediscovery motion for dismissal or summary judgment," citing Siegert v. Gilley, 500 U.S. 226, 236 (1991) (Kennedy, J., concurring in the judgment). This remark raised the possibility that heightened *pleading* might be required in unconstitutional-motive cases, even if heightened *proof* was not.

7.   *ASHCROFT V. IQBAL*

The Court imposed a heightened pleading requirement a decade later in Ashcroft v. Iqbal, 556 U.S. 662 (2009). The case involved a *Bivens* action brought by an alien detainee following the September 11 terrorist attacks. He claimed that the Attorney General and the Director of the FBI (among others) had discriminated against him on the basis of race, religion, and national origin by treating him as a person of "high interest" to be confined in a maximum security facility. The defendants invoked qualified immunity and moved to dismiss the claim. This claim required proof of purposeful discrimination by the Attorney General and the Director. These defendants could not be held liable on a theory of respondeat superior or deliberate in-difference. They could be held liable only for intentional discrimination in the exercise of their supervisory responsibilities.

Although the complaint alleged that the Attorney General and the Director had adopted the policy of detaining persons of "high interest" in maximum security facilities, it did not assert, apart from conclusory allegations, that they had done so for discriminatory reasons. The plaintiff's failure to make specific allegations of facts from which discriminatory motivation could be inferred led to the Court's dismissal of the complaint for failure to "state a claim to relief that is plausible on its face."

As an ordinary pleading matter, *Iqbal* is puzzling. Generally speaking, discriminatory intent is something that plaintiffs are allowed to allege quite generally under Federal Rule of Civil Procedure 9(b). Even if the plaintiff made more detailed allegations, there would be little chance of substantiating them without discovery. It seems clear, therefore, that *Iqbal* was not merely a pleading case but was heavily influenced by *Harlow*-like concerns about the administration of qualified immunity. Plaintiffs in unconstitutional-motivation cases now must be able to advance plausible allegations *before* discovery, and defendants can potentially avoid discovery when specific allegations cannot be stated. As the implementation of *Iqbal* in the lower courts becomes more clear, it may well convert the *suggestion* in *Crawford-El* that trial judges might require greater specificity in particular cases into a mandatory requirement of heightened pleading in all unconstitutional-motivation cases.[b]

8. APPEALABILITY OF IMMUNITY DENIALS: *MITCHELL V. FORSYTH*

In Mitchell v. Forsyth, 472 U.S. 511 (1985), former Attorney General John Mitchell was sued by a person whose telephone conversations had been intercepted in a "national security" wiretap. Mitchell claimed qualified immunity based on the uncertain legality of such wiretaps at the time of the

---

    b   *Iqbal* has been the subject of extensive commentary, including a Symposium in volume 14 of the Lewis & Clark Law Review featuring, among articles from various perspectives, Howard M. Wasserman, *Iqbal*, Procedural Mismatches, and Civil Rights Litigation, 14 Lewis & Clark L. Rev. 157 (2010) (arguing that *Iqbal* will lead to a substantial decrease in the enforcement of civil rights because of the specificity it requires for a plausible claim), and Sheldon Nahmod, Constitutional Torts, Over-Deterrence, and Supervisory Liability after *Iqbal*, 14 Lewis & Clark L. Rev. 279 (2010) (approving the conclusion, although not the reasoning, of the opinion in requiring proof of supervisors' intent when it is an element of the underlying constitutional violation). See also Gary S. Gildin, The Supreme Court's Legislative Agenda to Free Government from Accountability for Constitutional Deprivations, 114 Penn. St. L. Rev. 1333 (2010) (criticizing *Iqbal* as "the latest instance in a long line of cases in which the Supreme court, acting sua sponte, legislates a doctrine freeing government and its officials from accountability for proven violations of the Constitution"); Karen M. Blum, Section 1983 Litigation: Post-*Pearson* and Post-*Iqbal*, 26 Touro L. Rev. 433 (2010) (providing an early look at post-*Iqbal* experience in the lower courts); Mark R. Brown, Qualified Immunity and Interlocutory Fact-Finding in the Courts of Appeals, 114 Penn. St. L. Rev. 1317 (2010) (criticizing *Iqbal*, among other reasons, for embracing interlocutory appellate review of fact-finding associated with the new pleading requirements); Kit Kinports, *Iqbal* and Supervisory Immunity, 114 Penn. St. L. Rev. 1291 (2010) (criticizing *Iqbal* for rejecting supervisory liability and analyzing how qualified immunity should apply in such cases); James E. Pfander, *Iqbal*, *Bivens*, and the Role of Judge-Made Law in Constitutional Litigation, 114 Penn. St. L. Rev. 1387 (2010) (contrasting the judicial creativity evident in *Iqbal* and in qualified immunity cases generally with the disclaimer of judicial authority to allow recovery against federal officers under *Bivens*).

authorization. The District Court rejected this claim, holding that Mitchell should have anticipated the Supreme Court's subsequent rejection of such wiretaps in United States v. United States District Court (the *Keith* case), 407 U.S. 297 (1972). The District Court then granted summary judgment against Mitchell on the question of liability and scheduled a trial on damages.

The question was whether the trial court's rejection of the immunity defense was immediately appealable. Mitchell claimed that immediate appeal was authorized by the "collateral order" doctrine of Cohen v. Beneficial Industrial Loan Corp., 337 U.S. 541 (1949).[c] The Supreme Court agreed, with Justices Brennan and Marshall dissenting:

> [T]he *Harlow* Court refashioned the qualified immunity doctrine in such a way as to "permit the resolution of many insubstantial claims on summary judgment" and to avoid "subject[ing] government officials either to the costs of trial or to the burdens of broad-reaching discovery" in cases where the legal norms the officials are alleged to have violated were not clearly established at the time. Unless the plaintiff's allegations state a claim of violation of clearly established law, a defendant pleading qualified immunity is entitled to dismissal before the commencement of discovery. Even if the plaintiff's complaint adequately alleges the commission of acts that violated clearly established law, the defendant is entitled to summary judgment if discovery fails to uncover evidence sufficient to create a genuine issue as to whether the defendant in fact committed those acts. *Harlow* thus recognized an entitlement not to stand trial or face the other burdens of litigation, conditioned on the resolution of the essentially legal question whether the conduct of which the plaintiff complains violated clearly established law. The entitlement is an *immunity from suit* rather than a mere defense to liability; and like an absolute immunity, it is effectively lost if a case is erroneously permitted to go to trial. Accordingly, the reasoning that underlies the immediate appealability of an order denying absolute immunity indicates to us that the denial of qualified immunity should be similarly appealable: in each case, the district court's decision is effectively unreviewable on appeal from a final judgment.

On the merits, the Court held that Mitchell was entitled to summary judgment on his claim of qualified immunity.

9.   THE LIMITS OF *MITCHELL*: *JOHNSON V. JONES*

In an opinion by Justice Breyer, the Court unanimously limited the immediate appealability of trial court immunity denials in Johnson v. Jones, 515 U.S. 304 (1995). Jones, a diabetic, suffered an insulin seizure on a public

---

[c] *Cohen* held that a decision is "final" for purposes of appeal if it falls within "that small class which finally determines claims of right separable from, and collateral to, rights asserted in the action, too important to be denied review, and too independent of the cause itself to require that appellate consideration be deferred until the whole case is adjudicated." *Cohen* and its progeny are discussed in Chapter V.

street. He was arrested by police officers who thought he was drunk and later found himself in a hospital with several broken ribs. Suit was filed under § 1983 against five policemen whom he accused of using excessive force during the arrest and beating him at the police station.

Three of the officer-defendants moved for summary judgment on the ground that Jones had no evidence that they either beat him or were present while others did. Jones contested these factual assertions, and the District Court denied the summary judgment motion on the ground that the record revealed genuine issues of disputed fact. The three officers immediately appealed, but the Circuit Court distinguished *Mitchell* and refused to accept jurisdiction. The Supreme Court affirmed. It held that courts were required to separate a "reviewable determination (that a given set of facts violates clearly established law) from [an] unreviewable determination (that an issue of fact is 'genuine')." A "simple 'we didn't do it' case," in the Court's view, presented an easy illustration of an inappropriate interlocutory appeal.[d]

10. ANALOGOUS IMMUNITIES FOR FEDERAL OFFICIALS

Section 1983 applies in terms only to persons acting under color of state law. Under Bivens v. Six Unknown Named Agents of the Federal Bureau of Narcotics, 403 U.S. 388 (1971), and subsequent cases, however, damage actions may be brought against federal officers for violations of constitutional rights. In Butz v. Economou, 438 U.S. 478, 504 (1978), the Court concluded that it would be "untenable to draw a distinction for purposes of immunity law between suits brought against state officials under § 1983 and suits brought directly under the Constitution against federal officers." For most purposes, therefore, the immunities accorded state and federal officers are the same. Indeed, the two lines of cases are cited interchangeably.

There are, however, a few respects in which federal officers are treated specially. Members of Congress are protected by Art. I, § 6, which provides in part that senators and representatives "shall in all Cases, except Treason, Felony and Breach of the Peace, be privileged from Arrest during their Attendance at the Sessions of their respective Houses, and in going to and returning from the same; and for any Speech or Debate in either House, they shall not be questioned in any other Place." The privilege from arrest has been read narrowly to permit the operation against senators and congressmen of ordinary criminal laws, see Gravel v. United States, 408 U.S. 606 (1972), but the Speech or Debate Clause had been construed quite broadly. Generally speaking, the Speech or Debate Clause protects federal legislators and their aides from being prosecuted or punished in relation to any official acts.

---

[d]   The Court also ruled that state courts do not have to provide the opportunity for interlocutory appeal that would be available in federal courts under *Mitchell*. In Johnson v. Fankell, 520 U.S. 911 (1997), Justice Stevens wrote for a unanimous Court. "The right to have the trial court rule on the merits of the qualified immunity defense presumably has its source in § 1983," the Court said, "but the right to immediate appellate review of that ruling in a federal case has its source in § 1291. The former right is fully protected by Idaho. The latter right, however, is a federal procedural right that simply does not apply in a nonfederal forum."

Another special feature of the law governing federal officers is the president's absolute immunity from award of damages for official misconduct. See Nixon v. Fitzgerald, 457 U.S. 731 (1982). No comparable immunity extends to state executives. In *Nixon*, the Court, speaking through Justice Powell, found that the "president occupies a unique position in the constitutional scheme" and is "entrusted with supervisory and policy responsibilities of utmost discretion and sensitivity" on a wide range of matters: "In view of the visibility of his office and the effect of his actions on countless people, the president would be an easily identifiable target for suits for civil damages. Cognizance of this personal vulnerability frequently could distract a president from his public duties, to the detriment not only of the president and his office but also the nation that the presidency was designed to serve." The Court concluded, therefore, that the president should have an absolute immunity for all acts within the "outer perimeter" of presidential responsibility.

Justice White dissented in an opinion joined by Justices Brennan, Marshall, and Blackmun. The dissenters argued that the scope of presidential immunity should be determined by function, not office. Thus, while absolute immunity might be appropriate for certain acts (e.g., presidential participation in prosecutorial decisions), qualified immunity should be applied to others. In the view of the dissenters, absolute immunity effectively placed the president above the law.[e]

Aside from the somewhat broader immunity accorded federal legislators and the president's absolute immunity from damage actions, federal officials are treated the same as are their state and local counterparts under § 1983. Thus, federal judges and law enforcement officers and executive personnel generally are entitled to the same absolute or qualified immunity, as the case may be, as exists under § 1983, and the meaning of those levels of immunity is generally the same in both contexts.

Brosseau v. Haugen

Supreme Court of the United States, 2004.
543 U.S. 194.

■ PER CURIAM.

Officer Rochelle Brosseau, a member of the Puyallup, Washington, Police Department, shot Kenneth Haugen in the back as he attempted to flee from law enforcement authorities in his vehicle. Haugen subsequently filed this action in the United States District Court for the Western District of Washington pursuant to 42 U.S.C. § 1983. He alleged that the shot fired by Brosseau constituted excessive force and violated his federal constitutional rights. The District Court granted summary judgment to Brosseau after finding she was entitled to qualified immunity. The Court

---

[e]   The implications of *Nixon v. Fitzgerald* for President Clinton excited much comment when Paula Jones sued the President for alleged wrongs before he took office. In response, the President claimed executive immunity for pre-presidential conduct. The Supreme Court ultimately rejected that claim. Clinton v. Jones, 520 U.S. 681 (1997). Rather than recognize any legal immunity for unofficial acts, the Court relied on the sound discretion of district judges to protect sitting presidents from harassment and frivolous litigation.

of Appeals for the Ninth Circuit reversed. Following the two-step process set out in Saucier v. Katz, 533 U.S. 194 (2001), the Court of Appeals found, first, that Brosseau had violated Haugen's Fourth Amendment right to be free from excessive force and, second, that the right violated was clearly established and thus Brosseau was not entitled to qualified immunity. Brosseau then petitioned for writ of certiorari, requesting that we review both of the Court of Appeals' determinations. We grant the petition on the second, qualified immunity question and [summarily] reverse.

The material facts, construed in a light most favorable to Haugen, are as follows. On the day before the fracas, Glen Tamburello went to the police station and reported to Brosseau that Haugen, a former crime partner of his, had stolen tools from his shop. Brosseau later learned that there was a felony no-bail warrant out for Haugen's arrest on drug and other offenses. The next morning, Haugen was spray-painting his Jeep Cherokee in his mother's driveway. Tamburello learned of Haugen's whereabouts, and he and cohort Matt Atwood drove a pickup truck to Haugen's mother's house to pay Haugen a visit. A fight ensued, which was witnessed by a neighbor who called 911.

Brosseau heard a report that the men were fighting in Haugen's mother's yard and responded. When she arrived, Tamburello and Atwood were attempting to get Haugen into Tamburello's pickup. Brosseau's arrival created a distraction, which provided Haugen the opportunity to get away. Haugen ran through his mother's yard and hid in the neighborhood. Brosseau requested assistance, and, shortly thereafter, two officers arrived with a K-9 to help track Haugen down. . . .

An officer radioed from down the street that a neighbor had seen a man in her backyard. Brosseau ran in that direction, and Haugen appeared. He ran past the front of his mother's house and then turned and ran into the driveway. With Brosseau still in pursuit, he jumped into the driver's side of the Jeep and closed and locked the door. Brosseau believed that he was running to the Jeep to retrieve a weapon.

Brosseau arrived at the Jeep, pointed her gun at Haugen, and ordered him to get out of the vehicle. Haugen ignored her command and continued to look for the keys so that he could get the Jeep started. Brosseau repeated her commands and hit the driver's side window several times with her handgun, which failed to deter Haugen. On the third or fourth try, the window shattered. Brosseau unsuccessfully attempted to grab the keys and struck Haugen on the head with the barrel and butt of her gun. Haugen, still undeterred, succeeded in starting the Jeep. As the Jeep started or shortly after it began to move, Brosseau jumped back and to the left. She fired one shot through the rear driver's side window at a forward angle, hitting Haugen in the back. She later explained that she shot Haugen because she was " 'fearful for the other officers on foot who [she] believed were in the immediate area, [and] for the occupied vehicles in [Haugen's] path and for any other citizens who might be in the area.' "

Despite being hit, Haugen, in his words, " 'st[ood] on the gas' " . . . ; swerved across the neighbor's lawn; and continued down the street. After about a half block, Haugen realized that he had been shot and brought the Jeep to a halt. He suffered a collapsed lung and was airlifted to a hospital. He survived the shooting and subsequently pleaded guilty to the felony of "eluding." Wash. Rev. Code § 46.61.024 (1994). By so pleading, he admitted that he drove his Jeep in a manner indicating "a wanton or wilful disregard for the lives . . . of others." He subsequently brought this § 1983 action against Brosseau.

* * *

. . . As the Court of Appeals recognized, the constitutional question in this case is governed by the principles enunciated in Tennessee v. Garner, 471 U.S. 1 (1985), and Graham v. Connor, 490 U.S. 386 (1989). These cases establish that claims of excessive force are to be judged under the Fourth Amendment's "objective reasonableness" standard. Specifically, with regard to deadly force, we explained in *Garner* that it is unreasonable for an officer to "seize an unarmed, nondangerous suspect by shooting him dead." But "[w]here the officer has probably cause to believe that the suspect poses a threat of serious physical harm, either to the officer or to others, it is not constitutionally unreasonable to prevent escape by using deadly force."

We express no view as to the correctness of the Court of Appeals' decision on the constitutional question itself. We believe that, however that question is decided, the Court of Appeals was wrong on the issue of qualified immunity.

Qualified immunity shields an officer from suit when she makes a decision that, even if constitutionally deficient, reasonably misapprehends the law governing the circumstances she confronted. . . . It is important to emphasize that this inquiry "must be undertaken in light of the specific context of the case, not as a broad proposition." *Saucier*, 533 U.S. at 206. As we previously said in this very context:

> [T]here is no doubt that *Graham v. Connor* clearly establishes the general proposition that use of force is contrary to the Fourth Amendment if it is excessive under objective standards of reasonableness. Yet that is not enough. Rather, we emphasized in Anderson v. Creighton, 483 U.S. 635, 640 (1987), "that the right the official is alleged to have violated must have been 'clearly established' in a more particularized, and hence more relevant, sense: The contours of the right must be sufficiently clear that a reasonable official would understand that what he is doing violates that right.' " . . .

The Court of Appeals acknowledged this statement of law, but then proceeded to find fair warning in the general tests set out in *Graham* and *Garner*. In so doing, it was mistaken. . . .

We therefore turn to ask whether, at the time of Brosseau's actions, it was "clearly established" in this more "particularized" sense that she was violating Haugen's Fourth Amendment right. The parties point us to only a handful of cases relevant to the "situation [Brosseau] confronted": whether to shoot a disturbed felon, set on avoiding capture through vehicular flight, when persons in the immediate area are at risk from that flight.[4] Specifically, Brosseau points us to Cole v. Bone, 993 F.2d 1328 (8th Cir. 1993), and Smith v. Freland, 954 F.2d 343 (6th Cir. 1992).

In these cases, the courts found no Fourth Amendment violation when an officer shot a fleeing suspect who presented a risk to others. *Smith* is closer to this case. There, the officer and suspect engaged in a car chase, which appeared to be at an end when the officer cornered the suspect at the back of a dead-end residential street. The suspect, however, freed his car and began speeding down the street. At this point, the officer fired a shot, which killed the suspect. The court held the officer's decision was reasonable and thus did not violate the Fourth Amendment. It noted that the suspect, like Haugen here, "had proven he would do almost anything to avoid capture" and that he posed a major threat to, among others, the officers at the end of the street.

Haugen points us to Estate of Starks v. Enyart, 5 F.3d 230 (7th Cir. 1993), where the court found summary judgment inappropriate on a Fourth Amendment claim involving a fleeing suspect. There, the court concluded that the threat created by the fleeing suspect's failure to brake when an officer suddenly stepped in front of his just-started car was not a sufficiently grave threat to justify the use of deadly force.

These . . . cases taken together undoubtedly show that this area is one in which the result depends very much on the facts of each case. None of them squarely governs the case here; they do suggest that Brosseau's actions fell in the " 'hazy border between excessive and acceptable force.' " *Saucier*, 533 U.S. at 206. The cases by no means "clearly establish" that Brosseau's conduct violated the Fourth Amendment.

The judgment of the United States Court of Appeals for the Ninth Circuit is therefore reversed, and the case is remanded for further proceedings consistent with this opinion.

[The concurring opinion of Justice Breyer, joined by Justices Scalia and Ginsburg, is omitted.]

---

4   The parties point us to a number of other cases in this vein that postdate the conduct in question. These decisions, of course, could not have given fair notice to Brosseau and are of no use in the clearly established inquiry.

■ JUSTICE STEVENS dissenting.

In my judgment, the answer to the constitutional question presented by this case is clear: Under the Fourth Amendment, it was objectively unreasonable for Officer Brosseau to use deadly force against Kenneth Haugen in an attempt to prevent his escape. What is not clear is whether Brosseau is nonetheless entitled to qualified immunity because it might not have been apparent to a reasonably well trained officer in Brosseau's shoes that killing Haugen to prevent his escape was unconstitutional. In my opinion that question should be answered by a jury. . . .

An officer is entitled to qualified immunity, despite having engaged in constitutionally deficient conduct, if, in doing so, she did not violate "clearly established statutory or constitutional rights of which a reasonable person would have known." Harlow v. Fitzgerald, 457 U.S. 800, 818 (1982). The requirement that the law be clearly established is designed to ensure that officers have fair notice of what conduct is proscribed. See Hope v. Pelzer, 536 U.S. 730, 739 (2002). Accordingly, we have recognized that "general statements of the law are not inherently incapable of giving fair and clear warning," United States v. Lanier, 520 U.S. 259, 271 (1997), and have firmly rejected the notion that "an official action is protected by qualified immunity unless the very action in question has previously been held unlawful." Anderson v. Creighton, 483 U.S. 635, 640 (1987).

Thus, the Court's search for relevant case law applying the Tennessee v. Garner, 471 U.S. 1 (1985), standard to materially similar facts is both unnecessary and ill-advised. See *Hope*, 536 U.S. at 741 ("Although earlier cases involving 'fundamentally similar' facts can provide especially strong support for a conclusion that the law is clearly established, they are not necessary to such a finding").

Rather than uncertainty about the law, it is uncertainty about the likely consequences of Haugen's flight—or, more precisely, uncertainly about how a reasonable officer making the split-second decision to use deadly force would have assessed the foreseeability of a serious accident—that prevents me from answering the question of qualified immunity that this case presents. This is a quintessentially "fact-specific" question, not a question that judges should try to answer "as a matter of law." Although it is preferable to resolve the qualified immunity question at the earliest possible stage of litigation, this preference does not give judges license to take inherently factual questions away from the jury. . . .

In sum, the constitutional limits on an officer's use of deadly force have been well settled in this Court's jurisprudence for nearly two decades, and, in this case, Officer Brosseau acted outside of those clearly delineated bounds. Nonetheless, in my judgment, there is a genuine factual question as to whether a reasonably well-trained officer standing in Brosseau's shoes could have concluded otherwise, and the question plainly falls within the purview of the jury.

For these reasons, I respectfully dissent.

NOTES ON "CLEARLY ESTABLISHED LAW"

1. HOPE V. PELZER

Determining whether precedents create "clearly established" law has been a source of continuing debate and confusion. The most vexing problem is the level of generality at which the question is addressed. At some level of abstraction, almost all law is "clearly established." There are few fresh beginnings in the law, and even innovations are tied, rhetorically and analytically, to prior decisions. If, however, the question is considered in a particularistic, fact-intensive way, "clearly established" law will be hard to come by. Few cases are exactly like prior precedents, and lawyers are adept at exploiting the inevitable differences.

Perhaps the most restrictive approach was that of the Eleventh Circuit, which for many years restricted "clearly established" law to that captured in a local precedent "materially similar" to the case at hand.[a] Under that standard, almost any appreciable difference between the case at hand and prior precedents resulted in a finding of qualified immunity. This approach went too far for the Supreme Court, which disapproved the requirement of "materially similar" precedent in Hope v. Pelzer, 536 U.S. 730 (2002).

Hope concerned the Alabama Department of Corrections' use of a "hitching post" to punish state prison inmates who refused to work or disrupted work squads. (Alabama was apparently the only state to use this practice.) According to his complaint, Hope was handcuffed to a hitching post on two occasions. The first time, he was attached to the post for two hours. Due to his height, his arms were pinioned above his shoulders and "[w]henever he tried moving his arms to improve his circulation, the handcuffs cut into his wrists, causing pain and discomfort." The second time, Hope's shirt was removed and he remained tied to the post for seven hours. He was given water only once or twice, was denied any bathroom breaks, was taunted by guards, and suffered sunburn.

Hope filed a § 1983 suit against three guards involved in the first incident, one of whom was also involved in the second. Both the District Court and the Eleventh Circuit held that the guards were entitled to qualified immunity. The Court of Appeals agreed with Hope that the alleged conduct would violate the Eighth Amendment. Nonetheless, because the cases on which Hope relied, "though analogous," were not "materially similar," they did not create clearly established law.

The Supreme Court reversed. Justice Stevens's opinion for the Court agreed that Alabama's practices violated the Eighth Amendment. Given the facts as alleged by Hope, the guards' actions involved the "unnecessary and

---

[a] The Eleventh Circuit's former approach is described and criticized in Mark R. Brown, The Fall and Rise of Qualified Immunity: From *Hope* to *Harris*, 9 Nev. L.J. 185, 197–200 (2008). The general problem of reconciling the Court's desire that unmeritorious constitutional tort actions be resolved at an early stage and the inevitably fact-specific nature of many qualified immunity issues is explored in Alan K. Chen, The Facts about Qualified Immunity, 55 Emory L.J. 229 (2006).

wanton infliction of pain" that Whitley v. Albers, 475 U.S. 312 (1986), had held violative of the Cruel and Unusual Punishment Clause. With respect to qualified immunity, the Court held that the Eleventh Circuit's requirement that § 1983 plaintiffs point to a decision involving "materially similar" facts was a "rigid gloss on the qualified immunity standard . . . not consistent with our cases." Such a requirement, the Court stated, was not necessary "to ensure that before they are subjected to suit, officers are on notice their conduct is unlawful."

The Court drew a parallel to its decision in United States v. Lanier, 520 U.S. 259 (1997), which involved criminal prosecution under 18 U.S.C. § 242 of a state judge who sexually assaulted a number of women. Section 242 makes it a crime for a state official to "willfully" deprive a person of rights protected by the Constitution. Lanier argued that he had not received "fair warning" that his conduct violated the statute because no prior case had held that sexual assaults committed under color of state law violated the Fourth Amendment. The Supreme Court disagreed, noting that it had repeatedly upheld convictions under § 242 despite factual differences between the instant prosecutions and prior precedents:

> Our opinion in *Lanier* thus makes clear that officials can still be on notice that their conduct violates established law even in novel factual circumstances. Indeed, in *Lanier*, we expressly rejected a requirement that previous cases be "fundamentally similar." Although earlier cases involving "fundamentally similar" facts can provide especially strong support for a conclusion that the law is clearly established, they are not necessary to such a finding. The same is true of cases with "materially similar" facts. Accordingly, pursuant to *Lanier* the salient question that the Court of Appeals ought to have asked is whether the state of the law in 1995 gave respondents fair warning that their alleged treatment of Hope was unconstitutional.

The Court held that it did. It pointed to a 1974 court of appeals decision, binding on the Eleventh Circuit, that had held unconstitutional several forms of corporal punishment inflicted within the Mississippi prison system, including "handcuffing inmates to the fence and to cells for long periods of time, . . . and forcing inmates to stand, sit or lie on crates, stumps, or otherwise maintain awkward positions for prolonged periods":

> [For] the purpose of providing fair notice to reasonable officers administering punishment for past misconduct, [there is no] reason to draw a constitutional distinction between a practice of handcuffing an inmate to a fence for prolonged periods and handcuffing him to a hitching post for seven hours. The Court of Appeals' conclusion to the contrary exposes the danger of a rigid, overreliance on factual similarity. . . .

> The obvious cruelty inherent in this practice should have provided respondents with some notice that their alleged conduct violated Hope's constitutional protection against cruel and unusual

punishment. Hope was treated in a way antithetical to human dignity—he was hitched to a post for an extended period of time in a position that was painful, and under circumstances that were both degrading and dangerous.

Justice Thomas, joined by Chief Justice Rehnquist and Justice Scalia, dissented:

> In evaluating whether it was clearly established in 1995 that respondents' conduct violated the Eighth Amendment, the Court of Appeals properly noted that "it is important to analyze the facts in [the prior cases relied upon by petitioner where courts found Eighth Amendment violations], and determine if they are materially similar to the facts in the case in front of us." The right not to suffer from "cruel and unusual punishments" is an extremely abstract and general right. In the vast majority of cases, the text of the Eighth Amendment does not, in and of itself, give a government official sufficient notice of the clearly established Eighth Amendment law applicable to a particular situation. Rather, one must look to case law. . . .

> Previous litigation over Alabama's use of the restraining bar, however, did nothing to warn reasonable Alabama prison guards that attaching a prisoner to a restraining bar was unlawful, let alone that the illegality of such conduct was clearly established. In fact, the outcome of those cases effectively forecloses petitioner's claim that it should have been clear to respondents in 1995 that handcuffing petitioner to a restraining bar violated the Eighth Amendment. . . .

> [I]f the application of this Court's general Eighth Amendment jurisprudence to the use of a restraining bar was as "obvious" as the Court claims, one wonders how Federal District Courts in Alabama could have repeatedly arrived at the opposite conclusion, and how respondents, in turn, were to realize that these courts had failed to grasp the "obvious." . . .

2. REQUIRED SIMILARITY BETWEEN CHALLENGED CONDUCT AND PRIOR PRECEDENT: THE EXAMPLE OF EXCESSIVE FORCE

Use of deadly force by police officers—the act challenged in *Brosseau*—is a sufficiently common occurrence that there will be many opportunities for fleshing out the circumstances in which an officer's actions are deemed unreasonable. Yet no two cases are exactly alike, and the task of finding "clearly established" law in prior cases remains heavily dependent on the level of generality. If the question is framed abstractly, the law will be found to have been "clearly established," even though the officer could reasonably have believed his or her actions to be lawful. But if the question is asked too specifically, even egregious misconduct will be immunized unless something very similar has happened before. The cases illustrate extreme results in both directions.[b]

This problem is exacerbated in excessive force cases. According to the Supreme Court, claims of excessive force should be analyzed under a Fourth Amendment standard of "objective reasonableness." Graham v. Connor, 490 U.S. 386, 395 (1989). This test is not to be applied "with the 20/20 vision of hindsight," but under the totality of the circumstances known to the officer at the time. Under this approach, any reasonable misapprehensions that an officer might have—including mistakes about whether the suspect was armed, about the level of risk to the officer, about the danger to innocent people if escape was successful—are incorporated into the question of "objective reasonableness" that defines the constitutional violation. Given that the underlying right takes care of any reasonable mistakes that an officer may have made, the role of qualified immunity in providing *additional* protection for reasonable mistake seems problematic.

3.   SOURCES OF "CLEARLY ESTABLISHED" LAW

There has long been a lively debate about what decisions count in the search for "clearly established" law. Everyone agrees that the United States Supreme Court is decisive. In the absence of a Supreme Court ruling, the Circuit Courts of Appeal regard their own precedents as similarly decisive, as are decisions of the highest court of the state where the conduct occurred. Some, but by no means all, circuits are also willing to look to the weight of authority elsewhere.

Doubt was thrown on all these practices by the Supreme Court's unanimous per curiam opinion in Taylor v. Barkes, 575 U.S. ___, 135 S.Ct. 2042 (2015). Barkes hanged himself in his jail cell. His wife and children claimed that that his suicide was foreseeable and sued certain state officials for failure to supervise the private contractor that did intake screening at the facility. The Third Circuit found a clearly established right to "proper implementation of adequate suicide prevention controls" and denied qualified immunity. The Supreme Court unanimously reversed. The Court first noted that none of its decisions clearly established such a right, or even discussed it, then continued as follows: "The Third Circuit nonetheless found this right clearly established by two of its own decisions. . . . Assuming for the sake of argument that a right can be 'clearly established' by circuit precedent despite disagreement in the [other] courts of appeals, neither of the Third Circuit decisions relied on clearly established the right at issue."

What the Court assumed only "for the sake of argument" had not previously been doubted. Of course, given the Court's conclusion as to the unclarity of the Third Circuit precedents, its aside about the possible inadequacy of clear circuit precedents may not matter. Meanwhile, the whole issue of exactly what precedents count awaits further clarification.

---

[b]   See John C. Jeffries, Jr., What's Wrong with Qualified Immunity?, 62 U. Fla. L. Rev. 1 (2010) (analyzing this problem and discussing illustrative cases). For more comprehensive analysis of immunities under § 1983, see John C. Jeffries, Jr., The Liability Rule for Constitutional Torts, 99 Va. L. Rev. 207 (2013).

4. RETURN TO THE COMMON LAW?

In Ziglar v. Abbasi, 582 U.S. ___, 137 S.Ct. 615 (2017), the Supreme Court refused to allow a *Bivens* action against senior federal officials and prison wardens alleged to have subjected unauthorized aliens to intolerable conditions of confinement following the terrorist attacks of September 11, 2001. A secondary claim was made under 42 U.S.C. § 1985(3), which imposes liability on two or more persons who "conspire . . . for the purpose of depriving . . . any person or class of persons of the equal protection of the laws." The Court rejected this claim on grounds of qualified immunity. Specifically, the Court noted the suggestion in the cases that "officials employed by the same governmental department do not conspire when they speak to one another and work together in their official capacities." The Court did not adopt that conclusion but said that its viability meant that a rule to the contrary was not "clearly established" and that the defendants were therefore entitled to qualified immunity.

The majority's analysis was a standard and straightforward application of qualified immunity doctrine. A quite different approach was suggested by Justice Thomas, concurring in part and concurring in the judgment. Thomas endorsed qualified immunity only insofar as it followed common-law doctrine in 1871. He put absolute legislative and judicial immunity in this category, as well as the executive immunity for false arrest and imprisonment articulated in Pierson v. Ray, 386 U.S. 547 (1967). The general structure of immunity absent "clearly established" law, however, he criticized as an untethered exercise in judicial policy-making and called for a new course: "Until we shift the focus of our inquiry to whether immunity existed at common law, we will continue to substitute our own policy preferences for the mandates of Congress. In an appropriate case, we should reconsider our qualified immunity jurisprudence."

NOTES ON THE "ORDER OF BATTLE" IN CONSTITUTIONAL TORTS

1. UNNECESSARY MERITS ADJUDICATION

Wilson v. Layne, 526 U.S. 603 (1999), and Saucier v. Katz, 533 U.S. 194 (2001), imposed an unusual sequence of decision—often called the "order of battle"—for qualified immunity disputes. A court hearing a constitutional tort claim for money damages had to determine first whether a constitutional right had been violated. If so, the court then decided whether the defendant's conduct was nevertheless protected by qualified immunity. Under this procedure, courts adjudicated constitutional claims on the merits even when their resolution did not affect the ultimate outcome.

Wilson v. Lane is a good example. Plaintiffs claimed that their Fourth Amendment rights had been violated when police invited *Washington Post* reporters to accompany them on a lawful search. The Court ruled first that such media "ride-alongs" violated the Fourth Amendment. The Court then found that, since the unconstitutionality of such actions was not clearly established at the time, the defendants were protected by qualified immunity. Note that the second conclusion rendered the first unnecessary. Given that the law was not clearly established, the defendants would have prevailed against a claim for money damages whether or not their conduct violated the Constitution. Yet, *Wilson* and *Saucier* required that the merits of constitutional tort claims be decided before consideration of qualified immunity. Why?

An answer to these questions was attempted in John C. Jeffries, Jr., The Right-Remedy Gap in Constitutional Law, 109 Yale L.J. 87 (1999). Jeffries pointed out that the limitation on money damages imposed by the law of qualified immunity is a two-edged sword. On the one hand, qualified immunity reduces the incentives for government officers to comply with existing constitutional requirements. That is because some existing requirements will be found not "clearly established" on the facts of the case and therefore not sufficient to support damages liability. On the other hand, qualified immunity reduces the cost of broadening or clarifying constitutional doctrine. Since damages liability is triggered only by conduct violating "clearly established" rules, rules can be refined or clarified without risk of imposing potentially large damages liability for conduct of (previously) doubtful illegality. The result, Jeffries argued, is to facilitate the development of the law by allowing courts to impose new or refined constitutional requirements, without triggering liability for past conduct.

More importantly, a ruling on the merits would preclude qualified immunity in the next case. Without merits-first adjudication, the same issue could arise repeatedly, be repeatedly resolved on qualified immunity, and never produce an authoritative ruling on the merits. In that circumstance, the effective meaning of the constitutional right would be, not what judges thought it did or should mean, but what government officers could reasonably believe it meant. With repeated invocations of qualified immunity, rights could effectively be reduced to the lowest plausible misconception that an executive officer could reasonably entertain.

2.   *PEARSON V. CALLAHAN*

Whatever its advantages, the requirement of merits-first adjudication prompted widespread criticism. In Pearson v. Callahan, 555 U.S. 223 (2009), the Supreme Court overruled the mandatory sequencing.

The underlying dispute in *Pearson* was an interesting question of search-and-seizure law. Having learned from a confidential informant of Callahan's sale of methamphetamines, a Utah drug task force arranged for the informant to purchase drugs while wired. The informant did so and, after the drugs had been produced, signaled to the police, who entered Callahan's trailer, arrested him, and seized the drugs. His subsequent conviction was set aside by the Utah Supreme Court on the ground that the warrantless search violated the Fourth Amendment. Callahan then sued several officers, including Pearson, for damages under § 1983. The District Court upheld the officers' defense of qualified immunity on grounds that they could reasonably have believed the search authorized by the doctrine of "consent once removed." In the words of the Supreme Court, this doctrine authorizes "warrantless entry by police officers into a home when consent to enter has already been granted to an undercover agent or informant who has observed contraband in plain view." Consensual entry by the undercover agent is valid despite the pretense of wanting to purchase drugs. "Once-removed" kicks in when the agent calls on outside officers to enter and make the arrest. Although several circuits had endorsed this theory and none had squarely denied it, the Tenth Circuit concluded not only that the search was unlawful, but also that it violated "clearly established" constitutional law.[a]

If the Supreme Court had followed *Wilson* and *Saucier*, it would have had to endorse or reject this interpretation of the Fourth Amendment before invoking qualified immunity:

> The specific defendants sued in *Pearson* would have been protected by qualified immunity, but that defense would have become irrelevant to future cases. The asserted right against warrantless search, despite the undercover invitee's report of contraband in plain view, would have become either clearly established or clearly non-existent. If the former, money damages would have become routinely available; if the latter, there would have been no claim. One way or the other, qualified immunity would have been eliminated for consent-once-removed searches.

John C. Jeffries, Jr., Reversing the Order of Battle in Constitutional Torts, 2009 Sup. Ct. Rev. 115, 120–21.

> Instead, the Court skipped the merits and ruled unanimously that the officers were entitled to qualified immunity because the right against consent-once-removed searches, if it existed, was not clearly established. Most of Justice Alito's opinion for the Court detailed the defects of merits-first adjudication. Most obvious was the "substantial expenditure of scarce judicial resources on difficult questions that have no effect on the outcome of the case." Moreover, in some cases (not *Pearson*), the merits are so fact-bound that a decision resolving them would have little precedential effect. Similarly, the factual basis for adjudicating the merits may be obscure at the pleading stage, when qualified immunity claims are ideally resolved. The Court also worried that the briefing on the law might be inadequate and that judges who had already mentally decided on qualified immunity might not give the merits full consideration. And finally, the *Pearson* Court noted the potential difficulty of securing appellate review of merits rulings, when the defendants who wished to appeal such rulings had prevailed on qualified immunity. Note, however, that *Pearson* did not forbid merits-first adjudication, but only said that the lower courts "should have the discretion to decide whether that procedure is worthwhile in particular cases."

3.   *REICHLE V. HOWARDS*

The merits-avoidance approach of *Pearson v. Callahan* was repeated in Reichle v. Howards, 566 U.S. 658 (2012). At a meet-and-greet in a Colorado shopping mall, Howards told Vice President Cheney that his Iraq war policies were "disgusting" and touched (in what manner was disputed) the Vice

---

[a]   Specifically, the Tenth Circuit ruled that consent-once-removed suffices when outside officers are called by an undercover *officer* who was invited into the premises and sees the contraband but does not extend to similar actions by a confidential *informant*.

President on the shoulder. A Secret Service agent subsequently interviewed Howards, who falsely denied having touched Cheney. Howards was arrested and charged under state law, but the charge was dropped. Howards then sued the Secret Service agents (under *Bivens*) and the local officers (under § 1983), claiming that his First Amendment rights had been violated by a retaliatory arrest. The courts found that there had been probable cause to arrest Howards for making a materially false statement to a federal officer in violation of 18 U.S.C. § 1001. The question then became whether Howards could pursue a First Amendment claim based on allegedly retaliatory motive for an arrest, despite the existence of probable cause.

Tenth Circuit precedent said that he could. Arguably, however, that precedent had been called into question by the Supreme Court's decision in Hartman v. Moore, 547 U.S. 250 (2006), which held that a First Amendment claim for retaliatory *prosecution* could not proceed if the charges were supported by probable cause. The Tenth Circuit held that *Hartman* applied only to retaliatory prosecution, as distinct from arrest, and that Howards' claim of retaliatory motivation had raised a material factual dispute that could go to trial. The Supreme Court unanimously disagreed. Speaking through Justice Thomas, the Court concluded that *Hartman* had substantially unsettled the law on retaliatory arrest and that the defendants were therefore entitled to qualified immunity. Justices Ginsburg and Breyer concurred in the judgment on narrow grounds, and Justice Kagan did not participate.

Reichle and *Pearson* are similar. In both cases, the Tenth Circuit took an aggressively expansive view of "clearly established" law and a correspondingly narrow view of qualified immunity, and in both cases the Supreme Court unanimously reversed without reaching the merits of the constitutional claims. In both cases, the Court therefore left circuit splits intact, thereby precluding "clearly established" law in future cases on similar facts.

4.   APPEAL OF MERITS RULINGS BY PREVAILING PARTIES: *CAMRETA V. GREENE*

Of all the objections to *Saucier*, none attracted more attention than the question of appealability. Could a defendant who prevailed on qualified immunity nevertheless seek appellate review of an adverse ruling on the merits?

Pearson referred to the example of Bunting v. Mellen, 541 U.S. 1019 (2004). Cadets at the Virginia Military Institute challenged the practice of conducting a prayer before the evening meal. They sued Bunting, then Superintendent of VMI, for declaratory and injunctive relief, as well as nominal damages. The District Court enjoined Bunting from continuing to sponsor the prayer, but said he was entitled to qualified immunity on damages. Both sides appealed. Meanwhile, Bunting retired, and the cadets graduated. The Court of Appeals therefore vacated the injunction as moot but affirmed the finding of qualified immunity. That left VMI officials in the unusual situation of having prevailed on the only claim decided by the Court of Appeals but nevertheless being saddled with an adverse ruling on the unconstitutionality of the supper prayer. Under its traditional practice, the Supreme Court would not grant certiorari to a prevailing party, and in fact the Court did deny the petition, but several Justices commented on the "procedural tangle" of reviewing merits rulings at the behest of a prevailing party.

The issue returned to the Supreme Court in Camreta v. Greene, 563 U.S. 692 (2011) (reproduced as a main case in Section 3 of Chapter III). The case arose in the aftermath of suspected child abuse. Camreta, a state child protective services worker, and Alford, a deputy sheriff, interviewed a girl at her elementary school about allegations that she had been sexually abused by her father. The father was tried for that crime, but when the jury could not reach a verdict, the charges were dismissed. The girl's mother then sued the officials for damages, claiming a violation of her daughter's constitutional rights. The Ninth Circuit agreed, ruling that the officials had violated the Fourth Amendment by failing to obtain a warrant (or parental permission) to conduct the interview. The Ninth Circuit also ruled, however, that the defendants were protected by qualified immunity. As in *Bunting*, the prevailing defendants then sought Supreme Court review of the adverse ruling on the merits.

Speaking through Justice Kagan, the Court found that "this Court generally may review a lower court's constitutional ruling at the behest of a government official granted immunity." The Court noted first that 28 U.S.C. § 1254(1) authorized certiorari "upon the petition of *any* party" (emphasis by the Court). Article III presented no obstacle, so long as the case presented a genuine case or controversy. That would often be true "when immunized officials seek to challenge a ruling that their conduct violated the Constitution," because such a ruling would have prospective effect on their future conduct:

> The court in such a case says: "Although this official is immune from damages today, what he did violates the Constitution and he or anyone else who does that thing again will be personally liable." If the official regularly engages in that conduct as part of his job (as Camreta does), he suffers injury caused by the adverse constitutional ruling. So long as it continues in effect, he must either change the way he performs his duties or risk a meritorious damages action. Only by overturning the ruling on appeal can the official gain clearance to engage in the conduct in the future. He thus can demonstrate, as we demand, injury, causation, and redressability.

Moreover, Justice Kagan added, "qualified immunity cases [are] in a special category when it comes to this Court's review of appeals brought by winners":

> The constitutional determinations that prevailing parties ask us to consider in these cases are not mere dicta or "statements in opinions." They are rulings that have a significant future effect on the conduct of public officials—both the prevailing parties and their co-workers—and the policies of the government units to which they belong. And more: they are rulings self-consciously designed to produce this effect, by establishing controlling law and preventing invocations of immunity in later cases. And still more: they are rulings designed this way with this Court's permission, to promote

clarity—and observance—of constitutional rules. . . . [T]aken together, [these considerations] support bending our usual rule to
permit consideration of immunized officials' petitions.

Despite this general conclusion, the Court found that this particular
case had become moot and therefore declined to proceed to merits review.
The Court also noted, without further explanation, that it "need not decide
if an appellate court can also entertain an appeal from a party who has prevailed on immunity grounds."

Justice Sotomayor, joined by Justice Breyer, concurred in the judgment.
They agreed that the case was moot and declined to consider any issues beyond that determination.

Justice Kennedy, joined by Justice Thomas, dissented:

As today's decision illustrates, our recent qualified immunity
cases tend to produce decisions that are in tension with conventional principles of case-or-controversy adjudication. This Court
has given the Courts of Appeals "permission" to find constitutional
violations when ordering dismissal or summary judgment based on
qualified immunity. This invitation, as the Court is correct to note,
was intended to produce binding constitutional holdings on the
merits. The goal was to make dictum precedent, in order to hasten
the gradual process of constitutional interpretation and alter the
behavior of government defendants. The present case brings the
difficulties of that objective into perspective. In express reliance on
the permission granted in *Pearson*, the Court of Appeals went out
of its way to announce what may be an erroneous interpretation of
the Constitution; and, under our case law, the Ninth Circuit must
give that dictum legal effect as precedent in future cases. . . .

The Court's analysis appears to rest on the premise that the
reasoning of the decision below in itself causes Camreta injury. Until today, however, precedential reasoning of general applicability
divorced from a particular adverse judgment was not thought to
yield "standing to appeal." Parr v. United States, 351 U.S. 513, 516,
517 (1956) (opinion for the Court by Harlan, J.). . . .

The conclusion that precedent of general applicability cannot
in itself create standing to sue or appeal flows from basic principles.
Camreta's asserted injury is caused not by the Court of Appeals or
by respondent but rather by "the independent action of some third
party not before the court"—that is, by the still-unidentified private
plaintiffs whose lawsuits Camreta hopes to avoid. Lujan v. Defenders of Wildlife, 504 U.S. 555, 560–61 (1992) (internal quotation
marks omitted). This circumstance distinguishes the present case
from requests for declaratory or injunctive relief filed against officeholders who threaten legal enforcement. An inert rule of law
does not cause particular, concrete injury; only the specific threat
of its enforcement can do so. That is why the proper defendant in a
suit for prospective relief is the party prepared to enforce the relevant legal rule against the plaintiff. Without an adverse judgment

from which to appeal, Camreta has in effect filed a new declaratory judgment action in this Court against the Court of Appeals. This is no more consistent with Article III than filing a declaratory judgment action against this Court for its issuance of an adverse precedent or against Congress in response to its enactment of an unconstitutional law.

If today's decision proves to be more than an isolated anomaly, the Court might find it necessary to reconsider its special permission that the Courts of Appeals may issue unnecessary merits determinations in qualified immunity cases with binding precedential effect. . . .

There will be instances where courts discuss the merits in qualified immunity cases. It is sometimes a better analytic approach and a preferred allocation of judicial time and resources to dismiss a claim on the merits rather than to dismiss based on qualified immunity. And "[i]t often may be difficult to decide whether a right is clearly established without deciding precisely what the existing constitutional right happens to be." *Pearson*, 555 U.S. at 236 (internal quotation marks omitted). This Court should not superintend the judicial decisionmaking process in qualified immunity cases under special rules, lest it make the judicial process more complex for civil rights suits than for other litigation. It follows, however, that the Court should provide no special permission to reach the merits. If qualified immunity cases were treated like other cases raising constitutional questions, settled principles of constitutional avoidance would apply. So would conventional rules regarding dictum and holding. Judicial observations made in the course of explaining a case might give important instruction and be relevant when assessing a later claim of qualified immunity. But as dicta those remarks would not establish law and would not qualify as binding precedent.

. . . I would dismiss this case and note that our jurisdictional rule against hearing appeals by prevailing parties precludes petitioners' attempt to obtain review of judicial reasoning disconnected from a judgment.

5. BIBLIOGRAPHY

The merits-first "order of battle" requirement by *Wilson* and *Saucier* produced considerable commentary, both before and after *Pearson v. Callahan*. For judicial criticism of the requirement of merits adjudication, see Judge Pierre Leval, Judging under the Constitution: Dicta about Dicta, 81 N.Y.U. L. Rev. 1249, 1275–81 (2006), and an influential opinion by Judge Jeffrey Sutton in Lyons v. City of Xenia, 417 F.3d 565, 580 (6th Cir. 2005) (Sutton, J., concurring). For academic criticism, see Thomas Healy, The Rise of Unnecessary Constitutional Rulings, 83 N.C.L. Rev. 847 (2005) (arguing that "unnecessary" merits adjudication is improper as well as unwise); and Nancy Leong, The *Saucier* Qualified Immunity Experiment: An Empirical

Analysis, 36 Pepperdine L. Rev. 667 (2009) (concluding on the basis of empirical investigation that merits-first adjudication is unlikely to result in the clarification or development of constitutional rights). Cf. Paul W. Hughes, Not a Failed Experiment: *Wilson-Saucier* Sequencing and the Articulation of Constitutional Rights, 80 U. Colo. L. Rev. 401 (2009) (reaching the opposite conclusion, also on the basis of empirical investigation).

For pre-*Pearson* articles supporting merits-first adjudication, see John M.M. Greabe, *Mirabile Dictum!*: The Case for "Unnecessary" Constitutional Ruling in Civil Rights Damages Actions, 74 Notre Dame L. Rev. 403 (1999) (arguing against "merits by-pass" and in favor of "not-strictly-necessary" constitutional adjudication); Michael L. Wells, The "Order-of-Battle" in Constitutional Litigation, 60 S.M.U. L. Rev. 1539 (2005) (arguing that "deciding immunity issues first stunts the growth of substantive law to the detriment of the vindication and deterrent goals of constitutional tort law); and Sam Kamin, An Article III Defense of Merits-First Decisionmaking in Civil Rights Litigation: The Continued Viability of *Saucier v. Katz*, 16 Geo. Mason L. Rev. 53 (2008) (anticipating and criticizing *Pearson v. Callahan*).

For post-*Pearson* commentary, see Jack M. Beermann, Qualified Immunity and Constitutional Avoidance, 2009 Sup. Ct. Rev. 139 (exploring the problems of unguided judicial discretion in deciding whether to address the merits in constitutional tort cases and calling for legal standards to provide guidance and prevent strategic behavior); John C. Jeffries, Jr., Reversing the Order of Battle in Constitutional Torts, 2009 Sup. Ct. Rev. 115 (emphasizing that the costs of going straight to qualified immunity will not be high for rights defined in other contexts, but that for rights enforced through money damages, avoiding merits adjudication will dilute the meaning of constitutional protections and result in persistent underenforcement of constitutional rights). Finally, for analysis of post-*Pearson* experience, see Karen M. Blum, Section 1983 Litigation: Post-*Pearson* and Post-*Iqbal*, 26 Touro L. Rev. 433 (2010); Karen M. Blum, Qualified Immunity: Further Developments in the Post-*Pearson* Era, 27 Touro L. Rev. 243 (2011); Michael T. Kirkpatrick and Joshua Matz, Avoiding Permanent Limbo: Qualified Immunity and the Elaboration of Constitutional Rights from *Saucier* to *Camreta* (and Beyond), 80 Fordham L. Rev. 643 (2011).

For empirical investigation of the effects of *Pearson*, see Aaron L. Nielson and Christopher J. Walker, The New Qualified Immunity, 89 So. Calif. L. Rev. 1 (2015). Nielson and Walker analyzed 800 decisions of the courts of appeal and concluded that "concerns about constitutional stagnation, while often overstated, appear to have at least some empirical foundation." They also found large disparities among circuits in their readiness to address the merits in qualified immunity cases, "leading to a geographically uneven development of constitutional law." In response to these findings, Nielson and Walker suggest that merits-first adjudication be encouraged by requiring trial courts to state reasons for going straight to immunity. See also Aaron L. Nielson and Christopher J. Walker, Strategic Immunity, 66 Emory L.J. 55 (2016), which uses the same data base to identify "panel effects" demonstrating strategic behavior by judges. Specifically, Nielson and Walker find that "all Republican" panels reach to find no constitutional violation, while "all Democratic" panels reach to recognize new constitutional rights.

NOTES ON DAMAGES IMMUNITY AND THE GOALS OF SECTION 1983

1. INTRODUCTION

Damage awards against public officials serve several objectives. They compensate the victims of official misconduct and work to deter repetition of such misconduct in the future. Additionally, damage awards are one way of affirming legal rights and thus of educating the moral sentiments of the community. Obviously, these and other goals of damages under § 1983 are directly compromised by recognition of official immunity. Thus, the immunity decisions provide a good context for exploring the objectives that award of damages might be thought to vindicate and the costs associated with pursuing those objectives.

2. COMPENSATION

The Supreme Court has said that compensation of victims is "the basic purpose of a § 1983 damages award." Carey v. Piphus, 435 U.S. 247, 254 (1978). Yet many of the Court's decisions undercut § 1983 as a compensatory remedy.

One restrictive factor is the Eleventh Amendment protection of states and state agencies. See Edelman v. Jordan, 415 U.S. 651 (1974). If it speaks with sufficient clarity, Congress can override this immunity in the enforcement of individual rights, but the Court has not found the intent to do so in § 1983. Quern v. Jordan, 440 U.S. 332 (1979). It is also true, after Monell v. Department of Social Services, 436 U.S. 658 (1978) (a main case in the next Section), that local governments may be held directly liable for monetary damages under § 1983, but only in very restricted circumstances. In most cases compensation for official misconduct must be sought from the individual officer, rather than from the government itself. While officer defendants are almost always reimbursed by the government that employs them,[a] the naming of individuals as defendants has important implications.

In some cases, plaintiffs may have trouble identifying the persons who should be sued. Where injury results from systemic failure rather than misconduct, the necessity of proceeding against named individuals may prove especially burdensome. Defendants who face personal liability for government acts may well arouse the sympathy of juries. But most importantly, the

---

[a] Governments routinely protect their employees against damage liability, either by themselves providing defense counsel and indemnifying the employees against loss or, less commonly, by purchasing insurance. As no such arrangements are required by federal law, the availability of counsel and indemnification depends on the statutes and practices in each jurisdiction. For many years, some doubted the pervasiveness of indemnification, and the evidence for it was dated and sparse. See, e.g., Project, Suing the Police in Federal Court, 88 Yale L.J. 781 (1979) (reporting indemnification in an early survey); John C. Jeffries, Jr., In Praise of the Eleventh Amendment and Section 1983, 84 Va. L. Rev. 47 (1998) (providing anecdotal support for routine indemnification). At long last, there is now disciplined empirical work showing that, at least for police officers, indemnification virtually always occurs. See Joanna Schwartz, Police Indemnification, 89 N.Y.U. L. Rev. 885 (2014).

fact that § 1983 actions ordinarily must be brought against officers as individuals introduces the perceived unfairness of imposing personal liability for good faith error. Thus, the *Scheuer* Court identified as the first rationale for official immunity "the injustice, particularly in the absence of bad faith, of subjecting to liability an officer who is required, by the legal obligations of his position, to exercise discretion." The resulting grant of qualified immunity to individual officials sharply curtails the availability of money damages for injured plaintiffs and might be thought to undermine the compensatory rationale for the § 1983 remedy.[b]

3.   DETERRENCE

A second goal of money damages is to deter future misconduct. An award of damages against one official conveys to others a threat of similar treatment if they too misbehave. Any limitation on the award of damages will necessarily reduce the deterrent effect of liability under § 1983. Why has the Supreme Court nevertheless embraced immunity (usually qualified immunity) despite the drop in the incentives to avoid unconstitutional behavior?

Part of the answer lies in a fear of overdeterrence. To the extent that the standards of liability are uncertain or the mechanisms of enforcement unpredictable, the deterrence message will be unclear. Officials will have an incentive to avoid all acts that might lead to civil liability or to the necessity of litigation. This unintended inhibitory effect is what the *Scheuer* Court had in mind when it identified as the second rationale for official immunity "the danger that the threat of such liability would deter [the official's] willingness to execute his office with the decisiveness and the judgment required by the public good."

Of course, the problem of unintended deterrence is not unique to this context. In much the same way, ordinary tort liability will inhibit some non-tortious conduct that the actor finds difficult to segregate from potentially tortious activity. In most situations, society relies on private decision-makers to evaluate the expected costs and benefits of their actions, including possible liability, and to make decisions roughly congruent with the social interest. In the context of damage actions against government officials, however, several factors combine to raise the prospect that personal liability will induce government officials to engage in excessive defensive activity and thus to sacrifice the public good in favor of individual protection. These factors are detailed in an analysis of the working environment of the street-level official by Peter H. Schuck in Suing Government: Citizen Remedies for Official Wrongs 60–77 (1983).

The person most likely to be sued under § 1983 is, in Schuck's parlance, the "street-level official." Examples include police officers, prison authorities, public school officials, and welfare administrators. Because these officials personally and directly deliver basic government services, they constantly

---

[b]   Whether this limitation of liability by qualified immunity is consistent with the goal of compensation, properly understood, is a theoretical issue of some subtlety. It is presented most clearly in Owen v. City of Independence, 445 U.S. 622 (1980), which is a main case in the next Section of this Chapter. The role of fault in a compensatory regime is considered more closely at that point.

interact with individual citizens on matters of intense concern. Many of these interactions are non-consensual and thus are likely to be characterized by conflict and mutual suspicion. The goals that these officials are directed to pursue—maintaining order, educating students, and the like—are often complex and ambiguous, and the choice of means to attain them is irreducibly judgmental.

Moreover, the official often has a duty to act. While the private citizen is usually free to do nothing if that seems the best course, the public official may be commanded by law (or at least expected) to intervene on behalf of the public interest. Since government action is likely to be coercive, it is especially productive of conflict and harm. Indeed, virtually any choice of action or inaction risks harm to someone. The decision to discipline a student risks unfairness to that student; the decision not to discipline may impair the educational opportunities of others. The decision to arrest may violate the rights of the arrestee; the decision not to arrest may sacrifice the protection of the public.

Not only are such decisions potentially harmful to others; they are also likely to be attended by significant risk of error. Many officials must act quickly, in situations that border on emergency, and on the basis of sketchy information. Under such circumstances, it is difficult to capture appropriate decision-making in dependable rules. Not that the effort is lacking. As Schuck points out, the street-level official is typically required to administer and to abide by a host of rules, but rules "so voluminous, ambiguous, contradictory, and in flux that officials can only comply with or enforce them selectively." In short, says Schuck, the officials "are actually awash in discretion."

Most important of all, public officials are typically unable to appropriate to themselves the benefits that flow from their decisions. The costs of malfeasance or mistake can be visited upon the official by a suit for damages, but the benefits of good performance tend to run to the public at large. The resulting incentive structure may conduce to defensive, cost-minimizing behavior, even if it entails a net loss in social benefits. As Schuck explains, "[m]ost private actors would decide to incur any cost if the expected value of the correlative benefit were great enough," but government officials shy away from actions that would drive their personal costs above what Schuck calls their "duty threshold":

> The duty threshold, of course, varies from official to official, for it is defined by one's idiosyncratic attitudes toward (and trade-offs among) certain values and interests, some altruistic, some more narrowly self-interested . . .—feelings of professionalism; moral duty; programmatic mission; fear of criticism, discipline, or reprisals for self-protective behavior; concern for professional reputation; habituation to routine; personal convenience; and the like. Officials tend to orient their decisions about whether, when, and how to act less toward maximizing . . . net benefits, which they cannot appropriate, than toward minimizing (subject to their duty threshold) those costs that they would incur personally.

Among these costs is the risk of being sued. The magnitude of this risk depends not only on the expected cost of adverse judgments, but also on the expected cost of having to defend such actions and on the demoralization or other nonpecuniary cost of being sued. As Schuck points out, an important element of nonpecuniary cost is uncertainty—uncertainty concerning "the outcome of the case; its duration; its effect upon the official's creditworthiness; the circumstances under which the official may receive (or lose) free counsel and indemnification of any settlement or adverse judgment; the quality of legal representation that the defending agency will provide; and potential conflicts of interest on the part of the defending agency or assigned counsel." Id. at 69. Given the environments in which they work, decisions of street-level officials are likely to be especially risky. As Schuck concludes, these officials have strong incentives to minimize costs, including the risk of being sued, even if a strategy of cost-minimization means foregoing social benefits.

Finally, it is worth noting that the expected costs and benefits to officials of their own decisions are typically asymmetrical. Action is likely to be more costly than inaction. This imbalance is due in part to what Jerry Mashaw has termed a "cause of action" problem. See Jerry L. Mashaw, Civil Liability of Government Officers: Property Rights and Official Accountability, 42 Law & Contemp. Probs. 8 (1978). The individual who is injured by affirmative misconduct can usually state a cause of action against the responsible official. The harm to the citizen and its connection to the official's conduct are usually clear. By contrast, persons injured by an official's failure to act may find it more difficult to state a claim for relief. The connection between harm to the citizen and official inaction may be indirect and obscure, and causation therefore difficult to establish. Furthermore, enforcement authority is typically discretionary in nature. As a result, the official may be protected from liability for an omission by the absence of any duty to act. For these reasons, the likelihood of being sued for erroneous action exceeds the risk for erroneous inaction, and the incentives of government officials, given a realistic threat of civil liability, may therefore be skewed toward defensive behavior.

One problem with this argument is that it ignores the importance of employer indemnification in affecting officer incentives. While it is true that government officers ordinarily cannot appropriate to themselves the full benefits of good performance, it is also true that they do not personally bear the full costs of mistakes. Officer incentives may be *reduced*, but it does not necessarily follow that they would be *skewed*. As compared to actors in the private sector, government officers may simply have less to gain or lose.

This argument is considered in John C. Jeffries, Jr., In Praise of the Eleventh Amendment and Section 1983, 84 Va. L. Rev. 47 (1998), which nonetheless concludes that "the incentives of government officers are skewed, as compared to actors in the private sector, toward inaction, passivity, and defensive behavior." He identifies three contributing factors, the first of which is government employment law:

The tradition of the civil service, powerfully reinforced by doctrines of procedural due process, makes government workers hard to fire.

Generally, the absence of good performance is not a sufficient reason. Much more than their colleagues in private industry, government employees are protected against discharge for relative inefficiency or lack of productivity. For government workers, the risk of job loss is overwhelmingly linked to bad performance, to the provable act of misconduct or neglect that will justify a civil service termination. Government workers might, therefore, rationally be more concerned with avoiding mistakes than with maximizing social benefits.

A second factor is the psychological self-selection that may be practiced by government employees who value security more than potential gain:

Persons willing to take risks in pursuit of gains may gravitate toward private industry, where successful risk-taking is more likely to be rewarded. Those who place a premium on job security may be drawn to government work. If, as a result, government workers are relatively risk-averse, the skewed incentives toward defensiveness and inaction may be reinforced by psychological predisposition.

The third factor that Jeffries identifies, and to him the most important, is a political tendency to "give greater weight to costs that must be accounted for in the budget and to discount costs that fall elsewhere":

On-budget costs mean higher taxes, and the political penalties for raising taxes can be severe. Acts that gives rise to § 1983 claims trigger on-budget costs and are therefore subject to the political disincentives of higher taxes. Government inaction may be just as costly, but the burdens fall elsewhere. The failure to arrest a suspected criminal or to discipline an unruly student may have error costs just as great as would result from taking those actions, but those costs are born by subsequent crime victims and by other students. If, as seems likely, the political culture punishes on-budget costs more than those that are borne elsewhere, government managers may reinforce their workers' incentives toward caution and constraint.

Jeffries also argues that the risk of overdeterrence would be "manageable, or at any rate less acute, if constitutional law were precise and rule-like":

It is the combination of skewed incentives and constitutional indeterminacy that makes the risk of unintended deterrence so severe. An unconstitutional search and seizure may differ only slightly from good police work. Conduct on the right side of the line is not only legally permissible, but socially desirable, even essential to maintaining adequate order and security. The obvious response to strict liability based on uncertain standards is to draw well back from the danger zone. However tolerable that reaction may be in some contexts, in others it is very costly. By limiting damages liability to acts that clearly cross the line, qualified immunity moderates unintended deterrence.

In any event, the prospect of unintended deterrence of legitimate government activity has loomed very large in the debates over official immunities. It is chiefly on this ground that the Supreme Court has established, both under § 1983 and under analogous *Bivens*-type actions against federal officers, that virtually every government official is entitled to at least a qualified defense of good faith and reasonable belief against actions for money damages. The result is a corresponding diminution in the deterrence of official misconduct, as well as a restriction in the availability of compensation for persons injured thereby.[c]

James Pfander and Jonathan Hunt, Public Wrongs and Private Bills: Indemnification and Government Accountability in the Early Republic, 85 N.Y.U. L. Rev. 1862 (2010), provides an illuminating account of the practice of congressional indemnification of government officials sued for wrongdoing during the early republic and antebellum periods. The authors find that "nineteenth-century legislators viewed reimbursement of a well-founded claim more as a matter of right than as a matter of legislative grace," and that this helps explain why "[s]overeign immunity played only a modest role in the early republic's system of government accountability in tort." Under this historic regime, "[c]ourts were to decide whether the conduct in litigation was lawful and award damages against the officer if it was not; Congress was to decide whether the officer had acted for the government within the scope of his agency, in good faith, and in circumstances that suggested the government should bear responsibility for the loss." Such an approach, they note, "contrasts dramatically with the current law of official immunity," under which the courts apply a qualified immunity doctrine in an effort to calibrate the proper level of official incentives.

4.   QUALIFIED VS. ABSOLUTE IMMUNITY

Do the considerations discussed above suggest an explanation for the distinction between the absolute immunity from damages afforded judges, legislators, and prosecutors and the qualified immunity available to executive officials? Absolute immunity obviates the risk of inducing timidity in the exercise of official authority, but only at the cost of failure to deter abuse. Qualified immunity, on the other hand, may inhibit official illegality, but not

---

[c] The applicability to governments of general deterrence theory is challenged in Daryl Levinson, In Making Government Pay: Markets, Politics, and the Allocation of Constitutional Costs, 67 U. Chi. L. Rev. 345 (2000). Levinson argues that government officers do not necessarily respond to liability rules in the same way as private actors. "Because government actors respond to political, not market, incentives, we should not assume that government will internalize social costs just because it is forced to make a budgetary outlay." Moreover, even if government officers do respond to the prospect of money damages, deterrence will still fail if constitutional violations create benefits for a majority of citizens that outweigh the costs imposed on a few. Levinson's arguments suggest a profound skepticism about the utility of money damages in enforcing constitutional rights.

These ideas are examined in a Symposium in the Georgia Law Review. Included is a Foreword by Thomas A. Eaton, 35 Ga. L. Rev. 837 (2001), and an Afterword by Marshall Shapo, 35 Ga. L. Rev. 931 (2001). Articles in the Symposium include: Myriam E. Gilles, In Defense of Making Government Pay: The Deterrent Effect of Constitutional Tort Remedies, 35 Ga. L. Rev. 845 (2001); Brian J. Serr, Turning Section 1983's Protection of Civil Rights into an Attractive Nuisance: Extra-Textual Barriers in Municipal Liability under *Monell*, 35 Ga. L. Rev. 881 (2001); Bernard P. Dauenhauer and Michael L. Wells, Corrective Justice and Constitutional Torts, 35 Ga. L. Rev. 903 (2001). For another response to Levinson, see Mark R. Brown, Deterring Bully Government: A Sovereign Dilemma, 76 Tulane L. Rev. 149 (2001) (using game theory to argue that government can be deterred by the prospect of damages liability).

without some impairment of effective functioning of government. Does the comparison of these risks justify the different treatment, for example, of judges and executive officials? Peter Schuck concluded that it does not:

> [W]hen one contrasts the circumstances under which street-level officials must often act (momentarily; with broad discretion and little guidance; with little information; under great stress and with uncertainty; in unfriendly surroundings; under severe resource constraints) with the conditions under which judges typically decide (at their own speed; with discretion narrowed and guidance provided by precedent and the wording of statutes, as well as by voluminous records and briefs; enjoying great deference; in friendly surroundings; able to treat time and information as "free goods"), one must conclude that street-level officials would be far more vulnerable to litigation liability than judges, immunity rules being equal. If the slightest risk of suits against judges suffices to justify absolute immunity, a higher risk to street-level officials would seem to justify no less.

Peter H. Schuck, Suing Government: Citizen Remedies for Official Wrongs 90–91 (1983). Schuck suggested that executive officials should also be absolutely immune from damages liability, but this recommendation was tied to an accompanying recommendation for expanded governmental liability for official misconduct. In the absence of expanded direct liability of government, the argument for expanded immunity of officials would obviously be more problematic.

A more pointed comment was offered by Justice Rehnquist in Butz v. Economou, 438 U.S. 478, 517 (1978) (Rehnquist, J., dissenting). In disagreeing with the Court's decision to extend only qualified immunity to cabinet-level executive officers, Rehnquist commented:

> The ultimate irony of today's decision is that in the area of common-law official immunity, a body of law fashioned and applied by judges, absolute immunity within the federal system is extended only to judges and prosecutors functioning in the judicial system. Similarly, where this Court has interpreted 42 U.S.C. § 1983 in the light of common-law doctrines of official immunity, again only judges and prosecutors are accorded absolute immunity. If one were to hazard an informed guess as to why such a distinction in treatment between judges and prosecutors, on the one hand, and other public officials on the other, obtains, mine would be that those who decide the common law know through personal experience the sort of pressures that might exist for such decision-makers in the absence of absolute immunity, but may not know or may have forgotten that similar pressures exist in the case of nonjudicial public officials to whom difficult decisions are committed. But the cynical among us might not unreasonably feel that this is simply another unfortunate example of judges treating those who are not part of the judicial machinery as "lesser breeds without the law."

5. AFFIRMATION OF RIGHTS

A different kind of justification for damage judgments focuses on the symbolic and educative functions of affirming legal rights. Christina Whitman, Constitutional Torts, 79 Mich. L. Rev. 5, 21–25 (1980), has emphasized the symbolic message of providing a federal remedy for the protection of federal constitutional rights as an important justification for the "supplementary" cause of action provided by § 1983. One way of affirming the importance of federal rights (especially constitutional rights) and of demonstrating the federal commitment to protection of those rights is by an award of damages. In this view, the damage judgment has symbolic value independent of compensation and deterrent effect.

Obviously, affirmation of rights does not depend specifically on damage awards against public officials. The symbolic and educative value of vindicating the plaintiff's rights can be accomplished by any kind of judgment in plaintiff's favor, including injunctive or declaratory relief.

Perhaps the most important context for considering affirmation of rights as a goal of § 1983 damages actions is when a constitutional violation does not produce ordinarily compensable injuries. The question then arises whether the plaintiff should be able to recover for the value or importance of the rights themselves, without regard to his or her personal injury. Carey v. Piphus, 435 U.S. 247 (1978), held that damage judgment must be limited in amount to compensation for actual harm suffered; only nominal damages may be awarded to vindicate the declaration of rights.

Carey v. Piphus involved two children who had been suspended from school without procedural due process. The court of appeals ruled that the students were entitled to substantial damages without proof of injury. The Supreme Court reversed:

> [T]he Court of Appeals [held] that respondents are entitled to recover substantial—although unspecified—damages to compensate them for "the injury which is 'inherent in the nature of the wrong,'" even if their suspensions were justified and even if they fail to prove that the denial of procedural due process actually caused them some real, if intangible, injury.... [Petitioners argue] that such injury cannot be presumed to occur, and that plaintiffs at least should be put to their proof on the issue, as plaintiffs are in most tort actions.
>
> We agree with petitioners in this respect.... First, it is not reasonable to assume that every departure from procedural due process, no matter what the circumstances or how minor, inherently is ... likely to cause distress.... Moreover, where a deprivation is justified but procedures are deficient, whatever distress a person feels may be attributable to the justified deprivation rather than to deficiencies in procedure. But as the Court of Appeals held, the injury caused by a justified deprivation, including distress, is not properly compensable under § 1983. This ambiguity in causation ... provides additional need for requiring the plaintiff to convince

the trier of fact that he actually suffered distress because of the denial of procedural due process itself.

The same approach was followed in Memphis Community School District v. Stachura, 477 U.S. 299 (1986). Plaintiff was a school teacher who had been improperly suspended following parental complaints about sex education. He claimed violations of procedural due process and a First Amendment right of academic freedom. The trial judge instructed the jury that it could award not only ordinary compensatory and punitive damages, but also damages based on the value or importance of the constitutional right that had been violated:

> You may wish to consider the importance of the right in our system of government, the role which this right has played in the history of our republic, [and] the significance of the right in the context of the activities which the plaintiff was engaged in at the time of the violation of the right.

The Supreme Court disapproved the instruction. Speaking through Justice Powell, the Court found it impossible to square with *Carey*. Non-punitive damages under § 1983 must be designed to compensate for actual injuries, the Court said, not simply to vindicate a "jury's perception of the abstract 'importance' of a constitutional right." Justice Marshall concurred in the judgment, agreeing that the jury had been invited to base its award on improper speculation about matters wholly detached from the actual injury.

Together, *Carey* and *Stachura* make it very difficult to use § 1983 damage actions to vindicate solely dignitary interests. Is this restriction wise? Would it be better to allow damage awards based on criteria such as those articulated by the *Stachura* trial court?

6. FOOTNOTE ON IMMUNITY FROM PROSPECTIVE RELIEF

Although most immunity decisions involve damages, questions occasionally arise concerning official immunity from prospective relief. The traditional view, dating at least from Ex parte Young, 209 U.S. 123 (1908), is that unconstitutional acts by state officials may be enjoined. State legislators, however, have absolute immunity against § 1983 injunctions. Supreme Court of Virginia v. Consumers Union, 446 U.S. 719 (1980); Tenney v. Brandhove, 341 U.S. 367 (1951). This rule parallels the immunity from prospective relief granted federal legislators by the Speech or Debate Clause. See, e.g., Eastland v. United States Servicemen's Fund, 421 U.S. 491, 502–03 (1975). The immunity applies only to legislative acts, not to all acts done by legislators.

In Pulliam v. Allen, 466 U.S. 522 (1984), the Supreme Court held that the same rule did not extend to judges. Like legislators, judges are absolutely immune from award of damages for their official acts. Unlike legislators, however, judges can be sued for injunctive or declaratory relief where appropriate. *Pulliam* involved an unusual situation where suit was brought to enjoin a state magistrate from her practice of requiring bond for nonjailable offenses and incarcerating those who could not make bail. Because of the short duration of each pretrial detention and the recurring nature of the practice, there was no adequate alternative remedy available to the *Pulliam* plaintiff. Ordinarily, of course, appeal or habeas corpus would have been an "adequate" remedy sufficient to preclude equitable relief.

If injunctive relief had been limited to cases where there was no alternative remedy, *Pulliam* would have had little practical significance. Nonetheless, judges objected vigorously to the prospect of being sued, and Congress amended §§ 1983 and 1988 to overrule *Pulliam*. Section 1983 now provides that the person acting under color of state law:

> shall be liable to the party injured in an action at law, suit in equity, or other proper proceeding for redress, *except that in any action brought against a judicial officer for an act or omission taken in such officer's judicial capacity, injunctive relief shall not be granted unless a declaratory decree was violated or declaratory relief was unavailable.* (Emphasis added.)

Section 1988(b) now provides that the court may allow:

> a reasonable attorney's fee as part of the costs, *except that in any action brought against a judicial officer for an act or omission taken in such officer's judicial capacity, such officer shall not be held liable for any costs, including attorney's fees, unless such action was clearly in excess of such officer's jurisdiction.* (Emphasis added.)

SECTION 3. GOVERNMENTAL LIABILITY

INTRODUCTORY NOTE ON MONROE V. PAPE

In Monroe v. Pape, 365 U.S. 167 (1961) (the main case in Section 1), the plaintiffs sued not only Chicago police officers but also the city itself. *Monroe* held that § 1983 provided a federal cause of action against the officers even if their conduct was unauthorized by, or even in violation of, state law. *Monroe* also held, however, that the city of Chicago could not be sued. The basis for this conclusion, explained Justice Douglas, was the 1871 Congress's rejection of the Sherman Amendment:

> When the bill that became the Act of April 20, 1871, was being debated in the Senate, Senator Sherman of Ohio proposed an amendment which would have made "the inhabitants of the county, city, or parish" in which certain acts of violence occurred liable "to pay full compensation" to the person damaged or his widow or legal representative. The amendment was adopted by the Senate. The House, however, rejected it. The Conference Committee reported another version. The House rejected the Conference report. In a second conference the Sherman amendment was dropped.
>
> ... Mr. Poland, speaking for the House Conferees about the Sherman proposal to make municipalities liable, said:
>
>> We informed the conferees on the part of the Senate that the House had taken a stand on that subject and would not recede from it; that that section imposing liability upon towns and counties must go out or we should fail to agree.

The objection to the Sherman amendment stated by Mr. Poland was that "the House had solemnly decided that in their judgment Congress had no constitutional power to impose any obligation upon county and town organizations, the mere instrumentality for the administration of state law."

The *Monroe* Court expressly declined to consider policy arguments for or against municipal liability and also declined to reach the question whether Congress has the constitutional power to make municipalities liable for the acts of their officers. Instead, the Court rested squarely on its understanding of legislative intent:

> The response of the Congress to the proposal to make municipalities liable for certain actions being brought within federal purview by the Act of April 20, 1871, was so antagonistic that we cannot believe that the word "person" was used in this particular act to include them. Accordingly we hold that the motion to dismiss the complaint against the city of Chicago was properly granted.

On this point, *Monroe* was unanimous. Nevertheless, the issue was reconsidered in the next main case.

Monell v. Department of Social Services

Supreme Court of the United States, 1978.
436 U.S. 658.

■ MR. JUSTICE BRENNAN delivered the opinion of the Court.

Petitioners, a class of female employees of the Department of Social Services and of the Board of Education of the City of New York, commenced this action under 42 U.S.C. § 1983 in July, 1971. The gravamen of the complaint was that the board and the department had as a matter of official policy compelled pregnant employees to take unpaid leaves of absence before such leaves were required for medical reasons. Cf. Cleveland Board of Education v. LaFleur, 414 U.S. 632 (1974). The suit sought injunctive relief and backpay for periods of unlawful forced leave. Named as defendants in the action were the department and the commissioner, the board and its chancellor, and the city of New York and its mayor. In each case, the individual defendants were sued solely in their official capacities.

On cross-motions for summary judgment, the District Court for the Southern District of New York held moot petitioners' claims for injunctive and declaratory relief since the city of New York and the board, after the filing of the complaint, had changed their policies relating to maternity leaves so that no pregnant employee would have to take leave unless she was medically unable to perform her job. No one now challenges this conclusion. The court did conclude, however, that the acts complained of were unconstitutional under *LaFleur*. Nonetheless plaintiffs' prayers for backpay were denied because any such damages would come ultimately from the city of New York and, therefore, to hold otherwise would be to "circumven[t]" the immunity conferred on municipalities by Monroe v. Pape, 365 U.S. 167 (1961). . . .

I

In *Monroe v. Pape*, we held that "Congress did not undertake to bring municipal corporations within the ambit of [§ 1983]." The sole basis for this conclusion was an inference drawn from Congress's rejection of the "Sherman Amendment" to the bill which became the Civil Rights Act of 1871—the precursor of § 1983—which would have held a municipal corporation liable for damage done to the person or property of its inhabitants by *private* persons "riotously and tumultuously assembled."[8]

Although the Sherman Amendment did not seek to amend § 1 of the Act, which is now § 1983, and although the nature of the obligation created by that amendment was vastly different from that created by § 1, the Court nonetheless concluded in *Monroe* that Congress must have meant to exclude municipal corporations from the coverage of § 1 because " 'the House [in voting against the Sherman Amendment] had solemnly decided that in their judgment Congress had no constitutional power to impose any *obligation* upon county and town organizations, the mere instrumentality for the administration of state law,' " (emphasis added), quoting Rep. Poland. This statement, we thought, showed that Congress doubted its "constitutional power . . . to impose *civil liability* on municipalities" (emphasis added), and that such doubt would have extended to any type of civil liability.

A fresh analysis of debate on the Civil Rights Act of 1871, and particularly of the case law which each side mustered in its support, shows, however, that *Monroe* incorrectly equated the "obligation" of which Representative Poland spoke with "civil liability." . . .

House opponents of the Sherman Amendment—whose views are particularly important since only the House voted down the amendment—. . . argued that the local units of government upon which the amendment fastened liability were not obligated to keep the peace at state law and further that the federal government could not constitutionally require local governments to create police forces, whether this requirement was levied directly, or indirectly by imposing damages for breach of the peace on municipalities. The most complete statement of this position is that of Representative Blair:

> The proposition known as the Sherman Amendment . . . is entirely new. It is altogether without a precedent in this country. . . . That amendment claims the power in the general government to go into the states of this union and lay such obligations as it may please upon the municipalities, which are the creatures of the states alone. . . .

---

[8]   We expressly declined to consider "policy considerations" for or against municipal liability.

Here it is proposed not to carry into effect an obligation which rests upon the municipalities, but to create that obligation, and that is the provision I am unable to assent to. . . .

Now, only the other day, the Supreme Court . . . decided [in Collector v. Day, 78 U.S. (11 Wall.) 113 (1871)] that there is no power in the government of the United States, under its authority to tax, to tax the salary of a state officer. Why? Simply because the power to tax involves the power to destroy, and it was not the intent to give the government of the United States power to destroy the government of the states in any respect. It was also held in the case of Prigg v. Pennsylvania, 41 U.S. (16 Pet.) 539 (1842), that it is not within the power of the Congress of the United States to lay duties upon a state officer; that we cannot command a state officer to do any duty whatever, as such; and I ask . . . the difference between that and commanding a municipality, which is equally a creature of the state, to perform a duty.

Any attempt to impute a unitary constitutional theory to opponents of the Sherman Amendment is, of course, fraught with difficulties, not the least of which is that most members of Congress did not speak to the issue of the constitutionality of the amendment. Nonetheless, two considerations lead us to conclude that opponents of the Sherman Amendment found it unconstitutional substantially because of the reasons stated by Representative Blair: First, Blair's analysis is precisely that of Poland, whose views were quoted as authoritative in *Monroe*, and that analysis was shared in large part by all House opponents who addressed the constitutionality of the Sherman Amendment. Second, Blair's exegesis of the reigning constitutional theory of his day, as we shall explain, was clearly supported by precedent—albeit precedent that has not survived. . . .

Collector v. Day, cited by Blair, was the clearest and, at the time of the debates, the most recent pronouncement of a doctrine of coordinate sovereignty that, as Blair stated, placed limits on even the enumerated powers of the national government in favor of protecting state prerogatives. There, the Court held that the United States could not tax the income of Day, a Massachusetts state judge, because the independence of the states within their legitimate spheres would be imperiled if the instrumentalities through which states executed their powers were "subject to the control of another and distinct government." [And in] Kentucky v. Dennison, 65 U.S. (24 How.) 66 (1861), . . . the Court was asked to require Dennison, the Governor of Ohio, to hand over Lago, a fugitive from justice wanted in Kentucky, as required by § 1 of the Act of Feb. 12, 1793, which implemented Art. IV, § 2, cl. 2 of the Constitution. Mr. Chief Justice Taney, writing for a unanimous Court, refused to enforce that section of the act:

[W]e think it clear, that the federal government, under the Constitution, has no power to impose on a state officer, as such, any duty whatever, and compel him to perform it; for if it possessed this power, it might overload the officer with duties which would fill up all his time, and disable him from performing his obligations to the state, and might impose on him duties of a character incompatible with the rank and dignity to which he was elevated by the state.

The rationale of *Dennison*—that the nation could not impose duties on state officers since that might impede states in their legitimate activities—is obviously identical to that which animated the decision in *Collector v. Day*. And, as Blair indicated, municipalities as instrumentalities through which states executed their policies could be equally disabled from carrying out state policies if they were also obligated to carry out federally imposed duties. Although no one cited *Dennison* by name, the principle for which it stands was well known to Members of Congress, many of whom discussed *Day*, as well as a series of state supreme court cases in the mid-1860s which had invalidated a federal tax on the process of state courts on the ground that the tax threatened the independence of a vital state function. Thus, there was ample support for Blair's view that the Sherman Amendment, by putting municipalities to the Hobson's choice of keeping the peace or paying civil damages, attempted to impose obligations on municipalities by indirection that could not be imposed directly, thereby threatening to "destroy the government of the states."

If municipal liability under § 1 of the Civil Rights Act of 1871 created a similar Hobson's choice, we might conclude, as *Monroe* did, that Congress could not have intended municipalities to be among the "persons" to which that section applied. But that is not the case.

First, opponents expressly distinguished between imposing an obligation to keep the peace and merely imposing civil liability for damages on a municipality that was obligated by state law to keep the peace, but which had not in violation of the Fourteenth Amendment. Representative Poland, for example, reasoning from Contract Clause precedents, indicated that Congress could constitutionally confer jurisdiction on the federal courts to entertain suits seeking to hold municipalities liable for using their authorized powers in violation of the Constitution—which is as far as § 1 of the Civil Rights Act went:

> I presume . . . that where a state had imposed a duty [to keep the peace] upon [a] municipality . . . an action would be allowed to be maintained against them in the courts of the United States under the ordinary restrictions as to jurisdiction. But enforcing a liability, existing by their own contract, or by a state law, in the courts, is a very widely different thing from devolving a new duty or liability upon them by the national government, which has no power either to create or destroy them, and no power or control over them whatever. . . .

Second, the doctrine of dual sovereignty apparently put no limit on the power of the federal courts to enforce the Constitution against municipalities that violated it. . . . The limits of the principles defined in *Dennison* and *Day* are not so well defined in logic, but are clear as a matter of history. It must be remembered that the same Court which rendered *Day* also vigorously enforced the Contract Clause against municipalities—an enforcement effort which included various forms of "positive" relief, such as ordering that taxes be levied and collected to discharge federal-court judgments, once a constitutional infraction was found. Thus, federal judicial enforcement of the Constitution's express limits on state power, since it was done so frequently, must, notwithstanding anything said in *Dennison* or *Day*, have been permissible. . . . Since § 1 of the Civil Rights Act simply conferred jurisdiction on the federal courts to enforce § 1 of the Fourteenth Amendment—a situation precisely analogous to the grant of diversity jurisdiction under which the Contract Clause was enforced against municipalities—there is no reason to suppose that opponents of the Sherman Amendment would have found any constitutional barrier to § 1 suits against municipalities. . . .

From the foregoing discussion it is readily apparent that nothing said in the debates on the Sherman Amendment would have prevented holding a municipality liable under § 1 of the Civil Rights Act for its own violations of the Fourteenth Amendment. The question remains, however, whether the general language describing those to be liable under § 1—"any person"—covers more than natural persons. An examination of the debate on § 1 and application of appropriate rules of construction show unequivocally that § 1 was intended to cover legal as well as natural persons. . . .

In both Houses, statements of the supporters of § 1 corroborated that Congress, in enacting § 1, intended to give a broad remedy for violations of federally protected civil rights. Moreover, since municipalities through their official acts could, equally with natural persons, create the harms intended to be remedied by § 1, and, further, since Congress intended § 1 to be broadly construed, there is no reason to suppose that municipal corporations would have been excluded from the sweep of § 1. One need not rely on this inference alone, however, for the debates show that members of Congress understood "persons" to include municipal corporations.

Representative Bingham, for example, in discussing § 1 of the bill, explained that he had drafted § 1 of the Fourteenth Amendment with the case of Barron v. Mayor of Baltimore, 32 U.S. (7 Pet.) 243 (1833), especially in mind. "In [that] case the *city* had taken private property for public use, without compensation . . . , and there was no redress for the wrong. . . ." (Emphasis added.) Bingham's further remarks clearly indicate his view that such takings by cities, as had occurred in *Barron*, would be redressable under § 1 of the bill. More generally, and as Bingham's remarks confirm, § 1 of the bill would logically be the vehicle by which Congress provided redress for takings, since that section provided the only civil remedy for Fourteenth Amendment violations and that amendment unequivocally prohibited uncompensated takings. Given this purpose, it beggars reason to suppose that Congress would have exempted municipalities from suit, insisting instead that compensation for a taking come from an officer in his individual capacity rather than from the government unit that had the benefit of the property taken.

In addition, by 1871, it was well understood that corporations should be treated as natural persons for virtually all purposes of constitutional and statutory analysis. . . .

That the "usual" meaning of the word "person" would extend to municipal corporations is also evidenced by an act of Congress which had been passed only months before the Civil Rights Act was passed. The act provided that

> in all acts hereafter passed . . . the word "person" may extend and be applied to bodies politic and corporate . . . unless the context shows that such words were intended to be used in a more limited sense.

Municipal corporations in 1871 were included within the phrase "bodies politic and corporate" and, accordingly, the "plain meaning" of § 1 is that local government bodies were to be included within the ambit of the persons who could be sued under § 1 of the Civil Rights Act. . . .

II

Our analysis of the legislative history of the Civil Rights Act of 1871 compels the conclusion that Congress *did* intend municipalities and other local government units to be included among those persons to whom § 1983 applies.[54] Local governing bodies, therefore, can be sued directly under § 1983 for monetary, declaratory, or injunctive relief where, as here, the action that is alleged to be unconstitutional implements or executes a policy statement, ordinance, regulation, or decision officially adopted and promulgated by that body's officers. Moreover, although the touchstone of the § 1983 action against a government body is an allegation that official policy is responsible for a deprivation of rights protected by the Constitution, local governments, like every other § 1983 "person," by the very terms of the statute, may be sued for constitutional deprivations visited pursuant to governmental "custom" even though such a custom has not received formal approval through the body's official decisionmaking channels. . . .

---

[54] There is certainly no constitutional impediment to municipal liability. "The Tenth Amendment's reservation of nondelegated powers to the states is not implicated by a federal-court judgment enforcing the express prohibitions of unlawful state conduct enacted by the Fourteenth Amendment." For this reason, National League of Cities v. Usery, 426 U.S. 833 (1976), is irrelevant to our consideration of this case. Nor is there any basis for concluding that the Eleventh Amendment is a bar to municipal liability. See, e.g., Fitzpatrick v. Bitzer, 427 U.S. 445 (1976). Our holding today is, of course, limited to local government units which are not considered part of the state for Eleventh Amendment purposes.

On the other hand, the language of § 1983, read against the background of the same legislative history, compels the conclusion that Congress did not intend municipalities to be held liable unless action pursuant to official municipal policy of some nature caused a constitutional tort. In particular, we conclude that a municipality cannot be held liable *solely* because it employs a tortfeasor—or, in other words, a municipality cannot be held liable under § 1983 on a respondeat superior theory.

We begin with the language of § 1983 as passed:

> [A]*ny person who*, under color of any law, statute, ordinance, regulation, custom, or usage of any state, *shall subject, or cause to be subjected*, any person . . . to the deprivation of any rights, privileges, or immunities secured by the Constitution of the United States, shall, any such law, statute, ordinance, regulation, custom, or usage of the state to the contrary notwithstanding, be liable to the party injured in any action at law, suit in equity, or other proper proceeding for redress. . . . (Emphasis added.)

The italicized language plainly imposes liability on a government that, under color of some official policy "causes" an employee to violate another's constitutional rights. At the same time, the language cannot be easily read to impose liability vicariously on governing bodies solely on the basis of the existence of an employer-employee relationship with a tortfeasor. Indeed, the fact that Congress did specifically provide that A's tort became B's liability if B "caused" A to subject another to a tort suggests that Congress did not intend § 1983 liability to attach where such causation was absent.

Equally important, creation of a federal law of respondeat superior would have raised all the constitutional problems associated with the obligation to keep the peace, an obligation Congress chose not to impose because it thought imposition of such an obligation unconstitutional. To this day, there is disagreement about the basis for imposing liability on an employer for the torts of an employee when the sole nexus between the employer and the tort is the fact of the employer-employee relationship. Nonetheless, two justifications tend to stand out. First is the commonsense notion that no matter how blameless an employer appears to be in an individual case, accidents might nonetheless be reduced if employers had to bear the cost of accidents. Second is the argument that the cost of accidents should be spread to the community as a whole on an insurance theory.

The first justification is of the same sort that was offered for statutes like the Sherman Amendment: "The obligation to make compensation for injury resulting from riot is, by arbitrary enactment of statutes, affirmatory law, and the reason of passing the statute is to secure a more perfect police protection." (Sen. Frelinghuysen) This justification was obviously insufficient to sustain the amendment against perceived constitutional difficulties and there is no reason to suppose that a more general liability imposed for a similar reason would have been thought less constitutionally objectionable. The second justification was similarly put forward as a justification for the Sherman Amendment: "we do not look upon [the Sherman Amendment] as a punishment. . . . It is a mutual insurance." (Rep. Butler) Again, this justification was insufficient to sustain the amendment.

We conclude, therefore, that a local government may not be sued under § 1983 for an injury inflicted solely by its employees or agents. Instead, it is when execution of a government's policy or custom, whether made by its lawmakers or by those whose edicts or acts may fairly be said to represent official policy, inflicts the injury that the government as an entity is responsible under § 1983. Since this case unquestionably involves official policy as a moving force of the constitutional violation found by the District Court, we must reverse the judgment below. . . .

III

Although we have stated before that stare decisis has more force in statutory analysis than in constitutional adjudication because, in the former situation, Congress can correct our mistakes through legislation, we have never applied stare decisis mechanically to prohibit overruling our earlier decisions determining the meaning of statutes. . . .

[Justice Brennan gave four reasons why stare decisis should not be applied in this situation.

[First, *Monroe* "was a departure from prior practice." In support of this assertion, Brennan cited a number of cases in which injunctive relief had been sought against municipalities. "Moreover," he continued, "the constitutional defect that led to the rejection of the Sherman Amendment would not have distinguished between municipalities and school boards, each of which is an instrumentality of state administration." For this reason, prior cases decided both before and after *Monroe* holding school boards liable in § 1983 actions were inconsistent with *Monroe*.

[Second, "recent expressions of Congressional intent" indicated that a broad implementation of the principle of *Monroe* was unsound. Here he cited the rejection of efforts to strip the federal courts of jurisdiction over school boards, the enactment of legislation to assist school boards in complying with federal court decrees, and a passage in attorney-fee legislation indicating that Congress expected attorney fees in § 1983 suits to be collectable from state or local governments.

[Third, unlike in a commercial situation, "municipalities can assert no reliance claim." Surely, he said, *Monroe* cannot be read as allowing local governments to rely on their ability to adopt unconstitutional policies.

[And finally, he argued that even under the most stringent test for when a statutory interpretation should be overruled, *Monroe* qualified. It is "beyond doubt," he elaborated, that *Monroe* is wrong and "there is no justification" given the legislative history "for excluding municipalities from the 'persons' covered by § 1983."]

IV

Since the question whether local government bodies should be afforded some form of official immunity was not presented [or] briefed . . . we express no views on the scope of any municipal immunity beyond holding that municipal bodies sued under § 1983 cannot be entitled to an absolute immunity, lest our decision that such bodies are subject to suit under § 1983 "be drained of meaning."

no views expressed on immunity scope

V

For the reasons stated above, the judgment of the Court of Appeals is Reversed.

■ MR. JUSTICE POWELL, concurring. . . .

Few cases in the history of the Court have been cited more frequently than Monroe v. Pape, 365 U.S. 167 (1961), decided less than two decades ago. Focusing new light on 42 U.S.C. § 1983, that decision widened access to the federal courts and permitted expansive interpretations of the reach of the 1871 measure. But *Monroe* exempted local governments from liability at the same time it opened wide the courthouse door to suits against officers and employees of those entities—even where they act pursuant to express authorization. The oddness of that result and the weakness of the historical evidence relied on by the *Monroe* Court in support of it, are well demonstrated by the Court's opinion today. . . .

The Court correctly rejects a view of the legislative history that would produce the anomalous result of immunizing local government units from monetary liability for action directly causing a constitutional deprivation, even though such actions may be fully consistent with, and thus not remediable under, state law. No conduct of government comes more clearly within the "under color of" state law language of § 1983. It is most unlikely that Congress intended public officials acting under the command or the specific authorization of the government employer to be *exclusively* liable for resulting constitutional injury. . . .

[This is not] the usual case in which the Court is asked to overrule a precedent. Here considerations of stare decisis cut in both directions. On the one hand, we have a series of rulings that municipalities and counties are not "persons" for purposes of § 1983. On the other hand, many decisions of this Court have been premised on the amenability of school boards and similar entities to § 1983 suits. . . .

If now, after full consideration of the question, we continued to adhere to *Monroe*, grave doubt would be cast upon the Court's exercise of § 1983 jurisdiction over school boards. . . . Although there was an independent basis of jurisdiction in many of the school board cases because of the inclusion of individual public officials as nominal parties, the opinions of this Court make explicit reference to the school board party, particularly in discussions of the relief to be awarded. [T]he exercise of § 1983 jurisdiction over school boards . . . has been longstanding. Indeed, it predated *Monroe*. . . .

The Court of Appeals in this case suggested that we import, by analogy, the Eleventh Amendment fiction of *Ex parte Young* into § 1983. That approach . . . would require "a bifurcated application" of "the generic word 'person' in § 1983" to public officials "depending on the nature of the relief sought against them." A public official sued in his official capacity for carrying out official policy would be a "person" for purposes of injunctive relief, but a non-"person" in an action for damages. The Court's holding avoids this difficulty.

Finally, if we continued to adhere to a rule of absolute municipal immunity under § 1983, we could not long avoid the question whether "we should, by analogy to our decision in *Bivens*, imply a cause of action directly from the Fourteenth Amendment. . . ." In light of the Court's persuasive re-examination in today's decision of the 1871 debates, I would have difficulty inferring from § 1983 "an explicit congressional declaration" against municipal liability for the implementation of official policies in violation of the Constitution. Rather than constitutionalize a cause of action against local government that Congress intended to create in 1871, the better course is to confess error and set the record straight, as the Court does today. . . .

■ MR. JUSTICE STEVENS, concurring in part.

[Justice Stevens declined to join those portions of the majority opinion dealing with respondeat superior on the ground that discussion of that issue was "merely advisory" and "not necessary to explain the Court's decision."]

■ MR. JUSTICE REHNQUIST, with whom THE CHIEF JUSTICE joins, dissenting.

Seventeen years ago in Monroe v. Pape, 365 U.S. 167 (1961), this Court held that the 42nd Congress did not intend to subject a municipal corporation to liability as a "person" within the meaning of 42 U.S.C. § 1983. Since then, the Congress has remained silent, but this Court has reaffirmed that holding on at least three separate occasions. Today, the Court abandons this long and consistent line of precedents, offering in justification only an elaborate canvass of the same legislative history which was before the Court in 1961. . . .

I

[O]ur only task is to discern the intent of the 42nd Congress. That intent was first expounded in *Monroe*, and it has been followed consistently ever since. This is not some esoteric branch of the law in which congressional silence might reasonably be equated with congressional indifference. Indeed, this very year, the Senate has been holding hearings on a bill which would remove the municipal immunity recognized by *Monroe*. In these circumstances, it cannot be disputed that established principles of stare decisis require this Court to pay the highest deference to its prior holdings. *Monroe* may not be overruled unless it has been demonstrated "beyond doubt from the legislative history of the 1871 statute that [*Monroe*] misapprehended the meaning of the controlling provision," [quoting Justice Harlan's remark in his *Monroe* concurrence about overruling the interpretation of "under color of" law adopted in *Screws* and *Classic*]. The Court must show not only that Congress, in rejecting the Sherman Amendment, concluded that municipal liability was not unconstitutional, but also that in enacting § 1, it intended to impose that liability. I am satisfied that no such showing has been made.

II

Any analysis of the meaning of the word "person" in § 1983, which was originally enacted as § 1 of the Ku Klux Klan Act of April 20, 1871, must begin, not with the Sherman Amendment, but with the Dictionary Act. The latter act, which supplied rules of construction for all legislation, provided:

> That in all acts hereafter passed . . . the word "person" may extend and be applied to bodies politic and corporate . . . unless the context shows that such words were intended to be used in a more limited sense. . . .

There are . . . factors . . . which suggest that the Congress which enacted § 1983 may well have intended the word "person" "to be used in a more limited sense," as *Monroe* concluded. It is true that this Court had held that both commercial corporations and municipal corporations were "citizens" of a state within the meaning of the jurisdictional provisions of Article III. Congress, however, also knew that this label did not apply in all contexts, since this Court had held commercial corporations not to be "citizens" within the meaning of the privileges and immunities clause, U.S. Const., Art. IV, § 2. Thus, the Congress surely knew that, for constitutional purposes, corporations generally enjoyed a different status in different contexts. Indeed, it may be presumed that Congress intended that a corporation should enjoy the same status under the Ku Klux Klan Act as it did under the Fourteenth Amendment, since it had been assured that § 1 "was so very simple and really reenacting the Constitution." At the time § 1983 was enacted the only federal case to consider the status of corporations under the Fourteenth Amendment had concluded, with impeccable logic, that a corporation was neither a "citizen" nor a "person."

Furthermore, the state courts did not speak with a single voice with regard to the tort liability of municipal corporations. Although many members of Congress represented states which had retained absolute municipal tort immunity, other states had adopted the currently predominant distinction imposing liability for proprietary acts. Nevertheless, no state court had ever held that municipal corporations were always liable in tort in precisely the same manner as other persons.

The general remarks from the floor on the liberal purposes of § 1 offer no explicit guidance as to the parties against whom the remedy could be enforced. As the Court concedes, only Representative Bingham raised a concern which could be satisfied only by relief against governmental bodies. Yet he never directly related this concern to § 1 of the act. Indeed, Bingham stated at the outset, "I do not propose now to discuss the provisions of the bill in detail," and, true to his word, he launched into an extended discourse on the beneficent purposes of the Fourteenth Amendment. While Bingham clearly stated that Congress could "provide that no citizen in any state shall be deprived of his property by state law or the judgment of a state court without just compensation therefore," he never suggested that such a power was exercised in § 1.[4] . . .

Thus, it ought not lightly to be presumed, as the Court does today, that § 1983 "should prima facie be construed to include 'bodies politic' among the entities that could be sued." Neither the Dictionary Act, the ambivalent state of judicial decisions, nor the floor debate on § 1 of the act gives any indication that any Member of Congress had any inkling that § 1 could be used to impose liability on municipalities. . . .

The Court is probably correct that the rejection of the Sherman Amendment does not lead ineluctably to the conclusion that Congress intended municipalities to be immune from liability under all circumstances. Nevertheless, it cannot be denied that the debate on that amendment, the only explicit consideration of municipal tort liability, sheds considerable light on the Congress's understanding of the status of municipal corporations in that context. . . . Whatever the merits of the constitutional arguments against it, the fact remains that Congress rejected the concept of municipal tort liability on the only occasion in which the question was explicitly presented. Admittedly this fact is not conclusive as to whether Congress intended § 1 to embrace a municipal corporation within the meaning of "person," and thus the reasoning of *Monroe* on this point is subject to challenge. The meaning of § 1 of the Act of 1871 has been subjected in this case to a more searching and careful analysis than it was in *Monroe*, and it may well be that on the basis of this closer analysis of the legislative debates a conclusion contrary to the *Monroe* holding could have been reached when that case was decided 17 years ago. But the rejection of the Sherman Amendment remains instructive in that here alone did the legislative debates squarely focus on the liability of municipal corporations, and that liability was rejected. . . .

The decision in *Monroe v. Pape* was the fountainhead of the torrent of civil rights litigation of the last 17 years. Using § 1983 as a vehicle, the

---

[4]   It has not been generally thought, before today, that § 1983 provided an avenue of relief from unconstitutional takings. Those federal courts which have granted compensation against state and local governments have resorted to an implied right of action under the Fifth and Fourteenth Amendments. Since the Court today abandons the holding of *Monroe* chiefly on the strength of Bingham's arguments, it is indeed anomalous that § 1983 will provide relief only when a local government, not the state itself, seizes private property.

courts have articulated new and previously unforeseeable interpretations of the Fourteenth Amendment. At the same time, the doctrine of municipal immunity enunciated in *Monroe* has protected municipalities and their limited treasuries from the consequences of their officials' failure to predict the course of this Court's constitutional jurisprudence. None of the members of this Court can foresee the practical consequences of today's removal of that protection. Only the Congress, which has the benefit of the advice of every segment of this diverse nation, is equipped to consider the results of such a drastic change in the law. It seems all but inevitable that it will find it necessary to do so after today's decision. . . .

NOTES ON GOVERNMENTAL LIABILITY UNDER § 1983

1. QUESTIONS AND COMMENTS ON *MONELL*

Before *Monell*, damages could be obtained from a police officer who violated constitutional rights but not from the city that ordered the officer to do so. Justice Powell commented on the "oddness" of that result. There is something odd, is there not, in holding an agent exclusively liable for acts specifically authorized by, and perhaps even commanded by, the principal? And yet, exactly this situation prevails with respect to state officials. They can be sued for damages under § 1983, but the state itself is immune from suit. Does this make sense? Is there any justification for treating states and municipalities differently?[a]

As a practical matter, the issue of state or municipal liability for the *authorized* acts of its employees matters chiefly when the official cannot be held personally liable. Where liability can be imposed on the official as an individual, the government will have a strong incentive to indemnify its employees against loss incurred in implementing official policy. Not only may the government feel a moral obligation to hold its employee harmless for following orders; but it will also find that indemnification is necessary to recruit and retain qualified employees. Few would be so bold as to accept government office without protection against personal liability for government error. Perhaps for that reason, states almost always follow the policy of defending state officers in actions under § 1983 and reimbursing them for any damages assessed, despite the formal immunity of the Eleventh Amendment.

Monell held that municipalities could be sued under § 1983, but only for actions taken pursuant to an official policy or custom. The Court specifically rejected the theory of respondeat superior. In essence, the *Monell* Court adopted for municipalities the test proposed for all § 1983 defendants by Justice Frankfurter's dissent in *Monroe*. Why? Is that result compelled by the language of the statute? Is it indicated by the rejection of the Sherman

---

[a] See William D. Murphy, Reinterpreting "Person" in Section 1983: The Hidden Influence of *Brown v. Board of Education*, 9 Black L.J. 97 (1985). Murray contends that *Monell* was necessary to remove the "very serious danger" of derailing desegregation suits against school boards. By contrast, Murphy suggests, the exclusion of states from the concept of "person" in § 1983 has no large impact on desegregation litigation.

amendment? Is it consistent with the purposes of § 1983, as interpreted in *Monroe*.[b]

2.   STATE AS "PERSON" UNDER § 1983: *WILL V. MICHIGAN DEPARTMENT OF STATE POLICE*

Before *Monell,* the Court assumed that *Monroe*'s conclusion that municipalities were not "persons" under § 1983 also applied to states. When *Monell* reversed that rule for localities, the question arose whether states might also be held directly liable under § 1983.

The question is entangled with the Eleventh Amendment, which has been read to deprive federal courts of jurisdiction over damage actions against states, except when Congress makes a very clear statement of the intent to impose such liability pursuant to its powers under the Reconstruction-era amendments. In Quern v. Jordan, 440 U.S. 332 (1979), the Court ruled that § 1983 was not such a legislative override of Eleventh Amendment immunity. That settled the matter for federal courts, but since the Eleventh Amendment does not apply in state court, the question remained open whether states might be sued there under § 1983.

The Supreme Court answered that question in Will v. Michigan Department of State Police, 491 U.S. 58 (1989). *Will* held that "person" in § 1983 does not include states or state officials acting in their official capacities.[c] Writing for the Court, Justice White argued that the legislative intent to make states directly liable had not been shown with the clarity required to alter the "usual constitutional balance" between the states and the national government. Nothing in the history or purpose of § 1983 clearly showed such intent.[d]

3.   STATE OFFICIAL AS "PERSON" WHEN ACTING IN OFFICIAL CAPACITY: *HAFER V. MELO*

The decision in *Will* led to the grant of certiorari in Hafer v. Melo, 502 U.S. 21 (1991), "to address the question whether state officers may be held personally liable for damages under § 1983 based upon actions taken in their

---

[b]   On the historical basis for rejecting respondeat superior, see David Jacks Achtenberg, Taking History Seriously: Municipal Liability under 42 U.S.C. § 1983 and the Debate over Respondeat Superior, 73 Fordham L. Rev. 2183 (2005), and Ronald M. Levin, The Section 1983 Municipal Immunity Doctrine, 65 Geo. L.J. 1483 (1977). For speculation that *Monroe* reflected Justice Powell's untimely agreement with the Frankfurter position in *Monroe v. Pape*, see David Jacks Achtenberg, Frankfurter's Champion: Justice Powell, *Monell*, and the Meaning of "Color of Law," 80 Fordham L. Rev. 681 (2011).

[c]   For an article lamenting the result in that case, see William Burnham and Michael C. Fayz, The State as a "Non-Person" under Section 1983: Some Comments on *Will* and Suggestions for the Future, 70 Ore. L. Rev. 1 (1991). For an analysis of *Will* as legal pragmatism, see Gene R. Shreve, Symmetries of Access in Civil Rights Litigation: Politics, Pragmatism, and *Will,* 66 Ind. L.J. 1 (1990).

[d]   Subsequently, the Court relied on *Will* to conclude that an Indian tribe cannot sue under § 1983 to contest the seizure of tribal records by state law enforcement officers. The Court found that tribes, like states, are not "persons" who can sue or be sued under § 1983. Inyo County v. Paiute-Shoshone Indians of the Bishop Community of the Bishop Colony, 538 U.S. 701 (2003). See also Ngiraingas v. Sanchez, 495 U.S. 182 (1990) (territories).

official capacities." Shortly after her election as Auditor General of Pennsylvania, Hafer discharged Melo and several other employees. The employees sued under § 1983, seeking reinstatement and damages. The District Court read *Will* to preclude liability for employment decisions taken in Hafer's official capacity as Auditor General, but the Supreme Court (with Justice Thomas not participating) unanimously disagreed.

Speaking for the Court, Justice O'Connor distinguished between "personal capacity" and "official capacity" suits:

> In Kentucky v. Graham, 473 U.S. 159 (1985), the Court sought to eliminate lingering confusion about the distinction between personal-and official-capacity suits. We emphasized that official-capacity suits " 'generally represent only another way of pleading an action against an entity of which an officer is an agent.' " A suit against a state official in her official capacity therefore should be treated as a suit against the state. Indeed, when an official sued in this capacity in federal court dies or leaves office, her successor automatically assumes her role in the litigation. Because the real party in interest in an official-capacity suit is the governmental entity and not the named official, "the entity's 'policy or custom' must have played a part in the violation of federal law." For the same reason, the only immunities available to the defendant in an official-capacity action are those that the governmental entity possesses.

> Personal-capacity suits, on the other hand, seek to impose individual liability upon a government officer for actions taken under color of state law. Thus, "[o]n the merits, to establish personal liability in a § 1983 action, it is enough to show that the official, acting under color of state law, caused the deprivation of a federal right." *Graham*, 473 U.S. at 166. While the plaintiff in a personal-capacity suit need not establish a connection to governmental "policy or custom," officials sued in their personal capacities, unlike those sued in their official capacities, may assert personal immunity defenses such as objectively reasonable reliance on existing law.

The Court then turned to *Will:*

> *Will* itself makes clear that the distinction between official-capacity suits and personal-capacity suits is more than "a mere pleading device." State officers sued for damages in their official capacity are not "persons" for purposes of the suit because they assume the identity of the government that employs them. By contrast, officers sued in their personal capacity come to court as individuals. . . .

> Hafer seeks to overcome the distinction between official-and personal-capacity suits by arguing that § 1983 liability turns not on the capacity in which state officials are sued, but on the capacity in which they acted when injuring the plaintiff. Under *Will,* she asserts, state officials may not be held liable in their personal capacity for actions they take in their official capacity. [W]e find [this

view] both unpersuasive as an interpretation of § 1983 and fore-closed by our prior decisions.

Through § 1983, Congress sought "to give a remedy to parties deprived of constitutional rights, privileges and immunities by an official's abuse of his position." Monroe v. Pape, 365 U.S. 167, 172 (1961). Accordingly, it authorized suits to redress deprivations of civil rights by persons acting "under color of any [state] statute, or-dinance, regulation, custom, or usage." 42 U.S.C. § 1983. The requirement of action under color of state law means that Hafer may be liable for discharging respondents precisely because of her authority as Auditor General. We cannot accept the novel proposi-tion that this same official authority insulates Hafer from suit. . . .

We hold that state officials, sued in their individual capacities, are "persons" within the meaning of § 1983. [They are not] abso-lutely immune from personal liability under § 1983 solely by virtue of the "official" nature of their acts.

In the end—despite what the Court says—the distinction between a per-sonal-capacity suit and an official-capacity suit usually turns on the pleading. Generally speaking, a § 1983 plaintiff may choose whom to sue and in what capacity.

4.   COMMENT ON JUDICIAL METHODOLOGY UNDER § 1983

In holding that a municipality is a "person" within the meaning of § 1983, *Monell* overruled part of *Monroe v. Pape*. Although the two decisions reach opposite conclusions, they are alike in methodology. In both cases, the Supreme Court treated the issue as a straightforward exercise in statutory construction. Both decisions locate the question in the textual ambiguity of the word "person" as used in § 1983; both refer to the Dictionary Act; and both purport to resolve the issue by resort to legislative history. The decisions read that history differently, but both seem to regard it as dispositive. Nei-ther opinion discusses the policies involved nor acknowledges the relevance of such discussion. In fact, the *Monroe* Court specifically disavowed attention to the "policy considerations" for or against municipal liability.

Perhaps this is just as it should be. Section 1983 is an act of Congress, and a traditional means of resolving statutory ambiguity is to refer to the intent of the enacting legislature. Indeed, the Court might have opened itself to criticism if it had taken any other approach. Conventional wisdom would say that the Court's job in interpreting acts of Congress (at least in the ab-sence of constitutional infirmity) is to give effect to the statutory meaning, not to consult its own perceptions of sound public policy.

And yet there is something a bit unsettling about the relentless histo-ricity of the early § 1983 opinions. For one thing, the legislative history is often less clear than it is made out to be. In *Monroe* and *Monell*, for example, despite a seemingly thorough search, neither side was able to produce the "smoking gun" that clearly demonstrated legislative intent one way or the other—not for the meaning of "under color of" law and not for the scope of the word "person." If, for example, the 42nd Congress had considered and rejected a proposal to exclude municipalities from the coverage of the word "person," the debates might have been more illuminating. But in fact the legislative history reveals no occasion for this kind of focused and collective consideration of the issue. Instead, inferences are drawn from scattered statements of individual legislators, whose views may or may not have been representative and who may or may not have had this issue precisely in mind when they spoke. To treat such evidence as dispositive may be placing more reliance on history than it can fairly bear.[e]

Moreover, the uncertainty of historical reconstruction increases with remoteness in time. The legislators who spoke and voted in 1871 did so against a background of political experience and constitutional interpretation vastly different from what we know today. Projecting their views forward in time invites distortion. Ultimately, what the Court is asking is not merely what the 42nd Congress said with respect to the kinds of problems then before it, but also what it meant for the issues now at hand. The more radical the change between that day and this, the less likely that the question is susceptible to meaningful answer.

Finally, these problems are compounded by the accumulation of precedent. The original meaning of the statute may be obscured by layers of interpretation. Each decision builds on the others. At some point, the statutory scheme, although grounded in a legislative act, is more nearly the product of judicial construction. Finding original meaning becomes increasingly difficult as it is projected onto a pattern of legal regulation substantially remade by subsequent interpretation.

Whether these concerns warrant deemphasis of the traditional model of statutory interpretation is a matter of controversy, both on and off the Supreme Court. Some think that § 1983 should be treated as a specie of federal common law, with the Supreme Court setting the terms of federal court supervision of state officials as it thinks best, but leaving the matter open for Congressional correction. Others may think that the model of federal common law invites inappropriate innovation and that the wiser course is for the Court to stick close to the traditional tasks of statutory construction.

Whatever the merits of this debate, this much is clear: From *Monroe* on, the Supreme Court has tended to anchor its interpretations of § 1983 in the traditional mode. Many decisions are explained chiefly, if not exclusively, in terms of statutory language, legislative history, and original intent. Often the policy justifications for deciding an issue one way or the other are slighted or ignored or refracted through the historical prism of what the framers "must have thought." As a result, students of § 1983 are often left to uncover the underlying policies for themselves and to reach their own conclusions on the wisdom of the Court's judgments substantially unaided by judicial explication.

---

[e]   See Richard A. Matasar, Personal Immunities under § 1983: The Limits of the Court's Historical Analysis, 40 Ark. L. Rev. 741 (1987).

Owen v. City of Independence

Supreme Court of the United States, 1980.
445 U.S. 622.

■ MR. JUSTICE BRENNAN delivered the opinion of the Court.

Monell v. New York City Dept. of Social Services, 436 U.S. 658 (1978), overruled Monroe v. Pape, 365 U.S. 167 (1961), insofar as *Monroe* held that local governments were not among the "persons" to whom 42 U.S.C. § 1983 applies and were therefore wholly immune from suit under the statute. *Monell* reserved decision, however, on the question whether local governments, although not entitled to absolute immunity, should be afforded some form of official immunity in § 1983 suits. In this action brought by petitioner in the District Court for the Western District of Missouri, the Court of Appeals for the Eighth Circuit held that respondent city of Independence, Mo., "is entitled to qualified immunity from liability" based on the good faith of its officials: "We extend the limited immunity the District Court applied to the individual defendants to cover the city as well, because its officials acted in good faith and without malice." We granted certiorari. We reverse.

I

The events giving rise to this suit are detailed in the District Court's findings of fact. On February 20, 1967, Robert L. Broucek, then city manager of respondent city of Independence, Mo., appointed George D. Owen to an indefinite term as chief of police.[2] In 1972, Owen and a new city manager, Lyle W. Alberg, engaged in a dispute over petitioner's administration of the police department's property room. In March of that year, a handgun, which the records of the department's property room stated had been destroyed, turned up in Kansas City in the possession of a felon. This discovery prompted Alberg to initiate an investigation of the management of the property room. Although the probe was initially directed by petitioner, Alberg soon transferred responsibility for the investigation to the city's department of law, instructing the city counselor to supervise its conduct and to inform him directly of its findings.

Sometime in early April 1972, Alberg received a written report on the investigation's progress, along with copies of confidential witness statements. Although the city auditor found that the police department's records were insufficient to permit an adequate accounting of the goods contained in the property room, the city counselor concluded that there was no evidence of any criminal acts or of any violation of state or municipal law in the administration of the property room. Alberg discussed the results of the investigation at an informal meeting with several city council members and advised them that he would take action at an appro-

---

[2]   Under § 3.3(1) of the city's charter, the city manager has sole authority to "[a]ppoint, and when deemed necessary for the good of the service, lay off, suspend, demote, or remove all directors, or heads, of administrative departments and all other administrative officers and employees of the city. . . ."

priate time to correct any problems in the administration of the police department.

On April 10, Alberg asked petitioner to resign as chief of police and to accept another position within the department, citing dissatisfaction with the manner in which petitioner had managed the department, particularly his inadequate supervision of the property room. Alberg warned that if petitioner refused to take another position in the department his employment would be terminated, to which petitioner responded that he did not intend to resign.

On April 13, Alberg issued a public statement addressed to the mayor and the city council concerning the results of the investigation. After referring to "discrepancies" found in the administration, handling, and security of public property, the release concluded that "[t]here appears to be no evidence to substantiate any allegations of a criminal nature" and offered assurances that "[s]teps have been initiated on an administrative level to correct these discrepancies." Although Alberg apparently had decided by this time to replace petitioner as police chief, he took no formal action to that end and left for a brief vacation without informing the city council of his decision.

While Alberg was away on the weekend of April 15 and 16, two developments occurred. Petitioner, having consulted with counsel, sent Alberg a letter demanding written notice of the charges against him and a public hearing with a reasonable opportunity to respond to those charges. At approximately the same time, city councilman Paul L. Roberts asked for a copy of the investigative report on the police department property room. Although petitioner's appeal received no immediate response, the acting city manager complied with Roberts's request and supplied him with the audit report and the witness statements.

On the evening of April 17, 1972, the city council held its regularly scheduled meeting. After completion of the planned agenda, councilman Roberts read a statement he had prepared on the investigation.[5] Roberts

---

[5] Roberts's statement . . . in part recited:

On April 2, 1972, the city council was notified of the existence of an investigative report concerning the activities of the chief of police of the city of Independence, certain police officers and activities of one or more other city officials. On Saturday, April 15th for the first time I was able to see these 27 voluminous reports. The contents of these reports are astoundingly shocking and virtually unbelievable. They deal with the disappearance of two or more television sets from the police department and [a] signed statement that they were taken by the chief of police for his own personal use.

The reports show that numerous firearms properly in the police department custody found their way into the hands of others including undesirables and were later found by other law enforcement agencies.

Reports whow [sic] that narcotics held by the Independence Missouri chief of police have mysteriously disappeared. Reports also indicate money has mysteriously disappeared. Reports show that traffic tickets have been manipulated. The reports show inappropriate requests affecting the police court have come from high ranking police officials. Reports indicate that things have occurred causing the unusual release of felons. The reports show gross inefficiencies on the part of a few of the high ranking officers of the police department.

charged that petitioner had misappropriated police department property for his own use, that narcotics and money had "mysteriously disappeared" from his office, that traffic tickets had been manipulated, that high ranking police officials had made "inappropriate" requests affecting the police court, and that "things have occurred causing the unusual release of felons." At the close of his statement, Roberts moved that the investigative reports be released to the news media and turned over to the prosecutor for presentation to the grand jury, and that the city manager "take all direct and appropriate action" against those persons "involved in illegal, wrongful, or gross inefficient activities brought out in the investigative reports." After some discussion, the city council passed Roberts's motion with no dissents and one abstention.

City manager Alberg discharged the petitioner the very next day. Petitioner was not given any reason for his dismissal; he received only a written notice stating that his employment as chief of police was "[t]erminated under the provisions of section 3.3(1) of the city charter." Petitioner's earlier demand for a specification of charges and a public hearing was ignored, and a subsequent request by his attorney for an appeal of the discharge decision was denied by the city on the grounds that "there is no appellate procedure or forum provided by the charter or ordinances of the city of Independence, Missouri, relating to the dismissal of Mr. Owen."

The local press gave prominent coverage both to the city council's action and petitioner's dismissal, linking the discharge to the investigation. As instructed by the city council, Alberg referred the investigative reports and witness statements to the prosecuting attorney of Jackson County, Mo., for consideration by a grand jury. The results of the audit and investigation were never released to the public, however. The grand jury subsequently returned a "no true bill," and no further action was taken by either the city council or city manager Alberg.

II

Petitioner named the city of Independence, city manager Alberg, and the present members of the city council in their official capacities as defendants in this suit.[9] Alleging that he was discharged without notice of reasons and without a hearing in violation of his constitutional rights to

---

In view of the contents of these reports, I feel that the information in the reports backed up by signed statements taken by investigators is so bad that the council should immediately make available to the news media access to copies of all of these 27 voluminous investigative reports so the public can be told what has been going on in Independence. I further believe that copies of these reports should be turned over and referred to the prosecuting attorney of Jackson County, Missouri for consideration and presentation to the next grand jury. I further insist that the city manager immediately take direct and appropriate action, permitted under the charter, against such persons as are shown by the investigation to have been involved.

[9]   Petitioner did not join former councilman Roberts in the instant litigation. A separate action seeking defamation damages was brought in state court against Roberts and Alberg in their individual capacities. Petitioner dismissed the state suit against Alberg and reached a financial settlement with Roberts.

procedural and substantive due process, petitioner sought declaratory and injunctive relief, including a hearing on his discharge, backpay from the date of discharge, and attorney's fees. The District Court, after a bench trial, entered judgment for respondents.[10]

The Court of Appeals initially reversed the District Court. Although it agreed with the District Court that under Missouri law petitioner possessed no property interest in continued employment as police chief, the Court of Appeals concluded that the city's allegedly false public accusations had blackened petitioner's name and reputation, thus depriving him of liberty without due process of law. That the stigmatizing charges did not come from the city manager and were not included in the official discharge notice was, in the court's view, immaterial. What was important, the court explained, was that "the official actions of the city council released charges against [petitioner] contemporaneous and, in the eyes of the public, connected with that discharge."[12]

Respondents petitioned for review of the Court of Appeals' decision. Certiorari was granted, and the case was remanded for further consideration in light of our supervening decision in Monell v. New York City Dept. of Social Services, 436 U.S. 658 (1978). The Court of Appeals on the remand reaffirmed its original determination that the city had violated petitioner's rights under the Fourteenth Amendment, but held that all respondents, including the city, were entitled to qualified immunity from liability . . . stating:

> The Supreme Court's decisions in Board of Regents v. Roth, 408 U.S. 564 (1972), and Perry v. Sindermann, 408 U.S. 593 (1972), crystallized the rule establishing the right to a name-clearing hearing for a government employee allegedly stigmatized in the course of his discharge. The Court decided those two cases two months after the discharge in the instant case. Thus, officials of the city of Independence could not have been aware of [petitioner's] right to a name-clearing hearing in connection with the discharge. The city of Independence should not be charged with predicting the future course of constitutional law. . . . We extend the limited immunity the district court applied to the individual

---

[10] The District Court, relying on *Monroe v. Pape*, held that § 1983 did not create a cause of action against the city, but that petitioner could base his claim for relief directly on the Fourteenth Amendment. On the merits, however, the court determined that petitioner's discharge did not deprive him of any constitutionally protected property interest because, as an untenured employee, he possessed neither a contractual nor a de facto right to continued employment as chief of police. Similarly, the court found that the circumstances of petitioner's dismissal did not impose a stigma of illegal or immoral conduct on his professional reputation, and hence did not deprive him of any liberty interest. . . .

[12] As compensation for the denial of his constitutional rights, the Court of Appeals awarded petitioner damages in lieu of backpay. . . . [B]ecause petitioner had reached the mandatory retirement age during the course of the litigation, he could not be reinstated to his former position. Thus the compensatory award was to be measured by the amount of money petitioner would likely have earned to retirement had he not been deprived of his good name by the city's actions, subject to mitigation by the amounts actually earned, as well as by the recovery from Councilman Roberts in the state defamation suit. . . .

defendants to the city as well, because its officials acted in good faith and without malice. We hold the city not liable for actions it could not reasonably have known violated [petitioner's] constitutional rights.

We turn now to the reasons for our disagreement with this holding.

III

Because the question of the scope of a municipality's immunity from liability under § 1983 is essentially one of statutory construction, the starting point in our analysis must be the language of the statute itself. By its terms, § 1983 "creates a species of tort liability that on its face admits of no immunities." Imbler v. Pachtman, 424 U.S. 409, 417 (1976). Its language is absolute and unqualified; no mention is made of any privileges, immunities, or defenses that may be asserted. Rather, the act imposes liability upon "*every* person" who, under color of state law or custom, "subjects, or causes to be subjected, any citizen of the United States . . . to the deprivation of any rights, privileges, or immunities secured by the Constitution and laws." And *Monell* held that these words were intended to encompass municipal corporations as well as natural "persons."

Moreover, the congressional debates surrounding the passage of § 1 of the Civil Rights Act of 1871—the forerunner of § 1983—confirm the expansive sweep of the statutory language. . . .

However, notwithstanding § 1983's expansive language and the absence of any express incorporation of common-law immunities, we have, on several occasions, found that a tradition of immunity was so firmly rooted in the common law and was supported by such strong policy reasons that "Congress would have specifically so provided had it wished to abolish the doctrine." Pierson v. Ray, 386 U.S. 547, 555 (1967). . . . Subsequent cases have required that we consider the personal liability of various other types of government officials. . . .

In each of these cases, our finding of § 1983 immunity "was predicated upon a considered inquiry into the immunity historically accorded the relevant official at common law and the interests behind it." Where the immunity claimed by the defendant was well established at common law at the time § 1983 was enacted, and where its rationale was compatible with the purposes of the Civil Rights Act, we have construed the statute to incorporate that immunity. But there is no tradition of immunity for municipal corporations, and neither history nor policy [supports] a construction of § 1983 that would justify the qualified immunity accorded the city of Independence by the Court of Appeals. We hold, therefore, that the municipality may not assert the good faith of its officers or agents as a defense to liability under § 1983.

A

Since colonial times, a distinct feature of our nation's system of governance has been the conferral of political power upon public and municipal corporations for the management of matters of local concern.

As *Monell* recounted, by 1871, municipalities—like private corporations—were treated as natural persons for virtually all purposes of
constitutional and statutory analysis. In particular, they were routinely
sued in both federal and state courts. Local governmental units were
regularly held to answer in damages for a wide range of statutory and
constitutional violations, as well as for common-law actions for breach of
contract. And although, as we discuss below, a municipality was not
subject to suit for all manner of tortious conduct, it is clear that at the
time § 1983 was enacted, local governmental bodies did not enjoy the sort
of "good-faith" qualified immunity extended to them by the Court of
Appeals.

As a general rule, it was understood that a municipality's tort liability in damages was identical to that of private corporations and individuals: "There is nothing in the character of a municipal corporation which
entitles it to an immunity from liability for such malfeasances as private
corporations or individuals would be liable for in a civil action. . . ."
Thomas G. Shearman and Amasa A. Redfield, A Treatise on the Law of
Negligence § 120, p. 139 (1869).

. . . Under this general theory of liability, a municipality was deemed
responsible for any private losses generated through a wide variety of its
operations and functions, from personal injuries due to its defective sew-
ers, thoroughfares, and public utilities, to property damage caused by its
trespasses and uncompensated takings.

Yet in the hundreds of cases from that era awarding damages
against municipal governments for wrongs committed by them, one
searches in vain for much mention of a qualified immunity based on the
good faith of municipal officers. . . .

To be sure, there were two doctrines that afforded municipal corporations some measure of protection from tort liability. The first sought to
distinguish between a municipality's "governmental" and "proprietary"
functions; as to the former, the city was held immune, whereas in its exercise of the latter, the city was held to the same standards of liability as
any private corporation. The second doctrine immunized a municipality
for its "discretionary" or "legislative" activities, but not for those which
were "ministerial" in nature. A brief examination of the application and
rationale underlying each of these doctrines demonstrates that Congress
could not have intended them to limit a municipality's immunity under
§ 1983.

The governmental-proprietary distinction owed its existence to the
dual nature of the municipal corporation. On the one hand, the municipality was a corporate body, capable of performing the same "proprietary"
functions as any private corporation, and liable for its torts in the same
manner and to the same extent, as well. On the other hand, the municipality was an arm of the state, and when acting in that "governmental"
or "public" capacity, it shared the immunity traditionally accorded the
sovereign. But the principle of sovereign immunity—itself a somewhat

arid fountainhead for municipal immunity—is necessarily nullified when the state expressly or impliedly allows itself, or its creation, to be sued. Municipalities were therefore liable not only for their "proprietary" acts, but also for those "governmental" functions as to which the state had withdrawn their immunity. And, by the end of the 19th century, courts regularly held that in imposing a specific duty on the municipality either in the charter or by statute, the state had impliedly withdrawn the city's immunity from liability for the nonperformance or misperformance of its obligation. Thus, despite the nominal existence of an immunity for "governmental" functions, municipalities were found liable in damages in a multitude of cases involving such activities.

That the municipality's common-law immunity for "governmental" functions derives from the principle of sovereign immunity also explains why that doctrine could not have served as the basis for the qualified privilege respondent city claims under § 1983. First, because sovereign immunity insulates the municipality from unconsented suits altogether, the presence or absence of good faith is simply irrelevant. The critical issue is whether injury occurred while the city was exercising governmental, as opposed to proprietary, powers or obligations—not whether its agents reasonably believed they were acting lawfully in so conducting themselves. More fundamentally, however, the municipality's "governmental" immunity is obviously abrogated by the sovereign's enactment of a statute making it amenable to suit. Section 1983 was just such a statute. By including municipalities within the class of "persons" subject to liability for violations of the federal Constitution and laws, Congress—the supreme sovereign on matters of federal law—abolished whatever vestige of the state's sovereign immunity the municipality possessed.

The second common-law distinction between municipal functions—that protecting the city from suits challenging "discretionary" decisions—was grounded not on the principle of sovereign immunity, but on a concern for separation of powers. A large part of the municipality's responsibilities involved broad discretionary decisions on issues of public policy—decisions that affected large numbers of persons and called for a delicate balancing of competing considerations. For a court or jury, in the guise of a tort suit, to review the reasonableness of the city's judgment on these matters would be an infringement upon the powers properly vested in a coordinate and coequal branch of government. In order to ensure against any invasion into the legitimate sphere of the municipality's policymaking processes, courts therefore refused to entertain suits against the city "either for the nonexercise of, or for the manner in which in good faith it exercises, *discretionary powers* of a public or legislative character."

Although many, if not all, of a municipality's activities would seem to involve at least some measure of discretion, the influence of this doctrine on the city's liability was not as significant as might be expected.

For just as the courts implied an exception to the municipality's immunity for its "governmental" functions, here, too, a distinction was made that had the effect of subjecting the city to liability for much of its tortious conduct. While the city retained its immunity for decisions as to whether the public interest required acting in one manner or another, once any particular decision was made, the city was fully liable for injuries incurred in the execution of its judgment. Thus, the municipalities remained liable in damages for a broad range of conduct implementing their discretionary decisions.

Once again, an understanding of the rationale underlying the common-law immunity for "discretionary" functions explains why that doctrine cannot serve as the foundation for a good-faith immunity under § 1983. That common-law doctrine merely prevented courts from substituting their own judgment on matters within the lawful discretion of the municipality. But a municipality has no "discretion" to violate the federal Constitution; its dictates are absolute and imperative. And when a court passes judgment on the municipality's conduct in a § 1983 action, it does not seek to second-guess the "reasonableness" of the city's decision nor to interfere with the local government's resolution of competing policy considerations. Rather, it looks only to whether the municipality has conformed to the requirements of the federal Constitution and statutes. . . .

In sum, we can discern no "tradition so well grounded in history and reason" that would warrant the conclusion that in enacting § 1 of the Civil Rights Act, the 42nd Congress sub silentio extended to municipalities a qualified immunity based on the good faith of their officers. Absent any clearer indication that Congress intended so to limit the reach of a statute expressly designed to provide a "broad remedy for violations of federally protected civil rights," *Monell*, we are unwilling to suppose that injuries occasioned by a municipality's unconstitutional conduct were not also meant to be fully redressable through its sweep.

B

Our rejection of a construction of § 1983 that would accord municipalities a qualified immunity for their good-faith constitutional violations is compelled both by the legislative purpose in enacting the statute and by considerations of public policy. The central aim of the Civil Rights Act was to provide protection to those persons wronged by the " '[m]isuse of power, possessed by virtue of state law and made possible only because the wrongdoer is clothed with the authority of state law.' " *Monroe*, 365 U.S. at 184. By creating an express federal remedy, Congress sought to "enforce provisions of the Fourteenth Amendment against those who carry a badge of authority of a state and represent it in some capacity, whether they act in accordance with their authority or misuse it." Id. at 172.

How "uniquely amiss" it would be, therefore, if the government itself—"the social organ to which all in our society look for the promotion of liberty, justice, fair and equal treatment, and the setting of worthy norms and goals for social conduct"—were permitted to disavow liability for the injury it has begotten. A damages remedy against the offending party is a vital component of any scheme for vindicating cherished constitutional guarantees, and the importance of assuring its efficacy is only accentuated when the wrongdoer is the institution that has been established to protect the very rights it has transgressed. Yet owing to the qualified immunity enjoyed by most government officials, see Scheuer v. Rhodes, 416 U.S. 232 (1974), many victims of municipal malfeasance would be left remediless if the city were also allowed to assert a good-faith defense. Unless countervailing considerations counsel otherwise, the injustice of such a result should not be tolerated.[33]

Moreover, § 1983 was intended not only to provide compensation to the victims of past abuses, but to serve as a deterrent against future constitutional deprivations, as well. The knowledge that a municipality will be liable for all of its injurious conduct, whether committed in good faith or not, should create an incentive for officials who harbor doubts about the lawfulness of their intended actions to err on the side of protecting citizens' constitutional rights. Furthermore, the threat that damages might be levied against the city may encourage those in a policymaking position to institute internal rules and programs designed to minimize the likelihood of unintentional infringements on constitutional rights. Such procedures are particularly beneficial in preventing those "systemic" injuries that result not so much from the conduct of any single individual, but from the interactive behavior of several government officials, each of whom may be acting in good faith.[36]

Our previous decisions conferring qualified immunities on various government officials are not to be read as derogating the significance of the societal interest in compensating the innocent victims of governmental misconduct. Rather, in each case we concluded that overriding considerations of public policy nonetheless demanded that the official be given a measure of protection from personal liability. The concerns that justified those decisions, however, are less compelling, if not wholly inapplicable, when the liability of the municipal entity is at issue.

In *Scheuer v. Rhodes*, the Chief Justice identified the two "mutually dependent rationales" on which the doctrine of official immunity rested:

---

[33] The absence of any damages remedy for violations of all but the most "clearly established" constitutional rights could also have the deleterious effect of freezing constitutional law in its current state of development, for without a meaningful remedy, aggrieved individuals will have little incentive to seek vindication of those constitutional deprivations that have not previously been clearly defined.

[36] In addition, the threat of liability against the city ought to increase the attentiveness with which officials at the higher levels of government supervise the conduct of their subordinates. The need to institute system-wide measures in order to increase the vigilance with which otherwise indifferent municipal officials protect citizens' constitutional rights is, of course, particularly acute where the front-line officers are judgment-proof in their individual capacities.

(1) the injustice, particularly in the absence of bad faith, of subjecting to liability an officer who is required, by the legal obligations of his position, to exercise discretion; (2) the danger that the threat of such liability would deter his willingness to execute his office with the decisiveness and the judgment required by the public good.

The first consideration is simply not implicated when the damages award comes not from the official's pocket, but from the public treasury. It hardly seems unjust to require a municipal defendant which has violated a citizen's constitutional rights to compensate him for the injury suffered thereby. Indeed, Congress enacted § 1983 precisely to provide a remedy for such abuses of official authority. Elemental notions of fairness dictate that one who causes a loss should bear the loss.

It has been argued, however, that revenue raised by taxation for public use should not be diverted to the benefit of a single or discrete group of taxpayers, particularly where the municipality has at all times acted in good faith. On the contrary . . . it is the public at large which enjoys the benefits of the government's activities, and it is the public at large which is ultimately responsible for its administration. Thus, even where some constitutional development could not have been foreseen by municipal officials, it is fairer to allocate any resulting financial loss to the inevitable costs of government borne by all the taxpayers, than to allow its impact to be felt solely by those whose rights, albeit newly recognized, have been violated.[39]

The second rationale mentioned in *Scheuer* also loses its force when it is the municipality, in contrast to the official, whose liability is at issue. At the heart of this justification for a qualified immunity for the individual official is the concern that the threat of *personal* monetary liability will introduce an unwarranted and unconscionable consideration into the decision making process, thus paralyzing the governing official's decisiveness and distorting his judgment on matters of public policy. The inhibiting effect is significantly reduced, if not eliminated, however, when the threat of personal liability is removed. First, as an empirical matter, it is questionable whether the hazard of municipal loss will deter a public officer from the conscientious exercise of his duties; city officials routinely make decisions that either require a large expenditure of municipal funds or involve a substantial risk of depleting the public fisc.

---

[39] *Monell v. New York Dept of Social Services* indicated that the principle of loss-spreading was an insufficient justification for holding the municipality liable under § 1983 on a respondeat superior theory. Here, of course, quite a different situation is presented. Petitioner does not seek to hold the city responsible for the unconstitutional actions of an individual official "*solely* because it employs a tortfeasor." Rather, liability is predicated on a determination that "the action that is alleged to be unconstitutional implements or executes a policy statement, ordinance, regulation, or decision officially adopted and promulgated by the body's officers." In this circumstance—when it is the local government itself that is responsible for the constitutional deprivation—it is perfectly reasonable to distribute the loss to the public as a cost of the administration of government, rather than to let the entire burden fall on the injured individual.

More important, though, is the realization that consideration of the *municipality's* liability for constitutional violations is quite properly the concern of its elected or appointed officials. Indeed, a decisionmaker would be derelict in his duties if, at some point, he did not consider whether his decision comports with constitutional mandates and did not weigh the risk that a violation might result in an award of damages from the public treasury. As one commentator aptly put it: "Whatever other concerns should shape a particular official's actions, certainly one of them should be the constitutional rights of individuals who will be affected by his actions. To criticize § 1983 liability because it leads decisionmakers to avoid the infringement of constitutional rights is to criticize one of the statute's raisons d'etre."[41]

IV

In sum, our decision holding that municipalities have no immunity from damages liability flowing from their constitutional violations harmonizes well with developments in the common law and our own pronouncements on official immunities under § 1983. Doctrines of tort law have changed significantly over the past century, and our notions of governmental responsibility should properly reflect that evolution. No longer is individual "blameworthiness" the acid test of liability; the principle of equitable loss-spreading has joined fault as a factor in distributing the costs of official misconduct.

We believe that today's decision, together with prior precedents in this area, properly allocates these costs among the three principals in the scenario of the § 1983 cause of action: the victim of the constitutional deprivation; the officer whose conduct caused the injury; and the public, as represented by the municipal entity. The innocent individual who is harmed by an abuse of governmental authority is assured that he will be compensated for his injury. The offending official, so long as he conducts himself in good faith, may go about his business secure in the knowledge that a qualified immunity will protect him from personal liability for damages that are more appropriately chargeable to the populace as a whole. And the public will be forced to bear only the costs of injury inflicted by the "execution of a government's policy or custom, whether made by its lawmakers or by those whose edicts or acts may fairly be said to represent official policy." *Monell v. New York City Dept. of Social Services.*

Reversed.

■ MR. JUSTICE POWELL, with whom THE CHIEF JUSTICE, MR. JUSTICE STEWART, and MR. JUSTICE REHNQUIST joined, dissenting.

The Court today holds that the city of Independence may be liable in damages for violating a constitutional right that was unknown when the events in this case occurred. It finds a denial of due process in the city's

---

[41] Note, Developments in the Law: Section 1983 and Federalism, 90 Harv. L. Rev. 1133, 1224 (1977).

failure to grant petitioner a hearing to clear his name after he was discharged. But his dismissal involved only the proper exercise of discretionary powers according to prevailing constitutional doctrine. The city imposed no stigma on petitioner that would require a "name clearing" hearing under the Due Process Clause.

On the basis of this alleged deprivation of rights, the Court interprets 42 U.S.C. § 1983 to impose strict liability on municipalities for constitutional violations. This strict liability approach inexplicably departs from this Court's prior decisions under § 1983 and runs counter to the concerns of the 42nd Congress when it enacted the statute. The Court's ruling also ignores the vast weight of common-law precedent as well as the current state law of municipal immunity. For these reasons, and because this decision will hamper local governments unnecessarily, I dissent.

I

The Court does not question the District Court's statement of the facts surrounding Owen's dismissal. It nevertheless rejects the District Court's conclusion that no due process hearing was necessary because "the circumstances of [Owen's] discharge did not impose a stigma of illegal or immoral conduct on his professional reputation." Careful analysis of the record supports the District Court's view that Owen suffered no constitutional deprivation. . . .

Due process requires a hearing on the discharge of a government employee "if the employer creates and disseminates a false and defamatory impression about the employee in connection with his termination. . . ." Codd v. Velger, 429 U.S. 624, 628 (1977) (per curiam). This principle was first announced in Board of Regents v. Roth, 408 U.S. 564 (1972), which was decided in June 1972, 10 weeks *after* Owen was discharged. The pivotal question after *Roth* is whether the circumstances of the discharge so blackened the employee's name as to impair his liberty interest in his professional reputation.

The events surrounding Owen's dismissal "were prominently reported in local newspapers." Doubtless, the public received a negative impression of Owen's abilities and performance. But a "name clearing" hearing is not necessary unless the employer makes a public statement that "might seriously damage [the employee's] standing and associations in his community." *Roth*, 408 U.S. at 573. No hearing is required after the "discharge of a public employee whose position is terminable at the will of the employer when there is no public disclosure of the reasons for the discharge." Bishop v. Wood, 426 U.S. 341 (1976).

The City Manager gave no specific reason for dismissing Owen. Instead, he relied on his discretionary authority to discharge top administrators "for the good of the service." Alberg did not suggest that Owen "had been guilty of dishonesty, or immorality." *Roth*, 408 U.S. at 573. Indeed, in his "property room" statement of April 13, Alberg said that there was "no evidence to substantiate any allegations of a criminal nature." This exoneration was reinforced by the grand jury's refusal to initiate a prosecution in the matter. Thus, nothing in the actual firing cast such a stigma on Owen's professional reputation that his liberty was infringed.

The Court does not address directly the question whether any stigma was imposed by the discharge. Rather, it relies on the Court of Appeals' finding that stigma derived from the events "connected with" the firing. That court attached great significance to the resolution adopted by the city council at its April 17 meeting. But the resolution merely recommended that Alberg take "appropriate action," and the District Court found no "causal connection" between events in the city council and the firing of Owen. Two days before the council met, Alberg already had decided to dismiss Owen. Indeed, councilman Roberts stated at the meeting that the city manager had asked for Owen's resignation.

Even if the council resolution is viewed as part of the discharge process, Owen has demonstrated no denial of his liberty. Neither the city manager nor the council cast any aspersions on Owen's character. Alberg absolved all connected with the property room of any illegal activity, while the council resolution alleged no wrongdoing. That events focused public attention upon Owen's dismissal is undeniable; such attention is a condition of employment—and of discharge—for high government officials. Nevertheless, nothing in the actions of the city manager or the city council triggered a constitutional right to a name-clearing hearing.

The statements by councilman Roberts were neither measured nor benign, but they provide no basis for this action against the city of Independence. Under Monell v. New York City Dept. of Social Services, 436 U.S. 658, 691 (1978), the city cannot be held liable for Roberts's statements on a theory of respondeat superior. That case held that § 1983 makes municipalities liable for constitutional deprivations only if the challenged action was taken "pursuant to official municipal policy of some nature. . . ." As the Court noted, "a municipality cannot be held liable *solely* because it employs a tortfeasor. . . ." The statements of a single councilman scarcely rise to the level of municipal policy. . . .

The Court now finds unconstitutional stigma in the interaction of unobjectionable official acts with the unauthorized statements of a lone councilman who had no direct role in the discharge process. The notoriety that attended Owen's firing resulted not from any city policy, but solely from public misapprehension of the reasons for a purely discretionary dismissal. There was no constitutional injury.

II

Having constructed a constitutional deprivation from a valid exercise of governmental authority, the Court holds that municipalities are strictly liable for their constitutional torts. Until two years ago, municipal corporations enjoyed absolute immunity from § 1983 claims. *Monroe v. Pape.* But *Monell* held that local governments are "persons" within the meaning of the statute, and thus are liable in damages for constitutional violations inflicted by municipal policies. *Monell* did not address the question whether municipalities might enjoy a qualified immunity or good-faith defense against § 1983 actions.

After today's decision, municipalities will have gone in two short years from absolute immunity under § 1983 to strict liability. As a policy matter, I believe that strict municipal liability unreasonably subjects local governments to damages judgments for actions that were reasonable when performed. It converts municipal governance into a hazardous slalom through constitutional obstacles that are unknown and unknowable.

The Court's decision also impinges seriously on the prerogatives of municipal entities created and regulated primarily by the states. At the very least, this Court should not initiate a federal intrusion of this magnitude in the absence of explicit congressional action. Yet today's decision is supported by nothing in the text of § 1983. Indeed, it conflicts with the apparent intent of the drafters of the statute, with the common law of municipal tort liability, and with the current state law of municipal immunities.

A

1

. . . The Court today abandons any attempt to harmonize § 1983 with traditional tort law. It points out that municipal immunity may be abrogated by legislation. Thus, according to the Court, Congress "abolished" municipal immunity when it included municipalities "within the class of 'persons' subject to liability" under § 1983.

This reasoning flies in the face of our prior decisions under this statute. We have held repeatedly that "immunities 'well grounded in history and reason' [were not] abrogated 'by covert inclusion in the general language' of 1983." Imbler v. Pachtman, 424 U.S. 409, 418 (1976), quoting Tenney v. Brandhove, 341 U.S. 367, 376 (1951). The peculiar nature of the Court's position emerges when the status of executive officers under § 1983 is compared with that of local governments. State and local executives are personally liable for bad-faith or unreasonable constitutional torts. Although Congress had the power to make those individuals liable for all such torts, this Court has refused to find an abrogation of traditional immunity in a statute that does not mention immunities. Yet the Court now views the enactment of § 1983 as a direct abolition of traditional municipal immunities. Unless the Court is overruling its previous immunity decisions, the silence in § 1983 must mean that the 42nd Congress mutely accepted the immunity of executive officers, but silently rejected common-law municipal immunity. I find this interpretation of the statute singularly implausible.

2

Important public policies support the extension of qualified immunity to local governments. First, as recognized by the doctrine of separation of powers, some governmental decisions should be at least presumptively insulated from judicial review. . . . The allocation of public resources and the operational policies of the government itself are activities that lie peculiarly within the competence of executive and legislative bodies. When charting those policies, a local official should not have to gauge his employer's possible liability under § 1983 if he incorrectly—though reasonably and in good faith—forecasts the course of constitutional law. Excessive judicial intrusion into such decisions can only distort municipal decisionmaking and discredit the courts. Qualified immunity would provide presumptive protection for discretionary acts, while still leaving the municipality liable for bad faith or unreasonable constitutional deprivations. . . .

The Court now argues that local officials might modify their actions unduly if they face personal liability under § 1983, but that they are unlikely to do so when the locality itself will be held liable. This contention denigrates the sense of responsibility of municipal officers, and misunderstands the political process. Responsible local officials will be concerned about potential judgments against their municipalities for alleged constitutional torts. Moreover, they will be accountable within the political system for subjecting the municipality to adverse judgments. If officials must look over their shoulders at strict municipal liability for unknowable constitutional deprivations, the resulting degree of governmental paralysis will be little different from that caused by fear of personal liability.[9]

In addition, basic fairness requires a qualified immunity for municipalities. The good-faith defense recognized under § 1983 authorizes liability only when officials acted with malicious intent or when they "knew or should have known that their conduct violated the constitutional norm." The standard incorporates the idea that liability should not attach unless there was notice that a constitutional right was at issue. This idea applies to governmental entities and individual officials alike. Constitutional law is what the courts say it is, and—as demonstrated by today's decision and its precursor, *Monell*—even the most prescient lawyer would hesitate to give a firm opinion on matters not plainly settled. Municipalities, often acting in the utmost good faith, may not know or anticipate when their action or inaction will be deemed a constitutional violation.

---

[9]   The Court's argument is not only unpersuasive, but also is internally inconsistent. The Court contends that strict liability is necessary to "create an incentive for officials . . . to err on the side of protecting citizens' constitutional rights." Yet the Court later assures us that such liability will not distort municipal decisionmaking because "[t]he inhibiting effect is significantly reduced, if not eliminated . . . when the threat of personal liability is removed." Thus, the Court apparently believes that strict municipal liability is needed to modify public policies, but will not have any impact on those policies anyway.

The Court nevertheless suggests that, as a matter of social justice, municipal corporations should be strictly liable even if they could not have known that a particular action would violate the Constitution. After all, the Court urges, local governments can "spread" the costs of any judgment across the local population. The Court neglects, however, the fact that many local governments lack the resources to withstand substantial unanticipated liability under § 1983. Even enthusiastic proponents of municipal liability have conceded that ruinous judgments under the statute could imperil local governments. By simplistically applying the theorems of welfare economics and ignoring the reality of municipal finance, the Court imposes strict liability on the level of government least able to bear it. For some municipalities, the result could be a severe limitation on their ability to serve the public.

B

The Court searches at length—and in vain—for legal authority to buttress its policy judgment. Despite its general statements to the contrary, the Court can find no support for its position in the debates on the civil rights legislation that included § 1983. Indeed, the legislative record suggests that the members of the 42nd Congress would have been dismayed by this ruling. Nor, despite its frequent citation of authorities that are only marginally relevant, can the Court rely on the traditional or current law of municipal tort liability. Both in the 19th century and now, courts and legislatures have recognized the importance of limiting the liability of local governments for official torts. Each of these conventional sources of law points to the need for qualified immunity for local governments.

1

The modern dispute over municipal liability under § 1983 has focused on the defeat of the Sherman Amendment during the deliberations on the Civil Rights Act of 1871. Senator Sherman proposed that local governments be held vicariously liable for constitutional deprivations caused by riots within their boundaries. As originally drafted, the measure imposed liability even if municipal officials had no actual knowledge of the impending disturbance. The amendment, which did not affect the part of the Civil Rights Act that we now know as § 1983, was approved by the Senate but rejected by the House of Representatives. After two revisions by conference committees, both houses passed what is now codified as 42 U.S.C. § 1986. The final version applied not just to local governments but to all "persons," and it imposed no liability unless the defendant knew that a wrong was "about to be committed."

Because Senator Sherman initially proposed strict municipal liability for constitutional torts, the discussion of his amendment offers an invaluable insight into the attitudes of his colleagues on the question now before the Court. Much of the resistance to the measure flowed from doubts as to Congress's power to impose vicarious liability on local governments. But opponents of the amendment made additional arguments that strongly support recognition of qualified municipal immunity under § 1983.

First, several legislators expressed trepidation that the proposal's strict liability approach could bankrupt local governments. . . .

Most significant, the opponents objected to liability imposed without any showing that a municipality knew of an impending constitutional deprivation. Senator Sherman defended this feature of the amendment as a characteristic of riot acts long in force in England and this country. But Senator Stevenson argued against creating "a corporate liability for personal injury which no prudence or foresight could have prevented." In the most thorough critique of the amendment, Senator Thurman carefully reviewed the riot acts of Maryland and New York. He emphasized that those laws imposed liability only when a plaintiff proved that the local government had both notice of the impending injury and the power to prevent it.

> Is not that right? Why make the county, or town, or parish liable when it had no reason whatsoever to anticipate that any such crime was about to be committed, and when it had no knowledge of the commission of the crime until after it was committed? What justice is there in that?

These concerns were echoed in the House of Representatives. . . .

Partly in response to these objections, the amendment as finally enacted conditioned liability on a demonstration that the defendant knew that constitutional rights were about to be denied. . . .

These objections to the Sherman Amendment apply with equal force to strict municipal liability under § 1983. Just as the 42nd Congress refused to hold municipalities vicariously liable for deprivations that could not be known beforehand, this Court should not hold those entities strictly liable for deprivations caused by actions that reasonably and in good faith were thought to be legal. The Court's approach today, like the Sherman Amendment, could spawn onerous judgments against local governments and distort the decisions of officers who fear municipal liability for their actions. Congress's refusal to impose those burdens in 1871 surely undercuts any historical argument that federal judges should do so now.

The Court declares that its rejection of qualified immunity is "compelled" by the "legislative purpose" in enacting § 1983. One would expect powerful documentation to back up such a strong statement. Yet the Court notes only three features of the legislative history of the Civil Rights Act. Far from "compelling" the Court's strict liability approach, those features of the congressional record provide scant support for its position.

First, the Court [relies on] statements by Congressmen attesting to the broad remedial scope of the law. In view of our many decisions recognizing the immunity of officers under § 1983, those statements plainly shed no light on the congressional intent with respect to immunity under the statute. Second, the Court cites Senator Stevenson's remark that frequently "a statutory liability has been created against municipal corporations for injuries resulting from a neglect of corporate duty." The Senator merely stated the unobjectionable proposition that municipal immunity could be qualified or abolished by statute. This fragmentary observation provides no basis for the Court's version of the legislative history.

Finally, the Court emphasizes the lack of comment on municipal immunity when opponents of the bill did discuss the immunities of government officers. "Had there been a similar common-law immunity for municipalities, the bill's opponents would have raised the spectre of its destruction as well." This is but another example of the Court's continuing willingness to find meaning in silence. This example is particularly noteworthy because the very next sentence in the Court's opinion concedes: "To be sure, there were two doctrines that afforded municipal corporations some measure of protection from tort liability." Since the opponents of the Sherman Amendment repeatedly expressed their conviction that strict municipal liability was unprecedented and unwise, the failure to recite the theories of municipal immunity is of no relevance here. In any event, that silence cannot contradict the many contemporary judicial decisions applying that immunity.

2

The Court's decision also runs counter to the common law in the 19th century, which recognized substantial tort immunity for municipal actions. Nineteenth-century courts generally held that municipal corporations were not liable for acts undertaken in their "governmental," as opposed to their "proprietary," capacity. Most states now use other criteria for determining when a local government should be liable for damages. Still, the governmental/proprietary distinction retains significance because it was so widely accepted when § 1983 was enacted. It is inconceivable that a Congress thoroughly versed in current legal doctrines would have intended through silence to create the strict liability regime now imagined by this Court.

More directly relevant to this case is the common-law distinction between the "discretionary" and "ministerial" duties of local governments. This Court wrote in Harris v. District of Columbia, 256 U.S. 650, 652 (1921): "[W]hen acting in good faith municipal corporations are not liable for the manner in which they exercise their discretionary powers." The rationale for this immunity derives from the theory of separation of powers. . . .

That reasoning, frequently applied in the 19th century, parallels the theory behind qualified immunity under § 1983. This Court has recognized the importance of preserving the autonomy of executive bodies entrusted with discretionary powers. *Scheuer v. Rhodes* held that executive officials who have broad responsibilities must enjoy a "range of discretion [that is] comparably broad." Consequently, the immunities available under § 1983 [vary] directly with "the scope of discretion and responsibility of the office. . . ." Strict municipal liability can only undermine that discretion.[18] . . .

3

Today's decision also conflicts with the current law in 44 states and the District of Columbia. All of those jurisdictions provide municipal immunity at least analogous to a "good faith" defense against liability for constitutional torts. Thus, for municipalities in almost 90 per cent of our jurisdictions, the Court creates broader liability for constitutional deprivations than for state-law torts. . . .

C

The Court turns a blind eye to this overwhelming evidence that municipalities have enjoyed a qualified immunity and to the policy considerations that for the life of this republic have justified its retention. This disregard of precedent and policy is especially unfortunate because suits under § 1983 typically implicate evolving constitutional standards. A good-faith defense is much more important for those actions than in those involving ordinary tort liability. The duty not to run over a pedestrian with a municipal bus is far less likely to change than is the rule as to what process, if any, is due the bus driver if he claims the right to a hearing after discharge.

The right of a discharged government employee to a "name clearing" hearing was not recognized until our decision in *Roth*. That ruling was handed down 10 weeks after Owen was discharged and eight weeks after the city denied his request for a hearing. By stripping the city of any immunity, the Court punishes it for failing to predict our decision in *Roth*. As a result, local governments and their officials will face the unnerving prospect of crushing damages judgments whenever a policy valid under current law is later found to be unconstitutional. I can see no justice or wisdom in that outcome.

NOTES ON OWEN V. CITY OF INDEPENDENCE

1.   THE DUE PROCESS ISSUE

In *Owen* the former police chief sought and received compensation for the period following his wrongful discharge. But why, exactly, was the discharge wrongful? The Court did not hold that Owen had a right to continued employment. As a discretionary employee, he was subject to termination for virtually any reason. The problem was apparently not the discharge itself but rather the accompanying publicity. Of course, coverage by the media would have been beyond the city's power to control, so the crucial error seems

---

[18] The Court cannot wash away these extensive municipal immunities. . . . The Court takes some solace in the absence in the 19th century of a qualified immunity for local governments. That absence, of course, was due to the availability of absolute immunity for governmental and discretionary acts. . . .

to have been the public dissemination by city officials of statements harmful to Owen's reputation. Far and away the most injurious were the remarks of councilman Roberts, remarks that even the dissent admitted were "neither measured nor benign."

Does *Owen* suggest that the city should have prevented those communications? Would the necessity for a hearing have been avoided if the city manager had refused to allow public disclosure of the charges in the investigative report? Or would it have been necessary as well to muzzle councilman Roberts? How could this have been done?

Suppose that Owen had been discharged without adverse publicity. Suppose further that Owen then went to a neighboring town and applied for appointment as chief of police. If an officer of that town telephoned the city manager of Independence and asked for a candid evaluation of Owen's character and abilities and for an explanation of the reasons for his dismissal, what would be the appropriate response? Should the city manager respond, or would it be wiser to refuse to cooperate?

One answer might be that a municipality should make no effort to restrict the flow of information to the public but should simply be prepared to grant a "name-clearing hearing" to any employee whose reputation is injured as a result. This seems to be the Court's position in *Owen*. Presumably, after councilman Roberts's remarks, the city should have held a hearing at which Owen would have had a chance to defend his record.

What would such a hearing look like? To what decision would it lead? Would the hearing officer attempt to adjudicate, whether, as Councilman Roberts alleged, narcotics and money had "mysteriously disappeared"? Or whether "inappropriate requests" to the police court had in fact been made by "high ranking police officials"? Or whether, as Councilman Roberts concluded, the investigative reports were "astoundingly shocking and virtually unbelievable"? By what standards would such issues be resolved? And if the determination were favorable to Owen, what relief would be given? Would he get his job back, or would he receive merely some sort of official certification of good character?

Perhaps the Court envisions that the "name-clearing hearing" would not lead to any decisional outcome but would merely present an opportunity for the airing of views. Suppose such a hearing is held, and Owen makes a wide-ranging defense of his conduct in office. What should the city officials do in response? Should they say anything? Does the hearing officer simply thank Owen for his time and allow the city to get on with the business of selecting a new Chief of Police? If so, the "name-clearing hearing" would be little more than a press conference. The value to Owen would depend on the willingness of the media to give coverage and sympathetic attention to his side of the story. Of course, the media could do that without an official proceeding, and the city's role in mediating between Owen and the press is at best obscure.

2. THE IMMUNITY ISSUE

The *Owen* opinion illustrates the familiar amalgam of statutory language, legislative history, common-law background, and public policy. Which of these factors seems to have been the most influential in *Owen*? Which should have been? What are the appropriate inferences to be drawn from legislative silence on the subject of immunities? Should the answer hinge on the law of municipal immunity as it stood in 1871? If so, which side seems to have the better of the argument?

Within its sphere, *Owen* imposes strict enterprise liability on local governments. Yet if *Owen* is a step toward enterprise liability, it is only a small step. Absent congressional action, states and state agencies remain immune under the Eleventh Amendment. Individual officers at all levels have the defense of qualified immunity, which severely limits the indirect liability of the governments that employ them. And local governments, who alone among § 1983 defendants can be held strictly liable, can be sued only for acts done pursuant to an official policy or custom. *Owen* is, therefore, the exception rather than the rule. Should it be? Or should the whole scheme of individual, fault-based liability be discarded in favor of a much expanded strict liability imposed directly on government?

3.   THE SIGNIFICANCE OF FAULT

The defense of qualified immunity means that liability under § 1983 generally is fault-based. *Owen* is exceptional in embracing a form of strict liability (if only for a limited class of cases).

This position is widely endorsed by academic commentators, many of whom favor strict liability either of the officer defendant or the government employer. See, e.g., Akhil Reed Amar, Of Sovereignty and Federalism, 96 Yale L.J. 1425 (1987) (insisting on the "remedial imperative" of governmental liability); George A. Bermann, Integrating Governmental and Officer Tort Liability, 77 Colum. L. Rev. 1175 (1977) (endorsing direct governmental liability with a right of indemnification against miscreant officials); Mark R. Brown, Correlating Municipal Liability and Official Immunity under Section 1983, 1989 U. Ill. L. Rev. 625, 631 (arguing that governmental liability and officer immunity should be inversely correlated to eliminate any gap between right and remedy); Mark R. Brown, The Demise of Constitutional Prospectivity: New Life for *Owen*?, 79 Iowa L. Rev. 273, 311–12 (1994) (concluding that immunity is inappropriate even for violations of newly declared constitutional rights); Harold S. Lewis, Jr. & Theodore Y. Blumoff, Reshaping Section 1983's Asymmetry, 140 U. Pa. L. Rev. 755, 756 (1992) (arguing for strict respondeat superior liability); Susanah M. Mead, 42 U.S.C. § 1983 Municipal Liability: The *Monell* Sketch Becomes a Distorted Picture, 65 N.C. L. Rev. 517, 538 (1987) (arguing for strict respondeat superior liability); Jon O. Newman, Suing the Lawbreakers: Proposals to Strengthen the Section 1983 Damage Remedy for Law Enforcers' Misconduct, 87 Yale L.J. 447 (1978) (calling for damages actions directly against state and federal governments); Laura Oren, Immunity and Accountability in Civil Rights Litigation: Who Should Pay?, 50 U. Pitt. L. Rev. 935, 1000–02 (1989) (arguing for strict respondeat superior liability); Peter H. Schuck, Suing Government: Citizen Remedies for Official Wrongs (1983) (arguing that enterprise liability would facilitate effective compensation).

The arguments for or against strict enterprise liability are generally instrumental in nature. That is, they turn on perceptions of efficient deterrence of constitutional violations, the fear of inhibiting the legitimate exercise of government power, and the like. Additionally, the issue has a noninstrumental aspect, concerned not with efficiency and deterrence but with fairness and justice. It is this latter aspect of the problem to which Justice Brennan referred when he found no "injustice" in imposing strict liability: "It hardly seems unjust to require a municipal defendant which has violated a citizen's constitutional rights to compensate him for the injury suffered thereby. . . . Elemental notions of fairness dictate that one who causes a loss should bear the loss."

This position has been attacked as a misunderstanding of the normative basis for compensation. See John C. Jeffries, Jr., Compensation for Constitutional Torts: Reflections on the Significance of Fault, 88 Mich. L. Rev. 82 (1989). Putting instrumental concerns to one side, Jeffries argues from principles of "corrective justice" that not only causation of injury, but also proof of fault[a] should be required:

> Just as causation identifies why this plaintiff is entitled to recover, fault identifies why *this defendant* is obliged to pay. Causation itself is inadequate to this task, for there are, in the nature of things, many causes of any injury. The plaintiff's own conduct, for example, is usually, if not always, a but-for cause of plaintiff's injury. Other causal antecedents abound, and there is nothing inherent in the concept of causation (as distinct from external limitations imposed in the name of causation) to say which causes count. The showing of fault fills this gap. It identifies the causal antecedent that will be regarded as legally significant. It singles out a particular defendant—one whose *wrongful* act has caused the plaintiff's injury—to make good the plaintiff's loss.

> More simply, fault supplies the moral dimension to the causal relationship. While causation traces a physical connection between doer and sufferer, it provides in itself no moral basis for coercing compensation.

Whatever the merits of argument about the conceptual significance of fault in municipal liability under § 1983, it is clear that the issue has practical consequences only in some cases. Mostly, they involve situations where local government has failed to anticipate changes—or at least clarification—in the law. When governmental policy violates a settled rule of constitutional law, qualified immunity (even if it were available) would provide no defense. A qualified immunity defense (if available) could be made out only if it would have been reasonable at the time to regard the policy as consistent with constitutional limitations. The chief effect of *Owen*, therefore, is to impose

---

[a] The fault requirement recognized by the defense of qualified immunity must be distinguished from the analytically separate issue of a fault requirement in the underlying constitutional violation. Some constitutional rights are defined in such a way that their violation requires proof of something like specific intent. The proof of discriminatory purpose required by the equal protection right against racial discrimination is an example. This is quite different from the fault involved in the failure to know about a clearly established constitutional right.

additional liability on local governments in cases where uncertainties or ambiguities in the law make it reasonable for the locality not to foresee that its policy would be struck down. Do "[e]lemental notions of fairness" require compensation in that situation?

4.   SUBSEQUENT RETROACTIVITY CASES

One way to look at *Owen* is that it imposed retroactive liability on the municipality for violating the requirement of a name-clearing hearing subsequently announced in Board of Regents v. Roth, 408 U.S. 564 (1972), and Perry v. Sindermann, 408 U.S. 593 (1972). In decisions since *Owen*, the Supreme Court first flirted with, then backed away from, an approach that would have made some constitutional decisions apply only prospectively.

American Trucking Associations, Inc. v. Smith, 496 U.S. 167 (1990), was a refund suit filed in state court by Arkansas taxpayers. They claimed that a highway use tax enacted in 1983 was unconstitutional. In 1987, the Supreme Court held in American Trucking Associations, Inc. v. Scheiner, 483 U.S. 266 (1987), that similar taxes imposed by Pennsylvania were unconstitutional. *Smith*, which was then pending in the Supreme Court, was remanded to the Arkansas Supreme Court for reconsideration in light of *Scheiner*. The Arkansas Supreme Court ruled that *Scheiner* should apply only prospectively. The case then came back to the Supreme Court. The judgment was for the most part affirmed, with the Court divided four-one-four.

Justice O'Connor wrote for a plurality of herself, Chief Justice Rehnquist, and Justices White, and Kennedy. Since *Scheiner* "established a new principle of law in the area of our dormant commerce clause jurisprudence" she thought it should not apply retroactively. Her analysis was a three-part inquiry derived from Chevron Oil Co. v. Huson, 404 U.S. 97 (1971):

> First, the decision to be applied nonretroactively must establish a new principle of law, either by overruling clear past precedent on which litigants may have relied, or by deciding an issue of first impression whose resolution was not clearly foreshadowed. Second, . . . we must . . . weigh the merits and demerits in each case by looking to the prior history of the rule in question, its purpose and effect, and whether retrospective operation will further or retard its operation. Finally, we [must] weig[h] the inequity imposed by retroactive application, for where a decision of this Court could produce substantial inequitable results if applied retroactively, there is ample basis in our cases for avoiding the injustice or hardship by a holding of nonretroactivity.

Justice O'Connor found inequity in applying *Scheiner* retroactively, since "the state promulgated and implemented its tax scheme in reliance" on the old law and a "refund, if required by state or federal law, could deplete the state treasury, thus threatening the state's current operations and future plans."

As to the seemingly contrary lesson of *Owen*, O'Connor said:

> Our delineation of the scope of liability under a statute designed to permit suit against government entities and officials

provides little guidance for determining the fairest way to apply our own decisions. Indeed, the policy concerns involved are quite distinct. In *Owen*, we discerned that according municipalities a special immunity from liability for violations of constitutional rights would not best serve the goals of § 1983, even if those rights had not been clearly established when the violation occurred. Such a determination merely makes municipalities, like private individuals, responsible for anticipating developments in the law. We noted that such liability would motivate each of the city's elected officials to "consider whether his decision comports with constitutional mandates and . . . weigh the risk that a violation might result in an award of damages from the public treasury." This analysis does not apply when a decision clearly breaks with precedent, a type of departure which, by definition, public officials could not anticipate nor have any responsibility to anticipate.

Justice Scalia concurred in the result. He thought prospective decisionmaking "incompatible with the judicial role," but concurred on the ground that *Scheiner* had been wrongly decided.

The dissenters, in an opinion by Justice Stevens, would have applied *Scheiner* to all cases then still pending on direct review. The dissent dealt with *Owen* in a footnote:

> Our decision in *Owen* is necessarily predicated upon the view that a court should apply the law in effect at the time of decision in considering whether the state has violated the Constitution. Although the plurality is technically correct that *Owen* did not hold that constitutional decisions should always apply "retroactively," that case, and the Congress that enacted § 1983, surely did not contemplate that state actors could achieve through the judicially crafted doctrine of retroactivity, the immunity not only from damages but also from liability denied them on the floors of Congress.

Three years later, the *Smith* plurality's suggestion that "new" constitutional rulings might apply only prospectively was rejected. In Harper v. Virginia Department of Taxation, 509 U.S. 86 (1993), the Court confronted another question of the effect a prior decision declaring state taxes invalid. This time the Court applied its prior ruling retroactively. Speaking through Justice Thomas, the majority seemed hostile to any notion of non-retroactivity in constitutional law: "When this Court applies a rule of federal law to the parties before it, that rule is the controlling interpretation of federal law and must be given full retroactive effect in all cases still open on direct review and as to all events, regardless of whether such events predate or postdate our announcement of the rule." Justice O'Connor, joined by Chief Justice Rehnquist, dissented.

The upshot of all this seems to be that *Owen* is restored to its apparent scope. Retroactive application of new constitutional rulings means, under *Owen*, that localities will be held liable for failing to anticipate such rulings, even in circumstances where individual defendants would have enjoyed the defense of qualified immunity.[b]

5. FEDERAL GOVERNMENTAL LIABILITY

An attempt to extend the rule of *Owen* to suits against the federal government was rejected in FDIC v. Meyer, 510 U.S. 471 (1994). Meyer was an executive in a savings and loan association. When the association failed, federal authorities took over and carried out their general policy of firing the senior management of failed thrifts. Meyer claimed that his termination without a hearing violated procedural due process and brought *Bivens* actions against both the official immediately responsible for his termination and the Federal Savings and Loan Insurance Corporation (FSLIC), whose duties were later assumed by the Federal Deposit Insurance Corporation (FDIC).

The jury found in favor of the defendant official on grounds of qualified immunity but held the federal agency, which presumably had no such immunity, liable in the amount of $130,000. A unanimous Supreme Court ruled that *Bivens* actions would not lie against federal agencies. The effect is to remit *Bivens* plaintiffs to suits against federal officers, with the attendant limitations of qualified immunity. Direct governmental liability is limited to localities.

INTRODUCTORY NOTES ON "OFFICIAL POLICY"

1. INTRODUCTION

Monell limited governmental liability to acts done pursuant to official policy or custom. This requirement has proved troublesome. The issue is clear where, as in *Monell,* the decision is taken pursuant to a rule or regulation of general applicability. More difficult questions arise when governmental liability is sought for a single act or decision by government officials. No one could contend that the Supreme Court's treatment of this issue has been clear.

The cases fall into two categories. The first concerns when the act of a government agent can properly be attributed to the agency itself. This issue is addressed in the note on *Pembaur* below and in the main case that follows, *City of St. Louis v. Praprotnik.* The second category concerns whether the government can be held liable for the omission of failing to train its officials properly. This issue is addressed in *City of Canton v. Harris,* which is discussed in the notes following *Praprotnik.*

2. *PEMBAUR V. CITY OF CINCINNATI*

Pembaur v. City of Cincinnati, 475 U.S. 469 (1986), arose from an investigation of alleged welfare fraud in Dr. Pembaur's medical clinic. A grand

---

[b]   For analysis of *Smith* and *Harper,* see Mark R. Brown, The Demise of Constitutional Prospectivity: New Life for *Owen?,* 79 Iowa L. Rev. 273 (1994).

jury issued subpoenas for two of Pembaur's employees, both of whom failed to appear. The prosecutor then obtained warrants ordering their arrest.

When deputy sheriffs arrived at the clinic to execute the warrants, Pembaur locked the door separating the reception area from the rest of the clinic and refused to let them in. After consulting with the Cincinnati police, the deputies called their supervisor to ask for instructions. The supervisor told them to call William Whalen, assistant prosecutor of the county, and to follow his directions. Whalen conferred with his superior and relayed the instruction to "go in and get" the recalcitrant witnesses. When advised of these instructions, the city police officers on the scene obtained an axe and chopped down the door. The deputies then entered and searched for the witnesses. They arrested two individuals who fit the descriptions in the warrants but turned out to be the wrong persons.

Four years later, Steagald v. United States, 451 U.S. 204 (1981), ruled that, absent exigent circumstances, the police cannot enter an individual's home or business without a search warrant, merely because they are seeking to execute an arrest warrant for a third person. *Steagald* was conceded to apply retroactively, and thus became the basis for Pembaur's § 1983 action against all involved. The issue that ultimately came to the Supreme Court was the liability of the county for the actions of its officers.

At trial, the evidence showed no prior instance when the sheriff had been denied access to property in an attempt to arrest a third person. There was no written or general policy on the issue. The county's liability therefore turned on its responsibility for the decision of its officials on this particular occasion. Speaking for the Court, Justice Brennan said:

> The Deputy Sheriffs who attempted to serve the [arrest warrants] at petitioner's clinic found themselves in a difficult situation. Unsure of the proper course of action to follow, they sought instructions from their supervisors. The instructions they received were to follow the orders of the County Prosecutor. The prosecutor made a considered decision based on his understanding of the law and commanded the officers forcibly to enter petitioner's clinic. That decision directly caused the violation of petitioner's Fourth Amendment rights.

> Respondent argues that the County Prosecutor lacked authority to establish municipal policy respecting law enforcement practices because only the County Sheriff may establish policy respecting such practices. Respondent suggests that the County Prosecutor was merely rendering "legal advice" when he ordered the Deputy Sheriffs to "go in and get" the witnesses. Consequently, the argument concludes, the action of the individual Deputy Sheriffs in following this advice and forcibly entering petitioner's clinic was not pursuant to a properly established municipal policy.

> We might be inclined to agree with respondent if we thought that the prosecutor had only rendered "legal advice." However, the Court of Appeals concluded, based upon its examination of Ohio law, that both the County Sheriff and the County Prosecutor could

establish county policy under appropriate circumstances, a conclusion that we do not question here. Ohio Rev. Code Ann. § 309.09 provides that county officers may "require . . . instructions from [the County Prosecutor] in matters connected with their official duties." Pursuant to standard office procedure, the Sheriff's office referred this matter to the Prosecutor and then followed his instructions. The Sheriff testified that his Department followed this practice under appropriate circumstances and that it was "the proper thing to do" in this case. We decline to accept respondent's invitation to overlook this delegation of authority by disingenuously labeling the prosecutor's clear command mere "legal advice." In ordering the Deputy Sheriffs to enter petitioner's clinic the County Prosecutor was acting as the final decisionmaker for the county, and the county may therefore be held liable under § 1983.

Justice White concurred to suggest that municipal liability was proper *only* because the search was not clearly illegal at the time it was made. If controlling law had plainly prohibited the search, he argued, the local officers could "not be said to have the authority to make contrary policy": "Had the sheriff or prosecutor in this case failed to follow an existing warrant requirement, it would be absurd to say that he was nevertheless executing county policy in authorizing the forceful entry. . . ." Here, however, the sheriff and the prosecutor exercised the discretion vested in them, and the decision they made therefore became "county policy." Justice O'Connor briefly endorsed these views in an opinion concurring in part and concurring in the judgment. Justice Stevens reiterated his belief that county liability could be based on respondeat superior.

Justice Powell, joined by Chief Justice Burger and Justice Rehnquist, dissented. He argued that "no official county policy could have been created solely by an off-hand telephone response from a busy County Prosecutor":

Proper resolution of this case calls for identification of the applicable principles for determining when policy is created. The Court today does not do this, but instead focuses almost exclusively on the status of the decisionmaker. Its reasoning is circular: it contends that policy is what policymakers make, and policymakers are those who have authority to make policy. . . .

In my view, the question whether official policy—in any normal sense of the term—has been made in a particular case is not answered by explaining who has final authority to make policy. The question here is not "*could* the County Prosecutor make policy?" but rather, "*did* he make policy?" By focusing on the authority granted to the official under state law, the Court's test fails to answer the key federal question presented. The Court instead turns the question into one of state law. . . . Here the Court of Appeals found that "both the County Sheriff and the County Prosecutor had authority under Ohio law to establish county policy under appropriate circumstances." Apparently that recitation of authority is all that is needed under the Court's test because no discussion is offered to demonstrate that the sheriff or the prosecutor actually used that authority to establish official county policy in this case. . . .

In my view, proper resolution of the question whether official policy has been formed should focus on two factors: (i) the nature of the decision reached or the action taken, and (ii) the process by which the decision was reached or the action was taken.

Focusing on the nature of the decision distinguishes between policies and mere ad hoc decisions. Such a focus also reflects the fact that most policies embody a rule of general applicability. That is the tenor of the Court's statement in *Monell* that local government units are liable under § 1983 when the action that is alleged to be unconstitutional "implements or executes a policy statement, ordinance, regulation, or decision officially adopted and promulgated by the body's officers." The clear implication is that policy is created when a rule is formed that applies to all similar situations. . . .[6] When a rule of general applicability has been approved, the government has taken a position for which it can be held responsible.

Another factor indicating that policy has been formed is the process by which the decision at issue was reached. Formal procedures that involve, for example, voting by elected officials, prepared reports, extended deliberation or official records indicate that the resulting decisions taken "may fairly be said to represent official policy." Owen v. City of Independence, 445 U.S. 622 (1980), provides an example. . . .

Applying these factors to the instant case demonstrates that no official policy was formulated. Certainly, no rule of general applicability was adopted. The Court correctly notes that the sheriff "testified that the Department had no written policy respecting the serving of [arrest warrants] on the property of third persons and that the proper response in any given situation would depend upon the circumstances." Nor could he recall a specific instance in which entrance had been denied and forcibly gained. The Court's result today rests on the implicit conclusion that the prosecutor's response—"go in and get them"—altered the prior case-by-case approach of the Department and formed a new rule to apply in all similar cases. Nothing about the Prosecutor's response to the inquiry over the phone, nor the circumstances surrounding the response, indicates that such a rule of general applicability was formed.

Similarly, nothing about the way the decision was reached indicates that official policy was formed. The Prosecutor, without time for thoughtful consideration or consultation, simply gave an off-the-cuff answer to a single question. There was no *process* at all.

---

[6]   The focus on a rule of general applicability does not mean that more than one instance of its application is required. The local government unit may be liable for the first application of a duly constituted unconstitutional policy.

The Court's holding undercuts the basic rationale of *Monell* and unfairly increases the risk of liability on the level of government least able to bear it. I dissent.

City of St. Louis v. Praprotnik

Supreme Court of the United States, 1988.
485 U.S. 112.

■ JUSTICE O'CONNOR announced the judgment of the Court and delivered an opinion, in which CHIEF JUSTICE REHNQUIST, JUSTICE WHITE, and JUSTICE SCALIA join.

This case calls upon us to define the proper legal standard for determining when isolated decisions by municipal officials or employees may expose the municipality itself to liability under 42 U.S.C. § 1983.

I

The principal facts are not in dispute. Respondent James H. Praprotnik is an architect who began working for petitioner city of St. Louis in 1968. For several years, respondent consistently received favorable evaluations of his job performance, uncommonly quick promotions, and significant increases in salary. By 1980, he was serving in a management-level city planning position at petitioner's Community Development Agency (CDA).

The Director of CDA, Donald Spaid, had instituted a requirement that the agency's professional employees, including architects, obtain advance approval before taking on private clients. Respondent and other CDA employees objected to the requirement. In April 1980, respondent was suspended for 15 days by CDA's Director of Urban Design, Charles Kindleberger, for having accepted outside employment without prior approval. Respondent appealed to the city's Civil Service Commission, a body charged with reviewing employee grievances. Finding the penalty too harsh, the commission reversed the suspension, awarded respondent back pay, and directed that he be reprimanded for having failed to secure a clear understanding of the rule.

The commission's decision was not well received by respondent's supervisors at CDA. Kindleberger later testified that he believed respondent had lied to the commission, and that Spaid was angry with respondent.

Respondent's next two annual job performance evaluations were markedly less favorable than those in previous years. In discussing one of these evaluations with respondent, Kindleberger apparently mentioned his displeasure with respondent's 1980 appeal to the Civil Service Commission. Respondent appealed both evaluations to the Department of Personnel. In each case, the department ordered partial relief and was upheld by the city's Director of Personnel or the Civil Service Commission.

In April 1981, a new mayor came into office, and Donald Spaid was replaced as Director of CDA by Frank Hamsher. As a result of budget cuts, a number of layoffs and transfers significantly reduced the size of CDA and of the planning section in which respondent worked. Respondent, however, was retained.

In the spring of 1982, a second round of layoffs and transfers occurred at CDA. At that time, the city's Heritage and Urban Design Division (Heritage) was seeking approval to hire someone who was qualified in architecture and urban planning. Hamsher arranged with the Director of Heritage, Henry Jackson, for certain functions to be transferred from CDA to Heritage. This arrangement, which made it possible for Heritage to employ a relatively high-level "city planning manager," was approved by Jackson's supervisor, Thomas Nash. Hamsher then transferred respondent to Heritage to fill this position.

Respondent objected to the transfer, and appealed to the Civil Service Commission. The commission declined to hear the appeal because respondent had not suffered a reduction in his pay or grade. Respondent then filed suit in federal district court, alleging that the transfer was unconstitutional. The city was named as a defendant, along with Kindleberger, Hamsher, Jackson (whom respondent deleted from the list before trial), and Deborah Patterson, who had succeeded Hamsher at CDA.

At Heritage, respondent became embroiled in a series of disputes with Jackson and Jackson's successor, Robert Killen. Respondent was dissatisfied with the work he was assigned, which consisted of unchallenging clerical functions far below the level of responsibilities that he had previously enjoyed. At least one adverse personnel decision was taken against respondent, and he obtained partial relief after appealing that decision.

In December 1983, respondent was laid off from Heritage. The lay off was attributed to a lack of funds, and this apparently meant that respondent's supervisors had concluded that they could create two lower-level positions with the funds that were being used to pay respondent's salary. Respondent then amended the complaint in his lawsuit to include a challenge to the layoff. He also appealed to the Civil Service Commission, but proceedings in that forum were postponed because of the pending lawsuit and have never been completed.

The case went to trial on [the theory] that respondent's First Amendment rights had been violated through retaliatory actions taken in response to his appeal of his 1980 suspension. . . . The jury returned special verdicts exonerating each of the three individual defendants, but finding the city liable. . . . Judgment was entered on the verdicts, and the city appealed. A panel of the Court of Appeals for the Eighth Circuit [affirmed by a divided vote].

The Court of Appeals found that the jury had implicitly determined that respondent's layoff from Heritage was brought about by an unconstitutional city policy. Applying a test under which a "policymaker" is one whose employment decisions are "final" in the sense that they are not subjected to de novo review by higher-ranking officials, the Court of Appeals concluded that the city could be held liable for adverse personnel decisions taken by respondent's supervisors. In response to petitioner's contention that the city's personnel policies are actually set by the Civil Service Commission, the Court of Appeals concluded that the scope of review before that body was too "highly circumscribed" to allow it fairly to be said that the commission, rather than the officials who initiated the actions leading to respondent's injury, were the "final authority" responsible for setting city policy. . . .

We granted certiorari and we now reverse.

II

[Part II of Justice O'Connor's opinion concluded that the legal standard for municipal liability had been properly presented for review.]

III

A

. . . In the years since *Monell* was decided, the Court has considered several cases involving isolated acts by government officials and employees. We have assumed that an unconstitutional governmental policy could be inferred from a single decision taken by the highest officials responsible for setting policy in that area of the government's business. See Owen v. City of Independence, 445 U.S. 622 (1980); Newport v. Fact Concerts, Inc., 453 U.S. 247 (1981). At the other end of the spectrum, we have held that an unjustified shooting by a police officer cannot, without more, be thought to result from official policy. Oklahoma City v. Tuttle, 471 U.S. 808 (1985).

Two terms ago, in Pembaur v. Cincinnati, 475 U.S. 469 (1986), we undertook to define more precisely when a decision on a single occasion may be enough to establish an unconstitutional municipal policy. Although the Court was unable to settle on a general formulation, Justice Brennan's plurality opinion articulated several guiding principles. First, a majority of the Court agreed that municipalities may be held liable under § 1983 only for acts for which the municipality itself is actually responsible, "that is, acts which the municipality has officially sanctioned or ordered." Second, only those municipal officials who have "final policymaking authority" may by their actions subject the government to § 1983 liability. Third, whether a particular official has "final policymaking authority" is a question of *state law*. Fourth, the challenged action must have been taken pursuant to a policy adopted by the official or officials responsible under state law for making policy *in that area* of the city's business.

The Courts of Appeals have already diverged in their interpretation of these principles. Today, we set out again to clarify the issue that we last addressed in *Pembaur*.

B

We begin by reiterating that the identification of policymaking officials is a question of state law. "Authority to make municipal policy may be granted directly by a legislative enactment or may be delegated by an official who possesses such authority, and of course, whether an official had final policymaking authority is a question of state law." *Pembaur*, 475 U.S. at 483 (plurality opinion).[1] Thus, the identification of policymaking officials is not a question of federal law and it is not a question of fact in the usual sense. The states have extremely wide latitude in determining the form that local government takes, and local preferences have led to a profusion of distinct forms. . . . Without attempting to canvass the numberless factual scenarios that may come to light in litigation, we can be confident that state law (which may include valid local ordinances and regulations) will always direct a court to some official or body that has the responsibility for making law or setting policy in any given area of a local government's business.[2]

We are not, of course, predicting that state law will always speak with perfect clarity. We have no reason to suppose, however, that federal courts will face greater difficulties here than those that they routinely address in other contexts. We are also aware that there will be cases in which policymaking responsibility is shared among more than one official or body. In the case before us, for example, it appears that the mayor or aldermen are authorized to adopt such ordinances relating to personnel administration as are compatible with the City Charter. See St. Louis City Charter, Art. XVIII, § 7(b). The Civil Service Commission, for its part, is required to "prescribe . . . rules for the administration and enforcement of the provisions of this article, and of any ordinance adopted in pursuance thereof, and not inconsistent therewith." § 7(a). Assuming

---

[1] Unlike Justice Brennan, we would not replace this standard with a new approach in which state law becomes merely "an appropriate starting point" for an "assessment of a municipality's actual power structure." Municipalities cannot be expected to predict how courts or juries will assess their "actual power structures," and this uncertainty could easily lead to results that would be hard in practice to distinguish from the results of a regime governed by the doctrine of respondeat superior. It is one thing to charge a municipality with responsibility for the decisions of officials invested by law, or by a "custom or usage" having the force of law, with policymaking authority. It would be something else, and something inevitably more capricious, to hold a municipality responsible for every decision that is perceived as "final" through the lens of a particular factfinder's evaluation of the city's "actual power structure."

[2] Justice Stevens, who believes that *Monell* incorrectly rejected the doctrine of respondeat superior, suggests a new theory that reflects his perceptions of the congressional purposes underlying § 1983. This theory would apparently ignore state law, and distinguish between "high" officials and "low" officials on the basis of an independent evaluation of the extent to which a particular official's actions have "the potential of controlling governmental decisionmaking," or are "perceived as the actions of the city itself." Whether this evaluation would be conducted by judges or juries, we think the legal test is too imprecise to hold much promise of consistent adjudication or principled analysis. We can see no reason, except perhaps a desire to come as close as possible to respondeat superior without expressly adopting that doctrine, that could justify introducing such unpredictability into a body of law that is already so difficult. . . .

that applicable law does not make the decisions of the commission reviewable by the mayor and aldermen, or vice versa, one would have to conclude that policy decisions made either by the mayor and aldermen or by the commission would be attributable to the city itself. In any event, however, a federal court would not be justified in assuming that municipal policymaking authority lies somewhere other than where the applicable law purports to put it. And certainly there can be no justification for giving a jury the discretion to determine which officials are high enough in the government that their actions can be said to represent a decision of the government itself.

As the plurality in *Pembaur* recognized, special difficulties can arise when it is contended that a municipal policymaker has delegated his policymaking authority to another official. If the mere exercise of discretion by an employee could give rise to a constitutional violation, the result would be indistinguishable from respondeat superior liability. If, however, a city's lawful policymakers could insulate the government from liability simply by delegating their policymaking authority to others, § 1983 could not serve its intended purpose. It may not be possible to draw an elegant line that will resolve this conundrum, but certain principles should provide useful guidance.

First, whatever analysis is used to identify municipal policymakers, egregious attempts by local governments to insulate themselves from liability for unconstitutional policies are precluded by a separate doctrine. Relying on the language of § 1983, the Court has long recognized that a plaintiff may be able to prove the existence of a widespread practice that, although not authorized by written law or express municipal policy, is "so permanent and well settled as to constitute a 'custom or usage' with the force of law." Adickes v. S.H. Kress & Co., 398 U.S. 144, 167–68 (1970). That principle . . . ensures that most deliberate municipal evasions of the Constitution will be sharply limited.

Second, as the *Pembaur* plurality recognized, the authority to make municipal policy is necessarily the authority to make *final* policy. When an official's discretionary decisions are constrained by policies not of that official's making, those policies, rather than the subordinate's departures from them, are the act of the municipality. Similarly, when a subordinate's decision is subject to review by the municipality's authorized policymakers, they have retained the authority to measure the official's conduct for conformance with *their* policies. If the authorized policymakers approve a subordinate's decision and the basis for it, their ratification would be chargeable to the municipality because their decision is final.

C

Whatever refinements of these principles may be suggested in the future, we have little difficulty concluding that the Court of Appeals applied an incorrect legal standard in this case. . . .

The city cannot be held liable under § 1983 unless respondent proved the existence of an unconstitutional municipal policy. Respondent does not contend that anyone in city government ever promulgated, or even articulated, such a policy. Nor did he attempt to prove that such retaliation was ever directed against anyone other than himself. Respondent contends that the record can be read to establish that his supervisors were angered by his 1980 appeal to the Civil Service Commission; that new supervisors in a new administration chose, for reasons passed on through some informal means, to retaliate against respondent two years later by transferring him to another agency; and that this transfer was part of a scheme that led, another year and a half later, to his lay off. Even if one assumes that all this was true, it says nothing about the actions of those whom the law established as the makers of municipal policy in matters of personnel administration. The mayor and aldermen enacted no ordinance designed to retaliate against respondent or against similarly situated employees. On the contrary, the city established an independent Civil Service Commission and empowered it to review and correct improper personnel actions. Respondent does not deny that his repeated appeals from adverse personnel decisions repeatedly brought him at least partial relief, and the Civil Service Commission never so much as hinted that retaliatory transfers or lay offs were permissible. Respondent points to no evidence indicating that the commission delegated to anyone its final authority to interpret and enforce the following policy set out in article XVIII of the city's charter, § 2(a):

> Merit and fitness. All appointments and promotions to positions in the service of the city and all measures for the control and regulation of employment in such positions, and separation therefrom, shall be on the sole basis of merit and fitness. . . .

The Court of Appeals concluded that "appointing authorities," like Hamsher and Killen were authorized to establish employment policy for the city with respect to transfers and layoffs. To the contrary, the City Charter expressly states that the Civil Service Commission has the power and the duty:

> To consider and determine any matter involved in the administration and enforcement of this [Civil Service] article and the rules and ordinances adopted in accordance therewith that may be referred to it for decision by the director [of personnel], or on appeal by any appointing authority, employee, or taxpayer of the city, from any act of the director of any appointing authority. The decision of the commission in all such matters shall be final, subject, however, to any right of action under law of the state or of the United States.

. . . A majority of the Court of Appeals panel determined that the Civil Service Commission's review of individual employment actions gave too much deference to the decisions of appointing authorities like Hamsher and Killen. Simply going along with discretionary decisions made by one's subordinates, however, is not a delegation to them of the authority to make policy. It is equally consistent with a presumption that the subordinates are faithfully attempting to comply with the policies that are supposed to guide them. It would be a different matter if a particular decision by a subordinate was cast in the form of a policy statement and expressly approved by the supervising policymaker. It would also be a different matter if a series of decisions by a subordinate official manifested a "custom or usage" of which the supervisor must have been aware. In both those cases, the supervisor could realistically be deemed to have adopted a policy that happened to have been formulated or initiated by a lower-ranking official. But the mere failure to investigate the basis of a subordinate's discretionary decisions does not amount to a delegation of policymaking authority, especially where (as here) the wrongfulness of the subordinate's decision arises from a retaliatory motive or other unstated rationale. In such circumstances, the purposes of § 1983 would not be served by treating a subordinate employee's decision as if it were a reflection of municipal policy.

Justice Brennan's opinion, concurring in the judgment, finds implications in our discussion that we do not think necessary or correct. We nowhere say or imply, for example, that "a municipal charter's precatory admonition against discrimination or any other employment practice not based on merit and fitness effectively insulates the municipality from any liability based on acts inconsistent with that policy." Rather, we would respect the decisions, embodied in state and local law, that allocate policymaking authority among particular individuals and bodies. Refusals to carry out stated policies could obviously help to show that a municipality's actual policies were different from the ones that had been announced. If such a showing were made, we would be confronted with a different case than the one we decide today.

Nor do we believe that we have left a "gaping" hole in § 1983 that needs to be filled with the vague concept of "de facto final policymaking authority." Except perhaps as a step towards overruling *Monell* and adopting the doctrine of respondeat superior, ad hoc searches for officials possessing such "de facto" authority would serve primarily to foster needless unpredictability in the application of § 1983.

IV

[T]he decision of the Court of Appeals is reversed, and the case is remanded for further proceedings consistent with this opinion.

It is so ordered.

■ JUSTICE KENNEDY took no part in the consideration or decision of this case.

■ JUSTICE BRENNAN, with whom JUSTICE MARSHALL and JUSTICE BLACKMUN join, concurring.

[T]his case at bottom presents a relatively straightforward question: whether respondent's supervisor at the Community Development

Agency, Frank Hamsher, possessed the authority to establish final employment policy for the city of St. Louis such that the city can be held liable under 42 U.S.C. § 1983 for Hamsher's allegedly unlawful decision to transfer respondent to a dead-end job. Applying the test set out two terms ago by the plurality in Pembaur v. Cincinnati, 475 U.S. 469 (1986), I conclude that Hamsher did not possess such authority and I therefore concur in the Court's judgment reversing the decision below. I write separately, however, because I believe that the commendable desire of today's plurality to "define more precisely when a decision on a single occasion may be enough" to subject a municipality to § 1983 liability has led it to embrace a theory of municipal liability that is both unduly narrow and unrealistic, and one that ultimately would permit municipalities to insulate themselves from liability for the acts of all but a small minority of actual city policymakers.

I

. . . The District Court instructed the jury that generally a city is not liable under § 1983 for the acts of its employees, but that it may be held to answer for constitutional wrongs "committed by an official high enough in the government so that his or her actions can be said to represent a government decision." . . . The Court of Appeals for the Eighth Circuit [affirmed, reasoning] that the city could be held accountable for an improperly motivated transfer and layoff if it had delegated to the responsible officials, either directly or indirectly, the authority to act on behalf of the city, and if the decisions made within the scope of this delegated authority were essentially final. Applying this test, the court noted that under the City Charter, "appointing authorities," or department heads, such as Hamsher could undertake transfers and layoffs subject only to the approval of the Director of Personnel, who undertook no substantive review of such decisions and simply conditioned his approval on formal compliance with city procedures. Moreover, because the Civil Service Commission engaged in highly circumscribed and deferential review of layoffs and, at least so far as this case reveals, no review whatever of lateral transfers, the court concluded that an appointing authority's transfer and layoff decisions were final.

Having found that Hamsher was a final policymaker whose acts could subject petitioner to § 1983 liability, the court determined that the jury had ample evidence from which it could find that Hamsher transferred respondent in retaliation for the latter's exercise of First Amendment rights, and that the transfer in turn precipitated respondent's layoff. . . .

II

. . . In concluding that Frank Hamsher was a policymaker, the Court of Appeals relied on the fact that the city had delegated to him "the authority, either directly or indirectly, to act on [its] behalf," and that his actions within the scope of this delegated authority were effectively final. In *Pembaur,* however, we made clear that a municipality is not liable merely because the official who inflicted the constitutional injury had the final authority to *act* on its behalf; rather, as four of us explained, the official in question must possess "final authority to establish municipal policy with respect to the [challenged] action." Thus, we noted, "[t]he fact that a particular official—even a policymaking official—has discretion in the exercise of particular functions does not, without more, give rise to municipal liability based on an exercise of that discretion." [J]ust as in Owen v. City of Independence, 445 U.S. 622 (1980), and Newport v. Fact Concerts, 453 U.S. 247 (1981), we deemed it fair to hold municipalities liable for the isolated, unconstitutional acts of their legislative bodies, regardless of whether those acts were meant to establish generally applicable "policies," so too in *Pembaur* four of us concluded that it is equally appropriate to hold municipalities accountable for the isolated constitutional injury inflicted by an executive final municipal policymaker, even though the decision giving rise to the injury is not intended to govern future situations. In either case, as long as the contested decision is made in an area over which the official or legislative body *could* establish a final policy capable of governing future municipal conduct, it is both fair and consistent with the purposes of § 1983 to treat the decision as that of the municipality itself, and to hold it liable for the resulting constitutional deprivation.

In my view, *Pembaur* controls this case. As an "appointing authority," Hamsher was empowered under the City Charter to initiate lateral transfers such as the one challenged here, subject to the approval of both the Director of Personnel and the appointing authority of the transferee agency. The charter, however, nowhere confers upon agency heads any authority to establish city *policy,* final or otherwise, with respect to such transfers. Thus, for example, Hamsher was not authorized to promulgate binding guidelines or criteria governing how or when lateral transfers were to be accomplished. Nor does the record reveal that he in fact sought to exercise any such authority in these matters. There is no indication, for example, that Hamsher ever purported to institute or announce a practice of general applicability concerning transfers. Instead, the evidence discloses but one transfer decision—the one involving respondent—which Hamsher ostensibly undertook pursuant to a city-wide program of fiscal restraint and budgetary reductions. At most, then the record demonstrates that Hamsher had the authority to determine how best to *effectuate* a policy announced by his superiors, rather than the power to *establish* that policy. . . . Because the court identified only one unlawfully motivated municipal employee involved in respondent's transfer and layoff, and because that employee did not possess final policymaking authority with respect to the contested decision, the city may not be held accountable for any constitutional wrong respondent may have suffered.

III

These determinations, it seems to me, are sufficient to dispose of this case, and I therefore think it unnecessary to decide, as the plurality does, who the actual policymakers in St. Louis are. I question more than the mere necessity of these determinations, however, for I believe that in the course of passing on issues not before us, the plurality announces legal principles that are inconsistent with our earlier cases and unduly restrict the reach of § 1983 in cases involving municipalities.

The plurality begins its assessment of St. Louis's power structure by asserting that the identification of policymaking officials is a question of state law, by which it means that the question is neither one of federal law nor of fact, at least "not in the usual sense." Instead, the plurality explains, courts are to identify municipal policymakers by referring exclusively to applicable state statutory law. Not surprisingly, the plurality cites no authority for this startling proposition, nor could it, for we have never suggested that municipal liability should be determined in so formulaic and unrealistic a fashion. In any case in which the policymaking authority of a municipal tortfeasor is in doubt, state law will naturally be the appropriate starting point, but ultimately the factfinder must determine where such policymaking authority actually resides, and not simply "where the applicable law purports to put it." . . . While the jury instructions in this case were regrettably vague, the . . . identification of municipal policymakers is an essentially factual determination "in the usual sense," and is therefore rightly entrusted to a properly instructed jury.

Nor does the "custom or usage" doctrine adequately compensate for the inherent inflexibility of a rule that leaves the identification of policymakers exclusively to state statutory law. That doctrine, under which municipalities and states can be held liable for unconstitutional practices so well settled and permanent that they have the force of law has little if any bearing on the question whether a city has delegated de facto final policymaking authority to a given official. A city practice of delegating final policymaking authority to a subordinate or mid-level official would not be unconstitutional in and of itself, and an isolated unconstitutional act by an official entrusted with such authority would obviously not amount to a municipal "custom or usage." Under *Pembaur,* of course, such an isolated act *should* give rise to municipal liability. Yet a case such as this would fall through the gaping hole the plurality's construction leaves in § 1983, because state statutory law would not identify the municipal actor as a policymaking official, and a single constitutional deprivation, by definition, is not a well settled and permanent municipal practice carrying the force of law.

For these same reasons, I cannot subscribe to the plurality's narrow and overly rigid view of when a municipal official's policymaking authority is "final." Attempting to place a gloss on *Pembaur*'s finality requirement, the plurality suggests that whenever the decisions of an official are subject to some form of review—however limited—that official's decisions are nonfinal. Under the plurality's theory, therefore, even where an official wields policymaking authority with respect to a challenged decision, the city would not be liable for that official's policy decision unless *reviewing* officials affirmatively approved both the "decision and the basis for it." Reviewing officials, however, may as a matter of practice never invoke their plenary oversight authority, or their review powers may be highly circumscribed. Under such circumstances, the subordinate's decision is in effect the final municipal pronouncement on the subject. Certainly a § 1983 plaintiff is entitled to place such considerations before the jury, for the law is concerned not with the niceties of legislative draftsmanship but with the realities of municipal decisionmaking, and any assessment of a municipality's actual power structure is necessarily a factual and practical one.

Accordingly, I cannot endorse the plurality's determination, based on nothing more than its own review of the city charter, that the mayor, the aldermen, and the CSC are the only policymakers for the city of St. Louis. While these officials may well have policymaking authority, that hardly ends the matter; the question before us is whether the officials responsible for respondent's allegedly unlawful transfer were final policymakers. As I have previously indicated, I do not believe that CDA Director Frank Hamsher possessed any policymaking authority with respect to lateral transfers and thus I do not believe that his allegedly improper decision to transfer respondent could, without more, give rise to municipal liability. Although the plurality reaches the same result, it does so by reasoning that because others could have reviewed the decisions of Hamsher and Killen, the latter officials simply could not have been final policymakers.

This analysis, however, turns a blind eye to reality, for it ignores not only the lower court's determination, nowhere disputed, that CSC review was highly circumscribed and deferential, but that in this very case the commission *refused* to judge the propriety of Hamsher's transfer decision because a lateral transfer was not an "adverse" employment action falling within its jurisdiction. . . . Because the plurality's mechanical "finality" test is fundamentally at odds with the pragmatic and factual inquiry contemplated by *Monell,* I cannot join what I perceive to be its unwarranted abandonment of the traditional factfinding process in § 1983 actions involving municipalities.

Finally, I think it necessary to emphasize that despite certain language in the plurality opinion suggesting otherwise, the Court today need not and therefore does not decide that a city can only be held liable under § 1983 where the plaintiff "prove[s] the existence of an unconstitutional municipal policy." . . . That question is certainly not presented by this case, and nothing we say today forecloses its future consideration. . . .

■ JUSTICE STEVENS, dissenting.

If this case involved nothing more than a personal vendetta between a municipal employee and his superiors, it would be quite wrong to impose liability on the City of St. Louis. In fact, however, the jury found the top officials in the city administration relying on pretextual grounds, had taken a series of retaliatory actions against respondent because he had testified truthfully on two occasions, one relating to personnel policy and the other involving a public controversy of importance to the mayor and the members of his cabinet. No matter how narrowly the Court may define the standards for imposing liability upon municipalities in § 1983 litigation, the judgment entered by the District Court in this case should be affirmed.

In order to explain why I believe that affirmance is required by this Court's precedents,[1] it is necessary to begin with a more complete statement of the disputed factual issues that the jury resolved in respondent's favor. . . .

The City of St. Louis hired respondent as a licensed architect in 1968. During the ensuing decade, he was repeatedly promoted and consistently given "superior" performance ratings. In April of 1980, while serving as the Director of Urban Design in the Community Development Agency (CDA), he was recommended for a two-step salary increase by his immediate superior.

Thereafter, on two occasions he gave public testimony that was critical of official city policy. In 1980 he testified before the Civil Service Commission (CSC) in support of his successful appeal from a 15-day suspension. In that testimony he explained that he had received advance oral approval of his outside employment and voiced his objections to the requirement of prior written approval. The record demonstrates that this testimony offended his immediate superiors at the CDA.

In 1981 respondent testified before the Heritage and Urban Design Commission (HUD) in connection with a proposal to acquire a controversial rusting steel sculpture by Richard Serra. In his testimony he revealed the previously undisclosed fact that an earlier city administration had rejected an offer to acquire the same sculpture, and also explained that the erection of the sculpture would require the removal of structures on which the city had recently expended about $250,000. This testimony offended top officials of the city government, possibly including the mayor, who supported the acquisition of the Serra sculpture, as well as respondent's agency superiors. They made it perfectly clear that they

---

[1]   This would, of course, be an easy case if the Court disavowed its dicta in part II of its opinion in Monell v. N.Y. City Dept. of Social Services, 436 U.S. 658, 691–95 (1978). Like many commentators who have confronted the question, I remain convinced that Congress intended the doctrine of respondeat superior to apply in § 1983 litigation. Given the Court's reiteration of the contrary ipse dixit in *Monell* and subsequent opinions, however, I shall join the Court's attempt to draw an intelligible boundary between municipal agents' actions that bind and those that do not. . . .

believed that respondent had violated a duty of loyalty to the mayor by expressing his personal opinion about the sculpture. . . .

After this testimony respondent was the recipient of a series of adverse personnel actions that culminated in his transfer from an important management level professional position to a rather menial assignment for which he was "grossly overqualified" and his eventual layoff. [E]vidence in the record amply supports the conclusion that respondent was first transferred and then laid off, not for fiscal and administrative reasons, but in retaliation for his public testimony before the CSC and HUD. It is undisputed that respondent's right to testify in support of his civil service appeal and his right to testify in opposition to the city's acquisition of the Serra sculpture were protected by the First Amendment to the federal Constitution. Given the jury's verdict, the case is therefore one in which a municipal employee's federal constitutional rights were violated by officials of the city government. . . .

In Monell v. New York Dept. of Social Services, 436 U.S. 658 (1978), [and subsequent cases], . . . the Court has permitted a municipality to be held liable for the unconstitutional actions of its agents when those agents: enforced a rule of general applicability, *Monell*; were of sufficiently high stature and acted through a formal process, Owen v. City of Independence, 445 U.S. 622 (1980); or were authorized to establish policy in the particular area of city government in which the tort was committed, Pembaur v. Cincinnati, 475 U.S. 469 (1986). Under these precedents, the City of St. Louis should be held liable in this case.

Both *Pembaur* and the plurality and concurring opinions today acknowledge that a high official who has ultimate control over a certain area of city government can bind the city through his unconstitutional actions even though those actions are not in the form of formal rules or regulations. Although the Court has explained its holdings by reference to the nonstatutory term "policy," it plainly has not embraced the standard understanding of that word as covering a rule of general applicability. Instead it has used that term to include isolated acts not intended to be binding over a class of situations. But when one remembers that the real question in cases such as this is not "what constitutes city policy?" but rather "when should a city be liable for the acts of its agents?", the inclusion of single acts by high officials makes sense, for those acts bind a municipality in a way that the misdeeds of low officials do not.

Every act of a high official constitutes a kind of "statement" about how similar decisions will be carried out; the assumption is that the same decision would have been made, and would again be made, across a class of cases. Lower officials do not control others in the same way. Since their actions do not dictate the responses of various subordinates, those actions lack the potential of controlling governmental decisionmaking; they are not perceived as the actions of the city itself. If a county police officer had broken down Dr. Pembaur's door on the officer's own initiative, this would have been seen as the action of an overanxious officer, and would not have sent a message to other officers that similar actions would be countenanced. . . . Here, the mayor, those working for him, and the agency heads are high-ranking officials; accordingly, we must assume that their actions have city-wide ramifications, both through their similar response to a like class of situations, and through the response of subordinates who follow their lead.

Just as the actions of high-ranking and low-ranking municipal employees differ in nature, so do constitutional torts differ. . . . [T]he typical retaliatory personnel action claim pits one story against another; although everyone admits that the transfer and discharge of respondent occurred, there is sharp, and ultimately central, dispute over the reasons—the motivation—behind the actions. *The very nature of the tort is to avoid a formal process. Owen*'s relevance should thus be clear. For if the Court is willing to recognize the existence of municipal policy in a non-rule case as long as high enough officials engaged in a formal enough process, it should not deny the existence of such a policy merely because those same officials act "underground," as it were. It would be a truly remarkable doctrine for this Court to recognize municipal liability in an employee discharge case when high officials are foolish enough to act through a "formal process," but not when similarly high officials attempt to avoid liability by acting on the pretext of budgetary concerns, which is what the jury found based on the evidence presented at trial. . . .

Whatever difficulties the Court may have with binding municipalities on the basis of the unconstitutional conduct of individuals, it should have no such difficulties binding a city when many of its high officials—including officials directly under the mayor, agency heads, and possibly the mayor himself—cooperate to retaliate against a whistleblower for the exercise of his First Amendment rights.

I would affirm the judgment of the Court of Appeals.

NOTES ON "OFFICIAL POLICY"

1. QUESTIONS AND COMMENTS ON *PRAPROTNIK*

The opinions in *Praprotnik* suggest three ways of identifying acts that trigger municipal liability. Justice O'Connor looks to state law. Does that mean, as Justice Brennan charged, that a municipality could insulate itself against liability by "precatory statements" against unconstitutional policies? By providing adequate internal review of personnel decisions? How would—or should—a court distinguish between self-protective window dressing and genuine attempts to do the right thing?

Justice Brennan would distinguish between final authority to act on behalf of the municipality and final authority to make official policy with respect to that act. Is this distinction clear? Does it aim at something important, or is it mere characterization?

Finally, Justice Stevens suggests that municipalities should be liable for the acts of high-ranking officials. Why? Does the rank of the official necessarily correlate with the official status of that person's actions? Why should the decisive factor be the position held by the *person* who acted unlawfully rather than the relation between the government and the unlawful act?

2.   ADDITIONAL COMMENTS ON *PRAPROTNIK*

The history of *Praprotnik* reveals something of a paradox: the jury exonerated each of the individual defendants, yet found the city liable. How could this be?

If no individual acted with an impermissible motive—that is, if the jury found that none of the individual defendants acted in retaliation for Praprotnik's exercise of his First Amendment rights—how could the city have committed a constitutional violation that requires such a motive? In any case where the underlying constitutional claim requires proof of a wrongful state of mind—for example, claims of racial discrimination under the Fourteenth Amendment, unconstitutional prison conditions under the Eighth Amendment, or retaliation under the First Amendment—it seems incontrovertible that the plaintiff must show that there is *someone* who acted with the requisite intent. Moreover, it should follow that the individuals who so acted would be liable for money damages. It would be highly unusual for actors motivated by an illicit objective to be protected by the defense of qualified immunity.

The fact that the jury found in favor of each of the individual defendants while finding against the city therefore suggests an inconsistency. The jury may have believed that there was impermissible retaliation, but was unwilling to impose monetary liability on individual officials. This possibility suggests that the jury may have undercompensated the plaintiff because they thought (often incorrectly, in light of indemnification practices) that it would be unfair to force public officials to pay for what seems to be the government's responsibility. Alternatively, the jury might have found no First Amendment violation, but felt sympathy for the plaintiff and saw the city as a deep pocket against whom liability could be imposed without fault. Does this suggest that the atmospherics of cases like *Praprotnik* may be driving some of the Court's attempts to limit governmental liability?

3.   THE SIGNIFICANCE OF STATE LAW: *MCMILLIAN V. MONROE COUNTY*

The role of state law assumed center stage in McMillian v. Monroe County, 520 U.S. 781 (1997). Walter McMillian was convicted of murder and later released when the state courts found that the authorities had suppressed exculpatory evidence. McMillian then brought a § 1983 action against (among others) the sheriff of Monroe County and the county itself. Ultimately, a divided Supreme Court ruled that in matters of law enforcement, the sheriff was not a final policymaker for the county.

The basis for this ruling was a detailed analysis of Alabama law, which revealed that, insofar as they were engaged in law enforcement, county sheriffs were in fact state officers. Speaking for the Court, Chief Justice Rehnquist examined a variety of state constitutional provisions and statutes dealing with sheriffs. The Court placed particular weight on the state Constitution, adopted in 1901, which added county sheriffs to a list of statewide officers constituting "executive department" of the state. This action responded to reports that sheriffs were allowing mobs to abduct and lynch prisoners. The 1901 Constitution made such "neglect" by sheriffs an impeachable offense and moved the impeachment authority from the county courts (where sheriffs had influence) to the state supreme court. Based on these provisions, the state supreme court had "held unequivocally that sheriffs are state officers, and that tort claims brought against sheriffs based on their official acts therefore constitute suits against the state, not against the sheriff's county." The Court was not concerned about the possibility that such conclusions could be manipulated to preclude liability, as the state constitutional provisions at issue long predated *Monell*.

Justice Ginsburg, joined by Justices Stevens, Souter, and Breyer, dissented. She focused on the facts that the county voters elected the sheriff, that county taxpayers paid his salary, and that the sheriff had broad authority to set law enforcement policy within the county. Nevertheless, she did not regard the majority's "Alabama-specific" approach as very consequential. In other states, sheriffs were still clearly local policymakers.

4. APPEALABILITY OF POLICYMAKER STATUS

The Court held unanimously in Swint v. Chambers County Commission, 514 U.S. 35 (1995), that the denial of a summary judgment motion on whether a given individual is a "policymaker" for a municipal entity is not immediately appealable under the "collateral order" doctrine of Cohen v. Beneficial Industrial Loan Corp., 337 U.S. 541 (1949). The Court distinguished the denial of summary judgment on claims by individuals to qualified immunity, which are immediately appealable (as immunities from suit) under Mitchell v. Forsyth, 472 U.S. 511 (1985).

In *Swint*, two individuals had filed proper interlocutory appeals under *Mitchell v. Forsyth*. The County Commission unsuccessfully argued as an alternative theory that the Circuit Courts should have discretion to exercise "pendent appellate jurisdiction" over its nonliability claim. Since the two types of claims were entirely unrelated ("The individual defendants' qualified immunity turns on whether they violated clearly established law; the County Commission's liability turns on the allocation of law enforcement power in Alabama."), the Court saw no basis for the exercise of such power. For criticism of this aspect of *Swint* and argument in favor of pendent appellate jurisdiction applicable to all categories of interlocutory review, see Joan Steinman, The Scope of Appellate Jurisdiction: Pendent Appellate Jurisdiction before and after *Swint*, 49 Hastings L.J. 1337 (1998).

5. BIBLIOGRAPHY

The Court's decisions on the conditions for imposing governmental liability under § 1983 spawned an enormous literature in the 1980s and 1990s. The subject has received less attention recently. Those who wish to research the topic should consult two symposia published in 1999, one in volume 48 of the DePaul Law Review and the other in volume 31 of the Urban Lawyer. These symposia contain articles from a variety of perspectives and citations to the voluminous earlier literature. For more recent work, see Fred Smith, Local Sovereign Immunity, 116 Colum. L. Rev. 409 (2016), which argues that the combination of stringency in determining whether a violation was caused by municipal policy or custom and the immunities available to individual officers creates a de facto rule of "local sovereign immunity."

NOTES ON FAILURE TO TRAIN AS "OFFICIAL POLICY"

1. INTRODUCTION

Pembaur and *Praprotnik* ask when the act of a government agent can properly be attributed to the principal. A second line of cases deals with whether the government's failure to train its subordinate officials can be characterized as "official policy or custom" under *Monell.*

2. *OKLAHOMA CITY V. TUTTLE*

In Oklahoma City v. Tuttle, 471 U.S. 808 (1985), a rookie police officer shot and killed Albert Tuttle as he tried to leave the scene of a reported robbery. The officer had already determined that the report was fictitious, and there seemed little reason to suspect that Tuttle was guilty of anything more serious than making the false report. Tuttle's widow sued both the officer and the city under § 1983. Her theory was that the city had a "policy" of inadequate training, which was responsible for the officer's precipitate reaction. The instructions allowed the jury to infer from a "single, unusually excessive use of force" that the officer's misconduct was "attributable to inadequate training or supervision amounting to 'deliberate indifference' or 'gross negligence' on the part of the officials in charge." The jury found in favor of the officer but returned a verdict against the city for $1.5 million.

This judgment was overturned by the Supreme Court. Speaking for a plurality of four, Justice Rehnquist said that proof of a single incident would not be enough to hold a municipality liable under *Monell,* "unless proof of the incident includes proof that it was caused by an existing, unconstitutional municipal policy, which policy can be attributed to a municipal policymaker." Rehnquist doubted whether a policy, not in itself unconstitutional, could ever support liability under *Monell* but said that "[a]t the very least there must be an affirmative link between the policy and the particular constitutional violation alleged." Justices Brennan, Marshall, and Blackmun concurred in the judgment on the ground that policy could not properly be inferred from a single act of police misconduct. Justice Stevens dissented in favor of municipal liability based on respondeat superior.

3. *CITY OF CANTON V. HARRIS*

The Court returned to the failure-to-train issue in City of Canton v. Harris, 489 U.S. 378 (1989). Geraldine Harris was arrested by officers of the Canton Police Department and brought to the police station in a patrol wagon. On two occasions she slumped to the floor, but no medical aid was summoned. After an hour, she was released and taken by her family to a hospital, where she was diagnosed as suffering from emotional ailments. She was hospitalized for a week and subsequently received outpatient treatment.

Mrs. Harris sued the city for, inter alia, failure to provide medical care. A municipal regulation authorized shift commanders to determine, in their discretion, whether a detainee needed medical care. There was also testimony suggesting that the shift commanders did not receive specialized training to make such determinations. A jury found for the plaintiff on the theory that the failure to train the shift commanders properly amounted to an official policy responsible for a constitutional violation.

In an opinion by Justice White, the Court held that a municipality could be held liable under § 1983 for failure to train its employees, but only under very limited circumstances. "We hold . . . that the inadequacy of police training may serve as the basis for § 1983 liability only where the failure to train amounts to deliberate indifference to the rights of persons with whom the police come into contact." Only in that circumstance, said the Court, did the failure to train reflect the kind of "deliberate" or "conscious" choice that constituted official policy under *Monell*. The case was remanded to the Court of Appeals to determine whether the evidence was sufficient to warrant a new trial under the "deliberate indifference" standard.

Justice Brennan concurred. Justices O'Connor, Scalia, and Kennedy agreed with the Court's analysis but dissented on the narrow ground that the evidence was insufficient to warrant a new trial.

4. QUESTIONS AND COMMENTS ON *HARRIS*

The *Harris* Court apparently was unanimous about the *standards* that should govern municipal liability for failure to train, though the Justices disagreed about application of those standards to the facts of the case. The Court embraced the oxymoron "deliberate indifference" as the governing concept. Is the central feature of this inquiry subjective or objective? Does it seek to determine what municipal policymakers were actually thinking about the constitutional rights at stake or what they *should have* thought based on external indicators? If the latter, what kinds of external indicators would be sufficient?

Recall that *Owen v. City of Independence* held, over the dissents of Justices Powell (replaced by Kennedy), Burger (replaced by Scalia), Stewart (replaced by O'Connor), and Rehnquist, that municipal government enjoys no qualified immunity from § 1983 liability and, in Justice Powell's words, "may be liable in damages for violating a constitutional right that was unknown when the events . . . occurred." Does *Harris* constitute the revenge of the *Owen* dissenters? How does the standard for determining municipal liability for failure to train differ from the standard that would apply if municipal government were entitled to a qualified immunity defense?

5. CONNICK V. THOMPSON

City of Canton v. Harris contemplated that municipal liability for failure to train would ordinarily rest on a pattern of constitutional violations, which would make "the need for more or different training . . . so obvious, and the inadequacy so likely to result in the violation of constitutional rights, that the policymakers of the city can reasonably be said to have been deliberately indifferent to the need." *Canton*, however, preserved the possibility that deliberate indifference could be found without a pattern of violations. The example given in footnote 10 of that opinion was a failure to provide any training to police officers on the use of deadly force to arrest fleeing felons. In that situation, said the Court, the "need to train officers in the constitutional limitations on the use of deadly force can be said to be 'so obvious' that failure to do so could properly be characterized as 'deliberate indifference' to constitutional rights." 489 U.S. 378, 390 n.10 (1989).

Connick v. Thompson, 563 U.S. 51 (2011), raised the question preserved in *Canton*: When, absent a pattern of similar violations, can the risk of a constitutional violation be so obvious that the failure to train for it amounts to deliberate indifference? John Thompson was charged with murder and an unrelated armed robbery. He was convicted of the robbery, despite exculpatory evidence that should have been, but was not, revealed by the prosecution as required by Brady v. Maryland, 373 U.S. 83 (1963). Because of the armed robbery conviction, Thompson did not testify at his murder trial, where he was again convicted and sentenced to death. Some 18 years later, the *Brady* violation was discovered, the armed robbery conviction vacated, and the murder conviction reversed. Thompson was retried for murder but acquitted. He then sued Harry F. Connick, the Orleans Parish District Attorney, in his official capacity, claiming that the district attorney's office was responsible for the *Brady* violation based on a deliberately indifferent failure to train. He recovered $14 million, plus $1 million in attorney's fees.

The Supreme Court reversed. Speaking through Justice Thomas, the Court held that Connick was entitled to judgment as a matter of law because Thompson had not proved that the district attorney was "on actual or constructive notice of, and therefore deliberately indifferent to, a need for more or different *Brady* training":

> A pattern of similar constitutional violations by untrained employees is "ordinarily necessary" to demonstrate deliberate indifference for purposes of failure to train. Bd. of Comm'rs of Bryan County v. Brown, 520 U.S. 397, 409 (1997). . . . Without notice that a course of training is deficient in a particular respect, decisionmakers can hardly be said to have deliberately chosen a training program that will cause violations of constitutional rights.

The possibility of failure-to-train liability based on a single incident, as contemplated in *Canton*, did not apply:

Failure to train prosecutors in their *Brady* obligations does not fall within the narrow range of *Canton*'s hypothesized single-incident liability. The obvious need for specific legal training that was present in the *Canton* scenario is absent here. Armed police must sometimes make split-second decisions with life-or-death consequences. There is no reason to assume that police academy applicants are familiar with the constitutional constrains on the use of the deadly force. And, in the absence of training, there is no way for novice officers to obtain the legal knowledge they require. Under those circumstances, there is an obvious need for some form of training. In stark contrast, legal "[t]raining is what differentiates attorneys from average public employees" [quoting from the opinion of Clement, J., in the Fifth Circuit].

Attorneys are trained in the law and equipped with the tools to interpret and apply legal principles, understand constitutional limits, and exercise legal judgment. . . . In light of this regime of legal training and professional responsibility, recurring constitutional violations are not the "obvious consequence" of failing to provide prosecutors with formal in-house training about how to obey the law. Prosecutors are not only equipped but are also ethically bound to know what *Brady* entails and to perform legal research when they are uncertain. A district attorney is entitled to rely on prosecutors' professional training and ethical obligations in the absence of specific reason, such as a pattern of violations, to believe that those tools are insufficient to prevent future constitutional violations. . . . A licensed attorney making legal judgment, in his capacity as a prosecutor, about *Brady* material simply does not present the same "highly predictable" constitutional violation as *Canton*'s untrained officer.

Justice Scalia, joined by Justice Alito, joined the opinion of the Court, but wrote separately to make an additional point. Scalia reviewed the instructions of the trial court, which basically required to jury to find (1) that Connick knew his prosecutors would confront *Brady* issues, (2) that compliance with *Brady* would involve difficult choices, and (3) that wrong choices would often result in deprivations of constitutional rights. Scalia said:

That theory of deliberate indifference would repeal the law of *Monell* in favor of the Law of Large Numbers. *Brady* mistakes are inevitable. So are all species of error routinely confronted by prosecutors: authorizing a bad warrant; losing a *Batson* claim [Batson v. Kentucky, 476 U.S. 79 (1986)]; crossing the line in closing argument; or eliciting hearsay that violates or violates the Confrontation Clause. Nevertheless, we do not have "de facto respondeat superior liability," *Canton*, 489 U.S. at 392, for each such violation under the rubric of failure-to-train simply because the municipality does not have a professional education program covering the specific violation in sufficient depth.

Justices Ginsburg, Breyer, Sotomayor, and Kagan dissented. Speaking through Justice Ginsburg, the dissenters challenged many aspects of the majority's understanding of the case. Justice Ginsburg recounted several *Brady* problems in Thompson's prosecutions (though not amounting to a pattern of similar violations), explored other instances of prosecutorial shoddiness, and identified "multiple shortfalls" in prosecutorial performance. Based on her detailed review of the record, Ginsburg found "abundant evidence" to support the jury's finding of deliberate indifference.

Much of the dispute between the majority and dissent in *Connick* is specific to, and indeed deeply embedded in, the facts of that case. Nonetheless, the opinions do reveal strongly divergent perspectives on failure to train. The majority appears preoccupied with the risk that liability for failure to train will degenerate into "de facto respondeat superior." The dissent is concerned with the evident injustice to this plaintiff and with the evidence of prosecutorial sloppiness or misconduct. In this particular instance, the *Brady* violation seemed to have been the result of deliberate and unethical concealment by an individual prosecutor, who had since died. Even had he been alive, however, the individual prosecutor would have been absolutely immune from liability for this flagrant misconduct. Thus, the plaintiff in *Connick* was defeated both by a restrictive understanding of "deliberate indifference" and by the rule of absolute immunity for individual officers. If change is needed, which would be the better route to a different result?

SECTION 4. FOR WHAT WRONGS?

SUBSECTION A. CONSTITUTIONAL RIGHTS ENFORCEABLE UNDER § 1983

INTRODUCTORY NOTE ON THE RELATIONSHIP OF RIGHTS AND REMEDIES

As the Supreme Court has repeatedly said, § 1983 "is not itself a source of substantive rights, but a method for vindicating federal rights elsewhere conferred by those parts of the United States Constitution and federal statutes that it describes." Baker v. McCollan, 443 U.S. 137, 144 n.3 (1979). For the most part, questions concerning the definition and scope of the underlying substantive rights being enforced in § 1983 actions have to this point been set aside.

Nonetheless, the remedial context in which the Supreme Court is asked to define constitutional rights can influence the scope of the rights it recognizes.[a] In some areas of constitutional law, the potential availability of monetary damages under § 1983 has played a relatively small role in the evolution of the substantive rights. For example, the meaning of equal protection under the Fourteenth Amendment has been developed largely through lawsuits seeking declaratory or injunctive relief. Similarly, although

---

[a]   See generally Daryl J. Levinson, Rights Essentialism and Remedial Equilibration, 99 Colum. L. Rev. 857 (1999).

the antecedents to the Fourth Amendment lay in common-law trespass actions against government officials, the contours of modern protections against unreasonable searches have been developed largely through motions to exclude evidence from use in criminal prosecution. In other areas, however, the potential of liability has significantly influenced the Court's decisionmaking.

Broadly speaking, the Court has two ways of accommodating a concern that money damages may adversely affect the behavior of public officials and, through them, the quality of government operations. One is to adopt transsubstantive rules that limit the availability of damages as a *remedy*. The doctrines of absolute and qualified immunity are examples of this approach. So, too, is the rejection of respondeat superior liability in *Monell* cases. The other way, which is the broad topic of this Subsection, is to cabin the underlying substantive right. The Court's treatment of cases under the Due Process Clause of the Fourteenth Amendment offers the best illustration of remedial concerns that seem to have affected the delineation of substantive rights.

There are three sorts of § 1983 claims that might be brought under the Due Process Clause. First, as a formal matter, the various guarantees of the Bill of Rights are made applicable to the states by way of incorporation in Fourteenth Amendment due process. Thus, a plaintiff might bring suit under § 1983 for violation by a state public official of rights to freedom of speech or freedom from unreasonable searches and seizures based on the First and Fourth Amendments, respectively, as incorporated in the Due Process Clause of the Fourteenth. Second, the Supreme Court has recognized a substantive component to due process that bars certain governmental actions "regardless of the fairness of the procedures used to implement them." Daniels v. Williams, 474 U.S. 327, 331 (1986). An example is the individual who is denied the substantive due process right to reproductive autonomy under Roe v. Wade, 410 U.S. 113 (1973). She too could bring suit under § 1983 to vindicate rights derived from the Fourteenth Amendment. Finally, due process provides a guarantee of fair procedures whenever a state deprives individuals of "life," "liberty," or "property." It is with respect to this last category—"procedural due process"—that the delineation of the right has become bound up especially closely with remedial concerns.

Doctrinally, the question whether a governmental actor has denied procedural due process can be divided into three separate concerns: First, has a cognizable "life," "liberty," or "property" interest been denied? Second, was the loss of that protected interest fairly attributable to the "state" as opposed to a private actor? Third, if the state did deprive an individual of life, liberty, or property, was it done "without due process of law"?

The Supreme Court's decision in *Paul v. Davis*, the next principal case, focuses on the definition of a constitutionally cognizable "liberty" interest. In reading the case, consider how much the Court's reasoning about the right was driven by concerns about the damages remedy.

Paul v. Davis

Supreme Court of the United States, 1976.
424 U.S. 693.

■ MR. JUSTICE REHNQUIST delivered the opinion of the Court.

We granted certiorari in this case to consider whether respondent's charge that petitioners' defamation of him, standing alone and apart from any other governmental action with respect to him, stated a claim for relief under 42 U.S.C. § 1983 and the Fourteenth Amendment. For the reasons hereinafter stated, we conclude that it does not.

Petitioner Paul is the Chief of Police of the Louisville, Ky., Division of Police, while petitioner McDaniel occupies the same position in the Jefferson County, Ky., Division of Police. In late 1972 they agreed to combine their efforts for the purpose of alerting local area merchants to possible shoplifters who might be operating during the Christmas season. In early December petitioners distributed to approximately 800 merchants in the Louisville metropolitan area a flyer, which began as follows:

TO: BUSINESS MEN IN THE METROPOLITAN AREA

The Chiefs of the Jefferson County and City of Louisville Police Departments, in an effort to keep their officers advised on shoplifting activity, have approved the attached alphabetically arranged flyer of subjects known to be active in this criminal field.

This flyer is being distributed to you, the business man, so that you may inform your security personnel to watch for these subjects. These persons have been arrested during 1971 and 1972 or have been active in various criminal fields in high density shopping areas.

Only the photograph and name of the subject is shown on this flyer, if additional information is desired, please forward a request in writing. . . .

The flyer consisted of five pages of "mug shot" photos, arranged alphabetically. Each page was headed:

NOVEMBER 1972
CITY OF LOUISVILLE
JEFFERSON COUNTY
POLICE DEPARTMENTS
ACTIVE SHOPLIFTERS

In approximately the center of page two there appeared photos and the name of the respondent, Edward Charles Davis III.

Respondent appeared on the flyer because on June 14, 1971, he had been arrested in Louisville on a charge of shoplifting. He had been arraigned on this charge in September 1971, and, upon his plea of not guilty, the charge had been "filed away with leave [to reinstate]," a disposition which left the charge outstanding. Thus, at the time petitioners caused the flyer to be prepared and circulated respondent had been charged with shoplifting but his guilt or innocence of that offense had never been resolved. Shortly after circulation of the flyer the charge against respondent was finally dismissed by a judge of the Louisville Police Court.

At the time the flyer was circulated respondent was employed as a photographer by the Louisville Courier-Journal and Times. The flyer, and respondent's inclusion therein, soon came to the attention of respondent's supervisor, the Executive Director of Photography for the two newspapers. This individual called respondent in to hear his version of the events leading to his appearing in the flyer. Following this discussion, the supervisor informed respondent that although he would not be fired, he "had best not find himself in a similar situation" in the future.

Respondent thereupon brought this § 1983 action in the District Court for the Western District of Kentucky, seeking redress for the alleged violation of rights guaranteed to him by the Constitution of the United States. [R]espondent sought damages as well as declaratory and injunctive relief. The District Court [dismissed the complaint], ruling that "[t]he facts alleged in this case do not establish that plaintiff has been deprived of any right secured to him by the Constitution of the United States."

Respondent appealed to the Court of Appeals for the Sixth Circuit which recognized that, under our decisions, for respondent to establish a claim cognizable under § 1983 he had to show that petitioners had deprived him of a right secured by the Constitution of the United States, and that any such deprivation was achieved under color of law. The Court of Appeals concluded that respondent had set forth a § 1983 claim "in that he has alleged facts that constitute a denial of due process of law." In its view our decision in Wisconsin v. Constantineau, 400 U.S. 433 (1971), mandated reversal of the District Court.

I

Respondent's due process claim is grounded upon his assertion that the flyer, and in particular the phrase "Active Shoplifters" appearing at the head of the page upon which his name and photograph appear, impermissibly deprived him of some "liberty" protected by the Fourteenth Amendment. His complaint asserted that the "active shoplifter" designation would inhibit him from entering business establishments for fear of being suspected of shoplifting and possibly apprehended, and would seriously impair his future employment opportunities. Accepting that such consequences may flow from the flyer in question, respondent's complaint would appear to state a classical claim for defamation actionable in the courts of virtually every state. Imputing criminal behavior to an individual is generally considered defamatory per se, and actionable without proof of special damages.

Respondent brought his action, however, not in the state courts of Kentucky, but in a United States District Court for that state. He asserted not a claim for defamation under the laws of Kentucky, but a claim that he had been deprived of rights secured to him by the Fourteenth Amendment of the United States Constitution. Concededly if the same allegations had been made about respondent by a private individual, he would have nothing more than a claim for defamation under state law. But, he contends, since petitioners are respectively an official of city and of county governments, his action is transmuted into one for deprivation by the state of rights secured under the Fourteenth Amendment. . . .

If respondent's view is to prevail, a person arrested by law enforcement officers who announce that they believe such person to be responsible for a particular crime in order to calm the fears of an aroused populace, presumably obtains a claim against such officers under § 1983. And since it is surely far more clear from the language of the Fourteenth Amendment that "life" is protected against state deprivation than it is that reputation is protected against state injury, it would be difficult to see why the survivors of an innocent bystander mistakenly shot by a policeman or negligently killed by a sheriff driving a government vehicle, would not have claims equally cognizable under § 1983.

It is hard to perceive any logical stopping place to such a line of reasoning. Respondent's construction would seem almost necessarily to result in every legally cognizable injury which may have been inflicted by a state official acting under "color of law" establishing a violation of the Fourteenth Amendment. We think it would come as a great surprise to those who drafted and shepherded the adoption of that amendment to learn that it worked such a result, and a study of our decisions convinces us they do not support the construction urged by respondent.

II

The result reached by the Court of Appeals, which respondent seeks to sustain here, must be bottomed on one of two premises. The first is that the Due Process Clause of the Fourteenth Amendment and § 1983 make actionable many wrongs inflicted by government employees which had heretofore been thought to give rise only to state-law tort claims. The second premise is that the infliction by state officials of a "stigma" to one's reputation is somehow different in kind from the infliction by the same official of harm or injury to other interests protected by state law, so that an injury to reputation is actionable under § 1983 and the Fourteenth Amendment even if other such harms are not. We examine each of these premises in turn.

A

The first premise would be contrary to pronouncements in our cases on more than one occasion with respect to the scope of § 1983 and of the Fourteenth Amendment. In the leading case of Screws v. United States, 325 U.S. 91 (1945), the Court considered the proper application of the criminal counterpart of § 1983, likewise intended by Congress to enforce the guarantees of the Fourteenth Amendment. In his opinion for the Court plurality in that case, Mr. Justice Douglas observed:

> Violation of local law does not necessarily mean that federal rights have been invaded. The fact that a prisoner is assaulted, injured, or even murdered by state officials does not necessarily mean that he is deprived of any right protected or secured by the Constitution or laws of the United States.

After recognizing that Congress's power to make criminal the conduct of state officials under the aegis of the Fourteenth Amendment was not unlimited because that amendment "did not alter the basic relations between the states and the national government," the plurality opinion observed that Congress should not be understood to have attempted

> to make all torts of state officials federal crimes. It brought within [the criminal provision] only specified actions done "under color" of law and then only those acts which deprived a person of some right secured by the Constitution or laws of the United States.

This understanding of the limited effect of the Fourteenth Amendment was not lost in the Court's decision in Monroe v. Pape, 365 U.S. 167 (1961). There the Court was careful to point out that the complaint stated a cause of action under the Fourteenth Amendment because it alleged an unreasonable search and seizure violative of the guarantee "contained in the Fourth Amendment [and] made applicable to the states by reason of the Due Process Clause of the Fourteenth Amendment." Respondent, however, has pointed to no specific constitutional guarantee safeguarding the interest he asserts has been invaded. Rather, he apparently believes that the Fourteenth Amendment's Due Process Clause should ex proprio vigore extend to him a right to be free of injury wherever the state may be characterized as the tortfeasor. But such a reading would make of the Fourteenth Amendment a font of tort law to be superimposed upon whatever systems may already be administered by the states. We have noted the "constitutional shoals" that confront any attempt to derive from congressional civil rights statutes a body of general federal tort law, Griffin v. Breckenridge, 403 U.S. 88, 101–02 (1971); a fortiori the procedural guarantees of the Due Process Clause cannot be the source for such law.

B

The second premise upon which the result reached by the Court of Appeals could be rested—that the infliction by state officials of a "stigma" to one's reputation is somehow different in kind from infliction by a state official of harm to other interests protected by state law—is equally untenable. The words "liberty" and "property" as used in the Fourteenth Amendment do not in terms single out reputation as a candidate for special protection over and above other interests that may be protected by state law. While we have in a number of our prior cases pointed out the frequently drastic effect of the "stigma" which may result from defamation by the government in a variety of contexts, this line of cases does not establish the proposition that reputation alone, apart from some more tangible interests such as employment, is either "liberty" or "property" by itself sufficient to invoke the procedural protection of the Due Process Clause. As we have said, the Court of Appeals, in reaching a contrary conclusion, relied primarily upon Wisconsin v. Constantineau, 400 U.S. 433 (1971). We think the correct import of that decision, however, must be derived from an examination of the precedents upon which it relied, as well as consideration of other decisions by this Court, before and after *Constantineau*, which bear upon the relationship between governmental defamation and the guarantees of the Constitution. While not uniform in their treatment of the subject, we think that the weight of our decisions establishes no constitutional doctrine converting every defamation by a public official into a deprivation of liberty within the meaning of the Due Process Clause of the fifth or Fourteenth Amendment.

[At this point the Court reviewed pre-*Constantineau* decisions, focusing on Joint Anti-Fascist Refugee Committee v. McGrath, 341 U.S. 123 (1951), in which the Court "examined the validity of the Attorney General's designation of certain organizations as 'Communist' on a list which he furnished to the Civil Service." The *McGrath* Court was badly split and produced no majority opinion, but several Justices indicated that mere injury to reputation would not violate due process. For example, Justice Jackson noted that "the mere designation as subversive deprives the organizations themselves of no legal right or opportunity":

> By it they are not dissolved, subjected to any legal prosecution, punished, penalized or prohibited from carrying on any of their activities. Their claim of injury is that they cannot attract audiences, enlist members, or obtain contributions as readily as before. These, however, are sanctions applied by public disapproval, not by law.

Justice Jackson nevertheless concluded that, owing to the disqualification of their members from public employment, the organizations had stated a claim upon which relief could be granted.

[Three *McGrath* dissenters would have held that the official listing of the organizations as "Communist" did not deprive them of property or liberty:

> It may be assumed that the listing is hurtful to their prestige, reputation and earning power. It may be such an injury as would entitle organizations to damages in a tort action against persons not protected by privilege. . . . This designation, however, does not prohibit any business of the organizations, subject them to any punishment, or deprive them of liberty of speech or other freedom.

[Justice Rehnquist summarized the various opinions in *McGrath* by saying that "at the least six of the eight Justices who participated in that case viewed any 'stigma' imposed by the official action of the Attorney General of the United States, divorced from its effect on the legal status of an organization or a person, such as loss of tax exemption or loss of government employment, as an insufficient basis for invoking the Due Process Clause of the Fifth Amendment." On this reading, *McGrath* and related cases supported two propositions:]

The Court has recognized the serious damage that could be inflicted by branding a government employee as "disloyal," and thereby stigmatizing his good name. But the Court has never held that the mere defamation of any individual, whether by branding him disloyal or otherwise, was sufficient to invoke the guarantees of procedural due process absent an accompanying loss of government employment.[4] . . .

It was against this backdrop that the Court in 1971 decided *Constantineau*. There the Court held that a Wisconsin statute authorizing the practice of "posting" was unconstitutional because it failed to provide procedural safeguards of notice and an opportunity to be heard, prior to an individual's being "posted." Under the statute "posting" consisted of forbidding in writing the sale or delivery of alcoholic beverages to certain persons who were determined to have become hazards to themselves, to their family, or to the community by reason of their "excessive drinking." The statute also made it a misdemeanor to sell or give liquor to any person so posted.

There is undoubtedly language in *Constantineau*, which is sufficiently ambiguous to justify the reliance upon it by the Court of Appeals:

---

[4] We cannot agree with the suggestion of our Brother Brennan, dissenting, that the actions of these two petitioner law enforcement officers come within the language used by Mr. Justice Harlan in his dissenting opinion in Jenkins v. McKeithen, 395 U.S. 411, 433 (1969). They are not by any conceivable stretch of the imagination, either separately or together, "an agency whose sole or predominant function, without serving any other public interest, is to expose and publicize the names of persons it finds guilty of wrongdoing." Indeed, the actions taken by these petitioners in this case fall far short of the more formalized proceedings of the Commission on Civil Rights established by Congress in 1957, the procedures of which were upheld against constitutional challenge by this Court in Hannah v. Larche, 363 U.S. 420 (1960). There the Court described the functions of the Commission in this language:

> It does not adjudicate. It does not hold trials or determine anyone's civil or criminal liability. It does not issue orders. Nor does it indict, punish, or impose any *legal sanctions*. It does not make determinations depriving anyone of his life, liberty, or property. In short, the Commission does not and cannot take any affirmative action which will affect an individual's *legal rights*. The only purpose of its existence is to find facts which may subsequently be used as the basis for legislative or executive action. (Emphasis supplied.)

Addressing itself to the question of whether the Commission's "proceedings might irreparably harm those being investigated by subjecting them to public opprobrium and scorn, the distinct likelihood of losing their jobs, and the possibility of criminal prosecutions," the Court said that "even if such collateral consequences were to flow from the Commission's investigations, they would not be the result of any affirmative determinations made by the Commission, and they would not affect the legitimacy of the Commission's investigative function."

Yet certainly where the state attaches "a badge of infamy" to the citizen, due process comes into play. "[T]he right to be heard before being condemned to suffer grievous loss of any kind, even though it may not involve the stigma and hardships of a criminal conviction, is a principle basic to our society."

Where a person's good name, reputation, honor, or integrity is at stake *because of what the government is doing to him*, notice and an opportunity to be heard are essential. (Emphasis supplied.)

The last paragraph of the quotation could be taken to mean that if a government official defames a person, without more, the procedural requirements of the Due Process Clause of the Fourteenth Amendment are brought into play. If read that way, it would represent a significant broadening of the holdings of [*McGrath* and similar cases], relied upon by the *Constantineau* Court. We should not read this language as significantly broadening those holdings without in any way adverting to the fact if there is any other possible interpretation of *Constantineau*'s language. We believe there is.

We think that the italicized language in the last sentence quoted, "because of what the government is doing to him," referred to the fact that the government action taken in that case deprived the individual of a right previously held under state law—the right to purchase or obtain liquor in common with the rest of the citizenry. "Posting," therefore, significantly altered his status as a matter of state law, and it was alteration of legal status which, combined with the injury resulting from the defamation, justified the invocation of procedural safeguards. The "stigma" resulting from the defamatory character of the posting was doubtless an important factor in evaluating the extent of harm worked by that act, but we do not think that such defamation, standing alone, deprived Constantineau of any "liberty" protected by the procedural guarantees of the Fourteenth Amendment.

This conclusion is reinforced by our discussion of the subject a little over a year later in Board of Regents v. Roth, 408 U.S. 564 (1972). There we noted that "the range of interests protected by procedural due process is not infinite," and that with respect to property interests they are,

of course, . . . not created by the Constitution. Rather, they are created and their dimensions are defined by existing rules or understandings that stem from an independent source such as state law—rules or understandings that secure certain benefits and that support claims of entitlement to those benefits.

While *Roth* recognized that governmental action defaming an individual in the course of declining to rehire him could entitle the person to notice and an opportunity to be heard as to the defamation, its language is quite inconsistent with any notion that a defamation perpetrated by a government official but unconnected with any refusal to rehire would be actionable under the Fourteenth Amendment:

> The state, *in declining to rehire the respondent*, did not make any charge against him that might seriously damage his standing and associations in his community. . . .
>
> Similarly, there is no suggestion that the state, *in declining to re-employ the respondent*, imposed on him a stigma or other disability that foreclosed his freedom to take advantage of other employment opportunities.

Thus it was not thought sufficient to establish a claim under § 1983 and the Fourteenth Amendment that there simply be defamation by a state official; the defamation had to occur in the course of the termination of employment. Certainly there is no suggestion in *Roth* to indicate that a hearing would be required each time the state in its capacity as employer might be considered responsible for a statement defaming an employee who continues to be an employee.

This conclusion is quite consistent with our most recent holding in this area, Goss v. Lopez, 419 U.S. 565 (1975), that suspension from school based upon charges of misconduct could trigger the procedural guarantees of the Fourteenth Amendment. While the Court noted that charges of misconduct could seriously damage the student's reputation, it also took care to point out that Ohio law conferred a right upon all children to attend school, and that the act of the school officials suspending the student there involved resulted in a denial or deprivation of that right.

III

It is apparent from our decisions that there exists a variety of interests which are difficult of definition but are nevertheless comprehended within the meaning of either "liberty" or "property" as meant in the Due Process Clause. These interests attain this constitutional status by virtue of the fact that they have been initially recognized and protected by state law,[5] and we have repeatedly ruled that the procedural guarantees of the Fourteenth Amendment apply whenever the state seeks to remove or significantly alter that protected status. In Bell v. Burson, 402 U.S. 535 (1971), for example, the state by issuing drivers' licenses recognized in its citizens a right to operate a vehicle on the highways of the state. The Court held that the state could not withdraw this right without giving petitioner due process. In Morrissey v. Brewer, 408 U.S. 471 (1972), the

---

[5]   There are other interests, of course, protected not by virtue of their recognition by the law of a particular state, but because they are guaranteed in one of the provisions of the Bill of Rights which has been "incorporated" into the Fourteenth Amendment. Section 1983 makes a deprivation of such rights actionable independently of state law. See Monroe v. Pape, 365 U.S. 167 (1961).

Our discussion in part III is limited to consideration of the procedural guarantees of the Due Process Clause and is not intended to describe those substantive limitations upon state action which may be encompassed within the concept of "liberty" expressed in the Fourteenth Amendment. Cf. part IV, infra.

state afforded parolees the right to remain at liberty as long as the conditions of their parole were not violated. Before the state could alter the status of a parolee because of alleged violations of these conditions, we held that the Fourteenth Amendment's guarantees of due process of law required certain procedural safeguards.

In each of these cases, as a result of the state action complained of, a right or status previously recognized by state law was distinctly altered or extinguished. It was this alteration, officially removing the interest from the recognition and protection previously afforded by the state, which we found sufficient to invoke the procedural guarantees contained in the Due Process Clause of the Fourteenth Amendment. But the interest in reputation alone which respondent seeks to vindicate in this action in federal court is quite different from the "liberty" and "property" recognized in those decisions. Kentucky law does not extend to respondent any legal guarantee of present enjoyment of reputation which has been altered as a result of petitioners' actions. Rather his interest in reputation is simply one of a number which the state may protect against injury by virtue of its tort law, providing a forum for vindication of those interests by means of damages actions. And any harm or injury to that interest, even where as here inflicted by an officer of the state, does not result in a deprivation of any "liberty" or "property" recognized by state or federal law, nor has it worked any change of respondent's status as theretofore recognized under the state's laws. For these reasons we hold that the interest in reputation asserted in this case is neither "liberty" nor "property" guaranteed against state deprivation without due process of law. . . .

IV

Respondent's complaint also alleged a violation of a "right to privacy guaranteed by the first, fourth, fifth, ninth, and Fourteenth Amendments." . . . While there is no "right of privacy" found in any specific guarantee of the Constitution, the Court has recognized that "zones of privacy" may be created by more specific constitutional guarantees and thereby impose limits upon government power. See Roe v. Wade, 410 U.S. 113, 152–53 (1973). Respondent's case, however, comes within none of these areas. . . . In *Roe* the Court pointed out that the personal rights found in this guarantee of personal privacy must be limited to those which are "fundamental" or "implicit in the concept of ordered liberty" as described in Palko v. Connecticut, 302 U.S. 319 (1937). The activities detailed as being within this definition were ones very different from that for which respondent claims constitutional protection—matters relating to marriage, procreation, contraception, family relationships, and child rearing and education. In these areas it has been held that there are limitations on the state's power to substantively regulate conduct.

Respondent's claim is far afield from this line of decisions. He claims constitutional protection against the disclosure of the fact of his arrest on a shoplifting charge. His claim is based, not upon any challenge to the state's ability to restrict his freedom of action in a sphere contended to be "private," but instead on a claim that the state may not publicize a record of an official act such as an arrest. None of our substantive privacy decisions hold this or anything like this, and we decline to enlarge them in this manner.

None of respondent's theories of recovery [was] based upon rights secured to him by the Fourteenth Amendment. Petitioners therefore were not liable to him under § 1983. The judgment of the Court of Appeals is reversed.

■ MR. JUSTICE STEVENS took no part in the consideration or decision of this case.

■ MR. JUSTICE BRENNAN with whom MR. JUSTICE MARSHALL concurs and MR. JUSTICE WHITE concurs in part, dissenting.

I dissent. The Court today holds that police officials, acting in their official capacities as law enforcers, may on their own initiative and without trial constitutionally condemn innocent individuals as criminals and thereby brand them with one of the most stigmatizing and debilitating labels in our society. If there are no constitutional restraints on such oppressive behavior, the safeguards constitutionally accorded an accused in a criminal trial are rendered a sham, and no individual can feel secure that he will not be arbitrarily singled out for similar ex parte punishment by those primarily charged with fair enforcement of the law. The Court accomplishes this result by excluding a person's interest in his good name and reputation from all constitutional protection, regardless of the character of or necessity for the government's actions. The result, which is demonstrably inconsistent with our prior case law and unduly restrictive in its construction of our precious bill of rights, is one in which I cannot concur. . . .

The stark fact is that the police here have officially imposed on respondent the stigmatizing label "criminal" without the salutary and constitutionally mandated safeguards of a criminal trial. The Court concedes that this action will have deleterious consequences for respondent [but finds] no infringement of constitutionally protected interests. This is because, the Court holds, neither a "liberty" nor a "property" interest was invaded by the injury done respondent's reputation and therefore no violation of § 1983 or the Fourteenth Amendment was alleged. I wholly disagree. . . .

There is no attempt by the Court to analyze the question as one of reconciliation of constitutionally protected personal rights and the exigencies of law enforcement. No effort is made to distinguish the "defamation" that occurs when a grand jury indicts an accused from the "defamation" that occurs when executive officials arbitrarily and without trial declare a person an "active criminal." Rather, the Court by mere fiat and with no analysis wholly excludes personal interest in reputation

from the ambit of "life, liberty, or property" under the fifth and Fourteenth Amendments, thus rendering due process concerns *never*
applicable to the official stigmatization, however arbitrary, of an individual. The logical and disturbing corollary of this holding is that no due
process infirmities would inhere in a statute constituting a commission
to conduct ex parte trials of individuals, so long as the only official judgment pronounced was limited to the public condemnation and branding
of a person as a Communist, a traitor, an "active murderer," a homosexual, or any other mark that "merely" carries social opprobrium. The
potential of today's decision is frightening for a free people.[9] That decision
surely finds no support in our relevant constitutional jurisprudence.

"In a Constitution for a free people, there can be no doubt that the
meaning of 'liberty' must be broad indeed." Board of Regents v. Roth, 408
U.S. 564, 572 (1972). "Without doubt, it denotes not merely freedom from
bodily restraint but also the right of the individual . . . generally to enjoy
those privileges long recognized . . . as essential to the orderly pursuit of
happiness by free men." Meyer v. Nebraska, 262 U.S. 390, 399 (1923).[10]
Certainly the enjoyment of one's good name and reputation has been recognized repeatedly in our cases as being among the most cherished of
rights enjoyed by a free people, and therefore as falling within the concept of personal "liberty."

[A]s Mr. Justice Stewart has reminded us, the individual's
right to the protection of his own good name

reflects no more than our basic concept of the essential dignity and worth of every human being—a concept at the root
of any decent system of ordered liberty. The protection of
private personality, like the protection of life itself, is left
primarily to the individual states under the Ninth and 10th
Amendments. But this does not mean that the right is entitled to any less recognition by this Court as a basic of our
constitutional system. Rosenblatt v. Baer, 383 U.S. 75, 92

---

[9]   Today's holding places a vast and arbitrary power in the hands of federal and state officials. It is not difficult to conceive of a police department, dissatisfied with what it perceives to
be the dilatory nature or lack of efficacy of the judicial system in dealing with criminal defendants, publishing periodic lists of "active rapists," "active larcenists," or other "known criminals."
The hardships resulting from the official stigmatization—loss of employment and educational
opportunities, creation of impediments to professional licensing, and the imposition of general
obstacles to the right of all free men to the pursuit of happiness—will often be as severe as
actual incarceration, and the Court today invites and condones such lawless action by those who
wish to inflict punishment without compliance with the procedural safeguards constitutionally
required of the criminal justice system.

[10]   One of the more questionable assertions made by the Court suggests that "liberty" or
"property" interests are protected only if they are recognized under state law or protected by
one of the specific guarantees of the Bill of Rights. To be sure, the Court has held [in *Roth*] that
"[p]roperty interests are not created by the Constitution. . . ." However, . . . we have never restricted "liberty" interests in the manner the Court today attempts to do. [T]he content of
"liberty" . . . has never been thought to depend on recognition of an interest by the state or federal government, and has never been restricted to interests explicitly recognized by other
provisions of the Bill of Rights. . . .

> (1966) (concurring opinion). Gertz v. Robert Welch, Inc., 418
> U.S. 323, 341 (1974).

We have consistently held that

> "[W]here a person's good name, reputation, honor, or integrity is at stake because of what the government is doing to him, notice and an opportunity to be heard are essential." Wisconsin v. Constantineau, 400 U.S. 433 (1971).

Board of Regents v. Roth, 408 U.S. 564, 573 (1972). In the criminal justice system, this interest is given concrete protection through the presumption of innocence and the prohibition of state-imposed punishment unless the state can demonstrate beyond a reasonable doubt, at a public trial with the attendant constitutional safeguards, that a particular individual has engaged in proscribed criminal conduct. . . .[12]

Today's decision marks a clear retreat from Jenkins v. McKeithen, 395 U.S. 411 (1969), a case closely akin to the factual pattern of the instant case, and yet essentially ignored by the Court. *Jenkins*, which was also an action brought under § 1983, both recognized that the public branding of an individual implicates interests cognizable as either "liberty" or "property," and held that such public condemnation cannot be accomplished without procedural safeguards designed to eliminate arbitrary or capricious executive action. *Jenkins* involved the constitutionality of the Louisiana Labor-Management Commission of Inquiry, an executive agency whose "very purpose . . . is to find persons guilty of violating criminal laws without trial or procedural safeguards, and to publicize those findings."

> [T]he personal and economic consequences alleged to flow from such actions are sufficient to meet the requirement that appellant prove a legally redressable injury. . . . Appellant's allegations go beyond the normal publicity attending criminal prosecution; he alleges a concerted attempt publicly to brand him a criminal without trial.

. . . Although three Justices in dissent would have dismissed the complaint for lack of standing, since there were no allegations that the appellant would be investigated, called as a witness, or named in the Commission's findings, they nevertheless observed:

> [There is] a constitutionally significant distinction between two kinds of government bodies. The first is an agency whose sole or predominant function, without serving any other public interest, is to expose and publicize the names of persons it finds guilty of wrongdoing. To the extent that such a determination—

---

[12] The Court's insensitivity to these constitutional dictates is particularly evident when it declares that because respondent had never been brought to trial, "his guilt or innocence of that offense [shoplifting] has never been resolved." It is hard to conceive of a more devastating flouting of the presumption of innocence. . . . Moreover, even if a person was once convicted of a crime, that does not mean that he is "actively engaged" in that activity now.

whether called a "finding" or an "adjudication"—finally and directly affects the substantial personal interests, I do not doubt that the Due Process Clause may require that it be accompanied by many of the traditional adjudicatory procedural safeguards.

Thus, although the Court was divided on the particular procedural safeguards that would be necessary in particular circumstances, the common point of agreement, and the one that the Court today inexplicably rejects, was that the official characterization of an individual as a criminal affects a constitutional "liberty" interest.

The Court, however, relegates its discussion of *Jenkins* to a dissembling footnote. First, the Court ignores the fact that the Court in *Jenkins* clearly recognized a constitutional "liberty" or "property" interest in reputation sufficient to invoke the strictures of the Fourteenth Amendment. It baffles me how, in the face of that holding, the Court can come to today's conclusion by reliance on the fact that the conduct in question does not "come within the language" of the *dissent* in *Jenkins*. Second, and more important, the Court's footnote manifests the same confusion that pervades the remainder of its opinion; it simply fails to recognize the crucial difference between the question whether there is a personal interest in one's good name and reputation that is constitutionally cognizable as a "liberty" or "property" interest within the Fourteenth and Fifth Amendment Due Process Clauses, and the totally separate question whether particular government action with respect to that interest satisfies the mandates of due process. Although the dissenters in *Jenkins* thought that the Commission's procedures complied with due process, they clearly believed that there was a personal interest that had to be weighed in reaching that conclusion. The dissenters in *Jenkins*, like the Court in Hannah v. Larche, 363 U.S. 420 (1960), held the view that in the context of a *purely investigatory, factfinding agency*, full trial safeguards are not required to comply with due process. But that question would never have been reached unless there were some constitutionally cognizable personal interest making the inquiry necessary—the interest in reputation that is affected by public "exposure." The Court, by contrast, now implicitly repudiates a substantial body of case law and finds no such constitutionally cognizable interest in a person's reputation, thus foreclosing any inquiry into the procedural protections accorded that interest in a given situation. . . .

Moreover, Wisconsin v. Constantineau, 400 U.S. 433 (1971), which was relied on by the Court of Appeals in this case, did not rely at all on the fact asserted by the Court today as controlling—namely, upon the fact that "posting" denied Ms. Constantineau the right to purchase alcohol for a year. Rather, *Constantineau* stated: "The *only* issue present here is whether the label or characterization given a person by 'posting,' though a mark of serious illness to some, is to others such a stigma or badge of disgrace that procedural due process requires notice and an opportunity to be heard." (Emphasis supplied.) In addition to the statements quoted by the Court, the Court in *Constantineau* continued:

> "Posting" under the Wisconsin act may to some be merely the mark of an illness, to others it is a stigma, an official branding of a person. The label is a degrading one. Under the Wisconsin act, a resident of Hartford is given no process at all. This appellee was not afforded a chance to defend herself. She may have been the victim of an official's caprice. Only when the whole proceedings leading to the pinning of an unsavory label on a person are aired can oppressive results be prevented. . . . "[T]he right to be heard before being condemned to suffer grievous loss of any kind, *even though it may not involve the stigma and hardships of a criminal conviction*, is a principle basic to our society." (Emphasis supplied.)

There again, the fact that governmental stigmatization of an individual implicates constitutionally protected interests was made plain.[15]

Thus, *Jenkins* and *Constantineau*, and the decisions upon which they relied, are cogent authority that a person's interest in his good name and reputation falls within the broad term "liberty" and clearly require that the government afford procedural protections before infringing that name and reputation by branding a person as a criminal. . . . The Court's approach . . . is to water down our prior precedents by reinterpreting them as confined to injury to reputation that affects an individual's employment prospects or, as "a right or status previously recognized by state law [that the state] distinctly altered or extinguished." The obvious answer is that such references in those cases (when there were such references) concerned the particular fact situations presented, and in nowise implied any limitation upon the application of the principles announced. Discussions of impact upon future employment opportunities were nothing more than recognition of the logical and natural consequences flowing from the stigma condemned.

---

[15] Even more recently in Goss v. Lopez, 419 U.S. 565 (1975), we recognized that students may not be suspended from school without being accorded due process safeguards. We explicitly referred to the "liberty interest in reputation" implicated by such suspensions based upon the fact that suspension for certain actions would stigmatize the student. . . . The Court states that today's holding is "quite consistent" with *Goss* because "Ohio law conferred a right upon all children to attend school, and . . . the act of the school officials suspending the student there involved resulted in a denial or deprivation of that right." However, that was only one-half of the holding in *Goss*. The Ohio law established a *property* interest which the Court held could not be deprived without according a student due process. However, the Court also specifically recognized that there was an independent *liberty* interest implicated in the case, not dependent upon the statutory right to attend school, but based . . . on the fact that suspension for certain conduct could affect a student's "good name, reputation, honor, or integrity."

Similarly, [t]he Court in *Roth* . . . was focusing on stigmatization as such. . . . The fact that a stigma is imposed by the government in terminating the employment of a government employee . . . does not detract from the fact that the operative "liberty" concept relates to the official stigmatization of the individual, whether imposed by the government in its status as an employer or otherwise.

Moreover, the analysis has a hollow ring in light of the Court's acceptance of the truth of the allegation that the "active shoplifter" label would "seriously impair [respondent's] future employment opportunities." This is clear recognition that an official "badge of infamy" affects tangible interests of the defamed individual and not merely an abstract interest in how people view him; for the "badge of infamy" has serious consequences in its impact on no less than the opportunities open to him to enjoy life, liberty, and the pursuit of happiness. It is inexplicable how the Court can say that a person's status is "altered" when the state suspends him from school, revokes his driver's license, fires him from a job, or denies him the right to purchase a drink of alcohol, but is in no way "altered" when it officially pins upon him the brand of a criminal, particularly since the Court recognizes how deleterious will be the consequences that inevitably flow from its official act. Our precedents clearly mandate that a person's interest in his good name and reputation is cognizable as a "liberty" interest within the meaning of the Due Process Clause, and the Court has simply failed to distinguish those precedents in any rational manner in holding that no invasion of a "liberty" interest was effected in the official stigmatizing without any "process" whatsoever.

I had always thought that one of this Court's most important roles is to provide a formidable bulwark against governmental violation of the constitutional safeguards securing in our free society the legitimate expectations of every person to innate human dignity and sense of worth. It is a regrettable abdication of that role and a saddening denigration of our majestic bill of rights when the Court tolerates arbitrary and capricious official conduct branding an individual as a criminal without compliance with constitutional procedures designed to ensure the fair and impartial ascertainment of criminal culpability. Today's decision must surely be a short-lived aberration.[18]

NOTES ON "LIBERTY" AND "PROPERTY" PROTECTED BY DUE PROCESS

1. INTRODUCTION

The Due Process Clause of the Fourteenth Amendment protects "life, liberty, or property" against deprivation without due process of law. This formulation covers a wide range of interests. At one time, the criterion for

---

[18] In light of my conviction that the state may not condemn an individual as a criminal without following the mandates of the trial process, I need not address the question whether there is an independent right of privacy which would yield the same result. Indeed, privacy notions appear to be inextricably interwoven with the considerations which require that a state not single out an individual for punishment outside the judicial process. Essentially, the core concept would be that a state cannot broadcast even such factual events as the occurrence of an arrest that does not culminate in a conviction when there are no legitimate law enforcement justifications for doing so. . . .

Mr. Justice White does not concur in this footnote.

determining whether a particular interest was protected was simply its "importance" to the individual. See, e.g., Bell v. Burson, 402 U.S. 535 (1971). This approach proved so inclusive that, in the words of one authority, "there seems to have been an overriding consensus that every individual 'interest' worth talking about [was] encompassed within the 'liberty' and 'property' secured by the Due Process Clause and thus entitled to some constitutional protection. . . ." Henry Paul Monaghan, Of "Liberty" and "Property," 62 Cornell L. Rev. 405, 406–07 (1977).

Then the Supreme Court took a new approach. In Board of Regents v. Roth, 408 U.S. 564 (1972), the Court for the first time rejected a procedural due process claim on the ground that the interest at issue (continued employment as a non-tenured teacher) was not "life, liberty, or property." *Roth* emphasized that the nature of the interest invaded, not simply its importance to the individual, was the critical threshold question triggering due process protection. This led to the development of a catalogue of "protectible interests." In subsequent years, the Court rejected several procedural due process claims under this rubric. *Paul v. Davis* is an early and controversial decision in that line.

The modern emphasis on defining "liberty" and "property" has led to some interesting interactions of state and federal law. On the one hand, the Due Process Clause of the Fourteenth Amendment is part of the federal Constitution, and it meaning is presumptively determined by federal law. On the other hand, the "liberty" and "property" interests that due process protects are defined, at least in part, by state law. Often, it is not clear which body of law determines the content of these terms.

The resulting inquiry is potentially circular. The federal Constitution overrides state law in requiring certain procedures for deprivation of "liberty" or "property." Yet the antecedent question of the existence of such interests is controlled, at least in the first instance, by state law. The risk is that states may define such interests so narrowly that the consequent federal procedural protection becomes, at least in certain contexts, unimportant.[a]

2.   QUESTIONS AND COMMENTS ON *PAUL V. DAVIS*

The Court held that Davis had no cognizable "liberty interest" in his reputation. The Court's motivation for taking that position was clearly the desire to avoid "mak[ing] of the Fourteenth Amendment a font of tort law to

---

[a]   This prospect prompted one commentator to argue that "liberty" and "property" should be treated as federal common law, adopted by the federal courts to enforce federal rights and therefore subject to minimum federal standards. See Robert Jerome Glennon, Jr., Constitutional Liberty and Property: Federal Common Law and § 1983, 51 So. Calif. L. Rev. 355 (1978).

Due process is not the only context where specification of the underlying right limits § 1983 claims. Susan R. Klein, *Miranda* Deconstitutionalized: When the Self-Incrimination Clause and the Civil Rights Act Collide, 143 U. Pa. L. Rev. 417 (1994), reports that "[t]he vast majority of courts hearing the issue have held that a *Miranda* violation is not a proper basis for a § 1983 claim." The usual basis for this conclusion is that *Miranda* does not define a constitutional right but only states a prophylactic rule designed to protect one. In this reasoning, a violation of *Miranda* is not a violation of a constitutional right and is, therefore, also not a "deprivation of any rights, privileges, or immunities secured by the Constitution and laws."

be superimposed upon whatever systems may already be administered by the states."

But is the Court correct in saying that Davis lost neither liberty nor property? Is not one central idea of the tort of defamation the notion that individuals enjoy a property interest in their reputations?[b] If this is correct, was Davis's real problem that he alleged deprivation of liberty rather than property? This seems implausible, given the Court's articulated concern not to create a "font of tort law." In fact, most torts involve the deprivation of some "property" or "liberty" the plaintiff would otherwise enjoy. Is there any way for the Court to acknowledge that a plaintiff enjoys a liberty or property interest protected by tort law without finding that its impairment by a person acting under color of state law constitutes a violation of the Due Process Clause?

In this connection, it may be useful to consider how the Court would have responded to a lawsuit seeking only prospective relief. Suppose that § 1983 did not exist and that Davis had sought only an injunction removing his name from the list of "active shoplifters" on the grounds that he had never been adjudicated to be a shoplifter. Could he have obtained relief in federal court? Is it plausible that the Supreme Court would have dismissed the lawsuit on the ground that Davis suffered no cognizable injury from having his name on such a list? Other than the remedy sought, what is the difference between that hypothetical lawsuit and the case Davis actually brought?

Consider also the observation in Rodney Smolla, The Displacement of Federal Due Process Claims by State Tort Remedies: *Parratt v. Taylor* and *Logan v. Zimmerman Brush Co.*, 1982 U. Ill. L. Rev. 831, that "[t]he critics of *Paul v. Davis* have never explained satisfactorily how a § 1983 action is in any substantive law sense an improvement on the law of libel." Is such an explanation possible? Is it necessary?

Academic reaction to the *Paul v. Davis* opinion has been largely hostile. In particular, the opinion was criticized for its disingenuous treatment of precedent. See 90 Harv. L. Rev. 293, 324–28 (1976) (concluding that it is "simply impossible" to reconcile *Paul* with prior decisions); Henry Paul Monaghan, Of "Liberty" and "Property," 62 Cornell L. Rev. 405, 423–29 (1977) (describing as "wholly startling" the Court's re-rationalization of its earlier cases).

Additionally, the decision has been criticized on the merits. Monaghan, for example, found it "an unsettling conception of 'liberty' that protects an individual against state interference with his access to liquor but not with his reputation in the community." See also Frank McClellan and Phoebe Northcross, Remedies and Damages for Violations of Constitutional Rights, 18 Duq. L. Rev. 409, 422–33 (1980) (criticizing the blanket removal of reputation from protected liberty interests as "unwise and short-sighted").

Despite the widespread criticism of *Paul v. Davis*, there have been occasional indications of sympathy for the Court's concern to limit the intrusion of federal civil rights actions into state tort law. Commentators who have

---

[b]   See Robert C. Post, The Social Foundations of Defamation Law: Reputation and the Constitution, 74 Calif. L. Rev. 691, 693–99 (1986) (collecting sources taking this view).

taken this position have looked for alternate rationales that might support the result. Of particular interest is the suggestion that *Paul* might have been based, not on a restrictive concept of protected "liberty" interests, but on a curtailment of the availability of remedies under § 1983.

The most prominent of these suggestions appears in the Monaghan article. Monaghan identified *Paul v. Davis* and other restrictive due process decisions as responses to the "staggering array of complaints" brought under § 1983. "Rightly or wrongly," he observed, "a majority of the present Court is struggling to place limits on the federal superintendence of the operations of state and local government, a struggle which has occurred largely in the context of '§ 1983' actions." In Monaghan's view, that effort was "understandable, if not acceptable," but the Court erred in addressing the problem by narrowing the scope of procedural due process. Instead, he speculated, perhaps it would have been better to read § 1983 "less than literally . . . so as not to embrace all the interests encompassed by the 'liberty' (and 'property') of the Due Process Clause."

This suggestion was echoed by Gerald Gunther, who noted that "a limiting statutory interpretation [of § 1983] would have made the Court's extensive discussion of constitutionally protected liberty interests unnecessary." Gerald Gunther, Cases and Materials on Constitutional Law 581 (11th ed. 1985).

What kind of limiting statutory construction might Monaghan and Gunther have had in mind? One possibility was suggested by Melvyn Durchslag in Federalism and Constitutional Liberties: Varying the Remedy to Save the Right, 54 N.Y.U. L. Rev. 723, 734–48 (1979). Durchslag argued that the federalism concern vindicated in *Paul v. Davis* should have been handled through an elaboration of official immunity under § 1983 rather than by redefinition of the underlying constitutional right.[c]

Of these several perspectives on *Paul v. Davis*, which is the most plausible? Is the decision simply wrong, or does it address a genuine problem? And if the latter, is the problem better addressed by a restrictive formulation of the underlying right or by a limiting construction of § 1983? And if the latter, what would that be?

3. *DESHANEY V. WINNEBAGO COUNTY DEPT. OF SOCIAL SERVICES*

The Court made another controversial determination of "liberty" interests in what has come to be known as the "Poor Joshua" case,[d] DeShaney v. Winnebago County Dept. of Social Services, 489 U.S. 189 (1989). Joshua DeShaney was four years old when he was beaten by his father and left with

---

[c]   For a reinterpretation of *Paul*, see Barbara E. Armacost, Race and Reputation: The Real Legacy of *Paul v. Davis*, 85 Va. L. Rev. 569 (1999) (arguing that much of the "scholarly hand-wringing" is misdirected, because most of the claims excluded from due process by *Paul* are redirected to other constitutional "homes"). For commentary on an analogous problem, see Barbara Kritchevsky, The Availability of a Federal Remedy under 42 U.S.C. § 1983 for Prosecution under an Unconstitutional State Statute: The Sixth Circuit Struggles in *Richardson v. City of South Euclid*, 22 U. Tol. L. Rev. 303 (1991).

[d]   The phrase comes from the last paragraph of Justice Blackmun's dissent, which begins: "Poor Joshua! Victim of repeated attacks by an irresponsible, bullying, cowardly, and intemperate father. . . ."

"brain damage so severe that he is expected to spend the rest of his life confined to an institution for the profoundly retarded." He had been the victim of repeated abuse since the time, 26 months earlier, when the county social service authorities had first been contacted on his behalf. There were at least three hospitalizations during this period and, though some efforts were made to create a more protective home environment, the authorities refused coercive intervention. Joshua and his mother[e] brought a § 1983 action in federal court against the county, its department of social services, and various department officials. The complaint "alleged that respondents had deprived Joshua of his liberty without due process of law, in violation of his rights under the Fourteenth Amendment, by failing to intervene to protect him against a risk of violence at his father's hands of which they knew or should have known." The District Court granted summary judgment for the defendants and the Court of Appeals affirmed. The Supreme Court also affirmed.

In contrast to *Paul v. Davis*, where the Court held that the plaintiff had not experienced the impairment of a liberty interest in the first place, Joshua had undeniably been deprived of liberty. The *DeShaney* Court focused on the second component of the due process inquiry, whether the deprivation was properly chargeable to the *state* or whether it was only his father, a private actor, who was responsible for the deprivation.

Though describing the facts as "undeniably tragic," Chief Justice Rehnquist's opinion for the Court held:

> [N]othing in the language of the Due Process Clause itself requires the state to protect the life, liberty, and property of its citizens against invasion by private actors. The clause is phrased as a limitation on the state's power to act, not as a guarantee of certain minimum levels of safety and security. It forbids the state itself to deprive individuals of life, liberty, or property without "due process of law," but its language cannot fairly be extended to impose an affirmative obligation on the state to ensure that those interests do not come to harm through other means. . . . As a general matter, then, we conclude that a state's failure to protect an individual against private violence simply does not constitute a violation of the Due Process Clause.[f]

It was argued that that a duty to protect "may arise out of certain 'special relationships' created or assumed by the state with respect to particular individuals." Prior cases had held, for example, that such duties arose with respect to persons in prison or involuntarily committed:

---

[e] Joshua's parents were divorced in Wyoming. Custody was awarded to the father, who later moved to Wisconsin, remarried, and was again divorced. The father was tried and convicted of child abuse.

[f] The Chief Justice had previously noted that the claim was "one invoking the substantive rather than the procedural component of the Due Process Clause; petitioners do not claim that the state denied Joshua protection without according him appropriate procedural safeguards, but that it was categorically obligated to protect him in these circumstances."—[Footnote by eds.]

But these cases afford petitioners no help. Taken together, they stand only for the proposition that when the state takes a person into its custody and holds him there against his will, the Constitution imposes upon it a corresponding duty to assume some responsibility for his safety and general well-being. The rationale for this principle is simple enough: when the state by the affirmative exercise of its power so restrains an individual's liberty that it renders him unable to care for himself, and at the same time fails to provide for his basic human needs—e.g., food, clothing, shelter, medical care, and reasonable safety—it transgresses the substantive limits on state action set by the Eighth Amendment and the Due Process Clause. The affirmative duty to protect arises not from the state's knowledge of the individual's predicament or from its expressions of intent to help him, but from the limitation which it has imposed on his freedom to act on his own behalf. In the substantive due process analysis, it is the state's affirmative act of restraining the individual's freedom to act on his own behalf—through incarceration, institutionalization, or other similar restraint of personal liberty—which is the "deprivation of liberty" triggering the protections of the Due Process Clause, not its failure to act to protect his liberty interests against harms inflicted by other means.

The Court concluded:

Judges and lawyers, like other humans, are moved by natural sympathy in a case like this to find a way for Joshua and his mother to receive adequate compensation for the grievous harm inflicted upon them. But before yielding to that impulse, it is well to remember once again that the harm was inflicted not by the state of Wisconsin, but by Joshua's father. The most that can be said of the state functionaries in this case is that they stood by and did nothing when suspicious circumstances dictated a more active role for them. In defense of them it must also be said that had they moved too soon to take custody of the son away from the father, they would likely have been met with charges of improperly intruding into the parent-child relationship, charges based on the same Due Process Clause that forms the basis for the present charge of failure to provide adequate protection.

The people of Wisconsin may well prefer a system of liability which would place upon the state and its officials the responsibility for failure to act in situations such as the present one. They may create such a system, if they do not have it already, by changing the tort law of the state in accordance with the regular law-making process. But they should not have it thrust upon them by this Court's expansion of the Due Process Clause of the Fourteenth Amendment.[2]

---

[2]   Petitioners also argue that the Wisconsin child protection statutes gave Joshua an 'entitlement' to receive protective services in accordance with the terms of the statute, an

Justice Brennan, joined by Justices Marshall and Blackmun, dissented. Justice Brennan stated that he "would focus first on the action that Wisconsin *has* taken with respect to Joshua and children like him, rather than on the actions that the state had failed to take." He saw the prison and involuntary commitment cases as establishing the principle that "if a state cuts off private sources of aid and then refuses aid itself, it cannot wash its hands of the harm that results from its inaction." Here the state had "cut off private sources of aid" by monopolizing the path of relief open to persons in Joshua's situation:

> In these circumstances, a private citizen, or even a person working in a government agency other than [the Department of Social Services (DSS)], would doubtless feel that her job was done as soon as she had reported her suspicions of child abuse to DSS. Through its child-welfare program, in other words, the state of Wisconsin has relieved ordinary citizens and governmental bodies other than the department of any sense of obligation to do anything more than report their suspicions of child abuse to DSS. If DSS ignores or dismisses these suspicions, no one will step in to fill the gap. Wisconsin's child-protection program thus effectively confined Joshua DeShaney within the walls of Randy DeShaney's violent home until such time as DSS took action to remove him. Conceivably, then, children like Joshua are made worse off by the existence of this program when the persons and entities charged with carrying it out fail to do their jobs.

> It simply belies reality, therefore, to contend that the state "stood by and did nothing" with respect to Joshua. Through its child-protection program, the state actively intervened in Joshua's life and, by virtue of this intervention, acquired even more certain knowledge that Joshua was in grave danger. These circumstances, in my view, plant this case solidly within the tradition of cases like [those governing prisons and involuntary commitments].

Justice Brennan added that liability could not be found in cases where the failure to intervene resulted from "the sound exercise of professional judgment." "Moreover," he continued, "that the Due Process Clause is not violated by merely negligent conduct, see Daniels v. Williams, 474 U.S. 327 (1986), and Davidson v. Cannon, 474 U.S. 344 (1986), means that a social worker who simply makes a mistake of judgment under what are admittedly complex and difficult conditions will not find herself liable in damages under § 1983."[g]

---

entitlement which would enjoy due process protection against state deprivation under our decision in Board of Regents v. Roth, 408 U.S. 564 (1972). But this argument is made for the first time in petitioners' brief to this Court: it was not pleaded in the complaint, argued to the Court of Appeals as a ground for reversing the District Court, or raised in the petition for certiorari. We therefore decline to consider it here.

[g]   For a sampling of the many prominent articles critical of *DeShaney*, see Jack M. Beermann, Administrative Failure and Local Democracy: The Politics of *DeShaney*, 1990 Duke L.J. 1078 (exploring the idea of a constitutional obligation on government to protect the weak and helpless); Karen M. Blum, *Monell, DeShaney,* and *Zinermon*: Official Policy, Affirmative Duty, Established State Procedure and Local Government Liability under Section 1983, 24 Creighton

4. THEORIES OF LIABILITY AFTER *DeShaney*

After *DeShaney*, there remain two theories for holding governments or public officials liable for not preventing tortious acts by private parties. First, the government is responsible when the injury occurs while the plaintiff is in state custody or when the government has a special relationship with the plaintiff. See, e.g., Youngberg v. Romeo, 457 U.S. 307 (1982) (involuntarily committed mental patients have a substantive due process right to protection from harm); Farmer v. Brennan, 511 U.S. 825 (1994) (deliberate indifference to a known risk of injury to a prisoner can give rise to a claim under the Eighth Amendment). Lower courts have refused to extend this reasoning to children in schools, though some have argued that they are in custody because of compulsory school attendance laws. See generally Daniel B. Weddle, Bullying in Schools: The Disconnect Between Empirical Research and Constitutional, Statutory, and Tort Duties to Supervise, 77 Temp. L. Rev. 641 (2004).

Second, the state is liable when the danger of an injury at private hands is "state created." For examples of cases holding government officials liable under this theory, see Monfils v. Taylor, 165 F.3d 511 (7th Cir. 1998) (holding a police officer liable for the murder of a confidential informant when he released a tape recording of the victim's call to the police, despite the victim's repeated entreaties not to reveal his identity); Kniepp v. Tedder, 95 F.3d 1199 (3rd Cir. 1996) (holding that the plaintiff had a § 1983 claim for brain damage suffered in a fall after being abandoned by a police officer who had stopped her while she was intoxicated). Generally, courts have required a fairly tight causal nexus between the government action and the injury. See, e.g., Martinez v. California, 444 U.S. 277, 284–85 (1980) (refusing to hold state officials liable under § 1983 for the plaintiff's murder by a parolee five months after his release from prison). See generally Laura Oren, Safari Into the Snake Pit: The State-Created Danger Doctrine, 13 Wm. & Mary Bill of Rights J. 165 (2005).

L. Rev. 1 (1990) (examining *DeShaney*'s impact on substantive due process claims against local governments); Thomas Eaton and Michael Wells, Government Inaction as a Constitutional Tort: *DeShaney* and Its Aftermath, 66 Wash. L. Rev. 107 (1991) (arguing that the decision does not categorically bar affirmative obligations on government but invites attention to the state's role in putting the individual at risk); Sheldon H. Nahmod, State Constitutional Torts: *DeShaney*, Reverse-Federalism and Community, 26 Rutgers L.J. 949 (1995) (noting that the federalism concerns supporting judicial restraint in cases such as *Paul v. Davis* and *DeShaney* are not applicable to state constitutional torts, which might be developed to deal with such situations). For a rare (if measured) defense of *DeShaney*, see Barbara E. Armacost, Affirmative Duties, Systemic Harms, and the Due Process Clause, 94 Mich. L. Rev. 982 (1996) (arguing that judicial refusal to impose liability for governmental failure-to-protect reflects an understandable reluctance to involve the courts in "second-guessing political decisions about the use of limited community resources").

SUBSECTION B. THE ROLE OF STATE LAW

INTRODUCTORY NOTES ON PARRATT V. TAYLOR AND ITS PROGENY

1.   *PARRATT V. TAYLOR*

The plaintiff in Parratt v. Taylor, 451 U.S. 527 (1981), was a prison in-mate who ordered $23.50 worth of hobby materials. When they arrived, he was in segregation and was not permitted to receive them. The materials were therefore signed for by two employees of the prison hobby center. When Taylor was released from segregation, the packages were nowhere to be found.

Taylor filed a § 1983 damages action against the warden and the hobby manager of the prison. He claimed that the defendants had negligently de-prived him of property without due process of law in violation of the Fourteenth Amendment. The District Court granted Taylor's motion for summary judgment and the Circuit Court affirmed. The Supreme Court granted certiorari and reversed. Justice Rehnquist's opinion for the Court made three main points:

(i)   Mental Elements of § 1983

A preliminary issue was whether § 1983 required proof of intentional or reckless wrongdoing or allowed recovery for negligence. Justice Rehnquist answered that "§ 1983, unlike its criminal counterpart, 18 U.S.C. § 242, has never been found by this Court to contain a state-of-mind requirement." Of course, proof of a particular state of mind may still be required to make out the underlying constitutional violation. A good example is the equal protec-tion guarantee against racial discrimination, which requires proof of a discriminatory purpose. Washington v. Davis, 426 U.S. 229 (1976). But the § 1983 plaintiff has no obligation to establish the defendant's state of mind unless required as a part of the underlying constitutional violation.

(ii)   Negligent Deprivation of Due Process

In *Parratt v. Taylor*, the underlying constitutional claim was based on procedural due process. This raised the question whether negligent behavior by state officials could "deprive" Taylor of property without due process of law. Rehnquist's answer was brief and unelaborated:

> Unquestionably, respondent's claim satisfies three prerequi-sites of a valid due process claim: the petitioners acted under color of state law; the hobby kit falls within the definition of property; and the alleged loss, even though negligently caused, amounted to a deprivation.[a]

---

[a]   Justice Powell disagreed. He argued:

   [T]he question is whether intent is required before there can be a "deprivation" of life, liberty, or property. . . . I would not hold that . . . a negligent act, causing unin-tended loss of or injury to property, works a deprivation in the constitutional sense. . . . A "deprivation" connotes an intentional act denying something to someone, or, at the

(iii) *The Process Due*

The Court continued:

> Standing alone, however, these three elements do not establish a violation of the Fourteenth Amendment. Nothing in that amendment protects against all deprivations of life, liberty, or property by the state. The Fourteenth Amendment protects only against deprivations "without due process of law." Our inquiry therefore must focus on whether the respondent has suffered a deprivation of property without due process of law. In particular, we must decide whether the tort remedies which the state of Nebraska provides as a means of redress for property deprivations satisfy the requirements of procedural due process.

The case therefore turned on whether Nebraska's postdeprivation tort remedy sufficed. The Court found that it did and accordingly that Taylor "has not alleged a violation of the Due Process Clause of the Fourteenth Amendment":

> The fundamental requirement of due process is the opportunity to be heard and it is an "opportunity which must be granted at a meaningful time and in a meaningful manner." Armstrong v. Manzo, 380 U.S. 545, 552 (1965). However, . . . we have rejected the proposition that "at a meaningful time and in a meaningful manner" *always* requires the state to provide a hearing prior to the initial deprivation of property. This rejection is based in part on the impracticability in some cases of providing any preseizure hearing. . . . Indeed, in [many] cases it is not only impracticable, but impossible, to provide a meaningful hearing before the deprivation. That does not mean, of course, that the state can take property without providing a meaningful postdeprivation hearing. The prior cases which have excused the prior-hearing requirement have rested in part on the availability of some meaningful opportunity subsequent to the initial taking for a determination of rights and liabilities.

The Court added these concluding remarks:

> Our decision today is fully consistent with our prior cases. To accept respondent's argument that the conduct of the state officials in this case constituted a violation of the Fourteenth Amendment would almost necessarily result in turning every alleged injury which may have been inflicted by a state official acting under "color of law" into a violation of the Fourteenth Amendment cognizable under § 1983. It is hard to perceive any logical stopping place to such a line of reasoning. Presumably, under this rationale any

---

very least, a deliberate decision not to act to prevent a loss. The most reasonable interpretation of the Fourteenth Amendment would limit due process claims to such active deprivations. [S]uch a rule would avoid trivializing the right of action provided in § 1983. That provision was enacted to deter real *abuses* by state officials in the exercise of governmental powers. It would make no sense to open the federal courts to lawsuits where there has been no affirmative abuse of power, merely a negligent deed by one who happens to be acting under color of state law.—[Footnote by eds.]

party who is involved in nothing more than an automobile accident with a state official could allege a constitutional violation under § 1983. Such reasoning "would make of the Fourteenth Amendment a font of tort law to be superimposed upon whatever systems may already be administered by the states." Paul v. Davis, 424 U.S. 693, 701 (1976). We do not think that the drafters of the Fourteenth Amendment intended the amendment to play such a role in our society.[b]

2. *HUDSON V. PALMER* AND INTENTIONAL WRONGDOING

In *Parratt v. Taylor,* Justice Blackmun suggested that postdeprivation remedies might not be adequate in cases of intentional wrongdoing. Hudson v. Palmer, 468 U.S. 517 (1984), addressed this question.

Hudson was an officer at a correctional institution. He conducted a "shakedown" search of inmate Palmer's cell, where he discovered a ripped pillowcase. Disciplinary proceedings were brought against Palmer, who was made to pay for the pillowcase. Subsequently, Palmer filed a § 1983 action claiming, inter alia, that Hudson himself had ripped the pillowcase—that is, that he had intentionally and without justification destroyed noncontraband personal property during the shakedown. Hudson denied the allegation and won a summary judgment, which in due course was affirmed by the Supreme Court. Indeed, on this issue, the decision was unanimous. In opinion by Chief Justice Burger, the Court said:

> While *Parratt* is necessarily limited by its facts to negligent deprivations of property, it is evident, as the Court of Appeals recognized, that its reasoning applies as well to intentional deprivations of property. The underlying rationale of *Parratt* is that when deprivations of property are effected through random and unauthorized conduct of a state employee, predeprivation procedures are simply "impracticable" since the state cannot know when such deprivations will occur. We can discern no logical distinction between negligent and intentional deprivations of property insofar as the "practicability" of affording pre-deprivation process is concerned. The state can no more anticipate and control in advance the random and unauthorized intentional conduct of its employees than it can anticipate similar negligent conduct. . . .

> Accordingly, we hold that an unauthorized intentional deprivation of property by a state employee does not constitute a viola-

---

[b]   Justices Stewart, White, and Blackmun wrote separately but concurred in the Court's opinion. Justice Powell concurred in the result on the rationale, as noted above, that no "deprivation" of property in the constitutional sense had occurred. Justice Marshall concurred in part and dissented in part. He agreed that "in cases involving claims of *negligent* deprivation of property without due process of law, the availability of an adequate postdeprivation cause of action for damages under state law may preclude a finding of a violation of the Fourteenth Amendment." But he thought that "prison officials have an affirmative obligation to inform a prisoner who claims that he is aggrieved by official action about the remedies available under state law" and that "[i]f they fail to do so, then they should not be permitted to rely on the existence of such remedies as adequate alternatives to a § 1983 action for wrongful deprivation of property."— [Footnote by eds.]

tion of the procedural requirements of the Due Process Clause of the Fourteenth Amendment if a meaningful postdeprivation remedy for the loss is available.

3.   DANIELS V. WILLIAMS AND THE MEANING OF "DEPRIVATION"

Parratt and *Hudson* gave rise to speculation about the continued viability of state sovereign immunity for garden-variety torts by state employees. Traditionally, states have asserted the right to claim sovereign immunity in their own courts when sued for torts committed by their employees. An attempt to evade this restriction by resort to federal court would be precluded by the Eleventh Amendment. As a result, garden-variety torts by government employees traditionally have been subject to compensation by the state only to the extent that the state has waived sovereign immunity.

Parratt and *Hudson* suggested a way around such restrictions. If a state fails to provide an adequate compensatory remedy for the tortious acts of its employees, perhaps those actions become procedural due process violations. Injured individuals could bring suit under § 1983 by characterizing the tort claim as an instance of procedural inadequacy. Of course, the action must be brought against the employee rather than directly against the state, but that may not matter, as states typically indemnify their employees.

The Court rejected this line of reasoning in Daniels v. Williams, 474 U.S. 327 (1986). Daniels was a prisoner in the Richmond, Virginia, City Jail. He tripped over a pillow allegedly left on a staircase by Williams, a corrections officer. Daniels asserted that the resulting injury was a "deprivation" of his "liberty" interest in freedom from bodily hurt. Since sovereign immunity blocked ordinary tort recovery, Daniels claimed that he had no adequate state remedy and therefore that the deprivation of liberty was without due process of law and hence compensable under § 1983.

The Supreme Court disagreed. In an opinion by Justice Rehnquist, the Court adopted Justice Powell's position in *Parratt* that "the Due Process Clause is simply not implicated by a *negligent* act of an official causing unintended loss of or injury to life, liberty, or property." *Parratt v. Taylor* was explicitly overruled "to the extent that it states that mere lack of due care by a state official may 'deprive' an individual of life, liberty or property under the Fourteenth Amendment." The Court reasoned that the Due Process Clause was "intended to secure the individual from the arbitrary exercise of the powers of government," not to provide a federal remedy for ordinary negligence:

> We think that the actions of prison custodians in leaving a pillow on the prison stairs, or mislaying an inmate's property, are quite remote from [constitutional concerns]. Far from an abuse of power, lack of due care suggests no more than a failure to measure up to the conduct of a reasonable person. To hold that injury caused by such conduct is a deprivation within the meaning of the Fourteenth Amendment would trivialize the centuries-old principle of due process of law.

Justices Marshall, Blackmun, and Stevens concurred in the result.

4.   *DAVIDSON V. CANNON*

Despite *Daniel's* holding that merely negligent deprivation does not violate due process, it seems clear that intentional torts are compensable under § 1983 if the state does not provide an adequate postdeprivation procedure, and it remains possible that recklessness or some other intermediate form of culpability may suffice. Division on these matters arose in a companion case to *Daniels,* Davidson v. Cannon, 474 U.S. 344 (1986). Davidson sued state prison officials for failure to protect him from another inmate. Prior to the assault, the victim had sent a note to prison authorities warning of the possibility, but they neglected to take timely action. The Court, with Justice Rehnquist again writing, rejected this claim on the authority of *Daniels.* Justice Stevens concurred in the result.

In dissent, Justice Brennan agreed that "merely negligent conduct . . . does not constitute a deprivation of liberty under the Due Process Clause" but asserted that "official conduct which causes personal injury due to recklessness or deliberate indifference, does deprive the victim of liberty within the meaning of the Fourteenth Amendment." In a separate dissent, Justice Blackmun, joined by Justice Marshall, agreed that mere negligence *"ordinarily"* would not be actionable under § 1983, but argued that in some cases, governmental negligence was the kind of abuse of power at which the Due Process Clause was aimed:

> It is one thing to hold that a commonplace slip and fall, or the loss of a $23.50 hobby kit, does not rise to the dignified level of a constitutional violation. It is a somewhat different thing to say that negligence that permits anticipated inmate violence resulting in injury, or perhaps leads to the execution of the wrong prisoner, does not implicate the Constitution's guarantee of due process. . . . It seems to me that when a state assumes sole responsibility for one's physical security and then ignores his call for help, the state cannot claim that it did not know a subsequent injury was likely to occur. [O]nce the state has taken away an inmate's means of protecting himself from attack by other inmates, a prison official's negligence in providing protection can amount to a deprivation of the inmate's liberty. . . .

Justice Blackmun also argued that the record might support a finding of recklessness, which in his view "must be sufficient" to cause a deprivation under the Fourteenth Amendment, even if negligence is not.

5.   QUESTIONS AND COMMENTS ON *PARRATT* AND ITS PROGENY

Parratt and its progeny settled that procedural due process is not violated by merely negligent deprivations. These cases also settled that adequate state-law remedies can satisfy due process, at least in cases of random and unauthorized deprivations, and thus cure any constitutional violation that might otherwise occur in the acts of individual government employees. Logan v. Zimmerman Brush Co., 455 U.S. 422 (1982), however, emphasized that deprivation of property pursuant to established state procedures could violate due process, regardless of postdeprivation remedies. As the next main case shows, the line between these propositions is anything but bright.

Zinermon v. Burch

Supreme Court of the United States, 1990.
494 U.S. 113.

■ JUSTICE BLACKMUN delivered the opinion of the Court.

I

Respondent Darrell Burch brought this suit under 42 U.S.C. § 1983 against the 11 petitioners, who are physicians, administrators, and staff members at Florida State Hospital (FSH) in Chattahoochee, and others. Respondent alleges that petitioners deprived him of his liberty, without due process of law, by admitting him to FSH as a "voluntary" mental patient when he was incompetent to give informed consent to his admission. Burch contends that in his case petitioners should have afforded him procedural safeguards required by the Constitution before involuntary commitment of a mentally ill person, and that petitioners' failure to do so violated his due process rights.

Petitioners argue that Burch's complaint failed to state a claim under § 1983 because, in their view, it alleged only a random, unauthorized violation of the Florida statutes governing admission of mental patients. Their argument rests on Parratt v. Taylor, 451 U.S. 527 (1981), and Hudson v. Palmer, 468 U.S. 517 (1984), where this Court held that a deprivation of a constitutionally protected property interest caused by a state employee's random, unauthorized conduct does not give rise to a § 1983 procedural due process claim, unless the state fails to provide an adequate postdeprivation remedy. The Court in those two cases reasoned that in a situation where the state cannot predict and guard in advance against a deprivation, a postdeprivation tort remedy is all the process the state can be expected to provide, and is constitutionally sufficient.

[The District Court granted petitioners' motion to dismiss], pointing out that Burch did not contend that Florida's statutory procedure for mental health placement was inadequate to ensure due process, but only that petitioners failed to follow the state procedure. Since the state could not have anticipated or prevented this unauthorized deprivation of Burch's liberty, the District Court reasoned, there was no feasible predeprivation remedy, and, under *Parratt* and *Hudson,* the state's postdeprivation tort remedies provided Burch with all the process that was due him.

On appeal, an Eleventh Circuit panel affirmed the dismissal [but after a rehearing en banc the Court of Appeals] reversed the District Court, and remanded the case. . . . This Court granted certiorari to resolve the conflict—so evident in the divided views of the judges of the Eleventh Circuit—that has arisen in the Court of Appeals over the proper scope of the *Parratt* rule.

Because this case concerns the propriety of a [motion to dismiss], the question before us is a narrow one. We decide only whether the *Parratt* rule necessarily means that Burch's complaint fails to allege any deprivation of due process, because he was constitutionally entitled to nothing more than what he received—an opportunity to sue petitioners in tort for his allegedly unlawful confinement. The broader questions of what procedural safeguards the Due Process Clause requires in the context of an admission to a mental hospital, and whether Florida's statutes meet these constitutional requirements, are not presented in this case. Burch did not frame his action as a challenge to the constitutional adequacy of Florida's mental health statutes. Both before the Eleventh Circuit and in his brief here, he disavowed any challenge to the statutes themselves, and restricted his claim to the contention that petitioners' failure to provide constitutionally adequate safeguards in his case violated his due process rights.[21]

II

A

For purposes of review of a [motion to dismiss], the factual allegations of Burch's complaint are taken as true. Burch's complaint, and the medical records and forms attached to it as exhibits, provide the following factual background:

On December 7, 1981, Burch was found wandering along a Florida highway, appearing to be hurt and disoriented. He was taken to Apalachee Community Mental Health Services (ACMHS) in Tallahassee. ACMHS is a private mental health care facility designated by the state to receive patients suffering from mental illness. Its staff in their evaluation forms stated that, upon his arrival at ACMHS, Burch was hallucinating, confused, psychotic, and believed he was "in heaven." His face and chest were bruised and bloodied, suggesting that he had fallen or had been attacked. Burch was asked to sign forms giving his consent to admission and treatment. He did so. He remained at ACMHS for three days, during which time the facility's staff diagnosed his condition as paranoid schizophrenia and gave him psychotropic medication. On December 10, the staff found that Burch was "in need of longer-term stabilization" and referred him to FSH, a public hospital owned and operated by the state as a mental health treatment facility. Later that day, Burch

---

[21] Inasmuch as Burch does not claim that he was deprived of due process by an established state procedure, our decision in Logan v. Zimmerman Brush Co., 455 U.S. 422 (1982), is not controlling. In that case, the plaintiff challenged not a state official's error in implementing state law, but "the 'established state procedure' that destroys his entitlement without according him proper procedural safeguards."

Burch apparently concedes that, if Florida's statutes were strictly complied with, no deprivation of liberty without due process would occur. If only those patients who are competent to consent to admission are allowed to sign themselves in as "voluntary" patients, then they would not be deprived of any liberty interest at all. And if all other patients—those who are incompetent and those who are unwilling to consent to admission—are afforded the protections of Florida's involuntary placement procedures, they would be deprived of their liberty only after due process.

signed forms requesting admission and authorizing treatment at FSH. He was then taken to FSH by a county sheriff.

Upon his arrival at FSH, Burch signed other forms for voluntary admission and treatment. One form, entitled "Request for Voluntary Admission," recited that the patient requests admission for "observation, diagnosis, care and treatment of [my] mental condition," and that the patient, if admitted, agrees "to accept such treatment as may be prescribed by members of the medical and psychiatric staff in accordance with the provisions of expressed and informed consent." Two of the petitioners, Janet V. Potter and Marjorie R. Parker, signed this form as witnesses. Potter is an accredited records technician; Parker's job title does not appear on the form.

On December 23, Burch signed a form entitled "Authorization for Treatment." This form stated that he authorized "the professional staff of [FSH] to administer treatment, except electroconvulsive treatment"; that he had been informed of "the purpose of treatment; common side effects thereof; alternative treatment modalities; approximate length of care," and of his power to revoke consent to treatment; and that he had read and fully understood the authorization. Petitioner Zinermon, a staff physician at FSH, signed the form as the witness.

On December 10, Doctor Zinermon wrote a "progress note" indicating that Burch was "refusing to cooperate," would not answer questions, "appears distressed and confused," and "related that medication has been helpful." A nursing assessment form dated December 11 stated that Burch was confused and unable to state the reason for his hospitalization and still believed that "[t]his is heaven." Petitioner Zinermon on December 29 made a further report on Burch's condition, stating that, on admission, Burch had been "disoriented, semi-mute, confused and bizarre in appearance and thought . . . not cooperative to the initial interview," and "extremely psychotic, appeared to be paranoid and hallucinating." The doctor's report also stated that Burch remained disoriented, delusional, and psychotic.

Burch remained at FSH until May 7, 1982, five months after his initial admission to ACMHS. During that time, no hearing was held regarding his hospitalization and treatment.

After his release, Burch complained that he had been admitted inappropriately to FSH and did not remember signing a voluntary admission form. His complaint reached the Florida Human Rights Advocacy Committee of the state's Department of Health and Rehabilitation Services. The committee investigated and replied to Burch by letter dated April 4, 1984. The letter stated that Burch in fact had signed a voluntary admission form, but that there was "documentation that you were heavily medicated and disoriented on admission and . . . you were probably not competent to be signing legal documents." The letter also stated that, at a meeting of the committee with FSH staff on August 4, 1983, "hospital administration was made aware that they were very likely asking medicated clients to make decisions at a time when they were not mentally competent."

In February 1985, Burch filed a complaint in the United States District Court for the Northern District of Florida. He alleged, among other things, that ACMHS and the 11 individual petitioners, acting under color of Florida law, and "by and through the authority of their respective positions as employees at FSH ... as part of their regular and official employment at FSH, took part in admitting plaintiff to FSH as a 'voluntary' patient." Specifically, he alleged:

> Defendants, and each of them, knew or should have known that plaintiff was incapable of voluntary, knowing, understanding and informed consent to admission and treatment at FSH. Nonetheless, defendants, and each of them, seized plaintiff and against plaintiff's will confined and imprisoned him and subjected him to involuntary commitment and treatment for the period from December 10, 1981, to May 7, 1982. For said period of 149 days, plaintiff was without the benefit of counsel and no hearing of any sort was held at which he could have challenged his involuntary admission and treatment at FSH.

> ... Defendants, and each of them, deprived plaintiff of his liberty without due process of law in contravention of the Fourteenth Amendment to the United States Constitution. Defendants acted with willful, wanton and reckless disregard of and indifference to plaintiff's Constitutionally guaranteed right to due process of law.

B

Burch's complaint thus alleges that he was admitted and detained at FSH for five months under Florida's statutory provisions for "voluntary" admission. These provisions are part of a comprehensive statutory scheme under which a person may be admitted to a mental hospital in several different ways.

First, Florida provides for short-term emergency admission. If there is reason to believe that a person is mentally ill and likely "to injure himself or others" or is in "need of care or treatment and lacks sufficient capacity to make a responsible application on his own behalf," he may immediately be detained for up to 48 hours. A mental health professional, a law enforcement officer, or a judge may effect an emergency admission. After 48 hours, the patient is to be released unless he "voluntarily gives express and informed consent to evaluation or treatment," or a proceeding for court-ordered evaluation or involuntary placement is initiated.

Second, under a court order a person may be detained at a mental health facility for up to five days for evaluation, if he is likely "to injure himself or others" or if he is in "need of care or treatment which, if not provided, may result in neglect or refusal to care for himself and ... such neglect or refusal poses a real and present threat of substantial harm to his well-being." Anyone may petition for a court-ordered evaluation of a person alleged to meet these criteria. After five days, the patient is to be released unless he gives "express and informed consent" to admission and treatment, or unless involuntary placement proceedings are initiated.

Third, a person may be detained as an involuntary patient, if he meets the same criteria as for evaluation, and if the facility administrator and two mental health professionals recommend involuntary placement. Before involuntary placement, the patient has a right to notice, a judicial hearing, appointed counsel, access to medical records and personnel, and an independent expert examination. If the court determines that the patient meets the criteria for involuntary placement, it then decides whether the patient is competent to consent to treatment. If not, the court appoints a guardian advocate to make treatment decisions. After six months, the facility must either release the patient, or seek a court order for continued placement by stating the reasons therefor, summarizing the patient's treatment to that point, and submitting a plan for future treatment.

Finally, a person may be admitted as a voluntary patient. Mental hospitals may admit for treatment any adult "making application by express and informed consent," if he is "found to show evidence of mental illness and to be suitable for treatment." "Express and informed consent" is defined as "consent voluntarily given in writing after sufficient explanation and disclosure . . . to enable the person . . . to make a knowing and willful decision without any element of force, fraud, deceit, duress, or other form of constraint or coercion." A voluntary patient may request discharge at any time. If he does, the facility administrator must either release him within three days, or initiate the involuntary placement process. At the time of his admission and each six months thereafter, a voluntary patient and his legal guardian or representatives must be notified in writing of the right to apply for a discharge.

Burch, in apparent compliance with [the Florida statutes], was admitted by signing forms applying for voluntary admission. He alleges, however, that petitioners violated this statute in admitting him as a voluntary patient, because they knew or should have known that he was incapable of making an informed decision as to his admission. He claims that he was entitled to receive the procedural safeguards provided by Florida's involuntary placement procedure, and that petitioners violated his due process rights by failing to initiate this procedure. The question presented is whether these allegations suffice to state a claim under § 1983, in light of *Parratt* and *Hudson*.

III

A

To understand the background against which this question arises, we return to the interpretation of § 1983 articulated in Monroe v. Pape,

365 U.S. 167 (1961). In *Monroe,* this Court rejected the view that § 1983 applies only to violations of constitutional rights that are authorized by state law. . . . Thus, overlapping state remedies are generally irrelevant to the question of the existence of a cause of action under § 1983. A plaintiff, for example, may bring a § 1983 action for an unlawful search and seizure despite the fact that the search and seizure violated the state's Constitution or statutes, and despite the fact that there are common-law remedies for trespass and conversion. . . .

This general rule applies in a straightforward way to two of the three kinds of § 1983 claims that may be brought against the state under the Due Process Clause of the Fourteenth Amendment. First, the clause incorporates many of the specific protections defined in the Bill of Rights. A plaintiff may bring suit under § 1983 for state officials' violation of his rights to, e.g., freedom of speech or freedom from unreasonable searches and seizures. Second, the Due Process Clause contains a substantive component that bars certain arbitrary, wrongful government actions "regardless of the fairness of the procedures used to implement them." Daniels v. Williams, 474 U.S. 327, 331 (1986). As to these two types of claims, the constitutional violation actionable under § 1983 is complete when the wrongful action is taken. A plaintiff, under *Monroe v. Pape,* may invoke § 1983 regardless of any state-tort remedy that might be available to compensate him for the deprivation of these rights.

The Due Process Clause also encompasses a third type of protection, a guarantee of fair procedure. A § 1983 action may be brought for a violation of procedural due process, but here the existence of state remedies is relevant in a special sense. In procedural due process claims, the deprivation by state action of a constitutionally protected interest in "life, liberty, or property" is not in itself unconstitutional; what is unconstitutional is the deprivation of such an interest *without due process of law*. The constitutional violation actionable under § 1983 is not complete when the deprivation occurs; it is not complete unless and until the state fails to provide due process. Therefore, to determine whether a constitutional violation has occurred, it is necessary to ask what process the state provided, and whether it was constitutionally adequate. This inquiry would examine the procedural safeguards built into the statutory or administrative procedure of effecting the deprivation, and any remedies for erroneous deprivations provided by statute or tort law.

In this case, . . . [Burch's claim] falls within the third, or procedural, category of § 1983 claims based on the Due Process Clause.

B

Due process, as this Court often has said, is a flexible concept that varies with the particular situation. To determine what procedural protections the Constitution requires in a particular case, we weigh several factors:

First, the private interest that will be affected by the official action; second, the risk of an erroneous deprivation of such interest through the procedures used, and the probable value, if any, of additional or substitute procedural safeguards; and finally, the government's interest, including the function involved and the fiscal and administrative burdens that the additional or substitute procedural requirement would entail.

Mathews v. Eldridge, 424 U.S. 319, 335 (1976).

Applying this test, the Court usually has held that the Constitution requires some kind of a hearing *before* the state deprives a person of liberty or property. . . . In some circumstances, however, the Court has held that a statutory provision for a postdeprivation hearing, or a common-law tort remedy for erroneous deprivation, satisfies due process.

This is where the *Parratt* rule comes into play. *Parratt* and *Hudson* represent a special case of the general *Mathews v. Eldridge* analysis, in which postdeprivation tort remedies are all the process that is due, simply because they are the only remedies the state could be expected to provide. In *Parratt,* a state prisoner brought a § 1983 action because prison employees negligently had lost materials he had ordered by mail.[14] The prisoner did not dispute that he had a postdeprivation remedy. Under state law, a tort-claim procedure was available by which he could have recovered the value of the materials. This Court ruled that the tort remedy was all the process the prisoner was due, because any predeprivation procedural safeguards that the state did provide, or could have provided, would not address the risk of *this kind* of deprivation. The very nature of a negligent loss of property made it impossible for the state to predict such deprivations and provide predeprivation process. . . .

Given these special circumstances, it was clear that the state, by making available a tort remedy that could adequately redress the loss, had given the prisoner the process he was due. Thus, *Parratt* is not an exception to the *Mathews* balancing test, but rather an application of that test to the unusual case in which one of the variables in the *Mathews* equation—the value of predeprivation safeguards—is negligible in preventing the kind of deprivation at issue. Therefore, no matter how significant the private interest at stake and the risk of its erroneous deprivation, the state cannot be required constitutionally to do the impossible by providing predeprivation process.

In *Hudson,* the Court extended this reasoning to an intentional deprivation of property. . . . The Court pointed out: "The state can no more anticipate and control in advance the random and unauthorized intentional conduct of its employees than it can anticipate similar negligent conduct." Of course, the fact that the guard's conduct was intentional meant that he himself could "foresee" the wrongful deprivation, and could

---

[14] *Parratt* was decided before this Court ruled, in Daniels v. Williams, 474 U.S. 327, 336 (1986), that a negligent act by a state official does not give rise to § 1983 liability.

prevent it simply by refraining from his misconduct. Nonetheless, the Court found that an individual state employee's ability to foresee the deprivation is "of no consequence," because the proper inquiry under *Parratt* is "whether the *state* is in a position to provide for predeprivation process" (emphasis added).

C

Petitioners argue that the dismissal [of the complaint] was proper because, as in *Parratt* and *Hudson,* the state could not possibly have provided predeprivation process to prevent the kind of "random, unauthorized" wrongful deprivation of liberty Burch alleges, so the postdeprivation remedies provided by Florida's statutory and common law necessarily are all the process Burch was due.[15]

Before turning to that issue, however, we must address a threshold question raised by Burch. He argues that *Parratt* and *Hudson* cannot apply to his situation, because those cases are limited to deprivations of property, not liberty.

Burch alleges that he was deprived of his liberty interest in avoiding confinement in a mental hospital without either informed consent or the procedural safeguards of the involuntary placement process. Petitioners do not seriously dispute that there is a substantial liberty interest in avoiding confinement in a mental hospital. Burch's confinement at FSH for five months without a hearing or any other procedure to determine either that he validly had consented to admission, or that he met the statutory standard for involuntary placement, clearly infringes on this liberty interest.

Burch argues that postdeprivation tort remedies are *never* constitutionally adequate for a deprivation of liberty, as opposed to property, so the *Parratt* rule cannot apply to this case. We, however, do not find support in precedent for a categorical distinction between a deprivation of liberty and one of property. . . .

It is true that *Parratt* and *Hudson* concerned deprivations of property. It is also true that Burch's interest in avoiding six months' confinement is of an order different from inmate Parratt's interest in mail-order materials valued at $23.50. But the reasoning of *Parratt* and *Hudson* emphasizes the state's inability to provide predeprivation process because of the random and unpredictable nature of the deprivation, not the fact that only property losses were at stake. In situations where the state feasibly can provide a predeprivation hearing before taking property, it generally must do so regardless of the adequacy of a postdeprivation tort

---

[15] Burch does not dispute that he had remedies under Florida law for unlawful confinement. Florida's mental health statutes provide that a patient confined unlawfully may sue for damages. ("Any person who violates or abuses any rights or privileges of patients" is liable for damages, subject to good-faith immunity but not immunity for negligence). Also, a mental patient detained at a mental health facility, or a person acting on his behalf, may seek a writ of habeas corpus to "question the cause and legality of such detention and request . . . release." Finally, Florida recognizes the common-law tort of false imprisonment.

remedy to compensate for the taking. Conversely, in situations where a predeprivation hearing is unduly burdensome in proportion to the liberty interest at stake, or where the state is truly unable to anticipate and prevent a random deprivation of a liberty interest, postdeprivation remedies might satisfy due process. Thus, the fact that a deprivation of liberty is involved in this case does not automatically preclude application of the *Parratt* rule.

To determine whether, as petitioners contend, the *Parratt* rule necessarily precludes § 1983 liability in this case, we must ask whether predeprivation procedural safeguards could address the risk of deprivations of the kind Burch alleges. To do this, we examine the risk involved. The risk is that some persons who come into Florida's mental health facilities will apparently be willing to sign forms authorizing admission and treatment, but will be incompetent to give the "express and informed consent" required for voluntary placement. . . . Persons who are mentally ill and incapable of giving informed consent to admission would not necessarily meet the statutory standard for involuntary placement, which requires either that they are likely to injure themselves or others, or that their neglect or refusal to care for themselves threatens their well-being. The involuntary placement process serves to guard against the confinement of a person who, though mentally ill, is harmless and can live safely outside an institution. Confinement of such a person not only violates Florida law, but also is unconstitutional. O'Connor v. Donaldson, 422 U.S. 563, 575 (1975) (there is no constitutional basis for confining mentally ill persons involuntarily "if they are dangerous to no one and can live safely in freedom"). Thus, it is at least possible that if Burch had had an involuntary placement hearing, he would not have been found to meet the statutory standard for involuntary placement, and would not have been confined at FSH. . . .

We now consider whether predeprivation safeguards would have any value in guarding against the kind of deprivation Burch allegedly suffered. Petitioners urge that here, as in *Parratt* and *Hudson,* such procedures could have no value at all, because the state cannot prevent its officials from making random and unauthorized errors in the admission process. We disagree.

The Florida statutes, of course, do not allow incompetent persons to be admitted as "voluntary" patients. But the statutes do not direct any member of the facility staff to determine whether a person is competent to give consent, nor to initiate the involuntary placement procedure for every incompetent patient. A patient who is willing to sign forms but incapable of informed consent certainly cannot be relied on to protest his "voluntary" admission and demand that the involuntary placement procedure be followed. The staff are the only persons in a position to take notice of any misuse of the voluntary admission process, and to ensure that the proper procedure is followed.

Florida chose to delegate to petitioners a broad power to admit patients to FSH, i.e., to effect what, in the absence of informed consent, is a substantial deprivation of liberty. Because petitioners had state authority to deprive persons of liberty, the Constitution imposed on them the state's concomitant duty to see that no deprivation occur without adequate procedural protections.

It may be permissible constitutionally for a state to have a statutory scheme like Florida's, which gives state officials broad power and little guidance in admitting mental patients. But when those officials fail to provide constitutionally required procedural safeguards to a person whom they deprive of liberty, the state officials cannot then escape liability by invoking *Parratt* and *Hudson*. It is immaterial whether the due process violation Burch alleges is best described as arising from petitioners' failure to comply with state procedures for admitting involuntary patients, or from the absence of a specific requirement that petitioners determine whether a patient is competent to consent to voluntary admission. Burch's suit is neither an action challenging the facial adequacy of a state's statutory procedures, nor an action based only on state officials' random and unauthorized violation of state laws. Burch is not simply attempting to blame the state for misconduct by its employees. He seeks to hold state officials accountable for their abuse of their broadly delegated, uncircumscribed power to effect the deprivation at issue.

This case, therefore, is not controlled by *Parratt* and *Hudson,* for three basic reasons:

First, petitioners cannot claim that the deprivation of Burch's liberty was unpredictable. Under Florida's statutory scheme, only a person competent to give informed consent may be admitted as a voluntary patient. There is, however, no specified way of determining, before a patient is asked to sign admission forms, whether he is competent. It is hardly unforeseeable that a person requesting treatment for mental illness might be incapable of informed consent, and that state officials with the power to admit patients might take their apparent willingness to be admitted at face value and not initiate involuntary placement procedures. Any erroneous deprivation will occur, if at all, at a specific, predictable point in the admission process—when a patient is given admission forms to sign.

This situation differs from the state's predicament in *Parratt*. While it could anticipate that prison employees would occasionally lose property through negligence, it certainly "cannot predict precisely when the loss will occur." Likewise, in *Hudson*, the state might be able to predict that guards occasionally will harass or persecute prisoners they dislike, but cannot "know when such deprivations will occur."

Second, we cannot say that predeprivation process was impossible here. Florida already has an established procedure for involuntary placement. The problem is only to ensure that this procedure is afforded to all patients who cannot be admitted voluntarily, both those who are unwilling and those who are unable to give consent.

In *Parratt*, the very nature of the deprivation made predeprivation process "impossible." It would do no good for the state to have a rule telling its employees not to lose mail by mistake, and it "borders on the absurd to suggest that a state must provide a hearing to determine whether or not a corrections officer should engage in negligent conduct." *Daniels*, 474 U.S. at 342 n.19 (Stevens, J., concurring in judgments). In *Hudson*, the errant employee himself could anticipate the deprivation since he intended to effect it, but the state still was not in a position to provide predeprivation process, since it could not anticipate or control such random and unauthorized intentional conduct. Again, a rule forbidding a prison guard from maliciously destroying a prisoner's property would not have done any good; it would be absurd to suggest that the state hold a hearing to determine whether a guard should engage in such conduct.

Here, in contrast, there is nothing absurd in suggesting that, had the state limited and guided petitioners' power to admit patients, the deprivation might have been averted. Burch's complaint alleges that petitioners "knew or should have known" that he was incompetent, and nonetheless admitted him as a voluntary patient in "willful, wanton, and reckless disregard" of his constitutional rights. Understood in context, the allegation means only that petitioners disregarded their duty to ensure that the proper procedures were followed, not that they, like the prison guard in *Hudson*, were bent upon effecting the substantive deprivation and would have done so despite any and all predeprivation safeguards. Moreover, it would indeed be strange to allow state officials to escape § 1983 liability for failing to provide constitutionally required procedural protections, by assuming that those procedures would be futile because the same state officials would find a way to subvert them.

Third, petitioners cannot characterize their conduct as "unauthorized" in the sense the term is used in *Parratt* and *Hudson*. The state delegated to them the power and authority to effect the very deprivation complained of here, Burch's confinement in a mental hospital, and also delegated to them the concomitant duty to initiate the procedural safeguards set up by state law to guard against unlawful confinement. . . .

We conclude that petitioners cannot escape § 1983 liability by characterizing their conduct as a "random, unauthorized" violation of Florida law which the state was not in a position to predict or avert, so that all the process Burch could possibly be due is a postdeprivation damages remedy. Burch, according to the allegations of his complaint, was deprived of a substantial liberty interest without either valid consent or an involuntary placement hearing, by the very state officials charged with the power to deprive mental patients of their liberty and the duty to implement procedural safeguards. Such a deprivation is foreseeable, due to the nature of mental illness, and will occur, if at all, at a predictable point in the admission process. Unlike *Parratt* and *Hudson,* this case does not represent the special instance of the *Mathews* due process analysis where postdeprivation process is all that is due because no predeprivation safe-guards would be of use in preventing the kind of deprivation alleged.

We express no view on the ultimate merits of Burch's claim; we hold only that his complaint was sufficient to state a claim under § 1983 for violation of his procedural due process rights.

The judgment of the Court of Appeals is affirmed.

It is so ordered.

■ JUSTICE O'CONNOR, with whom THE CHIEF JUSTICE, JUSTICE SCALIA, and JUSTICE KENNEDY join, dissenting.

Without doubt, respondent Burch alleges a serious deprivation of lib-erty, yet equally clearly he alleges no violation of the Fourteenth Amendment. The Court concludes that an allegation of state actors' wan-ton, unauthorized departure from a state's established policies and procedures, working a deprivation of liberty, suffices to support a proce-dural due process claim even though the state provides adequate post-deprivation remedies for that deprivation. The Court's opinion unneces-sarily transforms well-established procedural due process doctrine and departs from controlling precedent. I respectfully dissent.

Parratt v. Taylor, 451 U.S. 527 (1981), and *Hudson v. Palmer*, 468 U.S. 517 (1984), should govern this case. Only by disregarding the gist of Burch's complaint—that state actors' wanton and unauthorized depar-ture from established practice worked the deprivation—and by trans-forming the allegations into a challenge to the adequacy of Florida's ad-missions procedures can the Court attempt to distinguish this case from *Parratt* and *Hudson.*

Burch alleges a deprivation occasioned by petitioners' contravention of Florida's established procedures. Florida allows the voluntary admis-sion process to be employed to admit to its mental hospitals only patients who have made "application by express and informed consent for admis-sion," and requires that the elaborate involuntary admission process be used to admit patients requiring treatment and incapable of giving such consent. Burch explicitly disavows any challenge to the adequacy of those established procedural safeguards accompanying Florida's two avenues of admission to mental hospitals. . . .

Parratt and *Hudson* should readily govern procedural due process claims such as respondent's. Taken together, the decisions indicate that for deprivations worked by such random and unauthorized departures from otherwise unimpugned and established state procedures the state provides the process due by making available adequate postdeprivation remedies. . . .

Application of *Parratt* and *Hudson* indicates that respondent has failed to state a claim allowing recovery under 42 U.S.C. § 1983. Petition-ers' actions were unauthorized: they are alleged to have wrongly and without license departed from established state practices. Florida officials in a position to establish safeguards commanded that the voluntary admission process be employed only for consenting patients and that the involuntary hearing procedures be used to admit unconsenting patients. Yet it is alleged that petitioners "with willful, wanton and reckless disregard of and indifference to" Burch's rights contravened both commands. As in *Parratt,* the deprivation "occurred as a result of the unauthorized failure of agents of the state to follow established state procedure." The wanton or reckless nature of the failure indicates it to be random. The state could not foresee the particular contravention and was hardly "in a position to provide for predeprivation process," *Hudson,* 468 U.S. at 534, to ensure that officials bent upon subverting the state's requirements would in fact follow those procedures. For this wrongful deprivation resulting from an unauthorized departure from established state practice, Florida provides adequate postdeprivation remedies, as two courts below concluded, and which the Court and respondent do not dispute. *Parratt* and *Hudson* thus should govern this case and indicate that respondent has failed to allege a violation of the Fourteenth Amendment.

The allegedly wanton nature of the subversion of the state procedures underscores why the state cannot in any relevant sense anticipate and meaningfully guard against the random and unauthorized actions alleged in this case. The Court suggests that the state could foresee "that a person requesting treatment for mental illness might be incapable of informed consent." While foreseeability of that routine difficulty in evaluating prospective patients is relevant in considering the general adequacy of Florida's voluntary admission procedures, *Parratt* and *Hudson* address whether the state can foresee and thus be required to forestall the deliberate or reckless departure from established state practice. Florida may be able to predict that over time some state actors will subvert its clearly implicated requirements. Indeed, that is one reason that the state must implement an adequate remedial scheme. But Florida "cannot predict precisely when the loss will occur," *Parratt,* 451 U.S. at 541, and the Due Process Clause does not require the state to do more than establish appropriate remedies for any wrongful departure from its prescribed practices.

The Court attempts to avert the force of *Parratt* and *Hudson* by characterizing petitioners' alleged failures as only the routine but erroneous application of the admissions process. According to the Court, Burch suffered an "erroneous deprivation" and the "risk of deprivations of the kind Burch alleges" is that incompetent "persons who come into Florida's mental health facilities will apparently be willing to sign forms," prompting officials to "mak[e] random and unauthorized errors in the admission process." The Court's characterization omits petitioners' alleged wrongful state of mind and thus the nature and source of the wrongful deprivation.

A claim of negligence will not support a procedural due process claim, see Daniels v. Williams, 474 U.S. 327 (1986), and it is an unresolved issue whether an allegation of gross negligence or recklessness suffices. Id. at 334 n.3. Respondent, if not the Court, avoids these pitfalls. According to Burch, petitioners "knew" him to be incompetent or were presented with such clear evidence of his incompetence that they should be charged with such knowledge. Petitioners also knew that Florida law required them to provide an incompetent prospective patient with elaborate procedural safeguards. Far from alleging inadvertent or negligent disregard of duty, respondent alleges that petitioners "acted with willful, wanton and reckless disregard of and indifference" to his rights by treating him without providing the hearing that Florida requires. That is, petitioners did not bumble or commit "errors" by taking Burch's "apparent willingness to be admitted at face value." Rather, they deliberately or recklessly subverted his rights and contravened state requirements.

The unauthorized and wrongful character of the departure from established state practice makes additional procedures an "impracticable" means of preventing the deprivation. "The underlying rationale of Parratt is that when deprivations of property are effected through random and unauthorized conduct of a state employee, predeprivation procedures are simply 'impracticable' since the state cannot know when such deprivations will occur." Hudson, 468 U.S. at 533. The Court suggests that additional safeguards surrounding the voluntary admission process would have quite possibly reduced the risk of deprivation. This reasoning conflates the value of procedures for preventing error in the repeated and usual case (evaluated according to the test set forth in Mathews v. Eldridge, 424 U.S. 319 (1976)) with the value of additional predeprivation procedures to forestall deprivations by state actors bent upon departing from or indifferent to complying with established practices. Unsurprisingly, the Court is vague regarding how its proffered procedures would prevent the deprivation Burch alleges, and why the safeguards would not form merely one more set of procedural protections that state employees could willfully, recklessly and wantonly subvert. Indeed, Burch alleges that, presented with the clearest evidence of his incompetence, petitioners nonetheless wantonly or recklessly denied him the protections of the state's admission procedures and requirements. The state actor so indifferent to guaranteed protections would be no more prevented from working the deprivation by additional procedural requirements than would the mail handler in Parratt or the prison guard in Hudson. In those cases, the state could have, and no doubt did, provide a range of predeprivation requirements and safeguards guiding both prison searches and care of packages. . . . In all three cases, the unpredictable, wrongful departure is beyond the state's reasonable control. Additional safeguards designed to secure correct results in the usual case do not practicably forestall state actors who flout the state's command and established practice.

Even indulging the Court's belief that the proffered safeguards would provide "some" benefit, *Parratt* and *Hudson* extend beyond circumstances in which procedural safeguards would have had "negligible" value. In *Parratt* and *Hudson* additional measures would conceivably have had some benefit in preventing the alleged deprivations. A practice of barring individual or unsupervised shakedown searches, a procedure of always pairing or monitoring guards, or a requirement that searches be conducted according to "an established policy" (the proposed measure rejected as unnecessary in *Hudson*) might possibly have helped to prevent the type of deprivation considered in *Hudson*. More sensible staffing practices, better training, or a more rigorous tracking procedure may have averted the deprivation at issue in *Parratt*. In those cases, like this one, the state knew the exact context in which the wrongful deprivation would occur. Yet the possibility of implementing such marginally beneficial measures, in light of the type of alleged deprivation, did not alter the analysis. The state's inability to foresee and to forestall the wrongful departure from established procedures renders additional predeprivation measures "impracticable" and not required by the dictates of due process.

Every command to act imparts the duty to exercise discretion in accord with the command and affords the opportunity to abuse that discretion. The *Mathews* test measures whether the state has sufficiently constrained discretion in the usual case, while the *Parratt* doctrine requires the state to provide a remedy for any wrongful abuse. The Court suggests that this case differs from *Parratt* and *Hudson* because petitioners possessed a sort of delegated power. Yet petitioners no more had the delegated power to depart from the admission procedures and requirements than did the guard in *Hudson* to exceed the limits of his established search and seizure authority, or the prison official in *Parratt* wrongfully to withhold or misdeliver mail. Petitioners' delegated duty to act in accord with Florida's admissions procedures is akin to the mailhandler's duty to follow and implement the procedures surrounding delivery of packages, or the guard's duty to conduct the search properly. . . .

The suggestion that the state delegated to petitioners insufficiently trammeled discretion conflicts with positions that the Court ostensibly embraces. The issue whether petitioners possessed undue discretion is bound with and more properly analyzed as an aspect of the adequacy of the state's procedural safeguards, yet the Court claims Burch did not present this issue and purports not to decide it. . . .

The Court's decision . . . undermines two of this Court's established and delicately related doctrines, one articulated in *Mathews* and the other articulated in *Parratt*. As the Court acknowledges, the procedural component of the Due Process Clause requires the state to formulate procedural safeguards and adequate postdeprivation process sufficient to satisfy the dictates of fundamental fairness and the Due Process Clause. Until today, the reasoning embodied in *Mathews* largely determined that standard and the measures a state must establish to prevent a deprivation of a protected interest from amounting to a constitutional violation. *Mathews* employed the now familiar three-part test (considering the nature of the private interest, efficacy of additional procedures, and governmental interests) to determine what predeprivation procedural safeguards were required of the state. That test reflects a carefully crafted accommodation of conflicting interests, weighed and evaluated in light of what fundamental fairness requires. *Parratt* drew upon concerns similar to those embodied in the *Mathews* test. For deprivations occasioned by wrongful departures from unchallenged and established state practices, *Parratt* concluded that adequate postdeprivation process meets the requirements of the Due Process Clause because additional predeprivation procedural safeguards would be "impracticable" to forestall these deprivations. The *Mathews* and *Parratt* doctrines work in tandem. State officials able to formulate safeguards must discharge the duty to establish sufficient predeprivation procedures, as well as adequate postdeprivation remedies to provide process in the event of wrongful departures from established state practice. The doctrines together define the procedural measures that fundamental fairness and the Constitution demand of the state.

The Court today discovers an additional realm of required procedural safeguards. Now, all procedure is divided into three parts. In place of the border clearly dividing the duties required by *Mathews* from those required by *Parratt,* the Court marks out a vast terra incognita of unknowable duties and expansive liability of constitutional dimension. The *Mathews* test, we are told, does not determine the state's obligation to provide predeprivation procedural safeguards. Rather, to avoid the constitutional violation a state must have fully circumscribed and guided officials' exercise of power and provided additional safeguards, without regard to their efficacy or the nature of the governmental interests. Even if the validity of the state's procedures is not directly challenged, the burden is apparently on certain state actors to demonstrate that the state sufficiently constrained their powers. Despite the many cases of this Court applying and affirming *Mathews,* it is unclear what now remains of the test. And the *Parratt* doctrine no longer reflects a general interpretation of the Due Process Clause or the complement of the principles contained in *Mathews.* It is, instead, displaced when the state delegates certain types of duties in certain inappropriate ways. This resulting "no-man's land" has no apparent boundaries. We are provided almost no guidance regarding what the Due Process Clause requires, how that requirement is to be deduced, or why fundamental fairness imposes upon the states the obligation to provide additional safeguards of nearly any conceivable value. We are left only with the implication that where doubt exists, liability of constitutional dimension will be found. Without so much as suggesting that our prior cases have warned against such a result, the Court has gone some measure to " 'make of the Fourteenth Amendment a font of tort law to be superimposed upon whatever systems may already be administered by the states.'" *Parratt*, 451 U.S. at 544 (quoting Paul v. Davis, 424 U.S. 693, 701 (1976)). . . .

The Court believes that Florida's statutory scheme contains a particular flaw. That statutory omission involves the determination of competence in the course of the voluntary admission process, and the Court signals that it believes that these suggested additional safeguards would not be greatly burdensome. The Court further believes that Burch's complaint and argument properly raise these issues and that adopting the additional safeguards would provide relevant benefit to one in Burch's position. The traditional *Mathews* test was designed and, until today, has been employed to evaluate and accommodate these concerns. . . . That test holds Florida to the appropriate standard and, given the Court's beliefs set out above, would perhaps have yielded a result favoring respondent. While this approach, if made explicit, would have required a strained reading of respondent's complaint and arguments, that course would have been far preferable to the strained reading of controlling procedural due process law that the Court today adopts. Ordinarily, a complaint must state a legal cause of action, but here it may be said that the Court has stated a novel cause of action to support a complaint.

I respectfully dissent.

NOTES ON THE ROLE OF STATE LAW

1.   QUESTIONS AND COMMENTS ON *ZINERMON*

Why did the plaintiff in *Zinermon* disclaim the argument that Florida's statutory commitment procedures provided constitutionally inadequate safeguards? Consider the implications of such a claim for a damages remedy.

As a state entity, the Florida State Hospital was immune from suit under Edelman v. Jordan, 415 U.S. 651 (1974), and Will v. Michigan Department of State Police, 491 U.S. 58 (1989). Thus, the plaintiff could not seek money damages from the state. Given the unavailability of the state as a defendant, the plaintiff might have worried that claiming that the individual defendants acted pursuant to an unconstitutional state policy would set the stage for a successful assertion of qualified immunity: the individual defendants would claim that they conformed to a state policy that they reasonably could have believed to be lawful. Thus, the plaintiff had a strong practical incentive to allege instead that the individual defendants acted in an unauthorized fashion.

What would a sensible plaintiff's lawyer have done if the hospital been a municipal, rather than a state institution? Would the case have evolved differently?

2.   QUESTIONS AND COMMENTS ON THE ADEQUACY OF STATE LAW

Zinermon makes it clear that *Parratt* did not signal a general return to the position advocated by Justice Frankfurter in *Monroe v. Pape*. As Justice

Blackmun said, "for two of the three kinds of § 1983 claims that may be brought . . . under the Due Process Clause of the Fourteenth Amendment," the presence or absence of a state remedy is irrelevant. Specifically, for violations of the Bill of Rights or of the "substantive components" of the Due Process Clause, § 1983 provides remedial protection quite irrespective of any "process" provided by the state. It is only the third kind of claim—generalized interferences with liberty or property not covered by these more specific provisions—with which *Parratt* and its progeny are concerned. Once a person has been "deprived" of an identifiable "liberty" or "property" interest by state action, § 1983 will provide a remedy if the state has not provided adequate procedural protections.

If *Parratt* and *Hudson* were right in looking to the adequacy of state law remedies to determine whether there has been a due process violation, should the same approach be applied in *Zinermon*? Are the Court's grounds for distinguishing the earlier precedents persuasive? Could *Parratt* and *Hudson* be re-analyzed in the terms suggested by *Zinermon*?

Finally, is it possible that the approach of *Parratt* and *Hudson* should have been applied in *Paul v. Davis*? This question has been raised in Rodney Smolla, The Displacement of Federal Due Process Claims by State Tort Remedies: *Parratt v. Taylor* and *Logan v. Zimmerman Brush Co.*, 1982 U. Ill. L. Rev. 831. According to Smolla, "[t]he critics of *Paul v. Davis* have never explained satisfactorily how a § 1983 action is in any substantive law sense an improvement on the law of libel." Under this analysis, the state's provision of an adequate postdeprivation remedy would satisfy due process, and leave the injured plaintiff with no federal claim to pursue. Is this analysis persuasive? What would be its application to *DeShaney*?[a]

SUBSECTION C. NON-CONSTITUTIONAL RIGHTS ENFORCEABLE UNDER § 1983

Maine v. Thiboutot

Supreme Court of the United States, 1980.
448 U.S. 1.

■ MR. JUSTICE BRENNAN delivered the opinion of the Court.

This case presents two related questions arising under 42 U.S.C. §§ 1983 and 1988. Respondents brought this suit in the Maine Superior Court alleging that petitioners, the state of Maine and its Commissioner of Human Services, violated § 1983 by depriving respondents of welfare benefits to which they were entitled under the federal Social Security Act, specifically 42 U.S.C. § 602(a)(7). The petitioners present two issues:

---

[a] *Parratt* and its progeny generated an enormous literature. For two of the more recent articles, see Larry Alexander, Constitutional Torts, the Supreme Court, and the Law of Non-contradiction: An Essay on *Zinermon v. Burch*, 87 Nw. U. L. Rev. 576 (1993), and Richard H. Fallon, Jr., Some Confusions about Due Process, Judicial Review, and Constitutional Remedies, 93 Colum. L. Rev. 309 (1993).

(1) whether § 1983 encompasses claims based on purely statutory violations of federal law, and (2) if so, whether attorney's fees under § 1988 may be awarded to the prevailing party in such an action.[1]

I

Respondents, Lionel and Joline Thiboutot, are married and have eight children, three of whom are Lionel's by a previous marriage. The Maine Department of Human Services notified Lionel that, in computing the aid to families with dependent children (AFDC) benefits to which he was entitled for the three children exclusively his, it would no longer make allowance for the money spent to support the other five children, even though Lionel is legally obligated to support them. Respondents, challenging the state's interpretation of 42 U.S.C. § 602(a)(7), exhausted their state administrative remedies and then sought judicial review of the administrative action in the state Superior Court. By amended complaint, respondents also claimed relief under § 1983 for themselves and others similarly situated. The Superior Court's judgment enjoined petitioners from enforcing the challenged rule and ordered them to adopt new regulations, to notify class members of the new regulations, and to pay the correct amounts retroactively to eligible class members.[2] The court, however, denied respondents' motion for attorney's fees. The Supreme Judicial Court of Maine concluded that respondents had no entitlement to attorney's fees under state law, but were eligible for attorney's fees pursuant to the Civil Rights Attorneys' Fees Awards Act of 1976. We granted certiorari. We affirm.

II

Section 1983 provides:

> Every person who, under color of any statute, ordinance, regulation, custom, or usage, of any state or territory, subjects, or causes to be subjected, any citizen of the United States or other person within the jurisdiction thereof to the deprivation of any rights, privileges, or immunities secured by the Constitution *and laws*, shall be liable to the party injured in an action at law, suit in equity, or other proper proceeding for redress. (Emphasis added.)

The question before us is whether the phrase "and laws," as used in § 1983, means what it says, or whether it should be limited to some subset of laws. Given that Congress attached no modifiers to the phrase, the plain language of the statute undoubtedly embraces respondents' claim that petitioners violated the Social Security Act.

---

[1] Petitioners also argue that jurisdiction to hear § 1983 claims rests exclusively with the federal courts. Any doubt that state courts may also entertain such actions was dispelled by Martinez v. California, 444 U.S. 277, 283–84 n.7 (1980). There, while reserving the question whether state courts are *obligated* to entertain § 1983 actions, we held that Congress has not barred them from doing so.

[2] The state did not appeal the judgment against it.

Even were the language ambiguous, however, any doubt as to its meaning has been resolved by our several cases suggesting, explicitly or implicitly, that the § 1983 remedy broadly encompasses violations of federal statutory as well as constitutional law. Rosado v. Wyman, 397 U.S. 397 (1970), for example, "held that suits in federal court under § 1983 are proper to secure compliance with the provisions of the Social Security Act on the part of participating states." Edelman v. Jordan, 415 U.S. 651, 675 (1974). Monell v. New York City Dept. of Social Services, 436 U.S. 658 (1978), as support for its conclusion that municipalities are "persons" under § 1983, reasoned that "there can be no doubt that § 1 of the Civil Rights Act [of 1871] was intended to provide a remedy, to be broadly construed, against all forms of official violation of federally protected rights." Similarly, Owen v. City of Independence, 445 U.S. 622 (1980), in holding that the common-law immunity for discretionary functions provided no basis for according municipalities a good-faith immunity under § 1983, noted that a court "looks only to whether the municipality has conformed to the requirements of the federal Constitution and statutes." . . . Greenwood v. Peacock, 384 U.S. 808, 829–30 (1966), observed that under § 1983 state "officers may be made to respond in damages not only for violations of rights conferred by federal equal civil rights laws, but for violations of other federal constitutional and statutory rights as well." . . .

While some might dismiss as dictum the foregoing statements, numerous and specific as they are, our analysis in several § 1983 cases involving Social Security Act claims has relied on the availability of a § 1983 cause of action for statutory claims. Constitutional claims were also raised in these cases, providing a jurisdiction base, but the statutory claims were allowed to go forward, and were decided on the merits, under the court's pendent jurisdiction. In each of the following cases § 1983 was necessarily the exclusive statutory cause of action because, as the Court held in *Edelman v. Jordan*, the Social Security Act affords no private right of action against a state. [Citations omitted.]

In the face of the plain language of § 1983 and our consistent treatment of that provision, petitioners nevertheless persist in suggesting that the phrase "and laws" should be read as limited to civil rights or equal protection laws. Petitioners suggest that when § 1 of the Civil Rights Act of 1871, which accorded jurisdiction and a remedy for deprivations of rights secured by "the Constitution of the United States" was divided by the 1874 statutory revision into a remedial section, Rev. Stat. § 1979, and jurisdictional sections, Rev. Stat. §§ 563(12) and 629(16), Congress intended that the same change made in § 629(16) be made as to each of the new sections as well. Section 629(16), the jurisdictional provision for the circuit courts and the model for the current jurisdictional provision, 28 U.S.C. § 1343(3), applied to the deprivation of rights secured by "the Constitution of the United States, or of any right secured by any law providing for equal rights." On the other hand, the remedial provision, the predecessor of § 1983, was expanded to apply to deprivations of rights secured by "the Constitution and laws" and § 563(12), the provision granting jurisdiction to the district courts, to deprivations of rights secured by "the Constitution of the United States, or of any right secured by any law of the United States."

We need not repeat at length the detailed debate over the meaning of the scanty legislative history concerning the addition of the phrase "and laws." See Chapman v. Houston Welfare Rights Org., 441 U.S. 600 (1979). One conclusion which emerges clearly is that the legislative history does not permit a definitive answer. There is no express explanation offered for the insertion of the phrase "and laws." On the one hand, a principal purpose of the added language was to "ensure that federal legislation providing specifically for equality of rights would be brought within the ambit of the civil action authorized by that statute." Id. at 637 (Powell, J., concurring). On the other hand, there are no indications that that was the only purpose, and Congress's attention was specifically directed to this new language. Representative Lawrence, in a speech to the House of Representatives that began by observing that the revisers had very often changed the meaning of existing statutes, referred to the civil rights statutes as "possibly [showing] verbal modifications bordering on legislation." He went on to read to Congress the original and revised versions. In short, Congress was aware of what it was doing, and the legislative history does not demonstrate that the plain language was not intended.[5] Petitioners' arguments amount to the claim that had Congress been more careful, and had it fully thought out the relationships among the various sections,[6] it might have acted differently. That argument, however, can best be addressed to Congress, which, it is important to note, has remained quiet in the face of our many pronouncements on the scope of § 1983.

III

Petitioners next argue that, even if this claim is within § 1983, Congress did not intend statutory claims to be covered by the Civil Rights Attorneys' Fees Awards Act of 1976, which added the following sentence to 42 U.S.C. § 1988 (emphasis added):

---

[5]   In his concurring opinion in Chapman v. Houston Welfare Rights Org., 441 U.S. 600 (1979), Mr. Justice Powell's argument proceeds on the basis of the flawed premise that Congress did not intend to change the meaning of existing laws when it revised the statutes in 1874. He assumed that Congress had instructed the revisers not to make changes, and that the revisers had obeyed those instructions. In fact, the second section of the statute creating the revision commission mandated that the commissioners "mak[e] such alterations as may be necessary to reconcile the contradictions, supply the omissions, and amend the imperfections of the original text." Furthermore, it is clear that Congress understood this mandate to authorize the commission to do more than merely "copy and arrange in proper order, and classify in heads the actual text of statutes in force." . . .

[6]   There is no inherent illogic in construing § 1983 more broadly than § 1343(3) was construed in *Chapman v. Houston Welfare Rights Org.* It would only mean that there are statutory rights which Congress has decided cannot be enforced in the federal courts unless 28 U.S.C. § 1331(a)'s $10,000 jurisdictional amount is satisfied. [The jurisdictional amount for § 1331 was repealed in 1980.—Addition to footnote by eds.]

> In *any action* or proceeding *to enforce* a provision of §§ 1981, 1982, 1983, 1985, and 1986 of this title . . . , the court, in its discretion, may allow the prevailing party, other than the United States, a reasonable attorney's fee as part of the costs.

Once again, given our holding in part II, the plain language provides an answer. The statute states that fees are available in *any* § 1983 action. Since we hold that this statutory action is properly brought under § 1983, and since § 1988 makes no exception for statutory § 1983 actions, § 1988 plainly applies to this suit.

The legislative history is entirely consistent with the plain language. As was true with § 1983, a major purpose of the Civil Rights Attorneys' Fees Act was to benefit those claiming deprivations of constitutional and civil rights. Principal sponsors of the measure in both the House and the Senate, however, explicitly stated during the floor debate that the statute would make fees available more broadly. Representative Drinan explained that the act would apply to § 1983 and that § 1983 "authorizes suits against state and local officials based upon federal statutory as well as constitutional rights. . . ." Senator Kennedy also included a Social Security Act case as an example of the cases "enforc[ing] the rights promised by Congress or the Constitution" which the act would embrace. In short, there can be no question that Congress passed the Fees Act anticipating that it would apply to statutory § 1983 claims.

Several states, participating as amicus curiae, argue that even if § 1988 applies to § 1983 claims alleging deprivations of statutory rights, it does not apply in state courts. There is no merit to this argument. [We have] held that § 1983 actions may be brought in state courts. Representative Drinan described the purpose of the Civil Rights Attorneys' Fees Act as "authoriz[ing] the award of a reasonable attorney's fee in actions brought in state or federal courts." And Congress viewed the fees authorized by § 1988 as "an integral part of the remedies necessary to obtain" compliance with § 1983. It follows from this history and from the supremacy clause that the fee provision is part of the § 1983 remedy whether the action is brought in federal or state court.

Affirmed.

■ MR. JUSTICE POWELL, with whom THE CHIEF JUSTICE and MR. JUSTICE REHNQUIST join, dissenting.

The Court holds today, almost casually, that 42 U.S.C. § 1983 creates a cause of action for deprivations under color of state law of any federal statutory right. Having transformed purely statutory claims into "civil rights" actions under § 1983, the Court concludes that 42 U.S.C. § 1988 permits the "prevailing party" to recover his attorney's fees. These two holdings dramatically expand the liability of state and local officials and may virtually eliminate the "American rule" in suits against those officials.

The Court's opinion reflects little consideration of the consequences of its judgment. It relies upon the "plain" meaning of the phrase "and laws" in § 1983 and upon this Court's assertedly "consistent treatment" of that statute. But the reading adopted today is anything but "plain" when the statutory language is placed in historical context. Moreover, until today this Court never had held that § 1983 encompasses all purely statutory claims. Past treatment of the subject has been incidental and far from consistent. The only firm basis for decision is the historical evidence, which convincingly shows that the phrase the Court now finds so clear was—and remains—nothing more than a shorthand reference to equal rights legislation enacted by Congress. To read "and laws" more broadly is to ignore the lessons of history, logic, and policy. . . .

I

Section 1983 provides in relevant part that "[e]very person who, under color of [state law] subjects . . . any . . . person . . . to the deprivation of any rights, privileges, or immunities secured by the Constitution and laws, shall be liable to the party injured. . . ." The Court asserts that "the phrase 'and laws' . . . means what it says," because "Congress attached no modifiers to the phrase. . . ." Finding no "definitive" contrary indications in the legislative history of § 1983, the Court concludes that that statute provides a remedy for violations of the Social Security Act. The Court suggests that those who would read the phrase "and laws" more narrowly, should address their arguments to Congress.

If we were forbidden to look behind the language in legislative enactments, there might be some force to the suggestion that "and laws" must be read to include all federal statutes.[1] But the "plain meaning" rule is not as inflexible as the Court imagines. . . . We have recognized consistently that statutes are to be interpreted " 'not only by a consideration of the words themselves, but by considering, as well, the context, the purposes of the law, and the circumstances under which the words were employed.' " . . .

Blind reliance on plain meaning is particularly inappropriate where, as here, Congress inserted the critical language without explicit discussion when it revised the statutes in 1874. Indeed, not a single shred of evidence in the legislative history of the adoption of the 1874 revision mentions this change. Since the legislative history also shows that the revision generally was not intended to alter the meaning of existing law, this Court previously has insisted that apparent changes be scrutinized with some care. . . .

---

[1]   The "plain meaning" of "and laws" may be more elusive than the Court admits. One might expect that a statute referring to all rights secured either by the Constitution or by the laws would employ the disjunctive "or." . . .

In contrast, a natural reading of the conjunctive "and" in § 1983 would require that the right at issue be secured both by the Constitution and by the laws. In 1874, this would have included the rights set out in the Civil Rights Act of 1866, which had been incorporated in the Fourteenth Amendment and re-enacted in the Civil Rights Act of 1870. . . .

II

The origins of the phrase "and laws" in § 1983 were discussed in detail in two concurring opinions last term. Compare Chapman v. Houston Welfare Rights Org., 441 U.S. 600, 623 (Powell, J., concurring) with id. at 646 (White, J., concurring in judgment). I shall not recount the full historical evidence presented in my *Chapman* opinion. Nevertheless, the Court's abrupt dismissal of the proposition that "Congress did not intend to change the meaning of existing laws when it revised the statutes in 1874" reflects a misconception so fundamental as to require a summary of the historical record.

A

Section 1983 derives from § 1 of the Civil Rights Act of 1871, which provided a cause of action for deprivation of constitutional rights only. "Laws" were not mentioned. The phrase "and laws" was added in 1874, when Congress consolidated the laws of the United States into a single volume under a new subject-matter arrangement. Consequently, the intent of Congress in 1874 is central to this case.

In addition to creating a cause of action, § 1 of the 1871 act conferred concurrent jurisdiction upon "the district or circuit courts of the United States. . . ." In the 1874 revision, the remedial portion of § 1 was codified as § 1979 of the Revised Statutes, which provided for a cause of action in terms identical to the present § 1983. The jurisdictional portion of § 1 was divided into § 563(12), conferring district court jurisdiction, and § 629(16), conferring circuit court jurisdiction. Although §§ 1979, 563(12), and 629(16) came from the same source, each was worded differently. Section 1979 referred to deprivations of rights "secured by the Constitution and laws"; § 563(12) described rights secured "by the Constitution of the United States, or . . . by any law of the United States"; and § 629(16) encompassed rights secured "by the Constitution of the United States, or . . . by any law providing for equal rights of citizens of the United States." When Congress merged the jurisdiction of circuit and district courts in 1911, the narrower language of § 629(16) was adopted and ultimately became the present 28 U.S.C. § 1343(3).

B

In my view, the legislative history unmistakably shows that the variations in phrasing were inadvertent, and that each section was intended to have precisely the same scope. Moreover, the only defensible interpretation of the contemporaneous legislative record is that the reference to "laws" in each section was intended "to do no more than ensure that federal legislation providing specifically for equality of rights would be brought within the ambit of the civil action authorized by [§ 1979]." Careful study of the available materials leaves no serious doubt that the Court's contrary conclusion is completely at odds with the intent of Congress in 1874.

The Court holds today that the foregoing reasoning is based on a "flawed premise," because Congress instructed the revision commission to change the statutes in certain respects. But it is the Court's premise that is flawed. The revision commission, which worked for six years on the project, submitted to Congress a draft that did contain substantive changes. But a joint congressional committee, which was appointed in early 1873 to transform the draft into a bill, concluded that it would be "utterly impossible to carry the measure through, if it was understood that it contained new legislation." Therefore, the committee employed Thomas Jefferson Durant to "strike out . . . modifications of the existing law" "wherever the meaning of the law had been changed." On December 10, 1873 Durant's completed work was introduced in the House with the solemn assurance that the bill "embodies the law as it is."

The House met in a series of evening sessions to review the bill and to restore original meaning where necessary. During one of these sessions, Representative Lawrence delivered the speech upon which the Court now relies. Lawrence explained that the revisers often had separated existing statutes into substantive, remedial, and criminal sections to accord with the new organization of the statutes by topic. He read both the original and revised versions of the civil rights statutes to illustrate the arrangement, and "possibly [to] show verbal modifications bordering on legislation." After reading § 1979 without mentioning the addition of "and laws," Lawrence stated that "[a] comparison of all these will present a fair specimen of the manner in which the work has been done, and from these all can judge of the accuracy of the translation." Observing that "[t]his mode of classifying . . . to some extent duplicates in the revision portions of statutes" that previously were one, Lawrence praised "the general accuracy" of the revision. Nothing in this sequence of remarks supports the decision of the Court today. There was no mention of the addition of "and laws" nor any hint that the reach of § 1983 was to be extended. If Lawrence had any such intention, his statement to the House was a singularly disingenuous way of proposing a major piece of legislation.

In context, it is plain that Representative Lawrence did not mention changes "bordering on legislation" as a way of introducing substantive changes in § 1 of the 1871 act. Rather, he was emphasizing that the revision was not intended to modify existing statutes, and that his reading might reveal errors that should be eliminated. No doubt Congress "was aware of what it was doing." It was meeting specially in one last attempt to detect and strike out legislative changes that may have remained in the proposed revision despite the best efforts of Durant and the joint committee. No representative challenged those sections of the revised statutes that derived from § 1 of the Civil Rights Act of 1871. That silence reflected the understanding of those present that "and laws" did not alter the original meaning of the statute.[6] The members of Congress who participated in the year long effort to expunge all substantive alterations from the revised statutes evince no intent whatever to enact a far-reaching modification of § 1 of the Civil Rights Act of 1871. The relevant evidence, largely ignored by the Court today, shows that Congress painstakingly sought to avoid just such changes.

III

The legislative history alone refutes the Court's assertion that the 43rd Congress intended to alter the meaning of § 1983. But there are other compelling reasons to reject the Court's interpretation of the phrase "and laws." First, by reading those words to encompass every federal enactment, the Court extends § 1983 beyond the reach of its jurisdictional counterpart. Second, that reading creates a broad program for enforcing federal legislation that departs significantly from the purposes of § 1983. Such unexpected and plainly unintended consequences should be avoided whenever a statute reasonably may be given an interpretation that is consistent with the legislative purpose.

A

The Court acknowledges that its construction of § 1983 creates federal "civil rights" for which 28 U.S.C. § 1343(3) supplies no federal jurisdiction. The Court finds no "inherent illogic" in this view. But the gap in the Court's logic is wide indeed in light of the history and purpose of the civil rights legislation we consider today. Sections 1983 and 1343(3) derive from the same section of the same act. As originally enacted the two sections were necessarily coextensive. And this Court has emphasized repeatedly that the right to a federal forum in every case was viewed as a crucial ingredient in the federal remedy afforded by § 1983. . . . Since § 1343(3) covers statutory claims only when they arise under laws providing for the equal rights of citizens, the same limitation necessarily is implicit in § 1983. The Court's decision to apply that statute without regard to the scope of its jurisdictional counterpart is at war with the plainly expressed intent of Congress.

B

The Court's opinion does not consider the nature or scope of the litigation it has authorized. In practical effect, today's decision means that state and local governments, officers, and employees now face liability whenever a person believes he has been injured by the administration of *any* federal-state cooperative program, whether or not that program is related to equal or civil rights. . . .

Even a cursory survey of the United States code reveals that literally hundreds of cooperative regulatory and social welfare enactments may

---

[6]   The addition of "and laws" did not change the meaning of § 1 because Congress assumed that that phrase referred only to federal equal rights legislation. In 1874, the only such legislation was contained in the 1866 and 1870 Civil Rights Acts, which conferred rights also secured by the recently adopted Fourteenth Amendment.

be affected. The states now participate in the enforcement of federal laws governing migrant labor, noxious weeds, historic preservation, wildlife conservation, anadromous fisheries, scenic trails, and strip mining. Various statutes authorize federal-state cooperative agreements in most aspects of federal land management. In addition, federal grants administered by state and local governments now are available in virtually every area of public administration. Unemployment, Medicaid, school lunch subsidies, food stamps, and other welfare benefits may provide particularly inviting subjects of litigation. Federal assistance also includes a variety of subsidies for education, housing, health care, transportation, public works, and law enforcement. Those who might benefit from these grants now will be potential § 1983 plaintiffs.

No one can predict the extent to which litigation arising from today's decision will harass state and local officials; nor can one foresee the number of new filings in our already overburdened courts. But no one can doubt that these consequences will be substantial. And the Court advances no reason to believe that any Congress—from 1874 to the present day—intended this expansion of federally imposed liability on state defendants.

Moreover, state and local governments will bear the entire burden of liability for violations of statutory "civil rights" even when federal officials are involved equally in the administration of the affected program. Section 1983 grants no right of action against the United States, and few of the foregoing cooperative programs provide expressly for private actions to enforce their terms. Thus, private litigants may sue responsible federal officials only in the relatively rare case in which a cause of action may be implied from the governing substantive statute. Cf. Transamerica Mtg. Advisors v. Lewis, 444 U.S. 11 (1979); Touche Ross & Co. v. Redington, 442 U.S. 560 (1979). It defies reason to believe that Congress intended—without discussion—to impose such a burden only upon state defendants.

Even when a cause of action against federal officials is available, litigants are likely to focus efforts upon state defendants in order to obtain attorney's fees under the liberal standard of 42 U.S.C. § 1988. There is some evidence that § 1983 claims already are being appended to complaints solely for the purpose of obtaining fees in actions where "civil rights" of any kind are at best an afterthought. . . .

IV

The Court finally insists that its interpretation of § 1983 is foreordained by a line of precedent so strong that further analysis is unnecessary. It is true that suits against state officials alleging violations of the Social Security Act have become commonplace in the last decade. The instant action follows that pattern. Thus, the Court implies, today's decision is a largely inconsequential reaffirmation of a statutory interpretation that has been settled authoritatively for many years.

This is a tempting way to avoid confronting the serious issues presented by this case. But the attempt does not withstand analysis. Far from being a long-accepted fact, purely statutory § 1983 actions are an invention of the last 20 years. And the Court's seesaw approach to § 1983 over the last century leaves little room for certainty on any question that has not been discussed fully and resolved explicitly by this Court. Yet, until last term, neither this Court nor any justice ever had undertaken—directly and thoroughly—a consideration of the question presented in this case. . . .

The issue did not arise with any frequency until the late 1960s, when challenges to state administration of federal social welfare legislation became commonplace. The lower courts responded to these suits with conflicting conclusions. Some found § 1983 applicable to all federal statutory claims. Others refused to apply it to statutory rights. Yet others believed that § 1983 covered some but not all rights derived from nonconstitutional sources. Numerous scholarly comments discussed the possible solutions, without reaching a consensus. . . .

The Court quotes the statement in Edelman v. Jordan, 415 U.S. 651, 675 (1974), that Rosado v. Wyman, 397 U.S. 397 (1970), " 'held that suits in federal court under § 1983 are proper to secure compliance with the provisions of the Social Security Act on the part of participating states.' " If that statement were true, the confusion remaining after Rosado is simply inexplicable. In fact, of course, Rosado established no such proposition of law. The plaintiffs in that case challenged a state welfare provision on constitutional grounds premising jurisdiction upon § 1343(3), and added a pendent statutory claim. This Court held first that the District Court retained its power to adjudicate the statutory claim even after the constitutional claim, on which § 1343(3) jurisdiction was based, became moot. The opinion then considered the merits of the plaintiffs' argument that New York law did not comport with the Social Security Act. Although the Court had to assume the existence of a private right of action to enforce that act, the opinion did not discuss or purport to decide whether § 1983 applies to statutory claims.

Rosado is not the only case to have assumed sub silentio that welfare claimants have a cause of action to challenge the adequacy of state programs under the Social Security Act. As the Court observes, many of our recent decisions construing the act made the same unspoken assumption. It does not necessarily follow that the Court in those cases assumed that the cause of action was provided by § 1983 rather than the Social Security Act itself. But even if it did, these cases provide no support for the Court's ruling today. "[W]hen questions of jurisdiction have been passed on in prior decisions sub silentio, this Court has never considered itself bound when a subsequent case finally brings the jurisdictional issue before us." Hagans v. Lavine, 415 U.S. 528, 535 n.5 (1974). This rule applies with even greater force to questions involving the availability of a cause of action, because the question whether a cause of action exists—unlike the existence of federal jurisdiction—may be assumed without being decided. Thus, the Court's ruling finds no support in past cases in which the issue was not squarely raised. . . .

The Court also relies upon "numerous and specific" dicta in prior decisions. But none of the cited cases contains anything more than a bare assertion of the proposition that is to be proved. Most say much less than that. For example, the Court occasionally has referred to § 1983 as a remedy for violations of "federally protected rights" or of "the federal Constitution and statutes," Monell v. New York City Dept. of Social Services, 436 U.S. 658, 700–01 (1978); Owen v. City of Independence, 445 U.S. 622, 649, 650 (1980). These generalized references merely restate the language of the statute. They shed no light on the question whether all or only some statutory rights are protected. To the extent they have any relevance to the issue at hand, they could be countered by the frequent occasions on which the Court has referred to § 1983 as a remedy for constitutional violations without mentioning statutes. But the debate would be meaningless, for none of these offhand remarks provides the remotest support for the positions taken in this case.

The only remaining decision in the Court's "consistent" line of precedents are Greenwood v. Peacock, 384 U.S. 808, 829–30 (1966), and Edelman v. Jordan, 415 U.S. 651, 675 (1974). In each case, the Court asserted—without discussion and in the course of disposing of other issues—that § 1983's coverage of statutory rights extended beyond federal equal rights laws. Neither contains any discussion of the question; neither cites relevant authority. Nor has this Court always uncritically assumed the proposition for which *Greenwood* and *Edelman* now are said to stand. On the same day the Court decided *Edelman*, it refused to express a view on the question whether § 1983 creates a cause of action for purely statutory claims. Hagans v. Lavine, 415 U.S. 528, 534 n.5 (1974). The point was reserved again in Southeastern Community College v. Davis, 442 U.S. 397, 404–05 n.5 (1979).

To rest a landmark decision of this Court on two statements made in dictum without critical examination would be extraordinary in any case. In the context of § 1983, it is unprecedented. Our decisions construing the civil rights legislation of the Reconstruction era have repudiated "blind adherence to the principle of stare decisis. . . ." As Mr. Justice Frankfurter once observed, the issues raised under § 1983 concern "a basic problem of American federalism" that "has significance approximating constitutional dimension." *Monroe*, 365 U.S. at 222 (dissenting opinion). Although Mr. Justice Frankfurter's view did not prevail in *Monroe*, we have heeded consistently his admonition that the ordinary concerns of stare decisis apply less forcefully in this than in other areas of the law. E.g., *Monell v. New York City Dept. of Social Services*. Against this backdrop, there is no justification for the Court's reliance on unexamined dicta as the principal support for a major extension of liability under § 1983.

V

In my view, the Court's decision today significantly expands the con-cept of "civil rights" and creates a major new intrusion into state sovereignty under our federal system. There is no probative evidence that Congress intended to authorize the pervasive judicial oversight of state officials that will flow from the Court's construction of § 1983. Although today's decision makes new law with far-reaching consequences, the Court brushes aside the critical issues of congressional intent, national policy, and the force of past decisions as precedent. I would reverse the judgment of the Supreme Judicial Court of Maine.

NOTES ON NON-CONSTITUTIONAL RIGHTS ENFORCEABLE UNDER § 1983

1.   CHAPMAN V. HOUSTON WELFARE RIGHTS ORG.

As the *Thiboutot* opinions mention, the issue before the Court was first extensively examined in Chapman v. Houston Welfare Rights Org., 441 U.S. 600 (1979). That case involved claims that state welfare regulations violated the Social Security Act. The question was whether federal courts had juris-diction over such claims under the jurisdictional counterpart to § 1983, 28 U.S.C. § 1343(3).[a] Section 1343(3) confers subject matter jurisdiction on fed-eral district courts over actions to redress the deprivation under color of law "of any right, privilege or immunity secured by the Constitution of the United States or by any Act of Congress *providing for equal rights* of citizens or of all persons within the jurisdiction of the United States" (emphasis added). The Court held that this statute did not include claims of incompatibility between state welfare regulations and the Social Security Act.[b]

Speaking for the Court, Justice Stevens's opinion was joined by Chief Justice Burger, and Justices Blackmun, Powell, and Rehnquist. The majority considered and rejected several theories for bringing such claims within the coverage of § 1343(3). First, the Court held that "secured by the Constitu-tion," as these words are used in § 1343(3), did not include rights secured by the Supremacy Clause of Article VI. To hold otherwise would go too far, for every federal right is "secured" against state interference by the Supremacy Clause. If that suffices, every conceivable federal claim against a state agent would be "secured by the Constitution" within the meaning of § 1343(3) and the additional language providing for jurisdiction over claims "secured . . . by any Act of Congress providing for equal rights" would be rendered superflu-ous and without meaning.

---

[a]   Today, any claim based on federal law could be brought under 28 U.S.C. § 1331, but at the time of *Chapman* that statute required a minimum jurisdictional amount of more than $10,000, which this claim did not satisfy. The alternative jurisdictional basis of § 1343(3) there-fore mattered.

[b]   The Court also found no jurisdiction under 28 U.S.C. § 1343(4), a provision which origi-nated in the Civil Rights Act of 1957 and which gives the district courts jurisdiction over actions to enforce "any Act of Congress providing for the protection of civil rights, including the right to vote." Because of its different origin, the meaning of § 1343(4) has no relevance to the interpre-tation of § 1983.

Second, the Court also held that the Social Security Act was not itself a law "providing for equal rights" within the meaning of § 1343(3). If it were, then § 1343(3) would indirectly be given the broader scope of the "and laws" language of § 1983. The Court rejected this construction, noting that § 1983 does not secure any rights, equal or otherwise, but merely provides a cause of action for rights secured elsewhere. The Court found it unnecessary to decide whether §§ 1983 and 1343(3) covered the same behavior, but concluded that the limiting language in the latter could not be ignored.

In a dissent joined by Justices Brennan and Marshall, Justice Stewart argued that § 1983 was in fact an "act of Congress providing for equal rights" and therefore that § 1343(3) created federal jurisdiction for every claim brought under § 1983. Stewart pointed to *Rosado v. Wyman* and other cases treating § 1983 as the source of a cause of action to enforce the Social Security Act and rejected as anomalous the "conclusion that Congress intended § 1983 to create some causes of action which could not be heard in a federal court under § 1343(3)." That conclusion would be contrary to the Court's understanding that "the common origin of §§ 1983 and 1343(3) in § 1 of the 1871 Act suggests that the two provisions were meant to be, and are, complementary." The correct result, he argued, would be to bring the two provisions into alignment by reading § 1983 as a law "providing for equal rights" under § 1343(3) and thereby extending the jurisdictional statute to all causes of action under § 1983.

By far the most elaborate opinions in *Chapman* were the concurrences of Justices Powell and White. Powell, joined by Chief Justice Burger and Justice Rehnquist, argued that §§ 1983 and 1343(3) should be read as having the same scope and that the better interpretation would be to limit § 1983 to the reach of its jurisdictional counterpart. Powell supported this claim by an extensive review of the legislative history, the highlights of which are restated in his *Thiboutot* dissent.

Justice White concurred in the result. He concluded that §§ 1983 and 1343(3) were in fact not coextensive. White argued that the majority's construction of § 1343(3) was "compelled" by the "plain terms of that statute and the absence of any overriding indication in the legislative history that these plain terms should be ignored." At the same time, White found nothing in the history of § 1983 indicating that its equally "plain terms" should not also be given effect. White argued that the history of revision and recodification of various civil rights statutes yielded so many "ambiguities, contradictions, and uncertainties" that there was "no satisfactory basis" for overriding the literal terms of these laws. He concluded, therefore, that §§ 1983 and 1343(3) "cannot be read as though they were but one statute," but that each should be accorded the meaning indicated by its language. Ironically, although Justice White was alone in finding that §§ 1983 and 1343(3) should be read independently, it was his position that ultimately prevailed in *Thiboutot*.

2.   QUESTIONS AND COMMENTS ON *MAINE V. THIBOUTOT*

The broad authorization of suit in *Thiboutot* makes an interesting comparison with decisions dealing with "implied" causes of action under federal statutes. See Chapter II, Section 2. In these cases, courts have been asked to supplement the remedies created by Congress for the enforcement of federal regulatory statutes. Typically, Congress has established an administrative agency with specified enforcement powers but has not explicitly provided that persons injured by violations of the regulatory standards can bring suit. Starting in the mid-1970s, the Court became increasingly restrictive of attempts to read into such statutes private remedies they do not expressly provide. Today, the courts are reluctant to add a private right of action to a federal regulatory structure unless the legislative history suggests that Congress actually intended such a remedy. By contrast, *Thiboutot* reads § 1983 to authorize a private right of action for all violations of all federal statutes by state and local officials. Are these developments inconsistent?

The potential reach of *Thiboutot* is suggested by an appendix to Justice Powell's dissent. The appendix lists a number of federal statutes that do not provide for private enforcement but that typically will involve state and local officials in their administration. The examples fall into three broad categories: (1) joint federal-state regulatory programs—e.g., the Historic Sites, Buildings, and Antiquities Act, the Fish and Wildlife Coordination Act, and the Surface Mining Control and Reclamation Act; (2) resource management programs administered cooperatively by federal and state agencies—e.g., laws involving the administration of national parks and forest lands, the construction and management of water projects, and oil leasing; and (3) federal grant programs that either subsidize state or local activities or provide matching funds for state and local programs that meet federal standards.

Of these categories, the last is most important. It includes not only the welfare, unemployment, and medical assistance programs administered under the Social Security Act, but also grant programs under the Food Stamp Act, the Small Business Investment Act, the National School Lunch Act, and Public Works and Economic Development Act, the Energy Conservation and Production Act, the Developmentally Disabled Assistance and Bill of Rights Act, and the Urban Mass Transportation Act, among others. These statutes typically provide only for enforcement by federal agencies, but *Thiboutot* says that they may also be enforced by private damage actions under § 1983. The potential significance is hard to overstate. As noted in Richard B. Cappalli, Federal Grants and the New Statutory Tort: State and Local Officials Beware!, 12 Urb. Law. 445, 446 (1980):

> [W]hen state and local officials act (and many hospital, university, and nonprofit organization officials), the likelihood of finding an applicable federal standard of conduct is great. The officials are involved in a program activity which is aided by the federal government. The aid carries a series of standards imposed by the grant statute and its implementing regulations. While these standards are usually expressed at a high level of generality, they are readily usable in evaluating the "legality" of the officials' conduct in a wide variety of circumstances."

The enforcement of grant-in-aid standards by private damage actions raises a number of potential problems. See generally Cass R. Sunstein, Section 1983 and the Private Enforcement of Federal Law, 49 U. Chi. L. Rev. 394, 416–18 (1982). In some instances, Congress may have intended that the specified enforcement mechanism be exclusive. The addition of a private right of action may lead to over-enforcement of the federal standards. In some cases, the provision of a judicial remedy may invade agency specialization in the elaboration of statutory standards. Judicial enforcement, which tends to be decentralized and which depends on the agenda of private litigants, may also impair an agency's ability to devise a consistent and coordinated policy of enforcement. And finally, judicial supervision may diminish the political accountability of those who administer federal programs.

For all of these reasons, judicial enforcement of federal statutes under § 1983 may provide needed judicial oversight of state compliance with federal statutes, but in other instances may be disruptive of federal regulatory objectives. After *Thiboutot*, questions arose about whether and to what extent the courts would attempt to integrate the expansive approach of that decision with the potentially more restrictive policies and enforcement structures of the particular statutory schemes being enforced.

3. *NATIONAL SEA CLAMMERS*

In Middlesex County Sewerage Authority v. National Sea Clammers Association, 453 U.S. 1 (1981), an organization of commercial fisherman sued various governmental authorities to stop the discharge of sewage and other pollutants into New York Harbor and the Hudson River. The plaintiffs sought injunctive and declaratory relief, as well as damages. Among other grounds, the plaintiffs alleged that the pollution violated the Federal Water Pollution Control Act and the Marine Protection, Research, and Sanctuaries Act. Both statutes authorize "citizen suits," but only after 60-days' notice to both federal and state authorities and to the alleged violators and only for prospective relief.

Plaintiffs failed to give the required notice, and the District Court entered summary judgment on that ground. The Court of Appeals reversed on the theory that the statutorily authorized citizen suits were not the only causes of action available to these plaintiffs. Both statutes had "savings clauses" that preserved "any right which any person (or class of persons) may have under any statute or common law." The Court of Appeals reasoned that the savings clauses preserved implied rights of action that were not burdened by procedural requirements.

The Supreme Court reversed. Speaking through Justice Powell, the Court reiterated the now established doctrine that the existence of a private right of action to enforce the provisions of a federal regulatory statute turns chiefly on legislative intent. The Court examined the statutes in question and concluded that the legislative provision of "unusually elaborate enforcement mechanisms," including citizen suits for injunctive relief, precluded any finding of implied authorization of additional judicial remedies. The Court then turned to the question whether an "*express* congressional authorization of private suits under these acts" might be found in § 1983. In an analysis that closely tracked the rejection of implied rights of action, the Court concluded that the express statutory remedies showed "not only that

Congress intended to foreclose implied private actions but also that it intended to supplant any remedy that otherwise would be available under § 1983."

Justice Stevens, joined by Justice Blackmun, dissented. Stevens argued that the question was "not whether Congress 'intended to preserve the § 1983 right of action,' but rather whether Congress intended to withdraw that right of action." As he explained in a footnote, "Because the § 1983 plaintiff is invoking an express private remedy that is, on its face, applicable any time a violation of a federal statute is alleged, see *Maine v. Thiboutot*, the burden is properly placed on the defendant to show that Congress, in enacting the particular substantive statute at issue, intended an exception to the general rule of § 1983."

4.   SUBSEQUENT DECISIONS

In subsequent years, the Supreme Court rendered a series of decisions, usually on closely divided votes, that sometimes allowed § 1983 actions to enforce federal statutes and sometimes did not. In Wright v. Roanoke Redevelopment and Housing Authority, 479 U.S. 418 (1987), low-income tenants sued a public housing authority, alleging that they had been overbilled for their utilities in violation of a federal rent ceiling. The question was whether the federal rent ceiling could be enforced via § 1983. Speaking through Justice White, the Court ruled five-four that "the remedial mechanisms provided [are not] sufficiently comprehensive and effective to raise a clear inference that Congress intended to foreclose a § 1983 cause of action for the enforcement of tenants' rights secured by federal law." The *Wright* Court insisted that § 1983 would be available absent "express provision or other specific evidence from the statute itself that Congress intended to foreclose . . . private enforcement." Under that standard, very few federal statutes will be found to have foreclosed a private right of action under § 1983. Indeed, one might ask whether even the statutes in *Sea Clammers* met that test. O'Connor, Rehnquist, Powell, and Scalia dissented.

For another decision following *Wright* and distinguishing *Sea Clammers*, again on a five-four split, see Wilder v. Virginia Hospital Association, 496 U.S. 498 (1990). On the other hand, the Court also rendered decisions denying damages remedies under § 1983. See, e.g., Suter v. Artist M., 503 U.S. 347 (1992) (finding that the Adoption Assistance and Child Welfare Act of 1980 did not confer on its beneficiaries a private right to enforce federal standards); Blessing v. Freestone, 520 U.S. 329 (1997) (ruling that the Social Security Act provisions requiring substantial compliance with federal regulations regarding child support did not create any individually enforceable rights). In neither of these cases was there specific evidence that Congress affirmatively intended to foreclose enforcement under § 1983. As interpretations of the underlying statutes, these decisions may well have made sense, but they did not chart any clear course regarding the availability of § 1983.

5.   *SMITH V. ROBINSON*

Smith v. Robinson, 468 U.S. 992 (1984), presented the unusual case of the remedies provided by a federal statute arguably precluding the use of

§ 1983 to enforce a *constitutional* right. The case involved the right of a handicapped child to a "free appropriate public education." The plaintiffs claimed this right under four different theories: state law, a provision of the federal Education of the Handicapped Act (EHA), a provision of the federal Rehabilitation Act of 1973, and the Equal Protection Clause of the Fourteenth Amendment. Plaintiffs prevailed on the EHA theory. That statute provides an express remedy, enforceable in federal court, for the rights it protects.

The question then was whether the plaintiffs were entitled to attorney's fees. The EHA does not authorize attorney's fees. But the plaintiffs had also asserted a constitutional claim under § 1983, and plaintiffs who prevail in § 1983 actions, or who assert a "substantial but unaddressed" § 1983 claim and who prevail on other grounds, are entitled to attorney's fees under 42 U.S.C. § 1988. See Maher v. Gagne, 448 U.S. 122 (1980).

In an opinion by Justice Blackmun, the Court had "little difficulty concluding that Congress intended the EHA to be the exclusive avenue through which a plaintiff may assert an equal protection claim to a publicly financed education." Although the Court could "not lightly conclude that Congress intended to preclude reliance on § 1983 for a substantial equal protection claim, . . . § 1983 is a statutory remedy and Congress retains the authority to repeal it or replace it with an alternative remedy." The "crucial consideration" was what Congress intended, and here the Court thought Congress clearly intended to make the EHA remedy exclusive. It followed that attorney's fees were not available under § 1988. Justice Brennan, joined by Justices Marshall and Stevens, dissented.

Is there a case to be made that the standard by which to determine whether federal statutory remedies preclude assertion of a constitutional right under § 1983 should be different from the standard that should control whether such provisions preclude statutory enforcement via § 1983? For argument to this effect, see Rosalie Berger Levinson, Misinterpreting "Sounds of Silence": Why Courts Should Not "Imply" Congressional Preclusion of § 1983 Constitutional Claims, 77 Fordham L. Rev. 775 (2008).

6. *GONZAGA UNIVERSITY V. DOE*

The Supreme Court attempted to resolve the continuing confusion over the legacy of *Maine v. Thiboutot* in Gonzaga University v. Doe, 536 U.S. 273 (2002). The case concerned the Family Educational Rights and Privacy Act of 1974 (FERPA), 20 U.S.C. § 1232g, which prohibits federal funding of schools that permit the release of students' records without written consent. Doe alleged that Gonzaga, a private university in Washington state, violated FERPA by revealing allegations of sexual misconduct by an employee to state officials involved in teacher certification. The employee sued in state court under § 1983, and the state courts agreed that Gonzaga had acted under color of state law in helping the state officials. A jury awarded both compensatory and punitive damages, and the Washington Supreme Court affirmed.

The United States Supreme Court reversed. The opinion by Chief Justice Rehnquist began by noting that FERPA was enacted under Congress's

Spending Clause power—that is, Congress required privacy of personal information as a condition of receiving federal funds, rather than as a direct legislative command. In Pennhurst State School and Hospital v. Halderman, 451 U.S. 1 (1981), the Court had held that federal funding provisions create individually enforceable rights only when Congress manifests an "unambiguous" intent to create them. Otherwise, the Court stated, the remedy "for state noncompliance with federally imposed conditions is not a private cause of action for noncompliance but rather action by the Federal Government to terminate funds to the State."

The Court recognized that prior decisions had caused "uncertainty" in the lower courts. Some decisions allowed plaintiffs to enforce statutory rights under § 1983 so long as they fell "within the general zone of interest that the statute is intended to protect; something less than what is required for a statute to create rights enforceable directly from the statute itself under an implied private right of action. Fueling this uncertainty is the notion that our implied private right of action cases have no bearing on the standards for discerning whether a statute creates rights enforceable by § 1983." In *Gonzaga University*, the Court rejected this approach:

> We now reject the notion that our cases permit anything short of an unambiguously conferred right to support a cause of action brought under § 1983. Section 1983 provides a remedy only for the deprivation of "rights, privileges, or immunities secured by the Constitution and laws" of the United States. Accordingly, only "rights," not "benefits" or "interests," may be enforced under that section. This being so, we further reject the notion that our implied right of action cases are separate and distinct from our § 1983 cases. To the contrary, our implied right of action cases should guide the determination of whether a statute confers rights enforceable under § 1983.

> We have recognized that whether a statutory violation may be enforced through § 1983 "is a different inquiry than that involved in determining whether a private right of action can be implied from a particular statute." Wilder v. Virginia Hospital Association, 496 U.S. 498, 508, n.9 (1990). But the inquiries overlap in one meaningful respect—in either case we must first determine whether Congress intended to create a federal right. Thus we have held that "the question whether Congress . . . intended to create a private right of action [is] definitively answered in the negative" where "a statute by its terms grants no private rights to any identifiable class." Touche Ross & Co. v. Redington, 442 U.S. 560, 576 (1979). For a statute to create such private rights, its text must be "phrased in terms of the persons benefited." Cannon v. University of Chicago, 441 U.S. 677, 692, n.13 (1979). . . . But even where a statute is phrased in such explicit rights-creating terms, a plaintiff suing under an implied right of action still must show that the statute manifests an intent "to create not just a private right but also a private remedy." Alexander v. Sandoval, 532 U.S. 275, 286 (2001).

Plaintiffs suing under § 1983 do not have the burden of showing an intent to create a private remedy because § 1983 generally
supplies a remedy for the vindication of rights secured by federal
statutes. Once a plaintiff demonstrates that a statute confers an
individual right, the right is presumptively enforceable by § 1983.
But the initial inquiry—determining whether a statute confers any
right at all—is no different from the initial inquiry in an implied
right of action case, the express purpose of which is to determine
whether or not a statute "confers rights on a particular class of persons." California v. Sierra Club, 451 U.S. 287, 294 (1981). . . .

Accordingly, where the text and structure of a statute provide
no indication that Congress intends to create new individual rights,
there is no basis for a private suit, whether under § 1983 or under
an implied right of action.

The Court found that FERPA did not contain the kind of rights-creating
language that could support a § 1983 claim. It did not contain "individually
focused terminology"—for example, that "no person shall be subjected to" violations of FERPA. Instead, FERPA had an "aggregate focus," referring to
institutional policies and requiring that funds recipients "comply substantially." The conclusion that FERPA's nondisclosure provisions do not confer
enforceable rights was "buttressed by the mechanism that Congress chose to
provide for enforcing those provisions." The Court noted Congress's express
direction to the Secretary of Education to "deal with violations" and the extensive administrative complaint structure the Secretary had created and
found that "[t]hese administrative procedures squarely distinguish this case
from Wright v. Roanoke Redevelopment and Housing Authority, 479 U.S.
418 (1987), and *Wilder*, where an aggrieved individual lacked any federal
review mechanism."

Finally, the Court pointed to statutory language providing that "except
for the conduct of hearings, none of the functions of the Secretary under this
section shall be carried out in any of the regional offices" of the Department
of Education. 20 U.S.C. § 1232g(g). The legislative history showed that Congress had provided for "centralized review" because of concern that
"regionalizing the enforcement of [FERPA] may lead to multiple interpretations. . . ." 120 Cong. Rec. 39863 (1974) (joint statement). "It is implausible,"
the Court concluded, "to presume that the same Congress nonetheless intended private suits to be brought before thousands of federal-and state-
court judges, which could only result in the sort of 'multiple interpretations'
the Act explicitly sought to avoid."

Justice Breyer, joined by Justice Souter, concurred in the judgment.
They agreed that congressional intent was the key issue in determining
whether an individual could bring suit under § 1983, and that FERPA manifested no such intent, but they would not have adopted a presumption that
Congress intended to create a right only if the text or structure of a statute
showed an "unambiguous" intent.

Justice Stevens, joined by Justice Ginsburg, dissented. He argued that
the FERPA did contain rights-creating language. He also disagreed with

what he saw as the Court's "needlessly borrowing from cases involving implied rights of action":

> [O]ur implied right of action cases "reflect a concern, grounded in separation of powers, that Congress rather than the courts controls the availability of remedies for violations of statutes." Wilder v. Virginia Hospital Association, 496 U.S. 498, 509, n.9 (1990). However, imposing the implied right of action framework upon the § 1983 inquiry is not necessary: The separation-of-powers concerns present in the implied right of action context "are not present in a § 1983 case," because Congress expressly authorized private suits in § 1983 itself. Id.

7.   *CITY OF PALOS VERDES V. ABRAMS*

The restrictive approach of *Gonzaga University* was reaffirmed in City of Palos Verdes v. Abrams, 544 U.S. 113 (2005). Plaintiff Abrams sued his locality, claiming that the denial of a zoning permit for a radio antenna on his property violated restrictions imposed on localities by the Telecommunications Act of 1996. Writing for a nearly unanimous Court, Justice Scalia began with the familiar admonition that the statute must create individually enforceable rights in the class of beneficiaries to which the plaintiff belongs. That showing, however, creates only a rebuttable presumption that the right is enforceable under § 1983. The presumption is rebutted if the defendant shows that Congress "did not intend" that the newly created right be enforceable under § 1983, and a lack of congressional intent is the "ordinary inference" from a different statutory enforcement scheme. In the case of the Telecommunications Act, individual enforcement is explicitly authorized but on a shorter timetable, arguably without compensatory damages, and certainly without attorneys fees. These differences in remedy precluded application of § 1983, absent legislation indication of a purpose to provide that relief. Justice Breyer, joined by Justices O'Connor, Souter, and Ginsburg, concurred to say that context would sometimes be important in determining whether Congress intended to exclude enforcement under § 1983. Only Justice Stevens dissented.

8.   COMMENTARY AND BIBLIOGRAPHY

Many commentators argue that a § 1983 remedy should be presumptively available to enforce federal statutes, absent "clear evidence" of an affirmative congressional intent to withdraw it. See, e.g., Paul Wartelle and Jeffrey Hadley Louden, Private Enforcement of Federal Statutes: The Role of the Section 1983 Remedy, 9 Hast. Con. L. Q. 487, 543 (1982). In practice, this approach would read *Thiboutot* very broadly, for it would be rare indeed to find express indication of a legislative intent to preclude enforcement under § 1983. A decidedly different approach appears in George D. Brown, Whither *Thiboutot*?: Section 1983, Private Enforcement, and the Damages Dilemma, 33 DePaul L. Rev. 31 (1983). Brown concluded that "the Supreme Court's decision to apply, in a cursory fashion, a plain meaning approach to an exceedingly complex area was doomed from the start" and suggested that the Supreme Court should "admit the mistake and start over."

An intermediate position is advanced by Cass Sunstein in Section 1983 and the Private Enforcement of Federal Law, 49 U. Chi. L. Rev. 394 (1982). Sunstein is reluctant to apply § 1983 across the board, but equally unwilling to say that statutory specification of other remedies implied repeals other remedies. The right test, he suggests, is to ask whether there is "manifest inconsistency" between the statutory enforcement scheme and a private right of action. If so, the § 1983 remedy should be precluded, notwithstanding the absence of explicit legislative intent to accomplish that result. If not, a damage action under § 1983 should be freely available.

Sunstein goes on to categorize the contexts in which such manifest inconsistency is likely to exist. Clearest of all are statutes, such as those involved in *Sea Clammers*, that create independent private causes of action against state officials. In Sunstein's view, preclusion of § 1983 in such cases is equally justified, whether the private right of action arising from the underlying statute is express or implied.

Second, preclusion of § 1983 may be indicated where the statute involves open-ended substantive standards. In such a case, Congress may be relying on agency specialization to spell out what the law requires. Further, Congress may desire that the agency's policies be subject to influence by politically accountable branches of government. In such circumstances, the courts may "seriously distort" the regulatory scheme by interpreting statutory standards in advance of agency determination. Judicial review of agency decisions does not pose the same danger, for the courts ordinarily defer to non-arbitrary agency action.

Third, preclusion of § 1983 may be justified where the federal statute demands consistency and coordination in enforcement. Only an administrative agency can develop and implement a coherent system of enforcement priorities. He argues that judicial enforcement at the behest of private litigants is inevitably decentralized and potentially disruptive. Therefore, private actions should be precluded whenever "it appears that a rational enforcement scheme requires the exercise of prosecutorial discretion."

9. SECTION 1983 ACTIONS TO ENFORCE FEDERAL PREEMPTION OF STATE LAW

Can § 1983 be used to recover damages for state regulation that is unlawful only because it is preempted by federal law? The answer, it seems, is: "Usually, but perhaps not always."

(i) Golden State Transit Corp. v. Los Angeles

In 1986 the Supreme Court ruled that Los Angeles could not condition renewal of a taxi franchise on settlement of a labor dispute between the cab company and its union. That condition, said the Court, interfered with the company's right under the National Labor Relations Act to use economic weapons in collective bargaining. The company then sued the city for money damages under § 1983. A divided Supreme Court upheld the company's claim, but in terms that did not comprehend all claims based on federal preemption of state law. Golden State Transit Corp. v. City of Los Angeles, 493 U.S. 103 (1989).

In an opinion by Justice Stevens, the majority reasoned that the cab company was "the intended beneficiary of a statutory scheme that prevents governmental interference with the collective-bargaining process." Because the NLRA created rights in both labor and management, not only against each other but also against the state, the cab company could enforce those rights by a damages action under § 1983. In other cases, however, a private party might be only an incidental beneficiary of a federal scheme intended to benefit the general public. In that circumstance, damages under § 1983 would not be available, although the litigant may have the right to enjoin the preempted state regulation under the general equitable powers of the federal courts.

Justice Kennedy, joined by Chief Justice Rehnquist and Justice O'Connor, dissented. He argued that § 1983 should not be interpreted to authorize money damages "when the only wrong committed by the state or its local entities is misapprehending the precise location of the boundaries between state and federal power."

(ii) Dennis v. Higgins

Golden State was followed in Dennis v. Higgins, 498 U.S. 439 (1991). Dennis was the owner of a motor carrier. He filed suit in a Nebraska state court against the Director of the Nebraska Department of Motor Vehicles, arguing that a particular tax on motor carriers violated the negative Commerce Clause. One of the claims asserted was based on § 1983. The trial court held the tax unconstitutional on the asserted ground, and enjoined its future collection. But the court dismissed the § 1983 claim. The state Supreme Court affirmed the dismissal of the § 1983 claim on the ground, inter alia, that "the Commerce Clause does not establish individual rights against government, but instead allocates power between the state and federal governments."

The Supreme Court reversed in an opinion by Justice White. The issue was whether the Commerce Clause served only the abstract goals of promoting national economic and political unity, or whether it was also designed to benefit individuals. The Court held that the clause "of its own force imposes limitations on state regulation of commerce, and is the source of a right of action in those injured by regulations that exceed such limitations" and that it therefore confers "rights, privileges, or immunities" within the meaning of those words as used in § 1983.

Justice Kennedy, joined by Chief Justice Rehnquist, dissented. He argued that the majority decision "compounds the error of *Golden State*."

APPENDIX A

THE CONSTITUTION OF THE UNITED STATES OF AMERICA

We the People of the United States, in Order to form a more perfect Union, establish Justice, insure domestic Tranquility, provide for the common defence, promote the general Welfare, and secure the Blessings of Liberty to ourselves and our Posterity, do ordain and establish this Constitution for the United States of America.

ARTICLE I.

SECTION 1. All legislative Powers herein granted shall be vested in a Congress of the United States, which shall consist of a Senate and House of Representatives.

SECTION 2. The House of Representatives shall be composed of Members chosen every second Year by the People of the several States, and the Electors in each State shall have the Qualifications requisite for Electors of the most numerous Branch of the State Legislature.

No Person shall be a Representative who shall not have attained to the Age of twenty five Years, and been seven Years a Citizen of the United States, and who shall not, when elected, be an Inhabitant of that State in which he shall be chosen.

Representatives and direct Taxes shall be apportioned among the several States which may be included within this Union, according to their respective Numbers, which shall be determined by adding to the whole Number of free Persons, including those bound to Service for a Term of Years, and excluding Indians not taxed, three fifths of all other Persons. The actual Enumeration shall be made within three Years after the first Meeting of the Congress of the United States, and within every subsequent Term of ten Years, in such Manner as they shall by Law direct. The Number of Representatives shall not exceed one for every thirty Thousand, but each State shall have at Least one Representative; and until such enumeration shall be made, the State of New Hampshire shall be entitled to chuse three, Massachusetts eight, Rhode Island and Providence Plantations one, Connecticut five, New York six, New Jersey four, Pennsylvania eight, Delaware one, Maryland six, Virginia ten, North Carolina five, South Carolina five, and Georgia three.

When vacancies happen in the Representation from any State, the Executive Authority thereof shall issue Writs of Election to fill such Vacancies.

The House of Representatives shall chuse their Speaker and other Officers; and shall have the sole Power of Impeachment.

SECTION 3. The Senate of the United States shall be composed of two Senators from each State, chosen by the Legislature thereof, for six Years; and each Senator shall have one Vote.

Immediately after they shall be assembled in Consequence of the first Election, they shall be divided as equally as may be into three Classes. The Seats of the Senators of the first Class shall be vacated at the Expiration of the second Year, of the second Class at the Expiration of the fourth Year, and of the third Class at the Expiration of the sixth Year, so that one third may be chosen every second Year; and if Vacancies happen by Resignation, or otherwise, during the Recess of the Legislature of any State, the Executive thereof may make temporary Appointments until the next Meeting of the Legislature, which shall then fill such Vacancies.

No Person shall be a Senator who shall not have attained to the Age of thirty Years, and been nine Years a Citizen of the United States, and who shall not, when elected, be an Inhabitant of that State for which he shall be chosen.

The Vice President of the United States shall be President of the Senate, but shall have no Vote, unless they be equally divided.

The Senate shall chuse their other Officers, and also a President pro tempore, in the Absence of the Vice President, or when he shall exercise the Office of President of the United States.

The Senate shall have the sole Power to try all Impeachments. When sitting for that Purpose, they shall be on Oath or Affirmation. When the President of the United States is tried, the Chief Justice shall preside: And no Person shall be convicted without the Concurrence of two thirds of the Members present.

Judgment in Cases of Impeachment shall not extend further than to removal from Office, and disqualification to hold and enjoy any Office of honor, Trust or Profit under the United States: but the Party convicted shall nevertheless be liable and subject to Indictment, Trial, Judgment and Punishment, according to Law.

SECTION 4. The Times, Places and Manner of holding Elections for Senators and Representatives, shall be prescribed in each State by the Legislature thereof; but the Congress may at any time by Law make or alter such Regulations, except as to the Places of chusing Senators.

The Congress shall assemble at least once in every Year, and such Meeting shall be on the first Monday in December, unless they shall by Law appoint a different Day.

SECTION 5. Each House shall be the Judge of the Elections, Returns and Qualifications of its own Members, and a Majority of each shall constitute a Quorum to do Business; but a smaller Number may adjourn from day to day, and may be authorized to compel the Attendance of absent Members, in such Manner, and under such Penalties as each House may provide.

Each House may determine the Rules of its Proceedings, punish its Members for disorderly Behaviour, and, with the Concurrence of two thirds, expel a Member.

Each House shall keep a Journal of its Proceedings, and from time to time publish the same, excepting such Parts as may in their Judgment require Secrecy; and the Yeas and Nays of the Members of either House on any question shall, at the Desire of one fifth of those Present, be entered on the Journal.

Neither House, during the Session of Congress, shall, without the Consent of the other, adjourn for more than three days, nor to any other Place than that in which the two Houses shall be sitting.

SECTION 6. The Senators and Representatives shall receive a Compensation for their Services, to be ascertained by Law, and paid out of the Treasury of the United States. They shall in all Cases, except Treason, Felony and Breach of the Peace, be privileged from Arrest during their Attendance at the Session of their respective Houses, and in going to and returning from the same; and for any Speech or Debate in either House, they shall not be questioned in any other Place.

No Senator or Representative shall, during the Time for which he was elected, be appointed to any civil Office under the Authority of the United States, which shall have been created, or the Emoluments whereof shall have been encreased during such time; and no Person holding any Office under the United States, shall be a Member of either House during his Continuance in Office.

SECTION 7. All Bills for raising Revenue shall originate in the House of Representatives; but the Senate may propose or concur with amendments as on other Bills.

Every Bill which shall have passed the House of Representatives and the Senate, shall, before it become a Law, be presented to the President of the United States; If he approve he shall sign it, but if not he shall return it, with his Objections to that House in which it shall have originated, who shall enter the Objections at large on their Journal, and proceed to reconsider it. If after such Reconsideration two thirds of that House shall agree to pass the Bill, it shall be sent, together with the Objections, to the other House, by which it shall likewise be reconsidered, and if approved by two thirds of that House, it shall become a Law. But in all such Cases the Votes of both Houses shall be determined by Yeas and Nays, and the Names of the Persons voting for and against the Bill shall be entered on the Journal of each House respectively. If any Bill shall not be returned by the President within ten Days (Sunday excepted) after it shall have been presented to him, the Same shall be a Law, in like Manner as if he had signed it, unless the Congress by their Adjournment prevent its Return, in which Case it shall not be a Law.

Every Order, Resolution, or Vote to which the Concurrence of the Senate and House of Representatives may be necessary (except on a question of Adjournment) shall be presented to the President of the United States; and before the Same shall take Effect, shall be approved by him, or being disapproved by him, shall be repassed by two thirds of the Senate and House of Representatives, according to the Rules and Limitations prescribed in the Case of a Bill.

SECTION 8. The Congress shall have Power To lay and collect Taxes, Duties, Imposts and Excises, to pay the Debts and provide for the common Defence and general Welfare of the United States; but all Duties, Imposts and Excises shall be uniform throughout the United States;

To borrow Money on the credit of the United States;

To regulate Commerce with foreign Nations, and among the several States, and with the Indian Tribes;

To establish an uniform Rule of Naturalization, and uniform Laws on the subject of Bankruptcies throughout the United States;

To coin Money, regulate the Value thereof, and of foreign Coin, and fix the Standard of Weights and Measures;

To provide for the Punishment of counterfeiting the Securities and current Coin of the United States;

To establish Post Offices and post Roads;

To promote the Progress of Science and useful Arts, by securing for limited Times to Authors and Inventors the exclusive Right to their respective Writings and Discoveries;

To constitute Tribunals inferior to the supreme Court;

To define and punish Piracies and Felonies committed on the high Seas, and Offences against the Law of Nations;

To declare War, grant Letters of Marque and Reprisal, and make Rules concerning Captures on Land and Water;

To raise and support Armies, but no Appropriation of Money to that Use shall be for a longer Term than two Years;

To provide and maintain a Navy;

To make Rules for the Government and Regulation of the land and naval Forces;

To provide for calling forth the Militia to execute the Laws of the Union, suppress Insurrections and repel Invasions;

To provide for organizing, arming, and disciplining, the Militia, and for governing such Part of them as may be employed in the Service of the United States, reserving to the States respectively, the Appointment of the Officers, and the Authority of training the Militia according to the discipline prescribed by Congress;

To exercise exclusive Legislation in all Cases whatsoever, over such District (not exceeding ten Miles square) as may, by Cession of particular States, and the Acceptance of Congress, become the Seat of the Government of the United States, and to exercise like Authority over all Places purchased by the Consent of the Legislature of the State in which the Same shall be, for the Erection of Forts, Magazines, Arsenals, dock-Yards, and other needful Buildings;—And

To make all Laws which shall be necessary and proper for carrying into Execution the foregoing Powers, and all other Powers vested by this Constitution in the Government of the United States, or in any Department or Officer thereof.

SECTION 9. The Migration or Importation of such Persons as any of the States now existing shall think proper to admit, shall not be prohibited by the Congress prior to the Year one thousand eight hundred and eight, but a Tax or duty may be imposed on such Importation, not exceeding ten dollars for each Person.

The Privilege of the Writ of Habeas Corpus shall not be suspended, unless when in Cases of Rebellion or Invasion the public Safety may require it.

No Bill of Attainder or ex post facto Law shall be passed.

No Capitation, or other direct, Tax shall be laid, unless in Proportion to the Census or Enumeration herein before directed to be taken.

No Tax or Duty shall be laid on Articles exported from any State.

No Preference shall be given by any Regulation of Commerce or Revenue to the Ports of one State over those of another; nor shall Vessels bound to, or from, one State, be obliged to enter, clear, or pay Duties in another.

No Money shall be drawn from the Treasury, but in Consequence of Appropriations made by Law; and a regular Statement and Account of the Receipts and Expenditures of all public Money shall be published from time to time.

No Title of Nobility shall be granted by the United States: And no Person holding any Office of Profit or Trust under them, shall, without the Consent of the Congress, accept of any present, Emolument, Office, or Title, of any kind whatever, from any King, Prince or foreign State.

SECTION 10. No State shall enter into any Treaty, Alliance, or Confederation; grant Letters of Marque and Reprisal; coin Money; emit Bills of Credit; make any Thing but gold and silver Coin a Tender in Payment of Debts; pass any Bill of Attainder, ex post facto Law, or Law impairing the Obligation of Contracts, or grant any Title of Nobility.

No State shall, without the Consent of the Congress, lay any Imposts or Duties on Imports or Exports, except what may be absolutely necessary for executing its inspection Laws: and the net Produce of all Duties and Imposts, laid by any State on Imports or Exports, shall be for the Use of the Treasury of the United States; and all such Laws shall be subject to the Revision and Controul of the Congress.

No State shall, without the Consent of Congress, lay any Duty of Tonnage, keep Troops, or Ships of War in time of Peace, enter into any Agreement or Compact with another State, or with a foreign Power, or engage in War, unless actually invaded, or in such imminent Danger as will not admit of delay.

ARTICLE II.

SECTION 1. The executive Power shall be vested in a President of the United States of America. He shall hold his Office during the Term of four Years, and, together with the Vice President, chosen for the same Term, be elected, as follows:

Each State shall appoint, in such Manner as the Legislature thereof may direct, a Number of Electors, equal to the whole Number of Senators and Representatives to which the State may be entitled in the Congress: but no Senator or Representative, or Person holding an Office of Trust or Profit under the United States, shall be appointed an Elector.

The Electors shall meet in their respective States, and vote by Ballot for two Persons, of whom one at least shall not be an Inhabitant of the same State with themselves. And they shall make a List of all the Persons voted for, and of the Number of Votes for each; which List they shall sign and certify, and transmit sealed to the Seat of the Government of the United States, directed to the President of the Senate. The President of the Senate shall, in the Presence of the Senate and House of Representatives, open all the Certificates, and the Votes shall then be counted. The Person having the greatest Number of Votes shall be the President, if such Number be a Majority of the whole Number of Electors appointed; and if there be more than one who have such Majority, and have an equal Number of Votes, then the House of Representatives shall immediately chuse by Ballot one of them for President; and if no Person have a Majority, then from the five highest on the List the said House shall in like Manner chuse the President. But in chusing the President, the Votes shall be taken by States, the Representation from each State having one Vote; a quorum for this Purpose shall consist of a Member or Members from two thirds of the States, and a Majority of all the States shall be necessary to a Choice. In every Case, after the Choice of the President, the Person having the greatest Number of Votes of the Electors shall be the Vice President. But if there should remain two or more who have equal Votes, the Senate shall chuse from them by Ballot the Vice President.

The Congress may determine the Time of chusing the Electors, and the Day on which they shall give their Votes; which Day shall be the same throughout the United States.

No Person except a natural born Citizen, or a Citizen of the United States, at the time of the Adoption of this Constitution, shall be eligible to the Office of President; neither shall any Person be eligible to that Office who shall not have attained to the Age of thirty five Years, and been fourteen Years a Resident within the United States.

In Case of the Removal of the President from Office, or of his Death, Resignation, or Inability to discharge the Powers and Duties of the said Office, the Same shall devolve on the Vice President, and the Congress may by Law provide for the Case of Removal, Death, Resignation or Inability, both of the President and Vice President, declaring what Officer shall then act as President, and such Officer shall act accordingly, until the Disability be removed, or a President shall be elected.

The President shall, at stated Times, receive for his Services, a Compensation, which shall neither be encreased nor diminished during the Period for which he shall have been elected, and he shall not receive within that Period any other Emolument from the United States, or any of them.

Before he enter on the Execution of his Office, he shall take the following Oath or Affirmation:—"I do solemnly swear (or affirm) that I will faithfully execute the Office of President of the United States, and will to the best of my Ability, preserve, protect and defend the Constitution of the United States."

SECTION 2. The President shall be Commander in Chief of the Army and Navy of the United States, and of the Militia of the several States, when called into the actual Service of the United States; he may require the Opinion, in writing, of the principal Officer in each of the executive Departments, upon any Subject relating to the Duties of their respective Offices, and he shall have Power to grant Reprieves and Pardons for Offences against the United States, except in Cases of Impeachment.

He shall have Power, by and with the Advice and Consent of the Senate, to make Treaties, provided two thirds of the Senators present concur; and he shall nominate, and by and with the Advice and Consent of the Senate, shall appoint Ambassadors, other public Ministers and Consuls, Judges of the supreme Court, and all other Officers of the United States, whose Appointments are not herein otherwise provided for, and which shall be established by Law: but the Congress may by Law vest the Appointment of such inferior Officers, as they think proper, in the President alone, in the Courts of Law, or in the Heads of Departments.

The President shall have Power to fill up all Vacancies that may happen during the Recess of the Senate, by granting Commissions which shall expire at the End of their next Session.

SECTION 3. He shall from time to time give to the Congress Information of the State of the Union, and recommend to their Consideration such Measures as he shall judge necessary and expedient; he may, on extraordinary Occasions, convene both Houses, or either of them, and in Case of Disagreement between them, with Respect to the Time of Adjournment, he may adjourn them to such Time as he shall think proper; he shall receive Ambassadors and other public Ministers; he shall take Care that the Laws be faithfully executed, and shall Commission all the Officers of the United States.

SECTION 4. The President, Vice President and all Civil Officers of the United States, shall be removed from Office on Impeachment for, and Conviction of, Treason, Bribery, or other high Crimes and Misdemeanors.

ARTICLE III.

SECTION 1. The judicial Power of the United States, shall be vested in one supreme Court, and in such inferior Courts as the Congress may from time to time ordain and establish. The Judges, both of the supreme and inferior Courts, shall hold their Offices during good Behaviour, and shall, at stated Times, receive for their Services, a Compensation, which shall not be diminished during their Continuance in Office.

SECTION 2. The judicial Power shall extend to all Cases, in Law and Equity, arising under this Constitution, the Laws of the United States, and Treaties made, or which shall be made, under their Authority;—to all Cases affecting Ambassadors, other public Ministers and Consuls;—to all Cases of admiralty and maritime Jurisdiction;—to Controversies to which the United States shall be a Party;—to Controversies between two or more States;—between a State and Citizens of another State;—between Citizens of different States;—between Citizens of the same State claiming Lands under Grants of different States, and between a State, or the Citizens thereof, and foreign States, Citizens or Subjects.

In all Cases affecting Ambassadors, other public Ministers and Consuls, and those in which a State shall be Party, the Supreme Court shall have original Jurisdiction. In all the other Cases before mentioned, the supreme Court shall have appellate Jurisdiction, both as to Law and Fact, with such Exceptions, and under such Regulations as the Congress shall make.

The Trial of all Crimes, except in Cases of Impeachment, shall be by Jury; and such Trial shall be held in the State where the said Crimes shall have been committed; but when not committed within any State, the Trial shall be at such Place or Places as the Congress may by Law have directed.

SECTION 3. Treason against the United States, shall consist only in levying War against them, or in adhering to their Enemies, giving them Aid and Comfort. No Person shall be convicted of Treason unless on the Testimony of two Witnesses to the same overt Act, or on Confession in open Court.

The Congress shall have Power to declare the Punishment of Treason, but no Attainder of Treason shall work Corruption of Blood, or Forfeiture except during the Life of the Person attainted.

ARTICLE IV.

SECTION 1. Full Faith and Credit shall be given in each State to the public Acts, Records, and judicial Proceedings of every other State. And the Congress may by general Laws prescribe the Manner in which such Acts, Records and Proceedings shall be proved, and the Effect thereof.

SECTION 2. The Citizens of each State shall be entitled to all Privileges and Immunities of Citizens in the several States.

A Person charged in any State with Treason, Felony, or other Crime, who shall flee from Justice, and be found in another State, shall on Demand of the executive Authority of the State from which he fled, be delivered up, to be removed to the State having Jurisdiction of the Crime.

No Person held to Service or Labour in one State, under the Laws thereof, escaping into another, shall, in Consequence of any Law or Regulation therein, be discharged from such Service or Labour, but shall be delivered up on Claim of the Party to whom such Service or Labour may be due.

SECTION 3. New States may be admitted by the Congress into this Union; but no new State shall be formed or erected within the Jurisdiction of any other State; nor any State be formed by the Junction of two or more States, or Parts of States, without the Consent of the Legislatures of the States concerned as well as of the Congress.

The Congress shall have Power to dispose of and make all needful Rules and Regulations respecting the Territory or other Property belonging to the United States; and nothing in this Constitution shall be so construed as to Prejudice any Claims of the United States, or of any particular State.

SECTION 4. The United States shall guarantee to every State in this Union a Republican Form of Government, and shall protect each of them against Invasion; and on Application of the Legislature, or of the Executive (when the Legislature cannot be convened) against domestic Violence.

ARTICLE V.

The Congress, whenever two thirds of both Houses shall deem it necessary, shall propose Amendments to this Constitution, or, on the Application of the Legislatures of two thirds of the several States, shall call a Convention for proposing Amendments, which, in either Case, shall be valid to all Intents and Purposes, as Part of this Constitution, when ratified by the Legislatures of three fourths of the several States, or by Conventions in three fourths thereof, as the one or the other Mode of Ratification may be proposed by the Congress; Provided that no Amendment which may be made prior to the Year One thousand eight hundred and eight shall in any Manner affect the first and fourth Clauses in the Ninth Section of the first Article; and that no State, without its Consent, shall be deprived of its equal Suffrage in the Senate.

ARTICLE VI.

All Debts contracted and Engagements entered into, before the Adoption of this Constitution, shall be as valid against the United States under this Constitution, as under the Confederation.

This Constitution, and the Laws of the United States which shall be made in Pursuance thereof; and all Treaties made, or which shall be made, under the Authority of the United States, shall be the supreme Law of the Land; and the Judges in every State shall be bound thereby, any Thing in the Constitution or Laws of any State to the Contrary notwithstanding.

The Senators and Representatives before mentioned, and the Members of the several State Legislatures, and all executive and judicial Officers, both of the United States and of the several States, shall be bound by Oath or Affirmation, to support this Constitution; but no religious Test shall ever be required as a Qualification to any Office or public Trust under the United States.

ARTICLE VII.

The Ratification of the Conventions of nine States, shall be sufficient for the Establishment of this Constitution between the States so ratifying the Same.

* * *

ARTICLES IN ADDITION TO, AND AMENDMENT OF, THE CONSTITUTION OF THE UNITED STATES OF AMERICA, PROPOSED BY CONGRESS, AND RATIFIED BY THE SEVERAL STATES, PURSUANT TO THE FIFTH ARTICLE OF THE ORIGINAL CONSTITUTION.

AMENDMENT I [1791].

Congress shall make no law respecting an establishment of religion, or prohibiting the free exercise thereof; or abridging the freedom of speech, or of the press; or the right of the people peaceably to assemble, and to petition the Government for a redress of grievances.

AMENDMENT II [1791].

A well regulated Militia, being necessary to the security of a free State, the right of the people to keep and bear Arms, shall not be infringed.

AMENDMENT III [1791].

No Soldier shall, in time of peace be quartered in any house, without the consent of the Owner, nor in time of war, but in a manner to be prescribed by law.

AMENDMENT IV [1791].

The right of the people to be secure in their persons, houses, papers, and effects, against unreasonable searches and seizures, shall not be violated, and no Warrants shall issue, but upon probable cause, supported by Oath or affirmation, and particularly describing the place to be searched, and the persons or things to be seized.

AMENDMENT V [1791].

No person shall be held to answer for a capital, or otherwise infamous crime, unless on a presentment or indictment of a Grand Jury, except in cases arising in the land or naval forces, or in the Militia, when in actual service in time of War or public danger; nor shall any person be subject for the same offence to be twice put in jeopardy of life or limb; nor shall be compelled in any criminal case to be a witness against himself, nor be deprived of life, liberty, or property, without due process of law; nor shall private property be taken for public use, without just compensation.

AMENDMENT VI [1791].

In all criminal prosecutions, the accused shall enjoy the right to a speedy and public trial, by an impartial jury of the State and district wherein the crime shall have been committed, which district shall have been previously ascertained by law, and to be informed of the nature and cause of the accusation; to be confronted with the witnesses against him; to have compulsory process for obtaining Witnesses in his favor, and to have the Assistance of Counsel for his defence.

AMENDMENT VII [1791].

In Suits at common law, where the value in controversy shall exceed twenty dollars, the right of trial by jury shall be preserved, and no fact tried by a jury, shall be otherwise re-examined in any Court of the United States, than according to the rules of the common law.

AMENDMENT VIII [1791].

Excessive bail shall not be required, nor excessive fines imposed, nor cruel and unusual punishments inflicted.

AMENDMENT IX [1791].

The enumeration in the Constitution, of certain rights, shall not be construed to deny or disparage others retained by the people.

AMENDMENT X [1791].

The powers not delegated to the United States by the Constitution, nor prohibited by it to the States, are reserved to the States respectively, or to the people.

AMENDMENT XI [1798].

The Judicial power of the United States shall not be construed to extend to any suit in law or equity, commenced or prosecuted against one of the United States by Citizens of another State, or by Citizens or Subjects of any Foreign State.

AMENDMENT XII [1804].

The Electors shall meet in their respective states and vote by ballot for President and Vice-President, one of whom, at least, shall not be an inhabitant of the same state with themselves; they shall name in their ballots the person voted for as President, and in distinct ballots the person voted for as Vice-President, and they shall make distinct lists of all persons voted for as President, and of all persons voted for as Vice-President, and of the number of votes for each, which lists they shall sign and certify, and transmit sealed to the seat of the government of the United States, directed to the President of the Senate;—The President of the Senate shall, in the presence of the Senate and House of Representatives, open all the certificates and the votes shall then be counted;—The person having the greatest number of votes for President, shall be the President, if such number be a majority of the whole number of Electors appointed; and if no person have such majority, then from the persons having the highest numbers not exceeding three on the list of those voted for as President, the House of Representatives shall choose immediately, by ballot, the President. But in choosing the President, the votes shall be taken by states, the representation from each state having one vote; a quorum for this purpose shall consist of a member or members from two-thirds of the states, and a majority of all the states shall be necessary to a choice. And if the House of Representatives shall not choose a President whenever the right of choice shall devolve upon them, before the fourth day of March next following, then the Vice-President shall act as President, as in the case of the death or other constitutional disability of the President—The person having the greatest number of votes as Vice-President, shall be the Vice-President, if such number be a majority of the whole number of Electors appointed, and if no person have a majority, then from the two highest numbers on the list, the Senate shall choose the Vice-President; a quorum for the purpose shall consist of two-thirds of the whole number of Senators, and a majority of the whole number shall be necessary to a choice. But no person constitutionally ineligible to the office of President shall be eligible to that of Vice-President of the United States.

AMENDMENT XIII [1865].

SECTION 1. Neither slavery nor involuntary servitude, except as a punishment for crime whereof the party shall have been duly convicted, shall exist within the United States, or any place subject to their jurisdiction.

SECTION 2. Congress shall have power to enforce this article by appropriate legislation.

AMENDMENT XIV [1868].

SECTION 1. All persons born or naturalized in the United States, and subject to the jurisdiction thereof, are citizens of the United States and of the State wherein they reside. No State shall make or enforce any law which shall abridge the privileges or immunities of citizens of the United States; nor shall any State deprive any person of life, liberty, or property, without due process of law; nor deny to any person within its jurisdiction the equal protection of the laws.

SECTION 2. Representatives shall be apportioned among the several States according to their respective numbers, counting the whole number of persons in each State, excluding Indians not taxed. But when the right to vote at any election for the choice of electors for President and Vice President of the United States, Representatives in Congress, the Executive and Judicial officers of a State, or the members of the Legislature thereof, is denied to any of the male inhabitants of such State, being twenty-one years of age, and citizens of the United States, or in any way abridged, except for participation in rebellion, or other crime, the basis of representation therein shall be reduced in the proportion which the number of such male citizens shall bear to the whole number of male citizens twenty-one years of age in such State.

SECTION 3. No person shall be a Senator or Representative in Congress, or elector of President and Vice President, or hold any office, civil or military, under the United States, or under any State, who, having previously taken an oath, as a member of Congress, or as an officer of the United States, or as a member of any State legislature, or as an executive or judicial officer of any State, to support the Constitution of the United States, shall have engaged in insurrection or rebellion against the same, or given aid or comfort to the enemies thereof. But Congress may by a vote of two-thirds of each House, remove such disability.

SECTION 4. The validity of the public debt of the United States, authorized by law, including debts incurred for payment of pensions and bounties for services in suppressing insurrection or rebellion, shall not be questioned. But neither the United States nor any State shall assume or pay any debt or obligation incurred in aid of insurrection or rebellion against the United States, or any claim for the loss of emancipation of any slave; but all such debts, obligations and claims shall be held illegal and void.

SECTION 5. The Congress shall have power to enforce, by appropriate legislation, the provisions of this article.

AMENDMENT XV [1870].

SECTION 1. The right of citizens of the United States to vote shall not be denied or abridged by the United States or by any State on account of race, color, or previous condition of servitude.

SECTION 2. The Congress shall have power to enforce this article by appropriate legislation.

AMENDMENT XVI [1913].

The Congress shall have power to lay and collect taxes on incomes, from whatever source derived, without apportionment among the several States, and without regard to any census or enumeration.

AMENDMENT XVII [1913].

The Senate of the United States shall be composed of two Senators from each State, elected by the people thereof, for six years; and each Senator shall have one vote. The electors in each State shall have the qualifications requisite for electors of the most numerous branch of the State legislatures.

When vacancies happen in the representation of any State in the Senate, the executive authority of such State shall issue writs of election to fill such vacancies: *Provided*, That the legislature of any State may empower the executive thereof to make temporary appointments until the people fill the vacancies by election as the legislature may direct.

This amendment shall not be so construed as to affect the election or term of any Senator chosen before it becomes valid as part of the Constitution.

AMENDMENT XVIII [1919].

SECTION 1. After one year from the ratification of this article the manufacture, sale, or transportation of intoxicating liquors within, the importation thereof into, or the exportation thereof from the United States and all territory subject to the jurisdiction thereof for beverage purposes is hereby prohibited.

SECTION 2. The Congress and the several States shall have concurrent power to enforce this article by appropriate legislation.

SECTION 3. This article shall be inoperative unless it shall have been ratified as an amendment to the Constitution by the legislatures of the several States, as provided in the Constitution, within seven years from the date of the submission hereof to the States by the Congress.

AMENDMENT XIX [1920].

The right of citizens of the United States to vote shall not be denied or abridged by the United States or by any State on account of sex.

Congress shall have power to enforce this article by appropriate legislation.

AMENDMENT XX [1933].

SECTION 1. The terms of the President and Vice President shall end at noon on the 20th day of January, and the terms of Senators and Representatives at noon on the 3d day of January, of the years in which such terms would have ended if this article had not been ratified; and the terms of their successors shall then begin.

SECTION 2. The Congress shall assemble at least once in every year, and such meeting shall begin at noon on the 3d day of January, unless they shall by law appoint a different day.

SECTION 3. If, at the time fixed for the beginning of the term of the President, the President elect shall have died, the Vice President elect shall become President. If a President shall not have been chosen before the time fixed for the beginning of his term, or if the President elect shall have failed to qualify, then the Vice President elect shall act as President until a President shall have qualified; and the Congress may by law provide for the case wherein neither a President elect nor a Vice President elect shall have qualified, declaring who shall then act as President, or the manner in which one who is to act shall be selected, and such person shall act accordingly until a President or Vice President shall have qualified.

SECTION 4. The Congress may by law provide for the case of the death of any of the persons from whom the House of Representatives may choose a President whenever the right of choice shall have devolved upon them, and for the case of the death of any of the persons from whom the Senate may choose a Vice President whenever the right of choice shall have devolved upon them.

SECTION 5. Sections 1 and 2 shall take effect on the 15th day of October following the ratification of this article.

SECTION 6. This article shall be inoperative unless it shall have been ratified as an amendment to the Constitution by the legislatures of three-fourths of the several States within seven years from the date of its submission.

AMENDMENT XXI [1933].

SECTION 1. The eighteenth article of amendment to the Constitution of the United States is hereby repealed.

SECTION 2. The transportation or importation into any State, Territory, or possession of the United States for delivery or use therein of intoxicating liquors, in violation of the laws thereof, is hereby prohibited.

SECTION 3. This article shall be inoperative unless it shall have been ratified as an amendment to the Constitution by conventions in the several States, as provided in the Constitution, within seven years from the date of the submission hereof to the States by the Congress.

AMENDMENT XXII [1951].

SECTION 1. No person shall be elected to the office of the President more than twice, and no person who has held the office of President, or acted as President, for more than two years of a term to which some other person was elected President shall be elected to the office of the President more than once. But this Article shall not apply to any person holding the office of President when this Article was proposed by the Congress, and shall not prevent any person who may be holding the office of President, or acting as President, during the term within which this Article becomes operative from holding the office of President or acting as President during the remainder of such term.

SECTION 2. This article shall be inoperative unless it shall have been ratified as an amendment to the Constitution by the legislatures of three-fourths of the several States within seven years from the date of its submission to the States by the Congress.

AMENDMENT XXIII [1961].

SECTION 1. The District constituting the seat of Government of the United States shall appoint in such manner as the Congress may direct:

A number of electors of President and Vice President equal to the whole number of Senators and Representatives in Congress to which the District would be entitled if it were a State, but in no event more than the least populous State; they shall be in addition to those appointed by the States, but they shall be considered, for the purposes of the election of President and Vice President, to be electors appointed by a State; and they shall meet in the District and perform such duties as provided by the twelfth article of amendment.

SECTION 2. The Congress shall have power to enforce this article by appropriate legislation.

AMENDMENT XXIV [1964].

SECTION 1. The right of citizens of the United States to vote in any primary or other election for President or Vice President, for electors for President or Vice President, or for Senator or Representative in Congress, shall not be denied or abridged by the United States or any State by reason of failure to pay any poll tax or other tax.

SECTION 2. The Congress shall have power to enforce this article by appropriate legislation.

AMENDMENT XXV [1967].

SECTION 1. In case of the removal of the President from office or of his death or resignation, the Vice President shall become President.

SECTION 2. Whenever there is a vacancy in the office of the Vice President, the President shall nominate a Vice President who shall take office upon confirmation by a majority vote of both Houses of Congress.

SECTION 3. Whenever the President transmits to the President pro tempore of the Senate and the Speaker of the House of Representatives his written declaration that he is unable to discharge the powers and duties of his office, and until he transmits to them a written declaration to the contrary, such powers and duties shall be discharged by the Vice President as Acting President.

SECTION 4. Whenever the Vice President and a majority of either the principal officers of the executive departments or of such other body as Congress may by law provide, transmit to the President pro tempore of the Senate and the Speaker of the House of Representatives their written declaration that the President is unable to discharge the powers and duties of his office, the Vice President shall immediately assume the powers and duties of the office as Acting President.

Thereafter, when the President transmits to the President pro tempore of the Senate and the Speaker of the House of Representatives his written declaration that no inability exists, he shall resume the powers and duties of his office unless the Vice President and a majority of either the principal officers of the executive department or of such other body as Congress may by law provide, transmit within four days to the President pro tempore of the Senate and the Speaker of the House of Representatives their written declaration that the President is unable to discharge the powers and duties of his office. Thereupon Congress shall decide the issue, assembling within forty-eight hours for that purpose if not in session. If the Congress, within twenty-one days after receipt of the latter written declaration, or, if Congress is not in session, within twenty-one days after Congress is required to assemble, determines by two-thirds vote of both Houses that the President is unable to discharge the powers and duties of his office, the Vice President shall continue to discharge the same as Acting President; otherwise, the President shall resume the powers and duties of his office.

AMENDMENT XXVI [1971].

SECTION 1. The right of citizens of the United States, who are eighteen years of age or older, to vote shall not be denied or abridged by the United States or by any State on account of age.

SECTION 2. The Congress shall have power to enforce this article by appropriate legislation.

AMENDMENT XXVII [1992].

No law varying the compensation for the services of the Senators and Representatives shall take effect until an election of Representatives shall have intervened.

APPENDIX B

SELECTED FEDERAL STATUTES

I. Title 18, U.S.C.:

§ 3231. District courts

The district courts of the United States shall have original jurisdiction, exclusive of the courts of the States, of all offenses against the laws of the United States.

Nothing in this title shall be held to take away or impair the jurisdiction of the courts of the several States under the laws thereof.

II. Title 28, U.S.C.:

§ 1251. Original jurisdiction

(a) The Supreme Court shall have original and exclusive jurisdiction of all controversies between two or more States.

(b) The Supreme Court shall have original but not exclusive jurisdiction of:

(1) All actions or proceedings to which ambassadors, other public ministers, consuls, or vice consuls of foreign states are parties;

(2) All controversies between the United States and a State;

(3) All actions or proceedings by a State against the citizens of another State or against aliens.

§ 1254. Courts of appeals; certiorari; certified questions

Cases in the courts of appeals may be reviewed by the Supreme Court by the following methods:

(1) By writ of certiorari granted upon the petition of any party to any civil or criminal case, before or after rendition of judgment or decree;

(2) By certification at any time by a court of appeals of any question of law in any civil or criminal case as to which instructions are desired, and upon such certification the Supreme Court may give binding instructions or require the entire record to be sent up for decision of the entire matter in controversy.

§ 1257. State courts; certiorari

(a) Final judgments or decrees rendered by the highest court of a State in which a decision could be had, may be reviewed by the Supreme Court by writ of certiorari where the validity of a treaty or statute of the United States is drawn in question or where the validity of a statute of any State is drawn in question on the ground of its being repugnant to the Constitution, treaties, or laws of the United States, or where any title, right, privilege, or immunity is specially set up or claimed under the Constitution or the treaties or statutes of, or any commission held or authority exercised under, the United States.

(b) For purposes of this section, the term "highest court of s State" includes the district of Columbia Court of Appeals.

§ 1291. Final decisions of district courts

The courts of appeals (other than the United States Court of Appeal for the Federal Circuit) shall have jurisdiction of appeals from all final decisions of the district courts of the United States, the United States District Court for the District of the Canal Zone, the District Court of Guam, and the District Court of the Virgin Islands, except where a direct review may be had in the Supreme Court. The jurisdiction of the United States Court of Appeals for the Federal Circuit shall be limited to the jurisdiction described in sections 1292(c) and (d) and 1295 of this title.

§ 1292. Interlocutory decisions

(a) Except as provided in subsections (c) and (d) of this section, the courts of appeals shall have jurisdiction of appeals from:

(1) Interlocutory orders of the district courts of the United States . . . or of the judges thereof, granting, continuing, modifying, refusing or dissolving injunctions, or refusing to dissolve or modify injunctions, except where a direct review may be had in the Supreme Court . . .

(b) When a district judge, in making in a civil action an order not otherwise appealable under this section, shall be of the opinion that such order involves a controlling question of law as to which there is substantial ground for difference of opinion and that an immediate appeal from the order may materially advance the ultimate termination of the litigation, he shall so state in writing in such order. The Court of Appeals which would have jurisdiction of an appeal of such action may thereupon, in its discretion, permit an appeal to be taken from such order, if application is made to it within ten days after the entry of the order: *Provided, however,* That application for an appeal hereunder shall not stay proceedings in the district court unless the district judge or the Court of Appeals or a judge thereof shall so order. . . .

(e) The Supreme Court may prescribe rules, in accordance with section 2072 of this title, to provide for an appeal of an interlocutory decision to the courts of appeals that is not otherwise provided for under subsection (a) [or] (b) . . . .

§ 1331. Federal question

The district courts shall have original jurisdiction of all civil actions arising under the Constitution, laws, or treaties of the United States.

§ 1332. Diversity of citizenship; amount in controversy; costs

(a) The district courts shall have original jurisdiction of all civil actions where the matter in controversy exceeds the sum or value of $75,000, exclusive of interest and costs, and is between—

(1) citizens of different States;

(2) citizens of a State and citizens or subjects of a foreign state, except that the district courts shall not have original jurisdiction under this subsection of an action between citizens of a State and citizens or subjects of a foreign state who are lawfully admitted for permanent residence in the United States and are domiciled in the same State;

(3) citizens of different States and in which citizens or subjects of a foreign state are additional parties; and

(4) a foreign state, defined in section 1603(a) of this title, as plaintiff and citizens of a State or of different States.

(b) Except when express provision therefor is otherwise made in a statute of the United States, where the plaintiff who files the case originally in the Federal courts is finally adjudged to be entitled to recover less than the sum or value of $75,000, computed without regard to any setoff or counterclaim to which the defendant may be adjudged to be entitled, and exclusive of interest and costs, the district court may deny costs to the plaintiff and, in addition, may impose costs on the plaintiff.

(c) For the purposes of this section and section 1441 of this title—

(1) a corporation shall be deemed to be a citizen of every State and foreign state by which it has been incorporated and of the State or foreign state where it has its principal place of business, except that in any direct action against the insurer of a policy or contract of liability insurance, whether incorporated or unincorporated, to which action the insured is not joined as a party-defendant, such insurer shall be deemed a citizen of—

(A) every State and foreign state of which the insured is a citizen;

(B) every State and foreign state by which the insurer has been incorporated; and

(C) the State or foreign state where the insurer has its principal place of business; and

(2) the legal representative of the estate of a decedent shall be deemed to be a citizen only of the same State as the decedent, and the legal representative of an infant or incompetent shall be deemed to be a citizen only of the same State as the infant or incompetent. . . .

(e) The word "States", as used in this section, includes the Territories, the District of Columbia, and the Commonwealth of Puerto Rico.

§ 1335. Interpleader

(a) The district courts shall have original jurisdiction of any civil action of interpleader or in the nature of interpleader filed by any person, firm, or corporation, association, or society having in his or its custody or possession money or property of the value of $500 or more, or having issued a note, bond, certificate, policy of insurance, or other instrument of value or amount of $500 or more, or providing for the delivery or payment or the loan of money or property of such amount or value, or being under any obligation written or unwritten to the amount of $500 or more, if

(1) Two or more adverse claimants, of diverse citizenship as defined in subsection (a) or (d) of section 1332 of this title, are claiming or may claim to be entitled to such money or property, or to any one or more of the benefits arising by virtue of any note, bond, certificate, policy or other instrument, or arising by virtue of any such obligation; and if (2) the plaintiff has deposited such money or property or has paid the amount of or the loan or other value of such instrument or the amount due under such obligation into the registry of the court, there to abide the judgment of the court, or has given bond payable to the clerk of the court in such amount and with such surety as the court or judge may deem proper, conditioned upon the compliance by the plaintiff with the future order or judgment of the court with respect to the subject matter of the controversy.

(b) Such an action may be entertained although the titles or claims of the conflicting claimants do not have a common origin, or are not identical, but are adverse to and independent of one another.

§ 1341. Taxes by States

The district courts shall not enjoin, suspend or restrain the assessment, levy or collection of any tax under State law where a plain, speedy and efficient remedy may be had in the courts of such State.

§ 1342. Rate orders of State agencies

The district courts shall not enjoin, suspend or restrain the operation of, or compliance with, any order affecting rates chargeable by a public utility and made by a State administrative agency or a rate-making body of a State political subdivision, where:

(1) Jurisdiction is based solely on diversity of citizenship or repugnance of the order to the Federal Constitution; and,

(2) The order does not interfere with interstate commerce; and,

(3) The order has been made after reasonable notice and hearing; and,

(4) A plain, speedy and efficient remedy may be had in the courts of such State.

§ 1343. Civil rights and elective franchise

(a) The district courts shall have original jurisdiction of any civil action authorized by law to be commenced by any person:

(1) To recover damages for injury to his person or property, or because of the deprivation of any right or privilege of a citizen of the United States, by any act done in furtherance of any conspiracy mentioned in section 1985 of Title 42;

(2) To recover damages from any person who fails to prevent or to aid in preventing any wrongs mentioned in section 1985 of Title 42 which he had knowledge were about to occur and power to prevent;

(3) To redress the deprivation, under color of any State law, statute, ordinance, regulation, custom or usage, of any right, privilege or immunity secured by the Constitution of the United States or by any Act of Congress providing for equal rights of citizens or of all persons within the jurisdiction of the United States;

(4) To recover damages or to secure equitable or other relief under any Act of Congress providing for the protection of civil rights, including the right to vote.

(b) For purposes of this section—

(1) the District of Columbia shall be considered to be a State; and

(2) any Act of Congress applicable exclusively to the District of Columbia shall be considered to be a statute of the District of Columbia.

§ 1345. United States as plaintiff

Except as otherwise provided by Act of Congress, the district courts shall have original jurisdiction of all civil actions, suits or proceedings commenced by the United States, or by any agency or officer thereof expressly authorized to sue by Act of Congress.

§ 1350. Alien's action for tort

The district courts shall have original jurisdiction of any civil action by an alien for a tort only, committed in violation of the law of nations or a treaty of the United States.

§ 1359. Parties collusively joined or made

A district court shall not have jurisdiction of a civil action in which any party, by assignment or otherwise, has been improperly or collusively made or joined to invoke the jurisdiction of such court.

§ 1361. Action to compel an officer of the United States to perform his duty

The district courts shall have original jurisdiction of any action in the nature of mandamus to compel an officer or employee of the United States or any agency thereof to perform a duty owed to the plaintiff.

§ 1367. Supplemental jurisdiction

(a) Except as provided in subsections (b) and (c) or as expressly provided otherwise by Federal statute, in any civil action of which the district courts have original jurisdiction, the district courts shall have supplemental jurisdiction over all other claims that are so related to claims in the action within such original jurisdiction that they form part of the same case or controversy under Article III of the United States Constitution. Such supplemental jurisdiction shall include claims that involve the joinder or intervention of additional parties.

(b) In any civil action of which the district courts have original jurisdiction founded solely on section 1332 of this title, the district courts shall not have supplemental jurisdiction under subsection (a) over claims by plaintiffs against persons made parties under Rule 14, 19, 20, or 24 of the Federal Rules of Civil Procedure, or over claims by persons proposed to be joined as plaintiffs under Rule 19 of such rules, or seeking to intervene as plaintiffs under Rule 24 of such rules, when exercising supplemental jurisdiction over such claims would be inconsistent with the jurisdictional requirements of section 1332.

(c) The district courts may decline to exercise supplemental jurisdiction over a claim under subsection (a) if—

(1) the claim raises a novel or complex issue of State law,

(2) the claim substantially predominates over the claim or claims over which the district court has original jurisdiction,

(3) the district court has dismissed all claims over which it has original jurisdiction, or

(4) in exceptional circumstances, there are other compelling reasons for declining jurisdiction.

(d) The period of limitations for any claim asserted under subsection (a), and for any other claim in the same action that is voluntarily dismissed at the same time as or after the dismissal of the claim under subsection (a), shall be tolled while the claim is pending and for a period of 30 days after it is dismissed unless State law provides for a longer tolling period.

(e) As used in this section, the term "State" includes the District of Columbia, the Commonwealth of Puerto Rico, and any territory or possession of the United States.

§ 1369. Multiparty, multiforum jurisdiction

(a) In general.—The district courts shall have original jurisdiction of any civil action involving minimal diversity between adverse parties that arises from a single accident, where at least 75 natural persons have died in the accident at a discrete location, if—

    (1) a defendant resides in a State and a substantial part of the accident took place in another State or other location, regardless of whether that defendant is also a resident of the State where a substantial part of the accident took place;

    (2) any two defendants reside in different States, regardless of whether such defendants are also residents of the same State or States; or

    (3) substantial parts of the accident took place in different States.

(b) Limitation of jurisdiction of district courts.—The district court shall abstain from hearing any civil action described in subsection (a) in which—

    (1) the substantial majority of all plaintiffs are citizens of a single State of which the primary defendants are also citizens; and

    (2) the claims asserted will be governed primarily by the laws of that State.

(c) Special rules and definitions.—For purposes of this section—

    (1) minimal diversity exists between adverse parties if any party is a citizen of a State and any adverse party is a citizen of another State, a citizen or subject of a foreign state, or a foreign state as defined in section 1603(a) of this title;

    (2) a corporation is deemed to be a citizen of any State, and a citizen or subject of any foreign state, in which it is incorporated or has its principal place of business, and is deemed to be a resident of any State in which it is incorporated or licensed to do business or is doing business;

    (3) the term "injury" means—

        (A) physical harm to a natural person; and

        (B) physical damage to or destruction of tangible property, but only if physical harm described in subparagraph (A) exists;

    (4) the term "accident" means a sudden accident, or a natural event culminating in an accident, that results in death incurred at a discrete location by at least 75 natural persons; and

    (5) the term "State" includes the District of Columbia, the Commonwealth of Puerto Rico, and any territory or possession of the United States.

(d) Intervening parties.—In any action in a district court which is or could have been brought, in whole or in part, under this section, any person with a claim arising from the accident described in subsection (a) shall be permitted to intervene as a party plaintiff in the action, even if that person could not have brought an action in a district court as an original matter.

(e) Notification of judicial panel on multidistrict litigation.—A district court in which an action under this section is pending shall promptly notify the judicial panel on multidistrict litigation of the pendency of the action.

§ 1390. Scope

(a) Venue defined.—As used in this chapter, the term "venue" refers to the geographic specification of the proper court or courts for the litigation of a civil action that is within the subject-matter jurisdiction of the district courts in general, and does not refer to any grant or restriction of subject-matter jurisdiction providing for a civil action to be adjudicated only by the district court for a particular district or districts.

(b) Exclusion of certain cases.—Except as otherwise provided by law, this chapter shall not govern the venue of a civil action in which the district court exercises the jurisdiction conferred by section 1333, except that such civil actions may be transferred between district courts as provided in this chapter.

(c) Clarification regarding cases removed from State courts.—This chapter shall not determine the district court to which a civil action pending in a State court may be removed, but shall govern the transfer of an action so removed as between districts and divisions of the United States district courts.

§ 1391. Venue generally

(a) Applicability of section.—Except as otherwise provided by law—

(1) this section shall govern the venue of all civil actions brought in district courts of the United States; and

(2) the proper venue for a civil action shall be determined without regard to whether the action is local or transitory in nature.

(b) Venue in general.—A civil action may be brought in—

(1) a judicial district in which any defendant resides, if all defendants are residents of the State in which the district is located;

(2) a judicial district in which a substantial part of the events or omissions giving rise to the claim occurred, or a substantial part of property that is the subject of the action is situated; or

(3) if there is no district in which an action may otherwise be brought as provided in this section, any judicial district in which any

defendant is subject to the court's personal jurisdiction with respect to such action.

(c)   Residency.—For all venue purposes—

(1)   a natural person, including an alien lawfully admitted for permanent residence in the United States, shall be deemed to reside in the judicial district in which that person is domiciled;

(2)   an entity with the capacity to sue and be sued in its common name under applicable law, whether or not incorporated, shall be deemed to reside, if a defendant, in any judicial district in which such defendant is subject to the court's personal jurisdiction with respect to the civil action in question and, if a plaintiff, only in the judicial district in which it maintains its principal place of business; and

(3)   a defendant not resident in the United States may be sued in any judicial district, and the joinder of such a defendant shall be disregarded in determining where the action may be brought with respect to other defendants.

(d)   Residency of corporations in States with multiple districts.—For purposes of venue under this chapter, in a State which has more than one judicial district and in which a defendant that is a corporation is subject to personal jurisdiction at the time an action is commenced, such corporation shall be deemed to reside in any district in that State within which its contacts would be sufficient to subject it to personal jurisdiction if that district were a separate State, and, if there is no such district, the corporation shall be deemed to reside in the district within which it has the most significant contacts.

(e)   Actions where defendant is officer or employee of the United States—

(1)   In general.—A civil action in which a defendant is an officer or employee of the United States or any agency thereof acting in his official capacity or under color of legal authority, or an agency of the United States, or the United States, may, except as otherwise provided by law, be brought in any judicial district in which (A) a defendant in the action resides, (B) a substantial part of the events or omissions giving rise to the claim occurred, or a substantial part of property that is the subject of the action is situated, or (C) the plaintiff resides if no real property is involved in the action. Additional persons may be joined as parties to any such action in accordance with the Federal Rules of Civil Procedure and with such other venue requirements as would be applicable if the United States or one of its officers, employees, or agencies were not a party.

(2)   Service.—The summons and complaint in such an action shall be served as provided by the Federal Rules of Civil Procedure except that the delivery of the summons and complaint to the officer or agency as required by the rules may be made by certified mail

beyond the territorial limits of the district in which the action is brought.

(f) Civil actions against a foreign state—A civil action against a foreign state as defined in section 1603(a) of this title may be brought—

(1) in any judicial district in which a substantial part of the events or omissions giving rise to the claim occurred, or a substantial part of property that is the subject of the action is situated;

(2) in any judicial district in which the vessel or cargo of a foreign state is situated, if the claim is asserted under section 1605(b) of this title;

(3) in any judicial district in which the agency or instrumentality is licensed to do business or is doing business, if the action is brought against an agency or instrumentality of a foreign state as defined in section 1603(b) of this title; or

(4) in the United States District Court for the District of Columbia if the action is brought against a foreign state or political subdivision thereof.

(g) Multiparty, multiforum litigation—A civil action in which jurisdiction of the district court is based upon section 1369 of this title may be brought in any district in which any defendant resides or in which a substantial part of the accident giving rise to the action took place.

§ 1397. Interpleader

Any civil action of interpleader or in the nature of interpleader under section 1335 of this title may be brought in the judicial district in which one or more of the claimants reside.

§ 1404. Change of venue

(a) For the convenience of parties and witnesses, in the interest of justice, a district court may transfer any civil action to any other district or division where it might have been brought or to any district or division to which all parties have consented.

(b) Upon motion, consent or stipulation of all parties, any action, suit or proceeding of a civil nature or any motion or hearing thereof, may be transferred, in the discretion of the court, from the division in which pending to any other division in the same district. Transfer of proceedings in rem brought by or on behalf of the United States may be transferred under this section without the consent of the United States where all other parties request transfer.

(c) A district court may order any civil action to be tried at any place within the division in which it is pending.

(d) Transfers from a district court of the United States to the District Court of Guam, the District Court for the Northern Mariana Islands, or the District Court of the Virgin Islands shall not be permitted under this section. As otherwise used in this section, the term "district court" includes the District Court of Guam, the District Court for the Northern Mariana Islands, and the District Court of the Virgin Islands, and the term "district" includes the territorial jurisdiction of each such court.

§ 1406. Cure or waiver of defects

(a) The district court of a district in which is filed a case laying venue in the wrong division or district shall dismiss, or if it be in the interest of justice, transfer such case to any district or division in which it could have been brought.

(b) Nothing in this chapter shall impair the jurisdiction of a district court of any matter involving a party who does not interpose timely and sufficient objection to the venue.

(c) As used in this section, the term "district court" includes the District Court of Guam, the District Court for the Northern Mariana Islands, and the District Court of the Virgin Islands, and the term "district" includes the territorial jurisdiction of each such court.

§ 1441. Removal of civil actions

(a) Generally.—Except as otherwise expressly provided by Act of Congress, any civil action brought in a State court of which the district courts of the United States have original jurisdiction, may be removed by the defendant or the defendants, to the district court of the United States for the district and division embracing the place where such action is pending.

(b) Removal based on diversity of citizenship.—

(1) In determining whether a civil action is removable on the basis of the jurisdiction under section 1332(a) of this title, the citizenship of defendants sued under fictitious names shall be disregarded.

(2) A civil action otherwise removable solely on the basis of the jurisdiction under section 1332(a) of this title may not be removed if any of the parties in interest properly joined and served as defendants is a citizen of the State in which such action is brought.

(c) Joinder of Federal law claims and State law claims.—

(1) If a civil action includes

(A) a claim arising under the Constitution, laws, or treaties of the United States (within the meaning of section 1331 of this title), and

(B) a claim not within the original or supplemental jurisdiction of the district court or a claim that has been made nonremovable by statute, the entire action may be removed if the action would be removable without the inclusion of the claim described in subparagraph (B).

(2)   Upon removal of an action described in paragraph (1), the district court shall sever from the action all claims described in paragraph (1)(B) and shall remand the severed claims to the State court from which the action was removed. Only defendants against whom a claim described in paragraph (1)(A) has been asserted are required to join in or consent to the removal under paragraph (1).

(d)   Actions against foreign States.—Any civil action brought in a State court against a foreign state as defined in section 1603(a) of this title may be removed by the foreign state to the district court of the United States for the district and division embracing the place where such action is pending. Upon removal the action shall be tried by the court without jury. Where removal is based upon this subsection, the time limitations of section 1446(b) of this chapter may be enlarged at any time for cause shown.

(e)   Multiparty, multiforum jurisdiction.—

(1)   Notwithstanding the provisions of subsection (b) of this section, a defendant in a civil action in a State court may remove the action to the district court of the United States for the district and division embracing the place where the action is pending if—

(A)   the action could have been brought in a United States district court under section 1369 of this title; or

(B)   the defendant is a party to an action which is or could have been brought, in whole or in part, under section 1369 in a United States district court and arises from the same accident as the action in State court, even if the action to be removed could not have been brought in a district court as an original matter.

The removal of an action under this subsection shall be made in accordance with section 1446 of this title, except that a notice of removal may also be filed before trial of the action in State court within 30 days after the date on which the defendant first becomes a party to an action under section 1369 in a United States district court that arises from the same accident as the action in State court, or at a later time with leave of the district court.

(2)   Whenever an action is removed under this subsection and the district court to which it is removed or transferred under section 1407(j) has made a liability determination requiring further proceedings as to damages, the district court shall remand the action to the State court from which it had been removed for the determination of damages, unless the court finds that, for the convenience of parties and witnesses and in the interest of justice, the action should be retained for the determination of damages.

(3)   Any remand under paragraph (2) shall not be effective until 60 days after the district court has issued an order determining liability and has certified its intention to remand the removed action

for the determination of damages. An appeal with respect to the liability determination of the district court may be taken during that 60-day period to the court of appeals with appellate jurisdiction over the district court. In the event a party files such an appeal, the remand shall not be effective until the appeal has been finally disposed of. Once the remand has become effective, the liability determination shall not be subject to further review by appeal or otherwise.

(4) Any decision under this subsection concerning remand for the determination of damages shall not be reviewable by appeal or otherwise.

(5) An action removed under this subsection shall be deemed to be an action under section 1369 and an action in which jurisdiction is based on section 1369 of this title for purposes of this section and sections 1407, 1697, and 1785 of this title.

(6) Nothing in this subsection shall restrict the authority of the district court to transfer or dismiss an action on the ground of inconvenient forum.

(f) Derivative removal jurisdiction.—The court to which a civil action is removed under this section is not precluded from hearing and determining any claim in such civil action because the State court from which such civil action is removed did not have jurisdiction over that claim.

§ 1442. Federal officers or agencies sued or prosecuted

(a) A civil action or criminal prosecution that is commenced in a State court and that is against or directed to any of the following may be removed by them to the district court of the United States for the district and division embracing the place wherein it is pending:

(1) The United States or any agency thereof or any officer (or any person acting under that officer) of the United States or of any agency thereof, in an official or individual capacity, for or relating to any act under color of such office or on account of any right, title or authority claimed under any Act of Congress for the apprehension or punishment of criminals or the collection of the revenue.

(2) A property holder whose title is derived from any such officer, where such action or prosecution affects the validity of any law of the United States.

(3) Any officer of the courts of the United States, for or relating to any act under color of office or in the performance of his duties.

(4) Any officer of either House of Congress, for or relating to any act in the discharge of his official duty under an order of such House.

(b) A personal action commenced in any State court by an alien against any citizen of a State who is, or at the time the alleged action accrued was, a civil officer of the United States and is a nonresident of such State, wherein jurisdiction is obtained by the State court by personal service of process, may be removed by the defendant to the district court of the United States for the district and division in which the defendant was served with process.

(c)   Solely for purposes of determining the propriety of removal under subsection (a), a law enforcement officer, who is the defendant in a criminal prosecution, shall be deemed to have been acting under the color of his office if the officer—

(1)   protected an individual in the presence of the officer from a crime of violence;

(2)   provided immediate assistance to an individual who suffered, or who was threatened with, bodily harm; or

(3)   prevented the escape of any individual who the officer reasonably believed to have committed, or was about to commit, in the presence of the officer, a crime of violence that resulted in, or was likely to result in, death or serious bodily injury.

(d)   In this section, the following definitions apply:

(1)   The terms "civil action" and "criminal prosecution" include any proceeding (whether or not ancillary to another proceeding) to the extent that in such proceeding a judicial order, including a subpoena for testimony or documents, is sought or issued. If removal is sought for a proceeding described in the previous sentence, and there is no other basis for removal, only that proceeding may be removed to the district court.

(2)   The term "crime of violence" has the meaning given that term in section 16 of title 18.

(3)   The term "law enforcement officer" means any employee described in subparagraph (A), (B), or (C) of section 8401(17) of title 5 and any special agent in the Diplomatic Security Service of the Department of State.

(4)   The term "serious bodily injury" has the meaning given that term in section 1365 of title 18.

(5)   The term "State" includes the District of Columbia, United States territories and insular possessions, and Indian country (as defined in section 1151 of title 18).

(6)   The term "State court" includes the Superior Court of the District of Columbia, a court of a United States territory or insular possession, and a tribal court.

§ 1442a. Members of armed forces sued or prosecuted

A civil or criminal prosecution in a court of a State of the United States against a member of the armed forces of the United States on account of an act done under color of his office or status, or in respect to which he claims any right, title, or authority under a law of the United States respecting the armed forces thereof, or under the law of war, may at any time before the trial or final hearing thereof be removed for trial into the district court of the United States for the district where it is pending in the manner prescribed by law, and it shall thereupon be entered on the docket of the district court, which shall proceed as if the cause had been originally commenced therein and shall have full power to hear and determine the cause.

§ 1443. Civil rights cases

Any of the following civil actions or criminal prosecutions, commenced in a State court may be removed by the defendant to the district court of the United States for the district and division embracing the place wherein it is pending:

(1) Against any person who is denied or cannot enforce in the courts of such State a right under any law providing for the equal civil rights of citizens of the United States, or of all persons within the jurisdiction thereof;

(2) For any act under color of authority derived from any law providing for equal rights, or for refusing to do any act on the ground that it would be inconsistent with such law.

§ 1447. Procedure after removal generally . . .

(c) . . . If at any time before final judgment it appears that the district court lacks subject matter jurisdiction, the case shall be remanded. . . .

(d) An order remanding a case to the State court from which it was removed is not reviewable on appeal or otherwise, except that an order remanding a case to the State court from which it was removed pursuant to section 1442 or 1443 of this title shall be reviewable by appeal or otherwise. . . .

§ 1651. Writs

(a) The Supreme Court and all courts established by Act of Congress may issue all writs necessary or appropriate in aid of their respective jurisdictions and agreeable to the usages and principles of law.

(b) An alternative writ or rule nisi may be issued by a justice or judge of a court which has jurisdiction.

§ 1652. State laws as rules of decision

The laws of the several states, except where the Constitution or treaties of the United States or Acts of Congress otherwise require or provide, shall be regarded as rules of decision in civil actions in the courts of the United States, in cases where they apply.

§ 1738. State and Territorial statutes and judicial proceedings; full faith and credit

The Acts of the legislature of any State, Territory, or Possession of the United States, or copies thereof, shall be authenticated by affixing the seal of such State, Territory or Possession thereto.

The records and judicial proceedings of any court of any such State, Territory or Possession, or copies thereof, shall be proved or admitted in other courts within the United States and its Territories and Possessions by the attestation of the clerk and seal of the court annexed, if a seal exists, together with a certificate of a judge of the court that the said attestation is in proper form.

Such Acts, records and judicial proceedings or copies thereof, so authenticated, shall have the same full faith and credit in every court within the United States and its Territories and Possessions as they have by law or usage in the courts of such State, Territory or Possession from which they are taken.

§ 2071. Rule-making power generally

(a) The Supreme Court and all courts established by Act of Congress may from time to time prescribe rules for the conduct of their business. Such rules shall be consistent with Acts of Congress and rules of practice and procedure prescribed under section 2072 of this title. . . .

§ 2072. Rules of procedure and evidence; power to prescribe

(a) The Supreme Court shall have the power to prescribe general rules of practice and procedure and rules of evidence for cases in the United States district courts (including proceedings before magistrate judges thereof) and courts of appeals.

(b) Such rules shall not abridge, enlarge or modify any substantive right. All laws in conflict with such rules shall be of no further force or effect after such rules have taken effect. . . .

§ 2111. Harmless error

On the hearing of any appeal or writ of certiorari in any case, the court shall give judgment after an examination of the record without regard to errors or defects which do not affect the substantial rights of the parties.

§ 2201. Creation of remedy

(a) In a case of actual controversy within its jurisdiction, except with respect to Federal taxes other than actions brought under section 7428 of the Internal Revenue Code of 1986, a proceeding under section 505 or 1146 of title 11, or in any civil action involving an antidumping or countervailing duty proceeding regarding a class or kind of merchandise of a free trade area country (as defined in section 516A(f)(10) of the Tariff Act of 1930), as determined by the administering authority, any court of the United States, upon the filing of an appropriate pleading, may declare the rights and other legal relations of any interested party seeking such declaration, whether or not further relief is or could be sought. Any such declaration shall have the force and effect of a final judgment or decree and shall be reviewable as such. . . .

§ 2202. Further relief

Further necessary or proper relief based on a declaratory judgment or decree may be granted, after reasonable notice and hearing, against any adverse party whose rights have been determined by such judgment.

§ 2241. Power to grant writ

(a) Writs of habeas corpus may be granted by the Supreme Court, any justice thereof, the district courts and any circuit judge within their respective jurisdictions. The order of a circuit judge shall be entered in the records of the district court of the district wherein the restraint complained of is had.

(b) The Supreme Court, any justice thereof, and any circuit judge may decline to entertain an application for a writ of habeas corpus and may transfer the application for hearing and determination to the district court having jurisdiction to entertain it.

(c) The writ of habeas corpus shall not extend to a prisoner unless—

(1) He is in custody under or by color of the authority of the United States or is committed for trial before some court thereof; or

(2) He is in custody for an act done or omitted in pursuance of an Act of Congress, or an order, process, judgment or decree of a court or judge of the United States; or

(3) He is in custody in violation of the Constitution or laws or treaties of the United States; or

(4) He, being a citizen of a foreign state and domiciled therein is in custody for an act done or omitted under any alleged right, title, authority, privilege, protection, or exemption claimed under the commission, order or sanction of any foreign state, or under color thereof, the validity and effect of which depend upon the law of nations; or

(5) It is necessary to bring him into court to testify or for trial.

(d) Where an application for a writ of habeas corpus is made by a person in custody under the judgment and sentence of a State court of a State which contains two or more Federal judicial districts, the application may be filed in the district court for the district wherein such person is in custody or in the district court for the district within which the State court was held which convicted and sentenced him and each of such district courts shall have concurrent jurisdiction to entertain the application. The district court for the district wherein such an application is filed in the exercise of its discretion and in furtherance of justice may transfer the application to the other district court for hearing and determination.

(e) (1) No court, justice, or judge shall have jurisdiction to hear or consider an application for a writ of habeas corpus filed by or on behalf of an alien detained by the United States who has been determined by the United States to have been properly detained as an enemy combatant or is awaiting such determination.

(2) Except as provided in paragraphs (2) and (3) of section 1005(e) of the Detainee Treatment Act of 2005 (10 U.S.C. 801 note), no court, justice, or judge shall have jurisdiction to hear or consider any other action against the United States or its agents relating to any aspect of the detention, transfer, treatment, trial, or conditions of confinement of an alien who is or was detained by the United States and has been determined by the United States to have been properly detained as an enemy combatant or is awaiting such determination.

§ 2242. Application

Application for a writ of habeas corpus shall be in writing signed and verified by the person for whose relief it is intended or by someone acting in his behalf.

It shall allege the facts concerning the applicant's commitment or detention, the name of the person who has custody over him and by virtue of what claim or authority, if known.

It may be amended or supplemented as provided in the rules of procedure applicable to civil actions.

If addressed to the Supreme Court, a justice thereof or a circuit judge it shall state the reasons for not making application to the district court of the district in which the applicant is held.

§ 2243. Issuance of writ; return; hearing; decision

A court, justice or judge entertaining an application for a writ of habeas corpus shall forthwith award the writ or issue an order directing the respondent to show cause why the writ should not be granted, unless it appears from the application that the applicant or person detained is not entitled thereto.

The writ, or order to show cause shall be directed to the person having custody of the person detained. It shall be returned within three days unless for good cause additional time, not exceeding twenty days, is allowed.

The person to whom the writ or order is directed shall make a return certifying the true cause of the detention.

When the writ or order is returned a day shall be set for hearing, not more than five days after the return unless for good cause additional time is allowed.

Unless the application for the writ and the return present only issues of law the person to whom the writ is directed shall be required to produce at the hearing the body of the person detained.

The applicant or the person detained may, under oath, deny any of the facts set forth in the return or allege any other material facts.

The return and all suggestions made against it may be amended, by leave of court, before or after being filed.

The court shall summarily hear and determine the facts, and dispose of the matter as law and justice require.

§ 2244. Finality of determination

(a) No circuit or district judge shall be required to entertain an application for a writ of habeas corpus to inquire into the detention of a person pursuant to a judgment of a court of the United States if it appears that the legality of such detention has been determined by a judge or court of the United States on a prior application for a writ of habeas corpus, except as provided in section 2255.

(b) (1) A claim presented in a second or successive habeas corpus application under section 2254 that was presented in a prior application shall be dismissed.

(2) A claim presented in a second or successive habeas corpus application under section 2254 that was not presented in a prior application shall be dismissed unless—

(A) the applicant shows that the claim relies on a new rule of constitutional law, made retroactive to cases on collateral review by the Supreme Court, that was previously unavailable; or

(B) (i)   the factual predicate for the claim could not have been discovered previously through the exercise of due diligence; and

(ii) the facts underlying the claim, if proven and viewed in light of the evidence as a whole, would be sufficient to establish by clear and convincing evidence that, but for constitutional error, no reasonable factfinder would have found the applicant guilty of the underlying offense.

(3) (A) Before a second or successive application permitted by this section is filed in the district court, the applicant shall move in the appropriate court of appeals for an order authorizing the district court to consider the application.

(B) A motion in the court of appeals for an order authorizing the district court to consider a second or successive application shall be determined by a three-judge panel of the court of appeals.

(C) The court of appeals may authorize the filing of a second or successive application only if it determines that the application makes a prima facie showing that the application satisfies the requirements of this subsection.

(D) The court of appeals shall grant or deny the authorization to file a second or successive application not later than 30 days after the filing of the motion.

(E) The grant or denial of an authorization by a court of appeals to file a second or successive application shall not be appealable and shall not be the subject of a petition for rehearing or for a writ of certiorari.

(4) A district court shall dismiss any claim presented in a second or successive application that the court of appeals has authorized to be filed unless the applicant shows that the claim satisfies the requirements of this section.

(c) In a habeas corpus proceeding brought in behalf of a person in custody pursuant to the judgment of a State court, a prior judgment of the Supreme Court of the United States on an appeal or review by a writ of certiorari at the instance of the prisoner of the decision of such State court, shall be conclusive as to all issues of fact or law with respect to an asserted denial of a Federal right which constitutes ground for discharge in a habeas corpus proceeding, actually adjudicated by the Supreme Court therein, unless the applicant for the writ of habeas corpus shall plead and the court shall find the existence of a material and controlling fact which did not appear in the record of the proceeding in the Supreme Court and the court shall further find that the applicant for the writ of habeas corpus could not have caused such fact to appear in such record by the exercise of reasonable diligence.

(d) (1) A 1-year period of limitation shall apply to an application for a writ of habeas corpus by a person in custody pursuant to the judgment of a State court. The limitation period shall run from the latest of—

(A) the date on which the judgment became final by the conclusion of direct review or the expiration of the time for seeking such review;

(B) the date on which the impediment to filing an application created by State action in violation of the Constitution or laws of the United States is removed, if the applicant was prevented from filing by such State action;

(C) the date on which the constitutional right asserted was initially recognized by the Supreme Court, if the right has been newly recognized by the Supreme Court and made retroactively applicable to cases on collateral review; or

(D) the date on which the factual predicate of the claim or claims presented could have been discovered through the exercise of due diligence.

(2)   The time during which a properly filed application for State post-conviction or other collateral review with respect to the pertinent judgment or claim is pending shall not be counted toward any period of limitation under this subsection.

§ 2253. Appeal

(a)   In a habeas corpus proceeding or a proceeding under section 2255 before a district judge, the final order shall be subject to review, on appeal, by the court of appeals for the circuit in which the proceeding is held. . . .

(c)   (1)   Unless a circuit justice or judge issues a certificate of appealability, an appeal may not be taken to the court of appeals from—

(A)   the final order in a habeas corpus proceeding in which the detention complained of arises out of process issued by a State court; or

(B)   the final order in a proceeding under section 2255.

(2)   A certificate of appealability may issue under paragraph (1) only if the applicant has made a substantial showing of the denial of a constitutional right.

(3)   The certificate of appealability under paragraph (1) shall indicate which specific issue or issues satisfy the showing required by paragraph (2).

§ 2254. State custody; remedies in Federal courts

(a)   The Supreme Court, a Justice thereof, a circuit judge, or a district court shall entertain an application for a writ of habeas corpus in behalf of a person in custody pursuant to the judgment of a State court only on the ground that he is in custody in violation of the Constitution or laws or treaties of the United States.

(b)   (1)   An application for a writ of habeas corpus on behalf of a person in custody pursuant to the judgment of a State court shall not be granted unless it appears that—

(A)   the applicant has exhausted the remedies available in the courts of the State; or

(B)   (i)   there is an absence of available State corrective process; or

(ii)   circumstances exist that render such process ineffective to protect the rights of the applicant.

(2)   An application for a writ of habeas corpus may be denied on the merits, notwithstanding the failure of the applicant to exhaust the remedies available in the courts of the State.

(3)   A State shall not be deemed to have waived the exhaustion requirement or be estopped from reliance upon the requirement unless the State, through counsel, expressly waives the requirement.

(c)   An applicant shall not be deemed to have exhausted the remedies available in the courts of the State, within the meaning of this section, if he has the right under the law of the State to raise, by any available procedure, the question presented.

(d)   An application for a writ of habeas corpus on behalf of a person in custody pursuant to the judgment of a State court shall not be granted with respect to any claim that was adjudicated on the merits in State court proceedings unless the adjudication of the claim—

(1)   resulted in a decision that was contrary to, or involved an unreasonable application of, clearly established Federal law, as determined by the Supreme Court of the United States; or

(2)   resulted in a decision that was based on an unreasonable determination of the facts in light of the evidence presented in the State court proceeding.

(e)   (1)   In a proceeding instituted by an application for a writ of habeas corpus by a person in custody pursuant to the judgment of a State court, a determination of a factual issue made by a State court shall be presumed to be correct. The applicant shall have the burden of rebutting the presumption of correctness by clear and convincing evidence.

(2)   If the applicant has failed to develop the factual basis of a claim in State court proceedings, the court shall not hold an evidentiary hearing on the claim unless the applicant shows that—

(A)   the claim relies on—

(i)   a new rule of constitutional law, made retroactive to cases on collateral review by the Supreme Court, that was previously unavailable; or

(ii)   a factual predicate that could not have been previously discovered through the exercise of due diligence; and

(B)   the facts underlying the claim would be sufficient to establish by clear and convincing evidence that but for constitutional error, no reasonable factfinder would have found the applicant guilty of the underlying offense. . . .

(h)   Except as provided in section 408 of the Controlled Substances Act, in all proceedings brought under this section, and any subsequent proceedings on review, the court may appoint counsel for an applicant who is or becomes financially unable to afford counsel, except as provided by a rule promulgated by the Supreme Court pursuant to statutory authority. Appointment of counsel under this section shall be governed by section 3006A of title 18.

(i)   The ineffectiveness or incompetence of counsel during Federal or State collateral post-conviction proceedings shall not be a ground for relief in a proceeding arising under section 2254.

§ 2255. Federal custody; remedies on motion attacking sentence

(a)   A prisoner in custody under sentence of a court established by Act of Congress claiming the right to be released upon the ground that the sentence was imposed in violation of the Constitution or laws of the United States, or that the court was without jurisdiction to impose such sentence, or that the sentence was in excess of the maximum authorized by law, or is otherwise subject to collateral attack, may move the court which imposed the sentence to vacate, set aside or correct the sentence.

(b)   Unless the motion and the files and records of the case conclusively show that the prisoner is entitled to no relief, the court shall cause notice thereof to be served upon the United States attorney, grant a prompt hearing thereon, determine the issues and make findings of fact and conclusions of law with respect thereto. If the court finds that the judgment was rendered without jurisdiction, or that the sentence imposed was not authorized by law or otherwise open to collateral attack, or that there has been such a denial or infringement of the constitutional rights of the prisoner as to render the judgment vulnerable to collateral attack, the court shall vacate and set the judgment aside and shall discharge the prisoner or resentence him or grant a new trial or correct the sentence as may appear appropriate.

(c)   A court may entertain and determine such motion without requiring the production of the prisoner at the hearing.

(d)   An appeal may be taken to the court of appeals from the order entered on the motion as from the final judgment on application for a writ of habeas corpus.

(e)   An application for a writ of habeas corpus in behalf of a prisoner who is authorized to apply for relief by motion pursuant to this section, shall not be entertained if it appears that the applicant has failed to apply for relief, by motion, to the court which sentenced him, or that such court has denied him relief, unless it also appears that the remedy by motion is inadequate or ineffective to test the legality of his detention.

(f)   A 1-year period of limitation shall apply to a motion under this section. The limitation period shall run from the latest of—

(1)   the date on which the judgment of conviction becomes final;

(2)   the date on which the impediment to making a motion created by governmental action in violation of the Constitution or laws of the United States is removed, if the movant was prevented from making a motion by such governmental action;

(3)   the date on which the right asserted was initially recognized by the Supreme Court, if that right has been newly recognized

by the Supreme Court and made retroactively applicable to cases on collateral review; or

(4) the date on which the facts supporting the claim or claims presented could have been discovered through the exercise of due diligence.

(g) Except as provided in section 408 of the Controlled Substances Act, in all proceedings brought under this section, and any subsequent proceedings on review, the court may appoint counsel, except as provided by a rule promulgated by the Supreme Court pursuant to statutory authority. Appointment of counsel under this section shall be governed by section 3006A of title 18.

(h) A second or successive motion must be certified as provided in section 2244 by a panel of the appropriate court of appeals to contain—

(1) newly discovered evidence that, if proven and viewed in light of the evidence as a whole, would be sufficient to establish by clear and convincing evidence that no reasonable factfinder would have found the movant guilty of the offense; or

(2) a new rule of constitutional law, made retroactive to cases on collateral review by the Supreme Court, that was previously unavailable.

§ 2283. Stay of State court proceedings

A court of the United States may not grant an injunction to stay proceedings in a State court except as expressly authorized by Act of Congress, or where necessary in aid of its jurisdiction, or to protect or effectuate its judgments.

III. Title 42, U.S.C.:

§ 1983. Civil action for deprivation of rights

Every person who, under color of any statute, ordinance, regulation, custom, or usage, of any State or Territory or the District of Columbia, subjects, or causes to be subjected, any citizen of the United States or other person within the jurisdiction thereof to the deprivation of any rights, privileges, or immunities secured by the Constitution and laws, shall be liable to the party injured in an action at law, suit in equity, or other proper proceeding for redress, except that in any action brought against a judicial officer for an act or omission taken in such officer's judicial capacity, injunctive relief shall not be granted unless a declaratory decree was violated or declaratory relief was unavailable. For the purposes of this section, any Act of Congress applicable exclusively to the District of Columbia shall be considered to be a statute of the District of Columbia.